THE
PUB
GUIDE 2014

AA Lifestyle Guides

Published by AA Publishing, a trading name of AA Media Limited, whose registered office is Fanum House, Basing View, Basingstoke RG21 4EA. Registered number 06112600.
A CIP catalogue for this book is available from the British Library.

17th edition September 2013.
© AA Media Limited 2013.

Assessments of AA inspected establishments are based on the experience of the Hotel and Restaurant Inspectors on the occasion(s) of their visit(s) and therefore descriptions given in this guide necessarily contain an element of subjective opinion which may not reflect or dictate a reader's own opinion on another occasion. See pages 8–9 for a clear explanation of how, based on our Inspectors' inspection experiences, establishments are graded. If the meal or meals experienced by an Inspector or Inspectors during an inspection fall between award levels the restaurant concerned may be awarded the lower of any award levels considered applicable.

AA Media Limited strives to ensure accuracy of the information in this guide at the time of printing. Nevertheless, the Publisher cannot be held responsible for any errors or omissions, or for changes in the details given in this guide, or for the consequences of any reliance on the information provided by the same. This does not affect your statutory rights. Due to the constantly evolving nature of the subject matter the information is subject to change. AA Media Limited will gratefully receive any advice from our readers of any necessary updated information.

Please contact:
Advertising Sales Department: advertisingsales@theAA.com
Editorial Department: lifestyleguides@theAA.com
AA Hotel and B&B Scheme Enquiries: 01256 844455

Website addresses are included in some entries and specified by the respective establishment. Such websites are not under the control of AA Media Limited and as such AA Media Limited has no control over them and will not accept any responsibility or liability in respect of any and all matters whatsoever relating to such websites including access, content, material and functionality. By including the addresses of third party websites the AA does not intend to solicit business or offer any security to any person in any country, directly or indirectly.

Every effort has been made to trace the copyright holders, and we apologise in advance for any unintentional omissions or errors. We would be pleased to apply any corrections in a following edition of this publication. Photographs in the gazetteer are provided by the establishments.

Typeset/Repro: Servis Filmsetting Ltd, Stockport.
Printed and bound by Printer Trento SRL, Trento
Directory compiled by the AA Lifestyle Guides Department and managed in the Librios Information Management System.

Pub descriptions have been contributed by the following team of writers: David Ashby, Phil Bryant, Neil Coates, Marie-Claire Dillon, David Hancock, Carina Simon, Mark Taylor and Jenny White.

ISBN: 978-0-7495-7476-5
A04961

Maps prepared by the Mapping Services Department of AA Publishing.

Maps © AA Media Limited 2013.

Contains Ordnance Survey data © Crown copyright and database right 2013. Licence number 100021153.

Information on National Parks in England provided by the Countryside Agency (Natural England).

Information on National Parks in Scotland provided by Scottish Natural Heritage.

Information on National Parks in Wales provided by The Countryside Council for Wales.

Contents

Welcome to the Guide	4
How to Use the Guide	6
AA Classifications and Awards	8
AA Pub of the Year	10
A Fruitful Revival: Britain's cider industry	12
National Parks: running a pub in 'Britain's breathing spaces'	18
England	24
Channel Islands	528
Isle of Man	529
Scotland	530
Wales	556
Beer Festivals	590
Cider Festivals	596
County Maps	598
Atlas Section	601
Index of Pubs	628

We aim to bring you the country's best pubs, selected for their atmosphere, good beer and great food. Updated every year, this popular and well established guide includes lots of old favourites, plus many new and interesting destinations for drinking and eating across England, Scotland and Wales.

Who's in the Guide?

We make our selection by seeking out pubs that are worth making a detour for – 'destination' pubs – where publicans show real enthusiasm for their trade and offer a good selection of well-kept drinks and good food. We also choose neighbourhood pubs which are supported by locals and prove attractive to passing motorists or walkers. Our selected pubs make no payment for their inclusion in the guide*; they appear entirely at our discretion.

That Special Place

We find pubs that offer something special: pubs where the time-honoured values of a convivial environment for conversation while supping or eating have not been forgotten. They may be attractive, interesting, unusual or in a good location. Some may be very much a local pub or they may draw customers from further afield, while others appear because they are in an exceptional place. Interesting towns and villages, eccentric or historic buildings, and rare settings can all be found within this guide.

Tempting Food

We look for menus that show a commitment to home cooking, that make good use of local produce wherever possible, and offer an appetising range of freshly prepared dishes. Pubs presenting well-executed traditional dishes like ploughman's or pies, or those offering innovative bar or restaurant food, are all

in the running. In keeping with recent trends in pub food, we are keen to include those where particular emphasis is placed on imaginative modern dishes. Occasionally we include pubs that serve no food, or just snacks, but are distinctive in other ways.

Pick of the Pubs

Some of the pubs included in the guide are particularly special, and we have highlighted these as Pick of the Pubs. For 2014 over 700 pubs have been selected using the personal knowledge of our editorial team, our AA inspectors, and suggestions from our readers. These pubs have a more detailed description, and this year over 140 have chosen to enhance their entry by

purchasing two photographs as part of a full-page entry.

Beer and cider festivals

As well as keeping their ales and ciders in tip-top condition throughout the year, many of the pubs in this guide hold beer and cider festivals, either just one a year or on several occasions. If they have told us that they do, we have indicated these events in the pub entries, and where possible have also mentioned the month/s of the year or bank holidays when they are held. You'll find lists of these festivals at the back of the guide.

* Once chosen for the guide, pubs may decide to enhance their text entry or include advertising for which there is a charge.

Tell us what you think

We welcome your feedback about the pubs included, and about the guide itself. We would also be pleased to receive suggestions about good pubs you have visited that do not feature in this guide. A Readers' Report form appears at the back of the guide, so please write in or e-mail us at lifestyleguides@theaa.com. The pubs also feature on the AA website, theAA.com, and on the AA apps, along with our inspected restaurants, hotels and bed & breakfast accommodation.

1 LOCATION

Guide order Country; county; town or village. Pubs are listed under their town or village name alphabetically within their county, within their country. There is a county map at the back of the guide. Some village pubs prefer to be listed under the nearest town, in which case the village name appears in their address.

2 MAP REFERENCE

Each town or village is given a map reference – the map page number and a two-figure reference based on the National Grid. For example: **Map 4 SU09**

4 refers to the page number of the map section at the back of the guide

SU is the National Grid lettered square (representing 100,000sq metres) in which the location will be found

0 is the figure reading across the top and bottom of the map page

9 is the figure reading down at each side of the map page

London Maps: A Central London map and a Greater London map follow the map section at the back of the guide. The pub location will either appear on Plan 1 or Plan 2.

3 PUB NAME

Where the name appears in italic type the information that follows has not been confirmed by the pub for 2014.

4 AA STARS/DESIGNATORS

★★★ Star rating under AA Hotel or B&B Schemes (see page 8) followed by a designator (ie INN) which shows the type of hotel or B&B.

◉ AA Rosette award for food excellence (see page 9).

5 ADDRESS AND CONTACT DETAILS

6 DIRECTIONS

Brief details are given on how to find the pub.

7 DESCRIPTION

8 OPENING TIMES

Times are given for when the pub is open, and closed, followed by bar and restaurant opening times.

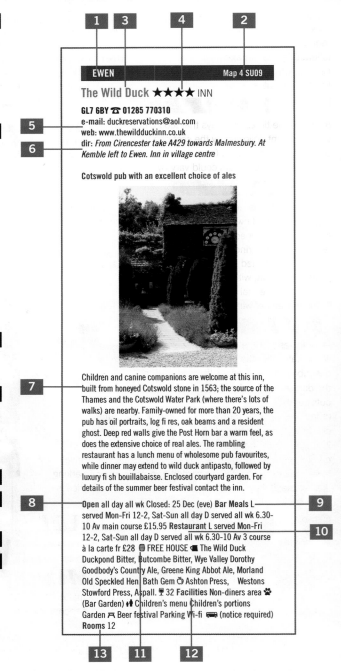

1 **3** **4** **2**

EWEN   Map 4 SU09

The Wild Duck ★★★★ INN

5
GL7 6BY ☎ 01285 770310
e-mail: duckreservations@aol.com
web: www.thewildduckinn.co.uk
6
dir: *From Cirencester take A429 towards Malmesbury. At Kemble left to Ewen. Inn in village centre*

Cotswold pub with an excellent choice of ales

7
Children and canine companions are welcome at this inn, built from honeyed Cotswold stone in 1563; the source of the Thames and the Cotswold Water Park (where there's lots of walks) are nearby. Family-owned for more than 20 years, the pub has oil portraits, log fi res, oak beams and a resident ghost. Deep red walls give the Post Horn bar a warm feel, as does the extensive choice of real ales. The rambling restaurant has a lunch menu of wholesome pub favourites, while dinner may extend to wild duck antipasto, followed by luxury fi sh bouillabaisse. Enclosed courtyard garden. For details of the summer beer festival contact the inn.

8
Open all day all wk Closed: 25 Dec (eve) **Bar Meals** L
served Mon-Fri 12-2, Sat-Sun all day D served all wk 6.30-10 Av main course £15.95 **Restaurant** L served Mon-Fri 12-2, Sat-Sun all day D served all wk 6.30-10 Av 3 course à la carte fr £28 ⊕ FREE HOUSE ◀ The Wild Duck Duckpond Bitter, Butcombe Bitter, Wye Valley Dorothy Goodbody's Country Ale, Greene King Abbot Ale, Morland Old Speckled Hen, Bath Gem ♂ Ashton Press, Westons Stowford Press, Aspall. ♟ 32 **Facilities** Non-diners area ☙ (Bar Garden) ♟ Children's menu Children's portions Garden ⊟ Beer festival Parking Wi-fi ▣ (notice required) **Rooms** 12

9
10
13 **11** **12**

9 BAR MEALS

Indicates the times and days that bar food can be ordered, followed by the average price of a main course (as supplied to us by the pub). Please be aware that last orders could vary by up to 30 minutes.

10 RESTAURANT

Indicates the times and days that food can be ordered from the restaurant, followed by the cost of a fixed price menu and a 3-course à la carte meal (as supplied to us by the pub). Please be aware that last orders could vary by up to 30 minutes.

11 BREWERY AND COMPANY

⊕ indicates the name of the brewery to which the pub is tied, or the company that owns it. FREE HOUSE is shown if the pub is independently owned and run.

◧ indicates the principal beers sold by the pub. The pub's top cask or hand-pulled beers are listed. Many pubs have a much greater selection, with several guest beers each week.

ŏ indicates the real ciders sold by the pub.

♟ the number of wines available by the glass.

12 FACILITIES

⊼ indicates that the pub serves food outside

❀ indicates that the pub has told us they are happy to be described as dog friendly. If possible we also show whereabouts the dogs are accepted (i.e. bar, restaurant, garden and/or outside area).

♦♦ indicates that the pub welcomes children and if they offer a children's menu and/or children's portions.

Further information in this section shows if the pub has a non-diners' area; holds a beer festival and/or a cider festival; has a children's play area, a garden or outside area; if parking is available; if they accept coach parties, and if prior notice is required; if Wi-fi is available.

13 ROOMS

The number of bedrooms is only shown if the pub's accommodation is rated by the AA.

NOTES

⊛ As so many establishments take one or more of the major credit or debit cards, we only indicate if a pub does not accept any cards.

AA Classifications & Awards

Many of the pubs in this guide offer accommodation. Where a Star rating appears next to an entry's name in the guide, the establishment has been inspected by the AA under common Quality Standards agreed between the AA, VisitBritain, VisitScotland and VisitWales. These ratings are for the accommodation, and ensure that the establishment meets the highest standards of cleanliness, with an emphasis on professionalism, proper booking procedures and prompt and efficient services. Some of the pubs in this guide offer accommodation but do not belong to an AA rating scheme; in this case reference to the accommodation is not included in their entry.

AA recognised establishments pay an annual fee that varies according to the classification and the number of bedrooms. The establishments receive an unannounced inspection from a qualified AA inspector who recommends the appropriate classification. Return visits confirm that standards are maintained; the classification is not transferable if an establishment changes hands.

The annual *AA Hotel Guide* and *AA Bed & Breakfast Guide* give further details of recognised establishments and the classification schemes. Details of AA recognised hotels, guest accommodation, restaurants and pubs are also available at **theAA.com,** and on AA apps.

AA Hotel Classification

Hotels are classified on a 5-point scale, with one star ★ being the simplest, and five stars offering a luxurious service at the top of the range. The AA's top hotels in Britain and Ireland are identified by red stars. (★) In addition to the main **Hotel** (HL) classification which applies to some pubs in this guide, there are other categories of hotel which may be applicable to pubs, as follows:

Town House Hotel (TH) – A small, individual city or town centre property.

Country House Hotel – (CHH) Quietly located in a rural area.

Small Hotel (SHL) – Owner managed with fewer than 20 bedrooms.

AA Guest Accommodation

Guest accommodation is also classified on a scale of one to five stars, with one ★ being the most simple, and five being more luxurious. Gold stars (★) indicate the very best B&Bs, Guest Houses, Farmhouses, Inns, Restaurant with Rooms and Guest Accommodation in the 3, 4 and 5 star ratings. A series of designators appropriate to the type of accommodation offered is also used, as follows:

Inn (INN) – Accommodation provided in a fully licensed establishment. The bar will be open to non-residents and food is provided in the evenings.

Bed & Breakfast (B&B) – Accommodation provided in a private house, run by the owner and with no more than six paying guests.

Guest House (GH) – Accommodation provided for more than six paying guests and run on a more commercial basis than a B&B. Usually more services, for example dinner, provided by staff as well as the owner.

Farmhouse (FH) – B&B or guest house rooms provided on a working farm or smallholding.

Restaurant with Rooms (RR) – Destination restaurant offering overnight accommodation. The restaurant is the main business and is open to non-residents. A high standard of food should be offered, at least five nights a week. A maximum of 12 bedrooms. Most Restaurants with Rooms have been awarded AA Rosettes for their food.

Guest Accommodation (GA) – Any establishment which meets the entry requirements for the Scheme can choose this designator.

U A small number of pubs have this symbol because their Star classification was not confirmed at the time of going to press.

Rosette Awards

Out of the thousands of restaurants in the British Isles, the AA identifies, with its Rosette Awards, around 2,000 as the best. What to expect from restaurants with AA Rosette Awards is outlined here; for a more detailed explanation of Rosette criteria please see **theAA.com**

◉ Excellent local restaurants serving food prepared with care, understanding and skill and using good quality ingredients.

◉◉ The best local restaurants, which consistently aim for and achieve higher standards and where a greater precision is apparent in the cooking. Obvious attention is paid to the selection of quality ingredients.

◉◉◉ Outstanding restaurants that demand recognition well beyond their local area.

◉◉◉◉ Amongst the very best restaurants in the British Isles, where the cooking demands national recognition.

◉◉◉◉◉ The finest restaurants in the British Isles, where the cooking stands comparison with the best in the world.

The prestigious annual awards for the AA Pub of the Year for England, Scotland and Wales have been selected with the help of our AA inspectors; we have chosen three very worthy winners. These pubs stand out for being great all-rounders, combining a convivial atmosphere, well kept beers and ciders, excellent food, and of course, a warm welcome from the friendly and efficient hosts and their staff.

ENGLAND

THE ELVEDEN ★★★★★
ELVEDEN, SUFFOLK page 403

A great place to visit for all the family, and the dog

This delightful pub is part of a Guinness family enterprise and is located on the Elveden Estate in a lovely part of Suffolk. Having been completely revamped in 2011 it now offers a contemporary bar, dining room and four luxury bedrooms. The friendly staff couldn't be more welcoming to families and visitors with dogs. In winter there'll be blazing fires to settle by, and when the weather's warmer the extensive patio area is ideal for alfresco dining, especially for those with children. They say a pint of Guinness here will be as good as it is in Emerald Isle, but the bar also has a great range of cask ales, bottled beers and wines to choose from; the menus are based on the plentiful supply of quality produce from the estate and farm, and children will delight in their own 'fawn-size' dishes. Whether here just for the day or stopping overnight, a visit wouldn't be complete without calling into the very impressive estate shops and taking a country woodland walk.

SCOTLAND

THE SHEEP HEID INN
CITY OF EDINBURGH page 539

A true Scottish welcome at this historic inn

Tucked away along narrow roads on the edge of Holyrood Park, is one of Edinburgh's oldest pubs, dating back to 1360. It's been a favourite place of refreshment for many including monachs and poets over the years, and today's visitors can still look forward to a very warm welcome.

The restored interior reveals much charm with roaring fires, old beams and a skittle alley. Every day of the week heralds a different social event – a return to retro dining on Mondays, ladies' night on Wednesdays, and platters of roasted meat for Sunday lunch being just three of the seven. Unpretentious AA Rosette cooking that includes tapas-style sharing plates, also draws the crowds. In summer there's nothing better than finding a seat in the beer garden with a pint of Harviestoun Bitter & Twisted or a glass of chilled white wine in hand. Championing in particular Baron Phillipe de Rothschild wines, the pub offers a Rothschild's wine flight, comprising three (from a choice of six) 50ml glasses, to help you decide just what your tastebuds like best.

WALES

THE GROES INN
CONWY, CONWY page 561

Historic pub with views of Snowdonia

It's said that The Groes Inn was the first house to be licensed in Wales – starting life as a two storey building in the 15th century. Extended, modernised and rerooted over the following centuries, the creeper-clad and flower bedecked building has an enviable location in the Conwy Valley with views over its beautiful gardens to the River Conwy and as far as Snowdonia in the distance.

Expect to find beamed ceilings, roaring fires, rambling rooms and artifacts such as careworn settles and military hats with a connection to the Duke of Wellington (the Iron Duke's grandson witnessed the purchase of the inn in 1889). Real ales from the Great Orme brewery are a highlight as is the AA Rosette cooking that focuses on produce from the nearby estates and seafood supplied directly from Anglesey boats and Conwy's quayside. Choosing to stay in one of the stylish en suite bedrooms surely adds extra temptation to indulging in the real ales and excellent wines that accompany an evening meal here.

Fruitful revival

Mark Taylor takes a look at the revival of Britain's cider industry

If you'd walked into a pub ten years ago, chances were the only cider available would be one of the big brands such as Blackthorn or Strongbow, or perhaps cans of Natch collecting dust on the bottom shelf. Fast-forward a decade and the choice of apple (and pear) tipple has never been more extensive, whether it's on draught or in a bottle.

Sales of cider are proving lucrative and pubs have embraced the resurgence of the centuries-old beverage to the extent that many establishments in this guide now hold their own annual cider festivals, such as The Fleece Inn at Bretforton, Worcestershire, where more than 40 ciders can be sampled.

Much of cider's recent renaissance is the result of what the industry likes to call the 'Magners effect'. Thanks to a major advertising campaign, Magners Original Vintage Cider served over ice became the must-have tipple in the summer of 2005. It sparked renewed interest in a drink that until then had suffered for years from an image problem and declining sales.

Until the Magners effect, cider was often regarded as a cheap, strong drink favoured by students and red-nosed characters sitting on park benches – tipplers perhaps characterised in the 1976 chart-topper *I Am A Cider Drinker* by The Wurzels. This Somerset band became famous for other songs such as *Drink Up Thy Zider* and *Combine Harvester*, and their image synonymous with a boozy straw-chewing country bumpkin perched on a stool in the village pub, nursing a pint of cloudy scrumpy cider.

While there may still be a few rural pubs selling locally-made ciders to such a clientele, the discerning cider drinker of today is more likely to be a smartly attired, high-earning young professional ➡

Andrew Quinlan and Neil MacDonald at Orchard

than a mud-splattered farmer with a tractor parked outside.

Whereas years ago, the choice of cider on offer in pubs was limited to the mass-produced big brands, these days the selection is much broader, as more and more artisan ciders appear on the market.

Large independent cider makers such as Thatchers of Somerset and Aspall of Suffolk may be the major players, but there are many smaller and rapidly expanding new brands on the scene.

And it's not just in the traditional cider heartland of Somerset – new producers are popping up all over the UK, making excellent new ciders in varying quantities. Pop into The Riverside Inn at

Aymestrey in Herefordshire, for example, and you'll be able to order a glass of Brook Farm Medium Dry made in nearby Wigmore. Stop off at the Caesars Arms in Creigiau near Cardiff and you can enjoy a pint of locally produced Gwynt y Ddraig Orchard Gold.

Seven centuries of cider making

Cider has been enjoyed in the UK since the 13th century, according to writer, historian and amateur cider-maker James Russell, author of *The Naked Guide to Cider*.

"Cider as we know it, was almost certainly brought to this country by the Normans in the wake of the Conquest

in 1066," says Russell, who makes his own cider on a very small scale at his urban Bristol home. Before that, cider drinkers had to get by with thin stuff made by cutting up apples – or crab apples – and soaking the pieces in water, before pressing the semi-fermented fruit through sackcloth.

"The Norman Conquest brought an influx of new technology. They had special cider apples, and – most importantly – they had mills that could crush the fruit in bulk. This expertise had travelled from Moorish Spain along the Atlantic seaboard of France, and was centred on the monasteries. Battle Abbey in Sussex was founded after the Norman victory at

Hastings, and by the early 13th century it was making money from sales of cider. Sussex is still a major cider-making county, so much so that the National Collection of Cider and Perry is located at Middle Farm, Firle, near Lewes."

English cider enjoyed a glorious reputation in the 17th and 18th centuries, when the gentry drank it instead of wine. Charles II liked to drink his cider from elaborately engraved glasses – he wasn't called the Merrie Monarch for nothing.

So when and why did cider go out of fashion and start to get such a bad reputation? According to Russell, there was a combination of reasons.

Out of favour

"Things went downhill in the 19th century, partly because the very best apple varieties went into decline, and partly because the wealthy went back to drinking wine again. What did for cider's reputation was the imposition of new taxes in the 1970s and the growing fashion for imported lager. The only cider makers who could make a living were the big industrial concerns, whose products were not always the finest.

"Meanwhile, small-scale farm cider making dwindled as farm workforces shrank and the tractor took over from the horse. A lot of expertise was lost, and cider making suffered as a result."

Whilst acknowledging the 'Magners effect' as one reason for cider's revival in 2005, Russell thinks it coincided with an increased consumer interest in provenance and quality when it comes to both food and drink.

"Ask people in the cider business and they will tell you that the resurgence began with the advertising campaign run by Magners a decade ago, which was based around images of beautiful

"Being less fattening than beer but sweeter, and less alcoholic than wine, cider is an ideal modern drink."

traditional orchards – people loved it.

Then there was the whole business of putting ice in the cider, which the drinking public also responded to.

"At the same time the 'local and organic' movement was becoming established, and small-scale cider makers began marketing their products in this way. Many had started production in the 1990s and were now in a position to expand rapidly as the market grew.

"All at once you had a situation where lager drinkers would try Magners, enjoy it, then look around for something a bit more interesting. Producers like Thatchers of Somerset and Westons of Herefordshire responded with beautifully packaged ciders aimed at younger people, and particularly at women. Being less fattening than beer but sweeter, and less alcoholic than wine, cider is an ideal modern drink."

The artisans make a showing

"Meanwhile, the ciders and perries being made by the best artisan producers – Once Upon a Tree, Oliver's and Gregg's Pit in Herefordshire – are absolutely world class, and far more reasonably priced than the equivalent wines."

Cider was of such a high quality and packaged in such attractive bottles that many were good enough for the dinner table, something helped along by endorsement from celebrity chefs such as Hugh Fearnley-Whittingstall and Mark Hix, both of whom have used cider and perry extensively in their regional, seasonal dishes.

One of the newest names on the cider scene is Orchard Pig, started by friends Andrew Quinlan and Neil MacDonald in Somerset in 2007.

With ciders such as Truffler, Reveller and Charmer appearing in more and ⇨

"West Country bittersweet cider apples give certain tannins, which play on parts of the taste buds a culinary apple just won't hit."

more pubs across the UK, Orchard Pig has become one of the most successful of the new wave of artisan cider makers – not bad for a business that started by accident when they made a batch of cider from home-grown apples to drink at a hog roast with friends.

"We got such great comments about our first 'test' batch, we decided to bottle it and continue as a hobby, until at 25,000 bottles it got a little out of hand. With the help of a business loan, it became a proper business and the rest is history," says Quinlan.

Much of Orchard Pig's appeal – apart from the striking and contemporary packaging and branding – is the fact they use West Country cider apples, many locally grown and are based on a farm that has made cider since the 1850s.

Quinlan says: "We've always been dedicated to taste, everything we have done from day one has revolved around this, so once people have tried our ciders, they realise they are onto a winner.

"With more and more landlords and publicans looking for a high quality premium product to complement their venue or menu, we fit the bill. Drinkers also like the fact we use traditional apple varieties because they want a drink with character.

"We have a variety of still and sparkling, bottled and draught ciders. The pubs lead with Reveller. A medium lightly sparkling cider at 4.5% abv, it's the most accessible cider for those drinkers who are looking for a cider away from the ordinary, but also one that's a little bit cheeky.

"There has been a shift in using culinary apples rather than cider apples, though this is quite often down to juicing properties of fruit and what is easiest to grow. West Country bittersweet cider apples give certain tannins, which play on parts of the taste buds a culinary apple just won't hit."

The future for cider

With cider makers dotted around the UK, from Kent to southern Scotland and all points West, the future of this traditional tipple is as rosy as the apples being picked to make them.

But what does the future hold and is there a danger that the cider bubble might burst? Not according to James Russell.

"The big news in the cider world at the moment is what's happening in America, where cider – they call it 'hard cider' – is just beginning to take off. Canny British producers are making deals with American cider makers and distributors, and the possibilities are incredible.

"In Britain, meanwhile, cider continues to grow in popularity. I'm not sure I'd agree that this is a bubble, since cider and perry have been staples of British culture for centuries. I'd say that the situation before Magners came along was unusual, and that normality has now been restored.

National Parks

Running a pub in 'Britain's breathing spaces' By Phil Bryant

There are 15 National Parks in Britain, from the Grampians in Scotland to Dartmoor in Cornwall. Covering 22,660 square kilometres, they are visited by some 80 million people a year, which is good news for scores of inns and pubs that are located in the National Parks.

After serving last orders on 30th March 2011, hundreds of pub landlords and landladies in Hampshire, and West and East Sussex thought about getting some shuteye. Next morning, 1st April, they woke up somewhere else, yet they hadn't travelled an inch. How? They were now in the South Downs National Park, a 100-mile stretch of southern England between Winchester and Eastbourne. The National Parks Authority's newest 'breathing space' had come into being.

The Peak District National Park was the first, created in April 1951. It was followed by the Lake District, whose beauty had been openly celebrated at least since 1775, when the poet Thomas Gray called Grasmere "an unsuspected paradise." The romantic poet William Wordsworth described it as "the loveliest spot that man hath ever found", and by 1810 he was calling the Lake District "a sort of national property".

Other romantic poets too, like Byron and Coleridge, wrote about the inspirational beauty of Britain's 'untamed' countryside, although in reality it was mostly farmed or managed in some way. During the second half of the 19th century there was growing awareness that industrialisation and urbanisation were threatening our more remote areas, but not until 1931 did the government first recommend their protection through designation as national parks. Nothing came of it, though.

In the mid-Forties, the government began examining long-term land use, and 'nature preservation' became part of the post-war reconstruction effort. In 1947 a committee, chaired by Sir Arthur Hobhouse, proposed the creation of twelve national parks in England and Wales. As a result, the National Parks and Access to the Countryside Act was passed two years later. ⇨

"I definitely think being in the park is to our advantage. Our customers often remark about the natural beauty of the area"

By 1957, in addition to those covering the Peak District and the Lake District, national parks had also been established in Snowdonia, Dartmoor, the Pembrokeshire Coast, the North York Moors, the Yorkshire Dales, Exmoor, Northumberland and, lastly, the Brecon Beacons. Another 32 years then passed before a special Act of Parliament gave the Norfolk and Suffolk Broads similar landscape protection, but with the additional statutory purpose of protecting the interests of navigation.

Further special legislation created Loch Lomond & The Trossachs and Cairngorms National Parks in 2002 and 2003 respectively, with New Forest following in 2005, and the South Downs in 2011, even though Hobhouse had earmarked the last two for designation sixty or so years earlier.

Popular with walkers and cyclists

Inns and pubs within a national park recognise the valuable additional marketing opportunities it gives them. One such is **The Inn at Inverbeg**, a popular resting place for travellers for 200 years and now in Loch Lomond & The Trossachs National Park. General manager Andrew Hepburn says: "I think people find it easier to decide on visiting a particular inn or pub, if it's in a national park. In our case, we benefit from the park authority's tourism strategy, in that it both encourages and welcomes tourists, while at the same time carefully manages their impact."

Deep in the Lake District National Park at Hawkshead, between Coniston Water and Windermere, is **The Queen's Head Inn & Restaurant**, owned by Val Edwards and Jane Harvey. A stone's throw from their door is William Wordsworth's old school, still housing the desk on which he carved his name. The inn, surrounded by stunning landscape and traditional Lakeland villages, attracts visitors from all over the world, and Val and Jane's staff are expected to be knowledgeable about walks, cycle trails and other outdoor activities for guests keen to explore.

Val identifies distinct seasons: "Our busier periods tend to be during the school holidays, although September and October are equally full with perhaps more affluent, mature guests and diners seeking a quieter stay. During the winter Hawkshead returns to being a very quiet village, often cut off by heavy snows, although this doesn't deter the more experienced walkers and cyclists."

Being in a park is an advantage

When Walter and Irene Kershaw first saw **The Pheasant Inn at Falstone** in the Northumberland National Park in 1985, they fell in love with it. Now largely retired, they leave day-to-day management to their son Robin, who says: "I definitely think being in the park is to our advantage. Our customers often remark about the natural beauty of the area, without necessarily mentioning the park, but perhaps appreciating how unspoilt these rural backwaters are". The opening in 2008 of Kielder Observatory nearby, which takes advantage of England's darkest skies, has brought a new stream of star-gazing visitors to the inn, especially during the quieter winter months.

About 500 feet above sea level in North Yorks Moors National Park is the charming, 19th-century **Hawnby Inn**, which Dave and Kath Young have run for 14 years. The park, says their website, makes the inn "the perfect base from which to explore this stunning area, ⇨

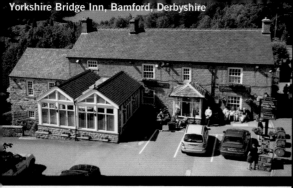
Yorkshire Bridge Inn, Bamford, Derbyshire

The Pheasant, Falstone, Northumberland

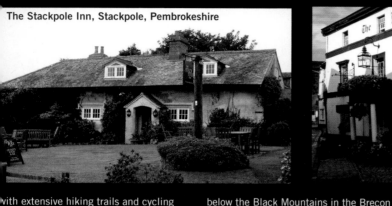
The Stackpole Inn, Stackpole, Pembrokeshire

The Bear Hotel, Crickhowell, Powys

with extensive hiking trails and cycling routes right from our door." And, it adds, the location also makes it a favourite for families, weddings, romantic getaways and, in winter, shooting parties.

In 2012, the Peak District National Park Authority awarded its coveted Environmental Quality Mark to the **Yorkshire Bridge Inn**, in Derbyshire's Hope Valley. Helen Illingworth, who owns the inn with her husband John, says: "We're very lucky to be able to live and work in such a stunning location. The park is a major selling point. Good weather definitely influences the number of visitors, although walkers are always out and about. But as we are quite high up, we can suffer if it snows heavily."

There are three National Parks in Wales – Snowdonia, the Brecon Beacons and Pembrokeshire Coast. In Crickhowell

below the Black Mountains in the Brecon Beacons, is the 15th-century **Bear Hotel**, which Judith Hindmarsh and her son Steve have run since 1978. "Being here has been brilliant for us," says Steve, "not least because for a long time it was the closest national park to London, so we've always had a lot of Londoners, particularly at weekends. There's so much to do here – walking, cycling, gliding, orienteering, climbing, all kinds of country pursuits – so we're busy all year round."

Near the town of Pembroke, Gary and Rebecca Evans run **The Stackpole Inn**, a traditional free house that also happens to be in the National Trust's Stackpole Estate, a listed, designed landscape and internationally important nature reserve. Rebecca has lived in the area all her life: "I never get tired of it. I walk my two lust dogs every day and the I always

something different to see. With the coastal path only fifteen minutes away, walkers come in all year round and many of them comment on how beautiful the area is."

The pretty Somerset village of Exford lies in the middle of Exmoor National Park, where Sara and Dan Whittaker, together with Christopher Kirkbride, run the 17th-century **Crown Hotel**. The inn's website gives the full promotional treatment to Exmoor's beautiful valleys, fast-flowing streams, heather-clad moorland and coastline, where Britain's highest cliffs can be found. "We love being here," enthuses Sara. "Exmoor isn't the largest or busiest National Park, but that's what makes it special. You can go back in time to the good old days before commercialism and get away from it all. Wall and shooters provide year-round trade. In fact, our busiest months are September, October and November."

Shaped over centuries

Further south, in Devon, is what Richard Edlmann calls the "quintessentially English" village of North Bovey. In 2011, Dartmoor National Park's 50th anniversary year, Richard took over the 13th-century **Ring of Bells**. "The village is a great base for walking and exploring the park, which is packed with places to visit and things to do. I'm proud that the pub is still going strong, thanks to great support from locals, who help provide a warm welcome to all our visitors".

Shaped over centuries by free-roaming ponies, cattle and pigs, the landscape of the New Forest National Park in Hampshire is like no other. In its south-eastern corner is **The East End Arms**, owned by John Illsley, a founding member of top British pop band, Dire Straits. On a day-to-day basis the pub is managed by Danielle Ball, who says: "Being in the National Park certainly brings in the visitors, especially walkers and cyclists – even as we speak, there are lots of bikes in the garden. We also get a lot of boaters up from Lymington".

Finally, we reach the South Downs National Park, where Clare Winterbottom and Francis Joyce own **The Thomas Lord** pub in the Hampshire village of West Meon. The pub is named after the founder of Lord's cricket ground, who is buried in the local churchyard. Clare and Francis arrived in October 2012, too late to witness any change arising from designation of the South Downs as a national park the previous year, but already well aware of its huge appeal. On the pub's website, for example, they extol "the stunning scenery to be enjoyed year-round, on foot or by cycle, in the nearby rolling countryside of the lovely Meon Valley". Says Clare: "Groups of walkers often arrive for an early coffee, study the lunch menu, order and then return later."

Also in the South Downs National Park, in the village of Poynings in West Sussex, is the late 19th-century **Royal Oak**, whose general manager, Nick Jerrim, comments: "Visitors often remark on the beauty of the locality. We've always benefited from walkers, cyclists and dog-owners, but it's nice to know that the area now has the added protection and status of being a National Park."

As Nick suggests, the South Downs were, just like all the others, popular areas to visit long before the addition of the words 'National Park'. But what these words do, beyond ensuring their future, is to give their many inns and pubs, particularly those special enough to be in this guide, a further valuable marketing tool, one that should help protect their futures too.

The Broads

The National Parks

England
The Broads
Dartmoor
Exmoor
Lake District
New Forest
Northumberland
North York Moors
Peak District
South Downs
Yorkshire Dales

Scotland
Cairngorms
Loch Lomond & The Trossachs

Wales
Brecon Beacons
Pembrokeshire Coast
Snowdonia

England

BEDFORDSHIRE

BEDFORD
Map 12 TL04

The Embankment

6 The Embankment MK40 3PD ☎ 01234 261332
e-mail: embankment@peachpubs.com
dir: *From M1 junct 13, A421 to Bedford. Left onto A6 to
town centre. Into left lane on river bridge. Into right lane
signed Embankment. Follow around St Paul's Square into
High St, into left lane. Left onto The Embankment*

Mock-Tudor riverside pub with a hospitable atmosphere

On the edge of Bedford's beautifully landscaped
Embankment gardens, this imposing pub sits behind an
outdoor terrace overlooking the River Great Ouse. Dating
from 1891, the building has been renovated and its
Victorian features brought back to life: the open fire,
antique mirrors, vintage tables, sofas in racing green and
silk lampshades. Food choices range from deli boards to
full meals, such as wood pigeon Kiev with a pomegranate
and bacon salad, followed by sun-dried tomato gnocchi,
confit peppers, basil purée and a parmesan crisp, and
finishing with pineapple upside down cake. Change of
landlord.

Open all day all wk Closed: 25 Dec **Bar Meals** L served all
wk 12-6 D served all wk 6-10 Av main course £13 food
served all day **Restaurant** L served all wk 12-6 D served
all wk 6-10 Fixed menu price fr £12 Av 3 course à la carte
fr £24 food served all day ⊕ PEACH PUBS ◀ Wells Eagle
IPA & Bombardier, Young's ♂ Aspall. ⛾ 16
Facilities Non-diners area ♣ (Bar Outside area) ♦♦
Children's portions Outside area ⅋ Parking Wi-fi
▭ (notice required)

The Park Pub & Kitchen

PICK OF THE PUBS

98 Kimbolton Rd MK40 2PA ☎ 01234 273929
e-mail: info@theparkbedford.co.uk
dir: *M1 junct 14, A509 follow Newport Pagnell signs, then
A422, A428 onto A6. right into Tavistock St (A600). Left
into Broadway, 1st left into Kimbolton Rd. Pub 0.5m*

Smart, bright, and spacious, a stylish mix of old and new

Built in the 1900s, this fine-looking pub is a stone's
throw from Bedford Park, just a little way out of town. If
you expect the smartly decorated exterior to promise
similar treatment inside, you won't be disappointed,
because the interior, with its fireplaces, flagstone floors
and beamed ceilings looks and feels very good. Beyond
the wrap-around bar are a spacious conservatory, relaxing
conservatory and airy garden room leading to an outdoor
area, where heaters permit comfortable drinking and
dining in less than heatwave conditions. In the bar is
Eagle IPA from the town's Wells and Young's brewery,
whose other flagship brew, Bombardier, is also on duty.
Menus reflect local sourcing, with daily fish specials
made from top-quality, market-fresh fish, and main
dishes such as steak and coriander burger with Swiss
cheese, bacon and house tomato chutney; or slow-roasted

pork collar with prune stuffing, osso buco, saffron risotto
and winter greens.

Open all day all wk **Bar Meals** L served Mon-Sat 12-3,
Sun 12-8 D served Mon-Sat 6-10, Sun 12-8 **Restaurant** L
served Mon-Sat 12-3, Sun 12-8 D served Mon-Sat 6-10,
Sun 12-8 ⊕ CHARLES WELLS ◀ Bombardier, Eagle IPA
♂ Symonds. ⛾ 33 **Facilities** Non-diners area ♦♦ Children's
portions Garden ⅋ Parking Wi-fi ▭ (notice required)

The Three Tuns

57 Main Rd, Biddenham MK40 4BD ☎ 01234 354847
e-mail: enquiries@threetunsbiddenham.com
dir: *On A428 from Bedford towards Northampton 1st left
signed Biddenham. Into village, pub on left*

Thatched pub with food of a high standard

In a pretty village, this stone-built pub has a large
garden with a patio and decking, and a separate
children's play area. Owner Chris Smith worked for French
celebrity chef Jean-Christophe Novelli for a number of
years and now produces dishes such as roast partridge
cooked in rosemary and juniper berry salt; wild and field
mushroom crumble; and banana tarte Tatin with coconut
and tarragon parfait. Each dish on the à la carte is
matched with a recommended wine. The two-course set
menu is excellent value. In the garden is a long-disused,
possibly haunted, morgue, the oldest building
hereabouts.

Open all wk 12-3 5.30-late (Fri-Sat all day Sun12-6) **Bar
Meals** L served Tue-Sun 12-2.30 D served Tue-Sat 6-9.30
Av main course £12-£14 **Restaurant** L served Tue-Sat
12-2.30, Sun 12-4 D served Tue-Sat 6-9.30 Av 3 course à
la carte fr £20 ⊕ GREENE KING ◀ IPA, Guinness, Guest
ale ♂ Aspall. ⛾ 16 **Facilities** Non-diners area ♦♦
Children's portions Play area Family room Garden ⅋
Parking Wi-fi ▭

BOLNHURST
Map 12 TL05

The Plough at Bolnhurst ⊛

PICK OF THE PUBS

Kimbolton Rd MK44 2EX ☎ 01234 376274
e-mail: theplough@bolnhurst.com
dir: *On B660 N of Bedford*

Tudor inn with notable food and wine

Six miles north of Bedford, this whitewashed 15th-century
country inn has a fresh, country-style decor coupled with
original features such as thick walls, low beams and
great open fires. The impressive choice of real ales and
inspired wine list are matched by a delicious menu
prepared by Raymond Blanc-trained Martin Lee and his
team of skilled chefs. The menu is driven by the freshest
local and regional produce and specialist foods gathered
from all corners. The result is an ever-changing choice of
unique dishes, which have gained The Plough an AA
Rosette. Start with roast pigeon breast, pickled onions,
crispy celeriac and chilli flakes with red wine sauce,
followed by roast fillet of monkfish, cannellini bean purée
with chorizo and confit red pepper. Steamed syrup
pudding makes a tempting dessert but do leave room for

the cheeseboard, with its astonishing choice of British,
Italian and French varieties.

Open Tue-Sat 12-3 6.30-11 (Sun 12-3) Closed: 1 Jan,
2wks Jan, Mon & Sun eve **Bar Meals** L served Tue-Sun
12-2 D served Tue-Sat 6.30-9.30 Av main course £18
Restaurant L served Tue-Sun 12-2 D served Tue-Sat
6.30-9.30 Fixed menu price fr £20 Av 3 course à la carte
fr £30 ⊕ FREE HOUSE ◀ Adnams Southwold Bitter,
Potton Village Bike, Fuller's London Pride, Hopping Mad
Brainstorm, Church End Goat's Milk ♂ Aspall Harry
Sparrow. ⛾ 13 **Facilities** Non-diners area ♦♦ Children's
portions Garden Parking Wi-fi ▭

BROOM
Map 12 TL14

The Cock

23 High St SG18 9NA ☎ 01767 314411
e-mail: broom@camelotinns.fsnet.co.uk
dir: *Off B658 SW of Biggleswade. 1m from A1*

Step back in time for good real ales

Unspoilt to this day with its intimate quarry-tiled rooms
with latched doors and panelled walls, this 17th-century
establishment is known as 'The Pub with no Bar'. Real
ales are served straight from casks racked by the cellar
steps. A straightforward pub-grub menu includes burgers,
jackets, sandwiches, omelettes and ploughman's. More
substantial offerings are scampi and chicken nuggets.
There are also veggie options (Stilton and vegetable
crumble; curry and rice) and specials (sirloin steak; half a
roast chicken). A skittle room is available for hire.

Open all day all wk **Bar Meals** L served all wk 12-2.30
D served Mon-Sat 6-9 **Restaurant** L served all wk 12-2.30
D served Mon-Sat 6-9 ⊕ GREENE KING ◀ Abbot Ale, IPA,
Guest ales. **Facilities** Non-diners area ♣ (Bar Garden) ♦♦
Children's menu Children's portions Play area Family
room Garden ⅋ Parking ▭ (notice required)

EATON BRAY
Map 11 SP92

The White Horse

Market Square LU6 2DG ☎ 01525 220231
e-mail: tom-dunnell@hotmail.co.uk
dir: *A5 N of Dunstable onto A505, left in 1m, follow signs*

Traditional warm and cosy inn

Independently owned and managed, this 300-year-old
village inn with picnic tables out front retains its
reputation for great home-cooked food and well-kept real
ales, including Sharp's Doom Bar and Greene King IPA.
Oak beams and horse brasses add to the traditional
charms of the interior. Typical starters might be tian of
smoked salmon and crab, and Stilton-stuffed
mushrooms, while chicken or vegetable curry, and Whitby
Bay scampi make filling main courses. Coq au vin or tuna
Niçoise might appear as specials. Traditional desserts
include Eton Mess and Bakewell tart. There is a good
value fixed-price lunch menu.

Open all wk 11.30-3 6.30-11 (Fri-Sun 11.30-11.30) **Bar
Meals** L served all wk 12-2.15 D served all wk 7-9.30 Av
main course £10 **Restaurant** L served all wk 12-2.15
D served all wk 7-9.30 Fixed menu price fr £6 Av 3 course

Save on hotels. Book at **theAA.com/hotel**

BEDFORDSHIRE 27 **ENGLAND**

à la carte fr £25 ⊕ PUNCH TAVERNS ◀ Greene King IPA, Morland Old Speckled Hen, Sharp's Doom Bar Ö Aspall. ♚ 10 **Facilities** Non-diners area ♦♦ Children's menu Children's portions Play area Family room Garden ⊼ Parking Wi-fi

HARROLD   Map 11 SP95

The Muntjac

71 High St MK43 7BJ ☎ 01234 721500
e-mail: muntjacharrold@hotmail.co.uk
dir: *Telephone for directions*

Free house with an Indian restaurant

This 17th-century former coaching inn is quite happy to be a little unorthodox. Independently run Harrold's Indian Cuisine restaurant offers dishes cooked to order to eat in or take away, its extensive menu featuring all the popular fish, meat, poultry and vegetarian dishes, as well as the less often encountered tandoori chicken mossallam, duck Darjeeling, and tawa specialities cooked using a traditional iron plate. A few English dishes are also available. The bar serves fine wines and Ringwood Best, Abbot Ale, and regularly-changing guest ales from local breweries.

Open all wk Mon-Thu 5.30-11 (Fri 12.30-12 Sat 12-12 Sun 12.30-10.30) ⊕ FREE HOUSE ◀ Ringwood Best Bitter, Greene King Abbot Ale, Guest ales Ö Symonds Founders Reserve. **Facilities** ♦♦ Children's portions Garden Parking **Notes** ⊗

IRELAND   Map 12 TL14

The Black Horse

SG17 5QL ☎ 01462 811398
e-mail: cctaverns@aol.com
dir: *From S: M1 junct 12, A5120 to Flitwick. Onto A507 by Redbourne School. Follow signs for A1, Shefford (cross A6). Left onto A600 towards Bedford*

Traditional and modern comfortably combined

A mix of light and dark beams, an inglenook fire and low ceilings combine with a bright, airy, chic interior in this 17th-century inn. The flower-rich garden and courtyard dining are popular in warmer weather. Grab a pint of Adnams, or choose from the excellent wine list, and settle down to appreciate the tempting range of dishes – maybe pan-fried pigeon breast with wild mushrooms, baby spinach and potato; pan-fried free range chicken breast with a Calvados and blackcurrant glaze, served with sautéed celeriac, fennel, garden peas and buttered tagliolini pasta; and a dessert of lemon spotted dick. Individual dietary requirements are catered for.

Open all wk 12-3 6-12 (Sun 12-6) Closed: 25-26 Dec, 1 Jan **Bar Meals** L served Mon-Sat 12-2.30, Sun 12-5 D served Mon-Sat 6.30-10 Av main course £10-£15 **Restaurant** L served Mon-Sat 12-2.30, Sun 12-5 D served Mon-Sat 6.30-10 Fixed menu price fr £12.95 ⊕ FREE HOUSE ◀ Adnams, Sharp's Doom Bar, Shepherd Neame Spitfire Ö Westons Stowford Press. ♚ 20 **Facilities** Non-diners area ♦♦ Children's portions Garden ⊼ Parking Wi-fi ▄▄ (notice required)

KEYSOE   Map 12 TL06

The Chequers

Pertenhall Rd, Brook End MK44 2HR ☎ 01234 708678
e-mail: chequers.keysoe@tesco.net
dir: *On B660, 7m N of Bedford. 3m S of Kimbolton*

Classic pub grub in a peaceful country pub

This peaceful 15th-century country pub has been in the same safe hands for over 25 years. No games machines, pool tables or jukeboxes disturb the simple pleasures of well-kept ales and great home-made food. The menu offers pub stalwarts like ploughman's; home-made steak-and-ale pie; pan-fried trout; glazed lamb cutlets and a variety of grilled steaks; and a blackboard displays further choice plus the vegetarian options. For a lighter option try the home-made chicken liver pâté or soup, fried brie with cranberries, or plain or toasted sandwiches.

Open Wed-Sun 11.30-2.30 6.30-11 (Mon 11.30-2.30) Closed: Mon eve & Tue **Bar Meals** L served Wed-Mon 12-2 D served Wed-Sun 6.30-9 ⊕ FREE HOUSE ◀ Hook Norton Hooky Bitter, Fuller's London Pride Ö Westons Stowford Press. **Facilities** Non-diners area ♦♦ Children's menu Children's portions Play area Family room Garden Parking ▄▄ (notice required) **Notes** ⊗

LINSLADE   Map 11 SP92

The Globe Inn

Globe Ln, Old Linslade LU7 2TA ☎ 01525 373338
e-mail: 6458@greeneking.co.uk
dir: *N of Leighton Buzzard*

Canalside pub that's a hive of activity

A very homely old pub, creaking with the character of the small Georgian farmhouse and stables it once was; beams, log fires, partial weatherboarding and a wrinkly roof line. Fronting the Grand Union Canal at the end of a no-through lane, it's a marvellous place to linger watching boating activity, supping on Greene King beers and choosing from a Pandora's Box of meals, varying from traditional meaty favourites like grilled pork chop to chicken fajitas, vegetarian lentil shepherd's pie, and smoked salmon and king prawn salad. There's a well-appointed restaurant, and children are made welcome with a play area in the tree-shaded garden.

Open all day all wk 11-11 **Bar Meals** L served all wk 11-11 D served all wk 11-11 food served all day **Restaurant** L served all wk 11-11 D served all wk 11-11 food served all day ⊕ GREENE KING ◀ Abbot Ale & IPA, Morland Old Speckled Hen Ö Aspall. ♚ 16 **Facilities** Non-diners area ❖ (Bar Garden) ♦♦ Children's menu Children's portions Play area Garden ⊼ Beer festival Parking ▄▄

NORTHILL   Map 12 TL14

The Crown

2 Ickwell Rd SG18 9AA ☎ 01767 627337
e-mail: enquiries@crownnorthill.co.uk
dir: *In village centre, adjacent to church*

Greene King pub with a wide-ranging menu

A delightful 16th-century pub with smart, modern interior decor. Greene King ales are well kept, and Doughty's Brasserie is undoubtedly a major attraction. Dig into sharing deli boards or sub rolls and panini with the likes of 21-day hung roast topside of beef, spring onions and horseradish mayo. Or how about mains such as chargrilled calves' liver and bacon, colcannon potatoes, caramelised onions and red wine sauce? The garden has plenty of tables for alfresco eating, and a children's play area.

Open all day all wk **Bar Meals** L served Mon-Fri 12-2.30, Sat 12-10, Sun 12-6 D served Mon-Fri 6.30-10, Sat 12-10, Sun 12-6 Av main course £8 **Restaurant** L served Mon-Fri 12-2.30, Sat 12-10 Sun 12-6 D served Mon-Fri 6.30-10, Sat 12-10, Sun 12-6 Av 3 course à la carte fr £30 ⊕ GREENE KING ◀ IPA & Abbot Ale, Morland Old Speckled Hen, Hardys & Hansons Olde Trip, Guest ales Ö Aspall. ♚ 9 **Facilities** Non-diners area ♦♦ Children's menu Children's portions Play area Garden Parking Wi-fi ▄▄

ODELL   Map 11 SP95

The Bell

Horsefair Ln MK43 7AU ☎ 01234 720254
dir: *Telephone for directions*

A fine example of a traditional village pub

Stone walls, open fireplaces and exposed beams provide the character for this 16th-century thatched village pub, with a spacious garden leading down to the River Ouse adding even more. But it doesn't stop there, not when you factor in the quality home-cooked food, such as ricotta and tomato tortellini; beef enchiladas; breaded fillet of haddock with home-made tartare sauce; and Irish beef stew. Sandwiches, baguettes and omelettes are also served at lunchtime. There is a summer beer festival.

Open all wk Mon-Thu 11.30-3 5-11.30 (Fri-Sun all day) **Bar Meals** L served Mon-Sat 11.30-2.30, Sun 12-7.30 D served Mon-Sat 6-9, Sun 12-7.30 ⊕ GREENE KING ◀ IPA, Abbot Ale, Seasonal ales Ö Westons Stowford Press. ♚ 8 **Facilities** Non-diners area ❖ (Bar Restaurant Garden) ♦♦ Children's menu Children's portions Garden ⊼ Beer festival Parking ▄▄

OLD WARDEN Map 12 TL14

Hare and Hounds

PICK OF THE PUBS

SG18 9HQ ☎ 01767 627225
e-mail: thehareandhounds@hotmail.co.uk
dir: *From Bedford on A306 right (or left from A600) to Old Warden. Also accessed from Biggleswade rdbt on A1*

Smart village inn with contemporary menus

Located beneath wooded hills in a peaceful corner of Bedfordshire, this elegant village dining pub reflects the eye-catching, somewhat ornate architectural style here at Old Warden estate village; the local Shuttleworth Estate is now world-renowned for the collection of vintage aircraft and automobiles at the nearby aerodrome. The interiors of the bar and the three chic dining rooms feature timbered walls, warm red and cream colours and fresh flowers; clean, crisp lines and contemporary furnishings. Wines include some from the local Warden Abbey vineyard, whilst beers come courtesy of Wells and Young's; Eagle IPA a regular favourite. Provenance of the food is particularly important to chef/patron Jago Hurt; his web of local suppliers guarantee the freshest produce, exampled by Summerhill Farm-shop sausages accompanied by rich red wine, bacon, red onion and mushroom casserole. The British cheese board is exceptional.

Open Tue-Sat 12-3 6-11 (Sun 12-10.30) Closed: 25 & 26 Dec, 1 Jan, Mon (ex BHs) **Bar Meals** L served all wk 12-2 D served all wk 6.30-9 **Restaurant** L served Mon-Sat 12-2, Sun 12-3.30 D served Mon-Sat 6.30-9 ⊕ CHARLES WELLS ◀ Eagle IPA, Young's Ö Aspall. ♟ 13 **Facilities** Non-diners area ♣ (Bar Garden) ♦♦ Children's portions Family room Garden ⋒ Parking

---

SALFORD Map 11 SP93

The Swan

PICK OF THE PUBS

2 Warendon Rd MK17 8BD ☎ 01908 281008
e-mail: swan@peachpubs.com
dir: *M1 junct 13, follow signs to Salford*

Smart gastro-pub with a new look

In this attractive village setting you'll find the tile-hung, Edwardian-era Swan, which has seen a change of landlord, a new kitchen garden and smokehouse, and a transformed interior featuring earthy green tones. The lively bar with its comfy leather armchairs makes you feel instantly at home, as does the eating area, where the big French doors can be thrown open to the garden. Peer through the feature window into the kitchen to watch the chefs preparing dishes from top, locally supplied or home-grown ingredients. Sandwiches, snacks and deli boards are available throughout the day. Lunch or dinner main courses include seared tuna loin, 28-day-aged chargrilled steaks and ox cheek and ale pie. The good value set menu is available Monday to Thursday and a sensibly priced wine list offers plenty by the glass. The restored barn with a large central dining table can be

used for a private dinner. There's a busy social calendar of events.

Open all day all wk 11am-mdnt (Sun 12-10.30) Closed: 25 Dec **Bar Meals** L served all wk 12-6 D served Mon-Sat 6-9.45, Sun 6-9.30 Av main course £16 food served all day **Restaurant** L served all wk 12-3 D served Mon-Sat 6-9.45, Sun 6-9.30 Fixed menu price fr £14 ⊕ PEACH PUBS ◀ Sharp's Doom Bar Ö Aspall. ♟ 12 **Facilities** Non-diners area ♣ (Bar Garden) ♦♦ Children's portions Garden ⋒ Parking Wi-fi ▭

SOULDROP Map 11 SP96

The Bedford Arms

High St MK44 1EY ☎ 01234 781384
e-mail: thebedfordarms@tiscali.co.uk
dir: *From Rushden take A6 towards Bedford. In 6m right into Stocking Lane to Souldrop. Pub 50mtrs on right*

Children welcome at this village free house

The time-honoured hallmarks of low beams, open fireplace, horse brasses, tankards and bar skittles are all present and correct in this over 300-year-old pub. On the bar counter, pump badges declare the presence of, among others, Hopping Mad's Brainstorm from Olney and Evershed's real cider. Shelves are laden with china, and artworks are for sale in the cottage-style dining room, where a good selection of pub dishes includes chicken or beef jalfrezi; liver, bacon and onions; triple-tail scampi; and signature dishes of steak and ale pie, and leek and Stilton bread and butter pudding. Play boules in the garden.

Open 12-3 6-11 (Fri-Sat 12-11 Sun 12-10) Closed: Mon (ex BHs) **Bar Meals** L served Tue-Sat 12-2, Sun 12-4 D served Tue-Sat 6.30-9 **Restaurant** L served Tue-Sat 12-2, Sun 12-4 D served Tue-Sat 6.30-9 ⊕ FREE HOUSE ◀ Phipps NBC Red Star, Greene King IPA, Black Sheep, Hopping Mad Brainstorm, Guest ale Ö Westons Stowford Press, Evershed's Cider. ♟ 11 **Facilities** Non-diners area ♦♦ Children's menu Children's portions Garden ⋒ Parking

---

SOUTHILL Map 12 TL14

The White Horse

High St SG18 9LD ☎ 01462 813364
e-mail: whitehorsesouthill@live.co.uk
dir: *Telephone for directions*

Pub with family appeal in pretty village

A country pub with traditional values, happily accommodating the needs of children in the large patio gardens, and those who like to sit outside on cool days enjoying a well-kept pint (the patio has heaters). Offering traditional English food, fish, vegetarian and children's dishes, grilled steaks are a big draw in the restaurant but other main courses from the extensive menu include rack of barbecue spare ribs; home-made game or fisherman's pie; plus choices from the chef's specials board. Salads, ploughman's, sandwiches, baguettes and wraps are also available.

Open all wk 11.30-3 6-11 (Sat 11.30-11 Sun 12-10.30) Closed: 26 Dec **Bar Meals** L served Mon-Fri 12-2, Sat-Sun

all day D served Mon-Fri 6-9.30, Sat-Sun all day **Restaurant** L served Mon-Fri 12-2, Sat-Sun all day D served Mon-Fri 6-9.30, Sat-Sun all day ⊕ ENTERPRISE INNS ◀ Greene King IPA, Banks & Taylor Golden Fox, Sharp's Doom Bar. ♟ 8 **Facilities** Non-diners area ♦♦ Children's menu Play area Garden ⋒ Parking Wi-fi ▭ (notice required)

STANBRIDGE Map 11 SP92

The Five Bells

Station Rd LU7 9JF ☎ 01525 210224
e-mail: fivebells@fullers.co.uk
dir: *Off A505 E of Leighton Buzzard*

A stylish and relaxing setting

The Five Bells is a whitewashed 400-year-old village inn, which has been delightfully renovated and revived. The bar features lots of bare wood as well as comfortable armchairs and polished, rug-strewn floors. The modern decor extends to the bright, airy 75-cover dining room with its oak beams and paintings. There's also a spacious garden with patio and lawns. The inn uses local suppliers where possible to offer farm-assured chicken and beef, and sustainable seafood. The menu typically includes dishes such as Woburn Abbey venison burger, and slow-cooked pressed Suffolk pork belly, which are complemented by light lunches and blackboard daily specials.

Open all day all wk 11-11 (Sun 12-10.30) **Bar Meals** L served Mon-Sat 12-10, Sun 12-9 D served Mon-Sat 12-10, Sun 12-9 food served all day **Restaurant** food served all day ⊕ FULLER'S ◀ Fuller's London Pride, George Gale & Co Seafarers, Guest Ale Ö Aspall. ♟ 8 **Facilities** ♣ (Bar Garden) ♦♦ Children's menu Children's portions Garden ⋒ Parking ▭

STUDHAM Map 11 TL01

The Bell in Studham NEW

Dunstable Rd LU6 2QG ☎ 01582 872460
e-mail: info@thebellinstudham.co.uk
dir: *M1 junct 9, A5 towards Dunstable. Left onto B4540 to Kensworth, B4541 to Studham*

Something for everyone in haunted old inn

The 500-year-old Bell makes two claims, neither likely to be challenged: it's in Bedfordshire's southernmost village, and it's the county's highest pub, which accounts for the panoramic views from the garden. Among several ghosts are Ted and his dog in the cellar bar; maybe Ted can't keep away from the locally brewed real ales and ten wines by the glass. Home-made English classics include fish and triple-cooked chips with 'lashings of vinegar', and traditional Sunday roasts. Weekday lunchtime deals cover pie of the day, pastas, and Italian thin-crust pizzas (also 'to go'). Check the summer beer and cider festival dates.

Open all day all wk **Bar Meals** L served Mon-Fri 12-2.30, Sat-Sun all day D served Mon-Fri 6-9.30, Sat-Sun all day **Restaurant** L served Mon-Fri 12-2.30, Sat-Sun all day D served Mon-Fri 6-9.30, Sat-Sun all day ⊕ FREE HOUSE

Save on hotels. Book at **theAA.com/hotel**

BEDFORDSHIRE – BERKSHIRE 29 **ENGLAND**

⬛ Greene King IPA, Guest ales. ⬗ 10
Facilities Non-diners area ☀ (Bar Garden) ⬥ Children's portions Garden ⌂ Beer festival Cider festival Parking Wi-fi ▭ (notice required)

The Anchor Inn

1 Dunstable Rd LU7 9PU ☎ **01525 211404**
dir: *Exit A5 at Tilsworth. In 1m pub on right at 3rd bend*

Classic Victorian country dining pub with a garden that's great for kids

The only pub in a Saxon village, The Anchor dates from 1878. Alan the landlord and his son, Vincent the chef, pride themselves on their fresh food and well-kept beers and guest ales. An acre of garden includes patio seating for alfresco dining, an adventure playground and a barbecue. A current menu lists the likes of sausage and mash; Thai chicken curry; pan-fried salmon steak; gnocchi and button mushrooms; and pie of the day. Also available are a selection of tortilla wraps and baguettes.

Open all day all wk 12-11.30 **Bar Meals** L served all wk 12-5 D served all wk 5-10 Av main course £12 food served all day **Restaurant** L served all wk 12-5 D served all wk 5-10 Av 3 course à la carte fr £25 food served all day ⊕ GREENE KING ⬛ IPA & Abbot Ale, Guest ales.
Facilities Non-diners area ⬥ Children's menu Children's portions Play area Garden ⌂ Parking Wi-fi ▭ (notice required)

The Birch at Woburn

20 Newport Rd MK17 9HX ☎ **01525 290295**
e-mail: ctaverns@aol.com
dir: *Telephone for directions*

Serious about good, locally sourced food

Close to Woburn Abbey and the Safari Park, this smart family-run establishment is located opposite Woburn Championship Golf Course and a short hop from junction 13 of the M1. The pub has built its reputation on friendly service and freshly cooked food; the kitchen team is passionate about sourcing ingredients from local farms and estates. The menu offers a range of English and continental dishes, and there is a griddle area where customers can select their steaks and fish, which are then cooked to your liking by the chefs.

Open 12-3 6-12 Closed: 25-26 Dec, 1 Jan, Sun eve **Bar Meals** L served all wk 12-2.30 D served Mon-Sat 6-10 **Restaurant** L served all wk 12-2.30 D served Mon-Sat 6-10 ⊕ FREE HOUSE ⬛ Fuller's London Pride, Adnams. ⬗ 12 **Facilities** Non-diners area ⬥ Children's portions Parking ▭ (notice required)

The Black Horse

1 Bedford St MK17 9QB ☎ **01525 290210**
e-mail: blackhorse@peachpubs.com
dir: *In town centre on A4012*

Georgian coaching inn serving seasonal fare

Right in the middle of the pretty village of Woburn, this 18th-century inn cuts an elegant figure. Behind the Georgian frontage, the original coaching inn feel of the cosy bar has been retained and complemented with a chic, relaxed dining area where seasonal, locally sourced food drives the all-day menus. Cornish mack bap, lettuce and tartare sauce makes a light lunch or start with potted rabbit and smoked bacon, sweet pickled onions, toasted walnut salad and rustic bread before Jimmy Butler's free-range bangers and mash and onion gravy, and salted fudge Valrhona chocolate mousse and banana ice cream to finish.

Open all day all wk 11-11 (Sat 11am-11.30pm) Closed: 25 Dec **Bar Meals** L served all wk 12-6 D served all wk 6-9.45 food served all day **Restaurant** L served all wk 12-3 D served all wk 6-9.45 ⊕ PEACH PUBS ⬛ Greene King IPA & Abbot Ale, Morland Old Golden Hen, Guest ale ♂ Aspall. ⬗ 10 **Facilities** Non-diners area ☀ (Bar Garden) ⬥ Children's portions Garden ⌂ Wi-fi ▭

The Tavistock Bar & Lounge

The Inn at Woburn, George St MK17 9PX
☎ **01525 290441**
e-mail: inn@woburn.co.uk
dir: *M1 junct 13, left signed Woburn. In Woburn left at T-junct*

Convivial bar for a drink and meal after a Woburn Abbey visit

Part of The Inn at Woburn, a coaching inn once used by mail coaches travelling from London to the north, The Tavistock Bar offers an informal setting in which to enjoy Wells Bombardier and Eagle real ales, and a wide range of wines, including 28 by the glass. In addition, an all-day bar menu offers light snacks and meals features sandwiches, wraps, salads, pie of the day, grilled sirloin steak, and salmon and crab Thai fish cake. Less often encountered favourites are eggs Florentine and Benedict.

Open all day all wk **Bar Meals** L served all wk 12-10 D served all wk 12-10 food served all day **Restaurant** L served all wk 12-2 D served all wk 6.30-9.30 ⊕ FREE HOUSE ⬛ Wells Bombardier, Eagle IPA. ⬗ 28 **Facilities** Non-diners area ⬥ Children's menu Children's portions Outside area Parking Wi-fi ▭ (notice required)

Hinds Head

Wasing Ln RG7 4LX ☎ **0118 971 2194**
e-mail: hindshead@fullers.co.uk
dir: *M4 junct 12, A4 towards Newbury, left on A340 towards Basingstoke, 2m to village*

Charming pub with many original features

This 17th-century inn with its distinctive clock and bell tower still incorporates the village lock-up, which was last used in 1865. The former brewhouse behind the pub creates an additional dining area. The menu features home-made British choices with international influences. Dishes range from a meze board to share; country pie of the week; rice noodle salad with prawns; leek and cheese crumble; honey-glazed roast salmon; and lunchtime jackets and sandwiches.

Open all wk Mon-Thu 11-11 (Fri-Sat 11am-mdnt Sun 11-10.30) **Bar Meals** L served Mon-Sat 12-3, Sun 12-6 D served Mon-Sat 6-9, Sun 12-6 **Restaurant** L served Mon-Sat 12-3, Sun 12-6 D served Mon-Sat 6-9, Sun 12-6 ⊕ FULLER'S ⬛ London Pride & ESB, Guest ales ♂ Aspall. ⬗ 12 **Facilities** Non-diners area ☀ (Bar Garden) ⬥ Children's menu Children's portions Family room Garden ⌂ Parking Wi-fi

The Bell Inn

RG8 9SE ☎ **01635 578272**
dir: *Just off B4009 (Newbury to Streatley road)*

Well-kept local ales in timewarp setting

Beginning life as a manor house in 1340, The Bell has reputedly been in the same family for 200 years: ask Mr Macaulay, the landlord - he's been here for over three decades. A 300-year-old, one-handed clock still stands in the taproom 'keeping imperfect time', and the rack for the spit-irons and clockwork roasting jack are still over the fireplace. One might be surprised to discover that an establishment without a restaurant can hold its own in a world of smart gastro-pubs. But The Bell survives thanks to hot, filled rolls and cracking pints of Arkell's plus local farmhouse ciders.

Open Tue-Sat 11-3 6-11 (Sun 12-3 7-10.30) Closed: 25 Dec, Mon (open BH Mon L only) **Bar Meals** L served Tue-Sat 11-2.30, Sun 12-2.30 D served Tue-6-9.30, Sun 7-9 ⊕ FREE HOUSE ⬛ Arkell's Kingsdown Special Ale & 3B, West Berkshire Old Tyler & Maggs' Magnificent Mild, Guest ales ♂ Upton's Farmhouse, Tutts Clump, Lilley's Pear & Apple. **Facilities** Non-diners area ☀ (Bar Garden) ⬥ Garden Parking **Notes** 🐾

ASCOT — Map 6 SU96

The Thatched Tavern

Cheapside Rd SL5 7QG ☎ 01344 620874
e-mail: enquiries@thethatchedtavern.co.uk
dir: *Follow Ascot Racecourse signs. Through Ascot 1st left (Cheapside). 1.5m, pub on left*

Modern grub in a historic pub

En route to Windsor Castle, Queen Victoria's carriage was allegedly sometimes spotted outside this 400-year-old, flagstone-floored, low-ceilinged pub, while what the history books call 'her faithful servant' John Brown knocked a few back inside. The sheltered garden makes a fine spot to enjoy a Fuller's real ale, a glass of wine and, for lunch, ciabatta like sausage and red onion marmalade or a ploughman's. For something more substantial try smoked haddock, spring onion and Atlantic prawn fishcake with parsley sauce, then free-range chicken breast on wilted spinach and dauphinoise potatoes with a chorizo and Puy lentil sauce.

Open all wk Mon-Thu 12-3 5.30-11 (Fri-Sun all day) **Bar Meals** L served Mon-Sat 12-2.30 Av main course £13 **Restaurant** L served Mon-Sat 12-2.30, Sun 12-3 D served Mon-Sat 7-9.45, Sun 7-9 Fixed menu price fr £16.50 Av 3 course à la carte fr £23 ⊕ FREE HOUSE ◀ Fuller's London Pride, Guinness Ö Westons Stowford Press. ☕ 11
Facilities Non-diners area ❖ Children's portions Garden Parking Wi-fi

---

ASHMORE GREEN — Map 5 SU56

The Sun in the Wood

Stoney Ln RG18 9HF ☎ 01635 42377
e-mail: suninthewood@wadworth.co.uk
dir: *From A34 at Robin Hood Rdbt left to Shaw, at mini rdbt right then 7th left into Stoney Ln 1.5m, pub on left*

Country pub surrounded by woodland

The Sun is a country pub and restaurant surrounded by beautiful mature woodland. A new look to the interior has been introduced to the lounge bar and restaurant, and beams and tables were stripped back to their natural hue. The menu proffers reliable starters such as Scottish smoked salmon and prawn mayonnaise salad; a typical main course from the carte is turkey, ham and leek pie; and home-made puddings cater for most allergy sufferers.

Open all wk 12-3 6-11 (Sat 12-11 Sun 12-8) **Bar Meals** L served Mon-Fri 12-2.30, Sat 12-9.30, Sun 12-5 D served Mon-Fri 6-9.30, Sat 12-9.30, Sun 12-5 **Restaurant** L served Mon-Fri 12-2.30, Sat 12-9.30, Sun 12-5 D served Mon-Fri 6-9.30, Sat 12-9.30, Sun 12-5 ⊕ WADWORTH ◀ 6X, Henry's Original IPA, The Bishop's Tipple Ö Westons Stowford Press. ☕ 15
Facilities Non-diners area ❖ (Bar) ❖ Children's menu Children's portions Play area Garden Parking Wi-fi

---

BOXFORD — Map 5 SU47

The Bell at Boxford

Lambourn Rd RG20 8DD ☎ 01488 608721
e-mail: paul@bellatboxford.com
dir: *M4 junct 14, A338 towards Wantage. Right onto B4000 to x-rds, signed Boxford. Or from A34 junct 13 towards Hungerford, right at rdbt onto B4000. At x-rds right to Boxford. Pub signed*

Seafood specials in a pretty mock-Tudor setting

At the heart of the lovely Lambourn Valley, close to Newbury Racecourse, this mock-Tudor country pub, boasts a period main bar in the part of the building dating back to the 17th century. Alfresco dining in flower-laden heated terraces offers hog roasts and barbecues and there's a good range of local ales, and now also Stowford Press cider on draught; all 60 wines on the list are available by the glass. Feast on seafood specials, beef and ale pie topped with three cheese mash or thin crust or rolled crust pizzas, also available to take away.

Open all day all wk **Bar Meals** L served Mon-Sat 12-2 (pizza Mon-Sat 2.30-7), Sun 12-9 D served Mon-Sat 7-10.30 (pizza 6.30-10.30), Sun 7-9.30 food served all day **Restaurant** L served Mon-Sat 12-2.30, Sun 12-7 D served Mon-Sat 7-9.30, Sun 7-9 ⊕ FREE HOUSE ◀ Wadworth The Bishop's Tipple, 6X & Henry's Original IPA, Guinness, West Berkshire Good Old Boy Ö Westons Stowford Press, Lilley's Apples & Pears. ☕ 60
Facilities Non-diners area ❖ (Bar Garden) ❖ Children's portions Garden Parking Wi-fi ▭ (notice required)

BRAY — Map 6 SU97

The Crown Inn ◉◉
PICK OF THE PUBS

High St SL6 2AH ☎ 01628 621936
dir: *M4 junct 8, A308(M) signed Maidenhead (Central). At next rdbt, right onto A308 signed Bray & Windsor. 0.5m, left onto B3028 signed Bray. In village, pub on left*

Cosy inn in Thames-side village

Half-timbered outside, this Tudor building explodes with the character of long gone days inside, with heavy beaming, open fires and all the trimmings. Originally two cottages, it's been an inn for several centuries; its name possibly deriving from regular visits here made by King Charles II when enjoying meetings with Nell Gwynn nearby. Assignations today are firmly rooted in the desire to enjoy the dishes that have gained the Heston Blumenthal-owned pub two AA Rosettes for the distinctly traditional English menu. Diners (restaurant bookings essential, but not for bar meals) may commence with a starter such as crispy cauliflower with cheese sauce and Henderson's relish, setting the standard for mains the like of chargrilled Hereford sirloin steak with marrowbone

sauce, or fillet of hake with charred leeks, celeriac purée and cep sauce, finishing with Earl Grey pannacotta. The enclosed courtyard is sheltered by a spreading vine, and there's a large garden in which to quaff Caledonian Flying Scotsman bitter.

Open all day all wk **Bar Meals** L served Mon-Fri 12-2.30, Sat 12-3, Sun 12-8 D served Mon-Thu 6-9.30, Fri-Sat 6-10, Sun 12-8 **Restaurant** L served Mon-Fri 12-2.30, Sat 12-3, Sun 12-8 D served Mon-Thu 6-9.30, Fri-Sat 6-10, Sun 12-8 ⊕ STAR PUBS & BARS ◀ Courage Best & Directors, Caledonian Flying Scotsman. ☕ 19
Facilities Non-diners area ❖ (Bar Garden Outside area) ❖ Children's menu Children's portions Garden Outside area ▭ Parking Wi-fi ▭ (notice required)

The Hinds Head ◉◉
PICK OF THE PUBS

See Pick of the Pubs on opposite page

BURCHETT'S GREEN — Map 5 SU88

The Crown

Burchett's Green Rd SL6 6QZ ☎ 01628 826184
e-mail: thecrown@thecrownburchettsgreen.co.uk
dir: *From Maidenhead take A4 towards Reading. At mini rdbt right signed Burchett's Green. Pub in village centre*

Homely pub with a secluded garden

This traditional brick-built village local dating from 1848 has a reputation for imaginative pub food cooked from local seasonal ingredients, including home-grown salads, herbs and vegetables. As well as lunchtime sandwiches, the seasonal menu could deliver pressed ham hock and parsley terrine; slow-cooked pork belly with mash and greens; Mediterranean vegetable lattice; and crumbled pear and coriander seed cake. The atmosphere is pubby and informal – bag a table by the blazing fire in the homely bar or eat in the garden alongside the vegetable patches. The landlords are classic car enthusiasts and welcome several car clubs on a regular basis.

Open 12-3 6-12 (Sat 12-4 6-12 Sun 12-9) Closed: Mon L **Bar Meals** L served Tue-Sun 12-3 D served Mon-Sat 6-9 Av main course £13 **Restaurant** L served Tue-Sat 12-2.30, Sun 12-3.30 D served Mon-Sat 6.30-9 Av 3 course à la carte fr £22 ⊕ GREENE KING ◀ Morland Original & Old Speckled Hen Ö Aspall. ☕ 10
Facilities Non-diners area ❖ (Bar Garden) ❖ Children's portions Garden ▭ Parking Wi-fi ▭ (notice required)

PICK OF THE PUBS

The Hinds Head ◉◉

BRAY   Map 6 SU97

High St SL6 2AB ☎ 01628 626151
e-mail: info@hindsheadbray.com
web: www.hindsheadbray.com
dir: *M4 junct 8/9 take Maidenhead Central exit. Next rdbt take Bray/Windsor exit. 0.5m, B3028 to Bray*

Old-English fare with a modern twist

Heston Blumenthal's younger sibling to his eponymous Fat Duck restaurant has, not surprisingly, become a gastronomic destination, yet the striking 15th-century building remains very much a village local. Its origins are a little obscure, with some saying it was used as a royal hunting lodge and others as a guest house for the local Abbot of Cirencester. What is known is that Queen Elizabeth II dined with European royalty at the pub in 1963. Expect an informal atmosphere in the traditional bar, with its beams, sturdy oak panelling, log fires, leather chairs, and pints of Rebellion available at the bar. On the ground floor is the main restaurant, while upstairs are two further dining areas, the Vicars Room, and the larger Royal Room. Having worked alongside the team in the Tudor kitchens at Hampton Court Palace, Heston rediscovered the origins of

British cuisine, and has reintroduced some classic recipes that echo the pub's Tudor roots. Top-notch ingredients are used in gutsy dishes that are cooked simply and delivered in an unfussy manner by head chef Kevin Love. Take bar snacks or starters like devils on horseback; or soused mackerel, pickled lemon and horseradish with main courses taking in oxtail and kidney pudding; or roast Cornish cod, wilted chard and mussel both. Room should be left for a memorable pudding, perhaps Quaking pudding, or treacle tart with milk ice cream. Well selected, widely sourced wines complete the picture. Booking for meals may be required. Dogs are welcome in the bar area.

Open all wk 11.30-11 (Sun 12-7) **Closed:** 25 Dec **Bar Meals** L served Mon-Sat 12-2.30, Sun 12-4 D served Mon-Sat 6.30-9.30 **Restaurant** L served Mon-Sat 12-2.30, Sun 12-4 D served Mon-Sat 6.30-9.30 ⊕ **FREE HOUSE** 🍺 Rebellion IPA & Seasonal ales, Windsor & Eton Seasonal ale ♻ Tutts Clump. 🍷 15 **Facilities** Non-diners area 🐾 (Bar) 🧒 Children's menu Parking 🚌 (notice required)

CHIEVELEY — Map 5 SU47

The Crab at Chieveley ★★★★ RR ◉◉

North Heath, Wantage Rd RG20 8UE ☎ 01635 247550
e-mail: info@crabatchieveley.com
dir: *M4 junct 13. 1.5m W of Chieveley on B4494*

Experience fresh seafood without a trip to the coast

This lovely old thatched dining pub has an award-winning seafood restaurant, which makes it the perfect place to break a tedious M4 journey or chill out on a summer evening. Specialising in fish dishes and with fresh deliveries daily, the continuously-changing menu in the maritime-themed restaurant offers mouth-watering starters such as Carlingford Loch oysters, followed by catch of the day, venison loin, bouillabaisse or Cornish lobster thermidor. The interesting dessert menu has treacle and pistachio tart with apricot purée and pistachio anglaise. Boutique bedrooms complete the package. Dogs are welcome.

Open all day all wk 11am-mdnt **Bar Meals** L served all wk 12-2.30 D served all wk 6-9.30 **Restaurant** L served all wk 12-2.30 D served all wk 6-9.30 ⊕ FREE HOUSE ◀ Sharp's Doom Bar, Greene King Abbot Ale, Shepherd Neame Spitfire Ò Savanna. ♀ 20
Facilities Non-diners area ✿ (Bar Garden) ♦ Children's menu Children's portions Garden ⚲ Parking Wi-fi **Rooms** 14

COLNBROOK — Map 6 TQ07

The Ostrich

High St SL3 0JZ ☎ 01753 682628
e-mail: enquiries@theostrichcolnbrook.co.uk
dir: *M25 junct 14 towards Poyle. Right at 1st rdbt, over next 2 rdbts. Left at sharp right bend into High St. Left at mini rdbt, pub on left*

900 years of hospitality and still going strong

Close to Heathrow and just minutes from the motorway, stands, surprisingly, one of England's oldest pubs. Dating from 1106 and once a coaching inn on the old London-Bath road, the vast and rambling Ostrich oozes history, with its heavily timbered façade, cobbled courtyard and an interior filled with wonky oak beams, massive fireplaces and crooked stairs. Cross Oak Inns have revamped it in contemporary style, so expect glass doors, a steel bar, chunky furnishings and vibrant colours. Equally modern, the menu takes in chicken terrine with rustic bread, pork belly with cider jus, and milk chocolate fondant.

Open all wk 12-3 5-11 (Sun all day) **Bar Meals** L served all wk 12-2.30 D served all wk 6-9.30 **Restaurant** L served all wk 12-2.30 D served all wk 6-9.30 ⊕ FREE HOUSE ◀ Sharp's Doom Bar, Windsor & Eton, Twickenham Fine Ales, Binghams Ò Westons Stowford Press. ♀ 10 **Facilities** Non-diners area ♦ Children's menu Children's portions Garden ⚲ Parking Wi-fi ▄ (notice required)

COOKHAM — Map 6 SU88

The White Oak ◉◉ NEW

The Pound SL6 9QE ☎ 01628 523043
e-mail: info@thewhiteoak.co.uk
dir: *From A4 E of Maidenhead take A4094 signed Cookham. Left into High St (B4447) signed Cookham Rise/Cookham Dean. Pass through common. Left at mini-rdbt, pub on right*

Seasonal menus and accomplished cooking

The arrival of chef Clive Dixon (ex-Blumenthal's Hinds Head) at this Thames Valley gastro-pub took the menu and cooking to another level and it's now the favoured eaterie in this affluent Berkshire village. In a cool, contemporary, yet relaxed setting discerning diners can tuck into some accomplished modern British dishes, accompanied by some select wines, or a pint of Abbot Ale. Daily menus brim with seasonal produce, so perhaps start with oak-smoked pollock with crab mayonnaise, shaved fennel and lemon, then choose Cornish lamb fillet with garlic greens and mustard mash, or lobster and crab burger. To finish, try the hot brioche doughnuts with raspberry purée and vanilla sauce.

Open all wk **Bar Meals** L served Mon-Sat 12-2.30, Sun 12-3.30 D served Mon-Sat 6.30-10, Sun 5.30-9 Av main course £16.50 **Restaurant** L served Mon-Sat 12-2.30, Sun 12-3.30 D served Mon-Sat 6.30-10, Sun 5.30-9 Fixed menu price fr £15 Av 3 course à la carte fr £29 ⊕ GREENE KING ◀ Abbot Ale, Morland Old Speckled Hen Ò Aspall. ♀ 24 **Facilities** Non-diners area ♦ Children's menu Children's portions Garden ⚲ Parking Wi-fi

COOKHAM DEAN — Map 5 SU88

The Chequers Brasserie

PICK OF THE PUBS

Dean Ln SL6 9BQ ☎ 01628 481232
e-mail: info@chequersbrasserie.co.uk
dir: *From A4094 in Cookham High St towards Marlow, over rail line. 1m on right*

Historic pub with an established brasserie

Tucked away between Marlow and Maidenhead, The Chequers is in one of the prettiest villages in the Thames Valley. Striking Victorian and Edwardian villas around the green set the tone, whilst the surrounding wooded hills and dales have earned Cookham Dean a reputation as a centre for wonderful walks. Wooden beams, an open fire and comfortable seating welcome drinkers to the small bar, perhaps to sample Rebellion's fine ales. Dining takes place in the older part of the building, or in the conservatory; a private dining room can be reserved for parties. The menus of expertly prepared dishes are based on fresh, quality ingredients enhanced by careful use of cosmopolitan flavours. A starter of pan-fried red mullet with couscous and harissa dressing could be followed by sweet potato, red pepper and chickpea risotto; or a platter of pork served with apple purée and crackling. Dogs are welcome in the garden only.

Open all wk Mon-Thu 12-3 5.30-11 (Fri-Sat 12-11.30 Sun 12-6) **Bar Meals** L served Mon-Sat 12-2.30, Sun 12-5 D served Mon-Thu 6.30-9.30, Fri-Sat 6.30-10 Av main course £15.95 **Restaurant** L served Mon-Sat 12-2.30, Sun 12-5 D served Mon-Thu 6.30-9.30, Fri-Sat 6.30-10 Fixed menu price fr £15 Av 3 course à la carte fr £27.50 ⊕ FREE HOUSE ◀ Rebellion IPA & Smuggler, Guinness Ò Westons Stowford Press. ♀ 14 **Facilities** Non-diners area ✿ (Garden) ♦ Children's portions Garden ⚲ Parking Wi-fi ▄

CRAZIES HILL — Map 5 SU78

The Horns

PICK OF THE PUBS

RG10 8LY ☎ 0118 940 6222
dir: *Off A321 NE of Wargrave*

Pretty black timbered pub with barn restaurant

Head to the secluded garden for summer alfresco options In the peaceful village of Crazies Hill, The Horns is a beautifully restored 16th-century pub with oak beams, terracotta walls and stripped wooden floors. There are three interconnecting rooms full of old pine tables, warmed by open fires; the main dining room is in an elegantly converted barn, which was added 200 years ago. The tranquil atmosphere makes it a great place to enjoy a pint of Oxford Gold or one of the dozen wines offered by the glass. Alternatively, you can eat and drink outside in the secluded garden when the weather is fine. The evening menu might offer starters of ham hock terrine, crispy duck salad or smoked mackerel pâté, while main courses encompass favourites such as slow-braised shin of beef with mash; roasted cod with braised baby gem and sautéed wild mushrooms; or guinea fowl wrapped in Parma ham with Puy lentils and fondant potatoes.

Open all wk 12-3 5-11 (Sat-Sun all day) **Bar Meals** L served Mon-Sat 12-2.30, Sun 12-3.30 D served Tue-Sat 6.30-9.30 **Restaurant** L served Mon-Sat 12-2.30, Sun 12-3.30 D served Tue-Sat 6.30-9.30 ⊕ BRAKSPEAR ◀ Bitter, Oxford Gold, Marston's Pedigree. ♀ 12 **Facilities** Non-diners area ✿ (Bar Garden) ♦ Children's menu Children's portions Play area Family room Garden ⚲ Parking Wi-fi ▄

EAST GARSTON — Map 5 SU37

The Queen's Arms Country Inn ★★★★ INN

PICK OF THE PUBS

RG17 7ET ☎ 01488 648757
e-mail: info@queensarmshotel.co.uk
dir: *M4 junct 14, 4m onto A338 to Great Shefford, then East Garston*

Stylish pub in the heart of racehorse country

Pleasantly located in the Lambourn Valley, home to over 2,000 racehorses and more than 50 racing yards, this charming pub acts as quasi-headquarters for British racing, with owners, trainers and jockeys among its clientele. The oldest part of this inn started life as a farmer's cottage in the 18th century, becoming licensed around 1856, the year of Queen Victoria's Silver Jubilee. Several years ago it joined the small and select group of Miller's Collection inns. The welcome is warm and the setting is stylishly traditional. So with a glass of Henry's IPA in hand, and a listening ear tuned for an indiscreet racing tip, take your time over your choice from the menu. The innovative English country dishes are prepared from fresh ingredients, all sourced as locally as possible, with game high on the list of the head chef's favourite ingredients. Book ahead for one of the elegant bedrooms.

Open all day all wk 11am-mdnt Closed: 25 Dec **Bar Meals** L served Mon-Sat 12-2.30, Sun 12-3.30 D served Mon-Sat 6.30-9.30 **Restaurant** L served Mon-Sat 12-2.30, Sun 12-3.30 D served Mon-Sat 6.30-9.30 ⊕ FREE HOUSE ◀ Wadworth Henry's Original IPA, Guinness, Guest ales ♂ Westons Stowford Press. **Facilities** Non-diners area ♥ (Bar Garden) ♦ Children's portions Garden ☞ Parking Wi-fi ▬ **Rooms** 8

FRILSHAM   Map 5 SU57

The Pot Kiln ◉◉

PICK OF THE PUBS

RG18 0XX ☎ 01635 201366
e-mail: admin@potkiln.org
dir: *From Yattendon follow Pot Kiln signs, cross over motorway. 0.25m, pub on right*

Recommended for their local game dishes

Chef-patron Mike Robinson is renowned for shooting much of the game he crafts into extraordinary dishes at this 18th-century country pub. The Pot Kiln may take some finding but the rewards of fine food and good beer make the journey worth it. It could be the commitment to real ale, with three on tap at any one time, from the award-winning West Berkshire Brewery (which originated at the pub, since relocated), but like-as-not it's the exceptional food which draws crowds to this former kiln-workers' old beerhouse secluded along back lanes in beautiful unspoilt countryside. Signature dishes include mallard breast and sherry braised leg with brioche croûton, seared foie gras or spiced shoulder and rack of lamb with fondant potatoes, apricot and spinach. Local trout and crayfish from the River Kennet may also feature. The small public bar serves excellent bar food including the pub's famous venison burgers and venison steak sandwiches.

Open Mon & Wed-Fri 12-3 6-11 (Sat-Sun 12-11) Closed: 25 Dec, Tue **Bar Meals** L served Wed-Mon 12-2.30 D served Wed-Mon 6.30-8.30 **Restaurant** L served Wed-Mon 12-2 D served Wed-Mon 7-9 ⊕ FREE HOUSE ◀ Brick Kiln, West Berkshire Mr Chubb's Lunchtime Bitter & Maggs' Magnificent Mild ♂ Thatchers, Cotswold. **Facilities** Non-diners area ♥ (Bar Garden) ♦ Children's menu Children's portions Play area Garden ☞ Parking Wi-fi

HERMITAGE   Map 5 SU57

The White Horse of Hermitage

Newbury Rd RG18 9TB ☎ 01635 200325
e-mail: whoh@btconnect.com
dir: *5m from Newbury on B4009. From M4 junct 13 follow signs for Newbury Showground, right into Priors Court Rd, left at mini rdbt, pub approx 50yds on right*

Good home-cooked food and a warm welcome

A family friendly pub dating back at least 160 years, The White Horse has achieved a solid reputation for its pub food, using the freshest and finest local produce to create a daily menu that typically includes burgers, pies, steaks and dishes such as smoked haddock fishcakes followed by lemon and paprika chicken. The interior bar and restaurant is contemporary in decor, and outside you choose between the Mediterranean-style patio or the large garden, which is equipped with swings, a bouncy castle and animal enclosures.

Open all day summer (Mon 5-11 Tue-Thu 12-3 5-11 Fri-Sat 12-11 Sun 12-10 winter) Closed: Mon L (ex BHs) **Bar Meals** L served Tue-Sat 12-3 D served Mon-Thu 5-9, Fri-Sat 5-9.30, Sun 12-6 **Restaurant** L served Tue-Sat 12-3 D served Mon-Thu 5-9, Fri-Sat 5-9.30, Sun 12-6 ⊕ GREENE KING ◀ Abbot Ale & IPA, Guinness, Guest ales ♂ Westons Stowford Press. ▾ 9 **Facilities** Non-diners area ♥ (Bar Garden) ♦ Children's menu Children's portions Play area Garden ☞ Beer festival Cider festival Parking Wi-fi ▬ (notice required)

HOLYPORT   Map 6 SU87

The Belgian Arms NEW

SL6 2JR ☎ 01628 634468
e-mail: reservations@thebelgianarms.com
dir: *M4 junct 8, A308(M). At rdbt take A330 signed Ascot. At Holyport village green left signed Bray & Windsor. 1st left into Holyport Rd. Belgian Arms on right*

Earthy decor, friendly staff and classy food

The name of this wisteria-draped village pub, just off the green and overlooking the pond, begs the question - what's the connection with Belgium? Apparently, during the First World War many local men fought in Flanders and so its name was changed from The Eagle as a tribute to them. Today's reputation is founded on executive chef Dominic Chapman's British food, featuring fresh, daily-delivered produce, often from artisan suppliers. Menus typically feature steak béarnaise; stews; roast Berkshire roe deer; Scottish salmon and mussel pie; and Sunday roasts. Crisp pig's ears with aïoli is a bar snack favourite.

Open all day all wk 11-11 (Sun 12-7) **Bar Meals** L served Mon-Sat 12-2.30, Sun 12-3.30 D served Mon-Thu 6.30-9.30, Fri-Sat 6-10 Av main course £15 **Restaurant** L served Mon-Sat 12-2.30, Sun 12-3.30 D served Mon-Thu 6.30-9.30, Fri-Sat 6-10 Av 3 course à la carte fr £25 ⊕ BRAKSPEAR ◀ Brakspear Best, Marston's Pedigree ♂ Symonds. ▾ 12 **Facilities** Non-diners area ♥ (Bar Garden) ♦ Children's menu Children's portions Garden ☞ Parking Wi-fi

The George on the Green

SL6 2JL ☎ 01628 628317
e-mail: natalie@thegeorgeonthegreen.com
dir: *M4 junct 8/9, at rdbt 2nd exit onto A308(M). At rdbt 3rd exit onto A308. At rdbt take 2nd exit signed Holyport. Pub in village centre*

Traditional landmark inn on the village green

Facing the vast, eponymous green, this low-beamed 16th-century pub may possibly have played host to Charles II and Nell Gwynne when the actress lived locally. Today's locals can look forward to great beers from Rebellion Brewery in nearby Marlow Bottom coupled with a selective, well thought-out menu; maybe baked crab gratin to start, then smoked chicken, leek and butternut squash risotto, or slow-roasted half shoulder of lamb with sweet potato boulangère. From outside tables, views stretch across the green to the tree-shaded village duck pond.

Open 12-3 5-11 (Sat 12-11 Sun 12-6) Closed: Mon **Bar Meals** L served Tue-Fri 12-2.30, Sat-Sun 12-4 D served Tue-Fri 5.30-9, Sat-Sun 12-4 **Restaurant** L served Tue-Fri 12-2.30, Sat-Sun 12-4 D served Tue-Fri 5.30-9, Sat-Sun 12-4 ◀ Rebellion Mutiny & IPA, Fuller's London Pride ♂ Thatchers Gold. **Facilities** Non-diners area ♦ Children's portions Garden Parking ▬

HUNGERFORD   Map 5 SU36

The Crown & Garter ★★★★ INN

PICK OF THE PUBS

Inkpen Common RG17 9QR ☎ 01488 668325
e-mail: gill.hern@btopenworld.com
dir: *From A4 to Kintbury & Inkpen. At village store left into Inkpen Rd, follow signs for Inkpen Common 2m*

Family-run free house with 'interesting' past

Inkpen Beacon, at 975 feet, is the highest chalk hill in England. On its summit stands a replica of Combe Gibbet where, in 1676, double-murderers George Broomham and Dorothy Newman were hanged, their bodies later being laid out in the Gibbet Barn at this traditional coaching and sheep drovers' inn. Today a family-run free house, its historic charm is best seen in the bar, where there's a huge inglenook fireplace and criss-crossing beams, and where Gibbet Ale, specially brewed in Enborne by Two Cocks Brewery, and West Berkshire's Good Old Boy are on tap. In addition to the bar, eat in the candlelit, wood-panelled restaurant, on the patio, or under an oak tree in the garden. From a daily-changing menu come starters of chicken liver parfait with cranberry sauce; and mains of smoked hake with Welsh rarebit, poached egg and hollandaise sauce; and spinach and cheese tortelloni.

Open 12-3 5.30-11 (Sun 12-5 7-10.30) Closed: Mon L & Tue L **Bar Meals** L served Wed-Sat 12-2, Sun 12-2.30 D served Mon-Sat 6.30-9 **Restaurant** L served Wed-Sat 12-2, Sun 12-2.30 D served Mon-Sat 6.30-9 ⊕ FREE HOUSE ◀ Crown & Garter Gibbet Ale, West Berkshire Good Old Boy, Guinness ♂ Westons Stowford Press. ▾ 9 **Facilities** Non-diners area Garden ☞ Parking Wi-fi **Rooms** 9

HUNGERFORD *continued*

The Pheasant Inn ★★★★ INN

Ermin St, Shefford Woodlands RG17 7AA
☎ **01488 648284**
e-mail: info@pheasantinnlambourn.co.uk
dir: *M4 junct 14, A338 towards Wantage. Left onto B4000 towards Lambourn*

Welcoming atmosphere, chic interior and good food

Originally called The Paraffin House because it was licensed to sell fuel alongside ale, this old drovers' retreat in the Lambourn Valley is a notable food pub with 11 contemporary bedrooms. Its interior retains original features such as beams, wood-panelling and a stone floor. Food choices include sharing boards crammed with the likes of houmous, tzatziki, olives and pitta bread, or full meals such as crispy salt and pepper squid with garlic mayonnaise followed by chicken and leek pie with mash and green vegetables, with ginger pannacotta and poached rhubarb for dessert. Wash it down with Ramsbury Gold or Symonds Founders Reserve cider. Change of hands.

Open all day all wk Closed: 25 Dec **Bar Meals** L served all wk 12-2.30 D served Mon-Sat 6.30-9.30, Sun 6.30-8.30 **Restaurant** L served all wk 12-2.30 D served Mon-Sat 6.30-9.30, Sun 6.30-8.30 ⊕ FREE HOUSE ◀ Ramsbury Gold, Upham Punter ♨ Symonds Founders Reserve. ♟ 12 **Facilities** Non-diners area ♣ (Bar Restaurant Garden) ♦ Children's portions Garden Parking Wi-fi ▭ Rooms 11

The Swan Inn ★★★★ INN

Craven Rd, Lower Green, Inkpen RG17 9DX
☎ **01488 668326**
e-mail: enquiries@theswaninn-organics.co.uk
web: www.theswaninn-organics.co.uk
dir: *S on Hungerford High St, past rail bridge, left to Hungerford Common, right signed Inkpen*

Recommended for their home-reared beef

Surrounded by fine walking country just below Combe Gibbet and Walbury Hill in the North Wessex Downs, this 17th-century village free house is presided over by organic beef farmers Mary and Bernard Harris. The beamed interior has old photographic prints and open fires. Almost everything on the menu is prepared using their own fresh produce; meats are 100% organic and butchered on the premises; all beef is supplied by their organic farm in Inkpen. Fresh pasta and bread are cooked

daily on the premises; even the wine is organic. The menu offers traditional English favourites and classic Italian dishes, such as home-made ravioli; minced beef and onion pie; chilli con carne; pan-fried swordfish steak with spicy tomato sauce; vegetable lasagne. There is an organic farm shop and butchery attached to the pub, and ten en suite bedrooms are available. An attractive terraced garden sets the scene for alfresco summer dining.

Open all wk 12-2.30 7-11 (Sat 12-11 Sun 12-4) Closed: 25-26 Dec **Bar Meals** L served all wk 12-2.30 D served all wk 7-9.30 Av main course £12 **Restaurant** L served Mon-Fri 12-2.30, Sat-Sun 12-3 D served Wed-Sat 7-9.30 Av 3 course à la carte fr £22 ⊕ FREE HOUSE ◀ Butts Traditional, Jester & Blackguard Porter, Guest ales. **Facilities** Non-diners area ♦ Children's menu Children's portions Play area Garden Outside area ☂ Parking Wi-fi ▭ (notice required) **Rooms** 10

HURLEY   Map 5 SU88

The Olde Bell Inn ★★★★★ INN @@
NEW

High St SL6 5LX ☎ **01628 825881**
e-mail: oldebellreception@coachinginn.co.uk
dir: *M4 junct 8/9 follow Henley signs. At rdbt take A4130 towards Hurley. Right to Hurley, inn 800yds on right*

Historic, yet modern inn with excellent food

Parts of this smart village inn date to 1135, when it was a guest house for pilgrims to a nearby priory. Heritage seeps from its very framework; the charming old bar has seen a republican plot (appropriately, Rebellion beers are sold here) and wartime visits by Churchill and Eisenhower. Today's visitors are drawn by the superb accommodation and accomplished ever-changing menus that are firmly based on produce from local farmers and suppliers. Look out for a starter of smoked ham hock terrine; or English asparagus, soft boiled quail's egg, white truffle oil and new potatoes as prelude to slow-roasted belly of Dingley Dell pork with Puy lentils, Alsace bacon and cider sauce; or pan-baked skate wing, brown shrimp, bubble-and-squeak with nut brown butter. Desserts will be a temptation too - perhaps baked white chocolate and vanilla cheesecake with raspberry ripple ice cream; or coconut pannacotta and Malibu-marinated pineapple; for the less sweet-toothed there is an excellent cheeseboard. The terrace and wildflower meadow-style beer garden are delightful.

Open all day all wk 10am-11pm **Bar Meals** L served Mon-Sat 12.30-2.30, Sun 12-3.30 D served Mon-Sat 6-10, Sun 6.30-9 **Restaurant** L served Mon-Sat 12.30-2.30, Sun 12-3.30 D served Mon-Sat 6-10, Sun 6.30-9 Fixed menu price fr £12.50 Av 3 course à la carte fr £29.50 ⊕ FREE HOUSE ◀ Rebellion, Cottage. ♟ 10 **Facilities** Non-diners area ♣ (Bar Garden) ♦ Children's menu Children's portions Play area Garden ☂ Parking Wi-fi ▭ **Rooms** 48

HURST   Map 5 SU77

The Green Man

Hinton Rd RG10 0BP ☎ **0118 934 2599**
e-mail: phil@thegreenman.uk.com
dir: *Off A321, adjacent to Hurst Cricket Club*

Enjoy good food and drink in relaxed 17th-century pub

Built from timbers of decommissioned ships from Porstmouth, the pub gained its first licence in 1602, and Brakspear purchased a 1,000 year lease on the building in 1646. The old black beams, low in places, are still to be seen and you'll find open fires, hand-drawn beer and good food. The seasonal main menu offers the likes of spicy Cajun chicken breast, Mexican beef chilli, game pie, and pan-fried sea bass fillet. There are weekend specials, such as oven-baked lemon sole or grilled Gressingham duck breast. The garden, open to fields and woodland, includes a children's play area.

Open all wk 11-3 5.30-11 (Sat-Sun all day) **Bar Meals** L served all wk 12-2.30 D served all wk 6-9.30 **Restaurant** L served all wk 12-2.30 D served all wk 6-9.30 ⊕ BRAKSPEAR ◀ Bitter & Seasonal ales, Wychwood Hobgoblin ♨ Addlestones. ♟ 8 **Facilities** Non-diners area ♦ Children's menu Children's portions Play area Garden ☂ Parking Wi-fi

KINTBURY   Map 5 SU36

The Dundas Arms

53 Station Rd RG17 9UT ☎ **01488 658263**
e-mail: info@dundasarms.co.uk
dir: *M4 junct 13, A34 to Newbury, A4 towards Hungerford, left to Kintbury. Pub 1m*

A perfect place to while away time watching boats go by

On the banks of both the Kennet & Avon Canal and the River Kennet itself, this late 18th-century free house is now under new ownership. The bar offers beers from West Berkshire and Ramsbury breweries and Orchard Pig ciders. You can watch narrowboats on the canal from the auberge-style restaurant, and choose a starter of rillettes of pork, cornichons, house pickles and toast, followed by slow roasted belly of English assured pork, black pudding, mash, spring greens and grain mustard. Leave a little room for an indulgent home-made lemon curd meringue pie. By all means, take your drinks and food outside to the patio or canalside jetty.

Open all day all wk **Bar Meals** L served Mon-Sat 12-2.30, Sun 12-9 (summer all day) D served Mon-Thu 6-9, Fri-Sat 6-10, Sun 12-9 (summer all day) **Restaurant** L served Mon-Sat 12-2.30, Sun 12-9 (summer all day) D served Mon-Thu 6-9, Fri-Sat 6-10, Sun 12-9 (summer all day) ⊕ FREE HOUSE ◀ West Berkshire Good Old Boy, Ramsbury Gold, Flack Manor, Upham Punter ♨ The Orchard Pig. ♟ **Facilities** Non-diners area ♦ Children's menu Family room Garden Outside area ☂ Parking

KNOWL HILL   Map 5 SU87

Bird In Hand Country Inn
PICK OF THE PUBS

Bath Rd RG10 9UP ☎ 01628 826622 & 822781
e-mail: info@birdinhand.co.uk
dir: *On A4, 5m W of Maidenhead, 7m E of Reading*

Friendly country pub

When George III lived at Windsor Castle, he sometimes stopped off at this part-14th-century inn. Today it's run by Caroline Shone, a member of the third generation of her family to do so. The choice of real ales in the wood-panelled bar, the oldest part of the pub, runs to five guests, and that's in addition to Binghams locally brewed Twyford Tipple. The 50-bin wine list includes a white and a rosé from nearby Stanlake Park vineyard. In the attractive restaurant, which overlooks a courtyard and fountain, the menu (this also applies in the bar) offers baguettes and paninis; jacket potatoes, omelettes, pizzas and vegetarian meals, with typical mains of scampi and chips; steak-and-kidney pudding; yellow Thai chicken curry; and chargrills. Specials include seafood fettuccine; grilled beef teriyaki; and Mediterranean vegetable lasagne. Beer festivals take place in June and November.

Open all day all wk **Bar Meals** Av main course £10.95 food served all day **Restaurant** L served all wk 12-2.30 D served all wk 6.30-10 ⊕ FREE HOUSE ◀ Binghams Twyford Tipple, 5 Guest ales ♻ Thatchers. ♟ 20 **Facilities** Non-diners area ♥ (Bar Garden) ♦ Children's menu Children's portions Garden ⌨ Beer festival Parking Wi-fi ▦

LECKHAMPSTEAD   Map 5 SU47

The Stag

Shop Ln RG20 8QG ☎ 01488 638436
dir: *6m from Newbury on B4494*

A great spot after a country walk

The white-painted Stag lies just off the village green in a sleepy downland village, close to the Ridgeway long-distance path and Snelsmore Common, home to nightjar, woodlark and grazing Exmoor ponies. Inside old black-and-white photographs tell of village life many years ago. Surrounding farms and growers supply all produce, including venison, pheasant and fresh river trout. Other possibilities are venison and redcurrant sausages with butternut squash mash; pork loin with creamy mushroom sauce; or traditional beer-battered fish and chips with mushy peas. There are around 20 red and white wines, among them varieties from Australia, California and France.

Open 12-3 6-11 Closed: Sun eve & Mon L **Bar Meals** L served Tue-Sat 12-2, Sun 12-3.30 D served Tue-Sat 6-9 Av main course £10 **Restaurant** L served Tue-Sat 12-2, Sun 12-3.30 D served Tue-Sat 6-9 ⊕ FREE HOUSE ◀ Morland Original, West Berkshire Good Old Boy, Guest ales ♻ Aspall. **Facilities** Non-diners area ♥ (Bar Garden Outside area) ♦ Children's menu Children's portions Garden Outside area ⌨ Parking Wi-fi ▦ (notice required)

MARSH BENHAM   Map 5 SU46

The Red House

RG20 8LY ☎ 01635 582017
e-mail: info@theredhousepub.com
dir: *From Newbury A4 towards Hungerford. Pub signed. in approx 3m. Left onto unclassified road to Marsh Benham*

Thatched country pub with gluten-free menu specialities

Tucked away in the verdant Kennet Valley, trim thatched roofs cap this tranquil retreat just a modest stroll (dog walkers welcome) from the Kennet & Avon Canal. Indulge in a beer from the respected West Berkshire brewery whilst contemplating views from the sheltered beer garden, or slumber beside the log fire, anticipating your choice from the kitchen overseen by experienced French chef-patron Laurent Lebeau. His essentially British menu might include braised ox cheeks in red wine with celeriac mash or, from the thoughtful gluten-free menu, south coast bream fillets and roasted root vegetables. As for the wines, Laurent chooses well.

Open all day all wk **Bar Meals** L served all wk 12-10 D served all wk 12-10 food served all day **Restaurant** L served all wk 12-10 D served all wk 12-10 food served all day ⊕ FREE HOUSE ◀ West Berkshire Good Old Boy & Mr Chubb's Lunchtime Bitter, Guest ales ♻ Westons Stowford Press. **Facilities** Non-diners area ♥ (Bar Garden) ♦ Children's menu Children's portions Garden ⌨ Parking Wi-fi ▦ (notice required)

MONEYROW GREEN   Map 6 SU87

The White Hart

SL6 2ND ☎ 01628 621460
e-mail: admin@thewhitehartholyport.co.uk
dir: *2m S from Maidenhead. M4 junct 8/9, follow Holyport signs then Moneyrow Green. Pub by petrol station*

Perfect stop for Windsor visitors

The close proximity to the M4 makes this traditional 19th-century coaching inn a popular spot for those heading to nearby Maidenhead and Windsor. The wood-panelled lounge bar is furnished with leather Chesterfields, and quality home-made food and real ales can be enjoyed in a cosy atmosphere with an open fire. Typical mains are mushroom Stroganoff; tuna niçoise salad; and baked sea bass. Sandwiches, baguettes and jacket potatoes are offered at lunchtime. There are large gardens to enjoy in summer with a children's playground and petanque pitch. Time a visit for the August cider and beer festival.

Open all day all wk **Bar Meals** L served all wk 12-2.30 D served all wk 6-9 **Restaurant** L served all wk 12-2.30 D served all wk 6-9 ⊕ GREENE KING ◀ IPA, Morland Old Speckled Hen, Guest ales ♻ Westons Stowford Press. **Facilities** Non-diners area ♥ (Bar Garden) ♦ Play area Garden ⌨ Beer festival Cider festival Parking Wi-fi ▦ (notice required)

OAKLEY GREEN   Map 6 SU97

The Greene Oak ◉ NEW

SL4 5UW ☎ 01753 864294
e-mail: info@thegreeneoak.co.uk
dir: *M4 junct 8, A308(M) signed Maidenhead Central. At rdbt take A308 signed Bray & Windsor. Right into Oakley Green Rd (B3024) signed Twyford. Pub on left*

Thriving gastro-pub near Windsor

The first of Henry Cripps's trio of gastro-pubs stands close to Windsor and draws an affluent dining crowd. They love the relaxed feel of the stylish and contemporary surroundings and are wowed by the imaginative modern food on the daily changing menus, and the excellent choice of wines. Kick off a memorable meal with seared pigeon breast with braised leg and wild mushroom fricassée, follow with pan-fried monkfish with pea and bacon risotto and parmesan, or beef Wellington for two with fat chips and jus, leaving room for pear and almond tarte Tatin with caramel sauce.

Open all wk **Bar Meals** L served Mon-Sat 12-2.30, Sun 12-3.30 D served Mon-Sat 6.30-9.30, Sun 5.30-9.30 Av main course £15 **Restaurant** L served Mon-Sat 12-2.30, Sun 12-3.30 D served Mon-Sat 6.30-9.30, Sun 5.30-9.30 Fixed menu price fr £15 Av 3 course à la carte fr £27 ⊕ FREE HOUSE ◀ Greene King IPA & Abbot Ale, Morland Old Speckled Hen ♻ Aspall. ♟ 26 **Facilities** Non-diners area ♦ Children's menu Children's portions Garden ⌨ Parking Wi-fi ▦ (notice required)

PALEY STREET   Map 5 SU87

The Royal Oak Paley Street ◉◉◉
PICK OF THE PUBS

Littlefield Green SL6 3JN ☎ 01628 620541
e-mail: info@theroyaloakpaleystreet.com
dir: *From Maidenhead take A330 towards Ascot for 2m, turn right onto B3024 signed Twyford, 2nd pub on left*

Top-notch, award-winning food

Sir Michael Parkinson, the former TV chat-show host, and his son Nick first saw this 17th-century, oak-beamed pub in 2001. Although Dad was sceptical, Nick saw the potential of running it, and how right he was; now Dad eats here frequently. Its calm elegance is partly due to the artworks on the walls, and partly to the large planters, white pebbles and waterfall in the garden. Head chef Dominic Chapman numbers three AA Rosettes among his collection of awards for exemplary British food, such as Blackface Cornish lamb shepherd's pie with hispi cabbage; diver-caught Orkney scallops with celeriac purée and hazelnut vinaigrette; lasagne of wild rabbit with wood blewits and chervil; and Taleggio cheese, artichoke, melted onion and radicchio tart. Desserts are expressed more prosaically: Cox's apple tart with vanilla ice cream; and soufflé of raspberries, for instance. Some 25 wines are by the glass, while Fuller's real ales are on handpump.

Open all wk 12-3 6-11 (Sun 12-4) **Bar Meals** L served Mon-Sat 12-3, Sun 12-4 D served Mon-Sat 6-11 Av main

continued

PALEY STREET *continued*

course £28 **Restaurant** L served Mon-Sat 12-2.30, Sun 12-3.30 D served Mon-Thu 6.30-9.30, Fri-Sat 6.30-10 Fixed menu price fr £25 Av 3 course à la carte fr £45 ⊕ FULLER'S ◀ London Pride, George Gale & Co Seafarers. ♀ 25 **Facilities** Non-diners area ♦♦ Garden Parking

---

PEASEMORE — Map 5 SU47

The Fox at Peasemore NEW

Hill Green Ln RG20 7JN ☎ 01635 248480
dir: *M4 junct 13, A34 signed Oxford. Immediately left onto slip road signed Chieveley, Hermitage & Beedon. At T-junct left, through Chieveley to Peasemore. Left at phone box, pub signed*

Stylish, newly refurbished village pub

The dust having settled following a complete refurbishment by Philip and Lauren Davison (licensees from the Sun in the Wood, Ashmore Green), Peasemore's village pub reopened. Their extensive efforts have left The Fox still charming and rustic, but with elegant modern touches. The bar serves West Berkshire's Good Old Boy, while on the main menu are peppered venison steak; slow-cooked lamb shank; pan-fried fillet of sea bass; and nut roast and wild mushroom strudel. Pub classics are beer-battered haddock; chicken and vegetable curry; and local sausages and mash. Opposite the pub is the village cricket ground.

Open 12-3 6-11 (Sat-Sun 12-late) Closed: Mon **Bar Meals** L served Tue-Sun 12-2 D served Tue-Sun 6-9 **Restaurant** L served Tue-Sun 12-2 D served Tue-Sun 6-9 ⊕ FREE HOUSE ◀ West Berkshire Good Old Boy. ♀ 14 **Facilities** Non-diners area ♣ (Bar Garden Outside area) ♦♦ Children's menu Children's portions Garden Outside area ♬ Parking ▭ (notice required)

READING — Map 5 SU77

The Flowing Spring

Henley Rd, Playhatch RG4 9RB ☎ 0118 969 9878
e-mail: info@theflowingspringpub.co.uk
dir: *3m N of Reading on A4155 towards Henley*

Cosy country pub at the edge of the Chilterns

A midsummer beer festival promising a dozen ales, live music and barbecue is one of a myriad of exciting events that take place throughout the year at this rural Fuller's establishment. Unusually the pub is on the first floor, which slopes steeply from one end of the bar to the other; the verandah overlooks Thames Valley countryside. Its quirky character notwithstanding, the pub has been recognised for its well-kept ales and cellar, and the menu of no-nonsense pub favourites is backed by a comprehensive range of vegetarian, gluten-free and dairy-free options. The huge garden is bounded by streams.

Open all day Closed: Mon **Bar Meals** L served Tue-Sun 12-2.30 D served Tue-Sat 6-9 **Restaurant** L served Tue-Sun 12-2.30 D served Tue-Sat 6-9 ⊕ FULLER'S ◀ London Pride & ESB, George Gale & Co Seafarers, Guest ale ♂ Aspall. ♀ 10 **Facilities** Non-diners area ♣ (Bar

Restaurant Garden) ♦♦ Children's portions Play area Garden ♬ Beer festival Cider festival Parking Wi-fi ▭ (notice required)

The Shoulder of Mutton

Playhatch RG4 9QU ☎ 0118 947 3908
e-mail: shoulderofmutton@hotmail.co.uk
dir: *From Reading follow signs to Caversham, then onto A4155 to Henley-on-Thames. At rdbt left to Binfield Heath, pub on left*

Village pub that is true to its name

This rustic inn with an airy conservatory restaurant draws a dedicated crowd keen to share chef-proprietor Alan Oxlade's passion for the finest foodstuffs and local Loddon ale. The pub specialises in mutton dishes (of course) and is proud to be a member of HRH The Prince of Wales' Mutton Renaissance Club. The signature dish is Welsh organic mountain mutton, slow roasted for seven hours; some dishes take up to two days of precision cooking. Everything on the menu has an inventive name: 'Titan's Crust' is a vegetarian tarte Tatin, 'Goosey Goosey Gander' a free-range goose breast served with a port and redcurrant sauce. The walled garden is a popular retreat.

Open 12-3 6-11 (Mon & Sun 12-3 Sat 12-3 6.30-11) Closed: 26 Dec, 2 Jan, Sun eve, Mon eve **Bar Meals** L served all wk 12-2 D served Tue-Sat 6.30-9 Av main course £14 **Restaurant** L served all wk 12-2 D served Tue-Sat 6.30-9 Av 3 course à la carte fr £26 ⊕ GREENE KING ◀ IPA, Loddon Hullabaloo ♂ Aspall. **Facilities** Non-diners area ♣ (Garden) ♦♦ Children's portions Garden ♬ Parking ▭ (notice required)

RUSCOMBE — Map 5 SU77

Buratta's at the Royal Oak

Ruscombe Ln RG10 9JN ☎ 0118 934 5190
e-mail: enquiries@burattas.co.uk
dir: *From A4 (Wargrave rdbt) take A321 to Twyford (signed Twyford/Wokingham). Straight on at 1st lights, right at 2nd lights onto A3032. Right onto A3024 (Ruscombe Rd which becomes Ruscombe Ln). Pub on left on brow of hill*

Relaxed pub with its own antiques shop

Originally a one-bar pub, the Royal Oak has been extended over the years and the old cottage next door is now the kitchen. With Binghams Brewery and Fuller's London Pride as resident ales, the relaxed restaurant offers a wide range of meals, from hearty bar snacks and sandwiches to regularly changing à la carte choices such as crayfish cocktail followed by pan-fried sea bass with sautéed garlic, balsamic tomatoes and chive mash. The large garden, complete with resident ducks, is dog friendly. The pub even has its own antiques shop and nearly everything in the pub is for sale.

Open Tue-Sat 12-3 6-11 (Sun-Mon 12-3) Closed: Sun eve & Mon eve **Bar Meals** L served all wk 12-2.30 D served Tue-Sat 7-9.30 Av main course £13-£14 **Restaurant** L served all wk 12-2.30 D served Tue-Sat 7-9.30 Av 3 course à la carte fr £27 ⊕ ENTERPRISE INNS ◀ Fuller's London Pride, Binghams, Guest ales. ♀ 12

Facilities Non-diners area ♣ (Bar Restaurant Garden) ♦♦ Children's menu Children's portions Garden ♬ Parking Wi-fi ▭ (notice required)

SINDLESHAM — Map 5 SU76

The Walter Arms

Bearwood Rd RG41 5BP ☎ 0118 977 4903
e-mail: mail@thewalterarms.com
dir: *A329 from Wokingham towards Reading. 1.5m, left onto B3030. 5m, left into Bearwood Rd. Pub 200yds on left*

Welcoming pub with interesting menu of global dishes

A typically solid Victorian building built about 1850 by John Walter III, grandson of the man who founded *The Times* newspaper. The idea was that it should be a working men's club for the workers on the Bearwood Estate, where Walter lived. Now a popular dining pub, the seasonal menus offer traditional English dishes, such as pan-roasted rump of lamb, and beer-battered sustainable haddock; as well as pasta, stone-baked pizzas and oriental- and Arabian-style 'smörgåsbord'. The beer garden is a good spot for a pint of London Pride or Courage Best.

Open all day all wk **Bar Meals** L served Mon-Fri 12-3, Sat 12-10, Sun 12-9 D served Mon-Fri 6-10, Sat-Sun all day **Restaurant** L served Mon-Fri 12-3, Sat 12-10, Sun 12-9 D served Mon-Fri 6-10, Sat-Sun all day ⊕ FREE HOUSE ◀ Fuller's London Pride, Courage Best, Guest ale ♂ Westons Stowford Press. **Facilities** Non-diners area ♦♦ Children's menu Children's portions Garden ♬ Parking

---

SONNING — Map 5 SU77

The Bull Inn

High St RG4 6UP ☎ 0118 969 3901
e-mail: bullinn@fullers.co.uk
dir: *From Reading take A4 towards Maidenhead. Left onto B4446 to Sonning*

Welcoming olde-worlde inn

Two minutes' walk from the River Thames in the pretty village of Sonning, this black-and-white timbered inn can trace its roots back 600 years or so; it can also boast visits by former owner Queen Elizabeth I and a mention in Jerome K Jerome's classic novel *Three Men in a Boat*. With Fuller's ales on tap, comfy leather chairs and log fires in the grate, The Bull charms locals and visitors alike. It's a great place to eat too, with an interesting menu of British and world cuisine. Dishes could include a Greek meze platter, popcorn tiger prawns, chilli con carne, and sweet and sour pigs' cheeks.

Open all day all wk 11-11 **Bar Meals** L served all wk 10-9.30 D served all wk 6.30-9.30 food served all day **Restaurant** L served all wk 10-9.30 D served all wk 6.30-9.30 food served all day ⊕ FULLER'S ◀ London Pride, Chiswick Bitter, Discovery & Organic Honey Dew, George Gale & Co HSB, Guest ale. ♀ 24 **Facilities** Non-diners area ♣ (Bar Garden) ♦♦ Children's portions Garden ♬ Parking Wi-fi ▭

Save on hotels. Book at theAA.com/hotel

BERKSHIRE 37 ENGLAND

STANFORD DINGLEY — Map 5 SU57

The Old Boot Inn

RG7 6LT ☎ 0118 974 4292
e-mail: johnintheboot@hotmail.co.uk
dir: M4 junct 12, A4/A340 to Pangbourne. 1st left to Bradfield. Through Bradfield, follow Stanford Dingley signs

Peaceful situation and well known for good food

Oak beams and half-timbering feature inside this cottagey inn remote along lanes in the peaceful Pang Valley. The rustic theme continues with log fires and an enormous beer garden rolling back to merge with pastureland backed by wooded hills. The modern conservatory restaurant is light and airy; just the place to moor up with a pint of local Dr Hexter's beer and seek inspiration on the menus. Old school bar meals are the tip of the iceberg, complemented by an à la carte selection and robust specials, perhaps roast chump of lamb with black pudding, red wine jus and seasonal vegetables.

Open all wk 11-3 6-11 (Sat-Sun all day) **Bar Meals** L served all wk 12-2 D served all wk 7-9 **Restaurant** L served all wk 12-2 D served all wk 7-9 ⊕ FREE HOUSE ⬛ Bass, West Berkshire Dr Hexters, Fuller's London Pride Ŏ Westons Stowford Press. 🍷 10
Facilities Non-diners area 🐾 (Bar Garden) ᛙ Children's menu Children's portions Play area Garden 🎋 Parking Wi-fi 🚌 (notice required)

SWALLOWFIELD — Map 5 SU76

The George & Dragon

PICK OF THE PUBS

Church Rd RG7 1TJ ☎ 0118 988 4432
e-mail: dining@georgeanddragonswallowfield.co.uk
dir: M4, junct 11, A33 towards Basingstoke. Left at Barge Ln to B3349 into The Street, right into Church Rd

Friendly country pub dating back to the 17th century

Formerly a farm, this country pub and restaurant looks very much the part with its low, stripped beams, log fires, rug-strewn floors and warm earthy tones. It has been under the same ownership for the last 20 years, and regular customers know what to expect from the internationally inspired seasonal menus, sourced extensively from local suppliers. Starters that may be available are herbed spinach and button mushroom pancake with mornay sauce; and soy- and chilli-braised octopus with pineapple, orange and tomato salsa. Typical main courses include local venison loin steak with haggis mash and redcurrant jus; baked meatballs in a rich Barolo wine tomato sauce, with zesty gremolata and pasta; and monkfish on sweet potato bubble-and-squeak. The garden overlooks beautiful countryside and makes a great place to head for after walking the long-distance Blackwater Valley Path, which follows the river from its source in Rowhill Nature Reserve to Swallowfield.

Open all day all wk **Bar Meals** L served Mon-Sat 12-2.30, Sun 12-3 D served Mon-Sat 7-9.30, Sun 7-9 **Restaurant** L served Mon-Sat 12-2.30, Sun 12-3 D served Mon-Sat 7-9.30, Sun 7-9 ⊕ FREE HOUSE ⬛ Fuller's London Pride, Ringwood Best Bitter, Sharp's Doom Bar Ŏ Thatchers Gold. **Facilities** Non-diners area ᛙ Children's menu Children's portions Garden 🎋 Parking

WALTHAM ST LAWRENCE — Map 5 SU87

The Bell

The Street RG10 0JJ ☎ 0118 934 1788
e-mail: info@thebellwalthamstlawrence.co.uk
dir: On B3024 E of Twyford. From A4 turn at Hare Hatch

Good ciders and beers at very old inn

This 14th-century free house is renowned for its ciders and an ever-changing range of real ales selected from small independent breweries. The building was given to the community in 1608 and profits from the rent still help village charities. Iain and Scott Ganson have built a local reputation for good food where everything possible is made on the premises, including all charcuterie and preparation of game. Start with yellow split pea soup with Bell beer bread or Welsh rarebit, then continue with pan-fried trout with Puy lentils, rainbow chard and horseradish dressing; or confit of pork belly with fondant potato, haricot beans, spinach and salsa verde. Don't miss the annual summer beer festival.

Open all wk 12-3 5-11 (Sat 12-11 Sun 12-10.30) **Bar Meals** L served Mon-Fri 12-2, Sat-Sun 12-3 D served all wk 6-9.30 ⊕ FREE HOUSE ⬛ Binghams Twyford Tipple, 5 Guest ales Ŏ Pheasant Plucker, Westons Old Rosie. 🍷 19
Facilities Non-diners area 🐾 (Bar Restaurant Garden) ᛙ Children's menu Children's portions Play area Garden 🎋 Beer festival Parking

WHITE WALTHAM — Map 5 SU87

The Beehive

Waltham Rd SL6 3SH ☎ 01628 822877
e-mail: beehivepub@aol.com
dir: M4 junct8/9, A404, follow White Waltham signs

A cracking country local in an idyllic village setting

With a smart, contemporary interior, this red-brick pub features an extension which gives easy access to the front patio overlooking the cricket pitch. Renowned for its relaxing atmosphere and choice of real ales, which includes a local Loddon brew, The Beehive is also a great place to eat. In addition to its lunchtime bar menu of burgers, jackets, salads and sandwiches, fresh seasonal dishes may feature seared scallops with bacon and chorizo; chicken supreme stuffed with haggis and wrapped in smoked ham; and Thai-style salmon fishcakes with sweet chilli dipping sauce.

Open all wk 11-3 5-11 (Sat 11am-mdnt Sun 12-10.30) Closed: 26 Dec **Bar Meals** L served Mon-Fri 12-2.30, Sat 12-9.30, Sun 12-8.30 D served Mon-Fri 5-9.30, Sat 12-9.30, Sun 12-8.30 **Restaurant** L served Mon-Fri 12-2.30, Sat 12-9.30, Sun 12-8.30 D served Mon-Fri

5-9.30, Sat 12-9.30, Sun 12-8.30 ⊕ ENTERPRISE INNS ⬛ Fuller's London Pride, Greene King Abbot Ale, Rebellion, Brakspear, Loddon guest ale. 🍷 14
Facilities Non-diners area 🐾 (Bar Garden) ᛙ Children's menu Children's portions Garden Parking Wi-fi 🚌 (notice required)

WINKFIELD — Map 6 SU97

Rose & Crown

Woodside, Windsor Forest SL4 2DP ☎ 01344 882051
e-mail: enquiries@roseandcrownwoodside.com
dir: M3 junct 3, from Ascot Racecourse on A332 take 2nd exit from Heatherwood Hosp rdbt, 2nd left

Tucked away pub with tranquil garden for alfresco dining

Run by the Fielder family for the past two years, this 200-year-old traditional pub comes complete with old beams and low ceilings and is hidden down a country lane with a peaceful garden overlooking open fields. A typical menu includes tapas; chorizo in white wine; spicy BBQ chicken wings; calamari with tartare sauce. To follow maybe pork and leek sausages with mash; surf and turf steak with garlic tiger king prawns; spicy beef chilli or a locally sourced steak chargrilled to your liking. Wash it all down with a well-kept pint of Old Speckled Hen.

Open all day all wk **Bar Meals** L served Mon-Fri 12-3, Sat 12-10, Sun 12-8 D served Tue-Sat 6-9.30, Sun 12-8 Av main course £6-£9 **Restaurant** L served Mon-Fri 12-3, Sat 12-10, Sun 12-8 D served Tue-Sat 6-9.30, Sun 12-8 Fixed menu price fr £9.95 Av 3 course à la carte fr £19.95 ⊕ GREENE KING ⬛ IPA, Abbot Ale, Morland Old Speckled Hen & Original, Guest ale. 🍷 12 **Facilities** Non-diners area 🐾 (Bar) ᛙ Children's menu Children's portions Play area Garden 🎋 Beer festival Cider festival Parking Wi-fi 🚌

WINTERBOURNE — Map 5 SU47

The Winterbourne Arms

RG20 8BB ☎ 01635 248200
e-mail: mail@winterbournearms.com
dir: M4 junct 13 into Chieveley Services, follow Donnington signs to Winterbourne. Right into Arlington Ln, right at T-junct, left into Winterbourne

Idyllic pub with large gardens

Steeped in 300 years of history, warmth and charm, yet only five minutes from the M4, this pretty village pub once housed the village bakery and shop. The Winterbourne's real ales may include local Whistle Wetter, while 12 wines served by the glass and 20 more by the bottle make for a comprehensive list. The traditional and modern British menus and daily-changing specials offer boned chicken leg stuffed with mozzarella and bacon served on a ham and pea risotto, which can be enjoyed by candlelight or alfresco in summer. Local game is served in season.

Open all wk 12-3 6-11 (Sun 12-10.30) **Bar Meals** L served all wk 12-2.30 D served all wk 6-10 Av main

continued

WINTERBOURNE *continued*

course £15 **Restaurant** L served all wk 12-2.30 D served all wk 6-10 Av 3 course à la carte fr £20 ⊕ FREE HOUSE ◀ Winterbourne Whistle Wetter, Ramsbury Gold, Guinness. ☗ 12 **Facilities** Non-diners area ☙ (Bar Garden) ♦️ Children's portions Garden ⚲ Parking ☜ (notice required)

WOOLHAMPTON Map 5 SU56

The Rowbarge NEW

Station Rd RG7 5SH ☎ 0118 971 2213
e-mail: rowbarge@brunningandprice.co.uk
dir: *From A4 (Bath Rd) at Midgham into Station Rd, signed to station & pub. Over rail crossing, over canal, pub on right*

Revitalised pub by the Kennet Canal

Since the early 18th-century this pub alongside a busy lock on the Kennet & Avon Canal has undergone the occasional change, but its most recent major refurbishment was more of a reincarnation, one that restored its truly traditional character. The bar serves half a dozen cask ales — King John and Saxon Archer among them — Aspall cider and 16 wines by the glass. For something light, try smoked haddock kedgeree, or a rump steak sandwich; main meals include calves' liver and bacon; baked salmon Wellington; and pan-fried parmesan gnocchi. The canal towpath borders the large garden. October is beer festival time.

Open all day all wk **Bar Meals** L served all wk 12-10 D served all wk 12-10 Av main course £12 food served all day **Restaurant** L served all wk 12-10 D served all wk 12-10 Av 3 course à la carte fr £22 food served all day ⊕ BRUNNING & PRICE ◀ Original, Andwell King John, Three Castles Saxon Archer, Guest ales Ö Aspall. ☗ 16 **Facilities** Non-diners area ☙ (Bar Garden) ♦️ Children's menu Children's portions Garden ⚲ Beer festival Parking Wi-fi ☜ (notice required)

WOKINGHAM Map 5 SU86

The Broad Street Tavern

29 Broad St RG40 1AU ☎ 0118 977 3706
e-mail: broadstreettavern@wadworth.co.uk
dir: *In town centre, adjacent to Pizza Express*

Town pub with interesting food options

Housed in a handsome detached period building fronted by elegant railings, this town-centre watering hole offers leather armchairs and sofas in the bar, and an extensive decked garden area with a summer bar and barbecue. Snacks range from organic baguettes to tapas dishes such as beer battered chicken strips; crispy filo prawns; and spicy fishcakes. More filling classics include pie of the day; a sliders board; home-made beer and cheddar soup; and eggs Benedict. Four beer festivals are hosted every year. Children are only allowed in for Sunday lunches.

Open all day all wk Closed: 25 Dec **Bar Meals** L served all wk 12-2.30 D served all wk 6-9.30 ⊕ WADWORTH ◀ 6X, Henry's Original IPA, The Bishop's Tipple Ö Westons Old

Rosie. ☗ 17 **Facilities** Non-diners area ☙ (Bar Garden) Garden ⚲ Beer festival Wi-fi ☜ (notice required)

YATTENDON Map 5 SU57

The Royal Oak Hotel

PICK OF THE PUBS

The Square RG18 0UG ☎ 01635 201325
e-mail: info@royaloakyattendon.com
web: www.royaloakyattendon.co.uk
dir: *M4 junct 12, A4 to Newbury, right at 2nd rdbt to Pangbourne then 1st left. From junct 13, A34 N 1st left, right at T-junct. Left then 2nd right to Yattendon*

Village pub with generous home-cooked food

Part of a row of 16th-century cottages, deep in shooting country, The Royal Oak wears its history well. This was where Oliver Cromwell and his Roundheads planned their strategy for the second Battle of Newbury in 1664 and their adversary, King Charles I, sought refuge here after the fighting was over. Log fires in the bar, oak beams, quarry-tiled and wood floors in the adjoining lounge and dining rooms, add to the character. Owner Rob McGill offers tip-top real ales from the West Berkshire Brewery in the village, including Mr Chubb's Lunchtime Bitter. From the regularly changing menu, order a sandwich or dive straight into the main menu with rabbit and mustard pie or steamed ham hock and onion pudding. Round off with treacle tart and clotted cream. French windows lead to a walled rear garden with vine-laden trellis, plus a boules piste, making a perfect spot in summer.

Open all day all wk **Bar Meals** L served Mon-Fri 12-2.30, Sat-Sun 12-3 D served Mon-Thu 6.30-9.30, Fri-Sat 6.30-10, Sun 6.30-9 Av main course £15 **Restaurant** L served Mon-Fri 12-2.30, Sat-Sun 12-3 D served Mon-Thu 6.30-9.30, Fri-Sat 6.30-10, Sun 6.30-9 Fixed menu price fr £12.95 Av 3 course à la carte fr £27.50 ⊕ FREE HOUSE ◀ West Berkshire Good Old Boy & Mr Chubb's Lunchtime Bitter, Guest ale Ö Westons Stowford Press. ☗ 10 **Facilities** Non-diners area ☙ (Bar Restaurant Garden) ♦️ Children's menu Children's portions Garden ⚲ Parking Wi-fi

The Albion

Boyces Av, Clifton BS8 4AA ☎ 0117 973 3522
e-mail: info@thealbionclifton.co.uk
dir: *From A4 take B3129 towards city centre. Right into Clifton Down Rd. 3rd left into Boyces Ave*

Popular from brunch through to the evening

This handsome Grade II listed coaching inn dates from the 17th century. Now owned by the St Austell Brewery, it's a popular place to enjoy West Country ales and ciders, as well as being a top gastro-pub. In the enclosed courtyard you can order jugs of Pimm's in summer or sip mulled cider under heaters in the winter. The modern British cooking uses local produce in dishes such as braised pork belly, scallops and chorizo purée; pan-fried hake with sauerkraut, gnocchi, champagne velouté and clams. Brunch and Sunday lunch menus are also available. There is an annual beer and cider festival in May.

Open all day 12-12 (Sat 11am-mdnt Sun 11-11) Closed: 25-26 Dec, Mon L **Bar Meals** L served Tue-Fri 12-3, Sat 11-3, Sun 11-3.30 D served Tue-Sat 7-10 Av main course £16 **Restaurant** L served Tue-Fri 12-3, Sat 11-3, Sun 11-3.30 D served Tue-Sat 7-10 Av 3 course à la carte fr £30 ⊕ ST AUSTELL BREWERY ◀ Otter Bitter, Dartmoor, Tribute, Trelawny Ö Thatchers Cheddar Valley, Thatchers Gold. ☗ 12 **Facilities** Non-diners area ☙ (Bar Garden) ♦️ Children's portions Garden ⚲ Beer festival Cider festival Wi-fi ☜ (notice required)

Cornubia

142 Temple St BS1 6EN ☎ 0117 925 4415
e-mail: philjackithecornubia@hotmail.co.uk
dir: *Opposite Bristol Fire Station*

One of Bristol's best kept secrets

Hidden among tall office buildings in the centre of Bristol, this welcoming Georgian pub was originally built as two houses. The pub's name is the Latinised version for Cornwall. Local workers love it, not just because of its convenience, but also for its choice of changing real ales, including its own Cornubia, two draught ciders and a serious collection of malts and bottled beers. Weekday lunchtime bar snacks include baguettes, Phil's specials of the day, and the pub's famous pork pies. There is a raised decking area at the front and live entertainment every week.

Open all day 12-11 Closed: 25-26 Dec, 1 Jan, Sun **Bar Meals** L served Mon-Sat 12-2.30 ⊕ FREE HOUSE ◀ Cornubia, Guest ales Ö Thatchers Cheddar Valley & Gold, Guest ciders. **Facilities** Non-diners area ☙ (Bar Garden) Garden ⚲ Parking Wi-fi ☜ (notice required)

Highbury Vaults

164 St Michaels Hill, Cotham BS2 8DE
☎ 0117 973 3203
e-mail: highburyvaults@youngs.co.uk
dir: *A38 to Cotham from inner ring dual carriageway*

Ever popular unpretentious city escape

A classic little city pub which oozes the character of a Victorian drinking house; lots of dark panelled nooks and crannies, dim lighting, impressive original bar and a cosmopolitan crowd of locals, many of whom retreat from their labours in academia and medicine at this corner of the university area of Bristol. Condemned Victorian prisoners took their last meals here; today's crowd are more fortunate, revelling in beers such as Bath Ales and chowing down on no-nonsense pub fare like fish pie, sausage and mash or burgers. Other benefits include no music or fruit machines and a heated garden terrace.

Open all day all wk 12-12 (Sun 12-11) Closed: 25 Dec eve, 26 Dec L, 1 Jan L **Bar Meals** L served Mon-Fri 12-2, Sat 12-2.30, Sun 12-3 D served Mon-Fri 5.30-8.30 Av main course £7.50 ⊕ YOUNG'S ◄ London Gold & Bitter, Bath Gem, St Austell Tribute, Guest ales ♂ Addlestones, Thatchers Gold. **Facilities** Non-diners area ♦♦ Garden ⋒ Wi-fi ▭ (notice required) **Notes** ⊛

The Kensington Arms

PICK OF THE PUBS

35-37 Stanley Rd BS6 6NP ☎ 0117 944 6444
e-mail: info@thekensingtonarms.co.uk
dir: *From Redland Rail Station into South Rd, then Kensington Rd. 4th right into Stanley Rd*

Local produce drives the menu here

A Victorian corner pub in the backstreets of Bristol's leafy and sought-after Redland district, this upmarket bar and dining room is packed with mismatched antique furniture and Victorian prints. In the dining room, complete with views into the open kitchen, the modern British food utilises the very best local produce and the menu changes daily, with meat from the region's farms and fish delivered daily from Cornwall. In the bar, try a raised venison pie with your pint of London Glory. Typical restaurant dishes in the evening are starters of duck hearts on toast; or whole roast quail and aïoli. These might be followed by Cornish cod with Puy lentils, Savoy cabbage and red wine sauce; game pie with buttered spinach or 30 day dry-aged rib of beef for two to share. Finish with pear and frangipane tart; chocolate marquise and black cherries or a selection of artisan cheeses.

Open all day all wk Closed: 25 & 26 Dec **Bar Meals** L served Mon-Fri 12-3, Sat 10-3 D served Mon-Sat 6-10 **Restaurant** L served Mon-Fri 12-3, Sat 10-3, Sun 12-4 D served Mon-Sat 6-10 ⊕ GREENE KING ◄ IPA Gold, London Glory, Morland ♂ Westons Stowford Press, Thatchers Gold. ♥ 14 **Facilities** Non-diners area ♣ (Bar Restaurant Outside area) ♦♦ Children's portions Outside area ⋒ Wi-fi ▭ (notice required)

Robin Hood's Retreat

197 Gloucester Rd BS7 8BG ☎ 0117 924 8639
e-mail: info@robinhoodsretreat.co.uk
dir: *At main rdbt at Broad Mead take Gloucester Rd exit, St Pauls; leads into Gloucester Rd (A38)*

A Bristol favourite setting a trend for the city

In the heart of Bristol, this Victorian red-brick pub is popular with real ale lovers, who usually have several to choose from. The interior has been superbly appointed, with original features retained and with the addition of richly coloured wood panelling and furniture. There's plenty of attention to detail in the food too, which is all prepared on the premises. Favourites are slow-cooked British dishes such as braised brisket of salt beef with toffee carrots and dripping roast potatoes, and several seafood options.

Open all wk Mon-Wed 12-11 (Thu-Sat 12-12 Sun 12-10.30) Closed: 25 Dec **Bar Meals** L served Mon-Sat 12-2.30, Sun 12-4 D served Mon-Sat 6-9, Sun 6.30-9 **Restaurant** L served Mon-Sat 12-2.30, Sun 12-4 D served Mon-Sat 6-9, Sun 6.30-9 ⊕ ENTERPRISE INNS ◄ Sharp's Doom Bar, St Austell Tribute, Adnams Lighthouse, Butcombe ♂ Westons Stowford Press, Addlestones Cloudy. ♥ 15 **Facilities** Non-diners area ♦♦ Children's portions Garden ⋒

BUCKINGHAMSHIRE

AMERSHAM   Map 6 SU99

Hit or Miss Inn

Penn Street Village HP7 0PX ☎ 01494 713109
e-mail: hit@ourpubs.co.uk
dir: *M25 junct 18, A404 (Amersham to High Wycombe road) to Amersham. Past crematorium on right, 2nd left into Whielden Ln (signed Winchmore Hill). 1.25m, pub on right*

A dining pub that is certainly a hit

Overlooking the cricket ground from which its name is taken, this is an 18th-century cottage-style dining pub. It has a beautiful country garden with lawn, patio and picnic tables for warmer days, while inside you'll find fires, old-world beams, Badger ales and a warm welcome from landlords Michael and Mary Macken, who have been running the pub for ten years. Options on the menu range from tempting sandwiches and baked potatoes to dishes like veal cutlet, pork tenderloin, rib-eye steak, and turkey schnitzel. There are daily specials, Sunday roasts and a children's menu, too. There is a village beer festival in mid-July.

Open all day all wk 11-11 (Sun 12-10.30) **Bar Meals** L served Mon-Fri 12-2.30, Sat 12-3, Sun 12-8 D served Mon-Sat 6.30-9.30, Sun 12-8 Av main course £12 **Restaurant** L served Mon-Fri 12-2.30, Sat 12-3, Sun 12-8 D served Mon-Sat 6.30-9.30, Sun 12-8 ⊕ HALL & WOODHOUSE ◄ Badger Dorset Best, Tanglefoot, K&B Sussex, Badger Firkin Fox ♂ Westons Stowford Press. ♥ 10 **Facilities** Non-diners area ♣ (Bar Restaurant Garden) ♦♦ Children's menu Children's portions Garden ⋒ Beer festival Parking Wi-fi ▭ (notice required)

AYLESBURY   Map 11 SP81

The King's Head

Market Square HP20 2RW ☎ 01296 718812
e-mail: info@farmersbar.co.uk
dir: *Access on foot only. From Market Square access cobbled passageway. Pub entrance under archway on right*

Brewery tap for the Chiltern microbrewery

Henry VIII reputedly wooed Anne Boleyn when staying at this well-preserved coaching inn dating from 1455. Today, The King's Head is the award-winning brewery tap for the Chiltern Brewery, one of the oldest microbreweries in the country. In addition, there is a special weekly gravity beer, served from a wooden cask atop the bar. Enjoy a pint in the ancient cobbled courtyard; or dine on beef cobbler, roasted vegetable parcel or fish and chips. Rothschild's supplies the wines from its former family seat at nearby National Trust-owned Waddesdon Manor. Contact the pub for details of the beer festivals.

Open all day all wk 11-11 (Sun 12-10.30) Closed: 25 Dec **Bar Meals** L served Mon-Fri 12-2, Sat-Sun 12-3 ⊕ FREE HOUSE/CHILTERN BREWERY ◄ Beechwood Bitter, Chiltern Ale, 300s Old Ale ♂ Westons Stowford Press & Wyld Wood Organic. ♥ 11 **Facilities** Non-diners area ♦♦ Children's menu Children's portions Garden ⋒ Beer festival ▭ (notice required)

BEACONSFIELD   Map 6 SU99

The Royal Standard of England

PICK OF THE PUBS

Brindle Ln, Forty Green HP9 1XT ☎ 01494 673382
e-mail: theoldestpub@btinternet.com
dir: *A40 to Beaconsfield, right at church rdbt onto B474 towards Penn, left onto Forty Green Rd, 1m*

Inn with memorable beers and game dishes

A ghostly drummer boy haunts the car park of this gabled, idyllic pub tucked away in The Chilterns on a site where ale has been provided since Saxon times, making this the oldest freehouse in England. They do serve spirits here, but many visit to quaff the ales flowing from the pub's own microbrewery, complementing other beers brewed in these chalk hills and a range of Somerset farm ciders and Herefordshire perry; there's a summer beer festival, too. Hearty food is the order of the day on the quality menus, served amid the striking leaded windows, magpie collection of artefacts, ancient pillars and beams and flagstone floors, warmed in winter by log-burners and an inglenook. Comfort zone pub classics include fish pie or Elwy Valley Welsh lamb shoulder with roasted peppers and onion, followed perhaps by treacle tart with ginger. Keep an eye on the specials boards for seasonal game, rabbit, pigeon or venison dishes.

Open all day all wk 11-11 **Bar Meals** food served all day **Restaurant** food served all day ⊕ FREE HOUSE ◄ Chiltern Ale, Brakspear Bitter, Britannia Pale & Golden, Guest ales ♂ Cotswold, The Orchard Pig, Westons Perry. ♥ 11 **Facilities** Non-diners area ♣ (Bar Restaurant Garden) ♦♦ Children's portions Family room Garden Beer festival Parking Wi-fi ▭

PICK OF THE PUBS

The Royal Oak

BOVINGDON GREEN   Map 5 SU88

Frieth Rd SL7 2JF ☎ 01628 488611
e-mail: info@royaloakmarlow.co.uk
web: www.royaloakmarlow.co.uk
*dir: A4155 from Marlow. 300yds right
signed Bovingdon Green. 0.75m, pub on
left*

Successful pub strong on seasonality

'Dogs, children and muddy boots
welcome' is the friendly motto at this
little old whitewashed pub, just up the
hill from town on the edge of Marlow
Common. It stands in sprawling, flower-
filled gardens and is one of the well-
regarded Salisbury Pubs mini-empire in
and around the Chilterns.* Inside, it's
spacious yet cosy, with dark floorboards,
rich fabrics, and a wood-burning stove.
All this sets the tone for early evening
regulars gathered round a challenging
crossword with a pint of Rebellion from
Marlow, or Tutts Clump draught cider
from West Berkshire. The imaginative
modern British and international menu,
put together with good food ethics in
mind, is designed to appeal to all,
beginning with 'small plates', such as
Trealy Farm charcuterie with walnut
remoulade and poached pear; and home
tea-smoked salmon with fennel, sesame
seeds and blood orange dressing. Main
courses cover ground from roast duck
breast with five spice noodle stir-fry, hot
and sour tamarind jus and roast

peanuts; and local pork sausage and
black pudding cassoulet with spring
onion mash; to feta with sweet potato
gnocchi, spinach and toasted hazelnut
pesto. Perhaps treat yourself to white
chocolate cheesecake with honeycomb
and spiced apricots to finish. An
exclusively European wine list has over
20 by the glass and a wide choice of
pudding wines, including one from
Worcestershire. Outside there's a sunny
summer terrace, pétanque piste and, if
you're lucky, red kites wheeling around
in the sky.

*Alford Arms, Hemel Hempstead, Hertfordshire;
and in Buckinghamshire, The Swan Inn, Denham;
The Old Queens Head, Penn.

Open all day all wk 11-11 (Sun
12-10.30) Closed: 25-26 Dec **Bar**

Meals L served Mon-Fri 12-2.30, Sat
12-3, Sun 12-4 D served Sun-Thu
6.30-9.30, Fri-Sat 6.30-10 **Restaurant** L
served Mon-Fri 12-2.30, Sat 12-3, Sun
12-4 D served Sun-Thu 6.30-9.30, Fri-
Sat 6.30-10 ⊕ SALISBURY PUBS LTD
🍺 Rebellion IPA, Smuggler Ŏ Thatchers,
Tutts Clump. ♇ 22 **Facilities** Non-
diners area 🐾 (Bar Garden) ♟
Children's portions Garden ⊼ Parking
Wi-fi

Save on hotels. Book at theAA.com/hotel

BUCKINGHAMSHIRE   41   ENGLAND

BLEDLOW
Map 5 SP70

The Lions of Bledlow

Church End HP27 9PE ☎ **01844 343345**
web: www.lionsofbledlow.co.uk
dir: M40 junct 6, B4009 to Princes Risborough, through Chinnor into Bledlow

Lovely old pub often in the spotlight

This lovely old free house dates back to the 1500s and is often used as a filming location for dramas such as *Midsomer Murders*, *Miss Marple* and *Restless*. Low beams and careworn flooring give the pub a timeless feeling, underlined by the steam trains chugging past on the heritage railway beyond the village green. Ramblers who drop down from the wooded Chiltern scarp can fill up on generously filled baguettes and rustic home-made meals like beef lasagne with garlic bread; and hot smoked mackerel fillets with salad and boiled potatoes, boosted by daily-changing specials.

Open all wk 11.30-3 6-11 (Sun 12-4 7-10.30 BHs & summer wknds all day) **Bar Meals** L served all wk 12-2.30 D served Mon-Sat 6.30-9.30, Sun 7-9 **Restaurant** L served all wk 12-2.30 D served Mon-Sat 6.30-9.30, Sun 7-9 ⊕ FREE HOUSE ◀ Wadworth 6X, Guest ales ⬙ Westons Stowford Press. ☂ 12 **Facilities** Non-diners area ♦♦ Children's menu Children's portions Family room Garden ⊟ Parking 🚐

BLETCHLEY
Map 11 SP83

The Crooked Billet ☺
PICK OF THE PUBS

2 Westbrook End, Newton Longville MK17 0DF
☎ **01908 373936**
e-mail: john@thebillet.co.uk
dir: M1 junct 13, follow signs to Buckingham. 6m, signed at Bottledump rdbt to Newton Longville

A high-end destination dining pub

Just down the road from the Bletchley Park is this magnificently thatched village pub. Timbers from a sailing vessel surplus to requirements around the time of Sir Francis Drake were recycled to create the core of the building. The soul of the once rural alehouse remains; crackling winter log fires (the house bacon is smoked in the inglenook) cast flickering shadows across oak beams; and there are huge lawned gardens. Top sommelier John Gilchrist and wife/chef Emma took on the run-down Billet more than a decade ago. Emma's menus are based on the finest, freshest ingredients from small, local

specialist producers and suppliers, and the emphasis is on taste and modern presentation; a cosmopolitan mix of contemporary and classical with English and French influences. The carte selection reads like a gastronome's wish list; all meals are matched to particular wines. Typical dishes could be pan-fried scallops with sweet potato purée; and crispy suckling pig and bacon.

Open 12-2.30 5.30-11 (Sun 12-4 7-10.30) Closed: 27-28 Dec, Mon **Bar Meals** L served Tue-Sat 12-2, Sun 12-4 D served Tue-Thu 7-9, Fri-Sat 7-9.30 **Restaurant** L served Tue-Sat 12-2, Sun 12-4 D served Tue-Thu 7-9, Fri-Sat 7-9.30 ⊕ GREENE KING ◀ Ruddles Best, Abbot Ale, IPA, Guest ales ⬙ Aspall. ☂ 200 **Facilities** Non-diners area ♦♦ Children's portions Garden ⊟ Parking

BOVINGDON GREEN
Map 5 SU88

The Royal Oak
PICK OF THE PUBS

See Pick of the Pubs on opposite page

BRILL
Map 11 SP61

The Pheasant Inn

Windmill St HP18 9TG ☎ **01844 239370**
e-mail: info@thepheasant.co.uk
dir: In village centre, by windmill

Stunning views from Brill's popular inn

Occupying a fine hilltop position on the edge of Brill Common, with impressive views over the Vale of Aylesbury and the Chilterns, this 17th-century beamed inn stands next to Brill Windmill, one of the oldest postmills in the country. A simple menu offers hearty modern pub dishes, including starters of spiced potted beef with horseradish cream, and main courses like venison with game chips and cranberry jus; and pot-roasted lamb shank with root vegetables and mash. Salads, filled baps and ploughman's lunches are served at lunchtime – best enjoyed in the garden in summer.

Open all day all wk 12-11 (Fri-Sat 12-12 Sun 12-10.30) **Bar Meals** L served Mon-Sat 12-2, Sun 12-6 D served all wk 6.30-9 Av main course £12 **Restaurant** L served all wk 12-2 D served all wk 6.30-9 Av 3 course à la carte fr £25 ⊕ FREE HOUSE ◀ St Austell Tribute, 2 Guest ales ⬙ Thatchers. **Facilities** Non-diners area ♦♦ Children's portions Garden ⊟ Parking Wi-fi 🚐 (notice required)

BUCKINGHAM
Map 11 SP63

The Old Thatched Inn

Main St, Adstock MK18 2JN ☎ **01296 712584**
e-mail: manager@theoldthatchedinn.co.uk
web: www.theoldthatchedinn.co.uk
dir: Telephone for directions

Spacious pub with plenty of original character

Once called the Chandos Arms, this lovely 17th-century thatched inn still boasts traditional beams and inglenook fireplace. The spacious interior consists of a formal conservatory and a bar with comfy furniture and a welcoming, relaxed atmosphere. Using the freshest, seasonal ingredients from local and regional suppliers, the evening menu takes in smoked mackerel rillette with cucumber and dill salad; and braised lamb neck fillet with roasted root vegetables and minted red wine gravy. Typical lunchtime dishes include pan-fried fillet of pollock with chorizo and potato hash; and Cumberland sausages with mash and onion gravy.

Open all day all wk Closed: 26 Dec **Bar Meals** L served Mon-Fri 12-2.30, Sat 12-3, Sun 12-9 D served Mon-Sat 6-9.30, Sun 12-9 Av main course £13.95 **Restaurant** Fixed menu price fr £13.95 Av 3 course à la carte fr £25 ⊕ FREE HOUSE ◀ Hook Norton Hooky Bitter, Morland Old Speckled Hen, Fuller's London Pride, Timothy Taylor ⬙ Aspall. ☂ 14 **Facilities** Non-diners area ❀ (Bar) ♦♦ Children's menu Children's portions Outside area ⊟ Parking Wi-fi

See advert on page 42

CHALFONT ST PETER
Map 6 TQ09

The Greyhound Inn
PICK OF THE PUBS

See Pick of the Pubs on page 43

A great atmosphere awaits you at Buckinghamshire's favourite owner-managed gastropub, the Old Thatched Inn, in the picturesque village of Adstock.

Our passion is freshly made, delicious food that is, where possible sourced locally and doesn't break the bank. Our delightful stylish listed Inn dates back to 1702 and oozes character and atmosphere – a perfect backdrop for our great food and friendly service.

So come and discover this hidden rural gem in Adstock, between Buckingham, Milton Keynes and Winslow. Nearby attractions: Stowe Gardens and Silverstone Race Track... Come enjoy...

- 5 Real Ales
- Home-made food
- Extensive menus
- Daily specials

The Old Thatched Inn, Main Street, Adstock, (bet. Buckingham & Winslow), Buckinghamshire, MK18 2JN

PICK OF THE PUBS

The Greyhound Inn

CHALFONT ST PETER Map 6 TQ09

SL9 9RA ☎ 01753 883404
e-mail: reception@thegreyhoundinn.net
web: www.thegreyhoundinn.net
dir: *M40 junct 1/M25 junct 16, follow signs for Gerrards Cross, then Chalfont St Peter*

14th-century coaching inn with good food

On the London Road and set beside the River Misbourne, this historic coaching inn has been at the heart of Chalfont St Peter since the 14th century. Over the years, it has welcomed many a traveller, including Winston Churchill, Oliver Cromwell and local landowner Judge Jeffreys, who held his famous assizes here in the 1680s before sending his victims to the gallows. Much of the pub's original character has been retained, including the massive beams supporting the weight of the inn, plus the huge brick chimneys. These days, visitors and villagers can establish a presence in the imposing panelled, flagstoned bar or chic restaurant, and chinwag with the locals over a pint of London Pride or one of the ten wines available by the glass. A continental-style menu of light dishes and sandwiches includes sirloin steak sandwich with fried onions, or chicken liver parfait with red onion marmalade on toasted brioche. For those with larger appetites, look forward to choosing from the extensive modern British menu, where a starter of pea and goats' cheese tart with rocket salad and red pepper coulis, or a sharing platter of fish or meat whets the appetite for steak and ale pie with bubble-and-squeak; squid ink linguine with clams, crayfish, shallot and roasted cherry tomato sauce; or grilled corn-fed chicken breast with chorizo potatoes and thyme sauce. Make sure you leave some room for one of the tempting desserts: apple tart with vanilla ice cream and Calvados raisins, perhaps, or chocolate fondant with candied orange and clotted cream.

Open all day all wk Mon-Wed 6.30am-10.30pm (Thu 6.30am-11.30pm Fri-Sat 6.30am-1am Sun 8.30am-10.30pm) **Bar Meals** L served Mon-Sat 12-2.30, Sun 12-6 D served Mon-Sat 6-9.30 Av main course £16 **Restaurant** L served Mon-Sat 12-2.30, Sun 12-6 D served Mon-Sat 6-9.30 Av 3 course à la carte fr £25 ⊕ ENTERPRISE INNS ◀ Fuller's London Pride, Sharp's Doom Bar, Adnams. 🍷 10 **Facilities** Non-diners area 🐾 (Bar Garden) 👪 Children's menu & portions Garden ⛩ Parking Wi-fi

CHEDDINGTON
Map 11 SP91

The Old Swan

58 High St LU7 0RQ ☎ 01296 668226
e-mail: oldswancheddington@btconnect.com
dir: *From Tring towards Marsworth take B489, 0.5m. Left towards Cooks Wharf onto Cheddington, pub on left*

Medieval charm in the Vale of Aylesbury

This stunning, neatly thatched 600-year-old free house nestles in the shadow of The Chilterns close to the Grand Union Canal. It's known not only for its real ales and traditional character but also for its food. Using locally sourced ingredients and game, fish and seafood supplies from sustainable south-coast fisheries, the menus offer a wide selection of modern dishes. A freshly prepared entrée of miniature smoked salmon, sea bass and prawn trio paves the way for chilli beef with coconut and herb rice or lamb's liver in red wine jus. Children are made very welcome and there's a good play area in the attractive garden.

Open all day all wk **Bar Meals** L served Mon-Thu 12-3, Fri-Sat 12-5, Sun 12-4 D served Mon-Thu 6-9, Fri-Sat 6-9.30 Av main course £12 **Restaurant** L served Mon-Thu 12-3, Fri-Sat 12-5, Sun 12-4 D served Mon-Thu 6-9, Fri-Sat 6-9.30 Fixed menu price fr £12 Av 3 course à la carte fr £23 ⊞ FREE HOUSE ◀ Tring Side Pocket for a Toad & Ridgeway Ů Westons Old Rosie, Thatchers Gold. ♟ 20 **Facilities** Non-diners area ♣ (Bar Garden) ♦ Children's portions Play area Garden ⊼ Beer festival Cider festival Parking Wi-fi ⛟ (notice required)

CHENIES
Map 6 TQ09

The Red Lion
PICK OF THE PUBS

See Pick of the Pubs on opposite page

CHESHAM
Map 6 SP90

The Black Horse Inn

Chesham Vale HP5 3NS ☎ 01494 784656
e-mail: enquiries@black-horse-inn.co.uk
dir: *A41 from Berkhamsted, A416 through Ashley Green, 0.75m before Chesham right to Vale Rd, at bottom of Nashleigh Hill, 1m, inn on left*

Traditional Chilterns' pub without modern intrusions

This 500-year-old pub is set in some beautiful valley countryside and is ideal for enjoying a cosy, traditional environment without electronic games or music. During the winter there are roaring log fires to take the chill off those who may spot one of the resident ghosts. An ever-changing menu includes an extensive range of snacks, while the main menu features hearty lamb casserole; baked fillet of sea bass with prawns in garlic butter; home-made pies; and steaks. In summer, eat in the large garden.

Open 12-3 6-11 (Sun 12-6) Closed: Sun eve **Bar Meals** L served Mon-Sat 12-2, Sun 12-3 D served Mon-Sat 6-9 **Restaurant** L served Mon-Sat 12-2, Sun 12-3 D served Mon-Sat 6-9 ⊞ PUNCH TAVERNS ◀ Tring Side Pocket for a Toad, Fuller's London Pride, 2 Guest ales Ů Westons Stowford Press. **Facilities** Non-diners area ♣ (Bar Garden) ♦ Children's portions Garden ⊼ Beer festival Parking Wi-fi ⛟ (notice required)

The Swan

Ley Hill HP5 1UT ☎ 01494 783075
e-mail: swanleyhill@btconnect.com
dir: *1.5m E of Chesham by golf course*

A warm welcome and a cosy fire

Set in the delightful village of Ley Hill, this beautiful 16th-century pub this was once the place where condemned prisoners would drink a 'last and final ale' on the way to the nearby gallows. During World War II, Glen Miller and Clark Gable cycled here for a pint from the Air Force base at Bovingdon. These days, it is a free house offering a warm welcome, real ales and good food, plus a large inglenook fireplace and original beams. Tiger prawns sautéed in garlic, chilli and ginger butter; home-made steak-and-kidney pie; and belly pork with crackling, apple purée and red wine jus are typical choices. Look out for the Bank Holiday beer festival in August.

Open 12-2.30 5.30-11 (Sun 12-4) Closed: Mon eve **Bar Meals** L served all wk 12-2.30 D served Tue-Sat 6.30-9.30 **Restaurant** L served all wk 12-2.30 D served Tue-Sat 6.30-9.30 ⊞ FREE HOUSE ◀ St Austell Tribute, Timothy Taylor Landlord, Tring Side Pocket for a Toad, Guest ales. **Facilities** Non-diners area ♦ Children's menu Garden ⊼ Beer festival Parking ⛟ (notice required)

CUBLINGTON
Map 11 SP82

The Unicorn ◉◉

High St LU7 0LQ ☎ 01296 681261
e-mail: theunicornpub@btconnect.com
dir: *2m N of A418 (between Aylesbury & Leighton Buzzard). In village centre*

Top Aylesbury Vale village free house

That the 17th-century Unicorn overflows with character is not surprising, given its low-beamed bar, wooden floors and real fires. Even the mismatched furniture plays its part. Relax, maybe in the secluded garden, with a pint of Sharp's Doom Bar or Shepherd Neame Spitfire. Two AA Rosettes recognise the inventive dishes on the seasonal menus, such as (from a spring sample) starters of duck and spring onion filo parcel with chilli tomato chutney; and pickled mackerel with apple, and watercress and radish cream; and main courses of steamed sea trout with salsify, sprouting broccoli and rapeseed dill emulsion; pan-roast beef fillet with garlic potato cream bake, olives, green beans and rosemary jus; and wild garlic and nettle pearl barley with goats' cheese and truffle oil. Finish with poached rhubarb, custard and shortbread. Events include quiz nights, live music, and

May and August Bank Holiday beer festivals featuring 12 real ales and ciders.

Open all day all wk 10.30am-11pm (Fri-Sat 10.30am-mdnt) **Bar Meals** food served all day **Restaurant** L served Mon-Sat 12-2, Sun 12-3 D served Mon-Sat 6.30-9, Sun 6.30-8.30 ⊞ FREE HOUSE ◀ Sharp's Doom Bar, Shepherd Neame Spitfire Ů Westons Stowford Press, Thatchers. **Facilities** Non-diners area ♦ Children's menu Children's portions Play area Garden ⊼ Beer festival Parking Wi-fi ⛟ (notice required)

CUDDINGTON
Map 5 SP71

The Crown
PICK OF THE PUBS

Spurt St HP18 0BB ☎ 01844 292222
e-mail: david@anniebaileys.com
dir: *Off A418 between Aylesbury & Thame*

Atmospheric pub offering a modern menu with international influences

The picturesque village of Cuddington and its thatched and whitewashed listed pub have featured in the TV series *Midsomer Murders*. The Crown's atmospheric interior includes a locals' bar and several low-beamed dining areas lit by candles in the evening. Fuller's London Pride, Adnams and guest ales are on tap, and there's also an extensive wine list and Symonds cider. Fish dishes are a major attraction, and might include smoked haddock with pancetta and a cheddar and leek potato cake; and fillet of bream with pak choi, chilli and sticky rice and an Asian vinaigrette. Among other modern, internationally influenced options are confit of chicken with roasted Mediterranean vegetables and a basil risotto; and slow-cooked Greek-style lamb shoulder with roasted aubergine and baby new potatoes. Look to the blackboard for daily specials or the set menu for good value options. A compact patio area provides outside seating.

Open all wk 12-3 6-11 (Sun all day) **Bar Meals** L served all wk 12-2.15 D served Mon-Sat 6.30-9.15 **Restaurant** L served all wk 12-2.15 D served Mon-Sat 6.30-9.15 ⊞ FULLER'S ◀ London Pride & ESB, Adnams, Guest ales Ů Symonds. ♟ 12 **Facilities** Non-diners area ♦ Children's portions Garden ⊼ Parking Wi-fi ⛟ (notice required)

Save on hotels. Book at **theAA.com/hotel**

BUCKINGHAMSHIRE 45 ENGLAND

PICK OF THE PUBS

The Red Lion

CHENIES   Map 6 TQ09

WD3 6ED ☎ **01923 282722**
e-mail:
theredlionchenies@hotmail.co.uk
web: www.theredlionchenies.co.uk
dir: *Between Rickmansworth &*
Amersham on A404, follow signs for
Chenies & Latimer

Very much a pub for everyone

Set in the Chess Valley, in a picture-
book village, complete with a pretty
green and an ancient parish church,
and just up the lane from Chenies
Manor. The unassuming, white-painted
Red Lion's owners Mike and Heather
Norris have over 25 years' experience
behind them, and they firmly believe the
17th-century inn's popularity stems
from being a pub that serves good food,
not a restaurant that serves beer.
Expect a plain, simply furnished main
bar, a charming, snug dining area
housed in the original cottage to the
rear with a tiled floor, old inglenook and
rustic furniture, a restaurant, and Mike
talking passionately about his real ales.
Lion's Pride, brewed by Rebellion, is
available here and here alone; other
local beers come from Vale Brewery in
Haddenham. Heather cooks everything,
including fresh daily pastas; bangers
with bubble-and-squeak; big chunks of
oven-baked leg of lamb (much like
Greek kleftiko); roast pork belly on leek
and potato mash; game pie; fishcakes

with horseradish and beetroot dip;
Orkneys rump steak; curries; poached
haddock with peppered red wine sauce;
and sausage, apple and cheddar pie.
Speaking of pies, brace yourself for the
famous lamb version, which a visiting
American serviceman once declared
beat a rival pub's pies hands down.
Ever since, its entry on the menu has
acquired an additional adjective every
time it is rewritten. Today, therefore, it
reads (take a deep breath) 'The
awesome, internationally acclaimed,
world-renowned, aesthetically and
palatably pleasing, not knowingly
genetically modified, hand-crafted,
well-balanced, famous, original Chenies
lamb pie'. Outside, on the pub's sunny
side, is a small seating area.

Open all wk Mon-Fri 11-2.30 5.30-11
(Sat 11-11 Sun 12-10.30) Closed: 25
Dec **Bar Meals** L served Mon-Fri 12-2
D served Mon-Fri 7-10 Sat 11-10 Sun
12-9 **Restaurant** L served Mon-Fri 12-2
D served Mon-Fri 7-10 Sat 11-10 Sun
12-9 🛢 FREE HOUSE 🍺 Wadworth 6X,
Rebellion Lion's Pride, Vale Best Bitter,
Guest ales 🍏 Thatchers Gold. 🍷 10
Facilities Garden Outside area 🅿
Parking

PICK OF THE PUBS

The Swan Inn

DENHAM   Map 6 TQ08

Village Rd UB9 5BH ☎ 01895 832085
e-mail: info@swaninndenham.co.uk
web: www.swaninndenham.co.uk
dir: *A40 onto A412. 200yds follow
'Denham village' sign. Through village,
over bridge, last pub on left*

Good beer and good food both prove a draw

In the picturesque village of Denham,
this Georgian, double-fronted inn
covered in wisteria feels tucked away in
the country and yet it's surprisingly
close to London and motorways. It's one
of the well-regarded Salisbury Pubs
mini-empire in and around the
Chilterns.* The traditional country inn's
large log fire and collection of rather
interesting pictures picked up at
auction give it a really homely feel.
Outside, a secluded terrace and large
gardens are ideal for families. Locals
help to maintain a thriving bar trade,
drawn in by well-kept Marlow Rebellion
IPA and guests, perhaps Caledonian's
Flying Scotsman. However, the food also
attracts a following: fresh seasonal
produce underpins a menu and daily
specials that feature more than a few
old favourites, some with a twist. For a
starter, look to the 'small plates' section
of the menu for juniper-spiced fillet beef
carpaccio with classic Waldorf salad.
Then, among the 'big plates' you'll find
plenty of variety, from braised pigs'

cheeks with black-and-white pudding,
pea mash and grain mustard gravy; and
poached salmon fillet with bok choy,
cavolo nero, ginger, chilli and noodle
stir fry; to borlotti bean, chestnut
mushroom and root vegetable stew with
a parsley dumpling and beetroot crisps.
Among the puddings are lemon curd
and treacle tart with salted caramel ice
cream. An exclusively European wine list
includes 22 by the glass and a wide
choice of pudding wines. A private
dining room is also available for family
occasions or business meetings.

*Alford Arms, Hemel Hempstead, Hertfordshire;
and in Buckinghamshire, The Royal Oak,
Bovingdon Green; The Old Queens Head, Penn.

Open all day all wk 11-11 (Sun
12-10.30) Closed: 25-26 Dec **Bar**

Meals L served Mon-Fri 12-2.30, Sat
12-3, Sun 12-4 D served Sun-Thu
6.30-9.30, Fri-Sat 6.30-10 **Restaurant** L
served Mon-Fri 12-2.30, Sat 12-3, Sun
12-4 D served Sun-Thu 6.30-9.30, Fri-
Sat 6.30-10 ⊕ SALISBURY PUBS LTD
◖ Rebellion IPA, Caledonian Flying
Scotsman Ö Thatchers. ♟ 22
Facilities Non-diners area ❖ (Bar
Garden) ♦ Children's portions Garden
⊼ Parking Wi-fi

Save on hotels. Book at theAA.com/hotel

BUCKINGHAMSHIRE 47 ENGLAND

DENHAM
Map 6 TQ08

The Falcon Inn ★★★★ INN

Village Rd UB9 5BE ☎ 01895 832125

e-mail: mail@falcondenham.com

dir: M40 junct 1, follow A40/Gerrards Cross signs. Approx 200yds, right into Old Mill Rd. Pass church on right, enter village. Pub opposite village green

The heart and soul of a conservation village

Barely 17 miles as the crow flies, yet central London seems light years away from this lovely 16th-century coaching inn opposite the village green. Expect well-kept Brakspear, Timothy Taylor and Wells real ales, and Lilley's Star Gazer cider in summer. Brasserie food includes pan-fried sea bass; stuffed chicken with chorizo and mozzarella; and mixed grill, namely lamb and pork chops, rump and gammon steaks, sausage, mushrooms, tomatoes and fries. The menu also lists pub classics such as beer-battered cod; and ham, egg and chips. Check the daily specials too. Other attractions are a south-facing terraced garden and four beamed bedrooms.

Open all day all wk Bar Meals L served Mon-Sat 11-3, Sun 12-6 D served Mon-Sat 5-9.30, Sun 12-6 Av main course £8 Restaurant L served Mon-Sat 11-3, Sun 12-6 D served Mon-Sat 5-9.30, Sun 12-6 Av 3 course à la carte fr £20 ⊕ ENTERPRISE INNS ◄ Timothy Taylor Landlord, Wells Bombardier, Brakspear, Ö Westons Stowford Press, Lilley's Star Gazer. ☑ 10 Facilities Non-diners area ♣ (Bar Garden) ♦ Children's portions Family room Garden ⨅ Beer festival Cider festival Wi-fi ⨿ (notice required) Rooms 4

The Swan Inn

PICK OF THE PUBS

See Pick of the Pubs on opposite page

DORNEY
Map 6 SU97

The Palmer Arms

Village Rd SL4 6QW ☎ 01628 666612

e-mail: chrys@thepalmerarms.com

dir: From A4 take B3026, over M4 to Dorney

Refurbished community pub with a suntrap garden

Built in the 15th century with wooden beams and open fires, this family-friendly pub in the pretty conservation village of Dorney is just a short stroll from the Thames Path and Boveney Lock. Refurbished in 2013 with contemporary decor and furnishings, head chef Justin Brown is also a new addition. He creates modern and classic British dishes, which can be accompanied by wines from the comprehensive list. Venison and black pudding sausage roll may precede a main of pan-fried breast of guinea fowl. There is a lighter lunch menu, roasts on Sundays and tasting menu evenings. A summer beer festival features local beers and ciders.

Open all day all wk 11am-11.30pm (Sun 12-10.30) Bar Meals food served all day Restaurant food served all day

⊕ GREENE KING ◄ Abbot Ale & IPA, Guinness Ö Aspall. ☑ 18 Facilities Non-diners area ♣ (Bar Garden) ♦ Children's menu Children's portions Play area Garden ⨅ Beer festival Parking ⨿

EASINGTON
Map 5 SP61

Mole and Chicken

PICK OF THE PUBS

HP18 9EY ☎ 01844 208387

e-mail: enquiries@themoleandchicken.co.uk

dir: M40 juncts 8 or 8a, A418 to Thame. At rdbt left onto B4011 signed Long Crendon & Bicester. In Long Crendon right into Carters Lane signed Dorton & Chilton. At T-junct left into Chilton Rd signed Chilton. Approx 0.75m to pub

Breathtaking views and good food

On the border between Oxfordshire and Buckinghamshire, this attractive pub has magnificent views across rolling countryside from its terraced garden. Built in 1831 as part of the workers' estate, it later became the village store and pub, selling only beer and cider until 1918. Inside it's all exposed beams, unusual flagged floors, and comfy sofas where you can sit with a glass of something to make your menu choices. The atmosphere is friendly and relaxed and local Old Hooky and Vale Best ales are served on tap. The seasonal menu typically offers an appetiser of houmous and toast ahead of white onion soup and a main course of confit duck leg with merguez sausage stew and roast garlic mash. For dessert, perhaps warm chocolate fondant with honeycomb ice cream. There's also a selection of bar dishes – maybe pork belly Thai curry or steak and onion sandwich.

Open all day all wk Bar Meals L served all wk 12-2.30 Restaurant L served all wk 12-2.30 D served all wk 6-9 ⊕ FREE HOUSE ◄ Hook Norton Old Hooky, Vale Best Bitter. ☑ 15 Facilities Non-diners area ♦ Children's menu Children's portions Garden ⨅ Parking Wi-fi

FARNHAM COMMON
Map 6 SU98

The Foresters

The Broadway SL2 3QQ ☎ 01753 643340

e-mail: info@theforesterspub.com

dir: Telephone for directions

Well-chosen dishes in an eclectic setting

This handsome 1930s building has an interior where old meets new – crystal chandeliers and log fires, real ales and cocktails, glass-topped tables and wooden floors, Chesterfields and velvet thrones. Opt for a starter of tomato, mozzarella and basil terrine, or one of the 'mini dishes' – perhaps mini shepherd's pie or battered haloumi. Typical main dishes include Duke of Berkshire pork with ruby red and Savoy cabbage and Calvados jus; and corn-fed chicken breast stuffed with langoustine mousse served with squid ink gnocchi and spinach foam. Choose something sweet from the list of 'dessert tapas'. There are front and rear gardens.

Open all day all wk Bar Meals L served all wk 12-3 D served all wk 6.30-10 Restaurant L served all wk 12-3

D served all wk 6.30-10 ⊕ PUNCH TAVERNS ◄ Fuller's London Pride, Young's, Guest ales Ö Thatchers Gold. Facilities Non-diners area ♦ Children's menu Children's portions Garden ⨅ Parking Wi-fi ⨿ (notice required)

FARNHAM ROYAL
Map 6 SU98

The Emperor

Blackpond Ln SL2 3EG ☎ 01753 643006

e-mail: bookings@theemperorpub.co.uk

dir: Telephone for directions

A pub for all seasons

Off the beaten track, this village inn with an attractive whitewashed façade is over 100 years old. Polished wood floors and original beams run through the bar, conservatory and refurbished barn, and there is a log fire in winter and alfresco tables in the summer. Bought by actor Dennis Waterman and his friend Martin Flood in 2012, The Emperor also has a new front of house manager and head chef. Their aim is to create a friendly local pub with traditional values. British favourites based on fresh seasonal fare, together with a handful of pizzas, drive the new menu, which might include Mediterranean vegetable linguine and corn-fed chicken with wild mushroom sauce.

Open all day all wk Bar Meals L served Mon-Sat 12-3, Sun 12-6 D served Mon-Sat 6-10, Sun 12-6 Av main course £12 Restaurant L served Mon-Sat 12-3, Sun 12-6 D served Mon-Sat 6-10, Sun 12-6 Av 3 course à la carte fr £25 ⊕ ORIGINAL PUB CO LTD ◄ Fuller's London Pride, Rebellion, 3 Guest ales. ☑ 8 Facilities Non-diners area ♣ (Bar Garden) ♦ Children's menu Children's portions Garden ⨅ Parking Wi-fi ⨿ (notice required)

FRIETH
Map 5 SU79

The Prince Albert

RG9 6PY ☎ 01494 881683

dir: 4m N of Marlow. Follow Frieth road from Marlow. Straight across at x-rds on Fingest road. Pub 200yds on left

A peaceful retreat and traditional pub grub

There's no television, jukebox or electronic games in this cottagey Chiltern Hills pub. What you get instead, surprise, surprise, is just good conversation, probably much as when it was built in the 1700s. In the bar, low beams, a big black inglenook stove, high-backed settles and lots of copper pots and pans; an alternative place to enjoy a pint of Brakspears is a seat in the garden, while admiring the woods and fields. A short menu sources locally for traditional pub food: sandwiches; filled jacket potatoes; Hambleden Valley sausages and mash; gammon steak, egg and chips; and smoked salmon with prawn salad.

Open all day all wk 11-11 (Sun 12-10.30) Bar Meals L served Mon-Sat 12.15-2.30, Sun 12.30-3 D served Fri-Sat 7.30-9.30 ⊕ BRAKSPEAR ◄ Bitter, Seasonal ales. ☑ 9 Facilities Non-diners area ♣ (Bar Garden) ♦ Children's portions Garden ⨅ Parking

GERRARDS CROSS — Map 6 TQ08

The Three Oaks NEW

Austenwood Ln SL9 8NL ☎ 01753 899016
e-mail: info@thethreeoaksgx.co.uk
dir: *From A40 at lights take B416 (Packhorse Rd) signed Village Centre. Over railway. Left signed Gold Hill into Austenwood Ln. Pub on right*

Contemporary gastro-pub with relaxed feel

Henry Cripps expanded his mini gastro-pub empire in the Thames Valley to three pubs in 2011 following the refurbishment of the Three Oaks in the heart of affluent Gerrards Cross. Like the other two 'Oaks' (the White Oak & Greene Oak in Berkshire), the result is a stylish dining venue with a smart, contemporary feel, yet the vibe is relaxed and informal. Drop by for a pint of local Rebellion Ale or a glass of unoaked Chardonnay and tuck into the cracking value set lunch menu, or perhaps ham hock terrine with piccalilli, followed by chargrilled lemon and thyme chicken with hand-cut chips and truffle mayonnaise, and then crème brûlée. There's a super terrace for alfresco dining, and don't miss the summer beer festival.

Open all wk **Bar Meals** L served Mon-Sat 12-2.30, Sun 12-3.30 D served Mon-Sat 6.30-9.30, Sun 5.30-9 Av main course £13.50 **Restaurant** L served Mon-Sat 12-2.30, Sun 12-3.30 D served Mon-Sat 6.30-9.30, Sun 5.30-9 Fixed menu price fr £15 Av 3 course à la carte fr £27 ⬤ Fuller's London Pride, Rebellion & IPA Ö Aspall. ♥ 24 **Facilities** Non-diners area ♦♦ Children's menu Children's portions Garden ⋒ Beer festival Parking Wi-fi �"" (notice required)

GREAT HAMPDEN — Map 5 SP80

The Hampden Arms

HP16 9RQ ☎ 01494 488255
dir: *M40 junct 4, A4010, right before Princes Risborough. Great Hampden signed*

Home-cooked food at lovely countryside inn

The large garden of this mock-Tudor free house on the wooded Hampden Estate sits beside the common, where you might watch a game of cricket during the season. Chef-proprietor Constantine Lucas includes some Greek signature dishes such as kleftiko and Greek salad alongside more traditional choices such as breaded chicken escalope; steak, ale and mushroom pie; and mixed pepper and aubergine risotto; blackboard specials add to the choices. Guest ales support regular brews from Adnams and Vale Brewery. The pub has a secure beer garden

Open all wk 12-3 6-12 **Bar Meals** L served Mon-Sat 12-2, Sun 12-3 D served Mon-Sat 6-9.30, Sun 7-9.30 ⊕ FREE HOUSE ⬤ Adnams Southwold Bitter, Vale, Fuller's London Pride, Guest ales Ö Addlestones. **Facilities** Non-diners area ♦♦ Children's menu Children's portions Family room Garden Parking

GREAT MISSENDEN — Map 6 SP80

The Nags Head ★★★★ INN ⍟

PICK OF THE PUBS

See Pick of the Pubs on opposite page

The Polecat Inn

PICK OF THE PUBS

170 Wycombe Rd, Prestwood HP16 0HJ
☎ 01494 862253
e-mail: polecatinn@btinternet.com
dir: *On A4128 between Great Missenden & High Wycombe*

The large garden is a big draw here

The Polecat, with its flower baskets and partial timber framing, dates back to the 17th century. The pub's beautiful three-acre garden, set amidst rolling Chilterns' countryside, is part of its great attraction. John Gamble bought the closed and dilapidated pub over 20 years ago, renovating and extending it to create an attractive free house, while retaining many original features. The small low-beamed rooms radiating from the central bar give many options when it comes to choosing where to eat or sup a pint of Ringwood Best Bitter. Dishes are prepared from local ingredients, including herbs from the garden. Lunchtime snacks are backed by a main menu with plenty of choices, from a starter of potted smoked mackerel to main courses such as roast parsnip bake, seafood cassoulet and beef Wellington; and for pudding, sherry trifle. Daily blackboard specials add to the choices.

Open 11-2.30 6-11 (Sun 12-3) Closed: 25-26 Dec, 1 Jan, Sun eve **Bar Meals** L served all wk 12-2 D served Mon-Sat 6.30-9 ⊕ FREE HOUSE ⬤ Marston's Pedigree, Morland Old Speckled Hen, Brakspear Bitter, Ringwood Best Bitter Ö Thatchers Gold. ♥ 16 **Facilities** Non-diners area ♦♦ Children's portions Play area Family room Garden ⋒ Parking �"" (notice required)

GROVE — Map 11 SP92

Grove Lock

LU7 0QU ☎ 01525 380940
e-mail: grovelock@fullers.co.uk
dir: *From A4146 (S of Leighton Buzzard) take B4146 signed Ivinghoe & Tring. Pub 0.5m on left*

Perfect atmosphere in summer and winter

This pub is situated next to Lock 28 on the Grand Union Canal, and is less than a mile from the scene of the 1963 Great Train Robbery. Its lofty open-plan bar has leather sofas, assorted tables and chairs and canal-themed artworks. The restaurant, once the lock-keeper's cottage, serves breaded chicken Caesar salad; butternut squash risotto; sausages and mash; and smoked belly of pork. Plenty of outdoor seating means you can watch the barges, while enjoying a pint of Fuller's. Catch a summer barbecue and hog roast.

Open all day all wk Mon-Sat 11-11 (Sun 11-10.30) **Bar Meals** L served Mon-Sat 12-9 D served Sun 12-7 food served all day **Restaurant** L served Mon-Sat 12-9 D served Sun 12-7 food served all day ⊕ FULLER'S ⬤ London Pride, Chiswick Bitter, Organic Honey Dew Ö Aspall. ♥ 14 **Facilities** Non-diners area ♦♦ Children's menu Children's portions Garden ⋒ Parking Wi-fi

HAMBLEDEN — Map 5 SU78

The Stag & Huntsman Inn ★★★★ INN

RG9 6RP ☎ 01491 571227
dir: *5m from Henley-on-Thames on A4155 towards Marlow, left at Mill End towards Hambleden*

Lovingly restored inn retaining old world charm

Close to the glorious beech-clad Chilterns, this 400-year-old brick and flint village pub has featured in countless films and television series. Ever-changing guest ales are served in the public bar, larger lounge bar and cosy snug. Food is available in the bars as well as the dining room, from an extensive menu of home-made pub favourites prepared with local seasonal produce. Opt for the likes of pan-fried fillet of salmon; rib-eye steak; or oven-roasted peppers filled with spiced couscous. Hambleden Estate game features strongly when in season, and there is a pizza and barbecue menu to enjoy in the garden during the summer months.

Open all wk 11-11 **Bar Meals** L served all wk 12-2.30 D served all wk 6-9 ⊕ FREE HOUSE ⬤ Rebellion, Sharp's, Loddon, Guest ales Ö Westons Stowford Press. **Facilities** 🐾 (Bar Garden) ♦♦ Garden ⋒ Parking �"" **Rooms** 9

Save on hotels. Book at **theAA.com/hotel**

BUCKINGHAMSHIRE 49 ENGLAND

PICK OF THE PUBS

The Nags Head ★★★★ INN ✿

GREAT MISSENDEN   Map 6 SP80

London Rd HP16 0DG ☎ **01494 862200**
e-mail: goodfood@nagsheadbucks.com
web: www.nagsheadbucks.com
dir: *N of Amersham on A413, left at
Chiltern hospital into London Rd signed
Great Missenden*

Anglo-French dishes at a charming pub

It has been over five years since the
Michaels family restored this 15th-
century inn tucked away in the sleepy
valley of the River Misbourne in the
picturesque Chiltern Hills. As they did
with such success at the Bricklayers
Arms in Flaunden, Hertfordshire (see
entry), the family has helped this former
coaching inn to gain a formidable
reputation for food and hospitality.
Originally three small cottages, features
include low oak beams and an inglenook
fireplace, which have been carefully
retained as a backdrop for the stylish
new bar. The late Roald Dahl used to be
a regular here and the dining room is
decorated with limited edition prints by
the children's author, who drew
inspiration from the pub for his famous
book *Fantastic Mr Fox*. Food is taken
seriously here, and executive head chef
Claude Paillet sources the finest
ingredients from local suppliers
wherever possible, for a menu that

fuses English with French. Lunch and
dinner menus may offer starters like
chicken liver parfait with mixed nut
crumble, or mushroom feuillette. Main
courses range from partridge breast
with confit legs, braised Puy lentils and
wild mushroom tarragon jus, to lamb
shank cooked in local ale with spinach
and wild rocket. Leave room for perhaps
lemon tart with cherry ice cream, or
poires Belle Hèléne. In summer, relax
over a drink or a meal whilst gazing out
over the Chiltern Hills from the pub's
lovely informal garden. Alternatively,
stay overnight in one of the five
beautifully refurbished and
contemporary bedrooms. Booking for
meals may be required.

Open all day all wk Closed: 25 Dec **Bar
Meals** L served Mon-Sat 12-2.30, Sun
12-3.30 D served all wk 6.30-9.30
Restaurant L served Mon-Sat 12-2.30,
Sun 12-3.30 D served all wk 6.30-9.30
⊕ FREE HOUSE ◼ Fuller's London Pride,
Rebellion, Tring, Vale ♂ Aspall. ♟ 19
Facilities Non-diners area ✿ (Bar
Garden) ♛ Children's portions Garden
☒ Parking Wi-fi **Rooms** 5

HEDGERLEY — Map 6 SU98

The White Horse

SL2 3UY ☎ 01753 643225
dir: *Telephone for directions*

One for the beer festival follower

An ale drinker's paradise if ever there was one, parts of which date back 500 years. With three beer festivals a year (Easter, Spring Bank Holiday and August Bank Holiday) and barely a pause between them, this pub can almost claim to run a single year-long celebration, with over 1,000 real ales consumed annually. Real cider and Belgian bottled beers augment the already mammoth range. A large well-kept garden at the rear hosts summer barbecues; otherwise the menu of home-cooked pub favourites ranges from a salad bar with quiches, sandwiches and ploughman's, through to curries, chilli, pasta dishes, pies and steaks (lunchtime only).

Open all wk 11-2.30 5-11 (Sat 11-11 Sun 11-10.30) **Bar Meals** L served Mon-Fri 12-2, Sat-Sun 12-2.30 ⊕ FREE HOUSE ◀ 8 Rotating ales ♂ 3 Guest ciders. ☻ 10 **Facilities** Non-diners area ♥ (Bar Garden) ♦ Children's portions Family room Garden ⋒ Beer festival Parking ➡

HIGH WYCOMBE — Map 5 SU89

The Sausage Tree

Saffron Rd HP13 6AB ☎ 01494 452204
e-mail: sausagetreepub@hotmail.co.uk
dir: *M40 junct 4, A404 signed Town Centre & Amersham. At rdbt 2nd exit signed Beaconsfield, Amersham, A404. At rdbt 2nd exit signed Beaconsfield. Left into Stuart Rd, left into Easton Terrace, left into Saffron Rd*

Chilterns' pub specialising in sausages

For a mind-boggling choice of sausages made from exotic meats or unusual ingredients, perhaps, pork, banana and honey, then look no further than this pub on the outskirts of High Wycombe. Deciding just which types of sausage to tuck into is difficult: pheasant and whisky; hot garlic; tipsy turkey, or kangaroo are just a few examples. Maybe plump instead for one of the 100 speciality beers on offer, or a pint of local Rebellion Ale, with a 16oz rump steak or a seafood kebab cooked at your table on fearsomely hot volcanic rock platters.

Open 12-3 6-11 Closed: Sun **Bar Meals** L served Mon-Sat 12-3 D served Mon-Sat 6-11 Av main course £15 **Restaurant** L served Mon-Sat 12-3 D served Mon-Sat 6-11 ⊕ ENTERPRISE INNS ◀ Rebellion Ales. ☻ **Facilities** Outside area ⋒ Parking Wi-fi

KNOTTY GREEN — Map 6 SU99

The Red Lion Knotty Green NEW

Penn Rd HP9 2TN ☎ 01494 680888
e-mail: info@myredlion.com
dir: *M40 junct 2, A355 signed Beaconsfield. At 2nd mini rdbt right onto A355 signed Amersham. Over railway, left into Ledborough Ln signed Penn. At T-junct right on B474 Hazlemere & Penn. Pub on left*

Delightful country pub with a literary past

The gallery of original Noddy prints and library of Enid Blyton books in the Snuggery is explained by the fact that the famous children's author lived most of her life in the hamlet, and this old pub was her local. From a menu declaring, somewhat tongue in cheek, "The finest food in all of Knotty Green!", dining possibilities include salmon and watercress Wellington; spicy Mexican chicken; mushroom or seafood risotto; a selection of pizzas; lemon sponge pudding and Belgian waffles. At the front, there's decking with tables and chairs.

Open all wk 12-3 5-11 (Mon 5-11, Fri 12-3 5-1am, Sat 12-12, Sun 12-8) **Bar Meals** L served Tue-Fri 12-3, Sat 12-9, Sun 12-5 D served Tue-Thu 5-8.30, Fri 6-9.30, Sat 12-9, Sun 12-5 Av main course £7.95 **Restaurant** L served Tue-Fri 12-3, Sat 12-9, Sun 12-5 D served Tue-Thu 5-8.30, Fri 6-9.30, Sat 12-9, Sun 12-5 ⊕ PUNCH TAVERNS ◀ Young's, Wells Bombardier ♂ Westons Stowford Press. ☻ 10 **Facilities** Non-diners area ♥ (Bar Garden) ♦ Children's menu Children's portions Garden ⋒ Parking Wi-fi ➡ (notice required)

LACEY GREEN — Map 5 SP80

The Whip Inn

Pink Rd HP27 0PG ☎ 01844 344060
dir: *1m from A4010 (Princes Risborough to High Wycombe road). Adjacent to windmill*

Traditional pub popular with walkers and cyclists

Standing high above the Vale of Aylesbury in the heart of the Chiltern Hills, the beer garden of this 200-year-old pub overlooks the Lacey Green windmill. Ramblers on the Chiltern Way join locals in appreciating some of 800 different real ales offered each year, as well as real Millwhites cider. A robust menu of home-made classic favourites such as ham, egg and chips and chargrilled steaks seals the deal at this rustic, music- and fruit-machine-free country inn. The Whip holds a beer festival twice a year in May and September.

Open all day all wk **Bar Meals** L served all wk 12-2.30 D served all wk 6.30-9 **Restaurant** L served all wk 12-2.30 D served all wk 6.30-9 ⊕ FREE HOUSE ◀ Over 800 guest ales a year ♂ Thatchers, Millwhites. ☻ 22 **Facilities** Non-diners area ♦ Children's menu Children's portions Garden ⋒ Beer festival Parking

LANE END — Map 5 SU89

Grouse & Ale

High St HP14 3JG ☎ 01494 882299
e-mail: info@grouseandale.co.uk
dir: *On B482 in village*

Smart pub with modern menus

For nearly a century before a major refurbishment a few years ago this had been The Clayton Arms, named after Sir Robert Clayton who, in 1679, built it to live in on becoming Lord Mayor of London. One of the draws is the cosy bar and dining area, where you can relax with the papers and a pint of Adnams Broadside or Caledonian Deuchars. The menu lists modern pub food such as chicken saltimbocca; beer-battered haddock; pork tenderloin; and spiced lentil and root vegetable hotpot. Daily specials supplement the main menu. The suntrap courtyard can be a good place to eat.

Open all day all wk **Bar Meals** L served Mon-Sat 12-2.30, Sun 12-4 D served Mon-Sat 6-9.30 **Restaurant** L served Mon-Sat 12-2.30, Sun 12-4 D served Mon-Sat 6-9.30 ◀ Adnams Broadside, Caledonian Deuchars IPA, Courage. ☻ 27 **Facilities** Non-diners area ♥ (Bar Outside area) ♦ Children's menu Children's portions Outside area ⋒ Parking Wi-fi

LITTLE KINGSHILL — Map 6 SU89

The Full Moon

Hare Ln HP16 0EE ☎ 01494 862397
e-mail: email@thefullmoon.info
dir: *SW of Great Missenden, accessed from either A413 or A4128*

Perfect for post-walk ales and meals

A popular post-ramble refuelling stop, especially as both dogs and children are warmly welcomed inside, this pub has a wealth of wonderful walks through the Chiltern Hills radiating from its doorstep. It is noted for its tip-top Fuller's London Pride and the weekly-changing guest ales, and the pub throngs during the mid July beer festival. Walking appetites will be satisfied with one of the sharing platters, a rib-eye steak sandwich or hearty mains like bison tournedos Rossini; sausages with mash, red onion confit and onion gravy; or slow-roasted pork belly with mashed potatoes and green beans.

Open all day all wk **Bar Meals** L served all wk 12-3 D served all wk 6-10 **Restaurant** L served all wk 12-3 D served all wk 6-10 ⊕ PUNCH TAVERNS ◀ Fuller's London Pride, Young's, Adnams, Guest ale ♂ Aspall. ☻ 21 **Facilities** Non-diners area ♥ (Bar Garden) ♦ Children's menu Children's portions Play area Garden ⋒ Beer festival Parking ➡ (notice required)

| LONG CRENDON | Map 5 SP60 |

The Angel Inn 🏵

PICK OF THE PUBS

47 Bicester Rd HP18 9EE ☎ 01844 208268
e-mail: info@angelrestaurant.co.uk
dir: *M40 junct 7, A418 to Thame, B4011 to Long Crendon. Inn on B4011*

Great food in an exceptional village inn

Nestled in the Vale of Aylesbury and close to the rippling Chiltern Hills, Long Crendon was a medieval centre for lace-making. Much olde-worlde atmosphere remains to beguile visitors, including the old Courthouse, picturesque ranges of cottages and the gabled Angel Inn. This old coaching stop retains much of its character, with original fireplaces and wattle-and-daub walls alongside modern features including an airy conservatory, dressed with tasteful natural materials and fabrics throughout. There's a particular emphasis on seafood dishes here, but such don't overshadow classic British dishes which together have gained head chef Trevor Bosch an AA Rosette. Drawn from various menus, starters may include twice baked Oxford Blue cheese soufflé, leading to eye-catching mains the like of angel fish pie with sauté spinach and cheddar mash or herb crusted chump of lamb on cassoulet of beans. The wine list exceeds 100 bins, with beers including local Vale brewery's Wychert.

Open all day Closed: 1-2 Jan, Sun eve **Bar Meals** L served all wk 12-2.30 D served Mon-Sat 7-9.30 Av main course £10.50 **Restaurant** L served all wk 12-2.30 D served Mon-Sat 7-9.30 Fixed menu price fr £14.95 Av 3 course à la carte fr £28 ⊕ FREE HOUSE ◀ Morrells Oxford Blue, Vale Wychert, Brakspear. ♟ 18 **Facilities** Non-diners area ♦♦ Children's portions Garden ⊞ Parking Wi-fi

| MARLOW | Map 5 SU88 |

The Hand & Flowers 🏵🏵🏵🏵

PICK OF THE PUBS

126 West St SL7 2BP ☎ 01628 482277
e-mail: reservations@thehandandflowers.co.uk
dir: *M4 junct 9, A404 to Marlow, A4155 towards Henley-on-Thames. Pub on right*

A gastronomic hotspot close to the Thames

An unassuming 18th-century pub on the outskirts of this upmarket town, The Hand & Flowers quickly became a destination for food-lovers after Tom and Beth Kerridge bought the lease in 2005. Despite gaining three AA Rosettes in its first year, the pub remains a relaxed and unpretentious place, with flagstone floors, old beams and timbers, roaring winter log fires, walls lined with striking modern art and leather banquettes. A small bar area serves decent real ale, while the friendly, knowledgeable service also helps to set the tone of the place. Tom's cooking is broadly modern British, underpinned by classical French techniques; simplicity, flavour and skill are at the top of his agenda. The seasonally-changing menu is built around top-notch produce. Start with salmon tartare with poppy seed crackers and continue

with tenderloin of Wiltshire pork with pickled mustard leaf. Be wowed by desserts such as pistachio cake with melon sorbet and marzipan. Tom Kerridge has been awarded AA Chefs' Chef of the Year for 2013-2014.

Open 12-2.30 6.30-9.30 (Sun 12-3.30) Closed: 24-26 Dec, 1 Jan Dinner, Sun eve **Bar Meals** L served Mon-Sat 12-2.30, Sun 12-3.15 D served Mon-Sat 6.30-9.30 Av main course £27 **Restaurant** L served Mon-Sat 12-2.30, Sun 12-3.15 D served Mon-Sat 6.30-9.30 Fixed menu price fr £15 Av 3 course à la carte fr £40 ⊕ GREENE KING ◀ Abbot Ale, Morland Old Speckled Hen, Rebellion Roasted Nuts Ò Aspall & Perronelle's Blush. ♟ 17 **Facilities** ♦♦ Children's portions Garden ⊞ Parking

The Kings Head

Church Rd, Little Marlow SL7 3RZ ☎ 01628 484407
e-mail: clive.harvison@sky.com
dir: *M40 junct 4, A4040 S, then A4155 towards Bourne End. Pub 0.5m on right*

Good range of real ales

This charming 16th-century pub with a large garden is only a few minutes' walk from the Thames Path. The open-plan interior features original beams and log fires. A great selection of ales awaits visitors to The Kings Head, including a couple from the Rebellion brewery in Marlow. As well as sandwiches, baguettes, paninis and jacket potatoes, the food includes substantial salads, steaks, chicken curry, chilli con carne, wholetail scampi and slow-roasted lamb shank. Tell staff you've parked the car, go for a walk and return for a meal.

Open all day all wk Closed: 26 Dec **Bar Meals** L served Mon-Sat 12-2.15, Sun 12-7 D served Mon-Sat wk 6.30-9.30, Sun 12-7 **Restaurant** L served Mon-Sat 12-2.15, Sun 12-7 D served Mon-Sat wk 6.30-9.30, Sun 12-7 ⊕ ENTERPRISE INNS ◀ Fuller's London Pride, Timothy Taylor Landlord, Adnams Broadside, Rebellion IPA & Smuggler Ò Aspall. ♟ 13 **Facilities** Non-diners area ♦♦ Children's menu Children's portions Garden ⊞ Parking 🚌 (notice required)

| MEDMENHAM | Map 5 SU88 |

The Dog and Badger

Henley Rd SL7 2HE ☎ 01491 571362
e-mail: info@thedogandbadger.com
dir: *On A4155, midway between Marlow & Henley-on-Thames*

14th-century pub on the brow of a wooded hill

This whitewashed family-run inn was built around 1390 as a meeting house in the grounds of Medmenham Abbey and is surrounded by peaceful Chiltern countryside between Marlow and Henley. Since then, visitors have included the noted Satanist James Dashwood, and Nell Gwynn, who is said to have met certain admirers at the pub. Modern-day visitors can be assured of a friendly welcome, good real ales and a menu of 'snack-wiches' and home-cooked dishes such as cod fricassée, wild mushroom linguine, and pan-fried stuffed chicken. Puddings include chocolate fondue to share and apple crumble. There are roasts on Sundays. A beer festival takes place in May.

Open 12-3 6-11 Closed: Sun eve **Bar Meals** L served Mon-Thu 12-2, Fri-Sat 12-2.30, Sun 12-3 (Sun 12-4 summer) D served Mon-Thu 6-9, Fri-Sat 6-10 **Restaurant** L served Mon-Thu 12-2, Fri-Sat 12-2.30, Sun 12-3 (Sun 12-4 summer) D served Mon-Thu 6-9, Fri-Sat 6-10 ⊕ ENTERPRISE INNS ◀ Rebellion IPA, Fuller's London Pride. ♟ 9 **Facilities** 🐾 (Bar Restaurant Garden) ♦♦ Children's portions Garden ⊞ Beer festival Parking Wi-fi 🚌 (notice required)

| MILTON KEYNES | Map 11 SP83 |

The Swan Inn

Broughton Rd, Milton Keynes Village MK10 9AH ☎ 01908 665240
e-mail: info@theswan-mkvillage.co.uk
dir: *M1 junct 14 towards Milton Keynes. Pub off V11 or H7*

Rustic rural charm with orchard garden

In the heart of the original Milton Keynes village, the beautiful 13th-century Swan Inn offers everything you could wish for from an ancient thatched pub. The interior is an eclectic mix of traditional charm and contemporary chic; it has flagstone floors, an open fire in the inglenook in winter keeps things cosy, and an orchard garden for those warmer days. The open-plan kitchen creates simple yet creative dishes such as ham hock terrine with spiced pear chutney, piccalilli dressing and toasted ciabatta, followed by slow-roasted pork belly with truffle mash and creamed wild mushroom, with banoffee crème brûlée and coconut shortbread for pudding.

Open all day all wk Mon-Thu 11-11 (Fri-Sat 11-mdnt Sun 12-10.30) **Bar Meals** L served Mon-Thu 12-3, Fri-Sat 12-10, Sun 12-8 D served Mon-Thu 6-9.30, Fri-Sat 12-10, Sun 12-8 **Restaurant** L served Mon-Thu 12-3, Fri-Sat 12-10, Sun 12-8 D served Mon-Thu 6-9.30, Fri-Sat 12-10, Sun 12-8 ⊕ FRONT LINE INNS ◀ Wells Bombardier, Young's, Guest ales Ò Symonds. ♟ 34 **Facilities** Non-diners area 🐾 (Bar Garden) ♦♦ Children's portions Garden ⊞ Cider festival Parking Wi-fi 🚌 (notice required)

MOULSOE
Map 11 SP94

The Carrington Arms

Cranfield Rd MK16 0HB ☎ **01908 218050**
e-mail: enquiries@thecarringtonarms.co.uk
dir: *M1 junct 14, A509 to Newport Pagnell 100yds, turn right signed Moulsoe & Cranfield. Pub on right*

Village inn with superb 'choose your own' counter

Set in the picturesque village of Moulsoe, this Grade II listed building dates from 1860. Since the Dodman family took over the pub a few years ago they created a 'Best of British' restaurant offering seasonal menus. Customers can choose their own cuts of meat, fish and seafood from a special counter, or plump for meals such as Southern style pork with bacon macaroni cheese, pork nuggets and sweetcorn purée followed by poached sea trout fillet with new potatoes, crab bonbons and sprouting broccoli. Finish with a lemon thyme pannacotta. There's a summer beer and cider festival featuring local breweries and a barbecue.

Open all day all wk 12-11 **Bar Meals** L served all wk 12-10 D served all wk 12-10 Av main course £14.50 food served all day **Restaurant** L served all wk 12-2.30 D served all wk 6-10 Av 3 course à la carte fr £20 ⊕ FREE HOUSE ◙ Fuller's London Pride, Marston's Pedigree, Guest ales Ò Aspall, Westons. ♥ 10
Facilities Non-diners area ♥ Children's menu Garden ♬ Beer festival Cider festival Parking Wi-fi ⛺

OVING
Map 11 SP72

The Black Boy

Church Ln HP22 4HN ☎ **01296 641258**
dir: *4.6m N of Aylesbury*

16th-century pub with wonderful views

Oliver Cromwell and his soldiers camped in The Black Boy's huge garden after sacking nearby Bolebec Castle during the Civil War. Today, the 16th-century pub is a rural oasis, with spectacular views over the Vale of Aylesbury to Stowe School and beyond. At lunch wash down a seafood platter to share, beer-battered fish with chunky chips and tartare sauce, or lamb and apricot casserole, with a pint of local Vale Best Bitter. Evening extras may include sea bass with lemon and herb sauce, and pan-fried duck with wild mushroom and red wine sauce. Good value set and Sunday lunch menus.

Open 12-3 6-11 (Sat all day Sun 12-5) Closed: Mon **Bar Meals** L served Tue-Sat 12-2, Sun 12-3 D served Tue-Thu 6.30-9, Fri-Sat 6-9.30 Av main course £10 **Restaurant** L served Tue-Sat 12-2, Sun 12-3 D served Tue-Thu 6.30-9, Fri-Sat 6-9.30 ⊕ FREE HOUSE ◙ Vale Best Bitter, Sharp's Doom Bar, Guest ales Ò Thatchers Gold. ♥ 10
Facilities Non-diners area ♥ (Bar Garden) ♦ Children's menu Children's portions Garden ♬ Parking Wi-fi ⛺ (notice required)

PENN
Map 6 SU99

The Old Queens Head

PICK OF THE PUBS

See Pick of the Pubs on opposite page

PRESTON BISSETT
Map 11 SP62

The White Hart

Pound Ln MK18 4LX ☎ **01280 847969**
dir: *2.5m from A421*

Thatched pub in a peaceful location

A pretty 18th-century, timbered and whitewashed village pub, The White Hart has three unpretentious low-beamed rooms, log fires and a simple matchboarded bar front. Outside is a secluded garden and patio. Regular real ales include Hooky Bitter, The Rev. James and Doom Bar, while a small but considered menu offers ham, egg and chips; sirloin steak; pan-fried sea bass; roast vegetable lasagne; and Sunday roasts. Home-made bread-and-butter pudding, lemon sorbet and cheesecake are characteristic desserts. A beer festival is held on Spring Bank Holiday.

Open 12-2.30 6-11 (Sat-Sun 12-11) Closed: Mon **Bar Meals** L served Tue-Sun 12-2.30 D served Tue-Sun 6-11 **Restaurant** L served Tue-Sun 12-2.30 D served Tue-Sun 6-10 ⊕ FREE HOUSE ◙ Hook Norton Hooky Bitter & Old Hooky, Timothy Taylor Landlord, Brains The Rev. James, St Austell Tribute, Sharp's Doom Bar.
Facilities Non-diners area ♥ (Bar Restaurant Garden) ♦ Children's menu Children's portions Garden Beer festival Parking ⛺

RADNAGE
Map 5 SU79

The Three Horseshoes Inn

Horseshoe Rd, Bennett End HP14 4EB ☎ **01494 483273**
e-mail: threehorseshoe@btconnect.com
dir: *M40 junct 5, A40 towards High Wycombe, after unrestricted mileage sign turn left signed Radnage (Mudds Bank). 1.8m, 1st left into Bennett End Rd, inn on right*

European flavours in a renovated pub

When chef-patron Simon Crawshaw bought this beautiful old building in 2005, he knew it would be something special. Down a leafy lane, it is truly traditional – worn flagstones, blackened beams and original inglenook fireplace. On his modern English and European menus he typically offers rillette of poached and smoked Scottish salmon with home-made Hovis loaf, then roast rump of lamb with ratatouille, Suffolk kale and gratin potatoes and red wine jus. Enjoy Marlow's Rebellion ale in the bar or in the lovely garden.

Open 12-3 6-11 (Mon 6-11 Sat all day Sun 12-6) Closed: Sun eve, Mon L **Bar Meals** L served Tue-Sat 12-2.30, Sun 12-3 D served Mon-Sat 6-9 Av main course £16.50 **Restaurant** L served Tue-Sat 12-2.30, Sun 12-3 D served Mon-Sat 6-9 Av 3 course à la carte fr £30 ⊕ FREE HOUSE ◙ Rebellion, Brakspear Oxford Gold. ♥ 12
Facilities Non-diners area ♥ (Bar Garden) ♦ Children's portions Garden ♬ Parking Wi-fi ⛺ (notice required)

SEER GREEN
Map 6 SU99

The Jolly Cricketers ⊚

24 Chalfont Rd HP9 2YG ☎ **01494 676308**
dir: *M40 junct 2, A355 signed Beaconsfield A40, Amersham. At Pyebush rdbt 1st exit, A40 signed Beaconsfield, Amersham, A355. At rdbt, A355 signed Amersham. Right into Longbottom Ln signed Seer Green. Left into Bottom Ln, right into Orchard Rd, left into Church Rd, right into Chalfont Rd*

Top notch food in a homely setting

Chris Lillitou and Amanda Baker's 19th-century, wisteria-clad free house in the heart of the picture-perfect Seer Green appeals to all-comers: locals chatting over pints of Marlow's Rebellion IPA, quiz addicts on Sunday nights, live jazz fans, beer festival-goers, dog-walkers. The AA-Rosette menu has traditional leanings; a pint of prawns; chopped liver with brioche; and pressed ox tongue with pickled shallots, English mustard and lambs lettuce are typical starters. Follow with steak- and-kidney pie with cabbage and mash, or ale-braised ham with colcannon and parsley sauce. For dessert, maybe Bramley apple crumble with hazelnuts, cinnamon and vanilla ice cream. Beer festival Easter weekend and August Bank Holiday.

Open all day all wk Mon-Thu 12-11.30 (Fri-Sat 12-12 Sun 12-10.30) **Bar Meals** L served Mon-Sat 12-2.30 D served Mon-Sat 6.30-9 Av main course £15 **Restaurant** L served Mon-Fri 12-2.30, Sat-Sun 12-3.30 D served Mon-Sat 6.30-9 Av 3 course à la carte fr £26 ⊕ FREE HOUSE ◙ Rebellion IPA, Fuller's London Pride, Chiltern Beechwood Bitter, Vale VPA Ò Millwhites, Artisan bottle selection. ♥ 16 **Facilities** Non-diners area ♥ (Bar Restaurant Garden) ♦ Children's menu Children's portions Garden ♬ Beer festival Parking Wi-fi

PICK OF THE PUBS

The Old Queens Head

PENN   Map 6 SU99

Hammersley Ln HP10 8EY
☎ **01494 813371**
e-mail: info@oldqueensheadpenn.co.uk
web: www.oldqueensheadpenn.co.uk
dir: *B474 into School Rd, 500yds, left into Hammersley Ln*

Appetising food and well-kept ales

Between the delightful villages of Penn and Tylers Green and with lovely walks in beech woodland on its doorstep, this old pub has bags of character and atmosphere. It's one of the well-regarded Salisbury Pubs mini-empire in and around the Chilterns.* The timber-built dining room dates from 1666 (word of the Great Fire of London clearly hadn't reached here) when it was constructed as a barn, and although it has seen several additions since then, the cosy corners, undulating floors and real fires are reminders of its history. The owners have spent time at local auctions carefully selecting old furniture and pictures in keeping with the age of the pub. A sunny terrace overlooks the village church, and there's a large garden in which to eat and drink or you could settle by the fire with a pint of Ruddles County or a mug of hot chocolate. The kitchen team has created a modern British menu with starters of grilled herb polenta with slow-roast red pepper, rocket and herb oil; and potted

home-smoked mackerel with toasted brioche and beetroot and horseradish relish. Main course options are similarly mouthwatering: slow-cooked lamb shoulder with roast garlic mash, purple sprouting broccoli and roasting juices; and pheasant, leek and mushroom puff pastry pie with Koffman cabbage. For pudding, consider a banoffee pot with Chantilly cream or a plate of English cheeses. The wine list includes 22 by the glass and a separate pudding wine selection.

*Alford Arms, Hemel Hempstead, Hertfordshire; and in Buckinghamshire, The Swan Inn, Denham; The Royal Oak, Bovingdon Green.

Open all day all wk 11-11 (Sun 12-10.30) Closed: 25-26 Dec **Bar Meals** L served Mon-Fri 12-2.30, Sat

12-3, Sun 12-9 D served Mon-Thu 6.30-9.30, Fri-Sat 6.30-10 **Restaurant** L served Mon-Fri 12-2.30, Sat 12-3, Sun 12-9 D served Mon-Thu 6.30-9.30, Fri-Sat 6.30-10 🏠 SALISBURY PUBS LTD ◀ Greene King Ruddles County & IPA, Guinness Ö Aspall. ♟ 22 **Facilities** Non-diners area ✿ (Bar Garden) ♦♦ Children's portions Garden ⩩ Parking Wi-fi

SKIRMETT
Map 5 SU79

The Frog

PICK OF THE PUBS

RG9 6TG ☎ **01491 638996**
e-mail: info@thefrogatskirmett.co.uk
dir: Exit A4155 at Mill End, pub in 3m

Lots of local produce on the menu

At the heart of the Chilterns Area of Outstanding Natural Beauty, the Hamble Brook flows behind this 18th-century coaching inn. In summer the garden is a relaxing place to be, perhaps resting after a ramble to the famous windmill on nearby Turville Hill. Winter warmth is guaranteed in the charming public bar where oak beams, bare floorboards and leather seating combine with colourful textiles to create a welcoming atmosphere. Where better to settle with a pint of Rebellion or Sharp's? Head chef and co-owner Jim Crowe has developed excellent relationships with his suppliers, resulting in superb fresh local produce to satisfy the most discerning of palates. Jim's cooking style is adventurous yet classic, with modern takes on British and European dishes. Take your choice between two dining rooms, both appealing yet quite different from each other, with contemporary design that manages to highlight the historical nature of this lovely building.

Open 11.30-3 6-11 Closed: 25 Dec, Sun eve (Oct-Apr) **Bar Meals** L served all wk 12-2.30 D served all wk 6.30-9.30 **Restaurant** L served all wk 12-2.30 D served all wk 6.30-9.30 ⊕ FREE HOUSE ◀ Leaping Frog, Rebellion IPA, Sharp's Doom Bar, Wadworth Henry's Original IPA Ŏ Thatchers. ♟ 15 **Facilities** Non-diners area ❖ (Bar Garden) ♦ Children's menu Children's portions Family room Garden ♬ Parking ☛

TURVILLE
Map 5 SU79

The Bull & Butcher

PICK OF THE PUBS

RG9 6QU ☎ **01491 638283**
e-mail: info@thebullandbutcher.com
dir: M40 junct 5, follow Ibstone signs. Right at T-junct. Pub 0.25m on left

A quintessentially English pub in the Chilterns

Built in 1550, this village pub received its first licence in 1617 after workmen building the nearby church refused to continue without refreshments. Originally known as the 'Bullen Butcher' – a reference to Henry VIII and his second wife Anne Boleyn – the name was later adapted to its modern form. You'll soon feel at home in the relaxed atmosphere of the Windmill Lounge or the Well Bar, where a 50-foot well discovered in 1999 now features as a table. Original beams and large open fires add to the pub's charm; there's also a large garden and patio area, as well as a function room that's perfect for family or corporate occasions. On the seasonal menu, pub favourites might be pan-fried chicken breast or beer-

battered haddock. More adventurous tastes might opt for duck and port pâté followed by mushroom, hazelnut, brie and cranberry Wellington. Typical puds include glazed lemon tart.

Open all day summer 12-11 (Sat noon-1am) winter 12-3 5.30-11 Closed: Closed Mon in winter **Bar Meals** L served Mon-Sat 12-2.30, Sun 12-3 D served Mon-Sat 6-9.30 **Restaurant** L served Mon-Sat 12-2.30, Sun 12-3 D served Mon-Sat 6-9.30 ⊕ BRAKSPEAR ◀ Bitter & Oxford Gold, Guest ales Ŏ Symonds. ♟ 36 **Facilities** Non-diners area ❖ (Bar Garden) ♦ Children's menu Garden ♬ Parking Wi-fi ☛ (notice required)

WEST WYCOMBE
Map 5 SU89

The George and Dragon Hotel

High St HP14 3AB ☎ **01494 535340**
e-mail: georgeanddragon@live.co.uk
dir: On A40

Delightful timber-framed hotel reached through a cobbled archway

After hard a day touring the West Wycombe Caves, and stately houses at Cliveden and Hughenden, relax at this traditional coaching inn located in a National Trust village. The 14th-century inn was once a hideout for highwaymen stalking travellers between London and Oxford; indeed, one unfortunate guest, robbed and murdered here, is rumoured still to haunt its corridors. Reliable real ales include St Austell Tribute and Skinner's Smugglers. The varied menu offers freshly-prepared dishes cooked to order such as beef and ale pie; beer-battered haddock; a button mushroom, brie and cranberry filo parcel; and succulent rib-eye steaks.

Open all wk 12-12 (Fri-Sat noon-1am Sun 12-11.30) ⊕ ENTERPRISE INNS ◀ St Austell Tribute, Skinner's Smugglers Ale. **Facilities** ❖ (Bar Restaurant Garden) ♦ Play area Family room Garden Parking Wi-fi

WHEELER END
Map 5 SU89

The Chequers Inn

Bullocks Farm Ln HP14 3NH ☎ **01494 883070**
e-mail: landlord@chequerswheelerend.co.uk
dir: 4m N of Marlow

Families welcome at this Fuller's pub

This picturesque 16th-century inn, with its low-beamed ceilings, roaring winter fires and two attractive beer gardens, is ideally located for walkers on the edge of Wheeler End Common (families and dogs are welcome). Lunchtime dishes include pub favourites such as spaghetti bolognaise or bangers and mash with gravy; and there's a sandwich menu too. Typical evening choices are spicy chicken wings with blue cheese dressing; bacon and Stilton beefburger with chips; or pie of the day.

Open 12-3 6-11 (Sat 12-11 Sun 12-6 winter) Closed: Sun eve, Mon L **Bar Meals** L served Tue-Thu 12-2, Fri-Sun 12-3 D served Tue-Thu & Sat 6-9, Fri 6-9.30 **Restaurant** L served Tue-Thu 12-2, Fri-Sun 12-3 D served Tue-Thu &

Sat 6-9, Fri 6-9.30 ⊕ FULLER'S ◀ London Pride & ESB, George Gale & Co Seafarers, Guest ale Ŏ Aspall. ♟ 12 **Facilities** Non-diners area ❖ (Bar Garden) ♦ Children's menu Children's portions Garden ♬ Parking Wi-fi ☛ (notice required)

WOOBURN COMMON
Map 6 SU98

Chequers Inn ★★★ HL ◉◉

PICK OF THE PUBS

Kiln Ln HP10 0JQ ☎ **01628 529575**
e-mail: info@chequers-inn.com
dir: M40 junct 2, A40 through Beaconsfield towards High Wycombe. Left into Broad Ln, signed Taplow/Burnham/Wooburn Common. 2m to pub

Peaceful dining inn above the Thames Valley

Old and new blend seamlessly in this extended coaching inn, the heart of which is firmly fixed in the 17th century where hand-tooled oak posts support and break up the interior dispersed across timeworn flagged and wooden floors around the open fire and original bar. In contrast, the newly refurbished lounge is light, airy and chic, dressed with leather sofas and chairs, low tables, greenery and an open fire. The patio and flowery garden are sheltered by a magnificent old oak tree, making the most of the wooded Chiltern countryside of the Thames Valley, whilst the luxury accommodation comprises 17 individually designed rooms with antique pine furniture. Beers from the local Rebellion brewery feature at the bar, where the solid menu covers good pubby stalwarts like haddock, chips and mushy peas. The two AA Rosette restaurant menu features ever-changing dishes such as pan-fried duck breast, red cabbage and fondant potato; and dark chocolate delice, jasmine tea, cream and shortbread.

Open all day all wk 12-12 **Bar Meals** L served Mon-Fri 12-2.30, Sat 12-10, Sun 12-9.30 D served Mon-Thu 6-9.30, Fri 6-10, Sat 12-10, Sun 12-9.30 Av main course £9.95-£10.95 **Restaurant** L served all wk 12-2.30 D served all wk 7-9.30 Fixed menu price fr £17.95 Av 3 course à la carte fr £28.85 ⊕ FREE HOUSE ◀ Rebellion IPA, Hardys & Hansons Olde Trip, Fuller's, London Pride Ŏ Westons Stowford Press. ♟ 14 **Facilities** Non-diners area ♦ Children's menu Children's portions Garden ♬ Parking Wi-fi **Rooms** 17

CAMBRIDGESHIRE

BABRAHAM　　　　Map 12 TL55

The George Inn at Babraham

PICK OF THE PUBS

High St CB22 3AG ☎ 01223 833800
e-mail: info@thegeorgebabraham.co.uk
dir: *In High St, just off A11/A505 & A1307*

Traditional inn with enjoyable home cooking

This 18th-century coaching inn occupies an enviable position in the picturesque village of Babraham at the rural heart of Cambridgeshire, just four miles from Cambridge. Exposed beams and brickwork characterise most areas, lending a friendly and relaxed air to the place; a mix of leather sofas and solid oak furniture add to the appeal. Devastated by fire some years ago, the pub was restored to its former glory and the kitchen has established a good reputation for enjoyable home-cooked food, making the inn a destination dining venue. A typical menu might offer sautéed wild mushrooms on toasted brioche; stir-fried crispy duck with noodles and plum sauce; and chocolate and pear sponge pudding. An attractive rear patio with heaters and parasols leads to a garden, and special culinary and music events are hosted throughout the year.

Open all day all wk 12-11 (Sun 12-5) **Bar Meals** L served all wk 12-2 D served Mon 6-8, Tue-Sat 5.30-9 Av main course £10 **Restaurant** L served Mon-Fri 12-2, Sat-Sun 12-3 D served Mon 6-8, Tue-Sat 5.30-9 Av 3 course à la carte fr £19 ⊕ GREENE KING ◀ IPA, Morland Old Speckled Hen, Guest ale ♂ Aspall. **Facilities** Non-diners area ♦ Children's menu Children's portions Garden ⚞ Parking Wi-fi ⛟

BALSHAM　　　　Map 12 TL55

The Black Bull Inn ★★★★ INN ◉
NEW

27 High St CB21 4DJ ☎ 01223 893844
e-mail: info@blackbull-balsham.co.uk
dir: *From S: M11 junct 9, A11 towards Newmarket, follow Balsham signs. From N: M11 junct 10, A505 signed Newmarket (A11), onto A11, follow Balsham signs*

Transformed inn for excellent food and a good night's sleep

An AA Rosette for food and four AA stars for accommodation are just two of the awards acquired by this 16th-century pub, run by the same team as The Red Lion in nearby Hinxton. The bar serves East Anglian real ales and ciders, sandwiches, baguettes, hot meals and four types of shortcrust pastry pie. The restaurant is in an adjoining converted barn, where main dishes, depending on the season, may include roast breast and confit leg of partridge; lemon sole paupiettes; and beetroot risotto. Out front is a tree-lined sandstone patio, and at the back a south-facing beer garden.

Open all wk 11-3 5.30-11 (Sat 11-11 Sun 12-10.30) **Bar Meals** L served Mon-Thu 12-2, Fri-Sun 12-2.30 D served

Mon-Thu 6.30-9, Fri-Sat 6.30-9.30, Sun 7-9 Av main course £14 **Restaurant** L served Mon-Thu 12-2, Fri-Sun 12-2.30 D served Mon-Thu 6.30-9, Fri-Sat 6.30-9.30, Sun 7-9 Fixed menu price fr £13 Av 3 course à la carte fr £26 ⊕ FREE HOUSE ◀ Woodforde's Wherry, Adnams Southwold Bitter, Greene King IPA, Brandon Rusty Bucket, Nethergate ♂ Aspall & Harry Sparrow. ⚐ 12 **Facilities** Non-diners area ♣ (Bar Garden) ♦ Children's menu Children's portions Garden ⚞ Beer festival Parking Wi-fi ⛟ (notice required) **Rooms** 5

BARRINGTON　　　　Map 12 TL34

The Royal Oak

31 West Green CB22 7RZ ☎ 01223 870791
e-mail: info@royaloakbarrington.co.uk
dir: *From Barton off M11, S of Cambridge*

Quintessential English pub by village green

One of the oldest thatched and timbered pubs in England, this rambling 16th-century building overlooks a 30-acre village green. With a pretty 'chocolate-box' image on the outside, the smart interior is now contemporary in design; the menu lists the classic dishes for which the pub has long been known, such as pie of the day, toad-in-the-hole, beer battered haddock, and aubergine parmigana. Alongside this is a collection of salads and sandwiches, and a choice of ales that includes Twitchell and Adnams.

Open all wk 12-3 6-11 (Sun 12-11) **Bar Meals** L served all wk 12-2 D served all wk 6-9.30 **Restaurant** L served all wk 12-2 D served Mon-Sat 6-9.30, Sun 7-9 ⊕ FREE HOUSE ◀ Woodforde's, Buntingford Twitchell, Adnams, O'Hanlon's Royal Oak ♂ Aspall, Thatchers Gold. ⚐ 8 **Facilities** Non-diners area ♣ (Bar Garden) ♦ Children's menu Children's portions Garden ⚞ Parking Wi-fi ⛟ (notice required)

BOURN　　　　Map 12 TL35

The Willow Tree NEW

29 High St CB23 2SQ ☎ 01954 719775
e-mail: contact@thewillowtreebourn.com
dir: *From Royston on A1188, right on B1046 signed Bourn. Pub in village on right*

Shabby chic candlelit restaurant and bar serving East Anglian ales

A certain chemistry is at work in this village pub just off Ermine Street, the old Roman road from London to York. Head chef Craig Galvin-Scott, you see, is married to front-of-house manager, Shaina, and after they bought it in late 2012 they set about creating the shabby-chic (their word) interior, with a candlelit restaurant and bar. It soon began attracting awards. Seasonal menus feature lamb rump with braised Savoy cabbage, cream and bacon; sea bass with Jerusalem artichoke; and roulade with chard, ricotta and root vegetable. In the garden stands a graceful willow tree from which the inn takes its name.

Open all day all wk **Bar Meals** L served all wk 12-3 D served all wk 5.30-9.30 Av main course £12 **Restaurant** L served all wk 12-3 D served all wk

5.30-9.30 Av 3 course à la carte fr £27 ⊕ FREE HOUSE ◀ Milton Pegasus, Woodforde's Wherry ♂ Addlestones, Aspall. ⚐ 49 **Facilities** Non-diners area ♣ (Garden) ♦ Children's menu Children's portions Garden ⚞ Beer festival Cider festival Parking Wi-fi ⛟ (notice required)

BROUGHTON　　　　Map 12 TL27

The Crown Inn

Bridge Rd PE28 3AY ☎ 01487 824428
e-mail: info@thecrowninnrestaurant.co.uk
dir: *A141 from Huntingdon towards Warboys. Left to Broughton*

Picturesque inn at the heart of the community

In the mid-19th century, this village inn incorporated a saddler's shop, thatched stables and piggeries. Today it focuses on being a popular pub and restaurant in a thriving local community. The bar offers real ales from Suffolk and national breweries, and you'll also find Aspall cider. The restaurant combines a traditional pub look with contemporary design, and it's here you'll be able to eat modern European dishes cooked using the best sustainable fish caught by day boats, the highest quality meats and excellent seasonal vegetables. Menus change regularly, so you may find one offering seared pigeon breast; roast cod on a bed of sautéed celeriac; and cappuccino and hazelnut praline gâteau.

Open all wk Mon-Sat 11.30-3 6.30-11 (Sun 11.30-8) ⊕ FREE HOUSE ◀ Nethergate Sweeney Todd, Timothy Taylor Landlord, Adnams Southwold Bitter, Guest ales ♂ Aspall. **Facilities** ♣ (Bar Garden) ♦ Children's menu Children's portions Play area Garden Parking

CAMBRIDGE　　　　Map 12 TL45

The Anchor

Silver St CB3 9EL ☎ 01223 353554
e-mail: 7614@greeneking.co.uk
dir: *Telephone for directions*

Waterside pub appealing to students and visitors alike

This attractive pub is situated at the end of the medieval lane that borders Queens' College in the heart of this university city. Hard by the bridge over the River Cam, in fine weather the riverside patio is an ideal spot for enjoying one of a range of Greene King ales and guest beers, while watching the activities on the water. The more adventurous can hire a punt for a leisurely trip to Grantchester (of Rupert Brooke and Jeffrey Archer fame), and on return sample a choice of hearty meals from a range that includes lasagne, home-made pies and roast beef.

Open all wk Mon-Thu & Sun 11-11 (Fri-Sat 11am-mdnt) ⊕ GREENE KING ◀ IPA, Abbot Ale & St Edmunds, Morland Old Speckled Hen, Guest ales ♂ Aspall. **Facilities** ♦ Children's menu

CAMBRIDGE *continued*

Cambridge Blue

PICK OF THE PUBS

85 Gwydir St CB1 2LG ☎ 01223 471680
dir: *In city centre. Access by car to Gwydir St from Mill Rd only (no access by car from Norfolk St). Gwydir St parking available*

Global beer list along with pub food classics

A friendly 1860s backstreet pub, built to serve the terrace that housed railway workers, with an unexpected large suntrap garden and an amazing range of beers, from 200 bottled beers from around the world to a mind-boggling choice of 14 real ales from microbreweries on handpump in the taproom – try a pint of Oakham Inferno or Woodforde's Wherry. Inside are two real fires, lots of memorabilia and a lively, buzzy vibe. Good-value pub grub made on the premises comes in the form of steak-and-kidney pie; fish pie; sausages and mash; a daily curry; and a range of filled ciabatta sandwiches and jacket potatoes (plus there are always vegetarian options). February, June and October beer festivals.

Open all day all wk Mon-Sat 12-11 (Sun 12-10.30) **Bar Meals** L served Mon-Sat 12-10, Sun 12-9 food served all day ⊕ FREE HOUSE ◀ Woodforde's Wherry, Oakham Inferno, Guest ales ♂ Pickled Pig, Thatchers. ♀ 8 **Facilities** Non-diners area ♣ (Bar Garden) ♦♦ Children's portions Family room Garden ♬ Beer festival Wi-fi

Free Press

Prospect Row CB1 1DU ☎ 01223 368337
e-mail: craig.bickley@ntlworld.com
dir: *Telephone for directions*

Popular haunt for those who enjoy a lack of electronic noise

A pub for over 120 years, the Free Press gets its name from the time when part of it was a printing press which produced a free Cambridge newspaper. Now a haunt for students, academics, locals and visitors, this atmospheric and picturesque backstreet pub near the city centre has open fires and a beautiful walled garden – but no music, mobile phones or gaming machines. Punters are attracted by first-rate real ales and great home-made food such as toasted ciabattas; seafood platter; lamb's liver and bacon with bubble-and-squeak and gravy.

Open all wk 12-2.30 6-11 (Fri-Sat 12-11 Sun 12-3 7-10.30) Closed: 25-26 Dec, 1 Jan **Bar Meals** L served Mon-Fri 12-2, Sat-Sun 12-2.30 D served Mon-Sat 6-9, Sun 7-9 ⊕ GREENE KING ◀ IPA & Abbot Ale, XX Mild, Guest ales ♂ Westons Stowford Press & Old Rosie. ♀ 10 **Facilities** Non-diners area ♣ (Bar Garden) ♦♦ Children's portions Garden ♬ ⬛

The Old Spring

1 Ferry Path CB4 1HB ☎ 01223 357228
e-mail: theoldspring@hotmail.co.uk
dir: *Just off Chesterton Rd, (A1303) in city centre, near Midsummer Common*

Neighbourhood pub with a lengthy and varied menu

You'll find this bustling pub in the leafy suburb of De Freville, just a short stroll from the River Cam and its many boatyards, which makes its splendid decked patio popular as a post-workout refreshment spot for rowers. The bright and airy interior offers rug-covered wooden floors, comfy sofas and large family tables. Sip a pint of Abbot Ale, one of several real ales on tap, or one of 20 wines by the glass while choosing from over a dozen main courses plus specials, perhaps red Thai black tiger prawn curry, steak frites, corned beef hash, pan-seared halibut steak, or vegetable pappardelle pasta.

Open all day all wk 11.30-11 (Sun 12-10.30) **Bar Meals** L served Mon-Fri 12-2.30, Sat-Sun 12-4 D served Mon-Sun 6-9.30 Av main course £10-£12 ⊕ GREENE KING ◀ IPA & Abbot Ale, Hardys & Hansons Olde Trip, Morland Old Speckled Hen, Guest ales ♂ Aspall. ♀ 20 **Facilities** Non-diners area ♦♦ Children's menu Children's portions Garden ♬ Parking Wi-fi

The Punter

3 Pound Hill CB3 0AE ☎ 01223 363322
e-mail: info@thepuntercambridge.co.uk
dir: *Telephone for directions*

Seasonal food and local ales

Two minutes' walk from the city centre, this beautifully renovated coaching house is popular with visitors, locals and students alike. Drinkers can enjoy local ales alongside diners tucking into well-priced rustic food among the eclectic mix of pine furniture. Serving bar snacks, a three-course set menu and a daily-changing seasonal menu, dishes might include venison and pork terrine with home-made pickle; half roast guinea fowl with truffle mash, spinach and wild mushrooms; and chocolate terrine with rhubarb compôte. In the delightful courtyard garden pots of home-grown produce are sold.

Open all day all wk Closed: 25 Dec **Bar Meals** L served all day **Restaurant** L served Mon-Fri 12-3, Sat-Sun all day D served Mon-Fri 6-10, Sat-Sun all day ⊕ PUNCH TAVERNS ◀ M T Head Punter's Special Ale ♂ Addlestones. ♀ 13 **Facilities** Non-diners area ♣ (Bar Restaurant) ♦♦ Children's portions ♬ Wi-fi

The Black Horse

35 Park St CB23 8DA ☎ 01954 782600
e-mail: deniseglover@hotmail.co.uk
dir: *A14 junct 30, follow signs for Dry Drayton. In village turn right to pub. Signed*

Renowned for its ales and good food

Just five miles from Cambridge, The Black Horse has been at the heart of this quiet village for more than 300 years. Gary and Denise Glover and chef Marcello Silveira have built a reputation for notable food. Many local ales are showcased in the bar, and local suppliers dominate the menu in the restaurant. A starter of pan-seared pigeon breast, black pudding and game jus might be followed by Aldeburgh stone bass with green lentils, spinach and mussel sauce. The pub holds an annual beer festival over St George's Day weekend.

Open 12-3 6-11 (Sun 12-4) Closed: Mon **Bar Meals** L served Tue-Sat 12-2, Sun 12-4 D served Tue-Sat 6-9.30 **Restaurant** L served Tue-Sat 12-2, Sun 12-4 D served Tue-Sat 6-9.30 ⊕ FREE HOUSE ◀ Black Horse, Adnams, Guest ale ♂ Aspall. **Facilities** Non-diners area ♣ (Bar Garden) ♦♦ Children's portions Garden ♬ Beer festival Parking Wi-fi

The John Barleycorn

PICK OF THE PUBS

3 Moorfield Rd CB2 4PP ☎ 01223 832699
e-mail: info@johnbarleycorn.co.uk
dir: *Exit A505 into Duxford*

Traditional and comfortable village pub

If you need somewhere to relax after a day's racing at Newmarket, head for this thatched and whitewashed former coach house built in 1660. It took the name John Barleycorn in the mid-19th century and during World War II was a favourite watering hole for the brave young airmen of Douglas Bader's Duxford Wing. Step through the door into the softly lit bar with a rustic mix of country furniture, large brick fireplace, old tiled floor, cushioned pews and hop-adorned low beams. It's a cosy place in which to enjoy a hearty home-cooked meal, washed down with a refreshing pint of Greene King IPA or Abbot Ale. You can nibble on a bowl of olives or share a charcuterie board while making your menu selections: kipper and whisky pâté perhaps, followed by Dingley Dell maple-glazed rump of pork. Summer alfresco eating can be enjoyed on the flower-festooned rear patio. Change of hands.

Open all day all wk **Bar Meals** L served all wk D served all wk food served all day **Restaurant** food served all day ⊕ GREENE KING ◀ Greene King IPA, Abbot Ale, Ruddles Best & Ruddles County, Morland Old Speckled Hen. ♀ 12 **Facilities** Non-diners area ♣ (Bar Restaurant Garden) ♦♦ Children's menu Children's portions Play area Garden ♬ Parking Wi-fi ⬛ (notice required)

ELSWORTH   Map 12 TL36

The George & Dragon

41 Boxworth Rd CB23 4JQ ☎ 01954 267236
e-mail: info@georgeanddragon-elsworth.co.uk
dir: *SE of A14 between Cambridge & Huntingdon*

Agreeable beer selection and satisfying food

Set in a pretty village just outside Cambridge, this pub offers a friendly, relaxed environment, great beers and a wide range of satisfying food for locals and visitors alike. Aberdeen Angus steaks and fish fresh from Lowestoft are a draw here on the seasonal menu. Look out for wedges of breaded brie; hot potted crab with chilli; chicken and wild mushroom Stroganoff; and home-made fish pie. Friday night is steak night, Wednesday night is fish and chip supper, and there are special menus for occasions such as Valentine's Day, St George's Day and Mother's Day.

Open all wk 11-2.30 6-11 (Sun 12-10.30) **Bar Meals** L served Mon-Sat 12-2, Sun 12-8.30 D served Mon-Sat 6-9.30, Sun 12-8.30 **Restaurant** L served Mon-Sat 12-2, Sun 12-8.30 D served Mon-Sat 6-9.30, Sun 12-8.30 ⊕ FREE HOUSE ◀ Greene King IPA, Morland Old Speckled Hen, Guest ales ♻ Aspall. ♟ 13 **Facilities** Non-diners area ♣ (Bar Garden) ♦♦ Children's menu Children's portions Garden ⋒ Parking 🚌

ELTON   Map 12 TL09

The Crown Inn ★★★★★ INN

PICK OF THE PUBS

8 Duck St PE8 6RQ ☎ 01832 280232
e-mail: inncrown@googlemail.com
dir: *A1(M) junct 17, W on A605 signed Oundle/ Northampton. In 3.5m right to Elton, 0.9m left signed Nassington. Inn 0.3m on right*

Thatched stone inn oozing character and charm

The 17th-century Crown is tucked away behind a towering chestnut tree in the unspoilt village of Elton. Click open the door latch to reveal oak beams and natural stone aplenty, with a crackling winter fire in the inglenook. Golden Crown Bitter — locally brewed by the Tydd Steam brewery — takes pole position amongst the real ales at the bar, supported by Weston's Old Rosie and Glebe Farm ciders. Chef-patron Marcus Lamb places great emphasis on the food, with the finest local ingredients forming the basis for the freshly prepared traditional British favourites and dishes with a twist. Bar lunches feature sandwiches, baguettes and omelettes, as well as pub classics. In the evening, pan-fried breast of pigeon with glazed figs, confit shallot and smoked bacon might herald slow-roasted belly of rare-breed pork, fondant potato, braised red cabbage and chicory, and a Calvados jus.

Open all day all wk 12-11 **Bar Meals** L served Mon-Sat 12-2 D served Mon-Fri 6.30-9 **Restaurant** L served Sun 2-3 D served Mon-Sat 6.30-9 ⊕ FREE HOUSE ◀ Tydd Steam Golden Crown Bitter, Greene King IPA, Black Sheep, Digfield, Oakham, Adnams ♻ Westons Old Rosie, Glebe Farm. ♟ 8 **Facilities** Non-diners area ♣ (Bar) ♦♦ Children's menu Children's portions Outside area ⋒ Parking Wi-fi 🚌 (notice required) **Rooms** 5

ELY   Map 12 TL58

The Anchor Inn ★★★★ INN ◉

PICK OF THE PUBS

See Pick of the Pubs on page 58

FEN DITTON   Map 12 TL46

Ancient Shepherds

High St CB5 8ST ☎ 01223 293280
e-mail: ancientshepherds@hotmail.co.uk
dir: *From A14 take B1047 signed Cambridge/Airport*

Popular pub in a peaceful riverside village

Three miles from Cambridge, this heavily beamed pub is a popular dining destination away from the bustle of the city. Built as three cottages in 1540, it was named after the ancient order of Shepherds who once met here. The pub is free of music, darts and pool, and is a cosy place to sup a pint of London Pride beside one of the inglenook fires. The bar lunch menu offers an extensive range of filled baguettes as well as jackets and snacks. In the restaurant, follow Greek salad with fillet of plaice stuffed with prawns, and apple strudel for dessert. Specials could include oyster, mushroom and champagne risotto.

Open 12-2.30 6-11 Closed: 25-26 Dec, 1 Jan, Sun eve & Mon **Bar Meals** L served Tue-Sat 12-2, Sun 12-2.30 **Restaurant** L served Tue-Sat 12-2, Sun 12-2.30 D served Tue-Sat 6.30-9 ⊕ PUNCH TAVERNS ◀ Adnams Southwold Bitter, Greene King IPA, Fuller's London Pride ♻ Aspall. ♟ 8 **Facilities** Non-diners area ♣ (Bar Garden) ♦♦ Children's portions Garden ⋒ Parking Wi-fi

FENSTANTON   Map 12 TL36

King William IV

High St PE28 9JF ☎ 01480 462467
e-mail: kingwilliamfenstanton@btconnect.com
dir: *Off A14 junct 27 between Cambridge & Huntingdon*

Rustic village inn with good food

This rambling 17th-century village pub features oak beams, old brickwork and a wonderful central fireplace. Lunchtime offerings include a range of hot and cold sandwiches but also light bites such as roast confit duck leg with an oriental salad, or parmesan, leek and thyme tart with red onion jam. Diners looking for something more substantial can choose from classic grilled dishes such as spatchcock chicken, or enjoy Moroccan spiced stuffed chicken leg or pan-roasted mackerel. There is live music on Wednesday evenings and twice monthly at Sunday lunchtimes.

Open all wk Mon-Thu 12-3 5-11 (Fri-Sun all day) **Bar Meals** L served all wk 12-2.30 D served Mon-Thu 6-9, Fri-Sat 6-9.30 **Restaurant** L served all wk 12-2.30 D served Mon-Thu 6-9, Fri-Sat 6-9.30 ⊕ GREENE KING ◀ IPA, Guest ales ♻ Aspall. ♟ 13 **Facilities** Non-diners area ♣ (Bar Garden) ♦♦ Children's portions Garden ⋒ Parking Wi-fi 🚌 (notice required)

FORDHAM   Map 12 TL67

White Pheasant

CB7 5LQ ☎ 01638 720414
e-mail: whitepheasant@hotmail.com
dir: *From Newmarket A142 to Ely, approx 5m to Fordham. Pub on left in village*

An attractive place to relax

This 18th-century building stands in a fenland village between Ely and Newmarket. In recent years its considerable appeal has been subtly enhanced by improvements that preserve its period charm. You can enjoy locally brewed ale, a glass of wine, home-made lemonade or strawberryade while perusing the menus. Food is taken seriously here, with quality, presentation and flavour taking top priority, using produce sourced as locally as possible. Starters could be free-range chicken terrine with cranberry and chervil; crispy whitebait with garlic salt, lemon and tartare sauce. Following on with pan-fried Suffolk-reared beef fillet, wild mushrooms and red wine with thick-cut chips; roasted Gressingham duck breast, braised red cabbage with rapeseed oil mash; and buffalo mozzarella, plum tomato and parmesan gratin tart. Honey and lavender pannacotta with white chocolate, honeycomb and strawberries could be among the desserts.

Open 12-3 6-11 (Sun 12-4) Closed: Mon **Bar Meals** L served Tue-Sat 12-2.30, Sun 12-3 D served Tue-Sat 6-9.30 **Restaurant** L served Tue-Sat 12-2.30, Sun 12-3 D served Tue-Sat 6-9.30 ⊕ FREE HOUSE ◀ Nethergate, Adnams ♻ Aspall Harry Sparrow. ♟ 12 **Facilities** Non-diners area ♦♦ Children's portions Garden Parking 🚌

GREAT CHISHILL   Map 12 TL43

The Pheasant

24 Heydon Rd SG8 8SR ☎ 01763 838535
dir: *Off B1039 between Royston & Saffron Walden*

17th-century free house with inglenook and plenty of beams

Stunning views and roaring log fires characterise this traditional, beamed village free house, where Nethergate and Woodforde's are a couple of the real ale choices. There are no gaming machines or piped music to disturb the friendly, sociable bar, and children under 14 are not allowed in. In summer, bird song holds sway in the idyllic pub garden. Freshly made sandwiches come complete with chips and salad garnish, or there is a deal to include home-made soup as well. Home-made dishes like four-rib rack of lamb; calves' liver and bacon; and wild mushroom and tarragon linguine cater for larger appetites.

Open all wk 12-3 6-11 (Sat-Sun all day) **Bar Meals** L served all wk 12-2 D served all wk 6-9.30 **Restaurant** L served all wk 12-2 D served all wk 6-9.30 ⊕ FREE HOUSE ◀ Fuller's London Pride, Woodforde's Wherry, Nethergate ♻ Westons Stowford Press. ♟ 8 **Facilities** Non-diners area ♣ (Bar Garden) Garden ⋒ Parking Wi-fi 🚌 (notice required)

PICK OF THE PUBS

The Anchor Inn ★★★★ INN ❀

ELY Map 12 TL58

Sutton Gault CB6 2BD ☎ **01353 778537**
e-mail: anchorinn@popmail.bta.com
web: www.anchorsuttongault.co.uk
dir: *From A14, B1050 to Earith, take
B1381 to Sutton. Sutton Gault on left*

Riverside inn set in the fens

In 1630 the Earl of Bedford engaged the Dutch engineer Cornelius Vermuyden to drain the surrounding lawless and disease-ridden fens for agricultural use; The Anchor was constructed on the bank of the New Bedford River (or 'The Hundred Foot Drain') to accommodate Vermuyden's workforce and has been a pub ever since. Today, low beams, dark wood panelling, scrubbed pine tables on gently undulating tiled floors, antique prints and winter log fires lend character to the cosy, intimate atmosphere of this family-run free house, which changed hands in 2012. New beers include ales from the East Anglian Nethergate Growler and BlackBar breweries. Modern British cuisine is the strength here, with an emphasis on seasonal and traditional ingredients, featuring as much local produce as possible: Brancaster oysters and mussels, Cromer crab, venison from the Denham Estate and marsh samphire. These ingredients are combined with a light, individual touch to create flavoursome, unfussy dishes. Grilled dates wrapped in bacon with a

mustard cream sauce makes an interesting starter, which could be followed by spicy polenta and carrot cake with goats' cheese cream, pumpkin seed pesto and a radish salad; or roast rump of lamb with dauphinoise potatoes, purple sprouting broccoli and a lamb jus. Desserts may include vanilla latte pannacotta with white chocolate coffee beans and shortbread; and mixed berry posset with star anise syrup and a cinnamon tuile. There are roasts at Sunday lunchtimes, and summer meals can be enjoyed on the terrace overlooking the river. En suite accommodation is available for those who wish to explore East Anglia – the cathedral cities of Ely and Cambridge are both within easy reach.

Open Mon-Fri 12-2.30 7-10.30 (Sat 12-3 6.30-11 Sun 12-4 6.30-10) Closed: 25-26 Dec eve **Restaurant** L served Mon-Sat 12-2, Sun 12-2.30 D served Mon-Fri 7-9, Sat 6.30-9.30, Sun 6.30-8.30 ⊕ FREE HOUSE ◗ Nethergate Old Growler, BlackBar Bitter. ♟ 10 **Facilities** Non-diners area ⅋ Children's portions Garden ⟗ Parking Wi-fi 🚐 (notice required) **Rooms** 4

GREAT WILBRAHAM — Map 12 TL55

The Carpenters Arms NEW

10 High St CB21 5JD ☎ 01223 882093
e-mail: contact@carpentersarmsgastropub.co.uk
dir: *Village E of Cambridge*

Traditional free house, microbrewery and French-inspired food

A beer house since 1729, this now smartly refurbished pub restaurant is still brewing — today they're called Carpenter's Cask Best Bitter and Sixteen Strides, a hoppy pale ale. Other beers are also on draft, as are Ipswich microbrewery lager Calvors, and Aspall cider. Landlords Rick and Heather Hurley previously ran an award-winning restaurant in France, so expect French — eg tartiflette — Catalan, Italian and even Thai dishes on the menus. Other possibilities include chicken forestière; fillet steak; fish of the day; and vegetable strudel, while Sunday roasts remain decidedly English. A Suffolk white features among the world-sourced wine list.

Open 11.30-3 6.30-11 **Closed:** 26 Dec, 1 Jan, 1wk Nov & 1wk Feb, Sun eve & Tue **Bar Meals** L served Wed-Mon 12-2.30 D served Wed-Sat & Mon 7-9 Av main course £9.95 **Restaurant** L served Wed-Mon 12-2.30 D served Wed-Sat & Mon 7-9 Av 3 course à la carte fr £25 ⊕ FREE HOUSE ◖ Carpenter's Cask, Greene King IPA Ŏ Aspall. **Facilities** Non-diners area ♦ Children's portions Garden Outside area ⊼ Parking ▥ (notice required)

HEMINGFORD GREY — Map 12 TL27

The Cock Pub and Restaurant

PICK OF THE PUBS

See Pick of the Pubs on page 60

HILDERSHAM — Map 12 TL54

The Pear Tree Inn

High St CB21 6BU ☎ 01223 891680
e-mail: peartreeinn@btconnect.com
dir: *5m E of Cambridge, take A1307 to Haverhill, turn left to Hildersham*

Children, muddy boots and dogs all welcome

In a tranquil setting opposite the village green and close to a Roman road with excellent walks nearby, The Pear Tree has been a pub for more than 200 years. It became a free house in 2011 and offers a range of East Anglian real ales. The inn has undergone several changes over the last year, including a refurbishment, new landlord and new menu. Home-cooked, locally sourced food encompasses confit of pork with celeriac coleslaw; risotto or pie of the day; and roast salmon fillet with a herb and lemon cream sauce. Tuesday is fish and chip day. There's a lovely outdoor decking area.

Open 12-2.30 6-11 (Sun 12-3) **Closed:** Mon **Bar Meals** L served Tue-Sun 12-2 D served Tue-Sat 6.30-9 ⊕ FREE HOUSE ◖ Adnams Broadside, Woodforde's Wherry Ŏ Aspall. **Facilities** Non-diners area ♥ (Bar Garden) ♦

Children's menu Children's portions Garden ⊼ Parking Wi-fi ▥ (notice required)

HILTON — Map 12 TL26

The Prince of Wales ★★★ INN

Potton Rd PE28 9NG ☎ 01480 830257
e-mail: bookings@thehiltonpow.co.uk
dir: *On B1040 between A14 & A428 S of St Ives*

Popular inn in the heart of rural Cambridgeshire

The Prince of Wales is a traditional, 1830s two-bar village inn with four comfortable bedrooms. To drink, choose from Adnams, Timothy Taylor Landlord or a guest ale. Food options range from bar snacks to full meals, among which are grills, fish, curries brought in from a local Indian restaurant, and daily specials, such as lamb hotpot. Home-made puddings include crème brûlée and sherry trifle. The village's 400-year-old grass maze was where locals used to escape the devil.

Open 12-2.30 6-11 **Closed:** Mon L **Bar Meals** L served Tue-Sun 12-2 D served all wk 7-9 **Restaurant** L served Tue-Sun 12-2 D served all wk 7-9 ⊕ FREE HOUSE ◖ Timothy Taylor Landlord, Adnams, Guest ales Ŏ Aspall. ♥ 9 **Facilities** Non-diners area ♥ (Bar Garden) ♦ Children's menu Children's portions Garden ⊼ Parking Wi-fi ▥ **Rooms** 4

HINXTON — Map 12 TL44

The Red Lion Inn ★★★★ INN ⍟

PICK OF THE PUBS

32 High St CB10 1QY ☎ 01799 530601
e-mail: info@redlionhinxton.co.uk
dir: *N'bound only: M11 junct 9, towards A11, left onto A1301. Left to Hinxton. Or M11 junct 10, A505 towards A11/Newmarket. At rdbt take 3rd exit onto A1301, right to Hinxton*

Rambling inn in conservation village with super garden

This 16th-century, pink-washed free house and restaurant sits in a pretty and peaceful village with an award-winning walled garden with dovecote, arbour and a patio overlooking the church. Some customers like to eat informally on settles in the bar, where the ceilings are low, and green Chesterfield sofas sit on the wooden floors; others prefer the loftier ceilings and pegged oak rafters of the restaurant. Locally sourced, modern British menus apply throughout offering honey and mustard glaze hand-cut ham; pan-fried bream; poached and grilled multibird of chicken, pheasant and pigeon; and wild mushroom open ravioli. The real ales are also locally sourced: Adnams Bitter, Greene King IPA and Brandon Rusty Bucket are permanent fixtures, with other East Anglian microbreweries supplying on a rotational basis. A beer festival is held in late summer. Guest rooms have a fresh, contemporary feel and are set apart in a private garden area.

Open all day all wk **Bar Meals** L served Mon-Thu 12-2, Fri-Sun 12-2.30 D served Mon-Thu 6.30-9, Fri-Sat

6.30-9.30, Sun 7-9 Av main course £11 **Restaurant** L served Mon-Thu 12-2, Fri-Sun 12-2.30 D served Mon-Thu 6.30-9, Fri-Sat 6.30-9.30, Sun 7-9 Fixed menu price fr £14 Av 3 course à la carte fr £28 ⊕ FREE HOUSE ◖ Greene King IPA, Woodforde's Wherry, Brandon Rusty Bucket, Adnams, Guest ales Ŏ Aspall Harry Sparrow. ♥ 13 **Facilities** Non-diners area ♥ (Bar Garden) ♦ Children's portions Garden ⊼ Beer festival Cider festival Parking Wi-fi ▥ (notice required) **Rooms** 8

HISTON — Map 12 TL46

Red Lion

27 High St CB24 9JD ☎ 01223 564437
dir: *M11 junct 14, A14 towards. Exit at junct 32 onto B1049 for Histon*

Village pub with good choice of real ales

A pub since 1836, this popular village local on Cambridge's northern fringe has been run by Mark Donachy for almost two decades. A dyed-in-the-wool pub man, Mark's real ales include Oakham Bishops Farewell, as well as Pickled Pig Porker's Snout cider. There are also over 30 different Belgian bottled beers. The bar offers food at lunchtime and in the evenings. Expect cheerful service, winter log fires and a good-sized neat garden. Time a visit for the Easter or early September beer festivals.

Open all day all wk 10.30am-11pm (Fri 10.30am-mdnt Sun 12-11) **Bar Meals** L served Mon-Sat 12-2.30, Sun 12.30-5 D served Tue-Thu & Sat 6.30-10 ⊕ FREE HOUSE ◖ Batemans XB, Tring Blonde, Oakham Bishops Farewell Ŏ Pickled Pig Porker's Snout, Westons Perry. **Facilities** Non-diners area ♦ Children's portions Family room Garden ⊼ Beer festival Parking Wi-fi ▥ (notice required) **Notes** ⍟

HOLYWELL — Map 12 TL37

The Old Ferryboat Inn ★★★ INN

Back Ln PE27 4TG ☎ 01480 463227
e-mail: 8638@greeneking.co.uk
dir: *From Cambridge on A14 right onto A1096, right onto A1123, right to Holywell*

Great hospitality at inn steeped in history

Renowned as England's oldest inn, built some time in the 11th century, but with a hostelry history that goes back to the sixth. In a tranquil setting beside the Great Ouse River, The Old Ferryboat has immaculately maintained thatch, white stone walls, a cosy interior and bags of charm and character. It's a pleasant place — despite the resident ghost of a lovelorn teenager — in which to enjoy grilled pork chop and apple fritter; British beef and Ruddles ale pie; chicken tikka masala; or a surf 'n' turf burger. There are seven en suite bedrooms.

Open all wk 11-11 (Sun 12-10.30) **Bar Meals** L served all wk 12-10 D served all wk 12-10 food served all day **Restaurant** L served all wk 12-10, D served all wk 12-10 food served all day ⊕ OLD ENGLISH INNS & HOTELS ◖ Greene King IPA & XX Mild, Morland Old Speckled Hen, Guest ales Ŏ Aspall. ♥ 18 **Facilities** Non-diners area ♥ (Bar Restaurant Garden) ♦ Garden ⊼ Parking ▥ **Rooms** 7

PICK OF THE PUBS

The Cock Pub and Restaurant

HEMINGFORD GREY — Map 12 TL27

47 High St PE28 9BJ ☎ 01480 463609
e-mail: cock@cambscuisine.com
web: www.cambscuisine.com
dir: *Between A14 juncts 25 & 26 follow village signs*

Modern British cooking in a charming village close to the River Ouse

Although it's only a mile away from the busy A14, it feels like a world away. In the charming village of Hemingford Grey stands The Cock, a pretty 17th-century pub dozing on the main street among thatched, timbered and brick cottages; the ideal place to relax with peaceful views across the willow-bordered Great Ouse river. Other than the peaceful location, the detour is well worth taking as the food on offer is excellent — the set lunch menu is a steal. The stylishly revamped interior comprises a contemporary bar for drinks only, and a restaurant with bare boards, dark or white-painted beams, wood-burning stoves, and church candles on an eclectic mix of old dining tables. Cooking is modern British, with the occasional foray further afield, and fresh local produce is used in preparing the short, imaginative carte, while daily deliveries of fresh fish dictate the chalkboard menu choice. A typical meal might kick off with rabbit, spinach and soused carrot salad; duck parcel with sweet and sour cucumber; or poached pear and blue cheese salad. Follow with artichoke and truffle risotto with pecorino cheese and rocket; beef Wellington with potato bake, roast carrots and celeriac; or sausages (made by the owner) and mash; then round off with sticky toffee pudding, marmalade sponge, or a plate of unusual cheeses. The wine list specialises in the Languedoc-Roussillion area and the choice of real ales favours local micro-breweries, perhaps Great Oakley Wagtail, Oldershaw Best Bitter and Brewster's Hophead. There is a beer festival every August Bank Holiday weekend.

Open all wk 11.30-3 6-11 **Restaurant** L served all wk 12-2.30 D served all wk 6.15-9.30 ⊕ FREE HOUSE ◀ Brewster's Hophead, Great Oakley Wagtail, Oldershaw Best Bitter, Nethergate IPA ♂ Cromwell. ♟ 18 **Facilities** Non-diners area ♦♦ Children's portions Garden ⋒ Beer festival Parking 🚐 (notice required)

HORNINGSEA — Map 12 TL46

The Crown & Punchbowl

CB5 9JG ☎ 01223 860643
e-mail: info@thecrownandpunchbowl.co.uk
dir: *Telephone for directions*

Friendly coaching inn with seasonal menus

Dating back to 1764, the tiled and whitewashed Crown & Punchbowl stands in a little one-street village. Soft colours and wooden floors create a warm atmosphere, while in the low-beamed restaurant innovative influences are at play in dishes created with the finest, locally sourced ingredients: pan-seared scallops with curried parsnip purée, pineapple, chilli jam and curry tuile; and herb-crusted cod supreme, Brancaster mussel and vegetable chowder, parsley and pine nut pesto. The pudding menu is equally appealing, with the likes of blood orange and almond Battenberg, spiced orange and cardamom ice cream; and Bramley apple and sultana samosa, milk purée, apple sorbet, apple crisps and crushed hazelnuts.

Open Mon-Sun 12-3 Mon-Sat 6.30-9.30 Closed: Sun eve & BHs eve **Bar Meals** Av main course £16 **Restaurant** L served all wk 12-3 D served Mon-Sat 6.30-9.30 Av 3 course à la carte fr £30 ⊕ FREE HOUSE ◀ Thwaites Original Ö Aspall. **Facilities** Non-diners area ♦♦ Children's portions Garden ⊫ Parking Wi-fi

KEYSTON — Map 11 TL07

Pheasant Inn ◉◉
PICK OF THE PUBS

Village Loop Rd PE28 0RE ☎ 01832 710241
e-mail: info@thepheasant-keyston.co.uk
dir: *0.5m from A14, clearly signed, 10m W of Huntingdon, 14m E of Kettering*

Skilfully prepared British cuisine and well chosen wines

The Pheasant is a beautiful, whitewashed and thatched pub in a sleepy farming village. Following a five-year gap, in 2012 John and Julia Hoskins bought back this 16th-century inn, which their family first acquired in 1964. The large bar, which serves Adnams and Nene Valley, is a traditional and unspoilt mixture of oak beams, stripped boards, large open fires and simple wooden furniture. The airy Garden Room opens to a sunny patio and herb garden beyond. Chef-patron is Simon Cadge, who relies greatly on local producers and suppliers, leaving only smoked fish from Uig Lodge on the Isle of Lewis, and fine British cheeses from Neal's Yard Dairy in London to travel any great distance. Interesting flavours are at work in a starter of feta, blood orange, dandelion and walnut salad. Continue with pan-fried sea trout with gnocchi, braised fennel, leeks and brown shrimps; or traditional Keyston beefburger and hand-cut chips. John, a Master of Wine, compiles the wine list.

Open 12-3 6-11 (Sun 12-5) Closed: Mon & Sun eve **Bar Meals** L served Tue-Sat 12-2 D served Tue-Sat 6.30-9.30

Av main course £11 **Restaurant** L served Tue-Sat 12-2, Sun 12-3.30 D served Tue-Sat 6.30-9.30 Fixed menu price fr £15 Av 3 course à la carte fr £25 ⊕ FREE HOUSE ◀ Adnams Broadside, Nene Valley NVB Ö Aspall. ☻ 16 **Facilities** Non-diners area ♣ (Bar Restaurant Garden) ♦♦ Children's menu Children's portions Garden Parking Wi-fi ▄▄ (notice required)

KIMBOLTON — Map 12 TL16

The New Sun Inn

20-22 High St PE28 0HA ☎ 01480 860052
e-mail: newsuninn@btinternet.com
dir: *From A1 N take B645 for 7m. From A1 S take B661 for 7m. From A14 take B660 for 5m*

Tapas and traditional fare

Its pink-washed, profusely flower-basketed frontage makes this 17th-century inn easy to spot from a distance. Serving Wells Bombardier, Eagle IPA and a weekly guest, it also offers bar, conservatory and formal restaurant dining, from hot and cold tapas, to comprehensive lunch and evening menus featuring favourites like steak-and-kidney pudding. Other weekly changing possibilities are hake in pancetta with baby squid and chorizo; chargrilled chicken cassoulet; and goats' cheese, red onion and pine nut tart. Malteser cheesecake is a possible dessert. Themed events include lunch with the landlord and landlady.

Open all wk Mon-Thu 11.30-2.30 6-11 (Fri-Sun & mid Jun to mid Sep all day) ⊕ CHARLES WELLS ◀ Bombardier & Eagle IPA, Guest ales Ö Aspall. **Facilities** ♣ (Bar Garden) ♦♦ Children's portions Garden

LITTLE WILBRAHAM — Map 12 TL55

Hole in the Wall ◉
PICK OF THE PUBS

2 High St CB21 5JY ☎ 01223 812282
e-mail: info@holeinthewallcambridge.com
dir: *Telephone for directions*

Enjoyable food from a Masterchef finalist

The name of this 16th-century village pub and restaurant between Cambridge and Newmarket comes from the days when farm workers used to collect their jugs of beer through a hole in the wall so as not to upset the gentry in the bar. Since 2010, the heavily timbered pub has been owned by former Masterchef finalist Alex Rushmer, who has turned it into an award-winning venture. Customers can drink Elgood's Cambridge Bitter, Milton's Sparta, and Woodforde's Nelson's Revenge and Wherry in the hop-adorned bar. The first-class modern British cooking is prepared from fresh local produce and includes turkey, bacon and leek pie; and local venison sausages, mash and red cabbage at lunch and, in the evening, Keen's Cheddar and onion rarebit tart; or Blythburgh pork chop with potato and butternut mash, cider and mustard sauce. Finish with passion fruit posset or rice pudding, apple compôte and crumble.

Open 11.30-3 6.30-11 Closed: 2wks Jan, 25 Dec, Mon, Tue L, Sun eve **Bar Meals** L served Wed-Sun 12-2 D served Tue-Sat 7-9 Av main course £16 **Restaurant** L served Wed-Sun 12-2 D served Tue-Sat 7-9 Fixed menu price fr £14 Av 3 course à la carte fr £30 ⊕ FREE HOUSE ◀ Woodforde's Wherry & Nelson's Revenge, Elgood's Cambridge Bitter, Milton Sparta. ☻ 10 **Facilities** Non-diners area ♦♦ Children's portions Garden ⊫ Parking Wi-fi

MADINGLEY — Map 12 TL36

The Three Horseshoes
PICK OF THE PUBS

High St CB23 8AB ☎ 01954 210221
e-mail: 3hs@btconnect.com
dir: *M11 junct 13, 1.5m from A14*

Picturesque location and globally inspired dishes

This pretty thatched inn draws in the punters thanks to a lovely conservatory restaurant with views of the garden plus a small bustling bar offering real ales, ciders and an impressive 22 wines by the glass. Longstanding chef-patron Richard Stokes shows off his flair in modern dishes with global, often Italian, influences and exciting flavour combinations. Ingredients are sourced with care and dishes are available in child-sized portions too. Kick off perhaps with smoked eel, tare, green tea, wasabi cotta, sesame purée, edamame beans and coriander cress; or frozen foie gras, Riesling gelée, lychee and peanut butter. Mains might poached hake, piquillo peppers, saffron and pimenton sauce, saffron puffed rice, mussels, spinach, butter beans and chorizo crumbs. Puddings are equally creative – how about passion fruit 'snow egg', coconut marshmallow, white chocolate and vanilla custard and passion fruit granita to finish?

Open all wk 11.30-3 6-11 (Sun 11.30-3 6-9.30) **Bar Meals** L served Mon-Fri 12-2, Sat-Sun 12-2.30 D served all wk 6.30-9.30 Av main course £12 **Restaurant** L served all wk 12-2.30 D served Mon-Sat 6.30-9.30 Av 3 course à la carte fr £35 ⊕ FREE HOUSE ◀ Adnams Southwold Bitter, Hook Norton Old Hooky, Smiles Best Bitter, City of Cambridge Hobson's Choice, Guest ales Ö Westons Stowford Press. ☻ 22 **Facilities** Non-diners area ♦♦ Children's portions Garden Outside area ⊫ Parking Wi-fi ▄▄ (notice required)

NEWTON
Map 12 TL44

The Queen's Head

Fowlmere Rd CB22 7PG ☎ **01223 870436**
dir: *6m S of Cambridge on B1368, 1.5m off A10 at Harston, 4m from A505*

No nonsense food and good beer in old fashioned pub

The same family has owned and operated this tiny and very traditional village pub for some 50 years. Unchanging and unmarred by gimmickry, the stone-tiled bars, replete with log fires, pine settles and old school benches, draw an eclectic clientele, from Cambridge dons to local farm workers. They all come for tip-top Adnams ale direct from the drum, the friendly, honest atmosphere and straightforward pub dishes. Food is simple – at lunch, soup, sandwiches and Aga-baked potatoes. In the evening, just soup, toast and beef dripping, and cold platters. Village tradition is kept alive with time-honoured pub games – dominoes, table skittles, shove ha'penny and nine men's Morris.

Open all wk 11.30-2.30 6-11 (Sun 12-2.30 7-10.30) Closed: 25-26 Dec **Bar Meals** L served all wk 12-2.15 D served all wk 7-9.30 ⊕ FREE HOUSE ◀ Adnams Southwold Bitter, Broadside, Fisherman, Regatta ♂ Crones. ♚ 9 **Facilities** Non-diners area ☺ (Bar Outside area) ♙ Children's portions Family room Outside area ⋔ Parking **Notes** ⊜

OFFORD D'ARCY
Map 12 TL26

The Horseshoe Inn

90 High St PE19 5RH ☎ **01480 810293**
e-mail: info@theoffordshoe.co.uk
dir: *Between Huntingdon & St Neots. 1.5m from Buckden on A1*

Inventive cooking close to the river

Built by a yeoman farmer in 1626, this spruced up pub-restaurant stands close to the River Ouse in a sleepy village just off the A1. Famished travellers keen to escape the faceless services will find two comfortable bars serving good local real ales – try a pint of Nethergate Old Growler – and an imaginative changing menu. Chef-patron Richard Kennedy offers lunchtime pub classics like roast ham, double egg and chips or haggis and potato croquette, poached egg and crispy leeks followed by tandoori butter fried fillet of sea bream, saffron potatoes, fine beans and coconut. A midsummer beer festival is held on the green.

Open all day all wk 12-11 Closed: 2-4 Jan **Bar Meals** L served Mon-Sat 12-2.30 D served Mon-Sat 6-9.30 Av main course £14.50 **Restaurant** L served all wk 12-2.30 D served Mon-Sat 6-9.30 Fixed menu price fr £11.95 Av 3 course à la carte fr £25 ⊕ FREE HOUSE ◀ Adnams Southwold Bitter, Nethergate Old Growler, Potton Shannon IPA. ♚ 17 **Facilities** Non-diners area ☺ (Bar Garden) ♙ Children's portions Play area Garden ⋔ Beer festival Parking Wi-fi ➤ (notice required)

PETERBOROUGH
Map 12 TL19

The Brewery Tap

80 Westgate PE1 2AA ☎ **01733 358500**
e-mail: brewerytap.manager@oakagroup.com
dir: *Opposite bus station*

Award-winning brewpub with American style and local ales

Located in the old labour exchange on Westgate, this striking American-style pub is home to the multi-award winning Oakham Brewery and it is one of the largest brewpubs in Europe. Visitors can see the day-to-day running of the brewery through a glass wall spanning half the length of the bar. As if the appeal of the 12 real ales and the vast range of bottled beers was not enough, Thai chefs beaver away producing delicious snacks, soups, salads, stir-fries and curries. Look out for live music nights, and DJs on Saturday nights.

Open all day all wk 12-10.30 (Fri-Sat 12-late Sun 12-11) Closed: 25-26 Dec, 1 Jan **Bar Meals** L served Mon-Thu 12-2.30, Fri-Sat 12-10.30, Sun 12-3.30 D served Mon-Thu 5.30-10.30, Fri-Sat 12-10.30, Sun 5.30-9.30 **Restaurant** L served Fri-Sat 12-5.30 D served Wed-Sat 5.30-10.30 ⊕ FREE HOUSE ◀ Oakham Inferno, Citra, JHB & Bishops Farewell, Elgood's Black Dog, 7 Guest ales ♂ Westons 1st Quality, Old Rosie & Traditional. ♚ 10 **Facilities** Non-diners area ☺ (Bar) ♙ Wi-fi ➤

Charters Bar & East Restaurant

Upper Deck, Town Bridge PE1 1FP
☎ **01733 315700 & 315702 (bkgs)**
e-mail: charters.manager@oakagroup.com
dir: *A1/A47 towards Wisbech, 2m to city centre & town bridge (River Nene). Barge moored at Town Bridge (west side)*

Moored barge on the River Nene

The largest floating real ale emporium in Britain can be found moored in the heart of Peterborough. The 176-foot converted barge promises 'brews, blues and fine views'. It motored from Holland across the North Sea in 1991, and is now a haven for real-ale and cider-lovers. Twelve hand pumps dispense a continually changing repertoire of cask ales, while entertainment, dancing, live blues music and an Easter beer festival are regular features. The East part of the name applies to the oriental restaurant on the upper deck which offers a comprehensive selection of pan-Asian dishes.

Open all day all wk 12-11 (Fri-Sat noon-2am) Closed: 25-26 Dec, 1 Jan **Bar Meals** L served all wk 12-2.30 **Restaurant** L served Mon-Sat 12-2.30, Sun 12-3.30 D served Sun-Thu 5.30-10.30, Fri-Sat 5.30-11 ⊕ FREE HOUSE ◀ Oakham JHB, Bishops Farewell, Citra, Inferno & Scarlet Macaw, Guest ales ♂ Westons Old Rosie & Traditional. ♚ 10 **Facilities** Non-diners area ☺ (Bar Garden) ♙ Garden ⋔ Beer festival Parking Wi-fi ➤ (notice required)

REACH
Map 12 TL56

Dyke's End

CB25 0JD ☎ **01638 743816**
dir: *Telephone for directions*

At the heart of village life

Located in the centre of the village, overlooking the green, this pub was saved from closure by villagers in the 1990s. They ran it as a co-operative until 2003, when it was bought by Frank Feehan, who further refurbished and extended it. Frank's additions included the Devil's Dyke microbrewery, which continues to be run by owners Catherine and George Gibson. The pub has a strong local following for its food and beers. The menu is seasonal with daily-changing specials, although pub favourites like beer-battered haddock and steak frites are always popular.

Open 12-2.30 6-11 (Sat-Sun 12-11) Closed: Mon L **Bar Meals** L served Tue-Sun 12-2 D served all wk 7-9 ⊕ FREE HOUSE ◀ Devil's Dyke, Thwaites Wainwright, Adnams Southwold Bitter ♂ Aspall. ♚ 8 **Facilities** Non-diners area ☺ (Bar Garden) ♙ Children's portions Play area Family room Garden ⋔ Parking Wi-fi

SPALDWICK
Map 12 TL17

The George NEW

5-7 High St PE28 0TD ☎ **01480 890293**
e-mail: info@thegeorgespaldwick.co.uk
dir: *In village centre. Just off A14 junct 18. 5m W of Huntingdon*

Village centre inn gaining high praise

Dating from 1679, this former coaching inn is today a successful pub and restaurant with 21st-century credentials, yet which has retained its rustic charm and character. Proving the point is the bar, with its low ceilings and wooden floor, serving local real ales and snacks from sandwiches to light meals, such as home-made chilli with wild rice. In the restaurant, dishes similarly making use of free-range or organic meats, biodynamic vegetables and other locally supplied produce include chargrilled Aberdeenshire steak; pan-fried sea bass; and Mediterranean Wellington. Tables on the lawns and a terraced patio are popular on fine days.

Open all wk 11.30-3 5.30-11 (Sat 11.30am-mdnt Sun 12-10.30) **Bar Meals** L served Mon-Sat 12-2.30, Sun 12-7 D served Mon-Sat 6-9, Sun 12-7 **Restaurant** L served Mon-Sat 12-2.30, Sun 12-7 D served Mon-Sat 6-9, Sun 12-7 ◀ Woodforde's Wherry, Timothy Taylor Landlord, Black Sheep ♂ Aspall. ♚ 9 **Facilities** Non-diners area ♙ Children's menu Children's portions Garden Outside area ⋔ Beer festival Cider festival Parking Wi-fi ➤ (notice required)

Save on hotels. Book at **theAA.com/hotel**

CAMBRIDGESHIRE 63 **ENGLAND**

The Rose at Stapleford

81 London Rd CB22 5DG ☎ 01223 843349
e-mail: info@rose-stapleford.co.uk
dir: *Telephone for directions*

Great home cooked food and accredited ales

Paul and Karen Beer have made a success of The George & Dragon at Elsworth (see entry) and they're also weaving their magic at The Rose, a traditional village pub close to Cambridge and Duxford Imperial War Museum. Expect a stylish interior, replete with low beams and inglenook fireplaces, and extensive menus that draw on local Suffolk produce, particularly meat, with fish from Lowestoft. As well as a good selection of seafood appetisers, typical main dishes include home-made vegetable curry; warm Cajun chicken salad; wild mushroom Stroganoff; and beef lasagne.

Open all wk 11-2.30 6-11 (Sun 12-10.30) **Bar Meals** L served Mon-Sat 12-2, Sun 12-8.30 D served Mon-Sat 5.30-9.30, Sun 12-8.30 **Restaurant** L served Mon-Sat 12-2, Sun 12-8.30 D served Mon-Sat 5.30-9.30, Sun 12-8.30 ⊕ CHARLES WELLS ◀ Wells Bombardier Courage Directors Ö Aspall. ♈ 13 **Facilities** Non-diners area ♦↑ Children's menu Children's portions Garden ⋒ Parking ▤

The Bell Inn Hotel ★★★ HL ⊛

PICK OF THE PUBS

Great North Rd PE7 3RA ☎ 01733 241066
e-mail: reception@thebellstilton.co.uk
dir: *From A1(M) junct 16 follow signs for Stilton. Hotel on main road in village centre*

Handsome stone inn with historic Stilton pedigree

A Bell Inn has stood here since 1500, although this one is mid 17th century and it is reputedly the oldest coaching inn on the old Great North Road, with an impressive stone façade, a splendid inn sign and a fine original interior with an upbeat feel. It once welcomed (or maybe not!) highwayman Dick Turpin, as well as Lord Byron and Clark Gable, who was stationed nearby in 1943. Modern British dishes in the Galleried Restaurant include cannon of lamb; assiette of duck; and basil linguine with deconstructed ratatouille. In the Bar/Bistro try coq au vin, or local pork chops with apricot chutney and black pudding jus. Famous as the birthplace of Stilton cheese, the pub has just started making their own again called Bell Blue and the Stilton cheese sampler is a must to try. All the en-suite bedrooms are round the old courtyard — two are four-posters.

Open all wk 12-2.30 6-11 (Sat 12-3 6-12 Sun 12-11) **Closed:** 25 Dec **Bar Meals** L served Mon-Sat 12-2.30, Sun 12-3 D served all wk 6-9.30 Av main course £13 **Restaurant** L served Sun 12-2 D served Mon-Sat 7-9.30 Fixed menu price fr £24.50 Av 3 course à la carte fr £29.50 ⊕ FREE HOUSE ◀ Greene King IPA, Oakham Bishops Farewell, Morland Old Speckled Hen, Digfield Fool's Nook Ö Aspall. ♈ 8 **Facilities** Non-diners area ♦↑ Children's menu Children's portions Garden ⋒ Parking Wi-fi ▤ (notice required) **Rooms** 22

The Lazy Otter

Cambridge Rd CB6 3LU ☎ 01353 649780
e-mail: thelazyotter@btconnect.com
dir: *Telephone for directions*

Welcoming waterside focal point amidst the Fens

A pub here has served fenland watermen for several centuries; today's bustling incarnation is popular with leisure boaters on the River Ouse, which glides past the extensive beer garden, from which are cracking views over the rich farmland. Barley from these acres goes into the good range of East Anglian beers, including the house ale from Milton Brewery; an annual beer and cider festival is also held. The contemporary restaurant has modern dishes like gnocchi in Stilton, spinach and pea creamy sauce; traditionalists can savour rich home-made pies and smoked haddock and poached egg.

Open all day all wk 7am-11pm (Sun 8.30am-10.30pm) **Bar Meals** food served all day **Restaurant** food served all day ⊕ FREE HOUSE ◀ Adnams Broadside, Greene King IPA, Milton Lazy Otter, Milton Tiki, Guest ales Ö Westons Stowford Press & Old Rosie. ♈ 10 **Facilities** Non-diners area ♥ (Bar Restaurant Garden) ♦↑ Children's menu Children's portions Play area Garden ⋒ Beer festival Cider festival Parking Wi-fi ▤

The Red Lion

47 High St CB6 3LD ☎ 01353 648132
e-mail: redlion@charnwoodpubco.co.uk
dir: *Exit A10 between Cambridge & Ely into Stretham. Left into High St, pub on right*

Busy local with traditional food

In the village of Stretham ten miles north of Cambridge, this former coaching inn has a busy locals' bar where you can enjoy a pint of Adnams beer or Pickled Pig cider with bar meals such as a chicken fajita wrap with chips and salad or a whole baked camembert with crusty bread. Alternatively, head to the conservatory-style restaurant for traditional home-made favourites such as battered fish and chips; lasagne; steak and ale pie; home-cooked ham, eggs and chips; or one of the steaks from the grill, served with chips and salad.

Open all day all wk **Bar Meals** L served all wk 12-2.30 D served all wk 6-9 Av main course £8.95 **Restaurant** L served all wk 12-2.30 D served all wk 6-9 Fixed menu price fr £8.95 ⊕ CHARNWOOD PUB CO ◀ Greene King IPA, Wychwood Hobgoblin, Adnams, Marston's Ö Pickled Pig. ♈ 8 **Facilities** Non-diners area ♥ (Bar Garden) ♦↑ Children's menu Children's portions Garden ⋒ Parking Wi-fi ▤ (notice required)

The White Hart ★★★★ INN

Main St PE9 3BH ☎ 01780 740250
e-mail: info@whitehartufford.co.uk
dir: *From Stamford take B1443 signed Barnack. Through Barnack, follow signs to Ufford*

Creative menus, local ales and a warm welcome

Salvaged cast-iron railway signs and old agricultural tools embellish the bar of this 17th-century country inn, serving Aspall Suffolk Cyder and four real ales. An extensive wine list reflects the help of Master of Wine, John Atkinson. Locally sourced produce including game finds its way onto the seasonal menus, perhaps alongside traditional Lincolnshire sausages, mash and onion gravy; Thai-style seafood casserole; and wild mushroom, spinach and smoked Lincolnshire Poacher cheese risotto. Four individually styled bedrooms are in the main building, two in the converted cart shed.

Open all day all wk Mon-Thu 9am-11pm (Fri-Sat 9am-mdnt Sun 9-9) **Bar Meals** L served Mon-Sat 12-2.30, Sun 12-6 D served Mon-Sat 6-9.30 **Restaurant** L served Mon-Sat 12-2.30, Sun 12-6 D served Mon-Sat 6-9.30 ⊕ FREE HOUSE ◀ Black Sheep, Sharp's Doom Bar, Castle Rock Harvest Pale, Adnams Ö Aspall. ♈ 10 **Facilities** Non-diners area ♥ (Bar Garden) ♦↑ Children's menu Children's portions Play area Garden ⋒ Parking Wi-fi ▤ (notice required) **Rooms** 6

CHESHIRE

ALDFORD   Map 15 SJ45

The Grosvenor Arms

PICK OF THE PUBS

Chester Rd CH3 6HJ ☎ 01244 620228
e-mail: grosvenor.arms@brunningandprice.co.uk
dir: *On B5130, S of Chester*

Enjoyable food with broad appeal

Dating from 1864 and designed by John Douglas, who designed around 500 buildings, many of them in Cheshire, this Brunning & Price pub is a 'delight of higgledy-piggledy rooflines and soft, warm Cheshire brick'. The spacious, open-plan interior includes an airy conservatory and a panelled, book-filled library. Outside, a terrace leads into a small but pleasing garden, and on out to the village green. The range of real ales from small breweries around the country changes all the time so it's no wonder the locals are fond if it. On the bistro-style menu, starters may feature pork and chorizo meatballs in tomato sauce or salmon, watercress and fennel salad. They might precede main courses of venison cottage pie with sweet braised red cabbage or Malaysian vegetable, cashew and coconut curry with coriander rice. Leave room for bread and butter pudding with apricot sauce and clotted cream.

Open all day all wk **Bar Meals** L served Mon-Thu 12-9.30, Fri-Sat 12-10, Sun 12-9 D served Mon-Thu 12-9.30, Fri-Sat 12-10, Sun 12-9 Av main course £14 food served all day ⊕ FREE HOUSE/BRUNNING & PRICE ◀ Original Bitter, Weetwood Eastgate Ale, Phoenix, Guest ales ♂ Westons Stowford Press, Aspall. ₹ 20 **Facilities** Non-diners area ♣ (Bar Garden) ♦ Children's menu Children's portions Garden ⊟ Parking Wi-fi

ALLOSTOCK   Map 15 SJ77

The Three Greyhounds Inn NEW

Holmes Chapel Rd WA16 9JY ☎ 01565 723455
e-mail: info@thethreegreyhoundsinn.co.uk
dir: *S from Allostock on A50. Right on B5082 signed Northwich. Over M6, pub on right*

A real find at a rural crossroads

Cheshire Cat Pubs have restored this 300-year-old former farmhouse, transforming it from a rough drinking boozer into a stylishly eclectic dining pub. Doors were pushed open in October 2012 to reveal a warren of atmospheric rooms, replete with exposed beams, rugs on wooden floors, crackling log fires in brick fireplaces, fat candles on old dining tables, and a host of quirky touches to make you smile. Come for a choice of five local ales and over 50 brandies behind the bar, and some cracking pub food – seafood sharing plate; potted beef with stout piccalilli; cod loin with shrimp butter; duck leg and haricot bean stew; apple and Calvados crumble, and an imaginative choice of sandwiches. Book ahead for the memorable Sunday lunches. Dogs are welcome in the snug and the garden.

Open all day all wk **Bar Meals** L served all wk 12-9.30 D served all wk 12-9.30 Av main course £12 food served all day **Restaurant** food served all day ⊕ FREE HOUSE ◀ Almighty Allostock Ale, Byley Bomber, Merlins Gold, Three Greyhound Bitter, Weetwood Ales Cheshire Cat. ₹ 15 **Facilities** Non-diners area ♣ (Bar Garden) ♦ Children's portions Garden ⊟ Parking Wi-fi 🚗 (notice required)

ASTON   Map 15 SJ64

The Bhurtpore Inn

PICK OF THE PUBS

See Pick of the Pubs on opposite page

BROXTON   Map 15 SJ45

Egerton Arms

Whitchurch Rd CH3 9JW ☎ 01829 782241
e-mail: egertonarms@woodwardandfalconer.com
dir: *On A41 between Whitchurch & Chester*

Spacious pub with sun-trap garden

A little gem in the heart of the rolling Cheshire plains, where the aim is to cosset customers with a combination of lovely ales, a wide selection of wines, food that hits the spot, and excellent service from the enthusiastic and friendly staff. With a pint of Piffle in hand, choosing a dish to tickle your taste buds is not a problem – the menu covers all preferences, from toad-in-the-hole to warm duck salad or vegetable burrito. The spacious gardens are another bonus, and occasional special events represent excellent value.

Open all day all wk Closed: 25 Dec ⊕ WOODWARD & FALCONER PUBS LTD ◀ Woodward & Falconer Piffle, Weetwood Eastgate Ale, Theakston. **Facilities** ♦ Children's menu Children's portions Play area Garden Parking

BUNBURY   Map 15 SJ55

The Dysart Arms

PICK OF THE PUBS

Bowes Gate Rd CW6 9PH ☎ 01829 260183
e-mail: dysart.arms@brunningandprice.co.uk
dir: *Between A49 & A51, by Shropshire Union Canal*

Well defined English hostelry

A classic English village pub with open fires, lots of old oak, full-height bookcases and a pretty garden with views to two castles and the neighbouring parish church. Built as a farmhouse in the mid-18th century and licensed since the late 1800s, it once functioned simultaneously as a farm, an abattoir and a pub; the abattoir building was demolished by a German bomber on its way home from 'rearranging' the Liverpool docks. The hostelry is named after local landowners, the Earls of Dysart, whose coat of arms is above the door. An ever-changing line-up of ales is served in the central bar, around which are several airy rooms perfect for drinking and eating. Snacks

include a home-made fish finger butty; starters may list venison carpaccio with candied red cabbage; and main courses range from breast of pheasant with bacon and chestnut hash cake, to a pine nut-encrusted hake fillet.

Open all day all wk 11.30-11 (Sun 12-10.30) **Bar Meals** L served Mon-Sat 12-9.30, Sun 12-9 D served Mon-Sat 12-9.30, Sun 12-9 Av main course £12 food served all day **Restaurant** L served Mon-Sat 12-9.30, Sun 12-9 D served Mon-Sat 12-9.30, Sun 12-9 food served all day ⊕ BRUNNING & PRICE ◀ Original Bitter, Weetwood Best Cask, Guest ales ♂ Aspall. ₹ 18 **Facilities** Non-diners area ♣ (Bar) ♦ Children's portions Garden ⊟ Parking

BURLEYDAM   Map 15 SJ64

The Combermere Arms

SY13 4AT ☎ 01948 871223
e-mail: combermere.arms@brunningandprice.co.uk
dir: *From Whitchurch take A525 towards Nantwich, at Newcastle/Audlem/Woore sign, turn right at junct. Pub 100yds on right*

Classic coaching inn with impressive menu

Local shoots, walkers and town folk frequent this classic 17th-century country inn. Full of character and warmth, it has three roaring fires and a wealth of oak, nooks and crannies, pictures and old furniture. Food options range from light bites such as a rump steak sandwich to full meals – maybe garlic wild mushrooms on toasted brioche followed by steak-and-kidney pudding with mash, buttered greens and gravy. You could finish with chocolate and chilli tart with an orange and mint salad. There is a great choice of real ales and ciders, an informative wine list and impressive cheese board.

Open all day all wk 11.30-11 **Bar Meals** Av main course £12.95 food served all day **Restaurant** food served all day ⊕ FREE HOUSE/BRUNNING & PRICE ◀ Original Bitter, Woodlands Oak Beauty, Weetwood Cheshire Cat, St Austell Tribute, Morland Old Speckled Hen ♂ Westons Stowford Press, Thatchers Green Goblin, Aspall. ₹ 20 **Facilities** Non-diners area ♦ Children's menu Children's portions Garden ⊟ Parking Wi-fi

BURWARDSLEY   Map 15 SJ55

The Pheasant Inn ★★★★★ INN

PICK OF THE PUBS

See Pick of the Pubs on page 66

Save on hotels. Book at **theAA.com/hotel**

CHESHIRE 65 ENGLAND

PICK OF THE PUBS

The Bhurtpore Inn

ASTON Map 15 SJ64

Wrenbury Rd CW5 8DQ
☎ **01270 780917**
e-mail: simonbhurtpore@yahoo.co.uk
web: www.bhurtpore.co.uk
dir: *Just off A530 between Nantwich &*
Whitchurch. Follow Wrenbury signs at
x-rds in village

Friendly traditional inn with real community spirit

A pub since at least 1778, when it was called the Queen's Head. It subsequently became the Red Lion, but it was Lord Combermere's success at the Siege of Bhurtpore in India in 1826 that inspired the name that has stuck. Simon and Nicky George came across it in 1991, boarded-up and stripped-out. Simon is a direct descendant of Joyce George, who leased the pub from the Combermere Estate in 1849, so was motivated by his family history to take on the hard work of restoring the interior. Since then, 'award winning' hardly does justice to the accolades heaped upon this hostelry. In the bar, 11 ever-changing real ales are always available, mostly from local micro-breweries, as are real ciders, continental draught lagers and around 150 of the world's bottled beers. An annual beer festival, reputedly Cheshire's largest, is in its 18th year, with around 130 real ales. The pub has also been shortlisted five times for the 'National Whisky Pub

of the Year' award, and there is a long soft drinks menu. Recognition extends to the kitchen too, where unfussy dishes of classic pub fare are prepared. Among the hearty British ingredients you'll find seasonal game, such as venison haunch on cabbage with smoked bacon and cream; and rabbit loin with a pork and black pudding stuffing. Curries and balti dishes are always on the blackboard. Vintage vehicles bring their owners here on the first Thursday of the month, and folk musicians play on the third Tuesday.

Open all wk 12-2.30 6.30-11.30 (Fri-Sat 12-12 Sun 12-11) Closed: 25-26 Dec, 1 Jan **Bar Meals** L served Mon-Fri 12-2 D served Mon-Fri 6.30-9.30, Sat 12-9.30, Sun 12-9 **Restaurant** L served

Mon-Fri 12-2 D served Mon-Fri 6.30-9.30, Sat 12-9.30, Sun 12-9 ⊕ FREE HOUSE ◀ Salopian Golden Thread, Abbeydale Absolution, Weetwood Oast-House Gold, Hobsons Twisted Spire, Hobsons Mild Ŏ Thatchers Cheddar Valley, Moonshine, Westons Old Rosie. ♀ 12 **Facilities** Non-diners area ✿ (Bar Garden) ♦ Children's portions Garden Outside area ⋒ Beer festival Parking 🚐 (notice required)

PICK OF THE PUBS

The Pheasant Inn ★★★★★ INN

BURWARDSLEY   Map 15 SJ55

CH3 9PF ☎ **01829 770434**
e-mail: info@thepheasantinn.co.uk
web: www.thepheasantinn.co.uk
dir: *A41 (Chester to Whitchurch), 4m,
left to Burwardsley. Follow 'Cheshire
Workshops' signs*

A great find in rural Cheshire

In a peaceful corner of Cheshire lie the Peckforton Hills, a sandstone ridge liberally covered by thick woodlands. High on their west-facing slopes is this some 300-year-old former farmhouse and barn, where only five families have been licensees since it first became an alehouse. It stands high enough for there to be panoramic views taking in the Cheshire Plain, the Welsh hills and even the distant tower of Liverpool Cathedral, yet Chester, whose cathedral is also visible, is only 15 minutes' drive away. Among those who know it well are the walkers on the Sandstone Trail long-distance footpath from Frodsham on the Mersey to Whitchurch in Shropshire. On a summer's day the obvious place to be is outside in the flower-filled courtyard or on the terrace, but if the winter weather dictates otherwise, there are big open fires waiting. Four real ales, usually drawn from the Weetwood Brewery near Tarporley, are always on tap in the wooden-floored, heftily-beamed bar, and well chosen wines too. The kitchen makes extensive use of

produce from local estates, with the menu in the restaurant offering a wide choice of modern British and European dishes. Perhaps start with potted shrimps; curried parsnip soup, or confit Goosnargh duck leg with braised butter beans, then follow with roast rump of Welsh lamb, Savoy cabbage, celeriac fondant and red wine reduction; Weetwood ale, steak and mushroom pie; or chilli and crab linguine. The specials board adds to the tempting choices. If planning to stay overnight, there is comfortable en suite accommodation in both the main building and the ivy-clad stable wing.

Open all day all wk **Bar Meals** L & D food served all wk, all day **Restaurant** L & D food served all wk, all day ⊕ FREE HOUSE ◧ Weetwood Old Dog Premium Bitter, Eastgate Ale & Best Cask Bitter, Guest ale ♂ Kingstone Press. **Facilities** Non-diners area 🐾 👬 Children's menu Children's portions Garden 🎋 Parking Wi-fi 🚌 (notice required) **Rooms** 12

PICK OF THE PUBS

The Cholmondeley Arms

CHOLMONDELEY   Map 15 SJ55

SY14 8HN ☎ 01829 720300
e-mail: info@cholmondeleyarms.co.uk
web: www.cholmondeleyarms.co.uk
dir: *On A49, between Whitchurch & Tarporley*

Friendly inn with imaginative menus and 140 gins

Set in rolling Cheshire countryside virtually opposite Cholmondeley Castle on the A49, and still part of the Vicount's estate, is this red-brick former schoolhouse (closed 1982). Quirky and eclectic, it's surely one of England's more unique pubs, the decor and artefacts, including family heirlooms, educational memorabilia, bell tower without and blackboards within add tremendously to the atmosphere of the cavernous interior. No longer a draughty institute, owners Tim and Mary Bird have created a warm and inviting interior, with fat church candles on old school desks, fresh flowers, glowing log fires and a relaxing atmosphere. After exploring the local countryside, visiting nearby Cholmondeley Castle, country seat of Lord and Lady Cholmondeley or the fabulous ruins at Beeston, stapled to Cheshire's hilly sandstone spine, it's the perfect place to unwind, sup a pint of Shropshire Gold or Cholmondeley Best (only micro-brewery beers from a 30-mile radius can be found on the five hand pumps), or delve into the mind-boggling list of over 140 different gins behind the bar. Allow time to taste some of the best produce from Cheshire's burgeoning larder, including seasonal game from the estate. Nibble and natter over a pork pie with piccalilli, or pint of prawns, then start with a seafood sharing plate, pastrami cured salmon with crispy poached egg; or little Yorkshire puddings, pulled pork, crackling and brandy apple sauce. The 'Old School Favourites' mains take in a classic burger with chips and fennel coleslaw; venison, parsnip and lingonberry pudding with smoky bacon lentils; local ale battered haddock, chips and minted 'not so mushy' peas; leaving room for custard and gingerbread tart with roasted rhubarb — school meals were never like this!

Open all day all wk **Bar Meals** food served all day all wk 12-9.30 **Restaurant** food served all day all wk 12-9.30 ⊕ FREE HOUSE ◀ Cholmondeley Best Bitter, Salopian Shropshire Gold, 3 Guest ales. **Facilities** Non-diners area ❀ (Bar Restaurant Garden) ⅰ Children's portions Garden ⊼ Beer festival Parking Wi-fi ☞ (notice required)

CHESTER   Map 15 SJ46

The Brewery Tap

52-54 Lower Bridge St CH1 1RU ☎ 01244 340999
e-mail: drink@the-tap.co.uk
dir: *From B5268 in Chester into Lower Bridge St towards river*

Great ale in historic city surroundings

In 2008 the Spitting Feathers Brewery breathed new life into this historic pub situated in part of Gamul House, named after Sir Francis Gamul, a wealthy merchant and mayor of Chester who built it in 1620. This is reputedly where Charles I stayed when his troops were defeated at Rowton Moor, shortly before the king's final flight to Wales. Relax with a Thirstquencher ale and enjoy the pub's numerous period details, then choose from a menu of hearty pub favourites such as smoked mackerel, beetroot and horseradish; braised beef and Old Wavertonian pie, pickled red cabbage and fat chips.

Open all day all wk Closed: 25-26 Dec **Bar Meals** L served all wk 12-9.30 D served all wk 12-9.30 Av main course £9.95 food served all day ⊕ FREE HOUSE/SPITTING FEATHERS ◀ Thirstquencher, Old Wavertonian Stout Ò Gwynt y Ddraig Black Dragon. ☂ 14
Facilities Non-diners area ♦♦ Wi-fi

Old Harkers Arms

1 Russell St CH3 5AL ☎ 01244 344525
e-mail: harkers.arms@brunningandprice.co.uk
dir: *Close to railway station, on canal side*

A buzzy city watering hole

Housed in a former Victorian chandler's warehouse beside the Shropshire Union Canal, the tall windows, lofty ceilings, wooden floors and bar constructed from salvaged doors make this one of Chester's more unusual pubs. The bar offers over 100 malt whiskies and ales from a range of breweries. The daily-changing menu runs from light dishes such as crab linguine through to main courses like mixed bean and sweet potato cassoulet; and honey-glazed ham. The pub holds events such as 'Pudding, Pie and Great British Beers Week' in February, where over 20 ales are available during the week. A beer festival is also held in October.

Open all day all wk 11.30-11 (Sun 12-10.30) Closed: 25 Dec **Bar Meals** L served all wk 12-9.30 D served all wk 12-9.30 **Restaurant** L served all wk 12-9.30 D served all wk 12-9.30 ⊕ FREE HOUSE/BRUNNING & PRICE ◀ Brunning & Price Original Bitter, Weetwood Cheshire Cat, Flowers Original, Titanic Stout, Spitting Feathers, Hawkshead Ò Westons Wyld Wood Organic & Old Rosie, Aspall, Thatchers. ☂ 15 **Facilities** Non-diners area ♣ (Bar Restaurant Outside area) Outside area ⋈ Beer festival Wi-fi

CHOLMONDELEY   Map 15 SJ55

The Cholmondeley Arms

PICK OF THE PUBS

See Pick of the Pubs on page 67

CHRISTLETON   Map 15 SJ46

Ring O'Bells

Village Rd CH3 7AS ☎ 01244 335422
e-mail: info@ringobellschester.co.uk
dir: *Village 3m from Chester between A51 towards Nantwich & A41 towards Whitchurch*

A welcoming Chester-fringe pub

Wine tastings, live music and lunchtime networking meetings are among the events that draw drinkers and diners to this spruced-up village pub. And therein lies much of the appeal. The bar stocks real ale from Chester's Spitting Feathers brewery, as well as representatives from Liverpool Organic and Weetwood. Take your pick of outdoor dining areas - perhaps the decked suntrap terrace for a bacon, brie and cranberry sandwich, or a freshly-baked Siciliana pizza. Good use of local produce is also evident on seasonal menus listing linguine carbonara; braised winter vegetable and pearl barley stew; and beer-battered cod with hand-cut chips.

Open all day all wk **Bar Meals** L served Mon-Fri 12-3, Sat-Sun 12-5 D served Mon-Thu 5-9, Fri-Sat 5-9.30, Sun 5-8 Av main course £12 **Restaurant** L served Mon-Fri 12-3, Sat-Sun 12-5 D served Mon-Thu 5-9, Fri-Sat 5-9.30, Sun 5-8 Av 3 course à la carte fr £22 ⊕ TRUST INNS ◀ Spitting Feathers, Weetwood, Liverpool Organic. ☂ **Facilities** Non-diners area ♣ (Bar Restaurant Garden) ♦♦ Children's menu Children's portions Play area Garden ⋈ Parking Wi-fi ⇌ (notice required)

CONGLETON   Map 16 SJ86

Egerton Arms Country Inn ★★★★ INN

Astbury Village CW12 4RQ ☎ 01260 273946
e-mail: egertonastbury@totalise.co.uk
dir: *1.5m SW of Congleton off A34, by St Mary's Church*

Good pub food in delightful village

A buzzing, family-run village local with a good name for dependable real ales and freshly prepared fodder. Set at the edge of one of Cheshire's picture-perfect villages, near the ancient church and flowery green, the Egerton Arms enjoys views from the peaceful beer garden onto the nearby Bosley Cloud Hill. Take a stroll along the paths there or stroll along the Macclesfield Canal towpath. The restaurant offers a good selection including steak-and-kidney suet pudding, fresh sardines with lime and coriander butter, and a variety of baguettes and sandwiches. Stay awhile in the comfortable accommodation and you may meet the ghost, a local lady murdered next door in 1922. Dogs are welcome outside and children inside and out until 9pm.

Open all day all wk **Bar Meals** L served Mon-Sat 11.30-2, Sun 12-8 D served Mon-Sat 6-9, Sun 12-8 Av main course

£10.50 **Restaurant** L served Mon-Sat 12-1.45, Sun 12-8 D served Mon-Sat 6.30-8.45, Sun 12-8 ⊕ ROBINSONS ◀ Unicorn, Dizzy Blonde, Double Hop, Seasonal ales. ☂ 12 **Facilities** Non-diners area ♣ (Garden) ♦♦ Children's menu Children's portions Play area Garden ⋈ Parking Wi-fi **Rooms** 6

The Plough At Eaton ★★★★ INN

Macclesfield Rd, Eaton CW12 2NH ☎ 01260 280207
e-mail: theploughinn@hotmail.co.uk
dir: *On A536 (Congleton to Macclesfield road)*

Popular inn with barn restaurant

Set well back from the main road in the hamlet of Eaton, this 400-year-old Cheshire-brick inn is a far cry from its genesis as a farmers' local in a farmhouse. It's now a popular destination gastro-pub with a very accomplished menu, available throughout the very traditional interior or in the restaurant housed in a remarkable cruck barn moved here from Wales. From bar snacks such as grilled fresh sardines, the choice of dishes balloons to include pink roasted duck breast, with additional changing specials. Beers are largely from local Cheshire craft breweries. Handy for visiting Gawsworth Hall and Macclesfield's museums, the comfortable, en suite rooms are in a separate annexe.

Open all day all wk 11am-mdnt **Bar Meals** L served Mon-Thu 12-2.30, Fri-Sat 12-9.30, Sun 12-8 D served Mon-Thu 6-9.30, Fri-Sat 12-9.30, Sun 12-8 **Restaurant** L served Mon-Thu 12-2.30, Fri-Sat 12-9.30, Sun 12-8 D served Mon-Sat 6-9.30, Fri-Sat 12-9.30, Sun 12-8 ⊕ FREE HOUSE ◀ Hydes, Storm, Flowers, Guest ales. ☂ 10 **Facilities** Non-diners area ♦♦ Children's menu Garden ⋈ Parking ⇌ **Rooms** 17

COTEBROOK   Map 15 SJ56

Fox & Barrel

Foxbank CW6 9DZ ☎ 01829 760529
e-mail: info@foxandbarrel.co.uk
web: www.foxandbarrel.co.uk
dir: *On A49, 2.8m N of Tarporley*

Countryside pub offering a warm welcome and excellent food

The rather cute explanation for the pub's name is that a fox being chased by the local hunt ran into the cellar, where the landlord gave it sanctuary. And who's to say otherwise? Restored and refreshed features include a huge open log fire, old beams and half-panelled walls; the snug bar is the perfect spot for a pint of Weetwood. Classic pub food with an adventurous angle includes roasted Gressingham duck breast with parsnip, new potatoes and pear tarte Tatin; venison and rabbit suet pudding; and honey roasted butternut squash with horseradish gnocchi, pine nuts and blue cheese glaze. Outside is a secluded landscaped garden surrounded by unspoilt Cheshire countryside.

Fox & Barrel

Open all day all wk Closed: 25-26 Dec pm, 31 Dec am, 1 Jan pm **Bar Meals** Av main course £13.95 food served all day **Restaurant** Av 3 course à la carte fr £21 ⊕ FREE HOUSE ◀ Weetwood Eastgate Ale, Caledonian Deuchars IPA. ♀ 20 **Facilities** Non-diners area ☼ (Bar Garden) ♦♦ Children's portions Garden ⊼ Parking Wi-fi

---

DELAMERE   Map 15 SJ56

The Fishpool Inn **NEW**

Fishpool Rd CW8 2HP ☎ 01606 883277
e-mail: info@thefishpoolinn.co.uk

Strikingly transformed gastro-pub

The family-owned Nelson Hotels group's multi-million pound spend on an old country inn has sympathetically transformed it into a striking gastro-pub. Open since February 2013, newly evident are an oak-framed, sandstone extension, hundreds of freshly planted trees, shrubs and plants, a sun-terrace and a quaint log cabin (the office of a dog-training school, which was already here). Local real ales are kept in optimum condition in a new cellar nine feet underground. From an open-display kitchen comes seasonal, regionally sourced, modern British and European cooking, including charcoal-oven grills; woodstone-fired pizzas; assiette of fish; roast half-duck; and vegetable moussaka.

Open all day all wk **Bar Meals** L served Mon-Thu 12-9.30, Fri-Sat 12-10, Sun 12-9 D served Mon-Thu 12-9.30, Fri-Sat 12-10, Sun 12-9 food served all day **Restaurant** L served Mon-Thu 12-9.30, Fri-Sat 12-10, Sun 12-9 D served Mon-Thu 12-9.30, Fri-Sat 12-10, Sun 12-9 food served all day ⊕ FREE HOUSE ◀ Weetwood Ales Best Bitter & Eastgate, Guest ales Ŏ Herefordshire Cider. ♀ 14 **Facilities** Non-diners area ☼ (Bar Garden Outside area) ♦♦ Children's menu Children's portions Garden Outside area ⊼ Parking Wi-fi 🚌 (notice required)

FARNDON   Map 15 SJ45

The Farndon ★★★★ INN

High St CH3 6PU ☎ 01829 270570
e-mail: enquiries@thefarndon.co.uk
dir: *From Wrexham take A534 towards Nantwich. Follow signs for Farndon on left*

Fine food in the tranquil Dee Valley

This most imposing magpie inn commands Farndon's High Street as it winds down to the ancient, haunted stone bridge across the River Dee, which forms the England/Wales border. Coaches stopped here en route between the Midlands and Holyhead; centuries of hospitality are continued in the contemporary, comfy interior, a relaxing mix of colour-washed walls and modern furnishings all warmed by a seasonal roaring fire. Cheshire beers such as Weetwood accompany an impressive menu; a ballottine of pheasant starter followed by local venison and red wine casserole a typical choice from the regularly changing fare. Five boutique guest bedrooms complete the picture.

Open all wk 5-11 (Sat 12-11 Sun 12-10.30) **Bar Meals** L served Sat-Sun 12-9.30 D served Mon-Fri 6-9, Sat-Sun 12-9.30 Av main course £12 **Restaurant** D served Mon-Thu 6-9, Fri 6-9.30, Sat 12-9.30, Sun 12-8 Av 3 course à la carte fr £25 ⊕ FREE HOUSE ◀ Timothy Taylor Landlord, Weetwood Cheshire Cat & Eastgate Ale, Spitting Feathers Thirstquencher, Sandstone. **Facilities** Non-diners area ☼ (Bar) ♦♦ Children's menu Children's portions Garden ⊼ Parking Wi-fi 🚌 (notice required) **Rooms** 5

GAWSWORTH   Map 16 SJ86

Harrington Arms

Church Ln SK11 9RJ ☎ 01260 223325
dir: *From Macclesfield take A536 towards Congleton. Turn left for Gawsworth*

Lovely pub on a working farm

Part farmhouse, part pub, the little-changed interior comprises a main bar serving Robinsons real ales and quirky rooms with open fires and rustic furnishings. Memorable for its impression of timelessness, it dates from 1664 and has been licensed since 1710. On offer is good pub food made extensively from the wealth of local produce, some from the pub's own fields, including home-made cottage pie; rib-eye, sirloin and gammon steaks; scampi and chips; vegetarian sausage and mash; and daily specials. Early October sees the annual conker championship here.

Open all wk 12-3 5-11.30 (Sun 12-4 7-11) Closed: 25 Dec ⊕ ROBINSONS ◀ Unicorn, 1892, Build a Rocket Boys!, Dizzy Blonde & Seasonal ale, Guinness Ŏ Westons Stowford Press. **Facilities** ♦♦ Children's portions Garden Parking

---

GOOSTREY   Map 15 SJ77

The Crown **NEW**

111 Main Rd CW4 8DE ☎ 01477 532128
e-mail: info@thecrowngoostrey.co.uk
web: www.thecrowngoostrey.co.uk
dir: *In village centre. Follow Goostrey signs either from A50, or from A535 in Tremlow Green*

Spruced up village pub with crowd-pleasing food

The owners of the Boat at Erbistock, near Wrexham (see entry), added the 18th-century Crown to their select portfolio of pubs in 2012 and, following sympathetic refurbishment, have successfully breathed new life into this community local. There are oak beams, crackling winter fires, warm hues throughout, and an extensive modern menu. From home-made pork scratchings, best accompanied by a pint of local Weetwood Best, the choices include scotch egg with brown sauce and lamb shank with roasted root vegetables; plum and apple crumble; and all-day sandwiches — try the sirloin steak with blue cheese and caramelised onions.

Open all day all wk **Bar Meals** Av main course £10 food served all day **Restaurant** food served all day ⊕ FREE HOUSE ◀ Jennings Cumberland Ale, Weetwood Ales Best Bitter & Cheshire Cat, Timothy Taylor Landlord Ŏ Hereford Dry. ♀ 10 **Facilities** Non-diners area ☼ (Bar Garden) ♦♦ Children's menu Children's portions Garden Parking Wi-fi 🚌 (notice required)

PICK OF THE PUBS

The Dog Inn

KNUTSFORD   Map 15 SJ77

Well Bank Ln, Over Peover WA16 8UP
☎ **01625 861421**
e-mail: info@thedogpeover.co.uk
web: www.thedogpeover.co.uk
dir: *S from Knutsford take A50. Turn into Stocks Ln at The Whipping Stocks pub. 2m*

Friendly inn with good food and local ales

Now under new ownership, this inn started life as a row of cottages and then became a grocer's, shoemaker's and farmstead, which were later united as a public house in 1860. Before you go in, enjoy the pub sign, because there cannot possibly be another in Britain featuring a boxer dog with a turquoise ice-pack on its head! Colourful flowerbeds, tubs and hanging baskets create quite a display in summer, while year-round appeal derives from the cask-conditioned Cheshire ales from Hydes in Manchester and Weetwood in Tarporley, and an array of malt whiskies. There's an interesting choice of food too, prepared from produce sourced largely within Cheshire and which might appear on the menu as scallops with carrot purée, vanilla ice cream and crisp bacon; poached rabbit ragout on tagliatelle; grilled lamb cutlets, rosemary polenta chips and spiced tomato and minted yoghurt dips; and curried crab fritters with avocado and sun-blushed tomato salad. Ever-popular desserts include strawberry cheesecake, sticky toffee pudding and Cheshire dairy ice creams. For something lighter, choose from the excellent range of sandwiches or go for a slice of home-made pork pie with a pickled egg and piccalilli. On the first Sunday in August the pub is the venue for the Over Peover Gooseberry Show, when you can find out what possesses grown men and women to try and grow Cheshire's biggest gooseberry. Given the pub's name, it should come as no surprise to learn that dogs are welcome, except of course in the restaurant.

Open all day all wk **Bar Meals** Av main course £10 food served all day **Restaurant** food served all day ⊕ FREE HOUSE ◀ Weetwood Best Bitter & Cheshire Cat, Hydes. ♟ 10 **Facilities** Non-diners area ❖ (Bar Garden) ♟ Children's menu Children's portions Garden ⋒ Beer festival Parking Wi-fi ▥

GREAT BUDWORTH — Map 15 SJ67

George and Dragon NEW

High St CW9 6HF ☎ **01606 892650**
e-mail: thegeorge-dragon@btinternet.com
dir: *From M6 junct 19 or M56 junct 10 follow signs for Great Budworth*

Village local steeped in history

Painstakingly restored three years ago, this charming inn's many original features include a stone tablet in the bar dated 1722 and inscribed 'Nil nimium cupito' ('I desire nothing to excess'). Also visible is a verse above a door written by local Astley Hall estate-owner, Rowland Egerton-Warburton, who had the inn remodelled in 1875. Regular real ales are Lees Bitter from Manchester and the pub's own Great Budworth Bitter, the latter used to flavour the home-made steak, ale and mushroom pie. Other dishes include 'hot off the griddle' steaks, ribs and mixed grills; lamb rogan josh; and traditional fish and chips.

Open all day all wk **Bar Meals** L served all wk 11.30-3, snacks 3-5 D served all wk 5-10 Av main course £11.95 **Restaurant** L served all wk 11.30-3 D served all wk 5-9.30 Av 3 course à la carte fr £22.95 ⊕ J W LEES ◀ Lees Bitter, Great Budworth Best Bitter. ⚑ 12 **Facilities** Non-diners area ♦♦ Children's menu Children's portions Outside area ⌘ Parking Wi-fi ▦ (notice required)

HANDLEY — Map 15 SJ45

The Calveley Arms

Whitchurch Rd CH3 9DT ☎ **01829 770619**
e-mail: calveleyarms@btconnect.com
dir: *5m S of Chester, signed from A41. Follow signs for Handley & Aldersey Green Golf Course*

Old inn, old beams, great beer

The spruced-up old coaching inn, first licensed in 1636, stands opposite the church with views of the distant Welsh hills. Chock full of old timbers, jugs, pots, pictures, prints and ornaments, the rambling bars provide an atmospheric setting in which to sample some cracking beers and decent pub food. Typically, tuck into lunchtime filled baguettes (hot beef), steak-and-kidney pie, sirloin steak with pepper sauce, speciality salads, and a good selection of pasta dishes. There are spacious gardens to enjoy in summer.

Open all wk 12-3 6-11 (Sun 12-3 7-11) **Bar Meals** L served all wk 12-3 D served Mon-Sat 6-9, Sun 7-9 ⊕ ENTERPRISE INNS ◀ Castle Eden Ale, Marston's Pedigree, Theakston Black Bull Bitter, Wells Bombardier, Greene King IPA, Black Sheep ○ Aspall. **Facilities** Non-diners area ♦♦ Children's portions Play area Garden Parking ▦

HAUGHTON MOSS — Map 15 SJ55

The Nags Head

Long Ln CW6 9RN ☎ **01829 260265**
e-mail: roryk1@ournagshead.co.uk
dir: *Exit A49 S of Tarporley at Beeston/Haughton sign into Long Ln. 2.75m to pub*

Home-cooked food deep in the countryside

You can't miss this typical Cheshire black and white pub, especially from the Nantwich direction, because it will face you head on just before a bend. Dating from 1628, it was once the village smithy and still has its low ceilings and old beams, exposed brickwork, and open log fires, although the interior has now been opened up and re-floored with slate; outside are spacious landscape gardens and a bowling green. Landlords Rory and Debbie Keigan provide a broad range of home-cooked food, such as roasted guinea fowl breast; boneless lamb shoulder; Icelandic cod; and blue cheese and broccoli pasta.

Open all day all wk 11am-mdnt **Bar Meals** L served all wk 12-10 D served all wk 12-10 Av main course £10 food served all day **Restaurant** L served all wk 12-10 D served all wk 12-10 Fixed menu price fr £8.25 Av 3 course à la carte fr £20 food served all day ⊕ FREE HOUSE ◀ Flowers IPA, Sharp's Doom Bar, Weetwood, Guest ales ○ Kingstone Press. ⚑ 14 **Facilities** Non-diners area ♣ (Bar Garden) ♦♦ Children's menu Children's portions Play area Garden ⌘ Parking Wi-fi ▦ (notice required)

KETTLESHULME — Map 16 SJ97

Swan Inn

SK23 7QU ☎ **01663 732943**
e-mail: the.swan.kettleshulme@googlemail.co.uk
dir: *On B5470 between Whaley Bridge (2m) & Macclesfield (5m)*

Charming village pub once saved from closure

The Swan is a glorious, tiny 15th-century village inn huddled in the shadow of the craggy Windgather Rocks in the Cheshire Peak District. A consortium of locals bought the place over six years ago to save it from closure. Now safe and thriving in private hands again, the eclectic and international menu has interesting dishes such as 'stifado', a Greek rabbit stew slow-cooked with red wine, cinnamon, shallots and currants; and chicken jambonette, a chicken leg stuffed with duck and sausage meat, wrapped in proscuitto ham and smoky bacon. Local craft beers keep ramblers and locals very contented, especially at the pub's beer festival on the first weekend in September.

Open all wk Mon 5-11 Tue-Sun all day Closed: 25-26 Dec, 1 Jan, Mon L **Bar Meals** L served Tue 12-8.30, Wed & Sat 12-9, Thu-Fri 12-7, Sun 12-4 D served Tue 12-8.30, Wed & Sat 12-9, Thu-Fri 12-7, Sun 12-4 ⊕ FREE HOUSE ◀ Marston's, Marble, Thornbridge, Phoenix. **Facilities** Non-diners area ♣ (Bar Garden) ♦♦ Children's portions Garden ⌘ Beer festival Parking Wi-fi

KNUTSFORD — Map 15 SJ77

The Dog Inn

PICK OF THE PUBS

See Pick of the Pubs on opposite page

LACH DENNIS — Map 15 SJ77

The Duke of Portland

Penny's Ln CW9 7SY ☎ **01606 46264**
e-mail: info@dukeofportland.com
dir: *M6 junct 19, A556 towards Northwich. Left onto B5082 to Lach Dennis*

Recommended for the use of local produce

There was a change of hands here in June 2012 but this family-run pub continues to make a name for itself through a committed use of local and regional produce from across the Cheshire and Lancashire area. In the bar, enjoy a pint of Jennings Cocker Hoop or Cumberland Ale or one of the ten wines by the glass. The kitchen's top-drawer local suppliers are listed on the menus, which might include beef, Guinness and mushroom pie; risotto of smoked haddock with lemon, mint and pea; and classic coq au vin. A sunny, landscaped garden complements the attractive building.

Open all day all wk **Bar Meals** L served all wk 12-5.30 D served all wk 5.30-9.30 Av main course £12 food served all day **Restaurant** L served all wk 12-5.30 D served all wk 5.30-9.30 Fixed menu price fr £10.95 Av 3 course à la carte fr £23 food served all day ⊕ MARSTON'S ◀ Banks's Original, Brakspear Oxford Gold, Jennings Cocker Hoop & Cumberland Ale, Marston's Pedigree ○ Thatchers Gold. ⚑ 10 **Facilities** Non-diners area ♣ (Bar Garden) ♦♦ Children's menu Children's portions Garden ⌘ Parking Wi-fi ▦

MARTON — Map 16 SJ86

The Davenport Arms

PICK OF THE PUBS

Congleton Rd SK11 9HF ☎ **01260 224269**
e-mail: info@thedavenportarms.co.uk
dir: *2m from Congleton on A34*

Charming pub with pleasing home-made dishes

Dating back to the 18th century, this former farmhouse is steeped in history and enjoys a picturesque location opposite the oldest half-timbered church still in use in Europe. Inside, many period details make for a comfortable atmosphere. Pull up a leather armchair or sofa clad with cushions to the roaring fire in the traditional bar, and choice from the good selection of real ales and nine wines by the glass. In warmer times, the large garden is a big draw. There's something for everyone on the crowd-pleasing menu, all freshly made on the premises using local ingredients. You could start with home-made fishcake, citrus mayonnaise and sweet chilli dip; or black pudding stack with creamed leeks and bacon before trying perhaps chicken breast stuffed with

continued

MARTON *continued*

haggis, Skirlie potatoes, fresh vegetables and whisky and thyme sauce. There are also regularly changing chef's specials and curry nights on Tuesdays.

Open 12-3 6-12 (Fri-Sun 12-12) **Closed:** Mon L (ex BHs) **Bar Meals** L served Tue-Fri 12-2.30, Sat 12-9, Sun 12-8 D served Tue-Fri 6-9, Sat 12-9, Sun 12-8 Av main course £11 **Restaurant** L served Tue-Fri 12-2.30, Sat 12-9, Sun 12-8 D served Tue-Fri 6-9, Sat 12-9, Sun 12-8 Av 3 course à la carte fr £22 ⊕ FREE HOUSE ◑ Copper Dragon, Storm, Theakston, Beartown, Courage Directors, Wincle. ♚ 9 **Facilities** Non-diners area ♦♦ Children's menu Play area Garden ⚑ Parking Wi-fi ⛶ (notice required)

The Bulls Head

Mill Ln WA16 7HX ☎ 01565 873345
e-mail: info@thebullsheadpub.com
web: www.thebullsheadpub.com
dir: *From Knutsford take A537, A5085 to Mobberley*

A 200-year history of offering pub hospitality

The sister pub to the Cholmondeley Arms (see entry) this little gem, tucked away in sleepy Mobberley, thrives as a community local and destination for cracking real ales from Cheshire microbreweries and wholesome home-cooked food. Smart traditional rooms provide a comfortable and convivial setting for savouring delicious Sunday roasts, ale-battered haddock, a classic burger with hand-cut chips and fennel coleslaw, and sticky whisky toffee pudding. Wheat free and gluten free dishes are available. There's a super summer garden and don't miss the June beer festival.

Open all day all wk **Bar Meals** food served all day **Restaurant** food served all day ⊕ FREE HOUSE ◑ Bulls Head Bitter, Mobberley Wobbly Ale, 1812 Overture Ale, Blonde Bull. ♚ 16 **Facilities** Non-diners area ❤ (Bar Restaurant Garden) ♦♦ Children's portions Garden ⚑ Beer festival Parking Wi-fi ⛶ (notice required)

The Goshawk

Station Rd CH3 8AJ ☎ 01928 740900
e-mail: goshawk@woodwardandfalconer.com
dir: *A51 from Chester onto A54. Left onto B5393 towards Frodsham. Into Mouldsworth, pub on left*

Old railway inn popular with cyclists and walkers

This sturdy inn has a hint of Edwardian grandeur whilst benefiting from contemporary comforts; print-clad walls and dado rails, comfy sofas and open fires. Its village setting makes the most of the area's delights, including the many miles of footpaths, cycle trails and meres of nearby Delamere Forest; Chester is just one stop away on the train. Local ales from Weetwood draw an appreciative crowd, whilst the wide-ranging menu is matched by an extensive wine list. Tempting main courses are sesame-rolled tuna steak with oriental noodles; and the Goshawk steak burger. There's a good choice of vegetarian dishes. The terrace and large grassy beer garden offer views across the heart of Cheshire.

Open all day all wk 12-11 (Sun 12-10.30) **Closed:** 25 Dec & 1 Jan ⊕ WOODWARD & FALCONER PUBS LTD ◑ Piffle, Weetwood Eastgate Ale & Best Bitter, Guest ales. **Facilities** ♦♦ Children's menu Children's portions Play area Family room Garden Parking

The Thatch Inn

Wrexham Rd, Faddiley CW5 8JE ☎ 01270 524223
dir: *Follow signs for Wrexham from Nantwich, inn on A534 in 4m*

Pretty inn with plenty of beams and fires

Believed to be the oldest (and one of the prettiest) pubs in south Cheshire, the black-and-white Thatch Inn has a three-quarter acre garden, while inside there are plentiful oak beams, and open fires in winter. Starters might be black pudding and streaky bacon stack with creamy wholegrain mustard sauce, or traditional prawn cocktail with a mixed leaf salad. For your main course, maybe oven roasted pork fillet with carrot and parsnip mash, Parmentier potatoes and carrot and orange scented jus. Finish with chocolate praline and vanilla cheesecake with Cheshire Farm ice cream. Children have their own menu.

Open Mon-Tue 5.30-11, Wed-Thu 12-3 5.30-11, Fri-Sat 12-11, Sun 12-10.30 **Closed:** Mon L & Tue L **Bar Meals** L served Wed-Fri 12-3, Sat 12-9, Sun 12-8.30 D served Mon-Fri 5.30-9, Sat 12-9, Sun 12-8.30 ⊕ ENTERPRISE INNS ◑ Weetwood Eastgate Ale, Salopian Shropshire Gold. **Facilities** Non-diners area ♦♦ Children's menu Play area Garden ⚑ Parking ⛶

The Wizard Inn

Macclesfield Rd SK10 4UB ☎ 01625 584000
e-mail: wizardrestaurant@googlemail.com
dir: *On B5087 between Alderley Edge & Macclesfield. Adjacent to National Trust car park*

Family and dog friendly with good food to suit all

In National Trust woodlands below the red sandstone escarpment of Alderley Edge, The Wizard has all the country-pub hallmarks – stone floors, beams, scrubbed wood tables. Only the finest locally and responsibly sourced ingredients go into modern classics and specials, such as chargrilled rump steak with garlic prawns and triple-cooked beef-dripping chips; roast salmon with wild mushrooms, green kale and walnut pesto; and chicken curry with basmati and tomato and red onion salsa. The wine list is admirably brief; Pouilly Fumé is 'Fresh, light and bone dry', for example.

Open all wk 12-3 5.30-11 (Sat 12-11 Sun 12-10) **Closed:** 25 Dec ⊕ FREE HOUSE ◑ Storm Ale Force, Thwaites Wainwright. **Facilities** ❤ (Bar Restaurant Garden) ♦♦ Children's portions Garden Parking Wi-fi

The Red Lion ★★★ INN

277 Chester Rd, Hartford CW8 1QL ☎ 01606 74597
e-mail: cathy.iglesias@tesco.net
dir: *From A556 take Hartford exit. Red Lion at 1st junct on left next to church*

Popular village inn with stylish accommodation

This engaging inn was the village fire station until a century or so ago, and many artefacts remain from that time. Hunker down with a pint of Black Sheep, tuck in to hearty pub grub like home-made lamb hotpot, or take on the locals at darts or dominoes. This is a thriving community local where visitors to the nearby Delamere Forest or Oulton Park motor-racing circuit can also bed down in the en suite accommodation here. Log fires in winter, and at the back there is an enclosed beer garden.

Open all day all wk **Bar Meals** L served Mon-Sat 12-2 D served Mon-Sat 6-8 **Restaurant** L served Mon-Sat 12-2 D served Mon-Sat 6-8 ⊕ PUNCH TAVERNS ◑ Marston's Pedigree, Black Sheep, John Smith's Cask. ♚ 9 **Facilities** Non-diners area ❤ (Bar Garden) ♦♦ Family room Garden ⚑ Parking Wi-fi **Rooms** 3

The Boat House

1 The Parade CH64 6RN ☎ 0151 336 4187
e-mail: rachel.stubbs@woodwoodandfalconer.com
dir: *On B5135, 3m from Heswall*

Striking building on a nature reserve

With magnificent views across the Dee Estuary to Wales, this striking black-and-white timbered pub is a haven for both bird-watchers and seafood-lovers. Thirsty twitchers head straight for the bar and a pint of Piffle. If food is the

Save on hotels. Book at **theAA.com/hotel**

CHESHIRE 73 ENGLAND

priority, look to the airy dining room with views across salt marshes, or take a seat in the cosy modernised bars. Freshly supplied fish and seafood are the major attraction here, with plenty of lovingly prepared dishes. Look out for the flooding, about four times a year, when high tide reaches the pub's walls.

Open all day all wk 11-11 (Sun 11-10.30) Closed: 25 Dec, 1 Jan ⊕ FREE HOUSE ◀ John Smith's, Morland Old Speckled Hen, Woodward & Falconer Piffle, Weetwood Eastgate Ale. **Facilities** ♦♦ Children's portions Garden Parking Wi-fi

---

The Ship Hotel

The Parade CH64 6SA ☎ 0151 336 3931
e-mail: info@the-shiphotel.co.uk
dir: A540 (Chester towards Neston) left then immediately right onto B5136 (Liverpool Rd). In Neston town centre, left onto B5135. Follow to The Parade in Parkgate, hotel 50yds on right

Free house with fine views of the Welsh mountains

Parkgate's port is now silted up, but the views from The Parade across what is now the RSPB's Dee Estuary bird reserve to the Welsh coast don't change. With 18th-century origins, The Ship was regularly visited by Lord Nelson and his mistress Lady Hamilton, who had been born in nearby Neston. Real ale names to conjure with in the contemporary bar include Trapper's Hat from Wirral brewery Brimstage and Weetwood Oast-House Gold, also from Cheshire. Enjoy home-made food by the fire, with options such as pheasant wrapped in pancetta; Cumberland sausage and mash; surf and turf; Thai green curry, and specials.

Open all day all wk **Bar Meals** L served all wk 12-2.30 D served all wk 6-8.30 Av main course £11 **Restaurant** L served all wk 12-2.30 D served all wk 6-8.30 ⊕ FREE HOUSE ◀ Brimstage Trapper's Hat, Weetwood Oast-House Gold, Jennings Cumberland Ale, Tatton Gold. **Facilities** Non-diners area ♦♦ Children's menu Children's portions Outside area ⌂ Parking Wi-fi ⌘ (notice required)

The Smoker

WA16 0TY ☎ 01565 722338
e-mail: thesmokerinn@aol.com
dir: From M6 junct 19 take A556 W. Pub 1.75m on left

British and international cuisine in the countryside

Just over 400 years old, this thatched coaching inn was named after the Prince Regent's racehorse that won the 25 Guineas at Epsom in 1790. A trio of beamed and wood-panelled connecting rooms all have impressive period fireplaces, deep sofas, cushioned settles, Windsor chairs and collections of copper kettles. The menu here and in the separate restaurant features steaks and other chargrills; home-made chicken, mushroom and ham pie; minted and marinated lamb shank; lightly battered North Sea cod; and mushroom Stroganoff. Robinsons real ales

include Hannibal's Nectar and Long Kiss Goodnight. Children have their own play area in the large garden.

Open all wk 10-3 6-11 (Sun 10am-10.30pm) **Bar Meals** L served Mon-Sat 10-2.30, Sun 10-9 D served Mon-Sat 6-9.30, Sun 10-9 **Restaurant** L served Mon-Sat 10-2.30, Sun 10-9 D served Mon-Sat 6-9.30, Sun 10-9 ⊕ ROBINSONS ◀ Unicorn, Old Stockport, Dizzy Blonde, Hannibal's Nectar, Long Kiss Goodnight ♂ Westons Stowford Press. ₹ 10 **Facilities** Non-diners area ♦♦ Children's menu Children's portions Play area Garden Parking

---

The Legh Arms

The Village SK10 4DG ☎ 01625 829130
e-mail: legharms@hotmail.co.uk
dir: On A538 (New Road)

Serving good food all day every day

Trendy Prestbury is popular with premiership footballers and they're lucky to have the gabled and part-timbered Legh Arms on their doorstep. Fine ales from Robinsons Brewery nearby are dispensed at the bar with its oak beams and roaring fires and where simpler fare is on offer, such as salads, sharing platters, sandwiches and pub favourites. For a celeb-spotting special dinner, eat in the restaurant, where dishes use herbs from the pub's own walled garden. Pork chop served with Dijon and cider sauce and a leek and potato cake might fit the bill. The beer garden has a wood-burning stove for cooler nights.

Open all day all wk **Bar Meals** food served all day **Restaurant** L served Mon-Fri 12-2, Sat-Sun 12-10 D served Sat 12-10, Sun 12-9.30 ⊕ ROBINSONS ◀ Robinsons 1892, Robinsons Hatters, Unicorn. ₹ **Facilities** Non-diners area ❀ (Garden) ♦♦ Children's portions Garden ⌂ Parking Wi-fi

---

The Yew Tree Inn

Long Ln CW6 9RD ☎ 01829 260274
e-mail: info@theyewtreebunbury.com
dir: 400mtrs from A49

Beer is taken seriously at this village pub

Built by the Earl of Crewe, this is a sympathetically refurbished 19th-century pub. Inside, the original beams and open fires are a reminder of the pub's history, while the terrace is a more modern addition and perfect for summer dining. Up to eight real ales are available and the Easter beer festival, from Good Friday to Easter Monday, shouldn't be missed. As well as Westons Stowford Press, there is a guest cider on handpump. A seasonal menu is driven by local produce and might include beer-battered haddock, braised beef brisket, or pan-seared lamb's liver.

Open all day all wk **Bar Meals** L served Mon-Fri 12-2.30, Sat 12-10, Sun brunch 11-1, Sun 12-8 D served Mon-Thu 6-9.30, Fri 6-10, Sat 12-10, Sun 12-8 Av main course £12 **Restaurant** L served Mon-Fri 12-2.30, Sat 12-10, Sun brunch 11-1, Sun 12-8 D served Mon-Thu 6-9.30, Fri

6-10, Sat 12-10, Sun 12-8 Av 3 course à la carte fr £25 ⊕ FREE HOUSE ◀ Stonehouse Station Bitter, 7 Guest ales ♂ Westons Stowford Press, Guest Cider. ₹ 14 **Facilities** Non-diners area ❀ (Bar Garden Outside area) ♦♦ Children's menu Children's portions Garden Outside area ⌂ Beer festival Parking Wi-fi ⌘ (notice required)

The Bunbury Arms

Little Stanney Ln CH2 4HW ☎ 01244 301665
e-mail: bunburyarmschester@gmail.com
dir: From M53/M56 junct 11/15 take A5117. 1st left into Little Stanney Ln

Much loved alehouse with good food

In a small wooded hamlet, this traditional alehouse developed a fine reputation under the ownership of Alan Frain, who had run the pub since the '70s and who sadly passed away in 2011. Now in the experienced hands of his wife Janet, it continues to pride itself on its hospitality and good food. Inside, expect an open fire, TV, board games and darts, not forgetting an award-winning selection of real ales and extensive wine list. Typical dishes include black pudding and chorizo sautéed in red wine, on a spicy croûte; steak, ale and mushroom pie; and Thai green curry. Handy for the Cheshire Oaks retail outlet, Chester Zoo and Blue Planet Aquarium.

Open all day all wk **Bar Meals** L served all wk 12-6 D served Mon-Thu 6-9, Fri-Sat 6-9.30 Av main course £10 food served all day **Restaurant** L served Mon-Sat 12-6, Sun 12-8 D served Mon-Thu 6-9, Fri-Sat 6-9.30, Sun 12-8 food served all day ⊕ FREE HOUSE ◀ Robinsons Unicorn, JW Lees Coronation Street, Joseph Holt, Cains. ₹ 26 **Facilities** Non-diners area ❀ (Bar Garden) ♦♦ Children's menu Children's portions Garden ⌂ Beer festival Parking Wi-fi ⌘ (notice required)

The Hanging Gate Inn

Meg Ln, Higher Sutton SK11 0NG ☎ 01260 252238
dir: From S of Macclesfield take A523 (signed Leek). At lights left into Byron's Ln signed Sutton, Langley & Wincle. Bear left into Jarman, left onto Ridge Hill, becomes Meg Lane. 2nd right to pub on left

Stunning views and a warm welcome

Clinging to the hillside high above Rossendale, The Hanging Gate boasts breathtaking views across Cheshire into Wales. An old drovers' inn dating from 1661, the pub marks the spot where poachers on the Royal Macclesfield Forest were hanged. Quaff a pint of local ale in one of the three unspoilt rooms or tuck into regional produce, perhaps pheasant with smoked bacon, red wine sauce, and bubble-and-squeak. On a fine day bag a seat in the garden.

Open all wk 12-3 6-11 (Sat-Sun 12-11) ⊕ HYDES BREWERY ◀ Original, Manchester Finest, Craft Ales. **Facilities** ❀ (Bar Garden) ♦♦ Children's menu Children's portions Family room Garden Parking Wi-fi

SUTTON LANE ENDS *continued*

Sutton Hall

PICK OF THE PUBS

Bullocks Ln SK11 0HE ☎ 01260 253211
e-mail: sutton.hall@brunningandprice.co.uk
dir: *A523 from Macclesfield. At lights left into Byron's Ln (signed Sutton, Langley & Wincle) to village. Pub on left*

Former manor house turned spacious pub

The family seat of the Earls of Lucan, this striking half-timbered and gritstone manor house is surrounded by its own estate. Dating from the 16th century, but considerably added to since, it conceals a wealth of nooks and crannies, a snug, a library and seven different dining areas, with terraces and gardens outside. The Macclesfield Canal runs nearby, while in the other direction are the steeply wooded hills and crags of Macclesfield Forest. As part of the Brunning & Price chain of dining pubs, it offers the company's own Original Bitter alongside Lord Lucan, a local brew whose whereabouts are no mystery; the wine list is well compiled and there are over 100 whiskies. A typical starter is potted smoked mackerel, crayfish and apple and fennel salad. Sample mains include honey-roast duck breast; pan-fried sea bass with chorizo, caper and tomato dressing; and Moroccan spiced pepper with couscous, aubergine and okra salad.

Open all day all wk 11.30-11 (Sun 12-10.30) **Bar Meals** L served Mon-Sat 12-10, Sun 12-9.30 D served Mon-Sat 12-10, Sun 12-9.30 food served all day **Restaurant** L served Mon-Sat 12-10, Sun 12-9.30 D served Mon-Sat 12-10, Sun 12-9.30 food served all day ⊕ FREE HOUSE/ BRUNNING & PRICE ◀ Brunning & Price Original Bitter, Flowers Original, Wincle Lord Lucan Ŏ Aspall, Westons Wyld Wood Organic. ☗ 21 **Facilities** ✿ (Bar Garden) ♦♦ Children's portions Play area Garden ⨅ Parking

---

SWETTENHAM Map 15 SJ86

The Swettenham Arms

PICK OF THE PUBS

Swettenham Ln CW12 2LF ☎ 01477 571284
e-mail: info@swettenhamarms.co.uk
dir: *M6 junct 18 to Holmes Chapel, then A535 towards Jodrell Bank. 3m right (Forty Acre Lane) to Swettenham (NB do not use postcode for Sat Nav; enter Swettenham Road)*

A sure-fire hit with both drinkers and diners

Don't rely on your Sat Nav, or you may well end up in the middle of the local ford, but that said this pub's well worth the search. Opposite the church and festooned with flowers in the summer, this 600-year-old building is a former nunnery. The pub has been owned by the Cunninghams for 20 years now, and they have retained the traditional features of the polished copper bar, three open fireplaces and shiny brasses. Head chef Thomas Lüdecke is in his fourth year, and the seasonal menu is as modern as the pub is traditional. Home-grown vegetables, bee hives and the pub's own hens enrich the menu choices, from satisfying pub classics such as beef Wellington to restaurant-style pheasant breast stuffed with a smoked bacon and leek mousse. The banqueting suite overlooking the stunning lavender meadow to the rear of the pub can be hired for weddings. Wander in the adjoining 33-acre Quinta Arboretum, where there are plenty of easy-walking and wheelchair-friendly routes.

Open all day all wk 11.30am-close **Bar Meals** L served Mon-Fri 12-2.30, Sat-Sun 12-6 D served Mon-Sat 6-9.30, Sun 6-8.30 **Restaurant** L served Mon-Fri 12-2.30, Sat-Sun 12-6 D served Mon-Sat 6-9.30, Sun 6-8.30 ⊕ FREE HOUSE ◀ Timothy Taylor Landlord, Sharp's Doom Bar, Bollington Best, Courage Directors, Moorhouse's Pride of Pendle, Slater's Top Totty, Hydes, Black Sheep, Beartown Ŏ Addlestones. ☗ 12 **Facilities** Non-diners area ✿ (Bar Garden) ♦♦ Children's menu Garden ⨅ Parking Wi-fi ➡ (notice required)

TARPORLEY Map 15 SJ56

Alvanley Arms Inn ★★★★ INN

Forest Rd, Cotebrook CW6 9DS ☎ 01829 760200
e-mail: info@alvanleyarms.co.uk
dir: *On A49, 1.5m N of Tarporley*

Local produce on the menus

Under new owners, this lovely 16th-century former coaching inn has links to the Cotebrook Shire Horse Centre next door, so expect a horse-themed decor – rosettes, harnesses and horseshoes – in the traditional oak-beamed bar. Hand-pulled ales complement a range of freshly prepared dishes, based on ingredients from local family businesses. Dishes range from starters of cod and pancetta fish cake; and wholetail scampi, to main courses of traditional steak and ale pie; and the chef's curry of the day. Lighter options such as baguettes are available at lunchtime. Renovations uncovered original beams in the individually designed bedrooms.

Open all wk 12-3 5.30-11.30 (Sat-Sun 12-11) **Bar Meals** L served Mon-Fri 12-2, Sat-Sun 12-9 D served Mon-Fri 6-9, Sat-Sun 12-9 **Restaurant** L served Mon-Fri 12-2, Sat-Sun 12-9 D served Mon-Fri 6-9, Sat-Sun 12-9 ⊕ ROBINSONS ◀ Unicorn, Guest ales. ☗ 12 **Facilities** Non-diners area ♦♦ Children's menu Children's portions Garden ⨅ Parking Wi-fi ➡ (notice required) **Rooms** 7

The Swan, Tarporley

50 High St CW6 0AG ☎ 01829 733838
e-mail: info@theswantarporley.co.uk
web: www.theswantarporley.co.uk
dir: *From junct of A49 & A51 into Tarporley. Pub on right in village centre*

Full of nook-and-cranny-imbued character

A 500-year-old coaching inn on the Shrewsbury to Chester road, this sympathetically restored hostelry is one of the most historic inns in the area. It's been home to the Tarporley Hunt Club, known as the Green Collars, since it was formed in 1762. Regulars favour the open-fired Pantry Bar with its regional ales, but the Hayes and Pickering Rooms are also welcoming, the latter for locally sourced steak burger, cheese and onion pie, and roast duck; or be tempted by afternoon toast and cakes. There's also a good choice of sandwiches.

Open all day all wk **Bar Meals** L served Mon-Fri 7am-9pm, Sat 8am-9pm, Sun 8-8 D served Mon-Fri 7am-9pm, Sat 8am-9pm, Sun 8-8 Av main course £10 food served all day **Restaurant** L served Mon-Fri 7am-9pm, Sat 8am-9pm, Sun 8-8 D served Mon-Fri 7am-9pm, Sat 8am-9pm, Sun 8-8 food served all day ⊕ FREE HOUSE ◀ Weetwood Best Bitter & Eastgate Ale, Timothy Taylor Landlord, Guest ale Ŏ Hereford Dry. ☗ 10 **Facilities** Non-diners area ♦♦ Children's menu Children's portions Garden ⨅ Parking Wi-fi ➡ (notice required)

Save on hotels. Book at **theAA.com/hotel**

CHESHIRE 75 ENGLAND

PICK OF THE PUBS

The Bear's Paw ★★★★★ INN

WARMINGHAM   Map 15 SJ76

School Ln CW11 3QN ☎ 01270 526317
e-mail: info@thebearspaw.co.uk
web: www.thebearspaw.co.uk
dir: *M6 junct 18, A54, A533 towards Sandbach. Follow signs for village*

Refined gastro-pub cooking

With its prominent central gable and some nods towards typical Cheshire black-and-white half-timbering, this stylish 19th-century gastro inn has clearly had a lot of money spent on it. Acres — well it seems like acres — of reclaimed antique oak flooring, leather sofas surrounding two huge open fireplaces, bookshelves offering plenty of choice for a good read, and more than 200 pictures and archive photos lining the oak-panelled walls. The bar, in which stands a carved wooden bear with a salmon in its mouth, offers a half dozen cask ales from local micro-breweries, including the somewhat appropriate Beartown in Congleton, Weetwood in Tarporley, and Tatton in Knutsford, as well as Hereford dry cider. Whether you're sitting out front looking across to the churchyard or in the clubby interior, there's plenty of comfortable dining space in which to sample wholesome, locally sourced food from wide-ranging daily menus that expertly blend the classic with the modern. Take, for example, starters like Hesketh Bank beetroot with goats'

cheese and candied walnuts; and main dishes such as steak, Weetwood ale and onion pie, garden peas and hand-cut chips; or gigolette of chicken thigh with chorizo, button mushrooms, button onions, sauté new potatoes and chive velouté. Great for sharing are the imaginative deli boards, which come laden with local cheeses, charcuterie or pickled and smoked fish, and don't miss the Sunday roast lunches. For something lighter, think in terms of a filled jacket potato, or a sandwich, baguette or wrap. The Bear's Paw offers distinctive boutique-style en suite bedrooms.

Open all day all wk **Bar Meals** L served Mon-Thu 12-9.30, Fri-Sat 12-10, Sun 12-8 D served Mon-Thu 12-9.30, Fri-Sat

12-10, Sun 12-8 **Restaurant** L served Mon-Thu 12-9.30, Fri-Sat 12-10, Sun 12-8 D served Mon-Thu 12-9.30, Fri-Sat 12-10, Sun 12-8 🛢 FREE HOUSE
🍺 Weetwood Best Bitter & Cheshire Cat, Spitting Feathers, Beartown, Tatton
🍏 Hereford Dry Cider. 🍷 10
Facilities Non-diners area 🐾 👫 Children's menu Children's portions Garden 🎋 Parking Wi-fi 🚌 (notice required) **Rooms** 17

TUSHINGHAM CUM GRINDLEY   Map 15 SJ54

Blue Bell Inn

SY13 4QS ☎ 01948 662172
dir: *A41, 4m N of Whitchurch, signed Bell O' the Hill*

Old pub with a unique tale of haunting

This inn reputedly has a ghost duck, whose spirit is sealed in a bottle buried in the bottom step of the cellar. A lovely black-and-white, timber-framed building that oozes character with its abundance of beams, open fires and horse brasses, the oldest part dates to approximately 1550, and the main building was completed in 1667. It even has one of the largest working chimneys in Cheshire and a priest hole, while curios that have been discovered from within the wall structure are on display. A menu of hearty, home-cooked pub food includes curries, steak and chips, and chilli with garlic bread.

Open 12-3 6-11.30 Closed: Mon (ex BHs) ⊕ FREE HOUSE ◀ Salopian Shropshire Gold, Oakham JHB, Guest ales ♻ Thatchers Cheddar Valley, Westons Old Rosie.
Facilities ❧ (Bar Garden) ♦ Children's portions Family room Garden Parking

WARMINGHAM   Map 15 SJ76

The Bear's Paw ★★★★★ INN ◉

PICK OF THE PUBS

See Pick of the Pubs on page 75

WINCLE   Map 16 SJ96

The Ship Inn

Barlow Hill SK11 0QE ☎ 01260 227217
e-mail: garybparker@btconnect.com
dir: *From Buxton towards Congleton on A54 left into Barlow Hill at x-rds, follow signs for Wincle (0.75m) & Swythamley & brown signs to pub (Spoon & Fork)*

Popular Peak District destination

The adjoining villages of Danebridge and Wincle straddle the River Dane, which here in the western Peak District National Park divides Cheshire from Staffordshire. The park's moors, lush woodland and drystone-walled pastures are a favourite with walkers, many of whom beat a path to this 17th-century, pink-hued pub with a flagstoned taproom serving JW Lees' Manchester-brewed Coronation Street ale. New owners maintain the interesting and regularly-changing menu, perhaps on the day you visit offering crab, prawn and chorizo risotto; peppered sirloin steak in Madeira sauce; red Thai chicken curry; and haloumi cheese and vegetable stack. Splendid views from the beer garden.

Open Tue-Fri 12-3 5.30-11 Sat-Sun all day Closed: Mon (ex BHs) **Bar Meals** L served Tue-Fri 12-2.30, Sat 12-9.30, Sun 12-5 D served Tue-Thu 6-9, Fri-Sat 6-9.30 **Restaurant** L served Tue-Fri 12-2.30, Sat 12-9.30, Sun 12-5 D served Tue-Thu 6-9, Fri-Sat 6-9.30 ⊕ J W LEES ◀ Bitter, Coronation Street. ♥ 13
Facilities Non-diners area ❧ (Bar Restaurant Garden) ♦ Children's menu Children's portions Family room Garden ⌂ Parking Wi-fi ☕ (notice required)

WRENBURY   Map 15 SJ54

The Dusty Miller

CW5 8HG ☎ 01270 780537
dir: *Telephone for directions*

Transformed former corn mill on Llangollen Canal

This beautifully converted 18th-century corn mill is beside the Llangollen Canal in the rural village of Wrenbury. The pub's large arched windows offer views of passing boats, while a black-and-white lift bridge, designed by Thomas Telford, completes the picture-postcard setting. With a good choice of real ales, the menu, which mainly relies on ingredients from the region, offers pan-fried king scallops with pea purée; braised shallot and fig tarte Tatin; roasted chicken supreme; pan-fried salmon with new potatoes; and 28-day matured rib-eye steak.

Open 12-12 Closed: Mon in winter ⊕ FREE HOUSE ◀ Robinsons Unicorn, Old Tom & Dizzy Blonde, Guest ales ♻ Westons Stowford Press & Traditional.
Facilities ❧ (Bar Restaurant Garden) ♦ Children's menu Children's portions Garden Parking

CORNWALL & ISLES OF SCILLY

ALTARNUN   Map 2 SX28

Rising Sun Inn **NEW**

PL15 7SN ☎ 01566 86636
e-mail: risingsuninn@hotmail.co.uk
dir: *From A30 follow Altarnun signs onto unclassified road. Through Altarnun & Treween to T-junct. Inn 100yds on left*

Moorland free house worth leaving the A30 for

It's still fine to arrive by horse at this inviting, 18th-century moorland inn – there's a hitching post in the car park. On horseback could be the best way home, too, given the real ales from the village's Penpont brewery (which celebrates its birthday at a beer festival here in mid November), Skinner's Betty Stogs, and also Cornish Orchards and Press Gang ciders. Lunch and dinner dishes include Fowey River mussels and fries; and Cornish ham with free-range eggs, while others in the evening include 'crispy skin' roast duck-leg confit; cider-braised pressed belly of pork; and roasted vegetable and potato frittata.

Open all wk 12-2.30 5.30-11 (Sat 12-11 Sun & BHs 12-10.30) **Bar Meals** L served all wk 12-2 D served all wk 6-9 **Restaurant** D served all wk 6-9 ⊕ FREE HOUSE ◀ Penpont St. Nonna's, Skinner's Betty Stogs, Guest ales ♻ Cornish Orchards, Skinner's Press Gang.
Facilities Non-diners area ❧ (Bar Garden) ♦ Children's menu Children's portions Garden ⌂ Beer festival Parking Wi-fi ☕ (notice required)

BLISLAND   Map 2 SX17

The Blisland Inn

PL30 4JF ☎ 01208 850739
dir: *5m from Bodmin towards Launceston. From A30 follow Blisland signs. 2.5m to pub*

A Bodmin refuge especially for excellent ales

Beside one of Cornwall's few remaining village greens, this old stone inn hosts a beer festival each May when milds are promoted, augmenting the Cornish bitters, local ciders and countless guest beers that have gained the pub national recognition. Inside there's no jukebox or fruit machines, but beams, toby jugs, local photos, a huge collection of barometers and a slate floor produce a timeless atmosphere. Reliable pub grub includes home-made chicken and ham pie and bowls of thick soup, ideal for warming up after walking on nearby Bodmin Moor.

Open all day all wk ⊕ FREE HOUSE ◀ Sharp's, Skinner's, Guest ales ♻ Cornish Orchards, Winkleigh, Haye Farm.
Facilities ♦ Children's portions Family room Garden

BODINNICK   Map 2 SX15

The Old Ferry Inn NEW

PL23 1LX ☎ 01726 870237
e-mail: info@oldferryinn.co.uk
dir: *From Liskeard on A38 to Dobwalls, left at lights onto A390. After 3m left onto B3359 signed Looe. Right signed Lerryn/Bodinnick/Polruan for 5m*

Traditional Cornish pub with splendid estuary views

Daphne du Maurier wrote many of her novels at 'Ferryside', the house next door to this 400-year-old inn by the River Fowey. You can watch people messing about in boats from one of the sun terraces, stay in the bar among the nautical memorabilia, or cosy up in the stone-walled snug. A long list of snacks includes Cornish Pasties, while among the mains are cod in Sharp's ale batter; wholetail scampi and chips; roast chicken breast with local cider, cream and apple sauce; and wild mushroom and thyme penne pasta. The adjacent ferry carries cars over to Fowey town.

Open all day all wk **Bar Meals** L served all wk 12-3 D served all wk 6-9.15 Av main course £15 **Restaurant** L served all wk 12-3 D served all wk 6-9.15 Av 3 course à la carte fr £28 ∰ FREE HOUSE ◀ Sharp's Cornish Coaster Ö Haye Farm, Sharp's Orchard Cornish Cider. **Facilities** Non-diners area ❄ (Bar Outside area) ✦ Children's menu Family room Outside area ⌂ Parking Wi-fi ▭ (notice required)

BOLVENTOR   Map 2 SX17

Jamaica Inn

PL15 7TS ☎ 01566 86250
e-mail: enquiry@jamaicainn.co.uk
dir: *Follow A30 from Exeter. 10m after Launceston take Bolventor road, follow signs*

Famous inn with smuggling and literary connections

The setting for Daphne du Maurier's famous novel of the same name, this 18th-century inn stands high on Bodmin Moor. Its Smugglers Museum houses fascinating artefacts, while the Daphne du Maurier room honours the great writer. The place is big on atmosphere, with a cobbled courtyard, beamed ceilings and roaring fires, plus a children's play area and beautiful gardens. Breakfasts, mid-morning snacks and lunches provide an inviting choice, while the evening menu offers steaks, fish, chicken and vegetarian options.

Open all day all wk 9am-11pm (Tue-Thu 3-11 Fri-Sun 12-11 winter) ∰ FREE HOUSE ◀ Jamaica Inn Ale, Sharp's Doom Bar, St Austell Tribute. **Facilities** ✦ Play area Garden Parking

BOSCASTLE   Map 2 SX09

Cobweb Inn

The Bridge PL35 0HE ☎ 01840 250278
e-mail: cobweb.inn@virgin.net
dir: *In village centre*

Freshly prepared food in Cornish tourist spot

Built in the 1600s, this immense, five-storey stone edifice was once a bonded warehouse where customs agents guarded taxable imported goods. Rumour has it that despite this, one could drink illicitly in the beamed, flag-floored back room; today the bottle- and jug-festooned bar, where Cornwall-brewed real ales and farm ciders can be ordered without subterfuge. Eat here or in the charming white-painted restaurant, where seafood, steaks, pasties and a great deal more feature on the extensive menu and daily specials boards.

Open all day all wk ∰ FREE HOUSE ◀ Sharp's Doom Bar, St Austell Tribute, Tintagel Harbour Special, Guest ales Ö Healey's Cornish Rattler, Westons Stowford Press. **Facilities** ✦ Children's menu Children's portions Family room Garden Parking Wi-fi

---

The Wellington Hotel ★★★ HL ◉◉

PICK OF THE PUBS

The Harbour PL35 0AQ ☎ 01840 250202
e-mail: info@wellingtonhotelboscastle.com
dir: *A30/A395 at Davidstow follow Boscastle signs. B3266 to village. Right into New Rd*

Popular pub and restaurant on the coast

Nestling on one of England's most stunning coastlines at the end of a glorious wooded valley where the rivers Jordan and Valency meet, this listed 16th-century coaching inn with its castellated tower was renamed in 1852 in honour of the Duke of Wellington. Known affectionately as 'The Welly' by both locals and loyal guests, it was fully restored after devastating floods a few years ago, but retains much of its original charm, including beamed ceilings and real log fires. The traditional Long Bar, complete with minstrels' gallery, proffers a good selection of Cornish ales and ciders, malt whiskies and bar snacks, together with a menu that makes the most of fresh, local ingredients: seafood fettuccine, forest mushroom ragout, and fish and chips. The fine dining restaurant, The Waterloo, has been awarded two AA Rosettes and offers main courses such as halibut served with oxtail, cockles, bok choy and udon noodles.

Open all day all wk 11-11 **Bar Meals** L served Mon-Fri 12-3, Sat-Sun 12-9 D served Mon-Fri 6-9, Sat-Sun 12-9 Av main course £12.50 **Restaurant** D served Wed-Sun 6.30-10.30 Av 3 course à la carte fr £37.50 ∰ FREE HOUSE ◀ St Austell Tribute, Sharp's Doom Bar Ö Sharp's Orchard. **Facilities** Non-diners area ❄ (Bar Garden Outside area) ✦ Children's menu Children's portions Garden Outside area ⌂ Parking Wi-fi ▭ (notice required) **Rooms** 14

CADGWITH   Map 2 SW71

Cadgwith Cove Inn

TR12 7JX ☎ 01326 290513
e-mail: garryandhelen@cadgwithcoveinn.co.uk
dir: *A3083 from Helston towards Lizard. Left to Cadgwith*

Former smugglers' haunt under new ownership

Miraculously, Cadgwith remains a largely unspoilt fishing hamlet on the rugged Lizard coastline. A visit to this 300-year-old pub, familiar to anyone who watched *The Fisherman's Apprentice* on TV, will illustrate why it once appealed to smugglers. Relics in the atmospheric, simply furnished bars attest to a rich seafaring history; the cove itself is just across the old pilchard cellar from its sunny front patio. Traditional favourites include fish and chips; Cove crab salad; roast belly of pork; and mushroom Stroganoff. Folk music nights are Tuesdays, and the Cadgwith Singers tip up every Friday. A beer festival is planned.

Open all day all wk **Bar Meals** L served all wk 12-2 D served all wk 7-9 Av main course £9.70 food served all day **Restaurant** L served all wk 12-2 D served all wk 7-9 Fixed menu price fr £15.70 Av 3 course à la carte fr £19.70 food served all day ∰ PUNCH TAVERNS ◀ Sharp's, Skinner's, Guest ales Ö Westons Stowford Press, Thatchers. ♥ 9 **Facilities** Non-diners area ❄ (Bar Restaurant Outside area) ✦ Children's menu Children's portions Outside area ⌂ Parking Wi-fi ▭

CALLINGTON   Map 3 SX36

Manor House Inn

Rilla Mill PL17 7NT ☎ 01579 362354
e-mail: jackie.cole67@googlemail.com
dir: *5m from Callington, just off B3257*

A change of hands at this market town inn

Standing by the River Lynher on the edge of Bodmin Moor, this former granary once supplied the neighbouring mill. As we went to press we were informed of a change of ownership; the pub continues to serve real ales and ciders, and in the new owner's own words "serve proper food".

Open Mon 5-11 Tue-Fri 11-3 5-11 (Sat-Sun all day) Closed: Mon L **Bar Meals** L served Tue-Sun 12-2 D served Tue-Sun 6-9 ∰ FREE HOUSE ◀ Sharp's Own, Special, Guest ale Ö Thatchers Gold, Westons, Healey's Cornish Rattler. **Facilities** Non-diners area ❄ (Bar) ✦ Children's portions Garden ⌂ Beer Festival Parking ▭ (notice required)

CONSTANTINE   Map 2 SW72

Trengilly Wartha Inn

PICK OF THE PUBS

See Pick of the Pubs on page 78

PICK OF THE PUBS

Trengilly Wartha Inn

CONSTANTINE   **Map 2 SW72**

Nancenoy TR11 5RP ☎ 01326 340332
e-mail: reception@trengilly.co.uk
web: www.trengilly.co.uk
dir: *Telephone for detailed directions*

Hidden Cornish gem with locally sourced food

Since William and Lisa Lea arrived at Trengilly Wartha they have established it as one of Cornwall's leading inns. The Cornish name of this friendly free house means a settlement above the trees — although it actually lies at the foot of a densely wooded valley. Originally built as a small farmstead in the late 18th century, the building was sold for just £300 in 1946. Over the next decade, the Ballamy family renovated and extended the building with help from German prisoners of war, who installed the double staircase. Today the black-beamed bar with its cricketing memorabilia offers Skinner's Cornish Knocker amongst other local ales and ciders. There's also an extensive wine list with 15 varieties offered by the glass, and over 40 malt whiskies. Meanwhile, the menu includes locally sourced Cornish produce wherever possible. Expect classic lunchtime fare, including a range of traditional ploughman's with home-made granary bread, pickles and chutneys; and hot dishes like Tywardreath sausages, mustard mash and gravy. Fish and

seafood feature strongly in the restaurant, with starters like Falmouth River mussels, or smoked whiting with herb butter. Main course fish dishes might include wild sea bass, or fillet of brill with sundried tomato and baby spinach. Meat-eaters and vegetarians will also find plenty of choice — pork fillet with prune, apple and brandy sauce; and leek, broccoli and mushroom pancakes are typical choices, whilst home-made sweets are offered on the chalkboard. A pretty beer garden and vine-shaded pergola complete the picture, surrounded by the three meadows that formed part of the original smallholding.

Open all wk 11-3 6-12 **Bar Meals** L served all wk 12-2.15 D served all wk

6.30-9.30 **Restaurant** L served all wk 12-2.15 D served all wk 6.30-9.30 ⊕ **FREE HOUSE** ◀ Skinner's Cornish Knocker & Betty Stogs, Sharp's Doom Bar & Eden Ale, Penzance Potion No 9, Guest ales ♂ Henley's Cornish Rattler, Thatchers Gold. ♟ 15 **Facilities** Non-diners area ❤ (Bar Garden) ♦♦ Children's menu Children's portions Play area Family room Garden ☴ Parking Wi-fi 🚐

The Finnygook Inn

PL11 3BQ ☎ **01503 230338**
e-mail: eat@finnygook.co.uk
dir: *10m W of Tamar Bridge take A374 S. In 3m right signed Crafthole & follow pub signs. From Torpoint take A374, 5m to Antony. Left in Antony, 1m to T-junct. 3m to Crafthole*

Refurbished coaching inn serving peninsula-brewed beers

They say the ghost of smuggler Silas Finny walks abroad on the cliffs and byways hereabouts; so, too, do ramblers and visitors seeking to share the St Austell and Penpont beers, and tempting fodder available at this 16th-century pub. Located in a hamlet above Portwrinkle's cove-nibbled coast, The Finnygook serves seafood dishes, such as grilled Cornish sardines and crab linguine, backed by a host of reliable pub favourites (sausages with bubble-and-squeak, beefburger, and treacle sponge for dessert) taken by the log fire, in the library room or on the terrace with distant views up the Tamar estuary.

Open all day Closed: Mon in Nov-Mar **Bar Meals** L served all wk 12-9 (Nov-Mar Tue-Sun 12.30-2.30) D served all wk 12-9 (Nov-Mar Tue-Sun 6-9) Av main course £11 **Restaurant** L served all wk 12-9 (Nov-Mar Tue-Sun 12.30-2.30) D served all wk 12-9 (Nov-Mar Tue-Sun 6-9) Fixed menu price fr £10 Av 3 course à la carte fr £20 ⊕ FREE HOUSE ◀ Sharp's Doom Bar, St Austell Tribute & Proper Job, Penpont Cornish Arvor, Dartmoor. ♟ 10 **Facilities** Non-diners area ❀ (Bar Garden) ♦♦ Children's menu Children's portions Garden ᚒ Parking Wi-fi ⛟ (notice required)

The Smugglers' Den Inn

Trebellan TR8 5PY ☎ **01637 830209**
e-mail: info@thesmugglersden.co.uk
web: www.thesmugglersden.co.uk
dir: *From Newquay take A3075 to Cubert x-rds, then right, then left signed Trebellan, 0.5m*

Classic pub selection focusing on Cornish provenance

Look to the blackboard for fish specials in this thatched 16th-century pub situated less than 15 minutes from Newquay; the table d'hôte menu includes catch of the day too. Popular with locals and visitors alike, the pub comprises a long bar, family room, children's play area, courtyards and huge beer garden. Local suppliers are

listed at the bottom of the no-nonsense modern menu, where a salt and chilli squid could be followed by a slow-roasted shoulder of Cornish lamb. A real ale and pie festival is held over the May Day Bank Holiday weekend.

The Smugglers' Den Inn

Open all wk 11.30-3 6-11 (Sat 11-3 6-12 Sun & summer open all day) Closed: 25 Dec 12-3 **Bar Meals** L served all wk 12-2.30 (winter 12-2) D served all wk 6-9.30 (winter Sun-Thu 6-9, Fri-Sat 6-9.30) **Restaurant** L served all wk 12-2.30 (winter 12-2) D served all wk 6-9.30 (winter Sun-Thu 6-9, Fri-Sat 6-9.30) ⊕ FREE HOUSE ◀ Sharp's Doom Bar, St Austell Tribute, Guest ales Ö Healey's Cornish Rattler, Thatchers Gold. ♟ 10 **Facilities** Non-diners area ❀ (Bar Garden) ♦♦ Children's menu Play area Family room Garden ᚒ Beer festival Parking Wi-fi ⛟

See advert on page 80

The Borough Arms

PL31 2RD ☎ **01208 73118**
e-mail: borougharms@hotmail.co.uk
dir: *From A30 take A389 to Wadebridge, pub approx 1m from Bodmin*

Welcome refreshment in a Cornish valley

One of England's best loved recreational trails, the Camel Trail, skims past this considerably updated Victorian railway pub in the Cornish countryside outside Bodmin. Trains carrying china clay along the old line have been replaced by cyclists and ramblers, accessing the pub car park directly from the trail to indulge in a range of West Country real ales and ever-reliable pub grub. Steaks, barbecue pork ribs and fish and chips revive flagging lovers of the outdoors, or try the carvery. Families are well catered for, with a new children's play area to burn off extra calories.

Open all day all wk **Bar Meals** L served all wk 12-9 D served all wk 12-9 food served all day **Restaurant** L served all wk 12-9 D served all wk 12-9 food served all day ⊕ ST AUSTELL BREWERY ◀ Tribute, Dartmoor, Bass. **Facilities** Non-diners area ❀ (Bar Garden) ♦♦ Children's menu Children's portions Play area Family room Garden ᚒ Parking Wi-fi ⛟

The Punchbowl & Ladle

Penelewey TR3 6QY ☎ **01872 862237**
e-mail: punchbowlandladle@googlemail.com
dir: *From Truro take A39 towards Falmouth, after Shell garage at Playing Place rdbt follow King Harry Ferry signs. 0.5m, pub on right*

Cornish comforts in a thatched retreat

Flowers adorn the exterior of this gorgeous old pub close to the King Harry Ferry. Local rumour has it that the bar fireplace was used to burn contraband when customs officers dropped by. Head for the suntrap walled garden or patio with a glass of St Austell Proper Job beer or Cornish Rattler cider. Alternatively, settle down on the comfortable sofas in the cosy low-beamed bar and await your choice from the menu, which uses ingredients sourced from local Cornish suppliers and features great comfort dishes such as home-made fisherman's pie, ploughman's, and penne pasta in a tomato and basil sauce. Jackets, salads and sandwiches are also on offer.

Open all day all wk **Bar Meals** L served Mon-Sat 12-2.30, Sun 12-3 D served all wk 6-9 ⊕ ST AUSTELL BREWERY ◀ Tribute, Proper Job & Trelawny Ö Healey's Cornish Rattler. ♟ 16 **Facilities** Non-diners area ❀ (Bar Garden) ♦♦ Children's menu Children's portions Garden ᚒ Parking Wi-fi ⛟

The Ship Inn

Trafalgar Square PL23 1AZ ☎ **01726 832230**
e-mail: shipinnfowey@hotmail.com
dir: *From A30 take B3269 & A390*

Very old inn situated in Fowey's narrow streets

One of Fowey's oldest buildings, The Ship was built in 1570 by John Rashleigh, who sailed to the Americas with Walter Raleigh. Given Fowey's riverside position, assume a good choice of fish, including peppered smoked mackerel, breaded scampi, and Ship Inn fish pie. Other options include chilli con carne or local butcher's sausages and mash. St Austell ales, real fires and a long tradition of genial hospitality add the final touches.

Open all day all wk 11am-mdnt (Fri-Sat 11am-1am) ⊕ ST AUSTELL BREWERY ◀ Tribute & Proper Job, Dartmoor IPA Ö Healey's Cornish Rattler & Pear Rattler. **Facilities** ❀ (Bar) ♦♦ Children's menu Children's portions Family room

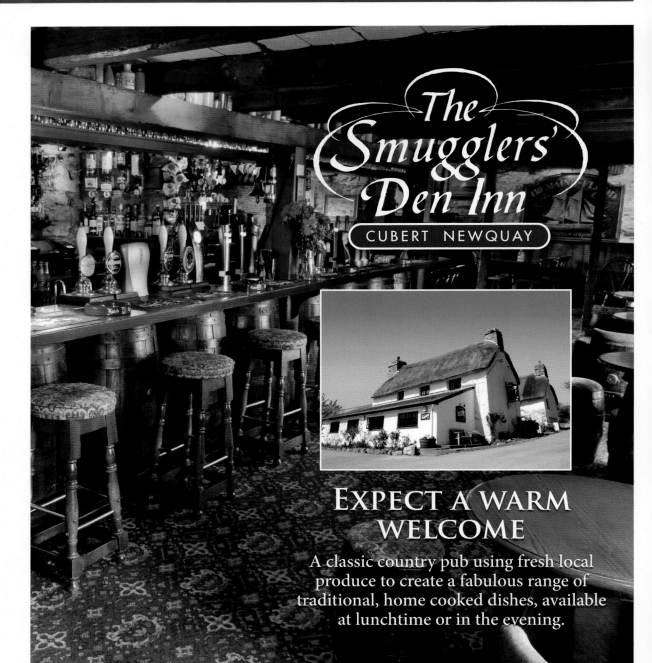

The Smugglers' Den Inn

CUBERT NEWQUAY

EXPECT A WARM WELCOME

A classic country pub using fresh local produce to create a fabulous range of traditional, home cooked dishes, available at lunchtime or in the evening.

Trebellan, Cubert, Newquay, Cornwall, TR8 5PY

Tel: (01637) 830209 *www.thesmugglersden.co.uk*

GUNNISLAKE   Map 3 SX47

The Rising Sun Inn

Calstock Rd PL18 9BX ☎ 01822 832201
dir: From Tavistock take A390 to Gunnislake. Left after lights into Calstock Rd. Inn approx 500mtrs on right

Charming inn in a lovely Cornish valley

Overlooking the stunning Tamar Valley, this traditional two-roomed picture-postcard pub is a popular stop for walkers, wildlife enthusiasts and cyclists; great walks start and finish from the pub. In warmer weather, enjoy a pint of real ale in the award-winning gardens or order from the simple menu of locally sourced, home-cooked food, perhaps chicken liver pâté, or soup of the day to start, and a warm duck salad or vegetable lasagne to follow.

Open all wk 12-3 5-11 **Bar Meals** L served all wk 12-3 D served all wk 5-9 ⊕ FREE HOUSE ◀ Skinner's Betty Stogs, St Austell Tribute, Otter, Dartmoor Legend, Dartmoor Jail Ale, Guest ales ♂ Westons Stowford Press, Thatchers. ♥ 25 **Facilities** Non-diners area ❀ (Bar Garden) ♦❙ Children's menu Children's portions Garden ⊼ Parking

GUNWALLOE   Map 2 SW62

The Halzephron Inn

PICK OF THE PUBS

TR12 7QB ☎ 01326 240406
e-mail: halzephroninn@tiscali.co.uk
dir: 3m S of Helston on A3083, right to Gunwalloe, through village. Inn on left

Breathtaking views and mouthwatering food

Perched high above Gunwalloe Fishing Cove, this 500-year-old, rugged stone inn commands an enviable position, with stunning views across Mount's Bay to Penzance. The name of the inn derives from Als Yfferin, old Cornish for 'Cliffs of Hell', an appropriate description for this hazardous stretch of Atlantic coastline. The two interconnecting bars feature attractive checked fabrics, padded wall benches, warming log fires, fishing memorabilia, and original watercolours of Cornish scenes. The monthly changing à la carte and twice-daily changing specials utilise the best Cornish produce available, including fresh seafood. Everything is home made, with the likes of salmon and dill fishcakes among the starters. Main courses include cottage pie, and baked fillet of hake topped with a herb crust and served with spring greens, parsley mash and chunky tomato sauce. On sunny days bag a front bench and savour a pint of Skinner's Betty Stogs while looking out to St Michael's Mount.

Open all wk 11-3 6-11 Closed: 25 Dec **Bar Meals** L served all wk 12-2 D served all wk 7-9 **Restaurant** L served all wk 12-2 D served all wk 7-9 ⊕ FREE HOUSE ◀ Sharp's Own, Doom Bar & Special, St Austell Tribute, Skinner's Betty Stogs, Lizard Kernow Gold ♂ Healey's Cornish Rattler, Skinner's Press Gang, Skreach. ♥ 9 **Facilities** Non-diners area ❀ (Bar Garden) ♦❙ Children's menu Children's portions Play area Family room Garden ⊼ Parking Wi-fi

GWEEK   Map 2 SW72

Black Swan ★★★★ INN **NEW**

TR12 6TU ☎ 01326 221502
e-mail: info@blackswangweek.co.uk
dir: In village centre

Refurbished inn with home-cooked food and Cornish beers

Located in the picturesque village of Gweek, a stone's throw from the popular National Seal Sanctuary, this delightful inn has been restored to its former glory. Cuisine is sourced with care, and local produce is used whenever possible; an extensive blackboard menu showcases pub classics and favourites. Not to be missed is a selection of Cornish Ales, along side the landlord's own, named after his dog 'Hamish'. Look out for details of their beer and mussel festival in the Autumn. If you'd like to stay over the pub has stylish bedrooms delightfully named Raspberry, Blackberry, Gooseberry and Mulberry.

Open all day all wk **Bar Meals** Av main course £12 food served all day **Restaurant** food served all day ⊕ PUNCH TAVERNS ◀ Sharp's Doom Bar, Hamish Cornish Ale ♂ Thatchers, Pirate's Potion. **Facilities** Non-diners area ♦❙ Children's menu Children's portions Garden ⊼ Beer festival Parking Wi-fi ▭ (notice required) **Rooms** 4

GWITHIAN   Map 2 SW54

The Red River Inn **NEW**

1 Prosper Hill TR27 5BW ☎ 01736 753223
e-mail: louisa.saville@googlemail.com
dir: Exit A30 at Loggans Moor rdbt, follow Hayle signs. Immediately take 3rd exit at mini rdt onto B3301 signed Gwithian. 2m to pub in village centre

A village pub that offers something for everyone

The name of this 200-year-old pub recalls the colour of the village river when it was mined locally. Close by runs the South West Coastal Path, and the beach is popular with surfers who, even in their wetsuits, are warmly welcomed here. Among its attractions are up to five, ever-changing Cornish real ales, an Easter weekend beer and cider festival, and food that ranges from fresh crab sandwiches and haloumi salad to fresh sea bass, steaks and Middle Eastern, Mexican and Indonesian dishes. Burgers are named Firebolt and Stinky Pig. An in-house shop sells artisan bread, pastries and farm produce.

Open 12-11 summer (Tue-Fri 12-2 5.30-11 Sat-Sun 12-11 winter) Closed: Mon (winter only) **Bar Meals** L served 12-2 D served 6-9 **Restaurant** L served 12-2 D served 6-9 ⊕ FREE HOUSE ◀ Sharp's Own, Courage Directors, Timothy Taylor Landlord, Hop Back Summer Lightning ♂ Sharp's Orchard, Thatchers Gold, Healey's Cornish Rattler, Cornish Orchards. **Facilities** Non-diners area ❀ (Bar Restaurant Garden) ♦❙ Children's menu Children's portions Garden ⊼ Beer festival Cider festival Parking Wi-fi ▭ (notice required)

HELFORD PASSAGE   Map 2 SW72

The Ferryboat Inn

TR11 5LB ☎ 01326 250625
e-mail: manager@ferryboatinnhelford.com
dir: In village centre, 1st turn after Trebah Gardens

Wonderful views and great seafood

There are fabulous views over the Helford estuary from this waterside pub, which dates back 300 years. Whether it's a plate of oysters and a glass of fizz on the sunny, south-facing terrace or braised beef with horseradish mash by the warmth of the granite fireplace inside, this is a venue for all weathers. Everything is made on the premises and the Ferryboat burger is especially popular. The pub is owned by Wright Brothers, custodians of the Duchy of Cornwall's oyster farm, so the quality of the shellfish and seafood speaks for itself. Try beer battered Cornish haddock with chips, tartare sauce and mushy peas.

Open all day Closed: Mon (low season) **Restaurant** L served all wk 12-2.30 D served all wk 6-8.30 ⊕ ST AUSTELL ◀ Tribute, Dartmoor ♂ Healey's Cornish Rattler. **Facilities** Non-diners area ❀ (Bar Restaurant Outside area) ♦❙ Children's menu Children's portions Outside area ⊼ Parking Wi-fi ▭ (notice required)

HELSTON   Map 2 SW62

The Queens Arms ★★★ INN

Breage TR13 9PD ☎ 01326 573485
e-mail: chris-brazier@btconnect.com
dir: Village off A394 (Penzance to Helston). Pub adjacent to church

Home-cooked food and DIY barbecues

It's not so apparent from outside, but this is a 15th-century pub where the workmen building St Breaca's Church lived. Its age is more obvious indoors, particularly in the beamed, open-fired bar, where real ales include Penzance Brewing's Potion No 9. Simple home-cooked food makes good use of local produce, including allotment-grown vegetables. Bar and restaurant menus offer breaded wholetail scampi, chips and peas; Thai green chicken curry and rice; and roasted vegetables with fruited couscous. Added attractions are a DIY barbecue, children's play area and two en suite double rooms.

Open all wk Mon-Thu 11.30-3 5-11.30 (Fri-Sun 11.30-11.30) ⊕ PUNCH TAVERNS ◀ Sharp's Doom Bar, Penzance Potion No 9 ♂ Addlestones. **Facilities** ♦❙ Children's menu Children's portions Play area Garden Parking Wi-fi **Rooms** 2

KINGSAND
Map 3 SX45

The Halfway House Inn

Fore St PL10 1NA ☎ 01752 822279
e-mail: info@halfwayinn.biz
dir: *From Torpoint Ferry or Tamar Bridge follow signs to Mount Edgcumbe*

Cosy village inn on former border crossing

So named because the pub stands at the point that once marked the spot of the Devon and Cornwall border, this friendly inn has been serving locals and visitors since 1850. Hidden amongst the narrow lanes and colourful houses of a quaint fishing village, the stone-walled bar offers plenty of original fireplaces and beams, all of which makes for a relaxing place to enjoy a pint of Betty Stogs. Alternatively, you can tuck into locally caught mackerel, sea bass and crab in the cosy restaurant.

Open all wk **Bar Meals** L served all wk 11-2 D served all wk 6-9 **Restaurant** L served all wk 11-2 D served all wk 6-9 ⊕ FREE HOUSE ◀ Sharp's Doom Bar & Own, Skinner's, Betty Stogs, Guinness Ö Westons Stowford Press & Old Rosie. ♀ 12 **Facilities** Non-diners area ✿ (Bar) ♦♦ Children's menu Children's portions Wi-fi

LANLIVERY
Map 2 SX05

The Crown Inn
PICK OF THE PUBS

PL30 5BT ☎ 01208 872707
e-mail: thecrown@wagtailinns.com
dir: *Signed from A390. Follow brown sign approx 1.5m W of Lostwithiel*

One of Cornwall's oldest pubs

In a moorland village above a tributary of the Fowey River is this former longhouse, with characteristic thick stone walls, low beams, granite and slate floors, open fires and an unusual bread oven. Much of the present building dates from the 12th century, when it housed the stonemasons constructing the nearby church. The pub has been extensively but sympathetically restored over the years; at one point the work uncovered a deep well, now covered by glass, under the porch. With the sea only a few miles away, expect a menu offering plenty of fresh fish and seafood, as well as other local produce. A popular main course is Cornish ale-battered fish with chips, crushed peas and home-made tartare sauce. At lunchtime, enjoy a fresh Fowey crab sandwich or a proper Cornish pasty. Doom Bar ale comes from Sharp's in Rock and Betty Stogs (a character in Cornish folklore) from Skinner's of Truro. There is a lovely garden. Change of hands.

Open all day all wk **Bar Meals** food served all day **Restaurant** food served all day ⊕ FREE HOUSE ◀ Sharp's Doom Bar, Skinner's Betty Stogs, Guest ales Ö Westons 1st Quality. **Facilities** Non-diners area ✿ (Bar Garden) ♦♦ Children's menu Children's portions Garden ☎ Parking Wi-fi ▬ (notice required)

LOOE
Map 2 SX25

The Ship Inn ★★★ INN

Fore St PL13 1AD ☎ 01503 263124
dir: *In town centre*

Busy pub on a narrow street

This lively St Austell Brewery-owned pub stands on a corner in the heart of this charming old fishing town, a minute's walk from the working harbour. Locals and tourists join together in the appreciation of a pint of Tribute, and select their favourites from the menu – a burger or hot baguette for some, while others go for steak-and-ale pie or hunter's chicken. A quiz is held on Mondays throughout the year, live bands play regularly, and well-equipped bedrooms are available for those wanting to tarry awhile.

Open all day all wk **Bar Meals** food served all day ⊕ ST AUSTELL BREWERY ◀ Tribute, Tinners, HSD Ö Healey's Cornish Rattler. ♀ **Facilities** Non-diners area ✿ (Bar) ♦♦ Children's menu Children's portions Family room **Rooms** 8

LUDGVAN
Map 2 SW53

White Hart

Churchtown TR20 8EY ☎ 01736 740574
e-mail: info@whitehartludgvan.co.uk
dir: *From A30 take B3309 at Crowlas*

Lovely Cornish pub with a chalkboard full of home-made dishes

Standing opposite the church, the White Hart is one of the oldest pubs in Cornwall and retains the peaceful atmosphere of a bygone era. There are splendid views across St Michael's Mount, and a great selection of real ales is sold from the back of the bar. The food is as popular as ever, with choices such as duck stir-fry with egg noodles; roasted salmon fillet with mustard butter crust; and grilled goats' cheese with portabello mushroom and red pepper salad.

Open all wk 12-3 6-late **Bar Meals** L served all wk 12-2.30 D served all wk 6-9.30 **Restaurant** L served all wk 12-2.30 D served all wk 6-9.30 ⊕ PUNCH TAVERNS ◀ Sharp's Doom Bar, Skinner's Betty Stogs, Hamish Traditional Cornish Ale Ö Thatchers. ♀ 8 **Facilities** Non-diners area ♦♦ Children's portions Garden ☎ Parking ▬

LUXULYAN
Map 2 SX05

The Kings Arms **NEW**

Bridges PL30 5EF ☎ 01726 850202
e-mail: kingsarmsbridges@gmail.com
dir: *From A30 at Innis Downs junct take A39 signed St Austell. Left signed Luxulyan. Over railway & river. Inn on right at bottom of hill*

Well-kept beers, good pub grub and a friendly welcome

Walkers, cyclists, families, dog owners - all are most welcome at this stone-built village pub. Owned by St Austell Brewery, it offers their HSD, Trelawny and Tribute real ales, an occasional guest, and Thatchers Heritage and Cheddar Valley ciders; wine drinkers have a choice of 11 by the glass. The menu offers a selection of no-nonsense snacks and main meals that should leave everybody happy - steak-and-kidney pudding; Cornish sausages; surf and turf; cod Mornay; rabbit casserole; fisherman's and cottage pies; and vegetarian options. A takeaway service includes home-made pizzas.

Open all day all wk **Bar Meals** L served Mon-Sat 12-8, Sun 12-2 D served Mon-Sat 12-8, Sun 6-8 **Restaurant** L served Mon-Sat 12-8, Sun 12-2 D served Mon-Sat 12-8, Sun 6-8 ⊕ ST AUSTELL BREWERY ◀ HSD, Tribute, Trelawny, Proper Job Ö Thatchers Heritage & Cheddar Valley. ♀ 11 **Facilities** Non-diners area ✿ (Bar Restaurant Garden) ♦♦ Children's menu Children's portions Garden ☎ Parking Wi-fi ▬ (notice required)

MANACCAN
Map 2 SW72

The New Inn

TR12 6HA ☎ 01326 231323
e-mail: penny@stmartin.wanadoo.co.uk
dir: *7m from Helston*

Pretty pub, well worth seeking out

This thatched village pub, deep in Daphne du Maurier country near the Helford River, dates back to Cromwellian times, although obviously Cromwell forbade his men to drink here. Attractions include the homely bars and large, natural garden full of flowers. At lunchtime you might opt for a roast beef and horseradish sandwich, in the evening perhaps fillets of monkfish sautéed in a creamy Pernod sauce or steak and Stilton pie. There are separate menus dedicated to crab dishes and steaks.

Open all wk 12-3 6-11 (Sat-Sun all day in summer) ⊕ PUNCH TAVERNS ◀ Sharp's Doom Bar Ö Westons Stowford Press. **Facilities** ✿ (Bar Garden) ♦♦ Children's menu Play area Garden Parking

Save on hotels. Book at **theAA.com/hotel**

CORNWALL & ISLES OF SCILLY 83 **ENGLAND**

Godolphin Arms

TR17 0EN ☎ 01736 710202
e-mail: enquiries@godolphinarms.co.uk
dir: *From A30 just outside Penzance follow Marazion signs. Pub 1st large building on right in Marazion, opposite St Michael's Mount*

Pub with direct access to a large sandy beach

Standing atop the sea wall at the end of the causeway to St Michael's Mount, there are superb views across the bay from the traditional bar, restaurant and beer terrace of the Godolphin Arms. The sea is so close that it splashes at the windows in winter as you watch the fishing boats returning with their catch. Seafood from the Newlyn fish market is listed on the daily specials board; crab in particular is a speciality. Other options include traditional pub favourites like bangers and mash, or sample a Cornish cream tea in the afternoon. The Goldolphin offers Cornish ales and ciders.

Open all day all wk 8am-mdnt ⊕ FREE HOUSE ◀ St Austell Tribute, Sharp's Doom Bar, Skinner's Betty Stogs Ö Healey's Cornish Rattler, Cornish Orchard. **Facilities** ◀ Garden Parking

The Ship Inn

Fore St PL26 6UQ ☎ 01726 843324
dir: *7m S of St Austell*

A popular tavern a few steps from the harbour

This 400-year-old inn stands just a few yards from Mevagissey's picturesque fishing harbour, so the choice of fish and seafood dishes comes as no surprise on a menu of home-cooked dishes: moules marinière, beer-battered cod, and oven-baked fillet of haddock topped with prawns and Cornish Tiskey cheese. The popular bar has low-beamed ceilings, flagstone floors and a strong nautical feel.

Open all day all wk 11am-mdnt **Bar Meals** L served all wk 12-3 D served all wk 6-9 ⊕ ST AUSTELL BREWERY ◀ St Austell Ö Healey's Cornish Rattler. ⬥ 8 **Facilities** Non-diners area ⬥ (Bar) ◀ Children's menu

The Plume of Feathers ★★★★ INN

PICK OF THE PUBS

TR8 5AX ☎ 01872 510387
e-mail: theplume@hospitalitycornwall.com
dir: *From A30 follow Mitchell signs*

Friendly atmosphere in a historic inn

This charming 16th-century coaching inn is set in the quiet leafy village of Mitchell. It has a rich history – John Wesley preached about Methodism here while Sir Walter Raleigh lived close by – and is a welcoming place to eat and drink today, thanks to its beamed ceilings, real fires

and local artwork. The airy conservatory is also an appealing place to dine while seven stylish bedrooms provide the perfect overnight retreat. Local Cornish produce takes centre stage on the modern British menu and there's always a good showing of fish and locally reared meats. You might find Cornish crab and sweet potato fritters, lemongrass and coriander beurre blanc to start, followed by a chargrilled Cornish beefburger or oven-roasted fillet of local hake, chickpea, lime and herb crust, pak choi, noodles with coconut and coriander reduction. A beer garden, Cornish real ales and a beer festival in May all prove an additional draw.

Open all day all wk 9am-11pm/mdnt (25 Dec 11-4) **Bar Meals** L served all wk 12-6 D served all wk 6-10 food served all day **Restaurant** L served all wk 12-6 D served all wk 6-10 food served all day ⊕ FREE HOUSE ◀ Sharp's Doom Bar, John Smith's Extra Smooth, Skinner's Ö Cornish Orchards. **Facilities** Non-diners area ⬥ (Bar Garden) ◀ Play area Garden ⌂ Beer festival Parking **Rooms** 7

The Miners Arms

TR5 0QF ☎ 01872 552375
e-mail: minersarms@live.co.uk
dir: *From A30 at Chiverton Cross rdbt take A3075 signed Newquay. At Pendown Cross left onto B3284 signed Perranporth. Left, left again to Mithian*

Fascinating history at centuries' old pub

The curiously light interior of this historic 16th-century pub adds yet another layer of mystery to the legends of its past. Over the centuries it has served as a courthouse, a venue for inquests, a smugglers' lair and even a house of ill repute. Relax beneath the low-beamed ceilings while admiring the wall paintings of Elizabeth I, and choose from the menu of dishes freshly cooked to order from local produce: hake topped with pesto; steak of the day; vegetable tagine; and the Miners fish pie is a must.

Open all day all wk 12-11.30 ⊕ PUNCH TAVERNS ◀ Sharp's Doom Bar, Guest ales Ö Westons Stowford Press. **Facilities** ⬥ (Bar) ◀ Children's menu Children's portions Garden Parking

The Bush Inn

PICK OF THE PUBS

EX23 9SR ☎ 01288 331242
dir: *Exit A39, 3m N of Kilkhampton, 2nd right into Shop. 1.5m to Crosstown, pub on left*

Great local food close to dramatic coastal path

A 13th-century free house set in an isolated cliff-top hamlet between Bude and Hartland on a dramatic stretch of the north Cornish coast, The Bush Inn was a natural haunt for smugglers a couple of centuries ago. The historic interior features flagstone floors, old stone fireplaces and a 'leper's squint', a tiny window through which food scraps were passed for the needy. Cornish

ales are on tap, and menus featuring local produce are served all day, every day. The pub's kitchen garden is productive, and beef comes from the inn's own farm in Morwenstow. Venison and pheasant from local shoots are used in robust winter warmers, while summer days are ideal for a beetroot and Cornish Yarg salad or fillet of salmon with caper and anchovy butter. The large garden overlooking the beautiful Tidna Valley and Atlantic Ocean has wooden play equipment for children. Look out for the beer and cider festival.

Open all day all wk 11am-12.30am **Bar Meals** L served all wk D served all wk Av main course £14 food served all day **Restaurant** L served all wk D served all wk food served all day ⊕ FREE HOUSE ◀ St Austell HSD & Tribute, Skinner's Betty Stogs Ö Thatchers, Cornish Orchards. ⬥ 9 **Facilities** Non-diners area ⬥ (Bar Garden) ◀ Children's menu Children's portions Play area Garden ⌂ Beer festival Cider festival Parking Wi-fi ▭

The Pandora Inn

PICK OF THE PUBS

See Pick of the Pubs on page 84

The Lewinnick Lodge Bar & Restaurant ★★★★ RR

Pentire Headland TR7 1NX ☎ 01637 878117
e-mail: thelodge@hospitalitycornwall.com
dir: *From Newquay take Pentire Rd 0.5m, pub on right*

Recommended for its fresh fish and stunning views

An 18th-century cottage stood on the rugged Pentire Headland here, until the present owners built a contemporary bar and restaurant, which must have one of the best coastal vistas in the county. These panoramic Atlantic views are to be had from the terrace (which overhangs the ocean) and the floor-to-ceiling restaurant windows. With a reputation for modern British food, The Lewinnick offers a starter of roasted wood pigeon breast, followed perhaps by tiger prawn linguine - one of its signature dishes. Clotted cream rice pudding makes an indulgent dessert.

Open all day all wk **Bar Meals** L served all wk 12-5 D served all wk 5-10 food served all day **Restaurant** L served all wk 12-5 D served all wk 5-10 food served all day ⊕ FREE HOUSE ◀ Sharp's Doom Bar, Skinner's Betty Stogs Ö Cornish Orchards. ⬥ 8 **Facilities** Non-diners area ⬥ (Bar Garden) ◀ Children's menu Children's portions Garden ⌂ Parking Wi-fi ▭ **Rooms** 10

PICK OF THE PUBS

The Pandora Inn

MYLOR BRIDGE   Map 2 SW83

Restronguet Creek TR11 5ST
☎ **01326 372678**
e-mail: info@pandorainn.com
web: www.pandorainn.com
dir: *From Truro/Falmouth follow A39, left at Carclew, follow signs to pub*

Historic waterside inn

Until the early 20th century, the tidal Restronguet Creek played an important part in the export of tin and copper. Overlooking the water is this 13th-century inn, named after the ship sent to Tahiti in 1790 to bring back the mutinous crew of Capt Bligh's HMS *Bounty*. Unfortunately, the Pandora sank with considerable loss of life on the Great Barrier Reef and its captain was eventually court-martialled. He subsequently bought the inn. Thatched, with low-beamed ceilings and flagstone floors, it was badly damaged by fire in 2011, but reopened a year later after careful restoration. The ground floor is largely unchanged, but it's a different story upstairs, where although ugly 1970s additions disappeared for good, a combination of listed building status and the wishes of long-term proprietors John Milan and Steve Bellman ensured the rest was restored using only traditional materials and building methods. An example is the vaulted dining area, where green-oak beams have been wooden-pegged the medieval

way. A few scorched sections of timber serve as reminders of what was lost. In the kitchen chef Tom Milby knows the area like the back of his oven glove and sources the freshest produce from local farmers, growers and fishermen. "What can be better than buying fish and shellfish off the boat as they land it on the Pandora's own pontoon?", he asks. Dine on that very pontoon, at a table by the water's edge, or in one of the series of little rooms inside, perhaps on seared Cornish scallops and langoustines, followed by slow-roasted pork belly, or home-smoked chicken breast. Alternatively, start with Mylor-smoked mackerel fillet, then pan-fried Cornish lamb's liver and bacon. Real ales come from the St Austell Brewery, and the ciders are Cornish Rattler.

Open all day all wk 10.30am-11pm **Bar Meals** L served all wk 10.30-9.30 D served all wk 10.30-9.30 food served all day **Restaurant** food served all day ⊕ ST AUSTELL BREWERY ◀ HSD, Tribute, Proper Job & Trelawny Ŏ Healey's Cornish Rattler & Pear Rattler. ⬗ 17 **Facilities** Non-diners area 🐾 (Bar) ♦ Children's menu & portions Outside area ⋔ Parking Wi-fi 🚐

PAR
Map 2 SX05

The Britannia Inn & Restaurant ★★★★ INN NEW

St Austell Rd PL24 2SL ☎ 01726 812889
e-mail: info@britanniainn.com
dir: On A390 between St Austell & St Blazey

A family-owned inn with large garden

Three generations of the Rawlings family have so far held the keys to this 16th-century free house, where Sharp's Doom Bar and St Austell Tribute real ales, and Healey's Rattler cider declare its loyalty to the Royal Duchy. The three dining areas do likewise by offering prime-cut Cornish steaks and other locally sourced dishes, typically battered cod and chips; lamb rogan josh with chickpeas and spinach; home-made beef stew with herb dumplings; and pesto chicken with penne pasta and red peppers. Special deals are available on Tuesday grill nights. Guest rooms are named after Cornish locations.

Open all day all wk **Bar Meals** L served all wk 12-9
D served all wk 12-9 food served all day **Restaurant** L
served all wk 12-2.30 D served all wk 6-9 ⊕ FREE HOUSE
◖ Sharp's Doom Bar, St Austell Tribute, Bass
Ỏ Thatchers Gold, Healey's Cornish Rattler. ₸
Facilities Non-diners area ♦♦ Children's menu Children's
portions Play area Family room Garden ㅈ Parking Wi-fi
🚌 (notice required) **Rooms** 5

The Royal Inn ★★★★ INN

66 Eastcliffe Rd PL24 2AJ ☎ 01726 815601
e-mail: info@royal-inn.co.uk
dir: A3082 Par, follow brown tourist signs for 'Newquay Branch line' or railway station. Pub opposite rail station

Welcoming pub on the Rail Trail

Originally frequented by travellers and employees of the Great Western Railway, this 19th-century inn was named after a visit by King Edward VII to a local copper mine. The pub is now on the Atlantic Coast Line of the 'Rail Ale Trail', and the building is much extended, with an open-plan bar serving a variety of real ales. Leading off are the dining areas which comprise a cosy beamed room and conservatory. The long bar menu offers everything from pizzas and burgers to salads and omelettes. The restaurant menu includes ham hock terrine, whole lemon sole with spicy prawn butter; and steaks with all the trimmings. Fifteen comfortable rooms are available.

Open all day all wk 11.30-11 (Sun 12-10.30) **Bar Meals** L
served all wk 12-2 D served all wk 6.30-9 **Restaurant** L
served all wk 12-2 D served all wk 6.30-9 ⊕ FREE HOUSE
◖ Sharp's Doom Bar & Special, Wells Bombardier,
Shepherd Neame Spitfire, Cotleigh Barn Owl Ỏ Healey's
Cornish Rattler, Thatchers Gold. ₸ 13
Facilities Non-diners area ♣ (Bar Garden) ♦♦ Children's
menu Children's portions Garden ㅈ Parking Wi-fi 🚌
Rooms 15

PENZANCE
Map 2 SW43

The Coldstreamer Inn ★★★ INN ◉

Gulval TR18 3BB ☎ 01736 362072
e-mail: info@coldstreamer-penzance.co.uk
dir: From Penzance take B3311 towards St Ives. In Gulval right into School Ln. Pub in village centre

Expect the best local produce at this traditional village inn

Young Tom Penhaul is cooking up a storm at this unassuming inn tucked away in a sleepy village close to Penzance and the heliport. In keeping with the contemporary dining room – smart decor, pine tables, wooden floors – menus are modern and evolve with the seasons, with quality, fresh local produce key to Tom's innovative dishes. Tuck into squid and red wine stew or smoked haddock croquettes to start; then follow with lemon sole, parsley potatoes, greens, prawns and wild mushrooms; or squash, sage and Cornish feta arancini. Round things off with some warm almond cake and poached pear or dark chocolate mousse with orange curd and praline. Excellent light lunches, a cracking bar with local ales and traditional bar games, and contemporary bedrooms complete the picture.

Open all day all wk **Bar Meals** L served all wk 12-3
D served all wk 6-9.30 (summer), 6-9 (winter) Av main
course £10-£14 **Restaurant** L served all wk 12-3 D served
all wk 6-9.30 (summer), 6-9 (winter) Fixed menu price fr
£14.50 Av 3 course à la carte fr £21 ⊕ PUNCH TAVERNS
◖ Skinner's Ginger Tosser, Bays Topsail, Guest ale. ₸ 12
Facilities Non-diners area ♣ (Bar Outside area) ♦♦
Children's menu Children's portions Outside area ㅈ Wi-fi
🚌 (notice required) **Rooms** 3

Dolphin Tavern ★★★ INN

Quay St TR18 4BD ☎ 01736 364106
e-mail: dolphin@tiscali.co.uk
dir: From rail station follow road along harbour. Tavern on corner opposite Scilonian Ferry Terminal

Interesting history and fish always on the menu

Sir Walter Raleigh is said to have smoked the first pipe of tobacco in England at this lovely 16th-century pub, the central part of which was once used as a courtroom by Judge Jeffreys. These days, the Dolphin serves great home-made food accompanied by a full range of St Austell beers, plus accommodation. Fresh, locally caught fish features on the daily specials board, and the menu offers a tempting selection of meat, vegetarian and children's dishes. A typical menu might feature steak and ale pie or Newlyn crab salad.

Open all day all wk Closed: 25 Dec **Bar Meals** food served
all day **Restaurant** food served all day ⊕ ST AUSTELL
BREWERY ◖ HSD, Tinners Ale, Tribute Ỏ Healey's Cornish
Rattler. ₸ 10 **Facilities** Non-diners area ♦♦ Children's
menu Children's portions Play area Family room Garden
Wi-fi 🚌 **Rooms** 2

The Turks Head Inn

Chapel St TR18 4AF ☎ 01736 363093
e-mail: turks@fsmail.net
dir: Telephone for directions

Historic tucked-away town pub

This popular terraced side-street local is the oldest pub in Penzance, dating from around 1233, and was the first in the country to be given the Turks Head name. Sadly, a Spanish raiding party destroyed much of the original building in the 16th century, but an old smugglers' tunnel leading directly to the harbour still exists. Wash down hearty pub food – steaks, burgers, fish pie – or perhaps seafood broth, green Thai monkfish curry or braised lamb shank, with a cracking pint of Sharp's Doom Bar, best enjoyed in the sunny flower-filled garden. Don't miss the annual beer festival.

Open all day all wk **Bar Meals** L served all wk 12-2.30
D served all wk 6-10 Av main course £9.95 **Restaurant** L
served all wk 12-2.30 D served all wk 6-10 Fixed menu
price fr £10 Av 3 course à la carte fr £21 ⊕ PUNCH
TAVERNS ◖ Sharp's Doom Bar, Turk's Head Ale
Ỏ Westons Old Rosie. ₸ 12 **Facilities** Non-diners area
♣ (Bar Restaurant Garden) ♦♦ Children's menu Children's
portions Family room Garden ㅈ Beer festival Wi-fi
🚌 (notice required)

PERRANUTHNOE
Map 2 SW52

The Victoria Inn ★★★ INN ◉

PICK OF THE PUBS

TR20 9NP ☎ 01736 710309
e-mail: enquiries@victoriainn-penzance.co.uk
dir: Exit A394 (Penzance to Helston road), signed Perranuthnoe

Ancient pub in coastal village

With a history spanning nine centuries, this striking, pink-washed village inn is probably Cornwall's oldest public house. Decorated with seafaring memorabilia, its typically Cornish, stone-walled bar attracts families strolling up from Perran Sands and walkers from the South West Coast Path. Cornish real ales, lager and cider have a complete monopoly in the wood-fire-warmed, softly lit bar; outside is a Mediterranean-style patio garden. Chef-proprietor Stewart Eddy (who runs the pub with his wife, Anna) cooks AA Rosette-standard local fish, seafood, meats and other quality dishes featuring on a menu listing honey-roasted duck breast and confit leg; slow-cooked pork belly and roasted pork fillet with black pudding; Provençal fish stew; and roasted tomatoes, aubergines and olives with crispy polenta. Lunch possibilities are chargrilled rib-eye steak; St Buryan pork sausages with bubble-and-squeak; and ham, free-range eggs and chips. Overnight guests can stay in smart en suite bedrooms.

Open 12-3 6.30-11 (Jun-Sep all day) Closed: 25-26 Dec,
1 Jan, 1wk Jan, Sun eve & Mon (off season) **Bar Meals** L
served Mon-Sat 12-2, Sun 12-3 D served all wk 6.30-9
Restaurant L served Mon-Sat 12-2, Sun 12-2.30 D served

continued

PERRANUTHNOE *continued*

all wk 6.30-9 ⊕ FREE HOUSE ◀ Sharp's Doom Bar, St Austell Tribute, Skinner's Betty Stogs, Cornish Chough Serpentine ♂ Healey's Cornish Orchards.
Facilities Non-diners area ♦️ Children's menu Children's portions Garden ⌠ Parking Wi-fi **Rooms** 2

PHILLEIGH
Map 2 SW83

Roseland Inn

TR2 5NB ☎ **01872 580254**
dir: *From Truro take A39 towards Falmouth. Left onto B3289 towards St Mawes. Left at sharp right bend for Philleigh*

Traditional Cornish pub with welcoming, cosy interior

Phil and Debbie Heslip take pride in the quality of their home-prepared modern British cooking at this highly appealing, rural 16th-century inn. The character of the interior owes much to the low-beamed ceilings, brassware, paintings and prints. Phil brews his ornithologically themed Cornish Shag, Chough to Bits and High-as-a-Kite beers on site. So, in winter cosy up to the fire for a drink or a meal prepared using the best of local Cornish produce, or in warmer weather head outside to the picnic tables. Just to the west is the famous King Harry Ferry over the River Fal.

Open all wk 11-3 6-11.30 ⊕ PUNCH TAVERNS ◀ Skinner's Betty Stogs, Roseland Cornish Shag, High-as-a-Kite & Chough to Bits ♂ Westons Stowford Press. **Facilities** ♦️ Children's menu Children's portions Garden Parking Wi-fi

---

POLKERRIS
Map 2 SX05

The Rashleigh Inn

PL24 2TL ☎ **01726 813991**
e-mail: jonspode@aol.com
dir: *Off A3082 outside Fowey*

Right on the beach

Once a coastguard station, this 300-year-old pub at the end of a no-through road to Polkerris beach faces west, so watching the sun set over St Austell Bay is a delight. In the bar there's a good selection of real ales from Cornwall and elsewhere, real cider, local organic soft drinks and a water bowl and Bonio biscuits for visiting dogs. Good, locally sourced food is typically slow-roasted Cornish belly pork; pan-fried fillet of wild sea bass; roasted darnes of gurnard; mushroom ravioli; and tapas, served on a slate platter.

Open all day all wk **Bar Meals** L served all wk 12-3, snacks 3-5 D served all wk 6-9 **Restaurant** L served all wk 12-3, snacks 3-5 D served all wk 6-9 ⊕ FREE HOUSE ◀ Timothy Taylor Landlord, Skinner's Betty Stogs, St Austell HSD, Otter Bitter, Black Sheep Best Bitter, Young's Special ♂ Westons Stowford Press, Addlestones. ☻ 11 **Facilities** Non-diners area ♣ (Bar Garden) ♦️ Children's menu Children's portions Garden ⌠ Parking Wi-fi

---

POLPERRO
Map 2 SX25

Old Mill House Inn

Mill Hill PL13 2RP ☎ **01503 272362**
e-mail: enquiries@oldmillhouseinn.co.uk
dir: *Telephone for directions*

Local food and ale in a 17th-century pub

In the heart of historic Polperro, this old inn was once the house and storage area of a grain mill built in the early 17th century. It has survived serious flood damage in the past – photographs recording the disaster can be seen on the walls. Here you can sample well-kept local ales and cider beside a log fire in the bar, or sit out over lunch in the riverside garden during fine weather. Local ingredients appear on the menu where you might find a seafood platter for sharing; trio of Cornish sausages and mash or home-made game pie. A beer festival is held on the first weekend in October.

Open all day all wk 10am-12.30am (Sun 10am-11.30pm) **Bar Meals** Av main course £5.50 **Restaurant** D served all wk 5.30-9 in season Av 3 course à la carte fr £16 ⊕ FREE HOUSE ◀ Skinner's Mill House Ale, Sharp's Doom Bar ♂ Westons Stowford Press & Cornish Orchards. **Facilities** Non-diners area ♣ (Bar Restaurant Garden) ♦️ Children's menu Children's portions Garden ⌠ Beer festival Wi-fi

---

PORT GAVERNE
Map 2 SX08

Port Gaverne Hotel

PICK OF THE PUBS

PL29 3SQ ☎ **01208 880244**
e-mail: graham@port-gaverne-hotel.co.uk
dir: *Signed from B3314, S of Delabole via B3267, E of Port Isaac*

Plenty of local fish and seafood on the menu

Walkers from the Heritage Coastal Path are always pausing for a pint of St Austell Tribute or Cornish Orchard cider in the small beer garden of this delightful 17th-century inn. The secluded cove just down from the pub is where women once loaded sea-bound ketches with slate from the great quarry at Delabole. But after the railway arrived in 1893, sea trade declined and tranquility returned to the port. The bar has slate floors (naturally), low wooden beams and the customary log fire. Locally supplied produce includes plenty of fresh fish, destined to appear, for example, as crab and prawn terrine with Marie Rose sauce, or whole grilled lemon sole topped with lemon and capers. Other possibilities include baked breast of chicken with root vegetable purée and a mushroom cream sauce or baked stuffed aubergine topped with goats' cheese. Home-made puddings are supplemented with Cornish ice creams.

Open all day all wk **Bar Meals** L served all wk 12-2.30 D served all wk 6-9 Av main course £9.95 **Restaurant** D served all wk 7-9 ⊕ FREE HOUSE ◀ Sharp's Doom Bar & Cornish Coaster, St Austell Tribute ♂ Cornish Orchards. ☻ 9

Facilities Non-diners area ♣ (Bar Garden) ♦️ Children's menu Children's portions Garden Parking Wi-fi ▭

PORTHLEVEN
Map 2 SW62

The Ship Inn

TR13 9JS ☎ **01326 564204**
e-mail: theshipinnporthleven@gmail.com
dir: *From Helston follow signs to Porthleven, 2.5m. On entering village continue to harbour. Take W road by side of harbour to inn*

Unspoilt pub in an unspoilt fishing port

Dating from the 17th century, this smugglers' inn is actually built into the cliffs, and is approached by a flight of stone steps. During the winter, two log fires warm the interior, while the flames of a third flicker in the separate Smithy children's room. Expect a good selection of locally caught fish and seafood, such as crab and prawn mornay, or the smoked fish platter, all smoked in Cornwall. The pub has declared itself a 'chip-free zone'.

Open all day all wk 11.30-11.30 (Sun 12-10.30) **Bar Meals** L served all wk 12-2 D served all wk 6.30-9 ⊕ FREE HOUSE ◀ Courage Best, Sharp's Doom Bar, Guest ales ♂ Cornish Orchards. **Facilities** Non-diners area ♣ (Bar Restaurant Garden) ♦️ Children's menu Family room Garden ⌠

PORT ISAAC
Map 2 SW98

The Slipway **NEW**

Harbour Front PL29 3RH ☎ **01208 880264**
e-mail: slipway@portisaachotel.com
dir: *From A39 take B3314 signed Port Isaac. Through Delabole & Pendoggett, right onto B3267. 2m to Port Isaac, pass Co-op on right, 100mtrs into Back Hill (one way) to harbour (NB no parking by hotel; car park at top of village)*

Harbourside pub noted for fish and seafood

With a reputation for seriously good fresh fish and seafood, this 16th-century, one-time ship's chandlery could hardly be closer to Port Isaac's tiny harbour. Cornish Orchards cider, and real ales from Tintagel and Sharp's breweries are on handpump in the bar, while in the heavy-beamed, galleried restaurant locally sourced dishes include bouillabaisse; whole roasted plaice; Cornish sirloin and venison steaks; and wild mushroom and rocket tagliatelle. On summer evenings the covered terrace overlooking the harbour is the perfect place to dine and enjoy music from the local bands.

Open all day all wk Closed: 25 Dec **Bar Meals** L served all wk 12-2.30 D served all wk 6.30-8.30 (9 summer) **Restaurant** L served all wk 12-2.30 D served all wk 6.30-8.30 (9 summer) ◀ Tintagel Harbour Special, Sharp's Doom Bar ♂ Cornish Orchards. **Facilities** Non-diners area ♣ (Bar Outside area) ♦️ Children's menu Children's portions Outside area ⌠ Wi-fi

PORTREATH	Map 2 SW64

Basset Arms

Tregea Ter TR16 4NG ☎ 01209 842077
e-mail: bassettarms@btconnect.com
dir: *From Redruth take B3300 to Portreath. Pub on left near seafront*

Local seafood a specialty

Built as a pub to serve harbour workers, at one time this early 19th-century Cornish stone cottage served as a mortuary for ill-fated seafarers, so there are plenty of ghost stories! Tin-mining and shipwreck paraphernalia adorn the low-beamed interior of the bar where you can wash down a meal with a pint of Skinner's real ale. The menu makes the most of local seafood, such as seafood stew; and home-made fish pie, but also provides a wide selection of alternatives, including steak and ale pie; gammon steak with pineapple, egg, chips and peas; and home-made mushroom Stroganoff.

Open all day all wk 11-11 (Fri-Sat 11am-mdnt Sun 11-10.30) **Bar Meals** L served all wk 12-2, Summer 12-3 D served all wk 6-9, Summer 5-9 **Restaurant** L served all wk 12-2, Summer 12-3 D served all wk 6-9, Summer 5-9 ⊕ FREE HOUSE ◀ Sharp's Doom Bar, Skinner's ♻ Thatchers Gold. **Facilities** Non-diners area ♥ (Bar Outside area) ◀ Children's menu Children's portions Play area Outside area ♔ Parking ⬛ (notice required)

RUAN LANIHORNE	Map 2 SW84

The Kings Head

TR2 5NX ☎ 01872 501263
e-mail: contact@kings-head-roseland.co.uk
dir: *3m from Tregony Bridge on A3078*

Country pub with delightful summer garden

This traditional country pub set deep in the Roseland countryside has a warm and welcoming atmosphere. Roaring winter fires, beamed ceilings and mulled wine contrast with summer days relaxing on the terrace with a jug of Pimm's, a pint of Betty Stogs or Stowford Press cider. Whatever the time of year, the chef responds with seasonal dishes using the best of local produce, ranging from duo of Cornish sausages and prime Cornish steaks to Mediterranean chicken, and fish pie. Look out for the signature dish, too – slow-roasted Terras Ruan duckling with pepper sauce.

Open 12-2.30 6-11 Closed: Sun eve, Mon (Oct-Etr) **Restaurant** L served all wk 12.30-2 D served all wk 6.30-9 ⊕ FREE HOUSE ◀ Skinner's Kings Ruan & Betty Stogs ♻ Westons Stowford Press. ♚ 9 **Facilities** Non-diners area ◀ Garden ♔ Parking

ST AGNES	Map 3 SW75

Driftwood Spars ★★★★ GA

PICK OF THE PUBS

Trevaunance Cove TR5 0RT ☎ 01872 552428
e-mail: info@driftwoodspars.co.uk
dir: *A30 onto B3285, through St Agnes, down steep hill, left at Peterville Inn, follow Trevaunance Cove sign*

Ideal for coastal path walkers

Complete with its own smugglers' tunnel, this family-run pub occupies a 300-year-old tin miners' store, chandlery and sail loft adjacent to the South West Coastal Path in the stunning Trevaunance Cove. Altogether this establishment comprises 15 bedrooms (some with stunning sea views); a dining room with sea view; two beer gardens; three bars sparkling with real fires, old brass and lanterns; a microbrewery; and a shop. Among the seven hand-pulled real ales are some of the 11 quality beers brewed on site, including Driftwood Spars Montol, a 35-bin wine list, 35 malts and an impressive selection of 'alcoholic curiosities'. On the menu, seafood figures strongly and the Sunday roast comes highly recommended. Tempting desserts might include saffron bread-and-butter pudding with vanilla bean ice cream. There is a mini beer festival mid-March and on May Day Bank Holiday weekend.

Open all day all wk 11-11 (Fri-Sat 11am-1am 25 Dec 11am-2pm) **Bar Meals** L served all wk 12-2.30 D served all wk 6.30-9.30 (winter 6.30-8.30) ⊕ FREE HOUSE ◀ Driftwood Spars Montol, Sharp's Doom Bar, Guest ales ♻ Healey's Cornish Rattler, Thatchers, Cornish Orchards. ♚ 9 **Facilities** Non-diners area ♥ (Bar Garden) ◀ Children's menu Children's portions Garden Outside area ♔ Beer festival Parking Wi-fi ⬛ (notice required) **Rooms** 15

ST BREWARD	Map 2 SX07

The Old Inn & Restaurant

Churchtown, Bodmin Moor PL30 4PP ☎ 01208 850711
e-mail: theoldinn@macace.net
dir: *A30 to Bodmin. 16m, right just after Temple, follow signs to St Breward. B3266 (Bodmin to Camelford road) turn to St Breward, follow brown signs*

Ancient inn high on the moor

On the edge of Bodmin Moor, this is not just Cornwall's highest inn (720ft above sea level), it's one of the oldest too, having been built in the 11th century for monks to live in. It's believed to have been a pub since the 15th century, although records only go back to 1806. You can see ancient granite fireplaces and sloping ceilings in the bars, where Sharp's Doom Bar and Orchard cider are in the line-up. Mixed grills, over 25 daily changing specials, a pie of the day, locally caught fish, and all-day Sunday carvery are served in the bars, spacious restaurant or large garden. Cream teas are also a speciality.

Open all day all wk **Bar Meals** L served Sun-Fri 11-2, Sat 11-9 D served Sun-Fri 6-9, Sat 11-9 **Restaurant** L served Mon-Fri 11-2, Sat-Sun 12-9 D served Mon-Fri 6-9, Sat-

Sun 12-9 ⊕ FREE HOUSE ◀ Sharp's Doom Bar & Special, Guest ales ♻ Sharp's Orchard. ♚ 15 **Facilities** Non-diners area ♥ (Bar Garden) ◀ Children's menu Children's portions Family room Garden Parking Wi-fi ⬛

ST EWE	Map 2 SW94

The Crown Inn

PL26 6EY ☎ 01726 843322
e-mail: phigham@fsmail.co.uk
dir: *From St Austell take B3273. At Tregiskey x-rds turn right. St Ewe signed on right*

Picture-postcard village inn

This pretty 16th-century village inn is only a mile away from the famous 'Lost Gardens of Heligan'. Rest and refuel by the fire in the traditional bar or relax in the peaceful flower-festooned garden in summer. Quaff a pint of St Austell ale and tuck into a hearty lunchtime bar snack or look to the board for evening specials like pan-fried kidneys with pepper sauce; hake with mussels, crushed potatoes and fish cream; or seared lamb rump with sweet potato mash and minted gravy.

Open all wk 12-2.30 5.30-close (summer all day) ⊕ ST AUSTELL BREWERY ◀ Tribute, Tinners Ale & Proper Job, Guest ale ♻ Healey's Cornish Rattler. **Facilities** ♥ (Bar Garden) ◀ Children's menu Children's portions Play area Family room Garden Parking Wi-fi

ST IVES	Map 2 SW54

The Queens ★★★★ INN ⊚

2 High St TR26 1RR ☎ 01736 796468
e-mail: info@queenshotelstives.com
dir: *5min walk from St Ives Station*

Winning combination of fine food and stylish accommodation

There's an easy-going mix of chic, contemporary design with a nod to times past in this thriving gastro-pub at the heart of the old town. It's worth the stroll from the harbour or the resort's beaches to discover this solid granite-built, late-Georgian building, where local art works vie for attention with local cider, Cornish beers and a great menu inspired by the wealth of the county's larder. Herb-roasted hake; Newlyn crab, or beef, venison and pheasant pie example the mains; a chalkboard holds much additional promise. Some of the ten stylish bedrooms have views over Carbis Bay.

Open all day all wk **Bar Meals** L served Mon-Sat 12-2.30, Sun 12-4 D served Mon-Sat 6.30-9.30 Av main course £12 ⊕ ST AUSTELL BREWERY ◀ Tribute, HSD ♻ Healey's Cornish Rattler. ♚ 16 **Facilities** Non-diners area ♥ (Bar Restaurant) ◀ Children's portions Wi-fi ⬛ (notice required) **Rooms** 10

ST IVES *continued*

The Sloop Inn ★★★ INN

The Wharf TR26 1LP ☎ **01736 796584**
e-mail: sloopinn@btinternet.com
dir: On St Ives harbour by middle slipway

Famous St Ives inn by picturesque harbour

A trip to St Ives wouldn't be complete without visiting this 700-year-old pub perched right on the harbourside. Slate floors, beamed ceilings and nautical artefacts dress some of the several bars and dining areas, whilst the cobbled forecourt is an unbeatable spot for people- and harbour-watching, preferably with a pint of local Doom Bar. The menu majors on local seafood, from line-caught St Ives Bay mackerel and fries to home-made Newlyn cod, smoked haddock and smoked bacon fishcakes. Most of the comfortably appointed bedrooms overlook the pretty bay.

Open all day all wk **Bar Meals** L served all wk 12-3 D served all wk 5-10 **Restaurant** D served Mon-Sat 6-10 ⊕ ENTERPRISE INNS ◀ Sharp's Doom Bar ⁑ Thatchers Gold. **Facilities** Non-diners area ❖ Outside area ⋒ Wi-fi ▭ (notice required) **Rooms** 18

The Watermill

Lelant Downs, Hayle TR27 6LQ ☎ **01736 757912**
e-mail: watermill@btconnect.com
dir: Exit A30 at junct for St Ives/A3074, turn left at 2nd mini rdbt

Converted mill with food to suit everyone

Set in extensive gardens on the old St Ives coach road, with glorious valley views towards Trencrom Hill, The Watermill is a cosy, family-friendly pub and restaurant created in the 18th-century Lelant Mill. The old mill machinery is still in place and the iron waterwheel continues to turn, gravity fed by the mill stream. Downstairs is the old beamed bar and wood-burning stove, while upstairs in the open-beamed mill loft is the atmospheric restaurant where steaks and fish (sea bass, sardines and mackerel perhaps) are specialities. There are beer festivals in June and November with live music all weekend.

Open all day all wk 12-11 **Bar Meals** L served all wk 12-2.30 D served all wk 6-9 **Restaurant** D served all wk 6-9 ⊕ FREE HOUSE ◀ Sharp's Doom Bar, Skinner's Betty Stogs, Guest ales ⁑ Healey's Cornish Rattler. **Facilities** Non-diners area ❖ (Bar Garden) ❦ Children's menu Play area Garden ⋒ Beer festival Parking ▭

Star Inn

TR19 7LL ☎ **01736 788767**
dir: Telephone for directions

A Cornish star for beer and music

Plenty of tin-mining and fishing stories are told at this town pub near Land's End. It dates back a few centuries, and was reputedly built to house workmen constructing the 15th-century church. John Wesley is believed to have been among the Star's more illustrious guests over the years, but these days the pub is most likely to be recognised for having featured in several television and film productions due to its immense charm and character. A choice of local St Austell beers is served, but there is no food. There's live music in a whole range of styles, including folk.

Open all day all wk 11am-12.30am ⊕ ST AUSTELL BREWERY ◀ HSD, Tinners Ale, Tribute, Dartmoor, Proper Job ⁑ Healey's Cornish Rattler. **Facilities** ❖ (Bar Garden) ❦ Family room Garden **Notes** ⊛

The Wellington

Market Square TR19 7HD ☎ **01736 787319**
e-mail: wellington.hotel@ymail.com
dir: Take A30 to Penzance, then A3071 W of Penzance to St Just

A good place to relax after exploring the western peninsula

Standing in the market square of the historic mining town of St Just, this family-run inn makes an ideal base for visiting Land's End and St Ives, as well as exploring the spectacular beaches and countryside – walking, climbing and bird-watching. Low ceilings, solid stonework and a secluded walled garden help evoke the atmosphere of Cornwall as it once was. St Austell beers and Cornish Rattler cider are served in the bar, while the menu offers a selection of grills, pasta dishes, sandwiches, daily specials, traditional pub dishes, and the popular Welly burger – either beef or vegetarian.

Open all day all wk ⊕ ST AUSTELL BREWERY ◀ Dartmoor, Tribute, HSD ⁑ Healey's Cornish Rattler. **Facilities** ❦ Children's menu Children's portions Play area Garden Wi-fi

---

St Kew Inn

Churchtown PL30 3HB ☎ **01208 841259**
e-mail: stkewinn@btconnect.com
dir: From Wadebridge N on A39. Left to St Kew

A chocolate-box village pub

Built in the 15th-century, in summer the pretty façade of this stone-built pub is enhanced with flower tubs and creepers. Inside, traditional features include a huge open fire. Cornish St Austell beers and Rattler cider are the prime refreshments, while menus proffer carefully sourced and prepared British dishes (often featuring fish

---

and seafood) with cosmopolitan touches. Choose between four eating areas – five if you include the garden – when ordering your lunchtime snack of potted brown shrimp. Alternatively, in the evening try the pork Stroganoff with noodles or the Porthilly mussels, followed by marmalade pudding with custard. Set menus are available.

Open all wk 11-3 5.30-11 (summer all day) **Bar Meals** L served all wk 12-2, summer all day D served all wk 6-9, summer all day **Restaurant** L served all wk 12-2, summer all day D served all wk 6-9, summer all day ⊕ ST AUSTELL BREWERY ◀ Tribute, HSD, Proper Job ⁑ Healey's Cornish Rattler. **Facilities** Non-diners area ❖ (Bar Garden) ❦ Children's menu Children's portions Family room Garden ⋒ Parking Wi-fi

The Victory Inn

PICK OF THE PUBS

Victory Hill TR2 5DQ ☎ **01326 270324**
e-mail: contact@victory-inn.co.uk
dir: A3078 to St Mawes. Pub adjacent to harbour

Seafood takes top billing on the menus

Named after Nelson's flagship, this friendly fishermen's local near the harbour adopts a modern approach to its daily lunch and dinner menus. You may eat downstairs in the traditional bar, or in the modern and stylish first-floor Seaview Restaurant (white walls, white linen and wicker chairs), with a terrace that looks across the town's rooftops to the harbour and the River Fal. High on the list of ingredients is fresh seafood – all from Cornish waters – the choice changing daily to include crab risotto, fisherman's pie, and beer-battered cod and hand-cut chips, with chicken breast cordon bleu, lamb shank Provençale, and curry or casserole of the day among the other favourites. Wines are all carefully chosen and excellent in quality, as are the real ales from Cornwall's own Roseland, Sharp's and Skinner's breweries. There is outside seating with views over the harbour. Booking for meals is definitely advisable in the summer.

Open all day all wk 11am-mdnt **Bar Meals** L served all wk 12-3 D served all wk 6-9.30 **Restaurant** L served all wk 12-3 D served all wk 6-9.30 ⊕ PUNCH TAVERNS ◀ Roseland Cornish Shag, Skinner's Betty Stogs, Sharp's Doom Bar ⁑ Westons Stowford Press, Thatchers Heritage. **Facilities** Non-diners area ❖ (Bar Garden) ❦ Children's menu Children's portions Garden ⋒ Wi-fi ▭

The Falcon Inn ★★★★ INN

PICK OF THE PUBS

See Pick of the Pubs on opposite page

PICK OF THE PUBS

The Falcon Inn ★★★★ INN

ST MAWGAN   Map 2 SW86

TR8 4EP ☎ 01637 860225
e-mail:
thefalconinnstmawgan@gmail.com
web: www.thefalconinnstmawgan.co.uk
dir: *From A30 (8m W of Bodmin) follow
signs to Newquay Airport. Turn right
200mtrs before airport terminal into
St Mawgan, pub at bottom of hill*

Traditional Cornish village inn

This wisteria-clad, stone-built inn
situated in the Vale of Lanherne is just
four miles from Newquay. It can trace
its ancestry back as far as 1758, but is
thought to be even older. By 1813 the
pub had been renamed more than once,
and in about 1880 it changed again to
The Falcon Inn, an allusion to the nearby
estate's coat of arms. Throughout much
of the 20th century the inn was run by
members of the Fry family; the present
innkeepers are David Carbis and Sarah
Lawrence. The Falcon's interior is cosy
and relaxed, with flagstone floors and
log fires in winter; there's a large
attractive garden, magnificent magnolia
tree and cobbled courtyard for alfresco
summer dining. An ever-changing
selection of predominantly West Country
real ales is augmented by Old Rosie
cider, and a dozen wines are served by
the glass. Lunchtime brings snacks like
Cornish pasty and spicy Indonesian crab

cakes, plus an appetising range of
sandwiches. There's also a good choice
of home-made hot dishes such as
breaded scampi, and a different soup,
pâté, pie, fish and curry every day. The
evening menu is served in the more
formal restaurant; main courses include
seafood linguine, jambalaya, rump
steak and roast loin of pedigree pork.
Slow-roasted leg of lamb with butternut
squash mash and red wine gravy; or
West Country mussels could be on the
specials menu. Comfortable,
individually furnished en suite
bedrooms are also available, and events
like charity quiz nights run throughout
the year. Contact the pub for details of
the beer festival.

Open all wk 11-3 6-11 (Jul-Aug all day)
Closed: 25 Dec (open 12-2) **Bar Meals** L
served all wk 12-2 D served all wk 6-9
Restaurant L served all wk 12-2
D served all wk 6-9 ⊕ FREE HOUSE
🍺 Rotating Real Ales ⚘ Westons Old
Rosie. ♟ 12 **Facilities** Non-diners area
🐾 (Bar Garden) 🧒 Children's menu
Children's portions Garden 🎪 Beer
festival Parking Wi-fi 🚌 (notice
required) **Rooms** 3

ST MERRYN — Map 2 SW87

The Cornish Arms

PICK OF THE PUBS

Churchtown PL28 8ND ☎ 01841 532700
e-mail: reservations@rickstein.com
dir: *From Padstow follow signs for St Merryn then Churchtown*

Simple British pub food the Rick Stein way

In the village of St Merryn, just outside Padstow, this ancient village pub is part of the Stein portfolio. Situated across the road from the parish church and overlooking a peaceful valley, the pub has remained very much the village boozer much to happiness of the locals who had worried that it might become a fancy gastro-pub. Replete with slate floors, beams and roaring log fires, the pub oozes character and they have kept the food offering equally traditional. The chalkboard lists simple pub classics prepared from fresh produce: scampi in a basket, mussels and chips, local rump steaks, followed perhaps by apple pie or treacle tart. Wash it down with a glass of Chalky's Bark, named after Rick's much-missed, rough-haired Jack Russell. Check with the pub for details of themed nights and the beer and mussels festival in March.

Open all day all wk 11-11 **Bar Meals** L served all wk 12-2.30 D served all wk 6-8.30 Av main course £11 **Restaurant** L served all wk 12-2.30 D served all wk 6-8.30 Av 3 course à la carte fr £18.80 ⊕ ST AUSTELL BREWERY ◀ Tribute, Proper Job, Trelawny, Chalky's Bite, Chalky's Bark ♂ Healey's Cornish Rattler. ♀ 16 **Facilities** Non-diners area ❖ (Bar Restaurant Garden) ♦♦ Children's menu Children's portions Garden ⌂ Beer festival Parking Wi-fi ⊟

SALTASH — Map 3 SX45

The Crooked Inn ★★★★ INN

Stoketon Cottage, Trematon PL12 4RZ
☎ 01752 848177
e-mail: info@crooked-inn.co.uk
dir: *Telephone for directions*

Family-run inn with good food and great children's facilities

Overlooking the lush Lyher Valley and run by the same family for more than 25 years, this delightful inn once housed staff from Stoketon Manor, whose ruins lie on the other side of the courtyard. It is set in ten acres of lawns and woodland, yet only 15 minutes from Plymouth. There is an extensive menu including evening specials with plenty of fresh fish and vegetarian dishes. The children's playground has friendly animals, swings, slides, a trampoline and a treehouse. The spacious bedrooms are individually designed and decorated.

Open all day all wk 11-11 (Sun 12-10.30) Closed: 25 Dec **Bar Meals** L served all wk 11-2.30 D served all wk 6-9.30 ⊕ FREE HOUSE ◀ St Austell HSD, Dartmoor Jail Ale, Guest ales ♂ Thatchers Gold, Addlestones. **Facilities** Non-diners area ❖ (Bar Restaurant Garden) ♦♦ Children's menu Play area Garden ⌂ Parking Wi-fi ⊟ **Rooms** 18

SENNEN — Map 2 SW32

The Old Success Inn

Sennen Cove TR19 7DG ☎ 01736 871232
e-mail: oldsuccess@staustellbrewery.co.uk
dir: *Telephone for directions*

On the doorstep of a beautiful Cornish beach

Once the haunt of smugglers and now a focal point for the Sennen Lifeboat crew, this 17th-century inn enjoys a glorious location overlooking Cape Cornwall. Its name comes from the days when fishermen gathered here to count their catch and share out their 'successes'. Fresh local seafood is to the fore, and favourites include Tribute-battered catch of the day and Cornish fish pie. Non-fishy choices include Cajun-style chicken, goats' cheese tart, Cornish pasty with chips, and casserole of the day.

Open all wk Mon-Sat 10am-11pm (Sun 11-10.30) ⊕ ST AUSTELL BREWERY ◀ Tribute, HSD, Proper Job, Trelawny ♂ Healey's Cornish Rattler. **Facilities** ❖ (Bar Garden) ♦♦ Children's menu Children's portions Garden Parking Wi-fi

TORPOINT — Map 3 SX45

Edgcumbe Arms

PICK OF THE PUBS

Cremyll PL10 1HX ☎ 01752 822294
dir: *Telephone for directions*

A 15th-century pub right on the Tamar estuary

Next to Mount Edgcumbe Country Park and close to the foot ferry from Plymouth, this inn offers glorious views from its bow window seats and waterside terrace, which take in Drakes Island, the Royal William Yard and the marina. Real ales from St Austell like Proper Job, plus Cornish Rattler cider, and quality home-cooked food are served in a series of rooms (the same extensive menu is offered throughout), which are full of character with American oak panelling and flagstone floors. Dishes are a mixture of international and traditional British: crab and prawn cakes or ham hock terrine to start, followed by lamb moussaka, beef cannelloni or chicken and Stilton pie. Vegetarian options might be sweet potato and Mediterranean vegetable tagine or bubble-and-squeak. Sandwiches, loaded potato skins and platters are also available. The inn has a first-floor function room with sea views, and a courtyard garden.

Open all day 11-11 Closed: Jan- Feb Mon & Tue eve **Bar Meals** L served 12-5 D served 12-9 Av main course £9 food served all day **Restaurant** food served all day ⊕ ST AUSTELL BREWERY ◀ Tribute, Proper Job, Trelawny ♂ Healey's Cornish Rattler. ♀ 10 **Facilities** Non-diners area ❖ (Bar Garden) ♦♦ Children's menu Children's portions Garden ⌂ Parking Wi-fi ⊟ (notice required)

TREBARWITH — Map 2 SX08

The Mill House Inn

PICK OF THE PUBS

PL34 0HD ☎ 01840 770200
e-mail: management@themillhouseinn.co.uk
dir: *From Tintagel take B3263 S, right after Trewarmett to Trebarwith Strand. Pub 0.5m on right*

Popular for good food and live entertainment

Set in seven acres of woodland on the north Cornish coast, The Mill House is half a mile from the surfing beach at Trebarwith Strand, one of the finest in Cornwall, while also nearby is Tintagel Castle. The log fires in this atmospheric stone building – a charming former corn mill dating from 1760 - warm the residents' lounge and slate-floored bar, where wooden tables and chapel chairs help create a relaxed, family-friendly feel. Locally brewed real ales are supplied by Sharp's and Tintagel breweries, and the ciders are Cornish Orchards and Cornish Rattler. Lunches, evening drinks and barbecues are particularly enjoyable out on the attractive terraces, while a more intimate dinner in the Millstream Restaurant might involve Porthilly mussels in cider, garlic and tarragon cream, followed by pan-fried fillet of red gurnard, steamed crab pappardelle with roasted chilli, capsicum and salsa verde. Regular live events feature local musicians and comedians.

Open all day all wk 11-11 (Fri-Sat 11am-mdnt Sun 12-10.30) **Bar Meals** L served Mon-Sat 12-2.30, Sun 12-3 D served all wk 6.30-8.30 **Restaurant** D served all wk 6.30-9 ⊕ FREE HOUSE ◀ Sharp's Doom Bar, Tintagel Cornwall's Pride, Sharp's Cornish Coaster ♂ Cornish Orchards, Healey's Cornish Rattler. **Facilities** Non-diners area ❖ (Bar Garden) ♦♦ Children's menu Children's portions Play area Family room Garden ⌂ Parking Wi-fi ⊟ (notice required)

The Port William

Trebarwith Strand PL34 0HB ☎ 01840 770230
e-mail: portwilliam@staustellbrewery.co.uk
dir: *From A39 onto B3314 signed Tintagel. Right onto B3263, follow Trebarwith Strand signs, then brown Port William signs*

Stunning location by the sea

Occupying one of the best locations in Cornwall, this former harbourmaster's house lies directly on the coastal path, 50 yards from the sea, which means the views are amazing. There is an entrance to a smugglers' tunnel at the rear of the ladies' toilet! Focus on the daily-changing specials board for such dishes as artichoke and roast pepper salad, warm smoked trout platter, and spinach and ricotta tortellini.

Open all wk 10am-11pm (Sun 10am-10.30pm) ⊕ ST AUSTELL BREWERY ◀ Tribute & Trelawny, Guest ales ♂ Healey's Cornish Rattler. **Facilities** ❖ (Bar Garden) ♦♦ Children's menu Children's portions Family room Garden Parking Wi-fi

TREBURLEY   Map 3 SX37

The Springer Spaniel
PICK OF THE PUBS

PL15 9NS ☎ 01579 370424
e-mail: enquiries@thespringerspaniel.org.uk
dir: *On A388 halfway between Launceston & Callington*

Local produce drives the seasonal menu

Roger and Lavinia Halliday's traditional hostelry offers local ales, delicious food, fine wines and friendly service. The inviting bar is furnished with high-backed wooden settles, farmhouse-style chairs and a wood-burning stove, whilst flickering candles in the evenings add to the romantic atmosphere of the restaurant. In summer the landscaped, sheltered garden is a great place to relax and enjoy the sun with a pint of Betty Stogs, or one of the half dozen wines by the glass. The fact that food is such a big draw here is partly down to where it comes from: fresh fish and seafood from Cornish waters; meat, game and dairy produce from local farmers and country estates; grass-fed pedigree South Devon cattle and Lleyn sheep from the owners' 100-hectare organic farm. A meal might begin with Tregida smoked mackerel, before a main course of steamed venison and wild mushroom pudding or grilled whole sole.

Open all wk 12-2.30 6-10.30 **Bar Meals** L served all wk 12-1.45 D served all wk 6.15-8.45 **Restaurant** L served all wk 12-1.45 D served all wk 6.15-8.45 ⊕ FREE HOUSE ◀ Sharp's Doom Bar, Skinner's Betty Stogs, Guest ale ♂ Thatchers, Cornish Orchards.
Facilities Non-diners area ❖ (Bar Garden) ♦❙ Children's menu Children's portions Family room Garden ⊓ Parking

TREGADILLETT   Map 3 SX28

Eliot Arms

PL15 7EU ☎ 01566 772051
dir: *From Launceston take A30 towards Bodmin. Then follow brown signs to Tregadillett*

Creeper covered inn with lots of nostalgia

The extraordinary decor in this charming creeper-clad coaching inn, dating back to 1625, includes Masonic regalia, horse brasses and grandfather clocks. It was believed to have been a Masonic lodge for Napoleonic prisoners, and even has its own friendly ghost. Customers can enjoy real fires in winter and lovely hanging baskets in summer. Food, based on locally sourced meat and fresh fish and shellfish caught off the Cornish coast, is served in the bar or bright and airy restaurant. Expect home-made soups, pie and curry of the day; steak and chips; chargrills; and home-made vegetarian dishes.

Open all day all wk 11.30-11 (Fri-Sat 11.30am-mdnt Sun 12-10.30) **Bar Meals** L served all wk 12-2 D served all wk 6-9 Av main course £8.95 **Restaurant** L served all wk 12-2 D served all wk 6-9 ⊕ FREE HOUSE ◀ St Austell Tribute, Caledonian Flying Scotsman, Theakston XB. ▾ 9
Facilities Non-diners area ♦❙ Children's menu Children's portions Family room Outside area Parking Wi-fi ▭ (notice required)

TRESCO (ISLES OF SCILLY)   Map 2 SV81

The New Inn ★★★★ INN ❀
PICK OF THE PUBS

New Grimsby TR24 0QQ ☎ 01720 422849
e-mail: newinn@tresco.co.uk
dir: *By New Grimsby Quay*

A must visit island treasure

Nowadays, as the only pub on the island, this has to be, as landlord Robin Lawson says, the 'Best Pub on Tresco'. It is very much the social hub of the island's community. Everywhere you look is maritime history, much of it, such as the signboard, mahogany bar and wall-planking, salvaged from wrecks. An AA Rosette recognises the quality of food - served from the same menu wherever you dine - in the quiet restaurant, the livelier Driftwood Bar, the Pavillion, or outside. Accompany a lunchtime beefburger with a pint of Scillonian real ale or Cornish Rattler cider. For dinner, seek out Scilly crab salad; seared salmon fillet with couscous salad; or butternut squash, Cornish goats' cheese and sage risotto; finish with sticky toffee sponge or dark chocolate fondant. Traditional roasts are served on Sundays. There are beer festivals in mid May and early September, and a cider festival in June. Some of the stylish rooms available have ocean views.

Open all wk all day (Apr-Oct) phone for winter opening **Bar Meals** L served all wk 12-2.15 D served all wk 6.30-9 **Restaurant** D served all wk 6.30-9 ⊕ FREE HOUSE/ TRESCO ESTATE ◀ Skinner's Betty Stogs, Tresco Tipple, Ales of Scilly Scuppered & Firebrand, St Austell Proper Job, Tintagel Harbour Special ♂ Healey's Cornish Rattler & Pear Rattler. ▾ 13 **Facilities** Non-diners area ♦❙ Children's menu Children's portions Garden ⊓ Beer festival Cider festival Wi-fi **Rooms** 16

TRURO   Map 2 SW84

Old Ale House

7 Quay St TR1 2HD ☎ 01872 271122
e-mail: jamie@oahtruro.com
dir: *In town centre*

City pub with live music, quiz and games nights

This traditional city centre pub right next to the main bus station in Truro offers a large selection of Skinner's real ales and guest beers, as well as live music and various quiz and games nights. The extensive menus include 'huge hands of hot bread' (quarter or half a bloomer covered in a topping of your choice and baked), sandwiches and the pub's famous skillets – perhaps the five-spice chicken, the Cantonese prawns or the sizzling beef. Beer festival between March and May.

Open all wk 11-11 (Fri-Sat 11am-1am Sun 12-10.30) Closed: 25-26 Dec, 1 Jan **Bar Meals** L served all wk 12-2.30 Av main course £6.20 **Restaurant** L served all wk 12-2.30 ⊕ ENTERPRISE INNS ◀ Skinner's Kiddlywink, Shepherd Neame Spitfire, Greene King Abbot Ale, Fuller's London Pride, Courage, Guest ales ♂ Skreach. ▾ 9 **Facilities** Non-diners area ♦❙ Children's portions Beer festival ▭ (notice required)

The Wig & Pen

Frances St TR1 3DP ☎ 01872 273028
e-mail: wigandpentruro@hotmail.com
dir: *In city centre near Law Courts*

Friendly city centre pub where everything is made in-house

Tim and Georgie Robinson's city-centre pub has both an L-shaped ground floor bar and a bar in the basement, which in the evenings becomes Quills restaurant. Food is freshly made in-house, from the modern pub classics and specials on the menu to the crisps and pork scratchings that go with Trelawny and Tribute beers. The diner's challenge is choosing between chicken schnitzel with mash; king prawn, salmon and lemon and rocket risotto; herb-crusted rack of lamb with Jerusalem artichoke dauphinoise; and baked red onions, toasted spiced couscous and grilled sweet potato. Watch the world go by from the sun terraces.

Open all day all wk Closed: 25-26 Dec, 1 Jan **Bar Meals** L served all wk 12-2.30 D served all wk 6-9.30 Av main course £10 **Restaurant** D served 7-9 Av 3 course à la carte fr £27.50 ⊕ ST AUSTELL BREWERY ◀ Tribute, HSD, Trelawny ♂ Healey's Cornish Rattler & Pear Rattler. ▾ 16 **Facilities** Non-diners area ❖ (Bar Garden) ♦❙ Children's portions Garden ⊓ ▭ (notice required)

VERYAN   Map 2 SW93

The New Inn

TR2 5QA ☎ 01872 501362
e-mail: info@newinn-veryan.co.uk
dir: *From St Austell take A390 towards Truro, in 2m left to Tregony. Through Tregony, follow signs to Veryan*

Traditional home cooking and good ales

This unspoiled, part-thatched pub started life as a pair of cottages in the 16th-century. In the centre of a pretty village on the Roseland Peninsula, The New Inn has open fires, a beamed ceiling, a single bar serving St Austell ales and a warm, welcoming atmosphere. Sunday lunch is a speciality; other choices during the week might include home-made vegetable chilli, hand-carved Cornish ham, local beer-battered fish or wholetail breaded scampi. Traditional puddings take in apple crumble, chocolate fudge cake and sticky toffee pudding – some served with Cornish clotted cream.

Open all day all wk 12-3 5.30-11 (Sun 7-11) Closed: 25 Dec **Bar Meals** L served all wk 12-2 D served Mon-Sat 6.30-9, Sun 7-9 **Restaurant** L served all wk 12-2 D served Mon-Sat 6.30-9, Sun 7-9 ⊕ ST AUSTELL BREWERY ◀ Tribute, Proper Job, Dartmoor ♂ Healey's Cornish Rattler. ▾ **Facilities** Non-diners area ❖ (Bar Restaurant Garden) ♦❙ Children's menu Children's portions Garden ⊓ Wi-fi ▭ (notice required)

WADEBRIDGE
Map 2 SW97

The Quarryman Inn

Edmonton PL27 7JA ☎ 01208 816444
e-mail: thequarryman@live.co.uk
dir: *Off A39 opposite Royal Cornwall Showground*

Tucked away in the Cornish countryside

Close to the famous Camel Trail, this friendly
18th-century free house has evolved from a courtyard of
cottages once home to slate workers from the nearby
quarry. Several bow windows, one of which features a
stained-glass quarryman panel, add character to this
unusual inn. The pub's menus change everyday but their
signature dishes are chargrilled steaks served on sizzling
platters and fresh local seafood; puddings are on the
blackboard. Meals and drinks can be enjoyed outside in
the slate courtyard in summer, or by a roaring fire in
colder months.

Open all day all wk 12-11 Closed: 25 Dec **Bar Meals** L
served all wk 12-2.30 D served all wk 6-9 ⊕ FREE HOUSE
◀ Timothy Taylor Landlord, Sharp's, Skinner's, Otter,
Guest ales ♂ Westons Stowford Press.
Facilities Non-diners area ♦♦ Children's menu Children's
portions Garden ⌂ Parking Wi-fi ☎ (notice required)

The Swan Hotel

9 Molesworth St PL27 7DD ☎ 01208 812526
e-mail: reservations@smallandfriendly.co.uk
dir: *In centre of Wadebridge on corner of Molesworth St
& The Platt*

**Family friendly, extensive menu and carvery five
days a week**

Bursting with life and at the heart of the local
community, this white-painted town-centre corner hotel
is an ideal base for exploring north Cornwall and the
nearby Camel Trail. Popular with families, the main bar
provides a comfortable place to relax and enjoy a drink or
a meal. Typical pub food in the Cygnet restaurant
includes locally smoked salmon; Cornish ham, egg and
chips; local crab cakes; and beer-battered fish and chips
with peas. There's also a good selection from the grill and
a carvery from Wednesdays to Sundays.

Open all day all wk **Bar Meals** L served all wk 12-9 Food
served all day **Restaurant** D served all wk 6.30-9 ⊕ ST
AUSTELL BREWERY ◀ Tribute & Proper Job, Guinness
♂ Healey's Cornish Rattler. ₹ 13
Facilities Non-diners area ✿ (Bar Outside area) ♦♦
Children's menu Children's portions Family room Outside
area ⌂ Wi-fi ☎ (notice required)

WIDEMOUTH BAY
Map 2 SS20

Bay View Inn

Marine Dr EX23 0AW ☎ 01288 361273
e-mail: thebayviewinn@aol.com
dir: *On Marine Drive adjacent to beach in Widemouth Bay*

Ocean views and good food

Dating back around 100 years, this welcoming, family-
run pub was a guest house for many years before
becoming an inn in the 1960s. True to its name, the pub
has fabulous views of the rolling Atlantic from its
restaurant and the large raised decking area outside. The
menu makes excellent use of local produce, as in the
signature dish of fish pie; and sea bass fillets with
Florentine potatoes and tiger prawn and saffron sauce.
Other choices include home-made pies, casseroles and
burgers.

Open all day all wk **Bar Meals** L served Mon-Fri 12-2.30,
Sat-Sun 12-9 D served Mon-Fri 5.30-9, Sat-Sun 12-9
Restaurant L served Mon-Fri 12-2.30, Sat-Sun 12-9
D served Mon-Fri 5.30-9, Sat-Sun 12-9 ⊕ FREE HOUSE
◀ Skinner's Betty Stogs & Spriggan Ale, Sharp's Doom
Bar ♂ Thatchers. ₹ 14 **Facilities** Non-diners area ✿ (Bar
Garden) ♦♦ Children's menu Children's portions Play area
Garden ⌂ Parking Wi-fi ☎ (notice required)

ZENNOR
Map 2 SW43

The Tinners Arms

PICK OF THE PUBS

TR26 3BY ☎ 01736 796927
e-mail: tinners@tinnersarms.com
dir: *Take B3306 from St Ives towards St Just. Zennor
approx 5m*

Timeless medieval village inn

Built of granite in 1271 for masons working on ancient

St Senara's church next door, famous for its richly carved
Mermaid Chair. Many may welcome the fact that the only
pub in the village has no TV, jukebox or fruit machine, nor
can a mobile phone signal reach it. Its closeness to the
South West Coastal Path almost guarantees that muddy-
booted walkers will be found among its clientele, enjoying
the timelessness of its stone floors, low ceilings,
cushioned settles, winter open fires and the revivifying
effect of one of the Cornish real ales or Burrow Hill cider
from Somerset. Based on ingredients from local suppliers,
the dinner menu offers lightly curried medallions of
monkfish; pan-fried lamb's liver and bacon; and garlic-
roasted Portobello mushrooms with couscous salad.
Sandwiches and light meals are available at lunchtime.
Outside is a large terrace with sea views.

Open all day all wk **Bar Meals** L served all wk 12-3
D served all wk 6.30-9 (ex Sun & Mon eve winter) ⊕ FREE
HOUSE ◀ Zennor Mermaid, St Austell Tinners Ale, Sharp's
Own ♂ Burrow Hill. ₹ 10 **Facilities** Non-diners area
✿ (Bar Restaurant Garden) ♦♦ Children's menu Children's
portions Garden ⌂ Parking

CUMBRIA

AMBLESIDE
Map 18 NY30

Drunken Duck Inn ★★★★★ INN ⊛⊛

PICK OF THE PUBS

See Pick of the Pubs on opposite page

Wateredge Inn

Waterhead Bay LA22 0EP ☎ 015394 32332
e-mail: stay@wateredgeinn.co.uk
dir: *M6 junct 36, A591 to Ambleside, 5m from Windermere
station*

**Family-run inn on the shores of Lake
Windermere**

The Wateredge Inn was converted from two 17th-century
fishermen's cottages, and now offers a stylish bar and
restaurant. With large gardens and plenty of seating
running down to the lakeshore, the inn has been run by
the same family for nearly 30 years. The lunch menu
offers sandwiches, salads, pub classics and slates –
platters of smoked fish, charcuterie or cheese and
antipasti. Meanwhile the dinner menu has choices
ranging from local Cumberland sausage and mash to
seared fillet of salmon with a tomato, chilli and tarragon
salsa. Specials and a children's menu are also available.

Open all day all wk 10.30am-11pm Closed: 23-26 Dec
Bar Meals L served Mon-Fri 12-2.30, Sat-Sun 12-4
D served all wk 6-9 ⊕ FREE HOUSE ◀ Theakston,
Barngates Tag Lag & Cat Nap, Watermill Collie Wobbles
♂ Symonds. ₹ 15 **Facilities** Non-diners area ✿ (Bar
Garden) ♦♦ Children's menu Children's portions Garden ⌂
Parking Wi-fi

APPLEBY-IN-WESTMORLAND
Map 18 NY62

The Royal Oak Appleby

Bongate CA16 6UN ☎ 017683 51463
e-mail: jan@royaloakappleby.co.uk
dir: *M6 junct 38, B6260 to Appleby-in-Westmorland.
Through square, over bridge, right onto B6542, pub in
0.25m. Or from A66 take B6542 through Appleby, pub
on left*

A traditional inn, a popular all-rounder

Parts of this former coaching inn date back to 1100, with
17th-century additions. The building provides a classic
dog-friendly tap-room with blackened beams, an oak-
panelled lounge with open fire, and a comfortable
restaurant. The modern British menu uses the best of
local ingredients and features dishes with rack of lamb with a
garlic, rosemary and redcurrant gravy; stuffed chicken
breast with Cumberland sausage and wrapped in bacon;
and spinach and ricotta cannelloni. Enjoy your visit with
a pint of Hawkshead.

Open all day all wk 8am-mdnt ⊕ FREE HOUSE
◀ Hawkshead, Black Sheep, Timothy Taylor, Copper
Dragon. **Facilities** ✿ (Bar Garden) ♦♦ Children's menu
Children's portions Garden Parking Wi-fi

PICK OF THE PUBS

Drunken Duck Inn ★★★★★ INN ✿✿

AMBLESIDE   Map 18 NY30

Barngates LA22 0NG ☎ 015394 36347
e-mail: info@drunkenduckinn.co.uk
web: www.drunkenduckinn.co.uk
dir: *From Kendal on A591 to Ambleside,
then follow Hawkshead sign. In 2.5m
inn sign on right, 1m up hill*

Stunning location for a traditional Lakeland inn

High above Ambleside, the 17th-century
Duck stands at a lonely crossroads close
to Tarn Hows, with wonderful views of
the fells towards Lake Windermere. It
has been in the same ownership since
the mid-1970s, although the amusing
title dates from Victorian times, when a
landlady found her ducks seemingly
dead in the road. Unaware that they
were merely sozzled from drinking beer
that had leaked into their feed, she
started plucking them for the pot. Then,
of course, they started to recover and
legend has it that, full of remorse, she
knitted them waistcoats to wear until
their feathers grew back. Beer is still
brewed here, in the adjoining Barngates
Brewery, using water drawn from the
fells, and is served – check out the
Cracker Ale, or Chesters Strong & Ugly
– in the oak-floored bar, with its old oak
beams hung with Kentish hops, bar top
made from black slate quarried less
than a mile away at Brathay, and oak
settles covered with local Herdwick
wool. Sketches, prints, fox masks and

enamel signs all add to the atmosphere,
along with candlelight and a log fire.
Excellent, locally sourced ingredients
are behind the two-AA Rosette food
served in three informal restaurant
areas, with lunchtime bringing soup,
salads and sandwiches, as well as hot
dishes like lamb suet pudding, spiced
red cabbage and mash; roasted salmon,
caper tomato and brown shrimp butter;
and Cullen skink with poached hen's
egg. At dinner, begin with king scallops
with Jerusalem artichoke and white
balsamic; then veal blanquette with
mash, parsley purée, onion soubise and
roasted garlic, or sea bass fillet with
king oyster mushroom, salsify and cep
jus. On the pudding menu may appear
blood orange and thyme soufflé with
yoghurt ice cream. Each bedroom comes

with antique furniture, prints and
designer fabrics.

Open all day all wk Closed: 25 Dec
Bar Meals L served all wk 12-4
Restaurant D served all wk 6-9.30
🛢 FREE HOUSE ◀ Barngates Cracker
Ale, Chesters Strong & Ugly, Tag Lag,
Cat Nap, Mothbag & Westmorland Gold,
Guest ale. 🍷 17 **Facilities** Non-
diners area 🐾 ♦ Children's portions
Garden 🎋 Parking Wi-fi **Rooms** 17

APPLEBY-IN-WESTMORLAND *continued*

Tufton Arms Hotel

PICK OF THE PUBS

Market Square CA16 6XA ☎ 017683 51593
e-mail: info@tuftonarmshotel.co.uk
dir: *In town centre*

Elegant coaching inn with its own house ale

This 16th-century inn, rebuilt in Victorian times with tall ceilings, is now Grade II listed. The interior displays co-owner Teresa Milsom's design skills with its attractive wallpapers, engravings and prints, heavy drapes and period furniture, all harmonising contentedly with contemporary fabrics, soft tones and modern lighting. On handpump in the bar are Cumberland Corby and the house beer, Tufton Arms Ale. At the heart of the hotel, overlooking a cobbled mews courtyard, is the Conservatory Restaurant, where David Milsom and his kitchen team's cuisine is complemented by a serious wine list. Typical dishes made from top-quality fresh local ingredients are wild mushroom and baby spinach tagliatelle; salmon and prawn chowder; slow-cooked lamb shank in a Madeira gravy; and home-made blackberry and apple crumble. The fixed-price menu could feature Serrano ham and honeydew melon then pan-fried loin of veal served with vegetable rice and pak choi.

Open all day all wk 7.30am-11pm Closed: 25-26 Dec **Bar Meals** L served all wk 12-2 D served all wk 6-9 **Restaurant** L served all wk 12-2 D served all wk 6-9 ⊕ FREE HOUSE ◀ Tufton Arms Ale, Cumberland Corby Ale. ☗ 15 **Facilities** Non-diners area ❀ (Bar Outside area) ♦♦ Children's portions Outside area ♯ Parking Wi-fi ⇔

BARBON   Map 18 SD68

The Barbon Inn

LA6 2LJ ☎ 015242 76233
e-mail: info@barbon-inn.co.uk
dir: *3.5m N of Kirkby Lonsdale on A683*

Family-run inn down narrow country lanes

Sitting happily in the Lune Valley, between the River Lune and the looming fells rising to Whernside, this whitewashed small village inn oozes the character only centuries of heritage can generate. The cosy Coach Lamp bar is particularly welcoming, with its vast fireplace and old furnishings. The Oak Room restaurant is equally enticing; secure one of the polished old settles and contemplate the very best that Cumbria, Yorkshire and Lancashire can provide, from grand beers brewed in Dent and Kirkby Lonsdale to pan-fried breast of pheasant, grouse and pigeon with dauphinoise potatoes, pancetta and juniper sauce.

Open all wk 12-2 6-11 (Sun 12-2 6-10.30) Closed: 25 Dec ⊕ FREE HOUSE ◀ York, Dent, Tirril, Kirkby Lonsdale ♂ Addlestones. **Facilities** ♦♦ Children's menu Children's portions Garden Parking Wi-fi

---

BASSENTHWAITE   Map 18 NY23

The Pheasant ★★★ HL ⑱

PICK OF THE PUBS

See Pick of the Pubs on opposite page

BEETHAM   Map 18 SD47

The Wheatsheaf at Beetham

PICK OF THE PUBS

LA7 7AL ☎ 015395 62123
e-mail: info@wheatsheafbeetham.com
dir: *On A6 5m N of junct 35*

Penny starters and desserts at traditional country inn

Jean and Richard Skelton, owners of this one-time farm and later coaching inn, make a remarkable offer: a starter and dessert for 1p each, when you order a main course. That's probably much the same as a farm labourer would have paid the farmer's wife for a meal here back in the early 1600s, from when the building dates. So, what do those pennies get you? All five starters on the menu qualify, including garlic mushrooms with toasted artisan bread; and smoked mackerel with potato salad. Among the main courses are haddock and prawn pie; pan-fried pork fillet on black pudding mash; and potato, leek and Shropshire Blue pie. Then it's back to the penny desserts offer with Eton Mess; and lemon tart with Chantilly cream. For a pre-meal pint, the Old Tap Bar offers Thwaites Wainwright, Tirril Queen Jean and Cross Bay Nightfall, and an impressive range of malt whiskies.

Open all day all wk 12-11 Closed: 25 Dec **Bar Meals** L served Mon-Sat 12-9, Sun 12-8.30 D served Mon-Sat 12-9, Sun 12-8.30 food served all day **Restaurant** food served all day ⊕ FREE HOUSE ◀ Thwaites Wainwright, Tirril Queen Jean, Cross Bay Nightfall ♂ Kingstone Press. **Facilities** Non-diners area ♦♦ Children's menu Children's portions Outside area ♯ Parking Wi-fi ⇔ (notice required)

BOOT   Map 18 NY10

Brook House Inn ★★★★ INN

PICK OF THE PUBS

CA19 1TG ☎ 019467 23288
e-mail: stay@brookhouseinn.co.uk
dir: *M6 junct 36, A590 follow Barrow signs. A5092, then A595. Pass Broughton-in-Furness, right at lights to Ulpha. Cross river, next left signed Eskdale to Boot. (NB not all routes to Boot are suitable in bad weather conditions)*

Tranquil location for tempting, home-made food

Few locations can rival this: Lakeland fells rise behind the inn to England's highest peak, whilst golden sunsets illuminate tranquil Eskdale. Footpaths wind to nearby Stanley Ghyll's wooded gorge with its falls and red squirrels, and the charming La'al Ratty narrow gauge railway steams to and from the coast. It's a magnet for ramblers and cyclists, so a small drying room for wet adventurers is greatly appreciated. Up to seven real ales are kept, including Yates Best Bitter and Langdale from Cumbrian Legendary Ales, and an amazing selection of 175 malt whiskies. Home-made food prepared from Cumbria's finest showcases the menus, so temper the drizzle with a warming bowl of home-made soup, or prawns in garlic butter spiced tomato chutney, followed by duck breast with orange and plum sauce; chicken Madras; or perhaps one of the vegetarian dishes such as Moroccan vegetable and bean casserole with rice and pine nut and apricot salad. Raspberry meringues or coffee torte with espresso sauce make a fine finish. This great community pub also takes a full role in the famous Boot Beer Festival each June.

Open all day all wk Closed: 25 Dec **Bar Meals** food served all day **Restaurant** L served by arrangement D served 6-8.30 ⊕ FREE HOUSE ◀ Hawkshead Bitter, Jennings Cumberland Ale, Cumbrian Legendary Langdale, Yates Best Bitter, Guest ales ♂ Westons Old Rosie. ☗ 10 **Facilities** Non-diners area ♦♦ Children's menu Family room Garden ♯ Beer festival Parking Wi-fi ⇔ Rooms 8

BORROWDALE   Map 18 NY21

The Langstrath Country Inn

CA12 5XG ☎ 017687 77239
e-mail: info@thelangstrath.com
dir: *B5289 past Grange, through Rosthwaite, left to Stonethwaite. Inn on left after 1m*

Picturesque village inn a favourite with ramblers

Nestling in the stunning Langstrath Valley in the heart of the Lakes, this lovely family-run 16th-century inn was originally a miner's cottage. It is an ideal base for those attempting England's highest peak, Scafell Pike; the inn also sits on the coast-to-coast and Cumbrian Way walks. The restaurant is ideally positioned to maximise the spectacular views. Here hungry ramblers enjoy high-quality Lakeland dishes based on local ingredients. A typical choice could include black pudding and chorizo salad; and smoked cod and Cumbrian cheddar fishcakes. Local cask-conditioned ales include some from the Keswick Brewery.

Open 12-10.30 Closed: Jan, Mon **Bar Meals** L served Tue-Sun 12-2.30 D served Tue-Sun 6-9 **Restaurant** L served Tue-Sun 12-2.30 D served Tue-Sun 6-9 ⊕ FREE HOUSE ◀ Jennings Bitter & Cocker Hoop, Hawkshead Bitter, Black Sheep, Keswick Thirst Rescue ♂ Thatchers Gold. ☗ 9 **Facilities** Non-diners area ♦♦ Children's menu Children's portions Garden ♯ Parking Wi-fi ⇔ (notice required)

PICK OF THE PUBS

The Pheasant ★★★ HL ✿

BASSENTHWAITE   Map 18 NY23

CA13 9YE ☎ 017687 76234
e-mail: info@the-pheasant.co.uk
web: www.the-pheasant.co.uk
dir: *A66 to Cockermouth, 8m N of Keswick on left*

Accomplished food in peaceful Lake District setting

At the foot of the Sale Fell and close to Bassenthwaite Lake, this 17th-century former coaching inn occupies a peaceful spot in the Lake District and is surrounded by lovely gardens. Once a farmhouse, the pub today combines the role of traditional Cumbrian hostelry with that of an internationally renowned modern hotel. Even so, you still sense the history the moment you walk through the door – the legendary foxhunter John Peel, whose "view halloo would awaken the dead", according to the song, was a regular here. In the warmly inviting bar, with polished parquet flooring, panelled walls and oak settles, hang two of Cumbrian artist and former customer Edward H Thompson's paintings. Here, order a pint of Coniston Bluebird or Hawkshead Red, or cast your eyes over the extensive selection of malt whiskies. The high standard of food, recognised by an AA Rosette, is well known for miles around; meals are served in the attractive beamed restaurant, bistro, bar and lounges overlooking the gardens. Light lunches served in the lounge and bar include open sandwiches, ploughman's and home-made pork pies, as well as main courses such as fish and chips; or smoked Cumbrian ham with fried hen's egg and triple cooked chips. A three-course dinner in the restaurant could feature seared scallops, crisp chicken wings and Jerusalem artichoke; roast rack of Cumbrian lamb, shank ragout, confit potato, heirloom carrot and braised little gem; and rum and raisin cheesecake, sour cherry ice cream, rum soaked raisins. Treat the family to afternoon tea with home-made scones and rum butter. Booking for meals may be required.

Open all wk Mon-Thu 11-2.30 5.30-10.30 (Fri-Sat 11-2.30 5.30-11 Sun 12-2.30 6-10.30) Closed: 25 Dec
Bar Meals L served all wk 12-2 D served all wk 6-9 **Restaurant** L served Sun 12.30-1.30 D served all wk 7-8.30
⊕ FREE HOUSE ◖ Coniston Bluebird, Jennings, Cumberland Ale, Hawkshead Red ♂ Thatchers Gold. ♟ 12
Facilities Non-diners area 🐾 (Bar Garden) ⅰ Children's menu Children's portions Garden 🎋 Parking Wi-fi
Rooms 15

BOWLAND BRIDGE　Map 18 SD48

Hare & Hounds Country Inn

PICK OF THE PUBS

LA11 6NN ☎ 015395 68333
e-mail: info@hareandhoundsbowlandbridge.co.uk
dir: M6 junct 36, A590 signed Barrow. Right onto A5074 signed Bowness & Windermere. Approx 4m at sharp bend left & follow Bowland Bridge sign

Fabulous views and local produce

Very much at the heart of the community, this 17th-century coaching inn even hosts the Post Office on Tuesday and Thursday afternoons. In the pretty little hamlet of Bowland Bridge, not far from Bowness, the pub has gorgeous views of Cartmel Fell. A traditional country-pub atmosphere is fostered by the flagstone floors, exposed oak beams and ancient pews warmed by open fires. Strong links with local food producers result in exclusively reared pork and lamb featuring on the menu and Hare of the Dog beer – brewed for the pub by Tirril Brewery – is a permanent fixture at the bar. Visit at lunchtime and take your pick from sandwiches and salads or hearty meals such as lamb meatballs with mint dressing and home-made apricot chutney, followed by beef and ale pie. Finish with home-made chocolate terrine and raspberry coulis. Time a visit for the late May bank holiday beer festival.

Open all day all wk 12-11 **Bar Meals** L served Mon-Fri 12-2, Sat 12-9, Sun 12-8.30 D served Mon-Fri 6-9, Sat 12-9, Sun 12-8.30 Av main course £11 ⊕ FREE HOUSE ◀ Tirril, Coniston, Ulverston, Hawkshead, Kirkby Lonsdale Ŏ Cowmire Hall. ♥ 10 **Facilities** Non-diners area ✿ (Bar Garden) ♦ Children's menu Children's portions Garden ☍ Beer festival Parking Wi-fi ➡ (notice required)

BRAITHWAITE　Map 18 NY22

Coledale Inn

CA12 5TN ☎ 017687 78272
e-mail: info@coledale-inn.co.uk
dir: M6 junct 40, A66 signed Keswick. Approx 18m. Exit A66, follow Whinlatter Pass & Braithwaite sign, left on B5292. In Braithwaite left at pub sign, over stream bridge to inn

An atmospheric place to finish a walk

Originally a woollen mill, the Coledale Inn dates from around 1824 and had stints as a pencil mill, a guest house and a private house before becoming the inn it is today. The interior is attractively decked out with Victorian prints, furnishings and antiques, whilst footpaths leading off from the large gardens make it ideal for exploring the nearby fells. Two homely bars serve a selection of local ales while traditional lunch and dinner menus are served in the dining room. Typical choices include Thai cod and prawn fish cake with sweet chilli dip; local sausages with mash and onion gravy; and apple and rhubarb crumble.

Open all day all wk **Bar Meals** L served all wk 12-2 D served all wk 6-9 Av main course £10.95

Restaurant Fixed menu price fr £13.50 Av 3 course à la carte fr £19.95 ⊕ FREE HOUSE ◀ Cumberland Corby Ale, Hesket Newmarket, Yates, Keswick, Tirril. ♥ 8 **Facilities** Non-diners area ✿ (Bar Garden) ♦ Children's menu Children's portions Play area Garden ☍ Parking Wi-fi ➡ (notice required)

The Royal Oak ★★★★ INN

CA12 5SY ☎ 017687 78533
e-mail: tpfranks@hotmail.com
dir: M6 junct 40, A66 towards Keswick, approx 18m (bypass Keswick), exit A66 left onto B5292 to Braithwaite. Pub in village centre

Delightful country pub surrounded by beautiful landscapes

Surrounded by high fells and beautiful scenery, The Royal Oak is set in the centre of the village and is the perfect base for walkers. The interior is all oak beams and log fires, and the menu offers hearty pub food, such as slow-roasted pork belly on apple mash; home-made fish pie; and slow-roasted lamb rump with mint gravy, all served alongside local ales, such as Sneck Lifter or Cumberland Ale. Visitors can extend the experience by staying over in the comfortable en suite bedrooms.

Open all day all wk **Bar Meals** L served all wk 12-2 D served all wk 6-9 Av main course £10 **Restaurant** L served all wk 12-2 D served all wk 6-9 ⊕ MARSTON'S ◀ Jennings Lakeland Stunner, Cumberland Ale, Cocker Hoop, Sneck Lifter. ♥ 8 **Facilities** Non-diners area ♦ Children's menu Children's portions Garden ☍ Parking Wi-fi ➡ **Rooms** 10

BRAMPTON　Map 21 NY56

Blacksmiths Arms ★★★★ INN

Talkin Village CA8 1LE ☎ 016977 3452
e-mail: blacksmithsarmstalkin@yahoo.co.uk
dir: From M6 take A69 E, after 7m straight on at rdbt, follow signs to Talkin Tarn then Talkin Village

Attractive free house serving good home-cooked food

With cartwheels lined up outside, this former smithy faces a small green by the crossroads in the centre of the village. On its doorstep is northern Cumbria's wildly beautiful countryside. The menu of good, traditional home cooking makes extensive use of fresh local produce for steak-and-kidney pie; chicken curry; rainbow trout; and spinach and ricotta cannelloni. Likely contenders as blackboard specials are tangy-sauced chicken Formentera; loin of lamb; and fillet of salmon. Two of the real ales come from the Geltsdale Brewery in neighbouring Brampton. There's a beer garden, and out front a couple of tables with seating.

Open all wk 12-3 6-12 **Bar Meals** L served all wk 12-2 D served all wk 6-9 Av main course £9.95 **Restaurant** L served all wk 12-2 D served all wk 6-9 Av 3 course à la carte fr £20 ⊕ FREE HOUSE ◀ Geltsdale Cold Fell, Yates, Brampton, Black Sheep. ♥ 16 **Facilities** Non-diners area ♦ Children's menu Children's portions Garden ☍ Parking Wi-fi **Rooms** 8

BROUGHTON-IN-FURNESS　Map 18 SD28

Blacksmiths Arms

PICK OF THE PUBS

Broughton Mills LA20 6AX ☎ 01229 716824
e-mail: blacksmithsarms@aol.com
dir: A593 from Broughton-in-Furness towards Coniston, in 1.5m left signed Broughton Mills, pub 1m on left

Ancient pub surrounded by quiet fells and farms

Originally a farmhouse and then an inn and blacksmith's (hence the name), this whitewashed Lakeland pub dates from 1577 and stands in the secluded Lickle Valley, with miles of glorious walks radiating from the front door. The interior remains largely unchanged, with oak-panelled corridors, slate floors, oak-beamed ceilings and log fires. The Lanes own and run the Blacksmiths, Michael dividing his time between the kitchen and the bar, and Sophie running front of house. The bar is reserved for drinking only, with ales from Cumberland, Barngates and Tirril and Westons Old Rosie cider. The Lanes use only suppliers who guarantee quality produce for their menus. Apart from lunchtime sandwiches, there are options such as Cajun-spiced chicken salad and roasted pork tenderloin. The evening menu typically features honey-roast breast of duck and roasted rump of lamb. The sheltered, flower-filled front patio garden is great for alfresco dining. Catch the beer festival during the first weekend in October.

Open all wk Mon 5-11 Tue-Fri 12-2.30 5-11 (Sat-Sun 12-11) Closed: 25 Dec, Mon L **Bar Meals** L served Tue-Sun 12-2 D served Tue-Sun 6-9 Av main course £11.95 **Restaurant** L served Tue-Sun 12-2 D served Tue-Sun 6-9 Fixed menu price fr £12.95 Av 3 course à la carte fr £24 ⊕ FREE HOUSE ◀ Cumberland Corby Blonde, Barngates Cracker Ale, Tirril Ŏ Westons Old Rosie. **Facilities** Non-diners area ♦ Children's menu Garden ☍ Beer festival Parking

BUTTERMERE　Map 18 NY11

Bridge Hotel

CA13 9UZ ☎ 017687 70252
e-mail: enquiries@bridge-hotel.com
dir: M6 junct 40, A66 to Keswick. Continue on A66 to avoid Keswick centre, exit at Braithwaite. Over Newlands Pass, follow Buttermere signs. (NB if weather is bad follow Whinlatter Pass via Lorton). Hotel in village

A good start or finish to a Cumbrian walk

Surrounded by the Buttermere Fells in an outstandingly beautiful area, this 18th-century former coaching inn is set between Buttermere and Crummock Water with lovely walks right on the doorstep. Good food and real ales are served in the character bars, and a four-course dinner in the dining room might include cushion of Fellside lamb on dauphinoise potatoes with root vegetables and rosemary and redcurrant jus, or roast breast of Gressingham duck on apple and potato rösti.

Open all day all wk 10.30am-11.30pm ⊕ FREE HOUSE ◀ Jennings Cumberland Ale, Smooth Bitter & Corby Blonde, Guinness. **Facilities** ♦ Children's menu Children's portions Garden Parking Wi-fi

Oddfellows Arms

CA7 8EA ☎ 016974 78227
e-mail: info@oddfellows-caldbeck.co.uk
dir: *Telephone for directions*

Hearty Lake District pub food

Caldbeck's famous resident, the huntsman John ("D'ye ken…") Peel lies in the churchyard opposite this 17th-century coaching inn. In fresh hands since April 2012, it serves Jennings real ales, lunchtime snacks – typically jacket potatoes and sandwiches – and offers a menu on which representative dishes include salmon and haddock fishcakes; traditional Cumberland sausage ring; Herdwick lamb cobbler; and cheese ploughman's. From the garden you can admire the dramatic northern fells of the Lake District National Park, before hitting the Cumbrian Way, which passes the front door, or pedalling off to the Reivers cycling route from Whitehaven to Tynemouth two miles away.

Open all day all wk **Bar Meals** L served all wk 12-2 D served all wk 6-8.30 Av main course £8.50-£9 **Restaurant** L served all wk 12-2 D served all wk 6-8.30 Av 3 course à la carte fr £18 ⊕ MARSTON'S ◀ Jennings Bitter, Cumberland Ale. ♀ 13 **Facilities** Non-diners area ♣ (Bar Garden) ♦♦ Children's menu Children's portions Garden ⊼ Parking Wi-fi 🚐 (notice required)

The Cavendish Arms

PICK OF THE PUBS

LA11 6QA ☎ 015395 36240
e-mail: info@thecavendisharms.co.uk
dir: *M6 junct 36, A590 signed Barrow-in-Furness. Cartmel signed. In village take 1st right*

Cosy retreat in a medieval village

A babbling stream flows past the tree-lined garden of this 450-year-old coaching inn situated within Cartmel's village walls, its longest-surviving hostelry. Many traces of its history remain, from the mounting block outside the main door to the bar itself, which was once the stables. Low, oak-beamed ceilings, uneven floors, antique furniture and an open fire create a traditional, cosy atmosphere, and outside. As well as Cumbrian ales, the food owes much to its local origins. The menu changes every six weeks, listing lunchtime sandwiches and starters such as mixed game pâté. Then move on to oven-baked fillet of hake or tagliatelle primavera. Desserts include banoffee crunch sundae and blackcurrant fool. The owners have teamed up with a local company that offers carriage tours of the village. This popular area is ideal for walking, horse riding, and visiting Lake Windermere. Contact the pub for details of the beer festival.

Open all day all wk 9am-11pm **Bar Meals** L served all wk 12-9 D served all wk 12-9 food served all day **Restaurant** L served all wk 12-9 D served all wk 12-9 food served all day ⊕ STAR PUBS & BARS ◀ Caledonian Deuchars IPA, Jennings Cumberland Ale, Cumberland

Corby Ale, Theakston, Guest ales. ♀ 8
Facilities Non-diners area ♣ (Bar Garden) ♦♦ Children's menu Children's portions Garden ⊼ Beer festival Parking Wi-fi 🚐

The Masons Arms

Strawberry Bank LA11 6NW ☎ 015395 68486
e-mail: info@masonsarms.info
dir: *M6 junct 36, A590 towards Barrow. Right onto A5074 signed Bowness/Windermere. 5m, left at Bowland Bridge. Through village, pub on right*

Attractive inn in a beautiful spot

An atmospheric, charmingly decorated pub with a stunning location overlooking the Winster Valley and beyond, The Masons Arms has an atmospheric interior with low, beamed ceilings, old fireplaces and quirky furniture. Waiting staff manoeuvre through the busy bar, dining rooms and heated, covered terraces carrying popular dishes such as warm pitta bread and home-made houmous to nibble; chicken liver pâté with fig and apple chutney to start; and a main course of creamy chicken, ham and leek pie with buttered peas and a choice of potato. Wash it down with a pint of Thwaites Wainwright or Hawkshead Bitter.

Open all day all wk **Bar Meals** L served Mon-Fri 12-2.30, Sat-Sun 12-9 D served Mon-Fri 6-9, Sat-Sun 12-9 **Restaurant** L served Sat-Sun 12-9 D served Mon-Fri 6-9, Sat-Sun 12-9 ⊕ FREE HOUSE/INDIVIDUAL INNS LTD ◀ Thwaites Wainwright, Hawkshead Bitter ♂ Cowmire Hall, Kingstone Press. ♀ 12 **Facilities** Non-diners area ♦♦ Children's menu Children's portions Garden ⊼ Parking Wi-fi

Pig & Whistle NEW

Aynsome Rd LA11 6PL ☎ 015395 36482
e-mail: info@pigandwhistlecartmel.co.uk
dir: *M6 junct 36, A590 towards Barrow. Left at Cartmel sign, pub in village centre*

A genuine local with first-class food

The co-landlord here with Penny Tapsell is Simon Rogan, one of the UK's most accomplished chefs. The pub has long been his local, and he intends it to remain just that – a local. His short but perfectly formed menu offers five remarkably good value-for-money dishes, namely: roast beef with all the trimmings; venison cottage pie with celeriac mash; crispy suckling pig with cabbage and cider gravy; breaded haddock with mushy peas; and roast butternut squash risotto. Real ale drinkers may run into a Dizzy Blonde in the bar – it's one of Robinsons of Stockport's seasonal brews.

Open all wk Summer 12-11 (Winter Mon-Thu 4-11 Fri-Sun 12-11) **Bar Meals** L served Wed-Sat 12-2 D served Wed-Sat 5.30-8.30 Av main course £8.95 **Restaurant** L served Wed-Sat 12-2, Sun 12-8.30 D served Wed-Sat 5.30-8.30, Sun 12-8.30 Fixed menu price fr £18.50 Av 3 course à la carte fr £18.50 ⊕ ROBINSONS ◀ Dizzy Blonde, Hartleys Cumbria Way ♂ Westons Stowford Press.
Facilities Non-diners area ♣ (Bar Restaurant Garden) ♦♦ Children's menu Garden ⊼ Wi-fi 🚐

George and Dragon

PICK OF THE PUBS

CA10 2ER ☎ 01768 865381
e-mail: enquiries@georgeanddragonclifton.co.uk
dir: *M6 junct 40, A66 towards Appleby-in-Westmorland, A6 S to Clifton*

Historic pub majoring on local produce

This lovely pub is more peaceful today than it was in 1745, when the retreating army of Bonnie Prince Charlie was defeated in the nearby village of Clifton. Set on the historic Lowther Estate near Ullswater; the ruined castle-mansion is set at the heart of pasture, woodland and fells alongside the rushing River Lowther and pretty village of Askham. Meticulously renovated by owner Charles Lowther, it is now a traditional inn with contemporary comforts. The appealing menu majors on the bountiful produce of the estate. Beef is from pedigree Shorthorns; pork from home-reared rare breed stock; game and most fish from local waters. Settle in with a pint of Lancaster Blonde and secure a starter of pigeon, pear and walnut salad with buttermilk and blue cheese dressing, followed by roast whole partridge, parsnip purée, braised cabbage and golden raisin sauce. There is a secluded courtyard and garden.

Open all day all wk Closed: 26 Dec **Bar Meals** L served all wk 12-2.30 D served all wk 6-9 **Restaurant** L served all wk 12-2.30 D served all wk 6-9 ⊕ FREE HOUSE ◀ Lancaster Blonde, Hawkshead Bitter, Eden Gold ♂ Westons Stowford Press. ♀ 17
Facilities Non-diners area ♣ (Bar Garden) ♦♦ Children's menu Children's portions Garden ⊼ Parking Wi-fi

The Trout Hotel ★★★★ HL

Crown St CA13 0EJ ☎ 01900 823591
e-mail: enquiries@trouthotel.co.uk
dir: *In town centre*

Popular hostelry overlooking the Derwent

The Trout is a popular black-and-white Grade II listed hotel at the quieter end of the Georgian town centre, right next door to Wordsworth's childhood home. At the bar several Jennings ales are backed by guests from Corby Brewery. Throughout the comprehensive menu The Trout's small army of local suppliers are referenced, so diners know the ingredients are locally sourced and fresh. A typical choice could be blue poppy seed Highgate chicken breast or Wilson's beef fajitas. Round things off with warm chocolate orange tart. In summer, meals and drinks can be enjoyed in the gardens overlooking the River Derwent.

Open all day all wk **Bar Meals** L served all wk 12-9.30 D served all wk 12-9.30 Av main course £12.95 food served all day **Restaurant** L served Sun 12-2 D served all wk 7-9.30 Fixed menu price fr £19.50 Av 3 course à la carte fr £29.85 ⊕ FREE HOUSE ◀ Jennings Cumberland Ale, Cooper Hoop, Corby Blonde ♂ Thatchers. ♀ 24
Facilities Non-diners area ♦♦ Children's menu Children's portions Garden ⊼ Parking Wi-fi 🚐 **Rooms** 49

CONISTON — Map 18 SD39

The Black Bull Inn & Hotel

PICK OF THE PUBS

1 Yewdale Rd LA21 8DU ☎ 015394 41335 & 41668
e-mail: i.s.bradley@btinternet.com
dir: *M6 junct 36, A590. 23m from Kendal via Windermere & Ambleside*

Classic Lakeland pub with own microbrewery

From outside the inn in the very heart of Coniston, lanes and paths tumble one way to the fabulous lake and in the other direction swiftly up into the stunning mountains which hem-in this part of Lakeland. Should this leave you stuck for choice as to which way to turn, tarry a while with a pint of Bluebird or Blacksmiths bitter brewed at the rear of the pub; drink in grand views from the outside tables or contemplate the exploits of Donald Campbell seeking the world water-speed record on the lake 45 years ago, recalled in photos and artefacts in the main bar where Campbell himself took sustenance. Early birds can tuck in to a full breakfast here before hitting the peaks; daytime diners can look forward to hearty snacks such as sautéed mushroom rarebit, home-cooked fish dishes using local sea and game fish and at least two vegetarian options from the regularly changing specials board.

Open all day all wk **Bar Meals** L served all wk 12-9 D served all wk 12-9 food served all day **Restaurant** L served all wk 12-2 D served all wk 6-9 ⊕ FREE HOUSE ◄ Coniston Bluebird Bitter, Bluebird Premium XB, Old Man Ale, Winter Warmer Blacksmiths Ale, Special Oatmeal Stout ♻ Broadoak Premium Perry & Moonshine, Gwynt y Ddraig Haymaker, Guest ciders. ♟ 10 **Facilities** Non-diners area ♣ (Bar Garden) ♦♦ Children's menu Children's portions Family room Garden ⊓ Parking Wi-fi ▄▄ (notice required)

CROOK — Map 18 SD49

The Sun Inn

LA8 8LA ☎ 01539 821351
dir: *Off B5284*

Just the place for refreshments when out walking

An oak-beamed, open fire-warmed country pub that has evolved over time from a row of early 18th-century cottages. Handpumps in the bar dispense Coniston Bluebird and Hawkshead, and seasonal menus feature a fine range of starters and light snacks, as well as locally sourced dishes such as Cajun chicken with garlic mayonnaise dip; grilled lamb's liver and bacon; and spinach and ricotta cannelloni. The restaurant carte and specials boards have their share of interesting dishes too, with medallions of pork; grilled salmon fillet; and mushroom Stroganoff.

Open all wk Mon-Fri 12-2.30 6-11 (Sat 12-11 Sun 12-10.30) ⊕ STAR PUBS & BARS ◄ Coniston Bluebird Bitter, Thwaites Wainwright, Hawkshead, Theakston. **Facilities** ♦♦ Children's menu Children's portions Garden Parking

CROSTHWAITE — Map 18 SD49

The Punch Bowl Inn ★★★★★ INN ◉◉

See Pick of the Pubs on opposite page

ELTERWATER — Map 18 NY30

The Britannia Inn

PICK OF THE PUBS

LA22 9HP ☎ 015394 37210
e-mail: info@britinn.co.uk
dir: *In village centre*

Well placed for the Lake District's top attractions

Built as a farmhouse and cobbler's, this whitewashed free house in the Langdale Valley is nearly 500 years old and became an inn some 200 years ago. A short drive away are Ambleside, Grasmere, Windermere, Hawkshead and Coniston, while walks and mountain-bike trails head off in all directions from the front door. With slate walls several feet thick, the bar area is essentially a series of small, cosy rooms with low-beamed oak ceilings and winter coal fires. Bar staff pull pints of Dent Aviator, Jennings Bitter and guest beers nineteen to the dozen, as well as the house special brewed by Coniston. An even wider selection of real ales is available during the two-week beer festival in mid-November. The inn offers a wide choice of fresh, home-cooked food, with an evening meal typically featuring grilled haggis, chicken and leek pie, and Cumberland sausage. Dine alfresco in the garden and take in the views of the village and tarns.

Open all day all wk 10.30am-11pm **Bar Meals** L served all wk 12-9.30 D served all wk 12-9.30 food served all day **Restaurant** D served all wk 6-9 ⊕ FREE HOUSE ◄ Jennings Bitter, Coniston Bluebird Bitter & Britannia Inn Special Edition, Dent Aviator, Hawkshead Bitter, Guest ales. **Facilities** Non-diners area ♣ (Bar Garden) ♦♦ Children's menu Children's portions Garden ⊓ Beer festival Parking Wi-fi ▄▄ (notice required)

ESKDALE GREEN — Map 18 NY10

Bower House Inn

PICK OF THE PUBS

CA19 1TD ☎ 019467 23244
e-mail: info@bowerhouseinn.co.uk
dir: *4m off A595, 0.5m W of Eskdale Green*

Old world charm and Cumbrian favourites

Hidden away in the fabulously unspoilt Eskdale Valley, this traditional Lake District hotel has been serving locals and walkers since the 17th century. Less than four miles from the main Cumbria coast road, it is ideally placed for visitors heading to the western lakes. Inside, oak beams, ticking clocks and crackling log fires create a comfortable setting to enjoy a pint of Bower House bitter in the bar, which opens out on to an attractive enclosed garden. The restaurant is a charming room with candlelit tables, exposed stone, log fires and equestrian pictures. Here, typical starters may include hand-pressed Cumberland terrine with tomato chutney, which might be followed by pan-fried duck breast with burnt orange sauce, fondant potato and vegetables or local Cumberland sausages with mash, peas and onion gravy. Dog-lovers may want to time a visit to coincide with the UK's largest annual meeting of Staffordshires in May.

Open all day all wk **Bar Meals** L served all wk 12-2.30 D served all wk 6-9 **Restaurant** L served all wk 12-2.30 D served all wk 6-9 ⊕ FREE HOUSE ◄ Bower House Ale, Guest ales. **Facilities** Non-diners area ♣ (Bar Garden) ♦♦ Children's menu Children's portions Play area Garden ⊓ Parking Wi-fi ▄▄ (notice required)

FAUGH — Map 18 NY55

The String of Horses Inn

CA8 9EG ☎ 01228 670297
e-mail: info@stringofhorses.com
dir: *M6 junct 43, A69 towards Hexham. In approx 5m right at 1st lights at Corby Hill/Warwick Bridge. 1m, through Heads Nook, in 1m sharp right. Left into Faugh. Pub on left down hill*

Traditional coaching inn in historic area

Close to Hadrian's Wall in the peaceful village of Faugh, this traditional 17th-century Lakeland inn may be tucked away but it's just ten minutes from Carlisle. There are oak beams, wood panelling, old settles and log fires in the restaurant, where imaginative pub food is on offer, and in the bar, where you'll find real ales from Brampton Brewery. Grilled duck breast with fig and port sauce; beef casserole and mash; Moroccan lamb tagine; and Spanish-style sea bass with mussels, king prawns and chorizo admirably represent what's on a typical menu.

Open Tue-Sun 6-11 Closed: Mon **Bar Meals** D served Tue-Sun 6-8.45 **Restaurant** D served Tue-Sun 6-8.45 ⊕ FREE HOUSE ◄ Brampton Best, Geltsdale Cold Fell. ♟ 8 **Facilities** Non-diners area ♦♦ Children's menu Outside area Parking Wi-fi ▄▄ (notice required)

PICK OF THE PUBS

The Punch Bowl Inn ★★★★★ INN

CROSTHWAITE   Map 18 SD49

LA8 8HR ☎ **015395 68237**
e-mail: info@the-punchbowl.co.uk
web: www.the-punchbowl.co.uk
dir: *M6 junct 36, A590 towards Barrow, A5074, follow Crosthwaite signs. Pub by church*

Luxury Lake District inn and restaurant

Very much a destination dining inn, The Punch Bowl stands alongside the village church in the delightfully unspoilt Lyth Valley. The slates on the bar floor were found beneath the old dining room and complement the Brathay slate bar top and antique furniture, while in the restaurant are polished oak floorboards, comfortable leather chairs and an eye-catching stone fireplace. Two rooms off the bar add extra space to eat or relax with a pint and a daily paper in front of an open fire. Head chef Scott Fairweather focuses on the best local and seasonal produce and has two AA Rosettes to show for his expertise. Sourcing extensively from the area's estates, farms and coastal villages, the lunch and dinner menus in both the bar and the restaurant might begin with baked Loch Fyne scallops, leeks pancetta and gruyère; or a crab pancake, pickled fennel and saffron mayonnaise. For a main course, possibly rack of lamb with boulangère potatoes, roast artichokes and a tarragon jus;

roast fillet of salmon, saffron potatoes, tenderstem broccoli, black tiger prawns and curry-infused oil; or butternut squash risotto, amaretti, parmesan and star anise oil. And for dessert, why not round things off with toffee soufflé and banana and lime ice cream; or cranberry custard tart with yoghurt sorbet and a florentine? The owners are great supporters of Cumbrian micro-breweries, witness Westmorland Gold from Barngates, and Bluebird from the Coniston brewery. In addition to a good list of dessert wines, champagne is available by the glass. Individually furnished guest rooms with free-standing roll-top baths are available.

Open all day all wk **Bar Meals** L served Mon-Fri 12-9, Sat-Sun 12-4 D served

Mon-Fri 12-9, Sat-Sun 5.30-9 Av main course £14.95 **Restaurant** L served Mon-Fri 12-9, Sat-Sun 12-4 D served Mon-Fri 12-9, Sat-Sun 5.30-9 Av 3 course à la carte fr £28.50 ⊕ FREE HOUSE ◀ Barngates Westmorland Gold, Coniston Bluebird Bitter, Winster Valley Old School Ŏ Thatchers Gold. ♟ 14 **Facilities** Non-diners area ♣ ♟ Children's menu Children's portions Garden ⋒ Parking Wi-fi **Rooms** 9

GRASMERE   Map 18 NY30

The Travellers Rest Inn

Keswick Rd LA22 9RR ☎ 015394 35604
e-mail: stay@lakedistrictinns.co.uk
dir: *A591 to Grasmere, pub 0.5m N of Grasmere*

Traditional old world charm and a mountain backdrop

Located on the edge of picturesque Grasmere and handy for touring and exploring the ever-beautiful Lake District, The Travellers Rest has been a pub for more than 500 years. Inside, a roaring log fire complements the welcoming atmosphere of the beamed and inglenook bar area. Along with ales like Sneck Lifter, an extensive menu of traditional home-cooked fare is offered, ranging from Westmorland terrine and eggs Benedict, to wild mushroom gratin and rump of Lakeland lamb.

Open all day all wk 12-11 ⊕ FREE HOUSE ◀ Jennings Bitter, Cocker Hoop, Cumberland Ale & Sneck Lifter, Guest ales. **Facilities** ❄ (Bar Garden) ♦ Children's menu Children's portions Family room Garden Parking Wi-fi

GREAT LANGDALE   Map 18 NY20

The New Dungeon Ghyll Hotel ★★★ HL

LA22 9JX ☎ 015394 37213
e-mail: enquiries@dungeon-ghyll.com
dir: *From Ambleside follow A593 towards Coniston for 3m, at Skelwith Bridge right onto B5343 towards 'The Langdales'*

Spectacularly located walkers' inn

Set in a spectacular spot at the foot of the Langdale Pikes and Pavey Ark, this traditional stone building was once a farmhouse before being transformed into a hotel in 1832. Full of character and charm, the rustic bar is popular with walkers returning from the fells. Local specialities are served in the bar and smart dining room. Typical dishes include game spring rolls with hoi sin and soy dipping sauce; pan-fried venison haunch with parsnip fondant and cranberry, thyme and port sauce; and sticky toffee pudding with ice cream. Real ales include Thwaites Original, Langdale Tup and Wainwright.

Open all day all wk **Bar Meals** L served all wk 12-9 food served all day **Restaurant** D served all wk 6-8.30 ⊕ FREE HOUSE ◀ Thwaites Original, Langdale Tup, Wainwright Ö Kingstone Press. ♟ 8 **Facilities** Non-diners area ♦ Children's menu Children's portions Garden ♬ Parking Wi-fi ⟷ **Rooms** 22

GREAT SALKELD   Map 18 NY53

The Highland Drove Inn and Kyloes Restaurant

PICK OF THE PUBS

CA11 9NA ☎ 01768 898349
e-mail: highlanddrove@kyloes.co.uk
dir: *M6 junct 40, A66 E'bound, A686 to Alston. 4m, left onto B6412 for Great Salkeld & Lazonby*

Convivial pub with high quality food

This 300-year-old country inn is named after the original Highland cattle that were bred in the Western Isles and then driven over the short channels of water to the mainland. Nestling on an old drove road by a village church deep in the lovely Eden Valley, the pub is a great all-rounder with a reputation for high-quality food, and it is still where locals come to enjoy the wide range of cask-conditioned real ales and a good selection of wines. Inside, there's an attractive brick and timber bar, old tables and settles in the main bar area, and a lounge with log fire and tartan fabrics. The upstairs restaurant has a unique hunting lodge feel, with a verandah and lovely country views. Menus reflect the availability of local game and fish, and meat from herds reared and matured in Cumbria.

Open all wk Tue-Sun 12-2 6-late Closed: 25 Dec, Mon L **Bar Meals** L served Tue-Sun 12-2 D served all wk 6-9 **Restaurant** L served Tue-Sun 12-2 D served all wk 6-9 ⊕ FREE HOUSE ◀ Theakston Black Bull Bitter, Best & Traditional Mild, John Smith's Cask & Smooth, Guest ale. ♟ 10 **Facilities** Non-diners area ♦ Children's menu Children's portions Garden ♬ Parking Wi-fi ⟷

GREAT URSWICK   Map 18 SD27

General Burgoyne NEW

Church Rd LA12 0SZ ☎ 01229 586394
e-mail: dropusaline@generalburgoyne.com
dir: *M6 junct 36, A590 towards Barrow-in-Furness. Through Ulverston, left after Swarthmoor signed Great Urswick, 1.5m to pub*

Traditional country pub fast making a big impression

Gentleman Johnny was a British army officer, politician and dramatist, infamous for surrendering his men to the enemy during the American War of Independence. A skull – not Burgoyne's – found during renovations in 1995 is displayed in the fire-warmed bar, where Robinsons beers are served, and the comprehensive menu includes pub classics and sandwiches. In the modern Orangery Restaurant, look for braised featherblade of Lakeland beef; pan-fried rainbow trout; potato and chick pea dhal with roast chicken breast, or without for vegetarians. For pie 'n' peas night, go on a Wednesday. Walkers, cyclists, bikers and dogs are always welcome.

Open all day 12-11 Closed: 1st wk Jan, Mon **Bar Meals** L served Wed-Sat 12-6, Sun 12-8 D served Tue-Sat 6-9, Sun 12-8 Av main course £11.95 food served all day **Restaurant** L served Wed-Sat 12-2, Sun 12-8 D served

Tue-Sat 6-9, Sun 12-8 Av 3 course à la carte fr £25 ⊕ ROBINSONS ◀ Dizzy Blonde, Hartleys Cumbria Way. ♟ 9 **Facilities** Non-diners area ❄ (Bar Outside area) ♦ Children's menu Children's portions Outside area ♬ Parking Wi-fi ⟷ (notice required)

HAWKSHEAD   Map 18 SD39

Kings Arms ★★★ INN

The Square LA22 0NZ ☎ 015394 36372
e-mail: info@kingsarmshawkshead.co.uk
dir: *M6 junct 36, A590 to Newby Bridge, right at 1st junct past rdbt, over bridge, 8m to Hawkshead*

Homely inn in Beatrix Potter village

In the charming square at the heart of this virtually unchanged Elizabethan Lakeland village, made famous by Beatrix Potter who lived nearby, this 16th-century inn throngs in summer. In colder weather, bag a table by the fire in the traditional carpeted bar, quaff a pint of Hawkshead Bitter and tuck into lunchtime light bites such as hot Cumberland sausage with a jacket potato and gravy or evening meals along the lines of smoked trout with cream cheese toasts followed by game and smoked bacon casserole. Look out for the carved figure of a king in the bar. Cosy, thoughtfully equipped bedrooms are available.

Open all day all wk 11am-mdnt **Bar Meals** L served all wk 12-2.30 D served all wk 6-9.30 **Restaurant** L served all wk 12-2.30 D served all wk 6-9.30 ⊕ FREE HOUSE ◀ Hawkshead Gold & Bitter, Coniston Bluebird, Cumbrian Legendary, Guest ales. **Facilities** Non-diners area ❄ (Bar) ♦ Children's menu Children's portions Outside area ♬ Beer festival Wi-fi ⟷ (notice required) **Rooms** 8

The Queen's Head Inn & Restaurant ★★★★ INN

PICK OF THE PUBS

Main St LA22 0NS ☎ 015394 36271
e-mail: info@queensheadhawkshead.co.uk
dir: *M6 junct 36, A590 to Newby Bridge, 1st right, 8m to Hawkshead*

The ideal base for exploring the southern Lakes

On the village's main street and surrounded by fells and forests, the 17th-century Queen's Head is a stone's throw from Esthwaite Water. Hawkshead has impressive literary links – William Wordsworth attended the local grammar school, and Beatrix Potter lived just up the road. Behind the pub's flower-bedecked exterior, low oak-beamed ceilings, wood-panelled walls, slate floors and welcoming fires create a relaxed, traditional setting. Real ales and an extensive wine list promise excellent refreshment, while the menu brims with fresh, quality local produce. At lunchtime sandwiches served with French fries and salad refuel the ramblers. In the evening you might start with ballotine of rabbit or pan-fried king scallops; follow with duo of south Lakeland pheasant or pan-seared plaice fillet. Vegetarians may plump for a dish of gnocchi, blue cheese, Greek yoghurt and pine nut sauce. Puddings are

Save on hotels. Book at **theAA.com/hotel**

CUMBRIA 101 ENGLAND

written on the blackboard. The en suite guest rooms are individually styled.

Open all day all wk 11am-11.45pm (Sun 12-11.45) **Bar Meals** L served Mon-Sat 12-2.30, Sun 12-5 D served all wk 6-9 **Restaurant** L served Mon-Sat 12-2.30, Sun 12-5 D served all wk 6-9 ⊕ ROBINSONS ◀ Double Hop, Hartleys Cumbria Way, Guest ale. ♚ 11 **Facilities** Non-diners area ♥ (Bar Garden) ♦ Children's menu Family room Garden ♯ Wi-fi ▬ (notice required) **Rooms** 13

The Sun Inn ★★★★ INN

Main St LA22 0NT ☎ 015394 36236
e-mail: rooms@suninn.co.uk
dir: *N on M6 junct 36, A591 to Ambleside, B5286 to Hawkshead. S on M6 junct 40, A66 to Keswick, A591 to Ambleside, B5286 to Hawkshead*

A popular hostelry in a busy village

This listed 17th-century coaching inn is at the heart of the charming village where Wordsworth went to school. Inside are two resident ghosts – a giggling girl and a drunken landlord – and outside is a paved terrace with seating. The wood-panelled bar has low, oak-beamed ceilings, and hill walkers and others will enjoy the log fires, real ales and locally sourced food. Choices range from steak and vegetable Westmorland pie; vegetable bake; and Lancashire hotpot to venison burger and fillet of plaice. There are modern bedrooms, including a four-poster room.

Open all day all wk 10am-mdnt ⊕ FREE HOUSE ◀ Cumbrian Legendary Loweswater Gold, Jennings, Guest ale. **Facilities** ♥ (Bar Garden) ♦ Children's menu Children's portions Garden Wi-fi **Rooms** 8

KESWICK	Map 18 NY22

Farmers Arms

Portinscale CA12 5RN ☎ 017687 72322
e-mail: thefarmers.arms@hotmail.co.uk
dir: *M6 junct 40, A66, bypass Keswick. After B5289 junct left to Portinscale*

A rural community pub with mountain views

Set in the pretty village of Portinscale, about a mile from Keswick, this 18th-century pub has traditional decor with an open fire. A warm welcome awaits the locals and touring visitors, who can expect good quality, well-kept ales, and traditional home-cooked food. Typical of the menu are cod goujons with a sweet chilli mayonnaise; Cumberland sausage with gravy; and lamb and mint suet pudding. Favourites from the dessert menu such as ginger pudding round things off nicely. Look out for live music and quiz nights. The beer garden to the rear has views of the mountains.

Open all day all wk ⊕ MARSTON'S ◀ Jennings Bitter, Cumberland Ale, Cocker Hoop & Sneck Lifter, Guest ale. **Facilities** ♥ (Bar Garden) ♦ Children's menu Children's portions Family room Garden Parking Wi-fi

The George ★★★★ INN

3 St John's St CA12 5AZ ☎ 017687 72076
e-mail: rooms@thegeorgekeswick.co.uk
dir: *M6 junct 40, A66, filter left signed Keswick, pass pub on left. At x-rds left into Station St, inn 150yds on left*

Imposing coaching inn with plenty of character

Keswick's oldest coaching inn is a handsome 17th-century building in the heart of this popular Lakeland town. Restored to its former glory, retaining its traditional black panelling, Elizabethan beams, ancient settles and log fires, it makes a comfortable base from which to explore the fells and lakes. Expect to find local Jennings ales on tap and classic pub food prepared from local ingredients. Typical dishes include trio of Cumbrian pork, seafood pasta, venison casserole, cow (steak) pie, apple crumble cheesecake, and sticky toffee pudding. There are 12 comfortable bedrooms available.

Open all day all wk **Bar Meals** L served Mon-Thu 12-2.30, Fri-Sun 12-5 D served all wk 5.30-9 **Restaurant** L served Mon-Thu 12-2.30, Fri-Sun 12-5 D served all wk 5.30-9 ⊕ JENNINGS ◀ Cumberland Ale, Sneck Lifter & Cocker Hoop, Guest ales. ♚ 10 **Facilities** Non-diners area ♥ (Bar Garden) ♦ Children's menu Garden Parking ▬ **Rooms** 12

PICK OF THE PUBS

The Inn at Keswick ★★★★ INN

KESWICK   Map 18 NY22

Main St CA12 5HZ ☎ **017687 74584**
e-mail: relax@theinnkeswick.co.uk
web: www.theinnkeswick.co.uk
dir: *M6 junct 40, A66 to Keswick town centre to war memorial x-rds. Left into Station St. Inn 100yds*

Popular inn at the heart of walking country

Located on the corner of Keswick's vibrant market square, this large yet friendly 18th-century coaching inn combines contemporary comfort with charming reminders of its place in local history. It is understandably popular with walkers – it's within a few strides of England's three highest peaks; dogs are permitted in the bar and some of the bedrooms, an important consideration for many. Lancaster Bomber is one of the award-winning Thwaites ales on tap, and Kingstone Press cider is popular too. The wine selection is small but perfectly formed, with some bottles coming in below the £20 mark. The kitchen's careful sourcing of ingredients from ethical suppliers ensures sustainability as well as freshness, and local artisans such as Thornby Moor Dairy are supported and named on the menu. The slight price premium for these policies is all but unnoticeable, as the menu represents excellent value for money. From noon until teatime, hot sandwiches such as tuna savoury with

cheddar are available, alongside cold sandwiches, light dishes such as tiger prawn tempura, and home comforts such as beefsteak and ale pie topped with puff pastry. Deli boards showing off a selection of local cheeses or meats are great for sharing. In the evening the chargrill is fired up, producing a delicious range of beef, gammon and chicken main courses. Alternatively, go for the hotpot of Fellside lamb topped with sliced potatoes – the inn's best-selling dish. For those with a nagging sweet tooth, a plate of warm treacle tart with clotted cream should hit the spot. If you book to stay in one of the 19 en suite rooms, a wholesome Cumbrian breakfast will set you up for the ramble you have planned.

Open all day all wk 9am-mdnt **Bar Meals** L served Mon-Sat 11-10, Sun 12-9 D served Mon-Sat 11-10, Sun 12-9 food served all day **Restaurant** food served all day 🍺 THWAITES INNS OF CHARACTER 🍺 Wainwright, Original, Lancaster Bomber 🍏 Kingstone Press. **Facilities** 🐾 (Bar) 👶 Children's menu Children's portions 🚌 **Rooms** 19

Save on hotels. Book at theAA.com/hotel

CUMBRIA 103 ENGLAND

The Horse & Farrier Inn

PICK OF THE PUBS

Threlkeld Village CA12 4SQ ☎ 017687 79688
e-mail: info@horseandfarrier.com
dir: *M6 junct 40, A66 signed Keswick, 12m, right signed Threlkeld. Pub in village centre*

A must for Lakeland walkers

Built in 1688, this lovely Lakeland inn is situated at the foot of Blencathra on the ancient route between Keswick and Penrith. With views across Skiddaw and Helvellyn, it's little wonder that it's a hot spot for serious walkers. Within the thick, whitewashed stone walls of this long, low building you'll find slate-flagged floors, beamed ceilings and crackling log fires, with hunting prints decorating the traditional bars and panelled snug. The inn has an excellent reputation for good food and the chefs make full use of local and seasonal produce. The lunchtime bar menu has all the old favourites, from home-roasted Cumbrian ham sandwiches to chilli con carne. In the restaurant, starters could be a pork, bacon and herb terrine; or hot oak-smoked fillet of Scottish salmon. Main courses take in Whitby scampi and chips; traditional Cumberland sausages and slow-braised lamb shoulder.

Open all day all wk 7.30am-mdnt **Bar Meals** L served all wk 12-9 D served all wk 12-9 Av main course £9.50 food served all day **Restaurant** L served all wk 12-9 D served all wk 12-9 Av 3 course à la carte fr £25 food served all day ⊕ JENNINGS ◀ Bitter, Cocker Hoop, Sneck Lifter & Cumberland Ale, Guest ale. ♟ 10
Facilities Non-diners area ❄ (Bar Garden) ♦♦ Children's menu Children's portions Family room Garden ⚲ Parking Wi-fi ⛟ (notice required)

The Inn at Keswick ★★★★ INN

PICK OF THE PUBS

See Pick of the Pubs on opposite page
See advert on page 101

The Kings Head

PICK OF THE PUBS

Thirlspot CA12 4TN ☎ 017687 72393
e-mail: stay@lakedistrictinns.co.uk
dir: *M6 junct 40, A66 to Keswick then A591, pub 4m S of Keswick*

Lovely valley views south of Keswick

Helvellyn, the third highest peak in England, towers above this 17th-century coaching inn; the long, whitewashed building and its delightful beer garden enjoy great views of the surrounding fells, while indoors the traditional bar features old beams and an inglenook fireplace. In addition to several regulars from the Cumberland brewery, there are guest real ales and a fine selection of wines and malt whiskies. In the refurbished bar, paninis, sandwiches and jacket potatoes head the lunchtime options, which also feature a deli board and ploughman's. It's in the restaurant, which looks out to the glacial valley of St Johns in the Vale, that dinner might begin with local Cumberland sausage and mash; and haddock in Jennings beer batter; and end with sticky toffee pudding. From Monday to Saturday chargrilled steaks, ham, pork and salmon extend the daily range.

Open all day all wk 11-11 **Bar Meals** L served all wk 12-9.30 D served all wk 12-9.30 Av main course £9.95 food served all day **Restaurant** D served all wk 7-8.30 Av 3 course à la carte fr £25 ⊕ FREE HOUSE ◀ Jennings Bitter, Cumberland Ale, Sneck Lifter & Cocker Hoop, Guest ales. ♟ 9 **Facilities** Non-diners area ❄ (Bar Garden) ♦♦ Children's menu Family room Garden ⚲ Parking Wi-fi ⛟

Pheasant Inn

Crosthwaite Rd CA12 5PP ☎ 017687 72219
dir: *On A66 Keswick rdbt towards town centre, 60yds on right*

Local food and ales, an ideal stop after a Lakeland walk

An open-fired, traditional Lakeland inn, owned by Jennings Brewery, so expect their regular range on tap, and a monthly guest. For the seasonal menus, the kitchen produces home-cooked, locally sourced food, including starters of whitebait with smoked paprika sauce; and "gooey" baked camembert with ciabatta dipping sticks and chilli, red onion and tomato relish. Follow with a favourite like red Thai chicken and mango curry, or a chef's speciality, such as prime Cumbrian rump steak; pan-fried swordfish marinated in basil and lemon; or oven-roasted chicken supreme on fettuccine pasta.

Open all day all wk Closed: 25 Dec ⊕ JENNINGS ◀ Bitter, Cumberland Ale, Cocker Hoop & Sneck Lifter, Guest ale. **Facilities** ❄ (Bar Garden) ♦♦ Children's menu Garden Parking

The Swinside Inn

Newlands Valley CA12 5UE ☎ 017687 78253
e-mail: booking@swinsideinn.com
dir: *1m from A66, signed Newlands/Swinside*

Enjoy the views from this traditional Lake District inn

Situated at the entrance to the quiet Newlands Valley, in the heart of the Lake District, The Swinside Inn is a listed building dating back to about 1642. From the pub there are superb views of Causey Pike and Cat Bells among other landmarks. The pub has a lounge bar and landscaped beer garden, plus a cosy themed bar, The Refuge Bar, with a pool table, TV and games. You'll also find traditional open fires and oak-beamed ceilings. The extensive bar menu may offer lamb Henry, Cumberland sausage, Swinside chicken, and fresh grilled Borrowdale trout.

Open all day all wk ⊕ STAR PUBS & BARS ◀ Jennings Cumberland Ale, John Smith's Extra Smooth, Caledonian Deuchars IPA, Guest ales. **Facilities** ❄ (Bar Garden) ♦♦ Children's menu Children's portions Family room Garden Parking Wi-fi

KIRKBY LONSDALE   Map 18 SD67

The Pheasant Inn

PICK OF THE PUBS

Casterton LA6 2RX ☎ 01524 271230
e-mail: info@pheasantinn.co.uk
dir: *M6 junct 36, A65 for 7m, left onto A683 at Devils Bridge, 1m to Casterton centre*

Peaceful inn with lovely views of the fells

Below the fell on the edge of the beautiful Lune Valley is this sleepy hamlet with its whitewashed 18th-century coaching inn. The staff and new owners, the Wilson family, ensure a warm welcome in the newly refurbished bar and stylish oak-panelled dining room. Guest ales and beers from Tirril, and a broad choice of wines can be sampled while perusing the interesting menu of quality seasonal produce sourced from the valley farms. Dishes may include rosemary skewers of cod, salmon and king prawns in a chilli and lime dressing to start, followed by slow-cooked shoulder of pork; pan-roasted cod with saffron and herb risotto and chorizo; and butter bean, wild mushroom and leek pie. Chocolate and honeycomb cheesecake is a tempting dessert. In fine weather you can sit outside on the lawn. The inn is perfectly situated for exploring the Dales, the Trough of Bowland and the Cumbrian Lakes.

Open all day all wk Closed: 2wks mid-Jan **Bar Meals** L served all wk 12-2 D served all wk 6-9 **Restaurant** L served Sun 12-2.30 D served Mon-Sat 6-9, Sun 6-8.30 ⊕ FREE HOUSE ◀ Theakstons, Tirril, Guest ales. ♟ 8 **Facilities** Non-diners area ❄ (Bar Garden Outside area) ♦♦ Children's menu Children's portions Garden Outside area ⚲ Parking Wi-fi ⛟ (notice required)

PICK OF THE PUBS

Three Shires Inn ★★★★ INN

LITTLE LANGDALE Map 18 NY30

LA22 9NZ ☎ 015394 37215
e-mail: enquiry@threeshiresinn.co.uk
web: www.threeshiresinn.co.uk
dir: *Exit A593, 2.3m from Ambleside at 2nd junct signed 'The Langdales'. 1st left 0.5m. Inn in 1m*

Perfect provender in a perfect setting

Set beside the winding lane that squeezes from Little Langdale towards the daunting Wrynose and Hard Knott Passes, England's steepest roads, this slate-built Lake District institution is a hugely popular stop-over for those seeking the ultimate combination of superb Lakeland beers, tasty Cumbrian fare and supremely comfortable accommodation. Personally run by the Stephenson family since 1983, it has a blazing fire in the traditional beamed bar during the winter months, while the landscaped garden with its magnificent fell views is the place to savour a pint of local real ale in summer. Everyone — including families with children and dogs — is welcomed in the bar, where amiable staff serve excellent ales from respected microbreweries like Hawkshead, Coniston and Ennerdale. The food is freshly prepared using local Lakeland ingredients. Lunchtime ciabattas and nibbles accompany mains like creamy chicken, leek and tarragon pie or sun-blushed tomato and

pine nut pasta, with a regular changing infusion of blackboard specials. An evening meal may commence with grilled scallops in toasted hazelnut butter, or pea and gorgonzola risotto, followed by a main dish of fillets of sea bass, steamed coconut and herb rice, sauté pak choi and Thai mussel broth; Lakeland rib-eye steak; or pan-fried pheasant breast, a leg meat burger, celeriac and potato purée, roasted beetroot with a port and red wine sauce. Finish with chocolate pancake with chocolate ice cream and white chocolate sauce. Booking ahead for an evening meal is recommended.

Open all wk 11-3 6-10.30 Dec-Jan, 11-10.30 Feb-Nov (Fri-Sat 11-11)
Closed: 25 Dec **Bar Meals** L served all

wk 12-2 (except 24-25 Dec) D served all wk 6-8.45 (except mid-wk Dec-Jan) **Restaurant** D served all wk 6-8.45 (except mid-wk Dec-Jan) ⊞ FREE HOUSE ◗ Cumbrian Legendary Melbreak Bitter, Jennings Bitter & Cumberland Ale, Coniston Old Man Ale, Hawkshead Bitter, Ennerdale Blonde. **Facilities** Non-diners area ☙ (Bar Garden) ♦♦ Children's menu Garden ⊼ Parking Wi-fi **Rooms** 10

KIRKBY LONSDALE *continued*

The Sun Inn ★★★★★ RR ◉

PICK OF THE PUBS

Market St LA6 2AU ☎ 01524 271965
e-mail: email@sun-inn.info
dir: *M6 junct 36, A65 for Kirkby Lonsdale. In 5m left signed Kirkby Lonsdale. Left at next T-junct. Right at bottom of hill*

Welcoming inn serving hearty food

Located next to the church in the pretty market town of Kirkby Lonsdale, this 17th-century free house is a short stroll from the famous Ruskin's View. There are natural stone walls, oak floors, log fires and furniture hand-made by the landlady's father, a cabinet maker. Some of the chairs were previously used on the RMS *Mauretania*. The selection of cask ales is backed by an extensive wine choice. 'Meats, fishes, loaves and dishes' is the carte for starter-size meals for nibbling and include the likes of grilled sardines on toasted sourdough and home-made pork scratchings with vintage cider apple purée. The restaurant menu changes seasonally. Starters may be haggis and black pudding with mustard mash, while hearty main courses such as beef brisket bourguignon and celeriac mash keep the customers satisfied. Eleven bedrooms make The Sun an ideal base from which to explore the Lake District and Yorkshire Dales.

Open all wk Mon 3-11, Tue-Sun 10am-11pm **Bar Meals** L served Tue-Sun 12-10 D served Mon 4-10, Tue-Sun 12-10 food served all day **Restaurant** L served Tue-Sat 12-6, Sun 12-2.30 D served Sun-Thu 6.30-9, Fri-Sat 6.30-9.30 ⊕ FREE HOUSE ◀ Kirkby Lonsdale Radical, Thwaites Wainwright, Hawkshead Bitter. ☗ 9
Facilities Non-diners area ☙ (Bar) ◖ Children's portions Wi-fi **Rooms** 11

The Whoop Hall ★★ HL

Skipton Rd LA6 2HP ☎ 01524 271284
e-mail: info@whoophall.co.uk
dir: *M6 junct 36, A65. Pub 1m SE of Kirkby Lonsdale*

Comfy inn in stunning countryside

Set in the gorgeous Lune Valley with fells rising to over 2,000-ft just up the lane, this considerately modernised 400-year-old coaching inn and hotel is a grand base for exploring the nearby Yorkshire Dales National Park. Yorkshire also provides beers such as Black Sheep and excellent local produce used on the enticing menus in the restaurant and bistro bar. Slow cooked pork belly with braised leeks and cider jus or roasted chump of lamb with bubble-and-squeak satisfy major appetites; or snack on stone baked pizzas or hot deli sandwiches while sitting on the terrace. 24 individually styled rooms encourage a lingering visit.

Open all wk **Bar Meals** L served all wk 12-9 D served all wk 12-9 Av main course £8 food served all day **Restaurant** L served all wk 12-9 D served all wk 12-9 food served all day ⊕ FREE HOUSE ◀ Jennings Cumberland Cream & Cumberland Ale, Black Sheep ☗ Thatchers Gold. ☗ 14 **Facilities** Non-diners area ☙ (Bar Garden) ◖ Play area Family room Garden ☴ Parking ☵ **Rooms** 24

LITTLE LANGDALE   Map 18 NY30

Three Shires Inn ★★★★ INN

PICK OF THE PUBS

See Pick of the Pubs on opposite page

LOWESWATER   Map 18 NY12

Kirkstile Inn ★★★★ INN

PICK OF THE PUBS

See Pick of the Pubs on page 106

LOW LORTON   Map 18 NY12

The Wheatsheaf Inn

CA13 9UW ☎ 01900 85199 & 85268
e-mail: j.williams53@sky.com
dir: *From Cockermouth take B5292 to Lorton. Right onto B5289 to Low Lorton*

Good beers, good food and good views

Occasionally, landlord Mark Cockbain crosses the lane from his white-painted, 17th-century pub to look for salmon and trout in the River Cocker. For visitors it's the panoramic views of the lush Vale of Lorton from the child-friendly beer garden that matter. The quaint, open-fired bar looks like a gamekeeper's lodge: "We like our locals to feel at home," says Mark's wife, Jackie. Real ales from Jennings in Cockermouth also help in that respect. On the menu are cottage pie; salmon en papillote; gammon and sirloin steaks; chicken, leek and Stilton pie; and vegetable curry. The end of March is beer festival time.

Open Tue-Sun Closed: Mon & Tue eve in Jan & Feb **Bar Meals** L served Fri 12-2, Sat 12-3, Sun 12-8.30 D served Mon-Sat 6-8.30, Sun 12-8.30 Av main course £11 **Restaurant** L served all wk D served Mon-Sat 6-8.30, Sun 12-8.30 Fixed menu price fr £9.95 ⊕ MARSTON'S ◀ Pedigree, Jennings Bitter & Cumberland Ale, Brakspear Oxford Gold. **Facilities** Non-diners area ☙ (Bar Garden) ◖ Children's menu Children's portions Family room Garden Beer festival Parking ☵

LUPTON   Map 18 SD58

The Plough Inn ★★★★★ INN ◉

PICK OF THE PUBS

Cow Brow LA6 1PJ ☎ 015395 67700
e-mail: info@theploughatlupton.co.uk
dir: *M6 junct 36, A65 towards Kirkby Lonsdale. Pub on right in Lupton*

A top-notch food at rejuvinated inn

Located in the hills between Kendal and Kirkby Lonsdale, the immense limestone whaleback of Farleton Fell rises behind this inn. In 2009 the owners of the renowned Punch Bowl at Crosthwaite (see entry) took on the failing Plough and transformed it into a dining establishment with wood-burning stoves, stunning oak beams, antique

---

furniture and quirky stuffed creatures. Local beers, including Kirkby Lonsdale Monumental and Coniston Bluebird, are available to deserving ramblers who've tackled the fell. The menu delivers with a punch, from small plate 'tidbits and tasters' (crispy fried whitebait; parmesan risotto balls with salsa) to full meals such as prawn and apple cocktail followed by lemon and herb roasted chicken breast, with lemon meringue pie for dessert. Besides the traditional British options there are internationally inspired dishes such as asparagus and ricotta tortellini. Wash it down with a wine kept in the rustic 'wine caves' viewable to the rear. Afternoon tea and accommodation are also available.

Open all day all wk **Bar Meals** L served all wk 12-9 D served all wk 12-9 Av main course £12.95 food served all day **Restaurant** L served all wk 12-9 D served all wk 12-9 Av 3 course à la carte fr £21.95 food served all day ⊕ FREE HOUSE ◀ Kirkby Lonsdale Monumental, Jennings Cumberland Ale, Coniston Bluebird Bitter ☗ Thatchers Gold. ☗ 14 **Facilities** Non-diners area ☙ (Bar Garden) ◖ Children's menu Children's portions Garden ☴ Parking Wi-fi **Rooms** 5

MILNTHORPE   Map 18 SD48

The Cross Keys

1 Park Rd LA7 7AB ☎ 015395 62115
e-mail: stay@thecrosskeyshotel.co.uk
dir: *M6 junct 35, to junct 35A then A6 N to Milnthorpe; or M6 junct 36, A65 towards Kendal. At Crooklands left onto B6385 to Milnthorpe. Pub at x-rds in village centre*

Village centre pub with a good range of local ales

Levens Hall, Leighton Moss Nature Reserve and Morecambe Bay are all within reach of this imposing former coaching inn. Set in the heart of Milnthorpe village, it makes a good pitstop for cask-conditioned ales and hearty pub food. Menus offer sandwiches, salads and pub favourites like roast topside of beef in a giant Yorkshire pudding; fresh fish and chips; beef Madras curry; and burgers. Puddings are a speciality – look out for the local favourite, sticky toffee.

Open all day all wk ⊕ ROBINSONS ◀ Dizzy Blonde, Hartleys XB, Veltins, Guest ale ☗ Westons Stowford Press. **Facilities** ◖ Children's menu Children's portions Garden Parking Wi-fi

NEAR SAWREY   Map 18 SD39

Tower Bank Arms

PICK OF THE PUBS

See Pick of the Pubs on page 107

PICK OF THE PUBS

Kirkstile Inn ★★★★ INN

LOWESWATER Map 18 NY12

CA13 0RU ☎ **01900 85219**
e-mail: info@kirkstile.com
web: www.kirkstile.com
dir: *Telephone for detailed directions*

Traditional pub set among woods, fells and lakes

Stretching as far as the eye can see, the woods, fells and lakes are as much a draw today as they must have been in the inn's infancy some 400 years ago. The beck below meanders under a stone bridge, oak trees fringing its banks with the mighty Melbreak towering impressively above. Tucked away next to an old church, this classic Cumbrian inn stands just half a mile from the Loweswater and Crummock lakes and makes an ideal base for walking, climbing, boating and fishing. The whole place has an authentic, traditional and well-looked-after feel – whitewashed walls, low beams, solid polished tables, cushioned settles, a well-stoked fire and the odd horse harness remind you of times gone by. You can call in for afternoon tea, but better still would be to taste one of the Cumbrian Legendary Ales – Loweswater Gold, Grasmoor Dark Ale, Esthwaite Bitter - brewed by landlord Roger Humphreys in Esthwaite Water near Hawkshead. Traditional pub food is freshly prepared using local produce and the lunchtime menu brims with wholesome dishes that will satisfy the most hearty appetites. Look for Lakeland steak and ale pie, deep-fried hake fillet in Kirkstile beer batter, or goats' cheese, spinach and roasted vegetable lasagne. If you're in need of a lighter meal, tuck into baguettes, sandwiches, tortilla wraps, omelettes, jacked potatoes or salads. Evening additions and daily specials may take in chicken breast stuffed with Cumberland sausage, wrapped in bacon; pork tenderloin with bubble-and-squeak; or mixed game pudding in suet pastry with shallot and port sauce. Leave room for hot sticky toffee pudding with toffee sauce and local vanilla ice cream.

Open all day all wk Closed: 25 Dec

Bar Meals L served all wk 12-2, light menu 2-4.30 D served all wk 6-9 Av main course £8-£12
Restaurant D served all wk 6-9 Av 3 course à la carte fr £17 ⊕ FREE HOUSE ◾ Cumbrian Legendary Loweswater Gold, Esthwaite Bitter, Grasmoor Dark Ale, Langdale ♂ Westons Stowford Press. ♟ 9 **Facilities** Non-diners area ♦♦ Children's menu & portions Family room Garden Beer festival Parking **Rooms** 10

Save on hotels. Book at **theAA.com/hotel**

CUMBRIA 107 ENGLAND

PICK OF THE PUBS

Tower Bank Arms

NEAR SAWREY Map 18 SD39

LA22 0LF ☎ 015394 36334
e-mail:
enquiries@towerbankarms.co.uk
web: www.towerbankarms.co.uk
dir: *On B5285 SW of Windermere. 1.5m from Hawkshead*

Rustic pub popular with Beatrix Potter fans

This 17th-century village pub on the west side of Lake Windermere is owned by the National Trust (although run independently), as is Beatrix Potter's old home, Hill Top, which is situated just behind the inn. Once known as The Blue Pig and later The Albion, it has been the Tower Bank Arms for over a century and Potter illustrated it perfectly in her *Tale of Jemima Puddleduck,* although history appears not to record whether she ever slipped in for a drink during a break from sketching! The literary connection brings out the Peter Rabbit fan club in force, particularly in summer, so the delightfully unspoilt rustic charm of this little treasure may be easier to appreciate out of season. In the low-beamed, slate-floored main bar there's an open log fire, fresh flowers and ticking grandfather clock, and local brews on handpump from the Hawkshead and Barngates breweries. The full lunch and dinner menus are available throughout all areas. Hearty country food makes good use of local

produce, whether a snack, such as a Lakeland ham sandwich or chicken liver pâté, or main dish, perhaps slow-braised shoulder of Cumbrian lamb; beef and ale stew; or roast belly pork with black pudding. Daily specials could feature locally reared rib-eye steak, and 'surf and turf'. Desserts include sticky toffee pudding, bread-and-butter pudding, and banana and gingerbread sundae. From the garden you are treated to a panorama of farms, fells and fields.

Open all wk (all day Etr-Oct) Closed: one wk in mid Jan **Bar Meals** L served all wk 12-2 D served Mon-Sat 6-9, Sun & BHs 6-8 (Mon-Thu in winter) Av main course £12.75 **Restaurant** D served Mon-Sat 6-9, Sun & BHs 6-8 (Mon-Thu in winter) Av 3 course à la carte fr £21.15

⊕ FREE HOUSE ◀ Barngates Tag Lag & Cat Nap, Hawkshead Bitter & Brodie's Prime ♻ Westons Wyld Wood Organic Vintage, Country Perry. ♟ 10 **Facilities** Non-diners area ♣ (Bar Garden) ♦♦ Children's portions Garden ⊼ Parking Wi-fi ▭▭ (notice required)

OUTGATE — Map 18 SD39

Outgate Inn

LA22 0NQ ☎ 015394 36413
e-mail: info@outgateinn.co.uk
dir: M6 junct 36, by-passing Kendal, A591 towards Ambleside. At Clappersgate take B5285 to Hawkshead, Outgate 3m

Traditional Cumbrian inn with welcoming atmosphere

Once owned by a mineral water manufacturer and now part of Robinsons and Hartleys Brewery, this 17th-century Lakeland inn is full of traditional features including oak beams and a real fire in winter. The secluded beer garden at the rear is a tranquil place to enjoy the summer warmth. Food options include salads and light bites such as a beefburger or ham, egg and chips; and hearty options such as braised blade of beef, horseradish mash with port jus; or grilled chicken wrapped in bacon with bubble-and-squeak and red wine and thyme sauce. Home-made Baileys and chocolate cheesecake is a typical dessert. Gluten-free menu available.

Open all day all wk **Bar Meals** L served all wk 12-5.30 D served all wk 5.30-8.45 food served all day **Restaurant** L served all wk 12-5.30 D served all wk 5.30-8.45 food served all day ⊕ ROBINSONS ◀ Dizzy Blonde, Hartleys XB. **Facilities** Non-diners area ❄ (Bar Garden) ♦ Children's menu Children's portions Garden ⋀ Parking Wi-fi ⛟ (notice required)

PENRITH — Map 18 NY53

Cross Keys Inn

Carleton Village CA11 8TP ☎ 01768 865588
e-mail: crosskeys@kyloes.co.uk
dir: From A66 in Penrith take A686 to Carleton Village, inn on right

Traditional food and lovely views

This much-refurbished old drovers' and coaching inn at the edge of Penrith offers sweeping views to the nearby North Pennines from the upstairs restaurant where timeless, traditional pub meals are the order of the day; Scottish wholetail battered scampi or Cumberland lamb hotpot for example. Kyloes Grill here is particularly well thought of, with only Cumbrian meats used. Beers crafted in nearby Broughton Hall by Tirril Brewery draw an appreciative local clientele, warming their toes by the ferocious log-burner or laying a few tiles on the domino tables.

Open all wk Mon-Fri 12-2.30 5-12 (Sat-Sun all day) **Bar Meals** L served Mon-Sat 12-2.30 **Restaurant** L served all wk 12-2.30 D served Sun-Thu 6-9, Fri-Sat 5.30-9 ⊕ FREE HOUSE ◀ Tirril 1823, Guest ale. ☘ 10 **Facilities** Non-diners area ❄ (Bar Garden) ♦ Children's menu Children's portions Garden ⋀ Parking Wi-fi ⛟ (notice required)

RAVENSTONEDALE — Map 18 NY70

The Black Swan ★★★★ INN

PICK OF THE PUBS

CA17 4NG ☎ 015396 23204
e-mail: enquiries@blackswanhotel.com
dir: M6 junct 38 take A685 E towards Brough

Award-winning inn with a local pride ethos

A previous winner of the AA Pub of the Year for England, The Black Swan is set in a pretty conservation village, nestling below Wild Boar Fell beside the frothy headwaters of the River Eden. The enterprising owners of this family-run residential inn have placed themselves right at the heart of the community; their on-site village store was opened by HRH Prince Charles in 2008. The imposing Victorian inn's tranquil riverside garden is home to red squirrels, which you might spot after you've walked the Howgill Fells, explored the Lakes or toured the Yorkshire Dales, all of which are on the doorstep. The ever-changing selection of northern beers includes the likes of Dent, Hawkshead and Tirril. Reliance on local produce is also evident in the choice of dishes, with all meat traceable. The menu might include a starter of beef carpaccio, a precursor to pan-fried monkfish wrapped in Cumbrian pancetta with a prawn and chilli risotto.

Open all day all wk 8am-11.30pm **Bar Meals** food served all day **Restaurant** food served all day ⊕ FREE HOUSE ◀ Black Sheep Ale & Best Bitter, Dent, Tirril, Hawkshead, Hesket Newmarket, Cumberland, Guinness, Guest ales ☘ Thatchers Gold. ☘ **Facilities** Non-diners area ❄ (Bar Garden) ♦ Children's menu Children's portions Garden Parking Wi-fi ⛟ (notice required) **Rooms** 14

The Fat Lamb Country Inn ★★★★ INN

PICK OF THE PUBS

Crossbank CA17 4LL ☎ 015396 23242
e-mail: enquiries@fatlamb.co.uk
dir: On A683 between Sedbergh & Kirkby Stephen

Old fashioned hospitality in idyllic countryside

High above the green meadows of Ravenstonedale in the furthest corner of old Westmorland, this 350-year-old stone coaching inn has its own nature reserve – seven acres of open water and wetlands, surrounded by flower-rich meadows. From The Fat Lamb's gardens, your gaze will fall on some of England's most precious and remote countryside, so it's no surprise that ramblers and country-lovers choose to stay here. An open fire in the traditional Yorkshire range warms the bar in winter, where visitors and locals mingle and natter. Snacks and meals are served both here and in the traditional and relaxed restaurant, which is decorated with old prints and plates. Start with pressed chicken and pistachio terrine, and follow perhaps with pan-fried sea bass fillet on a shrimp risotto. Alternatively, check out the day's specials board or five-course set menu. Whatever you choose, it will have been prepared on site using the best available local ingredients.

Open all day all wk **Bar Meals** L served all wk 12-2 D served all wk 6-9 Av main course £10.95 **Restaurant** L served all wk 12-2 D served all wk 6-9 Fixed menu price fr £25 ⊕ FREE HOUSE ◀ Black Sheep Best Bitter ☘ Westons Stowford Press. **Facilities** Non-diners area ❄ (Bar Garden) ♦ Children's menu Children's portions Play area Garden ⋀ Parking Wi-fi ⛟ (notice required) **Rooms** 12

The King's Head NEW

CA17 4NH ☎ 015396 23050
e-mail: enquiries@kings-head.com
dir: M6 junct 38, A685 towards Kirkby Stephen. Approx 7m, right to Ravenstonedale. Pub 200yds on right

Set in beautiful rolling Cumbrian countryside

It's hard to believe that this old whitewashed pub was closed for three years, re-opening in 2011 following major refurbishment. There are real fires in the restaurant, where a three-course lunch or evening meal might be 'Taste of the Lakes' smoked haddock; venison and cranberry pie, with braised cabbage and chips; and home-made warm treacle tart with vanilla ice cream. Vegetarians will find dishes such as beetroot risotto, and potato and smoked cheese suet pudding. Three regularly-changing real ales and eight wines by the glass are served in the open-plan bar. Cyclists will appreciate the lock-up facility for their bikes.

Open all day all wk Closed: 25 Dec **Bar Meals** L served all wk 12-9, 12-2.30 Oct-Etr D served all wk 12-9, 6-9 Oct-Etr Av main course £12 **Restaurant** L served all wk 12-9, 12-2.30 Oct-Etr D served all wk 12-9, 6-9 Oct-Etr Av 3 course à la carte fr £23 ⊕ FREE HOUSE ◀ 3 Guest ales regularly changing. ☘ 8 **Facilities** Non-diners area ❄ (Bar Garden) ♦ Children's menu Children's portions Garden ⋀ Parking Wi-fi ⛟ (notice required)

SANTON BRIDGE — Map 18 NY10

Bridge Inn NEW

CA19 1UX ☎ 019467 26221
e-mail: info@santonbridgeinn.com
dir: From A595 at Gosforth follow Eskdale & Wasdale sign. Through Santon to inn on left. Or inn signed from A595 S of Holmkirk

A "reet good welcome" awaits visitors to this country inn

The Lake District was formed, not by ice or volcanic action, but by large moles and eels. Actually, that's a lie, one of the many told in this comfortable old inn at the annual World's Biggest Liar competition, held every November. No doubt pints of Jennings Sneck Lifter and guest ales help to inspire such outrageous fibbing. Main courses include home-made steak-and-kidney pie; deep-fried haddock in Cocker Hoop beer batter; griddled gammon steak; and Kenyan Coast msetto (aubergine moussaka, mozzarella cheese and naan bread). The inn is licensed for civil marriages, when, hopefully, "I do" is not a lie!

Open all day all wk **Bar Meals** L served all wk 12-2.30 D served all wk 5.30-9 Av main course £9.50

Save on hotels. Book at theAA.com/hotel

CUMBRIA 109 ENGLAND

Restaurant L served all wk 12-2.30 D served all wk 5.30-9 Av 3 course à la carte fr £18 ⊕ JENNINGS ◀ Cumberland Ale, Sneck Lifter & Cocker Hoop. ☘ 10 **Facilities** Non-diners area ❖ (Bar Outside area) ♦♦ Children's menu Children's portions Family room Outside area ⏞ Parking Wi-fi ⛟ (notice required)

SEATHWAITE   Map 18 SD29

Newfield Inn

LA20 6ED ☎ 01229 716208
dir: *From Broughton-in-Furness take A595 signed Whitehaven & Workington. Right signed Ulpha. Through Ulpha to Seathwaite, 6m (NB do not use Sat Nav)*

Classic walkers' pub with view-filled garden

Tucked away in the peaceful Duddon Valley, Wordsworth's favourite, is Paul Batten's 16th-century cottage-style pub. Hugely popular with walkers and climbers, the slate-floored bar regularly throngs with parched outdoor types quaffing pints of Cumberland Ale and Jennings Bitter. Served all day, food is hearty and traditional and uses local farm meats; the choice ranges from fresh rolls, salads and lunchtime snacks like double egg and chips, to beef lasagne, grilled T-bone steak, and pear and chocolate crumble. Retreat to the garden in summer and savour cracking southern fells views, or come for the beer festival in October.

Open all day all wk **Bar Meals** Av main course £9.50 food served all day **Restaurant** food served all day ⊕ FREE HOUSE ◀ Cumberland Corby Ale, Jennings Cumberland Ale, Jennings Sneck Lifter, Barngates Cat Nap. ☘ 8 **Facilities** Non-diners area ❖ (Bar Garden) ♦♦ Children's portions Play area Garden ⏞ Beer festival Parking ⛟

SIZERGH   Map 18 SD48

The Strickland Arms

PICK OF THE PUBS

LA8 8DZ ☎ 015395 61010
e-mail: thestricklandarms@yahoo.co.uk
dir: *From Kendal A591 S. At Brettargh Holt junct left, at rdbt 3rd exit onto A590 (dual carriageway) signed Barrow. Follow brown signs for Sizergh Castle. Into right lane, turn right across dual carriageway. Pub on left*

Popular spot after exploring the southern lakes

Beside the lane leading to the National Trust's Sizergh Castle and just a stride from paths alongside the lively River Kent, this slightly severe-looking building (also NT-owned) slumbers amidst low hills above the Lyth Valley at the southern fringe of the Lake District National Park. The essentially open-plan interior is contemporary-Edwardian, with high ceilings, flagstoned floors, grand fires and Farrow & Ball finish to the walls, creating an instantly

welcoming atmosphere. Changing hands in June 2012, the inn now offers dishes such as potted Morecambe Bay shrimps; black pudding fritters; and Welsh rarebit. Then you can choose a salad or pasta dish; a mixed grill, a steak, or a classic such as lamb hotpot; steak pie; or Westmorland sausages with butter mash and onion gravy.

Open all wk Mon-Thu 12-3 5.30-11 (Fri-Sun all day) & (all day in summer) Closed: 25 Dec **Bar Meals** L served Mon-Fri 12-2, Sat 12-2.30, Sun 12-8.30 D served Mon-Sat 6-9, Sun 12-8.30 **Restaurant** L served Mon-Fri 12-2, Sat 12-2.30, Sun 12-8.30 D served Mon-Sat 6-9, Sun 12-8.30 ⊕ FREE HOUSE ◀ Thwaites Lancaster Bomber, Coniston Bluebird Bitter, Cumbrian Legendary Loweswater Gold, Kirkby Lonsdale Monumental, Bowness Bay Swan Blond ⚙ Kingstone Press. ☘ 9 **Facilities** Non-diners area ❖ (Bar Restaurant Garden) ♦♦ Children's menu Children's portions Garden ⏞ Beer festival Parking Wi-fi ⛟

TEMPLE SOWERBY   Map 18 NY62

The Kings Arms ★★★★ INN

CA10 1SB ☎ 017683 62944
e-mail: enquiries@kingsarmstemplesowerby.co.uk
dir: *M6 junct 40, E on A66 to Temple Sowerby. Inn in town centre*

Hostelry at the heart of the village

This 400-year-old coaching inn, just a few miles from Penrith, was where William Wordsworth and Samuel Coleridge, in 1799, set off for their exploration of the Lake District. The kitchen serves a mix of old pub-grub favourites, including chicken liver parfait, whitebait with bread and butter, and steak and ale pie; and modern dishes such as bacon and Stilton rarebit, slow roasted pork belly and mushroom Stroganoff. There is a good choice of vegetarian choice, a children's menu and the desserts are home made.

Open all wk 10-3 6-11 **Bar Meals** L served all wk 12-2 D served all wk 6-9 Av main course £10.50 **Restaurant** L served all wk 12-2 D served all wk 6-9 ⊕ FREE HOUSE ◀ Black Sheep, Guest ales ⚙ Westons Stowford Press. **Facilities** Non-diners area ❖ (Bar Garden) ♦♦ Children's menu Children's portions Garden ⏞ Parking Wi-fi ⛟ (notice required) **Rooms** 8

TIRRIL   Map 18 NY52

Queen's Head Inn

CA10 2JF ☎ 01768 863219
e-mail: margarethodge567@btinternet.com
dir: *A66 towards Penrith then A6 S towards Shap. In Eamont Bridge turn right just after Crown Hotel. Tirril in 1m on B5320*

Country inn with a poetic past

On the edge of the Lake District National Park, this traditional English inn dates from 1719 and is chock-full of beams, flagstones and memorabilia. While enjoying a pint of Unicorn, Cumbria Way or Dizzy Blonde in the bar, look for the Wordsworth Indenture, signed by the great poet himself, his brother, Christopher, and local wheelwright John Bewsher, to whom the Wordsworths sold the pub in 1836. A meal in the bar or restaurant might include bacon and black pudding salad; oven-baked chicken stuffed with Blengdale Blue and spinach; and chocolate and orange tart.

Open all day all wk Sun-Thu 12-11 (Fri-Sat 12-12) ⊕ ROBINSONS ◀ Unicorn & Dizzy Blonde, Hartleys Cumbria Way & XB, Guest ales ⚙ Westons Stowford Press. **Facilities** ❖ (Bar) ♦♦ Children's portions Parking

---

TORVER   Map 18 SD29

Church House Inn

LA21 8AZ ☎ 01539 441282
e-mail: churchhouseinn@hotmail.co.uk
dir: *A539 from Coniston towards Broughton-in-Furness. Inn on left in Torver before junct with A5084 towards Ulverston*

Centuries old hospitality under the Old Man of Coniston

Footpaths wind to the bank of Coniston Water whilst the ridges of the Coniston Horseshoe mountains rise steeply from sloping pastures opposite. Sitting plum in the middle, the 15th-century Church House Inn revels in this idyllic location, offering a great range of Lakeland beers and satisfying meals sourced from local farms and estates; Cumberland tattie hotpot based on slow-braised Herdwick lamb hits the spot, enjoyed in the olde-worlde rambling interior or sheltered beer garden.

Open all day all wk 10.30am-mdnt ⊕ ENTERPRISE INNS ◀ Hawkshead Bitter & Lakeland Gold, Barngates Tag Lag, Cumbrian Legendary Loweswater Gold. **Facilities** ❖ (Bar Garden) ♦♦ Children's portions Family room Garden Parking Wi-fi

TROUTBECK — Map 18 NY40

Queen's Head ★★★★ INN

PICK OF THE PUBS

Townhead LA23 1PW ☎ 015394 32174
e-mail: reservations@queensheadtroutbeck.co.uk
dir: M6 junct 36, A590, A591 towards Windermere, right at mini rdbt onto A592 signed Penrith/Ullswater. Pub 2m on left

Old Lakeland inn with a reputation for international cooking

This 17th-century inn stands in the valley of Troutbeck, which, bordered by impressive fells criss-crossed by footpaths, is a real magnet for ramblers. Nooks and crannies, a log fire throughout the year, and low beams stuffed with old pennies by farmers on their way home from market all help to make this smart coaching inn hard to beat in the traditional stakes. The bar is even a four-poster bed which once saw service in Appleby Castle. Look below bar counter level at the carved panelling while ordering a pint of Dizzy Blonde. The kitchen team create accomplished international dishes, with a typical first course of duck, orange and smoked bacon gâteau on a roasted chestnut purée with crispy sage leaves. Main courses of note include bobotie, a South African dish of minced lamb, almonds and apricots topped with brandy custard. Well-behaved dogs on leads are allowed on the slated area in the bar, and there are toys and games for young children.

Open all day all wk Bar Meals food served all day Restaurant food served all day ⊕ ROBINSONS ◀ Dizzy Blonde, Old Tom & Double Hop, Hartleys Cumbria Way & XB. ♟ 8 Facilities Non-diners area ❀ (Bar Outside area) ♦ Children's menu Children's portions Outside area ☞ Parking Wi-fi ⚊ Rooms 15

ULVERSTON — Map 18 SD27

Farmers Arms Hotel

Market Place LA12 7BA ☎ 01229 584469
e-mail: roger@thefarmers-ulverston.co.uk
dir: In town centre

A warm welcome and crowd-pleasing pub grub

Perhaps the oldest inn in the Lake District, there's a hospitable welcome here at the Farmers Arms, whether in the traditionally decorated restaurant with its oak beams and impressive views of the Crake Valley or in the 14th-century stable bar complete with a log fire and original slate floors. The wide-ranging menus include basket meals like quarter chicken with chips; sautéed mushrooms and creamy Stilton hot baguette; a variety of steaks plus lots of crowd-pleasers such as ploughman's lunch and locally sourced Cumberland sausage. Local ales include Hawkshead Bitter and there's both beer and cider festivals annually.

Open all day all wk Bar Meals L served all wk 9-3 D served all wk 6-9 ⊕ FREE HOUSE ◀ Hawkshead Bitter,

John Smith's, Courage Directors, Yates Ö Symonds. ♟ 12 Facilities Non-diners area ♦ Children's menu Children's portions Garden ☞ Beer festival Cider festival Wi-fi ⚊ (notice required)

Old Farmhouse NEW

Priory Rd LA12 9HR ☎ 01229 480324
e-mail: oldfarmhouse@hotmail.com
dir: From A590 in Ulverston take A5087 signed Bardsea. Pub on right

Community focused pub in a converted barn

Located just south of the town and a short distance from Morecambe Bay, the Old Farmhouse is a busy community pub housed within a beautifully converted barn. It has a separate snooker room, a lively bar with a big screen for live sports, and a very popular restaurant in the main barn area. From the extensive traditional menu choose a classic like their award-winning Cumberland pie, or pork cutlets with mushroom and pancetta sauce from the grill section. Specials may include lamb rump with redcurrant jus, and leave room for the apple and cinnamon crumble. Local Cumbrian ales and a sun-trap courtyard garden complete the picture.

Open all day all wk Bar Meals food served all day Restaurant food served all day ⊕ FREE HOUSE ◀ Ulverston Harvest Moon, Lancaster Blonde, Cumberland, Sharp's Doom Bar, Copper Dragon. ♟ 9 Facilities Non-diners area ❀ (Bar Garden Outside area) ♦ Children's menu Children's portions Garden Outside area ☞ Parking Wi-fi ⚊

The Stan Laurel Inn

31 The Ellers LA12 0AB ☎ 01229 582814
e-mail: thestanlaurel@aol.com
dir: M6 junct 36, A590 to Ulverston. Straight on at Booths rdbt, left at 2nd rdbt in The Ellers, pub on left after Ford garage

Local ales and hearty food

When the old market town of Ulverston's most famous son – the comic actor Stan Laurel – was born in 1890, this town-centre pub was still a farmhouse with two cottages surrounded by fields and orchards. Owners Trudi and Paul Dewar serve a selection of locally brewed real ales and a full menu of traditional pub food plus a specials board. Take your pick from starters such as pork, chicken and apricot terrine; Greek salad; or battered black pudding. Among tasty mains are steak and ale pie; vegetable and Stilton crumble; and a selection from the grill.

Open Mon 7pm-11pm Tue-Thu 12-2.30 6-11 Fri-Sat 12-2.30 6-12 Sun 12-11.30 Closed: Mon L Bar Meals L served Tue-Sat 12-2, Sun 12-8 D served Tue-Sat 6-9, Sun 12-8 Restaurant L served Tue-Sat 12-2, Sun 12-8 D served Tue-Sat 6-9, Sun 12-8 ⊕ FREE HOUSE ◀ Thwaites Original, Ulverston, Barngates, Salamander. Facilities Non-diners area ♦ Children's menu Children's portions Outside area ☞ Parking Wi-fi

WASDALE HEAD — Map 18 NY10

Wasdale Head Inn ★★★ INN

CA20 1EX ☎ 019467 26229
e-mail: reception@wasdale.com
dir: From A595 follow Wasdale signs. Inn at head of valley

Welcoming inn surrounded by record breakers

Dramatically situated at the foot of England's highest mountain, adjacent to England's smallest church and not far from the deepest lake, this Victorian inn is reputedly the birthplace of British climbing – photographs decorating the oak-panelled walls reflect the passion for this activity. It is also allegedly the home of the World's Biggest Liar, but hopefully that doesn't extend to the menu. Expect local ales and hearty food such as goulash soup followed by shepherd's pie with a golden cheesy topping or Thai green vegetable curry. A beer festival on the first Sunday in October is a great reason to hang up the climbing boots for a day and maybe stay over in one of the comfortable bedrooms.

Open all day all wk Bar Meals L served all wk 12-8.30 D served all wk 12-8.30 food served all day Restaurant D served Wed-Sun 6-8 ⊕ FREE HOUSE ◀ Cumbrian Legendary Ales Loweswater Gold & Esthwaite Bitter, Great Gable Yewbarrow & Iron Awe, Jennings Ö Westons. Facilities Non-diners area ❀ (Bar Restaurant Garden) ♦ Children's menu Children's portions Garden ☞ Beer festival Parking Rooms 20

WINDERMERE — Map 18 SD49

The Angel Inn

Helm Rd LA23 3BU ☎ 015394 44080
e-mail: rooms@the-angelinn.com
dir: From Rayrigg Rd (parallel to lake) into Crag Brow, right into Helm Rd

Modern decor, modern menus and lake views

Just five minutes' walk from Lake Windermere, in the centre of Bowness-on-Windermere, this family-owned and run gastro-pub offers plenty of city-chic style. Unusual local ales vie with international beers at the bar, and good food based on local produce is available throughout the day from a choice of menus: sandwiches and light lunches; starters, nibbles and salads; cheese plates or main courses – try wild boar and apple sausage or Cumbrian Fellbred steak – desserts and a children's menu. In summer customers can enjoy the gardens and grounds; the terrace offers fantastic views.

Open all day all wk 9am-11pm Closed: 25 Dec ⊕ FREE HOUSE ◀ Coniston Bluebird Bitter, Hawkshead Bitter, Tirril Old Faithful, Stringers West Coast Blond, Jennings Cumberland Ale. Facilities ♦ Children's menu Children's portions Garden Parking Wi-fi

Eagle & Child Inn

Kendal Rd, Staveley LA8 9LP ☎ 01539 821320
e-mail: info@eaglechildinn.co.uk
dir: *M6 junct 36, A590 towards Kendal then A591 towards Windermere. Staveley approx 2m*

Free house with a riverside beer garden

Surrounded by miles of excellent walking, cycling and fishing country in a quiet village, this friendly inn shares the same name with several pubs in Britain, which refers to a legend of a baby found in an eagle's nest during the time of King Alfred. The rivers Kent and Gowan meet at the pub's gardens with its picnic tables for outdoor eating and local-ale drinking. Dishes include ingredients from village suppliers, such as slow-roasted lamb shank, Cumberland sausage or chicken breast wrapped in smoked bacon. Interesting vegetarian choices might be Malaysian vegetable curry or vegetable and chickpea casserole.

Open all day all wk **Bar Meals** L served Mon-Fri 12-2.30, Sat-Sun 12-3 D served all wk 6-9 Av main course £10 ⊕ FREE HOUSE ◀ Hawkshead Bitter, Yates Best Bitter, Tirril, Coniston, Dent Ŏ Westons, Cowmire Hall Ancient Orchard, Cumbrian. ♚ 10 **Facilities** Non-diners area ♣ (Bar Restaurant Garden) ♦♦ Children's menu Children's portions Garden ♠ Parking Wi-fi ━━

WINSTER   Map 18 SD49

The Brown Horse Inn

LA23 3NR ☎ 015394 43443
e-mail: steve@thebrownhorseinn.co.uk
dir: *On A5074 between Bowness-on-Windermere & A590 (Kendal to Barrow-in-Furness road)*

An inn of many talents

The beautiful and tranquil Winster Valley is a perfect location for this 1850s inn full of original features. Despite all the time-worn charm, the decor has a subtly modern edge on account of a refurbishment. The inn is virtually self-sufficient: vegetables and free-range meat come from the owners' surrounding land, and ales are brewed on site. The innovative cooking is a contemporary take on traditional fare and dinner could see a starter of lobster custard, sea salt croûte, pistachio and parmesan; mains range from home-made pie of the week to mixed grill of lamb with fondant potatoes and minted hollandaise.

Open all day all wk **Bar Meals** L served all wk 12-2 D served all wk 6-9 Av main course £15.95 **Restaurant** L served all wk 12-2 D served all wk 6-9 ⊕ FREE HOUSE ◀ Winster Valley Best Bitter, Old School, Hurdler, Chaser. ♚ 12 **Facilities** Non-diners area ♣ (Bar Outside area) ♦♦ Children's menu Children's portions Outside area ♠ Parking Wi-fi ━━ (notice required)

WORKINGTON   Map 18 NY02

The Old Ginn House

Great Clifton CA14 1TS ☎ 01900 64616
e-mail: enquiries@oldginnhouse.co.uk
dir: *Just off A66, 3m from Workington & 4m from Cockermouth*

Converted farm building offering good food

When this was a farm, ginning was the process by which horses were used to turn a grindstone that crushed grain. It took place in the rounded area known today as the Ginn Room and which is now the main bar, serving Jennings and Coniston beers. The dining areas, all butter yellow, bright check curtains and terracotta tiles, rather bring the Mediterranean to mind, although the extensive menu and specials are both cosmopolitan and traditional. Take your pick from steak and ale pie; pasta carbonara; salmon fillet and prawns; Cumberland sausage and mash; or mushroom Stroganoff. Salads, jackets, and other lite-bites also available.

Open all day all wk Closed: 24-26 Dec, 1 Jan **Bar Meals** L served all wk 12-2 D served all wk 6-9.30 **Restaurant** L served all wk 12-2 D served all wk 6-9.30 ⊕ FREE HOUSE ◀ Jennings Bitter, John Smith's, Coniston Bluebird Bitter. **Facilities** Non-diners area ♦♦ Children's menu Children's portions Garden ♠ Parking ━━ (notice required)

YANWATH   Map 18 NY52

The Yanwath Gate Inn

PICK OF THE PUBS

CA10 2LF ☎ 01768 862386
e-mail: enquiries@yanwathgate.com
dir: *Telephone for directions*

Known for its Cumbrian craft beers and good food

Between the North Pennines and the hills and moors bounding Ullswater is this former 17th-century toll gate, or 'yat', on the long road from Kendal to Scotland. Today's incarnation as a pub and restaurant is a place where 'free range' and 'organic' are the watchwords. Lunch and evening menus will vary, and content depends on seasonal or specialist availability, with the Eden Valley providing much of the produce. For main course, perhaps try pan-roasted goose breast with bubble-and-squeak, ginger and honey jus; or sweet potato, shallot and banana tarte Tatin. Leave room for orange pannacotta with pickled lemons. To accompany, there's authentic Trappist beer, an excellent list of wines, or indulge in a beer from one of the reliable craft breweries within a few miles of the inn.

Open all day all wk **Bar Meals** L served all wk 12-2.30 D served all wk 6-9 **Restaurant** L served all wk 12-2.30 D served all wk 6-9 ⊕ FREE HOUSE ◀ Tirril, Barngates, Yates Ŏ Westons Old Rosie. ♚ 12 **Facilities** Non-diners area ♣ (Bar Garden) ♦♦ Children's menu Garden ♠ Parking Wi-fi

DERBYSHIRE

ASHOVER   Map 16 SK36

The Old Poets Corner

Butts Rd S45 0EW ☎ 01246 590888
e-mail: enquiries@oldpoets.co.uk
dir: *From Matlock take A632 signed Chesterfield. Right onto B6036 to Ashover*

Thriving pub with ten real ales

It's no wonder that ale and cider aficionados flock to this traditional village local; it dispenses eight ciders, and ten cask ales including choices from the Ashover Brewery behind the pub. The March and October beer festivals see these numbers multiply. There's live music here twice a week, quizzes, special events and Sunday night curries. Hearty home-cooked pub dishes range from creamy garlic mushrooms on sourdough bread to braised liver and onions in a rich gravy made with the pub's own Coffin Lane Stout. Walk it off in the scenic Derbyshire countryside.

Open all day all wk **Bar Meals** L served Mon-Fri 12-2, Sat-Sun 12-3 D served Mon-Thu 6.30-9, Fri-Sat 6-9.30, Sun 7-9 **Restaurant** L served Mon-Fri 12-2, Sat-Sun 12-3 D served Mon-Thu 6.30-9, Fri-Sat 6-9.30, Sun 7-9 ⊕ FREE HOUSE ◀ Ashover, Oakham, Guest ales Ŏ Broadoak Perry & Moonshine, Westons Old Rosie. **Facilities** Non-diners area ♣ (Bar Restaurant Outside area) ♦♦ Family room Outside area ♠ Beer festival Parking ━━ (notice required)

BAKEWELL   Map 16 SK26

The Bull's Head

PICK OF THE PUBS

Church St, Ashford-in-the-Water DE45 1QB ☎ 01629 812931
dir: *Off A6, 2m N of Bakewell, 5m from Chatsworth Estate*

Congenial, family-run coaching inn

In Debbie Shaw's family for 60 years, this popular 17th-century coaching inn has an abundance of oak beams, as well as open fires, carved settles, and jazz playing quietly in the background. While they've been at this Robinsons Brewery-owned house, landlords Debbie and husband Carl have picked up a number of impressive accolades. Carl, you see, is also the chef, producing not just the meals but the breads, chutneys and even the cheese biscuits, everything in fact that might accompany or follow a meal. His menus always list steak and Unicorn ale pie; other possibilities include baked red mullet with fennel, tomatoes and leeks; and wild mushroom Stroganoff vol-au-vent. The new Supper Club offers a choice of seven dishes at £7 each if ordered before 7pm. A snack in the attractive beer garden, followed by a game of boules could be fun.

Open all wk 12-3 6-11 (Sun 12-3.30 7-10.30) **Bar Meals** L served Mon-Sat 12-2, Sun 12-2.30 D served Mon-Sat 6.30-9, Sun 7-9 (ex Thu & Sun in winter) ⊕ ROBINSONS ◀ 1892, Build a Rocket Boys!, Unicorn. **Facilities** Non-diners area ♦♦ Children's portions Play area Family room Garden ♠ Parking

BAKEWELL *continued*

The Monsal Head Hotel

PICK OF THE PUBS

Monsal Head DE45 1NL ☎ 01629 640250
e-mail: enquiries@monsalhead.com
dir: *A6 from Bakewell towards Buxton. 1.5m to Ashford. Follow Monsal Head signs, B6465 for 1m*

Extensive range of local ales on draught

Only a few minutes from Chatsworth House and the famous railway viaduct at Monsal Head, the hotel's Stables bar reflects its earlier role as the home of railway horses collecting passengers from Monsal Dale station. It has a rustic ambience with an original flagstone floor, seating in horse stalls and a log fire – the perfect place to enjoy a range of cask ales from microbreweries such as Oakwell of Barnsley. The Longstone restaurant is spacious and airy with large windows to appreciate the views, again with an open fire in the colder weather. Although the menu has influences from around the world, it demonstrates an extensive use of local produce. Breakfasts and morning coffee are available everyday, and the same menu is offered in the bar, restaurant and the large outdoor seating area.

Open all day all wk 8am-mdnt **Bar Meals** L served Mon-Sat 12-9.30, Sun 12-9 D served Mon-Sat 12-9.30, Sun 12-9 food served all day **Restaurant** L served Mon-Sat 12-9.30, Sun 12-9 D served Mon-Sat 12-9.30, Sun 12-9 food served all day ⊕ FREE HOUSE ◀ Oakwell Barnsley Bitter, Bradfield, Buxton, Wincle ♻ Addlestones. ♟ 17 **Facilities** Non-diners area ♣ (Bar Garden) ♦ Children's menu Children's portions Garden Outside area ⏢ Parking ▤ (notice required)

BAMFORD   Map 16 SK28

Yorkshire Bridge Inn

PICK OF THE PUBS

See Pick of the Pubs on opposite page
See advert below

BARROW UPON TRENT   Map 11 SK32

Ragley Boat Stop

Deepdale Ln, Off Sinfin Ln DE73 1HH ☎ 01332 703919
e-mail: pippa@king-henrys-taverns.co.uk
dir: *Telephone for directions*

Canalside pub ideal for watching the world go by

This timbered and whitewashed free house features a lovely garden sloping down to the Trent and Mersey Canal. A huge balcony overlooking the canal and the grassy garden complete with picnic benches are both great spots for a quiet drink. The smart, spacious interior is cool and contemporary with muted colours, stripped wood and plenty of comfy sofas. The menu of freshly prepared dishes has choices to suit every appetite. Beef in all its forms is a major attraction; alternatively international flavours abound in dishes such as vegetable fajitas, chicken korma, swordfish steak, and a Cajun chicken and ribs combo.

Open all day all wk 11.30-11 **Bar Meals** L served all wk 12-10 D served all wk 12-10 food served all day **Restaurant** L served all wk 12-10 D served all wk 12-10 food served all day ⊕ FREE HOUSE/KING HENRY'S TAVERNS ◀ Greene King IPA, Marston's Pedigree, Guinness. ♟ 16 **Facilities** Non-diners area ♦ Children's menu Children's portions Garden Parking ▤

BEELEY   Map 16 SK26

The Devonshire Arms at Beeley ★★★★ INN ◉◉

PICK OF THE PUBS

Devonshire Square DE4 2NR ☎ 01629 733259
e-mail: res@devonshirehotels.co.uk
dir: *B6012 towards Matlock, pass Chatsworth House. After 1.5m turn left, 2nd entrance to Beeley*

Up-to-the-minute inn with a rich history

This handsome 18th-century village inn is surrounded by classic Peak District scenery and stands on the Chatsworth Estate. It became a thriving coaching inn; Charles Dickens was a frequent visitor; and it is rumoured that King Edward VII often met his mistress Alice Keppel here. The comfortably civilised and neatly furnished interior comprises three attractive beamed rooms, with flagstone floors, roaring log fires, antique settles and farmhouse tables; the rustic taproom is perfect for walkers with muddy boots. In contrast, the brasserie dining room is modern, bright and colourful, with stripey chairs and bold artwork. Come for beers brewed at Chatsworth's brewery and some sublime modern British food (two AA Rosettes) cooked by chef-patron Alan Hill. Using estate-reared and -grown produce, dishes include classics like beer-battered haddock and chips; beef cobbler; tempura skate wing with lobster sauce; and Chatsworth venison spit-roasted over the fire. There are wonderful walks from the front door.

Open all day all wk **Bar Meals** L served all wk 12-3 D served all wk 6-9.30 **Restaurant** L served all wk 12-3 D served all wk 6-9.30 ⊕ FREE HOUSE/DEVONSHIRE HOTELS & RESTAURANTS ◀ Peak Chatsworth Gold, Thornbridge Jaipur, Theakston Old Peculier ♻ Aspall. ♟ 10 **Facilities** Non-diners area ♦ Children's menu Children's portions Garden ⏢ Parking Wi-fi **Rooms** 8

PICK OF THE PUBS

Yorkshire Bridge Inn

BAMFORD   Map 16 SK28

Ashopton Rd S33 0AZ ☎ **01433 651361**
e-mail: info@yorkshire-bridge.co.uk
web: www.yorkshire-bridge.co.uk
dir: *From Sheffield A57 towards Glossop,
left onto A6013, pub 1m on right*

In the heart of wonderful Peak District walking country

Named after the old packhorse bridge over the River Derwent, this early 19th-century free house is only a short distance away from the Ladybower Reservoir. Between 1935 and 1943, when it was created, two local villages were drowned and during periods of drought it's possible to see the remains of one of them. It was in 1943 that the RAF's 617 Squadron, known as 'The Dambusters', used Ladybower and two other nearby reservoirs for testing Barnes Wallis's famous bouncing bombs, later to destroy two important German dams. Back inside, views from the beamed and chintz-curtained bars take in the peak of Whin Hill, making it a jolly good spot for enjoying a pint of Peak Bakewell Best or Farmers Bitter or one of the 11 wines by the glass, and good-quality pub food made with fresh local produce. Sandwiches are all freshly prepared, with fillings from home-baked ham to hot tuna melt. Main meal starters include Thai cod and prawn fishcakes, and a sharing platter in which nachos with melted cheese,

jalapeño peppers and baked spare ribs marinated in barbecue sauce are just a pointer to what will arrive on the plate. Next could come slow-roasted Derbyshire belly pork; roast chicken breast with Yorkshire pudding and sausage; freshly battered catch of the day; or one of the various salad platters. If you've walked to one of the reservoirs and back, look to the grill for a calorie-replacing T-bone, sirloin or gammon steak, cooked to your liking without demur from a chef who doesn't insist on doing it his way. Chocolate mousse, and daily-changing hot sponges finish a meal off well. A beer and cider festival is held in mid-May. Nearby attractions include Chatsworth, Haddon Hall, Dovedale, Buxton and Bakewell.

Open all day all wk **Bar Meals** L served Mon-Sat 12-2, Sun 12-8.30 D served Mon-Thu 6-9, Fri-Sat 6-9.30, Sun 12-8.30 ⊞ FREE HOUSE ◖ Peak Ales Bakewell Best Bitter, Bradfield Farmers Blonde & Farmers Bitter, Abbeydale Moonshine ♂ Thatchers. ♟ 11
Facilities Non-diners area ♦♦ Children's menu Children's portions Garden ⴕ Beer festival Cider festival Parking Wi-fi ⛟ (notice required)

BIRCHOVER
Map 16 SK26

The Druid Inn

PICK OF THE PUBS

Main St DE4 2BL ☎ 01629 653836
dir: From A6 between Matlock & Bakewell take B5056 signed Ashbourne. Approx 2m left to Birchover

Ever changing menu of good food

Although the pub has been here since 1607, it has gained a reputation for high-quality food for the last few years. Utilising plenty of Peak District produce, the menu combines traditional with contemporary dishes, all of which can be enjoyed in one of the four dining areas. Lunch and maybe a pint of Abbeydale Absolution in the bar and snug; a more formal meal in the upper or lower restaurant; or outside on the terrace, from where you can survey the surrounding countryside. The constantly evolving menu ranges from light bites and sandwiches to two- and three-course meals. A starter such as jellied pig's head with piccalilli and sourdough bread could precede Chatsworth Estate fallow deer stew with Yorkshire stump and juniper dumplings. End with Yorkshire blue cheese, pannacotta and Pontefract cake ice cream. Children and dogs are welcome too.

Open all day all wk noon-late **Bar Meals** L served Mon-Sat 12-9, Sun 12-8 D served Mon-Sat 12-9, Sun 12-8 food served all day **Restaurant** L served Mon-Sat 12-9, Sun 12-8 D served Mon-Sat 12-9, Sun 12-8 food served all day ⊕ FREE HOUSE ◀ Abbeydale Absolution, Guest ales. ♛ 10 **Facilities** Non-diners area ✿ (Bar Garden) ⬥ Children's menu Children's portions Family room Garden ⋒ Parking (notice required)

Red Lion Inn

PICK OF THE PUBS

Main St DE4 2BN ☎ 01629 650363
e-mail: red.lion@live.co.uk
dir: 5.5m from Matlock, off A6 onto B5056

Good beer plus Sardinian dishes on the menu

Built in 1680, the Red Lion started life as a farmhouse and gained its first licence in 1722; its old well, now glass-covered, still remains in the taproom. Follow a walk to nearby Rowter Rocks, a gritstone summit affording stunning valley and woodland views, cosy up in the oak-beamed bar with its exposed stone walls, scrubbed oak tables, worn quarry-tiled floor, and welcoming atmosphere. Quaff a pint of locally brewed Nine Ladies or one of the other real ales on tap that change weekly, and refuel with a plate of home-cooked food prepared from predominantly local ingredients. Start with a Sardinian speciality from owner Matteo Frau's homeland, perhaps a selection of cured meats, cheese and olives, then follow with pork loin medallions with lemon, caper and sage butter, or field mushroom tart Tatin with Birchover blue cheese. Don't miss the mid-July beer festival.

Open 12-2.30 6-11.30 (Sat & BH Mon 12-12 Sun 12-11) Closed: Mon in winter ex BHs **Bar Meals** L served Mon-Fri 12-2.30, Sat 12-9, Sun-12-8 D served Mon-Fri 6-9, Sat

12-9, Sun-12-8 Av main course £9.50 **Restaurant** L served Mon-Fri 12-2.30, Sat 12-9, Sun-12-8 D served Mon-Fri 6-9, Sat 12-9, Sun-12-8 Fixed menu price fr £7.95 Av 3 course à la carte fr £12.50 ⊕ FREE HOUSE ◀ Peak Swift Nick, Nine Ladies, Peakstones Rock, Buxton, Thornbridge, Ichinusa (Sardinian) ♂ Westons Perry & Old Rosie. **Facilities** Non-diners area ⬥ Children's portions Garden Beer festival Parking

BONSALL
Map 16 SK25

The Barley Mow

The Dale DE4 2AY ☎ 01629 825685
e-mail: david.j.wragg@gmail.com
dir: S from Matlock on A6 to Cromford. Right onto A5012 (Cromwell Hill). Right into Water Ln (A5012). Right in Clatterway towards Bonsall. Left at memorial into The Dale. Pub 400mtrs on right

Good food, real ales and fast fowl

There are several reasons to visit this intimate, former lead miner's cottage: Bonsall is apparently Europe's UFO capital; the pub hosts the World Championship Hen Races; and landlords Colette and David display an unshakeable commitment to Peak District and other regional real ales, as their bank holiday beer festivals help to confirm. The simple menu is all about home-cooked pub grub, such as ham, egg and chips; scampi and chips; extra-mature rump steak; chicken curry; sausages and mash; beef chilli; and gammon steak.

Open 6-11 (Sat-Sun 12-11) Closed: Mon (ex BHs) **Bar Meals** L served Sat-Sun 12-3 D served all wk 6-9 Av main course £8.95 ⊕ FREE HOUSE ◀ Thornbridge, Whim, Abbeydale, Blue Monkey ♂ Hecks, Westons Perry. ♛ 10 **Facilities** Non-diners area ✿ (Bar) ⬥ Children's menu Children's portions Outside area ⋒ Beer festival Parking Wi-fi

BRASSINGTON
Map 16 SK25

Ye Olde Gate Inn

PICK OF THE PUBS

Well St DE4 4HJ ☎ 01629 540448
e-mail: info@oldgateinnbrassington.co.uk
dir: 2m from Carsington Water off A5023 between Wirksworth & Ashbourne

Cosy inn popular with locals and visitors alike

Sitting beside an old London to Manchester turnpike in the heart of Brassington, a hill village on the southern edge of the Peak District, this venerable inn dates back to 1616. Aged beams (allegedly salvaged from the wrecked Armada fleet), a black cast-iron log burner, an antique clock, charmingly worn quarry-tiled floors and a delightful mishmash of polished furniture give the inn plenty of character – as does the reputed ghost. Hand-pumped Jennings Cumberland takes pride of place behind the bar, alongside other Marston's beers and guest ales. The menu offers firm lunchtime favourites, such as home-made curry; or a range of filled baguettes. In the evening you may find a fillet of pork in pepper sauce served with rice; poached salmon fillet with a prawn and white wine

sauce; or duck breast served with an orange and Cointreau sauce. Desserts range from a traditional apple crumble to a black cherry and white chocolate torte.

Open Tue eve-Sun Closed: Mon (ex BHs), Tue L **Bar Meals** L served Wed-Sat 12-1.45, Sun 12.30-2.45 D served Tue-Sat 6.30-8.45 ⊕ MARSTON'S ◀ Pedigree, Jennings Cumberland Ale, Guest ales. **Facilities** Non-diners area ⬥ Children's portions Family room Garden ⋒ Parking

CASTLETON
Map 16 SK18

The Peaks Inn

How Ln S33 8WJ ☎ 01433 620247
e-mail: info@peaksinn.com
dir: On A6187 in centre of village

Plenty on offer at this Peak District magnet

Here's where to aim for after climbing Lose Hill, or walking along the Hope Valley. Standing below Peveril Castle, this 17th-century, stone-built pub is a real magnet, seducing visitors with its leather armchairs, open log fires and locally brewed cask beers, real ciders and plenty of wines by the glass; alternative places to recover are the restaurant/coffee shop and raised sun terrace. Regional ingredients are used to good effect in Whitby wholetail scampi; Peaks Inn 'famous' square pie of the day; and even in spiced Nile perch with vegetable couscous; and Mediterranean vegetable pasta and pesto. The pub hosts a July beer festival.

Open all day all wk Closed: 25 Dec, 1st 2wks Jan **Bar Meals** L served Mon-Fri 12-3, Sat 12-8.30, Sun 12-4 D served Mon-Fri 5.30-8.30, Sat 12-8.30 **Restaurant** L served Sun 12-4 D served Mon-Fri 5.30-8.30 ⊕ PUNCH TAVERNS ◀ Kelham Island Easy Rider, Castle Rock Harvest Pale, Guest ales ♂ Westons Old Rosie & Stowford Press. ♛ 9 **Facilities** Non-diners area ✿ (Bar Garden) ⬥ Children's portions Garden ⋒ Beer festival Parking Wi-fi (notice required)

Ye Olde Nags Head

Cross St S33 8WH ☎ 01433 620248
e-mail: info@yeoldenagshead.co.uk
dir: A625 from Sheffield, W through Hope Valley, through Hathersage & Hope. Pub on main road

A warm welcome and crowd-pleasing food

Situated in the heart of the Peak District National Park, close to Chatsworth House and Haddon Hall, this traditional 17th-century coaching inn continues to welcome thirsty travellers. Miles of wonderful walks and country lanes favoured by cyclists bring visitors seeking a warm welcome and refreshment in the cosy bars warmed by open fires. The interior is a successful mix of contemporary and traditional, a theme also reflected in the menu: expect stone-baked pizzas, beef, ale and potato pie and The Nags mighty mixed grill. There's also a beer festival in the summer.

Open all day all wk **Bar Meals** L served all wk 12-9 D served all wk 12-9 Av main course £9 food served all day **Restaurant** L served all wk 12-9 D served all wk 12-9

Save on hotels. Book at theAA.com/hotel

DERBYSHIRE 115 ENGLAND

food served all day ⊕ FREE HOUSE ◄ Timothy Taylor Landlord, Buxton Kinder Sunset, Kelham Island Riders on the Storm, Black Sheep, Sharp's Doom Bar, Bradfield Farmers Blonde, Guinness Ö Westons Old Rosie. Facilities Non-diners area ✿ (Bar) ◕ Children's menu Children's portions Beer festival Parking Wi-fi ➡ (notice required)

CHELMORTON — Map 16 SK16

The Church Inn ★★★★ INN

SK17 9SL ☎ 01298 85319
e-mail: justinsatur@tiscali.co.uk
dir: *From A515 or A6 take A5270 between Bakewell & Buxton. Chelmorton signed*

A good all-rounder worth discovering

A narrow no-through-road ends here in secluded Chelmorton amidst a remarkable landscape of tiny medieval walled fields and hidden, wildflower-rich deep limestone dales. The Church Inn, too, is tiny and hidden; take the time discover it to relish the memorable mix of regional and microbrewery beers (try a Thornbridge) and an eclectic menu of pub favourites (surf 'n turf) and home-crafted specials which may include rabbit pie or vegetable Wellington. Bag a table in the patio garden to appreciate the exquisite location, opposite Derbyshire's highest church, or chinwag and warm up by the bar's roaring wood-burner.

Open all wk 12-3 6-12 (Fri-Sun 12-12) Bar Meals L served Mon-Thu 12-2.30, Fri-Sun 12-9 D served Mon-Thu 6-9, Fri-Sun 12-9 Av main course £9.50 Restaurant L served Mon-Thu 12-2.30, Fri-Sun 12-9 D served Mon-Thu 6-9, Fri-Sun 12-9 ⊕ FREE HOUSE ◄ Marston's Burton Bitter & Pedigree, Adnams Southwold Bitter, Local ales. Facilities Non-diners area ✿ (Bar Garden) ◕ Children's menu Children's portions Garden ⊼ Wi-fi ➡ (notice required) Rooms 4

CHESTERFIELD — Map 16 SK37

Red Lion Pub & Bistro

PICK OF THE PUBS

Darley Rd, Stone Edge S45 0LW ☎ 01246 566142
e-mail: dine@redlionpubandbistro.co.uk
dir: *Telephone for directions*

Innovative food close to good walking country

Dating back to 1788, the Red Lion has seen many changes but it has retained much of its character. Located on the edge of the beautiful Peak District National Park, the original wooden beams and stone walls are now complemented by discreet lighting and comfy leather armchairs which add a contemporary edge. Striking black-and-white photographs decorate the walls, whilst local jazz bands liven up the bar on Thursday evenings. Meals are served in the bar and bistro, or beneath umbrellas in the large garden. Seasonal produce drives the menu and the chefs make everything, from sauces to the chips. Typical choices might start with ham hock and black pudding croquette with soft boiled quail's egg and pineapple carpaccio, followed by pan-roasted

Gressingham duck breast, hazelnuts, parsnip and apple purée, raspberry and vinegar dressing and creamed potatoes. Leave space for roasted apple millefeuille with toffee apple ice cream and salted caramel.

Open all day all wk Bar Meals L served Sun-Thu 12-9, Fri-Sat 12-9.30 D served Sun-Thu 12-9, Fri-Sat 12-9.30 food served all day Restaurant L served Sun-Thu 12-9, Fri-Sat 12-9.30 D served Sun-Thu 12-9, Fri-Sat 12-9.30 food served all day ⊕ FREE HOUSE ◄ Guest ales. ♉ Facilities Non-diners area ◕ Children's menu Children's portions Garden ⊼ Parking Wi-fi ➡ (notice required)

CHINLEY — Map 16 SK08

Old Hall Inn

PICK OF THE PUBS

See Pick of the Pubs on page 116

DALBURY — Map 10 SK23

The Black Cow ★★★★ INN ◉ NEW

The Green DE6 5BE ☎ 01332 824297
e-mail: info@blackcow.co.uk
dir: *From A52 (W of Derby) take B5020 signed Mickleover. On left bend right signed Long Ln & Longford. Left signed Lees Dalbury. Pub on left in village. (NB if using Sat Nav follow directions not postcode)*

Recommended for its hospitality, accommodation and cuisine

Facing the village green and its iconic red telephone box, this free house champions real ales from county-based Dancing Duck, Mansfield and Mr Grundy's breweries. In the restaurant, award-winning head chef Jaswant Singh's seasonal menus might feature red Thai vegetable stir-fry; spicy meatballs in tomato parsley sauce with melted cheddar and pasta; and breaded scampi with home-made chips. Since this is Derbyshire, expect Bakewell tart with crème anglaise to make an appearance. Tastefully decorated guest rooms offer free Wi-fi. A small store/farm shop even sells ramblers' and cyclists' requirements.

Open all wk 12-3 5-close (Sat & Sun 12-close) Bar Meals L served Mon-Fri 12-2, Sat 12-9.30, Sun 12-4 D served Mon-Thu 6-9, Fri 6-9.30, Sat 12-9.30 Restaurant L served Mon-Fri 12-2, Sat 12-9.30, Sun 12-4 D served Mon-Thu 6-9, Fri 6-9.30, Sat 12-9.30 ⊕ FREE HOUSE ◄ Guest real ales. ♉ 10 Facilities Non-diners area ◕ Children's menu Children's portions Play area Family room Garden Outside area ⊼ Beer festival Parking Wi-fi ➡ (notice required) Rooms 5

DERBY — Map 11 SK33

The Alexandra Hotel

203 Siddals Rd DE1 2QE ☎ 01332 293993
e-mail: alexandrahotel@castlerockbrewery.co.uk
dir: *150yds from rail station*

Victorian railway hotel with an excellent choice of real ales

This small hotel was built in 1871 and is named after the Danish princess who married the Prince of Wales, later Edward VII. It was also known as the Midland coffee house after the Midland Railway company, one of Derby's major employers. It is noted for its real ales with between six and eight pumps on the go at any one time; real ciders, and bottled and draught continental beers complete the line-up at the bar. Simple food offerings include pies and filled rolls.

Open all day all wk 12-11 (Fri 12-12 Sat 11am-mdnt) Bar Meals food served all day ⊕ CASTLE ROCK ◄ Harvest Pale Ö Westons Old Rosie. Facilities Non-diners area ✿ (Bar Outside area) ◕ Outside area Parking Wi-fi

The Brunswick Inn

1 Railway Ter DE1 2RU ☎ 01332 290677
e-mail: thebrunswickinn@btconnect.com
dir: *From rail station turn right. Pub 100yds*

Rich in history and real ales

'A True Ale House and Brewery' it says on the sign outside this Grade II listed pub, which the Midland Railway built in the 1840s. It has no fewer than 16 handpumps, six for Brunswick ales brewed on the premises, the rest for guest beers. Real ciders are brought up from the cellar. Bar lunches are typically ploughman's, steak-and-ale pie, and chilli and cheese (either cheddar or Stilton), which is billed on the menu as 'cha-cha-cha'. There's a beer festival during the first weekend in October.

Open all day all wk Bar Meals L served Mon-Wed 11.30-2.30, Fri-Sat 11.30-5, Sun 12-4 ⊕ BRAMPTON ◄ Brunswick, Guest ales Ö Westons Old Rosie & 1st Quality. Facilities Non-diners area ✿ (Bar Garden) ◕ Children's portions Family room Garden ⊼ Beer festival ➡ Notes ◉

PICK OF THE PUBS

Old Hall Inn

CHINLEY Map 16 SK08

Whitehough SK23 6EJ ☎ 01663 750529
e-mail: info@old-hall-inn.co.uk
web: www.old-hall-inn.co.uk
dir: *B5470 W from Chapel-en-le-Frith. Right into Whitehough Head Ln. 0.8m to inn*

An ideal spot for serious walkers

Prime Peak District walking country lies all around this family-run, 16th-century pub attached to Whitehough Hall. Within easy reach are the iconic landscape features of Kinder Scout, Mam Tor and Stanage Edge, all very popular with climbers and fell-walkers, who head here and refreshment following their exertions. The good news is that there's a drinks list as long as your arm because the inn is a strong supporter of local breweries, and the popular bar delivers beers from Kelham Island, Red Willow, Thornbridge and many more, with Sheppy's from Somerset among the real ciders and perries. These are backed by all manner of bottled beers, particularly Belgian wheat, fruit and Trappist varieties, a remarkable choice of malts and gins and around 80 wines. The food is greatly sought after too and the pub opens into the Minstrels' Gallery restaurant in the old manor house, where a short seasonal menu and daily specials offer freshly made 'small plates' of smoked salmon with salsa verdi; smoked duck, walnut, rocket and

parmesan salad; or chicken liver, bacon and port pâté with onion marmalade. Larger options are steaks, cooked six ways from blue to well done; oven-roasted chicken supreme with spicy tuscan bean cassoulet, topped with crème fraîche; Cumberland sausages and mash; steak-and-kidney pudding; and French trimmed pork loin with apple sauce, Mac Burnham's black pudding fritter and cider sauce. Desserts, some accompanied by Hilly Billy ice cream from nearby Blaze Farm, are all home-made, as are all the chutneys, pickles and sauces.

Open all day all wk **Bar Meals** L served Mon-Sat 12-2, Sun 12-7.30 D served Mon-Thu 5-9, Fri-Sat 5-9.30, Sun 12-7.30 Av main course £10

Restaurant L served Mon-Sat 12-2, Sun 12-7.30 D served Mon-Thu 5-9, Fri-Sat 5-9.30, Sun 12-7.30 Av 3 course à la carte fr £15 ⊕ FREE HOUSE
◗ Marston's, Thornbridge, Phoenix, Abbeydale, Storm, Kelham Island, Red Willow Ở Thatchers, Sheppy's, Westons.
♟ 12 **Facilities** Non-diners area ♟♦
Children's menu & portions Garden ☲
Beer festival Parking Wi-fi 🚐

DOE LEA　　Map 16 SK46

Hardwick Inn

Hardwick Park S44 5QJ ☎ 01246 850245
e-mail: hardwickinn@hotmail.co.uk
dir: M1 junct 29, A6175. 0.5m left signed Stainsby/
Hardwick Hall. After Stainsby, 2m, left at staggered junct.
Follow brown tourist signs

Step back in time at this village inn

Dating from the 15th century and built of locally quarried
sandstone, this striking building was once the lodge for
Hardwick Hall (NT) and stands at the south gate of
Hardwick Park, not far from Chesterfield. Owned by the
Batty family for three generations, the pub has a
rambling interior and features period details such as
mullioned windows, oak beams and stone fireplaces.
Traditional food takes in a popular daily carvery roast, a
salad bar, hearty home-made pies, pot roasts and
casseroles, as well as selections of fish and vegetarian
dishes. A handy pitstop for M1 travellers.

Open all day all wk **Bar Meals** Av main course £10 food
served all day **Restaurant** food served all day ⊕ FREE
HOUSE ◀ Theakston Old Peculier & XB, Bess of Hardwick,
Black Sheep, Peak Ales Chatsworth Gold Ö Addlestones.
♟ 10 **Facilities** Non-diners area ❤ (Bar Garden) ♦️
Children's menu Children's portions Play area Family
room Garden 🎋 Parking 🚌

ELMTON　　Map 16 SK57

The Elm Tree NEW

S80 4LS ☎ 01909 721261
e-mail: enquiries@elmtreeelmton.co.uk
dir: M1 junct 30, A616 signed Newart through 5 rdbts.
Through Clowne, right at staggered x-rds into Hazelmere
Rd to Elmton

Contemporary dining pub with a passion for local produce

Food is very much the focus at this refurbished
17th-century pub tucked away in pretty Elmton. Chef-
patron Chris Norfolk is passionate about sourcing
seasonal and fully traceable produce from local suppliers,
including fruit and vegetables from neighbour's gardens,
and everything, from bread, pasta and pastry, is made on
the premises. Changing menus (served all day) may
deliver game terrine with apple chutney, liver and bacon
with thyme gravy, their award-winning burger (topped
with Stilton and jalapeño peppers), and blueberry
frangipane tart. There's a contemporary feel in the stone-
floored bar and 'The Library' private dining room and four
real ales on tap – don't miss the May beer festival.

Open all day Closed: Tue **Bar Meals** L served Mon, Wed-
Sat 12-9, Sun 12-6 D served Mon, Wed-Sat 12-9, Sun
12-6 food served all day **Restaurant** L served Mon, Wed-
Sat 12-9, Sun 12-6 D served Mon, Wed-Sat 12-9, Sun
12-6 food served all day ⊕ PUNCH TAVERNS ◀ ◀ Black
Sheep, Kelham Island Easy Rider, Elm Tree Bitter
Ö Westons Old Rosie & Perry. **Facilities** Non-diners area
❤ (Bar Garden) ♦️ Children's portions Play area Garden
🎋 Beer festival Parking 🚌 (notice required)

EYAM　　Map 16 SK27

Miners Arms

Water Ln S32 5RG ☎ 01433 630853
dir: Off B6521, 5m N of Bakewell

Children, dogs and walkers all welcome

This welcoming 17th-century inn and restaurant was
built just before the plague hit Eyam; the village tailor
brought damp cloth from London and hung it to dry in
front of the fire so releasing the infected fleas. The pub
gets its name from the local lead mines of Roman times.
Now owned by Greene King, there's always the option to
pop in for a pint of their IPA or Ruddles Best bitter, or
enjoy a meal. A beer festival is held three times a year.

Open all wk Mon 12-3 5.30-12 Tue-Sun 12-12 **Bar
Meals** L served Mon-Sat 12-2, Sun 12-3 D served Mon
6-8, Tue-Fri 6-9, Sat 7-9 **Restaurant** L served Mon-Sat
12-2, Sun 12-3 D served Mon 6-8, Tue-Fri 6-9, Sat 7-9
⊕ GREENE KING ◀ IPA, Ruddles Best, Guest ales
Ö Westons Old Rosie. **Facilities** Non-diners area ❤ (Bar
Garden) ♦️ Children's menu Children's portions Garden 🎋
Beer festival Parking Wi-fi 🚌 (notice required)

FENNY BENTLEY　　Map 16 SK14

Bentley Brook Inn ★★★ INN

PICK OF THE PUBS

DE6 1LF ☎ 01335 350278
e-mail: all@bentleybrookinn.co.uk
dir: 2m N of Ashbourne at junct of A515 & B5056

Former farmhouse noted for seasonal menus

Completely restored, this substantial farmhouse was
created in 1805 from the shell of a medieval building
that served the local manor. The impressive gabled,
timbered frontage surveys the three acres of gardens and
grounds, where beer fans will revel in the annual beer
festival, held in late May or early June. Settle by the
central open log fire in the bar and play dominoes, cards
or chess, or peruse the menu. In the restaurant, which
overlooks the terrace and garden, locally sourced,
seasonal menus might offer starters of tempura prawns
with chill jam or deep-fried whitebait dusted with
paprika. Main dishes take in home-made steak-and-ale
pie with suet pastry crust; rib-eye steak with pepper
sauce and hand-cut chips; and ale battered haddock and
chips. Eleven bedrooms make this inn the ideal base for
exploring the peaceful Derbyshire Dales.

Open all day all wk 12-12 Closed: 25 Dec **Bar Meals** L
served all wk 12-9 D served all wk 12-9 Av main course
£9.95 food served all day **Restaurant** L served all wk
12-9 D served all wk 12-9 food served all day ⊕ FREE
HOUSE ◀ Leatherbritches Dr Johnson, Falstaff, Nutbrook
Brewery Ö Addlestones. ♟ 10 **Facilities** Non-diners area
❤ (Bar Garden) ♦️ Children's menu Children's portions
Play area Family room Garden 🎋 Beer festival Parking
Wi-fi 🚌 **Rooms** 11

The Coach and Horses Inn

DE6 1LB ☎ 01335 350246
e-mail: coachandhorses2@btconnect.com
dir: On A515 (Ashbourne to Buxton road), 2.5m from
Ashbourne

17th-century coaching inn offering good, honest cooking

A cosy refuge in any weather, this family-run,
17th-century coaching inn stands on the edge of the Peak
District National Park. Besides the beautiful location, its
charms include stripped wood furniture and low beams,
real log-burning fires plus a welcoming and friendly
atmosphere. Expect a great selection of real ales and
good home cooking that is hearty and uses the best of
local produce. Expect local specials and dishes like
chicken breast wrapped in bacon with a Stilton sauce;
poached salmon fillet with a cream, white wine and
seafood sauce; or spicy vegetable and chilli bean
casserole on rice, with Haloumi. Hot and cold sandwiches
and baguettes provide lighter options.

Open all day all wk 11-11 (Sun 12-10.30) **Bar Meals** food
served all day **Restaurant** food served all day ⊕ FREE
HOUSE ◀ Marston's Pedigree, Oakham JHB, Peak Swift
Nick, Whim Hartington Bitter, Derby.
Facilities Non-diners area ♦️ Children's menu Family
room Garden 🎋 Parking 🚌 (notice required)

FOOLOW　　Map 16 SK17

The Bulls Head Inn ★★★★ INN

S32 5QR ☎ 01433 630873
e-mail: wilbnd@aol.com
dir: Just off A623, N of Stoney Middleton

Traditional English country pub serving good food

In an upland village surrounded by a lattice-work of dry-
stone walls, this 19th-century former coaching inn is the
epitome of the English country pub. Well, with open fires,
oak beams, flagstone floors, great views and good food
and beer, it has to be. The bar serves Black Sheep and
Peak Ales, lunchtime snacks and sandwiches, while main
meals include Cumberland sausages and Yorkshire
pudding; beef Wellington with red wine gravy; sea bream
fillets with lemon butter; Mediterranean vegetable hotpot;
and even ostrich steak with brandied game gravy. The
bedrooms are well equipped.

Open 12-3 6.30-11 (Sun all day) Closed: Mon (ex BHs)
Bar Meals L served Tue-Sun 12-2 D served Tue-Sun

continued

FOOLOW *continued*

6.30-9 **Restaurant** L served Tue-Sun 12-2 D served Tue-Sun 6.30-9 ⊕ FREE HOUSE ◫ Black Sheep, Peak, Adnams, Tetley. **Facilities** Non-diners area ✿ (Bar) ♦ Children's menu Children's portions ⊨ Parking ⛟ **Rooms** 3

FROGGATT
Map 16 SK27

The Chequers Inn ★★★★ INN ◉

PICK OF THE PUBS

Froggatt Edge S32 3ZJ ☎ 01433 630231
e-mail: info@chequers-froggatt.com
dir: *On A625, 0.5m N of Calver*

Excellent food and hospitality in hillside village

Originally four stone cottages, with origins in the 16th century, this traditional country inn hugs the wooded hillside below Froggatt Edge. Popular with walkers, the gritstone escarpment can be reached by a steep, wild woodland footpath from the pub's elevated secret garden. The comfortable interior of wooden floors, antiques and blazing log fires is perfect for a relaxing pint of Kelham Island Easy Rider, or Bakewell Best Bitter, brewed on the nearby Chatsworth Estate by Peak Ales. The traditional pub menu includes favourites such as beer-battered haddock; and beef and ale pie, both home-made of course. In addition, there's an ever-changing selection of blackboard specials, such as Moroccan-spiced rump of Derbyshire lamb with Bombay potatoes; roast loin of cod with sea scallop and potato gratin; and breast of local pheasant with confit leg ravioli. A vegetarian option is stuffed gnocchi with baby vegetables and grilled cherry tomatoes.

Open all day all wk Closed: 25 Dec **Bar Meals** L served Mon-Fri 12-2.30, Sat 12-9.30, Sun 12-9 D served Mon-Fri 6-9.30, Sat 12-9.30, Sun 12-9 ⊕ FREE HOUSE ◫ Kelham Island Easy Rider, Peak Bakewell Best Bitter, Wells Bombardier, Bradfield Farmers Blonde, Guest ales. ☷ 10 **Facilities** ♦ Children's menu Children's portions Garden ⊨ Parking Wi-fi **Rooms** 6

GREAT HUCKLOW
Map 16 SK17

The Queen Anne Inn ★★★ INN

SK17 8RF ☎ 01298 871246
e-mail: angelaryan100@aol.com
dir: *A623 onto B6049, exit at Anchor pub towards Bradwell, 2nd right to Great Hucklow*

Great hospitality in a country setting

The sheltered south-facing garden of this traditional country free house has stunning open views. The inn dates from 1621; a licence has been held for over 300 years, and the names of all the landlords are known. Inside you'll find an open fire in the stone fireplace, good food made using locally sourced produce, and an ever-changing range of cask ales. The inn has an AA Dinner Award in recognition of the quality of the food on offer; popular choices include sea bass fillet with parmesan crust; steak-and-kidney pudding; and steamed mussels

with freshly baked bread. There is a child-friendly south-facing garden and two guest bedrooms are available.

Open 12-2.30 5-11 (Fri-Sun 12-11) Closed: Mon ⊕ FREE HOUSE ◫ Tetley's Cask, Local guest ales ⚮ Westons Stowford Press. **Facilities** ✿ (Bar Garden) ♦ Children's menu Children's portions Family room Garden Parking **Rooms** 2

GRINDLEFORD
Map 16 SK27

The Maynard ★★★ HL ◉◉

PICK OF THE PUBS

Main Rd S32 2HE ☎ 01433 630321
e-mail: info@themaynard.co.uk
dir: *M1 junct 30, A619 into Chesterfield, then onto Baslow. A623 to Calver, right into Grindleford*

Peak District hotel with a fine dining restaurant

Situated in the heart of the Peak District National Park, close to Bakewell and Buxton, this former coaching inn is now an imposing stone hotel. It stands below the steep, wooded crags of Froggatt Edge and overlooks Grindleford and the Derwent Valley beyond. The capacious beer garden offers stunning panoramas across moorland and river valley. Continuing the Peakland theme, beer from Chatsworth's own estate brewery may be sampled in the Longhaw Bar with its leather sofas and log fires, where a good-value bar menu might include braised lamb shank or local gammon steak. For some of the best cuisine around, however, head for the contemporary Maynard Restaurant which has gained two AA Rosettes and offers seasonal, locally sourced dishes. A purple sprouting broccoli spring roll or pan-seared king scallops might be followed by herb-crusted loin of cod with giant couscous, salsa verde and confit radishes.

Open all day all wk **Bar Meals** L served all wk 12-2 D served all wk 7-9 **Restaurant** L served all wk 12-2 D served all wk 7-9 ⊕ FREE HOUSE ◫ Abbeydale Moonshine, Peak Bakewell Best Bitter. **Facilities** Non-diners area ♦ Children's menu Garden ⊨ Parking Wi-fi ⛟ **Rooms** 10

HARDSTOFT
Map 16 SK46

The Shoulder at Hardstoft ★★★★★ INN ◉◉

Deep Ln S45 8AF ☎ 01246 850276
e-mail: info@thefamousshoulder.co.uk
dir: *From B6039 follow signs for Hardwick Hall. 1st right into car park*

Top-notch menu in Derbyshire countryside inn

Just ten minutes from the M1, this 300-year-old pub is an ideal base for exploring the Peak District and Sherwood Forest. Peak Ales' Bakewell Best Bitter is one of the local beers available in the bar, with its open log fires. The kitchen sources all ingredients within 15 miles of the pub where possible, with the exception of fish, which is from sustainable sources. In the restaurant (with 2 AA Rosettes), look forward to a smoked goose breast starter, a taster for mains such as loin and liver of venison with

beetroot and celeriac rosette, or home-made braised chicken leg and leek pie.

Open all day all wk **Bar Meals** food served all day **Restaurant** food served all day ⊕ FREE HOUSE ◫ Peak Bakewell Best Bitter, Thornbridge Jaipur, Greene King Abbot Ale. ☷ 10 **Facilities** Non-diners area ✿ (Bar Restaurant) ♦ Children's portions ⊨ Parking Wi-fi ⛟ (notice required) **Rooms** 4

HARTSHORNE
Map 10 SK32

The Mill Wheel ★★★★ INN ◉

Ticknall Rd DE11 7AS ☎ 01283 550335
e-mail: info@themillwheel.co.uk
dir: *From A511 between Burton upon Trent & Ashby-de-la-Zouch take A514 at Woodville signed Derby. 1.8m to Hartshorne*

A good base while exploring this lovely area

Many trades have used this old building over the centuries; today it's a feel-good, rustic free house in an attractive setting not too far from the National Trust's remarkable Calke Abbey. The powerful wheel which has powered bellows, grindstones and hoists only momentarily diverts attention from the eclectic menu devised by Colin Brown. Signature dishes include pan-fried breast of pheasant with crisp confit leg, beetroot mash and port wine jus, or fillets of sea bass in a sage, pine nut and smoked bacon risotto. With modern bedrooms for overnighters, complete the treat with a Hop Back or Mill Wheel bitter or two.

Open all wk (Sat-Sun all day) **Bar Meals** L served Mon-Fri 12-2.30, Sat 12-9.15, Sun 12-8 D served Mon-Thu 6-9.15, Fri 6-9.30, Sat 12-9.15, Sun 12-8 Av main course £9.95 **Restaurant** L served Mon-Fri 12-2.30, Sat 12-9.15, Sun 12-8 D served Mon-Thu 6-9.15, Fri-Sat 6-9.30, Sun 12-7 ⊕ FREE HOUSE ◫ Mill Wheel Bitter, Greene King Abbot Ale, Hop Back Summer Lightning, Marston's Pedigree, Bass. ☷ 8 **Facilities** Non-diners area ♦ Children's menu Children's portions Garden ⊨ Parking Wi-fi ⛟ **Rooms** 4

HASSOP
Map 16 SK27

The Old Eyre Arms

DE45 1NS ☎ 01629 640390
e-mail: nick@eyrearms.com
dir: *On B6001 N of Bakewell*

A perfect Peak District escape

In a plum village-edge location between the formality of Chatsworth's vast estate, bold gritstone edges and the memorable wooded limestone dales of Derbyshire's River Wye, this comfortably unchanging, creeper-clad old inn ticks all the right boxes for beers and food too. Real ales from Peak Ales and Bradfield breweries couldn't be more local, whilst all meals are prepared in-house: kick off with a prawn skewer with chilli and lemon butter, and follow with Old English rabbit pie with cider and bacon, or aubergine and mushroom lasagne to take the chill off a long ramble. Oak beams and furnishing and log fires complete the picture.

Save on hotels. Book at theAA.com/hotel

DERBYSHIRE 119 ENGLAND

Open all wk 11-3 6.30-11 Closed: 25-26 Dec, 2wks in Jan **Bar Meals** L served all wk 12-2 D served all wk 6.30-9 ⊕ FREE HOUSE ◄ Peak Ales Swift Nick & Chatsworth Gold, Black Sheep Ale, Bradfield Farmers Blonde ♂ Westons Stowford Press. ♚ 9 **Facilities** Non-diners area ♦♦ Children's menu Children's portions Garden ⚞ Parking

HATHERSAGE — Map 16 SK28

Millstone Inn

Sheffield Rd S32 1DA ☎ 01433 650258
e-mail: enquiries@millstoneinn.co.uk
dir: *Telephone for directions*

Real ales with wonderful views

Striking views over the picturesque Hope Valley are afforded from this former coaching inn, set amid the beauty of the Peak District yet convenient for the city of Sheffield. The atmospheric bar serves six traditional cask ales all year round and the menu offers a good choice of dishes prepared from local produce, including a popular Sunday carvery of freshly roasted joints.

Open all day all wk 11.30-11 ⊕ FREE HOUSE ◄ Timothy Taylor Landlord, Black Sheep, Guest ales.
Facilities ♣ (Bar Restaurant Garden) ♦♦ Garden Parking

The Plough Inn ★★★★ INN ◉

PICK OF THE PUBS

See Pick of the Pubs on page 120

The Scotsmans Pack Country Inn

School Ln S32 1BZ ☎ 01433 650253
e-mail: scotsmans.pack@btinternet.com
dir: *From A6187 in Hathersage turn at church into School Lane*

A warm welcome for locals and visitors alike

Set in the beautiful Hope Valley on one of the old packhorse trails used by Scottish 'packmen', this traditional inn is a short walk from Hathersage church and Little John's Grave. The pub offers hearty dishes such as lamb's liver and bacon or rabbit casserole, best washed down with a pint of Jennings Cumberland. Weather permitting, head outside onto the sunny patio, next to the trout stream. A perfect base for walking and touring the Peak District.

Open all wk 11-3 6-12 (Fri-Sun all day) ⊕ MARSTON'S ◄ Pedigree, Jennings Cumberland Ale, Mansfield Original Bitter. **Facilities** ♦♦ Children's menu Children's portions Family room Garden Parking Wi-fi

---

HAYFIELD — Map 16 SK08

The Royal Hotel

Market St SK22 2EP ☎ 01663 742721
e-mail: enquiries@theroyalhayfield.co.uk
dir: *From A624 follow Hayfield signs*

Village centre pub on the Peak District border

Up in the High Peak, below the windswept plateau of Kinder Scout, the hotel, now in new hands, dates from 1755. Its period charm still very evident, one place to relax with a pint of Thwaites Wainwright or Lancaster Bomber is the oak-panelled, log-fired Windsor Bar. Another is the family lounge, popular with the local cricket team, whose ground is next door. The dining room carte keeps things simple: sausage and mash; tender beef and ale pie; and breaded wholetail scampi. Bar meals can be served on the patio overlooking the moorland. Visit first weekend in October for the beer festival.

Open all day all wk 9am-mdnt **Bar Meals** L served Mon-Fri 12-2.30, Sat 12-9, Sun 12-6 D served Mon-Fri 6-9, Sat 12-9, Sun 12-6 **Restaurant** L served Mon-Fri 12-2.30, Sat 12-9, Sun 12-6 D served Mon-Fri 6-9, Sat 12-9, Sun 12-6 ⊕ FREE HOUSE ◄ Thwaites Wainwright & Lancaster Bomber ♂ Westons Stowford Press, Scrumpy. ♚ **Facilities** Non-diners area ♣ (Bar Garden) ♦♦ Children's menu Children's portions Family room Garden ⚞ Beer festival Parking Wi-fi 🚐 (notice required)

HOGNASTON — Map 16 SK25

The Red Lion Inn

Main St DE6 1PR ☎ 01335 370396
e-mail: enquiries@redlionhognaston.org.uk
web: www.redlionhognaston.org.uk
dir: *From Ashbourne take B5035 towards Wirksworth. Approx 5m follow Carsington Water signs. Turn right to Hognaston*

Worth finding off the beaten track

In a village of old cottages close to the huge Carsington Water, this very traditional pub fronting the main street bursts with antique furniture spread liberally around an open-fire warmed interior originating in the 17th century. Beams, bare brick, old photos and bric-a-brac add further character to this peaceful retreat in fine walking and cycling country. Settle into a settle with a pint of bitter perhaps from Wincle brewery and home in on a tasty menu crafted from top-notch Derbyshire produce; slow-braised pheasant, hare, venison and rabbit pie takes the eye. The garden has a boules court.

Open all wk 12-2.30 6-11 **Bar Meals** L served all wk 12-2.30 D served all wk 6.30-9 summer, 6-8.30 winter Av main course £11 **Restaurant** L served all wk 12-2.30 D served all wk 6.30-9 summer, 6-8.30 winter Av 3 course à la carte fr £20 ⊕ FREE HOUSE ◄ Marston's Pedigree, Greene King Ruddles County, Black Sheep, Wincle, Timothy Taylor Landlord. ♚ 10 **Facilities** Non-diners area ♣ (Bar Garden) ♦♦ Children's portions Garden ⚞ Parking Wi-fi

---

HOPE — Map 16 SK18

Cheshire Cheese Inn

Edale Rd S33 6ZF ☎ 01433 620381
e-mail: laura@thecheshirecheeseinn.co.uk
dir: *On A6187 between Sheffield & Castleton, turn at Hope Church into Edale Rd*

Country inn with a rich history

Originally a farm, this 17th-century inn used to provide salt-carriers crossing the Pennines to Yorkshire with overnight lodgings, for which they paid in cheese. In the unspoilt atmosphere of today's pub payment is made the conventional way, but cheese with tomato, onion or pickle makes a good sandwich with a locally brewed real ale. Other home-made food includes main meals such as gammon steak with fried egg and chips; steak-and-kidney pudding; beer-battered Grimsby haddock; and large Yorkshire pud with local sausages. Dogs are welcome in the inn and beer garden.

Open Tue-Sun 12-3 6-late (Sat-Sun all day) Closed: Mon (out of season) ⊕ ENTERPRISE INNS ◄ Peak Swift Nick, Bradfield Farmers Blonde, Kelham Island Easy Rider ♂ Addlestones. **Facilities** ♣ (Bar Garden) ♦♦ Children's portions Family room Garden Parking Wi-fi

---

INGLEBY — Map 11 SK32

The John Thompson Inn & Brewery

DE73 7HW ☎ 01332 862469
e-mail: nick@johnthompsoninn.com
dir: *From A38 between Derby and Burton upon Trent take A5132 towards Barrow upon Trent. At mini rdbt right onto B5008 (signed Repton). At rdbt 1st exit into Brook End. Right into Milton Rd. Left, left again to Ingleby*

Friendly brewpub serving hearty lunches

A pub since 1968, this 15th-century former farmhouse took its name from licensee and owner John Thompson. Now run by son Nick, it is a traditional brewpub set in idyllic countryside beside the banks of the River Trent with views of the neighbouring National Forest. Inside, a wealth of original features make it an atmospheric place to enjoy a pint of home-brewed JTS XXX and tuck into lunches ranging from sandwiches to a roast beef carvery or a trio of cheese and pasta broccoli bake. Finish with home-made bread and butter pudding.

Open Tue-Fri 11-2.30 6-11 (Sat-Sun 11-11 Mon 6-11) Closed: Mon L **Bar Meals** L served Tue-Sun 12-2 Av main course £7.95 **Restaurant** L served Tue-Sun 12-2 ⊕ FREE HOUSE ◄ John Thompson JTS XXX, St Nick's, Gold, Rich Porter. ♚ 9 **Facilities** Non-diners area ♦♦ Children's portions Family room Garden Parking Wi-fi 🚐

PICK OF THE PUBS

The Plough Inn ★★★★ INN

HATHERSAGE Map 16 SK28

Leadmill Bridge S32 1BA
☎ 01433 650319 & 650180
e-mail:
sales@theploughinn-hathersage.co.uk
web:
www.theploughinn-hathersage.co.uk
dir: *M1 junct 29, take A617W, A619, A623, then B6001 N to Hathersage*

Riverside award-winner

The 16th-century Plough stands in nine acres by the River Derwent where the 18th-century, three-arched Leadmill Bridge carries the Derwent Valley Heritage Way over the rapids that disturb the otherwise gently flowing waters. Inside, smart red tartan carpets work well with the open fires and wooden beams of the bar, which serves hand-pulled Adnams, Black Sheep and Timothy Taylor ales. An extensive British menu features locally sourced starters such as mussel and saffron chowder; and rillette of confit salmon and crab, beef tomato, caperberries and lemon with chive oil. Next choose from the best part of 20 main courses, including fillet of British beef with lyonnaise potatoes, slow-roast shallots, spinach and roast garlic cream; chargrilled sea bream with marinated cherry tomatoes, sweet potato, wild rocket and salsa verde; and red pepper couscous with vegetable tagine and grilled haloumi. If you prefer, there's traditional pub grub too, typically seared lamb's liver with grilled back bacon; and ale-battered cod, with lighter meals served until 5.30pm. Roast meats are only part of the Sunday line-up, with dishes featuring lemon sole, pork medallions, chicken and pissaladière also on offer. The Plough's well-stocked cellar combines Old and New World wines, from France to Chile one way, and New Zealand the other. Guests may stroll through the landscaped grounds before retiring to one of the bedrooms in the inn itself, or in the converted barn across the cobbled courtyard.

Open all day all wk 11-11 (Sun 12-10.30) Closed: 25 Dec **Bar Meals** Av main course £14 food served all day **Restaurant** Fixed menu price fr £24 Av 3 course à la carte fr £27.50 food served all day ⊕ FREE HOUSE ◄ Adnams, Black Sheep, Timothy Taylor, Bass Extra Smooth. ♀ 15 **Facilities** Non-diners area ❖ ♦ Children's menu & portions Garden ⋒ Parking Wi-fi **Rooms** 5

Save on hotels. Book at theAA.com/hotel

DERBYSHIRE 121 ENGLAND

KIRK IRETON
Map 16 SK25

Barley Mow Inn

DE6 3JP ☎ 01335 370306
dir: *Telephone for directions*

Step back in time at this traditional pub

Built on the edge of the Peak District National Park by the Storer family of yeomen farmers in the 16th century, the building became an inn during the early 1700s. The imposing free house has remained largely unchanged over the years, and has been run by Mary Short since 1976. Six nine-gallon barrels of beer stand behind the bar, with cheese and pickle or salami rolls and bar snacks on offer at lunchtime. Tea and coffee is always available. Close to Carsington Water, there are good walking opportunities on nearby marked paths.

Open all wk 12-2 7-11 (Sun 12-2 7-10.30) Closed: 25 Dec, 1 Jan ⊕ FREE HOUSE ◄ Blue Monkey, Dancing Duck, Leatherbritches, Storm, Whim Hartington Bitter ♂ Thatchers. **Facilities** Non-diners area ♥ (Bar Garden) ♦♦ Garden Parking **Notes** ⊗

LITTLE HAYFIELD
Map 16 SK08

Lantern Pike

45 Glossop Rd SK22 2NG ☎ 01663 747590
e-mail: tomandstella@lanternpikeinn.co.uk
dir: *On A624, between Glossop and Chapel-en-le-Frith*

Welcoming pub in hilly terrain

Set in a tiny mill village at the edge of the Kinder Scout moors and below the shapely Lantern Pike hill, site of an Armada beacon, the sublime views from the beer garden of the wooded Peak District hills are reason enough to seek out this fine pub. Add a well-considered selection of real ales and an ever-changing menu – perhaps fresh fillet of red snapper, or griddled loin of pork in Stilton sauce – and it's little wonder that this ultra-traditional 170-year-old inn is a highly popular destination for diners and outdoor pursuits enthusiasts alike. Unique 'Coronation Street' ephemera add fascination for the faithful.

Open Mon 5-12, Tue-Fri 12-3 5-12 (Sat-Sun all day) Closed: 25 Dec, Mon L **Bar Meals** L served Tue-Fri 12-2.30, Sat-Sun 12-8.30 D served Mon 5-8, Tue-Fri 5-8.30, Sat-Sun 12-8.30 **Restaurant** L served Tue-Fri 12-2.30, Sat-Sun 12-8.30 D served Mon 5-8, Tue-Fri 5-8.30, Sat-Sun 12-8.30 ⊕ ENTERPRISE INNS ◄ Timothy Taylor Landlord, Castle Rock Harvest Pale, Ossett Silver King. **Facilities** Non-diners area ♦♦ Children's menu Children's portions Garden ⋔ Parking Wi-fi ⇌ (notice required)

LITTON
Map 16 SK17

Red Lion Inn

SK17 8QU ☎ 01298 871458
e-mail: theredlionlitton@hotmail.co.uk
dir: *Just off A623 (Chesterfield to Stockport road), 1m E of Tideswell*

Cosy, traditional community pub

The Red Lion is a beautiful, traditional pub on the village green, very much at the heart of the local community. It became a pub in 1787 when it was converted from three farm cottages. With its wood fires, selection of well-kept real ales and friendly atmosphere, it's a favourite with walkers and holiday-makers too. The menu offers hearty pub food at reasonable prices, such as Thai fishcakes with sweet chilli dip to start; Derbyshire lamb hotpot; steak-and-kidney pie; or South African bobotie to follow; and apple and berry crumble with custard to finish. A gluten-free menu is available. The pub, being small, is not ideal for children, but there's seating on the village green.

Open all day all wk **Bar Meals** L served Mon-Sat 12-9, Sun 12-8 D served Mon-Sat 12-9, Sun 12-8 food served all day **Restaurant** food served all day ⊕ ENTERPRISE INNS ◄ Abbeydale Absolution, 2 Guest ales. ¶ 10 **Facilities** Non-diners area ♥ (Bar Restaurant) Outside area ⋔

MATLOCK
Map 16 SK35

The Red Lion ★★★ INN

65 Matlock Green DE4 3BT ☎ 01629 584888
dir: *From Chesterfield, A632 into Matlock, on right just before junct with A615*

An all rounder in the heart of Derbyshire's county town

This friendly, family-run free house makes a good base for exploring local attractions like Chatsworth House, Carsington Water and Dovedale. Spectacular walks in the local countryside help to work up an appetite for bar lunches, or great tasting home-cooked dishes in the homely restaurant. On Sunday there's a popular carvery with freshly cooked gammon, beef, pork, lamb and turkey. In the winter months, open fires burn in the lounge and games room, and there's a boules area in the attractive beer garden for warmer days. Some of the ales from the bar were brewed on the Chatsworth Estate. There are six comfortable bedrooms.

Open all day all wk **Bar Meals** L served Tue-Fri 12-2 **Restaurant** L served Sun 12-2.45, Sun Carvery 12-7 D served Tue-Sat 6-9 ⊕ FREE HOUSE ◄ Morland Old Speckled Hen, Peak, Guest ales. **Facilities** Non-diners area Children's menu Children's portions Garden ⋔ Parking Wi-fi ⇌ **Rooms** 6

MELBOURNE
Map 11 SK32

The Melbourne Arms ★★★ INN

92 Ashby Rd DE73 8ES ☎ 01332 864949 & 863990
e-mail: info@melbournearms.co.uk
dir: *M1 junct 23A, A453 signed East Midlands (airport) to Isley Walton, right signed Melbourne, pass Donington Park to Melbourne*

An Indian restaurant in a pub

Mr and Mrs Kumar's Cuisine India restaurant has been part of this 18th-century inn on the outskirts of the Georgian market town of Melbourne for 16 years. Indian food lovers will expect the menu to offer a huge choice – and it does, from traditional bhuna and Kashmiri curries to balti dishes, and from vegetable jalfrezi to tandoori mushrooms. You can, however, also eat English food. Two bars serve Marston's Pedigree, and there's a coffee lounge. Popular with families, because of its modern, thoughtfully equipped bedrooms, many of which have views of the countryside.

Open all day all wk Closed: 26 Dec **Bar Meals** L served all wk 12-3 D served all wk 3-11 Av main course £7 food served all day **Restaurant** L served all wk 12-3.30 D served all wk 3.30-11.30 Av 3 course à la carte fr £16 food served all day ⊕ FREE HOUSE/DARSHANTI UK LTD ◄ Marston's Pedigree. **Facilities** Non-diners area ♦♦ Children's menu Children's portions Play area Family room Garden Outside area ⋔ Parking Wi-fi ⇌ **Rooms** 10

MIDDLE HANDLEY
Map 16 SK47

Devonshire Arms

Lightwood Ln S21 5RN ☎ 01246 434800
e-mail: enquiries@devonshirearmsmiddlehandley.com
dir: *B6052 from Eckington towards Chesterfield. 1.5m*

Great local beers and thoughtful menu

In the shade of a huge chestnut tree, this old stone village watering hole was subtly upgraded a few years ago, evolving into a contemporary dining pub twinned with the feel of a time-honoured local. The stylish interior displays original features including a grandfather clock and open fireplace. Modern, locally-sourced British dishes are the backbone of the busy kitchen's output; a good mix of pub classics and inspirations such as Moss Valley belly pork slow cooked overnight in cloudy cider, with apple and potato terrine. There's a solid wine list, or indulge in Sheffield's tasty Kelham Island beers.

Open all day all wk **Bar Meals** L served Mon-Fri 12-3, Sat 12-9, Sun 12-6 D served Mon-Fri 5-9, Sat 12-9, Sun 12-6 **Restaurant** L served Mon-Fri 12-3, Sat 12-9, Sun 12-6 D served Mon-Fri 5-9, Sat 12-9, Sun 12-6 ⊕ FREE HOUSE ◄ Bradfield Farmers Blonde, Kelham Island Pride of Sheffield, Peak Chatsworth Gold, Guest ales ♂ Addlestones. ¶ 10 **Facilities** Non-diners area ♥ (Bar Outside area) ♦♦ Children's menu Children's portions Outside area ⋔ Parking Wi-fi

MILLTOWN
Map 16 SK36

The Nettle Inn

S45 0ES ☎ **01246 590462**
e-mail: marcus.sloan@thenettleinn.co.uk
dir: *Telephone for directions*

Local ales and good menu choices at this traditional inn

A 16th-century hostelry on the edge of the Peak District, this inn has all the traditional charm you could wish for, from flower-filled hanging baskets to log fires and a stone-flagged taproom floor. Expect well-kept ales such as Bakewell Best, and impressive home-made food using the best of seasonal produce. Typical bar options are Armstrong's chicken and leek pie or chargrilled pork chop and plenty of sandwiches, while on the restaurant menu dishes such as wild salmon roulade or roast broccoli and rosemary filo parcel may tempt.

Open all wk 12-2.30 5.30-11 (Sun 12-10) ⊕ FREE HOUSE ◀ Peak Swift Nick, Bakewell Best Bitter, DPA.
Facilities ♦♦ Children's menu Children's portions Garden Parking Wi-fi

PILSLEY
Map 16 SK27

The Devonshire Arms at Pilsley ★★★ INN

High St DE45 1UL ☎ **01246 583258**
e-mail: res@devonshirehotels.co.uk
dir: *From A619, in Baslow, at rdbt take 1st exit onto B6012. Follow signs to Chatsworth, 2nd right to Pilsley*

Traditional inn on the Chatsworth Estate

Here is a fabulous old stone pub nestling in an estate village amidst the rolling parkland surrounding Chatsworth House, the 'Palace of The Peaks'. It's also an ideal base for visiting Matlock Bath and Castleton. There are open fires, Peak Ales from the estate's brewery and meats, game and greens from the adjacent estate shop, all sourced from these productive acres at the heart of the Peak District. A mixed grill, corned beef hash or minted lamb hotpot is a filling repast after a day's exploration of the area. Stop over at the luxurious accommodation designed by the Duchess of Devonshire.

Open all day all wk **Bar Meals** L served all wk 12-2.30 D served all wk 5-9 ⊕ FREE HOUSE ◀ Thornbridge Jaipur, Peak Chatsworth Gold, Guest ales. ♀ 12
Facilities Non-diners area ♦♦ Children's menu Children's portions ♫ Parking Wi-fi **Rooms** 7

ROWSLEY
Map 16 SK26

The Grouse & Claret ★★★★ INN

Station Rd DE4 2EB ☎ **01629 733233**
dir: *On A6 between Matlock & Bakewell*

Angling connections and colourful menus at this popular pub

A venue popular with local anglers, this 18th-century pub takes its name from a fishing fly. Situated at the gateway to the Peak District National Park, it is handy for visits to

the stately homes of Haddon Hall and Chatsworth House. After quenching the thirst with a pint of Marston's, the colourful menu promises a selection of well-priced and tasty pub meals: garlic mushrooms; pâté in a pot; pork rump in plum sauce; and Creole chicken are typical. Parents look on enviously as their offspring consume toffee apple wedges from the children's menu.

Open all day all wk **Bar Meals** L served Mon-Sat 12-9, Sun 12-8 D served Mon-Sat 12-9, Sun 12-8 Av main course £8.95 food served all day **Restaurant** L served Mon-Sat 12-9, Sun 12-8 D served Mon-Sat 12-9, Sun 12-8 food served all day ⊕ MARSTON'S ◀ Pedigree, Bank's Bitter, Jennings Cumberland Ale. ♀ 16
Facilities ♦♦ Children's menu Children's portions Play area Garden ♫ Parking Wi-fi 🚌 **Rooms** 8

SHARDLOW
Map 11 SK43

The Old Crown Inn

Cavendish Bridge DE72 2HL ☎ **01332 792392**
e-mail: jamesvize@hotmail.co.uk
dir: *M1 junct 24, A50 signed Stoke (& Shardlow). Take slip road signed B6540. At rdbt right, follow Shardlow sign. Left at Cavendish bridge sign to inn.*

Traditional inn with regular evening events

Up to nine real ales are served at this family-friendly pub on the south side of the River Trent, where there's a beer festival twice a year. Built as a coaching inn during the 17th century, it retains its warm and atmospheric interior. Several hundred water jugs hang from the ceilings, while the walls display an abundance of brewery and railway memorabilia. Traditional food is lovingly prepared by the landlady; main meals focus on pub classics such as home-made steak-and-kidney pie; ham, eggs and chips; lasagne; curry; steaks; and daily specials. Monday night is quiz night; folk music every Tuesday; curry night on Wednesdays.

Open all day all wk 11am-11.30pm (Fri-Sat 11am-12.30am Sun 11-11) **Bar Meals** L served Tue-Fri 12-2, Sat 12-8, Sun 12-3 D served Tue-Fri 5-8, Sat 12-8 **Restaurant** L served Tue-Fri 12-2, Sat 12-8, Sun 12-3 D served Tue-Fri 5-8, Sat 12-8 ⊕ MARSTON'S ◀ Pedigree & Old Empire, Jennings Cocker Hoop, Guest ales.
Facilities Non-diners area ♥ (Bar Restaurant) ♦♦ Children's menu Children's portions Play area Garden ♫ Beer festival Parking 🚌 (notice required)

STANTON IN PEAK
Map 16 SK26

The Flying Childers Inn

Main Rd DE4 2LW ☎ **01629 636333**
dir: *From A6 (between Matlock & Bakewell) follow Youlgrave signs. Onto B5056 to Ashbourne. Follow Stanton in Peak signs*

Enchanting old-style village pub

Above this instantly likeable, charmingly old-fashioned village pub looms Stanton Moor, riddled with Neolithic stone monuments. At the heart of a pretty old Peak District estate village, The Flying Childers was named after a champion racehorse owned by the 4th Duke of Devonshire. Little log fires warm the cosy, beamed

interior, where settles and magpie-furniture fit an absolute treat. The lunchtime-only menu is small but perfectly formed; hot roast pork filled cobs with stuffing and roast potatoes or maybe a rabbit and vegetable casserole, all with locally sourced ingredients. Local real ales, a beer garden and a great welcome for canine companions, too.

Open all wk 12-2 7-11 (Mon-Tue 7pm-11pm Sat-Sun 12-3 7-11) **Bar Meals** L served Wed-Sun 12-2 ⊕ FREE HOUSE ◀ Wells Bombardier, Guest ales.
Facilities ♥ (Bar Garden) ♦♦ Garden Parking Notes ⊛

TIDESWELL
Map 16 SK17

The George ★★★ INN

Commercial Rd SK17 8NU ☎ **01298 871382**
e-mail: info@georgeinn.co.uk
dir: *A619 to Baslow, A623 towards Chapel-en-le-Frith, 0.25m*

Charming coaching inn with traditional food

Set in the shadow of St John the Baptist's church (known locally as the Cathedral of the Peak), this delightful stone-built coaching inn dates from 1730 and is conveniently placed for exploring the National Park and visiting Buxton, Chatsworth and Eyam. The simple, unfussy menu focuses on traditional pub fare — lunchtime sandwiches and full meals such as mushroom and Stilton crumble followed by traditional rag pudding with gravy, and sticky toffee pudding for dessert. There's also a good selection from the grill, ranging from steaks to a fish medley or Cajun chicken.

Open all day all wk **Bar Meals** L served all wk 12-2.30 D served all wk 6-9 Av main course £6.95 **Restaurant** L served all wk 12-2.30 D served all wk 6-9 Fixed menu price fr £12 Av 3 course à la carte fr £17 ⊕ GREENE KING ◀ Morland Old Golden Hen, Guest ale ♂ Aspall.
Facilities Non-diners area ♥ (All areas) ♦♦ Children's menu Children's portions Garden Outside area ♫ Parking Wi-fi 🚌 (notice required) **Rooms** 4

Three Stags' Heads

Wardlow Mires SK17 8RW ☎ **01298 872268**
dir: *At junct of A623 (Baslow to Stockport road) & B6465*

Pottery and a pint under the same roof

A remarkable survivor, this unspoilt and rustic 17th-century moorland longhouse stands in renowned walking country and features a stone-flagged bar and huge range fire. The bar counter, a 1940s addition, sells Abbeydale beers, including the heady Black Lurcher and Brimstone bitter, and several real ciders. Hearty food includes pea and ham soup, chicken casserole, roast partridge and bread-and-butter pudding. Note the restricted opening hours, which allow owners Geoff and Pat Fuller time to make pottery, which you can buy. Sorry, it's not a pub for children.

Open all day Sat-Sun 12-12 (Fri 6-12) Closed: Mon-Thu (ex BHs) ⊕ FREE HOUSE ◀ Abbeydale Matins, Absolution, Black Lurcher, Brimstone ♂ Dunkertons Black Fox, Hecks Kingston Black, Gawtkin Yarlington Mill.
Facilities Parking **Notes** ⊛

DEVON

ASHBURTON   Map 3 SX77

The Rising Sun

Woodland TQ13 7JT ☎ 01364 652544
e-mail: admin@therisingsunwoodland.co.uk
*dir: From A38 E of Ashburton take lane signed Woodland/
Denbury. Pub on left, approx 1.5m*

Family friendly pub with large garden near Dartmoor

This former drovers' pub is now in the hands of the capable Reynolds family who are keen to put this family – and dog - friendly pub firmly on the map. Surrounded by gorgeous countryside, and with a large garden in which to sup a pint of Dartmoor Jail Ale, you're on the edge of Dartmoor National Park. Renowned for their home-made pies, there's also a chargrill for steaks, gammon and burgers, and also Sunday roasts and sandwiches at lunchtime. Super local cheeseboards are offered and children can choose from their own menu. Beer Festival in early summer – ring pub for date.

Open 12-3 6-11 (Sun 12-3 6.30-11) Closed: 25 Dec, Mon L **Bar Meals** L served Tue-Sat 12-2.15, Sun 12-2.30 D served Mon-Sat 6-9.15, Sun 6.30-9.15 **Restaurant** L served Tue-Sat 12-2.15, Sun 12-2.30 D served Mon-Sat 6-9.15, Sun 6.30-9.15 ⊕ FREE HOUSE ◀ Dartmoor Jail Ale, Guest ales ☉ Thatchers Gold. **Facilities** Non-diners area ❖ (Bar Restaurant Garden) ♦♦ Children's menu Children's portions Garden ⊼ Beer festival Parking Wi-fi ▭ (notice required)

AVONWICK   Map 3 SX75

The Turtley Corn Mill
PICK OF THE PUBS

TQ10 9ES ☎ 01364 646100
e-mail: eat@turtleycornmill.com
dir: From A38 at South Brent/Avonwick junction, take B3372, then follow signs for Avonwick, 0.5m

Local produce in an idyllic setting

Set among six acres of gardens and fields in the South Hams on the edge of Dartmoor, this sprawling old free house began life as a corn mill, then spent many years as a chicken hatchery before being converted to a pub. The site is bordered by a river and includes a lake complete with ducks and its own small island, whilst the interior is light and fresh with old furniture and oak and slate floors. You'll find plenty of newspapers and books to browse through while enjoying a whisky or supping a pint of Dartmoor Jail Ale. The daily-changing modern British menus for breakfast/brunch, lunch and dinner are extensively based on local produce from around the pub's idyllic location. Typical main-course choices include beef and Guinness pie; chilli braised belly pork and smoked haddock and salmon fishcakes.

Open all day all wk Closed: 25 Dec **Bar Meals** L served all wk 12-10 D served all wk 12-10 Av main course £13 food served all day **Restaurant** L served all wk 12-10 D served

all wk 12-10 Fixed menu price fr £11.95 Av 3 course à la carte fr £25 food served all day ⊕ FREE HOUSE ◀ Dartmoor Jail Ale, St Austell Tribute, Sharp's Doom Bar, Guest ales ☉ Thatchers. ♈ 10 **Facilities** Non-diners area ❖ (Bar Restaurant Garden) ♦♦ Children's portions Garden ⊼ Parking Wi-fi

AXMOUTH   Map 4 SY29

The Harbour Inn
PICK OF THE PUBS

Church St EX12 4AF ☎ 01297 20371
dir: In main street opposite church, 1m from Seaton

Daily-changing blackboard menus of local produce

A pebble's throw from the Axe Estuary in the picturesque village of Axmouth, this cosy, oak-beamed harbourside inn is a popular place for walkers and birdwatchers to refuel. Local ingredients are sourced for the food here and the bar and bistro menu offers comforting classics like local butcher's ham sandwiches; half a pint of king prawns; and smoked haddock and Somerset cheddar fishcakes. From a daily updated blackboard menu, you might want to consider oven-roasted salmon fillet with roasted fennel, caper and lemon butter sauce; breaded plaice fillets with peas and triple-fried chips; or steak and Poachers Ale pie. Leave room for apple and blackberry oat crunch crumble with vanilla custard; or banana Eton Mess with butterscotch sauce, meringue and honeycomb ice cream. The Harbour makes a great stop if you are walking the South West Coastal Path between Lyme Regis and Seaton.

Open all wk 11-11 (Fri-Sat 11am-mdnt Sun 11-10.30) **Bar Meals** L served all wk 12-9.30 D served all wk 12-9.30 food served all day **Restaurant** L served all wk 12-9.30 D served all wk 12-9.30 food served all day ⊕ HALL & WOODHOUSE ◀ Badger First Gold, Tanglefoot, K&B Sussex ☉ Badger Applewood, Westons Stowford Press. **Facilities** Non-diners area ❖ (Bar Garden) ♦♦ Children's menu Children's portions Play area Garden ⊼ Parking ▭

The Ship Inn

EX12 4AF ☎ 01297 21838
dir: 1m S of A3052 between Lyme & Sidmouth. Signed to Seaton at Boshill Cross

Locally sourced fare popular with visitors and locals

Built soon after the original Ship burnt down on Christmas Day 1879, this creeper-clad family-run inn is able to trace its landlords back to 1769. Well-kept real ales and draught cider complement an extensive menu, including daily blackboard specials featuring local fish and game cooked with home-grown herbs. Typical choices include sausages and mash with red onion gravy; mushroom Stroganoff; and whole baked trout with new potatoes. The pub has a skittles alley, and there are long views over the Axe estuary from the beer garden.

Open all wk 12-3 5.30-11 ⊕ FREE HOUSE ◀ Otter Bitter, Guinness ☉ Westons Stowford Press, Sheppy's. **Facilities** ❖ (Bar Garden) ♦♦ Children's menu Children's portions Garden Parking Wi-fi

BAMPTON   Map 3 SS92

Exeter Inn ★★★ INN NEW

EX16 9DY ☎ 01398 331345
e-mail: exeter_inn@btconnect.com
dir: From Bampton take B3227 (Brook St) signed Tiverton A396. Approx 1.2m to pub on rdbt (junct with A396)

Historic inn and restaurant in the upper Exe Valley

Traditional flagstones, oak beams and real log fires make a comfortable setting for relaxing with a Somerset- or Devon-sourced real ale or cider served straight from the barrel. The menu pulls in influences from many parts of the world, thus there's mild chicken curry as a bar snack; and main dishes of crispy chilli beef stir fry; Mediterranean vegetable tart with mozzarella; and, from nearer home, whole baked local trout with crayfish and lemon butter. Grills, snacks, paninis, sandwiches and children's meals add to the tally. Guests staying overnight will find both Devon coasts, Exmoor and Dartmoor easily reachable.

Open all day all wk **Bar Meals** L served all wk 12-2.30 D served all wk 5.30-9 Av main course £10 **Restaurant** L served all wk 12-2.30 D served all wk 5.30-9 Av 3 course à la carte fr ££20 ⊕ PUNCH TAVERNS ◀ Exmoor, Cotleigh ☉ Thatchers, Addlestones. **Facilities** Non-diners area ❖ (Bar Outside area) ♦♦ Children's menu Children's portions Outside area ⊼ Parking Wi-fi ▭ (notice required) **Rooms** 12

BEER   Map 4 SY28

Anchor Inn ★★★★ INN

Fore St EX12 3ET ☎ 01297 20386
e-mail: 6403@greeneking.co.uk
dir: A3052 towards Lyme Regis. At Hangmans Stone take B3174 into Beer. Pub on seafront

Enjoy sea views and sample fresh fish

A traditional inn overlooking the bay in the picture-perfect Devon village of Beer, this pretty colour-washed pub is perfectly situated for walking the Jurassic coastline. Fish caught by local boats features strongly on the menu, and the tempting starters might include a crabmeat pot with mixed leaves and granary bread, followed by home-made steak and Guinness pie; whole sea bass on king prawn and vegetable stir-fry; or wild mushroom and spinach risotto. Six comfortable guest rooms are also available.

Open all day all wk 8am-11pm **Bar Meals** L served Sun-Thu 11-9, Fri-Sat 11-9.30 D served Sun-Thu 11-9, Fri-Sat 11-9.30 **Restaurant** L served Mon-Fri 12-2.30, Sat-Sun 12-3 D served Sun-Thu 6-9, Fri-Sat 6-9.30 ⊕ GREENE KING ◀ IPA & Abbot Ale, Otter Ale ☉ Aspall. ♈ 14 **Facilities** Non-diners area ❖ (Bar Garden) ♦♦ Children's menu Garden ⊼ Wi-fi ▭ (notice required) **Rooms** 6

BEESANDS — Map 3 SX84

The Cricket Inn ★★★★ INN ⚜

PICK OF THE PUBS

TQ7 2EN ☎ 01548 580215
e-mail: enquiries@thecricketinn.com
dir: From Kingsbridge take A379 towards Dartmouth. At
Stokenham mini rdbt turn right to Beesands

This seaside inn is a must for seafood-lovers

In a small South Hams fishing village, The Cricket Inn
first opened its doors in 1867 and has since survived
storms, a World War II bomb and a mudslide. Refitted and
extended in 2003 and 2010 respectively, the inn
encompasses a dog-friendly bar serving West Country
ales, an AA-Rosette restaurant with sea views, and bright
and airy accommodation. The Cricket is just metres from
the sloping beach and clear waters of Start Bay and the
head chef works closely with local fishermen who bring
their catch straight to the kitchen door. From the lunch
menu, sample diver-caught Beesands scallops with
celeriac purée, boneless chicken wings and curried
lentils; or hand-picked Start Bay crab sandwiches.
Choices at dinner could be chicken and ham hock pie; the
'almost world famous' seafood pancake; and slow-cooked
smoked duck, all made with produce from the Devonshire
countryside and its waters.

Open all wk 11-3 6-11 (May-Sep all day) **Bar Meals** L
served all wk 12-2.30 D served all wk 6-8.30 Av main
course £11 **Restaurant** L served all wk 12-2.30 D served
all wk 6-8.30 ⊕ HEAVITREE ◀ Otter Ale & Bitter, St
Austell Tribute Ő Aspall, Heron Valley, Thatchers. ▼ 12
Facilities Non-diners area ♣ (Bar Restaurant) ♦♦
Children's menu Children's portions Outside area ⋒
Parking Wi-fi **Rooms** 8

BICKLEIGH — Map 3 SS90

Fisherman's Cot

EX16 8RW ☎ 01884 855237
e-mail: fishermanscot.bickleigh@marstons.co.uk
dir: Telephone for directions

Riverside hostelry popular with locals and visitors alike

Well-appointed thatched inn by Bickleigh Bridge over the
River Exe with food all day and beautiful gardens, just a
short drive from Tiverton and Exmoor. The Waterside Bar
is the place for doorstep sandwiches, pies, snacks and
afternoon tea, while the restaurant incorporates a carvery
(on Sunday) and carte menus. Expect dishes such as
farmhouse pâté; deep-fried baby squid; Thai red fish
curry; slow-cooked pork shank; steak and Exeter Ale pie;
and forest fruit crumble. Children's menu available.

Open all day all wk 11-11 (Sun 12-10.30) ⊕ MARSTON'S
◀ Wychwood Hobgoblin, Ringwood. **Facilities** ♣ (Bar
Garden) ♦♦ Children's menu Children's portions Garden
Parking

BIGBURY-ON-SEA — Map 3 SX64

Pilchard Inn

Burgh Island TQ7 4BG ☎ 01548 810514
e-mail: reception@burghisland.com
dir: From A38 exit Modbury, then follow signs for Bigbury
& Burgh Island

Take the 'sea tractor' to reach this inn

You can't simply park the car or even lean the bike
against a wall here because this 14th-century smugglers'
inn is on Burgh Island, cut off by the sea twice a day.
Depending on the tide, you walk here or ride the 'sea
tractor'. Expect Devon-brewed ales, beams, flagstones
and log fires, picnic tables by the water's edge and lovely
coastal views. Friday night curry apart (booking
advisable), food is served only at lunchtime in the form of
baguettes and bagels. Typical fillings are Brixham crab
and spring onion; Mendip Hills cheddar and real ale
chutney; and Burgh Island smoked salmon.

Open all day all wk **Bar Meals** L served all wk 12-3
Restaurant D served Fri 7-9 (curry buffet) ⊕ FREE HOUSE
◀ Pilchard Ale, The South Hams Eddystone & Devon Pride
Ő Thatchers Gold, Heron Valley. ▼ 10
Facilities Non-diners area ♣ (Bar Garden) ♦♦ Garden ⋒

BLACKAWTON — Map 3 SX85

The Normandy Arms ★★★★ INN ⚜

PICK OF THE PUBS

Chapel St TQ9 7BN ☎ 01803 712884
e-mail: info@normandyarms.co.uk
dir: From Dartmouth take A3122 towards Halwell. Right
at Forces Tavern to Blackawton

At the heart of a South Hams village

Training exercises for the 1944 Normandy landings took
place on nearby Slapton Sands, thus the name of this
16th-century free house. In Torcross there's a now-
recovered Sherman tank that sank in this action.
Essentially, the pub's character comes from the beamed
and slate-floored bar and the relaxing dining room, both
with log-burning stoves. Through the bar pumps flow
Otter Ale and Thatchers Cheddar Valley cider, with
periodic local and regional guest ales. New proprietor
Andrew West-Letford was head chef at highly-rated
establishments in south-east England before coming
here to draw up internationally-flavoured lunch and
evening menus that rely on top-quality South Hams
ingredients. Try roasted brill with brown shrimps and
wilted spinach; loin of Blackawton lamb with celeriac,
roasted shallots and potato pancakes; and chicken
supreme with roasted pumpkin and Alsace bacon. Among
his desserts is hot chocolate mousse with white chocolate
ice cream. Enjoy a family evening in the south-facing
garden.

Open Mon-Sat 12-3 5.30-11 (Sun 11.30-5.30) Closed:
2 Jan-1 Feb, Sun eve & Mon **Bar Meals** L served Tue-Sat
12-2.30, Sun 12.30-4 D served Tue-Sat 6.30-9.30
Restaurant L served Tue-Sat 12-2.30, Sun 12.30-4
D served Tue-Sat 6.30-9.30 ⊕ FREE HOUSE ◀ Otter Ale

Ő Thatchers Cheddar Valley. ▼ 12
Facilities Non-diners area ♣ (Bar Restaurant Garden) ♦♦
Children's portions Garden ⋒ Parking Wi-fi **Rooms** 4

BRAMPFORD SPEKE — Map 3 SX99

The Lazy Toad Inn with Rooms

PICK OF THE PUBS

EX5 5DP ☎ 01392 841591
e-mail: thelazytoadinn@btinternet.com
dir: From Exeter take A377 towards Crediton 1.5m, right
signed Brampford Speke

Excellent food at stylish country inn near Exeter

There's much to commend this 19th-century country inn
situated in a thatched village in peaceful countryside
with riverside walks. Polished slate tiles surround a bar
which dispenses ales from Otter as well as tasty ciders
from Sandford Orchards. Behind the pub Clive and Mo
Walker's smallholding supplies the soft fruit, herbs,
vegetables, lamb and eggs to the kitchen, while meat
and fish are cured in the pub smokery. Farming
implements jostle with bistro-style art and an eclectic
mix of tables and chairs make for a modern country
atmosphere. Settle by the fire and study a daily-changing
menu that feature starters like breast of Cornish wood
pigeon, wild mushroom sauce, roasted home-grown
artichokes and parsnip crisps; and mains such as slow-
roasted belly of pork, fondant potato, and prune and
trotter sauce. Excellent vegetarian options too and a
pretty cobbled courtyard and garden at the rear.

Open 11.30-2.30 6-11 (Sun 12-3) Closed: 3wks Jan, Sun
eve & Mon **Bar Meals** L served Tue-Sun 12-2 D served
Tue-Sat 6.30-9 ⊕ FREE HOUSE ◀ Otter Ale, Toads Tipple
Ő Sandford Orchards Devon Red & Devon Mist. ▼ 12
Facilities Non-diners area ♦♦ Children's menu Children's
portions Family room Garden ⋒ Parking Wi-fi

BRANSCOMBE — Map 4 SY18

The Fountain Head

EX12 3BG ☎ 01297 680359
e-mail: thefountainhead@btconnect.com
dir: From Seaton on A3052 towards Sidmouth left at
Branscombe Cross to pub

Often packed with walkers and locals

This 500-year-old forge and cider house is a true rural
survivor, tucked away in a peaceful village just a short
walk from the coastal path. The traditional worn
flagstones, crackling log fires, rustic furnishings, village-
brewed beers from Branscombe Vale, and the chatty
atmosphere (no intrusive music or electronic games here)
charm both locals and visitors. Hearty pub food includes
Moroccan-style vegetable stew; chicken supreme stuffed
with smoked cheese and bacon; and home-cooked honey-
roast ham, double egg and chips. There's a spit-roast
and barbecue every Sunday evening between July and
September. Don't miss the midsummer beer festival.

Open all wk 11-3 6-11 (Sun 12-10.30) **Bar Meals** L
served all wk 12-2 D served all wk 6.30-9 Av main course

Save on hotels. Book at theAA.com/hotel

DEVON 125 ENGLAND

£10 **Restaurant** L served all wk 12-2 D served all wk 6.30-9 ⊕ FREE HOUSE ◀ Branscombe Vale Branoc, Jolly Geff, Summa That ⚙ Westons. **Facilities** Non-diners area ❖ (Bar Restaurant Garden) ⅰ Children's menu Children's portions Family room Garden ⌂ Beer festival Parking ☎ (notice required)

The Masons Arms

PICK OF THE PUBS

EX12 3DJ ☎ 01297 680300
e-mail: masonsarms@staustellbrewery.co.uk
dir: Exit A3052 towards Branscombe, down hill, Masons Arms at bottom of hill

Ancient pub close to the sea

Located in the picturesque village of Branscombe, the inn is just a ten-minute stroll from the beach; its peaceful gardens have sea views across a picturesque valley. This creeper-clad pub dates from 1360, when it was a cider house squeezed into the middle of a row of cottages. Back then it was a smugglers' haunt and its interior has barely changed since those days: slate floors, stone walls, ships' beams, an old jail railing and a huge open fireplace used for spit roasts on Sundays all add to the time-warp charm. Five real ales such as Otter and Proper Job are always available, including several that are locally brewed, plus ciders such as Copper Press. Food is a serious business here; where possible all ingredients are grown, reared or caught locally, especially lobster and crab. A three-day beer festival is held in the middle of July.

Open all day all wk 11-11 (Sun 12-10.30) **Bar Meals** L served all wk 12-2.15 D served all wk 6.30-9 **Restaurant** L served all wk 12-2.15 D served all wk 6.30-9 ⊕ ST AUSTELL BREWERY ◀ Tribute & Proper Job, Otter ⚙ St Austell Copper Press, Thatchers Gold, Healey's Pear Rattler. ☂ 14 **Facilities** Non-diners area ❖ (Bar) ⅰ Children's menu Children's portions Outside area ⌂ Beer festival Parking Wi-fi

BRAUNTON   Map 3 SS43

The Williams Arms

Wrafton EX33 2DE ☎ 01271 812360
e-mail: info@williamsarms.co.uk
dir: On A361 between Barnstaple & Braunton

Family owned free house with popular carvery

This postcard-pretty thatched free house beside the popular Tarka Trail dates back to the 16th century and has been owned by the Squire family since the mid-70s. Its prime location sees weary walkers, cyclists and local diners pile in for the pub's famous daily carvery, which always features locally reared meat and seasonal vegetables. Alternatively, you can try Devon scallops in white wine and cream sauce; steak and real ale pie or lighter options like prawn salad or roast turkey panini, perfect washed down with a pint of Sharp's Doom Bar. The carvery proves very popular.

Open all day all wk 8.45am-11pm **Bar Meals** food served all day **Restaurant** L served Mon-Sat 12-2, Sun 12-3

D served all wk 6-9 ⊕ FREE HOUSE ◀ Worthington's Creamflow, Sharp's Doom Bar, Guinness, Exmoor Ales Gold ⚙ Thatchers. ☂ 10 **Facilities** Non-diners area ⅰ Children's menu Children's portions Play area Garden ⌂ Parking Wi-fi ☎ (notice required)

BRENDON   Map 3 SS74

Rockford Inn

EX35 6PT ☎ 01598 741214
e-mail: enquiries@therockfordinn.com
dir: A39 through Minehead follow signs to Lynmouth. Left to Brendon

Popular Exmoor hideaway

Standing alongside the East Lyn River in the tucked-away Brendon Valley, this traditional 17th-century free house stands in the heart of Exmoor and is handy for several walking routes. Thatchers ciders complement local cask ales such as Barn Owl and Devon Darter, and there's a choice of good home-made pub meals. Chicken and leek pie, River Exe moules marinière and slow-braised beef are typical menu choices; the specials board changes daily. Eat in the garden in warm weather, or head inside to the open fire when the weather changes.

Open all day Closed: Mon L **Bar Meals** L served Tue-Sun 12-3 D served Tue-Sun 6-8.30 ⊕ FREE HOUSE ◀ Cotleigh Barn Owl & 25, St Austell Tribute, Clearwater Proper Ansome, Devon Darter & Real Smiler, Exmoor ⚙ Thatchers, Addlestones. **Facilities** Non-diners area ❖ (Bar Restaurant Garden) ⅰ Children's menu Children's portions Garden ⌂ Parking Wi-fi

BRIDFORD   Map 3 SX88

The Bridford Inn

EX6 7HT ☎ 01647 252250
e-mail: info@bridfordinn.co.uk
web: www.bridfordinn.co.uk
dir: Telephone for directions

Inn with wonderful valley views

On the edge of Dartmoor above the beautiful Teign Valley, this village inn and shop was converted from three 17th-century cottages, and its elevated position provides glorious views over the area. Oak beams supporting the ceiling are timbers left over from construction of the replica Pilgrim Fathers' ship, The Mayflower. Menus offer grilled steak-and-kidney pie; roast chicken with lemon and thyme and mushroom risotto. The bar serves Jail Ale from Dartmoor Brewery. Look out for the pub's bank holiday beer and cider festivals in May and August.

The Bridford Inn

Open 12-3 5-11 (Fri 12-3 5-12, Sat 12-12, Sun 12-11) Closed: Tue L **Bar Meals** L served Mon & Wed-Fri 12-2, Sat 12-3, Sun 12-4 D served Mon & Wed-Sat 7-9 Av main course £9.95 ⊕ FREE HOUSE ◀ Dartmoor Jail Ale, Sharp's Doom Bar ⚙ Sandford Orchards, Thatchers Gold. **Facilities** Non-diners area ❖ (Bar Garden) ⅰ Children's menu Children's portions Garden ⌂ Beer festival Cider festival Parking Wi-fi ☎ (notice required)

BUCKFASTLEIGH   Map 3 SX76

Dartbridge Inn

Totnes Rd TQ11 0JR ☎ 01364 642214
e-mail: 6442@greeneking.co.uk
dir: From Exeter A38, take 1st Buckfastleigh turn, then left to Totnes. Inn on left

Comprehensive menu with cask ales on tap

Wooden floors, leather chairs, sofas and real fires define the ambience in the spacious bar of the Dartbridge, where various guest ales vie for your trade. Outside, there are views through trees to the River Dart, and a prettily furnished terrace with parasols where you can dine alfresco. The menus comprise salads, gourmet burgers, lunchtime sandwiches, Black Angus steaks, and pub favourites made with good-quality produce, such as beef and Ruddles ale pie; chicken fajitas; Suffolk pork sausages with Devon cheddar mash; and lentil shepherd's pie. A children's menu and specials are also available.

Open all day all wk ⊕ OLD ENGLISH INNS ◀ Greene King IPA & Abbot Ale, Morland Old Speckled Hen, Guest ales. **Facilities** ⅰ Children's menu Children's portions Garden Parking Wi-fi

BUCKLAND MONACHORUM — Map 3 SX46

Drake Manor Inn ★★★★ INN

The Village PL20 7NA ☎ **01822 853892**
e-mail: drakemanor@drakemanorinn.co.uk
dir: Off A386 near Yelverton

12th-century masons' house well-known for a warm welcome and good food

In the 12th century, when nearby St Andrew's church was being built, the masons needed a house to live in. Today's licensee of that now very old house is Mandy Robinson, who prides herself on running a 'proper pub', with a menu of locally-sourced delights. Look out for smoked haddock and spring onions fishcakes or breaded baby scallops with lemon and cracked pepper to start; followed by pork steak with Stilton and cream sauce and cider and apple compôte; or aubergine and spiced Mediterranean vegetable stack topped with brie. The sunny cottage garden is appealing, and the en suite room may invite you to stay overnight.

Open all wk Mon-Thu 11.30-2.30 6.30-11 (Fri-Sat 11.30-11.30 Sun 12-11) **Bar Meals** L served all wk 12-2 D served Mon-Sat 7-10, Sun 7-9.30 Av main course £6.50-£9.95 **Restaurant** L served all wk 12-2 D served Mon-Sat 7-10, Sun 7-9.30 Av 3 course à la carte fr £22 ⊕ PUNCH TAVERNS ◀ John Smith's, Sharp's Doom Bar, Otter Bitter ◊ Addlestones, Thatchers Gold. ♥ 9 **Facilities** Non-diners area ❀ (Bar Garden) ♦ Children's portions Family room Garden ⊼ Parking **Rooms** 1

BUTTERLEIGH — Map 3 SS90

The Butterleigh Inn

EX15 1PN ☎ **01884 855433**
e-mail: thebutterleighinn1@btconnect.com
dir: M5 junct 28, B3181 signed Cullompton. In Cullompton High St right signed Butterleigh. 3m to pub

Regularly changing real ales and home-made food

Set in a delightful village opposite the 13th-century St Matthew's church and in the heart of the rolling Devon countryside, the 400-year-old Butterleigh is a traditional free house. There is a mass of local memorabilia throughout this friendly local, where customers can choose from a selection of changing real ales including Dartmoor Jail Ale, ciders including Devon Scrumpy from Sandford Orchards, and around 15 malt whiskies. Expect home-made dishes such as turkey and pork pie; curry of the day; lamb chops; broccoli, leek and Stilton bake; and steaks from the grill. On fine days, the garden with its huge flowering cherry tree is very popular.

Open 12-2.30 6-11 (Fri-Sat 12-2.30 6-12 Sun 12-3) Closed: Sun eve, Mon L **Bar Meals** L served Tue-Sat 12-2 D served Tue-Sat 7-9 **Restaurant** L served Tue-Sat 12-2 D served Tue-Sat 7-9 ⊕ FREE HOUSE ◀ Cotleigh Tawny Ale, Otter Ale & Amber, Dartmoor IPA & Jail Ale, Guest ale ◊ Sandford Orchards Devon Scrumpy, Sheppy's, Winkleigh Sam's. **Facilities** Non-diners area ❀ (Bar Garden) ♦ Children's menu Children's portions Garden ⊼ Parking Wi-fi

CHAGFORD — Map 3 SX78

Sandy Park Inn

PICK OF THE PUBS

TQ13 8JW ☎ **01647 433267**
e-mail: info@sandyparkinn.co.uk
dir: From A30 exit at Whiddon Down, left towards Moretonhampstead. Inn 3m

Lovely thatched pub with a timeless quality

In a beautiful setting near the River Teign on the edge of Dartmoor, this inn attracts locals and travellers alike, while dogs are frequently to be found slumped in front of the fire. Homely horse brasses and sporting prints adorn the walls of the beamed bar, where you can choose from an eclectic wine list and a good range of traditional local ales like Otter Bitter and Dartmoor Jail Ale. Whether you eat in the bar, snug or candlelit dining room, menus of home-made dishes change with the seasons, blending pub classics with modern fusion and vegetarian options; a range of gourmet stone-baked pizzas is especially popular. Sample dishes are honey-glazed goats' cheese, oven-roasted fillet of hake, pan-fried lamb steak, and vanilla cheesecake. Sandwiches and salads are perfect for summer lunchtimes, when they can be served in the garden with its views towards the Castle Drogo estate and deer park.

Open all day all wk **Bar Meals** L served all wk 12-2.30 D served all wk 6-9 **Restaurant** L served all wk 12-2.30 D served all wk 6-9 ⊕ FREE HOUSE ◀ Otter Bitter, Dartmoor IPA, Dartmoor Jail Ale ◊ Thatchers. **Facilities** Non-diners area ❀ (Bar Garden) ♦ Children's menu Children's portions Family room Garden ⊼ Parking Wi-fi ▭

CLAYHIDON — Map 4 ST11

The Merry Harriers

PICK OF THE PUBS

Forches Corner EX15 3TR ☎ **01823 421270**
e-mail: peter.gatling@btinternet.com
dir: M5 junct 26, A38 signed Wellington. At next rdbt left signed Exeter/A38. Left into Ford St (follow brown pub sign). At next x-rds left signed Merrie Harriers 1.5m

Village inn with locally sourced food

Originally a Devon longhouse dating from the 15th century, this delightful free house is set in beautiful countryside high on the Blackdown Hills. The pub stands on the spot of notorious Forches Corner, which was the scene of ambushes during the 17th-century Monmouth Rebellion. The black-and-white building features beamed ceilings, a cosy inglenook and attractive dining areas. Peter and Angela Gatling have worked tirelessly to build the local drinks trade and expand the food operation. More than 90 per cent of kitchen ingredients come from the surrounding hills or further afield in the West Country. A bar lunch might feature pan-fried fillet of rainbow trout on chive potato cake, or for lighter appetites there are filled baguettes and ploughman's. In the evening you could try pan-braised pork chop with cider and apples

and mustard mash, or local steak-and-kidney pie. The large garden is popular during the summer.

Open 12-3 6.30-11 Closed: Sun eve & Mon **Bar Meals** L served Tue-Sat 12-2, Sun 12-2.15 D served Tue-Sat 6.30-9 Av main course £10 **Restaurant** L served Tue-Sat 12-2, Sun 12-2.15 D served Tue-Sat 6.30-9 Av 3 course à la carte fr £18 ⊕ FREE HOUSE ◀ Otter Head & Amber, Cotleigh Harrier, Exmoor Gold, St Austell Tinners ◊ Thatchers Gold, Bollhayes. ♥ 14 **Facilities** Non-diners area ❀ (Bar Garden) ♦ Children's menu Children's portions Play area Family room Garden ⊼ Parking Wi-fi ▭ (notice required)

CLEARBROOK — Map 3 SX56

The Skylark Inn

PL20 6JD ☎ **01822 853258**
e-mail: skylvic@btinternet.com
dir: 5m N of Plymouth on A386 towards Tavistock. Take 2nd right signed Clearbrook

Set in the Dartmoor National Park

Originally used by miners in the 18th century, The Skylark is just ten minutes from Plymouth. The village and surrounding area are ideal for cyclists and walkers. Children are welcome at this attractive pub and there is a special play area for them. Local ales and good wholesome food are served in the beamed bar with its large fireplace and wood-burning stove. Dishes include sizzling steaks, Mediterranean-style tuna, prawn salad, stuffed bell pepper, and classics like breaded scampi and barbecued ribs. Jackets and baguettes are also on offer. There is a beer festival on the August Bank Holiday and monthly charity quiz nights.

Open all wk 11.30-3 6-11.30 (Sat-Sun all day) **Bar Meals** L served Mon-Fri 12-2, Sat-Sun all day D served Mon-Fri 6.30-9, Sat-Sun all day Av main course £4.50 **Restaurant** L served Mon-Fri 12-2, Sat-Sun all day D served Mon-Fri 6.30-9, Sat-Sun all day ⊕ UNIQUE PUB CO LTD ◀ Otter Ale, St Austell Tribute, Dartmoor. **Facilities** Non-diners area ❀ (Bar Garden) ♦ Children's menu Children's portions Play area Family room Garden ⊼ Beer festival Parking ▭ (notice required)

CLOVELLY — Map 3 SS32

Red Lion Hotel ★★ HL

PICK OF THE PUBS

The Quay EX39 5TF ☎ **01237 431237**
e-mail: redlion@clovelly.co.uk
dir: From Bideford rdbt, A39 to Bude, 10m. At Clovelly Cross rdbt right, pass Clovelly Visitor Centre entrance, bear left. Hotel at bottom of hill

Excellent home-cooked food in unspoilt fishing village

This charming whitewashed hostelry sits right on the quay in Clovelly, the famously unspoilt 'village like a waterfall', which descends down broad steps to a 14th-century harbour. Guests staying in the whimsically decorated bedrooms can fall asleep to the sound of

Save on hotels. Book at **theAA.com/hotel**

DEVON 127 **ENGLAND**

waves lapping the shingle. Originally a beerhouse for fishermen and other locals, the Red Lion has plenty of character and offers Cornish ales such as Sharp's Doom Bar in its snug bar, where you can rub shoulders with the locals. Alternatively, you could settle in the Harbour Bar, and sample the home-cooked food, the modern seasonal menu specialising in fresh seafood, which is landed daily right outside the door. Choose pan-fried John Dory or poached brill with creamy mushroom sauce, or opt for Clovelly Estate venison and game dishes, or pork fillet with smoked bacon, apple purée and red wine jus. There is an annual beer festival late May Bank Holiday.

Open all day all wk **Bar Meals** L served all wk 12-2.30 D served all wk 6-8.30 **Restaurant** D served all wk 7-9 ⊕ FREE HOUSE ◀ Sharp's Doom Bar, Clovelly Cobbler, Guinness ☼ Thatchers, Winkleigh, Westons Stowford Press. **Facilities** ❧ (Bar) ♦ Children's menu Children's portions Family room Beer festival Parking Wi-fi ▭ **Rooms** 17

COCKWOOD
Map 3 SX98

The Anchor Inn

EX6 8RA ☎ 01626 890203
dir: *Off A379 between Dawlish & Starcross*

Waterside pub specialising in seafood

Originally a Seamen's Mission, this 450-year-old inn overlooks a small landlocked harbour on the River Exe and was once the haunt of smugglers. There is even a friendly ghost with his dog. In summer, customers spill out onto the verandah and harbour wall, while real fires, nautical bric-a-brac and low beams make the interior cosy in winter. For fish-lovers, the comprehensive menu will make decisions difficult – there are 28 different ways to eat mussels, countless fresh oyster and scallop dishes and fish platters. Meat-eaters and vegetarians are not forgotten. Beer festivals twice a year around Halloween and Easter.

Open all day all wk 11-11 (Sun 12-10.30 25 Dec 12-2) **Bar Meals** food served all day **Restaurant** food served all day ⊕ HEAVITREE ◀ Otter Ale, St Austell Tribute, Adnams Broadside, 3 Guest ales. ₱ 10 **Facilities** Non-diners area ❧ (Bar) ♦ Children's menu Outside area ▭ Beer festival Parking ▭ (notice required)

COLEFORD
Map 3 SS70

The New Inn ★★★★ INN

PICK OF THE PUBS

EX17 5BZ ☎ 01363 84242
e-mail: enquiries@thenewinncoleford.co.uk
dir: *From Exeter take A377, 1.5m after Crediton left for Coleford, 1.5m to inn*

Local ales and food in secluded Devon valley

The attractive 13th-century building with thatched roof makes a perfect home for this friendly inn. The ancient slate-floored bar with its old chests and polished brass blends effortlessly with fresh white walls, original oak beams and simple wooden furniture in the dining room.

Set beside the River Cole, the garden is perfect for alfresco summer dining, when you can ponder on the pub's history: it was used by travelling Cistercian monks long before Charles I reviewed his troops from a nearby house during the English Civil War. Menus change regularly, and special events such as 'fish fest week' or 'sea shanty night' are interspersed throughout the year. Home-made bar food includes a range of soups, omelettes and platters, while a larger meal might include chicken, ham and mushroom pie, or whole grilled sea bass served with an orange and lemon butter sauce. The pub's Amazon Blue parrot, called Captain, has been a famous fixture here for nearly 30 years, greeting bar regulars and guests booking into the six well-appointed bedrooms.

Open all wk 12-3 6-11 Closed: 25-26 Dec **Bar Meals** L served all wk 12-2 D served all wk 6-9.30 **Restaurant** L served all wk 12-2 D served all wk 6-9.30 ⊕ FREE HOUSE ◀ Sharp's Doom Bar, Otter Ale ☼ Winkleigh Sam's. ₱ 20 **Facilities** Non-diners area ❧ (Bar Garden) ♦ Children's menu Children's portions Garden ▭ Parking Wi-fi **Rooms** 6

DARTMOUTH
Map 3 SX85

Royal Castle Hotel ★★★ HL

PICK OF THE PUBS

11 The Quay TQ6 9PS ☎ 01803 833033
e-mail: lucyjonas@royalcastle.co.uk
dir: *In town centre, overlooking inner harbour*

Privately owned historic pub and hotel

Commanding a prime site overlooking the Dart estuary, this handsome old coaching inn was originally four Tudor houses built on either side of a narrow lane, which now forms the lofty hallway. Features include period fireplaces, spiral staircases, oil paintings and priest holes. A supporter of Taste of the West's 'buy local' campaign, the hotel offers a seasonal menu that includes South Devon mussels marinière; fillet steak tartare; chargrilled haloumi with roasted Mediterranean vegetables, as well as Dartmoor venison, South Hams beef and Dartmouth crab. As well as great river views, the Grill Room restaurant upstairs offers Chateaubriand for two. Lunchtime sandwiches and ploughman's are available in the pubby Harbour Bar, while in the Galleon lounge you'll find plenty of daily specials and firm favourites like battered cod and chips; a different pie every week; trio of local sausages with mash and onion gravy; and roast belly pork with crackling.

Open all day all wk 8am-11.30pm **Bar Meals** L served all wk 11.30-10 D served all wk 11.30-10 food served all day **Restaurant** L served all wk 12-2 D served all wk 6-10 ⊕ FREE HOUSE ◀ Dartmoor Jail Ale, Otter Amber, Sharp's Doom Bar ☼ Thatchers Gold, Orchard's. ₱ 29 **Facilities** Non-diners area ❧ (Bar) ♦ Children's menu Children's portions Family room Parking Wi-fi ▭ (notice required) **Rooms** 25

DENBURY
Map 3 SX86

The Union Inn

Denbury Green TQ12 6DQ ☎ 01803 812595
e-mail: enquiries@theunioninndenbury.co.uk
dir: *2m from Newton Abbot, signed Denbury*

Old and new come together in this village inn

Overlooking the village green, The Union Inn is at least 400 years old and counting. Inside are the original stone walls that once rang to the hammers of the blacksmiths and cartwrights who worked here many moons ago. The bar area has comfy leather sofas while the decor throughout is a mix of traditional and contemporary. Choose from the tapas and bar snack menu, the restaurant menu or the daily specials. Mouth-watering starters could include quail stuffed with pancetta or barbecued chicken wings. Follow with vegetable filo roulade; slow-cooked belly of Devon pork; seafood linguine; or the Union Inn burger.

Open all wk 12-3 6-11.30 (Thu-Sun 12-11) ⊕ ENTERPRISE INNS ◀ Otter Bitter, Hunter's Denbury Dreamer, Guest ales ☼ Westons. **Facilities** ❧ (Bar Restaurant Garden) ♦ Children's menu Children's portions Garden Parking Wi-fi

DITTISHAM
Map 3 SX85

The Ferry Boat

Manor St TQ6 0EX ☎ 01803 722368
e-mail: simonfbi@hotmail.co.uk
dir: *Telephone for directions*

Arrive at this riverside pub by boat

The only pub situated on the River Dart, this family-friendly inn dates back 300 years and the pontoon outside the entrance guarantees popularity with the boating fraternity. Tables at the front of the pub enjoy views across the river to Greenway House and Gardens, the National Trust property that was once Agatha Christie's home. With its year-round selection of four or five real ales, and open log fires crackling in the grates in winter, this really is a pub for all seasons. Menus of home-cooked food vary seasonally, based on fresh fish and seafood, and local meats and cheeses. A barbecue event in summer could feature local musicians.

Open all day all wk Closed: 25 Dec ⊕ PUNCH TAVERNS ◀ Otter Ale, Dorset Jurassic, Sharp's Doom Bar, Guest ales ☼ Addlestones, Westons Old Rosie & Stowford Press. **Facilities** ❧ (Bar) ♦ Children's menu Children's portions Family room

DODDISCOMBSLEIGH — Map 3 SX88

The Nobody Inn ★★★★ INN

PICK OF THE PUBS

EX6 7PS ☎ 01647 252394
e-mail: info@nobodyinn.co.uk
dir: *3m SW of Exeter Racecourse (A38)*

Renowned for its extensive wine selection

Although difficult to find, this famous Devon inn is worth searching for. Set in rolling countryside between the Haldon Hills and the Teign Valley, the inn can be traced back to 1591, although it was another two centuries before it became a hostelry. The pub acquired its unusual name after an unfortunate incident following the innkeeper's death in 1952. His corpse was accidentally left in the mortuary while the funeral took place around an empty coffin with 'no body'. The present owners — only the fifth since 1838 — have ensured that the pub retains its traditional low ceilings, blackened beams, inglenook fireplace and antique furniture. Here you can sample some 260 wines and 230 whiskies in addition to the range of real ales. Fresh fish, delivered daily from Brixham, can be found on the regularly changing menu. A typical dinner might be Sharpham Brie soufflé, pan-fried sea bass and sticky ginger pudding. Attractive bedrooms are available.

Open all day all wk 11-11 (Sun 12-10.30) **Bar Meals** L served Mon-Sat 12-2, Sun 12-3 D served Mon-Thu 6.30-9, Fri-Sat 6.30-9.30, Sun 7-9 Av main course £10.95 **Restaurant** D served Tue-Thu 6.30-9, Fri-Sat 6.30-9.30 Av 3 course à la carte fr £25 ⊕ FREE HOUSE ◀ Branscombe Vale Nobody's Bitter, Guest ales ♉ Brimblecombe's, St Austell Copper Press, Thatchers Gold. ♟ 28 **Facilities** Non-diners area ♦♦ Children's portions Garden ⌨ Parking Wi-fi **Rooms** 5

DOLTON — Map 3 SS51

Rams Head Inn

South St EX19 8QS ☎ 01805 804255
e-mail: ramsheadinn@btopenworld.com
dir: *8m from Torrington on A3124*

Traditional pub in Devon's lovely countryside

This 15th-century free house has retained much of its original character with huge old fireplaces, bread ovens and pot stands. The inn's central location places it on many inland tourist routes, whilst the Tarka Trail and Rosemoor Gardens are both nearby. Expect a selection of cask ales on tap, accompanied by popular and traditional meals on the restaurant menu, served at lunchtime and in the evening.

Open 10-3 6-11 (Fri-Sat 12-12 Sun 12-4 6-11) Closed: Mon winter **Bar Meals** L served all wk 12-2.30 D served Mon-Sat 6.30-9 Av main course £8 **Restaurant** L served all wk 12-2.30 D served Mon-Sat 6.30-9 Fixed menu price fr £10 Av 3 course à la carte fr £15 ⊕ FREE HOUSE ◀ Country Life Golden Pig, Sharp's Own ♉ Winkleigh. ♟ 14 **Facilities** Non-diners area ♥ (Bar Outside area) ♦♦ Garden Outside area ⌨ Parking Wi-fi ▭

EAST ALLINGTON — Map 3 SX74

The Fortescue Arms

TQ9 7RA ☎ 01548 521215
e-mail: info@fortescue-arms.co.uk
dir: *Telephone for directions*

Pretty free house in a South Hams village

This charming old country inn was taken over by a friendly new family in 2012. The flagstone-floored bar now offers three real ales from Dartmoor Brewery as well as Thatchers cider. The bar menu includes moules frites, a British cheeseboard and sandwiches. In the restaurant, expect the likes of goats' cheese tower with a baby leaf salad, followed by lamb three ways (rack, confit shoulder and marinated rump). For dessert, maybe warm treacle tart with an orange tuile, clotted cream and orange passion sorbet; or chocolate fondant with chocolate sorbet and espresso sauce. There are roasts on Sundays.

Open all day Closed: Mon L (open in holidays) **Bar Meals** Av main course £12 food served all day **Restaurant** Fixed menu price fr £8 Av 3 course à la carte fr £25 food served all day ⊕ FREE HOUSE ◀ Dartmoor Legend, IPA & Jail Ale, Guinness ♉ Thatchers. ♟ **Facilities** Non-diners area ♥ (Bar Restaurant Garden) ♦♦ Children's menu Children's portions Garden ⌨ Parking Wi-fi ▭ (notice required)

EXETER — Map 3 SX99

The Hour Glass

21 Melbourne St EX2 4AU ☎ 01392 258722
e-mail: ajpthehourglass@yahoo.co.uk
dir: *M5 junct 30, A370 signed Exeter. At Countess Weir rdbt 3rd exit onto Topsham Rd (B3182) signed City Centre. In approx 2m left into Melbourne St*

Quirky end-of-terrace pub with friendly staff

This distinctively shaped backstreet pub has built up a reputation for its friendly service and inventive food, not to mention its impressive range of local real ales. Expect beams, wood floors, an open fire and resident cats in the bar, where handpulled pints of Otter Bitter or Exeter Ferryman; can be enjoyed with curried eggs and watercress; or lamb, quince and Rioja stew with anchovy dumplings.

Open 12-3 5-close (Sat-Sun all day Mon 5-close) Closed: 25-26 Dec, Mon L **Bar Meals** L served Tue-Fri 12.30-2.30, Sat-Sun 12.30-3 D served Mon-Sat 7-9.30, Sun 6-9 **Restaurant** L served Tue-Fri 12.30-2.30, Sat-Sun 12.30-3 D served Mon-Sat 7-9.30, Sun 6-9 ⊕ ENTERPRISE INNS ◀ Otter Bitter, Exeter Ferryman, Bath SPA ♉ Burrow Hill. ♟ 24 **Facilities** Non-diners area Wi-fi

Red Lion Inn

Broadclyst EX5 3EL ☎ 01392 461271
dir: *On B3181 (Exeter to Cullompton road)*

Tucked away in a quiet corner of the Killerton Estate

You'll find the Red Lion in a 16th-century listed building set at the heart of a delightful village in the National Trust's Killerton Estate. The interior has a wealth of beams and warming open fires, where pints of Stormstay and Yellow Hammer are cheerfully served and supped. The typical menu may offer lamb's liver, onion and bacon casserole; pot roasted lamb shank; grilled sea bass; or Exmoore ale rabbit stew. Treat yourself to a home-made pud afterwards. Vegetarians and coeliacs are catered for, as are the canine contingent, who have their own bar menu.

Open all wk 11-3.30 5.30-11.30 (Sat 11am-11.30pm Sun 12-11) **Bar Meals** L served Mon-Fri 12-2.30, Sat-Sun 12-9 D served Mon-Fri 6-9, Sat-Sun 12-9 Av main course £5-£10 **Restaurant** L served Mon-Fri 12-2.30, Sat-Sun 12-9 D served Mon-Fri 6-9, Sat-Sun 12-9 Av 3 course à la carte fr £25 ⊕ FREE HOUSE ◀ Fuller's London Pride, O'Hanlon's Yellow Hammer & Stormstay, Otter Ale ♉ Thatchers, Gaymers. ♟ 8 **Facilities** Non-diners area ♥ (Bar Garden) ♦♦ Children's menu Children's portions Garden ⌨ Parking ▭ (notice required)

EXTON — Map 3 SX98

The Puffing Billy

PICK OF THE PUBS

Station Rd EX3 0PR ☎ 01392 877888
e-mail: enquiries@thepuffingbilly.co.uk
dir: *A376 signed Exmouth, through Ebford. Follow signs for pub, right into Exton*

Smart modern setting for seasonal British food

On the east side of the Exe Estuary, close to Exeter and Exmouth, the traditional looking 16th-century whitewashed building that is the Puffing Billy has a smart modern bar and restaurant. A good selection of 15 wines by the glass plus local ales like Bays Topsail and O'Hanlon's Yellow Hammer tempt those coming for a drink while the kitchen turns out modern British food in tune with the seasons. They make the most of the local larder, particularly fish from the estuary and Devon coast and beef and venison from Dartmoor. Expect the likes of sweet potato fondants with Norsworthy goats' cheese rarebit to start, then perhaps pan-fried brill with River Exe mussels and saffron tagliatelle. Grand Marnier baba with cranberry and walnut compôte is a decadent way to finish. There's also a good value set menu and a specials board.

Open all wk 12-3 6-11 (Apr-Sep all day) **Bar Meals** L served Mon-Sat 12-2 Av main course £7.95 **Restaurant** L served Mon-Sat 12-2, Sun 12-2.30 D served Mon-Sat 6.30-9.30, Sun 6-9 Fixed menu price fr £14.95 Av 3 course à la carte fr £24 ⊕ FREE HOUSE ◀ Otter Bitter, Bays Topsail, O'Hanlon's Yellow Hammer. ♟ 15 **Facilities** Non-diners area ♥ (Bar Garden) ♦♦ Children's menu Children's portions Garden ⌨ Parking Wi-fi ▭ (notice required)

GEORGEHAM
Map 3 SS43

The Rock Inn

Rock Hill EX33 1JW ☎ **01271 890322**
e-mail: therockgeorgeham@gmail.com
dir: *From A361 at Braunton follow Croyde Bay signs. Through Croyde, 1m to Georgeham. Pass shop & church. Inn on right*

A mixture of dining options at this popular inn

A great watering hole for walkers and cyclists, this old inn is also handy for the famous surfing beaches at Woolacombe. Its friendly atmosphere, comprising a mix of happy banter from the locals and gentle jazz played at lunchtime, adds to the enjoyment of a pint selected from the five ales on offer. Choose between the traditional bar, the slightly more contemporary lower bar, or a bright conservatory decorated with local art. The tasty menu is hard to resist, extending from a light lunch of Dave Wong's salt and pepper chilli squid, to dinner dishes such as the Rock's fish pie.

Open all day all wk 11am-mdnt **Bar Meals** L served all wk 12-2.30 D served all wk 6-9.30 **Restaurant** L served all wk 12-2.30 D served all wk 6-9.30 ◖ Timothy Taylor Landlord, Exmoor Ale, Fuller's, St Austell Tribute, Sharp's Doom Bar, Otter ♂ Thatchers Gold. ⚑ 12
Facilities Non-diners area ♦♦ Children's menu Children's portions Garden ⧥ Parking Wi-fi ▭

HARBERTON
Map 3 SX75

The Church House Inn

TQ9 7SF ☎ **01803 863707**
e-mail: info@churchhouseharberton.co.uk
dir: *From Totnes take A381 S. Turn right for Harberton, pub by church in village centre*

Family-run, country inn with a long history

Nestling in the beautiful South Devon countryside, this 13th-century free house is tucked away but easily accessible from Totnes. With high oak beams and a cosy atmosphere, The Church House was built around 1100 to accommodate monks constructing the church next door. Among its historic features is a fine medieval oak screen separating the long bar with its wood burners from the comfortable family room. Popular favourites on the menu include home-made chicken liver pâté; grilled scallop and tiger prawn kebab; poached salmon; and gammon steak with pineapple or egg.

Open all wk all day (Mon-Tue 12-3 6-11) ⊕ FREE HOUSE ◖ Dartmoor Jail Ale, Skinner's Betty Stogs ♂ Addlestones, Sandford Devon Mist, Westons.
Facilities ♣ (Bar) ♦♦ Children's menu Children's portions Parking Wi-fi

HAYTOR VALE
Map 3 SX77

The Rock Inn ★★★★ INN ◉

PICK OF THE PUBS

TQ13 9XP ☎ **01364 661305**
e-mail: inn@rock-inn.co.uk
dir: *A38 from Exeter, at Drum Bridges rdbt take A382 for Bovey Tracey, 1st exit at 2nd rdbt (B3387), 3m left to Haytor Vale*

An oasis of calm and comfort on wild Dartmoor

Sheltering below the Haytor Rocks, this beamed and flagstoned 18th-century coaching inn occupies a stunning location just inside Dartmoor National Park, with wonderful surrounding walks. The traditional interior is full of character with antique tables, settles, prints and paintings, a grandfather clock, and pieces of china over the two fireplaces, where logs crackle constantly on winter days. After a day walking on the moor, healthy appetites can be satisfied with some solid modern British cooking, using top-notch local produce in attractively presented dishes of steamed River Teign mussels, pan-roasted venison saddle, or rump steak with hand-cut chips. Leave room for a Bakewell tart or iced coffee parfait. Meals can be enjoyed alfresco in the courtyard or in the peaceful garden across the lane. West Country cheese is a particular feature, alongside wine from the Sharpham Vineyard in Totnes and local ales, including Dartmoor Jail Ale or IPA.

Open all day all wk 11-11 (Sun 12-10.30) Closed: 25-26 Dec **Bar Meals** L served all wk 12-2 **Restaurant** D served all wk 7-9 ⊕ FREE HOUSE ◖ Dartmoor Jail Ale, IPA ♂ Luscombe. ⚑ 12 **Facilities** Non-diners area ♣ (Garden) ♦♦ Children's menu Children's portions Family room Garden ⧥ Parking Wi-fi **Rooms** 9

HOLSWORTHY
Map 3 SS30

The Bickford Arms

Brandis Corner EX22 7XY ☎ **01409 221318**
e-mail: info@bickfordarms.com
dir: *On A3072, 4m from Holsworthy towards Hatherleigh*

Traditional pub with a diverse menu

This pub stood on the Holsworthy to Hatherleigh road for 300 years before it was gutted by fire in 2003. Although totally rebuilt, it has retained much period charm, with beams, a welcoming bar and two fireplaces. The bar serves international beers, local real ales and ciders. Choose from the same menu in the bar and restaurant – perhaps free-range Devon duck breast with redcurrant and red wine sauce, or home-made steak-and-ale pie. All food is prepared with locally sourced ingredients. On Sunday summer evenings, the beer garden hosts popular barbecues.

Open all wk 11-11 **Bar Meals** L served all wk 12-2.30 D served all wk 6-9 ⊕ FREE HOUSE ◖ Sharp's Doom Bar, Dartmoor Legend, St Austell Tribute ♂ Healey's Cornish Rattler. **Facilities** Non-diners area ♣ (Bar Garden) ♦♦ Children's menu Children's portions Garden ⧥ Parking Wi-fi ▭ (notice required)

HONITON
Map 4 ST10

The Holt ◉◉

PICK OF THE PUBS

178 High St EX14 1LA ☎ **01404 47707**
e-mail: enquiries@theholt-honiton.com
dir: *Telephone for directions*

One for fans of Otter ales

A holt is where otters live, and the significance of this is that in 1990 the parents of its joint owners, Joe and Angus McCaig, established the Otter Brewery in nearby Luppitt. It draws its water from the River Otter, and its full range of real ales is served in the bar, while Honiton's own Norcotts is among the ciders. Off the bar is an open-plan kitchen, while upstairs is a candlelit dining area. Head chef Angus has earned two AA Rosettes for his regularly changing menus that showcase local suppliers at length. Tapas are served at lunchtime and in the evening, and daily specials supplement main dishes such as grilled fillet of gurnard with samphire and smoked prawns; and beef casserole with mushrooms and crispy dumplings. The in-house smokery is kept busy. Live music, films and beer festivals ensure there is usually something happening.

Open 11-3 5.30-12 Closed: 25-26 Dec, Sun & Mon **Bar Meals** L served Tue-Sat 12-2 D served Tue-Sat 6.30-9 Av main course £14.50 **Restaurant** L served Tue-Sat 12-2 D served Tue-Sat 6.30-9.30 ⊕ FREE HOUSE ◖ Otter Bitter, Ale, Bright, Amber, Head ♂ Sheppy's, Thatchers Gold, Norcotts Cider. ⚑ 9 **Facilities** Non-diners area ♦♦ Children's portions Beer festival Wi-fi ▭

IDDESLEIGH
Map 3 SS50

The Duke of York

PICK OF THE PUBS

EX19 8BG ☎ **01837 810253**
e-mail: john@dukeofyorkdevon.co.uk
dir: *Telephone for directions*

Picture-perfect Devon inn in secluded village

It was in this thatched, Devon cob inn, in a tiny village of similarly jaw-droppingly pretty cottages, that local author Michael Morpurgo tentatively started his novel *War Horse* whilst chatting to veterans enjoying the pub's enticing range of west country cider and ales – Cotleigh is a favoured brew – stillaged behind the bar. He's not the only writer whose pilgrims visit the secluded Torridge Valley here; the well-known Tarka Trail, named for the otter in Henry Williamson's novel, passes the pub door. Around 640 years old, the inn oozes that indefinable aura of such maturity; huge inglenooks, timeworn wooden tables, ancient beams and pillars radiating from a bar hugely popular with the scattered local community and visitors tacking the fishing and rambling opportunities here. There's a well-balanced menu of robust Devon fare on offer; scallops wrapped in crispy bacon dents the appetite, followed up with grilled sea bass on a bed of pine nuts; local pork and pheasant also feature.

continued

IDDESLEIGH *continued*

Open all day all wk 11-11 **Bar Meals** L served all wk 11-10 D served all wk 11-10 food served all day ⊕ FREE HOUSE ◙ Adnams Broadside, Cotleigh Tawny Owl, Guest ales ♂ Winkleigh. ♀ 10 **Facilities** Non-diners area ❤ (Bar Garden) ♦♦ Children's menu Children's portions Garden Beer festival Wi-fi ▭

The George & Dragon

5 Fore St EX34 9ED ☎ 01271 863851
e-mail: linda.quinn5@btinternet.com
dir: *Telephone for directions*

Close to the harbour and serving traditional pub grub

The oldest pub in town, The George & Dragon dates from 1360 and is reputedly haunted. The food is of the simple, no-nonsense variety – typical examples include home-cooked boozy beef, chicken curry, mixed grills, and home-cooked crab from the harbour when available. There are no fruit machines or pool table, but if you are lucky there will be a little home-produced background music, along with a good choice of real ales and ciders.

Open all day all wk 10am-mdnt (Sun 12-12) ⊕ PUNCH TAVERNS ◙ Shepherd Neame Spitfire, Skinner's Betty Stogs, Exmoor Ale. **Facilities** ❤ (Bar) ♦♦ Children's menu Children's portions **Notes** ⊜

The Old Inn

EX13 7RB ☎ 01297 32096
e-mail: pub@oldinnkilmington.co.uk
web: www.oldinnkilmington.co.uk
dir: *From Axminster on A35 towards Honiton. Pub on left in 1m*

Delightful and well-kept thatched Devon longhouse offering classic pub meals

Duncan and Leigh Colvin's thatched Devon longhouse dates from 1650, when it was a staging house for changing post horses, and stands beside the A35 just west of Axminster. Weary travellers will find a cosy, beamed interior with a relaxed atmosphere, crackling log fires, and a fine range of local ales on tap. Order a pint of Otter to accompany a traditional pub meal, perhaps a Devon beef ploughman's lunch; ham, egg and chips; fish pie; or a daily chalkboard special like sea bass on sweet potato and fennel risotto. The south-facing garden is the venue for the Spring and August Bank Holiday beer festivals.

The Old Inn

Open all wk 11-3 6-11 Closed: 25-26 Dec **Bar Meals** L served all wk 12-2 D served all wk 6-9 **Restaurant** L served all wk 12-2 D served all wk 6-9 ⊕ FREE HOUSE ◙ Otter Bitter, Branscombe Vale Branoc & Drayman's Best ♂ Ashton Still. ♀ 10 **Facilities** Non-diners area ❤ (Bar Garden) ♦♦ Children's menu Children's portions Garden ☗ Beer festival Parking ▭ (notice required)

The Crabshell Inn

Embankment Rd TQ7 1JZ ☎ 01548 852345
e-mail: info@thecrabshellinn.com
dir: *A38 towards Plymouth, follow signs for Kingsbridge*

Gourmet pizzas and great views

The Crabshell is a traditional sailors' watering hole on the Kingsbridge estuary – you can moor up to three hours either side of high tide. As you would expect, the views from the outside tables – with a glass of Proper Job or Thatchers Gold in hand – and from the first-floor restaurant are unbeatable. As well as a good selection of salads, meat, poultry and fish dishes using locally sourced ingredients, the pub has introduced a gourmet pizza menu. Made with thin sourdough bases, there are more than a dozen mouthwatering toppings to choose from: quattro formaggi (four cheeses), fiorentina (spinach and egg), and 'go figa' (gorgonzola, fig, pancetta and cherry tomatoes).

Open all day all wk **Bar Meals** L served all wk 12-3, all day Jul-Aug D served all wk 6-9, all day Jul-Aug Av main course £12 **Restaurant** L served all wk 12-3, all day Jul-Aug D served all wk 6-9, all day Jul-Aug ⊕ FREE HOUSE ◙ Sharp's Doom Bar & Cornish Coaster, Otter Ale, St Austell Proper Job ♂ Thatchers Gold. ♀ **Facilities** Non-diners area ❤ (Bar Restaurant Garden) ♦♦ Children's menu Children's portions Play area Family room Garden ☗ Parking Wi-fi ▭

Barn Owl Inn

Aller Mills TQ12 5AN ☎ 01803 872130
e-mail: barnowl.allermills@hall-woodhouse.co.uk
dir: *Telephone for directions*

Ideally placed for Torbay and Devon's attractions

Flagged floors, a black-leaded range and oak beams are amongst the many charming original features at this 16th-century former farmhouse. The renovated building, which is handy for Dartmoor and the English Riviera towns, also boasts a high-vaulted converted barn with a minstrels' gallery. Lunchtime snacks include toasties, wraps and baguettes, while the main menu features plenty of traditional pub favourites all washed down with a pint of Tanglefoot or Badger First Gold.

Open all day all wk 11-11 (Sun 12-10.30) ⊕ HALL & WOODHOUSE ◙ Badger First Gold, Tanglefoot. **Facilities** ❤ (Bar Garden) ♦♦ Children's menu Children's portions Garden Parking

Bickley Mill Inn

PICK OF THE PUBS

TQ12 5LN ☎ 01803 873201
e-mail: info@bickleymill.co.uk
dir: *From Newton Abbot take A380 towards Torquay. Right at Barn Owl Inn, follow brown tourist signs*

Once a flour mill, now a charming foodie pub mixing old and new

A short drive from Torquay and Newton Abbot, this former 14th-century flour mill occupies an enviably secluded location in the wooded Stoneycombe Valley. Now a family-owned free house, the spacious property blends old and new in a fresh contemporary style. It comprises an attractive bar with roaring log fires and comfy sofas, and a restaurant separated into three areas – The Fireside, The Mill Room and The Panel Room. While perusing the appealing menu enjoy a pint of Otter or Teignworthy ale. Dishes are freshly prepared using quality produce from the local area. Fish from Brixham is a feature of the daily specials, along with regulars slow-braised lamb shank, minted pea purée, champ and rosemary jus; supreme of chicken, wild mushroom, leek and Madeira sauce; and pan-fried sea bass fillets with creamy mashed potato, crayfish and cucumber butter. There is outside decking and a tranquil garden.

Open all day all wk **Bar Meals** L served Mon-Sat 12-2.30, Sun 12-3 D served Mon-Sat 6-9, Sun 6-8 **Restaurant** L served Mon-Sat 12-2.30, Sun 12-3 D served Mon-Sat 6-9, Sun 6-8 ⊕ FREE HOUSE ◙ Otter Ale, Teignworthy, Bays. ♀ 12 **Facilities** Non-diners area ❤ (Bar Garden) ♦♦ Children's menu Children's portions Garden ☗ Parking Wi-fi ▭

KINGS NYMPTON   Map 3 SS61

The Grove Inn

PICK OF THE PUBS

EX37 9ST ☎ 01769 580406
e-mail: enquiry@thegroveinn.co.uk
dir: 2.5m from A377 (Exeter to Barnstaple road). 1.5m
from B3226 (South Molton road)

Classic English village pub

The Grove has everything one expects of an English pub:
thatched, whitewashed, beamed ceilings, stone walls,
rustic furnishings, flagstone floors and winter log fires. It
is, of course, a listed building, just like many others in
this secluded village. Moreover, it works closely with
nearby farmers to provide the fresh, seasonal produce we
all demand these days – count the local farm names on
the various menus. There's a good selection of grills,
while among the specials may be north Devon fish pie;
wild venison burger with Devon Blue cheese, wild garlic
leaf and Parma ham; and vegetable tagine with herbed
couscous. An accompanying drink could be one of the 26
wines by the glass, a pint from Great Torrington's
Clearwater brewery – Devon Dympsy, for example – or a
Sam's Dry cider from Winkleigh. Afterwards, investigate
the collection of 65 single malts. A beer and cider festival
takes place in July.

Open 12-3 6-11 (BH 12-3) **Closed:** Sun D & Mon L (ex
BHs) **Bar Meals** L served Tue-Sat 12-2 Av main course
£12 **Restaurant** L served Tue-Sat 12-2, Sun 12-3
D served Mon summer 6.45-9, Tue-Sat 6.45-9 Av 3 course
à la carte fr £22 ⊕ FREE HOUSE ◀ Exmoor Ale, Sharp's
Own, Clearwater Devon Dympsy & Devon Darter, Skinner's
Betty Stogs Ò Winkleigh & Sam's Dry. ₹ 26
Facilities Non-diners area ❤ (Bar Restaurant Garden) ♦♦
Children's menu Children's portions Garden ♫ Beer
festival Cider festival Wi-fi ☞ (notice required)

KINGSTON   Map 3 SX64

The Dolphin Inn

TQ7 4QE ☎ 01548 810314
e-mail: info@dolphininn.eclipse.co.uk
dir: From A379 (Plymouth to Kingsbridge road) take
B3233 signed Bigbury-on-Sea, at x-rds straight on to
Kingston. Follow brown inn signs

Off the beaten track for precious tranquillity

Church stonemasons lived here in the 15th century, and
later it was taken over by fishermen and their families.
Now run by the previous owner's business partner, the inn
is close to the beautiful Erme estuary and the popular
surfing beaches of the South Hams. Teignworthy's Spring
Tide is one of several real ales, alongside Haye Farm cider
from Cornwall. Home-made food includes traditional
steak-and-kidney pie; wild boar with hog's pudding
croquettes; fish and seafood specials; and vegetarian tart
of the week. A circular walk from the pub takes in
woodland, the estuary and the South West Coast Path.

Open 12-3 6-11 (Sun 12-3 7-10.30) **Closed:** Sun eve
winter **Bar Meals** L served Mon-Fri 12-2, Sat-Sun 12-2.30

D served all wk 6-9, closed Sun eve winter Av main course
£10.95-£14.95 **Restaurant** L served Mon-Fri 12-2, Sat-
Sun 12-2.30 D served all wk 6-9, closed Sun & Mon eve
winter ⊕ PUNCH TAVERNS ◀ Exmoor Ale, Teignworthy
Spring Tide, Sharp's Doom Bar, Otter, Timothy Taylor
Landlord Ò Haye Farm, Thatchers.
Facilities Non-diners area ❤ (Bar Restaurant Garden) ♦♦
Children's menu Children's portions Play area Family
room Garden ♫ Parking Wi-fi

LIFTON   Map 3 SX38

The Arundell Arms ★★★ HL ◉◉

PICK OF THE PUBS

PL16 0AA ☎ 01566 784666
e-mail: reservations@arundellarms.com
dir: 1m from A30 dual carriageway, 3m E of Launceston

Renowned for country pursuits

Escape the hurly-burly with a pint of Dartmoor Jail Ale in
the Courthouse Bar, a former police station incorporated
into this famous hotel, whilst allowing the extraordinary
range of country pursuits and activities here detain you
further. Walkers and horse-riders can enjoy some of
Devon's most unspoilt countryside, Dartmoor's bristling
tors are a short drive away whilst the inn's fishing beats
on the Tamar and tributaries attract fly-fishers. Local
farms and estates host shoots, as well as raising
livestock that features across the menus of the three
dining areas, and has earned the inn's Master Chef
Steven Pidgeon two AA Rosettes. The bar meals reflect the
care taken in selecting the finest local produce; The
Courthouse dishes and regularly-changing specials
incorporate the best pub food traditions, with home-made
fishcakes; ham, egg and chips or a warming beef
Stroganoff just the ticket after a day spent indulging in
the great outdoors. Excess energy can be burnt off playing
alley skittles.

Open all wk 12-3 6-11 **Bar Meals** L served all wk 12-2
D served all wk 6-9.30 Av main course £8.95 ⊕ FREE
HOUSE ◀ St Austell Tribute, Dartmoor Jail Ale, Guest ales
Ò Thatchers, Healey's Cornish Rattler. ₹ 9
Facilities Non-diners area ❤ (Bar Garden) ♦♦ Children's
menu Children's portions Garden ♫ Parking Wi-fi
Rooms 24

LUSTLEIGH   Map 3 SX78

The Cleave Pub

TQ13 9TJ ☎ 01647 277223
e-mail: ben@thecleavelustleigh.com
dir: From Newton Abbot take A382, follow Bovey Tracey
signs, then Moretonhampstead signs. Left to Lustleigh

Delightful thatched pub beside the village
cricket pitch

Set on the edge of Dartmoor National Park, and dating
from the 16th century, this thatched, family-run pub is
the only one in the village and is adjacent to the cricket
pitch. It has a traditional snug bar, with beams, granite
flooring and log fire; to the rear, formerly the old railway
station waiting room, is now a light and airy dining area

---

leading to a lovely cottage garden. The pub/bistro has
gained a reputation for an interesting and varied menu.
Dishes include Ligurian fish stew; River Teign mussels;
sausages in ale gravy with bubble-and-squeak; or hand
made pumpkin ravioli with sage butter and balsamic
onions. The Cleave hosts regular films, quizzes, Wii
nights, comedy nights and live music.

Open all day all wk 11-11 **Bar Meals** L served all wk
D served all wk food served all day **Restaurant** L served
all wk D served all wk food served all day ⊕ HEAVITREE
◀ Otter Ale, Bitter Ò Aspall. **Facilities** Non-diners area
❤ (Bar Restaurant Garden) ♦♦ Children's menu Children's
portions Garden ♫ Parking Wi-fi ☞ (notice required)

LUTON (NEAR CHUDLEIGH)   Map 3 SX97

The Elizabethan Inn

Fore St TQ13 0BL ☎ 01626 775425
e-mail: elizabethaninn@btconnect.com
web: www.elizabethaninn.co.uk
dir: Between Chudleigh & Teignmouth

Good honest Devon food and drink

Known locally as the Lizzie, this smart, welcoming
16th-century free house attracts diners and drinkers
alike. There's a great selection of West Country ales like
Dartmoor IPA to choose from, as well as Thatchers Gold
and local Reddaway's Farm cider. Sit beside a log fire in
winter or in the pretty beer garden on warmer days. The
pub prides itself on using the best local ingredients. The
bar menu includes salad bowls, omelettes, risottos and
traditional dishes, while the daily specials boards might
offer River Teign mussels, home-made lamb and mint
sausages, and vegetable terrine. A take-away menu is
available. A beer festival is held in June.

Open all wk 12-3 6-11.30 (Sun all day) (Sat all day BST)
Closed: 25-26 Dec, 1 Jan **Bar Meals** L served Mon-Sat
12-2, Sun 12-9 D served Mon-Sat 6-9.30, Sun 12-9 Av
main course £13 **Restaurant** L served Mon-Sat 12-2, Sun
12-9 D served Mon-Sat 6-9.30, Sun 12-9 ⊕ FREE HOUSE
◀ Fuller's London Pride, Teignworthy Reel Ale, Otter Ale,
Dartmoor IPA, St Austell Tribute Ò Thatchers Gold,
Reddaway's Farm. ₹ 11 **Facilities** Non-diners area
❤ (Bar Garden) ♦♦ Children's menu Children's portions
Garden ♫ Beer festival Parking Wi-fi

PICK OF THE PUBS

California Country Inn

MODBURY　　　　　　　Map 3 SX65

California Cross PL21 0SG
☎ **01548 821449**
e-mail:
enquiries@californiacountryinn.co.uk
web: www.californiacountryinn.co.uk
dir: *On B3196 (NE of Modbury)*

A real find in the South Hams area

This centuries-old inn stands in some of
the most tranquil countryside in
southern England, just a few miles from
Dartmoor to the north and the cliffs and
estuaries of the coast to the south. In
fact, this Area of Outstanding Natural
Beauty encompasses the hills and vales
which can be seen from the pub's
landscaped gardens. Dating from the
14th century, its unusual name is
thought to derive from local adventurers
in the mid-19th century who heeded the
call to 'go west' and waited at the
nearby crossroads for the stage to take
them on the first part of their journey to
America's west coast. They must have
suffered wistful thoughts of home when
recalling their local pub, with its
wizened old beams, exposed dressed-
stone walls and a fabulous, huge stone
fireplace. Old rural prints and
photographs, copper kettles, jugs,
brasses and many other artefacts add
to the rustic charm of the whitewashed
pub's atmospheric interior. A family-run
free house, the beers on tap are likely to
include Sharp's and St Austells', the

wine list has award-winning Devon
wines from nearby Sharpham Vineyard,
and the good-value house wines come
from Chile. Having won accolades as a
dining pub, head chef Tim Whiston's
food is thoughtfully created and
impressively flavoursome. Most
ingredients are sourced from the bounty
of the local countryside and waters, with
meats from a supplier in nearby
Loddiswell. Meals can be taken from the
bar menu, but why not indulge in the à
la carte menu from the inn's dining
room? Appetising starters include crispy
belly pork, tempura scallop with pickled
vegetables and beetroot crisps. The
main course selection may include local
guinea fowl (leg confit and pan-fried
breast) with creamed wild mushrooms,
or pan-fried sea bass fillets.

Open all day all wk **Bar Meals** L served
Mon-Sat 12-2, Sun 12-2.30 D served
Mon-Sat 6-9, Sun 6-8.30 **Restaurant** L
served Sun 12-2 D served Wed-Sun 6-9
⊕ FREE HOUSE ◀ Otter Bitter, Sharp's
Doom Bar, St Austell Tribute
Ö Addlestones, Thatchers Gold, Westons
Old Rosie. **Facilities** Non-diners area
❖ (Bar Garden) ✦ Children's menu
Children's portions Family room Garden
ᵝ Parking Wi-fi 🚌

LYDFORD   Map 3 SX58

Dartmoor Inn @@

PICK OF THE PUBS

EX20 4AY ☎ 01822 820221
e-mail: info@dartmoorinn.co.uk
dir: On A386 S of Okehampton

Elegance with a dash of Scandinavia and New England

Owners Karen and Philip Burgess have made their mark at this distinctive free house, which Charles Kingsley almost certainly described in his novel Westward Ho! The stylish, restrained decor extends through the cosy dining rooms and small bar, where real ales and high-class pub classics are on offer. Food is based on seasonal ingredients, sourced locally, and turned into top-notch dishes. In the New England-style restaurant you might start with corned beef terrine with mustard dressing, followed by pan-fried lamb's kidneys, bacon, black pudding and red wine sauce. After your meal, you can even browse for beautiful accessories and homeware in the inn's own boutique.

Open all day 11-3 6-11 Closed: Sun eve, Mon L (ex BHs) **Bar Meals** L served Tue-Sun 12-2.30 D served Mon-Sat 6.30-9.15 **Restaurant** L served Tue-Sun 12-2.30 D served Mon-Sat 6.30-9.15 ⊕ FREE HOUSE ◀ Otter Ale, St Austell Tribute ♂ St Austell Copper Press.
Facilities Non-diners area ❤ (Bar Restaurant Garden) ♦♦ Garden ⊓ Parking

LYMPSTONE   Map 3 SX98

The Globe Inn

The Strand EX8 5EY ☎ 01395 263166
dir: Telephone for directions

A stone's throw from the river estuary

This friendly beamed village pub in the estuary village of Lympstone has a good local reputation for food and drink. Well-kept Otter and London Pride are the ales on offer in the bar, while the menu offers fresh seafood and seasonal produce in traditional dishes such as lamb's liver, bacon and onion; home-made fish pie and seafood platters to share. On Sundays, the traditional roasts are especially popular. Occasional music nights and Tuesday is quiz night. There's no food on Mondays.

Open all day all wk 11-11 **Bar Meals** L served Tue-Sat 11.45-2.15, Sun 12-2 D served Tue-Sat 5.45-9.15 **Restaurant** L served Tue-Sat 11.45-2.15, Sun 12-2 D served Tue-Sat 5.45-9.15 ⊕ HEAVITREE ◀ Fuller's London Pride, Otter, Wadworth Henry's Original IPA ♂ Aspall, Addlestones. ₹ 10 **Facilities** Non-diners area ❤ (Bar) ♦♦ Wi-fi

LYNMOUTH   Map 3 SS74

Rising Sun Hotel ★★ HL @

PICK OF THE PUBS

Harbourside EX35 6EG ☎ 01598 753223
e-mail: reception@risingsunlynmouth.co.uk
dir: M5 junct 25 follow Minehead signs. A39 to Lynmouth

Historic inn with literary connections

Overlooking Lynmouth's tiny harbour and bay is this 14th-century thatched smugglers' inn. In turn, overlooking them all, are Countisbury Cliffs, the highest in England. The building's long history is evident from the uneven oak floors, crooked ceilings and thick walls. Literary associations are plentiful: R D Blackmore wrote some of his wild Exmoor romance, Lorna Doone, here; the poet Shelley is believed to have honeymooned in the garden cottage, and Coleridge stayed too. Immediately behind rises Exmoor Forest and National Park, home to red deer, wild ponies and birds of prey. With moor and sea so close, game and seafood are in plentiful supply; appearing in dishes such as braised pheasant with pancetta and quince and Braunton greens; and roast shellfish — crab, mussels, clams and scallops in garlic, ginger and coriander. At night the oak-panelled, candlelit dining room is an example of romantic British innkeeping at its best.

Open all day all wk 11am-mdnt Closed: 25 Dec **Bar Meals** L served all wk 12-2.30 D served all wk 6-9 **Restaurant** D served all wk 7-9 ⊕ FREE HOUSE ◀ Exmoor Gold, Fox, Antler, Ale ♂ Thatchers Gold, Addlestones.
Facilities Non-diners area ❤ (Bar) Outside area ⊓ 🚐 **Rooms** 14

MARLDON   Map 3 SX86

The Church House Inn

Village Rd TQ3 1SL ☎ 01803 558279
dir: Take Torquay ring road, follow signs to Marldon & Totnes, follow brown signs to pub

Grade II listed, 18th-century inn with contemporary touches

Built as a hostel for the stonemasons of the adjoining village church, this ancient country inn dates from 1362. It was rebuilt in 1740 and many features from that period still remain, including beautiful Georgian windows; some of the original glass is intact despite overlooking the cricket pitch. These days it has an uncluttered, contemporary feel with additional seating in the garden. As well as sandwiches, the lunch menu includes Dartmouth smoked fish platter; aubergine and lentil moussaka; and cauliflower roulade. Typical evening offerings are slow-roasted shoulder of lamb, and wild turbot.

Open all wk 11.30-2.30 5-11 (Fri-Sat 11.30-2.30 5-11.30 Sun 12-3 5.30-10.30) **Bar Meals** L served all wk 12-2 D served all wk 6.30-9.30 **Restaurant** L served all wk 12-2 D served all wk 6.30-9.30 ⊕ FREE HOUSE ◀ St Austell Dartmoor & Tribute, Teignworthy Gundog. ₹ 12

Facilities Non-diners area ❤ (Bar Garden) ♦♦ Children's portions Garden Parking

MEAVY   Map 3 SX56

The Royal Oak Inn

PL20 6PJ ☎ 01822 852944
e-mail: info@royaloakinn.org.uk
dir: B3212 from Yelverton to Princetown. Right at Dousland to Meavy, past school. Pub opposite village green

At the heart of the community in Dartmoor village

This traditional 15th-century inn is situated by a village green within Dartmoor National Park. Flagstone floors, oak beams and a welcoming open fire set the scene at this free house popular with cyclists and walkers. Local cask ales, ciders and fine wines accompany the carefully sourced ingredients in a menu ranging from lunchtime light bites to steak-and-ale pie; home-cooked ham, egg and chips; or local bangers and mash. Look out for cider and beer festivals during the year.

Open all wk Mon-Fri 11-3 6-11 (Sat-Sun & Apr-Oct all day 11-11) **Bar Meals** L served Mon-Fri 12-2.30, Sat-Sun 12-3 D served all wk 6-9 **Restaurant** L served Mon-Fri 12-2.30, Sat-Sun 12-3 D served all wk 6-9 ⊕ FREE HOUSE ◀ Dartmoor Jail Ale & IPA, St Austell Tribute, Sharp's Doom Bar, Guest ales ♂ Westons Old Rosie, Sandford Orchards Devon Red. ₹ 12
Facilities Non-diners area ❤ (Bar) ♦♦ Children's menu Children's portions Garden ⊓ Beer festival Cider festival 🚐

MODBURY   Map 3 SX65

California Country Inn

PICK OF THE PUBS

See Pick of the Pubs on opposite page

NEWTON ABBOT   Map 3 SX87

The Wild Goose Inn

Combeinteignhead TQ12 4RA ☎ 01626 872241
dir: From A380 at Newton Abbot rdbt take B3195 (Shaldon road) signed Milber, 2.5m to village, right at pub sign

Flying the flag for West Country ales and ciders

Set in the heart of Combeinteignhead at the head of a long valley, this charming free house boasts a sunny walled garden, overlooked by the ancient village church. The former farmstead was originally licensed as the Country House Inn in 1840 and renamed in the 1960s when nearby geese began intimidating the pub's customers. A good range of West Country real ales and ciders accompanies home-made pub food prepared from local ingredients. The lunch menu lists roast hake with a chorizo and white bean cassoulet, while an example from the à la carte is pork belly, braised lentils, choucroute

continued

NEWTON ABBOT *continued*

and sage jus. There is a beer festival every May Day weekend.

Open all wk 11-3 5.30-11 (Sun 12-3 7-11) **Bar Meals** L served Tue-Sun 12-2.30 D served Tue-Sat 6-9, Sun 7-9 **Restaurant** L served Tue-Sun 12-2.30 D served Tue-Sat 6-9, Sun 7-9 ⊕ FREE HOUSE ◀ Otter Ale, Skinner's Best Bitter, Teignworthy, Branscombe Vale, Exe Valley, Cotleigh, Sharp's Ŏ Skinner's Press Gang, Wiscombe Suicider, Milltop Gold. ♊ 10 **Facilities** Non-diners area ♦ Children's menu Children's portions Family room Garden ⋿ Beer festival Parking

---

NEWTON ST CYRES Map 3 SX89

The Beer Engine

EX5 5AX ☎ 01392 851282
e-mail: info@thebeerengine.co.uk
dir: *From Exeter take A377 towards Crediton. Signed from A377 towards Sweetham. Pub opposite rail station, over bridge*

Popular railway brewpub

This pretty whitewashed free house originally opened as a railway hotel in 1852. It sits opposite the Tarka Line on the banks of the River Creedy, much favoured by dogs and their walkers. Home to one of Devon's leading microbreweries, it produces ales with names such as Rail Ale and Sleeper Heavy. Freshly baked bread uses the wort (beer yeast) from the brewery; dishes may include a home-made fishcake with sweet chilli sauce and fresh bread; fresh haddock in Beer Engine batter; and chicken curry with rice. Vegetarians will rejoice in the range of soups and bakes.

Open all day all wk Tue-Sat 11-11 (Sun 12-10.30 Mon 11-10.30) **Bar Meals** L served all wk 12-2.15 D served Tue-Sat 6.30-9.15, Sun-Mon 6.30-8.15 Av main course £10.95 **Restaurant** L served all wk 12-2.15 D served Tue-Sat 6.30-9.15, Sun-Mon 6.30-8.15 ⊕ FREE HOUSE ◀ The Beer Engine Piston Bitter, Rail Ale, Sleeper Heavy, Silver Bullet Ŏ Westons Stowford Press, Dragons Tears. ♊ 9 **Facilities** Non-diners area ♣ (Bar Garden) ♦ Children's portions Garden ⋿ Parking Wi-fi ▭ (notice required)

NORTH BOVEY Map 3 SX78

The Ring of Bells Inn

PICK OF THE PUBS

TQ13 8RB ☎ 01647 440375
e-mail: mail@ringofbells.net
dir: *1.5m from Moretonhampstead off B3212. 7m S of Whiddon Down junct on A30*

Dog-friendly Dartmoor village pub

Dating back to the 13th-century, this thatched Dartmoor pub was originally built to house the stonemasons building the parish church. Overlooking the village green, The Ring of Bells (now under new ownership) draws Dartmoor visitors and walkers in for good food and regularly changing guest ales. The kitchen uses fresh, locally sourced produce and menus reflect the changing

seasons with both traditional and contemporary dishes; suppliers are proudly listed. Served in cosy low-beamed bars, with heavy oak doors, rustic furnishings, crackling winter log fires and evening candlelight, the daily menu may list grilled goats' cheese and onion tart, and local mussels as starters, followed by main dishes such as sweet potato and chickpea falafels with pitta bread and tzatziki; chunky fish soup, saffron rouille, granary bread and chips; and confit duck leg, pak choi, beetroot and Asian-spiced jus. Round off with pineapple tarte Tatin with stem ginger ice cream.

Open all day all wk Closed: 25 Dec drinks only **Bar Meals** L served all wk 12-2.30 D served all wk 6-9 Av main course £12.95 **Restaurant** L served all wk 12-2.30 D served all wk 6-9 Av 3 course à la carte fr £25 ⊕ FREE HOUSE ◀ St Austell Tribute, Teignworthy Reel Ale, Guest ales Ŏ Thatchers, Devon Mist. ♊ 12 **Facilities** Non-diners area ♣ (Bar Garden) ♦ Children's menu Children's portions Family room Garden ⋿ Wi-fi ▭ (notice required)

NOSS MAYO Map 3 SX54

The Ship Inn

PICK OF THE PUBS

PL8 1EW ☎ 01752 872387
e-mail: ship@nossmayo.com
dir: *5m S of Yealmpton. From Yealmpton take B3186, then follow Noss Mayo signs*

Superb waterside location

This waterside free house is a popular haunt for sailing enthusiasts and occupies a lovely spot on Noss Mayo's tidal waterfront on the south bank of the stunning Yealm estuary. The deceptively spacious building, renovated using reclaimed local stone and English oak, remains cosy thanks to its wooden floors, old bookcases, log fires and local pictures. Regional ales such as Dartmoor IPA are complemented by an ever-changing menu of home-made dishes majoring on local produce. Order home-baked Devon ham, free-range egg and chips, or haddock fillet fried in real ale batter with chips and mushy peas from the bar menu; or dive into the main menu for dishes such as rump of lamb with dauphinoise potatoes, or sea bass fillets on crushed new potatoes with olives and salsa verde. Round off with apple and plum crumble with custard. Walkers, too, throng the bar, and dogs are allowed downstairs.

Open all day all wk **Bar Meals** L served Mon-Sat 12-9.30, Sun 12-9 D served Mon-Sat 12-9.30, Sun 12-9 food served all day **Restaurant** L served Mon-Sat 12-9.30, Sun 12-9 D served Mon-Sat 12-9.30, Sun 12-9 food served all day ⊕ FREE HOUSE ◀ Dartmoor Jail Ale & IPA, St Austell Tribute & Proper Job, Otter, Palmers. ♊ 13 **Facilities** Non-diners area ♣ (Bar Garden) ♦ Children's portions Garden ⋿ Parking

---

OTTERY ST MARY Map 3 SY19

The Talaton Inn

Talaton EX5 2RQ ☎ 01404 822214
dir: *A30 to Fairmile, then follow signs to Talaton*

Black and white timbered, traditional inn

This well-maintained, timber-framed 16th-century inn is run by a brother and sister partnership. There is a good selection of real ales (Otter Ale, Otter Bright) and malts, and a fine collection of bar games. The regularly-changing evening blackboard menu might include brie wedges with cranberry dip; surf and turf; tuna steak au poivre; or gammon and egg. At Sunday lunchtimes (booking advisable), as well as the popular roast, there is also a pie and vegetarian choice. Lunchtime special deals available. There is a patio for summer dining and themed food nights.

Open 12-3 7-11 Closed: Mon (winter) **Bar Meals** L served Tue-Sun 12-2 D served Tue-Sat 7-9 Av main course £8.25 **Restaurant** L served Tue-Sun 12-2 D served Tue-Sat 7-9 Fixed menu price fr £5 Av 3 course à la carte fr £12.50 ⊕ FREE HOUSE ◀ Otter Ale & Bright, Guest ale Ŏ Westons Stowford Press. **Facilities** Non-diners area ♦ Children's portions Outside area ⋿ Parking ▭ (notice required)

PARRACOMBE Map 3 SS64

The Fox & Goose

PICK OF THE PUBS

See Pick of the Pubs on opposite page

PLYMOUTH Map 3 SX45

The Fishermans Arms

31 Lambhay St, The Barbican PL1 2NN
☎ 01752 661457
e-mail: info@thefishermansarms.com
dir: *At top of Lambhay Hill turn right, pass large car park, 2nd right into Lambhay St*

Traditional pub in the Barbican area

One wall of this city-centre pub in the historic Barbican area is the only surviving part of Plymouth Castle, which was demolished in the 15th century. Devoid of modern-day intrusions, it's a bustling local with log fires, regular quiz nights, tip-top St Austell ales, and excellent food. Dishes range from moules frites to steak, mushroom and ale pie. There is even a 3ft wide tunnel underneath the bar of Plymouth's second oldest pub, which runs to the shoreline — smugglers perhaps?

Open all wk Mon 6-11 Tue-Thu 12-3 6-11 (Fri-Sun all day from 12) **Bar Meals** L served Tue-Sat 12-2, Sun 12-3 D served Tue-Sat 6.30-9.30 **Restaurant** L served Tue-Sat 12-2, Sun 12-3 D served Tue-Sat 6.30-9.30 ⊕ ST AUSTELL BREWERY ◀ Tribute, Proper Job & Trelawny Ŏ Healey's Cornish Rattler. ♊ 12 **Facilities** Non-diners area ♣ (Bar) ♦ Children's portions ▭ (notice required)

Save on hotels. Book at **theAA.com/hotel**

DEVON 135 ENGLAND

PICK OF THE PUBS

The Fox & Goose

PARRACOMBE   Map 3 SS64

EX31 4PE ☎ **01598 763239**
e-mail:
info@foxandgooseinnexmoor.co.uk
web: www.foxandgooseinnexmoor.co.uk
dir: *1m from A39 between Blackmoor
Gate & Lynton. Follow Parracombe signs*

Relaxed atmosphere in Exmoor hostelry

This imposing Victorian building was once just a couple of tiny thatched cottages serving the local farming community. Transformation into a hotel took place when a narrow-gauge railway arrived in 1898 to link Parracombe with the outside world, represented by Lynton and Barnstaple. The line closed in the 1930s, although a short section was reopened a few years ago. Decorating the pub's interior are farm memorabilia, a scarf-wearing stag's head and photographs of villagers who now drink in more celestial surroundings; here beer-drinkers have a choice of local Cotleigh and Exmoor, Otter from South Devon and cider from Winkleigh, just north of Dartmoor. Good home-made food comes from constantly changing blackboard menus that are likely to feature seasonal game from surrounding farms and estates, as well as fish and shellfish caught off the north Devon coast. Examples include bouillabaisse; pan-fried skate wing with

brown shrimp and capers; brill fillets poached in red wine; and roast cod wrapped in bacon with Puy lentils. Among the meat choices are trio of venison sausages with creamy mash and gravy; fillet steak with sautéed mushrooms and cherry vine tomatoes; and confit of duck with juniper and port sauce. For vegetarians there are mushroom Stroganoff with cream, mustard and Cognac; and pearl barley risotto with roasted squash and sage. To follow, there's a good board of South West cheeses; brioche bread-and-butter pudding; and lemon posset with vanilla sablé biscuits. Pizzas are also available – either to eat in or take away. Children and dogs are welcome and, if they want, they can let off steam in the paved courtyard garden overlooking the river.

Open all wk 12-2.30 6-11 (Sun 12-2.30 7-10.30; summer all day) Closed: 25 Dec **Bar Meals** all wk 12-2 Mon-Sat 6-9, Sun 7-9 **Restaurant** all wk 12-2 Mon-Sat 6-9, Sun 7-9 ⊕ FREE HOUSE ◀ Cotleigh Barn Owl, Exmoor Fox, Otter Ale, Sharp's Doom Bar, Guinness Ŏ Winkleigh. ♟ 10 **Facilities** ✿ (Bar) ♦♦ Children's menu Children's portions Outside area ⊼ Parking Wi-fi

PLYMTREE — Map 3 ST00

The Blacksmiths Arms

EX15 2JU ☎ **01884 277474**
e-mail: blacksmithsplymtree@yahoo.co.uk
dir: *From A373 (Cullompton to Honiton road) follow Plymtree signs. Pub in village centre*

Well-kept ales and locally-sourced food

Alan and Susie Carter have been at the helm for the past six years and the pub has become the hub of this idyllic Devon village. A traditional free house with exposed beams and log fire, it has a reputation for serving quality food using local ingredients, and is known for generous portions of classics like game pie and local steaks. Up to 14 well-kept local ales include Otter Amber, and there is a fine selection of wines. A beer festival is held in July every even-numbered year. A large beer garden and alfresco dining area complete the picture.

Open Tue-Fri 6-11 (Sat 12-11 Sun 12-10 (Sun 12-4 Oct-Mar)) Closed: Mon **Bar Meals** L served Sat-Sun 12-2 D served Tue-Sun 6-9 **Restaurant** L served Sat-Sun 12-2 D served Tue-Sun 6-9 FREE HOUSE O'Hanlon's Yellow Hammer, Otter Amber, St Austell Proper Job & Tribute, Sharp's Doom Bar Westons Stowford Press. 8 **Facilities** Non-diners area (Bar Restaurant Garden) Children's menu Children's portions Play area Family room Garden Beer festival Parking Wi-fi (notice required)

PORTGATE — Map 3 SX48

The Harris Arms

PICK OF THE PUBS

EX20 4PZ ☎ **01566 783331**
e-mail: info@theharrisarms.co.uk
dir: *From A30 at Broadwoodwidger/Roadford Lake follow signs to Lifton then Portgate*

Rural pub with a passion for local produce

Not far off the A30 just before Devon turns into Cornwall, this 16th-century inn is an accessible spot for honest food with substance and style and certainly lives up to its promotional strapline: 'Eat real food and drink real wine'. In the bar the real ales are from Devon – Bays Best and Holsworthy Tamar Sauce; so too is Sam's Poundhouse real cider. The menu is very much locally sourced, from Port Isaac fresh fish to West Country artisan cheeses. Typically, start with slow-cooked pork cheeks with sweet potato and mushroom hash and a sage and cider sauce, then follow with venison bourguignon with creamy mash, or confit duck leg. Fish, game, vegetarian and other dishes are chalked up daily and pub classics, such as ham, egg and chips, get a look in too. Enjoy a steak sandwich outside on the decked patio and admire the view of Brent Tor in the distance.

Open 12-3 6.30-11 Closed: Sun eve & Mon **Bar Meals** L served Tue-Sun 12-2 D served Tue-Sat 6.30-9 Av main course £13.95 **Restaurant** L served Tue-Sun 12-2 D served Tue-Sat 6.30-9 Fixed menu price fr £10.95 (2 courses 6.30-7.30) Av 3 course à la carte fr £23.95 FREE HOUSE Bays, Fry's Brewery, Holsworthy Winkleigh Sam's Poundhouse. 20 **Facilities** Non-diners area (Bar Garden) Children's menu Children's portions Garden Outside area Parking

POSTBRIDGE — Map 3 SX67

Warren House Inn

PL20 6TA ☎ **01822 880208**
dir: *On B3212 between Moretonhampstead & Princetown*

Timeless Dartmoor pub

Built in 1845 to service the local tin mining industry, the Warren House Inn now stands alone and isolated high on Dartmoor. It has no mains services - it uses generators for electricity and gravity-fed water from a spring - but the fire in the hearth is said to have been burning continuously since the day the pub first opened. Four real ales and scrumpy cider are served, along with a menu of good home-cooked food: hearty soups, a selection of pies (including rabbit of course), beef and lamb raised on the moor, and vegetables supplied by local farms.

Open all day all wk 11-11 (winter Mon-Tue 11-5) **Bar Meals** L served all wk 12-9, Mon-Tue in winter 12-4.30 D served all wk 12-9 Av main course £10.50 food served all day **Restaurant** L served all wk 12-9, Mon-Tue in winter 12-4.30 D served all wk 12-9 food served all day FREE HOUSE Otter Ale, Sharp's Doom Bar, Guest ales Countryman Cider, Thatchers Gold. **Facilities** Non-diners area (Bar Garden) Children's menu Family room Garden Parking

RATTERY — Map 3 SX76

Church House Inn

TQ10 9LD ☎ **01364 642220**
e-mail: ray.hardy@btconnect.com
web: www.thechurchhouseinn.co.uk
dir: *1m from A38 (Exeter to Plymouth road) & 0.75m from A385 (Totnes to South Brent road)*

Centuries of conversation and hospitality

Tracing its history as far back as 1028, this venerable inn burgeons with brasses, bare beams, large fireplaces and other historic features. Some customers encounter the wandering spirit of a monk; fortunately he seems to be friendly. In the character dining room, dishes include deep-fried camembert with a cranberry sauce followed by venison sausages with spicy mash, peas and gravy. Fresh fish (local trout grilled in butter; monkfish with a brandy cream and mushroom sauce) features strongly. For dessert, maybe choose pecan pie. There is a large lawn beer garden and patio where you can enjoy a pint of Dartmoor Ale in warmer months.

Open all wk 11-2.30 6-11 (Sun 12-3 6-10.30) **Bar Meals** L served Mon-Sat 11.30-2, Sun 12-2 D served all wk 6.30-9 **Restaurant** L served Mon-Sat 11.30-2, Sun 12-2 D served all wk 6.30-9 FREE HOUSE Dartmoor Jail Ale & Legend, Church House Bitter, Guest ale Thatchers Gold. 10 **Facilities** Non-diners area (Bar Garden) Children's menu Children's portions Garden Parking (notice required)

ROCKBEARE — Map 3 SY09

Jack in the Green Inn

PICK OF THE PUBS

See Pick of the Pubs on opposite page

SALCOMBE — Map 3 SX73

The Victoria Inn

PICK OF THE PUBS

Fore St TQ8 8BU ☎ **01548 842604**
e-mail: info@victoriainn-salcombe.co.uk
dir: *In town centre, overlooking estuary*

Excellent local seafood

Tim and Liz Hore run this friendly and inviting pub in the centre of town, keeping the log fire roaring in winter, and in milder weather welcoming mums, dads, children and pets to the huge family garden with its shady terrace and enclosed children's play area. The bar presents St Austell ales, in addition to a range of wines and spirits. The first-floor restaurant gives stunning views of the pretty harbour and fishing boats bringing in the catch of the day. So in addition to the excellent fish and chips on offer expect to find starters such as Salcombe brown crab bisque; and warm smoked duck salad with walnuts and raspberry dressing; and a main dish of a home-made curry; or local pork tenderloin, Lyonnaise potatoes, seasonal vegetables and red wine reduction.

Open all day all wk 11.30-11 Closed: 25 Dec **Bar Meals** L served all wk 12-9 D served all wk 12-9 food served all day **Restaurant** L served all wk 12-9 D served all wk 12-9 food served all day ST AUSTELL BREWERY Tribute, Dartmoor, Proper Job Healey's Cornish Rattler. 20 **Facilities** Non-diners area (Bar Garden) Children's menu Children's portions Play area Garden Wi-fi

Save on hotels. Book at theAA.com/hotel

DEVON 137 ENGLAND

PICK OF THE PUBS

Jack in the Green Inn ❀❀

ROCKBEARE   Map 3 SY09

London Rd EX5 2EE ☎ **01404 822240**
e-mail: info@jackinthegreen.uk.com
web: www.jackinthegreen.uk.com
dir: *M5 junct 29, A30 towards Honiton,*
left signed Rockbeare

Top notch pub food for everyone

This white-painted, roadside pub has been run for two decades by rugby aficionado Paul Parnell. The empty plates and contented smiles of diners (and two AA Rosettes) testify to the Jack's well-deserved reputation for upmarket modern pub food, but Paul dislikes the term 'gastro-pub' as he doesn't want people, especially families, to think that it's purely a dining venue, and drive on by. What he offers is good West Country brews on tap and, in the restaurant, a simple philosophy of serving the best Devon produce in stylish surroundings. A makeover has introduced a new bar and refreshed paintwork, carpets and furnishings to create a clean, contemporary atmosphere, enhancing the bright low-beamed rooms with their soft leather chairs and wood-burning stove. Local artisan producers underpin chef Matthew Mason's innovative menus with punchy flavours, be it the local shoots which supply the game, or the growers of salad leaves and seasonal vegetables who are just six miles away. Pressed to label the food style, Paul and

Matthew would say modern British, exemplified by dishes like herb-crusted beef fillet, shallot purée, balsamic vinegar and olive oil; and belly of pork with pineapple, ginger and chilli salsa. The more traditional pub grub selection offers venison cottage pie, ploughman's lunch and braised faggot. The three-course 'Totally Devon' menu is good value, but why not push the boat out and go for the six-course tasting menu? Look to the chalkboard for daily specials like roast wood pigeon or grilled lemon sole. Head pastry chef Harriet Pecover creates the tasty 'sweets and treats'. Dine alfresco in the spacious rear courtyard in summer.

Open all wk 11-3 5.30-11 (Sun 12-11)
Closed: 25 Dec-5 Jan **Bar Meals** L

served Mon-Sat 12-2, Sun 12-9 D served Mon-Sat 6-9.30, Sun 12-9 **Restaurant** L served Mon-Sat 12-2, Sun 12-9 D served Mon-Sat 6-9.30, Sun 12-9 ⊕ FREE HOUSE ◀ Otter Ale & Amber, Sharp's Doom Bar, Butcombe Bitter ♂ Dragon Tears, Luscombe, St Georges. ♉ 12 **Facilities** Non diners area ⚬ Children's menu Children's portions Family room Outside area ⚲ Parking Wi-fi 🚌 (notice required)

SANDFORD — Map 3 SS80

The Lamb Inn

The Square EX17 4LW ☎ 01363 773676
e-mail: thelambinn@gmail.com
web: www.lambinnsandford.co.uk
dir: *A377 from Exeter to Crediton. 1st right signed Sandford & Tiverton. Left, left again, up hill. 1.5m left into village square*

A thriving community local

Mark Hildyard has worked hard at making this 16th-century former coaching inn a cracking all-round pub. Set in a sleepy Devon village, the pub's upstairs room is used as an art gallery, cinema (screenings most weekends), theatre, venue for open-mic nights and a meeting room for village groups. Downstairs, expect to find three log fires, candles on scrubbed tables, local Sandford Orchards cider and an imaginative chalkboard menu. Using the best Devon produce, top-notch dishes may include Creedy Carver chicken and bacon salad; and roasted monkfish with Serrano ham and a vanilla butter sauce. Everyone is welcome, including dogs and walkers in muddy boots. Contact the pub for details of the beer festivals.

Open all day all wk 11am-11.30pm **Bar Meals** food served all day **Restaurant** L served all wk 12.30-2.15 D served all wk 6.30-9.15 ⊕ FREE HOUSE ◖ Otter Bitter, O'Hanlon's Yellow Hammer, Dartmoor Jail Ale & Legend, Skinner's Ô Sandford Orchards. ♈ 9 **Facilities** Non-diners area ☺ (Bar Restaurant Garden) ◗ᐦ Children's portions Garden ⊨ Beer festival Wi-fi ▭ (notice required)

SHEBBEAR — Map 3 SS40

The Devil's Stone Inn

EX21 5RU ☎ 01409 281210
e-mail: churst1234@btinternet.com
dir: *From Okehampton right opposite White Hart, follow A386 towards Hatherleigh. At rdbt outside Hatherleigh take Holsworthy road to Highampton. Just after Highampton right, follow signs to Shebbear*

A village pub with an interesting history

A farmhouse before it became a coaching inn some 400 years ago, this inn is reputedly one of England's top dozen most haunted pubs. That does not deter the country sports lovers who use it as a base for their activities; it is especially a haven for fly-fishermen, with beats, some of which the pub owns, on the middle and upper Torridge. The pub's name comes from the village tradition of the turning the Devil's Stone (situated opposite the pub), which happens every year on 5th November. The beamed and flagstone-floored interior has several open fires. Locally sourced and home-cooked food, a selection of real ales and ciders, a games room, separate dining room and large garden complete the picture.

Open all wk 12-3 6-11 (Fri-Sun all day fr 12) **Bar Meals** L served all wk 12-2.30 D served all wk 6-9.30 Av main course £6.95 **Restaurant** L served all wk 12-2.30 D served all wk 6-9.30 Fixed menu price fr £3.50 Av 3 course à la carte fr £18 ⊕ FREE HOUSE ◖ Sharp's Doom Bar, St Austell Tribute, Black Prince & HSD Ô Healey's Cornish Rattler, Thatchers Gold. **Facilities** Non-diners area ☺ (Bar Garden) ◗ᐦ Children's menu Children's portions Play area Garden ⊨ Parking Wi-fi ▭ (notice required)

SIDBURY — Map 3 SY19

The Hare & Hounds

Putts Corner EX10 0QQ ☎ 01404 41760
e-mail: contact@hareandhounds-devon.co.uk
web: www.hareandhounds-devon.co.uk
dir: *From Honiton take A375 signed Sidmouth. In approx 0.75m pub at Seaton Rd x-rds*

Traditional whitewashed free house serving classic pub dishes

Behind the whitewashed walls of this traditional Devon free house you'll find a comfortable interior with wooden beams and winter log fires. There's also a large garden and a newly completed extension which both enjoy fantastic views down the valley to the sea at Sidmouth. Besides the daily carvery, the extensive menu features

classic pub dishes and snacks. Main course options include spaghetti bolognaise and steak-and-kidney pudding, as well as fish dishes and vegetarian options. The permanent cask ales are brewed less than ten miles away by the Otter Brewery.

Open all day all wk 10am-11pm (Sun 11-10.30) **Bar Meals** L served Mon-Sat 12-9 D served Mon-Sat 12-9 **Restaurant** L served all wk 12-9 D served all wk 12-9 ⊕ FREE HOUSE ◖ Otter Bitter & Ale, Guest ales Ô Wiscombe Suicider. **Facilities** Non-diners area ☺ (Bar Garden) ◗ᐦ Children's menu Children's portions Play area Garden ⊨ Parking Wi-fi

SIDMOUTH — Map 3 SY18

Blue Ball Inn

PICK OF THE PUBS

See Pick of the Pubs on opposite page

Dukes ★★★★ INN

PICK OF THE PUBS

The Esplanade EX10 8AR ☎ 01395 513320
e-mail: dukes@sidmouthinn.co.uk
dir: *Exit A3052 to Sidmouth, left onto Esplanade*

Relaxed, informal dining on the Regency esplanade

A stone's throw from the sea in Sidmouth's town centre, this contemporary family-friendly inn has a stylish and lively interior, a continental feel in the bar and public areas, and comfortable en suite bedrooms. In fine weather, the patio garden, which overlooks the sea, is a great place in which to bask in the sun with a pint of Otter Ale. If it's chilly, relax inside on one of the comfortable leather sofas, perhaps with an award-winning Christopher Piper wine, all of which are by the bottle or glass. Menu choices feature fresh fish from Brixham and prime meats and game from West Country farms. Lunchtime brings sandwiches and lighter pub favourites, while in the evening expect medallions of tenderloin pork, Puy lentil moussaka, and pan-fried sea bass fillet. Pizzas are also always available. Dukes has received an AA Dinner Award and also holds a green tourism award. A beer festival takes place during the first week of August.

Open all day all wk **Bar Meals** L served Sun-Thu 12-9, Fri-Sat 12-9.30 D served Sun-Thu 12-9, Fri-Sat 12-9.30 Av main course £10 **Restaurant** L served Sun-Thu 12-9, Fri-Sat 12-9.30 D served Sun-Thu 12-9, Fri-Sat 12-9.30 ⊕ FREE HOUSE ◖ Branscombe Vale Branoc & Summa That, Otter Ale, Ô Sandford Orchard, Annings Fruit Cider. ♈ 20 **Facilities** Non-diners area ☺ (Bar Garden) ◗ᐦ Children's menu Children's portions Garden ⊨ Beer festival Parking Wi-fi ▭ (notice required) **Rooms** 13

Save on hotels. Book at **theAA.com/hotel**

DEVON 139 **ENGLAND**

PICK OF THE PUBS

Blue Ball Inn

SIDMOUTH　　　　**MAP 3 SY18**

Stevens Cross, Sidford EX10 9QL
☎ **01395 514062**
e-mail:
enquiries@blueballinnsidford.co.uk
web: www.blueballinnsidford.co.uk
dir: *M5 junct 30, A3052, through Sidford towards Lyme Regis, inn on the left*

Thatched pub with a warm welcome and a wide selection of fresh fish

Postcard-pretty under its thatched roof, the 14th-century cob-and-flint Blue Ball in Sidford is popular with locals and visitors alike. Lovingly maintained, colourful and attractive gardens surround the inn and there is a large car park, a skittle alley and meeting and function facilities for up to 80 people. A wide selection of freshly prepared food from traditional beer battered fish and chips and steak and kidney pudding to a wide range of fresh fish including crab, lobster, sole and mussels; in addition there are many other dishes from the regularly changing specials board. The wine list ranges from new world and more traditional choices that will suit

all pockets. The real ales include local Otter Bitter, St Austell Tribute, Sharp's Doombar and Bass, and the ciders are Thatchers Gold and Taunton traditional cider. For those who prefer a soft drink there's a varied selection which includes products from the local area The inn is within easy reach of the M5, A303 and Exeter, and just minutes from stunning walks inland and along the coast. Families are very welcome here. Accommodation is available.

Open all day all wk Closed: 25 Dec eve
🍺 Otter Bitter, St Austell Tribute, Sharp's Doom Bar, Bass, Guest ale
🍏 Thatchers Gold **Facilities** Non-diners area 🐾 ♦️ Children's portions Garden 🪑 Parking Wi-fi Accommodation

PICK OF THE PUBS

The Tower Inn

SLAPTON Map 3 SX84

Church Rd TQ7 2PN ☎ 01548 580216
e-mail: towerinn@slapton.org
web: www.thetowerinn.com
dir: *Exit A379 S of Dartmouth, left at
Slapton Sands*

West Country ales and seasonal
menus

Tucked up a narrow driveway behind
cottages and the church in this unspoilt
Devon village, the ancient ivy-clad tower
(which gives this charming 14th-
century inn its name) looms hauntingly
above the pub. It is all that remains of
the old College of Chantry Priests — the
pub was built to accommodate the
artisans who constructed the monastic
college. Six hundred years on and this
truly atmospheric village pub continues
to welcome guests and the appeal, other
than its peaceful location, is the
excellent range of real ales on tap and
the eclectic choice of modern pub grub
prepared from locally sourced
ingredients, which include smoked fish
from Dartmouth, quality Devon-reared
beef, and fresh fish and crab landed at
Brixham. Expect hearty lunchtime
sandwiches alongside the ploughman's
platter laden with pork pie, cheddar
cheese, home-made relish and crusty
bread; and Thai fishcakes. A typical
evening meal may take in carpaccio of
Exmoor venison with rocket, olive
tapenade and parmesan; followed by

pork belly with curly kale and sage jus;
or pan-fried wild sea bass with braised
fennel, crab dumplings and a crab
bisque. Round off with apple and
blueberry crumble with vanilla ice
cream and wash down with a pint of
Otter or St Austell Proper Job. Stone
walls, open fires, low beams, scrubbed
oak tables and flagstone floors
characterise the welcoming interior, the
atmosphere enhanced at night with
candlelit tables. There's a splendid
landscaped rear garden, perfect for
summer alfresco meals. Visitors
exploring Slapton Ley Nature Reserve
and Slapton Sands should venture
inland to seek out this ancient inn.

Open 12-2.30 (12-3 summer) 6-11
Closed: 1st 2wks Jan, Sun eve during

Winter **Bar Meals** L served all wk
12-2.30 D served all wk 6.30-9.30 Av
main course £12.95 **Restaurant** L
served all wk 12-2.30 D served all wk
6.30-9.30 Av 3 course à la carte fr
£25.95 ⊕ FREE HOUSE ◀ Butcombe
Bitter, Otter Bitter, St Austell Proper Job,
ⵁ Addlestones, Sharp's Orchard.
Facilities Non-diners area 🐾 👫
Children's menu & portions Garden 🎍
Beer festival Parking Wi-fi 🚌

Save on hotels. Book at **theAA.com/hotel**

DEVON 141 **ENGLAND**

SLAPTON	Map 3 SX84

The Tower Inn

PICK OF THE PUBS

See Pick of the Pubs on opposite page

SOURTON	Map 3 SX59

The Highwayman Inn

EX20 4HN ☎ 01837 861243
e-mail: info@thehighwaymaninn.net
web: www.thehighwaymaninn.net
dir: *On A386 (Okehampton to Tavistock road). From Exeter, exit A30 towards Tavistock. Pub 4m from Okehampton, 12m from Tavistock*

One of a kind pub, crammed with objects both eccentric and obscure

The Highwayman is a fascinating and unique place, full of legend, strange architecture, eccentric furniture and obscure bric-à-brac, with roots going back to 1282. John 'Buster' Jones began creating his vision in 1959 – features include part of a galleon, wood hauled from Dartmoor's bogs, and Gothic church arches; the entrance is through the old Okehampton to Launceston coach. The pub is now run by his daughter Sally. Popular with holidaymakers and international tourists, The Highwayman refreshes one and all with drinks that include real farmhouse cider and interesting bottled beers from local breweries; great pasties and pies are always available, and for residents only a more extensive menu featuring lobster thermidor and duck á l'orange is offered.

Open 11.30-2 6-10.30 (Sun 12-2 7-10.30) Closed: 25-28 Dec, Mon eve it is advisable to check with pub that it is open **Bar Meals** L served all wk 12-1.45 D served all wk 6-9 ⊕ FREE HOUSE ◀ Marston's Pedigree, Wychwood Hobgoblin, Sharp's Doom Bar, Shepherd Neame Spitfire ♂ Grays. **Facilities** Non-diners area ♨ (Bar Restaurant Garden) Family room Garden ⊼ Parking Wi-fi **Notes** ⊛

SOUTH POOL	Map 3 SX74

The Millbrook Inn

PICK OF THE PUBS

TQ7 2RW ☎ 01548 531581
e-mail: info@millbrookinnsouthpool.co.uk
dir: *A379 from Kingsbridge to Frogmore. In Frogmore right signed South Pool. 2m to village*

Local seafood a specialty here

In summer when the tide is high, this quaint 16th-century village pub attracts boat owners from Salcombe and Kingsbridge. Set at the head of South Pool creek on the Salcombe estuary, the draw is chef Jean Phillipe Bidart's famous paellas, and barbecues in the pretty front courtyard and the tiny rear terrace overlooking a babbling brook and fields. JP's imaginative pub food, which draws on local, seasonal ingredients, notably oysters from Bigbury Bay, Start Bay crab, fish caught off the South Hams coast, local estate game, and allotment-grown vegetables. White-painted under its natural stone roof, The Millbrook has two cosy beamed bars with open fires and traditional pub decor, and a charming little dining room where booking is essential. Ian Dent and Diana Hunt are welcoming hosts, and the pub throngs with locals quaffing Red Rock ales.

Open all day all wk 12-11 (Sun 12-10.30) **Bar Meals** L served all wk 12-2 D served all wk 7-9 **Restaurant** L served Mon-Sat 12-2, Sun 12-3 D served all wk 7-9 ⊕ FREE HOUSE ◀ Red Rock, Millbrook, Guest ales ♂ Thatchers Heritage & Gold. ☻ 10 **Facilities** Non-diners area ♨ (Bar Restaurant Garden) Children's portions Garden Outside area ⊼ Wi-fi

SOWTON	Map 3 SX99

The Black Horse Inn

Old Honiton Rd EX5 2AN ☎ 01392 366649
e-mail: blackhorse@wadworth.co.uk
dir: *On old A30 from Exeter towards Honiton, 0.5m from M5 junct 29; 1m from Exeter International Airport. Inn between Sowton & Clyst Honiton*

Good food within easy reach of Exeter

This Wadworth-owned village pub has a relaxed atmosphere and is the perfect setting to enjoy a menu that uses plenty of produce from local suppliers. At lunch, jacket potatoes, paninis and ploughman's offer a lighter option, but there's also steak-and-kidney suet pudding; fish pie and a trio of sausages and mash for those with a bigger appetite. Try the local ale while sitting on the terrace on warmer days.

Open all day all wk 11-11 (Sun 11-10.30) **Bar Meals** L served Mon-Thu 11.45-2.30, Fri-Sun 11.45-9.30 D served Mon-Thu 6-9.30, Fri-Sun 11.45-9.30 **Restaurant** L served Mon-Thu 11.45-2.30, Fri-Sun 11.45-9.30 D served Mon-Thu 6-9.30, Fri-Sun 11.45-9.30 ⊕ WADWORTH ◀ Henry's Original IPA & 6X, Guest ales ♂ Thatchers. ☻ 11 **Facilities** Non-diners area ♨ (Bar Garden) Children's menu Garden ⊼ Parking Wi-fi ⛽

SPARKWELL	Map 3 SX55

The Treby Arms ◉◉ NEW

PICK OF THE PUBS

1 Newton Row PL7 5DD ☎ 01752 837363
e-mail: trebyarms@hotmail.co.uk

Village pub with a 'Masterchef' winning formula

Since chef-patron Anton Piotrowski became joint winner of BBC's Masterchef The Professionals in 2012, business has been brisk at his 17th-century pub, set in small village between Dartmoor and Plymouth. In fact, the interest in the pub, which has been transformed into a vibrant gastro-pub, is such that it is essential to book a table to experience Anton's inspired cooking. Using fresh seasonal produce, including locally-caught fish, estate game and village allotment vegetables, the daily menu may offer mackerel with squid and crab risotto and crab fritters, followed by Devon Ruby rib-eye steak with wild garlic mash and béarnaise; or bream with tomato broth, surf clams, shaved fennel and potato purée. To finish, try the cherry iced parfait with apricot soup, mint crisp and nectarine salad. Splash out and sample Anton's special 10-course Masterchef tasting menu.

Open 12-3 6-11 Closed: 25-26 Dec & 1-2 Jan, Mon **Bar Meals** L served Tue-Sun 12-3 D served Tue-Sun 6-9 **Restaurant** L served Tue-Sun 12-3 D served Tue-Sun 6-9 ⊕ FREE HOUSE ◀ St Austell Tribute, Dartmoor Jail Ale & IPA ♂ Thatchers, Harry's Cider. **Facilities** Non-diners area ♨ (Bar Outside area) Children's portions Outside area ⊼ Parking Wi-fi

SPREYTON	Map 3 SX69

The Tom Cobley Tavern

PICK OF THE PUBS

EX17 5AL ☎ 01647 231314
dir: *From A30 at Whiddon Down take A3124 N. 1st right after services, 1st right over bridge*

Fabulous views and a huge range of ales

This whitewashed Dartmoor village pub draws the crowds due to its associations with the Widecombe Fair. It was from this pub, one day in 1802, that Thomas Cobley and his companions set forth for the fair, an event immortalised in song, and his cottage still stands in the village. It remains a traditional village local; the unspoilt main bar has a roaring log fire, cushioned settles, and a vast range of 20 tip-top real ales straight from the cask, for which it has won many awards. The pub also offers a great range of real ciders. Typically, order a pint of Dartmoor Jail Ale to accompany some hearty pub food, which ranges from simple bar snacks to pies, salads, curries and fish dishes, as well as a good vegetarian selection. Summer alfresco drinking can be enjoyed on the pretty flower-decked terrace or in the rear garden with its far-reaching views.

Open 12-3 6-11 (Sun 12-4 7-11 Mon 6.30-11 Fri-Sat 12-3 6-1am) Closed: Mon L **Bar Meals** L served Tue-Sun 12-2 D served all wk 7-9 **Restaurant** L served Tue-Sun

continued

SPREYTON ***continued***

12-2 D served all wk 7-9 FREE HOUSE Cotleigh Tawny Ale, Teignworthy Gundog, Sharp's Doom Bar, St Austell Tribute & Proper Job, Dartmoor Jail Ale & Legend, Holsworthy Ales Winkleigh, Westons Stowford Press, Healey's Berry Rattler & Pear Rattler, Sandford Orchards, Gwynt y Ddraig, Lilley's. **Facilities** Non-diners area (Bar Garden) Children's menu Children's portions Garden Parking (notice required)

STAVERTON — Map 3 SX76

Sea Trout Inn

TQ9 6PA ☎ 01803 762274
e-mail: info@theseatroutinn.co.uk
dir: *From A38 take A384 towards Totnes. Follow Staverton & Sea Trout Inn sign*

Long, white-painted pub offering a modern British menu

Apart from the occasional puff of a steam train drifting across the pretty Dart Valley from the South Devon Railway, this character village inn is the epitome of tranquillity. Dating back 600 years, the Sea Trout ticks all the boxes for the authentic country pub, from the delightful locals' bar to the stylish restaurant, where trying to choose from the modern British menu can be agonising; slow-roast pork belly with chorizo bubble-and-squeak, or perhaps Massaman seafood curry, with well-kept Palmers ales the icing on the cake.

Open all day all wk **Bar Meals** L served Mon-Fri 12-2, Sat 12-2.30, Sun 12-3 D served Mon-Thu 6-9, Fri-Sat 6-9.30, Sun 6.30-9 Av main course £11.95 **Restaurant** L served Mon-Fri 12-2, Sat 12-2.30, Sun 12-3 D served Mon-Thu 6-9, Fri-Sat 6-9.30, Sun 6.30-9 Av 3 course à la carte fr £24 PALMERS 200, Copper Ale, Best Bitter & Dorset Gold Thatchers. **Facilities** Non-diners area (Bar Garden) Children's menu Children's portions Garden Parking Wi-fi

STOKE FLEMING — Map 3 SX84

The Green Dragon Inn

Church Rd TQ6 0PX ☎ 01803 770238
e-mail: pcrowther@btconnect.com
dir: *Off A379 (Dartmouth to Kingsbridge coast road) opposite church*

A haven of boating memorabilia

Opposite the village church, this South Hams pub has many seafaring connections, being only two miles from Dartmouth. Although there has been a building on this site since the 12th century, the first recorded landlord took charge in 1607. The current landlord has decorated the interior in a seafaring theme with charts and sailing pictures. Local beers such as Otter and Exmoor slake the thirst of walkers, whilst the great-value menu can satisfy the largest of appetites with hearty baguettes, hand-picked crab, cottage pie, Glamorgan sausages, surf 'n' turf burger or a West Country sirloin steak.

Open all wk 11.30-3 5.30-11 (Sun 12-3.30 6.30-10.30) Closed: 25-26 Dec **Bar Meals** L served all wk 12-2 D served all wk 6.30-8.30 HEAVITREE Otter Ale, Exmoor Ale, Guest Ales Aspall, Addlestones. 10 **Facilities** Non-diners area (Bar Garden) Children's menu Children's portions Play area Garden Parking

TAVISTOCK — Map 3 SX47

Peter Tavy Inn

Peter Tavy PL19 9NN ☎ 01822 810348
e-mail: chris@wording.freeserve.co.uk
dir: *From Tavistock take A386 towards Okehampton. In 2m right to Peter Tavy*

Dartmoor inn recommended for its pies

It is thought this inn was originally built in the 15th century as a Devon longhouse for the stonemasons rebuilding the village church. On the western flanks of Dartmoor, it is likely that it became a pub by the early 17th century and a further floor was added. It is now as much a draw for its range of local real ales and ciders as it is for its food, much of it sourced locally. The pies are popular main dishes, while there are always vegetarian and vegan options like spicy African sweet potato and spinach stew. Wash down seafood gumbo with pints of Otter Bright.

Open all wk 12-3 6-11 (Sun 12-3 6-10.30); all day Etr-Autumn Closed: 25 Dec **Bar Meals** L served all wk 12-2 D served all wk 6.30-9 **Restaurant** L served all wk 12-2 D served all wk 6.30-9 FREE HOUSE Dartmoor Jail Ale, Otter Bright, Branscombe Vale Drayman's Best Bitter Winkleigh Sam's Poundhouse & Crisp. 9 **Facilities** Non-diners area (Bar Restaurant Garden) Children's menu Children's portions Garden Parking Wi-fi

THURLESTONE — Map 3 SX64

The Village Inn

TQ7 3NN ☎ 01548 563525
dir: *Take A379 from Plymouth towards Kingsbridge, at Bantham rdbt take B3197, right signed Thurlestone, 2.5m*

Popular country pub offering fresh seafood

Just minutes from the beach and coastal path, The Village Inn was built in the 16th century using timbers salvaged from a wrecked Spanish Armada ship. A popular village pub, it is under the same ownership as the nearby Thurlestone Hotel. Expect traditional country pub decor, good service from the Grose family, well-kept ales and decent food. In addition to sandwiches and salads, classic dishes are the fish and seafood platter; and the pork and leek sausages with black pudding. Look to the blackboards for daily specials.

Open all wk 11.30-3 6-11.30 (Sat-Sun & summer all day) **Bar Meals** L served Mon-Fri 12-2.30, Sat-Sun 12-9 D served Mon-Fri 6-9, Sat-Sun 12-9 FREE HOUSE Palmers Best Bitter, Sharp's Doom Bar, Guest ale Heron Valley. **Facilities** Non-diners area (Bar Restaurant Outside area) Children's menu Children's portions Outside area Parking Wi-fi (notice required)

TIPTON ST JOHN — Map 3 SY09

The Golden Lion Inn

PICK OF THE PUBS

See Pick of the Pubs on opposite page

TOPSHAM — Map 3 SX98

Bridge Inn

PICK OF THE PUBS

Bridge Hill EX3 0QQ ☎ 01392 873862
e-mail: su3264@eclipse.co.uk
dir: *M5 junct 30 follow Sidmouth signs, in approx 400yds right at rdbt onto A376 towards Exmouth. In 1.8m cross mini rdbt. Right at next mini rdbt to Topsham. 1.2m, cross River Clyst. Inn on right*

True brewing heritage with royal approval

This 'museum with beer' is substantially 16th century, although its constituent parts vary considerably in age. Most of the fabric is local stone, while the old brewhouse at the rear is traditional Devon cob. Four generations of the same family have run it since great-grandfather William Gibbings arrived in 1897, and it remains eccentrically and gloriously old fashioned – mobile phones are definitely out. Usually around ten real ales from local and further-flung breweries are served straight from their casks, the actual line-up varying by the week. There are no lagers and only a few wines, two from a local organic vineyard. Traditional, freshly prepared lunchtime bar food includes granary ploughman's, pork pies, veggie or meat pasties, and sandwiches, all made with local ingredients. Queen Elizabeth II visited in 1998; it is believed this is the only time she has officially stepped inside an English pub.

Open all wk 12-2 6-10.30 (Sun 12-2 7-10.30) **Bar Meals** L served all wk 12-2 FREE HOUSE Branscombe Vale Branoc, Adnams Broadside, Exe Valley, O'Hanlon's, Teignworthy, Jollyboat Plunder. **Facilities** Non-diners area (Bar Garden) Garden Parking Wi-fi **Notes**

PICK OF THE PUBS

The Golden Lion Inn

TIPTON ST JOHN Map 3 SY09

EX10 0AA ☎ 01404 812881
e-mail: info@goldenliontipton.co.uk
web: www.goldenliontipton.co.uk
dir: *Telephone or visit website for directions*

Mediterranean slant to excellent menus

Michelle and Francois Teissier are currently celebrating their tenth year at the helm of this welcoming Devon village pub. So many things contribute to its traditional feel – the low wooden beams and stone walls, the winter log fire, the art-deco prints and Tiffany lamps, not to mention the paintings by Devonian and Cornish artists. And there's the bar, of course, where locally brewed Otter ales are the order of the day. Chef-patron Franky (as everyone calls him) trained in classical French cooking at a prestigious establishment in the Loire Valley, a grounding that accounts today for his rustic French, Mediterranean and British menus. Their delights may include moules frites; slow roasted lamb shank; escargots; crevettes in garlic butter; spinach and mushroom filled crêpes; chicken Xerez in light creamy sherry sauce. Given that the genteel seaside town of Sidmouth is just down the road, the seafood specials depend totally on that day's catch – cod, hake and sea bass are all candidates. Tempting white and granary

bread sandwiches are filled with fresh Lyme Bay crab, mature cheddar or home-cooked ham. The Sunday lunch menu offers roast West Country beef with Yorkshire pudding; roast lamb with mint sauce; and winter vegetable crêpe. As Franky sums up: 'When Michelle and I took over in 2003, our aim was to create a friendly, inviting village pub offering great value, high-quality food made from the freshest ingredients; with our combination of rustic French dishes and traditional British food with a Mediterranean twist, there's something for everyone!' Outside there is a grassy beer garden and walled terrace area with tumbling grapevines. On summer evenings you can listen to jazz.

Open all wk 12-2.30 6-11 (Sun 12-2.30 7-10.30) **Bar Meals** L served all wk 12-2 D served Mon-Sat 6.30-8.30, Sun 7-8.30 **Restaurant** L served all wk 12-2 ⊕ HEAVITREE ◼ Bass, Otter Ale & Bitter. ☷ 12 **Facilities** Non-diners area ⚤ Children's menu Children's portions Garden ⋒ Parking ▭ (notice required)

PICK OF THE PUBS

The Cary Arms ★★★★★ INN

Babbacombe Beach TQ1 3LX
☎ **01803 327110**
e-mail: enquiries@caryarms.co.uk
web: www.caryarms.co.uk
dir: *On entering Teignmouth, at bottom of hill at lights, right signed Torquay/ A379. Cross River Teign. At mini rdbt follow Babbacombe/Seafront signs. Pass Babbacombe Model Village, through lights, left into Babbacombe Downs Rd, left into Beach Rd*

Beachside inn that has it all

Right on the beach, the rambling and whitewashed Cary Arms is a real find in Babbacombe Bay. This 'boutique inn' is so much more than just a pub; unwind in the beamed bar with its original stone walls, perhaps with a pint of Doom Bar or Otter Ale in hand, contemplating the stunning views across the bay; stay in one of the luxury sea-facing bedrooms; and sample the delicious gastro-pub food from the daily-changing menu. The informal bar is perfect for playing a board game and relaxing after a bracing walk or a day on the beach. If it's a glorious summer's day, you will unquestionably wish to eat in the terraced gardens that lead down to the water's edge; this is when the barbecue and wood-fired oven come into their own. The watchwords in the kitchen are freshness and seasonality, underpinned by a respect for the local

pastures and waters. Catch of the day will be a must for fish-lovers — perhaps grilled skate wing with new potatoes, green beans and caper butter — but the menu reflects coast and country in equal measure. Hard to resist are chicken, mushroom and tarragon terrine with red onion jam and toasted brioche; and roasted guinea fowl supreme stuffed with chicken mousse, Parma ham, thyme-roasted potatoes and celeriac purée. The barbecue is often booked by groups, and a menu is available for the 'nippers'. If staying over, the bedrooms are classic and cool with echoes of New England beachside-chic, and most have a private terrace or balcony overlooking the sea.

Open all day all wk 12-11 **Bar Meals** L served all wk 12-3 D served all wk 6.30-9 Av main course £14 ⊕ FREE HOUSE ◀ Otter Ale, Bays Topsail, Sharp's Doom Bar ♂ Sheppy's, Sandford Devon Mist. ♟ 14 **Facilities** Non-diners area ❖ ♦♦ Children's menu Children's portions Family room Garden ☷ Wi-fi **Rooms** 8 (plus 4 self-catering cottages)

Save on hotels. Book at **theAA.com/hotel**

DEVON 145 ENGLAND

Start Bay Inn

TQ7 2TQ ☎ 01548 580553
e-mail: clair@startbayinn.co.uk
dir: *Between Dartmouth & Kingsbridge on A379*

14th-century pub serving the very freshest seafood

Located on the beach and with a freshwater reserve on its other side, the patio of this 14th-century inn overlooks the sea. The fishermen working from Start Bay deliver their catch direct to the kitchen; so does a local crabber, who leaves his catch at the back door to be cooked and picked by the pub. The former landlord (father of landladies Clair and Gail) continues to dive for scallops. Be in no doubt therefore about the freshness of the seafood on the specials board. Look also for Dartmouth Smokehouse products, locally sourced steaks, burgers from the village butcher, and Salcombe Dairy ice creams. Ploughman's, sandwiches and jackets are also available.

Open all day all wk 11.30-11 **Bar Meals** L served all wk 11.30-2.15 D served all wk 6-9.30 winter, 6-10 summer Av main course £10 ⊕ HEAVITREE ◀ Bass, Otter Ale & Bitter, St Austell Tribute ♻ Heron Valley. ♟ 8 **Facilities** Non-diners area ⬩♦ Children's menu Children's portions Family room Garden ⊼ Parking

The Cary Arms ★★★★★ INN

PICK OF THE PUBS

See Pick of the Pubs on opposite page

The Durant Arms ★★★★ INN

PICK OF THE PUBS

Ashprington TQ9 7UP ☎ 01803 732240
e-mail: info@durantarms.co.uk
dir: *From Totnes take A381 towards Kingsbridge, 1m, left for Ashprington*

Local wines served here

The 18th-century Durant Arms stands in the shadow of a beautiful 16th-century church and has stunning views of the River Dart. Off the tourist trail in a popular part of Devon and situated in the heart of a sleepy, picturesque village, the pub is located just outside Totnes, in the heart of the South Hams. Formerly known as The Ashprington Inn, a flagged entrance leads into the small main bar, which is fitted out in a traditional style, with work by local artists on display alongside the horse brasses, ferns and cheerful red velvet curtains – the perfect place to enjoy local Sharpham Vineyard wines or local real ales and ciders. Bedrooms are well appointed and attractively decorated and the food is cooked to order, using locally sourced ingredients wherever possible for the daily-changing blackboard menu. The little courtyard to the rear provides a cosy spot to linger over a summer meal.

Open all day all wk **Bar Meals** L served all wk 12-2 D served all wk 7-9.15 **Restaurant** L served all wk 12-2 D served all wk 7-9.15 ⊕ FREE HOUSE ◀ St Austell Tribute, Dartmoor ♻ Somersby. ♟ 22 **Facilities** Non-diners area ⬩♦ Children's menu Children's portions Family room Outside area ⊼ Parking Wi-fi ▭ **Rooms** 7

Royal Seven Stars Hotel

The Plains TQ9 5DD ☎ 01803 862125
e-mail: enquiry@royalsevenstars.co.uk
dir: *From A382 signed Totnes, left at 'Dartington' rdbt. Through lights towards town centre, through next rdbt, pass Morrisons car park on left. 200yds on right*

Town centre favourite

In the heart of Totnes, this Grade II listed property has three character bars and a grand ballroom. In the champagne bar, an addition to the TQ9 brasserie, is where bubbly is served by the glass or bottle from 5pm onwards, along with cocktails and wines. Excellent local brews and ciders are always on tap. Quality food at affordable prices is another strength – expect the likes of Thai marinated beef shortribs with Thai noodle salad; chicken breast in Parma ham filled with seasonal mushrooms, with sautéed potatoes, fine beans and hollandaise sauce; and steaks from the grill.

Open all day all wk **Bar Meals** L served all wk 11-9.30 D served all wk 11-9.30 food served all day **Restaurant** L served Sun 12-2.30 D served all wk 6.30-9.30 ⊕ FREE HOUSE ◀ Sharp's Doom Bar, Bays Gold, Courage Best, Dartmoor Legend & Jail Ale ♻ Thatchers, Orchard's, Ashridge. ♟ 26 **Facilities** Non-diners area ❤ (Bar Outside area) ⬩♦ Children's menu Children's portions Family room Outside area ⊼ Beer festival Cider festival Parking Wi-fi

Rumour

30 High St TQ9 5RY ☎ 01803 864682
dir: *Follow signs for Totnes castle/town centre. On main street up hill above arch on left. 5 min walk from rail station*

Stylish bar serving exciting European food

Named after Fleetwood Mac's landmark 1977 album, this 17th-century building at the top of the high street has had a chequered history including stints as a milk bar, restaurant and wine bar. Food offerings include an extensive hand-made pizza menu alongside light bites and brunch-style offerings and a more formal à la carte menu that could proffer ricotta and sage gnocchi with wilted spinach, butternut squash and pine nuts, or beef bourguignon with mashed potato and greens. Typical desserts might include pain perdu with spiced plums and vanilla ice cream or a retro Black Forest gateau.

Open all wk Mon-Sat 10am-11pm (Sun 6-10.30) **Bar Meals** L served Mon-Sat 12-3 D served Mon-Sat 6-10, Sun 6-9 **Restaurant** L served Mon-Sat 12-3 D served Mon-Sat 6-10, Sun 6-9 ⊕ FREE HOUSE ◀ Erdinger, Dartmoor Jail Ale, Hunter's, Quercus ♻ Thatchers. ♟ 12 **Facilities** Non-diners area ⬩♦ Children's portions Wi-fi

Steam Packet Inn ★★★★ INN

St Peter's Quay TQ9 5EW ☎ 01803 863880
e-mail: steampacket@buccaneer.co.uk
web: www.steampacketinn.co.uk
dir: *Exit A38 towards Plymouth, 18m. A384 to Totnes, 6m. Left at mini rdbt, pass Morrisons on left, over mini rdbt, 400yds on left*

Popular inn on the River Dart

Named after the passenger, cargo and mail steamers that once plied the Dart, this riverside pub (alongside which you can moor your boat) with four en suite guest rooms offers great views, particularly from the conservatory restaurant and heated waterside patio, where there is plenty of seating. A real log fire warms the bar in the colder months. The mainly traditional choices at lunch and dinner might include plaice goujons, gammon steak, lamb rump and Mexican fajitas. There are daily fish specials on the blackboard. Look out for the four-day beer festival in mid-May, occasional live music and summer barbecues.

Open all day all wk **Bar Meals** L served Mon-Fri 12-2.30, Sat 12-3, Sun 12-8 D served Mon-Sat 6-9.30, Sun 12-8 Av main course £10.95 **Restaurant** L served Mon-Fri 12-2.30, Sat 12-3, Sun 12-8 D served Mon-Sat 6-9.30, Sun 12-8 ⊕ FREE HOUSE/BUCCANEER ◀ Sharp's Doom Bar, Dartmoor Jail Ale, Guest ale ♻ Westons Stowford Press & GL, Ashridge. ♟ 11 **Facilities** Non-diners area ❤ (Bar Garden) ⬩♦ Children's menu Garden ⊼ Beer festival Parking Wi-fi ▭ (notice required) **Rooms** 4

The White Hart Bar & Restaurant

PICK OF THE PUBS

Dartington Hall TQ9 6EL ☎ 01803 847111
e-mail: bookings@dartingtonhall.com
dir: *A38 onto A384 towards Totnes. Turn at Dartington church into Dartington Hall Estate*

British tapas in a medieval setting

Part of the splendid 14th-century Dartington Hall Estate and deer park, The White Hart is surrounded by landscaped gardens and even has its own cinema located in a renovated medieval barn. Ancient tapestries, crackling fires, flagstones, Gothic chandeliers and limed oak settles characterise the interior, which was refurbished in spring 2013. Local Devon and Cornish real ales are available in the bar together with Thatchers draught cider, and there's a patio for the warmer weather. The exciting new British tapas menu lists regularly changing, creative dishes made from the best

continued

TOTNES continued

local produce: mini cottage pie, goats' cheese terrine, seared king scallops and crispy whitebait are just a few. Children are welcome and are encouraged to sample the tapas with the rest of the family. The daily-changing bar and restaurant menu uses fresh, seasonal ingredients from south Devon and the estate itself – single-suckled beef, grass-reared lamb, additive-free and free-range chickens and eggs, and fish.

Open all day all wk 12-11 **Bar Meals** L served all wk 12-9 D served all wk 12-9 food served all day **Restaurant** L served all wk 12-9 D served all wk 12-9 food served all day ⊕ FREE HOUSE ◀ St Austell Tribute, Local guest ales ♻ Thatchers. ♟ 10 **Facilities** Non-diners area ♦↑ Children's menu Children's portions Garden ⋒ Parking Wi-fi ▭ (notice required)

TRUSHAM   Map 3 SX88

Cridford Inn

PICK OF THE PUBS

TQ13 0NR ☎ 01626 853694
e-mail: reservations@vanillapod-cridfordinn.com
web: www.vanillapod-cridfordinn.com
dir: From A38 exit at junct for Teign Valley, right, follow Trusham signs for 4m

Historic pub near Dartmoor with great food

Medieval masons' marks are still visible above the bar in this heritage gem of a pub with over a thousand years of history packed into its rough stone walls and thatched roof. In summer sip a pint of local Teignworthy bitter on the terrace beneath mature trees and look out at the Teign Valley a short step from Dartmoor National Park. Food comes with an excellent local pedigree and seasonal flavour and you can eat in either the bar or the renowned Vanilla Pod restaurant: start with smoked Torbay mackerel pâté with rocket and parmesan salad before moving on to pan-fried supreme of Crediton chicken filled with chorizo sausage served with fragrant smoked paprika and tomato sauce, and finish with one of chef Ian's stunning desserts. There are great vegetarian options, lite bites and a new outside pizza oven. Beer festival in June.

Open all wk 11-3 6.15-11 (Sat 11-11 Sun 12-10.30) **Bar Meals** L served Mon-Fri 12-2.30, Sat & Sun (Mar-Sep) all day, Sun (Oct-Feb) 12-3 D served all wk 7-9.30 Av main course £11 **Restaurant** L served Sun 12-2 D served Tue-Sat 7-9.30 ⊕ FREE HOUSE ◀ Sharp's Doom Bar, Dartmoor Legend & Dragon's Breath, Teignworthy, Bays ♻ Thatchers. ♟ 10 **Facilities** Non-diners area ♣ (Bar Garden Outside area) ♦↑ Children's menu Children's portions Family room Garden Outside area ⋒ Beer festival Parking Wi-fi ▭ (notice required)

TUCKENHAY   Map 3 SX85

The Maltsters Arms

TQ9 7EQ ☎ 01803 732350
e-mail: maltsters@tuckenhay.com
dir: A381 from Totnes towards Kingsbridge. 1m, at hill top turn left, follow signs to Tuckenhay, 3m

Ideal location for enjoying a drink or meal by the river

A late 18th-century stone inn which refreshed busy locals working in commodities such as lime, paper, cider, roadstone and malt before these industries petered out in the 1940s. Overlooking the picturesque Bow Creek, it's a lovely spot for a sparkling pint of local cider and a plate of delectable food. Bar snacks include Bigbury Bay oysters, while the main menu embraces River Teign mussels; Yonder Park Farm bangers with black peppered mash; and a West Country cheese selection. Summertime special events and barbecues are followed by a beer festival in September.

Open all day all wk Mon-Thu & Sun 9am-11pm (Fri-Sat 9am-mdnt) **Bar Meals** L served Mon-Sat 12-2.30, Sun 12.30-3 D served all wk 6.30-9.30 **Restaurant** L served Mon-Sat 12-2.30, Sun 12.30-3 D served all wk 6.30-9.30 ⊕ FREE HOUSE ◀ Dartmoor IPA, Otter Ale, Sambrook's Wandle ♻ Thatchers Gold. ♟ 10 **Facilities** Non-diners area ♣ (Bar Restaurant Garden) ♦↑ Children's menu Children's portions Family room Garden ⋒ Beer festival Parking Wi-fi

TYTHERLEIGH   Map 4 ST30

The Tytherleigh Arms

EX13 7BE ☎ 01460 220214
e-mail: tytherleigharms@gmail.com
dir: Equidistant from Chard & Axminster on A358

Local produce at a smart 16th-century inn

This 16th-century coaching inn on the borders of Devon, Dorset and Somerset still retains plenty of original features, including beamed ceilings and huge fires, which makes for a lovely setting if you are popping in for a pint of Branoc ale, or making a beeline for the daily-changing menu. Local produce drives the menu, whether it's potted Lyme Bay crab, home-made West Country burger or Tytherleigh fish pie topped with Somerset cheddar mash.

Open 11-4 6-12 Closed: 25 Dec, Sun eve winter **Bar Meals** L served Mon-Fri 12-2.30, Sat 12-3, Sun 12-4 D served Mon-Fri 6-9.30, Sat 6-10, Sun 6-9 **Restaurant** L served Mon-Fri 12-2.30, Sat 12-3, Sun 12-4 D served Mon-Fri 6-9.30, Sat 6-10, Sun 6-9 ⊕ FREE HOUSE ◀ Otter Ale & Bitter, Branscombe Vale Branoc ♻ Thatchers Gold, Westons Wyld Wood Organic. ♟ 10 **Facilities** Non-diners area ♣ (Bar Garden) ♦↑ Children's portions Garden ⋒ Parking Wi-fi ▭ (notice required)

WIDECOMBE IN THE MOOR   Map 3 SX77

The Old Inn

TQ13 7TA ☎ 01364 621207
e-mail: oldinn.widecombe@hall-woodhouse.co.uk
dir: From Bovey Tracey take B3387 to Widecombe in the Moor

Country pub for all weathers

This 14th-century pub in the heart of a quintessential village is the start and finishing point for several excellent Dartmoor walks. A pub for all seasons, enjoy the five log fires when the weather turns cold or sit outside in the beer garden with its water features. Cask ales include seasonal guests, with plenty of wines by the glass. Lunchtime brings jacket potatoes and baguettes with a range of fillings, while those with heartier appetites can tuck into gourmet burgers; Somerset chicken and ham hock pie or vegetable curry.

Open all wk all day (ex 26 Dec & 1 Jan close 4pm) Closed: 25 Dec - open for bookings only **Bar Meals** food served all day **Restaurant** food served all day ⊕ HALL & WOODHOUSE ◀ Badger, Guest ales ♻ Badger Applewood, Westons Stowford Press. ♟ 23 **Facilities** Non-diners area ♣ (Bar Restaurant Garden) ♦↑ Children's menu Children's portions Garden ⋒ Parking Wi-fi ▭

The Rugglestone Inn

PICK OF THE PUBS

TQ13 7TF ☎ 01364 621327
e-mail: enquiries@rugglestoneinn.co.uk
dir: From village centre take road by church towards Venton. Inn down hill on left

Pretty, wisteria-clad Dartmoor pub

Originally a cottage, this unaltered Grade II listed building was converted to an inn around 1832. In the picturesque village of Widecombe in the Moor, the pub is surrounded by tranquil moorland and streams; the Rugglestone itself rises behind the pub, whilst Widecombe's famous church acts as a beacon for ramblers and riders seeking out the inn's rural location. Cosy little rooms, wood-burners and beers such as Teignworthy's Rugglestone Moor and farmhouse ciders such as Ashridge, tapped straight from barrels stillaged behind the snug bar, draw an appreciative crowd of regulars and visitors. The filling fare is a decent mix of classic pub staples and savoury dishes aimed at taking away the winter nip or fulfilling a summer evening's promise in the streamside garden. Hot pork baps with apple sauce; steak and Stilton pie; and oven-baked trout with lemon and garlic are all part of the Dartmoor experience.

Open all wk Mon-Thu 11.30-3 6-11.30 Fri 11.30-3 5-12 Sat 11.30am-12pm Sun 12-11 & BH **Bar Meals** L served all wk 12-2 D served all wk 6.30-9 **Restaurant** L served all wk 12-2 D served all wk 6.30-9 ⊕ FREE HOUSE ◀ O'Hanlon's Yellow Hammer, Otter Bitter, Teignworthy Rugglestone Moor, Dartmoor Legend ♻ Ashton Press, Lower Widdon Farm, Ashridge, North Hall Manor. ♟ 10 **Facilities** Non-diners area ♣ (Bar Restaurant Garden) ♦↑ Children's menu Children's portions Garden ⋒ Parking ▭ (notice required)

Save on hotels. Book at **theAA.com/hotel**

DEVON 147 ENGLAND

PICK OF THE PUBS

The Digger's Rest

WOODBURY SALTERTON   Map 3 SY08

EX5 1PQ ☎ 01395 232375
e-mail: bar@diggersrest.co.uk
web: www.diggersrest.co.uk
dir: *2.5m from A3052. Signed from Westpoint Showground*

Picturesque thatched pub offering the best of seasonal produce

This picturesque free house is just a few minutes' drive from the Exeter junction of the M5, and stands in the delightful east Devon village of Woodbury Salterton. The Digger's Rest is more than 500-years-old and with its thatched roof, thick stone and cob walls, heavy beams and log fire was originally a cider house. Today the choice on the bar is much wider but cider is still well represented with Westons Scrumpy and Stowford Press. Real ales feature Otter Bitter from Devon with guest appearances from other West Country brewers such as Bays and Palmers. Wine fans will appreciate the wine list which has been created by the independent Wine Merchant, Tanners of Shrewsbury. The food menus are created to make the best of seasonal produce. Sourcing locally plays a big role in freshness and quality control, and English and West Country organic produce is used wherever possible. The kitchen is also committed to supporting farmers who

practise good husbandry. Menus feature fish landed at Brixham and Looe, West Country beef hung for 21 days and pork from a farm just up the road. As well as the main menu there is a blackboard which features special dishes the chef has created from prime cuts or rarer seasonal ingredients he has sought out. Many of the dishes can be served as smaller portions for children and there is also a children's menu. Whether you want to check your emails (free Wi-fi), have a drink, snack or a full meal, you will find a warm welcome at The Digger's Rest. It's also worth checking the website for details of food clubs, quizzes and events.

Open all wk 11-3 5.30-11 (Sun 12-3.30 5.30-10.30) **Bar Meals** L served all wk 12-2 D served Mon-Sat 6-9, Sun 6-8.30 ⊕ FREE HOUSE ◀ Otter Bitter, Bays Topsail, Palmers Copper Ale Ō Westons & Stowford Press. ♟ 11 **Facilities** Non-diners area ❖ (Bar Garden) ♦♦ Children'smenu Children's portions Garden ᙏ Parking Wi-fi 🚌 (notice required)

WINKLEIGH — Map 3 SS60

The Kings Arms

Fore St EX19 8HQ ☎ 01837 83384
e-mail: kingsarmswinkleigh@googlemail.com
dir: *Village signed from B3220 (Crediton to Torrington road)*

Ancient country inn with traditional British menus

Scrubbed pine tables, wooden settles and wood-burning stoves set the scene in this thatched pub. The freshly made, locally sourced food (including meat from the village butcher) ranges from lighter options such as ploughman's and omelettes, to hearty dishes like fish pie, gammon steak, beef lasagne, scampi and a mixed grill. Pudding options are hazelnut meringues with raspberries and cream; Baileys and chocolate flake cheesecake; and warm chocolate brownie with chocolate sauce and vanilla ice cream. The village's own Winkleigh cider is available, together with local Otter Bitter and Sharp's Doom Bar.

Open all day all wk 11-11 (Sun 12-10.30) **Bar Meals** L served Mon-Sat 11-9.30, Sun 12-9 D served Mon-Sat 11-9.30, Sun 12-9 food served all day **Restaurant** L served Mon-Sat 11-9.30, Sun 12-9 D served Mon-Sat 11-9.30, Sun 12-9 food served all day ⊕ ENTERPRISE INNS ◀ Sharp's Doom Bar, Otter Bitter ♂ Winkleigh. **Facilities** Non-diners area ♣ (Bar Restaurant Garden) ♦ Children's portions Garden ♬

WOODBURY SALTERTON — Map 3 SY08

The Digger's Rest

PICK OF THE PUBS

See Pick of the Pubs on page 147

YEALMPTON — Map 3 SX55

Rose & Crown

PICK OF THE PUBS

Market St PL8 2EB ☎ 01752 880223
e-mail: info@theroseandcrown.co.uk
dir: *Telephone for directions*

Top dining near captivating countryside

There's a cool, airy, bistro-like atmosphere in this classy dining pub at the heart of the South Hams. Close to the pretty Yealm Estuary and just a few miles from the enticing wilderness of southern Dartmoor, foodies make a bee-line to sample Simon Warner's contemporary British cooking. Village locals and beer-lovers can sample beers from the St Austell Brewery stable, perhaps in the quirky walled courtyard garden with its fishpond and fountain, but it is as a destination dining pub that the Rose & Crown shines out. The menu proffers traditional classics with an extra touch of class, allowing the kitchen's focus on quality and local supply to be maintained. From the pub grub menu comes Cornish lamb hotpot; the carte menu greatly expands the temptation, perhaps the seared scallops, crab and salmon ravioli starter followed by duck

breast with roasted shallots, beetroot and sweet potato tart, finishing on peanut butter mousse with caramelised bananas.

Open all day all wk **Bar Meals** L served all wk 12-2.30 D served all wk 6.30-9.30 Av main course £11 **Restaurant** L served all wk 12-2.30 D served all wk 6.30-9.30 Av 3 course à la carte fr £30 ⊕ ST AUSTELL BREWERY ◀ Tribute, HSD & Proper Job ♂ Thatchers Gold, Symonds. **Facilities** Non-diners area ♣ (Bar Garden) ♦ Children's menu Children's portions Garden ♬ Parking Wi-fi ▭ (notice required)

DORSET

ASKERSWELL — Map 4 SY59

The Spyway Inn ★★★★ INN

DT2 9EP ☎ 01308 485250
e-mail: spywayinn@sky.com
dir: *From A35 follow Askerswell sign, then follow Spyway Inn sign*

Oak beams, cask ales and stunning views

Handy for Dorchester and Bridport, this old beamed country inn offers magnificent views of the glorious Dorset countryside. Close to West Bay and an ideal base to explore the Jurassic Coast World Heritage Site at nearby West Bay, the pub boasts a landscaped, sloping beer garden with a pond and stream. It all makes for a lovely setting to enjoy a glass of Otter Ale and sample locally sourced, home-cooked fare like minted lamb chops with mash and vegetables or home-made fish pie. Accommodation is also available.

Open all wk 12-3 6-close **Bar Meals** L served all wk 12-3 D served all wk 6.30-9 **Restaurant** L served all wk 12-3 D served all wk 6.30-9 ⊕ FREE HOUSE ◀ Otter Ale, Bitter ♂ Seasonal. ♥ **Facilities** Non-diners area ♦ Children's menu Children's portions Play area Garden ♬ Parking Wi-fi ▭ (notice required) **Rooms** 3

BLANDFORD FORUM — Map 4 ST80

The Anvil Inn ★★★★ INN

Salisbury Rd, Pimperne DT11 8UQ ☎ 01258 453431
e-mail: theanvil.inn@btconnect.com
dir: *Telephone for directions*

Very old inn offering good food and accommodation

A thatched, 16th-century inn with parts dating back even further, whose two bars offer a range of real ales, including Palmers Copper, and light meals. The charming beamed restaurant with log fire offers a full menu using Dorset produce, such as fresh fish landed on the nearby coast. Try the haddock and spring onion fishcakes; the Mediterranean vegetable lasagne; or maybe the home-made steak-and-ale pie (with shortcrust pastry, of course). The garden's lovely, especially by the fish pond. There are plenty of walks in the surrounding area and the Anvil Inn welcomes dogs.

Open all day all wk **Bar Meals** L served all wk 12-8.45 D served all wk 12-8.45 food served all day **Restaurant** L

served all wk 12-8.45 D served all wk 12-8.45 food served all day ⊕ FREE HOUSE ◀ Fuller's London Pride, Palmers Copper Ale, Butcombe Bitter, Guinness ♂ Addlestones, Ashton Press. ♥ 9 **Facilities** Non-diners area ♣ (Bar Garden) ♦ Children's menu Children's portions Garden ♬ Parking Wi-fi **Rooms** 12

BOURTON — Map 4 ST73

The White Lion Inn

High St SP8 5AT ☎ 01747 840866
e-mail: office@whitelionbourton.co.uk
dir: *Off A303, opposite B3092 to Gillingham*

Popular inn with a good choice of dishes and beers

Dating from 1723, The White Lion is a beautiful, stone-built, creeper-clad Dorset inn. The bar is cosy, with beams, flagstones and an open fire, and serves a range of real beers and ciders. Imaginative menus draw on the wealth of quality local produce, and dishes range from twice-baked cheddar soufflé or duck rillette to Moroccan tagine or roast venison. There a cider festival in July.

Open all wk Mon-Thu 12-3 5-11 (Fri-Sun all day) **Bar Meals** L served Mon-Sat 12-2.30, Sun 12-3.30 D served all wk 6-9 Av main course £10 **Restaurant** L served Mon-Sat 12-2.30, Sun 12-3.30 D served all wk 6-9 ⊕ FREE HOUSE/ADMIRAL TAVERNS ◀ Otter Amber, Sharp's Doom Bar, St Austell Tribute ♂ Thatchers, Rich's Farmhouse. **Facilities** Non-diners area ♣ (Bar Garden) ♦ Children's menu Children's portions Garden Cider festival Parking Wi-fi ▭

BRIDPORT — Map 4 SY49

The Shave Cross Inn ★★★★★ INN

PICK OF THE PUBS

Shave Cross, Marshwood Vale DT6 6HW
☎ 01308 868358
e-mail: roy.warburton@virgin.net
dir: *From Bridport take B3162. In 2m left signed 'Broadoak/Shave Cross', then Marshwood*

Caribbean food in the heart of Hardy country

Off the beaten track down narrow lanes in the beautiful Marshwood Vale, deep in Thomas Hardy country, this thatched 14th-century cob-and-flint inn was once a resting place for pilgrims and other monastic visitors on their way to Whitchurch Canonicorum to visit the shrine to St Candida and St Cross. While they were at the inn they had their tonsures trimmed, hence the pub's name. Step inside cosy bar to find low beams, stone floors, a huge inglenook fireplace, rustic furnishings, and local Dorset ale on tap, as well as real farm ciders. The food here is both unusual and inspirational, with a strong Caribbean influence together with dishes originating as far afield as Fiji. A starter of jerk chicken salad with plantin, crispy bacon and aïoli might be followed by a main course of hot and spicy Cuban seafood bouillabaisse or Jamaican jerk pork tenderloin with pineapple compôte. Accommodation available.

Save on hotels. Book at theAA.com/hotel

DORSET 149 ENGLAND

Open 11-3 6-11.30 Closed: Mon (ex BHs) **Bar Meals** L served Tue-Sun 12-2.30 D served Tue-Sat 6-8.30 Sun 6-8 **Restaurant** L served Tue-Sun 12-2.30 D served Tue-Sat 6-8.30 Sun 6-8 (closed Sun eve winter) ⊕ FREE HOUSE ◀ Branscombe Vale Branoc, Dorset, Local guest ales Ö Westons Old Rosie, Thatchers, Pitfield Thunderbolt. ⬙ 8 **Facilities** Non-diners area ♣ (Bar Garden) ♦♦ Children's menu Children's portions Play area Garden Parking Wi-fi ▥ **Rooms** 7

The West Bay

Station Rd, West Bay DT6 4EW ☎ **01308 422157**
e-mail: enquiries@thewestbayhotel.co.uk
dir: From A35 (Bridport by-pass) take B3157 (2nd exit) towards West Bay. After mini rdbt 1st left (Station Road). Pub on left

Local fish and seafood a speciality

Built in 1739, this traditional bar/restaurant lies at the foot of East Cliff, part of the impressive World Heritage Jurassic Coast, and in the picturesque harbour of West Bay. The pub specialises in fish and seafood with the latest catch shown as blackboard specials. Perhaps choose Thai crab cakes with sweet chilli prawn butter; then bouillabaisse with a hot baguette. For meat-eaters there's a good choice of steaks or maybe pot-roasted pork belly and cider jus. Palmers Brewery in Bridport furnishes the real ales, or you can ring the changes with a pint of Thatchers Gold cider.

Open all wk Mon-Thu 12-3 6-11 (Fri-Sun all day) ⊕ PALMERS ◀ Best Bitter, Copper Ale, 200 & Tally Ho!, Guinness Ö Thatchers Gold. **Facilities** ♦♦ Children's portions Garden Parking

Stapleton Arms

PICK OF THE PUBS

Church Hill SP8 5HS ☎ **01963 370396**
e-mail: relax@thestapletonarms.com
dir: 3.5m from Wincanton in village centre

Imaginative food in a relaxed setting

A stylish and unstuffy country pub tucked away in a pretty village on the Somerset, Wiltshire and Dorset border, the Stapleton Arms has an elegant dining room, secluded garden and a spacious bar offering real ales such as Butcombe and Moor Revival. In addition, the specialist cider and apple juice list includes draught ciders like Thatchers Cheddar Valley and Harry's Farmhouse Cider. The freshest seasonal ingredients from local producers lie behind an innovative modern menu that runs from nibbles (black pudding and marmalade Scotch egg) to full meals such as piri piri squid with chilli and lime may followed by the pub's own salt beef with parsley mash and glazed carrots. You could finish with rhubarb trifle and sorbet. As well as regular beer tastings, festivals and events, there are some great walks in the area, and picnics and maps are provided by the helpful staff.

Open all wk 11-3 6-11 (Sun 12-10.30) **Bar Meals** L served all wk 12-3 D served all wk 6-10 Av main course £14

Restaurant L served all wk 12-3 D served all wk 6-10 Av 3 course à la carte fr £28 ⊕ FREE HOUSE ◀ Moor Revival, Butcombe Ö Thatchers Cheddar Valley & Gold, The Orchard Pig, Ashton Press, Harry's Farmhouse Cider, Guest ciders. ⬙ 30 **Facilities** Non-diners area ♣ (Bar Garden) ♦♦ Children's menu Children's portions Play area Garden ⊟ Beer festival Parking Wi-fi ▥ (notice required)

Fox & Hounds Inn

Duck St DT2 0JH ☎ **01300 320444**
e-mail: lizflight@yahoo.co.uk
dir: On A37, between Dorchester & Yeovil, follow signs to Cattistock

Popular inn in pretty Dorset village

Expect a bar full of locals, children, dogs and even chickens under foot at this attractive pub. Situated in a picturesque village, the 17th-century inn has a welcoming and traditional atmosphere engendered by ancient beams, open fires in winter and huge inglenooks, one with an original bread oven. Palmers ales are on tap, along with Taunton cider, while home-made meals embrace Lyme Bay scallop and smoked bacon salad; vine tomato, fennel and basil pie; and lamb shank with redcurrant and rosemary sauce. Regular events include folk music and poetry.

Open 12-2.30 6-11 Closed: Mon L **Bar Meals** L served Tue-Sun 12-2 D served Tue-Sat 7-11 Av main course £9.95 **Restaurant** L served Tue-Sun 12-2 D served Tue-Sat 7-11 ⊕ PALMERS ◀ Best Bitter, Copper Ale, 200, Dorset Gold Ö Taunton Traditional, Thatchers Gold, Sheppy's. **Facilities** Non-diners area ♣ (Bar Restaurant Garden) ♦♦ Children's portions Play area Garden ⊟ Parking Wi-fi ▥ (notice required)

Winyard's Gap Inn

Chedington Ln DT8 3HY ☎ **01935 891244**
e-mail: enquiries@winyardsgap.com
dir: 5m S of Crewkerne on A356

Extravagant views, craft ciders and seasonal produce

Situated beside National Trust woodlands in a corner of the Dorset Area of Outstanding Natural Beauty, the old inn's garden commands an extraordinary view across Somerset from the eponymous gap in the sinuous chalk hills. The two counties provide the wherewithal for the August cider festival here, whilst beers from Exmoor and Otter breweries anoint the bar, with its solid rustic seating and tables and a log-burner for the winter nip. The ploughman's lunch takes in the cheeses of the area, or tackle a Dorset-caught sea bass with samphire and crayfish butter sauce. The bargain OAP weekday lunch is popular.

Open all wk 11.30-3 6-11 (Sat-Sun 11.30-11) Closed: 25-26 Dec **Bar Meals** L served Mon-Sat 12-2 D served all wk 6-9 Av main course £13 **Restaurant** L served all wk 12-2 D served all wk 6-9 Av 3 course à la carte fr £28

⊕ FREE HOUSE ◀ Sharp's Doom Bar, Dorset Piddle, Exmoor Ale, Otter Ale Ö Thatchers Gold, Westons Old Rosie & 1st Quality, Dorset Nectar. ⬙ 12 **Facilities** Non-diners area ♣ (Bar Garden) ♦♦ Children's menu Children's portions Garden ⊟ Cider festival Parking Wi-fi ▥ (notice required)

The Chetnole Inn

DT9 6NU ☎ **01935 872337**
e-mail: enquiries@thechetnoleinn.co.uk
dir: A37 from Dorchester towards Yeovil. Left at Chetnole sign

Tranquil village pub with garden overlooking fields

Bright, airy and hung with hop-bines, the interior of snug, bar and restaurant melds well into this flagstone-floored old village-centre inn opposite a pretty church deep in Thomas Hardy country. Plenty of walks thread their way through the rich countryside; it's handy, too, for the historic town of Sherbourne. West Country meats and Bridport-landed seafood fill the British menu. Choose perhaps one of the chef's pies or roast fillet of cod with Puy lentils and bacon and enjoy at a table in the tree-shaded garden, home to the pub's two giant rabbits. Butcombe beers may feature; there's a regular beer festival here.

Open 12-3 6.30-close Closed: Sun eve & Mon (Sep-Apr) **Bar Meals** L served all wk 12-2 D served Mon-Sat 6.30-9 **Restaurant** L served all wk 12-2 D served Mon-Sat 6.30-9 ⊕ FREE HOUSE ◀ Sharp's Doom Bar, Otter Ale, Butcombe Ö Thatchers. ⬙ 12 **Facilities** Non-diners area ♣ (Bar Garden) ♦♦ Children's menu Children's portions Play area Garden ⊟ Beer festival Parking Wi-fi ▥ (notice required)

The Anchor Inn

Seatown DT6 6JU ☎ **01297 489215**
dir: On A35 turn S in Chideock opposite church & follow single track road for 0.75m to beach

Set in a little cove beneath Golden Cap

A former smugglers' haunt, The Anchor enjoys an incredible setting in a cove surrounded by National Trust land. The large sun terrace and cliffside beer garden overlooking the beach make it a premier destination for throngs of holidaymakers in the summer, while on winter weekdays it is blissfully quiet. The menu starts with snacks and light lunches – three types of ploughman's, salads and a range of sandwiches and baguettes might take your fancy. For something more substantial choose beer-battered catch of the day, bangers and mash, or butternut squash and aubergine curry accompanied with one of the Palmers real ales.

Open all wk 11.30-10.30 **Bar Meals** L served all wk 12-9 D served all wk 12-9 food served all day **Restaurant** food served all day ⊕ PALMERS ◀ 200, Best Bitter, Copper Ale Ö Thatchers Gold. **Facilities** Non-diners area ♣ (Bar Restaurant Garden) ♦♦ Children's menu Children's portions Family room Garden ⊟ Parking

PICK OF THE PUBS

The Cock & Bottle

EAST MORDEN Map 4 SY99

BH20 7DL ☎ **01929 459238**
e-mail: cockandbottle@btconnect.com
web: www.cockandbottlemorden.co.uk
dir: *From A35 W of Poole right onto
B3075, pub 0.5m on left*

Local beer and a menu to suit all

Parts of this old Dorset longhouse were built about 400 years ago; the pub was originally cob-walled and, though it was sheathed in brick some time around 1800, it retained its thatched roof until the mid-60s. Today, the unspoilt interiors with their low-beamed ceilings and a wealth of nooks and crannies are redolent of a bygone age. The lively locals' bar is simply furnished and comfortably rustic, with a large wooden settle on which to while away a winter's evening with a game of dominoes beside the cosy log fire. The fine range of real ales from the nearby Hall & Woodhouse brewery is also available in the lounge bar, and a modern restaurant at the back completes the picture. Fresh game and fish feature strongly on the ever-changing menu, which ranges from light lunches, bar meals and Sunday roasts to pub favourites like steak-and-kidney pudding or lamb shank. The carte menu choices might include a starter of local dressed crab, or deep-

fried brie wedges with a Cumberland sauce. Moving on, rabbit pie with root vegetable and mushroom sauce; and grilled wild sea bass with crushed new potatoes, rocket and horseradish crème fraîche are typical main course options. Home-made desserts like orange and spiced rum crème brûlée; or dark and white chocolate terrine with a fruit coulis make a fitting finale to the meal. Lovely pastoral views over the surrounding farmland include the pub's paddock, which occasionally hosts vintage car and motorcycle meetings during the summer. Well-behaved dogs are welcome. Booking for meals may be required.

Open all wk 11.30-2.30 6-11 (Sun 12-3 7-10.30) **Bar Meals** L served all wk 12-2 D served Mon-Sat 6-9, Sun 7-9 **Restaurant** L served all wk 12-2 D served Mon-Sat 6-9, Sun 7-9 ⊕ HALL & WOODHOUSE ◼ Badger Dorset Best & Tanglefoot, Guest ale. **Facilities** Non-diners area ❤🛉 Children's menu Children's portions Play area Garden ⊓ Parking 🚍

Save on hotels. Book at **theAA.com/hotel**

DORSET 151 **ENGLAND**

CHRISTCHURCH   Map 5 SZ19

The Ship In Distress

66 Stanpit BH23 3NA ☎ 01202 485123
e-mail: shipindistress@rocketmail.com
dir: *Telephone for directions*

Community pub with lots of seafood

The seafood menu at this 300-year-old smugglers' pub reflects the closeness of Mudeford Quay and the English Channel. Nautical memorabilia is everywhere, so bag a seat by the woodburner with a pint of Ringwood Best Bitter or Fortyniner and traditional fish and chips or cottage pie; alternatively, head into the restaurant for salmon and scallion fishcake; fruits de mer; locally caught lobster; or whole Dorset crab. The full carte, including steaks, is on the blackboard. In summer enjoy the Shellfish Bar on the suntrap terrace.

Open all day all wk 11am-mdnt (Sun 11-11) **Bar Meals** L served Mon-Fri 12-2, Sat-Sun 12-2.30 D served Sun-Thu 6.30-9, Fri-Sat 6.30-9.30 **Restaurant** L served Mon-Fri 12-2, Sat-Sun 12-2.30 D served Sun-Thu 6.30-9, Fri-Sat 6.30-9.30 ⊕ PUNCH TAVERNS ◀ Dartmoor Jail Ale, Dorset Jurassic, St Austell Tribute, Ringwood Best Bitter & Fortyniner, Adnams Broadside, Guest ales ♻ Westons Stowford Press. **Facilities** Non-diners area ♣ (Bar Garden) ♦♦ Children's menu Children's portions Garden ⌁ Parking Wi-fi ▭ (notice required)

CHURCH KNOWLE   Map 4 SY98

The New Inn

BH20 5NQ ☎ 01929 480357
e-mail: maurice@newinn-churchknowle.co.uk
dir: *From Wareham take A351 towards Swanage. At Corfe Castle right for Church Knowle. Pub in village centre*

A warm welcome and now a carvery too

Landlord Maurice Estop, whose family have run this part-thatched, stone-built, 16th-century village inn for over 25 years, is only the fourth licensee in the last 150 years. Still in place are the old inglenook fireplaces and a brick alcove that used to be the kitchen oven from its days as a farmhouse. Real ales include Jurassic and changing guests, and there are draught ciders too. The new carvery is available alongside fresh home-cooked food includes catch of the day, roasts, traditional pies, sandwiches and home-made desserts. The Purbeck Lounge is tailor-made for family dining. Booking may be required for Sunday lunches and on some evenings.

Open 10-3 6-11 (10-3 5-11 summer) Closed: Mon Jan-Mar **Bar Meals** L served all wk 12-2.15 D served all wk 6-9.15 (5-9.15 summer) **Restaurant** L served all wk 12-2.15 D served all wk 6-9.15 (5-9.15 summer) ⊕ PUNCH TAVERNS ◀ Dorset Jurassic, St Austell Tribute, Guest ales ♻ Westons Old Rosie, Stowford Press & Traditional. ☗ 10 **Facilities** Non-diners area ♣ (Garden Outside area) ♦♦ Children's menu Children's portions Family room Garden Outside area ⌁ Parking Wi-fi ▭ (notice required)

CORFE CASTLE   Map 4 SY98

The Greyhound Inn

The Square BH20 5EZ ☎ 01929 480205
e-mail: eat@greyhoundcorfe.co.uk
dir: *A35 to Dorchester, 5m, left onto A351 to Corfe Castle*

Timeless village inn below castle ruins

Time drifts gently backwards at this eye-catching old village coaching inn. Supping Purbeck cider or a Doom Bar bitter in the secluded garden, your ruminations are interrupted by trains on the nearby heritage line, steam from which drifts through the commanding castle ruins above. A June medieval beer festival continues the theme, adding to annual seafood and sausage festivals. The menu is similarly comforting; with locally sourced ingredients to the fore in home-made dishes like braised belly pork spiced red cabbage in cider and sage gravy, or a light starter of pheasant cake with sweet chilli jam.

Open all day all wk 11am-1am **Bar Meals** Av main course £10 food served all day **Restaurant** Fixed menu price fr £18 Av 3 course à la carte fr £14 food served all day ⊕ ENTERPRISE INNS ◀ Sharp's Doom Bar, Hop Back Summer Lightning, Timothy Taylor Landlord, Guest ale ♻ Westons Stowford Press & Wyld Wood Organic Vintage, Thatchers, Purbeck Joe's. ☗ 9 **Facilities** Non-diners area ♣ (Bar Restaurant Garden) ♦♦ Children's menu Children's portions Play area Family room Garden ⌁ Beer festival Wi-fi ▭ (notice required)

CRANBORNE   Map 5 SU01

The Inn at Cranborne ★★★★ INN NEW

5 Wimborne St BH21 5PP ☎ 01725 551249
e-mail: info@theinnatcranborne.co.uk
dir: *On B3078 between Fordingbridge & Wimborne Minster*

Hearty food and Dorset ales in a delightful village

Jane Gould searched long and hard for somewhere to turn into her vision of a traditional English country pub. Since finding this 17th-century inn, she has skilfully transformed it into a must-visit destination in Cranborne Chase, nearly 400 square miles of rolling chalk downland. The inn's own Fleur Ale, brewed specially by Hall & Woodhouse, shares bar space with Dorset and Somerset ciders. Choose a table near one of the wood-burning stoves for something hearty from the daily-changing menu, such as grilled sea bass fillet; rump of local lamb; or a special, like sun-blushed tomato and rocket risotto.

Open all day Closed: Mon (bar & rest) **Bar Meals** L served Tue-Fri 12-2, Sat 12-2.30, Sun 12-4 D served Tue-Thu 6-9, Fri-Sat 6-9.30 Av main course £13.95 **Restaurant** L served Tue-Fri 12-2, Sat 12-2.30, Sun 12-4 D served Tue-Thu 6-9, Fri-Sat 6-9.30 Fixed menu price fr £19.95 Av 3 course à la carte fr £25 ⊕ HALL & WOODHOUSE ◀ Badger First Gold, The Fleur ♻ Westons Stowford Press, Badger Pearwood & Applewood. ☗ 10 **Facilities** Non-diners area ♦♦ Children's portions Garden ⌁ Parking Wi-fi ▭ (notice required) **Rooms** 8

EAST MORDEN   Map 4 SY99

The Cock & Bottle

PICK OF THE PUBS

See Pick of the Pubs on opposite page

EVERSHOT   Map 4 ST50

The Acorn Inn ★★★★ INN ◉

PICK OF THE PUBS

See Pick of the Pubs on page 153
See advert on page 152

FARNHAM   Map 4 ST91

The Museum Inn

PICK OF THE PUBS

DT11 8DE ☎ 01725 516261
e-mail: enquiries@museuminn.co.uk
dir: *From Salisbury take A354 to Blandford Forum, 12m. Farnham signed on right. Pub in village centre*

A great mix of tip-top ales and quality food

This part-thatched country pub lies in Cranborne Chase, where kings used to hunt, and where, in the 19th-century, General Augustus Pitt Rivers pioneered modern archaeological fieldwork. He built the inn for visitors to a small museum, now gone, where he displayed his finds. The interior features the original inglenook fireplace, flagstone floors, a fashionable mismatch of furniture and a book-filled sitting room for relaxing with a pint of London Pride or 6D Best. New landlord Gary Brewer took over in autumn 2012 and is passionate about his ales, while head chef Jenny Jones provides dishes created with quality seasonal ingredients, many sourced from local estates and farms. If shepherd's pie or beer-battered fish doesn't take your fancy, begin with Loch Duart salmon mousse, continue with slow-roasted pork belly and grainy mustard mash, and finish with rhubarb crumble served with crème anglaise. Local game often features on the specials board.

Open all day all wk **Bar Meals** L served Mon-Fri 12-2, Sat 12-2.30, Sun 12-3 D served all wk 7-9.30 **Restaurant** L served Sun 12-3 D served Fri-Sat 7-9.30 ⊕ FREE HOUSE ◀ Sixpenny 6D Best, Fuller's London Pride, Guest ale ♻ The Orchard Pig. ☗ 12 **Facilities** Non-diners area ♣ (Bar Restaurant Garden) ♦♦ Children's menu Children's portions Garden ⌁ Parking Wi-fi ▭ (notice required)

FERNDOWN
Map 5 SU00

The Kings Arms NEW

77 Ringwood Rd, Longham BH22 9AA ☎ **01202 577490**
e-mail: thekingsarmslongham@yahoo.co.uk
dir: *On A348*

Free house with an increasingly popular restaurant

All too seldom do closed-down pubs reopen, but this one did and, having done so, quickly became a resounding success. Locally, it's known for its British classics, especially steaks and other locally sourced pub food prepared by chef Mark Miller, a veteran of over 25 years with plenty of silverware in his cabinet. From his main menu come pan-fried calves' liver; chicken Boursin; bouillabaisse; and spinach and ricotta tortellini, while among his specials are medallions of beef fillet; duo of pork; and pan-fried sea bass. The bar usually keeps up to six real ales.

Open all day all wk **Bar Meals** L served Mon-Sat 11.30-9, Sun 12-9 D served Mon-Sat 11.30-9, Sun 12-9 Av main course £9.95-£13.95 food served all day **Restaurant** Fixed menu price fr £10.95 Av 3 course à la carte fr £25 food served all day ⊕ FREE HOUSE ◀ Ringwood, Butcombe, Otter, Fuller's ♻ Westons Stowford Press. ♟ 14 **Facilities** ❄ (Bar Outside area) ♦♦ Children's menu Children's portions Outside area �🏠 Parking Wi-fi ☜

FONTMELL MAGNA
Map 4 ST81

The Fontmell NEW

SP7 0PA ☎ **01747 811441**
e-mail: info@thefontmell.com
dir: *Halfway between Shaftesbury & Blandford Forum, on A350*

Smartly refurbished inn with seasonally inspired menus

On the A350, between Shaftesbury and Blandford Forum, is the former Crown pub and adjoining long-closed

brewery, where the eponymous metal beer bottle cap was invented. Its well-stocked bar sells Orchard Pig cider and local real ales such as Mallyshag – it's what they call a caterpillar on the Isle of Wight. Featuring on chef/patron Tom Shaw's frequently changing menu might be crab and Armagnac soup; seafood tapas; duo of lamb; and tandoori-style monkfish and tiger prawn curry. His Ladies at Lunch menu includes lighter options and salads. Film-shows take place most Sunday evenings in the dining room.

Open all day all wk **Bar Meals** L served all wk 12-2.30 D served all wk 6-9 Av main course £15 **Restaurant** L served all wk 12-2.30 D served all wk 6-9 Fixed menu price fr £15.50 Av 3 course à la carte fr £30 ⊕ FREE HOUSE ◀ Keystone Mallyshag, Seasonal ale ♻ The Orchard Pig. ♟ 13 **Facilities** Non-diners area ❄ (Bar Garden) ♦♦ Children's menu Children's portions Garden �🏠 Parking Wi-fi

GILLINGHAM
Map 4 ST82

The Kings Arms Inn

East Stour Common SP8 5NB ☎ **01747 838325**
e-mail: nrosscampbell@aol.com
dir: *4m W of Shaftesbury on A30*

Family-run pub with a Scottish flavour

Scottish touches – paintings by artist Mavis Makie, quotes by Robert Burns, the presence of haggis, skirlie and cranachan on the menus, and a wide choice of single malts – reflect the origin of this inn's landlord and landlady. A 200-year-old, family-run village free house where Victorian fireplaces sit comfortably alongside modern wooden furniture and subtly coloured fabrics, it offers an extensive choice of dishes ranging from hand-rolled shredded duck leg and red pepper spring rolls with plum sauce to slow roast belly pork on bubble-and-squeak with black pudding, cider sauce, apple fritter and crackling. Doom Bar, Tribute and Greene King IPA are on tap.

Open all wk 12-3 5.30-11.30 (Sat-Sun 12-12) **Bar Meals** L served Mon-Sat 12-2.30, Sun 12-9.15 D served Mon-Sat 5.30-9.15, Sun 12-9.15 **Restaurant** L served Mon-Sat 12-2.30, Sun 12-9.15 D served Mon-Sat 5.30-9.15, Sun 12-9.15 ⊕ FREE HOUSE ◀ Sharp's Doom Bar, Greene King IPA, St Austell Tribute. ♟ **Facilities** Non-diners area ❄ (Bar Garden) ♦♦ Children's menu Children's portions Family room Garden �🏠 Parking Wi-fi ☜ (notice required)

GUSSAGE ALL SAINTS
Map 4 SU01

The Drovers Inn

BH21 5ET ☎ **01258 840084**
dir: *A31 Ashley Heath rdbt, right onto B3081 follow signs*

A warm welcome, real ale and home-cooked food

A rural 16th-century pub with a fine terrace and wonderful views from the garden, so it's something of a surprise to know it was rescued from closure in 2000. The interior retains plenty of traditional appeal with flagstone floors and oak furniture. Landlord Jason is proud of the welcome he provides – ensuring, for example, that drinkers are never moved from tables to accommodate diners. Ales from Ringwood include seasonal guests, and the menu features carefully chosen rare-breed meats, vegetables from New Covent Garden via a local supplier, and fresh seafood from Poole.

Open all wk 12-3 6-12 (Sat-Sun & BH all day) Closed: 26 Dec ⊕ RINGWOOD BREWERY ◀ Best Bitter, Old Thumper, Fortyniner & Seasonal ales, Guest ales ♻ Thatchers Gold & Traditional. **Facilities** ❄ (Bar Restaurant Garden) ♦♦ Children's menu Children's portions Garden Parking Wi-fi

Save on hotels. Book at **theAA.com/hotel**

DORSET 153 **ENGLAND**

PICK OF THE PUBS

The Acorn Inn ★★★★ INN ✿

EVERSHOT | Map 4 ST50

DT2 0JW ☎ 01935 83228
e-mail: stay@acorn-inn.co.uk
web: www.acorn-inn.co.uk
dir: *From A37 between Yeovil & Dorchester, follow Evershot & Holywell signs, 0.5m to inn*

An excellent base for exploring Hardy Country

With window boxes and an unusual porch, this pretty 16th-century inn is attractively set at the heart of a quaint, historic village next to the church. Surrounded by unspoilt rolling countryside, the traditional Acorn was the model for Thomas Hardy's 'Sow and Acorn' in *Tess of the d'Urbervilles*, and it is believed that the infamous Judge Jeffreys used one of the rooms as a court. Oak-panelled bars with flagstone floors and blazing log fires in carved Hamstone fireplaces and elegantly decorated dining areas adorned with paintings offer a relaxed and civilised atmosphere for savouring some imaginative food. Proud of its sustainability and focus on using local, seasonal produce, the restaurant's modern British repertoire takes in confit leg of Gressingham duck with vanilla mash, seasonal vegetables and a red wine jus; and oven-baked aubergine parmigiana topped with grated parmesan and served on a tossed salad. The lunch and bar menus offer lighter

options, including sandwiches, twice-baked Somerset cheddar soufflé, deep-fried whitebait, ploughman's and traditional bar meals like venison sausages and beer-battered fish. Those with a sweet tooth should leave room for warm treacle tart or a selection of local cheeses. To drink, there's Otter and Doom Bar on tap, 11 wines by the glass and 100 malt whiskies. The pub also features a lovely old skittle alley and beer garden. The Acorn is handy for exploring the beautiful Dorset coastline, and many of the comfortable bedrooms, named after places in Hardy's novels, boast four-poster beds. There are some wonderful walks from the front door so don't forget to pack your boots.

Open all day all wk 11am-11.30pm

Bar Meals L served all wk 12-2 D served all wk 7-9 Av main course £12.95 **Restaurant** L served all wk 12-2 D served all wk 7-9 Av 3 course à la carte fr £30 ⊞ FREE HOUSE ◀ Sharp's Doom Bar, Otter ♂ Thatchers Gold & Traditional. ♉ 11 **Facilities** Non-diners area ✿ (Bar Garden) ♐ Children's portions Family room Garden ☎ Parking Wi-fi 🚌 (notice required) **Rooms** 10

KING'S STAG — Map 4 ST71

The Greenman

DT10 2AY ☎ 01258 817338
dir: *E of Sherborne on A3030*

Country pub known for its Sunday roasts

Legend has it that King's Stag in the Blackmore Vale owes its name to Henry III's favourite white hart, hunted down and killed by a local nobleman. Built around 1775 and full of oak beams, the pub has five separate dining areas where you can order anything from a snack to a banquet. The Sunday carvery offers a choice of five meats and eight vegetables – booking is essential. Children will enjoy the play area while parents can relax and enjoy a drink.

Open all wk 11-3 5.30-11 ⊕ ENTERPRISE INNS ◀ 2 Guest ales. **Facilities** ❤ (Bar Garden) ◀ Play area Family room Garden Parking

LODERS — Map 4 SY49

Loders Arms

DT6 3SA ☎ 01308 422431
dir: *Off A3066, 2m NE of Bridport*

Perfect stop for Dorset coast walkers

Tucked away in a pretty village near the Dorset coast, this 17th-century, creeper-covered local has a patio and garden with lovely views over Boarsbarrow Hill. Child-and dog-friendly, it also boasts a long cosy bar with warming winter fires or in the homely dining room, where there is a focus on local sourcing on the broad menu. A starter of smoked haddock chowder might be followed by a trio of local venison sausages on mustard mash or home-made fish pie. Children and vegetarians get their own menus.

Open all wk **Bar Meals** L served all wk 12-2 D served all wk 6.30-9 **Restaurant** L served all wk 12-2 D served all wk 6.30-9 ⊕ PALMERS ◀ Copper Ale, Best Bitter, 200 ♻ Thatchers Gold. **Facilities** Non-diners area ❤ (Bar Restaurant Garden) ◀ Children's menu Children's portions Garden ⋈ Parking Wi-fi

LOWER ANSTY — Map 4 ST70

The Fox Inn

DT2 7PN ☎ 01258 880328
e-mail: fox@anstyfoxinn.co.uk
dir: *A35 from Dorchester towards Poole for 4m, exit signed Piddlehinton/Athelhampton House, left to Cheselbourne, then right. Pub in village opposite post office*

Refurbished pub with extensive garden and patio area

Built more than 250 years ago, The Fox Inn was once the home of Charles Hall, who went on to co-found the Hall & Woodhouse Brewery. After the pub was refurbished the main restaurant was augmented by a light and airy garden eatery. Badger beers are, naturally enough, served in the bar. Change of hands in May 2013.

Open all day all wk ⊕ HALL & WOODHOUSE ◀ Badger Tanglefoot, Dorset Best, Seasonal ale. **Facilities** ◀ Children's menu Children's portions Garden Parking Wi-fi **Rooms** 11

LYME REGIS — Map 4 SY39

The Mariners ★★★★ INN ◉

Silver St DT7 3HS ☎ 01297 442753
e-mail: enquiries@hotellymeregis.co.uk
dir: *A35 onto B3165 (Lyme Rd). Mariners is pink building opposite road to The Cobb (Pound Rd)*

Try the local seafood specials

Once a coaching inn in the 17th-century, this restored property in the heart of the town is steeped in Lyme's fossil history, having once been home to the Philpot sisters, famed as collectors in the early 19th century. Beatrix Potter is said to have stayed here too, reputedly writing *The Tale of Little Pig Robinson* – The Mariners is pictured in the book. The building combines traditional character with modern style. Simple menus feature the best of local seafood and other quality ingredients in dishes such as slow roasted Dorset belly pork with apple purée and curly kale, and cappuccino mousse. Only bottled beers are available.

Open all day all wk **Bar Meals** L served all wk 12-2 D served all wk 6.30-9 **Restaurant** L served all wk 12-2 D served all wk 6.30-9 ⊕ FREE HOUSE ◀ Otter Bright, Mighty Hop Mighty Red IPA & Mariners Ale ♻ Thatchers Gold. ♇ 9 **Facilities** Non-diners area ❤ (Bar Garden) ◀ Children's menu Children's portions Garden ⋈ Parking Wi-fi ⛟ **Rooms** 14

Pilot Boat Inn

Bridge St DT7 3QA ☎ 01297 443157
dir: *Telephone for directions*

Centrally located seaside pub

Old smuggling and sea rescue tales are associated with this busy town-centre pub, close to the seafront. Along with Palmers ales, there is a good range of food on regularly changing menus. Traditional recipes using local ingredients include steak-and-kidney pie and Dorset chicken in a cider and apple sauce. Sandwiches, salads and cold platters are also offered, plus local crab, real scampi and chips, and other fresh fish from Lyme Bay as available. There are always good vegetarian options, such as three bean casserole, and butternut squash and goats' cheese lasagne.

Open all day all wk Closed: 25 Dec ⊕ PALMERS ◀ Best Bitter, 200, Bridport Bitter. **Facilities** ❤ (Bar Restaurant Garden) ◀ Children's menu Children's portions Garden

MILTON ABBAS — Map 4 ST80

The Hambro Arms

DT11 0BP ☎ 01258 880233
e-mail: info@hambroarms.co.uk
dir: *From A354 (Dorchester to Blandford road), exit at Milborne St Andrew to Milton Abbas*

Community-owned pub in a unique village setting

Picture-perfect Milton Abbas village was built in 1780, replacing a nearby medieval village which offended the privacy-seeking landowner the Earl of Dorchester, who had it demolished. The charming Hambro Arms was part of the package and thrives in its role at the heart of the community, which nowadays owns the long, thatched, whitewashed pub. Beers from Ringwood and a variety of guest breweries lead the wet-trade, whilst chef Fred Gallo caters for the inner-man with pub classics like faggots and mash or modern dishes such as truffle and walnut risotto. There's a beer festival each July.

Open all wk 11.30-3 6-11 (Sat-Sun 11.30-11.30) **Bar Meals** L served Mon-Fri 12-2.30, Sat-Sun 12-3 D served Mon-Thu 6-9, Fri-Sat 6-9.30 Av main course £10-£15 **Restaurant** L served Mon-Fri 12-2.30, Sat-Sun 12-3 D served Mon-Thu 6-9, Fri-Sat 6-9.30 ⊕ FREE HOUSE ◀ Sharp's Doom Bar, Ringwood, Guest ales ♻ Westons Stowford Press. ♇ 8 **Facilities** Non-diners area ◀ Children's menu Garden ⋈ Beer festival Parking Wi-fi ⛟

MOTCOMBE — Map 4 ST82

The Coppleridge Inn ★★★ INN

SP7 9HW ☎ 01747 851980
e-mail: thecoppleridgeinn@btinternet.com
web: www.coppleridge.com
dir: *Take A350 towards Warminster for 1.5m, turn left at brown tourist sign. Follow signs to inn*

Former farm in beautiful surroundings

Chris and Di Goodinge took over this 18th-century farmhouse and farm almost 25 years ago and converted it into the pub you see today. As well as retaining the flagstone floors and log fires, the Goodinge's have kept the farm's 15 acres of meadow and woodland, where they raise their own cattle. The bar offers a wide range of real ales, as well as constantly changing old favourites and specials like sweet potato fritter with mango chutney, roasted honey-glazed ham, chicken supreme, and pork and lemongrass burger. Ten spacious bedrooms are situated around a converted courtyard and there is a secure children's playground.

Open all wk 11-3 5-11 (Sat 11am-mdnt Sun 12-11) **Bar Meals** L served all wk 12-2.30 D served all wk 6-9 Av main course £11.50 **Restaurant** L served all wk 12-2.30 D served all wk 6-9 Av 3 course à la carte fr £22.45 ⊕ FREE HOUSE ⬛ Butcombe Bitter, Wadworth 6X, Fuller's London Pride, Sharp's Doom Bar, Ringwood Best Bitter ♙ Ashton Press. ♟ 10 **Facilities** Non-diners area ✿ (Bar Garden) ♙♦ Children's menu Children's portions Play area Family room Garden ♒ Parking Wi-fi 🚌 (notice required) **Rooms** 10

NETTLECOMBE   Map 4 SY59

Marquis of Lorne

DT6 3SY ☎ 01308 485236
e-mail: info@themarquisoflorne.co.uk
dir: From A3066 (Bridport-Beaminster road) approx 1.5m N of Bridport follow Loders & Mangerton Mill signs. At junct left past Mangerton Mill, through West Milton. 1m to T-junct, straight over. Pub up hill, approx 300yds on left

Recommended for its interesting menus

In a picturesque hamlet and close to the market town of Bridport, The Marquis of Lorne is surrounded by beautiful views. Built as a farmhouse in the 16th century and converted into a pub in 1871, it is now run by Steve and Tracey Brady. They have renewed the focus on local produce throughout the menus, and locally brewed Palmers ales are on tap. Crab with pink grapefruit and a green apple salad makes an interesting starter, while international influences are at play in a main course of sticky beef with Indonesian-style salad. Look out for special dinner evenings. The attractive gardens are family friendly, too.

Open all wk 12-2.30 6-11 **Bar Meals** L served all wk 12-2 D served all wk 6-9 **Restaurant** L served all wk 12-2 D served all wk 6-9 ⊕ PALMERS ⬛ Copper Ale, Best Bitter, 200. **Facilities** Non-diners area ✿ (Bar Garden) ♙♦ Children's menu Children's portions Play area Garden ♒ Parking Wi-fi 🚌 (notice required)

NORTH WOOTTON   Map 4 ST61

The Three Elms

DT9 5JW ☎ 01935 812881
dir: From Sherborne take A352 towards Dorchester then A3030. Pub 1m on right

Village store, post office...and pub

Incorporating a shop and post office, this family-friendly pub near the beautiful Blackmore Vale has become the heart of the community. The bar is well stocked with weekly changing guest real ales and ciders, and freshly cooked pub classics served at candlelit tables include West Country mixed grill, chilli con carne, and spinach and ricotta cannelloni. Among the 'two for £10' deals are chicken, beef and veggie burgers, fishcakes and lasagne. Takeaways are available, too. The large beer garden hosts summer barbecues and beer festivals.

Open all day all wk 11-11 (Sun 12-10.30) Closed: 26 Dec **Bar Meals** L served Mon-Sat 12-2.30, Sun 12-3 D served Mon-Sat 6-9.30, Sun 6-9 **Restaurant** L served Mon-Sat 12-2.30, Sun 12-3 D served Mon-Sat 6-9.30, Sun 6-9 ⊕ FREE HOUSE ⬛ St Austell Tribute, Guest ale ♙ Thatchers & Gold, St Austell Copper Press. **Facilities** Non-diners area ✿ (Bar Restaurant Garden) ♙♦ Children's menu Children's portions Play area Garden ♒ Beer festival Parking Wi-fi 🚌

OSMINGTON MILLS   Map 4 SY78

The Smugglers Inn

DT3 6HF ☎ 01305 833125
e-mail: smugglersinn.weymouth@hall-woodhouse.co.uk
dir: 7m E of Weymouth towards Wareham, pub signed

Coastal inn with an interesting past

Set on the cliffs at Osmington Mills with the South Coast Footpath running through the garden, the inn has beautiful views across Weymouth Bay. In the late 18th century (the inn dates back to the 13th century) it was the base of infamous smuggler Pierre La Tour who fell in love with the publican's daughter, Arabella Carless, who was shot dead while helping him to escape during a raid. Things are quieter now and you can enjoy a pint of Tanglefoot or one of the guest ales like Pickled Partridge. On the menu typical dishes are smoked haddock Benedict; venison sausages and mash; and steak and Tanglefoot pie.

Open all wk 11-11 (Sun 12-10.30) **Bar Meals** L served Mon-Sat 12-9.30, Sun 12-9 D served Mon-Sat 12-9.30, Sun 12-9 food served all day **Restaurant** L served Mon-Sat 12-9.30, Sun 12-9 D served Mon-Sat 12-9.30, Sun 12-9 food served all day ⊕ HALL & WOODHOUSE ⬛ Badger Tanglefoot, Guest ale. **Facilities** Non-diners area ✿ (Bar Restaurant Garden) ♙♦ Children's menu Children's portions Play area Garden ♒ Parking 🚌

PIDDLEHINTON   Map 4 SY79

The Thimble Inn

DT2 7TD ☎ 01300 348270
e-mail: thethimbleinn@gmail.com
dir: A35 W'bound, right onto B3143, Piddlehinton in 4m

Thatched inn by the river

This friendly village local with open fires, traditional pub games and good food cooked to order was taken over by new landlord Stuart Payne and landlady Heather Solonya in early 2012. The pub stands in a pretty valley on the banks of the River Piddle, and the riverside patio is popular in summer. Along with Palmers beers on tap, dishes from the menu range from Dorset brown crab fishcakes with lime and sweet chilli sauce as a starter, to Honeybrook pork and leek sausages with onion gravy and mash.

Open 11.30-2.30 6-11 Closed: Mon **Bar Meals** L served Tue-Sun 11.30-2 D served Tue-Sun 6.30-9 **Restaurant** L served Tue-Sun 11.30-2 D served Tue-Sun 6.30-9 ⊕ PALMERS ⬛ Copper Ale, Best Bitter, 200 ♙ Thatchers

Gold. **Facilities** Non-diners area ✿ (Bar Restaurant Garden) ♙♦ Children's menu Children's portions Garden ♒ Parking Wi-fi 🚌

PIDDLETRENTHIDE   Map 4 SY79

The Piddle Inn

DT2 7QF ☎ 01300 348468
e-mail: piddleinn@aol.com
dir: 7m N of Dorchester on B3143, in village centre

Delightful village inn with riverside patio area

Ramblers and visitors exploring the Dorset Area of Outstanding Natural Beauty just north of historic Dorchester can enjoy good food and local ales at The Piddle Inn. This idyllic, partly creeper-clad village inn is secluded in the valley of the eponymous chalk stream that courses behind the pub. Relax with gravity-dispensed beers from Dorset Piddle Brewery and indulge in meals created from the best local produce.

Open all wk 12-11.30 **Bar Meals** L served Mon-Sat 12-2, Sun 12-3 D served all wk 6-9.30 Av main course £8 **Restaurant** L served Mon-Sat 12-2, Sun 12-3 D served all wk 6-9.30 ⊕ FREE HOUSE ⬛ St Austell Tribute, Sharp's Doom Bar, Greene King, Dorset Piddle ♙ Thatchers Gold, Westons Stowford Press. **Facilities** Non-diners area ✿ (Bar Garden) ♙♦ Children's menu Children's portions Garden ♒ Parking Wi-fi 🚌 (notice required)

The Poachers Inn

DT2 7QX ☎ 01300 348358
e-mail: info@thepoachersinn.co.uk
dir: 6m N from Dorchester on B3143. At church end of village

Good range of food and garden with swimming pool

Located in the pretty little village of Piddletrenthide in the heart of Thomas Hardy country, this 17th-century riverside pub is perfectly situated for exploring west Dorset and the Jurassic Coast. The kitchen makes good use of Dorset suppliers to create both classic pub meals (scampi, pie of the day, gourmet burger, lamb cutlets) and contemporary alternatives (butternut squash and Mediterranean vegetable risotto) for the extensive menu. Relax with a glass of Butcombe Bitter in the beer garden, which even has a heated swimming pool to enjoy throughout the summer. Details of three circular walks are available at the bar.

Open all day all wk 8am-mdnt **Bar Meals** L served all wk 12-2.30 D served all wk 6-9.30 **Restaurant** L served all wk 12-2.30 D served all wk 6-9.30 ⊕ FREE HOUSE ⬛ Sharp's Doom Bar, St Austell Tribute, Butcombe Bitter ♙ Thatchers Gold. ♟ 9 **Facilities** Non-diners area ✿ (Bar Garden) ♙♦ Children's menu Children's portions Garden ♒ Parking Wi-fi 🚌 (notice required)

PLUSH
Map 4 ST70

The Brace of Pheasants ★★★★ INN

DT2 7RQ ☎ 01300 348357
e-mail: info@braceofpheasants.co.uk
dir: *A35 onto B3143, 5m to Piddletrenthide, then right to Mappowder & Plush*

Village inn popular with walkers

Tucked away in a fold of the hills in the heart of Hardy's beloved county, this pretty 16th-century thatched village inn is an ideal place to start or end a walk. With its welcoming open fire, oak beams and fresh flowers, it is the perfect setting to enjoy a selection of real ales and ciders and 18 wines by the glass. Food options might include pan-fried lamb's kidneys with mustard cream sauce or local venison steak with red wine reduction. The inn offers eight en suite bedrooms, four above the pub and four in the old skittle alley.

Open all wk 12-3 7-11 Closed: 25 Dec **Bar Meals** L served all wk 12-2.30 D served all wk 7-9 **Restaurant** L served all wk 12-2.30 D served all wk 7-9 ⊕ FREE HOUSE ◀ Sharp's Doom Bar, Flack Manor Flack's Double Drop, Palmers, Sunny Republic Ö Westons Traditional, Purbeck Dorset Draft, Cider by Rosie. ☗ 18
Facilities Non-diners area ❤ (Bar Restaurant Garden) ⦁ Children's portions Garden ♫ Parking Wi-fi 🚐 (notice required) **Rooms** 8

POOLE
Map 4 SZ09

The Guildhall Tavern

15 Market St BH15 1NB ☎ 01202 671717
e-mail: sewerynsevfred@aol.com
dir: *Near the Quay (multi-storey parking nearby)*

French-style seafood in a former cider house

In the heart of Poole's old town and just two minutes' walk from its historic quay, the Guildhall Tavern is impressively appointed without losing any of its traditional charm. The menu reflects the owners' Gallic roots and the emphasis is firmly on fresh fish and seafood, so you could start with pan-fried tiger prawns, followed by gratin de crabe (gratin of crab meat, fish flakes, mussels, prawns and cockles in a white wine sauce). Other main course options might include home-made quiche or boeuf bourguignon. There is also a set menu. French themed evenings are held monthly, with a special menu, live music and a quiz.

Open Tue-Sat Closed: 1st 2wks Nov, Mon, Sun **Bar Meals** L served Tue-Sat 11.30-3 **Restaurant** L served Tue-Sat 11.30-3 D served Tue-Sat 6-10 ⊕ FREE HOUSE ◀ Ringwood Best Bitter. ☗ 12 **Facilities** Non-diners area ⦁ Children's menu Children's portions Family room Parking Wi-fi 🚐

The Rising Sun

3 Dear Hay Ln BH15 1NZ ☎ 01202 771246
e-mail: paul@risingsunpoole.co.uk
dir: *On A350 rdbt in town centre (parking adjacent)*

Popular pub in busy town centre

This 18th-century pub just off the High Street in Poole has a warm and relaxing atmosphere, whether you are popping in for a pint of Doom Bar in the elegant lounge bar, or heading for the charming restaurants. The menus successfully combine traditional pub classics with more adventurous dishes and make sound use of fresh local ingredients. Starters might be Thai crab cakes and sweet chilli dip; or smoked mackerel with saffron new potato salad, and to follow beef Madras curry; burgers (including the vegetarian goats' cheese burger); or British shellfish linguine. Specials are chalked on the blackboards daily.

Open all day 11-11 Closed: 25-26 Dec, Sun **Bar Meals** L served Mon-Sat 12-2.30 D served Mon-Sat 6-9.30 **Restaurant** L served Mon-Sat 12-2.30 D served Mon-Sat 6-9.30 ⊕ FREE HOUSE ◀ Sharp's Doom Bar, Otter Bitter, Greene King IPA, Guest ale Ö Westons Stowford Press, Aspall. ☗ 12 **Facilities** Non-diners area Garden ♫ Wi-fi

---

POWERSTOCK
Map 4 SY59

Three Horseshoes Inn ★★★★ INN ◉

PICK OF THE PUBS

DT6 3TF ☎ 01308 485328
e-mail: threehorseshoespowerstock@live.co.uk
dir: *3m from Bridport off A3066 (Beaminster road)*

Great reputation for creative cuisine

To locals it's The Shoes, a pretty, late-Victorian inn belonging to Palmers, a part-thatched brewery in nearby Bridport. The pub patio and terraced garden look out over the village, above which rises Eggardon Iron Age hill fort. The food, accredited with one AA Rosette, owes much to a devotion to seasonal, locally sourced ingredients, some from the garden and some foraged from the surrounding hedgerows. Daily-changing menus lean towards game dishes in the winter and fresh fish in the summer, with such starters as rabbit and vegetable broth; wild boar Scotch quail egg with crispy pig's ears; and curried crab salad. This rather inventive approach continues with mains of gurnard and clam stew with chorizo and butter beans; local wood pigeon with braised lettuce, peas and bacon; and truffled risotto with cavolo nero, mushrooms, parmesan and walnut pesto. Two of the spacious en suite guest rooms look out over a valley.

Open 12-3 6.30-11.30 (Sun 12-3 6.30-10.30) Closed: Mon L **Bar Meals** L served Tue-Sat 12-2.30, Sun 12-3 D served all wk 6.30-9.30 **Restaurant** L served Tue-Sat 12-2.30, Sun 12-3 D served all wk 6.30-9.30 ⊕ PALMERS ◀ Best Bitter, Copper Ale, Tally Ho! Ö Thatchers Gold & Traditional. **Facilities** Non-diners area ❤ (Bar Garden) ⦁ Children's menu Children's portions Garden ♫ Parking Wi-fi **Rooms** 3

PUNCKNOWLE
Map 4 SY58

The Crown Inn

Church St DT2 9BN ☎ 01308 897711
e-mail: email@thecrowninndorset.co.uk
dir: *From A35, into Bride Valley, through Litton Cheney. From B3157, inland at Swyre*

Chocolate-box thatched inn

This picturesque 16th-century pub, now with a new landlord, was once the haunt of smugglers on their way from nearby Chesil Beach to visit prosperous customers in Bath. There's a traditional, welcoming atmosphere within the rambling, child- and dog-friendly bars with their log fires, comfy sofas and low beams. Home-cooked food ranges from Dorset cream teas, tapas slates, jackets and sandwiches to seasonally changing dishes like crab, coriander and chilli pancakes; honey-roast ham with bubble-and-squeak; and Mediterranean stuffed aubergine. Accompany your meal with a glass of real ale or one of the wines by the glass. The lovely garden overlooks the Bride Valley.

Open 11-3 5-11 Closed: Sun eve in winter **Bar Meals** L served Mon-Sat 12-2.30, Sun 12-5 D served Mon-Sat 6-9 Av main course £10 **Restaurant** Av 3 course à la carte fr £20 ⊕ PALMERS ◀ Best Bitter, 200, Copper Ale, Seasonal ales Ö Thatchers Gold. **Facilities** Non-diners area ❤ (Bar Restaurant Garden) ⦁ Children's menu Children's portions Garden ♫ Parking Wi-fi 🚐 (notice required)

SHAPWICK
Map 4 ST90

The Anchor Inn

West St DT11 9LB ☎ 01258 857269
e-mail: anchor@shapwick.com
dir: *From Wimborne or Blandford Forum take B3082. Pub signed*

Village-owned pub with great local food

The village owns this welcoming pub lock, stock and barrel. In 2006 it was saved from redevelopment by a group of 18 villagers who clubbed together to purchase the freehold, then bought back the lease in 2011. A family-run affair, it offers Cider by Rosie, an award-winning Dorset craft brew. Food-wise there are some surprising 'pub classics' such as pan-fried Irish white pudding with a grain mustard rarebit topping, plus à la carte options like smoked eel with horseradish cream, beetroot coulis and chive and potato salad, and salt and vinegar battered haddock with chips, tartare sauce and pea purée.

Open all day Closed: Sun eve **Bar Meals** L served Mon-Sat 12-3, Sun 12-4 D served Mon-Sat 6-9.30 Av main course £9 **Restaurant** L served Mon-Sat 12-3, Sun 12-4 D served Mon-Sat 6-9.30 Fixed menu price fr £11.50 Av 3 course à la carte fr £21 ⊕ FREE HOUSE ◀ Ringwood Best Bitter, Sharp's Doom Bar, Local guest ales Ö The Orchard Pig, Cider by Rosie, Westons Stowford Press. ☗ 20 **Facilities** Non-diners area ❤ (Bar Restaurant Garden) ⦁ Children's menu Children's portions Garden ♫ Parking Wi-fi 🚐 (notice required)

Save on hotels. Book at theAA.com/hotel

DORSET 157 ENGLAND

SHERBORNE
Map 4 ST61

The Kings Arms ★★★★★ INN

PICK OF THE PUBS

North Rd, Charlton Horethorne DT9 4NL
☎ 01963 220281
e-mail: admin@thekingsarms.co.uk
dir: On A3145, N of Sherborne. Pub in village centre

Enjoyable food in elegant gastro-pub

On the Somerset and Dorset border, three miles from the historic market towns of Sherborne and Wincanton, this elegant Edwardian building has been transformed into a chic country pub and modern restaurant with boutique-style accommodation. Locals and visitors head to the bar for the West Country ales, including Kings Arms Tipple, and for Lawrence's cider from nearby Corton Denham. A wide walkway leads past a theatre-style kitchen to the Georgian-mirrored dining room, from where doors lead to an extensive dining terrace overlooking a croquet lawn. The cooking style is both traditional and modern British, with additional influences from around the world, thus the day's lunch menu might lead to something light like a chicken Caesar salad or fish burger. Main courses, either at lunch or in the evening, might include roast rump of lamb with colcannon, roasted root vegetables and rosemary jus, or local steaks cooked on the Josper grill.

Open all day all wk **Bar Meals** L served all wk 12-2.30 D served Mon-Thu 7-9.30, Fri-Sat 7-10, Sun 7-9 **Restaurant** L served all wk 12-2.30 D served all wk Mon-Thu 7-9.30, Fri-Sat 7-10, Sun 7-9 ⊕ FREE HOUSE ◀ Kings Arms Tipple, Sharp's Doom Bar, Butcombe Ö Lawrence's. ♥ 13 **Facilities** Non-diners area ♣ (Bar Garden) ♦♦ Children's menu Children's portions Garden ♬ Parking Wi-fi ☷ (notice required) **Rooms** 10

SHROTON OR IWERNE COURTNEY
Map 4 ST81

The Cricketers

PICK OF THE PUBS

See Pick of the Pubs on page 158

STRATTON
Map 4 SY69

Saxon Arms

DT2 9WG ☎ 01305 260020
e-mail: rodsaxonlamont1@yahoo.co.uk
dir: 3m NW of Dorchester on A37. Pub between church & village hall

Thatched flint-stone pub serving good food

Popular with villagers as much as visiting fishermen, cycling clubs and ramblers, this handsome, thatched flint-stone free house is ideally situated for riverside walks. Flagstone floors, a wood-burning stove and solid oak beams create a comfortable setting for a traditional English inn that offers a friendly welcome, a range of well-kept real ales and simple, carefully cooked food. Menu choices include braised Dorset shoulder of lamb with garlic mash and redcurrant jus; pheasant breast on

red cabbage with sweet raspberry vinegar sauce; chargrilled pork tenderloin with bubble-and-squeak; and roasted butternut squash and chargrilled artichoke tagliatelle. There's also a deli counter and a selection of baguettes and jackets.

Open all wk 11-3 5.30-late (Fri-Sun 11am-late) **Bar Meals** L served Mon-Thu 11-2.15, Fri-Sat 11.30-9.30, Sun 12-9 D served Mon-Thu 6-9.15, Fri-Sat 11.30-9.30, Sun 12-9 Av main course £10.95 **Restaurant** L served Mon-Thu 11-2.15, Fri-Sat 11.30-9.30, Sun 12-9 D served Mon-Thu 6-9.15, Fri-Sat 11.30-9.30, Sun 12-9 Fixed menu price fr £10.95 Av 3 course à la carte fr £20 ⊕ FREE HOUSE ◀ Fuller's London Pride, Palmers Best Bitter, Greene King Abbot Ale & Ruddles, Otter, Ringwood, Timothy Taylor, Butcombe, Guest ales Ö Westons Stowford Press, Guest ciders. ♥ 15 **Facilities** Non-diners area ♣ (Bar Garden) ♦♦ Children's menu Children's portions Garden ♬ Parking Wi-fi ☷ (notice required)

STUDLAND
Map 5 SZ08

The Bankes Arms Hotel

Watery Ln BH19 3AU ☎ 01929 450225
dir: B3369 from Poole, take Sandbanks chain ferry, or A35 from Poole, A351 then B3351

Creeper-clad, 16th-century pub close to Studland Bay

Standing above the wide sweep of Studland Bay, this 16th-century creeper-clad inn was once a smugglers' dive. Nowadays the pub hosts an annual four-day festival in mid-August, featuring live music and some 200 beers and ciders that include award-winning ales from its own Isle of Purbeck brewery. Fresh fish and seafood salads are a speciality, but slow-braised lamb shank with rosemary mash; chilli con carne; and a daily curry are other examples from the menu.

Open all day all wk 11-11 (Sun 11-10.30) Closed: 25 Dec **Bar Meals** L served all wk 12-3 (summer & BH 12-9) D served all wk 6-9 (summer & BH 12-9) ⊕ FREE HOUSE ◀ Isle of Purbeck Fossil Fuel, Studland Bay Wrecked, Solar Power, Thermal Cheer, Harry's Harvest Ö Westons Old Rosie, Thatchers Cheddar Valley, Broadoak. **Facilities** Non-diners area ♣ (Bar Restaurant Garden) ♦♦ Children's menu Garden ♬ Beer festival Wi-fi ☷

SYDLING ST NICHOLAS
Map 4 SY69

The Greyhound Inn ★★★★ INN ◉

PICK OF THE PUBS

DT2 9PD ☎ 01300 341303
e-mail: info@dorsetgreyhound.co.uk
dir: From A37 (Yeovil to Dorchester road), exit at staggered x-rds signed Sydling St Nicholas & Cerne Abbas

Good food in the heart of Hardy country

Deep in Thomas Hardy country, this 17th-century pub is tucked away among pastel-hued flint and stone houses in a valley formed by Sydling Water. Relax in the open-plan

bar with a pint of Butcombe or a glass of draught Cornish Orchards cider. There are four areas to eat in: the bar, with its open fire; the conservatory with oak, fruitwood and scrubbed wood tables and a deep Chesterfield; the restaurant and the suntrap front terrace. The food is fresh and menus change every day. Fish, the pub's strength, is ordered the night before from the quaysides in Weymouth and Bridport, and there's usually game in season. As one of The Greyhound's partners is a vegetarian, the veggie alternatives are more imaginative than in some other places. Also on the menu could be Gressingham duck breast, dauphinoise potato, orange jus; whole gilt-head bream with Savoy cabbage and mussel broth.

Open 11-3 6-11 Closed: Sun eve **Bar Meals** L served Mon-Sat 12-2, Sun 12-2.30 D served Mon-Sat 6-9 **Restaurant** L served Mon-Sat 12-2, Sun 12-2.30 D served Mon-Sat 6-9 ⊕ FREE HOUSE ◀ St Austell Tinners Ale, Butcombe, Guest ales Ö Cornish Orchards. ♥ 12 **Facilities** Non-diners area ♣ (Bar Restaurant Garden) ♦♦ Children's menu Children's portions Play area Garden ♬ Parking Wi-fi **Rooms** 6

TARRANT MONKTON
Map 4 ST90

The Langton Arms ★★★★ INN

PICK OF THE PUBS

DT11 8RX ☎ 01258 830225
e-mail: info@thelangtonarms.co.uk
dir: A31 from Ringwood, or A357 from Shaftesbury, or A35 from Bournemouth

Thatched inn with great food and ales

Close to the village church and surrounded by countryside immortalised in Thomas Hardy's novels, this pretty 17th-century thatched inn has two bars, the Farmers and the Carpenters, both relaxing places for drinking from an ever-changing supply of outstanding real ales. The carte menu and traditional pub dishes are served in the bars, as well as in the Stables restaurant and conservatory. Expect choice West Country traditional fare made from local produce and vegetables grown in the vegetable patch: ham hock terrine with grain mustard mayonnaise; grilled rump steak with all the trimmings; and baked aubergine filled with ratatouille and topped with mozzarella are typical of the wide-ranging choices. There's also a choice of light bites and sharing platters, and a children's menu. All the comfortable and well-equipped bedrooms are on the ground floor, situated around an attractive courtyard.

Open all day all wk **Bar Meals** L served Mon-Fri 12-2.30, Sat-Sun all day D served Mon-Thu 6-9.30, Fri 6-10, Sat-Sun all day **Restaurant** L served Mon-Fri 12-2.30, Sat-Sun all day D served Mon-Thu 6-9.30, Fri 6-10, Sat-Sun all day ⊕ FREE HOUSE ◀ Local guest ales Ö Thatchers, Westons Stowford Press. **Facilities** Non-diners area ♦♦ Children's menu Children's portions Play area Family room Garden ♬ Parking Wi-fi ☷ **Rooms** 6

PICK OF THE PUBS

The Cricketers

SHROTON OR IWERNE COURTNEY | Map 4 ST81

DT11 8QD ☎ 01258 860421
e-mail: info@thecricketersshroton.co.uk
web: www.heartstoneinns.co.uk
dir: *7m S of Shaftesbury on A350, turn right after Iwerne Minster. 5m N of Blandford Forum on A360, past Stourpaine, in 2m left into Shroton*

Free house and restaurant in secluded gardens

Under Hambledon Hill, where General Wolfe trained his troops before his assault on Quebec in 1759, lies what maps show as both Iwerne Courtney and Shroton; ask locals for the latter when looking for this early 20th-century pub and you'll be pointed in the right direction. Built to replace a much earlier establishment, over the years it has become not only a real community local, but also a popular pit-stop for walkers on the Wessex Way, who, since the path passes conveniently right by, are rarely so unwise as to wander through without stopping for Joe and Sally Grieves' genuine hospitality. In the light, open-plan interior, where in winter there's a cosy log-burner, the real ales are Butcombe and Otter, while wine-drinkers will find up to 9 by the glass; there's no separate restaurant. The menu changes seasonally and makes use of locally sourced, home-cooked ingredients to offer starters such as

Lyme Bay scallops; Mediterranean meze platter; and deep-fried whitebait. Main dishes include rack of ribs with dips, skinny fries and salad; black treacle-brushed pork tenderloin with white bean mash and cider and apple sauce; and beer-battered cod and chips. For vegetarians there's Moroccan vegetable tagine; three-bean chilli; and gnocchi puttanesca. Baguettes and jacket potatoes are served at lunchtime, and on Sunday a choice of roast meats is always on offer. Specials are forever changing. Events include occasional summer barbecues and a beer festival weekend with live music. The pub is proud of its long association with the Shroton Cricket Club, from which it takes its name.

Open all wk 12-3 6-11 (Sun 12-10.30)
Bar Meals L served all wk 12-2.30 D served Mon-Thu 6.30-9, Fri-Sat 6.30-9.30 ⊕ FREE HOUSE ◀ Butcombe, Otter Bitter ♻ Westons Stowford Press. ♆ 9 **Facilities** Non-diners area ♦♦ Children's menu Children's portions Garden ⋒ Beer festival Parking Wi-fi 🚌 (notice required)

PICK OF THE PUBS

Rose & Crown Trent ★★★★★ INN

TRENT   Map 4 ST51

DT9 4SL ☎ 01935 850776
e-mail: dine@roseandcrowntrent.co.uk
web: www.roseandcrowntrent.co.uk
dir: *Just off A30 between Sherborne & Yeovil*

Innovative cooking in a timeless Dorset village inn

Located on the Ernest Cook Trust estate that surrounds Trent village, this idyllic ivy-clad 14th-century inn was revived by former landlord Buff Biggins, whose legend lives on in the pub to this day. Originally built to house builders of the Saint Andrew's church spire in this conservation village, today's structure owes more to its days as a farmhouse in the 18th century, but a few centuries aren't important when you can still enjoy the beams and flagstone floors of this Dorset gem. The lounge has a large, log-surrounded open fire and comfortable leather sofa; the main bar looks out over the fields, and from the restaurant you can survey the valley. Alternatively, the weather might be good enough to make the garden your destination. Quality local produce lies behind essentially traditional British food such as starters of slow-cooked pig's head, malt glazed jowl, rhubarb textures and pork juices; or Lyme Bay scallops with onion nuggets, cauliflower purée, pressed potato and black pudding. Follow these with risotto of

woodland mushroom, tarragon and chestnut with parmesan dumplings; or monkfish, lentil and smoked bacon ragout with spinach purée, shrimp garlic bread. Leave room for one of the innovative desserts — perhaps hazelnut cake, milk chocolate cream, Horlicks foam, lemon mascarpone, candied lemon and brandy snap. For those in search of a lighter bite at lunch, there is a ploughman's and sandwiches, as well as more traditional fish and chips; faggots with bubble-and-squeak; and beef and mushroom pie. Wadworth keeps the bar supplied with 6X and their other best-sellers, with ciders arriving from Thatchers and Westons.

Open 12-3 6-11 (Sat-Sun 12-11)
Closed: Mon **Bar Meals** L served

Tue-Sun 12-3 D served Tue-Sat 6-9
Restaurant L served Tue-Sun 12-3
D served Tue-Sat 6-9 ⊞ WADWORTH
🍺 6X, Henry's Original IPA, Horizon & Bishop's Tipple, Guest ale ♂ Westons Stowford Press, Thatchers Gold. 🍷 8
Facilities Non-diners area 🐾 👫
Children's menu Children's portions Family room Garden ⅋ Parking Wi-fi
🚌 (notice required) **Rooms** 3

TRENT
Map 4 ST51

Rose & Crown Trent ★★★★★ INN

PICK OF THE PUBS

See Pick of the Pubs on page 159

WEST BEXINGTON
Map 4 SY58

The Manor Hotel

DT2 9DF ☎ 01308 897660
e-mail: relax@manorhoteldorset.com
dir: On B3157, 5m E of Bridport. In Swyre turn opposite The Bull Inn into No Through Road

Cosy old pub overlooking Chesil Beach

Overlooking the Jurassic Coast's most famous feature, Chesil Beach, parts of this 16th-century manor house are thought to date from the 11th century. It offers an inviting mix of flagstones, Jacobean oak panelling, roaring fires and a cosy cellar bar serving Otter ales and locally sourced dishes. Eat in the Manor Restaurant or in the Cellar Bar. With a pint of Otter Ale in hand study the chalkboards displaying modern British dishes; perhaps Italian meatballs followed by a home-made fish or turkey and leek pie. The large free car park is a bonus.

Open all wk 11.30-3 6-10 Closed: 1st 2wks Jan **Bar Meals** L served all wk 12-2 D served Mon-Sat 6.30-9, Sun 6-8 **Restaurant** L served all wk 12-2 D served all wk 6-9 ⊕ FREE HOUSE ◀ Otter Ale & Bitter ♂ Thatchers Gold, Lilley's. **Facilities** Non-diners area ✿ (Bar Garden) ♦️ Children's menu Garden ⌐ Parking Wi-fi ▭ (notice required)

WEST LULWORTH
Map 4 SY88

The Castle Inn

Main Rd BH20 5RN ☎ 01929 400311
e-mail: office@lulworthinn.com
dir: Follow village signs from A352 (Dorchester to Wareham road). Inn on right on B3070 through West Lulworth. Car park opposite

Thatched free house with a wide range of ciders

In the heart of the Purbecks near Lulworth Cove, this 16th-century pub offers 13 real ciders, six regularly changing real ales and 15 single malt whiskies (complete with a booklet of tasting notes). The dog-friendly Castle is a traditional thatched inn with a wide-ranging menu of home-made dishes and daily specials. A selection includes chicken Stroganoff, chilli pasta bake, tuna steak, Dorset sausages and Mexican chip butty. Outside, you'll find large landscaped gardens packed with plants, and in summer there's a giant outdoor chess set.

Open all wk 12-2.30 7-11 Closed: 25 Dec ⊕ FREE HOUSE ◀ Sharp's, Isle of Purbeck, Dorset Piddle, Palmers, Plain, Flack Manor ♂ Westons Old Rosie, 1st Quality & Country Perry, Hecks Kingston Black & Blakeney Red.
Facilities ✿ (Bar Restaurant Garden) ♦️ Children's menu Children's portions Garden Parking Wi-fi

Lulworth Cove Inn

Main Rd BH20 5RQ ☎ 01929 400333
e-mail: lulworthcoveinn@hall-woodhouse.co.uk
dir: From A352 (Dorchester to Wareham road) follow Lulworth Cove signs. Inn at end of B3070, opposite car park

A short stroll from Lulworth Cove and the Jurassic Coast

Lulworth Cove's famous horseshoe bay is just steps away from the front door of this inn. It was once a distribution point for the mail service arriving by stagecoach, plus many smugglers stories can be heard. Ramblers can sate their appetites from the extensive menu, which features light bites, filled baguettes and jacket potatoes, as well as main course dishes like glazed chicken supreme; chilli roast salmon; Moroccan vegetables with couscous; and pork and apple sausages.

Open all day all wk ⊕ HALL & WOODHOUSE ◀ Badger ♂ Westons Stowford Press. **Facilities** ✿ (Bar Restaurant Garden) ♦️ Children's menu Children's portions Garden Wi-fi

WEST STOUR
Map 4 ST72

The Ship Inn

SP8 5RP ☎ 01747 838640
e-mail: mail@shipinn-dorset.com
dir: On A30, 4m W of Shaftesbury (4m from Henstridge)

Combining old and new in a rural setting

Walkers can explore the footpaths, which pass through the picturesque Dorset countryside surrounding this coaching inn built in 1750. The main bar has a traditional flagstone floor, low ceiling and log fire, while the lounge bar has stripped oak floorboards and chunky farmhouse furniture. Both offer a selection of beers and ciders, with weekly-changing guest ales. Menus include daily-changing specials such as oven-roasted salmon supreme with a cream of spinach and leek sauce. Home-made desserts may include dark chocolate and brandy torte. Outside there's a suntrap patio and large child-friendly garden.

Open all wk 12-3 6-11.30 ⊕ FREE HOUSE ◀ Palmers IPA, Sharp's Doom Bar, Ringwood Fortyniner ♂ Thatchers Cheddar Valley & Heritage, Westons Stowford Press. **Facilities** ✿ (Bar Garden) ♦️ Children's menu Children's portions Garden Parking Wi-fi

WEYMOUTH
Map 4 SY67

The Old Ship Inn

7 The Ridgeway DT3 5QQ ☎ 01305 812522
e-mail: info@theoldshipupwey.co.uk
dir: 3m from Weymouth town centre, at bottom of The Ridgeway

Weymouth views and real ales

Thomas Hardy refers to this 400-year-old pub in his novel *Under the Greenwood Tree*, and copper pans, old clocks and a beamed open fire create a true period atmosphere. Expect a good selection of real ales of tap, perhaps Dorset

Jurassic, Otter and Sharp's Doom Bar, with Addlestones cloudy cider as an alternative. A frequently changing menu of good home-cooked pub food offers smoked haddock fishcake with tartare sauce, slow-braised ham hock with winter vegetable broth, alongside classics like toad-in-the-hole; and ale battered fish and chips. On sunny days bag a bench in the garden and enjoy the views across Weymouth.

Open all wk **Bar Meals** L served Mon-Sat 12-2.30, Sun 12-6 D served Mon-Sat 6-9 Av main course £10 ⊕ PUNCH TAVERNS ◀ Sharp's Doom Bar, Ringwood Best Bitter, Dorset Jurassic, Otter, Guest ales ♂ Addlestones, Westons Stowford Press. ♟ 13 **Facilities** Non-diners area ✿ (Bar Garden) ♦️ Children's menu Children's portions Garden ⌐ Parking Wi-fi ▭

The Red Lion NEW

Hope Square DT4 8TR ☎ 01305 786940
e-mail: info@theredlionweymouth.co.uk
dir: Opposite Brewers Quay

Rums, real ale and extensive food choices

Smack opposite the old Devenish Brewery in the heart of Weymouth, the former brewery tap has long been a famous ale house, popular with locals and visitors, and with strong links with the local RNLI – it's the lifeboat crew's nearest pub. Refurbished in 2012, expect a comfortably rustic feel to the rambling rooms, with wood floors, candles on scrubbed tables, eclectic furnishings, period fireplaces, walls adorned with lifeboat pictures and artefacts, newspapers to peruse, and a cracking bar serving 80 rums, five ales, and traditional ciders. To eat, there are platters to share, big bowls of mussels served with crusty bread, fresh dressed crab and classic likes steak and ale pie.

Open all day all wk 11-11 (Fri-Sat 11am-mdnt Sun 12-10.30) **Bar Meals** L served all wk 12-3, Apr-Sep all day D served all wk 6-9, Apr-Sep all day Av main course £11 food served all day ⊕ FREE HOUSE ◀ Otter Brewery Life Boat Ale, Dorset Jurassic, Sharp's Doom Bar, Ringwood Best ♂ Westons Traditional Scrumpy & Country Perry. ♟ 12 **Facilities** Non-diners area ♦️ Children's portions Outside area ⌐ Wi-fi ▭ (notice required)

WIMBORNE ST GILES
Map 5 SU01

The Bull Inn

Coach Rd BH21 5NF ☎ 01725 517300
e-mail: bullwsg@btconnect.com
dir: From Salisbury take A354 towards Blandford Forum. Left onto B3081. Follow signs to Wimborne St Giles

Quality produce from the surrounding area

Situated in the heart of the Shaftesbury Estate on the edge of Cranborne Chase, there are three shoots within a five-minute drive of this pub, plus chalkwater stream fishing in the village. Much of the local produce ends up on the menu – pigeon breast with smoked black pudding and apple salad might be followed by pork belly with bubble-and-squeak and rocket – all washed down with local Badger ales.

Save on hotels. Book at theAA.com/hotel

DORSET – DURHAM, CO 161 ENGLAND

Open all wk 12-3 6-11 ⊕ HALL & WOODHOUSE ◆ Badger Tanglefoot, K&B Sussex, Hopping Hare ⊘ The Orchard Pig. **Facilities** ◾ Children's portions Garden Parking Wi-fi

---

WINTERBORNE ZELSTON   Map 4 SY89

Botany Bay Inne

DT11 9ET ☎ 01929 459227
dir: *A31 between Bere Regis & Wimborne Minster*

A change of hands at this main road pub

The pub was built by the Hall & Woodhouse brewery in the 1920s to replace one in the village the local squire found offensive. Initially called the General Allenby, its name was changed in the 1980s in belated recognition of prisoners from Dorchester jail awaiting transportation to Australia. No such threat hangs over today's visitors here. As we went to press we were informed of a change of hands.

Open all wk 10-3 6-11 **Bar Meals** L served all wk 12-2.15 D served all wk 6-9 **Restaurant** L served all wk 12-2 D served all wk 6-9 ⊕ HALL & WOODHOUSE ◆ Badger First Gold & Tanglefoot, Guest ales.
Facilities Non-diners area ❧ (Bar Garden) ◾ Children's menu Children's portions Garden 🅿 Parking 🚌 (notice required)

WORTH MATRAVERS   Map 4 SY97

The Square and Compass

BH19 3LF ☎ 01929 439229
dir: *Between Corfe Castle & Swanage. From B3069 follow signs for Worth Matravers*

Lovely pub with beer but no bar and limited food

Little has changed at this stone-built pub for the past century, during which time it has been run by the same family. This tucked-away inn boasts a simple interior with no bar, just a serving hatch and an abundance of flagstone floors, oak panels and a museum of local artefacts and fossils from the nearby Jurassic Coast. Award-winning West Country beers and ciders come straight from the barrel and food is limited to just pasties and pies. On the first Saturday in October there's a beer and pumpkin festival, and in early November there's a cider festival.

Open all wk 12-3 6-11 (summer & Fri-Sun 12-11) ⊕ FREE HOUSE ◆ Palmers Copper Ale & Dorset Gold, RCH Pitchfork, Hop Back Summer Lightning ⊘ Hecks Farmhouse, Seasonal home-produced.
Facilities Non-diners area ❧ (All areas) ◾ Garden Outside area Beer festival Cider festival 🚌 **Notes** ⊛

DURHAM, CO

AYCLIFFE   Map 19 NZ22

The County ★★★★ RR

13 The Green, Aycliffe Village DL5 6LX ☎ 01325 312273
e-mail: info@thecountyaycliffevillage.com
web: www.thecountyaycliffevillage.com
dir: *A1 (M) junct 59, off A167 into Aycliffe Village*

Picturesque village green setting and celebrity visitors

Prettily perched on the village green, the Hairy Bikers filmed on location here in 2012 and in 2000 Tony Blair wined and dined then French president Jacques Chirac at The County. The smart restaurant and terrace is a lovely place to eat, as is the homely bar where you can sup a pint of Black Sheep or The County's own brew. With superb local produce on the doorstep, expect the likes of warm caramelised red onion and Mordon Farm feta cheese tartlet, then roast pheasant, roast garlic and thyme mashed potato, sautéed cep mushrooms and jus, with spiced treacle sponge with dairy custard to finish.

Open all wk 12-3 6-11 (Sun all day) Closed: 25-26 Dec, 1 Jan **Bar Meals** L served Mon-Sat 12-2, Sun 12-9 D served Mon-Sat 6-9, Sun 12-9 **Restaurant** L served Mon-Sat 12-2, Sun 12-9 D served Mon-Sat 6-9, Sun 12-9 ⊕ FREE HOUSE ◆ Cocker Hoop, Black Sheep, Yorkshire Dales, Hawkshead ⊘ Thatchers Green Goblin. 🍷 10
Facilities Non-diners area ◾ Children's portions 🅿 Parking **Rooms** 7

BARNARD CASTLE   Map 19 NZ01

The Morritt Arms Hotel ★★★★ HL ◉◉

PICK OF THE PUBS

Greta Bridge DL12 9SE ☎ 01833 627232
e-mail: relax@themorritt.co.uk
dir: *On A1(M) at Scotch Corner take A66 towards Penrith, in 9m exit at Greta Bridge. Hotel over bridge on left*

Country house atmosphere

This fine building dates from the late 17th century, when it served Carlisle- and London-bound coach travellers. Traditionally a fine-dining venue, the restaurant has been brought bang up to date with vibrant colours, a touch of black leather, comfortable armchairs, silk blinds over window seats and works by local artists. This association with art began in 1946, when local portraitist Jack Gilroy painted the mural of Dickensian characters you'll find in the bar. Here, the two AA-Rosette menu opens with a

---

seafood platter, before featuring Mediterranean vegetable risotto; Neasham pork and leek sausages; and beer-battered cod. In the restaurant, venison loin with beetroot risotto; butter-fried plaice fillets; and wild mushroom and vegetable Wellington may well appear. Major Morritt beer, named after the hotel's former owner and namesake, was introduced at the pub's first cask ale festival in 2010. En suite bedrooms help to make this a popular function and wedding choice.

Open all day all wk 7am-11pm (Sun 7am-10.30pm) **Bar Meals** food served all day **Restaurant** L served all wk 12-3 D served all wk 7-9.30 ⊕ FREE HOUSE ◆ Morritt Arms Major Morritt, Timothy Taylor Landlord, Thwaites. 🍷 19 **Facilities** Non-diners area ◾ Children's menu Children's portions Play area Family room Garden Beer festival Parking Wi-fi 🚌 **Rooms** 26

BOLDRON   Map 19 NZ01

The George & Dragon Inn

DL12 9RF ☎ 01833 638215
e-mail: georgeanddragon_boldron@yahoo.com
dir: *Boldron signed from A66*

A very warm welcome and hearty Italian inspired dishes

Famished A66 travellers should take note of this free house in sleepy Boldron, a picture-book village located just two miles from historic Barnard Castle. Ales from local microbreweries and daily-changing, seasonally inspired menus await, the latter featuring an award-winning cheeseboard and salmon smoked on the premises. Look out for Milanese style breaded local pork cutlets, pan-fried with crunchy broccoli, chilli, spinach and lemon olive oil; and rich beef blade ragout. The early May beer festival champions local brews and fine cheeses. Wonderful surrounding walks too.

Open 11-2.30 5-11 Closed: Tue **Bar Meals** L served Mon & Wed-Sun 11-2.30 D served Mon & Wed-Sun 5-9 **Restaurant** L served Mon & Wed-Sun 11-2.30 D served Mon & Wed-Sun 5-9 ⊕ FREE HOUSE ◆ The Consett Ale Works Steel Town, Allendale Golden Plover & Wagtail, Wall's Brewing Co. **Facilities** Non-diners area ❧ (Bar Garden) ◾ Children's portions Garden 🅿 Beer festival Parking Wi-fi 🚌 (notice required)

CHESTER-LE-STREET   Map 19 NZ25

The Moorings Hotel

Hett Hill DH2 3JU ☎ 0191 370 1597
e-mail: info@themooringsdurham.co.uk
dir: *A1(M) junct 63 to Chester-le-Street. Take B6313. Hotel on left*

Tranquil Tees Valley setting

Handy both for the fascinating open air museum at Beamish and the historic heart of Chester-le-Street, this thriving hotel bar attracts much custom from ramblers and riders enjoying the glorious countryside along the valley of the River Tees. Thirsts are quenched by beers from Mordue or the respected microbrewery at the

continued

CHESTER-LE-STREET *continued*

Beamish complex, whilst keen appetites can be sated by dishes created from the freshest local produce. The menu of modern classics ranges across the spectrum, from breaded cod, haddock and crayfish tail fishcakes on ratatouille to sirloin steak with garlic butter tiger prawns, finishing with warm scotch pancakes with chocolate sauce.

Open all day all wk **Bar Meals** L served all wk 11.30-9.30 D served all wk 11.30-9.30 Av main course £10 food served all day **Restaurant** L served Sun 11.30-4 D served Thu-Sat 6.30-9.30 Fixed menu price fr £14.45 Av 3 course à la carte fr £25 ⊕ FREE HOUSE ◀ The Stables Beamish Hall Bitter, Malvern Hills Black Pear. **Facilities** ◀ Children's menu Family room Garden Outside area ⊼ Parking Wi-fi ⇎ (notice required)

COTHERSTONE   Map 19 NZ01

The Fox and Hounds

DL12 9PF ☎ 01833 650241
e-mail: ianswinburn999@btinternet.com
dir: *4m W of Barnard Castle. From A66 onto B6277, signed*

Picturesque village setting

At the heart of beautiful Teesdale and just a stone's throw from the river's wooded gorge, The Fox and Hounds is huddled above one of the village greens in pretty Cotherstone. Beams, open fires and thickly cushioned wall seats tempt you to linger at this 360-year-old coaching inn, admiring the local photographs and country pictures while you sip a pint of Black Sheep or Symonds cider. From the menu, tuck in to dishes made from the best of fresh, local ingredients: Wensleydale and hazelnut pâté with caramelised onion relish; steak, black pudding and Black Sheep ale pie; and pan-fried lamb's liver in rich gravy.

Open all wk 12-2.30 6.30-11 (Sun 12-2.30 6.30-10.30) Closed: 25-26 Dec **Bar Meals** L served all wk 12-2 D served all wk 6.30-9 **Restaurant** L served all wk 12-2 D served all wk 6.30-9 ⊕ FREE HOUSE ◀ Black Sheep Best Bitter & Ale, The Village Brewer Bull Premium Bitter, York Yorkshire Terrier, Daleside ☼ Aspall, Symonds. **Facilities** Non-diners area ◀ Children's menu Children's portions Outside area ⊼ Parking Wi-fi ⇎ (notice required)

DURHAM   Map 19 NZ24

Victoria Inn

86 Hallgarth St DH1 3AS ☎ 0191 386 5269
dir: *In city centre*

Traditional red brick, street pub at the heart of the city

This unique listed inn has scarcely changed since it was built in 1899 – not a jukebox, pool table or television to be found. Just five minutes' walk from the cathedral, it has been carefully nurtured by the Webster family for over three decades. Small rooms warmed by coal fires and a congenial atmosphere include the tiny snug, where a portrait of Queen Victoria still hangs above the upright piano. You'll find a few simple snacks to tickle the taste buds, but it's the cracking well-kept local ales, single malts, and over 40 Irish whiskies that are the main attraction.

Open all wk 11.45-3 6-11 ⊕ FREE HOUSE ◀ Wylam Gold Tankard, Durham Magus, Big Lamp Bitter, Hill Island. **Facilities** Non-diners area ❖ (Bar Restaurant) ◀ Family room Parking Wi-fi ⇎

FIR TREE   Map 19 NZ13

Duke of York Inn

DL15 8DG ☎ 01388 767429
e-mail: theduke-firtree@yahoo.co.uk
dir: *On A68, 12m W of Durham. From Durham take A690 W. Left onto A68 to Fir Tree*

Friendly staff, modern interior and good food

On the tourist route (A68) to Scotland, the Duke of York is a former drovers' and coaching inn dating from 1749. It is appointed inside and out to a high standard, keeping the traditional country feel with contemporary touches. Beers include Black Sheep Best Bitter and Camerons Smooth, and menus include goats' cheese crostini; chicken tagliatelle; fish and seafood pie; and Whitby scampi with hand-cut chips. Look out for the beer festival – call the pubs for the dates.

Open all day all wk **Bar Meals** L served all wk 12-9 D served all wk 12-9 food served all day **Restaurant** L served all wk 12-9 D served all wk 12-9 food served all day ⊕ CAMERONS BREWERY ◀ Smooth, Black Sheep Best Bitter, John Smith's, Guinness. **Facilities** Non-diners area ❖ (Bar Garden) ◀ Children's menu Children's portions Garden ⊼ Beer festival Parking Wi-fi ⇎

FROSTERLEY   Map 19 NZ03

The Black Bull Inn

DL13 2SL ☎ 01388 527784
dir: *From A68 onto A689 towards Stanhope. Left into Frosterley. Inn adjacent to railway station*

Great ales with bells on

Uniquely, this family-run, independent country pub has its own church bells – not to mention a great range of real ales to enjoy after a spot of bell-ringing. Located next to Weardale steam railway station, it has cosy, music-free rooms, a stone-flagged bar and open fires in Victorian ranges. The ad hoc beer festivals demonstrate unwavering backing for local microbreweries, while the kitchen is equally supportive of the regional suppliers behind the food. A meal might take in potted North Shields crab; herb crusted lamb shoulder with apricot and walnut stuffing, dauphinoise potatoes and rosemary jus; and raspberry and white chocolate cheesecake.

Open all day Closed: 1 Jan for 5wks, Sun eve, Mon, Tue **Bar Meals** L served Wed-Sun 12.30-2.30 D served Wed-Sat 7-9 **Restaurant** L served Wed-Sun 12.30-2.30 D served Wed-Sat 7-9 ⊕ FREE HOUSE ◀ Allendale, Wylam, Consett, York, Jarrow ☼ Wilkins Farmhouse, Westons. **Facilities** ❖ (Bar Garden) ◀ Children's portions Garden ⊼ Beer festival Cider festival Parking Wi-fi ⇎ (notice required)

HURWORTH-ON-TEES   Map 19 NZ30

The Bay Horse

45 The Green DL2 2AA ☎ 01325 720663
e-mail: mail@thebayhorsehurworth.com
dir: *From A66 at Darlington Football Club rdbt follow Hurworth sign*

Fine dining in pretty Tees Valley village

Savvy diners may get bitter and twisted at the bar in this sublime gastro-pub; its one of the real ales there to satisfy devotees seeking out the culinary magic conjured up by talented chef-proprietors Jonathan Hall and Marcus Bennett. The ancient pub underwent a comprehensive transformation a few years ago, retaining considerable character enhanced by carefully chosen period furnishings. Thoroughly modern cuisine sets this ambience off to a tee; starters based on roasted pigeon breast or smoked eel merely a hint of the creative mains; perhaps daube of beef with colcannon or roasted salmon with creamed clams may satisfy, taken in the bar or restaurant.

Open all day all wk Closed: 25-26 Dec **Bar Meals** L served Mon-Sat 12-2.30, Sun 12-4 D served all wk 6-close Av main course £16.95 **Restaurant** L served Mon-Sat 12-2.30, Sun 12-4 D served all wk 6-close Fixed menu price fr £16.95 Av 3 course à la carte fr £30.95 ⊕ FREE HOUSE ◀ Harviestoun Bitter & Twisted, Jennings Cumberland Ale. ♟ 12 **Facilities** Non-diners area ◀ Children's menu Garden ⊼ Parking Wi-fi

HUTTON MAGNA　　　Map 19 NZ11

The Oak Tree Inn ◉◉

PICK OF THE PUBS

DL11 7HH ☎ **01833 627371**
dir: *From A1 at Scotch Corner take A66 W. 6.5m, right for Hutton Magna*

18th-century, free house offering excellent cooking with a pedigree

At this whitewashed, part 18th-century free house run by Alastair and Claire Ross, expect great food, a superb selection of drinks and a warm welcome. Alastair previously spent 14 years in London working at The Savoy, Leith's and, more recently, a private members' club on The Strand. The AA two-Rosette cuisine in the simply furnished dining room is based around the finest local ingredients, and dishes change daily depending on produce available. The refined cooking style combines classic techniques and modern flavours: you could start with steamed Shetland mussels; tempura lemon sole with pea risotto; cauliflower, parmesan and thyme soup, or warm pork belly and vegetable salad. After that, maybe fillet of wild sea bass with brown shrimp, chorizo and vegetable broth; saddle of lamb with Provençale vegetables; or roast beef fillet with cabbage and bacon potatoes. As well as fine real ales, there's a menu of bottled beers from around the globe, and a list of over 20 malt whiskies.

Open 6-11 (Sun 5.30-10.30) Closed: Xmas & New Year, Mon **Bar Meals** Av main course £21 **Restaurant** D served Tue-Sun 6-9 Av 3 course à la carte fr £33 ⊕ FREE HOUSE ◀ Wells Bombardier, Timothy Taylor Landlord, Copper Dragon. ♚ 10 **Facilities** Non-diners area Parking

LONGNEWTON　　　Map 19 NZ31

Vane Arms ★★★★ INN

Darlington Rd TS21 1DB ☎ **01642 580401**
e-mail: thevanearms@hotmail.com
web: www.vanearms.com
dir: *W end of village, just off A66 midway between Stockton-on-Tees & Darlington*

Village pub with two beer festivals

This previously abandoned 18th-century pub is now loved once again after being bought by villagers Jill and Paul Jackson. There's no jukebox, pool or gaming machine, and the TV is on only for special events; background music

plays quietly in the lounge. Sensibly priced pub grub includes truffled chicken liver parfait, pasta carbonara, and dark chocolate mousse. Grill night is Tuesday, French is the cuisine on Wednesday evening, roasts on Sunday, and there is a Black Sheep beer festival in October and a mini beer festival in July. A large garden looks towards the Cleveland Hills and the North Yorkshire Moors. Accommodation is available.

Open all wk Tue-Thu 12-2 5-11 (Mon 5-11 Fri-Sat 12-2 5-12 Sun 12-11) **Restaurant** L served Tue-Sat 12-2, Sun 12-4 D served Mon-Sat 5-8.30 ⊕ FREE HOUSE ◀ Black Sheep Best Bitter, Guest ales Ŏ Hereford Dry. **Facilities** Non-diners area ✿ (Garden) ♦♦ Children's portions Garden ⋒ Beer festival Parking Wi-fi ☞ (notice required) **Rooms** 4

MIDDLESTONE　　　Map 19 NZ23

Ship Inn

Low Rd DL14 8AB ☎ **01388 810904**
e-mail: tony.theshipinn@googlemail.com
dir: *On B6287 (Kirk Merrington to Coundon road)*

A true locals' pub with great countryside views

A bustling local that knows how to generate community loyalty, not least through an ever-changing real ale portfolio. The lounge is all nautical memorabilia and walls festooned with old beer pump clips. Twenty-three miles from the sea and at 550 feet above sea level the rooftop patio offers excellent views over the Tees Valley and Cleveland Hills. Home-cooked food is served in the bar, using locally reared beef, pork and lamb, with dishes such as corned beef pie and award-winning pork and leek sausages. Look out for regular themed evenings.

Open all wk 4-11 (Fri-Sun 12-11) ⊕ FREE HOUSE ◀ 6 Guest ales Ŏ Westons. **Facilities** ✿ (Bar) ♦♦ Children's menu Children's portions Play area Family room Parking Wi-fi

NEWTON AYCLIFFE　　　Map 19 NZ22

Blacksmiths Arms

Preston le Skerne, (off Ricknall Lane) DL5 6JH ☎ **01325 314873**
dir: *Exit A167 (dual carriageway) at Gretna Green pub signed Great Stanton, Stillington & Bishopton, into Ricknall Ln. Blacksmiths Arms 0.5m*

Large dining pub in a rural setting serving good food

Enjoying an excellent reputation locally as a good dining pub, this former smithy dates from the 1700s, and is still relatively isolated in its farmland setting. The menu offers starters of crispy battered chicken with sweet chilli dip; king prawns with watercress and garlic sautéed potatoes; or potted mushrooms in a chardonnay cream sauce. Requiring their own page on the menu are fish dishes such as green-lipped mussels, slow-roasted pesto salmon, and grilled swordfish with prawn sauce. There's also a page of chef's specialities, good selection of

vegetarian dishes and a gluten-free menu. There is an ever-changing selection of real ales served in the bar.

Open 11.30-2.30 6-11 Closed: 1 Jan, Mon **Bar Meals** L served Tue-Sun 11.30-2 D served Tue-Sun 6-9 **Restaurant** L served Tue-Sun 11.30-2 D served Tue-Sun 6-9 ⊕ FREE HOUSE ◀ Guest ales. ♚ 10 **Facilities** Non-diners area ♦♦ Children's menu Play area Garden ⋒ Parking ☞ (notice required)

ROMALDKIRK　　　Map 19 NY92

Rose & Crown ★★★ HL ◉◉

PICK OF THE PUBS

See Pick of the Pubs on page 164

SEAHAM　　　Map 19 NZ44

The Seaton Lane Inn ★★★★ INN

Seaton Ln SR7 0LP ☎ **0191 581 2036**
e-mail: info@seatonlaneinn.com
dir: *S of Sunderland on A19 take B1404 towards Houghton-le-Spring. In Seaton turn left for pub*

Traditional pub with stylish, contemporary interior and good food

With a traditional bar area as well as a stylish restaurant and lounge, this boutique-type inn offers four real ales to keep the regulars happy, served from the central bar. The menu proffers many pub favourites – hot sandwiches such as the traditional BLT are served with chunky chips; pasta dishes, tortilla wraps and warm salads are all here as well as a good selection of main courses. A sample evening menu features braised shoulder of lamb on champ mash with rich minted jus; salmon marinated in teriyaki sauce with onions, peppers and tomatoes; and chunky beef cottage pie. Bedrooms are modern, spacious and smartly furnished.

Open all day all wk **Bar Meals** L served all wk 7am-9.30pm D served all wk 7am-9.30pm Av main course £7 food served all day **Restaurant** L served all wk 7am-9.30pm D served all wk 7am-9.30pm Fixed menu price fr £10.95 Av 3 course à la carte fr £20 food served all day ⊕ FREE HOUSE ◀ Timothy Taylor Landlord, Wells Bombardier, Caledonian Deuchars IPA, Sharp's Doom Bar. ♚ 10 **Facilities** Non-diners area ✿ (Bar Garden) ♦♦ Children's menu Children's portions Garden Outside area ⋒ Parking Wi-fi ☞ **Rooms** 18

PICK OF THE PUBS

Rose & Crown ★★★ HL ◉◉

ROMALDKIRK Map 19 NY92

DL12 9EB ☎ 01833 650213
e-mail: hotel@rose-and-crown.co.uk
web: www.rose-and-crown.co.uk
dir: *6m NW from Barnard Castle on B6277*

Teesdale dining pub under new ownership

Overlooking the village's old stocks and water pump, this creeper-clad stone-built coaching inn stands on the village green, while next door is the Saxon church known as 'The Cathedral of the Dale'. Step inside the 18th-century pub to be greeted by fresh flowers, varnished oak panelling, old beams, and gleaming copper and brass artefacts, then enter the quirky little bar and you'll encounter oak settles, a vast dog grate, old prints, carriage lamps and rural curios. In the secluded lounge you can retire to a wing-backed chair and be lulled by the ticking of a grandfather clock, with maybe a glass of Thwaites Wainwright or Black Sheep. Wines by the glass are listed on blackboards, while the bar and brasserie menu features haddock goujons, lamb's liver and bacon, and slow-cooked confit of chicken. Another option is a meal in the more formal panelled restaurant lit by candles. The

chefs rely on produce from Teesdale's farms and sporting estates, and fish from east coast to create the restaurant's daily-changing menu. This could start with seared mackerel fillet with roasted fennel and walnut salad; or chicken liver pâté and port and orange sauce. Then for mains, pan-fried corn-fed chicken breast with chicken roulade, sweet potato cake, spinach, celeriac purée and tarragon cream; and goats' cheese crostini served with cherry tomatoes and a rocket salad. Perhaps round things off with crème brûlée or local cheeseboard.

Open all day all wk Closed: 24-26 Dec **Bar Meals** L served all wk 12-2.30 D served all wk 7-9.30 **Restaurant** D served all wk 7-9 ⊕ FREE HOUSE ◄ Black Sheep Best Bitter, Thwaites Wainwright ⎊ Kingston. ♈ 9 **Facilities** Non-diners area ⊪ Children's menu Children's portions Outside area ⊼ Parking Wi-fi **Rooms** 12

STANLEY   Map 19 NZ15

The Stables Pub and Restaurant ★★★★ CHH

Beamish Hall Hotel, Beamish DH9 0YB
☎ 01207 288750 & 233733
e-mail: info@beamish-hall.co.uk
dir: A693 to Stanley. Follow signs for Beamish Hall Country House Hotel & Beamish Museum. Left at museum entrance. Hotel on left 0.2m after golf club. Pub within hotel grounds

Own-brewed beer and delicious food

The stone-floored, beamed bar is the perfect spot to sample the pub's own real ales, brewed on site at their microbrewery. The beer festival in the third week of September will get you even more closely acquainted, while a cider festival is held during the second weekend of December. The pub has been creatively moulded from the estate workshops of a stunning country mansion and has excellent accommodation. Regional producers supply the best local ingredients from which are crafted exemplary meals. Snack on open ravioli of smoked haddock, peas, tomato, chervil and fish cream; or sink into pan-fried lamb rump, lentils, fine beans, Chantenay carrots and apple purée.

Open all day all wk Mon-Thu 11-11 (Fri-Sat 11am-mdnt Sun 11-10.30) **Bar Meals** L served Mon-Thu 12-9, Fri-Sat 12-9.30, Sun 12-8 D served Mon-Thu 12-9, Fri-Sat 12-9.30, Sun 12-8 food served all day **Restaurant** food served all day ⊕ FREE HOUSE ◀ The Stables Beamish Hall Bitter, Beamish Burn Brown Ale, Old Miner Tommy, Silver Buckles Ŏ Gwynt y Ddraig Haymaker & Farmhouse Pyder. ♥ **Facilities** Non-diners area ♥ (Garden) ♦ Children's menu Children's portions Play area Garden ⊞ Beer festival Cider festival Parking Wi-fi ▭ **Rooms** 42

WINSTON   Map 19 NZ11

The Bridgewater Arms

DL2 3RN ☎ 01325 730302
e-mail: paul.p.grundy@btinternet.com
dir: Exit A67 between Barnard Castle & Darlington, onto B6274 into Winston

Former schoolhouse serving fresh seafood

Set in a former schoolhouse, this Grade II listed pub is decorated with original photographs of the building and its pupils. It prides itself on offering high quality, simple meals made with local produce, particularly seafood. Chicken liver, black pudding, apple and Stilton salad followed by roast rack of lamb with a leek and potato cake and rosemary gravy is a typical meal, while fishy offerings could include langoustines split and grilled in garlic butter; and monkfish wrapped in bacon on a curried prawn risotto. Afterwards, the historic Winston Bridge and beautiful views to the church are a short stroll away.

Open 12-2.30 6-11 Closed: 25-26 Dec, Sun & Mon **Bar Meals** L served Tue-Sat 12-2 D served Tue-Sat 6-9 Av main course £20 **Restaurant** L served Tue-Sat 12-2 D served Tue-Sat 6-9 ⊕ GREENE KING ◀ IPA, Timothy Taylor Landlord, Morland Old Speckled Hen Ŏ Aspall. ♥ 15 **Facilities** Non-diners area ♦ Children's portions Garden ⊞ Parking Wi-fi

ESSEX

ARKESDEN   Map 12 TL43

Axe & Compasses

PICK OF THE PUBS

See Pick of the Pubs on page 166

AYTHORPE RODING   Map 6 TL51

Axe & Compasses

Dunmow Rd CM6 1PP ☎ 01279 876648
e-mail: axeandcompasses@msn.com
dir: From A120 follow signs for Dunmow

Nostalgic pub with great home cooking

The owners of this weather-boarded, 17th-century pub like to create a 'nostalgic pub experience'. In the bar, ales from small regional brewers such as Nethergate, are backed by Westons ciders. David Hunt, a skilled self-taught chef, uses the best of seasonal produce and loves to offer dishes such as chicken liver and brandy parfait; pigeon breast with bacon lardons, Savoy cabbage, Puy lentils and game gravy; and a choice of five home-made pies. The pub also serves breakfast daily and offers a great range of bar snacks such as pork crackling with warm apple sauce or a home-made Scotch egg.

Open all day all wk 11am-11.30pm (Sun 12-11) **Bar Meals** L served Mon-Sat 12-2.30, Sun 12-8 D served Mon-Sat 6-9.30, Sun 12-8 Av main course £10.95 food served all day **Restaurant** L served Mon-Sat 12-2.30, Sun 12-8 D served Mon-Sat 6-9.30, Sun 12-8 ⊕ FREE HOUSE ◀ Brentwood Best, Nethergate Old Growler, Crouch Vale Brewers Gold, Woodforde's Wherry, Saffron Ŏ Westons Old Rosie, Herefordshire Country Perry. ♥ 15 **Facilities** Non-diners area ♥ (Bar Garden) ♦ Children's menu Children's portions Garden ⊞ Parking Wi-fi ▭

BLACKMORE   Map 6 TL60

The Leather Bottle

PICK OF THE PUBS

The Green CM4 0RL ☎ 01277 823538 & 821891
e-mail: leatherbottle@tiscali.co.uk
dir: M25 junct 8 onto A1023, left onto A128, 5m. Left onto Blackmore Rd, 2m. Left towards Blackmore, 2m. Right then 1st left

Gastro-pub with an emphasis on freshly cooked food

There has been a pub here for over 400 years, but when the original building burned down in 1954 this was the replacement two years later. The stone-floored bar is a cosy, welcoming place to savour East Anglian real ales and cider, while the restaurant is smart, with modern furnishings, and an airy conservatory opens on to a spacious garden with covered patio. The cuisine is a blend of European and traditional English, prepared with top-quality ingredients mainly from local suppliers. Lunchtime options include lamb's liver and bacon; pan-fried salmon; and pie of the day, while typical evening

dishes are roasted lamb shank; something from the extensive steak board selection; prawn and asparagus salad; and mozzarella and roasted vegetable terrine. Mixed berry Eton Mess, and poached figs with spiced honey and cinnamon cream are tasty-sounding desserts. The first Monday of every month is Jazz Night.

Open all day all wk **Bar Meals** L served Mon-Sat 12-2, Sun 12-4 D served Tue-Sat 7-9 Av main course £12.95 **Restaurant** L served Mon-Sat 12-2, Sun 12-4 D served Tue-Sat 7-9 Fixed menu price fr £10.95 Av 3 course à la carte fr £23 ⊕ FREE HOUSE ◀ Adnams Southwold Bitter & Broadside, Sharp's Doom Bar, Woodforde's Wherry, Cottage Cactus Jack Ŏ Aspall, Westons Old Rosie. ♥ 9 **Facilities** Non-diners area ♥ (Bar Garden) Children's portions Garden Parking ▭

BURNHAM-ON-CROUCH   Map 7 TQ99

Ye Olde White Harte Hotel

The Quay CM0 8AS ☎ 01621 782106
e-mail: whitehartehotel@gmail.com
dir: Along high street, right before clocktower, right into car park

Quayside hotel with an olde worlde atmosphere

Situated on the waterfront overlooking the River Crouch, the hotel dates from the 17th century and retains many original features, including beams and fireplaces. It also has its own private jetty. Enjoy fresh local produce and fish in The Waterside Restaurant, or eat in the bar or on the terrace. The dining room offers a wide range of starters, as well as main course options that include vegetarian dishes and a daily roast. The bar menu might feature lasagne and salad; or locally caught skate with new potatoes and vegetables.

Open all day all wk **Bar Meals** L served all wk 12-2.15 D served all wk 6.30-9 **Restaurant** L served all wk 12-2.15 D served all wk 7-9 ⊕ FREE HOUSE ◀ Adnams Southwold Bitter, Crouch Vale Brewers Gold. **Facilities** ♥ (Bar Outside area) ♦ Children's portions Outside area Parking ▭

PICK OF THE PUBS

Axe & Compasses

ARKESDEN Map 12 TL43

High St CB11 4EX ☎ **01799 550272**
e-mail: axeandcompasses@mail.com
web: www.axeandcompasses.co.uk
dir: *From Buntingford take B1038
towards Newport, left for Arkesden*

Lovely inn with Greek dishes on the menus

The Axe & Compasses is the centrepiece of this sleepy, picture-postcard village, whose narrow main street runs alongside gentle Wicken Water, spanned by a succession of footbridges that give access to white, cream and pink-washed cottages. The thatched central part of the pub dates from 1650; the right-hand extension was added during the early 19th century and is now the public bar. It's run by Themis and Diane Christou from Cyprus, who between them have knocked up a good few awards for the marvellous things they do here. Easy chairs and settees, antique furniture, clocks and horse brasses fill their comfortable lounge and, in winter, there's an open fire. The pumps of Greene King hold sway in the bar, and it's with a pint of Olde Trip that you can have a sandwich or light meal, such as monkfish served on a roasted red pepper sauce. In the softly lit restaurant area, which seats 50 on various levels, and where agricultural implements adorn the old beams, the slightly Greek-influenced menus offer a

good selection of starters, including flat field mushrooms baked with garlic, thyme, lemon juice and olive oil; and avocado, bacon and blue cheese crostini. There's a good choice of main courses too, examples being moussaka; supreme of chicken Kiev with mushroom duxelles in puff pastry and wholegrain mustard cream; tender rump of lamb with mint and red wine gravy; grilled halibut steak with creamed leeks; and fried spinach and potato cakes with tomato and basil sauce. Rounding off the menu are desserts from the trolley, such as trifle of the day, and summer pudding. The wine list is easy to navigate, with house reds and whites coming in at modest prices. On fine days many drinkers and diners head for the patio.

Open all wk 12-2.30 6-11 (Sun 12-3 6-10.30) **Bar Meals** L served all wk 12-2 D served all wk 6.30-9.15 **Restaurant** L served all wk 12-2 D served all wk 6.30-9.15 ⊕ GREENE KING ◖ IPA, Hardys & Hansons Olde Trip, Guest ale ♂ Thatchers Gold. ♀ 14 **Facilities** Non-diners area ♦♦ Children's portions Outside area ⋒ Parking ▭▭

Save on hotels. Book at **theAA.com/hotel**

ESSEX 167 ENGLAND

The Bell Inn

PICK OF THE PUBS

Saint James St CO9 3EJ ☎ 01787 460350
e-mail: hedinghambell@zoho.com
web: www.hedinghambell.co.uk
dir: *On A1124 N of Halstead, right to Castle Hedingham*

Honest pub grub in a traditional local

Situated in the charming medieval village of Castle Hedingham, The Bell has been run by the Ferguson family for over 40 years. A 15th-century former coaching inn, it remains a traditional pub serving good quality real ales and honest food using local ingredients. Exposed stone walls, heavy beams and real log fires create a welcoming atmosphere in which to enjoy a Mighty Oak Maldon Gold or one of the guest ales. The annual July beer festival that showcases up to 15 ales proves popular, as is live music every Friday night and jazz on the last Sunday of the month. The Turkish chef puts his stamp on the menu, with Mediterranean fish nights on Mondays, and Turkish stone-baked pizzas on Wednesdays. Otherwise, enjoy unpretentious pub classics like garlic mushrooms and granary toast; chicken and ham hock pie or grilled lamb chops, with sticky toffee pudding for afters.

Open all wk 11.45-3 6-11 (Fri-Sat 12-12 Sun 12-11) Closed: 25 Dec eve **Bar Meals** L served Mon-Fri 12-2, Sat-Sun 12-2.30 D served Sun-Mon 7-9, Tue-Sat 7-9.30 Av main course £9.95 ⊕ GRAY & SONS ◀ Mighty Oak Maldon Gold & IPA, Adnams Southwold Bitter, Guest ale Ö Aspall, Delvin End, Pheasant Plucker. **Facilities** Non-diners area 🐾 (Bar Garden) ♦ Children's menu Children's portions Play area Family room Garden ⌁ Beer festival Parking Wi-fi 🚌 (notice required)

The Swan Inn

CO6 2DD ☎ 01787 222353
e-mail: swan@cipubs.com
dir: *Pub visible just off A1124 (Colchester to Halstead road), from Colchester 1st left after viaduct*

Medieval pub with attractive riverside gardens

Under the constant gaze of a magnificent railway viaduct and surrounded by beautiful countryside, this 14th-century, low-beamed free house has a well-founded reputation for food, especially fresh fish. Other typical dishes include toad-in-the-hole; lamb's liver and bacon; and Mediterranean vegetable lasagne. The River Colne

runs through the gardens where, as in the sheltered courtyard, you can enjoy a meal. The bar serves plenty of wines by the glass and well-kept Adnams real ale.

Open all wk 11-3 6-11 (Sat 11-11 Sun 12-10.30) ⊕ FREE HOUSE ◀ Adnams Southwold Bitter & Broadside, Guest Ale Ö Aspall. **Facilities** ♦ Children's menu Children's portions Play area Garden Parking Wi-fi

Admiral J McHardy

37 Arbour Ln CM1 7RG ☎ 01245 256783
e-mail: admiraljmchardy@gmail.com
dir: *Telephone for directions*

White clapboard alehouse with a stylish interior

Now owned by Fireside Pubs & Restaurants, this late 19th-century pub has been renamed for the first Chief Constable of Essex, who was appointed in 1840. The new team's philosophy is 'to provide the best the customer can expect', guaranteeing that all produce is locally sourced and of a high quality. The chic decor is a stylish mix of traditional and contemporary while the menu offers predominantly classic pub dishes and grills - perhaps barbecue rack of ribs, grilled chicken burger in a ciabatta roll, and salmon, chorizo and broad bean fishcakes. There is a front patio and more secluded rear garden for alfresco dining. Enquire about the beer festival.

Open all day all wk 11-11 (Sun 11-10.30) **Bar Meals** L served Mon-Sat 11-9, Sun 11-8 D served Mon-Sat 11-9, Sun 11-8 food served all day ⊕ FREE HOUSE ◀ Sharp's Doom Bar, Guest ales. 🍷 12 **Facilities** Non-diners area ♦ Children's menu Children's portions Garden ⌁ Beer festival Parking Wi-fi 🚌

The Red Cow

11 High St SG8 8RN ☎ 01763 838792
e-mail: thepub@theredcow.com
dir: *M11 junct 10, A505 towards Royston. 2m, pass pet creamtorium, 1st left signed Chrishall. 3.5m, pub in village centre*

Recommended for their game dishes

Conveniently positioned between Saffron Walden and Royston, this 500-year-old thatched pub is very much the hub of the community in this pretty village. In the bar the real ales and cider are all East Anglian; on the menu are soups, sandwiches, jacket potatoes and other pub favourites. The seasonally changing restaurant carte typically offers battered oysters with saffron aïoli, which might be followed by trio of pork with black pudding, herb mash and cider jus. In the game season, a special set menu might include pheasant soup and roast partridge. Look out for regular beer festivals between June and August.

Open 12-3 6-12 (Sat 12-12 Sun 12-11) Closed: Mon **Bar Meals** L served Tue-Sun 12-3 D served Tue-Thu 6-9, Fri-Sat 6-9.30 **Restaurant** L served Tue-Sun 12-3 D served Tue-Thu 6-9, Fri-Sat 6-9.30 ⊕ FREE HOUSE ◀ Adnams

Southwold Bitter, Woodforde's Wherry & Nelson's Revenge Ö Aspall Harry Sparrow. **Facilities** Non-diners area 🐾 (Bar Garden) ♦ Children's menu Children's portions Play area Garden ⌁ Beer festival Parking Wi-fi 🚌 (notice required)

The Cricketers

PICK OF THE PUBS

CB11 4QT ☎ 01799 550442
e-mail: info@thecricketers.co.uk
dir: *M11 junct 10, A505 E, A1301, B1383. At Newport take B1038*

Famous dining pub in rural Essex

In the lovely village of Clavering with its thatched cottages, winding lanes, extensive woodland and farmland is The Cricketers. The pub has served the community for almost 500 years; all the signs are here — the beams, a forest of wooden pillars, old fireplaces, while outside a wisteria surrounds the door and tables dot a rose-fringed garden. The seasonally changing dishes are expertly prepared by head chef Justin Greig and his team. Meats are properly hung, the fish is always fresh, and local organic produce is used wherever possible. Jamie Oliver, son of landlords Trevor and Sally (over 30 years here), supplies the vegetables and herbs from his certified organic garden nearby. Begin with spicy venison patties or rack of sticky ribs. A salad or pasta dish might follow, or you could try confit leg of duck or chicken supreme. The extensive wine list changes regularly and features excellent house wines and a popular Connoisseurs' Selection, while beers are mostly East Anglian. Children are particularly welcome.

Open all day all wk Closed: 25-26 Dec **Bar Meals** L served all wk 12-2 D served all wk 6.30-9.30 **Restaurant** L served Mon-Sat 12-2, Sun 12-8 D served Mon-Sat 6.30-9.30, Sun 12-8 ⊕ FREE HOUSE ◀ Adnams Broadside & Southwold Bitter, Tetley's Bitter, Greene King IPA, Woodforde's Wherry & Norfolk Nog Ö Aspall. 🍷 17 **Facilities** Non-diners area ♦ Children's menu Children's portions Family room Garden ⌁ Parking Wi-fi 🚌 (notice required)

The Rose & Crown Hotel ★★★ HL

East St CO1 2TZ ☎ 01206 866677
e-mail: info@rose-and-crown.com
dir: *M25 junct 28, A12 N. Follow Colchester signs*

Ancient, black-and-white oak-framed hotel

Just a few minutes' stroll from Colchester Castle, this beautiful timber-framed building dates from the 14th century and is believed to be the oldest hotel in the oldest town in England. The Tudor bar with its central roaring fire is a great place to relax with a drink. Food is served in the Oak Room or the Tudor Room brasserie, an informal alternative serving classic bar food. Typically, start with ham hock terrine or a sharing platter of shellfish, then

continued

COLCHESTER continued

follow with pork belly with butterbean, pancetta and chorizo cassoulet. Leave room for warm pear and almond tart. Accommodation is available.

Open all wk ⊕ FREE HOUSE ◀ Rose & Crown Bitter, Tetley's Bitter, Adnams Broadside. **Facilities** ♦↑ Family room Parking Wi-fi **Rooms** 39

| DEDHAM | Map 13 TM03 |

Marlborough Head Inn ★★★ INN

Mill Ln CO7 6DH ☎ 01206 323250
e-mail: jen.pearmain@tiscali.co.uk
dir: E of A12, N of Colchester

Comfortable and cosy inn serving hearty food

Tucked away in glorious Constable Country, this 16th-century building was once a clearing-house for local wool merchants. In 1660, after a slump in trade, it became an inn. Today it is as perfect for a pint, sofa and newspaper as it is for a good home-cooked family meal. Traditional favourites such as steak, Guinness and mushroom pie; and lamb shank with red wine and rosemary appear on the menu, plus fish is given centre stage on Fridays. There is a terrace and walled garden to enjoy in the warmer weather. Three en suite bedrooms are available.

Open all day all wk 11.30-11 **Bar Meals** food served all day **Restaurant** food served all day ⊕ PUNCH TAVERNS ◀ Greene King IPA, Woodforde's Wherry, Nethergate Growler Ⓞ Aspall. ⓨ 12 **Facilities** Non-diners area ✿ (Bar Garden) ♦↑ Children's menu Children's portions Family room Garden Parking Wi-fi 🚌 (notice required) **Rooms** 3

The Sun Inn ★★★★ INN ◉

PICK OF THE PUBS

High St CO7 6DF ☎ 01206 323351
e-mail: office@thesuninndedham.com
dir: From A12 follow signs to Dedham for 1.5m, pub on High Street

A centuries-old inn with Mediterranean-influenced cuisine

Independently owned and run, this lovely old inn has a smart, yellow-painted exterior. Inside are two informal bars, an open dining room, a snug oak-panelled lounge, three open fires, and exposed timbers and beams. Outside is a suntrap terrace and walled garden overlooked by the church tower; so take your pick of where to enjoy a quiet pint of real ale or a glass of wine. Locally sourced seasonal ingredients drive the daily-changing menu of traditional Mediterranean-style dishes, many with a strong Italian influence. In spring, choose a starter of marinated sea bream fillet with baby fennel, lemon, olive oil and capers; in summer a dessert of peaches in Pinot Nero with star anise and vanilla ice cream; while autumn sees roasted game bird of the day; and in winter a hearty venison casserole might prove very tempting. The bar menu offers sandwiches and more. If you can't tear

yourself away, stay in an en suite guest room, all with large comfy beds.

Open all day all wk 11-11 Closed: 25-27 Dec **Bar Meals** L served Mon-Thu 12-2.30, Fri-Sun 12-3 D served Sun-Thu 6.30-9.30, Fri-Sat 6.30-10 Av main course £8.75 **Restaurant** L served Mon-Thu 12-2.30, Fri-Sun 12-3 D served Sun-Thu 6.30-9.30, Fri-Sat 6.30-10 Fixed menu price fr £15.50 Av 3 course à la carte fr £25 ⊕ FREE HOUSE ◀ Crouch Vale Brewers Gold, Adnams Broadside, 2 Guest ales Ⓞ Aspall. ⓨ 25 **Facilities** Non-diners area ✿ (Bar Garden) ♦↑ Children's menu Children's portions Garden ⋒ Parking Wi-fi **Rooms** 7

| FEERING | Map 7 TL82 |

The Sun Inn

Feering Hill CO5 9NH ☎ 01376 570442
e-mail: sunninnfeering@live.co.uk
dir: On A12 between Colchester & Witham. Village 1m

Ancient pub with two annual beer festivals

A pretty pub dating from 1525 with heavily carved beams to prove it, this Grade II listed building has two inglenook fireplaces and a large garden and courtyard. The traditional bar, which sells Shepherd Neame's real ales, has no TV or games machines. Home-cooked pub classics are backed by mains like herb-crusted rump of lamb with celeriac mash, wilted spinach and a rich meat jus. From May to September wood-fired pizzas are available. Three roasts, together with other options, are offered on Sundays. Over 40 real ales and ciders are showcased at May and October beer festivals.

Open all wk Sat-Sun all day **Bar Meals** L served Mon-Sat 12-2.30, Sun 12-8 D served Mon-Sat 6-9.30, Sun 12-8 **Restaurant** L served Mon-Sat 12-2.30, Sun 12-8 D served Mon-Sat 6-9.30, Sun 12-8 ⊕ SHEPHERD NEAME ◀ Master Brew, Spitfire & Bishops Finger, Guest ales Ⓞ Thatchers Heritage. ⓨ 12 **Facilities** Non-diners area ✿ (Bar Garden) ♦↑ Children's menu Children's portions Garden ⋒ Beer festival Parking 🚌 (notice required)

| FELSTED | Map 6 TL62 |

The Swan at Felsted

PICK OF THE PUBS

Station Rd CM6 3DG ☎ 01371 820245
e-mail: info@theswaninnfelsted.co.uk
dir: M11 junct 8, A120 signed Felsted. Pub in village centre

Pride of place in attractive village

Venture through the door of this red-brick and timbered building and a stylish gastro-pub awaits. Rebuilt after a disastrous fire in the early 1900s, the building was formerly the village bank, then a run-down boozer. In 2002 it was rescued and refurbished by Jono and Jane Clark. With polished wood floors, leather sofas and colourful modern art, it successfully balances traditional pub attributes with a quality dining experience. Locals come for cracking Greene King ales and over a dozen world wines served by the glass; if sharing a bottle, allow

time to peruse the 80-plus choices on the list. Seasonally changing food menus champion locally sourced produce, offering an imaginative selection of modern European dishes that remain in touch with their pub roots. Starters include goats' cheese and apple mousse, and rabbit terrine. Main courses cater to all tastes: roasted duck breast; gnocchi served with pesto and purple sprouting broccoli; or beer-battered haddock and chips. There is a courtyard garden to enjoy in the warmer months.

Open all day all wk 12-10 (Fri-Sat 12-11) **Bar Meals** L served Mon-Sat 12-2.30, Sun 12-5 D served all wk 5.30-9 **Restaurant** L served Mon-Sat 12-2.30, Sun 12-5 D served all wk 5.30-9 ⊕ GREENE KING ◀ IPA, Guinness, Guest ale Ⓞ Aspall. ⓨ 14 **Facilities** Non-diners area ✿ (Bar Restaurant Outside area) ♦↑ Children's menu Children's portions Outside area ⋒ Beer festival Parking

| FINGRINGHOE | Map 7 TM02 |

The Whalebone

Chapel Rd CO5 7BG ☎ 01206 729307
e-mail: vicki@thewhaleboneinn.co.uk
dir: Telephone for directions

British cuisine and breathtaking views

This Grade II listed 18th-century free house enjoys beautiful views from its position at the top of the Roman River Valley. Its name comes from the bones of a locally beached whale, which were once fastened above the door of the pub. Wooden floors, exposed beams, bespoke furniture, a roaring fire and unique artwork all combine to create a feeling of warmth and character. Hearty British fare is prepared from local ingredients, along with Adnams and Sharp's ales. A lunchtime snack can be enjoyed in one of the garden pavilions. The carte menu options include pan-fried red snapper to chargrilled rib-eye steak and roast topside of local beef.

Open all wk 12-3 5.30-11 (Sat 12-11 Sun 12-10.30) **Bar Meals** L served Mon-Sat 12-2.30, Sun 12-6.30 D served Mon-Thu 6.30-9, Fri-Sat 6.30-9.30, Sun 12-6.30 Av main course £12.95 **Restaurant** L served Mon-Sat 12-2.30, Sun 12-6.30 D served Mon-Thu 6.30-9, Fri-Sat 6.30-9.30, Sun 12-6.30 ⊕ FREE HOUSE ◀ Adnams, Woodforde's Wherry, Sharp's Doom Bar, 4 Guest ales Ⓞ Aspall. ⓨ 13 **Facilities** Non-diners area ✿ (Bar Restaurant Garden) ♦↑ Children's menu Children's portions Play area Family room Garden ⋒ Parking 🚌 (notice required)

Save on hotels. Book at **theAA.com/hotel**

ESSEX **169** ENGLAND

FULLER STREET
Map 6 TL71

The Square and Compasses

CM3 2BB ☎ **01245 361477**
e-mail: info@thesquareandcompasses.co.uk
web: www.thesquareandcompasses.co.uk
dir: From A131 (Chelmsford to Braintree) take Great
Leighs exit, enter village, right into Boreham Rd. Left
signed Fuller St & Terling. Pub on left

A prominent feature of village life

Known locally as The Stokehole, this beautifully restored
17th-century village pub is set in lovely countryside but is
just ten minutes from Chelmsford. Originally two farm
cottages, the privately owned and run free house still
retains its original beams and inglenook fireplaces, with
antique furnishings. The locally sourced food is
straightforward, served alongside a good selection of
ciders and ales. As well as pub classics, the daily-
changing specials might include Cromer crab cake,
28-day-hung fillet steak with haggis, and orange and
passionfruit tart. There is a picket fenced front garden
affording views of the Essex Way, and Mediterranean-
style decking area. A beer festival is held in June.

Open all wk 11.30-3 5.30-11 (Sat-Sun 12-11) **Bar
Meals** L served Mon-Fri 12-2, Sat 12-2.30, Sun 12-6
D served Mon-Sat 6.30-9.30 **Restaurant** L served Mon-Fri
12-2, Sat 12-2.30, Sun 12-6 D served Mon-Sat 6.30-9.30
⊕ FREE HOUSE ◀ Farmers Ales A Drop of Nelsons Blood,
Square and Compasses Stokers Ale, Dark Star Hophead
Ö Westons. ☐ 14 **Facilities** Non-diners area ✿ (Bar
Garden) ✦ Children's portions Garden ⊐ Beer festival
Parking

GESTINGTHORPE
Map 13 TL83

The Pheasant ★★★★★ INN ◉ **NEW**

Audley End, Church St CO9 3AU ☎ **01787 465010**
e-mail: thepheasantpb@aol.com
dir: Off B1058 between Castle Hedingham & Sudbury

Superb garden-to-table produce based food

A charming gastro-pub with a proven reputation for real
ales and food, owned by James and Diana Donoghue.
James used to design gardens (even winning a bronze
medal at Chelsea) and his fingers are still green, as
demonstrated by the pub's raised vegetable beds, which
provide organic fruit and vegetables for the restaurant.
He keeps bees too, using the honey in dressings and
salads. Starters typically include pigeon and beetroot
remoulade; and goats' cheese and onion tart, followed by
mains of pan-fried calves' liver and bacon; best loin of
cod in Mauldons beer batter; and Spanish vegetable
frittata.

Open all day all wk **Bar Meals** L served all wk 12-2.30
D served all wk 6.30-9.30 **Restaurant** L served all wk
6.30-9.30 Fixed menu price fr £18 Av 3 course à la carte
fr £25 ⊕ FREE HOUSE ◀ Adnams Southwold Bitter,
Sleaford Pleasant Pheasant Ö Aspall.
Facilities Non-diners area ✿ (Bar Garden Outside area)
✦ Children's portions Garden Outside area ⊐ Parking
Wi-fi ➾ (notice required) **Rooms** 5

GOLDHANGER
Map 7 TL90

The Chequers Inn

Church St CM9 8AS ☎ **01621 788203**
e-mail: chequersgoldhang@aol.com
dir: From B1026, 500mtrs to village centre

'Low' pub in a riverside village

Built in 1410, The Chequers can be found next to the
church in picturesque Goldhanger, on the River
Blackwater. The pub name comes from a chequerboard
used by the tax collector in the pub many, many years
ago. At around 30 feet above sea level, it reputedly has
the 'lowest' bar in Britain, where you can enjoy a pint of
Adnams Broadside. Several rooms decorated with farming
and fishing implements surround the bar area. Pride is
taken in the preparation and presentation of food, which
includes crispy chicken fillets with a lemon and herb
butter; and Somerset brie and beetroot chutney tart.
There are beer festivals in March and September.

Open all day all wk **Bar Meals** L served all wk 12-3
D served Mon-Sat 6.30-9 **Restaurant** L served all wk 12-3
D served Mon-Sat 6.30-9 ⊕ PUNCH TAVERNS ◀ Young's
Bitter, Crouch Vale Brewers Gold, Sharp's Doom Bar,
Timothy Taylor Landlord, Adnams Broadside Ö Westons
Traditional & Perry. ☐ 13 **Facilities** Non-diners area ✦
Children's menu Children's portions Garden ⊐ Beer
festival Parking Wi-fi ➾

GOSFIELD
Map 13 TL72

The Green Man

The Street CO9 1TP ☎ **01787 273608**
e-mail: info@thegreenmangosfield.co.uk
dir: Take A131 N from Braintree then A1017 to village

Dining pub with international cuisine

Close to the picturesque Gosfield Lake, this pink-washed
medley of buildings houses a welcoming village dining
pub. At lunchtime, enjoy a pint of Greene King IPA with a
choice of crusty filled baguettes, or dishes such as
breaded scampi and chips. Using the best of local
produce, the dinner menu is based around classic British
and international fare and offers the likes of asparagus
spears topped with Serrano ham; swordfish steak with a
soy, lime and chilli dressing; and toffee pecan meringue
cheesecake.

Open all day all wk ⊕ GREENE KING ◀ IPA & Abbot Ale,
Guest ales Ö Aspall, Kopparberg. **Facilities** ✦ Children's
menu Children's portions Garden Parking Wi-fi

GREAT TOTHAM
Map 7 TL81

The Bull at Great
Totham ★★★★ RR ◉◉

PICK OF THE PUBS

2 Maldon Rd CM9 8NH ☎ **01621 893385**
e-mail: reservations@thebullatgreattotham.co.uk
dir: Exit A12 at Witham junct to Great Totham

A highly regarded destination gastro-pub and restaurant

The Bull, overlooking the cricket green, is a 16th-century
coaching inn, proud holder of two AA Rosettes. It offers
not far short of 20 fine wines by the glass, real ales from
Adnams, Greene King and guest brewers, and a bar menu
of baguettes, spicy chicken wings, and beer-battered
haddock. Named after the ancient tree in the lavender-
filled garden is the fine-dining Willow Room, where you
might start with crisp-fried local duck egg, winter
vegetables and caramelised onion, then follow with baked
skate wing and caper beurre noisette; or seared salmon
fillet with spring greens and celeriac mash. If you're a
vegetarian, the burnt spinach lasagne with slow-cooked
egg and pumpkin purée might take your fancy. Finish in
style with cherry and almond frangipane with white
chocolate ice cream. Musical and themed dining evenings
and other events are held frequently.

Open all day all wk **Bar Meals** L served Mon-Fri 12-2.30
(light bites till 5.30), Sat 12-10, Sun 12-6.45 D served
Mon-Thu 5.30-9, Fri 5.30-10, Sat 12-10 Av main course
£12.50-£15 food served all day **Restaurant** L served Wed-
Sat 12-2.30, Sun 12-6.45 D served Wed-Sat 5.30-9 Fixed
menu price fr £12.95 Av 3 course à la carte fr £24.95
⊕ FREE HOUSE ◀ Adnams, Greene King, Guest ale. ☐ 17
Facilities Non-diners area ✿ (Garden) ✦ Children's
menu Children's portions Play area Garden Outside area
⊐ Parking ➾ (notice required) **Rooms** 4

GREAT YELDHAM
Map 13 TL73

The White Hart ★★★★ RR ◉◉

PICK OF THE PUBS

Poole St CO9 4HJ ☎ 01787 237250
e-mail: mjwmason@yahoo.co.uk
dir: *On A1017 between Haverhill & Halstead*

Character old inn with contemporary cooking

Highwaymen were once locked up in a small prison beneath the stairs of this impressive 500-year-old timber-framed inn. Situated on the border of Essex and Suffolk, The White Hart enjoys a setting within 4.5 acres of gardens, close to Heddingham Castle, the Colne Valley and Newmarket. With its blend of traditional and contemporary, it's a popular wedding venue on the one hand, and a great place to sample Brandon Rusty Bucket on the other. The hard work put in by the establishment's owner, Matthew Mason, has resulted in many awards, including two AA Rosettes for the food. The express bar menu lists favourites such as Cumberland sausage ring with cheddar mash and onion gravy, while the à la carte choice includes ballotine of Yeldham wood pigeon among its starters, and Auberies Estate roast loin of venison as a main course. For dessert there's baked Alaska or warm pear frangipane. Eleven en suite and fully equipped rooms complete the picture.

Open all day all wk ⊕ FREE HOUSE ◀ Adnams Southwold Bitter, Black Sheep, Brandon Rusty Bucket, Sharp's Doom Bar Ö Aspall. **Facilities** ₦ Children's menu Children's portions Play area Garden Parking Wi-fi **Rooms** 11

HASTINGWOOD
Map 6 TL40

Rainbow & Dove

Hastingwood Rd CM17 9JX ☎ 01279 415419
e-mail: rainbowanddove@hotmail.co.uk
dir: *Just off M11 junct 7*

Little pub with a varied history

Dating back to at least the 16th century, Rainbow & Dove was a farmhouse, staging post, village shop and post office before it became a pub. English Heritage has given it Grade II historical building status. There are cask-conditioned real ales, a selection of whiskies and a good wine list. Menus revolve around fresh seasonal produce. Fish from Billingsgate Market is bought, delivered and cooked all on the same day, so you may find skate, sea bass and bream on the blackboard. Other dishes include roasted garlic, broad bean and asparagus risotto; and chicken curry. An Oktoberfest-inspired beer festival is held over the last weekend in October.

Open Mon-Sat 11.30-3.30 6-11 (Sun 12-5) Closed: Sun eve **Bar Meals** L served Mon-Sat 12-2.30, Sun 12-3.30 D served Mon-Sat 6.30-9 Av main course £5.50 **Restaurant** L served Mon-Sat 12-2.30, Sun 12-3.30 D served Mon-Sat 6.30-9.30 Fixed menu price fr £7.25 ⊕ FREE HOUSE ◀ Rainbow & Dove, Adnams Broadside, Sharp's Doom Bar, Guest ales Ö Aspall. ₱ 10 **Facilities** Non-diners area ❄ (Bar Garden) ₦ Children's menu Children's portions Garden ⊼ Beer festival Parking ▦ (notice required)

HATFIELD BROAD OAK
Map 6 TL51

The Duke's Head

High St CM22 7HH ☎ 01279 718598
e-mail: info@thedukeshead.co.uk
web: www.thedukeshead.co.uk
dir: *M11 junct 8, A120 towards Great Dunmow. Right into B183 to Hatfield Broad Oak. Pub on left at 1st bend in village*

Welcoming child- and dog-friendly pub

On a corner, behind a white-painted picket fence, stands this 185-year-old village pub. Spacious, and with two wood-burning fires, it has a large catchment area, with customers drawn particularly by the seasonal British menu devised by Marco Pierre White protégé, chef/proprietor Justin Flodman. Justin's Sunday roasts are not alone in enjoying county-wide fame: among his specials is black treacle bacon chop with mustard mash and Puy lentil and chorizo ragout, while other attractions are local game; shellfish and seafood; Doom Bar beer-battered haddock fillet; slow-cooked Barnston beef cobbler; Moroccan-spiced Chiltern lamb shank; and sweet potato and pumpkin gnocchi.

Open all wk 12-3 5-11.30 (Fri-Sun all day) Closed: 25-26 Dec **Bar Meals** L served Mon-Fri 12-2.30, Sat 10.30-10, Sun 12-9 D served Mon-Thu 6.30-9.30, Fri 6.30-10, Sat 10.30-10, Sun 12-9 **Restaurant** L served Mon-Fri 12-2.30, Sat 10.30-10, Sun 12-9 D served Mon-Thu 6.30-9.30, Fri 6.30-10, Sat 10.30-10, Sun 12-9 ⊕ ENTERPRISE INNS ◀ Greene King IPA, Sharp's Doom Bar, Timothy Taylor Landlord Ö Aspall. ₱ 25 **Facilities** Non-diners area ❄ (Bar Garden) ₦ Children's menu Children's portions Play area Garden ⊼ Parking ▦ (notice required)

HATFIELD HEATH
Map 6 TL51

The Thatcher's **NEW**

Stortford Rd CM22 7DU ☎ 01279 730270
e-mail: info@thethatcherspub.co.uk
dir: *In village on A1060 (Bishop's Stortford road)*

Charming old pub serving home-made food

A pretty, thatched 16th-century pub overlooking the village green with oak beams and a welcoming inglenook wood-burning stove. The dishes are all prepared on the premises and might start with smoked haddock rarebit, pigeon pâté with beetroot chutney or deep-fried breaded Cornish brie, port and cranberry compôte, followed by a venison duo of roasted loin and a venison and vegetable pie, dauphinoise potatoes and braised red cabbage; Essex lamb rump, ratatouille, fondant potatoes and rosemary and redcurrant sauce, or pan-fried pancetta wrapped cod loin with broad bean and pea risotto. Also enjoy a pint from the Nethergates Brewery just 30 miles up the road.

Open all wk 11.30-3.30 5.30-11 (Sat-Sun all day) **Bar Meals** L served all wk 12-2 D served all wk 6-9 **Restaurant** L served all wk 12-2 D served all wk 6-9 ⊕ FREE HOUSE ◀ St Austell Tribute, Nethergate, Mighty Oak, Adnams. ₱ 11 **Facilities** Non-diners area ₦ Children's portions Family room Garden ⊼ Parking ▦ (notice required)

HORNDON ON THE HILL
Map 6 TQ68

Bell Inn & Hill House

PICK OF THE PUBS

High Rd SS17 8LD ☎ 01375 642463
e-mail: info@bell-inn.co.uk
dir: *M25 junct 30/31 signed Thurrock*

Historic inn with a quirky talking point

In the same family since 1938, this 15th-century coaching inn had a chequered and gruesome past – one local landowner was burnt at the stake for heresy behind the pub. Look out for the first-floor gallery that runs above the courtyard; from here luggage would have been transferred to and from the top of the London stagecoaches. In the wood-panelled bar, regular brews like Greene King IPA are backed by a selection of changing guest ales. The lunchtime bar menu offers sandwiches and light meals but booking is essential in the bustling restaurant, where the daily-changing modern British menu with an international twist is driven by the best seasonal produce. A typical meal might be pork shoulder wontons; pan-fried veal chop with balsamic roast shallots, blackberries and blue cheese; and mango and raspberry mousse. You might notice the hot cross buns hanging from the original king post that supports the ancient roof timbers. Every year the oldest willing villager hangs another, an unusual tradition that dates back 100 years to when the pub happened to change hands on a Good Friday.

Open all wk Mon-Fri 11-3 5.30-11 (Sat 11-3 6-11 Sun 12-4 7-10.30) Closed: 25-26 Dec **Bar Meals** L served all wk 12-1.45 D served Mon-Fri 6.30-9.45, Sat 6-9.45, Sun 7-9.45 Av main course £9.50 **Restaurant** L served Mon-Sat 12-1.45, Sun 12-2.30 D served Mon-Sat 6.30-9.45, Sun 7-9.45 Av 3 course à la carte fr £30 ⊕ FREE HOUSE ◀ Greene King IPA, Crouch Vale Brewers Gold, Sharp's Doom Bar, Bass, Guest ales. ₱ 16 **Facilities** Non-diners area ❄ (Bar Garden) ₦ Children's portions Garden ⊼ Parking Wi-fi

INGATESTONE　　　　Map 6 TQ69

The Red Lion

Main Rd, Margaretting CM4 0EQ ☎ **01277 352184**
dir: *From Chelmsford take A12 towards Brentwood. Margaretting in 4m*

A proper English pub

Emphatically a traditional inn and not a restaurant (although it does sell quality food), the 17th-century Red Lion is best described as a 'quintessential English pub'. The bar is decorated in burgundy and aubergine, the restaurant in coffee and cream. From an extensive menu choose prawn tostada; home-made balti curry; or classic moules marinière. Every Thursday you can get two steaks and a bottle of wine for £25. Wash it down with a pint of Greene King IPA or guest ales, and look out for Mr Darcy and Mr Gray, the house donkeys.

Open all wk 12-11 (Sun 12-6) **Bar Meals** L served all wk 12-3 D served Mon-Sat 6-9 **Restaurant** L served all wk 12-3 D served Mon-Sat 6-9 ⊕ GREENE KING ◀ IPA, Guest ales ○ Westons Stowford Press. ♀ 14
Facilities Non-diners area ♦♦ Children's menu Children's portions Play area Garden ⊨ Parking Wi-fi ▭ (notice required)

LANGHAM　　　　Map 13 TM03

The Shepherd and Dog

Moor Rd CO4 5NR ☎ **01206 272711**
dir: *A12 from Colchester towards Ipswich, take 1st left signed Langham*

20th-century country pub with good food from a varied menu

Set in the attractive village of Langham deep in Constable Country on the Suffolk/Essex border, this 1928 free house has all the classic styling of an English country pub. Widely renowned for its food, it serves an extensive variety of meat, fish and poultry dishes, plus a vegetarian selection and a children's menu. A typical meal could take in deep-fried brie with cranberry sauce followed by home-made chicken curry, beer-battered cod, or maybe rump steak and peppercorn sauce.

Open all wk **Bar Meals** L served Mon-Fri 12-3, Sat-Sun 12-9.30 D served Mon-Fri 6-9.30, Sat-Sun 12-9.30 Av main course £3.50-£5 **Restaurant** L served Mon-Fri 12-3, Sat-Sun 12-9.30 D served Mon-Fri 6-9.30, Sat-Sun 12-9.30 Fixed menu price fr £8.95 Av 3 course à la carte fr £13.95 ⊕ FREE HOUSE ◀ Greene King IPA & Abbot Ale, Guest ales. **Facilities** Non-diners area ♦♦ Children's menu Children's portions Garden Parking ▭

LITTLE BRAXTED　　　　Map 7 TL81

The Green Man

Green Man Ln CM8 3LB ☎ **01621 891659 & 07971 064378**
e-mail: info@thegreenmanlittlebraxted.com
dir: *From A12 junct 22 take unclassified road (Little Braxted Ln) through Little Braxted. Straight ahead into Kelvedon Rd. Right into Green Man Ln*

Classic village local in hands of a Masterchef

Take the Kelvedon road northbound from the village centre to find this unspoilt brick-and-tiled, Greene King pub. Dating from the early 1700s, it has a traditional interior with collections of beer tankards, horse brasses and old woodworking tools. Outside is a tree-shaded rear garden, which new owner, Masterchef Stephen Hurley, has ambitious plans for. His concise menu lists such dishes as lamb shank in red wine and mint gravy; beef lasagne with jacket potato; and Thai green chicken curry. Other attractions are Nethergate, Hydes and guest ales, and beer and cider festivals (please contact the pub for dates).

Open all wk Mon-Sat 11.30-3 5-11 (Sun 12-7) **Bar Meals** L served Mon-Sat 12-2.30, Sun 12-6 D served Mon-Sat 6-9 Av main course £9 **Restaurant** L served Mon-Sat 12-2.30, Sun 12-6 D served Mon-Sat 6-9 ⊕ GREENE KING ◀ IPA, Abbot Ale & Abbot Reserve, Nethergate, Hydes, Guest ales. ♀ 9
Facilities Non-diners area ❀ (Bar Garden) ♦♦ Children's menu Children's portions Garden ⊨ Beer festival Cider festival Parking Wi-fi ▭ (notice required)

LITTLE BURSTEAD　　　　Map 6 TQ69

The Dukes Head

Laindon Common Rd CM12 9TA ☎ **01277 651333**
e-mail: enquiry@dukesheadlittleburstead.co.uk
dir: *From Basildon take A176 (Noah Hill Rd) N toward Billericay. Left into Laindon Common Rd to Little Burstead. Pub on left*

Welcoming pub known for its themed food events

Smart interiors and a friendly team characterise the atmosphere in this large hostelry between Brentwood and Basildon. Chunky wood tables, leather-upholstered stools and relaxing armchairs surround the open fire in the bar area, where the ales vie for selection with an excellent range of wines served by the glass. Modern British food ranges from pizzas and pastas to the chef's daily specials.

Open all day all wk ⊕ MITCHELLS & BUTLERS ◀ Fuller's London Pride, Sharp's Doom Bar, Adnams.
Facilities ❀ (Bar Garden) ♦♦ Children's menu Children's portions Garden Parking

LITTLEBURY　　　　Map 12 TL53

The Queens Head Inn Littlebury

High St CB11 4TD ☎ **01799 520365**
e-mail: info@queensheadinnlittlebury.co.uk
dir: *M11 junct 9A, B184 towards Saffron Walden. Right onto B1383, S towards Wendens Ambo*

Popular community pub with large beer garden and good home-made food

A beautiful family-run former coaching inn with open fires, exposed beams and one of only two remaining full-length settles in England. Very much at the centre of the local community, the pub runs darts and football teams and pétanque competitions; a large beer garden with bouncy castle confirms its family-friendly credentials. The kitchen aims to produce good home-made pub grub at realistic prices, with a menu of popular favourites from pizzas to pies, ciabattas to curries.

Open all day all wk Mon 10am-11pm Tue-Thu 8am-11pm Fri 8am-1am Sat 9am-1am Sun 9am-11pm **Bar Meals** L served Tue-Sat 12-3, Sun 12-4 D served Tue-Sat 6-9 Av main course £8.95 **Restaurant** L served Tue-Sat 12-3, Sun 12-4 D served Tue-Sat 6-9 ⊕ GREENE KING ◀ IPA, Guest ale ○ Westons Stowford Press, Aspall. ♀ 9
Facilities Non-diners area ❀ (Bar Garden) ♦♦ Children's menu Children's portions Play area Garden ⊨ Beer festival Parking Wi-fi ▭ (notice required)

LITTLE CANFIELD　　　　Map 6 TL52

The Lion & Lamb

CM6 1SR ☎ **01279 870257**
e-mail: info@lionandlamb.co.uk
dir: *M11 junct 8, B1256 towards Takeley & Little Canfield*

Perfect for a pre-flight meal

Built as a coaching inn on what used to be the main East Coast road, this traditional country pub and restaurant is ideal for business or leisure. Now bypassed, travellers on the way to Stansted Airport seek it out for a last English pint before their trip, relaxing in the large and well-furnished garden. Inside are oak beams, winter log fires and plenty of real ales. A typical meal might be wild mushroom risotto with pesto and shaved parmesan followed by slow-roasted pork belly stuffed with apricots and sage, mashed sweet potato with a rich wine sauce. Finish with spotted dick.

Open all day all wk 11-11 **Bar Meals** Av main course £5-£12 food served all day **Restaurant** food served all day ⊕ GREENE KING ◀ IPA & St Edmunds, St Austell, Guest ales. ♀ 11 **Facilities** Non-diners area ♦♦ Children's menu Children's portions Play area Garden ⊨ Parking Wi-fi ▭

LITTLE DUNMOW — Map 6 TL62

Flitch of Bacon

The Street CM6 3HT ☎ 01371 820323
dir: B1256 to Braintree for 10m, exit at Little Dunmow, 0.5m, pub on right

Traditional family pub in the countryside

A charming 15th-century country inn, looking out over the fields, whose name refers to the ancient gift of half a salted pig, or 'flitch', to couples who have been married for a year and a day, and 'who have not had a cross word'. There are always two guest ales in addition to Greene King IPA. Children are welcome.

Open Mon eve-Sun Closed: Mon L ⊕ FREE HOUSE ◀ Greene King IPA, Guest ales. **Facilities** ⁜ Children's portions Family room Garden Wi-fi **Notes** ⊜

LITTLEY GREEN — Map 6 TL71

The Compasses NEW

CM3 1BU ☎ 01245 362308
e-mail: compasseslittleygreen@googlemail.com

Unspoilt country local deep in rural Essex

Ridley Brewery's former tap fell on hard times following the closure of the brewery and sale of the pub estate in 2005. Joss Ridley left London and a top job and snapped up the pub in 2008 to revive the family link and hasn't looked back. The traditional inn stands in a sleepy hamlet and thrives selling tip-top ales straight from the barrel, including Bishop Nick, brewed by Joss's brother Neilon, and fresh, hearty pub food. Using local ingredients, the menu and chalkboard specials include filled 'huffer' baps, pea and mushroom risotto, and beer battered cod and chips. The interior is timeless and unspoilt, the garden large and peaceful. Perhaps time your visit for the August Bank Holiday beer festival.

Open all wk 12-3 5.30-11.30 (Thu-Sun all day) **Bar Meals** L served Mon-Fri 12-2.30, Sat-Sun 12-5 D served Sun-Fri 7-9.30, Sat 5-9.30 **Restaurant** L served Mon-Fri 12-2.30, Sat-Sun 12-5 D served Sun-Fri 7-9.30, Sat 5-9.30 ⊕ FREE HOUSE ◀ Adnams, Bishop Nick, Green Jack, Crouch Vale, Mighty Oak Ò Gwynt y Ddraig, Westons, Burnard's. **Facilities** Non-diners area ⁜ (Bar Restaurant Garden) ⁜ Children's portions Garden ⋈ Beer festival Parking Wi-fi ⛟ (notice required)

MANNINGTREE — Map 13 TM13

The Mistley Thorn ⊛⊛

PICK OF THE PUBS

High St, Mistley CO11 1HE ☎ 01206 392821
e-mail: info@mistleythorn.co.uk
dir: From Ipswich A12 junct 31 onto B1070, follow signs to East Bergholt, Manningtree & Mistley. From Colchester A120 towards Harwich. Left at Horsley Cross. Mistley in 3m

Recommended for its excellent seafood dishes

Overlooking the estuary of the River Stour, this former coaching inn was built in 1723. The village was intended to become a fashionable saltwater spa, but it never quite took off. Inside, all the public spaces are light and airy with high ceilings, having received a makeover in 2013. Co-owner and executive chef Sherri Singleton, who hails from California, also runs the Mistley Kitchen cookery school next door. Outside the Thorn, a hanging sign says 'Oysters', a hefty hint of what's in store, those from Mersea Island being available year-round and Colchester natives when in season. With seafood a speciality, the two AA Rosette menus change daily to reflect availability: a starter of chargrilled day-boat squid might be followed by cioppino, a Californian-Italian seafood stew. And for dessert, chocolate and espresso terrine with chocolate ice cream. Real ales come from the Adnams and Mersea Island breweries.

Open all wk 12-2.30 6.30-9 (Sat-Sun all day) **Bar Meals** L served Mon-Fri 12-2.30, Sat-Sun 12-5 D served Mon-Fri 6.30-9.30, Sat-Sun 6-9.30 Av main course £7.95 **Restaurant** L served Mon-Fri 12-2.30, Sat-Sun 12-5 D served Mon-Fri 6.30-9.30, Sat-Sun 6-9.30 Fixed menu price fr £10.50 Av 3 course à la carte fr £21.50 ⊕ FREE HOUSE ◀ Adnams Southwold Bitter, Mersea Island. ⏰ 17 **Facilities** Non-diners area ⁜ (Bar Restaurant) ⁜ Children's menu Children's portions Parking Wi-fi

MARGARETTING TYE — Map 6 TL60

The White Hart Inn

Swan Ln CM4 9JX ☎ 01277 840478
e-mail: liz@thewhitehart.uk.com
dir: From A12 junct 15, B1002 to Margaretting. At x-rds in Margaretting left into Maldon Rd. Under rail bridge, left. Right into Swan Ln, follow Margaretting Tye signs. Follow to pub on right

Weatherboarded pub holding two popular beer festivals

Parts of this pub, sitting proudly on a green known locally as Tigers Island, are 250 years old. Landlady Liz and her team revel in offering a great choice of the best regional and local beers and ciders. The pub's interior, all matchboarding, old pictures, brewery memorabilia, dark posts, pillars, beams and fireplaces, oozes character, while the solidly traditional menu and specials board shout quality. Start with an Italian meat platter, and move on to lamb's liver and bacon casserole; grilled extra mature rib-eye steak; or roasted sea bass fillets served on couscous.

Open all wk 11.30-3 6-12 (Sat-Sun 12-12) Closed: 25 Dec ⊕ FREE HOUSE ◀ Adnams Southwold Bitter & Broadside, Mighty Oak IPA & Oscar Wilde Mild, Red Fox Hunter's Gold Ò Aspall, Black Rat, Rekorderlig. **Facilities** ⁜ (Bar Garden) ⁜ Children's menu Family room Garden Parking Wi-fi

MOUNT BURES — Map 13 TL93

The Thatchers Arms

Hall Rd CO8 5AT ☎ 01787 227460
e-mail: hello@thatchersarms.co.uk
dir: From A12 onto A1124 towards Halstead. Right immediately after Chappel Viaduct. 2m, pub on right

Bustling rural pub with well thought out menus

There's something for all-comers at this cheery country pub in the lovely Stour Valley. Challenge the quoits beds in the large beer garden, or ramble paths that Constable may once have walked; there's even a small cinema here. Popular with locals and visitors, up to five real ales (and twice-yearly beer festivals) slake the thirst of hop-lovers, whilst diners may choose from a sheaf of enticing menus, perhaps tempting with home-made venison and bacon burgers; alternatively home-smoked saddle of rabbit with wild mushroom and tarragon risotto accompanied by beer cured bacon lardons should satisfy. Slimmers and food allergy sufferers are also well catered for here.

Open 12-3 6-11 (Sat-Sun all day) Closed: Mon **Bar Meals** L served Tue-Sat 12-2.30, Sun 12-8 D served Tue-Sat 6-9, Sun 12-8 **Restaurant** L served Tue-Sat 12-2.30, Sun 12-8 D served Tue-Sat 6-9, Sun 12-8 ⊕ FREE HOUSE ◀ Adnams Southwold Bitter, Crouch Vale Brewers Gold, Guest ales. ⏰ 10 **Facilities** Non-diners area ⁜ (Bar Restaurant Garden) ⁜ Children's portions Garden ⋈ Beer festival Parking Wi-fi ⛟ (notice required)

MOUNTNESSING — Map 6 TQ69

The George & Dragon

294 Roman Rd CM15 0TZ ☎ 01277 352461
e-mail: enquiry@thegeorgeanddragonbrentwood.co.uk
dir: In village centre

Flavoursome food in a laid-back gastro-pub

Spruced-up in true contemporary gastro-pub style, the interior of this 18th-century former coaching inn successfully blends bold artwork, colourful leather chairs and chunky modern tables with preserved original wooden floors, exposed beams and brick fireplaces. In this relaxed and convivial setting tuck into Mediterranean-inspired British dishes from an extensive menu that should please all tastes and palates. There are sharing platters, salads and pasta dishes, a selection of stone-baked pizzas and main courses like calves' liver with champ and red wine jus; and sea bass with sweet potato and aubergine tagine.

Open all day all wk ⊕ MITCHELLS & BUTLERS ◀ Fuller's London Pride, Adnams Broadside Ò Aspall Harry Sparrow. **Facilities** ⁜ Children's portions Garden Parking

NEWNEY GREEN　　　　　　Map 6 TL60

The Duck Pub & Dining

CM1 3SF ☎ 01245 421894
e-mail: theduckinn1@btconnect.com
dir: *From Chelmsford take A1060 (Sawbridgeworth). Straight on at mini rdbt, 4th left into Vicarage Rd (signed Roxwell & Willingate), left into Hoe St, becomes Gravelly Ln, left to pub*

Peace and quiet at a quintessential country inn

Formed from two agricultural cottages, this 17th-century inn is nestled in the tiny hamlet of Newney Green. Fully restored by the current owners, the friendly Duck offers up to six real ales, including weekly guests, and menus that reflect the region's produce. Choose from the extensive menu in the beamed dining room, from classics like steak-and-ale pie and scampi and chips, to game casserole with dumplings, and lamb shank braised in honey and mint. Soak up the sun in the garden with its children's play area. There is an August Bank Holiday beer festival.

Open all day Closed: Mon **Bar Meals** L served Tue-Sun 12-9.30 D served Tue-Sun 12-9.30 Av main course £13 food served all day **Restaurant** L served Tue-Sun 12-9.30 D served Tue-Sun 12-9.30 Fixed menu price fr £15 Av 3 course à la carte fr £15 food served all day ⊕ FREE HOUSE ◀ Woodforde's Wherry, Adnams Broadside, Sharp's Doom Bar, Guest ales. ♚ 14
Facilities Non-diners area ♦♦ Children's menu Children's portions Play area Family room Garden ⚲ Beer festival Parking Wi-fi ☛

NORTH FAMBRIDGE　　　　　Map 7 TQ89

The Ferry Boat Inn

Ferry Ln CM3 6LR ☎ 01621 740208
dir: *From Chelmsford take A130 S, then A132 to South Woodham Ferrers, then B1012. Turn right to village*

Traditional riverside village inn

Believed to have been an inn for at least 200 years, the current owners of this 500-year-old, weatherboarded inn beside a yacht haven on the River Crouch arrived in April 2012. Known locally as the FBI, it started out as three fishermen's cottages, whose low beams and winter fires add character to the bars selling Greene King ales and Aspall cider. Menu choices include baguettes, jacket potatoes and burgers; steak-and-kidney pudding; Somerset pork loin steaks; scampi and chips; and vegetarian cheddar pie. Next door is a 600-acre Essex Wildlife Trust nature reserve, a winter feeding ground for Brent geese.

Open all day all wk **Bar Meals** L served all wk 12-2 D served all wk 7-9.30 **Restaurant** L served all wk 12-2 D served all wk 7-9.30 ⊕ FREE HOUSE ◀ Greene King IPA & Abbot Ale, Morland Ö Aspall. **Facilities** Non-diners area ♣ (Bar Garden) ♦♦ Children's menu Children's portions Family room Garden ⚲ Parking ☛ (notice required)

PATTISWICK　　　　　　　Map 13 TL82

The Compasses at Pattiswick

PICK OF THE PUBS

Compasses Rd CM77 8BG ☎ 01376 561322
e-mail: info@thecompassesatpattiswick.co.uk
dir: *A120 from Braintree towards Colchester. After Bradwell 1st left to Pattiswick*

Destination pub, an ideal rural retreat

Years ago, two farm workers' cottages were amalgamated to form this friendly pub, still surrounded by the meadows and pocket woodlands of the Holifield Estate. The pub's owners source some of the raw materials for their menu direct from the estate. Support for local producers is at the centre of the pub's ethos, with minimising food miles being a guiding principle. Hearty rural recipes and uncomplicated cooking allow the dishes to do the talking. The main menu is supplemented by a daily specials board, allowing the chefs to take full advantage of seasonal produce. The dinner menu might feature toad-in-the-hole; Mediterranean vegetable linguine; and roast mutton shepherd's pie. The wine list is very comprehensive and features some exclusive Bordeaux and Burgundies. A roaring log fire makes a welcoming sight in winter after a local walk, while in summer the large garden is inviting. Families are very well catered for here, with a play area and toy box to keep little diners entertained.

Open all wk 11-3 5.30-11 (Sat 11-3 5.30-12 Sun 12-4 5.30-9) **Bar Meals** L served all wk 12-3 D served Mon-Thu 5.30-9.30, Fri-Sat 5.30-9.45, Sun 5.30-9 **Restaurant** L served Mon-Sat 12-3 D served Mon-Thu 5.30-9.30, Fri-Sat 5.30-9.45, Sun 5.30-9 ⊕ FREE HOUSE ◀ Woodforde's Wherry, Adnams Broadside, St Austell Tribute Ö Aspall. ♚ 13 **Facilities** Non-diners area ♦♦ Children's menu Children's portions Play area Garden Parking Wi-fi

PELDON　　　　　　　　　Map 7 TL91

The Peldon Rose

Colchester Rd CO5 7QJ ☎ 01206 735248
e-mail: enquiries@thepeldonrose.co.uk
dir: *On B1025 Mersea Rd, just before causeway*

Historic inn, modern food

Contraband was once big business at this early 15th-century inn, understandably given its proximity to The Strood, which bridges the network of channels and creeks separating mainland Essex from Mersea Island. You can easily imagine the smugglers in the original-beamed bar with its leaded windows, but less so in the contemporary conservatory leading to the garden. A well-deserved reputation for good food begins with regularly changing menus offering chicken and chorizo terrine; and beetroot-cured salmon as starters, and main courses of Thai-style vegetable linguine; Moroccan-style lamb tagine; and beer-battered fish and chips. Chef's quiche of the day makes an ideal light lunch.

Open all day all wk Closed: 25 Dec **Bar Meals** L served all wk 12-2.30 D served all wk 6.30-9 **Restaurant** L served all wk 12-2.30 D served all wk 6.30-9 Av 3 course à la carte fr £20 ⊕ FREE HOUSE ◀ Adnams Southwold Bitter, Woodforde's Wherry Ö Aspall. ♚ 15
Facilities Non-diners area ♦♦ Children's menu Children's portions Garden ⚲ Parking ☛ (notice required)

RICKLING GREEN　　　　　Map 12 TL52

The Cricketers Arms NEW

CB11 3YG ☎ 01799 543210
e-mail: info@thecricketersarmsricklinggreen.co.uk
dir: *M11 junct 10, A505 E. 1.5m, right onto B1301, 2.2m, right onto B1383 at rdbt. Through Newport to Rickling Green. Right into Rickling Green Rd, 0.2m to pub, on left*

Classic village green pub – perfect for cricket fans

Well-placed for Saffron Walden and Stansted Airport, Cosy Pubs' flagship inn enjoys a peaceful position overlooking the village green and cricket pitch in sleepy Rickling Green. The rambling bar and dining rooms have a comfortable, contemporary feel, with squashy sofas by the log fire providing the perfect winter evening refuge for tucking into scallops with spicy chorizo, roast partridge with onion and bacon jus, and bread-and-butter pudding. Arrive early on summer weekends to bag a table on the terrace – a popular spot in which to relax with a pint of Doom Bar and watch an innings or two.

Open all day all wk **Bar Meals** L served Mon-Thu 12-3, Fri-Sat 12-10, Sun 12-8 D served Mon-Thu 6-10, Fri-Sat 12-10, Sun 12-8 Av main course £6.50 **Restaurant** L served Mon-Thu 12-2, Fri-Sat 12-10, Sun 12-8 D served Mon-Thu 6-10, Fri-Sat 12-10, Sun 12-8 Av 3 course à la carte fr £29.50 ⊕ PUNCH TAVERNS ◀ Sharp's Doom Bar, Woodforde's Wherry, Guest ale Ö Addlestones. ♚ 10
Facilities Non-diners area ♣ (Bar Garden Outside area) ♦♦ Children's menu Children's portions Garden Outside area ⚲ Parking Wi-fi ☛ (notice required)

SAFFRON WALDEN — Map 12 TL53

Old English Gentleman NEW

11 Gold St CB10 1EJ ☎ 01799 523595
e-mail: goodtimes@oldenglishgentleman.com
dir: *M11 junct 9a, B184 signed Saffron Walden. Left at High St lights into George St, 1st right into Gold St (one-way system)*

A warm, friendly town-centre local

Regulars call Jeff and Cindy Leach's 19th-century, town centre pub the OEG, an informality which the top-hatted dandy on the sign over the front door might frown upon. Ancient tobacco pipes line a wall of the central bar area, which extends into a dining space with a log burner and air conditioning, while outside is a heated patio garden. Resident ales Adnams Southwold and Woodforde's Wherry are backed up by changing guests and Aspall Suffolk cider, a portfolio that earns customers' respect. Hearty main meals include beer-battered catch of the day; piri piri chicken breast; and sausages and mash.

Open all day all wk **Bar Meals** L served all wk 12-2.30 **Restaurant** L served all wk 12-2.30 ◀ Woodforde's Wherry, Adnams Southwold Bitter, 2 Guest ales Ö Aspall. ♀ 10 **Facilities** Non-diners area ❤ (Bar Outside area) ♦♦ Outside area ♬ Wi-fi

STANSTED AIRPORT

See Little Canfield

STOCK — Map 6 TQ69

The Hoop ◉

21 High St CM4 9BD ☎ 01277 841137
e-mail: thehoopstock@yahoo.co.uk
web: www.thehoop.co.uk
dir: *On B1007 between Chelmsford & Billericay*

Traditional pub with a focus on food

This 15th-century free house on Stock's village green is every inch the traditional country pub, offering a warm welcome, authentic pub interiors and a pleasing absence of music and fruit machines. There's an emphasis on food here, with dishes ranging from traditional chicken and vegetable terrine to native lobster ravioli with carrot and anise purée, aubergine, tomato and basil. You could finish with chocolate fondant. The annual beer festival (late May) has been going from strength to strength for over 30 years; you'll have over 100 real ales to choose from, not to mention fruit beers, perries and more.

Open all day all wk **Bar Meals** L served Mon-Fri 12-2.30, Sat 12-9.30, Sun 12-5 D served Mon-Thu 6-9, Fri 6-9.30, Sat 12-9.30 Av main course £10 **Restaurant** L served Tue-Fri 12-2, Sun 12-3 D served Tue-Sat 6-9 Av 3 course à la carte fr £25 ⊕ FREE HOUSE ◀ Adnams Southwold Bitter, Crouch Vale Brewers Gold, Young's, Wibblers, Guest ales Ö Thatchers Gold. ♀ 12 **Facilities** Non-diners area ❤ (Bar Garden) ♦♦ Children's portions Garden ♬ Beer festival Wi-fi

WOODHAM MORTIMER — Map 7 TL80

Hurdlemakers Arms

Post Office Rd CM9 6ST ☎ 01245 225169
e-mail: info@hurdlemakersarms.co.uk
dir: *From Chelmsford A414 to Maldon/Danbury. 4.5m, through Danbury into Woodham Mortimer. Over 1st rdbt, 1st left, pub on left. Behind golf driving range*

Family-run pub with a great beer festival

Previously two cottages, this 400-year-old listed building in the sleepy village of Woodham Mortimer became a pub in 1837. The beamed interior still retains its open log fire and many original features, and ale-lovers will be delighted by the range of real ales such as Mighty Oak and Farmers. Home-made dishes might include Tuscan vegetable tart, roast or pie of the day, grilled steaks and beer-battered cod. There are weekend summer barbecues in the large garden, and a beer festival takes place on the last weekend of June, when there are over 25 ales and ciders to sample.

Open all day all wk 12-11 (Sun 12-9) **Bar Meals** L served Mon-Fri 12-3, Sat 12-9.30, Sun 12-8 D served Mon-Fri 6-9.30, Sat 12-9.30, Sun 12-8 **Restaurant** L served Mon-Fri 12-3, Sat 12-9.30, Sun 12-8 D served Mon-Fri 6-9.30, Sat 12-9.30, Sun 12-8 ⊕ GRAY & SONS ◀ Mighty Oak, Farmers, Wibblers, Guest ales Ö Westons Old Rosie & Wyld Wood Organic. ♀ 8 **Facilities** Non-diners area ♦♦ Children's menu Children's portions Play area Garden ♬ Beer festival Parking Wi-fi 🚌

GLOUCESTERSHIRE

ALDERTON — Map 10 SP03

The Gardeners Arms

Beckford Rd GL20 8NL ☎ 01242 620257
e-mail: gardeners1@btconnect.com
dir: *Telephone for directions*

Tapas, fresh fish and seasonal specials

A pub since the 16th century, this pretty, family-run, thatched free house is popular with walkers, cyclists and car clubs. You can play boules in the large beer garden, and traditional games in the stone-walled bar, where Cotswold Way numbers among the real ales. Starters include tapas; pub classics take in ham, egg and chips; and pork and leek sausages and mash; and for vegetarians there's broccoli and cauliflower carbonara bake. Fresh fish and seasonal specials change regularly. Spring Bank Holiday and Boxing Day both kick off five-day beer festivals, while the cider drinkers' turn is on August Bank Holiday.

Open all wk 9.30-2 6-10 (Fri 9.30-2 5.30-12 Sat 9.30-2 5.30-11 Sun 10-10) Closed: 3 days in Jan **Bar Meals** L served all wk 12-2 D served all wk 6-10 **Restaurant** L served Mon-Sat 12-2, Sun all day (until 8) D served all wk 6-10 ⊕ FREE HOUSE ◀ Sharp's Doom Bar, Butcombe Bitter, Prescott Track Record, Wickwar Cotswold Way, Local guest ales Ö Westons Stowford Press. **Facilities** Non-diners area ❤ (Bar Garden) ♦♦ Children's menu Children's portions Garden ♬ Beer festival Cider festival Parking 🚌 (notice required)

ALMONDSBURY — Map 4 ST68

The Bowl

16 Church Rd BS32 4DT ☎ 01454 612757
e-mail: bowlinn@sabrain.com
dir: *M5 junct 16 towards Thornbury. 3rd left onto Over Ln, 1st right onto Sundays Hill, next right onto Church Rd*

Village inn with six ales and fine food

The Bowl sits on the edge of the Severn Vale, hence its name. Part of this pretty, whitewashed building dates from 1147, when monks were building the church, so it was getting on when it became an inn in 1550. It has an atmospheric interior with exposed stonework and a wood-burner for winter warmth. The freshly prepared food includes seared scallops, minted pea purée and crispy prosciutto; lamb rump, red wine and redcurrant jus, green beans and garlic potatoes; good charcuterie and cheese boards too. There's Thatchers Gold cider and The Rev. James ale, with more at the beer festival in late summer.

Open all day all wk **Bar Meals** L served Mon-Fri 12-2.30, Sat 12-9.30, Sun 12-7 D served Mon-Fri 6-9.30, Sat 12-9.30, Sun 12-7 Av main course £10 **Restaurant** L served Mon-Fri 12-2.30, Sat 12-9.30, Sun 12-7 D served Mon-Fri 6-9.30, Sat 12-9.30, Sun 12-7 ⊕ BRAINS ◀ Bitter & The Rev. James, St Austell Tribute, Butcombe Ö Thatchers Gold. ♀ 16 **Facilities** Non-diners area ♦♦ Children's menu Children's portions Outside area ♬ Beer festival Parking Wi-fi

PICK OF THE PUBS

The Old Passage Inn ★ ★ ★ ★ RR

ARLINGHAM Map 4 SO71

Passage Rd GL2 7JR ☎ 01452 740547
e-mail: oldpassage@btconnect.com
web: www.theoldpassage.com
dir: *A38 onto B4071 through Arlingham.*
Through village to river

Famous for its seafood and river views

Overlooking the River Severn and set against the backdrop of the Forest of Dean, this was once the site of the ford across the River. This seafood restaurant-with-rooms on the riverbank once provided refreshment to ferry passengers across the tidal river but now attracts people from afar for its quality food and air of tranquillity. Eating in the open and airy dining room, or on the popular riverside terrace in summer is a delight. A selection of oysters and pre-starters such as soft shell crab with spicy kumquat chutney or North Atlantic prawns and mayonnaise act as a delicious curtain-raiser to the main menu. Head chef Mark Redwood uses only the freshest fish and seafood and keeps things simple to let the ingredients shine, whether it's lobster from Cornwall or oysters from Essex. Dishes may include scallop thermidor, spinach, cream sherry sauce; seared scallops with belly pork, spiced lentils, cauliflower purée, rum soaked raisins and lime syrup; brill fillet poached in red wine, braised gem lettuce, celeriac purée; or lobsters from the pub's own seawater tank — try one grilled with parsley and garlic butter. Carnivores will not be disappointed with seared breast of pigeon, celeriac gratin, pickled wild mushrooms and beetroot salad; and local sirloin of beef, balsamic cherry tomatoes, mushrooms, hand-cut chips and béarnaise sauce. Leave room for the local Cerney Ash goats' cheese or chocolate brownie with yoghurt ice cream.

Open 10-3 7-close Closed: 25 Dec, Jan-Feb Tue & Wed eve, Sun eve & Mon **Bar Meals** L served Tue-Sat 12-2, Sun 12-3 D served Tue-Sat 7-9 **Restaurant** L served Tue-Sat 12-2, Sun 12-3 D served Tue-Sat 7-9 ⊕ FREE HOUSE ♥ 12 **Facilities** Non-diners area ♦♦ Children's portions Garden ⋈ Parking Wi-fi **Rooms** 3

ARLINGHAM — Map 4 SO71

The Old Passage Inn ★★★★ RR ◉◉

PICK OF THE PUBS

See Pick of the Pubs on page 175

ASHLEWORTH — Map 10 SO82

The Queens Arms

PICK OF THE PUBS

The Village GL19 4HT ☎ 01452 700395
web: www.queensarmsashleworth.co.uk
dir: *From Gloucester N on A417 for 5m. At Hartpury, right at Broad St to Ashleworth. Pub 100yds past village green*

Free house offering an interesting menu

Set in a rural village between rolling hills and the River Severn, this is 16th-century inn is owned by Tony and Gill Burreddu. Although they have made alterations over the years, they have kept the original beams and iron fireplaces, simply complementing them with comfortable armchairs, antiques and a gallery of local artists' work. As a free house, The Queens Arms offers ales from a range of breweries including Sharp's and Timothy Taylor. With a loyal customer base, Tony and Gill have built a reputation for imaginative food made from the best local produce. The ever-changing menus have featured crab-stuffed red snapper; roasted partridge served with game chips; and tomato bredie, a South African lamb stew. From the peaceful garden behind 200-year-old clipped yews, enjoy views of the surrounding hills, in one hand a pint of Spitfire or a dry white wine; in the other a ping pong ball for amusing Talulah, the pub cat.

Open 12-3 7-11 Closed: 25-26 Dec & 1 Jan, Sun eve & Mon (ex BHs wknds) **Bar Meals** L served Tue-Sun 12-2 D served Tue-Sat 7-9 Av main course £12.95 **Restaurant** L served Tue-Sun 12-2 D served Tue-Sat 7-9 Av 3 course à la carte fr £22.50 ⊕ FREE HOUSE ◾ Timothy Taylor Landlord, Donnington BB, Brains The Rev. James, Shepherd Neame Spitfire, Sharp's Doom Bar, Brecon Brewing Gold Beacons ♂ Westons Stowford Press. ⚲ 14 **Facilities** Non-diners area ♦♦ Garden ⊟ Parking

BARNSLEY — Map 5 SP00

The Village Pub ★★★★★ INN ◉

PICK OF THE PUBS

GL7 5EF ☎ 01285 740421
e-mail: reservations@thevillagepub.co.uk
dir: *On B4425 4m NE of Cirencester*

Stylish Cotswold inn with food to match

Beautifully refurbished by the team behind neighbouring Barnsley House Country Hotel, The Village Pub manages to be both the local and a chic pub-restaurant, without becoming just another Cotswold tourist honeypot. Polished flagstones, oak floorboards, exposed timbers and open fireplaces are all there in spades, and the civilised atmosphere continues in each of the five rambling dining rooms, all sporting an eclectic mix of furniture, rug-strewn floors, oil paintings, cosy settles and warm terracotta walls. Modern British pub food draws a discerning dining crowd, with daily menus featuring quality local ingredients, some organic, like the vegetables from the Barnsley House gardens. Chef Graham Grafton's modern European menus include slow roast pork belly with roast vegetables and apple sauce, and orange steamed pudding and custard. Half portions are available for 'younger clientele'.

Open all wk 11-11 (Sun 11-10) **Bar Meals** L served Mon-Fri 12-2.30, Sat-Sun 12-3 D served Mon-Thu 6-9.30, Fri-Sat 6-10, Sun 6-9 ⊕ FREE HOUSE ◾ Hook Norton Hooky Bitter, Butcombe Gold, Guest ales ♂ Ashton Press. ⚲ 10 **Facilities** Non-diners area ♣ (Bar) ♦♦ Children's portions Outside area ⊟ Parking Wi-fi **Rooms** 6

BERKELEY — Map 4 ST69

The Malt House ★★★ INN

Marybrook St GL13 9BA ☎ 01453 511177
e-mail: the-malthouse@btconnect.com
web: www.themalthouse.uk.com
dir: *M5 junct 13/14, A38 towards Bristol. Pub on main road towards Sharpness*

Village charm in the pretty Vale of Berkeley

At the heart of historic Berkeley, close to the remarkable castle and the Edward Jenner (the pioneer immunologist) Museum, this village free house is a popular place with walkers on the spectacular Severn Way along the nearby estuary shoreline; comfy accommodation and good food tempt overnight stops here. Ease into the copiously beamed old bar and consider a menu rich with modern British dishes - steak and ale pie; lamb shank, or halibut steak with sweet chilli dip will satisfy; there's a good vegetarian selection including nut roast and a specials board with a great sausage choice.

The Malt House

Open all wk Mon-Thu 6-11 (Fri 5-12 Sat 12-12 Sun 12-3) **Bar Meals** L served Sat-Sun 12-2 D served Mon-Sat 6.30-8.30 **Restaurant** L served Sat-Sun 12-2 D served Mon-Sat 6.30-8.30 ⊕ FREE HOUSE ◾ Theakston Best Bitter ♂ Westons Stowford Press, Thatchers Gold. **Facilities** Non-diners area ♦♦ Children's menu Children's portions Garden ⊟ Parking Wi-fi 🚌 (notice required) **Rooms** 9

BIBURY — Map 5 SP10

Catherine Wheel ★★★★ INN

Arlington GL7 5ND ☎ 01285 740250
e-mail: info@catherinewheel-bibury.co.uk
dir: *On B4425, W of Bibury*

Welcoming Cotswold stone building offering a pleasing menu

This former blacksmith's has changed hands many times since J Hathaway opened it as an inn in 1856 but a warm welcome, good ales and quality food remain its hallmarks. The beautiful Cotswold-stone building, stable courtyard and orchard date back to the 15th century and plenty of historical features remain. The short but appetising menu might include seared scallops with crispy duck confit, squash purée and red wine syrup; pot-roasted chicken with truffle mash, smoked bacon, shallots and peas; and king prawn and mussel spaghetti. There is a beer festival held every August Bank Holiday.

Open all day all wk 9am-11pm **Bar Meals** L served Mon-Fri 12-3, Sat 12-9.30, Sun 12-9 D served Mon-Fri 6-9.30, Sat 12-9.30, Sun 12-9 food served all day **Restaurant** L served Mon-Fri 12-3, Sat 12-9.30, Sun 12-9 D served Mon-Fri 6-9.30, Sat 12-9.30, Sun 12-9 food served all day ⊕ FREE HOUSE/WHITE JAYS LTD ◾ Sharp's Doom Bar, Hook Norton ♂ Westons Stowford Press. **Facilities** Non-diners area ♣ (Bar Garden) ♦♦ Children's menu Children's portions Garden ⊟ Beer festival Parking Wi-fi 🚌 **Rooms** 4

Save on hotels. Book at theAA.com/hotel

GLOUCESTERSHIRE 177 ENGLAND

BIRDLIP
Map 10 SO91

The Golden Heart

Nettleton Bottom GL4 8LA ☎ 01242 870261
e-mail: info@thegoldenheart.co.uk
dir: *On A417 (Gloucester to Cirencester road). 8m from Cheltenham. Pub at base of dip in Nettleton Bottom*

Traditional pub with stunning views

A traditional 17th-century Cotswold-stone inn that was once a drovers' resting place, this lovely pub boasts stunning views of the valley from the terraced gardens. The main bar is divided into four cosy areas with log fires and traditional built-in settles. Excellent local ales and ciders are backed by a good selection of wines, while the extensive menus demonstrate commitment to local produce, particularly prize-winning meat from the region. Perhaps try beef, ale and vegetable pie; game pot suet pudding or the more exotic kangaroo, black cherry and sweet potato casserole. Vegetarian, vegan and gluten-free options are available.

Open all wk 11-3 5.30-11 (Fri-Sun & summer holidays open all day) Closed: 25 Dec **Bar Meals** L served Mon-Sat 12-3, Sun all day D served Mon-Sat 6-10, Sun all day **Restaurant** L served Mon-Sat 12-3, Sun all day D served Mon-Sat 12-3, Sun all day ⊕ FREE HOUSE ◀ Otter Bitter, Cotswold Way, Cotswold Lion, Brakspear ♂ Westons, Henney's, Thatchers. ☻ 10 **Facilities** Non-diners area ♨ (Bar Restaurant Garden) ♦ Family room Garden ⊼ Parking Wi-fi ▭

BLAISDON
Map 10 SO71

The Red Hart Inn

GL17 0AH ☎ 01452 830477
dir: *Take A40 (NW of Gloucester) towards Ross-on-Wye. At lights left onto A4136 signed Monmouth. Left into Blaisdon Lane to Blaisdon*

Village inn with tranquil country views

On the fringe of the Forest of Dean, this old whitewashed pub exudes the charm of a village local, all flagstoned floor, log fire, low beams and friendly pub dog to-boot. Four guest ales whet the whistle of passing ramblers, whilst those dining out will appreciate the quality pork raised by the pub's owners; sampled in the slow roast belly with black pudding, sage mash and cider cream sauce. Specials introduce dishes featuring venison or pheasant to the well-balanced menu, taken in the bar or restaurant. The sunny garden is a good place to sit with a glass of local cider.

Open all wk 12-3 6-11.30 (Sun 12.30-4 7-11) **Bar Meals** L served 12-2.15 D served 6.30-9.30 **Restaurant** L served 12-2.15 D served 6.30-9.30 ⊕ FREE HOUSE ◀ 4 Guest ales ♂ Westons Stowford Press, Traditional & 1st Quality. **Facilities** Non-diners area ♦ Children's menu Children's portions Play area Garden ⊼ Parking Wi-fi ▭

BLEDINGTON
Map 10 SP22

The Kings Head Inn ★★★★ INN ⊛

PICK OF THE PUBS

The Green OX7 6XQ ☎ 01608 658365
e-mail: info@kingsheadinn.net
dir: *On B4450, 4m from Stow-on-the-Wold*

A perfect country retreat

Facing the village green, this stone-built pub dating back to the 15th century is the quintessential Cotswold inn. Much of the original structure has survived, leaving low-beamed ceilings, flagstone floors, exposed stone walls, and inglenook fireplace. Archie and Nicola Orr-Ewing have worked hard to earn an excellent reputation built on well-kept real ales, an extensive wine list and wonderful local produce in the kitchen. In the bar, Hook Norton Hooky Bitter appears alongside guest ales from local microbreweries, organic cider, local lagers, over 25 malt whiskies, and 11 wines served by the glass. The menu is concise but some of the starters can be served as main courses, so choice is more than ample: salmon ballottine with beetroot coleslaw and dill crème fraîche might be followed by roast loin of roe deer with crushed root vegetables, boulangère potatoes and a juniper reduction. Apple crumble is one of the popular desserts.

Open all day all wk Closed: 25-26 Dec **Bar Meals** L served Mon-Fri 12-2, Sat-Sun 12-2.30 D served Sun-Thu 7-9, Fri-Sat 6.30-9.30 Av main course £14 **Restaurant** L served Mon-Fri 12-2, Sat-Sun 12-2.30 D served Sun-Thu 7-9, Fri-Sat 6.30-9.30 Av 3 course à la carte fr £24.50 ⊕ FREE HOUSE ◀ Hook Norton Hooky Bitter, Purity Gold, Vale VPA, Wye Valley, Brakspear ♂ Westons Stowford Press. ☻ 11 **Facilities** Non-diners area ♦ Children's menu Children's portions Garden ⊼ Parking Wi-fi **Rooms** 12

BOURTON-ON-THE-HILL
Map 10 SP13

Horse and Groom

PICK OF THE PUBS

GL56 9AQ ☎ 01386 700413
e-mail: greenstocks@horseandgroom.info
dir: *2m W of Moreton-in-Marsh on A44*

Handsome inn offering food that's worth a detour for

Owned and run by the Greenstock brothers since 2005, this Cotswold stone pub is both a serious dining destination and a friendly place for a drink. The handsome Grade II listed Georgian building combines a contemporary feel with plenty of original period features. The beer selection mixes local brews such as Cotswold Wheat Beer and over 20 carefully selected wines are served by the glass. The blackboard menu changes daily, providing plenty of appeal for even the most regular of diners. With committed local suppliers backed up by the pub's own vegetable patch, the kitchen has plenty of good produce to work with. A typical menu might feature Dexter beef, ale and mustard pie or pan-fried local pigeon breasts, creamed celeriac purée, chorizo and thyme; and puds such as banana and pecan sponge pudding. In

summer, head for the mature garden with its panoramic hilltop views.

Open 11-3 6-11 Closed: 25 Dec, Sun eve **Bar Meals** L served all wk 12-2 D served Mon-Sat 7-9 Av main course £14 **Restaurant** L served all wk 12-2 D served Mon-Sat 7-9 Av 3 course à la carte fr £20.75 ⊕ FREE HOUSE ◀ Wye Valley Bitter, Purity Pure UBU, Goffs Jouster, Cotswold Wheat Beer, Stroud Organic ♂ Hogan's. ☻ 21 **Facilities** Non-diners area ♦ Children's portions Garden ⊼ Parking Wi-fi

BROCKHAMPTON
Map 10 SP02

Craven Arms Inn

GL54 5XQ ☎ 01242 820410
e-mail: cravenarms@live.co.uk
dir: *From Cheltenham take A40 towards Gloucester. In Andoversford, at lights, left onto A436 signed Bourton & Stow. Left, follow signs for Brockhampton*

Secluded village setting in fine walking country

Inside and out, this set-back, gabled old village inn glows with mellow honeyed stone; log fires, beams and mullioned windows add to the charm of its setting beneath the gently undulating horizon of the Cotswolds themselves. A selection of real ales, plus ciders and perry from regional orchards attract drinkers, who also appreciate the annual July beer festival here. Diners can self-cook their fish and steaks on grill-stones at the table, or appreciate either the good old-fashioned comfort food or modern dishes like pan-fried sea bass with roasted Mediterranean vegetables or wild mushroom, apricot and goats' cheese loaf. There's a gluten free menu, too.

Open 12-3 6-11 Closed: Sun eve & Mon **Bar Meals** L served Tue-Sun 12-2.30 D served Tue-Thu 6.30-9, Fri-Sat 6.30-9.30 **Restaurant** L served Tue-Sun 12.30-2.30, Sun 12.30-3 D served Tue-Thu 6.30-9, Fri-Sat 6.30-9.30 ⊕ FREE HOUSE ◀ Otter, Butcombe ♂ Westons Stowford Press, Dunkertons. ☻ 9 **Facilities** Non-diners area ♨ (Bar Garden) ♦ Children's portions Garden ⊼ Beer festival Parking Wi-fi ▭ (notice required)

CHEDWORTH
Map 5 SP01

Hare & Hounds ★★★★ INN

PICK OF THE PUBS

Foss Cross GL54 4NN ☎ 01285 720288
e-mail: stay@hareandhoundsinn.com
dir: *On A429 (Fosse Way), 6m from Cirencester*

Built of mellow Cotswold stone with atmosphere to match

A memorable mix of old-world character and contemporary cuisine; creepers cling to the sharply-pitched roofline of the 14th-century inn, the old inn sign swings beneath a shady oak, and a string of open fires welcomes ramblers from the countless local walks, visitors to the nearby Roman villa complex or fans of the turf breaking away from Cheltenham's racecourse just a

continued

CHEDWORTH *continued*

few miles distant. The interior is an eclectic marriage of original features and modern chic; the ideal foundation for relaxing with a glass of locally brewed Arkell's bitter to accompany the excellent menu which is strong on seafood dishes with a nod to world cuisine. Grilled fillet of halibut on a bed of mild spiced celeriac, or spiced tofu and grilled haloumi cheese on an oriental vegetable stir-fry could be on the regularly updated menu here. In summer eat alfresco in the suntrap garden or stay over in one of the smart and comfortable rooms.

Open all wk Mon-Sat 11.30-2.30 6-close (Sun 11.30-2.30 7-close) **Bar Meals** L served all wk 12-2.30 D served Mon-Sat 6.30-9.30, Sun 7-9 **Restaurant** L served all wk 12-2.30 D served Mon-Sat 6.30-9.30, Sun 7-9 ARKELL'S 2B, 3B, Moonlight Westons Stowford Press. 8 **Facilities** Non-diners area (Bar Restaurant Garden) Children's menu Children's portions Family room Garden Parking Wi-fi **Rooms** 10

CHELTENHAM Map 10 SO92

The Gloucester Old Spot

Tewkesbury Rd, Piff's Elm GL51 9SY 01242 680321
e-mail: eat@thegloucesteroldspot.co.uk
dir: *On A4019 on outskirts of Cheltenham towards Tewkesbury*

Traditional pub with enthusiastic owners

Former leaseholders Simon and Kate Daws, who also own another Cheltenham pub, The Royal Oak Inn (see entry), purchased this traditional farming pub in 2012. Now a free house, it ticks all the boxes with its quarry tile floors, roaring log fires, farmhouse furnishings and real ales such as Wye Valley. Local ciders and perries are on offer at the bar and there is a May Day Bank Holiday cider festival, too. The baronial dining room takes its inspiration from the local manor, and game and rare-breed pork make an appearance on a menu that includes braised rabbit and black pudding cannelloni; and Old Spot pork loin steak with hand-cut chips.

Open all day all wk Closed: 25-26 Dec **Bar Meals** L served all wk 12-2 D served Mon-Sat 6-9 **Restaurant** L served Mon-Sat 12-2, Sun all day D served Mon-Sat 6-9 FREE HOUSE Timothy Taylor Landlord, Purity Mad Goose, Wye Valley HPA Thatchers, Westons Stowford Press, Black Rat, Gwynt y Ddraig. **Facilities** Non-diners area (Bar Garden) Children's menu Children's portions Garden Beer festival Cider festival Parking Wi-fi (notice required)

The Royal Oak Inn

The Burgage, Prestbury GL52 3DL 01242 522344
e-mail: eat@royal-oak-prestbury.co.uk
dir: *From town centre follow signs for Winchcombe/Prestbury & Racecourse. In Prestbury follow brown signs for inn from Tatchley Ln*

Welcoming pub recommended for its beer and cider festivals

On the outskirts of Cheltenham and close to the town's famous racecourse, this 16th-century pub was once owned by England cricket legend Tom Graveney. In 2012 former leaseholders Simon and Kate, who have been here for over a decade, bought the free house and continue to offer their hospitality. The couple now own The Gloucester Old Spot, Cheltenham (see entry), too. Enjoy well-kept local cask ales, real ciders and delicious food in the snug, the comfortable dining room or the heated patio overlooking a pretty beer garden. Menus include braised lamb shank, pork belly, vegetable curry, pan-fried duck breast and lunchtime filled ciabattas. There is a beer festival at Whitsun and an August Bank Holiday cider festival.

Open all day all wk Closed: 25 Dec **Bar Meals** L served Mon-Sat 12-2, Sun 12-9 **Restaurant** L served Mon-Sat 12-2, Sun 12-9 D served Mon-Sat 6.30-9, Sun 12-9 FREE HOUSE Timothy Taylor Landlord, Purity Mad Goose, Butcombe Bitter Thatchers, Westons Stowford Press, Black Rat Perry. **Facilities** Non-diners area Children's menu Children's portions Garden Beer festival Cider festival Parking Wi-fi

CHIPPING CAMPDEN Map 10 SP13

The Bakers Arms

Broad Campden GL55 6UR 01386 840515
e-mail: info@bakersarmscampden.co.uk
dir: *1m from Chipping Campden*

Sublime Cotswold pub with friendly welcome

Ease into the compact little bar here, squeeze into a space near the eye-catching inglenook and live the Cotswold dream, with local Stanney Bitter mirroring the colour of the mellow thatched stone cottages in this picture-postcard hamlet. The patio, terrace and garden are all ideal on summer evenings in this most tranquil spot, lost amidst lanes and tracks below tree-fringed hilltops. The traditional, well-considered menu may offer a creamy beetroot risotto starter with chicken, ham and leek pie or lamb shank to follow; the intimate dressed-stone walled restaurant area is a peaceful retreat from the popular bar. Please note that opening times in January and February differ from those at other times of year. Please contact the pub for details.

Open 11.30-2.30 5.30-11 (Fri-Sat 11.30-11 Sun 12-10.30, Jan/Feb Fri 11.30-2.30 5.30-11 Sat 11.30-11 Sun 12-8) Closed: 25-26 Dec & 31 Dec eve, Sun eve & Mon L Jan-Feb **Bar Meals** L served Mon-Fri 12-2, Sat 12-2.30, Sun 12-4, Jan/Feb Sun 12-3 D served Mon-Sat 6-9, Jan/Feb Tue-Sat 6-8.30 **Restaurant** L served Mon-Fri 12-2, Sat 12-2.30, Sun 12-4, Jan/Feb Sun 12-3 D served Mon-Sat 6-9, Jan/Feb Tue-Sat 6-8.30 FREE HOUSE Stanway Stanney Bitter, Wickwar, Wye Valley, Purity Thatchers Heritage. **Facilities** Non-diners area (Bar Garden) Children's menu Children's portions Play area Garden Parking Wi-fi (notice required)

Eight Bells

PICK OF THE PUBS

Church St GL55 6JG 01386 840371
e-mail: neilhargreaves@bellinn.fsnet.co.uk
web: www.eightbellsinn.co.uk
dir: *In town centre*

A true Cotswold experience

Originally built in the 14th century to house the stonemasons who constructed nearby St James' church, this lovely inn was rebuilt in the 17th century and was used to store the peel of eight bells that were hung in the church tower. The cobbled entranceway leads into two atmospheric beamed bars with open fireplaces and, in the floor of one, a surviving priest's hole; outside is an enclosed courtyard and terraced garden overlooking the almshouses and church. Enjoy the Hook Norton and Purity real ales and freshly prepared, locally sourced, seasonal dishes, such as spicy meatballs and spaghetti; chicken liver parfait; supreme of chicken wrapped in Parma ham; roasted butternut squash and tomato risotto; and toad-in-the-hole. Home-made puddings tempt with chocolate crème brûlée; apple and cinnamon sponge pudding served with custard; and lemon posset with a red berry coulis and shortbread. Specials, a prix-fixe menu and a children's menu are also available.

Open all day all wk 12-11 (Sun 12-10.30) Closed: 25 Dec **Bar Meals** L served Mon-Thu 12-2, Fri-Sat 12-2.30, Sun 12-9 D served Mon-Thu 6.30-9, Fri-Sat 6.30-9.30, Sun 12-9 **Restaurant** L served Mon-Thu 12-2, Fri-Sat 12-2.30, Sun 12-9 D served Mon-Thu 6.30-9, Fri-Sat 6.30-9.30, Sun 12-9 FREE HOUSE Hook Norton Hooky Bitter, Purity Pure UBU & Gold, Goffs Jouster, Wye Valley HPA Westons Old Rosie, Westons 1st Quality & Stowford Press. 8 **Facilities** Non-diners area (Bar) Children's menu Children's portions Garden Wi-fi

PICK OF THE PUBS

Seagrave Arms ★★★★ INN ❀

CHIPPING CAMPDEN   Map 10 SP13

Friday St, Weston Subedge GL55 6QH
☎ **01386 840192**
e-mail: info@seagravearms.co.uk
web: www.seagravearms.co.uk
dir: *A44 onto B4081 to Chipping Campden. Left at junct with High St. 0.5m, straight on at x-rds to Weston Subedge. Left at T-junct*

Log fires, flagstones, local ales and a warm welcome

A Grade II listed former farmhouse dating from around 1740, which has been sympathetically restored to retain many of its original features, the Cotswold-stone Seagrave Arms offers open log fires in winter and a sheltered courtyard for alfresco dining in the summer. Set in a delectable honey-stoned village between the verdant Vale of Evesham and the golden scarp of the Cotswolds, it's perfectly located for exploring the surrounding area; Stately Broadway Tower is on the horizon, the delights of Snowshill and Hidcote Manor and Garden are just a short distance away. Touring visitors are equally captivated by the Georgian inn's luxurious accommodation. At the bar, outstanding beers from Purity and Cotswold breweries slake the thirst of locals and ramblers diverting from the nearby Cotswold Way footpath. With the bountiful foodstuffs of the Cotswolds to choose from, the proprietors revel in

selecting the best local and sustainable produce. You could start with smoked ham hock rillettes with mustard pickles and spiced apple relish, and continue with Cotswold game casserole, creamy mash and purple sprouting broccoli. Local fish and steaks make regular appearances on the specials board. For vegetarians there's sage-roasted butternut squash and feta linguine. The lunchtime bar menu has favourites like fish pie, Oxford Blue cheese rarebit and beer-battered haddock. Appealing desserts could be chocolate and orange cappuccino mousse, or rhubarb crumble with home-made ginger ice cream. Alternatively you could finish with a selection of cheeses from nearby villages. Wash it down with a sprightly Gloucestershire wine from Three Choirs

Vineyard. The Sunday roasts prove to be very popular.

Open all day Closed: Mon **Bar Meals** food served all day **Restaurant** L served Tue-Sun 12-3 D served Tue-Sun 6-9.15 ⊞ FREE HOUSE ◀ Hook Norton, Cotswold, Purity ♻ Westons Stowford Press. ☕ 13 **Facilities** Non-diners area ♣ ⅰ Children's portions Garden Parking Wi-fi **Rooms** 6

CHIPPING CAMPDEN *continued*

The Kings ★★★★ RR ◉◉
PICK OF THE PUBS

The Square GL55 6AW ☎ 01386 840256
e-mail: info@kingscampden.co.uk
dir: *Telephone for directions*

Award-winning cuisine in a town centre pub

A lovely old townhouse facing the square of one of England's prettiest towns. Sympathetically restored, yet packed with character, the oldest parts include the 16th-century stone mullioned windows on the first floor. The bar offers at least two real ales, including local Hook Norton, as well as daily papers and traditional pub games, but no noisy gaming machines. Bar snacks include a good range of sandwiches and baguettes, while main meals are served in the informal bar brasserie or more formal two AA-Rosette restaurant overlooking the square. The packed menu offers some imaginative delights: tian of Salcombe crab with cherry tomatoes and herb crème fraîche; braised shank of Lighthorne lamb with dauphinoise potatoes, roast root vegetables and rosemary sauce; and risotto of the day. The large grassed garden and dining terrace is good to find in a town centre pub. Individually decorated bedrooms offer period features with plenty of modern comforts.

Open all day all wk 7am-11pm (Sat-Sun 8am-11pm) ⊕ FREE HOUSE ◀ Hook Norton Hooky Bitter ♂ Thatchers Gold. **Facilities** ♦♦ Children's menu Children's portions Garden Parking Wi-fi **Rooms** 19

Noel Arms Hotel ★★★ HL
PICK OF THE PUBS

High St GL55 6AT ☎ 01386 840317
e-mail: reception@noelarmshotel.com
dir: *On High St, opposite Town Hall*

Delightful inn with its own curry club

The Noel Arms is one of the oldest hotels in the Cotswolds, a place where traditional appeal has been successfully preserved and interwoven seamlessly with contemporary comforts. Charles II reputedly stayed in this golden Cotswold-stone 16th-century coaching inn. It was through the carriage arch that packhorse trains used to carry bales of wool, the source of Chipping Campden's prosperity, to Bristol and Southampton. Absorb these details of the hotel's history while sipping a pint of Hook Norton in front of the log fire in Dover's Bar; read the papers over a coffee and pastry in the coffee shop; and enjoy brasserie-style food in the restaurant. An alternative to the modern English dishes is brought by Indunil Upatissa who creates his trademark curries daily, and enthusiasts arrive for his Curry Club on the last Thursday evening of every month.

Open all day all wk **Bar Meals** food served all day **Restaurant** L served all wk 12-3 D served all wk 6-9.30 ⊕ FREE HOUSE ◀ Hook Norton Hooky Bitter, Wye Valley Butty Bach, Purity Gold & Pure UBU, Guinness ♂ Westons Stowford Press. ▾ **Facilities** Non-diners area ♣ (Bar) ♦♦ Children's menu Children's portions Outside area ♬ Parking Wi-fi ⛟ **Rooms** 28

Seagrave Arms ★★★★ INN ◉
PICK OF THE PUBS

See Pick of the Pubs on page 179

The Volunteer Inn

Lower High St GL55 6DY ☎ 01386 840688
e-mail: info@thevolunteerinn.net
dir: *From Shipston on Stour take B4035 to Chipping Campden*

Cotswold character and cuisine with a twist

The beautiful, honey-coloured Cotswold stone glowing beside Chipping Campden's main street continues within; the convivial, log-fire warmed stone floored bar a welcoming retreat for guests hunting through the town's antique shops or pausing on a stroll along the Cotswold Way footpath. Once a recruiting centre for volunteer militia, today's clients sign on for some very interesting dishes from the Maharaja Restaurant located here; Jalali hash is a roasted duck, red onion and peppers combination, or perhaps venison tikka would be the dish to try with a pint of Doom Bar bitter. The grassy beer garden is a quiet town centre retreat.

Open all wk Mon-Thu 3-12 (Fri-Sun 11am-late) **Bar Meals** Av main course £10 **Restaurant** D served all wk 5-10.30 ⊕ FREE HOUSE ◀ Sharp's Doom Bar. **Facilities** Non-diners area ♦♦ Children's portions Play area Family room Garden Wi-fi ⛟

CIRENCESTER   Map 5 SP00

The Crown of Crucis ★★★ HL
PICK OF THE PUBS

Ampney Crucis GL7 5RS ☎ 01285 851806
e-mail: reception@thecrownofcrucis.co.uk
dir: *On A417 to Lechlade, 2m E of Cirencester*

Quintessential Cotswold coaching inn

Overlooking the village cricket green, this 16th-century former coaching inn retains its historical charm while feeling comfortably up-to-date. The name 'Crucis' refers to the Latin cross in the nearby churchyard. The pub stands beside Ampney Brook in the heart of the Cotswolds, and the quiet stream meandering past the lawns creates a perfect picture of quintessential rural England. With its traditional beams, log fires and warm, friendly atmosphere, the busy bar offers a large selection of draught and real ales, including their own Crown Bitter, and a choice of wines by the glass. Bar food is served all day and ranges from sandwiches, salads and pastas, to dishes from the grill and stove: ham hock hash with fried free-range eggs and watercress; piri piri chicken, salad and chips; pan-fried calves' liver with black pudding, mash and red wine gravy. The restaurant offers a fine dining menu.

Open all day all wk 8am-11pm Closed: 25 Dec **Bar Meals** L served all wk 12-5 D served all wk 5-10 Av main course £12 food served all day ⊕ FREE HOUSE ◀ Crown Bitter, Sharp's Doom Bar & Seasonal ales, Wickwar ♂ Westons Stowford Press. ▾ 17

Facilities Non-diners area ♣ (Bar Garden) ♦♦ Children's menu Garden ♬ Parking Wi-fi ⛟ (notice required) **Rooms** 25

The Fleece at Cirencester ★★★★★ INN

41 Market Place GL7 2NZ ☎ 01285 658507
e-mail: relax@thefleececirencester.co.uk
web: www.thefleececirencester.co.uk
dir: *In centre of Cirencester*

Home-cooked food in the Cotswolds

In the heart of Cirencester (known as the capital of the Cotswolds), this 16th-century pub with rooms is reputed to be where Charles II disguised himself as a manservant when in hiding. The bar, restaurant and lounge were completely refurbished early in 2012 but The Fleece's charms have been retained. Settle by one of the log fires with a pint of Wainwright, and select from the menu that mixes the traditional with the modern using produce from trusted ethical suppliers. Start with a deli board, followed by steak from the chargrill or Gloucester Old Spot sausages. Toffee, pecan and banana sundae is for 'afters'. Afternoon tea is also served.

Open all day all wk **Bar Meals** L served all wk 12-6 D served Mon-Sat 6-9.30, Sun 6-8.30 Av main course £12-£18 food served all day **Restaurant** L served all wk 12-6 D served Mon-Sat 6-9.30, Sun 6-8.30 Av 3 course à la carte fr £25 food served all day ⊕ THWAITES ◀ Wainwright, Guest ales ♂ Kingstone Press. ▾ 9 **Facilities** Non-diners area ♣ (Bar Garden) ♦♦ Children's menu Children's portions Garden ♬ Parking Wi-fi **Rooms** 28

See advert on opposite page

Save on hotels. Book at **theAA.com/hotel**

GLOUCESTERSHIRE 181 ENGLAND

CLEARWELL
Map 4 SO50

The Wyndham Arms ★★★ HL ◉

The Cross GL16 8JT ☎ 01594 833666
e-mail: dine@thewyndhamhotel.co.uk
dir: *M4 junct 21 onto M48 for Chepstow. Exit at junct 2 signed A48/Chepstow. At rdbt take A48 towards Gloucester. Take B4228 to Coleford & The Forest of Dean. 10m, through St Briavels, in 2m Clearwell signed on left*

Cosy hotel between the Forest of Dean and the Wye Valley

Open log-burners and oak flooring create the sort of rustic charm that's ideal for enjoying a pint of Kingstone's real ales, brewed at nearby Tintern, or Severn Cider from Newnham. In the domed stone vaults of the Old Spot Country Restaurant, the AA has awarded a Rosette for the classic British food, sometimes given a contemporary tweak as in marinated chump of lamb with spiced red wine jus; goats' cheese and roasted vegetable tart with polenta 'chips'; seafood risotto; and red pepper, beans and chilli burger. The Wyndham's accommodation is perfect for Clearwell Castle, a popular wedding venue.

Open all day all wk Closed: early Jan **Bar Meals** L served Mon-Sat 12-2, Sun 12-2.30 D served all wk 6.30-9 Av main course £10 **Restaurant** L served Mon-Sat 12-2, Sun 12-2.30 D served all wk 6.30-9 Av 3 course à la carte fr £25 ⊕ FREE HOUSE ◖ Kingstone Humpty's Fuddle IPA, Kingstone Gold Fine Ale ♂ Severn. ☗ 10
Facilities Non-diners area ❄ (Bar Outside area) ⊪ Children's menu Children's portions Outside area ⊞ Parking Wi-fi **Rooms** 18

CLEVE HILL
Map 10 SO92

The Rising Sun ★★★ INN

GL52 3PX ☎ 01242 676281
e-mail: 9210@greeneking.co.uk
dir: *On B4632, 4m N of Cheltenham*

Hilltop inn offering stunning vistas

On a clear day you can see south Wales from this Victorian property on Cleeve Hill, which also boasts views across Cheltenham and the Malverns. Whether you are staying overnight or just popping in to relax, settle in the nicely modernised bar or, in summer, out in the garden, which is well furnished with trestle tables and benches. Food ranges from sandwiches and wraps to traditional English favourites served both at lunch and dinner, including a choice of Black Angus steaks, gourmet burgers and classics like chicken and mushroom pie.

Open all day all wk ⊕ GREENE KING ◖ IPA, Abbot Ale ♂ Aspall. **Facilities** ⊪ Children's menu Children's portions Family room Garden Parking Wi-fi **Rooms** 24

CLIFFORD'S MESNE
Map 10 SO72

The Yew Tree

PICK OF THE PUBS

GL18 1JS ☎ 01531 820719
e-mail: unwind@yewtreeinn.com
dir: *From Newent High Street follow signs to Clifford's Mesne. Pub at far end of village on road to Glasshouse*

Hard-to-find pub with stunning views

This former cider press is tucked away up a little lane on the slopes of National Trust's May Hill, Gloucestershire's highest point, from where you can see the Welsh mountains, the Malvern Hills and the River Severn. The pub has a quarry-tiled floor and winter log fires, and offers a good choice of local real ales from breweries like Wye Valley and Cotswold Spring, and ciders from Lyne Down and Three Choirs. As for the food, the emphasis is on tasty home cooking using seasonal local produce, with daily-changing menus and specials. Starters could include salmon and scallop terrine or artichoke and feta salad. For a main course, think about cider-cured bacon steak on caramelised celeriac and cider cream sauce, or perhaps Hereford sirloin steak. Home-made desserts include strawberries and champagne mousse. Time a visit for the October beer and cider festival.

Open 12-2.30 6-11 (Sun 12-5) Closed: Mon, Tue L, Sun eve **Bar Meals** L served Wed-Sat 12-2 D served Tue-Sat 6-9 Av main course £15 **Restaurant** Av 3 course à la carte fr £25 ⊕ FREE HOUSE ◖ Wye Valley HPA, Cotswold Spring Stunner, Sharp's Own, Gloucester Mariner, Local ales ♂ Westons Stowford Press, Lyne Down, Severn Cider & Perry, Swallowfield Cider & Perry, Three Choirs. ☗ 12
Facilities Non-diners area ❄ (Bar Restaurant Garden) ⊪ Children's menu Children's portions Play area Garden ⊞ Beer festival Cider festival Parking Wi-fi

COATES
Map 4 SO90

The Tunnel House Inn

PICK OF THE PUBS

See Pick of the Pubs on page 182

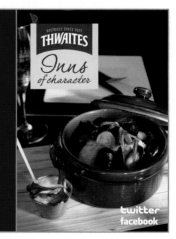

PICK OF THE PUBS

The Tunnel House Inn

COATES   Map 4 SO90

Tarlton Rd GL7 6PW ☎ 01285 770280
e-mail: info@tunnelhouse.com
web: www.tunnelhouse.com
dir: *A433 from Cirencester towards Tetbury, 2m, right towards Coates, follow brown inn signs*

Delightful Cotswold village inn

Down an unmade track, this rural inn was built for the navvies who spent five years constructing the two-mile long Sapperton Tunnel on the now-disused Thames and Severn Canal. The inn overlooks the entrance to the tunnel which hasn't been navigated by a barge since 1911. Three winter log fires warm the curio-filled bar, where oddities include an upside-down table suspended from the ceiling. Food, all home cooked, is served every day from noon onwards and you may eat in the bar or restaurant, starting perhaps with pheasant, lardons and plum mixed leaf salad with redcurrant and balsamic reduction; or potted salt beef served with toasted brioche, pickled onions and gherkins. A typical spring menu might offer main courses of goats' cheese-and thyme-stuffed chicken breast, wrapped in smoked bacon, with creamy red pesto linguine; baked smoked haddock stuffed with spinach and pine nuts on a bed of lemon and thyme risotto; and wild mushroom, leek and blue cheese puff pastry pie with sweet

potato wedges and parsnip crisps. Apple and red berry crumble with crème anglaise may appear on the desserts list, while Cotswold ice creams almost certainly will. At lunchtime eat more simply with a hot panini or a mature cheddar or Stilton ploughman's. The garden is tailor-made for relaxing with a pint of one of the mostly local real ales — typically from Uley, Wye Valley and Hook Norton breweries — or a Somerset or Herefordshire real cider, while enjoying the views over the fields. A beer festival in August, a children's play area and delightful walks add to the pub's popularity.

Open all day all wk noon-late **Bar Meals** L served 12-9.30 D served 12-9.30 Av main course £8 food served

all day **Restaurant** Av 3 course à la carte fr £22 food served all day ⊕ FREE HOUSE 🛢 Uley Old Spot & Bitter, Wye Valley Bitter, Stroud Budding Pale Ale, Hook Norton, Butcombe ⚲ Healey's Cornish Rattler, Black Rat, Westons Wyld Wood Organic. 🍷 9 **Facilities** Non-diners area 🐾 (All areas) 🚻 Children's menu Children's portions Play area Family room Garden Outside area 🏕 Beer festival Parking Wi-fi 🚐

Save on hotels. Book at theAA.com/hotel

GLOUCESTERSHIRE 183 ENGLAND

PICK OF THE PUBS

The Green Dragon Inn ★★★★ INN

COWLEY Map 10 SO91

Cockleford GL53 9NW ☎ 01242 870271
e-mail: green-dragon@buccaneer.co.uk
web: www.green-dragon-inn.co.uk
dir: *Telephone for directions*

Cotswolds inn featuring Mouseman furniture

With a pretty, rose-and creeper-covered Cotswold-stone façade, this building was recorded as an inn in 1675. However, it was 1710 before Robert Jones, a churchwarden, became the first landlord, splitting his time between pew and pump for the next 31 years. In summer the secluded patio garden overlooking a lake is an obvious spot to head for. Step inside the stone-flagged Mouse Bar and you will notice that each piece of English oak furniture features a carved mouse, the trademark of Robert Thompson, the Mouseman of Kilburn. He died in 1955, but North Yorkshire craftsmen continue the tradition. There's even one of the little beggars running along the edge of the bar in front of the Butcombe, Hook Norton and Sharp's beer pumps. Light meals and sandwiches are available at lunchtime. On the dinner menu, evening starters include minted lamb koftas with a banana and coconut curry sauce; and warm pigeon breast, smoked bacon and quail's egg salad. To follow could be steak-and-kidney suet pudding with

mushy peas; Cajun-spiced salmon steak with a mixed green salad and yellow chilli jam; or wild mushroom and baby spinach risotto with parmesan shavings and fresh basil. The children's menu will prove to be a hit too. The comfortable and individually furnished en suite bedrooms, and the St George's Suite (which has its own sitting room overlooking Cowley lakes) make The Green Dragon an ideal base for exploring the Cotswolds. Perhaps start by heading for the local Miserden Gardens and Chedworth Roman Villa.

Open all day all wk Closed: 25 Dec eve & 1 Jan eve **Bar Meals** L served Mon-Fri 12-2.30, Sat 12-3, Sun 12-3.30 D served all wk 6-10 Av main course £15.95 **Restaurant** L served Mon-Fri

12-2.30, Sat 12-3, Sun 12-3.30 D served all wk 6-10 Av 3 course à la carte fr £27.50 ⊕ FREE HOUSE/ BUCCANEER ◀ Hook Norton, Butcombe, Sharp's Doom Bar, Guest ale ⊘ Westons Stowford Press. **Facilities** Non-diners area ♦ Children's menu Outside area ⋈ Parking Wi-fi 🚌 **Rooms** 9

COLESBOURNE
Map 10 SP01

The Colesbourne Inn

PICK OF THE PUBS

GL53 9NP ☎ 01242 870376
e-mail: colesbourneinn@wadworth.co.uk
dir: Midway between Cirencester & Cheltenham on A435

Georgian country inn full of character

North of Cirencester in a picturesque Cotswold Valley, this handsome, stone-built inn is just a short meadow walk from the source of the Thames. It sits in two acres of grounds, which include a fine terrace and garden where you can sit with a pint of Wadworth 6X and savour the glorious country views. Dating back to 1827, the inn has been sympathetically restored and oozes historic charm and character in its bar and dining area, where you'll find original beams and roaring log fires aplenty. The seasonal menus combine traditional pub classics, including fish and chips with beer-batter and mushy peas, and honey-and mustard-glazed Cotswold ham with free-range egg and chips, with modern ideas, perhaps confit duck leg with orange, pomegranate and ginger jus; a natural smoked haddock and spring onion fishcake with creamed vegetables and fries; or roasted pumpkin curry with basmati rice and a naan bread.

Open all day all wk **Bar Meals** L served all wk 12-2.30 D served Mon-Sat 6-9.30, Sun 6-9 **Restaurant** L served all wk 12-2.30 D served Mon-Sat 6-9.30, Sun 6-9 ⊕ WADWORTH ◀ 6X, Henry's Original IPA, Horizon ♂ Westons Stowford Press. ☗ 20
Facilities Non-diners area ♦ Children's portions Garden Parking Wi-fi ☐ (notice required)

COWLEY
Map 10 SO91

The Green Dragon Inn ★★★★ INN

PICK OF THE PUBS

See Pick of the Pubs on page 183

CRANHAM
Map 10 SO81

The Black Horse Inn

GL4 8HP ☎ 01452 812217
dir: A46 towards Stroud, follow signs for Cranham

A great rest-stop for walkers

Near the Cotswold Way and the Benedictine Prinknash Abbey, in a small village surrounded by woodland and commons, this inn is popular with walkers, the cricket team and visiting Morris dancers. Mostly home-cooked traditional pub food includes cottage pie; roast pork, beef or turkey; kleftiko (half-shoulder of slow-cooked lamb in red wine, lemon and herbs); haggis and bacon; and roast vegetable, cranberry and goats' cheese nut roast. Among the real ales are Butcombe, Sharp's and Otter, and there are good ciders too in the cosy, open-fire-warmed bar.

Open 12-2 6.30-11 (Sun 12-2 8.30-11) Closed: 25 Dec, Mon (ex BHs L) ⊕ FREE HOUSE ◀ Sharp's Doom Bar, Otter, Butcombe, Guest ales ♂ Thatchers Gold, Westons Stowford Press & Country Perry. **Facilities** ☙ (Bar Garden) ♦ Children's portions Garden Parking

DURSLEY
Map 4 ST79

The Old Spot Inn

PICK OF THE PUBS

Hill Rd GL11 4JQ ☎ 01453 542870
e-mail: steveoldspot@hotmail.co.uk
dir: From Tetbury on A4135 (or Uley on B4066) into Dursley, round Town Hall. Straight on at lights towards bus station, pub behind bus station. From Cam to lights in Dursley immediately prior to pedestrianised street. Right towards bus station

Excellent beer at popular village local

This classic 18th-century free house is a former real ale pub of the year, so it's worth visiting to sample the regularly changing, tip-top real ales on handpump and to savour the cheerful buzzing atmosphere, as The Old Spot is a cracking community local. It sits smack on the Cotswold Way and was once three terraced farm cottages known as 'pig row.' It's apt, then that it should take its name from the Gloucestershire Old Spot pig. As well as organising three real ale festivals a year, landlord Steve Herbert organises a host of events, including brewery visits, cricket matches and celebrity chef nights. Devoid of modern-day intrusions, the rustic and traditional low-beamed bars are havens of peace, with just the comforting sound of crackling log fires and the hubbub of chatting locals filling the rambling little rooms. Food is wholesome and home made, ranging from ploughman's lunches and doorstep sandwiches to a pork and apple burger; haddock and chive fishcakes; or chicken fajitas. Puddings include treacle tart and white chocolate cheesecake. There's also a pretty garden for summer alfresco sipping.

Open all day all wk 11-11 (Sun 12-11) **Bar Meals** L served all wk 12-3 D served Mon only 6-9 **Restaurant** L served all wk 12-3 D served Mon only 6-9 ⊕ FREE HOUSE ◀ Old Ric, Session, Guest ales ♂ Westons 1st Quality. ☗ 8 **Facilities** Non-diners area ♦ Children's portions Family room Garden ☶ Beer festival Parking Wi-fi ☐

EBRINGTON
Map 10 SP14

The Ebrington Arms ★★★★ INN ◉◉

PICK OF THE PUBS

GL55 6NH ☎ 01386 593223
e-mail: reservations@theebringtonarms.co.uk
dir: From Chipping Campden on B4035 towards Shipston on Stour. Left to Ebrington signed after 0.5m

Award-winning food served at this quintessential village pub

Built in 1640, this award-winning Cotswold gem has an abundance of character thanks to the heavy beams and original flagstones in both the bar and Old Bakehouse dining room, and the large inglenook fireplaces, which recall the building's days as the village bakery. Very much the hub of community life, it's where lucky locals (and visitors too, of course) are spoilt for choice with several real ales, some from nearby breweries like Stroud and Uley, while cider-drinkers can enjoy Robinsons. As for the food, chef James Nixon, having grown up in the area, knows how to get his hands on the best freshly harvested, organic produce, as most of it is grown or reared in fields around the pub. That his culinary talents are recognised with two AA Rosettes should therefore come as no surprise. Music, games and quiz nights, and occasional themed dinner are held. En suite bedrooms are available.

Open all day all wk noon-close **Bar Meals** L served Mon-Sat 12-2.30, Sun 12-3.30 D served Mon-Thu 6-9, Fri-Sat 6-9.30, Sun 6-8.30 **Restaurant** L served Mon-Sat 12-2.30, Sun 12-3.30 D served Mon-Thu 6-9, Fri-Sat 6-9.30, Sun 6-8.30 ⊕ FREE HOUSE ◀ Uley Bitter, Stroud Budding Pale Ale, North Cotswold Windrush Ale, Prescott Hill Climb ♂ Robinsons Flagon.
Facilities Non-diners area ☙ (Bar Garden) ♦ Children's portions Garden ☶ Parking Wi-fi ☐ **Rooms** 3

The Inn at Fossebridge

With stunning riverside gardens, elegant furnishings and fantastic food, the *Inn at Fossebridge* is at the pinnacle of fine country living and set in a charming hamlet of the same name deep in the Cotswolds.

A charming Cotswold retreat with nine elegant en-suite bedrooms, a resident's lounge, numerous large open log fires and a superb flagstone floor in the dining pub. The Inn, a family run free house, serves well kept local cask ales and is open every day for lunch and dinner.

The two traditional Cotswold bars and dining pub (one with a dart's board and stag's head), are located in the oldest part of the building, divided by stone archways. They are a wonderful retreat, rustic and cosy, with flagstone floors, beamed ceilings, two open log fires, a log burning stove and mellow Cotswold stone walls.

The hotel's enthusiastic Head Chef and his team create high quality food which they describe as the very best in pub food. Enjoy local ales, fine wine and excellent food, combined with high levels of comfort and service. Our daily special's and creative menus offer dishes using fresh, award winning local and seasonal produce, from light lunches, Fossebridge classics.

As well as the à la carte menu served daily for lunch and dinner in our dining pub, *The Bridge Restaurant* is located within the hotel with beautiful views across the terrace and gardens beyond. The seasonal a la carte menu changes weekly and the restaurant is open for dinner every Thursday, Friday and Saturday evening.

Stow Rd, Fossebridge, Nr Circencester, Gloucestershire GL54 3JS • **Tel:** 01285 720721
Website: www.fossebridgeinn.co.uk • **Email:** info@fossebridgeinn.co.uk

EWEN — Map 4 SU09

The Wild Duck ★★★★ INN

GL7 6BY ☎ 01285 770310
e-mail: duckreservations@aol.com
web: www.thewildduckinn.co.uk
dir: *From Cirencester take A429 towards Malmesbury. At Kemble left to Ewen. Inn in village centre*

Cotswold pub with an excellent choice of ales

Children and canine companions are welcome at this inn, built from honeyed Cotswold stone in 1563; the source of the Thames and the Cotswold Water Park (where there's lots of walks) are nearby. Family-owned for more than 20 years, the pub has oil portraits, log fires, oak beams and a resident ghost. Deep red walls give the Post Horn bar a warm feel, as does the extensive choice of real ales. The rambling restaurant has a lunch menu of wholesome pub favourites, while dinner may extend to wild duck antipasto, followed by luxury fish bouillabaisse. Enclosed courtyard garden. For details of the summer beer festival contact the inn.

Open all day all wk Closed: 25 Dec (eve) **Bar Meals** L served Mon-Fri 12-2, Sat-Sun all day D served all wk 6.30-10 Av main course £15.95 **Restaurant** L served Mon-Fri 12-2, Sat-Sun all day D served all wk 6.30-10 Av 3 course à la carte fr £28 ⊕ FREE HOUSE ◄ The Wild Duck Duckpond Bitter, Butcombe Bitter, Wye Valley Dorothy Goodbody's Country Ale, Greene King Abbot Ale, Morland Old Speckled Hen, Bath Gem ♂ Ashton Press, Westons Stowford Press, Aspall. ♥ 32
Facilities Non-diners area ♣ (Bar Garden) ♦♦ Children's menu Children's portions Garden ⋒ Beer festival Parking Wi-fi ▭ (notice required) **Rooms** 12

FOSSEBRIDGE — Map 5 SP01

The Inn at Fossebridge ★★★★ INN

PICK OF THE PUBS

See Pick of the Pubs on opposite page
See advert on page 185

FRAMPTON MANSELL — Map 4 SO90

The Crown Inn ★★★★ INN

PICK OF THE PUBS

GL6 8JG ☎ 01285 760601
e-mail: enquiries@thecrowninn-cotswolds.co.uk
dir: *A419 halfway between Cirencester & Stroud*

A perfect Cotswold inn to while away the hours

Once a simple cider house, this classic Cotswold-stone inn is full of old-world charm, with honey-coloured stone walls, beams and open fireplaces where log fires are lit in winter. A handsome 17th-century inn right in the heart of the village, it is surrounded by the peace and quiet of the Golden Valley. There is also plenty of seating in the large garden for the warmer months. Gloucestershire beers, such as Stroud Organic and Laurie Lee's Bitter, are usually showcased alongside others from the region, and a good choice of wines by the glass is served in the restaurant and three inviting bars. Fresh local food with lots of seasonal specials may include black olive tapenade, or mini mackerel cake with grilled chicory to start, followed by fish, chips and garden peas; Gloucester Old Spot sausages; or steak salad. Comfortable annexe bedrooms are well appointed.

Open all day all wk 12-11 **Bar Meals** L served Mon-Sat 12-2.30, Sun 12-8.30 D served Mon-Sat 6-9.30, Sun 12-8.30 **Restaurant** L served Mon-Sat 12-2.30, Sun 12-8.30 D served Mon-Sat 6-9.30, Sun 12-8.30 ⊕ FREE HOUSE ◄ Butcombe Bitter, Uley Laurie Lee's Bitter, Stroud Organic, Guest ales ♂ Ashton Press, Westons Stowford Press. ♥ 16 **Facilities** Non-diners area ♣ (Bar Restaurant Garden) ♦♦ Children's portions Garden ⋒ Parking Wi-fi ▭ **Rooms** 12

GLOUCESTER — Map 10 SO81

Queens Head

Tewkesbury Rd, Longford GL2 9EJ ☎ 01452 301882
e-mail: queenshead@aol.com
dir: *On A38 (Tewkesbury to Gloucester road) in Longford*

A cracking line-up at the locals' bar

This pretty 250-year-old half-timbered pub/restaurant is just out of town, but cannot be missed in summer when it is festooned with hanging baskets. Inside, a lovely old flagstone-floored locals' bar proffers a great range of real ales and ciders. The owners, at the helm since 1995, believe in giving their diners high-quality, freshly prepared food that is great value for money. Menus tempt with modern British food: duck and orange pâté; braised shoulder of Herefordshire beef; and the ever-popular Longford lamb – slow-roasted in chef's own secret gravy. Smart casual dress and no children under 12 years.

Open all wk 11-3 5.30-11 **Bar Meals** L served all wk 12-2 D served all wk 6.30-9.30 **Restaurant** D served all wk 6.30-9.30 ⊕ FREE HOUSE ◄ Wye Valley Butty Bach, Brains The Rev. James, Skinner's Betty Stogs, Otter, Butcombe Gold ♂ Ashton Press, Westons Stowford Press. ♥ **Facilities** Non-diners area Parking Wi-fi

GREAT BARRINGTON — Map 10 SP21

The Fox

PICK OF THE PUBS

OX18 4TB ☎ 01451 844385
e-mail: info@foxinnbarrington.com
dir: *From Burford take A40 towards Northleach. In 3m right signed The Barringtons, pub approx 0.5m on right*

Owner's dream of a pub come true

Set in the picturesque Windrush Valley, this busy centuries-old former coaching house is at the heart of this pretty village. Popular with walkers, cyclists and with those attending Cheltenham racecourse, this quintessential Cotswold inn is built of mellow local stone. There's a lot new here - new chefs with new menus, a new conservatory dining bar, a barbecue and alfresco eating area, and the garden's also had a makeover. The inn offers a range of well-kept Donnington beers and a concise wine list. Quality produce from local suppliers dominates the menus – typical dishes are Clive Porter's sausage and mash with red onion marmalade, onion rings and red wine jus; grilled local Bibury trout, new potatoes and fresh vegetables; and twice slow roasted belly of pork. Don't miss the sticky toffee pudding and vanilla ice cream. The garden overlooks the River Windrush and on warm days it's a perfect summer watering hole and base for lovely walks and cycle rides.

Open all day all wk 11am-close **Bar Meals** L served Mon-Fri 12-2.30, Sat-Sun all day D served Mon-Fri 6.30-9.30, Sat-Sun all day **Restaurant** L served Mon-Fri 12-2.30, Sat-Sun all day D served Mon-Fri 6.30-9.30, Sat-Sun all day ⊕ DONNINGTON ◄ BB, SBA ♂ Westons Stowford Press & Perry, Addlestones. **Facilities** Non-diners area ♣ (Bar Garden) ♦♦ Children's portions Garden ⋒ Parking Wi-fi

GUITING POWER — Map 10 SP02

The Hollow Bottom

GL54 5UX ☎ 01451 850392
e-mail: hello@hollowbottom.com
dir: *Telephone for directions*

Cosy country pub with a horseracing theme

Often frequented by Cheltenham race-goers, this 18th-century Cotswold free house is decorated with all manner of horseracing memorabilia – from badges and silks to framed newspaper cuttings. Its nooks and crannies are warmed by a blazing log fire and lend themselves to planning an intimate drink or meal; there's also a separate dining room, plus outside tables for fine weather. In addition to real ales and ciders, the bar proffers a grand selection of malt whiskies, wines and champagne. If you're after a snack, baked potatoes and freshly made baguettes have a choice of fillings. Other dishes of typical pub fare extend from home-made pie or roast of the day to wholetail scampi.

Open all day all wk 9am-12.30am ⊕ FREE HOUSE ◄ Hollow Bottom Best Bitter, Donnington SBA, Guest ale ♂ Thatchers Gold & Cheddar Valley. **Facilities** ♦♦ Children's menu Children's portions Play area Garden Parking Wi-fi

PICK OF THE PUBS

The Inn at Fossebridge ★★★★ INN

FOSSEBRIDGE   Map 5 SP01

Stow Rd GL54 3JS ☎ **01285 720721**
e-mail: info@fossebridgeinn.co.uk
web: www.fossebridgeinn.co.uk
*dir: M4 junct 15, A419 towards
Cirencester, A429 towards Stow. Pub
approx 6m on left (in a dip)*

A delightful Cotswold's inn

A 17th-century award-winning, family-
run free house with accommodation, set
in four acres of riverside gardens with a
lake. Records show that there has been
a building here on the ancient Fosseway
since at least 1634; in 1749 it became a
coaching inn, the Lord Chedworth's
Arms, his lordship being the wealthy
local landowner after whom the old bar
is named. Stone archways divide the
restaurant from the two bar areas, each
featuring exposed beams, stone walls,
flagstone flooring and an open fire.
Whichever you choose, there are real
ales to weigh up, including Hook
Norton's Hooky and Cotswold Lion, and
Bath Ales SPA. Offering both lunch and
dinner options, the seasonal menu may
feature pan-fried pigeon breast, Puy
lentils, pancetta crisps; or a
Fossebridge duck Scotch egg to start,
followed by fish of the day with triple
cooked chips; roast rump of beef, truffle
mash, panache of vegetables and
Madeira jus; or River Fowey moules
marinière with crusty bread.
Alternatively, a sandwich or baguette

with Coln Valley smoked salmon and
cream cheese is a good bet for a lighter
option. There are Fossebridge Classics
too, such as sausages of the day with
creamy mash and red onion gravy; and
chargrilled home-made burger. A
vegetarian option might be risotto
primavera, Cerney goats' cheese with
red vein sorrel. Among the home-made
puddings there might be hot cross bun
pudding and vanilla sauce, or honey
roasted figs, clotted cream and quince
jelly. The bedrooms are appointed to a
high standard.

Open all day all wk 12-12 (Sun 12
-11.30) **Bar Meals** L served Mon-Fri 12
-2.30, Sat 12-3, Sun 12-3.30 D served
Thu-Sat 6-9.30 Apr-Sep, 6-9 Oct-Mar Av
main course £14.50 **Restaurant** L

served Mon-Fri 12-2.30, Sat 12-3, Sun
12-3.30 D served all wk 6-9.30 Apr-Sep,
all wk 6-9 Oct-Mar Av 3 course à la
carte fr £28 ⊕ FREE HOUSE ◀ Hook
Norton Hooky Bitter, Bath Ales SPA,
Cotswold Lion ♂ Westons Stowford
Press, Bath Ciders Bounders.
Facilities Non-diners area ✿ ♦
Children's menu & portions Play area
Garden ⊼ Parking Wi-fi ▭ (notice
required) **Rooms** 9

Map 4 ST77

The Bull at Hinton

PICK OF THE PUBS

See Pick of the Pubs on opposite page

Map 5 SU29

The Trout Inn

St Johns Bridge GL7 3HA ☎ 01367 252313
e-mail: chefpjw@aol.com
dir: *A40 onto A361 then A417. From M4 junct 15, A419, then A361 & A417 to Lechlade*

Extensive menu served in an ancient inn

When workmen constructed a new bridge over the Thames in 1220, they built an almshouse to live in. It became an inn in 1472, and its flagstone floors and beams now overflow into the old boathouse. The extensive menu features meat, fish and vegetarian options, as well as pizzas, filled jacket potatoes and burgers. This family-friendly pub offers smaller portions for children, who also have their own separate menu. The large garden often hosts live jazz, and there's a beer festival in June.

Open all wk 10-3 6-11 (summer all wk 10am-11pm) Closed: 25 Dec **Bar Meals** L served all wk 12-2 D served all wk 7-10 **Restaurant** L served all wk 12-2 D served all wk 7-10 ⊕ ENTERPRISE INNS ◀ Courage Best, Sharp's Doom Bar & Cornish Coaster, Guest ales. ☎ 15 **Facilities** Non-diners area ❀ (Bar Garden) ♦ Children's menu Children's portions Play area Family room Garden Beer festival Parking Wi-fi ▭ (notice required)

Map 4 ST89

The Royal Oak

1 The Street GL8 8UN ☎ 01666 890250
e-mail: info@royaloakleighterton.co.uk
dir: *M4 junct 18, A46 towards Stroud. After Dunkirk left, continue on A46. Right signed Leighterton*

Majors on local seasonal produce

Set in a picture-postcard Cotswold village, close to Westonbirt Arboretum, Paul and Antonia Whitbread's pub thrives as a popular dining venue. The bright, contemporary bar and dining room successfully blends exposed beams, open fires and antiques with modern furnishings. Enjoy a pint of Bath Ales or Hook Norton ale with a lunchtime sandwich or platter or dive into the main menu. Food is classic British and everything is made on the premises from local ingredients. Typically, tuck into lobster ravioli and vermouth butter sauce; game casserole with juniper berry dumplings; ginger and cinnamon sponge, warm poached apples and whipped cream.

Open all wk 12-3 5.30-11 (Sat 12-11 Sun 12-10.30) **Bar Meals** L served Mon-Fri 12-2, Sat 12-2.30, Sun 12-3 D served Mon-Fri 6-9, Sat 6-9.30 **Restaurant** L served Mon-Fri 12-2, Sat 12-2.30, Sun 12-3 D served Mon-Fri 6-9, Sat 6-9.30 ⊕ FREE HOUSE ◀ Otter Ale, Bath Barnsey, Wye Valley, Bath Ales Gem, Hook Nortons Hooky

◯ Westons Stowford Press, Sherston. ☎ 10 **Facilities** Non-diners area ❀ (Bar Garden) ♦ Children's menu Children's portions Garden ▭ Parking Wi-fi ▭ (notice required)

Map 4 ST58

White Hart

BS35 1NR ☎ 01454 412275
e-mail: whitehart@youngs.co.uk
dir: *M48 junct 1, follow Thornbury signs (B4461), 3m, 1st left to Littleton-on-Severn*

Classic Cotswold inn with a lovely garden

Secluded in a hamlet close to the Severn Estuary, views from the shrubby, suntrap beer garden of this lovely 17th-century inn encompass the distant wooded ridge of the Forest of Dean. Defiantly olde worlde with all the timeless trimmings, the enchanting beamed interior draws in beer-lovers to sample Bath Ales and Thatchers cider, whilst diners can expect a wide choice from an inspiring menu featuring their famous 8oz hanger steak; potted Gloucester ham; and goats' cheese and mushroom Wellington; with a local fruit crumble to finish.

Open all day all wk 12-11 (Fri-Sun 12-12) ⊕ YOUNG'S ◀ Bitter & Special, Bath Gem, Guest ales ◯ Thatchers Heritage & Gold, Addlestones. **Facilities** ❀ (Bar Garden) ♦ Children's menu Children's portions Family room Garden Parking

Map 10 SO93

The Hobnails Inn

GL20 8NQ ☎ 01242 620237
e-mail: enquiries@thehobnailsinn.co.uk
dir: *M5 junct 9, A46 towards Evesham then B4077 to Stow-on-the-Wold. Inn 1.5m on left*

Medieval inn benefiting from a beautiful rural setting

Dating from the 13th century, this charming Cotswold building is one of the oldest inns in the county. Its idyllic rural setting and lovely large garden attract summer visitors, while log fires warm the interior in winter. The philosophy here is to serve wholesome meals using seasonal produce, so settle into one of the leather sofas with a pint and a menu. Perhaps a 'big bap' – a 7-inch fresh bap filled with liver and onions, for example – will suffice. Alternatively the lunchtime carvery is backed by a great selection of classic English dishes.

Open all wk 12-3 5.30-11 (Sun all day) ⊕ ENTERPRISE INNS ◀ Fuller's London Pride ◯ Westons Stowford Press. **Facilities** ❀ (Bar Garden) ♦ Children's menu Children's portions Garden Parking Wi-fi

Map 10 SO61

The Glasshouse Inn

May Hill GL17 0NN ☎ 01452 830529
e-mail: glasshouseinn@gmail.com
dir: *Off A40 between Gloucester & Ross-on-Wye*

Gimmick-free traditional pub

The Glasshouse gets its name from Dutch glassmakers who settled locally in the 16th century but its origins can be traced back further, to 1450. A gimmick-free traditional pub, it is located in a fabulous rural setting with a country garden and an elegant interior. The inn serves a range of real ales including Butcombe and Sharp's Doom Bar, plus home-cooked dishes such as fish pie; cod and chips; beef curry; steak-and-kidney served in Yorkshire puddings; and chilli. At lunch you can choose from a range of sandwiches, ploughman's lunches or basket meals of chips with the likes of scampi or sausage.

Open 11.30-3 7-11 (Sun 12-3) Closed: Sun eve **Bar Meals** L served all wk 12-2 D served Mon-Sat 7-9 (booking required for parties of 6 or more) ⊕ FREE HOUSE ◀ Sharp's Doom Bar, Butcombe ◯ Westons Stowford Press. ☎ 12 **Facilities** Garden Parking Wi-fi

Map 10 SP22

The Fox

PICK OF THE PUBS

GL56 0UR ☎ 01451 870555 & 870666
e-mail: info@foxinn.net
dir: *A436 from Stow-on-the-Wold, right to Lower Oddington*

Creeper-clad pub with a delightful garden

Set in a quintessential Cotswold village and dating back to the 17th century, this stone-built, creeper-clad free house, is now under new ownership. The interior boasts polished flagstone floors, beams, log fires and antique furniture that creates a period feel. The daily-changing menus take full advantage of fresh, local produce. Typical starters include spinach and parmesan risotto; baked crab gratin; and beetroot, feta and pinenut salad. Followed by mains of pan-fried calves' liver, mash and onion and bacon gravy; and honey and mustard baked ham with parsley sauce. In summer, there's a terrace for alfresco dining, as well as a pretty, traditional cottage garden.

Open all wk 12-2.30 6-11 or 12 (Sun 12-3.30 7-10.30) Closed: 25 Dec **Bar Meals** L served Mon-Sat 12-2.30, Sun 12-3 D served Mon-Fri 6.30-9.30, Sat 6.30-10, Sun 7-9 **Restaurant** L served Mon-Sat 12-2.30, Sun 12-3 D served Mon-Fri 6.30-9.30, Sat 6.30-10, Sun 7-9 ⊕ FREE HOUSE ◀ Hook Norton Hooky Bitter, Donnington SBA, Dark Star The Art of Darkness, Wickwar Rite Flanker ◯ Aspall. ☎ 15 **Facilities** Non-diners area ♦ Children's portions Garden ▭ Parking Wi-fi

Save on hotels. Book at **theAA.com/hotel**

GLOUCESTERSHIRE 189 ENGLAND

PICK OF THE PUBS

The Bull at Hinton

HINTON Map 4 ST77

SN14 8HG ☎ **0117 937 2332**
e-mail:
reservations@thebullathinton.co.uk
web: www.thebullathinton.co.uk
dir: *From M4 junct 18, A46 to Bath 1m,*
turn right 1m, down hill. Pub on right

Break an M4 journey for this sleepy-village inn

Like so many old buildings, this 17th-
century, stone-built former farmhouse
and dairy has its fair share of ghosts —
look out for the lady in grey! It stands on
the southern edge of the Cotswolds and
became an inn just over 100 years ago;
today it's just five minutes' drive from
the M4. Run with charm and personality
by David and Elizabeth White, it's full of
original character, with a beamed bar
and dining room, in which you'll find
inglenook fireplaces, flagstone floors,
old pews and big oak tables, candlelit in
the evenings. Food is freshly prepared
from high quality, mostly local,
producers and suppliers, although fish
and seafood comes up daily from
St Mawes in Cornwall. Short, seasonal
menus list classics like beef and ale
shortcrust pastry pie with bubble-and-
squeak; supreme of chicken stuffed with
cherry tomatoes and mozzarella
wrapped in Parma ham; and monkfish
and Serrano ham kebabs, steamed rice
and brown shrimp sauce. A chalkboard
offers imaginative specials that by

making full use of seasonal produce
change frequently and, during the
winter, for example, those partial to
pheasant, partridge and venison should
be in luck. Another possibility is spicy
seafood spaghetti, with sea bass,
clams, prawns and mussels; and for
vegetarians, warm goats' cheese salad
with couscous and Mediterranean
vegetables. For dessert, try the banana-
coconut crème brûlée. The suntrap
south-facing terrace and garden is the
perfect spot for a pint of 6X, Henry's IPA,
Bishop's Tipple or Summersault from
Wadworth of Devizes.

Open 12-3 6-12 (Sat-Sun & BH open all
day) Closed: Mon L (ex BH) **Bar Meals** L
served Tue-Fri 12-2, Sat 12-9.30, Sun
12-8.30 (BHs 12-8) D served Mon-Fri

6-9, Sat 12-9.30, Sun 12-8.30 (BHs
12-8) **Restaurant** L served Tue-Fri 12-2,
Sat 12-9.30, Sun 12-8.30 (BHs 12-8)
D served Mon-Fri 6-9, Sat 12-9.30, Sun
12-8.30 (BHs 12-8) ⊕ WADWORTH
🍺 6X, Henry's Original IPA, Bishop's
Tipple & Summersault, Guest ale
Ö Thatchers Gold, Westons Stowford
Press. ☺ 11 **Facilities** Non-diners area
🍴 Children's menu Play area Garden ⊼
Parking Wi-fi 🚐 (notice required)

PICK OF THE PUBS

The Weighbridge Inn

MINCHINHAMPTON   Map 4 SO80

GL6 9AL ☎ **01453 832520**
e-mail: enquiries@2in1pub.co.uk
web: www.2in1pub.co.uk
dir: *On B4014 between Nailsworth & Avening*

Recommended for its freshly made pies

Parts of this whitewashed free house date back to the 17th century, when it stood adjacent to the original packhorse trail between Bristol and London. While the trail is now a footpath and bridleway, the road in front (now the B4014) became a turnpike in the 1820s. The innkeeper at the time ran both the pub and the weighbridge for the local woollen mills – serving jugs of ale in between making sure tolls were paid. Associated memorabilia and other rural artefacts from the time are displayed around the inn, which has been carefully renovated to retain original features, like exposed brick walls and open fires. Up in the restaurant, which used to be the hayloft, the old roof timbers reach almost to the floor. The inn prides itself on its decent ales and ciders, and the quality of its food, with everything cooked from scratch. Fish lovers could start with potted shrimps or a fish sharing board. Otherwise, the Mediterranean medley is sure to get the taste buds going. The hearty main courses include beef hot pot, broccoli

and cauliflower cannelloni, and chicken chasseur. Lighter meals are available as salads, omelettes, jacket potatoes and filled baguettes. The Weighbridge is also the home of 'the famous 2 in 1 pies', one half containing a filling of your choice from a selection of seven (such as pork, bacon and celery) and topped with pastry, the other half home-made cauliflower cheese – all cooked to order and available to take away or even bake at home. Typical desserts are banana crumble and chocolate cheesecake. From the patios and sheltered landscaped garden the Cotswolds are in full view.

Open all day all wk 12-11 (Sun 12-10.30) Closed: 25 Dec **Bar Meals** L served all wk 12-9.30 D served all wk

12-9.30 food served all day **Restaurant** L served all wk 12-9.30 D served all wk 12-9.30 food served all day ⊕ FREE HOUSE ◀ Wadworth 6X, Uley Old Spot, Palmers Best Bitter ♂ Westons Bounds, Thatchers Gold, Wicked Witch. ♀ 15 **Facilities** Non-diners area ♦ Children's menu Children's portions Family room Garden Parking Wi-fi 🚌

Save on hotels. Book at theAA.com/hotel

GLOUCESTERSHIRE 191 ENGLAND

MARSHFIELD   Map 4 ST77

The Catherine Wheel

39 High St SN14 8LR ☎ 01225 892220
e-mail: roo@thecatherinewheel.co.uk
dir: *M4 junct 18, A46 signed Bath. Left onto A420 signed Chippenham. Right signed Marshfield*

Traditional Cotswold inn with sunny patio

On the edge of the Cotswolds, this mainly 17th-century inn has the expected exposed brickwork and large open fireplaces offset by a simple, stylish decor. Menus are also simple and well presented, with favourites at lunchtime including steak-and-kidney pie; and jacket potatoes. In the evening look forward to potted smoked mackerel, lemon and herb pâté or tomato and goats' cheese tartlets, followed perhaps by venison stew and thyme dumplings or fish pie. A small but sunny patio is a lovely spot for a summertime pint of Butcombe Bitter or Thatchers cider.

Open all day all wk **Bar Meals** L served Mon-Fri 12-2, Sat-Sun 12-3 D served Mon-Thu 6.30-9, Fri-Sat 6.30-9.30, Sun 6-8.30 **Restaurant** L served Mon-Fri 12-2, Sat-Sun 12-3 D served Mon-Thu 6.30-9, Fri-Sat 6.30-9.30, Sun 6-8.30 ⊕ FREE HOUSE ◀ Butcombe Bitter, Sharp's Doom Bar, Local guest ale Ö Ashton Press, Thatchers. ♥ **Facilities** Non-diners area ♣ (Bar Garden) ♦♦ Children's portions Garden ⋈ Parking Wi-fi ▬ (notice required)

The Lord Nelson Inn

1 & 2 High St SN14 8LP ☎ 01225 891820
e-mail: thelordnelsoninn.@btinternet.com
dir: *M4 junct 18, A46 towards Bath. Left at Cold Ashton rdbt towards Marshfield & Chippenham*

Log fires in winter, patio in summer

In a conservation village on the edge of the Cotswolds and surrounded by wonderful walks, this 16th-century former coaching inn draws a loyal local crowd for good home-made food and quality cask ales. A spacious bar that provides a chance to mix with the locals, a candlelit restaurant, log fires in winter and a patio for summer use complete its attractions. With the food emphasis on simplicity and quality, the varied menus take in light bar lunches (ham, egg and chips), hearty evening dishes like pheasant with red wine and redcurrant gravy, and a very popular Sunday carvery.

Open all wk 12-2.30 5-11 (Fri-Sun 12-11) **Bar Meals** L served Mon-Sat 12-2, Sun 12-3 D served Mon-Sat 6.30-9, Sun 6-8.30 **Restaurant** L served Mon-Sat 12-2, Sun 12-3 D served Mon-Sat 6.30-9, Sun 6-8.30 ⊕ ENTERPRISE INNS ◀ Greene King IPA, Bath Gem, Sharp's Doom Bar Ö Thatchers Gold. ♥ 9 **Facilities** Non-diners area ♦♦ Children's menu Children's portions Play area Garden ⋈ Wi-fi ▬ (notice required)

MEYSEY HAMPTON   Map 5 SP10

The Masons Arms

28 High St GL7 5JT ☎ 01285 850164
e-mail: info@masonsarms.biz
dir: *6m E of Cirencester off A417, beside village green*

At the heart of village life

This is a quintessential 17th-century stone-built Cotswold inn, nestled alongside the green in the heart of the village. The hub of the community and welcoming to visitors, it offers something for everyone, from a warming log fire in the large inglenook to the range of well-kept Arkell's ales and Westons cider served in the convivial beamed bar. Good value home-made food could include local smoked trout salad or Gloucestershire pork loin with chips. Worth noting if visiting the Cotswold Water Park nearby.

Open 12-2 5.30-11 (Sat 12-11 Sun 12-10) Closed: Mon ⊕ ARKELL'S ◀ 3B, 2B, Kingsdown, Moonlight Ö Westons Stowford Press. **Facilities** ♣ (Bar Garden) ♦♦ Children's portions Garden Wi-fi

MINCHINHAMPTON   Map 4 SO80

The Weighbridge Inn

PICK OF THE PUBS

See Pick of the Pubs on opposite page

MORETON-IN-MARSH   Map 10 SP23

The Red Lion Inn

GL56 0RT ☎ 01608 674397
e-mail: info@theredlionlittlecompton.co.uk
dir: *Between Chipping Norton & Moreton-in-Marsh on A44*

A good place to enjoy pub games and seasonal food

A pretty Cotswold-stone building quietly located on the edge of the village, this is one of 15 pubs owned by Donnington Brewery – a family concern that has been brewing since 1865. Set in a large mature garden, the building has exposed stone walls and beams, inglenook fireplaces and real fires. Public bar games include darts, dominoes, a jukebox and pool table. The restaurant offers a seasonal menu and sensibly priced daily-changing specials.

Open all wk 12-3 6-12 ⊕ DONNINGTON ◀ BB, SBA. **Facilities** ♣ (Bar Garden) ♦♦ Children's portions Garden Parking Wi-fi

NAILSWORTH   Map 4 ST89

The Britannia

Cossack Square GL6 0DG ☎ 01453 832501
e-mail: pheasantpluckers2003@yahoo.co.uk
dir: *From A46 S'bound right at town centre rdbt. 1st left. Pub directly ahead*

Former manor house with a brasserie-style menu

Occupying a delightful position on the south side of Nailsworth's Cossack Square, The Britannia is a stone-built, 17th-century building. The interior is bright and uncluttered, while outside you'll find a pretty garden with plenty of tables, chairs and parasols for sunny days. The menu offers an interesting blend of modern British and continental food, with ingredients bought from both local suppliers and London's Smithfield Market. Go lightly with just a starter, perhaps moules marinière; or plunge into hearty mains such as chargrilled rump steak or confit pork belly. Other options include stone-baked pizzas and impressive meat-free options. Great wines, too.

Open all wk 11-11 (Fri-Sat 11am-mdnt Sun 11-10.30) Closed: 25 Dec ⊕ FREE HOUSE ◀ Sharp's Doom Bar, Buckham, Otter, Guest ales Ö Thatcher's Gold, Westons Stowford Press. **Facilities** ♣ (Bar Garden) ♦♦ Garden Parking

Tipputs Inn

Bath Rd GL6 0QE ☎ 01453 832466
e-mail: pheasantpluckers2003@yahoo.co.uk
dir: *A46, 0.5m S of Nailsworth*

Impeccably decorated pub-restaurant

Mellow Cotswold stone and stripped floorboards blend nicely with modern, clean-lined furniture in this 17th-century inn, while a giant candelabra adds a touch of grandeur. The Tipputs is owned by Nick Beardsley and Christophe Coquoin, who are responsible for creating the menus for all their Gloucestershire food pubs (such as The Britannia, also in Nailsworth), plus they select and import some ingredients and wines from France. There are dishes for every eventuality, starting with tapas-style appetisers and starters and extending through to pub classics (fish and chips; home-made burger and chips), classy options and South Indian cuisine.

Open all wk 10.30am-11pm ⊕ FREE HOUSE ◀ Otter Ale, Stroud Ö Westons Stowford Press. **Facilities** ♦♦ Children's menu Garden Parking

NETHER WESTCOTE   Map 10 SP22

The Feathered Nest Country Inn ★★★★★ INN ◉◉◉

PICK OF THE PUBS

See Pick of the Pubs on page 192

PICK OF THE PUBS

The Feathered Nest Country Inn ★★★★★ INN ✿✿✿

NETHER WESTCOTE   Map 10 SP22

OX7 6SD ☎ **01993 833030**
e-mail: info@thefeatherednestinn.co.uk
web: www.thefeatherednestinn.co.uk
dir: *A424 between Burford &*
Stow-on-the-Wold, follow signs

Award-winning food in a beautiful rural location

In the picturesque village of Nether Westcote on the border of Gloucestershire and Oxfordshire, The Feathered Nest has marvellous views over the Evenlode Valley. Originally an old malthouse, the pub has been updated and thoughtfully furnished whilst retaining the original character, especially in the cosy log-fired bar, where local and award-winning real ales are on offer. Herbs and vegetables are grown in the kitchen garden, with local produce forming the backbone of the menus. As well as bar snacks, the three-AA Rosette, modern British cuisine brings a daily set lunch menu for relaxed eating in the bar, and on the garden terrace (shaded by a sycamore tree) when the weather allows. Dishes could include mussel chowder, sea bream and peanut butter mousse. The seasonal à la carte offers a modern take on classic combinations, such as red mullet with artichoke and vegetable broth, fennel pollen, caper berries and olives; and venison loin with potato

dumplings, sauerkraut, quince, blackcurrant and a cocoa bean sauce. For simpler tastes there's a selection from the charcoal grill; maybe 28-day aged South Devon rib-eye steak with fries, bearnaise sauce and mixed leaf salad. Be sure to leave room for desserts such as passionfruit parfait with caramel sauce and pine nuts. Afternoon tea and Sunday lunch are also served. Individually decorated bedrooms furnished with antiques and comfortable beds are available; the pub makes an excellent base from which to explore the countryside and the quaint and charming villages nearby. Look out for enjoyable events running throughout the year, including a pie and pint tasting evening, live jazz, and a quiz night. Booking for meals recommended.

Open all day Closed: 25 Dec, Mon **Bar Meals** L served Tue-Sat 12-2.30, Sun 12-3.30 D served Tue-Sat 6.30-9.30 **Restaurant** L served Tue-Sat 12-2.30, Sun 12-3.30 D served Tue-Sat 6.30-9.30 ⊕ FREE HOUSE ⬛ Rotating Local Ales ♂ Thatchers Gold. ♟ 19 **Facilities** Non-diners area ❄ (Bar Garden) ♦♦ Children's menu Children's portions Family room Garden ⩎ Parking Wi-fi **Rooms** 4

NEWENT　　　Map 10 SO72

Kilcot Inn ★★★★ INN **NEW**

Ross Rd, Kilcot GL18 1NA ☎ 01989 720707
e-mail: info@kilcotinn.com
dir: *M50 junct 3, B4221 signed Newent. Approx 2m to pub on left*

Renovated country inn offering great hospitality

This delightful inn has the best traditions of hospitality, food and drink. From the selection of real ales and local ciders on tap to the high quality produce used in the dishes in the bar and restaurant there is something for everyone. Their menu might include Italian meat antipasti or smoked bacon and chorizo risotto for starters, followed by a home-made game, chicken and ham or vegetable pie; pan cooked Gloucester Old Spot pork loin, or grilled sirloin steak. Outdoor seating is available, including a pleasant garden area to the rear. The four stylish bedrooms are appointed to a high standard.

Open all day all wk **Bar Meals** L served all wk 12-3 D served all wk 6-9 **Restaurant** L served all wk 12-3 D served all wk 6-9 ⊕ FREE HOUSE ◀ Wye Valley Butty Bach, Marston's EPA ♻ Westons Stowford Press, Old Rosie & Country Perry. **Facilities** Non-diners area ❄ (Bar Garden Outside area) ♦ Children's portions Garden Outside area ⊨ Parking Wi-fi ▄ (notice required) **Rooms** 4

NEWLAND　　　Map 4 SO50

The Ostrich Inn

PICK OF THE PUBS

GL16 8NP ☎ 01594 833260
e-mail: kathryn@theostrichinn.com
dir: *Follow Monmouth signs from Chepstow (A466), Newland signed from Redbrook*

Huge range of real ales here

On the western edge of the Forest of Dean and adjoining the Wye Valley in a pretty village, the 13th-century Ostrich is thought to have taken its name from the family emblem of the Probyns, local landowners in previous centuries; it retains many of its ancient features, including a priest hole. With its warm welcome, The Ostrich is a thriving social centre for the village. An open log fire burns in the large lounge bar throughout the winter, and customers can relax immediately in the friendly atmosphere with a pint of their chosen brew. And what a choice. Eight cask-conditioned real ales such as Butty Bach are served at any one time; real ciders, too, are strongly represented. Diners settle down in the small and intimate restaurant, in the bar or out in gardens.

Open all wk 12-3 (Mon-Fri 6.30-11.30 Sat 6-11.30 Sun 6.30-10.30) **Bar Meals** L served all wk 12-2.30 D served Sun-Fri 6.30-9.30, Sat 6-9.30 **Restaurant** L served all wk 12-2.30 D served Sun-Fri 6.30-9.30, Sat 6-9.30 ⊕ FREE HOUSE ◀ Wye Valley Butty Bach, Uley Pigs Ear, Hook Norton Old Hooky, Adnams, Guest ales ♻ Westons Stowford Press & Old Rosie, Ty Gwyn, Severn Cider. **Facilities** Non-diners area ❄ (Bar Garden) ♦ Garden ⊨

NORTH CERNEY　　　Map 5 SP00

Bathurst Arms

PICK OF THE PUBS

GL7 7BZ ☎ 01285 831281
e-mail: james@bathurstarms.com
dir: *5m N of Cirencester on A435*

Convivial Cotswold dining pub

Whether for just a simple drink or snack, three-course lunch or dinner, pull in to this creeper-covered, 17th-century pub by the River Churn on the Earl of Bathurst's estate. The flagstoned and beamed bar is hugely appealing, even when the log fires aren't lit, but if the weather's kind the pretty riverside garden is equally pleasant. Prepared from locally sourced ingredients, are grilled mackerel fillet with pesto; and home-made cottage pie, while dinner suggestions might include pan-roasted duck breast; lightly grilled gilt-head bream fillet; slow-cooked Gloucestershire Old Spot pork belly; and roasted aubergine stuffed with vegetable ragout. For those who can manage a dessert, try steamed apricot and raisin pudding with toffee sauce; and poached blackberries with lemon curd, marshmallow and Chantilly cream. Box Steam's Golden Bolt and Wickwar's Cotswold Way await real ale drinkers, with many more at the January, April, July and October beer festivals.

Open all day all wk **Bar Meals** L served all wk 12-2 D served all wk 6-9 Av main course £15 **Restaurant** L served all wk 12-2 D served all wk 6-9 Fixed menu price fr £15 Av 3 course à la carte fr £23 ⊕ FREE HOUSE ◀ Box Steam Golden Bolt, Wickwar Cotswold Way ♻ Westons Stowford Press, Cotswold. ☗ 15 **Facilities** Non-diners area ❄ (Bar Garden) ♦ Children's menu Children's portions Garden ⊨ Beer festival Parking Wi-fi ▄ (notice required)

NORTHLEACH　　　Map 10 SP11

The Wheatsheaf Inn

West End GL54 3EZ ☎ 01451 860244
e-mail: reservations@cotswoldswheatsheaf.com
dir: *Just off A40 between Oxford & Cheltenham*

Stylish pub worth seeking out

A beautiful Cotswold-stone 17th-century inn on the square of the pretty former wool town of Northleach, The Wheatsheaf is everything anyone could wish for, with flagstone floors, beams, log fires and a vibrant, smartened-up feel throughout. It's the perfect place for enjoying bracing walks then chilling out in the bar with the papers or sampling some seriously good food. Monthly menus evolve with the season and may take in roast breast of chicken, borlotti bean and vegetable broth and salsa verde; calves' liver with sage and balsamic onions; Black Forest sundae.

Open all day all wk **Bar Meals** L served all wk 12-3 D served all wk 6-10 **Restaurant** L served all wk 12-3 D served all wk 6-10 ⊕ FREE HOUSE ◀ Fuller's London Pride ♻ Dunkertons. ☗ 10 **Facilities** Non-diners area ❄ (Bar Restaurant Garden) ♦ Children's menu Children's portions Play area Garden ⊨ Parking Wi-fi ▄ (notice required)

OLDBURY-ON-SEVERN　　　Map 4 ST69

The Anchor Inn

Church Rd BS35 1QA ☎ 01454 413331
e-mail: info@anchorinnoldbury.co.uk
dir: *From N A38 towards Bristol, 1.5m then right, village signed. From S A38 through Thornbury*

Homely inn in tranquil Severnside village

Set beside a tree-lined pill (stream) that meanders down to the nearby Severn Estuary, this family-friendly pub is on the Severn Way footpath and a popular stopping place for ramblers. Parts of the stone-built inn are nearly 500 years old, and an olde-worlde welcome is assured for travellers to this charming, out-of-the-way village. Appetite-busters on the good-value bar and dining room menu include pan-fried pheasant breast or crispy pork belly and black pudding with creamed cabbage and bacon. Reliable real ales include guests like Severn Sins, plus there's a good range of bottled cider and perry.

Open all wk 11.30-2.30 6-11 (Sat 11.30am-mdnt Sun 12-10.30) **Bar Meals** L served Mon-Fri 12-2, Sat 12-2.30, Sun 12-3 D served all wk 6-9 Av main course £9.95 **Restaurant** L served Mon-Fri 12-2, Sat 12-2.30, Sun 12-3 D served all wk 6-9 Fixed menu price fr £9.95 Av 3 course à la carte fr £19.95 ⊕ FREE HOUSE ◀ Bass, Butcombe Bitter, Otter Bitter, Guest ales ♻ Ashton Press, Sheppy's, Ashton Still. ☗ 16 **Facilities** Non-diners area ♦ Children's menu Family room Garden ⊨ Parking

PAINSWICK　　　Map 4 SO80

The Falcon Inn

New St GL6 6UN ☎ 01452 814222
e-mail: info@falconpainswick.co.uk
dir: *On A46 in centre of Painswick, opposite St Mary's church*

Historic inn with wide-ranging menus

In the heart of the town and opposite the church with its iconic 99 yew trees, this small hotel, restaurant and pub dates from 1554 but spent over 200 years as a courthouse. Expect a good choice of local real ales, including Hook Norton and tasty, home-cooked meals any time of day. An evening meal might offer pan-seared pigeon breast with pickled beetroot and parsnip purée; rack of lamb with garlic roasted new potatoes and red wine jus to follow; and rhubarb and apple crumble for dessert. A blackboard offers daily specials, steaks and pies.

Open all day all wk 10am-11pm **Bar Meals** L served all wk 12-3 D served all wk 7-9.30 **Restaurant** D served all wk 6-9.30 ⊕ PARSNIP INNS LTD ◀ Sharp's Doom Bar, Hook Norton, Guest ale ♻ Weston Stowford Press. ☗ 10 **Facilities** Non-diners area ❄ (All areas) ♦ Children's menu Children's portions Garden Outside area ⊨ Parking Wi-fi ▄ (notice required)

PICK OF THE PUBS

The Bell at Sapperton

GL7 6LE ☎ 01285 760298
e-mail: info@bellsapperton.co.uk
web: www.bellsapperton.co.uk
dir: *From A419 between Cirencester &
Stroud follow Sapperton signs*

Welcoming Cotswolds pub with a passion for local produce

Built of mellow Cotswold stone and set
in an idyllic village close to Cirencester
Park, the 300-year-old Bell's traditional
features (including exposed stone walls,
polished flagstones and bare boards,
beamed ceilings, open fireplaces) were
renovated in early 2013. The pub's new
licensee and new menu continue to
impress local walkers, families,
drinkers, diners and even horse riders
– the pub provides facilities for horses
to be tied up and watered. On warmer
days, there's a secluded rear courtyard
and a landscaped front garden for
alfresco dining. Civilised in every way,
The Bell attracts discerning folk for its
Hook Norton and Stroud ales, and its
innovative, home-made pub food,
served throughout four cosy dining
areas, each with their own individual
character. Menus change with the
seasons, but all are founded on fresh
produce from known suppliers and local
farms. The chef oversees the kitchen
garden, where vegetables and salads
are grown, and customers are welcome
to swap their own home-grown produce

for discounts or credit at the pub.
Walkers calling in for a snack might
tuck into a ham hock and pea tart or a
steak, onion and rocket sandwich,
perhaps washed down with a pint of
local Premium Cotswold Lager.
Meanwhile, serious diners can choose
from starters of cuttlefish and
watermelon, Brixham lobster fishcakes,
and salad Niçoise. Main course options
include monkfish in squid ink with
buttered spinach, cauliflower, bacon
and saffron potatoes; Longhorn beef
burger and chips; braised lamb shank
with confit of vegetables, potato purée
and garlic sauce; and lentil shepherd's
pie. Look out for the daily specials.
Leave room for rhubarb Eton Mess or
rum baba with drunken figs.

Open all wk 11-3 6.30-11 (Sun
12-10.30) Closed: 25 Dec **Bar Meals** L
served all wk 12-2.15 D served all wk
7-9.30 ⊞ FREE HOUSE ◛ Otter Bitter,
Hook Norton Hooky Bitter, Butcombe,
Stroud Budding ♻ Westons Stowford
Press. ♟ 12 **Facilities** Non-diners area
❤ ⭧ Children's menu Children's
portions Garden Parking Wi-fi

Save on hotels. Book at theAA.com/hotel

GLOUCESTERSHIRE 195 ENGLAND

PAXFORD
Map 10 SP13

The Churchill Arms ★★★★ INN ◉◉
PICK OF THE PUBS

GL55 6XH ☎ 01386 594000
e-mail: info@thechurchillarms.com
dir: *2m E of Chipping Campden, 4m N of Moreton-in-Marsh*

A perfect base for exploring the Cotswolds

Close to the historical wool town of Chipping Campden, this unpretentious 17th-century pub is the quintessential Cotswold inn. Nestled among honey-stone cottages in the chocolate-box village of Paxford, the pub draws an eclectic mix of customers, including drinkers, foodies and muddy walkers - the starting point of the Cotswold Way is a short stroll away. The setting for savouring the imaginative food and tip-top ales is suitably cosy with a rustic interior - expect flagstones, a beamed ceiling and large inglenook fireplace with wood-burning stove. The kitchen makes sound use of quality local supplies, and prepares innovative modern British dishes that evolve with the seasons, with clever twists on pub classics. Hook Norton, Purity and Wye Valley ales are on tap, among others, and an impressive list of wines ensures there's a tipple to suit every taste and pocket. Four comfortable en suite rooms complete the picture.

Open all wk 11-3 6-11 Closed: 25 Dec **Bar Meals** L served all wk 12-2 D served all wk 7-9 **Restaurant** L served all wk 12-2 D served all wk 7-9 ⊕ ENTERPRISE INNS ◀ Hook Norton Hooky Bitter, Wye Valley Butty Bach, Fuller's London Pride, Purity Mad Goose ♻ Westons Stowford Press. ☐ 9 **Facilities** Non-diners area ♦♦ Children's menu Children's portions Garden ♬ Wi-fi ▄ (notice required) **Rooms** 4

POULTON
Map 5 SP00

The Falcon Inn

London Rd GL7 5HN ☎ 01285 851597 & 850878
e-mail: bookings@falconinnpoulton.co.uk
dir: *From Cirencester 4m E on A417 towards Fairford*

Informal atmosphere and locally brewed cask ales

Owned by husband and wife Gianni Gray and Natalie Birch, this 300-year-old village pub places a welcome emphasis on real ales and good food. Contemporary furnishings blend with original features and log fires to create an informal pub for locals who want to sup a pint of Hooky or one of the rotating guests beers. Diners will be tempted by hot-smoked salmon fillet with roast beetroot, cucumber and horseradish; braised beef cheek, herb and truffle gnocchi, roasted root vegetables and seasonal greens; and chocolate fondant with honeycomb and pistachio ice cream.

Open Tue-Sat 12-3 5-11 (Sun 12-4) Closed: 25 Dec, Mon **Bar Meals** L served Tue-Sat 12-2.30, Sun 12-3 D served Tue-Sat 6-9 Av main course £12.50 **Restaurant** L served Tue-Sat 12-2.30, Sun 12-3 D served Tue-Sat 6-9 Fixed menu price fr £12.50 Av 3 course à la carte fr £20.50

⊕ FREE HOUSE ◀ Hook Norton Hooky Bitter, Guest ale ♻ Westons Stowford Press. ☐ 11 **Facilities** Non-diners area ♦♦ Children's menu Children's portions Garden ♬ Parking Wi-fi

SAPPERTON
Map 4 SO90

The Bell at Sapperton
PICK OF THE PUBS

See Pick of the Pubs on opposite page

SHEEPSCOMBE
Map 4 SO81

The Butchers Arms
PICK OF THE PUBS

See Pick of the Pubs on page 196

SOMERFORD KEYNES
Map 4 SU09

The Bakers Arms

GL7 6DN ☎ 01285 861298
e-mail: enquiries@thebakersarmssomerford.co.uk
dir: *Exit A419 signed Cotswold Water Park. Cross B4696, 1m, follow signs for Keynes Park & Somerford Keynes*

Chocolate-box Cotswold pub

The beautiful Bakers Arms dates from the 17th century and was formerly the village bakery; it still has its low-beamed ceilings and inglenook fireplaces. Only a stone's throw from the Thames Path and Cotswold Way, the pub is a convenient watering hole for walkers. The mature gardens are ideal for alfresco dining, while discreet children's play areas and heated terraces add to its broad appeal. The home-cooked food on offer runs along the lines of baguettes, specials and pub favourites – pasta bake, marinated rack of pork ribs, quiche of the day and Butcombe ale-battered fish and chips.

Open all day all wk 11-11 (Sun 12-10.30) **Bar Meals** L served 12-9 D served 12-9 food served all day **Restaurant** L served 12-9 D served 12-9 food served all day ⊕ ENTERPRISE INNS ◀ Butcombe Bitter, Stroud Budding, Sharp's Doom Bar ♻ Thatchers Gold, Westons Stowford Press. **Facilities** Non-diners area ❀ (Bar Restaurant Garden) ♦♦ Children's menu Children's portions Play area Garden ♬ Parking ▄ (notice required)

STONEHOUSE
Map 4 SO80

The George Inn

Peter St, Frocester GL10 3TQ ☎ 01453 822302
e-mail: paul@georgeinn.co.uk
dir: *M5 junct 13, onto A419 at 1st rdbt 3rd exit signed Eastington, left at next rdbt signed Frocester. Approx 2m on right in village*

Family-run, 18th-century rural inn

Look in vain for a fruit machine or jukebox in this family-run, former coaching inn which has a history going back to 1716; instead, enjoy what makes a pub good – a sensible choice of real ales and locally sourced, home-made food, which here means bacon-wrapped chicken breast, faggots, filled omelettes, and fish pie. The lovely courtyard garden is overlooked by the original coaching stables, while the Cotswold Way and a network of leafy paths help guide visitors to the August Bank Holiday village beer festival. There's a Sunday carvery, and a function room that seats up to 60.

Open all day all wk 7.30am-mdnt **Bar Meals** L served all wk 12-9.30 D served all wk 12-9.30 Av main course £7.95 food served all day **Restaurant** L served all wk 12-9.30 D served all wk 12-9.30 food served all day ⊕ ENTERPRISE INNS ◀ Sharp's Doom Bar, Timothy Taylor, 3 Guest ales ♻ Westons Old Rosie & Stowford Press, Thatchers Gold. ☐ 10 **Facilities** Non-diners area ❀ (Bar Garden) ♦♦ Children's menu Children's portions Play area Family room Garden ♬ Beer festival Parking Wi-fi ▄

STOW-ON-THE-WOLD
Map 10 SP12

The Unicorn

Sheep St GL54 1HQ ☎ 01451 830257
e-mail: reception@birchhotels.co.uk
dir: *Telephone for directions*

Terrific Cotswold market town setting

In the main square of Stow-on-the-Wold, this eye-catching 17th-century property is built from honey-coloured limestone and bedecked with abundantly flowering window boxes. The interior is stylishly presented with Jacobean pieces, antique artefacts and open log fires. Food is served in the oak-beamed bar, the stylish contemporary restaurant or in the secluded garden if the weather is fine. Typical dishes include duck and port pâté with red onion marmalade; knuckle of lamb braised with root vegetables in a rich sauce; home-made meringue with red berries and cream. Freshly made sandwiches are also available.

Open all day all wk **Bar Meals** L served all wk 12-2 D served all wk 7-9 Av main course £13 **Restaurant** L served all wk 12-2 D served all wk 7-9 Fixed menu price fr £12.50 Av 3 course à la carte fr £24 ⊕ FREE HOUSE ◀ Hook Norton Lion Pride of the Cotswolds ♻ Westons, Symonds. **Facilities** Non-diners area ♦♦ Children's menu Children's portions Garden ♬ Parking Wi-fi ▄

PICK OF THE PUBS

The Butchers Arms

SHEEPSCOMBE   Map 4 SO81

GL6 7RH ☎ **01452 812113**

e-mail: mark@butchers-arms.co.uk
web: www.butchers-arms.co.uk
dir: *1.5m S of A46 (Cheltenham to Stroud road), N of Painswick*

Rural Cotswolds gem with stunning views

Tucked into the western scarp of the Cotswolds and reached via narrow winding lanes, pretty Sheepscombe radiates all of the mellow, sedate, bucolic charm you'd expect from such a haven. The village pub, dating from 1670 and a favourite haunt of *Cider with Rosie* author Laurie Lee, lives up to such expectations and then some. Views from the gardens are idyllic whilst within is all you'd hope for: log fires, clean-cut rustic furnishings, village chatter backed up by local beers from Prescotts of Cheltenham Brewery. Walkers, riders and locals all beat a path to the door beneath the pub's famous carved sign showing a butcher supping a pint of ale with a pig tied to his leg. The pub takes its name from its association with Henry VIII's Royal Deer Park, which was located nearby, when deer carcasses were hung in what is now the bar. The fulfilling fodder here includes locally sourced meats, including beef from Beech Farm; the beef, ale and mushroom pie is a perennial favourite, as is the home-made burger — try one with a blue

cheese and chorizo topping. Alternative main courses take in ham, egg and chips and specials like seared tuna steak with fresh mango and pineapple salsa, and a smoked bacon chop with sautéed potatoes, warm onion, fennel and apple slaw and apple and sage jus. Nibblers can graze on a delicious bacon, West Country brie and cranberry sandwich, others can share a baked camembert or a huge fish platter, while those thinking of tucking into the memorable Sunday roasts should book well ahead. To drink, there's a cracking range of ales, and a traditional farmhouse scrumpy cider.

Open all wk 11.30-2.30 6.30-11 (Sat 11.30-11.30 Sun 12-10.30) **Bar Meals** L served Mon-Fri 12-2.30, Sat-Sun all day D served Mon-Sat 6.30-9.30, Sun 6.30-8

(ex Sun Jan & Feb) **Restaurant** L served Mon-Fri 12-2.30, Sat-Sun all day D served Mon-Sat 6.30-9.30, Sun 6.30-8 (ex Sun Jan & Feb) ⊕ FREE HOUSE ◀ Otter Bitter, Butcombe Bitter, St Austell Proper Job, Wye Valley Dorothy Goodbody's Ale, Bath Ales Gem ⑤ Westons Stowford Press & Traditional Scrumpy. **Facilities** Non-diners area ❤ (Bar Garden) ♦♦ Children's menu & portions Garden ♎ Parking Wi-fi

Save on hotels. Book at **theAA.com/hotel**

GLOUCESTERSHIRE 197 **ENGLAND**

STOW-ON-THE-WOLD *continued*

White Hart Inn

The Square GL54 1AF ☎ 01451 830674
e-mail: info@theoldbutchers.com
dir: *From A429 into market square. Inn on left*

Cosy bars and warming fires

Some of the mellow stone buildings in this lovely Cotswold town date to the 12th century, including parts of the White Hart. Two cosy bars benefit from open fires, and an atmospheric dining room serves lunchtime snacks such as a Lincolnshire poacher and piccalilli sandwich. For dinner, you could start with Cornish scallops with chorizo; follow with local pheasant cooked with cloves and cinnamon; and round off with chocolate marquis. There's a spacious car park.

Open all day all wk Closed: 1wk May & 1wk Oct ⊕ ARKELL'S ◄ 3B, 2B, Kingsdown ♂ Westons Stowford Press. **Facilities** ◑ Children's menu Children's portions Garden Parking Wi-fi

STROUD   **Map 4 SO80**

Bear of Rodborough Hotel ★★★ HL

PICK OF THE PUBS

Rodborough Common GL5 5DE ☎ 01453 878522
e-mail: info@bearofrodborough.info
dir: *From M5 junct 13 follow signs for Stonehouse then Rodborough*

Surrounded by 300 acres of National Trust land

Located amidst the rolling, windswept grassland of Rodborough Common with its far-reaching views of the Stroud Valley and Severn Vale, and cattle roaming free in the summer months, this 17th-century former alehouse takes its name from the bear-baiting that used to take place near by. Head to the bar for a pint of Wickwar before seeking a seat on the York stone terrace or in the gardens with their walled croquet lawn. The bar menu has many delights, such as afternoon tea, sharing platters and ploughman's, and fond favourites: blackened Cajun chicken, vegetable lasagne and honey-glazed ham. Look to the Library restaurant for a more formal affair, where you can try smoked haddock fishcake, seared loin of venison, and chocolate and cardamom mousse, all the while enjoying panoramas of the Cotswold countryside. Guest rooms are distinctively furnished and decorated with rich fabrics.

Open all day all wk 10.30am-11pm **Bar Meals** L served all wk 12-9.30, light menu all wk 12-9.30 D served all wk 6.30-9.30, light menu all wk 12-9.30 Av main course £16-£18 food served all day **Restaurant** L served Sun 12.30-3 D served all wk 7-9 Fixed menu price fr £28 ⊕ FREE HOUSE ◄ Butcombe, Stroud, Wickwar ♂ Ashton Press. ♈ 10 **Facilities** Non-diners area ♣ (Bar Garden) ◑ Children's menu Children's portions Play area Garden Parking Wi-fi ➡ (notice required) **Rooms** 46

The Ram Inn

South Woodchester GL5 5EL ☎ 01453 873329
dir: *A46 from Stroud to Nailsworth, right after 2m into South Woodchester, follow brown tourist signs*

A change of hands at this 17th-century inn

In winter the warmth from its huge fireplace might prove more appealing than standing on the terrace of this 17th-century Cotswold-stone inn, admiring the splendid views. Originally a farm, it became an alehouse in 1811 and is still full of historic little gems. Typical dishes are starters of deep-fried camembert with redcurrant jelly; or a chicken kebab with garlic mayonnaise; then a main course of spinach and feta goujons; a 10oz gammon steak, or chicken breast or 8oz rump steak all served with mushrooms and onion rings. Children have their own choices and gluten-free diets can be catered for.

Open all day all wk **Bar Meals** L served Mon-Fri 12-2, Sat-Sun 12-3 D served all wk 6-9 Av main course £12 **Restaurant** L served Mon-Fri 12-2, Sat-Sun 12-3 D served all wk 6-9 ⊕ FREE HOUSE ◄ Butcombe Bitter, Bath SPA, Guest ales ♂ Westons Stowford Press, Lilley's Crazy Goat. **Facilities** Non-diners area ♣ (Bar Restaurant Garden) ◑ Children's portions Family room Garden Parking Wi-fi ➡ (notice required)

Rose & Crown Inn

The Cross, Nympsfield GL10 3TU ☎ 01453 860240
dir: *M5 junct 13, off B4066, SW of Stroud*

Offering stunning views over the River Severn

Occupying a central position in the village, this imposing 400-year-old coaching inn of honey-coloured local stone could well be the highest pub in the Cotswolds. The closeness of the Cotswold Way makes it a popular stop for hikers and bikers. Inside, the inn's character is preserved with natural stone, wood panelling, a lovely open fire and local Stroud Organic and Wickwar Cotswold Way real ales. In the galleried restaurant, the owners offer fresh, home-made food cooked to order. In the large garden, children will enjoy the playground area, which has a swing, slides and a climbing bridge.

Open all day all wk 11.30-11 (Sun 12-9) ⊕ FREE HOUSE ◄ Stroud Organic, Sharp's Doom Bar, Wickwar Cotswold Way ♂ Westons Stowford Press, Aspall. **Facilities** ♣ (Bar Garden) ◑ Children's menu Children's portions Play area Garden Parking

The Woolpack Inn

Slad Rd, Slad GL6 7QA ☎ 01452 813429
e-mail: info@thewoolpackinn-slad.com
dir: *2m from Stroud, 8m from Gloucester*

Popular with ale fans, walkers and discerning diners

Close to the Cotswold Way in the beautiful Slad Valley, this friendly local is a favourite with walkers (muddy boots are not frowned upon). Laurie Lee of *Cider With Rosie* fame used to be a regular at The Woolpack too. Although ale aficionados make a detour here to sample the Uley Pigs Ear, the food is of equal importance. Meat is sourced within a 14-mile radius, and fruit and vegetables come from Cirencester or locals' gardens. A starter of white bean, thyme and truffle oil soup with home-made bread might be followed by pot roast pork belly with fondant potato, braised white cabbage, black pudding and cider gravy.

Open all day all wk 12-12 **Bar Meals** L served Mon-Sat 12-2, Sun 12-3.30 D served Tue-Sat 6.30-9 **Restaurant** L served Mon-Sat 12-2, Sun 12-3.30 D served Tue-Sat 6.30-9 ⊕ FREE HOUSE ◄ Uley Pigs Ear, Old Spot & Bitter, Stroud Budding, Butcombe Bitter ♂ Westons Old Rosie & Stowford Press. **Facilities** Non-diners area ♣ (Bar Restaurant Garden) ◑ Children's portions Garden Parking Wi-fi

TETBURY   **Map 4 ST89**

Gumstool Inn

PICK OF THE PUBS

Calcot Manor GL8 8YJ ☎ 01666 890391
e-mail: reception@calcotmanor.co.uk
dir: *3m W of Tetbury at A4135 & A46 junct*

Gastro-pub food and good wine choices

Part of Calcot Manor Hotel, a stone farmhouse originally built by Cistercian monks in the 14th century, this stylish country inn is now a popular free house. The buzzy and comfortable Gumstool Inn has a real country-pub atmosphere and stocks a good selection of ales such as Butcombe Bitter, and local ciders including Ashton Press. An excellent choice of wines is offered by the glass or bottle. The food here is of top-notch gastro-pub quality and there is a pronounced use of local suppliers. Kick off with starters smoked chicken Caesar salad or devilled lamb's kidneys on toast. Among the main courses may be found roasted pork belly with apple sauce, carrots and spring cabbage; and slow braised lamb hot pot with root vegetables. In the summer, grab a table on the pretty, flower-filled sun terrace, while winter evenings are warmed with cosy log fires. Booking for meals recommended.

Open all day all wk **Bar Meals** L served all wk 12-2.30 D served Mon-Sat 5.30-9.30, Sun 5.30-9 **Restaurant** L served Mon-Sat 12-2.30, Sun 12-4 D served Mon-Sat 5.30-9.30, Sun 5.30-9 ⊕ FREE HOUSE ◄ Butcombe Bitter, Sharp's Doom Bar ♂ Ashton Press. ♈ 26 **Facilities** Non-diners area ◑ Children's menu Children's portions Play area Family room Garden Parking Wi-fi ➡ (notice required)

TETBURY *continued*

The Priory Inn ★★★ SHL

PICK OF THE PUBS

London Rd GL8 8JJ ☎ 01666 502251
e-mail: info@theprioryinn.co.uk
dir: *M4 junct 17, A429 towards Cirencester. Left into B4014 to Tetbury. Over mini rdbt into Long St, pub 100yds after corner on right*

The true taste of the Cotswolds at its best

Parts of this thriving gastro-pub and hotel date from the 16th century, when it was a stable block and grooms' cottages for the neighbouring priory. The beers are from microbreweries like Wickwar; white wine and sparkling rosé spring from a vineyard at Malmesbury whilst the freshest of menu ingredients come from sources based strictly within 30 miles of the inn. Such happy coincidence of extraordinary suppliers ensures that visitors here may confidently settle into the traditional, bare-boarded, beamed bar or more contemporary lounge and restaurant, anticipating starters like smoked Bibury trout fishcake; and seared West Country venison haunch with blackberry and sage jus from the modern rustic menu. Children have the opportunity to create a personalised wood-fired pizza. The May Day Bank Holiday beer and cider festival is popular.

Open all day all wk 7am-11pm (Fri 7am-mdnt Sat 8am-mdnt Sun 8am-11pm) **Bar Meals** L served Mon-Thu 12-3, Fri-Sun & BH all day (bkfst served all wk 7-10.30) D served Mon-Thu 5-10, Fri-Sun & BH all day **Restaurant** L served Mon-Thu 12-3, Fri-Sun & BH all day (bkfst served all wk 7-10.30) D served Mon-Thu 5-10, Fri-Sun & BH all day Av 3 course à la carte fr £21 ⊕ FREE HOUSE ◀ Uley Bitter, Stroud, Guest ale Ö Thatchers Gold, Cotswold, Guest cider. ☂ 13
Facilities Non-diners area ◀▮ Children's menu Children's portions Play area Family room Garden ⊼ Beer festival Cider festival Parking **Rooms** 14

Snooty Fox Hotel ★★★ SHL

Market Place GL8 8DD ☎ 01666 502436
e-mail: res@snooty-fox.co.uk
dir: *In town centre opposite covered market hall*

Draw up a chair by the log fire

Occupying a prime spot in the heart of Tetbury, this 16th-century coaching inn and hotel retains many of its original features. Sit in a leather armchair in front of the log fire with a pint of Wadworth 6X and order from the extensive bar menu – eggs Benedict or a bowl of mussels maybe. Alternatively, head for the restaurant and enjoy the likes of pan-fried scallops with cauliflower purée and crisp black pudding followed by slow-roast lamb shank with leeks, bacon, creamed mash and onion sauce. Traditional puddings include Cambridge burnt cream, and rhubarb and apple crumble.

Open all day all wk **Bar Meals** L served all wk 12-3, snacks 3-6 D served all wk 6-9.30 Av main course £10 food served all day **Restaurant** L served all wk 12-3 D served all wk 6-9.30 Av 3 course à la carte fr £25 ⊕ FREE HOUSE ◀ Wadworth 6X, Butcombe Bitter Ö Ashton Press. **Facilities** Non-diners area ◀▮ Children's menu Children's portions Outside area ⊼ Wi-fi ▄ (notice required) **Rooms** 12

The Trouble House

PICK OF THE PUBS

Cirencester Rd GL8 8SG ☎ 01666 502206
e-mail: contact@troublehousetetbury.co.uk
dir: *On A433 between Tetbury & Cirencester*

Bistro classics in historic Cotswold pub

Named after a series of unfortunate events at the pub, namely agricultural riots, two suicides and a disastrous fire, this historic inn stands beside the A433 between Tetbury and Cirencester. Since it was taken over by Shane and Liam Parr (ex-Calcot Manor), the pub has continued to thrive as a destination dining pub with a rustic-chic interior that includes scrubbed tables, wooden floors, pastel-painted walls and three warming log fires. Liam's modern British cooking draws restaurant tourists across the Cotswolds for a table – so booking is advisable. In addition to the printed menu there's a favourites board offering the likes of Fowey mussel and smoked haddock chowder or chargrilled bavette steak with rösti potato, spinach and Café de Paris butter. Other options could include wild mushroom risotto followed by coq au vin with truffle mash. Finish with steamed lemon and raisin sponge and honey ice cream.

Open 11.30-3 6.30-11 Closed: 25 Dec, Sun eve, Mon (ex BHs L) **Bar Meals** L served Tue-Sun 12-2 D served Tue-Sat 7-9.30 Av main course £15 **Restaurant** L served Tue-Sun 12-2 D served Tue-Sat 7-9.30 Av 3 course à la carte fr £30 ⊕ WADWORTH ◀ 6X, Henry's Original IPA Ö Westons Stowford Press. ☂ 12
Facilities Non-diners area ◀ (Bar Garden Outside area) ◀▮ Children's portions Garden Outside area ⊼ Parking

TORMARTON | Map 4 ST77

Best Western Compass Inn

GL9 1JB ☎ 01454 218242
e-mail: info@compass-inn.co.uk
dir: *M4 junct 18, A46 N towards Stroud. After 200mtrs 1st right towards Tormarton. Inn in 300mtrs*

Country inn convenient for exploring the Cotswolds

A charming 18th-century creeper-clad inn, set in six acres of grounds in the heart of the Gloucestershire countryside, right on the Cotswold Way. Light bites and more filling meals can be taken in the bar where real ales and cider are served. In the restaurant, dishes might include home-made chicken Kiev; grilled lamb in mint marinade; spinach and ricotta tortellini; and breaded wholetail scampi.

Open all day all wk 7am-11pm (Sat-Sun 8am-11pm) Closed: 25-26 Dec ⊕ FREE HOUSE ◀ Fuller's London Pride, Bass, Butcombe Ö Ashton Press. **Facilities** ◀▮ Children's menu Children's portions Garden Parking Wi-fi

UPPER ODDINGTON | Map 10 SP22

The Horse and Groom Inn

PICK OF THE PUBS

GL56 0XH ☎ 01451 830584
e-mail: info@horseandgroom.uk.com
dir: *1.5m S of Stow-on-the-Wold, just off A436*

Enticing Cotswold-stone inn

Owner operated for the past decade, this 16th-century inn is situated in a conservation village in the Evenlode Valley. The pub boasts polished flagstones, beams and an inglenook log fire – what more could you ask for? Well, you could add the grapevines outside and the pleasure of dining on the terrace or in the walled gardens. Then there's the bar, offering an ever-changing choice of real ales from regional breweries, local cider and lagers from the Cotswold Brewing Co, and over 20 wines by the glass. The kitchen's commitment to neighbourhood sourcing of ingredients is impressive: bread, for instance, is made daily from locally milled flour, meats are from a Chipping Norton butcher's, and venison is from the Adlestrop Estate a mile away. Peruse the imaginative menus, typically featuring duck liver and brandy pâté; trio of pork, apple and leek sausages; baked fillets of sea bass with an Oriental broth; and dark chocolate tart.

Open all wk 12-3 5.30-11 (Sun 12-3 6.30-10.30) **Bar Meals** L served all wk 12-2 D served Mon-Sat 6.30-9, Sun 7-9 **Restaurant** L served all wk 12-2 D served Mon-Sat 6.30-9, Sun 7-9 ⊕ FREE HOUSE ◀ Wye Valley Bitter & HPA, Wickwar BOB, Goffs Tournament, Box Steam Chuffin Ale, Prescott Hill Climb Ö Cotswold. ☂ 25
Facilities Non-diners area ✿ (Bar Restaurant Garden) ◀▮ Children's menu Children's portions Garden ⊼ Parking Wi-fi

The White Hart Inn and Restaurant

High St GL54 5LJ ☎ 01242 602359
e-mail: info@whitehartwinchcombe.co.uk
dir: *In centre of Winchcombe on B4632*

Town pub specialising in wine

Popular with walkers, this 16th-century inn offers the perfect place to unwind in the cosy bar or intimate restaurant. The White Hart is in the heart of Winchcombe just outside Cheltenham, a small historic town set in the Cotswold countryside. There is a wine shop as well as the bar and restaurant. Specialising in an amazing choice of wines, there are also plenty of real ales, and simple and unpretentious British food sourced from local suppliers. Main dishes include Cotswold venison stew, roasted root vegetable tart and steamed sea bream.

Open all day all wk 10am-11pm (Fri-Sat 10am-mdnt Sun 10am-10.30pm) **Bar Meals** L served all wk 12-3, bar snacks all day food served all day **Restaurant** L served all wk 12-3 D served Sun-Thu 6-9.30, Fri-Sat 6-10 ⊕ ENTERPRISE INNS ◀ Wadworth 6X, Morland Old Speckled Hen, Butcombe, Otter, Guest ales ♻ Westons Stowford Press, Addlestones. ♟ 8
Facilities Non-diners area ❀ (Bar Garden) ♦ Children's menu Children's portions Garden ⊞ Parking Wi-fi

The Old Fleece

Bath Rd, Rooksmoor GL5 5NB ☎ 01453 872582
e-mail: pheasantpluckers2003@yahoo.co.uk
dir: *2m S of Stroud on A46*

Delightful dining pub set amid beautiful countryside

With miles of footpaths to explore right on the doorstep of this 18th-century Cotswold-stone coaching inn, you can walk to Rodborough, Minchinhampton and Selsley commons, or go one step further and connect eventually with the scenic Cotswold Way. The interior includes wooden floors, wood panelling and exposed stone, and the bar serves well-kept Tom Long and Buckham Bitter, which can also be enjoyed on the sun-warmed terrace. The comprehensive bistro menu of British and continental dishes ranges from classics such as Old Spot sausage and mash with onion gravy, to the likes of whole sea bream with braised fennel.

Open all day all wk 11-11 (Sun 11-10.30) ⊕ PHEASANT PLUCKERS LTD ◀ Buckham Bitter, Stroud Tom Long, Guest ales ♻ Ashton Still. **Facilities** ♦ Parking

The Victoria

PICK OF THE PUBS

See Pick of the Pubs on page 200

The Rams Head Inn

OL3 5UN ☎ 01457 874802
e-mail: info@ramsheaddenshaw.co.uk
dir: *M62 junct 22, A672 towards Oldham, 2m to inn*

A gastro-pub, farm shop and tea room

At 1,212 feet above sea level, this 450-year-old family-owned country inn has fabulous moorland views and is just two miles from the M62. Log fires and collections of memorabilia are features of the interior, which includes The Pantry, an in-house farm shop, deli, bakery and tea room selling everything from cheeses to chocolates. Game and seafood figure strongly on the menu, with dishes ranging from Whitby crab spring roll to pheasant breast wrapped in bacon. There are also plenty of vegetarian options. Finish with the inn's 'famed' sticky toffee pudding. There's a garden area to the rear of the inn with bench seating and panoramic views.

Open Tue-Fri 12-2.30 5.30-10 (Sat 12-10.30 Sun 12-8.30) Closed: 25-26 Dec, 1 Jan, Mon (ex BHs) **Bar Meals** L served Tue-Fri 12-2.30, Sat 12-10 Sun 12-8.30 D served Tue-Thu 5.30-8.30, Fri 5.30-9.30, Sat 12-10, Sun 12-8.30 Av main course £10 **Restaurant** L served Tue-Fri 12-2.30, Sat 12-10 Sun 12-8.30 D served Tue-Thu 5.30-8.30, Fri 5.30-9.30, Sat 12-10, Sun 12-8.30 Fixed menu price fr £11.95 Av 3 course à la carte fr £20.95 ⊕ FREE HOUSE ◀ Timothy Taylor Landlord, Black Sheep Best Bitter, Theakston Old Peculier ♻ Thatchers Gold. ♟ 16 **Facilities** Non-diners area ♦ Children's portions Garden ⊞ Parking Wi-fi ▦ (notice required)

The Metropolitan

PICK OF THE PUBS

2 Lapwing Ln M20 2WS ☎ 0161 438 2332
e-mail: info@the-metropolitan.co.uk
dir: *M60 junct 5, A5103, right into Barlow Moor Rd, left into Burton Rd. Pub at x-rds. Right into Lapwing Ln for car park*

Airy Victorian railway hotel turned gastro-pub

A former Victorian railway hotel, the 'Met' is well situated in the leafy suburb of West Didsbury. Originally a hotel for passengers riding the old Midland Railway into Manchester, the pub still punches above its weight architecturally - look in particular at the decorative floor tiling, the ornate windows and the delicate plasterwork.

During the latter part of the 20th century the building became very run down, but it was given a sympathetic renovation in the late 90s, reopening as a gastro-pub. Its huge, airy interior is filled with antique tables and chairs, and deep sofas, which suit the mainly young, cosmopolitan clientele. Sup Timothy Taylor Landlord and Caledonian Deuchars IPA ales, and to eat at lunchtime there's sandwiches and locally sourced steaks in addition to an all-day menu featuring smoked haddock Scotch egg, baked fillet of hake with a red pepper crust and Manchester tart with caramelised banana ice cream. The heated outside Stable Bar is popular in all weathers.

Open all day all wk 10am-11.30pm (Fri-Sat 10am-mdnt) Closed: 25 Dec **Bar Meals** L served Mon-Thu 12-9.30, Fri-Sat 12-10, Sun 12-9 D served Mon-Thu 12-9.30, Fri-Sat 12-10, Sun 12-9 food served all day **Restaurant** L served Mon-Thu 12-9.30, Fri-Sat 12-10, Sun 12-9 D served Mon-Thu 12-9.30, Fri-Sat 12-10, Sun 12-9 Fixed menu price fr £9.95 Av 3 course à la carte fr £20 food served all day ⊕ ENTERPRISE INNS ◀ Timothy Taylor Landlord, Caledonian Deuchars IPA, Guinness ♻ Westons, Rekorderlig. ♟ 28 **Facilities** Non-diners area ♦ Children's menu Children's portions Outside area ⊞ Parking Wi-fi ▦ (notice required)

The White House

Blackstone Edge, Halifax Rd OL15 0LG
☎ 01706 378456
dir: *On A58, 8m from Rochdale, 9m from Halifax*

A favourite with walkers and cyclists

Known as The White House for over 100 years, this 17th-century coaching house has been in the same hands for almost 30 of them. On the Pennine Way, 1,300 feet above sea level, it has panoramic views of the moors and Hollingworth Lake far below. Not surprising then, that it attracts walkers and cyclists who rest up and sup on Black Sheep and Exmoor Gold. A simple menu of pub grub ranges from sandwiches and salads, to grills, international and vegetarian dishes, and traditional mains such as home-made steak-and-kidney pie, and haddock and prawn Mornay.

Open all wk Mon-Sat 12-3 6-10 (Sun 12-10.30) Closed: 25 Dec **Bar Meals** L served Mon-Sat 12-2, Sun 12-9 D served Mon-Sat 6.30-9.30, Sun 12-9 **Restaurant** L served Mon-Sat 12-2, Sun 12-9 D served Mon-Sat 6.30-9.30, Sun 12-9 ⊕ FREE HOUSE ◀ Timothy Taylor Landlord, Theakston Best Bitter, Exmoor Gold, Black Sheep, Phoenix, Moorhouse's. **Facilities** Non-diners area ♦ Children's menu Parking ▦

PICK OF THE PUBS

The Victoria

ALTRINCHAM Map 15 SJ78

Stamford St WA14 1EX
☎ **0161 613 1855**
e-mail: the.victoria@yahoo.co.uk
web: www.thevictoria-altrincham.co.uk
dir: *From rail station cross main road, right. 2nd left into Stamford St*

Restored tavern with hearty food

Tucked away behind the main shopping street in the trendy Stamford Quarter of Altrincham, this compact, one-roomed street-corner pub was restored to its original glory when it reopened in 2006. Just a step or two away from Altrincham's shops and galleries, and handy too for the nearby Metrolink tram and rail interchange, this once dilapidated town-centre drinking den was transformed into an airy food-driven pub of choice; a stylish wood-panelled drawing-room area set for dining twinned with a chic, slate-floored area fronting the bar, where bar stools offer refuge for those intent simply on a restful pint of Waggle Dance or Old Speckled Hen. Owners Rachel Wetherill and Kevin Choudhary playfully dubbed one room the 'Gin Palace and Dining Room'; here their aim was to offer a tranquil, adults' retreat where home-cooked imaginative British food with a strong traditional influence takes the lead - and it's paid dividends. The menu changes every six to eight weeks to reflect seasonal availability; typical

starters might include pea and ham soup; curried lamb's kidneys; or cask ale and smoked bacon mussels. These could be followed by seared pigeon breast served on smoked bacon, walnut and parsley hash with creamed greens; slow-cooked chicken in red wine, thyme and bacon with saffron potatoes; and Blackstick Blue cheese and leek filo pasties. For dessert, maybe warm Eccles cake with custard or lemon meringue ice cream sundae. On Sundays traditional roasts are available. Hand-pulled cask ales are always available, and for drivers there is a temperance bar featuring locally produced drinks such as sarsaparilla and dandelion and burdock.

Open all day all wk 12-11 (Sun 12-6)

Closed: 26 Dec & 1 Jan **Bar Meals** L served Mon-Sat 12-3 D served Mon-Sat 5.30-9.30 Av main course £15.50 **Restaurant** L served Mon-Sat 12-3, Sun 12-4 D served Mon-Sat 5.30-9.30 Fixed menu price fr £13.95 Av 3 course à la carte fr £25 ⊞ FREE HOUSE ◀ Morland Old Speckled Hen, Wells Waggle Dance ♻ Westons Wyld Wood Organic. ⬤ 10 **Facilities** Non-diners area ⬤ Children's portions

MANCHESTER   Map 16 SJ89

Dukes 92

14 Castle St, Castlefield M3 4LZ ☎ 0161 839 8642
e-mail: info@dukes92.com
dir: *In Castlefield town centre, off Deansgate*

Relaxed contemporary dining in restored canalside building

Originally a block of 19th-century stables for horses delivering food from barges to the warehouses opposite, this beautifully restored canalside building reopened as a contemporary bar and grill over 20 years ago. The interior is full of surprises, with minimalist decor downstairs and an upper gallery displaying local artistic talent. At the bar you'll find Moorhouse's ales, cocktails and 15 wines by the glass. A grill restaurant is supplemented by a lunchtime bar menu and pizza range; choices from the renowned cheese and deli counter, displaying over 40 British and European savoury products, are served with freshly baked granary bread.

Open all day all wk Closed: 25-26 Dec, 1 Jan **Bar Meals** L served all wk 12-5.30 D served all wk 5.30-10 food served all day **Restaurant** L served Mon-Thu 12-10, Fri 12-10.30, Sat 12-11, Sun 12-5.30 D served Mon-Thu 12-10, Fri 12-10.30, Sat 12-11, Sun 5.30-9.30 food served all day ⊕ FREE HOUSE ◀ Moorhouse's ♂ Kopparberg. ♀ 15 **Facilities** Non-diners area ♦ Children's menu Children's portions Garden ♫ Parking ▭

Marble Arch

73 Rochdale Rd M4 4HY ☎ 0161 832 5914
dir: *In city centre (Northern Quarter)*

A hit since Victorian times

Built in 1888 by celebrated architect Alfred Darbyshire for Manchester brewery B&J McKenna, and celebrating 125 years in 2013, the Marble Arch is part of the award-winning organic Marble Brewery. A listed building famous for its sloping floor, glazed brick walls and barrel-vaulted ceiling, it is a fine example of Manchester's Victorian heritage. Now an established favourite with beer aficionados and offering six regular ales and eight seasonal house beers, the pub offers a well-considered menu, from traditional bar meals of fish and chips to rabbit cassoulet. Deli plates are also available. It hosts its own beer festivals.

Open all day all wk Closed: 25 Dec **Bar Meals** L served Mon-Sat 12-8.45, Sun 12-7.45 D served Mon-Sat 12-8.45, Sun 12-7.45 **Restaurant** L served Mon-Sat 12-8.45, Sun 12-7.45 D served Mon-Sat 12-8.45, Sun 12-7.45 ⊕ FREE HOUSE ◀ Marble Manchester Bitter, Lagonda IPA, Ginger Marble ♂ Moonshine. ♀ 10 **Facilities** ♦ Garden ♫ Beer festival

MARPLE BRIDGE   Map 16 SJ98

Hare & Hounds

19 Mill Brow SK6 5LW ☎ 0161 427 4042
e-mail: haremillbrow@gmail.com
dir: *From A626 in Marple Bridge (at lights at river bridge) follow Mellor signs into Town St. 1st left into Hollins Ln. Right at T-junct into Ley Ln. Pub 0.25m on left*

Idyllic rural retreat in lovely countryside

Tucked away in a secluded hamlet in the crinkly hills fringing the Peak District, this comfortable community local first opened its doors in 1805. It retains much character of days gone by and is a popular stop with ramblers exploring the countless paths threading the ridges, moors and wooded cloughs hereabouts. Roaring winter fires take away the chill; or settle down with a glass of Robinsons' Stockport-brewed beers in the summery garden and anticipate freshly cooked mains such as lamb loin with asparagus, peppers, confit tomato and garlic; or Cheddar cheese and spring onion pie, with chocolate and mango coulis-topped egg custard to finish.

Open all wk 5-12 (Fri 12-3 5-12 Sat-Sun 12-12) **Bar Meals** L served Fri-Sat 12-2, Sun 1-7 D served Mon-Sat 6-9.30 Av main course £12-£15 **Restaurant** L served Fri-Sat 12-2, Sun 1-7 D served Mon-Sat 6-9.30 Fixed menu price fr £12.95 Av 3 course à la carte fr £25 ⊕ ROBINSONS ◀ Unicorn, Hatters, Dizzy Blonde, Seasonal Ales ♂ Westons Stowford Press. **Facilities** Non-diners area ♣ (Bar Restaurant Garden) ♦ Children's portions Garden Parking Wi-fi

MELLOR   Map 16 SJ98

The Moorfield Arms ★★★★ INN

Shiloh Rd SK6 5NE ☎ 0161 427 1580
e-mail: info@moorfieldarms.com
dir: *From Marple station down Brabyns Brow to lights. Right into Town St. 3m, left into Shiloh Rd. 0.5m, pub on left*

Lovely views and good food

This old pub dates from 1640 and retains plenty of old-world charm and atmosphere. With stunning views of Kinder Scout and Lantern Pike, The Moorfield Arms makes an ideal Peak District base and is popular with fell walkers. The extensive menu includes fish specials and slow-roasted lamb in mint gravy and finished with fresh rosemary from the pub's own herb garden. When the sun makes an appearance, head for the garden terrace. Situated in a barn conversion, the en suite rooms are comfortable and stylish.

Open Tue-Sat 12-2.30 6-12 (Sun 12-9) Closed: Mon **Bar Meals** L served Tue-Sat 12-2, Sun 12-9 D served Tue-Fri 6.30-9, Sat 6-9, Sun 12-9 **Restaurant** L served Tue-Sat 12-2, Sun 12-9 D served Tue-Fri 6.30-9, Sat 6-9, Sun 12-9 ⊕ FREE HOUSE ◀ Wychwood Hobgoblin, Marston's EPA. ♀ 12 **Facilities** Non-diners area ♦ Children's menu Garden ♫ Parking ▭ **Rooms** 4

OLDHAM   Map 16 SD90

The Roebuck Inn

Strinesdale OL4 3RB ☎ 0161 624 7819
e-mail: sehowarth1@hotmail.com
dir: *From Oldham Mumps Bridge take Huddersfield Rd (A62), right at 2nd lights into Ripponden Rd (A672), 1m right at lights into Turfpit Ln, 1m*

Country pub not far from Oldham

A thousand feet up in Strinedale on the edge of Saddleworth Moor, this traditionally styled inn provides a menu with plenty of choice. Starters include Bury black pudding with hot mustard sauce, and smoked salmon and prawns, then comes a long list of main courses, including fillet of beef Stroganoff; fajitas with sour cream and guacamole; roast half-duck with orange stuffing; and deep-fried haddock in batter. Vegetarians could well find an option like spinach and ricotta tortellini with roasted peppers. Beers come from the Black Sheep Brewery in Masham.

Open all wk 12-3 5-11 (Fri-Sun 12-11) **Bar Meals** L served all wk 12-2.15 D served all wk 5-9.15 **Restaurant** L served all wk 12-2.15 D served all wk 5-9.15 ⊕ FREE HOUSE ◀ Black Sheep. ♀ 9 **Facilities** Non-diners area ♣ (Bar Garden) ♦ Children's menu Children's portions Play area Garden Parking Wi-fi ▭

The White Hart Inn ☺

51 Stockport Rd, Lydgate OL4 4JJ ☎ 01457 872566
e-mail: bookings@thewhitehart.co.uk
dir: *From Manchester A62 to Oldham. Right onto bypass, A669 through Lees. In 500yds past Grotton, at brow of hill right onto A6050*

Grade II listed coaching inn with award-winning gardens

High on the hillside overlooking Oldham and Manchester, The White Hart is owned by Charles Brierley, who converted the ground floor into a smart bar and brasserie, and who also put together the wine list after months of research. There's been a pub on this site since 1788, when its vast cellars were used for brewing beer using water from the well. The inn has retained its period charm with beams, exposed stonework and open fireplaces, blending these with contemporary decor. The kitchen team believe in creating 'meals, not sculptures on a plate' and in making good use of local ingredients to offer cosmopolitan dishes. Sample tuna sashimi, followed by slow-cooked rabbit leg, and vanilla cheesecake in the rustic brasserie. Book the contemporary restaurant for the seven-course chef's choice tasting menu. There's also an intimate library dining area.

Open all day all wk Closed: 26 Dec **Bar Meals** L served Mon-Sat 12-2.30, Sun 1-8 D served Mon-Sat 6-9.30, Sun 1-8 **Restaurant** L served Sun 1-3.30 D served Mon & Wed-Sat 6.30-9.30 ⊕ FREE HOUSE ◀ Timothy Taylor Landlord & Golden Best, JW Lees Bitter, Copper Dragon ♂ Westons Stowford Press. ♀ 12 **Facilities** Non-diners area ♦ Children's menu Garden ♫ Parking Wi-fi

SALFORD
Map 15 SJ89

The King's Arms NEW

11 Bloom St M3 6AN ☎ **0161 839 8726**
e-mail: kingsarmssalford@gmail.com
dir: Telephone for detailed directions

Late-Victorian corner pub where many people meet

For over a century, three main buildings occupied this street - the municipal gas offices, a hostel and this 1870s pub. Having survived major redevelopment all around, it has become a popular hostelry, as well as a venue for art exhibitions, fringe festivals, film screenings and poetry nights. Even the local knitters and crocheters' club meets here. Six hand pumps dispense an ever-changing range of mostly local real ales, and there are guest ciders and continental bottled beers too. A year-round menu offers sandwiches and all-day breakfasts; five-bean chilli; chicken, bacon and mushroom pie; and beer-battered fish and chips.

Open all day all wk **Bar Meals** L served Fri-Sun 12-8 D served Fri-Sun 12-8 Av main course £5-£8 food served all day **Restaurant** food served all day ⊕ FREE HOUSE ◀ 6 changing guest ales ☼ 2 changing guest ciders. ♀ **Facilities** ✿ (Bar Restaurant Garden) ♦♦ Garden ⌂ Wi-fi ⊖ (notice required)

STOCKPORT
Map 16 SJ89

The Arden Arms

23 Millgate SK1 2LX ☎ **0161 480 2185**
e-mail: steve@ardenarms.com
dir: M60 junct 27 to town centre. Across mini rdbt, at lights turn left. Pub on right of next rdbt behind Asda

Timeless gem with interesting real ales

In the centre of Stockport, this Grade II listed late-Georgian coaching inn retains its unspoilt multi-roomed layout and original tiled floors. The building was last modernised in 1908, giving drinkers the opportunity to order from the traditional curved bar before settling down by the coal fire in the tiny snug. Outside, the large cobbled courtyard is used for alfresco dining and summer concerts. The lunch menu has an extensive list of hot and cold sandwiches and daily-changing specials, while a cheese and onion pie or pan-fried lamb chops may be dinner options. There's always a traditional Sunday roast, as well as jazz nights and charity quizzes.

Open all wk 12-12 Closed: 25-26 Dec, 1 Jan **Bar Meals** L served Mon-Fri 12-2.30, Sat-Sun 12-4 **Restaurant** D served Wed-Sun 5.30-8 ⊕ ROBINSONS ◀ Unicorn, Hatters, Double Hop, Dizzy Blonde, Seasonal ales ☼ Westons Stowford Press. ♀ 9 **Facilities** Non-diners area ✿ (Bar Restaurant Garden) ♦♦ Garden ⌂ Wi-fi

The Nursery Inn

Green Ln, Heaton Norris SK4 2NA ☎ **0161 432 2044**
e-mail: nurseryinn@hydesbrewery.com
dir: Green Ln off Heaton Moor Rd. Pass rugby club on Green Ln, at end on right. Narrow cobbled road, pub 100yds on right

1930s pub with its own bowling green

The hub of the community, The Nursery Inn is an unspoilt Grade II listed hostelry, which can be located down a cobbled lane. In the spacious multi-roomed interior, including the oak-panelled lounge, you can drink beers from Hydes and enjoy some good value, home-cooked lunchtime snacks (the kitchen is closed in the evening). Sandwiches, toasties, jacket potatoes and pub-grub mains like gammon, scampi and rib-eye steak are available. The pub's well-used bowling green is to the rear. Eight guest real ales on handpump are served at the three annual beer festivals.

Open all day all wk **Bar Meals** L served Tue-Fri 12-2.30, Sat-Sun 12-4 **Restaurant** L served Tue-Sun 12-2.30 ⊕ HYDES BREWERY ◀ Original, Jekyll's Gold & Seasonal ales, Guest ales. **Facilities** Non-diners area ✿ (Bar Garden) ♦♦ Children's portions Garden ⌂ Beer festival Parking Wi-fi

WALMERSLEY
Map 15 SD81

The Lord Raglan

Nangreaves BL9 6SP ☎ **0161 764 6680**
dir: M66 junct 1, A56 to Walmersley. Left into Palantine Drive, left into Ribble Drive, left into Walmersley Old Rd to Nangreaves

Recommended for its own microbrewery beers

The rambling, stone-built Lord Raglan is set beside a cobbled lane high on the moors above Bury, at the head of a former weaving hamlet, where lanes and tracks dissipate into deep, secluded gorges rich in industrial heritage. Beers brewed at the on-site Leyden microbrewery may be taken in the garden, where the throaty cough of steam engines on the East Lancashire Railway echoes off the River Irwell's steep valley sides below the towering Peel Monument. Reliable, traditional pub grub and changing specials take the edge off walkers' appetites. Try the chicken and mushroom pie, hot steak sandwich, or grilled halibut steak served with a lime and tomato salsa. There are beer festivals in the summer and autumn.

Open all wk 12-2.30 6-11 (Fri 12-2.30 5-11 Sat-Sun all day) **Bar Meals** L served Mon-Fri 12-2, Sat 12-9, Sun 12-8 D served Mon-Thu 6-9, Fri 5-9, Sat 12-9, Sun 12-8 **Restaurant** L served Mon-Fri 12-2, Sat 12-9, Sun 12-8 D served Mon-Thu 6-9, Fri 5-9, Sat 12-9, Sun 12-8 ⊕ FREE HOUSE ◀ Leyden Nanny Flyer, Crowning Glory, Light Brigade, Black Pudding ☼ Wilce's Herefordshire. ♀ 10 **Facilities** ✿ (Bar Garden) ♦♦ Children's menu Children's portions Garden Beer festival Parking Wi-fi ⊖

HAMPSHIRE

ALTON
Map 5 SU73

The Anchor Inn ★★★★★ RR ◉◉

PICK OF THE PUBS

Lower Froyle GU34 4NA ☎ **01420 23261**
e-mail: info@anchorinnatlowerfroyle.co.uk
dir: From A31 follow Bentley signs

Quintessentially English inn with award-winning cuisine

This old, tile-hung rural inn is part of the Miller's Collection of period inns. The low ceilings, wooden floors, exposed beams and open fires all give clues to the age of the 16th-century farmhouse that forms the nucleus of the building. In fact, even during the last 60 years very little can have changed in the intimate snug and saloon bar. The beers are local, with Alton's Pride from the town's Triple fff brewery and King John from Andwell, near Basingstoke. The acclaimed restaurant (with two AA Rosettes) is run by Kevin Chandler, a passionate believer in the 'nose-to-tail' philosophy that ensures no part of an animal is wasted. His regularly changing menus offer simply cooked, local seasonal food. Begin dinner with a guinea fowl, chicken and wild mushroom terrine. For a main, opt for fillet of sea bass with roasted gnocchi. Working closely with Kevin and his team is wine expert Vincent Gasnier, a Master Sommelier. There are five beautifully designed guest rooms.

Open all day all wk Closed: 25 Dec **Bar Meals** L served all wk 12-2.30 D served all wk 6.30-9.30 Av main course £14 **Restaurant** L served Mon-Sat 12-2.30, Sun 12-4 D served Mon-Fri 6.30-9.30, Sat 6.30-10, Sun 7-9 Av 3 course à la carte fr £30 ⊕ FREE HOUSE/MILLER'S COLLECTION ◀ Triple fff Alton's Pride, Andwell King John ☼ Westons Stowford Press. ♀ 9 **Facilities** Non-diners area ♦♦ Children's menu Children's portions Garden ⌂ Parking Wi-fi ⊖ **Rooms** 5

AMPFIELD
Map 5 SU42

White Horse at Ampfield

Winchester Rd SO51 9BQ ☎ **01794 368356**
e-mail: whitehorseinn@hotmail.co.uk
dir: From Winchester take A3040, then A3090 towards Romsey. Ampfield in 7m. Or M3 junct 13, A335 (signed Chandler's Ford). At lights right onto B3043, follow Chandler's Ford Industrial Estate then Hursley signs. Left onto A3090 to Ampfield

Traditional village inn once frequented by pilgrims

With roots as a pilgrims' inn in the 16th century, the timber-framed White Horse is the only pub in the village in which The Rev W. Awdry, Thomas the Tank Engine's creator, lived as a boy. The building is home to three large inglenooks, the one in the public bar having an iron fireback decorated with the crest of Charles I and hooks on which to hang bacon sides for smoking. Typical dishes are pan-fried monkfish with chorizo and bean cassoulet;

Save on hotels. Book at theAA.com/hotel

HAMPSHIRE 203 ENGLAND

mixed game hotpot; and aubergine and lentil moussaka with 'Greek-style' sweet potato.

Open all day all wk 11-11 (Sun 12-9) ⊕ GREENE KING ◀ Morland Old Speckled Hen, Wadworth 6X, Ringwood Best Bitter. **Facilities** ◦◦ Children's menu Children's portions Play area Garden Parking Wi-fi

AMPORT
Map 5 SU34

The Hawk Inn NEW

SP11 8AE ☎ 01264 710371
e-mail: info@hawkinnamport.co.uk
dir: Telephone for directions

Both modern and traditional British food

Some may remember this lovingly restored village pub as The Amport Arms; some may guess that its new name is a nod towards the nearby Hawk Conservancy, where falconers fly birds of prey. In a light and spacious interior, the bar offers Ramsbury Gold real ale and Aspall cider, while a meal at one of the widely-spaced tables could feature grilled chicken Caesar salad; burger with smoked Applewood cheddar, bacon and fries; fresh salmon and samphire linguine in cream and tarragon sauce; or aubergine, red pepper, spring onion and goats' cheese quesadilla with guacamole.

Open all day all wk Closed: 25 Dec **Bar Meals** L served all wk 7.30am-10am, 12-2.30 D served all wk 6-9.45 Av main course £14 **Restaurant** L served all wk 7.30am-10am, 12-2.30 D served all wk 6-9.45 Av 3 course à la carte fr £25 ⊕ FREE HOUSE ◀ Ramsbury Gold ♂ Aspall. ♀ 14 **Facilities** Non-diners area ♣ (Bar Outside area) ◦◦ Children's menu Children's portions Outside area Parking Wi-fi

ANDOVER
Map 5 SU34

Wyke Down Country Pub & Restaurant

Wyke Down, Picket Piece SP11 6LX ☎ 01264 352048
e-mail: info@wykedown.co.uk
dir: 3m from Andover town centre on A303 follow signs for Wyke Down Caravan Park

Converted barn and conservatory dining

A diversified farm on the outskirts of Andover, this establishment combines a pub/restaurant with a golf driving range, but still raises its own beef cattle. The pub started in a barn over 25 years ago and the restaurant was built some years later. A typical meal might be chef's own chicken liver pâté with onion marmalade and warm toast followed by steamed pudding filled with steak, bacon, onion and London Pride. Other choices include plenty from the grill and international favourites such as curry and Cajun chicken.

Open all wk 12-3 6-11 Closed: 25 Dec-2 Jan **Bar Meals** L served all wk 12-2 D served all wk 6-8 **Restaurant** L served all wk 12-2 D served all wk 6-8 ⊕ FREE HOUSE ◀ Fuller's London Pride. **Facilities** Non-diners area ◦◦ Children's menu Children's portions Play area Garden Parking (notice required)

BALL HILL
Map 5 SU46

The Furze Bush Inn

Hatt Common, East Woodhay RG20 0NQ
☎ 01635 253228
e-mail: info@furzebushinn.co.uk
dir: From Newbury take A343 (Andover Road), pub signed

Hearty food in a handy location

A popular rural free house, this is a perfect place for refreshment following a day at the Newbury Races, walking the Berkshire Downs, or visiting Highclere Castle, the location for the TV series Downton Abbey. The bar menu features a good range of traditional favourites, such as home-made soup with a granary roll and butter or steak and ale pie, plus other pub classics including lasagne and curry with rice and naan bread. There's a large front garden, a children's play area and a rear patio with huge TV and parasols – perfect for summer drinking.

Open all day all wk **Bar Meals** L served Mon-Fri 12-3, Sat 12-9, Sun 12-8.30 D served Mon-Fri 5-9, Sat 12-9, Sun 12-8.30 **Restaurant** L served Mon-Fri 12-3, Sat 12-9, Sun 12-8.30 D served Mon-Fri 5-9, Sat 12-9, Sun 12-8.30 ⊕ FREE HOUSE ◀ Fuller's London Pride, Greene King Abbot Ale & IPA. **Facilities** Non-diners area ◦◦ Children's menu Play area Garden Beer festival Parking Wi-fi

BAUGHURST
Map 5 SU56

The Wellington Arms ◉◉

PICK OF THE PUBS

See Pick of the Pubs on page 204

BEAULIEU
Map 5 SU30

The Drift Inn

Beaulieu Rd SO42 7YQ ☎ 023 8029 2342
e-mail: bookatable@driftinn.co.uk
dir: From Lyndhurst take B3056 (Beaulieu Rd) signed Beaulieu. Cross railway line, inn on left

Family-friendly New Forest inn

Part of the New Forest Hotels group, the inn is surrounded by the glorious New Forest. The word 'drift' refers to the centuries-old, twice a year, round-up of the 3,000-plus free-wandering ponies. Beers from Ringwood on the western side of the forest and a guest ale are served in the bar, while in the restaurant a competitively priced menu lists Thai-style green vegetable curry; New Forest steak; and haddock and chips. Outside are two children's play areas and large gardens, although no one minds if you come inside wearing walking boots and with your dog in tow.

Open all wk **Bar Meals** L served all wk 12-9 D served all wk 12-9 food served all day **Restaurant** L served all wk 12-9 D served all wk 12-9 food served all day ⊕ FREE HOUSE ◀ Ringwood Best Bitter, Old Thumper & Boondoggle, Guest ales ♂ Thatchers. ♀ **Facilities** Non-diners area ♣ (Bar Restaurant Garden) ◦◦ Children's menu Children's portions Play area Garden Beer festival Parking Wi-fi

BEAUWORTH
Map 5 SU52

The Milburys

SO24 0PB ☎ 01962 771248
dir: A272 towards Petersfield, 6m, turn right for Beauworth

Popular community pub with great views and traditional pub grub

Dating from the 17th century and taking its name from the Bronze Age barrow nearby, this rustic hill-top pub is noted for its massive, 250-year-old treadmill that used to draw water from the 300-ft well in the bar. In summer, sweeping views across Hampshire can be savoured from the lofty garden. Inside you will find a great selection of real ales which you can enjoy by the warming winter fires. Traditional pub food, such as steak-and-ale pie and battered cod, is served all week in the bar and restaurant. There's a skittle alley, and rallies and club meetings are held here.

Open all wk **Bar Meals** L served all wk 12-2 D served all wk 6-9 **Restaurant** L served all wk 12-2 D served all wk 6-9 ⊕ FREE HOUSE ◀ Milburys Best, Goddards Ale of Wight, Hop Back Summer Lightning & Crop Circle ♂ Westons Stowford Press. **Facilities** Non-diners area ♣ (Bar Garden) ◦◦ Children's menu Children's portions Play area Family room Garden Parking

BENTLEY
Map 5 SU74

The Bull Inn

GU10 5JH ☎ 01420 22156
e-mail: enquiries@thebullinnbentley.co.uk
dir: 2m from Farnham on A31 towards Winchester

Period details and an extensive menu

Exposed beams, real fires and plenty of alfresco seating make this 15th-century coaching inn well worth a visit. There's also a great selection of food. Lunch brings ploughman's, jacket potatoes and sharing baskets of, perhaps, breaded whitebait, tartare sauce and brown bread and butter. Main meals include Guinness moules à la marinière or 'Bull sizzlers' of duck strip stir-fry with plum sauce, rice and prawn crackers. There's a decent selection of wines, including Châteauneuf du Pape, while beers include Fuller's London Pride and Ringwood Best Bitter.

Open all day all wk 11-11 (Sun 12-10.30) Closed: 1 Jan **Bar Meals** L served Mon-Sat 12-2.30, Sun 12-4.30 D served Mon-Sat 6-9.30 Av main course £9.50 **Restaurant** L served Mon-Sat 12-2.30, Sun 12-4.30 D served Mon-Sat 6-9.30 Fixed menu price fr £9.95 Av 3 course à la carte fr £22 ⊕ ENTERPRISE INNS ◀ Fuller's London Pride, St Austell Tribute, Ringwood Best Bitter ♂ Aspall. ♀ 9 **Facilities** Non-diners area ♣ (Bar Garden) ◦◦ Children's menu Children's portions Garden Parking Wi-fi (notice required)

PICK OF THE PUBS

The Wellington Arms ❀❀

BAUGHURST　　　　　Map 5 SU56

Baughurst Rd RG26 5LP
☎ **0118 982 0110**
e-mail: hello@thewellingtonarms.com
web: www.thewellingtonarms.com
dir: *From A4, E of Newbury, through Aldermaston. At 2nd rdbt 2nd exit signed Baughurst, left at T-junct, pub 1m*

Drawing discerning diners from miles around

Lost down a maze of lanes in peaceful countryside between Basingstoke and Newbury is the smart, whitewashed 'Welly', a former hunting lodge for the Duke of Wellington. Inside are wooden tables, tiled floors and attractively patterned curtains and blinds. Jason King and Simon Page have worked wonders with the place since taking over some nine years ago. Their ethos is simple: local, well-priced and delicious food. Jason's award-winning, daily chalkboard menus offer plenty of interest and imagination and much of the produce is organic, local or home-grown. Salad leaves, herbs and vegetables are grown in the pub's polytunnel and raised vegetable beds, free-range eggs come from their rare-breed and rescue hens, and there are also rare-breed sheep, Tamworth pigs and two beehives. This might translate to a starter of country-style terrine of local rabbit and wood pigeon with green

tomato chutney. Follow with roast rack of home-reared lamb, bashed root vegetable mash with crab apple jelly; or baked fillet of Brixham cod with oven-dried tomatoes, black olives and crushed new potatoes. Vegetarians will like the twice-baked goats' cheese soufflé, braised leeks, pinenuts and parmesan. One of the Wellington's home-made ice creams (gingerbread, dark chocolate, marmalade) or sorbets (mango, raspberry, blackcurrant) will make the perfect finish. Although the small dining room has been extended, booking is still advisable, or maybe just arrive early to secure a table. The well-tended garden is an extension for diners in the summer too; if the weather is on the chilly side, just ask for a cosy mohair rug to keep you warm.

Open 12-3.30 6-11 Closed: Sun eve
Restaurant L served all wk 12-1.30
D served Mon-Sat 6-9.30 ⊕ FREE
HOUSE ◨ Wadworth 6X, West Berkshire
Good Old Boy, Two Cocks Brewery
Roundhead ♂ Tutts Clump. ♟ 11
Facilities ❀ ☗ Children's portions
Garden ㅠ Parking Wi-fi

The Sun Inn

Bentworth, Hampshire GU34 5JT • **Tel:** 01420 562338
Website: www.thesuninnbentworth.co.uk • **Email:** info@thesuninnbentworth.co.uk

Hidden down a lane on the edge of Bentworth Village in Hampshire, *The Sun Inn* is a pretty flower-adorned and unspoilt rural free-house dating back to the 17th century when it was a pair of traditional cottages.

The landlady Mary Holmes has been at *The Sun* for the past 13 years and has ensured the pub has kept its original character. The brick and board floors are laid with a rustic mix of scrubbed pine tables, benches and settles, the original beams are hung with sparkling horse brasses, while the walls are adorned with plates and prints depicting the history of the village of Bentworth.

Nestle in front of one of the three crackling log fires warming each of the interlinked rooms. Peruse a magazine, enjoy the fresh flowers and relax in a cosy candlelit atmosphere with friendly helpful service. A thriving free house, the Sun offers a selection of real ales from around the local Hampshire area all on hand pump. These include *Andwells Resolute, Hogsback T.E.A, Bowman's Swift One* and *Ringwood Best*. As well as local real ales there is a wide range of guest beers including *Fuller's London Pride, Timothy Taylor's Landlord,* and *Sharps Doombar,* plus many more regular favourites.

As well as *The Sun*'s charm and extensive range of real ales and lagers, this freehouse really comes into its own by serving hearty home-cooked dishes that make a trip to this pub well worth the visit. Dishes range from ploughman's lunches, home-made soups and sandwiches to more filling options such as beer-battered cod, calves liver and bacon, tiger prawns and scallops in garlic butter, steak and Guinness pie, and half-shoulder of lamb with redcurrant and mint jelly. Game is also served in season including venison, partridge and pheasant.

If that is not enough to fill you up indulge in some of the home-made puddings like apple and rhubarb crumble, warm chocolate brownie, sticky toffee pudding, banoffee pie or strawberry and white chocolate cheesecake. When visiting *The Sun Inn* you will be sure to receive a warm and friendly welcome from Mary and her team.

BENTWORTH — Map 5 SU64

The Sun Inn

PICK OF THE PUBS

See Pick of the Pubs on opposite page
See advert on page 205

BISHOP'S WALTHAM — Map 5 SU51

The Hampshire Bowman NEW

Dundridge Ln SO32 1GD ☎ 01489 892940
e-mail: hampshirebowman@uwclub.net
dir: *From Bishop's Waltham on B3035 towards Corhampton. Right signed Dundridge. 1.2m to Pub*

Rustic rural gem lost down lanes

A true rural local, set in ten acres beside a country lane in rolling downland, this unassuming Victorian pub remains delightfully old fashioned. In the beamed, simply furnished and brick-floored bar you'll find time-honoured pub games and barrels of beer on racks behind the bar. Ale-lovers come for foaming pints of Bowman Swift One or Wallops Wood, or a glass or heady Black Dragon cider, best enjoyed in the rambling orchard garden. Soak it up with a traditional bar meal, perhaps ham, egg and chips, liver and bacon with mash and shallot jus; or fish and chips. Don't miss the July and December beer festivals.

Open all day all wk **Bar Meals** L served Mon-Thu 12-2, Fri-Sun 12-9 D served Mon-Thu 6-9, Fri-Sun 12-9 Av main course £9 **Restaurant** L served Mon-Thu 12-2, Fri-Sun 12-9 D served Mon-Thu 6-9, Fri-Sun 12-9 Av 3 course à la carte fr £18 ⊕ FREE HOUSE ◀ Bowman Ales Swift One & Wallops Wood, Guest ales ☉ Gwynt y Ddraig Black Dragon, Lilley's Sunset, Guest ciders.
Facilities Non-diners area ❄ (Bar Restaurant Garden) ♦♦ Children's menu Children's portions Play area Garden ⋒ Beer festival Cider festival Parking Wi-fi ➡ (notice required)

BOLDRE — Map 5 SZ39

The Hobler Inn

Southampton Rd, Battramsley SO41 8PT
☎ 01590 623944
e-mail: hedi@alcatraz.co.uk
dir: *From Brockenhurst take A337 towards Lymington. Pub on main road*

New Forest pub popular with families

On the main road between Brockenhurst and Lymington, The Hobler, now under new ownership, has a large grassed area and trestle tables ideal for families visiting the New Forest. The Hobler Inn is more London wine bar than local with stylish leather furniture, but still serves a well-kept pint of Ringwood. The food, served all day, is locally sourced and freshly cooked.

Open all day all wk **Bar Meals** food served all day **Restaurant** food served all day ⊕ ENTERPRISE INNS ◀ Ringwood Best Bitter, Timothy Taylor. ♈ 10 **Facilities** Non-diners area ♦♦ Children's menu Garden Parking Wi-fi ➡ (notice required)

The Red Lion

PICK OF THE PUBS

Rope Hill SO41 8NE ☎ 01590 673177
dir: *M27 junct 1, A337 through Lyndhurst & Brockenhurst towards Lymington, follow Boldre signs*

15th-century pub for all seasons

Mentioned in the Domesday Book, the Red Lion sits at the crossroads in the ancient village of Boldre. The rambling interior contains cosy, beamed rooms, log fires and rural memorabilia; the rooms glow with candlelight on antique copper and brass. Expect a genuinely warm welcome and traditional values, with Ringwood ales on offer at the bar. The kitchen places an emphasis on traditional meals made using the very best of the forest's produce. Typical starters include home-made venison pâté; and prawn and smoked salmon cocktail. There's an impressive selection of fish and vegetarian dishes, such as crab and spring onion fishcakes; or vegetable and lentil 'cottage pie', while meat lovers could plump for pan-fried lamb rump with sweet potato mash and rosemary and mint sauce. In the summer, you can enjoy full table service outside on the herb patio.

Open all wk 11-3 5.30-11 (Sun 12-8) (summer Sat 11-11) Closed: 25 Dec **Bar Meals** L served Mon-Sat 12-2.30, Sun 12-8 (summer Sat 12-9.30) D served Mon-Sat 6-9.30 Sun 12-8 (summer Sat 12-9.30) **Restaurant** L served Mon-Sat 12-2.30, Sun 12-8 (summer Sat 12-9.30) D served Mon-Sat 6-9.30 Sun 12-8 (summer Sat 12-9.30) ⊕ FREE HOUSE ◀ Ringwood Best Bitter & Fortyniner, Brakspear Oxford Gold, Guinness, Guest ales ☉ Thatchers Gold. ♈ 15 **Facilities** Non-diners area ❄ (Bar Garden) ♦♦ Children's portions Garden ⋒ Parking ➡ (notice required)

BRANSGORE — Map 5 SZ19

The Three Tuns Country Inn ◉

PICK OF THE PUBS

Ringwood Rd BH23 8JH ☎ 01425 672232
e-mail: threetunsinn@btconnect.com
dir: *1.5m from A35 Walkford junct. 3m from Christchurch & 1m from Hinton Admiral railway station*

Thatched New Forest pub with a huge garden

This picture-perfect, 17th-century inn has a riot of flowers outside in the spring and summer. There are five distinct public areas: a comfortable lounge bar with a winter log fire; an oak-beamed snug, similarly warmed, and with biscuits and water for the dog; a large terrace with a water feature for alfresco dining; a south-facing garden, with over 2,500 square metres of lawn (on sunny days out comes the barbecue) and surrounded by fields, trees and grazing ponies; and finally, the 60-seat restaurant. The menus offer something for everyone: if there's time for just a pint of Ringwood Best and a light bar snack, then maybe what will do the trick is oxtail and Dorset snail pie. Or, for those with more time to spend, perhaps rack of lamb with cheese, aubergine, tomato and creamed potatoes. For pudding, try the tempting New Forest ice

cream. A barn provides space for functions and a beer festival is held in September.

Open all day all wk 11-11 (Sun 12-10.30) **Bar Meals** L served Mon-Fri 12-2.15, Sat-Sun 12-9.15 D served Mon-Fri 6.30-9.15, Sat-Sun 12-9.15 **Restaurant** L served Mon-Fri 12-2.15, Sat-Sun 12-9.15 D served Mon-Fri 6.30-9.15, Sat-Sun 12-9.15 ⊕ ENTERPRISE INNS ◀ St Austell Tribute, Ringwood Best Bitter & Fortyniner, Exmoor Gold, Otter Bitter, Timothy Taylor ☉ Thatchers Gold & Katy, New Forest Traditional. ♈ 9 **Facilities** Non-diners area ❄ (Bar Garden) ♦♦ Children's menu Children's portions Garden ⋒ Beer festival Parking Wi-fi ➡ (notice required)

BROCKENHURST — Map 5 SU30

The Filly Inn ★★★★ INN NEW

Lymington Rd SO42 7UF ☎ 01590 623449
e-mail: info@thefillyinn.co.uk
dir: *On A337, 1m S of Brockenhurst towards Lymington*

A gem in the heart of the New Forest

Facing the open heathland of the New Forest National Park, this one-time coaching inn is run by Claire and Steve Lee who, since taking over, have given it a real shot in the arm. Their dog, Claude, has decided that his contribution is curling up in the bar and observing the humans drinking their local ales and ciders. Seasonal menus list freshly prepared Hampshire-sourced dishes from pickled eggs to home-made puddings, a range that includes ploughman's platters; steak and ale pie; beer-battered fish and chips; and award-winning cheeses and pork pies. Outside, is an enclosed terrace and an ample garden.

Open all day all wk **Bar Meals** L served Mon-Fri 12-3, Sat-Sun all day D served Mon-Fri 6-9, Sat-Sun all day **Restaurant** L served Mon-Fri 12-3, Sat-Sun all day D served Mon-Fri 6-9, Sat-Sun all day ⊕ PUNCH TAVERNS ◀ Rotating Guest Ales. ♈ 11 **Facilities** Non-diners area ❄ (Bar Restaurant Garden) ♦♦ Children's menu Children's portions Garden ⋒ Parking Wi-fi ➡ (notice required) **Rooms** 5

Save on hotels. Book at **theAA.com/hotel**

HAMPSHIRE 207 ENGLAND

PICK OF THE PUBS

The Sun Inn

BENTWORTH Map 5 SU64

Sun Hill GU34 5JT ☎ 01420 562338
e-mail: info@thesuninnbentworth.co.uk
web: www.thesuninnbentworth.co.uk
dir: *From A339 between Alton &*
Basingstoke follow Bentworth signs

A step back in time for hearty food

Just as you think you're about to leave the village behind, this pretty, foliage-covered, rural free house comes into view. Dating from the 17th century, when it was built as a pair of traditional cottages, little can have changed inside in recent years, which is how landlady Mary Holmes intends things to stay. The floors in the three interlinked rooms are laid with brick and board; the furniture is a mix of scrubbed pine tables, benches and settles; the old ceiling beams are hung with horse brasses; and assorted prints and plates decorate the walls. Log fires may be burning, while tasteful cosmetic touches – magazines, fresh flowers, flickering candlelight – enhance the period feel still further. Apart from The Sun's overall charm, people come here for its good selection of real ales, including from Andwell, Sharp's, Fuller's, Ringwood and Stonehenge breweries, as well as Aspall cider. They come too for the extensive range of hearty home-cooked dishes, which run from ploughman's, home-made soup and sandwiches, to tiger

prawns and scallops in garlic butter; chicken breast in Stilton and walnut sauce; steak, mushroom and ale pie; and Yorkshire pudding with vegetable sausages. Game in season includes pheasant, and venison cooked in Guinness with pickled walnuts. The uncomplicated desserts are typically warm chocolate brownie, banoffee pie, and treacle tart. There's a lot to see and do in the area: in Selborne, there's the house where naturalist Gilbert White lived and where the Oates (of Scott's ill-fated 1911-12 Antarctic expedition fame) Collection is now found, and Jane Austen's House at Chawton is an easy drive too. A ride on the Watercress Line from Alton about 15 minutes away takes you on a 10-mile steam train journey through the Hampshire countryside.

Open all wk 12-3 6-11 (Sun 12-10.30)
Bar Meals L served all wk 12-2 D served all wk 7-9.30 ⊞ FREE HOUSE ◀ Andwell Resolute, Ringwood Fortyniner, Sharp's Doom Bar, Stonehenge Pigswill, Fuller's London Pride, Black Sheep ♂ Aspall.
♟ 12 **Facilities** Non-diners area ❤ (Bar Garden) ♦ Children's menu Children's portions Family room Garden ☴ Parking

BURGHCLERE — Map 5 SU46

Marco Pierre White The Carnarvon Arms

PICK OF THE PUBS

Winchester Rd, Whitway RG20 9LE ☎ 01635 278222
e-mail: info@thecarnarvonarmshotel.com
dir: *M4 junct 13, A34 S to Winchester. Exit A34 at Tothill Services, follow Highclere Castle signs. Pub on right*

Fine dining in a relaxed country-pub environment

Originally a coaching inn for travellers to neighbouring Highclere Castle (the setting for ITV's period drama *Downton Abbey*), home to the present Lord and Lady Carnarvon, this Grade II listed building constructed in the 1800s is steeped in history. It was the 5th Earl of Carnarvon who famously opened Tutankhamun's tomb in 1922. Following a restoration by Marco Pierre White and his team, The Carnarvon Arms is now a modern country inn, decorated with an eclectic mix of artefacts and art. At the bar, try The Governor, a British beer created in collaboration with JW Lees, or a cider of the same name from Westons. The kitchen team prepare Marco's culinary creations, including fried duck egg and Stornoway black pudding in brioche; kipper pâté with whisky; caramelised honey-roast belly of pork; and smoked haddock with poached eggs. Finish with Mr White's rice pudding or Cambridge burnt cream with fresh raspberries.

Open all day all wk 8am-11.30pm (Fri-Sat 8am-12.30am) **Bar Meals** L served all wk 12-3 D served all wk 6-9.30 Av main course £9.95 **Restaurant** L served all wk 12-3 D served all wk 6-9.30 Fixed menu price fr £18.50 Av 3 course à la carte fr £28.50 ⊕ FREE HOUSE ◀ JW Lees The Governor, Guest ales Ò Westons The Governor. ₹ 15 **Facilities** Non-diners area ❄ (Bar) ❉ Children's menu Children's portions Outside area ⌱ Parking Wi-fi ▄ (notice required)

BURLEY — Map 5 SU20

The Burley Inn

BH24 4AB ☎ 01425 403448
e-mail: info@theburleyinn.co.uk
dir: *4m SE of of Ringwood*

Favoured forest village setting

A great base from which to explore the tracks, paths and rides of the surrounding New Forest National Park, this imposing Edwardian edifice, in neat grounds behind picket fencing, is one of a small local chain of dining pubs combining the best of local real ales – Flack Manor and Itchen Valley breweries often feature - with homely, traditional pub grub from an extensive menu. Toast wintery toes before log fires or relax on the decking patio, looking forward to olde English fish pie or venison casserole, with key lime pie to finish, whilst idly watching free-roaming livestock amble by on the village lanes.

Open all day all wk **Bar Meals** L served all wk 12-10 D served all wk 12-10 food served all day **Restaurant** L served all wk 12-10 D served all wk 12-10 food served all day ⊕ FREE HOUSE ◀ Ringwood Best Bitter & Fortyniner, Guest ales Ò Thatchers. ₹ 10 **Facilities** Non-diners area ❄ (Bar) Children's menu Children's portions Outside area ⌱ Parking Wi-fi ▄

CADNAM — Map 5 SU31

Sir John Barleycorn

Old Romsey Rd SO40 2NP ☎ 023 8081 2236
e-mail: sjb@alcatraz.co.uk
dir: *From Southampton M27 junct 1 into Cadnam*

The oldest inn in the New Forest

The name of this friendly thatched establishment comes from a folksong celebrating the transformation of barley to beer. Now owned by Fuller's, it is formed from three 12th-century cottages, one of which was once home to the charcoal burner who discovered the body of King William Rufus. Beers on offer are Fuller's London Pride and HSB, while ciders are represented by Westons Stowford Press and Old Rosie. The menu has something for everyone with quick snacks and sandwiches, a children's menu and traditional dishes like New Forest sausages, honey-roast ham, and fillet of sea bass. More inventive options are chicken and pea risotto, and smoked mackerel salad.

Open all day all wk 11-11 **Bar Meals** Av main course £12 food served all day **Restaurant** food served all day ⊕ FULLER'S ◀ London Pride, George Gale & Co HSB Ò Westons Stowford Press & Old Rosie. ₹ 10 **Facilities** Non-diners area ❉ Children's menu Garden ⌱ Parking ▄ (notice required)

CHALTON — Map 5 SU71

The Red Lion

PICK OF THE PUBS

PO8 0BG ☎ 023 9259 2246
e-mail: redlionchalton@fullers.co.uk
dir: *Just off A3 between Horndean & Petersfield. Follow signs for Chalton*

Traditional English pub with South Downs views

The Red Lion is said to be the oldest pub in Hampshire, dating back to 1147, when it was used as a residential workshop for the builders at St Michael's church opposite. It retains an olde worlde English charm, from the thatched roof and whitewashed exterior to the brass knick-knacks, timbered beams and roaring fires inside. The expansive garden features stunning panoramic views of the South Downs, a lovely place to enjoy one of the Fuller's ales on offer – Seafarers, HSB or London Pride plus there are guest ales and a beer festival at the end of July. The tempting thrice-weekly changing menu uses local ingredients where possible. Duck and pork terrine, cranberries, pistachios, red onion chutney and toasted bloomer might precede pan-fried calves' liver bacon, chive mash and onion gravy or a pub classic of ham, egg, chips and beans.

Open all day all wk 11.30-11 (Sun 12-10.30) **Bar Meals** Av main course £10.95 food served all day

Restaurant food served all day ⊕ FULLER'S ◀ London Pride, George Gale & Co Seafarers & HSB, Guest ales Ò Kopparberg, Aspall. ₹ 20 **Facilities** Non-diners area ❄ (Bar Garden) ❉ Children's menu Children's portions Garden ⌱ Beer festival Parking Wi-fi ▄ (notice required)

CHARTER ALLEY — Map 5 SU55

The White Hart Inn

White Hart Ln RG26 5QA ☎ 01256 850048
e-mail: enquiries@whitehartcharteralley.com
dir: *M3 junct 6, A339 towards Newbury. Right signed Ramsdell. Right at church, then 1st left into White Hart Ln*

Good pub food and reliable ales

When this free house opened in 1818, on the northern edge of the village overlooking open farmland and woods – just as today – it must have delighted the woodsmen and coach drivers visiting the farrier next door. Real ale pumps lined up on the herringbone-patterned, brick-fronted bar include Moor's Revival, Triple fff's Moondance and a couple from Bowman's. The menu changes daily to offer typical locally sourced dishes as steak and Stilton pie; Scottish salmon supreme; rump steak burger; traditional cottage pie; and spinach and mushroom penne pasta. A patio leads into an attractive garden. Contact the inn for its occasional beer festival dates.

Open 12-2.30 7-11 (Sun 12-10.30) Closed: 25-26 Dec, 1 Jan, Mon L **Bar Meals** L served Tue-Sun 12-2 D served Tue-Sat 7-9 Av main course £12.50 **Restaurant** L served Tue-Sun 12-2 D served Tue-Sat 7-9 ⊕ FREE HOUSE ◀ Triple fff Moondance, Bowman Swift One & Wallops Wood, Moor Revival. **Facilities** Non-diners area ❄ (Bar Garden) ❉ Children's menu Children's portions Family room Garden ⌱ Beer festival Parking Wi-fi ▄ (notice required)

CHAWTON — Map 5 SU73

The Greyfriar

Winchester Rd GU34 1SB ☎ 01420 83841
e-mail: hello@thegreyfriar.co.uk
web: www.thegreyfriar.co.uk
dir: *Just off A31 near Alton. Access to Chawton via A31/A32 junct. Follow Jane Austen's House signs. Pub opposite*

Old fashioned values and family-friendly

Opposite Jane Austen's House Museum stands this 16th-century pub, once a terrace of cottages. As well as

its friendly atmosphere and delightful village setting, the south-facing suntrap garden is another draw. The pub is Fuller's-owned and offers London Pride and Seafarers along with great food. A sample menu includes Japanese breaded prawns or baked Tunworth cheese for two (Hampshire's answer to camembert) to start, followed by smoked mackerel fishcakes, braised lamb shank, 10-hour roasted belly pork, vegetable linguine, gammon steak or steak-and-ale pie. Sandwiches and jackets are also available for lunch.

Open all day all wk 12-11 (Sun 12-10.30) **Bar Meals** L served Mon-Sat 12-2.30, Sun 12-7 D served Mon-Sat 6-9.30 **Restaurant** L served Mon-Sat 12-2.30, Sun 12-7 D served Mon-Sat 6-9.30 ⊕ FULLER'S ◣ London Pride, Geoge Gale & Co Seafarers, Seasonal ales Ō Aspall. **Facilities** Non-diners area ❧ (Bar Restaurant Garden) ♦ Children's portions Garden ⊼ Parking Wi-fi ⛟ (notice required)

CHERITON   Map 5 SU52

The Flower Pots Inn

SO24 0QQ ☎ 01962 771318
dir: *A272 towards Petersfield, left onto B3046, pub 0.75m on right*

Popular village pub with its own microbrewery

Known almost universally as The Pots, this pub used to be a farmhouse and home to the head gardener of nearby Avington Park. These days, local beer drinkers know the pub well for its award-winning Flower Pots Bitter and Goodens Gold, brewed across the car park in the microbrewery. Simple home-made food includes hearty filled baps, toasted sandwiches, jacket potatoes, cheese and meat ploughman's and different hotpots – chilli con carne, lamb and apricot, steak and ale, spicy mixed bean. A large, safe garden, with a covered patio, allows children to let off steam (under 14s are not allowed in the bar). The pub holds a beer festival in August.

Open all wk 12-2.30 6-11 (Sun 12-3 7-10.30) **Bar Meals** L served all wk 12-1.45 D served Mon-Sat 7-8.45 ⊕ FREE HOUSE ◣ Flower Pots Bitter, Goodens Gold Ō Westons Old Rosie. **Facilities** Non-diners area ❧ (Bar Garden) ♦ Children's portions Garden Beer festival Parking **Notes** ⊛

CLANFIELD   Map 5 SU71

The Rising Sun Inn ★★★ INN **NEW**

North Ln PO8 0RN ☎ 023 9259 6975
e-mail: enquiries@therisingsunclanfield.co.uk
dir: *A3(M) then A3 towards Petersfield. Left signed Clanfield. Follow brown inn signs*

Traditional village inn just inside the South Downs National Park

Although it looks two centuries old, the flint-faced Rising Sun was built in 2003. Apparently, in 1960, its predecessor was constructed in one day, even serving its first pint at 6pm. Today's bar serves Fuller's HSB, Ringwood Best, guest ales and Old Rosie cider. The menu focuses on pub classics such as beef stew and dumplings; beer-battered cod; and fisherman's pie, with support from chicken chasseur, pasta carbonara, and leek and potato bake. Tuesday night is steak night, curries are Thursday and it's Friday for music. The B&B accommodation is popular with walkers and cyclists on the South Downs Way.

Open all day all wk **Bar Meals** food served all day **Restaurant** food served all day ⊕ ENTERPRISE INNS ◣ George Gale & Co HSB, Ringwood Best Bitter, Guest ales Ō Westons Old Rosie. **Facilities** Non-diners area ❧ (All areas) ♦ Children's menu Children's portions Garden Outside area ⊼ Beer festival Parking Wi-fi ⛟ (notice required) **Rooms** 3

CRAWLEY   Map 5 SU43

The Fox and Hounds

SO21 2PR ☎ 01962 776006
e-mail: foxandhoundscrawley@hotmail.co.uk
dir: *A34 onto A272 then 1st right into Crawley*

Attractive village pub known for its range of wines

Rebuilt in impressive mock-Tudor style in 1910, this popular inn serves a well-to-do village close enough to affluent Winchester to attract its citizens too. Dining tables grouped round a central bar soon fill up for well prepared chicken with Stilton and mushroom sauce; cod with basil and parmesan crust; home-made pies; and mushroom Stroganoff. To drink, there are 36 wines by the glass and the beers come from Ringwood and Wychwood. Just down the road is a proper village duck pond.

Open all wk 11-3 6-11 (Sun 12-6) **Bar Meals** L served Mon-Sat 12-2.30, Sun 12-8 D served Mon-Sat 6.30-9.30, Sun 12-8 **Restaurant** L served Mon-Sat 12-2.30, Sun 12-4 D served Mon-Sat 6.30-9.30, Sun 12-4 ⊕ ENTERPRISE INNS ◣ Ringwood Best Bitter, Salisbury English Ale, Sharp's Doom Bar, Wychwood Hobgoblin, Guest ales Ō Westons Stowford Press, Symonds. ♚ 36 **Facilities** Non-diners area ❧ (Bar Garden) ♦ Children's menu Children's portions Play area Garden ⊼ Parking ⛟

CROOKHAM VILLAGE   Map 5 SU75

The Exchequer

Crondall Rd GU51 5SU ☎ 01252 615336
e-mail: bookings@exchequercrookham.co.uk
dir: *M3 junct 5, A287 towards Farnham for 5m. Left to Crookham Village*

Welcoming dining pub with top-notch ales

Amongst the quiet villages of north Hampshire in the beautiful setting of Crookham Village, this whitewashed free house is just a stone's throw from the A287. With a new landlord, The Exchequer serves carefully chosen wines and local ales straight from the cask, and offers a great seasonal menu with dishes featuring the best local produce. Start with a sharing board of meze or perhaps a sweet pepper and goats' cheese tart. Main course dishes include crushed new potato, salmon and smoked haddock fishcake; and roast chicken breast wrapped in Parma ham and stuffed with pâté. Leave room for blackberry and apple crumble with custard. Sandwiches and pub classics are available at lunchtime.

Open all wk 12-3 6-11 (Fri-Sun 12-11) **Bar Meals** L served Tue-Fri 12-2, Sat 12-2.30, Sun 12-8 D served Tue-Fri 6-9, Sat 6-9.30, Sun 12-8 **Restaurant** L served Tue-Fri 12-2, Sat 12-2.30, Sun 12-8 D served Tue-Fri 6-9, Sat 6-9.30, Sun 12-8 ⊕ FREE HOUSE ◣ Andwell, Hogs Back TEA, Ringwood Fortyniner Ō Thatchers, Surrey Garden Cider. ♚ 10 **Facilities** Non-diners area ♦ Children's menu Children's portions Garden ⊼ Parking Wi-fi

DOWNTON   Map 5 SZ29

The Royal Oak

Christchurch Rd SO41 0LA ☎ 01590 644999
e-mail: kathy@theroyaloakdownton.co.uk
dir: *On A337 between Lymington & Christchurch*

Close to the New Forest and the coast

Fronted by a white-painted picket fence, this pub on the edge of the New Forest is a mile from the beach at Lymington, from where you can look across the Solent to the Isle of Wight and its famed Needles. Although changing hands in June 2102 the inn still offers Ringwood's Best Bitter, the stronger Fortyniner and guest ales. The long menu has something to suits all tastes and appetites; rope grown mussels; pork chop with colcannon mash; and sticky toffee pudding give an idea of what's in store.

Open all day all wk 11am-11.30pm **Bar Meals** L served Mon-Fri 12-2.30, Sat-Sun all day D served Mon-Fri 6-9.30, Sat-Sun all day **Restaurant** L served Mon-Fri 12-2.30, Sat-Sun all day D served Mon-Fri 6-9.30, Sat-Sun all day ⊕ ENTERPRISE INNS ◣ Ringwood Best Bitter & Fortyniner, Guest ales Ō Thatchers Gold. ♚ 9 **Facilities** Non-diners area ❧ (Bar Garden) ♦ Children's menu Children's portions Garden ⊼ Parking Wi-fi ⛟

DROXFORD
Map 5 SU61

The Bakers Arms ⊛

PICK OF THE PUBS

High St SO32 3PA ☎ 01489 877533
e-mail: enquiries@thebakersarmsdroxford.com
dir: *10m E of Winchester on A32 between Fareham & Alton. 7m SW of Petersfield. 10m inland from Portsmouth*

Local produce used to create award-winning food

With an enviable position in the pretty Meon Valley in a lovely corner of rural Hampshire, this unpretentious, white-painted pub and restaurant is a perfect place to refuel. It has been opened up inside but still oozes country charm and character, the staff are friendly, and the locals clearly love the place. Over the big log fire a blackboard menu lists the simple, well cooked and locally sourced food, while in the bar customers make short work of its barrels of Wallops Wood from the village's own Bowman Brewery. They can snack, too, on home-made Cornish pasties, pickled eggs and onions, and hot filled baguettes. But the kitchen cooks to AA Rosette standard, so make the most of your visit if you're just passing through (much of the produce is grown or shot by the owner): roasted pigeon breast salad with pancetta and walnut dressing; fillet of gurnard with saffron and lemon risotto; and chocolate and fudge brownie with butterscotch ice cream will make you wish every village had a pub like this.

Open 11.45-3 6-11 (Sun 12-3) Closed: Sun eve & Mon **Bar Meals** L served Tue-Sun 12-2 D served Tue-Sat 7-9 **Restaurant** L served Tue-Sun 12-2 D served Tue-Sat 7-9 ⊕ FREE HOUSE ◀ Bowman Swift One, Wallops Wood ♡ Westons Stowford Press. ♟ 11
Facilities Non-diners area ♣ (Bar Restaurant Garden) ♦♦ Children's portions Garden ⊟ Parking Wi-fi

DUMMER
Map 5 SU54

The Queen Inn

Down St RG25 2AD ☎ 01256 397367
e-mail: richardmoore49@btinternet.com
dir: *From M3 junct 7 follow Dummer signs*

Country inn just off the M3

You can dine by candlelight in the restaurant at this low-beamed, 16th-century inn with a huge open log fire. The main menu offers a wide choice: steaks and burgers; fillet of beef medallions; teriyaki salmon; curry of the day; and warm bacon, mushroom and asparagus salad. Or at lunchtime there are savouries like Welsh rarebit and flame-grilled chicken ciabatta. Children are encouraged to have small adult portions, but have their own menu if all entreaties fail. There's a good real ale line-up, including Courage Best, London Pride and guests.

Open all wk 11-3 6-11 (Sun 12-3 7-10.30) **Bar Meals** L served all wk 12-2.30 D served Mon-Sat 6.30-9.30, Sun 7-9 **Restaurant** L served all wk 12-2.30 D served Mon-Sat 6.30-9.30, Sun 7-9 ⊕ ENTERPRISE INNS ◀ Courage Best, Fuller's London Pride, Morland Old Speckled Hen, Guest ales. **Facilities** Non-diners area ♦♦ Children's menu Children's portions Garden Parking Wi-fi

The Sun Inn

A30 Winchester Rd RG25 2DJ ☎ 01256 397234
e-mail: thesuninndummer@hotmail.co.uk
dir: *M3 junct 7, A30 (Winchester Rd) towards Basingstoke. Left onto A30 towards Winchester. Inn on right*

Well worth leaving the M3 for

Now in new hands, the Sun has stood for many years alongside the main coaching route from London to Exeter, today's A30. Passing traffic is not a problem since most West Country travellers now use the M3, accessible from nearby junction 7. Locally brewed Alton's Pride and Moondance from Triple fff take pole position in the bar, alongside Symonds cider, while in the restaurant the well conceived menu lists open-roasted chicken breast with pine nut and potato purée; pan-fried sea bream with roasted fennel and poached salsify; and classic home-made shepherd's pie. A lovely garden lies at the back.

Open all wk 12-11 **Bar Meals** L served all wk 12-3 D served Mon-Sat 6-9 Av main course £13.95 **Restaurant** L served all wk 12-3 D served Mon-Sat 6-9 Av 3 course à la carte fr £26.95 ⊕ FREE HOUSE ◀ Triple fff Alton's Pride & Moondance ♡ Symonds. ♟ 9
Facilities Non-diners area ♣ (Bar Garden) ♦♦ Children's menu Children's portions Play area Garden ⊟ Parking Wi-fi

DUNBRIDGE
Map 5 SU32

The Mill Arms ★★★★ INN

Barley Hill SO51 0LF ☎ 01794 340401
e-mail: millarms@btconnect.com
dir: *From Romsey take A3057 signed Stockbridge & Winchester. Left onto B3084 through Awbridge to Dunbridge. Pub on left before rail crossing*

Smart country pub offering good food not far from the River Test

This attractive 18th-century inn is situated in the heart of the Test Valley and close to the River Test, one of the finest chalk streams in the world. Not surprisingly, the pub is popular with fly fishermen the world over. A traditional country inn with wood and stone floors, oak beams and open fires, the menus combine old favourites and contemporary dishes. An excellent grill menu showcases local produce including buffalo and rare-breed pork, and wood-fired pizzas are available to eat in or takeaway. There's also a function room, a skittle alley and large landscaped gardens.

Open 12-2.30 6-11 (Sat 12-11 Sun 12-5) Closed: 25 Dec, Sun eve & Mon lunch & dinner **Bar Meals** L served Tue-Fri 12-2.30, Sat 12-9.30, Sun 12-4 D served Tue-Thu 6-9, Fri-Sat 6-9.30 Av main course £10 **Restaurant** L served Tue-Fri 12-2.30, Sat 12-9.30, Sun 12-4 D served Tue-Thu 6-9, Fri-Sat 6-9.30 Av 3 course à la carte fr £20 ⊕ ENTERPRISE INNS ◀ Flack Manor Flack's Double Drop, Sharp's Doom Bar, Ringwood ♡ Addlestones. ♟ 10
Facilities Non-diners area ♣ (Bar Garden) ♦♦ Children's menu Children's portions Garden ⊟ Beer festival Parking Wi-fi (notice required) **Rooms** 6

EAST BOLDRE
Map 5 SU30

Turfcutters Arms

Main Rd SO42 7WL ☎ 01590 612331
e-mail: enquiries.turfcutters@gmail.com
dir: *From Beaulieu take B3055 towards Brockenhurst. Left at Hatchet Pond onto B3054 towards Lymington, turn left, follow signs for East Boldre. Pub approx 0.5m*

Off the beaten track and offering good value food

Five miles south of Beaulieu, this New Forest pub, easily recognised by its white picket fence, attracts cyclists, ramblers, dog-walkers and locals all year round. In winter the open fires warm the cockles, while the lovely garden comes into its own in summer. Good beer including Ringwood and draught ciders such as Thatchers complement a menu of unpretentious pub grub including baguettes, jacket potatoes and main meals such as fish pie; chilli con carne; pie of the day and ham, eggs and chips. Children have their own menu, and canine treats are handed out at the bar. Time a visit for the annual beer festival.

Open all day all wk **Bar Meals** L served all wk 12-3 D served all wk 6-9 **Restaurant** L served all wk 12-3 D served all wk 6-9 ⊕ ENTERPRISE INNS ◀ Ringwood Best Bitter, Fortyniner, Boondoggle ♡ Thatchers Gold.
Facilities Non-diners area ♣ (Bar Restaurant Garden) ♦♦ Children's menu Children's portions Play area Garden ⊟ Beer festival Parking Wi-fi (notice required)

EAST END
Map 5 SZ39

The East End Arms

PICK OF THE PUBS

Main Rd SO41 5SY ☎ 01590 626223
e-mail: manager@eastendarms.co.uk
dir: *From Lymington towards Beaulieu (past Isle of Wight ferry), 3m to East End*

Striking all the right notes

Reached along lanes threading through the southern edge of the New Forest National Park, with The Solent just a short stroll south and the delightful Bucklers Hard nearby, the East End Arms is a reliable outlet for beers from Hampshire breweries such as Andwell or Ringwood drawn by gravity straight from the cask. It's a happy mix of community village inn and restaurant, which where possible draws on local produce and offers a daily-changing menu. A tempting starter can be seared scallops with New Forest artichoke purée and a poached quail's egg; leaving room perhaps for tagliatelle of New Forest wild mushrooms with baby spinach and truffle oil; local sausage, mash and gravy or steamed rope-grown mussels. The bright and airy restaurant has some photos of musicians on the walls, reflecting the pub's ownership by Dire Straits' bass player John Illsley; the inviting Foresters Bar is pleasingly old-fashioned, with flagstoned floors, roaring fire and village craic.

Open all wk 11.30-3 6-11 (Fri-Sun 11.30-11) **Bar Meals** L served Mon-Sat 12-2.30 **Restaurant** L served all wk

Save on hotels. Book at theAA.com/hotel

HAMPSHIRE 211 ENGLAND

12-2.30 D served Mon-Sat 7-9.30 ⊕ FREE HOUSE
◄ Ringwood Best Bitter & Fortyniner, Andwell's,
Jennings, Cottage Ŏ Thatchers & Katy.
Facilities Non-diners area ❀ (Bar Garden) ⦁ Children's
portions Garden ⊨ Parking Wi-fi

EAST MEON
Map 5 SU62

Ye Olde George Inn

Church St GU32 1NH ☎ 01730 823481
e-mail: yeoldegeorge@live.co.uk
dir: S of A272 (Winchester/Petersfield). 1.5m from
Petersfield turn left opposite church

Medieval inn set in a lovely village

In the beautiful countryside of the Meon Valley, the
setting for this delightful 15th-century coaching inn is
hard to beat. The village boasts a magnificent Norman
church where tapestry designs similar to Bayeux can be
found. If you want heavy beams, inglenook fireplaces and
wooden floors, look no further – they're all here, creating
an ideal atmosphere for a choice of Hall & Woodhouse
ales and Westons cider. The monthly changing menus
reflect the seasons, with lighter dishes in the summer
and hearty, warming food in the winter – such as roast
rump of lamb Wellington with sweet potato gratin, pea
purée and rosemary jus. There are tables outside in the
pretty patio garden.

Open all wk 11-3 6-11 (Sun 11-10) Closed: 25 Dec **Bar
Meals** L served Mon-Sat 12-2.30, Sun 12-3 D served
Mon-Sat 6.30-9.30, Sun 6.30-9 Av main course £12.95
Restaurant L served Mon-Sat 12-2.30, Sun 12-3 D served
Mon-Sat 6.30-9.30, Sun 6.30-9 Fixed menu price fr
£16.50 ⊕ HALL & WOODHOUSE ◄ Badger First Gold, K&B
Sussex, Tanglefoot Ŏ Westons Stowford Press. ⬥ 9
Facilities Non-diners area ❀ (Bar Garden) ⦁ Children's
menu Children's portions Garden ⊨ Parking Wi-fi ▬

EASTON
Map 5 SU53

The Chestnut Horse

SO21 1EG ☎ 01962 779257
e-mail: info@thechestnuthorse.com
dir: M3 junct 9, A33 towards Basingstoke, then B3047.
2nd right, 1st left

Hidden away in an idyllic Itchen Valley village

This gem of a 16th-century pub has an abundance of
traditional English character and atmosphere; old
tankards hang from the low-beamed ceilings in the two
bar areas, and a large open fire is the central focus
through the winter months. Award-winning beers, such as
Pickled Partridge and Chestnut Horse Special can be
enjoyed in the bar or the garden. Typical à la carte choices
are Hampshire venison casserole with sage and onion
cobbler; roasted butternut loaf with sweet crispy kale; and
coq au vin. You can walk off any excesses on one of the
enjoyable countryside walks that start at the front door.

Open all wk 12-3.30 5.30-11 (Fri-Sat 12-11.30 Sun
12-10.30) ⊕ HALL & WOODHOUSE ◄ Badger First Gold &
Pickled Partridge, Chestnut Horse Special Ŏ Westons
Stowford Press. **Facilities** ❀ (Bar Garden) ⦁ Children's
portions Garden Parking Wi-fi

EAST STRATTON
Map 5 SU54

Northbrook Arms

SO21 3DU ☎ 01962 774150
e-mail: northbrookarms@hotmail.com
dir: Follow brown pub sign from A33, 4m S of junct with
A303

Social centre of a small but perfectly formed village

Memo to Hollywood: if you need an English pub location,
look no further. Bang opposite the village green and
architecturally perfect, it endears itself to local bar-
proppers with six real ales and four ciders, a May beer
festival, and a September cider celebration. The compact
menu gets the thumbs up too, with dishes such as
blackened mackerel fillet with beetroot pickle and roasted
root vegetables; and spicy pork belly strips with cider and
sage jus and black pudding mash. The bar menu offers
pub classics and sandwiches. Newish landlord Jon
Coward plans a much-needed village shop in his old
wood store.

Open all day all wk **Bar Meals** L served all wk 11.30-2
D served all wk 5-9.30 Av main course £10 **Restaurant** L
served all wk 11.30-2 D served all wk 5-9.30 Fixed menu
price fr £10 ⊕ FREE HOUSE ◄ Otter, Bowman Swift One,
Flower Pots Cheriton Pots, Flack Manor Flack's Double
Drop, Amber Sharp's Cornish Coaster Ŏ Aspall, Westons
Old Rosie, Thatchers, Mr Whiteheads. ⬥ 10
Facilities Non-diners area ❀ (All areas) ⦁ Children's
portions Play area Garden Outside area ⊨ Beer festival
Cider festival Parking Wi-fi ▬ (notice required)

EVERSLEY
Map 5 SU76

The Golden Pot

PICK OF THE PUBS

See Pick of the Pubs on page 212

EXTON
Map 5 SU62

The Shoe Inn

Shoe Ln SO32 3NT ☎ 01489 877526
e-mail: theshoeexton@googlemail.com
dir: Exton on A32 between Fareham & Alton

Good food with many ingredients from the pub's own garden

On warmer days, you can enjoy views of Old Winchester
Hill from the garden of this popular pub in the heart of
the Meon Valley. Food is key – local ingredients include
those from its ever-expanding herb and organic vegetable
garden. A typical selection of dishes could include local
Southdown lamb's liver, bacon, onion gravy and mashed
potato; slow-cooked Oxford Sandy belly pork with Savoy
cabbage and cider jus. The bar offers well-kept Wadworth
ales, weekly changing guest ales, and over a dozen wines
served by the glass. There is a beer festival each year.

Open all wk 11-3 6-11 (Sat-Sun all day) Closed: 25 Dec
Bar Meals L served all wk 12-2.15 **Restaurant** L served
all wk 12-2.15 D served all wk 6-9 ⊕ WADWORTH ◄ 6X,
Henry's Original IPA, The Bishop's Tipple, Guest ales
Ŏ Westons Stowford Press. ⬥ 13 **Facilities** ❀ (Bar
Restaurant Garden) ⦁ Children's menu Children's
portions Garden ⊨ Beer festival Parking

FORDINGBRIDGE
Map 5 SU11

The Augustus John ★★ INN

116 Station Rd SP6 1DG ☎ 01425 652098
e-mail: enquiries@augustusjohnfordingbridge.co.uk
dir: 12m S of Salisbury on A338 towards Ringwood

Good stop off close to the New Forest

After 14 years as a member of staff, Lorraine Smallwood
took over this former station pub some five years ago. The
Welsh post-impressionist painter Augustus John was a
regular here, although today it's the Ringwood real ales
and food that continues to attract locals and visitors. A
typical menu might include lamb braised with mint; pan-
fried pork fillet flamed with brandy and apricots; the
chef's casserole of the day; or grilled salmon fillet with
lemon and saffron sauce. Time a visit for the May Bank
Holiday beer festival.

Open all wk 11.30-3 6.30-11.30 (Sun 12-3 7-11.30) **Bar
Meals** L served all wk 12-2.30 D served Mon-Sat 6.30-9,
Sun 7-9 (booking advised Fri-Sun) **Restaurant** L served
all wk 12-2.30 D served Mon-Sat 6.30-9, Sun 7-9
(booking advised Fri-Sun) ⊕ MARSTON'S ◄ Ringwood
Best Bitter & Fortyniner, Guest ale Ŏ Thatchers Gold.
Facilities Non-diners area ❀ (Bar Garden) ⦁ Children's
menu Children's portions Garden ⊨ Beer festival Parking
Wi-fi ▬ (notice required) **Rooms** 4

PICK OF THE PUBS

The Golden Pot

EVERSLEY Map 5 SU76

Reading Rd RG27 0NB
☎ 0118 973 2104
e-mail: jcalder@golden-pot.co.uk
web: www.golden-pot.co.uk
dir: *Between Reading & Camberley on B3272 approx 0.25m from Eversley cricket ground*

Innovative home prepared food incorporating local produce

This well-established free house dates back to the 1700s and is set in the heart of the village but benefits from being within easy reach of the M3 and M4. The pub offers a fine selection of real ales from such brewers as Upham, Hammerpot and Church End; with nine wines are sold by the glass, from an extensive and carefully sourced list of bottles arranged by country. A double-sided warming fire connects the bar and restaurant, while outside the Snug and Vineyard, surrounded by colourful tubs and hanging baskets, are just the ticket for summer relaxation. Monday evenings see live music performed for appreciative audiences, while they tuck into home-cooked food in addition to a unique and innovative rösti menu. At lunchtime, a range of baguettes and a separate children's menu runs alongside the main menu, which might kick off with Barkham blue, pear and walnut tart; or seared Shetland scallops and tiger prawns with pea purée, crispy bacon and black pudding. Options for main course might include venison and smoked bacon meatballs with curly kale and parsnip mash and red onion gravy; or roast corn-fed chicken breast with sage and onion pudding, confit shallots, sautéed mushrooms, spinach and sherry sauce, with pumpkin and mascarpone cannelloni being one of the meat-free choices. The specials board might also include a home-made pie of the day. To finish, choose perhaps spiced apple tarte Tatin with salted caramel dairy ice cream, or walnut and date steamed suet pudding with toffee sauce and custard. Dogs are welcome in the bar area and the garden.

Open 11.30-3 5.30-10.30 Closed: 25-26 & 31 Dec, 1 Jan, Sun eve

Bar Meals L served all wk 12-2 D served Mon-Sat 6-9 **Restaurant** L served all wk 12-2 D served Mon-Sat 6-9 FREE HOUSE Andwell, Bowman, Ascot, Rebellion, Windsor & Eton, Upham Ale, Church End, Dorset Piddle, Longdog Ales, Hammerpot Ales Rekorderlig. 9 **Facilities** Non-diners area (Bar Garden) Children's menu Children's portions Garden Parking Wi-fi

Save on hotels. Book at **theAA.com/hotel**

HAMPSHIRE 213 **ENGLAND**

HAMBLE-LE-RICE	Map 5 SU40

The Bugle ◉

PICK OF THE PUBS

High St SO31 4HA ☎ 023 8045 3000
e-mail: manager@buglehamble.co.uk
dir: *M27 junct 8, follow signs to Hamble. In village centre turn right at mini rdbt into one-way cobbled street, pub at end*

Contemporary food in lovingly-restored riverside inn

Matthew Boyle, owner of The White Star Tavern in Southampton (see entry) rescued this famous waterside pub from proposed demolition in 2005 and lovingly refurbished it using traditional methods and materials. Old features include exposed beams and brickwork, natural flagstone floors and the wonderful oak bar, plus there's a large heated terrace with lovely views over the River Hamble - perfect for outdoor dining. A pint of locally-brewed ale makes an ideal partner for one of the deli boards (great for sharing), a roast beef, horseradish crème fraîche and rocket sandwich, or a pub classic like fish pie with buttered greens. From the dining room menu, go for ham hock terrine with home-made piccalilli to start, then order the whole Torbay sole with garlic sauté potatoes and bisque vièrge, and round off with a seasonal fruit crumble with thick custard. For private dining, there's the Captain's Table upstairs.

Open all day all wk Mon-Thu 11-11 (Fri-Sat 11-mdnt Sun 12-10.30) **Bar Meals** L served Mon-Thu 12-2.30, Fri 12-3, Sat 12-4, Sun 12-9 D served Mon-Thu 6-9.30, Fri-Sat 6-10, Sun 12-9 **Restaurant** L served Mon-Thu 12-2.30, Fri 12-3, Sat 12-4, Sun 12-9 D served Mon-Thu 6-9.30, Fri-Sat 6-10, Sun 12-9 ⊕ FREE HOUSE ◀ Itchen Valley, Rotating local ales. ⬤ 10 **Facilities** Non-diners area ◗◖ Children's portions Outside area ⋒ Wi-fi ▭

HANNINGTON	Map 5 SU55

The Vine at Hannington

PICK OF THE PUBS

RG26 5TX ☎ 01635 298525
e-mail: info@thevineathannington.co.uk
dir: *Hannington signed from A339 between Basingstoke & Newbury*

A favourite with walkers and cyclists

Given the nature of North Hampshire's rolling chalk downland, you can expect rambling and cycling devotees to patronise this gabled Victorian inn. It used to be the Wellington Arms because it stands on what was once the Iron Duke's estate, but was renamed in 1960 after the Vine & Craven Hunt, whose kennels are nearby. A wood-burning stove heats the spacious, traditionally furnished bar areas and conservatory, where rural artefacts pop up here and there. Real ales coming from Sharp's and guest ales. Seasonal menus and daily specials feature marinated lamb and vegetable kebab, saffron rice and tomato and chilli sauce; medallions of beef with red wine, tarragon and mushroom sauce; and spinach and ricotta

cannelloni. Many of the herbs, salads and vegetables used in the kitchen are grown in the large garden, where there's also a children's play area.

Open 12-3 6-11 (Sat-Sun all day) Closed: 25 Dec, Mon **Bar Meals** L served Tue-Sat 12-2, Sun 12-7 D served Tue-Sat 6-9 **Restaurant** L served Tue-Sat 12-2, Sun 12-7 D served Tue-Sat 6-9 ⊕ PUNCH TAVERNS ◀ Sharp's Doom Bar, Guest ales ⬤ Aspall. ⬤ 11 **Facilities** Non-diners area ❀ (Bar Restaurant Garden) ◗◖ Children's menu Children's portions Play area Family room Garden ⋒ Beer festival Parking Wi-fi ▭ (notice required)

HARTLEY WINTNEY	Map 5 SU75

The Cricketers **NEW**

The Green RG27 8QB ☎ 01252 842166
e-mail: info@thecricketers-hartleywintney.co.uk
dir: *M3 junct 4A, A327 signed to Reading & Blackwater. Left onto A30 signed Hartley Wintney*

One for all, especially cricket fans

You don't have to like cricket to enjoy this handsome village pub, but if you do, you'll know that the pitch over the road has been continually played on longer than any other in the world. Menus reveal a strong county affinity, explicitly the starters of smoked fillet of Hampshire trout; and glazed goats' cheese with candied figs and Secretts Farm red chicory. Loyalty continues with Meon Valley sirloin steak; and locally-foraged mushrooms on toast, while from neighbouring Isle of Wight comes herb-crusted lamb; and from Berkshire, free-range pork belly, although pan-fried North Atlantic sea bass inevitably extends the catchment area.

Open all day all wk **Bar Meals** L served all wk 12-3 D served all wk 6-10 Av main course £15 **Restaurant** L served all wk 12-3 D served all wk 6-10 Av 3 course à la carte fr £25 ⊕ THE NEW PUB COMPANY ◀ Theakston Old Peculier, Courage Best Bitter, Thwaites Wainwright ⬤ Symonds. ⬤ 18 **Facilities** Non-diners area ❀ (Bar Garden) ◗◖ Children's portions Garden ⋒ Parking Wi-fi

HAVANT	Map 5 SU70

The Royal Oak

19 Langstone High St, Langstone PO9 1RY
☎ 023 9248 3125
e-mail: 7955@greeneking.co.uk
dir: *Telephone for directions*

Rustic waterside pub serving classic fare

Smack on the water's edge and originally a row of cottages used in conjunction with the adjacent old mill, this historic 16th-century pub enjoys stunning views across Langstone Harbour. An individual rustic charm characterises the unspoilt interior, with flagstone floors, exposed beams and winter fires contrasting with the waterfront benches (arrive early!) and secluded rear garden for alfresco summer drinking. Extensive menus list traditional pub dishes, the choice ranging from rump steak ciabatta and battered haddock and chips to beef and red wine casserole and dark chocolate and walnut brownie. Wash down with a pint of Abbot Ale.

Open all day all wk 11-11 **Bar Meals** L served all wk D served all wk food served all day **Restaurant** L served all wk D served all wk food served all day ⊕ GREENE KING ◀ IPA, Ruddles County & Best Abbot Ale, Morland Old Speckled Hen ⬤ Aspall. ⬤ 16 **Facilities** Non-diners area ◗◖ Children's menu Children's portions Family room Garden ⋒ Wi-fi

HAWKLEY	Map 5 SU72

The Hawkley Inn

Pococks Ln GU33 6NE ☎ 01730 827205
e-mail: info@hawkleyinn.co.uk
dir: *From A3 (Liss rdbt) towards Liss on B3006. Right at Spread Eagle, in 2.5m left into Pococks Ln*

Quirky interior but seriously good food

The inn sign saying 'Free Hoose' owes something to the moose head hanging over one of the fires, and indeed the pub decor is quite quirky. With ten beer engine, the Hawkley is well known by real ale enthusiasts and cider lovers. Menus change daily, so you may be lucky to find Asain spiced fishcakes; Stilton mushroom pot; rustic cassoulet; and a 'Firkin', 'Chickin' or Mirkin burger. Sandwiches, toasties and ploughman's too.

Open all wk Mon-Fri 12-3 5.30-11 (Sat-Sun all day) ⊕ FREE HOUSE/WEYBOURNE INNS ◀ 7 Constantly changing ales, Guest ales ⬤ Mr Whitehead's, Westons Bounds. **Facilities** ❀ (Bar Restaurant Garden) ◗◖ Children's portions Garden Wi-fi

HERRIARD — Map 5 SU64

The Fur & Feathers

Herriard Rd RG25 2PN ☎ 01256 384170
e-mail: bookings@thefurandfeathers.co.uk
web: www.thefurandfeathers.co.uk
dir: *From Basingstoke take A339 towards Alton. After Herriard follow pub signs. Turn left to pub*

Bag a table in the garden when the weather allows

Its high-ceilinged Victorian proportions translate into light and airy accommodation for drinkers and diners, and comfort too, with log-burning fireplaces at each end of the bar. Purpose-built 120 years ago for local farm workers, The Fur & Feathers has to this day obligations in the upkeep of the church roof. In the bar, a trio of ales are rotated, and menus of modern British cooking are perused. Typical dishes are Hampshire pork loin steaks with apple, celery and sultana compôte; and Indonesian curry made with local venison. A large garden hosts entertainment, and is home to chickens laying eggs for the pub's kitchen.

Open Tue-Thu 12-3 6-11 (Fri-Sat 12-11 Sun 12-6) Closed: 1wk end of Dec, Sun eve & Mon **Bar Meals** Av main course £14 **Restaurant** L served Tue-Sat 12-2.30, Sun 12-3 D served Tue-Sat 6.30-9 ⊕ FREE HOUSE ◼ Local ales, rotating Flack Manor Flack's Double Drop, Hogs Back TEA, Sharp's Doom Bar, Itchen Valley Fagins ☼ Mr Whitehead's. ♚ 11 **Facilities** Non-diners area ♦♦ Children's menu Children's portions Garden ⊓ Parking Wi-fi ▰ (notice required)

See advert on opposite page

HOLYBOURNE — Map 5 SU74

The White Hart Hotel

139 London Rd GU34 4EY ☎ 01420 87654
dir: *From M3 junct 5 follow Alton signs (A339). In Alton take A31 towards Farnham. Follow Holybourne signs*

Change of ownership at this village pub

The village of Holybourne is steeped in history: an old Roman fort lies under the cricket field, and the village also stands on the Pilgrims' Way. Rebuilt in the 1920s on the site of the original inn, The White Hart was refurbished to create a comfortable, welcoming setting for a well-kept pint of Greene King IPA or a hearty meal.

Open all day all wk **Bar Meals** L served all wk 12-3, Sun 12-5 D served Mon-Sat 5-10 Av main course £10 **Restaurant** L served all wk 12-3, Sun 12-5 D served Mon-Sat 5-10 Av 3 course à la carte fr £22 ⊕ GREENE KING ◼ IPA, Morland Old Speckled Hen, 3 Guest ales ☼ Holybourne Cider. ♚ 10 **Facilities** Non-diners area ♣ (Bar Garden) ♦♦ Children's menu Children's portions Play area Garden ⊓ Parking Wi-fi ▰ (notice required)

HOOK — Map 5 SU75

Crooked Billet

London Rd RG27 9EH ☎ 01256 762118
e-mail: richardbarwise@aol.com
web: www.thecrookedbillethook.co.uk
dir: *M3 junct 5, B3349 signed Hook. At 3rd rdbt right onto A30 towards London, pub on left 0.5m*

Guest ales and riverside garden

At first sight this family- and dog-friendly free house looks quite old; in fact it dates from only 1935, although a hostelry has been here since the 1600s. Richard and Sally Saunders have owned it for more than 25 years, so keeping their customers happy is second nature. Beer drinkers know they will always be greeted by new guest ales, with more at the August Bank Holiday beer festival. Food includes favourites like home-made chilli; chicken curry; gammon steak with egg or pineapple; various salads; and fresh fish specials. The lovely riverside garden has a children's play area.

Open all wk Mon-Fri 11.30-3 6-12 (Sat 11.30am-mdnt Sun 12-10) **Bar Meals** L served Mon-Sat 12-2.30, Sun 12-8 D served Mon-Fri 6.30-9.30, Sat 6.30-10 ⊕ FREE HOUSE ◼ Courage Best Bitter, Sharp's Doom Bar, Andwell, Dark Star, Guest ales ☼ Thatchers Green Goblin. **Facilities** Non-diners area ♣ (Bar Garden) ♦♦ Children's menu Children's portions Play area Garden ⊓ Beer festival Parking Wi-fi ▰ (notice required)

The Hogget Country Pub & Eating House

London Rd, Hook Common RG27 9JJ ☎ 01256 763009
e-mail: home@hogget.co.uk
dir: *M3 junct 5, A30, 0.5m, between Hook & Basingstoke*

Value for money just off the M3

Having passed the five-year milestone, the Hogget's reputation for good food and service continues to grow. Ringwood Best is the session beer, while the stronger candidates are either Ringwood 49er, Marston's Pedigree or Wychwood Hobgoblin. Carefully prepared English favourites include braised ox cheek; fillet of sea bass; gourmet burgers; and ham, egg and chips, but you'll also find chorizo and chicken breast with grilled mozzarella; Asian noodles with spring onion, carrots and cabbage; and fried eggs with warm tortilla and slow-cooked tomato sauce chilli, aka huevos rancheros. Thursday and Friday steak nights in winter become fish nights in summer.

Open all wk 12-3 5.30-11 (Sat 12-11 Sun 12-10.30) Closed: 25-26 Dec **Bar Meals** L served all wk 12-2.30 D served all wk 5.30-9 Av main course £12 **Restaurant** L served all wk 12-2.30 D served all wk 5.30-9 Av 3 course à la carte fr £23 ⊕ MARSTON'S ◼ Ringwood Best Bitter, Wychwood Hobgoblin, Guest ales ☼ Thatchers Gold. ♚ 12 **Facilities** Non-diners area ♣ (Bar Outside area) ♦♦ Children's menu Children's portions Outside area ⊓ Parking Wi-fi

HURSLEY — Map 5 SU42

The Dolphin Inn

SO21 2JY ☎ 01962 775209
dir: *Telephone for directions*

16th-century coaching inn close to South Downs National Park

Like most of the village, this old coaching inn with magnificent chimneys once belonged to the Hursley Estate, which is now owned by IBM. It was built between 1540 and 1560, reputedly using timbers from a Tudor warship called HMS *Dolphin* (today's less glamorous 'ship' is a shore establishment in Gosport). On tap in the beamed bars are Ringwood Best, Hop Back Summer Lightning, George Gale & Co HSB and Green Goblin oak-aged cider. In addition to sandwiches, baguettes and jacket potatoes, favourites include Hursley-made faggots; lamb's liver and bacon; scampi and chips; and macaroni cheese.

Open all day all wk Mon-Sat 11-11 (Sun 12-10.30) **Bar Meals** L served Mon-Sat 12-2.30, Sun 12-8.30 D served Mon-Thu 6-9, Fri-Sat 6.30-9.30, Sun 12-8.30 ⊕ ENTERPRISE INNS ◼ Hop Back Summer Lightning, George Gale & Co HSB, Ringwood Best Bitter ☼ Thatchers & Green Goblin. ♚ 12 **Facilities** Non-diners area ♣ (Bar Garden) ♦♦ Children's menu Children's portions Play area Family room Garden ⊓ Parking ▰ (notice required)

The Fur & Feathers

Herriard, Basingstoke RG25 2PN • Tel: 01256 384170

Website: www.thefurandfeathers.co.uk • **Email:** bookings@thefurandfeathers.co.uk

Formally The New Inn, *The Fur and Feathers* has seen many changes in its rich past. Not least the last three years having seen the pub revert from brewery ownership to a family run "Free House" and now recognised as a destination eatery of the highest order.

Fran and her small team of chefs cook up a cornucopia of delightful meals utilising Hampshire Beef, Lamb and pork along with local, from the village, game, vegetables and world renowned cheese! Yes cheese that ranks in the top fifty in the world after this years super-gold at the world cheese awards and made right here in Herriard.

The *Fur and Feathers* maintains its "pub" status and is defiantly a pub that serves great food rather than a restaurant that serves beer. The beer also has a local theme with three out of the four hand pumps usually offering Hampshire brewed beer. The wine list also boasts it's local credentials with a fantastic fiz by the glass or bottle from Danebury Vineyards along with their two still white wines.

Tall Victorian ceilings with huge sash windows allow the light to flood in producing a light and airy atmosphere by day and wood-fired log burners produce a warm and cosy feel by night. Fitted out with wooden floors, stripped pine tables and many pictures of the village past adds to the comfortable homely atmosphere.

Only a short ride, roughly 15 minutes, from Basingstoke or Alton *The Fur and Feathers* finds itself close to many tourist attractions and major population centres but far enough away to place you firmly in the north Hampshire countryside, surrounded by working farms producing Milk, Meat and Grain.

HURSLEY continued

The Kings Head

Main Rd SO21 2JW ☎ **01962 775208**
e-mail: info@kingsheadhursley.co.uk
dir: *On A3090 between Winchester & Romsey*

A winning mix of modernity and tradition

Close to historic Winchester and with pleasant walks nearby, The Kings Head was bought, a few years ago, by five local farming families who extensively refurbished it with decor and furniture to reflect its Georgian origins. The 'Taste of Hampshire Menu', available Monday to Friday lunchtime in addition to sandwiches and pub classics, offers pan-fried fillet of red mullet with tabouleh salad and saffron aïoli to start; followed by braised daube of Hampshire beef, choucroute cabbage and creamed piper potatoes; and bread-and-butter pudding with vanilla custard. The dinner menu includes Shetland mussels, confit belly of pork, and curried monkfish. Two guest ales change on a weekly basis. Beer festivals are held on August Bank Holiday and in December.

Open all day all wk 7.30am-11pm **Bar Meals** L served Mon-Sat 12-2, Sun 12-3 D served all wk 6-9 Av main course £13.50 **Restaurant** L served Mon-Sat 12-2, Sun 12-3 D served Sun-Thu 6-9, Fri-Sat 6-9.30 Fixed menu price fr £12.50 Av 3 course à la carte fr £12.50 ⊕ FREE HOUSE ◀ Bowman Ales Wallops Wood, Sharp's Doom Bar, Ringwood, 2 Guest ales ♉ Thatchers Gold. ♟ 10 **Facilities** Non-diners area ✿ (Bar Garden) ♦ Children's menu Children's portions Garden ✄ Beer festival Parking Wi-fi ➡ (notice required)

IBSLEY Map 5 SU10

Old Beams Inn

Salisbury Rd BH24 3PP ☎ **01425 473387**
e-mail: oldbeams@alcatraz.co.uk
dir: *On A338 between Ringwood & Salisbury*

Thatched pub on the edge of the New Forest

Old Beams, now under new ownership, is a beautiful centuries-old thatched and timber-framed village inn located south of Fordingbridge, with views of lovely countryside. It has a beer garden with a decked area and patio, and a cosy old-world interior. The wide ranging menu offers something for everyone from fish dishes, pasta, roasts, grills, salads to sandwiches, ploughman's and Welsh rarebits.

Open all wk 11am-11.30pm **Bar Meals** food served all day **Restaurant** food served all day ⊕ ALCATRAZ ◀ Morland Old Speckled Hen. ♟ 10 **Facilities** Non-diners area ♦ Children's menu Garden ✄ Parking Wi-fi ➡ (notice required)

LEE-ON-THE-SOLENT Map 5 SU50

The Bun Penny

36 Manor Way PO13 9JH ☎ **023 9255 0214**
e-mail: bar@bunpenny.co.uk
web: www.bunpenny.co.uk
dir: *From Fareham take B3385 to Lee-on-the-Solent. Pub 300yds before High St*

Classic country free house a short walk from the waterfront

A short walk from the waterfront, this former farmhouse occupies a prominent position on the road into Lee-on-the-Solent. Every inch a classic country free house, it has a large patio at the front and an extensive back garden that's ideal for summer relaxation, while real fires and cosy corners are welcome in winter. Otter beer is sold direct from the cask, backed by hand-pulls including ales from the local Oakleaf Brewery. A typical meal might be paprika-crusted calamari with garlic mayonnaise and sweet chilli dip followed by fillet of pork Wellington, roasted root vegetables with a light scrumpy sauce.

Open all day all wk 11-11 (Fri-Sat 11am-mdnt Sun 12-10.30) **Bar Meals** L served Mon-Sat 12-2.30, Sun 12-9 D served Mon-Sat 6-9, Sun 12-9 Av main course £9.95 **Restaurant** L served Mon-Sat 12-2.30, Sun 12-7 D served Mon-Sat 6-9, Sun 12-7 ⊕ FREE HOUSE ◀ Otter Bitter, Oakleaf Hole Hearted, Guest ales ♉ Westons. ♟ 13 **Facilities** Non-diners area ✿ (Bar Garden) ♦ Children's menu Children's portions Garden ✄ Parking Wi-fi ➡ (notice required)

LINWOOD Map 5 SU10

The High Corner Inn

BH24 3QY ☎ **01425 473973**
e-mail: highcorner@wadworth.co.uk
dir: *From A338 (Ringwood to Salisbury road) follow brown tourist signs into forest. Pass Red Shoot Inn, 1m, down gravel track at Green High Corner Inn*

Modernised, family-friendly New Forest inn

Down a gravel track a mile from the village of Linwood, this rambling, early 18th-century inn began life as a farm and is set in seven beautiful acres of woodland. A quiet hideaway in winter, mobbed in summer, it is popular with families with its numerous bar-free rooms, flower-filled terrace, large forest garden, an outdoor adventure playground and miles of surrounding forest and heathland walks and cycle trails. The beamed bars, replete with the full range of Wadworth ales on tap, are very agreeable settings for sampling an extensive range

of traditional home-cooked meals, bar snacks, daily specials and a Sunday carvery.

Open all wk Mon-Fri 12-3 6-11 (Sat 11-11 Sun 11-10.30 all day summer & school holidays) ⊕ WADWORTH ◀ 6X, Horizon, Henry's Original IPA, Seasonal Ales ♉ Westons, Thatchers Gold. **Facilities** ✿ (Bar Restaurant Garden) ♦ Children's menu Play area Garden Parking

LISS Map 5 SU72

The Jolly Drover ★★★★ INN

London Rd, Hillbrow GU33 7QL ☎ **01730 893137**
e-mail: thejollydrover@googlemail.com
dir: *From station in Liss at mini rdbt right into Hill Brow Rd (B3006) signed Rogate, Rake, Hill Brow. At junct with B2071, pub opposite*

Just out of town at the top of the hill

This pub was built in 1844 by Mr Knowles - a drover - to offer cheer and sustenance to other drovers on the old London road. For 17 years it has been run by Anne and Barry Coe, who welcome all-comers with a large log fire, secluded garden, a covered and heated patio, a choice of real ales such as London Pride, and home-cooked food. The same menu is served in the bar and restaurant. Dishes include local award-winning sausages, gammon steaks, ham and mushroom pie, fried egg and chips, and beef lasagne. Gluten-free and vegetarian choices are also available.

Open all wk 10.30-2.30 5.30-11 (Sat 10.30-3 5.30-11 Sun 12-3) **Bar Meals** L served Mon-Sat 12-2.15, Sun 12-2.30 D served Mon-Sat 7-9.30 **Restaurant** L served Mon-Sat 12-2.15, Sun 12-2.30 D served Mon-Sat 7-9.30 ⊕ ENTERPRISE INNS/WHITBREAD ◀ Fuller's London Pride, Sharp's Doom Bar, Timothy Taylor Landlord. ♟ **Facilities** Non-diners area ♦ Children's portions Garden ✄ Parking Wi-fi ➡ (notice required) **Rooms** 6

LITTLETON Map 5 SU43

The Running Horse ★★★★ INN ◉◉

PICK OF THE PUBS

88 Main Rd SO22 6QS ☎ **01962 880218**
e-mail: runninghorseinn@btconnect.com
dir: *3m from Winchester, 1m from Three Maids Hill, signed from Stockbridge Rd*

Attractive food-led pub

Just three miles from Winchester, this smart whitewashed inn is especially popular with those who, despite the city's many good eating establishments, prefer the quieter surroundings of a village. The bar's limestone counter, stripped wooden floor, leather tub chairs and original fireplace draw those who enjoy real ales, such as Sharp's Doom Bar and local Upham Classic. The focus on good eating helped The Running Horse to gain two AA Rosettes for its contemporary cuisine, examples of which include pan-fried Brixham red mullet, home-made lobster tortellini and lobster bisque; eight-hour slow-braised ox cheek with Savoy cabbage, fondant potato, baby fennel and a red wine and anise jus; and classics like home-made prime beefburger and chips. There are roasts on Sundays. The rear garden and front patio are large and peaceful — perfect for both dining and drinking. Beautifully appointed overnight accommodation is in a courtyard behind the main building.

Open all day all wk **Bar Meals** L served Mon-Sat 12-2, Sun 12-4 D served Mon-Sat 6-9.30, Sun 6-8 **Restaurant** L served Mon-Sat 12-2, Sun 12-4 D served Mon-Sat 6-9.30, Sun 6-8 ⊕ FREE HOUSE ◀ Sharp's Doom Bar, Upham Classic ♂ Aspall. ♀ 14 **Facilities** Non-diners area ♦↑ Children's menu Children's portions Garden ⌐ Parking Wi-fi ▭ (notice required) **Rooms** 9

LOCKERLEY   Map 5 SU22

Kings Arms at Lockerley NEW

PICK OF THE PUBS

Romsey Rd SO51 0JF ☎ 01794 340332
e-mail: info@kingsarmsatlockerley.co.uk
dir: *From Romsey A3057 towards Stockbridge. Left onto B3064 signed Lockerley. Approx 4m to Lockerley*

Revitalised village pub with short seasonal menus

Lockerley's local was closed and in a sorry state in 2011, then ex Hotel du Vin chef and respected pub operator Lucy Townsend got hold of keys. With her boundless energy and enthusiasm she has injected new life into the 18th-century brick pub, which stands just off the village green and a short drive from Mottisfont Abbey and the glorious Test Valley. Expect a classy look to the bar and dining room, with warm heritage hues, big mirrors and local artwork on panelled walls, glowing candles on an eclectic mix of old dining tables, and rugs on stone-tiled floors. A civilised setting for sampling Chris Heather's modern British cooking, his short seasonal menu perhaps offering crispy ham hock, deep-fried duck egg and truffle mayonnaise, rib-eye steak, hand-cut chips, roasted tomato and garlic butter, and chocolate terrine. Candlelit pods in the garden offer a unique summer alfresco dining experience.

Open all day all wk **Bar Meals** L served all wk 12-2.30 summer (all wk 12.30-2.30 winter) D served all wk 6.30-9.30 summer (all wk 6.30-9 winter) Av main course £14 **Restaurant** L served all wk 12-2.30 D served all wk 6.30-9.30 summer (all wk 6.30-9 winter) Av 3 course à la carte fr £25 ⊕ PUNCH TAVERNS ◀ Ringwood Best Bitter, Sharp's Doom Bar, Guest ale ♂ Westons Stowford Press. ♀ 14 **Facilities** Non-diners area ♥ (Bar Garden) ♦↑ Children's portions Garden ⌐ Parking Wi-fi ▭ (notice required)

LONGPARISH   Map 5 SU44

The Plough Inn ◉◉

PICK OF THE PUBS

SP11 6PB ☎ 01264 720358
e-mail: eat@theploughinn.info
dir: *M3 junct 8, A303 towards Andover. In approx 6m take B3048 towards Longparish*

A popular stop for walkers, fishermen and cyclists

Dating to 1721, this charming inn was taken over and refurbished by chef James Durrant and his wife Louise in 2012. It stands close to the centre of Longparish, just a few minutes' drive from Andover and remains a traditional country pub but with a contemporary feel. The nearby River Test is one of southern England's finest chalk streams and the Test Way footpath runs through the inn's car park, so it is a perfect place to slake your thirst after a walk, cycle ride or spot of fishing. Expect ales from Timothy Taylor and Ringwood, and a food offering from James and his team that is simple, flavoursome and unpretentious. Quality seasonal produce is used to create dishes such as Cornish mussels with cider, bacon and crème fraîche; and braised pork belly with rhubarb purée, black pudding croquettes and potato and egg hash. The attractive garden is great for summer dining and for the children to play in.

Open Mon-Thu 12-3.30 6-11 (Fri-Sat all day Sun 12-6) Closed: Sun eve **Bar Meals** L served Mon-Sat 12-2.30, Sun 12-4.30 D served Mon-Sat 6-9.30 Av main course £15 **Restaurant** L served Mon-Sat 12-2.30, Sun 12-4.30 D served Mon-Sat 6-9.30 Fixed menu price fr £15 Av 3 course à la carte fr £30 ⊕ ENTERPRISE INNS ◀ Timothy Taylor Landlord, Ringwood Best Bitter, Hogs Back ♂ Aspall, Thatchers, Westons. ♀ 12 **Facilities** Non-diners area ♦↑ Children's menu Children's portions Garden Parking Wi-fi ▭ (notice required)

LOWER SWANWICK   Map 5 SU40

Old Ship

261 Bridge Rd SO31 7FN ☎ 01489 575646
e-mail: simonoldship@gmail.com
dir: *Telephone for directions*

By the marina on the busy River Hamble

A 17th-century inn of great character on the banks of the River Hamble, the Old Ship has been an overall winner of Fareham in Bloom. It's popular with sailing types and families with dogs — the waterside patio is a great draw in summer. Inside are open fires in winter, dark wood panelling and beams, and a bar serving well-kept Fuller's

beers. The spacious candlelit restaurant has a high-vaulted ceiling and nautical paraphernalia. Here home-cooked dishes include all the family favourites, from ploughman's and jackets to lasagne or Cajun chicken.

Open all day all wk **Bar Meals** L served Mon-Fri 12-2.15, Sat-Sun 12-9.15 D served Mon-Fri 6.30-9.15, Sat-Sun 12-9.15 **Restaurant** L served Mon-Fri 12-2.15, Sat-Sun 12-9.15 D served Mon-Fri 6.30-9.15, Sat-Sun 12-9.15 ⊕ MERLIN INNS/FULLER'S ◀ Fuller's London Pride, George Gale & Co HSB, Guest ale. ♀ 8 **Facilities** Non-diners area ♥ (Bar Restaurant Garden) ♦↑ Children's menu Children's portions Family room Garden ⌐ Parking Wi-fi ▭

LOWER WIELD   Map 5 SU64

The Yew Tree

PICK OF THE PUBS

SO24 9RX ☎ 01256 389224
dir: *Take A339 from Basingstoke towards Alton. Turn right for Lower Wield*

Good selection of fine wines and local ales

The eponymous, 650-year-old yew tree was just getting into its stride when this free house started serving real ale in 1845. Set in wonderful countryside, opposite a picturesque cricket pitch, the popular landlord's simple mission statement promises 'Good honest food; great local beers; fine wines (lots of choice); and, most importantly, good fun for one and all'. Triple fff Moondance is the house beer, with 20 guest ale brewers on rotation, including Bowman Ales and Hogs Back. Most of the food is sourced from Hampshire or neighbouring counties, and the menu reflects the seasons while keeping the regular favourites 'to avoid uproar'. Sample dishes include lightly spiced vegetable tart; basil-marinated salmon fillet; and half a shoulder of lamb. Follow with chocolate and orange truffle cake. The wines are mainly New World, but with some classic Burgundies and plenty available by the glass. There is an annual cricket match and sports day in summer, and 'silly' quiz nights in winter.

Open Tue-Sat 12-3 6-11 (Sun all day) Closed: 1st 2wks Jan, Mon **Bar Meals** L served Tue-Sun 12-2 D served Tue-Sat 6.30-9, Sun 6.30-8.30 Av main course £10.50 **Restaurant** L served Tue-Sun 12-2 D served Tue-Sat 6.30-9, Sun 6.30-8.30 ⊕ FREE HOUSE ◀ Flower Pots Cheriton Pots, Bowman Swift One, Triple fff Moondance, Hogs Back TEA, Hop Back GFB, Andwell Gold Muddler. ♀ 14 **Facilities** Non-diners area ♥ (Bar Garden) ♦↑ Children's menu Children's portions Garden Parking

LYMINGTON — Map 5 SZ39

Mayflower Inn

Kings Saltern Rd SO41 3QD ☎ 01590 672160
e-mail: manager@themayflowerlymington.co.uk
dir: *A337 towards New Milton, left at rdbt by White Hart, left to Rookes Ln, right at mini rdbt, pub 0.75m*

Mock-Tudor inn serving good food, right next to the yacht haven

A favourite with yachtsmen and dog walkers, this solidly built mock-Tudor inn overlooks the Lymington River, with glorious views to the Isle of Wight. There's a magnificent garden with splendid sun terraces where visitors can enjoy a pint of Goddards Fuggle-Dee-Dum, and an on-going summer barbecue in fine weather. Menu prices are reasonable, with dishes that range from light bites like lemon and pepper monkfish goujons or a sharing platter, to main courses of black bean chicken stir-fry, or sea bass fillet with prawn and saffron risotto.

Open all day all wk **Bar Meals** food served all day **Restaurant** food served all day ⊕ ENTERPRISE INNS/ COASTAL INNS & TAVERNS LTD ◀ Ringwood Best Bitter, Fuller's London Pride, Wadworth 6X, Goddards Fuggle-Dee-Dum ♂ Thatchers. ♟ 9 **Facilities** Non-diners area ✿ (Bar Garden) ♦♦ Children's menu Children's portions Play area Garden ⋒ Parking Wi-fi ▭

The Walhampton Arms

Walhampton Hill SO41 5RE ☎ 01590 673113
e-mail: enquiries@walhamptonarms.co.uk
web: www.walhamptonarmslymington.co.uk
dir: *From Lymington take B3054 towards Beaulieu. Pub in 2m*

Order a meal from the popular carvery

New owners took over here in February 2013 but they have continued with the pub's popular and excellent value carvery. Originally a farm building in the early 19th-century that included a model dairy supplying Walhampton Estate, this friendly pub serves real ales from Ringwood, with guest ales from local microbreweries throughout the year. The steaks and surf 'n' turf are two reasons why people flock to the carvery but other popular dishes may include lamb's liver and bacon; steak and ale pie or the chef's curry with rice. Children too will find all their favourites on their own menu.

Open all day all wk 11–11 (Sun 12-10.30) **Bar Meals** L served Tue-Sat 12-9, Sun-Mon 12-8 D served Tue-Sat 12-9, Sun-Mon 12-8 **Restaurant** L served Tue-Sat 12-9, Sun-Mon 12-8 D served Tue-Sat 12-9, Sun-Mon 12-8 ⊕ FREE HOUSE ◀ Ringwood Best Bitter, Otter Bitter, Guest ales. ♟ 10 **Facilities** Non-diners area ✿ (Bar Outside area) ♦♦ Children's menu Children's portions Outside area ⋒ Parking Wi-fi ▭ (notice required)

LYNDHURST — Map 5 SU30

New Forest Inn

Emery Down SO43 7DY ☎ 023 8028 4690
e-mail: info@thenewforestinn.co.uk
dir: *M27 junct 1 follow signs for A35/Lyndhurst. In Lyndhurst follow signs for Christchurch, turn right at Swan Inn towards Emery Down*

18th-century inn with large garden

New Forest ponies occasionally wander into this traditional local, a distraction that only serves to enhance its friendly atmosphere. At least two guest ales back incumbents Fortyniner and Flack's Double Drop; Thatchers Green Goblin cider is also on tap. The double-sided, A3 menu showcases a multitude of items — doorstep sandwiches, snacks, chargrills, classics, salads, vegetarian and chef's choices. In there somewhere are chicken with bacon, smoked cheese and barbecue sauce; country faggots with mash, peas and fried onions; beer-battered haddock and chips; and vegetable frittata. Beer and cider festivals are, respectively, on July's second weekend and March's last.

Open all day all wk **Bar Meals** Av main course £11 food served all day **Restaurant** Fixed menu price fr £8.95 food served all day ⊕ ENTERPRISE INNS ◀ Ringwood Fortyniner, Flack Manor Flack's Double Drop, Guest ales ♂ Thatchers Gold, Thatchers Green Goblin. ♟ 12 **Facilities** Non-diners area ✿ (Bar Restaurant Garden) ♦♦ Children's menu Children's portions Garden ⋒ Beer festival Cider festival Parking Wi-fi ▭ (notice required)

The Oak Inn

Pinkney Ln, Bank SO43 7FE ☎ 023 8028 2350
e-mail: oakinn@fullers.co.uk
dir: *From Lyndhurst signed A35 to Christchurch, follow A35 for 1m, left at Bank sign*

Reliable oasis on New Forest trails

At the heart of the National Park, patrons enjoying Gales ales in the garden of this bare-boarded, bric-a-brac full country pub may idly watch local residents' pigs snuffling for acorns, New Forest ponies grazing or even fallow deer fleetingly flitting amidst the trees. It's a popular stop with cyclists and walkers exploring the Forest's tracks, breaking for a while to partake of the enticing menu which is strong on meals prepared using produce of the parish; perhaps a doorstop sandwich with New Forest ham and Loosehanger cheese, or pheasant and chestnut gnocchi with parsnip crisps as a main. Booking meals is advised.

Open all wk Mon-Fri 11.30-3.30 6-11 (Sat 11.30-11 Sun 12-10.30) **Bar Meals** L served Mon-Fri 12-2.30, Sat 12-9.30, Sun 12-9 D served Mon-Fri 6-9.30, Sat 12-9.30, Sun 12-9 **Restaurant** L served Mon-Fri 12-2.30, Sat 12-9.30, Sun 12-9 D served Mon-Fri 6-9.30, Sat 12-9.30, Sun 12-9 ⊕ FULLER'S ◀ London Pride, George Gale & Co HSB & Seafarers ♂ Aspall. ♟ 12
Facilities Non-diners area ✿ (Bar Restaurant Garden) ♦♦ Children's menu Children's portions Garden ⋒ Parking Wi-fi

MAPLEDURWELL — Map 5 SU65

The Gamekeepers

PICK OF THE PUBS

Tunworth Rd RG25 2LU ☎ 01256 322038 & 07786 998994
e-mail: info@thegamekeepers.co.uk
dir: *M3 junct 6, A30 towards Hook. Right across dual carriageway after The Hatch pub. Pub signed*

Victorian pub featuring an indoor well

This pub was a house belonging to shoemaker Joseph Phillips and his wife, Elizabeth, until Joseph turned the building into an inn called the Queen's Head. In the dining room, two bricks, one each side of the fireplace, are marked with the couple's initials and the date 1854. Acquiring its current name in 1973, it still displays much of its 19th-century origin through its low beams, flagstone floors and even an indoor well; outside, a large garden overlooks the north Hampshire countryside. Relax on a leather sofa with a pint of real ale, and choose your meal from the daily-changing menu and fish and game specials, starting maybe with moules marinière. Main courses to look out for are the slow-cooked game hotpot; oven-baked fish pie; and chargrilled pork, beer and watercress sausages with chive mash. Apple crumble, sticky toffee pudding, crème brûlée, chocolate brownies and a Hampshire cheeseboard are some of the desserts.

Open all wk Mon-Fri 11-3 5.30-12 (Sat 11am-mdnt Sun 11-11) Closed: 31 Dec, 1 Jan **Bar Meals** L served Mon-Fri 11-2.30, Sat-Sun 11-9.30 D served Mon-Fri 5.30-9, Sat-Sun 11-9.30 Av main course £18-£20 **Restaurant** L served Mon-Fri 11-2.30, Sat-Sun 11-9.30 D served Mon-Fri 5.30-9, Sat-Sun 11-9.30 Av 3 course à la carte fr £35 ⊕ FREE HOUSE ◀ Andwell Gold Muddler, Ruddy Darter, Resolute & King John, Firkin Fox ♂ Westons Stowford Press. ♟ 10 **Facilities** Non-diners area ✿ (Bar Garden) ♦♦ Children's portions Garden ⋒ Parking Wi-fi ▭ (notice required)

Save on hotels. Book at **theAA.com/hotel**

HAMPSHIRE 219 ENGLAND

PICK OF THE PUBS

The Fox

NORTH WALTHAM
Map 5 SU54

RG25 2BE ☎ 01256 397288
e-mail: info@thefox.org
web: www.thefox.org
dir: *M3 junct 7, A30 towards Winchester.
North Waltham signed on right. Take
2nd signed road*

Family-friendly pub with a large garden

Built as three farm cottages in 1624, a feature of the bar in this peaceful village pub is its collection of miniatures — over 1,100 so far, and counting. It's an easy place to get to whether travelling on the A303 or the M3. The Fox welcomes families, as you might guess from the children's adventure play area in the extensive beer garden which blazes with colour in summer when the pretty flower borders and hanging baskets are in bloom. In the bar, landlord Rob MacKenzie serves well-looked after real ales from Sharp's, Brakspear, West Berkshire and a guest brewery, and an impressive malt whisky selection among which you'll find the relatively scarce Auchentoshan, Dalmore and Singleton. Bar snacks include barbecued ribs, scampi and 'Fox' beef burger. Rob's wife Izzy is responsible for the monthly menus and daily specials board in the tartan-carpeted restaurant, which list the house specialities of cheese soufflé, and Hampshire venison served with glazed shallots, field

mushrooms, spinach, creamed swede and sauté potatoes. Among typical main courses there might be pan-fried chicken breast schnitzel topped with Napoletana sauce and melted cheese; Mediterranean vegetable stack served on a rösti; and baked sea bass fillets with ginger and coriander, served with new potatoes and sugar snaps. Home-made desserts are tempting too — there's red berry Pavlova, Malteser parfait, and clafoutis, a baked chocolate pudding with a hot fondant centre and butterscotch sauce. The Fox's events calendar features monthly wine tasting dinners.

Open all day all wk 11-11 Closed: 25 Dec **Bar Meals** L served all wk 12-2.30 D served all wk 6-9.30 **Restaurant** L

served all wk 12-2.30 D served all wk 6-9.30 ⊕ FREE HOUSE ◀ West Berkshire Good Old Boy, Brakspear, Sharp's Doom Bar, Guest ale Ö Aspall (& 10 bottled ciders) ⏰ 14
Facilities Non-diners area ❀ (Bar Garden) ⅋ Children's menu Children's portions Play area Garden ⋔ Beer festival Parking ⛟ (notice required)

MICHELDEVER   Map 5 SU53

The Dove Inn

Andover Rd, Micheldever Station SO21 3AU
☎ **01962 774288**
e-mail: info@the-dove-inn.co.uk
dir: *M3 junct 8 merge onto A303, take exit signed
Micheldever Station, follow station signs onto Andover
Rd, on left*

Crisp Georgian lines and period charm

An imposing, Grade II listed former railway and
stagecoach hotel of late-Georgian origins, with three bars
and two restaurants which reflect this heritage, a heady
mix of bare-board floors, robust beams to the ceilings,
open fires and impressive period furnishings and decor.
Constantly changing real ales and a reliable wine list
accompany the diverse choice of home-made dishes;
braised wood pigeon with cider sauce and shallot confit
to start, teamed with hazelnut and butternut squash
ravioli or Hampshire venison burger as a main. There's a
modest beer garden here, and a vine-dressed patio; a
beer festival is planned.

Open all wk 11-3 5.30-11 (Sat-Sun all day) **Bar Meals** L
served Mon-Fri 12-2, Sat-Sun 12-2.30 D served Mon-Thu
6.30-9, Fri-Sat 6-9.30, Sun 6-8 **Restaurant** L served
Mon-Fri 12-2, Sat-Sun 12-2.30 D served Mon-Thu 6.30-9,
Fri-Sat 6-9.30, Sun 6-8 ⊕ FREE HOUSE ◀ Guest ales. ♥ 9
Facilities Non-diners area ❄ (Bar Garden) ♦♦ Children's
menu Children's portions Garden ⊼ Beer festival Parking
Wi-fi ➡ (notice required)

Half Moon & Spread Eagle

Winchester Rd SO21 3DG ☎ **01962 774339**
dir: *From Winchester take A33 towards Basingstoke. In
5m left after small car garage. Pub 0.5m on right*

Smart inn offering a great choice of dishes

Once known as the Dever Arms, this much improved
former drovers' inn overlooks the cricket green in the
heart of a pretty thatched and timbered Hampshire
village. The pub comprises three smartly furnished
interconnecting rooms and it has a genuine feel of a
locals' pub. An extensive menu takes in starters of pork
and apple rillette, main courses of pan-seared chicken
breast with red wine sauce, bacon, mushrooms and
onions. Gourmet sandwiches and bar meals are also on
offer and takeaway fish and chips is available every day.

Open all day 12-11 Closed: Mon **Bar Meals** L served Tue-
Sun 12-9 D served Tue-Sun 12-9 food served all day
⊕ GREENE KING ◀ Guest ales ♂ Aspall, Thatchers. ♥ 16
Facilities Non-diners area ❄ (Bar Garden) ♦♦ Children's
menu Children's portions Play area Garden ⊼ Parking
Wi-fi ➡ (notice required)

NEW ALRESFORD   Map 5 SU53

The Bell Inn

12 West St SO24 9AT ☎ **01962 732429**
e-mail: info@bellalresford.com
dir: *In village centre*

Small, family-run free house in charming town centre

A well-restored former coaching inn in Georgian
Alresford's main street, where Hampshire real ales hold
their own against contenders from Cornwall and Devon,
and over 18 wines are available by the glass. The bar
dining area and candlelit restaurant offer fresh, locally
sourced pork, ale and watercress sausages and mash;
lamb shank with roast carrots and swede; pan-seared
king scallops; and roast Gressingham duck breast. A two-
courses-for-£10 meal could begin with grilled goats'
cheese salad with walnut dressing, then Thai green
chicken curry and basmati rice. Station Road opposite the
inn leads to the famous Watercress Line.

Open all day Closed: Sun eve **Bar Meals** L served all wk
12-3 D served Mon-Sat 6-9 Av main course £14
Restaurant L served Mon-Sat 12-3, Sun 12-4 D served
Mon-Sat 6-9 Fixed menu price fr £10 Av 3 course à la
carte fr £25 ⊕ FREE HOUSE ◀ Sharp's Doom Bar, Itchen
Valley Winchester Ale, Andwell Resolute, Upham Ale, Otter
♂ Mr Whitehead's Heart of Hampshire. ♥ 18
Facilities Non-diners area ❄ (Bar) ♦♦ Children's menu
Children's portions Outside area ⊼ Parking Wi-fi
➡ (notice required)

NORTHINGTON   Map 5 SU53

The Woolpack Inn

PICK OF THE PUBS

Totford SO24 9TJ ☎ **01962 734184**
e-mail: info@thewoolpackinn.co.uk
dir: *From Basingstoke take A339 towards Alton. Under
motorway, turn right (across dual carriageway) onto
B3036 signed Candovers & Alresford. Pub between Brown
Candover & Northington*

Welcoming country inn with cracking food and local ales

Set in stunning Hampshire countryside, this Grade II
listed drovers' inn has been sympathetically smartened
up, creating a sense of calm modernity while still
retaining the classic feel of a country pub. Standing in a
tiny hamlet in the peaceful Candover Valley, The
Woolpack (now under new ownership) welcomes walkers
and their dogs, families, cyclists and foodies. Ales
change weekly but include one named after The
Woolpack, while an up-market wine list will please the
cognoscenti. Eat in the traditional bar, where rugs on
tiled or wood floors and a roaring log fire create a relaxing
atmosphere; alternatives are the smart dining room or a
heated terrace. The bar menu proffers classics such as
pie of the day or bangers and mash with onion gravy.
Typical dining room main courses are confit pork belly,
smoked bacon and potato gratin; or spiced winter

vegetable hotpot, carrot and onion fritters and garlic
flatbread.

Open all day all wk **Bar Meals** L served all wk 12-3
D served Mon-Sat 6-9, Sun 6-8.30 Av main course £11.23
Restaurant L served all wk 12-3 D served Mon-Sat 6-9 Av
3 course à la carte fr £24.65 ⊕ FREE HOUSE ◀ The
Woolpack Ale, Palmers Copper Ale, Weekly changing Guest
ale ♂ Thatchers Gold. ♥ 11 **Facilities** Non-diners area
❄ (Bar Restaurant Garden) ♦♦ Children's menu Children's
portions Play area Garden ⊼ Parking Wi-fi ➡ (notice
required)

NORTH WALTHAM   Map 5 SU54

The Fox

PICK OF THE PUBS

See Pick of the Pubs on page 219

OLD BASING   Map 5 SU65

The Crown

The Street RG24 7BW ☎ **01256 321424**
e-mail: sales@thecrownoldbasing.com
dir: *M3 junct 6 towards Basingstoke. At rdbt right onto
A30. 1st left into Redbridge Ln, to T-junct. Right into The
Street, pub on right*

Village local with well-kept ales

Just outside Basingstoke is the picturesque village of Old
Basing, in the heart of which is The Crown. Reliable and
popular national ales are backed by local Andwell's King
John and a good wine list. The management takes great
pride in the fact that every dish is prepared from scratch
in the pub's kitchen. Food takes the form of bar snacks
like filled rolls, salads and deli boards. On the main
menu, a typical choice could be a starter of Cornish
pollock goujons followed by slow-braised beef in red wine,
bacon lardons, mushrooms and crispy bone marrow. Look
out for the annual beer festival.

Open all wk 11.30-2.30 5-11 (Fri-Sat 11.30-11.30 Sun
11.30-10) Closed: 1 Jan **Bar Meals** L served Mon-Thu
12-2, Fri-Sun 12-2.30 D served Mon-Thu 6-9, Fri-Sat
6-9.30 Av main course £9 **Restaurant** L served Mon-Thu
12-2, Fri-Sun 12-2.30 D served Mon-Thu 6-9, Fri-Sat
6-9.30 Av 3 course à la carte fr £30 ⊕ ENTERPRISE INNS
◀ Sharp's Doom Bar, Fuller's London Pride, Andwell King
John ♂ Thatchers Gold. ♥ 9 **Facilities** Non-diners area
❄ (Bar Garden) ♦♦ Children's menu Children's portions
Garden ⊼ Beer festival Parking Wi-fi ➡ (notice
required)

OVINGTON   Map 5 SU53

The Bush

PICK OF THE PUBS

See Pick of the Pubs on opposite page

PICK OF THE PUBS

The Bush

OVINGTON   Map 5 SU53

SO24 ORE ☎ 01962 732764
e-mail: thebushinn@wadworth.co.uk
web: www.thebushinn.co.uk
dir: *A31 from Winchester towards Alton & Farnham, approx 6m, left to Ovington. 0.5m to pub*

Old world charm by the Itchen

Located just off the A31 on a peaceful lane, this unspoilt 17th-century rose-covered cottage enjoys an enviable picturesque setting, close to one of Hampshire's famous chalk trout streams — the River Itchen. Gentle riverside strolls are very popular, as are the rustic bars and bench-filled garden of this one-time refreshment stop on the Pilgrim's Way between Winchester and Canterbury, both of which are often crammed with people replenishing their energy after a walk, especially on fine summer weekends. Don't expect to find a jukebox or fruit machine; the intimate, softly lit and atmospheric rooms boast dark-painted walls, an assortment of sturdy tables, chairs and high-backed settles and a wealth of old artefacts, prints and stuffed fish. On cold winter nights the place to sit with a pint of traditional ale is in front of the roaring log fire. The regularly-changing menu is based on the freshest food available, including local farm cheeses, meats from Wiltshire, Hampshire and Scotland, and fish from the Dorset and Cornish

coasts. Choices range from sandwiches, ploughman's lunches and other bar snacks, through to satisfying meals such as chicken liver pâté with grape chutney, or local smoked trout mousse; followed by Chinese-style braised belly pork with spring onions, pak choi and apple purée; and a daily seasonal special like Italian sausages on cannellini bean and potato mash, or vegetarian baked potato stuffed with leek and gruyère cheese on tomato sauce. Finish with sticky toffee pudding with caramel sauce, or Valrhona dark chocolate and raspberry crème brûlée. Real ales keep their end up too, with Wadworth 6X and guest ales.

Open all wk Mon-Fri 11-3 6-11 Sat 11-11 Sun 12-10.30 (summer hols Mon-

Sat 11-11 Sun 12-10.30) **Bar Meals** L served Mon-Fri 12-2.30, Sat-Sun 12-9.30, summer hols Mon-Sat 12-9, Sun 12-9.30 D served Mon-Fri 6-9.30, Sat-Sun 12-9.30, summer hols Mon-Sat 12-9, Sun 12-9.30 ⊕ WADWORTH ◀ 6X, Henry's Original IPA, Horizon, Guest ales Ö Thatchers Gold, Thatchers Traditional. ♟ 19 **Facilities** Non-diners area ❖ ♦♦ Children's menu Children's portions Family room Garden ⋒ Parking Wi-fi

The Old Drum ★★★★ INN ⊛ NEW

16 Chapel St GU32 3DP ☎ 01730 300544
e-mail: info@theolddrum.co.uk
dir: *From A3 follow town centre signs (Winchester Rd).
At mini-rdbt, 2nd exit. Over rail crossing, 3rd right into
Chapel St. Pub on right*

A contemporary pub in the centre of town

Two school-friends, now in their fifties, and their wives
have transformed Petersfield's oldest pub, rediscovering
en route original 16th-century features, including a
superb beamed ceiling and, of perhaps less pulse-racing
potential, a tongue-and-groove 60s ceiling. The bar where
author H G Wells once sat with a pint of mild now serves
five frequently-changing, locally micro-brewed real ales.
The food too has moved considerably on from H G's
pickled-egg-if-he-was-lucky days to include AA Rosette-
standard, locally sourced venison haunch with beer-
battered haggis; sea bass with onion bhaji, dhal, spiced
cauliflower and spinach; and butternut squash cannelloni
with Brighton Blue cheese sauce.

Open 10-3 5-11 Closed: 25 Dec, 1st wk Jan, Sun eve **Bar
Meals** L served Mon-Sat 12-2, Sun 12-3 D served Mon-
Sat 6.30-9.30 **Restaurant** L served Mon-Sat 12-2, Sun
12-3 D served Mon-Sat 6.30-9.30 ⊕ FREE HOUSE ◀ Dark
Star Hophead, American Pale Ale & The Art of Darkness,
Bowman Ales Wallops Wood, Suthwyk Ales Liberation,
Triple fff Moondance ♉ Westons Bounds. ♟ 12
Facilities Non-diners area ♣ (Bar Restaurant Garden) ♦♦
Children's portions Garden ♫ Beer festival Wi-fi **Rooms** 2

The Trooper Inn

PICK OF THE PUBS

Alton Rd, Froxfield GU32 1BD ☎ 01730 827293
e-mail: info@trooperinn.com
dir: *From A3 follow A272 Winchester signs towards
Petersfield (NB do not take A272). 1st exit at mini rdbt for
Steep. 3m, pub on right*

Ideal for visitors to South Downs National Park

Said to have been a recruiting centre at the outset of the
First World War, this 17th-century free house stands in
the heart of the countryside at one of Hampshire's
highest points. The inn backs onto Ashford Hangers
National Nature Reserve, and is also well positioned for
the South Downs National Park, Jane Austen's Chawton
and Gilbert White's Selborne. Inside the pub, expect
winter log fires, a spacious bar and a charming
restaurant with a vaulted ceiling and wooden settles.
Expect seasonal country cooking with fresh fish and
game, much of it from local suppliers and producers.
Slow-roasted lamb shoulder with honey and mint gravy,
creamy mash and spring greens; and free-range chicken,
green olive and preserved lemon tagine are typical main
course choices. The resident vegetarian chef creates
dishes like pine nut and caper stuffed roasted red
peppers. Bar meals such as mussels and chips are also
served.

Open 12-3 6-11 Closed: 25-26 Dec & 1 Jan, Sun eve &
Mon L **Bar Meals** L served Tue-Sat 12-2, Sun 12-2.30
D served Mon-Fri 6.30-9, Sat 7-9.30 **Restaurant** L served
Tue-Sat 12-2, Sun 12-2.30 D served Mon-Fri 6.30-9, Sat
7-9.30 ⊕ FREE HOUSE ◀ Ringwood Best Bitter, Ballards,
Local guest ales. **Facilities** Non-diners area ♣ (Bar
Restaurant Garden) ♦♦ Children's menu Children's
portions Garden ♫ Parking Wi-fi ▭ (notice required)

The White Horse Inn

Priors Dean GU32 1DA ☎ 01420 588387
e-mail: details@pubwithnoname.co.uk
dir: *A3/A272 to Winchester/Petersfield. In Petersfield left
to Steep, 5m then right at small x-rds to East Tisted, take
2nd drive on right*

Former forge with excellent beers

Originally used as a forge for passing coaches, this
splendid 17th-century farmhouse is also known as the
'Pub With No Name' as it has no sign. The blacksmith
sold beer to the travellers while their horses were
attended to. Today there is an excellent range of beers
including No Name Strong. Menus offer the likes of red
onion, feta and olive tart; duck breast with red cabbage
and pork reduction; and a selection of burgers and
sharing platters. The pub holds a beer festival every June
and a cider festival in September.

Open all day all wk 12-12 **Bar Meals** L served Mon-Fri
12-2.30, Sat-Sun all day D served Mon-Fri 6-9.30, Sat-
Sun all day Av main course £13.95 **Restaurant** L served
Mon-Fri 12-2.30, Sat-Sun all day D served Mon-Fri
6-9.30, Sat-Sun all day Fixed menu price fr £22.95
⊕ FULLER'S ◀ London Pride, George Gale & Co Seafarers,
No Name Best & No Name Strong, Ringwood Fortyniner,
Sharp's Doom Bar. ♟ 10 **Facilities** Non-diners area
♣ (Bar Garden) ♦♦ Children's menu Children's portions
Family room Garden ♫ Beer festival Cider festival
Parking ▭

Purefoy Arms ⊛⊛

PICK OF THE PUBS

Alresford Rd RG25 2EJ ☎ 01256 389777
e-mail: info@thepurefoyarms.co.uk
dir: *On B3046, S of Basingstoke*

Fabulous food in secluded village setting

Heavy on the bare brick and chunky wooden furnishings,
there's an air of quiet sophistication to this convivial
dining pub beside the handkerchief village green. The
menus astonish. Settle into a fireside Chesterfield, with a
glass of the local brew or a chilled South African
chardonnay perhaps, to study the hand written menus
and then struggle to decide which of Andres Alemany's
creative, award-winning dishes to opt for. Just to give an
idea of what's on offer - start with razor clams and confit
onion; or oxtail, duck and pistachio terrine with toasted
brioche, progressing then to Burgundy truffle risotto;
poached hake, piquillo pepper, paella rice and mussels;
or roast partridge with Koffman cabbage, garlic and
thyme potatoes, accompanied by fine wines from the

100-bin list. If dropping in for lunch there is an excellent
short 'Simple Lunch' menu of two or three courses. On a
lovely summer's evening you could relax in the garden
and just order a drink and some tapas-style nibbles.

Open 12-3 6-11 (Sun 12-4) Closed: 26 Dec & 1 Jan, Sun
eve & Mon **Bar Meals** L served Tue-Sat 12-3, Sun 12-4
D served Tue-Sat 6-10 **Restaurant** L served Tue-Sat 12-3,
Sun 12-4 D served Tue-Sat 6-10 ⊕ FREE HOUSE ◀ Flack
Manor Flack's Double Drop, Itchen Valley ♉ Westons
Bounds. ♟ 17 **Facilities** Non-diners area ♣ (Bar
Restaurant Garden) ♦♦ Children's menu Children's
portions Garden ♫ Parking Wi-fi ▭ (notice required)

The Star Inn

12 Market Place BH24 1AW ☎ 01425 473105
e-mail: thestarringwood@yahoo.co.uk
dir: *From A31 follow market place signs*

Specialising in Thai and Asian cuisine

Ian Pepperell, the landlord of this 470-year-old pub on
the square has played a character in BBC Radio 4's *The
Archers* for over 15 years. Away from his radio career he
pulls pints of Ringwood Best for locals and helps serve
the authentic Thai and oriental food that dominates the
menu. Typical dishes include salt and pepper squid,
deep-fried sea bass with chilli sauce, chicken in black
bean sauce, and aromatic crispy duck. At lunch, you can
also tuck into rib-eye steak and chips and tuna
mayonnaise sandwiches.

Open all day all wk Closed: 1 Jan ⊕ ENTERPRISE INNS
◀ Ringwood Best Bitter, Hop Back Summer Lightning,
Fuller's London Pride, Black Sheep, Brains ♉ Black Rat,
Thatchers Green Goblin. **Facilities** ♣ (Bar Garden)
Garden Wi-fi

The Rose & Thistle

SP6 3NL ☎ 01725 518236
e-mail: enquiries@roseandthistle.co.uk
dir: *Follow Rockbourne signs from either A354 (Salisbury
to Blandford Forum road) or A338 at Fordingbridge*

Pretty, quintessentially English pub

Originally two 17th-century thatched cottages, The Rose
& Thistle stands at the top of a fine main street lined
with picture-postcard period houses. Long, low and
whitewashed, the pub has a stunning rose arch, hanging
baskets round the door, and a quaint dovecote in the
glorious front garden. The charming beamed bars boast
attractive country-style fabrics and two huge fireplaces
for blazing winter warmth – perfect after a breezy
downland walk. Expect a relaxing atmosphere, Palmers
Copper Ale on tap and a selection of quality dishes from
lunchtime bar snacks like Welsh rarebit to more formal
options such as slow-cooked pork belly with herb-crusted
black pudding.

Open all wk 11-3 6-11 (Sat 11-11 Sun 12-8) **Bar Meals** L
served all wk 12-2.30 D served Mon-Sat 7-9.30
Restaurant L served all wk 12-2.30 D served Mon-Sat

Save on hotels. Book at **theAA.com/hotel**

HAMPSHIRE 223 ENGLAND

7-9.30 ⊕ FREE HOUSE ◀ Ringwood Best, Sharp's Doom Bar, Butcombe Bitter Ö Westons, Black Rat. ♀ 12 **Facilities** Non-diners area ◆◆ Children's portions Garden ⋒ Parking Wi-fi ⊑ (notice required)

ROCKFORD Map 5 SU10

The Alice Lisle

Rockford Green BH24 3NA ☎ 01425 474700
e-mail: alicelisle@fullers.co.uk
dir: *From Ringwood A338 towards Fordingbridge. 1m, turn right into Ivy Ln. At end, left, cross cattle grid. Inn on left*

Well known for its summer beer festivals

A picturesque, red-brick pub with a beautiful garden overlooking Blashford Lakes to the rear and Rockford Green to the front. Lady Alice Lisle, who lived down the road, was beheaded in 1685 for harbouring fugitives, following the failure of the Monmouth Rebellion. With the majority of produce sourced from New Forest Marque suppliers, choose from a menu including crab, fennel and chilli linguine; River Test trout fillet; gammon steak, chips and free-range eggs; and tomato and basil gnocchi. A Fuller's house, it hosts beer festivals in the summer.

Open all day all wk 10.30am-11pm **Bar Meals** L served Mon-Fri 12-2.30, Sat 12-3, Sun 12-6 D served Mon-Fri 6-9, Sat 5-9 **Restaurant** L served Mon-Fri 12-2.30, Sat 12-3, Sun 12-6 D served Mon-Fri 6-9, Sat 5-9 ⊕ FULLER'S ◀ London Pride, George Gale & Co Seafarers & HSB Ö New Forest Traditional. ♀ 10 **Facilities** ✿ (Bar Garden) ◆◆ Children's menu Children's portions Play area Garden ⋒ Beer festival Parking Wi-fi ⊑ (notice required)

ROMSEY Map 5 SU32

The Cromwell Arms ★★★★ RR

23 Mainstone SO51 8HG ☎ 01794 519515
e-mail: dining@thecromwellarms.com
dir: *From Romsey take A27 signed Ringwood, Bournemouth, Salisbury. Cross River Test, pub on right*

Offering locally sourced food and ales

With Broadlands, former home of Lord Mountbatten and current home of Lord and Lady Brabourne, as its neighbour, The Cromwell Arms derives its name from Romsey's links with the English Civil War. It offers fresh, home-cooked food and attentive service with some unique twists on traditional gastro-pub favourites. Typical locally sourced dishes are home-made game terrine with spiced apple chutney; and twice-baked cheese and mushroom soufflé with new potatoes and mixed leaves. Its Hampshire-skewed offering of real ales includes Double Drop from the town's Flack Manor brewery, and a diverse selection of wines.

Open all day all wk **Bar Meals** L served Mon-Fri 12-3, Sat-Sun 12-9.30 D served Mon-Fri 6-10, Sat-Sun 12-9.30 **Restaurant** L served Mon-Fri 12-3, Sat-Sun 12-9.30 D served Mon-Fri 6-10, Sat-Sun 12-9.30 ⊕ FREE HOUSE ◀ Flack Manor Flack's Double Drop, Andwell Ruddy Darter, Ringwood Best Bitter Ö Thatchers Gold. ♀ 17

Facilities Non-diners area ◆◆ Children's menu Children's portions Garden ⋒ Parking Wi-fi ⊑ (notice required)
Rooms 10

The Three Tuns ⊛

58 Middlebridge St SO51 8HL ☎ 01794 512639
e-mail: manager@the3tuns.co.uk
dir: *From Romsey bypass (A27) follow town centre sign. Left into Middlebridge St*

Award-winning pub run by top team in market town

A stone's throw from the market square this 300-year-old Grade II listed pub holds an AA rosette. Smart wood panelling, vintage chandeliers and botanical prints blend well with low oak beams and open fireplaces to give a traditional yet upbeat ambience. A simple British menu features many local ingredients for seasonal classics, sharing platters and Sunday roasts: how about a main of pan-fried lamb's liver with bubble-and-squeak, buttered greens and crispy bacon followed by fruit crumble and custard. For a quiet fireside pint, there's Ringwood or a guest.

Open all wk 12-3 5-11 (Fri-Sun 12-11) summer all day (Sun 11-10.30) Closed: 25 Dec **Bar Meals** L served Mon-Thu 12-2.30, Fri-Sun 12-3 D served Mon-Thu 6-9, Fri-Sat 6-9.30 Av main course £12 **Restaurant** L served Mon-Thu 12-2.30, Fri-Sun 12-3 D served Mon-Thu 6-9, Fri-Sat 6-9.30 Av 3 course à la carte fr £20 ⊕ ENTERPRISE INNS ◀ Ringwood Best Bitter, Flack Manor Flack's Double Drop, 2 Guest ales Ö Westons Stowford Press. ♀ 11 **Facilities** Non-diners area ◆◆ Children's portions Garden ⋒ Parking Wi-fi

ROTHERWICK Map 5 SU75

The Coach and Horses

The Street RG27 9BG ☎ 01256 768976
e-mail: ian027@btinternet.com
dir: *Follow brown signs from A32 (Hook to Reading road)*

A cosy and unpretentious atmosphere

Close to the church in Rotherwick – a picturesque village that has appeared in TV's *Midsomer Murders* – parts of this smart, cream-washed inn can be traced back to the 17th century. With log fires in winter, board games, exposed brickwork and red-and-black tiled or wooden floors, the interior is pleasingly traditional. The south-facing garden with views of fields is a draw in the summer as a place for a relaxed pint of ale, an afternoon tea or a sensibly priced meal of breaded mushrooms, oxtail stew and baked vanilla cheesecake. Look out for visiting Morris dancers throughout the summer.

Open 12-3 5.30-11 (Sat 12-11 Sun 12-6) Closed: Sun eve & Mon **Bar Meals** L served Tue-Sat 12-3, Sun 12-4 (booking advisable Sun) D served Tue-Sat 6-9 ⊕ HALL & WOODHOUSE ◀ Badger First Gold, Pickled Partridge, Firkin Fox, Fursty Ferret Ö Westons Stowford Press. **Facilities** Non-diners area ✿ (Bar Restaurant Garden) ◆◆ Children's menu Children's portions Garden ⋒ Parking Wi-fi ⊑ (notice required)

ST MARY BOURNE Map 5 SU45

The Bourne Valley Inn

SP11 6BT ☎ 01264 738361
e-mail: enquiries@bournevalleyinn.com
dir: *Telephone for directions*

Peaceful Victorian pub boasting a riverside garden

This popular, traditional inn is an oasis of tranquillity surrounded by fields on the outskirts of St Mary Bourne. Built around the end of the 19th century, it was known as The Railway Inn, due to its proximity to the now vanished railway line and station. Smartly furnished throughout, it has a large character bar with plenty of guest ales and a more intimate dining area, as well as a riverside garden abounding with wildlife where children can let off steam in the special play area. At lunch you could enjoy a 'country pub classic' such as shepherd's pie; line caught fish; and Boars Hill sausages and mash.

Open all day all wk ⊕ FREE HOUSE ◀ Guest ales. **Facilities** ✿ (Bar Garden) ◆◆ Children's menu Children's portions Play area Garden Parking Wi-fi

SELBORNE Map 5 SU73

The Selborne Arms

High St GU34 3JR ☎ 01420 511247
e-mail: info@selbornearms.co.uk
dir: *From A3 take B3006, pub in village centre*

Microbrewery delights in a friendly village pub

The massive chimney appearing to block the way in to this simply furnished village pub is known as a baffle entry. Once inside, you'll find homely bars with hop-strewn beams, a huge fireplace, up to seven (in summer) real ales from microbreweries, and Mr Whitehead's cider. Keen supporters of Hampshire Fare (a community interest company), the kitchen prepares steamed oxtail and kidney pudding; Blackmoor pigeon faggot on bubble-and-squeak; and whole grilled plaice. The village, overlooked by glorious beech 'hangers', is where naturalist Gilbert White lived in the 18th century.

Open all wk 11-3 6-11 (Sat-11-11 Sun 12-11) ⊕ FREE HOUSE ◀ Courage Best Bitter, Ringwood Fortyniner, Suthwyk Old Dick, Local guest ales Ö Mr Whitehead's. **Facilities** ◆◆ Children's menu Children's portions Play area Garden Parking

PICK OF THE PUBS

The Plough Inn

SPARSHOLT Map 5 SU43

Woodman Ln SO21 2NW
☎ 01962 776353
dir: *B3049 from Winchester towards Salisbury, left to Sparsholt, 1m*

Ever popular inn down a country lane

Built as a coach house to serve Sparsholt Manor opposite, this popular village pub just a few miles from Winchester has been a popular local alehouse for more than 150 years. Inside, the main bar and dining areas blend harmoniously together, with farmhouse-style pine tables, wooden and upholstered seats, and miscellaneous agricultural implements, stone jars, wooden wine box end-panels and dried hops. Wadworth of Devizes supplies all the real ales, and there's a good wine selection. Lunchtime regulars know that 'doorstep' is a most apt description for the great crab and mayonnaise, beef and horseradish and other sandwiches, plus good soups and chicken liver parfait. The dining tables to the left of the entrance look over open fields to wooded downland, and it's at this end of the pub you'll find a daily-changing blackboard offering dishes such as salmon and crab fishcakes with saffron sauce; lamb's liver and bacon with mash and onion gravy; beef, ale and mushroom pie; and whole baked

camembert with garlic and rosemary. The menu board at the right-hand end of the bar offers the more substantial venison steak with celeriac mash and roasted beetroot; roast pork belly with bubble-and-squeak, five spice and sultana gravy; chicken breast filled with goats' cheese mousse; and fillet of sea bass with olive mash. Puddings include sticky toffee pudding and crème brûlée. The Plough is very popular, so it's best to book for any meal. The delightful flower- and shrub-filled garden has plenty of room for children to run around and play in. There's a jazz night on the first Sunday in August and carol singing with Father Christmas on 23rd December.

Open all wk 11-3 6-11 (Sun 12-3 6-10.30) Closed: 25 Dec **Bar Meals** L served all wk 12-2 D served Sun-Thu 6-9, Fri-Sat 6-9.30 **Restaurant** L served all wk 12-2 D served Sun-Thu 6-9, Fri-Sat 6-9.30 ⊕ WADWORTH ◄ Henry's Original IPA, 6X, Old Timer, JCB. ♥ 15 **Facilities** Non-diners area ❤ (Bar Garden) ♦♦ Children's menu Children's portions Play area Family room Garden ⊓ Parking

Save on hotels. Book at **theAA.com/hotel**

HAMPSHIRE 225 **ENGLAND**

SILCHESTER
Map 5 SU66

Calleva Arms

Little London Rd, The Common RG7 2PH
☎ **0118 970 0305**
dir: *A340 from Basingstoke, signed Silchester.*

Village pub close to a famous archaeological site

Named for the nearby Calleva Atrebatum, a Roman town whose surviving walls are some of the best preserved in Britain, this 19th-century pub overlooking the common is the perfect starting (or finishing) point for walks. Two bar areas, with a log burner in the middle, lead to a pleasant conservatory and large enclosed garden. A comprehensive menu lists grilled steaks with fries; salads such as chicken Caesar; traditional choices like barbecued pork ribs; and vegetarian options. Baguettes and paninis are added to the lunchtime selection.

Open all wk 11-3 5.30-11 (Sat 11am-11.30pm Sun 12-11) **Bar Meals** L served all wk 12-2 D served all wk 6.30-9 **Restaurant** L served all wk 12-2 D served all wk 6.30-9 ⊕ FULLER'S ◀ London Pride, George Gale & Co HSB, Guinness Ŏ Aspall. ♥ 10 **Facilities** Non-diners area ❖ (Bar Garden) ♦ Children's portions Garden ♬ Parking Wi-fi ▄▄ (notice required)

SOUTHAMPTON
Map 5 SU41

The White Star Tavern, Dining & Rooms ★★★★★ INN ◉◉

28 Oxford St SO14 3DJ ☎ **023 8082 1990**
e-mail: reservations@whitestartavern.co.uk
dir: *M3 junct 13, A33 to Southampton. Follow Ocean Village & Marina signs*

Seasonal cooking amid ocean liner decor

Named after the famous White Star Line shipping company that used to set sail from Southampton, this stylish gastro-pub with rooms is set in cosmopolitan Oxford Street. The restaurant provides modern British cooking typified by smoked salmon fishcake, buttered spinach, watercress beurre blanc; free-range Hampshire pork belly, champ cake and cider gravy; New Forest strawberries with vanilla ice cream, black pepper and balsamic. Watch the world go by from the pavement tables, or stay a little longer in one of 13 smart and comfortable bedrooms.

Open all day all wk 7am-11pm (Fri 7am-mdnt Sat 8.30am-mdnt Sun 8.30am-10.30pm) Closed: 25 Dec ⊕ ENTERPRISE INNS ◀ Fuller's London Pride, Bowman Swift One, Ringwood. **Facilities** ♦ Children's menu Children's portions Wi-fi **Rooms** 13

SPARSHOLT
Map 5 SU43

The Plough Inn
PICK OF THE PUBS

See Pick of the Pubs on opposite page

STEEP
Map 5 SU72

Harrow Inn
PICK OF THE PUBS

GU32 2DA ☎ **01730 262685**
dir: *From A272 in Petersfield to Sheet, left opposite church (School Ln), then over A3 by-pass bridge. Inn signed on right*

Real ales, hearty food and serious charity fund raiser

This 16th-century tile-hung gem is situated in a lovely rural location and has changed little over the years. The McCutcheon family has run it since 1929; sisters Claire and Nisa, both born and brought up here, are now the third generation with their names over the door. Tucked away off the road, it comprises two tiny bars - the 'public' is Tudor, with beams, tiled floor, inglenook fireplace, scrubbed tables, wooden benches, tree-trunk stools and a 'library'; the saloon (or Smoking Room, as it is still called) is Victorian. Beers are dispensed from barrels, there is no till and the toilets are across the road. Food is in keeping: ham and pea soup; hot Scotch eggs (some days); cheddar ploughman's; and various quiches. The large garden has plenty of tables surrounded by country-cottage flowers and fruit trees. Quiz nights raise huge sums for charity, for which Claire's partner Tony grows and sells flowers outside. Ask about the Harrow Cook Book, a collection of customers' recipes on sale for charity.

Open 12-2.30 6-11 (Sat 11-3 6-11 Sun 12-3 7-10.30) Closed: Sun eve in winter **Bar Meals** L served all wk 12-2 D served all wk 7-9 ⊕ FREE HOUSE ◀ Ringwood Best Bitter, Hop Back GFB, Bowman, Dark Star Hophead, Flack Manor Flack's Double Drop Ŏ Thatchers Heritage. **Facilities** Non-diners area ❖ (Bar Garden Outside area) Garden Outside area ♬ Parking **Notes** ◉

STOCKBRIDGE
Map 5 SU33

Mayfly

Testcombe SO20 6AZ ☎ **01264 860283**
dir: *Between A303 & A30, on A3057*

Famous pub on the River Test

Standing right on the banks of the swiftly flowing River Test, the Mayfly is an iconic drinking spot. Inside the beamed old farmhouse with its traditional bar and bright conservatory you'll find a choice of draught ciders and up to six real ales. All-day bar food might include smoked haddock and spring onion fishcakes; stuffed roasted peppers with herb couscous; or pork chops with caramelised apple glaze. Arrive early on warm summer days to grab a bench on the large riverside terrace.

Open all day all wk 10am-11pm **Bar Meals** L served all wk 11.30-9 D served all wk 11.30-9 food served all day **Restaurant** food served all day ⊕ FREE HOUSE ◀ George Gale & Co Seafarers Ŏ Aspall, Thatchers Green Goblin & Gold. ♥ 20 **Facilities** Non-diners area ❖ (Bar Restaurant Garden) ♦ Children's portions Garden ♬ Parking ▄▄

The Peat Spade Inn ★★★★ INN ◉
PICK OF THE PUBS

Longstock SO20 6DR ☎ **01264 810612**
e-mail: info@peatspadeinn.co.uk
dir: *Telephone for directions*

Timeless inn famous for its fishing connections

Located between Winchester and Salisbury, The Peat Spade is a reminder of a bygone England and its country sport traditions. Perched on the banks of the River Test in a corner of Hampshire countryside famed for being the fly-fishing capital of the world, the unusual paned windows overlook the peaceful village lane and idyllic heavily thatched cottages at this striking, red-brick and gabled Victorian pub. You will find a relaxed atmosphere in the cosy fishing- and shooting-themed bar and dining room; a simple daily-changing menu lists classic English food combined with flavoursome European ingredients. The kitchen uses locally-sourced produce, including allotment-grown fruit and vegetables, and game from the Leckford Estate. To drink there are local cask ales such as Flack's Double Drop, and a small but innovative wine list which includes a choice of two champagnes served by the glass. In summer, retire to the super terrace.

Open all day all wk 11-11 (Sun 11-10.30) Closed: 25 Dec **Bar Meals** L served all wk 12-2.30 D served all wk 6.30-9.30 **Restaurant** L served all wk 12-2.30 D served all wk 6.30-9.30 ⊕ FREE HOUSE/MILLER'S COLLECTION ◀ Flack Manor Flack's Double Drop, Guest ales. ♥ 11 **Facilities** Non-diners area ❖ (Bar Garden) ♦ Children's menu Children's portions Garden ♬ Parking Wi-fi ▄▄ (notice required) **Rooms** 8

The Three Cups Inn ★★★ INN
PICK OF THE PUBS

High St SO20 6HB ☎ **01264 810527**
e-mail: manager@the3cups.co.uk
dir: *M3 junct 8, A303 towards Andover. Left onto A3057 to Stockbridge*

Charming pub with low beams and a river in the garden

The pub's name apparently comes from an Old English phrase for a meeting of three rivers, although there's only one river here. That river happens to be the Test, generally regarded as the birthplace of modern fly fishing. One of these channels flows through the delightful rear garden of this 15th-century, timber-framed building, where brown trout may be spotted from the patio. The low-beamed bar to the right of the front door can be warmed by the centrally placed log fire; Itchen Valley and Flower Pots - Hampshire real ales - and a guest, are served here. You can eat in the bar, but the main, candlelit dining area is at the other end of the building. Modern European and traditional selections blend fresh regional ingredients to create starters such as smoked salmon and crème fraîche terrine with citrus dressing; and main courses of rabbit leg braised in sherry, saffron, Savoy cabbage and wild mushroom tortellini. Accommodation

continued

STOCKBRIDGE *continued*

suites provide Egyptian cotton sheets and real ground coffee.

Open all day all wk 10am-11pm (Fri-Sun 8am-11pm) **Bar Meals** L served all wk 12-2.30 D served all wk 6-9.30 **Restaurant** L served all wk 12-2.30 D served all wk 6-9.30 Fixed menu price fr £10 ⊕ FREE HOUSE ◀ Itchen Valley Fagins, Young's Bitter, Flower Pots, Guest ales Ŏ Westons Stowford Press. ▼ **Facilities** Non-diners area ✿ (Bar Garden) ♦ Children's menu Children's portions Garden ⋈ Beer festival Cider festival Parking Wi-fi 🚐 **Rooms** 8

SWANMORE   Map 5 SU51

The Rising Sun

Hill Pound SO32 2PS ☎ 01489 896663
dir: *M27 junct 10, A32 through Wickham towards Alton. Left into Bishop's Wood Rd, right at x-rds into Mislingford Rd to Swanmore*

Homely haunted pub

Tucked in the heart of the beautiful Meon Valley, this 17th-century coaching inn has winter fires, low beams, uneven floors and lots of nooks and crannies. In summer, enjoy a pint of Hop Back Summer Lightning or Sharp's Doom Bar in the secluded rear garden. Home-cooked food makes good use of locally sourced ingredients in simple snacks such as a sandwiches and salads through to full meals along the lines of home-made chicken liver pâté with Cumberland sauce and melba toast followed by smoked haddock and spring onion fishcakes with salad and new potatoes. Look out for the resident ghost!

Open all wk Mon-Sat 11.30-3 5.30-11 (Sun 12-4 5.30-10.30) **Bar Meals** L served Mon-Sat 12-2, Sun 12-2.30 D served Mon-Sat 6-9, Sun 6-8.30 Av main course £4.55-£17.20 **Restaurant** L served Mon-Sat 12-2, Sun 12-2.30 D served Mon-Sat 6-9, Sun 6-8.30 Fixed menu price fr £8.50 Av 3 course à la carte fr £25 ⊕ FREE HOUSE ◀ Sharp's Doom Bar, Palmers, Hop Back Summer Lightning, Timothy Taylor Landlord Ŏ Westons Stowford Press. ▼ 13 **Facilities** Non-diners area ♦ Children's menu Children's portions Garden ⋈ Parking 🚐 (notice required)

TANGLEY   Map 5 SU35

The Fox Inn

SP11 0RU ☎ 01264 730276
e-mail: info@foxinntangley.co.uk
dir: *From rdbt (junct of A343 & A3057) in Andover follow station signs (Charlton Rd). Through Charlton & Hatherden to Tangley*

Local ales and spicy treats in rural seclusion

Curiously, a former chef to the Thai Royal Family now dedicates his skills to providing a startling menu to pub-goers who adventure along the country lanes that cross outside this secluded inn in the North Wessex Downs Area

of Outstanding Natural Beauty. Their reward is a superb setting beside coppice woodland with relaxing views across sloping arable fields that stretch to the horizons. This 300-year-old brick and flint cottage has been a pub since 1830; inside it is largely furnished in a casual-contemporary style featuring an unusual log-end bar design, where guests may enjoy a wide choice of genuine Thai dishes and some fine local beers.

Open all day all wk 12-11 (Sun 12-10.30) Closed: 25 Dec, 1 Jan **Bar Meals** L served all wk 12-2.30 D served Mon-Sat 6-9.30, Sun 6-8 Av main course £8.95 **Restaurant** L served all wk 12-2.30 D served all wk 6-9.30 Av 3 course à la carte fr £20 ⊕ FREE HOUSE ◀ Ramsbury, Flack Manor Flack's Double Drop, Upham Punter. ▼ 12 **Facilities** Non-diners area ✿ (Bar Restaurant Garden) ♦ Children's menu Children's portions Garden ⋈ Parking Wi-fi 🚐 (notice required)

TICHBORNE   Map 5 SU53

The Tichborne Arms

PICK OF THE PUBS

SO24 0NA ☎ 01962 733760
e-mail: tichbornearms@xln.co.uk
dir: *Pub signed from B3046, S of A31 between Winchester & Alresford*

Exceptional beers in secluded country inn

This very striking inter-war thatched pub stands on a site that has hosted inns since the early 15th century. In a settlement of thatched cottages close to the lively River Itchen and within the South Downs National Park, it's handy for both the Watercress Line steam railway and the charming cathedral city of Winchester. A Stephen Fry film *The Tichborne Claimant* tells the curious story of Victorian intrigue that brought the family, after which village and inn are named, to the headlines. Inside the inn are countless artefacts, antiques and taxidermy set in part-panelled, rustically furnished rooms, with log-burners and a stand-up piano. Owner Patrick Roper cooks to order from short daily menus, typically featuring fillet of sea bream with a creamy prawn sauce; medallions of pork tenderloin with an apple and cider sauce, or mushroom tagliatelle. Beers from carefully selected microbreweries like Downton and real ciders may be enjoyed in the tree-shaded garden, also host to a beer festival each third weekend in August.

Open all wk 11.45-3 6-11.30 (Sat open all day) **Bar Meals** L served all wk 12-2 D served all wk 6-9 **Restaurant** L served all wk 12-2.30 D served all wk 6-9 ⊕ FREE HOUSE ◀ Sharp's, Downton, Hop Back, Palmers, Bowman Ŏ Mr Whitehead's Cirrus Minor & Strawberry. ▼ 10 **Facilities** Non-diners area ✿ (Bar Restaurant Garden) ♦ Children's portions Garden ⋈ Beer festival Parking Wi-fi 🚐

UPPER FROYLE   Map 5 SU74

The Hen & Chicken Inn

GU34 4JH ☎ 01420 22115
e-mail: info@henandchicken.co.uk
dir: *2m from Alton, on A31 adjacent to petrol station*

Character coaching inn off the A31

Highwaymen, hop-pickers and high clergy have all supped and succoured here in this noble, three-storey Georgian road house. They'd still recognise some of the comfortably traditional interior - timeless panelling, beams, old tables and inglenook; maybe, too, the little wooden barn in a corner of the grassy garden, stood on its painted staddle stones. The reliable country menu is strong on local produce and vegetables from the garden; nibble on roast wild garlic and rosemary studded focaccia prior to calves' liver and bacon with parsley mash, whilst the carvery is a particular favourite. Badger beers include Tanglefoot.

Open all day all wk 11-11 (Sun 12-9) **Bar Meals** L served all wk 12-9 D served all wk 12-9 food served all day **Restaurant** L served all wk 12-9 D served all wk 12-9 food served all day ⊕ HALL & WOODHOUSE ◀ Badger Tanglefoot, K&B Sussex Ŏ Westons Stowford Press. **Facilities** Non-diners area ✿ (Bar Garden) ♦ Children's menu Children's portions Play area Garden ⋈ Parking Wi-fi 🚐 (notice required)

WARNFORD   Map 5 SU62

The George & Falcon ★★★★ INN

Warnford Rd SO32 3LB ☎ 01730 829623
e-mail: reservations@georgeandfalcon.com
dir: *M27 junct 10, A32 signed Alton. Approx 10.5m to Warnford*

Country inn with modern cuisine

The lively little River Meon slides past the garden of this imposing inn, first recorded over 400 years ago. The cosy, fire-warmed snug is the place to settle with a pint of Ringwood Fortyniner and reflect on a grand winter walk on nearby Old Winchester Hill; or discover the terrace and consider the enticing modern British menu. Seared scallops and white pudding whet the appetite for mains which include local pheasant breast braised in Somerset cider with wild mushrooms and pancetta, or chilli and black pudding-stuffed lamb with port and rosemary jus. Six en suite residential rooms complete the scene.

Open all day all wk 11-11 (Oct-Mar 11-3 6-11) **Bar Meals** L served all wk 11-3 D served all wk 6-9 Av main course £10.95 **Restaurant** L served all wk 12-3 D served all wk 6-9 Av 3 course à la carte fr £24 ⊕ MARSTON'S ◀ Ringwood Best Bitter, Fortyniner Ŏ Thatchers Gold. ▼ 9 **Facilities** Non-diners area ✿ (Bar Restaurant Garden) ♦ Children's menu Children's portions Family room Garden ⋈ Parking Wi-fi 🚐 (notice required) **Rooms** 6

Save on hotels. Book at theAA.com/hotel

HAMPSHIRE 227 ENGLAND

WARSASH
Map 5 SU40

The Jolly Farmer Country Inn

29 Fleet End Rd S031 9JH ☎ 01489 572500
e-mail: mail@thejollyfarmeruk.com
dir: *M27 junct 9, A27 (Fareham), right into Warsash Rd. 2m, left into Fleet End Rd*

Locally caught seafood a speciality

Martin and Cilla O'Grady have been running the show here since 1983, and their enthusiasm is as strong as ever. Old farming implements decorate the rustic-style bars, while outside are a patio, beer garden and children's play area. The comprehensive menu ranges from locally caught seafood dishes, sandwiches, salads, grills and pub favourites, to home-made dishes like confit of duck in orange and black cherry jus; grilled fresh haddock with prawn, garlic and herb sauce; and vegetable tikka masala. Daily chalkboard lunch, dinner and Sunday lunch specials, such as Catch-of-the-Day, and dishes for children, extend the options.

Open all day all wk 11-11 **Bar Meals** L served Mon-Fri 12-2.30, Sat-Sun all day D served Mon-Fri 6-10, Sat-Sun all day Av main course £9.95 **Restaurant** L served all wk 12-2.30 D served all wk 6-10 ◀ Fuller's London Pride, George Gale & Co HSB & Seafarers, Worthington's. ♥ 14 **Facilities** Non-diners area ❖ (Bar Garden) ♦❖ Children's menu Children's portions Play area Family room Garden ⋒ Parking Wi-fi ▥ (notice required)

WELL
Map 5 SU74

The Chequers Inn

RG29 1TL ☎ 01256 862605
e-mail: thechequers5@hotmail.co.uk
dir: *From Odiham High St into King St, becomes Long Ln. 3m, left at T-junct, pub 0.25m on top of hill*

Locally renowned little cracker

The features that many visitors to this charming pub remember are its low-beamed bar, log fires and scrubbed tables, all of course in keeping with its 15th-century origins. Since arriving in 2012, landlady Jane Bergeman and her kitchen team have maintained a reputation for nourishing contemporary dishes and British classics, represented by chilli and sesame calamari; seafood pancake; Cajun chicken burger; pan-fried calves' liver and bacon; and vegetable pasta bake, while game goes great guns in season. A pint of Badger tastes every bit as good out front under the grapevines as it does in the rear garden overlooking the countryside.

Open all wk 12-3 6-11 (Sat 12-11 Sun 12-10.30) **Bar Meals** L served Mon-Fri 12-2, Sat 12-3, Sun 12-6 D served Mon-Thu 6.30-9, Fri-Sat 6.30-9.30 **Restaurant** L served Mon-Fri 12-2, Sat 12-3, Sun 12-6 D served Mon-Thu 6.30-9, Fri-Sat 6.30-9.30 ⊕ HALL & WOODHOUSE ◀ Badger First Gold & Tanglefoot, Guinness, Seasonal ales Ö Westons Stowford Press. ♥ 8 **Facilities** Non-diners area ❖ (Bar Garden Outside area) ♦❖ Children's portions Garden Outside area ⋒ Parking Wi-fi ▥ (notice required)

WEST MEON
Map 5 SU62

The Thomas Lord ◉◉

PICK OF THE PUBS

High St GU32 1LN ☎ 01730 829244
dir: *M3 junct 9, A272 towards Petersfield, right at x-roads onto A32, 1st left*

Award-winning food in village inn with impressive cricketing connections

There has been a change of hands at this beautifully restored pub in the pretty village of West Meon close to Winchester. Now part of the Upham Pub Company, The Thomas Lord was named after the founder of Lord's Cricket Ground, who retired to West Meon in 1830 and is buried in the churchyard. The bar is decorated with cricketing memorabilia and is the setting for well-kept Upham ales, and a sophisticated range of wines. The pub's own garden supplies the kitchen with herbs, salads and vegetables, as do local farms and small-scale producers. The pub even has its own free-range hens. The result is a menu of seasonal delights which has gained head chef Fran Joyce two AA Rosettes. A typical meal might start with braised ox cheek, beetroot, carrot and walnut salad, followed by roasted crown of partridge, confit leg, curried squash purée, lentil jus and sultanas.

Open all day all wk **Bar Meals** L served Mon-Fri 12-2.30, Sat 12-3, Sun 12-4 D served Mon-Thu 6-9.30, Fri-Sat 6-10, Sun 6-9 Av main course £11 **Restaurant** L served Mon-Fri 12-2.30, Sat 12-3, Sun 12-4 D served Mon-Thu 6-9.30, Fri-Sat 6-10, Sun 6-9 Av 3 course à la carte fr £25 ⊕ FREE HOUSE ◀ Upham Ales, Ringwood Best Bitter Ö Thatchers Cheddar Valley. ♥ 15 **Facilities** Non-diners area ❖ (Bar Garden) ♦❖ Children's portions Garden ⋒ Parking Wi-fi ▥

WEST TYTHERLEY
Map 5 SU22

The Black Horse

The Village SP5 1NF ☎ 01794 340308
e-mail: info@theblackhorsepublichouse.co.uk
dir: *In village centre*

Ideal spot for walkers and cyclists

This traditional 17th-century former coaching inn is the perfect spot to rest and refuel. Located on the Clarendon Way, the popular walking/cycling trail between Winchester and Salisbury, it's a proper village community pub, replete with skittle alley, regular quiz nights and locals supping pints of Hop Back and Flower Pots ales by the blazing fire in the oak-beamed main bar. Food ranges from lunchtime filled ciabatta sandwiches to curries, pie of the day, burgers and main courses like tarragon chicken or creamy vegetable risotto. There is also a good-value and extensive Sunday lunch menu.

Open 12-3 6-11 (Sun 12-8) Closed: 2 days after New Year BHs, Mon L & Tue L **Bar Meals** L served Wed-Sun D served Tue-Sun **Restaurant** L served Wed-Sun D served Tue-Sun ⊕ FREE HOUSE ◀ Hop Back, Stonehenge, Bowman, Flower Pots Ö Westons 1st Quality. ♥ 8 **Facilities** Non-diners area ❖ (Bar Restaurant Garden) ♦❖

Children's menu Children's portions Play area Garden ⋒ Parking Wi-fi ▥ (notice required)

WICKHAM
Map 5 SU51

Greens Restaurant & Bar

The Square PO17 5JQ ☎ 01329 833197
dir: *M27 junct 10, A32 to Wickham*

Still going strong in charming village

With a black-and-white-timbered upper storey, Greens stands prominently on a corner of Wickham's medieval market square, the second largest in England. Owners Frank and Carol Duckworth opened here in 1985 and still use their original tag line – 'Nothing is too much trouble'. Head chef Joe Middleton changes the modern British menus seasonally to include starters like pan-fried chicken breast with warm salad of Alresford watercress, Brussels sprout leaves, wild mushrooms and chestnut dressing. Sample main dishes include duo of Hampshire free-range pork with black pudding mash, caramelised rhubarb and apple purée, crackling and thyme jus; pan-seared king scallops with apple and celeriac salad and pancetta lardons; and wild mushroom and spinach risotto with Old Winchester cheese and rocket salad. Ladies Who Lunch have their own club. Bowmans, in nearby Droxford, supplies two of its award-winning ales, while Spitfire comes from Faversham's Shepherd Neame.

Open 10-3 6-11 (Sat 11-11 Sun & BH 12-5 May-Sep all day) Closed: 19-20 May, Sun eve & Mon **Bar Meals** L served Tue-Sat 12-2.30, Sun 12-5 D served Tue-Sat 6-9.30 Av main course £13.24 **Restaurant** L served Tue-Fri 12-2.30, Sat 12-9.30 Sun 12-5 D served Tue-Sat 6-9.30 Fixed menu price fr £10.95 Av 3 course à la carte fr £30 ⊕ FREE HOUSE ◀ Bowman Wallops Wood & Swift One, Shepherd Neame Spitfire. ♥ 12 **Facilities** Non-diners area ♦❖ Children's portions Garden ⋒

WINCHESTER
Map 5 SU42

The Bell Inn

83 St Cross Rd S023 9RE ☎ 01962 865284
dir: *M3 junct 11, B3355 towards city centre. Approx 1m pub on right*

Community local close to pretty water meadows

Close to the 12th-century Hospital of St Cross & Almshouse of Noble Poverty, this community local is now run by David and Kerry Hicks. Greene King ales and good value food are served in the main bar, pine-furnished lounge and walled garden. Daily specials include pan-fried sirloin steak; oven-roasted chicken supreme stuffed with mozzarella and chorizo; pan-seared salmon fillet; and wild mushroom risotto. There's a children's selection too. A walk through the River Itchen water meadows leads to Winchester College and the city centre.

Open all day all wk 11-11 (Fri-Sat 12-12 Sun 12-10.30) ⊕ GREENE KING ◀ Ruddles Best, Belhaven Grand Slam, Morland Old Speckled Hen Ö Westons Stowford Press. **Facilities** ❖ (Bar Garden) ♦❖ Children's menu Children's portions Play area Garden Parking Wi-fi

WINCHESTER *continued*

The Black Boy NEW

1 Wharf Hill SO23 9NQ ☎ 01962 861754
e-mail: enquiries@theblackboypub.com
dir: *Off Chesil St (B3300)*

Traditional pub with the emphasis firmly on local ales

This old fashioned whitewashed pub in the ancient capital of Wessex is a decidedly beer-led hostelry. As well as three regular regional ales from the Cheriton, Ringwood and Hop Back breweries, The Black Boy offers two Hampshire guests, perhaps from Triple fff or Itchen Valley. A small selection of good French wines is also available. The interior features old wooden tables and a quirky decor with all manner of objects hanging from the ceiling, while the short daily menu on the blackboard could include sandwiches, home-made burgers and fish and chips. There is a sheltered garden with patio heaters.

Open all day all wk **Bar Meals** L served Wed-Sun 12-2 D served Tue-Sat 7-9 Av main course £10 ⊕ FREE HOUSE 🍺 Flower Pots Cheriton Pots, Ringwood Best Bitter, Bowman Ales Swift One, Hop Back Summer Lightning, Guest Ales ♂ Westons Stowford Press.
Facilities Non-diners area ❀ (All areas) ♦ Garden Outside area ⊼ Wi-fi

The Golden Lion

99 Alresford Rd SO23 0JZ ☎ 01962 865512
e-mail: derekandbrid@thegoldenlionwinchester.co.uk
web: www.thegoldenlionwinchester.co.uk
dir: *From Union St in town centre follow 'All other routes' sign. At rdbt 1st exit into High St. At rdbt 1st exit into Bridge St (B3404) signed Alton/Alresford, (becomes Alresford Rd)*

Charming flower bedecked pub

Winners of Winchester in Bloom awards for multiple years, bedecked with flower baskets, Brid and Derek Phelan's 1932-built, delightfully cottage-style pub is on Winchester's eastern fringe. As well as Irish charm, expect main and specials menus offering plenty of straightforward hearty pub meals. Lasagne, home-baked ham, battered hake fillet, steak-and-ale pie, and chargrilled lamb cutlets all feature. Soft cushions are

provided in the 'treasure chest' by the back door for those sitting in the large beer garden.

The Golden Lion

Open all wk Mon-Sat 11.30-3 5.30-11 (Sun 12-10.30) **Bar Meals** L served all wk 12-2.30 D served all wk 6-9 **Restaurant** L served all wk 12-2.30 D served all wk 6-9 ⊕ WADWORTH 🍺 6X, Henry's Original IPA, Seasonal ales ♂ Westons Stowford Press. ☗ **Facilities** Non-diners area ❀ (Bar Restaurant Garden) ♦ Children's menu Children's portions Garden ⊼ Parking Wi-fi 🚌 (notice required)

See advert on opposite page

The Green Man NEW

53 Southgate St SO23 9EH ☎ 01962 866809
e-mail: greenmanwinchester@gmail.com
dir: *Telephone for directions*

Cool and quirky town centre treasure

Jayne Gillin appears to have the midas touch with pubs in Winchester, sprucing up and reinvigorating fading boozers with style and panache and the Green Man, located opposite the city's tiny cinema, is no exception. Expect a funky retro vibe in the bar — wood floors, comfy chairs and intimate booths — a Gothic-style upstairs dining room with rich fabrics, candelabras and chandeliers, and in the Outhouse, the revamped old skittle alley, a chic and cool venue for private parties with platter suppers, pitchers of wine and buckets of beer served at a huge refectory table. Food in the bar takes in pig's cheeks with lentil and potato stew; macaroni cheese; and platters of charcuterie and cheeses, best washed down with a pint of Morlands.

Open all day all wk Closed: 25-26 Dec **Bar Meals** L served all wk 12-3 D served all wk 6-10 Av main course £11 **Restaurant** D served Thu-Sat 6-10 Fixed menu price fr £24.95 ⊕ GREENE KING 🍺 St Edmunds, Morland ♂ Aspall. ☗ 16 **Facilities** Non-diners area Wi-fi

The Old Vine ★★★★ INN

8 Great Minster St SO23 9HA ☎ 01962 854616
e-mail: reservations@oldvinewinchester.com
dir: *M3 junct 11, follow St Cross & City Centre signs. 1m, right at Green Man pub right into St Swithun St, bear left into Symonds St (one-way). Left into Little Minster St (NB for Sat Nav use SO23 9HB)*

Cathedral views and top hospitality

An elderly vine rambles all over the street frontage of this elegant pub, built on Saxon foundations in the 18th century. Directly opposite is Winchester's fine cathedral and the City Museum. Ringwood Best is the house real ale, with three local guests keeping it company in the oak-beamed bar, where you can eat sandwiches, salads and light meals. Freshly prepared, in the restaurant are, typically, crispy wholetail scampi; Japanese-style Scottish salmon fillet with sesame seed crust; and ricotta and spinach cannelloni with pine nut, sultana, shallot and garlic sauce. At the back is a flower-filled patio.

Open all day all wk Closed: 25 Dec **Bar Meals** L served Mon-Thu 12-2.30, Fri-Sun 12-6 D served Mon-Sat 6.30-9.30, Sun 6.30-9 Av main course £12 **Restaurant** L served Mon-Thu 12-2.30, Fri-Sun 12-3 D served Mon-Sat 6.30-9.30, Sun 6.30-9 ⊕ ENTERPRISE INNS 🍺 Ringwood Best Bitter, Guest ales. ☗ 11 **Facilities** Non-diners area ❀ (Bar Outside area) ♦ Family room Outside area ⊼ Wi-fi **Rooms** 5

The Westgate Inn ★★★ INN

2 Romsey Rd SO23 8TP ☎ 01962 820222
e-mail: wghguy@yahoo.co.uk
dir: *On corner of Romsey Rd & Upper High St, opposite Great Hall & Medieval West Gate*

Top of the hill landmark hostelry

Standing boldly on a street corner, the curving, Palladian-style façade of this 1860s inn overlooks the city's medieval Westgate. A well-known interest in real ales and ciders is backed up by an annual beer festival. Full English breakfasts and mid-morning brunches are followed by made-to-order lunchtime sandwiches, soups and uncomplicated three-egg omelettes with various fillings; bangers and mash; Spanish-style shepherd's pie with chorizo and patatas bravas; and 21-day aged Hampshire steaks, which landlords Guy and Helen Carpenter reckon are the best in the world. Attractive and good-sized accommodation is available.

Open all day all wk 12-11.30 **Bar Meals** L served all wk 7-2.30 D served all wk 6-9.30 Av main course £8.50 **Restaurant** L served all wk 12-2.30 D served all wk 6-9.30 ⊕ MARSTON'S 🍺 Burton Bitter, Jennings Cumberland Ale, Banks's Original, Guest ales ♂ Thatchers Gold, Green Goblin.
Facilities Non-diners area ♦ Children's menu Children's portions Beer festival Wi-fi **Rooms** 8

Save on hotels. Book at **theAA.com/hotel**

HAMPSHIRE 229 ENGLAND

The Golden Lion

99 Alresford Road, Winchester, Hampshire, SO23 0JZ

Tel: 01962 865512
Web: www.thegoldenlionwinchester.co.uk
E-mail: derekandbrid@thegoldenlionwinchester.co.uk

We warmly invite you to *The Golden Lion Pub*, Winchester, for our cosy vintage style interiors, excellent home cooked food and great Irish welcome! We are located just on the eastern edge of the city, within very easy reach of the M3, the A272 and the A34, just a 10 minute walk into the beautiful heart of the city with all of its historic attractions and wealth of independent shops. We have a large car park as well as patio areas and beer gardens to the front and back, including a special enclosed area for doggies to have a run. We are a TV and gaming machine free zone so that you can relax in our friendly atmosphere and enjoy our great background music, and we also welcome children who are eating with their parents/guardians.

We are very proud to have received many awards for the services that we offer, including 'The Casque Mark' and 'The Beer Master Award' for our real ales, the certification of 'Excellent' for our food hygiene and we have won many First Prizes for our floral displays and hanging baskets. We were also very honoured to have been awarded the Wadworth Brewery 'Best Pub of the Year' award. We were delighted to recieve the Quality Assured Award in Hampshire Hospitality Awards 2011/2012.

We have regular live music sessions such as Bluegrass music on the last Tuesday and Irish music on the second Thursday evening of each month.

We are really pleased to receive regular visitors who return again and again for the traditional home-cooked food and the constantly changing daily specials menus – so much so that we would recommend booking a table to avoid disappointment! We can also offer to arrange all your party booking requirements, whether you are planning a formal sit-down meal, a more casual finger buffet or a barbecue in the summer under our recently installed canopied 'Garden Room'.

We very much look forward to welcoming you very soon!

WINCHESTER *continued*

The Wykeham Arms ★★★★ INN ◉◉

PICK OF THE PUBS

75 Kingsgate St SO23 9PE ☎ 01962 853834
e-mail: wykehamarms@fullers.co.uk
dir: *Near Winchester College & Winchester Cathedral*

Buzzing gastro-pub in the heart of the city

Packed with character and always buzzing with activity, this handsome 270-year-old brick building draws an eclectic mix of customers, from businessmen and barristers, clergy and college dons to tourists and local drinkers and diners. Located in the oldest part of the city between the cathedral close and Winchester's famous college, the rambling series of bars and eating areas are furnished with old pine tables and college desks, four welcoming log fires and an impressive collection of hats, pictures and military memorabilia. From the modern, seasonal menus, order a starter of brown shrimp and River Teign mussel bouillabaisse, perhaps followed by fillet of wild boar, Jerusalem artichoke, potato fondant and sage-roasted apple. Finish off with hibiscus-infused pineapple and roast hazelnut ice cream. Light meals might be a ploughman's or roast apple and pickled beetroot salad. Wash down with a pint of HSB, or one of 20 excellent wines by the glass.

Open all day all wk **Bar Meals** L served all wk 12-3 D served all wk 6-9.30 Av main course £12 **Restaurant** L served all wk 12-3 D served all wk 6-9.30 Fixed menu price fr £13 Av 3 course à la carte fr £30 ⊕ FULLER'S ◀ London Pride, Geoge Gale & Co HSB & Seafarers, Flower Pots Goodens Gold, Guest ales Ŏ Westons. ♟ 20 **Facilities** Non-diners area ♣ (Bar) Outside area ♠ Parking Wi-fi **Rooms** 14

HEREFORDSHIRE

AYMESTREY | Map 9 SO46

The Riverside Inn

PICK OF THE PUBS

HR6 9ST ☎ 01568 708440
e-mail: theriverside@btconnect.com
dir: *On A4110, 18m N of Hereford*

Good walks, fishing and excellent refreshments

Built in 1580 the pub is midway along the Mortimer Trail and good walks and fishing are on the doorstep. A wood-panelled interior with low beams and log fires is a cosy bastion and there are ales such as Wye Valley Butty Back and Three Tuns XXX as well as Brook Farm and Robinsons Flagon cider. Visitors are encouraged to stroll in the vegetable, fruit and herb plots above the riverside beer garden to see that food here is 'truly seasonal and truly local'. Dishes are classic British with a twist with constantly changing menus: begin with gravad lax cured River Lugg trout and smoked trout mousse, beetroot relish and lemon dressing. A main course of seared breast of guinea fowl braised celeriac, Savoy cabbage, smoked bacon and rosemary sauce followed by lemon and almond tart with elderflower ice cream would keep anyone happy.

Open Tue-Sat 11-3 6-11 (Sun 12-3) Closed: 26 Dec & 1 Jan, Sun eve, Mon L, Mon eve in winter **Bar Meals** L served Tue-Sat 11-3, Sun 12-3 D served Tue-Sat 6-11 ⊕ FREE HOUSE ◀ Wye Valley Bitter & Butty Bach, Hobsons Best Bitter, Three Tuns XXX Ŏ Brook Farm Medium Dry, Westons Stowford Press, Robinsons Flagon. **Facilities** Non-diners area ♣ (Bar Restaurant Garden) ♦ Children's portions Garden ♠ Parking Wi-fi ➡ (notice required)

BODENHAM | Map 10 SO55

England's Gate Inn ★★★★ INN

HR1 3HU ☎ 01568 797286
e-mail: englandsgate@btconnect.com
dir: *From Hereford take A49 towards Leominster, right onto A417 at Bosey Dinmore hill, pub 2.5m on right*

Old inn with a popular festival

A pretty black-and-white coaching inn dating from around 1540, with atmospheric beamed bars and blazing log fires in winter. A picturesque beer garden attracts a good summer following, and so does the food. The menu features such dishes as slow-roasted shank of Ledbury lamb with parsnip and cardamom purée in red wine jus; baked fillet of cod topped with a garlic and herb crumble; or wholemeal pancakes filled with spinach and cream cheese served with ratatouille.

Open all day all wk ⊕ FREE HOUSE ◀ Wye Valley Bitter & Butty Bach, Wood's Shropshire Lad, Guest ales. **Facilities** ♦ Children's menu Children's portions Garden Parking Wi-fi **Rooms** 7

BRINGSTY COMMON | Map 10 SO75

Live and Let Live

WR6 5UW ☎ 01886 821462
e-mail: theliveandletlive@tiscali.co.uk
dir: *From A44 (Bromyard to Worcester road) turn at pub sign (black cat) onto track leading to common. At 1st fork bear right. Pub 200yds on right*

Ancient cider house offering local ales and ciders

One of the oldest buildings in the area is this 16th-century thatched cider house. Amidst bracken and old orchards on Bringsty Common, the timber-framed pub reopened following an extensive renovation. Local Oliver's cider is joined by beers from Herefordshire breweries. Bar meals and the intimate Thatch Restaurant major on seasonal food from the home area. A typical main course option is chicken breast stuffed with sun-dried tomatoes, topped with melted mozzarella and served with duchess potatoes, fresh vegetables and a home-made cheese sauce. A four-day beer and cider festival runs over the Easter weekend, when live music adds to the entertainment.

Open Tue-Thu 12-2.30 5.30-11 (Fri-Sun & summer all day) Closed: Mon (ex BHs) **Bar Meals** L served Tue-Sun 12-2 (12-4 summer) D served Tue-Sun 6-9 (5-9 summer) **Restaurant** D served Tue-Sun 6-9 ⊕ FREE HOUSE ◀ Wye Valley, Hobsons Ŏ Thatchers, Oliver's. **Facilities** Non-diners area ♦ Children's portions Garden ♠ Beer festival Parking ➡ (notice required)

CAREY | Map 10 SO53

Cottage of Content

HR2 6NG ☎ 01432 840242
dir: *From x-rds on A49 between Hereford & Ross-on-Wye, follow Hoarwithy signs. In Hoarwithy branch right, follow Carey signs*

Cracking inn secluded in Wye Valley

Lost along narrow lanes in bucolic countryside close to the meandering River Wye, this pretty streamside inn has been licensed for 529 years. Now, as then, local ciders and beers flow from the bar in the lovingly updated interior, which boasts log fire and flagged floors, with heavy timbering and pubby furnishings. Making the most of the Herefordshire setting; locally smoked salmon is a favourite starter, prior to lightly smoked pheasant breast wrapped in bacon and herbs on tomato cassoulet. From the sloping, family-friendly grassy garden are relaxing views across the tranquil countryside.

Open 12-2 6.30-11 (times vary summer & winter) Closed: 1wk Feb, 1wk Oct, Sun eve, Mon, Tue L (winter only) **Bar Meals** L served Tue-Sat 12-2 **Restaurant** L served Tue-Sun 12-2 D served Tue-Sat 6.30-9 ⊕ FREE HOUSE ◀ Wye Valley Butty Bach, Hobsons Best Bitter Ŏ Ross-on-Wye, Carey Organic, Westons Stowford Press. **Facilities** Non-diners area ♦ Children's menu Children's portions Garden ♠ Parking ➡ (notice required)

Save on hotels. Book at theAA.com/hotel

HEREFORDSHIRE 231 ENGLAND

CLIFFORD
Map 9 SO24

The Castlefields NEW

HR3 5HB ☎ 01497 831554
e-mail: info@thecastlefields.co.uk
dir: On B4352 between Hay-on-Wye & Bredwardine

Traditional country pub and restaurant in Golden Valley

After hours spent browsing in nearby Hay-on-Wye, the 'Town of Books', a ten-minute drive will get you to this family-run, 16th-century former coach-house. The interior is furnished with elegantly modern tables and chairs, although a reminder of the pub's long life is the glass-covered, 39ft-deep well. Home-cooked, locally-sourced food served all day includes roast half-duck with orange sauce; pan-fried liver and crispy bacon; tagliatelle carbonara; wholetail scampi; and lots of grills. Wednesday is curry night and traditional roasts are served on Sundays. Rev James and his companions, Doom Bar and Butty Bach, will be in the bar.

Open all day Closed: Mon (Nov-Feb) **Bar Meals** Av main course £5.95 food served all day **Restaurant** Av 3 course à la carte fr £16.95 food served all day ⊕ FREE HOUSE ◀ Sharp's Doom Bar, Brains The Rev. James, Wye Valley Butty Bach. ❦ **Facilities** Non-diners area ♦♦ Children's menu Children's portions Play area Garden ⩍ Parking Wi-fi 🚌 (notice required)

CRASWALL
Map 9 SO23

The Bulls Head

HR2 0PN ☎ 01981 510616
e-mail: info@thebullsheadcraswall.co.uk
dir: From A465 at Pandy follow Walterstone, Oldcastle & Longtown signs. In Longtown follow Craswall sign. Village in 11m

Weekend only refuelling stop

You'll find this old drovers' inn south of Hay-on-Wye in a remote spot at the foot of the Black Mountains. Only open at weekends, it is popular with walkers and riders, who tie their horses at the rail outside. Real ales and farmhouse ciders are served through the hole in the wall servery in the bar with its flagstone floors and log fires. There is a Mediterranean feel to the menu, which might take in soup au pistou; Italian style meatballs; ragu of boar with chestnuts and creamed polenta; and clementine cake for dessert.

Open Fri-Sun 12-3 7-late Closed: Mon-Thu (please telephone in Jan & Feb for wknd opening times) **Bar Meals** L served Fri-Sun 12-2.30 D served Fri-Sat 7-8.30 Av main course £15 **Restaurant** L served Fri-Sun 12-2.30 D served Fri-Sat 7-8.30 Av 3 course à la carte fr £26 ⊕ FREE HOUSE ◀ Wye Valley Butty Bach & Bitter ♂ Gwatkin's Farmhouse, Westons Old Rosie, Dunkertons Premium Organic & Black Fox. **Facilities** Non-diners area ♣ (Bar Garden) ♦♦ Garden Wi-fi

DORSTONE
Map 9 SO34

The Pandy Inn

PICK OF THE PUBS

HR3 6AN ☎ 01981 550273
e-mail: info@pandyinn.co.uk
dir: Exit B4348, W of Hereford. Inn in village centre

Lovely views from the large garden

Just a few miles from Hay-on-Wye, The Pandy is an ideal stop when touring the Brecon Beacons or the picturesque Golden Valley. Reputed to be one of the oldest inns in the county, Richard de Brito, one of the four Norman knights who murdered Thomas à Becket in 1170, is said to have built The Pandy to house workers. Much later, Oliver Cromwell is known to have taken refuge here during the Civil War. The ancient hostelry is delightfully situated opposite the village green; the large garden has views of Dorstone Hill. The interior retains some original flagstone floors and beams. In the dog-friendly bar you'll find Wye Valley Butty Bach, or a pint of Stowford Press cider if you prefer. Bar food takes the form of baguettes, and pizzas can be ordered in two sizes. In the restaurant, there is a short but excellent range of dishes.

Open Tue-Fri 12-3 6-11 (Sat 12-11 Sun 12-3 6.30-10.30) Closed: Mon **Bar Meals** L served Tue-Sun 12-2 **Restaurant** L served Tue-Sun 12-2 D served Tue-Sun 6.30-9 ⊕ FREE HOUSE ◀ Wye Valley Butty Bach, Golden Valley Brewers Choice ♂ Westons Stowford Press. **Facilities** Non-diners area ♣ (Bar Garden) ♦♦ Children's menu Children's portions Play area Garden ⩍ Parking Wi-fi 🚌

EARDISLEY
Map 9 SO34

The Tram Inn NEW

Church Rd HR3 6PG ☎ 01544 327251
e-mail: info@thetraminn.co.uk
dir: On A4111 at junct with Woodeaves Rd

Friendly free house with a long tradition of hospitality

This traditional black and white timbered, 16th-century inn has wood burning stoves to welcome you in the winter and a garden for enjoying a pint and a meal in the warmer months, and the chance for a game of petanque too. Carte and set menus offer dishes such as chicken and duck liver pâté; roasted sweet potato soup; spinach and goats' cheese pasty; Herefordshire steak and ale pie; roast topside of Willersley beef (served pink); and pan roasted hake and salmon fillets. Blackboard special add to the choices. Desserts are tempting – warmed Eccles cake slice with custard, or boozy banoffee pie with butterscotch ice cream. A family and dog friendly pub.

Open 12-3 6-12 (Fri-Sat 12-3 6-12.30 Sun 12-3 7-11) Closed: Mon (ex BHs) **Bar Meals** L served Tue-Sun 12-3 D served Tue-Sat 6-9 **Restaurant** L served Tue-Sun 12-3 D served Tue-Sat 6-9 ⊕ FREE HOUSE ◀ Wye Valley Butty Bach, Hobsons Best Bitter ♂ Westons Stowford Press, Dunkertons Organic. **Facilities** Non-diners area ♣ (Bar Garden) ♦♦ Children's portions Play area Garden ⩍ Parking 🚌 (notice required)

GARWAY
Map 9 SO42

Garway Moon Inn ★★★★ INN NEW

HR2 8RQ ☎ 01600 750270
e-mail: info@garwaymooninn.co.uk
dir: From Hereford S on A49. Right onto A466, right onto B4521. At Broad Oak turn right to Garway

Eat, drink and relax in this privately owned country inn

In 2007, the Bolderson family bought this substantial former farm building, dating from around 1750, overlooking Garway Common. 'We plan to be here for a long time,' they say. A Hereford brewery supplies real ale and ciders, while Wye Valley provides its popular Butty Bach. Traditional, home-made pub food sourced from ethically sound suppliers has helped gain an AA Dinner Award for seasonal menus offering black pudding and chorizo potato cake; fish chowder; pheasant pie; and roasted beetroot risotto. Check out the mid-week lunch, and evening burger and curry deals. The smart guest rooms are named after long-closed local pubs.

Open Mon & Wed 6pm-late (Thu-Fri 12-3 6-late Sat-Sun noon-late) Closed: Tue **Bar Meals** L served Thu-Sun 12-2 D served Wed-Mon 6-9 **Restaurant** L served Thu-Sun 12-2 D served Wed-Mon 6-9 ⊕ FREE HOUSE ◀ Wye Valley Butty Bach & HPA ♂ Westons Stowford Press. **Facilities** Non-diners area ♣ (Bar Garden) ♦♦ Children's menu Children's portions Family room Garden ⩍ Parking Wi-fi 🚌 (notice required) **Rooms** 3

HAMPTON BISHOP
Map 10 SO53

The Bunch of Carrots

HR1 4JR ☎ 01432 870237
e-mail: bunchofcarrots@buccaneer.co.uk
dir: From Hereford take A4103, A438, then B4224

Child-friendly riverside pub offering local ales

Named after a rock formation in the River Wye that runs beside this family-friendly free house, the pub's interior boasts real fires, old beams and flagstone floors. Outside there's a garden and children's play area, making this an ideal place in which to sample a pint of Wye Valley Bitter. The extensive menu of pub favourites offers baguettes and hand-cut sandwiches as well as hot dishes like fish pie and peas; or slow-roast belly pork and crackling. There's also a daily specials board, carvery and children's menu.

Open all day all wk ⊕ FREE HOUSE ◀ Wye Valley Bitter, Sharp's Doom Bar, Courage Best Bitter ♂ Westons Stowford Press. **Facilities** ♦♦ Children's menu Play area Garden Parking Wi-fi

HOARWITHY — Map 10 SO52

The New Harp Inn

HR2 6QH ☎ 01432 840900
e-mail: newharpinn@btinternet.com
dir: *From Ross-on-Wye take A49 towards Hereford. Turn right for Hoarwithy*

A real country pub

The New Harp's slogan reads: 'Kids, dogs and muddy boots all welcome' – and it's certainly popular with locals, fishermen, campers and visitors to the countryside. Situated on the River Wye in an Area of Outstanding Natural Beauty, the pub has extensive gardens and a real babbling brook. Begin your visit with a local real ale or the home-produced cider. The menu includes starters such as chicken liver pâté, and balsamic-glazed goats' cheese on a pesto croûton, then moves on to mains like wild boar sausages, and Hereford rump steak. There's also a board for specials. Look out for Bank Holiday beer festivals and a cider festival on the August Bank Holiday.

Open all wk 12-3 6-11 (Fri-Sun all day) **Bar Meals** L served Mon-Fri 12-3, Sat-Sun all day D served Mon-Fri 6-9, Sat-Sun all day Av main course £12 **Restaurant** L served Mon-Fri 12-3, Sat-Sun all day D served Mon-Fri 6.30-9.30, Sat-Sun all day ⊕ FREE HOUSE ◀ Wye Valley Butty Bach, Butcombe, Holden's, Otter ♻ Broome Farm, Westons Stowford Press & Gold Label, New Harp Reserve. ♚ 10 **Facilities** Non-diners area ♥ (Bar Garden) ♦♦ Children's menu Children's portions Garden ♛ Beer festival Cider festival Parking Wi-fi ▄

KILPECK — Map 9 SO43

The Kilpeck Inn

HR2 9DN ☎ 01981 570464
e-mail: booking@kilpeckinn.com
web: www.kilpeckinn.com
dir: *From Hereford take A465 S. In 6m at Belmont rdbt left towards Kilpeck. Follow church & inn signs*

A warm welcome awaits at this green inn

Kilpeck is renowned for its Romanesque church, a few minutes' walk from this 250-year-old, whitewashed pub. In autumn 2012, the management was taken over by Julian Vaughn, who is supported by experienced chef

Ross Williams. The bar stocks local real ales, and draught cider from Westons in Much Marcle. Smoked haddock chowder; vegetable and goats' cheese terrine; and roast rack of Marches lamb number among the typical locally sourced dishes. Commendably green, the pub uses a wood-pellet burner for underfloor heating; rainwater to flush the loos; and solar panels for hot water.

Open 12-2.30 5.30-11 (Sun 12-5.30) Closed: 25 Dec, Sun eve **Bar Meals** L served Mon-Sat 12-2, Sun 12-3 D served Mon-Sat 6-9 **Restaurant** L served Mon-Sat 12-2, Sun 12-3 D served Mon-Sat 7-9 ⊕ FREE HOUSE ◀ Butcombe Bitter, Wye Valley Butty Bach, Golden Valley .410 ♻ Westons Stowford Press. ♚ 9 **Facilities** Non-diners area ♦♦ Children's portions Garden ♛ Parking Wi-fi ▄ (notice required)

KIMBOLTON — Map 10 SO56

Stockton Cross Inn

HR6 0HD ☎ 01568 612509
e-mail: mb@ecolots.co.uk
dir: *From A49 take A4112 between Leominster & Ludlow*

Chocolate-box pretty, inside and out

Standing at a lonely crossroads where witches were allegedly hanged, this black-and-white former drovers' inn is picture-book pretty, and is regularly photographed by tourists as well as appearing on calendars and chocolate boxes. Landlord Mike Bentley keeps a good range of ales, including local Wye Valley Butty Bach, and regular guest ales. A typical meal could include devilled whitebait with home-made tartare sauce; slow-roasted belly pork with black pudding mash and red wine gravy; and apple crumble with custard. Lunchtime snacks include sandwiches and salads; in summer, enjoy them in the pretty garden.

Open 12-3 7-11 Closed: Sun eve & Mon **Bar Meals** L served Tue-Sun 12-2 D served Tue-Sat 7-9 Av main course £11 **Restaurant** L served Tue-Sun 12-2 D served Tue-Sat 7-9 ⊕ FREE HOUSE ◀ Wye Valley Butty Bach & HPA, Guest ales ♻ Robinsons Flagon, Westons Stowford Press. ♚ 8 **Facilities** Non-diners area ♦♦ Children's menu Children's portions Garden ♛ Parking Wi-fi

KINGTON — Map 9 SO25

The Stagg Inn and Restaurant ◉◉

PICK OF THE PUBS

Titley HR5 3RL ☎ 01544 230221
e-mail: reservations@thestagg.co.uk
dir: *Between Kington & Presteigne on B4355*

Fusion of village local and fine-dining restaurant

Part medieval, part early Victorian and with a bit from the 1970s, this highly acclaimed gastro-pub stands where two sheep-droving roads met. Then called The Balance

because wool was weighed there, it was renamed The Stag's Head by local 19th-century reformer Eliza Greenly after her family crest, the extra 'g' worming its way in later. Locals drink, eat and chat, undisturbed by music, amidst a collection of 200 pub jugs in the small bar and at farmhouse tables in the dining rooms. Real ales are Ludlow Gold and Wye Valley, and also from the Marches come draught and bottled ciders, and flavoured vodkas. Awarded two AA Rosettes, Roux-trained local boy Steve Reynolds produces 72-hour-cooked ox-cheek with smoked tongue and spinach; Herefordshire rump steak with roast cherry tomatoes and béarnaise sauce; and sea bass fillet with mushroom duxelle and charred leeks. Separately listed vegetarian dishes include pumpkin and cashew nut risotto.

Open Tue-Sat 12-3 6.30-10.30 (Sun 12-3) Closed: 25-27 Dec, 2wks Nov, 2wks Jan & Feb, Sun eve & Mon **Bar Meals** L served Tue-Sat 12-2 D served Tue-Sat 6.30-9 Av main course £11 **Restaurant** L served Tue-Sun 12-2 D served Tue-Sat 6.30-9 Av 3 course à la carte fr £30 ⊕ FREE HOUSE ◀ Ludlow Gold, Wye Valley Butty Bach ♻ Dunkertons, Westons, Ralph's, Robinsons. ♚ 12 **Facilities** Non-diners area ♥ (Bar Garden) Children's menu Children's portions Garden ♛ Parking Wi-fi

LEDBURY — Map 10 SO73

Prince of Wales

Church Ln HR8 1DL ☎ 01531 632250
e-mail: pebblewalk@gmail.com
dir: *M50 junct 2, A417 to Ledbury. Pub in town centre behind Market House (black & white building) on cobbled street (parking nearby)*

Black and white half-timbered inn offering home-made pies and excellent local beers

In an enchanting spot hidden between Ledbury's memorable half-timbered market house and the ancient church, a cobbled alley lined by eye-catching medieval houses hosts this cracking little pub. All low beams with bags of character, folk nights add to the craic at this half-timbered gem, where home-made pies or pork and beef sausages from an award-winning local butcher are firm favourites on the traditional pub menu. The local theme continues, with Westons Bounds scrumpy from neighbouring Much Marcle and beers from Wye Valley Brewery just down the road complementing a huge range of guest ales.

Open all day all wk **Bar Meals** L served all wk 12-2.30 D served all wk 6-8.30 ⊕ FREE HOUSE ◀ Hobsons Best Bitter, Wye Valley Butty Bach & HPA, Otter Bitter, Guest ales ♻ Westons Bounds. **Facilities** Non-diners area ♦♦ Children's menu Outside area ♛ Wi-fi ▄ (notice required)

The Talbot

14 New St HR8 2DX ☎ 01531 632963
e-mail: talbot.ledbury@wadworth.co.uk
dir: From A449 in Ledbury into Bye St, 2nd left into Woodley Rd, over bridge to junct, left into New St. Pub on right

Beautiful inn in historic town

This higgledy-piggledy marvel is one of the stars of Ledbury's extensive suite of amazing half-timbered buildings. Parts of it date back to 1550; the interior of the coaching inn oozes the character of great age, with fine beams and panelling in the refined dining room. Holes caused by musket shot fired during a Civil War skirmish are just another quirky talking point of the gabled building, where Wadworth's beers and local organic perry slake the thirst of ramblers fresh from the challenging local countryside. Indulge in tasty platters, large grills or chicken, ham and leek pie, perhaps sat in the sun-trap courtyard garden.

Open all day all wk **Bar Meals** L served all wk 12-3 D served all wk 5.30-9 **Restaurant** L served all wk 12-3 D served all wk 5.30-9 ⊕ WADWORTH ◀ 6X, Henry's Original IPA & Wadworth guest ales, Wye Valley Butty Bach Ỗ Westons Stowford Press, Wyld Wood Organic & Perry. ♀ 15 **Facilities** Non-diners area Children's portions Garden ♬ Wi-fi

The Trumpet Inn

Trumpet HR8 2RA ☎ 01531 670277
e-mail: trumpet@wadworth.co.uk
dir: 4m from Ledbury, at junct of A438 & A417

Beamed inn dating from the Middle Ages

This former coaching inn and post house takes its name from the days when mail coaches blew their horns on approaching the crossroads. A traditional black and white building, it dates back to the late 14th century. The cosy bars feature a wealth of exposed beams, with open fireplaces and a separate dining area. There is camembert or fisherman's platters to share, and main courses like Mr Waller's trio of sausages with mash and onion gravy; Angus beefburgers; or risotto or pie of the day to choose from.

Open all day all wk **Bar Meals** L served Mon-Sat 12-2.30, Sun 12-9 D served Mon-Sat 6-9, Sun 12-9 **Restaurant** L served Mon-Sat 12-2.30, Sun 12-9 D served Mon-Sat 6-9, Sun 12-9 ⊕ WADWORTH ◀ 6X, Henry's Original IPA Ỗ Westons Stowford Press. **Facilities** Non-diners area ♦♦ Garden Parking Wi-fi 🚌

LEOMINSTER **Map 10 SO45**

The Grape Vaults

Broad St HR6 8BS ☎ 01568 611404
e-mail: jusaxon@tiscali.co.uk
dir: Telephone for directions

In the heart of the town centre

This unspoilt, 15th-century pub is so authentic that even its fixed seating is Grade II listed. Its many charms include a small, homely bar complete with a coal fire. A good selection of real ale is a popular feature, and includes microbrewery offerings. The unfussy food encompasses favourites like cottage pie, lasagne, chicken curry and various fresh fish and vegetarian choices. There are also plenty of jackets, baguettes, omelettes and other lighter meals available. No jukebox, gaming machines or alcopops! There is live music every Sunday and in December a beer festival takes place on the same day as the Victorian street market.

Open all day all wk 11-11 **Bar Meals** L served all wk 12-2 D served Mon-Sat 5.30-9 ⊕ PUNCH TAVERNS ◀ Ludlow Best, Mayfields, Wood's, Malvern Hills, Guest ales Ỗ Westons Stowford Press. ♀ 10 **Facilities** Non-diners area ❀ (Bar Restaurant) ♦♦ Children's portions Beer festival Wi-fi **Notes** ☺

MADLEY **Map 9 SO43**

The Comet Inn

Stoney St HR2 9NJ ☎ 01981 250600
e-mail: thecometinn-madley@hotmail.co.uk
dir: 6m from Hereford on B4352

Hearty food served in converted cottages with plenty of character

Set at a crossroads deep in rural Herefordshire, the space-age parabolic dishes of the Madley Earth Station and the distant smudge of the Black Mountains provide contrasting skylines visible from the large grounds of this convivial local. Within, it retains much of the character of the old cottages from which it was converted over 100 years ago. Vicky Willison, the enthusiastic and welcoming owner, serves a select range of Herefordshire- and Worcestershire-brewed beers to accompany simple and hearty home-cooked pub food in the conservatory off the main bar, with smaller portions for smaller appetites if required. There is a large garden with children's play area.

Open all wk 12-3 6-11 (Fri-Sun & BHs all day) **Bar Meals** food served all day **Restaurant** food served all day ⊕ FREE HOUSE ◀ Wye Valley, St George's, Hereford Ỗ Westons Stowford Press, Gold Label & Vintage. **Facilities** Non-diners area ♦♦ Children's menu Children's portions Play area Garden ♬ Parking Wi-fi 🚌 (notice required)

ORLETON **Map 9 SO46**

The Boot Inn

SY8 4HN ☎ 01568 780228
e-mail: thebootinn@villagegreeninns.com
web: www.thebootinnorleton.co.uk
dir: Follow A49 S from Ludlow (approx 7m) to B4362 (Woofferton), 1.5m off B4362 turn left. Inn in village centre

Atmospheric hostelry with many tall tales

A black and white, half-timbered, 16th-century village inn characterised by a large inglenook fireplace, oak beams, mullioned windows, and exposed wattle-and-daub. Herefordshire real ales and Robinsons cider accompany dishes such as slow-cooked belly pork; line-caught sea bass; and wild mushroom and spinach linguine. In the back room is a painting from which the figure of one-time regular Joe Vale was obliterated after arguing with the landlord. Occasionally, old Joe's ghost returns.

Open all wk 12-3 5.30-11 (Sat-Sun all day) **Bar Meals** L served Mon-Sat 12-2, Sun 12-3.30 D served all wk 6.30-9 **Restaurant** L served Mon-Sat 12-2, Sun 12-3.30 D served all wk 6.30-9 ⊕ VILLAGE GREEN INNS ◀ Hobsons Best Bitter, Wye Valley, Local guest ales Ỗ Robinsons, Westons Stowford Press. **Facilities** Non-diners area ❀ (Bar Garden) ♦♦ Children's menu Play area Garden ♬ Cider festival Parking 🚌

PICK OF THE PUBS

The Saracens Head Inn ★★★★ INN

SYMONDS YAT (EAST)   Map 10 SO51

HR9 6JL ☎ 01600 890435
e-mail:
contact@saracensheadinn.co.uk
web: www.saracensheadinn.co.uk
dir: *A40 onto B4229, follow Symonds Yat East signs, 2m*

Former cider mill in an unrivalled location

Occupying a stunning position on the east bank of the River Wye where it flows into a steep wooded gorge on the edge of the Royal Forest of Dean, The Saracens Head can be reached by the inn's own ferry, which still operates by hand, just as it has for the past 200 years. Symonds Yat East ('yat' being the local name for a gate or pass) was named after Robert Symonds, a Sheriff of Herefordshire in the 17th century, and has been designated an Area of Outstanding Natural Beauty. There's a relaxed atmosphere throughout the 16th-century inn, from the bar (serving Wye Valley ales), the cosy lounge and stylish dining room, and two sunny terraces overlooking the Wye. Seasonal menus and daily specials boards offer both the traditional and modern: Carmarthenshire venison carpaccio with rocket, parmesan and basil oil could be followed by a home-made pie of the day or beer-battered Brixham cod fillet, triple-cooked chips and mushy peas. If you come at lunchtime, try the local version of a ploughman's – the ferryman's lunch. Main courses at dinner might include confit Welsh lamb shoulder cassoulet; or a savoury baked spinach cheesecake. Complete your meal with one of the desserts on the blackboard or you might opt for a slate of three local cheeses – Hereford Hop, Per Las and Celtic Promise – served with grapes, crackers, and quince and rose petal jelly. A stay in one of the ten en suite bedrooms is a must if you're exploring this area.

Open all day all wk Closed: 25 Dec **Bar Meals** L served all wk 12-2.30 D served all wk 6.30-9 **Restaurant** L served all wk 12-2.30 D served all wk 6.30-9 ⊞ FREE HOUSE ◀ Wye Valley HPA & Butty Bach, Otley 01, Mayfields Copper

Fox, Kingstone Gold Fine Ale, Sharp's Doom Bar ⚘ Westons Wyld Wood Organic & Stowford Press, Lyne Down Roaring Meg. ♀ 10 **Facilities** Non-diners area ♟ Children's menu Children's portions Garden ⋒ Parking Wi-fi **Rooms** 10

Save on hotels. Book at **theAA.com/hotel**

HEREFORDSHIRE 235 ENGLAND

PEMBRIDGE Map 9 SO35

New Inn

Market Square HR6 9DZ ☎ **01544 388427**
dir: *From M5 junct 7 take A44 W through Leominster towards Llandrindod Wells*

Traditional inn for good beer and home-cooked food

Formerly a courthouse and jail, and close to the last battle of the War of the Roses, this 14th-century black and white timbered free house has been under the same ownership for 29 years. Worn flagstone floors and winter fires characterise the cosy bar, and in summer customers spill out into the pub's outdoor seating area in the Old Market Square. Don't expect to find any background music or a TV screen. Home-cooked English fare, using local produce, might include seafood stew with crusty bread; beef steak-and-ale pie; or leek, mushroom and Shropshire Blue cheese croustade with salad.

Open all wk 11-2.30 6-11 (summer 11-3 6-11) Closed: last wk Feb **Bar Meals** L served all wk 12-2 D served all wk 6.30-9 **Restaurant** L served all wk 12-2 D served all wk 6.30-9 ⊕ FREE HOUSE ◾ Hobsons Town Crier, Sharp's Doom Bar, Hook Norton, Three Tuns, Ludlow Ŏ Westons Stowford Press & Wyld Wood Organic, Dunkertons. ♈ 10 **Facilities** Non-diners area ◗◖ Children's portions Family room Garden Parking

STAPLOW Map 10 SO64

The Oak Inn

PICK OF THE PUBS

HR8 1NP ☎ **01531 640954**
e-mail: oakinn@wyenet.co.uk
dir: *M50 junct 2, A417 to Ledbury. At rdbt take 2nd exit onto A449, then A438 (High St). Take B4214 to Staplow*

17th-century drinkers' pub in the heart of rural Herefordshire

Two miles north of Ledbury and close to the Malvern Hills, this black-and-white free house is the only pub to abutt the Hereford to Gloucester Canal, which closed in 1881 but is now undergoing restoration. The three cosy bar areas have log-burning stoves, flagstone floors and old wooden beams adorned with hops. The Oak welcomes locals and visitors alike with a choice of two local real ales and two guests. As befits a former cider house, fermented apple juice is also a major strength here: Westons and Robinsons are both near by. The rustic restaurant area has an open-plan kitchen serving traditional dishes prepared with care and using locally sourced ingredients. The lunchtime sandwiches and grilled ciabatta melts are mouthwateringly good. Otherwise, you could opt for a sharing platter or a main of fish pie or a slow-cooked Herefordshire steak. The owners describe their pub as 'definitely dog-friendly'.

Open all day all wk **Bar Meals** L served all wk 12-2.30 D served all wk 6.30-9.30 Av main course £16.50 **Restaurant** L served Mon-Sat 12-2.30, Sun 12-3 D served Mon-Sat 6.30-9.30, Sun 6.30-9 ⊕ FREE HOUSE ◾ Wye Valley Bitter, Bathams Best Bitter, Guest ales Ŏ Westons Stowford Press, Robinsons. **Facilities** Non-diners area ♥ (Bar Restaurant Garden) ◗◖ Children's portions Garden ⋔ Parking Wi-fi

SYMONDS YAT (EAST) Map 10 SO51

The Saracens Head Inn ★★★★ INN

PICK OF THE PUBS

See Pick of the Pubs on opposite page
See advert below

PICK OF THE PUBS

The Mill Race

HR9 5QS ☎ **01989 562891**
e-mail: enquiries@millrace.info
web: www.millrace.info
dir: *B4234 from Ross-on-Wye to Walford. Pub 3m on right*

The best local produce, direct from its own nearby farm

There's another Walford in the north of the county, so make sure you've put the right postcode into your Sat Nav. It lies on the banks of the River Wye, just upstream from the picturesque gorge at Symonds Yat, and the Forest of Dean. Standing majestically on the other bank is Goodrich Castle, home to 'Roaring Meg', the only surviving Civil War mortar, which the Parliamentarians used to breach its walls. The pub's interior is suitably cosy and welcoming, with a beamed and flagstone-floored bar and rustically furnished dining areas. Warm up in winter by one of the log fires, or in summer relax on the terrace and watch the buzzards drifting overhead. At nearby Bishopwood is the pub's own 1,000-acre farm estate, which together with a dedicated supply chain of local producers, allows landlord Luke Freeman and his team to dedicate their days to producing the award-winning food that is highly regarded within the Herefordshire Slow Food movement. Lunch and evening menus vary; a typical midday meal might begin

with slow-roasted confit of duck leg hash and quails' egg, with partridge with white bean, tomato and wild mushroom to follow. In the evening, consider a starter of smoked rainbow trout, horseradish and potato salad; followed by pollack, mussels, spicy chorizo and squid stew; or venison loin with sloe gin jelly. Wednesday night is fish night, while on Tuesday and Thursday the outdoor pizza oven is fired up to produce unusual English-style pizzas, such as Featherstone Flyer (pheasant and chestnuts) and Hopcraft Hot One (sweet chilli and jalapeño peppers). Wines from Herefordshire are on the globe-spanning list.

Open all wk 11-3 5-11 (Sat-Sun all day) **Bar Meals** L served Mon-Fri 12-2, Sat

12-2.30, Sun all day D served Mon-Sat 6-9, Sun all day **Restaurant** L served Mon-Fri 12-2, Sat 12-2.30, Sun all day D served Mon-Sat 6-9.30, Sun all day ⊕ FREE HOUSE ◖ Wye Valley Bitter & Butty Bach, Butcombe, Guinness ♂ Westons Stowford Press, Lyne Down Roaring Meg. ♟ 25 **Facilities** Non-diners area ♦♦ Children's menu Children's portions Garden ⊼ Parking Wi-fi 🚌

TILLINGTON — Map 9 SO44

The Bell

HR4 8LE ☎ 01432 760395
e-mail: glenn@thebellinntillington.co.uk
dir: From A4103 (N Hereford) follow Tillington sign

Village pub with something for everybody

Among blossoming fruit trees (in the spring, that is) this traditional, newly refurbished village pub has been run since 1988 by the Williams family. With two bars, one with an open fire and a screen for sporting events, dining room, extensive gardens, patio and grassed play area, it offers something for everybody. Home-made ciders are served alongside Herefordshire ales and Sharp's Doom Bar. Prepared from locally-sourced ingredients are sandwiches, light lunches, and dishes such as roast pigeon with juniper and forest fruits; seafood chowder; home-reared pork; and Madras curry with chicken, lamb, prawn or vegetable. Fish specials are offered every Wednesday night.

Open all day all wk **Bar Meals** L served Mon-Fri 12-2.30, Sat all day, Sun 12-3 D served Mon-Fri 6-9.30, Sat all day Av main course £12 **Restaurant** L served Mon-Fri 12-2.30, Sat all day, Sun 12-3 D served Mon-Fri 6-9.30, Sat all day ◀ Sharp's Doom Bar, Hereford Best Bitter, Local ales. **Facilities** Non-diners area ♦♦ Children's menu Play area Garden ⌁ Parking Wi-fi

WALFORD — Map 10 SO52

The Mill Race

PICK OF THE PUBS

See Pick of the Pubs on opposite page

WALTERSTONE — Map 9 SO32

Carpenters Arms

HR2 0DX ☎ 01873 890353
e-mail: carpentersarms1@btinternet.com
dir: Exit A465 between Hereford & Abergavenny at Pandy

Step back in time inside the cosy Carpenters

Half a mile from the Welsh border, this 300-year-old free house has been owned by the Watkins for three generations. Located on the edge of the Black Mountains and overlooked by Offa's Dyke, there's plenty of character in the pub. You'll find beams, antique settles and a leaded range with open fires that burn all winter; a perfect cosy setting for enjoying a pint of Ramblers Ruin. Popular food options include salmon and leek pie; lamb cutlet with a redcurrant and rosemary sauce; and vegetarian cannelloni. Ask about the large choice of home-made desserts. There are a few tables outside which can be a suntrap in summer.

Open all day all wk 12-11 Closed: 25 Dec **Bar Meals** food served all day ⊞ FREE HOUSE ◀ Wadworth 6X, Breconshire Golden Valley & Ramblers Ruin ♂ Westons. **Facilities** Non-diners area ♦♦ Children's portions Play area Family room Garden Parking ▭ Notes ⊛

WELLINGTON — Map 10 SO44

The Wellington

HR4 8AT ☎ 01432 830367
e-mail: jpgsurman@gmail.com
dir: Exit A49 into village centre. Pub 0.25m on left

Country pub ideal for families

The garden of this pub is sunny and secure, an ideal venue for the beer festival held here in early June. If the weather is inclement, the pub's restaurant and conservatory are also at the disposal of family groups. Here, a typical lunch could comprise potted crab, cottage pie topped with cheddar mash, and sticky toffee pudding. Dinner choices include seared scallops, pancetta and apple and mustard sauce; steak au poivre and chunky chips; and chocolate pudding cake with clotted cream. Ales are local, coming from Wye Valley Brewery in Herefordshire and Hobsons in Shropshire. Change of hands.

Open 12-2.30 5.30-11 Closed: Mon **Bar Meals** L served Tue-Sat 12-2 D served Tue-Sat 6-9 **Restaurant** L served Tue-Sat 12-2, Sun 12-2.30 D served Tue-Sat 6-9 ⊞ FREE HOUSE ◀ Wye Valley Butty Bach & HPA, Hobsons, Guest ales ♂ Westons. ♟ 9 **Facilities** Non-diners area 🐾 (Bar Garden) ♦♦ Children's portions Garden ⌁ Beer festival Parking Wi-fi ▭ (notice required)

WEOBLEY — Map 9 SO45

Ye Olde Salutation Inn

PICK OF THE PUBS

Market Pitch HR4 8SJ ☎ 01544 318443
e-mail: info@salutation-inn.com
dir: A44, then A4112, 8m from Leominster

Timber-framed free house run by a chef-proprietor

Known to locals as 'the Sal', this 17th-century black-and-white pub is in the heart of the medieval village of Weobley. The inn, sympathetically converted from an old alehouse and adjoining cottage, is the perfect base for exploring the Welsh Marches and the Black-and-White Villages Trail. The book capital of Hay-on-Wye and the cathedral city of Hereford are close by, as are the Wye Valley and Black Mountains. Chef-proprietor Stuart Elder took over a couple of years ago, 12 years after he worked here as a chef for the previous owners. Chef's specials and old favourites are served in the traditional lounge bar with its welcoming atmosphere and cosy inglenook fireplace. The inn's restaurant offers a range of tempting dishes created with the use of locally sourced ingredients. Start, perhaps, with deep-fried artichoke hearts in a light batter. Continue with half a roast duck with orange and ginger sauce; and finish with lemon tart and raspberry sorbet.

Open all day all wk 12-11 (Sun 12-10.30) **Bar Meals** L served all wk 12-3 D served all wk 6-9.30 Av main course £13 **Restaurant** L served all wk 12-3 D served all wk 6-9.30 Fixed menu price fr £13.50 Av 3 course à la carte fr £25 ⊞ FREE HOUSE ◀ Wye Valley Butty Bach, Wood's,

Hobsons ♂ Westons Stowford Press, Robinsons. **Facilities** Non-diners area ♦♦ Children's portions Outside area ⌁ Parking Wi-fi ▭ (notice required)

WINFORTON — Map 9 SO24

The Sun Inn **NEW**

HR3 6EA ☎ 01544 327677
e-mail: richard23457@btinternet.com
dir: In village centre on A438 (Hereford to Brecon road)

Small, intimate pub with a friendly atmosphere

Ever since taking over this pub in 2006 owners Gail and Richard Greenwood and their chefs have been seeking out the local Herefordshire food producers to create the monthly changing menus. 'Local' really doesn't get much closer than the pork and lamb from the chef's own farm and beef from less than a mile away; fish travels a little further but is fresh from Cornwall. With that in mind perhaps choose new season Hay-on-Wye lamb loin chop, vodka mint jelly, lamb and mint jus from a spring menu; or on another occasion pan-fried scallops in brandy; slow roasted pork belly and soured apple compôte with crispy crackling.

Open 12-2 6.30-last orders Closed: Sun eve & Mon (tue Oct-Apr) **Bar Meals** L served Tue-Sat 12-2, Sun 12-3, Wed-Sun 12-2 winter D served Tue-Sat 6.30-9, Wed-Sat 6.30-9 winter **Restaurant** L served Tue-Sat 12-2, Sun 12-3, Wed-Sun 12-2 winter D served Tue-Sat 6.30-9, Wed-Sat 6.30-9 winter ◀ Wye Valley Butty Bach, Brecon Gold Beacons ♂ Gwatkin, Westons Old Rosie. **Facilities** Non-diners area ♦♦ Children's menu Children's portions Garden ⌁ Parking Wi-fi

WOOLHOPE

Map 10 SO63

The Butchers Arms ✪

PICK OF THE PUBS

HR1 4RF ☎ 01432 860281
e-mail: food@butchersarmswoolhope.co.uk
dir: From Hereford take B4224 towards Ross-on-Wye.
Follow signs for Woolhope on left in Fownhope

Award winning cuisine in pretty surroundings

Dating from the 16th century, this classic Herefordshire half-timbered inn once wore several hats - village butcher, bakery and brewery. With a stream-bordered garden in an Area of Outstanding Natural Beauty at the foot of Marcle Ridge, this is the heart of cider country, so expect local marques Gwatkin and Dragon Orchard at the bar, as well as Wye Valley cask ales. There's also a well-considered wine list, with 10 by the glass and carafe, to match renowned chef-patron Stephen Bull's menu. Awarded one AA Rosette for quality, typical dishes include spinach and green chilli pancakes; Longhorn beef and chorizo meatballs with rosemary and garlic polenta chips; and fillet of Cornish hake with brown shrimp and tomato herb cream. Look out too for Chepstow duck and Kentchurch venison. If you're tall, the rather low ceilings mean 'duck or grouse'; better still, borrow one of the pub's hard hats.

Open 12-2.30 6.30-11 Closed: Sun eve, Mon (ex BHs) **Bar Meals** L served Tue-Sat 12-2, Sun 12-2.15 D served Tue-Sat 7-9 **Restaurant** L served Tue-Sat 12-2, Sun 12-2.15 D served Tue-Sat 7-9 Av 3 course à la carte fr £20 ⊕ FREE HOUSE ◀ Local ales ◯ Westons Stowford Press, Oliver's, Dragon Orchard, Gwatkin. ♈ 10 **Facilities** Non-diners area ✿ (Bar Restaurant Garden) ♦♦ Children's portions Garden ⋔ Parking Wi-fi

The Crown Inn

HR1 4QP ☎ 01432 860468
e-mail: menu@crowninnwoolhope.co.uk
dir: B4224 to Mordiford, left after Moon Inn. Pub in village centre

Locally sourced food and great choice of ciders and perries

A traditional village free house with large gardens, The Crown Inn is popular with walkers and well supported by locals and visitors alike. Excellent food and drink are a priority here, with good ales as well as 24 local ciders and perries. Daily specials include trout fishcakes with garlic mayonnaise; cider-braised ham with free-range eggs and chunky chips; pheasant Kiev with sweet potato mash and stir-fried cabbage. There is an outside summertime music in the garden on Saturday nights and a May Day Bank Holiday beer and cider festival.

Open all wk 12-2.30 6.30-11 (Sat-Sun all day) **Bar Meals** L served all wk 12-2 D served all wk 6.30-9 Av main course £11 **Restaurant** L served all wk 12-2 D served all wk 6.30-9 ⊕ FREE HOUSE ◀ Wye Valley HPA, Hobsons Best Bitter, Guest ales ◯ Westons Stowford Press, Country Perry & Bounds, Local ciders. ♈ 8 **Facilities** Non-diners area ♦♦ Children's menu Children's portions Garden ⋔ Beer festival Cider festival Parking Wi-fi ⊖ (notice required)

HERTFORDSHIRE

ALDBURY

Map 6 SP91

The Greyhound Inn

19 Stocks Rd HP23 5RT ☎ 01442 851228
e-mail: greyhound@aldbury.wanadoo.co.uk
dir: Telephone for directions

A traditional village inn offering good food in a relaxed atmosphere

The village's ancient stocks and duck pond are popular with film-makers who frequently use Aldbury as a location, allowing the pub's customers the chance to witness every clap of the clapperboard. In the oak-beamed restaurant, the comprehensive menu includes salads and platters, as well as king prawn and crab linguine; roasted duck breast with lime scented rice and sweet pepper and aubergine jam; or confit of pork belly on mash and bok choi. Among the desserts are baked figs with mascarpone cheese, and warm almond and treacle tart with custard. The bar snacks are a local legend, especially when accompanied by Badger Best or Tanglefoot ale.

Open all day all wk 11.30-11 (Sun 12-10.30) Closed: 25 Dec **Bar Meals** L served all wk 12-2.30 D served all wk 6.30-9.30 **Restaurant** L served all wk 12-2.30 D served all wk 6.30-9.30 ⊕ HALL & WOODHOUSE ◀ Badger Dorset Best, Tanglefoot, K&B Sussex. ♈ 13 **Facilities** Non-diners area ✿ (Bar Garden) ♦♦ Family room Garden Parking Wi-fi ⊖

The Valiant Trooper

Trooper Rd HP23 5RW ☎ 01442 851203
e-mail: valianttrooper@gmx.co.uk
dir: A41 at Tring junct, follow rail station signs 0.5m, at village green turn right, 200yds on left

Delicious dishes in the Chilterns

Named in honour of the Duke of Wellington who allegedly discussed strategy with his troops here, this old pub has been enjoyed by lucky locals for centuries. Located in the quintessential Chilterns village of Aldbury, beneath the beech woods of Ashridge Park, the Trooper's bar proffers six real ales and beer festivals usually take place on Bank Holidays. Bar food encompasses jackets, sandwiches, ploughman's and pub favourites. The restaurant menu features more creative dishes like braised spring vegetable medley with shredded ham hock and parmesan served with cheddar scones and wholegrain mustard.

Open all day all wk 12-11 (Sun 12-10.30) **Bar Meals** L served Mon-Fri 12-3, Sat 12-9, Sun 12-4 D served Mon-Fri 6-9, Sat 12-9 **Restaurant** L served Mon-Fri 12-3, Sat 12-9, Sun 12-4 D served Mon-Fri 6-9, Sat 12-9 ⊕ FREE HOUSE ◀ Fuller's London Pride, Tring Side Pocket for a Toad & Ridgeway, Guest Ales ◯ Lilley's Apples & Pears, Millwhite. **Facilities** Non-diners area ✿ (Bar Garden) ♦♦ Children's menu Children's portions Play area Family room Garden Beer festival Parking Wi-fi ⊖

ARDELEY

Map 12 TL32

Jolly Waggoner

SG2 7AH ☎ 01438 861350
e-mail: adrian@churchfarmardeley.co.uk
dir: From Stevenage take B1037, through Walkern, in 2m right to Ardeley

Ancient village pub with a 'one-mile menu'

All meat on the Jolly Waggoner's menu, including heritage varieties and rare breeds, is traditionally reared at Church Farm across the road, together with over 100 different vegetables, fruits and herbs. Church Farm took on the stewardship of this 500-year-old pub in 2011, which means that the food on offer is truly local, being sourced from within a one-mile radius. Start with garlic mushrooms or smoked duck breast, and continue with pan-roasted partridge breast or bean, tomato and caramelised onion pie from the market menu. Regular beers are Buntingford and Fuller's London Pride. The annual beer festival takes place in August.

Open all day all wk 12-11.30 (Fri-Sat noon-12.30am) **Bar Meals** L served Mon-Fri 12-2, Sat 12-9, Sun 12-7 D served Mon-Fri 6.30-9, Sat 12-9, Sun 12-7 Av main course £12.50 **Restaurant** L served Mon-Fri 12-2, Sat 12-9, Sun 12-7 D served Mon-Fri 6.30-9, Sat 12-9, Sun 12-7 Av 3 course à la carte fr £24.75 ⊕ FREE HOUSE ◀ Thwaites Highwayman, Fuller's London Pride, Adnams Broadside, Dark Star, Buntingford, Red Squirrel RSX ◯ Aspall. ♈ 13 **Facilities** Non-diners area ✿ (Bar Garden) ♦♦ Children's menu Children's portions Garden ⋔ Beer festival Parking Wi-fi ⊖

AYOT GREEN

Map 6 TL21

The Waggoners ✪

Brickwall Close AL6 9AA ☎ 01707 324241
e-mail: laurent@thewaggoners.co.uk
dir: Ayot Green on unclassified road off B197, S of Welwyn

Modern French cuisine in the Hertfordshire countryside

Close to the large, traditional village green and with good English real ales flowing in the beamed bar, it comes as a surprise that the menu has a strong French bent to it. Cue the Gallic owners, whose culinary skills have gained an AA Rosette for their inspired cuisine at this former waggoners' and coaching stop in the low Hertfordshire hills. An enterprising entrée may be a courgette ball stuffed with pork and sea spice aubergine, followed by slow cooked ox cheeks with orange mashed potato, mixed vegetables and Guardian sauce. The wine list stretches to 50 bins.

Open all day all wk **Bar Meals** L served all wk 12-2.45 D served all wk 6.30-9.30 **Restaurant** L served all wk 12-2.45 D served all wk 6.30-9.30 ⊕ PUNCH TAVERNS ◀ Fuller's London Pride, St Austell Tribute, Adnams Broadside, Greene King Abbot Ale & IPA, Sharp's Doom Bar. ♈ 50 **Facilities** Non-diners area ✿ (Bar Garden) ♦♦ Children's portions Garden ⋔ Parking Wi-fi ⊖ (notice required)

BARLEY   Map 12 TL43

The Fox & Hounds

High St SG8 8HU ☎ **01763 849400**
e-mail: foxandhoundsbarley@hotmail.co.uk
dir: A505 onto B1368 at Flint Cross, pub 4m

Historic pub with a reputation for good micro-brewery ales

This 16th-century former hunting lodge is set in a beautiful and historic village in north Hertfordshire. Expect a wealth of exposed beams, fireplaces, wood-burners, original flooring and more nooks and crannies than you can shake a stick at. The pub has made a name for itself by serving top-quality real ales from micro-breweries and offering home-cooked food in the dedicated restaurant. A typical menu might include home-made beef lasagne and chicken curry. Child- and dog-friendly.

Open all day all wk 12-11 (Fri- Sat 12-12) ⊕ FREE HOUSE ◄ Adnams Southwold Bitter, Flowers IPA, Woodforde's Wherry, Falstaff Phoenix, Greene King Abbot Ale ♂ Lyne Down Roaring Meg. **Facilities** ❤ (Bar Garden) ♦↑ Children's menu Children's portions Play area Garden Parking Wi-fi

BERKHAMSTED   Map 6 SP90

The Old Mill

London Rd HP4 2NB ☎ **01442 879590**
e-mail: oldmill@peachpubs.com
dir: At east end of London Rd in Berkhamsted centre

Historic waterside pub buzzing throughout the week

Occupying a plum spot on the Grand Union Canal, this is a great place to enjoy a pint of Greene King IPA and a deli board, either while relaxing on big leather sofas in the low-beamed bar or outside in the canal-side garden. The restored pub retains many of its original Georgian and Victorian features; a reclaimed millstone and historic photographs of mill machinery reflect the building's past. Menus in the comfortable dining room showcase the best seasonal ingredients — perhaps pan-fried cod fillet with a lobster spring roll, spring vegetables and garlic and ginger broth. From the sheltered courtyard you can watch the mill-race crashing over the weir. Change of landlord.

Open all day all wk Closed: 25 Dec **Bar Meals** L served all wk 12-6 D served all wk 6-10 Av main course £15 food served all day **Restaurant** L served all wk 12-6 D served all wk 6-10 Fixed menu price fr £12 Av 3 course à la carte fr £25 food served all day ⊕ PEACH PUBS ◄ Greene King IPA, Morland Old Speckled Hen, Tring Side Pocket for a Toad ♂ Aspall. ♀ 16 **Facilities** Non-diners area ❤ (Bar Garden) ♦↑ Children's portions Garden ⊞ Parking Wi-fi ▬ (notice required)

BRAUGHING   Map 12 TL32

The Golden Fleece NEW

20 Green End SG11 2PG ☎ **01920 823555**
e-mail: pub@goldenfleecebraughing.co.uk
dir: A10 N from Ware. At rdbt right onto B1368 signed Braughing. Approx 1m to village

Lovingly restored village inn en-route to Cambridge

This Grade II-listed Georgian coaching inn was closed for a decade until Peter and Jessica Tatlow bought it at auction and reopened it in 2010 after a major renovation. Their hard work has clearly paid off as the pub has quickly gained a good reputation for its local real ales and ciders, but also its food, which specialises in gluten- and dairy-free dishes. Carrot and orange soup followed by venison, apple and thyme burger are typical choices and the monthly tapas night is a popular fixture on the last Wednesday of the month.

Open all wk 11.30-3 5.30-11 (Fri 11.30-3 5.30-12 Sat 11.30am-mdnt Sun 12-10) Closed: 25 Dec **Bar Meals** L served Mon-Sat 12-2.30, Sun 12-6 D served Mon-Thu 6-9, Fri-Sat 7-10, Sun 12-6 **Restaurant** L served Mon-Sat 12-2.30, Sun 12-6 D served Mon-Thu 6.30-9, Fri-Sat 7-10, Sun 12-6 ⊕ FREE HOUSE ◄ Adnams, Nethergate, Buntingford ♂ Aspall Harry Sparrow. ♀ 15 **Facilities** Non-diners area ♦↑ Children's menu Children's portions Garden ⊞ Parking Wi-fi ▬ (notice required)

BUNTINGFORD   Map 12 TL32

The Sword Inn Hand ★★★★ INN

Westmill SG9 9LQ ☎ **01763 271356**
e-mail: welcome@theswordinnhand.co.uk
dir: Off A10 1.5m S of Buntingford

Welcoming travellers since the 14th century

Midway between London and Cambridge, this old inn provides an excellent stopping off point. Inside are the original oak beams, flagstone floors and open fireplace; outside is a large garden and pretty patio. As a free house, there is a varied selection of real ales from the likes of Greene King, Sharp's and Timothy Taylor. Fresh produce is delivered daily for a good selection of bar snacks including salads, omelettes, sandwiches and light dishes. Taken from a typical evening menu are mozzarella-stuffed peppers with couscous; basil-crusted salmon fillet with Mediterranean vegetables; and calves' liver and bacon. Luxury accommodation is available.

Open all wk 12-3 5-11 (Sun Sep-Apr 12-7 May-Aug 12-10) **Bar Meals** L served Mon-Sat 12-2.30, Sun 12-4 D served Mon-Sat 6.30-9.30 **Restaurant** L served Mon-Sat 12-2.30, Sun 12-4 D served Mon-Sat 6.30-9.30 ⊕ FREE HOUSE ◄ Greene King IPA, Young's Bitter, Timothy Taylor Landlord, Sharp's Doom Bar, Guest ales ♂ Westons Stowford Press. ♀ 9 **Facilities** Non-diners area ♦↑ Children's menu Children's portions Play area Garden ⊞ Parking Wi-fi ▬ **Rooms** 4

COTTERED   Map 12 TL32

The Bull at Cottered

SG9 9QP ☎ **01763 281243**
e-mail: cordell39@btinternet.com
dir: On A507 in Cottered between Buntingford & Baldock

Charming, traditional village local

Low beams, antique furniture, cosy fires and teamwork — four key things that sum up this member of the Greene King estate. Then, of course, there's the food. You can eat in one of two traditional bars with open fires, in the pretty beamed dining room, or in the large, well-kept gardens. Everything that can be is home-made, the brasserie-style cooking typified by starters of fresh Devon crab; and fried brie on warm cranberry sauce; then calves' liver with Roquefort cheese and horseradish sauce; breast of duck with honey and wholegrain mustard glaze; or omelette Arnold Bennett.

Open all wk 11.30-3 6.30-11 (Sun 12-10.30) **Bar Meals** L served Mon-Sat 12-2, Sun 12-4 D served Mon-Sat 6.30-9.30, Sun 6-9 Av main course £15 **Restaurant** L served Mon-Sat 12-2, Sun 12-4 D served Mon-Sat 6.30-9.30, Sun 6-9 Fixed menu price fr £22 Av 3 course à la carte fr £28 ⊕ GREENE KING ◄ IPA & Abbot Ale, Morland Old Speckled Hen. **Facilities** Non-diners area ♦↑ Children's portions Garden ⊞ Parking ▬

DATCHWORTH   Map 6 TL21

The Tilbury ☺

Walton Rd SG3 6TB ☎ **01438 815550**
e-mail: info@thetilbury.co.uk
dir: A1(M) junct 7, A602 signed Ware & Hertford. At Bragbury End right into Bragbury Ln to Datchworth

Elegant country pub serving British classics with a distinctive twist

A well selected wine list, real ales and a list of over 30 bottled beers are a nice introduction to this once-tired old village boozer, now turned into a notable dining pub by TV chef Paul Bloxham. Bare brick walls, wooden floors and interesting art suit the mood for the seasonally inspired modern British food. The fixed-price market menu represents special value, offering the likes of ham hock and salt beef terrine with toast and mustard pickle, followed by roast sea trout, cauliflower couscous, ratatouille and salsa verde. Deserts may include local honey pannacotta with a red wine poached pear.

Open 12-3 6-late Closed: Sun eve **Bar Meals** L served all wk 12-2 Av main course £9-£14 **Restaurant** D served Mon-Sat 6-9.30 Fixed menu price fr £13.95 Av 3 course à la carte fr £17.95 ⊕ BRAKSPEAR ◄ Bitter, Oxford Gold ♂ Westons Wyld Wood Organic, Symonds. ♀ 30 **Facilities** Non-diners area ♦↑ Children's menu Children's portions Garden Parking Wi-fi

PICK OF THE PUBS

The Bricklayers Arms ❀

FLAUNDEN   Map 6 TL00

Hogpits Bottom HP3 0PH
☎ **01442 833322**
e-mail: goodfood@bricklayersarms.com
web: www.bricklayersarms.com
dir: *M25 junct 18, A404 (Amersham road). Right at Chenies for Flaunden*

Country inn with Anglo-French cuisine

The creeper-clad Bricklayers Arms is a low, cottagey tiled pub formed from a pair of 18th-century cottages. It was in 1832 that Benskin's brewery converted the first of the cottages into an alehouse; the other joined it in the 1960s. Lost down leafy Hertfordshire lanes in a peaceful and inviting location, the pub has featured in many fictional films and TV programmes, and is a favourite with locals, walkers, horse-riders and, well, just about everyone. In summer, the flower-festooned garden is the perfect place to savour an alfresco pint or meal. An ivy-covered façade gives way to an immaculate interior, complete with low beams, exposed brickwork, candlelight and open fires. The award-winning restaurant is housed in a converted outbuilding and barn. Here you'll find a happy marriage of traditional English and French cooking. The Gallic influence comes from experienced head chef, Claude Pallait, and his team who use fresh organic produce from local

suppliers to create seasonal lunch and dinner menus, plus daily specials. For starters try goose rillette with Kentish pear chutney and rye toast; or charcuterie for two to share. To follow ox cheek slowly cooked in Tring Ale; or a duo of haunch venison steak and slowly cooked shoulder with cabbage and spring onion mash. But don't stop there, from the puddings perhaps choose raspberry Eton mess, or apple and rhubarb crumble. Opt for one of the 120 wines from all corners of the world and, in the summer, enjoy it with your lunch in the terraced garden.

Open all day all wk 12-11.30 (Sun 9.15am-10.30pm 25 Dec 12-3) **Bar Meals** L served Mon-Sat 12-2.30, Sun 12-3.30 D served Mon-Sat 6.30-9.30,

Sun 6.30-8.30 Av main course £17 **Restaurant** L served Mon-Sat 12-2.30, Sun 12-3.30 D served Mon-Sat 6.30-9.30, Sun 6.30-8.30 Fixed menu price fr £15 Av 3 course à la carte fr £29 ⊕ FREE HOUSE ◖ Tring Jack O'Legs, Sharp's Doom Bar, Rebellion Ŏ Aspall, Thatchers Gold. ♟ 20 **Facilities** Non-diners area ♣ ♦♦ Children's portions Garden ⋈ Parking Wi-fi

Save on hotels. Book at theAA.com/hotel

HERTFORDSHIRE 241 ENGLAND

The Beehive

SG13 8NB ☎ 01707 875959
e-mail: squirrell15@googlemail.com
dir: *B158 from Hertford towards Hatfield. Left signed Little Berkhamsted. Left at war memorial signed Epping Green*

Countryside pub with emphasis on fish dishes

This family-run free house has held its liquor licence for over 200 years and featured in the *Catweazel* TV series in the 1970s. These days it retains plenty of traditional charms including exposed beams, a real fire in winter and decked and grassed areas for sunnier days. The kitchen specialises in fresh fish from Billingsgate Market – maybe poached fish pie or sea bass fillets with basil pesto. Alternatives include steak, mushroom and ale pudding, and Thai green chicken curry. A constantly changing special board adds to the choices. At the bar you'll find two permanent ales and a changing guest.

Open all wk Mon-Sat 11.30-3 5.30-11 (Sun 11-11) **Bar Meals** L served Mon-Sat 12-2.30, Sun 12-4 D served Mon-Sat 6-9.30, Sun 6-8.30 **Restaurant** L served Mon-Sat 12-2.30, Sun 12-4 D served Mon-Sat 6-9.30, Sun 6-8.30 ⊕ FREE HOUSE ◀ Greene King IPA, Morland Old Speckled Hen, Guest ale. ☂ 8 **Facilities** Non-diners area ♦♦ Children's portions Garden ⋒ Parking Wi-fi ▭ (notice required)

The Bricklayers Arms ⍟

PICK OF THE PUBS

See Pick of the Pubs on opposite page

Alford Arms

PICK OF THE PUBS

See Pick of the Pubs on page 242

The Land of Liberty, Peace and Plenty

Long Ln WD3 5BS ☎ 01923 282226
e-mail: beer@landoflibertypub.com
dir: *M25 junct 17, follow Heronsgate signs. 0.5m, pub on right*

Top quality beers and ciders in single-bar pub

Named after a Chartist settlement established in Heronsgate in 1847, this pub is believed to have the second longest name in the British Isles. A traditional pub with a large garden and covered decked area, the cosy single bar has a buzz of conversation from locals. The focus here are the real ales and real ciders, all of which can be enjoyed with bar snacks of pork pies, pasties and pots of nuts. Please note that no children or the use of mobile phones are allowed in the bar. Regular events and beer festivals are held during the year.

Open all wk 12-11 (Fri 12-12 Sat 11am-mdnt) **Bar Meals** food served all day ⊕ FREE HOUSE ◀ 6 Guest ales ⍭ Millwhites, Westons. **Facilities** Non-diners area ☂ (Bar Garden) Garden ⋒ Beer festival Parking Wi-fi ▭ (notice required)

The Raven

SG5 3JB ☎ 01582 881209
e-mail: theraven@emeryinns.com
dir: *5m W of Hitchin. 5m N of Luton, just outside Barton-le-Clay*

Family friendly pub

This neat 1920s pub is named after Ravensburgh Castle in the neighbouring hills. Comfortable bars witness the serving of four weekly-changing guest ales, perhaps Fuller's London Pride or Greene King IPA, while outside a large garden with heated terrace and a play area ensure family friendliness. Extensive menus and blackboard specials embrace pub classics, salads, jackets, baguettes and wraps, vegetarian options, fish dishes and 'combination' meat plates like ribs and/or steak with Cajun chicken, and surf 'n' turf. So a three-course meal could see loaded potato skins, fillet of salmon salad, and chocolate and honeycomb sundae.

Open all day all wk **Bar Meals** Av main course £9.95 **Restaurant** Fixed menu price fr £15.95 Av 3 course à la carte fr £22 ⊕ FREE HOUSE ◀ Greene King IPA, Morland Old Speckled Hen, Fuller's London Pride, Timothy Taylor Landlord, Sharp's Doom Bar. ☂ 24 **Facilities** Non-diners area ♦♦ Children's menu Children's portions Play area Garden ⋒ Parking Wi-fi ▭ (notice required)

The Fox and Hounds

PICK OF THE PUBS

See Pick of the Pubs on page 243

The Nags Head

The Ford SG11 2AX ☎ 01279 771555
e-mail: paul.arkell@virgin.net
dir: *M11 junct 8, A120 towards Puckeridge & A10. Left at lights in Little Hadham. Pub 1m on right*

Along the country byways just south of Little Hadham

This warm and relaxed country pub was built in 1595 and still retains its traditional atmosphere, with an old bakery oven and a good range of real ales at the bar. Fish dishes such as poached skate wing with black butter and capers feature strongly on the full à la carte menu, which also includes a choice of steaks and vegetarian meals. At lunchtime, sandwiches and jacket potatoes offer a lighter alternative to hot main courses. Sit out the front on a good day and enjoy the countryside.

Open all wk 11.30-2.30 6-11 (Sun 12-10.30) **Bar Meals** L served Mon-Sat 12-2, Sun all day D served Mon-Sat 6-9, Sun all day Av main course £12 **Restaurant** L served Mon-Sat 12-2, Sun all day D served Mon-Sat 6-9, Sun all day ⊕ GREENE KING ◀ Abbot Ale, Ruddles County & IPA, Morland Old Speckled Hen, Marston's Pedigree. ☂ 12 **Facilities** Non-diners area ♦♦ Children's menu Children's portions Garden ⋒ Wi-fi ▭

The Sun at Northaw

1 Judges Hill EN6 4NL ☎ 01707 655507
e-mail: reservations@thesunatnorthaw.co.uk
dir: *M25 junct 24, A111 to Potters Bar. Right onto A1000, becomes High Street (B156). Follow to Northaw, pub on left*

Pretty inn with a skilled chef patron

A Grade II listed inn on a picturesque village green, The Sun has gained a reputation for its real ale, with up to seven available at any time. There is also an excellent wine list to complement cooking from chef and owner Oliver Smith, whose menus are driven by local, seasonal produce. An appetiser of pork crackling with apple sauce might precede a starter of razor clams with ramsons and smoked bacon, followed by a main course of hare and trotter pie with a suet crust and carrot and swede mash. Finish with Seville orange marmalade steamed pudding and custard.

Open 12-5 6-11 Closed: Sun eve & Mon **Bar Meals** L served Tue-Sat 12-4 D served Tue-Sat 6-10 **Restaurant** L served Tue-Sun 12-4 D served Tue-Sat 6-10 ⊕ FREE HOUSE ◀ Adnams, Buntingford, Saffron, Nethergate, Red Squirrel RSX ⍭ Millwhites, Aspall. ☂ 12 **Facilities** Non-diners area ☂ (Bar Garden) ♦♦ Children's menu Children's portions Garden ⋒ Parking Wi-fi

The Hoops Inn

SG10 6EF ☎ 01279 843568
e-mail: reservations@hoops-inn.co.uk
dir: *From Ware on B1004 towards Bishop's Stortford right onto unclassified road to Perry Green*

Stylish inn with links to sculptor Henry Moore

Once home to Henry Moore, Perry Green is dotted with his famous sculptures. This comfortable dining inn is part of the estate and it boasts a chic country decor, contemporary furnishings and Moore-inspired artefacts. The food here draws a crowd thanks to mains of poached sea trout with spring vegetables; or Cornish lamb with spring greens. Excellent Sunday roasts can be walked off by visiting the Moore Foundation's estate just across the village green. There is a large front terrace and back garden to enjoy in the warmer weather.

Open all day 11.30-11 Closed: Mon **Bar Meals** L served Tue-Sat 12-3, Sun 12-6 D served Tue-Sat 5-9.30 food served all day ⊕ FREE HOUSE ◀ Adnams Southwold Bitter, Guinness ⍭ Aspall. **Facilities** ♦♦ Children's portions Garden ⋒ Beer festival Parking ▭ (notice required)

PICK OF THE PUBS

Alford Arms

HEMEL HEMPSTEAD   Map 6 TL00

Frithsden HP1 3DD ☎ 01442 864480
e-mail: info@alfordarmsfrithsden.co.uk
web: www.alfordarmsfrithsden.co.uk
dir: *From Hemel Hempstead on A4146,
2nd left at Water End. 1m, left at
T-junct, right in 0.75m. Pub 100yds on
right*

Professional but relaxed pub with understated style

With a flower-filled garden overlooking
the green in the untouched hamlet of
Frithsden, this pretty Victorian pub is
surrounded by National Trust woodland
and has historic Ashridge Park on its
doorstep. It's one of four in the well-
regarded Salisbury Pubs mini-empire in
and around the Chilterns*. Cross the
threshold and you'll immediately pick up
on the warm and lively atmosphere,
derived from the buzz of conversation,
some soft jazz in the background, and
from the rich colours and eclectic mix of
old furniture and antique pictures in the
dining room and bar from Tring's well-
known salerooms. Also from Tring is real
ale called Side Pocket for a Toad, which
shares bar space with Rebellion IPA and
Sharp's Doom Bar. The seasonal menus
and daily specials are a balance of
modern British with more traditional
dishes, all prepared from fresh local
produce whenever possible. There's a
great choice of light dishes or 'small
plates', from the potted salt beef with

beetroot relish and chilli corn bread to
the baked smoked haddock and prawn
pancake with a spicy bisque sauce.
Equally imaginative main meals include
confit duck and Jerusalem artichoke
rösti with fried local duck egg, buttered
chard and caramelised onion jus; and
chickpea, potato, spinach and coconut
curry with chargrilled flatbread, sticky
rice and a red onion bhaji. Orange rice
pudding with a nutmeg glaze is one way
to finish, or there's also the plate of
British cheeses or home-made sorbets
and ice creams. Like all pubs in the
Salisbury group, they do great Sunday
roasts. *The Swan Inn, Denham; The Royal Oak,
Bovingdon Green; and The Old Queens Head, Penn
(all in Buckinghamshire).

Open all day all wk 11-11 (Sun
12-10.30) Closed: 25-26 Dec **Bar**

Meals L served Mon-Fri 12-2.30, Sat
12-3, Sun 12-4 D served Sun-Thu
6.30-9.30, Fri-Sat 6.30-10 **Restaurant** L
served Mon-Fri 12-2.30, Sat 12-3, Sun
12-4 D served Sun-Thu 6.30-9.30, Fri-
Sat 6.30-10 🛢 SALISBURY PUBS LTD
🍺 Rebellion IPA, Sharp's Doom Bar,
Tring Side Pocket for a Toad
🍏 Thatchers. ☻ 22 **Facilities** Non-
diners area ☺ ♦♦ Children's portions
Garden ⋈ Parking Wi-fi

Save on hotels. Book at theAA.com/hotel

HERTFORDSHIRE 243 ENGLAND

PICK OF THE PUBS

The Fox and Hounds

HUNSDON　　　　　　Map 6 TL41

2 High St SG12 8NH ☎ 01279 843999
e-mail: info@foxandhounds-hunsdon.co.uk
web: www.foxandhounds-hunsdon.co.uk
dir: *From A414 between Ware & Harlow take B180 in Stanstead Abbotts N to Hunsdon*

Mediterranean-inspired menu in a relaxing pub in a sleepy village

Owned and run by chef James Rix and wife Bianca, this renowned gastro-pub is set in a sleepy Hertfordshire village, but attracts food lovers from afar. The easy-going atmosphere is thanks to a cosy winter fire warming the old bar, liberally supplied with Victorian-style furnishings. There's no pressure to do anything other than enjoy a glass of Adnams, but resistance is futile when you see James's imaginative, Mediterranean-inspired menu, which changes daily and with the seasons. There's no doubt that the food side of the pub is the main draw here, and lunch and dinner can be taken in the bar or elegant, chandeliered dining room. James successfully combines traditional pub favourites (with a twist) with French and Italian influences, and his simply described dishes champion local produce. Expect interesting combinations of ingredients, bold flavours and difficulty in deciding. Kick off with deep-fried queenie scallops and tartare sauce or devilled lamb's kidneys

on toast; then ragout of braised hare with penne, or confit partridge breast and leg with duck fat potato cake and wild mushrooms; or splash out on a 32-day aged belted Scotch Black Angus, served with fat chips and béarnaise. Finish with hot chocolate pudding with espresso ice cream, or pear and almond tart with crème fraîche. There are regular 'days', including pie day on Wednesday in winter, and lobster night on Thursday in summer. The tree-shaded garden, together with the covered terrace is popular with drinkers and alfresco diners. Booking for meals is advised.

Open 12-4 6-11 Closed: 26 Dec, Sun eve, Mon & BHs eve (Tue after BHs) **Bar Meals** L served Tue-Sat 12-2.30, Sun

12-3.30 D served Tue-Sat 6-9.30 Av main course £15 **Restaurant** L served Sun 12-3.30 D served Fri-Sat 6-9.30 Fixed menu price fr £13.50 Av 3 course à la carte fr £27.50 ⊕ FREE HOUSE ◀ Adnams Southwold Bitter & Broadside, Guinness, Local ales ♂ Aspall. ♀ 9 **Facilities** Non-diners area ♣ (Bar Garden) ♙ Children's menu Children's portions Play area Garden ⊓ Parking Wi-fi

POTTEN END
Map 6 TL00

Martins Pond

The Green HP4 2QQ ☎ 01442 864318
dir: *A41 onto A416 signed Chesham, follow signs to Berkhamsted town centre. At lights straight over into Lower Kings Rd. Pass station, into Station Rd. Left at pub on opposite side of village green*

Innovative food and good walks directly from the pub

The unusual name refers to the village green where this welcoming pub is located. A section of Grim's Dyke, an ancient bank-and-ditch earthwork, is clearly visible nearby. By comparison the pub – dating from 1924 – is relatively new, but there's been a public house here since the 17th century. These days it's a good destination for home-cooked food such as crispy duck and filo parcels with spiced plums and red chard, followed by venison and smoked bacon meatballs with buttered Savoy cabbage and a red wine and cranberry gravy.

Open all day all wk Closed: 26 Dec **Bar Meals** L served Mon-Sat 12-2.30, Sun 12-7.30 D served Mon-Sat 6-9, Sun 12-7.30 **Restaurant** L served Mon-Sat 12-2, Sun 12-7.30 D served Mon-Sat 6-9, Sun 12-7.30 ⊕ FREE HOUSE ◀ Fuller's London Pride, Tetley's. ♟ 13 **Facilities** Non-diners area ❤ (Bar Garden) ♦ Children's portions Garden ⊓ Parking Wi-fi

POTTERS CROUCH
Map 6 TL10

The Holly Bush

AL2 3NN ☎ 01727 851792
e-mail: info@thehollybushpub.co.uk
dir: *Village accessed from A4147 & A405*

Country pub with old-world charm

Tucked away in a hamlet, The Holly Bush is a picturesque 17th-century pub with a large enclosed garden complete with wooden benches and tables. There is a delightfully welcoming atmosphere, with antique dressers, log fires and exposed beams setting the interior style. Traditional and modern pub fare is offered. At lunch there's ploughman's, baked potatoes, garden salads, deli platters, burgers and toasted sandwiches; while on the evening menu there might be meatballs in a tomato and basil sauce; brie, pesto and cherry tomato filo tart; and salmon, sweet potato, red pepper and coriander fishcakes. The pub is close to St Albans with its Roman ruins and good local walks.

Open all wk 12-2.30 6-11 (Sun 12-3) **Bar Meals** L served Mon-Sat 12-2, Sun 12-2.30 D served Wed-Sat 6-9 ⊕ FULLER'S ◀ London Pride, ESB, George Gale & Co Seafarers, Seasonal ales. **Facilities** Non-diners area Garden ⊓ Parking Wi-fi ⊜ (notice required)

SARRATT
Map 6 TQ09

The Cock Inn

Church Ln WD3 6HH ☎ 01923 282908
e-mail: enquiries@cockinn.net
dir: *M25 junct 18, A404 signed Chorleywood, Amersham. Right follow signs to Sarratt. Pass church on left, pub on right*

Oozing character and charm

A warm and friendly welcome is guaranteed at this traditional village inn standing opposite Sarratt's Norman church. Originally called the Cock Horse, the 17th-century pub is in the heart of the Chess Valley, an area favoured by walkers. It has head-cracking low beams, an inglenook fireplace and Hall & Woodhouse ales at the bar, while the ancient timbered barn houses the restaurant. Expect classic and imaginative pub dishes such as crispy whitebait, followed by horseshoe gammon or home-made steak and Badger Ale pie. Light bites and sandwiches are served in the bar or garden.

Open all day all wk **Bar Meals** L served Mon-Sat 12-2.30, Sun 12-6 D served Mon-Sat 6-9 **Restaurant** L served Mon-Sat 12-2.30, Sun 12-6 D served Mon-Sat 6-9 ⊕ HALL & WOODHOUSE ◀ Badger Tanglefoot, K&B Sussex ♂ Westons Stowford Press. **Facilities** Non-diners area ❤ (Bar Garden) ♦ Children's menu Children's portions Play area Garden ⊓ Parking ⊜ (notice required)

SHENLEY
Map 6 TL10

The White Horse, Shenley

37 London Rd WD7 9ER ☎ 01923 853054
e-mail: enquiry@whitehorseradlett.co.uk
dir: *M25 junct 22, B556 then B5378 to Shenley*

Village pub with an interesting menu

The White Horse belies its 170-year-old foundation as a village pub, offering contemporary comforts and dining at the fringe of this green-belt village, with country walks to the Hertfordshire Way from the door. Bright, light and cheerful inside, with some quirky decor, it's an ideal place to sup a Sharp's Doom Bar bitter over a Sunday roast or crack a bottle from the extensive wine list and indulge in soft shell crab with crispy calamari, soy, ginger and chilli dip followed by pork fillet wrapped in sage and prosciutto with pistachio and blue cheese sauce, with white chocolate brûlée for dessert.

Open all day all wk 11-11 ⊕ FREE HOUSE/MITCHELLS & BUTLERS ◀ Sharp's Doom Bar, Young's ♂ Aspall. **Facilities** ❤ (Bar Garden) ♦ Children's menu Children's portions Garden Parking

STAPLEFORD
Map 6 TL31

Papillon Woodhall Arms ★★★ INN

17 High Rd SG14 3NW ☎ 01992 535123
e-mail: info@papillon-woodhallarms.com
dir: *On A119, between A602 & Hertford*

Reliable and popular rural fringe inn

Nudging the fringe of Hertfordshire's pleasant countryside of pasture and copses, this handsome roadhouse has a long-established reputation as a destination dining pub. Good, pubby bar meals like beef Stroganoff or chicken, ham and leek pie accompany beers such as St Austell Tribute in the comfortably appointed, fire-warmed bar, whilst the thriving Papillon Restaurant side of the business pushes the culinary boat out. Anticipate a hot avocado starter with prawns and cheese fondue; then fresh skate wing with beurre noir, or saddle of venison with cinnamon black cherry sauce. Good value accommodation makes this ideal for a short break.

Open all wk 12-2 6.30-10.30 (Sun 12-2.30 6.30-10.30) **Bar Meals** L served all wk 12-2 D served Sun-Fri 6.30-10 **Restaurant** L served all wk 12-2 D served all wk 6.30-10 ⊕ FREE HOUSE ◀ Greene King IPA, Young's Special, St Austell Tribute, Black Sheep ♂ Aspall. ♟ 10 **Facilities** Non-diners area ❤ (Garden) ♦ Children's menu Children's portions Family room Garden ⊓ Parking Wi-fi ⊜ (notice required) **Rooms** 10

TRING
Map 6 SP91

The Cow Roast Inn

Cow Roast, London Rd HP23 5RF ☎ 01442 822287
e-mail: cowroastinn@btconnect.com
dir: *Between Berkhamstead & Tring on A4251*

Old coaching inn with an oriental twist

The classic interior of this venerable inn threads through a forest of timber posts, splaying out on timeworn flagstone floors to comfy asides with horse-brass bedecked log fire and drinking areas with pub games. In past centuries it was frequented by local farmers driving cattle to the London markets and navvies building the nearby Grand Union Canal. Today's guests appreciate beers from the local Tring Brewery and a restaurant specialising in Thai meals, whilst those with a less adventurous palate savour pub staples like fish pie or rack of ribs. There's a grand garden, and a beer festival is held.

Open all day all wk 12-close **Bar Meals** L served Tue-Sun 12-9 D served Tue-Sun 12-9 food served all day **Restaurant** L served Tue-Sat 12-3, Sun 12-5 D served Tue-Sat 5-9 ◀ Greene King Abbot Ale, Tring Side Pocket for a Toad, Guest ales ♂ Westons. **Facilities** Non-diners area ❤ (Bar Garden) ♦ Children's menu Children's portions Garden ⊓ Beer festival Parking Wi-fi ⊜ (notice required)

WELWYN　　　Map 6 TL21

The White Hart ★★★ HL ◉

2 Prospect Place AL6 9EN ☎ 01438 715353
e-mail: bookings@thewhiteharthotel.net
dir: *A1(M) junct 6. On corner of Prospect Place (just past fire station), at top of High St*

Elegant former coaching inn

Once on the A1 trunk road, long ago rerouted well to the east, this 17th-century coaching inn today stands in a much quieter Welwyn. Its old beams, stone flags and inglenook fireplace blend easily with contemporary wood floors, leather chairs and numerous framed pictures and prints. With an AA Rosette, the restaurant's monthly menus mix modern and traditional British styles to offer tempura battered fish and chips (in the bar); grilled saddle of lamb; individual venison Wellington; root vegetable stew; and goats' cheese and rosemary gnocchi. A Charles Wells pub, so expect Bombardier and Eagle IPA, with Aspall cider too.

Open all day all wk 7am-mdnt (Sun 9am-10.30pm) **Bar Meals** L served all wk 12-2.30 D served Mon-Sat 6.30-9.30, Sun 6-8.30 **Restaurant** L served all wk 12-2.30 D served Mon-Sat 6.30-9.30, Sun 6-8.30 ⊕ CHARLES WELLS ◖ Bombardier & Eagle IPA ⏣ Westons Stowford Press, Aspall. ♟ 15 **Facilities** Non-diners area ♦⦿ Children's menu Children's portions Parking Wi-fi
Rooms 13

WELWYN GARDEN CITY　　　Map 6 TL21

The Brocket Arms

Ayot St Lawrence AL6 9BT ☎ 01438 820250 & 07867 537718
e-mail: bookings@brocketarms.com
dir: *A1(M) junct 4 follow signs to Wheathampstead, then Shaw's Corner. Pub past Shaw's Corner on right*

Great ales in a traditional setting

Encircled by a picturesque village that was once home to George Bernard Shaw, The Brocket Arms dates in parts to 1378 when it was built as a monks' hostel; it became a tavern in the 1630s. Huge oak beams and hefty hearths greet you along with a great range of real ales and wines. Food options range from snacks such as a Scotch egg with home-made chutney through to full meals such as pan-seared scallops with caramelised cauliflower purée and parsnip crisp followed by pan-fried pork loin with black pudding mash, thyme jus and creamed leeks.

Open all day all wk 12-11 (Sun 12-10.30) **Bar Meals** L served all wk 12-2.30 D served Mon-Sat 5-9 **Restaurant** L served all wk 12-2.30 D served Mon-Sat 7-9 ⊕ FREE HOUSE ◖ Nethergate Brocket Bitter, Greene King IPA & Abbot Ale, Sharp's Doom Bar, Adnams Broadside, Black Sheep, Guest ales ⏣ Aspall. ♟ 18
Facilities Non-diners area ♣ (Bar Garden) ♦⦿ Children's menu Children's portions Play area Garden ⊨ Beer festival Parking Wi-fi ▭

WILLIAN　　　Map 12 TL23

The Fox ◉

PICK OF THE PUBS

SG6 2AE ☎ 01462 480233
e-mail: restaurant@foxatwillian.co.uk
dir: *A1(M) junct 9 towards Letchworth, 1st left to Willian, pub 0.5m on left*

Fine dining pub with a smart, contemporary interior

An imposing Georgian building sitting opposite the village pond and right next to the church, the 18th-century Fox is an award-winning destination, attracting locals, walkers and cyclists. It's overseen by Cliff Nye, known for his Norfolk pubs, so it's no surprise to discover that East Anglian ales and fresh fish are brought in from Norfolk, while other produce is sourced locally. Receiving a makeover in early 2013, a clean, crisp look defines the interior, while the laid-back bar, restaurant atrium, enclosed courtyard and two beer gardens are all pleasant places to settle down with the modern British menus. Snacks include sharing boards, sandwiches, tempura squid rings and confit chicken spring roll. For an AA Rosette meal in the restaurant, opt for smoked salmon and prawn linguine, or peppered fillet of venison. Look out for themed food nights, such as 'tapas the British way', and chefs' demonstrations.

Open all day all wk 12-11 (Fri-Sat 12-12 Sun 12-10.30) **Bar Meals** L served Mon-Fri 12-2, Sat 12-6, Sun 12-3 D served Mon-Fri 7-9 Av main course £14.95 **Restaurant** L served Mon-Sat 12-2, Sun 12-3 D served Mon-Thu 6.45-9, Fri-Sat 6.30-9.15 Av 3 course à la carte fr £28.45 ⊕ FREE HOUSE ◖ Adnams Southwold Bitter, Woodforde's Wherry, Sharp's Doom Bar, Brancaster, Guest ales ⏣ Aspall. ♟ 14 **Facilities** Non-diners area ♣ (Bar Garden) ♦⦿ Children's portions Garden ⊨ Parking Wi-fi

KENT

BEARSTED　　　Map 7 TQ85

The Oak on the Green

Bearsted Green ME14 4EJ ☎ 01622 737976
e-mail: headoffice@villagegreenrestaurants.com
dir: *In village centre*

Beefy treats beside the village green

Half a Kentish hop garden drapes the beams in this lively old pub, known for its thoughtful, quality menu and the sometimes unusual real ales. The oak-shaded terrace of this eye-catching gabled pub, which dates from 1665, overlooks a corner of the immense village green and cricket pitch, great for those long summer evenings. The kitchens were once the village goal; escaping from them today are freshly-prepared dishes with a distinct nod towards Scottish beef - the range of gastro-burgers is notable, or plump for a tournedos of beef Rossini, whilst seafood lovers should go for the skate wing perhaps.

Open all day all wk Closed: 25 Dec **Bar Meals** L served Mon-Sat 12-10.30, Sun 12-10 D served Mon-Sat 12-10.30, Sun 12-10 food served all day **Restaurant** L served Mon-Sat 12-10.30, Sun 12-10 D served Mon-Sat 12-10.30, Sun 12-10 food served all day ⊕ FREE HOUSE ◖ Fuller's London Pride & ESB, Ringwood Old Thumper, 1648 Bee-Head ⏣ Biddenden. **Facilities** Non-diners area ♣ (Bar Restaurant) ♦⦿ Children's menu Children's portions Outside area ⊨ Parking ▭

BENENDEN　　　Map 7 TQ83

The Bull at Benenden

PICK OF THE PUBS

The Street TN17 4DE ☎ 01580 240054
e-mail: enquiries@thebullatbenenden.co.uk
dir: *From A229 onto B2086 to Benenden. Or from Tenterden take A28 S towards Hastings. Right onto B2086*

Perfect pies below the Downs

A huge brick-built inglenook fireplace takes centre stage at one side of the bar in this appealing inn overlooking Benenden's green and village cricket pitch. Centre stage at the bar itself is the considered selection of local real ales sourced by mine host Mark; ales from Chiddingstone's Larkins brewery lead the hop assault, whilst Kentish cider also puts in an appearance. The Bull dates from 1601 and has striking and unusual chinoiserie windows. The interior boasts wooden floors, scrubbed tables and an eclectic array of antique furniture. The Bull could lay claim to being pie and pudding central, with some superb gourmet examples produced by the kitchen team: slow cooked local game suet crust or smokey haddock, hard boiled egg and spinach puff pastry just a taste of the individual creations here, in addition to a comprehensive pub grub selection. In summer, head outside to the secret garden.

Open all day all wk noon-2am **Bar Meals** L served Mon-Sat 12-2.30, Sun 12-4 D served Mon-Sat 6-9.20 **Restaurant** D served Fri-Sun 6-9.20 ⊕ FREE HOUSE

continued

BENENDEN *continued*

Dark Star Hophead, Rother Valley Level Best, Larkins, Harvey's, Guest ales Biddenden. **Facilities** (Bar Garden) Children's menu Children's portions Garden Parking (notice required)

BIDDENDEN
Map 7 TQ83

The Three Chimneys

PICK OF THE PUBS

Biddenden Rd TN27 8LW ☎ 01580 291472
dir: *From A262 midway between Biddenden & Sissinghurst, follow Frittenden signs. (Pub seen from main road). Pub immediately on left in hamlet of Three Chimneys*

Pretty Kentish pub with excellent food

Worth remembering if visiting nearby Sissinghurst Castle, this 15th-century timbered treasure has every natural advantage of being a classic country pub, its original, small-roomed layout and old-fashioned furnishings remain delightfully intact. There are old settles, low beams, wood-panelled walls, worn brick floors, crackling log fires, soft evening candlelight, and an absence of music and electronic games. Modern-day demand for dining space has seen the addition of the rear Garden Room and a tasteful conservatory, and drinkers and diners spill out onto the secluded heated side patio and vast shrub-filled garden, which are perfect for summer eating. Food, locally sourced, is seasonally bang up to date and listed on daily-changing chalkboards. Tuck into a hearty ploughman's lunch or salmon and smoked haddock fishcakes with tartare sauce, or something more substantial, perhaps roast duck with bubble-and-squeak and port jus, or pan-fried rib-eye steak with garlic butter. If you have room for afters, try the delicious sticky toffee pudding. Adnams ales and the heady Biddenden cider are tapped direct from cask.

Open all wk 11.30-3 5.30-11 (Sat-Sun 11.30-4 5.30-11) Closed: 25 Dec **Bar Meals** L served all wk 12-2.30 D served all wk 6.30-9.30 **Restaurant** L served all wk 12-2.30 D served all wk 6.30-9.30 ⊕ FREE HOUSE Harvey's Sussex Old Ale, Adnams Biddenden. 10 **Facilities** Non-diners area (Bar Garden) Children's portions Garden Parking

BOSSINGHAM
Map 7 TR14

The Hop Pocket

The Street CT4 6DY ☎ 01227 709866
dir: *Telephone for directions*

A warm welcome at this family-friendly village inn

Birds of prey and an animal corner for children are among the more unusual attractions at this family pub in the heart of Kent. Canterbury is only five miles away and the county's delightfully scenic coast and countryside are within easy reach. As this is a free house there is a good range of ales to accompany dishes like fish pie, supreme of chicken, spicy salmon, Cajun beef, chilli nachos and fish platter. There is also an extensive range of sandwiches and omelettes.

Open all wk 11-3 6-12 (Sat & Sun all day) **Bar Meals** L served all wk 12-2.30 D served Mon-Sat 7-9.30 **Restaurant** L served all wk 12-2.30 D served Mon-Sat 7-9.30 ⊕ FREE HOUSE Fuller's London Pride, Wadworth 6X, Adnams, Purity, Local Ales. **Facilities** Non-diners area (Bar Restaurant Garden) Children's portions Play area Garden Parking Wi-fi

BRABOURNE
Map 7 TR14

The Five Bells Inn

The Street TN25 5LP ☎ 01303 813334
e-mail: visitus@fivebellsinnbrabourne.com
dir: *5m E of Ashford*

In the heart of rolling countryside

Pilgrims and weary travellers once joined village locals at this 16th-century inn surrounded by orchards at the foot of the North Downs; now it is the perfect pitstop for walkers and cyclists, who can enjoy a glass of local beer, cider or wine. With a relaxed and informal atmosphere, the owners uphold good, simple country pub values. A wood-fired oven is central to the regularly changing menu, so typical choices could include stone-baked pizza, vegetable pasta bake, fishcakes, lamb rump, beefburger with oven-baked potato skins, and baked fillet of hake. As well as a selection of Kentish cheeses and ice creams, other puddings are listed on the blackboard.

Open all day all wk **Restaurant** food served all day ⊕ FREE HOUSE Goacher's, Hopdaemon, Brabourne Stout, Guest ales Biddenden. **Facilities** Non-diners area Children's portions Garden Outside area Parking Wi-fi (notice required)

BROOKLAND
Map 7 TQ92

Woolpack Inn

Beacon Ln TN29 9TJ ☎ 01797 344321
dir: *1.5m past Brookland towards Rye on A259*

Charming inn partly built from salvaged ships' timbers

Isolated down a lane deep in Kentish marshland, this 15th-century cottage oozes character. It's rumoured that at one time the Woolpack had a secret tunnel used by smugglers to escape the excise men; the old spinning wheel mounted on the bar ceiling was used to divide up their contraband. Open beams and a vast inglenook fireplace (you can sit in it!) add to the atmosphere. The chef makes extensive use of fresh produce including local game and fish. On the main menu, expect pub favourites like chicken Kiev, lamb shank and battered cod. There are barbecues in the two beer gardens on summer evenings.

Open all wk 11-3 6-11 (Sat 11-11 Sun 12-10.30 (open all day BH & school hols)) Shepherd Neame Spitfire, Master Brew. **Facilities** Children's menu Children's portions Play area Family room Garden Parking

CANTERBURY
Map 7 TR15

The Chapter Arms

New Town St, Chartham Hatch CT4 7LT ☎ 01227 738340
e-mail: info@chapterarms.com
dir: *A28 from Canterbury towards Ashford. Right signed Chartham Hatch. 1m to pub*

An acre of gardens and a talented kitchen team

This charming and picturesque free house was once three cottages owned by Canterbury Cathedral's Dean and Chapter – hence the name. It sits on the North Downs Way overlooking apple orchards and oast houses. The à la carte menu includes goats' cheese crostini served with beetroot salad; deep-fried whitebait; Kentish lamb rump; beer-battered plaice goujons; and mushroom and leek Stroganoff. Look out for the Spoofers' Bar, where you can enjoy a game of spoof; The Chapter Arms hosted the World Spoofing Championships in 2010 and was featured in Rory McGrath and Will Mellor's TV programme *Champions of the World* in 2013. A barbecue operates on Bank Holidays and for special events.

Open all wk 11-3 6-11 (Sun 12-5) **Bar Meals** L served all wk 12-2.30 D served Mon-Sat 6.30-9 **Restaurant** L served Mon-Sat 12-2.30, Sun 12-3 D served Mon-Sat 6.30-9 ⊕ FREE HOUSE Shepherd Neame Master Brew, Wells Bombardier, Greene King IPA, Adnams, Harvey's, Young's, Guest ales Thatchers. 10 **Facilities** Non-diners area (Bar Restaurant Garden) Children's menu Children's portions Play area Garden Parking Wi-fi

Save on hotels. Book at **theAA.com/hotel**

KENT 247 **ENGLAND**

PICK OF THE PUBS

Castle Inn

CHIDDINGSTONE   Map 6 TQ54

TN8 7AH ☎ 01892 870247
e-mail: info@castleinn-kent.co.uk
web: www.castleinn-kent.co.uk
dir: *1.5m S of B2027 between Tonbridge & Edenbridge*

Historic inn in film-set village

Arguably one of England's prettiest villages, Chiddingstone is a fine example of a Tudor one-street village. To ensure its preservation, the National Trust bought it in 1939, part of the deal included the Castle Inn, built in 1420 when it was known as Waterslip House. It was over three centuries later that two brothers opened it as the Five Bells. Timber-framed and tile-hung, the inn — indeed, the whole village — may seem familiar, because it has been the backdrop to numerous films requiring scenes of a rural England now largely vanished. The heavily beamed saloon bar serves beers from Larkin's, brewed a few hundred yards away, and Harveys from Lewes in neighbouring East Sussex; about 150 wines are on the wine list. Although chef John McManus is also the proprietor, it's really because of what he and his team do in the kitchen and restaurant that attracts the most attention. For a start, they ensure a good lunchtime range of bar snacks and main and light meals, from a ploughman's to smoked haddock fishcake, and specials too. There's also

plenty of choice at dinner: start maybe with oriental crispy duck salad; follow with rump of lamb, or smoked haddock fishcake; and finish with dark chocolate truffle sandwich. On Sundays a set three-course lunch might feature mosaic of local game terrine with home-made chutney and Groombridge granary bread; sirloin of Kentish beef with crispy roast potatoes, Yorkshire pudding and pan gravy; and apple and rhubarb crumble with traditional English custard. Behind the inn is a vine-hung courtyard with its own bar, then over a bridge are a beautifully tended lawn and flowerbeds.

Open all day all wk 11-11 (Sun 12-10.30) **Bar Meals** L served Mon-Fri 12-2, Sat-Sun 12-4 D served Mon-Sat

7-9.30 **Restaurant** L served Mon-Fri 12-2, Sat-Sun 12-4 D served Mon-Sat 7-9.30 ⊞ FREE HOUSE ◀ Larkins Traditional, Porter & Platinum Blonde, Harvey's Sussex ♂ Westons Stowford Press. ♟ 9 **Facilities** Non-diners area ♣ (Bar Garden) ♦ Children's menu Children's portions Garden ⋒ Wi-fi ⚌ (notice required)

The Dove Inn ◉

Plum Pudding Ln, Dargate ME13 9HB ☎ 01227 751360
e-mail: doveatdargate@hotmail.com
dir: *6m from Canterbury; 4m from Whitstable. Telephone for detailed directions*

Friendly village pub with great food

Tucked down the delightfully named Plum Pudding Lane in a sleepy hamlet surrounded by orchards and farmland, the unpretentious honeysuckle- and rose-clad Dove draws discerning diners from far and wide for its top-notch food. The interior is simple and relaxed with stripped wooden floors and scrubbed tables. Outside is a gorgeous cottage garden where, appropriately, a dovecote and doves present an agreeably scenic backdrop for an alfresco meal or quiet pint. The Dove's menu is sensibly short and draws on quality local ingredients, which are soundly handled, offering a balanced choice of contemporary rustic dishes. After breads and olives for nibbles, start with carpaccio of locally reared beef, horseradish and watercress; or pumpkin and sage risotto and truffle oil. For a main course try roasted cod, braised lentils and salsify with potato purée; or roasted marsh lamb, black cabbage, and pearl barley, leaving room for triple chocolate brownie and peanut butter ice cream.

Open 12-3 6-12 (Fri 12-12 Sun 12-5) Closed: Mon **Bar Meals** L served Wed-Sat 12-2.30 D served Wed-Sat 6.30-9 **Restaurant** L served Wed-Sun 12-2.30 D served Wed-Sat 7-9 ⊕ SHEPHERD NEAME ◀ Master Brew, Spitfire, Seasonal ales. **Facilities** Non-diners area ☻ (Bar Garden) ♦♦ Children's portions Garden ☐ Parking Wi-fi ▬ (notice required)

The Granville

Street End, Lower Hardres CT4 7AL ☎ 01227 700402
e-mail: info@thegranvillecanterbury.com
dir: *On B2068, 2m from Canterbury towards Hythe*

Ever-changing art at pub with contemporary character

As well as a striking feature central fireplace/flue, this light and airy pub not far from Canterbury displays an interesting series of roll-over art exhibitions and installations (lino cuts, photographs, sculptures). Ample parking, a patio and large beer garden where summer barbecues take place make this Shepherd Neame pub good for families and dogs, whilst locals head for the public bar. The kitchen team has a confident approach to utilising the best that Kent and the enfolding seas can provide. You could start with chicken liver parfait with toast and pickles, followed perhaps by coq au vin or roast salmon fillet with pea sauce and crispy pancetta.

Open 12-3 5.30-11 Closed: 26 Dec, Mon ⊕ SHEPHERD NEAME ◀ Master Brew, Seasonal ale. **Facilities** ☻ (Bar Garden) ♦♦ Children's portions Garden Parking Wi-fi

The Red Lion

High St, Stodmarsh CT3 4BA ☎ 01227 721339
e-mail: redlionstodmarsh@btconnect.com
dir: *From Canterbury take A257 towards Sandwich, left into Stodmarsh Rd to Stodmarsh*

Championing local produce and international flavours

Set in a tiny hamlet, The Red Lion has changed little since it was rebuilt after a fire in 1720. Surrounded by reed beds, which are home to marsh harriers, bearded tits and bitterns, the pub's interior, warmed by two large log fires, is adorned with traditional hop garlands, curios, antiques and a collection of international menus. From the kitchen expect a cosmopolitan and seasonally-changing menu blended with local produce. Salads come from allotments and gardens, meats from local farms, and wild mushrooms from surrounding woodland. Classic plates with a modern twist include deep-fried rabbit, fries and aïoli, or slow-cooked pork belly with butterbeans, chorizo and tomato. Outside is an extensive garden where an antique forge doubles as a barbecue during the summer months; here you'll find an abundance of flowers and hop bines, with ducks, chickens and rabbits wandering about.

Open 11.30-3 6-11 (Sat 11-11 Sun 12-5) Closed: Sun eve & Mon ⊕ FREE HOUSE ◀ Greene King IPA & Ruddles County, Morland Old Speckled Hen, Hopdaemon Golden Braid Ŏ Thatchers. **Facilities** ♦♦ Children's menu Children's portions Play area Family room Garden Parking Wi-fi

The Bowl Inn

Egg Hill Rd TN27 0HG ☎ 01233 712256
e-mail: info@bowl-inn.co.uk
dir: *M20 junct 8/9, A20 to Charing, then A252 towards Canterbury. Left at top of Charing Hill into Bowl Rd, 1.25m*

Popular inn especially with walkers and cyclists

Standing high on top of the North Downs in an Area of Outstanding Natural Beauty, this popular pub was originally built as a farmhouse in 1512. For over 20 years it has been run by the Paine family, who have retained the old-world charm courtesy of warming winter fires in the large inglenook fireplace. The well-priced menu includes bar snacks of spinach and feta cheese goujons, plus a main menu featuring cheese and ham ploughman's, sausage sandwiches and steak baps. An annual beer festival takes place in mid-July.

Open all wk Mon-Sat 12-12 Sun 12-11 (Mon-Thu 4-11 Fri-Sun 12-12 winter) **Bar Meals** L served all wk 12-9.30 (Mon-Thu 4-9.30, Fri-Sun 12-9.30 winter) D served all wk 12-9.30 (Mon-Thu 4-9.30, Fri-Sun 12-9.30 winter) food served all day ⊕ FREE HOUSE ◀ Fuller's London Pride, Adnams Southwold Bitter, Harvey's Sussex Best Bitter, Whitstable East India Pale Ale, Young's Bitter. **Facilities** Non-diners area ☻ (Bar Garden) ♦♦ Garden ☐ Beer festival Parking Wi-fi ▬ (notice required)

The Oak

5 High St TN27 0HU ☎ 01233 712612
e-mail: info@theoakcharing.co.uk
dir: *M20 junct 9, A20 towards Maidstone. 5m to Charing. Right into High St*

Contemporary cuisine in a picturesque inn

This gabled old inn in one of Kent's prettiest villages makes the most of its location, sourcing beers from Nelson, across the North Downs in Chatham, and harvesting produce from the bountiful surrounding acres of the 'Garden of England'. High-quality ingredients are sourced for the robust modern English menus. Fish from Hythe and Rye, pork and lamb from downland farms, and vegetables from local growers feature in dishes such as pan-seared fillet of smoked haddock on sautéed leeks with crème fraîche mash.

Open all wk 11-11 (Sun 12-10.30) **Bar Meals** L served Mon-Sat 12-2.30, Sun 12-4 D served all wk 6-9 **Restaurant** L served Mon-Sat 12-2.30, Sun 12-4 D served all wk 6-9 ⊕ FREE HOUSE ◀ Shepherd Neame Master Brew, Nelson Ŏ Thatchers Gold. **Facilities** Non-diners area ♦♦ Children's menu Children's portions Garden Parking Wi-fi

Castle Inn

See Pick of the Pubs on page 247

The White Horse

The Square CT4 8BY ☎ 01227 730355
e-mail: info@thewhitehorsechilham.co.uk
dir: *Take A28 from Canterbury then A252, in 1m turn left*

One of the most photographed pubs in Britain

The White Horse is situated opposite the 15th-century village square where the annual May Fair is held; the square is a delightfully haphazard mix of gabled, half-timbered houses, shops, and inns dating from the late Middle Ages, with the North Downs Way passing through. This flint and stone inn offers a traditional atmosphere and a wide selection of real ales from breweries like Sharp's, Greene King and Shepherd Neame. The modern cooking is based on fresh local produce, mainly organic. A meal might include chilli con carne and home-made steak-and-ale pie. The bar menu offers sandwiches and ploughman's. There is live music every Saturday.

Open all day all wk noon-close Closed: 25 Dec eve **Bar Meals** L served Mon-Fri 12-3, Sat all day, Sun 12-5 D served all wk 6-9 ⊕ ENTERPRISE INNS ◀ Shepherd Neame Master Brew, Greene King IPA, Sharp's Doom Bar, Guest ale Ŏ Thatchers Gold. **Facilities** Non-diners area ♦♦ Children's menu Children's portions Garden ☐ Beer festival ▬

Save on hotels. Book at theAA.com/hotel

KENT 249 ENGLAND

PICK OF THE PUBS

The Griffins Head

CHILLENDEN Map 7 TR25

CT3 1PS ☎ **01304 840325**
web: www.griffinsheadchillenden.co.uk
dir: *A2 from Canterbury towards Dover,*
then B2046. Village on right

Ancient inn with imaginative food

Dating from 1286, when Edward I was on the English throne, this fine black-and-white, half-timbered Wealden hall house is an architectural gem. It was once part of the estate of John de Chillenden and for centuries was a farm and brewhouse, until in 1766 it was granted a full licence to serve travellers on what then was the main road from Canterbury to Deal, although it's hard to believe today. The building you see is Tudor, constructed around the original wattle-and-daub walls, some of which can be seen in one of the three mercifully unspoilt flagstone-floored rooms. Here you can sit at old scrubbed pine tables and on recycled church pews and take in the exposed brick walls and beams above your head. Owned by Shepherd Neame, it has been managed for more than 27 years by Jerry and Karen Copestake, who have won awards as testament to how well they do things here. The constantly changing seasonal menu is typically English and specialises in game from local estates and locally caught fish, especially haddock, cod, sea bass and sea bream.

Typical dishes might include red wine-marinated shoulder of lamb; warm salads with steak and roasted vegetables; chicken and ham pie; beef bourguignon; and traditional pub favourites like lamb's or calves' liver and bacon. Desserts include apple crumble, and home-made ice creams flavoured with passionfruit, ginger, raspberry or strawberry. The pretty garden, full of rambling roses and clematis, is especially popular during summer weekend barbecues. On the first Sunday of every month vintage and classic car enthusiasts turn up in their Armstrong Siddeleys, Austin 7s, MG TCs and other venerable vehicles. Local cricketers like to meet here too. Children are not allowed indoors.

Open all day Closed: Sun pm **Bar Meals** L served all wk 12-2 D served Mon-Sat 7-9.30 **Restaurant** L served all wk 12-2 D served Mon-Sat 7-9.30 ⊕ SHEPHERD NEAME ◖ Shepherd Neame. ♟ 10 **Facilities** Non-diners area Garden Outside area ⪥ Parking

CHILLENDEN   Map 7 TR25

The Griffins Head

PICK OF THE PUBS

See Pick of the Pubs on page 249

CHIPSTEAD   Map 6 TQ55

George & Dragon NEW

39 High St TN13 2RW ☎ 01732 779019
e-mail: info@georgeanddragonchipstead.com
dir: *Telephone for directions*

Sincerity in everything is the watchword here

The delights of this 16th-century village gastro-pub are easily summarised: the welcoming open fires, the heavy oak beams and solid furnishings; the splendidly beamed upstairs restaurant; and the tree-house-inspired private dining room. Then there's Westerham Brewery's specially-produced George's Marvellous Medicine ale; and finally, the food, using top free-range or organic meats from farms in Kent and neighbouring counties, and sustainable fish from south-east coastal waters. Daily-changing menus list grilled skate wing with lemon and caper butter; seared haunch of Chart Farm venison with Jerusalem artichoke and truffle; and beetroot and goats' cheese risotto. One further delight is the summer beer festival.

Open all day all wk Closed: 1 Jan **Bar Meals** L served Mon-Fri 12-3, Sat-Sun 12-4 D served Mon-Sat 6-9.30, Sun 6-8.30 Av main course £8.95 **Restaurant** L served Mon-Fri 12-3, Sat-Sun 12-4 D served Mon-Sat 6-9.30, Sun 6-8.30 Fixed menu price fr £13.50 ⊕ FREE HOUSE ◀ Westerham George's Marvellous Medicine & Grasshopper ♂ Westons Stowford Press. ♀ 18 **Facilities** Non-diners area ✿ (Bar Garden) ♦️ Children's menu Children's portions Play area Garden ⊼ Beer festival Parking Wi-fi ▭ (notice required)

CRANBROOK   Map 7 TQ73

The George Hotel

Stone St TN17 3HE ☎ 01580 713348
e-mail: georgehotel@shepherd-neame.co.uk
dir: *From A21 follow signs to Goudhurst. At large rdbt take 3rd exit to Cranbrook (A229). Hotel on left*

Former courthouse offers brasserie and restaurant dining

One of Cranbrook's landmark buildings, the 14th-century George Hotel traditionally served visiting buyers of locally made Cranbrook cloth. Magistrates held court here for over 300 years, and today the sophisticated interior mixes period features with contemporary decor. Two separate menus have been created; the brasserie offers a take on classic English cuisine – grilled veal escalope with crushed sweet potatoes, grilled vegetables and a port jus, perhaps, while in the restaurant diners can sample modern English dishes like pan-roasted lamb noisettes with dauphinoise potatoes, chicory, red onion and apricot tatin and rosemary jus.

Open all day all wk Bar Meals L served all wk 12-3 D served Mon-Sat 6-9.30, Sun 6-9 Restaurant L served all wk 12-3 D served Mon-Sat 6-9.30, Sun 6-9 ⊕ SHEPHERD NEAME ◀ Master Brew, Spitfire ♂ Thatchers. ♀ 16 Facilities Non-diners area ✿ (Bar) ♦️ Children's menu Children's portions Outside area ⊼ Parking Wi-fi ▭ (notice required)

DARTFORD   Map 6 TQ57

The Rising Sun Inn ★★★ INN

Fawkham Green, Fawkham, Longfield DA3 8NL
☎ 01474 872291
web: www.risingsun-fawkham.co.uk
dir: *0.5m from Brands Hatch Racing Circuit & 5m from Dartford*

Traditional 16th-century pub opposite the village green

Standing on the green in a picturesque village not far from Brands Hatch, The Rising Sun is a 16th-century building, which has been a pub since 1702. Inside you will find a bar full of character, complete with inglenook log fire, and Inglenooks restaurant where home-made traditional house specials and a large fish menu, using the best local produce, are served. Among the mains you may find grilled and marinated lamb rump; pork fillet with Stilton, bacon and chives wrapped in Parma ham; teriyaki salmon on spinach; and bacon and onion pudding. There is also a front patio and garden for alfresco dining in warmer weather, plus comfortable en suite bedrooms if you would like to stay over.

Open all day all wk **Bar Meals** food served all day **Restaurant** L served all wk 12-3 D served all wk 6.30-9.30 ⊕ FREE HOUSE ◀ Courage Best & Directors, Fuller's London Pride, Timothy Taylor Landlord, Sharp's Doom Bar. ♀ 9 **Facilities** Non-diners area ♦️ Children's portions Garden ⊼ Beer festival Cider festival Parking Wi-fi **Rooms** 5

FAVERSHAM   Map 7 TR06

Albion Taverna

29 Front Brents ME13 7DH ☎ 01795 591411
e-mail: albiontaverna@yahoo.co.uk
dir: *Telephone for directions*

Mexican and English cook house on the waterfront

Located next to the Shepherd Neame Brewery near the Faversham swing bridge, the Albion Taverna looks directly onto the attractive waterfront area. The colourful menu is a combination of Mexican and English dishes. On the Mexican side are fajitas and quesadillas with a choice of fillings, nachos, buffalo wings, marinated ribs, chipotle meatballs and beef or bean chilli pots. English options include a lamb, mint and chilli burger; chargrilled steak and crab cake salad. Other treats are mussels cooked country style, Thai style or Mexican style. For dessert, try churros with dark chocolate fondue. There is an annual hop festival in early September.

Open all wk 12-3 6-11.30 (Sat-Sun 12-11.30) **Bar Meals** Av main course £11 **Restaurant** L served Mon-Fri 12-3, Sat-Sun 12-10 D served Mon-Fri 6-10, Sat-Sun 12-10 Fixed menu price fr £25 Av 3 course à la carte fr £26 ⊕ SHEPHERD NEAME ◀ Master Brew ♂ Thatchers Gold. ♀ **Facilities** Non-diners area ♦️ Children's menu Children's portions Play area Garden ⊼ Beer festival Parking Wi-fi ▭ (notice required)

Shipwright's Arms

PICK OF THE PUBS

Hollowshore ME13 7TU ☎ 01795 590088
dir: *A2 through Ospringe then right at rdbt. Right at T-junct then left opposite Davington School, follow signs*

Walk in the footsteps of pirates, smugglers and sailors

Although there has been a building on this site since the 13th century, the creekside Shipwright's Arms was first licensed in 1738 and has been a well-known spot for sailors and fishermen ever since. Once a popular haunt for pirates and smugglers, this homely brick and weatherboarded pub stands in a remote location on the Swale marshes. Best reached on foot or by boat, the effort in getting here is well rewarded as this charming, unspoilt tavern that oozes historic character. Step back in time in the relaxed and comfortable bars, which boast nooks and crannies, original timbers, built-in settles, well-worn sofas, wood-burning stoves, and a wealth of maritime artefacts. Locally-brewed Goacher's and Whitstable ales are tapped straight from the cask, and make for a perfect match for the simple, traditional bar food: hot smoked mackerel; mushroom Stroganoff; macaroni cheese; sausage, mash and peas; and fresh fish caught by the local trawler.

Open 11-3 6-10 (Sat-Sun 11-4 6-11 in winter; Sat 11-11 Sun 12-10.30 in summer) Closed: Mon (Oct-Mar) **Bar Meals** L served Mon-Sat 11-2.30, Sun 12-2.30 D served Tue-Sat 7-9 (no food Tue-Thu eve in winter) **Restaurant** L served Tue-Sat 11-2.30, Sun 12-2.30 D served Tue-Sat 7-9 (no food Tue-Thu eve in winter) ⊕ FREE HOUSE ◀ Goacher's, Hopdaemon, Whitstable, Local ales. ♀ 12 **Facilities** Non-diners area ♦️ Children's menu Children's portions Family room Garden ⊼ Parking ▭

Save on hotels. Book at **theAA.com/hotel**

KENT 251 **ENGLAND**

FORDCOMBE · Map 6 TQ54

Chafford Arms

TN3 0SA ☎ **01892 740267**
e-mail: chaffordarms@btconnect.com
dir: *On B2188 (off A264) between Tunbridge Wells, East Grinstead & Penshurst*

Attractive pub in the Weald serving local brews

This visually striking country inn, with multiple gables and tall chimneys has hints of Arts and Crafts about it. Set in The Weald high above the Medway Valley, close to Penshurst Place and handy for Hever Castle, fine walking on the Weald Way is rewarded by the prospect of beers from local microbreweries and a menu of comforting, home-made pub meals like fisherman's pie or Italian meatball linguine. Hunker down beside roaring log fires or rest awhile in the rose-scented garden, with great views of pretty countryside.

Open all day all wk 11am-mdnt ⊕ ENTERPRISE INNS ◀ Larkins Best Bitter, Harvey's Sussex Best Bitter. **Facilities** ❀ (Bar Garden) ♦♦ Children's menu Garden Parking

GOODNESTONE · Map 7 TR25

The Fitzwalter Arms

The Street CT3 1PJ ☎ **01304 840303**
e-mail: thefitzwalterarms@hotmail.co.uk
dir: *From A2 & B2046 follow Goodnestone Park Garden signs*

Stunning inn in memorable estate village

This charming village inn has been catering for travellers crossing north Kent since 1589. A true community local; loyal regulars welcome today's visitors heading for the renowned Goodnestone Gardens nearby, where Jane Austen was a regular guest at the great house. This attractive, brick-built inn boasts log fires, bar billiards, a tranquil church-side garden and some great beers from the nearby Shepherd Neame brewery; ample themes around which to plot a visit and investigate the seasonally-tilted menu of home-cooked fare. Mushroom risotto to start, and then pork belly, caramelised apple, black pudding and mustard seed jus are good menu examples; special diets can be accommodated.

Open Tue-Thu 12-3 6-11 (Mon 6-11 Fri-Sat noon-1am Sun 12-11) Closed: Mon (Tue L in winter) **Bar Meals** L served Tue-Sun 12-3 D served all wk 6-9 **Restaurant** L served Tue-Sun 12-3 D served all wk 6-9 ⊕ SHEPHERD NEAME ◀ Master Brew, Spitfire, Early Bird, Late Red, Kent. **Facilities** Non-diners area ♦♦ Children's portions Garden ⋔ Wi-fi 🚌 (notice required)

GOUDHURST · Map 6 TQ73

The Goudhurst Inn **NEW**

Cranbrook Rd TN17 1DX ☎ **01580 212605**
e-mail: enquiries@thegoudhurstinn.com
dir: *From A21 (or A228) take A262, follow Goudhurst signs. Pub on A262 in village*

Revitalised village pub with stunning views

Graeme and Lois Digham have breathed new life into the former Chequers Inn since they took over in 2011. You can't miss the striking blue exterior and the spruced up bar and dining area have a comfortable contemporary feel, perfect for a relaxing with a pint of Harvey's and a classic lunchtime bar meal – ham, egg and chips, Scotch egg with mustard mayonnaise, or Moroccan spiced lamb burger. Come in the evening for Rye bay scallops, lamb shoulder with truffle cream potato and port sauce, and baked chocolate tart. Dine alfresco and savour glorious Wealden views.

Open all day all wk **Bar Meals** L served all wk 12-2.30 D served all wk 6-9.30 Av main course £10 **Restaurant** L served all wk 12-2.30 D served all wk 6-9.30 Fixed menu price fr £15.95 Av 3 course à la carte fr £30 ⊕ ENTERPRISE INNS ◀ Harvey's, Timothy Taylor Landlord, Sharp's Doom Bar ♻ Symonds. ▾ **Facilities** Non-diners area ❀ (Bar Restaurant Garden) ♦♦ Children's menu Children's portions Play area Family room Garden ⋔ Parking Wi-fi 🚌 (notice required)

Green Cross Inn

TN17 1HA ☎ **01580 211200**
dir: *A21 from Tonbridge towards Hastings left onto A262 towards Ashford. 2m, Goudhurst on right*

Seafood is the draw at this dining pub

In an unspoiled corner of Kent, close to Finchcocks Manor, and originally built to serve the Paddock Wood–Goudhurst railway line, which closed in 1968, this thriving dining pub specialises in fresh seafood. Arrive early to bag a table in the dining room, prettily decorated with fresh flowers, and tuck into Cornish cock crab, sea bass with spring onions, ginger, soy sauce and white wine, or seafood paella, or go for the fillet steak pan-fried with peppercorns, brandy and cream, followed by pannacotta with raspberry coulis; all freshly prepared by the chef-owner who is Italian and classically trained.

Open all wk 12-3 6-11 Closed: Sun eve ⊕ FREE HOUSE ◀ Harvey's Sussex Best Bitter, Guinness ♻ Biddenden. **Facilities** ♦♦ Children's portions Garden Parking

The Star & Eagle ★★★★ INN

High St TN17 1AL ☎ **01580 211512**
e-mail: starandeagle@btconnect.com
dir: *Just off A21 towards Hastings. Take A262 into Goudhurst. Pub at top of hill adjacent to church*

Outstanding views and assured cooking

The vaulted stonework suggests that this rambling, big-beamed 14th-century building may once have been a monastery, and the tunnel from the cellars probably surfaces underneath the neighbouring parish church. Standing 400 feet above sea level, the Star & Eagle has breathtaking views of the orchards and hop fields that helped earn Kent the accolade 'The Garden of England'. Harvey's and Oxford Gold are the mainstays in the bar, and there's plenty of choice in wines served by the glass. While quaffing, unwind and enjoy choosing between the fine traditional and continental dishes prepared under the guidance of Spanish chef-proprietor Enrique Martinez. Typical dishes are king prawns sautéed in garlic, chilli and white wine; Spanish-style pot-roast shoulder of lamb; and boiled ham with free-range egg and bubble-and-squeak. Finish with whisky bread and butter pudding and cream. The ten bedrooms and the public rooms boast original features and much character.

Open all day all wk 11-11 (Sun 12-3 6.30-10.30) **Bar Meals** L served all wk 12-2.30 D served all wk 7-9.30 Av main course £15 **Restaurant** L served all wk 12-2.30 D served all wk 7-9.30 ⊕ FREE HOUSE ◀ Harvey's, Brakspear Oxford Gold, Wychwood Hobgoblin. ▾ 14 **Facilities** Non-diners area ♦♦ Children's menu Children's portions Family room Garden ⋔ Parking Wi-fi 🚌 **Rooms** 10

GRAVESEND · Map 6 TQ67

The Cock Inn

Henley St, Luddesdowne DA13 0XB ☎ **01474 814208**
e-mail: andrew.r.turner@btinternet.com
dir: *Telephone for directions*

Adults-only pub with cask conditioned English ales

Dating from 1713, this whitewashed free house in the beautiful Luddesdowne Valley has two traditional beamed bars with wood-burning stoves and open fires. Always available are seven well-kept real ales, Köstritzer and other German beers, and not a fruit machine, jukebox or television in sight. All food is ordered at the bar: expect filled submarine rolls, basket meals and home-made cod and chips; steak, mushroom and Irish stout pie; and spinach and ricotta ravioli. As an adults-only pub, no-one under 18 is allowed.

Open all day all wk 12-11 (Sun 12-10.30) **Bar Meals** L served all wk 12-3 ⊕ FREE HOUSE ◀ Adnams Southwold Bitter, Broadside & Lighthouse, Shepherd Neame Master Brew, Goacher's Real Mild Ale, Woodforde's Wherry. **Facilities** Non-diners area ❀ (Bar Restaurant Garden) Garden ⋔ Parking

HALSTEAD
Map 6 TQ46

Rose & Crown

Otford Ln TN14 7EA ☎ **01959 533120**
e-mail: info@roseandcrownhalstead.co.uk
dir: *M25 junct 4, follow A21, London (SE), Bromley, Orpington signs. At Hewitts Rdbt 1st exit onto A224 signed Dunton Green. At rdbt 3rd exit into Shoreham Ln. In Halstead left into Station Rd, left into Otford Ln*

Bustling community local

This handsome Grade II listed pub, nestled in the lee of the North Downs, is all a good village pub should be; traditional pub games including bat and trap, family friendly, supporting local microbreweries such as Tonbridge and Westerham (with no less than three beer festivals held each year) and a welcoming base for walks into the peaceful countryside on the doorstep. With lively bar, peaceful lounge, Stables Restaurant and tranquil garden to suit all tastes, home-made pub grub is the icing on the cake, from fish and chips through minted lamb shank to venison and ale pie.

Open all day all wk **Bar Meals** L served all wk 12-11 D served all wk 12-11 Av main course £7 food served all day **Restaurant** L served all wk 12-11 D served all wk 12-11 food served all day ⊕ FREE HOUSE ◀ Larkins Traditional, Whitstable East India Pale Ale, Guest ales Ö Westons. ♥ **Facilities** Non-diners area ❄ (Bar Garden Outside area) ♦ Children's menu Children's portions Play area Garden Outside area ♩ Beer festival Parking Wi-fi 🚌

HARRIETSHAM
Map 7 TQ85

The Pepper Box Inn

ME17 1LP ☎ **01622 842558**
e-mail: enquiries@thepepperboxinn.co.uk
dir: *From A20 in Harrietsham take Fairbourne Heath turn. 2m to x-rds, straight over, 200yds, pub on left*

Family-run inn with stunning views

High up on the Greensand Ridge this delightful 15th-century country pub enjoys far-reaching views over the Weald of Kent from its terrace. Run by the same family since 1958, it takes its name from an early type of pistol, a replica of which hangs behind the bar. Using the best local seasonal produce, food ranges from bar snacks of ham, egg and chips or chicken curry through to tiger prawns pan fried in garlic, chilli and ginger butter, followed by slow-roasted belly pork with cider, apples, thyme and mashed potatoes.

Open all wk 11-3 6-11 ⊕ SHEPHERD NEAME ◀ Master Brew, Spitfire, Late Red. **Facilities** Garden Parking

HAWKHURST
Map 7 TQ73

The Black Pig at Hawkhurst

Moor Hill TN18 4PF ☎ **01580 752306**
e-mail: enquiries@theblackpigathawkhurst.co.uk
dir: *On A229, S of Hawkhurst*

A success story in rural Kent

Mark and Lucy Barron-Reid's second entrerprise, a stylish community pub on Moor Hill, continues to thrive and gain praise for its locally sourced food. Like their first pub, the Bull at Benenden (see entry) a few miles east, the ethos is to specialise in food and drink from Kent and Sussex, so expect to find Copper Top ale from the Old Dairy Brewery in Rolvenden, and simple, home-cooked food – mixed seafood risotto, local rabbit burger, shoulder of lamb with mustard mash, garlic and rosemary jus, and a fish and seafood sharing platter. Wines are also sourced from local vineyards, and lagers from Whitstable and Tenterden.

Open all day all wk 11am-mdnt **Bar Meals** L served Mon-Sat 12-2.30, Sun 12-4 D served all wk 6.30-9.30 ⊕ FREE HOUSE ◀ Dark Star Hophead, Larkins Traditional, Old Dairy Copper Top, Harvey's Ö Biddenden. **Facilities** Non-diners area ❄ (Bar Garden) ♦ Children's menu Children's portions Garden ♩ 🚌

The Great House

Gills Green TN18 5EJ ☎ **01580 753119**
e-mail: enquiries@thegreathouse.net
dir: *Just off A229 between Cranbrook & Hawkhurst*

White clapboard free house in the heart of the Weald

A wonderfully atmospheric 16th-century free house with a network of exposed beams, log fires and stone floors. Three dining areas are complemented by an orangery opening on to a Mediterranean-style terrace, with Italian designer chairs, and a neat garden entered through a lychgate. The French chef creates traditional English and regional French brasserie-style dishes making full use of fresh, seasonal and, in the case of the meats, organic produce. For lunch, the long menu offers seared Bedgebury pigeon; tiger prawns and avocado salad; and Harvey's beer-battered haddock. In the evening think about slow-cooked Kentish vegetable casserole; roast whole red partridge with Puy lentils; or South East Coast halibut with tarragon mash. Desserts range from peach tarte Tatin to Amaretto crème brûlée. In the bar, one of the real ciders is from nearby Biddenden (the other is Aspall from Suffolk), and 70 world wines include some from Tenterden.

Open all day all wk 11.30-11 **Bar Meals** L served Mon-Fri 12-3, Sat-Sun 12-9.45 D served Mon-Fri 6-9.45, Sat-Sun 12-9.45 Av main course £14 **Restaurant** L served Mon-Fri 12-3, Sat-Sun 12-9.45 D served Mon-Fri 6-9.45, Sat-Sun 12-9.45 Av 3 course à la carte fr £26 ⊕ FREE HOUSE ◀ Harvey's, Guinness, Sharp's Doom Bar Ö Biddenden, Aspall. ♥ 20 **Facilities** Non-diners area ❄ (Bar Restaurant Garden) ♦ Children's menu Children's portions Garden ♩ Parking Wi-fi

HERNHILL
Map 7 TR06

The Red Lion

Crockham Ln ME13 9JR ☎ **01227 751207**
e-mail: enquiries@theredlion.org
web: www.theredlion.org
dir: *M2 junct 7, A299 signed Whitstable, Herne Bay & Ramsgate. Follow Fostall sign, up slip road. Right, signed Fostall & Hernhill. In Hernhill pub on left*

Historic pub by pretty village green

An eye-catching mix of crucks and half-timbering outside; within, a forest of hop-adorned beams and pillars characterise this rambling, medieval, flagstone floored inn next to the village green. The beer garden has views to distant wooded hills, a sheltered base in which to sup real ales from regional breweries, complemented by an August Bank Holiday beer festival. Fine, fulfilling pub grub includes medallions of pork in a tarragon cream sauce, sausage and mash or squid, mussel and prawn risotto from the weekly-changing specials board. Wednesday's see a pensioner's special lunchtime menu.

Open all wk 11.30-3 6-11 (Fri-Sat 12-11 Sun 12-10.30) **Bar Meals** L served Mon-Sat 12-3, Sun 12-8 D served Mon-Sat 6-9, Sun 12-8 Av main course £10 **Restaurant** L served Mon-Sat 12-3, Sun 12-8 D served Mon-Sat 6-9, Sun 12-8 Fixed menu price fr £10.75 Av 3 course à la carte fr £15.75 ⊕ FREE HOUSE ◀ Sharp's Doom Bar, Fuller's London Pride, Adnams Broadside. ♥ 12 **Facilities** Non-diners area ❄ (Bar Garden) ♦ Children's menu Children's portions Play area Family room Garden ♩ Beer festival Parking Wi-fi 🚌

See advert on opposite page

Save on hotels. Book at **theAA.com/hotel**

KENT 253 ENGLAND

Red Lion

Crockham Lane, Hernhill, Kent
Tel: 01227 751207
Website: www.theredlion.org
Email: enquiries@theredlion.org

A picturesque 14th century pub situated in a small village near the town of Faversham. Surrounded in history the pub dates back to the 1300s and still contains many original features. The pub offers a selection of traditional English food alongside the frequently changing seasonal specials. Facilities include an upstairs restaurant, available for dining or large functions, a front patio overlooking the church and village green, and a well-established pub garden with many historical features and a large play area for children.

HODSOLL STREET — Map 6 TQ66

The Green Man

TN15 7LE ☎ 01732 823575
e-mail: the.greenman@btinternet.com
dir: *On North Downs between Brands Hatch & Gravesend off A227*

Recommended for its fish dishes

This 300-year-old, family-run pub is loved for its decent food and real ales. It stands in the picturesque village of Hodsoll Street on the North Downs, surrounded by beautiful Kent countryside, with a large garden for warmer weather. Sharp's Doom Bar and Timothy Taylor Landlord are a couple of the four real ales on tap. Food is prepared to order using fresh local produce, and the evening menu includes a wide variety of fish, such as smoked haddock, whole sea bass, halibut steak and crab and prawn salad, as well as dishes like duck and bacon salad; steak-and-kidney filo parcel; and vegetable and Stilton crumble.

Open all wk 11-2.30 6-11 (Fri-Sun all day) **Bar Meals** L served Mon-Thu 12-2, Fri-Sun all day D served Mon-Thu 6.30-9.30, Fri-Sun all day **Restaurant** L served Mon-Thu 12-2, Fri-Sun all day D served Mon-Thu 6.30-9.30, Fri-Sun all day ⊕ HAYWOOD PUB COMPANY LTD ◀ Timothy Taylor Landlord, Harvey's, Sharp's Doom Bar, Guest ale ♂ Thatchers Gold. **Facilities** Non-diners area ♦♦ Children's menu Children's portions Play area Garden ⋒ Parking Wi-fi ⛟

HOLLINGBOURNE — Map 7 TQ85

The Dirty Habit NEW

PICK OF THE PUBS

Upper St ME17 1UW ☎ 01622 880880
e-mail: enquiries@thedirtyhabit.net
dir: *M20 junct 8, follow A20 signs, then Hollingbourne signs on B2163. Through Hollingbourne, pub on hill top on right*

Historic watering hole on the Pilgrims Way

There's been a pub on this site since the 11th century, when monks brewed ale here for pilgrims plodding from Winchester to the shrine of Thomas à Becket at Canterbury. Renovation has done wonders for the building, without losing any of its period charm. Look, for instance, at the long Georgian oak bar and panelling, and the Victorian furniture, all beautifully restored by skilled local craftsmen. Harvey's of Lewes is one of the real ales on tap, and there's cider from Biddenden too. The Monks Corner, with oak beams to the apex and a bread oven in the corner, is ideal for private dining, while outside is a quiet terrace. The kitchen prepares traditional favourites such as steak-and-kidney pie; fish and chips; 21-day-matured Kentish beef fillet; braised and roasted partridge; pan-fried salmon; wild mushroom risotto, and specialities including langoustines and lobster.

Open all day all wk **Bar Meals** Av main course £12.30 food served all day **Restaurant** Av 3 course à la carte fr £26 food served all day ⊕ ENTERPRISE INNS ◀ Harvey's,

Old Dairy Red Top, Timothy Taylor Landlord ♂ Biddenden, Aspall. ☖ 28 **Facilities** ♣ (Bar Restaurant Outside area) ♦♦ Children's menu Children's portions Outside area ⋒ Parking Wi-fi

ICKHAM — Map 7 TR25

The Duke William

The Street CT3 1QP ☎ 01227 721308 & 721244
e-mail: goodfood@dukewilliam.biz
dir: *A257 Canterbury to Sandwich. In Littlebourne left opposite The Anchor, into Nargate St. 0.5m right into Drill Ln, right into The Street*

Child-friendly village inn recommended for its Sunday lunches

This family-friendly, whitewashed free house is in the heart of Ickham village. Traditional, locally sourced and home-cooked food is the keynote here; the Sunday lunches are particularly popular. Menu choices might include fresh fish, venison or slow-roast pork, all served with local vegetables. Chicken liver pâté and rabbit casserole could appear on the daily specials menu. The lovely garden features a covered patio, as well as a children's play area with a swing and slide.

Open all day all wk **Bar Meals** L served all wk 12-3 D served all wk 6-10 **Restaurant** L served all wk 12-3 D served all wk 6-10 ⊕ FREE HOUSE ◀ Shepherd Neame Master Brew, Harvey's, Sharp's Doom Bar, Guest ale ♂ Symonds. ☖ 9 **Facilities** Non-diners area ♣ (Bar Garden) ♦♦ Children's menu Children's portions Play area Garden ⋒ Wi-fi ⛟ (notice required)

IDEN GREEN — Map 6 TQ73

The Peacock

Goudhurst Rd TN17 2PB ☎ 01580 211233
dir: *A21 from Tunbridge Wells to Hastings, onto A262, pub 1.5m past Goudhurst*

Family friendly inn

Dating from the 14th century, this Grade II listed former smugglers' haunt has exposed brickwork, low beams, an inglenook fireplace, and ancient oak doors. Kent's Best and Bishops Finger can be found among several ales in the convivial bar. Popular with families, The Peacock offers a wide range of traditional pub food made using produce from local farmers; maybe creamy garlic mushrooms on toast followed by ham, egg and chips or Cajun spiced chicken with sweet chilli dip. In summer enjoy the large enclosed garden with fruit trees and picnic tables on one side of the building. Beer festivals are held at varying times in the year.

Open all day all wk 12-11 (Sun 12-6) **Bar Meals** L served Mon-Fri 12-2.30, Sat all day, Sun 12-3 D served Mon-Fri 6-8.45, Sat all day Av main course £10 **Restaurant** L served Mon-Fri 12-2.30, Sat all day, Sun 12-3 D served Mon-Fri 6-8.45, Sat all day ⊕ SHEPHERD NEAME ◀ Master Brew, Kent, Bishops Finger, Seasonal ales. **Facilities** Non-diners area ♣ (Bar Garden) ♦♦ Children's menu Children's portions Family room Garden ⋒ Beer festival Parking Wi-fi ⛟ (notice required)

IGHTHAM — Map 6 TQ55

The Harrow Inn

PICK OF THE PUBS

Common Rd TN15 9EB ☎ 01732 885912
dir: *1.5m from Borough Green on A25 to Sevenoaks, signed Ightham Common, turn left into Common Rd. Inn 0.25m on left*

Worth seeking out for imaginative food

Tucked away down country lanes, yet easily accessible from both the M20 and M26, this creeper-hung, stone-built free house dates back to at least the 17th century. The two-room bar area has a great brick fireplace, open to both sides and piled high with logs, while the restaurant's vine-clad conservatory opens on to a terrace that's ideal for a pint of Loddon Hoppit or Gravesend Shrimpers and warm weather dining. Menus vary with the seasons, and seafood is a particular speciality: fish lovers can enjoy dishes such as crab and ginger spring roll; swordfish with Cajun spice and salsa; or pan-fried fillets of sea bass with lobster cream and spinach. Other main courses may include baked sausage with gammon, fennel, red onions and garlic; and tagliatelle with wild mushroom, fresh herb, lemongrass and chilli ragout. The car park is fairly small, but there is adequate street parking.

Open 12-3 6-11 Closed: 1wk between Xmas & New Year, Sun eve & Mon-Wed **Bar Meals** L served Thu-Sun 12-2 D served Thu-Sat 6-9 **Restaurant** L served Thu-Sun 12-2 D served Thu-Sat 6-9 ⊕ FREE HOUSE ◀ Loddon Hoppit, Gravesend Shrimpers. ☖ 9 **Facilities** Non-diners area ♦♦ Children's portions Family room Outside area Parking

IVY HATCH — Map 6 TQ55

The Plough at Ivy Hatch

PICK OF THE PUBS

High Cross Rd TN15 0NL ☎ 01732 810100
e-mail: info@theploughivyhatch.co.uk
dir: *Exit A25 between Borough Green & Sevenoaks, follow Ightham Mote signs*

The perfect spot for a lingering lunch or supper

This tile-hung 17th-century free house stands in a picturesque village, just a short walk from the National Trust's Ightham Mote. The bar offers beers from the Tonbridge Brewery and the wine list covers New and Old World. The modern British menus with European highlights are updated daily, driven by locally produced seasonal ingredients including seafood and game. The comfort food bar menu includes brunch (from 9am Mon-Fri) rump steak burger, ploughman's and ciabatta sandwiches. A starter from the main menu might be pressed oxtail terrine with caper salad. For the main course, expect dishes like pan-fried fillet of bream, confit leg of Barbary duck or Chart Farm venison pavé. Desserts include orange, almond and Amaretto drizzle cake. There is also a great sweet and savoury pancake menu. With lots of walks in the area, there's no need to worry about squelching back to the pub in muddy boots, as the terrace and garden are ideal for alfresco dining.

Open all wk all wk 9-3 6-11 (Sat 12-11 Sun 10-6) Closed:
1 Jan **Bar Meals** L served Mon-Sat 12-2.45, Sun 12-6
D served Mon-Sat 6-9.30 Av main course £14
Restaurant L served Mon-Sat 12-2.45, Sun 12-6 D served
Mon-Sat 6-9.30 Av 3 course à la carte fr £20 ⊕ FREE
HOUSE ◀ Tonbridge Coppernob, Tonbridge Rustic
◯ Westons Stowford Press. ☻ 10
Facilities Non-diners area ◀◀ Children's menu Children's
portions Garden ◚ Parking Wi-fi ▱ (notice required)

LAMBERHURST   Map 6 TQ63

The Vineyard

PICK OF THE PUBS

Lamberhurst Down TN3 8EU ☎ 01892 890222
e-mail: enquiries@thevineyard.com
dir: *From A21 follow brown Vineyard signs onto B2169
towards Lamberhurst. Left, continue to follow Vineyard
signs. Straight on at x-rds, pub on right*

Fine Kentish beers, Kentish wine and Kentish food

Built over 300 years ago; this country roadside inn was
totally refurbished in 2012. Elements of the pub of old are
reflected in the huge brick-built fireplace with piles of
logs ready for incineration and a quirky stuffed boar's
head mounted above. Leather sofas, wingback and
parlour chairs mix easily with the rustic look and chunky
wooden furniture, whilst the eye is taken by a mural
illustrating the well-established winemaking craft in the
area. The pub is next door to one of England's oldest
vineyards; there's a good list of bins here, whilst fans of
the hop are rewarded with a stillage behind the bar
sporting firkins from microbreweries such as Old Dairy.
From the kitchen comes a pleasing mix of top-notch
traditional English and regional French brasserie dishes:
scallop and squid fricassée with chorizo to start, then
roasted forest partridge with Puy lentils, or cyder braised
wild rabbit, leek and mushroom pie, finishing with
cranberry and clementine crumble.

Open all day all wk 11.30-11 **Bar Meals** L served Mon-Fri
12-6, Sat-Sun 12-9.30 D served Mon-Fri 6-9.45, Sat-Sun
12-9.30 Av main course £14.50 food served all day
Restaurant L served Mon-Fri 12-3, Sat-Sun 12-9.45
D served Mon-Fri 6-9.45, Sat-Sun 12-9.45 Av 3 course à
la carte fr £26 ⊕ FREE HOUSE ◀ Sharp's Doom Bar,
Harvey's, Old Dairy ◯ Aspall. ☻ 20
Facilities Non-diners area ❀ (Bar Garden) ◀◀ Children's
portions Garden ◚ Parking

LEIGH   Map 6 TQ54

The Greyhound Charcott

Charcott TN11 8LG ☎ 01892 870275
e-mail: ghatcharcott@aol.com
dir: *From Tonbridge take B245 N towards Hildenborough.
Left onto Leigh road, right onto Stocks Green road.
Through Leigh, right then left at T-junct, right into
Charcott (Camp Hill)*

True pub traditions at the heart of the village

This cosy pub has been welcoming locals and visitors for
around 120 years and you can expect a traditional
atmosphere in which music, pool table and fruit machine
have no place. Winter brings log fires, while in summer
you can relax in the garden with a pint of locally brewed
Westerham British Bulldog. From a changing menu begin
with home-made pork and brandy pâté with apple chutney
followed by braised lamb shank, mash and rosemary,
garlic and red wine gravy, or plaice fillet with lemon,
caper and shrimp butter. Snacks include ploughman's,
sandwiches and classics like cod and chips.

Open all wk 12-3 5.30-11 (Sat-Sun all day) **Bar Meals** L
served Mon-Sat 12-2, Sun 12-3 D served Mon-Sat
6.30-9.30 **Restaurant** L served Mon-Sat 12-2, Sun 12-3
D served Mon-Sat 6.30-9.30 ⊕ ENTERPRISE INNS
◀ Woodforde's Wherry, Westerham British Bulldog BB,
Harvey's ◯ Westons Stowford Press. ☻ 12
Facilities Non-diners area ◀◀ Children's portions Garden
Parking Wi-fi ▱ (notice required)

LEYSDOWN-ON-SEA   Map 7 TR07

The Ferry House Inn ★★★★ INN NEW

Harty Rd ME12 4BQ ☎ 01795 510214
e-mail: info@theferryhouseinn.co.uk
dir: *From A429 towards Sheppey. At rdbt take B2231 to
Eastchurch. From Eastchurch High St into Church Rd. At
rdbt into Rowetts Way signed Leysdown. Right into Harty
Ferry Rd to village*

In remotest Sheppey, but well worth finding

On the edge of the Swale estuary, this 16th-century pub
stands in three acres of terraced lawns offering views
over the water to Faversham, Whitstable and the North
Downs. Even major refurbishment has not upset its
character and charm - the open log fires, the wooden
beams, the solid oak floors. For many years it has been a
popular rendezvous for yachtsmen, and with AA rated
accommodation holidaymakers love it too. Membership of
Produced in Kent means locally sourced food, such as
fisherman's catch of the day; Ferry burger with smoked
cheese, chips and salad; and crispy mushroom risotto
cake.

Open Tue-Fri & Mon (Apr-Sep) 11-3 6.30-11 (Sat all day
Sun 11-5) Closed: 24-31 Dec, Mon (Oct-Mar) **Bar Meals** L
served Mon-Fri 12-2.30, Sat & Sun 12.30-4 D served Mon-
Sat 6.30-9 **Restaurant** L served Mon-Fri 12-2.30, Sat &
Sun 12.30-4 D served Mon-Sat 6.30-9 ⊕ FREE HOUSE
◀ Shepherd Neame Spitfire, Young's Special ◯ Sheppy's.
Facilities Non-diners area ❀ (Garden) ◀◀ Children's menu

Children's portions Play area Family room Garden ◚
Parking Wi-fi ▱ (notice required) **Rooms** 4

LINTON   Map 7 TQ75

The Bull Inn

Linton Hill ME17 4AW ☎ 01622 743612
e-mail: food@thebullatlinton.co.uk
dir: *S of Maidstone on A229 (Hastings road)*

Rural pub ideal for alfresco eating and drinking

Built in 1674, this part-timbered former coaching inn
stands high on the Greensand Ridge, with wonderful
views and sunsets over the Weald. The award-winning
garden includes two oak gazebos and a large decked area
for alfresco bistro dining and afternoon tea. Inside there
is an imposing inglenook fireplace, lots of beams and a
bar serving Shepherd Neame ales. The wide-ranging
menu offers hearty sandwiches and pub classics —
perfect sustenance for walkers tackling the Greensand
Way. You might find king prawn penne pasta, fajitas,
pork suet pudding and luxury fish pie, as well as a carvery
on Sundays.

Open all day all wk 11am-11.30pm (Sun 12-10.30) **Bar
Meals** L served all wk 12-9 D served all wk 12-9 Av main
course £9.95 food served all day **Restaurant** L served all
wk 12-9 D served all wk 12-9 Av 3 course à la carte fr
£25 food served all day ⊕ SHEPHERD NEAME ◀ Shepherd
Neame Master Brew, Kent's Best, Late Red ◯ Thatchers
Gold. **Facilities** Non-diners area ❀ (Bar Garden) ◀◀
Children's menu Children's portions Garden ◚ Parking
Wi-fi ▱

LOWER HALSTOW   Map 7 TQ86

The Three Tuns NEW

The Street ME9 7DY ☎ 01795 842840
e-mail: info@thethreetunsrestaurant.co.uk
dir: *From A2 between Rainham & Newington turn left,
follow Lower Halstow sign. At T-junct right signed Funton
& Iwade. Pub on right*

Quality dining, pub grub and Kentish real ales

Built in 1468 and licensed to sell an ale since 1764, Chris
and Carol Haines's traditional fire-warmed bar is
paradise for lovers of local real ales and cider. They stock
Millis's Kentish Best Bitter, Goacher's Real Mild and
Dudda's Tun cider, while August Bank Holiday sees the
Kentish Ale and Cider Festival, with a hog-roast, seafood
and live music. Farms supply much of the food on the
ever-changing restaurant menu, where items might
include pan-fried pheasant breast; Dover sole; and grilled
sirloin steak. A large beer garden with decking flanks a
stream that soon flows into nearby Halstow Creek.

Open all day all wk **Bar Meals** food served all day
Restaurant L served Mon-Sat 12-2, Sun 12-9 D served
Mon-Sat 6-9, Sun 12-9 ⊕ FREE HOUSE ◀ Millis Brewing
Co Kentish Best, Goacher's Real Mild Ale ◯ Dudda's Tun
Kentish Cider, Core Fruit Products Hard Core. ☻ 10
Facilities Non-diners area ❀ (Bar Garden) ◀◀ Children's
menu Children's portions Garden ◚ Beer festival Cider
festival Parking Wi-fi ▱ (notice required)

PICK OF THE PUBS

The Bottle House Inn

Coldharbour Rd TN11 8ET
☎ **01892 870306**
e-mail: info@thebottlehouseinnpenshurst.
co.uk
web: www.thebottlehouseinnpenshurst.co.uk
dir: *Telephone for directions*

Historic pub off the beaten track

Built as a farmhouse in 1492, this historic building formed part of a local estate during Henry VII's reign. A handsome, weatherboarded inn set down a country lane, it wasn't until 1806 that it was granted a licence to sell ales and ciders, later diversifying to function as a shop, farrier's and cobbler's too. Refurbishment in 1938 unearthed hundreds of old bottles, which inspired its unusual name. Later improvements included ancient oak beams sandblasted back to their natural colour, brickwork exposed and walls painted in neutral shades. At the copper-topped bar counter choose between Harvey's of Lewes and Chiddingstone-brewed Larkins hand-pumped beers, or a wine from one of the 11 served by the glass, then settle at a bench seat on the patio or in the garden. The menus in the stylish dining room change regularly to capitalise on the availability of seasonal produce, while the specials board changes daily. Light bites might include moules marinière or chicken, bacon and

avocado salad with honey and wholegrain mustard dressing. Starters are equally enticing – pork belly squares with parsnip purée and honey and mustard glaze or fig, Parma ham, walnut salad with cherry vinaigrette, for instance. Among the main courses are braised half shoulder of lamb with roasted root vegetables and dauphinoise potatoes; pan-fried fillet of cod on parmesan mash, wilted spinach, roasted cherry tomatoes and pesto dressing; and fisherman's pie. From the home-made desserts, you're likely to find raspberry and blueberry trifle or praline pannacotta with chocolate ice cream.

Open all day all wk 11-11 (Sun 11-10.30) Closed: 25 Dec **Bar Meals** L &

D served Mon-Sat 12-10, Sun & BH 12-9 Av main course £13 food served all day **Restaurant** L & D served Mon-Sat 12-10, Sun & BH 12-9 Fixed menu price fr £22.50 Av 3 course à la carte fr £22.50 food served all day ⊕ **FREE HOUSE** ◀ Harvey's Sussex Best Bitter, Larkins. ♟ 11 **Facilities** Non-diners area ♣ (Bar Garden) ♦ Children's menu & portions Garden ☰ Parking ⛟ (notice required)

Save on hotels. Book at **theAA.com/hotel**

KENT 257 **ENGLAND**

MAIDSTONE
Map 7 TQ75

The Black Horse Inn ★★★★ INN

Pilgrim's Way, Thurnham ME14 3LD ☎ 01622 737185
e-mail: info@wellieboot.net
web: www.wellieboot.net
dir: *M20 junct 7, A249, right into Detling. Opposite Cock Horse Pub turn onto Pilgrim's Way*

Charming free house on the Pilgrim's Way

Tucked beneath the North Downs on the Pilgrim's Way, this 18th-century former forge welcomes guests with an open log fire in the colder months. Dine in the conservatory restaurant that has stunning countryside views or in the cosy candlelit restaurant. Real ales change weekly and the kitchen uses local ingredients in fish or meat sharing plates, or in mains like haunch of Chart Farm venison with tomato relish, chunky chips and garlic mushrooms; a daily-changing specials board adds to the choices.

Open all day all wk **Bar Meals** L served all wk 12-6 D served all wk 6-10 food served all day **Restaurant** L served all wk 12-6 D served all wk 6-10 food served all day ⊕ FREE HOUSE ◀ Greene King IPA, Wychwood Hobgoblin, Westerham Grasshopper, Harvey's Sussex Best Bitter, Black Sheep ♂ Biddenden. ₹ 21
Facilities Non-diners area ⚘ (Bar Garden) ♦ Children's menu Children's portions Garden ⚑ Parking ▥ (notice required) **Rooms** 27

MARKBEECH
Map 6 TQ44

The Kentish Horse

Cow Ln TN8 5NT ☎ 01342 850493
dir: *3m from Edenbridge & 7m from Tunbridge Wells. 1m S of Hever Castle*

Country pub with a large garden welcoming all

Surrounded by Kent countryside, this pub is popular with ramblers, cyclists and families, as well as having a strong local following. Situated in four acres with views over Ashdown Forest, there is an extensive garden and children's play area. The menu is cooked simply from fresh ingredients, and can be served anywhere in the pub or garden. Real ales always available are Harvey's and locally-brewed Larkins.

Open all day all wk ⊕ FREE HOUSE ◀ Harvey's, Larkins.
Facilities ♦ Play area Garden Parking

NEWNHAM
Map 7 TQ95

The George Inn

44 The Street ME9 0LL ☎ 01795 890237
e-mail: hotchefpaul@msn.com
dir: *4m from Faversham*

Charming former farmhouse with regular events

Attractive country inn first licensed in 1718, after decades as a farm. It almost has its own bus — well, the timetable for the 344 from Sittingbourne shows it as a stop. Beams, wooden floors, inglenook and candlelit tables instil it with great character. Locally sourced food includes lunchtime home-made soups and ploughman's; at dinner, pan-fried sea bass; slow-roasted belly pork in cider; and juicy sirloin steaks. The pub calendar is full of events. James Pimm, inventor of the eponymous fruit cup, came from Newnham.

Open all wk 11.30-3 6.30-11 (Sun 11.30-6.30) Closed: 26 Dec ⊕ SHEPHERD NEAME ◀ Master Brew, Kent's Best, Seasonal ale ♂ Thatchers Gold. **Facilities** ♦ Children's menu Children's portions Garden Parking Wi-fi

PENSHURST
Map 6 TQ54

The Bottle House Inn
PICK OF THE PUBS

See Pick of the Pubs on opposite page

The Spotted Dog
PICK OF THE PUBS

Smarts Hill TN11 8EE ☎ 01892 870253
e-mail: thespotteddogpub@gmail.com
dir: *Off B2188 between Penshurst & Fordcombe*

Nestled in the folds of the Weald

This independently run weatherboarded inn started life as a row of cottages in the 15th-century, and is now a rambling building with open fires, a forest of low beams and oak-board floors. There are tiered beer gardens to the front and rear, the latter offering fantastic views in the summer. Kentish ales from Larkins and cider from Chiddingstone are just another excellent reason to stop here, along with the bang up-to-date menu, making the most of the produce grown in this richly endowed countryside. Sample a starter of deep-fried crispy duck rolls drizzled with hoi sin sauce, precursor to Thai green chicken curry; steak-and-kidney pie; or loin of lamb with a red wine, rosemary and redcurrant jus. These are enhanced by a daily-changing specials board and lunchtime baguettes, sandwiches and ploughman's. The Spotted Dog is close to two magnificent stately homes, Penshurst Place and Hever Castle.

Open all day Closed: Mon eve **Bar Meals** L served Mon-Fri 12-2.30, Sat 12-9 D served Tue-Fri 6-9, Sat 12-9 Av main course £10 **Restaurant** L served Mon-Fri 12-2.30, Sat 12-9, Sun 12-6 D served Tue-Fri 6-9, Sat 12-9 Fixed menu price fr £9.95 ⊕ FREE HOUSE ◀ Larkins Traditional, Harvey's, Guest ale ♂ Chiddingstone. **Facilities** Non-diners area ⚘ (Bar Garden Outside area) ♦ Children's menu Children's portions Garden Outside area ⚑ Parking Wi-fi ▥ (notice required)

PLUCKLEY
Map 7 TQ94

The Dering Arms
PICK OF THE PUBS

Station Rd TN27 0RR ☎ 01233 840371
e-mail: jim@deringarms.com
dir: *M20 junct 8, A20 to Ashford. Right onto B2077 at Charing to Pluckley*

Village dining inn worth seeking out

There's a touch of Victorian Gothic and 'Hammer' films about this eye-catching stone pub. Imposing part creeper-clad stone gables and arched windows mark out this building as something special; it was built as a hunting lodge and its grandeur remains inside, with open fires, bare boards, scrubbed old tables and a hop-bine dressed bar groaning with venerable hand-pumps. The separate clubroom has comfy settees, log-burner and a baby grand just itching to be played. It's a popular destination for lovers of seafood, with ever-changing and ever-evolving dishes filling the specials board. A starter of crayfish tails with chilli and lime beurre noisette could be followed by fillet of black bream with marsh samphire and beurre blanc or grilled skate wing with caper butter. The non-fish dishes are equally inspiring; guinea fowl casseroled in sherry and tarragon sauce might tempt. Drinkers are rewarded with a fine cellar, plus Kentish ales and cider to refresh the palate.

Open Mon-Fri 11.30-3.30 6-11 (Sat 9am-11pm Sun 12-4) Closed: 26-27 Dec, Sun eve **Bar Meals** L served Mon-Fri 12-2.30, Sat 12-3, Sun 12-4 D served Mon-Sat 6.30-9 **Restaurant** L served Mon-Fri 12-2.30, Sat 12-3, Sun 12-4 D served Mon-Sat 6.30-9 ⊕ FREE HOUSE ◀ Goacher's Best Dark Ale, Gold Star Ale, Old Ale ♂ Biddenden. ₹ 8 **Facilities** Non-diners area ⚘ (Bar Garden) ♦ Children's portions Family room Garden ⚑ Parking Wi-fi

ROLVENDEN — Map 7 TQ83

The Bull

1 Regent St TN17 4PB ☎ 01580 241212
e-mail: thebullinnkent@yahoo.com
dir: Just off A28, approx 3m from Tenterden

The beer garden overlooks the village cricket pitch

This handsome, tile hung village inn dates, in part, back to the 13th century and is located close to the walled garden that inspired Frances Hodgson Burnett's classic tale The Secret Garden. Handy, too, for steam trains of the Kent and East Sussex Railway, there's a welcome focus on local beers and produce, with a heart-warming, pubby menu enhanced by modern dishes like tempura prawns served with sweet chilli dipping sauce, followed by Moroccan lamb tagine and Mediterranean couscous or home-roasted ham with free-range eggs and hand-cut chips. There's a lovely beer garden overlooking the village cricket ground.

Open all day all wk **Bar Meals** L served all wk 12-3 D served all wk 6-10 Av main course £9.95 **Restaurant** L served all wk 12-3 D served all wk 6-10 ⊕ FREE HOUSE ◀ Red Top, Harvey's, Old Dairy Gold Top ♂ Westons Stowford Press. ☗ 12 **Facilities** Non-diners area ♣ (Bar Garden) ♦ Children's menu Children's portions Garden ♬ Beer festival Parking Wi-fi

ST MARGARET'S BAY — Map 7 TR34

The Coastguard

PICK OF THE PUBS

CT15 6DY ☎ 01304 853176
e-mail: bookings@thecoastguard.co.uk
dir: A258 between Dover & Deal follow St Margaret's at Cliffe signs. 2m, through village towards sea

Splendid coastal views and market-fresh food

The popular Heritage Coast footpath passes the door of this convivial waterside pub, whilst the watersport fans beach their kayaks here to indulge in a half of Gadds' The Ramsgate No 5 bitter or a sip of Rough Old Wife cider. Sitting on the suntrap terrace here, the hazy smudge on the horizon is likely to be the French coast, shimmering beyond the silently passing ferries and freighters. Crane your neck upwards and the view of Blighty's fine countryside is cut off by – well – Blighty's most famous natural feature; the White Cliffs of Dover. The food is renowned for its wonderful flavours, and all freshly made on the premises from local produce as far as possible. Many dishes have a story behind them: they might be based on an old Roman recipe, a reworked classic dish, or perhaps an original creation. The menus change twice daily, depending on what's available.

Open all day all wk 11-11 (Sun 11-10.30) **Bar Meals** L served all wk 12.30-2.45 D served all wk 6.30-8.45 **Restaurant** L served all wk 12.30-2.45 D served all wk 6.30-8.45 ⊕ FREE HOUSE ◀ Gadds' The Ramsgate No 5, Fyne, Adnams ♂ Kent, Rough Old Wife, Hogan's. **Facilities** Non-diners area ♦ Children's portions Garden ♬ Parking Wi-fi

SANDWICH — Map 7 TR35

George & Dragon Inn

Fisher St CT13 9EJ ☎ 01304 613106
e-mail: enquiries@georgeanddragon-sandwich.co.uk
dir: Between Dover & Canterbury

Charming family run pub serving modern British food

Built in 1446, ale was first sold here in 1549, but was only licensed under the name of George & Dragon in 1615. This town centre pub oozes charm and character, with its wood floors and open fires, and makes a welcome pit stop when exploring historic Sandwich on foot. Run by two brothers, you can refuel with a pint of well-kept Shepherd Neame Master Brew or a guest ale. On the monthly-changing evening menu, you might find butterbean and mushroom pâté with bread and onion marmalade, followed by pork loin on cabbage and leeks, bacon and cheddar mash and roasted apple sauce. Head outside to the picturesque suntrap courtyard in summer.

Open 11-3 6-11 (Sat 11-11 Sun 12-4) Closed: Sun eve **Bar Meals** L served all wk 12-2 D served Mon-Sat 6-9 Av main course £8-£13 **Restaurant** L served all wk 12-2 D served Mon-Sat 6-9 Av 3 course à la carte fr £24 ⊕ ENTERPRISE INNS ◀ Shepherd Neame Master Brew, Wantsum, Guest ales ♂ Aspall. ☗ 9 **Facilities** Non-diners area ♣ (Bar Garden) Garden ♬ Wi-fi

SELLING — Map 7 TR05

The Rose and Crown

Perry Wood ME13 9RY ☎ 01227 752214
e-mail: info@roseandcrownperrywood.co.uk
dir: From A28 right at Badgers Hill, left at end. 1st left signed Perry Wood

Pretty country pub with a long history

Goldings hops are draped around this rambling, low-beamed 16th-century inn, with exposed brickwork, inglenooks, horse brasses, corn dollies and a bar offering Harvey's Sussex, Adnams Southwold real ales and Biddenden cider. Descend to the restaurant, where the ghost of Hammond Smith, murdered after a boozy day in 1889, may join you, but don't let his presence detract from the pleasure of home-cooked Kent fish pie; lamb shank; chicken and carrot casserole; or brie, bacon and walnut jacket potato. The flower-festooned garden is made for summer eating and drinking.

Open 12-3 6.30-11 Closed: 25-26 Dec eve, 1 Jan eve, Mon eve **Bar Meals** L served all wk 12-2 D served Tue-Sat 6.30-9 **Restaurant** L served all wk 12-2 D served Tue-Sat 6.30-9 ⊕ FREE HOUSE ◀ Adnams Southwold Bitter, Harvey's Sussex Best Bitter, Guest ale ♂ Westons Stowford Press, Biddenden. **Facilities** Non-diners area ♣ (Bar Restaurant Garden) ♦ Children's menu Children's portions Play area Garden ♬ Parking ☗ (notice required)

SHIPBOURNE — Map 6 TQ55

The Chaser Inn

Stumble Hill TN11 9PE ☎ 01732 810360
e-mail: enquiries@thechaser.co.uk
dir: N of Tonbridge take A227 towards Shipbourne. Pub on left

Popular pub with famous connections

Once a haunt for stars such as Richard Burton and Elizabeth Taylor, the Chaser Inn is an informal, relaxed village inn, next to the church and overlooking the common. Well-kept real ales and plenty of wines by the glass are complemented by an extensive menu of sandwiches, light bites and main courses such as whole grilled plaice, caper and citrus butter; or steak and vegetable suet pudding. There is a lovely beer garden and the covered courtyard comes into its own in the winter months. The pub takes its name from its long association with the nearby Fairlawne racing stables.

Open all day all wk **Bar Meals** Av main course £6.95-£20.95 food served all day **Restaurant** food served all day ⊕ WHITING AND HAMMOND ◀ Greene King IPA & Abbot Ale, Morland Old Speckled Hen, Guest ales. ☗ 40 **Facilities** Non-diners area ♣ (Bar Garden) ♦ Children's portions Garden ♬ Parking Wi-fi ☗ (notice required)

SMARDEN — Map 7 TQ84

The Chequers Inn

PICK OF THE PUBS

The Street TN27 8QA ☎ 01233 770217
e-mail: spaldings@thechequerssmarden.com
dir: Through Leeds village, left to Sutton Valence/ Headcorn then left for Smarden. Pub in village centre

Ancient pub with courtyard and lovely gardens

The former weavers' village of Smarden has around 200 buildings of architectural and historical interest, one of which is the clapboarded 14th-century Chequers Inn. Its beautiful landscaped garden features a large carp pond and an attractive south-facing courtyard. Ales brewed by Sharp's, Fullers, Wadworth and the Old Dairy Brewery are served in the low-beamed bars. Seasonal ingredients are sourced locally for the menus of traditional and modern food. Typical of the restaurant choices are starters of mussels and squid in a spicy sauce with garlic bread; and main courses like pan-fried chicken stuffed with goats' cheese and wrapped in bacon. The bar menu, carte and children's menu are all served on Sundays too, when traditional beef, lamb and pork roasts are joined by gammon and turkey.

Open all day all wk **Bar Meals** L served all wk 12-3 D served all wk 6-9 **Restaurant** L served all wk 12-3 D served all wk 6-9 ⊕ FREE HOUSE ◀ Sharp's Doom Bar, Fullers London Pride, Wadworth 6X, Old Dairy ♂ Stowford Press. **Facilities** Non-diners area ♦ Children's menu Children's portions Garden ♬ Beer festival Parking Wi-fi ☗

SPELDHURST   Map 6 TQ54

George & Dragon

PICK OF THE PUBS

Speldhurst Hill TN3 0NN ☎ 01892 863125
e-mail: julian@speldhurst.com
dir: *Telephone for directions*

Ancient inn done up in fine style

The bar of this heavily-beamed village inn, built in the 13th century, serves some rather good local beers, namely Westerham Brewery's specially produced George's Marvellous Medicine; Larkins Bitter, brewed near Edenbridge; and Harvey's Sussex from Lewes. The seasonal menu promises organic, free-range and GM-free produce whenever possible, with as much as possible sourced locally, which means that Kent and Sussex place-names appear on the menu, including grilled Ashdown Forest heather-fed lamb chops; pan-seared Rye Bay scallops with broad bean salad and pancetta; Speldhurst pork sausages with mash and onion gravy; and roasted breast of Chevening Estate pheasant with confit leg. The menu's Cow Corner section lists Hereford sirloin and T-bone steaks, hung for 28 and 35 days respectively. A separate game menu offers seared local pigeon breasts with Puy lentils and smoked bacon. Representing UK wine growers is Grosvenor, a sparkling Chardonnay from Ridgeview in the South Downs village of Ditchling.

Open all day all wk **Bar Meals** L served all wk 12-2.30 D served Mon-Sat 7-9.45 Av main course £10.50 **Restaurant** L served Sat 12-3, Sun 12-4 D served Fri 7-10, Sat 6.30-10 Av 3 course à la carte fr £28.50 ⊕ FREE HOUSE ◀ Harvey's Sussex Best Bitter, Westerham George's Marvellous Medicine, Larkins Ŏ Westons Stowford Press. ₹ 11 **Facilities** Non-diners area ♦ Children's portions Family room Garden ⊼ Parking Wi-fi ▭

STALISFIELD GREEN   Map 7 TQ95

The Plough at Stalisfield Green NEW

ME13 0HY ☎ 01795 890256
e-mail: theplough@stalisfieldgreen.com
dir: *From A20 (dual carriageway) W of Charing follow Stalisfield Green signs. Approx 2m to village*

Downland pub with a passion for Kentish produce

The Plough is a splendid, 15th-century Kentish hall house situated by the green in an unspoilt hamlet high up on the North Downs. A real country pub, it enjoys far-reaching views across the Swale estuary and is worth seeking out for the array of Kentish drinks - microbrewery beers, ciders and juices - and modern pub food prepared from ingredients sourced from local farms and artisan producers. Daily menus evolve with the seasons, typically offering Rye Bay scallops, oxtail and beef shin pie, red gurnard with shrimps and brown butter; and steamed orange sponge. The mid-week set menu is a steal and worth the drive.

Open 12-3 6-11 (Sat 12-11 Sun 12-6) Closed: Mon **Bar Meals** L served Tue-Sun 12-2 D served Tue-Sat 6-9 Av

main course £13 **Restaurant** L served Tue-Sun 12-2 D served Tue-Sat 6-9 Fixed menu price fr £13.95 ⊕ FREE HOUSE ◀ Changing Guest ales. ₹ 9 **Facilities** Non-diners area ♣ (Bar Restaurant Garden) ♦ Children's portions Family room Garden ⊼ Parking ▭ (notice required)

STOWTING   Map 7 TR14

The Tiger Inn

TN25 6BA ☎ 01303 862130
e-mail: info@tigerinn.co.uk
dir: *Telephone for directions*

Classic village pub with rustic charm and hearty food

Lost down winding lanes in a scattered North Downs hamlet, the 250-year-old Tiger Inn oozes traditional character and rural charm. The front bar is delightfully rustic and unpretentious, with stripped oak floors, two warming wood-burning stoves, old cushioned pews, and scrubbed old pine tables. Mingle with the locals at the bar with a pint of Master Brew, then order a hearty meal from the inviting chalkboard menu – Romney Marsh rack of lamb with redcurrant jus, whole Dover sole, chicken, ham and leek pie with shortcrust pastry. In summer dine alfresco on the suntrap front terrace. There are super walks all around.

Open all day Closed: Tue **Bar Meals** L served Wed-Sun 12-9 D served Mon 4-9, Wed-Sun 12-9 Av main course £13 food served all day **Restaurant** L served Wed-Sun 12-9 D served Mon 4-9, Wed-Sun 12-9 food served all day ⊕ FREE HOUSE ◀ Shepherd Neame Master Brew, Harvey's, Old Dairy, Gadds', Hop Fuzz Ŏ Biddenden. ₹ 10 **Facilities** Non-diners area ♣ (Bar Garden) ♦ Children's menu Children's portions Garden ⊼ Parking Wi-fi ▭

TENTERDEN   Map 7 TQ83

White Lion Inn

57 High St TN30 6BD ☎ 01580 765077
e-mail: whitelion.tenterden@marstons.co.uk
dir: *On A28 (Ashford to Hastings road)*

Spruced up town centre inn

Beside the broad tree-lined street in Tenterden, 'the Jewel of the Weald', stands this renovated and rejuvenated inn, which combines many original features with a contemporary look and feel. Reasonably priced fresh food ranges from starters of baked camembert with onion jam to share, or salmon and crab cakes with tartare sauce, to mains such as steak, mushroom and ale pie; battered haddock and fat chips; or grilled salmon Niçoise. Look out for special offers on pub classics served all day. Reliable Marston's and Hobgoblin ales are the mainstay in the bar.

Open all wk 10am-11pm (wknds 10am-mdnt) **Bar Meals** L served Mon-Sat 12-10, Sun 12-9 D served Mon-Sat 12-10, Sun 12-9 food served all day **Restaurant** L served Mon-Sat 12-10, Sun 12-9 D served Mon-Sat 12-10, Sun 12-9 food served all day ⊕ MARSTON'S ◀ Pedigree, Jennings Cumberland Ale, Wychwood Hobgoblin Ŏ Symonds. **Facilities** Non-diners area ♦

Children's menu Children's portions Outside area ⊼ Parking Wi-fi ▭ (notice required)

TONBRIDGE   Map 6 TQ54

See also Penshurst

The Little Brown Jug NEW

Chiddingstone Causeway TN11 8JJ ☎ 01892 870318
e-mail: enquiries@thelittlebrownjug.co.uk
dir: *On B2027 between Tonbridge & Bough Beech*

Warm and welcoming village favourite

With three open fires on cold days, this village treasure always feels as warm as toast; even the Polynesian-style Little Brown Huts in the garden are heated, each seating up to ten for lunch or dinner (booking advised). Amenities of a more conventional kind include the bar, dispensing Chiddingstone-brewed Larkins beers, and the restaurant, which does a particularly good line in moules and fries; Stargazy fish pie; Highfield Farm shoulder of lamb; coq au vin; and vegetable Wellington. Events are a big thing here, with sausage and pie weeks, and the May and October three-day beer festivals.

Open all day all wk **Bar Meals** Av main course £6.95-£20.95 food served all day **Restaurant** food served all day ⊕ WHITING AND HAMMOND ◀ Greene King IPA & Abbot, Larkins, Guest ale Ŏ Thatchers. ₹ 40 **Facilities** ♣ (Bar Garden) ♦ Children's portions Play area Garden ⊼ Beer festival Parking Wi-fi ▭

TUDELEY   Map 6 TQ64

The Poacher

Hartlake Rd TN11 0PH ☎ 01732 358934
e-mail: enquiries@thepoachertudeley.co.uk
dir: *A21 S onto A26 E, at rdbt turn right. After 2m turn sharp left into Hartlake Rd, 0.5m on right*

Country pub with contemporary atmosphere and an up-to-date menu

Cross Oak Inns lavished money on this unassuming rural pub a while back and the result is impressive. Expect acres of wood floor, modern brown banquette seating, contemporary artwork on the walls, and a long, slate-fronted bar counter dispensing Doom Bar and local Tonbridge ales. Chunky low tables, a few plush stools and ultra-trendy striped chairs, and floor-to-ceiling wine chillers enhance the great 'bar' atmosphere. In keeping, food is bang up to date, so expect arancini risotto balls infused with star anise; sharing dishes of meat and cheese; sweet potato and coriander cakes with black olive houmous; or pork saltimbocca; and good puddings like white chocolate and pistachio parfait. Tudeley church is worth a visit to see the famous windows by Marc Chagall.

Open all wk 12-3.30 5.30-11 (Sun 12-10.30) Closed: 25 Dec **Bar Meals** L served all wk 12-2.30 D served all wk 6-9.30 Av main course £12 **Restaurant** L served all wk 12-2.30 D served all wk 6-9.30 Av 3 course à la carte fr £25 ⊕ FREE HOUSE ◀ Sharp's Doom Bar, Shepherd Neame Spitfire, Tonbridge Ŏ Thatchers Gold. ₹ 10 **Facilities** Non-diners area ♦ Children's menu Children's portions Garden ⊼ Parking Wi-fi ▭ (notice required)

TUNBRIDGE WELLS (ROYAL) — Map 6 TQ53

The Beacon ★★★★ INN

PICK OF THE PUBS

See Pick of the Pubs on opposite page

The Crown Inn

The Green, Groombridge TN3 9QH ☎ 01892 864742
e-mail: crown.inn.groombridge@gmail.com
dir: *Take A264 W of Tunbridge Wells, then B2110 S*

Good food and bags of character

In the 18th century this charming free house was the infamous headquarters for a gang of smugglers who hid their casks of tea in the passages between the cellar and Groombridge Place, later home to Sir Arthur Conan Doyle. Doyle made this 16th-century pub his local and today, its low beams and an inglenook fireplace are the setting for some great food and drink. Favourites include lamb's liver with crispy bacon and mash; Thai-style red chicken curry with rice, and daily specials based on fresh local produce. Eat alfresco during the summer months.

Open all day all wk **Bar Meals** L served Mon-Thu 12-2.30, Fri-Sat 12-9, Sun 12-6 D served Mon-Thu 6-9, Fri-Sat 12-9, Sun 12-6 **Restaurant** L served Mon-Thu 12-2.30, Fri-Sat 12-9, Sun 12-6 D served Mon-Thu 6-9, Fri-Sat 12-9, Sun 12-6 ⊕ FREE HOUSE ◀ Harvey's Sussex Best Bitter, Black Cat, Larkins ♂ Westons Stowford Press. **Facilities** Non-diners area ♣ (Bar Garden) ♦♦ Children's menu Children's portions Play area Garden ☴ Parking

The Hare on Langton Green

PICK OF THE PUBS

Langton Rd, Langton Green TN3 0JA ☎ 01892 862419
e-mail: hare@brunningandprice.co.uk
dir: *From Tunbridge Wells follow A264 towards East Grinstead. Pub on x-rds at Langton Green*

Imaginative daily-changing menus

In a well-to-do suburb of equally well-to-do Tunbridge Wells, overlooking the village green, the 'brewers-Tudor-style' Hare opened in 1901, replacing an 18th-century predecessor demolished a year earlier after a fire. Pub group Brunning and Price lease it from Greene King, so expect the usual Bury St Edmunds range, plus Biddenden Bushel and Aspall ciders. The extensive menu changes daily: an interesting way to start is with crispy duck egg, shredded duck, pickled mushrooms, asparagus and sherry vinaigrette; or vegetable pakora with raita and coconut and mango salad. Equally off the beaten track are mains of Malaysian fish stew (king prawns, cod, salmon, haddock and mussels) with sticky rice; and chilli and herb gnocchi with roasted pepper, grilled courgette, sweet potato and Bloody Mary dressing. For something closer to home, try braised shoulder of lamb with dauphinoise potato, baby carrots, parsnips and mint jus. There are also light bites and sandwiches.

Open all day all wk 12-11 (Fri-Sat 12-12 Sun 12-10.30) **Bar Meals** food served all day **Restaurant** food served all

day ⊕ BRUNNING & PRICE ◀ Greene King IPA, Ruddles Best & Abbot Ale, Morland Original, Hardys & Hansons Olde Trip ♂ Westons Old Rosie & Wyld Wood Organic, Aspall, Biddenden Bushel. ☗ 20 **Facilities** Non-diners area ♣ (Bar Garden) ♦♦ Children's menu Children's portions Garden Parking Wi-fi

WESTERHAM — Map 6 TQ45

The Fox & Hounds

Toys Hill TN16 1QG ☎ 01732 750328
e-mail: hickmott1@hotmail.com
dir: *From A25 in Brasted follow brown signs for pub into Chart Lane. 2m to pub*

Great alehouse, especially for dog owners

Chartwell, where Sir Winston Churchill lived, is not far from this late 18th-century alehouse surrounded by National Trust land high on Kent's Greensand Ridge. All food served in the bar and traditionally styled restaurant is made on the premises from locally sourced produce. A starter might be a king prawn salad with a tomato and ginger dressing, followed by chicken linguine, parmesan shavings and garlic bread. Specials could include pan-fried sea bass or salmon. Lunchtime filled rolls are available Tuesdays to Saturdays and there are hog roasts in summer. The landlord describes the pub as very dog friendly.

Open all day 10-3 6-11 (Sat 10am-11pm Sun 10-6) Closed: 25 Dec, Mon eve, Mon all day Oct-Etr **Bar Meals** L served Mon-Sat 12-2, Sun 12-3 D served Tue-Sat 6-9 **Restaurant** L served Mon-Sat 12-2, Sun 12-3 D served Tue-Sat 6-9 ⊕ GREENE KING ◀ IPA, Abbot Ale, Morland Original. ☗ 10 **Facilities** Non-diners area ♣ (Bar Garden) ♦♦ Children's menu Garden Outside area ☴ Parking Wi-fi ⮐ (notice required)

Grasshopper on the Green

The Green TN16 1AS ☎ 01959 562926
e-mail: info@grasshopperonthegreen.com
dir: *M25 junct 5, A21 towards Sevenoaks, then A25 to Westerham. Or M25 junct 6, A22 towards East Grinstead, A25 to Westerham*

Local brews and modern home-cooked cuisine

Overlooking Westerham's pretty green, the 700-year-old Grasshopper takes its name from the arms of local merchant Thomas Gresham, founder of London's Royal Exchange in 1565. The bar's low-beamed ceilings, hung with antique jugs, and its winter log fire are particularly appealing, as are Westerham brewery's Grasshopper and British Bulldog real ales. House specials include spicy chicken wrap; and home-made roasted vegetable lasagne, while regular cast members include grilled fresh tuna, lemon butter and capers; and slow-roasted lamb shank with red wine and rosemary jus. Ask long-term hosts Neale and Anne Sadlier for directions to Chartwell, Sir Winston Churchill's former home.

Open all day all wk **Bar Meals** L served all wk 12-9 D served all wk 12-9 Av main course £11 food served all day **Restaurant** L served all wk 12-9 D served all wk 12-9 food served all day ⊕ FREE HOUSE ◀ Adnams Broadside,

Harvey's Sussex Best Bitter, Courage Best Bitter, Westerham British Bulldog BB & Grasshopper. ☗ 12 **Facilities** Non-diners area ♣ (Bar Garden) ♦♦ Children's menu Children's portions Play area Garden ☴ Parking Wi-fi ⮐ (notice required)

WEST MALLING — Map 6 TQ65

The Farmhouse

PICK OF THE PUBS

97 The High St ME19 6NA ☎ 01732 843257
e-mail: enquiries@thefarmhouse.biz
dir: *M20 junct 4, S on A228. Right to West Malling. Pub in village centre*

Elegant gastro-pub showcasing local ingredients

Well positioned in the heart of the pretty old Kentish market town of West Malling, The Farmhouse is a handsome Elizabethan house offering a friendly welcome, in the stylish bar or two dining areas. Local seasonal ingredients are used to produce a range of menus with a strong French influence. Expect starters such as local game terrine with apple and raisin chutney; devilled lamb's kidneys with wild mushrooms; and spiced crab cakes with sweet chilli sauce; and mains like lamb rump, sautéed potatoes, butternut squash purée, curly kale, rosemary sauce; venison medallions, rösti potato, wild mushroom sauce; and beetroot and goats' cheese risotto. Puddings include Kentish apple and pear crumble with cinnamon custard; and coconut pannacotta. There are stone-baked pizzas and toasted paninis alongside the blackboard menu, which changes regularly. Outside is a pretty walled garden with an area of decking overlooking 15th-century stone barns.

Open all day all wk 11-11 **Bar Meals** L served Mon-Thu 12-3, Fri-Sat 12-9.45, Sun 12-9.30 D served Mon-Thu 6-9.45, Fri-Sat 12-9.45, Sun 12-9.30 Av main course £14.50 **Restaurant** L served Mon-Thu 12-3, Fri-Sat 12-9.45, Sun 12-9.30 D served Mon-Thu 6-9.30, Fri-Sat 12-9.45, Sun 12-9.30 Av 3 course à la carte fr £26.50 ⊕ ENTERPRISE INNS ◀ Harvey's, Guinness, Sharp's Doom Bar ♂ Biddenden, Aspall. ☗ 20 **Facilities** Non-diners area ♦♦ Children's portions Garden ☴ Parking Wi-fi

Save on hotels. Book at **theAA.com/hotel**

KENT 261 ENGLAND

PICK OF THE PUBS

The Beacon ★★★★ INN

TUNBRIDGE WELLS (ROYAL)   Map 6 TQ53

Tea Garden Ln TN3 9JH
☎ **01892 524252**
e-mail: info@the-beacon.co.uk
web: www.the-beacon.co.uk
dir: *From Tunbridge Wells take A264 towards East Grinstead. Pub 1m on left*

Extensive grounds, great views, good food

As the address suggests, there were tea gardens here in an area called Happy Valley. They were created about 1820, but the late Victorians presumably lost interest, because in 1895 Sir Walter Harris was able to buy the land and build a house, Rusthall Beacon, here. After a wartime spell as a hostel for Jewish refugees, in 1950 it became a hotel. Standing in nearly 17 acres, the building is jam-packed with impressive architectural features — moulded plaster ceilings and stained glass windows in particular. The bar offers a trinity of real ales — Harvey's Best, Larkins Traditional and Timothy Taylor Landlord, as well as Stowford Press draught cider and Westons Organic bottled pear cider. Take a pint out to the terrace and enjoy the terrific views. Food is served in the bar, the restaurant, or in one of three private dining rooms, where the menus take full advantage of local produce, not least the fruit, vegetables and herbs from The Beacon's own kitchen garden. Start perhaps with

goats' cheese pannacotta and roasted fig with apple and hazelnut salad; or Shetland mussels with creamy Stowford Press cider sauce and Rusbridge bread from nearby Southborough. For a main course, select from a list containing assiette of lamb - braised lamb shoulder, mini sphepherd's pie, lamb cutlet with rosemary crust - spinach and aubergine caviar; and Newhaven fish pie topped with mature cheddar and seasonal vegetables. There are plenty of others to choose from, as well as the daily specials board. A good wine list offers plenty of choice by the glass.

Open all day all wk 11-11 (Sun 12-10.30) **Bar Meals** L served Mon-Thu 12-2.30, Fri-Sun 12-9.30 D served Mon-Thu 6.30-9.30, Fri-Sun 12-9.30

Restaurant L served Mon-Thu 12-2.30, Fri-Sun 12-9.30 D served Mon-Thu 6.30-9.30, Fri-Sun 12-9.30 ⊕ FREE HOUSE ◀ Harvey's Sussex Best Bitter, Timothy Taylor Landlord, Larkins Traditional ○ Westons Stowford Press & Westons Wyld Wood Organic Pear. ♟ 12 **Facilities** Non-diners area ♦♦ Children's menu Children's portions Play area Garden ⟗ Parking Wi-fi 🚌 (notice required) **Rooms** 3

WHITSTABLE
Map 7 TR16

The Sportsman ◉◉

PICK OF THE PUBS

Faversham Rd, Seasalter CT5 4BP ☎ 01227 273370
e-mail: contact@thesportsmanseasalter.co.uk
dir: 3.5m W of Whitstable, on coast road between
Whitstable & Faversham

Chalkboard and changing menus focussing on seafood

Reached via a winding lane across open marshland from
Whitstable, and tucked beneath the sea wall, The
Sportsman has a rustic and welcoming interior, with
wooden floors and stripped pine furniture. There has been
an inn on this site since 1642, but the surrounding area
was entered in the Domesday Book as belonging to the
kitchens of Canterbury Cathedral. A plaque on the wall
commemorates the part played by the pub in a little
known World War II episode, the Battle of Graveney
Marshes: in 1940 a German Junkers 88 crashlanded near
the pub, where a platoon of London Irish Rifles was
billeted. After surrendering, the Germans were taken to
the pub for a pint to await the POW authorities. Today's
range of Shepherd Neame ales would certainly have gone
down well in 1940. The pub is renowned for its food and
the high standard of cooking is recognised with two AA
Rosettes. Fish and seafood feature strongly - maybe
pickled herrings and cabbage salad; followed by gurnard
fillet with a bouillabaisse sauce and green olive
tapenade. Alternatives might include crispy duck, smoked
chilli salsa and sour cream.

Open all wk 12-3 6-11 **Closed:** 25-26 Dec, 1 Jan
⊕ SHEPHERD NEAME ◂ Late Red, Master Brew, Original
Porter, Early Bird, Goldings Ale, Whitstable Bay
Ď Thatchers Gold. **Facilities** ♦♦ Children's portions Family
room Garden Parking

WROTHAM
Map 6 TQ65

The Bull ★★★★ INN ◉

Bull Ln TN15 7RF ☎ 01732 789800
e-mail: info@thebullhotel.com
dir: M20 junct 2, A20 (signed Paddock Wood, Gravesend
& Tonbridge). At rdbt 3rd exit onto A20 (signed Wrotham,
Tonbridge, Borough Green, M20 & M25). At rdbt take 4th
exit into Bull Ln (signed Wrotham)

Ancient pub featuring micro-beers and an aircraft theme

In a quiet country location, this attractive three-storey
building can be traced to 1385; it was first licensed under
Henry VII in 1495. More recently, World War II pilots
relaxed here; stamps on the restaurant ceiling mark
downed German planes, and dozens of pictures of
Spitfires decorate the place. Ales from the award-winning
Dark Star microbrewery are supported by a vast wine list.
Food follows classic lines, but as much as possible is
sourced from local growers and suppliers: Hartley Bottom
lamb and prune pie, and Woods Farm egg and cheese
omelette are just two examples. Why not stay over in one
of the bedrooms and try the circular walk from the pub?

Open all day all wk ⊕ FREE HOUSE ◂ Dark Star Partridge
Best Bitter, Hophead Ď Westons Stowford Press.
Facilities ♦♦ Children's portions Garden Parking Wi-fi
Rooms 11

WYE
Map 7 TR04

The New Flying Horse

Upper Bridge St TN25 5AN ☎ 01233 812297
e-mail: newflyhorse@shepherd-neame.co.uk
dir: Telephone for directions

Charming inn with an award-winning garden

With a 400-year-old history, this village inn charms with
its low ceilings, black beams, open brickwork and large
open fireplace. In winter snuggle up by the fire, savour a
pint of Late Red and select a couple of classics from the
menu, such as sea bass with fennel and red pepper
risotto; and roast pheasant with fondant potato and
parsnip crisps. Very much the village local it has a rare
bat and trap game, and a stunning World War II 'Soldier's
Dream of Blighty' garden which won an award at the
Chelsea Flower Show a few years ago.

Open all day all wk **Bar Meals** L served all wk 12-2
D served all wk 6-9 **Restaurant** L served all wk 12-2
D served all wk 6-9 ⊕ SHEPHERD NEAME ◂ Master Brew,
Spitfire & Late Red, Guest ales. ♥ 12
Facilities Non-diners area ♦♦ Children's menu Children's
portions Play area Garden Parking ▨

LANCASHIRE

ALTHAM
Map 18 SD73

The Walton Arms

Burnley Rd BB5 5UL ☎ 01282 774444
e-mail: walton-arms@btconnect.com
dir: M65 junct 8, A678, pub between Accrington &
Padiham

Popular pub serving good pub food

A long-established way-station on an ancient highway
linking Yorkshire and Lancashire, this sturdy, stone-built
dining pub oozes history. Pilgrims to Whalley Abbey called
at an inn here when Henry VII was king. Beams and
brasses, rustic furniture and slabbed stone floors
welcome today's pilgrims intent on sampling the
comprehensive menu, either as a bar meal or in the
atmospheric dining room. Typical choices include a pot of
button mushrooms with creamed blue cheese sauce
followed by hake fillet with a soft herb crust, new
potatoes and seasonal vegetables or the inn's 'famous'
shoulder of local lamb with roasted vegetables.

Open 12-2.30 5.30-11 (Sun 12-10.30) **Closed:** Mon **Bar
Meals** L served Tue-Sat 12-2, Sun 12-8.30 D served Tue-
Sat 6-9, Sun 12-8.30 **Restaurant** L served Tue-Sat 12-2,
Sun 12-8.30 D served Tue-Sat 6-9, Sun 12-8.30 ⊕ J W
LEES ◂ Bitter. ♥ 16 **Facilities** Non-diners area ♦♦
Children's menu Children's portions Outside area ⊓
Parking Wi-fi ▨ (notice required)

BARROW
Map 18 SD73

The Eagle at Barrow **NEW**

Clitheroe Rd BB7 9AQ ☎ 01254 825285
e-mail: info@theeagleatbarrow.co.uk
dir: Off A59, N of Whalley. Contact pub for detailed
directions

Successful pub with great interior

A lavish refurbishment six years ago launched the Eagle
on its upwardly mobile path. At its heart is the oak-
panelled public bar with a log fire, antique pews and
chairs, Bowland Brewery real ales, Swedish Rekorderlig
cider, and baby grand piano providing lively
entertainment on Friday and Saturday evenings. Taylor's
champagne bar is for those after a little more privacy.
The wide choice of food in the Brasserie, sourced from the
very best local produce, includes beef bourguignon;
steamed suet steak pudding; fish pie; and spiced
aubergine. Buy take-away award-winning sausages and
other regional treats from Berkins Deli in-house.

Open all day all wk **Bar Meals** L served Mon-Sat 12-2.30,
Sun 12-7.30 D served Mon-Sat 6-9 **Restaurant** L served
Mon-Dat 12-2.30, Sun 12-7.30 D served Mon-Sat 6-9.30
⊕ FREE HOUSE ◂ Bowland Hen Harrier & Sawly Tempted,
Courage Directors, Caledonian Deuchars IPA
Ď Rekorderlig. ♥ **Facilities** Non-diners area ♦♦ Children's
menu Children's portions Outside area ⊓ Parking Wi-fi

Save on hotels. Book at **theAA.com/hotel**

LANCASHIRE 263 **ENGLAND**

BASHALL EAVES · Map 18 SD64

The Red Pump Inn

Clitheroe Rd BB7 3DA ☎ 01254 826227
e-mail: info@theredpumpinn.co.uk
dir: *3m from Clitheroe, NW, follow 'Whitewell, Trough of Bowland & Bashall Eaves' signs*

Good honest food and northern ales

This 18th-century pub was formerly a coaching inn and the horses would quench their thirst from the old red pump now in the bar — hence the name. Real ale drinkers can quench their thirst from a northern line-up, including Tirril, Black Sheep and Moorhouse's. The kitchen team offer fuss-free, tasty food prepared from quality local-as-possible ingredients. Menus can change more often than seasonally in order to provide the freshest produce in dishes such as Lancashire ox-cheek pie; rabbit loin casserole with rabbit haggis, carrot mash and twice-fried chips; and linguine salsa verde. Children have their own menu.

Open 12-3 6-11 (Sun 12-9) Closed: 2wks early Jan, Mon (ex BHs) ⊕ FREE HOUSE ◀ Black Sheep, Moorhouse's, Tirril. **Facilities** ♦♦ Children's menu Children's portions Garden Parking Wi-fi

BILSBORROW · Map 18 SD53

Owd Nell's Tavern

Guy's Thatched Hamlet, Canal Side PR3 0RS
☎ 01995 640010
e-mail: info@guysthatchedhamlet.com
dir: *M6 junct 32 N on A6. In approx 5m follow brown tourist signs to Guy's Thatched Hamlet*

Old-world charm and family fun by the canal

Run by the same family for over 30 years this country-style tavern forms part of Guy's Thatched Hamlet, a cluster of eating and drinking venues beside the Lancaster Canal. Expect excellent ales, such as Owd Nell's Canalside Bitter or Pendle Witches Brew, and an authentic country pub ambience enhanced by flagged floors, fireplaces and low ceilings. All-day fare is typified by spicy nachos or potato wedges; followed by venison pie or dry-cured gammon steak; and finishing with banoffee pie. Children's menus are available. There are beer, cider, wine and oyster festivals in summer.

Open all day all wk 7am-2am Closed: 25 Dec **Bar Meals** L served all wk 12-9 D served all wk 12-9 food served all day **Restaurant** L served all wk 12-9 D served all wk 12-9 food served all day ⊕ FREE HOUSE ◀ Moorhouse's Premier Bitter & Pendle Witches Brew, Owd Nell's Canalside Bitter, Bowland, Copper Dragon, Black Sheep, Thwaites, Hart Ò Thatchers Heritage & Cheddar Valley. ♟ 20 **Facilities** Non-diners area ♥ (Bar Garden Outside area) ♦♦ Children's menu Children's portions Family room Garden Outside area ⚑ Beer festival Cider festival Parking Wi-fi 🚌 (notice required)

BLACKBURN · Map 18 SD62

Clog and Billycock ◉

PICK OF THE PUBS

Billinge End Rd, Pleasington BB2 6QB ☎ 01254 201163
e-mail: enquiries@theclogandbillycock.com
dir: *M6 junct 29 to M65 junct 3, follow Pleasington signs*

A great pit-stop for walkers

In a village at the fringe of Blackburn, its hillside setting is in pleasantly wooded countryside with walks from the door leading to Witton Country Park, Pleasington Old Hall and riverside rambles through the striking gorge of the River Darwen. From the same stable as The Three Fishes at Whalley and The Highwayman at Burrow, this busy dining inn serves Thwaites' ales, whilst the wine list stretches to over 35 bins. Marry this to the well-crafted menu and you've the start of a long friendship with this mid-Victorian inn, which is an engaging mix of contemporary and traditional styles, with a surprisingly airy interior. Lancashire produce steers the menu; commence with pork and black pudding Scotch egg and straw potatoes, and follow with Lancashire hot pot or rare-breed baked sticky pork ribs. Finish with Bramley apple pie and custard.

Open all wk 12-11 (Sun 12-10.30) Closed: 25 Dec **Bar Meals** L served Mon-Sat 12-2, Sun 12-8.30 (afternoon bites Mon-Sat 2-5.30) D served Mon-Thu 5.30-8.30, Fri-Sat 5.30-9, Sun 12-8.30, BHs 12-9 Av main course £13.75 food served all day **Restaurant** Av 3 course à la carte fr £24 ⊕ FREE HOUSE ◀ Thwaites Original, Wainwrights & Triple C Ò Kingstone Press. ♟ 11 **Facilities** Non-diners area ♥ (Bar Outside area) ♦♦ Children's menu Outside area ⚑ Parking Wi-fi

See advert on page 272

The Millstone at Mellor ★★★★★ INN ◉◉

PICK OF THE PUBS

See Pick of the Pubs on page 264
See advert below

PICK OF THE PUBS

The Millstone at Mellor ★★★★★ INN

BLACKBURN Map 18 SD62

Church Ln, Mellor BB2 7JR
☎ 01254 813333
e-mail: relax@millstonehotel.co.uk
web: www.millstonehotel.co.uk
dir: *M6 junct 31, A59 towards Clitheroe,
past British Aerospace. Right at rdbt
signed Blackburn/Mellor. Next rdbt 2nd
left. At top of hill on right*

Country-edge inn with superb cuisine

This handsome coaching inn stands in an old village at the edge of Mellor Moor above Blackburn. With the beautiful Ribble Valley and Forest of Bowland Area of Natural Beauty to the north, Pendle Hill nearby and the half-timbered wonder that is Samlesbury Hall just along the lanes, it's little wonder that this inn is a popular place. It's very much a village inn at the heart of the community, presided over by chef-patron Anson Bolton, whose culinary skills have repeatedly gained two AA Rosettes in recognition of his innovative take on classic dishes. Warm up by the log fire in the well-appointed bar or relax in the oak-panelled Miller's restaurant, perhaps picking at an opening nibble of black pudding fritters and chilli jam and pondering the attractive menu options. The selection of starters ranges from duck spring rolls to smoked haddock fishcake; or settle

for a ploughman's platter featuring Lancashire Blackstick's blue cheese, goats' cheese and baked brie. Mains reflect the strong tradition of good pub food, with a sturdy fish pie a popular option, whilst the Bowland steak, kidney and Thwaites Wainwright Ale suet pudding is a great winter warmer. Let your eyes drift to the 'Inn Season' specials board, drawing on the extravagant produce for which the Ribble Valley is widely renowned; 28-day aged Bowland steaks are also a favourite. Walkers passing from the local footpath network can expect beers from the local Thwaites brewery, founded over 200 years ago by Daniel Thwaite, who is buried in the churchyard near this, one of his first pubs.

Open all day all wk **Bar Meals** L served Mon-Sat 12-9.30, Sun 12-9 food served all day 🛢 THWAITES INNS OF CHARACTER 🍺 Lancaster Bomber, Original, Wainwright ♨ Kingstone Press. 🍷 10 **Facilities** Non-diners area 👬 Children's menu Children's portions Outside area 🪑 Parking Wi-fi **Rooms** 23

Save on hotels. Book at **theAA.com/hotel**

LANCASHIRE 265 ENGLAND

BLACKO — Map 18 SD84

Moorcock Inn

Gisburn Rd BB9 6NG ☎ 01282 614186
e-mail: jamesseemann@live.co.uk
dir: M65 junct 13, A682, inn halfway between Blacko & Gisburn

Country pub with many walks around

Beyond the folly of Blacko Tower, high on the road towards Gisburn on the Upper Admergill area, lies this family-run, 18th-century inn with traditional log fires and splendid views towards the Pendle Way. With Thwaites Wainwright and Kingstone Press cider served in the bar. There's a wide choice on the menu and specials board including salads and sandwiches, and vegetarian and children's meals. Main dishes are hearty and include lasagne, various steak, salads, sandwiches and vegetarian choices.

Open 12-2 6-9 (Sat 12-9 Sun 12-6) Closed: Mon eve **Bar Meals** L served Mon-Fri 12-2, Sat 12-9, Sun 12-6 D served Tue-Fri 6-9, Sat 12-9, Sun 12-6 **Restaurant** L served Mon-Fri 12-2, Sat 12-9, Sun 12-6 D served Tue-Fri 6-9, Sat 12-9, Sun 12-6 ⊕ FREE HOUSE ◀ Thwaites Wainwright, Lancaster Bomber Ŏ Kingstone Press. **Facilities** Non-diners area ✿ (Bar Restaurant Outside area) ⬤ Children's menu Children's portions Outside area ⋒ Parking ⬛

BURROW — Map 18 SD67

The Highwayman ⬤

PICK OF THE PUBS

LA6 2RJ ☎ 01524 273338
e-mail: enquiries@highwaymaninn.co.uk
dir: M6 junct 36, A65 to Kirkby Lonsdale. A683 S. Burrow approx 2m

Showcases the best local produce

This 18th-century coaching inn is now one of chef Nigel Haworth's thriving group of dining pubs. What you can expect here is craggy stone floors, warm solid wood furniture, log fires in winter and walled gardens in which to enjoy outdoor drinking and dining. Thwaites of Blackburn supply their cask ales, Kingstone Press sends its draught cider, and there is an extensive list of fine wines. The head chef and his team not only know the traditional specialities of the area but also how to give them that little contemporary nudge. Start with twice-baked Lancashire cheese soufflé and follow with slow-braised ox cheek and horseradish mash or fish pie. There are seasonal alternative menus, a very good children's menu and a gluten-free one too. The landscaped terraced gardens offer comfortable seating and outdoor heating, and the flowers and shrubs have been carefully chosen to help attract the butterflies and birds.

Open all day all wk 12-11 (Sun 12-10.30) Closed: 25 Dec **Bar Meals** L served Mon-Sat 12-2, Sun 12-8.30 (afternoon bites Mon-Sat 2-5.30) D served Mon-Thu 5.30-8.30, Fri-Sat 5.30-9, Sun 12-8.30, BHs 12-9 Av main course £12.75 food served all day **Restaurant** Av 3

course à la carte fr £24 ⊕ RIBBLE VALLEY INNS ◀ Thwaites Lancaster Bomber, Wainwrights & Nutty Black Ŏ Kingstone Press. ♛ 11 **Facilities** Non-diners area ✿ (Bar) ⬤ Children's menu Play area Garden ⋒ Parking

See advert on page 272

CARNFORTH — Map 18 SD47

The Longlands Inn and Restaurant

Tewitfield LA6 1JH ☎ 01524 781256
e-mail: info@longlandshotel.co.uk
dir: Telephone for directions

Confident cooking of local produce

Although very much Lancastrian, this traditional country inn is only minutes away from the Cumbria border. With its nooks and crannies, old beams and uneven floors, this family-run dog-friendly inn stands next to Tewitfield locks on the Lancaster Canal and is an ideal base for the Lake District. The bar, with Tirril ales on tap, rocks to live bands on Mondays while hungry music lovers consume plates of stone-baked pizzas and pasta. Otherwise look to the restaurant for good country cooking and local produce, with Lakeland steaks and Morecambe Bay shrimps on the appetising menu. Children are well catered for.

Open all day all wk 11-11 **Bar Meals** L served Mon-Fri 12-2.30, Sat 12-4, Sun 12-9 D served Mon-Sat 6-9.30, Sun 12-9 **Restaurant** L served Mon-Fri 12-2.30, Sat 12-4, Sun 12-9 D served Mon-Sat 6-9.30, Sun 12-9 ⊕ FREE HOUSE ◀ Tirril Old Faithful, Black Sheep, Bowland Hen Harrier, Old School Brewery. ♛ 9 **Facilities** Non-diners area ✿ (Bar Garden) ⬤ Children's menu Garden ⋒ Parking Wi-fi ⬛ (notice required)

CHIPPING — Map 18 SD64

Dog & Partridge

Hesketh Ln PR3 2TH ☎ 01995 61201
dir: M6 junct 31A, follow Longridge signs. At Longridge left at 1st rbdt, straight on at next 3 rdbts. At Alston Arms turn right. 3m, pub on right

Tudor pub with a restored barn restaurant

Dating back to 1515, this pleasantly modernised rural pub in the Ribble Valley enjoys delightful views of the surrounding fells. The barn has been transformed into a welcoming dining area, where home-made food on the comprehensive bar snack menu is backed by a specials board featuring fresh fish and game dishes. A typical menu shows a starter of deep-fried garlic mushrooms; then mains of braised pork chops with home-made apple sauce and stuffing or home-made steak-and-kidney pie.

Open 11.45-3 6.45-11 (Sat 11.45-3 6-11 Sun 11.45-10.30) Closed: Mon ⊕ FREE HOUSE ◀ Black Sheep, Tetley's, Guest ales. **Facilities** ⬤ Children's menu Children's portions Parking

CLITHEROE — Map 18 SD74

The Assheton Arms

PICK OF THE PUBS

Downham BB7 4BJ ☎ 01200 441227
e-mail: info@asshetonarms.com
dir: A59 to Chatburn, then follow Downham signs

Historic north west inn focusing on seafood

Originally a farmhouse brewing beer just for its farm workers, this pub became the George and Dragon in 1872, then in 1950 was renamed in honour of the contribution Ralph Assheton, Lord Clitheroe, made to the war effort during World War II. In December 2011 the inn was taken over by the family-owned and operated Seafood Pub Company. They made some sweeping changes, including the renovation of a disused two-level dining area, which is now in use once again. At the bar you'll find a great choice of real ales, as well as cider from Thatchers. Local sourcing is a priority here and the fish- and seafood-oriented menu is full of interest, with typical choices including king prawn sesame soldiers, Malaysian seafood curry, fish pie, and herb-crusted haddock. Besides the regular menu there are daily specials. The inn hosts a seafood festival in September.

Open all day all wk 12-10.30 (Fri-Sat 12-12) **Bar Meals** L served Mon-Sat 12-3, Sun 12-8 D served Mon-Thu 6-8.30, Fri-Sat 6-9, Sun 12-8 **Restaurant** L served Mon-Sat 12-3, Sun 12-8 D served Mon-Thu 6-8.30, Fri-Sat 6-9, Sun 12-8 ⊕ FREE HOUSE ◀ Thwaites Wainwright, Black Sheep, Hawkshead, Timothy Taylor Ŏ Thatchers Gold, Kopparberg. ♛ 10 **Facilities** Non-diners area ✿ (Bar Garden) ⬤ Children's menu Children's portions Garden ⋒ Parking Wi-fi ⬛ (notice required)

COLNE — Map 18 SD83

The Alma Inn ★★★★ INN

Emmott Ln, Laneshawbridge BB8 7EG ☎ 01282 857830
e-mail: reception@thealmainn.com
dir: M65, A6068 towards Keighley. At Laneshawbridge left into Emmott Ln. 0.5m, pub on left

Country inn serving local produce

Deep in Pendle's magnificent countryside, this 18th-century inn has been lovingly restored to preserve original features such as stone floors, original beams and real fires. It offers a relaxed and welcoming setting for drinking or dining. The menu is built around local produce including steak (served with a choice of sauces) and Pendle Forest lamb cutlets, maybe pan-fried and served with sweet potato fondant, tomato fondue and smoked Lancashire cauliflower cheese. Other options include sandwiches and filled crusty ciabattas. Finish with home-churned ice cream or vanilla rice pudding with home-made jam.

Open all day all wk **Bar Meals** L served all wk 12-9 D served all wk 12-9 food served all day **Restaurant** L served all wk 12-9 D served all wk 12-9 food served all day ⊕ FREE HOUSE ◀ Moorhouse's Pride of Pendle,

continued

COLNE continued

Lancaster Blonde, Guest ales ☼ Rekorderlig. ♟ 10
Facilities Non-diners area ✿ (Bar Garden) ♦︎ Children's
menu Children's portions Garden ⊢ Parking Wi-fi 🚐
Rooms 10

ELSWICK · Map 18 SD43

The Ship at Elswick

High St PR4 3ZB ☎ 01995 672777
e-mail: mail@theshipatelswick.co.uk
dir: *M55 junct 3, A585 signed Fleetwood. Right onto
Thistleton Rd (B5269)*

Former farmhouse in a quiet village, offering hearty food

In a quiet village on the Fylde and handy both for
Blackpool and the quieter resorts of Cleveleys and
Fleetwood, this former farmhouse is now a reliable village
local and dining inn. From Fleetwood come some of the
fish inhabiting the very traditional menu here; beef and
Guinness pie is another favourite or start with a plate of
Bury black pudding with poached egg hollandaise,
chorizo and rocket. There are also pasta choices, salads
and a Sunday roast. The owners are proud to use
Lancashire produce in most of their dishes, although the
standard beer is Yorkshire's Black Sheep Best Bitter!

Open all day all wk **Bar Meals** Av main course £10 food
served all day **Restaurant** Av 3 course à la carte fr £20
food served all day ⊕ PUNCH TAVERNS ◀ Jennings
Cumberland Ale, Black Sheep, Guest ales. ♟ 8
Facilities Non-diners area ♦︎ Children's menu Children's
portions Play area Garden ⊢ Parking Wi-fi 🚐

FENCE · Map 18 SD83

Fence Gate Inn

Wheatley Lane Rd BB12 9EE ☎ 01282 618101
e-mail: info@fencegate.co.uk
dir: *From M65 junct 13 towards Fence, 1.5m, pub set
back on right opposite T-junct for Burnley*

Village inn with a bustling brasserie

Once a private house, this imposing 300-year-old building
next to the village church only became an inn as recently
as 1982. At the edge of beautiful open countryside, the
pub's brasserie and dining suites reveal its function as a
foodie destination, but drinkers aren't forgotten, with a
wood-panelled bar featuring a grand log fire and high-
quality furnishings, where Lancashire-brewed beers are
the order of the day. The Lancashire theme continues with
the locally sourced food: Bowland beef steak burger,
pulled pork sandwich, chicken schnitzel, lamb kofta salad
and vegetable Thai green curry.

Open all day all wk noon-close **Bar Meals** L served Mon-
Sat 12-2.30, Sun 12-8 D served Mon-Sat 6-9, Sun 12-8
Restaurant L served Mon-Sat 12-2.30, Sun 12-8 D served
Mon-Sat 6-9, Sun 12-8 ⊕ FREE HOUSE ◀ Courage
Directors, Caledonian Deuchars IPA, Theakston,
Moorhouse's, Bowland, Guest ales ☼ Westons Stowford
Press. ♟ 10 **Facilities** Non-diners area ♦︎ Children's menu
Children's portions Garden Parking Wi-fi 🚐

FENISCOWLES · Map 18 SD62

Oyster & Otter
PICK OF THE PUBS

631 Livesey Branch Rd BB2 5DQ ☎ 01254 203200
e-mail: info@oysterandotter.co.uk
dir: *M65 junct 3, right at lights, right at mini rdbt into
Livesey Branch Rd*

A family-owned, seafood-led gastro-pub

The clapboard and stone exterior gives this Blackburn-
fringe pub more of a New England look than mill-town
Lancashire. Successful ex-Fleetwood fish wholesaler
Chris Neve, its owner, comes from a long line of North Sea
and Irish Sea trawlermen; his daughter Joycelyn studied
the coastal food industry in South America before
becoming head of operations here. The third lynch-pin is
executive chef Antony Shirley, formerly head chef at
Raffles in the West Indies. Fish starters include haddock
goujons with saffron and chilli mayo; and a platter of
king prawn sesame soldiers, Atlantic crevettes, pickled
cockles, smoked salmon and Maryland crab cakes. Main
courses include tikka-spiced monkfish with Bombay
potatoes and prawn and red onion bhaji; Malaysian
seafood curry; and fish pie. Alternatively, there's Pendle
Hill steak with slow-roasted tomatoes; Persian chicken
with jewelled rice and pomegranates; and gnocchi with
porcini mushroom cream, spinach and pine nuts. A
typical dessert is white chocolate and orange tiramisu.

Open all day all wk **Restaurant** L served Mon-Sat 12-3,
Sun 12-9 D served Mon-Thu 5-9, Fri-Sat 5-10, Sun 12-9
⊕ THWAITES ◀ Wainwright, Lancaster Bomber, Original
☼ Kingstone Press. ♟ 9 **Facilities** Non-diners area ♦︎
Children's menu Children's portions Garden ⊢ Parking
Wi-fi 🚐 (notice required)

FORTON · Map 18 SD45

The Bay Horse Inn
PICK OF THE PUBS

LA2 0HR ☎ 01524 791204
e-mail: yvonne@bayhorseinn.com
dir: *M6 junct 33 take A6 towards Garstang, turn left for
pub, approx 1m from M6*

Stylish family-run inn with impressive fireplace and imaginative menu

Tucked down a country lane on the edge of the Forest of
Bowland, the Wilkinson family has been at the helm of
this charming 18th-century pub for about 20 years. They
have continued to develop and improve the pub and its
extended gardens, which lead to open fields where
pheasants and deer can often be spotted. Mismatched
furniture and a handsome stone fireplace with roaring
winter log fires characterise the inn, which offers real
cask beers, as well as an extensive wine list. Chef Craig
Wilkinson specialises in simple, fresh and imaginative
dishes. A sample menu offers starters such as grilled
black pudding with celeriac, cured ham, apple purée and
brown sauce; or pigeon salad with asparagus, hazelnuts,
thyme and orange dressing. Follow on with cod loin,

butter beans, cream, pak choi and chorizo; or beef fillet
with blue cheese butter. Leave space for lemon posset,
sticky toffee pudding or an excellent Lancashire
cheeseboard.

Open 12-3 6-12 Closed: Mon (ex BHs L) **Bar Meals** L
served Tue-Sat 12-1.45, Sun 12-3 D served Tue-Sat 6-9
Restaurant L served Tue-Sat 12-1.45, Sun 12-3 D served
Tue-Sat 6-9 ⊕ FREE HOUSE ◀ Moorhouse's Pendle
Witches Brew, Black Sheep, Guest ale. ♟ 11
Facilities Non-diners area ✿ (Bar Garden) ♦︎ Children's
portions Garden ⊢ Parking Wi-fi

GRINDLETON · Map 18 SD74

Duke of York

Brow Top BB7 4QR ☎ 01200 441266
e-mail: info@dukeofyorkgrindleton.com
dir: *From A59 N of Clitheroe left to Chatburn. In Chatburn
right into Ribble Ln. Over river, right at T-junct. Pub at
brow of hill on left*

A leading Ribble Valley dining pub

Built of local stone, with an interior characterised by low
ceilings, stone-flagged floors and little nooks and
crannies, this creeper-clad village pub is at least 150
years old. Food takes the lead, although the bar still gets
its fair share of Lancaster Blonde real ale drinkers.
Driving things from the kitchen is chef/proprietor Michael
Heathcote, on whose daily menu appears a short, but
carefully chosen, choice of dishes, such as home-smoked
and beetroot-cured salmon; belly, fillet and shoulder of
pork; roasted breast of mallard; and lobster thermidor. A
seven-course Menu Surprise opens with langoustine
bisque. There's a lovely garden too.

Open 12-3 6-11 (Sun 12-3 5-11) Closed: 25 Dec, Mon (ex
BHs) **Bar Meals** L served Tue-Sun 12-2 D served Tue-Sat
6-9, Sun 5-7.30 Av main course £16.95 **Restaurant** L
served Tue-Sun 12-2 D served Tue-Sat 6-9, Sun 5-7.30
Fixed menu price fr £9.99 Av 3 course à la carte fr £31.95
⊕ PUNCH TAVERNS ◀ Timothy Taylor Landlord, Lancaster
Blonde. ♟ 20 **Facilities** Non-diners area ✿ (Bar Garden)
♦︎ Children's menu Children's portions Garden ⊢ Parking
Wi-fi 🚐 (notice required)

HESKIN GREEN · Map 15 SD51

Farmers Arms

85 Wood Ln PR7 5NP ☎ 01257 451276
e-mail: andy@farmersarms.co.uk
dir: *On B5250 between M6 & Eccleston*

Handsome family-run pub

This fine 17th-century pub used to be called the Pleasant
Retreat, but in 1902 the name was changed. Never mind,
because this long, creeper-covered building is still
pleasant, very pleasant actually, and its flagstoned Vault
Bar is still a retreat. Malcolm and Ann Rothwell have
been here for a quarter of a century, and now son Andrew
and his wife Sue are slowly taking over the helm. The
menu may include minted lamb cutlets or baked haddock
gratin, while the main menu features Cumberland
sausage, lasagne verdi, grills and steaks, and a selection

Save on hotels. Book at **theAA.com/hotel**

LANCASHIRE 267 **ENGLAND**

of salads, jacket potatoes and sandwiches. Hand-pulled real ales include Silver Tally, named after the token that miners would exchange for a lamp.

Open all day all wk ⊕ ENTERPRISE INNS ◖ Timothy Taylor Landlord, Marston's Pedigree, Prospect Silver Tally, Black Sheep, Tetley's. **Facilities** ✿ (Bar Garden) ⊕ Children's menu Children's portions Play area Garden Parking Wi-fi

HEST BANK
Map 18 SD46

Hest Bank Inn

2 Hest Bank Ln LA2 6DN ☎ **01524 824339**
e-mail: chef.glenn@btinternet.com
dir: *From Lancaster take A6 N, after 2m left to Hest Bank*

Historic inn with lots to offer

First licensed in 1554, this former coaching inn is awash with history: it was occupied by Cromwell's officers in the Civil War and later became the haunt of highwaymen. Comedian Eric Morecambe used to drink at the canalside Hest Bank, which offers cask ales and a wide selection of meals all day, with local suppliers playing an important role in maintaining food quality. The good value menu ranges from piri-piri chicken to steamed venison and beef pudding. Enjoy a pint of Thwaites Wainwright in the terraced garden. Wednesday evening is quiz night, while steak night is every Thursday. Call the pub for details of their beer festival.

Open all day all wk 11.30-11.30 (Sun 11.30-10.30) **Bar Meals** L served Mon-Sat 12-9, Sun 12-8 D served Mon-Sat 12-9, Sun 12-8 food served all day **Restaurant** L served Mon-Fri 12-3, Sat 12-9, Sun 12-8 D served Mon-Fri 5-9, Sat 12-9, Sun 12-8 ⊕ PUNCH TAVERNS ◖ Thwaites Wainwright, Black Sheep Best Bitter, Guest ales. **Facilities** Non-diners area ✿ (Bar Garden) ⊕ Children's menu Children's portions Play area Garden ⊼ Beer festival Parking Wi-fi ⊜ (notice required)

LANCASTER
Map 18 SD46

The Borough

3 Dalton Square LA1 1PP ☎ **01524 64170**
e-mail: vicki@theboroughlancaster.co.uk
web: www.theboroughlancaster.co.uk
dir: *Telephone for directions*

Superb Lancashire produce in town house pub

This Grade II Georgian pub with a Victorian frontage continues to go from strength to strength. Wooden floors, chunky tables, Chesterfield sofas, warm green hues and masses of light from a huge bay window create a friendly, relaxed vibe for enjoying a cracking range of Lancashire ales and a quality food offering. Using top-notch ingredients from local suppliers, including meat and eggs from surrounding farms, the seasonal menu may take in salt and pepper calamari, minted locally reared lamb Henry and summer berry jelly. Steaks from the grill and a real value 'school dinners' menu are also available.

Open all wk 12-11 (Fri noon-12.30am Sat 9am-12.20am) Closed: 25 Dec **Bar Meals** L served Sun-Thu 12-9, Fri-Sat 12-9.30 D served Sun-Thu 12-9, Fri-Sat 12-9.30 Av main course £11 **Restaurant** L served Sun-Thu 12-9, Fri-Sat 12-9.30 D served Sun-Thu 12-9, Fri-Sat 12-9.30 Av 3 course à la carte fr £20 ⊕ FREE HOUSE ◖ Borough IPA, Lancaster Amber, Young's Bitter, Wells Eagle IPA, Bowland Hen Harrier. ☿ 11 **Facilities** Non-diners area ✿ (Bar) ⊕ Children's menu Garden ⊼ Wi-fi ⊜ (notice required)

Penny Street Bridge ★★★ TH

PICK OF THE PUBS

See Pick of the Pubs on page 268
See advert below

The Stork Inn

Conder Green LA2 0AN ☎ **01524 751234**
e-mail: tracy@thestorkinn.co.uk
dir: *M6 junct 33 take A6 N. Left at Galgate & next left to Conder Green*

Traditional coaching inn with South African influences

The Stork is a white-painted coaching inn spread along the banks of the tidal Lune estuary, with a colourful 300-year-history that includes several name changes. The quaint sea port of Glasson Dock is a short walk along the Lancashire Coastal Way, and the Lake District and M6 are easily accessible. In the bar you will find local ales such as Lancaster Black, Amber and Blonde. Seasonal specialities join home-cooked English and South African food like pan-fried chicken breast topped with Lancashire cheese and bacon; Boerewors - lightly spiced pure beef farmer's sausage, served with sweet potato mash and a balsamic, red onion and tomato relish; and minted pea risotto.

Open all day all wk 8.30am-11pm **Bar Meals** L served all wk 12-9 (breakfast 8.30-11) D served all wk 12-9 food served all day **Restaurant** food served all day ⊕ ENTERPRISE INNS ◖ Timothy Taylor Landlord, Black Sheep, Lancaster Blonde, Amber Ales. ☿ 10 **Facilities** Non-diners area ✿ (Bar Restaurant Garden) ⊕ Children's menu Children's portions Play area Garden ⊼ Parking Wi-fi ⊜

PICK OF THE PUBS

Penny Street Bridge ★★★ TH

LANCASTER　　　Map 18 SD46

Penny St LA1 1XT ☎ 01524 599900
e-mail: relax@pennystreetbridge.co.uk
web: www.pennystreetbridge.co.uk
dir: *In city centre*

Quirkily elegant, canal-side, city centre townhouse offering the best of Lancashire produce

Right in the centre of the city, the listed Penny Street Bridge was once a Corporation Toll House. Demolished in 1901, it was then rebuilt as two separate pubs, which Thwaites Brewery joined together again in 2007 to create a smart town-house hotel, bar and brasserie. Its wonderfully high ceilings make it feel light and modern, although retained period features can be seen everywhere, from the listed staircase to the servant bell hooks, and from the stained-glass windows to the rather special wardrobe in one of the bedrooms that the owners can't, and wouldn't ever want to, move. The atmosphere is quirkily elegant, with wooden floors in the brasserie, mismatched tables and tub chairs in the traditional bar and grill, and a stylish, contemporary feel in the refurbished bedrooms. Chef Andrew Nixon and his team prepare all food on the premises. Served all day, their seasonal menus make the most of the excellent Lancashire produce available

locally, from smoked haddock fishcakes or tempura tiger prawns for a starter, to main courses such as steamed steak and ale pudding; Lancashire cheese, onion and potato pie; or lamb hotpot. Steaks aged for 28 days are seared on the charcoal grill and served with thick-cut chips and a Caesar side salad. Stone-baked pizzas made with fresh dough come with all the popular toppings, like pepperoni, or goats' cheese and red onion. For pudding, try the banoffee sundae, apple and blackberry crumble, or sticky toffee pudding. Opposite the pub is Penny Street Bridge itself, under which runs the Lancaster Canal on its 42-mile journey from Tewitfield to Kendal.

Open all day all wk 9am-mdnt **Bar Meals** food served all day **Restaurant** food served all day ⊕ THWAITES INNS OF CHARACTER ◀ Wainwright, Lancaster Bomber, Original ♂ Kingstone Press. ♜ 11 **Facilities** Non-diners area ♦♦ Children's menu Children's portions Garden ㅈ Parking Wi-fi 🚌 (notice required) **Rooms** 28

Save on hotels. Book at **theAA.com/hotel**

LANCASHIRE 269 **ENGLAND**

LANCASTER *continued*

The Sun Hotel and Bar

PICK OF THE PUBS

LA1 1ET ☎ 01524 66006
e-mail: info@thesunhotelandbar.co.uk
dir: *6m from M6 junct 33*

Famous for its hospitality over the centuries

The oldest building in Lancaster, The Sun was first
licensed as 'Stoop Hall' in 1680 as the town's premier
coaching inn. Generals from the occupying Jacobean
Army lodged here in 1745, and the artist JMW Turner
stayed whilst making sketches of Heysham in 1812.
Original features include a bottomless well and beautiful
old door. Owned by the Lancaster Brewery, the pub has a
wide selection of cask ales, world beers and wines. The
bar is frequented throughout the day; from hotel guests
and business breakfasters, to shoppers enjoying mid-
morning coffee or brunch, and customers tucking into the
locally sourced food at lunch and dinner, as well as wine
and ale connoisseurs. The experienced kitchen brigade
prepares sea bass Niçoise; baby carrot and fennel risotto;
and sausages and mash. The extensive cheese board
menu is especially popular, and also includes cold meats,
pâtés and fish. There is a patio for alfresco dining in
warmer weather, regular quiz nights and an annual beer
festival in the summer.

Open all day all wk from 7.30am-late **Bar Meals** L served
all wk 12-3 D served Sun-Thu 4-9, Fri-Sat 4-7 Av main
course £11 food served all day **Restaurant** L served all wk
12-3 D served Sun-Thu 4-9, Fri-Sat 4-7 food served all
day ⊕ FREE HOUSE ◀ Lancaster Amber & Blonde,
Thwaites Lancaster Bomber, Timmermans Strawberry
♻ Kingstone Press. ♟ 23 **Facilities** Non-diners area ♦♦
Children's menu Children's portions Garden ⏢ Beer
festival Wi-fi 🚐 (notice required)

The White Cross

Quarry Rd LA1 4XT ☎ 01524 33999
e-mail: twcpub@yahoo.co.uk
dir: *S on one-way system, left after Town Hall. Over canal
bridge, on right*

Enjoy good food as canal boats go by

Set in a 130-year-old former cotton mill warehouse on the
edge of the Lancaster Canal, The White Cross is a short
stroll from the city centre. A regularly changing selection
of up to 14 cask ales includes beers from Copper Dragon,
Timothy Taylor and Theakston breweries, but food is an
equal draw at this popular waterfront venue. Home-made
pork pies; lamb, mint and rosemary burgers; lasagne al
forno; and deli boards to share are typical menu choices.
A beer and pie festival takes place in late April.

Open all day all wk **Bar Meals** food served all day
Restaurant food served all day ⊕ ENTERPRISE INNS
◀ Copper Dragon Golden Pippin, Timothy Taylor Landlord,
Theakston Old Peculier ♻ Westons Stowford Press & Old
Rosie, Ribble Valley Gold. ♟ 13 **Facilities** Non-diners area
♦♦ Children's menu Children's portions Garden ⏢ Beer
festival Parking Wi-fi 🚐 (notice required)

LITTLE ECCLESTON   Map 18 SD44

The Cartford Inn

PICK OF THE PUBS

See Pick of the Pubs on page 270

See Pick of the Pubs on page 270

NEWTON-IN-BOWLAND   Map 18 SD65

Parkers Arms

PICK OF THE PUBS

BB7 3DY ☎ 01200 446236
e-mail: enquiries@parkersarms.co.uk
dir: *From Clitheroe take B6478 through Waddington to
Newton-in-Bowland*

Imaginative cooking and delightful countryside views

In a beautiful hamlet amidst the rolling hills of the
Trough of Bowland, this Georgian dining inn is just yards
from the River Hodder and enjoys panoramic views over
Waddington Fell. It celebrates its rural location by serving
the best of Lancashire produce. This includes ales from
the local breweries, meats raised on nearby moorland,
vegetables from Ribble Valley farms and fresh fish from
nearby Fleetwood. French chef-patron Stosie Madi even
forages for ingredients herself. The simple, but elegant,
modern dishes on the daily-changing, seasonal menu
include Goosnargh corn-fed chicken and leek pie; slow-
braised shin of Bowland beef in ale with creamed mash;
and fillet of sea bass with pea gnocchi and a lemon
reduction. For pudding could be 'Wet Nelly', a classic
north-west dessert originally created for Lord Nelson in
Liverpool and reworked by co-owner Kathy Smith.

Open 12-3 6-close (Sat-Sun & BH 12-close) Closed: Mon
Bar Meals L served Tue-Sun 12-3 D served Tue-Sun
6-8.30 Av main course £12 **Restaurant** L served Tue-Sun
12-3 D served Tue-Sun 6-8.30 Fixed menu price fr £13 Av
3 course à la carte fr £23 ⊕ FREE HOUSE/ENTERPRISE
Lease ♻ Westons Stowford Press.
Facilities Non-diners area ♣ (Bar Restaurant Garden) ♦♦
Children's menu Children's portions Garden ⏢ Parking
Wi-fi 🚐 (notice required)

PARBOLD   Map 15 SD41

The Eagle & Child

PICK OF THE PUBS

Maltkiln Ln, Bispham Green L40 3SG ☎ 01257 462297
web: www.ainscoughs.co.uk
dir: *3m from M6 junct 27. Take A5209 to Parbold. Right
onto B5246. 2.5m, Bispham Green on right*

Excellent alfresco dining potential in summer

A country dining pub in a pretty and peaceful location,
The Eagle & Child's outside seating is ideally positioned
to enjoy bowling on the green during the summer months.
The bar maintains its traditional atmosphere by offering
a choice of real ciders and regularly-changing guest ales
from a dozen nearby microbreweries; the annual early
May Bank Holiday beer festival attracts up to 2,000
people to a huge marquee in the pub grounds. Menus for
both bar and restaurant hinge on locally sourced and
organic produce when possible. Typical starters of sticky
chicken wings with lemon, thyme and garlic or crispy
duck salad might be followed by traditional Lancashire
hotpot or chicken and mushroom pie. The pub's unusual
name derives from a local legend that Lord Derby's
illegitimate son was discovered in an eagle's nest; a
more prosaic local title is the Bird and Bastard.

Open all wk 12-3 5.30-11 (Fri-Sun 12-11) **Bar Meals** L
served all wk 12-2 D served Sun-Thu 5.30-8.30, Fri-Sat
5.30-9 **Restaurant** L served all wk 12-2 D served Sun-Thu
5.30-8.30, Fri-Sat 5.30-9 ⊕ FREE HOUSE ◀ Moorhouse's
Black Cat, Thwaites Original, Southport Golden Sands,
Guest ales ♻ Kingstone Press, Farmhouse Cider Scrumpy.
Facilities Non-diners area ♣ (Bar Restaurant Garden) ♦♦
Children's menu Children's portions Family room Garden
⏢ Beer festival Parking 🚐 (notice required)

PICK OF THE PUBS

The Cartford Inn

LITTLE ECCLESTON   Map 18 SD44

PR3 0YP ☎ 01995 670166
e-mail: info@thecartfordinn.co.uk
web: www.thecartfordinn.co.uk
dir: *Off A586*

17th-century inn with eclectic interiors and excellent food

Set in an idyllic location adjoining a toll bridge across the tidal Rive Wyre, this award-winning 17th-century coaching inn enjoys extensive views over the countryside towards the Trough of Bowland and Beacon Fell. Owners Julie and Patrick Beaume have created a pleasing mix of traditional and gastro decor: the stylish and contemporary interior is an appealing blend of striking colours, natural wood and polished floors, whilst the smart open fireplace and an eclectic selection of furniture adds a comfortable and relaxed feel to the bar lounge. Thanks to a new extension, The Cartford now also includes the impressive River Lounge restaurant and an attractive dining terrace, where you can enjoy an imaginative range of dishes based on quality ingredients from local suppliers. Lunchtime sandwiches like cold poached salmon or Cumbrian cured ham and chutney come on Pebby's fresh bread and are served with organic crisps, whilst wooden platters are the showcase for local antipasti, Fleetwood seafood, and organic crudités. Cartford

favourites include Pilling Marsh lamb hotpot; and the ever-popular fish with chunky chips and marrowfat peas. Other main course options range from a braised and roasted pork belly, with sesame-roasted kale cabbage and egg noodles; to Cumberland sausages with mash and onion gravy. Orange and spiced fig cooked cheesecake; and chocolate fondant served with mascapone cream are just two of the choices for dessert. The Cartford Inn makes an ideal spot from which to explore the surrounding area; Lancaster, the Royal Lytham Golf Club, and Blackpool with its Winter Gardens and Grand Theatre are all within easy reach. Accommodation available.

Open all day Closed: 25 Dec, Mon L **Bar**

Meals L served Tue-Sat 12-2, Sun 12-8.30 D served Mon-Thu 5.30-9, Fri-Sat 5.30-10 **Restaurant** L served Tue-Sat 12-2, Sun 12-8.30 D served Mon-Thu 5.30-9, Fri-Sat 5.30-10 ⊕ FREE HOUSE ◪ Moorhouse's Pride of Pendle, Hawkshead Lakeland Gold, Theakston Old Peculier ♂ Westons. **Facilities** Non-diners area ⁂ Children's menu Children's portions Garden ⊼ Parking Wi-fi

PENDLETON · Map 18 SD73

The Swan with Two Necks

BB7 1PT ☎ 01200 423112
e-mail: swanwith2necks@yahoo.co.uk
dir: *Exit A59 between Whalley & Chatburn follow Pendleton signs, 0.5m to pub*

Charming 18th-century inn, set in a beautiful stone-built Lancashire village

Hidden away in the pretty village of Pendleton, The Swan with Two Necks is a traditional village inn dating back to 1722. Pendleton nestles under Pendle Hill, which is famous for its witches, and that's not the only curious piece of history attached to this place; the inn's name refers to the tradition of marking the necks of swans belonging to the Worshipful Company of Vintners with two 'nicks' to distinguish them from swans belonging to the king or queen. Of course you won't find swan on the menu here, but this pub is renowned for its ales and ciders, so be sure to try the likes of Phoenix Wobbly Bob or Dove Syke Ribble Valley Gold.

Open 12-3 6-11 (Sun 12-10.30) Closed: 25 Dec, Mon L **Bar Meals** L served Tue-Sat 12-1.45, Sun 12-6.30 D served Mon-Sat 6-8.30 ⊕ FREE HOUSE ◖ Phoenix Wobbly Bob, Copper Dragon Golden Pippin, Prospect Nutty Slack, Marble, Salamander Ö Westons Traditional & Country Perry, Ribble Valley Gold. ♀ 14
Facilities Non-diners area ♦♦ Children's menu Children's portions Garden ♬ Parking ▭ (notice required)

SAWLEY · Map 18 SD74

The Spread Eagle

PICK OF THE PUBS

BB7 4NH ☎ 01200 441202
e-mail: spread.eagle@zen.co.uk
dir: *Just off A159 between Clitheroe & Skipton, 4m N of Clitheroe*

Well-appointed trendy pub focusing on modern dishes

This handsome old stone inn stands on a quiet lane in the glorious Ribble Valley, flanked on one side by the impressive ruins of Sawley Abbey, and on other by the River Ribble. Inside, choose between the elegant, light-filled dining room with its lush river views through picture windows, or the charming 17th-century bar, where you'll find traditional stone-flagged floors, old oak furniture and roaring fires alongside trendy wallpaper, painted settles strewn with bright cushions, colourful upholstered chairs, eclectic objets d'art, and cool Farrow & Ball hues. All this adds up to a cosy and relaxing setting for savouring a pint of Timothy Taylor Landlord and some decent modern pub food. Served throughout the inn and changing daily, the menu may include scallops and black pudding with saffron and orange dressing; a classic steak-and-kidney pudding; rib-eye steak with garlic butter and hand-cut chips; and warm chocolate brownie with maple ice cream. Don your boots and walk it all off in the Bowland Hills.

Open all day all wk 11-11 (Sun 12-10.30) **Bar Meals** L served Mon-Sat 12-2, Sun 12-7.30 D served Mon-Sat 6-9.30, Sun 12-7.30 **Restaurant** L served Mon-Sat 12-2, Sun 12-7.30 D served Mon-Sat 6-9.30, Sun 12-7.30 ⊕ INDIVIDUAL INNS ◖ Thwaites Wainwright, Timothy Taylor Landlord, Moorhouse's Ö Kingstone Press. ♀ 16
Facilities Non-diners area ♣ (Bar Garden) ♦♦ Children's menu Children's portions Garden ♬ Parking ▭

TOCKHOLES · Map 15 SD62

The Royal Arms

Tockholes Rd BB3 0PA ☎ 01254 705373
dir: *M65 junct 4 follow Blackburn signs. Right at lights, 1st left. Up hill left at 3B's Brewery into Tockholes Rd. Pub in 3m on left*

Rich with pickings from Lancashire microbreweries

High in the West Pennine Moors is this appealing old stone pub nestled in a tiny fold of mill-workers' cottages. Walks from the door drop into Roddlesworth Woods or climb to the imposing Jubilee Tower on nearby Darwen Hill. There's an engaging hotchpotch of furnishings in the fire-warmed, flagstoned and beamed rooms together with fascinating old photos of the local villages in their mill-town heyday. Take a glass of Glen Top out to tables on the lawn and study the regularly changing menu of home-cooked goodies, including cheeky leeky pie (chicken, leek and onion) and some great spicy dishes.

Open all day Closed: Mon ◖ Rossendale Glen Top Bitter, Three B's, Guest ales. **Facilities** ♣ (Bar Restaurant

Garden) ♦♦ Children's menu Children's portions Garden Parking

TUNSTALL · Map 18 SD67

The Lunesdale Arms

LA6 2QN ☎ 015242 74203
e-mail: info@thelunesdale.co.uk
dir: *M6 junct 36. A65 Kirkby Lonsdale. A638 Lancaster. Pub 2m on right*

Welcoming pub showcasing locally sourced produce

Set in a small rural village in the beautiful Lune Valley, this bright and cheery pub has quite a reputation for its food, wines and fine regional beers (Black Sheep and Dent). It draws diners from far and wide for its daily-changing chalkboard menus that include bread baked on the premises, meat from local farms and organically grown vegetables and salads. Depending on the season and new ideas, you could see country terrine with medlar jelly; butternut squash, sage and Lancashire blue cheese risotto; and steak, Guinness and mushroom pie. In winter, cosy up by the wood-burning stove in the light and airy bar, with its comfortable sofas and local artwork.

Open 11-3 6-12 (Sat Sun & BH 11-4 6-1am) Closed: 25-26 Dec, Mon (ex BHs) ⊕ FREE HOUSE ◖ Dent Aviator, Black Sheep, Brysons, Guinness Ö Westons Stowford Press. **Facilities** ♣ (Bar Garden) ♦♦ Children's portions Family room Garden Parking

WADDINGTON · Map 18 SD74

Waddington Arms **NEW**

West View, Waddington Rd BB7 3HP ☎ 01200 423262
e-mail: info@waddingtonarms.co.uk
dir: *In village centre*

Menu featuring local specialities

There's some doubt about the age of James Warburton's imposing establishment, although knowing that it was a coaching inn points one in the right direction. In the bar and outside a nice touch is the cushioned wickerwork chairs, perfect for relaxing with a pint of Bowland Hen Harrier, Thwaites Wainwright or The Waddy from Moorhouse's. Dining is available throughout, including in two cosy side rooms off the main bar. Strong on local specialities, the menu offers Lancashire hotpot with pickled red cabbage; pork loin with black-pudding-crushed potatoes; pan-fried salmon fillet with sautéed potatoes and prawns; and wild mushroom risotto.

Open all day all wk **Bar Meals** L served Mon-Fri 12-2.30, Sat 12-9.30, Sun 12-9 D served Mon-Fri 6-9.30, Sat 12-9.30, Sun 12-9 Av main course £13 **Restaurant** L served Mon-Fri 12-2.30, Sat 12-9.30, Sun 12-9 D served Mon-Fri 6-9.30, Sat 12-9.30, Sun 12-9 Fixed menu price fr £22 Av 3 course à la carte fr £25 ◖ Bowland Hen Harrier, Thwaites Wainwright, Moorhouse's. ♀ 14
Facilities Non-diners area ♦♦ Children's menu Children's portions Play area Family room Garden ♬ Parking Wi-fi ▭ (notice required)

LOCAL HEROES

This part of the world attracts millions of visitors every year thanks, in no small part, to its magnificent scenery. But it's now also recognised as the food capital of Great Britain...home to the country's most gifted artisan producers and a group of famous pubs that has picked up a hatful of the nation's most coveted awards.

Ribble Valley Inns really puts the 'local' into locals. On the menu... traditional dishes with a contemporary twist, created by a Michelin Star chef using the finest, freshest ingredients sourced from the pick of the local farmers and suppliers.

This is food with roots, served in warm and welcoming surroundings...with log fires crackling in the winter, sprawling terraces to dine alfresco in the summer, and an impressive line-up of fine wines and guest beers to complete the picture.

Four stunning pubs...three in Lancashire and a fourth in Yorkshire. And just one promise. Whichever you choose you'll enjoy the real taste of the North!

RIBBLE VALLEY INNS...PUBS WITH A SERIOUS PEDIGREE
The multi award-winning RVI concept is the creation of
Northcote's Craig Bancroft and Nigel Haworth, Michelin Starred chef and
winner of BBC2's Great British Menu.

Save on hotels. Book at theAA.com/hotel

LANCASHIRE – LEICESTERSHIRE 273 ENGLAND

WHALLEY — Map 18 SD73

The Three Fishes ⊛

Mitton Rd, Mitton BB7 9PQ ☎ **01254 826888**
e-mail: enquiries@thethreefishes.com
web: www.thethreefishes.com
dir: M6 junct 31, A59 to Clitheroe. Follow Whalley signs, B6246, 2m

Stylish pub championing local food heroes

With Pendle Hill forming one horizon, Longridge Fell another, The Three Fishes is part of a landscape that inspired parts of JRR Tolkien's *Lord of the Rings* trilogy. For more than four centuries, travellers have been stopping here for refreshments. The menus are inspired by Nigel Haworth, chef-patron of Northcote, his renowned restaurant in nearby Langho, which like this pub is an associate company of Ribble Valley Inns. The restaurant relies extensively on trusted regional suppliers. Try potted Morecambe Bay shrimps with blade mace butter, or Goosnargh corn-fed chicken liver pâté as a starter, followed by a main course of cheese and onion pie; Lancashire hotpot; or baked North Sea cod with spring greens, new potatoes and hollandaise sauce. A six-variety Lancashire cheeseboard should go down well with cheese lovers, with the likes of rhubarb and apple crumble with custard one of several comforting puddings.

Open all day all wk 12-11 (Sun 12-10.30) Closed: 25 Dec **Bar Meals** L served Mon-Sat 12-2, Sun 12-8.30 (afternoon bites Mon-Sat 2-5.30) D served Mon-Thu 5.30-8.30, Fri-Sat 5.30-9, Sun 12-8, BHs 12-9 Av main course £13.75 food served all day **Restaurant** Av 3 course à la carte fr £24 ⊕ FREE HOUSE ◼ Bowland Hen Harrier, Wainwright Thwaites ♂ Stowford Press. 11 **Facilities** Non-diners area 🐾 (Bar Garden) 🍴 Children's menu Children's portions Garden ⋒ Parking

See advert on opposite page

WHEELTON — Map 15 SD62

The Dressers Arms

Briers Brow PR6 8HD ☎ **01254 830041**
e-mail: info@dressersarms.co.uk
dir: M61 junct 8, A674 to Blackburn. Follow sign for pub on right

Dog-friendly, welcoming fires and good pub grub

Until the 1960s, this was the smallest pub in Lancashire. The long, low, creeper-festooned old gritstone building is crammed with local photos, collectables and artefacts spread through a clutch of separate drinking areas; partly flagged floors are warmed by roaring fires in winter. Its appeal is enhanced by the choice of ales and a reliable raft of home-made pub grub: perhaps a hot sandwich of pan-fried chicken and bacon with melted cheese will hit the spot; otherwise look to the specials for a trio of lamb cutlets with port and rosemary sauce.

Open all day all wk **Bar Meals** food served all day **Restaurant** food served all day ⊕ FREE HOUSE ◼ The Dressers Arms Dressers Bitter, Black Sheep ♂ Westons. 20 **Facilities** Non-diners area 🐾 (Bar Restaurant Garden) 🍴 Children's menu Children's portions Family room Garden ⋒ Parking Wi-fi 🚌

WHITEWELL — Map 18 SD64

The Inn at Whitewell ★★★★★ INN ⊛

Forest of Bowland BB7 3AT ☎ **01200 448222**
e-mail: reception@innatwhitewell.com
dir: From B6243 follow Whitewell signs

Historic inn with spectacular valley views

Part of the Duchy of Lancaster Estate, the Inn at Whitewell is perched high on the banks of the River Hodder. Little of the wild beauty of the Forest of Bowland can have changed since the 1300s, when this stone inn was built as a small manor house for the keepers of the Royal forest. The somewhat eccentric interior is packed with random furnishings, antiques and pictures, a Bowman family passion. The kitchen produces consistently delicious food for the bar at lunch and supper, typically fish pie or grilled Goosnargh chicken thighs marinated in Thai-style aromatics, and also for the dining room in the evening, when you might choose a warm salad of pigeon breast; and fillet of pork with bubble-and-squeak and caramelised apples. The whole complex embraces 23 individually decorated bedrooms, a wine merchant, an art gallery and a shop selling home-made goodies.

Open all day all wk 10am-1am **Bar Meals** L served all wk 12-2 D served all wk 7.30-9.30 **Restaurant** D served all wk 7.30-9.30 ⊕ FREE HOUSE ◼ Timothy Taylor Landlord, Bowland, Copper Dragon, Moorhouse's, Hawkshead ♂ Dunkertons Premium Organic. 16 **Facilities** Non-diners area 🐾 (Bar Garden) 🍴 Children's portions Garden ⋒ Parking Wi-fi 🚌 (notice required) **Rooms** 23

LEICESTERSHIRE

BIRSTALL — Map 11 SK50

The White Horse

White Horse Ln LE4 4EF ☎ **0116 267 1038**
e-mail: info@thewhitehorsebirstall.co.uk
dir: M1 junct 21A, A46 towards Newark 5.5m. Exit A46 at Loughborough

Delivering the very best expected of a village inn

A former canal-worker's beerhouse whose tranquil garden was once a coal wharf serving the village of Birstall, The White Horse (formerly The Mulberry Tree) overlooks Watermead Country Park. Rebuilt in the 1920s, the pub has matured over the years into today's restful retreat offering reliable beers, good company and a sought-after range of dishes. Boaters and ramblers alike look forward to classic main courses such as a hand-made burger with chips and onion rings; gammon with egg and chips; or beef lasagne with dressed salad and garlic bread. Or follow the locals' lead and tuck in to the pie of the week with all the trimmings.

Open all wk winter 12-3 5.30-11 (Sun 12-10.30); summer all day everyday ⊕ TRUST INNS ◼ Timothy Taylor Landlord, Jennings Cumberland Ale, Guest ale. **Facilities** 🐾 (Bar Garden) 🍴 Children's menu Children's portions Play area Garden Parking

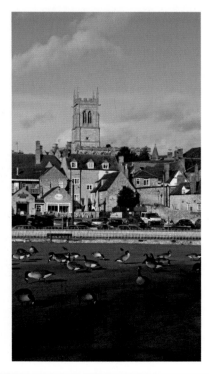

BREEDON ON THE HILL — Map 11 SK42

The Three Horseshoes

Main St DE73 8AN ☎ 01332 695129
e-mail: ian@thehorseshoes.com
dir: *5m from M1 junct 23a. Pub in village centre*

Welcoming old pub with a chocolate workshop next door

Originally a farrier's, the buildings here are around 250 years old; the pub has been here for at least a century, while the main kitchen, a farm shop and a chocolate workshop now occupy the smithy and stables in the courtyard. Inside, numerous original features and old beams are supplemented by antique furniture, and sea-grass matting completes the warm and welcoming atmosphere. Typical dishes start with smoked salmon with lemon mayonnaise or tomato and vodka soup, followed by blackened salmon with crème fraîche, duck breast with cabbage and whisky, or beef hot pot with Yorkshire pudding. Try some of the hand-made chocolates for dessert.

Open 10.30-2.30 5.30-11 (Sun 12-3) **Closed:** 25-26 & 31 Dec-1 Jan, Sun eve **Bar Meals** L served Mon-Sat 12-2 D served Mon-Sat 5.30-9.15 Av main course £7.50 **Restaurant** L served Mon-Sat 12-2, Sun 12-3 D served Mon-Sat 6.30-9.15 Av 3 course à la carte fr £26 ⊕ FREE HOUSE ◀ Marston's Pedigree, Guest ales. **Facilities** Non-diners area ❖ (Bar Garden) ♦♦ Children's portions Garden ⅋ Parking

BRUNTINGTHORPE — Map 11 SP68

The Joiners

Church Walk LE17 5QH ☎ 0116 247 8258
e-mail: stephen@thejoinersarms.co.uk
dir: *4m from Lutterworth*

Food-led village gastro-pub

Yesteryear's modest village pub is today's popular eating place, thanks to Stephen and Tracy Fitzpatrick. You'll find stripped oak beams, flagstone floors, an open fire and lots of brassware and candles. Menus change constantly, with ingredients sourced from wherever Stephen thinks best – beef from Scotland, seafood from Cornwall, black pudding from Clonakilty. A typical example lists monkfish in Parma ham, cherry tomato and basil gnocchi; Barbary duck breast with black cherry and brandy sauce; supreme of chicken with pea and smoked bacon risotto; and aubergine stuffed with ratatouille and mozzarella. Every Tuesday there's a three-course fixed-price 'Auberge Supper'.

Open 12-2 6.30-11 **Closed:** Mon **Bar Meals** L served Tue-Sun 12-2 **Restaurant** L served Tue-Sun 12-2 D served 6.30-9.30 ⊕ FREE HOUSE ◀ Sharp's Doom Bar, Marston's Pedigree. ♎ 16 **Facilities** Non-diners area Outside area ⅋ Parking ▭ (notice required)

BUCKMINSTER — Map 11 SK82

Tollemache Arms

48 Main St NG33 5SA ☎ 01476 860477
e-mail: info@tollemache-arms.co.uk
dir: *4m from A1, between Colsterworth & Melton Mowbray on B676*

Time a visit for pie night

This striking 18th-century building on the Tollemache Estate is situated in the beautiful village of Buckminster. Those looking to enjoy a drink are welcomed by the big oak bar which serves local Oakham ales, while diners can get comfy in the stylish, oak-floored dining room and library and enjoy the good modern British food. Using local seasonal produce, daily menus may feature mushroom and thyme soup; pork saltimbocca with spring onion potato cake; and Bakewell tart. Thursday evening is pie night. This is a community focused pub where dogs and children are welcome.

Open Tue-Sat 12-3 6-11 (Sun 12-4.30) **Closed:** 25, 27-29 Dec, Sun eve, Mon **Bar Meals** L served Tue-Sun 12-2 D served Tue-Sat 6.30-9 Av main course £11 **Restaurant** L served Tue-Sun 12-2 D served Tue-Sat 6.30-9 ⊕ FREE HOUSE ◀ Oakham Ales JHB, Guest Ale. **Facilities** Non-diners area ❖ (Bar Garden Outside area) ♦♦ Children's menu Children's portions Garden Outside area ⅋ Parking Wi-fi ▭ (notice required)

COLEORTON — Map 11 SK41

George Inn

Loughborough Rd LE67 8HF ☎ 01530 834639
e-mail: janice@jwilkinson781.orangehome.co.uk
web: www.georgeinncoleorton.co.uk
dir: *A42 junct 13 onto A512*

Relaxing country pub in National Forest

A comfortably refurbished and extended old local bristling with homely touches, with crackling log-burners in the main rooms and a tree-shaded beer garden looking over the rich pasturelands of this corner of Leicestershire. It's at the heart of extensive National Forest, whilst Calke Abbey is a leisurely drive away. Bright and airy inside, with colourwash and panelled walls and nooks and crannies to explore, Black Sheep or Adnams bitters may complement the sturdy menu. Kick in with goats' cheese and poached pear, following up with wild boar sausages or steak and ale pie with Stilton; some gluten-free options, too.

Open 12-3 5.30-11 (Fri-Sat 12-11 Sun 12-4) **Closed:** Sun eve, Mon **Bar Meals** L served Tue-Sat 12-2.30, Sun 12-3 D served Tue-Thu 6-9, Fri-Sat 6-9.30 **Restaurant** L served Tue-Sat 12-2.30, Sun 12-3 D served Tue-Thu 6-9, Fri-Sat 6-9.30 ⊕ FREE HOUSE ◀ Marston's Pedigree, Guest ales ☼ Thatchers Gold. ♎ 12 **Facilities** Non-diners area ♦♦ Children's menu Children's portions Play area Garden ⅋ Parking Wi-fi

EVINGTON — Map 11 SK60

The Cedars

Main St LE5 6DN ☎ 0116 273 0482
e-mail: pippa@king-henrys-taverns.co.uk
dir: *From Leicester take A6 towards Market Harborough. Left at lights, onto B667 to Evington. Pub in village centre*

'Something for everyone' menus

At The Cedars you can choose to eat in the restaurant with its panoramic windows overlooking the fountain and pond, dine alfresco in the gardens, or just enjoy a drink in the lounge bar with its leather sofas and relaxed atmosphere. The menu of freshly prepared dishes offers something for everyone – small and large appetites alike. Choose from steaks, grills and burgers, as well as traditional favourites such as fish pie, vegetarian options and international dishes like lamb rogan josh. Smaller plates include paninis, salads and jackets. For dessert, the chocolate fudge cake or pecan pie is a treat for those with a sweet tooth.

Open all day all wk 11.30-11 **Bar Meals** L served all wk 12-10 D served all wk 12-10 food served all day **Restaurant** L served all wk 12-10 D served all wk 12-10 food served all day ⊕ FREE HOUSE/KING HENRY'S TAVERNS ◀ Greene King IPA, Marston's Pedigree, Guinness. **Facilities** Non-diners area ♦♦ Children's menu Children's portions Garden Parking ▭

GRIMSTON — Map 11 SK62

The Black Horse

3 Main St LE14 3BZ ☎ 01664 812358
e-mail: amanda.wayne@sky.com
dir: *Telephone for directions*

Family pub in the countryside

The address of Amanda Sharpe's 16th-century coaching inn may well be Main Street, but Grimston's main street isn't even a B road. The pub overlooks the village green, and beyond that to the Vale of Belvoir, which locals pronounce 'Beaver', a tip that may help if ordering Belvoir Star Mild in the bar; real ales from Adnams, Marston's and St Austell should present no problem. Traditional main courses include sirloin, fillet and gammon steaks; chicken with Stilton and bacon; salmon supreme; and vegetarian specials. A daily-changing board lists fresh fish specials and more unusual dishes. The outdoor eating area is popular.

Open all wk 12-3 6-11 (Sun 12-6) **Bar Meals** L served Mon-Sat 12-2, Sun 12-3 D served Mon-Sat 6-9 **Restaurant** L served Mon-Sat 12-2, Sun 12-3 D served Mon-Sat 6-9 ⊕ FREE HOUSE ◀ Marston's Pedigree, St

Save on hotels. Book at theAA.com/hotel

LEICESTERSHIRE 275 ENGLAND

Austell Tribute, Belvoir Star Mild, Adnams, Guest ales Thatchers Gold. **Facilities** Non-diners area (Bar Garden) Children's menu Children's portions Garden

The Fox & Hounds

6 Somerby Rd LE15 8LY ☎ 01664 452129
dir: 4m from Oakham in Knossington

Cosy, inviting interior and good food

High quality food and helpful, friendly service are the hallmarks of this 500-year-old pub. Set in the village of Knossington close to Rutland Water, the building retains lots of traditional features, and the large rear garden and sitting area are ideal for alfresco summer dining. A typical lunch menu might include grilled lamb rump with ratatouille and tapenade; vegetable tart with Stilton; or salmon with roasted aubergine, red pepper and coriander salsa.

Open Tue-Fri 6-11 (Sat 6.30-11, Sun 12-4) Closed: 10 days in summer, Sun eve & Mon **Bar Meals** D served Tue-Sat 6.30-9 **Restaurant** L served Sun 12-3 D served Tue-Sat 6.30-9 ENTERPRISE INNS Fuller's London Pride. **Facilities** Non-diners area (Bar Garden Outside area) Children's portions Garden Outside area Parking Wi-fi (notice required)

The Almanack

15 Bathhouse Ln, Highcross LE1 4SA ☎ 0116 216 0705
e-mail: hello@thealmanack-leicester.co.uk
dir: In Highcross shopping centre (car parks nearby)

The talk of the town

This modern gastro-pub with dramatic floor-to-ceiling windows sits in the heart of Leicester's trendy Highcross restaurant quarter. Simultaneously hip and down-to-earth, the vintage-inspired interior features a gently curved, warm red-brick bar. Take a seat on one of the retro chairs or slide into a booth for a pint of Purity Gold or a guest ale and order from an extensive menu that includes deli boards, sandwiches and main dishes such as pan-fried Welsh sea bass with saffron potato salad and chilli, ginger and sesame sautéed pak choi; and chargrilled free-range chicken tikka skewer with chips.

Open all day all wk Closed: 25 Dec **Bar Meals** L served all wk 12-6 D served all wk 6-10 Av main course £11 food served all day **Restaurant** L served all wk 12-3 D served all wk 6-10 Fixed menu price fr £10 Av 3 course à la carte fr £21 FREE HOUSE/PEACH PUBS Purity Gold, Pure UBU, Guest ale Aspall. 16 **Facilities** Non-diners area (Bar Outside area) Children's menu Children's portions Outside area Wi-fi (notice required)

The Falcon Inn ★★★ INN

64 Main St LE12 5DG ☎ 01509 842416
e-mail: enquiries@thefalconinnlongwhatton.com
dir: Telephone for directions

Mediterranean spice in classic British pub

There's a taste of the Middle East to this traditional country inn in the shape of Lebanese-born proprietor Jad Otaki; the Mezzeh is akin to a tasting menu of some half dozen starters and four main courses. If spice is not your thing, you can plump for familiar bar meals such as home-made steak and ale pie; or salmon fillet in a cream, mushroom and seafood sauce. However, The Falcon is at heart an English pub, decked out with flower displays and hosting real ale drinkers on the striking heated rear terrace. Accommodation is available.

Open all day all wk **Bar Meals** L served Mon-Sat 12-2, Sun 12-4 D served Mon-Sat 6.30-9 **Restaurant** L served Mon-Sat 12-2, Sun 12-4 D served Mon-Sat 6.30-9 EVERARDS Tiger & Original, Guest ale. **Facilities** Non-diners area Children's portions Family room Garden Outside area Parking Wi-fi (notice required) **Rooms** 11

The Royal Oak ★★★★ INN

PICK OF THE PUBS

26 The Green LE12 5DB ☎ 01509 843694
e-mail: enquiries@theroyaloaklongwhatton.co.uk
dir: M1 junct 24, A6 to Kegworth. Right into Whatton Road (becomes Kegworth Ln) to Long Whatton. From Loughborough, A6 towards Kegworth. Left onto B5324, right into Hathern Rd leading to The Green

Stylish village inn with rooms

Ideally situated in a picturesque village close to Loughborough and East Midlands Airport, The Royal Oak is appointed to a high standard. An award-winning gastro-pub, offering high quality, locally sourced food, popular brews in the smart bar include Blue Monkey and a carefully selected wine list proffers nine by the glass. In the equally stylish restaurant diners can expect some tough decisions: will it be slow roasted belly of pork with crispy sage and onion hash, black pudding, bacon and apple boudin, cider poached pear and white onion sauce; duo of duck with parsnip dauphinoise, braised red cabbage and redcurrant reduction; or beetroot, goats' cheese and cranberry Wellington with wild mushrooms? Leave room for desserts such as chocolate and orange brownie with ice cream or Eton Mess. The impeccably furnished guest bedrooms are in a separate building.

Open all day all wk **Bar Meals** L served Mon-Sat 12-2.30, Sun 12-4 D served Mon-Sat 5.30-9.30 Av main course £11 **Restaurant** L served Mon-Sat 12-2.30, Sun 12-4 D served Mon-Sat 5.30-9.30 Fixed menu price fr £15 Av 3 course à la carte fr £25 FREE HOUSE St Austell Tribute, Bass, Blue Monkey, Sharp's Doom Bar, Guest ales Westons Old Rosie, Thatchers. 9 **Facilities** Non-diners area Children's portions Garden Beer festival Cider festival Parking Wi-fi **Rooms** 7

The Man at Arms

The Green, Bitteswell LE17 4SB ☎ 01455 552540
e-mail: pippa@king-henrys-taverns.co.uk
dir: From Lutterworth take Lutterworth Rd towards Ullesthorpe. Turn left at small white cottage. Pub on left after college on village green

Contemporary decor and hearty pub grub

Close to the market town of Lutterworth, this large village pub is named after a bequest by the Dowse Charity to the nearby village of Bitteswell in return for providing a 'man at arms' for times of war. It was the first pub bought by the King Henry's Taverns group; now, 28 years later, it has a smart, contemporary interior, all clean lines, wooden floorboards and high-backed leather seats, and shares a common menu with its sister pubs. Along with traditional favourites, there are international, fish and vegetarian dishes. Sizeable options include the Titanic challenge – a rump steak weighing some three pounds.

Open all day all wk 11.30-11 **Bar Meals** L served all wk 12-10 D served all wk 12-10 food served all day **Restaurant** L served all wk 12-10 D served all wk 12-10 food served all day FREE HOUSE/KING HENRY'S TAVERNS Greene King IPA, Wells Bombardier, Guinness, Bass. 16 **Facilities** Non-diners area Children's menu Children's portions Garden Parking

The Swan Inn

10 Loughborough Rd LE12 7AT ☎ 0116 230 2340
e-mail: danny.harwood@hotmail.com
dir: On A6 between Leicester & Loughborough

Beside the river with gardens

Originally built as two terraced cottages in 1688, this Grade II listed free house stands on the banks of the River Soar and has a secluded riverside garden, ideal for summer sipping and dining. Exposed beams, flagstone floors and roaring winter log fires characterise the cosy bar and dining areas. Fine wines and cask-conditioned beers from Theakston and Black Sheep accompany a varied, weekly-changing menu of British and European classics, as well as light lunches and snacks: salmon fillet with slow-cooked leeks in filo pastry, and duck breast with Savoy cabbage and pancetta are indicative of the standard.

Open all wk 12-2.30 5.30-11 (Fri 12-2.30 4.30-12 Sat 12-12 Sun 12-10.30) **Bar Meals** L served Mon-Sat 12-2, Sun 12-5 D served Mon-Sat 6.30-9.30 **Restaurant** L served Mon-Sat 12-2, Sun 12-5 D served Mon-Sat 6.30-9.30 FREE HOUSE Black Sheep Best Bitter, Theakston XB & Old Peculier, Morland Old Speckled Hen, Guest ales Westons Stowford Press, Guest ciders. **Facilities** Non-diners area (Bar Garden) Children's portions Garden Beer festival Parking

MOWSLEY
Map 11 SP68

The Staff of Life

PICK OF THE PUBS

Main St LE17 6NT ☎ 0116 240 2359
dir: *M1 junct 20, A4304 to Market Harborough. Left in Husbands Bosworth onto A5199. In 3m turn right to pub*

Fresh look at a charming village inn

Tucked away in the countryside, this pub has been in the same hands for over a decade and was spruced up in 2012. Were they to return, the former residents of this well-proportioned Edwardian house would surely be amazed by the transformation of their home into such an appealing community local. The bar has high-backed settles, a flagstone floor and a large woodburning stove. Look up to see not only a fine wood-panelled ceiling but also, not quite where you'd expect it, the wine cellar. In the dining area overlooking the garden, carefully prepared by dishes combine British and international influences: Peking duck pancakes could be followed by wild rabbit and prune faggots on spring onion mash. Desserts are created by Linda O'Neill, a former member of the Irish Panel of Chefs. A small patio area lies to the front with additional outside seating in the rear garden.

Open Mon-Sat 6-close (Sat 12-3 6-close Sun 12-10.30) Closed: Mon-Fri L **Bar Meals** L served Sat 12-2.15, Sun 12-3 D served Tue-Sat 6-9.15 **Restaurant** L served Sat 12-2.15, Sun 12-3 D served Tue-Sat 6-9.15 ⊕ FREE HOUSE ◀ Sharp's Doom Bar, Fuller's London Pride, Timothy Taylor. ▮ 19 **Facilities** Non-diners area ◆▮ Children's portions Garden ⊼ Parking ▭ (notice required)

OADBY
Map 11 SK60

Cow and Plough

PICK OF THE PUBS

Gartree Rd, Stoughton Farm LE2 2FB ☎ 0116 272 0852
e-mail: cowandplough@googlemail.com
dir: *From Leicester on A6 towards Oadby. Left at hospital sign at lights. At next rdbt follow Spire Hospital sign into Gartree Rd*

Former farm building famous for its pies

Housed in old Victorian farm buildings, the Cow and Plough continues to thrive, hosting functions and events including quarterly beer and cider festivals. The pub also brews its own award-winning Steamin' Billy beers, named in honour of the owners' Jack Russell terrier. The interior is decorated with historic inn signs and brewing memorabilia, providing a fascinating setting in which to enjoy food from the regularly changing menus. Typical choices include terrine of prawn and smoked salmon, or quail Scotch egg with pig's head croquettes followed by confit duck leg with celeriac pomme Anna, green beans

and red cabbage, or a vegetarian-friendly chargrilled vegetable tarte Tatin. A separate list of 'traditional dishes' offers the likes of lamb's liver and crispy bacon or a pie of the day (Thursday is pie night). Puddings continue in a traditional vein with the likes of lemon posset or baked blueberry and white chocolate cheesecake.

Open all day all wk **Bar Meals** L served Mon-Sat 12-2.30, Sun 12-5 D served Mon-Sat 6-9 Av main course £15 **Restaurant** L served Mon-Sat 12-2.30, Sun 12-5 D served Mon-Sat 6-9 Av 3 course à la carte fr £25 ⊕ FREE HOUSE ◀ Steamin' Billy Bitter & Skydiver, Fuller's London Pride, Batemans Dark Mild, Abbeydale, Belvoir ♉ Steamin' Billy Country Cider, Moonshine, Rekorderlig, Thatchers, Westons. ▮ 10 **Facilities** Non-diners area ❤ (Bar Outside area) ◆▮ Children's menu Children's portions Family room Outside area ⊼ Beer festival Parking Wi-fi ▭

SILEBY
Map 11 SK61

The White Swan

Swan St LE12 7NW ☎ 01509 814832
e-mail: tamiller56@googlemail.com
dir: *From Leicester towards Loughborough, right for Sileby; or take A46 towards Newark-on-Trent, left for Sileby*

A reputation for home-cooked food

Behind the unassuming exterior of this 1930s building, you'll find a free house of some character, with a book-lined restaurant and a homely bar with an open fire and pictures and knick-knacks adorning the walls. A wide selection of home-made rolls, baguettes and snacks is on offer; menus change weekly, and there are blackboard specials, too. Menu options might include a starter of duck and vegetable pancake rolls with hoi sin sauce; and a main of roast leg of lamb with Mediterranean vegetables. There are also fish and vegetarian dishes, such as king prawn linguine, and cheese and beetroot tartlets.

Open Tue-Sat 12-2 6-11 Sun 12-2 Closed: 27 Dec & 1 Jan, Sat L, Sun eve & Mon **Bar Meals** L served Tue-Sun 12-1.30 (ex Sat) D served Tue-Sat 7-8.30 Av main course £9 **Restaurant** L served Sun 12-1.30 D served Tue-Sat 7-8.30 Fixed menu price fr £12.50 Av 3 course à la carte fr £18 ⊕ FREE HOUSE ◀ Fuller's London Pride, Guest ales. ▮ 8 **Facilities** Non-diners area ◆▮ Children's menu Children's portions Outside area ⊼ Parking Wi-fi

SOMERBY
Map 11 SK71

Stilton Cheese Inn

High St LE14 2QB ☎ 01664 454394
web: www.stiltoncheeseinn.co.uk
dir: *From A606 between Melton Mowbray & Oakham follow signs to Pickwell & Somerby. Enter village, 1st right to centre, pub on left*

Great for real ales and whiskies

Customers say that entering this inn is like stepping back in time. An attractive 17th-century building made from mellow local sandstone, it stands in the centre of the village surrounded by beautiful countryside. Nearby is Melton Mowbray, famous for its pork pies and Stilton cheese — hence the pub's name. It enjoys a good reputation for its food, and for its great selections of real ales, wines and malt whiskies. A typical meal might include prawn cocktail followed by home-made cottage pie or other pub classics such as steak and chips or Somerby sausages with mash and onion gravy.

Open all wk 12-3 6-11 (Sun 12-3 7-11) **Bar Meals** L served all wk 12-2 D served Mon-Sat 6-9, Sun 7-9 Av main course £10 **Restaurant** L served all wk 12-2 D served Mon-Sat 6-9, Sun 7-9 ⊕ FREE HOUSE ◀ The Grainstore Ten Fifty, Brewster's Hophead, Belvoir Star, Oakham Ales JHB, Newby Wyke Kingston Topaz ♉ Westons Old Rosie & Bounds. ▮ 15 **Facilities** Non-diners area ◆▮ Children's menu Children's portions Family room Garden ⊼ Parking ▭ (notice required)

Save on hotels. Book at theAA.com/hotel

LEICESTERSHIRE 277 ENGLAND

STATHERN
Map 11 SK73

Red Lion Inn

PICK OF THE PUBS

Red Lion St LE14 4HS ☎ **01949 860868**
e-mail: info@theredlioninn.co.uk
dir: *From A1 (Grantham), A607 towards Melton, turn right in Waltham, right at next x-rds then left to Stathern*

An inn for all seasons

Located in the beautiful Vale of Belvoir, details like the flagstone bar, the elegant dining room and the comfortable lounge (complete with plenty of reading material) make this establishment stand out. The Red Lion has plenty to offer all year round: logs crackling in the stove in winter, 'country cocktails' in summer, Sunday lunches, cookery demonstrations and wine evenings. There's a great line-up of regional ales, farmhouse ciders and local fruit beers at the bar. Menus change seasonally in accordance with locally supplied produce, and offer a mix of classic pub food and innovative country cooking. Typical of chef Sean Hope's dishes are curried celeriac soup; pan-fried salmon, gnocchi, peas and mint; Marseille-style bouillabaisse; confit of duck leg, carrot, fennel, orange, star anise. Desserts reflect an attention to detail and are listed with suggested wines, ports and beers: Bakewell tart with almond cream; cappuccino mousse with Amaretto ice cream. There are good value set meals too.

Open 12-3 6-11 (Fri-Sat 12-11 Sun 12-7) Closed: Sun eve & Mon **Bar Meals** L served Tue-Sat 12-2, Sun 12-3 D served Tue-Thu 6-9, Fri 5.30-9.30, Sat 7-9.30 Av main course £15.50 **Restaurant** L served Tue-Sat 12-2, Sun 12-3 D served Tue-Thu 6-9, Fri 5.30-9.30, Sat 7-9.30 Fixed menu price fr £13.50 Av 3 course à la carte fr £28 ⊕ RUTLAND INN COMPANY LTD ◀ The Grainstore Red Lion Ale, Brewster's Marquis, Fuller's London Pride ♻ Aspall, Sheppy's. ♟ 8 **Facilities** Non-diners area ❧ (Bar Garden) ❖ Children's menu Children's portions Garden ⋔ Parking

SWITHLAND
Map 11 SK51

The Griffin Inn

174 Main St LE12 8TJ ☎ **01509 890535**
e-mail: thegriffininn@swithland.info
dir: *From A46 into Anstey. Right at rdbt to Cropston. Right at x-rds, 1st left, 0.5m to Swithland. Follow brown signs for inn*

Unpretentious food in a traditional walker's inn

Parts of this welcoming, traditional, family-run country inn date back to the 15th century. There are three cosy bar areas serving a range of real ales, two dining rooms, a skittle alley and large patio. Menus and a wide range of specials offer unfussy, good-value food including baked camembert, toasted onion bread and red onion chutney, pan-fried sea bass fillets, sautéed potatoes and steamed seasonal vegetables or smoked paprika, rocket and chorizo risotto. The area is popular with walkers heading for Swithland Woods, Beacon Hill and the Old John folly. There's also a steam railway nearby.

Open all day all wk **Bar Meals** L served Mon-Thu 12-2, Fri-Sun 12-9 D served Mon-Thu 6-9, Fri-Sun 12-9 Av main course £13 **Restaurant** L served Mon-Thu 12-2, Fri-Sun 12-9 D served Mon-Thu 6-9, Fri-Sun 12-9 ⊕ EVERARDS ◀ Adnams Southwold Bitter, 2 Guest ales ♻ Symonds, Local Cider, Guest Cider. ♟ 9 **Facilities** Non-diners area ❖ Children's portions Garden Parking Wi-fi ▭

THORPE LANGTON
Map 11 SP79

The Bakers Arms

Main St LE16 7TS ☎ **01858 545201**
dir: *Take A6 S from Leicester then left signed 'The Langtons', at rail bridge continue to x-rds. Straight on to Thorpe Langton. Pub on left*

Intimate thatched pub with great fish nights

A pretty thatched pub set in an equally pretty village, the Bakers Arms has the requisite low beams, rug-strewn quarry-tiled floors, large pine tables and open fires. Its weekly-changing menu of modern pub food has gained it a keen local following. Expect dishes like pan-fried scallops with Clonakilty black pudding and orange sauce; confit of duck with red pepper and ginger marmalade; and crêpes with apple and cinnamon. Fish lovers should be sure to visit on a Thursday, when fish specials might include hake with asparagus cream sauce. The area is popular with walkers, riders and mountain bikers.

Open 6.30-11 (Sat 12-2.30 6.30-11 Sun 12-2.30) Closed: 1-7 Jan, Sun eve, Mon **Restaurant** L served Sat-Sun 12-2.30 D served Tue-Sat 6.30-9.15 ⊕ FREE HOUSE ◀ Langton Bakers Dozen Bitter. ♟ 9 **Facilities** Non-diners area Garden ⋔ Parking Wi-fi

WELHAM
Map 11 SP79

The Old Red Lion

Main St LE16 7UJ ☎ **01858 565253**
e-mail: pippa@king-henrys-taverns.co.uk
dir: *NE of Market Harborough take B664 to Weston by Welland. Left to Welham*

Tranquil setting in rolling countryside

The airy, split-level, contemporary interior of today's pub blends well with vestiges of its origins as a coaching inn. Polished floorboards, leather seating and open fire are a welcome retreat for ramblers drifting in from the area's popular walking routes. Views from the windows stretch across this rural corner of Leicestershire where the River Welland meanders through rich pastureland. One of a small chain of local dining pubs; the menu covers all bases, from British classics such as steak and ale pie to a select choice of international dishes, with vegetarian options including mushroom, cranberry and brie Wellington. Beers include Marston's Pedigree.

Open all day all wk 11.30-11 **Bar Meals** L served all wk 12-10 D served all wk 12-10 food served all day **Restaurant** L served all wk 12-10 D served all wk 12-10 food served all day ⊕ FREE HOUSE/KING HENRY'S TAVERNS ◀ Greene King IPA, Marston's Pedigree, Guinness. ♟ 15 **Facilities** Non-diners area ❖ Children's menu Children's portions Outside area ⋔ Parking Wi-fi ▭

WOODHOUSE EAVES
Map 11 SK51

The Wheatsheaf Inn ★★★★ INN

Brand Hill LE12 8SS ☎ **01509 890320**
e-mail: richard@wheatsheafinn.net
dir: *M1 junct 22, follow Quorn signs*

Old village inn at heart of Charnwood Forest

A rambling, creeper dressed stone inn (it was a quarrymen's watering hole 200 years ago) with contemporary bed and breakfast accommodation, a comfortably traditional bar and 'Mess' dining area based on RAF connections. Charnwood Forest's stirring countryside is all around and the Great Central Railway (steam) is close-by. Explorers may choose to sit in the flowery courtyard garden, indulging in Timothy Taylor Landlord bitter and select from an ever-changing menu; smoked haddock cooked in white wine, cream and tomatoes or perhaps a risotto of wild mushrooms. There's a decent list of wines to accompany.

Open all wk Closed: Sun eve in winter **Bar Meals** L served Mon-Fri 12-2.30, Sat 12-2.30, Sun 12-3.30 D served Mon-Sat 6.30-9.15 Av main course £11 **Restaurant** L served Mon-Fri 12-2.30, Sat 12-2.30, Sun 12-3.30 D served Mon-Sat 6.30-9.15 ⊕ FREE HOUSE ◀ Greene King Abbot Ale, Timothy Taylor Landlord, Adnams Broadside, Tetley's Smoothflow, Marston's Pedigree, Guest ale. ♟ 16 **Facilities** Non-diners area ❧ (Bar Garden) ❖ Children's menu Children's portions Garden ⋔ Parking Wi-fi ▭ (notice required) **Rooms** 2

WYMESWOLD
Map 11 SK62

The Windmill Inn NEW

83 Brook St LE12 6TT ☎ 01509 881313
e-mail: info@thewindmillwymeswold.com
dir: *From A46 N of Six Hills left onto A606 signed Wymeswold. In village left into Church Ln, left into Brook St. Or from M1 junct 24, A6 signed Loughborough & Kegworth, A6006 to Wymeswold*

Spruced up local that loves families

Rescued and revived by the team behind the successful Curzon Arms in Woodhouse Eaves, the Windmill once again thrives as a village local. Expect a fresh, contemporary feel to the rambling bar and dining areas, with wood or stone tiled floors, wood-burning stoves, warm Farrow & Ball hues, and comfortable seating setting the informal scene. Monthly menus combine pub classics and grills with modern British dishes, perhaps mussels, leek and bacon broth followed by thyme-roasted chicken with garlic crushed potatoes and lemon sauce, and rhubarb crumble. Dogs and children (toy box in evidence) are really welcome here and there's a gorgeous garden for summer dining.

Open all wk 12-3 5-12 (Sat-Sun 12-11) **Bar Meals** L served Mon-Fri 12-2.30, Sat-Sun 12-5 D served Mon-Fri 5.30-9.30 Av main course £12 **Restaurant** L served Mon-Fri 12-2.30, Sat-Sun 12-5 D served Mon-Sat 5.30-9.30 Fixed menu price fr £12.50 Av 3 course à la carte fr £25 ⊕ FREE HOUSE ◀ Sharp's Doom Bar, Castle Rock Harvest Pale Ở Symonds. ♀ **Facilities** Non-diners area ♣ (Bar Garden Outside area) ♦♦ Children's menu Children's portions Family room Garden Outside area ⌒ Parking Wi-fi

WYMONDHAM
Map 11 SK81

The Berkeley Arms NEW

59 Main St LE14 2AG ☎ 01572 787587
e-mail: info@theberkeleyarms.co.uk
dir: *In town centre*

Locally sourced, freshly prepared meals and fine wines

Having fulfilled their long-held ambition to own a pub, Neil and Louise Hitchen have, in three short years, seen the appealing, stone-built Berkeley Arms go from strength to strength. Food is fresh and locally sourced, with a daily-changing carte, and bar, set lunch and dinner menus. Look for whole roasted partridge; fillet of cod with crab and herb crust; steak, kidney and ale pie; and Hambleton Bakery campanelle pasta with wild mushrooms. Rabbit, muntjac deer and pigeon also appear on the menu from time to time. Traditional two- and three- course lunches are served on Sundays.

Open 12-3 6-11 (Sun 12-5) Closed: 1st 2wks Jan & 1wk summer, Sun eve & Mon **Bar Meals** L served Tue-Sat 12-2 D served Tue-Sat 6.30-9.30 Av main course £10-£23 **Restaurant** L served Tue-Sat 12-2, Sun 12-3 D served Tue-Sat 6.30-9.30 Fixed menu price fr £18.95 Av 3 course à la carte fr £29.90 ⊕ FREE HOUSE ◀ Greene King IPA, Marston's Pedigree Ở Addlestones. ♀ 10 **Facilities** Non-diners area ♣ (Bar Garden) ♦♦ Children's portions Garden ⌒ Parking

LINCOLNSHIRE

ASWARBY
Map 12 TF03

The Tally Ho Inn

NG34 8SA ☎ 01529 455170
e-mail: info@thetallyhoinn.com
dir: *3m S of Sleaford on A15 towards Bourne & Peterborough*

Striking inn deep in the country

Set between fens and the rolling south Lincolnshire hills, this sturdy, gabled pub began life as a farmhouse on the country estate of Aswarby Hall, which surrounds the building; the old English garden, rambling amidst fruit trees, enjoys views across the landscaped parkland. Among sturdy pillars, beams and exposed stonework, dine in style on freshly prepared modern British dishes created by chef-proprietor John Blenkiron. Enticing small-plate starters feature pan-roasted scallops with peas, mint and crispy Serrano, setting the scene for braised lamb shank in Chianti. On the August Bank Holiday, the pub holds a family fun day with real ales, hog roast and live music.

Open 12-2.30 6-11 (Sun 12-3) Closed: Sun eve & Mon **Bar Meals** L served Tue-Sat 12-2, Sun 12-2.30 D served Tue-Thu 6-9, Fri-Sat 6-9.30 Av main course £14.50 **Restaurant** L served Tue-Sat 12-2, Sun 12-2.30 D served Tue-Thu 6-9, Fri-Sat 6-9.30 Fixed menu price fr £8.50 Av 3 course à la carte fr £42.50 ⊕ FREE HOUSE ◀ Timothy Taylor Landlord, Greene King Abbot Ale, Guest ales Ở Westons Wyld Wood Organic. **Facilities** Non-diners area ♦♦ Children's menu Children's portions Garden ⌒ Beer festival Parking Wi-fi ➡ (notice required)

BARNOLDBY LE BECK
Map 17 TA20

The Ship Inn

Main Rd DN37 0BG ☎ 01472 822308
e-mail: the_ship_inn@btinternet.com
dir: *M180 junct 5, A18 past Humberside Airport. At Laceby Junction rdbt (A18 & A46) straight over follow Skegness/Boston signs. Approx 2m turn left signed Waltham & Barnoldby le Beck*

Traditional village pub with coal fires and great seafood

Set in a picturesque village on the edge of the Lincolnshire Wolds, this 300-year-old inn has always attracted an interesting mix of customers, from Grimsby's seafarers to aviators from the county's World War II airstrips. The bar is filled with maritime bric-à-brac and serves a grand choice of ales such as Black Sheep or Tom Wood's, and there's also a beautiful garden. Seafood is a speciality so tuck into pan-fried cod cheeks with pea purée and chorizo, and then whole salt crusted sea bass, coriander and chilli rice and stir-fried vegetables.

Open 12-3 6-11 (Fri-Sat 12-3 6-12 Sun 12-5) Closed: 25 Dec, Sun eve **Bar Meals** L served Mon-Sat 12-2, Sun 12-5 D served Mon-Sat 6-9 **Restaurant** L served Mon-Sat 12-2, Sun 12-5 D served Mon-Sat 6-9 ⊕ FREE HOUSE/ INNOVATIVE SIGHT LTD ◀ Black Sheep Best Bitter, Tom

Wood's, Guinness Ở Thatchers Gold. ♀ 9 **Facilities** Non-diners area ♦♦ Children's portions Garden ⌒ Parking Wi-fi ➡ (notice required)

BELCHFORD
Map 17 TF27

The Blue Bell Inn

1 Main Rd LN9 6LQ ☎ 01507 533602
e-mail: bluebellbelchford@gmail.com
dir: *Off A153 between Horncastle & Louth*

Family-run traditional country free house

On the Viking Way, in the heart of the Lincolnshire Wolds, this pub attracts regular diners from as far away as Boston, Grimsby and Skegness. Locals come too, of course, to enjoy locally sourced, home-made food such as corn-fed chicken breast with roasted squash and creamed sweetcorn; wild fallow venison and red wine pie; steaks with onion rings, chips, tomatoes and mushrooms; and twice-baked Stilton cheese soufflé with Waldorf salad. Anyone just wanting a drink is welcome to settle into an armchair with a pint of Batemans XXXB, or a glass of French or New World wine.

Open all wk 11.30-2.30 6.30-11 Closed: 2nd & 3rd wk Jan **Bar Meals** L served all wk 12-2 D served all wk 6.30-9 **Restaurant** L served all wk 12-2 D served all wk 6.30-9 ⊕ FREE HOUSE ◀ Batemans XXXB, Greene King IPA, Guest ale. **Facilities** Non-diners area ♦♦ Children's menu Children's portions Garden ⌒ Parking Wi-fi

BOURNE
Map 12 TF02

The Wishing Well Inn

Main St, Dyke PE10 0AF ☎ 01778 422970
e-mail: wishingwell@hotmail.com
dir: *Take A15 towards Sleaford. Inn in next village*

Black and white timbered village pub

This Lincolnshire village free house started life in 1879 as a one-room pub called the Crown. Several extensions have since been sympathetically executed with recycled stone and timbers; the well that gives the pub its name, previously in the garden, is now a feature of the smaller dining room. Loyal customers return again and again to enjoy a comprehensive menu of traditional favourites in the warm and welcoming atmosphere. Outside, an attractive beer garden backs onto the children's play area, and there is a beer festival over the August Bank Holiday weekend.

Open all wk 11-3 5-11 (Fri-Sat 11am-mdnt Sun & summer all wk 11-11) **Bar Meals** L served Mon-Thu 12-2, Fri-Sun 12-9 D served Mon-Thu 5.30-9, Fri-Sun 12-9 ⊕ FREE HOUSE ◀ Greene King Abbot Ale, Greene King IPA, Shepherd Neame Spitfire, 3 Guest ales. **Facilities** Non-diners area ♦♦ Children's menu Children's portions Play area Garden ⌒ Beer festival Parking Wi-fi ➡ (notice required)

The Goat

155 Spalding Road, Deeping St James, Frognall PE6 8SA • Tel: 01778 347629
Website: www.thegoatfrognall.com • **Email:** Debbiestokes@thegoatfrognall.com

Located just outside of the growing village of Frognall, and set in countryside, this 17th-century free house has bags of traditional charm. There are wooden beams accompanied by historical artifacts and photographs, as well as an open fire and wood burner making it the perfect place to relax. After 10 years of hard work, Graham and Debbie, as well as their friendly staff pride themselves in providing a warm welcome to both locals and visitors.

The bar hosts a selection of drinks suitable for everyone, from cold lager and bottled ciders to a large selection of soft drinks. In addition we hold an ever-changing selection of award winning real ales and a large selection of Malt Whiskeys. Breweries often featured include: Batemans, Hopshackle, Elland, St Austel, Oakham ales and The Grainstore Brewery. The Pub is known by many for its range and care of strong ales and won a CAMRA award for this. Hosting an annual beer festival in the summer in our large beer garden with over 20 real ales and ciders *The Goat* attracts visitor from all over the county.

Our Food offering focuses on using fresh local produce to create traditional dishes. Seasonal Menu's and a range of specials, by our Head Chef, are created using locally sourced meat and products, and dishes can be adapted to specific dietary requirements.

Dishes range from starters of Garlic Bread and Breaded Brie wedges, and sharers such as Nachos. Main courses include traditional dishes such as Home Battered Fish & Chips, Pan Fried Rutland Water Trout and a fine selection of Homemade Burgers and Pies made using 100% beef.

The finishing touches are the desserts, featuring dishes such as Homemade Chocolate Brownie, Homemade Bread and Butter pudding and the decadent Goat To Share.

There is a Children's menu available, and family's are catered for, with a designated family area overlooking the spacious beer garden and children's play areas.

Bespoke menus are also available for private parties and can include buffets or bespoke menus. Booking for meals may be required.

CONINGSBY
Map 17 TF25

The Lea Gate Inn

Leagate Rd LN4 4RS ☎ 01526 342370
e-mail: theleagateinn@hotmail.com
dir: *Off B1192 just outside Coningsby*

The oldest licensed premises in the county

Dating from 1542, this was the last of the Fen Guide Houses that provided shelter before the treacherous marshes were drained. Among the oak-beamed pub's features are a priest's hole, low ceilings, a very old inglenook fireplace, extensive gardens and a yew tree dating from the 1600s. The same family have been running the pub since 1983 and they source their produce locally (including game in season). All food is home made, and dishes on the seasonal menu could include wild rabbit shortcrust pie, aubergine and courgette moussaka, pan-fried lemon sole, and beef Wellington.

Open all wk 11.30-3 6-11 (Sun 12-10.30) **Bar Meals** L served Mon-Sat 11.45-2, Sun 12-9 D served Mon-Sat 6-9 Av main course £8.95 **Restaurant** L served Mon-Sat 11.45-2, Sun 12-9 D served Mon-Sat 6-9 ⊕ FREE HOUSE ◀ Wells Bombardier, Black Sheep, Guest ales ♉ Thatchers Gold. ♟ **Facilities** Non-diners area ♣ (Bar Garden) ♦♦ Children's menu Children's portions Play area Garden ♬ Parking Wi-fi ▭

DRY DODDINGTON
Map 11 SK84

Wheatsheaf Inn

NG23 5HU ☎ 01400 281458
e-mail: wheatsheafdrydoddington@hotmail.co.uk
web: www.wheatsheaf-pub.co.uk
dir: *From A1 between Newark-on-Trent & Grantham. Turn into Doddington Ln for Dry Doddington*

Village inn with a good selection of ales on tap

The church, with its leaning tower, faces this pantile-roofed inn across the village green. No one's sure of the inn's age, but they can date the pre-Jurassic era stones used to build it as 200 million years old! Abbot, Batemans XB and Timothy Taylor Landlord are the regular real ales, with Lincolnshire easily the biggest contributor of produce on the menus. Enjoy a starter of pea, mint and crème fraîche risotto, followed by slow-braised shoulder of lamb; fish of the day; or honey-roasted pepper and goats' cheese tart, in the bar, restaurant or sheltered garden.

Open 12-3 5-11 (Sat-Sun 12-11) Closed: Mon **Bar Meals** L served Tue-Fri 12-2, Sat 12-2.30, Sun 12-3

FROGNALL
Map 12 TF11

The Goat

155 Spalding Rd PE6 8SA ☎ 01778 347629
e-mail: debbiestokes@thegoatfrognall.com
web: www.thegoatfrognall.com
dir: *A1 to Peterborough, A15 to Market Deeping, old A16 to Spalding, pub approx 1.5m from A15 & A16 junct*

Traditional country pub with guest ales and an extensive menu

With five different guest ales every week, beer and cider is taken seriously here and you might want to time a visit for the June beer festival. Families are equally welcome at this friendly country free house, which has an open fire, a large conservatory with its own courtyard and a child-friendly garden. The extensive menu has broad appeal and main courses include lamb and mint pie; beef in red wine; mushroom and pepper curry; and home-cooked ham salad.

Open all wk Mon-Thu 12-3 6-11.30 (Fri-Sat 12-11.30 Sun 12-11) Closed: 25 Dec, 1 Jan **Bar Meals** L served Mon-Thu 12-2, Fri-Sat 12-9.30, Sun 12-9 D served Mon-Thu 6.30-9.30, Fri-Sat 12-9.30, Sun 12-9 Av main course £9.95 **Restaurant** L served Mon-Thu 12-2, Fri-Sat 12-9.30, Sun 12-9 D served Mon-Thu 6.30-9.30, Fri-Sat 12-9.30, Sun 12-9 ⊕ FREE HOUSE ◀ Guest ales from

D served Tue-Fri 6-9, Sat 6-9.30 **Restaurant** L served Tue-Fri 12-2, Sat 12-2.30, Sun 12-3 D served Tue-Fri 6-9, Sat 6-9.30 ⊕ FREE HOUSE ◀ Timothy Taylor Landlord, Greene King Abbot Ale, Batemans XB ♉ Hogan's. ♟ 12 **Facilities** Non-diners area ♣ (Bar Garden) ♦♦ Children's menu Children's portions Garden ♬ Parking Wi-fi ▭ (notice required)

Elgood's, Batemans, Abbeydale, Nethergate, Hopshackle ♉ Westons Old Rosie, Moonshine, Thatchers Cheddar Valley. **Facilities** Non-diners area ♦♦ Children's menu Children's portions Play area Family room Garden ♬ Beer festival Parking ▭ (notice required)

See advert on page 279

FULBECK
Map 17 SK95

The Hare & Hounds NEW

The Green NG32 3JJ ☎ 01400 273322
e-mail: armsinn@yahoo.co.uk
dir: *On A607, N of Grantham*

Village pub with imaginative food

Overlooking an attractive village green, this is a 17th-century, Grade II listed pub where a log fire does the business in winter; on warmer days, an outside eating area awaits. The beer pumps in the bar announce Jennings Cumberland and a couple from the Marston's stable. The chef and his team work with only the best locally sourced ingredients, producing a typical three-course dinner of curried smoked haddock risotto with poached egg and crispy pancetta; breast of chicken with pan haggerty, green beans and wild mushroom sauce; and Baileys crème brûlée. Pub classics include Lincolnshire sausages with mash and onion gravy; and barbecued sticky ribs.

Open 12-2 5.30-11 (Sun 12-4) Closed: Sun eve **Bar Meals** L served Mon-Sat 12-2, Sun 12-3 D served Mon-Sat 6-9 **Restaurant** L served Mon-Sat 12-2, Sun 12-3 D served Mon-Sat 6-9 ◀ Jennings Cumberland Ale, Marston's Pedigree. ♟ 11 **Facilities** Non-diners area ♦♦ Children's menu Children's portions Family room Garden ♬ Parking Wi-fi

Save on hotels. Book at theAA.com/hotel

LINCOLNSHIRE 281 ENGLAND

GOSBERTON — Map 12 TF23

The Black Horse

66 Siltside, Gosberton Risegate PE11 4ET
☎ **01775 840995**
dir: *From Spalding take A16 towards Boston. Left onto A152. At Gosberton take B1397 to Gosberton Risegate. Pub set back from road*

Fenland local championing local food

Tucked away in a village amidst the Fens outside Spalding, this lovely creeper-clad pub is a showcase for Lincolnshire's wealth of food producers. Huddle up to the woodburning stove or catch the summer rays in the beer garden, sipping Black Sheep or Fuller's London Pride. The menu changes fortnightly and has Italian and Asian influences. Tuck into chicken liver pâté with caramelised onions; braised lamb shank with tomato and rosemary sauce; beer battered haddock and chips; and rib-eye steak with hand-cut chips and all the trimmings. Finish with rhubarb crumble and custard.

Open Tue-Thu 5.30-10.30 (Fri-Sat 12-11 Sun 12-10.30) Closed: Mon **Bar Meals** L served Fri-Sun 12-6 **Restaurant** L served Sun 12-6 D served Tue-Sat 6-9 ⊕ FREE HOUSE ◾ Black Sheep, Fuller's London Pride. **Facilities** Non-diners area ❀ (Bar Garden) ♦ Children's portions Garden ᗍ Parking Wi-fi 🚐

HOUGH-ON-THE-HILL — Map 11 SK94

The Brownlow Arms ★★★★★ INN ◉

High Rd NG32 2AZ ☎ **01400 250234**
e-mail: armsinn@yahoo.co.uk
dir: *Take A607 (Grantham to Sleaford road). Hough-on-the-Hill signed from Barkston*

Well-groomed inn featuring a landscaped terrace

At the heart of a pretty village, this 17th-century stone inn is named after former owner Lord Brownlow and it still has the look of a welcoming country house. In the convivial bar, enjoy a pint of Black Sheep as you make your menu choices. The modern, AA-Rosette dishes include a starter of beer-battered tiger prawns in a lime, chilli and coriander dressing, which might be followed by Barbary duck breast, petit pois, buttered mash and Madeira jus. Leave room for the individual cherry frangipane tart. The landscaped terrace encourages alfresco dining. Only children over eight years are accepted.

Open Tue-Sat 6pm-11pm, Sun L Closed: 25-27 Dec, 31 Dec-1 Jan, Mon, Sun eve **Restaurant** L served Sun 12-2.30 D served Tue-Sat 6.30-9 ⊕ FREE HOUSE ◾ Timothy Taylor Landlord, Black Sheep. ♏ 10 **Facilities** Non-diners area Garden ᗍ Parking Wi-fi **Rooms** 6

INGHAM — Map 17 SK98

Inn on the Green

34 The Green LN1 2XT ☎ **01522 730354**
web: www.innonthegreeningham.co.uk
dir: *From Lincoln take A15 signed Scunthorpe. Left into Ingham Ln signed Ingham, Cammeringham. Right onto B1398 (Middle St), left to Ingham*

Village pub offering some excellent pub food

Its name neatly summarises the position of this charming, ever popular Grade II listed country pub/restaurant. In addition to the choice of real ales, seasonal dishes using local produce are served throughout the pub's three bars — cosy entrance bar with sofas, front bar with roaring log fire, and another one upstairs; restaurant seating is at the rear on the ground and first floors. Staples include chicken liver pâté with homemade red onion marmalade. Daily-changing specials range from potted local rabbit with poached rhubarb and cider jelly to seared Atlantic halibut. Super desserts, all home made, and a range of vegetarian options complete the picture. Booking for meals is recommended.

Open 11.30-3 6-11 (Sat 11.30-11 Sun 12-10.30) (Sat 11.30-3 6-11 in winter) Closed: Mon **Bar Meals** L served Wed-Sat 12-2, Sun 12-4 D served Tue-Sat 6-9 **Restaurant** L served Wed-Sat 12-2, Sun 12-4 D served Tue-Sat 6-9 ⊕ FREE HOUSE ◾ Batemans XB, Black Sheep, Adnams Ỏ Westons Stowford Press. ♏ 9 **Facilities** Non-diners area ♦ Children's portions Garden ᗍ Parking 🚐 (notice required)

KIRKBY LA THORPE — Map 12 TF04

Queens Head

Church Ln NG34 9NU ☎ **01529 305743 & 307194**
e-mail: clrjcc@aol.com
web: www.thequeensheadinn.com
dir: *Pub signed from A17 (dual carriageway)*

Offering ales brewed in a windmill

Heavy beams, open log fires, antique furnishings and original watercolours - this destination dining pub ticks all the boxes when it comes to original features and traditional character. The French-trained chef-proprietor prepares everything on site, from breads to desserts, and local ingredients get star billing on the extensive seasonal menus. A smoked duck, chicken and avocado salad might make way for grilled sea bass or three nut, parsnip and sweet potato cakes. Wash it down with Lincolnshire ales from the 8 Sail Brewery, brewed in Heckington Windmill, or wines from a well-considered list.

Open all wk 12-3 6-11 (Sun 12-11) **Bar Meals** L served Mon-Sat 12-2.30, Sun 12-8.30 D served Mon-Fri 6-9.30, Sat 6-10, Sun 12-8.30 Av main course £8.95 **Restaurant** L served Mon-Sat 12-2.30, Sun 12-8.30 D served Mon-Fri 6-9.30, Sat 6-10, Sun 12-8.30 Fixed menu price fr £13.95 Av 3 course à la carte fr £25 ⊕ FREE HOUSE ◾ Batemans XB, 8 Sail Brewery, Guest ales. ♏ 9 **Facilities** Non-diners area ♦ Children's menu Children's portions Outside area ᗍ Parking Wi-fi 🚐 (notice required)

See advert on page 282

KIRTON IN LINDSEY — Map 17 SK99

The George

20 High St DN21 4LX ☎ **01652 640600**
e-mail: enquiry@thegeorgekirton.co.uk
dir: *From A15 take B1205, turn right onto B1400*

Country inn near Ermine Street

Lincoln and the Wolds are within easy reach of this extensively restored yet traditional pub. The 18th-century former coaching inn serves locally brewed Batemans ales and seasonally changing menus. Customers can dine in the comfortable bar area or in the informal restaurant. Favourite starters such as prawn cocktail, and bar meals such as lasagne with salad and hand-cut chips, are topped by regularly changing specials such as chicken schnitzel with a brandy and mushroom sauce; and game and blackcurrant pie.

Open all wk 5-11 (Sun 12-2.30) **Bar Meals** Av main course £5.95 **Restaurant** Fixed menu price fr £10.95
⊕ FREE HOUSE ◀ Batemans XB.
Facilities Non-diners area ♦ Children's menu Children's portions Play area Garden 🚍

LINCOLN — Map 17 SK97

Pyewipe Inn

Fossebank, Saxilby Rd LN1 2BG ☎ **01522 528708**
e-mail: enquiries@pyewipe.co.uk
dir: *From Lincoln on A57 past Lincoln/A46 Bypass, pub signed in 0.5m*

Waterside inn with home-made food

There's a great view of nearby Lincoln Cathedral from the grounds of this waterside inn, which takes its name from the local dialect for lapwing. Set in four wooded acres beside the Roman-built Fossedyke Navigation, it serves real ales and home-made, locally sourced food. Expect dishes such as partridge and black pudding stack with a red wine sauce; pork belly with a cider and grain mustard sauce and mash; or loin of cod poached in Thai broth with noodles and stir-fried vegetables. There is a beer garden and riverside patio where you can enjoy your meal and a cold beer.

Open all day all wk 11-11 ⊕ FREE HOUSE ◀ Guest ales.
Facilities ♦ Children's portions Garden Parking Wi-fi

The Victoria

6 Union Rd LN1 3BJ ☎ **01522 541000**
e-mail: jonathanjpc@aol.com
dir: *From city outskirts follow signs for Cathedral Quarter. Pub 2 mins' walk from all major up-hill car parks. Adjacent to West Gate of Lincoln Castle*

Good real ales in the city

Situated right next to the West Gate entrance of the castle and a short stroll from Lincoln Cathedral, a long-standing drinkers' pub with a range of real ales, including six changing guest beers, ciders and perries. As well as the fantastic views of the castle, the pub also offers great meals made from home-prepared food including hot baguettes and filled bacon rolls, Saturday breakfasts and Sunday lunches. House specials include sausage and mash, various pies, chilli con carne and home-made lasagne. Facilities include a large beer garden with children's play area. There are Halloween and winter beer festivals.

Open all day all wk 11am-mdnt (Fri-Sat 11am-1am Sun 12-12) **Bar Meals** L served all wk 12-2.30 Av main course £6.95 ⊕ BATEMANS ◀ XB, Timothy Taylor Landlord, Castle Rock Harvest Pale, Guest ales ♂ Westons.
Facilities Non-diners area ❤ (Bar Garden) ♦ Children's portions Play area Garden 🎋 Beer festival Wi-fi 🚍 (notice required)

The Queens Head

Kirkby La Thorpe, Sleaford, Lincolnshire NG34 9NU
Tel: 01529 305743 or 01529 307194 • Website: www.thequeensheadinn.com

John and Paul, proprietors for over 16 years, are delighted to welcome you to the Queens Head, Kirkby-La-Thorpe, one of Lincolnshire's finest traditional dining experiences.

Visitors to the Queens Head will experience the best in traditional English cuisine with a touch of modern flair and local theme. We offer local cask conditioned ales, a comprehensive wine list and many other drinks all set in luxurious informal surroundings.

We pride ourselves on the fact that all produce is sourced locally guaranteeing freshness, variety and choice. All food is homemade on the premises including many different types of bread, succulent sweets and with a fresh fish, meat & vegetable delivery every day.

We also have a large covered patio area which on a hot summer night is the perfect place for some alfresco dining under the stars or just to relax and have a drink with your friends.

We strongly advise that you pre-book your table (evenings in particular) as we do get very busy and don't like to disappoint customers.

We hope that every visit will be a pleasant surprise & look forward to welcoming you very soon!

Open Monday- Friday 12pm- 3pm & 6pm-11pm (Last meals served at 2.30pm & 9.30pm)

Saturday & Sundays Open all day from12noon (Meals served all day)

Save on hotels. Book at theAA.com/hotel

LINCOLNSHIRE 283 ENGLAND

Wig & Mitre

32 Steep Hill LN2 1LU ☎ 01522 535190
e-mail: email@wigandmitre.com
dir: *At top of Steep Hill, adjacent to cathedral & Lincoln Castle car parks*

Old fashioned values and contemporary cuisine

Ideally located between the castle and the cathedral in the upper part of the medieval city, the Wig & Mitre is a mix of architectural styles from the 14th century onwards. Owned and operated by the Hope family since 1977 (who also own Caunton Beck, Caunton, Nottinghamshire; see entry), it's a music-free zone: instead you'll find a reading room and, since it's not tied to a brewery, real ales from Batemans, Black Sheep and Young's. Food includes English breakfasts served until noon, all-day hot and cold sandwiches, and light meals. Turning to the main menu, you might start with smoked trout and horseradish pâté; then spiced fillet of salmon with couscous, tempura spring onions and coriander crème fraîche; or fillet steak, goose fat fondant potato, field mushroom, slow-roast tomato and sauce diablo. Under 'puds' the menu lists steamed butterscotch pudding and dark chocolate torte. Popular gourmet food and wine evenings are held regularly (booking essential).

Open all day all wk 8.30am-mdnt **Bar Meals** L served all wk 8.30am-10pm D served all wk 8.30am-10pm Av main course £10.50-£20 food served all day **Restaurant** L served all wk 8.30am-10pm D served all wk 8.30am-10pm Av 3 course à la carte fr £20 food served all day ⊕ FREE HOUSE ◀ Batemans XB, Young's London Gold, Black Sheep. ♥ 24 **Facilities** Non-diners area ♣ (Bar) ♦♦ Children's menu Children's portions

The Willoughby Arms

Station Rd NG33 4RA ☎ 01780 410276
e-mail: info@willoughbyarms.co.uk
dir: *B6121 (Stamford to Bourne road), at junct follow signs to Careby/Little Bytham, inn 5m on right*

Former railway property now a traditional inn

This beamed, traditional stone country inn started life as the booking office and waiting room for Lord Willoughby's private railway line. These days it has a fresher look whilst retaining its traditional charms. Expect a good selection of real ales - including several from local microbreweries - with great, home-cooked food available every lunchtime and evening. Dishes range from sirloin steak topped with a Diane sauce to chargrilled tuna steak with lemon butter. As well as a cosy bar with open fire, and a light and airy sun lounge, there is also a large beer garden with stunning views to enjoy on warmer days. August Bank Holiday beer festival.

Open all day all wk 12-11 **Bar Meals** L served Mon-Sat 12-2, Sun 12-3 D served all wk 6-9 Av main course £8.50 ⊕ FREE HOUSE ◀ Hopshackle Simmarillo, Abbeydale

Absolution ♂ Bristol Port, Broadoak Kingston Black. ♥ 10 **Facilities** Non-diners area ♣ (Bar Garden) ♦♦ Children's menu Children's portions Garden ♫ Beer festival Parking Wi-fi ▭ (notice required)

Red Lion Inn

PE23 4PG ☎ 01790 752271
e-mail: enquiries@redlioninnpartney.co.uk
dir: *On A16 from Boston, or A158 from Horncastle*

Sound reputation for good, home-cooked food

Here is a welcoming village inn especially to walkers and cyclists due to its location, just below the Lincolnshire Wolds; many inevitably more than ready for pint of Black Sheep, a draught of Westons 1st Quality cider, or a glass of chilled wine. The pub's solid reputation for home-cooked food can be attributed to dishes such as sweet and sour chicken with rice; moussaka; pheasant, venison and rabbit pie; cod and prawns in cheese sauce; and vegetable chilli. A formidable selection of desserts includes puddings, sponges, sundaes and tarts.

Open 12-2 6-11 (Sun 12-2 6-10.30) Closed: Mon **Bar Meals** L served Tue-Sun 12-2 D served Tue-Sun 6-9 **Restaurant** L served Tue-Sun 12-2 D served Tue-Sun 6-9 ⊕ FREE HOUSE ◀ Black Sheep, Guinness, Tetley's, Guest ales ♂ Westons 1st Quality. **Facilities** Non-diners area ♦♦ Children's portions Parking Wi-fi ▭ (notice required)

Red Lion Inn

PE23 4DS ☎ 01790 753727
dir: *A158 from Horncastle, through Hagworthingham, right at top of hill signed Raithby*

Quiet village setting, cosy in winter, garden in summer

This traditional beamed village pub, parts of which date back 300 years, is situated on the edge of the Lincolnshire Wolds, a great place for walking and cycling. Inside is a wealth of character with log fires providing a warm welcome in winter. Dine in one of the four bars or on the comfort of the restaurant. A varied menu of home-made dishes is prepared using fresh local produce - sea bass with stir-fried vegetables; roast guinea fowl with tomato, garlic and bacon; and medallions of beef with peppercorn sauce. Meals can be taken in the garden in the warmer months.

Open 12-2 6-11 (Mon 7-11) Closed: Mon L **Bar Meals** L served Tue-Sun 12-2 D served Tue-Sat 7-8.30 **Restaurant** L served Tue-Sun 12-2 D served Tue-Sun 7-8.30 ⊕ FREE HOUSE ◀ Thwaites, Batemans ♂ Thatchers Gold. **Facilities** Non-diners area ♦♦ Children's menu Children's portions Garden ♫ Parking ▭ (notice required)

The Bustard Inn & Restaurant ◉

44 Main St NG34 8QG ☎ 01529 488250
e-mail: info@thebustardinn.co.uk
dir: *A15 from Lincoln. Right onto B1429 for Cranwell, 1st left after village, straight across A17*

Grade II listed pub with its own house ale

Situated above Lincoln Edge, this imposing building dates from 1860 and is at the heart of the pretty stone-built estate village. Legend has it that the last indigenous great bustard specimen was shot nearby in 1845 by the local lord of the manor; the pub's name recalls this deed. In the beer garden and courtyard, locals indulge in the house beer Cheeky Bustard, brewed by a local micro. The renovated, light and airy interior is divided between the bar and an elegant restaurant, with dressed stone walls, beamed ceiling and tapestry chairs; an ornate oriel window looks out on to the lovely garden. Chef Phil Lowe's one AA-Rosette cuisine draws on local produce where possible. The bar menu features spicy Thai-style mussels, and beer-battered fish and chips. Meanwhile the daily à la carte menu might offer chicken and mushroom fricassée with truffle pasta; and fillet of beef in a Madeira sauce. There is live music most Wednesday nights and special food nights once a month.

Open 12-3 5.30-11 (Sun 12-3.30) Closed: 1 Jan, Sun eve, Mon **Bar Meals** L served Tue-Sat 12-2.30, Sun 12-3 D served Tue-Sat 6-9.30 Av main course £16 **Restaurant** L served Tue-Sat 12-2.30, Sun 12-3 D served Tue-Sat 6-9.30 Fixed menu price fr £8.95 Av 3 course à la carte fr £26 ⊕ FREE HOUSE ◀ Riverside Cheeky Bustard, Batemans Yella Belly Gold, Guinness, Guest ale ♂ Aspall. ♥ 13 **Facilities** Non-diners area ♦♦ Children's menu Children's portions Garden ♫ Parking Wi-fi ▭ (notice required)

Blue Cow Inn & Brewery

High St NG33 5QB ☎ 01572 768432
e-mail: enquiries@bluecowinn.co.uk
dir: *Between Stamford & Grantham on A1*

Own-brewed real ale and pub classics

Licensee Simon Crathorn has been brewing the award-winning Blue Cow Best Bitter at the small brewery here for more than ten years — ask for a free viewing, subject to availability. The pub was renamed 'blue' by erstwhile owner the Duke of Buckminster nearly 400 years ago, on account of his political allegiance to the Whigs. Low beams, flagstone floors and dressed-stone walls characterise the ancient interior, with crackling log fires to take the edge off the fenland breezes; any remaining chill may be generated by the pub's ghosts — a lady and a dog. Snacks, salads and sandwiches are offered, as well as mains like gammon steak, sausages and scampi.

continued

SOUTH WITHAM *continued*

Open all day all wk 11-11 **Bar Meals** L served all wk D served all wk food served all day **Restaurant** L served all wk (booking req Sun L) D served all wk food served all day ⊕ FREE HOUSE ◀ Blue Cow Best Bitter. ♀ 10 **Facilities** Non-diners area ✿ (Bar Restaurant Garden) ♦♦ Children's menu Children's portions Family room Garden ⋈ Parking Wi-fi ▭ (notice required)

The George of Stamford ★★★★ HL ◉

PICK OF THE PUBS

71 St Martins PE9 2LB ☎ **01780 750750**
e-mail: reservations@georgehotelofstamford.com
web: www.georgehotelofstamford.com
dir: *From Peterborough take A1 N. Onto B1081 for Stamford, down hill to lights. Hotel on left*

Historic coaching inn with traditional food

Although the exact date is unknown, The George dates back 1,000 years but the main block of this beautiful coaching inn was erected in 1597 by Lord Burghley, Elizabeth I's Lord High Treasurer. The London Room and York Bar were where passengers waited while one of the 'twenty up' and 'twenty down' daily stagecoaches changed horses. Today's visitors can have soup, a sandwich or snack in the bar or lounge, or a light meal in the Garden Room or cobbled courtyard, while in the magnificent oak-panelled restaurant, grilled Dover sole; omelette Arnold Bennett and seared calves' liver are the order of the day. Additionally, there are shellfish, pastas and cold buffets. Outside, over the old Great North Road, is the gallows sign that warned highwaymen to stay away; under the Cocktail Bar is a medieval crypt; and there's a walled Monastery Garden, which pilgrims walked in, but monks never did.

Open all day all wk 11-11 (Sun 12-11) **Bar Meals** L served all wk 12-2.30 **Restaurant** L served all wk 12-2.30 (Garden Room all wk 12-11) D served all wk 7-10.30 food served all day ⊕ FREE HOUSE ◀ Adnams Broadside, The Grainstore, Bass, Guest ales ♂ Aspall. ♀ 21 **Facilities** Non-diners area ♦♦ Children's portions Garden Outside area ⋈ Parking Wi-fi **Rooms** 47

The Tobie Norris

PICK OF THE PUBS

12 Saint Pauls St PE9 2BE ☎ **01780 753800**
e-mail: info@tobienorris.com
dir: *From A1 to Stamford on A6121, becomes West St, then East St. After right bend right into Saint Pauls St*

Three-storey pub specialising in stone-baked pizzas

Set over three storeys and with seven rooms in a medieval hall house dating back to 1280, this extensively restored building is named after Tobie or Tobias Norris, a 16th century bell-founder who lived here. Guest ales, usually from microbreweries, and Adnams Southwold Bitter, Castle Rock and Harvest Pale, complement the food. A whole menu is dedicated to the kitchen's stone-baked pizzas cooked in ovens imported from Italy, with a list of toppings so customers can get creative. The standard menu has lots of twists on old favourites as well as plenty more Italian influences. Start with a plate of antipasti before mains like wild game, ale and brown sugar pie or Tuscan sausage and smoked chicken lasagne. Puddings include cold banana and custard crumble with coffee ice cream and, in another nod to Italy, affogato. A large enclosed patio appeals on warmer days.

Open all day all wk **Bar Meals** L served all wk 12-2.30 D served Mon-Sat 6-9 ⊕ FREE HOUSE ◀ Adnams Southwold Bitter, Castle Rock Harvest Pale, Guest ales ♂ Aspall, Guest cider. ♀ 18 **Facilities** Non-diners area ✿ (Bar Garden) Garden ⋈ Wi-fi

---

The Jenny Wren Inn

East Ferry Rd DN17 3AS ☎ **01724 784000**
e-mail: info@jennywreninn.co.uk
dir: *Telephone for directions*

Italian dishes a specialty here

With an upstairs function room overlooking the River Trent, this beamed and wood-panelled former farmhouse has buckets of character. No better place then for the sampling of special cocktails and nibbles now served every evening; ale lovers can stick to the likes of Batemans. The pub gains much praise for its food, especially for dishes involving line-caught fresh fish. Otherwise the Italian head chef and his team create both traditional pub favourites and authentic pasta, to be enjoyed in the ground-floor lounge with open fire. Chicken Bologna and smoked haddock with mash and leek sauce are typical main courses.

Open all wk 12-3 5.45-10.30 (Fri-Sun 11.30-10.30) **Bar Meals** L served Mon-Thu 12-2, Fri-Sun 12-9 D served Mon-Thu 5.45-9, Fri-Sun 12-9 **Restaurant** L served Mon-Thu 12-2, Fri-Sun 12-9 D served Mon-Thu 5.45-9, Fri-Sun 12-9 ⊕ FREE HOUSE ◀ Morland Old Speckled Hen, Theakston, Batemans, Tom Wood's. **Facilities** Non-diners area ✿ (Bar Garden) ♦♦ Children's menu Children's portions Family room Garden Parking Wi-fi ▭

Kings Head Inn

Mill Rd LN12 1PB ☎ **01507 339798**
e-mail: lordandladyhutton@hotmail.co.uk
dir: *From A1031 between Mablethorpe & Theddlethorpe, turn left into Mill Rd. Pub on right*

Ultra low ceilings and old world charm

Two miles from the beach and close to a nature reserve, this thatched 16th-century inn is a sight for sore eyes. Inside are charming bars with traditional furnishings and very low ceilings. All food is locally sourced and vegetables are home grown. Fish is a speciality in the summer; game in the winter. Dishes range from Thai-style fishcakes with home-made sweet chilli sauce through to traditional favourites such as steak-and-ale pie or grilled steak with all the trimmings.

Open 12-3 6-11 (Sat 12-11 Sun 12-10.20 summer; Sun 12-5 winter) Closed: Mon (winter) ⊕ FREE HOUSE ◀ Batemans XB, Black Sheep ♂ Thatchers Gold, Skidbrooke. **Facilities** ✿ (Bar Garden) ♦♦ Children's portions Family room Garden Parking Wi-fi

---

The Penny Farthing Inn

4 Station Rd LN4 3SA ☎ **01526 378359**
dir: *From Sleaford take A153, left onto B1189. At junct with B1191 follow signs for Timberland*

A good retreat after exploring Lincoln

Located in a charming village just outside Lincoln, The Penny Farthing has a traditional pub style. It's a popular and friendly pub and is worth noting if you're looking for somewhere comfortable and informal after exploring Lincoln and its cathedral. From the seasonal dinner menu, try twice-baked cheese soufflé with a spinach and grain mustard velouté followed by oven-roasted belly pork with fennel and bacon in cider jus. Finish with baked chocolate tart and ice cream.

Open all day Closed: Mon ⊕ FREE HOUSE ◀ Shepherd Neame Spitfire, John Smith's, Timothy Taylor Landlord, Wells Bombardier. **Facilities** ♦♦ Children's portions Garden Parking Wi-fi

---

Village Limits Country Pub, Restaurant & Motel

Stixwould Rd LN10 6UJ ☎ **01526 353312**
e-mail: info@villagelimits.co.uk
dir: *At rdbt on main street follow Petwood Hotel signs. Motel 500yds past Petwood Hotel*

Tranquil location beside country park

Handily placed for the southern hills of the Lincolnshire Wolds and the Battle of Britain Flight aircraft heritage at nearby RAF Coningsby, the heart of the old Edwardian spa town is just a short walk away. This little country inn excels at offering beers from Tom Wood's and Dixon's and meals which champion the best of locally sourced ingredients. Lincolnshire Poacher cheese rarebit sets the scene for steamed mussels with tomato and chilli sauce or a creamy leek and Stilton crumble. Keep an eye on the specials board for the latest dishes.

Open 11.30-3 6.30-11 Closed: 26 Dec-2 Jan, Mon L **Bar Meals** L served Tue-Sun 11.30-2 D served all wk 6.30-9 Av main course £12 **Restaurant** L served Tue-Sun 11.30-2 D served all wk 6.30-9 ⊕ FREE HOUSE ◀ Batemans XB, Tom Wood's Best Bitter, Dixon's Major Bitter ♻ Thatchers. ♣ 8 **Facilities** Non-diners area ♦♦ Children's menu Children's portions Garden ♠ Parking Wi-fi

---

WOOLSTHORPE   Map 11 SK83

The Chequers Inn
PICK OF THE PUBS

Main St NG32 1LU ☎ 01476 870701
e-mail: justinnabar@yahoo.co.uk
dir: *Approx 7m from Grantham. 3m from A607, follow heritage signs to Belvoir Castle*

Charming cosy interior and tip-top food

The counties of Lincolnshire, Leicestershire and Nottinghamshire all meet not far from this 17th-century coaching inn next to the village cricket pitch, with Belvoir Castle clearly visible a mile or so away. Interior delights are the five real fires, a bar that does a good line in real ales and cider, including Timothy Taylor Landlord, Milestone's Loxley Ale and Aspall. Dine in the Snug & Bar, the contemporary Dining Room, or the Bakehouse Restaurant, where the oven from village bakery days remains in place. What you can expect here is excellent food, such as braised oxtail with white turnip purée, mash and onion gravy; hake with clams, pancetta and thyme risotto and red wine sauce. There are pub classics too, like salmon fishcakes, home-made pie and chicken, bacon, new potato, poached egg and hollandaise salad.

Open all day all wk **Bar Meals** L served Mon-Sat 12-2.30, Sun 12-4 D served Mon-Sat 6-9.30, Sun 6-8.30 Av main course £14 **Restaurant** L served Mon-Sat 12-2.30, Sun 12-4 D served Mon-Sat 6-9.30, Sun 6-8.30 Fixed menu price fr £17.50 Av 3 course à la carte fr £28 ⊕ FREE HOUSE ◀ Timothy Taylor Landlord, Sharp's Doom Bar, Milestone Loxley Ale ♻ Aspall. ♣ 30
Facilities Non-diners area ♣ (Bar Garden) ♦♦ Children's menu Children's portions Garden ♠ Parking Wi-fi ▭ (notice required)

LONDON
E1

Town of Ramsgate   PLAN 2 G3

62 Wapping High St E1W 2NP ☎ 020 7481 8000
e-mail: peter@townoframsgate.co.uk
dir: *Nearest tube station: Wapping*

River Thames gem full of history

Close to The City, this Grade II listed building dates back 500 years and is steeped in history. Press gangs used to work the area, imprisoning men overnight in the cellar, and Judge Jeffreys was caught here while trying to flee the country. The pub retains much of its original character with bric-à-brac and old prints. The owners serve a range of real ales and more than a dozen wines by the glass. Enjoy dishes such as cottage pie in the bar or on the terrace overlooking the River Thames.

Open all day all wk 12-12 (Sun 12-11) **Bar Meals** L served all wk 12-4 D served all wk 5-9 Av main course £9.50 ⊕ FREE HOUSE ◀ Fuller's London Pride, Adnams, Young's ♻ Aspall. ♣ 13 **Facilities** Non-diners area ♣ (Bar Garden) ♦♦ Garden ♠ Wi-fi ▭ (notice required)

E8

The Cat & Mutton   PLAN 2 G4

76 Broadway Market, Hackney E8 4QJ
☎ 020 7254 5599
e-mail: andy@catandmutton.co.uk
dir: *Telephone for directions*

Popular food pub

Used by workers on their way to London's livestock markets in the 17th century, this revamped pub was once known as the 'Cattle & Shoulder of Mutton'. Today, the building has been reinvented as one of East London's busiest food pubs. At scrubbed tables in trendy, gentrified surroundings, order deep fried herring roe with sauce gribiche; pan-fried duck breast with butternut purée, pancetta, greens and lavender; and Westmorland tart with whisky cream. Lunchtime brings lighter options such as linguine with courgette, chard, hazelnut and Cashel Blue. There are well-kept real ales and several wines are offered by the glass.

Open all day all wk 12-11 (Fri-Sat noon-1am) Closed: 25-26 Dec **Bar Meals** L served Mon-Fri 12-3 D served Mon-Sat 6.30-10 Av main course £13 **Restaurant** L served Mon-Sat 12-3, Sun 12-5 D served Mon-Sat 6-10 Fixed menu price fr £12.50 ⊕ SEAMLESS LTD ◀ Adnams Southwold Bitter, Shepherd Neame Spitfire, Caledonian Deuchars IPA, Harvey's Sussex ♻ Westons, Addlestones, Aspall. ♣ 12 **Facilities** Non-diners area ♣ (Bar Restaurant) ♦♦ Children's portions Outside area ♠ Wi-fi

---

E9

The Empress ◉   PLAN 2 G4
PICK OF THE PUBS

130 Lauriston Rd, Victoria Park E9 7LH
☎ 020 8533 5123
e-mail: info@theempressofindia.com
dir: *From Mile End Station turn right into Grove Rd, leads into Lauriston Rd*

Café, bar and restaurant offering friendly service

A classic, mid-Victorian East End corner pub, with Gothic revival windows at first-floor level, lofty ceilings and a long bar serving Foundation Bitter from East London Brewing's husband and wife team. Neighbourhood suppliers are important to The Empress, with meats and fish from Victoria Park suppliers Ginger Pig and Jonathan Norris respectively, and coffee from Nude, if you please, in Brick Lane. Head chef Elliott Lidstone's open kitchen options include weekend brunch (from 10am), lunch, dinner and all-day bar snacks. He changes his seasonal, classic British food menus frequently, examples of his output being razor clams with chorizo; squid with fregola (a Sardinian pasta); sirloin steak with chips and tarragon butter; and duck breast with pak choi, honey and soya. The weekend brunch menu's Full Empress – two eggs, bacon, mushrooms, slow-roasted tomatoes and toast – is popular. Sunday roasts are served until 9.30pm.

Open all day all wk Closed: 25-26 Dec **Bar Meals** food served all day **Restaurant** L served Tue-Fri 12-3, Sat 12.30-4, Sun 12.30-9 D served Mon-Sat 6-10, Sun 12.30-9 Av 3 course à la carte fr £23 ⊕ FREE HOUSE ◀ East London Foundation Bitter ♻ Hogan's. ♣ 19 **Facilities** Non-diners area ♣ (Bar Outside area) ♦♦ Children's menu Children's portions Outside area ♠ Wi-fi ▭

E14

The Grapes   PLAN 2 G3
PICK OF THE PUBS

76 Narrow St, Limehouse E14 8BP ☎ 020 7987 4396
e-mail: info@thegrapes.co.uk
dir: *Telephone for directions*

Dickensian pub on the Thames

In *Our Mutual Friend*, Charles Dickens immortalised this old Thames-side pub as the Six Jolly Fellowship Porters. While he might recognise the wood-panelled, Victorian long bar and The Dickens Snug, where as a child he reputedly danced on a table, much of surrounding Limehouse has changed beyond recognition. So too has the Isle of Dogs, as looking east from the small terrace over the river at the back to the skyscrapers of Canary Wharf proves. Cask-conditioned ales in the bar include Adnams, Marston's Pedigree, Timothy Taylor Landlord and guests, while in the tiny upstairs dining room the fresh seafood includes pan-seared scallops, chorizo and smoked chilli; grilled or crispy battered haddock fillet;

continued

E14 *continued*

and whole roasted sea bass. If you'd prefer steak and chips, or shepherd's pie, they're on the menu too. Salads, sandwiches and bar meals are always available, and there are traditional roasts on Sundays. Change of hands.

Open all day all wk 12-11 (Mon-Wed 12-3 5.30-11) Closed: 25-26 Dec, 1 Jan **Bar Meals** L served Mon-Sat 12-2.30, Sun 12-3.30 D served Mon-Sat 6.30-9.30 **Restaurant** L served Mon-Fri 12-2.30 D served Mon-Sat 6.30-9.30 ⊕ SPIRIT LEASED ◀ Marston's Pedigree, Timothy Taylor Landlord, Adnams, Guest ales ♂ Aspall. **Facilities** Non-diners area ✿ (Bar)

The Gun ◉ PLAN 2 G3

PICK OF THE PUBS

27 Coldharbour, Docklands E14 9NS ☎ 020 7515 5222
e-mail: info@thegundocklands.com
dir: *From South Quay DLR, east along Marsh Wall to mini rdbt. Turn left, over bridge then 1st right*

A surviving riverside gem

Once a dockers', stevedores' and boatmen's local, this old Thames-side pub was named after the cannon fired to celebrate the opening of West India Docks in 1802. Destroyed by fire in 2001, it reopened three years later following painstaking restoration work by owners Tom and Ed Martin, in close consultation with English Heritage. In the main bar London brewer Sambrook's Junction sits alongside Adnams Bitter, Otter Amber and Symonds cider. There is also a restaurant, two private dining rooms (one where Lord Nelson and Lady Hamilton secretly met), two snugs, and a riverside terrace overlooking the Millennium Dome. Snacks include Colchester rock oysters; devilled whitebait; and black pudding Scotch eggs, while the main menu offers pan-fried fillet of golden bream with Dorset crab mash; thyme-roasted Suffolk poussin; and sautéed potato gnocchi with kale and roast squash. Croatian, Greek and Lebanese wines feature among the 100-or-so listed.

Open all wk 11am-mdnt (Sun 11-11) Closed: 25-26 Dec **Bar Meals** L served Mon-Sat 12-3, Sun 12-4 D served Mon-Sat 6-10.30, Sun 6.30-9.30 Av main course £10.50 **Restaurant** L served Mon-Sat 12-3, Sun 12-4 D served Mon-Sat 6-10.30, Sun 6.30-9.30 Av 3 course à la carte fr £26 ⊕ ETM GROUP ◀ Sambrook's Brewery Junction Ale, Adnams Southwold Bitter, Otter Amber ♂ Symonds. ☗ 22 **Facilities** Non-diners area ♦ Children's portions Outside area ㅈ Wi-fi ▭ (notice required)

EC1

The Bleeding Heart Tavern ◉ PLAN 1 E4

PICK OF THE PUBS

19 Greville St EC1N 8SQ ☎ 020 7242 8238
e-mail: bookings@bleedingheart.co.uk
dir: *Close to Farringdon tube station, at corner of Greville St & Bleeding Heart Yard*

Historic city pub with great wines and rotisserie

Famed for the gruesome murder of Lady Elizabeth Hatton in 1626, the tavern dates from 1746 when Holborn had a boozer for every five houses and inns boasted that their customers could be 'drunk for a penny and dead drunk for twopence'. Prices have changed and the tavern is now open for breakfast, has a light lunchtime menu if you're pressed for time and keeps traditional ales from Adnams. Downstairs, the warm and comforting dining room features an open rotisserie and grill serving free-range organic British meat, game and poultry alongside an extensive wine list. Typical menu choices might start with a venison Scotch egg as a prelude to haddock Monte Carlo with spinach and mash, or spit-roast leg of Suffolk lamb with seasonal vegetables, roast potatoes and mint sauce. Good charcuterie, smoked and cured fish and desserts such as blackberry and apple crumble with custard.

Open all day 7am-11pm Closed: BHs, 10 days at Xmas, Sat-Sun **Bar Meals** food served all day **Restaurant** L served Mon-Fri 12-2.30 D served Mon-Fri 6-10.30 ⊕ FREE HOUSE ◀ Adnams Southwold Bitter, Broadside, Fisherman, May Day ♂ Aspall. ☗ 17 **Facilities** Non-diners area

---

The Coach & Horses PLAN 1 E5

PICK OF THE PUBS

26-28 Ray St, Clerkenwell EC1R 3DJ ☎ 020 7278 8990
e-mail: info@thecoachandhorses.com
dir: *From Farringdon tube station right into Cowcross St. At Farringdon Rd turn right, after 500yds left into Ray St. Pub at bottom of hill*

Archetypal Victorian gastro-pub in Clerkenwell

This restored, wood-panelled, late 19th-century pub was built to serve the myriad artisans, many of them Italian, who once lived in this area. At one time a secret passage led to the long-buried River Fleet, which still runs beneath the pub and is audible from a drain outside the entrance. Unsurprisingly, there are a few ghosts, including an old man and a black cat. Typical bar snacks include duck livers on toast; and scallops with Jerusalem artichoke purée and Morteau sausage, while in the Eduardo Paolozzi-artwork-decorated dining room the modern British menu lists reasonably priced dishes such as pearl barley orzotto with celeriac and baby turnips; braised beef rib with white onion purée and caramelised shallots; and red mullet with lobster bisque and winter vegetable minestrone. Enjoy with a pint of Fuller's London Pride, Burrow Hill or Bounders cider, or a glass of wine from the well-balanced list.

Open all wk 12-11 (Sat 6-11 Sun 12.30-5) Closed: 24 Dec-1st Mon in Jan, BHs **Bar Meals** L served Mon-Fri 12-3, Sun 1-4 D served Mon-Sat 6-10 Av main course £11.25 **Restaurant** L served Mon-Fri 12-3, Sun 1-4 D served Mon-Sat 6-10 Fixed menu price fr £16.50 Av 3 course à la carte fr £23 ⊕ PUNCH TAVERNS ◀ Timothy Taylor Landlord, Fuller's London Pride, Woodforde's Wherry, Brentwood BBC 2 ♂ Burrow Hill, Bath Ciders Bounders. ☗ 17 **Facilities** Non-diners area ✿ (Bar Restaurant Outside area) ♦ Children's portions Outside area ㅈ Beer festival Wi-fi ▭ (notice required)

The Eagle PLAN 1 E5

159 Farringdon Rd EC1R 3AL ☎ 020 7837 1353
dir: *Angel/Farringdon tube station. Pub at north end of Farringdon Rd*

One of trendy Clerkenwell's top establishments

Blazing a trail in the early 1990s and paving the way for what we now except as stylish gastro-pubs, The Eagle is still going strong – despite considerable competition. The lofty interior includes a wooden-floored bar and dining area, a mishmash of vintage furniture, and an open-to-view kitchen that produces a creatively modern, twice-daily changing menu and tapas selection which revel in bold, rustic flavours. Typical of the range are salt cod soup; Venetian-style calves' liver on toast with sweet onion, red wine vinegar and parsley; and rare grilled onglet with horseradish cream, roast potatoes and rocket.

Open all day 12-11 (Sun 12-5) Closed: BHs L (1wk Xmas), Sun eve ⊕ FREE HOUSE ◀ Wells Eagle IPA & Bombardier ♂ Westons, Addlestones. **Facilities** ✿ (Bar) ♦ Children's portions

---

The Jerusalem Tavern PLAN 1 E4

PICK OF THE PUBS

55 Britton St, Clerkenwell EC1M 5UQ ☎ 020 7490 4281
e-mail: thejerusalemtavern@gmail.com
dir: *100mtrs NE of Farringdon tube station; 300mtrs N of Smithfield*

Historic inn with St Peter's Brewery cask and bottled beers

Owned by Suffolk's St Peter's Brewery, this historic tavern has close links to Samuel Johnson, Oliver Goldsmith, David Garrick and the young Handel, who used to drink here on his visits to London. Named after the Priory of St John of Jerusalem, founded in 1140, the pub can be traced back to the 14th century, having occupied several sites in the area including part of St John's Gate. The current premises date from 1720 although the shop frontage dates from about 1810, when it was a workshop for Clerkenwell's various watch and clock craftsmen. Its dimly lit Dickensian bar, with bare boards, rustic wooden tables, old tiles, candles, open fires and cosy corners, is the perfect film set - which is what it has been on many occasions. A classic pub in every sense, it offers the full range of cask and bottled beers from St Peter's Brewery, as well as a range of simple pub fare.

Open all day 11-11 Closed: 25 Dec-1 Jan, Sat-Sun **Bar Meals** L served Mon-Fri 12-3 Av main course £9 ⊕ ST

Save on hotels. Book at **theAA.com/hotel**

LONDON 287 **ENGLAND**

PETER'S BREWERY ◄ St Peter's (full range) ♻ New Forest Traditional, Oliver's, Once Upon a Tree Tumpy Ground. **Facilities** Non-diners area ♣ (Bar) Outside area Wi-fi

The Peasant

PICK OF THE PUBS

PLAN 1 E5

240 Saint John St EC1V 4PH ☎ 020 7336 7726
e-mail: eat@thepeasant.co.uk
dir: Exit Angel & Farringdon Rd tube station. Pub on corner of Saint John St & Percival St

Restored Victorian pub with reputation for good food

With its mahogany horseshoe bar, mosaic floor and period chandeliers in the circus-memorabilia-filled restaurant, this beautifully restored, Grade II listed former gin palace still looks very Victorian. One of the trailblazers of the original gastro-pub movement, it is still very much a place for a drink as it is a destination for food. Real ales include Truman's Runner, a bitter that revives the name of one of that long-defunct brewery's favourites; there are good real ciders too, lots of bottled beers, and decent wines. Two menus are on offer: a carte for upstairs, and lighter meals in the bar. A typical dinner upstairs begins with salmon tempura with warm egg noodle salad, soya and wasabi dressing, and follows with braised pork cheeks and ham hock faggot with garlic sausage cassoulet. Beer festivals are in April and November.

Open all day all wk Closed: 24 Dec-2 Jan **Bar Meals** L served all wk 12-11 D served all wk 12-11 food served all day **Restaurant** D served Tue-Sat 6-11 ⊕ FREE HOUSE ◄ Wells Bombardier, Crouch Vale Brewers Gold, Truman's Runner, Guest ales ♻ Thatchers Pear & Katy, Aspall, The Orchard Pig. ♈ 15 **Facilities** Non-diners area ♦ Children's portions Garden Beer festival 🚌 (notice required)

Ye Olde Mitre

PLAN 1 E4

1 Ely Court, Ely Place EC1N 6SJ ☎ 020 7405 4751
e-mail: yeoldemitre@fullers.co.uk
dir: From Chancery Lane tube station exit 3 walk downhill to Holborn Circus, left into Hatton Garden. Pub in alley between 8 & 9 Hatton Garden

Historic, hidden away pub

Built in 1546, extended in 1781, in the shadow of the palace of the Bishops of Ely, this quirky historic corner pub is in Ely Court, off Hatton Garden. It is often used as a film location. Choose from at least five real ales in the magnificent wood-panelled rooms, with a range of bar snacks or 'English tapas' that includes toasted sandwiches, pork pies, Scotch eggs, sausage rolls, olives and picked eggs. Beer festivals are held in May, August and December, but the pub is closed at weekends and Bank Holidays.

Open all day Closed: 25 Dec, 1 Jan, BHs, Sat-Sun (ex 1st wknd Aug) **Bar Meals** L served Mon-Fri 11.30-9.30 D served Mon-Fri 11.30-9.30 food served all day ⊕ FULLER'S ◄ London Pride, Geoge Gale & Co Seafarers, Caledonian Deuchars IPA, Adnams Broadside, Guest ales ♻ Biddenden Bushels, Thatchers. ♈ 8 **Facilities** Non-diners area Garden 🌳 Beer festival Wi-fi

EC2

The Fox NEW

PLAN 1 F4

28-30 Paul St EC2A 4LB ☎ 020 7729 5708
e-mail: info@thefoxpublichouse.co.uk
dir: Nearest tube station: Old Street. Take exit 4 for City Road South, into City Rd. 2nd left into Epworth St, 500yds, pub on corner at junct with Paul St

Chill out with good food in this Shoreditch retreat

Not long ago, few visited Shoreditch for pleasure. Now, together with neighbouring Hoxton and Spitalfields, it is one of the capital's buzziest districts, with Victorian pubs like this thriving once more. Carefully selected wines and real ales - Harvey's Sussex and Otter, for example - and simple, straightforward food help to make it the place to head for after the shops and flower market of Columbia Road, the Asian bustle of Brick Lane, or a hard day at the office. Typically on the menu are linguine with mussels; Blackface lamb steak with celeriac mash; and cottage pie with cabbage.

Open all day all wk Closed: 25-28 Dec & BHs **Bar Meals** L served all wk 12-3 D served all wk 5-10 Av main course £10 **Restaurant** L served all wk 12-3 D served all wk 5-10 Fixed menu price fr £12 Av 3 course à la carte fr £25 ⊕ ENTERPRISE INNS ◄ Harvey's Sussex Best Bitter, Sharp's Doom Bar, Otter Bitter ♻ Addlestones. ♈ 13 **Facilities** Non-diners area ♣ (Bar) ♦ Outside area 🌳 Wi-fi

Old Dr Butler's Head

PLAN 1 F4

Mason's Av, Coleman St, Moorgate EC2V 5BT ☎ 020 7606 3504
e-mail: olddoctorbutlers@shepherdneame.co.uk
dir: Telephone for directions

Traditional pub in the heart of the City

Physician to James I, Butler was actually an old fraud whose home-brewed medicinal ale could only be sold at inns displaying his portrait on their sign. Although the pub is old, the wooden façade is probably Victorian and certainly older than the mock-Tudor buildings opposite. A Shepherd Neame house, it stocks their real ales in the bar, where you can tuck into steak-and-kidney suet pudding. Restaurant dishes include ale-battered cod and chips; 10oz mature rump steak; pan-fried calves' liver; and sausages and mash. Please note that, like some other City pubs, the ODBH closes at weekends.

Open all day Closed: Sat-Sun **Bar Meals** L served Mon-Fri 12-3 D served Mon-Fri 6-9 Av main course £8 **Restaurant** L served Mon-Fri 12-3 D served Bookings only Av 3 course à la carte fr £20 ⊕ SHEPHERD NEAME ◄ Spitfire, Bishops Finger, Master Brew, Kent's Best, Seasonal ale. ♈ 9 **Facilities** Non-diners area Outside area 🌳 Wi-fi 🚌

The Princess of Shoreditch NEW

PLAN 1 F4

76-78 Paul St EC2A 4NE ☎ 020 7729 9270
e-mail: info@theprincessofshoreditch.com
dir: Nearest tube station: Old Street

Well-known City gastro-pub

A pub since 1742, the former Princess Royal acquired its new name in 2010 following a major refurbishment that, say owners Scott and Maria Hunter, "made the old girl look better than ever". In the lively ground-floor bar beers change weekly, with regular supplies from London Fields brewery in Hackney, and real cider from Hogan's in Warwickshire. Food is served too, although for more formal dining (booking is recommended), climb the spiral staircase to the restaurant for dishes such as pan-fried pollock with cherry tomato and cannellini bean ragout; trio of lamb; and butternut squash, spinach and wild mushroom pie.

Open all day all wk Closed: 25-27 Dec **Bar Meals** L served Mon-Fri 12-3, Sat 12-4, Sun 12-8 D served Mon-Sat 6.30-10, Sun 12-8 **Restaurant** L served Tue-Fri 12-3, Sun 12-8 D served Mon-Sat 6.30-10, Sun 12-8 Av 3 course à la carte fr £21 ◄ Sharp's, London Fields, Hackney, Redemption ♻ Hogan's. ♈ 9 **Facilities** Non-diners area ♦ Outside area Wi-fi

EC4

The Black Friar

PLAN 1 E3

174 Queen Victoria St EC4V 4EG ☎ 020 7236 5474
dir: Opposite Blackfriars tube station

Stunning interior and an impressive range of beers

Space permitting, so much could be written about this 1875 pub and its later art nouveau interior celebrating the fanciful antics of the medieval Dominican monks, who once lived here, known as the Blackfriars. Real ales range from Adnams to Timothy Taylor, via Fuller's, Sharp's and St Austell, with solid sustenance of sandwiches and pies; Cumberland sausage and mash; salmon and broccoli fishcakes; and roasted vegetable risotto. On a triangular site by Blackfriars tube station, it's popular with City suits.

Open all day all wk Mon-Sat 10am-11pm (Sun 12-10.30) Closed: 25 Dec ⊕ MITCHELLS & BUTLERS ◄ Fuller's London Pride, St Austell Tribute, Sharp's Doom Bar, Adnams, Timothy Taylor ♻ Westons Wyld Wood Organic, Aspall. **Facilities** ♦ Garden

EC4 *continued*

The Old Bank of England PLAN 1 E4

194 Fleet St EC4A 2LT ☎ 020 7430 2255
e-mail: oldbankofengland@fullers.co.uk
dir: *By Courts of Justice*

Called to the bar in more ways than one

This magnificent building previously housed the Law Courts' branch of the Bank of England. Set between the site of Sweeney Todd's barbershop and his mistress's pie shop, it stands above the original bank vaults and the tunnels in which Todd butchered his unfortunate victims. Aptly, there's an extensive range of speciality pies including game, brandy and redcurrant, and lamb and red pepper, but other treats include roasted lemon and thyme chicken breast on a pearl barley broth, and caramelised onion and olive puff pastry tart.

Open all day Closed: BHs, Sat-Sun ⊕ FULLER'S ◀ London Pride, Chiswick Bitter, Discovery, ESB, Seasonal ales. **Facilities** Garden Wi-fi

The White Swan ☻ PLAN 1 E4

PICK OF THE PUBS

108 Fetter Ln, Holborn EC4A 1ES ☎ 020 7242 9696
e-mail: info@thewhiteswanlondon.com
dir: *Nearest tube: Chancery Lane. From station towards St Paul's Cathedral. At HSBC bank left into Fetter Ln. Pub on right*

Fresh fish arrives daily from Billingsgate

In the heart of the City, this handsome pub — formerly the old Mucky Duck — is spread across three floors, housing a traditional ground floor bar plus mezzanine and first-floor dining room. In the wood-panelled bar, enjoy a cosmopolitan selection of beers and lagers, and plenty of wines by the glass. Its fresh cream-coloured walls embrace leather-covered bar stools and mixed wooden tables, chairs and banquettes; beneath your feet there are reclaimed timber floorboards. Upstairs is the beautifully restored dining room with mirrored ceiling and linen-clad tables. Cooking is modern British in style: king scallop and Jersey Royal ceviche with hazelnuts is a sample springtime starter. Fish from Billingsgate each morning appears in mains such as cod, razor clams, leek and mousseron mushroom, sea shore vegetable dressing. An alternative is Herdwick lamb rump with minted broad beans, potato croquettes and shallot purée. To finish, the rhubarb pie and custard is excellent.

Open 11am-mdnt (Fri 11-1am) Closed: 25-26 Dec & BHs, Sat-Sun **Bar Meals** L served Mon-Fri 12-3 D served Mon-Fri 6-10 Av main course £13 **Restaurant** L served Mon-Fri 12-3 D served Mon-Fri 6-10 Fixed menu price fr £27 Av 3 course à la carte fr £27 ⊕ ETM GROUP ◀ Fuller's London Pride, Adnams, Guinness ♻ Addlestones. ☂ 12 **Facilities** ♦♦ Wi-fi 🚌 (notice required)

N1

The Albion PLAN 2 F4

10 Thornhill Rd, Islington N1 1HW ☎ 020 7607 7450
e-mail: info@the-albion.co.uk
dir: *From Angel tube station, cross road into Liverpool Rd past Sainsbury's, continue to Richmond Ave. Left. At junct with Thornhill Rd turn right. Pub on right*

Islington local with walled garden

In the heart of Islington, just off Upper Street in the Barnsbury conservation area, stands this Georgian gem of a pub. The spacious walled garden and wisteria-covered pergola draw the summer crowds — perfect for relaxed alfresco drinking and tucking into some cracking modern pub food prepared from top-notch British produce. The brasserie-style menu centres around the charcoal grill — whole mackerel, 28-day aged Galloway rib-eye steak — alongside chicken, leek and mushroom pie; smoked haddock fishcake with hollandaise; and treacle sponge with crème anglaise. Log fires warm the classic dark wood panels and tastefully furnished interior in winter.

Open all day all wk ⊕ PUNCH TAVERNS ◀ Ringwood Best Bitter, Caledonian Deuchars IPA ♻ Addlestones. **Facilities** ❅ (Bar Garden) ♦♦ Children's menu Children's portions Garden Wi-fi

The Barnsbury PLAN 2 F4

209-211 Liverpool Rd, Islington N1 1LX
☎ 020 7607 5519
e-mail: thebarnsburypub@hotmail.com
dir: *Telephone for directions*

Top quality ales and good English food

The Barnsbury, a 'free house and dining room' in the heart of Islington, is a welcome addition to the London scene. It's a gastro-pub where both the food and the prices are well conceived — and its walled garden makes it a secluded and sought-after summer oasis for alfresco relaxation. At least six guest ales are backed by an in-depth wine list. The food is cooked from daily supplies of fresh ingredients which have been bought direct from the market. Starter dishes range from smoked chicken and mango salad to a charcuterie board. Tempting mains might include pea and Stilton risotto; and seared tuna with roasted tomato and basil fusilli.

Open all day all wk 12-11 (Sun 12-10.30) Closed: 25-26 Dec, 1 Jan ⊕ FREE HOUSE ◀ Guest ales. **Facilities** ♦♦ Garden

The Charles Lamb PLAN 2 F4

16 Elia St, Islington N1 8DE ☎ 020 7837 5040
e-mail: food@thecharleslambpub.com
dir: *From Angel station turn left, at junct of City Rd turn left. Pass Duncan Terrace Gdns, left into Colebrooke Row. 1st right*

A really friendly London local

Named after a local writer who lived in Islington in the 1830s, this cracking neighbourhood pub thrives thanks to the hard work and dedication of Camille and MJ Hobby-Limon, who took over the former Prince Albert in 2005. Locals beat a path to the door for microbrewery ales and the hearty, home-cooked comfort food listed on the daily chalkboard menu. With inspiration from the Mediterranean, dishes may include Basque fish stew, wild mushroom and pearl barley risotto, and a rustic cassoulet. The pub hosts an annual Bastille Day event complete with petanque competition, and a Spring Bank Holiday beer festival.

Open all wk Mon & Tue fr 4 Wed-Sun fr noon Closed: 23 Dec-1 Jan **Bar Meals** L served Wed-Fri 12-3, Sat 12-4, Sun 12-6 D served Mon-Sat 6-9.30, Sun 7-9 ⊕ FREE HOUSE ◀ Dark Star Hophead, Triple fff Alton's Pride, Guest ales ♻ Thatchers. ☂ 9 **Facilities** Non-diners area ♦♦ Beer festival Wi-fi

The Drapers Arms ☻ PLAN 2 F4

PICK OF THE PUBS

44 Barnsbury St N1 1ER ☎ 020 7619 0348
e-mail: nick@thedrapersarms.com
dir: *Turn right from Highbury & Islington station, 10 mins along Upper St. Barnsbury St on right opposite Shell service station*

Hearty food and well-kept ales

Nick Gibson's handsome pub was built in the 1830 by the Drapers' livery company and it has been a popular Islington local ever since. The downstairs bar is illuminated by large picture windows, its unfussy interior furnished with a mix of squashy sofas and solid wooden tables. The pub serves local real ale and cider drinkers well, with Harvey's Sussex and Dark Star Hophead, plus Stowford Press and Orchard Pig cider. Thought clearly goes into the menus too, as testified by hearty starters like mussels, cider, cream and parsley; ox tongue, chicory, cornichons and mustard; and potted brown shrimps. The kitchen approaches mains in the same way, with confit duck leg, Puy lentils and Old Spot bacon; Barnsley lamb chop, purple sprouting broccoli and anchovy dressing; and lemon sole, creamed spinach and almonds. A typical dessert might be buttermilk pudding with blood orange. Look out for the August beer festival.

Open all day all wk Closed: 25-26 Dec **Bar Meals** L served Mon-Sat 12-3, Sun 12-4 D served Mon-Sat 6-11, Sun 6.30-9.30 **Restaurant** L served Mon-Sat 12-3, Sun 12-4 D served Mon-Sat 6-11, Sun 6.30-9.30 ⊕ FREE HOUSE ◀ Harvey's Sussex, Sambrook's Wandle, Truman's Runner, Dark Star Hophead, Windsor & Eton Windsor Knot, Cornish Crown Bitter ♻ Westons Stowford Press & Wyld Wood Organic, The Orchard Pig. ☂ 18

Facilities Non-diners area 🐾 (Bar Garden) 👶 Children's portions Garden 🍺 Beer festival Wi-fi

---

The Duke of Cambridge
PLAN 2 F4

PICK OF THE PUBS

30 Saint Peter's St N1 8JT ☎ 020 7359 3066
e-mail: duke@dukeorganic.co.uk
dir: *Telephone for directions*

Organic pub advocating sustainable and ethical values

Geetie Singh's obsession with achieving the lowest possible carbon footprint possible at her remarkable Islington gastro-pub, the first certified organic pub in Britain, has reached new heights. Everything possible is re-used or recycled and even the electricity is wind and solar generated. Sustainable, ethically-produced ingredients are approved by the Soil Association and Marine Conservation Society, and items such as bread, ice cream and pickles are all made on site. Beers from local microbreweries, real ciders such as Luscombe, and organic wines go hand-in-hand with a mouthwatering seasonal menu that may change twice daily, with 80 per cent of ingredients sourced from the Home Counties. A spring choice could be mussels in tomato, chorizo and ale sauce, followed by Dover sole with Savoy cabbage, pancetta and sautéed potatoes. The winter menu may offer beetroot and cumin seed soup with crème fraîche, followed by rabbit and red wine stew with bubble-and-squeak. To finish, there could be rhubarb fool with coconut macaroon.

Open all day all wk Closed: 24-26 & 31 Dec, 1 Jan **Bar Meals** L served Mon-Fri 12.30-3, Sat-Sun 12.30-3.30 D served Mon-Sat 6.30-10.30, Sun 6.30-10 **Restaurant** L served Mon-Fri 12.30-3, Sat-Sun 12.30-3.30 D served Mon-Sat 6.30-10.30, Sun 6.30-10 ⊕ FREE HOUSE 🍺 Pitfield SB Bitter, East Kent Goldings, Shoreditch Stout & Eco Warrior, St Peter's Best Bitter ♂ Westons, Dunkertons, Luscombe. 🍷 12 **Facilities** Non-diners area 🐾 (Bar) 👶 Children's portions 🚌

The House
PLAN 2 F4

63-69 Canonbury Rd N1 2DG ☎ 020 7704 7410
e-mail: maurkio@thehouseislington.com
dir: *Telephone for directions*

A historic house in leafy Islington, offering a seasonal British menu

Situated in Islington's prestigious Canonbury district but moments away from the hustle and bustle of Upper Street, this successful gastro-pub has featured in a celebrity cookbook and garnered plenty of praise since it opened its doors a few years ago. Expect a thoroughly modern, seasonal British menu at lunch and dinner. Typical dishes include almond crust brie cheese with cranberry compôte and pitta bread, or Poole mussels with Somerset cider and parsley to start; followed by venison pie with root vegetable mash, roast guineafowl breast with sweet potato fondant, or pan-fried sea bass with caramelised Jerusalem artichoke and langoustine bisque.

Leave room for rice pudding with autumn fruits and sloe gin, or baked vanilla cheesecake.

Open Mon-Thu 4-12 (Fri 12-12 Sat-Sun 10am-2am) Closed: Mon-Thu L (ex BHs) **Bar Meals** L served Fri 12-4, Sat-Sun 10-4 D served all wk 6-10.30 **Restaurant** L served Sat-Sun 10-4 D served Mon-Sat 6-10.30, Sun 6-10 ⊕ PUNCH TAVERNS 🍺 Sharp's Doom Bar, Guinness ♂ Aspall. 🍷 15 **Facilities** Non-diners area 🐾 (Bar Garden) 👶 Children's menu Children's portions Garden 🍺 Wi-fi 🚌

N6

The Flask
PLAN 2 E5

PICK OF THE PUBS

77 Highgate West Hill N6 6BU ☎ 020 8348 7346
e-mail: theflaskhighgate@london-gastros.co.uk
dir: *Nearest tube: Archway/Highgate*

Landmark gastro-pub with links to Dick Turpin

This Grade II listed pub, dating back to 1663 and made famous by Byron, Keats, Hogarth and Betjeman, has become a London landmark. High on Highgate Hill, it may now be a gastro-pub with a big reputation but its name was made long ago when Dick Turpin frequented it. It retains much of its character and cosy atmosphere and a maze of small rooms is served by two bars, one of which houses the original sash windows. Fuller's and guest real ales from newer London breweries such as Redemption are on offer alongside two dozen bottled ales and ciders, and some sensibly priced wines. Starters include smoked duck and celeriac remoulade, while typical mains are gammon, hispi, colcannon and parsley sauce; and whole sea bass with fennel and sauce vierge. For dessert, try chocolate and Guinness cake. The large front garden is especially popular in the summer.

Open all day all wk 12-11 (Sun 12-10.30) Closed: 25 Dec **Bar Meals** L served Mon-Fri 12-3, Sat-Sun 12-4 D served Mon-Sat 6-10, Sun 6-9 Av main course £12 ⊕ FULLER'S 🍺 London Pride, ESB, George Gale & Co Seafarers, Guest ales ♂ Aspall. 🍷 13 **Facilities** Non-diners area 🐾 (Bar Restaurant Garden) 👶 Garden 🍺 Wi-fi 🚌 (notice required)

NW1

The Chapel
PLAN 1 B4

48 Chapel St NW1 5DP ☎ 020 7402 9220
e-mail: thechapel@btconnect.com
dir: *By A40 Marylebone Rd & Old Marylebone Rd junct. Off Edgware Rd by tube station*

A popular child-friendly gastro-pub

The Chapel has a bright, open-plan interior of stripped floors and pine furniture, and boasts one of central London's largest enclosed pub gardens – great for the children to let off steam. Owners Alison McGrath and Lakis Hondrogiannis take delivery of the freshest produce for daily-changing menus featuring internationally influenced dishes, as well as Mediterranean antipasti and canapés. A sample dinner menu lists lamb koftas

---

with tzatziki; springbok Wellington with truffle mash and French beans; and warm chocolate and almond tart served with ice cream. Many wines are served by the glass.

Open all day all wk Closed: 25-26 Dec, 1 Jan, Etr **Restaurant** L served all wk 12-2.30, Sun 12.30-3 D served all wk 7-10 ⊕ FREE HOUSE/GREENE KING 🍺 IPA, Hardys & Hansons Olde Trip ♂ Aspall. 🍷 15 **Facilities** Non-diners area 🐾 (Bar Restaurant Garden) 👶 Children's menu Children's portions Garden 🍺 🚌 (notice required)

The Engineer
PLAN 2 E4

PICK OF THE PUBS

65 Gloucester Av, Primrose Hill NW1 8JH
☎ 020 7483 1890
e-mail: enquiries@theengineerprimrosehill.co.uk
dir: *Telephone for directions*

World beers and eclectic dishes in a relaxed atmosphere

Built by Isambard Kingdom Brunel in 1841, this unassuming street corner pub stands tucked away in a residential part of Primrose Hill close to Camden Market. It attracts a discerning dining crowd who relish its imaginative and well-prepared food and friendly, laid-back atmosphere. There is a spacious bar area, wood floors, sturdy wooden tables with candles, simple decor and cosy upstairs private dining rooms. A walled, paved and heated garden to the rear is popular in fine weather. In addition to cosmopolitan beers, the drinks list includes hand-crafted teas, freshly ground coffees, interesting wines, and a variety of whiskies. Regularly changing menus feature an eclectic mix of inspired home-made dishes using organic and free-range products. A typical Sunday lunch menu may feature rabbit terrine with piccalilli to start, followed by roast duck with plums and braised red cabbage, or lamb shoulder with confit garlic and mint sauce. Leave room for bitter chocolate pudding with malt ice cream.

Open all day all wk 9am-11pm (Sun & BH 9am-10.30pm) **Bar Meals** L served all wk 12-10 D served all wk 12-10 food served all day **Restaurant** L served Mon-Fri 12-3, Sat-Sun 12-4 D served all wk 6-10 ⊕ MITCHELLS & BUTLERS 🍺 Redemption, Sharp's Doom Bar ♂ Aspall Harry Sparrow. 🍷 19 **Facilities** Non-diners area 🐾 (Bar Garden) 👶 Children's menu Children's portions Family room Garden 🍺 Beer festival Cider festival Wi-fi 🚌

NW1 *continued*

The Globe
PLAN 1 B4

43-47 Marylebone Rd NW1 5JY ☎ 020 7935 6368
e-mail: globe.1018@thespiritgroup.com
dir: *At corner of Marylebone Rd & Baker St, opposite Baker St tube station*

Busy pub with good British food

Many famous and infamous characters have been patrons here including Charles Dickens. Built in 1735, the same year as the neighbouring Nash terraces, the pub retains much of its period charm, including William, the ghost of a former landlord. The first omnibus service from Holborn stopped here and the Metropolitan line was constructed under the road a few feet from the tavern. A good choice of real ales is offered alongside freshly cooked British pub food, such as bangers and mash, chicken tikka masala, Wiltshire cured ham, egg and chips, and steak-and-ale pie.

Open all day all wk 10am-11pm (Fri-Sat 10am-11.30pm Sun 10am-10.30pm) (Closed some eves after Wembley football matches) Closed: 25 Dec ⊕ PUNCH TAVERNS ◀ Greene King Abbot Ale, Wells Bombardier, Young's, Morland Old Speckled Hen, Guest ales. **Facilities** ⬢ Children's menu Children's portions Wi-fi

The Lansdowne
PLAN 2 E4

90 Gloucester Av, Primrose Hill NW1 8HX
☎ 020 7483 0409
e-mail: info@thelansdownepub.co.uk
dir: *Turn right from Chalk Farm tube station into Adelaide Rd, 1st left into Bridge Approach (on foot). Into Gloucester Av, 500yds. Pub on corner*

One of the first dining pubs in Primrose Hill

The Lansdowne comprises a light, spacious bar with high ceilings, an outdoor seating area and a slightly more formal upper dining room. All food is freshly prepared on the premises, using organic or free-range ingredients wherever possible, and portions are invariably generous. The daily-changing blackboard menu of vibrant Mediterranean cuisine offers a selection of pizzas in addition to home-cured bresaola with rocket, capers and parmesan; pan-fried sardines on toast with watercress; confit pork belly with prunes, potatoes and lardons; poached sea trout with crushed herb potatoes; polenta with roast pumpkin, buffalo mozzarella and walnuts.

Open all day all wk 12-11 (Sat 10am-11pm Sun 10am-10.30pm) ⊕ FREE HOUSE ◀ Wells Bombardier, Truman's ♻ Aspall. **Facilities** ⬢

The Prince Albert
PLAN 2 F4

163 Royal College St NW1 0SG ☎ 020 7485 0270
e-mail: info@princealbertcamden.com
dir: *From Camden tube station follow Camden Rd. Right into Royal College St, 200mtrs on right*

Organic food at character pub

Picnic tables furnish the small paved courtyard, while The Prince Albert's wooden floors and bentwood furniture make a welcoming interior for customers and their four-legged friends. Real ales there are, but you may fancy a refreshing Stowford Press cider for a change, and wine drinkers have plenty of choice. Bar snacks range from home-roasted nuts to crispy salt and pepper chicken wings, which also feature on the great-value set menu; these can be followed by Old English pork sausages or beer-battered haddock. Two or three times a year the pub holds a three-day real ale festival.

Open all day all wk 12-11 (Sun 12-10.30) **Bar Meals** L served Mon-Fri 12-3, Sat-Sun 12-5 D served Mon-Fri 6-10 **Restaurant** L served Mon-Sat 12-3, Sat-Sun 12-5 D served Mon-Fri 6-10 ⊕ FREE HOUSE ◀ Adnams Broadside, Kirin Ichiban, Black Sheep ♻ Westons Stowford Press. ♟20 **Facilities** Non-diners area ⬢ (Bar Garden) ⬢ Children's menu Children's portions Garden ♒ Beer festival Wi-fi

The Queens
PLAN 2 E4

49 Regents Park Rd, Primrose Hill NW1 8XD
☎ 020 7586 0408
e-mail: queens@youngs.co.uk
dir: *Nearest tube: Chalk Farm*

Historic and convivial pub

There's a traditional British menu at this cosy Victorian pub overlooking Primrose Hill. Located in one of London's most affluent and personality-studded areas, The Queens is steeped in celebrity history and is mentioned in many stars' autobiographies. The bar menu offers a range of sandwiches, supported by hot dishes like sausages, mash and onion gravy, and cod and chips in ale batter. Grab a seat on the terraced seating outdoors in good weather.

Open all day all wk 11-11 (Sun 12-10.30) ⊕ YOUNG'S ◀ Bitter & Special, Wells Bombardier, Guest ales. **Facilities** ⬢ Children's portions Wi-fi

The Holly Bush
PLAN 2 E4

Holly Mount, Hampstead NW3 6SG ☎ 020 7435 2892
e-mail: hollybush@fullers.co.uk
dir: *Nearest tube: Hampstead. Exit tube station into Holly Hill, 1st right*

Historic pub serving hearty food

Once the stables belonging to the home of English portraitist George Romney, The Holly Bush became a pub after his death in 1802. The building has been investigated by 'ghost busters', but more tangible 21st-century media celebrities are easier to spot these days. The original panelled walls remain, and there are chandeliers in the restaurant. Depending on your appetite, the menu offers beef, ale and mushroom pie; seared duck breast with red cabbage, new potatoes and fennel; and bar snacks of sausage rolls and Scotch eggs – perfect with a pint of London Pride or Seafarers.

Open all day all wk 12-11 (Sun 12-10.30) **Bar Meals** L served Mon-Fri 12-3, Sat 12-4, Sun 12-5 D served Mon-Sat 6-10, Sun 6-9 Av main course £12 **Restaurant** L served Mon-Fri 12-3, Sat 12-4, Sun 12-5 D served Mon-Sat 6-10, Sun 6-9 ⊕ FULLER'S ◀ London Pride & ESB, Butcombe, Seafarers ♻ Aspall. ♟10 **Facilities** Non-diners area ⬢ (Bar Restaurant) ⬢ Children's portions Outside area ♒ Beer festival Wi-fi 🚌 (notice required)

The Bull and Last
PLAN 2 E5

168 Highgate Rd NW5 1QS ☎ 020 7267 3641
e-mail: info@thebullandlast.co.uk
dir: *From Kentish Town tube station N into Highgate Rd (10 mins' walk)*

Tempting menus and many wines by the glass

A historic free house in a Grade II listed building, a stone's throw from Hampstead Heath. Children and dogs are welcome too, so this really is a relaxing place to sample a pint of Young's or one of the wines sold by the glass. Wondering whether to eat? A glance at the menu will make up your mind – who can resist mouthwatering starters like orecchiette (ear-shaped pasta) with chicken livers, or fish soup with rouille and gruyère croquettes? Move on to roast Cornish cod with oxtail ragout if you're determined to push the boat out.

Open all day all wk 12-11 (Fri-Sat 12-12 Sun 12-10.30) Closed: 24-25 Dec ⊕ FREE HOUSE/ETIVE PUBS LTD ◀ Hook Norton Hooky Bitter, Sharp's Doom Bar, Ringwood Best Bitter, Young's London Porter ♻ Addlestones. **Facilities** ⬢ (Bar) ⬢ Children's menu Children's portions Wi-fi

Dartmouth Arms
PLAN 2 E5

35 York Rise NW5 1SP ☎ 020 7485 3267
e-mail: dartmoutharms@faucetinn.com
dir: *5 mins' walk from Hampstead Heath, 2 mins from Tufnell Park tube station*

Hearty pub grub plus weekend breakfasts

This welcoming local close to Hampstead Heath is open for breakfast from 10am at weekends and will happily serve you a Virgin Mary (a Bloody Mary without the vodka) along with your bacon buttie. Quiz nights every Tuesday are perhaps a better time to sample ales by Adnams, Westerham and Young's, and there's a good choice of real ciders too. Sustenance comes in the form of hearty, upmarket pub food: parsnip and apple soup; Bridge Farm organic bangers with celeriac mash, roasting gravy and freshly battered onion rings; and apple crumble with crème anglaise are typical offerings.

Open all day all wk 11-11 (Fri 11am-mdnt Sat 10am-mdnt Sun 10am-10.30pm) ⊕ FREE HOUSE ◀ Westerham Finchcocks Original, Adnams, Young's ♻ Kingstone Press, Briska. **Facilities** ⬢ Children's menu Children's portions Wi-fi

Save on hotels. Book at theAA.com/hotel

LONDON 291 ENGLAND

The Lord Palmerston — PLAN 2 E5

33 Dartmouth Park Hill NW5 1HU ☎ 020 7485 1578
e-mail: lordpalmerston@geronimo-inns.co.uk
dir: *From Tufnell Park Station turn right. Up Dartmouth Park Hill. Pub on right, on corner of Chetwynd Rd*

Revamped pub with a focus on quality

A stylish London pub in the Dartmouth Park conservation area, the Lord Palmerston reopened following a major refurbishment programme that included extensive works to the kitchen, dining areas and garden. Food is taken seriously, with dishes including pork rillettes with cornichons and toast; wood pigeon with pearl barley, bacon, peas and red wine jus; and apple crumble with fresh cream. Other choices range from ale battered cod and chips to pickled walnut, Oxfordshire Blue, chicory and pear salad. As well as beer festivals in February and September, the pub holds weekly quiz nights and film screenings.

Open all day all wk 12-11 (Sun 12-10.30) **Bar Meals** L served Mon-Fri 12-3, Sat 12-4, Sun 12-5 D served Mon-Sat 6.30-10, Sun 6-8.30 Av main course £14 **Restaurant** L served Mon-Fri 12-3, Sat 12-4 D served Mon-Sat 6.30-10, Sun 6-9 Fixed menu price fr £24.50 ⊕ GERONIMO INNS LTD ◀ Adnams Southwold Bitter, Sharp's Doom Bar, Twickenham Naked Ladies, Purity Pure UBU, Redemption Ò Aspall. ₹ 24 **Facilities** Non-diners area ❤ (Bar Restaurant Garden) •♦ Children's portions Garden Beer festival Cider festival Wi-fi ━

NW6

The Salusbury Pub and Dining Room — PLAN 2 D4

50-52 Salusbury Rd NW6 6NN ☎ 020 7328 3286
e-mail: thesalusburypub@btconnect.com
dir: *100mtrs left from Queens Park tube & train station*

Fine English ales and inviting Italian food

In the hub of the Queen's Park community, this gastro-pub has a lively and vibrant atmosphere, offering draft beers and a London restaurant-style menu without the associated prices. The award-winning wine list boasts more than 100 wines, including mature offerings from the cellar. The owners stick to their successful formula of fantastic Italian food, great wines and consistent service. An antipasti starter of fritto of squid and mullet with aïoli sets the high standard; the treats continue with pheasant with cauliflower purée and parsnip crisps; halibut with Jerusalem artichokes, or pappardelle with duck ragu. An equally enticing set menu is also available.

Open all day 12-11 (Thu-Sat 12-12 Sun 12-10.30) Closed: 25-26 Dec, Mon L (ex BHs) **Bar Meals** L served Tue-Fri 12-3, Sat-Sun 12.30-3.30 D served all wk 7-10.15 Av main course £14 **Restaurant** L served Tue-Fri 12-3, Sat-Sun 12.30-3.30 D served all wk 7-10.15 Fixed menu price fr £30 Av 3 course à la carte fr £20 ⊕ FREE HOUSE ◀ St Austell Tribute, Greene King Abbot Ale, Moorland Old Speckled Hen Ò Aspall. ₹15 **Facilities** Non-diners area ❤ (Bar Outside area) •♦ Children's portions Family room Outside area ♬ Wi-fi ━ (notice required)

NW8

The New Inn — PLAN 2 E4

2 Allitsen Rd, St John's Wood NW8 6LA ☎ 020 7722 0726
e-mail: thenewinn@gmail.com
dir: *Exit A41 by St John's Wood tube station into Acacia Rd, last right, to end on corner*

British favourites meet international tapas

Colourful flower baskets and troughs break the lines of this street-corner pub, where pavement tables are a popular retreat for locals supping Abbot Ale, Aspall cider or a choice from the extensive wine list. This convivial Regency inn is well-placed for nearby Regent's Park and Lord's Cricket Ground. In the elegant restaurant, diners indulge in the sharing boards, the global tapas selection, fresh salads or a traditional main like bangers and mash or rack of ribs. Desserts include a tiramisu and home-made ice creams. There is a 'Little People's' menu, and a curry night every Wednesday.

Open all day all wk 11-11 (Fri-Sat 11-mdnt Sun 12-10.30) **Bar Meals** Av main course £12 food served all day **Restaurant** food served all day ⊕ GREENE KING ◀ Abbot Ale, IPA Ò Aspall, Kopparberg, Rekorderlig. ₹ 14 **Facilities** Non-diners area ❤ (Bar Restaurant) •♦ Children's menu Children's portions Wi-fi ━

The Salt House — PLAN 2 E4

63 Abbey Rd, St John's Wood NW8 0AE ☎ 020 7328 6626
e-mail: info@thesalthouse.co.uk
dir: *Turn right outside St John's Wood tube. Left into Marlborough Place, right into Abbey Rd, pub on left*

Pub with a commitment to quality, home-cooked food

A 'mere scuttle' from The Beatles' famous Abbey Road zebra crossing is how this 18th-century inn describes itself. It promises two things: to source excellent ingredients and to home cook them. With the exception of the odd bottle of ketchup, everything – including bread, buns and pasta – is made on site. Meats are accredited by the Rare Breed Survival Trust, and most fish is caught in Looe. Main courses include comfort dishes such as beer-battered fish and chips, and pork and leek sausages. Warm pear and almond tart with Chantilly cream is a nice finish. Outside heaters allow for alfresco dining even when the weather is inclement.

Open all day all wk 12-11 (Sat 12-12) ⊕ GREENE KING ◀ Abbot Ale, Guinness Ò Aspall. **Facilities** •♦ Family room

---

NW10

William IV Bar & Restaurant — PLAN 2 D4

786 Harrow Rd NW10 5JX ☎ 020 8969 5944
e-mail: info@williamivlondon.com
dir: *Nearest tube: Kensal Green*

Gastro-pub of great character

Character is everywhere in this large, rambling gastro-pub, happily co-existing with cosmopolitan Kensal Green's cafés, delis and antique shops. Music plays in the bar, but you can always chill out in the sofa area. Classic and modern European food is represented by duck breast with pickled cabbage, bok choy and anise jus; baked cod, chorizo and potato cake, green beans and sweet wine dressing; and courgette parcel stuffed with wild rice, and saffron cream sauce.

Open all day all wk 12-11 (Fri-Sun noon-1am) ⊕ FREE HOUSE ◀ Fuller's London Pride, Morland Old Speckled Hen, Guest ales Ò Aspall. **Facilities** •♦ Children's menu Children's portions Garden Wi-fi

---

SE1

The Anchor & Hope ⑳⑳ — PLAN 1 E3

36 The Cut SE1 8LP ☎ 020 7928 9898
e-mail: anchorandhope@btconnect.com
dir: *Nearest tube: Southwark & Waterloo*

Down-to-earth and lively gastro-pub

This pub remains unstuffy, and children, parents, and dogs are all welcome. As a result, the pavement tables are much sought after in fine weather. The Anchor & Hope's menu is a no-nonsense list of refreshingly unembroidered dishes, and may change twice daily according to demand. Expect robust, gutsy flavours in warm snail and bacon salad; Middlewhite faggots and chips; and warm pickled herring with potato and sour cream. The wine list is notable for its straightforward pricing approach; many half bottles are half the cost of full ones – a factor much appreciated by the pub's faithful diners.

Open all day Closed: BHs, Xmas, New Year, 2wks Aug, Sun eve, Mon L ⊕ CHARLES WELLS ◀ Bombardier & Eagle IPA, Young's, Erdinger, Kirin Ò Luscombe. **Facilities** ❤ (Bar Restaurant) •♦

SE1 continued

The Fire Station
PLAN 1 E3

150 Waterloo Rd SE1 8SB ☎ 020 7620 2226
e-mail: info@thefirestationwaterloo.com
dir: Turn right at exit 2 of Waterloo Station

Converted early-Edwardian fire station

The remarkable conversion of this former fire station has kept many of its former trappings intact, including the original brickwork, doors and red fire buckets. The bar offers draught and bottled beers as well as cocktails and wines. The rear dining room faces the open kitchen; there are breakfast, set lunch, Sunday, restaurant and pre-theatre menus to take your pick from, as well as bar snacks and light bites. Dishes are home-made, traditional British and European, for example bouillabaisse, and chicken, walnut and tarragon ballotine. The handy location close to Waterloo, the Old Vic Theatre and Imperial War Museum means it can get busy.

Open all day all wk 9am-mdnt (Sun 11-11) Closed: 25-26 Dec, 1 Jan ⊕ MARSTON'S ◀ EPA, Fuller's London Pride, Ringwood. Facilities ◆◆ Children's portions Wi-fi

---

The Garrison
PLAN 1 G2

PICK OF THE PUBS

99-101 Bermondsey St SE1 3XB ☎ 020 7089 9355
e-mail: info@thegarrison.co.uk
dir: From London Bridge tube station, E towards Tower Bridge 200mtrs, right onto Bermondsey St. Pub in 100mtrs

Friendly neighbourhood gastro-pub

No doubt this green-tiled, street-corner pub was once a popular local for generations of Surrey Docks stevedores. The docks are no more and Bermondsey has gone up-market, but were those old boys to return they'd no doubt be amazed by the pub's 21st-century restyling, based around an idiosyncratic mix of decorative themes and antique knick-knacks. The place pulsates from breakfast through to the evening, when the downstairs room doubles as a mini-cinema. Start the day with a 'full and proper' or 'full vegetarian' breakfast, or maybe smoked haddock with poached egg, potato pancake and hollandaise; for lunch, there's pan-roasted coley with Jerusalem artichoke and chervil root purée; or Somerset brie with roasted pepper and pesto sandwich. In the evening, check out smoked salmon kedgeree; braised ox cheek with roasted parsnips; or the day's steak special. Drinks include beers from Adnams, and Munich's Spaten-Franziskaner, as well as Dunkerton and Breton ciders.

Open all day all wk 8am-11pm (Fri 8am-mdnt Sat 9am-mdnt Sun 9am-10.30pm) Closed: 25-26 Dec Bar Meals L served Mon-Fri 12-3, Sat-Sun 12.30-4 D served Mon-Sat 6-10, Sun 6-9.30 Restaurant L served Mon-Fri 12-3, Sat-Sun 12.30-4 D served Mon-Sat 6-10, Sun 6-9.30 ⊕ FREE HOUSE ◀ Spaten-Franziskaner-Bräu Franziskaner Hefe-Weisse, Adnams, Staropramen Ö Thatchers Pear, Dunkertons. ▼ 17 Facilities Non-diners area Wi-fi

---

The George Inn
PLAN 1 F3

77 Borough High St SE1 1NH ☎ 020 7407 2056
e-mail: 7781@greeneking.co.uk
dir: From London Bridge tube station, take Borough High St exit, left. Pub 200yds on left

Unique former haunt of Charles Dickens

The coming of the nearby railway meant demolition of part of what is now London's sole surviving example of a 17th-century, galleried coaching inn, but what's left is impressive. National Trust-owned, it still features some very old woodwork, like the simple wall seats. Serving thirsty Londoners for centuries, the pub is mentioned in Dickens's Little Dorrit. As well as Greene King ales and rotating guests, George Inn Ale is the house beer. The pub grub includes a sharing fish slate, potted mackerel, chicken casserole, shepherd's pie, roasted vegetable and cheese filo parcel, and Toulouse sausages. There are various beer festivals throughout the year.

Open all day all wk 11-11 (Sun 12-10.30) Closed: 25-26 Dec Bar Meals L served Mon-Sat 11-10, Sun 12-10 D served Mon-Sat 11-10, Sun 12-10 Av main course £10 food served all day Restaurant L served Mon-Sat 11-10, Sun 12-10 D served Mon-Sat 11-10, Sun 12-10 food served all day ⊕ GREENE KING ◀ Royal London, Abbot Ale & IPA, Morland Old Speckled Hen, George Inn Ale, Guest ale Ö Aspall. Facilities Non-diners area ◆◆ Garden ♬ Beer festival Wi-fi ▭

The Market Porter
PLAN 1 F3

9 Stoney St, Borough Market, London Bridge SE1 9AA
☎ 020 7407 2495
dir: Close to London Bridge Station

A real ale pub with a Harry Potter connection

With as apt a name as you could wish for, this Borough Market pub is blessed with a really good atmosphere, especially on Thursdays, Fridays and Saturdays, when the retail market operates. A claim to fame is that a few years ago the inn was transformed into the Third Hand Book Emporium in one of the Harry Potter films. The exceptional choice of real ales includes the resident Harvey's, others changing up to nine times a day and some international sidekicks. Apart from sandwiches and bar snacks are dishes such as Cumberland sausage with mash and red onion marmalade; slow-braised belly of Middle English pork with thyme; and tuna Niçoise salad. On weekdays the pub opens its doors at 6am.

Open all day all wk ⊕ FREE HOUSE ◀ Harvey's Sussex Best Bitter, wide selection of international ales.

The Crooked Well NEW
PLAN 2 F3

16 Grove Ln, Camberwell SE5 8SY ☎ 020 7252 7798
e-mail: info@thecrookedwell.com
dir: Nearest station: Denmark Hill

Neighbourhood restaurant and bar is a Camberwell beauty

Set up and run by three friends, each with stacks of restaurant experience in the kitchen or front of house, this Victorian, street corner pub has rapidly earned some worthy plaudits for its food. A penchant for home-cooked British classics, such as rabbit and bacon pie (for two), still allows continental influences to not so much creep in as enter with brio – for example, roast lamb with spiced aubergine and tzatziki; rose-harissa-toasted couscous; and coley with tagliatelle and salsa verde. Regularly involved with community events, it holds mums' (and dads') mornings and jazz nights.

Open all day all wk Closed: 25-30 Dec Bar Meals L served Mon-Sat 12.30-3, Sun 12.30-4 D served Mon-Sat 6.30-10.30, Sun 7-9.30 Av main course £10 Restaurant L served Mon-Sat 12.30-3, Sun 12.30-4 D served Mon-Sat 6.30-10.30, Sun 7-9.30 Fixed menu price fr £10 Av 3 course à la carte fr £26 ⊕ PUNCH TAVERNS ◀ Sharp's Doom Bar Ö Westons Wyld Wood Organic. ▼ 10 Facilities Non-diners area ✿ (Bar Restaurant Outside area) ◆◆ Children's menu Children's portions Outside area ♬ Wi-fi ▭ (notice required)

The Cutty Sark Tavern
PLAN 2 G3

4-6 Ballast Quay, Greenwich SE10 9PD
☎ 020 8858 3146
dir: Nearest tube: Greenwich. From Cutty Sark ship follow river towards Millennium Dome (10 mins' walk)

A three-storey favourite with river views

There's been a tavern on Ballast Quay for hundreds of years. The current building dates back to the early 1800s when it was called the Union Tavern. It was renamed when the world famous tea-clipper was dry-docked upriver in 1954. Inside there are low beams, creaking floorboards, dark panelling and, from the large bow window in the upstairs bar, commanding views of the Thames, Canary Wharf and the Millennium Dome. Well-kept beers, wines by the glass and a wide selection of malts are all available, along with a choice of light bites, salads, classics like poacher's chicken, steak-and-ale pie and Hawaiian burger, as well as vegetarian and fish dishes, and a children's menu. Busy at weekends, especially on fine days.

Open all day all wk ⊕ FREE HOUSE ◀ Fuller's London Pride, George Gale & Co Seafarers, Butcombe. Facilities ◆◆ Children's menu Children's portions Garden

Save on hotels. Book at theAA.com/hotel

LONDON 293 ENGLAND

Greenwich Union Pub
PLAN 2 G3

56 Royal Hill SE10 8RT ☎ 020 8692 6258
e-mail: theunion@meantimebrewing.com
dir: *From Greenwich DLR & main station exit by main ticket hall, turn left, 2nd right into Royal Hill. Pub 100yds on right*

A beer-drinker's idea of heaven

In the heart of Greenwich's bustling Royal Hill, this pub's comfortable leather sofas and flagstone floors help to keep its original character intact. Interesting craft beers from the award-winning Meantime Brewing Co, along with lagers from around the world and a beer garden, make this a popular spot. The food is an eclectic range of traditional and modern dishes drawn from around the world. Everything is freshly prepared and sourced locally where possible: fish comes straight from Billingsgate Market, while bread comes from the Greenwich itself. The lunch menu includes sandwiches, and favourites like home-made 28-day-aged Angus beefburger, while at dinner you could opt for Welsh rarebit followed by kedgeree or three bean chilli. All courses, including dessert, can be accompanied by a recommended beer, so you could round off with sticky toffee pudding and a glass of Meantime Chocolate Porter.

Open all day all wk 12-11 (Sun 12-10.30) **Bar Meals** Av main course £12 food served all day **Restaurant** food served all day ⊕ FREE HOUSE ◀ Meantime Pale Ale, Pilsner, Yakima Red ⓸ Thatchers. **Facilities** ✿ (Bar Restaurant Garden) ♦♦ Garden ♫ Wi-fi

North Pole Bar & Restaurant
PLAN 2 G3

PICK OF THE PUBS

131 Greenwich High Rd, Greenwich SE10 8JA
☎ 020 8853 3020
e-mail: info@northpolegreenwich.com
dir: *Right from Greenwich rail station, pass Novotel. Pub on right*

The complete package in Greenwich

Dating from 1849, the name originated with the Victorian obsession for polar exploration, and North Pole Road adjoins the pub. It's a stylish, contemporary venue, offering a complete night out under one roof, with a bar, restaurant and basement club. Outside in the beer garden (which is also home to a shisha pipe lounge) is seating for 100 people. Refreshments range from international beers such as Staropramen to cocktails, while the all-day bar menu features tapas, platters, sandwiches, grills and salads. The Piano restaurant attracts both visitors and loyal locals with its seasonally changing, modern European à la carte and brasserie menus: ballotine of duck with foie gras and spicy fruit chutney; basil-infused gnocchi with wild mushrooms and baby spinach; and roasted salmon fillet with mixed peppers, aubergine fondue and a red pepper and basil sauce. Desserts range from star anise crème brûlée to treacle pudding.

Open all day all wk noon-2am **Bar Meals** L served all wk 12-10 D served all wk 12-10 Av main course £7 food served all day **Restaurant** L served Sat-Sun 12-5

D served all wk 6-10.30 Fixed menu price fr £16.95 Av 3 course à la carte fr £23.95 ⊕ FREE HOUSE ◀ Guinness, Staropramen, Greene King IPA ⓸ Aspall. ♥ 9
Facilities Non-diners area ✿ (Bar Restaurant Garden) ♦♦ Children's menu Children's portions Garden ♫ Wi-fi ▧ (notice required)

SE11

The Tommyfield NEW
PLAN 1 E1

185 Kennington Ln SE11 4EZ ☎ 020 7735 1061
e-mail: info@thetommyfield.co.uk
dir: *Nearest tube station: Kennington*

Transformed south London corner pub

Inspiration for what to call the former White Hart was the 150th anniversary in 2010 of the first British chip shop, in the famous Tommyfield Market in Oldham. Now part of the Renaissance Pubs group, the pub's padded seating runs around the sides of the large, wooden-floored open bar area, where Sambrook's beer bats for London breweries. With menus echoing Victorian chop houses, expect roasts and grills; sustainable fish from English waters; traditional pie and mash; wild boar and apple sausages; and pumpkin gnocchi. Children are well catered for. A popular fortnightly comedy night takes place upstairs.

Open all day all wk Closed: 25-26 Dec, 1 Jan **Bar Meals** L served all wk 12-3.30 D served all wk 6-10.30 Av main course £12.50 **Restaurant** L served all wk 12-3.30 D served all wk 6-10.30 Fixed menu price fr £18.50 Av 3 course à la carte fr £25 ⊕ FREE HOUSE ◀ Timothy Taylor, Sambrook's Wandle, Two Cocks Roundhead ⓸ Aspall. ♥ 18 **Facilities** Non-diners area ✿ (Bar Restaurant Outside area) ♦♦ Children's menu Children's portions Outside area Wi-fi ▧ (notice required)

SE21

The Crown & Greyhound
PLAN 2 F2

73 Dulwich Village SE21 7BJ ☎ 020 8299 4976
e-mail: enquiry@thecrownandgreyhound.co.uk
dir: *Nearest station: North Dulwich*

A warm welcome in Dulwich

With a history reaching back to the 18th century, The Crown & Greyhound (nicknamed The Dog) counts Charles Dickens and John Ruskin amongst its celebrated patrons. In the olden days, the pub was split in two - The Crown served the gentry while The Greyhound housed the labourers. Modern day customers will find three bars and a restaurant in the heart of peaceful Dulwich Village. The ever-changing menu might feature Shropshire roast chicken with herb butter and fries, and sticky toffee pudding for dessert. There are daily salads, pasta and fish dishes, too.

Open all day all wk 11-11 (Thu-Sat 11am-mdnt Sun 11-10.30) **Bar Meals** L served Mon-Sat 12-10, Sun 12-9 D served Mon-Sat 12-10, Sun 12-9 food served all day **Restaurant** L served Mon-Sat 12-10, Sun 12-9 D served Mon-Sat 12-10, Sun 12-9 food served all day ⊕ MITCHELLS & BUTLERS ◀ Harvey's Sussex Best Bitter,

Sharp's Doom Bar, Guest ales ⓸ Aspall. ♥ 20
Facilities Non-diners area ✿ (Bar Garden) ♦♦ Children's menu Children's portions Garden ♫ ▧ (notice required)

The Rosendale NEW
PLAN 2 F2

65 Rosendale Rd, West Dulwich SE21 8EZ
☎ 020 8761 9008
e-mail: info@therosendale.co.uk
dir: *Nearest station: West Dulwich*

Transformed mid-Victorian coach house

Owned by three former schoolmates who also run other South London pubs, every one, they say, an "all-too-forgettable place" until they came along and transformed them. They like keeping things simple but interesting, so the formidably-stocked bar might include Moor Nor' Hop, a Somerset-brewed, but also North American-style, pale ale, several real ciders, and a mind-boggling range of rums, tequilas and vodkas. Traditional British food, using top-quality ingredients, such as meats from the boys' own farm in Hampshire, includes bar snacks like Welsh rarebit, and the more substantial Orkney sirloin steak; honey-spiced Goosnargh duck; and roast butternut and ricotta ravioli.

Open all day all wk Closed: 26 Dec **Bar Meals** L served Mon-Fri 12-3.30, Sat 12-4, Sun 12-9 D served Mon-Thu 6-10, Fri-Sat 6-10.30, Sun 12-9 Av main course £9-£14.50 **Restaurant** L served Mon-Fri 12-3.30, Sat 12-4, Sun 12-9 D served Mon-Thu 6-10, Fri-Sat 6-10.30, Sun 12-9 Av 3 course à la carte fr £22.50 ⊕ RENAISSANCE PUBS ◀ Moor Nor' Hop, Adnams Ghost Ship, Harvey's Sussex Best Bitter, Timothy Taylor Landlord ⓸ Wilkins Farmhouse, Hecks, Sandford Orchards, Wilcox. ♥ 27
Facilities Non-diners area ✿ (Bar Garden) ♦♦ Children's menu Children's portions Play area Garden ♫ Wi-fi ▧

SE22

The Palmerston ◉
PLAN 2 F2

91 Lordship Ln, East Dulwich SE22 8EP
☎ 020 8693 1629
e-mail: info@thepalmerston.net
dir: *2m from Clapham, 0.5m from Dulwich Village, 10 mins' walk from East Dulwich station*

Smart London corner pub serving excellent modern food

A striking gastro-pub, heavy on the wood panelling, with much stripped floorboard and some great floor tiling. Occasional installations of photographic exhibitions add to the flair of this corner-plot destination dining pub in leafy Dulwich. Chef Jamie Younger's one AA Rosette results from his modern British menu with a Mediterranean twist. Start with fricassée of plaice in brioche with leeks, spinach and tarragon; follow with taleggio, Swiss chard and beetroot frittata or roast fillet of Cornish seabass with spinach, brown shrimp, dill and lemon butter sauce; and finish with spotted dick and rum custard. Affable locals pop in for some flavoursome beers, too, from the likes of Sharp's and Harvey's.

continued

SE22 continued

Open all day all wk Closed: 25-26 Dec, 1 Jan **Bar Meals** L served Mon-Fri 12-2.30, Sat-Sun 12-3.30 D served Mon-Sat 7-10, Sun 7-9.30 Av main course £11 **Restaurant** L served Mon-Fri 12-2.30, Sat-Sun 12-3.30 D served Mon-Sat 7-10, Sun 7-9.30 Fixed menu price fr £13.50 Av 3 course à la carte fr £27 ⊕ ENTERPRISE INNS ⬤ Sharp's Doom Bar, Harvey's, Timothy Taylor Landlord, Sambrook's Wandle ♻ Westons Stowford Press. ☂ 16
Facilities Non-diners area ⬤ Children's portions Outside area ⚲

SE23

The Dartmouth Arms   PLAN 2 G2

7 Dartmouth Rd, Forest Hill SE23 3HN
☎ 020 8488 3117
e-mail: mail@thedartmoutharms.com
dir: 800mtrs from Horniman Museum

Smart Georgian pub with modern British cuisine

The long-vanished Croydon Canal once ran behind this pub dating from 1815, and you can still see the towpath railings at the bottom of the car park. Behind the smart façade, bars serve snacks, traditional real ales, continental lagers, cocktails, coffees and teas, while the restaurant might offer grilled haloumi skewers or duck liver parfait as starters, and mains might be Shetland mussels in a cider, leek and cream sauce or pan-fried salmon with sun-dried tomato risotto and watercress. Puddings include vanilla pannacotta. There's a small, secluded garden.

Open all wk Closed: 25-26 Dec, 1 Jan **Bar Meals** food served all day **Restaurant** L served Mon-Sat 12-3.30, Sun 12-10 D served Mon-Sat 12-10.30, Sun 12-10 ⊕ ENTERPRISE INNS ⬤ Fuller's London Pride, Timothy Taylor Landlord, Sharp's Doom Bar ♻ Addlestones.
Facilities Non-diners area ⬤ Garden ⚲ Parking Wi-fi 🚌

SW1

The Buckingham Arms   PLAN 1 D2

62 Petty France SW1H 9EU ☎ 020 7222 3386
e-mail: buckinghamarms@youngs.co.uk
dir: Nearest tube: St James's Park

Forever popular for good beer and top pub food

This elegant Young's pub was known as the Black Horse until 1903 and retains much of its old charm including etched mirrors and period light fittings in the bar. Close to Buckingham Palace, it is popular with pretty much everyone: tourists, business people, politicians, media types and real ale fans. Expect a good range of simple pub food, including sharing platters, sandwiches and hearty favourites such as sausages and mash, steak-and-ale pie and West Country beef burgers.

Open all day 11-11 (Sat 12-6 Sun 12-6 summer) Closed: 25-26 Dec, Sun (winter) ⊕ YOUNG'S ⬤ Bitter, Wells Bombardier, Sambrook's Wandle. **Facilities** ⬤ (Bar) ⬤ Wi-fi

Nags Head   PLAN 1 B2

PICK OF THE PUBS

53 Kinnerton St SW1X 8ED ☎ 020 7235 1135
dir: Telephone for directions

Step back in time at this mew's pub

This pub was built in the early 19th century to cater for the footmen and stable hands who looked after the horses in these Belgravia mews. With its Dickensian frontage and an interior like a well-stocked bric-à-brac shop, the Nags Head stubbornly resists any contemporary touches. It's a mobile phone-free zone, too. Compact and bijou, it's located in a quiet mews near Harrods, its front and back bars connected by a narrow stairway and boasting wooden floors, panelled walls, and low ceilings. The walls are covered with photos, drawings, mirrors, helmets, model aeroplanes; there are even penny-slot machines. The atmosphere is best described as 'entertaining' if you're in the right frame of mind. The waist-high bar is another oddity, but the full Adnams range is served, along with a good value menu that includes salads, sandwiches, a daily roast and pie, and traditional pub favourites like chilli con carne and ploughman's.

Open all day all wk 11-11 **Bar Meals** L served all wk 11-9.30 food served all day **Restaurant** food served all day ⊕ FREE HOUSE ⬤ Adnams Southwold Bitter, Broadside, Fisherman, Regatta ♻ Aspall.
Facilities Non-diners area ☙ (Bar) ⬤

The Orange Public House & Hotel   PLAN 1 C1

37 Pimlico Rd SW1W 8NE ☎ 020 7881 9844
e-mail: reservations@theorange.co.uk
dir: Nearest tube stations: Victoria & Sloane Street

An ornate corner building offering rustic and uncomplicated food

Recognised for its approach to sustainability, The Orange comprises a number of light and airy adjoining rooms, which have a rustic Tuscan feel with their muted colours and potted orange trees on stripped wooden boards. Well-heeled locals quaff Adnams ales and Italian wines while selecting from menus of modern European dishes. Wood-fired pizzas and oven roasts lead the way, but the carte is full of good things: grilled English rose veal chop; line-caught cod with celeriac, apple, Puy lentils, kale and Madeira jus; and steak, ale and cheddar pie, to list but a few.

Open all day all wk 8am-11.30pm (Sun 8am-10.30pm) **Bar Meals** L served all wk 12-6 D served all wk 6-10 Av main course £17 food served all day **Restaurant** L served all wk 12-3 D served all wk 6-10 Av 3 course à la carte fr £32 ⊕ FREE HOUSE ⬤ Adnams, Meantime Wheat & Pale Ale ♻ Aspall. ☂ 15 **Facilities** Non-diners area ⬤ Children's menu Children's portions Wi-fi

The Thomas Cubitt   PLAN 1 C2

44 Elizabeth St SW1W 9PA ☎ 020 7730 6060
e-mail: reservations@thethomascubitt.co.uk
dir: Nearest stations: Victoria & Sloane Square

Distinguished pub in fashionable district

Norfolk-born builder Thomas Cubitt developed Belgravia as a stuccoed rival to swanky Mayfair. This exclusive, white-painted corner pub draws a discerning crowd to its country-house-style interior featuring open fireplaces, detailed panelling and a superb hand-made, oak counter. Floor-to-ceiling glass doors open out on to tables and chairs on the street. In the bar, where Adnams and Deuchars real ales are resident, enjoy Carlingford rock oysters; and corn-fed chicken Caesar salad: upstairs the dining room offers Highland venison Wellington; Isle of Gigha halibut fillet; and Fivemiletown goats' cheese and spinach pie. Booking is essential for the memorable Sunday roast.

Open all day all wk 12-11 (Sun 12-10.30) Closed: Xmas **Bar Meals** L served all wk all day D served all wk all day Av main course £15 food served all day **Restaurant** L served all wk 12-3.30 D served all wk 6-9.30 Av 3 course à la carte fr £38 ⊕ FREE HOUSE ⬤ Caledonian Deuchars IPA, Adnams ♻ Aspall. ☂ **Facilities** Non-diners area ⬤ Children's menu Children's portions ⚲ 🚌 (notice required)

The Wilton Arms   PLAN 1 B2

71 Kinnerton St SW1X 8ED ☎ 020 7235 4854
e-mail: wilton@shepherd-neame.co.uk
dir: Between Hyde Park Corner & Knightsbridge tube stations

Cosy pub serving Shepherd Neame ales

Known locally as The Village Pub, this early 19th-century hostelry's other name is a reference to the 1st Earl of Wilton. In summer it is distinguished by fabulous flower-filled baskets and window boxes. High settles and bookcases create cosy, individual seating areas in the air-conditioned interior, and a conservatory covers the old garden. Shepherd Neame ales, including Spitfire, accompany traditional pub fare: ploughman's, toasted sandwiches, burgers, sausages and mash with onion gravy; and a smoked salmon platter with brown bloomer bread are typical options. There's also a good choice of chicken dishes including garlic battered chicken goujons.

Open all day all wk Closed: 25-26 Dec, BHs **Bar Meals** L served Mon-Fri 12-4, Sat 12-3 D served Mon-Fri 5.30-9 ⊕ SHEPHERD NEAME ⬤ Spitfire & Bishops Finger, Oranjeboom. **Facilities** Non-diners area ☙ (Bar Outside area) ⬤ Children's portions Outside area ⚲ Wi-fi 🚌

Save on hotels. Book at theAA.com/hotel

LONDON 295 **ENGLAND**

SW3

The Admiral Codrington
PLAN 1 B2

17 Mossop St SW3 2LY ☎ 020 7581 0005
e-mail: admiral.codrington@333holdingsltd.com
dir: *Nearest tube stations: South Kensington & Sloane Square. Telephone for detailed directions*

Chic modern interior and tip-top ales

To habitués of this smart South Ken gastro-pub, it's The Cod, which explains the whimsical item on the menu – Admiral's cod, served with tomato, mushroom and herb crust. It's one of many modern British options that also include slow-cooked shoulder of lamb, root vegetables and rosemary, and three-cheese macaroni with crispy bacon. The restaurant's glass roof retracts to give 'alfresco' dining, and the heated beer garden has an all-weather awning. Snacks are available in the bar.

Open all day all wk 11.30am-mdnt (Fri-Sat 11.30am-1am Sun 12-10.30) ⊕ FREE HOUSE ◀ Shepherd Neame Spitfire, Black Sheep, Guinness ♂ The Orchard Pig. **Facilities** ♦♦ Children's menu Garden Wi-fi

The Builders Arms
PLAN 1 B1

PICK OF THE PUBS

13 Britten St SW3 3TY ☎ 020 7349 9040
e-mail: thebuildersarms@geronimo-inns.co.uk
dir: *From Sloane Square tube station into King's Rd. Right into Chelsea Manor St, at end right into Britten St, pub on right*

Modern English food with a twist

The Builders Arms is a stylish three-storey Georgian pub tucked away in the back streets of Chelsea, just off the Kings Road. It was built by the same crew that constructed St Luke's church over the way. Inside, leather sofas dot the spacious informal bar area, where you can enjoy a pint of Bombardier or Doom Bar. The Geronimo team are committed to using seasonal food, and have also developed a bespoke cheese, Stithians, which is only available in their pubs. The menu offers a wide range, from chicken liver parfait with tomato and apple chutney to a fillet steak open sandwich served with fries and red onion marmalade. Starters include wild mushrooms, brioche and truffle cream sauce, while a sample main course is mussels steamed with beer, celery and Oxford Blue sauce. There is an impressive number of wines by the glass. When the sun shines the outdoor terrace is hugely popular.

Open all wk Mon-Wed 11-11 Thu-Sat 11am-mdnt (Sun 12-10.30) **Restaurant** L served Mon-Fri 12-3, Sat 12-4, Sun 12-6 D served Mon-Wed 7-10, Thu-Sat 7-11, Sun 7-9 ⊕ GERONIMO INNS ◀ Wells Bombardier, Sharp's Doom Bar, Flowers IPA ♂ Aspall. ♚ 36 **Facilities** Non-diners area ☻ (Bar Restaurant) ♦♦ Children's portions Outside area ⋒ Wi-fi ▦

Coopers Arms
PLAN 1 B1

87 Flood St, Chelsea SW3 5TB ☎ 020 7376 3120
e-mail: coopersarms@youngs.co.uk
dir: *From Sloane Square tube station, into King's Rd. Approx 1m W, opposite Waitrose, turn left. Pub half way down Flood St*

Upmarket Chelsea pub offering a warm welcome

Tucked off the King's Road and close to the river, this pub sees celebrities rubbing shoulders with the aristocracy and blue collar workers. The stuffed brown bear, Canadian moose and boar bring a character of their own to the bar, where at least five real ales grace the pumps. Food is served here and in the quiet upstairs dining room, with a focus on fish and steak. The menu also offers a great home-made burger, pie of the day and salads. The interesting sharing platters include mini pies, vegetarian meze and charcuterie. There are quiz and live music nights, as well as a May beer festival.

Open all day all wk 12-11 (Sun 12-10.30) **Bar Meals** L served Mon-Fri 12-3, Sat 12-10, Sun 12-9 D served Mon-Fri 5-10, Sat 12-10, Sun 12-9 Av main course £11.50 **Restaurant** L served Mon-Fri 12-3, Sat 12-10, Sun 12-9 D served Mon-Fri 5-10, Sat 12-10, Sun 12-9 ⊕ YOUNG'S ◀ Special & Bitter, Wells Bombardier, Guinness. ♚ 15 **Facilities** Non-diners area ☻ (Bar Garden) ♦♦ Children's portions Garden Beer festival Wi-fi

The Pig's Ear
PLAN 1 A1

35 Old Church St SW3 5BS ☎ 020 7352 2908
e-mail: thepigsear@hotmail.co.uk
dir: *Telephone for directions*

Popular Chelsea gastro-pub

Corner gastro-pub off the King's Road specialises in real ales such as Pigs Ear and Sambrook's, as well as daily changing guests; you can also have Breton cider and Czech, Belgian and German bottled lagers. There's a traditional, timeless feel to the bar and the oak-panelled dining room on the first floor, where the British/French brasserie menu might offer a pork sharing board; Mediterranean fish soup; hand-chopped Scottish fillet steak tartare; line-caught whole sea bass en papillote; and risotto with seasonal wild mushrooms.

Open all day all wk ⊕ FREE HOUSE ◀ Uley Pigs Ear, Sambrook's, Duchess IPA, Guinness, Guest ales. **Facilities** ☻ (Bar) ♦♦ Children's portions Wi-fi

SW4

The Abbeville **NEW**
PLAN 2 F2

67-69 Abbeville Rd SW4 9JW ☎ 020 8675 2201
e-mail: info@theabbeville.co.uk
dir: *Nearest tube station: Clapham South*

Smart Clapham neighbourhood pub

The one-time Huguenot enclave around Abbeville Road lacked its own pub until local boys Nick Fox, Tom Peake and Mark Reynolds transformed a former restaurant into the pioneering member of today's Renaissance group of south London pubs; Massimo Tebaldi joined later as group executive chef. In style terms we're talking eccentric 16th-century paintings and mismatched furniture, although the long-legged bar chairs are clearly members of the same family. Timothy Taylor Landlord bitter hits the spot with the locals, while dishes include saffron risotto with seared scallops; chargrilled, marinated lamb rump salad; and chicken and wild mushroom ballottine with truffle dumplings.

Open all day all wk **Bar Meals** Av main course £14 food served all day **Restaurant** L served Mon-Fri 12-3.30, Sat 12-4, Sun 1-9 D served Mon-Fri 6-10.30, Sun 1-9 Av 3 course à la carte fr £25 ⊕ FREE HOUSE ◀ Timothy Taylor Landlord ♂ Aspall. ♚ 14 **Facilities** Non-diners area ☻ (Bar Restaurant Outside area) ♦♦ Children's menu Children's portions Outside area ⋒ Wi-fi

The Stonhouse **NEW**
PLAN 2 E2

165 Stonhouse St SW4 6BJ ☎ 020 7819 9312
e-mail: info@thestonhouse.co.uk
dir: *Nearest tube station: Clapham Common*

Modern local on a residential side street

Tucked discreetly away between Clapham's Old Town and its busy High Street is this impressively transformed corner local. In the elegant bar, Sambrook's Wandle and Timothy Taylor Landlord vie for real ale drinkers' attention, while cider fans can choose Aspall. In the log-fire-warmed dining area, the brasserie-style menu is skewed towards modern British food, in particular steaks, dishes featuring free-range chicken and pork from the pub's Hampshire farm, and sustainably sourced fish. Starters include pan-fried pigeon breast; and smoked mackerel pâté. For something different, try gnocchi with gorgonzola, sun-dried tomato and pine nuts. A partially-covered paved garden area lies outside.

Open all day all wk Closed: 25-26 Dec, 1 Jan **Bar Meals** L served Mon-Fri 12-3.30, Sat 11-4, Sun 11-9 D served Mon-Sat 6-10.30, Sun 11-9 Av main course £12.50 **Restaurant** L served Mon-Fri 12-3.30, Sat 11-4, Sun 11-9 D served Mon-Sat 6-10.30, Sun 11-9 Av 3 course à la carte fr £25 ⊕ PUNCH TAVERNS ◀ Timothy Taylor Landlord, Sambrook's Wandle ♂ Aspall. ♚ 19 **Facilities** Non-diners area ☻ (Bar Garden) ♦♦ Children's menu Children's portions Garden ⋒ Wi-fi ▦ (notice required)

SW6

The Atlas
PLAN 2 E3

PICK OF THE PUBS

16 Seagrave Rd, Fulham SW6 1RX ☎ 020 7385 9129
e-mail: reservations@theatlaspub.co.uk
dir: *2 mins walk from West Brompton tube station*

Traditional London pub with a walled garden

Just around the corner from West Brompton tube, The Atlas is one of only a handful of London pubs to have a walled garden. Located in a trendy part of town where a great many pubs have been reinvented to become diners or restaurants, here is a traditional, relaxed local that remains true to its cause with a spacious bar area split into eating and drinking sections. Typical menus might feature starters such as roast butternut squash soup with orange and sour cream; or crispy soft shell crab with guacamole and red pepper slaw. Tempting mains demonstrate some European influences in dishes such as roast guinea fowl with crispy polenta, cherry tomato and basil; and linguine alla 'genovese', green beans, potato, pesto and parmesan. There are good choices on the wine list, and The London Wine Academy holds wine workshops here.

Open all day all wk 12-12 Closed: 24-31 Dec **Bar Meals** L served Mon-Fri 12-2.30, Sat 12-4, Sun 12-10 D served Mon-Sat 6-10, Sun 12-10 ⊕ FREE HOUSE ◀ Fuller's London Pride, Guest ales ♂ Symonds. ♚ 15 **Facilities** Non-diners area ♦♦ Children's portions Garden ♬ Wi-fi ☞ (notice required)

The Harwood Arms ◉◉ NEW PLAN 2 E3

PICK OF THE PUBS

Walham Grove SW6 1QP ☎ 020 7386 1847
e-mail: admin@harwoodarms.com
dir: *Telephone for directions*

Tip-top dining pub in leafy Fulham

The combined talents of chef Brett Graham (The Ledbury, London) and TV chef Mike Robinson, who also owns the Pot Kiln in Berkshire (see entry), have transformed this neighbourhood pub in leafy Fulham into top dining venue. There's inspired British cooking but the Harwood remains a proper pub, with microbrewery ales on tap, a vibrant, friendly atmosphere, and a quiz night on Tuesdays. The kitchen's passion about provenance and seasonality of food is key to its success, and the pub is renowned for its game and wild food, predominantly from Berkshire, where Mike Robinson shoots on various estates. The short, ever-changing menu delivers warm salad of wood pigeon; roe deer haunch with tarragon, mustard and garlic potatoes; bream with cucumber, sea purslane and mussels; and fig tart with honey and thyme. Be sure to book ahead.

Open all day Closed: 24-27 Dec, 1 Jan, Mon until 5.30pm **Bar Meals** Av main course £19 **Restaurant** L served Tue-Sat 12-3, Sun 12-4 D served Mon-Sat 6.30-9.30, Sun 7-9 Av 3 course à la carte fr £35 ⊕ ENTERPRISE INNS ◀ Sambrook's Wandle, Bath Ales Gem, Hackney American Pale Ale. ♚ 20 **Facilities** Non-diners area ♦♦ Children's portions Wi-fi ☞ (notice required)

The Jam Tree
PLAN 2 E3

541 King's Rd SW6 2EB ☎ 020 3397 3739
e-mail: info@thejamtree.com
dir: *Nearest stations: Imperial Wharf & Fulham Broadway*

Quirky gastro-pub with a vibrant night life

Number two in The Jam Tree gastro-pub family, this Chelsea sibling echoes the quirkiness of the Kensington original. Antique mirrors, personalised artworks, old Chesterfields and mismatched furniture give the interior a decidedly individual look. The modern British menu with colonial undertones offers curries; thali, an Indian tasting platter; chicken or vegetable Madras; and beef rang dang. Other possibilities are slow-roasted duck leg; and seared scallops with Malay potato cake. A long cocktail list, barbecue, plasma screen and resident DJs are additional reasons for visiting.

Open all day all wk **Bar Meals** L served Mon-Fri 12-3, Sat-Sun 11-5 D served Mon-Fri 6-10, Sat 5-10, Sun 5-9 **Restaurant** L served Mon-Fri 12-3, Sat-Sun 11-5 D served Mon-Fri 6-10, Sat 5-10, Sun 5-9 ⊕ FREE HOUSE ◀ Timothy Taylor Landlord ♂ Symonds. ♚ 9 **Facilities** Non-diners area ♣ (Bar Restaurant Garden) ♦♦ Children's menu Children's portions Garden ♬ Wi-fi

The Sands End Pub
PLAN 2 E3

135-137 Stephendale Rd, Fulham SW6 2PR
☎ 020 7731 7823
e-mail: thesandsend@hotmail.co.uk
dir: *From Wandsworth Bridge Rd (A217) into Stephendale Rd. Pub 300yds at junct with Broughton Rd*

Local, seasonal produce drives the menu here

A stylish country pub in the city is how fashionable Fulham foodies regard this much-loved neighbourhood gem. Expect to find scrubbed farmhouse tables, wooden floors, locals quaffing pints of Black Sheep, chalkboard menus listing terrific bar snacks (the Scotch eggs are legendary) and a food philosophy built around the 'Field to Fork' mantra. The British seasonal cooking makes use of foraged produce and even vegetables from the pub's allotment, resulting in hearty and honest dishes like belly of pork with braised hispi cabbage and wholegrain mustard sauce; and apple and rhubarb crumble.

Open all day all wk Closed: 25 Dec **Bar Meals** L served all wk 12-3, snacks all day, brunch fr 10am wknds D served all wk 6-10.30 Av main course £15 food served all day **Restaurant** L served all wk 12-3 D served all wk 6-10.30 Fixed menu price fr £14.50 Av 3 course à la carte fr £32.50 ⊕ PUNCH TAVERNS ◀ St Austell Tribute, Sharp's Doom Bar, Black Sheep ♂ Aspall. ♚ 16 **Facilities** Non-diners area ♣ (Bar Restaurant Outside area) ♦♦ Children's portions Outside area ♬ Wi-fi

The White Horse
PLAN 2 E3

PICK OF THE PUBS

1-3 Parson's Green, Fulham SW6 4UL ☎ 020 7736 2115
e-mail: info@whitehorsesw6.com
dir: *140mtrs from Parson's Green tube*

Beer Academy at the 'Sloaney Pony'

With a triangular walled front terrace overlooking Parson's Green, the former late 18th-century coaching inn and Victorian gin palace is a substantial sandstone pub. It's a destination for lovers of British pub food and interesting real ales and wines, with a restaurant in the former coach house, an upstairs bar, and a luxurious private dining area. The interior is a pleasing blend of polished mahogany and wooden and flagstone floors, open fires and contemporary lighting. Every dish on the menu comes with a recommended beer to drink, such partnering forming part of the pub's Beer Academy Courses. For instance, a starter of ham hock and broad bean terrine is paired with Anchor Bock; and a main of sea bass, chickpeas, chorizo and squid should be washed down with a pint of Oakham JHB. It's good for Sunday brunch, summer barbecues and its four annual beer festivals – American, European, British and Old Ale.

Open all day all wk **Bar Meals** L served all wk 12-10.30 D served all wk 12-10.30 food served all day **Restaurant** food served all day ⊕ MITCHELLS & BUTLERS ◀ Adnams Broadside, Oakham JHB, Hobsons Best Bitter ♂ Aspall. ♚ 20 **Facilities** Non-diners area ♣ (Bar Garden) ♦♦ Children's portions Garden ♬ Beer festival Wi-fi

SW10

The Hollywood Arms
PLAN 1 A1

PICK OF THE PUBS

45 Hollywood Rd SW10 9HX ☎ 020 7349 7840
e-mail: hollywoodarms@youngs.co.uk
dir: *From Chelsea & Westminster Hospital in Fulham Rd into Hollywood Rd opposite, 200mtrs on right*

Gem of a pub with a considered approach to cooking

In the heart of Chelsea, this listed building dates back to the mid-17th century when it was the home of landowner Henry Middleton, who owned land in England, Barbados and America. The interior of this hidden treasure is elegantly appointed, its original charm complemented by rich natural woods, pastel shades and modern fabrics. The large upstairs lounge has elegant mouldings around the ceiling and large open fires, whilst the ground-floor pub and restaurant retains much of its traditional atmosphere. Here the chefs lovingly create dishes from scratch using high-quality ingredients. Small plates will produce diver-caught scallop gratin or potted Wiltshire rabbit on sourdough, while main courses offer game pie; Gressingham duck breast with rösti and spiced red cabbage; or whole baked sea bass with fennel, orange and caper salad. Classic puddings include treacle tart and apple crumble with custard.

Open all day all wk 12-11.30 (Thu-Sat 12-12 Sun 12-10.30) Bar Meals L served Mon-Fri 12-3, Sat-Sun 12-9 D served Mon-Fri 6-9, Sat-Sun 12-9 Restaurant L served Mon-Fri 12-3, Sat-Sun 12-9 D served Mon-Fri 6-9, Sat-Sun 12-9 ⊕ YOUNG'S ◀ Wells Bombardier, Youngs, Meantime Ŏ Aspall. ♟ 12 Facilities Non-diners area ❦ (Bar Restaurant) ♦ Children's portions ☰ Beer festival Cider festival Wi-fi ▭ (notice required)

Lots Road Pub and Dining Room
PLAN 2 E3

114 Lots Rd, Chelsea SW10 0RJ ☎ 020 7352 6645
e-mail: lotsroad@foodandfuel.co.uk
dir: 5-10 mins walk from Fulham Broadway Station

A star of the gastro-pub scene

Located opposite the entrance to Chelsea Harbour, this pub appeals to well-heeled locals with its relaxing vibe, attentive staff, great pub food, and a smart, comfortable, well-designed space, which segues smoothly between jaunty bar area and the more secluded dining room. There are real ales, an excellent wine list, and cocktails both quirky and classic. The menu offers a mix of seasonal pub classics and more innovative dishes, perhaps pumpkin and ginger soup; lamb shoulder shepherd's pie and curly kale; or root vegetable and butter bean lasagne and French beans. Don't miss Saturday brunch and the Sunday family roasts.

Open all day all wk 11-11 (Sun 12-10.30) ⊕ FOOD AND FUEL ◀ Sharp's Doom Bar, Wells Bombardier & Eagle IPA, Guinness. Facilities ♦ Children's menu Children's portions Wi-fi

SW11

The Bolingbroke Pub & Dining Room
PLAN 2 E2

172-174 Northcote Rd SW11 6RE ☎ 020 7228 4040
e-mail: info@thebolingbroke.com
dir: Nearest stations: Clapham South; Clapham Junction

Family-friendly dining pub

This refined dining pub stands in a road known colloquially as 'Nappy Valley', due to its popularity with well-heeled young families. Named after the first Viscount Bolingbroke, who managed to be both brilliant politician and reckless rake, the pub caters admirably for children and adults alike. Expect modern British fare along the lines of beetroot and goats' cheese tarte Tatin with balsamic glaze followed by braised beef cheeks with haggerty potatoes and red cabbage. Weekend brunch includes baked egg and soldiers for babies.

Open all day all wk Closed: 25-26 Dec Bar Meals L served Mon-Fri 12-3.30, Sat 10-4, Sun 12-9 D served Mon-Sat 6-10.30, Sun 12-9 Av main course £13 Restaurant L served Mon-Fri 12-3.30, Sat 10-4, Sun 12-9 D served Mon-Sat 6-10.30, Sun 12-9 ⊕ FREE HOUSE ◀ Timothy Taylor Landlord Ŏ Aspall, Westons Wyld Wood Organic. ♟ 13 Facilities Non-diners area ❦ (Bar Restaurant) ♦ Children's menu Children's portions Outside area ☰ Wi-fi ▭ (notice required)

The Fox & Hounds
PLAN 2 E2
PICK OF THE PUBS

66 Latchmere Rd, Battersea SW11 2JU
☎ 020 7924 5483
e-mail: foxandhoundsbattersea@btopenworld.com
dir: From Clapham Junction exit into High St turn left, through lights into Lavender Hill. After post office, left at lights. Pub 200yds on left

Known for its international wine list and Mediterranean food

This is one of those archetypal Victorian corner pubs that London still has in abundance but from the moment you step through the door you'll feel like one of the locals. Its style is simple: with bare wooden floors, an assortment of furniture, walled garden, extensive patio planting and a covered and heated seating area. Regulars head here for the good selection of real ales and an international wine list; the menu suggests the 'Wine of the Moment' with tasting notes, and Ales of the Week. Fresh ingredients are delivered daily from the London markets, enabling the Mediterranean-style menu and specials to change accordingly; all prepared in the open-to-view kitchen. So, you might start with saffron potato soup or squid and chorizo with prawns. Follow with roast spatchcock chicken with Parma ham; spinach and roast garlic risotto; rib-eye steak, roast potatoes and salsa verde; or pan-roasted salmon. A traditional British lunch is served on Sundays.

Open 12-3 5-11 (Mon 5-11 Fri-Sat 12-11 Sun 12-10.30) Closed: 24 Dec-1 Jan, Mon L Bar Meals L served Fri 12.30-3, Sat 12.30-4, Sun 12.30-10 D served all wk 6.30-10 ⊕ FREE HOUSE ◀ St Austell Tribute, Dark Star, Sambrook's, Guest ales Ŏ Aspall. ♟ 14 Facilities Non-diners area ♦ Children's portions Garden ☰ Wi-fi ▭ (notice required)

SW12

The Avalon NEW
PLAN 2 E2

16 Balham Hill SW12 9EB ☎ 020 8675 8613
e-mail: info@theavalonlondon.com
dir: Nearest tube station: Clapham South

Elegant, comfortable and relaxing

Named after the mythical isle of Arthurian legend, the attractions of this Balham member of the Renaissance group of south London pubs are far from fairytale. For example, there's a three-tiered rear garden that comes alive on summer days, the bar stocks Timothy Taylor Landlord, Sharp's Doom Bar and Aspall cider, and the wine list offers many by the glass. On top of that, house policy is to serve beef aged in-house, sustainable fish from English waters, and free-range pork and chicken from the group's farm. Bar meals include meze platter; Welsh rarebit; fish and chips; and croque monsieur.

Open all day all wk Closed: 26 Dec Bar Meals L served Mon-Fri 12-3.30, Sat 12-4, Sun 12-9 D served Mon-Sat 6-10.30, Sun 12-9 Av main course £11-£18 Restaurant L served Mon-Fri 12-3.30, Sat 12-4, Sun 12-9 D served Mon-Sat 6-10.30, Sun 12-9 Fixed menu price fr £28.50 ⊕ ENTERPRISE INNS ◀ Timothy Taylor Landlord, Sharp's

Doom Bar Ŏ Aspall. ♟ 15 Facilities Non-diners area ❦ (Bar Garden) ♦ Children's menu Children's portions Family room Garden ☰ Wi-fi

SW13

The Bull's Head
PLAN 2 D3

373 Lonsdale Rd, Barnes SW13 9PY ☎ 020 8876 5241
e-mail: jazz@thebullshead.com
dir: Telephone for directions

Riverside pub famous for authentic jazz and blues

The Thames-side setting of this imposing 17th-century pub would be a draw in itself, but what really pulls the crowds in are the top-class jazz and blue groups that have made the pub internationally famous over 50 years. Countless famous musicians have whet their whistles with the fine cask-conditioned ales from Wells and Young's – and so can you in the bustling bar. Traditional bar lunches include salt beef sandwiches; sausages, mash and onion gravy; and plum and apple crumble, while authentic Thai food is available throughout the pub in the evening.

Open all day all wk 12-12 Closed: 25 Dec ⊕ YOUNG'S ◀ Special, Bitter, Ramrod & Winter Warmer, Wells Bombardier, Guinness. Facilities ♦ Children's portions Family room Garden Wi-fi

The Idle Hour
PLAN 2 D2
PICK OF THE PUBS

62 Railway Side, Barnes SW13 0PQ ☎ 020 8878 5555
e-mail: theidlehour@aol.com
dir: From Mortlake High St (A3003) into White Hart Ln. 5th left into Railway Side (at rail crossing). Pub just past school

A good place for celebrity spotting

Being a little tricky to find doesn't fox the locals, nor apparently does it deter the custom of 'names' from music, film and TV, who frequent this mid 19th-century, Barnes-backwater free house. Although designed with a nod to tradition, that is, lots of candles and fresh flowers everywhere and a real fire in the winter, it's still modern and stylish. A bit quirky too - for proof, check any of the wrong-time-telling clocks. What confirms its pub status is that there are always at least ten draught beers, many more in bottles, a 'mind-boggling' array of spirits, and a carefully selected, almost entirely organic, wine list, many by the glass. The small, frequently changing menu makes use of mainly organic ingredients. A secluded garden doubles as a suntrap during the day and a romantic, candlelit spot for evening dining.

Open all wk 12-12 (Fri-Sat noon-1am) Closed: 25 Dec Bar Meals L served Mon-Fri 12-3, Sat-Sun 12.30-10.30 D served Mon-Fri 6-10, Sat-Sun 12.30-10.30 Restaurant L served Mon-Fri 12-3, Sat-Sun 12.30-10.30 D served Mon-Fri 6-10, Sat-Sun 12.30-10.30 ⊕ FREE HOUSE ◀ Harvey's Sussex Best Bitter, Sharp's Cornish Coaster Ŏ Addlestones. ♟ 15 Facilities Non-diners area ❦ (Bar Restaurant Garden) ♦ Garden ☰ Wi-fi

237 Lower Richmond Rd, Putney, London SW15 1HJ
Tel: 0208 788 0640   **Fax:** 01455 221 296
Website: www.thespencerpub.com
Email: info@thespencerpub.com

We at *The Spencer* pride ourselves on serving good food, excellent drinks and having friendly staff going above and beyond, to make your experience a truly memorable one. Our menu is full of British pub classics but also has a few contemporary dishes which makes for a mouth watering selection. We handpick the wines to complement the menu and our knowledgeable staffs are always on hand to give you advice.

Our focus is on you, our customer, and we try to ensure that your experience is an enjoyable one. The food is great value for money and the beers and wine are possibly some of the best selected in the area.

The Spencer is situated in the leafy backstreets of Putney, off the beaten track with a beautiful view of the common. There is plenty of space for all the family; children and dogs included. You can relax outside with a Pimm's in the all day sun or toast your feet during those cold winter evenings in front of our fire.

Save on hotels. Book at **theAA.com/hotel**

LONDON 299 **ENGLAND**

SW14

The Victoria
PLAN 2 C2

10 West Temple Sheen, East Sheen SW14 7RT
☎ **020 8876 4238**
e-mail: bookings@thevictoria.net
dir: *Nearest tube station: Richmond*

Family-friendly and a real charmer

Close to Richmond Park, The Victoria offers something for everyone, with a large conservatory dining room and a leafy garden with a safe children's play area. TV chef Paul Merrett and restaurateur Greg Bellamy are at the helm, so you can expect top culinary delights. Menus encompass casual bites like sausage roll or Angus beefburger, as well as main courses such as braised Cornish cuttlefish, tomato, chickpeas, rosemary and black ink aïoli; or Dingley Dell pork chop on champ with tarragon and grain mustard jus and red onion jam. Saturday brunch and Sunday lunch are particularly popular with families. Fuller's London Pride is on tap.

Open all day all wk **Bar Meals** L served Mon-Fri 12-10 D served Mon-Fri 12-10 Av main course £15.50 food served all day **Restaurant** L served Mon-Fri 12-2.30, Sat 12-3, Sun 12-5 D served Mon-Thu 6-10, Fri-Sat 6-10.30 Fixed menu price fr £12.50 Av 3 course à la carte fr £28 ⊕ ENTERPRISE INNS ◀ Fuller's London Pride, Timothy Taylor Landlord, Guest ale Ò Aspall. ♀ 28 **Facilities** Non-diners area ✿ (Bar Garden) ♦♦ Children's menu Children's portions Play area Garden ⴲ Parking Wi-fi

SW15

The Spencer
PLAN 2 D2

PICK OF THE PUBS

See Pick of the Pubs on page 300
See advert on opposite page

The Telegraph
PLAN 2 D2

Telegraph Rd, Putney Heath SW15 3TU
☎ **020 8788 2011**
e-mail: info@thetelegraphputney.co.uk
dir: *Nearest tube: East Putney. Nearest rail station: Putney High St*

A 'country pub' just minutes from the busy streets

This pub was close to an Admiralty telegraph station between London and Portsmouth, and has been involved in the sale of beer since before 1856. Although it's only five minutes from the hustle and bustle of Putney High Street, The Telegraph feels more like a country pub. Certainly the focus on well-kept real ales cannot be faulted, with Naked Ladies from Twickenham Fine Ales well worth a try. The menu, with its pub fare and contemporary European dishes, includes grazing boards and chicken, chorizo and haloumi skewers to start, and mains of braised lamb shank, roast duck breast, steaks and burgers.

Open all day all wk 11-mdnt **Bar Meals** L served Mon-Sat 12-9.30, Sun 12-9 D served Mon-Sat 12-9.30, Sun 12-9 food served all day **Restaurant** L served Mon-Sat 12-9.30, Sun 12-9 D served Mon-Sat 12-9.30, Sun 12-9 food served all day ◀ Sharp's Doom Bar, Twickenham Naked Ladies, Brakspear Bitter, Adnams Broadside. **Facilities** ♦♦ Children's menu Children's portions Garden Parking ⴲ

SW18

The Alma Tavern
PLAN 2 E2

499 Old York Rd, Wandsworth SW18 1TF
☎ **020 8870 2537**
e-mail: alma@youngs.co.uk
dir: *Opposite Wandsworth Town rail station*

A well-renovated Victorian town pub

Not far from the Thames or Wandsworth Common, the vivid green tiles covering part of the curving frontage of this street-corner inn can't fail to catch the eye, as do the belvedere tower and imposing balustrading. Step inside to appreciate the decorative plaster frieze, superb island bar, mosaics and feature mahogany staircase. The roomy bar has an interesting mix of highly polished wood and distressed tables, with plenty of perching posts; off this is a more peaceful dining room, where a combination of traditional pub grub and gastro-pub dishes attracts diners from a wide area. Beers from Young's and a good list of bins provide ample accompaniment.

Open all day all wk ⊕ YOUNG'S ◀ Sambrook's Wandle Ò Addlestones. **Facilities** ♦♦ Children's portions Wi-fi

The Earl Spencer
PLAN 2 E2

PICK OF THE PUBS

260-262 Merton Rd, Southfields SW18 5JL
☎ **020 8870 9244**
dir: *Exit Southfields tube station, into Replingham Rd, left at junct with Merton Rd, to junct with Kimber Rd*

Modern community and gastro-pub

Edwardian pubby grandeur, log fires and polished wood furnishings offer a relaxed, informal atmosphere at this gastro-pub less than fifteen minutes from the Wimbledon All England Tennis Club in SW19. The emphasis of the kitchen is the daily changing, seasonal menus with everything made on the premises including the bread. Kick off with pig's head terrine and stuffed pork belly with gribiche sauce; or warm smoked sprats, horseradish and mustard butter before progressing to grilled Toulouse sausages, mash, greens and white onion sauce; or herb-crumbed fillet of plaice with buttered new potatoes, fennel and caper slaw. Round off with ricotta doughnuts and butterscotch sauce. In warmer weather, simply unwind with a beer on the front patio. Change of ownership.

Open all wk 4-11 (Fri-Sat 11am-mdnt Sun 12-10.30) Closed: 25 & 26 Dec **Bar Meals** L served Fri-Sat 12.30-3, Sun 12.30-4 D served Mon-Sat 7-10.30, Sun 7-9.30 Av main course £13.95 ⊕ ENTERPRISE INNS ◀ Sambrook's Wandle, Otter, Harvey's Sussex Best Bitter, Sharp's Cornish Coaster, Rotating Guest Ales Ò Aspall, Westons Old Rosie & Wyld Wood Organic. ♀ 17 **Facilities** Non-diners area ✿ (Bar Garden) ♦♦ Garden Wi-fi

The Roundhouse
PLAN 2 E2

2 Northside, Wandsworth Common SW18 2SS
☎ **020 7326 8580**
e-mail: roundhouse@sabretoothvintners.com
dir: *Telephone for directions*

Recommended for its London microbrewery ales

Between Clapham Junction and Wandsworth, The Roundhouse has the ambience of a friendly local, with a round black walnut bar, open kitchen, and eclectic art on the walls. Ales come from two local microbreweries, including Battersea's Sambrook's - a Wandle ale named after a nearby river. The short, daily-changing menu may take in roast beetroot, feta, apple and caramelised pecan salad; pan-fried pollock, Jerusalem artichoke, purple sprouting broccoli and carrots; or roasted vegetable lasagne with a mixed leaf salad. Finish with chocolate cheesecake brownie and popcorn ice cream.

Open all day all wk Mon-Thu 12-11 (Fri-Sat 12-12 Sun 12-10.30) Closed: 25-26 Dec **Bar Meals** L served Mon-Fri 12-3, Sat 12-4, Sun 12-4.30 D served Mon-Sat 6-10, Sun 6.30-9 **Restaurant** L served Mon-Fri 12-3, Sat 12-4, Sun 12-4.30 D served Mon-Sat 6-10, Sun 6.30-9 ⊕ FREE HOUSE ◀ Sambrook's Wandle, Battersea Brownstone Ò Aspall. ♀ 15 **Facilities** Non-diners area ✿ (Bar Garden) ♦♦ Children's portions Garden ⴲ Wi-fi ⷇ (notice required)

PICK OF THE PUBS

The Spencer

SW15 **PLAN 2 D2**

237 Lower Richmond Rd, Putney SW15 1HJ ☎ 020 8788 0640

e-mail: info@thespencerpub.com
web: www.thespencerpub.com
dir: *Corner of Putney Common & Lower Richmond Rd, opposite Old Putney Hospital*

Well kept ales and family-friendly food

Formerly known as The Spencer Arms, this landmark pub occupies a lofty position on green and leafy Putney Common and its close proximity to the Thames Embankment makes it one of the best vantage points for watching the annual Oxford and Cambridge boat race. The beer garden here is part of the common and the pub's 25 picnic benches are hotly contested in the summer by those in search of an alfresco lunch. A light, bright and airy interior belies the rather traditional look of the place; revamped a few years ago, the emphasis is on good dining in a stylish environment where locals are still welcomed to sup at the bar, with Timothy Taylor Landlord and Fuller's London Pride among the pick of the beers. Meals, in the bar or restaurant area, are a modern take on traditional favourites, such as a starter of potted salmon with lemon, dill and chives, or classic prawn cocktail with Marie Rose sauce. Mains take on a seasonal look to

reflect the desire to use only the freshest ingredients; look for a ravioli of rocket and ricotta with sage butter; monkfish, butterfly prawns and chorizo brochettes with rice; or venison and juniper berry casserole with wild mushrooms and butternut squash. Typical desserts might include spiced apple and sultana crumble and custard or mango and passion fruit cheesecake. Sunday roasts and rotisserie free-range chickens are a favourite with families, and children get to choose from their own well-priced menu. An extensive breakfast menu (available 9am-noon from Monday to Saturday) is a popular option with early morning dog walkers and cyclists.

Open all day all wk Mon-Sat 9am-mdnt Sun 11-11.

Breakfast served Mon-Sat 9am-12.**Bar & Restaurant meals** served Mon-Sat 12-10, Sun 12-9. Bar Av main course £12; Restaurant Av 3 course à la carte fr £15 ⊞ FREE HOUSE ◀ Fuller's London Pride, Sharp's Doom Bar, Guinness, Timothy Taylor Landlord Ꝺ Symonds. ♟ 20 **Facilities** Non-diners area 🐾 ♦♦ Children's menu Children's portions Play area Garden 🎋 Wi-fi 🚐

Save on hotels. Book at **theAA.com/hotel**

LONDON 301 **ENGLAND**

SW18 *continued*

The Ship Inn PLAN 2 E2

PICK OF THE PUBS

41 Jew's Row SW18 1TB ☎ **020 8870 9667**
e-mail: theship@youngs.co.uk
dir: *From Wandsworth Bridge (S of river) into Jews Row (one way). Right at T-junct*

Conservatory bar favoured for its barbecues and live music

By its own admission, this late 18th-century Thames-side pub upriver from Wandsworth Bridge can't claim to be in one of London's most appealing locations, but it's fought hard to stay noticed and is really worth tracking down. An extensive renovation bringing new features is testament to this. Enter via the delightful, two-level, rose-covered terrace and you'll find a vibrant conservatory bar with bare floorboards, central wood-burning stove, motley collection of old wooden tables and chairs, and an open-plan kitchen that prepares jolly good pub food from high quality produce. On days when the barbecue is fired up, grab a pint of Young's or Sambrook's Wandle and enjoy chargrilled sirloin steak, braised shallots, hand-cut chips and watercress; seared guinea fowl, truffled mash, wilted greens and mushroom jus; or parsnip, tomato and goats' cheese gratin, Jerusalem artichoke and spinach fricassée. Tuesdays are given over to lively acoustic Irish music, and other bands play on Thursdays and Sundays; quiz night is Wednesday.

Open all day all wk Sun-Wed 11-11 (Thu-Sat 11am-mdnt) **Bar Meals** L served all wk 12-6 D served all wk 6-10 food served all day **Restaurant** L served Mon-Sat 12-4, Sun 12-5 D served Mon-Sat 6-10, Sun 7-10 ⊕ YOUNG'S & WELLS ◀ Wells Bombardier, Sambrook's Wandle, Young's & Seasonal ales Ŏ Addlestones, Aspall. ♀ 15 **Facilities** Non-diners area ♦ Children's menu Children's portions Garden ⊼ Wi-fi

---

W1

Duke of Wellington PLAN 1 B4

94a Crawford St W1H 2HQ ☎ **020 7723 2790**
e-mail: theduke@hotmail.co.uk
dir: *5 mins' walk from Baker Street Station*

Stylish decor and fine food

A refreshing mix of street-corner local and cosmopolitan restaurant is found here at the busy heart of Marylebone, amidst Georgian style terraces close to leafy Bryanston Square. Inspired interior design raises The Duke's profile, with gilt mirrors and an eye-catching Roman-style mural acting as foils to the dark-wood bar, rustic tables and fittings. The bright, first-floor restaurant is a tranquil escape and shares many dishes with the bar menu; smoked haddock with quails' eggs a starter before artichoke, sweet potato, chestnut and tomato crumble or chargrilled Galloway onglet steak with béarnaise sauce. Outside tables are popular with drinkers supping Doom Bar.

Open all day all wk Closed: 25 Dec-2 Jan **Bar Meals** L served all wk 12-4 D served all wk 6.30-10 Av main

course £14 **Restaurant** L served all wk 12-4 D served all wk 7-10 Av 3 course à la carte fr £28 ⊕ PUNCH TAVERNS ◀ Sharp's Doom Bar, Fuller's London Pride, Black Sheep Ŏ Addlestones. ♀ **Facilities** Non-diners area ♣ (Bar) ♦ Children's portions ⊼ Wi-fi ▦ (notice required)

French House PLAN 1 D4

49 Dean St, Soho W1D 5BG ☎ **020 7437 2477**
dir: *Nearest tube stations: Piccadilly Circus, Tottenham Court Road, Covent Garden. Pub at Shaftesbury Avenue end of Dean St*

The rich and famous beat a path to this Soho spot

This legendary Soho watering hole was patronised by General de Gaulle during the Second World War, and later by Dylan Thomas, Francis Bacon, Dan Farson and many other louche Soho habitués. Run by Lesley Lewis for over 20 years, the small, intimate and very atmospheric bar only serves half pints of Budvar, Leffe and Guinness. The upstairs is a second bar, offering more informal drinking space; this area is also used as an art gallery. Only lunchtime bar food is served.

Open all day all wk 12-11 (Sun 12-10.30) Closed: 25 Dec ⊕ FREE HOUSE ◀ Budweiser Budvar, Kronenbourg, Leffe, Meteor, Guinness. **Facilities** Wi-fi

---

The Grazing Goat PLAN 1 B4

6 New Quebec St W1H 7RQ ☎ **020 7724 7243**
e-mail: reservations@thegrazinggoat.co.uk
dir: *Behind Marble Arch tube station, off Seymour St*

Stylish London dining pub with plenty of character

Just minutes away from Oxford Street and Marble Arch, this classy, six-storey pub is full of period features including open fireplaces, oak floors and solid oak bars. The name is not mere whimsy; goats did once graze around here because the first Lady Portman was allergic to cow's milk. Expect modern British, seasonal cooking – maybe roasted celeriac soup or wild mushroom and spinach tart to start; followed by Petley Farm pork and ham hock pie or Highland game venison, with pear and hazelnut tart or rhubarb trifle for dessert. Floor-to-ceiling glass doors are opened in warmer weather for alfresco dining.

Open all day all wk 7.30am-11.30pm (Sun 7.30am-10.30pm) **Bar Meals** Av main course £17 food served all day **Restaurant** L served all wk 12-3 D served all wk 6-10 Av 3 course à la carte fr £32 ⊕ FREE HOUSE ◀ Sharp's Doom Bar, Caledonian Deuchars IPA Ŏ Aspall. ♀ 20 **Facilities** Non-diners area ♦ Children's portions ⊼ Wi-fi ▦ (notice required)

The Only Running Footman ⊛ NEW PLAN 1 C3

5 Charles St, Mayfair W1J 5DF ☎ **020 7499 2988**
e-mail: manager@therunningfootmanmayfair.com
dir: *Nearest tube station: Green Park*

Smart Mayfair pub - popular all year round

This central Mayfair pub's full name is 'I Am The Only Running Footman', recalling the manservants who would precede their aristocrat master's carriage, clearing riff-raff out of the way and paying tolls. By the early 1800s, only the 4th Duke of Queensbury's footman remained in service, so His Grace renamed this, their once-favourite pub, after him. The ground floor is traditionally pub-like, with removable windows to create an inside/outside feel in summer, but upstairs is an elegant restaurant serving slow-roast pork belly; fillet of wild halibut; fish stew; and venison loin from Holcot Estate, the pub's game farm in Northamptonshire.

Open all day all wk **Bar Meals** Av main course £17 food served all day **Restaurant** L served all wk 12-2.30 D served all wk 6.30-9.45 Fixed menu price fr £30 Av 3 course à la carte fr £25 ⊕ THE MEREDITH PUB GROUP ◀ Wells Bombardier, Greene King IPA, Young's Special Ŏ Aspall. ♀ 20 **Facilities** ♣ (Bar Outside area) ♦ Children's menu Children's portions Outside area ⊼ Wi-fi ▦ (notice required)

The Portman PLAN 1 B4

51 Upper Berkeley St W1H 7QW ☎ **020 7723 8996**
e-mail: manager@theportmanmarylebone.com
dir: *From Marble Arch into Great Cumberland Place, 3rd left into Upper Berkeley St*

Stylish central London pub with a seasonal British menu

Tucked between the hustle of Oxford Street and the elegant shops of Marylebone, prisoners once stopped here for a final drink on their way to the gallows at Tyburn Cross. These days, this friendly central London pub is the perfect place for weary shoppers to refuel on Rebellion Brewery ales and seasonal British classics served all day, 365 days a year. Seared Barbary duck breast with thyme rösti and cherry sauce or the pie of the day are popular choices, as are the steaks and Angus beef burgers.

Open all day all wk **Bar Meals** Av main course £14 food served all day **Restaurant** L served all wk 12-6 D served all wk 6-10 Fixed menu price fr £28 Av 3 course à la carte fr £24 food served all day ⊕ FREE HOUSE ◀ Rebellion, Guest ale Ŏ Aspall. ♀ 15 **Facilities** Non-diners area ♣ (Bar Outside area) ♦ Children's menu Children's portions Outside area ⊼ Wi-fi ▦ (notice required)

W2

The Cow
PLAN 2 E4

89 Westbourne Park Rd W2 5QH ☎ 020 7221 5400
e-mail: office@thecowlondon.co.uk
dir: *Telephone for directions*

Oysters and Guinness take centre stage

Popular with the Notting Hill glitterati, this atmospheric Irish gastro-pub has a bustling downstairs bar and a tranquil first-floor dining room. 'Eat heartily and give the house a good name' is the sound philosophy here, and the stars of the show are oysters and Guinness. Daily specials include seafood plates and platters; bowls of whelks and winkles; and 'Cow classics' such as Londoner sausages with mash and gravy; hand-made taglioni with crab, tomato and chilli; or fish stew with rouille and croûtons.

Open all day all wk Closed: 25 Dec ⊕ FREE HOUSE ◀ Fuller's London Pride, Courage Directors, De Koninck, Guinness.

The Prince Bonaparte
PLAN 2 E4

80 Chepstow Rd W2 5BE ☎ 020 7313 9491
e-mail: princebonaparte@realpubs.co.uk
dir: *Nearest tube: Notting Hill Gate or Westbourne Park*

Convivial atmosphere and excellent menus

The building, originally a gin house built in 1850, is noted for its airy and open-plan interior. It became a first-generation gastro-pub in the early 1990s, featuring a large half-moon bar fronted by high tables; lofty ceiling spaces, a skylight and theatre-style kitchen characterise the dining room. Guest ales and many bottled beers witness its credentials as a drinker's pub. High-quality produce likely to feature on the excellent menu may include Dover sole, lamb from Devon and New Forest venison.

Open all day all wk 12-11 (Sun 12-10.30) ⊕ FREE HOUSE/REAL PUBS ◀ Sharp's Doom Bar, 2 Guest ales ♂ Aspall. **Facilities** ♦♦ Children's portions Wi-fi

The Westbourne
PLAN 2 E4

101 Westbourne Park Villas W2 5ED ☎ 020 7221 1332
dir: *On corner of Westbourne Park Rd & Westbourne Park Villas*

Friendly atmosphere and daily-changing menus

Bare floorboards and a long green and zinc bar characterise this classic Notting Hill gastro-pub, much favoured by its bohemian and celebrity clientele. The popular terrace is a suntrap in summer and heated in winter, attracting many locals and visitors to enjoy good food and drinks in a unique atmosphere. Daily-changing imaginative dishes are listed on a large blackboard above the bar, using fresh ingredients from leading independent suppliers. Dishes might include Gloucester Old Spot pork loin chop with chorizo and black cabbage.

Open Tue-Sat 12-11 (Sun 12-10.30 Mon 5-11) Closed: 24 Dec-2 Jan, Mon L ⊕ FREE HOUSE ◀ Caledonian Deuchars IPA, Staropramen, Leffe, Hoegaarden, Flowers. **Facilities** ♦♦ Children's portions Garden Wi-fi

W4

Sam's Brasserie & Bar ⊛
Map 6 TQ27 | PLAN 2 D3

11 Barley Mow Passage, Chiswick W4 4PH
☎ 020 8987 0555
e-mail: info@samsbrasserie.co.uk
dir: *Behind Chiswick High Rd, off Heathfield Terrace*

All day eating in factory conversion

Once the Sanderson wallpaper factory, this large converted red-brick warehouse is a very unique space. Open all day from breakfast onwards, it covers all bases with its food and drink offering. Enjoy a pint of London Pride and rock oysters in the bar or tuck in to main menu choices such as grilled pork chop with black pudding mash, winter greens and cider jus in the buzzy brasserie. Don't miss the Sunday roasts.

Open all day all wk Closed: 25-26 Dec ⊕ FREE HOUSE ◀ Fuller's London Pride. **Facilities** ♦♦ Children's menu Children's portions Wi-fi

The Swan
PLAN 2 D3

PICK OF THE PUBS

1 Evershed Walk, 119 Acton Ln, Chiswick W4 5HH
☎ 020 8994 8262
e-mail: theswanpub@btconnect.com
dir: *Pub on right at end of Evershed Walk*

Mediterranean cuisine accompanied by recommended ales

A friendly gastro-pub, The Swan is the perfect spot for all seasons with its welcoming wood-panelled interior and a large lawned garden and patio for summertime refreshments. Good food is at the heart of the operation, and you can sit and eat wherever you like. The menu of modern, mostly Mediterranean cooking has a particular Italian influence, and vegetarians are not forgotten. Start perhaps with fried beef dumplings with sweet chilli relish; a vegetarian option could be baked goats' cheese bruschetta with Sicilian aubergine relish and pesto. Next comes the main course: roast poussin with lemon and thyme and sweet potato hash; or pheasant and wild mushroom risotto. If you still have an appetite, then finish off with pear and almond tart, or home-made ice cream. Real ale recommendations are shown on the menu.

Open all wk 5-11.30 (Sat 12-11.30 Sun 12-11) Closed: 24-31 Dec ⊕ FREE HOUSE ◀ Fuller's London Pride, Harvey's Sussex Best Bitter, St Austell Tribute, Otter Bitter, Guinness ♂ Westons Wyld Wood Organic. **Facilities** ♦♦ Children's portions Garden

W6

Anglesea Arms ⊛
PLAN 2 D3

PICK OF THE PUBS

35 Wingate Rd W6 0UR ☎ 020 8749 1291
e-mail: anglesea.events@gmail.com
dir: *Telephone for directions*

Cosy pub with award-winning food

Close to Ravenscourt Park tube station, this traditional corner pub is reputed to be where the Great Train Robbery was hatched back in the 1960s. Today, real fires and a relaxed atmosphere are the attraction of this intimate pub, together with a terrace where drinks and food can be served. Behind the Georgian façade, well-kept ales are dispensed from breweries as far apart as Suffolk and Cornwall, and the place positively buzzes with people eagerly seeking out the unashamedly gastro-pub food with one AA Rosette. Unusual dishes from the open kitchen shine out, including starters such as split pea and smoked ham soup. Mains may feature slow roast pork belly with mashed potato and red cabbage. Custard tart with white chocolate ice cream could be a pudding option, as could cheeses from Neal's Yard Dairy. There's a seriously impressive wine cellar here too, with 20 available by the glass.

Open all day all wk 11-11 (Sun 12-10.30) Closed: 25-27 Dec **Bar Meals** L served Mon-Sat 12.30-7, Sun 12.30-8.30 D served Mon 7-10, Tue-Sat 7-10.30, Sun 12.30-8.30 Av main course £15 food served all day **Restaurant** L served Mon-Fri 12.30-2.45, Sat 12.30-3, Sun 12.30-8.30 D served Mon-Sat 7-10.30, Sun 12.30-8.30 Av 3 course à la carte fr £30 ⊕ ENTERPRISE INNS ◀ Ringwood Fortyniner, St Austell Tribute, Sharp's Cornish Coaster, Otter Ale & Bitter, Woodforde's Wherry ♂ Westons Wyld Wood Organic, Gaymers, Aspall. ♚ 20 **Facilities** Non-diners area ♣ (Bar Garden) ♦♦ Children's portions Garden ☰

The Dartmouth Castle
PLAN 2 D3

PICK OF THE PUBS

26 Glenthorne Rd, Hammersmith W6 0LS
☎ 020 8748 3614
e-mail: dartmouth.castle@btconnect.com
dir: *Nearest tube station: Hammersmith. 100yds from Hammersmith Broadway*

Corner pub with a reputation for imaginative cooking

While it's very much a place to relax over a pint or two, the food is proving a great attraction at this corner pub. The monthly-changing menu ranges from imaginative sandwiches (mozzarella and slow-roast tomatoes with pesto; or marinated rump steak with onions, chilli and red wine) to gutsy Mediterranean fare that includes a wide range of canapé platters as well as main dishes like Spanish pork stew with chorizo, or fish stew with langoustines and tiger prawns. Vegetarians aren't forgotten either, with choices like linguine alla genovese or slow-roast tomato and saffron risotto. Typical desserts are apple and rhubarb crumble and home-made ice creams. The range of beers includes at least two real ales on tap at any one time, and there's a well-chosen international wine list with 15 available by the glass. There's also a beer garden for the summer months and a function room.

Open all day 12-11 (Sat 5-11 Sun 12-10.30) Closed: Etr, 23 Dec-2 Jan, Sat L **Bar Meals** L served Mon-Fri 12-2.30, Sun 12-9.30 D served Mon-Fri 6-10, Sat 6-10, Sun 12-9.30 ⊕ FREE HOUSE ◀ Sharp's Doom Bar, Sambrook's Wandle, Otter Bitter, Guest ales ♂ Aspall. ♈ 15 **Facilities** Non-diners area ☻ (Bar Restaurant Garden) ◀ Garden ⊼ Wi-fi

The Hampshire Hog **NEW**   PLAN 2 D3

225-227 King St W6 9JT ☎ 020 8748 3391
e-mail: info@the-hog.com
dir: *Nearest tube station: Hammersmith*

Passion and flair in downtown Hammersmith

After 17 years' experience in Hampstead, Abigail Osborne and Tamsin Olivier opened this stylish gastro-pub. Externally Victorian, right down to its street corner location, the interior is impressively contemporary, with wood floors, lots of white paint, quirky crockery and a conservatory. Typifying the carefully sourced food are pear and daikon salad with curly endive, dandelion, cashew nut cheese and pomegranate; tarragon and dried fruit-stuffed pork neck with celeriac purée, kale and lardons; and poached hake with chilli, coriander and lemongrass broth, corn and udon noodles. Brunch is served until midday and you can buy home-made food from the pub's pantry.

Open all day Closed: 25-26 Dec, Sun pm **Bar Meals** L served Mon-Sat 12-4, Sun & BHs 12.30-5 D served Mon-Sat 6.30-10.30 Av main course £15 **Restaurant** L served Mon-Sat 12-4, Sun & BHs 12.30-5 D served Mon-Sat 6.30-10.30 Av 3 course à la carte fr £28 ⊕ STAR PUBS & BARS ◀ Caledonian 80/- & Deuchars IPA. ♈ 14 **Facilities** Non-diners area ☻ (Bar Garden) ◀ Children's menu Children's portions Garden ⊼ Wi-fi ▭ (notice required)

The Stonemasons Arms   PLAN 2 D3

54 Cambridge Grove W6 0LA ☎ 020 8748 1397
e-mail: stonemasonsarms@london-gastros.co.uk
dir: *From Hammersmith tube station into King St, 2nd right into Cambridge Grove, pub at end*

Creative cooking and a tempting alfresco area

Fascinating menu options make this imposing corner pub, just a short hop from Hammersmith tube station, well worth finding; squid and octopus salad, herbed croutons and lemon oil might be a good place to start before white lamb stew, pearl barley, flageolet beans and carrots. The tasty eating options make the Stonemasons popular with local residents and business people alike. During warmer months a decking area can be used for alfresco dining, and there's a secluded, intimate restaurant area. The pub carries an ever-changing display of works by a local artist, and there are weekly quiz nights.

Open all day all wk 11-11 (Sun 12-10.30) Closed: 25-26 Dec **Bar Meals** L served Mon-Fri 12-3, Sat 12-10, Sun 12-9.30 D served Mon-Fri 6-10, Sat 12-10, Sun 12-9.30 **Restaurant** L served Mon-Fri 12-3, Sat 12-10, Sun 12-9.30 D served Mon-Fri 6-10, Sat 12-10, Sun 12-9.30 ⊕ FULLER'S ◀ London Pride & Organic Honey Dew, Guinness ♂ Aspall. ♈ 20 **Facilities** Non-diners area ◀ Children's portions Garden Wi-fi ▭

W8

The Mall Tavern ☻☻   PLAN 2 E3

71-73 Palace Gardens Ter, Notting Hill W8 4RU
☎ 020 7729 3374
e-mail: info@themalltavern.com
dir: *Nearest tube station: Notting Hill*

Stylish pub at the heart of Notting Hill life

A Victorian pub built in 1856 midway between Notting Hill and Kensington, The Mall was, and remains, a true locals' tavern — albeit a rather stylish, upmarket one. With two AA Rosettes, expect a hearty, playful and modern take on pub food — maybe gala pie with Hawaiian salad or chicken liver pâté with pickled onion to start; followed by fried kitchari with Indian onions and nigella seeds; or pollock fillet with cloud mushrooms, scorched shallots and oyster leaves. Finish off with cranberry cheesecake, warm chocolate 'finger of fudge' cake with clementines for dessert. Besides regular beers such as Sharp's Doom Bar and By the Horns Stiff Upper Lip, there's an impressive list of wines, with many available by the glass. Also on offer is a 'secret' kitchen table that allows up to 10 diners an interactive dining experience.

Open all day all wk Closed: 1wk Xmas **Bar Meals** L served 12-10 D served 12-10 Av main course £14 food served all day **Restaurant** L served 12-10 D served 12-10 Fixed menu price fr £10 Av 3 course à la carte fr £25 food served all day ⊕ ENTERPRISE INNS ◀ Sharp's Doom Bar, By The Horns Stiff Upper Lip, Nelson Pieces of Eight ♂ Addlestones, Aspall. ♈ 10 **Facilities** Non-diners area ☻ (Bar Restaurant Garden) ◀ Children's portions Garden ⊼ Wi-fi ▭ (notice required)

The Scarsdale   PLAN 2 E3

23A Edwardes Square, Kensington W8 6HE
☎ 020 7937 1811
e-mail: scarsdale@fullers.co.uk
dir: *From Kensington High Street tube station turn left. 0.5m (10 mins' walk) left into Edwardes St after Odeon Cinema*

19th-century character pub in quiet area

The Scarsdale is a 19th-century free-standing building with colourful hanging baskets and window boxes spilling into the small terraced patio, in a leafy road just off Kensington High Street. The Frenchman who developed the site was supposedly one of Bonaparte's secret agents, but more recently - the 1970s and 80s - the Scarsdale played a role as the local watering hole for Bodie and Doyle, in ITV's *The Professionals*. A typical restaurant menu offers duck leg confit with apple compôte; fillet of beef Wellington in puff pastry with pâté and red wine sauce; and spinach and ricotta tortellini with sundried tomato sauce. There is also an equally tempting bar menu, and an impressive wine list.

Open all day all wk 12-11 (Sun 12-10.30) Closed: 25-26 Dec **Bar Meals** Av main course £10 food served all day **Restaurant** L served all wk 12-3 D served all wk 6-10 Fixed menu price fr £21 Av 3 course à la carte fr £25 ⊕ FULLER'S ◀ London Pride & Bengal Lancer, George Gale & Co Seafarers, Butcombe. ♈ 20 **Facilities** Non-diners area ☻ (Bar Garden) Garden ⊼ Wi-fi

W9

The Waterway   PLAN 2 E4

54 Formosa St W9 2JU ☎ 020 7266 3557
e-mail: info@thewaterway.co.uk
dir: *From Warwick Avenue tube station into Warwick Av, turn left into Formosa St*

Canalside pub with a great range of drinks

Enjoying a lovely setting in Maida Vale, The Waterway offers great alfresco opportunities with is outdoor terrace, where popular barbecues are held in summer. In colder weather, the bar is a great place to relax with its sumptuous sofas and open fires. There is a good choice of drinks, including many wines and a couple of champagnes by the glass, as well as draught beers and non-alcoholic cocktails. The menus offer modern British and European food — gnocchi with wild mushrooms and roast chestnuts; grilled salmon with a warm pearl barley salad, red pepper coulis and rocket; and affogato to finish.

Open all day all wk 12-11 (Sat 10.30am-11pm Sun 11-10.30) **Bar Meals** L served all day D served all day Av main course £14 food served all day **Restaurant** L served Mon-Fri 12-3.30, Sat-Sun 12-4 D served Mon-Sat 6.30-10.30, Sun 6.30-10 Fixed menu price fr £16 Av 3 course à la carte fr £19.50 ⊕ ENTERPRISE INNS ◀ Sharp's Doom Bar, Fuller's London Pride, Skinner's Cornish Knocker ♂ Aspall. ♈ 16 **Facilities** Non-diners area ◀ Children's menu Children's portions Garden Wi-fi ▭

W11

Portobello Gold PLAN 2 E3

95-97 Portobello Rd, Notting Hill W11 2QB
☎ 020 7460 4900
e-mail: reservations@portobellogold.com
dir: *From Notting Hill Gate tube station follow signs to Portobello Market*

A touch of gold in Notting Hill

In the heart of famous Portobello Road Market, this quirky Notting Hill pub/wine bar/brasserie has been under the same ownership since 1985, and offers an interesting range of British ales and European beers (including a gluten-free choice), great wines and cocktails. Former US President Bill Clinton dropped into Portobello Gold with an entire motorcade, stayed an hour and left without paying! Many other famous visitors have called in or become regulars. Menus always list game and seafood, including sashimi, British mussels and Irish oysters. Dishes such as pasta, tortillas, burgers, bangers and steaks are all prepared from scratch on the premises. With the landlord's wife, Linda Bell, an established wine writer, 18 wines by the glass should be no surprise.

Open all day all wk **Bar Meals** L served all day D served all day Av main course £12 food served all day **Restaurant** L served all day D served all evening food served all day ⊕ HERMES UNIT TRUST ◀ Brakspear Oxford Gold, Harvey's Sussex, Meantime, Leffe, Freedom, Guinness ♥ Thatchers Gold, Katy & Spartan. ♟ 18 **Facilities** Non-diners area ♣ (Bar) ♦♦ Children's portions Wi-fi ▦ (notice required)

W14

The Albion PLAN 2 D3

121 Hammersmith Rd, West Kensington W14 0QL
☎ 020 7603 2826
e-mail: chris@downthealbion.com
dir: *Near Kensington Olympia & Barons Court tube stations*

Famous for its beer festival

Weary from wandering around Olympia and in need of refreshment? Then head across the road to The Albion for a pint of London Pride, Deuchers IPA or one of the many wines by the glass. A fine old pub that takes its name from HMS *Albion*, it has the look and feel of an old ship. The concise pub grub menu features a selection of burgers, Cajun chicken, wholetail scampi and sausages and mash. Jacket potatoes, sandwiches and omelettes are also on offer at lunchtime. The pub is well known for its Easter Music and Real Ale Festival. Change of ownership.

Open all day all wk **Bar Meals** L served all wk 11-3 D served all wk 5-10 Av main course £8.50 ◀ Caledonian Deuchars IPA, Fuller's London Pride, St Austell Tribute ♥ Symonds. ♟ 13 **Facilities** Non-diners area Garden ⊼ Beer festival Wi-fi ▦ (notice required)

The Cumberland Arms PLAN 2 D3

PICK OF THE PUBS

29 North End Rd, Hammersmith W14 8SZ
☎ 020 7371 6806
e-mail: thecumberlandarmspub@btconnect.com
dir: *From Kensington Olympia tube station turn left. At T-junct right into Hammersmith Rd. 3rd left into North End Rd, 100yds pub on left*

Gastro-pub with a locals' atmosphere

At the heart of cosmopolitan Hammersmith and handy for Olympia, this eye-catching gastro-pub, generously dressed with colourful summer hanging baskets and boxes, is a popular retreat for people-watching. Bag a bench beside the adjacent flowery enclave on sunny days or head indoors, where mellow furniture and stripped floorboards characterise its interior. Friendly staff, a comprehensive wine list and well-kept ales (Doom Bar, London Pride, Exmoor Gold) are the draw for those seeking after-work refreshment, but it is also a great place for sampling enticing Mediterranean-style cuisine from a regularly updated menu and specials selection. Starters range from soup or smoked trout with avocado salad to more unusual arancini – deep fried risotto balls with butternut squash and parmesan. Head then towards Tunisian lamb and prune tagine, ginger, coriander and tomato with herbed couscous salad; or perhaps saltimbocca of pork with butterbean and pepper salad and caramelised onions. Meal-sized 'Cumberland Sandwiches' include marinated rump steak with chilli, red wine and onions.

Open all day all wk 12-11 (Sun 12-10.30 Thu-Fri 12-12) Closed: 24 Dec-1 Jan **Restaurant** L served Mon-Sat 12-3, Sun 12.30-9.30 D served Mon-Sat 6-10 Sun 12.30-9.30 ⊕ FREE HOUSE ◀ Fuller's London Pride, Exmoor Gold, Sharp's Doom Bar, Staropramen. ♟ 16 **Facilities** Non-diners area ♣ (Bar Restaurant Garden) ♦♦ Children's portions Garden ⊼ Wi-fi ▦ (notice required)

WC1

The Bountiful Cow PLAN 1 E4

PICK OF THE PUBS

51 Eagle St, Holborn WC1R 4AP ☎ 020 7404 0200
e-mail: manager@roxybeaujolais.com
dir: *230mtrs NE from Holborn tube station, via Procter St. Walk through 2 arches into Eagle St. Pub between High Holborn & Red Lion Square*

Homage to the cow

The exotically-named Australian Roxy Beaujolais runs this 'public house devoted to beef', her second pub venture following her delightful Seven Stars behind the Law Courts. If pictures of cows, bullfights, cowgirls, diagrams of meat cuts and posters of cow-themed films are your thing, then you'll love this place too; jazzy but discreet music adds to an atmosphere halfway between funky bistro and stylish saloon. Ales are Adnams Southwold Bitter and Dark Star Hophead, cider is Aspall, and the short wine list includes several gutsy reds. Roxy's menus – she declares herself to be Head Cook – are based on

beef aged in-house from Smithfield Market, whose butchers have celebrated Christmas here for two years running. A starter of duck rillettes or octopus salad might precede all cuts of steaks; home-made sausages and mash; chargrilled sea bream; roast corn-fed chicken; or Welsh 'wizard' rarebit, with Guinness and Worcestershire sauce on focaccia.

Open all day 11-11 (Sat 12-11) Closed: 25-26 Dec, 1 Jan, Sun **Bar Meals** L served Mon-Sat 12-10.30 D served Mon-Sat 12-10.30 **Restaurant** L served Mon-Sat 12-10.30 D served Mon-Sat 12-10.30 ⊕ FREE HOUSE ◀ Adnams Southwold Bitter, Dark Star Hophead ♥ Aspall. ♟ **Facilities** Non-diners area ♦♦ ⊼ Wi-fi ▦ (notice required)

The Lady Ottoline **NEW** PLAN 1 E4

11A Northington St WC1N 2JF ☎ 020 7831 0008
e-mail: info@theladyottoline.com
dir: *Nearest tube station: Chancery Lane*

Smart Bloomsbury set piece

Scott and Maria Hunter (also owners of the Princess of Shoreditch – see entry) opened the doors here a few years ago following an extensive refurbishment. Named after Bloomsbury society hostess Lady Ottoline Morrell, this attractive corner pub, complete with log fire, serves four local ales, including Sambrook's, bottled craft beers and ciders, and nine wines by the glass. In the upstairs dining rooms, head chef Alan Irwin prepares simple, but awfully good, seasonally-based food such as roasted hen pheasant with casserole of leg; poached garlic chicken Kiev; and Crown Prince pumpkin risotto. Well-behaved children (until 6pm) are welcome in the pub.

Open all day all wk Closed: 25 Dec-2 Jan **Bar Meals** L served Mon-Fri 12-3, Sat 12-4, Sun 12-8 D served Mon-Sat 6.30-10, Sun 12-8 Av main course £14 **Restaurant** L served Tue-Fri 12-3, Sun 12-8 D served Mon-Sat 6.30-10, Sun 12-8 Av 3 course à la carte fr £21 ⊕ PUNCH TAVERNS ◀ Sharp's Doom Bar, Sambrook's, Redemption Pale Ale. ♟ 9 **Facilities** Non-diners area ♦♦ Children's portions Outside area ⊼ Wi-fi

The Lamb PLAN 1 D5

94 Lamb's Conduit St WC1N 3LZ ☎ 020 7405 0713
e-mail: lambwc1@youngs.co.uk
dir: *From Russell Square tube station, turn right, 1st right into Grenville St, 1st left into Guildford St, 1st right into Guildford Place (leads to Lamb's Conduit St)*

A gem of a pub once patronised by Dickens

First recorded in 1729, this building was 'heavily improved' between 1836 and 1876, and frequented by Charles Dickens when he lived nearby in Doughty Street (his residence is now home to the Dickens Museum). The distinctive green-tiled façade, very rare glass snob screens, dark polished wood, and original sepia photographs of music hall stars who performed at the nearby Holborn Empire, all contribute to the feeling of stepping back in time – as does the absence of television and fruit machines. Home-cooked bar food includes a vegetarian corner; a fish choice including traditional fish and chips; steaks from the griddle; plus pies and baked dishes from the stove.

Open all day all wk 12-11 (Thu-Sat 12-12 Sun 12-10.30) ⊕ YOUNG'S ◀ Young's (full range). **Facilities** ♦♦ Garden

---

Norfolk Arms   PLAN 1 D5

28 Leigh St WC1H 9EP ☎ 020 7388 3937
e-mail: info@norfolkarms.co.uk
dir: *Nearest tube stations: Russell Square, King's Cross & Euston*

Classic London corner pub offering international tapas choices

Located on a busy street corner in Bloomsbury, within five minutes' walk of St Pancras International, the Norfolk Arms is a London gastro-pub. Behind its Victorian frontage, the main bar and dining area are at ground level, with private dining on the first floor. The extensive and eclectic bar menu features British, European and Middle Eastern tapas: typical choices are stuffed vine leaves, Scotch egg, Valencian carrots and Serrano ham. The main menu includes oxtail stew and spicy Italian sausages. A great choice of beers and ten wines by the glass complete the picture.

Open all day all wk Closed: 25-26, 31 Dec & 1 Jan **Bar Meals** food served all day **Restaurant** food served all day ⊕ STAR PUBS & BARS ◀ Theakston XB, Greene King IPA. ♟ 10 **Facilities** Non-diners area ♦♦ Children's portions ♬ Wi-fi

---

WC2

The George   PLAN 1 E4

213 Strand WC2R 1AP ☎ 020 7353 9638
e-mail: enquiries@georgeinthestrand.com
dir: *Opposite Royal Courts of Justice*

Frequented by the good and the famous over many years

Facing the Royal Courts of Justice, The George was built as a coffee house in 1723, although the black-and-white façade is late Victorian. Once regulars included Horace Walpole and Samuel Johnson, today mingle with judges, barristers and court reporters over a pint of Sharp's Doom Bar, a lunchtime salad, an open sandwich or hot wrap. For something more substantial, try chargrilled rib-eye steak; smoked poached haddock with bubble-and-squeak; traditional Irish lamb stew with dumplings; or the roast carvery.

Open all day all wk Closed: 25-26 Dec ⊕ FREE HOUSE ◀ Sharp's Doom Bar, Hogs Back TEA, Sambrook's Wandle, Black Sheep, Purity Pure UBU, Adnams Southwold Bitter ♂ Aspall. **Facilities** ♦♦ Wi-fi

---

The Seven Stars   PLAN 1 E4

PICK OF THE PUBS

53 Carey St WC2A 2JB ☎ 020 7242 8521
e-mail: roxy@roxybeaujolais.com
dir: *From Temple tube station turn right. 1st left into Arundel St. Right into Strand (walking). Left into Chancery Lane. 1st left into Carey St*

A real one off - stylish saloon style and market driven dishes

The Seven Stars may never have seen better days in its four centuries of existence. Since Roxy Beaujolais took over this ancient Grade II listed pub behind the Royal Courts of Justice 12 years ago, delicate and undisruptive primping has produced nothing but accolades. Improvements have been managed with such tact by Roxy's architect husband that some think even his modern dumbwaiter is ancient. Strengthened by its ambience, The Seven Stars has bloomed into the ideal pub – the food is simple but well executed, the ales are kept perfectly, the wines are few but very good, and the staff are welcoming and efficient. The day's dishes, listed on the blackboard, change according to what's best in the market and what tickles Roxy's fancy. Examples are tuna kedgeree biryani; and hot smoked German sausages with sautéed potatoes.

Open all day all wk 11-11 (Sat 12-11 Sun 12-10.30) Closed: 25-26 Dec, 1 Jan **Bar Meals** L served Mon-Fri 12-9.30, Sat-Sun 1-9.30 D served Mon-Fri 12-9.30, Sat-Sun 1-9.30 **Restaurant** L served Mon-Fri 12-9.30, Sat-Sun 1-9.30 D served Mon-Fri 12-9.30, Sat-Sun 1-9.30 ⊕ FREE HOUSE ◀ Adnams Southwold Bitter & Broadside, Sambrook's Wandle, Sharp's Cornish Coaster ♂ Aspall. **Facilities** Non-diners area Wi-fi

---

The Sherlock Holmes   PLAN 1 D3

10 Northumberland St WC2N 5DB ☎ 020 7930 2644
e-mail: 7967@greeneking.co.uk
dir: *From Charing Cross tube station into Villiers St. Through 'The Arches' (runs underneath Charing Cross station) straight across Craven St into Craven Passage to Northumberland St*

Themed pub serving comforting pub grub

Painted black with etched glass windows and colourful hanging baskets, this traditional corner pub is chock-full of Holmes memorabilia, including photographs of Conan Doyle, mounted pages from manuscripts, and artefacts and pieces recording the adventures of the Master Detective. There's even a replica of Holmes' and Watson's sitting room and study. This split-level establishment has a bar on the ground floor and on the first floor an intimate covered roof garden and the restaurant. There's Sherlock Holmes Ale to drink, hot and cold bar food plus an à la carte menu offering traditional roast dinners, ham, egg and chips and home-made steak and mushroom in ale pie with cheesecake of the day for afters.

Open all day all wk Closed: 25-26 Dec **Bar Meals** food served all day **Restaurant** food served all day ⊕ GREENE KING ◀ Sherlock Holmes Ale & Abbot Ale, Morland Old Speckled Hen ♂ Aspall. ♟ 14 **Facilities** Non-diners area ♦♦ Outside area ♬ Wi-fi 🚐 (notice required)

GREATER LONDON

CARSHALTON   Map 6 TQ26

The Sun

4 North St SM5 2HU ☎ 020 8773 4549
e-mail: thesuncarshalton@googlemail.com
dir: *Off A232 (Croydon Rd) between Croydon & Sutton*

A great place for real ales

A popular stop after visiting Carshalton Ponds, this is very much a family-friendly pub. A beer festival is held every June; at other times there are always five ales on the go, including Timothy Taylor Landlord. Menus of rustic comfort food with European influences use the freshest, seasonal, free-range and organic produce: a meal could take in crispy belly pork with black pudding, pickled cauliflower and smoked apple chutney; pan-fried sea trout with celeriac rösti, creamed leek and Savoy cabbage; and lemon tart with clotted cream. Look out for wine and cheese specials on Thursdays and the supper club set menu on Wednesdays.

Open all day Closed: Mon until 5pm **Bar Meals** L served Tue-Fri 12-3, Sat 12-9.30, Sun 12-9 D served Mon Fri 6-9.30, Sat 12-9.30, Sun 12-9 Av main course £15 ⊕ FREE HOUSE ◀ Timothy Taylor Landlord, Rudgate Ruby Mild, Sharp's Doom Bar ♂ Westons, Addlestones. ♟ 14 **Facilities** Non-diners area ☸ (Bar Restaurant Garden) ♦♦ Children's menu Children's portions Play area Family room Garden ♬ Beer festival Wi-fi 🚐

CHELSFIELD   Map 6 TQ46

The Five Bells

PICK OF THE PUBS

BR6 7RE ☎ 01689 821044
dir: *From M25 junct 4 take A224 towards Orpington. In approx 1m turn right into Church Rd. Pub on left*

Country pub with live music and open mic nights

This whitewashed family-run pub is a Grade II listed building conveniently located just inside the M25, but also situated in a protected conservation village, with many lovely walks in the area. Dating from 1680, The Five Bells takes its name from the magnificent bells at the St Martin of the Tours church just up the road. There are two bars: one is a dog-friendly front bar boasting an original inglenook fireplace; the other houses the restaurant area. This in turn leads to the patio and extensive garden, which comes complete with a children's swing and play area. The seasonal menu complements the real ales and wines on offer: home-made steak-and-kidney pudding; honey-roast ham with eggs and chips; and vegetarian risotto are examples from a winter menu. Home-made pizzas are available at any time during pub opening hours, and beer festivals take place at Easter and in October along with regular live music, quizzes and other events.

Open all day all wk **Bar Meals** L served all wk 12-3 D served Thu-Sat 6.30-9 **Restaurant** L served all wk 12-3 D served Thu-Sat 6.30-9 ⊕ ENTERPRISE INNS ◀ Courage

continued

CHELSFIELD *continued*

Best, Sharp's Doom Bar, Guinness. ♦ 13
Facilities Non-diners area ☙ (Bar Garden) ♦♦ Children's menu Children's portions Play area Garden ⊨ Beer festival Parking Wi-fi ▄▄ (notice required)

HAM

Hand & Flower
PLAN 2 C2

24 Upper Ham Rd TW10 5LA ☎ 020 8332 2022
e-mail: info@handandflower.com
dir: *On A307*

Daily-changing menus and many different eating areas

Originally the old toll house on the turnpike opposite Ham Common, the revamped Hand & Flower stands a short stroll from Richmond Park. Follow a good summer walk with lunch in the stunning, award-winning garden, replete with pond, private dining area and secluded tables away from the bustling patio. On inclement days head indoors to the modern and spacious dining area for all-day food, the daily menu ranging from home-made burgers and sandwiches to dressed crab; Caesar salad; and sea bass with samphire, chilli and lime braised fennel, and vegetable and potato broth.

Open all day all wk ⊕ TOP TAVERNS LTD ◀ Fuller's London Pride, Harvey's. **Facilities** ♦♦ Children's menu Children's portions Garden Wi-fi

KINGSTON UPON THAMES

The Boaters Inn **NEW**
PLAN 2 C1

Canbury Gardens, Lower Ham Rd KT2 5AU
☎ 020 8541 4672
e-mail: enquiries@boaterskingston.com
dir: *Just off Lower Ham Rd*

Thames-side favourite for jazz, food and ale

Arrive early to bag one of the prized balcony seats at this stunning riverside pub and savour the view across the Thames, which is best enjoyed at sunset. The place heaves at weekends and on sunny days, with Thames-path walkers and cyclists, and boaters jostling with local diners for a table on the impressive alfresco terrace. The draw, other than the river, are the seven microbrewery ales on tap in the airy, wood-floored bar, the famous Sunday evening jazz sessions, and the fresh, modern pub food on offer. Daily menus may list rabbit ragout on toast, a ploughman's board to share, salmon and squid linguine, venison with orange marmalade, and sticky toffee pudding.

Open all day all wk **Bar Meals** Av main course £12–£15 **Restaurant** L served all day (12-3 Nov-Feb) D served all day (5-9.30 Nov-Feb) Fixed menu price fr £15 Av 3 course à la carte fr £24.50 ⊕ GREENE KING ◀ Sambrook's Wandle, Dark Star American Pale Ale & Hophead, Surrey Hills Shere Drop ♂ Westons Stowford Press, Aspall. ♦ 10 **Facilities** Non-diners area ☙ (Bar Restaurant Garden) ♦♦ Children's menu Children's portions Garden ⊨ Beer festival Cider festival Wi-fi ▄▄ (notice required)

MERSEYSIDE

BARNSTON
Map 15 SJ28

Fox and Hounds

Barnston Rd CH61 1BW ☎ 0151 648 7685
e-mail: ralphleech@hotmail.com
dir: *M53 junct 4, A5137 to Heswall. In Heswell at rdbt onto A551 signed Barnston*

Conservation area Edwardian delight

Built in 1911, the pub's Edwardian character is preserved in the leaded windows, pitch-pine woodwork and open fire. In the Snug, the original bar, are collections of bric-à-brac – 30 brewery clocks, 52 flying ducks and 85 brass ashtrays. A good variety of real ales includes Brimstage Trapper's Hat, from the heart of the Wirral. Liver and onions; beef hotpot; steak pie; and a vegetarian dish of the day are supplemented at lunchtime by paninis, light meals and salad platters. The traditional Sunday roasts feature topside of Welsh Black beef and Welsh lamb. Highly colourful in summer is the beautifully kept garden.

Open all day all wk 11-11 (Sun 12-10.30) **Bar Meals** L served Mon-Sat 12-2, Sun 12-3 D served Tue-Fri fr 5.30 Av main course £8.95 ⊕ FREE HOUSE ◀ Theakston Best Bitter & Old Peculier, Brimstage Trapper's Hat, Webster's, Guest ales ♂ Aspall. ♦ 12 **Facilities** Non-diners area ♦♦ Children's portions Family room Garden ⊨ Parking Wi-fi ▄▄ (notice required)

GREASBY
Map 15 SJ28

Irby Mill

Mill Ln CH49 3NT ☎ 0151 604 0194
e-mail: info@irbymill.co.uk
dir: *M53 junct 3, A552 signed Upton & Heswall. At lights onto A551 signed Upton & Greasby. At lights left into Arrowe Brook Rd. At rdbt 3rd exit into Mill Ln*

Former miller's cottage serving local produce

An eye-catching, solid, sandstone-block built old miller's cottage (the windmill was demolished in 1898, the pub opened in 1980) just a short jog from the airy heights of Thurstaston Common at the heart of The Wirral Peninsula. One of the area's best choices of real ales meets an exceptional, very pubby menu strong on Wirral produce – 'Muffs' sausage and mash comes with stewed peas, onion gravy and onion rings and could be followed by Nicholls of Parkgate ice cream. Popular with ramblers and Sunday diners, there's a suntrap grassy garden for summer; a log fire for the winter.

Open all day all wk **Bar Meals** L served Mon-Sat 12-9, Sun 12-8 D served Mon-Sat 12-9, Sun 12-8 Av main course £9 **Restaurant** L served Mon-Sat 12-9, Sun 12-8 D served Mon-Sat 12-9, Sun 12-8 ⊕ STAR PUBS & BARS ◀ Wells Bombardier, Greene King Abbot Ale, Jennings Cumberland Ale, Theakston Best Bitter, 4 Guest ales. ♦ 12 **Facilities** ☙ (Bar Garden) ♦♦ Children's menu Children's portions Garden Parking Wi-fi ▄▄

HIGHTOWN
Map 15 SD30

The Pheasant Inn

20 Moss Ln L38 3RA ☎ 0151 929 2106
dir: *From A565 take B5193, follow signs to Hightown*

A different event every day of the week

This attractive pub with a whitewashed wooden exterior is a former alehouse with a sunny garden. It's just minutes from Crosby Beach, where sculptor Antony Gormley's famous 100 cast-iron figures gaze out to sea. Surrounded by fields and golf courses, the pub retains an original brick in the restaurant wall dated 1719. In the bar these days you'll find Thwaites Wainwright alongside Aspall ciders. The menu is changed twice a year so expect dishes like pulled beef and bacon pie or a minted lamb burger. There are also the legendary Sunday platter, fish suppers on 'Fin and Fizz' Fridays, retro dining evenings and a menu just for the ladies on Wednesday nights.

Open all day all wk 12-11 (Sun 12-10.30) **Bar Meals** L served all wk 12-6 D served all wk 6-9.30 food served all day **Restaurant** L served all wk 12-6 D served all wk 6-9.30 food served all day ⊕ MITCHELLS & BUTLERS ◀ Thwaites Wainwright ♂ Aspall Draught & Organic. ♦ 30 **Facilities** Non-diners area ♦♦ Children's menu Garden ⊨ Parking Wi-fi

LIVERPOOL
Map 15 SJ39

The Monro **NEW**

92 Duke St L1 5AG ☎ 0151 707 9933
e-mail: mail.monro@themonrogroup.com
dir: *Telephone for detailed directions*

Elegant gastro-pub offering fresh, locally sourced food

In 1746, merchant John Bolton built himself a finely-proportioned house, which today is this popular city gastro-pub. Bolton later entered history as a combatant in Liverpool's last recorded duel (he was the victor). The elegance of the interior would make him feel very nostalgic, although he might struggle with the concept of naming beers Boondgood (Ringwood), Cocker Hoop (Jennings) and GingerBeard (Wychwood). Examples from a monthly-changing menu include duck bourgignon with pancetta lardons and port-wine-glazed silverskin onions; poached salmon and sea bass with pea linguine and garlic cream sauce; and vegetable Wellington. The Early Doors menu is for those short of time.

Open all day all wk Closed: 25-26 Dec, 1 Jan **Bar Meals** L served all wk 12-9.30 D served all wk 12-9.30 food served all day **Restaurant** L served all wk 12-9.30 D served all wk 12-9.30 food served all day ⊕ FREE HOUSE ◀ Ringwood Boondgoggle, Jennings Cocker Hoop, Wychwood GingerBeard ♂ Thatchers Katy. ♦ 10 **Facilities** Non-diners area ♦♦ Children's menu Children's portions Garden ⊨ Wi-fi ▄▄ (notice required)

NORFOLK

BAWBURGH   Map 13 TG10

Kings Head

PICK OF THE PUBS

Harts Ln NR9 3LS ☎ 01603 744977
e-mail: anton@kingshead-bawburgh.co.uk
dir: *From A47 take B1108 W towards Walton. Right signed Bawburgh*

Worth finding after exploring nearby Norwich

Opposite the village green and just yards from the River Yare, this 17th-century free house has bags of traditional charm. There are solid oak beams, bulging walls, wooden floors and comfy leather seating. Owners Anton and Pam Wimmer have been welcoming locals and visitors alike for 29 years now. The pub is named after King Edward VII who, says Anton, "invested the Edwardian era with a reputation for delicious if somewhat upholstered pleasures. We aim to continue this philosophy". Behind the bar are East Anglian ales and ciders, including Woodforde's Wherry. Head chef Dan Savage and second chef Leigh Taylor create monthly menus and daily-changing specials that are firmly rooted in the local markets — and they can make many of the dishes dairy- or gluten-free on request. Menus might include a starter of chickpea and chorizo stew, and main courses such as slow-braised shin of beef and horseradish suet pudding. Leave room for warm banana cake with caramel sauce.

Open all day all wk **Bar Meals** L served Mon-Sat 12-2, Sun 12-4, summer Sun 12-3 D served Mon-Sat 5.30-9, summer Sun 6-9 **Restaurant** L served Mon-Sat 12-2, Sun 12-4, summer Sun 12-3 D served Mon-Sat 5.30-9, summer Sun 6-9 ⊕ FREE HOUSE ◀ Adnams Southwold Bitter & Broadside, Woodforde's Wherry, Guest ale ♻ Aspall. ♟ 15 **Facilities** Non-diners area ♥ (Bar Garden) ♦ Children's menu Children's portions Garden ⋈ Parking Wi-fi ▦ (notice required)

BINHAM   Map 13 TF93

Chequers Inn

Front St NR21 0AL ☎ 01328 830297
dir: *On B1388 between Wells-next-the-Sea & Walsingham*

Home of the Front Street Brewery

Just a few miles from the north Norfolk coast, the Chequers is home to the Front Street Brewery, but even though they brew their own beer they still have guest ales together with an extensive range of foreign bottled beers such as Küppers Kölsch and Chimay Red Label, and a connoisseur's selection of rare and vintage beers. The pub has been owned by a village charity since the 1640s, and was originally a trade hall; many stones from the nearby Binham Priory were used in its construction. The daily-changing menu might include mixed bean and Mediterranean vegetable chilli or deep-fried catfish fillet.

Open all wk 11.30-2.30 6-11 (Fri-Sat 11.30-2.30 6-11.30 Sun 12-3 7-11) ⊕ FREE HOUSE ◀ Front Street Binham Cheer, Callums Ale & Unity Strong, Seasonal specials. **Facilities** ♦ Children's menu Children's portions Garden Parking Wi-fi

BLAKENEY   Map 13 TG04

The Blakeney White Horse

PICK OF THE PUBS

See Pick of the Pubs on page 308

The Kings Arms

Westgate St NR25 7NQ ☎ 01263 740341
e-mail: kingsarmsnorfolk@btconnect.com
dir: *From Holt or Fakenham take A148, then B1156 for 6m to Blakeney*

Very old pub in lovely seaside village

Tucked away in a popular fishing village close to the north Norfolk coastal path (Peddars Way), this thriving free house is the perfect refreshment stop following an invigorating walk, time spent birdwatching, or a boat trip to the nearby seal colony. An excellent selection of real ales, including Norfolk-brewed Woodforde's Wherry is backed by menus featuring locally caught fish and seasonal seafood — cod, prawn and bacon chowder; mussels in garlic cream sauce — together with braised pheasant with bacon jus; steak and Adnams ale suet pudding; and home-made lasagne.

Open all day all wk Closed: 25 Dec eve **Bar Meals** food served all day ⊕ FREE HOUSE ◀ Morland Old Speckled Hen, Woodforde's Wherry, Marston's Pedigree, Adnams Southwold Bitter. ♟ 10 **Facilities** Non-diners area ♥ (Bar Restaurant Garden) ♦ Children's menu Children's portions Play area Family room Garden Parking Wi-fi ▦

BRANCASTER   Map 13 TF74

The Ship Hotel

Main Rd PE31 8AP ☎ 01485 210333
e-mail: thebar@shiphotelnorfolk.co.uk
dir: *On A149 in village centre*

Nautical pub serving cracking food

Set in a prime coastal location close to Brancaster beach, TV chef and hotelier Chris Coubrough's stylish gastro-pub continues to attract walkers, beach bums and families with its appealing menus of modern pub food prepared from fresh produce sourced from local farmers and fisherman. Be tempted by smoked haddock, cockles and leek chowder or local venison casserole. Wash it down with a pint of Bitter Old Bustard in the gorgeous bar and dining rooms, where you can expect rug-strewn wood floors, wood-burning stoves, shelves full of books, quirky antiques, scrubbed wooden tables and a distinct nautical feel.

Open all day all wk **Bar Meals** L served 12-2.30 (school holidays, menu available 3-6) D served 6.30-9.30 **Restaurant** L served 12-2.30 (school holidays, menu available 3-6) D served 6.30-9.30 ⊕ FREE HOUSE/FLYING KIWI INNS ◀ Jo C's Norfolk Kiwi & Bitter Old Bustard, Adnams Southwold Bitter ♻ Aspall. ♟ 19 **Facilities** Non-diners area ♥ (Bar Garden) ♦ Children's menu Children's portions Garden ⋈ Parking Wi-fi ▦

BRANCASTER STAITHE   Map 13 TF74

The Jolly Sailors

PE31 8BJ ☎ 01485 210314
e-mail: info@jollysailorsbrancaster.co.uk
dir: *On A149 (coast road) midway between Hunstanton & Wells-next-the-Sea*

Children, muddy boots and dogs welcome

Focal point of the village, the 18th-century 'Jolly' is the brewery tap for the Brancaster microbrewery, both being run by father and son team, Cliff and James Nye. In the Harbour Snug you can look out over the water, read local books, and play darts and board games. The Nyes' Brancaster ales aren't obligatory — you'll also find Woodforde's and Adnams. Pub food is typified by open-fired pizzas; pie of the day; Cromer crab with salad; and spiced veggie burger. The beach-themed ice cream hut in the garden is an attraction. A beer, real cider and music festival begins in mid-June.

Open all wk Mon-Thu 12-3 6-11 Fri 12-3 5-11 (Mon-Fri all day spring & summer) Sat 12-11 Sun 12-10.30 **Bar Meals** L served (winter) Mon-Fri 12-2 (all day spring & summer), Sat-Sun 12-9 D served (winter) Mon-Fri 6-9 (all day spring & summer), Sat-Sun 12-9 Av main course £9.50 **Restaurant** Av 3 course à la carte fr £19.95 ⊕ FREE HOUSE ◀ Brancaster Best, The Wreck & Oyster Catcher, Woodforde's Wherry, Adnams, Guest ales ♻ Westons Stowford Press. ♟ 10 **Facilities** Non-diners area ♥ (Bar Garden) ♦ Children's menu Children's portions Play area Garden ⋈ Beer festival Parking Wi-fi ▦ (notice required)

PICK OF THE PUBS

The Blakeney White Horse

BLAKENEY   Map 13 TG04

4 High St NR25 7AL ☎ 01263 740574
e-mail: hello@blakeneywhitehorse.co.uk
web: www.blakeneywhitehorse.co.uk
dir: From A148 (Cromer to King's Lynn road) onto A149 signed to Blakeney

Popular pub in fishing village

Since the 17th century, this former coaching inn has been tucked away among Blakeney's flint-built fishermen's cottages, a short, steepish amble up from the small tidal harbour. All around are glorious views over creeks, the Glaven Valley estuary, acres of marram grass-covered dunes, sea lavender, samphire, mussel beds and, on the horizon, the shingle ridge of Blakeney Point, to which a little ferry will be pleased to take you. On the way you may well see Arctic terns, skylarks, redshanks, oyster catchers and thriving colonies of seals. Back in the pub, Francis and Sarah Guildea's tastefully refurbished, Adnams-stocked bar is stylish yet informal, the conservatory is naturally bright – both are eating areas, where the same menu and daily specials apply. Locally sourced food is a given, especially the lobster, crab and mussels from village fishermen, meats and game from Norfolk estates, soft fruit, salads, asparagus and free range eggs from local smallholders, while rod- and line-caught mackerel and sea bass find their way through the kitchen

door in summer. On the lunch menu there'll be filled bagels and baguettes with french fries; chargrilled haloumi with houmous, roasted red pepper and salad; and pie of the day. In the evening maybe a three-course dinner of smoked haddock fishcakes with beetroot rémoulade and poached egg; braised beef brisket with horseradish mash, wilted spinach, sautéed garlic, wild mushrooms and red wine jus; and gooseberry jam crème brûlée. Fish and seafood dishes continue with Morston mussels marinière; cataplana; and pan-fried cod fillet with dauphinoise potatoes, sautéed brown shrimps and crab bisque. A lighter options menu operates daily at lunchtime and there are traditional roasts on Sundays.

Open all day all wk 10.30am-11pm Closed: 25 Dec **Bar Meals** L served Mon-Sat 12-2, Sun 12-2.30 D served Mon-Sat 6-9, Sun 6.30-9 ⊞ ADNAMS ◖ Southwold Bitter, Broadside, Adnams Guest ales ♂ Aspall. ☗ 14
Facilities Non-diners area ❧ (Bar Restaurant) ♠ Children's menuChildren's portions Family room Outside area ⌂ Parking Wi-fi

BRANCASTER STAITHE *continued*

The White Horse ★★★ HL ⑨⑨

PICK OF THE PUBS

PE31 8BY ☎ 01485 210262
e-mail: reception@whitehorsebrancaster.co.uk
dir: *A149 (coast road), midway between Hunstanton & Wells-next-the-Sea*

Stylish inn on marshland coastline

From the airy conservatory restaurant, summer sun deck and elegant bedrooms at The White Horse, there are stunning vistas over glorious tidal marshes to Scolt Head Island, a four-mile long sandbar home to a nature reserve rich in birdlife. Reflecting the view, colours are muted and natural, and beach-found objects are complemented by contemporary artworks. Scrubbed pine tables and high-backed settles in the bar create a welcoming atmosphere, while alfresco dining in the sunken front garden is a popular warm-weather option, accompanied by local Brancaster Oyster Catcher. While the bar menu lists grills, salads and sandwiches, the extensive, daily-changing restaurant menu (with two AA Rosettes) champions the freshest local seafood, including seasonal fish and shellfish gathered at the foot of the garden. Typically, follow Brancaster mussels with chargrilled swordfish, lemon and herb new potatoes, red onion salad and salsa verde butter; or polenta, haloumi and Mediterranean vegetable stack. There are also good puddings — perhaps try the Amaretto chocolate torte.

Open all day all wk 11-11 (Sun 11-10.30) (open from 9am for breakfast) **Bar Meals** L served all wk 11-9 D served all wk 11-9 Av main course £14.50 food served all day **Restaurant** L served all wk 12-2 D served all wk 6.30-9 Av 3 course à la carte fr £28 ⊕ FREE HOUSE ◀ Adnams Ghost Ship, Woodforde's Wherry, Brancaster Best & Oyster Catcher, Guest ales Ö Aspall, Whin Hill. ⚑ 16 **Facilities** Non-diners area ❀ (Bar Garden) ♦♦ Children's menu Children's portions Garden ⊼ Parking Wi-fi **Rooms** 15

BURNHAM MARKET   Map 13 TF84

The Hoste ★★★★ HL ⑨⑨

PICK OF THE PUBS

The Green PE31 8HD ☎ 01328 738777
e-mail: reception@hoste.co.uk
dir: *Signed from B1155, 5m W of Wells-next-the-Sea*

One of Norfolk's most popular dining inns

North Norfolk's endless sandy beaches and beautiful countryside are virtually on the doorstep of this cream-painted, pantiled old village manor house. A hotel since 1651, it has also been a courthouse, livestock market, brothel and Horatio Nelson's Saturday morning local. A magnificent combination of top-notch two-AA Rosette food and boutique accommodation, there's a cosy bar, three main restaurants, lounge, conservatory and pretty walled garden behind the terrace restaurant. The all-East Anglian real ale line-up includes, appropriately, Nelson's Revenge from Woodforde, while the 150-bin list features

some of the world's finest wines. Examples of items on the seasonal modern British menus are Brancaster oysters, seafood chowder, gourmet burger, lamb bourguignon, and Gressingham duck breast. A vegetarian might home in on sweet potato, ricotta and sage open lasagne. A selection of Norfolk cheeses is offered as a dessert, as too is marmalade-glazed bread-and-butter-pudding. There was a change of hands in 2012.

Open all day all wk **Bar Meals** L served all wk 12-2 D served all wk 6-9 **Restaurant** L served all wk 12-2 D served all wk 6-9 ⊕ FREE HOUSE ◀ Adnams Broadside, Woodforde's Wherry & Nelson's Revenge. ⚑ 16 **Facilities** Non-diners area ❀ (Bar Garden) ♦♦ Children's menu Children's portions Garden Parking Wi-fi **Rooms** 34

BURNHAM THORPE   Map 13 TF84

The Lord Nelson

PICK OF THE PUBS

Walsingham Rd PE31 8HN ☎ 01328 738241
e-mail: enquiries@nelsonslocal.co.uk
dir: *B1355 (Burnham Market to Fakenham road), pub 9m from Fakenham & 1.75m from Burnham Market*

Soak up over 370 years of atmosphere

This pub started life in 1637 as The Plough and was renamed The Lord Nelson in 1798, to honour Horatio Nelson who was born in the village. Located opposite the delightful village cricket ground and bowling green, it has an atmospheric interior that has changed little over the past 370 plus years; you can even sit on Nelson's high-backed settle. Drinks are served from the taproom, with real ales drawn straight from the cask. In the cosy bar you can also partake in unique rum-based tipples such as Nelson's Blood. The kitchen aims to cook dishes with balance between flavours, so that the quality of the ingredients shines. A typical meal is farmhouse pâté with toast and red onion marmalade followed by pan-fried salmon in a green herb crust with beurre blanc and duchess potatoes, with apple pie and vanilla ice cream for dessert. Children will enjoy the huge garden. From May to September, weekend walking tours of Nelson's village are available.

Open all wk 12-3 6-11 (Jul-Aug 12-11) **Bar Meals** L served all wk 12-2.30 D served all wk 6-9 **Restaurant** L served all wk 12-2.30 D served all wk 6-9 ⊕ GREENE KING ◀ Abbot Ale, Woodforde's Wherry Ö Aspall. ⚑ 14 **Facilities** Non-diners area ❀ (Bar Garden) ♦♦ Children's menu Play area Garden ⊼ Parking Wi-fi ▭

BURSTON   Map 13 TM18

The Crown

Mill Rd IP22 5TW ☎ 01379 741257
e-mail: enquiries@burstoncrown.com
dir: *NE of Diss*

Locals' pub with inventive food

Steve and Bev Kembery have transformed their 16th-century pub by the green into a cracking community pub, drawing locals in for top-notch ale and food,

organising the village fête, hosting three beer festivals a year, and offering a weekly busker's night and regular theme nights. As well as a decent pint of Adnams, you can tuck into jerk chicken with lime and chilli mayonnaise baguettes or spinach and cream cheese pancakes in the bar or, from the à la carte, slow-roasted pulled pork shoulder with fennel and lemon infused yogurt and flatbread then braised beef cheeks with pears, chocolate and celeriac mash. Well worth finding.

Open all day all wk **Bar Meals** L served Mon-Sat 12-2, Sun 12-4 D served Mon-Sat 6.30-9 **Restaurant** L served Mon-Sat 12-2, Sun 12-4 D served Mon-Sat 6.30-9 ⊕ FREE HOUSE ◀ Adnams Southwold Bitter & Old Ale, Elmtree Burston's Cuckoo, Greene King Abbot Ale, Elgood's Ö Aspall, Burnards Norfolk Cider. **Facilities** Non-diners area ❀ (Bar Garden) ♦♦ Children's menu Children's portions Garden ⊼ Beer festival Parking Wi-fi ▭ (notice required)

CLEY NEXT THE SEA   Map 13 TG04

The George Hotel

PICK OF THE PUBS

High St NR25 7RN ☎ 01263 740652
e-mail: info@thegeorgehotelatcley.co.uk
dir: *On A149 through Cley next the Sea, approx 4m from Holt*

Village hotel popular with birdwatchers

The George's beer garden backs on to the salt marshes of the north Norfolk coast, which prove a paradise for birdwatchers. Indeed, this old hotel has been an ornithological focal point for many years. Ask to see its 'bird bible', a record of sightings kept by visiting observers. The welcoming bar is home to several real ales, including Yetman's from just along the coast at Holt. You can snack in the lounge bar or dine in the light, painting-filled restaurant. The daily-changing menu offers only the best of local fresh ingredients, and fish and seafood is a real strength. Sample dishes include seared pigeon breast with Puy lentils and a rocket salad; moules marinière; vegetarian risotto of the day; and venison sausage with dauphinoise potatoes and Savoy cabbage. Baked vanilla cheesecake is among the desserts. The village's famous mill and Blakeney Harbour are just a mile away.

Open all day all wk 10.30am-11.30pm **Bar Meals** L served Mon-Sat 12-2.15, Sun 12.30-2.30 D served Mon-Sat 6.30-9, Sun 6.30-8.30 **Restaurant** L served Mon-Sat 12-2.15, Sun 12.30-2.30 D served Mon-Sat 6.30-9, Sun 6.30-8.30 ⊕ FREE HOUSE ◀ Adnams Broadside, Woodforde's Wherry, Yetman's, Guest ales Ö Aspall. ⚑ 8 **Facilities** Non-diners area ❀ (Bar Restaurant Garden) ♦♦ Children's menu Garden ⊼ Parking Wi-fi ▭ (notice required)

CROMER
Map 13 TG24

The Red Lion Food and Rooms ★★★★ INN

Brook St NR27 9HD ☎ 01263 514964
e-mail: info@redlion-cromer.co.uk
dir: *From A149 in Cromer right into Church St, leads to Garden St. Right into Jetty St, left into Tucker St. Pub on corner of Brook St*

With an AA Dinner Award seafood is a must

Built in the 19th century, when Cromer was fast becoming a popular seaside resort, the Red Lion overlooks the pier and Blue Flag beach. Although used by the armed forces during World War II, it mercifully retains much of its Victorian interior. For real ale drinkers, the bar is heaven, with Bees Wobble, Humpty Dumpty Railway Sleeper and Adnams Broadside in the line-up (many more at the autumn beer festival). Coastal waters provide treats like Cromer crab thermidor and Morston mussels; others are Norfolk sausages and venison; braised lamb shank; and wild mushroom Stroganoff. Many of the bedrooms have sea views.

Open all day all wk **Bar Meals** L served all wk 12-2.30 D served all wk 6-9.30 **Restaurant** L served all wk 12-2.30 D served all wk 6-9.30 ⊕ FREE HOUSE ◄ Bees Wobble, Green Jack Lurcher Stout, Woodforde's Nelson's Revenge, Humpty Dumpty Railway Sleeper, Adnams Broadside. ♀ 14 **Facilities** Non-diners area ❤ (Bar) ♦♦ Children's menu Children's portions Beer festival Parking Wi-fi ☞ (notice required) **Rooms** 15

EAST RUDHAM
Map 13 TF82

The Crown Inn

The Green PE31 8RD ☎ 01485 528530
e-mail: reception@crowninnnorfolk.co.uk
dir: *On A148, 6m from Fakenham*

Popular pub on the village green

Part of TV chef Chris Coubrough's thriving Flying Kiwi mini-empire of pubs along the Norfolk coast, The Crown draws the crowds for its charming, spruced-up interior, which successfully blends traditional period features (low beams, rug-strewn wooden floor, open log fires) with contemporary comforts — cool Farrow & Ball colours, high-backed leather chairs at scrubbed tables, shelves of books, fresh flowers and chunky church candles. The menu changes every two weeks and lists good modern British dishes prepared from fresh Norfolk produce. Tuck into roast chump of lamb with roast Mediterranean vegetables, crispy polenta and black olive jus or a lunchtime sandwich. Expect proper children's food.

Open all day all wk ⊕ FREE HOUSE/FLYING KIWI INNS ◄ Adnams Southwold Bitter & Broadside, Flying Kiwi Homebrew Ö Aspall. **Facilities** ♦♦ Children's menu Children's portions Parking Wi-fi

EAST RUSTON
Map 13 TG32

The Butchers Arms

Oak Ln NR12 9JG ☎ 01692 650237
e-mail: info@thebutchersarms.biz
dir: *From A149 SE of North Walsham follow signs for Briggate, Honing & East Ruston. Oak Ln off School Rd*

Local ale and traditional food

A timeless village pub, without jukebox or pool table but with 'Mavis', a 1954 Comma fire engine, parked outside, this quintessential beamed pub started life as three terraced cottages in the early 1800s. Landlady Julie Oatham has been here for over 20 years, and ensures a welcoming atmosphere. Real ales from local breweries such as Adnams are served alongside traditional favourites of home-made cottage pie; beef chilli and a roast of the day. The desserts change daily but are of the comforting, traditional type. There is a beer garden and vine-covered patio for summer dining.

Open 12-2.30 6.30-11 Closed: Mon (Sep-Jun) **Bar Meals** L served all wk 12-2 D served all wk 7-8.30 **Restaurant** L served all wk 12-2 D served all wk 7-8.30 ⊕ FREE HOUSE ◄ Morland Old Speckled Hen, Greene King IPA, Adnams, Woodforde's. **Facilities** Non-diners area ❤ (Bar Garden) ♦♦ Children's menu Children's portions Garden ㅉ Parking Wi-fi ☞ (notice required) **Notes** ☺

EATON
Map 13 TG20

The Red Lion

50 Eaton St NR4 7LD ☎ 01603 454787
e-mail: admin@redlion-eaton.co.uk
dir: *Off A11, 2m S of Norwich city centre*

The menus offer a seemingly endless choice

This heavily beamed 17th-century coaching inn has bags of character, thanks to its Dutch gable ends, panelled walls, suit of armour and inglenook fireplaces. The covered terrace enables customers to enjoy one of the real ales or sample a glass from the wine list outside during the summer months. Everyone will find something that appeals on the extensive menus, which include plenty of fish options: pan-fried mackerel with a roast beetroot and feta salad; Cromer crab cakes with sweet chilli and lime mayonnaise; and Swannington lamb cutlets with chargrilled courgettes, tomatoes and basil butter. There's a light meals and snack menu too.

Open all day all wk **Bar Meals** L served all wk 12-2.15 D served all wk 6.15-9 **Restaurant** L served all wk 12-2.15 D served all wk 6.15-9 ◄ Adnams Southwold Bitter, Woodforde's Wherry, Fuller's London Pride. ♀ 10 **Facilities** Non-diners area ♦♦ Children's menu Children's portions Garden Parking Wi-fi

ERPINGHAM
Map 13 TG13

The Saracen's Head

Wolterton NR11 7LZ ☎ 01263 768909
e-mail: info@saracenshead-norfolk.co.uk
dir: *From A140, 2.5m N of Aylsham, left, through Erpingham. Pass Spread Eagle on left. Through Calthorpe, 0.5m, pub on right*

Country pub in a Tuscan farmhouse-style building

The privately owned Saracen's Head is deep among the fields down country lanes — and you do find yourself wondering why there's a pub in such a lonely spot. The answer is that it was once a coach house, built in 1806 for neighbouring Wolterton Hall. You may eat in one of the bars, where Suffolk and Norfolk real ales are on handpump, or in the restaurant, where sample dishes might be roast Norfolk pheasant with Calvados and cream; and baked Cromer crab with apple and sherry. For a really quiet drink or meal, sit out in the sheltered courtyard garden.

Open 11.30-3 6-11 (Sun 12-3 7-10.30) Closed: 25-29 Dec, Mon (ex BHs), Tue L (Oct-May) ⊕ FREE HOUSE ◄ Adnams Southwold Bitter, Woodforde's Wherry, Guest ales. **Facilities** ♦♦ Children's menu Children's portions Garden Parking

FAKENHAM
Map 13 TF92

The Wensum Lodge Hotel

Bridge St NR21 9AY ☎ 01328 862100
e-mail: enquiries@wensumlodge.fsnet.co.uk
dir: *In town centre*

Delightful riverside pub

Idyllically located by the River Wensum just three minutes' walk from Fakenham, this lovely pub has a stream flowing through its garden and offers guests free fishing on the river. The building dates from around 1700, and was originally the grain store for the adjoining mill. Fine ales are complemented by home-cooked food prepared from locally supplied ingredients, with baguettes, jacket potatoes and an all-day breakfast on the light bite menu, and a carte menu for heartier fare. An ideal base for cycling, birdwatching, fishing and horseracing.

Open all wk ⊕ FREE HOUSE ◄ Greene King Abbot Ale & IPA, Old Mill Traditional Bitter. **Facilities** Non-diners area ♦♦ Garden Parking ☞

Save on hotels. Book at theAA.com/hotel

NORFOLK 311 ENGLAND

GREAT MASSINGHAM   Map 13 TF72

The Dabbling Duck NEW

11 Abbey Rd PE32 2HN ☎ 01485 520827
e-mail: info@thedabblingduck.co.uk
dir: *From King's Lynn take either A148 or B1145 then follow Great Massingham signs. Or from Fakenham take A148 signed King's Lynn. Or from Swaffham take A1065 towards Cromer, then B1145 signed King's Lynn*

Stylish village-owned inn

Resurrected, after a period of closure, as the Dabbling Duck by a consortium of local businessmen and a tireless campaign by the local authority, the pub on Great Massingham's glorious green thrives as a community local and a stylish inn. Head for the high-backed settles by the raised log fire to peruse the papers with a pint of Wherry, or tuck into braised lamb shank with mash and mixed bean cassoulet, and treacle and pecan tart at a scrubbed table in one of the comfortably rustic dining areas. There are shelves groaning with books and board games, rugs on tiled floors and the atmosphere is informal and relaxed. The result is a cracking village pub.

Open all wk 12-11 **Bar Meals** L served all wk 12-2.30 D served all wk 6.30-9 **Restaurant** L served all wk 12-2.30 D served all wk 6.30-9 ⊕ FREE HOUSE ◀ Woodforde's Wherry, Beeston Worth the Wait ♂ Aspall. **Facilities** Non-diners area ❀ (Bar Garden Outside area) ♦♦ Children's menu Children's portions Play area Garden Outside area ⌂ Parking Wi-fi ▭ (notice required)

GREAT RYBURGH   Map 13 TF92

The Blue Boar Inn

NR21 0DX ☎ 01328 829212
e-mail: blueboarinn@ryburgh.co.uk
dir: *Off A1067, 4m S of Fakenham*

Good food in pretty Wensum Valley inn

Lots to see at this character, listed village inn; beyond the beer garden is a notable round-towered medieval church (once linked to the pub by a secret tunnel), whilst inside are quarry-tile floors, beams and a vast inglenook, spread through a jumble of levels marking alterations to this popular local pub over the centuries. It was used as a recruiting station during the Napoleonic Wars; all that's required of today's visitors is to enjoy the local Yetman's beers and indulge the richly varied, Norfolk-based menu, which may include cassoulet of chicken leg and sausage, or pot roast half guinea fowl.

Open 6-11 (Sun 12-6) Closed: Tue **Bar Meals** L served Sun 12-4.30 D served Wed-Sat & Mon 6.30-9 Av main course £10.95 **Restaurant** L served Sun 12-4.30 D served Wed-Sate & Mon 6.30-9 Av 3 course à la carte fr £25 ⊕ FREE HOUSE ◀ Adnams Southwold Bitter, Winter's Golden & Revenge, Guinness, Staropramen, Yetman's ♂ Addlestones, Westons Stowford Press, Aspall. ♥ 8 **Facilities** Non-diners area ♦♦ Children's menu Children's portions Play area Family room Garden ⌂ Parking Wi-fi ▭

HEVINGHAM   Map 13 TG12

Marsham Arms Coaching Inn

Holt Rd NR10 5NP ☎ 01603 754268
e-mail: info@marshamarms.co.uk
dir: *On B1149 N of Norwich airport, 2m through Horsford towards Holt*

Charming inn serving ales from the taproom

Victorian philanthropist and landowner Robert Marsham built the Marsham Arms as a roadside hostel for poor farm labourers. Although now updated, it retains some original features, including the wooden beams and large open fireplace. Real ales are served straight from the barrel. The seasonal menu uses fresh local produce, and there are always vegetarian and gluten-free options. Typical dishes include beer battered tiger prawns with a chilli dip; mushroom Stroganoff; and deep-filled shortcrust pie of the day with creamy mash, peas and gravy. There is a spacious garden with a paved patio. The inn holds a Green Tourism award.

Open all day all wk **Bar Meals** L served Mon-Fri 12-2.30, Sat-Sun all day D served Mon-Fri 6-9, Sat-Sun all day **Restaurant** L served Mon-Fri 12-2.30, Sat-Sun all day D served Mon-Fri 6-9, Sat-Sun all day ⊕ FREE HOUSE ◀ Adnams Southwold Bitter & Broadside, Woodforde's Wherry, Mauldons, Grain Best Bitter, Humpty Dumpty ♂ Aspall. ♥ **Facilities** Non-diners area ❀ (Bar Restaurant Garden) ♦♦ Children's menu Children's portions Garden ⌂ Parking Wi-fi ▭ (notice required)

HEYDON   Map 13 TG12

Earle Arms

The Street NR11 6AD ☎ 01263 587376
e-mail: theearlearms@gmail.com
dir: *Signed between Cawston & Corpusty on B1149 (Holt to Norwich road)*

One for fans of the turf

H", the landlord and chef, is responsible for the horse-racing memorabilia throughout this 16th-century, Dutch-gabled free house on the village green. As part-owner of a racehorse, he will gladly give you a tip, but says it's probably best not to go nap on it. The privately owned conservation village of Heydon is often used for filming, and many a star of the big and small screen has enjoyed the Earle's off-the-pier-fresh seafood; fillet of beef Marchand de Vin with vegetables; mixed bean chilli with rice; and game stew. A beer festival is held on St George's Day (23rd April).

Open 12-3 6-11 Closed: Mon **Bar Meals** L served Tue-Sun 12-2 D served Tue-Sun 6-8.30 **Restaurant** L served Tue-Sun 12-2 D served Tue-Sat 6-8.30 ⊕ FREE HOUSE ◀ Woodforde's Wherry, Adnams, Guest ales. ♥ 16 **Facilities** Non-diners area ♦♦ Children's menu Children's portions Garden ⌂ Beer festival Parking Wi-fi ▭

HINGHAM   Map 13 TG00

The White Hart Hotel

3 Market Place NR9 4AF ☎ 01953 850214
e-mail: whitehart@flyingkiwiinns.co.uk
dir: *In market square on B1108*

A gastro-pub drawing on the larder of East Anglia

One of several inns owned by TV chef Chris Coubrough, The White Hart stands in Hingham's picturesque Georgian market place. Elements of the old coaching inn remain in the beams and open fireplaces; however these traditional features are twinned with contemporary design ideals, resulting in a memorable mix of retro rustic and exotic touches. The Norfolk Kiwi beer here is brewed by Chris's wife Jo, and is also used in the fish batter. The modern British cuisine is suitably inspiring; crayfish, cucumber and avocado salad; and caramelised blood oranges with chocolate sorbet take the eye.

Open all day all wk **Bar Meals** L served all wk 12-2.30 D served all wk 6.30-9.30 Av main course £11.95 **Restaurant** L served Mon-Sat 12-2.30, Sun 12-8 D served Mon-Sat 6.30-9.30, Sun 12-8 ⊕ FREE HOUSE ◀ Adnams Southwold Bitter, Jo C's Norfolk Kiwi, Guest ale ♂ Aspall. ♥ **Facilities** ❀ (Bar) ♦♦ Children's menu Children's portions Outside area ⌂ Wi-fi

HOLT   Map 13 TG03

The Pigs

PICK OF THE PUBS

See Pick of the Pubs on page 312

HORSTEAD   Map 13 TG21

Recruiting Sergeant

Norwich Rd NR12 7EE ☎ 01603 737077
dir: *On B1150 between Norwich & North Walsham*

Regularly changing menu of local produce

The Recruiting Sergeant, a colour-washed brick and flint free house, has an enviable local reputation for food. Fresh local produce is the foundation of the ever-changing menu, which might include Binham Blue salad with pickled pears; toasted steak sandwich, red onion marmalade and chips; chargrilled Cajun spiced swordfish and king prawn brochettes on Caesar salad; and a giant bowl of Brancaster mussels.

Open all day all wk 11-11 (Sun 12-10.30) ⊕ FREE HOUSE ◀ Greene King Abbot Ale, Adnams, Woodforde's, Courage ♂ Aspall. **Facilities** ♦♦ Children's menu Children's portions Garden Parking

PICK OF THE PUBS

The Pigs

HOLT   Map 13 TG03

Norwich Rd, Edgefield NR24 2RL
☎ **01263 587634**
e-mail: info@thepigs.org.uk
web: www.thepigs.org.uk
dir: *On B1149*

Bustling village local with pig-inspired menus

Bought by three ambitious co-owners in 2006, this 17th-century country inn on the edge of a lovely village has been transformed into a thriving local and celebration of all things Norfolk, both on the plate and in the glass. The lovely tranquil setting at the fringe of the village allows for a peaceful garden, whilst locals barter their fresh fruit and vegetables over the bar for a pint or two, practise darts or bar billiards and quaff the Old Spot bitter brewed by local Wolf Brewery — what else. An impressively versatile menu emerges from the kitchen, utilising forgotten cuts of locally sourced meat and produce from the pub's adjoining allotment. If it's genuine 'nose to tail' dining you're looking for, the Honey, Colman's mustard and marmalade glazed pork ribs, followed by the slow-cooked belly of pork with smoky bacon beans, apple chutney, black pudding and crackling should fit the bill. Tapas-style starters called 'Iffits' also include devilled whitebait with gentleman's relish and lemon, thyme and garlic chicken wings

and are ideal for sharing. If pork-based treats aren't your thing, then venison and port casserole with honey and sage roasted root vegetables, Colman's mustard mash and cinnamon spiced red cabbage may tempt, along with fish options such as deep-fried line-caught haddock, mushy peas, beef dripping chips and tartare sauce. Leek, wild mushroom and pine nut pot barley stew is one of the meat-free choices. Leave room for one of the tempting desserts, perhaps sticky date pudding with toffee sauce and vanilla ice cream. A children's cookery school proves popular.

Open all day all wk 8am-11pm **Bar Meals** L served Mon-Sat 12-2.30, Sun & BH 12-9 D served Mon-Sat 6-9 Av main

course £12.50 **Restaurant** L served Mon-Sat 12-2.30, Sun & BH 12-9 D served Mon-Sat 6-9 Fixed menu price fr £20 Av 3 course à la carte fr £30 ⊕ FREE HOUSE 🍺 Woodforde's Wherry, Greene King Abbot Ale, Wolf Old Spot & Adnams Broadside ♂ Aspall. ♒ 17 **Facilities** Non-diners area 🐾 (Bar) 🚻 Children's menu & portions Play area Family room Outside area ⩑ Parking Wi-fi 🚐 (notice required)

Save on hotels. Book at **theAA.com/hotel**

NORFOLK 313 ENGLAND

HUNSTANTON
Map 12 TF64

The Ancient Mariner Inn ★★★★ HL

Golf Course Rd, Old Hunstanton PE36 6JJ
☎ **01485 536390**
e-mail: conference@lestrangearms.co.uk
dir: *Off A149, 1m N of Hunstanton. Left at sharp right bend by pitch & putt course*

Coastal setting with great views and local walks

Summer evenings can be spectacular here; when the sun sets across the sands of The Wash, the light matches the straws and golds of the real ales enjoyed by drinkers in the peaceful gardens, up to seven beers may be on tap. Equally enticing is the menu of modern pub classics such as fish pie or vegetarian Wellington; daily specials boost the choice. The appealing flint and brick inn is creatively incorporated into the stable block of a Victorian hotel, the stylish rooms of which are popular with visitors to the beautiful Norfolk Coast Area of Outstanding Natural Beauty. Live music is hosted on the last Friday of every month.

Open all day all wk **Bar Meals** L served all wk 12-9 D served all wk 12-9 food served all day **Restaurant** L served all wk 12-9 D served all wk 12-9 food served all day ⊕ FREE HOUSE ◀ Adnams, Theakston, Wychwood, Shepherd Neame, Sharp's, Woodforde's ♂ Symonds. ♈ 10 **Facilities** Non-diners area ❄ (Bar Garden) ♦ Children's menu Children's portions Play area Family room Garden ⊨ Beer festival Parking Wi-fi 🚗 (notice required)
Rooms 43

The King William IV Country Inn & Restaurant

Heacham Rd, Sedgeford PE36 5LU ☎ **01485 571765**
e-mail: info@thekingwilliamsedgeford.co.uk
web: www.thekingwilliamsedgeford.co.uk
dir: *A149 to Hunstanton, right at Norfolk Lavender in Heacham onto B1454, signed Docking. 2m to Sedgeford*

Food and drink to please all tastes

Tucked away in the village of Sedgeford, this free house has been an inn for 175 years. It's conveniently close to the north Norfolk coastline and the Peddars Way. Made cosy by winter log fires, it has four dining areas, plus a covered alfresco terrace where you may enjoy a local crab salad in the summer months. You'll find five real ales on tap, and extensive menus (including gluten free and vegetarian) to please everyone: cheese salad, or sautéed lamb's kidneys for starters, and parmesan-crusted sea bass in pesto sauce, and stuffed guinea fowl breast to

follow. Events include quiz Mondays, curry Tuesdays and piano Fridays.

The King William IV Country Inn & Restaurant

Open all day 11-11 (Sun 12-10.30) Closed: Mon L (ex BHs) **Bar Meals** L served Tue-Sat 12-2, Sun 12-2.30 D served all wk 6.30-9 **Restaurant** L served Tue-Sat 12-2, Sun 12-2.30 D served all wk 6.30-9 ⊕ FREE HOUSE ◀ Woodforde's Wherry, Adnams Southwold Bitter, Greene King Abbot Ale, Morland Old Speckled Hen, Guest ale ♂ Aspall Harry Sparrow. ♈ 9 **Facilities** Non-diners area ❄ (Bar Garden) ♦ Children's menu Children's portions Family room Garden ⊨ Parking Wi-fi 🚗 (notice required)

HUNWORTH
Map 13 TG03

The Hunny Bell
PICK OF THE PUBS

The Green NR24 2AA ☎ **01263 712300**
e-mail: hunnybell@animalinns.co.uk
dir: *From Holt take B1110. 1st right to Hunworth*

Tranquil valley pub with a lovely English garden

Set next to the green in pretty Hunworth in the peaceful Glaven Valley, just two miles south of Holt, this 18th-century gem of a pub provides a quiet haven away from the bustling beaches and villages on the coast. In-the-know foodies retreat from the salt marshes to the cosy snug and the rustic-chic beamed main bar, which successfully blend historic charm with a contemporary feel. From this blend you get real coffee, pints of Wherry and some imaginative pub food. Kick off with pressed Norfolk reared ham hock and green peppercorn terrine; follow with braised Stody Estate pheasant coq au vin with bubble-and-squeak, braised red cabbage and button mushrooms; and finish with the assiette of chocolate desserts. Walkers will find excellent lunchtime sandwiches. Outside, there's a terrace overlooking the green, as well as a charming old-world English garden. A beer festival is held in late August.

Open all wk 12-3 6-11 **Bar Meals** L served all wk 12-2.30 D served all wk 6-9 **Restaurant** L served all wk 12-2.30 D served all wk 6-9 ⊕ FREE HOUSE/ANIMAL INNS ◀ Woodforde's Wherry, Adnams, Greene King, Marston's Pedigree ♂ Aspall. ♈ 10 **Facilities** Non-diners area ♦ Children's menu Children's portions Garden ⊨ Beer festival Parking Wi-fi 🚗 (notice required)

INGHAM
Map 13 TG32

The Ingham Swan
PICK OF THE PUBS

Swan Corner, Sea Palling Rd NR12 9AB
☎ **01692 581099**
e-mail: info@theinghamswan.co.uk
dir: *From A149 through Stalham to Ingham*

Picture-postcard dining inn

This corner of Norfolk has an embarrassment of riches. Just a couple of miles away, at Hickling Broad, cranes and marsh harriers cause birdwatchers' hearts to flutter. The Swan itself is equally majestic; once part of Ingham Priory, just it and the adjoining church survived Henry VIII's dissolution. Along a country lane, this beautiful thatched building has been carefully transformed into a fine-dining restaurant whilst retaining the aura of a pub; visitors are always welcome at the very traditional bar for real ales from the local Woodforde's brewery. Chef-patron Daniel Smith trained at Le Gavroche in London and Blakeney's Morston Hall, and he sticks to his Norfolk roots with an inventive modern menu packed with seasonal local produce. To start perhaps, caramelised onion and Cashel Blue cheese tartlets with Serrano ham and wild roquette, leading to pan-fried halibut with chive risotto, diver-caught scallops, buttered samphire and brown shrimp butter sauce. The menu helpfully suggests wines to accompany.

Open all wk 11-3 6-11 Closed: 25-26 Dec **Bar Meals** Av main course £16 **Restaurant** L served Tue-Sun (all wk Apr-Oct) D served Tue-Sat (all wk Apr-Oct) Fixed menu price fr £13.95 Av 3 course à la carte fr £28 ⊕ FREE HOUSE ◀ Woodforde's Wherry, Nelson's Revenge, Nog, Sundew & Admiral's Reserve ♂ Aspall. ♈ 10 **Facilities** Non-diners area ♦ Children's portions Garden ⊨ Parking 🚗

ITTERINGHAM
Map 13 TG13

The Walpole Arms

NR11 7AR ☎ 01263 587258
e-mail: info@thewalpolearms.co.uk
web: www.thewalpolearms.co.uk
dir: *From Aylsham towards Blickling. After Blickling Hall take 1st right to Itteringham*

Revamped dining pub

Owned by a local farming family, this renowned rural dining venue is tucked away down narrow lanes on the edge of sleepy Itteringham, close to Blickling Hall (National Trust). Reopened in May 2012 following extensive refurbishment, its oak-beamed bar offers local Woodforde's and Adnams ales on tap, while menus champion top-notch meats and produce from the family farm and local artisan producers. Typical dishes include fried duck egg with black pudding and chorizo, spinach and toast; free-range chicken and ham hock pie with mash and greens; and cauliflower and lentil curry with pilau rice and a carrot and onion bhaji.

Open all wk 12-3 6-11 (Sat 12-11 Sun 12-5) **Bar Meals** L served Mon-Sat 12-2.30, Sun 12-3 D served Mon-Sat 6.30-9.15 **Restaurant** L served Mon-Sat 12-2.30, Sun 12-3 D served Mon-Sat 6.30-9.15 ⊕ FREE HOUSE ◀ Adnams Broadside & Southwold Bitter, Woodforde's Wherry, Guest ales Ō Aspall. ☗ 20
Facilities Non-diners area ❄ (Bar Garden) ♦♦ Children's menu Children's portions Garden ♠ Parking Wi-fi 🚐 (notice required)

KING'S LYNN
Map 12 TF62

The Stuart House Hotel, Bar & Restaurant ★★★ HL

35 Goodwins Rd PE30 5QX ☎ 01553 772169
e-mail: reception@stuarthousehotel.co.uk
dir: *Follow signs to town centre, pass under Southgate Arch, immediate right, in 100yds turn right*

Small independent hotel and free house

In a central, but nevertheless quiet location, this hotel and bar in attractive grounds is one of the town's favoured eating and drinking places. Top-notch East Anglian ales and traditional snacks are served in the bar, and there's a separate restaurant carte typically featuring Norfolk sausages with creamy mash and red onion gravy; pan-fried fillet of sea bass with herbed sauté potatoes; sweet chilli beef with noodles; and vegetable Kiev with garlic butter sauce. Daily specials, like everything else, are home cooked from fresh local

produce. Events include regular live music, murder mystery dinners and a July beer festival.

Open all wk 5-11 **Bar Meals** D served all wk 6-9.30 **Restaurant** D served all wk 7-9.30 ⊕ FREE HOUSE ◀ Oakham JHB, Timothy Taylor Landlord, Adnams, Woodforde's, Greene King. **Facilities** Non-diners area Children's portions Play area Garden Beer festival Parking Wi-fi 🚐 (notice required) **Rooms** 18

LARLING
Map 13 TL98

Angel Inn

PICK OF THE PUBS

NR16 2QU ☎ 01953 717963
e-mail: info@angel-larling.co.uk
dir: *5m from Attleborough, 8m from Thetford. 1m from station*

Family-run inn with well-kept ales

Run for more than 80 years by three generations of the Stammers family, this 17th-century former coaching on the edge of Breckland and Thetford Forest Park has a good local feel and offers visitors a warm welcome. In the heavily-beamed public bar, a jukebox, dartboard and fruit machine add to the traditional feel, while the oak-panelled lounge bar has dining tables with cushioned wheel-back chairs, a wood burner and a huge collection of water jugs. Five guest ales, including a mild, are served, as well as more than a hundred whiskies. Menus make good use of local ingredients, with lighter snacks including sandwiches, jacket potatoes, ploughman's, burgers and salads. Typically among the mains are chicken and mushroom Stroganoff; prawn Thai red curry; Whitby breaded scampi; and a vegetarian Stilton and mushroom bake. Each August the Angel hosts Norfolk's largest outdoor beer festival, with over 100 real ales and ciders.

Open all day all wk 10am-mdnt **Bar Meals** L served Sun-Thu 12-9.30, Fri-Sat 12-10 D served Sun-Thu 12-9.30, Fri-Sat 12-10 **Restaurant** L served Sun-Thu 12-9.30, Fri-Sat 12-10 D served Sun-Thu 12-9.30, Fri-Sat 12-10 Fixed menu price fr £20 Av 3 course à la carte fr £20 food served all day ⊕ FREE HOUSE ◀ Adnams Southwold Bitter, Caledonian Deuchars IPA, Timothy Taylor Landlord, Mauldons, Hop Back Ō Aspall. ☗ 10
Facilities Non-diners area ♦♦ Children's menu Children's portions Play area Garden ♠ Beer festival Parking Wi-fi 🚐

LETHERINGSETT
Map 13 TG03

The Kings Head

PICK OF THE PUBS

Holt Rd NR25 7AR ☎ 01263 712691
e-mail: manager@kingsheadnorfolk.co.uk
dir: *On A148, 1m from Holt. Pub on corner*

Vintage-chic gastro-pub recommended for its outdoor areas

Chris Coubrough's thriving Norfolk-based Flying Kiwi Inns snapped up this rather grand, manor-like building and revamped it in impressive style. Expect an elegant, rustic-chic feel throughout the rambling dining areas that radiate from the central bar, with rugs on terracotta tiles, squashy sofas and leather chairs fronting blazing winter log fires, feature bookcases, warm heritage hues, and an eclectic mix of old dining tables. The atmosphere is informal, the beer is East Anglian-brewed – try a pint of Adnams – and the food modern British and prepared from top-notch ingredients supplied by local farmers, fisherman and artisan producers. The pub has its own herd of Dexter cows. This translates to ham hock, pistachio and mustard terrine with piccalilli; Norfolk duck cassoulet; sea bass with shellfish bouillabaisse, saffron potatoes and garlic rouille; and vanilla pannacotta with rhubarb. This gastro-pub has superb alfresco areas including an excellent children's garden and a gravelled front terrace with posh benches and brollies.

Open all day all wk 11-11 **Bar Meals** L served Mon-Sat 12-2.30, Sun 12-8 D served Mon-Sat 6.30-9.30, Sun 12-8 **Restaurant** L served Mon-Sat 12-2.30, Sun 12-8 D served Mon-Sat 6.30-9.30, Sun 12-8 ⊕ FREE HOUSE/FLYING KIWI INNS ◀ Adnams Southwold Bitter, Jo C's Norfolk, Guest ales Ō Aspall. ☗ 14 **Facilities** Non-diners area ♦♦ Children's menu Children's portions Play area Garden ♠ Parking Wi-fi 🚐

MARSHAM
Map 13 TG12

The Plough Inn

PICK OF THE PUBS

Norwich Rd NR10 5PS ☎ 01263 735000
e-mail: enquires@ploughinnmarsham.co.uk
dir: *On A140, 10m N of Norwich, 1m S of Aylsham*

Countryside inn specialising in gluten- and wheat-free dishes

Whether you're touring the Norfolk Broads or on your way to Norwich Airport six miles away, the welcome at this 18th-century country hostelry will be warm, and experienced staff will ensure you enjoy your visit. Greene King IPA and Adnams are the ales on offer, together with a good range of wines. The restaurant uses local and seasonal produce if possible; the varied menus of modern British favourites are prepared in-house, and wheat- and gluten-free meals are a speciality. The range of lunchtime sandwiches, jacket potatoes and omelettes offer fillings to suit every palate. Tasty starters are home-made focaccia with olives, and chicken liver pâté. Main courses range from sirloin steak Stroganoff to fillet of salmon with a leek and potato cake, vegetables and a white wine sauce. Children are well catered for with their own menu. The carvery is popular on Sundays.

Open all wk 12-2.30 6-11 (all day summer) **Bar Meals** L served all wk 12-2.30 D served all wk 6-9 **Restaurant** L served all wk 12-2.30 D served all wk 6-9 ⊕ FREE HOUSE ◀ Greene King IPA, Adnams, John Smith's ○ Aspall. 🍷 10 **Facilities** Non-diners area ◀ Children's menu Children's portions Garden 🚗 Parking Wi-fi 🚐 (notice required)

MUNDFORD   Map 13 TL89

Crown Hotel

Crown Rd IP26 5HQ ☎ **01842 878233**
e-mail: info@the-crown-hotel.co.uk
dir: A11 to Barton Mills onto A1065 through Brandon to Mundford

Formerly a hunting lodge, currently a great pub with two restaurants

Originally a hunting lodge, this historic hillside inn on the edge of Thetford Forest dates back to 1652. Traditional, home-cooked food is served in the bars and two restaurants; perhaps pan-fried supreme of salmon with warm cherry tomato and basil salad or Jimmy Butler's slow-roasted pork belly with apple brandy sauce, baked apple and dauphinoise potatoes. In addition to the real ales and wines, there is a choice of over 50 malt whiskies. Being on a hill, the garden is on the first floor.

Open all day all wk 10.30am-mdnt **Bar Meals** L served all wk 12-3 D served all wk 6.30-10 **Restaurant** L served all wk 12-3 D served all wk 6.30-10 ⊕ FREE HOUSE ◀ Courage Directors, Greene King Ruddles County, Hardys & Hansons Olde Trip, Woodforde's Wherry, Guest ales. 🍷 9 **Facilities** Non-diners area 🐾 (Bar Garden) ◀ Children's portions Garden 🚗 Parking Wi-fi 🚐

NEWTON   Map 13 TF81

The George & Dragon

Swaffham Rd PE32 2BX ☎ **01760 755046**
e-mail: info@newtongeorge.co.uk
dir: 3m N of Swaffham on A1065

Traditional village inn in deepest Norfolk

If, like George Orwell, you could design your perfect pub (his was the fictitious Moon Under Water), then maybe this 1740-built, part-brick, part-flint, village inn will fit your bill. There's nothing imaginary about it: for a start, all the real ales are East Anglian, including the specially-brewed Newton Bitter. Locally sourced food is fresh and cooked to order, typically rib-eye steak with chips; South African bobotie and rice; slow-roast leg of duck with bubble-and-squeak; salmon and dill fishcakes; plus meat-free options. Phone the pub for jazz and Irish ceilidh nights dates. All this and three acres of garden.

Open 11-3 6-11 Closed: Sun eve & Mon L **Bar Meals** L served Tue-Sun 12-2 D served Mon-Sat 6-9 Av main course £10.50 **Restaurant** L served Tue-Sun 12-2 D served Mon-Sat 6-9 Av 3 course à la carte fr £20 ⊕ FREE HOUSE ◀ Newton Bitter, Guest ales ○ Aspall, Guest ciders. 🍷 13 **Facilities** Non-diners area 🐾 (Bar

Restaurant Garden) ◀ Children's menu Children's portions Play area Garden 🚗 Parking Wi-fi

---

NORWICH   Map 13 TG20

Adam & Eve

Bishopsgate NR3 1RZ ☎ **01603 667423**
e-mail: theadamandeve@hotmail.com
dir: Behind Anglican Cathedral, adjacent to Law Courts

Historic city-centre bolt hole

This enchanting, brick-and-flint built inn sits beneath trees at the fringe of the grounds of Norwich's Anglican Cathedral, the builders of which lodged at the pub, licensed since 1249. It's a refreshing step back in time, free of electronic diversions whilst rich with local beers from Humpty Dumpty and Wolf breweries; spirits here include ghosts of lingering, long-gone former locals. Who can blame them when the food is as rewarding as the ales; visitors resting on a tour of Norwich's finest can expect no-nonsense quality pub classics like filled large Yorkshire pudding, trawlerman's pie, home-made curry or chilli. The hanging basket displays are stunning.

Open all day all wk 11-11 (Sun 12-10.30) Closed: 25-26 Dec, 1 Jan **Bar Meals** L served Mon-Sat 12-7, Sun 12-5 ⊕ ENTERPRISE INNS ◀ Adnams Southwold Bitter, Theakston Old Peculier, Wolf Straw Dog, Humpty Dumpty ○ Aspall. 🍷 11 **Facilities** 🚗 Parking Wi-fi 🚐

The Mad Moose Arms
PICK OF THE PUBS

2 Warwick St NR2 3LB ☎ **01603 627687**
e-mail: madmoose@animalinns.co.uk
dir: 1m from A11

Ambitious cooking in a gastro-pub popular with the locals

Dating back to the late 1800s, this bustling neighbourhood pub offers the best of both worlds, with a welcoming ground-floor bar and an elegant upstairs dining room. Regulars know they can expect well-kept real ales and a bar menu offering a variety of interesting sandwiches, light meals and salads; and main dishes such as crispy chilli chicken with sesame stir-fried noodles or tomato and brie tarts with basil pesto. On the first floor is the elegant restaurant with chandeliers, sea green drapes, and a feature wall depicting a fairytale forest. Confident and ambitious cooking is typified by a starter of double baked goats' cheese soufflé, pickled beetroot and rocket salad. This might be followed by seared fillet of black bream, herb gnocchi, chorizo, spinach, tomato and anchovy dressing. Among the desserts consider chocolate fondant. There is a stylish outdoor patio for alfresco dining and beer festivals in May and October.

Open all day all wk 12-12 **Bar Meals** L served all wk 12-2 D served all wk 5.30-9 Av main course £9-£10 **Restaurant** D served Fri-Sat 6-9.30 Av 3 course à la carte fr £20 ⊕ FREE HOUSE/ANIMAL INNS ◀ Morland Old Speckled Hen, Greene King IPA ○ Aspall. 🍷 22 **Facilities** Non-diners area 🐾 (Bar Garden) ◀ Children's menu Children's portions Garden 🚗 Beer festival Wi-fi 🚐 (notice required)

Ribs of Beef

24 Wensum St NR3 1HY ☎ **01603 619517**
e-mail: roger@cawdron.co.uk
dir: From Tombland (in front of cathedral) turn left at Maids Head Hotel. Pub 200yds on right on bridge

City centre local providing cask ales and river views

Originally an alehouse back in the 18th century, between the 1960s and 80s, this building was used variously as an antiques shop, electrical store and fashion boutique before Roger and Anthea Cawdron relicensed it in 1985. They continue to welcome locals and holidaymakers cruising The Broads. The pub is valued for its comfy leather seats, range of cask ales, excellent wines and traditional English food using locally sourced produce. Breakfast is available until midday, whilst hearty choices like beef and ale stew, nut roast and wholetail scampi rub shoulders with sandwiches, burgers and jacket potatoes on the varied main menu. Sit outside on the jetty during the warmer months with its fabulous river views.

Open all day all wk 11-11 (Fri-Sat 11am-1am) **Bar Meals** L served Mon-Fri 12-2.30, Sat-Sun 12-5 Av main course £6.95 ⊕ FREE HOUSE ◀ Woodforde's Wherry, Adnams Southwold Bitter, Elgood's Black Dog, Oakham JHB, Fuller's London Pride ○ Kingfisher Norfolk Cider. 🍷 9 **Facilities** Non-diners area ◀ Children's menu Children's portions Family room Garden Outside area 🚗 Wi-fi 🚐 (notice required)

RINGSTEAD   Map 12 TF74

The Gin Trap Inn ★★★★ INN ⊛
PICK OF THE PUBS

6 High St PE36 5JU ☎ **01485 525264**
e-mail: thegintrap@hotmail.co.uk
dir: A149 from King's Lynn towards Hunstanton. In 15m turn right at Heacham for Ringstead

Fortifying walkers and cyclists on the Peddars Way

Dating from 1667 and sympathetically upgraded over the years, this attractive village inn is a comfy base from which to explore the north Norfolk coast. The pub is so called, as for many years it was packed with old gin traps, once used for snaring game. The rustic bar has exposed brickwork and beams, and a log-burning stove, plus there's an intimate dining room and modern conservatory. There's also a pretty walled garden for summer alfresco drinking and dining. Dog walkers, ramblers and cyclists pop in for the East Anglian ales and a meal to sustain them along the Peddars Way recreational path. The kitchen team takes pride in the provenance of the locally sourced produce that goes into the meals on its AA-Rosette gastro-pub menu. Most dishes are listed on the regularly changing blackboards, with pub favourites like fish pie, Holkham Estate beefburger and beer-battered haddock always on offer.

Open all day all wk 11.30-11 (11.30-2.30 6-11 in winter) **Bar Meals** L served Mon-Fri 12-2, Sat-Sun 12-2.30

continued

RINGSTEAD *continued*

D served Sun-Thu 6-9, Fri-Sat 6-9.30 **Restaurant** L served Mon-Fri 12-2, Sat-Sun 12-2.30 D served Sun-Thu 6-9, Fri-Sat 6-9.30 ⊕ FREE HOUSE ◀ Adnams Southwold Bitter, Woodforde's Wherry, Guest ales Ö Aspall. ♀ 10 **Facilities** Non-diners area ❖ (Bar Restaurant Garden) ♦♦ Children's menu Children's portions Garden ⊭ Parking Wi-fi ⊨ (notice required) **Rooms** 3

The Salthouse Dun Cow

Coast Rd NR25 7XA ☎ **01263 740467**
e-mail: salthouseduncow@gmail.com
dir: *On A149 (coast road). 3m E of Blakeney, 6m W of Sheringham*

An ideal retreat overlooking salt marsh scenery

In a quiet coastal village within an Area of Outstanding Natural Beauty, this traditional brick and flint pub probably originated as a cattle barn built around 1650. Today it overlooks some of Britain's finest salt marshes, so expect to share it, particularly the front garden, with birdwatchers and walkers. The interior decor reflects the surrounding farmland and seascapes. Local suppliers provide high quality produce for select menus prepared from scratch, especially fresh shellfish and game from local shoots. Samphire, asparagus and soft fruit are all sourced within five miles.

Open all day all wk ⊕ PUNCH TAVERNS ◀ Woodforde's Wherry, Adnams, Guest ales Ö Aspall. **Facilities** ❖ (Bar Restaurant Garden) ♦♦ Children's menu Children's portions Garden Parking Wi-fi

The Rose & Crown ★★ HL ⊛

PICK OF THE PUBS

Old Church Rd PE31 7LX ☎ **01485 541382**
e-mail: info@roseandcrownsnettisham.co.uk
dir: *10m N from King's Lynn on A149 signed Hunstanton. At Snettisham rdbt take B1440 to Snettisham. Left into Old Church Rd, inn on left*

Roses round the door and fresh seafood from the salt marshes

Anthony and Jeannette's splendid 14th-century inn was originally built to house the craftsmen who built the beautiful church up the road and is everything you'd expect from a Norfolk village inn. Beyond the rose-festooned façade lie twisting passages and hidden corners, leading to three charming bars, replete with heavy oak beams, uneven red-tiled floors, inglenook fireplaces, tip-top Adnams ale on tap, and an informal atmosphere. The menu makes good use of locally supplied produce – beef comes from cattle that grazed the nearby salt marshes; fishermen still in their waders deliver Brancaster mussels and Thornham oysters; and strawberries and asparagus are grown locally. Start with white onion and thyme velouté, follow with Jerusalem artichoke and wild mushroom risotto, or whole chargrilled

sea bass with new potatoes and olives, leaving room for orange syllabub with zabaglione ice cream and Italian meringue. Stylish bedrooms offer excellent accommodation and the pretty walled garden was once the village bowling green.

Open all day all wk **Bar Meals** L served Mon-Fri 12-2, Sat-Sun 12-5.30 D served Sun-Thu 6-9, Fri-Sat 6-9.30 Av main course £10 **Restaurant** L served Mon-Fri 12-2, Sat-Sun 12-5.30 D served Sun-Thu 6-9, Fri-Sat 6-9.30 ⊕ FREE HOUSE ◀ Adnams Southwold Bitter & Broadside, Bass, Fuller's London Pride, Greene King IPA. ♀ 12 **Facilities** Non-diners area ❖ (Bar Restaurant Garden) ♦♦ Children's menu Children's portions Play area Family room Garden ⊭ Parking Wi-fi **Rooms** 16

The Stiffkey Red Lion

44 Wells Rd NR23 1AJ ☎ **01328 830552**
e-mail: redlion@stiffkey.com
dir: *On A149, 4m E of Wells-next-the-Sea; 4m W of Blakeney*

A perfect spot for walkers and birdwatchers

Dating from the 17th century, this comfortable inn has been a house and even a doctor's surgery in its long life. Located on the north Norfolk coast, it is now a popular bolt-hole for walkers and birdwatchers stepping off the nearby salt marshes. Grab an old pew by one of the four log fires and warm up over a glass of Nelson's Revenge and locally sourced seasonal dishes such as salmon and crab fishcakes with home-made tartare sauce; home honey-roasted ham with egg and chips; and classic spotted dick for dessert. Children's meals are available.

Open all day all wk **Bar Meals** L served Mon-Sat 12-2.30, Sun 12-9 D served Mon-Sat 6-9, Sun 12-9 **Restaurant** L served Mon-Sat 12-2.30, Sun 12-9 D served Mon-Sat 6-9, Sun 12-9 ⊕ FREE HOUSE ◀ The Stiffkey Red Lion Stewkey Brew, Woodforde's Wherry & Nelson's Revenge. ♀ 12 **Facilities** Non-diners area ❖ (Bar Restaurant Garden) ♦♦ Children's menu Children's portions Garden ⊭ Parking Wi-fi

The Wildebeest

PICK OF THE PUBS

82-86 Norwich Rd NR14 8QJ ☎ **01508 492497**
e-mail: wildebeest@animalinns.co.uk
dir: *From A47 take A140, left to Dunston. At T-junct turn left, pub on right*

Perfect retreat from city hustle and bustle

A member of the Norfolk-based Animal Inns family, this charming village local has been trading for more than 20 years. Its trendy rustic-chic look comes from a satisfying combination of oak beams, wooden floors, chunky wooden tables, potted plants, log fires, rag-washed yellow walls and, outside, a patio with a giant umbrella. Although it's food-led, don't feel you shouldn't slip in for a pint or two of Adnams, an Aspall cider, or a glass of wine, 10 of

which are available by the glass. The kitchen takes a modern approach, as shown by Norfolk venison carpaccio with port and orange jelly, semi-dried grapes and black pepper ice cream; and pan-fried fillet of turbot with Puy lentil cream, clams and roasted salsify. Among the specials are pan-fried fillet of mullet with pepper and olive salad and pesto oil; and braised ox cheeks with buttered mash, seasonal vegetables and mushroom jus.

Open all wk all day (Etr-Sep) phone for winter opening **Bar Meals** L served all wk 12-2.30 D served all wk 6-9 Av main course £14 **Restaurant** L served all wk 12-2.30 D served all wk 6-9 Fixed menu price fr £15 Av 3 course à la carte fr £26 ⊕ FREE HOUSE ◀ Adnams Ö Aspall. ♀ 10 **Facilities** Non-diners area ♦♦ Children's menu Children's portions Garden ⊭ Parking

The Hare Arms

PICK OF THE PUBS

PE34 3HT ☎ **01366 382229**
e-mail: trishmc@harearms222.wanadoo.co.uk
dir: *From King's Lynn take A10 to Downham Market. After 9m village signed on left*

Attractive pub with a good vegetarian selection

Named after the Hare family, who have lived at Stow Hall since 1553, this ivy-clad pub has been run for the past 37 years by Trish and David McManus. No music drowns the conversation in the L-shaped bar and adjoining conservatory, which are both full of fascinating bygones the landlords have collected along the way. A large bar food menu is always available, supplemented by daily specials of, say, Cajun-spiced salmon fillet served with a minted yogurt dip. Starters on the restaurant menu could be pork terrine flavoured with brandy, garlic pistachio nuts and mixed herbs; and melon in a stem ginger dressing. Sample main courses include prime fillet steak topped with tiger prawns and garlic butter. There is a separate vegetarian menu with a good choice of dishes, from spring rolls to mozzarella and thyme risotto balls, and from nut cutlets to a penne pasta bake. Expect to see peacocks in the garden.

Open all wk 11-2.30 6-11 (Sat 11-11 Sun 12-10.30) Closed: 25-26 Dec **Bar Meals** L served Mon-Fri 12-2, Sun 12-2 D served Mon-Fri 6.30-10, Sat-Sun 12-10 Av main course £10 **Restaurant** D served Mon-Sat 7-9 Fixed menu price fr £21 Av 3 course à la carte fr £30 ⊕ GREENE KING ◀ Abbot Ale & IPA, Morland Old Speckled Hen, Guest ales Ö Aspall. ♀ 9 **Facilities** Non-diners area ♦♦ Children's menu Children's portions Family room Garden ⊭ Parking Wi-fi

Save on hotels. Book at **theAA.com/hotel**

NORFOLK 317 ENGLAND

PICK OF THE PUBS

The Orange Tree

THORNHAM   Map 12 TF74

High St PE36 6LY ☎ 01485 512213
e-mail:
email@theorangetreethornham.co.uk
web: www.theorangetreethornham.co.uk
dir: *Telephone for directions*

Contemporary dining pub in a coastal village

Standing in the centre of the village opposite the church, this family-run pub makes a useful stop for walkers on the ancient Peddars Way. Formerly a smugglers' haunt, the 400-year-old whitewashed inn has evolved over the years into the stylish country pub it is today. Develop an appetite with a stroll to the local staithe, where working fishing boats still come and go through the creeks of Brancaster Bay, before returning for meal and a pint of East Anglian-brewed ale. Chef Philip Milner makes the most of freshly landed local seafood, with innovative dishes like pan-fried lemon sole with a lemon, fennel and caper salad, anchovy and roasted red pepper aïoli. But it's not just the seafood that justifies his claim that the restaurant is the jewel in The Orange Tree's crown; the pub has a long-established relationship with local suppliers, and most of the meat is sourced from the Sandringham Estate. Traditional beef Wellington gets the celebrity treatment with wild mushroom crêpe, spinach and horseradish purée,

smoked garlic and potato rösti and salted caramel pastry. Meanwhile, dishes on the bar classics menu could include Moroccan preserved lemon, feta and chickpea burger; free-range chicken and wild mushroom pie; seafood spaghetti and Cumberland sausage ring. Look to the board for the daily sandwich selection. Leave space to sample the appetising selection of desserts, such as the delightfully themed 'Fairground': bubblegum pannacotta, baby toffee apples, candyfloss, butterscotch popcorn and chocolate covered honeycomb. Traditionalists might opt for sticky toffee pudding or a home-made ice cream or sorbet. Dogs get their own beer and menu, while children will love the climbing frame in the pub's garden.

Open all day all wk **Bar Meals** L served all wk 12-3 D served all wk 6-9.30 **Restaurant** L served all wk 12-3 D served all wk 6-9.30 ⊞ PUNCH TAVERNS 🍺 Woodforde's Wherry, Adnams Southwold Bitter, Crouch Vale Brewers Gold Ŏ Aspall. ♟ 21
Facilities Non-diners area 🐾 (Bar Garden) 🧒 Children's menu Children's portions Play area Garden ⊼ Parking Wi-fi 🚌

SWANTON MORLEY — Map 13 TG01

Darbys Freehouse

1&2 Elsing Rd NR20 4NY ☎ 01362 637647
e-mail: louisedarby@hotmail.co.uk
dir: From A47 (Norwich to King's Lynn) take B1147 to Dereham

A bit of a make-over at this country pub

A large country house, divided first into cottages in the late 19th century, then in 1988 converted into a pub. The pub was undergoing a refurbishment in the spring of 2013. The mostly locally supplied pub food includes dishes such as chorizo and mixed bean chilli pot with pastry crust; pork sausages with creamy mash, curly kale and onion gravy; sharing boards; and vegetarian and children's selections. Guest ales join Norfolk and Suffolk regulars.

Open all wk Mon-Thu 11.30-3 6-11 (Fri-Sat 11.30-11 Sun 12-10.30). Food served all day Sat-Sun ◑ Woodforde's Wherry, Adnams Broadside & Southwold Bitter, 2 Guest ales. **Facilities** ♦ Children's menu Children's portions Play area Family room Garden Parking

THOMPSON — Map 13 TL99

Chequers Inn

PICK OF THE PUBS

Griston Rd IP24 1PX ☎ 01953 483360
e-mail: richard@thompsonchequers.co.uk
dir: Exit A1075 between Watton & Thetford

Extensive countryside views from the garden

The Chequers takes its name from the cloth used for counting money, wages and rents in medieval times. Manorial courts, held here from at least 1724, dealt with rents, letting of land, and petty crime. Well off the beaten track, this splendid, long and low, thatched 17th-century inn is worth finding for its peaceful location and unspoilt charm. Beneath the steep-raked thatch of this ancient alehouse, once a row of several cottages, lies a series of low-ceilinged interconnecting rooms served by a long bar. Wonky wall timbers, low doorways, open log fires, a rustic mix of old furniture and farming implements characterise the atmospheric interior. Eat in the bar for a menu packed with pub favourites. The inn is an ideal base for exploring the heart of Norfolk and the Peddars Way National Trail. Dogs are welcome in the large rear garden, which offers picnic tables and children's play equipment.

Open all wk 11.30-3 6.30-11 **Bar Meals** L served all wk 12-2 D served all wk 6.30-9 **Restaurant** L served all wk 12-2 D served all wk 6.30-9 ⊕ FREE HOUSE ◑ Adnams Southwold Bitter, Wolf Ale, Greene King IPA Ö Thatchers, Aspall. ☻ 8 **Facilities** Non-diners area ♣ (Bar Garden) ♦ Children's menu Children's portions Play area Garden ⋏ Beer festival Parking Wi-fi ➡ (notice required)

THORNHAM — Map 12 TF74

Marco Pierre White The Lifeboat Inn

PICK OF THE PUBS

Ship Ln PE36 6LT ☎ 01485 512236
e-mail: reception@lifeboatinn.co.uk
dir: A149 from Hunstanton for approx 6m. 1st left after Thornham sign

Different dining areas and Marco inspired dishes

This rambling, 16th-century smugglers' inn, situated on the edge of a vast expanse of salt marsh, is a short stroll from sweeping beaches, renowned bird reserves, and bracing coastal path walks. The ramble of old rooms retain their original character, boasting low-beamed ceilings, rug-strewn tiled floors, low doors, half-panelled walls, five log-burning fires, and a rustic array of furniture, from carved oak tables to antique settles and pews. Antique oil lamps suspended from the ceiling and a wealth of nautical bric-à-brac enhance the charm, while the adjoining conservatory is renowned for its ancient vine and there's an adjacent walled patio garden. Food ranges from sausage and caramelised onion sandwiches, and starters like potted duck and salt and pepper calamari with lemon mayonnaise, to traditional fish and chips, braised lamb shank with roasted root vegetables and red wine jus, and grilled plaice with potted shrimps and lemon butter. It's perfectly placed for visiting Sandringham and Nelson's birthplace at Burnham Thorpe.

Open all day all wk **Bar Meals** L served all wk 12-2.30, 3-5.30 D served all wk 6-9.30 **Restaurant** L served Sun 12-2 D served all wk 7-9.30 ⊕ VICTORY INNS ◑ Greene King Abbot Ale & IPA, Woodforde's Wherry, Adnams, JW Lees The Governor, Guest ales Ö Aspall, Westons Stowford Press, Governor. ☻ 10 **Facilities** Non-diners area ♣ (Bar Garden) ♦ Children's menu Children's portions Play area Garden ⋏ Parking Wi-fi ➡ (notice required)

The Orange Tree

PICK OF THE PUBS

See Pick of the Pubs on page 317

TITCHWELL — Map 13 TF74

Titchwell Manor Hotel ★★★ HL ◉◉◉

PICK OF THE PUBS

PE31 8BB ☎ 01485 210221
e-mail: margaret@titchwellmanor.com
dir: A149 between Brancaster & Thornham

Sublime sea views and extraordinary cuisine

The north Norfolk coast fragments into a series of sandbank islands and marshes creating a memorable landscape, home for 200 bird species. Ramblers and twitchers work up healthy appetites here; which may be sated at the comfy mix of dining opportunities at Titchwell Manor. Once a marshland farmhouse, over 25 years Margaret and Ian Snaith have tastefully modernised

it, while their son Eric and his team are responsible for the three AA-Rosette cuisine in the elegant Conservatory overlooking the walled garden, the Eating Rooms and the bar; in summer the sea-view terrace is popular. The modern European menus feature starters like baked celeriac with liquorice granola, truffle custard and cranberry; or partridge breast with baked apple and turnip. Time then for mains of pheasant schnitzel with pickled cabbage spätzle, lardon and mushroom; or venison pudding confit shallot, whilst Brancaster shellfish are always popular. Some of the luxurious suites have sea views.

Open all day all wk **Bar Meals** L served all wk 12-5.30 D served all wk 6-9.30 Av main course £14 **Restaurant** L served all wk 12-2.30 D served all wk 6-9.30 Av 3 course à la carte fr £22 ⊕ FREE HOUSE ◑ Abbot Ale, Woodforde's Wherry Ö Aspall. ☻ 17 **Facilities** Non-diners area ♣ (Bar Garden) ♦ Children's menu Children's portions Garden ⋏ Parking Wi-fi ➡ (notice required) **Rooms** 26

WARHAM ALL SAINTS — Map 13 TF94

Three Horseshoes

PICK OF THE PUBS

NR23 1NL ☎ 01328 710547
dir: From Wells A149 to Cromer, then right onto B1105 to Warham

Honest pub food in traditional pub

This gem of a pub first opened its doors in 1725. Its rambling old rooms, including a gas-lit main bar, are stone floored with scrubbed wooden tables. A grandfather clock ticks away in one corner, and a curious green and red dial in the ceiling turns out to be a rare example of Norfolk Twister, an ancient pub game. Vintage posters, clay pipes, photographs and memorabilia adorn the walls, while down a step are old one-arm bandits. Woodforde's Sundew and Nelson's Revenge are served from the cask through a hole in the bar wall. Home-made soups, pies and puddings dominate the menu, so start with creamy mushroom or vegetable soup; follow with macaroni cheese bake for a light lunch, or chicken and rabbit pie if more hungry. Date and banana sponge or Marsh mud pie are served with custard or cream. A no-chips policy applies, incidentally. Outside is a beer garden and covered courtyard.

Open all wk 12-2.30 6-11 **Bar Meals** L served all wk 12-1.45 D served all wk 6-8 ⊕ FREE HOUSE ◑ Woodforde's Wherry, Sundew, Nelson's Revenge Ö Whin Hill. **Facilities** Non-diners area ♣ (Bar Garden) ♦ Children's portions Family room Garden ⋏ Parking ➡ (notice required)

Save on hotels. Book at **theAA.com/hotel**

NORFOLK 319 **ENGLAND**

WELLS-NEXT-THE-SEA — Map 13 TF94

The Crown Hotel

PICK OF THE PUBS

The Buttlands NR23 1EX ☎ 01328 710209
e-mail: reception@crownhotelnorfolk.co.uk
dir: 10m from Fakenham on B1105

Boutique inn on the coast

This 17th-century former coaching inn overlooks the tree-lined green known as The Buttlands. The Crown's striking contemporary decor blends effortlessly with its old-world charm and beneath the bar's ancient beams, East Anglian ales and Aspall real cider are on tap. Whether you eat in the bar, more formally in the restaurant, in the cheerful Orangery, or outside with its great views, the menus offer traditional favourites, the best of modern British cuisine, and internationally influenced dishes. Perhaps opt for baked feta polenta with a ratatouille sauce; or roast salmon fillet on a prawn, chickpea and broccoli broth from the main menu. The Crown Classics set menu changes every two weeks and could feature Holkham venison casserole or honey and mustard marinated goats' cheese salad. Desserts might include honey and thyme brûlée. A good few wines are available by the glass and there are a few half-bottles. Tuesday evening is seafood night.

Open all day all wk **Bar Meals** L served all wk 12-2.30 D served all wk 6.30-9.30 Av main course £13.50 **Restaurant** L served all wk 12-2.30 D served all wk 6.30-9.30 Fixed menu price fr £12.95 ⊕ FREE HOUSE/ FLYING KIWI INNS ◀ Adnams Southwold Bitter, Jo C's Norfolk Kiwi, Guest ale ⚬ Aspall. ♥ 14 **Facilities** Non-diners area ✿ (Bar Garden) ♦ Children's menu Children's portions Garden ⌂ Parking Wi-fi 🚗

The Globe Inn

The Buttlands NR23 1EU ☎ 01328 710206
e-mail: globe@holkham.co.uk
dir: In village centre

Seasonally inspired food not far from the quay

The Globe is a short stroll from the town's bustling quay and overlooks the leafy village green. It has a warm, welcoming bar and comfortable restaurant, with a sunny courtyard for alfresco drinking and dining. The menus take full advantage of the abundance of local produce from both land and sea – such as tender asparagus in early summer and game from the Holkham Estate in winter. Smoked mackerel pâté, horseradish crème fraîche and toast makes a delicious starter. To finish, share the Norfolk cheese selection with celery, quince jelly and biscuits.

Open all day all wk ⊕ ADNAMS ◀ Adnams ⚬ Aspall. **Facilities** ✿ (Bar Restaurant Garden) ♦ Children's menu Children's portions Garden Wi-fi

WEST BECKHAM — Map 13 TG13

The Wheatsheaf

Manor Farm, Church Rd NR25 6NX ☎ 01263 822110
e-mail: manager@thewheatsheafwestbeckham.co.uk
dir: 2m from Sheringham on A148, turn opposite Sheringham Park

Quiet village pub with home-cooked food

Situated in a quiet village just two miles from Sheringham and formerly known as the 'old manor farmhouse', this charming building was converted to a pub over 20 years ago and retains many original features. Sample one of the real ales from Woodforde's and relax in the bar, one of the restaurants or the large garden. All food is made on the premises using fresh local produce. From the bar menu, dishes might include prime beef lasagne or beer-battered haddock, while typical choices from the restaurant menu are roasted pepper and cashew Stroganoff; and slow-roasted belly pork with bubble-and-squeak.

Open 11.30-3 6.30-11.30 Closed: Mon ⊕ FREE HOUSE ◀ Woodforde's Wherry, Greene King IPA, Guest ales ⚬ Aspall. **Facilities** ♦ Children's menu Children's portions Play area Garden Parking

WESTON LONGVILLE — Map 13 TG11

The Parson Woodforde

Church St NR9 5JU ☎ 01603 881675
e-mail: manager@theparsonwoodforde.com
dir: From Norwich take A1067 (Fakenham road). After Morton turn left in Marl Hill Rd to Weston Longville

Good ales and Norfolk produce on the menus

Just a 20-minute drive from Norwich, in the village of Weston Longville, this pub started life as the Five Ringers back in 1845. Now it's a free house with a great selection of real ales and a restaurant. A range of local cask ales are on offer alongside a menu that showcases Norfolk produce in dishes such as a duo of braised lamb and shank with a fruit terrine and horseradish mash with thyme.

Open all day all wk Closed: 25 Dec (drinks only 12-2.30), Mon (Jan-Feb) ⊕ FREE HOUSE ◀ Grain Best Bitter, Wolf Straw Dog, Adnams Southwold Bitter, Winter's ⚬ Aspall. **Facilities** ♦ Children's menu Children's portions Garden Parking Wi-fi

WINTERTON-ON-SEA — Map 13 TG41

Fishermans Return

The Lane NR29 4BN ☎ 01493 393305
e-mail: enquiries@fishermansreturn.com
web: www.fishermansreturn.com
dir: 8m N of Great Yarmouth on B1159

Just round the corner from sandy beaches

This dog-friendly, 350-year-old brick and flint free house stands close to long beaches and National Trust land, making it the ideal spot to finish a walk. Guest ales support Woodforde's Norfolk Nog and Wherry behind the bar, whilst the menus range from popular favourites like omelettes and filled jacket potatoes to sirloin steak and three bean chilli. Look out for fish and seafood specials on the daily-changing blackboard, where freshly caught mackerel or sea bass may be on offer. The pub hosts a beer festival on August Bank Holiday.

Open all wk 11-2.30 5.30-11 (Sat-Sun 11-11) **Bar Meals** L served all wk 12-2.30 D served all wk 6-9 **Restaurant** L served all wk 12-2.30 D served all wk 6-9 ⊕ FREE HOUSE ◀ Woodforde's Wherry & Norfolk Nog, Guest ales ⚬ Westons Stowford Press & Old Rosie Scrumpy, Local ciders. ♥ 9 **Facilities** Non-diners area ✿ (Bar Restaurant Garden) ♦ Children's menu Children's portions Play area Family room Garden Beer festival Cider festival Parking Wi-fi 🚗

WIVETON — Map 13 TG04

Wiveton Bell ⊚

PICK OF THE PUBS

Blakeney Rd NR25 7TL ☎ 01263 740101
e-mail: enquiries@wivetonbell.co.uk
dir: From Blakeney take A149 towards Cley next the Sea. Right into Wiverton Rd

Tranquil country pub championing local fish and game

The stylishly spruced-up Bell, built in the 18th century, overlooks the peaceful village green and church in the sleepy hamlet of Wiveton, which stands just a mile inland from the glorious coastal salt marshes. Expect a chic interior, with earthy heritage-coloured walls, stripped beams, chunky tables and oak-planked floors. Further character is provided by the bold, contemporary oil paintings by local artists that line the walls of the cosy bar and conservatory dining room, where Yetman's ale (brewed up the road), Aspall cider and a carefully

continued

WIVETON *continued*

selected wine list hold sway. In winter, head for the tables close to the inglenook fireplace, mingle with the locals and walkers (wellies are welcome), and peruse the seasonal menu. Begin with smoked leg and breast of partridge, and follow with Brancaster mussels steamed in white wine or chicken and bacon carbonara. Don't miss the excellent Sunday roasts – booking essential.

Open all day all wk Closed: 25 Dec **Bar Meals** L served all wk 12-2.15 D served all wk 6-9 Av main course £12.95 **Restaurant** L served all wk 12-2.15 D served all wk 6-9.15 Av 3 course à la carte fr £23.50 ⊕ FREE HOUSE ◀ Woodforde's Wherry, Adnams Broadside, Yetman's ♻ Aspall. ▮ 17 **Facilities** Non-diners area ♦♦ Children's menu Children's portions Garden ⼧ Parking Wi-fi

WOODBASTWICK — Map 13 TG31

The Fur & Feather Inn

Slad Ln NR13 6HQ ☎ 01603 720003
dir: *From A1151 (Norwich to Wroxham road), follow brown signs for Woodforde's Brewery. Pub adjacent to Brewery*

An idyllic thatched country pub ideal for beer lovers

Eight real ales from Woodforde's Brewery next door are served straight from the cask here, with no jukebox, TV or pool table to disturb the peace. The pub was originally two farm cottages, and now boasts three cosy bar areas and a smart restaurant. Here you can enjoy traditional home-made English fare, with a great selection of pies, burgers and grills: lamb, garlic and rosemary pie; rib-eye steak with all the trimmings; and The Old Forge Burger, topped with hickory-smoked barbecue sauce and crispy bacon. An interesting vegetarian selection and a 'catch of the day' menu (where you select your fresh fish from the counter) complete the picture.

Open all day all wk **Bar Meals** L served 10-9 D served 10-9 Av main course £11 food served all day **Restaurant** L served 10-9 D served 10-9 Av 3 course à la carte fr £21 food served all day ◀ Woodforde's Wherry, Sundew, Iceni Norfolk Gold, Norfolk Nog, Nelson's Revenge, Once Bittern, Headcracker, Mardler's Mild. ▮ 12 **Facilities** Non-diners area ♦♦ Children's menu Garden ⼧ Parking Wi-fi ➡ (notice required)

ASHBY ST LEDGERS — Map 11 SP56

The Olde Coach House Inn

CV23 8UN ☎ 01788 890349
e-mail: info@oldecoachhouse.co.uk
dir: *M1 junct 18 follow A361/Daventry signs. Village on left*

Good food in a memorable village setting

This mellow stone inn nestles amidst thatched cottages in the lovely estate village here; until a century ago it was a farmhouse. Today it's an engaging mix of contemporary and rustic, with a strong emphasis on comfort; deep leather furnishings tempt you to linger by log fires, wondering at the function of the archaic rural artefacts on display. The courtyard dining area is a popular place to sample the extensive fare. Slow cooked lamb shank vies with tomato and shallot tart Tatin as typical mains, with an appealing self-selection grazing board offering a fulfilling alternative. Beers are from the Wells and Young's stable.

Open all wk Mon-Thu 12-3 5.30-11 (Fri-Sun all day) **Bar Meals** L served Mon-Sat 12-2.30, Sun 12-8 D served Mon-Sat 6-9.30, Sun 12-8 Av main course £12 **Restaurant** L served Mon-Sat 12-2.30, Sun 12-8 D served Mon-Sat 6-9.30, Sun 12-8 Fixed menu price fr £9.95 Av 3 course à la carte fr £25 ⊕ CHARLES WELLS ◀ Bombardier, Young's. ▮ 12 **Facilities** Non-diners area ♣ (Bar Garden) ♦♦ Children's menu Children's portions Play area Garden ⼧ Parking Wi-fi ➡ (notice required)

ASHTON — Map 11 SP74

The Old Crown

1 Stoke Rd NN7 2JN ☎ 01604 862268
e-mail: bex@theoldcrownashton.co.uk
dir: *M1 junct 15, A508 to Roade. 1m, left to Ashton*

Dining pub with innovative menus

A well-appointed homely village local in the small rural community of Ashton. A pub for over 300 years, its pretty, sheltered gardens are a popular choice for summer dining, or settle in to the beamed bar room and look forward to choosing from the well thought out, balanced menus while sipping a pint of well-kept ale. Perhaps start with deep-fried squid with aïoli, followed by ginger and soy marinated chicken breast with sticky coconut rice; or trio of lamb (cutlet, mini shepherd's pie and slow cooked shoulder); then spiced pecan and chocolate tart. There are regular events held throughout the year.

Open 12-3 6-11 (Sat 12-11.30 Sun 12-10.30) Closed: Mon **Bar Meals** L served Tue-Fri 12-2.30, Sat 12-9.30, Sun 12-4 D served Tue-Fri 6-9.30 ⊕ CHARLES WELLS ◀ Eagle IPA, Courage Directors, Young's. ▮ 10 **Facilities** Non-diners area ♦♦ Children's portions Garden Parking Wi-fi ➡ (notice required)

AYNHO — Map 11 SP53

The Great Western Arms

Station Rd OX17 3BP ☎ 01869 338288
e-mail: info@great-westernarms.co.uk
dir: *From Aynho take B4031 (Station Road) W towards Deddington. Turn right to pub*

Run by a young and friendly bunch

The Great Western Railway company disappeared in 1948, but its name lives on in this foliage-covered inn between the line it built to Birmingham, and the Oxford Canal. It's a Hook Norton pub, so the brewery's range of ales is well represented; ten wines are sold by the glass, and there's a packed whisky and spirit shelf. Good things on chef-patron René Klein's menus include his creamy chicken curry; venison, pheasant, cranberry and port pie; Cajun-dusted salmon fillet; and leek and cheese sausages. The pretty courtyard and garden has won Hook Norton's top award. Beer festival first weekend in October.

Open all day all wk Closed: 25 Dec **Bar Meals** L served all wk 12-3 D served all wk 6-9 Av main course £12.50 **Restaurant** L served all wk 12-3 D served all wk 6-9 ⊕ HOOK NORTON ◀ Hooky Bitter, Twelve Days, Cotswold Lion ♻ Westons Perry, Old Rosie & Stowford Press. ▮ 10 **Facilities** Non-diners area ♣ (Bar Garden) ♦♦ Children's menu Children's portions Garden ⼧ Beer festival Parking Wi-fi ➡ (notice required)

BULWICK — Map 11 SP99

The Queen's Head

PICK OF THE PUBS

Main St NN17 3DY ☎ 01780 450272
e-mail: info@thequeensheadbulwick.co.uk
dir: *Just off A43, between Corby & Stamford*

Village free house supporting local breweries

A 17th-century stone-built free house overlooking the village church, parts of The Queen's Head date back to 1400. The pub is a warren of small rooms with exposed wooden beams, four open fireplaces and flagstone floors. Relax by the fire or on the patio with a pint of real ale from the local Oakham or Rockingham breweries. Local shoots supply seasonal game such as teal, woodcock and partridge, and other ingredients often include village-grown fruit and vegetables brought in by customers and friends. Lunchtime brings a good selection of sandwiches, snacks and main dishes. The evening menu might feature local pork sausages with mash and white onion and grainy mustard sauce. The menu is backed by a comprehensive wine list. The Queen's Head also has a outdoor oven for outside dining.

Open 12-3 6-11 (Sun 12-7) Closed: Mon **Bar Meals** L served Tue-Sat 12-2, Sun 12-3 D served Tue-Sat 6-9 **Restaurant** L served Tue-Sat 12-2, Sun 12-3 D served Tue-Sat 6-9 ⊕ FREE HOUSE ◀ Rockingham, Oakham, Digfield Ales, Shepherd Neame. ▮ 9 **Facilities** Non-diners area ♣ (Bar Outside area) ♦♦ Children's portions Outside area ⼧ Parking ➡

Save on hotels. Book at theAA.com/hotel

NORTHAMPTONSHIRE 321 ENGLAND

CHACOMBE
Map 11 SP44

George and Dragon

Silver St OX17 2JR ☎ 01295 711500
e-mail: georgeanddragonchacombe@googlemail.com
dir: *M40 junct 11, A361 (Daventry road). Chacombe 1st right*

Traditional pub in a pretty village

Within easy reach of Silverstone racing circuit, this honey-stoned, 17th-century pub is tucked away beside the church. Situated in a conservation area, the pub retains a traditional, welcoming atmosphere: the three bars have an abundance of low beams, simple wooden chairs and settles, roaring log fires, and warm terracotta decor. The sun terrace to the rear is a good spot for sampling the ales in summer. The lunchtime menu offers sandwiches and baguettes; small bites such as soups, salads and fishcakes; and bigger plates like chilli con carne, beefburger and vegetable lasagne. The evening menu ups the ante with modern British cuisine.

Open all day all wk 12-11 ⊕ EVERARDS ◀ Tiger & Beacon, Guest ales. **Facilities** ♦♦ Children's menu Children's portions Garden Parking Wi-fi

CRICK
Map 11 SP57

The Red Lion Inn

52 Main Rd NN6 7TX ☎ 01788 822342
dir: *M1 junct 18, A428, 0.75m, follows signs for Crick from rdbt*

Village inn in the same hands for many years

An old gabled, thatched, coaching inn of mellow ironstone standing beside the pretty main street just a stone's throw from Crick's ancient church. Exposed beams, low ceilings and open fires characterise this village free-house, family-run for the past 33 years. Beers from Adnams or Wells example the varied range of real ales available here, with classic pub meals the order of the day.

Open all wk 11-2.30 6.15-11 (Sun 12-3 7-11) **Bar Meals** L served all wk 12-2 D served Mon-Sat 6.30-9 ⊕ FREE HOUSE ◀ Adnams Southwold Bitter, Wells Bombardier, Morland Old Speckled Hen, Guest ale. **Facilities** Non-diners area ❄ (Bar Restaurant Garden) ♦♦ Children's menu Children's portions Garden ⌂ Parking Wi-fi

EAST HADDON
Map 11 SP66

The Red Lion
PICK OF THE PUBS

Main St NN6 8BU ☎ 01604 770223
e-mail: nick@redlioneasthaddon.co.uk
dir: *Just off A428*

Top gastro-pub with its own cookery school

Since taking over, former Gary Rhodes chef Adam Gray and his partner Nick Bonner have put The Red Lion firmly on the map as a top destination gastro-pub. Such is the pub's reputation for culinary excellence that it even runs its own cookery school. Expect a high standard of food at this village pub, whether in snacks such as free-range pork Scotch egg, or potted mackerel with rhubarb and toasted spelt bread to begin; main dishes like braised red wine beef with carrots and creamy mash or poached organic salmon with red cabbage and wild mushrooms; and puddings along the lines of banana fool with toffee sauce. Accompany your meal with one of 14 wines served by the glass or a pint of Wells Bombardier. The landscaped gardens offer good views over rolling countryside.

Open all day 11-11 (Sun 11-3) Closed: Sun eve **Bar Meals** L served Mon-Sat 12-2.30, Sun 12-3 D served Mon-Fri 6-9, Sat 6-10 **Restaurant** L served Mon-Sat 12-2.30, Sun 12-3 D served Mon-Fri 6-9, Sat 6-10 ⊕ CHARLES WELLS ◀ Young's, Courage Directors. ♈ 14 **Facilities** Non-diners area ♦♦ Children's portions Garden ⌂ Parking Wi-fi

EYDON
Map 11 SP54

Royal Oak @ Eydon

6 Lime Av NN11 3PG ☎ 01327 263167
e-mail: info@theroyaloakateydon.co.uk
dir: *Telephone for directions*

Walkers, locals, children and dogs all very welcome

John Crossan's mellow stone pub dates back 300 years and stands in the heart of pretty Eydon. Innovative modern pub food draws discerning diners from far and wide but it's still very much hub of the village, welcoming walkers, dogs and local drinkers into the bar and dining areas. Come for pints of Hooky by the inglenook or for daily menus that champion local seasonal produce, including vegetables from the village allotments. Tuck into braised beef with roasted root vegetables or pan-fried sea bass with surf clam and crayfish velouté, followed by dark chocolate fondant, or opt for a cracking home-made burger from the short bar menu.

Open 12-3 6-11 (Sat 12-12 Sun 12-11) Closed: Mon L **Bar Meals** L served Tue-Sun 12-2 D served Tue-Sat 7-9, Sun 6.30-8.30 ⊕ FREE HOUSE ◀ Fuller's London Pride, Timothy Taylor Landlord, Hook Norton Hooky Bitter, Gueat ales Ở Westons Stowford Press. ♈ 16 **Facilities** Non-diners area ❄ (Bar Garden) ♦♦ Children's menu Children's portions Garden ⌂ Beer festival Parking Wi-fi ⊟ (notice required)

FARTHINGHOE
Map 11 SP53

The Fox

Baker St NN13 5PH ☎ 01295 713965
e-mail: enquiries@foxatfarthinghoe.co.uk
dir: *M40 junct 11, A422, towards Brackley. Approx 5.5m to Farthinghoe*

Relaxed village pub with friendly service and convenient for Silverstone

Only 12 miles from Silverstone, this Charles Wells pub brings its customers fresh, locally sourced food with friendly service and a relaxing village atmosphere. In practice this translates as a varied menu offering pub favourites such as glazed Cotswold ham, sticky BBQ ribs, kedgeree smoked haddock, and chef's fish pie, along with more exotic options such as chicken and chorizo linguine. Sandwiches and wraps are also available, and there is even a take-out menu. Ladies' Night on Wednesdays means three courses and a glass of wine for £16.50. Tuesday evening is curry night, Thursdays and Fridays have extra seafood dishes while a roast is offered every Sunday lunch.

Open all wk 12-3 6-11 (Fri-Sun 12-11) **Bar Meals** L served all wk 12-2.30 D served all wk 6-9.30 Av main course £15 **Restaurant** L served all wk 12-2.30 D served all wk 6-9.30 Fixed menu price fr £10 Av 3 course à la carte fr £32 ⊕ CHARLES WELLS ◀ Bombardier, Young's, Erdinger, Guest ale. ♈ 12 **Facilities** Non-diners area ♦♦ Children's portions Garden ⌂ Parking Wi-fi ⊟ (notice required)

FARTHINGSTONE
Map 11 SP65

The Kings Arms
PICK OF THE PUBS

Main St NN12 8EZ ☎ 01327 361604
e-mail: paul@kingsarms.fsbusiness.co.uk
dir: *M1 junct 16, A45 towards Daventry. At Weedon take A5 towards Towcester. Right signed Farthingstone*

Attractive village pub with wildlife loving garden

Tucked away in perfect walking country, this 300-year-old stone free house is close to the National Trust's Elizabethan mansion at Canon's Ashby. Paul and Denise Egerton grow their own salads and herbs in the pub's quirky garden, which is full of interesting recycled items, decorative trees and shrubs, and secluded corners; it is a haven for wildlife with 20 species of butterflies and 200 of moths, and 50 different types of birds all noted. The terrace is the place to enjoy alfresco drinking on warmer days with red kites and buzzards overhead; in winter, real fires warm the stone-flagged interior. The Kings Arms is mainly a drinkers' pub, with up to five real ales and Westons Old Rosie cider on tap. But bar lunches served at weekends feature quality fine foods such as a platter of fish from Loch Fyne, game casserole, salmon fishcakes, filled Yorkshire puds and speciality British cheeses.

Open 7-11.30 (Fri 6.30-12 Sat-Sun 12-4 7-11.30) Closed: Mon **Bar Meals** L served Sat-Sun 12-2.30 D served last Fri in month Av main course £8.50 ⊕ FREE HOUSE ◀ Skinner's Betty Stogs, Vale VPA, St Austell Trelawny, Silverstone Pitstop, Adnams Ở Westons Old Rosie. **Facilities** Non-diners area ❄ (Bar Restaurant Garden) ♦♦ Children's portions Family room Garden ⌂ Parking Wi-fi

FOTHERINGHAY — Map 12 TL09

The Falcon Inn

PICK OF THE PUBS

PE8 5HZ ☎ 01832 226254
e-mail: info@thefalcon-inn.co.uk
dir: *From A605 between Peterborough & Oundle follow Fotheringhay signs*

Popular locals' inn with designer garden

First the history: it was in this sleepy village that Richard III was born in 1452, and 115 years later Mary, Queen of Scots was beheaded. The attractive 18th-century, stone-built pub stands in gardens redesigned by award-winning landscape architect Bunny Guinness. It's a real local, the Tap Bar regularly used by the village darts team, their throwing arms lubricated by pints of Fool's Nook ale and Aspall cider. The menus in both the bar and charming conservatory restaurant rely extensively on locally sourced ingredients. In the winter, offerings from the restaurant are Portland crab; crayfish and saffron tart; and ham hock terrine to start. Mains might be rack of lamb with dauphinoise potato, baby vegetables and red wine jus. The bar menu has sandwiches and a selection of starters and mains, such as sautéed king prawns, and shin of beef. For dessert, there's lemon meringue pie or chocolate nemesis.

Open all day 12-11 (Mon-Sat 12-11 Sun 12-4 Jan-Mar) Closed: Sun eve Jan-Mar **Bar Meals** L served Mon-Sat 12-2, Sun 12-3 (Sun 12-4 Jan-Mar) D served Mon-Sat 6-9, (Sun 6-8.30 Apr-Dec) **Restaurant** L served Mon-Sat 12-2, Sun 12-3 (Sun 12-4 Jan-Mar) D served Mon-Sat 6-9, (Sun 6-8.30 Apr-Dec) ⊕ FREE HOUSE ◀ Greene King IPA, Digfield Fool's Nook, Fuller's London Pride, Guest ales Ŏ Aspall. ₹ 14 **Facilities** Non-diners area ❤ (Bar Restaurant Garden) ⭥ Children's menu Children's portions Garden ⏚ Beer festival Parking Wi-fi ▬ (notice required)

GRAFTON REGIS — Map 11 SP74

The White Hart

Northampton Rd NN12 7SR ☎ 01908 542123
e-mail: alan@pubgraftonregis.co.uk
dir: *M1 junct 15, A508 towards Milton Keynes*

Thatched pub offering a friendly welcome

This thatched, stone-built property dating from the 16th century is the focal point for a friendly village with around 100 residents. In 1464 Edward IV married Elizabeth Woodville in this historic place. The pub has been run by the same family for over 15 years and Alan the owner, is also the chef. Menus change frequently according to available produce. Typical choices include steak-and-kidney pie; lasagne; steaks served in a variety of ways; smoked haddock and broccoli baked in cheese sauce; and salmon and monkfish mornay on a bed of pesto tagliatelle. Well-kept ales and 14 wines by the glass complete the picture. The garden has a gazebo/band stand.

Open 12-2.30 6-11 Closed: Mon **Bar Meals** L served Tue-Sun 12-2 D served Tue-Sun 6-9.30 **Restaurant** D served Tue-Sun 6.30-9 ◀ Greene King, Abbot Ale, IPA Ŏ Aspall. ₹ 14 **Facilities** Non-diners area ❤ (Garden) ⭥ Children's portions Garden ⏚ Parking Wi-fi

GREAT OXENDON — Map 11 SP78

The George Inn

LE16 8NA ☎ 01858 465205
e-mail: info@thegeorgegreatoxendon.co.uk
dir: *A508 towards Market Harborough*

Village inn with an attractive conservatory restaurant

On the edge of the little village of Great Oxendon stands this old pub run by new chef-patron Allan Wiseman. At the welcoming bar, beers from Timothy Taylor and Adnams are supplemented by regular guest ales. The inn has been lovingly restored and refurbished over the years, retaining much character, with beams, open log fires and comfy furnishings. Choose the airy conservatory overlooking the gardens or sit outside on the sun-warmed patio in summer, and start with a smoked salmon platter or mushroom ragout on a toasted muffin with béarnaise sauce. Mains offer up steaks, sausages, breaded haddock, slow-braised shoulder of lamb and supreme of chicken.

Open 12-3 5.30-11 (Sun 12-3) Closed: 25 Dec, Sun eve **Bar Meals** L served all wk 12-2 D served Mon-Sat 6-9.30 Av main course £10.25 **Restaurant** L served all wk 12-2 D served Mon-Sat 6-9.30 Fixed menu price fr £11.95 Av 3 course à la carte fr £22.50 ⊕ FREE HOUSE ◀ Adnams Southwold Bitter, Timothy Taylor Landlord, Guest ales. ₹ 10 **Facilities** Non-diners area ❤ (Bar) ⭥ Children's portions Garden ⏚ Parking Wi-fi ▬ (notice required)

HARRINGWORTH — Map 11 SP99

The White Swan

Seaton Rd NN17 3AF ☎ 01572 747543
e-mail: thewhiteswanharringworth@gmail.com
dir: *From A47 between Uppingham & Duddington take B672 signed Coldacott & Seaton. Under Harringworth Viaduct to T-junct. Left signed Harringworth. Under viaduct again. Pub in village centre on left*

Ancient pub in a lovely valley setting

At the time of writing, this handsome, ironstone-built coaching inn was undergoing a major refurbishment and a new menu was being planned. Set in the verdant Welland Valley, close to where it is crossed by one of England's longest railway viaducts - all 82 arches of it - the 16th-century village inn has built up a good reputation over the years for the quality of the food and the beers.

Open Tue-Thu 12-3 6-11 (Fri-Sat 12-3 5.30-11 Sun 12-8) Closed: Mon **Bar Meals** L served Tue-Fri 12-2, Sat 12-3, Sun 12-7 D served Tue-Sat 6-9, Sun 12-7 **Restaurant** L served Tue-Fri 12-2, Sat 12-3, Sun 12-7 D served Tue-Sat 6-9, Sun 12-7 ◀ Guinness, Guest ales. **Facilities** Non-diners area ⭥ Children's menu Children's portions Garden Parking ▬

KILSBY — Map 11 SP57

The George

Watling St CV23 8YE ☎ 01788 822229
dir: *M1 junct 18, follow A361/ Daventry signs. Pub at rdbt junct of A361 & A5*

A great local with home-cooked food

A warm welcome and great local atmosphere characterise this village pub, which has a traditional public bar and a high-ceilinged wood-panelled lounge opening into a smarter but relaxed area with solidly comfortable furnishings. The lunch bar menu includes sandwiches, filled baguettes, faggots with spring onion mash and mushy peas; and home-made fishcakes. The evening menu majors on home-made, hearty dishes such as beef and real ale shortcrust pie; lasagne; and the generous chicken and bacon Caesar salad. A children's menu is always available. There is an attractive garden for sunny days.

Open all wk 11.30-3 5.30-11.30 (Sun 12-5 6-11) **Bar Meals** L served Mon-Sat 12-2, Sun 12-4 D served all wk 6-9 **Restaurant** L served Mon-Sat 12-2, Sun 12-4 D served all wk 6-9 ⊕ PUNCH TAVERNS ◀ Fuller's London Pride, Adnams Southwold Bitter, Timothy Taylor Landlord. ₹ 8 **Facilities** Non-diners area ⭥ Children's menu Children's portions Garden ⏚ Parking Wi-fi ▬

NASSINGTON — Map 12 TL09

The Queens Head Inn ★★★★ INN ◉

54 Station Rd PE8 6QB ☎ 01780 784006
e-mail: info@queensheadnassington.co.uk
dir: *Exit A1 at Wansford, follow Yarwell & Nassington signs. Through Yarwell. Pub on left in Nassington*

Traditional inn with great food

A stone-built inn with exposed beams and traditional furnishings, The Queens Head's name nods to the beheading of Mary, Queen of Scots at nearby Fotheringhay Castle in 1587. Proud of its AA Rosette, it offers favourites old and new, including chicken liver parfait with anchovy butter and tomato and red onion chutney; roast belly of pork with pea purée, potato fondant and cider and chive butter sauce; and apple tarte Tatin with honeyed ice cream. Dine outdoors in warmer weather. Stay in one of the nine en suite bedrooms.

Open all day all wk **Bar Meals** L served all wk 12-2 D served all wk 5.30-9.30 **Restaurant** L served all wk 12-2.30 D served Mon-Sat 5.30-9.30 ⊕ FREE HOUSE ◀ Greene King IPA, Oakham JHB Ŏ Jacques. ₹ 8 **Facilities** Non-diners area ❤ (Bar Garden) ⭥ Children's menu Children's portions Garden ⏚ Parking Wi-fi ▬ (notice required) Rooms 9

Save on hotels. Book at **theAA.com/hotel**

NORTHAMPTONSHIRE 323 ENGLAND

NORTHAMPTON
Map 11 SP76

Althorp Coaching Inn

Main St, Great Brington NN7 4JA ☎ **01604 770651**
e-mail: althorpcoachinginn@btconnect.com
dir: From A428 pass main gates of Althorp House, left
before rail bridge. Great Brington 1m

Listed thatched pub with old world charm

On the Althorp Estate, the Spencer ancestral home, this
16th-century stone coaching inn has original decor
throughout. A brick and cobbled courtyard is surrounded
by stable rooms, and the enclosed flower garden is a
peaceful spot in which to sample one of the real ales
from a wide selection that includes weekly changing
guest ales. The cellar restaurant specialises in traditional
English cooking based on locally sourced ingredients.
Look out for dishes such as slow-braised lamb casserole;
fillet of pork with an apricot and sage stuffing; and wild
mushroom Stroganoff. Contact the pub for details of the
beer festival.

Open all day all wk 11-11 (wknds 11am-mdnt) **Bar
Meals** L served Mon-Sat 12-3, Sun 12-5 D served Mon-
Thu 6.30-9.30, Fri-Sat 6.30-10 **Restaurant** L served Mon-
Sat 12-3, Sun 12-5 D served Sun-Thu 6.30-9.30, Fri-Sat
6.30-10 ⊕ FREE HOUSE ◀ Greene King IPA & Abbot Ale,
Fuller's London Pride, Cottage Puffing Billy, Tunnell Sweet
Parish Ale, 5 Guest ales Ö Farmhouse, Thatchers
Heritage. ▼ 10 **Facilities** Non-diners area ❤ (Bar Garden)
♦♦ Children's menu Children's portions Garden ⊼ Beer
festival Parking Wi-fi ▦ (notice required)

OUNDLE
Map 11 TL08

The Chequered Skipper

Ashton PE8 5LD ☎ **01832 273494**
e-mail: enquiries@chequeredskipper.co.uk
dir: A605 towards Oundle, at rdbt follow signs to Ashton.
1m, turn left into Ashton

Well know for their pizzas

Destroyed by fire in 1997, The Chequered Skipper has
been restored to its traditional thatched exterior
complemented by a contemporary interior. Located
opposite the green in the model village of Ashton, built
for the estate workers in the 1880s, the pub plays its part
well, with timeless oak floor and beams, and a collection
of butterfly display cases diverting attention from a bar
stocking locally brewed beers (two beer festivals a year).
The menu mixes speciality pizzas and traditional English
and European dishes – pork and liver pâté might be
followed by braised shoulder of lamb with dauphinoise
potatoes.

Open all wk 11.30-3 6-11 (Sat 11.30-11 Sun 11.45-11)
Bar Meals L served Mon-Fri 12-2, Sat 12-2.30, Sun 12-3
D served Mon-Sat 6.30-9.30, Sun 6.30-9 **Restaurant** L
served Mon-Fri 12-2, Sat 12-2.30, Sun 12-3 D served
Mon-Sat 6.30-9.30, Sun 6.30-9 ⊕ FREE HOUSE
◀ Rockingham Ale, Brewster's Hophead, Oakham. ▼ 8
Facilities Non-diners area ❤ (Bar Garden) ♦♦ Children's
portions Garden Beer festival Parking Wi-fi ▦ (notice
required)

SIBBERTOFT
Map 11 SP68

The Red Lion

PICK OF THE PUBS

43 Welland Rise LE16 9UD ☎ **01858 880011**
e-mail: andrew@redlionwinepub.co.uk
dir: From Market Harborough take A4304, through
Lubenham, left through Marston Trussell to Sibbertoft

A real passion for good wine

Since taking over this friendly 300-year-old free house,
Andrew and Sarah Banks have built up an impressive
reputation and a loyal following. The interior is an
appealing blend of contemporary and classic decor, with
oak beams, leather upholstery and a smartly turned-out
dining room. Wine is the owners' special passion; over
200 bins appear on the ever-growing wine list, 20 labels
are served by the glass, and wine festivals are held every
year. After tasting, all the wines can be bought at take-
home prices, avoiding the guesswork of supermarket
purchases. From the monthly-changing menu, deep-fried
paprika-dusted whitebait might precede half a pheasant
wrapped in bacon, before rounding off with a raspberry
and oatcake tower. Monday night is curry night and
roasts are served on Sundays. In fine weather, meals are
served in the quiet garden – a favourite with local
walkers and cyclists – and there's also a children's play
area.

Open 12-2 6.30-11 Closed: Mon L & Tue L, Sun eve **Bar
Meals** L served Wed-Sun 12-2 D served Mon-Sat
6.30-9.30 **Restaurant** L served Wed-Sun 12-2 D served
Mon-Sat 6.30-9.30 ⊕ FREE HOUSE ◀ Timothy Taylor
Landlord, Black Sheep, Adnams Ö Aspall, Thatchers.
▼ 20 **Facilities** Non-diners area ❤ (Garden) ♦♦ Children's
menu Children's portions Play area Garden ⊼ Parking
Wi-fi ▦ (notice required)

STOKE BRUERNE
Map 11 SP74

The Boat Inn

NN12 7SB ☎ **01604 862428**
e-mail: info@boatinn.co.uk
web: www.boatinn.co.uk
dir: In village centre, just off A508 & A5

Family-run free house on the Grand Union Canal

Just across the lock from the National Waterways
Museum, the busy Boat Inn has been run by the
Woodward family since 1877. Take your pick from the
selection of beers: Marston's Pedigree, Wychwood
Hobgoblin and Jennings Cumberland Ale are just a

---

couple. The all-day bar menu lists hot baguettes, light
bites, burgers, and main courses such as vegetable tart,
chicken Bruerne and steak-and-ale pie. For a more formal
experience overlooking the peaceful waters, the
Woodwards Restaurant offers à la carte and set menus,
including salmon goujons with coriander mayonnaise;
mushroom and tarragon strudel; and lemon curd ice
cream terrine.

Open all day all wk 9.30am-11pm (Sun
9.30am-10.30pm) **Bar Meals** L served all wk 9.30-9.30
D served all wk 9.30-9.30 Av main course £8 food served
all day **Restaurant** L served Tue-Sat 12-2, Sun 12-3
D served all wk 7-9 Fixed menu price fr £14.95 Av 3
course à la carte fr £25 ⊕ FREE HOUSE ◀ Banks's Bitter,
Marston's Pedigree, Frog Island Best Bitter, Marston's Old
Empire, Wychwood Hobgoblin, Jennings Cumberland Ale
Ö Thatchers Traditional. ▼ 10 **Facilities** Non-diners area
❤ (Bar Garden) ♦♦ Children's menu Children's portions
Garden ⊼ Parking ▦ (notice required)

THORNBY
Map 11 SP67

The Red Lion **NEW**

Welford Rd NN6 8SJ ☎ **01604 740238**
e-mail: enquiries@redlionthornby.co.uk
dir: A14 junct 1, A5199 towards Northampton. Pub on
left in village

An oasis just off the A14

Weary A14 travellers should take note of this 400-year-
old traditional pub, as it's just a mile from Junction 1 in
tiny Thornby. Rest and refuel in the glorious summer
garden, or bag a seat by the log fire in the comfortable
bar on cold winter days. Simon and Louise Cottle have
slowly refurbished the interior, and offer four ales on
handpump and a regularly changing menu of freshly
prepared dishes. From lunchtime filled baguettes (brie,
bacon and cranberry), the choice extends to lamb tagine
with saffron couscous and pan-fried sea bass with
ratatouille and home-made pesto. Linger and enjoy a
pudding, perhaps cherry Bakewell tart. Plans include an
annual beer festival.

Open all wk **Restaurant** L served Tue-Sat 12-2, Sun 12-5
D served Tue-Sat 6.30-9 ⊕ FREE HOUSE ◀ Adnams,
Black Sheep, The Grainstore, Purity Ö Westons Stowford
Press. **Facilities** Non-diners area ❤ (Bar Garden) ♦♦
Children's portions Garden ⊼ Beer festival Parking
▦ (notice required)

TITCHMARSH
Map 11 TL07

The Wheatsheaf at Titchmarsh

1 North St NN14 3DH ☎ **01832 732203**
e-mail: enquiries@thewheatsheafattitchmarsh.co.uk
dir: From A14 junct 13 take A605 towards Oundle, right
to Titchmarsh. Or from A14 junct 14 follow signs for
Titchmarsh

Pretty village pub with smart, modern interior

Darren and Amy Harding refurbished this stone-built
village pub with great consideration and its mix of

continued

TITCHMARSH *continued*

traditional and contemporary styles are in perfect balance. Greene King real ales are backed by others from Sharp's, Butcombe and regularly changing guests, and sandwiches are made on demand. Among the light snacks are pan-fried chilli and garlic meatballs, and leek and pea risotto, while for a typical main meal consider braised blade of beef; duck stir-fry with Asian style vegetables; or oven roasted chicken breast with a mushroom and marsala sauce. There's a chargrill too.

Open all wk 12-3 6-11 (Sat 12-11 Sun 12-8) **Bar Meals** L served Mon-Thu 12-2, Fri-Sat 12-2.30, Sun 12-5 D served Mon-Sat 6-9.30 **Restaurant** L served Mon-Thu 12-2, Fri-Sat 12-2.30, Sun 12-5 D served Mon-Sat 6-9.30 ⊕ FREE HOUSE ◀ Greene King IPA, Sharp's Doom Bar, Fuller's London Pride, Butcombe, Guest ales ♂ Aspall. ♀ 11 **Facilities** Non-diners area ♦♦ Children's menu Children's portions Garden ⨩ Parking Wi-fi ▭ (notice required)

TOWCESTER   Map 11 SP64

The Saracens Head ★★★ INN

219 Watling St NN12 7BX ☎ 01327 350414
e-mail: saracenshead.towcester@greeneking.co.uk
dir: *From M1 junct 15A, A43 towards Oxford. Take A5 signed Towcester*

400 years old and immortalised by Charles Dickens

This imposing building dates back over 400 years, and is featured in Charles Dickens' first novel, *The Pickwick Papers*. The same home comforts that Dickens enjoyed when visiting Towcester have been updated to modern standards, and discerning customers will find excellent service in the restored pub. Starters might be potted smoked mackerel; or shredded duck and hoisin spring rolls, followed by a main course of Suffolk-farmed pork sausages with mature cheddar mash and sautéed red onion gravy; or vegetable and cashew nut paella. Sandwiches, jackets, wraps and ciabattas are all available too.

Open all day all wk **Bar Meals** L served all wk 12-5 D served all wk 5-10 food served all day **Restaurant** L served all wk 12-5 D served all wk 5-10 food served all day ⊕ GREENE KING/OLD ENGLISH INNS ◀ Abbot Ale & IPA, Guest ale ♂ Aspall. ♀ 13 **Facilities** Non-diners area ♦♦ Children's menu Children's portions Garden ⨩ Beer festival Parking Wi-fi ▭ **Rooms** 21

WADENHOE   Map 11 TL08

The King's Head

PICK OF THE PUBS

Church St PE8 5ST ☎ 01832 720024
e-mail: aletha@wadenhoekingshead.co.uk
dir: *From A605, 3m from Wadenhoe rdbt. 2m from Oundle*

Pretty pub featuring a shaded riverside garden

Set in the unspoilt village of Wadenhoe, alongside the picturesque River Nene, this stone-built, partially thatched inn has been serving travellers since the 17th

century. In the summer, grab a seat in extensive riverside gardens in the shade of the ancient willow trees and watch the colourful narrow boats over a pint of King's Head Bitter; August also brings a beer festival. In winter, head for the comfortable bar with its quarry-tiled and bare-boarded floors, heavy oak-beamed ceilings, pine furniture and open log fires. The pub offers the most modern facilities but has lost none of its old world charm. The lunchtime menu offers sandwiches, pies and light bites such as home-made burger topped with cheddar cheese and chips or a ploughman's. In the evening you can feast like a king on warm pork and black pudding terrine with apple sauce, or roast chicken, tarragon and shallot pot pie, minted new potatoes and purple sprouting broccoli.

Open all day all wk 11-11 (Sun 12-10 winter 11-2.30 5.30-11 Sun 12-6) Closed: Sun eve in winter **Bar Meals** L served all wk 12-2.30 D served all wk 6-9 **Restaurant** L served all wk 12-2.30 D served all wk 6-9 ⊕ FREE HOUSE ◀ King's Head Bitter, Digfield Barnwell Bitter, Hogs Back BSA ♂ Kingstone Press. ♀ 15 **Facilities** Non-diners area ♦♦ Children's portions Garden ⨩ Beer festival Parking ▭

WESTON   Map 11 SP54

The Crown

PICK OF THE PUBS

Helmdon Rd NN12 8PX ☎ 01295 760310
e-mail: info@thecrownweston.co.uk
dir: *Accessed from A43 or B4525*

Historic pub serving quality real ales

This 16th-century inn pub is probably best known as the place where Lord Lucan was allegedly spotted enjoying a pint the day after the brutal murder of his children's nanny in 1974. He was never seen again. Robert Grover took over The Crown 12 years ago and he has ensured that his pub continues to feature prominently in the life of the local community by hosting regular events such as curry evenings. The pub is well known for its excellent beers, a short but elegant range of dishes based on high quality ingredients, welcoming staff and its family-friendly atmosphere. Real ales are a strength, at least four in number, and wines are reasonably priced. The kitchen flies the flag for local produce and the seasonal menus might kick off with chicken liver and cider pâté and move on to beef bourguignon. Round off with baked chocolate and ginger mousse.

Open all wk 6-11.30 (Fri-Sat 12-3.30 6-11.30 Sun 12-3.30 7-11) Closed: 25 Dec **Bar Meals** L served Fri-Sun 12-2.30 D served Tue-Sat 6-9.30 Av main course £10 ⊕ FREE HOUSE ◀ Greene King IPA, Hook Norton Best, Timothy Taylor Landlord, St Austell Tribute, Black Sheep ♂ Westons Stowford Press. **Facilities** Non-diners area ❄ (Bar Garden) ♦♦ Children's portions Family room Garden ⨩ Parking Wi-fi ▭ (notice required)

NORTHUMBERLAND

BARRASFORD   Map 21 NY97

The Barrasford Arms ⓐ

NE48 4AA ☎ 01434 681237
e-mail: contact@barrasfordarms.co.uk
dir: *From A69 at Hexham take A6079 signed Acomb & Chollerford. In Chollerford by church turn left signed Barrasford*

A destination food pub

Chef Tony Binks's village inn stands close to Hadrian's Wall deep in the glorious Northumbrian countryside, with spectacular views of the Tyne Valley. Despite the emphasis on food, it retains a traditional pub atmosphere, with local Wylam and Hadrian Border ales on tap in the time-honoured bar, which fills with locals and passing walkers and cyclists. Most beat a path to the door for Tony's short, imaginative, one-AA Rosette menus. For dinner, tuck into twice-baked cheddar soufflé; seared fillet of wild sea trout, shrimp, tomato and saffron broth; soft pistachio meringue, orange and vanilla mascarpone and strawberries. His set and Sunday lunches are great value.

Open 12-3 6-11 (Sat-Sun all day) Closed: 1st wk Jan, Mon L **Restaurant** L served Tue-Sun 12-2 D served Mon-Sat 6.30-9 Fixed menu price fr £12 Av 3 course à la carte fr £25 ⊕ FREE HOUSE ◀ Wylam Gold Tankard, Hadrian Border Gladiator. **Facilities** Non-diners area ♦♦ Children's portions Garden ⨩ Parking ▭ (notice required)

BEADNELL   Map 21 NU22

The Craster Arms ★★★★ INN NEW

The Wynding NE67 5AX ☎ 01665 720272
e-mail: michael@crasterarms.co.uk
dir: *Exit A1 at Brownieside signed Preston. Left at T-junct signed Seahouses. Right signed Beadnell village. Pub on left*

Within walking distance of beautiful beaches

In the 15th century, the English in this neck of the woods built small fortified watch towers to warn of Scottish invasions – this was one of them. Since becoming a pub in 1818 its role has widened to offer not just food, drink and accommodation, but a programme of live entertainment, the Crastonbury music festival, and a beer and cider festival (last weekend in July). Sandwiches, baguettes, paninis, salads and hot meals are available at lunchtime; in the evening there's braised lamb shank; Thai green chicken curry; seasonal blackboard specials; crab fishcake and other local seafood.

Open all day all wk **Bar Meals** Av main course £8.95 food served all day **Restaurant** food served all day ⊕ PUNCH TAVERNS ◀ Camerons Strongarm, Black Sheep, Mordue Workie Ticket ♂ Westons Traditional Scrumpy & Old Rosie. **Facilities** Non-diners area ❄ (Bar Garden) ♦♦ Children's menu Children's portions Garden ⨩ Beer festival Cider festival Parking Wi-fi ▭ **Rooms** 3

Save on hotels. Book at theAA.com/hotel

NORTHUMBERLAND 325 ENGLAND

PICK OF THE PUBS

The Pheasant Inn ★★★★ INN

Stannersburn NE48 1DD
☎ **01434 240382**
e-mail: stay@thepheasantinn.com
web: www.thepheasantinn.com
dir: *A69, B6079, B6320, follow signs for Kielder Water*

Perfect base for Northumbrian adventures

In the early 17th century, long, long before nearby Kielder Water and Kielder Forest were created, agricultural workers drank at a beer-house in Stannersburn. This ivy-clad country inn is that beer-house, now finding itself where the Northumberland National Park meets the Border Forest Park, and surrounded by verdant valleys, high moors and tranquil woodlands. It's well positioned too for cycle tracks, a sculpture trail, an observatory, endless walks and wildlife watching, including red squirrels. What you see today is what Irene and Robin Kershaw have achieved since they acquired it, then rather run down, in 1985. Most spaces in the two bars have been filled with historic Northumberland memorabilia, and on the exposed stone walls that support the blackened beams are photos of yesteryear's locals working at forgotten trades like blacksmithing and coalmining. In winter, log fires cast flickering shadows across the furniture. The restaurant, with terracotta-coloured walls and furnished in mellow pine, looks out over the countryside. Self-evidently it's where to enjoy Irene and Robin's daily-changing, traditional British food, all making the most of what Northumbria has to offer, such as slow-roasted local lamb with rosemary and redcurrant jus; grilled fresh salmon with hot pepper marmalade and crème fraîche; fresh dressed crab from the Northumberland coast; and Stilton and vegetable crumble with salad. Excellent beers from Wylam Brewery and Timothy Taylor might cloud the mind, but not the dark night skies, which make the area a mecca for astronomers. There is a tranquil stream-side garden.

Open 12-3 6.30-11 Closed: 25-27 Dec, Mon-Tue (Nov-Mar) **Bar Meals** L served

Mon-Sat 12-2.30 D served all wk 6-9 (Etr-Oct 6-8.30) Av main course £11 **Restaurant** L served Mon-Sat 12-2.30 D served Mon-Sat 6.30-8.30 Av 3 course à la carte fr £24.95 ⊕ FREE HOUSE ◀ Timothy Taylor Landlord, Wylam Gold Tankard, Rocket, Red Kite, Red Shot & Angel. **Facilities** Non-diners area ♦♦ Children's menu & portions Play area Family room Garden ⋒ Parking Wi-fi **Rooms** 8

BELFORD
Map 21 NU13

Blue Bell Hotel

Market Place NE70 7NE ☎ 01668 213543
e-mail: enquiries@bluebellhotel.com
dir: *From A1 halfway between Berwick-upon-Tweed & Alnwick follow Belford signs*

Worth leaving the busy A1 for

At one time a busy coaching inn in the village centre on the old London to Edinburgh road, the hotel and its fine gardens still attract the traveller. Unquestionably, the food has much to do with its appeal, with starters that include bacon, brie and black pudding salad; smoked salmon and dill fishcake; and local Adderstone Scotch egg, while the roll-call of main dishes includes chicken Kiev; pan-fried liver, red onions and bacon; Eyemouth fish pie; rib-eye and sirloin steaks; and tagliatelle pesto. A little further north, over a causeway, is Holy Island, but do check the times of the tides before visiting.

Open all day all wk 11am-mdnt **Bar Meals** L served all wk 12-2.30 D served all wk 6-9 **Restaurant** L served Sun 12-2.30 D served all wk 6-9 ⊕ FREE HOUSE ◀ Tetley's Smoothflow, Black Sheep, Guinness.
Facilities Non-diners area ◀ Children's menu Children's portions Play area Garden Parking Wi-fi ▭

CARTERWAY HEADS
Map 19 NZ05

The Manor House Inn
PICK OF THE PUBS

DH8 9LX ☎ 01207 255268
e-mail: themanorhouseinn@gmail.com
dir: *A69 W from Newcastle, left onto A68 then S for 8m. Inn on right*

One to head out of town for

When shopping in Newcastle or Durham palls and you fancy a drink or meal out of town, a 30-minute drive will get you to this former coaching inn. As the stone walls, low-beamed ceiling and massive timber support in the bar might suggest, it was built in the mid 18th century. From its lofty position, there are great views of both the Derwent Valley and reservoir. Jostling for real ale drinkers' attention are five contenders, among them Robinsons Dizzy Blonde and Copper Dragon's Golden Pippin. The restaurant is divided into two, the larger area welcoming families with children. Most produce is local and includes game and wild fish from hereabouts. Suggested dishes include Northumbrian black pudding with apple, soft poached egg and salad; rolled shoulder of Minsteracres lamb with rich redcurrant jus; tandoori rabbit legs; and North Sea haddock in crispy beer batter. Beer festivals are held throughout the year.

Open all day all wk 11-11 (Sun 12-10.30 Mon 12-11) Closed: 26 Dec **Bar Meals** L served Mon-Sat 12-9, Sun 12-8 D served Mon-Sat 12-9, Sun 12-8 Av main course £13 food served all day **Restaurant** D served Thu-Sat 6-9, Sun 12-8 Av 3 course à la carte fr £20 ⊕ ENTERPRISE INNS ◀ Morland Old Speckled Hen, Black Sheep, Sharp's Doom Bar, Robinsons Dizzy Blonde, Copper Dragon Golden

Pippin ☼ Westons Old Rosie. ♥ 8
Facilities Non-diners area ♣ (Bar Garden) ◀ Children's menu Children's portions Garden ▱ Beer festival Cider festival Parking Wi-fi ▭ (notice required)

CORBRIDGE
Map 21 NY96

The Angel of Corbridge

Main St NE45 5LA ☎ 01434 632119
e-mail: info@theangelofcorbridge.com
dir: *0.5m off A69, signed Corbridge*

Prime location in historic town

In the scenic Tyne Valley and handy for Hadrian's Wall, this reinvigorated old coaching inn has made a success in each area of its operation; there's a striking restaurant offering a solid English menu drawing on the producers of Northumbria (including their own lambs) and a traditional locals' bar, where beers from the local Wylam brewery are in evidence; the Angel also has a Martini bar. Typical dishes on the menu are a starter of black pudding, poached egg and pancetta; a main course of pan-seared lamb's liver with bacon, champ mashed potato and onion gravy. Tempting sandwiches (sliced local ham with home-made pease pudding) and strong puddings complete the deal.

Open all day all wk **Bar Meals** L served Mon-Sat 12-9, Sun 12-5 D served Mon-Sat 12-9 Av main course £12 **Restaurant** L served Mon-Sat 12-9, Sun 12-5 D served Mon-Sat 12-9 Av 3 course à la carte fr £20 ⊕ FREE HOUSE ◀ Timothy Taylor Landlord, Wylam Angel, Local alesl. ♥ 12 **Facilities** Non-diners area ◀ Children's menu Children's portions Outside area ▱ Parking Wi-fi ▭ (notice required)

CRASTER
Map 21 NU21

The Jolly Fisherman

Haven Hill NE66 3TR ☎ 01665 576461
e-mail: info@thejollyfishermancraster.co.uk
dir: *Exit A1 at Denwick. Follow Seahouses signs, then 1st sign for Craster*

Fine harbourside location

Now splendidly refurbished, the charm of this historic stone-flagged, low-beamed pub remains undimmed. When it's cold, relax by an open fire; at any time admire impressive Dunstanburgh Castle from the delightful beer garden. When the pub opened in 1847, Craster was a thriving fishing village; now only a few East Coast cobles leave harbour, mostly for the herring that, once smoked, become the famous kippers. House specialities are fresh fish stew; whole line-caught sea bass; breast of chicken in Serrano ham; and slow-roasted pepper with butternut squash and celeriac risotto. At the bar are Black Sheep and Mordue's Workie Ticket bitter.

Open all day all wk **Bar Meals** food served all day **Restaurant** food served all day ⊕ PUNCH TAVERNS ◀ Mordue Workie Ticket, Black Sheep, Timothy Taylor Landlord ☼ Symonds Scrumpy Jack. ♥ 12
Facilities Non-diners area ♣ (Bar Garden) ◀ Children's menu Children's portions Garden ▱ Parking Wi-fi ▭ (notice required)

FALSTONE
Map 21 NY78

The Pheasant Inn ★★★★ INN
PICK OF THE PUBS

See Pick of the Pubs on page 325

HALTWHISTLE
Map 21 NY76

Milecastle Inn

Military Rd, Cawfields NE49 9NN ☎ 01434 321372
e-mail: clarehind@aol.com
dir: *From A69 into Haltwhistle. Pub approx 2m at junct with B6318*

Ideal retreat while visiting Roman sites

A traditional pub decorated with horse brasses and local pictures, the Milecastle occupies a wonderfully remote and peaceful location high on the moorland edge. One horizon is serrated by the line of Hadrian's Wall and there are easy walks up the lane past Roman camps to reach Milecastle 42 beside the Wall at Cawfield Crags. Tasty beers from Newcastle's Big Lamp Brewery are ample reward for a breezy stroll, accompanied perhaps by game pâté with toast; chicken curry with rice and chips; or a choice of pies. A roaring winter fire takes the chill, or you could sit outside and enjoy the curlew-haunted countryside.

Open all day all wk 12-11 (12-3 6-10 Nov-Mar) ⊕ FREE HOUSE ◀ Big Lamp Prince Bishop, Sunny Daze.
Facilities ◀ Children's menu Children's portions Garden Parking Wi-fi

HAYDON BRIDGE
Map 21 NY86

The General Havelock Inn

Ratcliffe Rd NE47 6ER ☎ 01434 684376
e-mail: info@generalhavelock.co.uk
dir: *On A69, 7m W of Hexham*

Free house overlooking the River Tyne

Built in the 1760s, this riverside inn is named after a 19th-century British Army officer. The pub, with its restaurant in a converted stone barn, is a favourite with local showbusiness personalities. The real ales are all sourced from a 15-mile radius: Mordue Workie Ticket and Big Lamp Bitter are but two. Owner/chef Gary Thompson makes everything by hand, including the bread and ice cream. Local ingredients are the foundation of his dishes, which include steamed lemon sole in a crisp pasty pillow; chicken and mushroom pie; and warm walnut tart. In summer, the patio area is covered by a marquee.

Open 12-2.30 7-12 (Sun 12-10.30) Closed: Mon **Bar Meals** L served Tue-Sun 12-4 D served Tue-Sun 7-9 Av main course £10 **Restaurant** L served Tue-Sun 12-2 D served Tue-Sun 7-9 Av 3 course à la carte fr £20 ⊕ FREE HOUSE ◀ High House Farm Nel's Best, Geltsdale Cold Fell, Big Lamp Bitter, Mordue Workie Ticket, Cumberland Corby Blonde, Allendale. ♥ 15
Facilities Non-diners area ♣ (Bar Garden) ◀ Children's portions Family room Garden ▱ Wi-fi ▭ (notice required)

PICK OF THE PUBS

The Feathers Inn

HEDLEY ON THE HILL   Map 19 NZ05

NE43 7SW ☎ 01661 843607
e-mail: info@thefeathers.net
web: www.thefeathers.net
dir: *A695 towards Gateshead. In Stocksfield right into New Ridley Rd. Left at Hedley on the Hill sign to village*

Microbrewery ales and cracking food

This small, 200-year-old stone-built free house is set high above the Tyne Valley with splendid views across the Cheviot Hills. Once frequented by lead miners and cattle drovers, all visitors are charmed by the friendly and relaxed atmosphere created by owners Rhian Cradock and Helen Greer. It's also worth the detour for its rotating choice of microbrewery ales; relax and sup Wylam Red Kite or Northumberland Pit Pony beside a welcoming woodburning stove. Old oak beams, rustic settles and stone walls decorated with local photographs set the informal scene. There's a good selection of traditional pub games like shove ha'penny and bar skittles and you'll find a good collection of cookery books to browse through. Rhian's impressive daily menu makes sound use of the freshest local ingredients – including game from local shoots, rare-breed local cattle and Longhorn beef – to create great British classics as well as regional dishes from the north east. You could start with a mini game pie

with blackberry dressing and watercress salad, or home-made black pudding with a duck egg and devilled gravy. Typical main courses include seared peppered haunch of roe deer with creamed Northumbrian leeks and celeriac mash. Leave room for Yorkshire rhubarb and custard tart or apple, quince and almond cake. Families are welcome, and a small side room can be booked in advance if required. The annual beer and food festival takes place over Easter and includes a barrel race, egg jarping, barbecue and a farmers' market, while the cider festival is on the August Bank Holiday.

Open all wk 12-11 (Mon 6-11 Sun 12-10.30) Closed: No food served 1st 2wks Jan **Meals** L served Tue-Sat 12-2,

Sun 12-2.30 D served Tue-Sat 6-8.30 Av main course £15 ⊞ FREE HOUSE ◼ Mordue Workie Ticket, Fuller's London Pride, Northumberland Pit Pony, Orkney Red MacGregor, Hadrian Border Gladiator, Wylam Red Kite, The Consett Ale Works Red Dust ♂ Westons 1st Quality & Old Rosie. ♀ **Facilities** Non-diners area ♦♦ Children's portions ⋈ Beer festival Cider festival Parking Wi-fi

HEDLEY ON THE HILL — Map 19 NZ05

The Feathers Inn

PICK OF THE PUBS

See Pick of the Pubs on page 327

HEXHAM — Map 21 NY96

Battlesteads Hotel & Restaurant

PICK OF THE PUBS

See Pick of the Pubs on opposite page

Dipton Mill Inn

PICK OF THE PUBS

Dipton Mill Rd NE46 1YA ☎ 01434 606577
e-mail: ghb@hexhamshire.co.uk
dir: *2m S of Hexham on HGV route to Blanchland, B6306, Dipton Mill Rd*

Former mill with its own brewery

Rebuilt some 400 years ago, this former farmhouse has a pretty millstream running right through the gardens. It is surrounded by farmland and woods with footpaths for pleasant country walks, and Hadrian's Wall and other Roman sites are close by. The Dipton Mill is home to Hexhamshire Brewery ales, which include Devil's Water and Old Humbug. All dishes are freshly prepared from local produce where possible. Start with carrot and celery soup with a warm roll, followed by steak-and-kidney pie; chicken in sherry sauce or braised beef steak with tomato and peppers. A decent selection of vegetarian options includes tagliatelle with creamy basil sauce and fresh parmesan; cheese and tomato flan with salad; and ratatouille with couscous. Dessert brings comforting favourites such as chocolate brownie with ice cream or bread and butter pudding plus a good cheese selection. Salads, sandwiches and ploughman's are also always available.

Open 12-2.30 6-11 (Sun 12-3) Closed: 25 Dec, Sun eve **Bar Meals** L served all wk 12-2 D served Mon-Sat 6.30-8 Av main course £8 ⊕ FREE HOUSE ◀ Hexhamshire Shire Bitter, Old Humbug, Devil's Water, Devil's Elbow, Whapweasel, Blackhall English Stout ◑ Westons Old Rosie, Guest cider. ♥ 17 **Facilities** Non-diners area ♣ (Garden) ♦♦ Children's portions Garden ☒ ⛟ (notice required) **Notes** ⊛

Miners Arms Inn

Main St, Acomb NE46 4PW ☎ 01434 603909
e-mail: minersarms2012@gmail.com
dir: *2m W of Hexham on A69*

Traditional food in peaceful village pub

The Greenwell family took over this 18th-century village pub near Hadrian's Wall in 2012 and it's very much a family business with David and Elwyn helped by their two daughters. Among the choice of ales, local Wylam Gold Tankard is always available, with guest beers available

every week. Mainly locally sourced dishes, including haggis and black pudding with peppercorn sauce; and home-made steak and ale pie typify the traditional food. Visitors can enjoy the open-hearth fire, the sunny beer garden, or simply sit out front soaking up life in this peaceful village. Beer festivals are held occasionally.

Open all wk 4-12 (Sat-Sun 12-12) **Bar Meals** Av main course £8 ⊕ FREE HOUSE ◀ Wylam Gold Tankard, Yates Best Bitter, Guest ale. **Facilities** Non-diners area ♣ (Bar Garden) ♦♦ Children's menu Children's portions Garden ☒ Beer festival

---

Rat Inn

PICK OF THE PUBS

NE46 4LN ☎ 01434 602814
e-mail: info@theratinn.com
dir: *2m from Hexham, Bridge End (A69) rdbt, take 4th exit signed Oakwood. Inn 500yds on right*

Passionate about local food

An attractive, ivy-clad sandstone building, this former drovers' inn catered to farmers from the Borders on their way to the market in Hexham, which just up the road. Just how the Rat came by its name is shrouded in mystery — why not ask the locals for their theories? On sunny days soak up the spectacular views of the Tyne Valley from the glorious hillside garden. On cooler days retreat into the classic bar, where you'll find crackling log fires, a flagstone floor, old pews and benches and an impressive oak bar dispensing six guest ales, perhaps local Wylam Gold Tankard. Blackboard special wines are matched to seasonal dishes. Order from an interesting daily menu that bristles with locally sourced ingredients — meat, game and cheese are exclusively Northumbrian. In addition, herbs are grown in the garden, fish is cured in the pub, and everything is made from scratch, including pickles and puddings. Typically, tuck into pan-fried coley or roast rib of beef for two.

Open all day all wk **Bar Meals** L served Tue-Sat 12-2, Sun 12-3 D served Tue-Sat 6-9 Av main course £12.95 **Restaurant** L served Tue-Sat 12-2, Sun 12-3 D served Tue-Sat 6-9 Av 3 course à la carte fr £23 ⊕ FREE HOUSE ◀ Cumberland Corby Ale, High House Farm Nel's Best, Hexhamshire Shire Bitter, Timothy Taylor Landlord, Wylam Gold Tankard. ♥ **Facilities** Non-diners area ♦♦ Children's portions Garden Parking Wi-fi

---

LONGFRAMLINGTON — Map 21 NU10

The Anglers Arms

PICK OF THE PUBS

Weldon Bridge NE65 8AX ☎ 01665 570271 & 570655
e-mail: johnyoung@anglersarms.fsnet.co.uk
dir: *Take A697 N of Morpeth signed Wooler & Coldstream. 7m, left to Weldon Bridge*

Former coaching inn on the River Coquet

Commanding the picturesque Weldon Bridge over the River Coquet since the 1760s, this part-battlemented, former coaching inn on the road to Scotland is full of

knick-knacks and curios, pictures and fishing memorabilia. Timothy Taylor Landlord and Theakston Best Bitter are among the real ales to accompany bar meals like Chinese duck salad or traditional cod and chips. An old Pullman railway carriage provides a different dining experience, with silver service as standard, and dishes such as tournedos Flodden, which is prime fillet stuffed with Applewood cheese wrapped in bacon and coated in garlic sauce; grilled fillet of salmon with new potatoes, baby corn, green beans, rocket and chilli sauce; and stir-fried vegetable sizzler. The carefully tended half-acre of garden is perfect for alfresco dining and includes a children's play park. You can fish on the pub's own mile of River Coquet.

Open all day all wk 11-11 (Sun 12-10.30) **Bar Meals** L served all wk 12-9.30 D served all wk 12-9.30 food served all day **Restaurant** L served all wk 12-9.30 D served all wk 12-9.30 food served all day ⊕ FREE HOUSE ◀ Timothy Taylor Landlord, Morland Old Speckled Hen, Greene King Abbot Ale, Theakston Best Bitter. **Facilities** Non-diners area ♣ (Bar Garden) ♦♦ Children's portions Play area Family room Garden ☒ Parking ⛟ (notice required)

LONGHORSLEY — Map 21 NZ19

Linden Tree ★★★★ HL ⊚⊚

Linden Hall NE65 8XF ☎ 01670 500033
e-mail: lindenhall@macdonald-hotels.co.uk
dir: *From A1 onto A697, 1m N of Longhorsley*

The 19th-hole after a round of golf

The friendly and informal Linden Tree pub stands within the 450-acres surrounding of Linden Hall, the impressive Georgian mansion that is now a popular golf and country club. A sunny patio makes for a relaxed setting for lunch in summer and the brasserie-style menu makes good use of Scottish beef and lamb. Dishes might include Thai green curry mussels; 21-day aged Scottish beefburger with tomato relish and beef dripping chips; leg of lamb steak; battered haddock with chips and mushy peas or steak-and-ale pie. Round off a long day with a nightcap in the golfers' lounge.

Open all day all wk Mon-Sat 11-11 (Sun 11-10.30) **Bar Meals** L served all wk 12-5 D served all wk 5-9.30 Av main course £8.95 food served all day **Restaurant** L served all wk 12-5 D served all wk 5-9.30 Av 3 course à la carte fr £25 food served all day ⊕ FREE HOUSE ◀ Greene King IPA, Guinness, John Smith's. **Facilities** Non-diners area ♦♦ Children's menu Children's portions Play area Garden ☒ Parking ⛟ (notice required) **Rooms** 50

Save on hotels. Book at theAA.com/hotel

NORTHUMBERLAND 329 ENGLAND

PICK OF THE PUBS

Battlesteads Hotel & Restaurant

HEXHAM Map 21 NY96

Wark NE48 3LS ☎ 01434 230209
e-mail: info@battlesteads.com
web: www.battlesteads.com
dir: *10m N of Hexham on B6320 (Kielder road)*

Eco-friendly hotel specialising in home-grown and local produce

Outstanding green credentials, including a carbon-neutral heating system, account for some of the awards picked up by Richard and Dee Slade's hotel, restaurant and pub. Standing just a few miles north of Hadrian's Wall and close to Kielder Forest and Border Riever country, it was converted from an 18th-century farmhouse and is utterly charming – from the flower tubs and hanging baskets to Gilroy the cat, who long ago adopted the place as his home. Renowned for superb food, there are three dining options: a relaxed bar area, where Durham Magus and other regional real ales are on tap; the conservatory, with views of the secret walled garden; and the main restaurant where dark wood furnishings, low lighting and old British Railways travel posters create a more formal setting. Chef Eddie Shilton sources all the food from the two-acre gardens and polytunnels, or from no more than 25 miles away from the village. His style, primarily modern British with a smattering of international choices,

leads to seasonal game, Cumbrian beef, Northumbrian lamb, and fish and seafood from North Shields. Look out too for Louisiana chicken with a red onion, bacon and prawn cream sauce; confit of duck leg; and butternut squash risotto. Dee's desserts include award-winning whisky and marmalade bread-and-butter pudding; fruit Pavlova; and local cheeses that might be hard to find further south. There are over 25 organic, Fairtrade and biodynamic wines to choose from. Guests are encouraged to log the wildlife they see around the hotel, and someone who knows their birds has noted a leucistic, or albino, oystercatcher among the buzzards, ospreys and red kites. Richard is always pleased to conduct a tour of the hotel's green installations.

Open all day all wk **Bar Meals** L served all wk 12-3 D served all wk 6.30-9.30 **Restaurant** L served all wk 12-3 D served all wk 6.30-9.30 ⊞ FREE HOUSE ◪ Durham Magus, High House Farm Nel's Best, Guest ales Ŏ Thatchers Gold. ♟ 25 **Facilities** Non-diners area ♥ (Bar Garden) ♦♦ Children's portions Garden ⊼ Beer festival Parking Wi-fi 🚐 (notice required)

LOW NEWTON BY THE SEA — Map 21 NU22

The Ship Inn

The Square NE66 3EL ☎ 01665 576262
e-mail: forsythchristine@hotmail.com
dir: *NE from A1 at Alnwick towards Seahouses*

Good, simple food and home-brewed beers

There's a very salty tang about this pretty, late-1700s inn - of course there is, since it overlooks Newton Haven's sandy beach. Then there are the names of the real ales: Sea Coal, Sea Wheat, Ship Hop Ale and Sandcastles at Dawn, all in fact, with Dolly Day Dream brewed next door. The barrels then have to be rolled all of 15ft to the cellar; from here they are pumped to the small bar, where you can expect plenty of locally caught fresh and smoked fish; Buttercross Farm free-range bacon, mushroom and tomato stottie (flat loaf); vegetarian options, and old-fashioned possets and crumbles.

Open all wk seasonal variations, please telephone for details **Bar Meals** L served all wk 12-2.30 D served all wk 7-8 (some seasonal variations, please telephone for details) ⊕ FREE HOUSE ◀ The Ship Inn Sea Coal, Dolly Day Dream, Sea Wheat, Ship Hop Ale, Sandcastles at Dawn. **Facilities** ❀ (Bar Garden) ❖ Garden **Notes** ⊛

MILFIELD — Map 21 NT93

The Red Lion Inn

Main Rd NE71 6JD ☎ 01668 216224
e-mail: redlioninn@fsmail.net
web: www.redlionmilfield.co.uk
dir: *On A697, 9m S of Coldstream (6m N of Wooler)*

Historic inn serving comfort food and guest ales

Dating back to the 1700s, sheep drovers from the northern counties stayed at this stone building before it was used as a stopover for the mail stagecoach en route from Edinburgh and London. Well placed for salmon and trout fishing on the River Tweed and for shooting on the Northumberland estates, the Red Lion offers a relaxing atmosphere, good guest beers and wholesome food. Start with veal, wild mushroom and chorizo broth with potato dumplings before enjoying pan-fried breast of chicken, borders haggis, peppercorn sauce, creamed potato and vegetables; for pudding choose baked stuffed bramley apple, toffee sauce and vanilla ice cream. There's also a beer festival in June.

Open all wk 11-3 5-11 (Sat 11-11 Sun 11-10.30) (Apr-Nov all day) **Bar Meals** L served Mon-Fri 11-2, Sat-Sun 11-9 D served Mon-Fri 5-9, Sat-Sun 11-9 ⊕ FREE HOUSE

◀ Black Sheep, Guinness, Guest ales ♂ Thistly Cross, Westons. **Facilities** Non-diners area ❖ Children's menu Children's portions Garden ⋒ Beer festival Parking Wi-fi 🚌

NETHERTON — Map 21 NT90

The Star Inn

NE65 7HD ☎ 01669 630238
dir: *7m from Rothbury*

Old fashioned inn, tip-top cask ales but no food

Little has changed at this timeless gem since the Wilson-Morton family took over in 1917. Lost in superb remote countryside north of Rothbury, The Star retains many period features and the bar is like stepping into someone's living room, comfortable and quiet, with no intrusive fruit machines or piped music. Don't expect any food, just cask ales (Camerons Strongarm) in the peak of condition, served from a hatch in the entrance hall. A real find.

Open Tue-Wed & Sun 7.30pm-10.30pm (Fri-Sat 7.30pm-11pm) Closed: Mon, Thu ⊕ FREE HOUSE ◀ Guest ales. **Facilities** Non-diners area Outside area Parking 🚌 (notice required) **Notes** ⊛

NEWTON — Map 21 NZ06

Duke of Wellington Inn

NE43 7UL ☎ 01661 844446
e-mail: info@thedukeofwellingtoninn.co.uk
dir: *From Corbridge A69 towards Newcastle. 3m to village*

Hillside, traditional country pub

Just off the A69 near Corbridge, this early 19th-century pub overlooks the Tyne Valley and is a handy base for exploring the National Park and Hadrian's Wall. The building's original oak and stone are complemented by modern furniture and fabrics that create a comfortable pub offering local ales and enjoyable dishes such as English asparagus risotto; and pan-seared scallops with spiced chorizo and black pudding. There is a cycle and golf club store and boot room for visitors; and dogs are welcome in the bar.

Open all day all wk **Bar Meals** L served 12-9 food served all day **Restaurant** L served 12-9 food served all day ⊕ FREE HOUSE ◀ Hadrian Border Tyneside Blond, Timothy Taylor Landlord. ♀ 11 **Facilities** Non-diners area ❀ (Bar Garden) ❖ Children's menu Children's portions Garden ⋒ Parking Wi-fi 🚌 (notice required)

NEWTON-ON-THE-MOOR — Map 21 NU10

The Cook and Barker Inn ★★★★ INN

PICK OF THE PUBS

NE65 9JY ☎ 01665 575234
e-mail: info@cookandbarkerinn.co.uk
dir: *0.5m from A1 S of Alnwick*

Traditional Northumbrian inn with amazing views

Enjoying outstanding views of the Northumberland coast and the Cheviot Hills, The Cook and Barker is a traditional stone-built inn clad in creepers and flower baskets. Phil Farmer's long-established family business goes way beyond providing 'pub grub with rooms', thanks to his deployment of expert front-of-house and skilled kitchen teams. As he also runs Hope House Farm eight miles away, he has no trouble sourcing the organic beef, lamb and pork that feature on the wide-ranging bar and restaurant menus. These offer modern European cuisine focusing on seafood and 'forest and field' with the occasional oriental influence. Typically, start with cured Spanish ham with feta and watermelon; continue with Asian roasted monkfish and tempura prawns with an essence of crayfish and lobster; or roast rack of lamb with a roasted pear and redcurrant sauce. The cosy en suite bedrooms are smartly furnished, some with traditional features such as exposed beams.

Open all day all wk 12-11 **Bar Meals** L served all wk 12-2 D served all wk 6-9 **Restaurant** L served all wk 12-2 D served all wk 7-9 ⊕ FREE HOUSE ◀ Timothy Taylor Landlord, Black Sheep, Bass ♂ Kopparberg. **Facilities** Non-diners area ❖ Children's portions Garden ⋒ Parking Wi-fi 🚌 (notice required) **Rooms** 18

SEAHOUSES — Map 21 NU23

The Bamburgh Castle Inn ★★★ INN

NE68 7SQ ☎ 01665 720283
e-mail: enquiries@bamburghcastleinn.co.uk
dir: *A1 onto B1341 to Bamburgh, B1340 to Seahouses, follow signs to harbour*

Harbourside inn with superb Farne islands views

With its prime location on the quayside giving wraparound sea views as far as the Farne Islands, this is surely one of the best positioned pubs anywhere along Northumberland's stunning coast. Dating back to the 18th century, the inn has been transformed in more recent times to offer superb bar and dining areas plus seating outside. A beer festival is held in the garden every year, children and dogs are welcomed, and pub dishes of locally sourced food represent excellent value. Typical of these are venison and chilli pâté; home-made fishcakes; and Moroccan lamb steak.

Open all day all wk **Bar Meals** food served all day **Restaurant** food served all day ⊕ FREE HOUSE ◀ Hadrian Border Farne Island. ♀ 11 **Facilities** Non-diners area ❀ (Bar Restaurant Garden) ❖ Children's menu Children's portions Family room Garden ⋒ Beer festival Parking Wi-fi 🚌 (notice required) **Rooms** 29

Save on hotels. Book at theAA.com/hotel

NORTHUMBERLAND – NOTTINGHAMSHIRE 331

ENGLAND

The Olde Ship Inn ★★★★ INN

9 Main St NE68 7RD ☎ 01665 720200
e-mail: theoldeship@seahouses.co.uk
dir: *Lower end of main street above harbour*

Family-owned inn with a nautical theme

Set above the bustling old harbour of Seahouses, The Olde Ship is a stone-built residential inn. Built on a farm around 1745, it has been in the present owners' family for over 100 years, and has a long-established reputation for good food and drink in relaxing surroundings. Lit by stained-glass windows, the main saloon bar is full of character, with its wooden floor made from ships' decking. It offers whiskies as well as a selection of real ales, such as Farne Island and Nel's Best. The inn's corridors and boat gallery are an Aladdin's cave of antique nautical artefacts, ranging from a figurehead to all manner of ship's brasses and dials. Bar foods include locally caught seafood and home-made soups. In the evenings, starters like chicken liver pâté, and venison and pork terrine are followed by chilli bean stew, trio of mixed grilled fish, and steak-and-ale pie. The bedrooms have en suite bathrooms and are tastefully decorated; some have views of the Farne Islands.

Open all day all wk 11-11 (Sun 12-11) **Bar Meals** L served all wk 12-2.30 D served all wk 7-8.30 (no D late Nov-late Jan) **Restaurant** L served Sun 12-2 D served all wk 7-8.30 (no D late Nov-late Jan) ⊕ FREE HOUSE ◀ Greene King Ruddles, Courage Directors, Hadrian Border Farne Island, Morland Old Speckled Hen, High House Farm Nel's Best, Black Sheep, Theakston. ☗ 10 **Facilities** Non-diners area ☺ Children's menu Children's portions Family room Garden ⩋ Parking Wi-fi **Rooms** 18

The Kirkstyle Inn

CA8 7PB ☎ 01434 381559
e-mail: mail@andrewmarkland.plus.com
dir: *Just off A689, 6m N of Alston*

Wonderful views of the South Tyne Valley

Slaggyford has no shop or school, but when the South Tynedale Railway, currently being restored, reaches the village it will again have a station and its first trains since 1976. Thankfully, it already has the 18th-century Kirkstyle Inn, named after the stile into the adjacent churchyard and blessed with wonderful views of the river. In winter a log fire heats the bar, where among the real ales are Yates Best Bitter and a summer brew named after the inn. On the menu are local sausages with Alston honey mustard; shepherd's suet pudding; and breaded scampi. Fridays and Saturdays are Steak Nights.

Open 12-3 6-11 Closed: Mon (Tue in winter) **Bar Meals** L served Tue-Sun 12-2 D served Tue-Sun 6-8.30 Av main course £9.95 **Restaurant** L served Tue-Sun 12-2 D served Tue-Sun 6-8.30 Av 3 course à la carte fr £19.50 ⊕ FREE HOUSE ◀ Kirkstyle Ale, Yates Best Bitter, Guinness. **Facilities** Non-diners area ☺ (Bar Garden Outside area) ☖ Children's portions Garden Outside area ⩋ Parking Wi-fi ▭ (notice required)

The Boatside Inn

NE46 4SQ ☎ 01434 602233
e-mail: sales@theboatsideinn.com
web: www.theboatsideinn.com
dir: *From A69 W of Hexham, follow signs to Warden Newborough & Fourstones*

A traditional haven for walkers and cyclists

Standing beneath Warden Hill at the confluence of the North and South Tyne rivers, The Boatside is surrounded by woodland footpaths and bridleways, and has fishing rights on the river. The name of this stone-built country free house harks back to the days when a rowing boat ferried people across the river before the bridge was built. Black Sheep, Wylam and Mordue ales are on offer in the bar with its log fire and dart board. Meals are served in the conservatory, restaurant or snug, and include curry of the day, seasonal game casserole, seafood pie, Japanese stir-fry and mushroom Stroganoff. The Boatside welcomes children too.

Open all day all wk 11-11 (Sun 11-10.30) **Bar Meals** L served Mon-Sat 11-9, Sun 12-8 D served Mon-Sat 11-9, Sun 12-8 Av main course £9.95 food served all day **Restaurant** L served Mon-Sat 12-2.30, Sun 12-8 D served Mon-Sat 6-9, Sun 12-8 ⊕ FREE HOUSE ◀ Black Sheep, John Smith's, Mordue, Wylam. **Facilities** Non-diners area ☺ (Bar Garden) ☖ Children's menu Children's portions Garden ⩋ Parking Wi-fi ▭ (notice required)

The White Swan ◉

NE70 7HY ☎ 01668 213453
e-mail: dianecuthbert@yahoo.com
dir: *100yds E of A1, 10m N of Alnwick*

Award-winning cuisine just off the A1

This 200-year-old coaching inn stands near the original toll bridge over the Waren Burn. Formerly on the Great North Road, the building is now just a stone's throw from the A1. Inside, you'll find thick stone walls and an open fire for colder days; in summer, there's a small sheltered seating area outside, with further seats in the adjacent field. The Dukes of Northumberland once owned the pub, and its windows and plasterwork still bear the family crests. Visitors and locals alike enjoy the welcoming atmosphere, fine wines and Northumbrian ales. The modern British dishes are created from Northumbrian

produce and all prepared in-house; the bread, preserves and desserts are home made too. Try smoked chicken and mango slices served on a bed of salad; and Barbary duck breast with spicy red cabbage and a morel, cherry and Kirsch dressing. Vegetarians are well catered for, with interesting dishes like roasted bell peppers stuffed with spicy Puy lentils and glazed with Northumberland nettle cheese.

Open all wk Mon-Sat 12-2.30, 5.30-10 (Sun all day) **Bar Meals** L served all wk 12-2.30 D served all wk 6-9 Av main course £11.95 **Restaurant** L served all wk 12-2.30 D served all wk 6-9 Av 3 course à la carte fr £25 ⊕ FREE HOUSE ◀ Caledonian Flying Scotsman. ☗ 10 **Facilities** Non-diners area ☺ (Bar Garden) ☖ Children's menu Children's portions Garden Parking Wi-fi ▭

Victoria Hotel

Dovecote Ln NG9 1JG ☎ 0115 925 4049
e-mail: victoriabeeston@btconnect.com
dir: *M1 junct 25, A52 E. Turn right at Nurseryman PH, right opposite Rockaway Hotel into Barton St, 1st left, adjacent to railway station*

Excellent range of beers, ciders and whiskies

This free house combines a welcoming atmosphere with great food and a wide choice of traditional ales and ciders, continental beers and lagers, many wines by the glass and single malt whiskies. The Victoria dates from 1899 when it was built next to Beeston Railway Station, and the large, heated patio garden is still handy for a touch of train-spotting. Main courses could include cottage pie, Lincolnshire sausages or seafood risotto. There are just as many options for vegetarians: spicy burritos, moussaka, and individual hand-made wild mushroom and cheese pie. Check out the dates of the four annual beer festivals (cider also available) – end of January, Easter, last two weeks in July, and October.

Open all day all wk 10.30am-11pm (Sun 12-11) Closed: 26 Dec **Bar Meals** L served Sun-Tue 12-8.45, Wed-Sat 12-9.30 food served all day **Restaurant** L served Sun-Tue 12-8.45, Wed-Sat 12-9.30 food served all day ⊕ FREE HOUSE ◀ Batemans XB, Castle Rock Harvest Pale, Everards Tiger, Holden's Black Country Bitter, Blue Monkey, Kelham Island Best Bitter, Guest ales ◔ Thatchers Traditional, Broadoak, Biddenden Bushels. ☗ 25 **Facilities** Non-diners area ☺ (Bar Garden) ☖ Garden ⩋ Beer festival Parking Wi-fi

BLIDWORTH — Map 16 SK55

Fox & Hounds

Blidworth Bottoms NG21 0NW ☎ 01623 792383
e-mail: info@foxandhounds-pub.com
web: www.foxandhounds-pub.com
dir: From Ravenshead towards Blidworth on B6020, right to Blidworth

Revitalised country pub with theatrical leanings

A fusion of blues, creams, reds and a change of furniture and fabrics have revitalised the pub without damaging the traditional country-style character that stem from its early 19th-century origins. For nearly 100 years the locals have performed a 'Plough Play' in the pub every January, recalling the days when Blidworth Bottoms was a larger community with shops and a post office. The Greene King ales are reliable as ever, and the refreshed menu still delivers well-priced dishes of popular home-made favourites, such as beef casserole and herb dumplings or cottage pie.

Open all day all wk 11.30-11.30 (Fri-Sat 11.30am-mdnt) Bar Meals L served all wk 11.30-9 D served all wk 11.30-9 food served all day Restaurant food served all day ⊕ GREENE KING ◀ Morland Old Golden Hen, Hardys & Hansons Best Bitter & Olde Trip, Seasonal guest ales. ♈ 9 Facilities Non-diners area ✿ (Bar Garden) ♦♦ Children's menu Children's portions Play area Garden ᚙ Parking ▭

CAR COLSTON — Map 11 SK74

The Royal Oak NEW

The Green NG13 8JE ☎ 01949 20247
e-mail: rich-vicky@btconnect.com
dir: From Newark-on-Trent on A46 follow Mansfield, then Car Colston signs. From rdbt N of Bingham on A46 follow Car Colston sign. Left at next rdbt signed Car Colston

Good pub food and an intriguing past

Some experts attribute origins as a hosiery factory to this 200-year-old inn, citing as evidence its unusual vaulted brick ceiling, undoubtedly capable of supporting any weighty textile machinery above. Much older is the centurion, perhaps from the nearby Roman-British town of Margidunum, whose ghost you may run into. Normally on duty in the bar is owner Richard Spencer, dispensing his carefully tended Marston's, Brakspear and Wychwood real ales, while Vicky, his wife (a dab hand chef) is in the kitchen preparing dishes such as fresh beer-battered cod and haddock; shepherd's pie; ham salad; and sweet potato, chickpea and spinach curry.

Open all wk 11.30-3 5.30-11 (Fri-Sat 11.30-11 Sun 12-10.30) Bar Meals L served Mon-Sat 12-2.15, Sun 12-4 D served Mon-Sat 6-8.45 Av main course £9.75 Restaurant L served Mon-Sat 12-2.15, Sun 12-4 D served Mon-Sat 6-8.45 ⊕ MARSTON'S ◀ Marston's EPA & Burton Bitter, Brakspear Bitter, Wychwood Hobgoblin,. ♈ 13 Facilities Non-diners area ✿ (Bar Garden) ♦♦ Children's portions Garden ᚙ Parking Wi-fi ▭ (notice required)

CAUNTON — Map 17 SK76

Caunton Beck

PICK OF THE PUBS

NG23 6AB ☎ 01636 636793
e-mail: email@cauntonbeck.com
dir: 6m NW of Newark on A616 to Sheffield

A beautifully restored village pub-restaurant

Built as a cottage in the 16th-century, this family-owned pub's colourful rose arbour reflects the work of late 19th-century horticulturalist Samuel Reynolds Hole, the local vicar and later Dean of Rochester. Marston's, Batemans and Black Sheep real ales complement a worthy international wine list, a good few of which are by the glass. Like its sister establishment the Wig & Mitre in Lincoln (see entry), meals begin with breakfast and carry on throughout the day and evening, and can be taken outside on the terrace. A typical main meal would be sesame-crusted sea bass with Indian-spiced rice and Katsu curry sauce; followed by dark chocolate, mocha and hazelnut marquise. Daily specials are on the blackboard, while the children's menu offers macaroni cheese and sausage and mash; and, for that rarity, the truly health-conscious youngster, fresh raw vegetables. A full calendar of events includes 'meet the brewer' nights and gourmet food and wine evenings (booking essential).

Open all day all wk 8am-mdnt Bar Meals L served all wk 8am-10pm D served all wk 8am-10pm Av main course £11.50-£15 food served all day Restaurant L served all wk 8am-10pm D served all wk 8am-10pm Av 3 course à la carte fr £21 food served all day ⊕ FREE HOUSE ◀ Batemans GHA, Marston's Pedigree, Black Sheep, Guinness ♂ Thatchers. ♈ 24 Facilities Non-diners area ✿ (Bar Garden) ♦♦ Children's menu Children's portions Garden ᚙ Parking

COLSTON BASSETT — Map 11 SK73

The Martin's Arms

PICK OF THE PUBS

See Pick of the Pubs on opposite page

EDWINSTOWE — Map 16 SK66

Forest Lodge ★★★★ INN

4 Church St NG21 9QA ☎ 01623 824443
e-mail: reception@forestlodgehotel.co.uk
dir: A614 towards Edwinstowe, onto B6034. Inn opposite church

Lovingly restored coaching inn at the edge of Robin Hood's Sherwood

This 18th-century coaching inn stands on the edge of Sherwood Forest opposite the church where Robin Hood reputedly married Maid Marian. Sympathetically restored by the Thompson family over the past decade, it includes stylish accommodation and a comfortable restaurant and bar. Decent cask ales are always on tap in two beamed bars warmed by open fires. An impressive baronial-style dining hall is an ideal setting for wholesome fare such as roast rabbit loin, baby leeks, braised lettuce and red wine essence; followed by oak smoked haddock with champ potato, black pudding and cauliflower purée; or confit leg of guinea fowl with goose fat roast potatoes and Savoy cabbage.

Open all wk 11.30-3 5.30-11 (Fri 11.30-3 5-11 Sun 12-3 6-10.30) Closed: 1 Jan Bar Meals L served all wk 12-2.30 D served all wk 6-9.30 Restaurant L served all wk 12-2.30 D served all wk 6-9.30 ⊕ FREE HOUSE ◀ Wells Bombardier, Kelham Island Pale Rider & Easy Rider, Forest Lodge English Pale Ale. Facilities Non-diners area ♦♦ Children's menu Children's portions Garden ᚙ Parking Wi-fi ▭ (notice required) Rooms 13

Save on hotels. Book at **theAA.com/hotel**

NOTTINGHAMSHIRE 333 ENGLAND

PICK OF THE PUBS

The Martin's Arms

COLSTON BASSETT Map 11 SK73

School Ln NG12 3FD ☎ **01949 81361**
e-mail: martins_arms@hotmail.com
web: www.themartinsarms.co.uk
dir: *Exit A46 between Leicester &
Newark*

Traditional 18th-century pub with seasonally inspired menus

At the heart of village life since the 18th
century, this old pub takes its name
from Henry Martin, MP for Kinsale in
County Cork, who was the local squire
in the early 19th century. Situated
at the corner of a leafy cul-de-sac
by an old market cross owned by the
National Trust, it is surrounded by
ancient trees in the estate parkland
to which it belonged until 1990, when
the present owners, Jack Inguanta
and Lynne Strafford Bryan, bought it,
undertaking to maintain its character
and atmosphere. This they have clearly
managed to do, since much of the
interior will take you straight back in
time, especially the Jacobean fireplaces
and the period furnishings. The bar has
an impressive range of real ales, with
Castle Rock Harvest Pale waving the
flag for the county, while another local
'brew' is elderflower pressé from Belvoir
Fruit Farms. Bread, preserves, sauces,
terrines, soups, pasta and much, much
more are all made on site. Classic pub
dishes include beefburger with bacon,
Stilton and triple blanched chips; and

fish and chips with minted crushed
peas, tartare sauce and lemon salad,
while mains from a winter carte include
langoustine crumble with tomatoes and
paprika; braised pheasant blanquette
with pilaf rice; cassoulet of Skrei cod
with white haricot beans and smoked
bacon; and braised venison with
tagliatelle. Among the desserts are pear
and vanilla crumble or golden syrup
sponge with treacle ice cream. Prices for
a good number of the fine wines begin
at below £20. The one-acre garden
incorporates a croquet lawn. Booking for
meals may be required.

Open all wk 12-3.30 6-11 (Sun 12-5
7-11) Closed: 25 Dec eve, 26 Dec eve
Bar Meals L served Mon-Sat 12-2, Sun
12-2.30 D served Mon-Sat 6-9.30

Restaurant L served all wk 12-2 D
served Mon-Sat 7-9.30 ⊕ FREE HOUSE
◀ Marston's Pedigree, Bass, Greene
King IPA, Timothy Taylor Landlord,
Elgood's Black Dog, Castle Rock Harvest
Pale, Shepherd Neame Spitfire. ⟡
Facilities Non-diners area ᴥ Children's
portions Family room Garden ⋒ Parking
🚌 (notice required)

FARNDON
Map 17 SK75

The Farndon Boathouse ⊚

PICK OF THE PUBS

Off Wyke Ln NG24 3SX ☎ 01636 676578
e-mail: info@farndonboathouse.co.uk
dir: *From A46 rdbt (SW of Newark-on-Trent) take Fosse Way signed Farndon. Right into Main St signed Farndon. At T-junct right into Wyke Ln, follow Boathouse signs*

Award-winning riverside eaterie

Clad in wood, with chunky exposed roof trusses, stone floors, warehouse-style lighting, and an abundance of glass, this modern bar and eatery, in the style of an old boathouse, sits wonderfully well on the banks of the River Trent. Just how well you'll realise if you approach from the river in your cruiser, or watch a sunset through the extensively glazed frontage of the bar and restaurant. With the award of an AA Rosette, the food philosophy champions local sourcing and home preparation, with home-smoked meats, fish, spices and cheeses, for example, and herbs and leaves grown in the kitchen garden. Exciting dishes include smoked haddock on a kedgeree style risotto; Thai fish bowl; seared duck breast on a frittata of potato and Iberico Belota chorizo; and chargrilled Scotch steaks. Cask-conditioned real ales change frequently, and live music is played every Sunday evening.

Open all day all wk 10am-11pm **Bar Meals** L served Mon-Fri 12-2.30, Sat-Sun 12-3 D served all wk 6-9.30 **Restaurant** L served Mon-Fri 12-2.30, Sat-Sun 12-3 D served all wk 6-9.30 ⊕ FREE HOUSE ◀ Greene King IPA, Guest ales ♂ Thatchers. ♟ 46
Facilities Non-diners area ♦ Children's menu Children's portions Garden Parking Wi-fi ▭

HARBY
Map 17 SK87

Bottle & Glass

High St NG23 7EB ☎ 01522 703438
e-mail: email@bottleandglassharby.com
dir: *S of A57 (Lincoln to Markham Moor road)*

Village inn with historic links

Just seven miles west of Lincoln, this lovely old free house is situated in the peaceful village of Harby – most famous for being where Edward I's wife Eleanor reputedly died in 1290. Compact and convivial, with flagged floors and heavy beams, the pub offers great food, beginning with full English breakfast and with sandwiches and light meals available all day. Seasonal main dishes include line-caught cod, fondue of tomatoes, mussels, chorizo, pak choi and basil; or roast chicken, dauphinoise potatoes, girolles, spinach and cream sauce. The terrace is inevitably popular on sunny days.

Open all day all wk 10am-11pm **Bar Meals** L served Mon-Fri & Sun 10-9.30, Sat 10-10 D served Mon-Fri & Sun 10-9.30, Sat 10-10 Av main course £11.50-£32 food served all day **Restaurant** L served Mon-Fri & Sun 10-9.30, Sat 10-10 D served Mon-Fri & Sun 10-9.30, Sat 10-10 Av 3 course à la carte fr £21.50 food served all day

---

⊕ FREE HOUSE ◀ Young's Bitter & London Gold, Black Sheep, Guinness ♂ Thatchers Gold. ♟ 24
Facilities Non-diners area ♣ (Bar Garden) ♦ Children's menu Children's portions Garden ⋒ Parking

---

KIMBERLEY
Map 11 SK44

The Nelson & Railway Inn

12 Station Rd NG16 2NR ☎ 0115 938 2177
dir: *M1 junct 26, A610 to Kimberley*

Family-run former railway inn

This popular village pub has been run by the same family for over 43 years. Originally 17th-century with Victorian additions, it sits next door to the Hardys & Hansons Brewery that supplies many of the beers. Sadly the two nearby railway stations that once made it a railway inn are now derelict. Interesting brewery prints and railway signs decorate the beamed bar and lounge. A hearty menu of pub favourites includes ploughman's and hot rolls, as well as grills and pub classics like lasagne, scampi and chips and home-made steak and ale pie.

Open all day all wk 11am-mdnt **Bar Meals** L served Mon-Fri 12-2.30, Sat 12-9, Sun 12-6 D served Mon-Fri 5.30-9, Sat 12-9 **Restaurant** L served Mon-Fri 12-2.30, Sat 12-9, Sun 12-6 D served Mon-Fri 5.30-9, Sat 12-9 ⊕ GREENE KING ◀ Hardys & Hansons Best Bitter, Cool & Dark Mild, Guest ales. **Facilities** Non-diners area ♦ Children's menu Children's portions Family room Garden Beer festival Parking Wi-fi ▭

LAXTON
Map 17 SK76

The Dovecote Inn

Cross Hill NG22 0SX ☎ 01777 871586
e-mail: dovecote_inn@btconnect.com
dir: *Exit A1 at Tuxford through Egmanton to Laxton*

Superb local produce

This family-run, 18th-century pub has a delightful beer garden with views of the church, while the interior has a bar as well as three cosy wining and dining rooms. Like most of the village of Laxton, it is Crown Estate property, belonging to the Royal Family. The seasonal, home-cooked dishes could include chicken and liver brandy pâté with chutney and home-made bread; pan-fried haunch of local wild venison with a potato and black pepper cake, creamed sprouts with nutmeg and chestnuts and a brandy and raisin jus; and chocolate fondant. A beer festival is held on the last weekend in August.

Open all wk 11.30-3 5.30-11 (Sun 12-10.30) **Bar Meals** Av main course £12 **Restaurant** L served Mon-Sat 12-2, Sun 12.30-6 D served Mon-Sat 5.30-9 Av 3 course à la carte fr £20 ⊕ FREE HOUSE ◀ Castle Rock Harvest Pale, Everards Tiger, 2 Guest ales. ♟ 9
Facilities Non-diners area ♦ Children's menu Children's portions Garden ⋒ Beer festival Parking Wi-fi ▭ (notice required)

MORTON
Map 17 SK75

The Full Moon Inn

PICK OF THE PUBS

Main St NG25 0UT ☎ 01636 830251
e-mail: bookings@thefullmoonmorton.co.uk
dir: *Newark A617 to Mansfield. Past Kelham, turn left to Rolleston & follow signs to Morton*

Pretty red-brick pub with year-round appeal

Big flavours, no frills is the motto at this ivy-clad Trent Valley free house with a charming summer garden. William and Rebecca White have transformed the place into a contemporary and comfortable pub, exposing the old beams and brickwork from the original 18th-century cottages, and bringing in reclaimed panelling and furniture. The choice on hand-pull proves that William takes his real ales seriously, whilst Rebecca's forte is cooking. Her kitchen produces farm-fresh food, mostly locally sourced, for the breakfast, lunch and evening menus. The lunchtime selection includes omelettes or sandwiches, as well as a choice of starters and hot dishes like crab cakes and maple-roasted ham. The evening brings a more extensive modern British menu: a typical selection might begin with black pudding salad, followed by cod loin on a tomato and diced potato salsa. A takeaway menu features pies, burgers and fish and chips.

Open all wk fr 10am **Bar Meals** L served all wk 12-2.30 D served all wk 5.30-9 **Restaurant** L served all wk 12-2.30 D served all wk 5.30-9 ⊕ FREE HOUSE ◀ Wells Bombardier, Caythorpe Dover Beck Bitter, Abbeydale Moonshine, Guest ales. ♟ 8 **Facilities** Non-diners area ♣ (Bar Garden) ♦ Children's menu Children's portions Play area Family room Garden ⋒ Parking Wi-fi ▭

NEWARK-ON-TRENT
Map 17 SK75

The Prince Rupert

46 Stodman St NG24 1AW ☎ 01636 918121
e-mail: info@theprincerupert.co.uk
dir: *5 mins walk from Castle on entry road to Market Sq*

Brimming with character and charm

The 15th-century Prince Rupert oozes character and charm and is one of Newark's most historic pubs. Expect old beams, wood floors, crackling log fires and cosy corners in the series of small downstairs rooms; make sure you explore upstairs, as the ancient architectural features are stunning. To drink, there's Ufford Ales and Westons Vintage cider on tap, while menus take in pub classics and excellent stone-baked pizzas. There are regular live music events.

Open all day all wk 11am-mdnt (Fri-Sat 11am-1am Sun 12-12) Closed: 25 Dec ⊕ FREE HOUSE ◀ Ufford Ales Rupert's War Dog, Thornbridge Wild Swan & Jaipur, Blue Monkey ♂ Westons Wyld Wood Organic Vintage.
Facilities ♦ Garden Wi-fi

NOTTINGHAM Map 11 SK53

Fellows Morton & Clayton

54 Canal St NG1 7EH ☎ **0115 950 6795**
e-mail: office@fellowsmortonandclayton.co.uk
dir: *Telephone for directions*

Britain's canal heritage on a plate

The pub used to be the headquarters of FM&C, until 1948 the largest canal transportation company in England. From the Castle Wharf complex, the pub's cobbled courtyard overlooks the Nottingham Canal. A giant plasma screen might be showing a big sporting event while you tuck into a salad, pasta, burger, light meal or more substantial dish, such as hand-made pork faggots with Irish champ potato, peas and carrots; rolled and stuffed pork belly with crispy crackling, sweet potato mash and green beans; or beef and ale gravy pie. Nottingham EPA is one of the real ales.

Open all day all wk **Bar Meals** L served all wk 10-3 D served Thu-Sun 3-9 Av main course £8.50 food served all day ⊕ ENTERPRISE INNS ◄ Timothy Taylor Landlord, Fuller's London Pride, Nottingham EPA, St Austell Trelawny Ö Westons Scrumpy. **Facilities** Non-diners area Children's portions Garden ⚑ Parking Wi-fi 🚐 (notice required)

Ye Olde Trip to Jerusalem

PICK OF THE PUBS

1 Brewhouse Yard, Castle Rd NG1 6AD
☎ **0115 947 3171**
e-mail: 4925@greeneking.co.uk
dir: *In town centre*

Medieval gem with history aplenty

Castle Rock, upon which stands Nottingham Castle, is riddled with caves and passageways cut into the sandstone. The builders of this unusual pub made the most of this, incorporating some of the caves into the design of the inn, one of Britain's oldest- founded in AD1189. The name recalls that soldiers, clergy and penitents gathered here before embarking on the Crusade to the Holy Land – doubtless they drank to their quest at the castle's beerhouse before their trip to Jerusalem. Centuries of service impart instant appeal, from the magpie collection of furnishings in the warren of rooms to the unique Rock Lounge, and quirks such as the cursed galleon and the fertility chair. Beers from the Nottingham Brewery feature strongly, accompanying a reliable menu of old favourites like slow-cooked pork belly and Scottish scampi, to tapas style dishes, sharing plates, lighter mains and fish such as oven-baked cod, crayfish and spinach fishcakes. Several annual beer festivals.

Open all day all wk 11-11 (Fri-Sat 11am-mdnt) Closed: 25 Dec **Bar Meals** D served all wk 11-10 Av main course £9.95 food served all day ⊕ GREENE KING ◄ IPA & Abbot Ale, Morland Old Speckled Hen, Hardys & Hansons Olde Trip, Nottingham guest ales Ö Aspall. ☗ 13 **Facilities** Non-diners area ◖◗ Garden Beer festival Wi-fi 🚐 (notice required)

TUXFORD Map 17 SK77

The Mussel & Crab

Sibthorpe Hill NG22 0PJ ☎ **01777 870491**
e-mail: musselandcrab1@hotmail.com
web: www.musselandcrab.com
dir: *From Ollerton/Tuxford junct of A1 & A57. N on B1164 to Sibthorpe Hill. Pub 800yds on right*

A huge choice of seafood dishes

Landlocked Nottinghamshire may not offer sea views but Bruce and Allison Elliott-Bateman have turned this quirky pub into a renowned seafood restaurant since taking over in the late 1990s. Beautifully fresh fish and seafood dominate the menu, with food served in a multitude of rooms; the piazza room is styled as an Italian courtyard and the beamed restaurant is big on rustic charm. Over a dozen blackboards offer ever-changing fish dishes, as well as 'things that don't swim'. You could select rock oysters, chargrilled swordfish and a mini Baileys cheesecake, or whole camembert, duo of pork and crème brûlée.

Open all wk 11-3 6-11 **Bar Meals** L served Mon-Sat 11-2.30, Sun 11-3 D served Mon-Sat 6-10, Sun 6-9 Av main course £12 **Restaurant** L served Mon-Sat 11-2.30, Sun 11-3 D served Mon-Sat 6-10, Sun 6-9 Fixed menu price fr £10 Av 3 course à la carte fr £22 ⊕ FREE HOUSE ◄ Tetley's Smoothflow & Cask, Guinness. ☗ 16 **Facilities** Non-diners area ❀ (Bar Garden) ◖◗ Children's menu Family room Garden ⚑ Parking

OXFORDSHIRE

ADDERBURY Map 11 SP43

Red Lion ★★★ INN

The Green OX17 3LU ☎ **01295 810269**
e-mail: 6496@greeneking.co.uk
dir: *S of Banbury on A4260*

Historic inn overlooking the village green

A fine stone-built coaching inn overlooking the village green. Dating back to English Civil War times, it was once owned by the Royalists who, a tad sycophantically, called it The King's Arms. A list of landlords since 1690 is displayed inside, where age-blackened 'duck or grouse' beams, oak panelling and great big fireplaces set the scene for daily newspapers, real ales and good wines. Classic dishes include British beef and Ruddles ale pie; slow-cooked lamb shank; chicken tikka masala; and grilled sea bass fillets. Accommodation is provided in 12 individually designed rooms.

Open all day all wk 7am-11pm (Sat 8am-11.30pm Sun 8am-11pm) ⊕ GREENE KING ◄ Abbot Ale, Morland Old Speckled Hen, Guest ales. **Facilities** ◖◗ Children's menu Children's portions Garden Parking Wi-fi **Rooms** 12

BAMPTON Map 5 SP30

The Romany

Bridge St OX18 2HA ☎ **01993 850237**
e-mail: theromanyinnbampton@yahoo.co.uk
dir: *Telephone for directions*

A warm welcome and live entertainment

This 18th-century building of Cotswold stone was a shop until a couple of decades ago. Now a pretty inn, The Romany counts a beamed bar, log fires and intimate dining room among its many charms. The choice of food ranges from bar snacks and bar meals to a full carte, with home-made specials like lasagne, chicken Romany, or chilli and chips. There is also a good range of vegetarian choices. The garden might be just the spot to enjoy a pint of Hooky Bitter or London Pride. Regional singers provide live entertainment a couple of times a month.

Open all day all wk 12-12 ⊕ PUNCH TAVERNS ◄ Hook Norton Hooky Bitter, Fuller's London Pride, Guest ales. **Facilities** ◖◗ Children's menu Children's portions Play area Garden Wi-fi

BANBURY
Map 11 SP44

The Wykham Arms

Temple Mill Rd, Sibford Gower OX15 5RX
☎ 01295 788808
e-mail: info@wykhamarms.co.uk
web: www.wykhamarms.co.uk
dir: Between Banbury & Shipston-on-Stour off B4035

Thatched pub with a pretty courtyard

Named after William of Wykeham who in the 14th century was Bishop of Winchester, Chancellor of England and founder of Oxford colleges. He also built much of Windsor Castle, from which town, coincidentally, arrived proprietors and classically trained chefs Damian and Debbie Bradley to run this Cotswold-stone free house. They offer well-kept real ales (Wye Valley HPA and Purity Pure UBU among them), good wines and impressive food, typically corn-fed chicken breast in smoked bacon with ragout; pavé of Shetland salmon with red wine risotto; and confit of Warwickshire pork belly with bubble-and-squeak.

Open 12-3 6-11 Closed: 25 Dec, Mon (ex BHs) **Bar Meals** L served Tue-Sun 12-2.30 D served Tue-Sat 6-9.30 **Restaurant** L served Tue-Sun 12-2.30 D served Tue-Sat 6-9.30 ⊕ FREE HOUSE ◀ St Austell Tribute, Wye Valley HPA, Purity Pure UBU, Guinness ♂ Guest ciders. ☂ 20 **Facilities** Non-diners area ♦♦ Children's portions Family room Garden Outside area ⊐ Parking Wi-fi

See advert below

Ye Olde Reindeer Inn

47 Parsons St OX16 5NA ☎ 01295 264031
e-mail: yeoldereindeerinn@hotmail.com
dir: 1m from M40 junct 11, in town centre just off market square. Car park access via Bolton Rd

Town pub with interesting history

Cotswold-brewed beers from the renowned Hook Norton Brewery draw in a lively local clientele to this historic pub right at the core of old Banbury, just a stone's throw from the Cross of nursery-rhyme fame. Its origins go back to Tudor times, whilst from here in the Civil War Oliver Cromwell himself is believed to have directed his commanders in the richly panelled Globe Room. Weekly events include live music, steak nights and quizzes. Enjoy good, solid pub grub in the traditional, time-worn, classic interior or indulge in a game of Aunt Sally in the flower-decked courtyard.

Open all day all wk Sun-Thu 11am-11pm (Fri-Sat 11am-mdnt) Closed: 25 Dec **Bar Meals** L served all wk 12-3 D served Mon-Sat 6-9 Av main course £6.95 **Restaurant** L served all wk 12-3 D served Mon-Sat 6-9 ⊕ HOOK NORTON ◀ Hooky Bitter, Old Hooky, Hooky Lion, Hooky Mild ♂ Stowford Press. **Facilities** Non-diners area ♥ (All areas) ♦♦ Children's menu Children's portions Family room Garden Outside area ⊐ Beer festival Parking 🚌 (notice required)

BARNARD GATE
Map 5 SP41

The Boot Inn

OX29 6XE ☎ 01865 881231
e-mail: info@theboot-inn.com
dir: Off A40 between Witney & Eynsham

Where footwear is king

The Cotswolds start just west of ancient Eynsham, where Adelaide-born chef Craig Foster runs the low-beamed, stone-flagged Boot. His inn has a renowned celebrity footwear collection, among which are boots formerly worn by Kevin Pietersen, Stirling Moss and Jeremys -Clarkson, Irons and Paxman; no women seem to be represented. Inside, two open fires set the scene, while outside is a pleasant garden. Otter Ale from Devon, Doom Bar from Cornwall and Young's London Gold from Bedford are on tap, as is Symonds cider from Hereford. The wine list is good, too – look for those marked "Landlord's Choice". The lunch menu offers salads, omelettes and sandwiches, while main menu options include Loch Duart gravad lax; braised and pressed blade of beef; and courgette and feta cheese spring roll. Make a booking under the "Roll a Dice" promo and get up to 50 per cent off your bill.

Open all wk 12-3 6-11 (Sun 12-10) **Bar Meals** L served Mon-Sat 12-2.30, Sun 12-9 D served Mon-Sat 7-9.30, Sun 12-9 **Restaurant** L served Mon-Sat 12-2.30, Sun 12-9 D served Mon-Sat 7-9.30, Sun 12-9 ⊕ FREE HOUSE ◀ Young's London Gold, Otter Ale, Sharp's Doom Bar ♂ Symonds. ☂ 8 **Facilities** Non-diners area ♥ (Bar Garden) ♦♦ Children's menu Children's portions Garden ⊐ Parking Wi-fi 🚌 (notice required)

Save on hotels. Book at **theAA.com/hotel**

OXFORDSHIRE 337 ENGLAND

PICK OF THE PUBS

The Vines

BLACK BOURTON   Map 5 SP20

Burford Rd OX18 2PF ☎ 01993 843559
e-mail: info@vineshotel.com
web: www.vinesblackbourton.co.uk
dir: *A40 at Witney onto A4095 to Faringdon, 1st right after Bampton to Black Bourton*

Stylish village retreat with modern British food

Ahdy and Karen Gerges bought The Vines, already a highly regarded restaurant and bar, in 2002, and have never looked back. Built of Cotswold stone, as virtually everywhere is round here, it has been an inn since only the 1940s, when it apparently helped relieve pressure on the village local caused by the influx of American servicemen based around here. But beyond the Cotswold-stone façade, nowhere else has an interior like it. The striking murals and reliefs in the restaurant and bar are the legacy of John Clegg, who created it for a BBC television programme. Take it all in over a pint of Old Hooky in the spacious and comfortably furnished lounge, or make for the patio, where you can stop playing art critic and play a challenging game of Aunt Sally. The menus list an imaginative choice of internationally influenced modern British dishes, all freshly prepared using locally sourced produce. Typical examples from the starters listed on the

carte include Roquefort cheesecake with quince dressing; and smoked salmon soufflé and celeriac remoulade. Then among the mains could be rack of lamb on sweet potato and swede purée with rich Madeira jus and parsnip crisps; smoked haddock, cream cheese and caper risotto, with fresh dill, rocket and a soft poached egg; and hand-made Glamorgan sausages on a bed of creamy Savoy cabbage with parsley mashed potatoes. For dessert, try profiteroles with chocolate sauce; Eton Mess; and warm apple cake and custard. There's always a Sunday roast and a good selection of Old and New World wines.

Open all wk **Bar Meals** L served Tue-Sun 12-2 D served Mon-Sat 6-9, Sun 7-9 Av main course £13 **Restaurant** L served Sat-Sun 12-2 D served Mon-Sat 6-9 Av 3 course à la carte fr £25 ⊞ FREE HOUSE ◀ Hook Norton Old Hooky, Tetley's Smoothflow. **Facilities** Non-diners area ♦♦ Children's menu Children's portions Garden Parking Wi-fi

BECKLEY
Map 5 SP51

The Abingdon Arms

High St OX3 9UU ☎ 01865 351311
e-mail: bookings@abingdonarms.co.uk
dir: *M40 junct 8, follow signs at Headington rdbt for Beckley, then brown tourist signs*

Pretty pub with famous literary connections

Evelyn Waugh, author of *Brideshead Revisited*, once enjoyed the warm hospitality of the Abingdon Arms and the pub is just as welcoming today. Lewis Carroll, R D Blackmore and John Buchan all have connections to Beckley too. Set in a pretty village to the north of Oxford, the pub has been smartly updated but still retains a cosy and traditional atmosphere. Good food and beers from Brakspear have also helped put it on the map. A range of light meals is available at lunchtime, while dinner could feature rump of lamb wrapped in pancetta or king prawn and clam linguine. There are opportunities for many pleasant walks in the area.

Open all wk 12-3 6-11 (Sat-Sun all day) ⊕ BRAKSPEAR ◀ Bitter, Special, Oxford Gold & Guest ale, Wychwood Hobgoblin, Marston's Pedigree ♂ Symonds.
Facilities ♣ (Bar Garden) ♦ Children's menu Children's portions Play area Garden Parking Wi-fi

BLACK BOURTON
Map 5 SP20

The Vines

PICK OF THE PUBS

See Pick of the Pubs on page 337

BLOXHAM
Map 11 SP43

The Elephant & Castle

OX15 4LZ ☎ 01295 720383
e-mail: bloxhamelephant1@btconnect.com
dir: *Take A361 from Banbury towards Chipping Campden*

Traditional Cotswold stone coaching inn

Locals play Aunt Sally or shove-ha'penny in this 15th-century coaching inn's big wood-floored bar, whilst the lounge boasts a bar-billiards table and a large inglenook fireplace. External features include an arch that used to straddle the former Banbury to Chipping Norton turnpike; at night the gates of the pub were closed, and no traffic could get over the toll bridge. Today the menu offers toasties and baguettes, and favourites like scampi, crispy cod and vegetarian shepherd's pie. The bar serves seasonal and guest ales as well as Westons ciders. The beer festival in May is part of the Bloxfest Music Festival.

Open all wk 10-3 6-12 (Fri 10-3 5-2am Sat 10am-2am Sun 10am-mdnt) **Bar Meals** L served Mon-Sat 12-2 Av main course £6 **Restaurant** L served Mon-Sat 12-2 ⊕ HOOK NORTON ◀ Hooky Bitter & Seasonal ales, Guest ales ♂ Westons 1st Quality, Traditional, Old Rosie, Wyld Wood Organic Vintage, Bounds & Perry.
Facilities Non-diners area ♣ (Bar Restaurant Garden) ♦ Children's menu Children's portions Family room Garden ⊼ Beer festival Parking Wi-fi ▨

BRIGHTWELL BALDWIN
Map 5 SU69

The Lord Nelson Inn

PICK OF THE PUBS

OX49 5NP ☎ 01491 612497
e-mail: ladyhamilton1@hotmail.co.uk
dir: *Off B4009 between Watlington & Benson*

Pretty garden for alfresco dining

In Nelson's day the pub was simply known as the Admiral Nelson, but when, in 1797, the great man was elevated to the peerage, the pub's name was elevated too. In 1905, the inn was closed following complaints about over-indulgent estate workers but several years later, the building was bought by a couple who gave it a complete makeover, and The Lord Nelson finally reopened on Trafalgar Day, 1971. Now full of fresh flowers, candlelight and a splendid inglenook fireplace, it's just the place to relax after a country walk or a day at the office. And, during the summer, the pretty terraced garden with its weeping willow is popular for alfresco eating and drinking. All the food is freshly cooked, using local produce where possible. Starters might include tempura king prawns with sweet chilli dip, while main course options include half roast duck with spiced plum sauce and potatoes.

Open all wk 12-3 6-11 (Sun 12-10.30) (summer 11-3 6-11) Closed: 25 Dec **Bar Meals** L served Mon-Sat 12-3, Sun 12-3.30 D served Mon-Sat 6-10, Sun 7-9.30 **Restaurant** L served Mon-Sat 12-3, Sun 12-3.30 D served Mon-Sat 6-10, Sun 7-9.30 ⊕ FREE HOUSE ◀ Rebellion IPA, Adnams, Brakspear, Black Sheep ♂ Westons Stowford Press. ♟20 **Facilities** Non-diners area ♣ (Bar Garden) ♦ Children's portions Garden ⊼ Parking Wi-fi ▨ (notice required)

BRIGHTWELL-CUM-SOTWELL
Map 5 SU59

The Red Lion

The Street OX10 0RT ☎ 01491 837373
e-mail: enquiries@redlion.biz
dir: *From A4130 (Didcot to Wallingford road) follow Brightwell-cum-Sotwell signs. Pub in village centre*

Friendly village pub

Now under new ownership this picture-postcard thatched and timbered 16th-century village pub is not only pretty but also a cracking community local. Hearty, traditional pub food is freshly prepared from local produce. Look to the chalkboard for the famous short-crust pastry pies of the day, or the main menu for things like lasagne, pork tenderloin with black pudding and caramelised apple, or vegetable tagine. Don't miss the Sunday roast lunches. The pub holds a beer festival (with live music) for two days every summer. Behind the bar, beers come from the likes of West Berkshire, Loddon and Appleford breweries, while a choice of wine comes from the very local Brightwell Vineyard.

Open all wk 12-3 6-11 **Bar Meals** L served all wk 12-2 D served Tue-Sat 6.30-9 **Restaurant** L served all wk 12-2 D served Tue-Sat 6.30-9 ⊕ FREE HOUSE ◀ West

Berkshire Good Old Boy, Loddon Hoppit, Appleford Brightwell Gold ♂ Westons Stowford Press, Tutts Clump.
Facilities Non-diners area ♣ (Bar Garden) ♦ Children's menu Children's portions Garden ⊼ Beer festival Parking

BROUGHTON
Map 11 SP43

Saye and Sele Arms

Main Rd OX15 5ED ☎ 01295 263348
e-mail: mail@sayeandselearms.co.uk
dir: *From Banbury Cross take B4035 to Broughton. Approx 3m*

Peaceful retreat in historic village

Named after the family who own the astonishing, moated Broughton Castle at the edge of this attractive village; this charming, ironstone-built pub is itself over 400 years old. Beams in the cosy restaurant and bar sag with the weight of over 200 collectable water jugs; at the bar, beer lovers will find ales from Vale, Cottage and other micros, pleasing to quaff in the tree-shaded garden. There's a very strong, wide-ranging menu, featuring home-made shortcrust pies such as lamb and apricot from chef-patron Danny McGeehan, typically alongside mains like poached fresh salmon fillet with a sauce of shallots, tarragon, mushroom and white wine.

Open 11.30-2.30 7-11 (Sat 11.30-3 7-11 Sun 12-5) Closed: 25 Dec, Sun eve **Bar Meals** L served Mon-Sat 12-2 D served Mon-Sat 7-9.30 **Restaurant** L served Mon-Sat 12-2, Sun 12-3 D served Mon-Sat 7-9.30 ⊕ FREE HOUSE ◀ Adnams Southwold Bitter, Sharp's Doom Bar, 2 Guest ales ♂ Westons Stowford Press, Thatchers Dry. ♟9 **Facilities** Non-diners area ♦ Children's portions Garden ⊼ Parking ▨ (notice required)

BURCOT
Map 5 SU59

The Chequers

OX14 3DP ☎ 01865 407771
e-mail: enquiries@thechequers-burcot.co.uk
dir: *On A415 (Dorchester to Abingdon road) between Clifton Hampden & Dorchester*

Serious but unpretentious British classic food

Steven Sanderson's 400-year-old, thatched and timber-framed pub was once a staging post for boats on the river locals call the Isis, but which everyone else knows as the Thames. As chef, he devises straightforward British classics for his seasonal menus, using carefully chosen meats, fish from Devon and Cornwall markets, mussels from the Norfolk coast, and oysters from Loch Ryan in Scotland and from Jersey. Locals supply game during the winter, and neighbours' gardens and allotments also yield their bounty. Try Steven's roasted Cotswold lamb, or wild sea trout fillet; the wine list reflects his passionate oenological interest.

Open all day all wk 12-11 **Bar Meals** L served all wk 12-3 D served all wk 6.30-9.30 **Restaurant** L served all wk 12-3 D served all wk 6.30-9.30 ⊕ FREE HOUSE ◀ St Austell Tribute, Young's, Cottage, Loose Cannon Abingdon Bridge, Guest ales ♂ Aspall. ♟20
Facilities Non-diners area ♦ Children's menu Children's portions Garden ⊼ Parking Wi-fi ▨ (notice required)

Save on hotels. Book at **theAA.com/hotel**

OXFORDSHIRE 339 **ENGLAND**

BURFORD
Map 5 SP21

The Highway Inn

117 High St OX18 4RG ☎ **01993 823661**
e-mail: info@thehighwayinn.co.uk
dir: From A40 onto A361

Charming medieval pub in a picturesque Cotswold town

The best views of Burford's high street are to be enjoyed from this renovated inn's top-of-the-town position. Take in the bustling scene from pavement tables or retreat to the peace and quiet of the medieval rear courtyard. Dating to 1480, character and charm abound inside, from the low beams, open fires and nooks and crannies in the bar and dining areas to the unique cellar dining room, which is popular with parties and weddings. Monthly menus brim with local produce, from Dursley steaks to the pub's signature rack of ribs with chef's own sauce. Ask the pub for details of the beer festival.

Open all day all wk 12-11 Closed: 25-26 Dec, 1st 2wks Jan **Bar Meals** L served Mon-Sat 12-2.30, Sun 12-3 D served Sun-Thu 6-9, Fri-Sat 6-9.30 ⊕ FREE HOUSE ◀ Hook Norton Hooky Bitter, Wye Valley Butty Bach, Butcombe, Prescott ♂ Westons Stowford Press, Cotswold. ☗ 15 **Facilities** Non-diners area ❤ (Bar Garden) ♦♦ Children's menu Children's portions Family room Garden ⌂ Beer festival Wi-fi ▭ (notice required)

The Inn for All Seasons

PICK OF THE PUBS

The Barringtons OX18 4TN ☎ **01451 844324**
e-mail: sharp@innforallseasons.com
dir: 3m W of Burford on A40

Renowned for its selection of fresh fish

Starting life as two quarrymen's cottages, this 17th-century inn once witnessed the dispatch of Cotswold stone for buildings like St Paul's Cathedral. Many years after it became an inn owned by the Barrington Park Estate, in 1964 it was sold to Jeremy Taylor, who renamed the pub after *A Man for All Seasons*, a film he had worked on as a horse choreographer. The Sharp family have been here since taking over in the mid-1980s. Within lies a treasure trove of ancient oak beams, leather chairs and interesting memorabilia. The bar offers Wadworth ales and guests such as Sharp's Doom Bar, as well as an extensive wine list. Matthew Sharp selects seasonal local produce for his British-continental cuisine, and he also offers one of the best fresh fish boards in the area. Meat options include wild boar and sage pâté; and pan-seared loin of Barrington Estate venison. Round off, perhaps, with sticky toffee pudding. Meals can also be taken in the lovely beer garden.

Open all wk 11-2.30 6-11 (Fri-Sat 11-11) **Bar Meals** L served all wk 12-2.30 D served all wk 6.30-9.30 Av main course £12.50 **Restaurant** L served all wk 12-2.30 D served all wk 6.30-9.30 Av 3 course à la carte fr £28.50 ⊕ FREE HOUSE ◀ Wadworth 6X & Horizon, Sharp's Doom Bar ♂ Sharp's Orchard. ☗ 16 **Facilities** Non-diners area ❤ (Bar Garden) ♦♦ Children's menu Children's portions Play area Garden ⌂ Parking Wi-fi ▭

The Lamb Inn ★★★ SHL ◉◉

PICK OF THE PUBS

Sheep St OX18 4LR ☎ **01993 823155**
e-mail: info@lambinn-burford.co.uk
dir: M40 junct 8, follow A40 & Burford signs, 1st turn, down hill into Sheep St

Cotswold charm and style

In a grass-verged, tranquil side street in this attractive Cotswolds town, the 15th-century Lamb is a dyed-in-the-wool award winner, including two AA Rosettes. A welcoming atmosphere is generated by the bar's flagstone floor, log fire, cosy armchairs, gleaming copper, brass and silver and, last but not least, Hook Norton and Wickwar real ales. In fact, old-world charm and stylish interiors are a feature throughout. Take, for example, the elegant columns and mullioned windows of the courtyard-facing restaurant, where chef Sean Ducie presents contemporary English cooking, based extensively on local produce. Grilled haddock with garlic mash; pan-fried pheasant breast; 10-hour confit duck leg; and penne pasta with ratatouille sauce will give you an idea of what to expect. An extensive cellar offers over 100 wines.

Open all day all wk **Bar Meals** L served all wk 12-9.30 D served all wk 12-9.30 Av main course £11-£20 food served all day **Restaurant** L served all wk 12-2.30 D served all wk 7-9.30 Av 3 course à la carte fr £39 ⊕ FREE HOUSE ◀ Hook Norton Hooky Bitter, Wickwar Cotswold Way. ☗ 16 **Facilities** Non-diners area ❤ (Bar Garden) ♦♦ Children's menu Children's portions Garden ⌂ Parking Wi-fi **Rooms** 17

CASSINGTON
Map 5 SP41

The Chequers Inn

6 The Green OX29 4DG ☎ **01865 882620**
e-mail: info@chequersoxford.co.uk
dir: From Oxford take A40 towards Witney. Right to Cassington

Smart village inn near the church

Turn off the busy A40, and you'll find this imposing Cotswold-stone inn next to the church at the end of the village road. The interior is cosy yet stylish, with polished flagstone floors, winter log fires and wooden furniture adorned with pretty candles. Freshly prepared meals include starters of goats' cheese and caramelised plum crostini, or parsnip and sweet potato soup; followed by main courses of Thai chicken curry; honey and cider ham; and rib-eye steak with peppercorn sauce. There is a beautiful orangery, perfect for private parties and functions. Change of hands in July 2012.

Open all wk Mon-Thu 12-2.30 4.30-11 (Fri-Sat 12-11 Sun 12-10.30) **Bar Meals** L served Mon-Fri 12-2, Sat-Sun 12-3 D served all wk 6-9 **Restaurant** L served Mon-Fri 12-2, Sat-Sun 12-3 D served all wk 6-9 ⊕ FREE HOUSE ♂ Westons Stowford Press. ☗ 10 **Facilities** Non-diners area ♦♦ Children's menu Children's portions Outside area ⌂ Parking Wi-fi ▭ (notice required)

CAULCOTT
Map 11 SP52

Horse & Groom

Lower Heyford Rd OX25 4ND ☎ **01869 343257**
web: www.horseandgroomcaulcott.co.uk
dir: From Bicester take B3040 signed Witney. Through Middleton Stoney. Approx 2.3m to Caulcott

Picture-perfect classic village pub

A classic, thatched English village pub, built of local limestone; the interior is intimate, with wavy beams, settles, an inglenook, and a bar well supplied with real ales from Hook Norton, Vale and others, and ciders including Moles Black Rat. His Gallic origins aside, chef/owner Jerome Prigent's weekly-changing menus are essentially modern English (apart from croque monsieur as a lunchtime snack), such as grilled sirloin steak; venison burger; seared Cornish sea bass; and fresh egg tagliatelle. He devotes another menu entirely to sausages. A beer festival takes place during Bastille Day weekend in July.

Open 12-3 6-11 Closed: Mon eve **Bar Meals** L served Tue-Sun D served Tue-Sat Av main course £10 **Restaurant** L served Tue-Sun D served Tue-Sat Fixed menu price fr £12 Av 3 course à la carte fr £25 ⊕ FREE HOUSE ◀ Hook Norton Hooky Bitter, Sharp's Doom Bar, Vale Gravitas, St Austell Proper Job, White Horse Bitter ♂ Westons Old Rosie & Stowford Press, Moles Black Rat. **Facilities** Non-diners area Children's portions Garden ⌂ Beer festival Parking Wi-fi ▭ (notice required)

CHALGROVE — Map 5 SU69

The Red Lion Inn

PICK OF THE PUBS

The High St OX44 7SS ☎ 01865 890625
dir: *B480 from Oxford ring road, through Stadhampton, left then right at mini rdbt. At Chalgrove Airfield right into village*

Historic pub overlooking the village green

Other than the occasional quack of inquisitive ducks, the medieval village of Chalgrove may be tranquil these days but that wasn't the case in 1643 when Prince Rupert clashed with John Hampden's Parliamentarian forces during the First Civil War. The stream-side beer garden of this old inn overlooks the compact green at the heart of the village, where thatched cottages slumber not far from the church which is, unusually, owner of the pub. In the bar, select from the great range of draught beers complementing the appealing menu created from the best local ingredients by chef-patron Raymond Sexton. The choice may include salad of Serrano ham, buffalo mozzarella and sun-blushed tomatoes, an appetiser for sautéed lamb's liver and bacon with creamy mash and red onion gravy, or breast of Gressingham duck with rhubarb and ginger sauce. Finish with iced lemon meringue parfait courtesy of Suzanne Sexton, an accomplished pastry chef.

Open all wk 11.30-3 6-11 (Sat 11.30-3 6-1am Sun all day) Closed: 25 Dec **Bar Meals** L served Mon-Sat 12-2, Sun 12-3 D served Mon-Sat 6-9 **Restaurant** L served Mon-Sat 12-2, Sun 12-3 D served Mon-Sat 6-9 ⊕ FREE HOUSE ◀ Fuller's London Pride, Butcombe, Guest ale ○ Aspall, Westons Stowford Press.
Facilities Non-diners area ❄ (Bar Garden) ♦♦ Children's menu Children's portions Play area Garden ⊼ Wi-fi ▦ (notice required)

CHARLBURY — Map 11 SP31

The Bull Inn

PICK OF THE PUBS

Sheep St OX7 3RR ☎ 01608 810689
e-mail: info@bullinn-charlbury.com
dir: *M40 junct 8, A40, A44 follow Woodstock/Blenheim Palace signs. Through Woodstock take B4437 to Charlbury, pub at x-rds in town*

Imaginative cooking and Cotswold ales

A short hop from Woodstock, Blenheim Palace and the attractions of the Cotswolds, this handsome stone-fronted 16th-century free house presides over Charlbury's main street. Log fires burning in the inglenook fireplaces and the beamed interior add to the charming period character, as does the wooden-floored bar that offers a range of Cotswold ales by Goffs. A tastefully furnished lounge and dining room add to the relaxing space, while

outside the vine-covered terrace is a lovely backdrop for a drink or meal in summer. Sandwiches served at lunchtime from Tuesday to Saturday may suffice, but the main menu may prove tempting with a starter of Thai fishcake, Asian slaw and sweet chilli dressing and main courses like pan-fried Barbary duck breast, Puy lentils, candied red cabbage and bacon lardons or chicken casserole with chervil dumplings, baby onions and curly kale. Leave room for the jam roly-poly and home-made custard or selection of local cheeses.

Open 12-2.30 6-11 Closed: 25-26 Dec, Sun eve & Mon **Bar Meals** L served Tue-Fri 12-2, Sat-Sun 12-2.30 D served Tue-Sat 6.30-9 **Restaurant** L served Tue-Fri 12-2, Sat-Sun 12-2.30 D served Tue-Sat 6.30-9 ⊕ FREE HOUSE ◀ Goffs, Loddon ○ Thatchers Gold. ₹ 10 **Facilities** Non-diners area ♦♦ Children's portions Garden ⊼ Parking

CHECKENDON — Map 5 SU68

The Highwayman ⊛

PICK OF THE PUBS

Exlade St RG8 0UA ☎ 01491 682020
dir: *On A4074 (Reading to Wallingford road)*

Desirable food below Chiltern beech woods

The wooded hills of the Chilterns, criss-crossed by bridleways and footpaths, form a constant horizon drifting above the rural location of this attractive old building. Just a stone's throw away is the remarkable Maharaja's Well at nearby Stoke Row, a bracing circular ramble from the inn. Bare brick and beams predominate in the airy interior, interspersed by alcoves and warmed by log-burning stoves in this much updated 16th-century inn, where contented regulars sup beers supplied from the nearby Loddon brewery. The menu is eclectic and strong on locally sourced raw materials, gaining an AA Rosette. A speciality here is the pies; wild boar pie or venison cottage pie may tempt as a follow-up to a smoked mackerel pâté and whisky jelly starter. Alternatively a crisp snowy walk is well-rewarded with roasted chestnut and winter vegetable hotpot with potato rösti, whilst the steaks here are from the Royal Windsor Estate. A peaceful rear garden and suntrap terrace make for laid-back summer drinking.

Open 12-3 6-11 (Sun 12-6) Closed: Mon **Bar Meals** L served Tue-Sat 12-2, Sun 12-3 D served Tue-Sat 6-9 **Restaurant** L served Tue-Sat 12-2, Sun 12-3 D served Tue-Sat 6-9 ⊕ FREE HOUSE ◀ Fuller's London Pride, Loddon Hoppit, Butlers, Guest ale. ₹ 11 **Facilities** Non-diners area ❄ (Bar Garden) ♦♦ Children's portions Garden ⊼ Parking Wi-fi ▦ (notice required)

CHINNOR — Map 5 SP70

The Sir Charles Napier ⊛⊛⊛

PICK OF THE PUBS

Spriggs Alley OX39 4BX ☎ 01494 483011
dir: *M40 junct 6, B4009 to Chinnor. Right at rdbt in Spriggs Alley*

Outstanding cooking in the Chilterns

Elegant red kites – there are now 250 breeding pairs – soar over this sublime flint-and-brick dining inn, which is also just ten minutes from the M40. High amidst the beech woods of the Chiltern Hills in an Area of Outstanding Natural Beauty, the pub makes the most of this secluded locale, seasonal forays to the hedgerows and woods produce herbs, fungi and berries used in the inventive menus, whilst the plump local game finds its way into some of the extraordinary three AA-Rosette winning dishes here. Diners distribute themselves amidst a most eclectically furnished suite of rooms with comfy sofas set near warming winter log fires. Rabbit terrine with piccalilli and brioche gives a flavour of things to come; Cornish hake with bean ragout, cockles, mussels and clams, or lamb cutlets and hotpot with Savoy cabbage and shallot purée for example, accompanied by a choice from over 200 wines.

Open 12-4 6-12 (Sun 12-6) Closed: 25-26 Dec, Mon, Sun eve **Bar Meals** L served Tue-Fri 12-2.30 D served Tue-Fri 6.30-9 **Restaurant** L served Tue-Sat 12-2.30, Sun 12-3.30 D served Tue-Sat 6.30-10 Fixed menu price fr £17.50 Av 3 course à la carte fr £40 ⊕ FREE HOUSE ◀ Wadworth 6X, Henry's Original IPA. ₹ 12 **Facilities** Non-diners area ♦♦ Children's menu Children's portions Garden Parking Wi-fi

CHIPPING NORTON — Map 10 SP32

The Chequers

Goddards Ln OX7 5NP ☎ 01608 644717
e-mail: info@chequers-pub.com
dir: *In town centre, adjacent to theatre*

Traditional pub without gaming machines and jukebox

This traditional English pub stands next to Chipping Norton's popular theatre, making it ideal for pre-show drinks and suppers. The name dates back to 1750, but it's thought that an alehouse has stood on this site since the 16th century. Besides the cosy bar, there's a conservatory restaurant, formerly the old courtyard, serving locally sourced home-made dishes such as cauliflower, spinach and potato curry; a daily shortcrust pie; and rich venison stew.

Open all day all wk 11-11 (Fri-Sat 11am-mdnt Sun 11-10.30) Closed: 25 Dec ⊕ FULLER'S ◀ Chiswick Bitter, London Pride & ESB, George Gale & Co HSB. **Facilities** ♦♦ Children's menu Children's portions Wi-fi

Save on hotels. Book at **theAA.com/hotel**

OXFORDSHIRE 341 ENGLAND

PICK OF THE PUBS

Bear & Ragged Staff

CUMNOR   Map 5 SP40

28 Appleton Rd OX2 9QH
☎ **01865 862329**
e-mail:
enquiries@bearandraggedstaff.com
web: www.bearandraggedstaff.com
dir: A420 from Oxford, right onto B4017 signed Cumnor

Old World charm and modern menus

In typically tranquil Oxfordshire countryside, this 16th-century, stone-built dining pub has a rich history, not least having served as a billet for troops during the English Civil War. While the soldiers were here, Richard Cromwell, son of Oliver and Lord Protector of England, allegedly chiselled away the Royal Crest that once adorned the lintel above one of the doors in the bar, and Sir Walter Scott mentions this very Bear & Ragged Staff in his novel, *Kenilworth*. The chefs here take full advantage of the fresh, seasonal game available from local estates and shoots, since the surrounding woods and farmland teem with pheasant, partridge, deer, muntjac, rabbit, duck and pigeon. From the kitchen come hearty, country-style casseroles, stews, steaks, bangers and mash and other pub classics. Install yourself in one of the traditional bar rooms, all dressed stone and warmed by log fires, relax on the stone-flagged patio, or settle in the comfortable

restaurant and ask for the eminently manageable menu. Start with meze, charcuterie, crispy duck leg pancakes or home-made soup; then choose vegetable tagine; pork and wild boar faggots; chargrilled venison steak; market fish of the day; or butternut squash, brown cap mushrooms and spinach risotto. Pizzas from an authentic oven are another option. If, to follow, upside-down apple pudding with Calvados crème anglaise, or creamy rice pudding with red plum compôte fail to tick the right box, call for the cheeseboard, full of British classics with crackers, celery, chutney and grapes. The Bear has a climbing frame for children and dogs are welcome in the bar area.

Open all day all wk **Bar Meals** food served all day **Restaurant** food served all day ⊕ GREENE KING 🍺 Guest ales, Guinness Ö Aspall, Hogan's. 🍷 14 **Facilities** Non-diners area 🐾 (Bar Garden) 👶 Children's menu Children's portions Play area Garden Outside area 🎪 Parking Wi-fi 🚌 (notice required)

CHISELHAMPTON
Map 5 SU59

Coach & Horses Inn

PICK OF THE PUBS

Watlington Rd OX44 7UX ☎ 01865 890255
e-mail: enquiries@coachhorsesinn.co.uk
dir: *From Oxford on B480 towards Watlington, 5m*

Peace and quiet aplenty at this charming pub

This delightful 16th-century inn is set in peaceful countryside six miles south-east of Oxford. Inside you'll find roaring log fires, original exposed beams, an old bread oven and furniture styles that enhance the character of the building. A wide range of imaginative food is served, including a daily specials fish board; grills, poultry and game dishes are also perennial favourites.

Open all day all wk 11-11 (Sun 12-3.30 7-10.30) **Bar Meals** L served all wk 12-2 **Restaurant** L served all wk 12-2 D served Mon-Sat 7-9.30 ⊕ FREE HOUSE ◀ Hook Norton Hooky Bitter & Old Hooky, Sharp's Doom Bar, Loddon, Guest ales Ò Westons Stowford Press. ♟ 10 **Facilities** Non-diners area ♦♦ Children's menu Children's portions Garden ⊨ Parking Wi-fi

CHRISTMAS COMMON
Map 5 SU79

The Fox and Hounds

OX49 5HL ☎ 01491 612599
dir: *M40 junct 5, 2.5m to Christmas Common, on road towards Henley*

Dog- and child-friendly Chilterns pub

Standing high on the Chilterns escarpment in lovely countryside, this pretty pub dates from around 1645, and known by locals as the 'Top Fox' (because there's a Fat one in nearby Watlington). Inside there's a cosy inglenook fireplace to bag a seat by and enjoy a pint of Brakspears, or in warmer weather wander outside into the sun-trap garden. Its barn-style restaurant seats about 50 people, the bar another 25. A change of hands in 2013.

Open all day all wk 12-11 (Sun 12-10.30) **Bar Meals** L served Mon-Fri 12-2.30, Sat 12-3, Sun 12-4 D served Mon-Thu 7-9, Fri-Sat 7-9.30 **Restaurant** L served Mon-Fri 12-2.30, Sat 12-3, Sun 12-4 D served Mon-Thu 7-9, Fri-Sat 7-9.30 ⊕ BRAKSPEAR ◀ Bitter, Seasonal ales Ò Addlestones. ♟ 11 **Facilities** Non-diners area ♣ (Bar Restaurant Garden) ♦♦ Children's menu Children's portions Garden ⊨ Parking ▦ (notice required)

CHURCH ENSTONE
Map 11 SP32

The Crown Inn

PICK OF THE PUBS

Mill Ln OX7 4NN ☎ 01608 677262
dir: *Off A44, 15m N of Oxford*

Charming pub with all the right ingredients

This traditional rustic bar with a roaring fire is a lovely place to enjoy a pint of Hook Norton Hooky Bitter or

perhaps a local Cotswold Cider while the beamed dining room and expansive slate-floored conservatory are also attractive places to eat and drink on the edge of the Cotswolds. Run by chef Tony Warburton and his wife Caroline, this 17th-century stone free house also benefits from a sheltered back garden, which is a popular place to enjoy a spot of sunny weather. Home-made meals, simply prepared, make the best of what's on offer locally. You might find cream of lightly spiced parsnip soup or fishcakes with coriander and chilli mayonnaise to begin, or how about roast belly of Cotswold pork with apple sauce, crackling and cider gravy, or halibut fillet with spinach, chilli and herb butter?

Open all wk 12-3 6-11 (Sun 12-4) Closed: 26 Dec, 1 Jan **Bar Meals** L served all wk 12-2 D served Mon-Sat 7-9 **Restaurant** L served all wk 12-2 D served Mon-Sat 7-9 ⊕ FREE HOUSE ◀ Hook Norton Hooky Bitter, Timothy Taylor Landlord, Wychwood Hobgoblin Ò Cotswold. ♟ 8 **Facilities** Non-diners area ♦♦ Children's portions Garden Parking

CLIFTON
Map 11 SP43

Duke of Cumberland's Head

OX15 0PE ☎ 01869 338534
e-mail: info@thecliftonduke.com
dir: *A4260 from Banbury, then B4031 from Deddington*

Lovely old inn with popular dishes

Believed to be Elizabethan, this thatched stone pub commemorates Prince Rupert of the Rhine, who fought alongside his uncle, Charles I, at the nearby Battle of Edge Hill in 1642. Many old features survive, including the inglenook fireplace and low exposed beams. Three real ales are always on tap, as is Addlestones cider, and the whisky bar needs no explanation. Largely traditional pub favourites, sourced from local farmers, gamekeepers and suppliers, include pie of the day; slow-cooked pork belly; seafood linguine; and roasted butternut squash and sage risotto.

Open all wk 11-3 6-11 Closed: 25 Dec **Bar Meals** L served Mon-Sat 12-2.30, Sun 12-3 D served Mon-Thu 6.30-9, Fri-Sat 6.30-9.30 **Restaurant** L served Mon-Sat 12-2.30, Sun 12-3 D served Sun-Thu 6.30-9, Fri-Sat 6.30-9.30 ⊕ FREE HOUSE ◀ Hook Norton, Tring, Vale, Sharp's Doom Bar, Ramsbury Ò Addlestones. ♟ 11 **Facilities** Non-diners area ♣ (Bar Restaurant Garden) ♦♦ Children's menu Children's portions Garden ⊨ Parking Wi-fi

CUMNOR
Map 5 SP40

Bear & Ragged Staff

PICK OF THE PUBS

See Pick of the Pubs on page 341

The Vine Inn

11 Abingdon Rd OX2 9QN ☎ 01865 862567
dir: *A420 from Oxford, right onto B4017*

Well kept real ales and large garden

A vine does indeed clamber over the whitewashed frontage of this 18th-century village pub. In 1560, nearby Cumnor Place was the scene of the suspicious death of the wife of Lord Robert Dudley, favourite of Elizabeth I; the house was pulled down in 1810. There's a selection of rotating real ales in the carpeted bar, and a typical seasonal menu includes hunter chicken with chips, peas and grilled tomato; sausage and mash with onion gravy; and classic Greek salad, with blackboard specials extending the choice. Children love the huge garden.

Open all wk (Sat-Sun all day) ⊕ PUNCH TAVERNS ◀ Guest ales. **Facilities** ♦♦ Children's menu Children's portions Play area Garden Parking

DEDDINGTON
Map 11 SP43

Deddington Arms ★★★ HL ⚙

PICK OF THE PUBS

Horsefair OX15 0SH ☎ 01869 338364
e-mail: deddarms@oxfordshire-hotels.co.uk
dir: *M40 junct 11 to Banbury. Follow signs for hospital, then towards Adderbury & Deddington, on A4260*

Good country pub fare in a 16th-century inn

Overlooking Deddington's pretty market square, this striking 16th-century former coaching inn boasts a wealth of timbering, flagstone floors, numerous nooks and crannies, crackling winter log fires and sought-after window seats in the beamed bar. Here you can savour a pint of Black Sheep or Adnams ale while perusing the great value set lunch menu or the imaginative carte. Eat in the bar or head for the elegant dining room and kick off a one AA-Rosette meal with smoked salmon and dill roulade with watercress pesto, followed by braised lamb shank with creamed potatoes and minted peas, or a freshly made pizza (goats' cheese, red onion and rocket), and stem ginger crème brûlée. From the market lunch menu perhaps choose smoked ham and Stilton salad, and rabbit casserole with new potatoes. Accommodation includes 27 en suite bedrooms with cottage suites and four-poster luxury.

Open all day all wk 11am-mdnt (Sun 11-11) **Bar Meals** L served all wk 12-2.30 D served all wk 6.30-9.30 Av main course £12 **Restaurant** L served all wk 12-2.30 D served all wk 6.30-9.30 Fixed menu price fr £16 Av 3 course à la carte fr £18 ⊕ FREE HOUSE ◀ Black Sheep, Adnams, 2 Guest ales Ò Westons Stowford Press. ♟ 8 **Facilities** Non-diners area ♦♦ Children's menu Children's portions Parking Wi-fi ▦ (notice required) **Rooms** 27

DORCHESTER (ON THAMES)
Map 5 SU59

The George ★★ HL

PICK OF THE PUBS

See Pick of the Pubs on opposite page

Save on hotels. Book at **theAA.com/hotel**

OXFORDSHIRE 343 ENGLAND

PICK OF THE PUBS

The George ★★ HL

DORCHESTER (ON THAMES)   Map 5 SU59

25 High St OX10 7HH ☎ 01865 340404
e-mail:
georgedorchester@relaxinnz.co.uk
web: www.thegeorgedorchester.com
dir: *From M40 junct 7, A329 S to A4074 at Shillingford. Follow Dorchester signs. From M4 junct 13, A34 to Abingdon then A415 E to Dorchester*

Take a step back in time at this friendly inn

The multi-gabled, 15th-century George stands in the old town's picturesque high street, opposite the 12th-century Dorchester Abbey. Believed to be one of the country's oldest coaching inns, it has been a welcome haven for many an aristocrat, including Sarah Churchill, the first Duchess of Marlborough, while much later the non-aristocratic author D H Lawrence favoured it with his presence. Oak beams and inglenook fireplaces characterise the interior, while the elevated restaurant offers a secret garden with a waterfall. The Potboys Bar, apparently named after the Abbey bell-ringers, is a traditional taproom and therefore unquestionably the right place to enjoy a pint from one of the six breweries that make up The George's roll of honour while tucking into pasta carbonara with garlic bread; bangers and mash with gravy; or an 8oz rump steak with fat chips from the bar menu. Food is all locally sourced: the

Abbey gardens, for example, supply all the herbs, customers contribute the occasional home-grown vegetables, and local shoots provide pheasants. In Carriages Restaurant the menu offers confit of crisp belly pork with Puy lentils, local Toulouse sausages and crushed new potatoes; coq au vin with roasted garlic croûtons and celeriac mash; fresh and smoked fish pie with potato and cheddar cheese glaze; and butternut squash risotto with red onion, fresh herbs, white truffle oil and parmesan shavings. Expect white chocolate and marmalade bread-and-butter pudding with Disaronno custard, and Eton Mess for dessert. There are well-equipped bedrooms some with views of either the extensive gardens or the Abbey.

Open all day all wk 7am-mdnt **Bar Meals** L served all wk 12-3 D served all wk 6-9 **Restaurant** L served all wk 12-3 D served all wk 6-9 ⊕ CHAPMANS GROUP ◖ Wadworth 6X, Skinner's Betty Stogs, Fuller's London Pride, Sharp's Doom Bar, Hook Norton Ŏ Westons Stowford Press. **Facilities** Non-diners area ♦♦ Children's menu & portions Garden Outside area ⊼ Beer festival Parking Wi-fi 🚌 **Rooms** 24

DORCHESTER (ON THAMES) *continued*

The White Hart ★★★ HL

PICK OF THE PUBS

High St OX10 7HN ☎ 01865 340074
e-mail: whitehart@oxfordshire-hotels.co.uk
dir: *On A4074 (Oxford to Reading road)*

Smart hotel with a claim to fame

If this picture-perfect hotel looks familiar, that could be because it has played a starring role in the TV series *Midsomer Murders.* Set seven miles from Oxford in heart of historic Dorchester, it has welcomed travellers for around 400 years, and the bars attract locals, residents and diners alike. There is a great choice of real beers available. Log fires and candlelight create an intimate atmosphere for the enjoyment of innovative dishes prepared from fresh ingredients. A good-value fixed-price lunch is available Monday to Saturday, with a choice of three starters, mains and desserts. The carte menu doubles your choice and includes imaginative dishes such as pumpkin risotto or Thai-style fishcakes, followed by roasted loin of pork with braised red cabbage, caramelised apple and sweet potato crisps; fish and chips in beer-batter with crushed minted peas and hand-cut chips; or grilled peppered rump steak.

Open all day all wk 11am-mdnt (Sun 11-11) **Bar Meals** L served all wk 12-2.30 D served all wk 6.30-9.30 **Restaurant** L served all wk 12-2.30 D served all wk 6.30-9.30 ⊕ FREE HOUSE ◄ Adnams, Black Sheep ♂ Westons Stowford Press. ₹ 12
Facilities Non-diners area ♦♦ Children's portions Garden 듀 Parking ⌂ **Rooms** 28

EAST HENDRED   **Map 5 SU48**

Eyston Arms NEW

High St OX12 8JY ☎ 01235 833320
e-mail: info@eystonarms.co.uk
dir: *Just off A417 (Wantage to Reading road)*

A family-owned local favourite

Owned, appropriately, by the Eyston family, who have lived in the village since 1443, this old inn stands just north of the prehistoric track known as The Ridgeway. With some of its original look revealed by renovations, the pub greets its customers with a huge log fire, flagstone floor, simple polished tables, leather chairs and cartoons of its regulars. The bar stocks real ales from Wadworth and Oxfordshire neighbour, Hook Norton. Chef Maria Jaremchuk's ever-changing menus may feature cock-a-leekie pie; chargrilled rib-eye steak; and vegetarian pad Thai, while carefully cultivated contacts with south coast fishermen mean excellent fish specials.

Open all wk 11-3 6-11 (Fri-Sat 11-11) **Bar Meals** L served 12-2 D served 6.30-9.30 Av main course £12-£15 **Restaurant** L served 12-2 D served 6.30-9.30 Fixed menu price fr £12 ⊕ FREE HOUSE ◄ Hook Norton, Wadworth 6X ♂ Westons Stowford Press. **Facilities** Non-diners area ♨ (Bar Outside area) ♦♦ Children's portions Outside area 듀 Parking Wi-fi

---

FARINGDON   **Map 5 SU29**

The Lamb at Buckland

PICK OF THE PUBS

Lamb Ln, Buckland SN7 8QN ☎ 01367 870484
e-mail: thelambatbuckland@googlemail.com
dir: *Just off A420, 3m E of Faringdon*

Cotswold-stone inn with imaginative food

Tucked away in the beautiful village of Buckland in the Vale of the White Horse, just 15 minutes' drive from Oxford, this Cotswold stone inn dates from the 17th century. It is run by husband and wife Richard and Shelley Terry, and Christopher Green, all three of whom are trained chefs – although you'll find Shelley running front of house while the two men work in the kitchen. The trio are united in their objective: to offer good food in a pub atmosphere, with relaxed and friendly service. To this end local producers of both ales and food are called upon to stock the bar and larder, and many of the vegetables are grown in the kitchen garden next to the suntrap patio. Typical dishes are Bombay potato 'Scotch egg' with spiced carrot purée followed by 'posh chicken and chips' – pan-roasted breast of poussin with deep fried leg, corn fritter, bread sauce and fat chips.

Open all wk 11.30-3 6-11 Closed: Sun eve, Mon **Bar Meals** L served Tue-Sat 12-2, Sun 12-3 D served Tue-Sat 7-9 Av main course £12.95 **Restaurant** L served Tue-Sat 12-2, Sun 12-3 D served Tue-Sat 7-9 Av 3 course à la carte fr £23 ⊕ FREE HOUSE ◄ Brakspear Bitter, Ramsbury Gold, West Berkshire Good Old Boy, Loose Cannon Abingdon Bridge. ₹ 12 **Facilities** Non-diners area ♨ (Bar Restaurant Garden) ♦♦ Children's portions Garden 듀 Parking Wi-fi

---

The Trout at Tadpole Bridge ★★★★ INN ⍟

PICK OF THE PUBS

Buckland Marsh SN7 8RF ☎ 01367 870382
e-mail: info@troutinn.co.uk
dir: *A415 from Abingdon signed Marcham, through Frilford to Kingston Bagpuize. Left onto A420. 5m, right signed Tadpole Bridge. Or M4 (E'bound) junct 15, A419 towards Cirencester. 4m, onto A420 towards Oxford. 10m, left signed Tadpole Bridge*

Secluded riverside setting and a warm welcome

Just a few miles downstream from the head of navigation on The Thames, this lovely stone pub is popular both with adventurous boaters and with ramblers on the long distance Thames Path which threads along the bank. For culture tourists, William Morris' remarkable Kelmscott Manor is just up the road. Very secluded beside an ancient bridge, the huge garden stretches to the riverbank, a tranquil spot to sit, sup beers from local microbreweries like White Horse or local Cotswold cider and take in the views across rich rolling farmland. Comfy accommodation here encourages stay-overs by diners who head here for Gareth and Helen Pugh's well balanced menu, starting perhaps with smoked eel, wine jelly and

---

red pepper dressing, a tingling precursor to roasted suckling pig with spinach dauphinoise potatoes, or Gressingham duck breast with pear and potato cake, braised lettuce and beetroot and ginger purée. Booking ahead is recommended.

Open all wk 11.30-3 6-11 (Sat-Sun all day May-Sep all wk all day) Closed: 25-26 Dec **Bar Meals** L served all wk 12-2 D served all wk 7-9 Av main course £12.95 **Restaurant** L served all wk 12-2 D served all wk 7-9 Av 3 course à la carte fr £28 ⊕ FREE HOUSE ◄ Ramsbury Bitter, Young's Bitter, White Horse Wayland Smithy, Loose Cannon Abingdon Bridge ♂ Westons Stowford Press, Cotswold. ₹ 12 **Facilities** Non-diners area ♨ (Bar Restaurant Garden) ♦♦ Children's menu Children's portions Garden 듀 Parking Wi-fi **Rooms** 6

FERNHAM   **Map 5 SU29**

The Woodman Inn

SN7 7NX ☎ 01367 820643
e-mail: enquiries@thewoodmaninn.net
dir: *M4 junct 15, A419 towards Swindon. Right onto A420 signed Oxford/Shrivenham. Straight on at next 2 rdbts. At x-rds left onto B4508 to Fernham*

Old inn near famous landmark

An enticing mix of ultra-traditional old village bar wrapped around a tempting stillage, plus an eye-opening Tudor-style banqueting hall welcome guests to this pretty 400-year old pub. In a peaceful village in the Vale of White Horse, the famous Uffington white horse chalk figure is just a handful of miles away; the inn's reputation for fine ales and good food draws visitors from this notable landmark. Beers from the likes of Oakham breweries are richly supplemented in the annual beer festival here. Great lite-bite snacks satisfy; or indulge in honey roasted breast of duck, spring onion mash and cherry sauce.

Open all day all wk **Bar Meals** L served Mon-Fri 12-2, Sat-Sun 12-2.30 D served all wk 6.30-9.30 **Restaurant** L served Mon-Fri 12-2, Sat-Sun 12-2.30 D served all wk 6.30-9.30 ⊕ FREE HOUSE ◄ Timothy Taylor Landlord, Wadworth 6X, Wychwood Hobgoblin, Oakham, Bath, White Horse, Guest ales ♂ Aspall, Thatchers Cheddar Valley. **Facilities** Non-diners area ♨ (Bar Restaurant Garden) ♦♦ Children's menu Children's portions Family room Garden 듀 Beer festival Parking Wi-fi ⌂

Save on hotels. Book at **theAA.com/hotel**

OXFORDSHIRE 345 ENGLAND

PICK OF THE PUBS

The White Hart ❀❀

FYFIELD Map 5 SU49

Main Rd OX13 5LW ☎ **01865 390585**
e-mail: info@whitehart-fyfield.com
web: www.whitehart-fyfield.com
dir: *7m S of Oxford, just off A420
(Oxford to Swindon road)*

Confident cooking in picturesque village inn

Mark and Kay Chandler's 500-year-old former chantry house is steeped in history and has been a pub since 1580 when St John's College in Oxford leased it to tenants but reserved the right to 'occupy it if driven from Oxford by pestilence' – so far this has not been invoked! The building is breathtaking and boasts a grand hall with a 15th-century arch-braced roof, original oak beams, flagstone floors, and huge stone-flanked windows. For a table with a view there's still a splendid 30ft high mistrels' gallery overlooking the restaurant. Study the wonderful history and architecture over a pint of Loose Cannon Abingdon Bridge or Sharp's Doom Bar, or one of the 14 wines served by the glass in the character bar – in winter arrive early to bag the table beside the roaring fire. Awarded two AA Rosettes for his food, chef/owner Mark is steadfast in his pursuit of fresh, seasonal food from trusted local suppliers and their own kitchen garden provides a regular supply of fruit and vegetables. Mark's cooking reveals a

high level of technical skill and his menus change daily, perhaps featuring creamy cauliflower and truffle soup with cheese and pancetta scone; or home-cured salmon gravad lax with marinated cucumber salad among the starters. To follow, try slow roasted Kelmscott pork belly with apple, carrots, celeriac purée, cider jus and foot-long crackling; or pan-fried duck breast with sweet potatoes Anna, purée and crisps and rhubarb and star anise sauce; then perhaps a trio of lemon puddings. Fish, antipasti or mezze sharing boards are great for nibbles. The lunchtime set menu is great value.

Open 12-3 5.30-11 (Sat 12-11 Sun 12-10.30) Closed: Mon (ex BH) **Bar Meals** L served Tue-Sat 12-2.30, Sun 12-3

D served Tue-Sat 7-9.30 Av main course £16.75 **Restaurant** L served Tue-Sat 12-2.30, Sun 12-3 D served Tue-Sat 7-9.30 Fixed menu price fr £17 Av 3 course à la carte fr £25 ⊕ FREE HOUSE ◀ Sharp's Doom Bar, Loddon Hullabaloo, Loose Cannon Abingdon Bridge, Guest ales ♂ Thatchers Cheddar Valley, Thatchers Gold. ♟ 14 **Facilities** Non-diners area ♦♦ Children's menu Children's portions Play area Garden ⋒ Beer festival Parking Wi-fi 🚌

FILKINS Map 5 SP20

The Five Alls NEW

PICK OF THE PUBS

GL7 3JQ ☎ 01367 860875
e-mail: info@thefiveallsfilkins.co.uk
dir: *Between Lechlade & Burford, just off A361*

A class act in the Cotswolds

Respected restaurateurs Sebastian and Lana Snow upped-sticks and literally moved down the road from the Swan at Southrop to picture-postcard Filkins and this 18th-century gem in 2012. They haven't look back, gently refurbishing the interior, which now oozes warmth and style, with rugs on stone floors, flickering candles on old dining tables, and a leather Chesterfield fronting the log fire – the perfect spot to relax with a pint and the papers. The Snow's have reinvigorated the old pub - the bar bustles with locals, walkers and cyclists supping pints of Oxford Gold and tucking into proper bar snacks, while the Italian inspired modern British menu, which changes monthly and bristles with quality, locally sourced ingredients, draws diners from far and wide across the Cotswolds. Typically, follow wild mushroom gnocchi with roast confit lamb shoulder with aubergine parmigiana, roast garlic and spinach, leaving room for panettone bread-and-butter pudding with crème anglaise.

Open all day all wk **Bar Meals** L served all wk 12-2.30 D served Mon-Sat 6-9.30 Av main course £16 **Restaurant** L served all wk 12-2.30 D served Mon-Sat 6-9.30 Fixed menu price fr £15 Av 3 course à la carte fr £28 ⊕ FREE HOUSE ◀ Ringwood, Brakspear Oxford Gold, Wychwood Hobgoblin. **Facilities** Non-diners area ❄ (Bar Restaurant Garden) ◀ Children's menu Children's portions Play area Garden ⊞ Parking Wi-fi ➡

FRINGFORD Map 11 SP62

The Butchers Arms

OX27 8EB ☎ 01869 277363
e-mail: tg53@sky.com
dir: *4m from Bicester on A4421 towards Buckingham*

Charming pub next to the village green

Lark Rise to Candleford author Flora Jane Thompson was born at Juniper Hill, a couple of miles from this pretty, creeper-covered pub, and her first job was in the Post Office in Fringford. In her writings, Juniper Hill became Lark Rise, Fringford became Candleford Green, and Buckingham and Banbury metamorphosed into Candleford. Handpumps dispense Old Hooky, Doom Bar and Tring Brewery's bizarrely named Side Pocket for a Toad, while the menu offers a good traditional selection, including pie of the day; lemon sole; home-made curry; and liver, bacon and onions. You can watch the cricket from the patio and in mid-June there's a beer and cider festival.

Open all day all wk **Bar Meals** L served all wk 12-2.30 D served all wk 6.30-9 Av main course £9.95 **Restaurant** L served Mon-Sat 12-2.30, Sun 12-3.30 D served all wk 6.30-9 Fixed menu price fr £10.95

⊕ PUNCH TAVERNS ◀ Hook Norton Old Hooky, Sharp's Doom Bar, Tring Side Pocket for a Toad ♂ Thatchers Katy, Westons Stowford Press. **Facilities** Non-diners area ❄ (Bar) ◀ Children's menu Children's portions ⊞ Beer festival Cider festival Parking Wi-fi ➡ (notice required)

FULBROOK Map 10 SP21

The Carpenters Arms

Fulbrook Hill OX18 4BH ☎ 01993 823275
e-mail: bridgett.howard@ntlworld.com
dir: *From rdbt on A40 at Burford take A361 signed Chipping Norton. Pub on right 150mtrs from mini rdbt just after bridge*

Stylish pub with seasonally changing menus

Expect oodles of charm and character from this 17th-century stone pub; the warren of cosy, beautifully decorated and furnished rooms draws a cosmopolitan crowd, many of whom stop to enjoy the modern British cooking. Choices range from bar snacks such as game pie with mash and carrots to more ambitious dishes such as goats' cheese tian with tomato, basil and olives followed by rack of lamb with sautéed potatoes, asparagus, lemon and rosemary.

Open Wed-Fri 12-2.30 Tue-Thu 6-9 Fri-Sat 12-3 6-9.30 Sun 12-3 Closed: Sun eve, Mon, Tue L (winter) ⊕ GREENE KING ◀ IPA & Abbot Ale, Morland Old Speckled Hen ♂ Aspall. **Facilities** ❄ (Bar Restaurant Garden) ◀ Children's portions Garden Parking Wi-fi

FYFIELD Map 5 SU49

The White Hart ◉◉

PICK OF THE PUBS

See Pick of the Pubs on page 345

GORING Map 5 SU68

Miller of Mansfield ★★★★★ RR ◉◉

PICK OF THE PUBS

High St RG8 9AW ☎ 01491 872829
e-mail: reservations@millerofmansfield.com
dir: *From Pangbourne take A329 to Streatley. Right on B4009, 0.5m to Goring*

A beautiful focal point for the village

The stylishly renovated red-brick Georgian coaching inn in this attractive Thames-side village is in an Area of Outstanding Natural Beauty, making it the perfect bolt-hole for exploring the Thames Path (just along the road) and the Chiltern Hills. Despite being highly rated as a restaurant with rooms, the Miller of Mansfield remains a cracking pub. The bar is replete with shiny wooden floors, fat candles on scrubbed tables, blazing log fires and local ales like Good Old Boy. The kitchen focuses on freshness of ingredients, so expect seasonality in its take on modern British cooking. Suppliers are carefully sourced, and just about everything that can be is home made. In the Philippe Starck-influenced dining room,

each dish brims with flavour: lime and cracked black pepper marinated fillet of pork with ricotta, baby spinach mashed potato and a cider, apple and date purée. You can order Thai green curry, barbecued ribs and sandwiches from the all-day bar menu.

Open all day all wk 8am-11pm **Bar Meals** L served all wk 12-10 D served all wk 12-10 food served all day **Restaurant** L served all wk all day D served all wk all day ⊕ FREE HOUSE ◀ West Berkshire Good Old Boy, Rebellion IPA. **Facilities** Non-diners area ❄ (Bar Garden) ◀ Children's menu Children's portions Garden ⊞ Parking Wi-fi ➡ **Rooms** 13

GREAT TEW Map 11 SP42

The Falkland Arms

PICK OF THE PUBS

OX7 4DB ☎ 01608 683653
e-mail: falklandarms@wadworth.co.uk
dir: *Off A361, 1.25m, signed Great Tew*

Ancient inn replete with English character

Named after Lucius Carey, 2nd Viscount Falkland, who inherited the manor of Great Tew in 1629, this 500-year-old creeper-clad inn can be found nestling at the end of a charming row of Cotswold-stone cottages. The Falkland Arms is a classic: wooden floors, exposed beams, high-backed settles and low stools and an inglenook fireplace characterise the intimate bar, where a huge collection of beer and cider mugs and jugs hangs from the ceiling. Wadworth and guest ales, together with a meal, can be enjoyed in the bar or the lovely pub garden. Sharing plates, pork pie, baked camembert and home-made soup supplement the lunchtime menu of thick-cut bloomer sandwiches. In the evening, booking is essential for dinner in the small dining room. Expect pan-fried potato gnocchi with wild spinach and mushrooms; honey-roast Wiltshire ham; and chef's pie of the day. Being a genuine English pub, clay pipes and snuff are always on sale!

Open all day all wk **Bar Meals** L served all wk 12-2.30 D served all wk 6.30-9.30 Av main course £8.95 **Restaurant** L served all wk 12-2.30 D served all wk 6.30-9.30 Fixed menu price fr £10.95 ⊕ WADWORTH ◀ 6X, Henry's Original IPA & Horizon, Guest ales ♂ Westons Traditional, Stowford Press. ⌾ 14 **Facilities** Non-diners area ❄ (Bar Restaurant Garden) ◀ Children's portions Garden ⊞ Beer festival Wi-fi ➡ (notice required)

Save on hotels. Book at **theAA.com/hotel**

OXFORDSHIRE 347 ENGLAND

PICK OF THE PUBS

The Cherry Tree Inn ★★★★ INN ❀

HENLEY-ON-THAMES　　　Map 5 SU78

Stoke Row RG9 5QA ☎ 01491 680430
e-mail:
enquiries@thecherrytreeinn.co.uk
web: www.thecherrytreeinn.co.uk
dir: *B481 towards Reading & Sonning
Common 2m, follow Stoke Row sign*

British and European food in cleverly revamped old pub

Originally three flint cottages, the
400-year-old Cherry Tree reopened in
April 2012 following a comprehensive
re-fit. Among other things, this ensured
the new strong colours and modern,
comfortable furnishings looked good
alongside the original flagstone floors,
beamed ceilings and fireplaces.
Brakspear's Bitter, Oxford Gold and
seasonal ales are on hand-pump in the
bar, where there is also a good range of
malt whiskies, chilled vodkas and wines
by the glass. An eat-anywhere policy
means freedom to enjoy any of the
British and European dishes in the bar,
restaurant or large garden. Local
produce is used throughout the menu,
with items such as lobster, oysters and
game available in season. Billed as
'quintessentially English' dishes are
Hereford beef and Cornish oyster
shortcrust pastry pie; and roast Long
White ham with fried duck egg and
rough-cut chips. Other mains include
ratatouille profiteroles with parmesan
Mornay and roasted new potatoes;

daube of Hambleden wild venison with
thyme suet dumplings and beetroot; and
loin of line-caught black cod with plum
tomato stew and white bean cassoulet.
Chalkboards offer daily specials, and
Sunday roasts feature Scottish prime
beef, Yorkshire pudding, roast potatoes,
fresh vegetables and home-made
horseradish. Children may eat in the
dining rooms until 8pm, choosing from
a menu that includes grilled fresh
chicken and chips; pork and leek
sausages and mash; and fish and
chips. The large south-facing garden
makes fine-weather dining a pleasure.
All around is the Chilterns Area of
Outstanding Natural Beauty.

Open all wk 11-3 5-11 (Fri-Sat 11-11
Sun 12-10) Closed: 1 Jan **Bar Meals** L

served Mon-Fri 12-3, Sat 12-4, Sun
12-10 D served Mon-Sat 7-10 Av main
course £13 **Restaurant** L served Mon-Fri
12-3, Sat 12-4, Sun 12-10 D served
Mon-Sat 7-10 Fixed menu price fr £15
Av 3 course à la carte fr £22.50
⊕ BRAKSPEAR ◀ Bitter, Oxford Gold,
Seasonal ales ♂ Symonds. ♟ 12
Facilities Non-diners area ❤ (Bar
Garden) ♦ Children's menu Garden ⋒
Beer festival Parking **Rooms** 4

HAMPTON POYLE — Map 11 SP51

The Bell

PICK OF THE PUBS

OX5 2QD ☎ 01865 376242
e-mail: contactus@thebelloxford.co.uk
dir: *From N: exit A34 signed Kidlington, over bridge. At mini rdbt turn right, left to Hampton Poyle (before slip road to rejoin A34). From Kidlington: at rdbt (junct of A4260 & A4165) take Bicester Rd (Sainsbury's on left) towards A34. Left to Hampton Poyle*

Flagstone floors and old beams

A centuries-old inn that is independent and privately owned. The charms of its oak beams and time-worn flagstone floors are now complemented by a new dining area, with an open kitchen featuring an eye-catching wood-burning oven, from which are produced rustic pizzas and other dishes. These, along with burgers and salads, are served in the bar at any time, while in the restaurant a meal might start with creamy Windrush Valley goats' cheese, roast beetroot, toasted hazelnuts and grapefruit; continue with rare-breed Tamworth pork chop with shredded pork croquette and chive mash; and finish with warm treacle tart and honeycomb. Grilled fish and shellfish are accompanied by simple butter sauces. Should you have a well-behaved dog, it will be welcome to join you in the bar or out on the delightful south-facing terrace. Conveniently sited for Oxford, Bicester Village shopping outlet and Blenheim Palace.

Open all day all wk 7am-11pm **Bar Meals** L served Mon-Sat 12-2.30, Sun 12-3 D served Sun-Thu 6-9, Fri-Sat 6.30-9.30 **Restaurant** L served Mon-Sat 12-2.30, Sun 12-3 D served Sun-Thu 6-9, Fri-Sat 6.30-9.30 ⊕ FREE HOUSE ◀ Hook Norton Hooky Bitter, Wye Valley Butty Bach ⏃ Westons Stowford Press. ⬤ 10
Facilities Non-diners area ❀ (Bar Garden Outside area) ♦♦ Children's portions Family room Garden Outside area ☛ Parking Wi-fi ⬛ (notice required)

HARWELL — Map 5 SU48

The Hart of Harwell **NEW**

High St OX11 0EH ☎ 01235 834511
e-mail: info@hartofharwell.com
dir: *In village centre, accessed from A417 & A4130*

Face-lift puts village pub firmly on the map

Several old wells were found during renovations of this 15th to 16th-century pub, and one now serves as a dining table. You can peer down it while eating – an unusual diversion. The modern bar's stable of Greene King real ales is supplemented by regularly-changing guests. Sandwiches are served at lunchtime only, while the main menu covers both lunch and dinner, so either meal could feature a prawn and crayfish salad starter, followed by, say, pork fillet and black pudding mash with walnut and Stilton sauce; or perhaps ale-battered haddock fillet and hand-cut chips; and, to end, apricot-glazed bread and butter pudding.

Open all wk 12-3 5.30-11 (Fri-Sat 12-12 Sun 12-11) **Bar Meals** L served all wk 12-2.30 D served all wk 6-9.30 Av main course £13 **Restaurant** L served all wk 12-2.30 D served all wk 6-9.30 Av 3 course à la carte fr £22 ⊕ GREENE KING ◀ Morland Old Speckled Hen & Original, Hardys & Hansons Best Bitter ⏃ Aspall. ⬤ 24
Facilities Non-diners area ❀ (Bar Garden) ♦♦ Children's menu Children's portions Garden ☛ Parking Wi-fi

HENLEY-ON-THAMES — Map 5 SU78

The Cherry Tree Inn ★★★★ INN ◉

PICK OF THE PUBS

See Pick of the Pubs on page 347
See advert on opposite page

The Five Horseshoes

PICK OF THE PUBS

Maidensgrove RG9 6EX ☎ 01491 641282
e-mail: admin@thefivehorseshoes.co.uk
dir: *From Henley-on-Thames take A4130, 1m, take B480 signed Stonor. In Stonor left, through woods, over common, pub on left*

Popular for its summer hog roasts and barbecues

There's every chance of seeing red kites wheeling around above this 16th-century, brick and flint pub overlooking the Chiltern Hills. Its two snug bar areas are characterised by beams, wrought iron, brasswork, open fires, traditional pub games and Brakspear's real ales on the handpumps. To dine in the large conservatory restaurant is to enjoy an approach to traditional English dishes that often involves tweaking them to intensify the flavours, thus a menu typically begins with Cornish oysters and Bloody Mary sorbet; and whole baked camembert stuffed with almonds and rosemary. Of appeal to follow might be a main course of roast haunch of muntjac venison; herb-crusted fillet of wild sea bass; goats' cheese and ratatouille ravioli; or even a Chateaubriand for two. Pub classics include beer-battered haddock and chips and doorstep sandwiches. Dogs are welcome in the bar and two large beer gardens, the location for summer weekend barbecues and Bank Holiday hog roasts.

Open all wk 12-3.30 6-11 (Sat 12-11 Sun 12-6) ⊕ BRAKSPEAR ◀ Ordinary, Oxford Gold. **Facilities** ❀ (Bar Garden) ♦♦ Children's portions Garden Parking

The Little Angel

Remenham Ln RG9 2LS ☎ 01491 411008
e-mail: enquiries@thelittleangel.co.uk
web: www.thelittleangel.co.uk
dir: *M4 juncts 8 & 9, A404, A4130 to Henley, then towards Maidenhead. Pub on left*

Spacious and busy pub with an inviting interior

This large whitewashed pub just over Henley's famous bridge from the town gets pretty packed, especially at weekends. The chic interior features wooden floorboards, duck-egg blue tones with warming accents, an open fire, and spacious bar and dining areas. Other attractions are the well-compiled wine list, the Brakspear ales, and the exceptional modern menu, which is changed quarterly. Try corned beef and piccalilli terrine, chicken ballottine, and Belgian chocolate sponge. Sundays are "unbelievably busy" so booking is essential, but don't worry, lunch is served all day.

Open all day all wk 11-11 (Fri-Sat 11am-mdnt Sun 12-10) **Bar Meals** L served Mon-Fri 12-3, Sat-Sun all day D served Mon-Fri 7-10, Sat-Sun all day Av main course £11 **Restaurant** L served Mon-Fri 12-3, Sat-Sun all day D served Mon-Fri 7-10, Sat-Sun all day Av 3 course à la carte fr £21 ⊕ BRAKSPEAR ◀ Brakspear, Oxford Gold, Seasonal ales, Guinness ⏃ Symonds. ⬤ 11
Facilities Non-diners area ❀ (Bar Restaurant Garden) ♦♦ Children's menu Children's portions Garden ☛ Parking Wi-fi ⬛

See advert on page 350

Save on hotels. Book at **theAA.com/hotel**

OXFORDSHIRE 349 ENGLAND

The Cherry Tree Inn
Stoke Row South Oxfordshire

PUB | RESTAURANT | ROOMS

The Cherry Tree Inn is your quintessential English country pub at its very best. Beautifully situated in the Chiltern's in the picturesque South Oxfordshire village of Stoke Row, it is surrounded by the most enchanting beech woods & a slice of the country life.

With miles of walks, cycling, riding & outdoor pursuits & with 4 AA 4* letting rooms, a vibrant & busy bar & some of the best pub food around, it is a firm favourite in the area.

Just 10 minutes west of the historic town of Henley on Thames, it is perfectly positioned for those wanting a day trip, as part of a holiday in the area & most definitely for the well kept ales, wines & innovative food that delivers fresh pub classics alongside more foodie treats. They have a seasonally changing menu, daily scrummy specials, cracking bar bites & attract, businesses, couples, groups & locals alike.

Definitely worth a visit, especially in the spring & summer in their glorious garden. BBQ's, Live Music, Sporting Events & more will be found on their events calendar. This is a lovely pub!

OPEN EVERY DAY | DRINKS | LUNCH | DINNER
CASK ALES | WINES | CHAMPAGNE
SEASONAL MENU | DAILY SPECIALS BOARDS | SUNDAY ROASTS

www.thecherrytreeinn.co.uk | 01491 680 430

THE LITTLE ANGEL
Henley on Thames

Henley on Thames, a historic town in South Oxfordshire & just an hour from London is home to the famous Little Angel Pub. Situated just 80 yards from Henley Bridge & the famous Royal Regatta course on the River Thames, it is renowned the world over. One of the largest & most individual pubs in the area, the focus here is a cracking bar, fantastic food & good times. Open every day, all day & serving only the best local & seasonal food, this award winning pub is one of the busiest in the region & is as happy hosting thousands during regatta week in July, as it is a romantic table for two! A uniquely designed pub, it has several individual areas that can cater for parities of all sizes & with a large car park for its patrons, is highly prized in the town. Daily specials boards deliver some delicious foodie treats, as does the daily bar food offer, including enormous home made Scotch eggs that are superb. Cosy in the winter but equally loved for its large patio garden for al fresco dining or just drinks. Overlooking the quintessential Henley Cricket Club grounds, you could do worse than while away an afternoon with a good lunch, chilled bottle of rosé & good company. Whether you are enjoying a day trip, passing through or partaking in one of the large annual events in the town, you would not want to pass The Little Angel & not pop in. Their friendly & efficient staff will take great care of you.

The Little Angel Remenham Lane Henley On Thames Berks RG9 2LS
01491 411 008 enquiries@thelittleangel.co.uk www.thelittleangel.co.uk

HENLEY-ON-THAMES continued

The Three Tuns

5 The Market Place RG9 2AA ☎ **01491 410138**
e-mail: info@threetunshenley.co.uk
dir: In town centre. Parking nearby

Known for its warm and friendly service

Mark and Sandra Duggan turned this formerly run-down pub into a bustling drinking and dining spot. One of the oldest pubs in town, the cosy, matchboarded front bar has scrubbed tables, an open fire and a miscellany of artefacts, posters and prints. From the adjacent intimate dining room, a passageway leads to the suntrap terrace garden. Freshly sourced local produce (the butcher's only next door!) underpins menus both traditional and modern: Barkham Blue cheese soufflé, confit duck leg, and roast loin of cod, for example. There is live music every Sunday evening and comedy every first Thursday of the month.

Open all day 11.30-11 (Sat 11am-mdnt Sun 11-10) Closed: 25 Dec, Mon **Bar Meals** L served Tue-Fri 12-3, Sat-Sun 12-4 D served Tue-Sat 6-9.45 **Restaurant** L served Tue-Fri 12-3, Sat-Sun 12-4 D served Tue-Sat 6-9.45 Fixed menu price fr £10 Av 3 course à la carte fr £21 ⊕ BRAKSPEAR ◀ Special, Oxford Gold ♂ Westons Wyld Wood. ♥ 12 **Facilities** Non-diners area ❀ (Bar Garden) ♦❢ Children's portions Garden ♯

WhiteHartNettlebed

PICK OF THE PUBS

High St, Nettlebed RG9 5DD ☎ **01491 641245**
e-mail: whitehart@tmdining.co.uk
dir: On A4130 between Henley-on-Thames & Wallingford

History and tradition blends with stylish modernity

Royalist and parliamentary soldiers made a habit of lodging in local taverns during the English Civil War; this 15th-century inn reputedly billeted troops loyal to the King. During the 17th and 18th centuries the area was plagued by highwaymen, including the notorious Isaac Darkin, who was eventually caught, tried and hung at Oxford Gaol. These days the beautifully restored property is favoured by a stylish crowd who appreciate the chic bar and restaurant. Heading the beer list is locally-brewed Brakspear, backed by popular internationals and a small selection of cosmopolitan bottles. A typical three-course meal selection could comprise sweet potato and gruyère tartlet with rocket; spinach, feta and cumin spanakopita with baba ganoush; and lemon and thyme pannacotta with red wine poached pear.

Open all day all wk 7am-11pm (Sun 8am-10pm) **Bar Meals** L served Mon-Sat 12-3, Sun 12-8 D served Mon-Sat 6-10 **Restaurant** L served Mon-Sat 12-3, Sun 12-8 D served Mon-Sat 6-10 ⊕ BRAKSPEAR ◀ Brakspear, Guinness ♂ Symonds. ♥ 12 **Facilities** Non-diners area ❀ (Bar Garden) ♦❢ Children's menu Children's portions Play area Family room Garden ♯ Parking 🚐

The Muddy Duck NEW

PICK OF THE PUBS

Main St OX27 8ES ☎ **01869 278099**
e-mail: dishitup@themuddyduckpub.co.uk
dir: From Bicester towards Buckingham on A4421 left signed Fringford. Through Fringford, right signed Hethe, left signed Hethe

Rural pub and restaurant where quality matters

The Harris family say they are "shamelessly two-faced" about how they have created contrasting areas in their old, stone-built village pub. First, there's the refurbished pub itself, somewhere to enjoy a pint by the fire and have a snack or an uncomplicated meal, like ale-battered fish and chips; then, for the full dining experience is the Malthouse restaurant in a renovated, tin-roofed barn. Between the two is an open kitchen, the source of freshly prepared, simply worded dishes such as starters of Cornish crab, prawn and avocado, and wild mushroom and leek tart, while mains include steak of the day; Muddy Duck pie; honey- and thyme-roasted duck breast; halibut wrapped in pancetta, and other fish specials. For vegetarians, maybe shallot tarte Tatin. On the heated terrace, which overlooks the beer garden, stands a Tuscan wood-fired oven. The real ales are likely to include Hooky, Tribute and Landlord.

Open all day all wk 11-11 **Bar Meals** L served Mon-Sat 12-3, Sun 12-4 D served Mon-Sat 6-9 **Restaurant** L served Mon-Sat 12-3, Sun 12-4 D served Mon-Sat 6-9 ⊕ FREE HOUSE ◀ Timothy Taylor Landlord, St Austell Tribute, Hook Norton Hooky Bitter ♂ Westons Stowford Press. ♥ 10 **Facilities** Non-diners area ❀ (Bar Garden) ♦❢ Children's menu Children's portions Garden ♯ Parking Wi-fi

---

Rising Sun

Witheridge Hill RG9 5PF ☎ **01491 640856**
e-mail: info@risingsunwitheridgehill.co.uk
dir: From Henley-on-Thames take A4130 towards Wallingford. Take B481, turn right to Highmoor

Intimate, cottagey pub in the Chilterns

Next to the green in a Chilterns' hamlet, you approach this 17th-century pub through the garden. Inside, you'll notice the richly coloured walls, low-beamed ceilings, boarded floors and open fires. Chalkboards tell you which guest ales are accompanying regulars Brakspear's Ordinary and Oxford Gold, and Wyld Wood Organic, the incumbent cider. A tapas menu offers Cajun crayfish, black pudding, battered calamari rings and other appetisers. The three-section restaurant is a cosy place to dine on slow-cooked belly pork with black pudding mash; button mushroom and sweet potato curry; or roast sea bass fillet with rösti. Check dates of outdoor music events.

Open all wk Mon-Fri 12-3 5-11 (Sat 12-11 Sun 12-7) **Bar Meals** L served Mon-Fri 12-2, Sat-Sun 12-3 D served Mon-Sat 6.30-9 Av main course £13 **Restaurant** L served Mon-Fri 12-2, Sat-Sun 12-3 D served Mon-Sat 6.30-9 Av 3 course à la carte fr £25 ⊕ BRAKSPEAR ◀ Ordinary, Oxford Gold ♂ Westons Wyld Wood Organic. ♥ 10 **Facilities** Non-diners area ❀ (Bar Garden) ♦❢ Children's menu Children's portions Family room Garden ♯ Parking Wi-fi 🚐 (notice required)

The Plough Inn

GL7 3HG ☎ **01367 253543**
e-mail: josie.plough@hotmail.co.uk
dir: M4 junct 15, A419 towards Cirencester, then right onto A361 to Lechlade. A417 towards Faringdon, follow signs to Kelmscott

Picturesque village pub and River Thames walks

Dating from 1631, this attractive Cotswold-stone inn stands on the Thames Path a mere 600-yards from the river and midway between Radcot and Lechlade, making it a haven for walkers and boaters — own moorings for customers. It's also just a short walk from Kelmscott Manor, once home to William Morris. Exposed stone walls and flagstone floors set the scene for real ales and an extensive, hearty menu. Dishes range from tiger prawn, mussel and smoked salmon linguine to baked toad-in-the-hole. There's a beer, cider and music festival in August.

Open all day all wk 11.30-11 (Sun 11-11) **Bar Meals** L served all wk 12-3 D served all wk 7-10 Av main course £10.50 **Restaurant** L served all wk 12-3 D served all wk 7-10 Av 3 course à la carte fr £28.50 ⊕ FREE HOUSE ◀ Wye Valley, Hook Norton, Box Steam, Wickwar, Guest ales ♂ Thatchers, Westons Stowford Press. **Facilities** Non-diners area ♦❢ Children's menu Children's portions Garden ♯ Beer festival Cider festival Wi-fi 🚐 (notice required)

KINGHAM · Map 10 SP22

The Kingham Plough ★★★★ INN ◉◉

PICK OF THE PUBS

The Green OX7 6YD ☎ 01608 658327
e-mail: book@thekinghamplough.co.uk
dir: *B4450 from Chipping Norton to Churchill. 2nd right to Kingham, left at T-junct. Pub on right*

Warm and relaxing village pub with an imaginative and award-winning menu

Situated on the village green in a beautiful Cotswold village, this quintessential inn has a relaxing bar where you can enjoy one of the real ales and daily-changing bar snacks like snail and field mushrooms on toast, or Cotswold rarebit on sourdough toast. In the restaurant chef-proprietor Emily Watkins, who worked under Heston Blumenthal at The Fat Duck, changes the short menu daily to accommodate the deliveries from local farms, smallholdings and game estates. Expect innovative two AA-Rosette dishes like Cornish mackerel burger with beetroot muffin and beetroot and blood orange chutney; followed by pigeon breasts with roasted root vegetables and black cabbage; skirt steak with bone marrow butter and onion rings. For dessert have a spoon ready for clementine meringue pie or rice pudding 'doughnut' with plum jam and ice cream; or go for an exemplary local cheeseboard. Look out for events such as the annual farmers' market, cider festival, quiz nights and food tasting evenings.

Open all day all wk Closed: 25 Dec **Bar Meals** L served Mon-Sat 12-9, Sun 12-8 D served Mon-Sat 12-9, Sun 12-8 Av main course £10 food served all day **Restaurant** L served Mon-Sat 12-2, Sun 12-3 D served Mon-Sat 6.30-9 Av 3 course à la carte fr £40 ⊕ FREE HOUSE ◀ Wye Valley HPA, Purity Mad Goose, Cotswold Wheat Beer, Hook Norton Ŏ Ashton Press.
Facilities Non-diners area ❧ (Bar Garden) ♦ Children's menu Children's portions Garden ⚲ Parking Wi-fi **Rooms** 7

LANGFORD · Map 5 SP20

The Bell at Langford

GL7 3LF ☎ 01367 860249
dir: *From Swindon take A361 towards Lechlade & Burford. Through Lechlade, at rdbt right onto B4477 signed Carterton. Turn right for Langford*

Cotswold idyll with fine fishy menu

A long, rambling cottagey pub in a village of gorgeous honeyed Cotswold-stone houses and leafy byways, The Bell punches well above its weight on both character and food scales. Beams, inglenook, dressed stone and colourwash above flagstoned floors, with an eclectic mix of furnishings in both the bar and restaurant make this a firm favourite with repeat visitors who appreciate the rich menus here. Search out the fried breast of pigeon with sautéed gnocchi starter; prelude to mains with a distinct seafood bent, including fillet of hake with Mediterranean sausage cassoulet, or perhaps local Kelmscott pork and

herb sausages. Hook Norton beers are locally brewed favourites.

Open 12-3 7-11 (Fri 12-3 7-12 Sat 12-3 7-11.30) Closed: Sun eve & Mon **Bar Meals** L served Tue-Sun 12-1.45 D served Tue-Sat 7-9 **Restaurant** L served Tue-Sun 12-1.45 D served Tue-Sat 7-9 ⊕ FREE HOUSE ◀ Sharp's Doom Bar, St Austell Tribute, Hook Norton Ŏ Aspall, Thatchers Gold. ♥ 12 **Facilities** Non-diners area ❧ (Bar Restaurant Garden) ♦ Children's menu Children's portions Play area Garden ⚲ Parking ➠ (notice required)

LOWER SHIPLAKE · Map 5 SU77

The Baskerville ★★★★ INN

PICK OF THE PUBS

Station Rd RG9 3NY ☎ 0118 940 3332
e-mail: enquiries@thebaskerville.com
dir: *Just off A4155, 1.5m from Henley towards Reading, follow signs at War Memorial junct*

Variety and a relaxed atmosphere are key here

On the popular Thames Path is this modern-rustic pub of real quality. Walkers remove their muddy boots at the door before heading to the bar that's adorned with sporting memorabilia, and where pints of Loddon Hoppit, brewed two miles away, await. There is plenty of choice food-wise; whether it's the bar menu or the à la carte, the objective is to serve great food at reasonable prices in an unpretentious atmosphere. Modern British describes the kitchen's approach, with continental and Eastern influences evident in the sustainably sourced ingredients. For lunch, you could go for an open sandwich or savour seafood linguine. Typical evening choices might be rope-grown mussels steamed in a fragrant Thai sauce; and slow-cooked Oxfordshire pork belly. The wine list extends to 50 bins, and owner Allan Hannah betrays his origins with 40 malt whiskies. The pub boasts an attractive garden, where summer Sunday barbecues are a common fixture, plus comfortable accommodation.

Open all day all wk 11-11 (Sun 12-10.30) Closed: 25 Dec, 1 Jan **Bar Meals** L served Mon-Sat 12-6, Sun 12-3.30 D served Mon-Thu 6-9.30, Fri-Sat 6-10 Av main course £16.50 food served all day **Restaurant** L served Mon-Sat 12-6, Sun 12-3.30 D served Mon-Thu 6-9.30, Fri-Sat 6-10 Fixed menu price fr £14.95-£19.95 Av 3 course à la carte fr £25 food served all day ◀ Fuller's London Pride, Loddon Hoppit, Timothy Taylor Landlord, Sharp's Doom Bar Ŏ Thatchers. ♥ 12 **Facilities** Non-diners area ❧ (Bar Garden) ♦ Children's menu Children's portions Play area Garden ⚲ Parking Wi-fi **Rooms** 4

LOWER WOLVERCOTE · Map 5 SP40

The Trout Inn

195 Godstow Rd OX2 8PN ☎ 01865 510930
dir: *From A40 at Wolvercote rdbt (N of Oxford) follow signs for Wolvercote, through village to pub*

Utterly captivating waterside inn

Threaded into the structure of a very old building, The Trout was already ancient when Lewis Carroll, and later CS Lewis took inspiration here; centuries before it had been a hospice for Godstow Nunnery, on the opposite bank of the Thames. It featured in several episodes of *Inspector Morse*, and has long been a favourite with undergraduates. Its leaded windows, great oak beams, flagged floors and glowing fireplaces make it arguably the area's most atmospheric inn. On a summer day bag a table on the terrace by the fast flowing water to enjoy the comprehensive menu that has distinct Mediterranean lineage; there's a wide range of freshly made pastas and pizzas backed up by reliable modern British fare to choose from.

Open all day all wk 9am-close ⊕ FREE HOUSE ◀ Brakspear Oxford Gold & Bitter, Adnams Lighthouse, Sharp's Doom Bar, Guest ales Ŏ Aspall. **Facilities** ♦ Garden Parking

MARSH BALDON · Map 5 SU59

Seven Stars NEW

The Green OX44 9LP ☎ 01865 343337
e-mail: info@sevenstarsonthegreen.co.uk
dir: *From Oxford ring road onto A4074 signed Wallingford. Through Nuneham Courtenay. Left, follow Marsh Baldon signs*

Re-invigorated community-owned pub

Following three periods of closure in the past four years, exasperated Marsh Baldon residents dug deep into their pockets and bought the historic 350-year-old pub on the pretty village green. The doors of the new-look Seven Stars were pushed open in March 2013 to reveal a comfortable spruced up interior, local ales on tap and a modern pub menu offering a good range of dishes prepared from fresh local ingredients. Typical dishes include pea, spinach and mint risotto, sausages and mash, classic Sunday roasts, and specials like fish pie and sticky toffee pudding. For summer, there's a gorgeous garden and an August beer festival, and a new restaurant in a converted barn is due to open in late 2013.

Open all day all wk **Bar Meals** Av main course £8.95-£9.95 food served all day **Restaurant** food served all day ⊕ FREE HOUSE ◀ Fuller's London Pride, Loose Cannon Abingdon Bridge, White Horse Ŏ Aspall.
Facilities Non-diners area ❧ (Bar Restaurant Garden) ♦ Children's menu Children's portions Garden ⚲ Beer festival Parking Wi-fi ➠ (notice required)

Save on hotels. Book at **theAA.com/hotel**

OXFORDSHIRE 353 **ENGLAND**

| MIDDLETON STONEY | Map 11 SP52 |

Best Western The Jersey Arms ★★ HL

OX25 4AD ☎ **01869 343234**
e-mail: jerseyarms@bestwestern.co.uk
dir: *3m from junct 9/10 of M4. 3m from A34 on B430*

British food in a historic property

Until 1951, when a family called Ansell bought it, this 13th-century country inn belonged to the Jersey Estate. In 1985 the Ansells sold it to Donald and Helen Livingston, making them only its third set of owners since 1243. It is just three minutes from Bicester Shopping Village. Food can be taken in the Bar & Grill where the British menu is supplemented by daily specials. Start with salmon and coriander fishcake, then try slow-roasted shoulder of Oxfordshire pork with sage and onion sauce; chargrilled chicken, with onion, tomato and tarragon sauce; or savoury pancake stuffed with spinach and cream cheese.

Open all day all wk **Bar Meals** L served all wk 12-2 D served all wk 6.30-9 **Restaurant** L served all wk 12-2 D served all wk 6.30-9 ⊕ FREE HOUSE ◀ Flowers. ♟ 9 **Facilities** Non-diners area ♦♦ Children's menu Garden ⊼ Parking Wi-fi **Rooms** 20

| MILCOMBE | Map 11 SP43 |

The Horse & Groom Inn NEW

OX15 4RS ☎ **01295 722142**
e-mail: horseandgroominn@gmail.com
dir: *From A361 between Chipping Norton & Bloxham follow Milcombe signs. Pub at end of village*

A refurbished Cotswold pub

There's certainly been some changes at the 17th-century Horse & Groom, since it underwent a major update a couple of years ago, though there's still signs of the traditional elements as in the stone floor, wood-burning stove, snug area, darts and bar billiards for instance. A contemporary dining room seats 50, and the menus are bursting with dishes of local produce. Start of with potted Milcombe pheasant with pickles and toast, followed by a steak from Long Compton, or Mr Beadle's pork and leek sausages, mash, and rich onion gravy. Vegetarians have interesting choices too – cream of artichoke soup; butternut squash risotto, and Greek roasted vegetable casserole perhaps.

Open 12-3 6-11 (Sun 12-5) Closed: 25 Dec eve & 26 Dec, Sun eve **Bar Meals** L served Mon-Sat 12-2.30, Sun 12-4 D served Mon-Sat 6-9 Av main course £10 **Restaurant** L served Mon-Sat 12-2.30, Sun 12-4 D served Mon-Sat 6-9 Av 3 course à la carte fr £20 ⊕ PUNCH TAVERNS ◀ Sharp's Doom Bar, Hook Norton Hooky Bitter, Young's Bitter Ö Westons Stowford Press. ♟ 11 **Facilities** Non-diners area ♣ (Bar Outside area) ♦♦ Children's menu Children's portions Outside area ⊼ Parking Wi-fi ▰▰ (notice required)

| MURCOTT | Map 11 SP51 |

The Nut Tree Inn ◉◉

PICK OF THE PUBS

Main St OX5 2RE ☎ **01865 331253**
dir: *M40 junct 9, A34 towards Oxford. Left onto B4027 signed Islip. At Red Lion turn left. Right signed Murcott, Fencott & Charlton-on-Otmoor. Pub on right in village*

Family-run cracker between Oxford and Bicester

Local man Mike North always dreamt of owning the thatched, 15th-century free house overlooking the pond in Murcott, one of the 'Seven Towns' encircling the semi-wetland of Otmoor. So, in 2006 he and Imogen, now his wife, bought it. Oak beams, wood-burners and unusual carvings are the setting for an impressive portfolio of widely-sourced real ales and award-winning, modern British food. With 'free-range, wild and organic' as guiding principles, the Norths raise rare-breed pigs, and their own and villagers' gardens supply fruit and veg. In the new-look dining room a typical two-AA Rosette meal would be pan-fried Cornish mackerel with bacon and clam chowder; grilled fillet of Charolais beef; then hot prune and Armagnac soufflé. A seven-course tasting menu includes Puy lentil soup; olive oil-poached Scottish halibut; and Yorkshire rhubarb bavarois. Glasses of wine start at under £4, although you can pay three figures for a bottle if you wish.

Open all day Closed: 1wk from 27 Dec, Sun eve & Mon **Bar Meals** L served Tue-Sat 12-2.30, Sun 12-3 D served Tue-Sat 7-9 Av main course £10 **Restaurant** L served Tue-Sat 12-2.30, Sun 12-3 D served Tue-Sat 7-9 Fixed menu price fr £18 Av 3 course à la carte fr £38 ⊕ FREE HOUSE ◀ Vale Best Bitter, Fuller's London Pride, Brains The Rev. James, Shepherd Neame Spitfire, Oxfordshire Ales Pride of Oxford. ♟ 17 **Facilities** Non-diners area ♦♦ Children's portions Garden ⊼ Parking ▰▰ (notice required)

| NORTH HINKSEY VILLAGE | Map 5 SP40 |

The Fishes

OX2 0NA ☎ **01865 249796**
e-mail: fishes@peachpubs.com
dir: *From A34 S'bound (dual carriageway) left at junct after Botley Interchange, signed North Hinksey & Oxford Rugby Club. From A34 N'bound exit at Botley Interchange & return to A34 S'bound, then follow as above*

Victorian pub with a tranquil garden

A short walk from the centre of Oxford, this attractive tile-hung pub sits in three acres of wooded grounds running down to a stream. Delightfully tranquil and with lots of shade, this is an ideal place for a picnic (complete with rug and Pimm's) ordered at the bar or one of their regular barbecues. There is also a generously proportioned decking area and a lovely playground for the children. Real ales can be enjoyed in the cosy snug, which is often used for book clubs and dance classes, but you may well be tempted to eat the modern British food in the conservatory. Choices include free-range Cotswold chicken with potato rösti, wilted spinach and morel cream.

Open all day all wk Closed: 25 Dec **Bar Meals** L served all wk 12-6 D served all wk 6-10 Av main course £15 food served all day **Restaurant** L served all wk 12-6 D served all wk 6-10 Fixed menu price fr £12 Av 3 course à la carte fr £25 food served all day ⊕ PEACH PUBS ◀ Greene King IPA, Morland Old Speckled Hen, Guest ales Ö Aspall. ♟ 16 **Facilities** Non-diners area ♣ (Bar Garden) ♦♦ Children's portions Garden ⊼ Parking Wi-fi ▰▰ (notice required)

| NORTHMOOR | Map 5 SP40 |

The Red Lion NEW

OX29 5SX ☎ **01865 300301**
e-mail: redlion-northmoor@yahoo.co.uk
dir: *A420 from Oxford. At 2nd rdbt take 3rd exit onto A415. Left after lights into Moreton Ln. At end turn right, Pub on right*

A pretty pub offering a warm and friendly welcome

A pretty 17th-century pub with a large garden set on the skew in the middle of the village. Experts have deduced from the positioning of its wooden beams and open fireplaces that it was originally two cottages. Greene King owns it, so expect a guest ale alongside their usual range. Baguettes, ploughman's and filled jacket potatoes are served at lunchtime, while the main menu may start with bubble-and-squeak, free-range egg and bacon; and crab fishcakes with Thai sweet chilli sauce, before offering home-made pie; battered haddock and chips; and four-bean chilli with rice. Live music is often featured.

Open all wk 12-3 6-11 (Sat all day Sun 12-6) **Bar Meals** L served Mon-Sat 12-2.30, Sun 12-3.30 D served Mon-Sat 6-9 ⊕ GREENE KING ◀ Morland, IPA, 1 Guest ale Ö Symonds Scrumpy Jack. **Facilities** Non-diners area ♣ (Bar Garden Outside area) ♦♦ Children's menu Children's portions Garden Outside area ⊼ Beer festival Parking Wi-fi ▰▰ (notice required)

PICK OF THE PUBS

The Crown Inn

PISHILL   Map 5 SU78

RG9 6HH ☎ **01491 638364**
e-mail:
enquiries@thecrowninnpishill.co.uk
web: www.thecrowninnpishill.co.uk
dir: *A4130 from Henley-on-Thames,
right onto B480 to Pishill*

Coaching inn with thatched barn

A pretty 15th-century brick and flint
former coaching inn, The Crown has had
a colourful history. The building began
life in medieval times, serving ale to the
thriving monastic community, then
providing refuge to Catholic priests
escaping Henry VIII's tyrannical rule. It
contains possibly the country's largest
priest hole, in which one Father
Dominique met his end, and whose
ghost is occasionally seen around the
premises. Before going any further, how
should Pishill be pronounced? Old maps
show a second 's' in the name,
supporting the theory that farm-waggon
drivers used to stop at the inn having
made the long climb out of Henley-on-
Thames, and while the men topped
themselves up in the bar, the horses
would relieve themselves. Fast-forward
to the Swinging 60s, and the
neighbouring thatched barn housed a
nightclub hosting George Harrison,
Dusty Springfield and other big names
from the world of pop. Nowadays, the
barn is licensed for civil ceremonies, as
well as serving as a function room. In

the pub itself, the bar is supplied by
mostly local breweries, typically
Brakspear, Loddon, Rebellion, Vale and
West Berkshire. The menu always
includes sandwiches and ploughman's
at lunchtimes, and features fresh local
produce cooked to order. Lunch and
dinner are served every day and may be
enjoyed inside, where there are three log
fires, or in the picturesque garden
overlooking the valley. Depending on the
season, you might find lamb and kidney
hotpot with cauliflower cheese gratin;
fish brandade with vegetable and
chestnut crumble, and pink peppercorn
and dill hollandaise sauce; and red
onion, pine nut and blue cheese parcel
with roasted new potatoes, poached
pear and rocket salad. In late
September, there's a beer festival.

Open all wk 12-3 6-11 (Sun 12-10)
Closed: 25-26 Dec **Bar Meals** L served
all wk 12-2.30 D served all wk
6.30-9.30 Av main course £11
Restaurant L served all wk 12-2.30 D
served all wk 6.30-9.30 ⊞ FREE HOUSE
◀ Brakspear, West Berkshire, Loddon,
Rebellion **Facilities** Non-diners area 🐾
(Bar Garden) ♦♦ Children's portions
Garden ⋒ Beer festival Parking Wi-fi
🚌 (notice required)

Save on hotels. Book at theAA.com/hotel

OXFORDSHIRE 355 ENGLAND

OXFORD
Map 5 SP50

The Magdalen Arms

243 Iffley Rd OX4 1SJ ☎ 01865 243159
e-mail: info@magdalenarms.co.uk
dir: On corner of Iffley Rd & Magdalen Rd

Busy food pub with a boho vibe

Just a short stroll from Oxford city centre, this bustling food pub is run by the same team as Waterloo's hugely influential Anchor & Hope gastro-boozer. There is a similar boho feel to the place with its dark red walls and vintage furniture and the nose-to-tail menu will be familiar to anybody who knows the pub's London sibling. Expect the likes of rabbit and pork rillettes with cornichons and sourdough toast; pappardelle and huntsman's sauce; and warm treacle tart and cream. Real ales are complemented by a vibrant modern wine list.

Open 11-11 (Mon 5-11 Sun 12-10.30) Closed: BHs, 24-26 Dec, Mon L **Bar Meals** L served Tue-Sat 12-2.30, Sun 12-3 D served Mon-Sat 6-10, Sun 6-9.30 Av main course £12.80 **Restaurant** L served Tue-Sat 12-2.30, Sun 12-3 D served Mon-Sat 6-10, Sun 6-9.30 Av 3 course à la carte fr £24.50 ⊕ STAR PUBS & BARS ◀ Caledonian Deuchars IPA, Ringwood Fortyniner, Theakston Best Bitter Ó Symonds. ♀ 16 **Facilities** Non-diners area ♥ (Bar Garden) ♦♦ Children's portions Garden ♠ Beer festival Wi-fi ◼ (notice required)

The Oxford Retreat

1-2 Hythe Bridge St OX1 2EW ☎ 01865 250309
e-mail: info@theoxfordretreat.com
dir: In city centre. 200mtrs from rail station towards centre

Perched on the river close to the city centre

Smack beside the River Isis, the decked, tree-shaded waterside garden at this imposing gabled pub is the place to be seen and is best enjoyed after a day exploring the city of dreaming spires. Arrive early and relax sipping cocktails or a pint of London Pride, then order from the eclectic pub menu, tucking into potted pork with spicy chutney; a ham hock sharing plate served with home-made breads; a pepperoni pizza; or sirloin steak with dauphinoise potatoes and red wine jus. In winter retreat inside and cosy up around the log fire.

Open all wk 4-close (Fri & Sun noon-close Sat noon-3am) Closed: 25-26 Dec & 1 Jan ⊕ FREE HOUSE ◀ Fuller's London Pride, Guinness, Staropramen Ó Westons Wyld Wood Organic. **Facilities** ♦♦ Children's portions Garden Wi-fi

The Punter NEW

7 South St, Osney Island OX2 0BE ☎ 01865 248832
e-mail: info@thepunteroxford.co.uk
dir: Telephone for directions

Quirky Thames-side treasure

Feeling famished on your tour of the Dreaming Spires, then seek out this rustic-cool pub on Osney Island in the heart of the city – it enjoys a magnificent and very tranquil spot beside the River Thames. The decor is eclectic and interesting, with much to catch the eye, from rugs on flagstone floors and mismatched tables and chair to bold artwork on whitewashed walls. Come for a relaxing pint of Punter Ale by the river or refuel on something tempting from the daily menu – rabbit rillettes with spicy beetroot chutney, fish curry, venison steak with dauphinoise and braised red cabbage, or pork and leek sausages with mash and gravy.

Open all day all wk **Bar Meals** L served Mon-Fri 12-3, wknds all day D served Mon-Fri 6-10, wknds all day **Restaurant** L served Mon-Fri 12-3, wknds all day D served Mon-Fri 6-10, wknds all day ◀ The Punter Ale Ó Addlestones. ♀ 12 **Facilities** Non-diners area ♦♦ Children's portions Garden ♠ Wi-fi

Turf Tavern

4 Bath Place, off Holywell St OX1 3SU ☎ 01865 243235
e-mail: 8004@greeneking.co.uk
dir: Telephone for directions

The hidden haunt of dons and students over many centuries

A jewel of a pub, and consequently one of Oxford's most popular, although it's not easy to find, as it is approached through hidden alleyways, which, if anything, adds to its allure. Previously called the Spotted Cow, it became the Turf in 1842, probably in deference to its gambling clientele; it has also had brushes with literature, film and politics. The Turf Tavern is certainly one of the city's oldest pubs, with some 13th-century foundations and a 17th-century low-beamed front bar. Three beer gardens help ease overcrowding, but the 11 real ales and reasonably priced pub grub keep the students, locals and visitors flowing in.

Open all day all wk 11-11 Closed: 25 Dec **Bar Meals** L served all wk 11-9 D served all wk 11-9 food served all day ⊕ GREENE KING ◀ Guest ales Ó Westons Old Rosie. **Facilities** ♥ (Bar Garden) ♦♦ Garden ♠ Wi-fi ◼

PISHILL
Map 5 SU78

The Crown Inn
PICK OF THE PUBS

See Pick of the Pubs on opposite page

RAMSDEN
Map 11 SP31

The Royal Oak
PICK OF THE PUBS

See Pick of the Pubs on page 356

ROTHERFIELD PEPPARD
Map 5 SU78

The Unicorn

Colmore Ln, Kingwood RG9 5LX ☎ 01491 628674
e-mail: enquiries@unicornkingwood.co.uk
dir: Exit A4074 (Reading to Wallingford), follow Sonning Common & Peppard signs. Left in Peppard Common signed Stoke Row. Right into Colmore Ln at Unicorn sign

Popular, smart village pub

A village local set in the Chilterns, The Unicorn is five miles from Henley-on-Thames and Reading. Petitioning villagers saved the pub from closure and change of use. Now, with children and dogs welcome, expect to have to fight your way in on a Friday or Saturday evening, or during the beer festival, such is The Unicorn's reputation as a friendly drinking pub. It's also becoming known as a food destination, serving light lunches such as ploughman's or classic Welsh rarebit with salad and fries; and dinner highlights such as crab and sweetcorn risotto followed by luxury fish pie.

Open all wk 11-3 5.30-11 (Fri-Sat 11am-mdnt Sun 12-10) ⊕ BRAKSPEAR ◀ Bitter & Oxford Gold, Marston's Pedigree, Hook Norton Ó Westons Wyld Wood Organic, Symonds. **Facilities** ♥ (Bar Restaurant Garden) ♦♦ Children's portions Garden Parking Wi-fi

SHILTON
Map 5 SP20

Rose & Crown

OX18 4AB ☎ 01993 842280
dir: From A40 at Burford take A361 towards Lechlade on Thames. Right, follow Shilton signs on left. Or from A40 E of Burford take B4020 towards Carterton

Well-supported village local

A traditional Cotswold-stone inn dating back to the 17th century, whose two rooms retain their original beams and are warmed by a winter log fire. In the bar, two of Hook Norton's real ales are partnered by Young's Bitter and Ashton Press cider. As their pedigrees might lead you to expect, chef-landlord Martin Coldicott, who trained at London's Connaught Hotel, and head chef Jamie Webber, from The Ivy, prepare above average, but simply presented food, typically smoked haddock, salmon and prawn pie; venison with celeriac purée; and baked aubergine parmigiana with mozzarella. You may eat and drink in the garden if you prefer.

Open all wk 11.30-3 6-11 (Fri-Sun & BH 11.30-11) **Bar Meals** L served Mon-Fri 12-2, Sat-Sun & BH 12-2.45 D served all wk 7-9 Av main course £12.50 **Restaurant** L served Mon-Fri 12-2, Sat-Sun & BH 12-2.45 D served all wk 7-9 Av 3 course à la carte fr £25 ⊕ FREE HOUSE ◀ Hook Norton Old Hooky, Young's Bitter Ó Ashton Press. ♀ 10 **Facilities** Non-diners area ♥ (Bar Garden) ♦♦ Garden ♠ Parking

PICK OF THE PUBS

The Royal Oak

RAMSDEN Map 11 SP31

High St OX7 3AU ☎ 01993 868213
e-mail: jonoldham57@gmail.com
web: www.royaloakramsden.com
dir: *B4022 from Witney towards
Charlbury, right before Hailey, through
Poffley End*

Award-winning pub near many lovely walks

Built of Cotswold stone and facing Ramsden's fine parish church, this former 17th-century coaching inn is a popular refuelling stop for walkers exploring nearby Wychwood Forest and visitors touring the pretty villages and visiting Blenheim Palace. Whether you are walking or not, the cosy inn oozes traditional charm and character, with its old beams, warm fires and stone walls, and long-serving landlords John and Jo Oldham provide a very warm welcome. A free house, it dispenses beers sourced from local breweries, such as Hook Norton Hooky Bitter and Old Hooky, alongside Adnams Broadside and Young's Special. Somerset's Original Cider Company supplies the bar with Pheasant Plucker cider, alongside Westons Old Rosie from Herefordshire. With a strong kitchen team, the main menu, built on the very best of fresh local and seasonal ingredients, regularly features a pie of the week topped with puff pastry or the popular suet pudding; there are other pub

favourites such as oven-baked baby brie with tomato and herb crust; moules marinière; haunch of local venison steak, mash and piquant orange sauce; and pan-fried English calves' liver. Among the daily specials you may find roast local partridge, Armagnac sauce, caramelised apple and game chips; or chilli con carne. For a lighter bite try the devilled lamb's kidneys or the Kelmscott bacon salad. Carefully selected by the owner, the wine list has over 200 wines, specialising in those from Bordeaux and Languedoc, with 30 of them served by the glass. Every Thursday evening there is a special offer of steak, with a glass of wine and dessert included.

Open all wk 11.30-3 6.30-11 (Sun 11.30-3 7-10.30) Closed: 25 Dec

Bar Meals L served all wk 12-2 D served Mon-Sat 7-9.45, Sun 7-9 **Restaurant** L served all wk 12-2 D served Mon-Sat 7-9.45, Sun 7-9 ⊕ FREE HOUSE ◀ Hook Norton Old Hooky & Hooky Bitter, Adnams Broadside, Young's Special, Wye Valley ᘒ Westons Old Rosie, Pheasant Plucker. ♟ 30 **Facilities** Non-diners area ☙ (Bar Garden) ♦♦ Children's portions Garden Parking

SHIPTON-UNDER-WYCHWOOD   Map 10 SP21

The Shaven Crown Hotel

High St OX7 6BA ☎ 01993 830500
e-mail: relax@theshavencrown.co.uk
dir: *On A361, halfway between Burford & Chipping Norton*

Historic inn overlooking the picturesque village green and church

This 14th-century coaching inn was built by the monks of Bruern Abbey as a hospice for the poor. Following the Dissolution of the Monasteries, Elizabeth I used it as a hunting lodge before giving it to the village in 1580, when it became the Crown Inn. Thus it stayed until 1930, when a brewery with a sense of humour changed the name as homage to the familiar monastic tonsure. Its interior is full of original architectural features, like the Great Hall. Light meals and real ales are served in the bar, while the restaurant offers Cotswold ham, beef, lamb and venison pie; beer-battered fish and chips; and winter vegetable and bean hotpot.

Open all wk 11-3 5-11 (Sat-Sun 11-11) **Bar Meals** L served Mon-Fri 12-2, Sat 12-9.30, Sun 12-9 D served Mon-Fri 6-9.30, Sat 12-9.30, Sun 12-9 **Restaurant** L served Mon-Fri 12-2, Sat 12-9.30, Sun 12-9 D served Mon-Fri 6-9.30, Sat 12-9.30, Sun 12-9 ⊕ FREE HOUSE ◀ Hook Norton, Wye Valley, Goffs, Cottage ♻ Westons Stowford Press. ♟ 10 **Facilities** Non-diners area ❤ (Bar Garden) ♦ Children's menu Children's portions Garden ♬ Parking Wi-fi ⇔ (notice required)

STANDLAKE   Map 5 SP30

The Bell Inn NEW

21 High St OX29 7RH ☎ 01865 300784
e-mail: info@thebellstandlake.co.uk
dir: *From A415 in Standlake into High St, pub 500yds on right*

Thriving village pub close to the Thames

Experienced landlord Craig Foster, who owns the Boot in Barnard Gate took on the Bell, which stands tucked away in a sleepy village close to the River Thames, and hasn't looked back. Refurbished in a comfortably rustic style, it draws drinkers and diners in for its relaxed atmosphere, four real ales on tap, and the short imaginative lunch and dinner menus. Typically, tuck into mussels steamed with white wine, shallots and cream; braised blade of beef ; and chicken, leek and mushroom pie, with decent sandwiches (rare roast beef and mustard) on offer at lunchtimes. Ale buffs should take note of the August beer festival.

Open all day all wk **Bar Meals** food served all day **Restaurant** food served all day ⊕ FREE HOUSE ◀ Woodforde's Wherry, Skinner's Betty Stogs, Prescott Track Record ♻ Thatchers Gold. ♟ 8 **Facilities** Non-diners area ❤ (Bar Restaurant Garden) ♦ Children's menu Children's portions Family room Garden ♬ Beer festival Parking Wi-fi ⇔ (notice required)

STEEPLE ASTON   Map 11 SP42

The Red Lion

South Side OX25 4RY ☎ 01869 340225
e-mail: redlionsa@aol.com
dir: *0.5m off A4260 (Oxford Rd). Follow brown tourist signs for pub*

Lovely garden with valley views

Situated high in the beautiful north Oxfordshire village of Steeple Aston and close to Blenheim Palace and Banbury Cross, this unspoilt 18th-century pub is a popular place for thirsty walkers. From its pretty floral suntrap terrace, enjoy a pint of local Hook Norton beer as you enjoy the majestic view of the Cherwell Valley. The conservatory-style oak dining room offers dishes ranging from a range of thin-crust stone-baked pizzas to traditional favourites such as smoked salmon and pea risotto followed by gammon ham with fried free-range eggs and chips or chicken curry with rice and mango chutney.

Open all wk 12-3 5.30-11 (Sat 12-11 Sun 12-5) (Jun-Oct all day) Closed: Sun eve from 5pm **Bar Meals** L served all wk 12-2.30 D served Mon-Sat 6-9 **Restaurant** L served all wk 12-2.30 D served Mon-Sat 6-9 ⊕ HOOK NORTON ◀ Hooky Bitter, Lion & Mild ♻ Westons Stowford Press. ♟ 11 **Facilities** Non-diners area ❤ (Bar) ♦ Children's portions Outside area ♬ Parking Wi-fi ⇔ (notice required)

STOKE ROW   Map 5 SU68

Crooked Billet

PICK OF THE PUBS

RG9 5PU ☎ 01491 681048
dir: *From Henley towards Oxford on A4130. Left at Nettlebed for Stoke Row*

17th-century pub with plenty of character and an excellent menu

Built in 1642, the Crooked Billet was once the hideout of notorious highwayman Dick Turpin. Tucked away down a single track lane in deepest Oxfordshire, this charmingly rustic pub is now a popular hideaway for the well-heeled

and the well known. Many of its finest features are unchanged, including the low beams, tiled floors and open fires that are so integral to its character. Local produce and organic fare are the mainstays of the kitchen, to the extent that the chef-proprietor will even exchange a lunch or dinner for the locals' excess vegetables. Menu offerings include starters like seared mackerel with shredded cucumber pickle and chilli saffron salsa; or spinach and ricotta gnocchi. To follow, there's a good range of mains, including John Dory with seared diver scallops; pink carved venison with haggis, baby spinach and roast figs; or slow-roast honey and soy pork belly with steamed bok choi and sweet potato confit. Leave space for steamed syrup sponge or marmalade bakewell tart. The pub hosts music nights, wine tastings and other events.

Open all wk 12-3 7-12 (Sat-Sun 12-12) Closed: 25 Dec **Bar Meals** L served Mon-Fri 12-2.30, Sat 12-10.30, Sun 12-10 D served Mon-Fri 7-10, Sat 12-10.30, Sun 12-10 **Restaurant** L served Mon-Fri 12-2.30, Sat 12-10.30, Sun 12-10 D served Mon-Fri 7-10, Sat 12-10.30, Sun 12-10 ⊕ BRAKSPEAR ◀ Organic Best Bitter. ♟ 10 **Facilities** Non-diners area ♦ Children's portions Garden ♬ Parking

SWERFORD   Map 11 SP33

The Mason's Arms

Banbury Rd OX7 4AP ☎ 01608 683212
e-mail: admin@masons-arms.com
dir: *Between Banbury & Chipping Norton on A361*

Large beer garden ideal for families

Jamie Bailey and Louise Robertson arrived here in 2012 after running pubs in Shropshire. A 300-year-old, stone-built former Masonic lodge, this pub in the Cotswolds has retained its traditional, informal feel. Jamie's modern European cooking concentrates on local produce where possible and there is an emphasis on fish on the specials board, which might offer pan-fried tiger prawns with chilli and chorizo followed by pan-fried red mullet on crab meat and samphire linguine. Non-fish options include coq au vin or venison Wellington. The large garden has stunning views of the surrounding area.

Open all wk 10-3 6-11 (Sun 12-dusk) **Bar Meals** L served Mon-Sat 12-2.30, Sun 12-dusk D served Mon-Sat 7-9, Sun 12-dusk **Restaurant** L served Mon-Sat 12-2.30, Sun 12-dusk D served Mon-Sat 7-9, Sun 12-dusk ⊕ FREE HOUSE ◀ Wychwood Hobgoblin, Brakspear. ♟ 20 **Facilities** Non-diners area ❤ (Bar Garden) ♦ Children's menu Children's portions Garden ♬ Parking Wi-fi ⇔

SWINBROOK · Map 5 SP21

The Swan Inn ★★★★ INN ◉◉

PICK OF THE PUBS

OX18 4DY ☎ 01993 823339
e-mail: info@theswanswinbrook.co.uk
dir: *A40 towards Cheltenham, left towards Swinbrook, pub 1m before Burford*

Tranquility and class at Cotswold boutique inn

Hidden in the Windrush Valley you will find the idyllic village of Swinbrook where time stands still. Owners Archie and Nicola Orr-Ewing took on the lease of this dreamy, wisteria-clad stone pub from the Dowager Duchess of Devonshire, the last surviving Mitford sister, in 2007. The Swan is the perfect English country pub – it stands by the River Windrush near the village cricket pitch, overlooking unspoilt Cotswold countryside. It gets even better inside: the two cottage-style front rooms, replete with worn flagstones, crackling log fires, low beams and country furnishings, lead through to a cracking bar and classy conservatory extension. First-class pub food ranges from simple bar snacks to more substantial main courses of guinea fowl, apricot and chickpea tagine; and Cornish hake with a casserole of butter beans, tomato and chorizo. You won't want to leave, so book one of the stunning en suite rooms in the restored barn.

Open all wk (Closed afternoons Nov-Feb) Closed: 25 Dec **Bar Meals** L served Mon-Fri 12-2, Sat-Sun 12-2.30 D served Mon-Thu & Sun 7-9, Fri-Sat 7-9.30 **Restaurant** L served Mon-Fri 12-2, Sat-Sun 12-2.30 D served Mon-Thu & Sun 7-9, Fri-Sat 7-9.30 ⊕ FREE HOUSE ◖ Hook Norton, Guest ales ♉ Aspall, Westons Wyld Wood Organic & Stowford Press. ▾ 9 **Facilities** Non-diners area ♦↑ Children's menu Children's portions Garden ⌁ Parking Wi-fi **Rooms** 6

SYDENHAM · Map 5 SP70

The Crown Inn

PICK OF THE PUBS

Sydenham Rd OX39 4NB ☎ 01844 351634
dir: *M40 junct 6, B4009 towards Chinnor. Left onto A40. At Postcombe right to Sydenham*

Delightful village inn very much part of the community

In a small village below the scarp slopes of the Chilterns, this pretty 16th-century inn shows how careful refurbishment can successfully incorporate both traditional and modern styles. Old photographs, for example, hang contentedly alongside contemporary paintings. The menu is short – barely a dozen items are featured – but expect good things of those that are, such

as main courses of slow-roasted Moroccan spiced lamb shank pie with baked potato mash; seafood and chorizo risotto; and pan-fried pork escalope with avocado, mature cheddar and cream. Desserts include chocolate fondant and apple and almond tart. In the bar, a pint of Brakspear would go well with a ploughman's, omelette, baguette or pizza. The pub also hosts quizzes and live music.

Open 12-3 5.30-11 (Sat 12-11 Sun 12-3) Closed: Sun eve, Mon **Bar Meals** L served Tue-Sun 12-2.30 D served Tue-Sat 7-9.30 **Restaurant** L served Tue-Sun 12-2.30 D served Tue-Sat 7-9.30 ⊕ FREE HOUSE/THE SYDENHAM PUB CO ◖ Fuller's London Pride, Brakspear, Guinness, Guest ale ♉ Westons Stowford Press, Thatchers Gold. **Facilities** Non-diners area ♠ (Bar Restaurant Garden) ♦↑ Children's portions Garden ⌁ ⇛

TETSWORTH · Map 5 SP60

The Old Red Lion

40 High St OX9 7AS ☎ 01844 281274
e-mail: info@theoldredliontetsworth.co.uk
dir: *From Oxford ring road at Headington take A40. Follow A418 signs (over M40). Right onto A40 signed Milton Common & Tetsworth*

Village pub ideal for early birds

An airy, contemporary pub with traditional flourishes, ideal for trippers heading for the nearby Chilterns. Open for breakfast from 7am, birdwatchers pursuing red kites can stop by before hitting the hills, whilst cricketers inspecting the wicket on the adjacent village green pitch can take a leisurely mid-morning full-English. Not content with two restaurant areas and a bustling bar to run, the owners also host a village shop here. Beers from local microbreweries hit the spot, whilst timeless pub grub meals like sausage and mash fill the gap. Summer barbecues and the Sunday carvery are popular. There's a mini beer festival every Easter.

Open all day all wk 7am-10pm (Fri 7am-mdnt, Sat 8.30am-10pm, Sun 8am-4.30pm) **Bar Meals** L served all day open for breakfast Av main course £7 food served all day **Restaurant** L served all day open for breakfast ⊕ FREE HOUSE ◖ Loose Cannon Brewery, White Horse ♉ Thatchers Gold. **Facilities** Non-diners area ♦↑ Children's menu Children's portions Garden Outside area ⌁ Beer festival Parking Wi-fi ⇛

THAME · Map 5 SP70

The James Figg

21 Cornmarket OX9 2BL ☎ 01844 260166
e-mail: thejamesfigg@peachpubs.com
dir: *In town centre*

Buzzing market place pub with secret garden

An attractive 18th-century pub whose name celebrates England's first undisputed champion boxer who lived here 300 years ago. A traditional interior with dark wood floors, Ercol Windsor chairs, a double-sided open fire and a curving bar stocking ales such as Mad Goose and Vale Best Bitter. A list of snacks offers Scotch eggs, pork pies and breaded camember, while light options include sandwiches and a hot roast bap. If you're seeking something more substantial, look to a range of burgers, pizzas and classics such as honey-roasted ham, egg and chips. Beyond The Stables function room, you'll find a private garden.

Open all day all wk 11am-mdnt Closed: 25 Dec **Bar Meals** L served all wk 12-8.30, Sun 12-6 Av main course £8 food served all day **Restaurant** food served all day ⊕ FREE HOUSE/PEACH PUBS ◖ Vale Best Bitter, Purity Mad Goose, Sharp's Doom Bar ♉ Aspall. ▾ 10 **Facilities** Non-diners area ♠ (Bar Restaurant Garden) ♦↑ Children's portions Garden ⌁ Parking Wi-fi

The Thatch

29-30 Lower High St OX9 2AA ☎ 01844 214340
e-mail: thatch@peachpubs.com
dir: *In town centre*

Half-timbered pub with a sunny courtyard garden

In the heart of Thame's high street, the striking Thatch (thatched, of course) was originally a row of 16th-century cottages. It remains a cosy warren of rooms with inglenook fireplaces and antique furniture. If you make it past the bar without being tempted by coffee, cakes or a pint of Doom Bar, you'll find yourself in the restaurant overlooking the garden. The kitchen focuses on the best seasonal and responsibly sourced ingredients – a cold cuts deli board to share might be followed by a pumpkin, thyme and Stilton tart; twice-baked pork belly; or herb-crusted loin of venison. There is a beer festival during National Cask Ale Week.

Open all day all wk Closed: 25 Dec **Bar Meals** L served all wk 12-10 D served all wk 12-10 Av main course £14.35 food served all day **Restaurant** L served all wk 12-2.45 D served all wk 6-10 Av 3 course à la carte fr £25 ⊕ PEACH PUBS ◖ Vale Wychert, Sharp's Doom Bar, Hooky ♉ Aspall. ▾ 16 **Facilities** Non-diners area ♠ (Bar Garden) ♦↑ Children's portions Garden ⌁ Beer festival Parking Wi-fi ⇛ (notice required)

TOOT BALDON   Map 5 SP50

The Mole Inn ☺☺

PICK OF THE PUBS

OX44 9NG ☎ 01865 340001
e-mail: info@themoleinn.com
dir: *5m SE from Oxford city centre off B480*

A foodie destination with great service

The 300-year-old, Grade II listed Mole Inn has put the amusingly named village of Toot Baldon on the map with the exciting, two AA-Rosette-awarded culinary output of chef and host Gary Witchalls. His dedication in the kitchen is matched by the front-of-house professionalism of his wife, Jenny. Drinks are also a strength: try a pint of Hook Norton, Shepherd Neame Spitfire or The Mole's Pleasure - an ale developed together with Moodley's microbrewery, which is particularly suited to the pub's dry-aged steaks from Aberdeenshire. Pick from rib-eye, rump, sirloin or fillet steaks and then choose your sauce. Other options could include lightly curried risotto of natural smoked haddock with a poached egg; roast fillet of cod with celeriac mash, curly kale and warm seafood vinaigrette; and sticky date pudding with toffee sauce and cardamon ice cream. Leather sofas, stripped beams, solid white walls and terracotta floors provide the perfect background for a leisurely meal.

Open all day all wk 12-12 (Sun 12-11) Closed: 25 Dec
Restaurant L served Mon-Sat 12-2.30, Sun 12-4 D served Mon-Sat 7-9.30, Sun 6-9 ⊕ FREE HOUSE ◀ The Mole's Pleasure, Fuller's London Pride, Shepherd Neame Spitfire, Hook Norton, Guinness. ♟ 11 **Facilities** Non-diners area ♦♦ Children's menu Children's portions Garden ⊭ Parking

WEST HANNEY   Map 5 SU49

Plough Inn

Church St OX12 0LN ☎ 01235 868674
e-mail: info@ploughwesthanney.co.uk
dir: *From Wantage take A338 towards Oxford. Inn in 1m*

Friendly village inn

This thatched building dates back to around 1525 when it was built as an estate workers' cottage and became a pub almost 200 years ago. This is a friendly village inn, with log fires, roast chestnuts, mulled wine and Sharp's Doom Bar as the house beer. From the kitchen come home-cooked, seasonal dishes such as warmed Windrush trout pasta salad, as well as daily specials and snacks. Dining outside in the pretty walled garden is an option in summer, and beer festivals take place on May (Oxfordshire ales) and August (champion beers of Britain) Bank Holidays. As we went to press we learnt of a change of ownership.

Open all wk 12-3 6-12 (Sat-Sun all day) **Bar Meals** L served all wk 12-3 D served all wk 6-9 **Restaurant** L served all wk 12-2 D served all wk 6-9 ⊕ FREE HOUSE ◀ West Berkshire, Loddon, Vale, Wychwood, Sharp's Doom Bar ☼ Westons, Thatchers Gold. ♟ 10
Facilities Non-diners area ♣ (Bar Garden) ♦♦ Children's menu Children's portions Play area Garden ⊭ Beer festival Parking Wi-fi ▭

WESTON-ON-THE-GREEN   Map 11 SP51

The Ben Jonson

OX25 3RA ☎ 01869 351153
e-mail: dine@thebenjonsonpub.co.uk
dir: *M40 junct 9, A34 towards Oxford. 1st exit onto B430. At rdbt right into village. Pub on left*

Pretty village pub on a green

Dating from 1742, the pub was named after the English Renaissance dramatist, poet and actor, who reputedly stopped at the pub on his way to visit William Shakespeare in Stratford. There is a separate bar and dining area, as well as a secluded terrace garden and the food is sourced as locally as possible with all real ales from Oxfordshire, as are a number of wines. Simple, seasonal dishes on the daily-changing menu might include baguettes, ploughman's, Oxfordshire cheeses, starters of deep fried whitebait or chicken liver pâté, and mains of slow cooked duck leg or smoked haddock fishcakes.

Open all day all wk 12-11 **Bar Meals** L served all wk 12-9 D served all wk 12-9 food served all day **Restaurant** L served all wk 12-9 D served all wk 12-9 food served all day ⊕ FREE HOUSE ◀ Brakspear, Wychwood Hobgoblin, Hook Norton Old Hooky, White Horse. ♟ 14
Facilities Non-diners area ♦♦ Children's menu Children's portions Garden ⊭ Parking Wi-fi

WHEATLEY   Map 5 SP50

Bat & Ball Inn

28 High St, Cuddesdon OX44 9HJ ☎ 01865 874379
e-mail: info@batball.co.uk
dir: *Through Wheatley towards Garsington, turn left signed Cuddesdon*

Cricket themed village pub

No surprise that the bar here is packed to the gunnels with cricketing memorabilia, but the charm of this former coaching inn extends to beamed ceilings, flagstone floors and solid wood furniture warmed by an open log fire. The house ale 'LBW' is flanked by Marston's beers. A comprehensive seasonal menu, supplemented by daily specials, is likely to include the Bat burger, home made from steak and with a choice of toppings; and slow-braised shoulder of lamb. Look out for clay pigeon shoots, pig roasts, steak nights and sausage and mash evenings. The pub is in an ideal spot for walkers, and dogs are welcome too.

Open all day all wk **Bar Meals** L served Mon-Fri 12-2.30, Sat-Sun all day D served Mon-Fri 6-9.30, Sat-Sun all day **Restaurant** L served Mon-Fri 12-2.30, Sat-Sun all day D served Mon-Fri 6-9.30, Sat-Sun all day ⊕ MARSTON'S ◀ Pedigree, LBW Bitter, Guinness ☼ Thatchers Gold.
Facilities Non-diners area ♣ (Bar Garden) ♦♦ Children's menu Children's portions Garden ⊭ Parking Wi-fi ▭ (notice required)

WITNEY   Map 5 SP31

The Fleece

11 Church Green OX28 4AZ ☎ 01993 892270
e-mail: fleece@peachpubs.com
dir: *In town centre*

Flexible dining in an ex-brewery

Overlooking the village's beautiful church green in the heart of picturesque Witney, this fine Georgian building was once the home of Clinch's brewery. Nowadays, it serves food and drink from lunch through the afternoon to dinner plus well-kept ales are a big draw. Share an inventive deli board or spiced chickpea, red pepper and feta pitta and cumin crème fraîche roll or dig into mains like sea trout fishcake, spinach and chive butter sauce or free-range chicken breast, seasonal greens, cauliflower purée, roasted garlic and basil dressing.

Open all day all wk **Bar Meals** L served all wk 12-6.30 D served all wk 6.30-10 food served all day **Restaurant** L served all wk 12-2.30 D served all wk 6.30-10 food served all day ⊕ PEACH PUBS ◀ Greene King IPA, Morland Old Speckled Hen, Guest ale ☼ Aspall. ♟
Facilities Non-diners area ♣ (Bar) ♦♦ Children's portions ⊭ Parking Wi-fi

---

The Three Horseshoes

78 Corn St OX28 6BS ☎ 01993 703086
e-mail: thehorseshoeswitney@hotmail.co.uk
dir: *From Oxford on A40 towards Cheltenham take 2nd turn to Witney. At rdbt take 5th exit to Witney. Over flyover, through lights. At next rdbt take 5th exit into Corn St. Pub on left*

Friendly and historic town centre pub

Built of Cotswold stone, the historic Grade II listed building sits on Witney's original main street. A traditional family-run pub, it has a charming and stylish interior with stone walls, low ceilings, wood and flagstone floors, and blazing log fires in winter. An impressive selection of ales includes Ringwood Fortyniner and Wychwood Hobgoblin. Dishes range from simple sandwiches and a grill menu through to dishes such as Cornish crab cake with vanilla and lime mayonnaise, followed by Gressingham duck breast with fondant potato.

Open all day all wk 11am-12.30am ⊕ ADMIRAL TAVERNS ◀ Ringwood Fortyniner, Wychwood Hobgoblin, Brakspear Bitter, Hook Norton, White Horse ☼ Thatchers Green Goblin, Westons Stowford Press. **Facilities** ♦♦ Children's portions Garden Wi-fi

PICK OF THE PUBS

The Kings Arms ★★★ HL ✿

19 Market St OX20 1SU
☎ **01993 813636**
e-mail:
stay@kingshotelwoodstock.co.uk
web: www.kingshotelwoodstock.co.uk
dir: *In town centre*

Smart hotel with bags of style

This imposing Georgian free house and
hotel is in the middle of the charming,
historic town of Woodstock, less than
five minutes' walk from Blenheim
Palace, home of the Dukes of
Marlborough and birthplace of Winston
Churchill. The comfortable bar areas
have stripped wooden floors, a log-
burning stove and marble-topped
counters, where a guest real ale
accompanies regulars Brakspear Oxford
Gold, Wychwood Hobgoblin and Hook
Norton Hooky Bitter. The all-day bar
menu lists sandwiches, sharing boards
and cream teas. For rather more stylish
surroundings, go to the Atrium
Restaurant with its black-and-white
tiled flooring and high-backed leather
chairs, where the AA has awarded a
Rosette for the modern and classic
English cuisine. You might begin with
game terrine with pear chutney and
rustic toast; Cornish crab and dill
omelette; or Scottish scallops with
Jerusalem artichokes and hazelnut
dressing. A good choice of main dishes
includes pumpkin and Waterloo cheese

gâteau with a toasted seed salad;
Kelmscott Farm ham with free-range
eggs and chips; braised duck leg with
rich plum sauce, celeriac dauphinoise
and buttered chard; and pork belly with
roast squash, carrot purée and Bramley
apple gravy. And there are enough
desserts to keep anyone happy: treacle
and roast walnut tart with fresh cream;
decadent chocolate quartet (featuring
dark chocolate orange truffle, espresso
brûlée, white chocolate mousse and
dark chocolate cupcake); creamed rice
pudding and plum jam; and a range of
natural ice creams and sorbets. It
makes a good base from which to
explore Oxfordshire and the Cotswolds.

Open all day all wk **Bar Meals** L served
Mon-Fri 12-2.30, Sat 12-3, Sun all day

D served Mon-Sat 6.30-9, Sun all day
Restaurant L served Mon-Fri 12-2.30,
Sat 12-3, Sun all day D served Mon-Sat
6.30-9, Sun all day ⊕ FREE HOUSE
🛢 Brakspear Oxford Gold, Wychwood
Hobgoblin, Hook Norton Hooky Bitter,
Guest ales Ŏ Thatchers Green Goblin.
🍷 15 **Facilities** Non-diners area ♦♦
Children's portions 🎋 Wi-fi 🚐 (notice
required) **Rooms** 15

WOODSTOCK   Map 11 SP41

The Kings Arms ★★★ HL ⊛

PICK OF THE PUBS

See Pick of the Pubs on opposite page

WOOLSTONE   Map 5 SU28

The White Horse

SN7 7QL ☎ 01367 820726
e-mail: info@whitehorsewoolstone.co.uk
dir: *Exit A420 at Watchfield onto B4508 towards Longcot signed Woolstone*

Olde-worlde thatched Elizabethan pub

Following an invigorating Ridgeway walk across White Horse Hill, this black-and-white timbered village pub is the perfect rest and refuelling stop. Upholstered stools line the traditional bar, where a fireplace conceals two priest holes, visible to those who don't mind getting their knees dirty. Accompany a pint of Arkell's ale with an open lamb and minted gravy sandwich, or a lunchtime fire-roasted barbecue chilli pot. Evening extras may include confit belly of pork and butternut squash ravioli. The pub has a garden, and children and dogs are welcome throughout.

Open all day all wk 11-11 **Bar Meals** L served all wk 12-2.30 D served Mon-Sat 6-9 Av main course £9.95 **Restaurant** L served all wk 12-2.30 D served all wk 6-9 Av 3 course à la carte fr £26.95 ⊕ ARKELL'S ◀ Moonlight & Wiltshire Gold, Guinness, Arkell's 3B Ö Westons Stowford Press. **Facilities** Non-diners area ♥ (Bar Restaurant Garden) ♦ Children's portions Garden ⊫ Parking Wi-fi ⬛

WYTHAM   Map 5 SP40

White Hart

OX2 8QA ☎ 01865 244372
e-mail: whitehartwytham@wadworth.co.uk
dir: *Just off A34 NW of Oxford*

Smart gastro-pub that's been on TV

In a sleepy hamlet west of Oxford, this Cotswold-stone pub was featured in the *Inspector Morse* TV series. The pub, now is new hands, is more 'smart gastro-pub' than traditional village local, the bold interior blending flagged floors and big stone fireplaces with a contemporary style. You can pop in for a pint but this is predominantly a place to eat, and boasts an extensive wine list. In summer, dine alfresco on the Mediterranean-style terrace.

Open all wk 12-3 6-11 (Sat-Sun 12-11, all day everyday Apr-Oct) **Bar Meals** L served Mon-Fri 12-2.30, Sat 12-9, Sun 12-8 D served Mon-Fri 6-9, Sat 12-9, Sun 12-8 **Restaurant** L served Mon-Fri 12-2.30, Sat 12-9, Sun 12-8 D served Mon-Fri 6-9, Sat 12-9, Sun 12-8 ⊕ WADWORTH ◀ Henry's IPA & 6X, Guest ales Ö Westons Stowford Press. ♟ 15 **Facilities** Non-diners area ♦ Children's menu Garden ⊫ Beer festival Cider festival Parking Wi-fi

RUTLAND

BARROWDEN   Map 11 SK90

Exeter Arms

PICK OF THE PUBS

LE15 8EQ ☎ 01572 747247
e-mail: enquiries@exeterarmsrutland.co.uk
dir: *From A47 turn at landmark windmill, village 0.75m S. 6m E of Uppingham & 17m W of Peterborough*

Cracking country pub boasting a vast garden

In the heart of pretty Barrowden, overlooking the village green, duck pond and open countryside, this 17th-century stone building has seen many roles in its long life, including a smithy, a dairy and a postal collection point. Landlord Martin Allsopp brews ales such as Beech, Bevin, Owngear and Blackadder in the on-site microbrewery, and also offers a range of ten wines by the glass. Expect a traditional feel to the spacious bar and an informal atmosphere for enjoying some good pub food. At lunchtime, tuck into sandwiches or hearty pub classics. The more refined dinner menu could begin with mushroom bruschetta stuffed with red peppers and topped with brie, followed by smoked haddock with soft poached egg and spring onion mash; or chicken breast wrapped in Parma ham with a mushroom sauce. The garden is complete with a pétanque court for lazy summer days, while food is served on the front patio in warm weather.

Open 12-2.30 6-11 Closed: Sun eve, Mon L **Bar Meals** L served Tue-Sat 12-2 Av main course £10.95 **Restaurant** L served Sun 12-2 D served Tue-Sat 6.30-9 ⊕ FREE HOUSE ◀ Exeter Arms Beech, Bevin, Owngear, Hop Gear, Attitude Two, Pilot, Blackadder. ♟ 10 **Facilities** Non-diners area ♥ (Bar Garden) ♦ Garden ⊫ Parking Wi-fi ⬛ (notice required)

BRAUNSTON   Map 11 SK80

The Blue Ball

6 Cedar St LE15 8QS ☎ 01572 722135
dir: *From Oakham N on B640. Left onto Cold Overton Rd, 2nd left onto West Rd, onto Braunston Rd (becomes Oakham Rd). In village 2nd left into Cedar St. Pub on left opposite church*

Charming thatched pub, Rutland's oldest pub

'The warmest welcome at the oldest inn in Rutland county' is the proud claim at the 17th-century Blue Ball, only a few miles from Rutland Water. The pub makes a good stopping-off point for cyclists and walkers. Landlord Dominic Way certainly looks after his Marston's ales, as locals in the beamed and cosy bar will testify. Expect modern British cuisine like chicken and sun-blushed tomato risotto; and chilli- and lemon-marinated cod loin. There is a Sunday set menu and sandwiches at lunchtime (the bread is home baked). A Young Diners menu confirms the pub's family-friendly credentials.

Open 12-3 6-11 (Sat-Sun all day) Closed: 25 Dec, Mon **Bar Meals** L served Tue-Sun 12-1.45 D served Tue-Sun

6.30-9 Av main course £11.95-£16.95 **Restaurant** L served Tue-Sat 12-1.45, Sun 12-3 D served Tue-Sun 6.30-9 Fixed menu price fr £12.95 Av 3 course à la carte fr £23 ⊕ MARSTON'S ◀ EPA & Burton Bitter, Jennings Cumberland Ale Ö Thatchers. ♟ 10 **Facilities** Non-diners area ♦ Children's menu Children's portions Outside area ⊫ Wi-fi

CLIPSHAM   Map 11 SK91

The Olive Branch ★★★★ INN ⊛⊛

PICK OF THE PUBS

Main St LE15 7SH ☎ 01780 410355
e-mail: info@theolivebranchpub.com
dir: *2m from A1 at B664 junct, N of Stamford*

Tranquillity at the fringe of The Wolds

Investigate the bar here both for the tasty beers from the Grainstore brewery in nearby Oakham and the unusual nurdling chair, used in an archaic pub game involving throwing coins into the hole in the seat; just one of a range of eye-catching furniture and artefacts dappling the interior of this one-time terrace of farmworkers' cottages. Olives are a starter dish here, but the name derives from the local squire's peace-offering in opening this inn in 1890 to replace a favourite village pub closed by that same squire. This too closed in 1997, reopening in 1999 and gaining two AA Rosettes recognition for chef and co-owner Sean Hope, whose well-balanced menus are fiercely local in provenance. Enjoy honey roast pork belly, cider fondant and tender stem broccoli or Campanelli pasta with Cropwell Bishop Stilton, pickled walnuts and watercress. In winter indulge in chestnuts roasted in the pub's open fires.

Open all wk 12-3.30 6-11 (Sat 12-11 Sun 12-10.30) Closed: 25 Dec eve **Bar Meals** L served Mon-Fri 12-2, Sat 12-2 & 2.30-5.30, Sun 12-3 D served Mon-Sat 7-9.30, Sun 7-9 Av main course £16.95 **Restaurant** L served Mon-Sat 12-2, Sun 12-3 D served Mon-Sat 7-9.30, Sun 7-9 Fixed menu price fr £19.95 Av 3 course à la carte fr £26.75 ⊕ FREE HOUSE/RUTLAND INN COMPANY LTD ◀ The Grainstore Olive Oil, Timothy Taylor Landlord Ö Sheppy's Dabinett Apple, Oakwood Special & Cider with Honey, Bottle Kicking Scrambler. ♟ 27 **Facilities** Non-diners area ♥ (Bar Garden) ♦ Children's menu Children's portions Garden ⊫ Parking Wi-fi **Rooms** 6

COTTESMORE
Map 11 SK91

The Sun Inn NEW

25 Main St LE15 7DH ☎ 01572 812321
e-mail: suninncottesmore@btconnect.com
dir: Take B668 from Oakham to Cottesmore, or from A1 at
Stretton take B668 to Cottesmore

Good looks inside and out

With its well-trimmed thatched roof, whitewashed walls,
hanging baskets and flagstoned courtyard, the
17th-century Sun is as pretty as the proverbial picture.
The interior lends its weight too, thanks especially to the
beamed ceilings and stone-flagged floors. Despite being
The Who's former drinking haunt, there are no pinball
wizards in the bar, just Oakham and Everard's ales and a
wide range of meals, such as hot filled baps; lamb and
chickpea curry; and local pork and herb sausages with
mash. Other home-cooked possibilities include venison
and forest fruits in game gravy; fish pie; and wild
mushroom risotto.

Open 11.30-2.30 5-11 Closed: Sun eve in winter **Bar
Meals** L served all wk 12-2.30 D served all wk 6-9 Av
main course £9 **Restaurant** L served all wk 12-2.30
D served all wk 6-9 Av 3 course à la carte fr £20
⊕ EVERARDS ◀ Everards Tiger & Beacon, Oakham Ales
Ö Westons Scrumpy. **Facilities** Non-diners area ☻ (Bar
Garden) ♦♦ Children's menu Children's portions Garden ⌂
Parking Wi-fi ▭ (notice required)

EMPINGHAM
Map 11 SK90

The White Horse Inn

Main St LE15 8PS ☎ 01780 460221
e-mail: info@whitehorserutland.co.uk
dir: From A1 take A606 signed Oakham & Rutland Water.
From Oakham take A606 to Stamford

Stone-built pub on the shores of Rutland Water

Steve and Claire Glencross took over this 17th-century
former courthouse at the beginning of 2013 and have
completely refurbished the entire body of the pub,
revealing the period features such as wooden floors and
open fireplaces. The beamed bar, good selection of real
ales and friendly staff makes it an ideal place to relax
after a walk or cycle ride. The pub works closely with local
suppliers to ensure high-quality seasonal ingredients for
the menu of pub classics and more sophisticated choices,
such as sausages and mash, and honey-roast duck
breast with braised red cabbage.

Open all day all wk Closed: 25 Dec **Bar Meals** L served all
wk 12-9 D served all wk 12-9 food served all day
Restaurant L served all wk 12-9 D served all wk 12-9
food served all day ⊕ ENTERPRISE INNS ◀ John Smith's,
Timothy Taylor Landlord, Guiness, Guest ales. ♀ 14
Facilities Non-diners area ♦♦ Children's menu Children's
portions Garden ⌂ Parking ▭

EXTON
Map 11 SK91

Fox & Hounds

PICK OF THE PUBS

19, The Green LE15 8AP ☎ 01572 812403
e-mail: sandra@foxandhoundsrutland.co.uk
dir: Take A606 from Oakham towards Stamford, at
Barnsdale turn left, after 1.5m turn right towards Exton.
Pub in village centre

Perfect place to unwind and enjoy quality food

Traditional English and Italian food is the hallmark of
this imposing 17th-century free house, which stands
opposite the green amid the charming stone and
thatched cottages in the village centre. There's a
delightful walled garden, making this former coaching
inn a perfect spot for a sunny day. The pub has a
reputation for good food and hospitality, and is an ideal
stopping-off point for walkers and cyclists exploring
nearby Rutland Water and the surrounding area. Its menu
is the work of Italian chef-proprietor Valter Floris and his
team, and in the evenings there's an impressive list of
authentic, thin-crust pizzas. In addition, the main menu
features coq au vin with bacon, chestnut mushrooms,
Savoy cabbage and new potatoes; roasted pumpkin and
goats' cheese filo tartlets; and calves' liver with mash
and onion gravy. Good beers include Grainstore Ten Fifty.

Open all wk 11-3 6-11 (Sat-Sun all day) **Bar Meals** L
served Mon-Fri 12-2, Sat-Sun 12-9 D served Mon-Fri 6-9,
Sat-Sun 12-9 **Restaurant** L served Mon-Fri 12-2, Sat-Sun
12-9 D served Mon-Fri 6-9, Sat-Sun 12-9 ⊕ FREE HOUSE
◀ Greene King IPA, The Grainstore Ten Fifty, Phipps IPA
Ö Thatchers Gold. ♀ 10 **Facilities** Non-diners area ♦♦
Children's menu Children's portions Family room Garden
⌂ Parking Wi-fi ▭

GREETHAM
Map 11 SK91

The Wheatsheaf

1 Stretton Rd LE15 7NP ☎ 01572 812325
e-mail: enquiries@wheatsheaf-greetham.co.uk
dir: From A1 follow signs for Oakham onto B668 to
Greetham, pub on left

Homely refuge with an emphasis on locally
sourced food

Set sideways to the road, this 18th-century, stone-built
village pub is lovingly run by Carol and Scott Craddock.
Carol notched up more than 20 years working in several
renowned kitchens before coming to put her wide
experience to excellent use here. She changes her modern
British menu weekly, and cooks using locally sourced
meats and high quality sustainable fresh fish; she makes
bread daily, too. A typical lunch might feature roast
medium-rare rump of beef, while dinner could be pan-
fried whole tiger prawns with peri peri, either as a starter
or main course. Rutland-brewed real ales are served in
the bar.

Open 12-3 6-close (Fri-Sun all day) Closed: 1st 2 wks in
Jan, Mon (ex BHs) **Bar Meals** L served Tue-Fri 12-2, Sat
12-2.30, Sun 12-3 D served Tue-Sat 6.30-9 Av main

course £12 **Restaurant** L served Tue-Fri 12-2, Sat
12-2.30, Sun 12-3 D served Tue-Sat 6.30-9 ⊕ PUNCH
TAVERNS ◀ Greene King IPA, Oldershaw Newton's Drop,
Brewsters Decadence, Oakham Ales Inferno, Grainstore
Triple B. ♀ 11 **Facilities** Non-diners area ☻ (Bar Garden)
♦♦ Children's menu Children's portions Garden ⌂ Parking
Wi-fi ▭ (notice required)

LYDDINGTON
Map 11 SP89

The Marquess of Exeter ★★★★ INN ◉

52 Main St LE15 9LT ☎ 01572 822477
e-mail: info@marquessexeter.co.uk
dir: A1(N) exit towards Leicester/A4. At rdbt onto A47
towards Leicester. At Uppingham rdbt onto A6003/Ayston
Rd. Through Uppingham to Stoke Rd. Left into Lyddington,
left onto Main St. Pub on left

Smart village inn with great food

Run by renowned local chef Brian Baker, this old village
inn fits seamlessly into Lyddington's long, yellow-brown
ironstone streetscape. Stylish contemporary design works
well together with traditional pub essentials, to wit,
beams, flagstone floors and winter fires. Modern British
menus offer starters ranging from tom yum soup to
chicken liver parfait with fig chutney; and main courses
such as herb crumbed cod cheeks with frites and tartare
sauce; and Brian's signature sharing dish of grilled rib of
Derbyshire beef with frites and béarnaise sauce. Add a
shady garden and the mix is complete for an enjoyable
overnight stay, especially now that guest rooms have
been given the luxury treatment.

Open all day all wk **Bar Meals** L served Mon-Sat 12-2.30,
Sun 12-3 D served Mon-Sat 6.30-9.30, Sun 6-9
Restaurant L served Mon-Sat 12-2.30, Sun 12-3 D served
Mon-Sat 6.30-9.30, Sun 6-9 ⊕ MARSTON'S ◀ Pedigree,
Brakspear Ö Thatchers. ♀ 14 **Facilities** Non-diners area
♦♦ Children's menu Children's portions Garden ⌂ Parking
Wi-fi ▭ (notice required) **Rooms** 17

Old White Hart ★★★★ INN

51 Main St LE15 9LR ☎ 01572 821703
e-mail: mail@oldwhitehart.co.uk
dir: From A6003 between Uppingham & Corby take B672.
Pub on main street

17th-century inn in a rural conservation village

Owners Stuart and Holly East have been running this free
house opposite the village green for over 13 years. It is
constructed from honey-coloured sandstone like the
surrounding cottages, and has original beamed ceilings
and stone walls. On warm days customers take their pint
of Great Oakley bitter (this and more at the summer beer
festival), or Aspall cider out into the gardens or onto the
covered patio. Dishes served in the restaurants include
ham hock terrine, rib-eye steak, grilled pork chop, and
vegetarian choices. Half-price menu offers are available
Monday to Thursday. The inn also has a floodlit petanque
pitch. Accommodation is in converted cottages alongside
the pub.

Open all wk 12-3 6.30-11 (Sun 12-3 7-10.30) Closed:
25 Dec, 26 Dec eve **Bar Meals** L served Mon-Sat 12-2,

Sun 12-2.30 D served all wk 6.30-9 **Restaurant** L served Mon-Sat 12-2, Sun 12-2.30 D served all wk 6.30-9 ⊕ FREE HOUSE ◼ Greene King IPA, Timothy Taylor Landlord & Golden Best, The Grainstore, Great Oakley ◐ Aspall. 🍷 10 **Facilities** Non-diners area 🕯 Children's portions Play area Garden 🎗 Beer festival Parking Wi-fi ▥ (notice required) **Rooms** 10

MANTON   Map 11 SK80

The Horse and Jockey

2 St Marys Rd LE15 8SU ☎ 01572 737335
e-mail: enquiries@horseandjockeyrutland.co.uk
dir: Exit A6003 between Oakham & Uppingham signed Rutland Water South Shore. 1st left in Manton into St Marys Rd

Handy refuelling stop by Rutland Water

Cyclists and ramblers investigating the recreational tracks around Rutland Water can expect treats in the form of fine Rutland-brewed beers — including one created for the pub - and some robust pub food at this pleasing, stone-built village free house. Privately owned, the innate charm of the traditional, stone-floored, beamed interior complements the wholesome home-cooked menu which is strong on produce with local provenance. Steaks, curries, baked fish or roast loin of pork are amongst the pub favourites helping refuel visitors to the vast reservoir. Vegetarian options may include mushroom and red onion confit pudding and a specials board is also available.

Open all day all wk **Bar Meals** L served Mon-Fri 12-3 (Apr-Sep) 12-2.30 (Oct-Mar), Sat-Sun 12-9 D served Mon-Fri 6-9, Sat-Sun 12-9 **Restaurant** L served Mon-Fri 12-3 (Apr-Sep) 12-2.30 (Oct-Mar), Sat-Sun 12-9 D served Mon-Fri 6-9, Sat-Sun 12-9 ⊕ FREE HOUSE ◼ The Grainstore Cooking, Morland Old Speckled Hen, Guest ales ◐ Jollydale, Kopparberg. 🍷 12
Facilities Non-diners area 🐾 (Bar Garden) 🕯 Children's portions Garden 🎗 Parking Wi-fi ▥ (notice required)

OAKHAM   Map 11 SK80

The Finch's Arms

Oakham Rd, Hambleton LE15 8TL ☎ 01572 756575
e-mail: info@finchsarms.co.uk
dir: From Oakham take A606 signed Stamford. Turn right signed Upper Hambleton. Pub on left

Smart pub with extensive outside area

Beamed ceilings, cask ales and a small bustling bar characterise this traditional 17th-century free house, with magnificent views overlooking Rutland Water. Log fires warm the snug seating areas in winter, whilst in summer months there's an appealing outside terrace. Typical dishes in the Garden Room restaurant might include roast chicken with pea, smoked bacon and parmesan risotto; or baked Cornish cod with buttered cabbage and hazelnut crust.

Open all day all wk ⊕ FREE HOUSE/PROPER PUB COMPANY ◼ Timothy Taylor Landlord, Black Sheep.
Facilities 🕯 Children's portions Garden Parking Wi-fi

The Grainstore Brewery

Station Approach LE15 6RE ☎ 01572 770065
e-mail: enquiries@grainstorebrewery.com
dir: Adjacent to Oakham rail station

The largest brewery in the smallest county

One of the best brew pubs in Britain, the Grainstore Brewery is housed in a three-storey Victorian grain store next to Oakham railway station. Founded in 1995, Davis's brewing company uses the finest quality hops and ingredients to make the beers that can be sampled in the pub's taproom. Food is wholesome and straightforward, with the ales playing an important part in recipes for Rutland Panther chilli con carne and pork and Ten Fifty sausages. A full diary of events includes live music, the annual August Bank Holiday Rutland beer festival and the May Bank Holiday cider festival. Tours of the brewery can be arranged.

Open all day all wk Sun-Thu 11-11 (Fri-Sat 11am-mdnt)
Bar Meals L served all wk 11-3 Av main course £7.95 ⊕ FREE HOUSE ◼ The Grainstore Rutland Panther, Triple B, Ten Fifty, Silly Billy, Rutland Beast, Nip, Seasonal beers ◐ Sheppy's. **Facilities** Non-diners area 🐾 (Bar Garden) 🕯 Children's portions Garden 🎗 Beer festival Cider festival Parking Wi-fi ▥ (notice required)

SOUTH LUFFENHAM   Map 11 SK90

The Coach House Inn

3 Stamford Rd LE15 8NT ☎ 01780 720166
e-mail: thecoachhouse123@aol.com
dir: On A6121, off A47 between Morcroft & Stamford

Former stables serving well-kept real ales

Horses were once stabled here while weary travellers enjoyed a drink in what is now a private house next door. This elegantly appointed, attractive stone inn offers a comfortable 40-cover dining room and a cosy bar serving Adnams, Morland and Timothy Taylor Landlord. A short, appealing menu in the Ostler's Restaurant might feature chicken liver pâté with orange and cranberry chutney; and lamb shank with garlic mash, root vegetables and redcurrant jus. In the bar tuck into roast cod with hand-cut chips and pea purée; or beef and ale casserole.

Open 12-2 5-11 (Sat all day) Closed: 25 Dec, 1 Jan, Sun eve, Mon L **Bar Meals** L served Tue-Sat 12-2 D served Mon-Sat 6.30-9 **Restaurant** L served Tue-Sun 12-2 D served Mon-Sat 6.30-9 ⊕ FREE HOUSE ◼ Timothy Taylor Landlord, Morland Old Speckled Hen, Adnams, Greene King IPA, Guinness ◐ Aspall.
Facilities Non-diners area 🕯 Children's portions Garden 🎗 Parking Wi-fi ▥ (notice required)

STRETTON   Map 11 SK91

The Jackson Stops Country Inn

PICK OF THE PUBS

Rookery Rd LE15 7RA ☎ 01780 410237
e-mail: info@thejacksonstops.com
dir: From A1 follow Stretton signs

Timeless pub with seasonal dishes

The long, low, stone-built partly thatched building dates from 1721, and has plenty of appeal: stone fireplaces with log fires, exposed stone, quarry-tiled floors, scrubbed wood tables and five intimate dining rooms. In the timeless and beamed snug bar, the choice of real ales lifts the heart, boding well for the excellent value to be had from the dishes on the seasonally changing menu, all freshly prepared and cooked by the kitchen staff. Children can choose from their own menu or take smaller portions from the adult choice. And, if you were wondering about the pub's name: there can be few pubs in the country that have acquired their name by virtue of a 'For Sale' sign. One was planted outside the pub for so long during a previous change of ownership that the locals dispensed with the old name in favour of the name of the estate agent on the board.

Open 12-3.30 6-11 (Sun 12-5) Closed: Sun eve, Mon **Bar Meals** L served Tue-Sat 12-3, Sun 12-5 D served Tue-Sat 6.30-9.30 Av main course £11.45 **Restaurant** L served Tue-Sat 12-3, Sun 12-5 D served Tue-Sat 6.30-9.30 Fixed menu price fr £12.95 Av 3 course à la carte fr £25 ⊕ FREE HOUSE ◼ The Grainstore Cooking. 🍷 48
Facilities Non-diners area 🐾 (Bar Garden) 🕯 Children's menu Children's portions Garden 🎗 Parking ▥ (notice required)

WHITWELL   Map 11 SK90

The Noel @ Whitwell

Main Rd LE15 8BW ☎ 01780 460347
e-mail: info@thenoel.co.uk
dir: Between Oakham & Stamford on A606, N shore of Rutland Water

North shore village pub for everyone

The part-thatched village inn stands just a 15-minute stroll from the north shore of Rutland Water, so worth noting if you are walking or pedalling the lakeside trail and in need of refreshment. The friendly, spruced-up bar and dining room have stylish modern feel and feature flagstone floors, heritage colours and a warming winter log fires. Expect to find local Grainstore ales on tap and a wide-ranging menu listing pasta and salad dishes alongside shoulder of lamb with red wine gravy; beef bourguignon; and Cajun salmon with chilli dressing.

Open 12-3 6-close Closed: Mon **Bar Meals** L served Tue-Sat 12-2, Sun 12-3 D served Tue-Sat 6.30-9 **Restaurant** L served Tue-Sat 12-2, Sun 12-3 D served Tue-Sat 6.30-9 ⊕ ENTERPRISE INNS ◼ Greene King Ruddles County, The Grainstore Cooking ◐ Westons Stowford Press. 🍷 10
Facilities Non-diners area 🐾 (Bar Garden) 🕯 Children's menu Children's portions Garden 🎗 Parking Wi-fi ▥ (notice required)

PICK OF THE PUBS

Kings Arms ★★★★ INN ◎◎

WING   Map 11 SK80

Top St LE15 8SE ☎ 01572 737634
e-mail: info@thekingsarms-wing.co.uk
web: www.thekingsarms-wing.co.uk
dir: *1m off B6003 between Uppingham & Oakham*

Smoked produce is a speciality at this 17th-century free house

Dating from 1649, this attractive, stone-built free house has been run by the Goss family since 2004. James and Ali look after the kitchen and front-of-house, while parents David and Gisa Goss are always ready to lend a hand. The bar has flagstone floors, low-beamed ceilings, nooks, crannies, two open fires, and a wide selection of traditional cask ales. Lunchtime bar meals are supplemented in the two AA-Rosette restaurant by an à la carte menu and daily specials. There are artisanal overtones, which isn't at all surprising given the close links the Gosses have forged with local farmers, millers, smallholders, hunters and fishermen. On offer are dishes such as Glapthorpe duck liver parfait with air-dried duck breast, clementine salad and elderberry jelly; or roe deer saddle with celeriac purée. From the on-site smokehouse comes eel, trout, meats, black pudding and other products that owe much to James's skill with Swiss and Danish curing, smoking and air-drying techniques. On the 'classics'

menu might be Rutland shepherd's pie; beer-battered fish of the day; and baked home-smoked Cote Hill blue cheese with sourdough. Served at lunchtime only are freshly baked cobs with home made beef dripping chips, filled with roast Hambleton beef, Colston Basset Stilton, pork loin with apple compôte, or one filled with salad. Ice creams and sorbets are home made, often using seasonal windfall fruits and flowers. Eight spacious letting rooms with their own private entrance are set away from the pub. Booking for meals may be required.

Open Tue-Sun 12-3 6.30-11 (seasonal times) Closed: Sun eve, Mon, Tue L (Oct-Mar), Sun eve, Mon L (Apr-Sep) **Bar Meals** L served Tue-Sun 12-2.30 D served Tue-Sat 6.30-8.30 Av main

course £12.50 **Restaurant** L served Tue-Sun 12-2.30 D served Mon-Sat 6.30-8.30 Av 3 course à la carte fr £30 🛢 FREE HOUSE 🍺 Shepherd Neame Spitfire, The Grainstore Cooking, Marston's Pedigree ♻ Sheppy's, Jollydale, Stamford, Bottle Kicking. 🍷 33 **Facilities** Non-diners area 🐾 (Bar Garden) 🚼 Children's menu Children's portions Garden 🪧 Parking Wi-fi 🚌 (notice required) **Rooms** 8

WING   Map 11 SK80

Kings Arms ★★★★ INN ◉◉

PICK OF THE PUBS

See Pick of the Pubs on opposite page

SHROPSHIRE

ADMASTON   Map 10 SJ61

The Pheasant Inn at Admaston

TF5 0AD ☎ **01952 251989**
e-mail: info@thepheasantadmaston.co.uk
dir: *M54 junct 6 towards Whitchurch then follow B5063 towards Shawbirch & Admaston. Pub is on left of main rd*

Stylish country inn with good children's menu

Dating from the 19th century, this lovely old country pub offers a stylish interior decor and real fire, which add character to the dining areas. The large enclosed garden is ideal for families and there is a good menu for children under ten. Grown-ups certainly aren't overlooked, either — the kitchen uses the best local produce in dishes such as Shropshire Blue and caramelised onion horn, which might be followed by Wickstead aged sirloin steak with balsamic tomatoes, watercress salad and chips. Steamed chocolate pudding, and banana and pecan tart are just two options for dessert.

Open all day all wk 11-11 (Thu 11am-11.30pm Fri-Sat 11am-mdnt) **Bar Meals** L served Mon-Fri 12-2, Sat 12-9.15, Sun 12-7 **Restaurant** L served Mon-Fri 12-2, Sat 12-9.15, Sun 12-7 ⊕ ENTERPRISE INNS ◀ Salopian Shropshire Gold, Greene King IPA, Guinness. ₹ 10 **Facilities** Non-diners area ♦♦ Children's menu Children's portions Play area Garden ⌂ Parking Wi-fi ⛟

BASCHURCH   Map 15 SJ42

The New Inn

Church Rd SY4 2EF ☎ **01939 260335**
e-mail: eat@thenewinnbaschurch.co.uk
dir: *8m from Shrewsbury, 8m from Oswestry*

Shropshire beers plus the best local produce on the menus

Near the medieval church, this stylishly modernised old whitewashed village pub is a focal point for all things Welsh Marches, with beers from nearby Oswestry's Stonehouse brewery amongst five ales stocked, meats from the village's Moor Farm or Shrewsbury's renowned market, and cheeses from a Cheshire supplier. The parents of the former owners have taken over, so expect Gerry to be manning the pumps and Ann in charge of the kitchen. The tempting fare might include a starter of chicken liver parfait with red onion jam; followed by rump of Shropshire lamb, fondant potato, pea and mint purée with redcurrant sauce.

Open Tue-Fri 11-3 6-11 (Sat 11-11 Sun 12-11) Closed: 26 Dec, 1 Jan, Mon **Bar Meals** L served Tue-Sat 12-2, Sun 12-6 D served Tue-Sat 6-9 **Restaurant** L served Tue-Sat 12-2, Sun 12-6 D served Tue-Sat 6-9 ⊕ FREE HOUSE

◀ Banks's Bitter, Stonehouse Station Bitter, Hobsons Best Bitter, Guest ales Ŏ Thatchers Gold.
Facilities Non-diners area ♦♦ Children's menu Children's portions Garden ⌂ Beer festival Parking Wi-fi

BISHOP'S CASTLE   Map 15 SO38

The Three Tuns Inn

PICK OF THE PUBS

Salop St SY9 5BW ☎ **01588 638797**
e-mail: timce@talk21.com
dir: *From Ludlow take A49 through Craven Arms, then left onto A489 to Lydham, then A488 to Bishop's Castle, inn at top of the town.*

Historic inn renowned for its microbrewery ales

In a small market town near the Welsh border, in an Area of Outstanding Natural Beauty, stands this 17th-century inn. For over 350 years the pub and the adjoining, identically named brewery were run as a single business, and although ownership has now split, they continue to work together, which explains the array of Three Tuns real ales in the bar, including 1642, the golden bitter that commemorates the date of the inn's first brewing licence. The public, snug and lounge bars are free from piped music and games machines, although there's occasional live jazz, rock, classical music and Morris dancing in the garden or function room. In the oak-framed, glass-walled dining room the menu offers chargrilled Cajun chicken, venison stew, and Gressingham duck breast. For vegetarians, sweet potato and chickpea balti is a possibility. Dogs are welcome throughout. A beer festival over the second weekend of July involves all the town's pubs.

Open all day all wk **Bar Meals** L served all wk 12-3 D served Mon-Sat 7-9 **Restaurant** L served all wk 12-3 D served Mon-Sat 7-9 ⊕ STAR PUBS & BARS ◀ Three Tuns XXX, Solstice, Old Scrooge, Cleric's Cure, 1642. ₹ 12 **Facilities** Non-diners area ♣ (Bar Restaurant Garden) ♦♦ Children's menu Children's portions Garden Beer festival

BRIDGNORTH   Map 10 SO79

Halfway House Inn ★★★ INN

Cleobury Rd, Eardington WV16 5LS ☎ **01746 762670**
e-mail: info@halfwayhouseinn.co.uk
dir: *M54 junct 4, A442 to Bridgnorth. Or M5 junct 4, A491 towards Stourbridge. A458 to Bridgnorth. Follow tourist signs on B4363*

An olde-worlde coaching inn

This 17th-century coaching inn was renamed in 1823 after the very young Princess Victoria stopped here en route between Shrewsbury and Worcester; when she asked where she was, came the diplomatic reply, 'halfway there ma'am'. An original Elizabethan mural has been preserved behind glass for all to enjoy, and the pub is renowned for a good selection of regional real ales, 40 malts, and around 100 wines. The weekend lunch menu ranges from light bites to home-cooked pub classics, while the dinner menu has steaks from the grill, deep-

fried breaded brie, and chicken curry. Finish with warm chocolate fudge cake. Accommodation is available.

Open all wk 6-11.30 (Fri-Sat 11am-11.30pm Sun 11-9) Closed: Sun eve Nov-Mar **Bar Meals** L served Fri-Sun 12-2 D served Mon-Sat 6-9 Av main course £6.95 **Restaurant** L served Sat-Sun 12-7 D served Mon-Sat 6-9 Fixed menu price fr £16 Av 3 course à la carte fr £22.50 ⊕ FREE HOUSE ◀ Holden's Golden Glow, Wood's Shropshire Lad, Guinness Ŏ Westons Stowford Press. ₹ 10 **Facilities** Non-diners area ♣ (Bar Garden) ♦♦ Children's menu Children's portions Play area Garden ⌂ Parking Wi-fi ⛟ (notice required) **Rooms** 10

BURLTON   Map 15 SJ42

The Burlton Inn ★★★★ INN

PICK OF THE PUBS

SY4 5TB ☎ **01939 270284**
e-mail: enquiries@burltoninn.com
dir: *10m N of Shrewsbury on A528 towards Ellesmere*

A classy country gastro-pub with rooms

This pretty 18th-century inn stands on the road between Shrewsbury and Ellesmere, in the picturesque Salopian village of Burlton. Run by Paul and Lindsay Devaney, the pub has a charming dining area, a soft-furnished space for relaxation, and a traditional bar with wooden beams and a snug — the perfect place to enjoy a pint of Robinsons Unicorn and other seasonal bitters. Behind the main building are en suite guest rooms and the terrace, ideal for alfresco summer dining. Paul also performs the role of chef, creating dishes to please a broad range of tastes, from traditional pub food to contemporary fine dining. The menus offer nibbles such lamb koftas, followed perhaps by a starter of crayfish salad, and a main course of lamb shoulder casserole, roasted carrot and celeriac, and crusty bread. For dessert, try warm apple and cherry pie with vanilla custard. A separate children's menu offers the likes of crispy chicken or sausage and mash.

Open all wk 12-3 6-11 (Sun 12-5) Closed: 25 Dec **Bar Meals** L served Mon-Sat 12-2, Sun 12-3 D served Mon-Sat 6-9 Av main course £10 **Restaurant** L served Mon-Sat 12-2, Sun 12-3 D served Mon-Sat 6-9 Fixed menu price fr £8 Av 3 course à la carte fr £22 ⊕ ROBINSONS ◀ Build a Rocket Boys! & Unicorn, Hartleys Cumbria Way Ŏ Westons Stowford Press. ₹ 9 **Facilities** Non-diners area ♦♦ Children's menu Children's portions Garden ⌂ Parking Wi-fi **Rooms** 6

CARDINGTON — Map 10 SO59

The Royal Oak

SY6 7JZ ☎ 01694 771266
e-mail: inntoxicated@gmail.com
dir: *Turn right off A49 N of Church Stretton; 2m off B4371 (Church Stretton-Much Wenlock road)*

Historic pub in a conservation village

Set in a conservation village and reputedly the oldest continuously licensed pub in Shropshire, this free house can trace its roots to the 15th century. The rambling low-beamed bar with vast inglenook (complete with cauldron, black kettle and pewter jugs) and comfortable beamed dining room are refreshingly undisturbed by music, TV or games machines. Choose from the excellent cask ales and ponder your choice of sustenance: good-value home-made fare includes fried black pudding and bacon on mixed leaves; fish pie; and good meat-free options such as vegetable tagine with chickpeas.

Open 12-2.30 (Sun 12-3.30) Tue-Wed 6.30-11 (Thu-Sat 6.30-12 Sun 7-11) Closed: Mon **Bar Meals** L served Tue-Sat 12-2, Sun 12-2.30 D served Tue-Sat 6.30-9, Sun 7-9 Av main course £12.25 **Restaurant** L served Tue-Sat 12-2, Sun 12-2.30 D served Tue-Sat 6.30-9, Sun 7-9 Av 3 course à la carte fr £16.90 ⊞ FREE HOUSE ◀ Ludlow Best, Three Tuns XXX, Wye Valley Butty Bach, Salopian Hop Twister, Sharp's Doom Bar.
Facilities Non-diners area ❤ (Bar Outside area) ♦♦ Children's menu Outside area ⌁ Parking Wi-fi ⇒ (notice required)

CHURCH STRETTON — Map 15 SO49

The Bucks Head ★★★★ INN

42 High St SY6 6BX ☎ 01694 722898
e-mail: lnutting@btinternet.com
dir: *12m from Shrewsbury & Ludlow*

Traditional pub in the Shropshire Hills

The small market town of Church Stretton is sandwiched between the Long Mynd and Wenlock Edge, and the charming old Bucks Head is without doubt where to stay to explore these impressive landscape features. The pub is known for several essential things: its comfortable, AA four-star accommodation, its well-kept Banks's, Marston's and guest ales, and its restaurant. Where possible, the kitchen uses local fresh meat, poultry and vegetables for rib-eye, sirloin and rump steaks; Cajun chicken with sour cream; plaice fillet in breadcrumbs; beef or roasted vegetable lasagne; and cream cheese and broccoli bake.

Open all day all wk **Bar Meals** L served all wk 12-2.30 D served all wk 6-9 **Restaurant** L served all wk 12-2.30 D served all wk 6-9 ⊞ MARSTON'S ◀ Pedigree, Banks's Original & Bitter, 2 Guest ales. **Facilities** Non-diners area ♦♦ Children's menu Children's portions Garden ⌁ Wi-fi ⇒ (notice required) **Rooms 4**

CLAVERLEY — Map 10 SO79

The Woodman

Danford Ln WV5 7DG ☎ 01746 710553
dir: *On B4176 (Bridgnorth to Dudley road)*

In open countryside with a warm welcome

Village farms, butcher and baker supply much of the produce used in the well-respected dishes here at this sibling-run, three-storey Victorian inn. Outside a picturesque settlement deep in the east Shropshire countryside, the beer, too, comes from just down the lane in Enville, whilst the wine list spreads its wings worldwide. The contemporary interior is a comfy mix of village local and bistro, where dishes such as smoked duck breast terrine with plum and hoi sin dressing; and braised lamb shank, Savoy cabbage mash, and red wine and mint gravy could appear on the menus. Alfresco dining is a popular summer option, indulging in grand rural views to the ridge of Abbot's Castle Hill. Change of hands in March 2013.

Open all day 12-2.30 5.30-11 (Sun 12-4) Closed: Sun eve, Mon **Restaurant** L served Tue-Sat 12-2.30, Sun 12-4 D served Tue-Sat 6-9.30 ⊞ PUNCH TAVERNS ◀ Black Sheep, Enville Ale. ♛ 10 **Facilities** Garden ⌁ Parking Wi-fi

CLEOBURY MORTIMER — Map 10 SO67

The Crown Inn

PICK OF THE PUBS

Hopton Wafers DY14 0NB ☎ 01299 270372
dir: *On A4117 8m E of Ludlow, 2m W of Cleobury Mortimer*

Creeper-clad coaching inn with three restaurants

This 16th-century creeper-clad inn is in an ideal spot for walking in the lush countryside surrounding the small village of Hopton Wafers. The inn retains much of its original character and has an enviable reputation for good food made with ingredients sourced from regional producers. Eat in one of three eating areas: in the Shropshire Restaurant overlooking the countryside; in Poachers, with exposed beams, stonework and large inglenook fireplace; and in the Rent Room, which offers daily menus, light bites and specials - and more of those rural views. In Poachers, a typical meal might be pan-seared scallops and asparagus on a salad of radish and red onion with a lemon dressing; followed by fillet of beef on beetroot risotto with a port reduction. The wine list has been selected by a local merchant and includes a wide range of fine ports, Armagnacs and Cognacs.

Open all day all wk **Bar Meals** L served all wk 12-2.30 D served all wk 6-9 Av main course £12.50 **Restaurant** L served Mon-Fri 12.30-2, Sat 12-2.30, Sun 12-8 D served Mon-Fri 6-9, Sat 6-9.30, Sun 12-8 Fixed menu price fr £11.99 Av 3 course à la carte fr £29.95 ⊞ FREE HOUSE ◀ Hobsons Best Bitter, Guest ales. ♛ 25
Facilities Non-diners area ❤ (Bar Garden) ♦♦ Children's menu Children's portions Play area Garden Parking ⇒

CLUN — Map 9 SO38

The White Horse Inn

The Square SY7 8JA ☎ 01588 640305
e-mail: pub@whi-clun.co.uk
web: www.whi-clun.co.uk
dir: *On A488 in village centre*

Home to the Clun Brewery

In the beautiful Shropshire Hills, this gloriously unspoilt and unpretentious village inn oozes character with beams, wizened wood and slab floors. Two beers brewed in their own microbrewery, the Clun, together with others selected from Shropshire's many craft breweries provide the line-up at the bar. This 'green' pub offers visitors drawn to AE Housman's 'Quietest place under the sun' heart-warming pub grub, derived from very local suppliers. Main courses may include Cajun chicken fillet, cauliflower gratin, and beer-battered haddock. The traditional suet puddings are a speciality. Regular events take place here, including the Clun Valley beer festival on the first weekend in October.

Open all day all wk **Bar Meals** L served Mon-Sat 12-2, Sun 12.30-2.30 D served all wk 6.30-8.30 **Restaurant** L served Mon-Sat 12-2, Sun 12.30-2.30 D served all wk 6.30-8.30 ⊞ FREE HOUSE ◀ Clun Pale Ale & Citadel, Wye Valley Butty Bach, Hobsons Best Bitter, Salopian Shropshire Gold, Guest ales ♉ Westons 1st Quality, Robinsons Flagon. **Facilities** Non-diners area ❤ (Bar Garden) ♦♦ Children's menu Children's portions Garden ⌁ Beer festival Wi-fi ⇒ (notice required)

CRAVEN ARMS   Map 9 SO48

The Sun Inn

Corfton SY7 9DF ☎ 01584 861239
e-mail: normanspride@btconnect.com
dir: On B4368, 7m N of Ludlow

Family-run pub with an innovative microbrewery

Close to the towns of Ludlow and Bridgnorth, and the ramblers' paradise of Clee Hill and Long Mynd, this historic pub was first licensed in 1613. It has been run by the Pearce family since 1984 and since 1997 landlord Norman Pearce has been brewing the Corvedale ales in what was the pub's old chicken and lumber shed, using local borehole water; Mahorall cider, from just down the road, is another thirst-quenching option. Teresa Pearce uses local produce in a delicious array of traditional dishes — game hotpot, battered cod, lamb curry. There are also vegetarian and some vegan options. The pub holds a beer festival in May.

Open all wk 12-2.30 6-11 (Sun 12-3 7-11) **Bar Meals** L served Mon-Sat 12-2, Sun 12-2.45 D served Mon-Sat 6-9, Sun 7-9 Av main course £8.90 **Restaurant** L served Mon-Sat 12-2, Sun 12-2.45 D served Mon-Sat 6-9, Sun 7-9 ⊕ FREE HOUSE ◀ Corvedale Norman's Pride, Dark & Delicious, Katie's Pride, Farmer Rays ♂ Mahorall Farm. ♥ 8 **Facilities** Non-diners area ♣ (Bar Garden) ♦♦ Children's menu Children's portions Play area Garden ⊼ Beer festival Parking Wi-fi ▦ (notice required)

CRESSAGE   Map 10 SJ50

The Riverside Inn

Cound SY5 6AF ☎ 01952 510900
e-mail: info@theriversideinn.net
dir: On A458 7m from Shrewsbury, 1m from Cressage

Great river views from the conservatory and garden

This inn sits in three acres of gardens alongside the River Severn, offering customers delightful river views both outdoors and from a modern conservatory. Originally a vicarage for St Peter's church in the village, the building also housed a girls' school and a railway halt before becoming a pub in 1878. The pub is popular with anglers. The monthly-changing menu might open with melon and ginger cocktail or a smoked salmon roulade, followed perhaps by cod mornay or Burgundy chicken. Comforting desserts include home-made toffee cheesecake. Their own brew, Riverside Inn Bitter, is available in the cosy bar.

Open all wk Sat-Sun all day May-Sep ⊕ FREE HOUSE ◀ Riverside Inn Bitter, Guest ales. **Facilities** ♣ (Bar Garden) Garden Parking Wi-fi

HODNET   Map 15 SJ62

The Bear at Hodnet ★★★ INN

TF9 3NH ☎ 01630 685214
e-mail: reception@bearathodnet.co.uk
dir: At junct of A53 & A442 turn right at rdbt. Inn in village centre

Haunted, historic, former coaching inn

With old beams, open fireplaces and secret passages leading to the church, this black-and-white-timbered, former coaching inn was once known for its bear-baiting pit. In the 1680s, a landlord threw Jasper, a regular down on his luck, out into a bitterly cold night. Within hours both were dead, Jasper from hypothermia, the landlord from fright, as if he'd seen a ghost, which legend suggests was Jasper. New landlord Gregory Williams may have met him wandering an upstairs corridor. Food includes pan-fried sea trout; crispy-chicken salad; and rump or rib-eye steaks. The bar serves Shropshire Gold and Brew XI real ales.

Open all day all wk 12-11 (Sun 12-10.30) **Bar Meals** L served Mon-Thu 12-9, Fri-Sat 12-9.30, Sun 12-8.30 D served Mon-Thu 12-9, Fri-Sat 12-9.30, Sun 12-8.30 food served all day **Restaurant** L served Mon-Thu 12-9, Fri-Sat 12-9.30, Sun 12-8.30 D served Mon-Thu 12-9, Fri-Sat 12-9.30, Sun 12-8.30 food served all day ⊕ FREE HOUSE ◀ Salopian Shropshire Gold, Brew XI ♂ Westons Stowford Press. ♥ 10 **Facilities** Non-diners area ♣ (Bar Garden) ♦♦ Children's menu Children's portions Play area Garden ⊼ Parking Wi-fi ▦ (notice required) **Rooms** 9

IRONBRIDGE   Map 10 SJ60

The Malthouse

The Wharfage TF8 7NH ☎ 01952 433712
e-mail: mcdonald740@msn.com
dir: Telephone for directions

Live music and good food

In the Severn Gorge, within a mile of the famous Iron Bridge, the 18th-century Malthouse is known for its Friday and Saturday night live music. But for a different way to spend the evening try the restaurant, where candlelit tables and an extensive menu feature home-made steak and Guinness pie; king prawn linguine; braised shoulder of Shropshire lamb; and mushroom, pepper and spinach Stroganoff. There's pubbier grub too, such as thick pork sausages with black pudding mash. Brakspear, Wood's and Titanic make up the real ale portfolio.

Open all day all wk **Bar Meals** L served all wk 11-10 D served all wk 11-10 food served all day **Restaurant** L served all wk 11-10 D served all wk 11-10 food served all day ⊕ FREE HOUSE ◀ Wychwood Hobgoblin, Wood's Shropshire Lad, Brakspear, Titanic ♂ Thatchers Gold & Pear. ♥ 10 **Facilities** Non-diners area ♦♦ Children's menu Children's portions Garden ⊼ Parking Wi-fi ▦

LEEBOTWOOD   Map 15 SO49

Pound Inn

SY6 6ND ☎ 01694 751477
e-mail: info@thepound.org.uk
dir: On A49, 9m S of Shrewsbury

Contemporary interior at old thatched inn

An eye-catching pub in a memorable location. This thatched, 15th-century drovers' inn lies at the foot of the jagged, whaleback hills of mid-Shropshire, with The Lawley rising steeply beyond the garden. It is a happy mix of traditional village pub (it's the oldest building in the village) and smart dining destination draws in ramblers to sup Salopian Brewery beers and to try a taste of grilled ox tongue and cauliflower cheese fritter to start, followed by Shropshire sausages with cheddar mash or roast venison with butternut squash.

Open all wk 12-2.30 6-10.30 ◀ Wye Valley Butty Bach, Salopian Shropshire Gold ♂ Westons Stowford Press. **Facilities** ♦♦ Children's portions Garden Parking

LITTLE STRETTON   Map 15 SO49

The Ragleth Inn

Ludlow Rd SY6 6RB ☎ 01694 722711
e-mail: wendyjd65@hotmail.com
dir: From Shrewsbury take A49 towards Leominster. At lights in Church Stretton turn right. 3rd left into High St. Continue to Little Stretton. Inn on right

Country inn serving home-cooked favourites

This 17th-century country inn sits midway between Shrewsbury and Ludlow in beautiful countryside at the foot of the Long Mynd hills. The pretty, traditional exterior includes a large beer garden with plenty of wooden benches and a children's play area, matched within by two bars and a restaurant with oak beams, antiques and inglenook fireplaces. A good range of ales accompanies classic pub dishes such as garlic mushrooms with a crusty roll; home-made steak and ale pie; and filled baguettes. Specials include seafood cocktail followed by slow-roasted pork belly with sweet braised red cabbage and red wine sauce. All diets can be catered for.

Open all wk **Bar Meals** L served Mon-Sat 12-2.15, Sun all day D served Mon-Sat 6.30-9, Sun all day Av main course £9 **Restaurant** L served Mon-Sat 12-2.15, Sun all day D served Mon-Sat 6.30-9, Sun all day Av 3 course à la carte fr £22 ⊕ FREE HOUSE ◀ Greene King Abbot Reserve, Wye Valley Butty Bach, Hobsons, Three Tuns, Sharp's Doom Bar ♂ Westons Stowford Press, Thatchers Gold. **Facilities** Non-diners area ♣ (Bar Garden) ♦♦ Children's menu Children's portions Play area Garden ⊼ Parking Wi-fi ▦ (notice required)

LLANFAIR WATERDINE　　Map 9 SO27

The Waterdine

PICK OF THE PUBS

LD7 1TU ☎ 01547 528214
e-mail: info@waterdine.com
dir: *4.5m W of Knighton off B4355, turn right opposite Lloyney Inn, 0.5m into village, last on left*

Excellent food in an extravagant landscape

Just yards from the Welsh border and close to Offa's Dyke in the magnificent Shropshire Hills, the compact riverside inn offers sublime views along the deep Teme Valley. It originated as a Welsh longhouse, becoming a drovers' inn 450 years ago. The family of Lord Hunt, of Everest expedition fame, lived in the village, and some of the planning reputedly took place in the lounge bar. Today it serves an appealing range of real ales, ciders and wines; wood-burning stoves create a cosy atmosphere in winter. There are two dining rooms: the Garden Room looks out over the river, and the beamed Taproom has a massive oak mantle which displays burn marks from long-extinguished candles. The fixed-price menus change with the seasons and focus availability of game and meats; start with wild pigeon breast on celeriac purée, continuing with Mortimer Forest roe deer saddle with blackberry sauce leading to banana, walnut and butterscotch crumble. Booking is essential.

Open 12-3 7-11 Closed: 1wk winter, 1wk spring, Sun eve & Mon (ex BHs), Tue-Wed L **Bar Meals** L served Thu-Sun 12.15-1.30 **Restaurant** L served Thu-Sun 12.15-1.30 D served Tue-Sat 7-8.30 Fixed menu price fr £32.50 ⊕ FREE HOUSE ◀ Wood's Shropshire Legends, Parish Bitter, Shropshire Lad Ö Brook Farm.
Facilities Non-diners area ✦✦ Children's portions Garden Parking

LUDLOW　　Map 10 SO57

The Church Inn ★★★ INN

Buttercross SY8 1AW ☎ 01584 872174
dir: *In town centre, behind Buttercross*

Real ales and pies in a narrow town centre street

The inn stands on one of the oldest sites in Ludlow town centre, dating back some seven centuries, and through the ages has been occupied by a blacksmith, saddler, apothecary and barber-surgeon. These days it enjoys a reputation for providing a good range of up to ten real ales in the cosy bar areas alongside the pies for which it has become well known - there's a choice of 30 different pies at any one time. There are ten comfortable en suite bedrooms with smart modern bathrooms.

Open all day all wk **Bar Meals** L served Mon-Fri 12-2.30, Sat-Sun 12-3 D served Mon-Sat 6.30-9, Sun 6.30-8.30 ⊕ FREE HOUSE ◀ Hobsons Town Crier & Hobsons Mild, Weetwood, Wye Valley Bitter, Ludlow Gold & Boiling Well, Guest ales Ö Stowford, Aspall, Robinsons.
Facilities Non-diners area ✦✦ Children's menu ▭▭
Rooms 10

The Clive Bar & Restaurant with Rooms ★★★★★ RR ◉◉

PICK OF THE PUBS

Bromfield SY8 2JR ☎ 01584 856565
e-mail: info@theclive.co.uk
web: www.theclive.co.uk
dir: *2m N of Ludlow on A49, between Hereford & Shrewsbury*

Handsome Georgian building with classy bar and restaurant

Robert, later Lord, Clive was credited with securing India for the British crown and, for a while, he lived in this former farmhouse on the Earl of Plymouth's estate. Early in the 20th century it became The Clive Arms to cater for estate workers. Retaining original features that harmonise well with a 1990s refurbishment, it has a bright, modern bar serving Ludlow Gold and Hobsons Best Bitter, ciders from Dunkertons, Mahorall Farm and Thatchers, and light snacks. On a wall in the 18th-century lounge, where there's an enormous fireplace, is Clive's original coat of arms. An upper area leads to a sheltered courtyard with tables and parasols. The cuisine includes Shropshire venison Wellington; parmesan-crusted rack of lamb; monkfish in Parma ham; and roasted butternut squash risotto. Steamed Shetland mussels; lamb's liver and bacon; and wild mushroom tagliatelle take Sunday lunch beyond just traditional roasts. Tastefully converted period outbuildings provide accommodation.

Open all day all wk Closed: 25-26 Dec **Bar Meals** L served Mon-Fri 12-3, Sat-Sun 12-6.30 D served Mon-Sat 6.30-10, Sun 6.30-9.30 Av main course £10.95 **Restaurant** L served all wk 12-3 D served Mon-Sat 6.30-10, Sun 6.30-9.30 Av 3 course à la carte fr £30 ⊕ FREE HOUSE ◀ Hobsons Best Bitter, Ludlow Gold Ö Dunkertons, Mahorall Farm, Thatchers Old Rascal. ₹ 9
Facilities Non-diners area ✦✦ Children's portions Garden ⊼ Parking Wi-fi ▭▭ (notice required) **Rooms** 15

MARTON　　Map 15 SJ20

The Lowfield Inn

SY21 8JX ☎ 01743 891313
e-mail: lowfieldinn@tiscali.co.uk
dir: *From Shrewsbury take B4386 towards Montgomery. Through Westbury & Brockton. Pub on right in 13m just before Marton*

Successful modern interpretation of old village inn

In a stunning location below the crinkly west Shropshire Hills, this pub is a modern replacement for an old inn demolished in 2007. Whilst the ambience has altered, the atmosphere of a friendly village local is retained, with fierce dedication to supporting microbreweries dotted along the England/Wales border – Monty's and Three Tuns beers are regularly stocked. Modern British pub grub is the order of the day; black pudding and crispy bacon starter with duck breast Wellington to follow a typical choice. The eye-catching brick bar, comfy seating, slab floor, log-burner and duck pond add to the developing character of this new village favourite.

Open all day all wk **Bar Meals** L served all wk 12-9.30 D served all wk 12-9.30 food served all day **Restaurant** L served all wk 12-9.30 D served all wk 12-9.30 food served all day ⊕ FREE HOUSE ◀ Three Tuns XXX & 1642, Monty's Moonrise & Mojo, Wood's Shropshire Lad, Salopian Shropshire Gold Ö Inch's Stonehouse, Westons Old Rosie, Gwynt y Ddraig Dog Dancer. ₹ 18
Facilities Non-diners area ✿ (Bar Restaurant Garden) ✦✦ Children's menu Children's portions Garden ⊼ Parking Wi-fi ▭▭

The Sun Inn

SY21 8JP ☎ 01938 561211
e-mail: suninnmarton@googlemail.com
dir: *On B4386 (Shrewsbury to Montgomery road), in centre of Marton*

Convivial free house respected for its food

Probably about 300 years old, the attractive, stone-built Sun stands on a corner in a quiet hamlet. The Gartell family runs it very much as a convivial local, with darts, dominoes, regular quiz nights and Hobsons real ales from Cleobury Mortimer. It's well respected as a dining venue, with the Gartells offering modern British dishes such as slow-roast belly pork with Thai spice, coconut milk and egg noodles; free-range chicken breast stuffed with feta cheese, sun-dried tomato and basil; and blackboard fish specials. Offa's Dyke Path runs nearby on its 177-mile route from Sedbury Cliffs on the Severn estuary to Prestatyn.

Open 12-3 7-12 Closed: Sun eve, Mon, Tue L **Bar Meals** L served Wed-Sat 12-2.30 D served Tue-Fri from 7pm **Restaurant** L served Wed-Sun 12-2.30 D served Tue-Sat from 7pm ⊕ FREE HOUSE ◀ Hobsons Best Bitter, Guest ales. ₹ 8 **Facilities** Non-diners area ✦✦ Children's portions Garden ⊼ Parking ▭▭ (notice required)

PICK OF THE PUBS

The Crown Country Inn ★★★★ INN ◉◉

MUNSLOW   Map 10 SO58

SY7 9ET ☎ **01584 841205**
e-mail: info@crowncountryinn.co.uk
web: www.crowncountryinn.co.uk
dir: *On B4368 between Craven Arms &*
Much Wenlock

Dedication to serving excellent food

The Grade II listed Crown has stood in its lovely setting below the limestone escarpment of Wenlock Edge since Tudor times. An impressive three-storey building, it served for a while as a Hundred House, a type of court, where the infamous 'Hanging' Judge Jeffreys sometimes presided over proceedings. Could it be that the black-swathed Charlotte, whose ghost is sometimes seen in the pub, once appeared before him? The main bar retains its sturdy oak beams, flagstone floors and prominent inglenook fireplace, and on offer are beers from the Three Tuns Brewery. Owners Richard and Jane Arnold are well known for their strong commitment to good food, Richard being not only head chef but Shropshire's only Master Chef of Great Britain, a title he has cherished for many years. Meals based on top-quality local produce from trusted sources are served in the main bar, the Bay dining area, and the

Corvedale restaurant, the former court room. These may include dishes such as flaked ham hock and tomato terrine with hazelnut and paprika dressing; roast wood pigeon breast, warm beetroot chutney, rosemary polenta fritter and port wine syrup; and griddled rib-eye or Hereford sirloin steak. Sundays here are deservedly popular, when a typical lunch might start with cream and coriander soup; followed by roast fore rib of beef and Yorkshire pudding, or pave of Shetland salmon, with red wine and crayfish butter sauce; and to finish, Limoncello cheesecake, or Seville orange pannacotta. Three large bedrooms are in a converted Georgian stable block. Booking for meals may be required.

Open Tue-Sat 12-3.30 6.45-11 (Sun 12-3.30) Closed: Xmas, Sun eve, Mon **Bar Meals** L served Tue-Sun 12-2 D served Tue-Sat 6.45-8.45 Av main course £11 **Restaurant** L served Tue-Sun 12-2 D served Tue-Sat 6.45-8.45 Av 3 course à la carte fr £30 ⊕ FREE HOUSE 🛢 Three Tuns 1642.
Facilities Non-diners area 🍴 Children's portions Play area Garden 🚫 Parking 🚐 **Rooms** 3

MUCH WENLOCK
Map 10 SO69

The George & Dragon

2 High St TF13 6AA ☎ 01952 727312
e-mail: thegeorge.dragon@btinternet.com
dir: *On A458 halfway between Shrewsbury & Bridgnorth, on right of the High Street*

Good pub food and choice of ales

If you are looking for somewhere dog-friendly, with five cask ales and several draught ciders, and where newspapers are provided, this early 18th-century inn should do nicely. Over the fireplace in the bar, an oak beam features the initials of the Yates family, innkeepers from 1834 to 1958. On the menu are baguettes and light lunches, while in the evening choose from deep-fried breaded scampi; chicken breast wrapped in bacon, stuffed with garlic mushrooms; a selection of pies – beef in ale, traditional fish and Shropshire fidget (pork and apple) – and vegetarian options. Beer festivals on St Georges Day and at other times.

Open all day all wk 12-11 (Fri-Sat noon-mdnt) **Bar Meals** L served all wk 12-2.30 D served Mon-Tue, Thu-Sat 6-9 Av main course £7.95-£8.95 **Restaurant** L served all wk 12-2.30 D served Mon-Tue, Thu-Sat 6-9 ⊕ PUNCH TAVERNS ◀ Greene King Abbot Ale, Hobsons Best Bitter, St Austell Tribute, Guest ales Ō Westons Wyld Wood Organic, Thatchers Gold, Symonds Scrumpy Jack. **Facilities** Non-diners area ❤ (Bar Outside area) ♦♦ Children's menu Children's portions Outside area ⊼ Beer festival Wi-fi ▦

The Talbot Inn

High St TF13 6AA ☎ 01952 727077
e-mail: the_talbot_inn@hotmail.com
dir: *M54 junct 4, follow Ironbridge Gorge Museum signs, then Much Wenlock signs. Much Wenlock on A458, 11m from Shrewsbury, 9m from Bridgnorth*

Small and friendly 650-year-old pub

Enter this ancient pub down an alleyway and peek through the archway to see its delightful courtyard where you can sit outside in warmer weather. Built in 1361, originally as an abbot's house, The Talbot has also been an almshouse and a coaching inn. The cosy interior has oak beams, old fireplaces and welcoming staff. Most of the food is freshly prepared from local produce for extensive, regularly changing menus featuring sandwiches, salads, jacket potatoes, steaks, fish, filled Yorkshire puds and huge Sunday roasts. Look to the blackboards for the vegetarian options (red pepper and goats' cheese lasagne, vegetable curry) and a long list of desserts.

Open all day all wk 11am-2am **Bar Meals** L served all wk 12-2.30 D served Mon-Sat 6-9, Sun 6-8.30 **Restaurant** L served all wk 12-2.30 D served Mon-Sat 6-9, Sun 6-8.30 ⊕ FREE HOUSE ◀ Bass, Guest ales Ō Blackthorn. ♈ 11 **Facilities** Non-diners area ♦♦ Children's portions Garden ⊼ Parking ▦ (notice required)

MUNSLOW
Map 10 SO58

The Crown Country Inn ★★★★ INN ⑳⑳

PICK OF THE PUBS

See Pick of the Pubs on page 369

NORTON
Map 10 SJ70

The Hundred House ★★★★ INN ⑳⑳

PICK OF THE PUBS

Bridgnorth Rd TF11 9EE ☎ 01952 580240
e-mail: reservations@hundredhouse.co.uk
dir: *On A442, 6m N of Bridgnorth, 5m S of Telford centre*

Award-winning pub with quirky features

Surrounded by rolling Severn Valley countryside and just a ten-minute drive from Ironbridge Gorge and its many museums, this historic 14th-century pub has been run as a popular inn by the Phillips family for the past 25 years. Downstairs is an amazing interconnecting warren of lavishly decorated bars and dining rooms with old quarry-tiled floors, exposed brickwork, beamed ceilings and Jacobean oak panelling. Younger son Stuart Phillips continues to head kitchen operations, producing a mix of innovative new dishes and pub favourites with two AA Rosettes. The à la carte might offer griddled scallops with risotto cake, stir-fried vegetables, carrot and ginger oil, or rich Provençale fish soup, which might be followed by roast breast of free-range chicken stuffed with tarragon mousse served with tomato and wild mushroom sauce, or roast chump of Shropshire lamb with leek, parsnip and lamb cake with sautéed kidney and rosemary jus. Cookery classes are also available.

Open all day all wk 10am-11pm Closed: 25 Dec eve **Bar Meals** L served all wk 12-2.30 D served all wk 6-9.30 **Restaurant** L served Mon-Sat 12-2.30, Sun 12-9 D served Mon-Sat 6-9.30, Sun 12-9 ⊕ FREE HOUSE ◀ Ironbridge, Three Tuns, Ludlow Ō Rosie's. ♈ 10 **Facilities** Non-diners area ❤ (Bar Garden) ♦♦ Children's menu Children's portions Family room Garden ⊼ Parking Wi-fi ▦ (notice required) **Rooms** 9

OSWESTRY
Map 15 SJ22

The Bradford Arms ★★★★ INN

Llanymynech SY22 6EJ ☎ 01691 830582
e-mail: robinbarsteward@tesco.net
dir: *5.5m S of Oswestry on A483 in Llanymynech*

Tip-top ales at Welsh Borders pub

Once part of the Earl of Bradford's estate, between Oswestry and Welshpool, this 17th-century coaching inn is ideally situated for golfing, fishing and walking. It is well known as a community pub serving first-class real ales. Eating in the spotless, quietly elegant bar, dining rooms and conservatory is a rewarding experience, with every taste catered for. For lunch try oven-roast chicken supreme, giant filled Yorkshire pudding, or steak-and-kidney pudding; while a typical dinner menu features Stilton chicken, beef Stroganoff, fisherman's pie, and leek, mushroom and onion pancake. Comfortable accommodation is available.

Open all wk 11.30-3 5.30-12 **Bar Meals** L served all wk 11.30-2 Av main course £7.95 **Restaurant** L served all wk 11.30-2 D served all wk 5.30-9 Fixed menu price fr £7.95 Av 3 course à la carte fr £16.95 ⊕ FREE HOUSE ◀ Black Sheep Best Bitter, Tetley's Smoothflow, Guinness, 2 Guest ales Ō Gaymers. **Facilities** Non-diners area ❤ (Bar Outside area) ♦♦ Children's menu Children's portions Outside area ⊼ Parking Wi-fi ▦ (notice required) **Rooms** 5

PAVE LANE
Map 10 SJ71

The Fox

TF10 9LQ ☎ 01952 815940
e-mail: fox@brunningandprice.co.uk
dir: *1m S of Newport, just off A41*

Grand Edwardian pub offering Shropshire ales

Behind The Fox's smart exterior are spacious rooms and little nooks wrapped around a busy central bar, where there is an original wooden fireplace and plenty of Shropshire real ales demanding attention. The menu offers sandwiches and light meals (camembert quiche, goats' cheese rarebit), as well as grilled smoked haddock kedgeree, honey-glazed ham, falafel burger, and pork schnitzel. To finish, choose from ice cream, sorbet, cheese or traditional puddings like chocolate brownie. Enjoy the gently rolling countryside and wooded hills from the lovely south-facing terrace with its patio tables and large grassy area.

Open all day all wk 12-11 (Sun 12-10.30) **Bar Meals** food served all day **Restaurant** food served all day ⊕ FREE HOUSE/BRUNNING & PRICE ◀ Timothy Taylor Landlord, Wood's Shropshire Lad, Thwaites Original, Titanic Mild, Holden's Golden Glow. ♈ **Facilities** Non-diners area ❤ (Bar Garden) ♦♦ Children's portions Garden ⊼ Parking

Save on hotels. Book at **theAA.com/hotel**

SHROPSHIRE 371 ENGLAND

SHIFNAL
Map 10 SJ70

Odfellows Wine Bar

Market Place TF11 9AU ☎ **01952 461517**
e-mail: odfellows@gmail.com
web: www.odleyinns.co.uk
dir: *M54 junct 4, 3rd exit at rdbt, at next rdbt take 3rd exit, past petrol station, round bend under rail bridge. Bar on left*

Quirky and good value

No letters please, telling us we can't spell. The single 'd' is because Odley Inns own this slate-floored, town-centre café bar and restaurant, one of its three in Shropshire. And beer drinkers should not misinterpret the rest – a wine bar, yes, but there are six real ales, including its own brew and a good Belgian selection. Lunch in the elevated dining area and attractive conservatory includes sandwiches and light meals, and the evening menu lists grills; leek and mushroom gratin; Od fish pie; and bacon-wrapped pheasant breast. There's regular live music, and beer and cider festivals are in May and September.

Open all day all wk 12-12 Closed: 25-26 Dec, 1 Jan **Bar Meals** L served all wk 12-6 D served all wk 6-9 food served all day **Restaurant** L served all wk 12-6 D served all wk 6-9 food served all day ⊕ FREE HOUSE ◀ Salopian, Slater's, Hobsons, Joule's, Titanic ♂ Thatchers, Addlestones. ☂ 11
Facilities Non-diners area ♦ Children's menu Children's portions Garden ⏸ Beer festival Parking Wi-fi

SHREWSBURY
Map 15 SJ41

The Armoury

Victoria Quay, Victoria Av SY1 1HH ☎ **01743 340525**
e-mail: armoury@brunningandprice.co.uk
dir: *Telephone for directions*

Great beers and food in converted warehouse

Smack beside the River Severn, this former armoury building was converted by Brunning & Price and makes an impressive, large-scale pub with its vast warehouse windows. Inside, huge bookcases dominate the bar and restaurant area, where the modern monthly-changing menu is accompanied by a great range of real ales such as Salopian Shropshire Gold, local cider and a well-considered wine list. Typical dishes are scallops with pea purée; local venison with redcurrant and rosemary gravy; excellent sandwiches (roast beef, rocket and horseradish), and glazed lemon tart with mixed berry coulis for pudding.

Open all day all wk **Bar Meals** food served all day **Restaurant** food served all day ⊕ FREE HOUSE/BRUNNING & PRICE ◀ Salopian Shropshire Gold, Wood's Shropshire Lad, Hobsons Twisted Spire, Three Tuns XXX, Phoenix, Brunning & Price Original Bitter. ☂ 12
Facilities Non-diners area ♦ Children's menu Children's portions Garden Outside area ⏸ Wi-fi

Lion & Pheasant Hotel ★★★ TH ⚜⚜ NEW

50 Wyle Cop SY1 1XJ ☎ **01743 770345**
e-mail: info@lionandpheasant.co.uk
dir: *From S & E: pass abbey, cross river on English Bridge to Wyle Cop, hotel on left. From N & W: follow Town Centre signs onto one-way system to Wyle Cop. Hotel at bottom of hill on right*

Boutique hotel luxury in historic market town

The handsome façade of this family-owned hotel and free house graces medieval Wyle Cop, shortly before the street becomes English Bridge over the River Severn. A coolly elegant look is evident throughout, from the ground floor public areas to the spacious, well-equipped bedrooms upstairs. Just off the reception is the wood-floored café-style bar, which leads to the flagstoned Inglenook Bar, serving snacks and a full range of main meals. On the first floor is the split-level restaurant, where Cumbrian rose veal with onion soubise; seafood stew with spicy mussel and saffron sauce; and parmesan gnocchi help to maintain their two AA Rosette status.

Open all day all wk Closed: 25 Dec **Bar Meals** food served all day **Restaurant** food served all day ⊕ FREE HOUSE ◀ Salopian Shropshire Gold, 3 Guest ales ♂ Robinsons, Aspall. ☂ 13 **Facilities** Non-diners area ♦ Children's menu Children's portions Garden ⏸ Parking Wi-fi 🚌 (notice required) **Rooms** 22

The Mytton & Mermaid Hotel ★★★ HL ⚜⚜

PICK OF THE PUBS

Atcham SY5 6QG ☎ **01743 761220**
e-mail: reception@myttonandmermaid.co.uk
dir: *From M54 junct 7 signed Shrewsbury, at 2nd rdbt take 1st left signed Ironbridge/Atcham. In 1.5m hotel on right after bridge*

Riverside former coaching inn

Sir Clough Williams-Ellis, creator of the Italianate village of Portmeirion in North Wales, once lived in this Grade II listed property on the banks of the River Severn. Dating from 1735 it's tastefully decorated throughout, the interior recalling the atmosphere of long-past mail-coach days. There's a relaxed feel about the place, especially the bar, which features a wood floor, scrubbed tables, comfy sofas and an open log fire. Here, local real ales include Shropshire Gold and Hobsons Best, while county-sourced ingredients drive the seasonal, modern British menu in the two-AA Rosette restaurant. A starter of Severn and Wye smoked salmon could precede ballottine of free-range chicken; Wenlock Edge pork and leek sausage with cheesy mash; or sweet potato, aubergine and chickpea bhuna. For dessert, treacle tart with clotted cream ice cream, and blackberry Eton Mess are typical options. Opposite the hotel is the National Trust's Attingham Park.

Open all day all wk 7am-11pm Closed: 25 Dec **Bar Meals** L served all wk Brunch 9-12, Lunch 12-2.30, Afternoon 2.30-6 food served all day **Restaurant** L served Mon-Sat 12-2.30, Sun 12-9 D served Mon-Sat 7-10, Sun 12-9 ⊕ FREE HOUSE ◀ Wood's Shropshire Lad, Salopian Shropshire Gold, Hobsons Best Bitter, Wye Valley. ☂ 12 **Facilities** Non-diners area ♦ Children's menu Garden ⏸ Parking Wi-fi 🚌 (notice required) **Rooms** 18

STOTTESDON
Map 10 SO68

Fighting Cocks

1 High St DY14 8TZ ☎ 01746 718270
e-mail: sandrafc_5@hotmail.com
dir: *11m from Bridgnorth off B4376*

Deep-in-the-countryside pub and shop

According to a framed newspaper cutting on the pub wall, 'Nipper Cook' drank 30 pints of cider each night at this unassuming 18th-century rural free house. Today, this lively local hosts regular music nights, as well as an apple day each October and an annual beer festival in November. Expect home-made pâtés, curries, pies and puddings on the menu. The owners' neighbouring shop supplies local meats, home-made pies, sausages, and produce from the gardens.

Open all wk 6pm-mdnt (Fri 5pm-1am Sat 12-12 Sun 12-10.30) **Bar Meals** L served Sat-Sun 12-2.30 **Restaurant** L served Sat-Sun 12-2.30 D served Mon-Sat 7-9 ⊕ FREE HOUSE ◀ Hobsons Best Bitter, Town Crier & Mild, Wye Valley HPA & Bitter, Ludlow Gold Ö Westons Stowford Press, Robinsons Flagon.
Facilities Non-diners area ♦ Children's menu Garden Outside area ⌐ Beer festival Parking Wi-fi

WELLINGTON
Map 10 SJ61

The Old Orleton Inn

Holyhead Rd TF1 2HA ☎ 01952 255011
e-mail: aapub@theoldorleton.com
dir: *From M54 junct 7 take B5061 (Holyhead Rd), 400yds on left on corner of Haygate Rd & Holyhead Rd*

Grand views and wide-ranging menus

The old and new blend effortlessly throughout this 17th-century former coaching inn. Overlooking the famous Wrekin Hill, it is popular with walkers exploring the Shropshire countryside. Expect a relaxed and informal atmosphere, local Hobsons ales on tap and modern British food prepared from scratch. At lunch in the brasserie taking in soup, sandwiches, salad platters, chef's dish of the day and more. Evening choices include Bar Bites for a just a snack or three- course meals that might include port and juniper braised Shropshire lamb shank; and guinea fowl and oyster mushroom hot pot.

Open 12-3 5-11 Closed: 1st 2wks Jan, Sun eve **Bar Meals** L served Mon-Sat 12-2.30, Sun 12-4 D served Mon-Sat 6-9.30 Av main course £14 **Restaurant** L served Mon-Sat 12-2.30, Sun 12-4 D served Mon-Sat 6-9.30 Av 3 course à la carte fr £25 ⊕ FREE HOUSE ◀ Hobsons Best Bitter, Town Crier Ö Westons Stowford Press. ☍ 10
Facilities Non-diners area Garden ⌐ Parking Wi-fi ⎚ (notice required)

WENTNOR
Map 15 SO39

The Crown Inn

SY9 5EE ☎ 01588 650613
dir: *From Shrewsbury A49 to Church Stretton, follow signs over Long Mynd to Asterton, right to Wentnor*

A lovely village pub set in a beautiful landscape

Deep amid the Shropshire Hills, this inviting 16th-century timbered inn is popular with walkers who warm themselves at wood-burning stoves in winter and on the outside decking in the summer; here you can sup Three Tuns bitter and gaze at the Long Mynd's lofty ridge. The pub's homely atmosphere, enhanced by beams and horse brasses, makes eating and drinking here a pleasure. Meals are served in the bar or separate restaurant; expect pub classics like garlic mushrooms and chicken balti with rice, chips and naan bread.

Open all day all wk **Bar Meals** L served all wk 12-9.30 D served all wk 12-9.30 Av main course £8.75 food served all day **Restaurant** L served all wk 12-9.30 D served all wk 12-9.30 Fixed menu price fr £12.95 food served all day ⊕ FREE HOUSE ◀ Brains The Rev. James, Hobsons Old Henry, Three Tuns Ö Westons Scrumpy. ☍ 8
Facilities Non-diners area ❀ (Bar Garden) ♦ Children's menu Children's portions Play area Garden ⌐ Beer festival Parking Wi-fi ⎚ (notice required)

WHITCHURCH
Map 15 SJ54

Willeymoor Lock Tavern

Tarporley Rd SY13 4HF ☎ 01948 663274
dir: *2m N of Whitchurch on A49 (Warrington to Tarporley road)*

Canalside pub ideal for families and walkers

Watch narrow boats negotiating the lock from this much-extended former lock-keeper's cottage on the attractive and busy Llangollen Canal. In the bar, Shropshire Gold represents the county, teapots hang from low beams and there are open log fires. Competitively priced food includes plenty of fish and veggie dishes, as well as pub classics and meats from the grill: beef and onion pie, wholetail scampi, and vegetable chilli. The children's play area and large beer garden make this an ideal warm weather location, and it's a popular refreshment spot for walkers exploring the nearby Sandstone Trail and the Bishop Bennett Way.

Open all wk 12-2.30 6-11 (Sun 12-2.30 6-10.30) Closed: 25 Dec **Bar Meals** L served all wk 12-2 D served all wk 6-9 Av main course £7.50 **Restaurant** L served all wk 12-2 D served all wk 6-9 ⊕ FREE HOUSE ◀ Weetwood Eastgate Ale, Timothy Taylor Landlord, Greene King IPA, Morland Old Speckled Hen, Salopian Shropshire Gold, Stonehouse Ö Aspall, Westons. ☍ 9
Facilities Non-diners area ♦ Children's menu Play area Garden Outside area ⌐ Parking ⎚ (notice required)

SOMERSET

ASHCOTT
Map 4 ST43

Ring O'Bells

High St TA7 9PZ ☎ 01458 210232
e-mail: info@ringobells.com
dir: *M5 junct 23 follow A39 & Glastonbury signs. In Ashcott turn left, at post office follow church & village hall signs*

Traditional family-run village free house

Successfully run by the same family for over 25 years, this independent free house dates in parts from 1750, and the interior reflects this with beams, split-level bars, an old fireplace and a collection of bells and horse brasses. The pub is close to the Somerset Levels, RSPB reserve at Ham Wall and National Nature Reserve at Shapwick Heath. Local ales and ciders are a speciality, while all food is made on the premises. Expect good-value dishes and daily specials such as sticky slow-cooked belly pork; fresh whole lemon sole with parsley and lemon butter; or Somerset scrumpy chicken. Treat yourself to an ice cream sundae for dessert.

Open all wk 12-3 7-11 (Sun 7-10.30) Closed: 25 Dec **Bar Meals** L served all wk 12-2 D served all wk 7-10 Av main course £8-£10 **Restaurant** L served all wk 12-2 D served all wk 7-10 Av 3 course à la carte fr £20 ⊕ FREE HOUSE ◀ Guest ales Ö Wilkins Farmhouse, The Orchard Pig. ☍ 8
Facilities Non-diners area ❀ (Bar Garden) ♦ Children's menu Children's portions Play area Garden ⌐ Parking Wi-fi ⎚ (notice required)

ASHILL
Map 4 ST31

Square & Compass ★★★★ INN

Windmill Hill TA19 9NX ☎ 01823 480467
e-mail: squareandcompass@tiscali.co.uk
dir: *Exit A358 at Stewley Cross service station onto Wood Rd. 1m to pub in Windmill Hill*

Friendly rural pub with high-quality accommodation

Beautifully located overlooking the Blackdown Hills, this traditional family-owned country pub has been a labour of love for owners Chris and Janet Slow for over 15 years. A warm and friendly atmosphere pervades the bar with its hand-made settles and tables. Exmoor and St Austell ales head the refreshments list, while reasonably priced and freshly made meals are prepared in the state-of-the-art kitchen. In addition to classic pub dishes, grills and omelettes, the chef's specials may tempt with beef casserole and cheese dumplings; or breast of pheasant with an apple and cider sauce. The barn next door hosts weddings and regular live music, while eight bedrooms offer four-star accommodation.

Open 12-3 6.30-late (Sun 7-late) Closed: 25-26 Dec, Tue-Thu L **Bar Meals** L served Fri-Mon 12-2 D served all wk 7-9.30 **Restaurant** L served Fri-Mon 12-2 D served all wk 7-9.30 ⊕ FREE HOUSE ◀ St Austell Tribute & Trelawny, Exmoor. **Facilities** Non-diners area ❀ (Bar Garden) ♦ Children's menu Children's portions Garden ⌐ Parking Wi-fi **Rooms** 8

Save on hotels. Book at **theAA.com/hotel**

SOMERSET 373 ENGLAND

AXBRIDGE
Map 4 ST45

Lamb Inn

The Square BS26 2AP ☎ **01934 732253**
dir: *10m from Wells & Weston-Super-Mare on A370*

Plenty of pub favourites at this old inn

Parts of this rambling 15th-century building were once the guildhall, but when a new town hall was opened in 1830 it became an inn. Opposite is the medieval King John's Hunting Lodge, so christened in 1905 by an owner who chose to ignore the fact that John died over two centuries before it was built. The bars are heated by log fires and offer Butcombe ales; there's also a skittle alley and large terraced garden. Examples of pub favourites are beef and ale pie; chicken parmigiani; home-made curries; and salmon fillet supreme. Jacket potatoes, baguettes and sandwiches are available too.

Open all wk 11-3 6-11 (Thu-Sat 11am-11.30pm Sun 12-10.30) **Bar Meals** L served all wk 12-2.30 D served Mon-Sat 6-9 Av main course £8.75-£15 ⊕ BUTCOMBE ◀ Bitter & Gold, Guest ales ♻ Thatchers, Ashton Press. **Facilities** Non-diners area ❀ (Bar) Children's menu Children's portions Garden ⊟ Wi-fi ➠ (notice required)

BABCARY
Map 4 ST52

Red Lion

TA11 7ED ☎ **01458 223230**
e-mail: redlionbabcary@btinternet.com
dir: *Please telephone for directions*

Pretty pub with a great range of food

Rich colour-washed walls, heavy beams and simple wooden furniture characterise this beautifully appointed, thatched free house has. The bar offers a great selection of real ales, and you can dine there, in the restaurant or in the garden. The daily menus run from pub favourites such as shepherd's pie with cheesy mash and braised red cabbage or char-grilled steak with all the trimmings through to warm goats' cheese cheesecake with chorizo jam; and slow roasted belly pork with braised red cabbage, mustard mash and apple sauce. All bread is baked on the premises and local suppliers are used whenever possible.

Open all wk **Bar Meals** L served all wk 12-2.30 D served Mon-Sat 7-9.30 Av main course £10.75 **Restaurant** L served all wk 12-2.30 D served Mon-Sat 7-9.30 Av 3 course à la carte fr £28 ⊕ FREE HOUSE ◀ Teignworthy, Otter, Bays, Yeovil Ales ♻ Westons Stowford Press. ♟ 12 **Facilities** Non-diners area ❀ (Bar Garden) ♦♦ Children's portions Play area Garden ⊟ Parking Wi-fi ➠

BACKWELL
Map 4 ST46

The New Inn ◉

86 West Town Rd BS48 3BE ☎ **01275 462199**
e-mail: thenew-inn@yahoo.com
dir: *From Bristol A370 towards Weston-Super-Mare. Pub on right just after Backwell in West Town. Or from M5 junct 21, A370 towards Bristol*

Country pub with a lovely line in summer barbecues

This 18th-century country pub has a relaxed and welcoming atmosphere inside, and a rear garden perfect for summertime Sunday evening barbecues. A good selection of draught beers and ciders is sold at the bar, while attentive staff look after diners tucking into dishes that range from the traditional to the contemporary: pan-fried mackerel, soused beetroot and samphire, for example, could be followed by 28-day dry-aged West Country rib eye steak. Dogs are allowed in the bar and garden, and there is plenty of parking.

Open all day all wk 11.30am-12.30am **Bar Meals** food served all day **Restaurant** food served all day ⊕ ENTERPRISE INNS ◀ Bath Ales Gem, Butcombe ♻ Thatchers Gold, Westons Stowford Press. ♟ 12 **Facilities** Non-diners area ❀ (Bar Restaurant Garden) ♦♦ Children's menu Children's portions Play area Garden ⊟ Parking Wi-fi ➠ (notice required)

BATH
Map 4 ST76

The Chequers ◉

50 Rivers St BA1 2QA ☎ **01225 360017**
e-mail: info@thechequersbath.com
dir: *In city centre, near the Royal Crescent*

Smart city gastro-pub

Ferrying aristocrats around late 18th-century Bath gave sedan-chair carriers a powerful thirst. It was rectified here in 1776, among Bath's most fashionable residences. Run by the team behind the nearby Marlborough Tavern it offers Butcombe Bitter and Bath Gem, as well as several real ciders, including Westons Wyld Wood Organic. At the bar you can order a range of sandwiches and pub classics, while upstairs is a rather refined restaurant where, if you're after a little more solitude, you can enjoy pan-fried turbot with steamed mussels; duck egg, pea and Bath soft cheese omelette; and home-made prime beefburger.

Open all day all wk Closed: 25 Dec **Bar Meals** L served Mon-Sat 12-2.30, Sun 12-6 D served Mon-Sat 6-9.30, Sun 12-6 ⊕ ENTERPRISE INNS ◀ Butcombe Bitter, Bath Gem ♻ Westons Wyld Wood Organic, Addlestones, Symonds Founders Reserve. ♟ 19 **Facilities** Non-diners area ❀ (Bar Restaurant) ♦♦ Children's portions ⊟ Wi-fi ➠ (notice required)

The Garricks Head

7-8 St John's Place BA1 1ET ☎ **01225 318368**
e-mail: info@garricksheadpub.com
dir: *Adjacent to Theatre Royal. Follow Theatre Royal brown tourist signs*

City centre pub with a dining room and outside terrace

Once the home of Beau Nash, the celebrated dandy who put the spa city on the map, The Garricks Head is subsumed within the Theatre Royal, for whose customers it provides pre-show dining facilities. The bar has a lot to commend it: a selection of natural wines from Europe, four real ales, five Somerset ciders, and the largest selection of single malt whiskies in Bath. The food, locally sourced as far as possible, includes pub classics such as liver and bacon, and fish and chips, while the carte features roast venison; rib of beef for two; and duck with lentils.

Open all day all wk Closed: 25-26 Dec **Bar Meals** L served Mon-Sat 12-3, Sun 12-4 D served Mon-Sat 5.30-10, Sun 5.30-9 Av main course £12.95 **Restaurant** L served Mon-Sat 12-3, Sun 12-4 D served Mon-Sat 5.30-10, Sun 5.30-9 Fixed menu price fr £16.95 Av 3 course à la carte fr £24.50 ⊕ FREE HOUSE ◀ Otter Bitter, Palmers, Milk Street Funky Monkey ♻ The Orchard Pig. ♟ 20 **Facilities** Non-diners area ❀ (Bar Restaurant Garden) ♦♦ Children's portions Garden ⊟ Wi-fi ➠ (notice required)

The Hop Pole

PICK OF THE PUBS

7 Albion Buildings, Upper Bristol Rd BA1 3AR ☎ **01225 446327**
e-mail: hoppole@bathales.co.uk
dir: *On A4 from city centre towards Bristol. Pub opposite Royal Victoria Park*

An oasis of calm plus top notch beer and food

Phil Cotton has taken over at this delightful pub just off the River Avon towpath, opposite Royal Victoria Park. Described as both a country pub in the heart of a city, and as a 'secret oasis', it has a stripped-down, stylish interior and a lovingly restored, spacious beer garden, which Phil has refreshed with a grapevine canopy. Bath Ales, now elevated from microbrewery to regional brewery status, supplies many beers from its stable – here you'll find Barnsey (formerly Barnstormer), Gem and SPA. All food is home cooked, from the bar snacks to the main meals such as River Fowey mussels with cider and saffron sauce; honey and clove ham hock, piccalilli and cauliflower cheese; grilled cod with chorizo and haricot cassoulet; and grilled vegetable tart with rocket, parmesan shavings and potato salad. Children can be served smaller portions from the main menu.

Open all day all wk 12-11 (Fri-Sat 12-12) **Bar Meals** L served Mon-Sat 12-9.30, Sun 12-8 D served Mon-Sat 12-9.30, Sun 12-8 Av main course £10 **Restaurant** L served Mon-Sat 12-9.30, Sun 12-8 D served Mon-Sat 12-9.30, Sun 12-8 Fixed menu price fr £10 Av 3 course à la carte fr £20 ⊕ BATH ALES ◀ Gem, SPA, Barnsey, Guest

continued

BATH continued

ales ᵭ Bath Ciders Bounders, Bath Ciders Bounders Traditional. 🍷 16 **Facilities** Non-diners area 🐾 (Bar Garden) 🍴 Children's menu Children's portions Garden Outside area 🅿 Wi-fi 🚬 (notice required)

King William

PICK OF THE PUBS

36 Thomas St BA1 5NN ☎ 01225 428096
e-mail: info@kingwilliampub.com
dir: *At junct of Thomas St & A4 (London Rd), on left from Bath towards London. 15 mins walk from Bath Spa main line station*

An appealing city pub exuding charm and character

You could walk past this unassuming free house and scarcely give it a second look. Yet that would be a mistake, for within the plain Bath stone building lies a happy mix of destination dining inn and locals' pub, with a cosy snug and traditional bar beneath the memorable upstairs dining room. Real ale buffs will generally find a regular Palmers ale, supplemented by guest beers from local microbreweries such as Stonehenge, Milk Street and Yeovil. New head chef Scott Galloway creates traditional dishes with a contemporary twist from locally produced seasonal ingredients. The bar menu offers lighter dishes, but serious diners will seek out the inspiring daily-changing restaurant menu. A starter of brown crab and razor clams, pickled cauliflower and shellfish sauce might herald a main course of whole braised oxtail for two to share. Rhubarb trifle with ginger shortbread completes an evening of easy eating, with a good accompanying wine list.

Open all wk 12-3 5-close (Sat-Sun 12-close) Closed: 25 Dec **Bar Meals** L served Mon-Sun 12-3 D served Mon-Sat 6-10, Sun 6-9 **Restaurant** L served Sun 12-3 D served Wed-Sat 6-10 ⊕ FREE HOUSE ◀ Stonehenge Danish Dynamite, Palmers Dorset Gold, Milk Street Funky Monkey, Yeovil Ales Star Gazer ᵭ Pheasant Plucker, Westons Wyld Wood Organic, The Orchard Pig. 🍷 14 **Facilities** Non-diners area 🐾 (Bar) 🍴 Children's portions Wi-fi

The Marlborough Tavern ☺☺

PICK OF THE PUBS

35 Marlborough Buildings BA1 2LY ☎ 01225 423731
e-mail: info@marlborough-tavern.com
dir: *200mtrs from W end of Royal Crescent*

Well placed for Bath's best attractions

Just around the corner from the famous Royal Crescent, this 18th-century pub once looked after the needs of foot-weary sedan-chair carriers. Today's clientele will more likely need a break from the rigours of traipsing round Bath's shops, and fancy a drink and something to eat in the contemporary, retro and classic-style bar or courtyard. Butcombe, Timothy Taylor's Landlord, Cheddar Totty Pot dark porter and Addlestones cider occupy the handpumps, and 23 wines are sold by the glass. A typical

starter prepared from local seasonal and organic produce is pan-seared scallops with crispy Parma ham, celeriac and apple salad, and curried mayonnaise. Similarly, main dishes would be represented by pan-roasted Cornish hake with Toulouse sausage and haricot bean casserole, crispy squid, baby spinach and braised fennel; and Thai vegetable curry, chai rice, rice noodles and sautéed bok choi. Run by the same team as The Chequers nearby.

Open all day all wk 12-11 (Fri-Sat noon-12.30am) Closed: 25 Dec **Restaurant** L served Mon-Sat 12-2.30, Sun 12.30-4 D served Mon-Thu 6-9.30, Sun 6-9 ⊕ FREE HOUSE ◀ Butcombe Bitter, Timothy Taylor Landlord, Cheddar Totty Pot ᵭ Addlestones. 🍷 23 **Facilities** Non-diners area 🐾 (Bar Restaurant Garden) 🍴 Children's portions Garden 🅿 Wi-fi 🚬 (notice required)

The Star Inn

23 Vineyards BA1 5NA ☎ 01225 425072
e-mail: landlord@star-inn-bath.co.uk
dir: *On A4, 300mtrs from centre of Bath*

The city's oldest pub offering ales from its only brewery

Set amid glorious Georgian architecture and first licensed in 1760, the impressive Star Inn is one of Bath's oldest pubs and is of outstanding historical interest, with a rare and totally unspoiled interior. Original features in the four drinking areas include 19th-century Gaskell and Chambers bar fittings, a barrel lift from the cellar, and even complimentary pinches of snuff found in tins in the smaller bar! Long famous for its pints of Bass served from the jug, these days Abbey Ales from Bath's only brewery are also popular. Fresh filled rolls are available and free snacks on Sundays. A beer festival is held twice a year.

Open all wk 12-2.30 5.30-12 (Fri 12-2.30 5.30-1am Sat noon-1am Sun 12-12) ⊕ PUNCH TAVERNS ◀ Abbey Bellringer, Bath Star, Twelfth Night & White Friar, Bass ᵭ Abbey Ales Hells Bells. **Facilities** Non-diners area 🐾 (Bar Restaurant) 🍴 Beer festival Wi-fi 🚬

BAWDRIP
Map 4 ST33

The Knowle Inn

TA7 8PN ☎ 01278 683330
e-mail: peter@matthews3.wanadoo.co.uk
dir: *M5 junct 23 or A39 from Bridgwater towards Glastonbury*

A true community pub with amazing views

This 16th-century pub on the A39 nestles beneath the Polden Hills and has far-reaching views across Sedgemoor to the Quantocks and Blackdown Hills. The live music, skittles and darts are popular with locals, while the seafood specials and Mediterranean-style garden, complete with fish pond, attract visitors from further afield for summer alfresco meals. A full range of sandwiches and light meals is backed by pub favourites such as loaded potato skins, deep-fried plaice fillet, red bean and lentil chilli, seafood chowder, grilled steak with all the trimmings, and Malteser cheesecake.

Open all day all wk **Bar Meals** L served all wk 11-3 D served all wk 6-9 **Restaurant** L served all wk 11-3 D served all wk 6-9 ⊕ ENTERPRISE INNS ◀ Otter, Guest ales ᵭ Thatchers, Natch. **Facilities** Non-diners area 🐾 (Bar Garden) 🍴 Children's menu Children's portions Garden Parking Wi-fi 🚬 (notice required)

BECKINGTON
Map 4 ST85

Woolpack Inn ★★★★ INN

BA11 6SP ☎ 01373 831244
e-mail: 6534@greeneking.co.uk
dir: *Just off A36 near junct with A361*

Former coaching inn with smart interior

There has been a change of hands at this charming, stone-built coaching inn dating back to the 1500s. Standing in the middle of the village and a short drive from Bath, inside there's an attractive, flagstone floor in the bar and outside at the back, a delightful terraced garden. The lunch menu offers soup and sandwich platters, and larger dishes such as sausages and mash; burger; pies; steaks; and beer-battered cod and chips. The evening menu is extensive. Twelve en-suite bedrooms, including one four-poster room and one family room, are available.

Open all day all wk 11-11 (Sun 11-10) **Bar Meals** L served Mon-Sat 12-2.30, Sun 12-3 D served Mon-Sat 6-10, Sun 6-9 Av main course £8.49 **Restaurant** L served Mon-Sat 12-2.30, Sun 12-3 D served Mon-Sat 6-10, Sun 6-9 Av 3 course à la carte fr £9.95 ⊕ OLD ENGLISH INNS & HOTELS ◀ Greene King IPA & Abbot Ale, Butcombe, Guest ale ᵭ Westons Stowford Press. 🍷 14 **Facilities** Non-diners area 🐾 (Bar Garden) 🍴 Children's menu Children's portions Garden Parking Wi-fi 🚬 **Rooms** 12

BISHOPSWOOD
Map 4 ST21

Candlelight Inn

TA20 3RS ☎ 01460 234476
e-mail: info@candlelight-inn.co.uk
dir: *From A303 SW of Newtown, right a x-rds signed Bishopswood & Churchinford. Pub on right in village*

Remote pub with excellent food

Debbie and Tom have breathed new life into this rustic rural local tucked away deep in the Blackdown Hills. A 17th-century flint-built inn with wooden floors, crackling log fires and a warm and friendly atmosphere, locals gather here for tip-top pints of Exmoor or Branscombe ale drawn straight from the cask. Food will not disappoint, with everything made on the premises, including vegetables grown in the pub's garden. Follow pickled herring and potato salad with rump of English veal with chargrilled Mediterranean vegetables, leaving room for lemon curd sponge pudding and custard. Look out for occasional beer festivals.

Open 12-3 6-11 (Sun all day) Closed: 25-27 Dec, Mon **Bar Meals** L served Tue-Fri 12-2, Sat-Sun 12-2.30 D served Tue-Thu & Sun 7-9, Fri-Sat 7-9.30 **Restaurant** L served Tue-Fri 12-2, Sat-Sun 12-2.30 D served Tue-Thu &

Sun 7-9, Fri-Sat 7-9.30 ⊕ FREE HOUSE ◀ Otter Bitter, Bass, Exmoor, Branscombe ♂ Thatchers, Sheppy's, Tricky. ♈ 9 **Facilities** Non-diners area ♥ (Bar Garden) ♦♦ Children's portions Garden ♁ Beer festival Parking Wi-fi ▒ (notice required)

BLUE ANCHOR   Map 3 ST04

The Smugglers

TA24 6JS ☎ 01984 640385
e-mail: info@take2chefs.co.uk
web: www.take2chefs.co.uk
dir: *Off A3191, midway between Minehead & Watchet*

Welcoming pub between the sea and hills

'Fresh food, cooked well' is the simple philosophy at this friendly 300-year-old inn. It stands just yards from Blue Anchor Bay on one side, with a backdrop of the Exmoor Hills on the other. Head to the Cellar Bar for refreshment, and to order food. Starters and light bites include sardines and local mussels, while the stoves and grill proffer steaks, Lashford's award-winning sausages, and weekly specials such as lamb rump marinated in cider and honey. In fine weather families can eat in the large walled garden where children enjoy the bouncy castle.

Open 12-3 6-11 (Sat-Sun 12-11) (summer 12-close) Closed: Sun eve, Mon (Nov-Feb only) **Bar Meals** L served all wk 12-2.15 D served all wk 6-9 **Restaurant** L served all wk 12-2.15 D served all wk 6-9 ⊕ FREE HOUSE ◀ Otter Smuggled Otter & Ale, Boddingtons ♂ Westons Traditional. ♈ 8 **Facilities** Non-diners area ♥ (Bar Restaurant Garden) ♦♦ Children's menu Children's portions Play area Garden ♁ Parking Wi-fi ▒ (notice required)

CATCOTT   Map 4 ST33

The Crown Inn

1 The Nydon TA7 9HQ ☎ 01278 722288
e-mail: catcottcrownin@aol.com
dir: *M5 junct 23, A39 towards Glastonbury. Turn left to Catcott*

Venerable ale house with good home-cooked food

Originally a beer house serving local peat-cutters, this low-beamed, flagstoned pub in the Somerset levels is perhaps 400 years old. The winter log fire takes the chill off Bristol Channel winds; in summer the half-acre beer garden is great for families and sun worshippers. Food is plentiful, imaginative and home made; typical options include spicy battered chilli beef; lasagne; and

cheesecake. Look out for specials such as fish pie au gratin; game casserole; or teryaki belly pork. A good range of cask ales and ciders from regional suppliers completes the picture.

Open 12-2.30 6-late Closed: Mon L **Bar Meals** L served Tue-Sun 12-2 (booking advisable Sun) D served all wk 6-9 Av main course £10 **Restaurant** L served Tue-Sun 12-2 (booking advisable Sun) D served Sun-Thu 6-9, Fri-Sat 6-9.30 (booking advisable Fri-Sat) ⊕ FREE HOUSE ◀ Sharp's Doom Bar, St Austell Proper Job, Molegrip Core ♂ Pheasant Plucker, Thatchers Gold. ♈ 10 **Facilities** Non-diners area ♥ (Bar Garden) ♦♦ Children's menu Children's portions Play area Garden ♁ Parking Wi-fi ▒

CHEW MAGNA   Map 4 ST56

The Bear and Swan

PICK OF THE PUBS

South Pde BS40 8SL ☎ 01275 331100
dir: *A37 from Bristol. Turn right signed Chew Magna onto B3130. Or from A38 turn left on B3130*

Much loved by locals and visitors alike

The Victorians clearly didn't like the frontage of this early 18th-century pub, so they gave it one of their own. Inside, the oak-beamed rooms with scrubbed wooden floors and diverse collection of reclaimed tables, chairs and assorted artefacts all contribute to its warm and friendly atmosphere. It's owned by Fuller's, so expect London Pride, but you'll also find Butcombe Bitter, local real ciders and a list of well selected wines. The restaurant offers daily one-, two- and three-course menus with good choices of fish, game, seafood, meats and vegetarian dishes. You might care to start with wasabi tuna and tiger prawn satay with pepper salad; before moving on to aubergine rarebit with tomato, caper and pesto risotto; or baked cod with pancetta crust, fennel and rocket linguine and sweet roasted garlic velouté. The August Bank Holiday weekend cider festival also features a barbecue and live music.

Open all day Mon-Sat 12-11 (Sun 12-8) Closed: 25 Dec, Sun eve **Bar Meals** L served Mon-Sat 12-2.30, Sun 12-3 D served Mon-Sat 6.30-9.30 **Restaurant** L served Mon-Sat 12-2.30, Sun 12-3 D served Mon-Sat 6.30-9.30 ⊕ FULLER'S ◀ London Pride, Butcombe Bitter ♂ Ashton Press, Aspall, Symonds. ♈ 12 **Facilities** Non-diners area ♥ (Bar Garden) ♦♦ Children's portions Garden ♁ Cider festival Parking Wi-fi ▒ (notice required)

The Pony and Trap ◉◉

Knowle Hill, Newton BS40 8TQ ☎ 01275 332627
e-mail: josh@theponyandtrap.co.uk
dir: *Take A37 S from Bristol. After Pensford turn right at rdbt onto A368 towards Weston-Super-Mare. In 1.5m right signed Chew Magna & Winford. Pub 1m on right*

Country cottage pub-restaurant with award-winning cuisine

This 200-year-old building benefits from a stunning location, enjoying fantastic views across the Chew Valley. The Pony and Trap still feels like a rural local despite the acclaim it has achieved with its food. Committed to sourcing all ingredients as locally as possible, everything on the menu is made on the premises, right down to the bread and butter. Try haunch of venison with ox tongue, red cabbage and potato cake, followed by walnut and mocha mousse cake. An eight-course tasting menu is available. Fine wines, local real ales and a local cider sum up its appeal.

Open 12-3 6.30-12 (Sun all day) Closed: Mon (ex BHs & Dec) **Bar Meals** L served Tue-Sat 12-2.30, Sun 12-3.30 D served Tue-Sun 7-9.30 Av main course £15 **Restaurant** L served Tue-Sat 12-2.30, Sun 12-3.30 D served Tue-Sun 7-9.30 Av 3 course à la carte fr £27.95 ⊕ FREE HOUSE ◀ Butcombe Bitter, Sharp's Doom Bar, Guest ale ♂ Ashton Press. ♈ 26 **Facilities** Non-diners area ♦♦ Children's portions Garden Parking Wi-fi

---

CHURCHILL   Map 4 ST45

The Crown Inn

The Batch BS25 5PP ☎ 01934 852995
dir: *From Bristol take A38 S. Right at Churchill lights, left in 200mtrs, up hill to pub*

Rural village pub with lovely gardens

This gem of a pub was once a stop on what was then the Bristol to Exeter coach road. A good selection real ales is served straight from the cask in the two flagstone-floored bars, where open fires blaze on cold days. With a new landlord at the start of 2013, the freshly prepared bar lunches now include sandwiches, soups, salads and ploughman's, all made from the best local ingredients. In fact the beef comes straight from the fields that can be seen from the pub's windows. You can enjoy a meal in the beautiful gardens in warmer weather, perhaps beef casserole; chilli; or cauliflower cheese.

Open all day all wk 11-11 (Fri 11am-mdnt) **Bar Meals** L served all wk 12-2.30 ⊕ FREE HOUSE ◀ Palmers IPA, Bass, RCH PG Steam & Hewish IPA, Bath Gem, St Austell Tribute, Butcombe ♂ Thatchers, Ashton Press, Healey's Cornish Rattler, Bath Ciders Bounders. **Facilities** Non-diners area ♥ (Bar) ♦♦ Children's portions Garden ♁ Parking ▒ **Notes** ◉

CLAPTON-IN-GORDANO — Map 4 ST47

The Black Horse

PICK OF THE PUBS

Clevedon Ln BS20 7RH ☎ 01275 842105
e-mail: theblackhorse@talktalkbusiness.net
dir: M5 junct 19, 3m to village. 2m from Portishead, 10m from Bristol

Real ales, short lunchtime menu, families welcome

The bars on one of the windows of this attractive, whitewashed inn near Bristol are a reminder that the Black Horse's Snug Bar was once the village lock-up. Built in the 14th century, the traditional bar of this pub features low beams, flagstone floors, wooden settles, and old guns above the big open fireplace. Real ales served straight from the barrel include local Butcombe Best and Wadworth 6X, whilst cider fans will rejoice at the sight of Thatchers Heritage. The small kitchen in this listed building limits its output to traditional pub food served lunchtimes only (Monday to Saturday). The repertoire includes hot and cold filled baguettes and rolls; home-made soup of the day; pies and seasonal specials. The large rear garden includes a children's play area, and there's a separate family room.

Open all day all wk **Bar Meals** L served Mon-Sat 12-2 ⊕ ENTERPRISE INNS ◀ Courage Best Bitter, Wadworth 6X, Shepherd Neame Spitfire, Butcombe Bitter, Exmoor Gold, Otter Bitter ⚬ Thatchers Heritage. ♟ 8 **Facilities** Non-diners area ♦️ Play area Family room Garden Parking

CLUTTON — Map 4 ST65

The Hunters Rest ★★★★ INN

PICK OF THE PUBS

See Pick of the Pubs on opposite page

COMBE HAY — Map 4 ST75

The Wheatsheaf

PICK OF THE PUBS

BA2 7EG ☎ 01225 833504
e-mail: info@wheatsheafcombehay.co.uk
dir: From Bath take A369 (Exeter road) to Odd Down, left at park & ride & immediately right towards Combe Hay. 2m to thatched cottage, turn left

Grab a table in the tranquil garden

The Wheatsheaf was built in 1576 as a farmhouse, but not until the 18th century did it begin its life as an alehouse, and today its old persona rubs shoulders companionably with the new, country-chic interior. A long, whitewashed free house with a pantiled roof, the pub stands on a peaceful hillside. The building is decorated with flowers in summer, when the gorgeous south-facing garden makes an ideal spot for outdoor drinking and dining. In the stylishly decorated, rambling bar with its massive wooden tables, sporting prints and

open fires, the resident real ale is Butcombe Bitter and the ciders are Cheddar Valley and Ashton Press. The garden is home to free-range chickens and ducks, blissfully unaware of the importance of their various contributions to the daily menus prepared by head chef, Eddy Rains, who is wholly committed to the use of the freshest seasonal ingredients.

Open 10.30-3 6-11 (Sun 11-5.30) Closed: 25-26 Dec & 1st wk Jan, Sun eve, Mon (ex BHs) **Bar Meals** L served Tue-Sat 12-2.30 D served Tue-Sat 6.30-9.30 **Restaurant** L served Tue-Sun 12-2 D served Tue-Sat 6.30-9.30 ⊕ FREE HOUSE ◀ Butcombe Bitter, Guest ale ⚬ Thatchers & Cheddar Valley, Ashton Press. ♟ 13 **Facilities** Non-diners area ♣ (Bar Restaurant Garden) ♦️ Garden ☂ Parking Wi-fi

COMPTON DANDO — Map 4 ST66

The Compton Inn

Court Hill BS39 4JZ ☎ 01761 490321
e-mail: paul@huntersrest.co.uk
dir: From A368 between Chelwood & Marksbury follow Hunstrete & Compton Dando signs

Confident cooking in a picturesque location

A former farmhouse, the Grade II listed Compton Inn has only been a pub since World War II, but it has been sympathetically restored. Located in picturesque Compton Dando, with its imposing church and hump-backed bridge crossing the River Chew, it is only a few miles from the bustling city of Bristol. It's an ideal bolt-hole to enjoy local ale and cider, and well-cooked dishes like herb-crusted hake, lemon and chorizo crushed potatoes and ratatouille or Somerset faggots in onion gravy, mustard and spring onion mash and vegetables. For pudding try Bakewell tart and blackberry ice cream.

Open all day all wk **Bar Meals** L served Mon-Sat 12-2.15, Sun 12-6 D served Mon-Sat 6.15-9.15 Av main course £12.50 **Restaurant** L served Mon-Sat 12-2.15, Sun 12-6 D served Mon-Sat 6.15-9.15 ⊕ PUNCH TAVERNS ◀ Bath Ales Gem, Sharp's Doom Bar, Otter Bitter ⚬ Thatchers Traditional. ♟ 10 **Facilities** Non-diners area ♣ (Bar Restaurant Garden) ♦️ Children's menu Children's portions Garden ☂ Parking Wi-fi 🚌 (notice required)

CORTON DENHAM — Map 4 ST62

The Queens Arms ★★★★ INN ◉

PICK OF THE PUBS

DT9 4LR ☎ 01963 220317
e-mail: relax@thequeensarms.com
dir: A303 follow signs for Sutton Montis, South Cadbury & Corton Denham. Through South Cadbury, 0.25m, left, up hill signed Corton Denham. Left at hill top to village, approx 1m. Pub on right

The ideal place to relax after a ramble

This late 18th-century, stone-built former cider house is set in a web of lanes meandering through stunning countryside of grassy downs and gurgling trout streams. Beneath the old beams in the bar and separate dining

room are old scrubbed tables set with designer china, grand open fireplaces, and leather chairs and sofas. Outside, the sheltered terrace and sunny garden are perfect for outdoor eating and drinking. Owners Gordon and Jeanette Reid provide over 30 bottled world beers, draught ales from Pitney microbrewery Moor, and local farm ciders, scrumpy and apple juices. There's a great wine list, too. They champion animal welfare and high-quality local produce, measuring food in metres rather than miles. A starter of haggis ravioli sets the scene for mains of leek and saffron risotto, and honey-roast ham. A seven-course tasting menu is also on offer. Events include a beer festival, cider bus tour and film nights. Spacious guest rooms overlook the rolling countryside.

Open all day all wk **Bar Meals** L served all wk 12-3 D served Mon-Sat 6-10, Sun 6-9.30 Av main course £11 **Restaurant** L served all wk 12-3 D served Mon-Sat 6-10, Sun 6-9.30 Fixed menu price fr £27.50 Av 3 course à la carte fr £30 ⊕ FREE HOUSE ◀ Moor Revival & Nor'Hop, Guest ales ⚬ Thatchers Gold, Hecks, Wilkins Farmhouse, Burrow Hill, The Orchard Pig. ♟ 14 **Facilities** Non-diners area ♣ (Bar Garden) ♦️ Children's menu Children's portions Garden ☂ Beer festival Parking Wi-fi **Rooms** 8

CRANMORE — Map 4 ST64

Strode Arms

BA4 4QJ ☎ 01749 880450
e-mail: info@strodearms.co.uk
dir: S of A361, 3.5m E of Shepton Mallet, 7.5m W of Frome

Country pub in pretty setting

On warm days the terrace of this handsome stone coaching inn overflows with happy punters clutching well kept pints of Strong in the Arm or Henry's Original IPA as they gaze over the village duck pond. Inside all is reassuringly traditional with a spacious bar and a cosy country character with log fires. Starters include warm salad of black pudding, smoked bacon and crispy potatoes with dressed leaves and poached egg; mains include slow roasted feather blade of beef, roasted shallots, buttery garlic potato cake, local spinach and thyme jus. There's a good value menu for children as well.

Open all wk 11.30-3 6-11 **Bar Meals** L served all wk 12-2 D served Mon-Sat 6-9 Av main course £10 **Restaurant** L served all wk 12-2 D served Mon-Sat 6-9 ⊕ WADWORTH ◀ Henry's Original IPA, 6X, The Bishop's Tipple, Strong in the Arm, Wadworth Horizon ⚬ Westons Traditional. ♟ **Facilities** Non-diners area ♣ (Bar Garden) ♦️ Children's menu Children's portions Play area Family room Garden ☂ Parking Wi-fi 🚌 (notice required)

Save on hotels. Book at **theAA.com/hotel**

SOMERSET 377 ENGLAND

PICK OF THE PUBS

The Hunters Rest ★★★★ INN

CLUTTON　　　　　　　Map 4 ST65

King Ln, Clutton Hill BS39 5QL
☎ **01761 452303**
e-mail: info@huntersrest.co.uk
web: www.huntersrest.co.uk
dir: *On A37 follow signs for Wells through Pensford, at large rdbt left towards Bath, 100mtrs, right into country lane, pub 1m up hill*

Traditional country inn with excellent views

Dating from 1750, The Earl of Warwick's former hunting lodge offers far-reaching views across the Cam Valley to the Mendip Hills and the Chew Valley towards Bristol. When the estate was sold in 1872, the building became a tavern serving the growing number of coal miners working in the area, but all the mines closed long ago and the place has been transformed into a popular and attractive inn. Paul Thomas has been running the place for more than 25 years, during which time he has established a great reputation for good home-made food, real ales – typically Butcombe, Bath Gem and Otter – and a well-stocked wine cellar. The menu includes smoked trout and prawn salad; coarse chicken liver pâté on warm granary toast; giant pastries called oggies, which might come with a variety of fillings, such as beef steak and Stilton, mixed smoked fish, and cauliflower cheese; and the Hunter's

Smoky – a warming mix of smoked haddock, salmon and trout with cheese sauce. Other hot dishes include barbecued chicken with smoky BBQ sauce; beef lasagne; Somerset faggots and onion gravy; and from the specials blackboard a selection of daily-delivered, Brixham-landed sea bass and other fish; slow braised lamb shank with red wine and rosemary gravy, mash and buttered greens; and game casserole with herb dumplings. Finish with a popular dessert such as tarte au citron, or maple and walnut cheesecake. In summer you can sit out in the landscaped grounds, and if a longer visit is on the cards the inn has very stylish en suite bedrooms.

Open all day all wk **Bar Meals** L served

all wk 12-9.45 D served all wk 12-9.45 Av main course £10 food served all day **Restaurant** L served all wk 12-9.45 D served all wk 12-9.45 Av 3 course à la carte fr £25 food served all day ⊕ FREE HOUSE ◧ Bath Gem, Otter Ale, Butcombe Ŏ Broadoak, Thatchers. ♟ 10 **Facilities** Non-diners area ✿ 📍 Children's menu & portions Play area Family room Garden Parking Wi-fi 🚌 (notice required) **Rooms** 5

CREWKERNE
Map 4 ST40

The George Inn ★★★ INN

Market Square TA18 7LP ☎ 01460 73650
e-mail: georgecrewkerne@btconnect.com
dir: *Telephone for directions*

400 years of hospitality in busy market town

Situated in the heart of Crewkerne, The George has been welcoming travellers since 1541, though the present hamstone building dates from 1832, and the current landlord has held sway since 1994. Kingstone Press ciders sit alongside four real ales in the bar, while the kitchen produces an array of popular dishes for bar snacks and more substantial meals from the daily specials board. Vegetarian and vegan meals are always available. Comfortable en suite bedrooms are traditionally styled and include four-poster rooms.

Open all day all wk **Bar Meals** L served all wk 12-2 D served all wk 7-9 Av main course £8.50 **Restaurant** L served all wk 12-2 D served all wk 7-9 ⊕ FREE HOUSE ◄ St Austell Tribute, Dartmoor Legend, Boddingtons ♻ Thatchers Gold, Kingstone Press. ☿ 8
Facilities Non-diners area ⬥ Children's menu Children's portions Outside area �ⴹ Wi-fi ▭ **Rooms** 13

The Manor Arms

North Perrott TA18 7SG ☎ 01460 72901
dir: *From A30 (Yeovil/Honiton) take A3066 towards Bridport. North Perrott 1.5m*

A bastion of tradition in the country

On the Dorset/Somerset border, this 16th-century Grade II listed pub and its neighbouring hamstone cottages overlook the green in the conservation village of North Perrott. The inn has been lovingly restored and an inglenook fireplace, flagstone floors and oak beams are among the charming features inside. Dogs and children are welcome, there's a good beer garden for warmer days, and there are plenty of rambling opportunities on the doorstep. To accompany ales like Exmoor, and Ashton Press cider, expect wholesome traditional food such as cottage pie, pan-fried lamb's liver and beer-battered cod. There is also a specials board, and every month sees a different theme night.

Open 12-3 6-11 Closed: Sun eve **Bar Meals** L served all wk 12-2 D served Mon-Sat 6.30-9 **Restaurant** L served all wk 12-2 D served Mon-Sat 6.30-9 ⊕ FREE HOUSE ◄ Sharp's Doom Bar, Exmoor, Butcombe ♻ Ashton Press. **Facilities** Non-diners area ⬥ (Bar Garden) ⬥ Children's menu Children's portions Garden �ⴹ Parking Wi-fi

CROSCOMBE
Map 4 ST54

The Bull Terrier ★★★ INN

Long St BA5 3QJ ☎ 01749 343658
e-mail: barry.vidler@bullterrierpub.co.uk
dir: *Halfway between Wells & Shepton Mallet on A371*

One of Somerset's oldest pubs

This unspoiled village free house was first licensed in 1612, although the building itself is medieval. The fine beams in the bar, once the main hall, are original, the inglenook fireplace and ceiling being added in the 16th century. A real ale and a cider come from the Cheddar area. One menu is offered throughout, with Greenland prawn cocktail, and chunky chicken goujons among the ten starters. Included in the 25 main dishes are leg of English lamb; local sirloin and fillet steaks; fresh trout with almonds; and spinach and peanut stuffed pancakes. In suitable weather, enjoy the pretty walled garden.

Open all wk 12-2.45 7-late **Bar Meals** L served all wk 12-2 D served all wk 7-9 Av main course £9 **Restaurant** L served all wk 12-2 D served all wk 7-9 ⊕ FREE HOUSE ◄ Courage Directors, Marston's Pedigree, Morland Old Speckled Hen, Greene King Ruddles County, Cheddar ♻ Thatchers Cheddar Valley & Gold. ☿ 8
Facilities Non-diners area ⬥ (Bar Restaurant Garden) ⬥ Children's menu Children's portions Family room Garden ⴹ Parking ▭ **Rooms** 2

The George Inn

Long St BA5 3QH ☎ 01749 342306 & 345189
e-mail: pg@thegeorgeinn.co.uk
dir: *On A371 midway between Shepton Mallet & Wells*

Renovated pub with traditional food and two beer festivals

This 17th-century village pub has received ongoing renovations since the Graham family bought it 13 years ago. After flooding in July 2012, the pub underwent further updates and is now a great place to enjoy local ales such as Moor Revival in the bar with its large inglenook fireplace and family grandfather clock. There are real ciders too, including Thatchers Gold, and diners can enjoy locally sourced quality food, with daily specials complementing old favourites such as smoked haddock fishcakes, and fillet steak. The garden terrace incorporates an all-weather patio and children's area. There are beer festivals on the Spring Bank Holiday and in October.

Open all wk 12-3 6-11 **Bar Meals** L served Mon-Sat 12-2.15, Sun 12-2.30 D served all wk 6-9 Av main course £9-£11 **Restaurant** L served Mon-Sat 12-2.15, Sun 12-2.30 D served all wk 6-9 ⊕ FREE HOUSE ◄ Butcombe Bitter, Moor Revival, Blindmans, Hop Back Summer Lightning, Cheddar Ales Potholer ♻ Thatchers Cheddar Valley & Gold, The Orchard Pig, Bittersweet. ☿ 9
Facilities Non-diners area ⬥ (Bar Garden) ⬥ Children's menu Children's portions Play area Family room Garden ⴹ Beer festival Parking Wi-fi

DINNINGTON
Map 4 ST41

Dinnington Docks

TA17 8SX ☎ 01460 52397
e-mail: hilary@dinningtondocks.co.uk
dir: *S of A303 between South Petherton & Ilminster*

Traditional locals' pub in a small hamlet

Formerly known as the Rose & Crown, this traditional village pub on the old Fosse Way has been licensed for over 250 years and has no loud music, pool tables or fruit machines to drown out the conversation. Inside you will find pictures, signs and memorabilia of its rail and maritime past. Good-quality cask ales and farmhouse cider are served, and freshly prepared food including the likes of crab cakes, faggots, snapper, steak, and lamb shank for two feature on the menu. There's a quiz night every Sunday, and the pub is located in an ideal place for cycling and walking.

Open all wk 11.30-3 6-12 (Sat-Sun all day) ⊕ FREE HOUSE ◄ Butcombe Bitter, Guest ales ♻ Burrow Hill, Westons Stowford Press, Thatchers Gold. **Facilities** ⬥ Children's menu Children's portions Play area Family room Garden Parking

DITCHEAT
Map 4 ST63

The Manor House Inn

PICK OF THE PUBS

BA4 6RB ☎ 01749 860276
e-mail: landlord@manorhouseinn.co.uk
dir: *From Shepton Mallet take A371 towards Castle Cary, in 3m turn right to Ditcheat*

Local ales complement fine food in lovely Mendips setting

In the pretty village of Ditcheat, between Shepton Mallet and Castle Cary, this handsome red-brick, 17th-century free house belonged to the lord of the manor about 150 years ago when it was known as the White Hart. Convenient for the Royal Bath and West Showground and the East Somerset Steam Railway, it is also boasts views of the Mendips. Flagstone floors and warming log fires in winter add to the charm of the friendly bar, which serves local Butcombe Bitter and regular guest ales, Thatchers cider and up to nine wines by the glass. The seasonal menu may offer starters such as home-baked ratatouille with rich provençale sauce; and scallops in shells with lemon and lime dressing; followed by main courses of braised brisket of beef with creamy horseradish mash and rich Guinness sauce; or guinea fowl breast with spinach, fondant potato and Marsala sauce.

Open all day all wk Mon-Sat 12-11 (Sun 12-9) **Bar Meals** L served Mon-Sat 12-2.30, Sun 12-5 D served Mon-Thu 6.30-9, Fri-Sat 6.30-9.30 **Restaurant** L served Mon-Sat 12-2.30, Sun 12-5 D served Mon-Thu 6.30-9, Fri-Sat 6.30-9.30 ⊕ FREE HOUSE ◄ Butcombe Bitter, Guest ales ♻ Ashton Press, Thatchers Dry. ☿ 9
Facilities Non-diners area ⬥ Children's portions Garden ⴹ Parking Wi-fi ▭ (notice required)

DULVERTON
Map 3 SS92

Woods Bar and Restaurant ◉

4 Bank Square TA22 9BU ☎ 01398 324007
e-mail: woodsdulverton@hotmail.com
dir: *From Tiverton take A396 N. At Machine Cross take B3222 to Dulverton. Establishment adjacent to church*

Serious food and a friendly atmosphere

In the rural town of Dulverton on the edge of Exmoor, this is a bar and restaurant where food and drink are taken seriously, but without detriment to its friendly atmosphere. It's run by owners with a passion for wine – every bottle on the comprehensive list (up to £25) can be opened for a single glass. The cosy bar crackles with conversation while dishes of modern British cooking with a French accent leave the kitchen. Typical of these one AA-Rosette dishes are roast chicken supreme with rösti potato, Savoy cabbage, pancetta and Jerusalem artichoke and wild mushroom fricassée.

Open all wk 11-3 6-11.30 (Sun 12-3 7-11) **Bar Meals** L served all wk 12-2 D served all wk 6-9.30 Av main course £8 **Restaurant** L served all wk 12-2 D served all wk 7-9.30 Av 3 course à la carte fr £22 ⊕ FREE HOUSE ◖ St Austell Tribute, HSD, Dartmoor Ố Thatchers, Healey's Cornish Rattler. ☻ **Facilities** Non-diners area ❄ (Bar Restaurant Garden) ♦ Children's menu Children's portions Garden

DUNSTER
Map 3 SS94

The Luttrell Arms
PICK OF THE PUBS

High St TA24 6SG ☎ 01643 821555
e-mail: info@luttrellarms.fsnet.co.uk
dir: *From A39 (Bridgwater to Minehead), left onto A396 to Dunster (2m from Minehead)*

Historic setting for a drink or meal

The Abbots of Cleeve installed their guests in this substantial 15th-century building, built of local red sandstone, and it was Oliver Cromwell's headquarters during his siege of Dunster Castle, ancestral seat of the Luttrells. Now in fresh hands, the pub is one of Britain's oldest post-houses and retains its galleried courtyard, stone-mullioned windows, wood-panelled walls and open fireplaces. Over a pint of Sharp's Doom Bar or Thatchers Cheddar Valley cider, study the seasonal menu before dining in the main bar, in the restaurant, or outside. In addition to lunchtime sandwiches and baguettes, there's plenty to choose from: starters of carpaccio of beef with parmesan dressing; and pumpkin and bacon soup. Main courses include grilled gurnard with Niçoise salad; steak-and-kidney pie; the pub's 'famous' rack of barbecue ribs; and cauliflower cheese with jacket potato. From the garden you can look over medieval Dunster and see Exmoor National Park.

Open all day all wk 8am-11pm **Bar Meals** L served all wk 11.30-3, all day summer D served all wk 7-10 Av main course £9 **Restaurant** L served Sun 12-3 D served all wk 7-10 Fixed menu price fr £19.95 Av 3 course à la carte fr

£30 ⊕ FREE HOUSE ◖ Exmoor Ale, Sharp's Doom Bar, Guest ale Ố Thatchers Cheddar Valley. ☻ 12
Facilities Non-diners area ❄ (Bar Restaurant Garden) ♦ Children's menu Children's portions Family room Garden ⊼ Wi-fi ▭

The Stags Head Inn **NEW**

10 West St TA24 6SN ☎ 01643 821229
e-mail: info@stagsheadinnexmoor.co.uk
dir: *From A39 take A396 to Dunster. Pub on right*

Cosy, welcoming pub on edge of Exmoor

Dunster Castle dominates this historic village, the Gateway to Exmoor National Park. The inn itself is 16th century, as a fresco in a bedroom depicting Henry VIII as the devil confirms. The bar stocks Somerset real ciders and ales, including Wills Neck, named after the highest point in the Quantocks. Club sandwiches are served at lunchtime, while the main menu presents hake, salmon, prawn and smoked haddock pie; chicken rogan josh; chargrilled West Country sirloin steak; and baked venison and butternut squash in shortcrust pastry. This small inn has limited seating, so reservations for dinner and Sunday lunch are recommended.

Open 11.45-3.30 5.45-11 Closed: Wed L **Bar Meals** L served Thu-Tue 12-2.30 D served all wk 6-9 Av main course £10 ⊕ FREE HOUSE ◖ Exmoor Ale, Otter Ale, Quantock Wills Neck Ố Thatchers Gold.
Facilities Non-diners area ❄ (Bar Garden) ♦ Children's menu Garden ⊼ Cider festival Wi-fi ▭ (notice required)

EAST BOWER
Map 4 ST33

The Bower Inn **NEW**

Bower Ln TA6 4TY ☎ 01278 422926
e-mail: enquiries@thebowerinn.co.uk
dir: *M5 junct 23, A39 signed Glastonbury & Wells. Right at lights signed Bridgwater. Under motorway, left into Bower Ln to pub on right*

Attractive 18th-century building in a picturesque cottage garden

The Bower Inn was converted from a private family home to a restaurant in the 1980s, then following two years of closure, it attracted the attention of Peter and Candida Leaver, who purchased, renovated and reopened it in 2010. Business is good, both in the bar (mind the tiger!), where Somerset's Butcombe and Devon's Otter real ales are served, and in the contemporary restaurant, renowned for home-made food such as grilled pork loin steak with black pepper and cider sauce; fresh battered cod with pea purée; and spinach and ricotta tortellini in white wine cream sauce.

Open 12-3 6-11 Closed: Mon L **Bar Meals** L served Tue-Sun 12.30-2.30 D served Mon-Sat 6.30-9, Sun 6.30-8 **Restaurant** L served Tue-Sun 12.30-2.30 D served all wk 6.30-9 ⊕ FREE HOUSE ◖ Otter, Butcombe.
Facilities Non-diners area ❄ (Bar Garden) ♦ Children's menu Children's portions Garden ⊼ Parking Wi-fi ▭ (notice required)

EAST COKER
Map 4 ST51

The Helyar Arms ★★★ INN
PICK OF THE PUBS

Moor Ln BA22 9JR ☎ 01935 862332
e-mail: info@helyar-arms.co.uk
dir: *3m from Yeovil. Take A57 or A30, follow East Coker signs*

Sublime inn in idyllic Somerset village

Named after Archdeacon Helyar, a chaplain to Queen Elizabeth I, the inn sits at heart of a truly picturesque village of thatched houses trimmed by colourful cottage gardens. Peek through the stone mullioned windows of this partly 15th-century building and you'll glimpse a traditional village-style old bar warmed by open fires. Step inside to enjoy a beer from one of a number of West Country breweries regularly stocked; settle in and look forward to a menu which makes full use of local produce, including Somerset game and fish from the south Devon coast which often feature on the specials board. The à la carte includes starters of pan-fried crab cakes with chilli and lime mayonnaise; the main event may be a classic Brixham fish, chips, crushed peas and tartare sauce, whilst 28-day hung Somerset beef makes for excellent steaks. The six en suite rooms are a great base for ramblers exploring the tranquil countryside or visiting the NT's remarkable Montacute House.

Open all wk 11-3 6-11 Closed: 25 Dec eve **Bar Meals** L served all wk 12-2.30 D served all wk 6.30-9.30 Av main course £12 **Restaurant** L served all wk 12-2.30 D served all wk 6.30-9.30 ⊕ PUNCH TAVERNS ◖ Butcombe Bitter, Sharp's Doom Bar, Exmoor Ố Thatchers Gold, Taunton Original. **Facilities** Non-diners area ❄ (Bar Restaurant Garden) ♦ Children's portions Family room Garden ⊼ Parking Wi-fi ▭ (notice required) **Rooms** 6

EXFORD
Map 3 SS83

The Crown Hotel ★★★ HL ◉
PICK OF THE PUBS

TA24 7PP ☎ 01643 831554
e-mail: info@crownhotelexmoor.co.uk
dir: *From M5 junct 25 follow Taunton signs. Take A358 then B3224 via Wheddon Cross to Exford*

Dedicated to produce from the Southwest

A family-run 17th-century coaching inn in the heart of Exmoor National Park, The Crown is a comfy mix of elegance and tradition and remains a hotel to this day. With three acres of its own grounds and a tributary of the infant River Exe flowing through its woodland, it's popular with outdoor pursuits enthusiasts, but the cosy bar is also very much the social heart of the village; many of the patrons enjoy the Exmoor Ales from Wiveliscombe just down the road. The AA-Rosette cuisine promises much, especially with Exmoor's profuse organic produce on the doorstep and the kitchen's close attention to sustainable sources. Menus could tempt with twice-baked cheese soufflé; slow-roasted belly of pork on buttered cabbage with creamed potatoes, roasted root vegetables and red

continued

EXFORD continued

wine sauce; and sautéed potato gnocchi in a wild mushroom and cream sauce with globe artichokes, rocket and truffle oil.

Open all day all wk 12-11 **Bar Meals** L served all wk 12-2.30 D served all wk 5.30-9.30 Av main course £12 **Restaurant** D served all wk 7-9 Fixed menu price fr £27 ⊕ FREE HOUSE ◀ Exmoor Ale & Gold, Guest ales Ö Thatchers Gold, St Austell Copper Press. ♟ 10 **Facilities** Non-diners area ❖ (Bar Garden) ♦ Children's portions Garden ⊨ Parking Wi-fi ▄ (notice required) **Rooms** 16

FAULKLAND   Map 4 ST75

Tuckers Grave

BA3 5XF ☎ 01373 834230
dir: *From Bath take A36 towards Warminster. Turn right on A366, through Norton St Philip towards Faulkland. In Radstock, left at x-rds, pub on left*

The smallest pub in Somerset in a lovely countryside setting

Tapped Butcombe ale and Cheddar Valley cider draw local aficionados to this unspoilt rural gem, which was threatened with permanent closure a few years ago. Somerset's smallest pub has a tiny atmospheric bar with old settles but no counter, or music, television or jukebox either. Lunchtime sandwiches are available, and a large lawn with flower borders makes an attractive outdoor seating area, with the countryside adjacent. The 'grave' in the pub's name is the unmarked one of Edward Tucker, who hung himself here in 1747.

Open 11.30-3 6-11 (Sun 12-3 7-10.30) Closed: 25 Dec, Mon L ⊕ FREE HOUSE ◀ Fuller's London Pride, Butcombe Bitter Ö Thatchers Cheddar Valley. **Facilities** ♦ Family room Garden Parking **Notes** ⊜

FRESHFORD   Map 4 ST76

The Inn at Freshford

The Hill BA2 7WG ☎ 01225 722250
e-mail: landlord@theinnatfreshford.co.uk
dir: *1m from A36 between Beckington & Limpley Stoke*

Village inn that welcomes walkers, children and dogs

Popular with walkers and their dogs, this family-run 15th-century inn in the Limpley Stoke valley is ideally placed for strolling along the nearby Kennet & Avon Canal. The delights of Wiltshire's Box Steam Brewery take their turn in the bar. Here wooden floors, original beams and log fires add tremendous charm. The varied and contemporary menu changes weekly, but choices might include devilled kidneys on toast with fried egg; pan-fried medallions of venison; and puddings such as pear and cranberry frangipane tart.

Open all wk Mar-Dec all day; Jan-Feb Mon-Thu 10.30-3 6-11 Fri-Sat all day Sun 10.30-6 ⊕ FREE HOUSE ◀ Box Steam, Guest ale. **Facilities** ❖ (Bar Restaurant Garden) ♦ Children's menu Children's portions Garden Parking Wi-fi

HASELBURY PLUCKNETT   Map 4 ST41

The White Horse at Haselbury

PICK OF THE PUBS

North St TA18 7RJ ☎ 01460 78873
e-mail: whitehorsehaselbury@hotmail.co.uk
dir: *Just off A30 between Crewkerne & Yeovil on B3066*

French and British classics in a rural pub

New landlords, as of April 2013, Rebecca and Richard Robinson hail from the London restaurant scene with the move marking a homecoming for Rebecca, originally from Broadwinsor. It's easy to see the appeal of the pub in rural Somerset, which used to be a rope works and flax store and was then a cider house. Real ales and ciders are showcased in annual festivals but expect the likes of Otter Ale and Teignworthy beers and Thatchers and Burrow Hill cider on a regular basis. The menu takes inspiration from French and British classics and makes the most of the fantastic local produce, particularly the abundance of fine seafood from the Dorset coast. Bouride of Cornish mussels with brandard stuffed piquillo pepper and garlic croûtons might precede roast fillet of sea bass, fennel, blood orange and watercress salad. Richard and Rebecca pledge that the great British pub experience is important to them so they welcome those who just want home-made Scotch eggs and a pint as much as those seeking fine food and wine.

Open 12-2.30 6.30-11 Closed: Sun eve, Mon **Bar Meals** L served Tue-Sun 12-3 D served Tue-Sat 6.30-9.30 Av main course £13.95 **Restaurant** L served Tue-Sun 12-3 D served Tue-Sat 6.30-9.30 Fixed menu price fr £13.95 Av 3 course à la carte fr £25 ⊕ FREE HOUSE ◀ Palmers Best Bitter, Otter Ale, Teignworthy, Wadworth 6X, Sharp's Doom Bar, Butcombe Ö Thatchers, Burrow Hill. ♟ 10 **Facilities** Non-diners area ❖ (Garden) ♦ Children's menu Children's portions Garden ⊨ Beer festival Cider festival Parking Wi-fi ▄ (notice required)

HINTON BLEWETT   Map 4 ST55

Ring O'Bells

BS39 5AN ☎ 01761 452239
e-mail: ringobellshinton@butcombe.com
dir: *11m S of Bristol on A37 towards Wells. Turn right from either Clutton or Temple Cloud to Hinton Blewett*

A great walkers' pub with a welcoming atmosphere

On the edge of the Mendips, this 200-year-old inn describes itself as the 'archetypal village green pub' and offers good views of the Chew Valley. An all-year-round cosy atmosphere is boosted by a log fire in winter, and a wide choice of well-kept real ales. An extra dining area/function room has been added. There's always something going on, whether it's a tour of the brewery, pig racing night or fishing competitions. Good-value dishes include beer-battered haddock fillet with chips; pie of the day with mashed potato; or Ashton cider-braised pork belly and pork cheek on a black pudding mash. Baguettes, sandwiches, jacket potatoes and ploughman's are also available.

Open all wk Mon-Thu 12-3 5-11 (Fri-Sun all day summer Fri-Sun 12-3 4.30-12 winter) **Bar Meals** L served Fri-Sat 12-2.30, Sun 12-3 D served all wk 6-9 **Restaurant** L served Fri-Sat 12-2.30, Sun 12-3 D served all wk 6-9 ⊕ BUTCOMBE ◀ Fuller's London Pride, Butcombe, Adam Henson's Rare Breed, Guest ales Ö Ashton Press & Still. ♟ 8 **Facilities** Non-diners area ♦ Children's menu Children's portions Garden Parking Wi-fi ▄

HINTON ST GEORGE   Map 4 ST41

The Lord Poulett Arms

PICK OF THE PUBS

See Pick of the Pubs on opposite page

HOLCOMBE   Map 4 ST64

The Holcombe Inn ★★★★★ INN ◉

Stratton Rd BA3 5EB ☎ 01761 232478
e-mail: bookings@holcombeinn.co.uk
dir: *On A367 to Stratton-on-the-Fosse, take concealed left turn opposite Downside Abbey signed Holcombe, take next right, pub 1.5m on left*

Known for great food and glorious sunsets

From the lovely gardens of this 17th-century, Grade II listed country inn you can see Downside Abbey, home of a community of Benedictine monks. Log-fired, flagstone-floored and with tucked-away corners, this is where to find some of the county's top locally produced food, and recognised as such by an AA Rosette. Menus usually list Cotswold lager-battered haddock fillet; pan-seared John Dory; chargrilled loin of rabbit; and roasted cauliflower cheese omelette. Otter and Bath Gem real ales, and Thatchers and Orchard Pig real ciders are on tap and wines by the glass are plentiful. Catch a sunset – they can be rather special here.

Open all wk 12-3 6-11 (Fri-Sun all day) **Bar Meals** L served Mon-Thu 12-2.30, Fri-Sun all day D served Mon-Thu 6.30-9.30, Fri-Sun all day Av main course £9.95 **Restaurant** L served Mon-Thu 12-2.30, Fri-Sun all day D served Mon-Thu 6.30-9.30, Fri- Sun all day ⊕ FREE HOUSE ◀ Otter Ale, Bath Gem Ö Thatchers, The Orchard Pig, Hecks. ♟ 17 **Facilities** Non-diners area ♦ Children's menu Children's portions Garden ⊨ Parking Wi-fi ▄ **Rooms** 7

PICK OF THE PUBS

The Lord Poulett Arms

HINTON ST GEORGE   Map 4 ST41

High St TA17 8SE ☎ 01460 73149
e-mail:
reservations@lordpoulettarms.com
web: www.lordpoulettarms.com
dir: *2m N of Crewkerne, 1.5m S of A303*

Award-winning pub between the A30 and A303

A pub since 1680, there's that certain something about this handsome stone village inn that we do so well in Britain: thatched roof, secluded garden; wisteria-draped pergola tucked in next to an old Fives court. Then inside, a magpie-mix of polished antique furniture distributed judiciously across timeworn boarded floors, shiny flagstones and a vast fireplace pumping out the heat into tastefully decorated rooms. The feel is so quintessentially, dare we say it, English. The inner bar is popular with locals, not least because it dispenses pints of Branscombe Vale, Hop Back and Otter ales, and West Country ciders straight from the cask. Such a traditional interior does not mean you'll necessarily get traditional food, although if you want a grilled sirloin steak with Dorset mushrooms and Madeira cream, it could well be waiting for you to ask. Just as likely, though, are confit Creedy carver duck leg with five-spiced red cabbage and wasabi mash; tandoori-dusted megrim sole with sweet potato, curry oil and

pickled vegetables; and spelt spätzle with sprouting broccoli pesto and Laverstoke Park (Formula One champion Jody Scheckter's Hampshire farm) mozzarella. Puddings include Yorkshire rhubarb crumble and vanilla ice cream; Lord Poulett apple tarte Tatin; and a fine selection of West Country cheeses served with home-made oat cakes and chutney. The set two- and three-course Sunday lunches are good value. There's a decent wine list, too, and a summer weekend beer festival. For outdoor dining there are white metalwork tables and chairs in a lavender-fringed gravelled area reminiscent of somewhere French, and picnic-sets in a wild flower meadow.

Open all day all wk 12-11 Closed: 26

Dec, 1 Jan **Bar Meals** L served all wk 12-2.30, bar menu 3-6.30 D served all wk 7-9.15 Av main course £14 **Restaurant** L served all wk 12-2.30, bar menu 3-6.30 D served all wk 7-9.15 Av 3 course à la carte fr £19 ⊕ FREE HOUSE 🛢 Hop Back, Branscombe Vale, Otter, Dorset 🍎 Thatchers Gold, Burrow Hill. 🍷 14 **Facilities** Non-diners area 👫 Children's portions Garden 🎍 Beer festival Parking Wi-fi

HOLTON
Map 4 ST62

The Old Inn

BA9 8AR ☎ 01963 32002
e-mail: info@theoldinnholton.co.uk
dir: *From W into village, pub on left*

Go for the steaks and fish cooked on the grill

A change of hands in August 2012 saw the arrival of new owner Nick Hart, with Gordon Ramsay protégée Jason Porter heading up the kitchen of this restored 400-year-old coaching inn. Settle in front of the log fire with a pint of Wadworth ale or Thatchers cider, while choosing from a broad menu that incorporates light bites, sandwiches, steaks from the grill, or à la carte choices such as lamb's liver with crispy bacon on chive mash. Fresh fish is also a feature – look for pan-seared fillet of sea bass with potato terrine, wilted spinach, wood mushrooms and hazelnut cream.

Open 12-3 6-11 (Sat 12-11 Sun 12-6) Closed: Sun eve **Bar Meals** L served Mon-Sat 12-2, Sun 12-4 D served Mon-Sat 6-9 Av main course £14 **Restaurant** L served Mon-Sat 12-2, Sun 12-4 D served Mon-Sat 6-9.30 Fixed menu price fr £11.50 Av 3 course à la carte fr £24.50 ⊕ FREE HOUSE ◀ Wadworth Boundary, Butcombe, Cheddar, Wessex Kilmington Best ♻ Thatchers, Addlestones. **Facilities** Non-diners area ❖ (Bar Garden) ♦♦ Children's menu Children's portions Garden ⌁ Parking Wi-fi ⛺ (notice required)

HUISH EPISCOPI
Map 4 ST42

Rose & Crown (Eli's)

TA10 9QT ☎ 01458 250494
dir: *M5 junct 25, A358 towards Ilminster. Left onto A378. Huish Episcopi in 14m (1m from Langport). Pub near church in village*

The pub with no bar, but plenty of real ales

Locked in a glorious time-warp, this 17th-century thatched inn, affectionately known as Eli's, (named after the current landlord's grandfather) has been in the Pittard family for over 150 years. Don't expect to find a bar counter, there's just a flagstoned taproom where customers congregate among the ale and farmhouse cider casks. In a side room are a sit-up-and-beg piano, time-honoured pub games, old photos and fairly basic furniture. Home-made food includes popular steak-and-ale pie, sandwiches, jacket potatoes or pork cobbler. Regular Irish music evenings and monthly folk-singing evenings are fun.

Open all wk 11.30-3 5.30-11 (Fri-Sat 11.30-11.30 Sun 12-10.30) **Bar Meals** L served all wk 12-2 D served Mon-Sat 5.30-7.30 ⊕ FREE HOUSE ◀ Teignworthy Reel Ale, Glastonbury Mystery Tor, Hop Back Summer Lightning, Butcombe Bitter, Branscombe Vale Summa That ♻ Burrow Hill, Thatchers Gold. **Facilities** Non-diners area ❖ (Bar Garden) ♦♦ Play area Family room Garden ⌁ Parking ⛺ (notice required) **Notes** ⊕

ILCHESTER
Map 4 ST52

Ilchester Arms

The Square BA22 8LN ☎ 01935 840220
e-mail: mail@ilchesterarms.com
dir: *From A303 take A37 signed Ilchester/Yeovil, left at 2nd Ilchester sign. Hotel 100yds on right*

Smart hostelry close to A303

An elegant Georgian-fronted house with lots of character, this establishment was first licensed in 1686; attractive features include warming open fires and a lovely walled garden. Between 1962 and 1985 it was owned by the man who developed Ilchester cheese, and its association with good food continues: chef-proprietor Brendan McGee takes pride in producing modern British dishes such as breast of chicken filled with wild mushroom mousse; pan-fried medallions of pork tenderloin on a bed of baked sweet potato purée; and wild and forest mushroom casserole. Bank holiday beer and cider festivals are held - contact the pub for details.

Open all day all wk 7am-11pm Closed: 26 Dec **Bar Meals** L served Mon-Sat 12-2.30 D served Mon-Sat 7-9 Av main course £7.50 **Restaurant** L served all wk 12-2.30 D served Mon-Sat 7-9 Fixed menu price fr £13.95 Av 3 course à la carte fr £23 ⊕ FREE HOUSE ◀ Yeovil Ales, Bass Extra Smooth, Local Ales ♻ Thatchers Gold & Pear. ♈ 14 **Facilities** Non-diners area ❖ (Bar Garden) ♦♦ Children's menu Children's portions Play area Family room Garden ⌁ Beer festival Cider festival Parking Wi-fi ⛺

ILMINSTER
Map 4 ST31

New Inn ★★★★ INN

Dowlish Wake TA19 0NZ ☎ 01460 52413
dir: *From Ilminster follow Kingstone & Perry's Cider Museum signs, in Dowlish Wake follow pub signs*

Recommended for its home-cooked food and local cider

Deep in rural Somerset, this 350-year-old stone-built pub is tucked away in the village of Dowlish Wake, close to Perry's thatched Cider Mill and Museum. Inside are two bars (serving Perry's Cider, of course) with wood-burning stoves and a restaurant, where menus of home-cooked food capitalise on the quality and freshness of local produce. You could opt for a signature dish such as fillet of salmon in a prawn and butter glaze; or stick to pub favourites such as a giant Yorkshire pudding filled with pork sausages, new potatoes, vegetables and gravy. There are four guest rooms situated in an annexe overlooking the large secluded garden.

Open all wk 11.30-3 6-11 **Bar Meals** L served all wk 12-2.30 D served all wk 6-8.45 Av main course £7.50-£13 **Restaurant** L served all wk 12-2.30 D served all wk 6-8.45 ⊕ FREE HOUSE ◀ Butcombe Bitter, Otter Ale ♻ Thatchers Gold, Perry's. ♈ 10 **Facilities** Non-diners area ❖ (All areas) ♦♦ Children's menu Children's portions Garden Outside area ⌁ Parking Wi-fi ⛺ (notice required) **Rooms** 4

KILVE
Map 3 ST14

The Hood Arms ★★★★ INN

TA5 1EA ☎ 01278 741210
e-mail: info@thehoodarms.com
dir: *From M5 junct 23/24 follow A39 to Kilve. Village between Bridgwater & Minehead*

The Quantock Hills and the coast both on the doorstep

The Quantock Hills rise up behind this family-run 17th-century coaching inn, just an ammonite's throw from Kilve's fossil-rich beach. Real ales to enjoy in the beamed bar or in the garden include regulars from Otter and Palmers, guests Jurassic and Harbour Master, and local ciders, any of which will happily accompany a warm foccacia roll, jacket potato or something from the main menu, such as pheasant breast in streaky bacon; osso buco; sea bass fillets with crayfish and dill risotto; or mixed squash with pequillo peppers. Specials are chalked up daily. There are 12 stylish guest rooms, some with four-poster beds.

Open all day all wk ⊕ FREE HOUSE ◀ Otter Head, Palmers Copper Ale, Fuller's London Pride, Guinness, Guest ales ♻ Thatchers Gold. **Facilities** ❖ (Bar Restaurant Garden) ♦♦ Children's menu Children's portions Play area Family room Garden Parking Wi-fi **Rooms** 12

KINGSDON
Map 4 ST52

Kingsdon Inn

TA11 7LG ☎ 01935 840543
e-mail: enquiries@kingsdoninn.co.uk
dir: *A303 onto A372, right onto B3151, right into village, right at post office*

Former cider house with great food

Once a cider house, this pretty thatched pub is furnished with stripped pine tables and cushioned farmhouse chairs, and there are enough open fires to keep everywhere well warmed. The three charmingly decorated, saggy-beamed rooms have a relaxed and friendly feel. Hosts Adam Cain and Cinzia Iezzi have a wealth of experience in some of the UK's most respected pubs, and they have made food a key part of the Kingsdon's appeal. Menus make excellent use of seasonal, local and often organic produce - maybe chicken liver and port parfait with red onion compôte followed by pan-fried turbot with pea tortellini, baby vegetables and a light shellfish bisque.

Open all wk 12-3 6-11 (Sun 12-3 7-10.30) **Bar Meals** L served all wk 12-2 D served all wk 6.30-9 Av main course £12.95 ⊕ FREE HOUSE/GAME BIRD INNS ◀ Sharp's Doom Bar, Butcombe, Otter ♻ Thatchers, Ashton Press. ♈ 10 **Facilities** Non-diners area ❖ (Bar Garden) ♦♦ Children's menu Children's portions Garden ⌁ Parking Wi-fi ⛺ (notice required)

LANGLEY MARSH — Map 3 ST02

The Three Horseshoes

TA4 2UL ☎ 01984 623763
e-mail: mark_jules96@hotmail.com
dir: *M5 junct 25 take B3227 to Wiveliscombe. Turn right up hill at lights. From square, turn right, follow Langley Marsh signs, pub in 1m*

Traditional pub values with home-cooked food

Surrounded by beautiful countryside, this handsome 17th-century red sandstone pub has had only four landlords during the last century. It remains a free house, with traditional opening hours, a good choice of ales straight from the barrel and a warm, friendly welcome. The landlord's wife prepares home-cooked meals, incorporating local ingredients and vegetables from the pub garden. Popular with locals, walkers and cyclists, there's an enclosed garden with outdoor seating to enjoy in warmer weather.

Open 7pm-11pm (Sun 12-2.30) Closed: Sun eve, Mon, Tue-Sat L **Bar Meals** L served Sun 12-1.45 D served Tue-Sat 7-9 ⊕ FREE HOUSE ◀ Otter Ale, Exmoor Ale, Cotleigh 25, St Austell Tribute ♂ Thatchers Gold.
Facilities Non-diners area ♦♦ Outside area ⋒ Parking

LONG SUTTON — Map 4 ST42

The Devonshire Arms ★★★★ INN ◉

PICK OF THE PUBS

TA10 9LP ☎ 01458 241271
e-mail: mail@thedevonshirearms.com
dir: *Exit A303 at Podimore rdbt onto A372. 4m, left onto B3165*

Exceptional food and beers beside the village green

A handsome old gabled inn of mellow limestone, dressed by colourful wisteria and creepers, standing at the heart of the village at the fringe of the fabulous Somerset Levels, renowned for their wildlife. Also flowing from these watery levels is a great range of beers, some of which form the enticing centrepiece to the smart bar; Merlin's Magic and Cheddar Potholer just a brace of these ales, whilst apple lovers can sample Olde Harry's draught cider, brewed in the village. The walled courtyard garden is a suntrap dining area; tuck in to any of a superb suite of freshly prepared, largely locally sourced dishes whilst watching locals play boules or croquet here. Commence with wood pigeon breast salad with poached pear, hazelnuts and chicory; progressing then to beef and cep pie cooked in local ale, or sample River Fowey mussels cooked in Harry's cider.

Open all wk 12-3 6-11 Closed: 25-26 Dec, 1 Jan **Bar Meals** L served all wk 12-2.30 D served all wk 7-9.30 **Restaurant** D served all wk 7-9.30 ⊕ FREE HOUSE ◀ Cheddar Potholer, Moor Revival, Merlin's Magic, Otter Bitter ♂ Burrow Hill, Olde Harry's. ♟ 10
Facilities Non-diners area ♦♦ Children's menu Play area Garden ⋒ Parking Wi-fi **Rooms** 9

LOWER LANGFORD — Map 4 ST46

The Langford Inn ★★★★ INN

BS40 5BL ☎ 01934 863059
e-mail: langfordinn@aol.com
web: www.langfordinn.com
dir: *M5 junct 21, A370 towards Bristol. At Congresbury turn right onto B3133 to Lower Langford. Village on A38*

Traditional and international food

This acclaimed Mendip pub and restaurant is owned by Cardiff brewery Brains, so expect a decent pint of SA in the bar. It also offers accommodation in converted 17th-century barns. Brains beers are joined by local Butcombe ales in the bar, which is adorned with local memorabilia. The daily-changing menu proffers traditional dishes such as crispy whitebait, steak and chips or beef and ale pie; but masala chicken curry; sizzling beef and oyster sauce; and sizzling vegetable fajitas offer something different. There's a good choice of 24 wines by the glass to accompany your meal.

Open all day all wk **Bar Meals** L served 12-9 food served all day **Restaurant** L served 12-9 D served Fri-Sat 12-9.30 food served all day ⊕ BRAINS ◀ SA, Butcombe, Guinness ♂ Thatchers Gold & Katy. ♟ 24
Facilities Non-diners area ❀ (Bar Garden) ♦♦ Children's menu Children's portions Garden Parking Wi-fi ⬛ (notice required) **Rooms** 7

LOWER VOBSTER — Map 4 ST74

Vobster Inn ★★★★ INN ◉◉

PICK OF THE PUBS

BA3 5RJ ☎ 01373 812920
e-mail: info@vobsterinn.co.uk
dir: *4m W of Frome*

Historic village pub with Spanish twist

Raf and Peta Davila have quickly made their mark here since they arrived and have been awarded two AA Rosettes in the process. Set in four acres of glorious countryside in the pretty hamlet of Lower Vobster, it is believed the inn originated in the 16th-century and was used by King James II and his army of Royalists prior to the battle of Sedgemoor in 1685. For lunch, choose a filled baguette, ploughman's, or a steak. On the main menu you'll find rabbit pie; Cornish hake with salsa verde and Palourde clams; and a mixed grill comprising rib-eye, gammon, black pudding, sausage, hen's egg, onion rings and French fries. The tapas menu offers roast Catalan tomato bread and Spanish meatballs. All desserts are home made, with choices like chocolate pannacotta and orange and mango sorbet. Special events like paella night and pudding night are popular. Individually furnished bedrooms are available.

Open 12-3 6.30-11 Closed: Sun eve & Mon (ex BHs L) **Bar Meals** L served Tue-Sun 12-2 D served Tue-Sat 6.30-9 Av main course £11.95 **Restaurant** L served Tue-Sun 12-2 D served Tue-Sat 6.30-9 Av 3 course à la carte fr £23.50 ⊕ FREE HOUSE ◀ Butcombe Blond, Bitter ♂ Ashton Press, The Orchard Pig. ♟ 10 **Facilities** Non-diners area ♦♦ Children's menu Children's portions Family room Garden ⋒ Parking Wi-fi ⬛ (notice required) **Rooms** 4

MARTOCK — Map 4 ST41

The Nag's Head Inn

East St TA12 6NF ☎ 01935 823432
dir: *Telephone for directions*

Hamstone former cider house offering good grub, skittles and beer

This 16th-century former cider house is set in a lovely hamstone street in a picturesque south Somerset village. The large rear garden is partly walled and has pretty borders and trees. Ales, wines and home-cooked food are served in both the public and lounge/diner bars, where crib, dominoes, darts and pool are available. The pub also has a separate skittle alley. There's a poker evening on Thursday and Sunday evening is quiz night.

Open all wk 12-3 6-11 (Fri-Sun 12-12) **Bar Meals** L served all wk 12-2 D served Mon-Tue 6-8, Wed-Sat 6-9 Av main course £6.50 **Restaurant** L served all wk 12-2 D served Mon-Tue 6-8, Wed-Sat 6-9 Fixed menu price fr £7.95 Av 3 course à la carte fr £15 ⊕ FREE HOUSE ◀ Yeovil Ruby, Local Guest ales ♂ Thatchers Gold, Westons Stowford Press. **Facilities** Non-diners area ❀ (Bar Restaurant Garden) ♦♦ Children's menu Children's portions Family room Garden ⋒ Parking ⬛ (notice required)

MELLS Map 4 ST74

The Talbot Inn NEW

Selwood St BA11 3PN ☎ 01373 812254
e-mail: info@talbotinn.com
dir: *A362 from Frome towards Radstock. Left signed Mells, Hapsford & Great Elm. Right at T-junct in Mells. Inn on right*

Traditional yet stylish coaching inn

In coaching days, this 15th-century inn was the stop before Wells. Perhaps some passengers mistakenly alighted here in Mells, a bonus for the innkeepers of the day. It has a main bar, snug and map rooms, all open for classic pub food and Talbot Ale. Across a cobbled courtyard is the Coach House Grill Room, where chef Pravin Nayar's fish and meats are grilled over a charcoal fire and, on Sundays, whole roast chickens and suckling pigs are carved at table. His bar snacks – including deep-fried rabbit legs, and duck hearts on toast – are clearly no ordinary bar snacks.

Open all day all wk **Bar Meals** L served all wk 12-2.30 D served all wk 6-9.30 Av main course £13 **Restaurant** L served Mon-Sat 12-2.30, Sun 12-3 D served all wk 6-9.30 Av 3 course à la carte fr £25 ⊕ FREE HOUSE ◀ Butcombe, Talbot Ale, Moles Brewery Tap ♂ Ashton Press, The Orchard Pig, Westons Wyld Wood Organic. **Facilities** ♣ (Bar Restaurant Garden) ♦♦ Children's menu Children's portions Garden ⊟ Parking

MILVERTON Map 3 ST12

The Globe ★★★ INN ⊛

PICK OF THE PUBS

Fore St TA4 1JX ☎ 01823 400534
e-mail: info@theglobemilverton.co.uk
dir: *On B3187*

Contemporary inn close to the Quantocks

The Globe is very much part of the local community, thanks to Mark and Adele Tarry, who bought the freehold of this old coaching inn, with its clean-lined, contemporary interior sitting comfortably within the Grade II listed building. Local artists display their paintings on the walls of the restaurant and bar area, whilst a wood-burning stove and a sun terrace provide for all seasons. Expect tip-top local ales like Exmoor and Otter and heady cider from Sheppy's. The extensive menu makes good use of West Country produce and ranges from traditional steak-and-kidney pie and home-made burgers at lunchtime, to roasted vegetable and feta tart; roast lamb with garlic, fennel and redcurrant sauce; and lemon tart with raspberry cream. Everything is home made, including the bread and there is a carefully thought-out children's menu too. Stay over in one of the comfortable bedrooms and explore the Quantock Hills and Exmoor.

Open 12-3 6-11 (Fri-Sat 12-3 6-11.30) Closed: Sun eve, Mon L **Bar Meals** L served Tue-Sun 12-2 D served Mon-Sat 6.30-9 **Restaurant** L served Tue-Sun 12-2 D served Mon-Sat 6.30-9 ⊕ FREE HOUSE ◀ Exmoor Ale, Butcombe

Bitter, Otter Bitter, Guest ales ♂ Sheppy's. ♀ 9 **Facilities** Non-diners area ♦♦ Children's menu Outside area ⊟ Parking Wi-fi **Rooms** 3

MONKTON COMBE Map 4 ST76

Wheelwrights Arms NEW

BA2 7HB ☎ 01225 722287
e-mail: bookings@wheelwrightsarms.co.uk
dir: *SE of Bath*

Lovely valley and village setting for old pub

As pretty a pub in as pretty a village as you could wish for, dating from 1750 and a pub since 1850, with the annexe once used by local wheelwrights to keep carts rolling. You're only a stone's throw from Bath and near the canal so grab a pint of Butcombe and head for the wonderful snug or the sheltered garden. Pub classics to à la carte menus will satisfy all, plus steaks, sharing plates and ciabattas. And a seriously good wine list to wash it all down with.

Open all day all wk **Bar Meals** L served all wk 12-3 D served all wk 6-10 **Restaurant** L served all wk 12-3 D served all wk 6-10 Fixed menu price fr £12 Av 3 course à la carte fr £25.50 ⊕ FREE HOUSE ◀ Butcombe ♂ Honey's Midford Cider Honey & Daughter. ♀ 10 **Facilities** ♦♦ Children's portions Garden ⊟ Parking Wi-fi 🚐 (notice required)

MONTACUTE Map 4 ST41

The Kings Arms Inn

49 Bishopston TA15 6UU ☎ 01935 822255
e-mail: info@thekingsarmsinn.co.uk
dir: *From A303 onto A3088 at rdbt signed Montacute. Hotel in village centre*

17th-century village pub with cosy bar and good food

The hamstone-built, refurbished Kings Arms has stood in this picturesque village, at the foot of Mons Acutus (thus, supposedly, Montacute) since 1632. Along with cask ales and fine wines, you can eat in the fire-warmed bar or lounge, in the large beer garden, or in the restaurant. Starters include deep-fried whitebait, or duck and orange pâté, with main courses of chicken supreme with bacon, mushroom and shallot cream sauce; or battered cod and chips. A bar favourite is the succulent salt beef sandwich. There are plenty of events to watch out for.

Open all wk 7.30am-11pm **Bar Meals** L served all wk 12-3 D served all wk 6-9 **Restaurant** L served all wk 12-3 D served all wk 6-9 ⊕ GREENE KING ◀ Ruddles Best & IPA, Morland Old Speckled Hen, Timothy Taylor Landlord ♂ Aspall, Thatchers. ♀ 11 **Facilities** Non-diners area ♣ (Bar Garden) ♦♦ Garden Parking Wi-fi 🚐

The Phelips Arms

The Borough TA15 6XB ☎ 01935 822557
e-mail: thephelipsarms@hotmail.com
dir: *From Cartgate rdbt on A303 follow signs for Montacute*

Pub classics in a classic setting

About 1598 Sir Edward Phelips, Master of the Rolls and the prosecutor during the Gunpowder Plot trial, built Montacute House, now owned by the National Trust. Next door, overlooking the village square, stands this 17th-century hamstone building, offering well-kept Palmers beers and Thatchers Old Rascal cider. The main menu features chef's pie of the day; honey and mustard roasted ham and free-range eggs; Somerset sausage and creamy apple mash; and pasta arrabbiata. Sandwiches, baguettes and jacket potatoes are available too. The pub, with its beautiful walled garden, featured in the 1995 film *Sense and Sensibility*.

Open all wk 12-2.30 6-11 (Sun 12-6) Closed: 25 Dec **Bar Meals** L served Mon-Sat 12-2, Sun 12-4 D served Mon-Sat 6.30-9 **Restaurant** L served Mon-Sat 12-2, Sun 12-4 D served Mon-Sat 6.30-9 ⊕ PALMERS ◀ Best Bitter, 200, Copper Ale, Palmers Tally Ho! & Dorset Gold ♂ Thatchers Gold & Old Rascal. ♀ 10 **Facilities** Non-diners area ♣ (Bar Restaurant Garden) ♦♦ Children's menu Children's portions Garden Parking Wi-fi 🚐

NORTH CURRY Map 4 ST32

The Bird in Hand

1 Queen Square TA3 6LT ☎ 01823 490248
dir: *M5 junct 25, A358 towards Ilminster, left onto A378 towards Langport. Left to North Curry*

Low beams, warming fires, friendly service

Cheerful staff provide a warm welcome to this friendly 300-year-old village inn, which boasts large inglenook fireplaces, flagstone floors, exposed beams and studwork. The place is very atmospheric at night by candlelight, and the daily-changing blackboard menus feature local produce, including game casserole, curries and bubble-and-squeak with sausage, bacon, eggs and mushrooms. The à la carte menu always has three or four fresh fish dishes, steaks and home-made desserts.

Open all wk 12-3 6-11 (Fri 12-3 5.30-12 Sat 12-3 6-12) Closed: 25 Dec eve **Bar Meals** L served Mon-Sat 12-2, Sun 12-3 D served Sun-Thu 6.45-9, Fri-Sat 7-9.30 **Restaurant** L served Mon-Sat 12-2, Sun 12-3 D served Sun-Thu 6.45-9, Fri-Sat 7-9.30 ⊕ FREE HOUSE ◀ Otter Bitter & Ale, Exmoor Gold, Cotleigh Barn Owl, Butcombe Gold, Teignworthy Old Moggie, Hop Back ♂ Parsons Choice, Ashton Press, Thatchers Gold. ♀ 9 **Facilities** Non-diners area ♣ (Bar) ♦♦ Children's portions Outside area ⊟ Parking Wi-fi

Save on hotels. Book at **theAA.com/hotel**

SOMERSET 385 ENGLAND

NORTON ST PHILIP
Map 4 ST75

George Inn

PICK OF THE PUBS

High St BA2 7LH ☎ 01373 834224
e-mail: georgeinn@wadworth.co.uk
dir: *A36 from Bath to Warminster, 6m, right onto A366 to Radstock, village 1m*

Historic pub with a far-reaching reputation

Grade I listed, this truly remarkable building was built, so historians believe, in 1223 as temporary accommodation for Carthusian monks while they constructed Hinton Priory two miles away. In 1397, the Prior granted it a licence to sell ale, making it one of the country's oldest continuously licensed inns. When Wadworth, the Devizes brewery, carried out a major restoration, it uncovered medieval wall paintings, which are now preserved, as are other interesting features like the stone-tiled roof, massive doorway, turreted staircase, cobbled courtyard and open-air gallery. There are two menus, the carte and the more pocket-friendly and informal Monmouth's. For a lighter option, a selection of ciabattas is served until 6pm. Outside, you can eat in the ancient and atmospheric courtyard and from the beer garden watch cricket on the Mead.

Open all day all wk 11.30-11 (Sun 12-10.30) **Bar Meals** L served Mon-Fri 12-2.30, Sat 12-9.30, Sun 12-9 **D** served Mon-Thu 6-9, Fri 6-9.30, Sat 12-9.30, Sun 12-9 **Restaurant** L served Mon-Fri 12-2.30, Sat 12-9.30, Sun 12-9 D served Mon-Thu 6-9, Fri 6-9.30, Sat 12-9.30, Sun 12-9 ⊕ WADWORTH ◀ 6X, Henry's Original IPA, The Bishop's Tipple ♂ Westons Stowford Press, Thatchers Gold. ♟ **Facilities** Non-diners area ♣ (Bar Garden) ♦ Children's menu Children's portions Play area Garden ♫ Parking Wi-fi ⚌

NUNNEY
Map 4 ST74

The George at Nunney

Church St BA11 4LW ☎ 01373 836458
e-mail: info@thegeorgeatnunney.co.uk
dir: *0.5m N off A361, Frome/Shepton Mallet*

The hub of the village's lively community

With views of 14th-century moated castle ruins, and a babbling brook and waterfall directly opposite, this rambling inn has the added attractions of landscaped gardens and winter log fires. Run by the Hedges family since 2012, the stylish interior merges contemporary with traditional. The beamed bar has a choice of Wadworth ales, Thatchers cider and fine wines. The extensive à la carte menu changes with the seasons and mixes modern British dishes with Asian and Mediterranean influences: Greek meze, ham hock terrine, Somerset pork belly, stone-baked pizzas, king prawn linguine. Sandwiches are available at lunchtime and there are roasts on Sundays.

Open all day all wk **Bar Meals** L served all wk 12-2.30 D served all wk 7-9.30 **Restaurant** L served all wk

12-2.30 D served all wk 7-9.30 ⊕ WADWORTH ◀ Wadworth 6X, Henrys IPA & The Bishop's Tipple ♂ Thatchers Gold. ♟ 8 **Facilities** Non-diners area ♣ (Bar Restaurant Garden) ♦ Children's menu Children's portions Family room Garden ♫ Parking Wi-fi ⚌ (notice required)

OAKHILL
Map 4 ST64

The Oakhill Inn ★★★★ INN ⊛

PICK OF THE PUBS

Fosse Rd BA3 5HU ☎ 01749 840442
e-mail: info@theoakhillinn.com
dir: *On A367 between Stratton-on-the-Fosse & Shepton Mallet*

Mendips inn known for its excellent cooking

You can see the village church and Mendip Hills from the landscaped garden of this smart stone-built inn. The interior is attractively decorated with one of the deep duck-egg blue walls featuring an eye-catching display of over 20 clocks. Homage is paid to the village's former brewing tradition by rotating real ales from local microbreweries, including Devilfish in nearby Hemington. Alongside these are Palmers and Butcombe ales, draught lagers and local draught farmhouse ciders, including Pheasant Plucker. Head chef Neil Creese insists that his award-winning menus must conform to free-range and organic principles; his mantra "local food tastes better" means that he sources dairy products, eggs and organic beef from within three miles. Settle back with the seasonal menu and go for a three-course meal of rabbit and pistachio terrine, venison steak, and raspberry cheesecake. The bar menu offers a good choice of steaks, as well as ploughman's, fish and chips, and sandwiches. Accommodation is available.

Open all wk Mon-Fri 12-3 5-11 (Sat-Sun 12-12) **Bar Meals** L served all wk 12-3 D served all wk 6-9 **Restaurant** L served all wk 12-3 D served all wk 6-9 ⊕ FREE HOUSE ◀ Butcombe Bitter, Devilfish Devil Best, Palmers ♂ Pheasant Plucker, Lilley's Sunset. ♟ **Facilities** Non-diners area ♣ (Bar Restaurant Garden) ♦ Children's menu Children's portions Garden ♫ Parking Wi-fi ⚌ (notice required) **Rooms** 5

OVER STRATTON
Map 4 ST41

The Royal Oak

TA13 5LQ ☎ 01460 240906
e-mail: info@the-royal-oak.net
dir: *Exit A303 at Hayes End rdbt (South Petherton). 1st left after Esso garage signed Over Stratton*

Real ales and home-cooked food

With X-shaped tie-bar ends securing its aged hamstone walls, a thatched roof, blackened oak beams, flagstones, log fires, old church pews and settles, this 17th-century former farmhouse certainly looks like a textbook example of an English country pub. First licensed in the 1850s, the bar dispenses real ales from Hall & Woodhouse in Blandford, Dorset. With different prices for small or normal appetites, home-cooked dishes on the menu range from chicken tikka lahoori, via salmon en croute, to beef and bacon pie. Added attractions are the good value two-course set lunch menu, large patio, children's play area and barbecue.

Open Tue-Sun Closed: Mon **Bar Meals** L served Tue-Sun 12-2 D served Tue-Sun 6-9 **Restaurant** L served Tue-Sun 12-2 D served Tue-Sun 6-9 ⊕ HALL & WOODHOUSE ◀ Badger Dorset Best, Tanglefoot, K&B Sussex. **Facilities** Non-diners area ♣ (Bar Garden) ♦ Children's menu Children's portions Play area Family room Garden Parking

PITNEY
Map 4 ST42

The Halfway House

TA10 9AB ☎ 01458 252513
dir: *On B3153, 2m from Langport & Somerton*

Recommended for its excellent range of real ales

A delightfully old fashioned rural pub, The Halfway House has three homely rooms boasting open fires, books and games, but no music or electronic games. This free house is largely dedicated to the promotion of real ale, with an annual beer festival in March, and always eight to twelve tip-top ales at the bar, including Otter Ale, Moor Northern Star and Teignworthy. The home-cooked rustic fare is made using local ingredients. At lunchtime sandwiches, jacket potatoes, ploughman's and soups are served, while a great range of curries and specials are available for dinner (except Sundays when the pub is too busy with drinkers to prepare food).

Open all wk 11.30-3 5.30-11 (Fri-Sat 11.30-3 5.30-12 Sun all day) **Bar Meals** L served Mon-Sat 12-2.30, Sun 2-5 D served Mon-Sat 7-9.30 Av main course £8.50 ⊕ FREE HOUSE ◀ Butcombe Bitter, Otter Ale, Hop Back Summer Lightning, Moor Northern Star, Teignworthy ♂ Kingston Black, Burrow Hill, Wilkins Farmhouse, Gold Rush. ♟ 8 **Facilities** Non-diners area ♣ (Bar Garden) ♦ Children's portions Play area Garden Beer festival Parking Wi-fi

PORLOCK
Map 3 SS84

The Bottom Ship

Porlock Weir TA24 8PB ☎ **01643 863288**
e-mail: enquiries@shipinnporlockweir.co.uk
dir: *Telephone for directions*

Thatched inn at lovely Porlock Weir location

Enjoy superb views across the Bristol Channel to south Wales from the suntrap terrace at this thatched waterside pub, best enjoyed following a coastal path stroll. Exmoor ales are the mainstay in the beamed bar, with a couple of real ciders also on tap. Home-made food using fresh local produce includes most pub favourites, from deep-fried whitebait to steak-and-ale pie. Children have their own menu and dogs are welcome. Don't miss the music and ale festival in early July.

Open all day all wk **Bar Meals** L served all wk 12-3 D served all wk 6-8.30 ⊕ FREE HOUSE ◀ Exmoor Ale & Stag, Otter Bright, St Austell Trelawny Ŏ Thatchers Cheddar Valley, Dry & Gold, Cornish Orchard & Pear. **Facilities** Non-diners area ☻ (Bar Garden) ⁙ Children's menu Children's portions Garden ⋒ Beer festival Cider festival Parking 🚌

The Ship Inn

High St TA24 8QD ☎ **01643 862507**
e-mail: enquiries@shipinnporlock.co.uk
dir: *A358 to Williton, then A39 to Porlock. 6m from Minehead*

Picture-postcard inn with seafaring tales to tell

Reputedly one of the oldest inns on Exmoor, this 13th-century free house stands at the foot of Porlock's notorious hill, where Exmoor tumbles into the sea. In the past it's attracted the sinister attentions of Nelson's press gang, but now its thatched roof and traditional interior provide a more welcoming atmosphere. Regularly changing menus include an appealing selection of hot and cold baguettes, and hot dishes from sausage and mash to guinea fowl breast with crispy bacon and red wine jus. There's also a beer garden and children's play area.

Open all day all wk ⊕ FREE HOUSE ◀ St Austell Tribute & Proper Job, Exmoor Ale, Cotleigh Tawny Owl, Otter Ŏ Thatchers & Cheddar Valley. **Facilities** ☻ (Bar Garden) ⁙ Children's menu Children's portions Play area Garden Parking Wi-fi

RODE
Map 4 ST85

The Mill at Rode

BA11 6AG ☎ **01373 831100**
e-mail: info@themillatrode.co.uk
dir: *6m S of Bath*

Impressive riverside building with alfresco eating terrace

A converted grist mill on the banks of the beautiful River Frome, this magnificent multi-storeyed Georgian building sits in its own landscaped grounds in the rural hinterland south of Bath. The dining-terrace overhangs the rushing waters, a great location in which to indulge in local beers or select from the West Country-based menu; maybe terrine of local game with apple chutney and warm toast, followed by fillets of Cornish plaice stuffed with mushrooms and spinach and topped with a vintage cheddar sauce. A children's playroom offers grown-ups the chance of escape and have a peaceful chinwag.

Open all day all wk 12-11 Closed: 25 Dec **Bar Meals** L served all wk 12-9.30 D served all wk 12-9.30 food served all day **Restaurant** L served all wk 12-9.30 D served all wk 12-9.30 food served all day ⊕ FREE HOUSE ◀ Butcombe Bitter, Marston's Pedigree, Guinness, Guest ales Ŏ Black Rat, Ashton Press. ♟ 35 **Facilities** Non-diners area ⁙ Children's menu Children's portions Play area Family room Garden Parking Wi-fi 🚌

RUDGE
Map 4 ST85

The Full Moon at Rudge ★★★★ INN

BA11 2QF ☎ **01373 830936**
e-mail: info@thefullmoon.co.uk
dir: *From A36 (Bath to Warminster road) follow Rudge signs*

Cosy interior, good ales and ciders

Just seven miles from Longleat, this venerable 16th-century old cider house is located at the crossing of two old drove roads and enjoys great views of Westbury White Horse. Sympathetically updated, the pub retains its stone-floored rooms furnished with scrubbed tables. The modern menus change to reflect the seasons, with Barnsley lamb chop with rosemary jus or Somerset sirloin steak being examples of the fare. There is a large garden with a play area, and 17 comfortable bedrooms for those wishing to stay longer.

Open all day all wk 11.30-11 (Sun 12-10.30) **Bar Meals** L served Sun-Thu 12-2, Fri-Sat 12-9 D served Mon-Thu 6-9, Fri-Sat 12-9, Sun 7-9 **Restaurant** L served Sun-Thu 12-2, Fri-Sat 12-9 D served Mon-Thu 6-9, Fri-Sat 12-9, Sun 7-9 ◀ Butcombe Bitter, Otter, Guest ale Ŏ Thatchers Gold, Rich's Farmhouse. **Facilities** Non-diners area ⁙ Children's menu Play area Garden Parking Wi-fi 🚌 **Rooms** 17

SHEPTON BEAUCHAMP
Map 4 ST41

Duke of York

North St TA19 0LW ☎ **01460 240314**
e-mail: sheptonduke@tiscali.co.uk
dir: *N of A303 between Ilchester & Ilminster*

Traditional village pub with plenty of reasons to visit

Husband and wife team Paul and Hayley Rowlands have now been at the helm of this 17th-century free house for more than a decade. The bar stocks good West Country ales and local ciders, and the restaurant's traditional menu pleases locals and tourists alike with home-made pie of the day, southern fried chicken fillet, vegetable curry, beef lasagne, chargrilled steaks and lunchtime sandwiches. Gardens, a skittle alley, two steak nights a week, a Sunday carvery and a beer festival in September round off the attractions of this homely pub.

Open all day Mon 5.30-11 Tue-Sun 12-12 (Sep-Apr Mon 5.30-11 Tue-Wed 4-12 Thu-Sun 12-12) Closed: Mon L **Bar Meals** L served Tue-Sun 12-2 (Sep-Apr Thu-Sun 12-2) D served Tue-Sat 6.45-9 **Restaurant** L served Sun 12-2.30 D served Tue-Sat 6.45-9 ⊕ FREE HOUSE ◀ Teignworthy Reel Ale, Otter Ale Ŏ Thatchers Gold. ♟ 9 **Facilities** Non-diners area ☻ (Bar Garden) ⁙ Children's menu Children's portions Family room Garden Beer festival Parking Wi-fi 🚌 (notice required)

SHEPTON MALLET
Map 4 ST64

The Three Horseshoes Inn

PICK OF THE PUBS

Batcombe BA4 6HE ☎ **01749 850359**
e-mail: info@thethreehorseshoesinn.com
dir: *Take A359 from Frome to Bruton. Batcombe signed on right. Pub by church*

A dedicated team offering a warm welcome

This honey-coloured stone inn enjoys a peaceful position squirrelled away in the very rural Batcombe Vale, and the lovely rear garden overlooks the old parish church. The long and low-ceilinged main bar has exposed stripped beams, a huge stone inglenook with log fire, and is warmly and tastefully decorated, with pale blue walls hung with old paintings, creating a homely atmosphere. From gleaming handpumps on the bar come foaming pints of local brew. Menus draw on the wealth of fresh seasonal produce available locally, with lunches taking in cumin spiced lamb salad with new potatoes and fine beans, or Somerset ham and local eggs with chips. Choice at dinner extends to pan-fried bream with fennel and creamed leeks, or a more classic rib-eye steak and chips. Desserts include boozy orange parfait or a board of local cheeses.

Open all wk Mon-Fri 11-3 6-11 (Sat 11-11 Sun 12-10.30) **Bar Meals** L served all wk 12-2.30 D served Mon-Sat 6-9.30, Sun 6-9 **Restaurant** L served all wk 12-2.30 D served Mon-Sat 6-9.30, Sun 6-9 ⊕ FREE HOUSE ◀ Butcombe Bitter, Moor Revival Ŏ Rich's Farmhouse, Ashton Press. ♟ 8 **Facilities** Non-diners area ⁙ Children's menu Children's portions Garden Cider festival Parking Wi-fi

PICK OF THE PUBS

The Carpenters Arms

STANTON WICK Map 4 ST66

BS39 4BX ☎ 01761 490202
e-mail: carpenters@buccaneer.co.uk
web: www.the-carpenters-arms.co.uk
dir: *From A37 at Chelwood rdbt take*
A368 signed Bishop Sutton. Right to
Stanton Wick

Popular destination for good food and fine wines

Converted from a row of miners'
cottages (for there was a colliery at
neighbouring Pensford until 1955), this
charming stone-built, pantile-roofed
free house overlooks the Chew Valley.
It's well placed for visiting Bath, Bristol
and the smaller cathedral city of Wells,
but if you're already in one of these
cities, then this quiet hamlet is equally
well placed if you fancy pointing the car
the other way and heading for
somewhere rural. Beyond the flower-
hung exterior, in the rustic bar, you'll
find low beams, old pews, squashy
sofas, and precision-cut logs stacked
neatly from floor to ceiling in the large
fireplace. It all adds up to an appealing,
music-free, chatty atmosphere. For a
pint of Butcombe Bitter or Sharp's Doom
Bar, the bar is where you need to be,
although by all means take it outside to
the attractively landscaped patio. The
menus are changed regularly to make
the best of West Country, seasonal
produce, incorporated into a menu that
might feature goujons of salmon with

salad; fillet of sea bass on crispy
vegetable stir-fry; steak and mushroom
suet pudding; pan-fried chicken breast
wrapped in Parma ham; and vegetable
bake with goats' cheese. And then there
are the delicious home-made desserts,
especially the apple and blackberry
flapjack crumble with custard; and the
Bakewell tart with clotted cream. The
extensive wine list combines New and
Old World favourites, with a Chilean
pudding wine available by the half
bottle. Nearby Chew Valley Lake is an
established wildlife haven, where you
can walk the Grebe and Bittern nature
trails.

Open all day all wk 11-11 (Sun
12-10.30) Closed: 25-26 Dec **Bar
Meals** L served Mon-Sat 12-2.30, Sun

12-9 D served Mon-Thu 6-9.30, Fri-Sat
6-10, Sun 12-9 Av main course £14.95
Restaurant L served Mon-Sat 12-2.30,
Sun 12-9 D served Mon-Thu 6-9.30,
Fri-Sat 6-10, Sun 12-9 Av 3 course à la
carte fr £25.95 ⬛ FREE HOUSE
◀ Butcombe Bitter, Sharp's Doom Bar.
🍷 10 **Facilities** Non-diners area 👫
Children's menu Children's portions
Outside area 🪑 Parking 🚌 (notice
required)

SHEPTON MALLET *continued*

The Waggon and Horses

PICK OF THE PUBS

Frome Rd, Doulting Beacon BA4 4LA ☎ 01749 880302
e-mail: waggon.horses09@googlemail.com
dir: *1.5m NE of Shepton Mallet. From Shepton Mallet take A37 N towards Bristol. At x-rds right into Old Frome Rd (follow brown pub sign)*

Traditional home-cooked dishes in the Mendips

Sitting high in the Mendip Hills with views over Glastonbury is this pretty, whitewashed building with leaded windows. Once a coaching inn in the 18th century, it is now a family-run pub with a large enclosed garden, where drinks and meals can be enjoyed outside in fine weather. A varying range of local real beers and ciders are served alongside traditional home-cooked dishes. You could begin with prawns in filo pastry or a pot of mushrooms, bacon and cheese, followed by fillet of salmon in dill sauce, faggots in onion gravy or a rump, fillet, T-bone or sirloin steak. Baguettes, jacket potatoes, ploughman's and other light bites are available at lunchtime. Children are most welcome, and the building is accessible for wheelchairs. Other facilities include the skittle alley and a function room, plus there are regular (motor)bike nights and Italian food every Thursday evening.

Open all wk Mon-Sat 12-2.30 6-11 (Sun 12-3 6-10) **Bar Meals** L served Mon-Sat 12-2.30, Sun 12-3 D served Mon-Sat 6-9, Sun 6-8 Av main course £8.50 **Restaurant** L served Mon-Sat 12-2.30, Sun 12-3 D served Mon-Sat 6-9, Sun 6-8 ⊕ FREE HOUSE ◀ Wadworth 6X, Butcombe Ŏ Wilkins Farmhouse, Ashton Press. **Facilities** Non-diners area ✿ (Bar Garden) ⁏ Children's menu Children's portions Garden ☞ Parking ▭

SHEPTON MONTAGUE   Map 4 ST63

The Montague Inn

PICK OF THE PUBS

BA9 8JW ☎ 01749 813213
e-mail: info@themontagueinn.co.uk
dir: *From Wincanton take A371 towards Castle Cary, right signed Shepton Montague. Or from A359, S of Bruton left signed Shepton Montague*

A treasure amongst the country lanes of Somerset

Nestling in rolling unspoilt Somerset countryside on the edge of sleepy Shepton Montague, this 18th-century stone-built village inn is hidden down winding country lanes. Tastefully decorated throughout, with the homely bar featuring old dark pine and an open log fire, and a cosy, yellow-painted dining room, the focus and draw of this rural dining pub is the careful sourcing of local foods from artisan producers and the kitchen's imaginative seasonal menus. Expect to find cask ales from Bath Ales;

salads, fruit and vegetables from local farms, and free-range eggs from Blackacre Farm. This translates to lunchtime dishes like duck liver parfait and orange jelly; smoked haddock soufflé; and devilled chicken livers on toast. Evening specials might include rump of lamb with roasted garlic and parsley mash, ending with strawberry parfait and berry compôte. The attractive rear terrace with rural views is perfect for summer sipping. Families are most welcome.

Open 12-3 6-11.30 Closed: Sun eve & BHs eve **Bar Meals** L served all wk 12-2.30 D served Mon-Sat 7-9.30 **Restaurant** L served all wk 12-2.30 D served Mon-Sat 7-9.30 ⊕ FREE HOUSE ◀ Wadworth 6X & Henry's IPA, Bath Ales Gem, Guest ales Ŏ Thatchers Gold, Addlestones, Local Cider. ⬥ **Facilities** Non-diners area ⁏ Children's portions Family room Garden ☞ Cider festival Parking Wi-fi

---

STANTON WICK   Map 4 ST66

The Carpenters Arms

PICK OF THE PUBS

See Pick of the Pubs on page 387

STOGUMBER   Map 3 ST03

The White Horse

High St TA4 3TA ☎ 01984 656277
e-mail: info@whitehorsestogumber.co.uk
dir: *From Taunton take A358 to Minehead. In 8m left to Stogumber, 2m into village centre. Right at T-junct & right again. Pub opposite church*

Village local off the beaten track

This traditional free house on the edge of the Quantock Hills is ideally situated for walkers and visitors travelling on the West Somerset Steam Railway and who alight at Stogumber station. Formerly the village's Market Hall and Reading Room, the dining room is now the place to study a menu of home-cooked dishes such as Caribbean pork with apple, mango and ginger; steak-and-kidney pudding; or local gammon steak, egg and chips. Enjoy local ales such as Otter Bitter in the courtyard garden.

Open all day all wk **Bar Meals** L served all wk 12-2 D served all wk 7-9 Av main course £9 **Restaurant** L served all wk 12-2 D served all wk 7-9 ⊕ FREE HOUSE ◀ St Austell Proper Job, Otter Bitter, Local & Guest ales Ŏ Thatchers, Healey's Cornish Rattler, St Austell Copper Press. **Facilities** Non-diners area ✿ (Bar Restaurant Garden) ⁏ Children's menu Garden ☞ Parking Wi-fi ▭ (notice required)

STOKE ST GREGORY   Map 4 ST32

Rose & Crown

Woodhill TA3 6EW ☎ 01823 490296
e-mail: info@browningpubs.com
dir: *M5 junct 25, A358 towards Langport, left at Thornfalcon, left again, follow signs to Stoke St Gregory*

Family-run showcase for local food and ales

Bought by Ron and Irene Browning in 1979, this Somerset Levels pub is now run by sons Stephen and Richard and their other halves, making it very much a family-run concern. The brothers are also the chefs, responsible for its well-deserved reputation for good food, while partners Sally and Leonie look after front of house. Classic pub dishes appear alongside the more modern such as seared scallops with sweet chilli and lime, which might be followed by roasted West Country lamb rump with redcurrant sauce. West County real ales aplenty and farmhouse ciders in the bar include Exmoor Ale and Thatchers cider.

Open all wk 11-3 6-11 **Bar Meals** L served all wk 12-2 D served all wk 7-9 **Restaurant** L served all wk 12-2 D served all wk 7-9 ⊕ FREE HOUSE ◀ Exmoor Ale, Fox & Stag, Otter Ale, Butcombe, Wickwar, Guest ales Ŏ Thatchers Gold, Local cider. **Facilities** Non-diners area ⁏ Children's menu Children's portions Garden ☞ Parking Wi-fi ▭ (notice required)

STREET   Map 4 ST43

The Two Brewers ★★★★ INN

38 Leigh Rd BA16 0HB ☎ 01458 442421
e-mail: richard@thetwobrewers.co.uk
dir: *In town centre*

A country pub in a town

This stone inn successfully achieves a balance between town local and country pub. Behind the bar, which serves cask-conditioned ales like Courage Best bitter, is a collection of unusual pump-clips. Both alley skittles and boules in the enclosed garden are taken seriously. Guests staying over in the converted stable accommodation may plan visits to nearby Glastonbury Tor over a meal of freshly home-cooked goodies, such as crispy golden whitebait; the bestselling Ohio meat pie; steak and chips; or a simple jacket potato. Children's portions are available. Puddings include Somerset apple cake and hot chocolate fudge cake.

Open all wk Mon-Sat 11-3 6-11 (Sun 11.30-3 6-10.30) Closed: 25-26 Dec **Bar Meals** L served all wk 12-2 D served all wk 6-9 **Restaurant** L served all wk 12-2 D served all wk 6-9 ⊕ FREE HOUSE ◀ St Austell Tribute, Courage Best, 2 Guest ales Ŏ Westons Stowford Press. **Facilities** Non-diners area ⁏ Children's menu Children's portions Garden ☞ Parking Wi-fi **Rooms** 3

TAUNTON
Map 4 ST22

The Hatch Inn

Village Rd, Hatch Beauchamp TA3 6SG
☎ **01823 480245**
e-mail: melanie.1963@hotmail.co.uk
dir: M5 junct 25, S on A358 for 3m. Left to Hatch Beauchamp, pub in 1m

A growing reputation for quality pub food and ales

Taken over by a new landlord in 2012, The Hatch is undergoing refurbishment and has a new chef and new menu too. Surrounded by splendid Somerset countryside, the pub dates back to the mid-1800s and has its share of ghostly occupants. The inn prides itself on its friendly, community atmosphere and the quality of its wines and West Country beers, including St Austell and Butcombe. Wholesome home-made food is served, prepared from local produce, with a good choice of snacks and meals such as breaded whitebait, vegetable chilli, chicken korma and gammon steak. There's a takeaway menu as well.

Open all day all wk 12-3 5-11 (Thu 12-3 5-12 Fri-Sat 12-12 Sun 12-10.30) **Bar Meals** L served all wk 12-3 D served all wk 6-10 **Restaurant** L served all wk 12-3 D served all wk 6-10 ⊕ FREE HOUSE ◀ Yeovil Summerset, St Austell Tribute, Butcombe Ở Ashton Press. ♀ 9 **Facilities** Non-diners area ✿ (Bar Restaurant Outside area) ♦† Children's menu Children's portions Outside area ⋒ Parking Wi-fi ▭ (notice required)

TINTINHULL
Map 4 ST41

The Crown and Victoria Inn ★★★★ INN ◉

PICK OF THE PUBS

14 Farm St BA22 8PZ ☎ **01935 823341**
e-mail: info@thecrownandvictoria.co.uk
dir: 1m S of A303. Adjacent to Tintinhull Garden (NT)

Perfect for the family

Despite it's unusual name, Tintinhull is a normal village, although its pub is rather special. Three hundred years old, and run by Isabel Thomas and Mark Hilyard, it occupies an enviable position amidst the sweeping willow trees in its peaceful beer garden. The beer pumps belong exclusively to West Country real ales, such as Butcombe, Cheddar and Yeovil, while from the wine list, ten are sold by the glass. Locally sourced food, much of it organic and free-range, feature on the AA Rosette menus. Typical starters might include devilled whitebait with mayonnaise; and baked camembert with oregano and caramelised onion focaccia. Often among the mains are roasted guinea fowl breast with chipolata and chestnuts; succulent Somerset pork in spices with parsnip purée; and butternut squash couscous with prune and onion confit. Finish with canapés of West Country cheeses. Five spacious, well-equipped bedrooms complete the picture.

Open all wk 10-4 5.30-late **Bar Meals** L served all wk 12-2.30 D served Mon-Sat 6.30-9.30 **Restaurant** L served all wk 12-2.30 D served Mon-Sat 6.30-9.30 ⊕ FREE HOUSE ◀ Sharp's Doom Bar, Butcombe, Cheddar, Cotleigh, Yeovil Ở Ashton Press. ♀ 10 **Facilities** Non-diners area ♦† Children's menu Children's portions Garden ⋒ Parking Wi-fi ▭ **Rooms** 5

TRISCOMBE
Map 4 ST13

The Blue Ball Inn

PICK OF THE PUBS

TA4 3HE ☎ **01984 618242**
e-mail: enq@blueballinn.info
dir: From Taunton take A358 past Bishops Lydeard towards Minehead

Converted barn with a popular beer festival

Although the 18th-century Blue Ball is still down the same narrow lane in the Quantock Hills, some years ago it moved across the road to the pretty thatched barn, which was converted into a pub. The inn looks south to the Brendon Hills and serves regional ales such as Cotleigh Tawny Owl and Exmoor Gold, plus Thatchers and Mad Apple ciders. Lunch might consist of Blapas (Blue Ball tapas), followed by braised pork chop, and dark chocolate pudding to finish; or a filled country roll. The frequently changing dinner menu could offer carpaccio of venison, shaved fennel salad and blackberry dressing; breasts of Quantock pigeon, cabbage Charlotte, truffle potato purée and a little pigeon pie; and steamed treacle sponge, rhubarb and clotted cream. There is a separate Somerset cheese menu. On the first Saturday in September is Triscombefest, the beer and live music festival.

Open 12-3 6-11 (Fri-Sat 12-11 Sun 12-6) Closed: 25 Dec, 26 Dec eve, 1 Jan eve, Mon, Sun eve (winter only) **Bar Meals** Av main course £15 **Restaurant** L served Tue-Sat 12-2, Sun 12-3 D served Tue-Sat 7-9 Fixed menu price fr £25 Av 3 course à la carte fr £28 ⊕ FREE HOUSE ◀ Cotleigh Tawny Owl, Exmoor Gold & Stag, St Austell Tribute, Otter Head Ở Thatchers, Mad Apple. **Facilities** Non-diners area ✿ (Bar Garden) ♦† Children's portions Garden ⋒ Beer festival Parking Wi-fi ▭ (notice required)

WATERROW
Map 3 ST02

The Rock Inn

PICK OF THE PUBS

TA4 2AX ☎ **01984 623293**
dir: From Taunton take B3227. Waterrow approx 14m W. Or from M5 junct 27, A361 towards Tiverton, then A396 N, right to Bampton, then B3227 to Waterrow

Local produce drives the menus

This 400-year-old, half-timbered former smithy and coaching inn, occupies a picturesque spot in a lovely green valley beside the River Tone. In the bar, local farmers stand on the well-worn floors or sit at the scrubbed tables in front of a log fire drinking local brews with appropriate West Country-sounding names like Cotleigh Tawny and Sheppy's Taunton-made cider. You can eat in the dog-friendly bar or mount a few steps to the small, bistro-style restaurant where chunky tables are topped with church candles, and food is locally sourced, freshly prepared and cooked to order. Both eating areas share the same ever-changing menu, written up on blackboards and featuring the best cuts of West Country meat, fish delivered daily from Brixham and game from local shoots. There is also a private dining room for up to 14 people. Change of hands.

Open 12-3 6-11 (Sun 6-10.30) Closed: Mon L **Bar Meals** L served Tue-Sun 12-2.30 D served Mon-Thu 6.30-9, Fri-Sun 6.30-9.30 **Restaurant** L served Tue-Sun 12-2.30 D served Mon-Thu 6.30-9, Fri-Sun 6.30-9.30 ⊕ FREE HOUSE ◀ Cotleigh Tawny Owl & Barn Owl, Exmoor Gold Ở Sheppy's, Thatchers. ♀ 9 **Facilities** Non-diners area ✿ (Bar) ♦† Children's menu Children's portions Parking Wi-fi ▭

WEDMORE
Map 4 ST44

The George Inn NEW

Church St BS28 4AB ☎ **01934 712124**
e-mail: olivia@thegeorgewedmore.co.uk
dir: M5 junct 22, follow Bristol/Cheddar signs (A38). From dual carriageway right, follow signs for Mark, then Wedmore. Pub in village centre

Sophisticated makeover at pretty village inn

Gordon Stevens had renovated lots of old properties before taking over this former coaching inn, so restoring it to its former glory held no terrors. The result is an object lesson in 'refurbing', with retained original features mixing with old and new furniture and artwork. As it's a free house, expect cask ales from Butcombe and Sharp's, and Thatchers real cider. As you might hope, food is sourced as locally as possible and includes roasted Cornish plaice and home-made chips; pork, honey and cider sausages with mustard mash; lamb kofta curry; and slow-roasted tomato and garlic risotto.

Open all day all wk **Bar Meals** L served Mon-Fri 12-2, Sat-Sun 12-2.30 D served Mon-Sat 6-9 Av main course £8 **Restaurant** L served Mon-Fri 12-2, Sat-Sun 12-2.30 D served Mon-Sat 6-9 Av 3 course à la carte fr £21 ⊕ FREE HOUSE ◀ Butcombe, Sharp's Doom Bar, Wells Bombardier, Warwickshire Ở Thatchers. **Facilities** Non-diners area ✿ (Bar Garden Outside area) ♦† Children's menu Children's portions Play area Garden Outside area ⋒ Beer festival Parking Wi-fi ▭ (notice required)

WELLS   Map 4 ST54

The City Arms

69 High St BA5 2AG ☎ 01749 673916
e-mail: cityofwellspubcoltd@hotmail.com
dir: On corner of Queen St & Lower High St

Cathedral city gem with a colourful past

Once the city jail, this pink-washed pub then became an abattoir. Owner Penny Lee says some people would argue that it was therefore only a matter of time before it became a hostelry! A true free house, it offers seven real ales, some rarely encountered outside Somerset, three draught ciders, and a good choice of wines and champagnes by the glass. Fresh local produce is paramount, with the menu offering creamy fish pie; lean-cut steak and ale pie; home-cooked honey- and mustard-glazed ham; and vegetarian options. The weekly-changing specials board incorporates fresh fish and speciality dishes, such as Somerset chicken casserole.

Open all wk 9am-11pm (Fri-Sat 9am-mdnt Sun 10am-11pm) **Bar Meals** L served all wk 12-9.30 D served all wk 12-9.30 Av main course £7.50 food served all day ⊕ FREE HOUSE ◀ Cheddar Potholer, Butts Barbus barbus, Glastonbury Hedge Monkey & Golden Chalice, Sharp's Ⓞ Ashton Press, Aspall, Addlestones, Symonds, Soap Dodger. ♈ 10 **Facilities** Non-diners area ❖ (Bar Garden) ♦️ Children's menu Children's portions Family room Garden Wi-fi ▭

The Crown at Wells ★★★★ INN

Market Place BA5 2RP ☎ 01749 673457
e-mail: eat@crownatwells.co.uk
dir: On entering Wells follow signs for Hotels & Deliveries. Left at lights into Sadler St, left into Market Place. For hotel car park pass Bishop's Palace entrance, post office & town hall into car park

Coaching inn with claims to fame

A stone's throw from the magnificent cathedral and moated Bishop's Palace in England's smallest city, this 15th-century inn looks out onto the Market Place. The exterior will be familiar to movie buffs as it featured in the hit film Hot Fuzz. William Penn, a Quaker who preached from The Crown, later gave his name to Pennsylvania and the inn's comfortable Penn Bar. Bar menu choices, using local produce wherever possible, include spinach and ricotta tortellini; crispy battered haddock; and Belgian chocolate mousse. A restaurant, Anton's Bistrot, is also on site. There are 15 charming bedrooms and a heated courtyard.

Open all day all wk Closed: 25 Dec **Bar Meals** L served Sun-Tue & Thu-Fri 12-2, Wed & Sat 12-9 D served Mon-Sat 6-9.30, Sun 6-9 **Restaurant** L served Mon-Sat 12-2, Sun 12-2.30 D served Mon-Sat 6-9.30, Sun 6-9 ⊕ FREE HOUSE ◀ Sharp's Doom Bar, Glastonbury Holy Thorn, Butcombe Ⓞ Ashton Press. ♈ 11
Facilities Non-diners area ❖ (Garden) ♦️ Children's menu Children's portions Garden ⊞ Parking Wi-fi ▭ (notice required) **Rooms** 15

The Fountain Inn & Boxer's Restaurant

PICK OF THE PUBS

1 Saint Thomas St BA5 2UU ☎ 01749 672317
e-mail: eat@fountaininn.co.uk
dir: In city centre, at A371 & B3139 junct. Follow signs for The Horringtons. Inn on junct of Tor St & Saint Thomas St

Well placed for visiting this gem of a city

Wells Cathedral is a short walk away from the Lawrence family's attractive blue-shuttered pub with pretty window boxes. The interior is just as enticing, with a large open fire in the big, comfortable bar, interesting bric-à-brac, discreet music and board games. Boxer's restaurant upstairs is run by head chef Julie Pearce — here for 17 years and counting — who maintains her winning repertoire of high quality, home-cooked food for both restaurant and bar. Among the dinner favourites are 'Priddy (a nearby village) Good' steaks and sausages; slow-roasted lamb shank with fresh mint and port-wine jus; pan-fried escalope of salmon topped with saffron and dill cream sauce; and wild mushroom, pecan nut, blue cheese and cream tagliatelle. Some of these you'll also find at lunchtime, alongside baked local ham, duo of eggs and hand-cut chips. Finish on either occasion with apricot and almond tart with local clotted cream. Parking is available opposite.

Open all wk Mon-Sat 12-2.30 6-11 (Sun 12-2.30 7-11) Closed: 25-26 Dec **Bar Meals** L served all wk 12-2 D served Mon-Sat 6-9, Sun 7-9 **Restaurant** L served all wk 12-2 D served Mon-Sat 6-9, Sun 7-9 ⊕ PUNCH TAVERNS ◀ Butcombe Bitter, Sharp's Doom Bar. ♈ 23 **Facilities** Non-diners area ♦️ Children's menu Children's portions Parking ▭ (notice required)

WEST BAGBOROUGH   Map 4 ST13

The Rising Sun Inn

TA4 3EF ☎ 01823 432575
e-mail: jon@risingsuninn.info
dir: Telephone for directions

Family-run pub serving West Country ales

This traditional, 16th-century village pub lies in the picturesque Quantock Hills and is run by the Brinkman family, who have just added their son and his partner to the team. After a fire the inn was rebuilt around the cob walls and magnificent door; the decor is both bold and smart. A good choice of ales and food, both sourced from local suppliers, is on offer. Main courses include venison in a port and plum sauce; and oven-roasted lemon sole topped with shrimp butter. Among the many puddings are banoffee pie and vanilla and passionfruit cheesecake. A gallery restaurant above the bar is ideal for private functions.

Open all wk 10.30-3 6-11 **Bar Meals** L served all wk 12-2 D served all wk 6.30-9.30 **Restaurant** L served all wk 12-2 D served all wk 6.30-9.30 ⊕ FREE HOUSE ◀ Exmoor Ale, St Austell Proper Job, Butcombe. ♈
Facilities Non-diners area ❖ (Bar) ♦️ Children's portions Wi-fi

WEST CAMEL   Map 4 ST52

The Walnut Tree

PICK OF THE PUBS

Fore St BA22 7QW ☎ 01935 851292
e-mail: info@thewalnuttreehotel.com
dir: Exit A303 between Sparkford & Yeovilton Air Base at x-rds signed West Camel

A short hop from the busy main road

The A303 to the West Country can be a tedious drive, so it might be worth making a half-mile detour to this family-run village inn. The eponymous tree provides the terrace with welcoming dappled shade on warm sunny days, while inside the black-beamed, part-oak, part-flagstone-floored bar sets the scene. Otter real ales and Thatchers Gold cider can accompany lunchtime smoked haddock, prawn and pasta bake; Thai red chicken curry and basmati rice; or ham and mushroom omelette, chips and salad. The evening menu, served in the Rosewood Restaurant, changes seasonally to offer starters such as Cornish mussels in white wine cream, onion and garlic sauce; and baked figs with goats' cheese and Parma ham; followed perhaps by a main course of fillet of beef Rossini with pâté and rich Madeira sauce; or smoked haddock fillet with cheese and chive sauce.

Open 11-3 5.30-11 Closed: 25-26 Dec, 1 Jan, Sun eve, Mon L, Tue L **Bar Meals** L served Wed-Sun 12-2 D served Mon-Sat 6-9 **Restaurant** L served Wed-Sun 12-2 D served Mon-Sat 6-9 ⊕ FREE HOUSE ◀ Otter Ale, Bitter Ⓞ Thatchers Gold. ♈ 9 **Facilities** Non-diners area ♦️ Children's portions Garden Parking Wi-fi

WEST HATCH   Map 4 ST22

The Farmers Arms **NEW**

TA3 5RS ☎ 01823 480980
e-mail: farmersarmswh@gmail.com
dir: M5 junct 25, A358 towards Ilminster. Approx 2m follow West Hatch & RSPCA Centre signs. Continue following RSPCA signs & brown pub sign (ignore West Hatch sign). Pub at brow of hill on left

Traditional pub that's a walker's favourite retreat

A converted farmhouse dating from the 16th century in the countryside just a five-minute drive from Taunton. Walkers and riders are frequent visitors as the pub is on the 13.5 mile Neroche Staple Fitzpaine Herepath (meaning people's path). Either sit in the light and airy restaurant or in the beer garden to enjoy well kept Otter and Exmoor beers and food such as a starter of pork and wholegrain mustard terrine and apple purée, or tuna Thai fishcake. Then choose perhaps a main dish of bouillabaisse with grilled salmon, new potatoes, smoke paprika remoulade; or braised pork belly with bubble-and-squeak, honey roast beetroot, braised greens and cider sauce.

Open all day all wk 11am-11.30pm Closed: 25 Dec **Bar Meals** L served all wk 12-2, cream teas 3-5.30 D served all wk 6-9 Av main course £10 **Restaurant** L served all wk

12-2 D served all wk 6-9 Fixed menu price fr £9.95 Av 3 course à la carte fr £22.50 ⊕ FREE HOUSE ◄ Otter, Exmoor Ales ☉ Thatchers, Thatchers Gold. **Facilities** Non-diners area ❤ (Bar Garden Outside area) ♦♦ Children's portions Garden Outside area ⊼ Parking Wi-fi 🚐 (notice required)

WEST HUNTSPILL   Map 4 ST34

Crossways Inn ★★★★ INN

PICK OF THE PUBS

See Pick of the Pubs on page 392

WEST MONKTON   Map 4 ST22

The Monkton Inn

PICK OF THE PUBS

Blundells Ln TA2 8NP ☎ 01823 412414
dir: *M5 junct 25 to Taunton, right at Creech Castle for 1m, left into West Monkton, right at Procters Farm, 0.5m on left*

Pretty little pub offering hearty meals

A little bit tucked away on the edge of the village, this convivial pub is run by Peter and Val Mustoe who, for many years, lived in South Africa. Once inside you'll undoubtedly be struck by the polished floorboards, stone walls, log fire, leather sofas, smart dining furniture, in fact, by the whole set-up. At the bar you'll be able to order Exmoor and Sharp's real ales, as well as your food, but meals are served only in the restaurant or on the patio. Lunch could be Cape Malay chicken and apricot curry, or the more prosaic steak, egg and chips, while the dinner menu offers grilled fillet of springbok with a redcurrant sauce; pan fried pork tenderloin with apple and cider sauce; Somerset lamb cutlets with redcurrant and mint jus; or medley of mushrooms with rice and side salad. On Sundays expect roasts, fish and chips, a curry and chargrills.

Open all wk 12-3 6-11 **Bar Meals** L served all wk 12-2 D served all wk 6-9 Av main course £9.50 **Restaurant** L served all wk 12-2 D served all wk 6-9 ⊕ ENTERPRISE INNS ◄ Sharp's Doom Bar, Exmoor Gold, Otter Ale ☉ Thatchers Gold, Aspall. ♛ 10 **Facilities** Non-diners area ❤ (Bar Garden Outside area) ♦♦ Children's menu Children's portions Play area Garden Outside area ⊼ Parking 🚐 (notice required)

WEST PENNARD   Map 4 ST53

The Apple Tree Inn **NEW**

BA6 8ND ☎ 01749 890060
e-mail: theappletree.glastonbury@gmail.com

Family-oriented pub close to Glastonbury Tor

Although their 17th-century, stone-built roadside inn is still a relatively new venture for locally renowned chef Lee Evans and his wife Ally, it has already been highly praised. Intriguing artworks hang in the wood- and stone-floored bar and dining area, neatly cut logs are stacked either side of the open fire, and Somerset real ales and ciders are on handpump. A typical Lee menu offers deep-fried Somerset brie with Cumberland sauce; followed by braised blade of beef with parsley porridge and baby onions; and hand-made petits fours to follow. Treats on the bar await well-behaved dogs.

Open 12-3 6-11 Closed: 25-26 Dec, Mon **Bar Meals** L served Tue-Sun 12-2.30 D served Tue-Sun 6-9 Av main course £9.50 **Restaurant** L served Tue-Sun 12-1.45 D served Tue-Sun 6-9 Fixed menu price fr £5.95 Av 3 course à la carte fr £27.50 ⊕ FREE HOUSE ◄ Butcombe, Exmoor Ales Gold, Yeovil Ales Star Gazer, Palmers Copper Ale ☉ Ashton Press, Worley's, Hecks, Thatchers Gold. ♛ 10 **Facilities** Non-diners area ❤ (Bar Restaurant Garden) ♦♦ Children's menu Children's portions Garden ⊼ Parking 🚐 (notice required)

WHEDDON CROSS   Map 3 SS93

The Rest and Be Thankful Inn ★★★★ INN

TA24 7DR ☎ 01643 841222
e-mail: stay@restandbethankful.co.uk
dir: *5m S of Dunster*

Traditional pub on Exmoor's heights

Almost 1,000 feet up in Exmoor National Park's highest village, this early 19th-century coaching inn blends old-world charm with friendly hospitality. Today's travellers are welcomed with log fires warming the bar in winter; traditional entertainments of skittle alley and pool table are at the disposal of the energetic. Menus of carefully prepared pub favourites may include deep-fried brie wedges; Exmoor sausages in red onion gravy; a 'taste of the West' cheeseboard; and Somerset farmhouse ice creams. The popular Sunday carvery represents excellent value. Contact the pub for details of their beer festival.

Open all wk 10-3 6-close **Bar Meals** L served all wk 12-2 D served all wk 6.30-9 **Restaurant** L served all wk 12-2 D served all wk 6.30-9 ⊕ FREE HOUSE ◄ Exmoor Ale, St Austell Proper Job & Tribute, Sharp's Own, Guinness ☉ Thatchers, Thatchers Gold, St Austell Copper Press. ♛ 9 **Facilities** Non-diners area ♦♦ Children's menu Children's portions Garden Beer festival Parking Wi-fi 🚐 (notice required) **Rooms** 8

WINSFORD   Map 3 SS93

Royal Oak Inn

TA24 7JE ☎ 01643 851455
e-mail: enquiries@royaloakexmoor.co.uk
web: www.royaloakexmoor.co.uk
dir: *Follow Winsford signs from A396 (Minehead to Tiverton road)*

Local ales and seasonal produce in a delightful setting

Previously a farmhouse and dairy, the Royal Oak is a stunningly attractive thatched inn in one of Exmoor's prettiest villages, huddled beneath the rising moors beside the River Exe. Inside its all big fires, comfy chairs, restrained paraphernalia and restful decor, all the better to enjoy the twin treats of good honest Exmoor beers and rich local produce on the seasonal bar and restaurant menus, including slow-braised lamb shank with pan-fried gnocchi and red wine jus; butternut squash risotto cake; and deep-fried scampi in stout batter and chips.

Open all wk 11-3 6-11 **Bar Meals** L served all wk 12-2 D served all wk 6-9 **Restaurant** L served all wk 12-2 D served all wk 6-9 ⊕ ENTERPRISE INNS ◄ Exmoor Ale, Stag, Gold ☉ Thatchers. **Facilities** Non-diners area ♦♦ Children's menu Children's portions Garden ⊼ Parking Wi-fi

PICK OF THE PUBS

Crossways Inn ★★★★ INN

Withy Rd TA9 3RA ☎ 01278 783756
e-mail: info@crosswaysinn.com
web: www.crosswaysinn.com
dir: *M5 juncts 22 or 23 on A38*

Good beer and cider choices plus classic pub food

A family-run 17th century, tile-hung coaching inn ideally positioned for visitors to the Somerset Levels or walkers looking for a cosy respite from the rigours of the Mendip Hills. The Crossways Inn has benefited from major renovation work in recent years, including the revamped skittle alley and new state-of-the-art kitchen. Warmed by two open log fireplaces, the cosy, wavy-beamed interior has an array of fine old photos of the area. Draw close to the bar to inspect the ever-rotating selection of excellent beers, often from micro-breweries in Somerset, such as Moor and RCH. The beer choice increases significantly during the pub's popular August Bank Holiday beer festival. Cider drinkers are spoiled for choice, too, with Thatchers on tap and Rich's Cider created at a local farm just a couple of miles away. The classic food here also tends to be very locally sourced, like Somerset rump and sirloin steaks, which come with home-made peppercorn, Stilton or white wine and mushroom sauce. Cottage pie, sausages and mash, curry of the day, and scampi

and chips are all popular options, but you will need to check the specials board for the daily pie. The pasta section of the menu offers lasagne, spaghetti bolognese and, for vegetarians, roasted vegetable and four-cheese bake. Lighter meals include sandwiches, baguettes, ploughman's and jacket potatoes. Interesting desserts are toffee and Dime Bar crunch pie, and Alabama chocolate fudge cake. Under-10s can have a menu of their own. In summer, the large enclosed beer garden and children's play area comes into its own, as does the heated gazebo.

Open all day all wk **Closed:** 25 Dec **Bar Meals** L served all wk 12-2.30 D served all wk 6-9 **Restaurant** L served all wk 12-2.30 D served all wk 6-9

⊕ FREE HOUSE ◀ Exmoor Stag, Cotleigh Snowy, Sharp's Doom Bar, Otter Ale, RCH Double Header, Moor, Butcombe ♂ Thatchers Gold, Dry & Heritage, Rich's. ☒ 16 **Facilities** Non-diners area ❀ ♦ Children's menu Children's portions Play area Family room Garden ⊓ Beer festival Parking Wi-fi ═══ (notice required) **Rooms** 7

Save on hotels. Book at **theAA.com/hotel**

SOMERSET 393 ENGLAND

PICK OF THE PUBS

The Masons Arms ★★★★ INN

YEOVIL Map 4 ST51

41 Lower Odcombe BA22 8TX
☎ **01935 862591**
e-mail:
paula@masonsarmsodcombe.co.uk
web: www.masonsarmsodcombe.co.uk
dir: *A3088 to Yeovil, right to Montacute,*
through village, 3rd right after petrol
station to Lower Odcombe

Friendly village inn that brews its own beer

Originally a traditional cider house comprising three cottages, this thatched 16th-century inn used to be where thirsty masons from the local quarry were served. Believed to be the oldest building in the village, the pub has four thatched 'eyebrows' above its upper windows. Proprietors Drew and Paula saved the pub from closure when they took it on in 2005 and it has become the hub of the village. Drew is also a brewer and the bar serves pints from the pub's own micro-brewery, making it the only place you can enjoy pints of Odcombe No 1, Roly Poly and Half Jack. The owners have built strong green credentials, recycling anything and everything, and growing many of their own vegetables and fruit. The wine list reflects this commitment, with organic, vegetarian, biodynamic and fairly traded choices. When he's not brewing beer, Drew also runs the

kitchen, producing freshly prepared dishes for seasonal and daily-changing menus. Pub favourites might include a pie of the day or ham with free-range duck egg and chips, whilst the à la carte menu available at lunchtime and in the evening could start with scallops, black pudding, pea purée and wilted spinach and continue with a main course of apple and cumin stuffed pork tenderloin, fondant potato, buttered leeks and cider jus. Round things off with one of the home-made desserts — perhaps iced peanut butter parfait and chocolate sauce or lemon tart with raspberry sorbet. The comfortable en suite letting rooms are set back from the road and overlook the pretty garden.

Open all wk 12-3 6-12 **Bar Meals** L served all wk 12-2 D served all wk 6.30-9.30 Av main course £11 **Restaurant** L served all wk 12-2 D served all wk 6.30-9.30 ⊕ FREE HOUSE ◾ Odcombe No 1, Spring, Roly Poly, Winters Tail, Half Jack ♺ Thatchers Gold & Heritage. ♈ 8 **Facilities** Non-diners area 🐾 👬 Children's menu Children's portions Garden ⩌ Parking Wi-fi **Rooms** 6

WOOKEY
Map 4 ST54

The Burcott Inn

Wells Rd BA5 1NJ ☎ 01749 673874
e-mail: ian@burcottinn.co.uk
dir: *2m from Wells on B3139*

Homely stone-built inn with a friendly welcome

On the edge of a charming village just two miles from the cathedral city of Wells, the age of this 300-year-old pub is confirmed by the low-beamed ceilings, flagstone floors and log fires. Another notable feature is its copper-topped bar with five real ales and Addlestones cider on hand-pull. Here, you can have a snack or a daily special, while in the restaurant typical dishes include egg and prawn salad, grilled trout fillets, apricot chicken breast, sweet pepper and tomato tartlet, and rump steak. There are also specials board choices. The large enclosed garden enjoys views of the Mendip Hills.

Open 11.30-2.30 6-11 (Sun 12-3) Closed: 25-26 Dec, 1 Jan, Sun eve **Bar Meals** L served all wk 12-2 D served Tue-Sat 6.30-9 Av main course £10 **Restaurant** L served all wk 12-2 D served Tue-Sat 6.30-9 Av 3 course à la carte fr £20 ⊕ FREE HOUSE ◀ Teignworthy Old Moggie, RCH Pitchfork, Hop Back Summer Lightning, Cheddar Potholer, Butts Barbus barbus ☼ Addlestones. **Facilities** Non-diners area ♦ Children's menu Children's portions Family room Garden ⋈ Parking ⛟ (notice required)

WOOKEY HOLE
Map 4 ST54

Wookey Hole Inn ⊚

High St BA5 1BP ☎ 01749 676677
e-mail: mail@wookeyholeinn.com
dir: *Opposite Wookey Hole caves*

A top selection of beers and noteworthy cuisine

Opposite the famous caves, this family-run hotel, restaurant and bar is outwardly traditional, although the interior looks and feels very laid-back. Somerset and continental draught and bottled beers include Glastonbury's Love Monkey and fruity Belgian Früli; local Wilkins tempts cider-heads. There are plenty of lunchtime snacks and dishes such as wild boar burger, Greek salad and sweet chilli chicken stir-fry. The evening restaurant

menu could see Somerset chicken stuffed with red onion and sage, grain mustard mash, parsnip purée and chasseur sauce; and winter vegetable and cheese pithivier with gnocchi, tomato and sweet chilli sauce, and a rocket, parmesan and toasted seed salad.

Open all day all wk Closed: 25-26 Dec, Sun eve **Bar Meals** L served all wk 12-2.30 D served Mon-Sat 7-9.30 **Restaurant** L served all wk 12-2.30 D served Mon-Sat 7-9.30 ⊕ FREE HOUSE ◀ Glastonbury Love Monkey, Cheddar, Yeovil, Cottage ☼ Wilkins Farmhouse. **Facilities** Non-diners area ♣ (Bar Garden) ♦ Children's menu Children's portions Garden ⋈ Parking Wi-fi ⛟ (notice required)

YEOVIL
Map 4 ST51

The Half Moon Inn ★★★ INN

Main St, Mudford BA21 5TF ☎ 01935 850289
e-mail: enquiries@thehalfmoon.co.uk
dir: *A303 at Sparkford onto A359 to Yeovil, 3.5m on left*

Long menu with something for everyone

The exposed beams and flagstone floors retain the character of this painstakingly restored 17th-century village pub just north of Yeovil. Local East Street Cream ale is one of the beers on tap and there are ten wines by the glass to accompany the extensive menu of home-cooked food, which includes pub classics and main meals such as pork Stroganoff, venison casserole, and a mixed grill of sea bass, salmon and haddock. The large cobbled courtyard is ideal for alfresco dining and spacious, well-equipped bedrooms are also available.

Open all day all wk Closed: 25-26 Dec **Bar Meals** L served all wk 12-9.30 D served all wk 12-9.30 food served all day **Restaurant** L served all wk 12-9.30 D served all wk 6-9.30 food served all day ⊕ FREE HOUSE ◀ RCH Pitchfork, East Street Cream ☼ Westons Old Rosie & Perry. ♣ 10 **Facilities** Non-diners area ♦ Children's menu Children's portions Outside area ⋈ Parking Wi-fi **Rooms** 14

The Masons Arms ★★★★ INN
PICK OF THE PUBS
See Pick of the Pubs on page 393

See Pick of the Pubs on page 393

STAFFORDSHIRE

ALSTONEFIELD
Map 16 SK15

The George
PICK OF THE PUBS

DE6 2FX ☎ 01335 310205
e-mail: emily@thegeorgeatalstonefield.com
dir: *7m N of Ashbourne, signed Alstonefield to left off A515*

A pretty Peak District National Park pub

In a village above Dovedale, this attractive, stone-built pub offers a bar with a homely fire, historic artefacts, portraits of locals and a good choice of real ales. To one side is the snug, which, as the dining room, has lime-plastered walls and farmhouse furniture, with candlelight and fresh flowers adding an elegant touch. Emily Brighton, whose family has run The George for three generations, warmly welcomes all-comers, although asks walkers to leave their muddy boots at the door. The kitchen's passion for using locally sourced food has prompted the pub to create its own organic garden, which now produces abundant vegetables, salad leaves and herbs. A winter lunch menu might offer chicken liver parfait with toasted brioche; and trio of local sausages with onion marmalade, while dinner might start with Stilton beignet, sautéed mushrooms and spinach velouté; then market fish of the day with shrimps, mussels and parmentier potatoes.

Open all wk Mon-Fri 11.30-3 6-11 (Sat 11.30-11 Sun 12-9.30) Closed: 25 Dec **Bar Meals** L served all wk 12-2.30 D served Mon-Sat 7-9, Sun 6.30-8 Av main course £11-£28 **Restaurant** L served all wk 12-2.30 D served Mon-Sat 7-9, Sun 6.30-8 ⊕ MARSTON'S ◀ Burton Bitter & Pedigree, Jennings Cumberland Ale, Brakspear Oxford Gold, Guest ale, Banks's Sunbeam ☼ Thatchers. ♣ 10 **Facilities** Non-diners area ♣ (Bar Garden) ♦ Children's portions Garden Parking

The Watts Russell Arms
PICK OF THE PUBS
See Pick of the Pubs on opposite page

See Pick of the Pubs on opposite page

Save on hotels. Book at **theAA.com/hotel**

STAFFORDSHIRE 395 ENGLAND

PICK OF THE PUBS

The Watts Russell Arms

ALSTONEFIELD   Map 16 SK15

Hopedale DE6 2GD ☎ 01335 310126
e-mail: contact@wattsrussell.co.uk
web: www.wattsrussell.co.uk
dir: *Take A515 N towards Buxton. In 6.5m left to Alstonefield & Milldale. Cross River Dove, take left fork to Milldale. 1.5m to pub*

Informal and friendly pub with great walks on the doorstep

In the heart of the Peak District National Park, and within walking distance of the Dove and Manifold Valleys, this charming 18th-century stone-built inn was once a farmstead until it became a beer house called the New Inn. It was renamed in 1851 after the wife of wealthy industrialist Jesse Watts-Russell, whose father built the neo-Gothic Ilam Hall down the road. Husband and wife team Bruce and Chris Elliott run the pub, whose cosy interior gladdens all who enter, and dogs are very welcome in the terraced gardens and courtyard. At the bar, made from old oak barrels, Chris serves well-kept real ales from breweries all within a 25-mile radius, Thornbridge in Bakewell, for example; hand-crafted lagers from the Freedom Brewery in Abbots Bromley; single malts from a 15-strong selection; and eight wines by

the glass. In the kitchen, Bruce prepares everything from scratch, using mostly locally supplied produce and ingredients, and with prior notice most dietary requirements can be catered for. Chris and Bruce insist that theirs is not a 'gastro-pub', and that it's not a problem if you want a starter or a pudding on its own. At lunchtime there are 'roll your own' tortilla wraps and pancakes, soups, and hot plates such as salmon fillets and spirali bolognese, while typical in the evening would be breast of Gressingham duck cooked in cider and brandy; chicken cooked in tomato and red wine; and in season a winter casserole of beef, oxtail and venison. On Friday evenings there's 'tapas with a twist'.

Open Mon 12-2.30 Tue-Fri 12-10 (Sat 12-11 Sun 12-8) Closed: Mon eve **Bar Meals** L served Mon 12-2, Tue-Sat 12-4, Sun 12-7 D served Tue-Sat 7-9 ⊕ FREE HOUSE ◀ Guest ales. ♟ 8
Facilities Non-diners area ❤ (Bar Garden) ♦♦ Children's portions Garden ☴ Parking

ALTON · Map 10 SK04

Bulls Head Inn

High St ST10 4AQ ☎ 01538 702307
e-mail: janet@thebullsheadalton.co.uk
dir: M6 junct 14, A518 to Uttoxeter. Follow Alton Towers signs. Onto B5030 to Rocester, then B5032 to Alton. Pub in village centre

Family-run inn with a varied menu

This 18th-century coaching inn is handy for the Peak District, and Alton Towers theme park, which is less than a mile away. Oak beams and an inglenook fireplace set the scene for the old-world bar, where a rotating selection of real ales from three handpumps, and Addlestones cider are on offer. In the country-style dining room with its pine furniture and slate floor, the evening menu might include smoked salmon and pesto tagliatelle; oven-roasted lemon and thyme chicken leg; vegetable fajitas; pan-fried sea bass with stir-fried noodles; and curry or pie of the day.

Open all day all wk 11-11 **Bar Meals** L served all wk 12-2.30 D served all wk 6-9 Av main course £7.50 **Restaurant** L served all wk 12-2.30 D served all wk 6-9 Fixed menu price fr £8.95 ⊕ FREE HOUSE ◀ Bass, Greene King Abbot Ale & Ruddles County, Fuller's London Pride, Sharp's Doom Bar, Wells Bombardier, Hancock's ♂ Addlestones. ☗ 8 **Facilities** Non-diners area ♦♦ Children's menu Children's portions Garden ⊨ Parking Wi-fi

ANSLOW · Map 10 SK22

The Burnt Gate at Anslow

Hopley Rd DE13 9PY ☎ 01283 563664
e-mail: info@burntgate.co.uk
dir: From Burton upon Trent take B5017 towards Abbots Bromley. At top of Henhurst Hill turn right into Hopley Rd signed Anslow

Friendly free house; special diets catered for

There's a country-house feel to this hanging-basket bedecked village inn, set in pleasant countryside near Tutbury. Named after a tollhouse that was burned to the ground centuries ago, light oak beams and colour-washed walls brighten the interior, where patrons can look forward to locally brewed real ale and a generous menu crafted largely from Staffordshire-sourced materials; chicken breast stuffed with fresh spinach and mushrooms in Madeira sauce hits the spot. Vegans, vegetarians and coeliacs will be particularly pleased with the choices available here.

Open all day all wk Closed: 31 Dec ⊕ FREE HOUSE ◀ Marston's Pedigree, Guest ales. **Facilities** Children's menu Parking Wi-fi

BARTON-UNDER-NEEDWOOD · Map 10 SK11

The Waterfront

Barton Marina DE13 8DZ ☎ 01283 711500
e-mail: info@waterfrontbarton.co.uk
dir: Exit A38 onto B5016 towards Barton-under-Needwood. 1st left signed Barton Turn. 1st right into Barton Marina

Large modern pub overlooking a marina

This pub is part of a purpose-built marina complex, and is constructed with reclaimed materials to resemble a Victorian canalside warehouse. Overlooking busy moorings, it offers beers specially brewed for the pub and a fair few cocktails – best enjoyed outside on the terrace in sunny weather. Dine in the contemporary conservatory from an extensive menu of snacks, oven-fired pizzas, and old favourites like chicken tikka, Barnsley lamb chop, Caesar salad, rib-eye steak and Cajun chicken burger. The pub's beer festival is held during the first weekend in April. A walk along the Trent & Mersey towpath leads to the nearby National Memorial Arboretum, the UK's Centre of Remembrance.

Open all day all wk **Bar Meals** L served 10-6 D served 6-9.30 food served all day **Restaurant** L served Mon-Sat 12-3, Sun 12-8 D served Mon-Sat 6-9.30 ⊕ FREE HOUSE ◀ Waterfront Barton Pale & Marina Bitter, St Austell Tribute, Marston's Pedigree ♂ Thatchers. ☗ 20 **Facilities** Non-diners area ♦♦ Children's menu Children's portions Garden ⊨ Beer festival Parking Wi-fi ☎ (notice required)

CAULDON · Map 16 SK04

Yew Tree Inn

ST10 3EJ ☎ 01538 308348
dir: Between A52 & A523. 4.5m from Alton Towers

Quirky pub with lots to see

Alan East's 300-year-old pub is home to his amazing collection of antiques and curiosities, including a 3,000-year-old Grecian urn, several penny-farthings, polyphons, a pair of Queen Victoria's stockings, a crank handle telephone and a pub lantern. No wonder he's been nicknamed the Moorland Magpie. A snacks-only menu offers locally made, hand-raised pork pies, sandwiches, baps, quiches and desserts, all ready to be accompanied by a pint of Bass, Burton Bridge or Rudgate Ruby Mild.

Open all wk 10.30-2.30 6-12 (Sun 12-3 7-12) **Bar Meals** L served 10.30-2.30, Sun 12-3 ⊕ FREE HOUSE ◀ Burton Bridge, Bass, Rudgate Ruby Mild. **Facilities** Non-diners area ♣ (Bar) ♦♦ Family room Parking ☎ **Notes** ⊛

CHEADLE · Map 10 SK04

The Queens At Freehay

Counslow Rd, Freehay ST10 1RF ☎ 01538 722383
e-mail: mail@queensatfreehay.co.uk
dir: From Cheadle take A552 towards Uttoxeter. In Mobberley left, through Freehay to pub at next rdbt. Freehay also signed from B5032 (Cheadle to Denstone road)

Tucked away in a quiet village

Surrounded by mature trees and well-tended gardens, this 18th-century, family-run pub and restaurant has a refreshing, modern interior and it's just four miles from Alton Towers. Iconic draught Burton, Ringwood Fortyniner and the more local Alton Abbey are among the beers on handpump in the bar. With a good reputation for food, its main menu is supplemented by daily chef's specials on the fresh fish and meat boards. Expect Staffordshire black pudding or tomato, mozzarella and basil salad to start, followed by chicken fusilli pasta, pan-fried duck breast, Thai fishcakes, or mixed grill. Crusty rolls and light bites are lunchtime options.

Open all wk 12-3 6-11 (Sun 12-4 6.30-11) Closed: 25-26, 31 Dec-1 Jan **Bar Meals** L served Mon-Sat 12-2, Sun 12-2.30 D served Mon-Sat 6-9.30, Sun 6.30-9.30 Av main course £11.95 **Restaurant** L served Mon-Sat 12-2, Sun 12-2.30 D served Mon-Sat 6-9.30, Sun 6.30-9.30 Av 3 course à la carte fr £20 ⊕ FREE HOUSE ◀ Burton Ale, Peakstones Rock Alton Abbey, Wells Bombardier, Guinness, Marstons Pedigree, Ringwood Fortyniner. ☗ **Facilities** Non-diners area ♦♦ Children's portions Garden ⊨ Parking Wi-fi

COLTON · Map 10 SK02

The Yorkshireman

Colton Rd WS15 3HB ☎ 01889 583977
e-mail: theyorkshireman@wine-dine.co.uk
dir: From A51 rdbt in Rugeley follow rail station signs, under rail bridge, to pub

Try real ales from the local microbrewery

The pub's name comes from a scion of the White Rose county who was once landlord here although the heritage of this edge-of-town pub opposite Rugeley's Trent Valley railway station is lost in the mists of time. Many believe it may have been established as a tavern to serve the new railway in the 19th century and it's certainly seen a lot of life since those days, including a meeting place for farmers and soldiers. Walk through the doors today to find a panelled, wood-floored dining pub specialising in dishes using top Staffordshire produce and offering beers from a local microbrewery including, unusually, a lager. The eclectic furnishings are part of the charm, and the faux Stubbs paintings attract much comment. The seasonal menu is updated regularly, but a good range covering all the bases is assured.

Open all wk 12-2.30 5.30-10 (Sat 12-11 Sun 12-6) **Bar Meals** L served Mon-Sat 12-2.30, Sun 12-6 D served

Save on hotels. Book at **theAA.com/hotel**

STAFFORDSHIRE 397 **ENGLAND**

Mon-Sat 6-9 **Restaurant** L served Mon-Sat 12-2.30, Sun 12-6 Bistro menu Mon-Sat 12-2 D served Mon-Sat 6-9 ⊕ **FREE HOUSE** ◀ Blythe ○ Westons Stowford Press. ☗ 10 **Facilities** Non-diners area ❀ (Bar Garden) ⁑ Children's portions Garden ╦ Parking Wi-fi ▭

ECCLESHALL   Map 15 SJ82

The George

Castle St ST21 6DF ☎ 01785 850300
e-mail: vicki@slatersales.co.uk
dir: *From M6 junct 14 take A5013 to Eccleshall (6m)*

Slater's beers the big attraction here

Effectively this pub is the taphouse for the family microbrewery, whose Top Totty bitter received much media coverage in 2012 when it was withdrawn as a guest ale from a House of Commons bar, because its pump badge upset the shadow equalities minister. Dog-friendly and welcoming, The George serves snacks and light meals in both the open-fired bar and restaurant; among the choices could be grilled steaks; pork medallions in whisky and mushroom sauce; battered coley and hand-cut chips; and roast beetroot and asparagus risotto. A beer festival is held in the spring.

Open all day all wk 11am-1.30am (Fri-Sat 11am-2.30am Sun 12-12) **Bar Meals** L served Mon-Fri 12-3, Sat 12-9, Sun 12-6 D served Mon-Fri 6-9, Sat 12-9 Av main course £3.95 **Restaurant** L served Mon-Fri 12-3, Sat 12-9, Sun 12-6 D served Mon-Fri 6-9, Sat 12-9 ⊕ **SLATER'S ALES** ◀ Slater's Ales ○ Thatchers Gold. ☗ 10 **Facilities** Non-diners area ❀ (Bar Restaurant) ⁑ Children's menu Children's portions ╦ Beer festival Parking Wi-fi ▭

GREAT BRIDGEFORD   Map 10 SJ82

The Mill at Worston **NEW**

Worston Ln ST18 9QA ☎ 01785 282710
e-mail: info@themillatworston.co.uk
dir: *M6 junct 14, A5013 signed Eccleshall. 2m to Great Bridgeford. Turn right signed Worston Mill. Or from Eccleshall on A5013 towards Stafford. 3m to Great Bridgeford, turn left to Mill*

A restored corn mill now serving good food

Documents can trace a mill on this site from 1279. The building that now occupies this rural spot beside the River Sow dates from 1814, when it was in daily use as a corn mill. Visitors can still see the original wheel and gearing that powered the mill stone. Drop in for meals that range from ciabatta or baguette sandwiches, jacket potatoes and grills to home-made steak and ale pie, wild mushroom carbonara and roasted field mushrooms with Welsh rarebit, all washed down with a pint of Joule's Slumbering Monk perhaps? The pretty gardens, with duck pond, make a great place for alfresco eating in the warmer months.

Open all day all wk Closed: 26 Dec **Bar Meals** L served all wk 12-6 D served Mon-Thu 6-9, Fri-Sat 6-10 Av main course £9.95 food served all day **Restaurant** L served Sat-Sun 12-6 D served Wed-Thu 6-9, Fri-Sat 6-10 Fixed

menu price fr £8.95 Av 3 course à la carte fr £25 ⊕ **FREE HOUSE** ◀ Morland Old Speckled Hen, Joule's Slumbering Monk. ☗ 12 **Facilities** Non-diners area ⁑ Children's menu Children's portions Play area Garden ╦ Parking Wi-fi ▭ (notice required)

LEEK   Map 16 SJ95

Three Horseshoes Inn ★★★ HL ◉◉

Buxton Rd, Blackshaw Moor ST13 8TW
☎ 01538 300296
e-mail: enquiries@3shoesinn.co.uk
dir: *On A53, 3m N of Leek*

Award-winning food at well known inn

A family-run inn and country hotel in the Peak District National Park, the Three Horseshoes offers breathtaking views of the moorlands, Tittesworth reservoir and rock formations from the attractive gardens. Inside this creeper-covered inn are ancient beams, gleaming brass, rustic furniture and wood fires in the winter, with a good selection of real ales. Using the best Staffordshire produce, visitors can choose from wide ranging lunch and dinner menus: locally-reared roast meat in the bar carvery, the relaxed atmosphere of the brasserie offering modern British and Thai dishes, or Kirks Restaurant. Delicious afternoon teas are also available.

Open all day all wk **Bar Meals** food served all day **Restaurant** L served Sun 12.15-1.30 D served Mon-Sat 6.30-9 ⊕ **FREE HOUSE** ◀ Theakston XB, Courage Directors, Morland Old Speckled Hen, John Smith's. ☗ 12 **Facilities** Non-diners area ⁑ Children's menu Children's portions Play area Garden Parking ▭ **Rooms** 26

ONNELEY   Map 15 SJ74

The Wheatsheaf Inn ★★★★ INN

Bar Hill Rd CW3 9QF ☎ 01782 751581
e-mail: pub@wheatsheafpub.co.uk
web: www.wheatsheafpub.co.uk
dir: *On A525 between Madeley & Woore*

Attractive inn offering good regional ales

Starting life as a coaching inn in the 18th century, this whitewashed pub with flower-filled window boxes lies in the hamlet of Onneley. Although it has been modernised, the old beams and fires are still in place, making for a cosy setting to enjoy real ales from Staffordshire breweries like Titanic and Peakstones. Meat from the local farm appears on the menu, which includes whole baby chicken glazed with honey and mustard, beefburger and lamb steak. Look out for world food themed nights.

The pub adjoins a golf course, so don't forget to pack your clubs and maybe stay over in the guest rooms situated in converted stables.

Open all day all wk **Bar Meals** L served Mon-Sat 12-9 D served Mon-Sat 12-9 food served all day **Restaurant** L served Mon-Sat 12-9 D served Mon-Sat 12-9 food served all day ⊕ **FREE HOUSE** ◀ Wells Bombardier, Joule's, Titanic, Salopian, Peakstones, 2 Guest ales ○ Westons. ☗ 8 **Facilities** Non-diners area ❀ (Bar Garden) ⁑ Children's menu Children's portions Play area Family room Garden ╦ Parking Wi-fi **Rooms** 10

STAFFORD   Map 10 SJ92

The Holly Bush Inn

PICK OF THE PUBS

See Pick of the Pubs on page 398

STOURTON   Map 10 SO88

The Fox Inn

Bridgnorth Rd DY7 5BL ☎ 01384 872614 & 872123
e-mail: foxinnstourton@gmail.com
dir: *5m from Stourbridge town centre. On A458 (Stourbridge to Bridgnorth road)*

Forty-plus years behind the bar

Stefan Caron has been running this late 18th-century inn for more than 40 years. In unspoilt countryside on an estate once owned by Lady Jane Grey, it retains the style of an old country pub, with church pews in the bar, where Black Country brewers Bathams and Wye Valley put on a double act. Menus variously offer chicken balti; fresh tagliatelle; Tex Mex, a rib-eye steak with chilli and mozzarella; pie of the day with peas and chunky chips; and beer-battered cod with mushy peas. A large garden with weeping willow, gazebo and attractive patio area are the external attractions.

Open all wk 10.30-3 5-11 (Sat-Sun 10.30am-11pm) **Bar Meals** L served Mon-Sat 12-2.30 D served Tue-Sat 7-9.30 **Restaurant** L served Tue-Sat 12-2.30, Sun 12.30-5 D served Tue-Sat 7-9.30 ⊕ **FREE HOUSE** ◀ Bathams, Wye Valley HPA, Guinness ○ Robinsons, Thatchers. **Facilities** Non-diners area ❀ (Garden) ⁑ Children's menu Children's portions Garden ╦ Parking ▭

PICK OF THE PUBS

The Holly Bush Inn

STAFFORD Map 10 SJ92

Salt ST18 0BX ☎ 01889 508234
e-mail: geoff@hollybushinn.co.uk
web: www.hollybushinn.co.uk
dir: *Telephone for directions*

Ancient pub with the second oldest licence in England

This thatched inn is situated in the village of Salt, which has been a settlement since the Saxon period. It is thought to be only the second pub in the country to receive, back in Charles II's reign, a licence to sell alcohol, although the building itself may date from 1190; and when landlord Geoff Holland's son Joseph became a joint licensee at the age of 18 years and 6 days, he was the youngest person ever to be granted a licence. The pub's comfortably old-fashioned interior contains all the essential ingredients: heavy carved beams, open fires, attractive prints and cosy alcoves. The kitchen has a strong commitment to limiting food miles by supporting local producers, and to ensuring that animals supplying meat have lived stress-free lives. The main menu features traditional dishes such as steak and ale pie; battered cod with mushy peas; and beefburger with beer battered onion rings; but also included are the still-traditional-but-less-well-known, such as grilled pork chop with cheese, beer and mustard topping; and free range supreme of chicken with

Guinness. Specials change every session, but usually include Staffordshire oatcakes stuffed with bacon and cheese; hand-made pork, leek and Stilton sausages with fried eggs and chips; roast topside of beef; or ham with sweet Madeira gravy. Evening specials may offer home-smoked fillet of Blythe Field trout with horseradish sauce; warm pan-fried duck and pear salad; Scottish mussels steamed with cider and cream; rabbit casserole with dumplings; or slow-cooked mutton with caper sauce. Cheeses are all hand-made to old English recipes, while seasonal puddings include traditional bread-and-butter pudding, and apple crumble. During the warmer months hand-made pizzas are cooked in a wood-fired brick oven.

Open all day all wk 12-11 (Sun 12-10.30) Closed: 25-26 Dec **Bar Meals** L served Mon-Sat 12-9.30, Sun 12-9 Av main course £10.95 food served all day ⊕ FREE HOUSE ◀ Marston's Pedigree, Adnams, Guest ales. ☿ 12 **Facilities** Non-diners area ♦♦ Children's menu Children's portions Garden ㅈ Beer festival Parking Wi-fi

Save on hotels. Book at **theAA.com/hotel**

STAFFORDSHIRE 399 ENGLAND

PICK OF THE PUBS

The Crown Inn

WRINEHILL Map 15 SJ74

Den Ln CW3 9BT ☎ 01270 820472
e-mail: info@thecrownatwrinehill.co.uk
web: www.thecrownatwrinehill.co.uk
dir: *On A531, 1m S of Betley. 6m S of
Crewe; 6m N of Newcastle-under-Lyme*

Great ales and food at this family run free house

After 35 years at the helm Staffordshire's longest serving licensee Charles Davenhill has pulled his last pint at this 19th-century former coaching inn and handed over the reins to his eminently capable daughter and son-in-law, Anna and Mark Condliffe. With an open-plan layout the pub nevertheless retains its oak beams and famously large inglenook fireplace, always a welcome feature. The bar does a good line in well-kept real ales, with always a choice of seven, two each from Jennings and Marston's, one from Salopian Ales and every week two micro-brewery guests including their own 'Legend' ale; fifteen wines are offered by the glass. Food is a major reason for the success of The Crown, not just for its consistent quality but for the generosity of the portions. Regularly changing menus are jam-packed with choice: from modestly priced light meals, such as locally sourced pork and leek sausages, buttered mash and onion gravy; and breaded plaice fillets with chips, peas and home-made tartare

sauce, to head chef Steve's trademark piri-piri chicken; smoked haddock and salmon fishcakes. Anna, a vegetarian herself, recognises that choice should extend beyond mushroom Stroganoff, so alternatives such as roasted vegetable lasagne al forno with salad; and veggie burritos filled with courgettes, baby corn and mixed peppers in tomato sauce will always make a showing on the menus. For a puddings try home-made steamed chocolate sponge with a rich chocolate sauce and vanilla ice cream; or iced lemon brûlée. On their own menu children will find home-roasted ham with free-range egg and a pot of tomato dipping sauce and farfalle pasta with tomato sauce and cheese.

Open 12-3 6-11 (Sun 12-4 6-10.30) Closed: 25-26 Dec, Mon L **Bar Meals** L served Tue-Fri 12-2, Sat-Sun 12-3 D served Sun-Thu 6-9, Fri 6-9.30, Sat 6-10 Av main course £10 ⊕ FREE HOUSE ◂ Marston's Pedigree & Burton Bitter, Jennings Sneck Lifter, Legend, Salopian, Guest ales. ♟ 15
Facilities Non-diners area ♦♦ Children's menu Children's portions Outside area 🎋 Parking Wi-fi 🚌 (notice required)

SUMMERHILL — Map 10 SK00

Oddfellows in the Boat

The Boat, Walsall Rd WS14 0BU ☎ 01543 361692
e-mail: info@oddfellowsintheboat.com
dir: *A461 (Lichfield towards Walsall). At rdbt junct with A5 (Muckley Corner) continue on A461. 500mtrs, U-turn on dual carriageway back to pub*

An ale lover's dream

This light and airy pub with country pine furnishings once served bargees on the now-disused 'Curly Wyrley' Canal to the rear. Real ale lovers can enjoy what amounts to a rolling beer festival all year thanks to an ever-changing choice from local microbreweries. Locally sourced dishes are prepared in an open kitchen and chalked up daily. Typical choices include spicy sausage and white bean cassoulet; roasted Nile perch with crushed potato and pineapple salsa; and toffee and banana crumble. There is a large, attractive beer garden to enjoy on sunny days.

Open all wk 11-3 6-11 (Sun 12-11) Closed: 25 Dec **Bar Meals** L served Mon-Sat 12-2.15, Sun 12-8.15 D served Mon-Sat 6-9.30, Sun 12-8.15 Av main course £12.50 **Restaurant** L served Mon-Sat 12-2.15, Sun 12-8.15 D served Mon-Sat 6-9.30, Sun 12-8.15 Fixed menu price fr £12.50 Av 3 course à la carte fr £20 ⊕ FREE HOUSE ◼ 3 Guest ales. ♚ 13 **Facilities** Non-diners area ♦↟ Garden ♬ Beer festival Parking Wi-fi

TAMWORTH — Map 10 SK20

The Globe Inn ★★★ INN

Lower Gungate B79 7AT ☎ 01827 60455
e-mail: info@theglobetamworth.com
dir: *Telephone for directions*

Restored early 20th-century pub with a hearty menu of favourites

A popular meeting place in the 19th century, The Globe was rebuilt in 1901. The restored exterior shows off its original appearance, while interior decoration has followed design styles of the era – the elegant carved bar and fireplaces reinforce its period character; air conditioning in public areas and satellite television are two concessions to 21st-century living. Beers from large breweries, menus of pub grub, a function room, and en suite accommodation complete the picture. Food-wise expect wraps, ciabattas, sandwiches, burgers, and jackets as well as steak-and-kidney pie, cod and chips and cottage pie.

Open all day all wk 11-11 (Thu-Sat 11am-mdnt Sun 12-11) Closed: 25 Dec, 1 Jan **Bar Meals** L served all wk 11-2 D served Mon-Sat 6-9 **Restaurant** L served Mon-Sat 11-2, Sun 12-4 D served Mon-Sat 6-9, Sun 12-4 ⊕ FREE HOUSE ◼ Bass, Worthington's, Holden's Black Country Mild. **Facilities** Non-diners area ♦↟ Children's menu Children's portions Parking Wi-fi ▥ (notice required) **Rooms** 18

WETTON — Map 16 SK15

Ye Olde Royal Oak

DE6 2AF ☎ 01335 310287
e-mail: royaloakwetton@live.co.uk
dir: *A515 from Ashebourne towards Buxton, left in 4m signed Alstonfield. In Alstonfield follow Wetton sign*

Old pub in astonishing Peak District countryside

Set in a pretty village in the White Peak; this comfortably traditional pub has been here for over 250 years. Lanes plummet into the chasm of the nearby Manifold Valley with its famous ash woods and Thor's Cave, whilst byways thread through a landscape revealing the area's fascinating lead and copper mining heritage. Beers from microbreweries like Belvoir or Wincle help pass the time in the peaceful beer garden or sun lounge, where ravenous walkers and cyclists can look forward to home-cooked pub grub. Ham dishes are a particular favourite, or maybe aubergine and walnut bake will fill the gap.

Open 12-2 7-closing Closed: Mon-Tue in winter **Bar Meals** L served Wed-Sun 12-2 D served Wed-Sun 7-9 Av main course £8.50 ⊕ FREE HOUSE ◼ Belvoir Gordon Bennett, Wincle Sir Philip. **Facilities** Non-diners area ♚ (Bar Garden) ♦↟ Children's menu Family room Garden ♬ Parking ▥ (notice required)

WRINEHILL — Map 15 SJ74

The Crown Inn

PICK OF THE PUBS

See Pick of the Pubs on page 399

The Hand & Trumpet

Main Rd CW3 9BJ ☎ 01270 820048
e-mail: hand.and.trumpet@brunningandprice.co.uk
dir: *M6 junct 16, A351, follow Keele signs, 7m, pub on right in village*

Smart pub with alfresco area overlooking the water

A deck to the rear of this relaxed country pub overlooks sizeable grounds, which include a large pond. The pub has a comfortable interior with original floors, old furniture, open fires and rugs. Six cask ales and over 70 malt whiskies are offered, along with a locally sourced menu. Typical dishes are potted Mrs Kirkham's Lancashire cheese with chicory, grape and walnut salad; venison, pigeon and duck meatloaf with bubble-and-squeak. There is a beer festival in the last week of January and a cider festival and hog roast in August.

Open all day all wk 11.30-11 (Sun 11.30-10.30) **Bar Meals** L served all wk 12-10 D served all wk 12-10 Av main course £12.95 food served all day **Restaurant** L served all wk 12-10 D served all wk 12-10 food served all day ⊕ BRUNNING & PRICE ◼ Caledonian Deuchars IPA, Salopian Oracle, Merlin's Kings Ale ♂ Aspall. ♚ 12 **Facilities** Non-diners area ♚ (Bar Garden) ♦↟ Children's portions Garden ♬ Beer festival Cider festival Parking

SUFFOLK

ALDRINGHAM — Map 13 TM46

The Parrot and Punchbowl Inn & Restaurant

Aldringham Ln IP16 4PY ☎ 01728 830221
dir: *On B1122, 1m from Leiston, 3m from Aldeburgh, on x-rds to Thorpeness*

Former smugglers' haunt, now a welcoming pub and restaurant

If you thought bizarre pub names were a late 20th-century fad, think again. Originally called The Case is Altered, this 16th-century pink-washed smugglers' inn became The Parrot and Punchbowl in 1604 when Aldringham was a centre for smuggled contraband. East Anglian-brewed ales from Adnams and Woodforde's, and Suffolk's Aspall cider all feature in the bar line-up. The good-value menu offers crayfish cocktail, bangers and mash, home-made lasagne, sirloin steak with fries, grilled cod fillet and slow-braised lamb's liver. Daily specials and vegetarian meals also have very reasonable price tags. There are roasts on Sundays and quiz nights.

Open 12-2.30 6-11 (Sun 12-2) Closed: Mon Jan-Mar **Bar Meals** L served all wk 12-2 D served Mon-Sat 6.30-9 **Restaurant** L served all wk 12-2 D served Mon-Sat 6.30-9 ⊕ ENTERPRISE INNS ◼ Woodforde's Wherry, Adnams, Guest ale ♂ Aspall. **Facilities** Non-diners area ♚ (Bar Garden) ♦↟ Children's portions Play area Family room Garden ♬ Parking Wi-fi ▥

BRANDESTON — Map 13 TM26

The Queens Head ◉

PICK OF THE PUBS

The Street IP13 7AD ☎ 01728 685307
dir: *From A14 take A1120 to Earl Soham, then S to Brandeston*

Family- and dog-friendly hostelry in a sleepy village

Created from four cottages and first opened in 1811, this smart Adnams pub stands slightly off the beaten track deep in peaceful Suffolk countryside. A detour is well worthwhile to sample one of the cracking Southwold ales, or a meal prepared to AA-Rosette standard. Outside is a well-furnished summer garden, while inside the warm and richly coloured decor complements the traditional homely features of wood panelling, quarry-tiled floors and open log fires. The modern British menu, described as 'pub food with a twist', is based on local produce where possible, and bristles with interest. How often do you come across fricassée of golden beetroot, pak choi, russet apples and parmesan cream? Or mushroom raviolo, braised oxtail, pickled mushrooms and shallot purée? Sunday lunches are always popular and family-based events are organised throughout the year, including barbecues in the garden and a beer festival in June to coincide with the village fête.

Save on hotels. Book at **theAA.com/hotel**

SUFFOLK 401 ENGLAND

Open 12-3 6-12 (Sun 12-6) Closed: Sun eve, Mon **Bar Meals** L served Tue-Sat 12-2:30, Sun 12-3 D served Tue-Sat 6-9 **Restaurant** L served Tue-Sat 12-2, Sun 12-3 D served Tue-Sat 6-9 ⊕ ADNAMS ◄ Broadside, Southwold Bitter, Seasonal ales ⌁ Aspall. **Facilities** Non-diners area ✿ (Bar Garden) ♦ Children's menu Children's portions Garden ⋒ Beer festival Parking Wi-fi ▦

BROMESWELL　　　　　　Map 13 TM35

The British Larder NEW

Orford Rd IP12 2PU ☎ 01394 460310
e-mail: info@britishlardersuffolk.co.uk
dir: *From A12 take A1152 signed Orford, Rendlesham, Woodbridge & Melton. Over railway line, approx 1m to pub on left*

A pub passionate about Suffolk produce

Put firmly on Suffolk's culinary map a few years ago by ex-Gordon Ramsay chef Madalene Bonvini-Hamel and named after her hugely successful recipe blog, the British Larder champions local and seasonal produce sourced from Suffolk farms and artisan suppliers. Daily menus bristle with fresh local ingredients, from Orford smoked salmon as a starter, to Dingley Dell pork with creamy mash and apple sauce, Blaxhall pheasant Kiev, and High House Farm Cox's apple and walnut strudel. To drink, there's ale from Adnams and cider from Aspall, and the atmosphere throughout the contemporary bar and dining rooms is relaxed and informal.

Open 12-4 6-10 (Sat 12-11 Sun 12-10) Closed: Sun eve & Mon 2 Jan-1 Apr **Bar Meals** L served all wk 12-3 D served all wk 6-9 Av main course £15 **Restaurant** L served all wk 12-3 D served all wk 6-9 Fixed menu price fr £15 Av 3 course à la carte fr £26.25 ⊕ PUNCH TAVERNS ◄ Woodforde's Wherry, Adnams ⌁ Aspall. ☻ 37 **Facilities** Non-diners area ✿ (Bar Garden Outside area) ♦ Children's menu Children's portions Play area Garden Outside area ⋒ Parking Wi-fi ▦ (notice required)

BURY ST EDMUNDS　　　　　Map 13 TL86

The Nutshell

17 The Traverse IP33 1BJ ☎ 01284 764867
dir: *Telephone for directions*

Officially the smallest pub in Britain

Measuring just 15ft by 7ft, this unique pub has been confirmed as Britain's smallest by *Guinness World Records*; and somehow more than 100 people and a dog managed to fit inside in the 1980s. It has certainly become a tourist attraction and there's lots to talk about while you enjoy a drink – a mummified cat and the bar ceiling, which is covered with paper money. There have been regular sightings of ghosts around the building, including a nun and a monk who apparently weren't praying! No food is available, though the pub jokes about its dining area for parties of two or fewer.

Open all day all wk ⊕ GREENE KING ◄ IPA & Abbot Ale, Guest ales. **Facilities** Non-diners area Wi-fi ▦ **Notes** ☺

The Old Cannon Brewery ★★★ INN

PICK OF THE PUBS

See Pick of the Pubs on page 402

The Three Kings

Hengrave Rd, Fornham All Saints IP28 6LA
☎ 01284 766979
e-mail: thethreekings@keme.co.uk
dir: *A14 junct 42, B1106 to Fornham All Saints*

Family-run village pub and restaurant

An 18th-century coaching inn in Greene King's heartland, just two miles north of its Bury St Edmunds brewery. In 1173, Fornham was the site of the only documented pitched battle to have been fought in Suffolk. Family run, the pub has all the essentials – wood-panelled bars, restaurant, conservatory and courtyard. Bar food is mainly baguettes, sandwiches, wraps, salads and burgers, while the more adventurous main menu offers braised steak in red onion and balsamic jus; grilled smoked haddock; and Quorn chilli con carne. Pies and a vegetarian curry of the day feature as specials.

Open all day Closed: 26 Dec, 1 Jan, Sun eve **Bar Meals** L served all wk 12-2.30 D served Mon-Sat 6-9.30 **Restaurant** L served Sun Carvery 12.15-2 ⊕ GREENE KING ◄ Rotating Ales ⌁ Aspall. ☻ 18 **Facilities** ♦ Children's menu Children's portions Outside area ⋒ Parking Wi-fi ▦ (notice required)

CAVENDISH　　　　　　Map 13 TL84

Bull Inn

High St CO10 8AX ☎ 01787 280245
e-mail: knaffton@btinternet.com
dir: *A134 (Bury St Edmunds to Long Melford), right at green, pub 3m on right*

Warming fires, oak beams, good beers and good food

A fine double-fronted, probably Victorian façade masks the splendid 15th-century beamed interior of this pub in one of Suffolk's prettiest villages. The atmosphere's good, the beers are from Adnams and a guest brewery, and the food's jolly decent too, with a menu listing perhaps rustic steak, mushroom and Irish ale pie; beer-battered fish and chips; smoked salmon and crayfish tagliatelle; and Mediterranean vegetable lasagne. Sunday roast may be selected from joints of beef, pork, lamb, chicken and turkey. Dogs are welcome downstairs in the public bar and in the patio garden.

Open all wk 11-3 6.30-11 **Bar Meals** L served all wk 12-3 D served all wk 6.30-9 **Restaurant** L served all wk 12-3 D served all wk 6.30-9 ⊕ ADNAMS ◄ Southwold Bitter & Broadside, Guest ales ⌁ Aspall. **Facilities** Non-diners area ✿ (Bar Garden) ♦ Children's menu Children's portions Garden ⋒ Parking ▦ (notice required)

CHILLESFORD　　　　　　Map 13 TM35

The Froize Inn ◉

PICK OF THE PUBS

The Street IP12 3PU ☎ 01394 450282
e-mail: dine@froize.co.uk
dir: *On B1084 between Woodbridge (8m) & Orford (3m)*

Foodie heaven near coastal heaths

This brick-built inn, converted from medieval gamekeepers' cottages over 20 years ago, is just a short hop from the Suffolk Heritage Coast. The mantra of sustainability and low food miles drives the extraordinary dishes created by chef and owner David Grimwood; his tempting menus draw custom from far and wide. Starters on the hot table may include pan-fried pigeon breasts with blackcurrant dressing; or creamy parsnip and potato soup with truffle oil; the gastro-fest then advances with braised Suffolk Red Poll beefsteak with foraged mushrooms; devilled lamb's kidneys with little chipolatas; or grilled wing of Orford skate with lemon and cashew nuts. The Froize Inn champions the great British pudding, so don't miss out on a dish of their marmalade bread and butter pudding, or a little pot of chocolate and hazelnut mousse. On a summer evening arm yourself with a glass of South African Chardonnay or a pint of Adnams and relax in the newly planted memorial orchard beside the inn.

Open Tue-Sun Closed: Mon **Restaurant** L served Tue-Sun 12-2 D served Thu-Sat from 7pm ⊕ FREE HOUSE ◄ Adnams ⌁ Aspall. ☻ 12 **Facilities** ♦ Children's portions Garden ⋒ Parking Wi-fi ▦ (notice required)

PICK OF THE PUBS

The Old Cannon Brewery ★★★ INN

BURY ST EDMUNDS Map 13 TL86

86 Cannon St IP33 1JR
☎ **01284 768769**
e-mail: info@oldcannonbrewery.co.uk
web: www.oldcannonbrewery.co.uk
dir: *A14 junct 43, follow signs to town centre, left at 1st rdbt into Northgate St, 1st right into Cadney Ln, left at end into Cannon St, pub 100yds on left*

Revitalised gastro-pub with a micro-brewery

Brewing first began at this Victorian pub with its own adjacent brewery over 160 years ago. Now its an independent brewpub; the bar itself is dominated by two giant stainless steel brewing vessels, which are used to brew the ales dispensed from the gleaming handpumps. The brewer uses East Anglian-grown and malted barley, and choice hops; ale aficionados can choose between The Old Cannon Best Bitter or Gunner's Daughter which are augmented by a seasonal or special occasion beer. An August Bank Holiday beer festival and tours of the brewery are added attractions. In keeping with having a brewery inside the bar-cum-dining room, the decor is light and airy, with some walls painted in a rich, earthy colour, plus you can expect wooden floors and rustic scrubbed tables. In true brasserie style, the Brewery Kitchen serves 'cannon fodder', freshly prepared seasonal British fare,

always made from great local produce. Some starters and light dishes can be upped in size, such as moules marinière and Thai red curry. Other typical choices include pot-roasted ham hock with an apple, cider and mushroom sauce; and the pub's own pork and Gunner's Daughter ale sausages. The daily specials board offers more options. Overnight guests can stay in the converted old brewery, just across the courtyard. The pub is tucked away down Bury's back streets, so follow the directions carefully.

Open all day all wk 12-11 (Sun 12-10.30) **Bar Meals** L served all wk 12-9 D served all wk 12-9 Av main course £12 food served all day **Restaurant** L served all wk 12-9 D

served all wk 12-9 Fixed menu price fr £25 Av 3 course à la carte fr £25 food served all day ⊕ FREE HOUSE ◀ The Old Cannon Best Bitter, Gunner's Daughter, Hornblower & Seasonal ales, Adnams Southwold Bitter, Guest ales ⊘ Aspall, Aspall Perronelle's Blush. ♟ 12 **Facilities** Non-diners area Garden ⊼ Beer festival Parking Wi-fi **Rooms** 7

CRATFIELD   Map 13 TM37

The Cratfield Poacher

Bell Green IP19 0BL ☎ 01986 798206
e-mail: cratfieldpoacher@yahoo.co.uk
dir: B1117 from Halesworth towards Eye. At Laxfield right, follow Cratfield signs. Or, A143 from Diss towards Bungay. Right at Harleston onto B1123 towards Halesworth. Through Metfield, 1m, right, follow Cratfield signs

Family-run free house in rural location

A pub for the past 350 years, this handsome longhouse in deepest rural Suffolk is off the beaten track but well worth the detour. Boasting some impressive exterior plasterwork pargeting, it is just as charming inside, with low beams and tiled floors. There's always six draught beers available, often from the Adnams and Oakham breweries, plus local Aspall cider. Home-cooked food, such as smoked mackerel salad and shepherd's pie, with daily-changing specials complete the pleasing picture at this proper village local, which is the hub of the community.

Open 12-2.30 6-12 (Sat-Sun all day) Closed: Mon, Tue L **Bar Meals** L served Wed-Fri 12-2.30 (Sat-Sun all day) D served Tue-Fri 6-9 (Sat-Sun all day) Av main course £8.50 **Restaurant** L served Wed-Fri 12-2.30 (Sat-Sun all day) D served Tue-Fri 6-9 (Sat-Sun all day) Fixed menu price fr £8.50 Av 3 course à la carte fr £12.50 ⊕ FREE HOUSE ◀ Crouch Vale Brewers Gold, Oakham JHB, Earl Soham Victoria Bitter & Gannet Mild, Adnams Ö Aspall. **Facilities** Non-diners area ❤ (Bar Garden) ✦ Children's menu Children's portions Garden ⧢ Parking ▭ (notice required)

DENNINGTON   Map 13 TM26

Dennington Queen

The Square IP13 8AB ☎ 01728 638241
e-mail: denningtonqueen@yahoo.co.uk
dir: From Ipswich A14 to exit for Lowestoft (A12). Then B1116 to Framlingham, follow signs to Dennington

Village centre pub worth seeking out

A 16th-century inn with bags of old-world charm including open fires, a coffin hatch, a bricked-up tunnel to the neighbouring church and a ghost. Locally brewed Aspall cider accompanies real ales from Adnams, Black Sheep, Timothy Taylor and, from Woodbridge, Earl Soham. Suggestions from the modern British menu include Thai fishcakes with sweet chilli jam; calves' liver with champ mash, Bramfield bacon and red onion jus; and wild mushroom and smoked cheddar risotto. A typical daily special is spinach and pea linguine with salsa verde.

Open all wk 12-3 6-close **Bar Meals** L served all wk 12-2 D served all wk 6.30-9 **Restaurant** L served all wk 12-2 D served all wk 6.30-9 ⊕ FREE HOUSE ◀ Earl Soham Victoria Bitter, Timothy Taylor Landlord, Adnams, Black Sheep Ö Aspall. **Facilities** Non-diners area ✦ Children's menu Children's portions Garden ⧢ Parking ▭ (notice required)

DUNWICH   Map 13 TM47

The Ship at Dunwich ★★ SHL ⊚

PICK OF THE PUBS

See Pick of the Pubs on page 404

EARL SOHAM   Map 13 TM26

Victoria

The Street IP13 7RL ☎ 01728 685758
dir: From A14 at Stowmarket take A1120 towards Yoxford

Microbrewery beers at their best

This friendly, down-to-earth free house is a showcase for Earl Soham beers, which for many years were produced from a microbrewery behind the pub. Some ten years ago the brewery moved to the Old Forge building a few yards away, where production still continues. Inside this traditional pub, simple furnishings, bare floorboards and an open fire set the scene for traditional home-cooked pub fare, including ploughman's, jacket potatoes and macaroni cheese. Heartier meals include a variety of curries and casseroles, local sausages and mash, and gammon and eggs, followed by home-made desserts. A specials board and vegetarian dishes add to the choices.

Open all wk 11.30-3 6-11 **Bar Meals** L served all wk 12-2 D served all wk 7-10 Av main course £9 ⊕ FREE HOUSE/ EARL SOHAM BREWERY ◀ Earl Soham Victoria Bitter, Albert Ale, Brandeston Gold, Sir Roger's Porter Ö Aspall. **Facilities** Non-diners area ❤ (Bar Garden) ✦ Children's portions Garden ⧢ Parking ▭ (notice required)

ELVEDEN   Map 13 TL88

Elveden Inn ★★★★★ INN

AA PUB OF THE YEAR FOR ENGLAND 2013-2014

PICK OF THE PUBS

Brandon Rd IP24 3TP ☎ 01842 890876
e-mail: info@elvedeninn.com
dir: From Mildenhall take A11 towards Thetford. Left onto B1106, pub on left

Award-winning inn showcasing produce from the estate

Located on the Elveden Estate, home to a direct descendent of the Guinness family, this village inn reopened in 2011 after an expensive renovation to reveal a relaxed and contemporary bar and dining rooms, and four luxury bedrooms. Expect a family-friendly atmosphere, blazing log fires in winter, a tip-top pint of Guinness (of course), East Anglian ales on tap, and a modern pub menu that brims with produce sourced from the estate farm and surrounding area. Whether eating inside, or outside on the patio area, a meal could kick off with a fish, meat or vegetarian sharing platter; baby squid and mussels pan-fried with chilli and garlic; or quince pannacotta with parsnip crisps and beetroot coulis. Next might be haddock in Guinness batter with hand-cut chips; venison cottage pie; or poached pear,

Stilton and walnut tart. Children can choose from their own selection of 'fawn-size' portions. Don't miss the mid-June beer festival.

Open all day all wk **Bar Meals** L served all wk 12-9 D served all wk 12-9 food served all day **Restaurant** L served all wk 12-9 D served all wk 12-9 food served all day ⊕ FREE HOUSE ◀ Purity Mad Goose, Adnams Broadside, Southwold & East Green, Guiness Ö Aspall & Perronelle's Blush. ▪ 9 **Facilities** Non-diners area ❤ (Bar Restaurant Garden) ✦ Children's menu Children's portions Garden ⧢ Beer festival Parking Wi-fi ▭ (notice required) **Rooms** 4

EYE   Map 13 TM17

The White Horse Inn ★★★★ INN

Stoke Ash IP23 7ET ☎ 01379 678222
e-mail: mail@whitehorse-suffolk.co.uk
dir: On A140 between Ipswich & Norwich

Family run inn with good food

Midway between Norwich and Ipswich, this 17th-century coaching inn is set amid lovely Suffolk countryside. The heavily timbered interior accommodates an inglenook fireplace, two bars and a restaurant. An extensive menu is supplemented by lunchtime snacks, grills and daily specials from the blackboard. Try salmon pâté or smoked duck salad to start. Main courses include red pepper and goats' cheese lasagne; honey and mustard chicken; venison casserole; chicken Madras; and baked salmon with a sage and parmesan crust. There are 11 spacious motel bedrooms in the grounds, as well as a patio and secluded grassy area.

Open all day all wk 7am-11pm (Sat 8am-11pm Sun 8am-10.30pm) **Bar Meals** food served all day **Restaurant** food served all day ⊕ FREE HOUSE ◀ Greene King Abbot Ale, Adnams, Woodforde's Wherry Ö Aspall. **Facilities** Non-diners area ✦ Children's menu Children's portions Garden Parking Wi-fi ▭ **Rooms** 11

PICK OF THE PUBS

The Ship at Dunwich ★★ SHL ◉

DUNWICH   Map 13 TM47

Saint James St IP17 3DT
☎ **01728 648219**
e-mail: info@shipatdunwich.co.uk
web: www.shipatdunwich.co.uk
dir: N on A12 from Ipswich through Yoxford, right signed Dunwich

Coastal pub renowned for its fish and chips

Dunwich was at one time a medieval port of some size and importance, but then the original village was virtually destroyed by a terrible storm in 1326. Further storms and erosion followed and now the place is little more than a hamlet beside a shingle beach. Two minutes' stroll from the beach, The Ship at Dunwich is a well-loved old smugglers' inn overlooking the salt marshes and sea, and is popular with walkers and birdwatchers visiting the nearby RSPB Minsmere reserve. The Ship keeps Dunwich on the map with hearty meals and ales from Adnams, Woodfordes and St Peters – to name just a few. Its delightful unspoilt public bar offers nautical bric-à-brac, a wood-burning stove in a huge fireplace, flagged floors and simple wooden furnishings. Sympathetically spruced up in recent years, with the addition of clean, comfortable and contemporary-style bedrooms, it is locally renowned for its fish and chips, which include a choice of cod, whiting, plaice or hake.

Other dishes plough a traditional furrow. You could start with an English cheese and ale fondue with home-made seeded puff pastry sticks, or smoked mackerel pâté with dill soldiers and cucumber relish, followed perhaps by beef, mushroom and baby onion pie with herb mash; or twice-cooked crispy duck leg with home-made plum jam glaze, spring onion and smoked bacon croquettes. Desserts continue in a similar vein – maybe old English treacle tart or vanilla rice pudding with home-made jam. Look for the ancient fig tree in the garden, and take note of the inn's three annual beer festivals in spring, summer and autumn.

Open all day all wk **Bar Meals** L served all wk 12-3 D served all wk 6-9 Av main

course £13.50 **Restaurant** L served all wk 12-3 D served all wk 6-9 ⊕ FREE HOUSE ◀ Adnams Southwold Bitter, Humpty Dumpty, Brandon Rusty Bucket, Earl Soham, Green Jack, Grain Norfolk Brewery, Woodforde's, St Peter's ♻ Aspall. ⁊ 9 **Facilities** Non-diners area ❤ ♦ Children's menu Children's portions Family room Garden ⋒ Beer festival Parking Wi-fi **Rooms** 15

Save on hotels. Book at theAA.com/hotel

SUFFOLK 405 ENGLAND

FRAMLINGHAM
Map 13 TM26

The Station Hotel

Station Rd IP13 9EE ☎ **01728 723455**
e-mail: framstation@btinternet.com
dir: *Bypass Ipswich towards Lowestoft on A12. Approx 6m, left onto B1116 to Framlingham*

Known for its bold and flavoursome dishes

Built as part of the local railway in the 19th century, The Station Hotel has been a pub since the 1950s, outliving the railway which closed in 1962. Inside, you will find scrubbed tables and an eclectic mix of furniture. During the last decade it has established a fine reputation for its gutsy and earthy food listed on the ever-changing blackboard menu. A typical lunch could be kedgeree; dinner might include pot-roasted rabbit and bean stew; or pan-fried mullet with linguine clam chowder. A wood-fired pizza oven was installed in 2013. Several of the beers are supplied by Suffolk brewery, Earl Soham and there is a beer festival in mid-July.

Open all wk 12-2.30 5-11 (Sun 12-3 7-10.30) **Bar Meals** L served all wk 12-2 D served Sun-Thu 6.30-9, Fri-Sat 6.30-9.30 ⊕ FREE HOUSE ◀ Earl Soham Victoria Bitter, Albert Ale & Gannet Mild, Veltins, Crouch Vale, Guinness Ŏ Aspall. **Facilities** Non-diners area ✿ (Bar Garden) ♦♦ Children's portions Family room Garden Beer festival Parking ▦

FRAMSDEN
Map 13 TM15

The Dobermann Inn

The Street IP14 6HG ☎ **01473 890461**
dir: *S off A1120 (Stowmarket to Yoxford road). 10m from Ipswich on B1077 towards Debenham*

Thatched village inn with popular food

This pretty country pub was named by its current proprietor who is a prominent breeder and judge of Dobermanns. The thatched roofing, gnarled beams, open fire and assorted furniture reflect its 16th-century origins. With a selection of Adnams ales on offer and Mauldons Dickens bitter, food ranges from sandwiches, hearty ploughman's and salads to main courses featuring plenty of fish and vegetarian choices. Reliable favourites include chilli con carne, spicy nut loaf, Dover sole, and steak and mushroom pie.

Open 12-3 7-11 Closed: 25-26 Dec, Sun eve, Mon **Bar Meals** L served Tue-Sun 12-2 D served Tue-Sat 7-9 ⊕ FREE HOUSE ◀ Adnams Southwold Bitter, Old Ale & Broadside, Mauldons Dickens Ŏ Aspall. **Facilities** Non-diners area Garden Parking ▦ (notice required) **Notes** ⊛

GREAT BRICETT
Map 13 TM05

The Veggie Red Lion
PICK OF THE PUBS

Green Street Green IP7 7DD ☎ **01473 657799**
e-mail: janwise@fsmail.net
dir: *4.5m from Needham Market on B1078*

Smart country inn with innovative approach to meals

After several years as standard bearer in the field of specialist vegetarian and vegan destination dining pubs, Jan Wise's inspirational business continues to thrive deep in the Suffolk countryside, surrounded by rich farmland and coverts. Greene King beers are the staple on the bar, but it's the innovative menu that draws the discerning diner well off the beaten track. Jan's unfailing commitment to developing exquisite dishes has won accolades – you'll find no hint of anything that once grazed, swam or pecked; special diets are usually no problem either, and many dishes are gluten free. Settle down in the rustic beamed and colour-washed interior to experience the delightful difficulty of deciding just what treats to try. A visit might start with a Red Lion samosa, crafted from butternut squash, spinach and red lentils, advancing then to a main of mushroom, red wine and chestnut pie, boosted with parsnips and celeriac. Daily changing specials guarantee there's always something new to try.

Open 12-3 6-11 Closed: Sun eve & Mon **Bar Meals** L served Tue-Sun 12-2 D served Tue-Sat 6-9 ⊕ GREENE KING ◀ IPA, Morland Old Speckled Hen Ŏ Aspall. **Facilities** Non-diners area ♦♦ Children's menu Children's portions Play area Garden Parking Wi-fi

HALESWORTH
Map 13 TM37

The Queen's Head
PICK OF THE PUBS

The Street, Bramfield IP19 9HT ☎ **01986 784214**
e-mail: info@queensheadbramfield.co.uk
dir: *2m from A12 on A144 towards Halesworth*

Local produce gets star billing here

In the centre of Bramfield on the edge of the Suffolk Heritage Coast near Southwold, the enclosed garden of this lovely Grade II listed pub is overlooked by the thatched village church with its unusual separate round bell tower. The pub's interior is welcoming, with scrubbed pine tables, exposed beams, a vaulted ceiling in the bar and enormous fireplaces. In the same hands for two decades, the pub's landlord enthusiastically supports the 'local and organic' movement – reflected by a menu which proudly names the farms and suppliers from which the carefully chosen ingredients are sourced. There is nonetheless a definite cosmopolitan twist in dishes such as griddled Marlin steaks marinated in ginger, garlic, dill and soy sauce; leg of lamb steaks with rosemary, garlic and honey; and Dover sole with prawn and almond butter. Home-made puddings such as plum frangipane tart are tempting, as is the platter of three local cheeses.

Open all wk 10.30-2.30 6.30-11 (Sun 12-3 7-10.30) **Bar Meals** L served all wk 12-2 D served Mon-Fri 6.30-9.15, Sat 6.30-10, Sun 7-9 ⊕ ADNAMS ◀ Southwold Bitter, Broadside Ŏ Aspall. ☗ 8 **Facilities** Non-diners area ✿ (Bar Garden) ♦♦ Children's menu Children's portions Family room Garden Parking Wi-fi ▦ (notice required)

HAWKEDON
Map 13 TL75

The Queen's Head **NEW**
PICK OF THE PUBS

Rede Rd IP29 4NN ☎ **01284 789218**
dir: *From A143 at Wickham St, between Bury St Edmunds & Haverhill, follow Stansfield sign. At junct left signed Hawkedon. 1m to village*

Thriving village local with a butcher's shop

Off-the-beaten track by the green in a picture-book village deep in rural Suffolk, the Queen's Head is worth seeking out for its classic 15th-century character and charm – inglenook fireplace, stone floors, head-cracking timbers, scrubbed pine tables – and top-notch hearty pub food prepared from the best local ingredients. The pub rears its own livestock (Suffolk sheep and Dexter cattle) and, like the pork, venison, poultry and wild boar sourced from local farms, they are hung and butchered at the butcher's shop in the pub grounds. This may translate to venison carpaccio, pork chops with Stilton, pear and sage and pot-roasted beef with red wine and red onion marmalade, with butterscotch and almond pudding among the desserts. Sunday roast lunches, traditional bar snacks, and pizzas baked in the stone oven complete the culinary picture. A thriving community local, it also offers live music, a beer and cider festival in July, and game and wine tasting dinners.

Open all wk 5-11 (Fri-Sun 12-11) **Bar Meals** L served Fri-Sun 12-2.30 D served Wed-Thu 6-9, Fri-Sun 6.30-9 Av main course £14 **Restaurant** L served Fri-Sun 12-2.30 D served Wed-Thu 6-9, Fri-Sun 6.30-9 ⊕ FREE HOUSE ◀ Woodforde's Wherry, Adnams Ŏ Westons Old Rosie & Country Perry, Once Upon A Tree. **Facilities** Non-diners area ✿ (Bar Garden) ♦♦ Children's portions Garden Beer festival Cider festival Parking Wi-fi

HITCHAM
Map 13 TL95

The White Horse Inn

The Street IP7 7NQ ☎ 01449 740981
e-mail: lewis@thewhitehorse.wanadoo.co.uk
dir: *13m from Ipswich & Bury St Edmunds, 7m Stowmarket, 7m Hadleigh*

Friendly pub in the heart of the countryside

A blacksmith's forge was once attached to this 400-year-old inn, originally a staging post for London and Norwich coaches. In the late 17th century a notorious highwayman was arrested and tried in what nowadays is the public bar, found guilty and hanged from a nearby tree. Today, the bar is for more for hanging out, drinking Rattlesden Best and other Suffolk real ales, playing traditional pub games and enjoying regular live entertainment. Freshly prepared meals include jacket potatoes; ham or cheese ploughman's; butterflied chicken breast; salmon steak; and vegetarian Italian layer bake. In summer, barbecues are held in the garden.

Open all wk 12-3 6-11 **Bar Meals** L served all wk 12-2.30 D served all wk 6-9 **Restaurant** L served all wk 12-2.30 D served all wk 6-9 ⊕ FREE HOUSE ◀ Adnams Southwold Bitter & Fisherman, Rattlesden Best, Cox and Holbrook Stowmarket Porter Ŏ Aspall. ♟ **Facilities** Non-diners area ❀ (Bar Garden) ♦♦ Children's menu Children's portions Garden ⊼ Parking Wi-fi ▭ (notice required)

HOLBROOK
Map 13 TM13

The Compasses

Ipswich Rd IP9 2QR ☎ 01473 328332
e-mail: jayne.gooding@hotmail.co.uk
dir: *From A137 S of Ipswich, take B1080 to Holbrook, pub on left. From Ipswich take B1456 to Shotley. At Freston Water Tower right onto B1080 to Holbrook. Pub 2m right*

Proudly not a gastro-pub

On the spectacular Shotley peninsula bordered by the rivers Orwell and Stour, this traditional 17th-century country pub offers a simple, good-value menu. There's nothing self-consciously primped and styled about its interior or its food offerings; it prides itself on not being a gastro-pub but offering good value and plenty of choice. Typical starters include prawn cocktail and breaded mushrooms with garlic mayo. Follow this with minced beef and onion pie; crispy chicken mornay; or local sausages with egg and chips. There's a separate kids' menu and some good vegetarian choices such as Cajun five bean chilli.

Open 11.30-2.30 6-11 (Sun 12-3 6-10.30) Closed: 26 Dec, Tue eve **Bar Meals** L served all wk 12-2.15 D served Wed-Mon 6-9.15 **Restaurant** L served all wk 12-2.15 D served Wed-Mon 6-9.15 ⊕ PUNCH TAVERNS ◀ Adnams Southwold Bitter, Sharp's Doom Bar Ŏ Aspall. ♟ 12 **Facilities** Non-diners area ♦♦ Children's menu Children's portions Play area Garden ⊼ Parking Wi-fi ▭ (notice required)

HONEY TYE
Map 13 TL93

The Lion

CO6 4NX ☎ 01206 263434
e-mail: enquiries@lionhoneytye.co.uk
dir: *On A134 midway between Colchester & Sudbury*

A friendly pub with a good range of food

A traditional country dining pub, located in an Area of Outstanding Natural Beauty, The Lion has a walled beer garden for outside eating and drinking. The spacious restaurant is decorated in a modern, comfortable style and the bar has low-beamed ceilings and an open log fire. The bar menu offers a good choice of sandwiches, jackets and pub classics, while the main menu includes smoked salmon and potato rösti stack; tiger prawn spaghetti; roasted pepper filled with basil and vegetable couscous; and lamb meatballs in a tomato and mint cream sauce.

Open 12-3 6-11 (Sun 12-10.30) Closed: Mon **Bar Meals** L served Tue-Sat 12-2, Sun 12-8 D served Tue-Sat 6-9, Sun 12-8 **Restaurant** L served Tue-Sat 12-2, Sun 12-8 D served Tue-Sat 6-9, Sun 12-8 ◀ Adnams. ♟ 9 **Facilities** Non-diners area ♦♦ Children's menu Children's portions Garden ⊼ Parking ▭

INGHAM
Map 13 TL87

The Cadogan ★★★★ INN ◉

The Street IP31 1NG ☎ 01284 728443
e-mail: info@thecadogan.co.uk
dir: *A14 junct 42, 1st exit onto B1106. At rdbt take 1st exit (A134). 3m to Ingham. Pub on left*

A welcoming place to stay or dine

A friendly and inviting pub with seven en suite bedrooms for those who want to stay longer, The Cadogan sits just four miles from the centre of Bury St Edmunds. The kitchen places an emphasis on seasonality and local produce; lunchtime sandwiches and light bites are complemented by dinner options such as crackling and apple sauce to nibble; pressed ham hock terrine and homemade piccalilli to start; and a main course of smoked haddock rarebit with crushed potatoes and tomato sauce. Open all day, the pub has a large garden, with a children's play area, perfect for alfresco dining.

Open all day all wk Closed: 25-26 Dec & 31 Jan eve **Bar Meals** L served Mon-Sat 12-2.30, Sun 12-8.30 D served Mon-Sat 6-9.30, Sun 12-8.30 **Restaurant** L served Mon-Sat 12-2.30, Sun 12-8.30 D served Mon-Sat 6-9.30, Sun 12-8.30 ⊕ GREENE KING ◀ Abbot Ale, Brewshed Pale Ale Ŏ Aspall. ♟ 14 **Facilities** Non-diners area ♦♦ Children's menu Children's portions Play area Garden ⊼ Parking Wi-fi ▭ (notice required) **Rooms** 7

IPSWICH
Map 13 TM14

The Fat Cat

288 Spring Rd IP4 5NL ☎ 01473 726524
e-mail: fatcatipswich@btconnect.com
dir: *From A12 take A1214 towards town centre, becomes A1071 (Woodbridge Road East). At mini rdbt 2nd left into Spring Rd*

One for the beer lover

Good beer and conversation are the two main ingredients in this no-frills free house. The Fat Cat is a mecca for beer aficionados, with a friendly atmosphere in two homely bars and a raft of real ales served in tip-top condition from the taproom behind the bar. The head-scratching choice – up to 22 every day – come from Dark Star, Elgood's, Green Jack and a host of local microbreweries. Soak up the beer with simple bar snacks like beef and Guinness pasties, sausage rolls, pork pies and baguettes.

Open all day all wk **Bar Meals** food served all day ⊕ FREE HOUSE ◀ Adnams Old Ale, Dark Star Hophead, Elgood's Black Dog, Green Jack Gone Fishing, Crouch Vale Brewers Gold, Guest ales Ŏ Aspall. ♟ 8 **Facilities** Garden ▭ (notice required) **Notes** ◉

LAXFIELD
Map 13 TM27

The Kings Head (The Low House)

PICK OF THE PUBS

Gorams Mill Ln IP13 8DW ☎ 01986 798395
e-mail: lowhouse@keme.co.uk
dir: *On B1117*

Discover a real old pub with authentic atmosphere

This unspoilt thatched 16th-century alehouse is a rare Suffolk gem that oozes charm and character. Locals know it as The Low House because it lies in a dip below the churchyard. Tip-top Adnams ales are served straight from the cask in the original taproom – this is one of the few pubs in Britain which has no bar. Order a pint of Broadside and retire to an ancient fireplace with a horseshoe of high-backed settles with an oak table in the middle. Traditional lunchtime fare includes sandwiches and baguettes, perhaps a BLT or roast beef and horseradish. Home-cooked dishes range from classics like sausages with mash and onion gravy to slow-roasted Dingley Dell pork and lamb shank cooked in Guinness. Beer festivals in May and September are unforgettable occasions thanks to the beautiful situation of the pub overlooking the river; its grounds, now with rose gardens and an arbour, were formerly the village bowling green.

Open all wk 11am-close (winter 12-3 6-close) **Bar Meals** L served Mon-Sat 12-2, Sun 12-3 D served Mon-Sat 6.30-9 **Restaurant** L served Mon-Sat 12-2, Sun 12-3 D served Mon-Sat 6.30-9 ⊕ ADNAMS ◀ Southwold Bitter, Broadside & Ghost Ship ales, Guest ales Ŏ Aspall. ♟ 11 **Facilities** Non-diners area ❀ (Bar Garden) ♦♦ Children's portions Play area Family room Garden ⊼ Beer festival Parking Wi-fi ▭ (notice required)

LEVINGTON	Map 13 TM23

The Ship Inn

Church Ln IP10 0LQ ☎ 01473 659573
e-mail: theshipinnlevington@hotmail.co.uk
dir: *From A14 junct 58 take A1156 signed Levington. Left signed Levington Marina*

Thatched inn with a maritime theme

Overlooking the River Orwell, the timbers of this 13th-century inn are impregnated with the salt of the sea. The Ship stands within sight of the Suffolk marshes, where the hulks of beached sailing vessels were broken up for their precious beams. Families are welcome to enjoy the estuary views outside from the front seats or rear patio; however the interior is so full of maritime lamps, compasses and keepsakes that it's deemed as unsafe for children. The sophisticated menu changes daily and focuses on executing a select number of dishes well; these might include pan-fried sardines with tomato and coriander salsa; and confit of duck leg with red wine-braised cabbage and sweet potato fries.

Open all wk 11.30-3 6-11 (Sat 11.30-11 Sun 12-10.30) ⊕ ADNAMS ◀ Southwold Bitter & Broadside, Guest ale ♂ Aspall. **Facilities** ♦♦ Garden Parking Wi-fi

LIDGATE	Map 12 TL75

The Star Inn

PICK OF THE PUBS

The Street CB8 9PP ☎ 01638 500275
dir: *From Newmarket clocktower in High St follow signs towards Clare on B1063. Lidgate 7m*

Mediterranean dishes at horseracing fraternity favourite

Quintessential English pub dating back to the 14th-century. An important meeting place for local residents, the pub is popular with Newmarket trainers on race days, and with dealers and agents from all over the world during bloodstock sales. Originally two cottages, the two traditionally furnished bars still fit the old-world bill with heavy oak beams, log fires, pine tables and antique furniture, but the dishes on the menu are a mix of Spanish and British. On the Spanish side are starters like whole baby squid with garlic and chilli or fish soup, which might be followed by bean and chorizo stew. British tastes are also catered for, with dishes such as warm chicken liver salad; venison steaks in port; and pigs' cheeks. There's an extensive wine list, too, with a number of well-priced Riojas jostling for position alongside the real ales on tap.

Open 12-3 6-12 Closed: Mon **Bar Meals** L served Tue-Sat 12-2.30 D served Tue-Sat 6.30-9.30 **Restaurant** L served Tue-Sun 12-2.30 D served Tue-Sat 6.30-9.30 ⊕ FREE HOUSE ◀ Black Sheep, Marston's Pedigree, Timothy Taylor, Woodforde's Wherry ♂ Thatchers. **Facilities** Non-diners area ♦♦ Children's portions Garden ♬ Parking 🚐

LINDSEY TYE	Map 13 TL94

The Lindsey Rose

IP7 6PP ☎ 01449 741424
e-mail: thelindseyrose@hotmail.co.uk
dir: *From A12 between Ipswich & Sudbury take A1141 signed Lavenham. Ignore 1st sign for Lindsey, follow 2nd sign, then pub sign*

Lindsey's local for over 500 years

Set in the beautiful Suffolk countryside between Ipswich and Sudbury, The Lindsey Rose has been the village local for over 500 years. Local ales are stocked in the bar and also take centre stage at the pub's annual beer festival. The region's produce is also celebrated on the menu, which might include their famous Red Poll beefburger blue cheese, bacon and home-made chips; vegetable stir-fry, coriander omelette; and sticky toffee pudding. Children are very welcome here and get their own menu and activity area outside.

Open all wk 11-3 5.30-11 (Sun all day) **Bar Meals** L served Mon-Sat 12-2.30, Sun 12-3 D served Mon-Sat 6.30-9.30, Sun 7-9 **Restaurant** L served Mon-Sat 12-2.30, Sun 12-3 D served Mon-Sat 6.30-9.30, Sun 7-9 ⊕ FREE HOUSE ◀ Adnams Southwold Bitter, Mauldons ♂ Aspall. **Facilities** Non-diners area ♣ (Bar Restaurant Garden) ♦♦ Children's menu Children's portions Play area Garden ♬ Beer festival Parking Wi-fi 🚐 (notice required)

MELTON	Map 13 TM25

Wilford Bridge

Wilford Bridge Rd IP12 2PA ☎ 01394 386141
dir: *From A12 towards coast, follow signs to Bawdsey & Orford, cross rail lines, next pub on left*

Flower adorned, free house near Sutton Hoo

On the other side of the River Deben from the pub - over Wilford Bridge, in fact - is Sutton Hoo (National Trust), where the famous 7th-century ship-burial was found in 1939. Mike and Anne Lomas have been running this free house for the last 20 years, he specialising in classic English dishes, especially seafood, such as haddock, salmon and prawn pie; Shingle Street cod fillet; and plenty of shellfish, while from the chargrill come lamb and veal cutlets, steaks, and tournedos Rossini. In the bar, Adnams is joined by guest ales.

Open all day all wk ⊕ FREE HOUSE ◀ Adnams Southwold Bitter & Broadside, John Smith's, Guest ales ♂ Aspall. **Facilities** ♦♦ Children's menu Garden Parking

MILDENHALL	Map 12 TL77

The Bull Inn ★★★ HL ◉

PICK OF THE PUBS

The Street, Barton Mills IP28 6AA ☎ 01638 711001
e-mail: reception@bullinn-bartonmills.com
dir: *Exit A11 between Newmarket & Mildenhall, signed Barton Mills*

Ancient inn with a 21st-century makeover

With its fine gables, dormer windows and coaching courtyard, this rambling 16th-century building certainly has the look of a traditional roadside inn. However, step inside and be wowed by Cheryl, Wayne and Sonia's contemporary makeover, which successfully blends original oak beams, big fireplaces and wooden floors with funky fabrics, designer wallpapers and bold colours. The hub of the building (and village) is the bar, where you can peruse the menus with a tip-top pint of East Anglian ale, perhaps a local Humpty Dumpty brew. Menus evolve with the seasons and every effort is made to reduce 'food miles'. In the bar or delightful courtyard, tuck into MOO pie, a Norfolk steak-and-ale pie with creamy mash. Cooking changes in the restaurant, where a meal might feature the signature dish of fillet steak tower with a potato and tarragon croquette, red onion marmalade, roasted roots and peppercorn sauce.

Open all day all wk 8am-11pm **Bar Meals** L served Sun-Thu 12-9, Fri-Sat 12-9.30 (bkfst 8-12) D served Sun-Thu 12-9, Fri-Sat 12-9.30 Av main course £12 food served all day **Restaurant** L served Sun 12-4 D served all wk 6-9 Av 3 course à la carte fr £30 ⊕ FREE HOUSE ◀ Adnams Broadside, Greene King IPA, Brandon Rusty Bucket, Humpty Dumpty, Wolf ♂ Aspall. ♀ 11 **Facilities** Non-diners area ♦♦ Children's menu Children's portions Garden ♬ Parking Wi-fi 🚐 (notice required) **Rooms** 15

The Swan Inn ◉◉

PICK OF THE PUBS

The Street IP7 7AU ☎ 01449 741391
e-mail: carol@monkseleigh.com
dir: *On B1115 between Sudbury & Hadleigh*

Award-winning food in picturesque village setting

The oldest building in a settlement of venerable properties; a veritable jigsaw of thatch, colourwash and cottage gardens veneer the sloping green in this picture postcard village. Wealth came from the wool trade and the original inn may have been the manorial court before affluent wool merchants first dined out here. Vestiges of the original 14th-century building remain, including the old smoke hole, wattle-and-daub panels and some fine beams supporting the thatched roof. Today's bright and airy interior is the destination of choice for diners keen to share the culinary skills of chef-patron Nigel Ramsbottom, whose background at Miller Howe in Windermere and The Walnut Tree near Abergavenny is rewarded with two AA Rosettes here. Ever-changing dishes are seasonal, with a strong nod to Suffolk's superb range of suppliers. Look for chilled Suffolk asparagus with parmesan flakes to start; whole roast partridge with blueberry sauce, or skate grilled with butter and lemon take the eye as mains, with chocolate loaf and coffee sauce to finish.

Open 12-2 7-11 Closed: 25-26 Dec, 2wks in summer, Sun eve & Mon **Bar Meals** L served Tue-Sun 12-2 D served Tue-Sat 7-9 Av main course £14 **Restaurant** L served Tue-Sun 12-2 D served Tue-Sat 7-9 Fixed menu price fr £14.75 Av 3 course à la carte fr £26 ⊕ FREE HOUSE ◀ Greene King IPA, Adnams Southwold Bitter & Broadside Ö Aspall, Thatchers Katy, Savanna. ⬦ **Facilities** Non-diners area ◖ Children's portions Garden Parking ▭

Anchor Inn

PICK OF THE PUBS

26 Court St CO6 4JL ☎ 01206 262313
e-mail: info@anchornayland.co.uk
dir: *Follow A134 from Colchester towards Sudbury for 3.5m through Great Horkesley, at bottom of hill right into Horkesley Rd. Pub on right after bridge*

Eclectic modern dining in Constable Country

The inn, which enjoys a placid setting beside the alder-fringed meadows of the River Stour, is reputedly the last remaining place from which press-gangs recruited their 'volunteers' in this area. Today's customers can rest easy

here, recovering from strolls around the idyllic village which is close to the heart of 'Constable Country'. Having undergone a comprehensive yet sensitive refurbishment, The Anchor is a light, airy destination where local and regional ales change monthly (there are also twice-yearly beer festivals), with the riverside decking and garden the ideal spot to tarry a while. Head chef Ross Armstead presides over a progressive menu of pub favourites and modern European dishes, so anticipate shepherd's pie or sausage and mash; or graduate to mushroom-stuffed guinea fowl ballotine with white onion purée and parsley mash, or pan-roasted North Atlantic cod on a Merguez sausage cassoulet. The inn has a smokehouse, and meals on the à la carte menu often reflect this.

Open all wk Tue-Sun all day (Mon 11-3 5-11) **Bar Meals** L served Mon-Fri 12-2, Sat 12-2.30, Sun 12-4 D served Mon-Fri 6.30-9, Sat 6.30-9.30 Av main course £9.95 **Restaurant** L served Mon-Fri 12-2, Sat 12-2.30, Sun 12-4 D served Mon-Fri 6.30-9, Sat 6.30-9.30 Fixed menu price fr £12.50 Av 3 course à la carte fr £24.50 ⊕ FREE HOUSE/EXCLUSIVE INNS ◀ Greene King IPA, Adnams, Local & Guest ales Ö Aspall, Carter's. **Facilities** Non-diners area ❀ (Garden) ◖ Children's menu Children's portions Garden ▭ Beer festival Parking Wi-fi ▭ (notice required)

The Plough

IP29 4BE ☎ 01284 789208
dir: *On A143 between Bury St Edmunds & Haverhill*

Interesting menus in Suffolk's highest spot

Tucked away in the village on the green is this part-thatched, 16th-century pub easily identified by an old plough and a weeping willow at the front. On long-standing landlord Brian Desborough's ever-changing blackboard menu look for diced Highland beef in cream with wholegrain mustard and whisky sauce; minted local venison in chilli sauce with potato and cheese topping; and sea bass fillets in cream with bacon, butterbean and sweetcorn sauce. The bar serves Fuller's, Adnams, Ringwood and Sharp's ales and ten wines by the glass. At 128 metres above sea level, Rede is Suffolk's highest point - verified by the *Guinness Book of World Records*.

Open all wk 11-3 6-12 (Sun 12-3) **Bar Meals** L served all wk 12-2 D served Mon-Sat 6-9 **Restaurant** L served all wk 12-2 D served Mon-Sat 6-9 ⊕ ADMIRAL TAVERNS ◀ Fuller's London Pride, Ringwood Best Bitter, Sharp's Cornish Coaster, Adnams Ö Aspall. ⬦ 10 **Facilities** Non-diners area ◖ Children's portions Garden ▭ Parking Wi-fi ▭ (notice required)

Sibton White Horse Inn ★★★★ INN ◉

PICK OF THE PUBS

See Pick of the Pubs on opposite page

The Crown Inn

PICK OF THE PUBS

Bridge Rd IP17 1SL ☎ 01728 688324
e-mail: snapecrown@tiscali.co.uk
dir: *A12 from Ipswich towards Lowestoft, right onto A1094 towards Aldeburgh. In Snape right at x-rds by church, pub at bottom of hill*

A must for concert-goers

It must be the abundant old beams, brick floors, fine double settle and large inglenook fireplace that help make this 15th-century, former smugglers' inn so atmospheric. The absence of gaming machines and background music also contributes, and then, of course, there's the food. Teresa and Garry Cook know exactly where their produce comes from: they rear their own quail, poultry, Suffolk lamb, rare-breed pigs and Anglo-Nubian goats; they source Limousin beef from a nearby farm and game from local shoots. Orford fishermen do their bit too. From the Cook's allotment come vegetables and herbs, and they forage enthusiastically. So, menus are forever changing, but typical are cauliflower and caraway fritters; pigeon with black pudding; and smoked haddock fishcake. Pre- or post-concert meals are available for those going to Snape Maltings. Traditional folk music is played in the pub on the last Thursday evening of every month. The garden is spacious.

Open all wk 12-3 6-11 **Bar Meals** L served all wk 12-2.30 D served all wk 6-9.30 Av main course £10 **Restaurant** L served all wk 12-2.30 D served all wk 6-9.30 Av 3 course à la carte fr £20 ⊕ ADNAMS ◀ Southwold Bitter, Broadside, Seasonal ales Ö Aspall. ⬦ 12 **Facilities** Non-diners area ❀ (Bar Garden) ◖ Children's portions Garden ▭ Parking ▭ (notice required)

PICK OF THE PUBS

Sibton White Horse Inn ★★★★ INN

SIBTON   Map 13 TM36

Halesworth Rd IP17 2JJ
☎ **01728 660337**
e-mail: info@sibtonwhitehorseinn.co.uk
web: www.sibtonwhitehorseinn.co.uk
dir: *A12 at Yoxford onto A1120, 3m to Peasenhall. Right opposite butchers, inn 600mtrs*

Delightful, award-winning inn

Off the beaten track in the heart of the Suffolk countryside, but just five minutes from the A12 at Yoxford and ten miles from the coast, this rustic 16th-century inn retains much of its Tudor charm and incorporates stone floors, exposed brickwork and ships' timbers believed to have come from Woodbridge shipyard. A genuine free house, the bar with its raised gallery is the place to enjoy pints of Green Jack Trawlerboys or Woodforde's Once Bittern. There is a choice of dining areas to sample the award-winning food, while the secluded courtyard has a Mediterranean feel when the sun comes out. Owners Neil and Gill Mason are committed to producing high-quality food from fresh local ingredients – and, to prove it, they grow many of their own vegetables behind the pub. At lunch, you can order from the set menu or from the selection of light bites and sandwiches. The à la carte, available at both lunch and dinner, offers old favourites like chicken liver and brandy pâté, and 28-day-hung

steak with hand-cut chips. For something a little more special, there's pressed pigeon, ham hock and pheasant egg terrine with celeriac and carrot slaw and beetroot dressing; roast rump of lamb accompanied by mini moussaka, sautéed potatoes, ratatouille, spinach and red pepper coulis; or grilled fillet of mackerel with warm apricot and potato salad, smoked mackerel velouté and curry oil. Finish, perhaps, with apple tarte Tatin and nutmeg ice cream. Well-behaved children are welcome; only those over six are permitted in the evening.

Open 12-2.30 6.30-11 Closed: 26-27 Dec, Mon L **Bar Meals** L served Tue-Sat 12-2, Sun 12-2.30 D served Mon-Sat 7-9, Sun 7-8.30 Av main course £14

Restaurant L served Tue-Sat 12-2, Sun 12-2.30 D served Mon-Sat 7-9, Sun 7-8.30 Fixed menu price fr £13.25 Av 3 course à la carte fr £25 ⊕ FREE HOUSE ◀ Adnams Southwold Bitter, Woodforde's Once Bittern, Green Jack Trawlerboys Best Bitter ☼ Aspall. ♇ 9 **Facilities** Non-diners area ☙ (Bar Garden) ♦ Children's portions Garden ⨅ Beer festival Parking Wi-fi **Rooms** 6

SNAPE continued

The Golden Key

PICK OF THE PUBS

Priory Ln IP17 1SQ ☎ 01728 688510
dir: *Telephone for directions*

Dog-friendly, 16th-century, cottage-style pub

This delightful village pub is a five-minute walk from Snape Maltings, home of the well-known Concert Hall, one of the focal points of the annual Aldeburgh Festival. The pub's low beamed ceilings and log fires not only attest to its age, but also help to generate its comfortable feel, especially in the quarry-tiled main bar, where you'll find villagers enjoying their pints of Southwold-brewed Adnams Broadside and Explorer. The food, both in the bar and in the pine-furnished dining room, owes much to the immediate locality, with fish delivered daily from Aldeburgh, lamb from a neighbouring farm and game supplied by the Benhall Shoot. Among the typical dishes are Richardson Smokehouse Suffolk ham with egg and chips; lamb curry with braised rice, tomato and coriander salad; and vegetable moussaka. Pre- and post-concert dining is available, but please book. Annual beer festival.

Open all wk 12-3 6-11 (Sun all day) **Bar Meals** L served all wk 12-2.30 D served all wk 6-9 **Restaurant** L served all wk 12-2.30 D served all wk 6-9 ⊕ ADNAMS ◀ Southwold Bitter, Broadside, Explorer, Old Ale, Oyster Stout Ô Aspall. ♀ 15 **Facilities** Non-diners area ✿ (All areas) ♦♦ Children's portions Garden Outside area ⊓ Beer festival Parking Wi-fi ▄▄ (notice required)

Plough & Sail

Snape Maltings IP17 1SR ☎ 01728 688413
dir: *On B1069, S of Snape. Signed from A12*

New kids on the block

Local twins, Alex (front of house) and Oliver (chef) Burnside have re-opened this pink, pantiled old inn at the heart of the renowned Snape Maltings complex; it's handy for cultural and shopping opportunities and close to splendid coastal walks. The interior is a comfy mix of dining and avant-garde destination pub; local ales and a good bin of wines accompany a solid menu, featuring a game terrine with toast and onion jam, or spiced pear with sugared walnuts, Cashel Blue and chicory salad to start; followed with crisp pork belly with thyme rösti, carrot purée, greens and red wine jus; or butternut squash, spinach, wild mushroom and garlic risotto. Leave room for treacle tartlet with char-grilled satsumas and crème fraîche or Madeira poached pear with walnut parfait and sweet syrup.

Open all day all wk **Bar Meals** L served all wk 12-2.30 all day summer D served all wk 6-9 all day summer **Restaurant** L served all wk 12-2.30 all day summer D served all wk 6-9 all day summer ⊕ FREE HOUSE ◀ Adnams Broadside, Southwold Bitter, Ghost Ship, Guest ale Ô Aspall. ♀ 10 **Facilities** Non-diners area ✿ (Bar Garden) ♦♦ Children's menu Children's portions Garden ⊓ Parking Wi-fi ▄▄ (notice required)

The Duke's Head NEW

Slug's Ln NR32 5QR ☎ 01502 733931 & 730281
e-mail: dukeshead.somerleyton@googlemail.com
dir: *From A143 onto B1074 signed Lowestoft & Somerleyton. Pub signed from B1074*

Rural estate-owned gastro-pub

Owned by and overlooking the Somerleyton Estate, this spruced up pub stands tucked away down Slug's Lane on the edge of the village. Renowned locally for its imaginative seasonal menus, which champion game and meats reared on estate farms, it thrives as a gastro-pub and the rambling and very relaxed bar and dining areas fill early with diners in the know. Bare boards, beams and crackling log fires set the informal scene for savouring game terrine; pork belly with cider cream sauce; and white chocolate cheesecake from the dinner menu. There's an equally inviting brunch menu and a choice of sandwiches. Savour the views over a pint of Wherry in the garden in summer.

Open all day all wk **Bar Meals** L served 12-3 (winter), Mon-Sat all day, Sun 12-10.30 (Jul-Aug) D served 6.30-9 (winter), Mon-Sat all day, Sun 12-10.30 (Jul-Aug) Av main course £8.95 **Restaurant** L served 12-3 (winter), Mon-Sat all day, Sun 12-10.30 (Jul-Aug) D served 6.30-9 (winter), Mon-Sat all day, Sun 12-10.30 (Jul-Aug) ⊕ FREE HOUSE ◀ Adnams, Woodforde's Wherry, Guest ales in summer. ♀ 12 **Facilities** Non-diners area ✿ (Bar Garden) ♦♦ Children's menu Children's portions Play area Garden ⊓ Beer festival Cider festival Parking Wi-fi ▄▄ (notice required)

The Crown Hotel ★★ HL ⚫

PICK OF THE PUBS

The High St IP18 6DP ☎ 01502 722275
e-mail: crown.hotel@adnams.co.uk
web: www.adnamshotels.co.uk
dir: *A12 onto A1095 to Southwold. Hotel in town centre*

The flagship hotel for the Adnams Brewery

Centrally located in the seaside town of Southwold, The Crown dates back to the 18th century, when it was a coaching inn. Buzzing with lively informality, it is now a hotel owned by the Adnams Brewery (also based in Southwold), and offers a range of excellent ales on tap, as well as local Aspall cider. The high standard of cooking is recognised with an AA Rosette, and the hotel also holds a green award. The location brings seafood options such as roulade of lemon sole, pan-fried sea bream fillet, and roasted scallops. Other choices from 'land' and 'garden' might include confit Gressingham duck leg, roast rack of lamb, goats' cheese risotto, and savoury pear tarte Tatin. Warm chocolate and peanut butter brownie is among the excellent puddings. The Crown's 14 bedrooms are reached through twisting corridors and staircases.

Open all wk 8am-11pm (Sun 8am-10.30pm) **Bar Meals** L served Mon-Fri 12-2, Sat-Sun 12-2.30 D served Sun-Fri 6-9, Sat 6-9.30 (5.30-9.30 summer) Av main course £16 **Restaurant** L served Mon-Fri 12-2, Sat-Sun 12-2.30 D served Sun-Fri 6-9, Sat 6-9.30 (5.30-9.30 summer) Fixed menu price fr £19.95 ⊕ ADNAMS Ô Aspall. ♀ 20 **Facilities** Non-diners area ♦♦ Children's menu Children's portions Garden ⊓ Parking Wi-fi **Rooms** 14

The Randolph

PICK OF THE PUBS

41 Wangford Rd, Reydon IP18 6PZ ☎ 01502 723603
e-mail: reception@therandolph.co.uk
dir: *A12 onto A1095 towards Southwold. Left into Wangford Rd*

Impressive village pub just outside Southwold

Built in 1899 by the town's well-known Adnams Brewery, this hotel was named after Lord Randolph Churchill, Sir Winston's father and a keen huntsman like the brewery's directors. The light and airy lounge bar, with contemporary high-backed chairs and comfortable sofas, overlooks a sunny, enclosed garden. In the bar and restaurant a modern British menu offers starters of moules marinière; and smoked duck breast with beetroot and lemon salad and tzatziki; and mains of chicken, mushroom and ham suet pudding; chargrilled rib-eye and sirloin steaks; deep-fried, line-caught haddock in Adnams beer batter; and Moroccan vegetable tagine with lemon couscous. Specials have included blue cheese pannacotta with pickled walnuts, celery and apple salad; pan-fried fillet of sea bass in bacon; fricassée of pork fillet with chestnut mushrooms; and Sri Lankan salmon curry. Children under 12 have their choices.

Open all day all wk **Bar Meals** L served all wk 12-2 D served all wk 6.30-9 **Restaurant** L served all wk 12-2 D served all wk 6.30-9 ⊕ ADNAMS ◀ Southwold Bitter, Explorer, Old Ale, Adnams Ghost Ship Ô Aspall. **Facilities** Non-diners area ♦♦ Children's menu Children's portions Garden ⊓ Parking Wi-fi ▄▄ (notice required)

Save on hotels. Book at theAA.com/hotel

SUFFOLK 411 ENGLAND

The Angel Inn ★★★★ INN

PICK OF THE PUBS

CO6 4SA ☎ 01206 263245
e-mail: info@angelinnsuffolk.co.uk
dir: *From Colchester take A134 towards Sudbury, 5m to Nayland. Or from A12 between juncts 30 & 31 take B1068, then B1087 to Nayland*

Ancient coaching inn in Constable country

A 16th-century building that has been an inn for most of its existence, the Angel's modern facilities, like the air-conditioned conservatory, patio and sun terrace, harmonise happily with the ancient charm of its beamed bars, log fires and snug areas. The Well Room, with its lofty, timbered ceiling and 52-ft deep well, is a popular place for a meal, with modern British main course options including Aylesbury duck breast with dauphinoise potato, carrot and cumin, Savoy cabbage and wild mushrooms; wild sea bass with samphire, cauliflower purée, spiced cauliflower samosas and squid ink risotto balls; and pumpkin and goats' cheese strudel with fresh basil, artichoke purée and baby salad. The 35-bin wine list offers up to 12 by the glass, and real ales come mostly from small regional breweries. The village church appears in several of Constable's paintings, although apparently not always in the right place.

Open all day all wk 11-11 (Sun 11-10.30) **Bar Meals** L served Mon-Fri 12-3.30, Sat 12-9.30, Sun 12-9 D served Mon-Fri 6-9.30, Sat 12-9.30, Sun 12-9 Av main course £9.95 **Restaurant** L served Mon-Fri 12-3.30, Sat 12-9.30, Sun 12-9 D served Mon-Fri 6-9.45, Sat 12-9.30, Sun 12-9 Fixed menu price fr £15.95 Av 3 course à la carte fr £25 ⊕ FREE HOUSE/EXCLUSIVE INNS ◀ Adnams Southwold Bitter, Greene King, Nethergate, 2 Guest ales Ö Aspall. ⏹ 12 **Facilities** Non-diners area ❀ (Bar Garden) ⏺ Children's menu Children's portions Family room Garden Outside area ⛫ Parking Wi-fi ▭ (notice required) **Rooms** 6

The Crown ★★★ SHL ◉◉

PICK OF THE PUBS

CO6 4SE ☎ 01206 262001
e-mail: info@crowninn.net
dir: *Exit A12 signed Stratford St Mary & Dedham. Through Stratford St Mary 0.5m, left, follow signs to Higham. At village green left, left again, 2m, pub on right*

Delightful spot with award-winning food

In the heart of Constable country and within easy reach of the timeless villages of Lavenham, Kersey and Long Melford, this 16th-century free house sits above the Stour and Box river valleys on the Suffolk and Essex border. Stylishly appointed with a contemporary bar and informal dining areas, the pub also has 11 luxury en suite

bedrooms. Local produce underpins the modern British menu, with dishes freshly prepared to order. Lunch brings full meals and lighter options, or look to the chalkboard for the daily East Coast fish selection. An evening meal might begin with pheasant, rabbit and venison terrine with red onion marmalade, followed by confit duck and new potato hash with watercress and fried egg. Blood orange tart with citrus yogurt makes for a refreshing end to the meal. Every dish is given a wine match, and a decent selection of ales complements the superb wine list.

Open all day all wk 7.30am-11pm (Sun 8am-10.30pm) Closed: 25-26 Dec **Bar Meals** L served Mon-Sat 12-2.30, Sun 12-9 D served Mon-Thu 6-9.30, Fri-Sat 6-10, Sun 12-9 **Restaurant** L served Mon-Sat 12-2.30, Sun 12-9 D served Mon-Thu 6-9.30, Fri-Sat 6-10, Sun 12-9 ⊕ FREE HOUSE ◀ Adnams Southwold Bitter, Crouch Vale Brewers Gold, Woodforde's Wherry, Guest ales Ö Aspall. ⏹ 32 **Facilities** Non-diners area ⏺ Children's menu Children's portions Outside area ⛫ Parking Wi-fi **Rooms** 11

The Buxhall Crown

Mill Rd, Buxhall IP14 3DW ☎ 01449 736521
e-mail: mail@thebuxhallcrown.co.uk
dir: *B1115 from Stowmarket, through Great Finborough to Buxhall*

Charming rural pub with large secluded patio

Now in new hands, this 17th-century building has two bars, one very much in keeping with its origins, the other, the Mill Bar, dating from Georgian times. Bar snacks, light lunches and four-course meals are catered for, the menu changing in response to the seasons and the availability of locally sourced produce; breads, biscuits, ice creams and sorbets are all freshly made on the premises. To start, a mini-meze of cured meats, perhaps, or scallops with smoked pork belly; followed by three-rib rack of English lamb; extra-mature British rib-eye steak; or vegetarian pea and mint mousse.

Open 12-3 7-11 (Sat 12-3 6.30-11) Closed: Sun eve & Mon **Bar Meals** L served Tue-Sun 12-2 D served Tue-Fri 7-9, Sat 6.30-9 Av main course £16 **Restaurant** L served Tue-Sun 12-2 D served Tue-Fri 7-9, Sat 6.30-9 ⊕ FREE HOUSE ◀ Adnams Southwold Bitter, Adnams Broadside Ö Aspall. ⏹ 12 **Facilities** Non-diners area ❀ (Bar Restaurant Garden) ⏺ Children's portions Garden Parking Wi-fi ▭

The Ivy House

Wilby Rd IP21 5JN ☎ 01379 384634
e-mail: stenselthhome@aol.com
dir: *Telephone for directions*

Interesting ales and wines in a pretty pub

Around the corner from Stradbroke's main street, this Grade II listed thatched pub with wooden beams dates from the Middle Ages. Real ales on handpump and wine from the Adnams wine cellar are the draw here. The weekly-changing menu makes good use of local and seasonal produce to offer both British and Asian-style dishes, and in warmer weather you can sit outside at the front or in the garden. Typical options include teriyaki-marinated chicken skewers with salsa to start; and pan-fried calves' liver with Suffolk dry-cured bacon, mash and onion gravy as a main course. Leave room for dark chocolate cake with praline ice cream. Curries and other dishes are available to take away.

Open all wk 12-3 6-11 **Restaurant** L served all wk 12-2 D served all wk 6.30-9 ⊕ FREE HOUSE ◀ Adnams, Woodforde's, Buffy's Ö Aspall. **Facilities** Non-diners area ❀ (Bar Garden) Garden ⛫ Parking Wi-fi

Moon & Mushroom Inn

High Rd IP6 9LR ☎ 01473 785320
e-mail: moonandmushroom@gmail.com
dir: *Take B1077 (Westerfield road) from Ipswich. Approx 6m right to Swilland*

Tranquil escape in deepest Suffolk

The delightful sight of several firkins of East Anglian beer stillaged enticingly behind the bar welcomes drinkers to this 400-year-old free-house in the Suffolk countryside. Diners, too, relish the prospect of indulging in home-cooked specials such as wild rabbit pie or mushroom steamed pudding with four-mushroom sauce. The pub was reputedly a staging post for the despatch of convicts to Australia, and the records at Ipswich Assizes do indeed show that a previous landlord was deported for stealing two ducks and a pig. Today's guests are able to linger longer in the colourful cottagey interior or the fragrant rose garden here.

Open Tue-Sat (Sun L) Closed: Sun eve & Mon **Bar Meals** L served Tue-Sat 12-2, Sun 12-2.30 D served Tue-Sat 6.30-9 Av main course £9.95 **Restaurant** L served Tue-Sat 12-2, Sun 12-2.30 D served Tue-Sat 6.30-9 Fixed menu price fr £10 ⊕ FREE HOUSE ◀ Nethergate Suffolk County, Woodforde's Wherry & Admiral's Reserve, Wolf Ale & Golden Jackal Ö Aspall. **Facilities** Non-diners area ❀ (Bar Garden) ⏺ Children's portions Garden ⛫ Parking

PICK OF THE PUBS

The Westleton Crown ★★★ HL 🌹🌹

WESTLETON   Map 13 TM46

The Street IP17 3AD ☎ **01728 648777**
e-mail: info@westletoncrown.co.uk
web: www.westletoncrown.co.uk
dir: *A12 N, turn right for Westleton just
after Yoxford. Hotel opposite on entering
Westleton*

Classic dishes with a twist and and fine local ales

Standing opposite the parish church in
a peaceful village close to the RSPB's
Minsmere, this traditional coaching inn
dates back to the 12th century and
provides a comfortable base for
exploring Suffolk's glorious Heritage
Coast. The pub retains plenty of
character and rustic charm,
complemented by all the comforts of
contemporary living. On winter days
you'll find three crackling log fires, local
real ales including Brandon Rusty
Bucket and Adnams Southwold Bitter,
as well as a good list of wines (with 11
available by the glass). There's also an
extensive menu that includes innovative
daily specials and classic dishes with a
twist, freshly prepared from the best
local produce. Eat in the cosy bar, in the
elegant dining room, or in the garden
room. Sandwiches are made with a
choice of The Crown's own breads, and
served with sea-salted crisps and a
dressed salad. More substantial
appetites might choose from starters
like Blythburgh ham hock and parsley

with a beetroot and celeriac rémoulade
mayonnaise; or grilled sardines with a
potato and sage terrine and black olive
dressing. Follow up with main course
choices such as pan-fried fillet of
halibut with roasted salsify, parsley and
vanilla creamed potato and clementine
butter sauce; or suet pudding filled with
slow-cooked beef and mushrooms,
Lyonnaise potatoes and spinach. Save
some space for accomplished desserts
like baked pumpkin cheesecake with
chargrilled poached pears and vanilla
cream; or baked fig tarte Tatin with
vanilla and balsamic syrup ice cream.
Retire to one of the 34 comfortably and
individually styled bedrooms. Outside,
the large terraced gardens are floodlit in
the evening.

Open all day all wk 7am-11pm (Sun
7.30am-10.30pm) **Bar Meals** L served
all wk 12-2.30 D served all wk
6.30-9.30 **Restaurant** L served all wk
12-2.30 D served all wk 6.30-9.30
⊕ FREE HOUSE ◀ Adnams Southwold
Bitter, Brandon Rusty Bucket Ď Aspall
Harry Sparrow. ♟ 11 **Facilities** Non-
diners area 🐾 ♦️ Children's menu
Children's portions Garden ⅋ Parking
Wi-fi 🚌 (notice required) **Rooms** 34

Save on hotels. Book at **theAA.com/hotel**

SUFFOLK 413 ENGLAND

PICK OF THE PUBS

The White Horse ✿

WHEPSTEAD Map 13 TL85

Rede Rd IP29 4SS ☎ 01284 735760
web: www.whitehorsewhepstead.co.uk
*dir: From Bury St Edmunds take A143
towards Haverhill. Left onto B1066 to
Whepstead. In Whepstead right into
Church Hill, leads into Rede Rd*

Delightful East Anglian pub with a loyal following

This village pub was built as a
farmhouse in the early 17th century and
extended during the Victorian era. As it
is surrounded by rural public footpaths,
many people take advantage of pub's
short walk guides and then return here
for lunch or dinner. In 2009 Gary and Di
Kingscott refurbished the pub to the
great delight of the locals and
tremendously loyal staff. The bright,
spacious interior makes it a great space
for the display and sale of artworks by
local painters. The large, copper-topped
bar, open fire and comfortable wooden
chairs make you feel instantly at home,
while nostalgic touches like the Tuck
Shop – which sells ice cream, sweets
and chocolate – appeal to adults and
children alike. As well as reliable Suffolk
ales and real cider behind the bar, the
award-winning menus change on a
daily basis. Gary oversees the kitchen,
and his passion for great,
uncomplicated food is evident in every

dish. Quality seasonal ingredients are
locally sourced where possible and
always fresh; meat comes from the
butcher in the next village. Starters
could include the likes of smoked
haddock chowder and crusty bread; and
jellied ham hock terrine with home-
made piccalilli. Main course options
might be chicken, mushroom, wine and
tarragon open pie; or roast pumpkin
ravioli, toasted pine nuts and salad.
Chocolate truffle torte and baked apricot
cheesecake are among the dessert
choices. Di runs the front of house and
her years of experience ensure quick and
friendly service. Skye, the dog, can be
found snoozing in a corner when he is
not gently greeting customers.

Open 11.30-3 7-11 Closed: 25-26 Dec,
Sun eve **Bar Meals** L served all wk 12-2
D served Mon-Sat 7-9.30 Av main
course £12.95 **Restaurant** L served all
wk 12-2 D served Mon-Sat 7-9.30
🛢 FREE HOUSE ◀ Adnams Southwold
Bitter & Broadside, Guest Ale ♂ Aspall.
🍷 10 **Facilities** Non-diners area 👫
Children's portions Garden Parking 🚌

THORPENESS
Map 13 TM45

The Dolphin Inn

Peace Place IP16 4NA ☎ 01728 454994
e-mail: dolphininn@hotmail.co.uk
web: www.thorpenessdolphin.com
dir: *A12 onto A1094 & follow Thorpeness signs*

At the community's heart and close to never ending beaches

A stone's throw from the shingle of Suffolk's Heritage Coast and in a conservation area, this community-focused free house replaced a 1910 predecessor, destroyed by fire in 1995. At the bar are real ales from Adnams and Brandon, nearly 20 wines by the glass, and bourbons and single malts in abundance. Look forward to River Deben blue mussels with smoked bacon; oven-baked chicken breast with sweet potato mash; or wild mushroom with white wine and parmesan risotto. After a bracing walk on the beach sit beside the fire and tuck into one of their home-made pies; in summer barbecues are held in the huge garden.

Open 11-3 6-11 (Sat all day Sun 11-5) Closed: Sun eve & Mon in winter **Bar Meals** L served all wk 12-2.30 D served all wk 6.30-9.30 **Restaurant** L served all wk 12-2.30 D served all wk 6.30-9.30 ⊕ FREE HOUSE ◀ Adnams Southwold Bitter & Broadside, Brandon Rusty Bucket, Mauldons Midsummer Gold, Woodforde's Wherry ♂ Aspall. ☷ 18 **Facilities** Non-diners area ♣ (Bar Garden) ♦♦ Children's menu Children's portions Garden ⊓ Parking Wi-fi ▭

TUDDENHAM
Map 13 TM14

The Fountain

The Street IP6 9BT ☎ 01473 785377
e-mail: fountainpub@btconnect.com
dir: *From Ipswich take B1077 (Westerfield Rd) signed Debenham. At Westerfield turn right for Tuddenham*

Informal bistro-style eating in a 16th-century country pub

Only three miles north of Ipswich in the lovely village of Tuddenham St Martin, this 16th-century country pub combines old fashioned pub hospitality with an informal bistro-style restaurant. The menu changes frequently and there is an emphasis on local produce in dishes such as duck and spring onion samosas; braised Suffolk lamb shank; and glazed lemon tart with blackberry sorbet. Wash it all down with pints of Adnams ale or Aspall cider.

Open all wk 12-3 6-11 **Bar Meals** L served all wk 12-2 D served Mon-Fri 6-9, Sat 6-9.30 Av main course £11.95 **Restaurant** L served Mon-Sat 12-2, Sun 12-7 D served Mon-Fri 6-9, Sat 6-9.30 Fixed menu price fr £13.95 Av 3 course à la carte fr £22 ⊕ FREE HOUSE ◀ Adnams ♂ Aspall. ☷ 9 **Facilities** Non-diners area ♦♦ Children's menu Children's portions Garden ⊓ Parking Wi-fi

UFFORD
Map 13 TM25

The Ufford Crown NEW

High St IP13 6EL ☎ 01394 461030
e-mail: max@theuffordcrown.com
dir: *Just off A12 between Woodbridge & Wickham*

Friendly, family-run village pub and restaurant

Step though the doors of Max and Polly Durrant's handsome property and you'll find a spacious restaurant, cosy bar, stylish lounge area and, at the rear, a terrace and garden, where there's plenty to keep children amused. Adnams, Brandeston Gold and Australian Victoria Bitter badges adorn the real ale pumps, with Aspall cider alongside. Gifted chef Will Hardiman has a reputation for using all cuts of meat, including sweetbreads and ox cheeks, and Lowestoft-landed fish. Heavily reliant on seasonal produce from local suppliers, his menus feature chargrilled duck hearts with Asian salad; chicken, ham, mushroom and tarragon pie; and crispy Dingley Dell pork belly.

Open 12-3 5-11 (Sat-Sun all day) Closed: Tue (Winter) **Bar Meals** L served all wk 12.30-2 D served all wk 6.30-9 Av main course £13 **Restaurant** L served all wk 12.30-2 D served all wk 6.30-9 ⊕ FREE HOUSE ◀ Adnams Southwold Bitter, Earl Soham Brandeston Gold & Victoria Bitter ♂ Aspall. ☷ 15 **Facilities** Non-diners area ♣ (Bar Garden) ♦♦ Children's menu Children's portions Play area Garden ⊓ Parking Wi-fi ▭ (notice required)

WALBERSWICK
Map 13 TM47

The Anchor ◉◉

PICK OF THE PUBS

Main St IP18 6UA ☎ 01502 722112
e-mail: info@anchoratwalberswick.com
dir: *A12 onto B1387, follow Walberswick signs*

A family-friendly retreat with first-class food

Mark and Sophie Dawber are responsible for ensuring this striking Arts and Crafts pub on the Suffolk coast is more than just a village local. Mark, who oversees the drinks side, used to run a highly rated London pub, while Sophie, who once provided the catering on *Star Wars* film-sets, and whose family has long-standing local connections, runs the kitchen. The menu suggests a beer or wine to accompany each dish, thus Belgian Westmalle Tripel or Pinot Grigio are teamed with scallops, parsnip purée and pancetta salad; and Adnams Broadside or Sesti Grangiovese are recommended as accompaniments to Anchor pie with mustard mash. Similarly, partnerships are also proposed for West Mersea oysters; rib-eye steak; and saffron, tomato and fennel linguine. Dessert of treacle tart is paired with a Muscat. The adjoining wild

flower meadow is perfect for a picnic, especially during the mid-August beer festival.

Open all day all wk **Bar Meals** Av main course £13.25 food served all day **Restaurant** L served all wk 12-3 D served all wk 6-9 ⊕ ADNAMS ◀ Southwold Bitter, Broadside & Seasonal ales, Meantime Helles & Pale Ale, Bitburger, Guest ales ♂ Aspall. ☷ 22 **Facilities** Non-diners area ♦♦ Children's menu Children's portions Family room Garden ⊓ Beer festival Parking Wi-fi

The Bell Inn NEW

Ferry Rd IP18 6TN ☎ 01502 723109
dir: *From A12 take B1387 to Walberswick, after village green right down track*

Old inn where the menu captures top Suffolk produce

Six centuries old and going stronger than ever, the Bell stands close to the Southwold ferry, the Suffolk Coastal Path and the marshes. Character is certainly not in short supply, with oak-beamed ceilings, hidden alcoves, worn flagstone floors and open fires. Firm favourites on the menu are Brancaster mussels in cider; whole grilled Dover sole with lemon and herb butter; parmesan and garlic-crusted chicken schnitzel; and steak, mushroom and Adnams ale pie. Out back is a family-friendly garden overlooking a creek and the beach; here too is the Barn Café, offering everything for a picnic. Well-behaved dogs are welcome.

Open all day all wk **Bar Meals** L served all wk 12-2.30 D served all wk 6-9 Av main course £11 ⊕ ADNAMS ◀ Southwold Bitter, Broadside, Sole Star, Spindrift, Ghost Ship ♂ Aspall. ☷ 15 **Facilities** Non-diners area ♣ (Bar Garden) ♦♦ Children's menu Children's portions Family room Garden ⊓ Parking Wi-fi ▭ (notice required)

WESTLETON
Map 13 TM46

The Westleton Crown ★★★ HL ◉◉

PICK OF THE PUBS

See Pick of the Pubs on page 412

WHEPSTEAD
Map 13 TL85

The White Horse ◉

PICK OF THE PUBS

See Pick of the Pubs on page 413

Save on hotels. Book at **theAA.com/hotel**

SURREY 415 ENGLAND

SURREY

ABINGER
Map 6 TQ14

The Stephan Langton

PICK OF THE PUBS

Friday Street RH5 6JR ☎ 01306 730775 & 737129
e-mail: info@stephanlangtonpub.co.uk
dir: *Exit A25 between Dorking & Guildford at Hollow Ln. 1.5m, left into Friday Street*

A popular stop for walkers

This is prime Surrey walking country and a popular pitstop is The Stephan Langton, a 1930s building named after the first archbishop of Canterbury, who was supposedly born in Friday Street. Undulating mixed woodland surrounds this secluded hamlet at the base of Leith Hill, the highest summit in south-east England. Langton helped draw up the Magna Carta and a copy of the document is pinned to a wall in the rustic, bare-boarded bar. Equally unpretentious is the adjoining dining room, with its cream-washed walls, simple wooden tables and chairs, and open fires. Having conquered Leith Hill, relax on the suntrap patio and savour a thirst-quenching pint of locally brewed Hogs Back TEA. Peruse the short, inviting menu that hits the spot with lunchtime sandwiches and hearty main dishes. Changing daily specials make the most of local produce, much of it sourced from the surrounding Wooton Estate.

Open 11.30-3 5.30-11 (Sat 11-11 Sun 12-9) Closed: Mon L **Bar Meals** L served Tue-Sat 12-2.30, Sun 12-4 D served Tue-Sat 6.30-9.30 **Restaurant** L served Tue-Sat 12-2.30, Sun 12-4 D served Tue-Sat 6.30-9.30 ⊕ FREE HOUSE ◀ Hogs Back TEA, Sharp's Doom Bar, Morland Old Speckled Hen, Greene King IPA ♻ Thatchers Gold. **Facilities** Non-diners area ❤ (Bar) ♦ Children's portions Outside area ⊟ Parking ▬ (notice required)

The Volunteer

Water Ln, Sutton RH5 6PR ☎ 01306 730985
e-mail: volunteer247@btinternet.com
dir: *Between Guildford & Dorking, 1m S of A25*

Good spot for tip-top beer and good food

Enjoying a delightful rural setting with views over the River Mole, this popular village pub was originally farm cottages and first licensed about 1870. Under the ownership of Hall & Woodhouse, it remains an ideal watering hole for walkers who want to relax over a pint in the attractive three-tier pub garden, or in the bustling bar with its two fireplaces. Typical dishes include red Thai curry; chicken and asparagus pie; and the renowned Volunteer fish pie. Sandwiches, baguettes, melts, toasted sandwiches and jacket potatoes are all available too.

Open all wk 12-3 6-11 (Sat 12-11 Sun 12-4) **Bar Meals** L served Mon-Fri 12-2.30, Sat 12-9, Sun 12-3 D served Mon-Fri 6.30-9.30, Sat 12-9 **Restaurant** L served Mon-Fri 12-2.30, Sat 12-9, Sun 12-3 D served Mon-Fri 6.30-9.30, Sat 12-9 ⊕ HALL & WOODHOUSE ◀ Badger Tanglefoot,

K&B Sussex, Guest ales ♻ Westons Stowford Press. ☍ 9 **Facilities** Non-diners area ❤ (Bar Restaurant Garden) ♦ Children's menu Children's portions Garden ⊟ Parking Wi-fi ▬ (notice required)

ALBURY
Map 6 TQ04

The Drummond at Albury ★★★ INN

The Street GU5 9AG ☎ 01483 202039
e-mail: drummondarms@aol.com
dir: *6m from Guildford on A248*

Riverside pub in the heart of the Surrey Hills

This eye-catching village inn, which has hanging flower baskets outside in summer, was reopened a few years ago by the Duke of Northumberland whose family have historic links to the pub. Its pleasant beer garden backs onto River Tillingbourne. Expect a comforting mix of great local (from Hogs Back) and national real ales. In the conservatory restaurant, the best of modern and traditional British cooking is on offer – herb-roasted chicken breast, trout from the Albury Estate lakes, and the popular home-made Drummond pies. Individually appointed letting rooms make the pub a good base from which to explore the North Downs.

Open all day all wk 11-11 (Fri-Sat 11am-mdnt Sun 12-10.30) **Bar Meals** L served Mon-Fri 12-3, Sat 12-6, Sun 12-8 D served Mon-Sat 6-9.30, Sun 12-8 **Restaurant** L served Mon-Fri 12-3, Sat 12-6, Sun 12-8 D served Mon-Sat 6-9.30, Sun 12-8 ⊕ FREE HOUSE ◀ Courage Best Bitter, Fuller's London Pride, Hogs Back TEA, Adnams. ☍ 10 **Facilities** Non-diners area ❤ (Bar Garden) ♦ Children's portions Garden ⊟ Parking Wi-fi **Rooms** 9

William IV

Little London GU5 9DG ☎ 01483 202685
dir: *Off A25 between Guildford & Dorking (for detailed directions contact pub)*

16th-century free house on a quiet country lane

Deep in the wooded Surrey Hills yet only a few miles from Guildford, this 16th-century free house provides 'proper pub food' made from mostly local produce. Sometimes it's the free-range pork raised by landlord Giles written on the blackboards, but more usually it's liver and bacon, beer-battered cod and chips, or pan-fried Cajun chicken, all served in the bar and dining room. Young's and two Surrey breweries supply the real ales. It is great walking and riding country, and the attractive garden is ideal for post-ramble relaxation.

Open all wk 11-3 5.30-11 (Sat 11-11 Sun 12-11) **Bar Meals** L served all wk 12-2 D served Mon-Sat 7-9 ⊕ FREE HOUSE ◀ Young's, Hogs Back, Surrey Hills ♻ Westons Stowford Press, Addlestones. **Facilities** Non-diners area ❤ (Bar Garden) ♦ Children's portions Garden ⊟ Parking Wi-fi ▬ (notice required)

BETCHWORTH
Map 6 TQ25

The Red Lion

Old Rd, Buckland RH3 7DS ☎ 01737 843336
e-mail: info@redlionbetchworth.co.uk
dir: *Telephone for directions*

A favourite with walkers and cyclists

Set in 18 acres next to a cricket ground, the family-run Red Lion dates back to the 18th century, is home to a wisteria thought to be around 250 years old. Although only 15 minutes from Gatwick, the pub enjoys lovely rolling countryside views - the area is ideal for walkers. Sandwiches are listed on the bar menu, while starters from the à la carte menu could include crab spring rolls with sweet chilli dip; pasta topped with ratatouille; roasted salmon fillet with tarragon cream sauce; or home-cooked ham, free eggs and hand-cut chips. There are two unusual function areas: a fully air-conditioned cellar, and an outdoor area covered with a cedar shingle roof.

Open all day all wk 11am-11.30pm (Fri-Sat 11am-mdnt) **Bar Meals** L served Sun-Fri 12-2.30, Sat 12-4 **Restaurant** L served Mon-Fri 12-2.30, Sat-Sun 12-4 D served Mon-Thu 6.30-9, Fri-Sat 6.30-9.30, Sun 6.30-8 ⊕ PUNCH TAVERNS ◀ Adnams Southwold Bitter, Sharp's Doom Bar, Hogs Back TEA, Fuller's London Pride ♻ Addlestones, Westons Stowford Press. ☍ 9 **Facilities** Non-diners area ❤ (Bar Restaurant Garden) ♦ Children's menu Children's portions Garden ⊟ Parking Wi-fi ▬ (notice required)

BRAMLEY
Map 6 TQ04

Jolly Farmer Inn

High St GU5 0HB ☎ 01483 893355
e-mail: enquiries@jollyfarmer.co.uk
dir: *From Guildford take A281 (Horsham road). Bramley 3.5m S of Guildford*

Welcoming and friendly pub

A 16th-century coaching inn steeped in character and history, this friendly family-run free house clearly has a passion for beer. Besides the impressive range of Belgian bottled beers, you'll always find up to eight constantly-changing cask real ales on the counter. The pub offers a high standard of food all freshly cooked, with daily specials board featuring Scottish sirloin and vegetable stir-fry; home-made lasagne; Caesar salad and a full rack of barbecue pork ribs with chips and salad.

Open all day all wk 11-11 **Bar Meals** L served all wk 12-2.30 D served all wk 6-9.30 **Restaurant** L served all wk 12-2.30 D served all wk 6-9.30 ⊕ FREE HOUSE ◀ 8 Guest ales ♻ Westons Stowford Press, Aspall. ☍ 16 **Facilities** Non-diners area ❤ (Bar Garden) ♦ Children's menu Garden ⊟ Parking Wi-fi ▬ (notice required)

PICK OF THE PUBS

The Swan Inn ★★★★ INN ❀

CHIDDINGFOLD Map 6 SU93

Petworth Rd GU8 4TY ☎ 01428 684688
e-mail:
info@theswaninnchiddingfold.com
web: www.theswaninnchiddingfold.com
dir: *From A3 follow Milford/Petworth/
A283 signs. At rdbt 1st exit onto A283.
Slight right onto Guildford & Godalming
bypass. Right into Portsmouth Rd, left
(continue on A283), to Chiddingfold*

Cosmopolitan food and drink in stylish village inn

The owners of The Swan Inn ran a pub in
fashionable Knightsbridge for 20 years
before taking over here and they have
added luxurious boutique-style
accommodation to this lovely old village
inn. Nestling among the Surrey Hills in
the village of Chiddingfold between
Guildford and Petworth, The Swan is
typical of the coaching inns that used to
serve customers travelling to or from the
south coast. Rebuilt in the 1880s and
refurbished to a high standard in 2010,
The Swan today offers weary travellers a
friendly and relaxed welcome. In the bar,
temptations include local ales such as
Shere Drop brewed by the Surrey Hills
Brewery, and from an international list,
there are 16 wines served by the glass.
The menu also has broad appeal, with
top-notch produce such as Scottish
salmon, Parma ham and foie gras. A
typical meal might kick off with an
appetiser of roasted Provençal

vegetable and gruyère tart with rocket
and pesto salad or guinea fowl, pork
and chorizo terrine with apricot and
pomegranate chutney. They might be
followed by main course choices of
grilled sea bream with harissa,
couscous and a vegetable and chickpea
stew, or fillet of wild boar with celeriac
mash, black pudding, roasted apples
and wholegrain mustard sauce. Typical
desserts include apple and pear
frangipane tart with crème anglaise and
amaretti ice cream, or a selection of
home-made ice creams.

Open all day all wk 11-11 (Sun
12-10.30) **Bar Meals** L served all wk
12-3 D served Mon-Sat 6.30-10, Sun
6.30-9 Av main course £13.50
Restaurant L served all wk 12-3 D

served Mon-Sat 6.30-10, Sun 6.30-9 Av
3 course à la carte fr £27 ⊕ FREE
HOUSE ◀ Adnams Southwold Bitter,
Surrey Hills Shere Drop, Guest ale
Ŏ Hogan's, Aspall. ⚑ 16 **Facilities** Non-
diners area ❤ (Bar Garden) ♦♦
Children's menu Children's portions
Garden ⌿ Beer festival Parking Wi-fi
Rooms 10

BUCKLAND · Map 6 TQ25

The Jolly Farmers Deli Pub & Restaurant

Reigate Rd RH3 7BG ☎ 01737 221355
e-mail: info@thejollyfarmersreigate.co.uk
dir: *On A25 approx 2m from Reigate & 4m from Dorking*

Delightful deli, farm shop and pub combo

Beside the A25 between Reigate and Dorking, this unique free house may look like a traditional pub but step inside and you'll find a cracking deli/farmshop that showcases local foods and artisan producers smack next to the comfortable, wood-floored bar and restaurant. Choose from deli snacks such as a hand-made sausage roll with onion marmalade or Jolly Farmer picked eggs, or plump for a full meal — maybe deep fried baby squid followed by a gourmet burger with Jolly Farmers relish and real chips. Wash it down with a pint of Dark Star Hophead or WJ King Horsham Best.

Open all day all wk **Bar Meals** L served all wk all day D served all wk all day Av main course £9.95 food served all day **Restaurant** L served Mon-Fri 12-3, Sat 12-9.30, Sun 12-8.30 D served Sat 12-9.30, Sun 12-8.30 Av 3 course à la carte fr £21.50 ⊕ FREE HOUSE ◀ Dark Star Hophead, WJ King Horsham Best, Dorking DB Number One, Pilgrim Surrey Bitter. ♟ 14 **Facilities** Non-diners area ❀ (Bar Garden) ♦⊪ Children's menu Children's portions Play area Garden ⍲ Parking Wi-fi ▬ (notice required)

CHIDDINGFOLD · Map 6 SU93

The Crown Inn ★★★★★ INN

The Green GU8 4TX ☎ 01428 682255
e-mail: enquiries@thecrownchiddingfold.com
dir: *On A283 between Milford & Petworth*

Historic timbered inn, more than 700 years old

Set by the village green and church, this beautifully appointed inn is one of the county's oldest buildings. It oozes charm and character, featuring ancient panelling, open fires, distinctive carvings, huge beams, and eight comfortable bedrooms. In addition to the house beer, Crown Bitter, ales come from Surrey, Hampshire and London breweries. Food ranges from decent snacks like a seafood platter and smoked salmon ciabatta sandwich, to Crown favourites such as corned beef hash, and imaginative dishes, perhaps confit leg and roast breast of guinea fowl with Puy lentils and spinach or sweet potato, chickpea and shallot tagine.

Open all day all wk **Bar Meals** L served Mon-Sat 12-2.30, Sun 12-3 D served Mon-Sat 6.30-10, Sun 6.30-9 **Restaurant** L served Mon-Sat 12-2.30, Sun 12-3 D served Mon-Sat 6.30-10, Sun 6.30-9 ⊕ FREE HOUSE/FGH INNS ◀ Crown Bitter, Fuller's London Pride, Triple fff Moondance, Hop Back Summer Lightning. **Facilities** Non-diners area ♦⊪ Children's menu Children's portions Garden ⍲ Wi-fi ▬ **Rooms** 8

The Swan Inn ★★★★ INN ⦿

PICK OF THE PUBS

See Pick of the Pubs on opposite page

COLDHARBOUR · Map 6 TQ14

The Plough Inn

PICK OF THE PUBS

Coldharbour Ln RH5 6HD ☎ 01306 711793
e-mail: theploughinn@btinternet.com
dir: *M25 junct 9, A24 to Dorking. A25 towards Guildford. Coldharbour signed from one-way system*

Well established pub in pretty village

Known to date from 1641, the Abrehart family's old coaching inn gets much of its footfall from walkers and cyclists scaling nearby 965-ft Leith Hill, the highest point in south-eastern England. Earlier visitors were smugglers en route from the south coast to London, which may be why the resident ghost is a sailor. Another high point is the landlord's own microbrewery, producing Tallywhacker porter, Crooked Furrow bitter and the lighter Beautiful South, as well as Biddenden cider. The Abreharts' 25-year residency has produced a family-friendly place with big fires, a pretty garden and an evening steakhouse with a malt whisky bar serving 21-day, dry-aged local Aberdeen Angus steaks and other chargrills. On the menus expect lamb, mint and coriander sausages and mash with Merlot gravy; cod, haddock, prawn and salmon pie; and Mediterranean vegetable and goats' cheese tart. Home-made puddings include spotted dick and a daily crumble.

Open all day all wk 11.30am-mdnt Closed: 25 Dec **Bar Meals** L served Mon-Fri 12-2.30, Sat-Sun 12-3 D served Mon 7-9.30 **Restaurant** D served Tue-Sun 7-10 ⊕ FREE HOUSE ◀ Leith Hill Crooked Furrow, Tallywhacker & The Beautiful South, Shepherd Neame Spitfire ⦿ Biddenden. **Facilities** Non-diners area ♦⊪ Children's menu Children's portions Garden Parking Wi-fi ▬ (notice required)

COMPTON · Map 6 SU94

The Withies Inn

Withies Ln GU3 1JA ☎ 01483 421158
dir: *Telephone for directions*

Eclectically furnished old village inn

This low-beamed inn has slumbered beside the wooded common for five centuries, maturing into a popular, cosy village local enhanced by an intimate restaurant area, where home-made pâté can lead in to poached halibut with prawns and brandy sauce. Seasonal specials tumble from the menu; asparagus, grouse or wild duck may be available here. Comfort-food bar snacks range from filled jacket potatoes to fisherman's broth or a hot salt beef sandwich; tuck into sausage, mash and onion gravy after a stroll in the lovely surrounding countryside, or relax in the garden with a pint of TEA from the local Hogs Back Brewery.

Open 11-3 6-11 (Fri 11-11) Closed: Sun eve **Bar Meals** L served all wk 12-2.30 D served Mon-Sat 7-10 **Restaurant** L served all wk 12-2.30 D served Mon-Sat 7-10 ⊕ FREE HOUSE ◀ Hogs Back TEA, Greene King IPA, Adnams, Sharp's Doom Bar ⦿ Aspall. ♟ 12 **Facilities** Non-diners area ♦⊪ Children's portions Garden ⍲ Parking Wi-fi ▬ (notice required)

CRANLEIGH · Map 6 TQ03

The Richard Onslow

113-117 High St GU6 8AU ☎ 01483 274922
e-mail: hello@therichardonslow.co.uk
dir: *From A281 between Guildford & Horsham take B2130 to Cranleigh, pub in village centre*

A grand old tile-hung pub

In the heart of the village, this smart pub underwent a major refurbishment a few years ago, revealing its traditional character in the original brick inglenook and other carefully restored features while also benefiting from contemporary decor. Enjoy pints of ale from local independent breweries like Surrey Hills and take advantage of the fact that food is served all day starting with breakfast — to eat in or take away. The emphasis is firmly on seasonal produce, as much as possible being sourced locally. Just some of the options are deli boards, chargrilled steaks, the roast of the day and mains such as roasted monkfish fillet.

Open all day all wk Closed: 25 Dec **Bar Meals** L served all wk 12-6 D served all wk 6-10 Av main course £15 food served all day **Restaurant** L served all wk 12-6 D served all wk 6-10 Fixed menu price fr £12 Av 3 course à la carte fr £25 food served all day ⊕ PEACH PUBS ◀ Surrey Hills Shere Drop, Sharp's Doom Bar ⦿ Aspall. ♟ 16 **Facilities** Non-diners area ❀ (Bar Garden) ♦⊪ Children's portions Garden ⍲ Wi-fi ▬ (notice required)

DUNSFOLD
Map 6 TQ03

The Sun Inn

The Common GU8 4LE ☎ 01483 200242
e-mail: suninn@dunsfold.net
dir: *A281 through Shalford & Bramley, take B2130 to Godalming. Dunsfold on left after 2m*

Bags of traditional charm

A traditional 17th-century inn opposite the cricket green and village pond in a chocolate-box village, The Sun delivers a warm welcome, blazing fires and an array of real ales from the likes of Adnams, Harvey's and Sharp's. The home-made healthy eating dishes use produce from the inn's own vegetable garden. Typical starters include minestrone soup; crab and avocado salad; and nachos. Among the main courses you'll find Aberdeen Angus steakburgers; vegetarian spaghetti bolognese; and wholetail scampi and chips. Enjoy the quiz every Sunday evening, and look out for the special pie nights on Wednesdays.

Open all day all wk **Bar Meals** L served all wk 12-2.30 D served Mon-Sat 7-9.15, Sun 7-8.30 Av main course £8.95 **Restaurant** L served all wk 12-2.30 D served Mon-Sat 7-9.15, Sun 7-8.30 ⊕ PUNCH TAVERNS ◀ Sharp's Doom Bar, Harvey's Sussex, Adnams, Guest ales Ⓞ Westons Scrumpy. ♀ 10 **Facilities** Non-diners area ❖ (Bar Restaurant Garden) ♦♦ Children's menu Children's portions Garden ⋔ Parking Wi-fi ▭ (notice required)

EASHING
Map 6 SU94

The Stag on the River

Lower Eashing GU7 2QG ☎ 01483 421568
e-mail: bookings@stagonthereashing.co.uk
dir: *From A3 S'bound exit signed Eashing, 200yds over river bridge. Pub on right*

A good meeting place by the river

The river is the Wey, and this comfortable, well-appointed village inn on its banks takes full advantage, with a large beer garden and separate patio. Fixtures on handpump in the bar are Hogs Back TEA (Traditional English Ale) and Surrey Hills Shere Drop, named after a nearby village; others rotate. A seasonal menu might begin with fresh crab bruschetta in lime and chilli mayonnaise, or a charcuterie sharing board. Main courses include smoked haddock and prawn pie in spinach, bacon and mascarpone sauce; and supreme of chicken with dauphinoise potatoes.

Open all wk all day (ex Mon-Thu 3-5) Closed: 25 Dec ⊕ FREE HOUSE ◀ Hogs Back TEA, Surrey Hills Shere Drop, Guest ales. **Facilities** ❖ (Bar Garden) ♦♦ Children's menu Children's portions Garden Parking Wi-fi

EAST CLANDON
Map 6 TQ05

The Queens Head

The Street GU4 7RY ☎ 01483 222332
e-mail: mark.williams@redmistleisure.co.uk
dir: *4m E of Guildford on A246. Signed*

Smart village pub - eat and drink in or out

This bustling brick-built village pub close to the North Downs Way is a haven for ramblers and locals seeking the best local produce. Beer is courtesy of the nearby Surrey Hills Brewery, while the food majors on locally sourced seasonal produce including meat from a 100-acre working farm. A hearty plate of braised lamb shank with parsley mash, braised cabbage and rosemary jus will revive after a long winter walk, or share a fish board, including crayfish, Devon crab and smoked mackerel, in the tree-shaded garden.

Open all wk 12-3 6-11 (Sat 12-11 Sun 12-9) ⊕ FREE HOUSE ◀ Surrey Hills Shere Drop, Hogs Back TEA, Brakspear Oxford Gold, Shepherd Neame Spitfire, Sharp's Doom Bar. **Facilities** ♦♦ Children's menu Children's portions Garden Parking Wi-fi

EFFINGHAM
Map 6 TQ15

The Plough

Orestan Ln KT24 5SW ☎ 01372 458121
dir: *Between Guildford & Leatherhead on A246*

Hidden gem in the Surrey Hills

Smartly refurbished in December 2012 with neutral tones and a light and airy atmosphere, this pub probably dates from the mid-1870s, judging by the beamed interior. The Plough also acquired a beautiful orchard garden; there are plenty of tables in the garden and terrace, and Surrey Hills ramblers are often to be found here. Monthly-changing, freshly prepared contemporary and traditional British favourites include duck liver pâté; guinea fowl breast with fondant potato and root vegetable purée in a cider cream sauce; and sweet potato, courgette and red onion Stroganoff. Sunday roasts come with huge Yorkshire puds. The Plough is near Polesden Lacey, an opulent National Trust country house.

Open all wk 11.30-3 5.30-11 (Sun 12- 7) Closed: 25-26 Dec & 31 Dec eve **Bar Meals** L served Mon-Sat 12-2.30, Sun 12-5 D served Mon-Sat 7-10 Av main course £13.95 **Restaurant** L served Mon-Sat 12-2.30, Sun 12-5 D served Mon-Sat 7-10 ⊕ YOUNG'S ◀ Special & Winter Warmer, Wells Bombardier, Courage Directors, St Austell Tribute Ⓞ Westons Stowford Press. ♀ 16
Facilities Non-diners area ♦♦ Children's menu Children's portions Garden Parking Wi-fi

ELSTEAD
Map 6 SU94

The Woolpack

The Green, Milford Rd GU8 6HD ☎ 01252 703106
e-mail: info@woolpackelstead.co.uk
dir: *A3 S, take Milford exit, follow signs for Elstead on B3001*

Village local with an Italian flavour

Originally a wool exchange dating back to the 17th century, the attractive tile-hung Woolpack has been refurbished by new Italian owners, yet weaving shuttles and other artefacts relating to the wool industry remain appealing features, as do the open log fires, low beams, high-backed settles, and comfortable window seats. Cask-conditioned ales include local Hogs Back TEA and Ringwood Fortyniner. On the menu, starters such as smoked duck salad are followed by fish pie; rib-eye steak with chunky chips and peppercorn sauce; and broad bean, pea and leek risotto, plus there's a traditional bar and sandwich menu. The surrounding common land attracts ramblers galore, especially at lunchtime.

Open all wk 12-3 6-11 (Sun 12-10) **Bar Meals** L served Mon-Sat 12-3, Sun 12-8 D served Mon-Sat 6-9, Sun 12-8 Av main course £10 **Restaurant** L served Mon-Sat 12-3, Sun 12-8 D served Mon-Sat 6-9, Sun 12-8 Av 3 course à la carte fr £22 ⊕ PUNCH TAVERNS ◀ Ringwood Fortyniner, Hogs Back TEA, Sharp's Doom Bar Ⓞ Westons Stowford Press. ♀ **Facilities** Non-diners area ❖ (Bar Garden) ♦♦ Children's menu Children's portions Garden ⋔ Parking Wi-fi ▭ (notice required)

ENGLEFIELD GREEN
Map 6 SU97

The Fox and Hounds

Bishopsgate Rd TW20 0XU ☎ 01784 433098
e-mail: marketing@thefoxandhoundsrestaurant.com
dir: *With village green on left, left into Bishopsgate Rd*

Upmarket dining close to Windsor Great Park

Dating back to 1780, this pub is ideally situated next to the Bishopsgate entrance to Windsor Great Park in the village of Englefield Green. Enjoy a pint of Brakspear bitter in the stylish bar or enjoy a slap-up meal in the light and elegant conservatory restaurant. A starter of wild Cornish mussels with smoked bacon, cider and leek cream might be followed by twice cooked pork belly with caramelised pineapple, crispy squid and spring onion crushed potatoes. Leave room for dark chocolate and walnut tart or the tasting plate of puddings to share.

Open all day all wk 8am-11pm **Bar Meals** L served all wk 12-9.30 D served all wk 12-9.30 **Restaurant** L served all wk 12-3 D served Mon-Sat 6-9.30, Sun 6-9 ⊕ FREE HOUSE/ENTERPRISE INNS ◀ Brakspear Bitter, Brakspear Oxford Gold Ⓞ Symonds. ♀ 14 **Facilities** Non-diners area ❖ (Bar Garden) ♦♦ Children's menu Children's portions Garden ⋔ Parking Wi-fi ▭ (notice required)

Save on hotels. Book at **theAA.com/hotel**

SURREY 419 ENGLAND

The Bat and Ball Freehouse

Bat and Ball Lane, Boundstone, Farnham, Surrey GU10 4SA
www.thebatandball.co.uk

Tel: 01252 792108
E-mail: info@thebatandball.co.uk

The Bat and Ball Freehouse nestles in the bottom of the Bourne valley in Boundstone near Farnham. Over 150 years old, the Pub has a relaxed, rural feel, surrounded by woodland and wildlife, and is the focal point of 5 footpaths which connect to local villages. Customers can eat or drink throughout the Pub, patio area and the large south-facing garden (which backs onto the Bourne stream and has a popular children's play structure). All the food is cooked in-house and this is very much a pub that serves restaurant quality food and not a restaurant that sells beer! The bar area has both a traditional and modern style to it to provide for our differing customer tastes, both young and old, and we have a tempting selection of 6 well-kept Cask Ales.

FARNHAM — Map 5 SU84

The Bat & Ball Freehouse

PICK OF THE PUBS

See Pick of the Pubs on opposite page
See advert on page 419

The Spotted Cow at Lower Bourne

Bourne Grove, Lower Bourne GU10 3QT
☎ **01252 726541**
e-mail: thespottedcow@btinternet.com
web: www.thespottedcowpub.com
dir: *From Farnham town centre, cross rail line, onto B3001. Right into Tilford Rd, up hill, at lights straight on, Bourne Grove 3rd right*

Idyllic woodland and garden setting

Set in four acres of secluded, woodland-shaded grounds and two gardens, one of which is enclosed and especially suitable for young children, the Spotted Cow is a perfect place to unwind. Indulge in some of the great TEA beer from nearby Hogs Back Brewery and consider the ever-changing menu of tried-and-tested favourites, all made fresh on the premises. Sandwiches, jackets and ploughman's are on the bar lunch menu, while regularly-changing specials could include home-made spiced parsnip soup with chunky bread or breast of duck on crushed new potatoes with a port and cranberry sauce.

Open all wk 12-3 5.30-11 (Sat 12-11 Sun 12-10.30) **Bar Meals** L served Mon-Sat 12-2.30 D served Mon-Sat 6-9.15 **Restaurant** L served Mon-Sat 12-2.30, Sun 12-7 D served Mon-Sat 6-9.15 ⊕ FREE HOUSE ◀ Timothy Taylor Landlord, Hogs Back TEA, Otter ♂ Addlestones. **Facilities** Non-diners area ✿ (Bar Restaurant Garden) ♦♦ Children's portions Play area Garden ⊟ Parking Wi-fi

FETCHAM — Map 6 TQ15

The Bell

Bell Ln KT22 9ND ☎ **01372 372624**
e-mail: bellfetcham@youngs.co.uk
dir: *From A245 in Leatherhead take Waterway Rd (B2122). At rdbt 2nd exit into Guildford Rd (B2122). At mini rdbt right into Cobham Rd. Straight on at next 2 mini rdbts. Left into School Ln, left into Bell Ln*

Something for everyone whether inside or outdoors

The striking 1930s building in the pretty Mole Valley is one of Young's Brewery's 'flagship' dining pubs. Expect a smart terrace for alfresco drinking and dining, a light and airy wood-panelled restaurant, and a comfortable bar, replete with leather sofas and chairs. Using quality, seasonal produce, including vegetables from Secretts Farm and pork from Dingley Dell Farms, everything on the menus is cooked from scratch. The traditional British cuisine includes the likes roast Gressingham duck leg, and pan-fried sea bream on the main menu. Booking is essential for Sunday roasts.

Open all day all wk ⊕ YOUNG'S ◀ Special, Wells Bombardier, Guest ale ♂ Aspall. **Facilities** ♦♦ Children's portions Garden Parking Wi-fi

FOREST GREEN — Map 6 TQ14

The Parrot Inn

PICK OF THE PUBS

RH5 5RZ ☎ **01306 621339**
e-mail: drinks@theparrot.co.uk
dir: *B2126 from A29 at Ockley, signed Forest Green*

A 17th-century country pub in the Surrey Hills

Overlooking the village green and cricket pitch, this inviting, tile-hung country pub fulfils its external promise with a traditional bar straight out of a film-set, all low-beamed ceilings, flagstone floor and huge brass fireplace. French doors to the left lead to a sheltered, paved terrace; to the right is the restaurant. Diners should know that landlady Linda Gotto has a farm in Dorking, where she raises Middle White and Saddleback pigs, Shorthorn cattle and Dorset lamb, hogget and mutton, and her kitchen makes its own pies, preserves and charcuterie. Menu items employing these home-grown or home-made products are marked with a G, among them scallops with black pudding and sage; steak and ale crumble; lamb and chilli burger; and pork belly with cabbage, bacon and apple. Not so identified are cod, chorizo and white bean cassoulet; and chestnut and mushroom charlotte with butternut squash. An on-site farm shop opens daily.

Open all day all wk Closed: 25 Dec **Bar Meals** L served Mon-Sat 12-3, Sun 12-5 D served Mon-Sat 6-10 Av main course £14 **Restaurant** L served Mon-Sat 12-3, Sun 12-5 D served Mon-Sat 6-10 Av 3 course à la carte fr £26 ⊕ FREE HOUSE ◀ Ringwood Best Bitter & Old Thumper, Timothy Taylor Landlord, Dorking DB Number One, Young's. ♀ 14 **Facilities** Non-diners area ✿ (Bar Garden) ♦♦ Children's portions Garden ⊟ Parking Wi-fi

GUILDFORD — Map 6 SU94

The Boatman

Millbrook GU1 3XJ ☎ **01483 568024**
e-mail: contact@boatman-guildford.co.uk
web: www.boatman-guildford.co.uk
dir: *From Guildford take A281 towards Shalford. Pub on right*

Enjoyable food by the river

Set on the banks of the River Wey, this tranquil pub is just half a mile from Guildford and boasts lovely views across the river to parkland. Extensive terraced seating leads down to the water where you can enjoy a pint of Hogs Back or one of the 14 wines by the glass. Alternatively, there's a covered garden area if the weather is being unkind. Food served throughout the day centres on pub favourites: home-made fish pie; chicken stuffed with ham and smoked Swiss cheese; gammon, egg and chips; home-made vegetable lasagne.

Open all wk 12-11 (Sun 12-10.30) **Bar Meals** L served Mon-Sat 12-9.30, Sun 12-7 D served Mon-Sat 12-9.30, Sun 12-7 ⊕ FREE HOUSE ◀ Otter Bitter, Hogs Back TEA. ♀ 14 **Facilities** Non-diners area ♦♦ Children's menu Garden Parking Wi-fi

The Keystone

3 Portsmouth Rd GU2 4BL ☎ **01483 575089**
e-mail: drink@thekeystone.co.uk
dir: *From Guildford rail station turn right. Cross 2nd pedestrian crossing, downhill past Savills Estate Agents. Pub 200yds on left*

Relaxed atmosphere away from the busy High Street

Just off the bottom of Guildford's bustling High Street, this easy-going and unpretentious pub features squashy leather sofas, pub art and a secluded outdoor terrace. Along with real ales and cider, expect fairly priced, modern pub food including salads, steaks and pies. Main course options range from sweet potato, chickpea and red pepper curry to lime and coriander chicken breast with wild rice.

Open all day all wk 12-11 (Fri-Sat 12-12 Sun 12-5) Closed: 25-26 Dec, 1 Jan ⊕ PUNCH TAVERNS ◀ Wadworth 6X, Tiple fff Alton's Pride, Guest ales ♂ Westons Wyld Wood Organic, Addlestones. **Facilities** ♦♦ Children's menu Children's portions Garden Cider festival

Save on hotels. Book at **theAA.com/hotel**

SURREY 421 ENGLAND

PICK OF THE PUBS

The Bat & Ball Freehouse

FARNHAM   Map 5 SU84

15 Bat & Ball Ln, Boundstone GU10 4SA
☎ **01252 792108**
e-mail: info@thebatandball.co.uk
web: www.thebatandball.co.uk
dir: *From A31 (Farnham bypass) onto
A325 signed Birdworld. Left at Bengal
Lounge. At T-junct right, immediately
left into Sandrock Hill Rd. 0.25m left
into Upper Bourne Ln. Follow signs.*

Micro-brewery ales and internationally-inspired dishes

Tucked down a lane in a wooded valley
south of Farnham, this 150-year-old inn
is well worth seeking out – although it's
not that easy to find. Hops for the local
breweries in Farnham and Alton were
once grown in the valley, and originally
the hop-pickers were paid in the
building that eventually became the
pub. An enterprising tenant grasped the
business opportunity that presented
itself, and began to provide the pickers
with ale, relieving them of some of their
hard-earned cash! Very much a
community pub, the interior features
terracotta floors, oak beams, a roaring
fire and plenty of cricketing
memorabilia. The lovely garden has a
patio with picnic tables, a vine-topped
pergola and a children's play fort.
Expect several regularly changing cask-
conditioned ales, perhaps including
brews from local Bowman, Ballards,
Arundel and Weltons micro-breweries, a

good range of wines (eight by the glass)
and home-cooked food with
international flavours. Enjoy a sharing
platter laden with deli meats, pâté,
chutney, ricotta and bread; or a light
meal or starter of smoked salmon with
Asian-inspired coleslaw, tossed in
sesame, soy, ginger and coriander; or
Mexican nachos topped with crab meat,
salsa and cheese. The extensive choice
of main courses takes in rabbit madras
topped with crispy onions and served
with rice and naan; parsnip cakes with
warm giant couscous salad; creamy
smoked haddock and prawn fish pie;
and baked cod loin with slow-cooked
chorizo and a white bean, tomato and
garlic cassoulet. Don't miss the popular
Beer, Cider and Music Festival on the
second weekend in June.

Open all day all wk 11-11 (Sun
12-10.30) **Bar Meals** L served Mon-Sat
12-2.15, Sun 12-3 D served Mon-Sat
7-9.30, Sun 6-8.30 ⊕ FREE HOUSE
◀ Hogs Back TEA, Triple fff, Bowman,
Ballards, Andwell, Arundel, Weltons
Ŏ Westons Stowford Press, Aspall. ☘ 8
Facilities Non-diners area 🐾 ♟
Children's menu Children's portions
Play area Family room Garden ⋒ Beer
festival Parking Wi-fi

HASCOMBE
Map 6 TQ03

The White Horse

The Street GU8 4JA ☎ 01483 208258
e-mail: pub@whitehorsehascombe.co.uk
dir: *From Godalming take B2130. Pub on left 0.5m after Hascombe*

Village pub with many walks around

Surrounded by prime walking country, this 16th-century pub's flower-filled garden is a summer stunner. Other selling points include its traditional interior, impressive tally of real ales and ciders, popular family room and ample outdoor seating; then there's the high standard of food, with meats coming from organic pedigree breeds. A meal might take in ribollita (a rich Tuscan soup); Angus beef and ale pie, curly kale and chips; or baked cod, chickpea and chorizo stew; and lemon polenta cake.

Open all day all wk 11-11 (Fri-Sat 11am-1am Sun 11-10.30) Bar Meals L served Mon-Fri 12-3, Sat 12-10, Sun 12-4 D served Mon-Fri 6-10, Sat 12-10, Sun 6-9 Restaurant L served Mon-Fri 12-3, Sat 12-10, Sun 12-4 D served Mon-Fri 6-10, Sat 12-10, Sun 6-9 ⊕ FREE HOUSE ◀ Sharp's Doom Bar, Hogs Back TEA, Harvey's, Otter, Guest ales ♂ Hogan's. ♀ 11
Facilities Non-diners area ♥ (Bar Garden) ♦ Children's menu Children's portions Play area Family room Garden ⌂ Parking Wi-fi ▭ (notice required)

HASLEMERE
Map 6 SU93

The Wheatsheaf Inn ★★★ INN

Grayswood Rd, Grayswood GU27 2DE ☎ 01428 644440
e-mail: thewheatsheaf@aol.com
dir: *Exit A3 at Milford, A286 to Haslemere. Grayswood approx 7.5m N*

Woodland-edge setting in the Surrey Hills

A most distinctive part hang-tiled Edwardian pub with enough vegetation to give Kew a run for its money. The hanging-basket festooned verandah, creeper-covered pergola and patio and colourful garden just invite a lingering visit with a pint of Langham Hip Hop bitter to hand, relaxing after a walk in the enfolding Surrey Hills beloved by Tennyson. There's opportunity to stay overnight here in seven comfy rooms so creating an added excuse to engage with a wide-ranging menu of pub classics and thoughtful specials. Kick in on warmed brie with Cumberland sauce, leaving room for slow-braised pork belly on colcannon with cider and sage gravy.

Open all wk 11-3 6-11 (Sun 12-3 7-10.30) Bar Meals L served all wk 12-2 D served all wk 7-9.45 Restaurant L served all wk 12-2 D served all wk 7-9.45 ⊕ FREE HOUSE ◀ Fuller's London Pride, Sharp's Doom Bar, Greene King Abbot Ale, Langham Hip Hop ♂ Aspall.
Facilities Non-diners area ♥ (Bar Garden) ♦ Children's menu Children's portions Garden Parking Wi-fi Rooms 7

LEIGH
Map 6 TQ24

The Plough

Church Rd RH2 8NJ ☎ 01306 611348
e-mail: sarah@theploughleigh.wanadoo.co.uk
dir: *Telephone for directions*

Ramblers' retreat in the Surrey countryside

Some parts of this appealing, architecturally mixed building are known to date from the 15th century, whilst the popular locals' bar with its fire and traditional pub games is somewhat younger. Situated by a large green bordered by old houses and the medieval church, The Plough today is a cracking village pub. Beers from the Hall & Woodhouse list slake the thirst of walkers enjoying exploring the Surrey Weald, whilst the popular pub grub menu of bangers and mash or fish and chips is supplemented by chicken fillet, Black Forest ham or lamb steak dishes.

Open all wk 11-11 (Sun 12-11) Bar Meals food served all day Restaurant food served all day ⊕ HALL & WOODHOUSE ◀ Badger Dorset Best, Tanglefoot, K&B Sussex ♂ Symonds Scrumpy Jack. ♀ 11
Facilities Non-diners area ♥ (Bar Garden) ♦ Children's menu Children's portions Garden ⌂ Parking Wi-fi

The Seven Stars

PICK OF THE PUBS

Bunce Common Rd, Dawes Green RH2 8NP ☎ 01306 611254
e-mail: James@7starleigh.co.uk
dir: *S of A25 (Dorking to Reigate road)*

Timeless tavern with high quality food

Tucked away in the rural southern reaches of the Mole Valley, the charm of this early 17th-century, tile-hung tavern is enhanced by the absence of games machines, TV screens and piped music. The older bar is centred on an inglenook fireplace at one end and a log-burning stove at the other. It's a peaceful spot to enjoy a pint of Young's or Fuller's London Pride real ale and a glass of Aspall cider. The restaurant has its own bar, which is always available to use when open. The food served is of high quality and is prepared by a team of three chefs using local produce whenever possible. At the front is a garden for those with a drink, at the side a patio and garden for diners, and there's plenty of parking space.

Open all wk 12-11 (Sun 12-10.30) Bar Meals L served Mon-Thu 12-2.30, Fri-Sat 12-3, Sun 12-6 D served Mon-Thu 6-9, Fri-Sat 6.30-9.30 Restaurant L served Mon-Thu 12-2.30, Fri-Sat 12-3, Sun 12-6 D served Mon-Thu 6-9, Fri-Sat 6.30-9.30 ⊕ PUNCH TAVERNS ◀ Fuller's London Pride, Young's, Sharp's Doom Bar ♂ Aspall. ♀ 12
Facilities Non-diners area ♥ (Bar Garden) ♦ Children's portions Garden ⌂ Parking

LINGFIELD
Map 6 TQ34

Hare and Hounds

PICK OF THE PUBS

See Pick of the Pubs on opposite page

LONG DITTON
Map 6 TQ16

The Ditton

64 Ditton Hill Rd KT6 5JD ☎ 020 8339 0785
e-mail: goodfood@theditton.co.uk
dir: *Telephone for directions*

Community local in quiet suburb not far from Hampton Court

A 1930s building, it looks as though it was once two semi-detached houses but, whatever its origin, it has become a community local, with beers from Sharp's and Black Sheep. Looking over a typical menu, you'll find starters like smoked haddock Scotch egg on mixed leaves with a curried mayo or Parma ham, fig and goats' cheese mixed leaf salad; followed by pan-fried lamb's liver on mash with fried onions, bacon and cabbage; Suffolk belly pork on dauphinoise potatoes with sugar snap peas and roast apple; or pub classics like fish and chips or chicken curry. Summer barbecues are held in the large beer garden, and there's also a skittle alley with league nights every Monday.

Open all day all wk 12-11 Bar Meals L served Mon-Sat 12-9, Sun 12-5 D served Mon-Sat 12-9, Sun 12-5 food served all day Restaurant L served Mon-Sat 12-9, Sun 12-5 D served Mon-Sat 12-9, Sun 12-5 food served all day ⊕ ENTERPRISE INNS ◀ Sharp's Doom Bar, Black Sheep Best Bitter, Otter Bitter. ♀ 10
Facilities Non-diners area ♥ (Bar Garden) ♦ Children's menu Children's portions Play area Garden ⌂ Beer festival Parking Wi-fi ▭ (notice required)

MICKLEHAM
Map 6 TQ15

King William IV

Byttom Hill RH5 6EL ☎ 01372 372590
dir: *M25 junct 9, A24 signed Dorking, pub just before Mickleham*

Just the place after a long walk nearby

The King Billy, built in 1790 for local estate workers, has a panelled snug and larger back bar with an open fire, cast-iron tables and grandfather clock. The terraced garden is ideal for summer socialising and offers panoramic views of the Mole Valley, where earlier you might have been walking. Hogs Back TEA and Shere Drop are in the bar, with food such as tournedos Rossini; Thai-spiced free-range chicken; and Scottish fillet steak.

Open all wk 11.30-3 6-11 (Sun 12-10.30) ⊕ FREE HOUSE ◀ Hogs Back TEA, Surrey Hills Shere Drop ♂ Westons Stowford Press. Facilities ♦ Children's portions Garden Parking

Save on hotels. Book at **theAA.com/hotel**

SURREY 423 ENGLAND

PICK OF THE PUBS

Hare and Hounds

LINGFIELD　　　Map 6 TQ34

Common Rd RH7 6BZ ☎ 01342 832351
e-mail:
info@hareandhoundspublichouse.co.uk
web:
www.hareandhoundspublichouse.co.uk
dir: *From A22 follow Lingfield
Racecourse signs into Common Rd*

Charming and eccentric country pub with excellent menus

Not far from Lingfield Park racecourse, this 18th-century, pale blue-washed, country pub has adopted the fashionable shabby-chic look for its interior, all mismatched furniture, shelves full of old books, a stone rabbit sitting on what looks like an old packing case... but it's a style that works. The pub has made a good name for its modern and classic food, no doubt partly attributable to the fact that chef and owner Eric Payet incorporates into the menus tastes and flavours from his Indian Ocean island childhood home of Réunion. Further inspiration comes from Eric and his wife Tracy's many years of working in restaurants throughout France and the UK. Using local produce where possible, a meal may start with rice wine-cured mackerel with salted red cabbage and pink ginger gel; or warm stuffed ballotine of quail, Earl Grey tea, prune and hazelnut. This might be followed by fish and chips with pea tartare and curry salt; roast stone

bass fillet with confit celery, crosnes, chorizo powder and lemon curd; or braised blade of beef, crushed swede and confit potato, red wine jus and poached shallot. Among the possible ways to finish are rhubarb trifle with gingerbread mousse and custard ice cream; or warm apple and custard doughnut with blackberry and cider sorbet. Blackboards list light lunches, pub classics and brunch – perhaps croque monsieur, or indeed, croque madame; and baked egg coccotte. On a sunny day, the split-level decked garden is a good spot for a pint of Harvey's Sussex bitter, Doom Bar, or a glass of wine selected by Nick Hillman's merchant vintners' company in the village.

Open all day Closed: 1-5 Jan, Sun eve
Bar Meals L served Mon-Sat 12-2.30,
Sun 12-3 D served Mon-Sat 7-9.30
Restaurant L served Mon-Sat 12-2.30,
Sun 12-3 D served Mon-Sat 7-9.30
⊕ PUNCH TAVERNS ◼ Harvey's Sussex,
Guinness, Sharp's Doom Bar ♂ Westons
Stowford Press. ♀ 12 **Facilities** Non-
diners area ♦♦ Children's portions
Garden ♫ Parking

MICKLEHAM *continued*

The Running Horses

Old London Rd RH5 6DU ☎ 01372 372279
e-mail: info@therunninghorses.co.uk
dir: M25 junct 9, A24 towards Dorking. Left signed
Mickleham/B2209

Lovely country inn below Box Hill

Experts agree that the inn, now owned by Brakspear, was
built in the 16th century. It had an important role as a
coaching inn, but it also sheltered highwaymen - a tiny
ladder leading to the roof space was discovered during
alterations. The inn acquired its name in 1825 after two
horses, Colonel and Cadland, running in the Derby at
Epsom, passed the post together. They appear on the inn
sign, and the bars are named after them. Food ranges
from lunchtime sandwiches and ploughman's to
tandoori-marinated chicken; classic fish pie; and steak,
Guinness and mushroom pie.

Open all day all wk 12-11 (Sun 12-10.30) Closed: 25, 26
& 31 Dec eve, 1 Jan eve **Bar Meals** L served Mon-Fri
12-2.30, Sat-Sun 12-3 D served Mon-Sat 7-9.30, Sun
6.30-9 Av main course £15.95 **Restaurant** L served Mon-
Fri 12-2.30, Sat-Sun 12-3 D served Mon-Sat 7-9.30, Sun
6.30-9 Av 3 course à la carte fr £29.50 ⊕ BRAKSPEAR
◫ Fuller's London Pride, Ringwood ♻ Symonds. ♟ 9
Facilities Non-diners area ♣ (Bar Garden) ◈ Children's
portions Garden ⇌ Wi-fi

The Surrey Oaks

Parkgate Rd RH5 5DZ ☎ 01306 631200
e-mail: ken@surreyoaks.co.uk
dir: From A24 follow signs to Newdigate, at T-junct turn
left, pub 1m on left

Excellent beers in lovely country pub

Creepers wind up this partly hang-tiled little pub set
amidst copses at the village edge in deepest Surrey. It's
over 440 years old; until the 1850s it was the
wheelwright's shop, but today's visitors can build muscle
playing boules in the large garden or alley skittles. Loads
of character invests the interior, including a fine
inglenook and flagged floors in the bars. Regular beer
festivals complement the enticing, ever-changing
selection of real ales. Booking is highly recommended for
both restaurant and bar meals here, where enticing
dishes on the specials board may include pork fillet in
pear and cider sauce.

Open all wk 11.30-2.30 5.30-11 (Sat 11.30-3 6-11 Sun
12-9) **Bar Meals** L served Mon-Sat 12-2, Sun 12-2.30
D served Tue-Sat 6.30-9.30 **Restaurant** L served Mon-Sat
12-2, Sun 12-2.30 D served Tue-Sat 6.30-9.30
⊕ ADMIRAL TAVERNS ◫ Harvey's Sussex Best, Surrey
Hills Ranmore Ale, Guest ales ♻ Moles Black Rat,
Westons Country Perry. **Facilities** Non-diners area ♣ (Bar
Garden) ◈ Children's menu Children's portions Play area
Garden ⇌ Beer festival Parking Wi-fi ⇌ (notice
required)

The Inn on the Pond

Nutfield Marsh Rd RH1 4EU ☎ 01737 643000
e-mail: enquiries@theinnonthepondnutfield.co.uk
dir: From A25 E from Redhill, turn left after Nutfield
village & down Church Hill. 1m on left

Overlooking a conservation area

Part of the select Cross Oak Inns group, the beautifully
appointed Inn on the Pond lives up to its name – it
stands next to a duck pond, and the village cricket pitch
and overlooks Nutfield Marsh Nature Reserve (monthly
wildlife walks). Time your arrival for sunset and you can
savour a pint of Hogs Back TEA on the front terrace and
watch the sun sink into the Surrey Hills. Inside, there are
log fires, a contemporary decor and modern pub menus.

Open all wk 12-3 5.30-11 (all day Sat-Sun in summer)
Closed: 25 Dec ⊕ FREE HOUSE/CROSS OAK INNS ◫ Hogs
Back TEA, Sharp's Doom Bar, Pilgrim Progress, Tonbridge
Blonde Ambition ♻ Westons Stowford Press.
Facilities ♣ (Bar Garden) ◈ Children's menu Children's
portions Garden Parking

Bryce's at The Old School House ◉
PICK OF THE PUBS

RH5 5TH ☎ 01306 627430
e-mail: fish@bryces.co.uk
dir: 8m S of Dorking on A29

Championing seafood at a smart country inn

This Grade II listed former boarding school dates back to
1750, and owner Bill Bryce has been at the helm for over
20 years now. He is passionate about fresh fish and
offers a huge range, despite the land-locked location in
rural Surrey. These days, it's more of a restaurant than a
pub, although there is a bar with its own menu and a
range of real ales including Horsham Bitter. The dishes
on the restaurant menu are nearly all fish, with a few
specials for non-piscivores. Options to start include
grilled Cornish sardines, garlic and lemon butter; and
steamed mussels à la creme. Main courses include grilled
Scottish halibut, creamed cabbage, bacon and pinenuts;
or red snapper fillet, bok choi, ginger and sesame
dressing. Look to the blackboard for the home-made
desserts. You can also order takeaway fish and chips at
the bar.

Open 12-3 6-11 Closed: 25-26 Dec, 1 Jan, Sun pm Nov,
Jan-Feb **Bar Meals** L served all wk 12-2.30 D served all
wk 6-9.30 **Restaurant** L served all wk 12-2.30 D served
all wk 7-9.30 ⊕ FREE HOUSE ◫ Fuller's London Pride,
Weltons Horsham Bitter, John Smith's Extra Smooth. ♟ 15
Facilities Non-diners area ♣ (Bar) ◈ Children's portions
⇌ Parking ⇌ (notice required)

The Kings Arms Inn

Stane St RH5 5TS ☎ 01306 711224
e-mail: enquiries@thekingsarmsockley.co.uk
dir: M25 junct 9, A24 through Dorking towards Horsham,
A29 to Ockley

A warm welcome and lots of charm

Welcoming log fires, a priest hole, a friendly ghost and an
award-winning garden are just a few charms of this oak-
beamed 16th-century inn. In the picturesque village of
Ockley and overlooked by the tower of Leith Hill, it's an
ideal setting in which to enjoy a pint and wholesome food
after climbing the hill. Choices prepared by chef include
sandwiches, a Greek meze sharing plate, pie of the day;
and more adventurous dishes such as chicken liver
parfait followed by confit of duck with château potatoes,
spiced braised red cabbage, Morello cherries and orange
sauce.

Open all wk 12-3 6-11 ⊕ FREE HOUSE/CROSS OAK INNS
◫ WJ King Horsham Best, Sharp's Doom Bar, Hogs Back
TEA ♻ Westons Stowford Press. **Facilities** ◈ Children's
menu Children's portions Garden Parking Wi-fi

Fox & Hounds

Tilburstow Hill Rd RH9 8LY ☎ 01342 893474
e-mail: info@foxandhounds.org.uk
dir: 4m from M25 junct 6

Haunted country pub serving home-cooked food

Dating in part to 1368, the Fox & Hounds has been a pub
since 1601, and it is said that 17th-century pirate and
smuggler John Trenchman haunts the building; he died in
the building after being fatally wounded in an ambush
nearby. A large inglenook in the restaurant and a real fire
in the lower bar add to the old-world charm. Food-wise
there's plenty to choose from, including a starter of
crayfish and smoked salmon salad; jackets and
sandwiches; and mains ranging from applewood-smoked
ham to vegetarian pasta bake and whole sea bass. The
large garden offers rural views and home-grown
vegetables; marquees are erected in summer for alfresco
dining.

Open all day all wk **Bar Meals** L served all wk 12-9
D served all wk 12-9 food served all day **Restaurant** L
served all wk 12-9 D served all wk 12-9 food served all
day ⊕ GREENE KING ◫ Abbot Ale & IPA, Guest ales. ♟ 12
Facilities Non-diners area ♣ (Bar Garden) ◈ Children's
menu Children's portions Garden ⇌ Parking ⇌ (notice
required)

Save on hotels. Book at **theAA.com/hotel**

SURREY **425** ENGLAND

STOKE D'ABERNON · Map 6 TQ15

The Old Plough NEW

2 Station Rd KT11 3BN ☎ 01932 866419
e-mail: info@oldploughcobham.co.uk
dir: From A245 into Station Rd. Pub on corner

Friendly, smart and independently-owned community pub

A four-month overhaul in 2012 revitalised this 300-year-old pub, where Sherlock Holmes and Dr Watson 'stayed' in one of Sir Arthur Conan Doyle's novels. The makeover left the charming bar untouched, but happily gone is the old conservatory, replaced by a light, bright restaurant overlooking the garden. An extended and re-equipped kitchen is now capable of preparing fresh food all day (until 5.30pm in the bar), with main courses such as pan-fried calves' liver with crispy bacon; Scotch fillet steak with Blacksticks Blue cheese glaze; French fish stew; and vegetarian curry. Children are welcome in the restaurant area until 7.30pm.

Open all day all wk **Bar Meals** Av main course £13 food served all day **Restaurant** Fixed menu price fr £27.95 Av 3 course à la carte fr £22 food served all day ⊕ FULLER'S ◀ London Pride, Surrey Hills Shere Drop, George Gale & Co Seafarers Ö Aspall. ♟ 18 **Facilities** Non-diners area ♣ (Bar Garden) ♦♦ Children's menu Children's portions Garden ♬ Parking Wi-fi ▭

TILFORD · Map 5 SU84

The Duke of Cambridge

Tilford Rd GU10 2DD ☎ 01252 792236
e-mail: amy.corstin@redmistleisure.co.uk
dir: From Guildford on A31 towards Farnham follow Tongham, Seale, Runfield signs. Right at end, follow Eashing signs. Left at end, 1st right (signed Tilford St). Over bridge, 1st left, 0.5m

Family-friendly pub offering wholesome local fodder

Set among pine trees with a lovely garden and terrace, this attractive pub in the Surrey countryside welcomes all, children and dogs included. Expect Surrey ales and hearty local food with much of the seasonal produce on the menu coming from the neighbouring farm. Typical of the menu are deli boards; pan-seared rump of venison; pesto and butternut squash tagliatelle; and bangers and mash. In May fundraising for a local charity is the excuse for a beer and music festival. The Garden Bar & Grill is a summer feature (weather permitting), as well as garden parties and hog roasts.

Open all wk 11-3 5-11 (Sat 11-11 Sun 12-10.30) Closed: 25 Dec & 31 Dec eve **Restaurant** L served Mon-Fri 12-2.30, Sat 12-3.30, Sun 12-8.30 D served Mon-Thu 6-9, Fri-Sat 6-9.30, Sun 12-8.30 ⊕ FREE HOUSE/RED MIST LEISURE LTD ◀ Hogs Back TEA, Ringwood Fortyniner, Surrey Hills Shere Drop Ö Thatchers Gold. ♟ 15 **Facilities** ♣ (Bar Garden) ♦♦ Children's menu Children's portions Play area Garden ♬ Beer festival Parking Wi-fi

WEST CLANDON · Map 6 TQ05

The Onslow Arms NEW

The Street GU4 7TE ☎ 01483 222447
e-mail: info@onslowarmsclandon.co.uk
dir: On A247, S of railway line

Old favourite revived as a smart community local

For decades this 17th-century pub in affluent West Clandon operated more as a fine dining French restaurant than pub. Following a period of closure, new owners have spruced the old pub up and restored it as a smart community pub, where drinkers and diners are equally welcome. Come for pints of local Shere Drop ale in the informal bar, replete with squashy sofas in front of a blazing log fire, newspapers to peruse, and free Wi-fi. Equally pubby, food is served all day and throughout the pub, the varied lunchtime/afternoon menu offering crab, spring onion sandwiches, devilled kidneys, a gourmet burger, and fish stew. In the evening, settle into the beamed and wood-floored restaurant for a fish sharing board, rump steak with all the trimmings, and baked vanilla cheesecake.

Open all day all wk **Bar Meals** Av main course £13 food served all day **Restaurant** Fixed menu price fr £27.95 Av 3 course à la carte fr £22 food served all day ⊕ FREE HOUSE ◀ Surrey Hills Shere Drop, Sharp's Cornish Coaster, Hogs Back TEA Ö Westons Stowford Press. ♟ 18 **Facilities** Non-diners area ♣ (Bar Garden) ♦♦ Children's menu Children's portions Garden ♬ Parking Wi-fi ▭

WEST END · Map 6 SU96

The Inn @ West End

PICK OF THE PUBS

42 Guildford Rd GU24 9PW ☎ 01276 858652
e-mail: greatfood@the-inn.co.uk
dir: On A322 towards Guildford. 3m from M3 junct 3, just beyond Gordon Boys rdbt

Gastro-pub going from strength to strength

Gerry and Ann Price have created an establishment that out-manoeuvres many a competitor with weekly fish nights, monthly quizzes and special events linked to their expanding wine business. But this doesn't preclude anyone from simply enjoying a pint of Exmoor or Fuller's London Pride with the newspaper in the bar; on a fine evening the clematis-hung terrace overlooking the garden and boules pitch is a blissful spot. The modern interior is open plan with wooden floors, yellow walls, tasteful checks, crisp linen-clothed tables and an open fire. The kitchen team continues to make great use of the pub's fruit and vegetable garden in the creation of seasonal dishes. Organic Saddleback pork pâté with apple and walnut salad could precede a casserole of slowly cooked game with juniper, herbs and red wine. Home-made desserts such as rice pudding with caramelised apples round things off nicely.

Open all wk 11-3 5-11 (Sat 11-11 Sun 12-10.30) **Bar Meals** L served Mon-Sat 12-2.30, Sun 12-3 D served Mon-Sat 6-9.30, Sun 6-9 **Restaurant** L served Mon-Sat 12-2.30, Sun 12-3 D served Mon-Sat 6-9.30, Sun 6-9 ⊕ FREE HOUSE ◀ Fuller's London Pride, Exmoor, George Gale & Co Seafarers Ö Aspall. ♟ 15 **Facilities** Non-diners area ♣ (Bar Garden) Children's portions Garden ♬ Beer festival Parking Wi-fi

WEST HORSLEY · Map 6 TQ05

The King William IV

PICK OF THE PUBS

83 The Street KT24 6BG ☎ 01483 282318
e-mail: info@kingwilliam4th.com
dir: Off A246 (Leatherhead to Guildford road)

Relaxed and homely atmosphere in leafy Surrey

Named in honour of the monarch who relaxed England's brewing laws, this popular gastro-pub is situated in a leafy Surrey village. The business was started by a miller, Edmund Collins, who knocked two cottages together to create an alehouse. Many of the original Georgian features have been preserved, but there is also an airy conservatory restaurant and a large garden and terrace to the rear, with colourful tubs and floral baskets. It's popular with walkers and is close to the Royal Horticultural Society's Wisley Gardens. Local beers include Shere Drop and Courage Directors, plus a guest ale of the month, and a dozen wines are offered by the glass. The well-priced menu ranges from burgers and fish pie to platters, oven-baked salmon fillet and rump steak. Leave room for banoffee pie, chocolate fudge cake or crème brûlée.

Open all day all wk 11.30am-mdnt (Sun 12-10.30) **Bar Meals** L served all wk 12-3 D served Mon-Fri 6-9, Sat all day **Restaurant** L served all wk 12-3 D served Mon-Fri 6-9, Sat all day ⊕ ENTERPRISE INNS ◀ Surrey Hills Shere Drop, Courage Best & Directors, Sharp's Doom Bar, Greene King Ruddles, Guest ales. ♟ 12 **Facilities** Non-diners area ♣ (Bar Garden) ♦♦ Children's menu Children's portions Family room Garden ♬ Parking Wi-fi ▭

WINDLESHAM — Map 6 SU96

The Half Moon

Church Rd GU20 6BN ☎ 01276 473329
e-mail: c@sturt.tv
dir: *M3 junct 3, A322 follow Windlesham signs into New Rd; right at T-junct into Church Rd, pub on right*

Old-fashioned values and friendly service

Family-owned since 1909, Helga and Conrad Sturt's slate-floored, low-beamed, 17th-century free house offers the traditional country pub experience, including locally brewed Hogs Back real ale and Lilley's Bee Sting pear cider from Somerset. There's plenty of choice at lunchtime, while dinner options include Cumberland sausage with creamed potatoes, crispy leeks and onion jus; grilled fillet of sea bass with spicy tomato and king prawn sauce; ricotta, spinach and wild mushroom cannelloni; and local game in season. Go past the patio terrace into the well-kept beer garden with a children's play area. Check with the pub for beer festival dates.

Open 11-3 5-11 Closed: Sun after 7pm **Bar Meals** L served all wk 12-2.15 D served Mon-Sat 6-9.15 Av main course £10-£15 **Restaurant** L served all wk 12-2.15 D served Mon-Sat 6-9.15 Fixed menu price fr £15 Av 3 course à la carte fr £22 ⊕ FREE HOUSE ◀ Sharp's, Theakston, Fuller's, Timothy Taylor, Hogs Back, Palmers, Dark Star ♂ Lilley's Bee Sting Pear, Westons Old Rosie. ♟ 10 **Facilities** ♣ (Bar Garden) ♦ Children's menu Children's portions Play area Garden ⌖ Beer festival Parking Wi-fi ▄▄ (notice required)

SUSSEX, EAST

ALCISTON — Map 6 TQ50

Rose Cottage Inn

PICK OF THE PUBS

BN26 6UW ☎ 01323 870377
e-mail: ian@alciston.freeserve.co.uk
dir: *Off A27 between Eastbourne & Lewes*

Home-cooked food in a pretty cottage

Expect a warm welcome at this traditional village pub, housed in a 17th-century flint cottage complete with roses round the door and a lovely front garden. At the foot of the South Downs, ramblers will find it a good base for long walks in unspoilt countryside, especially along the old traffic-free coach road to the south. With its oak beams, and sloping walls and ceilings, the inn has been in the same family for over 40 years, and is well known for its good, home-cooked food, including organic vegetables and local meats, poultry and game. You might choose from the wide selection of fish, or opt for lamb casserole or rabbit and bacon pie from the daily specials. Classic pub dishes, salads and light bites are also available. When in season, fresh mussels are delivered from Scotland every Friday, and are then cooked in French or Italian style. The inn sells a number of items from local suppliers for customers to buy, including honey and eggs.

Open all wk 11.30-3 6.30-11 Closed: 25-26 Dec **Bar Meals** L served all wk 12-2 D served all wk 7-9.30 **Restaurant** L served all wk 12-2 D served all wk 7-9.30 ⊕ FREE HOUSE ◀ Harvey's Sussex Best Bitter, Dark Star ♂ Biddenden. ♟ 8 **Facilities** Non-diners area ♣ (Bar Garden) Garden Parking Wi-fi

ALFRISTON — Map 6 TQ50

George Inn

High St BN26 5SY ☎ 01323 870319
e-mail: info@thegeorge-alfriston.com
dir: *Telephone for directions*

Period inn in a lovely location

First licensed to sell beer as far back as 1397, this splendid Grade II listed flint and half-timbered inn is set in a picturesque village with the South Downs Way passing its front door. The heavy oak beams and ancient inglenook fireplace add plenty of character to the bar, whilst the kitchen serves delights such as rustic boards to share; crayfish, crab and salmon tian; grilled sardines with a rocket, red pepper and tomato salad; traditional coq-au-vin with mashed potatoes and vegetables and double-baked pistachio cheesecake with cherry compôte and crème anglaise to finish. A network of smugglers' tunnels leads from the pub's cellars.

Open all day all wk Closed: 25-26 Dec **Bar Meals** L served Sun-Thu 12-9, Fri-Sat 12-10 D served Sun-Thu 12-9, Fri-Sat 12-10 food served all day **Restaurant** L served Sun-Thu 12-9, Fri-Sat 12-10 D served Sun-Thu 12-9, Fri-Sat 12-10 food served all day ⊕ GREENE KING ◀ Abbot Ale, Hardys & Hansons Olde Trip, Dark Star Hophead ♂ Aspall.

♟ 9 **Facilities** Non-diners area ♣ (Bar Restaurant Garden) ♦ Children's menu Children's portions Garden ⌖ Wi-fi ▄▄

ASHBURNHAM PLACE — Map 6 TQ61

Ash Tree Inn

Brownbread St TN33 9NX ☎ 01424 892104
dir: *From Eastbourne take A271 at Boreham Bridge towards Battle. Next left, follow pub signs*

Popular country pub that welcomes walkers

Deep in the Sussex countryside on the delightfully named Brownbread Street, the 400-year-old Ash Tree is a hub of local activity, hosting everything from quiz nights to cricket club meetings. It boasts a warm and bright interior, replete with stripped wooden floors, four fireplaces (two of them inglenooks), exposed beams and a friendly local atmosphere. Expect to find Harvey's ale on tap and traditional home-cooked meals such as breaded tiger prawns with sweet chilli dip; or soup of the day followed by steak-and-kidney pudding; tagliatelle with bacon, mushroom and garlic cream sauce; or ham, free-range eggs and chips. Walkers and dogs are welcome.

Open 12-4 7-11 (Sat-Sun 11.30am-mdnt) Closed: Mon pm (Sun pm winter) **Bar Meals** L served Tue-Sun 12-3 D served Tue-Sat 7-9 **Restaurant** L served Tue-Sun 12-3 D served Tue-Sat 7-9 ⊕ FREE HOUSE ◀ Harvey's Sussex Best Bitter, Guest ales ♂ Westons Stowford Press. **Facilities** Non-diners area ♣ (Bar Restaurant Garden) ♦ Children's portions Garden ⌖ Parking Wi-fi ▄▄ (notice required)

BERWICK — Map 6 TQ50

The Cricketers Arms

PICK OF THE PUBS

BN26 6SP ☎ 01323 870469
e-mail: pbthecricketers@aol.com
dir: *Off A27 between Polegate & Lewes, follow signs for Berwick Church*

Popular with South Downs walkers

Previously two farmworkers' cottages dating from the 16th century, this flintstone building was an alehouse for 200 years, until around 50 years ago Harveys of Lewes, Sussex's oldest brewery, bought it and turned it into a 'proper' pub. The Grade II listed building, in beautiful cottage gardens, is close to many popular walks - the South Downs Way runs along the crest of the chalk scarp between here and the sea. Three beamed, music-free rooms with stone floors and open fires are simply furnished with old pine furniture. A short menu of home-made food includes king prawns in chilli oil, and peppered mackerel with horseradish mayonnaise as starters. Their home-made burger is an ever-popular main course, as are ham, egg and chips; and fresh dressed crab salad. Nearby is Charleston Farmhouse, the country rendezvous of the Bloomsbury Group of writers, painters and intellectuals, and venue for an annual literary festival.

Save on hotels. Book at **theAA.com/hotel**

SUSSEX, EAST 427 ENGLAND

Open all wk Mon-Fri 11-3 6-11 Sat 11-11 Sun 12-9 (May-Sep Mon-Sat 11-11 Sun 12-10.30) Closed: 25 Dec **Bar Meals** L served Oct-Apr Mon-Fri 12-2.15, Sat-Sun 12-9, May-Sep all wk 12-9 D served Oct-Apr Mon-Fri 6.15-9, Sat-Sun 12-9, May-Sep all wk 12-9 Av main course £10 **Restaurant** L served Oct-Apr Mon-Fri 12-2.15, Sat-Sun 12-9, May-Sep all wk 12-9 D served Oct-Apr Mon-Fri 6.15-9, Sat-Sun 12-9, May-Sep all wk 12-9 ⊕ HARVEYS OF LEWES ◀ Sussex Best Bitter, Armada Ale Ď Thatchers. �🍷 12 **Facilities** 🐾 (Bar Garden) ɨ📍 Children's portions Family room Garden 🗚 Parking 🚌 (notice required)

BLACKBOYS   **Map 6 TQ52**

The Blackboys Inn

Lewes Rd TN22 5LG ☎ 01825 890283
e-mail: info@theblackboys.co.uk
dir: *From A22 at Uckfield take B2102 towards Cross in Hand. Or from A267 at Esso service station in Cross in Hand take B2102 towards Uckfield. Village 1.5m*

Hamlet pub known for its Sunday roasts

This inn was named after the local charcoal-burners, or the soot-caked 'blackboys', with whom the 14th-century pub was once a favourite. Today's well-scrubbed visitors enjoy beers from Harvey's of Lewes in one of two bars, and in the restaurant, vegetables from the garden, game from local shoots, and fish from Rye and Hastings. Typical dishes include grilled mackerel, slow-braised lamb shank, and wild mushroom risotto. A function room is available for larger parties to hire. Outside are rambling grounds with resident ducks and an orchard. There are quiz nights and live music every month, as well as an annual beer festival – contact the pub for details.

Open all day all wk 12-11 (Sun 12-10) **Bar Meals** L served Mon-Sat 12-2.30, Sun 12-4 D served Mon-Sat 6-9.30 **Restaurant** L served Mon-Sat 12-2.30, Sun 12-4 D served Mon-Sat 6-9.30 ⊕ HARVEYS OF LEWES ◀ Sussex Best Bitter, Sussex Hadlow Bitter, Sussex Old Ale, Seasonal ales. ⍟ 15 **Facilities** Non-diners area 🐾 (Bar Restaurant Garden) ɨ📍 Children's menu Children's portions Garden 🗚 Beer festival Parking Wi-fi 🚌

BRIGHTON & HOVE   **Map 6 TQ30**

The Basketmakers Arms

12 Gloucester Rd BN1 4AD ☎ 01273 689006
e-mail: bluedowd@hotmail.co.uk
dir: *From Brighton station main entrance 1st left (Gloucester Rd). Pub on right at bottom of hill*

Leave The Lanes to the tourists and find this cracker

Peter Dowd has run his Victorian back-street local, tucked away in the bohemian North Laine area, with passion and pride for over 25 years. Quirky customer messages left in vintage tins on the walls have made the pub a local legend. Expect to find a splendid selection of Fuller's and guest real ales, around 100 malt whiskies and rarely seen vodkas, gins and bourbons. Food is all prepared from locally sourced produce, such as the fish which comes in daily from Sussex fishermen. Hot mains include seafood platter; rib-eye and rump steaks; and authentic beef or vegetarian Mexican chilli.

Open all day all wk 11-11 (Fri-Sat 11am-mdnt Sun 12-11) **Bar Meals** L served all wk 12-8.30 D served all wk 12-8.30 Av main course £8.95 food served all day ⊕ FULLER'S ◀ London Pride, ESB, Discovery & Bengal Lancer, George Gale & Co HSB & Seafarers, Guest ales. **Facilities** 🐾 (Bar Restaurant) ɨ📍 Outside area 🗚 Wi-fi

---

The Bell NEW

15-17 Belfast St BN3 3YS ☎ 01273 770773
e-mail: info@thebellhove.co.uk
dir: *From A259 (coast road) into Hove St (A2023). Right into Blatchington Rd at lights. 4th right into Haddington St, right into Malvern St, left into Belfast St to pub (one-way system)*

Popular side-street pub, known for friendly service

Once you find the side street, the vermillion- and white-painted façade of this smart, late-Victorian community pub quickly reveals its location. Another pointer, when it's warm, is the customers at the tables out front. A guest ale accompanies Bass and Lewes-brewed Harveys in the bar, where Happy Hour lasts all day on Mondays, and from 4-6pm on other weekdays. Describing his food as "stylish without pretence", chef Mark's two years' experience cooking for ravenous scientists at a research station in Antarctica comes in handy for jambalaya; wholetail Whitby scampi and chunky chips; and caramelised roasted fennel, shallot and goats' cheese tart.

Open all day all wk **Bar Meals** L served all wk 12-3 D served all wk 6-9.30 **Restaurant** L served all wk 12-3 D served all wk 6-9.30 ◀ Harvey's Sussex Best Bitter, Bass, Guest ale. **Facilities** Non-diners area ɨ📍 Children's portions Garden 🗚 Wi-fi 🚌 (notice required)

Preston Park Tavern

88 Havelock Rd BN1 6GF ☎ 01273 542271
e-mail: info@prestonparktavern.co.uk
web: www.prestonparktavern.co.uk
dir: *From N towards Brighton on A23, at Mill Rd rdbt take 2nd exit, continue on A23 (follow Brighton, then Town Centre signs). Left (one-way) into Stanford Ave, left into Havelock Rd*

Family-friendly pub with tempting food

Tucked away in the residential backstreets of Brighton, Preston Park Tavern is a light and airy gastro-pub with an open kitchen. At lunchtime, the hearty sandwiches are made with organic granary bread or home-made focaccia, and there are main courses of grilled plaice and a beef, horseradish and thyme burger. The evening menu moves up a gear with slow-roasted Sussex pork belly with kale and bacon rösti; and carrot, ginger and coriander fritters. Sunday lunches are worth booking for and the set lunch menu during the week is very good value. Children are welcomed and have their own menus. The pub also has a sustainability award.

Open all day all wk Closed: 25 Dec & 1 Jan **Bar Meals** L served Mon-Fri 12-2.30, Sat 12-4, Sun 12-6 D served Mon-Sat 6-9.45 Av main course £10-£14 **Restaurant** L served Mon-Fri 12-2.30, Sat 12-4, Sun 12-6 D served Mon-Sat 6-9.45 Fixed menu price fr £12.50 Av 3 course à la carte fr £25 ⊕ FREE HOUSE ◀ Harvey's Sussex Best Bitter, Long Man American Pale Ale, Long Man Sussex Pride Ď Westons Stowford Press. ⍟ 22 **Facilities** Non-diners area 🐾 (Bar Restaurant Garden) ɨ📍 Children's menu Children's portions Garden 🗚 Wi-fi

PICK OF THE PUBS

The Merrie Harriers

COWBEECH Map 6 TQ61

BN27 4JQ ☎ 01323 833108
e-mail:
ben@sussexcountrytaverns.co.uk
web: www.merrieharriers.co.uk
dir: *Off A271, between Hailsham &
Herstmonceux*

Modern British food in pretty country inn

Owned by Ben and Nicky West and a
brother-in-law, Gary Neate, this
attractive, white-painted clapboard
village inn is very much the hub of the
community. Built in 1624, its external
good looks are matched inside by the
wealth of oak beams, and a huge
inglenook fireplace that takes centre
stage in the bar area. Look out for the
female ghost who apparently wanders
around and likes looking out of the
kitchen window. Outside, the terrace
overlooks its own acre of the Weald
where the pub grows fruit and
vegetables, and the tug-of-war team
practises. Studying the modern British,
daily-changing menu should ideally
take place over one of the ten wines by
the glass or a pint of Harvey's, Timothy
Taylor or WJ King real ale. Ben's
commitment to cooking with locally
grown ingredients is evident wherever
you look: for example, the fish (Dover
sole, sea bass, crab, lobster and
scallops) are caught in The Channel off

Eastbourne and are always in demand,
especially on seafood nights. Then
there's the beef, the organic lamb and
the pork, all Sussex reared and bred,
while the game - roebuck deer,
pheasant, teal, wood pigeon and hare
- is all bought from or traded with local
gamekeepers. Ben uses traditional, but
often forgotten, cuts of meat, such as
crispy pig's cheeks and 21-day-aged
onglet steak. They also provide classic
pub dishes such as liver and bacon, fish
pie and ploughman's. The Merrie
Harriers is also renowned for its Sunday
lunch with a choice of roasts, served
with real gravy and horseradish from
the garden. Their beer and music
festival is held every August Bank
Holiday, and entrance is free.

Open all wk Mon-Thu 11.30-3 6-12 (Fri-
Sun all day) **Bar Meals** L served all wk
12-2.30 D served all wk 6.30-9
Restaurant L served all wk 12-2.30 D
served all wk 6.30-9 ⊕ FREE HOUSE
◀ Harvey's, Timothy Taylor, WJ King
Ŏ Westons Stowford Press. ♀ 10
Facilities Non-diners area ✿ (Bar
Garden) ♦ Children's menu Children's
portions Play area Garden Beer festival
Parking Wi-fi 🚌

Save on hotels. Book at **theAA.com/hotel**

SUSSEX, EAST 429 ENGLAND

CHELWOOD GATE — Map 6 TQ43

The Red Lion NEW

Lewes Rd RH17 7DE ☎ 01825 740265
e-mail: david@redlionchelwoodgate.co.uk
dir: On A275

Popular Ashdown Forest destination

An attractive pub built in the early 1800s that includes among its famous visitors Prime Minister Harold Macmillan and President John F Kennedy. Although it is owned by Kent brewer Shepherd Neame, Harveys of Lewes also gets a look in on the bar. A full menu is served in the conservatory dining room and on the patio, while a more limited selection applies at tables in the extensive gardens. Typical dishes are pan-fried sirloin of Sussex beef; skate wing with fresh winkles and beurre noisette; and herby couscous-stuffed pepper with roasted vegetables. For a special, maybe rump of lamb with lentils.

Open all day all wk summer all day (winter 12-3 5.30-11) **Bar Meals** L served all day summer Av main course £12.50 **Restaurant** L served all wk 12-2.30 D served all wk 6-9.30 Av 3 course à la carte fr £25 ⊕ SHEPHERD NEAME ◀ Spitfire, Harvey's Sussex Best Bitter.
Facilities Non-diners area ❈ (Bar Garden) ♦️ Children's menu Children's portions Garden ☞ Parking

CHIDDINGLY — Map 6 TQ51

The Six Bells

BN8 6HE ☎ 01825 872227
dir: E of A22 between Hailsham & Uckfield. Turn opposite Golden Cross pub

Popular pub with vintage car, music and jazz events

Inglenook fireplaces and plenty of bric-à-brac are to be found at this large free house, which is where various veteran car and motorbike enthusiasts meet on club nights. The jury in the famous 1852 Onion Pie Murder trial sat and deliberated in the bar before finding the defendant, Sarah Ann French, guilty. Exceptionally good-value bar food includes green lip mussels with salad and French bread; cauliflower and broccoli bake; rack of ribs; chicken curry; and spicy ravioli with salad. Enjoy the fortnightly popular folk and blues evenings.

Open all wk 10-3 6-11 (Fri-Sun all day) ⊕ FREE HOUSE ◀ Courage Directors, Harvey's Sussex Best Bitter.
Facilities ♦️ Family room Garden Parking

COWBEECH — Map 6 TQ61

The Merrie Harriers

PICK OF THE PUBS

See Pick of the Pubs on opposite page

DANEHILL — Map 6 TQ42

The Coach and Horses

PICK OF THE PUBS

RH17 7JF ☎ 01825 740369
e-mail: coachandhorses@danehill.biz
dir: From East Grinstead, S through Forest Row on A22 to junct with A275 (Lewes road), right on A275, 2m to Danehill, left into School Ln, 0.5m, pub on left

Country pub offering much more than beer

On the edge of Ashdown Forest, The Coach opened in 1847 and was then a simple alehouse with stabling. Today it is a pub and restaurant attracting both locals and those from further afield. Inside, vaulted ceilings, panelling and stone and wood flooring add to the charm. An enormous maple tree dominates the sunny, child-free terrace at the rear, while from the peaceful front garden, where children can play, you can see the South Downs. Drinkers can enjoy weekly-changing guest ales and local Danehill Black Pig cider. Local sourcing is the guiding principle wherever possible, such as fish from Seaford Bay and lamb from Danehill itself. Typical menu choices could include chicken and herb terrine; and pan-roasted fillet of sea bass. Those who like their pub classics are looked after with minced beef and onion pie, or Sussex rib-eye steak. A good-value light-lunch menu is also available.

Open all wk 11.30-3 6-11 (Sat-Sun 12-11) Closed: 26 Dec **Bar Meals** L served Mon-Fri 12-2.30, Sun 12-3 D served Mon-Fri 7-9, Sat 7-9.30 **Restaurant** L served Mon-Fri 12-2, Sun 12-3 D served Mon-Thu 7-9, Fri-Sat 7-9.30 ⊕ FREE HOUSE ◀ Sharp's Doom Bar, WJ King, Harvey's, Hammerpot, Guest ales Ò Westons Stowford Press, Black Rat, Black Pig. ♒ 8
Facilities Non-diners area ❈ (Bar Garden) ♦️ Children's menu Children's portions Play area Garden Parking Wi-fi

DITCHLING — Map 6 TQ31

The Bull ★★★★ INN

PICK OF THE PUBS

See Pick of the Pubs on page 430

EAST CHILTINGTON — Map 6 TQ31

The Jolly Sportsman ◉◉

Chapel Ln BN7 3BA ☎ 01273 890400
e-mail: info@thejollysportsman.com
dir: From Lewes take A275, left at Offham onto B2166 towards Plumpton, take Novington Ln, after approx 1m left into Chapel Ln

Award-winning rustic food and local ales to match

Isolated but well worth finding, Bruce Wass's dining pub enjoys a lovely garden setting on a peaceful dead-end lane looking out to the South Downs. The bar retains some of the character of a Victorian alehouse, with Dark Star and Harvey's on tap, while the dining room strikes a

cool, modern-rustic pose. Well-sourced food shines on daily-changing, two AA-Rosette menus, served throughout the pub, from rabbit pappardelle with chestnut mushroom, artichoke and wild garlic to roast turbot with béarnaise sauce. Good value fixed-price and children's menus are also available.

Open all wk (Sat & Summer all day) Closed: 25 Dec **Bar Meals** L served Mon-Sat 12-2.30, Sun 12-3.30 D served Sun-Thu 6.30-9.30, Fri-Sat 6.30-10 Av main course £15 **Restaurant** L served Mon-Sat 12.15-2.30, Sun 12.15-3.30 D served Mon-Thu 7-9.30, Fri-Sat 7-10, Sun 7-9 Fixed menu price fr £13.50 Av 3 course à la carte fr £25 ⊕ FREE HOUSE ◀ Dark Star Hophead, Harvey's Sussex Best Bitter Ò Westons. ♒ 14
Facilities Non-diners area ❈ (Bar Garden) ♦️ Children's menu Children's portions Play area Garden ☞ Parking Wi-fi

EAST DEAN — Map 6 TV59

The Tiger Inn

PICK OF THE PUBS

The Green BN20 0DA ☎ 01323 423209
e-mail: tiger@beachyhead.org.uk
dir: From A259 between Eastbourne & Seaford. Pub 0.5m

Downland village inn handy for the Seven Sisters

Just down from the famous Beachy Head, the popular beach at Birling Gap was formerly the haunt of smugglers, whose base of operation was today's Tiger Inn, hidden up a tranquil side valley. It sits beside a village green lined with picture-postcard cottages and enjoys wonderful downland views. The interior is quintessentially English too, with log fires, beams, stone floors and ancient settles. As brewery tap for the nearby Beachy Head microbrewery, the best of local beers are guaranteed, supplemented by a popular annual beer festival. Ramblers from the nearby coastal path join diners in seeking out the fulsome meals on the good, solid menu of pub favourites like sausage with mash and sweet roasted red onion gravy, or perhaps roasted salmon on fennel purée with a prawn and vermouth sauce, complemented by an ever-changing selection of specials.

Open all day all wk **Bar Meals** L served all wk 12-3 D served all wk 6-9 Av main course £8-£12 **Restaurant** L served all wk 12-3 D served all wk 6-9 ⊕ FREE HOUSE/ BEACHY HEAD BREWERY ◀ Legless Rambler & Original Ale, Harvey's Ò Westons Stowford Press. ♒ 10
Facilities Non-diners area ❈ (Bar Garden) ♦️ Children's portions Garden ☞ Beer festival Parking Wi-fi

PICK OF THE PUBS

The Bull ★★★★ INN

DITCHLING Map 6 TQ31

2 High St BN6 8TA ☎ 01273 843147
e-mail: info@thebullditchling.com
web: www.thebullditchling.com
dir: *A27 from Brighton onto A23, follow Pyecombe/Hassocks signs, then Ditchling signs, 3m*

Old inn with contemporary feel

This venerable 450-year-old inn started life as monks' lodgings. Today's cosy retreat is a far cry from those spartan days — The Bull's memorable interior pushes all the right buttons with open fires, wavy beams, leather sofas, cosy corners, candlelight, bare floorboards, scrubbed tables and a locals' bar brimming with good Sussex beers. Dominic and Vanessa Worral have toiled tirelessly to create the archetypal English village inn with a refreshing contemporary edge. The monks' draughty rooms have been replaced with individually designed guest accommodation, very popular with visitors to the South Downs National Park within which The Bull stands. The rounded tops of the hills rise steeply beyond the village to the commanding Ditchling Beacon; a self-guided walk from the pub will take you there, and the South Downs Way National Trail also crosses the Beacon. Brighton is just 15 minutes away by car. Sussex farms and estates provide the chefs with a panoply of delights with which to create their refreshingly modern gourmet British dishes. Typical 'small plate' starters could include Thai beef noodle salad with mirin dressing; and pan-seared scallops with roasted pancetta, sautéed kale and celeriac purée. Luxurious main courses take the form of ballotine of rabbit stuffed with prunes, smoked bacon and Puy lentil soup; or sea trout en papillote, with clams, fennel and sorrel. Vegetarian options are no less flavoursome. Desserts include spiced apple and pistachio clafoutis, and home-made ice creams. Wine-lovers will delight in a generous list which includes more than 23 served by the glass

Open all day all wk 11-11 (Sat 8.30am-11pm Sun 8.30am-10.30pm) **Bar Meals** L served Mon-Fri 12-2.30, Sat

12-9.30, Sun 12-9 (Sat-Sun bkfst 8.30-10.30am) D served Mon-Fri 6-9.30, Sat 12-9.30, Sun 12-9 ⊕ FREE HOUSE 🍺 Harvey's Sussex Best Bitter, Timothy Taylor Landlord, Hop Back Summer Lightning, Dark Star ♂ Westons Traditional. ♟ 23 **Facilities** Non-diners area 🍴 Children's menu Children's portions Play area Garden 🎋 Parking Wi-fi **Rooms** 4

Save on hotels. Book at theAA.com/hotel

SUSSEX, EAST 431 ENGLAND

ERIDGE GREEN — Map 6 TQ53

The Nevill Crest and Gun NEW

Eridge Rd TN3 9JR ☎ 01892 864209
e-mail: nevill.crest.and.gun@brunningandprice.co.uk
dir: *On A26 between Tunbridge Wells & Crowborough*

Intriguingly named pub with over 500 years of history

This uniquely named, tile-hung pub was built on land owned by the Nevill family, the Earls of Abergavenny, which explains the 'Crest'; a cannon that once stood outside accounts for the 'Gun'. The hamlet's balancing act on the Kent-Sussex border is reflected in the low-beamed, wooden-floored bar where Larkins and Black Cat real ales come from the former, Harvey's from the latter. A springtime daily-changing menu advocates pan-fried thyme polenta with mushrooms, parmesan and pine nut salad; roast leg of pork; harissa-baked salmon with lemon and coriander couscous; and roasted aubergine, goats' cheese and red pepper lasagne.

Open all day all wk **Bar Meals** Av main course £14 food served all day **Restaurant** food served all day ⊕ BRUNNING & PRICE ◀ Harvey's, Larkins, Black Cat Ŏ Biddenden. ⬤ 16 **Facilities** Non-diners area ❀ (Bar Garden Outside area) ♦ Children's portions Play area Garden Outside area ⊼ Beer festival Cider festival Parking Wi-fi ▥ (notice required)

EWHURST GREEN — Map 7 TQ72

The White Dog NEW

Village St TN32 5TP ☎ 01580 830264
e-mail: info@thewhitedogewhurst.co.uk
dir: *On A21 from Tonbridge towards Hastings, left after Hurst Green signed Bodiam. Straight on at x-rds, through Bodiam. Over rail crossing, left for Ewhurst Green*

Family-run country inn overlooking Bodiam Castle

This tile-hung village pub is either the first in, or the last out of the village, depending on which way you are travelling. Its age is more apparent from the interior, particularly the huge fireplace, old oak beams and stone floors. Four hand-pumps dispense regularly-changing, mostly Sussex real ales and some 20 wines are available by the glass. The seasonal menus show how dependent the kitchen is on the local area: for example, Rye Bay fish and mussel chowder; chargrilled chump of Romney Marsh lamb; and home-made gnocchi with fresh tomato and basil sauce, and Twineham Grange cheese.

Open all wk 12-3 5-11 (Fri-Sun 12-11) **Bar Meals** L served all wk 12-2.30 D served all wk 6.30-9.30 Av main course £9 **Restaurant** L served all wk 12-2.30 D served all wk 6.30-9.30 Fixed menu price fr £14 Av 3 course à la carte fr £24 ⊕ FREE HOUSE ◀ Harvey's, Sharp's Doom Bar, Regularly changing local ales. ⬤ 20 **Facilities** Non-diners area ❀ (Bar Garden Outside area) ♦ Children's menu Children's portions Play area Garden Outside area ⊼ Parking Wi-fi ▥ (notice required)

FLETCHING — Map 6 TQ42

The Griffin Inn

PICK OF THE PUBS

TN22 3SS ☎ 01825 722890
e-mail: info@thegriffininn.co.uk
dir: *M23 junct 10 to East Grinstead, then A22, then A275. Village signed on left*

Popular for its huge gardens and lovely country views

The unspoilt village of Fletching overlooks the Ouse Valley, and this imposing Grade II listed inn has landscaped gardens with views of the Ashdown Forest, Sussex Downs and 'Capability' Brown designed Sheffield Park Gardens. You might just hear a steam whistle, for the heritage Bluebell Railway is little more than a mile away. The 16th-century interior simply oozes charm from its beams, panelling, settles and log fires. The bar boasts handpumps dispensing the best of local ales, a generous wine list, and champagnes and dessert wines by the glass. Walkers and cyclists arriving to join destination diners will revel in the terrific menu, created from the freshest of local produce. Typical dishes include roasted Mediterranean vegetable bruschetta, roast rump of Romney Marsh lamb, Rye Bay plaice, and breast of guinea fowl. The Griffin has strong cricketing connections and has two of its own cricket teams.

Open all day all wk 12-11 (Sat 12-12) Closed: 25 Dec **Bar Meals** L served Mon-Fri 12-2.30, Sat-Sun 12-3 D served all wk 7-9.30 Av main course £12-£13 **Restaurant** L served Mon-Fri 12-2.30, Sat-Sun 12-3 D served Mon-Sat 7-9.30 Av 3 course à la carte fr £32 ⊕ FREE HOUSE ◀ Harvey's Sussex Best Bitter, WJ King, Hepworth & Co Ŏ Westons Stowford Press. ⬤ 16 **Facilities** Non-diners area ❀ (Bar Garden) ♦ Children's menu Children's portions Play area Garden ⊼ Parking Wi-fi

GUN HILL — Map 6 TQ51

The Gun

PICK OF THE PUBS

TN21 0JU ☎ 01825 872361
e-mail: enquiries@thegunhouse.co.uk
dir: *5m S of Heathfield, 1m off A267 towards Gun Hill. 4m off A22 between Uckfield & Hailsham*

First-class food in a charming setting

This black-and-white, 15th-century pub is tucked away in the heart of the Sussex countryside and was once the main courthouse serving the neighbouring towns and villages. Its wooden floors and beams, and hideaway places provide the perfect setting for quiet eating and drinking. A separate panelled dining room with a stunning fireplace is ideal for private parties. Dishes are seasonal and sourced from local suppliers. The fish and game deli boards are good to share with a gathering of friends. Main courses might include oven-roasted partridge with game chips, braised red cabbage, watercress, chestnuts and pancetta jus; and a vegetable

and chickpea ragout with herbed couscous. On sunny days, dine alfresco in the large garden (complete with wooden climbing frame and swings) or on the terrace, and enjoy the views across the countryside. Afternoon tea is available every day of the week (booking required).

Open all wk 11.30-3 5.30-11 (Sun 11.30-10.30) **Bar Meals** L served Mon-Sat 12-3, Sun 12-9.30 D served Mon-Sat 6-9.45, Sun 12-9.30 Av main course £14.50 **Restaurant** L served Mon-Sat 12-3, Sun 12-9.30 D served Mon-Sat 6-9.45, Sun 12-9.30 Av 3 course à la carte fr £26 ⊕ FREE HOUSE ◀ Sharp's Doom Bar, Harvey's, Guinness Ŏ Biddenden, Aspall. ⬤ 14 **Facilities** Non-diners area ❀ (All areas) ♦ Children's menu Children's portions Play area Garden Outside area ⊼ Parking Wi-fi

HARTFIELD — Map 6 TQ43

Anchor Inn

Church St TN7 4AG ☎ 01892 770424
e-mail: info@anchorhartfield.com
dir: *On B2110*

Friendly free house in the Ashdown Forest

This family-orientated pub is in the heart of 'Winnie the Pooh' country. It was built in 1465 and was at one time a workhouse before it became a pub in the late 19th century. Locals meet in the front bar with its stone floors and heavy wooden beams, whilst an inglenook fireplace and library area give the back bar a more intimate feel. As well as hot and cold snacks, main courses such as Moroccan mixed bean casserole and slow-braised lamb shank satisfy heartier appetites. Friday evening is steak night. The front verandah and large garden are a bonus on warm sunny days. Look out for the early summer beer and cider festival.

Open all day all wk **Bar Meals** L served Mon-Fri 12-3, Sat 12-10, Sun 12-9 D served Mon-Thu 6-9, Fri 6-10, Sat 12-10, Sun 12-9 **Restaurant** L served Mon-Fri 12-3, Sat 12-10, Sun 12-9 D served Mon-Thu 6-9, Fri 6-10, Sat 12-10, Sun 12-9 ⊕ FREE HOUSE ◀ Harvey's Sussex Best Bitter, Moorhouse's Black Cat, Larkins Ŏ Westons Stowford Press. **Facilities** Non-diners area ❀ (Bar Garden) ♦ Children's menu Children's portions Play area Garden ⊼ Beer festival Cider festival Parking Wi-fi ▥ (notice required)

The Hatch Inn

PICK OF THE PUBS

See Pick of the Pubs on page 432

PICK OF THE PUBS

The Hatch Inn

HARTFIELD Map 6 TQ43

Coleman's Hatch TN7 4EJ
☎ **01342 822363**
e-mail: nickad@mac.com
web: www.hatchinn.co.uk
dir: *A22 at Forest Row rdbt, 3m to Coleman's Hatch, right by church*

Award winning pub in the heart of Ashdown Forest

If AA Milne could populate Ashdown Forest with a bear called Winnie the Pooh, a tiger called Tigger and a kangaroo called Kanga, why shouldn't llamas and reindeer live here? Well, they do, on a farm in nearby Wych Cross, not far from this eye-catching old inn at the site of one of the medieval gates into what was then dense woodland with valuable iron and timber reserves. Built around 1430, the part-weatherboarded building may have been cottages for iron workers, although it has been a pub for nearly 300 years, it was no doubt much appreciated by the dry-throated charcoal burners who used to work in these parts, and even passing smugglers. Classic beams and open fires draw an appreciative crowd to sample beers from Fuller's, Larkins and Harvey's, and the food, a fusion of classic and modern, for which during the past 17 years proprietor Nicholas Drillsma and partner Sandy Barton have built an enviable reputation. Their daily-changing menus are complemented by

an extensive wine list, including ten by the glass. With plenty of local suppliers to draw on, fresh seasonal produce features in just about everything. Lunchtime mains include beef and chilli meatballs, fettucine and roasted vine tomato sauce; pan-fried skate wing with lime and caper butter; and slow roasted pork belly with apple mash and red wine reduction. A reservation is essential for evening dining where choices may include deep-fried calamari with aïoli or beetroot infused salmon gravadlax followed by wild mushroom, pea and spinach risotto or chargrilled fillet steak. Finish with dark rum and vanilla pannacotta with pecan shortbread, or pear tart Tatin with clotted cream.

Open all wk 11.30-3 5.30-11 (Sat-Sun all day) Closed: 25 Dec drinks only **Bar Meals** L served all wk 12-2.15 D served Mon-Thu 7-9.15, Fri-Sat 7-9.30 **Restaurant** L served all wk 12-2.15 D served Mon-Thu 7-9.15, Fri-Sat 7-9.30 🌐 FREE HOUSE 🍺 Harvey's & Sussex Old Ale, Fuller's London Pride, Sharp's Doom Bar, Larkins Ŏ Westons Stowford Press. ♟ 10 **Facilities** Non-diners area ♦♦ Children's portions Play area Garden

Save on hotels. Book at theAA.com/hotel

SUSSEX, EAST 433 ENGLAND

HEATHFIELD
Map 6 TQ52

Star Inn

Church St, Old Heathfield TN21 9AH ☎ **01435 863570**
e-mail: chappellhatpeg@aol.com
dir: *Old Heathfield SE of Heathfield assessed from B2096*

Stonemasons' inn with great views and a welcoming interior

Built as an inn for the stonemasons who constructed the 14th-century church, this creeper-clad stone building has a stunning summer garden that affords impressive views across the High Weald; a view once painted by Turner. Equally appealing is the atmospheric, low-beamed main bar with its rustic furnishings and huge inglenook fireplace – all very cosy and welcoming in winter. Note the unusual barrel-vaulted ceiling in the upstairs dining room and the chalkboard menu that lists fresh fish and seafood direct from the day boats in Hastings.

Open all day all wk **Bar Meals** L served Mon-Sat 12-2.30, Sun 12-3 D served Mon-Sat 7-9.30, Sun 6-8.30 Av main course £11.50 **Restaurant** L served Mon-Sat 12-2.30, Sun 12-3 D served Mon-Sat 7-9.30, Sun 6-8.30 Av 3 course à la carte fr £23 ⊕ FREE HOUSE ◀ Shepherd Neame Master Brew, Harvey's, Guest ale ⭕ Thatchers. ♚ 10
Facilities Non-diners area ❤ (All areas) ♦♦ Children's menu Children's portions Garden Outside area ⊟ Parking Wi-fi ⛟ (notice required)

ICKLESHAM
Map 7 TQ81

The Queen's Head

Parsonage Ln TN36 4BL ☎ **01424 814552**
dir: *Between Hastings & Rye on A259. Pub in village at x-rds near church*

A must for real ale lovers

This 17th-century tile-hung and oak-beamed pub enjoys magnificent views from its gardens of the Brede Valley and as far as the coast at Rye. The traditional atmosphere has been preserved, with vaulted ceilings, large inglenook fireplaces, split-level floors, church pews, antique farm implements, and a bar from the old Midland Bank in Eastbourne. Customers are kept happy with up to ten real ales, an annual beer festival on the first weekend in October, and menus ranging from salads, sandwiches and ploughman's to a comprehensive main menu selection which includes half a pint of prawns, home-made lamb and mint pie, Thai vegetable curry, and grilled pork chops.

Open all wk 11-11 (Sun 11-10.30) Closed: 25 & 26 Dec (eve) **Bar Meals** L served Mon-Fri 12-2.30, Sat-Sun 12-9.30 D served Mon-Fri 6-9.30, Sat-Sun 12-9.30 Av main course £9.50 ⊕ FREE HOUSE ◀ Rother Valley Level Best, Greene King Abbot Ale, Harvey's Sussex Best Bitter, Ringwood Fortyniner, Dark Star ⭕ Biddenden, Westons Old Rosie. ♚ 12 **Facilities** Non-diners area ❤ (Bar Restaurant Garden) ♦♦ Children's menu Children's portions Play area Garden ⊟ Beer festival Parking Wi-fi ⛟ (notice required)

LANGNEY
Map 6 TQ60

The Farm @ Friday Street NEW

15 Friday St BN23 8AP ☎ **01323 766049**
e-mail: enquiries@farmfridaystreet.com

Excellent find in Eastbourne's outer reaches

Although surrounded by the ever-expanding town, this Whiting & Hammond Group pub still looks like the elegant farmhouse it once was. Fishmongers call the kitchen daily to tell them what's looking good from the day's catch, while other possibilities are chicken, mushroom and ham shortcrust pastry pie; fillet of beef Stroganoff with pilau rice; braised oxtail suet pudding with black pudding mash; and gnocchi with quinoa, chestnut mushrooms, soft herbs and truffle cream. Desserts include sorbets; banoffee pie; and chocolate brownie. Sunday lunches, with live music, are hugely popular and beer festivals are held in June and August.

Open all day all wk **Bar Meals** Av main course £9 food served all day **Restaurant** Fixed menu price fr £10.95 Av 3 course à la carte fr £22.95 food served all day ⊕ ENTERPRISE INNS ◀ Harvey's, Fuller's London Pride, Sharp's Doom Bar, Timothy Taylor ⭕ Westons Old Rosie. ♚ **Facilities** Non-diners area ❤ (Bar Restaurant Garden) ♦♦ Children's portions Garden ⊟ Beer festival Parking Wi-fi

MAYFIELD
Map 6 TQ52

The Middle House

PICK OF THE PUBS

See Pick of the Pubs on page 434

MILTON STREET
Map 6 TQ50

The Sussex Ox

BN26 5RL ☎ **01323 870840**
e-mail: mail@thesussexox.co.uk
dir: *Off A27 between Wilmington & Drusillas. Follow brown signs to pub*

Views of the Long Man of Wilmington from the beer garden

A former slaughterhouse and butcher's dating from 1900, this pub retains its church pew seating and wood panelling. Drink deeply of old Sussex here, with the wonderful, matchboarded old bar rooms serving local ales and oozing character. Dine in the bar, the Garden Room, or the more formal Dining Room; the daily-changing menu relies on the best local ingredients. To start, perhaps Mediterranean vegetable terrine, then follow with free-range lemon chicken and thyme puff pastry pie. Bar snacks such as root vegetable crisps and spicy chicken skewers are also available, washed down with the pub's own Oxhead bitter from Dark Star Brewery.

Open all wk Mon-Fri 11.30-3 6-11 Sat 11.30-11 Sun 12-10.30 Closed: 25-26 Dec **Bar Meals** L served Mon-Fri 12-2, Sat-Sun 12-2.30 D served all wk 6-9 Av main course £10 **Restaurant** L served Mon-Fri 12-2, Sat-Sun 12-2.30 D served all wk 6-9 ⊕ FREE HOUSE ◀ Harvey's Sussex Best Bitter, Dark Star Oxhead, Long Man American Pale Ale ⭕ Kingstone Press. ♚ 17
Facilities Non-diners area ❤ (Bar Garden) ♦♦ Children's portions Family room Garden ⊟ Parking Wi-fi

OFFHAM
Map 6 TQ41

The Blacksmiths Arms ★★★★ INN

London Rd BN7 3QD ☎ **01273 472971**
e-mail: blacksmithsarms@shineadsl.co.uk
web: www.theblacksmithsarms-offham.co.uk
dir: *2m N of Lewes on A275*

Many reasons to visit this friendly inn

A hostelry since the mid-18th century, this free house in the South Downs National Park is just two miles from the lovely old town of Lewes. So that makes two reasons to visit, or even stay in the charming, high-quality accommodation. A third reason is Bernard and Sylvia Booker's flavoursome cooking using the best sustainably sourced local produce for lemon sole Walewska; steak-and-kidney pie; and spinach and ricotta cannelloni. And a fourth is Harvey's real ales in a bar with a log fire in the inglenook.

Open 12-3 6.30-10.30 Closed: Sun eve, Mon winter, Mon L summer **Bar Meals** L served Tue-Sun 12-2 **Restaurant** L served Tue-Sun 12-2 D served Tue-Sat 6.30-9 ⊕ FREE HOUSE ◀ Harvey's, Bitburger. ♚ 10
Facilities Non-diners area ♦♦ Children's portions Garden ⊟ Parking Wi-fi **Rooms** 4

PICK OF THE PUBS

The Middle House

MAYFIELD   Map 6 TQ52

High St TN20 6AB ☎ 01435 872146
e-mail:
info@themiddlehousemayfield.co.uk
web: www.themiddlehousemayfield.co.uk
dir: *E of A267, S of Tunbridge Wells*

Historic timber-framed hostelry

Once described as 'one of the finest
examples of a timber-framed building in
Sussex', this Grade I listed, 16th-
century village inn dominates Mayfield's
High Street. It has been here since
1575, when it was built for Sir Thomas
Gresham, Elizabeth I's Keeper of the
Privy Purse and founder of the London
Stock Exchange. The entrance hall
features a large ornately carved wooden
fireplace by master carver Grinling
Gibbons, wattle-and-daub infill, a
splendid oak-panelled restaurant and
secret priest holes. A private residence
until the 1920s, it is now a family-run
business. Real ale drinkers do well here,
with a handsome choice, including
Harvey's Sussex Best Bitter from Lewes
and Fuller's London Pride. As in all good
kitchens, the meats, poultry, game and
vegetables come from local farms and
producers. The bar menu includes
classic dishes of home-cooked smoked
gammon with two free-range fried eggs;
deep-fried wholetail scampi with chunky
chips; home-made sausages of the day;
fresh salads, vegetarian options and
children's healthy-eating options. For

something a little less traditional, try
pot-roast shank of local lamb tagine, or
roast boneless quail filled with mixed
forest mushrooms. The carte offers
whole large grilled Cornish sardines
with garlic butter; fanned marinated
duck breast with chorizo and sun-
blushed tomato risotto; and corn fritter
and harissa-roasted vegetable stack
with toasted feta cheese. And of the
desserts, special mention goes to pine
nut and maple pannacotta with roasted
blueberries, pistachio ice cream and
lavender honeycomb. It isn't just the
building that has been described in
superlative terms – the private chapel
in the restaurant is regarded as 'one of
the most magnificent in England'. Step
outside onto the lovely terraced gardens
to enjoy views of the rolling countryside.

Open all day all wk **Bar meals** L served
Mon-Fri 12-2, Sat 12-2.30 D served Mon-
Sat 6.30-9.30, Sun all day **Restaurant** L
served Tue-Sun 12-2 D served Tue-Sat
6.30-9 ⊕ FREE HOUSE ◧ Harvey's Sussex
Best Bitter, Greene King Abbot Ale, Black
Sheep Best Bitter, Theakston Best Bitter,
Adnams Southwold Bitter, Sharp's Doom
Bar, Fuller's London Pride ♂ Thatchers
Gold. ☐ 9 **Facilities** Non-diners area ☺
(Garden) ¶ Children's menu Children's
portions Play area Garden ⊭ Parking Wi-fi

Save on hotels. Book at theAA.com/hotel

SUSSEX, EAST 435 ENGLAND

PLUMPTON
Map 6 TQ31

Half Moon

Ditchling Rd BN7 3AF ☎ **01273 890253**
e-mail: info@halfmoonplumpton.com
dir: *A275 from Lewes. Left onto B2116 signed Plumpton. Pub on right in village*

Tucked away down the South Down lanes

Just ten minutes from Lewes and at the foot of the South Downs National Park, this lovely 200-year-old former coach house is all you could hope for when it comes to a typical English inn. Enjoy foaming pints of local Harvey's ales by the fire in the stone-walled bar. Alternatively, settle down in the well-appointed, antique-filled dining room for comforting dishes such as crispy fried pig's ears with garlic mayonnaise; seared red mullet fillet with cuttlefish and citrus salad; and roasted free range guinea fowl with garlic gnocchi, fresh broad beans and peas. For dessert, maybe coffee crème brûlée.

Open all day Closed: Sun eve **Bar Meals** L served all wk 12-6 D served Mon-Sat 6-9 Av main course £14 food served all day **Restaurant** L served all wk 12-3 D served Mon-Sat 6-9 Fixed menu price fr £13 Av 3 course à la carte fr £25 ⊕ FREE HOUSE ◀ Harvey's, WJ King, Hammerpot, Long Man ♂ Westons, Severn. ☘ 10 **Facilities** Non-diners area ❀ (Bar Restaurant Garden) ♦♦ Children's menu Children's portions Play area Family room Garden ⊼ Parking Wi-fi ⛟

RINGMER
Map 6 TQ41

The Cock

Uckfield Rd BN8 5RX ☎ **01273 812040**
e-mail: matt@cockpub.co.uk
web: www.cockpub.co.uk
dir: *Just off A26 approx 2m N of Lewes just outside Ringmer*

Step back in time at this historic pub

This 16th-century inn takes its name from a bygone era when a cock horse was a spare horse used by coachmen to pull heavy loads – immortalised in the nursery rhyme 'Ride a Cock Horse to Banbury Cross'. Once a mustering point during the Civil War, the interior of the main bar is pretty much unaltered since Cromwell's time, including oak beams, flagstone floors and a blazing fire in the inglenook. Harvey's, Hogs Back and guest ales

accompany a truly extensive menu of favourites and plenty of vegetarian and fish dishes, among which are chicken goujons, steak-and-ale pie, Greek salad, smoked haddock, and mushroom and red pepper Stroganoff.

The Cock

Open all wk 11-3 6-11.30 (Sun 11-11) Closed: 26 Dec **Bar Meals** L served Mon-Fri 12-2, Sat 12-2.30, Sun 12-9.30 D served Mon-Sat 6-9.30, Sun 12-9.30 Av main course £10.75 **Restaurant** L served Mon-Fri 12-2, Sat 12-2.30, Sun 12-9.30 D served Mon-Sat 6-9.30, Sun 12-9.30 Av 3 course à la carte fr £18.60 ⊕ FREE HOUSE ◀ Harvey's Sussex Best Bitter, Hogs Back, Rudgate Viking, Hammerpot Guest ales. ☘ 10 **Facilities** Non-diners area ❀ (Bar Garden) ♦♦ Children's menu Children's portions Play area Garden ⊼ Parking ⛟ (notice required)

See advert below

RUSHLAKE GREEN Map 6 TQ61

Horse & Groom

TN21 9QE ☎ **01435 830320**
e-mail: info@thehorseandgroom.eu
dir: Telephone for directions

An appealing pub-restaurant with rustic character

At the edge of the enormous green that gives the village its name, the Horse & Groom has a huge garden offering a grand prospect over the pretty East Sussex countryside, a much sought-after spot for summertime refreshment. Residents have supped here for over 230 years and the pub retains its heavy beams, hearth, brass and copper, and a restaurant complete with antique firearms. Drinkers delight in Harvey's and guest ales, whilst diners are rewarded by a fulfilling menu of home-cooked fare. Typical choices include fresh fillet of Hastings cod in chef's beer-batter or marinated duck breast with stir-fried vegetables. Change of landlord.

Open all wk 12-3.30 5.30-11 (Sat-Sun all day) **Bar Meals** L served Mon-Sat 12-2.30, Sun 12-5 D served Mon-Sat 6-9 **Restaurant** L served Mon-Sat 12-2.30, Sun 12-5 D served Mon-Sat 6-9 ⊕ SHEPHERD NEAME ◀ Harvey's Sussex Best Bitter, Guest ales Ŏ Thatchers Gold. **Facilities** Non-diners area ♦♦ Children's portions Garden ⋒ Parking Wi-fi ⇛

RYE Map 7 TQ92

The George Tap ★★★★ HL ◉

98 High St TN31 7JT ☎ **01797 222114**
e-mail: stay@thegeorgeinrye.com
dir: M20 junct 10, A2070 to Brenzett, A259 to Rye

Long-standing inn in pretty Sussex town

This town-centre inn can trace its origins back to 1575. Inside it offers a fascinating mix of old and new, with an exquisite original Georgian ballroom and plenty of antique and contemporary furnishings and locally produced art. In the bar, the draw is beers from Dark Star and Harvey's breweries and a tasty, light bar menu. Diners taking the one AA-Rosette meals can enjoy fruits of the sea from local boats; perhaps scallops with pea purée, confit garlic and poached quail egg yolk followed by classic fish and chips with mushy peas. Alternatively, try grilled lamb from the wood charcoal oven or classic steak frites.

Open all day all wk **Bar Meals** L served all wk 12-6 D served all wk 6-10 Av main course £12 food served all day **Restaurant** L served all wk 12-3 D served all wk 6-10 Av 3 course à la carte fr £25 ⊕ FREE HOUSE ◀ White Chilly Willy, Dark Star American Pale Ale, Harvey's Sussex Best Bitter Ŏ Biddenden Bushell. ♟ 15 **Facilities** Non-diners area ♦♦ Children's menu Children's portions Garden ⋒ Wi-fi ⇛ **Rooms** 34

Mermaid Inn ★★★ HL ◉◉

PICK OF THE PUBS

Mermaid St TN31 7EY ☎ **01797 223065**
e-mail: info@mermaidinn.com
dir: A259, follow signs to town centre, into Mermaid St

Atmospheric historical treasure serving top-notch food

One of the most famous and photographed of England's ancient inns, this venerable building was a haunt of seafarers from the Cinque Port harbour at the hill-foot. The sea long ago receded beyond the marshes but the aura of the smuggler's inn remains, with ships' timbers for beams and huge open fireplaces carved from French stone ballast dredged from Rye harbour. A vast inglenook where the infamous Hawkshurst gang warmed themselves also has a hidden priest hole; throughout, tasteful furnishings and antiques pave the way for an inspirational dining experience. British and French-style food is served in both the bar and linenfold-panelled, restaurant, and under sunshades on the patio. Seafood and local lamb feature strongly on all menus; a Mermaid fish casserole or fricassée of woodland mushrooms at the bar; braised shoulder of Romney Marsh lamb or pan-roasted smoked haddock at the table. Superb wines, local Harvey's beer and exceptional hotel bedrooms are the icing on the cake.

Open all day all wk 12-11 **Bar Meals** L served all wk 12-2.30 D served all wk 6-9 Av main course £11 **Restaurant** L served all wk 12-2.30 D served all wk 7-9.30 Fixed menu price fr £21 ⊕ FREE HOUSE ◀ Fuller's London Pride, Harvey's Ŏ Kingstone Press. ♟ 15 **Facilities** Non-diners area ♣ (Garden) ♦♦ Children's menu Children's portions Garden ⋒ Parking Wi-fi ⇛ (notice required) **Rooms** 31

The Ypres Castle Inn

PICK OF THE PUBS

Gun Garden TN31 7HH ☎ **01797 223248**
e-mail: info@yprescastleinn.co.uk
dir: Behind church & adjacent to Ypres Tower

One of the ancient town of Rye's best-kept secrets

The pretty Ypres Castle Inn, known as 'The Wipers' by the locals, sits beneath the ramparts of the Ypres Castle Tower and has been providing hospitality since 1640. It was once the haunt of local wool smugglers. Now under new management, the inn has a relaxed, friendly atmosphere and offers a reading room stocked with an eclectic literary mix and children's games. The bar, featuring the original timber frame of the building, serves local Harvey's Sussex Best Bitter, best enjoyed sitting next to the roaring log fire. From the garden there are magnificent views of Romney Marsh and the River Rother;

the Rye Bay fishing fleet which moors close by provides most of the seafood on the menu. Other options include Romney Marsh lamb hotpot and wild boar sausage and mash. Booking is advisable for the traditional Sunday roasts. There is live music on Friday nights, Sundays and in the garden in summer. Dogs are welcome – ask for a free dog treat.

Open all day all wk **Bar Meals** L served all wk 12-3 D served Mon-Sat 6-9 **Restaurant** L served all wk 12-3 D served Sat-Thu 6-9, Fri 6-8 ⊕ FREE HOUSE ◀ Harvey's Sussex Best Bitter, Timothy Taylor Landlord, Larkins Best Bitter, Adnams, Guest ales Ŏ Biddenden Bushell. ♟ 12 **Facilities** Non-diners area ♣ (Bar Garden) ♦♦ Children's menu Children's portions Garden ⋒ Wi-fi

SALEHURST Map 7 TQ72

Salehurst Halt

PICK OF THE PUBS

Church Ln TN32 5PH ☎ **01580 880620**
dir: 0.5m from A21 (Tunbridge Wells to Hastings road). Exit at Robertsbridge rdbt to Salehurst

Free house with hop growing connections

Built in the 1860s, when it was known as the Old Eight Bells. Legend puts the name change down to a church organist who commuted to the village from Bodiam, necessitating a new halt on the Robertsbridge to Tenterden line. Despite use by many a hop-picker thereafter, the steam railway eventually closed. Today the hop crop is sold to Harvey's in Lewes, and returned as one of the ales sold by the pub – its traditional cellar is much prized for maintaining ale in top condition. The hop-growing farm also supplies the pub's meats, including Buster's burgers; note that evening meals are only served from Wednesday to Saturday. The landscaped garden has a wonderful terrace with beautiful views over the Rother Valley; here a wood-fired pizza oven (and outdoor griddle weather permitting) runs almost continually during the summer, with orders taken at the garden counter. Before leaving, have a stroll around this picturesque hamlet and the 12th-century church.

Open Tue-Wed 12-3 6-11 (Thu-Sun 12-11) Closed: Mon **Bar Meals** L served Tue-Sun 12-2.30 D served Wed-Sat 7-9 ⊕ FREE HOUSE ◀ Harvey's Sussex Best Bitter, Dark Star, Old Dairy, Guest ales Ŏ Biddenden Bushels, East Stour. **Facilities** Non-diners area ♦♦ Children's portions Garden ⋒

Save on hotels. Book at theAA.com/hotel

SUSSEX, EAST 437 ENGLAND

The Peacock Inn

PICK OF THE PUBS

TN22 3XA ☎ 01825 762463
e-mail: enquiries@peacock-inn.co.uk
dir: *Just off A272 (Haywards Heath to Uckfield road) &
A26 (Uckfield to Lewes road)*

Pretty black and white pub with seasonally inspired menus

Mentioned in Samuel Pepys' diary, The Peacock Inn dates from 1567 but is these days more renowned for its food and its warm welcome. This traditional inn is full of old-world charm, both inside and out. Woodcote Bitter and a guest ale keeps beer-lovers happy, and there are eight wines by the glass. For the hungry there are starters such as crispy poached duck egg and ham hock, lambs lettuce; seared breast of wood pigeon, red wine and pancetta risotto; followed by braised pork belly, smoked pork rissoles, conference pears, onions, Madeira jus; or pan-fried south coast cod, crab ravioli, confit fennel, baby artichokes, lemon basil dressing. For the non-meat eaters there's wild mushroom and celeriac risotto. Leave room for desserts such as strawberry and rhubarb cheesecake with ginger parfait or peach pannacotta with champagne jelly. The large rear patio garden is a delightful spot in summer.

Open all wk 11-3 6-11 Closed: 25-26 Dec **Bar Meals** L served Mon-Sat 12-3, Sun 12-6 D served Mon-Sat 6-9.30 **Restaurant** L served Mon-Sat 12-3, Sun 12-6 D served Mon-Sat 6-9.30 ⊕ FREE HOUSE ◀ Harvey's Sussex Best Bitter, Hammerpot Woodcote Bitter, Guest ale. ☻ 8 **Facilities** Non-diners area ☻ (Bar Garden) ●↑ Children's menu Children's portions Garden ⋈ Parking

The Bull

Dunster Mill Ln TN5 7HH ☎ 01580 200586
e-mail: enquiries@thebullinn.co.uk
dir: *From M25 exit at Sevenoaks toward Hastings, right at x-rds onto B2087, right onto B2099 through Ticehurst, right for Three Legged Cross*

Home-cooked food and large family-friendly garden

The Bull started life as a 14th-century Wealden Hall House, reputedly one of the oldest dwelling places in the country, and is set in a hamlet close to Bewl Water. The interior features oak beams, inglenook fireplaces, quarry-tiled floors, and a mass of small intimate areas in the bar. The extensive gardens are popular with families who enjoy the duck pond, petanque pitch, aviary and children's play area. Menus offer pub favourites ranging from freshly baked baguettes and bar snacks to hearty dishes full of comfort, such as bangers and mash and treacle tart.

Open all day all wk 12-12 Closed: 25-26 Dec eve ⊕ FREE HOUSE ◀ Harvey's Sussex Best Bitter & Armada Ale, Timothy Taylor Landlord, Guest ales ♉ Westons Stowford Press. **Facilities** ☻ (Bar Garden) ●↑ Children's menu Children's portions Play area Garden Parking Wi-fi

The Bell **NEW**

PICK OF THE PUBS

High St TN5 7AS ☎ 01580 200234
e-mail: info@thebellinticehurst.com
dir: *From A21 follow signs for Ticehurst. Pub in village centre*

Village inn refurbished to make you smile

Following serious investment and a full-scale refurbishment, the doors of the new-look Bell were pushed open in late 2011 to reveal a cool, comfortable and very quirky pub. The authentic 16th-century charm of the building has been preserved in the bar, with its rustic wooden floors, sagging beams, and a blazing log fire in the huge brick inglenook. There's a cosy snug next door with leather Chesterfields and shelves of books, and beyond, the Stable with a Table, an inspired function room space with a long sunken table and benches, perfect for the regular debate evenings (Table Talks) and demonstration dinners. Funky design touches abound, from the top hat lampshades and pillar of books in the bar, to the tubas for urinals in the Gents and the stuffed squirrel that appears to hold up a ceiling. Beer and food is as local as you can get – wash down Weald smokery salmon, Sussex rib-eye steak with béarnaise sauce, or roast venison with cranberry sauce with a pint of Harvey's.

Open all day all wk **Bar Meals** L served all wk 12-6 D served all wk 6-9.30 food served all day **Restaurant** L served all wk 12-3 D served all wk 6-9.30 ⊕ FREE HOUSE ◀ Harvey's, Sharp's Doom Bar, Seasonal Guest ales ♉ Symonds. ☻ 12 **Facilities** Non-diners area ☻ (Bar Garden) ●↑ Children's menu Garden ⋈ Parking Wi-fi ▦ (notice required)

The Best Beech Inn

PICK OF THE PUBS

Best Beech Hill TN5 6JH ☎ 01892 782046
e-mail: info@thebestbeech.co.uk
dir: *7m from Tunbridge Wells. On A246 at lights left into London Rd (A26), left at mini rdbt onto A267, left, right onto B2100. At Mark Cross signed Wadhurst, 3m on right*

Welcoming country pub

Situated in the perfect country-pub setting - in an Area of Outstanding Natural Beauty near the Kent and Sussex border. Once a coaching house dating back to 1680, the pub has been sympathetically preserved the essential Victorian character of its heyday, with comfy chairs, exposed brickwork and open fireplaces. The atmosphere is relaxed and welcoming while the decor combines both old and new. The seasonal menus offer the freshest, most dynamic ingredients sourced from local suppliers. Starters might include chicken liver parfait, followed by main courses such as leek, mushroom and almond loaf, or game pie. Enjoy apple pie with rhubarb compôte or local Sussex cheeses for pudding. Sandwiches and children's choices are also available. The tip-top ales and great selection of wines can be enjoyed by the fire in winter or out on the terrace in summer.

Open all wk 12-11 (Mon 5-11) **Bar Meals** L served Tue-Sat 12-9, Sun 2-5 D served Tue-Sat 12-9 food served all day **Restaurant** L served Tue-Sat 12-9, Sun 2-5 D served Tue-Sat 12-9 food served all day ⊕ SHEPHERD NEAME ◀ Harvey's ♉ Thatchers Gold. ☻ 9 **Facilities** Non-diners area ●↑ Children's menu Children's portions Garden ⋈ Parking Wi-fi ▦ (notice required)

The Giants Rest

The Street BN26 5SQ ☎ 01323 870207
e-mail: giantsrest@hotmail.com
dir: *2m from Polegate on A27 towards Brighton*

Perfect after a long country walk

This family-owned Victorian free house has the famous chalk figure of the Long Man of Wilmington standing guard further up the lane and proves to be just the place to leave muddy boots at the door after a steep hill walk. The rustic wooden-floored bar is decorated with Beryl Cook prints. Take a seat at a pine table, each with its own wooden puzzle, and order some home-prepared food: chicken liver parfait with date and apple chutney; home-cooked ham with bubble-and-squeak and house chutney; and traditional fruit crumble are typical choices. Wash it down with beers from the Longman Brewery at Litlington just three miles down the road.

Open all wk 11-3 6-11 (Sat-Sun all day) **Bar Meals** L served Mon-Fri 11.30-2, Sat-Sun all day D served Mon-Fri 6.30-9, Sat-Sun all day **Restaurant** L served Mon-Fri 11.30-2, Sat-Sun all day D served Mon-Fri 6.30-9, Sat-Sun all day ⊕ FREE HOUSE ◀ Longman Best Bitter, Long Blonde, Old Man, American Pale Ale ♉ Westons Stowford Press. ☻ **Facilities** Non-diners area ☻ (Bar Restaurant Garden) ●↑ Children's portions Garden ⋈ Parking Wi-fi ▦

WITHYHAM   Map 6 TQ43

The Dorset Arms

PICK OF THE PUBS

TN7 4BD ☎ 01892 770278
e-mail: p-abbott@btconnect.com
dir: *4m W of Tunbridge Wells on B2110 between Groombridge & Hartfield*

Packed with historical features

The picture-postcard perfection of this centuries-old building is a jigsaw of ages and styles - slender chimney stacks, sharp gables, gleaming white weatherboarding and careworn tiles. Licensed some 200 years ago when it took the name of the local landowning family, once Earls of Dorset, the interior doesn't disappoint, with a comfy, period mix of flagstoned and oak-boarded floors, vast open fireplace, undulating beams, and magpie furniture. It remains at heart a true village local, with darts, good Sussex ales from Harvey's and a vibrant community atmosphere. The produce of the kitchen is also a major draw, with an extensive, daily-changing specials board complementing the respectable carte menu. Starters include goats' cheese crostini; and whitebait with salad. The main course options might be Thai green chicken curry; chargrilled pork chops, wholegrain mustard mash and cider reduction; and beer battered skinless cod fillet and triple cooked hand-cut chips. All desserts are home-made. Tables on the green outside allow summertime alfresco dining.

Open 12-3 6-11 (Sat-Sun all day) Closed: Mon Oct-May **Bar Meals** L served all wk 12-2.30, Sat-Sun all day D served all wk 6-9, Sat-Sun all day **Restaurant** L served all wk 12-2.30, Sat-Sun all day D served all wk 6-9, Sat-Sun all day ⊕ HARVEYS OF LEWES ◀ Sussex Best Bitter, Seasonal ales. **Facilities** Non-diners area ❅ (Bar Garden) ⏍ Children's menu Children's portions Garden ⌒ Parking Wi-fi

SUSSEX, WEST

AMBERLEY   Map 6 TQ01

The Bridge Inn

Houghton Bridge BN18 9LR ☎ 01798 831619
e-mail: bridgeamberley@btinternet.com
web: www.bridgeinnamberley.com
dir: *5m N of Arundel on B2139. Adjacent to Amberley rail station*

Reliable old inn in National Park village

Visiting the fascinating Amberley Museum and Heritage Centre, just over the road from this mellow free-house, is a good way of working up an appetite before investigating this charming period pub close to the River Arun. People are drawn in to the candlelit bar and log fires on cold winter evenings for real ales from the likes of Ballards and Harveys, and in summer to seek shade in the sheltered garden; from here they can appreciate the delightful countryside of the South Downs and contemplate meals from the solid pubby menu, with classics like battered cod fillet and chips. Mediterranean-inspired dishes often feature on the specials board.

Open all day all wk 11-11 (Sun 12-10.30) **Bar Meals** L served Mon-Fri 12-2.30, Sat-Sun 12-4 D served Mon-Sat 6-9, Sun 5.30-8 **Restaurant** L served Mon-Fri 12-2.30, Sat-Sun 12-4 D served Mon-Sat 6-9, Sun 5.30-8 ⊕ FREE HOUSE ◀ Skinner's Betty Stogs, Harvey's Sussex Best Bitter, Ballards Golden Bine, Guest ales ⏏ Westons Stowford Press. **Facilities** Non-diners area ❅ (Bar Garden) ⏍ Children's menu Children's portions Garden Outside area ⌒ Parking ☕ (notice required)

ASHURST   Map 6 TQ11

The Fountain Inn

PICK OF THE PUBS

BN44 3AP ☎ 01403 710219
e-mail: manager@fountainashurst.co.uk
dir: *On B2135 N of Steyning*

Traditional English pub with some famous admirers

The South Downs and the village duck pond are visible from the terrace of this 16th-century listed building, which comes complete with wonky floorboards, inglenook fireplaces, beams, rustic furnishings, a skittle alley and the smell of home cooking. Sir Laurence Olivier and author Hilaire Belloc were regulars, and Sir Paul McCartney loved the place so much he filmed part of the video for *Wonderful Christmas Time* here in 1979. Local beers from Harvey's accompany the tasty, freshly cooked pub food that attracts walkers, cyclists, locals and those from further afield. At lunchtime there are light bites, or at lunch or dinner you could opt for the full three courses; maybe bucket of whitebait followed by a chickpea and chilli burger or chicken pie, and apple and blackberry crumble for pudding. Look out for events including live music and comedy. Change of hands.

Open all day all wk 11-11 (Sun 11-10.30) **Bar Meals** L served Mon-Fri 12-2.30, Sat-Sun 12-9.30 D served Mon-Fri 6-9.30, Sat-Sun 12-9.30 Av main course £14 **Restaurant** L served Mon-Fri 12-2.30, Sat-Sun 12-9.30 D served Mon-Fri 6-9.30, Sat-Sun 12-9.30 Av 3 course à la carte fr £25 ⊕ ENTERPRISE INNS ◀ Harvey's Sussex, Sharp's Doom Bar, Fuller's, Seasonal & Guest ales ⏏ Westons Stowford Press. **Facilities** Non-diners area ❅ (Bar Garden) ⏍ Children's menu Children's portions Garden ⌒ Parking Wi-fi ☕ (notice required)

BALCOMBE   Map 6 TQ33

The Cowdray

RH17 6QD ☎ 01444 811280
e-mail: alexandandy@hotmail.co.uk
dir: *M23 junct 10a, B2036 towards Balcombe*

Revitalised pub aiming high

This once run-down village boozer has been transformed into a plushly upholstered dining pub. Inside you'll find wood floors, a fresh, crisp decor, and a pub menu that's a cut above average. Alex and Andy Owen, who previously worked for Gordon Ramsay, specialise in sourcing ingredients within Sussex if possible. Notable exceptions are the Scottish Angus and Longhorn beef cuts which appear on the separate rare-breeds steak menu. Other dishes might include pigeon with raisin purée, onion marmalade and mixed leaves; roasted lamb chump with honey-glazed root vegetables and dauphinoise potatoes; and tarte Tatin for pudding.

Open all day all wk Closed: 25 Dec eve ⊕ GREENE KING ◀ IPA, Morland Original, Guinness. **Facilities** ❅ (Bar Garden) ⏍ Children's menu Children's portions Play area Family room Garden Parking Wi-fi

Save on hotels. Book at theAA.com/hotel

SUSSEX, WEST 439 ENGLAND

BOSHAM
Map 5 SU80

The Anchor Bleu

High St PO18 8LS ☎ **01243 573956**
dir: *From A27 SW of Chichester take A259. Follow Fishbourne signs, then Bosham signs*

Harbourside pub with plenty of real ales

If you park your car opposite The Anchor Bleu, check the tide times at this 17th-century inn, as that area floods during most high tides. Flagstone floors, low beams, an open log fire and two terraces, one overlooking Chichester Harbour, add to the charm of this popular pub. A good choice of real ales is on offer, including Ringwood Fortyniner. Dishes are based on locally sourced, seasonal ingredients, such as Blackdown venison steak, salt and pepper squid, and brie and artichoke tartlet. Reservations for the evening are recommended but there are no bookings taken for lunch. Meals can be taken on the terraces during warmer weather.

Open all wk all day (11.30-3 6-11 Nov-Mar) **Bar Meals** L served Mon-Sat 12-3 Sun all day D served all wk 6.30-9.30 Av main course £8.95 **Restaurant** L served all wk 12-3 D served all wk 6.30-9.30 Fixed menu price fr £9.95 ⊕ ENTERPRISE INNS ◀ Sharp's Cornish Coaster & Doom Bar, Ringwood Fortyniner, Otter Ale, Hop Back Summer Lightning & TEA, Bath Gem ◊ Westons Stowford Press, Taunton Original. ♚ 10 **Facilities** Non-diners area ♦♦ Children's menu Children's portions Garden ⋒ ⛟ (notice required)

BURGESS HILL
Map 6 TQ31

The Oak Barn

Cuckfield Rd RH15 8RE ☎ **01444 258222**
e-mail: enquiries@oakbarnrestaurant.co.uk
web: www.oakbarnrestaurant.co.uk
dir: *Telephone for directions*

British produce in an idyllic setting

As its name suggests, this popular pub-restaurant occupies a 250-year-old barn that has been lovingly restored using salvaged timbers from wooden ships. Brimming with charm, the interior is rich in oak flooring, authentic wagon wheel chandeliers, and fine stained glass. Lofty raftered ceilings, a galleried restaurant, and leather chairs fronting a huge fireplace add to the atmosphere. Sup a pint of Harvey's and tuck into dishes constructed from seasonal British ingredients: grilled queen scallops to start, followed by pan-roasted baby chicken, and home-made pear and almond tart to finish. Outside is an enclosed courtyard and patios, with water features.

The Oak Barn

Open all day all wk 10am-11pm (Sun 11-11) **Bar Meals** L served all wk 12-2.30 D served all wk 6-9.30 Av main course £13.50 **Restaurant** L served all wk 12-2.30 D served all wk 6-9.30 Fixed menu price fr £13.50 Av 3 course à la carte fr £24 ⊕ FREE HOUSE ◀ Harvey's, Guinness. ♚ 8 **Facilities** Non-diners area ♦♦ Children's portions Garden ⋒ Parking Wi-fi

See advert on page 000

BURPHAM · Map 6 TQ00

George & Dragon ⊚

PICK OF THE PUBS

BN18 9RR ☎ 01903 883131
e-mail: sara.cheney@btinternet.com
dir: *Exit A27 1m E of Arundel signed Burpham, 2.5m, pub on left*

Home cooked locally sourced food in beautiful Sussex village

Tucked away down a long 'no through road', Burpham looks across the Arun Valley to the mighty Arundel Castle. There are excellent riverside and downland walks on the doorstep of this 300-year-old free house, and walkers are welcome in the bar. Step inside and you'll find beamed ceilings and modern prints on the walls, with worn stone flags on the floor. The original rooms have been opened out to form a large space that catches the late sunshine, but there are still a couple of alcoves with tables for an intimate drink. You'll also discover a small bar hidden around a corner. This is very much a dining pub, attracting visitors from far and wide. The à la carte menu and specials board offer a good choice of dishes between them: for starters you could try pan-seared scallops or Thai-marinated tiger prawns with noodles. Main courses might include chicken and wild mushroom pie, or seafood risotto. There are tables outside, ideal for whiling away an afternoon or evening in summer, listening to the cricket being played on the green.

Open all wk 12-3 6-11 **Bar Meals** L served Mon-Fri 12-2, Sat-Sun 12-3 D served all wk 6-9 **Restaurant** L served Mon-Fri 12-2, Sat 12-2.30, Sun 12-3 D served all wk 6-9 ⊕ FREE HOUSE ◀ Arundel, Guest ales ⚬ Aspall. **Facilities** Non-diners area ♦♦ Children's menu Garden ⊼ Parking ▥

BURY · Map 6 TQ01

The Squire & Horse

Bury Common RH20 1NS ☎ 01798 831343
e-mail: squireandhorse@btconnect.com
dir: *On A29, 4m S of Pulbrough, 4m N of Arundel*

Family-run free house with innovative menus

The original 16th-century building was extended several years ago, with old wooden beams and country fireplaces throughout. All the food is freshly cooked to order and sourced locally wherever possible. With the head chef originating from Australia there are innovative gastro-pub style dishes on offer here. These could include springbok Wellington with confit potato, or pork escalopes layered with ratatouille and three cheeses. You can also dine outside in the stylish seating area. There is a members' dining club to join with discounts throughout the year.

Open all wk 11-3 6-11 ⊕ FREE HOUSE ◀ Greene King IPA, Harvey's Sussex, Guest ales. **Facilities** ♦♦ Children's menu Garden Parking

CHARLTON · Map 6 SU81

The Fox Goes Free ★★★★ INN

PICK OF THE PUBS

See Pick of the Pubs on opposite page

CHICHESTER · Map 5 SU80

The Bull's Head ★★★★ INN

99 Fishbourne Road West PO19 3JP ☎ 01243 839895
e-mail: enquiries@bullsheadfishbourne.net
dir: *A27 onto A259, 0.5m on left*

Good range of well-kept real ales

Only three minutes' walk from Chichester harbour, this traditional roadside pub with large open fire has been a hostelry since some time in the 17th century, and before that it was a farmhouse. Its position just outside Chichester is perfect for visiting Fishbourne Roman Palace and Bosham harbour. Home-cooked food is based on locally sourced ingredients and baguettes and jacket potatoes are on offer as a lighter option. The pub serves five real ales all in tip-top condition. Live jazz is played every month and special events are hosted throughout the year.

Open all wk 11-3 5.30-11 (Sat-Sun all day) **Bar Meals** L served Mon-Fri 12-2, Sat 12-9.30, Sun 12-3 D served Mon-Fri 6-9, Sat 12-9.30, Sun 6-8.30 **Restaurant** L served Mon-Fri 12-2, Sat 12-9.30, Sun 12-3 D served Mon-Fri 6-9, Sat 12-9, Sun 6-8.30 ⊕ FULLER'S ◀ London Pride, Geoge Gale & Co Seafarers ⚬ Aspall. ₤ 10 **Facilities** Non-diners area ✿ (Bar) ♦♦ Children's portions Outside area ⊼ Parking Wi-fi ▥ (notice required) **Rooms** 4

The Earl of March ⊚

PICK OF THE PUBS

Lavant Rd, Lavant PO18 0BQ ☎ 01243 533993
e-mail: info@theearlofmarch.com
dir: *On A286, 1m N of Chichester*

Lots of style at former coaching inn

Named after the local landowning dynasty, The Earl nestles at the foot of the South Downs National Park and is an inspirational place to visit. William Blake wrote the words to 'Jerusalem' whilst sitting in the east-facing bay window here in 1803; today's visitors can enjoy much the same views that prompted his outpourings. The excellent choice of dishes is prepared from the bounty of local estates and the nearby Channel. A winter menu might have perhaps pan-seared scallops, langoustines, pork belly, pea purée, Selsey bisque; followed by whole roasted partridge, pomme Anna, mulled plums, quails egg, cep broth and pickled mushroom. Such dishes are crafted by Giles Thompson, former Executive Chef at London's Ritz Hotel and now proprietor of this delightful 18th-century coaching inn appointed in 'country plush' style.

Open all day all wk **Bar Meals** L served all wk 12-2.30 winter, 12-9 summer D served all wk 12-9 summer Av main course £18.50 **Restaurant** L served all wk 12-2.30

winter, Sun 12-3 summer D served Mon-Sat 5.30-9.30, Sun 6-9 Fixed menu price fr £18.50 Av 3 course à la carte fr £30 ⊕ ENTERPRISE INNS ◀ Hop Back Summer Lightning, Harvey's, Guest ale ⚬ Westons Stowford Press, Aspall. ₤ 31 **Facilities** Non-diners area ✿ (Bar Garden) ♦♦ Children's menu Children's portions Garden ⊼ Parking Wi-fi

Royal Oak Inn ★★★★★ INN ⊚

PICK OF THE PUBS

See Pick of the Pubs on page 442

COMPTON · Map 5 SU71

Coach & Horses

The Square PO18 9HA ☎ 023 9263 1228
dir: *On B2146 S of Petersfield, to Emsworth, in centre of Compton*

Appealing South Downs honeypot

David and Christiane Butler have run their 17th-century coaching inn in this pretty South Downs village since 1985. Popular with walkers, cyclists and, let's face it, anyone looking for good food and drink, its unspoiled Victorian bar, with two open fires, is widely known for championing local microbreweries like Dark Star, Ballards and Langham. The oldest part of the pub, with many exposed beams, is the restaurant, where David, who trained at The Ritz, serves chicken mushroom and tarragon pie; avocado and spinach bake; and crackling pork belly, and makes good use of local game and South Downs lamb.

Open all wk 11.30-3 6-11 **Bar Meals** L served all wk 12-2 D served all wk 7-9 **Restaurant** L served all wk 12-2 D served all wk 7-9 ⊕ FREE HOUSE ◀ Ballards Best Bitter, Hammerpot Bottle Wreck Porter, Guest ales ⚬ Thatchers, Appledram. **Facilities** Non-diners area ✿ (Bar Outside area) ♦♦ Children's portions Outside area ⊼ Parking Wi-fi ▥ (notice required)

CUCKFIELD · Map 6 TQ32

The Talbot

High St RH17 5JX ☎ 01444 455898
e-mail: info@thetalbotcuckfield.co.uk
dir: *B2036 into village centre*

Former staging-post inn with smart interior

At the heart of the historic village of Cuckfield. A contemporary pub and restaurant that prides itself on making the most of the local larder, whether it's Dark Star or Harvey's ales or seasonal dishes such as seared Newhaven scallops with parsnip purée and black pudding, or roasted field mushroom with home-smoked blue cheese. Such is the pub's commitment to local food, there is a monthly producers' market in the courtyard.

Open all day all wk ⊕ FREE HOUSE ◀ Harvey's Sussex Best Bitter, Dark Star, Guest ales. **Facilities** ✿ (Bar Garden) ♦♦ Children's menu Children's portions Garden Wi-fi

PICK OF THE PUBS

The Fox Goes Free ★★★★ INN

CHARLTON   Map 6 SU81

PO18 0HU ☎ 01243 811461
e-mail: enquiries@thefoxgoesfree.com
web: www.thefoxgoesfree.com
dir: *A286, 6m from Chichester towards Midhurst*

Friendly pub with William III, the racing world and the WI connections

Standing in unspoiled countryside at the foot of the South Downs, this lovely old brick and flint free house was a favoured hunting lodge of William III. With its three huge fireplaces, old pews and brick floors, the 15th-century building simply exudes charm and character. The pub, which hosted the first English Women's Institute meeting in 1915, lies close to the Weald and Downland Open Air Museum, where 50 historic buildings from around southern England have been reconstructed. Goodwood Estate is also close by, and The Fox attracts many customers during the racing season and the annual Festival of Speed. Away from the high life, you can watch the world go by from the solid timber benches and tables to the front, or relax under the apples trees in the lawned rear garden. Lest all this sounds rather extravagant, you'll find that The Fox is a friendly and welcoming drinkers' pub with a good selection of real ales that includes the eponymous Fox Goes Free bitter. Everything from the

chips to the ice cream is home-made and, whether you're looking for a quick bar snack or something more substantial, the daily-changing menus offer something for every taste. Bar meals include lasagne, sausages with bubble-and-squeak, and fish and chips with mushy peas; as well as a selection of ciabattas. Further choices may start with home-baked bread and marinated olives, or whole baked camembert, confit garlic and toasted fingers. Continue with meat and fish main courses such as chicken breast with grilled chorizo and pearl bailey; or roast monkfish with confit potatoes, pea puree and tomato coulis. Salads can be prepared for both small and large appetites, and there are some appealing vegetarian options, too.

Open all day all wk 11-11 (Sun 12-11) Closed: 25 Dec eve **Bar Meals** L served Mon-Fri 12-2.30, Sat-Sun 12-10 D served Mon-Fri 6.30-10, Sat-Sun 12-10 **Restaurant** L served all wk 12-2.30 D served all wk 6.30-10 ⊕ FREE HOUSE ◀ The Fox Goes Free, Ballards Best Bitter ♂ Addlestones, Westons Stowford Press. ♀ 10 **Facilities** Non-diners area ❀ ♦ Children's menu & portions Garden ⋔ Parking Wi-fi 🚌 **Rooms** 5

PICK OF THE PUBS

Royal Oak Inn ★★★★★ INN ✿

CHICHESTER　　　　　Map 5 SU80

Pook Ln, East Lavant PO18 0AX
☎ **01243 527434**
e-mail: info@royaloakeastlavant.co.uk
web: www.royaloakeastlavant.co.uk
dir: *2m N of Chichester. Exit A286 to East Lavant centre*

A smart dining pub with luxury accommodation

Starting life two centuries ago as a farmhouse, the Royal Oak is set within the South Downs National Park and is just up the hill from Goodwood racecourse; it is also perfectly situated for the nearby cathedral city of Chichester. The creeper-clad Georgian inn is at the heart of the beautiful, historic village of East Lavant and is known for offering great food to visitors and locals alike. The brick-lined restaurant and beamed bar achieve a crisp, rustic brand of chic: details include chunky wooden tables, leather chairs, open fires, fresh flowers, candles, and wine attractively displayed in alcoves set into the walls; local Sussex Gold and Horsham Best ales, whiskies and Gospel Green Champagne cider are among the thirst-quenchers on offer. The seasonal menu is an easy mix of modern European dishes and English classics with a twist, and much of the produce is grown by villagers in return for pints. The lovely patio is the perfect place to enjoy a trio of Selsey crab –

white crab meat with horseradish mayonnaise, brown crab mousse and a crab cake with a basil and vermouth foam – perhaps accompanied by one of the 20 wines by the glass. The specials board features the fish and meat dishes of the day, while the à la carte could list a starter of pan-roasted breast of wood pigeon with individual apple tarte Tatin, celeriac and truffle purée, lardons and a rich red wine dressing; and a main course of pithivier of garden vegetables and mushrooms on a bed of broccoli purée and served with tarragon cream. There are luxury guest rooms with large, comfortable beds and en suite bathrooms.

Open all day all wk 7am-11.30pm **Bar Meals** Av main course £9.95 food served

all day **Restaurant** L served all wk 12-2.30 D served Mon-Fri 6-9, Sat 6-9.30, Sun 6.30-9 Fixed menu price fr £16.95 Av 3 course à la carte fr £29 ⊕ FREE HOUSE ◀ Skinner's Betty Stogs, Sharp's Doom Bar, Arundel Sussex Gold, WJ King Horsham Best ♂ Gospel Green Champagne & Cidermakers, Thatchers Gold. ♟ 20 **Facilities** Non-diners area ♦♦ Children's portions Garden ⋒ Parking Wi-fi **Rooms** 8

Save on hotels. Book at theAA.com/hotel

SUSSEX, WEST 443 ENGLAND

DIAL POST
Map 6 TQ11

The Crown Inn

Worthing Rd RH13 8NH ☎ **01403 710902**
e-mail: crowninndialpost@aol.com
dir: *8m S of Horsham, off A24*

Family heritage at real ale gastro-pub

Front of house here is Penny Middleton, whose grandparents owned this tile-hung free house overlooking the village green in the late 60s and early 70s. That her sister and partner rear the pigs and lambs that end up in the kitchen strengthens the family involvement. Although it is food-led, if you just want a pint of bitter from the Bedlam, Devil's Dyke or Harveys brewery, that's absolutely fine. Penny's chef husband James makes everything on the premises, including coarse pork and chicken liver pâté; Harveys beer-battered haddock and hand-cut chips; gently spiced bean and vegetable casserole; and home-made blackcurrant sorbet.

Open all wk Mon-Sat 11-3 6-11 (Sun 12-4) **Bar Meals** L served all wk 12-2.15 D served Mon-Sat 6-9.15 Av main course £12 **Restaurant** L served all wk 12-2.15 D served Mon-Sat 6-9.15 Av 3 course à la carte fr £25 ⊕ FREE HOUSE ◀ Harvey's Sussex Best Bitter, Devil's Dyke Porter, Kissingate Best, Guest ale ♂ Thatchers Gold. ☲ 12 **Facilities** Non-diners area ❤ (Bar Restaurant Garden) ♦♦ Children's portions Garden ⊟ Parking Wi-fi 🚌 (notice required)

DUNCTON
Map 6 SU91

The Cricketers

GU28 0LB ☎ **01798 342473**
e-mail: info@thecricketersduncton.co.uk
dir: *On A285, 3m from Petworth, 8m from Chichester*

Ideal rest stop when exploring the South Downs

Named to commemorate its one-time owner John Wisden, the first-class cricketer and creator of the famous sporting almanac, this attractive whitewashed pub sits in beautiful gardens behind Goodwood. Dating to the 16th century, with an inglenook fireplace, the inn has hardly changed over the years. Well-kept real ales include Arundel Sussex Gold, while the blackboard menu offers lunchtime sandwiches and traditional favourites, home-cooked from locally sourced ingredients. Look for the likes of crackling pork hock, toad-in-the-hole, herb-crusted rack of lamb, crab salad, and Sussex Slipcote cheese risotto. Children are welcome and there's a menu to suit younger tastes.

Open all day all wk **Bar Meals** L served Mon-Thu 12-2.30, Fri-Sun 12-9 D served Mon-Thu 6-9, Fri-Sun 12-9 **Restaurant** L served Mon-Thu 12-2.30, Fri-Sun 12-9 D served Mon-Thu 6-9, Fri-Sun 12-9 ⊕ FREE HOUSE ◀ Triple fff Moondance, WJ King Horsham Best, Arundel Sussex Gold, Guest ale ♂ Thatchers & Heritage. **Facilities** Non-diners area ❤ (Bar Restaurant Garden) ♦♦ Children's menu Children's portions Play area Garden ⊟ Parking

EAST ASHLING
Map 5 SU80

Horse and Groom ★★★★ INN

PO18 9AX ☎ **01243 575339**
e-mail: info@thehorseandgroomchichester.co.uk
web: www.thehorseandgroomchichester.co.uk
dir: *3m from Chichester on B1278 towards Rowland's Castle*

Traditional inn with suntrap beer garden

This 400-year-old village inn with rooms retains much of its heritage; timber frames, oak beams and flagstone floors offer a comfy retreat. The pub has long been popular with visitors exploring Bosham Harbour, and the South Downs National Park to the north. In the bar, try ales such as Dark Star Hophead and Sharp's Doom Bar accompanied by a toasted ciabatta or baked potato, while in the restaurant, enjoy the extensive menu of mains and fish dishes. Choices include cottage pie, lamb cutlets, fillet steak and crab salad. If ordering from the set menu, pre-booking is required.

Open 12-3 6-11 (Sat all day Sun 12-6) Closed: Sun eve **Bar Meals** L served Mon-Sat 12-2.15, Sun 12-2.30 D served Mon-Sat 6.30-9.15 **Restaurant** L served Mon-Sat 12-2.15, Sun 12-2.30 D served Mon-Sat 6.30-9.15 ⊕ FREE HOUSE ◀ Hop Back Summer Lightning, Brewster's Hophead, Dark Star Hophead, Sharp's Doom Bar, Young's ♂ Westons Stowford Press, Addlestones. **Facilities** Non-diners area ❤ (Bar Garden) ♦♦ Children's menu Children's portions Garden ⊟ Parking Wi-fi **Rooms** 11

EAST DEAN
Map 6 SU91

The Star & Garter

PICK OF THE PUBS

PO18 0JG ☎ **01243 811318**
e-mail: thestarandgarter@hotmail.com
dir: *On A286 between Chichester & Midhurst. Exit A286 at Singleton. Village in 2m*

Nestling in charming downland village

Built as a pub from traditional Sussex flint in about 1740, The Star & Garter stands close to the village pond in the pretty downland village of East Dean. The interior is open and gives a light and airy atmosphere with original brickwork, antique panelling, scrubbed tables and a wood-burning stove. In the bar, two locally brewed real ales are served from the barrel alongside two ciders and a range of wines by the glass. Locally renowned for an excellent selection of fish and shellfish, the menu also includes fine meat and vegetarian dishes, plus sharing platters. Typical choices include roasted guinea fowl with creamy Shropshire Blue sauce; couscous-crusted goats' cheese with red onion salad; and pan-seared scallops with crispy pancetta and salad. A sunny sheltered patio, an original well and attractive lawned gardens complete the picture. Goodwood racecourse and motor racing venues are just a short hop by car.

Open all wk 11-3 6-11 (Fri 11-3 5-11 Sat-Sun all day) **Bar Meals** L served Mon-Fri 12-2.30, Sat-Sun all day D served Mon-Fri 6.30-9.30, Sat-Sun all day **Restaurant** L served Mon-Fri 12-2.30, Sat-Sun all day D served Mon-Fri 6.30-9.30, Sat-Sun all day ⊕ FREE HOUSE ◀ Arundel Castle, Sussex Gold, Guest ales ♂ Westons 1st Quality, Aspall. ☲ 11 **Facilities** Non-diners area ♦♦ Children's menu Children's portions Garden ⊟ Parking Wi-fi 🚌

EAST GRINSTEAD
Map 6 TQ33

The Old Dunnings Mill NEW

Dunnings Rd RH19 4AT ☎ **01342 326341**
e-mail: enquiries@theolddunningsmill.co.uk
dir: *From High St into Ship St. At mini rdbt right into Dunnings Rd. Pub on right*

Old meets new – and works

There are two parts to this pub: the original 16th-century flour mill, and the stylistically sympathetic 1970s addition, with wooden floors and a bar with an open fire. The front garden is fenced, and a stream, which powers a working water-wheel, runs under the covered decking with tables, chairs, gas-burners and potted plants. As it's a Harveys of Lewes pub, you'll find their Best and Hadlow real ales in the bar, while on the menu look for braised half-shoulder of Sussex lamb; pan-fried trout fillet; and penne pasta arrabbiata. The ODM holds beer festivals in June and September.

Open all day all wk **Bar Meals** L served all wk 12-9.30 D served all wk 12-9.30 food served all day **Restaurant** L served all wk 12-9.30 D served all wk 12-9.30 food served all day ⊕ HARVEYS OF LEWES ◀ Sussex Best Bitter, Sussex Hadlow Bitter ♂ Thatchers Gold Apple & Pear. ☲ 27 **Facilities** Non-diners area ❤ (Bar Garden) ♦♦ Children's portions Garden ⊟ Beer festival Parking Wi-fi 🚌 (notice required)

| ELSTED | Map 5 SU81 |

The Three Horseshoes

GU29 0JY ☎ 01730 825746
dir: A272 from Midhurst towards Petersfield, left in 2m
signed Harting & Elsted, 3m to pub on left

Game is a speciality here

With views across fields and woods, this 16th-century
former drovers' alehouse is one of those quintessential
English country pubs that Sussex specialises in. Tucked
below the steep scarp slope of the South Downs National
Park, expect unspoilt cottage-style bars, worn stone-
flagged floors, low beams, latch doors, a vast inglenook,
and a mix of antique furnishings. On fine days the
extensive rear garden, with roaming bantams, is hugely
popular. Tip-top real ales, including local Ballards, are
drawn from the cask, and a daily-changing blackboard
menu offers classic country cooking with game abundant
in season and treacle tart being a typical dessert.

Open all wk **Bar Meals** L served all wk 12-2 D served
Mon-Sat 6.30-9, Sun 7-8.30 **Restaurant** L served all wk
12-2 D served Mon-Sat 6.30-9, Sun 7-8.30 ⊕ FREE
HOUSE ◀ Ballards Best Bitter, Hop Back Summer
Lightning, Bowman Wallops Wood, Flower Pots.
Facilities Non-diners area ❤ (Bar Garden) ♦♦ Children's
portions Garden ⌗ Parking

| FERNHURST | Map 6 SU82 |

The Red Lion

The Green GU27 3HY ☎ 01428 643112
dir: Just off A286 midway between Haslemere & Midhurst

Tempting menu in South Downs village

In the dimpled shade of a huge maple, this attractive
stone-and-whitewashed inn overlooks a corner of the
green in this peaceful village set in the wooded hills of
the South Downs National Park. Cricketers from the
nearby ground amble here to enjoy Fuller's beers and
guest ales, settling in the oak-beamed, fire-warmed heart
of the 16th-century building to select from a menu finely
balanced between good pub grub (fish and chips, grills)
and enticing diversions such as chicken and chorizo
jambalaya or fillet of sea bass with asparagus and prawn
sauce. Finish with home-made marbled chocolate pot
perhaps.

Open all day all wk 11.30-11 (Sun 11.30-10.30) **Bar
Meals** L served all wk 12-3 D served all wk 6-9.30
Restaurant L served all wk 12-3 D served all wk 6-9.30
⊕ FULLER'S ◀ ESB, Chiswick Bitter & London Pride,
Guest ale Ò Aspall. ♙ 8 **Facilities** Non-diners area
❤ (Bar Garden) ♦♦ Children's menu Children's portions
Garden Parking 🚐

| GRAFFHAM | Map 6 SU91 |

The Foresters Arms

PICK OF THE PUBS

The Street GU28 0QA ☎ 01798 867202
e-mail: info@forestersgraffham.co.uk
dir: From Midhurst S on A285, left to Heyshott, straight
on to Graffham. From Petworth S on A286, turn right to
Graffham, left fork into village centre

A rural gem beneath the hills

Hidden away in a tranquil cul-de-sac village at the foot
of the South Downs, this 17th-century inn is worth
seeking out for post-walking and biking refreshment, or
following a day's antique hunting in Petworth and
Arundel. In the bar you'll find old beams, exposed stone
walls and a large smoke-blackened fireplace, as well as
tip-top ales from local Harvey's, Langham and Dark Star
breweries. The pub offers an imaginative short menu that
trawls the Mediterranean for inspiration and reflects the
seasons, making sound use of quality Sussex produce.
For a starter or light lunch try white onion and cider soup
or rib-eye beef and horseradish crème fraîche
sandwiches, both served with Farretti's Italian ciabatta
bread, or tuck into coq au vin; beefburger in focaccia with
hand-cut chips; or confit duck leg with red wine jus.
Leave room for spiced bread-and-butter pudding. Don't
miss the monthly Saturday live jazz evenings.

Open all wk 12-3 6-late (all day Sat-Sun in Jul-Aug) **Bar
Meals** L served all wk 12-2.30 D served Mon-Sat 6-9.15,
Sun 6-8 Av main course £12 **Restaurant** L served all wk
12-2.30 D served Mon-Sat 6-9.15, Sun 6-8 Av 3 course à
la carte fr £21 ⊕ FREE HOUSE ◀ Harvey's Sussex Best
Bitter, Dark Star Hophead, Langham seasonal ale
Ò Stowford Press. ♙ 17 **Facilities** Non-diners area
❤ (Bar Restaurant Garden) ♦♦ Children's menu Children's
portions Garden ⌗ Parking Wi-fi

| HALNAKER | Map 6 SU90 |

The Anglesey Arms at Halnaker

PICK OF THE PUBS

See Pick of the Pubs on opposite page

| HENLEY | Map 6 SU82 |

Duke of Cumberland Arms

GU27 3HQ ☎ 01428 652280
e-mail: info@thedukeofcumberland.com
dir: Between Haslemere & Midhurst, just off A286 S of
Fernhurst

'Pretty as a picture' inn with good beers and good food

Many fine words have been written about this beautiful,
15th-century pub perched on a wooded hillside in the
South Downs National Park. Inside are flagstones, brick
floors, scrubbed tables, and ales served straight from the
barrels Harvey's and Langham breweries deliver them in.
The first-rate menus impress at lunchtime with Sussex
venison ragout, and pan-seared scallop salad, and again
in the evening with confit free-range pork belly with apple
and Calvados glaze, and whole roasted Sussex partridge
with black pudding mash.

Open all day all wk ⊕ FREE HOUSE ◀ Harvey's Sussex,
Langham Best Bitter & Hip Hop Ò Westons Stowford
Press. **Facilities** ❤ (Bar Garden) ♦♦ Children's portions
Garden Parking Wi-fi

| HEYSHOTT | Map 6 SU81 |

Unicorn Inn

PICK OF THE PUBS

GU29 0DL ☎ 01730 813486
e-mail: unicorninnheyshott@hotmail.co.uk
dir: Telephone for directions

A favourite with walkers and cyclists; great views

Jenni Halpin's 18th-century free house stands in a sleepy
Sussex village and enjoys stunning views of the South
Downs from its beautiful, south-facing rear garden, the
perfect spot to relax on sunny day with a pint of Horsham
Best or Andwell King John . Being within a National Park,
it's a fair bet that you'll share the pub with walkers and
cyclists (and, of course, some locals) seeking out the
home-cooked food listed on seasonal menus that make
sound use of locally sourced produce. The bar, with
beams and a large log fire, is particularly atmospheric,
while the subtly lit, cream-painted restaurant is where
you can sample fresh fish from Selsey – try wild sea bass
fillet with white wine and chive sauce – or dishes likes
slow-roasted lamb shank with mash and a redcurrant
and rosemary sauce, or confit duck leg with elderberry
and balsamic sauce. Good sandwiches (roast beef and
horseradish) and popular Sunday lunches complete the
pleasing picture.

Open all day (Sun 12-4) Closed: 2wks Jan, Sun eve & Mon
(except BHs & Summer) **Bar Meals** L served Tue-Sat
12-2, Sun 12-2.30 D served Tue-Sat 7-9 **Restaurant** L
served Tue-Sat 12-2, Sun 12-2.30 D served Tue-Sat 7-9
⊕ FREE HOUSE ◀ WJ King Horsham Best, Andwell King
John Ò Westons Stowford Press.
Facilities Non-diners area ❤ (Bar Garden) ♦♦ Children's
menu Children's portions Garden ⌗ Parking 🚐 (notice
required)

Save on hotels. Book at theAA.com/hotel

SUSSEX, WEST 445 ENGLAND

PICK OF THE PUBS

The Anglesey Arms at Halnaker

HALNAKER   **Map 6 SU90**

PO18 0NQ ☎ 01243 773474
e-mail: info@angleseyarms.co.uk
web: www.angleseyarms.co.uk
dir: *From centre of Chichester 4m E on*
A285 (Petworth road)

Country pub with extensive gardens and fine dining

Standing on the Goodwood Estate, famous for its horse racing, the Festival of Speed and the Goodwood Revival is Jools and George Jackson's charming, red-brick Georgian country pub. The village name, in which the 'l' is silent, comes from the Old English for 'half an acre'. The Anglesey is set in its own two acres of landscaped grounds, which include a lovely tree-shaded beer garden. Head first to the wood-floored bar to enjoy hand-pulled Bowman Swift One or Black Sheep Best Bitter, or one of the unusual wines from small vineyards. The kitchen team makes skilful use of meats from traceable and organically raised animals, including meat from the Estate's farm, as well as locally caught sustainable fish and organic vegetables. The Anglesey has built a special reputation for its Sussex steaks, hung for at least 21 days. Hand-cut sandwiches and ploughman's are available at lunchtime along with a full menu including dressed Selsey crab salad and home-baked ham. For dinner in the period dining room with its

garden views, try a starter of duck and pork rillettes, baby fig and rocket salad, then follow with Thai-style red king prawn curry with basmati rice; or an organic beef burger served with blue cheese, onion rings and fries. At both lunch and dinner, blackboards list daily local meat and fish dishes. Desserts, such as chocolate orange bread-and-butter pudding, are all home made. On Sundays, in addition to traditional roasts, the menu offers dishes like crab and prawn linguine. Within a mile of the pub is the famous archaeological site, where in 1993 the 500,000 year-old shin-bone of Boxgrove Man was found.

Open all wk 11-3 5.30-11 (Fri-Sun 11-11) **Bar Meals** L served Mon-Sat 12-2.30, Sun 12-3 D served Mon-Sat

6.30-9.30 **Restaurant** L served Mon-Sat 12-2.30, Sun 12-3 D served Mon-Sat 6.30-9.30 🛢 PUNCH TAVERNS 🍺 Young's Bitter, Bowman Swift One, Black Sheep Best Bitter Ŏ Westons Stowford Press. 🍷 12 **Facilities** Non-diners area 🐾🚹 Children's portions Garden 🚗 Parking Wi-fi 🚐

HORSHAM Map 6 TQ13

The Black Jug

31 North St RH12 1RJ ☎ 01403 253526
e-mail: black.jug@brunningandprice.co.uk
dir: *Telephone for directions*

Recommended for its eclectic menu

'When our week's work is over, to the Jug we repair'. So begins some mid-Victorian doggerel about this attractive town-centre pub, which now has flower baskets adorning its façade. The 19th-century hostelry here burnt down and was rebuilt in the 1930s. Inside, you'll find classic wood panelling and wooden flooring, old furniture and bookcases; outside, a lovely plant-filled conservatory-cum-courtyard. All-day meals (from noon) are freshly prepared using local ingredients wherever possible: salt cod tortilla with a watercress and fennel salad; tandoori haloumi with a toasted coconut, fresh pineapple and lime and mint salad; and venison rump with potato gratin and a port reduction.

Open all day all wk **Bar Meals** L served Mon-Sat 12-10, Sun 12-9.30 D served Mon-Sat 12-10, Sun 12-9.30 food served all day **Restaurant** L served Mon-Sat 12-10, Sun 12-9.30 D served Mon-Sat 12-10, Sun 12-9.30 food served all day ⊕ BRUNNING & PRICE ◀ Harvey's Sussex, Caledonian Deuchars IPA, Theakston Old Peculier ♻ Westons Wyld Wood Vintage Cider, Gwynt y Ddraig Black Dragon. ♈ 15 **Facilities** Non-diners area ☜ (Bar Garden) ♦♦ Children's portions Garden ⊼

KINGSFOLD Map 6 TQ13

The Dog and Duck

Dorking Rd RH12 3SA ☎ 01306 627295
e-mail: info@thedoganduck.fsnet.co.uk
dir: *On A24, 3m N of Horsham*

Children and dogs very welcome

The Dog and Duck is a 16th-century family-run and family-friendly country pub. There's plenty of children's play equipment in the huge garden, and three very large fields encourage dogs and energetic owners to stretch their legs. In the summer a native American camp is set up, complete with tipis and camp fire. The rest of the year sees the diary chock-full of celebratory events, including the charity fundraising beer festival - contact the pub for details.

Open all wk 12-3 6-11 (Fri 12-3 6-12 Sat 12-12 Sun 12-10) **Bar Meals** L served all wk 12-2.30 (3pm Sun) D served Mon-Sat 6-9 **Restaurant** L served all wk 12-2.30 (3pm Sun) D served Mon-Sat 6-9 ⊕ HALL & WOODHOUSE ◀ Badger K&B Sussex, Dorset Best, Seasonal ales ♻ Westons Stowford Press. **Facilities** Non-diners area ☜ (Bar Garden) ♦♦ Children's menu Children's portions Play area Garden ⊼ Beer festival Parking ⇌ (notice required)

The Owl at Kingsfold

Dorking Rd RH12 3SA ☎ 01306 628499
e-mail: info@theowl-kingsfold.co.uk
web: www.theowl-kingsfold.co.uk
dir: *On A24, 4m N of Horsham*

In a hamlet just 20 minutes from the sea

A traditional country free house with wooden beams, flagstone floors and log burners. It occupies a prominent roadside site in the village, with plenty of parking and a garden with views to the Surrey Hills; composer Ralph Vaughan Williams reputedly arranged the 'Kingsfold Hymn' here. There are three real ales to choose from, while the frequently changing lunch menu might include West Sussex smokie or home-made liver pâté to start, followed by slow roasted shoulder of lamb; home-made stout and Stilton pie, or half a roast sticky lime chicken and chips; a specials board adds to the choices.

Open all day all wk **Bar Meals** food served all day **Restaurant** food served all day ⊕ FREE HOUSE ◀ Hogs Back TEA, St Austell Tribute, Harvey's Sussex ♻ Westons. ♈ 12 **Facilities** Non-diners area ♦♦ Children's menu Children's portions Garden ⊼ Parking Wi-fi

KIRDFORD Map 6 TQ02

The Half Moon Inn
PICK OF THE PUBS

RH14 0LT ☎ 01403 820223
e-mail: info@halfmoonkirdford.co.uk
dir: *Exit A272 at Wisborough Green, follow Kirdford signs*

Log fires and serious dining in unspoilt village

A bit off the beaten track, this red-tiled 16th-century village inn opposite the church is covered in climbing roses. The interior consists of an attractive bar with adjoining wooden-floored restaurant area, oak beams, tiled floors and several log fires in winter. Although drinkers are welcome, this is mainly a dining pub and the chef serves honest wholesome food with the menus reflecting the best of the season's ingredients. Try braised shin of beef with baby turnips, sugar snap peas and creamed potatoes or a classic cottage pie. Private dining is available and there are gardens to front and rear.

Open 12-3 6-11 Closed: Sun eve, Mon **Bar Meals** L served Tue-Sun 12-3 D served Tue-Sat 6-9.30 **Restaurant** L served Tue-Sun 12-3 D served Tue-Sat 6-9.30 ⊕ ENTERPRISE INNS ◀ Fuller's London Pride. **Facilities** Non-diners area ☜ (Bar Garden) ♦♦ Children's portions Garden ⊼ Parking

LAMBS GREEN Map 6 TQ23

The Lamb Inn

RH12 4RG ☎ 01293 871336 & 871933
e-mail: lambinnrusper@yahoo.co.uk
dir: *6m from Horsham between Rusper & Faygate. 5m from Crawley*

Unspoilt village local with a long list of ciders and beers

Landlords Ben and Chris run a successful modern business within the ancient framework of their unspoilt, rustic country pub. They serve some great local beers and ciders in the beamed bar – too many to list, sadly, but there's Weltons Old Cocky for one, while from Kent comes Biddenden real cider. As much as possible, menus feature locally sourced produce, typical dishes being roasted Suffolk duck with green peppercorn and orange sauce; chargrilled gammon steak; and king prawns in crispy filo pastry. Regulars often bring game in for the pot. The annual August beer festival draws a good crowd.

Open all wk Mon-Thu 11.30-3 5.30-11 (Fri-Sat 11.30-11 Sun 12-10.30) Closed: 25-26 Dec **Bar Meals** L served Mon-Thu 12-2, Fri-Sat 12-9.30, Sun 12-9 D served Mon-Thu 6.30-9.30, Fri-Sat 12-9.30, Sun 12-9 Av main course £12.50 **Restaurant** L served Mon-Thu 12-2, Fri-Sat 12-9.30, Sun 12-9 D served Mon-Thu 6.30-9.30, Fri-Sat 12-9.30, Sun 12-9 Fixed menu price fr £11 Av 3 course à la carte fr £25 ⊕ FREE HOUSE ◀ WJ King Kings Old Ale, Weltons Old Cocky, Langham LSD, Dark Star Hophead & Partridge Best Bitter ♻ Westons Stowford Press, Biddenden, Rekorderlig. ♈ 12 **Facilities** Non-diners area ☜ (Bar Outside area) ♦♦ Children's menu Children's portions Outside area ⊼ Beer festival Parking Wi-fi ⇌ (notice required)

LODSWORTH Map 6 SU92

The Halfway Bridge
Inn ★★★★★ INN ⊛
PICK OF THE PUBS

Halfway Bridge GU28 9BP ☎ 01798 861281
e-mail: enquiries@halfwaybridge.co.uk
dir: *Between Petworth & Midhurst, adjacent to Cowdray Estate & Golf Club on A272*

A main road attraction well worth stopping at

In 2000, a Dutch couple published a book about their favourite British road, the A272! Now in new hands, one of the road's attractions is this renovated, 17th-century traditional pub and contemporary dining inn, with beamed ceilings, bar stools made from whisky barrels, and log fires in the tastefully furnished public rooms. Outside is a peaceful patio and garden. Customers seeking a truly local pint will find real ales from Langham, brewed two minutes away. Also available in the bar are sausage and mash with onion gravy; chargrilled rib-eye steak sandwiches; and baked camembert with shallot jam and toasted ciabatta, while regularly-changing main menus feature Moroccan-style vegetable tagine and minted couscous; oven-roasted

Save on hotels. Book at theAA.com/hotel

SUSSEX, WEST 447 ENGLAND

rump of lamb; and monkfish and tiger prawn Thai green curry. Daily specials are on a blackboard. The pub stands on the 16,500-acre Cowdray Estate, home of British polo.

Open all day all wk 8am-11pm **Bar Meals** L served Mon-Sat 12-2.30 Av main course £7.50 **Restaurant** L served Mon-Fri 12-2.30, Sat-Sun 12-6 D served Mon-Thu 6-9.30, Fri-Sat 6-10, Sun 6-9 Fixed menu price fr £19.50 Av 3 course à la carte fr £32 ⊕ FREE HOUSE ◀ Sharp's Doom Bar, Long Man, Langham ♂ Thatchers. ♀ 25 **Facilities** Non-diners area ♣ (Bar Garden) ♦♦ Children's menu Children's portions Garden ⊟ Parking Wi-fi **Rooms** 7

The Hollist Arms

PICK OF THE PUBS

The Street GU28 9BZ ☎ 01798 861310
e-mail: info@thehollistarms.com
dir: *Between Midhurst & Petworth, exit A272, follow brown pub signs*

Traditional charm and character in idyllic setting

A family-friendly, 15th-century public house outside which, on the lawn, stands a grand old tree ringed by a bench. The pub overlooks the green in a picturesque village that is now within the South Downs National Park. Inglenook fireplaces, low beams and a blissful absence of games machines imbue it with traditional pub charm and character, but what differentiates it from others is the impression that the owners, Sally and Serge, have transplanted a bistro from rural France. A window table in the atmospheric dining room is rather popular, but alternatives are in the snug and several small rooms. Seasonal menus of home-cooked French and English food may feature bouillabaisse; falafel, guacamole and piperade salad; and venison steak with root vegetable gratin and juniper jus. Real ales come from Timothy Taylor and Lodsworth-brewed Langham. Well-behaved dogs usually find there's a tasty bone to gnaw on.

Open all day all wk 11-11 **Bar Meals** L served all wk 12-2.30 D served all wk 6-9 **Restaurant** L served all wk 12-2.30 D served all wk 6-9 ⊕ FREE HOUSE ◀ Timothy Taylor Landlord, Dark Star Best & Hophead, Langham ♂ Westons Stowford Press, Hogan's. ♀ 9 **Facilities** Non-diners area ♣ (Bar Restaurant Garden) ♦♦ Children's menu Children's portions Garden ⊟ Parking Wi-fi ▥ (notice required)

LOWER BEEDING   Map 6 TQ22

The Crabtree NEW

Brighton Rd RH13 6PT ☎ 01403 892666
e-mail: info@crabtreesussex.com
dir: *On A281 between Cowfold & Horsham, opposite South Lodge Hotel*

Family run pub in lovely Sussex countryside

Call in at The Crabtree and you'll be following in the footsteps of author and poet Hilaire Belloc who was often to be found here. The inn, originally built in 1539, is located in beautiful countryside which is where the pub

sources 90% of their produce. Trusty local companies supply meat from high welfare farms and the daily caught fish and shellfish comes via the harbour at nearby Shoreham. Start perhaps with dill cured local mackerel, pickled vegetables, horseradish cream and watercress; followed by rump of Sussex lamb, white bean purée, braised shoulder croquette, baby carrots and spring greens; or Blackmoor Estate pheasant breast, potato fondant, spiced red cabbage, and yellow raisin puree. Extensive bar snacks range from Carlingford oysters to Scotch egg with curried mayo.

Open all day all wk **Bar Meals** L served all wk 12-9 D served all wk 12-9 Av main course £14 food served all day **Restaurant** L served Mon-Sat 12-3, Sun 12-7 D served Mon-Sat 6-9, Sun 12-7 Fixed menu price fr £14 Av 3 course à la carte fr £30 ⊕ HALL & WOODHOUSE ◀ Badger Tanglefoot, K&B Sussex ♂ Westons Stowford Press. ♀ 20 **Facilities** Non-diners area ♣ (Bar Garden) ♦♦ Children's portions Garden ⊟ Parking Wi-fi

LURGASHALL   Map 6 SU92

The Noah's Ark

The Green GU28 9ET ☎ 01428 707346
e-mail: amy@noahsarkinn.co.uk
dir: *B2131 from Haslemere follow signs to Petworth/Lurgashall. A3 from London towards Portsmouth. At Milford take A283 signed Petworth. Follow signs to Lurgashall*

At the height of country chic

In a picturesque village beneath Blackdown Hill, this attractive 16th-century inn overlooks the cricket green. The pretty, shabby-chic interior is full of warmth thanks to the charm of old beams, a large inglenook fireplace, muted colours, pale wooden furniture, fresh flowers and the enthusiasm of its owners. In addition to the Greene King ales is a regularly changing guest, and the traditional British food with a contemporary twist uses seasonal ingredients carefully sourced from the best local suppliers. The menu is concise but enticing: a bowl of mussels with cider, bacon and crusty bread may precede a main course of roast guinea fowl supreme with truffle mash, leeks, sprouts and bacon.

Open all day all wk 11-11 (Sun 12-10 summer Sun 12-8 winter) **Bar Meals** L served Mon-Sat 12-2.30, Sun 12-3 D served Mon-Sat 7-9.30 Av main course £13 **Restaurant** L served Mon-Sat 12-2.30, Sun 12-3 D served Mon-Sat 7-9.30 Av 3 course à la carte fr £25 ⊕ GREENE KING ◀ IPA & Abbot Ale, Guest ale ♂ Westons Stowford Press. **Facilities** Non-diners area ♣ (Bar Garden) ♦♦ Children's portions Family room Garden ⊟ Parking Wi-fi ▥ (notice required)

MAPLEHURST   Map 6 TQ12

The White Horse

Park Ln RH13 6LL ☎ 01403 891208
dir: *5m SE of Horsham, between A281 & A272*

Village-brewed cider and local ales are a draw

This rural free house has been under the same family ownership for over 30 years and lies deep in the Sussex countryside. It offers a welcome haven free from music and fruit machines. Hearty home-cooked pub food and an enticing selection of five real ales are served over what is reputed to be the widest bar counter in Sussex. Sip a pint of Harvey's Sussex Best Bitter or King's Red River whilst admiring the rolling countryside from the large, quiet, south-facing garden. Village-brewed cider is a speciality.

Open 12-2.30 6-11 (Sun 12-3 7-11) Closed: Mon L **Bar Meals** L served Tue-Sun 12-2 D served Mon-Sat 6-9, Sun 7-9 ⊕ FREE HOUSE ◀ Harvey's Sussex Best Bitter, Weltons Pridenjoy, Dark Star Espresso, King's Red River ♂ JB, Local cider. ♀ 11 **Facilities** Non-diners area ♦♦ Children's menu Children's portions Play area Family room Garden ⊟ Parking Wi-fi ▥ (notice required) **Notes** ☺

NUTHURST   Map 6 TQ12

Black Horse Inn

PICK OF THE PUBS

Nuthurst St RH13 6LH ☎ 01403 891272
e-mail: enquiries@theblackhorseinn.com
dir: *4m S of Horsham, off A281, A24 & A272*

Blend of traditional and contemporary in a tranquil setting

The Black Horse's 18th-century features — stone-flagged floors, exposed wattle-and-daub walls, inglenook fire — have been combined with touches of contemporary style to create a truly relaxing dining pub. The lovely old building, half masked by impressive window boxes in summer, was originally part of a row of workers' cottages on the Sedgwick Park estate; it was first recorded as an inn in 1817. Today the hostelry's real ales and ciders are backed by a concise but complete menu of dishes from the kitchen. Lunch sees a range of open sandwiches competing with classic hot plates and specials. In the evening expect more complex fare such as forest mushroom lasagne, or loin of pork with dauphinoise potatoes. Home-made puddings follow simple but classic lines such as lemon meringue pie. On sunny days you can sit out on the terraces at the front and rear, or take drinks across the stone bridge over a stream into the delightful back garden.

Open all wk 12-3 6-11 (Sat 12-11 Sun 12-8.30 BH all day) **Bar Meals** L served Mon-Fri 12-2.30, Sat 12-8.30, Sun 12-6 D served Mon-Fri 6-8.30, Sat 12-8.30, Sun 12-6 **Restaurant** L served Mon-Fri 12-2.30, Sat 12-8.30, Sun 12-6 D served Mon-Fri 6-8.30, Sat 12-8.30, Sun 12-6 ⊕ FREE HOUSE/MR SMITHS PUBS ◀ Dark Star Hophead, Sharp's Doom Bar, Long Man Best Bitter, Young's, Guest ales ♂ Westons Stowford Press. **Facilities** Non-diners area ♦♦ Children's menu Children's portions Garden ⊟ Parking ▥

OVING — Map 6 SU90

The Gribble Inn

PO20 2BP ☎ 01243 786893
dir: *From A27 take A259. After 1m left at rdbt, 1st right to Oving, 1st left in village*

Pub and microbrewery with added extras

This charming 16th-century inn now contains a village store, coffee shop and microbrewery, as well as a pub, within its walls. It is a peaceful spot to sup any of the eight own-brewed real ales plus a choice of five or six seasonal extras; takeaway polypins are also sold. Named after local schoolmistress Rose Gribble, the inn has large open fireplaces, wood burners, low beams and no background music. From the daily-changing menu, enjoy traditional pub food such as beer-battered haddock or slow-roast pork belly. The inn hosts summer and winter beer festivals, and there is also a skittle alley, enjoyed by parties and works' social functions.

Open all day all wk 11-11 **Bar Meals** L served all wk 12-2 D served all wk 6.30-9.30 Av main course £10.95 **Restaurant** L served all wk 12-2 D served all wk 6.30-9.30 ⊕ HALL & WOODHOUSE ◀ Gribble Ale, Reg's Tipple, Pig's Ear, Fuzzy Duck, Plucking Pheasant, Mocha Mole & Sussex Quad Hopper, Flints Full Glory, Gribble Wobbler Ö Westons Stowford Press. ₹ 20 **Facilities** Non-diners area ❤ (Bar Garden) ✦ Children's menu Children's portions Family room Garden 뉴 Beer festival Parking 🚐

PETWORTH — Map 6 SU92

The Angel Inn ★★★★ INN

Angel St GU28 0BG ☎ 01798 344445 & 342153
e-mail: enquiries@angelinnpetworth.co.uk
web: www.angelinnpetworth.co.uk
dir: *From Petworth centre take A283 E towards Fittleworth, pub on left*

A real gem in a delightful town

Bowed walls, exposed beams, head-cracking doorways and sloping floors all testify to the Angel's medieval origins, especially in the bedrooms. So too do the ships' beams and three open fireplaces, one of which is used to spit-roast joints of meat. Petworth's Langham brewery supplies real ales, as does the one in Arundel, alongside guests. The modern British menu changes four times a year; there are also fortnightly and daily specials, such as pan-fried pigeon breast with grilled black pudding; braised shoulder of Southdown lamb; The Angel fish pie; and wild mushroom Stroganoff. The walled patio garden can be a real sun-trap.

The Angel Inn

Open all day all wk 10.30am-11pm (Sun 11.30-10.30) **Bar Meals** L served all wk 12-2.30 D served Mon-Sat 6.30-9.30, Sun 6-9 ⊕ FREE HOUSE ◀ Arundel, Langham, Guest ales Ö Aspall, Addlestones. ₹ 25 **Facilities** Non-diners area ❤ (Bar Garden) ✦ Children's menu Children's portions Garden 뉴 Parking Wi-fi **Rooms** 6

See advert on opposite page

POYNINGS — Map 6 TQ21

Royal Oak

PICK OF THE PUBS

See Pick of the Pubs on page 450

ROWHOOK — Map 6 TQ13

The Chequers Inn ◉

PICK OF THE PUBS

RH12 3PY ☎ 01403 790480
e-mail: thechequersrowhook@googlemail.com
dir: *Off A29 NW of Horsham*

Country pub run by a Master Chef

Operated by accomplished chef Tim Neal, member of the prestigious Master Chefs of Great Britain and holder of an AA Rosette, The Chequers is a striking, 400-year-old higgledy-piggledy pub. Expect to find a classic interior of flagstone floor, low beams, blazing fire in the inglenook and all the trimmings. The bar offers Harvey's Sussex on tap and an impressive wine list to partner the extensive bar menu (baked tomato, mozzarella and basil ciabatta; pan-fried sirloin steak), which may also be eaten in the inn's restaurant. Tim delights in using only the best local produce, taking this to the extreme by going native and sourcing seasonal wild mushrooms and even truffles from the generous woodlands near the hamlet of Rowhook. From the restaurant menu (also served in the bar), begin with bacon roly-poly with fried quail's egg, then follow with butternut squash and brie tart, or crispy hake fillet on a curried mussel and leek cream.

Open 11.30-3.30 6-11.30 (Sun 12-3.30) Closed: 25 Dec, Sun & BHs eve **Bar Meals** L served all wk 12-2 D served Mon-Sat 7-9 Av main course £10.50 **Restaurant** L served all wk 12-2 D served Mon-Sat 7-9 Av 3 course à la carte fr £31.50 ⊕ FREE HOUSE ◀ Harvey's Sussex, Guest ale Ö Thatchers Gold. ₹ 10 **Facilities** Non-diners area Children's portions Garden 뉴 Parking

SHIPLEY — Map 6 TQ12

The Countryman Inn

PICK OF THE PUBS

See Pick of the Pubs on page 451

George & Dragon

Dragons Green RH13 8GE ☎ 01403 741320
e-mail: info@georgeanddragonpubdragonsgreen.co.uk
dir: *Signed from A272 between Coolham & A24*

Renovated village pub with lots going on

Set amid beautiful Sussex countryside, this 17th-century cottage is a haven of peace and quiet, especially on balmy summer evenings when the garden is a welcome retreat. Its interior is all head-banging beams and inglenook fireplaces, with an excellent choice of real ales at the bar. Food-wise, expect pub classics such as sausage, mash and onion gravy; seared salmon fillet with new potatoes; and pesto chicken and bacon salad. Shipley is famous for its smock mill.

Open all wk 12-3 6-11 (Sat-Sun all day) **Bar Meals** L served all wk 12-2 D served Tue-Sat 6-9 **Restaurant** L served all wk 12-2 D served Tue-Sat 6-9 ⊕ FREE HOUSE ◀ Badger Dorset Best, Fursty Ferret & Pickled Partridge, Harvey's Sussex Best Bitter, Guest ale Ö Westons Stowford Press. ₹ 8 **Facilities** Non-diners area ✦ Children's portions Play area Family room Garden Parking Wi-fi 🚐

SINGLETON — Map 5 SU81

The Partridge Inn

PO18 0EY ☎ 01243 811251
e-mail: info@thepartridgeinn.co.uk
dir: *Telephone for directions*

Delightful country pub run by a former top London chef

Set within the picturesque Goodwood Estate in the South Downs village of Singleton, this pub dates back to the 16th century when it was part of a huge hunting park owned by the Fitzalan Earls of Arundel. Today, it is popular with walkers enjoying the rolling Sussex countryside and visitors to Goodwood for motor-and horse-racing. Now run by Giles Thompson, former executive head chef of The Ritz London, you can expect a friendly welcome and great food, from tempting sandwiches, salads and light bites to main courses of O'Hagan's seasonal sausages with pea mash and red onion gravy; steak, mushroom and ale pie; and roasted squash and sage risotto with truffle oil.

Open all wk Mon-Fri 12-3 6-11 (Sat-Sun all day) **Bar Meals** L served Mon-Fri 12-2, Sat-Sun 12-3 D served Mon-Thu & Sun 6-9, Fri-Sat 6-9.30 Av main course £17 **Restaurant** L served Mon-Fri 12-2, Sat-Sun 12-3 D served Mon-Thu & Sun 6-9, Fri-Sat 6-9.30 Av 3 course à la carte fr £25 ⊕ ENTERPRISE INNS ◀ Fuller's London Pride, Harvey's Sussex, Hop Back Summer Lightning Ö Westons Stowford Press. ₹ 15 **Facilities** Non-diners area ❤ (Bar Garden) ✦ Children's menu Children's portions Garden 뉴 Parking Wi-fi

The Angel Inn

Angel Street, Petworth GU28 0BG
Tel: 01798 344445 · **Website:** www.angelinnpetworth.co.uk
Email: enquiries@angelinnpetworth.co.uk

An inn where you can relax and unwind, the Angel Inn is just 300 yards from Golden Square, the centre of Petworth, one of Britain's most attractive market towns. The inn, which has medieval origins, has recently undergone a complete refurbishment. The unspoilt bar boasts ships beams, wooden and slate floors, stone walls and three fireplaces, one of which is used regularly to spit roast a joint of meat gently cooked over the fire. There are six comfortable bedrooms, all with an en suite bathroom or shower room. The Angel Inn is a warm and welcoming Inn; an idyllic base set in the South Downs National Park with much to see and do in the town or from which to explore the many interesting places nearby.

Eat In. Eat Out.

We refer to The Angel as a pub, that is to say a pub serving particularly good food. Ingredients are locally sourced where possible, much of our fish is landed at Littlehampton, and the Sussex Downs provide our lamb, along with much of the vegetables that we serve.

The Angel offers diners a choice of modern and classic British cuisine served throughout the three bar areas. When the weather allows meals are also served in the attractive paved garden. The menu is based on seasonal dishes, changing four times a year supplemented by a fortnightly menu and chef's specials which change daily.

Start with goat's cheese crème brûlée, creamy goats cheese on a layer of caramelised onion with a crunchy topping served with salad leaves; or smoked haddock, salmon and dill fish cake, served with a warm tartar sauce. Follow with a main course of braised shoulder of Southdown lamb, cooked slowly in a rosemary and thyme stock served with a redcurrant and port jus, with new potatoes; or roasted Mediterranean vegetable filo pastry tart, served with a mixed salad and your choice of a four cheese sauce or a tomato and basil sauce. Leave enough room for a dessert and coffee!

Don't be fooled by the relaxed, informal atmosphere; we take good food seriously.

PICK OF THE PUBS

Royal Oak

POYNINGS Map 6 TQ21

The Street BN45 7AQ ☎ **01273 857389**
e-mail: ropoynings@aol.com
web: www.royaloakpoynings.biz
dir: *From A23 onto A281 signed Henfield
& Poynings*

Dining pub in downland village

In a pretty South Downs National Park
village and close to the remarkable
Devil's Dyke, this award-winning pub
has been run by Paul Day and Lewis
Robinson for many years, with the help
of chef David Wharton. Occupying a
lovely spot handy for glorious downland
walks, the pub has plenty to offer all
year round. In summer, the wonderful
garden boasts excellent barbecue
facilities, serene rural views, and all-
day food. Beyond the handsome exterior
the contemporary decor inside is an
effortless blend of solid oak floors, old
beams hung with hop bines and
sumptuous sofas. In the bar, Sussex-
brewed Harvey's Sussex Best Bitter sits
alongside Westons cider and perry, and
an accessible wine list includes New
and Old World wines with up to 14
available by the glass. The menu
changes seasonally and is driven by
local produce. The broad range of meals
suits most appetites. Gregarious grazers
will appreciate the shared fish platter,
offering peppered smoked mackerel,
prawns, smoked salmon and marinated
anchovies with warm ciabatta; nibble

on tapas-style plates or a ciabatta
sandwich platter of roasted red pepper,
courgette, aubergine and houmous.
Main menu starters may feature Sussex
game terrine or Caerphilly cheese and
leek tart; quality openers for mains like
braised shin of beef, Guinness and wild
mushroom pie with horseradish mash;
chargrilled chicken breast with chorizo,
herb and mixed bean stew, or local pork
and leek sausages with onion jam and
truffled mash. A daily-changing
specials board enhances the choice
considerably, and there are regular
themed dish nights. Booking ahead for
meals is advised.

Open all day all wk 11-11 (Sun
12-10.30) **Bar Meals** L served all wk
12-9.30 D served all wk 12-9.30 food

served all day **Restaurant** L served all
wk 12-9.30 D served all wk 12-9.30 food
served all day ⊕ FREE HOUSE
🛢 Harvey's Sussex Best Bitter
Ö Westons Country Perry. 🍷 14
Facilities Non-diners area 🚻 Children's
menu Children's portions Play area
Garden 🎋 Parking Wi-fi 🚐 (notice
required)

Save on hotels. Book at theAA.com/hotel

SUSSEX, WEST 451 ENGLAND

PICK OF THE PUBS

The Countryman Inn

SHIPLEY MAP 6 TQ12

Countryman Ln RH13 8PZ
☎ **01403 741383**
e-mail: countrymaninn@btinternet.com
web: www.countrymanshipley.co.uk
dir: *A272 at Coolham into Smithers Hill Ln. 1m, left at T-junct*

Set in 3,500 acres of farmland that's getting back to nature

Alan Vaughan and his family have run this traditional rural free house since 1986. Surrounding it are 3,500 acres of farmland owned by the Knepp Castle Estate, now gradually returning to a more natural state since the introduction of fallow deer, free-roaming Tamworth pigs, Exmoor ponies and Longhorn cattle. Wild birds have also been encouraged to return, attracted by newly planted wild grasses. In the open log fire-warmed bar, you'll find cask-conditioned Harvey's and Dark Star ales, and more than 30 wines from around the world. Local game, free-range meats from local farms and vegetables from the pub's own garden make their appearance on the menu, alongside fish from the two nearest Sussex ports of Shoreham and Newhaven. Pub grub lovers will find what they're looking for in bangers 'n' mash; ham, egg and chips; and scampi and chips, for example, as well as sandwiches and baguettes, salads and platters. Typical

starters on the main menu include smoked salmon salad; pan-seared scallops with parsley butter and lardons or hoi sin lamb wrap; and to follow, mains of baked halloumi and tomato stack; chicken stuffed with cream cheese, wrapped in bacon and served with wild mushrooms; or red pepper and chickpea dhansak. Please note that very young children are not permitted in the restaurant, but if the weather's good enough they are welcome to eat in the garden, where the open-air kitchen serves ploughman's lunches with home-baked bread and other snacks, grills and shellfish. In the pub's own farm shop you can buy a wide range of food including free-range eggs, home-made preserves, pickles and relishes.

Open all wk 10-4 6-11 **Bar Meals** L served all wk 11.30-3.30 D served all wk 6-9.30 Av main course £14 **Restaurant** L served all wk 11.30-3.30 D served all wk 6-9.30 ⊕ FREE HOUSE 🍺 Harvey's, Dark Star, Guest ales ♻ Thatchers Gold. 🍷 18 **Facilities** Non-diners area Garden 🎋 Parking Wi-fi

SLINDON
Map 6 SU90

The Spur

BN18 0NE ☎ 01243 814216
e-mail: thespurslindon@btinternet.com
dir: From A27 take A29 signed Slindon

Pretty pub with lovely garden for alfresco drinking and eating

Set just outside the village of Slindon on top of the rolling South Downs, this 17th-century pub is a an ideal stopping-off point on a day out in the country. It has been praised for its friendly atmosphere and for generous portions of food. Outside are large pub gardens and a courtyard, inside is an open-plan bar and restaurant, warmed by crackling log fires. Daily-changing bar meals are on the blackboard, and may include lamb cutlets, steak-and-kidney pie, and fresh fish and shellfish. The restaurant menu changes every few months, and a typical selection of dishes from this includes seafood risotto, half shoulder of Southdown lamb, and goats' cheese and roasted pepper savoury cheesecake. A skittle alley and function room are also available.

Open all wk 11.30-3 6-11 (Sun 12-10) **Bar Meals** L served Mon-Sat 12-2, Sun 12-8 D served Mon-Tue 7-9, Wed-Sat 7-9.30, Sun 12-8 Av main course £11 **Restaurant** L served Mon-Sat 12-2, Sun 12-8 D served Mon-Tue 7-9, Wed-Sat 7-9.30, Sun 12-8 Fixed menu price fr £18.50 ⊕ FREE HOUSE ◀ Sharp's Doom Bar, Courage Directors ♂ Thatchers Gold. ♇ 10
Facilities Non-diners area ♥ (Bar Garden) ♦️ Children's menu Children's portions Garden ⊼ Beer festival Parking 🚐

STEDHAM
Map 5 SU82

Hamilton Arms/Nava Thai Restaurant

Hamilton Arms, School Ln GU29 0NZ ☎ 01730 812555
e-mail: hamiltonarms@hotmail.com
web: www.thehamiltonarms.co.uk
dir: Off A272 between Midhurst & Petersfield

Well known for the excellent Thai food

Smiling Thai staff serve authentic Thai food and beers in this whitewashed free house opposite the village common – but if you prefer you can opt for English bar snacks and ales, including the Hamilton's own draught Armless. Thai treats include favourites such as tom yam gai; chu chi gung (red prawn curry) and pud Thai. For £10 on Sundays, eat as much as you want from the Thai or English-roast buffets. Takeaways are available too. The

pub is home to the Mudita Trust, which helps abused and underprivileged children in Thailand.

Open all day Closed: Mon (ex BHs) **Bar Meals** L served Tue-Sun 12-2.30 D served Tue-Sun 6-10 **Restaurant** L served Tue-Sun 12-2.30 D served Tue-Sun 6-10 ⊕ FREE HOUSE ◀ Fuller's London Pride, Triple fff Alton's Pride, Hamilton Armless. ♇ 8 **Facilities** Non-diners area ♥ (Bar Garden) ♦️ Children's menu Children's portions Play area Garden ⊼ Parking Wi-fi 🚐

SUTTON
Map 6 SU91

The White Horse Inn
PICK OF THE PUBS

The Street RH20 1PS ☎ 01798 869221
e-mail: mail@whitehorse-sutton.co.uk
dir: From Petworth follow signs for Roman villa then to Sutton

Stylish pub deep in the countryside

In a sleepy village tucked beneath the South Downs amid a maze of the narrow lanes, this 250-year-old pub has been transformed into a stylish modern country inn. Being so handy for polo at Cowdray Park and racing at Goodwood, it makes a great watering hole at the end of a hard day's entertainment. Handpumps in the smart wooden-floored bar dispense the likes of local Harvey's and Adnams ales, while menus make good use of seasonal produce from local suppliers to create some imaginative and good-value dishes. Perhaps start with mussels grilled with garlic and herb butter, then follow with confit duck with dauphinoise, green beans and red wine jus, and round off with sticky toffee pudding with butterscotch sauce and vanilla ice cream. Lighter options include Sussex cheddar and pickle sandwiches; ham, egg and chips; and smoked chicken, avocado, chorizo and tomato salad. There's a super terrace and garden for summer alfresco meals.

Open all wk 11-3 6-11 **Bar Meals** L served all wk 11.30-2.30 D served all wk 6.30-9.30 **Restaurant** L served all wk 11.30-2.30 D served all wk 6.30-9.30 ⊕ ENTERPRISE INNS ◀ Sharp's Doom Bar, Fuller's London Pride, Harvey's, Adnams ♂ Westons Stowford Press. **Facilities** Non-diners area ♦️ Children's portions Garden Parking Wi-fi 🚐

TILLINGTON
Map 6 SU92

The Horseguards Inn ★★★★ INN ◉
PICK OF THE PUBS

GU28 9AF ☎ 01798 342332
e-mail: info@thehorseguardsinn.co.uk
dir: From Petworth towards Midhurst on A272. 1m, right signed Tillington. Inn 300mtrs up hill opposite church

Country comforts and character in a South Downs village

Beneath its steeply-pitched roof The Horseguards looks out over the landscaped acres of Petworth Park. The National Trust's most impressive art collection is held in

Petworth House, across the parkland where the Horse Guards Regiment grazed their steeds. Inside the 350-year-old inn is a series of tastefully appointed rooms with sagging beams, stripped floorboards, open fires (you can roast chestnuts on one), antique and pine furnishings, fresh flowers and candles. The rustic, tree-shaded garden, complete with chickens and straw bales, is popular with families. The restrained, seasonally-changing menu, often dressed with locally foraged hedgerow specialities, has gained an AA Rosette award. An opening gambit may be potato cake with smoked eel, treacle, bacon, beetroot and horseradish, setting the scene for pheasant breasts, root vegetable mash, greens, gravy and hawthorn jelly. Comfy, country-style bedrooms complete the village idyll.

Open all day all wk **Bar Meals** L served Mon-Fri 12-2.30, Sat 12-3, Sun 12-3.30 D served all wk 6.30-9 **Restaurant** L served Mon-Fri 12-2.30, Sat 12-3, Sun 12-3.30 D served all wk 6.30-9 ⊕ ENTERPRISE INNS ◀ Harvey's Sussex Best Bitter, Skinner's Betty Stogs, Staropramen, Guinness ♂ Westons Stowford Press. ♇ 16 **Facilities** Non-diners area ♥ (Bar Restaurant Garden) ♦️ Children's menu Children's portions Garden ⊼ Wi-fi 🚐 (notice required) **Rooms** 3

TROTTON
Map 5 SU82

The Keepers Arms ◉
PICK OF THE PUBS

GU31 5ER ☎ 01730 813724
e-mail: ss@keepersarms.co.uk
dir: 5m from Petersfield on A272 towards Midhurst, pub on right just after narrow bridge

Fabulous views of the South Downs

Perched above the A272, one of England's most delightful cross-country roads, this charming 17th-century free house is owned by Salvinia McGrath. Low ceilings, wooden floorboards and an open log fire greet you on entering the convivial bar, where the line-up of ales includes Dark Star, Ringwood, Uphams and Langham. Oak dining tables and comfortable upholstered chairs furnish the restaurant, whose look was inspired by a Scottish hunting lodge, thus the rich tartan fabrics. Real effort is made to source locally for the menus and blackboards that are likely to offer caramelised onion and goats' cheese tart; Parma ham, fig and rocket with parmesan; spiced Gressingham duck breast with Puy lentils and watercress salad; and pan-fried fillets of sea bass with truffle oil, crushed new potatoes, spinach and vanilla butter. There are views of the South Downs from both the restaurant and terrace.

Open 12-3.30 6-11 Closed: Mon (until mid May) **Bar Meals** L served all wk 12-2 D served all wk 7-9.30 Av main course £10 **Restaurant** L served all wk 12-2 D served all wk 7-9.30 Av 3 course à la carte fr £25 ⊕ FREE HOUSE ◀ Dark Star Hophead, Ringwood Best Bitter & Fortyniner, Ballards Best Bitter, Otter Ale, Uphams Ale, Langham ♂ Thatchers Gold. ♇ 8 **Facilities** Non-diners area ♥ (Bar Restaurant Garden) ♦️ Children's portions Garden Outside area ⊼ Parking Wi-fi

Save on hotels. Book at **theAA.com/hotel**

SUSSEX, WEST 453 ENGLAND

PICK OF THE PUBS

The Cat Inn

WEST HOATHLY　　　Map 6 TQ33

North Ln RH19 4PP ☎ 01342 810369
e-mail: thecatinn@googlemail.com
web: www.catinn.co.uk
dir: *A22 towards Forest Row onto B2110
signed Turners Hill. Left into Vowels Ln
signed West Hoathly. Left into Selsfield
Rd, into Chapel Row, right into North Ln*

Village hospitality at its best

Regional and county awards, and a top-to-bottom, inside-and-out paint job have been added to the CV of the 16th-century, tile-hung Cat. High on a spur of the Sussex Weald, the village is on the western edge of Ashdown Forest, an area interlaced with super walks and not far from the Bluebell Railway. Inside the old bar you'll find two inglenook fireplaces, oak beams, fine wooden panelling and floors, and the sort of buzzy atmosphere village pubs are so good at generating. Local breweries Black Cat (Groombridge), Dark Star (Partridge Green), Harveys (Lewes) and Larkins (Chiddingstone) provide the beers. The well-lit dining rooms are furnished with wooden dining chairs and tables on pale wood strip flooring, and throughout there are hops, china platters and brass and copper ornaments. Glass doors from the contemporary-style garden room open on to a terrace. Head chef Max Leonard makes good use of South Downs lamb, Sussex coast fish and seafood, estate

game and whatever else can be sourced locally, but he goes further afield for such dishes as Berkshire pork and chorizo burger; wild Norfolk moules marinière; and home-cured gravad lax and Loch Duart salmon. From closer to home are starters of High Weald ricotta, blood orange, beetroot, quinoa and rocket salad; West Hoathly game terrine; Rye Bay skate fillet with caper and cockle butter; and the Sussex vegetables that accompany his steak, mushroom and ale pie. Among Max's puddings are mango pannacotta with coconut meringue and exotic fruit salad; and white chocolate and apricot bread and butter pudding and custard.

Open all day 12-11.30 Closed: Sun eve
Bar Meals L served Mon-Thu 12-2, Fri-

Sun 12-2.30 D served Mon-Thu 6-9, Fri-Sat 6-9.30 Av main course £14
Restaurant L served Mon-Thu 12-2, Fri-Sun 12-2.30 D served Mon-Thu 6-9, Fri-Sat 6-9.30 Av 3 course à la carte fr £26 ⊕ FREE HOUSE ◼ Harvey's Sussex Best Bitter, Moorhouse's Black Cat, Larkins, Dark Star ♻ Westons Stowford Press. ♟ 10 **Facilities** Non-diners area ❀ (Bar Garden) ♠ Children's portions Garden ⊼ Parking (limited) Wi-fi

WALDERTON — Map 5 SU71

The Barley Mow

PO18 9ED ☎ 023 9263 1321
e-mail: info@thebarleymowpub.co.uk
dir: *B2146 from Chichester towards Petersfield. Turn right signed Walderton, pub 100yds on left*

Popular carvery and pretty garden

A favourite with walkers, cyclists and horse-riders out exploring the Kingley Vale nature reserve, this ivy-clad 18th-century pub was used by the local Home Guard as its HQ in World War II. It is famous locally for its skittle alley, which can be hired in combination with a buffet. The secluded, stream-bordered garden is a real sun trap, perfect for a pint of Old Thumper; in winter months the log fires crackle. The menu encompasses grills, fish dishes, salads and pub classics, as well as steaks served sizzling hot 'on the stone' for you to cook to your liking at your table. The Sunday carvery is very popular (booking advised).

Open all wk 11-3 6-11 (Sat 11-11 Sun 12-10.30) **Bar Meals** L served Mon-Sat 12-2.30, Sun all day D served all wk 6-9.30 **Restaurant** L served all wk 12-2.30 D served all wk 6-9.30 ⊕ FREE HOUSE ◀ Ringwood Old Thumper & Fortyniner, Fuller's London Pride, Harvey's Sussex Best Bitter, Sharp's Doom Bar, Adnams, Otter Ö Westons Stowford Press, Thatchers. ♥ 10
Facilities Non-diners area ♣ (Bar Garden) ♦♦ Children's menu Children's portions Garden Parking ☞ (notice required)

WARNINGLID — Map 6 TQ22

The Half Moon

The Street RH17 5TR ☎ 01444 461227
e-mail: info@thehalfmoonwarninglid.co.uk
dir: *1m from Warninglid/Cuckfield junct of A23 & 6m from Haywards Heath*

Family-owned country inn welcoming whatever the season

This picture-perfect Grade II listed building dates from the 18th century and has been sympathetically extended to preserve its traditional feel. Look out for the glass-topped well as you come in. Enjoy a pint of Harvey's or a real cider while perusing the menu, which offers specials and pub classics. Try oriental crispy pork balls with satay sauce and star anise drizzle; gnocchi in a wild mushroom and tarragon mustard cream; butternut squash falafel burger served with hand-cut chips; and chicken rogan josh served with onion bhaji, basmati rice, mango chutney and a poppadom. The pub garden is home to a 250-year-old cider press.

Open all wk 11.30-2.30 5.30-11 (Sat 11.30-11 Sun 11.30-10.30) ⊕ FREE HOUSE ◀ Harvey's Sussex & Old Ale, Dark Star Ö Symonds, Westons. **Facilities** ♣ (Bar Garden) ♦♦ Children's menu Children's portions Family room Garden Parking Wi-fi

WEST CHILTINGTON — Map 6 TQ01

The Queens Head

The Hollow RH20 2JN ☎ 01798 812244
e-mail: enquiries@thequeensheadsussex.co.uk
dir: *Telephone for directions*

Historic country pub with broad appeal

Named after Anne of Cleves, to whom Henry VIII gave nearby Nyetimber (now a vineyard) on divorcing her, this family-run, 16th-century country pub serves a good selection of local and more distantly brewed real ales in the beamed, low-ceilinged, open-fired bars. Locally sourced meals include prosciutto, fig and goats' cheese salad; pie of the day; beer battered cod and chips; and traditional pork sausages with mash. Comforting desserts include spotted dick and custard; and bread and butter pudding. Stone-baked and deep-pan pizzas are available at lunchtime and in the evening. Sandwiches, baguettes and ploughman's at lunchtime too.

Open all day all wk 12-11 (Mon 6-11 ex BH 12-11 Sun 12-10.30) Closed: 1 Jan **Bar Meals** L served Tue-Sat 12-2.30, Sun & BH 12-4 D served Tue-Sat 6-9.30 Av main course £9.95 **Restaurant** L served Tue-Sat 12-2.30, Sun & BH 12-4 D served Tue-Sat 6-9.30 Av 3 course à la carte fr £20 ⊕ ENTERPRISE INNS ◀ Harvey's Sussex Best Bitter, Fuller's London Pride, Timothy Taylor Landlord, Adnams Explorer, St Austell Tribute Ö Aspall.
Facilities Non-diners area ♣ (Bar Restaurant Garden) ♦♦ Children's menu Children's portions Garden ☴ Parking Wi-fi ☞ (notice required)

WEST HOATHLY — Map 6 TQ33

The Cat Inn

PICK OF THE PUBS

See Pick of the Pubs on page 453

WINEHAM — Map 6 TQ22

The Royal Oak

BN5 9AY ☎ 01444 881252
e-mail: theroyaloakwineham@sky.com
dir: *Between A272 (Cowfold to Bolney road) & B2116 (Hurst to Henfield road)*

Quintessential English country inn

Tucked away on a quiet country lane near Henfield, this part-tiled, black-and-white timbered cottage is a classic alehouse, a true rural survivor that has been serving the locals for hundreds of years. Dating from the 14th century, it has head-cracking low beams, a huge inglenook with warming winter fire, brick and stone-flagged floors, and time-honoured pub games. Bedlam and Dark Star ales are drawn straight from the drum and home-cooked pub food ranges from ploughman's boards to hearty Sussex beef, stout and mushroom pie with new potatoes and baby carrots. Extensive gardens are just the spot for summer alfresco drinking.

Open all wk 11-3 5.30-close (Sat 11-3 6-close Sun 11-3 7-close) **Bar Meals** L served all wk 12-2.30 D served all wk 7-9.30 **Restaurant** L served all wk 12-2.30 D served all wk 7-9.30 ⊕ FREE HOUSE ◀ Bedlam Brewery, Dark Star, Guest ales Ö Wobblegate. ♥ 20
Facilities Non-diners area ♣ (Bar Garden) ♦♦ Children's portions Garden Beer festival Parking Wi-fi ☞

WARWICKSHIRE

ALCESTER — Map 10 SP05

The Holly Bush

PICK OF THE PUBS

37 Henley St B49 5QX ☎ 01789 762482
e-mail: thehollybushpub@btconnect.com
dir: *M40 junct 15, A46 signed Warwick/Stratford. From Stratford take A46 to Redditch, follow Alcester signs*

Independent pub in a Roman market town

You wouldn't know it today, but Tracey-Jane Deffley's 16th-century town-centre pub used to have just one bar. Not that there's anything wrong with that, but look at it now, with two bars serving eight beers, including a couple from Purity Brewing in nearby Great Alne, and Hogan's cider, made in the Malvern Hills. Then there's the two dining rooms, and an award-winning, vegetable- and salad-producing garden. Among the contemporary and traditional dishes on offer are roasted Cajun chicken; rump of Warwickshire lamb; braised pork faggots; Irish sausage and mash; and butternut squash and spring greens risotto. Sandwich and fresh fish ideas appear on the specials board. Choosing a wine from the well-priced selection is simplified by refreshingly factual descriptions. Not only are the food and drink good, but the service is friendly too. Regular live music nights and beer and cider festivals in June and October.

Open all day all wk 12-12 (Fri-Sat noon-1am) **Bar Meals** L served Mon-Sat 12-2.30, Sun 12-3 D served Tue-Sat 6-9.30 Av main course £11 **Restaurant** L served Mon-Sat 12-2.30, Sun 12-3 D served Tue-Sat 6-9.30 Av 3 course à la carte fr £24 ⊕ FREE HOUSE ◀ Sharp's Doom Bar, Purity Gold, Black Sheep, Hobsons Town Crier, Guest ales Ö Hogan's, Local cider. ♥ 9
Facilities Non-diners area ♣ (Bar Garden) ♦♦ Children's menu Children's portions Garden ☴ Beer festival Cider festival Parking ☞ (notice required)

ALDERMINSTER — Map 10 SP24

The Bell

PICK OF THE PUBS

See Pick of the Pubs on opposite page

Save on hotels. Book at theAA.com/hotel

WARWICKSHIRE 455 ENGLAND

PICK OF THE PUBS

The Bell

ALDERMINSTER Map 10 SP24

CV37 8NY ☎ 01789 450414
e-mail: info@thebellald.co.uk
web: www.thebellald.co.uk
dir: *On A3400, 3.5m S of Stratford-upon-Avon*

Country pub chic with great food

Set in the heart of a picturesque village between Stratford-upon-Avon and Shipston on Stour, this striking Georgian coaching inn has been beautifully upgraded and refurbished by the Alscot Estate. The result is a refreshing mix of contemporary comforts and rustic charm, with the historic core of beamed ceilings, blazing log fires and flagged floors combining well with bold colours and stylish fabrics and the modern dining courtyard. The inn is located beside a grassy garden and a riverside meadow that ripples down to the River Stour is perfect for enjoying summer picnics. The restaurant oozes charm and is cunningly designed into quirky zones, each with its own distinct atmosphere. Time to enjoy a pint of Hook Norton or the inn's locally-brewed Alscot Ale and nibble on a self-selected grazing platter, perhaps laden with hams, olives, mozzarella, pesto, balsamic shallots, vine tomatoes and garlic focaccia, before considering the indulgent daily-changing menu.

Typically, begin with potted duck liver and orange pâté, carpaccio of smoked duck and pink grapefruit salad, then follow with slow roasted pork stuffed with pepperoni and sage, with crackling and pearl barley risotto. Round off with warm dark chocolate and fudge tart with strawberry ice cream, or a plate of local cheeses with home-made chutney. In the bar, sandwiches are served with hand-cut chips and salad, or you can try a Bell classic, perhaps the beef and thyme burger, or bangers and mash. Much of the produce is local, with vegetables and herbs harvested from Alscot's historic kitchen garden, and game and venison is reared on the estate.

Open all wk 9.30-3 6-11 (Fri-Sat 9.30am-11pm Sun 9.30-5) **Bar Meals** L served Mon-Fri 12-2, Sat 12-2.30, Sun 12-3 D served Mon-Thu 7-9, Fri-Sat 6-9 **Restaurant** L served Mon-Fri 12-2, Sat 12-2.30, Sun 12-3 D served Mon-Thu 7-9, Fri-Sat 6-9 ⊕ FREE HOUSE ◀ Hook Norton, Alscot Ale ♂ Hogan's. ▼ 12 **Facilities** Non-diners area ♦♦ Children's menu Garden ⋒ Parking Wi-fi ▥▥

ALVESTON   Map 10 SP25

The Baraset Barn

PICK OF THE PUBS

1 Pimlico Ln CV37 7RJ ☎ 01789 295510
e-mail: barasetbarn@lovelypubs.co.uk
dir: Telephone for directions

200-year old history with contemporary refinements

Barn is what it's called, because barn is what it was. Not any more, though. True, the original flagstones reflect its 200-year existence, but it is now a light and modern gastro-pub with a dramatic interior styled in granite, pewter and oak. Stone steps lead from the bar to the main dining area with brick walls and high oak beams, while the open mezzanine level offers a good view of the glass-fronted kitchen. The luxurious lounge is furnished with comfortable sofas for whiling away the morning with a coffee and the papers. The menu successfully blends classic British with Mediterranean ideas, such as sharing plates of tapas; starters of vodka- and beetroot-cured salmon, capers, sieved egg and horseradish crème fraîche; and spiced pumpkin and cauliflower fritters. Follow with Purity real ale-battered fish, chips, minted pea purée and sauce gribiche; or calves' liver and onions. The continental-style patio garden is made for outdoor dining.

Open all day 12-11 Closed: 25 Dec (open for food) & 1 Jan, Sun eve, Mon (Jan) **Bar Meals** L served all wk 12-2.30 D served Mon-Sat 6.30-9.30 **Restaurant** L served Mon-Sat 12-2.30, Sun 12-3.30 D served Mon-Sat 6.30-9.30 ⊕ FREE HOUSE ◀ Purity Pure UBU. **Facilities** Non-diners area ❀ (Bar Garden) ♦♦ Children's portions Garden ⚞ Parking Wi-fi ⛟

ARDENS GRAFTON   Map 10 SP15

The Golden Cross

PICK OF THE PUBS

Wixford Rd B50 4LG ☎ 01789 772420
e-mail: info@thegoldencross.net
dir: Telephone for directions

Pretty pub with prized faggots

This traditional 18th-century country inn is the place to come if you like faggots, because an old recipe that went walkabout has now been rediscovered, much to the delight of locals. With other traditional favourites they appear on the single menu served throughout, listing starters and light bites such as chicken liver pâté with onion marmalade and toasted farmhouse-style bread or smoked haddock and prawn risotto, perhaps followed by slow-roasted pork belly with mash, red cabbage and a roast shallot and cider gravy or spinach and feta filo pie. If you eat in the pastel-toned dining room take a good look at the attractive plasterwork on the ceiling, or if you prefer to stay in the rug-strewn, flagstone-floored bar, the hefty beams are worth more than a cursory glance. The real ales here come from Wells, Purity or a guest. The garden is large and safe, and the covered patio is heated.

Open all wk Mon-Fri 12-2.30 5-12 (Sat-Sun all day) **Bar Meals** L served all wk 12-2.30 D served all wk 5-9 **Restaurant** L served all wk 12-2.30 D served all wk 5-9 ⊕ CHARLES WELLS ◀ Bombardier, Purity, Guest ales ♂ Thatchers Heritage. ☗ 10 **Facilities** Non-diners area ❀ (Bar Garden) ♦♦ Children's menu Children's portions Garden ⚞ Parking Wi-fi ⛟ (notice required)

ASTON CANTLOW   Map 10 SP16

The King's Head

21 Bearley Rd B95 6HY ☎ 01789 488242
e-mail: info@thekh.co.uk
web: www.thekh.co.uk
dir: Exit A3400 between Stratford-upon-Avon & Henley-in-Arden. Follow Aston Cantlow signs

Rustic Tudor pub steeped in history

Flanked by a huge spreading chestnut tree and oozing historic charm, this impressive black-and-white timbered Tudor building has been appointed in a modern style. Tastefully rustic inside, with lime-washed low beams, huge polished flagstones, painted brick walls, old scrubbed pine tables and crackling log fires, it draws diners for innovative pub food. Tuck into grilled fillet of Cajun sea bass with a lime and coriander mash and carrot and ginger purée; trio of free range pork roast loin, braised belly and cheek bon bon or chargrilled Lashford's sausages and mash with onion gravy. There's a smart rear terrace and a cider bar serving up to seven traditional ciders.

Open all day all wk **Bar Meals** L served Mon-Sat 12-9.30, Sun 12-5 D served Mon-Sat 12-9.30, Sun 12-5 **Restaurant** L served Mon-Sat 12-9.30, Sun 12-5 D served Mon-Sat 12-9.30, Sun 12-5 food served all day ⊕ ENTERPRISE INNS ◀ Purity Gold & Pure UBU, Greene King Abbot Ale, M&B Brew XI ♂ Thatchers. ☗ 12 **Facilities** Non-diners area ❀ (Bar Garden) ♦♦ Children's menu Children's portions Garden ⚞ Parking Wi-fi ⛟ (notice required)

See advert on opposite page

BARFORD   Map 10 SP26

The Granville @ Barford

PICK OF THE PUBS

52 Wellesbourne Rd CV35 8DS ☎ 01926 624236
e-mail: info@granvillebarford.co.uk
dir: M40 junct 15, A429 signed Stow, left to Barford

Friendly and stylish village dining pub

Situated in the heart of Shakespeare country, this impressive brick building dates back to Georgian times. The comfortable dining pub benefits from stylish decor and warm, friendly service, which has made it a firm favourite with locals and visitors alike. Relax on the leather sofas in the lounge with a drink - a pint of Pure UBU perhaps, or choose from the accessible wine list. The Granville's ever-changing seasonal menus offer varied, interesting choices and good value. At lunch, the offering ranges from doorstep sandwiches and wraps to starters like linguine in a lightly spiced crab broth with spring onion, lime and coriander. An evening meal might begin with salmon and haddock fishcakes, wilted spinach, lemon and butter sauce, followed by North African spiced lamb patties, winter fruit saffron couscous, mint and cucumber yogurt. Enjoy alfresco dining in the spacious patio garden. There is a calendar of events to entertain customers.

Open all wk Mon-Thu 12-3 5-11 (Fri close 11.30 Sat 12-11.30 Sun 12-11) **Bar Meals** L served Mon-Fri 12-2.30, Sat 12-3, Sun 12-4 D served Mon-Sat 6-9.30 **Restaurant** L served Mon-Fri 12-2.30, Sat 12-3, Sun 12-4 D served Mon-Sat 6-9.30 ⊕ ENTERPRISE INNS ◀ Hook Norton Hooky Bitter, Fuller's London Pride, Pure UBU ♂ Thatchers Gold, Guest ciders. ☗ 17 **Facilities** Non-diners area ❀ (Bar Garden) ♦♦ Children's portions Play area Garden Parking Wi-fi ⛟

EDGEHILL   Map 11 SP34

The Castle Inn

OX15 6DJ ☎ 01295 670255
e-mail: castleinnedgehill@gmail.com
dir: M40 junct 11, A422 towards Stratford-upon-Avon. 6m to Upton House, next right, 1.5m to Edgehill

Two bars and far-reaching views

A man called Sanderson Miller built this curious, castellated property on top of Edgehill in 1742, right where Charles I had raised his standard before engaging with the Parliamentarians in the first major clash of the English Civil War. In 1922, 100 years after it became an alehouse, Hook Norton acquired it and the two bars still serve that brewery's own and guest ales today. Plentiful, traditional food includes pork, Stilton and mushroom bake; seafood platter; steak, mushroom and Hooky ale pie (aka Boozy Bullock); and veggie pie of the day.

Open all day all wk 11.30am-close ⊕ HOOK NORTON ◀ Hooky Bitter, Old Hooky, Hooky Dark & Hooky Gold, Guest ales ♂ Westons Old Rosie. **Facilities** ❀ (Bar Garden) ♦♦ Children's menu Children's portions Garden Parking

ETTINGTON — Map 10 SP24

The Chequers Inn

PICK OF THE PUBS

91 Banbury Rd CV37 7SR ☎ 01789 740387
e-mail: hello@the-chequers-ettington.co.uk
dir: *Take A422 from Stratford-upon-Avon towards Banbury. Ettington in 5m, after junction with A429*

Tastefully decorated country inn serving modern European fare

Thought to have once been a courthouse and probably named after the old Chequers tree that used to stand in front of the building, this locals' pub is an elegant place to eat and drink. The dining room is decorated in French style with ornate mirrors and chairs, rich tapestries and comfortable armchairs, while the spacious garden looks out over the kitchen's vegetable patch. Kick off proceedings with Chequers' Scotch duck egg with onion jam and Guinness, or pan-fried squid, chorizo and chilli with coriander salad. Mains continue in the modern European vein; how about Spanish-style fish stew with saffron potatoes and garlic bread or a British warmer of venison casserole, chestnut and herb dumplings, red cabbage and parsnip crisps or something familiar from the pub classics menu? The monthly fish night is also popular.

Open 12-3 5-11 (Sat 12-11 Sun 12-6) Closed: Sun eve, Mon **Bar Meals** L served Tue-Sat 12-2.30, Sun 12.30-3.30 D served Tue-Sat 6.30-9.30 **Restaurant** L served Tue-Sat 12-2.30, Sun 12.30-3.30 D served Tue-Sat 6.30-9.30 ⊕ FREE HOUSE ◀ Greene King IPA, Fuller's London Pride, St Austell Tribute ♂ Thatchers Gold. ☙ 8
Facilities Non-diners area ❖ (Bar Garden) ♦ Children's menu Children's portions Garden ⋒ Parking Wi-fi ☷ (notice required)

The Houndshill

Banbury Rd CV37 7NS ☎ 01789 740267
e-mail: info@thehoundshill.co.uk
dir: *On A422 SE of Stratford-upon-Avon*

Out in the country south east of Stratford

Family-run for over 30 years, this inn is set in 12 acres of garden and woodland in the beautiful Warwickshire countryside, and a perfect base for exploring popular tourist attractions such as Oxford, Blenheim, Stratford and the Cotswolds. The pleasant tree-lined garden is especially popular with families. Typical dishes include grilled sirloin steak with fries, tomatoes, mushrooms and peas; chilli con carne; home-made chicken curry; baked lasagne; or The Houndshill platter — smoked salmon, avocado, prawns, melon and cold poached salmon.

Open all wk 12-3 6-11 Closed: 24 Dec-1 Jan ⊕ FREE HOUSE ◀ Purity Gold & Pure UBU. **Facilities** ♦ Children's menu Children's portions Play area Garden Parking Wi-fi

FARNBOROUGH — Map 11 SP44

The Inn at Farnborough

PICK OF THE PUBS

OX17 1DZ ☎ 01295 690615
e-mail: enquiries@theinnfarnborough.co.uk
dir: *M40 junct 11 towards Banbury. Right at 3rd rdbt onto A423 signed Southam. 4m onto A423. Left onto single track road signed Farnborough. Approx 1m, right into village, pub on right*

Stylish pub with excellent food

This Grade II listed, 16th-century property used to be the Butcher's Arms, having once belonged to the butcher on the now National Trust-owned Farnborough Park Estate. Built of locally quarried, honey-coloured Hornton stone, tasteful restoration has ensured the retention of a fine inglenook fireplace and other original features. The bar serves Hook Norton real ales, locally made Hogan's cider, and plenty of wines served by the glass. The concise menu lists British pub classic dishes, and others with a Mediterranean influence, but quality ingredients and high culinary skills ensure impressive results whatever your choice. Starters include sautéed king scallops with crab and tarragon risotto; and among the mains are roast breast of Gressingham duck with spiced plum and star anise jus, rösti potato, carrot purée and winter roots; and chicken curry with lime, coriander and fragrant rice. Enjoy good coffee in the terraced garden or covered decking area.

Open all wk 10-3 6-11 (Sat-Sun all day) **Bar Meals** L served all wk 12-3 D served all wk 6-10 Av main course £15 **Restaurant** L served all wk 12-3 D served Mon-Fri 6-10, Sat-Sun 10am-mdnt Fixed menu price fr £11.95 Av 3 course à la carte fr £22 ⊕ FREE HOUSE ◀ Hook Norton Hooky Bitter ♂ Hogan's, Local ciders. ☙ 14
Facilities Non-diners area ❖ (Bar Garden) ♦ Children's menu Children's portions Play area Garden ⋒ Parking Wi-fi ☷ (notice required)

GAYDON — Map 11 SP35

The Malt Shovel

Church Rd CV35 0ET ☎ 01926 641221
e-mail: malt.shovel@btconnect.com
dir: *M40 junct 12, B4451 to Gaydon*

Village pub that gets it right

Richard and Debi Morisot's 16th-century village pub has a reputation for being friendly and reliable, qualities that have helped to make their venture a success. Another plus is the range of real ales, usually from Everards, Fuller's, Hook Norton, Timothy Taylor or Wadworth. Menu options include duck with orange, lemon and honey; wild boar and apple sausages; battered haddock; and four-cheese ravioli. If all you want is a lunchtime snack, there are chunky granary sandwiches, baguettes and hot paninis. Well-behaved children and dogs are welcome and can play with Molly, the Morisot's Jack Russell, and their springer spaniel, Rosie.

Open all wk 11-3 5-11 (Fri-Sat 11-11 Sun 12-10.30) **Bar Meals** L served all wk 12-2 D served all wk 6.30-9 Av main course £10 **Restaurant** L served all wk 12-2 D served all wk 6.30-9 Av 3 course à la carte fr £20 ⊕ ENTERPRISE INNS ◀ Fuller's London Pride, Timothy Taylor Landlord, Everards Tiger, Wadworth 6X, Hook Norton. ☿ 10 **Facilities** Non-diners area ❖ (Bar Outside area) ☖ Children's portions Outside area ⋒ Parking ▭ (notice required)

GREAT WOLFORD — Map 10 SP23

The Fox & Hounds Inn

CV36 5NQ ☎ 01608 674220
e-mail: enquiries@thefoxandhoundsinn.com
dir: *Off A44 NE of Moreton-in-Marsh*

Unspoilt village inn with a kitchen garden

This family-run pub is located in the heart of Warwickshire, surrounded by wonderful countryside. The quintessential English inn ambience of settles, log fires and beams festooned with hops is an ideal place to sup pints of Hook Norton or Purity ales. The busy kitchen uses local produce such as Dexter beef and seasonal game from local shoots. Herbs and vegetables come from the kitchen garden, and mushrooms are of the wild variety; only fresh fish comes from further afield. A typical selection from the modern British menu could include oxtail risotto, and slow-roast belly pork with home-made black pudding.

Open 12-2.30 6-11.30 (Sun 12-10.30) Closed: 1st 2wks Jan, Mon ⊕ FREE HOUSE ◀ Hook Norton Hooky Bitter, Purity, Guest ales ⓣ Westons Stowford Press. **Facilities** ☖ Children's portions Garden Parking

HENLEY-IN-ARDEN — Map 10 SP16

The Bluebell ◉◉

93 High St B95 5AT ☎ 01564 793049
e-mail: info@bluebellhenley.co.uk
dir: *Opposite police station on A3400 in town centre*

Innovative food in pub with plenty of character

Since taking over The Bluebell seven years ago, Leigh and Duncan Taylor have worked tirelessly to update and improve this 500-year-old former coaching inn on Henley-in-Arden's picturesque High Street. Be wowed by the stylish interior design, which combines original beams, worn flagstones and open fireplaces with bold colours and an eclectic mix of furnishings and fabrics. The bar and dining room ooze style and atmosphere and both throng with drinkers and diners choosing from seasonal menus brimming with local or home-grown produce. Typically, tuck into baked beetroot, ricotta, hazelnuts, mint, honey and white balsamic dressing; and Highland venison and chestnut pie.

Open all day Closed: Mon (ex BHs) **Bar Meals** L served Tue-Sat 12-2.30, Sun 12-3.30 D served Tue-Sat 6-9.30 **Restaurant** L served Tue-Sat 12-2.30, Sun 12-3.30 D served Tue-Sat 6-9.30 ⊕ FREE HOUSE ◀ Purity Pure UBU & Mad Goose, Church End What The Fox's Hat, Hook Norton Hooky Bitter ⓣ Hogan's. ☿ 16 **Facilities** Non-diners area ❖ (Bar Restaurant Garden) ☖ Children's portions Garden ⋒ Parking Wi-fi

HUNNINGHAM — Map 11 SP36

The Red Lion, Hunningham

PICK OF THE PUBS

Main St CV33 9DY ☎ 01926 632715
e-mail: info@redlionhunningham.co.uk
dir: *From Leamington Spa take B4453, through Cubbington to Weston under Wetherby. Follow Hunningham signs (turn sharp right as road bends left towards Princethorpe)*

Comic book decoration but a serious approach to food

Set in the heart of rural Warwickshire and beside a 14th-century bridge, this quirky country pub's beer garden leads down to the River Leam and offers views of sheep and cows grazing. The real fires, original features and an eclectic mix of tables and chairs are enhanced by contemporary touches such as framed vintage comic book covers; look out for the additional comments on the menus that should make you smile! Once settled in one of dining areas peruse the appealing, well-executed menu then pop up to the bar to place your order. Locally sourced produce drives the generous dishes - a winter menu included ham and lentil soup; potted chicken pâté with 'too much toast' as starters, followed by Buttercross Farm pork chop with bubble-and-squeak and parsley sauce; spicy Hatton sausage and chickpea casserole; smoked haddock and Thai red curry fishcakes and mixed salad. On August Bank Holiday park your car (and tent if you like) in one of two fields for the annual outdoor film and beer festival; look out for the other events that take place.

Open all day all wk **Bar Meals** L served all wk 12-9.30 D served all wk 12-9.30 food served all day **Restaurant** L served all wk 12-9.30 D served all wk 12-9.30 food served all day ⊕ GREENE KING ◀ IPA & Abbot Ale, Hook Norton Old Hooky, BrewDog Alpha Dog, Guest ales. ☿ 28 **Facilities** Non-diners area ❖ (Bar Restaurant Garden) ☖ Children's portions Garden ⋒ Beer festival Parking Wi-fi

ILMINGTON — Map 10 SP24

The Howard Arms

PICK OF THE PUBS

Lower Green CV36 4LT ☎ 01608 682226
e-mail: info@howardarms.com
dir: *Exit A429 or A3400, 9m from Stratford-upon-Avon*

Popular with walkers and ramblers

A stunning 400-year-old Cotswold-stone inn on the picturesque village green of Ilmington, The Howard Arms is the start and finish to a number of fabulous local walks and is popular with ramblers. A detailed guide of walks can be bought at the bar for a small donation, with all monies going to the church funds. The flagstoned bar and open-plan dining room create a civilised look without sacrificing period charm, and it is all imbued with an informal atmosphere and a log fire that burns for most of the year. Award-winning ales feature with famous local names to the area such as Purity and Hook Norton, while wine drinkers can choose from a carefully selected list of over 30 wines by the glass. Equally serious are the inn's efforts to source seasonal ingredients and always strive to use local suppliers.

Open all day all wk **Bar Meals** L served Mon-Fri 12-2.30, Sat-Sun 12-3 D served Mon-Sat 6.30-9.30, Sun 6.30-9 **Restaurant** L served Mon-Sat 12-2.30, Sat-Sun 12-3 D served Mon-Sat 6.30-9.30, Sun 6.30-9 ⊕ FREE HOUSE ◀ Warwickshire Lady Godiva, Wye Valley Bitter, Hook Norton Old Hooky, Purity ⓣ Hogan's. ☿ 30 **Facilities** Non-diners area ☖ Children's portions Garden ⋒ Parking Wi-fi ▭ (notice required)

KENILWORTH — Map 10 SP27

The Almanack

Abbey End North CV8 1QJ ☎ 01926 353637
e-mail: hello@thealmanack-kenilworth.co.uk
dir: *Exit A46 at Kenilworth & brown Castle sign, towards town centre. Left into Abbey Hill (B4104) signed Balsall Common. At rdbt into Abbey End. Opposite Holiday Inn*

Modern British gastro-pub

Inspired by the 1960s Kinks hit 'Autumn Almanac', the stylish interior harks back to the 60s with its retro Danish teak and rosewood furniture and original album covers on the walls. The huge island bar separates the lounge from the eatery and open kitchen. The pub is open all day for breakfast, coffee and cake, lunch and dinner; menu choices include deli boards, a daily roast, a selection from the chargrill, and full meals such as superfood salad followed by Cornish lamb medallions, dauphinoise potatoes, crushed carrots and pea shoots; with lemon

Save on hotels. Book at theAA.com/hotel

WARWICKSHIRE 459 ENGLAND

queen of puddings or crème brûlée for dessert. There's a special kids' menu, too.

Open all day all wk Closed: 25 Dec **Bar Meals** L served all wk 12-6 D served all wk 6-10 Av main course £15 **Restaurant** L served all wk 12-3 D served all wk 6-10 Fixed menu price fr £12 Av 3 course à la carte fr £25 ⊕ FREE HOUSE/PEACH PUBS ◀ Purity Pure UBU & Gold, Sharp's Doom Bar ♂ Aspall. ♟ 16 **Facilities** Non-diners area ❀ (Bar Outside area) ♦♦ Children's menu Children's portions Outside area ᗴ Wi-fi ▄▄ (notice required)

LAPWORTH　　　　　　　　　Map 10 SP17

The Boot Inn

PICK OF THE PUBS

Old Warwick Rd B94 6JU ☎ 01564 782464
e-mail: thebootinn@lovelypubs.co.uk
dir: *Telephone for directions*

Stylish country pub on the canal

Beside the Grand Union Canal in the unspoilt village of Lapworth, this lively and convivial 16th-century former coaching inn is reputedly haunted by a former waitress from the 19th century. Apart from its smart interior with its soft modern furnishings complementing the old-world feel, the attractive garden is a great place to relax or dine on warm days, while a canopy and patio heaters make it a comfortable place to sit even on cooler evenings. Being a free house, there is a good choice of real ales to enjoy – Fuller's London Pride or Purity Pure UBU maybe. But the main draw is the modern brasserie-style food. Choose a filled wrap, pitta or sandwich for lunch. For dinner, a starter of devilled kidneys on toast; or freshly made soup perhaps followed by a main of spit-roasted piri-piri chicken; confit of duck, fondant potato, wilted spinach and tomato compôte; or Thai vegetable curry. Children and 'well-natured' dogs are welcome, while the friendly staff can cater for any dietary requirements. The annual fireworks display attracts a huge crowd.

Open all day all wk 11-11 (Thu-Sat 11am-mdnt Sun 12-10.30) **Bar Meals** L served Mon-Sat 12-2.30, Sun 12-3 D served Mon-Fri 7-9.30, Sat 6.30-9.30, Sun 7-9 **Restaurant** L served Mon-Sat 12-2.30, Sun 12-3 D served Mon-Fri 7-9.30, Sat 6.30-9.30, Sun 7-9 ⊕ FREE HOUSE ◀ Fuller's London Pride, Purity Pure UBU, Marston's EPA ♂ Thatchers Gold, Westons Stowford Press. ♟ 9 **Facilities** Non-diners area ❀ (Bar Restaurant Garden) ♦♦ Children's menu Children's portions Garden ᗴ Parking ▄▄ (notice required)

LEAMINGTON SPA (ROYAL)　　　Map 10 SP36

The Moorings at Myton

Myton Rd CV31 3NY ☎ 01926 425043
e-mail: info@themoorings.co.uk
web: www.themoorings.co.uk
dir: *M40 junct 14 or 13, A452 towards Leamington Spa. At 4th rdbt after crossing canal, pub on left*

Anglo-French cuisine in waterside location

Raymond Blanc protégés Charles Harris and Nigel Brown have created a relaxed, New England-style interior that has enhanced the building's architectural features and made full use of its unique waterside location. A wide range of ales is on offer but wine buffs will be drawn to the excellent list with over a dozen by the glass. Trusted local suppliers are the cornerstone of the Anglo-French menu that includes soufflés, sharing plates, salads and steaks alongside main courses such as roasted breast of duck à l'orange and braised beef, mashed potatoes and bourguignon sauce.

Open all day all wk **Bar Meals** L served all wk 12-2.30 D served all wk 6-9.30 Av main course £13 **Restaurant** L served all wk 12-2.30 D served all wk 6-9.30 Av 3 course à la carte fr £25 ⊕ CHARLES WELLS ◀ Bombardier, Young's London Gold, Courage Directors, Warwickshire Darling Buds. ♟ 13 **Facilities** Non-diners area ❀ (Bar Garden) ♦♦ Children's menu Children's portions Family room Garden ᗴ Parking Wi-fi ▄▄ (notice required)

See advert on page 461

LONG COMPTON　　　　　　　Map 10 SP23

The Red Lion ★★★★ INN ◉

PICK OF THE PUBS

Main St CV36 5JS ☎ 01608 684221
e-mail: info@redlion-longcompton.co.uk
dir: *On A3400 between Shipston on Stour & Chipping Norton*

Cotswold character and award-winning cuisine

Just a couple of miles south of the old coaching inn, the Cotswolds reveals one of its secrets, The Rollright Stones. Their origin is wreathed in mystery, although tales of shape-shifting to form this eerie stone circle abound. There's no mystery as to why locals and visitors head for The Red Lion though; the promising combination of a traditional Cotswold inn and the AA Rosette guarantees a first rate experience. The lovely mix of beams, stone-flags and bare stone, colourwash and boarding evokes a timeless atmosphere, log fires and log-burners add that

extra winter appeal. The lavender-scented garden is a good mooring spot in which to quaff Hook Norton and other ales, anticipate the great menu based on Cotswold regional produce. Perhaps start with creamy wild mushroom ragout with garlic, rocket and toasted brioche; followed by their signature steak and Hook Norton ale pie. Five luxurious bedrooms are available to extend your stay.

Open all wk Mon-Thu 10-2.30 6-11 (Fri-Sun all day) **Bar Meals** L served Mon-Thu 12-2.30, Fri-Sun 12-9.30 D served Mon-Thu 6-9, Fri-Sun 12-9.30 Av main course £14.50 **Restaurant** L served Mon-Thu 12-2.30, Fri-Sun 12-9.30 D served Mon-Thu 6-9, Fri-Sun 12-9.30 ⊕ FREE HOUSE ◀ Hook Norton Hooky Bitter, Adnams, Timothy Taylor. ♟ 11 **Facilities** Non-diners area ♦♦ Children's menu Children's portions Play area Garden ᗴ Parking Wi-fi **Rooms** 5

MONKS KIRBY　　　　　　　　Map 11 SP48

The Bell Inn

Bell Ln CV23 0QY ☎ 01788 832352
e-mail: belindagb@aol.com
dir: *Off B4455 (Fosse Way)*

Timbered inn offering menus with strong Spanish influences

This quaint, timbered inn was once the gatehouse of a Benedictine priory and then a brewhouse cottage. The pine bar top came from a tree grown in Leire churchyard nearby. The Spanish owners describe their pub as "a corner of Spain in the heart of England". Mediterranean and traditional cuisine play an important role on the truly extensive menu. Enjoy a glass of Ruddles while taking time to make your choices. Lobster Zarzuela, monkfish al horno, solomillo Andalucia and grilled halibut all make a showing. Grills, pasta, and paella are all readily available.

Open all wk 12-3 6.30-10.30 Closed: 26 Dec, 1 Jan, Mon eve **Bar Meals** L served all wk 12-3 D served Tue-Sun 6.30-10.30 **Restaurant** L served all wk 12-3 D served Tue-Sun 6.30-10.30 ⊕ FREE HOUSE ◀ Greene King IPA, Ruddles. **Facilities** Non-diners area ❀ (Garden) ♦♦ Children's portions Garden Parking Wi-fi ▄▄

OFFCHURCH
Map 11 SP36

The Stag at Offchurch

Welsh Rd CV33 9AQ ☎ 01926 425801
e-mail: info@thestagatoffchurch.com
web: www.thestagatoffchurch.com
dir: *From Leamington Spa take A425 towards Southam. At Radford Semele left into Offchurch Ln to Offchurch*

Picturesque pub with progressive menu

A chocolate box thatched pub in a classic English village. This considerately modernised inn balances the atmosphere of times long-gone with contemporary flourishes that together attract a varied clientele of diners, ramblers and locals to the restaurant and bar (where Warwickshire Brewery ales feature). The imaginative menu offers plenty of choice – start with Lincolnshire Poacher cheese soufflé with white wine cream sauce, progressing then to pan-roasted cod with mashed potato, green beans, brown shrimp, clam and cider marinière; or Cornish spring lamb mixed grill with a red wine jus. Executive chef Nigel Brown, who has worked with Raymond Blanc, specialises in locally raised, 28-day dry-aged Aberdeenshire beef steaks.

Open all day all wk **Bar Meals** L served all wk 12-2.30 D served all wk 6-9.30 **Restaurant** L served all wk 12-2.30 D served all wk 6-9.30 ⊕ FREE HOUSE ◀ Hook Norton, Warwickshire ♂ Somersby Cider. ¶ 13 **Facilities** Non-diners area ♥ (Bar Garden) ♦♦ Children's menu Children's portions Garden ⊟ Parking Wi-fi

See advert on opposite page

OXHILL
Map 10 SP34

The Peacock

Main St CV35 0QU ☎ 01295 688060
e-mail: info@thepeacockoxhill.co.uk
dir: *From Stratford-upon-Avon take A422 towards Banbury. Turn right to Oxhill*

Destination pub in picturesque village

Yvonne Hamlett and Pam Farrell's objective is to run a classic English country pub. They can tick that one off, then. Their 16th-century, stone-built pub effortlessly combines its historic past with a relaxed modern atmosphere. Hand-pulled ales come from Purity, Timothy Taylor, Wye Valley and guests, and the popular food reflects the kitchen's focus on meats and vegetables from local farms, and fresh fish from Devon and Cornwall. Meal ideas include pie of the day; slow-cooked brisket of beef; duo of salmon and sea bass with dill beurre blanc; and roasted vegetables in tomato and white wine sauce with pasta.

Open all day all wk 12-11 **Bar Meals** L served Mon-Sat 12-2, Sun 12-8 D served Mon-Sat 6-9, Sun 12-8 **Restaurant** L served Mon-Sat 12-2, Sun 12-8 D served Mon-Sat 6-9, Sun 12-8 Fixed menu price fr £13.50 ◀ Timothy Taylor Golden Best, Wye Valley HPA & Butty Bach, Purity, Guest ales ♂ Thatchers Pear & Gold, Healey's Cornish Rattler. ¶ 12 **Facilities** Non-diners area ♦♦ Children's menu Children's portions Garden ⊟ Parking Wi-fi 🚌

PRESTON BAGOT
Map 10 SP16

The Crabmill

B95 5EE ☎ 01926 843342
e-mail: thecrabmill@lovelypubs.co.uk
dir: *M40 junct 16, A3400 towards Stratford-upon-Avon. Take A4189 at lights in Henley-in-Arden. Left, 1.5m pub on left*

Richly varied menu in converted cider mill

Handy for a pre-prandial stroll in superb countryside alongside the Stratford-upon-Avon Canal, this carefully renovated former rural mill, where crab apples were perhaps mashed into cider, is a fine destination gastro-pub presented in a modern rustic style. Colourwash, comfy seating and light beams offer an airy, informal interior. Contemporary dishes shine out from the extensive menu; commence with Somerset brie and leek tart before sampling a main of roast venison pave with celeriac dauphinoise, sautéed sprouts and bacon or braised belly of pork with truffle mash.

Open all day 11-11 Closed: Sun eve **Bar Meals** L served Mon-Thu 12-3, Fri-Sat 12-5, Sun 12-4 D served Mon-Sat 6.30-9.30 **Restaurant** L served Mon-Sat 12-2.30, Sun 12-4 D served Mon-Sat 6.30-9.30 ⊕ FREE HOUSE ◀ Greene King Abbot Ale, Purity Gold, St Austell Tribute, Fuller's London Pride ♂ Stowford Press. ¶ 14 **Facilities** Non-diners area ♥ (Bar Garden) ♦♦ Children's menu Children's portions Garden ⊟ Parking Wi-fi

PRIORS MARSTON
Map 11 SP45

The Hollybush Inn

PICK OF THE PUBS

Hollybush Ln CV47 7RW ☎ 01327 260934
e-mail: enquiries@hollybushatpriorsmarston.co.uk
dir: *From Southam take A425 towards Daventry, 1st right signed Priors Marston. 6m, left after war memorial, next left, 150yds left again*

Thriving and relaxed village local

Originally a farmhouse, The Hollybush only became a fully licensed pub in 1947. Set in the beautiful village of Priors Marston in the heart of Warwickshire, it's a warm hub of village social activity with a very relaxed atmosphere and real fires. The menus range from open sandwiches and sharing boards to a comprehensive main menu selection - perhaps a starter of peppered carpaccio of beef with a wild rocket and parmesan salad and fresh lemon juice; followed by pan-fried red mullet fillets with a rustic Italian ratatouille and sautéed potatoes. For those in search of pub classics, beer-battered haddock and chips; and ham, egg and chips are also on offer. Desserts could include profiteroles or sticky toffee pudding. Smaller portions can be ordered for most of the grown-up dishes.

Open all wk 12-3 5.30-11 (Sat-Sun 12-11) ⊕ PUNCH TAVERNS ◀ Morland Old Speckled Hen, Hook Norton, Fuller's ♂ Westons Stowford Press. **Facilities** ♦♦ Children's portions Garden Parking Wi-fi

SALFORD PRIORS
Map 10 SP05

The Bell at Salford Priors

Evesham Rd WR11 8UU ☎ 01789 772112
e-mail: info@thebellatsalfordpriors.com
dir: *From A46 (Bidford Island) towards Salford Priors. Through village. Pub on left*

High-quality yet informal dining

This black-and-white timber-framed pub draws diners for its rural location and the daily-changing menu that champions local seasonal produce. It is within striking distance of Stratford-upon-Avon, the Cotswolds and the NEC at Birmingham. Expect a warm welcome, glowing fires and three real ales on tap, including Sharp's Doom Bar. The dining room is decorated in the contemporary style and you can also eat alfresco, weather permitting. Typically, follow a whole baked camembert studded with walnuts, with chicken escalope served with a garlic, lemon and herb crème fraîche, and then passionfruit crème brûlée. There is a set lunch menu, roasts on Sunday and fish night every Friday.

Open all wk 12-3 6-close (Sat-Sun all day) **Bar Meals** L served all wk 12-2.30 D served all wk 6-9 **Restaurant** L served Mon-Fri 12-2.30, Sat-Sun all day D served Mon-Fri 6-9, Sat-Sun all day ⊕ ENTERPRISE INNS ◀ Wye Valley HPA, Sharp's Doom Bar, Wickwar BOB ♂ Westons Old Rosie. ¶ 10 **Facilities** Non-diners area ♥ (Bar Garden) ♦♦ Children's menu Children's portions Garden ⊟ Parking Wi-fi

Save on hotels. Book at **theAA.com/hotel**

WARWICKSHIRE 461 **ENGLAND**

SHREWLEY — Map 10 SP26

The Durham Ox Restaurant and Country Pub

PICK OF THE PUBS

Shrewley Common CV35 7AY ☎ 01926 842283
e-mail: enquiries@thedurhamox.com
dir: *M40 junct 15, A46 towards Coventry. 1st exit signed Warwick, left onto A4177. After Hatton Country World, pub signed, 1.5m*

Superior dining in a village pub

Named after an ox of epic proportions, this 300-year-old pub-restaurant is situated in the peaceful village of Shrewley, just four miles from Warwick and Leamington. Warm and inviting, its old beams, tiled floor, oak panelling, roaring fire and traditional hospitality combine with a city chic to give it that competitive edge. Success is in no small measure due to the restaurant, where impressive, seasonally changing classic and contemporary dishes are prepared. A meal might consist of a pigeon, spinach and mushroom pasty; slow-braised venison and Black Sheep ale casserole with braised red cabbage and thyme dumplings; and dark chocolate fondant. Potted kippers with cucumber pickle could appear on the specials list. For a real treat, your table could opt for the gourmet experience menu. Bar food includes snacks, sandwiches and hearty pub classics, such as spicy and sticky pork ribs. Extensive gardens incorporate a safe children's play area.

Open all wk 11-11 (Sun 12-10) **Bar Meals** L served Mon-Fri 12-2.30, Sat 12-9.30, Sun 12-6.30 D served Mon-Fri 6-9.30, Sat 12-9.30, Sun 12-6.30 **Restaurant** L served Mon-Fri 6-9.30, Sat 12-9.30, Sun 12-6.30 D served Mon-Fri 6-9.30, Sat 12-9.30, Sun 12-6.30 ⊕ GREENE KING ◀ Ruddles County & IPA, Greene King Abbot Ale, Morland Old Speckled Hen, Guest ales Ö Westons Stowford Press. ▼ 21 **Facilities** Non-diners area ❤ (Bar Garden Outside area) ♦▮ Children's menu Children's portions Play area Garden Outside area ⋒ Parking Wi-fi ▄ (notice required)

STRATFORD-UPON-AVON — Map 10 SP25

The One Elm

PICK OF THE PUBS

1 Guild St CV37 6QZ ☎ 01789 404919
e-mail: theoneelm@peachpubs.com
dir: *In town centre*

Quirky decor and a Mediterranean-style courtyard

Named after the elm tree that used to be a boundary marker of Stratford-on-Avon, the One Elm occupies a prime location in the town centre not far from the river and theatre. It mirrors the chic, contemporary look and style of menus to be found at other Peach Pubs, the innovative small pub group. Opening at 9.30am for coffee and breakfast, there's an informal, almost continental feel about the place, especially in the stylish front lounge area with its wood floor, bright painted walls, leather sofas and low tables displaying the day's newspapers. Beyond the central, open-to-view kitchen is the more formal dining area, while the upstairs seating area has an even grander feel. The menu is an eclectic list of modern pub food. Try herb pancakes with spinach and mushroom stuffing and gruyère cream sauce; Aberdeenshire cheeseburger with chips, onion rings and coleslaw; or a deli board to share. The secluded terrace gives you a feeling of being abroad.

Open all day all wk 9.30am-11pm (Thu 9.30am-mdnt Fri-Sat 9.30am-1am Sun 9.30am-10.30pm) Closed: 25 Dec **Bar Meals** L served all wk 12-6 D served all wk 6-10 food served all day **Restaurant** L served all wk 12-6 D served all wk 6-10 food served all day ⊕ FREE HOUSE/PEACH PUBS ◀ Purity Pure UBU & Gold, Sharp's Doom Bar Ö Aspall. ▼ 14 **Facilities** Non-diners area ❤ (Bar Garden) ♦▮ Children's menu Children's portions Garden ⋒ Parking Wi-fi ▄

STRETTON ON FOSSE — Map 10 SP23

The Plough Inn

GL56 9QX ☎ 01608 661053
e-mail: saravol@aol.com
dir: *From Moreton-in-Marsh, 4m on A429 N. From Stratford-upon-Avon, 10m on A429 S*

Traditional village pub with a French influence

A classic village pub built from mellow Cotswold stone, The Plough has the requisite exposed beams and real fire. Four real ales are usually on tap, ciders include Black Rat, and there's a good range of wines too. It's a family-run affair, with French chef and co-owner Jean-Pierre in charge of the kitchen; so expect traditional French dishes on the specials board. With a spit-roast in the inglenook fireplace in winter and spring, entertainment on Sunday evenings ranges from quizzes to folk music.

Open 11.30-2.30 6-11.30 (Sun 12-3) Closed: 25 Dec eve, Sun eve & Mon L (ex BHs) **Bar Meals** L served Tue-Sun 12-2 D served Tue-Sat 7-9 ⊕ FREE HOUSE ◀ Ansell's Mild, Shepherd Neame Spitfire, Hook Norton, Purity, Local ales Ö Thatchers Katy & Traditional, Black Rat. ▼ 9 **Facilities** Non-diners area ♦▮ Children's portions Play area Garden ⋒ Parking Wi-fi ▄ (notice required)

TANWORTH IN ARDEN — Map 10 SP17

The Bell Inn NEW

The Green B94 5AL ☎ 01564 742212
e-mail: thebell@realcoolbars.com
dir: *M42 junct 8, A435 signed Evesham. Left signed Portway & Tanworth (Penn Ln). To T-junct, left signed Tanworth. 1st right signed Tanworth. Inn in village centre*

A popular village pub once featured on TV

Older visitors might remember (or conveniently forget) a TV soap called *Crossroads*, many of whose outdoor scenes were shot in Tanworth, doubling as 'Kings Oak'. The pub overlooks the small village green and war memorial, and has stood here since the 17th century, so the cool grey tones of the thoroughly modern bar area might come as a surprise. Here lunchtime snacks and main meals include sandwiches and baguettes; Timothy Taylor ale-battered fish and chips; and home-made Arabic tapas. In the evening, try grilled Gressingham duck breast with Thai stir-fry; or pesto tagliatelle with mozzarella cheese and roasted Mediterranean vegetables.

Open all day all wk **Bar Meals** L served Mon-Sat 12-2.30, Sun 12-8 D served Mon-Sat 6.30-9, Sun 12-8 **Restaurant** L served Mon-Sat 12-2.30, Sun 12-8 D served Mon-Sat 6.30-9, Sun 12-8 ⊕ ENTERPRISE INNS ◀ Timothy Taylor Landlord Ö Thatchers Gold. ▼ **Facilities** Non-diners area ❤ (Bar Outside area) ♦▮ Children's menu Children's portions Outside area ⋒ Parking Wi-fi ▄ (notice required)

TEMPLE GRAFTON — Map 10 SP15

The Blue Boar Inn ★★★ INN

B49 6NR ☎ 01789 750010
e-mail: info@theblueboar.co.uk
dir: *From A46 (Stratford to Alcester) turn left to Temple Grafton. Pub at 1st x-rds*

Historic inn with Cotswolds views

The oldest part of this former ale house and now thriving village inn dates back to the early 1600s and includes a 35-foot deep well, now glassed over and illuminated, set into a flagstoned floor and home to goldfish. Warmth in the bar and restaurant comes from four open fires, while in the summer there is a patio garden with views of the Cotswold Hills. Extensive menus include steak from local Freeman's Farm, pork belly with cider jus, pub classics like chilli and coriander beefburger, and a steak and onion sandwich. Wash it down with a pint of Jennings or Wychwood Hobgoblin. There are 14 attractive bedrooms.

Open all day all wk **Bar Meals** L served all wk 12-3 D served all wk 6-10 Av main course £10 **Restaurant** L served Mon-Fri 12-3, Sat 12-10, Sun 12-9 D served Mon-Fri 6-10, Sat 12-10, Sun 12-9 Av 3 course à la carte fr £19 ⊕ MARSTON'S ◀ Pedigree, Wychwood Hobgoblin, Banks's Bitter, Jennings Ö Thatchers Gold. ▼ 10 **Facilities** Non-diners area ❤ (Bar Garden) ♦▮ Children's menu Children's portions Garden ⋒ Parking Wi-fi ▄ (notice required) **Rooms** 14

Save on hotels. Book at **theAA.com/hotel**

WARWICKSHIRE 463 ENGLAND

WARWICK   Map 10 SP26

The Rose & Crown

PICK OF THE PUBS

30 Market Place CV34 4SH ☎ **01926 411117**
e-mail: roseandcrown@peachpubs.com
dir: *M40 junct 15 follow signs to Warwick. Pass castle car park entrance up hill to West Gate, left into Bowling Green St, 1st right, follow one-way system to T-junct right into Market Place, pub visible ahead*

A vibrant and stylish gastro-pub

The flagship venture of the innovative Peach Pub Company created over a decade ago, The Rose & Crown continues to thrive. In a corner of Warwick's market place, there are a few tables outside to enjoy a spot of people-watching. The laid-back vibe and contemporary look sit well with period features and homely touches such as comfy leather sofas. The pub opens early for breakfast and offers a modern pub menu that's served all day. Deli boards offer a selection of small tapas-style portions, and the seasonal menu also offers a wide range of dishes to suit the occasion and time of day. There are sandwiches, salads, grills and roasts, and mains like herb-crusted Cornish lamb leg cannon with crushed minted potatoes, peas and baby onion jus. Puddings may include mixed berry knickerbocker glory. A beer festival is usually held at the end of May.

Open all day all wk Mon-Wed 7am-11pm (Thu 7am-11.30pm Fri 7am-12.30am Sat 8am-12.30am Sun 8am-10pm) Closed: 25 Dec **Bar Meals** L served all wk 12-6 D served Mon-Sat 6-10, Sun 6-9.30 Av main course £15 food served all day **Restaurant** L served all wk 12-6 D served Mon-Sat 6-10, Sun 6-9.30 Fixed menu price fr £12 Av 3 course à la carte fr £25 food served all day ⊕ FREE HOUSE/PEACH PUBS ◀ Purity Pure UBU & Gold, Sharp's Doom Bar ♻ Aspall. ♟16
Facilities Non-diners area ♣ (Bar Outside area) ♦ Children's portions Outside area ♫ Beer festival Wi-fi ▭ (notice required)

WELFORD-ON-AVON   Map 10 SP15

The Bell Inn

PICK OF THE PUBS

Binton Rd CV37 8EB ☎ **01789 750353**
e-mail: info@thebellwelford.co.uk
dir: *Telephone for directions*

An enjoyably civilised pub

The interior of this appealing, early 16th-century pub is chock-full of signs of its age. Each distinct space displays its own character, with flagstones in one, and oak flooring in another; there's antique wood panelling in the bar, and three open fires, one an inglenook. Legend has it that William Shakespeare, having been drinking here with the dramatist Ben Jonson, contracted fatal pneumonia after returning to Stratford-upon-Avon in the pouring rain. It's a matter owners Colin and Teresa Ombler leave others to debate, while they focus on providing quality drink and food. For example, there are always five real ales, including at least two local brews, and 16 wines served by the glass. Starters and light meals include avocado and crispy smoked bacon salad; and deep-fried brie with apricot and ginger compôte. Main courses include horseshoe gammon and pineapple; faggots with sage and onion gravy; and green Thai monkfish curry.

Open all wk 11.30-3 6-11 (Sat 11.30-11 Sun 12-10.30) **Bar Meals** L served Mon-Fri 11.30-2.30, Sat-Sun all day D served Mon-Thu 6-9.30, Fri 6-10, Sat-Sun all day Av main course £13.55 **Restaurant** L served Mon-Fri 11.30-2.30, Sat-Sun all day D served Mon-Thu 6-9.30, Fri 6-10, Sat-Sun all day Av 3 course à la carte fr £22.25 ⊕ ENTERPRISE INNS ◀ Wells Bombardier, Hobsons Best Bitter, Flowers Best Bitter & IPA, Purity Gold & Pure UBU, Hook Norton, Greene King IPA. ♟16
Facilities Non-diners area ♦ Children's menu Children's portions Garden ♫ Parking Wi-fi ▭ (notice required)

WITHYBROOK — Map 11 SP48

The Pheasant

Main St CV7 9LT ☎ 01455 220480
e-mail: thepheasant01@hotmail.com
web: www.thepheasanteatinghouse.com
dir: *7m NE of Coventry, on B4112*

Crowd-pleasing pub grub in an idyllic location

A warm welcome awaits you at this 17th-century inn, idyllically situated beside the brook where withies were once cut for fencing, hence the village's name, Withybrook. The Pheasant is a popular free house, cosy and full of character with an inglenook fireplace, farm implements and horse-racing photographs on display. The chalkboard flags up daily and seasonal specials, complementing a wealth of food choices from the extensive main menu. Take your pick from chef's special curry, fresh venison pie, sizzling skillets including Cajun chicken, Japanese breaded king prawns or broccoli and walnut lasagne. Save room for chocolate lumpy bumpy for afters. Outside, the benches on the patio area overlooking the Withy Brook can accommodate 100 people — perfect for a leisurely lunch or a thirst-quenching pint of real ale after a walk in the beautiful surrounding countryside.

Open all wk 11-3 6-11.30 (Sun & BH 11-11) Closed: 25-26 Dec **Restaurant** L served Mon-Sat 12-2, Sun 12-8.30/9 D served Mon-Sat 6-10, Sun 12-8.30/9 ⊕ FREE HOUSE ◀ Courage Directors, Theakston Best Bitter, John Smith's Extra Smooth, Young's Bitter. ☂ 16 **Facilities** Non-diners area ☙ (Garden) ♦♦ Children's menu Children's portions Garden ☴ Parking Wi-fi ▭ (notice required)

See advert on page 463

WEST MIDLANDS

BARSTON — Map 10 SP27

The Malt Shovel at Barston

PICK OF THE PUBS

See Pick of the Pubs on opposite page
See advert on page 466

BIRMINGHAM — Map 10 SP08

The Old Joint Stock

4 Temple Row West B2 5NY ☎ 0121 200 1892
e-mail: oldjointstock@fullers.co.uk
dir: *Opposite main entrance to St Philip's Cathedral, just off Colmore Row*

Great for pies or taking in a show

This impressively colonnaded building was designed by the same architect as part of St Philip's Cathedral opposite. Originally a library and later a bank, its high-Victorian Gothic interior incorporates an immense domed ceiling, stately-home fittings and towering mahogany island bar. Pies take up a chunk of the menu, which also features bloody Mary sardines with toast; bangers and mash with red wine gravy; and evening snacks such as cheese straws. Fuller's, the owner, has developed the second floor as an 80-seat theatre for productions from Shakespeare to fashion shows. A beer festival is held twice yearly.

Open all wk all day (Sun 12-5) **Bar Meals** L served all wk 12-5 D served Mon-Sat 5-10 Av main course £10.25 food served all day **Restaurant** L served all wk 12-5 D served Mon-Sat 5-10 Fixed menu price fr £12.95 food served all day ⊕ FULLER'S ◀ London Pride, ESB, Discovery. ☂ 16 **Facilities** Non-diners area ♦♦ Family room Outside area ☴ Beer festival Wi-fi ▭

CHADWICK END — Map 10 SP27

The Orange Tree

PICK OF THE PUBS

Warwick Rd B93 0BN ☎ 01564 785364
e-mail: theorangetree@lovelypubs.co.uk
dir: *3m from Knowle towards Warwick*

Informal modern pub with a diverse menu

Refurbished in 2012, The Orange Tree is part of the small Lovely Pubs chain in Warwickshire. It fits the brand with its wooden floors, unclothed tables, neutral-toned walls and light modern interiors coupled with old beams, antique mirrors and a relaxed pubby vibe. Outside, landscaped gardens are perfect for dining in the sunshine. On the extensive menu, (of which there is a separate vegetarian one, almost as long) comfort food options sit alongside globally influenced dishes and

there's a plat du jour and 'pud de jour' during the week. So try perhaps, gambas pil pil: pan-fried king prawns in garlic, chilli, saffron, paprika and parsley with aïoli crostini or a sharing plate, then pizza or pasta or chargrilled pork cutlet, pumpkin, wild mushroom and sage, amaretti crumble, fondant potato and cider sauce. Finish with a retro banana split, brought up to date with dulce de leche and amaretti biscuits.

Open all day all wk 11-11 **Bar Meals** L served Mon-Sat 12-2.30, Sun 12-7 D served Mon-Sat 6-9.30 Av main course £15 **Restaurant** L served Mon-Sat 12-2.30, Sun 12-7 D served Mon-Sat 6-9.30 Fixed menu price fr £8.95 Av 3 course à la carte fr £22 ⊕ FREE HOUSE ◀ Fuller's London Pride, Purity Pure UBU. ☂ 10 **Facilities** Non-diners area ☙ (Bar Garden) ♦♦ Children's portions Play area Garden ☴ Parking Wi-fi ▭ (notice required)

HAMPTON IN ARDEN — Map 10 SP28

The White Lion Inn

PICK OF THE PUBS

10 High St B92 0AA ☎ 01675 442833
e-mail: info@thewhitelioninn.com
dir: *M42 junct 6, A45 towards Coventry. At rdbt take A452 towards Leamington Spa. At rdbt take B4102 towards Solihull. Approx 2m to Hampton in Arden*

Former farmhouse serving international food

Licensed since at least 1836, this 17th-century timber-framed pub was originally a farmhouse. Landlord Chris Roach and partner FanFan draw on their considerable experience from managing (and, of course, visiting) many restaurants, bistros and gastro-pubs in England and France. The bright and modern interior is wood floored, decorated with fresh flowers and furnished with wicker chairs. The simple bistro-style, seasonal menu nods fairly vigorously across the English Channel, with items like classic French Paysanne salad; moules a la crème; and French boeuf bourguignon. Non-Gallic finds are likely to include home-made lasagne; Jamaica jerk chicken; smoked salmon and pea risotto; fish and chips; and a home-made cheeseburger. There are also sandwiches (toasted if preferred) and jacket potatoes. The traditional Sunday lunches are a must. The bar offers a good selection of real ales and ciders, including Brew XI, Mad Goose, Tribute and Doom Bar.

Open all day all wk noon-12.30am (Sun 12-10.30) **Bar Meals** L served all wk 12-2.30 D served all wk 6.30-9.30 **Restaurant** L served all wk 12-2.30 D served all wk 6.30-9.30 ⊕ PUNCH TAVERNS ◀ M&B Brew XI, Purity Mad Goose, St Austell Tribute, Sharp's Doom Bar, Hobsons ♺ Westons Stowford Press, Aspall. ☂ 9 **Facilities** Non-diners area ☙ (Bar Restaurant Garden) ♦♦ Children's menu Children's portions Garden ☴ Parking Wi-fi ▭ (notice required)

PICK OF THE PUBS

The Malt Shovel at Barston

BARSTON   Map 10 SP27

Barston Ln B92 0JP ☎ 01675 443223
e-mail:
themaltshovelatbarston@gmail.com
web: www.themaltshovelatbarston.com
dir: *M42 junct 5, A4141 towards Knowle.*
Left into Jacobean Ln, right at T-junct
(Hampton Ln). Left into Barston Ln,
0.5m

Smart, busy inn down the country lanes

The Malt Shovel is an airy, well-designed free house with modern soft furnishings and interesting artefacts. An early 20th-century, stylishly converted mill building, it sits comfortably in the countryside outside Solihull. Natural wood and pastel colours characterise the interiors and flowers decorate the unclothed tables in the tiled dining area. The bar is cosy and relaxed with winter log fires, and there's an attractive garden for outdoor dining; at weekends the restaurant in the adjacent converted barn is opened. The extensive choice of modern British dishes makes the best of fresh seasonal ingredients, and, predictably, the daily fish specials board is popular with lovers of seafood. A look through the imaginative menu finds starters like Jamaican spiced pork ribs with sweetcorn and sugared mango; and antipasto of cured meats with black grapes and truffle honey. Main course dishes are just as appetising: there's seared peppered tuna with celeriac, horseradish and enoki mushrooms; slow-cooked Moroccan spiced lamb shank, date couscous and apricot yoghurt; dry-aged Scottish sirloin with mustard glaze and home-made chips; and zucchini cannelloni stuffed with ricotta and sweet potato, duo of peas and truffle oil. As for desserts, you won't often come across raspberry and hibiscus flower cheesecake with pannacotta ice cream; or apricot and mascarpone crispy wonton with lime syrup and apple sorbet, so tuck in. A board of English and European cheeses with grapes, celery, apple and sultana chutney and crisp-bread will fill any remaining corners.

Open all day all wk **Bar Meals** L served Mon-Sat 12-2.30, Sun 12-4 D served Mon-Sat 6-9.30 Av main course £16.50 **Restaurant** L served Sun 12-4 D served Mon-Sat 7-9.30 Fixed menu price fr £26 🌐 FREE HOUSE ◀ St Austell Tribute, M&B Brew XI, Timothy Taylor Landlord. 🍷 12 **Facilities** Non-diners area 👫 Children's menu Children's portions Garden 🪑 Parking Wi-fi

SEDGLEY
Map 10 SO99

Beacon Hotel & Sarah Hughes Brewery
PICK OF THE PUBS

129 Bilston St DY3 1JE ☎ 01902 883380
dir: *Telephone for directions*

Enjoy a pint of ale brewed on the premises

Home of the Sarah Hughes Brewery and the famous Dark Ruby Mild, the Beacon Hotel is a restored Victorian tap house that has barely changed in 150 years. Proprietor John Hughes reopened the adjoining Sarah Hughes Brewery in 1987, 66 years after his grandmother became the licensee. The rare snob-screened island bar serves a simple taproom, with its old wall benches and a fine blackened range; a super cosy snug replete with a green-tiled marble fireplace, dark woodwork, velvet curtains and huge old tables; and a large smoke-room with an adjoining, plant-festooned conservatory. On a tour of the brewery you can see the original grist case and rare open-topped copper that add to the Victorian charm and give unique character to the brews. Flagship beers are Sarah Hughes Dark Ruby, Sedgley Surprise and Amber, with seasonal bitter and two guest beers from small microbreweries also available. Food in the pub is limited

to filled cob rolls but there is a designated children's room and play area, as well as a large garden.

Open all wk 12-2.30 5.30-11 (Sat-12-3 6-11 Sun 12-3 7-10.30) **Bar Meals** food served all day ⊕ FREE HOUSE ◀ Sarah Hughes Dark Ruby, Sedgley Surprise & Amber, Guest ales. **Facilities** Non-diners area ◀ Play area Family room Garden Outside area ♉ Parking ⛟ (notice required) **Notes** ⊜

WEST BROMWICH
Map 10 SP09

The Vine

Roebuck St B70 6RD ☎ 0121 553 2866
e-mail: bharat@thevine.co.uk
dir: *M5 junct 1, follow West Bromwich/A41 signs. 1st left into Roebuck St. Pub at end on corner*

Spicy meals near West Brom's football ground

Certainly not the most attractive approach road to this pub, but keep going. Beers from reliable well-loved stalwarts such as Bathams and Holdens help this thriving, edge-of-town free-house shine out. Equally adept at attracting customers to fill the surprisingly large open-plan interior and conservatory-style dining area is the remarkable menu created by Suki Patel, based around

a pick 'n mix of firm Indian favourites. Goat jalfrezi with massala chips – no problem; chicken, lamb and prawn bhuna and bullet naan – take a seat. The indoor barbecue is extremely popular, with chicken tikka particularly favoured. There's also a range of traditional pub grub dishes and some wonderful spicy vegetarian choices, like mutter paneer.

Open all wk 11.30-2.30 5-11 (Fri-Sat 12-11 Sun 12-10) **Bar Meals** L served Mon-Fri 11.30-2.30, Sat-Sun 12-10 D served Mon-Fri 5-10.30, Sat-Sun 12-10 Av main course £6 **Restaurant** L served Mon-Fri 11.30-2.30, Sat-Sun 12-10 D served Mon-Fri 5-10.30, Sat-Sun 12-10 ⊕ FREE HOUSE ◀ Bathams, Holden's, Wye Valley, Burton Bridge. **Facilities** Non-diners area ◀ Garden ♉ Wi-fi ⛟ (notice required)

Save on hotels. Book at **theAA.com/hotel**

WIGHT, ISLE OF 467 ENGLAND

WIGHT, ISLE OF

ARRETON
Map 5 SZ58

The White Lion

Main Rd PO30 3AA ☎ 01983 528479
e-mail: chrisandkatieiow@hotmail.co.uk
dir: *On A3056 (Blackwater to Shanklin/Sandown road)*

Traditional pub food and well-kept real ales

In the corner of the bar is a dole window, through which the landlord of this old coaching inn would, under the sheriff's watchful eye, pay the poor of the village. Maybe among them was George, the resident ghost. The lovely interior features oak beams, polished brass and open fires, while an outside seating area offers views of the downs. Well-kept beers and traditional pub grub are served all day, ranging from prawn cocktail; and deep-fried bread-crumbed brie wedges, to pork and ale sausages with mash and onion gravy; home-made chicken curry; and smoked haddock with spring onion fishcakes.

Open all day all wk **Bar Meals** L served all wk 12-9 D served all wk 12-9 food served all day **Restaurant** L served all wk 12-9 D served all wk 12-9 food served all day ⊕ ENTERPRISE INNS ◀ Sharp's Doom Bar, Timothy Taylor Landlord ♂ Westons Stowford Press, Thatchers Pear. **Facilities** Non-diners area ♥ (Bar Garden) ♦ Children's menu Children's portions Family room Garden ⋒ Parking ▄▄

BEMBRIDGE
Map 5 SZ68

The Crab & Lobster Inn ★★★★ INN

32 Forelands Field Rd PO35 5TR ☎ 01983 872244
e-mail: info@crabandlobsterinn.co.uk
web: www.crabandlobsterinn.co.uk
dir: *From High St in Bembridge, 1st left after Boots into Forelands Rd. At right bend, left into Lane End Rd, 2nd right into Egerton Rd. At T-junct left into Howgate Rd. Road bears right & becomes Forelands Field Rd, follow brown inn signs*

Great sea views and seafood at beamed inn

This Victorian spirit merchant's inn is bedecked with flower baskets in summer and the stunning coastal location beside Bembridge Ledge means the raised deck and patio is a perfect place to sup locally brewed Goddards Fuggle-Dee-Dum bitter whilst watching yachts and fishing boats out in the eastern approach to the Solent. Locally caught seafood is one of the pub's great attractions, with dishes such as baked crab ramekin,

moules marinière, pan-fried scallops and lobster salad. There are meat and vegetarian dishes too, and sandwiches at lunchtime. Some of the light and airy bedrooms have outstanding sea views.

The Crab & Lobster Inn

Open all day all wk 11-11 (Sun 11-10.30) **Bar Meals** L served all wk 12-2.30 (summer Sat-Sun & BH 2.30-5.30 limited menu) D served Sun-Thu 6-9, Fri-Sat 6-9.30 Av main course £8-£12 **Restaurant** L served all wk 12-2.30 (summer Sat-Sun & BH 2.30-5.30 limited menu) D served Sun-Thu 6-9, Fri-Sat 6-9.30 ⊕ ENTERPRISE INNS ◀ Sharp's Doom Bar, Goddards Fuggle-Dee-Dum, Greene King IPA, John Smith's ♂ Westons Stowford Press. ♟ 12 **Facilities** Non-diners area ♥ (Bar Garden) ♦ Children's menu Children's portions Garden ⋒ Parking Wi-fi **Rooms** 5

BONCHURCH
Map 5 SZ57

The Bonchurch Inn

Bonchurch Shute PO38 1NU ☎ 01983 852611
e-mail: gillian@bonchurch-inn.co.uk
dir: *Signed from A3055 in Bonchurch*

Family-run free house with an Italian emphasis

Tucked away in a secluded Dickensian-style courtyard, this small inn is in a quiet, off-the-road location. In fact, little has changed here since this former coaching inn and stables was granted its first licence in the 1840s. Food is available lunchtime and evenings in the bar; choices range from sandwiches and salads to plenty of fresh fish and traditional meat dishes. Italian specialities are a prominent feature on account of the owners' heritage; try one of the pizzas, the tagliatelle carbonara, or the king prawn portofino (mushrooms, Pernod, cream and rice). Desserts also have an Italian bias – perhaps zabaglione or tiramisù.

Open all wk 11-3 6.30-11 Closed: 25 Dec **Bar Meals** L served all wk 12-2 D served all wk 6.30-9 **Restaurant** D served all wk 7-8.45 ⊕ FREE HOUSE ◀ Courage Directors, Best Bitter. **Facilities** Non-diners area ♥ (Bar) ♦ Children's menu Children's portions Family room Outside area ⋒ Parking Wi-fi

COWES
Map 5 SZ49

Duke of York Inn ★★★ INN

Mill Hill Rd PO31 7BT ☎ 01983 295171
e-mail: bookings@dukeofyorkcowes.co.uk
dir: *In town centre*

Inn with a seafaring theme and seafood on the menu

This former coaching inn has been run by the same friendly family for over 40 years. Situated close to the centre of Cowes and the marina, the informal pub has a nautical theme running throughout. Everyone is made welcome here, even soggy, wet yachtsmen. Fuggle-Dee-Dum from the island's Goddards Brewery is just one real ale on offer. Quality home-cooked food with an emphasis on fresh seafood is available in the bar and restaurant and includes grilled sardines, seafood mixed grill, moules marinière, bangers and mash, and half a roast chicken, as well as daily blackboard specials and Sunday roasts. There are comfortable, individually decorated bedrooms.

Open all day all wk **Bar Meals** L served all wk 12-2.30 D served all wk 6-10 **Restaurant** L served all wk 12-2.30 D served all wk 6-10 ⊕ ENTERPRISE INNS ◀ Goddards Fuggle-Dee-Dum, Sharp's Doom Bar, Ringwood Best Bitter ♂ Westons 1st Quality & Old Rosie. **Facilities** Non-diners area ♥ (Bar Restaurant Outside area) ♦ Children's menu Children's portions Outside area ⋒ Parking Wi-fi ▄▄ **Rooms** 13

The Fountain Inn ★★★ INN

High St PO31 7AW ☎ 01983 292397
e-mail: 6447@greeneking.co.uk
dir: *Adjacent to Red Jet passenger ferry in town centre*

Quayside contentment at the heart of Cowes

An imposing foursquare Georgian building built to cater for travellers awaiting the mainland ferry that still plies from the dock behind the inn. Character oozes from the nooks and crannies peppering the public areas, where French King Charles X and family also took sustenance in 1830. The decking patio overlooking the bustling West Cowes Quay is a fine base at which to appreciate the Greene King beers or chow down on a robust menu of pub favourites like roasted cod loin, pan-seared black pearl scallops or Suffolk pork sausages with Cheddar mash. Some of the en suite bedrooms have sea views.

Open all day all wk **Bar Meals** L served all wk 12-9 D served all wk 12-9 food served all day **Restaurant** L served all wk 12-9 D served all wk 12-9 food served all day ⊕ GREENE KING ◀ IPA, Morland Old Speckled Hen, Greene King Abbot Reserve. ♟ **Facilities** Non-diners area ♥ (Bar Outside area) ♦ Children's menu Children's portions Outside area ⋒ Wi-fi **Rooms** 20

FISHBOURNE
Map 5 SZ59

The Fishbourne ★★★★ INN NEW

Fishbourne Ln PO33 4EU ☎ 01983 882823

e-mail: info@thefishbourne.co.uk

dir: *From East Cowes ferry terminal to rdbt. 3rd exit signed Ryde & Newport. At T-junct left onto A3021 signed Ryde & Newport. At next rdbt 1st exit signed Newport. At next rdbt 1st exit onto A3054 signed Ryde. Left at lights into Fishbourne Ln signed Portsmouth. Pass ferry terminal to pub*

Top quality eating in a pub environment

Time your ferry crossing to Portsmouth carefully and, since it's down the same cul-de-sac as the Wightlink terminal, you'll be able to visit this mock-Tudor dining pub. A design-savvy approach to furnishing is apparent in the spacious bar, where there are smart leather sofas, and in the elegant dining area, where lunchtime sees sandwiches, baguettes, seafood specialities, deli boards and sharing platters, as well as old favourites like fish and chips, and sausages and mash. Daily-changing blackboard specials may include local shellfish, halibut wrapped in Parma ham; and slow-roasted pork belly. The en suite bedrooms are newly refurbished.

Open all day all wk **Bar Meals** Av main course £12 food served all day **Restaurant** Fixed menu price fr £16.95 food served all day ⊕ ENTERPRISE INNS ◀ Ringwood, Sharp's Doom Bar ♂ Westons Stowford Press. ♀ 11 **Facilities** Non-diners area ♦♦ Children's portions Garden ⋒ Parking Wi-fi ⬛ **Rooms** 5

FRESHWATER
Map 5 SZ38

The Red Lion

PICK OF THE PUBS

Church Place PO40 9BP ☎ 01983 754925

dir: *In Old Freshwater follow signs for All Saints Church*

Peaceful village centre pub near harbour

Next to one of the oldest churches on the Isle of Wight, today's more modern Red Lion can trace its origins back to the 11th century. Walkers, golfers and visiting yachtsmen beat a path to the door for pints of Goddard's Special and Fuggle-Dee-Dum and the stories flow. The bar has settles and sofas around well-scrubbed pine tables, polished flagstones and winter fires. Many ingredients used are from the island and most of the herbs and some vegetables are grown in the pub's garden. So, mull over whether to start with crab and avocado cocktail or crispy duck salad: then ponder a main of braised lamb shank with minted gravy, or chicken breast stuffed with brie. Old favourites include steak and ale pie and lamb Madras. Finish with a fruit Pavlova and you'll be ready for a good walk down to Yarmouth harbour or a snooze in the garden.

Open all wk 11.30-3 5.30-11 (Sun 12-3 7-10.30) **Bar Meals** L served all wk 12-2 D served Mon-Sat 6.30-9, Sun 7-9 Av main course £12 **Restaurant** L served all wk 12-2 D served Mon-Sat 6.30-9, Sun 7-9 Av 3 course à la carte fr £20 ⊕ ENTERPRISE INNS ◀ Goddards Special Bitter &

Fuggle-Dee-Dum, Sharp's Doom Bar ♂ Thatchers. **Facilities** Non-diners area ♣ (Bar Garden) Garden ⋒ Parking

GODSHILL
Map 5 SZ58

The Taverners

PICK OF THE PUBS

High St PO38 3HZ ☎ 01983 840707

dir: *Telephone for directions*

All-in-one pub, eating house and shop

Islanders Lisa Choi and Roger Serjent run this village pub with an impressive commitment to keeping food and drink miles low. Meats and dairy products all come from Wight farmers, fish are from local waters, island fruit and vegetables are used when in season, and much else is locally caught, shot or foraged. Cheeses come from the award-winning Isle of Wight Cheese Company and breads and pastries are baked in-house. Ten wines by the glass, Taverners Own real ale and Godshill cider are sold in the bar. Traditional dishes are beef and ale pie in suet crust pastry; pork sausages with bubble-and-squeak; and beer-battered fish and chips. Daily specials have included braised lamb hearts stuffed with lamb mince; and wild mushroom risotto. An in-pub shop sells home-made foods from the kitchen, fine wines, and local products. In the garden, adjoining the vegetable plots, is a toddlers' play area.

Open all day all wk Closed: 1st 3wks Jan **Bar Meals** L served all wk 12-3 D served Sun-Thu 6-9, Fri-Sat 6-9.30 Av main course £12 **Restaurant** L served all wk 12-3 D served Sun-Thu 6-9, Fri-Sat 6-9.30 Av 3 course à la carte fr £22 ⊕ PUNCH TAVERNS ◀ Taverners Own, Sharp's Doom Bar, Brains The Rev. James, Black Sheep, Butcombe ♂ Westons Stowford Press, Godshill. ♀ 10 **Facilities** Non-diners area ♣ (Bar Garden) ♦♦ Children's menu Children's portions Play area Garden ⋒ Parking Wi-fi ⬛ (notice required)

HULVERSTONE
Map 5 SZ38

The Sun Inn at Hulverstone

Main Rd PO30 4EH ☎ 01983 741124

e-mail: lesleyblanchard@btconnect.com

dir: *Between Mottistone & Brook on B3399*

Village-edge inn in stunning location

All flagstones, floorboards, beams, settles and fires, this lovely ancient thatched pub occupies an enviable position in the gently rolling countryside towards the western tip of the island. With English Channel views from the pleasant garden here, customers can indulge in Wight-brewed beers from Goddards and choose from a menu almost entirely sourced from the island's own producers. The village bakery, farm shop, local fishmongers and cheesemaker ensure the produce is the freshest possible. Cue beer-battered cod; or chicken breast with bacon and Isle of Wight Blue cheese, whilst the specials board details the home-made pie of the day. Restaurant booking is advised.

Open all day all wk **Bar Meals** L served all wk 12-9 D served all wk 12-9 food served all day **Restaurant** L served all wk 12-9 D served all wk 12-9 food served all day ⊕ ENTERPRISE INNS ◀ Ringwood Fortyniner, Goddards Fuggle-Dee-Dum, Adnams Southwold Bitter, Otter Ale ♂ Weston Stowford Press. **Facilities** Non-diners area ♣ (Bar Garden) ♦♦ Children's portions Garden ⋒ Parking Wi-fi ⬛ (notice required)

NINGWOOD
Map 5 SZ38

Horse & Groom

Main Rd PO30 4NW ☎ 01983 760672

e-mail: info@horse-and-groom.com

web: www.horse-and-groom.com

dir: *On A3054 (Yarmouth to Newport road)*

Great for families with young children

Just a couple of miles west of Yarmouth on the Newport road, this large landmark pub is certainly family-friendly. There's a pleasant garden with a large children's play area, and an extensive and well-priced kids' menu. Food is served daily from noon until 9pm, and the offering ranges from baguettes and light bites to pub favourites like thick-cut roast local ham, egg and chips; home-made beef lasagne; vegetable curry, plus a specials board offering seasonal specialities. Four-footed family members are also welcome on the stone and wood floored indoor areas.

Open all day all wk **Bar Meals** L served all wk 12-9 D served all wk 12-9 food served all day **Restaurant** L served all wk 12-9 D served all wk 12-9 food served all day ⊕ ENTERPRISE INNS ◀ Ringwood, Goddards ♂ Westons Stowford Press. ♀ 13 **Facilities** Non-diners area ♣ (Bar Garden) ♦♦ Children's menu Children's portions Play area Garden ⋒ Parking Wi-fi ⬛ (notice required)

PICK OF THE PUBS

The New Inn

SHALFLEET   Map 5 SZ48

Main Rd PO30 4NS ☎ 01983 531314
e-mail: info@thenew-inn.co.uk
web: www.thenew-inn.co.uk
dir: *6m from Newport to Yarmouth on A3054*

Recommended for their seafood

One of the island's best-known dining pubs, The New Inn's name refers to how it rose phoenix-like from the charred remains of an older inn, which burnt down in 1743. Set on the National Trust-owned Newtown River estuary, this charming whitewashed pub is an absolute mecca for sailing folk. Original inglenook fireplaces, flagstone floors and low-beamed ceilings give the place bags of character. The waterside location sets the tone for the menu; the pub has a reputation for excellent seafood dishes, with lobster and cracked local crab usually available. Daily specials are chalked on blackboards around the place. Further fish options may include fillet of trout with capers, brown shrimp and chorizo butter; salad of lemon, garlic and herb marinated tiger prawns or fish pie. Meat lovers could try slow cooked leg of duck with bacon, lentils and red wine and thyme gravy or locally made beef and horseradish sausages with wholegrain mustard mash. Vegetarians can enjoy

the likes of crisp fried polenta with roast butternut squash and shallots, walnuts and extra virgin olive oil. There's also a list of dishes for 'smaller appetites', including beer-battered fish and chips; local 5oz rump steak and chips with peas or gnocchi with sautéed kale, almonds, cream and parmesan — but if it's a light lunch you're seeking, be sure to consider the best-selling hand-picked crabmeat sandwiches and baguettes or the ploughman's featuring local cheeses. At the bar you'll find Goddards Fuggle-Dee-Dum and Doom Bar among others, Thatchers Heritage cider and over 60 worldwide wines comprise one of the island's most extensive selections.

Open all day all wk **Bar Meals** L served all wk 12-2.30 D served all wk 6-9.30 **Restaurant** L served all wk 12-2.30 D served all wk 6-9.30 ⊕ ENTERPRISE INNS ◀ Goddards Fuggle-Dee-Dum, Sharp's Doom Bar ♂ Westons Stowford Press, Thatchers Heritage. ♟ 11 **Facilities** Non-diners area 🐾 (Bar Garden) 👶 Children's portions Garden ⋒ Parking

---

NITON
Map 5 SZ57

Buddle Inn

St Catherines Rd PO38 2NE ☎ 01983 730243
e-mail: sayhi@buddleinn.co.uk
dir: Take A3055 from Ventnor. In Niton take 1st left
signed 'to the lighthouse'

Popular with hikers and ramblers

Flanked by the English Channel on one side and the
coastal path on the other, this 16th-century, former cliff-
top farmhouse and smugglers' inn is one of the island's
oldest hostelries. The interior has the full traditional
complement - stone flags, oak beams and a large open
fire, great real ales on tap, and muddy boots are welcome.
Expect hearty home-made food such as spring onion and
smoked haddock fishcake, followed by the curry of the day
or beef bourguignon. Two beer festivals a year take place
in June and September. Change of hands.

Open all day all wk 11-11 (Sun 12-10.30) Bar Meals L
served all wk 12-9 D served all wk 12-9 food served all
day Restaurant L served all wk 12-9 D served all wk 12-9
food served all day ⊕ ENTERPRISE INNS ◀ Goddards
Fuggle-Dee-Dum, Ale of Wight & Winter Warmer, Sharp's
Doom Bar, Greene King Abbot Ale, Ō Thatchers Gold. ♀ 8
Facilities Non-diners area ♦♦ Children's menu Children's
portions Garden Outside area ♬ Beer festival Parking
Wi-fi ⊜ (notice required)

NORTHWOOD
Map 5 SZ49

Travellers Joy

85 Pallance Rd PO31 8LS ☎ 01983 298024
e-mail: tjoy@globalnet.co.uk
dir: Telephone for directions

Family-run haven for ale lovers

Just a little way inland from Cowes, this 300-year-old
alehouse offers eight real ales on handpump all year
round, including St Austell Tribute, and Timothy Taylor
Landlord. Don't expect words such as 'drizzled' or 'pan-
roasted' here because the home-cooked food is honest
and uncomplicated, but with all the trimmings — home-
made steak-and-kidney pie; a quarter chicken with
mushrooms, chips and peas; gammon steak, egg and
chips; or maybe home-made cottage pie with vegetables
are all typical choices. Children's portions are available.
Outside is a pétanque terrain and pets' corner.

Open all wk 12-2.30 5-11 (Fri-Sun 12-11.30) Bar Meals L
served all wk 12-2 D served all wk 6.30-9.30 ⊕ FREE
HOUSE ◀ Island Wight Gold, Courage Directors,
Caledonian Deuchars IPA, St Austell Tribute, Timothy
Taylor Landlord. Facilities Non-diners area ♣ (Bar
Garden) ♦♦ Children's menu Children's portions Family
room Garden ♬ Parking ⊜ (notice required)

ROOKLEY
Map 5 SZ58

The Chequers

Niton Rd PO38 3NZ ☎ 01983 840314
e-mail: richard@chequersinn-iow.co.uk
dir: Telephone for directions

A country pub at the heart of the island

While possessing many modern facilities, this family-
friendly country free house with log fires and a large
garden still retains a traditional character that recalls its
days as a customs and excise house in the 18th century.
Here since 1989, landlords Richard and Sue Holmes know
the names of all their predecessors back to 1799. A
reputation for good food at reasonable prices can be
attributed to a repertoire of bar snacks, children's dishes,
sandwiches, cold platters, grilled meats and main menu
items like fresh seafood specials; Godshill game sausage;
chicken and seafood stir-fry; and home-made vegetable
curry.

Open all day all wk Bar Meals food served all day
Restaurant food served all day ⊕ FREE HOUSE
◀ Ringwood Best Bitter & Fortyniner, Guest ales
Ō Thatchers. ♀ Facilities Non-diners area ♣ (Bar
Garden) ♦♦ Children's menu Children's portions Play area
Family room Garden ♬ Parking Wi-fi

SEAVIEW
Map 5 SZ69

The Boathouse ★★★★ INN

Springvale Rd PO34 5AW ☎ 01983 810616
e-mail: info@theboathouseiow.co.uk
web: www.theboathouseiow.co.uk
dir: From Ryde take A3055. Left onto A3330, left into
Puckpool Hill. Pub 0.25m on right

Watch the ocean liners from this seaside winner

In the rather chic and certainly aptly-named Seaview, the
powder-blue-painted Boathouse overlooks the eastern
Solent. The setting really is spectacular. Well-kept ales
and an extensive global wine listing complement specials
boards that make the most of freshly landed local fish.
Other choices include lunchtime baguettes and
sandwiches; Isle of Wight rump and sirloin steaks; whole
cracked crab salad; and leek and mustard crumble with

ratatouille. Children might like dishes such sausages
with chips and peas; and broccoli, tomato and pasta in
creamy blue cheese sauce with toasted nuts. Sea views
are available in some of the stylish en suite bedrooms.

Open all day all wk 9am-11pm Bar Meals L served all
week 12-2.30 D served all week 6-9.30 Restaurant L
served all wk 12-2.30 D served all wk 6-9.30 ⊕ PUNCH
TAVERNS ◀ Ringwood Best Bitter, Sharp's Doom Bar,
Bass, Greene King IPA Ō Westons Stowford Press. ♀ 11
Facilities Non-diners area ♦♦ Children's portions Garden
♬ Parking Wi-fi Rooms 4

The Seaview Hotel &
Restaurant ★★★ HL ⊛

PICK OF THE PUBS

High St PO34 5EX ☎ 01983 612711
e-mail: reception@seaviewhotel.co.uk
dir: B3330 from Ryde, left signed Puckpool, along
seafront, hotel on left

A ideal spot for Solent views

The Seaview Hotel's quiet location just a short stroll from
the seafront means that from selected vantage points,
particularly The Terrace, there are fantastic views of the
Solent. Warm and welcoming, The Pump Bar is a hidden
gem and perfect for ladies who lunch, old friends
spinning yarns or families chilling out; its decor reflects
the seaside location with a quirky selection of lobster
pots, oars, masts and other nautical memorabilia. At the
bar you'll find Isle of Wight ales and there's also an
extensive menu featuring ingredients from the hotel's
own farm. Expect a pleasing mix of traditional and
innovative dishes, including locally caught fresh fish and
seafood specials. Alternatives are chicken liver parfait
with onion chutney followed by beef pie or an old favourite
like ham, egg and chips. Classic desserts such as plum
crumble round things off nicely.

Open all wk 10-3 6-11 Bar Meals L served all wk 12-2.30
D served all wk 6.30-9.30 Av main course £9.95
Restaurant L served all wk 12-2.30 D served all wk
6.30-9.30 Av 3 course à la carte fr £27 ⊕ FREE HOUSE
◀ Island Ales, Yates Ō Westons Stowford Press.
Facilities Non-diners area ♣ (Bar Outside area) ♦♦
Children's menu Children's portions Outside area ♬ Wi-fi
Rooms 29

SHALFLEET
Map 5 SZ48

The New Inn

PICK OF THE PUBS

See Pick of the Pubs on page 469

SHORWELL　　　　Map 5 SZ48

The Crown Inn
PICK OF THE PUBS

Walkers Ln PO30 3JZ ☎ 01983 740293
e-mail: enquiries@crowninnshorwell.co.uk
web: www.crowninnshorwell.co.uk
dir: *Left at top of Carisbrooke High Street. Shorwell approx 6m*

Pretty village pub beside a delightful stream

A traditional country pub in a pretty village, parts of The Crown date from the 17th century, although its varying floor levels suggest many subsequent alterations. Log fires and antique furniture abound and if you're lucky you might glimpse the friendly female ghost who seems to disapprove of customers playing cards. Outside are a children's play area and a beautiful stream, whose trout grow fat exclusively for the herons it seems. Real ales include Sharp's Doom Bar and Adnams Broadside. Good use is made of locally sourced lamb, beef, game and fish on bi-annually revised menus that offer pub staples like fisherman's pie, curry and home-made beef lasagne, while further study reveals a good range of starters (maybe the chef's home-made pâté of the day or traditional prawn cocktail), a selection from the grill, hot and cold sharing platters, pizzas and a vegetarian selection offering the likes of vegetable curry and vegetable kebabs.

Open all day all wk **Bar Meals** L served all wk 12-9.30 D served all wk 12-9.30 food served all day **Restaurant** L served all wk 12-9.30 D served all wk 12-9.30 food served all day ⊕ ENTERPRISE INNS ◀ Sharp's Doom Bar, Adnams Broadside, Goddards, St Austell Tribute ♻ Westons Stowford Press. ♟ 12 **Facilities** Non-diners area ♣ (Bar Restaurant Garden) ♦ Children's menu Children's portions Play area Garden Parking Wi-fi ▭ (notice required)

WHIPPINGHAM　　　　Map 5 SZ59

The Folly

Folly Ln PO32 6NB ☎ 01983 297171
dir: *Telephone for directions*

Extensive menus and a large beer garden

The Folly stands beside the River Medina and you can, if you wish, travel here from Cowes on the pub's own waterbus. In the bar are timbers from the hull of an old barge, and even the restaurant tables are named after boats. The menus offer a wide choice of lighter bites – sandwiches, wraps, jacket potatoes and salads – as well as gourmet burgers, steaks and grills, and classic pub grub. In addition, there are sharing plates, daily specials and international mains such as aubergine gratin; chicken fajitas; and sweet potato, apricot, chickpea and red pepper skewers. Wednesday evening is 'Get Spicy' curry night.

Open all day all wk **Bar Meals** L served all wk 12-5 D served all wk 5-10 food served all day **Restaurant** L served all wk 12-5 D served all wk 5-10 food served all day ⊕ GREENE KING ◀ IPA, Morland Old Speckled Hen ♻ Aspall. ♟ 11 **Facilities** ♣ (All areas) ♦ Children's menu Children's portions Garden Outside area ⊼ Parking Wi-fi ▭

WILTSHIRE

ALDBOURNE　　　　Map 5 SU27

The Blue Boar

20 The Green SN8 2EN ☎ 01672 540237
e-mail: blueboar.green@btconnect.com
dir: *From Salisbury take B4192 to Aldbourne. Or M4 junct 14 take A338 to Hungerford, B4192 to Aldbourne & follow brown signs*

World World II connections in charmingly pretty village

A traditional, 16th-century pub with two open fires, The Blue Boar serves Wadworth and regularly-changing guest ales from a perfect location on the village green. Eating outside is a joy, with views of beautiful houses, the church and a Celtic cross. Typical home-prepared food includes baked camembert; ratatouille pancake; and steak-and-kidney pie. The bar menu has sandwiches, filled jackets and pub classics. Beer festivals are held in April and October. Enthusiasts periodically relive the days when America's 506th Parachute Infantry Regiment ('The Screaming Eagles') were billeted in the village during the Second World War.

Open all wk 11.30-3 5.30-11 (Fri-Sun 11.30-11) **Bar Meals** L served all wk 12-2 D served all wk 6.30-9.30 **Restaurant** L served Mon-Fri 12-2, Sat-Sun 12-2.30 D served all wk 6.30-9.30 ⊕ WADWORTH ◀ 6X & Henry's Original IPA, Guest ales ♻ Westons Stowford Press. **Facilities** Non-diners area ♦ Children's portions Garden ⊼ Beer festival Wi-fi ▭

The Crown Inn ★★★ INN

The Square SN8 2DU ☎ 01672 540214
e-mail: bookings@thecrownaldbourne.co.uk
dir: *M4 junct 15, N on A419, signed Aldbourne*

Classic village-square inn in popular rambling area

This imposing coaching inn has served the village for over 400 years, and retains much period feel in the well-beamed old bar. In the Second World War, American NCO's made it their mess-room and enjoyed local beers and food; today's regulars and visitors may indulge in White Horse or Bryden ales, whilst the home-prepared food majors on ingredients sourced from local suppliers. Pub-cured ham or sausage and mash are favourites, as are the home-made stone-baked pizzas. There are beer festivals each May and September and a cider festival is held in July.

Open all day all wk 12-12 **Bar Meals** Av main course £9.95 food served all day **Restaurant** Av 3 course à la carte fr £21 food served all day ⊕ ENTERPRISE INNS ◀ Shepherds Neame Spitfire, Ramsbury Gold, Sharp's Doom Bar, Guest ales ♻ Westons Stowford Press, Aspall. ♟ 16 **Facilities** Non-diners area ♣ (Bar Garden) ♦ Children's menu Children's portions Play area Garden ⊼ Beer festival Cider festival Parking Wi-fi ▭ **Rooms** 4

AXFORD | Map 5 SU27

Red Lion Inn

PICK OF THE PUBS

SN8 2HA ☎ 01672 520271
e-mail: info@redlionaxford.com
dir: *M4 junct 15, A346 to Marlborough centre. Left, follow Ramsbury signs. Inn 3m*

Eye-catching dining inn

This old inn has been welcoming travellers for over 400 years. From the flower-bedecked terrace (perfect for alfresco summer dining), divine views percolate to the river and this peaceful stretch of countryside. It's located in the North Wessex Downs Area of Outstanding Natural Beauty and close to the popular walks in the ancient Savernake Forest; ample opportunity to work up an appetite. Tables and chairs constructed from half-barrels and squashy sofas dot the timeworn parquet flooring of the convivial bar, at the heart of which is a huge inglenook fireplace. Settle in with a vintage from the wine list or a glass of Good Old Boy, and consider a menu which is strong on seasonal game and fish dishes with a contemporary European flavour. Choices include whole grilled trout with lemon and almonds with a stir-fry; braised rabbit with mustard; and roast beef salad.

Open all wk 12-3 6-11 **Bar Meals** L served Tue-Sat 12-2 D served Tue-Fri 6-9 **Restaurant** L served Tue-Sun 12-2 D served Tue-Sat 6-9 ⊕ FREE HOUSE ◀ Timothy Taylor Landlord, West Berkshire Good Old Boy ○ Westons Stowford Press. **Facilities** Non-diners area ♦ Children's portions Garden Parking Wi-fi ▬

BERWICK ST JOHN | Map 4 ST92

The Talbot Inn

The Cross SP7 0HA ☎ 01747 828222
dir: *From Shaftesbury take A30 towards Salisbury. Right to Berwick St John. Pub 1.5m*

Traditional pub with lots of character

The Talbot Inn used to be three cottages, one of them the village shop, before becoming an alehouse in 1835. Under new ownership, this typical old English country free house in the beautiful Chalke Valley dates from the 17th century and has the beams, low ceilings and huge inglenook fireplace so typical of its kind. Real ales plus good home-cooked food shown on the menus and specials board are on offer; try the crumbed butterfly prawns with sweet chilli dipping sauce or garlic mushrooms to start; followed by cooked ham, egg and chips; home-made lasagne or salmon and broccoli mornay.

Open 12-2.30 6.30-11 (Sun 12-4) Closed: Sun eve & Mon **Bar Meals** L served Tue-Sun 12-2 D served Tue-Sat 6.30-9 ⊕ FREE HOUSE ◀ Ringwood Best Bitter, Wadworth 6X, Sixpenny Handley IPA ○ Westons Stowford Press. **Facilities** ♣ (Bar Garden) ♦ Children's portions Garden Parking

BISHOPSTONE | Map 5 SU28

The Royal Oak

Cues Ln SN6 8PH ☎ 01793 790481
e-mail: royaloak@helenbrowningorganics.co.uk
dir: *M4 junct 15, A419 towards Swindon. At rdbt right into Pack Hill signed Wanborough. In Bishopstone left into Cues Ln. Pub on right*

Rustic, relaxed and friendly pub with its own farm

Organic farmer Helen Browning rescued the delightful Royal Oak from closure. The pub stands tucked away in a glorious village below the Wiltshire Downs. You can expect a cracking community atmosphere, Arkell's ales, Westons ciders, roaring logs fires and daily-changing menus. Almost 60 per cent of produce comes from Helen's own farm, with the rest sourced from three other local organic farms and allotments. A three-course dinner could be fillet steak carpaccio with rocket pesto; pork tenderloin with bacon, tabouleh, pak choi and date purée; and plum upside down cake with plum sauce and cream. The child-friendly garden has a Wendy house and rope swing.

Open all wk 12-3 6-11 (Sat 12-12 Sun 12-10) **Bar Meals** L served all wk 12-3 D served all wk 6-9.30 Av main course £15 ⊕ ARKELL'S ◀ Moonlight & 3B, Donnington SBA ○ Westons Old Rosie, Wyld Wood Organic & Perry. **Facilities** Non-diners area ♣ (All areas) ♦ Children's menu Children's portions Play area Garden Outside area ⊞ Parking Wi-fi ▬ (notice required)

BOX | Map 4 ST86

The Northey ★★★★★ INN

Bath Rd SN13 8AE ☎ 01225 742333
e-mail: thenorthey@ohhcompany.co.uk
web: www.ohhcompany.co.uk
dir: *A4 from Bath towards Chippenham, 4m. Between M4 juncts 17 & 18*

Contemporary inn close to Bath

The former station hotel, built by Brunel for his workers who were building Box Tunnel, was transformed from a shabby roadside drinking pub to a stylish inn by Mark Warburton. The contemporary interior makes good use of wood and flagstone flooring, high-backed oak chairs, leather loungers and handcrafted tables around the bar, where inviting sandwiches (smoked salmon with lemon

and chive mayonnaise) and pub classics like ham, egg and chips hold sway. The main menu ranges from potted duck with quince jelly; and rack of lamb with rosemary and olive crust to the pub's speciality fish dishes and great steaks. Swish bedrooms complete the picture.

The Northey

Open all day all wk Closed: 25 Dec **Bar Meals** food served all day **Restaurant** food served all day ⊕ FREE HOUSE ◀ Warburtons, Wadworth Horizon & 6X. ♀ 16 **Facilities** Non-diners area ♣ (Bar Garden) ♦ Children's menu Children's portions Garden ⊞ Parking Wi-fi **Rooms** 3

The Quarrymans Arms

Box Hill SN13 8HN ☎ 01225 743569
e-mail: pub@quarrymans-arms.co.uk
dir: *Telephone for directions*

Former miners' pub with excellent views

Superb views of the Box Valley can be enjoyed from this 300-year-old pub, from where you can also see Solsbury Hill. A display of Bath stone mining memorabilia bears witness to the years Brunel's navvies spent driving the Great Western Railway through Box Tunnel (spot the bar's replica fireplace) deep beneath the pub. The resultant honeycomb of Bath stone workings attract potholers and cavers, who slake their thirsts on local ales and ciders, and replace lost calories with local faggots; home-made curry; calves' liver, or something from the comprehensive vegetarian selection. 'Mini ale weeks' are held throughout the year.

Open all day all wk 11am-11.30pm **Bar Meals** L served all wk 11-3 D served all wk fr 6 Av main course £10 **Restaurant** L served all wk fr 11 D served all wk fr 6 Av 3 course à la carte fr £20 ⊕ FREE HOUSE ◀ Butcombe Bitter, Wadworth 6X, Moles Best, Local Guest ales ○ Westons Stowford Press, Black Rat, Guest cider. ♀ 13 **Facilities** Non-diners area ♣ (Bar Restaurant Garden) ♦ Children's menu Children's portions Family room Garden ⊞ Beer festival Cider festival Parking Wi-fi ▬ (notice required)

Save on hotels. Book at **theAA.com/hotel**

WILTSHIRE 473 **ENGLAND**

PICK OF THE PUBS

The Tollgate Inn ★★★★

BRADFORD-ON-AVON Map 4 ST86

Holt BA14 6PX ☎ 01225 782326
e-mail: laura@tollgateinn.co.uk
web: www.tollgateinn.co.uk
dir: *M4 junct 18, A46 towards Bath,
then A363 to Bradford-on-Avon, then
B3107 towards Melksham, pub on right*

Country free house in new hands

Standing just off the village green, this
stone-built, part 16th-century
amalgamation of a weaving shed and
chapel was taken over by Mark Hedges
and Laura Boulton in 2012, wanting to
bring it back to its country pub roots.
Set in 1.5 acres of countryside with a
garden and dining terrace, The Tollgate
is a five-minute drive from the Georgian
market town of Bradford-on-Avon. The
richly furnished, oak-floored main bar
area has a wood-burning stove and
comfy sofas, and serves real ciders and
real ales from, among others, small
local breweries like Moles and
Glastonbury. As well as a bar and
restaurant, the pub also has an on-site
deli, farm shop and café, where you can
go for soup or a sandwich. There are two
dining rooms, one upstairs in the
original chapel, once used by the
weavers working below. Here the classic
yet innovative menu changes with the
seasons, always with an emphasis on
local produce whose provenance is open
for inspection, with meat coming from
the farm just across the road. Fresh fish

is delivered daily from Brixham and
Lyme Bay, and vegetables from
Bromham, eight miles away. Crayfish
and crab tian with rich tomato fondue;
and smoked chicken and red pepper
terrine make appetising starters. Main
courses include honey- and lemon-
glazed breast of duck with creamed
leeks and cabbage, fondant potato and
a confit onion sauce; roast vegetable
ragout with horseradish, cheddar and
parsley dumplings; and 'forever
changing' trio of local sausages, creamy
mustard mash, sweet onion gravy and
seasonal vegetables. All main dishes
have suggested wines. There are
interesting puddings, such as rosemary
and raspberry tart.

Open 11.30-3 5.30-11 (Sun 11.30-3)

Closed: Sun eve, Mon **Bar Meals** L
served Tue-Sun 12-2 D served Tue-Sat
7-9 **Restaurant** L served Tue-Sun 12-2
D served Tue-Sat 7-9 ⊕ FREE HOUSE
◖ Moles Best, Sharp's Own & Doom
Bar, Glastonbury Mystery Tor, St Austell
Ö Thatchers Traditional, Ashton Press,
Lilley's Bee Sting Pear. ♟ 10
Facilities Non-diners area ♦♦ Children's
portions Garden ⋒ Parking Wi-fi
Rooms 4

BRADFORD-ON-AVON — Map 4 ST86

The Dandy Lion

35 Market St BA15 1LL ☎ 01225 863433
e-mail: Dandylion35@aol.com
dir: *Telephone for directions*

In bustling town near bridge over the River Avon

In the centre of the lovely market town of Bradford-on-Avon, this 18th-century inn was once a boot and shoe shop and a grocery. It is now a popular place for bar and restaurant offering well-kept Wadworth ales and continental lagers, together with a mix of traditional English and rustic European food. The bar menu offers hot filled flatbreads, light bites and 'things on toast', whilst the choice in the upstairs restaurant menu might include chicken Kiev; steak, mushroom and ale pie; and home-baked Wiltshire ham, free-range eggs and triple cooked chips.

Open all wk 11-3 6-11 (Fri-Sat 11-11 Sun 11.30-10.30) Closed: 25 Dec **Bar Meals** L served all wk 12-2.30 D served all wk 6-9.30 **Restaurant** D served Fri-Sat 7-9.30 ⊕ WADWORTH ◀ 6X, Henry's Original IPA, Seasonal ales ♂ Westons Stowford Press & Wyld Wood Organic. ♟ 21 **Facilities** Non-diners area ❄ (Bar) ♦♦ Children's portions

The Tollgate Inn ★★★★ INN

PICK OF THE PUBS

See Pick of the Pubs on page 473

BRINKWORTH — Map 4 SU08

The Three Crowns

PICK OF THE PUBS

SN15 5AF ☎ 01666 510366
e-mail: info@threecrownsbrinkworth.co.uk
dir: *From Swindon take A3102 to Royal Wootton Bassett, take B4042, 5m to Brinkworth*

Traditional village inn with food to match

The village sits in rich farming countryside on a low ridge above the River Avon; glimpses of Daunstey Vale catch the eye from the pub's secluded beer garden and tree-shaded patio, where heaters bring additional comfort as the evenings draw in. Lots of greenery inside and out here, with the conservatory restaurant festooned with potted plants and the little village green fronting this traditional old inn. It's a thriving community pub, hosting locals and their dogs, the local hunt when it meets, and families set on celebrating a special occasion. Amiable staff greets you in the beamed, fire-warmed old bar, where ales include London Pride. The menu has long been recognised for its ambition and variety. The mix of modern dishes and classics includes steak-and-kidney pudding; fish and chips with tartare sauce and mushy peas; fish pie or vegetable curry with rice.

Open all day all wk 10am-mdnt **Bar Meals** L served Mon-Sat 12-2.30, Sun 12-9 D served Mon-Sat 6-9.30, Sun 12-9 **Restaurant** L served Mon-Sat 12-2.30, Sun 12-9

D served Mon-Sat 6-9.30, Sun 12-9 ⊕ HERITAGE PROPERTIES ◀ Sharp's Doom Bar, Fullers London Pride ♂ Westons Stowford Press. ♟ 27
Facilities Non-diners area ❄ (Bar Garden) ♦♦ Children's menu Children's portions Play area Garden ⼊ Parking Wi-fi

BROAD CHALKE — Map 5 SU02

The Queens Head Inn

1 North St SP5 5EN ☎ 01722 780344
e-mail: ryan.prince@btinternet.com
dir: *A354 from Salisbury towards Blandford Forum, at Coombe Bissett right towards Bishopstone, pub in 4m*

Ivy clad village inn worth a detour to find

Located halfway along the Chalke Valley and just eight miles from Salisbury, this former cottage has been the hub of the village for 150 years. Low beams and an open fire add to the cosy ambience in the bar, where well-kept Badger ales are the main attraction. Fresh, locally sourced produce is used to create a traditional and seasonal range of dishes such as pan-fried whole trout glazed with lemon and parsley butter or steak-and-ale pie. Head out to the courtyard in warmer weather.

Open all wk 11-3 6-11 (Fri 11-3 6-12 Sat 11-11.30 Sun 12-8) ⊕ HALL & WOODHOUSE ◀ Badger Dorset Best, Tanglefoot, Hopping Hare, Pickled Partridge, Lemony Cricket, Fursty Ferret, Furkin Fox ♂ Westons Stowford Press. **Facilities** ♦♦ Children's menu Children's portions Family room Garden Parking Wi-fi

BROUGHTON GIFFORD — Map 4 ST86

The Fox

The Street SN12 8PN ☎ 01225 782949
e-mail: alexgeneen@gmail.com
dir: *From Melksham take B3107 towards Holt. Turn right to Broughton Gifford. Pub in village centre*

Showing a commitment to home-grown and home-reared produce

The excellent ales at this village pub are augmented in the summer months when it hosts a beer and cider festival. Food standards are high too. The owners raise their own chickens, ducks and pigs, tend an extensive vegetable and herb garden, and barter with villagers for wildfowl and other produce. Bread is either baked in the kitchen or provided by the ethical Thoughtful Bread Company. Plans are afoot to build a smokehouse in the grounds, as the pub already produces cured hams, charcuterie and sausages from its pigs. Typical of the menus are Cornish crab quiche; roasted pheasant crown; goats' cheese pesto ravioli; and lamb suet pudding.

Open 12-3 5-9.30 Closed: Mon L **Bar Meals** L served Tue-Sun 12-2.30 D served all wk 6.30-9.30 Av main course £16.95 **Restaurant** L served Tue-Sun 12-2.30 D served all wk 6.30-9.30 ⊕ FREE HOUSE ◀ Bath Gem, Otter Bitter, Butcombe Bitter, Fuller's London Pride. ♟ 18
Facilities Non-diners area ❄ (Bar Garden) ♦♦ Children's menu Children's portions Garden ⼊ Beer festival Cider festival Parking Wi-fi ⛍ (notice required)

BURCOMBE — Map 5 SU03

The Ship Inn

Burcombe Ln SP2 0EJ ☎ 01722 743182
e-mail: theshipburcombe@mail.com
web: www.theshipburcombe.co.uk
dir: *In Burcombe, off A30, 1m from Wilton & 5m W of Salisbury*

Riverside village pub run by passionate foodies

A 17th-century village pub with low ceilings, oak beams and a large open fire. In summer the riverside garden is where you'd enjoy a leisurely meal in the company of the resident ducks. Seasonal menu examples include starters like crab toasties with smoked chilli jam or pork, mustard and pistachio terrine with balsamic chutney; followed by mains of pressed pork belly with mash and red cabbage; confit duck leg with gratin dauphinoise and green beans; or home-made fishcakes with herbed fries. In the bar Wadworth 6X, Ringwood Best and Butcombe hold the fort on hand-pull.

Open all wk 11-3 6-11 **Bar Meals** L served all wk 12-2.30 D served all wk 6-9 Av main course £12 **Restaurant** L served all wk 12-2.30 D served all wk 6-9 Av 3 course à la carte fr £25 ⊕ ENTERPRISE INNS ◀ Wadworth 6X, Ringwood Best Bitter, Butcombe ♂ Thatchers Gold. ♟ 9
Facilities Non-diners area ❄ (Bar Garden) ♦♦ Children's menu Children's portions Garden ⼊ Parking Wi-fi ⛍ (notice required)

BURTON — Map 4 ST87

The Old House at Home ★★★★★ INN

SN14 7LT ☎ 01454 218227
e-mail: office@ohhcompany.co.uk
dir: *On B4039 NW of Chippenham*

Family-run, traditional ivy-clad free house offering a warm welcome

This ivy-clad, stone built free house dates from the early 19th century and is one of two run by the Warburton family (the other is The Northey Arms in Box). Dad David has been here for years and still happily pulls pints of Maiden Voyage, Wadworth 6X and Thatchers Gold in the low-beamed bar. The finest seasonal ingredients are used to create impressive menu favourites like venison casserole; peppered smoked haddock pilaf; lasagne verdi or home cooked, honey-glazed ham. The beautifully landscaped gardens feature a waterfall. Six high quality bedrooms are available in a stylish annexe.

Save on hotels. Book at theAA.com/hotel

WILTSHIRE 475 ENGLAND

Open all day all wk **Bar Meals** L served all wk 12-9.30
D served all wk 12-9.30 food served all day **Restaurant** L
served all wk 12-9.30 D served all wk 12-9.30 food served
all day ⊕ FREE HOUSE ◀ Ales of Scilly Maiden Voyage,
Wadworth 6X, Guest ales Ō Thatchers Gold & Traditional.
🍷 12 **Facilities** Non-diners area 😾 (Bar Restaurant
Garden) ♦ Children's menu Children's portions Garden ⋒
Parking Wi-fi 🚌 (notice required) **Rooms** 6

COLLINGBOURNE DUCIS   Map 5 SU25

The Shears Inn

The Cadley Rd SN8 3ED ☎ **01264 850304**
e-mail: info@theshears.co.uk
dir: *Just off A338 between Marlborough & Salisbury*

Delightful thatched pub with modern British menu

Dating from the 18th century, this traditional family-run
country inn was once a shearing shed for market-bound
sheep. The original part of the building is thatched, while
inside you'll find wooden and slate floors, low-beamed
ceilings and a large inglenook dominating the restaurant.
Typical choices from the tasty modern British menu may
include beer-battered haggis and black pudding; honey
and watercress sausages and mash; and lemon posset
with raspberry shortbread. The enclosed sunny garden is
an ideal venue for the annual cider festival held in late
summer.

Open 11-3 6-11 (Sat 11-11 summer, Sun fr 12) Closed:
Sun eve **Bar Meals** L served Mon-Sat 12-2, Sun 12-3.30
D served Mon-Sat 6-9.30 Av main course £9.95
Restaurant L served Mon-Sat 12-2, Sun 12-3.30 D served
Mon-Fri 7-9.15, Sat 7-9.30 Av 3 course à la carte fr £27
⊕ BRAKSPEAR ◀ Bitter, Wychwood Hobgoblin, Ringwood
Ales Ō Westons Wyld Wood Organic, Addlestones. 🍷 12
Facilities Non-diners area 😾 (Bar Restaurant Garden) ♦
Children's menu Children's portions Garden ⋒ Cider
festival Parking Wi-fi 🚌 (notice required)

CORTON   Map 4 ST94

The Dove Inn ★★★★ INN ◎

PICK OF THE PUBS

BA12 0SZ ☎ **01985 850109**
e-mail: info@thedove.co.uk
dir: *5m SE of Warminster. Exit A36 to Corton*

Refurbished pub in the heart of the countryside

Squirreled away in the delightful Wylye Valley, this
bustling 19th-century pub guarantees a warm welcome.
Now refurbished, many original features were restored
such as the striking central fireplace and flagstone and
oak floors. The appealing menu is based firmly on West
Country produce, with many ingredients coming from just
a few miles away. Popular lunchtime bar snacks give way
to a full evening carte featuring well-made and hearty
pub classics. Typical starters include crispy duck
pancakes, and king prawn and avocado cocktail. These
might be followed by a turkey, ham and leek pie, or
Moroccan-spiced braised lamb shank. Fish and chips,
and the famous Dove burger and chips are available to

take away, wrapped traditionally in newspaper. Children
get to choose from their own menu. The spacious garden
is the perfect spot for barbecues or a drink on summer
days while the bedrooms arranged around a courtyard
make The Dove an ideal touring base.

Open all day all wk **Bar Meals** food served all day
Restaurant L served all wk 12-3 D served all wk 6-9.30
⊕ FREE HOUSE ◀ Otter Bitter, Timothy Taylor Landlord,
Guest ale Ō Aspall. **Facilities** Non-diners area 😾 (Bar
Garden) ♦ Children's menu Children's portions Garden
Parking Wi-fi 🚌 (notice required) **Rooms** 7

CRICKLADE   Map 5 SU09

The Red Lion Inn ★★★★ INN ◎

74 High St SN6 6DD ☎ **01793 750776**
e-mail: info@theredlioninncricklade.co.uk
dir: *M4 junct 15, A419 towards Cirencester. Left onto
B4040 into Cricklade. Right at T-junct (mini-rdbt) into
High St. Inn on right*

On-site microbrewery and Saddleback pigs

Just off the Thames Path as it passes through historic
Cricklade, this early 17th-century pub retains many
historic features. Hop Kettle microbrewery in a barn
behind the pub adds to the line-up of real ales and
ciders, including Wadworth 6X and Mates Jackdaw.
Home-prepared restaurant food is noteworthy for using
locally foraged and wild ingredients, rare-breed meats
and sustainable fish. Customers can even swap fruit and
veg from their gardens for vouchers towards food and
drink. Opt for chicken liver parfait, breast of Cold Aston
pheasant, and rhubarb and pistachio Eton Mess. It's the
first weekend in June for the beer festival.

Open all day all wk **Bar Meals** L served Mon-Sat 12-2.30,
Sun 12-3 D served Mon-Thu 6.30-9 Av main course £9.95
Restaurant L served Tue-Sat 12-2.30, Sun 12-3 D served
Tue-Thu 6.30-9, Fri-Sat 6.30-9.30 Fixed menu price fr
£12.95 Av 3 course à la carte fr £22 ⊕ FREE HOUSE
◀ Hop Kettle North Wall & Pond Skipper, Wadworth 6X
Ō Mates Ravens Roost & Jackdaw. 🍷 9
Facilities Non-diners area 😾 (Bar Garden) ♦ Children's
menu Children's portions Garden ⋒ Beer festival Wi-fi
🚌 (notice required) **Rooms** 5

CRUDWELL   Map 4 ST99

The Potting Shed

The Street SN16 9EW ☎ **01666 577833**
e-mail: bookings@thepottingshedpub.com
dir: *On A429 between Malmesbury & Cirencester*

Welcoming dining pub

Dogs and children are welcome at this Cotswold dining
pub, which prides itself on offering good bitter,
interesting wine and a mix of creative and British food.
Light pastel shades and beams scrubbed down to their
natural hue characterise the appealing interior, where
typical dishes include braised lamb sweetbreads and
wild mushrooms on thyme toast; beef, mushroom and
Barnsey ale stew with buttered potatoes; and cinnamon,
honey and orange rice pudding. Food and drink can be

served outside; two acres of grounds allow plenty of
space for lawns, fruit trees and vegetable plots which
supply fresh produce for the kitchen.

Open all day all wk **Bar Meals** L served Mon-Sat 12-2.30,
Sun 12-3 D served Mon-Sat 7-9.30, Sun 7-9 Av main
course £15.95 **Restaurant** L served Mon-Sat 12-2.30, Sun
12-3 D served Mon-Sat 7-9.30, Sun 7-9 ⊕ ENTERPRISE
INNS ◀ Butcombe Bitter Ō Thatchers, Bath Ciders
Bounders. 🍷 **Facilities** Non-diners area 😾 (Bar
Restaurant Garden) ♦ Children's portions Garden ⋒
Parking Wi-fi 🚌 (notice required)

DEVIZES   Map 4 SU06

The Bear Hotel ★★★ HL ◎◎

The Market Place SN10 1HS ☎ **01380 722444**
e-mail: info@thebearhotel.net
dir: *In town centre, follow Market Place signs*

A Devizes landmark for many centuries

Slap bang in the heart of Devizes, close to the Wadworth
Brewery that owns it, this character coaching inn dates
from around 1559. Notable former guests include Judge
Jeffreys, George III and Harold Macmillan, all of whom
would have enjoyed the abundance of old beams and log
fires. With two AA Rosettes a meal here might include
pork and duck rillette followed by whole grilled plaice
with fine beans, new potatoes, parsley and caper butter.
On sunny days, grab a seat in the courtyard.

Open all day all wk 9.30am-11pm ⊕ WADWORTH ◀ 6X,
Henry's Original IPA, Old Timer, Malt & Hops, Boundary,
Horizon, Seasonal ales. **Facilities** 😾 (Bar Garden) ♦
Children's menu Children's portions Garden Parking Wi-fi
Rooms 25

The Raven Inn

Poulshot Rd SN10 1RW ☎ **01380 828271**
e-mail: theraveninnpoulshot@yahoo.co.uk
dir: *A361 from Devizes towards Trowbridge, left at
Poulshot sign*

A warm welcome and ever changing menus of home-cooked food

Worth noting if walking the Kennet & Avon Canal towpath
or visiting the famous Caen Hill flight of locks, this half-
timbered 18th-century pub is just a short walk away.
Divert for tip-top Wadworth ales and the weekly-changing
menu, which offers a mixture of modern pub classics and
more imaginative dishes. Expect to find the Raven burger,
ham, egg and chips, and steak-and-kidney pie alongside
rabbit braised in cider and grilled sole with lemon and
parsley butter. Leave room for warm chocolate brownie
with chocolate sauce. The pub is dog friendly.

Open 11.30-2.30 6-11 (Sun 12-3 6-10) Closed: Mon
(Oct-Etr) ⊕ WADWORTH ◀ 6X, Henry's Original IPA,
Horizon, Old Timer Ō Thatchers Gold. **Facilities** 😾 (Bar
Garden) ♦ Children's menu Children's portions Garden
Parking Wi-fi

DONHEAD ST ANDREW — Map 4 ST92

The Forester

PICK OF THE PUBS

Lower St SP7 9EE ☎ 01747 828038

e-mail: possums1@btinternet.com

dir: From Shaftesbury on A30 towards Salisbury. In approx 4.5m left, follow village signs

Traditional pub specialising in West Country seafood

Describing itself as very dog friendly, this lovely 15th-century pub is an ideal place to put your feet up after one of the long local walks, perhaps with your dog in tow. Close to Wardour Castle in a pretty little village, The Forester has warm stone walls, a thatched roof, original beams and an inglenook fireplace. An extension provides a restaurant plus a restaurant/meeting room, with double doors opening on to the lower patio area, where you can enjoy a regional ale in the summer. The restaurant has a reputation for excellent cuisine at reasonable prices and for using only the freshest ingredients. Dishes are constructed with a mix of traditional and cosmopolitan flavours, with seafood a speciality. Perhaps start with soft herring roe, pancetta, capers and parsley; follow with braised leg and confit shoulder of Wiltshire rabbit, mashed potato and winter vegetables. To finish, maybe try Seville orange tart with fennel sorbet or the artisan cheeseboard.

Open 12-2 6.30-11 Closed: 25-26 Dec, Sun eve **Bar Meals** L served all wk 12-2 D served Mon-Sat 7-9 Av main course £15.50 **Restaurant** L served all wk 12-2 D served Mon-Sat 7-9 Fixed menu price fr £19.50 Av 3 course à la carte fr £25 ⊕ FREE HOUSE ◀ Butcombe, Otter ♂ Westons Wyld Wood Organic. ☗ 15 **Facilities** Non-diners area ✿ (Bar Restaurant Garden) ◈ Children's menu Children's portions Garden ⊫ Parking Wi-fi

---

EAST CHISENBURY — Map 5 SU15

Red Lion Freehouse ★★★★★ GH

SN9 6AQ ☎ 01980 671124

e-mail: enquiries@redlionfreehouse.com

dir: From A303 take A345 N. Exit at Enford. Left at T-junct towards East Chisenbury. Pub 1m on right

Excellent food in rural village pub

A thatched building dating back to Tudor times, the Red Lion started life as a beer house run by Mrs Weeks. On the edge of Salisbury Plain and with fishing rights on the River Avon, the pub attracts country sports enthusiasts, not to mention locals tempted by guest ales and excellent food. Owned by two chefs with a background in top restaurants, everything is made on the premises using prime seasonal ingredients. You could start with warm crab tart; continue with roast rib of Wiltshire beef and end with Valrhona chocolate terrine. May Bank Holiday beer festival.

Open all day all wk **Bar Meals** L served Mon-Sat 12-2, Sun 12-3 D served all wk 6.30-9 **Restaurant** L served Mon-Sat 12-2, Sun 12-3 D served all wk 6.30-9 Fixed menu price fr £20 Av 3 course à la carte fr £32 ⊕ FREE

HOUSE ◀ Guest ales ♂ Ty Gwyn, Black Rat, Perry's. ☗ 10 **Facilities** Non-diners area ✿ (Bar Restaurant Garden) ◈ Children's portions Garden ⊫ Beer festival Parking Wi-fi **Rooms** 5

EAST KNOYLE — Map 4 ST83

The Fox and Hounds

PICK OF THE PUBS

See Pick of the Pubs on opposite page

EBBESBOURNE WAKE — Map 4 ST92

The Horseshoe

PICK OF THE PUBS

Handley St SP5 5JF ☎ 01722 780474

dir: Telephone for directions

Well-kept beers and home-made food

Dating from the 17th century, the family-run Horseshoe is a genuine old English pub in the pretty village of Ebbesbourne Wake. The original building has not changed much, except for a conservatory extension to accommodate more diners, and there's a lovely flower-filled garden. Beyond the climbing roses are two rooms adorned with simple furniture, old farming implements and country bygones, linked to a central servery where well-kept cask-conditioned ales are dispensed straight from their barrels — Bowman Swift One, Otter Bitter and Palmers Copper — plus real ciders too. Good-value traditional bar food is offered from a varied menu. Freshly prepared from local produce, dishes include local faggots in onion gravy; ham, egg and chips; lamb hotpot; and lunchtime sandwiches. The home-made pies are a firm favourite — venison and mushroom; chicken, ham and mushroom; steak-and-kidney; and game. Ice creams are provided by Buttercup Ice Cream in Wardour.

Open 12-3 6.30-11 (Sun 12-4) Closed: 26 Dec, Sun eve & Mon L **Bar Meals** L served Tue-Sat 12-2 D served Tue-Sat 7-9 **Restaurant** L served Sun 12-2.30 D served Tue-Sat 7-9 ⊕ FREE HOUSE ◀ Otter Bitter, Bowman Ales Swift One, Palmers Copper Ale, Guest ales ♂ Thatchers Gold. **Facilities** Non-diners area ✿ (Bar Garden) ◈ Children's portions Play area Garden ⊫ Parking

---

EDINGTON — Map 4 ST95

The Three Daggers ★★★★★ INN
NEW

Westbury Rd BA13 4PG ☎ 01380 830940

e-mail: hello@threedaggers.co.uk

dir: A36 towards Warminster, A350 to Westbury, A303 to Edington

Where locally sourced meals are kept simple

Opened as the Paulet Arms in 1750 by Harry Paulet, the Lord of Edington Manor, locals quickly christened it the Three Daggers, after the family's coat of arms. It has always been well known for its friendly atmosphere, for enjoying a good meal, and for its accommodation, as

---

today's five AA stars and a Dinner Award demonstrate. Box Steam, Stonehenge and Wadworth breweries supply their beers, and Thatchers its real cider. From the dinner menu come game pie; Downland Farm pork chop; Cornish lemon sole; and pan-fried gnocchi. In March there's a beer festival, and in September it's cider's turn.

Open all day all wk 8am-11pm **Bar Meals** L served Mon-Sat 12-2.30, Sun 12-8.30 D served Mon-Thu 6-9, Fri-Sat 6-9.30, Sun 12-8.30 Av main course £13 **Restaurant** L served Mon-Sat 12-2.30, Sun 12-8.30 D served Mon-Thu 6-9, Fri-Sat 6-9.30, Sun 12-8.30 Av 3 course à la carte fr £25 ⊕ FREE HOUSE ◀ Stonehenge Ales Pigswill, Wadworth Henry's Original IPA & The Bishop's Tipple, Box Steam ♂ Westons Stowford Press, Thatchers Heritage & Traditional. ☗ 12 **Facilities** Non-diners area ✿ (Bar Garden) ◈ Children's menu Children's portions Play area Garden ⊫ Beer festival Cider festival Parking Wi-fi ⊞ (notice required) **Rooms** 3

FONTHILL GIFFORD — Map 4 ST93

The Beckford Arms

PICK OF THE PUBS

See Pick of the Pubs on page 478

FROXFIELD — Map 5 SU26

The Pelican Inn

Bath Rd SN8 3JY ☎ 01488 682479

e-mail: enquiries@pelicaninn.co.uk

web: www.pelicaninn.co.uk

dir: On A4 midway between Marlborough & Hungerford

Locally sourced produce cooked simply

Terry and Kirsty took over this 17th-century roadside inn in late 2012 and they are keen to make this a village pub serving the local community. Just 300 yards from the Kennet & Avon Canal, it is a popular refuelling stop for walkers, cyclists and the boating fraternity, as well as weary A4 travellers. Expect Otter Bitter and local guest ales on tap, a raft of wines by the glass, and locally sourced food. The menu offers traditional pub favourites such as steak and Otter ale pie; roasted chicken breast filled with mushrooms and pancetta; local pork sausages and mash.

Open all day all wk 11-11 (Sun 12-10) **Bar Meals** L served all wk 12-9 D served all wk 12-9 food served all day **Restaurant** L served all wk 12-9 D served all wk 12-9 food served all day ⊕ FREE HOUSE ◀ Otter Bitter, Guest ales. ☗ 9 **Facilities** Non-diners area ✿ (Bar Garden) ◈ Children's menu Garden ⊫ Parking Wi-fi ⊞ (notice required)

Save on hotels. Book at **theAA.com/hotel**

WILTSHIRE 477 ENGLAND

PICK OF THE PUBS

The Fox and Hounds

EAST KNOYLE   Map 4 ST83

The Green SP3 6BN ☎ 01747 830573
e-mail: fox.hounds@virgin.net
web:
www.foxandhounds-eastknoyle.co.uk
dir: *From A303 follow Blandford/East
Knoyle signs onto A350, follow brown
pub signs*

Traditional pub with lovely views

This partly thatched and half-timbered,
rustic 15th-century inn makes the most
of its stunning Blackmore Vale location.
There are exceptional views from the
patio beer garden and nearby East
Knoyle village green across these
Wiltshire and Dorset boundary-lands,
where Sir Christopher Wren was born
and the family of Jane Seymour (Henry
VIII's third wife) were based. Hidden in a
timeless village on a greensand ridge,
the engaging exterior is well matched by
the atmospheric interior, with lots of
flagstone flooring, wood-burning fires
and restful stripped wood furniture.
Locals eager to partake of Thatchers
Cheddar Valley cider or Hop Back Crop
Circle rub shoulders with diners keen to
make the acquaintance of the eclectic
menu. Blackboard menus increase the
choice, dependant entirely on the
availability of the freshest local fare.
Starters might include deep-fried
rosemary and garlic-crusted brie
wedges with cranberry jelly or tempura-
battered king prawns with sweet chilli

dip. When it comes to main courses,
good, wholesome pub grub like fish pie;
chicken pie with chips and vegetables
and home-made sausages, mash and
gravy share the board with lamb shank
braised in red wine; slow-roasted belly
pork with an apple and cider sauce;
duck breast with damson sauce and
spring onion mash; or Thai green curry
with lemongrass-scented jasmine rice.
Stone-baked pizzas from a clay oven
and a comprehensive children's menu
add to the fray, whilst desserts include
fresh Dorset apple cake with golden
syrup and cream or chocolate and
raspberry tart with mascarpone cream.
There is also a gluten-free chocolate
fondant and ice cream.

Open all wk 11.30-3 5.30-11

Bar Meals L served all wk 12-2.30 D
served all wk 6-9 **Restaurant** L served
all wk 12-2.30 D served all wk 6-9
⊕ FREE HOUSE ◗ Hop Back Crop Circle
& Summer Lightning, Wickwar BOB,
Adnams Broadside, Palmers Dorset
Gold, St Austell Tribute, Butcombe
Ố Thatchers Cheddar Valley. ☙ 15
Facilities Non-diners area ❦ ♦♦
Children's menu Garden ⊼ Parking Wi-fi
🚌 (notice required)

PICK OF THE PUBS

The Beckford Arms

FONTHILL GIFFORD   Map 4 ST93

SP3 6PX ☎ 01747 870385
e-mail: info@beckfordarms.com
web: www.thebeckfordarms.com
dir: *From A303 (E of Wincanton) follow Fonthill Bishop sign. At T-junct in village right, 1st left signed Fonthill Gifford & Tisbury. Through Fonthill Estate arch to pub*

Stylish country pub on the edge of rolling parkland

Surely the approach to very few, if any, pubs is through an arch as impressive as the one on Lord Margadale's 10,000-acre Fonthill Estate. To be fair, that's not the only way of reaching the Georgian country coaching inn that reopened after a terrible fire in 2010. Today, you'd never know what damage the flames did, but in the parquet-floored bar is a reminder of the conflagration in the liquid form of Keystone's Beckford Phoenix real ale; other beers on tap are Dorset Piddle's Jimmy Riddle, Butcombe and Erdinger wheat beer, and one of the real ciders is Sheppy's. Available by the glass is Fonthill Glebe, a local crisp white wine. In winter the huge open fire is used to spit-roast suckling pigs and warm mulled wine. The restaurant's glass wall opens on to the terrace and pretty garden, where hammocks hang between the trees, you can play pétanque and children can do what children do. Deciding what to eat from the daily-

changing menu could prove pleasantly tricky: for example, do you start with cream of artichoke soup with chorizo and croutons, or chilli- and garlic-fried prawns on grilled bread with fennel and watercress salad? Then there are the mains: loin of venison with roasted shallots, bone marrow, parsnip purée and fried mushrooms; Newlyn pollock with mussels, white wine, potatoes, cream and purple sprouting broccoli; or poached hen's egg with creamed Puy lentils, chestnut mushrooms and Jerusalem artichokes. Among the bar meals are fish and chips with mushy peas, tartare sauce and lemon; and Tiny Thai snacks.

Open all day all wk **Bar Meals** L served all wk 12-2.30 D served all wk 6-9.30 Av

main course £14.50 **Restaurant** L served Mon-Sat 12-2.30, Sun 12-3 D served all wk 6-9.30 Av 3 course à la carte fr £25 ⊞ FREE HOUSE ◀ Keystone Beckford Phoenix, Dorset Piddle Jimmy Riddle, Butcombe, Erdinger ⚙ Ashton Press, Westons Wyld Wood Organic, Sheppy's. ♟ 12 **Facilities** Non-diners area ♣ ♦ Children's menu & portions Play area Garden ⌁ Parking Wi-fi

Save on hotels. Book at theAA.com/hotel

WILTSHIRE 479 **ENGLAND**

   Map 4 ST95

The Bell Inn

PICK OF THE PUBS

High St SN10 5TH ☎ **01380 813277**
e-mail: gary06weston@aol.com
dir: *From Salisbury take A360 towards Devizes, through West Lavington, 1st left after black & yellow striped bridge onto B3098. Right to Great Cheverell*

A TV star, and no wonder

Apparently mentioned in the Domesday Book, in far more recent times – namely the 18th century – The Bell became a drovers' inn. Even more recently, it achieved nationwide fame on TV's *Location, Location, Location.* Free-house status enables Gary and Lou Weston to offer Sharp's Doom Bar, Wadworth 6X and a guest ale in the log-fired bar, while home-cooked food is served in the elegant, oak-beamed restaurant. Starters include two types of meze – Mediterranean, with marinated olives, roasted artichoke and sun-dried tomatoes; and seafood, with breaded king prawns, whitebait and calamari. Main courses include pan-fried halibut; slow-roasted lamb shank; and local venison sausages. Finish a 24oz rump steak and earn a free dessert, most likely Marshfield Farm ice cream, rather than sticky toffee pudding. Pub classics like chicken tikka masala, and wholetail scampi also feature on the menu. The secluded garden and patio are well provided with seating.

Open all wk **Bar Meals** L served all wk 12-2.30 D served all wk 6-9 **Restaurant** L served all wk 12-2.30 D served all wk 6-9 ⊕ FREE HOUSE ◀ Wadworth 6X, IPA, Sharp's Doom Bar, Guest ale ♂ Westons Stowford Press. ♟ 16 **Facilities** Non-diners area ♦♦ Children's menu Children's portions Garden Parking Wi-fi 🚐

HANNINGTON   Map 5 SU19

The Jolly Tar

Queens Rd SN6 7RP ☎ **01793 762245**
e-mail: jolly.tar@sky.com
dir: *M4 junct 15, A419 towards Cirencester. At Bunsdon/Highworth sign follow B4109. Towards Highworth, left at Freke Arms, follow Hannington & Jolly Tar pub signs*

Local ales and a spacious garden

It may be far from the sea, but there's a nautical reason for this former farmhouse's name – a retired sea captain married into the Freke family, who once owned it. Old timbers and locally brewed Arkell's ales are served in its two bars, making this pretty inn an appealing destination. All food on the daily menu is freshly prepared; a meal could take in crispy chilli squid with garlic mayo followed by home-made steak and ale pie with chunky chips. The conservatory restaurant overlooks the sun terrace and spacious garden, replete with a children's play area.

Open 12-3 6-11 (Sun 12-3 7-11) Closed: Mon L (ex BHs) **Restaurant** L served Tue-Sun 12-2 D served Mon-Sat 6.30-9, Sun 7-9 ⊕ ARKELL'S ◀ 3B, Wiltshire Gold, Bees

---

Organic. ♟ 9 **Facilities** Non-diners area ♣ (Bar Garden) ♦♦ Children's menu Play area Garden 🚗 Parking Wi-fi

---

HEYTESBURY   Map 4 ST94

The Angel Coaching Inn

PICK OF THE PUBS

High St BA12 0ED ☎ **01985 840330**
e-mail: admin@angelheytesbury.co.uk
dir: *A303 onto A36 towards Bath, 8m, Heytesbury on left*

Refurbished dining pub in an upmarket village

Close to the River Wylye, Longleat and Warminster, and well placed for exploring Bath and Salisbury, The Angel is a 17th-century coaching inn tucked away in a sleepy village. Although these days it is more of a dining destination, it retains its traditional charm and character, and the atmosphere is relaxed and informal. Reserve a scrubbed pine table in the main beamed bar surrounded by fine prints and a roaring log fire in the inglenook; alternatively, relax into a deep sofa with a pint of Old Speckled Hen in the lounge before dining in the more modern and formal restaurant; summer alfresco meals can be enjoyed in the secluded courtyard garden. Menus change daily and typically offer a starter of wild boar belly and blood pudding salad, followed by crab and smoked trout risotto or a choice of steaks. Simpler lunchtime meals include egg muffins and sandwiches. Walk it all off with a stroll through the river valley and surrounding downland.

Open all day all wk **Bar Meals** L served all wk 12-2.30 D served all wk 6.30-9.30 Av main course £10 **Restaurant** L served all wk 12-2.30 D served all wk 6.30-9.30 Av 3 course à la carte fr £25 ⊕ GREENE KING ◀ London Glory, Morland Old Speckled Hen ♂ Thatchers Gold. ♟ 8 **Facilities** Non-diners area ♣ (Bar) ♦♦ Children's portions Outside area 🚗 Parking Wi-fi 🚐

HINDON   Map 4 ST93

Angel Inn

PICK OF THE PUBS

High St SP3 6DJ ☎ **01747 820696**
e-mail: info@angel-inn-at-hindon.co.uk
dir: *1.5m from A303, on B3089 towards Salisbury*

Rustic charm meets urbane sophistication

Just minutes from the ancient mounds and henges of Salisbury Plain, this beautifully restored 18th-century coaching inn offers many original features: wooden floors, beams and a huge stone fireplace. Outside is an attractive paved courtyard with garden furniture, where food can be served in fine weather. Behind the bar are Brakspear, Sharp's and Timothy Taylor ales. The pine country-style tables and chairs, together with the day's newspapers, lend a friendly and relaxed atmosphere, while an eclectic mix of traditional and modern British dishes characterises the brasserie-style menu. Dishes are based on quality seasonal ingredients and prepared using classical French techniques. A typical starter is pheasant and bacon terrine; main courses could be Loch

---

Duart salmon en croûte, or chicken supreme with white bean and chorizo stew. Lunchtime snacks are a ploughman's or Cajun chicken and cheese melt ciabatta. Desserts are on the blackboard, as are the day's specials.

Open all day all wk 11-11 (Sun 12-4) **Bar Meals** L served all wk 12-2.30 D served Mon-Sat 6-9.30 **Restaurant** L served all wk 12-2.30 D served Mon-Sat 6-9.30 ⊕ FREE HOUSE ◀ Timothy Taylor Landlord, Sharp's, Brakspear ♂ Thatchers Gold. ♟ 14 **Facilities** Non-diners area ♣ (Bar Garden Outside area) ♦♦ Children's portions Garden Outside area 🚗 Parking Wi-fi

---

The Lamb at Hindon ★★★★ INN ◉

PICK OF THE PUBS

High St SP3 6DP ☎ **01747 820573**
e-mail: info@lambathindon.co.uk
dir: *From A303 follow Hindon signs. At Fonthill Bishop right onto B3089 to Hindon. Pub on left*

Traditional, warm and welcoming historic coaching inn

The stone-built Lamb began trading as a beer house in the 12th century. By the late 18th it had become a coaching inn and even in 1870 was still providing 300 horses daily for long-distance coaches. Now under new management, the inn retains plenty of old-time character, thanks to its inglenook fireplaces, flagstone floors, heavy beams, and period furnishings and paintings. Where better then for a pint of Butcombe, or a malt whisky from one of Wiltshire's largest selections? Lunch and dinner menus, recognised with an AA Rosette, are broadly similar, the main difference being sandwiches on the former. Otherwise, it's a case of choosing between, for example, main courses of rare-breed pork sausages; 21-day-aged rib-eye steak; line-caught cod with mushy peas; and pickled Dorset mushroom risotto. Travellers caught in slow-moving traffic on the A303 nearby should turn off for breakfast, morning coffee or lunch. The accommodation includes four-poster bedrooms.

Open all day all wk 7.30am-11pm **Bar Meals** L served all wk 12-2.30 D served all wk 6.30-9.30 **Restaurant** L served all wk 12-2.30 D served all wk 6.30-9.30 ⊕ BOISDALE ◀ Young's Bitter, St Austell Tribute, Butcombe, Guest ale ♂ Westons Stowford Press. ♟ 10 **Facilities** Non-diners area ♣ (Bar Garden) ♦♦ Children's menu Children's portions Garden 🚗 Parking Wi-fi 🚐 (notice required) **Rooms** 19

HORNINGSHAM | Map 4 ST84

The Bath Arms at
Longleat ★★★★ INN ◉◉

PICK OF THE PUBS

BA12 7LY ☎ **01985 844308**
e-mail: enquiries@batharms.co.uk
dir: *Off B3092 S of Frome*

Quirky but stylish country inn within the Longleat Estate

Built in the 17th century, The Bath Arms occupies a prime position at one of the entrances to Longleat Estate and the famous Safari Park. The building became a public house with rooms in 1732 called the New Inn; it was later renamed the Weymouth Arms, and became the Marquess of Bath Arms in 1850. An ivy-clad stone inn, it features two fine beamed bars – one traditional with settles, old wooden tables and an open fire, and a bar for dining. The Wessex Brewery furnishes the public bar with its much-cherished Horningsham Pride ale, while most food is sourced within 50 miles of the pub. Simple menus focus on quality produce, with minimal use of international influences and an emphasis on traditional preserving methods – smoking, curing, potting and pickling. The lunchtime menu has traditional favourites such as traditional fish and chips, chicken Caesar salad and rib-eye steak, but these belie the kitchen team's culinary expertise which has won two AA Rosettes - revealed in dinner dishes such as pan-fried fillet of sea bass, brown shrimps and white bean cassoulet; and roasted guinea fowl with fondant potato, mushrooms and bacon. Stylish accommodation is available.

Open all day all wk **Bar Meals** L served all wk 12-2.30 D served Sun-Thu 7-9, Fri-Sat 7-9.30 **Restaurant** L served all wk 12-2.30 D served Sun-Thu 7-9, Fri-Sat 7-9.30 ⊕ WESSEX BREWERY ◀ Horningsham Pride & Golden Apostle, Guest ales ♂ Westons Stowford Press, Addlestones. ♟ 9 **Facilities** Non-diners area ♣ (Bar Garden) ♦♦ Children's menu Children's portions Garden ⼧ Beer festival Parking Wi-fi ☛ (notice required) **Rooms** 16

LACOCK | Map 4 ST96

The George Inn

4 West St SN15 2LH ☎ **01249 730263**
e-mail: thegeorgelacock@wadworth.co.uk
dir: *M4 junct 17, A350, S, between Chippenham & Melksham*

Step back in time at this historic gem

Steeped in history and much used as a film and television location, the beautiful National Trust village of Lacock includes this atmospheric inn. The George dates from 1361 and boasts a medieval ceiling, a low-beamed ceiling, mullioned windows, flagstone floors, plenty of copper and brass, and an old tread wheel by which a dog would drive the spit. Locals and visitors discuss the merits of the ale selection at the bar, while menus proffer a selection of steaks and flavoursome pies, with fish

options among the summertime specials; finish with home-made bread-and-butter pudding.

Open all wk 9-2.30 5-11 (Fri-Sat 9am-11pm Sun 9am-10.30pm) Closed: 25 Dec **Bar Meals** L served all wk 12-2 D served all wk 6-9 **Restaurant** L served all wk 12-2 D served all wk 6-9 ⊕ WADWORTH ◀ 6X, Henry's Original IPA, JCB, Henry's Smooth ♂ Westons Stowford Press. ♟ 9 **Facilities** Non-diners area ♦♦ Children's menu Children's portions Play area Garden Parking ☛

Red Lion Inn

1 High St SN15 2LQ ☎ **01249 730456**
e-mail: redlionlacock@wadworth.co.uk
dir: *M4 junct 17, A350, S, between Chippenham & Melksham*

Imposing Lacock village hostelry with large garden

A historic 18th-century inn at the heart of the National Trust village of Lacock, whose famous abbey has featured in many films. The pub's Georgian interior with large open fireplace and flagstone floors creates an atmosphere conducive to the enjoyment of Wadworth ales and a wondrous choice of real ciders. Home-cooked food follows traditional lines, from sharing boards of meats, fish or cheeses to main plates of wild boar and apple sausages; free-range chicken breast with a Stilton and bacon cream; or a Red Lion beefburger topped with red onion marmalade and goats' cheese.

Open all day all wk 8am-11pm (Sat 9am-11pm Sun 9am-10.30pm) ⊕ WADWORTH ◀ 6X, Henry's Original IPA, Horizon, Swordfish ♂ Westons Stowford Press, Thatchers Gold. **Facilities** ♦♦ Children's menu Children's portions Garden Parking Wi-fi

---

LIMPLEY STOKE | Map 4 ST76

The Hop Pole Inn

Woods Hill, Lower Limpley Stoke BA2 7FS
☎ **01225 723134**
dir: *Telephone for directions*

Cask ales in a real country pub atmosphere

Set in the beautiful Avon Valley, The Hop Pole dates from 1580 and takes its name from the hop plant that still grows outside the pub. Eagle-eyed film fans may recognise it as the hostelry in the 1993 film *The Remains of the Day*. A hearty menu includes Thai vegetable curry, home-made pies, fresh local trout, and steaks. Food can be enjoyed with one of the many ales, or one of the wines served by the glass.

Open all wk 11-2.30 6-11 (Sun 12-3 7-10.30) Closed: 25 Dec **Bar Meals** L served Mon-Sat 12-2, Sun 12-2.15 D served Mon-Thu 6-9, Fri-Sat 6-9.30, Sun 7-9 **Restaurant** L served Mon-Sat 12-2, Sun 12-2.15 D served Mon-Thu 6-9, Fri-Sat 6-9.30, Sun 7-9 ⊕ FREE HOUSE ◀ Sharp's Doom Bar, Bath Gem, Guest ales ♂ Westons Stowford Press. ♟ 11 **Facilities** Non-diners area ♣ (Bar Garden) ♦♦ Children's menu Children's portions Family room Garden ⼧ Parking Wi-fi

---

LOWER CHICKSGROVE | Map 4 ST92

Compasses Inn ★★★★ INN ◉

PICK OF THE PUBS

SP3 6NB ☎ **01722 714318**
e-mail: thecompasses@aol.com
dir: *On A30 (1.5m W of Fovant) 3rd right to Lower Chicksgrove. In 1.5m left into Lagpond Ln, pub 1m on left*

Picture-perfect thatched inn amid rolling countryside

You're bound to be charmed by this 14th-century inn situated in a tiny hamlet. An old cobbled path leads to the low latched door that opens into a delightful bar with worn flagstones, exposed stone walls and old beams. Snuggle up to the large inglenook fireplace or relax in the intimate booth seating, perfect on a winter's evening. You can be certain to find three or four local real ales on tap, perhaps from Wiltshire breweries Keystone or Stonehenge, and the wine list is comprehensive. Be sure to try the food: the kitchen team has won an AA Rosette for their freshly made seasonal dishes; these are written on a blackboard because they change so frequently. Examples of starters are duck liver parfait or beetroot-cured salmon. Main dishes could be pan-fried fillet of hake with a lemon, pea and tiger prawn risotto, or traditional cottage pie. Five bedrooms are available, providing an ideal base for exploring the area.

Open 12-3 6-11 (Sun 12-3 7-10.30) Closed: 25-26 Dec, Mon L Jan-Mar **Bar Meals** L served all wk 12-2 D served all wk 6.30-9 Av main course £15 **Restaurant** Av 3 course à la carte fr £24 ⊕ FREE HOUSE ◀ Keystone Large One, Stonehenge Spire Ale, Plain Inntrigue, Butcombe ♂ Thatchers Gold, Ashton Still. ♟ 8 **Facilities** Non-diners area ♣ (Bar Restaurant Garden) ♦♦ Children's menu Children's portions Garden ⼧ Parking Wi-fi ☛ **Rooms** 5

MALMESBURY | Map 4 ST98

The Smoking Dog

62 The High St SN16 9AT ☎ **01666 825823**
e-mail: smokindog@sabrain.com
dir: *5m N of M4 junct 17*

Peaceful town centre beer-garden retreat

At the foot of Malmesbury's pretty high street and handy for visiting the famous abbey here, this is a favourite with families, who appreciate the secure beer garden. The Cotswold stone inn is draped with hanging baskets, whilst inside the bar boasts a fine open fire, just the place to hunker down with a glass of Bath Gem beer and consider a fulfilling menu boasting starters such as dolcelatte and walnut tortellini leading to mains covering most bases, from pork loin chop with sticky harissa sauce to roasted fig, blue cheese and prosciutto salad. A popular beer and sausage festival enlivens the Spring Bank Holiday weekend.

Open all day all wk 12-11 (Fri-Sat 12-12 Sun 12-10.30) **Bar Meals** L served Mon-Sat 12-9, Sun 12-8.30 D served Mon-Sat 12-9, Sun 12-8.30 food served all day

Save on hotels. Book at **theAA.com/hotel**

WILTSHIRE 481 ENGLAND

Restaurant L served Mon-Sat 12-9, Sun 12-8.30 D served Mon-Sat 12-9, Sun 12-8.30 food served all day ⊕ BRAINS ◀ The Rev. James, Bath Ales Gem, Guest ales. ⬤ 11 **Facilities** Non-diners area ✿ (Bar Garden) ♦️ Children's menu Children's portions Garden ☂ Beer festival Wi-fi

The Vine Tree

PICK OF THE PUBS

Foxley Rd, Norton SN16 0JP ☎ **01666 837654**
e-mail: tiggi@thevinetree.co.uk
dir: *M4 junct 17, A429 towards Malmesbury. Turn left for village after 1m follow brown signs*

Former mill with great home cooking

This atmospheric pub used to be a mill; workers apparently passed beverages out through front windows to passing carriages - an early drive-through it would seem. These days, it is well worth seeking out for its interesting modern pub food and memorable outdoor summer dining. In the central bar a large open fireplace burns wood all winter, and there's a wealth of old beams, flagstone and oak floors. Ramblers and cyclists exploring Wiltshire's charms are frequent visitors, and the inn is situated on the official county cycle route. Cooking is modern British in style; you could start with pork crackling and apple sauce, then move on to savoury tarte Tatin made with red onions and goats' cheese. After that, perhaps pan-fried fillets of gilt head bream with a caper and parsley crushed new potato cake, followed by Cointreau crème brûlée. There are also great real ales and a terrific stock of wines, with a high number by the glass. In addition to the suntrap terrace, there's a two-acre garden with two boules pitches.

Open 12-3 6-12 (Sun 12-4) Closed: Sun eve **Bar Meals** L served Mon-Sat 12-2.30, Sun 12-3.30 D served Mon-Thu 7-9.30, Fri-Sat 7-10 Av main course £13.95 **Restaurant** L served Mon-Sat 12-2.30, Sun 12-3.30 D served Mon-Thu 7-9.30, Fri-Sat 7-10 Av 3 course à la carte fr £25.95 ⊕ FREE HOUSE ◀ St Austell Trelawny & Tribute, Uley Bitter, Stonehenge Pigswill, Guest ales ♂ Westons Stowford Press. ⬤ 40 **Facilities** Non-diners area ✿ (Bar Restaurant Garden) ♦️ Children's menu Children's portions Play area Garden ☂ Parking Wi-fi ▭ (notice required)

MARDEN Map 5 SU05

The Millstream

SN10 3RH ☎ **01380 848490**
e-mail: themillstreammarden@gmail.com
dir: *6m E of Devizes, N of A342*

Peaceful alfresco options here

Set in the heart of the Pewsey Vale, The Millstream is an attractive village pub near Devizes. Inside, the three fireplaces make for a cosy and romantic atmosphere in which to sip a regional Thatchers cider and refuel with a bar snack or a light lunch of salmon fishcakes with lemon mayonnaise or double baked cheese soufflé. More substantial meal options include medallions of pork with green peppercorn sauce; or king scallops and bacon salad with warm vinaigrette. The large garden is a wonderfully peaceful spot for an alfresco drink or meal.

Open all wk 12-3 6.30-11 **Bar Meals** L served all wk 12-2.30 D served all wk 6.30-9.30 **Restaurant** L served all wk 12-2.30 D served all wk 6.30-9.30 ⊕ WADWORTH ◀ 6X, IPA, Horizon ♂ Thatchers Gold. **Facilities** Non-diners area ✿ (Bar Garden) ♦️ Children's portions Play area Family room Garden ☂ Parking Wi-fi ▭ (notice required)

MARLBOROUGH Map 5 SU16

The Lamb Inn ★★★ INN

The Parade SN8 1NE ☎ **01672 512668**
e-mail: thelambinnmarlboro@fsmail.net
dir: *E along High St (A4) turn right into The Parade, pub 50yds on left*

Flower-bedecked pub with home-cooked food

Overlooking Marlborough's impressively wide main street, this coaching inn dates from 1673. It's a dog-friendly and welcoming hostelry today, but the dining room, converted from the stable, is reputed to be haunted since a woman was killed when pushed down the stairs. Landlady and chef Jackie Scott uses prime local ingredients including Wiltshire beef, pork from farms close by, game in season, and herbs and berries from the hedgerows. Expect the likes of pigeon and wild mushroom pâté; and a home-made cassoulet of smoked ham, garlic sausage, lamb and duck.

Open all day all wk ⊕ WADWORTH ◀ 6X, Guest ales. **Facilities** ✿ (Bar Restaurant Garden) ♦️ Children's portions Garden Wi-fi **Rooms** 6

MINETY Map 5 SU09

Vale of the White Horse Inn

PICK OF THE PUBS

SN16 9QY ☎ **01666 860175**
e-mail: info@valeofthewhitehorseinn.co.uk
dir: *On B4040 (3m W of Cricklade, 6m E of Malmesbury)*

Popular with the local community

An eye-catching and beautifully restored inn overlooking a large pond. Built in the early 1800s, the building's true history is something of a mystery, but it was registered by its current name in the 1881 census. Today, sitting under a parasol on the large raised terrace, it's hard to think of a better spot. The village bar is popular with the local community, drawn by a good selection of real ales and events such as skittles evenings, live music and quizzes. The ethos is to serve good home-cooked food at sensible prices. Upstairs, lunch and dinner are served in the stone-walled restaurant with its polished tables and bentwood chairs. The bar menu offers baguettes, ploughman's, nachos and daily specials. Most pub favourites will be found on the à la carte, ranging from chicken Caesar salad to home-made cottage pie and rib-eye steak. Mint chocolate chip cheesecake might tempt for dessert.

Open all wk 11.45-2.45 4.45-11 (Thu-Sat 11.45-11 Sun 11.45-10.30) **Bar Meals** L served all wk 12-2.30 D served all wk 6-9.15 **Restaurant** L served all wk 12-2.30 D served all wk 6-9.15 ⊕ FREE HOUSE ◀ Cotswold Spring

Stunner, Otter Bitter, Moles Best ♂ Westons Stowford Press, Pheasant Plucker, Broadoak. ⬤ 10 **Facilities** Non-diners area ✿ (Bar Garden) ♦️ Children's menu Children's portions Family room Garden ☂ Parking Wi-fi ▭

NEWTON TONY Map 5 SU24

The Malet Arms

SP4 0HF ☎ **01980 629279**
e-mail: info@maletarms.com
dir: *8m N of Salisbury on A338, 2m from A303*

Riverside inn ideal for a peaceful pint

Off the beaten track, in a quiet village on the River Bourne, this 17th-century inn was originally built as a dwelling house. Much later it became The Malet Arms after lord of the manor Sir Henry Malet. The pub is free of fruit machines and piped music, creating a peaceful atmosphere in which to enjoy local real ale, draught cider or a whisky. All the food on the ever-changing blackboard menu, from scampi to Thai chicken curry, is home cooked. Game is plentiful in season, often courtesy of the landlord. In fine weather you can sit in the garden where there is a children's play area. Look out for the beer festival in July.

Open all wk 11-3 6-11 (Sun 12-3 6-10.30) Closed: 25-26 Dec, 1 Jan **Bar Meals** L served all wk 12-2.30 D served all wk 6.30-10 Av main course £10.50 **Restaurant** L served all wk 12-2.30 D served all wk 6.30-10 ⊕ FREE HOUSE ◀ Ramsbury, Stonehenge, Triple fff, Palmers, Andwell ♂ Westons Old Rosie & Stowford Press, Ashton Press. ⬤ 9 **Facilities** Non-diners area ♦️ Children's menu Play area Garden Beer festival Parking

NUNTON Map 5 SU12

The Radnor Arms

SP5 4HS ☎ **01722 329722**
dir: *From Salisbury ring road take A338 to Ringwood. Nunton signed on right*

South of Salisbury, popular with locals and visitors alike

Not far from Salisbury this is a popular pub in the centre of Nunton dating from around 1750. In 1855 it was owned by the local multi-talented brewer/baker/grocer, and bought by Lord Radnor in 1919. Bar snacks are supplemented by an extensive fish choice and daily specials, which might include braised lamb shank, wild mushroom risotto, turbot with spinach or Scotch rib-eye fillet, all freshly prepared. There is a summer garden with rural views to enjoy, and the pub hosts an annual pumpkin competition in October.

Open all wk 11-3.30 6-11.30 **Bar Meals** L served all wk 12-2 D served all wk 6-9 **Restaurant** L served all wk 12-2 D served all wk 6-9 ⊕ FREE HOUSE ◀ Hook Norton Old Hooky, Sharp's Doom Bar, Downton Quadhop, Otter, Black Sheep ♂ Westons Stowford Press. **Facilities** Non-diners area ✿ (Bar Restaurant Garden) ♦️ Children's portions Play area Family room Garden ☂ Parking Wi-fi ▭

OAKSEY Map 4 ST99

The Wheatsheaf at Oaksey ◎◎

PICK OF THE PUBS

Wheatsheaf Ln SN16 9TB ☎ 01666 577348
e-mail: info@thewheatsheafatoaksey.co.uk
dir: *From Cirencester take A419 towards Swindon, follow B4696/South Cerney signs. Through water meadows to Oaksey. Or take A433 towards Tetbury, A429 through Kemble to Oaksey*

Innovative food and old-world charm

After several years at the helm, during which time he gained this sophisticated dining pub two AA Rosettes, chef-patron Tony Robson-Burrell handed the reins to his Ritz London-trained son Jack in November 2012. The origins of this mellow Cotswold-stone inn go back over 700 years. The huge old fireplace, beams, parquet floor and comfortably lived-in bar furniture are instantly welcoming, whilst in the restaurant area, Elizabethan England is replaced by inspiring, contemporary decor, light wood and striking prints. Handy for the Cotswold Water Park and Roman Cirencester, explorers chancing on The Wheatsheaf are rewarded with innovative dishes but also old-world charm. Enjoy a starter of Cornish mussels with smoked bacon and cider, and move on to braised shoulder of pork with Savoy cabbage, mash and smoked apple sauce. Alternatively, choose from nine gourmet burgers, washed down with pints of London Pride or Sharp's Doom Bar.

Open Tue-Fri 12-2 6-11 (Sat 12-11 Sun 12-6) Closed: Sun eve, Mon **Bar Meals** L served Tue-Sun 12-2 D served Tue-Sat 6.30-9 Av main course £9.50-£13 **Restaurant** L served Tue-Sun 12-2 D served Tue-Sat 6.30-9 Av 3 course à la carte fr £20 FREE HOUSE Sharp's Doom Bar, Fuller's London Pride, Timothy Taylor Landlord. 14 **Facilities** Non-diners area (Bar Garden) Children's menu Children's portions Garden Parking Wi-fi (notice required)

OGBOURNE ST ANDREW Map 5 SU17

Silks on the Downs

Main Rd SN8 1RZ ☎ 01672 841229
e-mail: silks@silksonthedowns.co.uk
web: www.silksonthedowns.co.uk
dir: *M4 junct 15, A346 towards Marlborough. Approx 6m to Ogbourne St Andrew. Pub on A346*

Village pub with a horseracing theme

A mile north of the bustling market town of Marlborough can be found this pub, tucked away in rolling downland. The free house's name reflects the racing heritage of the Berkshire Downs (whose western boundary is on the border with Wiltshire). Framed silks of leading racehorse owners and jockeys adorn the walls and the pub offers local Ramsbury ales, fine wines and an informal dining experience. There are filled freshly baked organic baguettes at lunchtime or classics like Thai chicken curry and venison sausages. Potted crab, Barbary duck breast and roasted vegetable tagliatelle are among the evening additions.

Open 12-3 6.30-11 Closed: 25 & 26 Dec, Sun eve **Bar Meals** L served Mon-Tue 12-2, Wed-Sun 12-2.30 D served Mon-Tue 7-9, Wed-Sat 7-9.30 Av main course £10.50 **Restaurant** L served Mon-Tue 12-2, Wed-Sun 12-2.30 D served Mon-Tue 7-9, Wed-Sat 7-9.30 FREE HOUSE Ramsbury Gold, Wadworth 6X & Henry's Original IPA Aspall. 11 **Facilities** Non-diners area Children's menu Children's portions Garden Parking Wi-fi

PEWSEY Map 5 SU16

The Seven Stars Inn

Bottlesford SN9 6LW ☎ 01672 851325
e-mail: info@thesevenstarsinn.co.uk
dir: *Off A345*

Handsome thatched inn with seven-acre gardens

Close to two of Wiltshire's famous white horses, this 16th-century free house lies in the heart of the Vale of Pewsey between Salisbury Plain and the Marlborough Downs, and is a 15-minute drive from the stone circles of Avebury. The bar maintains its original character with low beams and oak panelling, and you can expect local Wadworth 6X, Ramsbury Gold and guest ales on tap. The menu of home-made, no-frills classics could list a dry cured meat and sausage board, followed by roast pork belly, ale-battered haddock, or pan-fried wild mushroom gnocchi.

Open 12-3 6-11 Closed: Mon & Tue L **Bar Meals** L served Wed-Sun 12-3 D served Tue-Sat 6-9 **Restaurant** L served Wed-Sun 12-3 D served Tue- Sat 6-9 FREE HOUSE Wadworth 6X, Ramsbury Gold, Guest Ales Westons Stowford Press. **Facilities** Non-diners area (Bar Restaurant Garden) Children's menu Children's portions Garden Parking Wi-fi

PITTON Map 5 SU23

The Silver Plough

PICK OF THE PUBS

White Hill SP5 1DU ☎ 01722 712266
e-mail: info@silverplough-pitton.co.uk
dir: *From Salisbury take A30 towards Andover, Pitton signed. Approx 3m*

Pleasant, uncompromising village pub

There's a timeless atmosphere to this English country inn at the fringe of the Salisbury Downs. At its heart is an intricately moulded old dark-wood bar from which diverge rooms and a snug with rustic furniture, aged beams, log fires and country-style decor, whilst hop festoons remind that this is the place to get a reliable pint of First Gold or K & B Sussex from Hall & Woodhouse's Dorset brewery. Local produce is to the fore in the solidly traditional menu of pub favourites given a modern twist, such as a starter of chicken liver and brandy pâté with onion marmalade and melba toast. Mains may feature home-made hock, leek and cider pie with mash and seasonal vegetables, or baby rack of pork ribs slow-roasted with a barbecue and Jack Daniels sauce with corn on the cob, chips and salad. There's a traditional skittles alley here, too, and the gardens offer views over the villages' thatched roofs.

Open all wk 12-3 6-11 (Sun all day) **Bar Meals** L served all wk 12-2 D served all wk 6-9 Av main course £10.95 **Restaurant** L served Mon-Sat 12-2, Sun all day D served Mon-Sat 6-9, Sun all day Av 3 course à la carte fr £22 HALL & WOODHOUSE Badger Tanglefoot, First Gold & K&B Sussex, Guest ale Westons Stowford Press. 15 **Facilities** Non-diners area (Bar Garden) Children's menu Children's portions Family room Garden Parking Wi-fi (notice required)

Save on hotels. Book at **theAA.com/hotel**

WILTSHIRE 483 ENGLAND

RAMSBURY — Map 5 SU27

The Bell at Ramsbury ★★★★ INN ◉

The Square SN8 2PE ☎ **01672 520230**
e-mail: thebell@thebellramsbury.com
web: www.thebellramsbury.com
dir: *M4 junct 14, A338 to Hungerford. B4192 towards Swindon. Left to Ramsbury*

Country pub serving its own microbrewery ales

This 17th-century coaching inn occupies a lovely position at the centre of the village in the Kennet Valley on the Wiltshire/Berkshire border. The Bell has its own microbrewery, which supplies the light and airy bar with Ramsbury Gold and Bitter. Enjoy light meals such as fishcakes or Thai green curry in the cosy bar area with its wood-burners and comfortable sofas. Alternatively, book a table in the restaurant and order from a concise modern British à la carte that might include chicken and mushroom terrine, beetroot tagliatelle, Ramsbury Estate venison, and lemon meringue parfait.

The Bell at Ramsbury

Open all day all wk 12-11 (Sun 12-10) **Bar Meals** L served Mon-Sat 12-2.30 D served Mon-Sat 6-9, Sun 6-8 **Restaurant** L served all wk 12-2.30 D served Mon-Sat 6-9 ⊞ FREE HOUSE ◖ Ramsbury Bitter, Gold ◌ Thatchers Gold, Lilley's Apples & Pears. ☗ 12 **Facilities** Non-diners area ☙ (Bar Garden) ♦ Children's menu Children's portions Garden ☕ Parking Wi-fi **Rooms** 9

See advert below

ROWDE — Map 4 ST96

The George & Dragon ★★★★ RR ◉◉
PICK OF THE PUBS

High St SN10 2PN ☎ **01380 723053**
e-mail: thegandd@tiscali.co.uk
dir: *1m from Devizes, take A342 towards Chippenham*

Fish and seafood a specialty here

Narrowboaters from the nearby Kennet & Avon Canal enjoy coming here for a pint of Butcombe Bitter and Ringwood Fortyniner, especially after they've just navigated their way through the 29 locks of the Caen Flight. In 1917 the writer Edward Hutton said that Rowde had a 'curious inn', although whether, since there were then four inns in this Wiltshire village, he meant this 16th-century coaching inn isn't known. Not curious, but certainly interesting, is that the Tudor Rose of Elizabeth I is carved on the old beams in the cosy interior, with large open fireplaces, wooden floors, antique rugs and candlelit tables. The two-AA Rosette restaurant specialises in fresh fish and seafood, while other temptations include game terrine with home-made chutney and toast; roast loin of pork with apple sauce and crackling; and mushroom risotto with parmesan and truffle oil. Quality accommodation is provided in individually designed bedrooms.

Open 12-3 6.30-10 (Sat 12-4 6.30-10 Sun 12-4) Closed: Sun eve **Bar Meals** L served Mon-Fri 12-3, Sat-Sun 12-4 D served Mon-Sat 6.30-10 Av main course £13.75 **Restaurant** L served Mon-Fri 12-3, Sat-Sun 12-4 D served Mon-Sat 6.30-10 Fixed menu price fr £16.50 Av 3 course à la carte fr £19.50 ⊞ FREE HOUSE ◖ Butcombe Bitter, Sharp's Doom Bar, Bath Gem, Fuller's ESB & London Pride, Ringwood Fortyniner ◌ Ashton Press. ☗ 10 **Facilities** Non-diners area ♦ Children's menu Children's portions Garden Parking Wi-fi ☷ **Rooms** 3

SALISBURY
Map 5 SU12

The Cloisters

83 Catherine St SP1 2DH ☎ 01722 338102
e-mail: thecloisters83@gmail.com
dir: *In city centre, near cathedral*

A reputation for good honest food

Near the cathedral, the appropriately named Cloisters is a mid 18th-century pub. Its Victorian windows look into a beamed interior warmed by a pair of open fires. The choice of ales includes Hop Back Summer Lightning and a weekly changing guest ale. Thanks to a well-qualified chef, the menu will please everyone with its popular pub plates, from traditional fish and chips to ratatouille bake and the popular Cloisters beefburger, and the more modern dishes of penne pasta with chicken and pesto, and sea bass with mint, white wine and garlic. Booking is advised for the Sunday carvery.

Open all day all wk 11-10 (Thu-Sat 11am-mdnt Sun 12-10) **Bar Meals** L served Mon-Fri 11-3, Sat 11-9, Sun 12-9 D served Mon-Fri 6-9, Sat 11-9, Sun 12-9 Av main course £10 **Restaurant** L served Mon-Fri 11-3, Sat 11-9, Sun 12-9 D served Mon-Fri 6-9, Sat 11-9, Sun 12-9 ⊕ ENTERPRISE INNS ◀ Sharp's Doom Bar, Hop Back Summer Lightning, Guest ales. ♀ **Facilities** Non-diners area ♦♦ Children's menu Children's portions ☞ (notice required)

Old Mill ★★★ INN

Town Path SP2 8EU ☎ 01722 327517
e-mail: theoldmill@simonandsteve.com
dir: *From A338 onto A3094, take 3rd right*

Old world charm beside the River Nadder and water meadows

Just ten minutes from Salisbury Cathedral, this pub is split between two buildings: the flagstone bar, originally a Georgian yarn factory, and the restaurant, which is in a 15th-century former paper mill, England's first. You can see the mill races through a glass panel. Menus typically offer mixed game suet pudding, chargrilled rump steak, fish specials, and linguine pomodoro. The large beer garden straddles the River Nadder just before it joins the Avon. En suite guest rooms with original beams look across the water meadows.

Open all day all wk ⊕ GREENE KING ◀ IPA & Abbot Ale, Morland Old Speckled Hen ◔ Aspall. **Facilities** ❖ (Bar Garden) ♦♦ Children's menu Children's portions Garden Parking Wi-fi **Rooms** 11

The Wig and Quill

1 New St SP1 2PH ☎ 01722 335665
e-mail: enquiries@wigandquill.co.uk
dir: *On approach to Salisbury follow brown Old George Mall Car Park signs. Pub opposite car park*

Charming old pub close to the cathedral

New Street is very close to the cathedral, whose superlative spire soars skywards just behind this traditional city pub. In the roomy, beamed bar with its open fires, flagstone and wooden floored, enjoy a pint of 6X or a guest cider. From the menu choose between trio of local sausages and mash; warm chicken and bacon salad; and scampi and chips. Try apple pie or hot chocolate fudge cake for dessert. Lying behind the pub is a sheltered courtyard garden for the summer months.

Open all wk 10am-close **Bar Meals** L served all wk 12-3.30 D served all wk 6.30-8.45 **Restaurant** L served all wk 12-3.30 D served all wk 6.30-8.45 ⊕ WADWORTH ◀ 6X, The Bishop's Tipple, Henry's Original IPA & Horizon, Guest ales ◔ Westons Stowford Press, Guest ciders. ♀ 14 **Facilities** Non-diners area ♦♦ Children's menu Children's portions Garden ☞

SEEND
Map 4 ST96

Bell Inn

Bell Hill SN12 6SA ☎ 01380 828338
dir: *On A361 between Devizes & Semington*

Historic village pub serving a wide range of food

Under new management since September 2012, this lovely red-brick pub in the pretty village of Seend has panoramic views of Salisbury plain and the Westbury Valley. The restaurant offers pub classics alongside an à la carte that could include slow-cooked sticky belly pork with stir-fried vegetables; local venison sausages and mash; or roasted butternut and sweet potato curry. Oliver Cromwell and his troops reputedly enjoyed breakfast at this inn in 1645 before attacking nearby Devizes Castle. Its other claim to fame is that John Wesley opened the chapel next door and preached against the 'evils' of drink outside the pub.

Open all wk 12-2.30 5.30-11.30 **Bar Meals** L served all wk 12-2 D served all wk 5.30-9 Av main course £9.50 **Restaurant** L served all wk 12-2 D served all wk 5.30-9 Fixed menu price fr £11.50 ⊕ WADWORTH ◀ 6X, Henry's Original IPA, The Bishop's Tipple ◔ Westons Stowford Press. **Facilities** Non-diners area ❖ (Bar Garden) ♦♦ Children's menu Children's portions Play area Garden Parking Wi-fi ☞

SEMINGTON
Map 4 ST86

The Lamb on the Strand

99 The Strand BA14 6LL ☎ 01380 870263
e-mail: info@thelambonthestrand.co.uk
dir: *1.5m E on A361 from junct with A350*

Craft brews and interesting tapas

This popular dining pub began life as a farmhouse in the 18th-century, later developing into a beer and cider

house. Today, customers can choose a real ale from the Wiltshire craft brewery Box Steam, or a cider from Westons. Food is freshly prepared from locally sourced ingredients, with an appetising choice of hot dishes, salads and doorstep sandwiches at lunchtime. The Wiltshire tapas menu offers an interesting mix of British and global treats: chilli pickled onions with Wiltshire cheddar; Moroccan-spiced onion rings; and chorizo in red wine, brandy and parsley. The Lamb's own slow-cooked sticky ribs in a sweet, piquant sauce is typical of the modern British fare on the evening carte. Contact the pub for details of the beer festival.

Open all wk 12-3 6-11 **Bar Meals** L served all wk 12-3 D served all wk 6-9.30 Av main course £9.95 **Restaurant** L served all wk 12-3 D served all wk 6-9.30 Fixed menu price fr £9.95 ⊕ FREE HOUSE ◀ Box Steam, Guinness ◔ Bath Ciders Bounders, Westons Stowford Press. ♀ 15 **Facilities** Non-diners area ❖ (Bar Restaurant Garden) ♦♦ Children's menu Children's portions Play area Family room Garden ☎ Beer festival Parking Wi-fi ☞ (notice required)

SHERSTON
Map 4 ST88

The Rattlebone Inn

Church St SN16 0LR ☎ 01666 840871
e-mail: eat@therattlebone.co.uk
dir: *M4 junct 17, A429 to Malmesbury. 2m after passing petrol station at Stanton St Quentin, turn left signed Sherston*

Lots of events and country bistro dining

Named after the legendary Saxon warrior John Rattlebone, who is said to haunt this 16th-century Cotswolds pub, The Rattlebone boasts roaring winter fires and bags of character. A lively drinkers' pub, it offers real ales, organic cider and many wines by the glass. Its menus use local ingredients where possible and are best described as 'country bistro'. They proffer such delights as chargrilled marinated lamb steak served with couscous and chilli oil. Outside are three boules pistes, two gardens where summer barbecues are held, and a beautiful skittle alley. It's also the home of Mangold Hurling, a slightly insane West Country sport. There's live music every month and a cider festival in July.

Open all wk 12-3 5-11 (Fri 12-3 5-12 Sat 12-12 Sun 12-11) **Bar Meals** L served Mon-Sat 12-2.30, Sun 12-3 D served Mon-Sat 6-9.30 Av main course £10 **Restaurant** L served Mon-Sat 12-2.30, Sun 12-3 D served Mon-Sat 6-9.30 Fixed menu price fr £14 Av 3 course à la carte fr £20 ⊕ YOUNG'S ◀ Bitter, Wells Bombardier, St Austell Tribute ◔ Westons Stowford Press & Wyld Wood Organic, Thatchers Gold. ♀ 14 **Facilities** Non-diners area ❖ (Bar Garden) ♦♦ Children's portions Garden ☎ Cider festival Wi-fi ☞ (notice required)

Save on hotels. Book at theAA.com/hotel

WILTSHIRE 485 ENGLAND

STOURTON
Map 4 ST73

Spread Eagle Inn ★★★★ INN
PICK OF THE PUBS

BA12 6QE ☎ **01747 840587**
e-mail: enquiries@spreadeagleinn.com
dir: N of A303 off B3092

In the beautiful setting of the Stourhead Estate

This charming 19th-century inn is in an enviable position right at the heart of the 2,650-acre Stourhead Estate, one of the country's most loved National Trust properties. Before or after a walk through the magnificent gardens and landscapes, there is plenty on offer here, including real ales brewed in a nearby village and traditional countryside cooking using produce from local specialists in and around north Dorset, west Wiltshire and south Somerset. Even the simple ploughman's is prepared with local bread with a Dorset Blue cheese or Keene's mature cheddar served with home-made chutney. In the restaurant, expect oven-baked Cornish sea bass fillets with parmesan mash; free-range tarragon-stuffed chicken suprême with parmentier potatoes; and chef's crème brûlée to finish. The interior is smartly traditional, and in the bedrooms, antiques sit side by side with modern comforts.

Open all day all wk 9.30am-11pm **Bar Meals** L served all wk 12-3 D served all wk 7-9 **Restaurant** L served all wk 12-3 D served all wk 7-9 ⊕ FREE HOUSE ◀ Wessex Kilmington Best, Butcombe, Guest ales Ö Ashton Press. ♟ 8 **Facilities** ♦♦ Outside area ⊼ Parking ▭ **Rooms** 5

SWINDON
Map 5 SU18

The Weighbridge Brewhouse NEW

Penzance Dr SN5 7JL ☎ **01793 881500**
e-mail: info@weighbridgebrewhouse.co.uk
dir: M4 junct 16, follow Swindon Centre signs, then Outlet Car Park West signs

Striking pub and brewery in former railway building

Built in 1906, the former Great Western Railway Weighhouse was transformed by experienced operator Anthony Windle into a stunning new pub-restaurant concept, replete with microbrewery. Many original features have been retained and the old railway building boasts brick walls and lofty ceilings, with a vast bar at one end, dispensing the six home-brewed ales and 47 wines by the glass, and an airy, smart and very comfortable dining room at the other. Extensive monthly menus may deliver rack of lamb with red wine and cream sauce; beef, Stilton and ale pie; whole Dover sole; and interesting vegetarian options. Portions are very generous, so don't expect starters but, if you have room, there's chocolate fondant pudding to finish.

Open all day all wk Closed: 25-26 Dec **Bar Meals** Av main course £17 **Restaurant** L served Mon-Sat 12-2, Sun 12-8 D served Mon-Sat 6-9.30, Sun 12-8 Fixed menu price fr £12 Av 3 course à la carte fr £30 ⊕ FREE HOUSE ◀ Brinkworth Village, Weighbridge Best, Antsally's,

Pooley's Golden. ♟ 47 **Facilities** Non-diners area ♦♦ Children's menu Children's portions Outside area ⊼ Parking Wi-fi

TOLLARD ROYAL
Map 4 ST91

King John Inn
PICK OF THE PUBS

SP5 5PS ☎ **01725 516207**
e-mail: info@kingjohninn.co.uk
dir: On B3081 (7m E of Shaftesbury)

Stylish country pub with plenty of local produce

Rescued and revamped with style and flair by Alex and Gretchen Boon, this attractive Victorian pub stands in idyllic Tollard Royal, deep in unspoilt downland on the Wiltshire/Dorset border. Its airy, open-plan bar and dining areas are stylishly uncluttered and have an upmarket feel, featuring rugs on terracotta tiles, old pine tables, snug alcoves, warming winter log fires, and a solid oak bar. Peruse the daily papers, sup a pint of Wadworth 6X or delve in Alex's impressive list of wines by the glass, then tuck into some hearty, modern British food from the delicious daily menu that brims with local produce. Perhaps start with pig's head hash with fried egg and parsley sauce before moving on to turbot fillet with saffron linguine, mussels, bacon and smoked eel, then finish with pear frangipane tart. There's a super summer terrace for alfresco meals and a wine shop across the car park.

Open all wk 12-3 6-11 **Bar Meals** L served Mon-Fri 12-2.30, Sat-Sun 12-3 D served all wk 7-9.30 Av main course £16.95 **Restaurant** L served Mon-Fri 12-2.30, Sat-Sun 12-3 D served all wk 7-9.30 ⊕ FREE HOUSE ◀ Butcombe Bitter, Wadworth 6X, Guest ales Ö Ashton Press. ♟ 16 **Facilities** Non-diners area ✿ (Bar Restaurant Garden) Children's portions Garden ⊼ Parking Wi-fi

UPPER WOODFORD
Map 5 SU13

The Bridge Inn

SP4 6NU ☎ **01722 782323**
e-mail: enquiries@thebridgewoodford.co.uk
web: www.thebridgewoodford.co.uk
dir: From Salisbury take A360. Turn right for Middle Woodford & Upper Woodford. (Village between A360 & A345 5m N of Salisbury)

Quiet riverside pub with large garden and modern British menus

On a quiet lane running along the west side of the broad Wiltshire Avon, this charming pub has a large, grassy garden running down to the wide sweep of the river. Seasonal starter choices might include crab toasties with smoked chilli jam; or smoked salmon, cream cheese and chive pâté. Appearing among the half-dozen winter menu mains could be butternut squash and spinach risotto with gremolata; fish pie with cheesy mash; home-made fishcakes with herbed fries; and 28-day-aged Stokes Marsh farm rib-eye steak with chips, mushrooms and sautéed mange-tout. Diners can now watch the kitchen in action through the new Theatre Kitchen window.

Open all wk 11-3 6-11 **Bar Meals** L served all wk 12-2.30 D served all wk 6-9 Av main course £12 **Restaurant** L served all wk 12-2.30 D served all wk 6-9 Av 3 course à la carte fr £25 ⊕ ENTERPRISE INNS ◀ Hop Back Summer Lightning, Wadworth 6X, Ringwood Best Bitter Ö Thatchers Gold. ♟ 10 **Facilities** Non-diners area ✿ (Bar Garden) ♦♦ Children's menu Children's portions Garden ⊼ Parking Wi-fi ▭ (notice required)

UPTON LOVELL
Map 4 ST94

Prince Leopold Inn

BA12 0JP ☎ **01985 850460**
e-mail: princeleopold@live.co.uk
dir: From Warminster take A36 towards Salisbury 4.5m, left to Upton Lovell

Idyllic stream-side setting

Tucked away at the fringe of Salisbury Plain and named after Queen Victoria's youngest son, whose country retreat was nearby, this bustling village inn luxuriates in its enviable position beside the Wylye trout-stream and tree-dappled water meadows. Those in the know sup on local microbrewery beers in the peaceful waterside garden, or perhaps repair to the traditional, part-panelled interior, period snug or airy contemporary lounge, where a well-balanced menu of pub favourites may include pork

continued

UPTON LOVELL *continued*

and mushroom pie, slow roast belly pork with cider sauce or wild mushroom and spinach lasagne. The restaurant room has relaxing views over the river.

Open all wk 12-3 6-11 (Sat-Sun 12-11) Closed: 25 Dec **Bar Meals** L served Mon-Thu 12-2.30, Fri-Sat 12-3, Sun 12-4 D served Mon-Sat 6.30-9 Av main course £9 **Restaurant** L served Mon-Thu 12-2.30, Fri-Sat 12-3, Sun 12-4 D served Mon-Sat 6.30-9 Av 3 course à la carte fr £23 ⊕ FREE HOUSE ◀ Wadworth 6X, Butcombe, Plain Ales. ♥ **Facilities** Non-diners area ✿ (Bar Garden) ✦♦ Children's menu Children's portions Garden Parking Wi-fi ⊞ (notice required)

WARMINSTER　　　　　Map 4 ST84

The Angel Inn

PICK OF THE PUBS

Upton Scudamore BA12 0AG ☎ 01985 213225
e-mail: mail@theangelinn.co.uk
dir: *From Warminster take A350 towards Westbury or A36 towards Bath*

Modern British cooking down Wiltshire lanes

Entry to this 16th-century coaching inn is through a walled garden and terrace; here you may eat and drink, although the open fires and natural wood flooring of the interior might tempt you to stay inside. A free house, it serves Wadworth 6X, Butcombe and guest ales, and 10 wines by the glass. Lunchtime choices and specials include home-roasted gammon with fried eggs, minted peas and chips; and beer-battered fillet of pollock with hand-cut chips, crushed peas and tartare sauce. The modern British style of cooking continues at dinner with pan-seared breast of wood pigeon with glazed figs, black pudding purée and baby beetroot salad, followed perhaps by pan-roasted fillet of brill with pease pudding, bubble-and-squeak, and pea, clam and herb sauce. Longleat Safari & Adventure Park is five miles away, and Bath and Salisbury are also easily reached, although in opposite directions.

Open all wk 11-3 6-11 **Bar Meals** L served all wk 12-2 D served all wk 6-9 Av main course £12 **Restaurant** L served all wk 12-3 D served all wk 6-9.30 Fixed menu price fr £10 Av 3 course à la carte fr £25 ⊕ FREE HOUSE ◀ Wadworth 6X, Butcombe, John Smith's Extra Smooth, Guest ales. ♥ 10 **Facilities** Non-diners area ✦♦ Children's menu Children's portions Garden ⏚ Parking Wi-fi

The Bath Arms

Clay St, Crockerton BA12 8AJ ☎ 01985 212262
e-mail: batharms@aol.com
dir: *From Warminster on A36 take A350 towards Shaftesbury then left to Crockerton, follow signs for Shearwater*

Family- and dog-friendly pub on the Longleat Estate

Set on the Longleat Estate close to the Shearwater Lake, this whitewashed country pub attracts locals, walkers

and tourists. The garden has been landscaped to provide a pleasant spot for outdoor drinking and dining, and the Garden Suite, with views across the lawn, provides additional seating on busy weekends. Expect stylish food such as sticky beef with braised red cabbage; grilled salmon with fennel and rocket salad; and chicken breast with parsnip mash, beans and lentils. Baguettes are also available.

Open all day all wk 11-3 6-11 (Sat-Sun 11-11) ⊕ FREE HOUSE ◀ Wessex Crockerton Classic & Potters Ale, Guest ales. **Facilities** ✿ (Bar Garden) ✦♦ Children's portions Play area Garden Parking Wi-fi

The George Inn

Longbridge Deverell BA12 7DG ☎ 01985 840396
e-mail: info@the-georgeinn.co.uk
dir: *Telephone for directions*

A very popular spot on fine days

A 17th-century coaching inn overlooking the grassy banks of the River Wylye, The George is a very popular spot on fine days. Food served in the traditional, oak-beamed Smithy Bar and in the two restaurants reflects the seasons, so beef stew and dumplings, for example, is a typical winter dish. Other possibilities include chicken Madras and pan-seared salmon; there's also a dedicated steak menu and Sunday carvery. One of the real ales – Deverill's Advocate – is brewed in the village and is always in demand at the pub's August beer festival.

Open all day all wk 11-11 (Sun 12-10.30) Closed: 25 Dec fr 3, 26 Dec (1 Jan open 11-3) **Bar Meals** L served Mon-Thu 12-2.30, Fri-Sat 12-9.30, Sun 12-9 D served Mon-Thu 6-9.30, Fri-Sat 12-9.30, Sun 12-9 **Restaurant** L served Mon-Thu 12-2.30, Fri-Sat 12-9.30, Sun 12-9 D served Mon-Thu 6-9.30, Fri-Sat 12-9.30, Sun 12-9 ◀ Wadworth 6X, Wessex Deverill's Advocate, John Smith's Ò Thatchers Cheddar Valley. ♥ 11 **Facilities** ✿ (Bar Garden) ✦♦ Children's menu Children's portions Play area Garden ⏚ Beer festival Parking Wi-fi ⊞ (notice required)

WHITLEY　　　　　Map 4 ST86

Marco Pierre White The Pear Tree Inn ★★★★ INN

PICK OF THE PUBS

Top Ln SN12 8QX ☎ 01225 709131
e-mail: info@wheelerspeartree.com
dir: *A365 from Melksham towards Bath, at Shaw right onto B3353 to Whitley, 1st left*

Delightful country pub with chic interior

This wisteria-clad stone pub epitomises the best of modern interior design, from the beautifully crafted furniture to the positioning of the stone ginger beer jars. Even so, farmhouse character remains, from the flagstone floors to the grand open fires and eclectic collection of agricultural artefacts. Like other inns belonging to Mr White, it offers a carefully selected worldwide wine list and The Governor ale, named after the celebrity chef's family greyhound. Dine in the bar, restaurant or peaceful gardens on British and European dishes chosen from a

menu that differentiates itself by offering not starters, but hors d'oeuvres, such as Maxim's quail eggs; petit chou farci à l'ancienne (stuffed cabbage); and Wheeler's (of St James's) pea and ham soup. The quality continues with wing of skate with winkles and jus à la Parisienne; Mr Lamb's shepherd's pie; and caramelised honey-roast pork belly with Marco Polo glaze. Accommodation is available.

Open all day all wk bkfst-11pm **Bar Meals** L served Mon-Sat 12-2.30, Sun all day D served Mon-Sat 6-9.30, Sun all day **Restaurant** L served Mon-Sat 12-2.30, Sun all day D served Mon-Sat 6-9.30, Sun all day ◀ JW Lees The Governor, Wadworth 6X, Ò Thatchers Gold, Governor. ♥ **Facilities** Non-diners area ✦♦ Children's menu Garden Parking Wi-fi **Rooms** 6

WOOTTON RIVERS　　　　　Map 5 SU16

Royal Oak

PICK OF THE PUBS

SN8 4NQ ☎ 01672 810322
e-mail: royaloak35@hotmail.com
dir: *3m S from Marlborough*

Pretty thatched pub, a favourite with walkers

This much expanded 16th-century thatched and timbered pub is perfectly situated for Stonehenge, Bath and Winchester and for exploring the ancient oaks of Savernake Forest. Only 100 yards from the Kennet & Avon Canal and the Mid-Wilts Way, it has an interior as charming as the setting, with low, oak-beamed ceilings, exposed brickwork and wide open fireplaces. In the bar you'll find Wadworth 6X and guest ales, including local Ramsbury Bitter. The menus cover all manner of pubby favourites, including cottage pie with vegetables; local game pie with claret and juniper; surf 'n' turf; and a cheeseburger with home-made relish, salad and chips. Other options include a starter of pigeon terrine with fig compôte, followed perhaps by lamb cutlets with leek fondue. There's also a decent selection of international favourites ranging from pork goulash to Thai chicken curry with rice. To finish, maybe sherry trifle or apple crumble with fresh cream.

Open all wk 10-3 6-11 (Sat-Sun all day) **Bar Meals** L served Mon-Sat 12-2.30, Sun 12-8.30 D served Mon-Sat 6-9.30, Sun 12-8.30 **Restaurant** L served Mon-Sat 12-2.30, Sun 12-8.30 D served Mon-Sat 6-9.30, Sun 12-8.30 ⊕ FREE HOUSE ◀ Wadworth 6X, Local Guest ales Ò Westons Stowford Press. ♥ 9 **Facilities** Non-diners area ✿ (Bar Outside area) ✦♦ Children's menu Children's portions Family room Outside area ⏚ Parking Wi-fi ⊞ (notice required)

Save on hotels. Book at theAA.com/hotel

WORCESTERSHIRE 487 ENGLAND

WORCESTERSHIRE

BECKFORD
Map 10 SO93

The Beckford ★★★★ INN

Cheltenham Rd GL20 7AN ☎ 01386 881532
e-mail: enquiries@thebeckford.com
dir: *M5 junct 9, A46 towards Evesham, 5m to Beckford*

Cotswold country inn just off the A46

Midway between Tewkesbury and Evesham, this rambling Georgian country inn has the Cotswolds beckoning just to the east and shapely Bredon Hill rising immediately to the north. The Beckford is an enticing mix of contemporary comforts and traditional fixtures throughout the public areas and the comfortable bedrooms. A typical meal might include pan-seared scallops with spicy chorizo on a bed of leaves with a sweet balsamic reduction; chargrilled duck breast with home-made tipsy Oxford marmalade sauce laced with whisky and served with new potatoes; and creamy chocolate pannacotta with fruits of the forest compôte.

Open all day all wk ⊕ FREE HOUSE ◀ Fuller's London Pride, Courage Best Bitter, Wye Valley, Wickwar, Prescott Ŏ Westons Stowford Press. **Facilities** ❁ (Bar Garden) ♦¦ Children's menu Children's portions Garden Parking Wi-fi **Rooms** 13

BEWDLEY
Map 10 SO77

Little Pack Horse

31 High St DY12 2DH ☎ 01299 403762
e-mail: enquiries@littlepackhorse.co.uk
dir: *From Kidderminster follow ring road & Safari Park signs. Then follow Bewdley signs over bridge, turn left, then right, right at top of Lax Ln. Pub in 20mtrs*

Period inn offering local produce and pies

Officially dated back to 1532, making it the second oldest pub in Bewdley, the timber-framed inn was a carrier's pub and clearing house for goods in transit. Inside retains a period feel, thanks to low beams and roaring log fires. Hobsons Town Crier and Bewdley Worcestershire Way are popular local ales and the menu relies on local produce too - Wyre Forest charcuterie platter, and goats' cheese, artichoke and Worcestershire pear filo parcel being just two choices. They take their pies and savoury puddings seriously here – there's a wide selection including a traditional beer, Guinness and oyster suet pudding, and chicken, leek and bacon pie.

Open all wk 12-2.30 6-11.30 (Sat-Sun 12-12) **Bar Meals** L served Mon-Fri 12-2.15, Sat-Sun 12-4 D served Mon-Thu 6-9, Fri 6-9.30, Sat-Sun 5.30-9.30 Av main course £12 **Restaurant** L served Mon-Fri 12-2.15, Sat-Sun 12-4 D served Mon-Thu 6-9, Fri 6-9.30, Sat-Sun 5.30-9.30 Av 3 course à la carte fr £23 ⊕ PUNCH TAVERNS ◀ St Austell Tribute, Bewdley Worcestershire Way, Hobsons Town Crier Ŏ Thatchers Katy, Westons Stowford Press. ♚ 10 **Facilities** Non-diners area ❁ (Bar Garden Outside area) ♦¦ Children's menu Children's portions Family room Garden Outside area ⊼ Wi-fi ▭ (notice required)

The Mug House Inn & Angry Chef Restaurant ★★★★ INN ◎

PICK OF THE PUBS

12 Severnside North DY12 2EE ☎ 01299 402543
e-mail: drew@mughousebewdley.co.uk
dir: *A456 from Kidderminster to Bewdley. Pub in town on river*

Unrivalled riverside location

Although unusual as a pub name today, in the 17th century a 'mug house' was a popular term for an alehouse; one can see why. The Severnside address is a strong clue as to its location – right on that river, with just a narrow, cobbled road and some river's edge seating between it and the pub's flower-decked frontage. Bewdley Brewery's Worcestershire Sway may be on duty at the bar alongside regulars Timothy Taylor Landlord, Wye Valley HPA and Westons Traditional scrumpy. Food follows pub-classic lines: crusty cobs and chunky 'sarnies', jacket potatoes and Mug House platters at lunchtime, while AA Rosette-standard, 'Angry Chef (cause unknown!) Favourites' on the short restaurant carte might include house speciality of whole lobster halved and grilled; and chargrilled 10oz rib-eye steak. Accommodation is comfortable and thoughtfully furnished. A beer festival is held in the rear garden every May Day Bank Holiday.

Open all day all wk 12-11 **Bar Meals** L served Mon-Sat 12-2.30, Sun 12-5 **Restaurant** L served Mon-Sat 12.2.30, Sun 12-5 D served Mon-Sat 6.30-9 ⊕ PUNCH TAVERNS ◀ Bewdley Worcestershire Sway,Timothy Taylor Landlord, Wye Valley HPA, Guest ales Ŏ Westons Traditional. ♚ 10 **Facilities** Non-diners area ❁ (Bar Garden) Garden ⊼ Beer festival Wi-fi **Rooms** 7

Woodcolliers Arms ★★★ INN

76 Welch Gate DY12 2AU ☎ 01299 400589
e-mail: roger@woodcolliers.co.uk
dir: *3m from Kidderminster on A456*

17th-century free house with a Russian flavour

If you've never tried atbivnaya, you can at this 17th-century, family-run free house built on a hillside just across the river from the Severn Valley steam railway. Battered pork steak, it's one of the several dishes Russian chef Boris Rumba serves alongside largely locally sourced more traditional pub favourites, such as beef, chicken or mushroom Stroganoff (actually, this too is Russian in origin), sea bass fillet or steak. There's always a weekly-changing roll-call of local real ales on offer, and Herefordshire ciders. Comfortable accommodation includes the Secret Room, once blocked off and 'lost' for years.

Open all wk 5pm-12.30am (Sat 12.30-12.30 Sun 12.30-11) **Bar Meals** L served Sat-Sun 12.30-3 D served all wk 6-9 Av main course £8 **Restaurant** L served Sat-Sun 12.30-3 D served all wk 6-9 Av 3 course à la carte fr £20 ⊕ FREE HOUSE/OLIVERS INNS LTD ◀ Ludlow Gold, Three Tuns 1642, Kinver Edge Ŏ Thatchers Gold, Westons Old Rosie, Westons Country Perry. ♚ 14 **Facilities** Non-diners area ❁ (Bar) ♦¦ Outside area ⊼ Parking Wi-fi ▭ (notice required) **Rooms** 5

BRANSFORD
Map 10 SO75

The Bear & Ragged Staff

Station Rd WR6 5JH ☎ 01886 833399
e-mail: mail@bear.uk.com
dir: *3m from Worcester or Malvern, clearly signed from A4103 or A449*

Continuing to build a good reputation for good food

Easily reachable from both Malvern and Worcester, Gary Whitby and Lynda Williams' lovely old free house was built in 1861 as an estate rent office and stables. They bought it in 1997 and have fully renovated and extended it, while creating its reputation for good food and beers, such as Hobsons Twisted Spire (named after Cleobury Mortimer's parish church) and Sharp's Doom Bar. A typical meal might involve white crabmeat and crayfish tails, followed by braised brisket of Herefordshire beef. Blackboard specials include roast fillet of red bream. In addition to the bar and restaurant menus, there are weekend barbecues.

Open 11.30-2 6-11 Closed: 25 Dec eve, 1 Jan eve, Sun eve **Bar Meals** L served all wk 12-2 D served Mon-Sat 6.30-9 Av main course £12.50 **Restaurant** L served all wk 12-2 D served Mon-Sat 6.30-9.30 Av 3 course à la carte fr £25 ⊕ FREE HOUSE ◀ Hobsons Twisted Spire, Sharp's Doom Bar Ŏ Westons Stowford Press. ♚ 10 **Facilities** Non-diners area ❁ (Bar Garden) ♦¦ Children's menu Children's portions Garden ⊼ Parking Wi-fi ▭ (notice required)

BRETFORTON   Map 10 SP04

The Fleece Inn

PICK OF THE PUBS

The Cross WR11 7JE ☎ 01386 831173
e-mail: nigel@thefleeceinn.co.uk
web: www.thefleeceinn.co.uk
dir: From Evesham follow signs for B4035 towards Chipping Campden. Through Badsey into Bretforton. Right at village hall, past church, pub in open parking area

Ancient village inn with traditional menus

The first pub to be owned by The National Trust, The Fleece Inn was built as a longhouse in Chaucer's time and was owned by the same family until the death in 1977 of Lola Taplin – a direct descendent of the farmer who built it. A quintessential English pub, the beautiful timbered building was nearly lost in a tragic fire in 2004; a massive renovation followed, when its features and integrity were restored. Real ale devotees will admire one of England's oldest pewter collections as they order a pint of Uley Pigs Ear or Wye Valley Bitter; and cider lovers can try the home-brewed Ark cider. Families will enjoy the summer sunshine in the apple orchard while children use the play area. Typical dishes on the menu are lamb, pea and mint hotpot; chicken curry; and home-cooked ham, egg and chips. An ale and cider festival is held in October.

Open all wk 11-11 (Sep-May Mon-Tue 11-3 6-11 Wed-Sun 11-11) **Bar Meals** L served Mon-Sat 12-2.30, Sun 12-4 D served Mon-Sat 6.30-9, Sun 6.30-8.30 Av main course £8.95 ⊕ FREE HOUSE ◀ Uley Pigs Ear, Wye Valley Bitter ○ Thatchers Heritage, The Ark. ♀ 12 **Facilities** Non-diners area ◑ Children's menu Children's portions Play area Garden ⊼ Beer festival Cider festival Wi-fi ▭ (notice required)

BROADWAY   Map 10 SP03

Crown & Trumpet

Church St WR12 7AE ☎ 01386 853202
e-mail: info@cotswoldholidays.co.uk
dir: From High St follow Snowshill sign. Pub 600yds on left

Ideally placed for exploring the Cotswolds

Just behind the green in this internationally-known picture-postcard village is the Crown & Trumpet, a traditional, 17th-century, mellow-stone inn. The classic beamed bar is just the place for a pint of Cotswold Spring

Codrington Codger, or Stanway Cotteswold Gold bitter, or you can take it out into the peaceful patio garden; a winter alternative is a glass of mulled wine or a hot toddy by the fire. Classic pub food at lunch and dinner includes battered haddock; chilli con carne; pan-fried breast of chicken and chorizo; and vegetable lasagne. There's musical entertainment every Saturday evening, and monthly jazz and blues evenings. Booking for meals is recommended.

Open all wk 11-3 5-11 (Fri-Sat 11am-mdnt Sun 12-11) **Bar Meals** L served Mon-Fri 12-2.30, Sat-Sun 12-5 D served Mon-Fri 6-9.30, Sat-Sun 5-9.30 **Restaurant** L served Mon-Fri 12-2.30, Sat-Sun 12-5 D served Mon-Fri 6-9.30, Sat-Sun 5-9.30 ⊕ ENTERPRISE INNS ◀ Stroud Tom Long, Cotswold Spring Codrington Codger, Stanway Cotteswold Gold ○ Gwatkin. ♀ 9 **Facilities** Non-diners area ◑ (Bar Restaurant Garden) ◑ Children's menu Children's portions Garden ⊼ Beer festival Parking Wi-fi ▭ (notice required)

CLENT   Map 10 SO97

The Bell & Cross

PICK OF THE PUBS

Holy Cross DY9 9QL ☎ 01562 730319
dir: Telephone for directions

Good food near famous country park

Standing at the heart of a peaceful Worcestershire village, this character pub is the ideal culmination of a visit to the remarkable Clent Hills which rumble across the horizon just a mile from the Bell & Cross. Exploring the bald hills, wooded dingles and fabulous viewpoints can work up a healthy appetite; who better to help sate this than the former chef to the England football squad, host-patron Roger Narbett. (see also next entry) Head for the bar for a rolling selection of hand-pulled beers and an inviting log fire in winter; the extensive garden, or the covered and heated patio for comfortable alfresco dining on cooler nights. The imaginative menu opens with a substantial range of starters and lite-bites such as Loch Fyne oak-smoked salmon with vodka chantilly, or farmhouse confit duck rillette with pineapple and cracked black pepper salsa. Enticing mains include slow cooked free-range belly pork with smashed apples, spring cabbage and cider sauce; or tandoori spiced salmon fillet, cucumber salad and lime mayo. Booking is recommended.

Open all wk 12-3 6-11 (Sun 12-10.30) Closed: 25 Dec, 26 Dec eve, 1 Jan eve **Bar Meals** L served all wk 12-2 D served Mon-Sat 6.30-9.15 **Restaurant** L served Mon-Sat 12-2, Sun 12-7 D served Mon-Sat 6.30-9.15, Sun 12-7 ⊕ ENTERPRISE INNS ◀ Marston's Pedigree & Burton Bitter, Timothy Taylor Landlord, Guest ales. ♀ 15 **Facilities** Non-diners area ◑ (Bar Garden) ◑ Children's menu Children's portions Garden ⊼ Parking ▭ (notice required)

DROITWICH   Map 10 SO86

The Chequers

PICK OF THE PUBS

Kidderminster Rd, Cutnall Green WR9 0PJ ☎ 01299 851292
dir: Telephone for directions

Charming pub run by ex-England soccer chef

Roger Narbett used to be the England football team chef; his soccer memorabilia can be found in the Players Lounge of this charming pub he now runs with wife Joanne (see also previous entry). Its traditional look comes from the cranberry-coloured walls, open fire, church-panel bar and richly hued furnishings. Indeed, some might also make a case for including the range of real ales, such as Enville, Wye Valley HPA and Hook Norton in the bar, adjoining which is the country-style Garden Room with plush sofa and hanging tankards. The menus offer a wide choice, from sandwiches, deli platters and 'bucket food' to pub classics like faggots, mushy peas and cheesy mash. Among the top performers are grilled fillet of sea bream; Merlot-braised blade of Scottish beef; Malaysian chicken curry with sweet potato; and roasted pepper filled with parmesan risotto and Tuscan vegetables. How sorry England's finest must have been to see Roger go.

Open all day all wk Closed: 25 Dec, 26 Dec eve & 1 Jan eve **Bar Meals** L served Mon-Sat 12-2, Sun 12-2.30 D served all wk 6.30-9.15 **Restaurant** L served Mon-Sat 12-2, Sun 12-2.30 D served all wk 6.30-9.15 ⊕ FREE HOUSE ◀ Enville Ale, Greene King Ruddles, Wye Valley HPA, Timothy Taylor, Hook Norton, Otter Bitter. ♀ 15 **Facilities** Non-diners area ◑ (Bar Garden) ◑ Children's menu Children's portions Family room Garden ⊼ Parking Wi-fi ▭ (notice required)

The Honey Bee

Doverdale Ln, Doverdale WR9 0QB ☎ 01299 851620
e-mail: honey@king-henrys-taverns.co.uk
dir: From Droitwich take A442 towards Kidderminster. Left to Dovedale

Spacious, modern and friendly pub

Set in four and half acres of grounds, you can go fishing for carp in this pub's two lakes – and even have your meal brought to you. The garden also has a great play area for children and there is a patio for outdoor drinking and dining. The contemporary interior has plenty of areas in which to enjoy freshly prepared dishes which will satisfy small and large appetites alike. Choose from a good selection of steaks and grills, fish and seafood options like swordfish steak, traditional favourites such as half a roast chicken, and international and vegetarian dishes, perhaps vegetable fajitas.

Open all day all wk 11.30-11 **Bar Meals** L served all wk 12-10 D served all wk 12-10 food served all day **Restaurant** L served all wk 12-10 D served all wk 12-10 food served all day ⊕ FREE HOUSE/KING HENRY'S TAVERNS ◀ Greene King IPA, Marston's Pedigree, Guinness. ♀ 15 **Facilities** Non-diners area ◑ Children's menu Children's portions Play area Garden Parking ▭

PICK OF THE PUBS

The Boot Inn ★★★★ INN

FLYFORD FLAVELL | Map 10 SO95

Radford Rd WR7 4BS ☎ 01386 462658
e-mail: enquiries@thebootinn.com
web: www.thebootinn.com
dir: *A422 from Worcester towards Stratford. Turn right to village*

Friendly, family-run old coaching inn

Parts of this family-run, award-winning, traditional coaching inn can be traced back to the 13th century, and for evidence you need only to look at the heavy beams and slanting doorways. Keep an eye out too for the friendly ghost, age uncertain. The large bar area is comfortable, the pool table and TV having been banished to a separate room, while regulars like London Pride and Black Sheep, and an extensive wine list complement the varied and imaginative menus which change every six weeks. You can eat from the lunchtime sandwich and bar snack menu, from the extensive specials board, or from the full à la carte, but no matter which you choose, or indeed where – including the conservatory – only the best and freshest, mostly county-sourced, produce is used. A sample menu therefore may include starters of Portobello mushroom stuffed with crispy bacon and goats' cheese, and mango and crayfish salad; followed by something from the griddle, such as English steaks hung for 21 days; sea bass fillets with sizzled ginger, chilli, spring onion and hoi sin; pork rib-eye steak with walnut crust and cider apple sauce; roasted lamb shank with redcurrant and rosemary gravy; or chive savoury pancakes filled with roasted vegetables and melted brie. Sundays are devoted to roasts – beef, pork and turkey are served, along with the specials menu. Gardens and a shaded patio area are especially suited to summer dining. The comfortable en suite bedrooms in the converted coach house are furnished in antique pine and equipped with practical goodies.

Open all day all wk **Bar Meals** L served all wk 12-2 D served all wk 6.30-10 **Restaurant** L served all wk 12-2 D served all wk 6.30-10 🍺 PUNCH

TAVERNS 🍺 Fuller's London Pride, Black Sheep, Sharp's Doom Bar Ὸ Westons Stowford Press. 🍷 8 **Facilities** Non-diners area 🐾 (Bar Garden) 🚻 Children's menu Children's portions Garden ☂ Parking Wi-fi 🚌 (notice required) **Rooms** 5

DROITWICH *continued*

The Old Cock Inn

Friar St WR9 8EQ ☎ 01905 770754
e-mail: pub@oldcockinn.co.uk
dir: *M5 junct 5, A449 to Droitwich. Pub in town centre opposite theatre*

Town centre pub with unusual stained-glass windows

Three stained-glass windows, rescued from a church destroyed during the Civil War, are a feature of this charming pub, first licensed during the reign of Queen Anne. The stone carving with a frog emerging from its mouth above the front entrance is believed to portray Judge Jeffreys, who is said to have held one of his assizes here. A varied menu, including snacks, platters and more substantial dishes – salmon with a sweet chilli coating; pasta with roasted vegetables and pesto; lamb chop trio; and bacon, egg and chips - is supplemented by the daily specials.

Open 12-3 6-11 (Sun-Mon 12-6 Sat all day) Closed: Sun eve & Mon eve **Bar Meals** L served Tue-Sat 12-2.30 D served Tue-Sat 6-9 ⊕ MARSTON'S ◀ EPA, Guest ales ♻ Thatchers Heritage. **Facilities** Non-diners area ✿ (Bar Garden) ♦♦ Children's portions Garden ♫ Wi-fi ⬛ (notice required)

ELDERSFIELD Map 10 SO73

The Butchers Arms NEW

Lime St GL19 4NX ☎ 01452 840381
dir: *A417 from Gloucester towards Ledbury. After BP garage take B4211. In 2m take 4th left into Lime St*

A real beer-lovers' pub with a concise menu

Dating from the 16th century this is a pub which values its beer-drinking customers. The low-ceilinged, wooden-floored bar offers a good choice of regional beers served from the cask and is the hub of local life (although, sorry, it's not for the under-10s). The seasonal menu may be small, but it sure offers diversity: for example, cider-braised pig's cheek with fried bantam egg and crackling to start; then turbot roasted on the bone with lobster ravioli, fried green beans and buttered chard; and Seville orange marmalade pudding and Drambuie custard to finish. A spacious garden adds to its charm.

Open 12-2 7-11 Closed: 1wk Jan, 1 wknd Aug, 24-26 Dec, Sun eve & Mon (incl BHs) **Restaurant** L served Fri-Sun 12-1 D served Tue-Sat 7-9 Av 3 course à la carte fr £48 ⊕ FREE HOUSE ◀ Wye Valley Dorothy Goodbody's Golden Ale, St Austell Tribute, Wickwar Sunny Daze. ♥ 11 **Facilities** Garden Parking

---

FAR FOREST Map 10 SO77

The Plough Inn

Cleobury Rd DY14 9TE ☎ 01299 266237
e-mail: info@nostalgiainns.co.uk
dir: *On A417*

Top notch carvery operation in lovely countryside setting

The location in beautiful rolling countryside, the excellent range of locally brewed real ales, and one of the best carvery dining operations for miles draw local foodies to this family-owned, 18th-century coaching inn. It's also popular with walkers and cyclists, so arrive early to get the pick of the four roasted joints, perhaps leg of lamb, Far Forest venison, local pork and Scottish beef, all served with a choice of 12 vegetables. Alternatively, try ale-battered cod followed by Baileys profiteroles. The gorgeous summer garden comes with its own bar.

Open all wk 12-3 6-11 (Fri-Sat 12-11 Sun 12-10) **Bar Meals** L served Mon-Fri 12-2, Sat 12-9, Sun 12-6 D served Mon-Fri 6-9, Sat 12-9, Sun 12-6 **Restaurant** L served Mon-Fri 12-2, Sat 12-9, Sun 12-6 D served Mon-Fri 6-9, Sat 12-9 ⊕ FREE HOUSE ◀ Greene King Abbot Ale, Morland Old Speckled Hen, Morland Old Golden Hen ♻ Aspall, Westons Stowford Press, Robinsons Flagon. **Facilities** Non-diners area ♦♦ Children's menu Children's portions Garden ♫ Parking Wi-fi ⬛ (notice required)

FLADBURY Map 10 SO94

Chequers Inn

Chequers Ln WR10 2PZ ☎ 01386 860276
e-mail: 123_lee@live.co.uk
dir: *Off A44 between Evesham & Pershore*

River Avon walkers can refuel here

With its beams and open fire, this lovely old inn has bags of rustic charm. Tucked away in a pretty village with views of the glorious Bredon Hills, local produce from the Vale of Evesham provides the basis for home-cooked dishes such as jumbo crayfish and prawn cocktail; boiling ham with two eggs and chunky chips; and a range of home-made desserts. There is also a traditional Sunday carvery. The pretty walled garden enjoys outstanding views - a great setting for drinking or dining - and the nearby River Avon is ideal for walking.

Open 12-3 6-11 Closed: Sun eve **Bar Meals** L served Mon-Sat 12-2 D served Mon-Sat 6-9 Av main course £10 **Restaurant** L served all wk 12-2 D served Mon-Sat 6-9 Av 3 course à la carte fr £20 ⊕ ENTERPRISE INNS ◀ Sharp's Doom Bar, Black Sheep ♻ Westons Stowford Press, Aspall. ♥ **Facilities** Non-diners area ✿ (Bar Garden) ♦♦ Children's menu Children's portions Play area Garden ♫ Parking ⬛ (notice required)

FLYFORD FLAVELL Map 10 SO95

The Boot Inn ★★★★ INN

PICK OF THE PUBS

See Pick of the Pubs on page 489

HARTLEBURY Map 10 SO87

The White Hart NEW

The Village DY11 7TD ☎ 01299 250286
e-mail: skdiprose@fsmail.net
dir: *From Stourport-on-Severn take A4025 signed Worcester & Hartlebury. At rdbt take B4193. Pub in village centre*

Back on the map for really good food

Owner and top chef Simon Diprose now runs this traditional country pub which has gone from strength to strength since his arrival. The concise menus might begin with lightly curried cauliflower soup; whole baked camembert, rustic bread and caramelised onions; or goats' cheese and beetroot galette and walnut salad. Moving onto something more substantial there's spinach and ricotta tortellini; Mr Gough's honey roast ham and free range eggs; poached fillet of sea bass with tomato, chilli and ginger sauce; English rib eye steak, dauphinoise potatoes, fresh vegetables and barlotti bean and thyme sauce. At lunchtime you could opt for just filled baps, a ploughman's or a burger and chunky chips.

Open all day all wk **Bar Meals** L served Tue-Sat 12-3 Av main course £10 **Restaurant** L served Tue-Sun 12-3 D served Tue-Sat 6-9 Av 3 course à la carte fr £22 ⊕ PUNCH TAVERNS ◀ Timothy Taylor Landlord, Sharp's Doom Bar, Wye Valley HPA ♻ Westons Stowford Press & Wyld Wood. **Facilities** Non-diners area ✿ (Bar Garden) ♦♦ Children's menu Children's portions Garden ♫ Parking Wi-fi

---

KEMPSEY Map 10 SO84

Walter de Cantelupe Inn ★★★ INN

PICK OF THE PUBS

Main Rd WR5 3NA ☎ 01905 820572
dir: *4m S of Worcester city centre on A38. Pub in village centre*

Village pub known for its personal service

Just four miles from the centre of Worcester, this privately owned and run free house commemorates a 13th-century Bishop of said city, who was strongly against his parishioners' habit of brewing and selling ales as a way to raise church funds. With its whitewashed walls bedecked with flowers, parts of the inn date from the 17th century, as the wooden beams and stone floor testify. Outside, a walled and paved garden has been fragrantly planted with clematis, roses and honeysuckle, and its south-facing position can be a real suntrap. The menu is written up each day on a blackboard, with some produce being supplied by local villagers; choices appeal to both traditionalists and those seeking something more contemporary. You could begin with winter vegetable chowder, follow with braised lamb shank or steak-and-ale pie, and round off with apple crumble. Cask ales include a particularly well-kept Timothy Taylor Landlord. The pub also has accommodation.

Open Tue-Fri 5.30-11 Sat 12-11 Sun 12-9 Closed: 25-26 Dec, 1 Jan, Mon (ex BHs) **Bar Meals** L served Sun 12-5

D served Tue-Sat 6-9.30 **Restaurant** L served Sat 12-2.30, Sun 12-6 D served Tue-Sat 6.30-9 ⊕ FREE HOUSE ◀ Timothy Taylor Landlord, Cannon Royall Kings Shilling Ŏ Westons Stowford Press.
Facilities Non-diners area ❤ (Bar Outside area) ◑ Children's portions Outside area ⊼ Parking Wi-fi
Rooms 3

KNIGHTWICK   Map 10 SO75

The Talbot

PICK OF THE PUBS

WR6 5PH ☎ 01886 821235
e-mail: info@the-talbot.co.uk
dir: *A44 (Leominster road) through Worcester, 8m W right onto B4197 at River Teme bridge*

Family-run inn and brewery

Run by the Clift family for the past 30 years, The Talbot is a traditional 14th-century coaching inn on the bank of the River Teme. Surrounded by hop yards and meadows, this peaceful inn is also home to the Teme Valley Brewery, which uses locally grown hops in a range of curiously named cask-conditioned ales called This, That, T'Other and Wot. Nearly everything on the menus is made in-house, including bread, preserves, black pudding and raised pies. Salads, herbs and vegetables are grown in the large organic kitchen garden, and everything else comes from a local source, with the exception of fish, which arrives from Cornwall and Wales. The bar menu offers ploughman's, filled rolls and hot dishes, whilst in the restaurant, starters might include pig's head brawn with toast, followed by rose veal Stroganoff. Leave space for rhubarb tart. Beer festival held the second weekend in October.

Open all day all wk 7.30am-11.30pm **Bar Meals** L served all wk 12-9 D served all wk 12-9 food served all day **Restaurant** L served all wk 12-6.30 D served all wk 6.30-9 food served all day ⊕ FREE HOUSE ◀ Teme Valley This, That, T'Other & Wot, Hobsons Best Bitter Ŏ Kingstone Press, Robinsons. ♇ 12
Facilities Non-diners area ❤ (Bar Restaurant Garden) ◑ Children's portions Garden ⊼ Beer festival Parking Wi-fi 🚌

LOWER BROADHEATH   Map 10 SO85

The Dewdrop Inn

Bell Ln WR2 6RR ☎ 01905 640012
e-mail: enquiries@thedewdrop-inn.co.uk
dir: *From Worcester take A443 towards Kidderminster. Left onto B4202 towards Martley. Left into Bell Ln on entering Lower Broadheath. Pub 400yds on right*

One for classical music lovers perhaps

Sir Edward Elgar, one of England's greatest composers, was born in leafy Lower Broadheath; his birthplace museum is just a few minutes' walk from this country inn, whose top real ales are from Bewdley and Wye Valley breweries; the cider is Robinsons. The house policy of sourcing, where possible, produce from within a 30-mile radius results in bar and restaurant menus featuring classic dishes such as local lamb rump, and rib-eye and sirloin steaks; and Gressingham duck breast, while inevitably from further away will be beer-battered fish of the day, and possibly pan-fried shark steak.

Open all day all wk **Bar Meals** L served all wk 12-2.30 D served all wk 5.30-9 **Restaurant** L served all wk 12-2.30 D served all wk 5.30-9 ⊕ FREE HOUSE ◀ Bewdley Worcestershire Way, Wye Valley Ŏ Robinsons. **Facilities** Non-diners area ◑ Children's menu Children's portions Play area Garden ⊼ Parking Wi-fi 🚌 (notice required)

MALVERN   Map 10 SO74

The Inn at Welland

Drake St, Welland WR13 6LN ☎ 01684 592317
e-mail: info@theinnatwelland.co.uk
dir: *M50 junct 1, A38 follow signs for Upton upon Severn. Left onto A4104, through Upton upon Severn, 2.5m. Pub on right*

Stylish inn with panoramic views

Formerly known as The Anchor, this 17th-century country inn close to the Three Counties Showground is appointed to a high standard with an eclectic mix of smart, contemporary furnishings and rustic chic. There are spectacular views of the Malvern Hills from the stylish terrace, where you can dine alfresco in the warmer months; and the pub has a wood-burner and open fire for the winter. Food centres around seasonal local produce accompanied by Wye Valley or Malvern Hills ales, plus guests. Typical dishes might be pressed game terrine, followed by crisp confit of woodland pork belly. There is a good children's menu.

Open Tue-Sat 9.30am-11pm (Sun 9.30-6) Closed: Sun eve & Mon **Bar Meals** L served Tue-Sun 12-2.30 D served Tue-Sat 6.30-9.30 **Restaurant** L served Tue-Sun 12-2.30 D served Tue-Sat 6.30-9.30 ⊕ FREE HOUSE ◀ Otter Bitter, Wye Valley, Malvern Hills, Guest ales Ŏ Westons Stowford Press. ♇ 14 **Facilities** Non-diners area ◑ Children's menu Children's portions Garden ⊼ Parking Wi-fi

The Nag's Head

19-21 Bank St WR14 2JG ☎ 01684 574373
e-mail: enquiries@nagsheadmalvern.co.uk
dir: *Off A449*

An excellent choice of real ales

From this pub's garden, the looming presence of North Hill, northernmost top of the stunning Malvern Hills, takes the eye - if only momentarily - away from the panoply of delights at this enterprising free house. 'Real ale, real food, real people' is the motto at the Nag's Head. Fifteen real ales, many from local breweries, adorn the bar; eight are permanent fixtures and include three from the pub's own St George's microbrewery. The annual beer festival on St George's Day offers even more choice. The interior is dotted with snugs, log fires and a magpie's nest of artefacts to create a cosy atmosphere, and the marvellous menu features grilled Wiltshire trout and butternut squash and pepper tart.

Open all day all wk **Bar Meals** L served all wk 12-2 **Restaurant** D served all wk 6.30-8.30 ⊕ FREE HOUSE ◀ St George's Friar Tuck, Tennent's Charger, Holden's Dragon's Blood, Bathams, Banks's Ŏ Thatchers Gold, Westons 1st Quality. **Facilities** Non-diners area ❤ (Bar Restaurant Garden) ◑ Children's portions Garden ⊼ Beer festival Parking Wi-fi 🚌 (notice required)

The Wyche Inn ★★★★ INN

74 Wyche Rd WR14 4EQ ☎ 01684 575396
e-mail: thewycheinn@googlemail.com
dir: *1.5m S of Malvern. On B4218 towards Malvern & Colwall. Off A449 (Worcester to Ross/Ledbury road)*

Spectacular views and home-cooked food

Start or end a walk in the Malvern Hills in this traditional, dog-friendly country inn, probably the highest in Worcestershire. Indeed, the views from various nearby high points are quite something; from Malvern Beacon, for instance, you can see seven counties. Beers come from Hobsons and Wye Valley, while home-cooked dishes include pie of the day, chicken curry and battered cod. Themed food nights feature sirloin steak (Tuesday/Saturday) and mixed grill (Wednesday), and roast lunches are served on Sundays. Well-behaved pets are welcome in the six rooms.

Open all day all wk **Bar Meals** L served Mon-Fri 12-2.30, Sat 12-8.30, Sun 12-6 (winter Sat 12-2.30, Sun 12-3.30) D served Mon-Fri 6-8.30, Sat 12-8.30 (winter Sat 5-8.30) **Restaurant** L served Mon-Fri 12-2.30, Sat 12-8.30, Sun 12-6 (winter Sat 12-2.30, Sun 12-3.30) D served Mon-Fri 6-8.30, Sat 12-8.30 (winter Sat 5-8.30) ⊕ FREE HOUSE ◀ Hobsons Best Bitter, Wye Valley HPA. ♇ 9 **Facilities** Non-diners area ❤ (Bar Garden) ◑ Children's menu Children's portions Garden ⊼ Parking Wi-fi
Rooms 6

MARTLEY
Map 10 SO76

Admiral Rodney Inn ★★★ INN

Berrow Green, WR6 6PL ☎ 01886 821375
e-mail: rodney@admiral.fslife.co.uk
dir: M5 junct 7, A44 signed Leominster. Approx 7m at Knightwick right onto B4197. Inn 2m on left at Berrow Green

On the Worcester Way

An early 17th-century farmhouse situated on the Worcester Way, now with two bars serving Wye Valley Bitter and HPA as regular ales, three local guests, Robinsons Tenbury cider and, in summer, draught perry. Traditional pub food includes lunchtime sandwiches, baguettes and rump steak, fried egg and mushrooms. Mains in the evening might extend to faggots with mash; Cajun chicken quesadilla; and roasted Mediterranean vegetable pancake. Fish are a speciality on their own weekly changing menu. The large, separate dining room opens at weekends. Well-behaved dogs are welcome in the pub and in the en suite bedrooms.

Open all wk 12-3 5-11 (Mon 5-11 Sat 12-11 Sun 12-10.30) ⊕ FREE HOUSE ◀ Wye Valley Bitter, HPA, Local Guest ales (Black Pear, Malvern Hills, Kinver, Hobsons, Birds) Ö Westons Stowford Press, Robinsons. **Facilities** ♣ (Bar Garden) ♦ Children's menu Garden Parking Wi-fi **Rooms** 3

PERSHORE
Map 10 SO94

The Defford Arms

Upton Rd, Defford WR8 9BD ☎ 01386 750378
dir: From Pershore take A4104 towards Upton upon Severn. Pub on left in village

Revitalised village pub with much charm

Rescued from dereliction by Neil and Sue Overton in 2007, The Defford Arms stands testament to their efforts: they have eschewed music, gambling machines and TV in favour of old fashioned values. It's in a great location too, so days out at Croome Park, the Three Counties Showground at Malvern, Cheltenham Racecourse or Pershore's plum festival could all include a welcome break here. Expect traditional home-made food such as chicken liver pâté and red onion jam; cottage pie; and cinnamon bread-and-butter pudding.

Open all wk Mon 5.30-9 Tue 12-2.30 5.30-9.30 Wed 12-2.30 5.30-10 Thu 12-2.30 5.30-10.30 Fri 12-2.30 5.30-11 Sat 12-11.30 Sun 12-4 ⊕ FREE HOUSE ◀ Guest ales Ö Westons Stowford Press. **Facilities** ♣ (Bar Garden) ♦ Children's menu Children's portions Garden Parking

POWICK
Map 10 SO85

The Halfway House Inn

Bastonford WR2 4SL ☎ 01905 831098
e-mail: contact@halfwayhouseinnpowick.co.uk
dir: M5 junct 7, A4440 then A449

A warm welcome at this village pub

Standing halfway between Worcester and Malvern on the main road, this aptly named Georgian free house boasts winter log fires and a mature shady garden at the side. Steaks and seafood are a speciality, but the menu also features a good choice of fresh, locally sourced hot dishes such as pork medallions and black pudding on mashed potatoes with creamy, coarse-grain mustard. The extensive lunchtime menu offers salads, sandwiches and jacket potatoes, as well as hot dishes and a range of ploughman's.

Open 12-3 6-11 Closed: Mon-Tue **Bar Meals** L served Wed-Sun 12-2 D served Wed-Sat 6-9 **Restaurant** L served Wed-Sun 12-2 D served Wed-Sat 6-9 ⊕ FREE HOUSE ◀ Greene King Abbot Ale, Fuller's London Pride, St George's, Timothy Taylor Ö Westons Stowford Press. **Facilities** Non-diners area ♦ Children's menu Children's portions Garden ⊼ Parking Wi-fi (notice required)

YORKSHIRE, EAST RIDING OF

BARMBY ON THE MARSH
Map 17 SE62

The King's Head

High St DN14 7HT ☎ 01757 630705
e-mail: rainderpubcoltd@tiscali.co.uk
dir: M62 junct 37 follow A614/Bridlington/York/Howden signs. Left at A63. At rdbt 1st exit onto A614/Booth Ferry Rd towards Goole. At rdbt 4th exit on B1228/Booth Ferry Rd. Left, through Asselby to Barmby on the Marsh

Look out for their Yorkshire tapas menu

In the 17th century this pub served a ferry that crossed the Rivers Ouse and Derwent. Nowadays this family-run village pub is a place that appeals to all tastes; from the beamed bar through a bright, modern lounge to the cosy, intimate restaurant. Several members of the family are trained chefs and make the most of Yorkshire's burgeoning larder; braised beef with clementines and ginger wine served with herb cobbler and mash is just one of the tempting mains here. Their innovative Yorkshire tapas menu features haddock goujons, confit lamb croquettes, and baked mussels. There are great open sandwiches and a take-away deli menu (including ice creams), too.

Open Wed-Thu 12-2 5-11 (Mon-Tue 5-11 Fri 12-2 5-12 Sat 12-12 Sun 12-11) Closed: Mon L, Tue L **Bar Meals** L served Wed-Fri 12-2, Sat-Sun all day D served Wed-Thu 5-8.30, Fri 5-9, Sat-Sun all day **Restaurant** L served Sat-Sun all day D served Wed-Thu 5-8.30, Fri 5-9, Sat-Sun all day ⊕ FREE HOUSE ◀ Black Sheep Best Bitter, 3 Guest ales. **Facilities** Non-diners area ♦ Children's menu Children's portions Outside area ⊼ Parking Wi-fi (notice required)

BEVERLEY
Map 17 TA03

The Ferguson Fawsitt Arms & Country Lodge

East End, Walkington HU17 8RX ☎ 01482 882665
e-mail: admin@fergusonfawsitt.com
dir: M62 junct 38 onto B1230, left on A1034, right onto B1230, on left in centre of Walkington

Traditional inn where time stands still

Three miles from Beverley in the picturesque village of Walkington, there is a timeless quality to this Victorian pub named after two important local families. Parts of the pub used to form the village blacksmith's shop where carriage wheels were repaired. Open fires, dark-wood panelling, carved settles, beams and some decent tiling to the floor welcomes those set on sampling a pint of Black Sheep, or diners intent on a good Sunday roast, home-made steak pie from the carvery or a traditional pub meal from the bar food menu.

Open all day all wk 11-11 (Sun 12-11) **Bar Meals** L served all wk 12-9 D served all wk 12-9 food served all day **Restaurant** L served all wk 12-9 D served all wk 12-9 food served all day ⊕ FREE HOUSE ◀ Greene King Abbot Ale, Black Sheep, Guest ales. ♟ 10 **Facilities** Non-diners area ♦ Children's menu Children's portions Outside area ⊼ Parking Wi-fi

Green Dragon

51 Saturday Market HU17 8AA ☎ 01482 889801
dir: *Telephone for directions*

Popular meeting place with well kept cask ales

This historic Tudor-fronted inn has a sleek, stylish interior with polished wood floors, modern bar furniture and heritage colours on the walls. It is reputedly haunted by the ghost of a young Danish soldier who was executed after killing a comrade in a duel in 1689. Expect handpicked real ales from all over the UK and hearty, modern pub food such as chicken wings with piri-piri sauce; smoked haddock fishcakes with baby potatoes, mixed seasonal salad and tartare sauce; and Cumberland sausages and mash.

Open all day all wk **Closed:** 25 Dec ⊕ NICHOLSONS ◀ Leeds Pale, Thornbridge Pica Pica ♂ Westons Old Rosie, Aspall. **Facilities** ⊕ Children's menu Children's portions Garden

FLAMBOROUGH   Map 17 TA27

The Seabirds Inn

Tower St YO15 1PD ☎ 01262 850242
e-mail: philip.theseabirds@virgin.net
dir: *On B1255 E of Bridlington*

Village pub that keeps it simple

Just east of this 200-year-old village pub is the famous chalk promontory of Flamborough Head and its equally famed lighthouse. With the North Sea so close you'd expect plenty of fish, and there is, namely, spicy Whitby creel king prawns; deep-fried dusted whitebait; salmon steak Mornay; and battered haddock fillet. This is not a menu to overreach itself, instead keeping to staples like a good choice of steaks; chicken breast with bacon, barbecue sauce and cheese; gammon with egg and pineapple; and steamed suet pudding with spinach, pine nuts, mozzarella cheese and cherry tomatoes. Guest ales are on tap in the bar.

Open 12-3 6-11 **Closed:** Mon (winter) **Bar Meals** L served all wk 12-2 D served Sun-Fri 6-8.30, Sat 6-9.30 **Restaurant** L served all wk 12-2 D served Sun-Fri 6-8.30, Sat 6-9.30 ⊕ FREE HOUSE ◀ John Smith's, Tetley's Smoothflow, Guest ales. ♀ 9 **Facilities** Non-diners area ♥ (Bar Garden) Children's menu Children's portions Garden ⚘ Parking 🚐

HUGGATE   Map 19 SE85

The Wolds Inn ★★★ INN

YO42 1YH ☎ 01377 288217
e-mail: huggate@woldsinn.freeserve.co.uk
dir: *S off A166 between York & Driffield*

Yorkshire Wolds inn with hearty home-made food

Sixteenth century in origin, this family-run hostelry is, at 525 feet above sea level, the highest in the Yorkshire Wolds. Copper pans and gleaming brassware fill the wood-panelled interior, where the open fires still burn good old-fashioned coal. The restaurant is widely known for serving large portions of, among other things, locally sourced Barnsley chops; crispy fresh farm duckling; fillet of plaice; chicken breast stuffed with spinach; and Wolds Topper, "the mixed grill to remember". The overnight accommodation is particularly popular with those exploring the countryside and coast.

Open 12-2 6-11 (Sun 12-10.30) **Closed:** Mon (ex BHs) ⊕ FREE HOUSE ◀ Timothy Taylor Landlord & Golden Best, John Smith's ♂ Kingstone Press. **Facilities** ⊕ Children's menu Children's portions Garden Parking **Rooms** 3

LOW CATTON   Map 17 SE75

The Gold Cup Inn

YO41 1EA ☎ 01759 371354
dir: *1m S of A166 or 1m N of A1079, E of York*

Attractive, family-run country pub

Refurbished, but it's still quite clear that this charming, family-run free house is old - 300 years old, in fact. Giveaways are the low beams and open fireplaces in the bar, now complemented by new wooden floors, modern fabrics and wall-mounted coach-lamps. Bar meals are served every lunchtime (except Monday) and evening from the extensive menu. Equally extensive is the carte, whose options include roast loin of pork or beef with Yorkshire pudding; hot and spicy Cajun chicken with mint yoghurt dip; and breaded Whitby scampi. A paddock adjoining the large beer garden runs down to the River Derwent.

Open 12-2.30 6-11 (Sat-Sun 12-11) **Closed:** Mon L **Bar Meals** L served Tue-Fri 12-2.30, Sat-Sun 12-6 D served all wk 6-9 **Restaurant** L served Sun 12-8.30 D served Mon-Sat 6-9, Sun 12-8.30 ⊕ FREE HOUSE ◀ Theakston Black Bull. ♀ 11 **Facilities** Non-diners area ♥ (Bar Garden) ⊕ Children's menu Children's portions Play area Garden ⚘ Parking 🚐 (notice required)

LUND   Map 17 SE94

The Wellington Inn

19 The Green YO25 9TE ☎ 01377 217294
e-mail: tellmemore@thewellingtoninn.co.uk
dir: *On B1248 NE of Beverley*

Exciting food in quintessential village inn

Occupying a wonderfully rural location, this country pub is popular with locals and visitors alike, whether for a pint of real ale, a glass of wine, or a plate of decent food. Nicely situated opposite the picture-postcard village green, inside is a unique blend of old and new where you can choose from the traditional pub menu or from the carte in the more formal restaurant. Expect mouthwatering dishes like smoked duck breast, melon and pickled ginger salad with soy dressing, followed perhaps by mixed fish, crab, king prawn and scampi thermidor with basmati rice.

Open 12-3 6.30-11 **Closed:** Mon L **Bar Meals** L served Tue-Sun 12-2 D served Tue-Sat 6.30-9 **Restaurant** D served Tue-Sat 7-9 ⊕ FREE HOUSE ◀ Timothy Taylor Landlord, Black Sheep Best Bitter, John Smith's, Copper Dragon, Regular guest ale. ♀ 11 **Facilities** Non-diners area ⊕ Children's menu Children's portions Garden Parking Wi-fi

SANCTON   Map 17 SE83

The Star

King St YO43 4QP ☎ 01430 827269
e-mail: benandlindsey@thestaratsancton.co.uk
dir: *2m SE of Market Weighton on A1034*

Traditional local serving top-notch pub food

Built as a farmhouse and converted into a pub in 1710, the sandstone Star stands in a pretty Anglo-Saxon, Yorkshire Wolds village. Owner-chef Ben Cox and his wife Lindsey spruced up and extended the pub a few years ago, adding a stylish dining area, so expect stone floors, log-burning stoves and a modern feel. Ben is passionate about using local produce and his impressive dishes include a winter salad of sloe gin, juniper, pear and walnuts; haunch of roe deer; and hazelnut cheesecake. There's an excellent vegetarian menu and the set Yorkshire Lunch menu is a steal. The 'Little Star' kids' menu even has a choice of 'mocktails'.

Open 12-3 6-11 (Sun all day) **Closed:** Mon **Bar Meals** L served Tue-Sat 12-2, Sun 12-3 D served Tue-Sat 6-9.30, Sun 6-8 Av main course £11.95 **Restaurant** L served Tue-Sat 12-2, Sun 12-3 D served Tue-Sat 6-9.30, Sun 6-8 Fixed menu price fr £15.95 Av 3 course à la carte fr £34.95 ⊕ FREE HOUSE ◀ Black Sheep, Copper Dragon, Wold Top, Great Newsome ♂ Moorlands Farm. ♀ 21 **Facilities** Non-diners area ♥ (Garden) ⊕ Children's menu Children's portions Play area Garden ⚘ Parking

SOUTH DALTON — Map 17 SE94

The Pipe & Glass Inn @@

PICK OF THE PUBS

West End HU17 7PN ☎ 01430 810246
e-mail: email@pipeandglass.co.uk
dir: *Just off B1248 (Beverley to Malton road). 7m from Beverley*

Smart inn serving quality food and ales

Part 15th-century, part 17th, the inn occupies the site of the original gatehouse to Dalton Hall, family seat of Lord Hotham. James and Kate Mackenzie's transformation of their inn has helped to earn it two AA Rosettes, but it still feels like the village local, with Copper Dragon, Cropton, Wold Top and other locally brewed ales, and Moorlands cider in the bar. The restaurant is more contemporary in style and the conservatory looks out over the garden. James sources top-notch local and seasonal produce for modern British menus, which at lunchtime may feature fillet of English beef with roast shallots; and beetroot and Yellison Farm (in the Yorkshire Dales) goats' cheese tart. Evening possibilities include slow-cooked crispy lamb with mutton and kidney faggot; and a special of turbot fillet with monkfish cheek fritter and braised oxtail and horseradish sauce. The Hotham Room has its own kitchen for private dining.

Open all day 12-11 (Sun 12-10.30) Closed: 2wks Jan, Mon (ex BHs) **Bar Meals** L served Tue-Sat 12-2, Sun 12-4 D served Tue-Sat 6.30-9.30 **Restaurant** L served Tue-Sat 12-2, Sun 12-4 D served Tue-Sat 6.30-9.30 ⊕ FREE HOUSE ◀ Wold Top, Copper Dragon, Black Sheep, Cropton, John Smith's, York Ŏ Moorlands Farm. ☐ 15 **Facilities** ♦ Children's menu Children's portions Garden ☐ Parking Wi-fi

SUTTON UPON DERWENT — Map 17 SE74

St Vincent Arms

Main St YO41 4BN ☎ 01904 608349
e-mail: enquiries@stvincentarms.co.uk
dir: *From A64 follow signs for A1079. Turn right, follow signs for Elvington on B1228. Through Elvington to Sutton upon Derwent*

Welcoming black and white timbered pub

The pub is named after John Jervis, who was mentor to Admiral Lord Nelson and who became the first Earl of St Vincent in the 18th century. This is a warm family-run pub with an old fashioned welcoming atmosphere, minus music and gaming machines but with the addition of great food and an excellent selection of beers and wines. Lunches follow popular lines with salads, home-made lasagne, or large haddock with chips and mushy peas. Specials, served both at lunch and in the evening, may include gratin of queenie scallops; pan-fried Dover sole; or Toulouse sausages on parsley mash.

Open all wk 11.30-3 6-11 (Sun 12-3 6.30-10.30) ⊕ FREE HOUSE ◀ Timothy Taylor Landlord, Fuller's ESB & London Pride, York Yorkshire Terrier, Wells Bombardier, Old Mill Traditional Bitter. **Facilities** ♦ Garden Parking

YORKSHIRE, NORTH

AKEBAR — Map 19 SE19

The Friar's Head

Akebar Park DL8 5LY ☎ 01677 450201 & 450591
e-mail: info@akebarpark.com
dir: *From A1 at Leeming Bar onto A684, 7m towards Leyburn. Entrance at Akebar Park*

Stone-built Dales pub with a lovely conservatory

This 200-year-old pub lies in the heart of Wensleydale, known for its castles, abbeys and waterfalls. Located next to a golf course and at the entrance to Akebar Holiday Park, The Friar's Head overlooks beautiful countryside and has grounds where you can play bowls, croquet and pétanque. Inside you'll find exposed beams and stonework, and hand-pulled Yorkshire ales at the bar. The lush plants and vines of the Cloister conservatory dining room give it a tropical appearance; in the evening it looks magical in the candlelight. Typical dishes include pan-seared queen scallops, duck filo parcels, Cajun salmon and pasta bolognese.

Open all wk 10-3 6-11.30 (Fri-Sun 10am-11.30pm Jul-Sep) Closed: 25 Dec, 26 Dec eve **Bar Meals** L served all wk 12-2.30 D served all wk 6-9.30 **Restaurant** L served all wk 12-2.30 D served all wk 6-9.30 ⊕ FREE HOUSE ◀ John Smith's, Theakston Best Bitter, Black Sheep Best Bitter, Timothy Taylor Landlord. ☐ 12 **Facilities** Non-diners area ♦ Children's portions Garden ☐ Parking

ALDWARK — Map 19 SE46

The Aldwark Arms @@

YO61 1UB ☎ 01347 838324
dir: *From York ring road take A19 N. Left into Warehill Ln signed Tollerton & Helperby. Through Tollerton, follow Aldwark signs*

Refurbished gastro-pub that proves a real draw

Nestled in the Vale of York and extensively renovated a few years ago, this handsome pub has risen phoenix-like under its new guise as a dining inn dedicated to supporting farms and estates in the Hambleton area of Yorkshire. Sofas, open fires, wooden floors and a large garden terrace all draw locals to indulge in a pint of Timothy Taylor, while diners travel considerable distances to sample chef-patron Chris Hill's exceptional, two AA-Rosette restaurant menu — think mains of slow-cooked oxtail with honeyed root vegetables; and medallions of monkfish with a herb crust, Parma ham, scallops and shrimps. The cosy bar serves lighter meals like rump steak sandwich and French onion soup.

Open all day Closed: Mon ⊕ FREE HOUSE ◀ Timothy Taylor. **Facilities** ♦ Children's menu Children's portions Play area Garden Parking

APPLETON-LE-MOORS — Map 19 SE78

The Moors Inn

YO62 6TF ☎ 01751 417435
e-mail: enquiries@moorsinn.co.uk
dir: *On A170 between Pickering & Kirbymoorside*

Moors village pub with enjoyable home-cooked food

Situated in the North York Moors National Park, this 18th-century Grade II listed inn is a good choice for its location and home-cooked food. Taken over by the Frank family in 2012, the pub is set in a small village with lovely scenery in every direction; in summer you can sit in the garden and enjoy the splendid views. Dishes include braised lamb shank with mint gravy; mussels with white wine and cream; and Whitby scampi. Many of the vegetables are grown by the landlord. In addition to hand-pumped local ales, there is also a choice of wines by the glass.

Open all day all wk **Bar Meals** L served Mon-Sat 12.2.30 (light snacks all day) D served all wk 6.30-8.30 Av main course £12 **Restaurant** L served Mon-Sat 12-2.30, Sun 12-3 D served all wk 6.30-8.30 Fixed menu fr £16 Av 3 course à la carte fr £25 ⊕ FREE HOUSE ◀ Rudgate Viking, World Top, York Guzzler, Black Sheep Ŏ Westons Stowford Press. **Facilities** Non-diners area ❧ (Bar Garden Outside area) ♦ Children's portions Garden Outside area ☐ Parking ▭

APPLETREEWICK — Map 19 SE06

The Craven Arms

BD23 6DA ☎ 01756 720270
e-mail: info@craven-cruckbarn.co.uk
dir: *2m E of Burnsall off B6160*

Interesting blackboard menus

Originally a farm and later used as a weaving shed and courthouse, this 16th-century Dales pub has spectacular views of the River Wharfe and Simon's Seat. The building retains its original beams, flagstone floors, gas lighting and magnificent fireplace; the village stocks are still outside. Traditional real ales are served and there's a beer festival every October. The blackboard menu changes daily and offers plenty of choice - maybe sautéed rabbit kidneys in a wholegrain mustard sauce on toast; and locally-sourced venison steak with butternut squash purée, kale and rösti potato. A heather-thatched cruck barn to the rear serves as a restaurant and function room.

Open all day all wk **Bar Meals** L served Mon-Thu 12-2, Fri-Sun 12-5 D served Mon-Sat 6.30-9, Sun 6.30-8.30 Av main course £10 **Restaurant** L served all wk 12-2.30 D served Mon-Sat 6.30-9, Sun 6.30-8.30 Fixed menu price fr £10 ⊕ FREE HOUSE ◀ Dark Horse Cruck Barn Bitter & Hetton Pale Ale, Saltaire Raspberry Blonde, Moorhouse's Blond Witch & Black Witch Ŏ Kingstone Press, Ampleforth Abbey. **Facilities** Non-diners area ❧ (Bar Garden) ♦ Children's menu Children's portions Play area Garden ☐ Beer festival Parking Wi-fi

Save on hotels. Book at theAA.com/hotel

YORKSHIRE, NORTH 495 ENGLAND

ASENBY
Map 19 SE37

Crab & Lobster ★★★★★ RR ☺☺

PICK OF THE PUBS

Dishforth Rd YO7 3QL ☎ 01845 577286
e-mail: reservations@crabandlobster.co.uk
dir: *From A1(M) take A168 towards Thirsk, follow signs for Asenby*

Eclectic interiors and excellent food

This unique 17th-century thatched pub with its friendly bar is set amid seven acres of garden, lake and streams in the heart of the North Yorkshire countryside. Inside and out it is festooned with everything from old advertising signs to fishing nets, an Aladdin's cave of antiques and artefacts from around the world. Equally famous for its innovative two AA-Rosette cuisine and special gourmet extravaganzas, the menus show influences from France and Italy. Starters leave no doubt you are in seafood heaven: the pub's famous fish club sandwich; Loch Fyne smoked salmon, warm leek and horseradish pancakes; and grilled queenie scallops are just a few of the offerings. The theme continues into main courses with the likes of fish pie, roast monkfish with pancetta, leeks and lentils; lobster thermidor with scallops and prawns and Goan seafood curry. For those who prefer meat, the range of locally-sourced ingredients will not disappoint: honey and peppered duck breast with winter greens, confit and brown onion mash is just one example. Desserts such as sticky date and toffee banana pudding, or baked carrot cheesecake with frosted lemon creamed cheese, Grand Marnier and navel orange sauce are equally appealing. Accommodation is available.

Open all day all wk **Bar Meals** L served all wk 12-2.30 D served Sun-Fri 7-9, Sat 6.30-9.30 Av main course £17 **Restaurant** Fixed menu price fr £18.50 Av 3 course à la carte fr £35 ⊕ FREE HOUSE ◀ Copper Dragon Golden Pippin, John Smith's, Hambleton, Guinness. **Facilities** Non-diners area ◀● Children's portions Garden ⊼ Parking Wi-fi **Rooms** 14

ASKRIGG
Map 18 SD99

The King's Arms NEW

Main St DL8 3HQ ☎ 01969 650113
e-mail: info@kingsarmsaskrigg.co.uk
dir: *From A1 exit at Scotch Corner onto A6108, through Richmond, right onto B6270 to Leyburn. Follow Askrigg signs to Main St*

Stone-built Wensleydale inn on the Herriot Trail

Owned by North Yorkshire hotelier Charles Cody, this elegant, 18th-century coaching inn used to double as the fictional Drover's Arms, vet James Herriot's favourite watering hole in the BBC drama *All Creatures Great and Small*. There's a big Yorkshire inglenook fireplace in the oak-panelled bar, where photographs show cast members relaxing between takes. The food, written up daily on an impressive mirror behind the bar, is based on top quality produce, such as game from the surrounding moors, and fish fresh from Hartlepool. Look also for loin of local lamb; pan-fried salmon; and wild mushroom risotto.

Open all day all wk **Bar Meals** L served all wk 12-2.30 D served Mon-Sat 5.30-9, Sun 5.30-8 Av main course £14 **Restaurant** L served all wk 12-2.30 D served Mon-Sat 5.30-9, Sun 5.30-8 Av 3 course à la carte fr £23.50 ⊕ FREE HOUSE ◀ Black Sheep, Theakstons, Yorkshire Dales ♂ Thatchers Gold. ⬚ 13 **Facilities** Non-diners area ♣ (Bar Outside area) ◀● Children's menu Children's portions Outside area Wi-fi 🚌 (notice required)

AUSTWICK
Map 18 SD76

The Game Cock Inn

The Green LA2 8BB ☎ 015242 51226
e-mail: eric.coupey@hotmail.co.uk
dir: *A65 from Skipton or Kendal, then follow signs for Austwick*

Popular Yorkshire Dales pub at the heart of the community

A traditional Thwaites pub in a village below Oxenber Hill, capped with a magnificent limestone pavement. In the bar, winter log fires; outside a large garden with children's play area. Wherever possible, Eric Coupey, who runs the pub with his wife Maree, chooses local firms to supply fresh produce for his imaginative menus of English, French and Mediterranean dishes. The Gallic influence continues with Breton night on Tuesdays and French on Wednesdays; locally sourced steaks are Thursdays, and on Fridays you can take away fish, chips and mushy peas.

Open Tue-Fri 11.30-3 5-close (Sat-Sun all day) Closed: Mon ⊕ THWAITES ◀ Original, Lancaster Bomber, Wainwright & Nutty Black, Guest ales ♂ Kingstone Press. **Facilities** ♣ (Bar Garden) ◀● Children's menu Children's portions Play area Garden Parking Wi-fi

AYSGARTH
Map 19 SE08

The George & Dragon Inn

PICK OF THE PUBS

DL8 3AD ☎ 01969 663358
e-mail: info@georgeanddragonaysgarth.co.uk
dir: *On A684 midway between Leyburn & Hawes. Pub in village centre*

Perfect location for exploring Wensleydale

The George & Dragon Inn is a 17th-century Grade II listed building in a superb location in the Yorkshire Dales National Park, near the beautiful Aysgarth Falls. The area is perfect for walking, touring and visiting the many attractions, including Forbidden Corner, the Wensleydale Railway, and the cheese factory. The owners are proud to continue a centuries-long tradition of Yorkshire hospitality at the inn, with customers keeping cosy in winter by the fireside, and in summer enjoying their drinks and meals out on the furnished flower-filled patio. Well-kept real ales are served, and the inn has a great reputation for its traditional food, including steak pie and fish and chips. In the early evening a fixed-price menu meets the needs of ravenous walkers, while a broader à la carte choice comes into force after 7pm. Choices could be home-made chicken liver pâté with apple chutney;

Wensleydale pork sausages and mash; or braised pork belly, mash, choucroute and cider reduction.

Open all wk 12-close **Bar Meals** L served all wk 12-2 D served all wk 6-8.30, May-Sep 5.30-9 ⊕ FREE HOUSE ◀ Black Sheep Best Bitter, Theakston's Best Bitter, Yorkshire Dales, Guest ales ♂ Thatchers Gold. ⬚ 16 **Facilities** Non-diners area ♣ (Bar Garden) ◀● Garden ⊼ Parking 🚌

BEDALE
Map 19 SE28

The Castle Arms Inn ★★★★ INN

Meadow Ln, Snape DL8 2TB ☎ 01677 470270
e-mail: castlearms@aol.com
dir: *From A1 (M) at Leeming Bar take A684 to Bedale. At x-rds in town centre take B6268 to Masham. Approx 2m, turn left to Thorp Perrow Arboretum. In 0.5m left for Snape*

Great base for walking or cycling

In the sleepy village of Snape, this family-run 14th-century pub is a good starting point for walking and cycling, and visiting local stately homes, castles and film locations – particularly as it has bed and breakfast accommodation. The homely interior has exposed beams and horse brasses and a real fire in the bar, home to Brakspear and Jennings real ales. A meal in the restaurant selected from the ever-changing menu might feature smoked salmon salad; steak and ale pie with vegetables and chips; and an ice cream sundae for dessert. Afterwards, there is a range of liqueur coffees to tempt you.

Open all wk 12-3 6-12 **Bar Meals** L served all wk 12-2 D served all wk 7-9 (ex Sun winter) **Restaurant** L served all wk 12-2 D served all wk 7-9 (ex Sun winter) ⊕ MARSTON'S ◀ Jennings Bitter, Brakspear Bitter, Ringwood Boondoggle. **Facilities** Non-diners area ♣ (Bar Garden) ◀● Children's menu Children's portions Garden ⊼ Parking **Rooms** 9

BOROUGHBRIDGE
Map 19 SE36

The Black Bull Inn

PICK OF THE PUBS

See Pick of the Pubs on page 496

PICK OF THE PUBS

The Black Bull Inn

BOROUGHBRIDGE　　Map 19 SE36

6 St James Square YO51 9AR
☎ **01423 322413**
web: www.blackbullboroughbridge.co.uk
dir: A1(M) junct 48, B6265 E for 1m

Traditional inn offering true Yorkshire hospitality

Using a false name, highwayman Dick Turpin stayed at this ancient inn which stands in a quiet corner of the market square and was one of the main stopping points for travellers on the long road between London and the North. Today you have to turn off the A1(M), but it's well worth it to discover an inn built in 1258 that retains its ancient beams, low ceilings and roaring open fires, not to mention one that also gives houseroom to the supposed ghosts of a monk, a blacksmith, a cavalier and a small boy. Tony Burgess is the landlord and the man responsible for high standards that exclude anything electronic which makes a noise. The hot and cold sandwich selection in the bar is wide, while in the dining room expect a good choice of traditional pub food on menus offering lamb shank on creamy mash in port and honey gravy; salmon steak on fried noodles with spicy oriental sauce; Barnsley chop and other

grills; and Sizzlers, such as Mexican spiced vegetables in a hot sweet salsa sauce; and pan-fried duck breast topped with peppers, mushrooms, bamboo shoots and sweet and sour sauce. Frequently changing blackboard specials widen the choice to include halibut steak with smoked salmon and fresh prawns in white wine sauce; and wild button mushroom ragout with fresh salad. Possible followers are apple pie and custard; citrus lemon tart; or mixed ice creams, brandy snaps and fruit purées. In the bar, real ale drinkers will find favourites from Timothy Taylor, Cottage Brewery and Theakston, while the wine list shows all the signs of careful compilation.

Open all day all wk 11-11 (Fri-Sat 11am-mdnt Sun 12-11) **Bar Meals** L served all wk 12-2 D served all wk 6-9 **Restaurant** L served all wk 12-2 D served all wk 6-9 ⊕ FREE HOUSE ◖ John Smith's, Timothy Taylor Best Bitter, Wells Bombardier, Theakston, Cottage, Guest ale. ♟ 11 **Facilities** Non-diners area ❖ ◖ Children's menu Children's portions Parking 🚌

BOROUGHBRIDGE *continued*

Crown Inn Roecliffe ★★★★★ RR ◉

PICK OF THE PUBS

Roecliffe YO51 9LY ☎ 01423 322300
e-mail: info@crowninnroecliffe.co.uk
dir: *A1(M) junct 48, follow Boroughbridge signs. At rdbt
to Roecliffe*

Wonderful village pit stop just off the A1

Karl and Amanda have worked wonders on this handsome
16th-century former coaching inn beside Roecliffe's
neatly trimmed green. The striking green-painted pub has
been lovingly restored, with stone-flagged floors, oak
beams and crackling log fires featuring prominently in
the civilised bar and dining rooms. Local produce is
name-checked – farm meats, game shoots, Whitby fish
and crab, and kippers, salmon and haddock are smoked
in-house – and put to fine use on a clearly focused
modern British menu. Everything is home made, from
fresh chicken liver and foie gras parfait, rhubarb chutney
and toasted brioche for a starter, to roasted venison with
sliced port mulled pears and fried Jerusalem artichokes
for a main course. Delicious puddings may include a
chilled very lemony soufflé, or try a plate of Yorkshire and
French cheeses. The four elegant bedrooms, each with
sleigh beds, authentic antiques and free-standing baths,
are the icing on the cake.

Open all wk 12-3.30 5-12 (Sun 12-7) **Bar Meals** L served
Mon-Sat 12-2.30, Sun 12-7 D served Mon-Sat 6-9.30,
Sun 12-7 Av main course £15 **Restaurant** L served Mon-
Sat 12-2.30, Sun 12-7 D served Mon-Sat 6-9.30, Sun
12-7 Fixed menu price fr £16.95 Av 3 course à la carte fr
£30 ⊕ FREE HOUSE ◀ Timothy Taylor Landlord, Ilkley
Gold & Mary Jane, Theakston, Black Sheep. ♟ 30
Facilities Non-diners area ♣ (Bar Garden) ♦♦ Children's
menu Children's portions Garden ⋈ Parking Wi-fi
▭ (notice required) **Rooms** 4

BREARTON   Map 19 SE36

Malt Shovel Inn

PICK OF THE PUBS

See Pick of the Pubs on page 498
See advert below

BROUGHTON   Map 18 SD95

The Bull ◉

PICK OF THE PUBS

BD23 3AE ☎ 01756 792065
e-mail: enquiries@thebullatbroughton.com
dir: *3m from Skipton on A59, on right*

Destination dining in a timeless setting

The Bull is part of the historic Broughton Estate, 3,000
acres of prime Yorkshire turf owned by the Tempest
family for 900 years. The relaxed atmosphere of this
dining pub eases you seamlessly into a lost world. The
setting helps; the stunning mansion is close by and the
pedigree cattle graze pastures skirting the Aire Valley. A
dining pub it may be, but The Bull welcomes beer drinkers
with plenty of choice: try Hetton Pale Ale or Signal Main
Line. Award-winning chefs make the most of the carefully
selected local producers; provenance and traceability are
key to the ingredients used in the extensive modern
English menu. How better to start than with Nidderdale
chicken and bacon turnover? Main courses and grills
feature the famous beef – perhaps in the form of flat iron
steak or chargrilled burger. Alternatively you'll find
Lancashire hot pot and cheese and onion pie.

Open all day all wk 12-11 (Sun 12-10) Closed: 25 Dec
Bar Meals L served Mon-Sat 12-2, Sun 12-8.30 D served
Mon-Thu 5.30-8.30, Fri-Sat 5.30-9, Sun 12-8.30 Av main
course £13.75 **Restaurant** Av 3 course à la carte fr £24
⊕ FREE HOUSE ◀ Dark Horse Hetton Pale Ale, Copper
Dragon Golden Pippin, Settle Signal Main Line ♂ Westons
Stowford Press. ♟ 11 **Facilities** Non-diners area ♣ (Bar

Outside area) ♦♦ Children's menu Outside area ⋈ Parking
Wi-fi

See advert on page 272

BURNSALL   Map 19 SE06

The Devonshire Fell ★★★★ RR ◉◉

PICK OF THE PUBS

BD23 6BT ☎ 01756 729000
e-mail: manager@devonshirefell.co.uk
dir: *On B6160, 6m from Bolton Abbey rdbt, A59 junct*

Stylish inn with breathtaking views

This former Victorian club for gentlemen mill-owners sits
on the edge of the Duke of Devonshire's estate with
unparalleled views of the river, the picturesque village of
Burnsall and the Yorkshire Dales. Given the lineage and
the stunning setting, one would expect polished antiques
and a classic country-house feel, but the decor is bright
and lively, with vibrant colours, polished floorboards, and
bold, contemporary works of art throughout the relaxing,
open-plan lounge bar and conservatory restaurant and
the quirky, hugely individual boutique-style bedrooms.
Equally bang up-to-date are the modern, Mediterranean-
inspired dishes, which have been awarded two AA
Rosettes. A meal might include sea bass fillet with
Morecambe Bay brown shrimp and shellfish foam; honey-
roasted duck breast with champ potatoes, baby turnips
and blackberry sauce; and dark chocolate marquis with
basil ice cream and fresh raspberries. Simpler dishes like
fish and chips and sausage and mash are served in the
bar, alongside local Copper Dragon ales.

Open all day all wk **Bar Meals** L served Mon-Sat 12-2,
Sun 12-3 D served all wk 7-9 Av main course £12.50
Restaurant L served Mon-Sat 12-2, Sun 12-3 D served all
wk 7-9 Av 3 course à la carte fr £35 ⊕ FREE HOUSE/
DEVONSHIRE HOTELS & RESTAURANTS ◀ Copper Dragon
Scotts 1816 & Golden Pippin, Truman's. ♟ 10
Facilities Non-diners area ♦♦ Children's menu Children's
portions Garden ⋈ Parking Wi-fi ▭ (notice required)
Rooms 12

The Malt Shovel

Main Street, Brearton,
North Yorkshire HG3 3BX
Tel: 01423 862929

Website: www.themaltshovelbrearton.co.uk
Email: bleikers@themaltshovelbrearton.co.uk

The Malt Shovel has been offering hospitality and refreshment to locals and visitors for over four hundred years.

At the heart of the tiny North Yorkshire village of Brearton, just four miles from Harrogate and Knaresborough, *The Malt Shovel* has become a gastronomic destination in its own right. But it remains, above all, a local, family-run country Inn, offering excellent food, friendly service and the warmest of welcomes.

PICK OF THE PUBS

Malt Shovel Inn

BREARTON — Map 19 SE36

HG3 3BX ☎ **01423 862929**
e-mail: bleikers@
themaltshovelbrearton.co.uk
web: www.themaltshovelbrearton.co.uk
dir: *A61 onto B6165 towards
Knaresborough. Left, follow Brearton
signs. 1m to village*

Secluded country inn with thoughtful menu

Swiss-born Jürg Bleiker bought this
lovely 16th-century country pub having
previously set up and run Bleiker's
Smokehouse, now in the hands of his
two daughters and their husbands.
Parts of the original structure catch the
eye in the busy interior, where log fires
will draw you into the jigsaw of spaces
and corners. Big leather chairs and
pianos dot stone-flagged floors of the
bar, curiously named The Monkey; more
intimate settings in the Red Room and
the elegant Green Room all meld
together. With Jürg as head chef, front
of house is run by his wife Jane and son
D'Arcy and his wife Anna, both of whom
are internationally renowned operatic
soloists (check for dates of opera-with-
dinner evenings). Wine lovers will
appreciate the well-balanced list, while
beer drinkers can enjoy Black Sheep
Best, Timothy Taylor Landlord or a
guest; the cider is Aspall's. The menu is
regularly tweaked to make the most of
the seasonal largesse available from

the strong contingent of local suppliers,
guaranteeing both freshness and
traceability. Smoked dishes feature
strongly, often utilising the smokery on
the premises; the Malt Shovel Smokie
starter of flaked smoked haddock with
cream, whisky and crispy gruyère a case
in point. Mains include comfort dishes
like lamb hot pot or calves' liver, mash
and black bacon; or plump for
Nidderdale chicken breast with Serrano
ham, chorizo and herb gnocchi.
Accompanying organic vegetables are
sourced from the pub's own
smallholding. Jürg personally selects
and describes his wines on a list stating
that all house wines are served by the
500ml carafe, as well as by the glass.

Open 12-3 5.30-11 (Sun 12-4) Closed:

25 Dec, Sun eve, Mon **Bar Meals** L
served Wed-Sat 12-2, Sun 12-4 D
served Wed-Sat 6-9 Av main course
£12.95 **Restaurant** L served Wed-Sat
12-2, Sun 12-4 D served Wed-Sat 6-9
Fixed menu price fr £16 Av 3 course à la
carte fr £22.85 ⊕ FREE HOUSE ◼ Black
Sheep Best Bitter, Timothy Taylor
Landlord, Guest ale ♂ Aspall. ☙ 21
Facilities Non-diners area ☗ Children's
portions Garden ☴ Parking

BURNSALL *continued*

The Red Lion ★★ HL

PICK OF THE PUBS

By the Bridge BD23 6BU ☎ **01756 720204**
e-mail: info@redlion.co.uk
dir: *From Skipton take A59 E, then B6160 towards Bolton Abbey, Burnsall 7m*

Popular 16th-century pub by the river

This 16th-century ferryman's inn overlooks the River Wharfe as it gently curves under a magnificent five-arch bridge. Large gardens and terraces make it an ideal spot for sunny days; while for refuge on chillier days the interior is welcoming with its creaky sloping floors and beamed ceilings. The original 'one-up, one-down' structure, which is now the oak-panelled and floored main bar, is the focal point. Bar food includes lunchtime sandwiches and light meals such as ham hock terrine with shallot compôte; and shepherd's pie or pork belly with a spring vegetable and smoked bacon jardinière in the evening. The main menu ups the ante with the likes of Thai-style fish fritters, followed by oxtail and potato pie. If you are staying over in one of the bedrooms look out for the horse trough — it was easier to build the steps around it.

Open all day all wk 8am-11.30pm **Bar Meals** L served Mon-Fri 12-2.30, Sat 12-9.30, Sun 12-9 D served Mon-Fri 6-9.30, Sat 12-9.30, Sun 12-9 **Restaurant** L served Mon-Fri 12-2.30, Sat 12-9.30, Sun 12-9 D served Mon-Fri 6-9.30, Sat 12-9.30, Sun 12-9 ⊕ FREE HOUSE ◖ Timothy Taylor Golden Best, Theakston Best Bitter, Thwaites Ö Thatchers. ☘ 14 **Facilities** Non-diners area ♦♦ Play area Family room Garden ⊨ Parking **Rooms** 25

CALDWELL   Map 19 NZ11

Brownlow Arms

DL11 7QH ☎ **01325 718471**
e-mail: bookings@brownlowarms.co.uk
dir: *From A1 at Scotch Corner take A66 towards Bowes. Right onto B6274 to Caldwell. Or from A1 junct 56 take B6275 N. 1st left through Mesonby to junct with B6274. Right to Caldwell*

Family friendly country inn

Set in delightful rolling countryside between Barnard Castle and Darlington, this stone inn in the tiny village of Caldwell is a great place to seek out. With ten wines by the glass, plenty more bins and reliable Yorkshire real ales, time passes easily here. A blend of traditional and modern rooms is the setting for unpicking a phenomenally comprehensive, globally inspired menu. Start perhaps with Peking duck rolls with hoi sin sauce, or sizzling king prawn and chorizo tapas; followed by home-made suet steak-and-kidney pudding; lobster and scallop thermidor; or lemon chilli chicken with noodles.

Open all wk 5.30pm-10.30pm (Sat-Sun 12-11) **Bar Meals** L served Sat 12-9, Sun 12-8 D served Mon-Fri 5.30-9 **Restaurant** L served Sat 12-9, Sun 12-8 D served Mon-Fri 5.30-9 ⊕ FREE HOUSE ◖ Timothy Taylor Landlord, Black Sheep, John Smith's, Guinness. ☘ 10

Facilities Non-diners area ♦♦ Children's menu Children's portions Garden Parking Wi-fi

CARTHORPE   Map 19 SE38

The Fox & Hounds

PICK OF THE PUBS

DL8 2LG ☎ **01845 567433**
dir: *Off A1, signed on both N'bound & S'bound carriageways*

Vegetarians have their own extensive menu

In the sleepy village of Carthorpe, the cosy Fox and Hounds has been a country inn for over 200 years, and the old anvil and other tools from its time as a smithy are still evident. Landlady Helen Talyor's parents bought the pub thirty years ago, and in the her hands and that of her husband Vincent's, they have certainly established an excellent reputation for their food which comes from named suppliers and the daily delivery of fresh fish. A typical dinner could begin with grilled black pudding with roasted apple, followed by half roasted Gressingham duckling with orange sauce, parsley and thyme stuffing and apple sauce, and finish with bramble and almond tart. There is a separate vegetarian menu of dishes that can be chosen as a starter or a main, such as caramelised onion and goats' cheese tart. Beers include local Black Sheep, while the wine choice is global in scope. Home-made produce such as jams and chutneys are available to purchase.

Open Tue-Sun 12-3 7-11 Closed: 25 Dec & 1st 2wks Jan, Mon **Bar Meals** L served Tue-Sun 12-2 D served Tue-Sun 7-9.30 Av main course £13.95 **Restaurant** L served Tue-Sun 12-2 D served Tue-Sun 7-9.30 Fixed menu price fr £14.95 Av 3 course à la carte fr £25 ⊕ FREE HOUSE ◖ Black Sheep Best Bitter, Worthington's, Guest ale Ö Thatchers Gold. **Facilities** ♦♦ Children's portions Parking

CHAPEL LE DALE   Map 18 SD77

The Old Hill Inn

LA6 3AR ☎ **015242 41256**
dir: *From Ingleton take B6255 4m, pub on right*

An ancient Dales inn of great character

Beautiful views of the Dales await visitors to this former farmhouse, later a drovers' inn, parts dating from 1615, the rest from 1835. When Winston Churchill stayed here on huntin', shootin', fishin' holidays, he no doubt enjoyed the bar, which these days serves eminent Yorkshire real ales like Black Sheep and Dent Aviator. A family of four chefs run the inn (one of whom makes sculptures from sugar) producing lunchtime snacks of sandwiches and home-made burgers, and typical main dishes of beef and ale casserole; smoked haddock fishcakes; and specials of pan-fried fillet of sea bass; and venison steak.

Open Tue-Sun Closed: 24-25 Dec, Mon (ex BHs) **Bar Meals** L served Tue-Sat 12-2.30, Sun 12-3 D served Tue-Fri & Sun 6.30-8.45, Sat 6-8.45 **Restaurant** L served Tue-Sat 12-2.30, Sun 12-3 D served Tue-Fri & Sun 6.30-8.45,

Sat 6-8.45 ⊕ FREE HOUSE ◖ Black Sheep Best Bitter, Theakston Best Bitter, Dent Aviator, Guest beer Ö Thatchers Gold, Aspall. **Facilities** Non-diners area ♣ (Bar Garden) ♦♦ Children's menu Children's portions Garden Parking

COLTON   Map 16 SE54

Ye Old Sun Inn

PICK OF THE PUBS

See Pick of the Pubs on page 500

CRAYKE   Map 19 SE57

The Durham Ox

PICK OF THE PUBS

Westway YO61 4TE ☎ **01347 821506**
e-mail: enquiries@thedurhamox.com
web: www.thedurhamox.com
dir: *From A19 through Easingwold to Crayke. From market place left up hill, pub on right*

At the top of their game for many years

The finest of Yorkshire welcomes awaits you at this hilltop pub, which is set in the beautiful Howardian Hills, an Area of Outstanding Natural Beauty. The free house is named after an eponymous ox that was born in 1796 and grew to massive proportions; a print hanging in the bottom bar is dedicated to its first owner, the Rt Hon Lord Somerville. With its flagstone floors, exposed beams, oak panelling and roaring winter fires in the main bar, The Durham Ox ticks all the right boxes. Only the best real ales and produce make it to the starting block here. Sandwiches and pub classics like spiced sticky pork ribs provide everyday fare, whilst more discerning palates will also find plenty of choice; fish and game are especially well regarded. Start your meal with oak-smoked trout pâté, before moving on to slow-braised venison and Black Sheep ale casserole. Desserts are no less appealing, with dark chocolate fondant a typical choice.

Open all day all wk 12-11.30 (Sun 12-10.30) Closed: 25 Dec **Bar Meals** L served Mon-Sat 12-2.30, Sun 12-3 D served Mon-Sat 5.30-9.30, Sun 5.30-8.30 **Restaurant** L served Mon-Sat 12-2.30, Sun 12-3 D served Mon-Sat 5.30-9.30, Sun 5.30-8.30 ⊕ FREE HOUSE ◖ Timothy Taylor Landlord, Black Sheep Best Bitter. ☘ 10 **Facilities** Non-diners area ♦♦ Children's menu Children's portions Garden ⊨ Parking Wi-fi

PICK OF THE PUBS

Ye Old Sun Inn

COLTON   Map 16 SE54

Main St LS24 8EP ☎ **01904 744261**
e-mail: yeoldsuninn@hotmail.co.uk
web: www.yeoldsuninn.co.uk
dir: *Approx 3.5m from York, off A64*

Country pub that goes from strength to strength

Ashley and Kelly McCarthy took over this 17th-century country pub in 2004 and have worked hard in transforming its fortunes from a run-down local to a thriving inn. They added a new bar area and extended the dining area, allowing them more space to increase the excellent themed events and cookery demonstrations and classes that have proved so popular in recent years. The former deli to the rear of the pub has made way for Ashley's new state-of-the-art kitchen, with the deli now placed in the dining room, where diners can buy freshly baked bread, home-made jams and chutneys, fresh fish, and daily essentials. A marquee in the garden overlooks rolling countryside and is used for large functions, which includes a summer beer festival and regular farmers' markets. Ashley takes pride in sourcing food and ale from small local producers and suppliers, including salads from his own polytunnel, and his menus are innovative and exciting. Lunches include light bites such as sandwiches, salads and wraps, plus there's an excellent Sunday lunch menu

featuring locally sourced roasted meats, chef's specials and a dinner menu. Expect Yorkshire-style main courses such as braised beef cheeks with horseradish mash and casseroled vegetables; steak and Black Sheep Bitter pie with shortcrust pastry; or rack of Yorkshire lamb with bubble-and-squeak and red wine jus. Precede with roasted tomato and pesto soup and finish with upside-down plum sponge with home-made plum sorbet, or tuck into Ashley's tasting platter of desserts. All dishes come with a wine recommendation, or look to the handpumps: Rudgate Battle Axe or Timothy Taylor Landlord are among the choice of seven real ales.

Open all wk 12-2.30 6-11 (Sun

12-10.30) **Bar Meals** L served Mon-Sat 12-2, Sun 12-7 D served Mon-Sat 6-9.30 **Restaurant** L served Mon-Sat 12-2, Sun 12-7 D served Mon-Sat 6-9.30 ⊕ FREE HOUSE ◀ Timothy Taylor Landlord & Golden Best, Rudgate Battle Axe, Black Sheep, Ossett, Moorhouse's, Guest ale ♨ Aspall. ♟ 18 **Facilities** Non-diners area ♦♟ Children's menu Children's portions Garden ⊼ Beer festival Parking Wi-fi ▭

Save on hotels. Book at theAA.com/hotel

YORKSHIRE, NORTH 501 ENGLAND

CROPTON
Map 19 SE78

The New Inn

YO18 8HH ☎ 01751 417330
e-mail: info@croptonbrewery.com
dir: Telephone for directions

Microbrewery on site draws many real ale enthusiasts

On the edge of the North York Moors National Park, this family-run free house is fortunate to have the acclaimed Cropton microbrewery at the bottom of the garden. Popular with locals and visitors alike, the pub is a draw to ale lovers and there is an annual beer festival in November. Meals are served in the restored village bar and in the elegant Victorian restaurant: choices could include Yorkshire coast fishcakes or crisp belly pork with dauphinoise potatoes; an extensive range from the grill; plus lunchtime sandwiches and ciabatta rolls.

Open all day all wk 11-11 (Sun 11-10.30) **Bar Meals** L served all wk 12-2 D served all wk 6-9 **Restaurant** D served all wk 6-9 ⊕ FREE HOUSE ◀ Cropton Two Pints, Yorkshire Warrior, Blackout, Monkmans Slaughter, Yorkshire Moors Bitter & Honey Gold Ŏ Mr Whitehead's. **Facilities** Non-diners area ♣ (Bar Garden) ⬦ Children's menu Children's portions Play area Family room Garden ⊨ Beer festival Parking Wi-fi ▭ (notice required)

EAST WITTON
Map 19 SE18

The Blue Lion

PICK OF THE PUBS

DL8 4SN ☎ 01969 624273
e-mail: enquiries@thebluelion.co.uk
dir: From Ripon take A6108 towards Leyburn

Smart 18th-century village pub with imaginative food

This smart 18th-century coaching inn, tucked away in an unspoilt estate village close to Jervaulx Abbey, once frequented by drovers and travellers journeying through Wensleydale, has become one of North Yorkshire's finest inns, run by Paul and Helen Klein. The inn has an interior best described as rural chic with stacks of atmosphere and charm. The classic bar with its open fire and flagstone floor is a beer drinker's haven, where the best of North Yorkshire's breweries present a pleasant dilemma for the real ale lover. A blackboard displays imaginative but unpretentious bar meals, while diners in the candlelit restaurant can expect culinary treats incorporating a variety of Yorkshire ingredients, notably seasonal game. A memorable meal may comprise pan-fried king scallops with caramelised cauliflower and hazelnut dressing; or butternut squash and wild mushroom risotto with parmesan and truffle oil; followed by pancetta-wrapped pheasant breast with creamed cavolo nero, thyme and pearl barley jus, or poached halibut with samphire, caper, chive and vermouth velouté; and vanilla fudge parfait with caramelised figs and honey to finish.

Open all day all wk 11-11 Closed: 25 Dec **Bar Meals** L served all wk 12-2.15 D served all wk 7-9.30 **Restaurant** L served all wk 12-2.15 D served all wk 7-9.30 ⊕ FREE HOUSE ◀ Black Sheep Best Bitter & Riggwelter, Theakston Best Bitter, Worthington's Ŏ Thatchers Gold. ⬗ 12 **Facilities** Non-diners area ♣ (Bar Garden) ⬦ Children's portions Garden ⊨ Parking Wi-fi

The Cover Bridge Inn

DL8 4SQ ☎ 01969 623250
e-mail: enquiries@thecoverbridgeinn.co.uk
dir: On A6108 between Middleham & East Witton

Welcoming Wensleydale pub with well-kept draught ales

The Harringtons have now owned this magnificent little pub at one end of a venerable arched bridge on the River Cover for some 15 years. The pub's oldest part was probably built around 1670, to cater for the increasing trade on the drovers' route from Coverdale. Watch out for the cunning door-latch, which befuddles many a first-time visitor. The ancient interior rewards with wrinkled beams, a vast hearth and open log fires, settles and wholesome fodder, including home-made pies, daily specials, and their famous ham and eggs. Relax in the riverside garden with your choice from eight ales on tap, three of which are rotating guests.

Open all day all wk **Bar Meals** L served all wk 12-2 D served all wk 6-9 ⊕ FREE HOUSE ◀ Guest ales Ŏ Westons Old Rosie, Gwynt y Ddraig Happy Daze & Two Trees Perry. **Facilities** Non-diners area ♣ (Bar Garden) ⬦ Children's menu Children's portions Play area Garden ⊨ Parking ▭ (notice required)

EGTON
Map 19 NZ80

The Wheatsheaf Inn

PICK OF THE PUBS

YO21 1TZ ☎ 01947 895271
e-mail: info@wheatsheafegton.com
dir: Off A169, NW of Grosmont

Handsome pub at the centre of the community

This modest old pub is very popular with fishermen, as the River Esk runs along at the foot of the hill, and is a big draw for fly-fishers in particular. The pub sits back from the wide main road and it would be easy to drive past it, but that would be a mistake as the welcoming main bar is cosy and traditional, with low beams, dark green walls and comfy settles. The menu offers sandwiches, soup and hot focaccia rolls at lunchtime, as well as a range of light lunches, including wholetail Whitby scampi. In the evening, the supper menu might include a starter of lamb's kidneys with bacon, Madeira and redcurrant gravy and main courses such as chicken and smoked bacon puff pastry pie. There's a locals' bar too, but it only holds about a dozen people, so get there early.

Open 11.30-3 5.30-11.30 (Sat 11.30-11.30 Sun 11.30-11) Closed: Mon **Bar Meals** L served Tue-Sun 12-2

D served Tue-Sat 6-9 ⊕ FREE HOUSE ◀ Black Sheep Best Bitter & Golden Sheep, John Smith's, Timothy Taylor Landlord, Guest ales Ŏ Thatchers Gold. **Facilities** Non-diners area ⬦ Garden ⊨ Parking Wi-fi

EGTON BRIDGE
Map 19 NZ80

Horseshoe Hotel

YO21 1XE ☎ 01947 895245
e-mail: horseshoehotel@yahoo.co.uk
dir: From Whitby take A171 towards Middlesborough. Village signed in 5m

Riverside hotel champions local ingredients and ales

The Horseshoe, now under new ownership, is an 18th-century country house set in beautiful grounds by the River Esk, handy for visiting Whitby, Robin Hood's Bay, the North Yorkshire Moors Railway and TV's *Heartbeat* country. Inside the welcoming bar are oak settles and tables, local artists' paintings, and plates around the picture rails. Along with some great beers, such as Durham Brewery ale, local ingredients are used to create the varied menu, try wholetail scampi and chips or medallion of pork fillet with woodchopper sauce.

Open all wk 11.30-3 6.30-11 (Sat 11.30-11 Sun 12-10.30) **Bar Meals** L served all wk 12-2 D served all wk 6-9 Av main course £6.95 **Restaurant** L served all wk 12-2 D served all wk 6-9 ⊕ FREE HOUSE ◀ John Smith's Cask, Durham, Black Sheep, Theakston, Guest ales. **Facilities** Non-diners area ⬦ Children's menu Children's portions Family room Garden ⊨ Parking Wi-fi ▭ (notice required)

The Postgate

YO21 1UX ☎ 01947 895241
dir: Telephone for directions

Walkers, families and dogs are very welcome

Set in the Esk Valley within a stone's throw of the river, The Postgate is a typical North York Moors country inn; it played the part of the Black Dog in TV's *Heartbeat*. Being on the coast-to-coast trail, and becoming known as a food destination, the pub is popular with walkers who chat amiably with locals in the bar over their pints of Black Sheep. A myriad of food choices written on blackboards change with seasonal availability. Fresh fish and seafood are strengths, while hearty dishes of local lamb and mature beef are served with your choice of vegetables, potatoes or salads.

Open all wk 12-3 5.30-12 ⊕ PUNCH TAVERNS ◀ Timothy Taylor Landlord, Black Sheep Bitter. **Facilities** ♣ (Bar Garden) ⬦ Children's menu Children's portions Garden Parking Wi-fi

FELIXKIRK
Map 19 SE48

The Carpenters Arms NEW

YO7 2DP ☎ 01845 537369
e-mail: enquiries@thecarpentersarmsfelixkirk.com
web: www.carpentersarmsfelixkirk.com
dir: *From Thirsk take A170 towards Helmsley. Left signed Felixkirk, 2.25m to village*

Unpretentious village pub with lovely views

Felixkirk, in the Vale of Mowbray, has no shops, making this Provenance Inn owned pub the village's only retail establishment. To the east are the Hambleton Hills and the North Yorks Moors National Park, while west are the Yorkshire Dales. Bare stonework, slate flooring and rich red walls characterise the interior, and there's an open fire in the bar. The restaurant and tiered terrace offer the best views. Menu descriptions are simple: pan-seared salmon fillet; roasted chicken breast; sticky ribs; steak ciabatta. Check out The Magnificent Seven - seven main courses, including bangers and mash, each £7.

Open all day all wk **Bar Meals** L served Mon-Sat 12-2.30, Sun 12-3 D served Mon-Sat 6-9.30, Sun 6-8.30 Av main course £14.95 **Restaurant** L served Mon-Sat 12-2.30, Sun 12-3 D served Mon-Sat 6-9.30, Sun 6-8.30 Av 3 course à la carte fr £27.95 ⊕ PROVENANCE INNS ◖ Black Sheep Best Bitter, Timothy Taylor Landlord ♂ Aspall.
Facilities Non-diners area ✿ (Bar Garden) ♦♦ Garden ㅈ Parking Wi-fi ☞ (notice required)

GIGGLESWICK
Map 18 SD86

Black Horse Hotel

32 Church St BD24 0BE ☎ 01729 822506
e-mail: theblackhorse-giggle@tiscali.co.uk
dir: *Telephone for directions*

Village centre inn with pub favourites on the menu

Set next to the church and behind the market cross in the 17th-century main street, this traditional free house is as charming as Giggleswick itself. Down in the warm and friendly bar you'll find a range of hand-pulled ales, with local guest beer sometimes available. The menu of freshly prepared pub favourites ranges from hot sandwiches, home-made pizzas or giant filled Yorkshire puddings, to main course dishes like traditional lamb hotpot or horseshoe of local gammon.

Open 12-2.30 5.30-11 (Sat-Sun 12-11) Closed: Mon **Bar Meals** L served Tue-Sun 12-1.45 D served Tue-Sun 7-8.45 Av main course £8.50 **Restaurant** L served Sun 12-1.45

D served Tue-Sun 7-8.45 ⊕ FREE HOUSE ◖ Timothy Taylor Landlord & Golden Best, John Smith's.
Facilities Non-diners area ♦♦ Children's menu Children's portions Garden ㅈ Parking Wi-fi

GOATHLAND
Map 19 NZ80

Birch Hall Inn

Beck Hole YO22 5LE ☎ 01947 896245
e-mail: glenys@birchhallinn.fsnet.co.uk
dir: *9m from Whitby on A169*

One of the smallest bars in the country

Beck Hole is a tiny hamlet of nine cottages and a pub hidden in the steep Murk Esk Valley close to the North Yorkshire Moors (steam) Railway. This delightful little free house has just two tiny rooms separated by a sweet shop; no more than 30 people plus two small dogs have ever fitted inside with the door closed! The main bar offers well-kept local ales to sup beside an open fire in winter, including the pub's house ale, Beckwatter. In warm weather, food and drink can be enjoyed in the large garden, which has peaceful views. The local quoits team play on the village green on summer evenings. The pub has been under the same ownership for over 25 years and the simple menu features the local butcher's pies, old-fashioned flatcakes filled with ham, cheese, corned beef or farmhouse pâté, and home-made scones and buttered beer cake.

Open 11-3 7.30-11 (11-11 summer) Closed: Mon eve & Tue in winter **Bar Meals** L served food served during all opening hours ⊕ FREE HOUSE ◖ Birch Hall Inn Beckwatter, Black Sheep Best Bitter, Durham Black Velvet, York Guzzler. **Facilities** ✿ (Bar Garden) ♦♦ Family room Garden ㅈ **Notes** ⊗

GRASSINGTON
Map 19 SE06

Grassington House ★★★★★ RR ◉◉

5 The Square BD23 5AQ ☎ 01756 752406
e-mail: bookings@grassingtonhousehotel.co.uk
dir: *A59 into Grassington, in town square opposite post office*

A destination pub and restaurant with rooms

Whoever commissioned this private house in 1760 chose the site well, for John and Sue Rudden's elegant Georgian pub and restaurant stands imposingly in Grassington's cobbled square. Fresh local produce underpins a two AA-Rosette menu offering Goosnargh corn-fed chicken liver pâté; pan-roasted Bolton Abbey lamb cutlet, loin and braised belly; beer-battered Northumberland haddock; and taster slates of tapas-style nibbles. Thwaites Original and Wainwright, and Dark Horse Hetton Pale Ale are bar staples. Original Georgian architecture is complemented by splendidly refurbished rooms, convenient for the 2014 Tour de France, which will pass by Grassington on its circuitous way from Leeds to Harrogate.

Open all day all wk **Bar Meals** L served Mon-Fri 12-2.30, Sat 12-4, Sun 12-8 D served Mon-Sat 6-9.30, Sun 12-8 Av main course £16 **Restaurant** L served all wk 12-2.30 D served Mon-Sat 6-9.30, Sun 6-8.30 Fixed menu price fr

£16.50 Av 3 course à la carte fr £28 ⊕ FREE HOUSE ◖ Dark Horse Hetton Pale Ale, Thwaites Original & Wainwright. ☿ 14 **Facilities** Non-diners area ♦♦ Children's menu Children's portions Garden ㅈ Parking Wi-fi ☞ (notice required) **Rooms** 9

GREAT AYTON
Map 19 NZ51

The Royal Oak ★★★ INN

123 High St TS9 6BW ☎ 01642 722361
e-mail: info@royaloak-hotel.co.uk
dir: *Telephone for directions*

Enjoyable food served all day

Run by the Monaghan family since 1978, this 18th-century inn stands opposite the green in the village where explorer Captain James Cook attended school. Original features, including beamed ceilings and open fires in the public bar and restaurant, are very much part of its charm and character. An extensive range of food is available all day: from an evening menu come Yorkshire pudding filled with beef and mash; grilled salmon fillet with parsley butter; and crisp pork belly with mustard gravy. Banana butterscotch sundae is a typical dessert. Stay over in one of the five comfortable bedrooms.

Open all day all wk Closed: 25 Dec **Bar Meals** L served all wk 12-6 D served all wk 6-9.30 food served all day **Restaurant** L served all wk 12-2 D served all wk 6-9.30 ⊕ STAR PUBS & BARS ◖ John Smith's Smooth, Courage Directors, Theakston. ☿ 10 **Facilities** Non-diners area ✿ (Bar Garden) ♦♦ Children's menu Children's portions Garden ㅈ Wi-fi ☞ (notice required) **Rooms** 5

GREAT HABTON
Map 19 SE77

The Grapes Inn

YO17 6TU ☎ 01653 669166
e-mail: info@thegrapes-inn.co.uk
dir: *From Malton take B1257 towards Helmsley. In Amotherby right into Amotherby Ln. After Newsham Bridge right into Habton Ln & follow pubs signs. 0.75m to pub*

Great community pub with well-liked menu

The village pub was extended a few years ago to incorporate the old post office here in fertile Ryedale, between the Howardian Hills and the North Yorkshire Moors near the bustling market town of Malton. Cue the lively taproom, where beers from the Marston's list are popular with locals and visitors alike, and the cosy dining room, separated by a roaring log fire warming both rooms on a winter's evening. Chef-proprietor Adam Myers conjures up some enticing meals; roasted monkfish on pea, bacon and parmesan risotto or roasted vegetable and feta tart are just two of the hearty, home-cooked dishes here.

Open Tue-Fri 6pm-close (Sat 12-2 6-close Sun open all day) Closed: fr 2 Jan for 2wks, Mon **Bar Meals** L served Sat-Sun 12-2 D served Tue-Sat 6.30-8.30, Sun 6.30-8.30 **Restaurant** L served Sat-Sun 12-2 D served Tue-Sat 6.30-8.30, Sun 6.30-8.30 ⊕ MARSTON'S ◖ Ringwood Best Bitter, Wychwood Hobgoblin, Guest ales ♂ Thatchers Gold. **Facilities** Non-diners area ♦♦ Children's menu Children's portions Outside area ㅈ Parking

PICK OF THE PUBS

The Bridge Inn

GRINTON　　　Map 19 SE09

DL11 6HH ☎ 01748 884224
e-mail: atkinbridge@btinternet.com
web: www.bridgeinngrinton.co.uk
dir: *Exit A1 at Scotch Corner onto
A6108, through Richmond. Left onto
B6270 towards Grinton & Reeth*

A favourite with ramblers and discerning diners

A 13th-century riverside pub close to one of Yorkshire's finest old churches, known as the Cathedral of the Dales, The Bridge is located in Grinton, which has stood here for almost 1,000 years. Two of the Yorkshire Dales' wildest and prettiest dales meet in Grinton; Arkengarthdale and Swaledale collide in a symphony of fells, moors, waterfalls and cataracts. Lanes and tracks slope down from the heights, bringing ramblers and riders to appreciate the good range of northern beers that Andrew Atkin matches with his fine foods; York Brewery's Yorkshire Terrier being a case in point. Locals enjoy the bustling games room and beamed old bar serving baguettes and rye squares, whilst a more tranquil restaurant area caters for those after a more intimate meal experience. Resident chef John Scott is in charge of the food, his menu inspired by carefully chosen seasonal local game, meats, fish and other produce, including herbs plucked from the garden. Expect traditional English

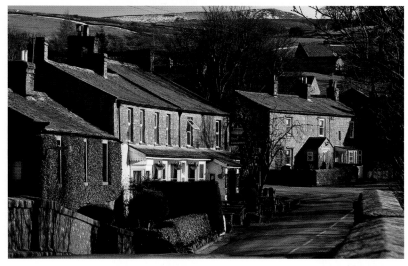

dishes with a modern twist, enhanced by daily-changing specials. Starters range from hot smoked salmon fillet with red chard, pickled cucumber, dill salad, poppy seed blinis and chive crème fraîche, to chicken tikka kebabs with a pepper, mixed bean and mint salad and a mango chutney dressing. Mains reflect a similar scope, running from homely slow-roasted pork belly or trio of Swaledale lamb to smoked haddock, salmon and king prawns in a creamy sauce and wrapped in a savoury pancake. Finish with Liz's ginger pudding and vanilla ice cream; blueberry and white chocolate cheesecake; or a selection of Swaledale cheeses with savoury biscuits and chutney. For entertainment there is musicians' night every Thursday.

Open all day all wk **Bar Meals** Av main course £10-£16 food served all day **Restaurant** food served all day ⊕ JENNINGS ◀ Cumberland Ale & Cocker Hoop, Caledonian Deuchars IPA, York Yorkshire Terrier, Adnams. **Facilities** Non-diners area ✿ (Bar Garden) ⅋ Children's menu Children's portions Garden Parking Wi-fi ▦

GREAT OUSEBURN — Map 19 SE46

The Crown Inn NEW

Main St YO26 9RF ☎ 01423 330013 & 330430
e-mail: liz@thecrown-inn.com
dir: *A59 onto B6265 towards Boroughbridge. After 3.5m right into Carrside Ln into Great Ouseburn. Right at x-rds. Pub 100mtrs on right*

Vale of York pub with very good food

The lights had been out for eight months when Paul and Liz Jackson first saw the Crown. Today, as testament both to their efforts and village support, this community local is going from strength to strength. There are six eating areas, including the bar, where the top-selling real ales are Black Sheep and Rudgate's Crown Blonde. Locally sourced steaks, pie of the day, and fish and chips are year-round staples, while the monthly-changing carte offers, for example, Yorkshire Dales rump of lamb with red wine and blackberries; roasted hake with chestnut mushroom velouté; and roasted pepper and vine tomato tarte Tatin.

Open 12-3 5-11 (Sun 12-8) Closed: Mon & Tue Bar Meals L served Wed-Sat 12-2.30, Sun 12-8 D served Wed-Sat 5-9.30 Av main course £10-£15 Restaurant L served Wed-Sat 12-2.30, Sun 12-8 D served Wed-Sat 5-9.30 Fixed menu price fr £13.50 Av 3 course à la carte fr £20 ⊕ FREE HOUSE ◀ Rudgate Crown Blonde, Black Sheep Best Bitter ☼ Aspall. ♀ 13
Facilities Non-diners area ♦️ Children's portions Outside area ⧖ Parking Wi-fi ☛ (notice required)

GREEN HAMMERTON — Map 19 SE45

The Bay Horse Inn

York Rd YO26 8BN ☎ 01423 330338
e-mail: enquiry@bayhorsegreenhammerton.co.uk
dir: *A1 junct 47 follow signs for A59 towards York. After 3m, turn left into village, on right opposite post office*

Hearty food in the Vale of York

This traditional inn is part of the original settlement of Green Hammerton, positioned on the old Roman road from York to Aldborough. The pub has served travellers and villagers for over 200 years; many features from those days remain in the beamed, fire-warmed interior. Reliable Yorkshire cask beers accompany home-made meals strong on local produce; excellent matured steaks, gammon and chicken grilled to order are always available. Daily-changing dishes include haunch of venison steak with pear, cranberry and port sauce; and pork fillet with cider and apple sauce. Outside is a garden and patio area.

Open all wk 11.30-2.30 5.30-12 (Sat 11.30am-mdnt Sun 11.30-8) ⊕ GREENE KING ◀ IPA, Timothy Taylor, Black Sheep, Guest ale. Facilities ❖ (Bar Garden) ♦️ Children's portions Garden Parking Wi-fi

GRINTON — Map 19 SE09

The Bridge Inn

PICK OF THE PUBS

See Pick of the Pubs on page 503

HARDRAW — Map 18 SD89

The Green Dragon Inn

DL8 3LZ ☎ 01969 667392
e-mail: info@greendragonhardraw.com
dir: *From Hawes take A684 towards Sedbergh. Right to Hardraw, approx 1.5m*

If you're in the area, don't miss this one

Entering the Bar Parlour is like stepping into a Tudor film-set, although parts of the inn are much older — 13th century, in fact. Gravestones, forming part of the floor, were washed away from the neighbouring churchyard during floods. In a wooded site behind is Hardraw Force, England's highest single-drop waterfall, which JMW Turner painted while staying here in 1816. The choice of real ales is good, and pub food includes home-made steak pie; giant Yorkshire pudding; and local game casserole. Beer festivals in June and July, a third with cider in October, and regular live folk music are all big draws.

Open all day all wk Bar Meals L served all wk 11.30-3 D served all wk 6-10 Av main course £9.95 ⊕ FREE HOUSE ◀ Timothy Taylor Landlord, Theakston Best Bitter & Old Peculier, Wensleydale, Yorkshire Dales ☼ Olivers, Gwatkins, Dunkertons, Ralph's. Facilities Non-diners area ❖ (Bar Garden) ♦️ Children's menu Children's portions Family room Garden ⧖ Beer festival Cider festival Parking Wi-fi ☛ (notice required)

HAROME — Map 19 SE68

The Star Inn ◉◉

PICK OF THE PUBS

YO62 5JE ☎ 01439 770397
e-mail: reservations@thestarinnatharome.co.uk
dir: *From Helmsley take A170 towards Kirkbymoorside 0.5m. Turn right for Harome*

Renowned gastro-pub

This 14th-century thatched gem sits in a beautiful village on the fringe of the North Yorkshire Moors National Park. Great local walks and a properly pubby bar are worth the journey alone and both locals and visitors can revel in Copper Dragon or Cropton's Two Chefs whilst eagerly awaiting the call to dine. Andrew Pern's daily-changing seasonal menu crafted largely from local produce has made this one of the jewels in England's gastro-pub crown. Treat yourself to grilled black pudding with pan-fried foie gras, salad of Pickering watercress, apple and vanilla chutney and scrumpy reduction before moving on to grilled fillet of sea bass with smoked eel croquettes, fresh horseradish and Lindisfarne oyster velouté. Finish with baked soufflé of forced Yorkshire rhubarb with stem ginger syrup. In the bar the quick of eye might spot the

trademark carved mice on the oak furniture created by 'Mouseman' Thompson's works in nearby Kilburn.

Open all wk 11.30-3 6.30-11 (Mon 6.30-11 Sun 12-11) Closed: 1 Jan, Mon L Bar Meals L served Tue-Sat 11.30-2, Sun 12-6 D served Mon-Sat 6.30-9.30 Av main course £20 Restaurant L served Tue-Sat 11.30-2, Sun 12-6 D served Mon-Sat 6.30-9.30 Fixed menu price fr £20 Av 3 course à la carte fr £30 ⊕ FREE HOUSE ◀ Theakston Best Bitter, Black Sheep, Copper Dragon, Hambleton, Cropton ☼ Westons Stowford Press, Ampleforth Abbey. ♀ 24 Facilities Non-diners area ♦️ Children's menu Children's portions Garden ⧖ Parking ☛ (notice required)

HAWES — Map 18 SD88

The Moorcock Inn

Garsdale Head LA10 5PU ☎ 01969 667488
e-mail: admin@moorcockinn.com
dir: *On A684, 5m from Hawes, 10m from Sedbergh at junct with B6259 for Kirkby Stephen*

Old inn surrounded by open countryside

At the tip of Wensleydale, this 18th-century inn stands alone in open countryside, although it is only three-quarters of a mile from Garsdale Station. Inside is a traditional blend of original stonework, bright colours and comfortable sofas. Savour a glass of local real ale from the Tirril Brewery, draught lager or one of the 50 malt whiskies, and enjoy the spectacular views from the garden. Home-cooked lunches include jackets, sandwiches and pub classics. For dinner, start with whitebait, brown bread, lemon and aïoli, then tuck into steak, mushroom and ale pie or a vegetarian choice of sweet potato and aubergine curry.

Open 12-12 Mar-Oct (Mon-Fri 12-3 6-12 Sat-Sun 12-12 Nov-Feb) Closed: 25 Dec Mon & Wed in Nov & Jan Bar Meals L served all wk 12-3 D served until 9pm food served all day Restaurant L served all wk 12-3 D served until 9pm food served all day ⊕ FREE HOUSE ◀ Copper Dragon, Theakston, Tirril Ales, Nine Standards Brewery, Cumberland Corby Ale, Dent, Wensleydale, Guest ales ☼ Thatchers. ♀ 52 Facilities Non-diners area ❖ (Bar Restaurant Garden) ♦️ Children's menu Children's portions Garden ⧖ Parking Wi-fi ☛ (notice required)

HAWNBY — Map 19 SE58

The Inn at Hawnby ★★★★ INN ◉

PICK OF THE PUBS

YO62 5QS ☎ 01439 798202
e-mail: info@innathawnby.co.uk
dir: *Off B1257 between Stokesley & Helmsley*

Stunning views and first-rate food

In the heart of the North Yorkshire Moors at the top of a hill in the village of Hawnby, this charming 19th-century former drovers' inn with rooms offers panoramic country views. Run by hands-on and welcoming proprietors Kathryn and David Young, it offers the award-winning, one AA-Rosette cuisine that majors on local produce. Dishes such as ham hock terrine with piccalilli dressing

Save on hotels. Book at **theAA.com/hotel**

YORKSHIRE, NORTH 505 ENGLAND

and toast; roast duck breast with purple sprouting broccoli, fondant potato and classic reform sauce; or fillet of pork wrapped in Parma ham with parsnip purée, spinach and garlic mash can be enjoyed with a pint of light and quaffable Hawnby Hops ale brewed especially for the pub. Puddings include hot fruit waffle with vanilla ice cream and grenadine; and lemon and blueberry posset. For designated drivers, there's even free water from the inn's own spring. If you would like to stay over, there are nine comfortable rooms.

Open all wk 10-3 6-11 (Fri-Sun all day) Closed: 25 Dec **Bar Meals** L served all wk 12-2 D served all wk 7-9 Av main course £15 **Restaurant** L served all wk 12-2 D served all wk 7-9 Av 3 course à la carte fr £25 ⊕ FREE HOUSE ◙ Timothy Taylor Landlord, Black Sheep, Hawnby Hops, Great Newsome Arden ale Ö Westons Stowford Press. ♚ 8 **Facilities** Non-diners area ❖ (Bar Garden) ♦❙ Children's menu Children's portions Garden ⋒ Parking Wi-fi ▦ (notice required) **Rooms** 9

HELPERBY
Map 19 SE46

The Oak Tree Inn NEW

Raskelf Rd YO61 2PH ☎ **01423 789189**
e-mail: enquiries@theoaktreehelperby.com
web: www.theoaktreehelperby.com
dir: *A19 from York towards Thirsk. After Easingwold left signed Helperby. Approx 5m to village*

No-nonsense pub food at newly refurbished village inn

Depending on how you approach the village, the signs say either Helperby Brafferton or Brafferton Helperby, an apparent confusion which to locals probably makes perfect sense. Major refurbishment has revived this member of the Provenance Inn group, giving it a spacious new bar for informal dining, and a barn extension overlooking the rear courtyard for more formal meals. You'll find the same menu as in sister pubs in Felixkirk and Marton, offering unfussy mains such as slow-braised venison; Moroccan spiced chicken supreme; Yorkshire steaks; and Black Sheep beer-battered fish and chips.

Open all day all wk **Bar Meals** L served Mon-Sat 12-2.30, Sun 12-3 D served Mon-Sat 5.30-9.30, Sun 5.30-8.30 Av main course £12.95 **Restaurant** L served Mon-Sat 12-2.30, Sun 12-3 D served Mon-Sat 5.30-9.30, Sun 5.30-8.30 Fixed menu price fr £14.95 Av 3 course à la carte fr £22.95 ⊕ PROVENANCE INNS ◙ Black Sheep Best Bitter, Timothy Taylor Landlord Ö Aspall. **Facilities** Non-diners area ❖ (Bar Outside area) ♦❙ Children's menu Children's portions Outside area ⋒ Parking Wi-fi ▦ (notice required)

HIGH GRANTLEY
Map 19 SE26

The Grantley Arms

HG4 3PJ ☎ **01765 620227**
e-mail: vsails2@aol.com
dir: *From Ripon on B6265 towards Pateley Bridge (pass Fountains Abbey) take 2nd right signed Grantley. 0.5m pub on left*

Hands-on approach pays off

On the edge of the Yorkshire Dales National Park, three miles from Fountains Abbey and five from the market town of Ripon, is this 17th-century inn that Valerie Sails and Eric Broadwith have run since 2001. They can usually be found front-of-house, either in the bar, home of some excellent Yorkshire real ales, or in the intimate restaurant, where crisp linen cloths cover the tables. With virtually everything made in the pub's own kitchen, start with smoked haddock fillet, diced vegetables, parsley and potato chowder, then rare-breed belly pork with apple sauce and red wine jus, and coconut mousse to finish.

Open 12-3 5.30-11 (Sun 12-3.30 5.30-11) Closed: 2wks Nov, Mon **Bar Meals** L served Tue-Sat 12-2, Sun 12-3.30 D served Tue-Sun 5.30-9 **Restaurant** L served Tue-Sat 12-2, Sun 12-3.30 D served Tue-Sun 5.30-9 ⊕ FREE HOUSE ◙ Theakston, Hambleton, Great Newsome, Old Mill Ö Thatchers Gold. ♚ 10 **Facilities** Non-diners area ♦❙ Children's menu Children's portions Outside area ⋒ Parking Wi-fi ▦ (notice required)

HOVINGHAM
Map 19 SE67

The Malt Shovel

Main St YO62 4LF ☎ **01653 628264**
e-mail: info@themaltshovelhovingham.com
dir: *18m NE of York, 5m from Castle Howard*

Roadside village pub

Tucked away in the Duchess of Kent's home village, the stone-built 18th-century Malt Shovel offers a friendly atmosphere with well-kept ales and food prepared from quality local ingredients. There are two dining rooms where you can enjoy starters of whitebait with lime and chili mayonnaise, chicken liver pâté with chutney, or black pudding and apple fritters, followed by swordfish with tomato and anchovy sauce, mustard chicken, or chickpea curry. There is also a large beer garden at the rear of the pub where you can sit and enjoy a pint or two in lovely surroundings.

Open all wk winter 11.30-2 6-11 (Sun & summer 11.30-2.30 5.30-11) **Bar Meals** L served Mon-Sat 11.30-2 (winter) 11.30-2.30 (summer), Sun 12-2.30 D served Mon-Sat 6-9 (winter) 5.30-9 (summer), Sun 5.30-8 **Restaurant** L served Mon-Sat 11.30-2 (winter) 11.30-2.30 (summer), Sun 12-2.30 D served Mon-Sat 6-9 (winter) 5.30-9 (summer), Sun 5.30-8 ⊕ PUNCH TAVERNS ◙ Copper Dragon Golden Pippin, Theakston Best Bitter, Black Sheep, Guest ale. **Facilities** Non-diners area ❖ (Bar Garden) ♦❙ Children's menu Children's portions Garden ⋒ Parking ▦ (notice required)

The Worsley Arms Hotel
PICK OF THE PUBS

Main St YO62 4LA ☎ **01653 628234**
e-mail: enquiries@worsleyarms.co.uk
dir: *On B1257 between Malton & Helmsley*

A magnificent base for exploring North Yorkshire

Built by Sir William Worsley in 1841, this village hotel and pub form part of the Worsley family's historic Hovingham Hall Estate, birthplace of the Duchess of Kent, and currently home to her nephew. Hambleton Stallion from nearby Thirsk, and Black Sheep from Masham are on tap in the Cricketers' Bar (the local team has played on the village green for over 150 years). You can eat here or in the restaurant; lunch and afternoon tea are also served in the large walled garden. Lunchtime choices could include traditional mains like Wensleydale gammon steak, and a selection of sandwiches; while the à la carte lists pan-fried sea bass with a crab and king prawn risotto; and confit of braised lamb shank. A short drive from the market town of Pickering, the hotel is also well placed for visiting York, the Dales and Castle Howard. The pub hosts regular wine evenings, monthly quizzes and a supper club.

Open all day all wk 11-11 **Bar Meals** L served all wk 12-2 D served all wk 6.30-9 Av main course £14 **Restaurant** L served Sun 12-2.30 D served all wk 6.30-9 Av 3 course à la carte fr £27.50 ⊕ FREE HOUSE ◙ Hambleton Stallion, Black Sheep. ♚ 20 **Facilities** Non-diners area ❖ (Bar Garden) ♦❙ Garden ⋒ Parking ▦ (notice required)

HUBBERHOLME
Map 18 SD97

The George Inn

BD23 5JE ☎ **01756 760223**
dir: *From Skipton take B6265 to Threshfield. B6160 to Buckden. Follow signs for Hubberholme*

Family-owned Dales inn with bags of charm

Stunningly located beside the River Wharfe in the Yorkshire Dales National Park, this pub was built in the 1600s as a farmstead and still has flagstone floors, stone walls, mullioned windows and an open fire. To check if the bar is open, look for a lighted candle in the window. Beers are local, coming from the Black Sheep and Yorkshire Dales breweries. Enjoy your pint on the terrace in the summer months. The evening menu includes a starter of red bell pepper filled with ratatouille, a main of Dales lamb chops, and a dessert of home-made Bakewell tart. There's a slightly reduced lunch menu with the addition of baguettes.

Open 12-3 6-11 Closed: Dec-Jan, Mon **Bar Meals** L served Tue-Sun 12-2 D served Tue-Sun 6-8 Av main course £10 ⊕ FREE HOUSE ◙ Black Sheep, Yorkshire Dales Ö Thatchers Gold. **Facilities** ♦❙ Children's menu Outside area ⋒ Parking **Notes** ⊛

KILBURN — Map 19 SE57

The Forresters Arms Inn

The Square YO61 4AH ☎ 01347 868386
e-mail: admin@forrestersarms.com
dir: From Thirsk take A170, after 3m turn right signed Kilburn. At Kilburn Rd junct, turn right, inn on left in village square

Sturdy coaching inn with hearty food

Next door to the famous Robert Thompson craft carpentry workshop, the Forresters Arms has fine examples of his early work, with the distinctive trademark mouse evident in both bars. A sturdy stone-built former coaching inn still catering for travellers passing close by the famous White Horse of Kilburn on the North York Moors, it has log fires, cask ales and good food. Dishes include salmon fishcakes with salad and herb mayonnaise; a home-made burger with crispy bacon and Applewood cheese; and traditional fish and chips. There's also a specials board and a selection of lunchtime snacks.

Open all day all wk 9am-11pm Bar Meals L served Mon-Fri 12-3, off season 12-2.30, Sat-Sun all day D served all wk 6-9, off season 6-8 Restaurant L served Mon-Fri 12-3, off season 12-2.30, Sat-Sun all day D served all wk 6-9, off season 6-8 ⊕ ENTERPRISE INNS ◀ John Smith's Cask, Guest ales ♂ Symonds Founder Reserve.
Facilities Non-diners area ❀ (Bar Garden) ❦ Children's menu Children's portions Garden ☂ Beer festival Parking Wi-fi ☞ (notice required)

KIRBY HILL — Map 19 NZ10

The Shoulder of Mutton Inn

DL11 7JH ☎ 01748 822772
e-mail: info@shoulderofmutton.net
dir: From A1 (Scotch Corner junct) take A66. In approx 6m follow signs for Kirby Hill on left

Picture-postcard village inn

Most buildings in this pretty hamlet are clustered round the green, diagonally opposite the ivy-clad, 18th-century inn. From its garden and sheltered patio the views over Holmedale are alone worth coming here for, while other obvious attractions are the open log fires warming the traditional bar, the local Daleside ales, and the stone-walled, beamed restaurant. Here seasonal, home-cooked food includes smoky haddock linguine; Gressingham duck breast with plum, orange and ginger sauce; and game pie with mushrooms and black pudding bubble-and-squeak. Hearty bar snacks are a good alternative. A beer festival is held over the August Bank Holiday.

Open all wk 6-11 (Sat-Sun 12-3 6-11) Bar Meals L served Sat-Sun 12-2 D served Wed-Sun 6.30-9 Av main course £10-£15 Restaurant L served Sun 12-2 D served Wed-Sun 6.30-9 Av 3 course à la carte fr £28 ⊕ FREE HOUSE ◀ Daleside, Guest ales ♂ Thatchers.
Facilities Non-diners area ❦ Garden Beer festival Parking

KIRKBY FLEETHAM — Map 19 SE29

The Black Horse Inn ★★★★★ RR ◉◉

Lumley Ln DL7 0SH ☎ 01609 749010
e-mail: gm@blackhorsekirkbyfleetham.com
dir: Signed from A1 between Catterick & Leeming Bar

Charming and successful inn

Legend has it that Dick Turpin eloped with his lady from this village pub in the Swale valley, just off the vast village green; the inn was named after the outlaw's steed in celebration. The pub garden adjoins fields, and the interior, including the seven character bedrooms, is appointed to create a pleasing mix of tradition and comfort. No surprise then that locals and visitors are encouraged to tarry a while, to sup a grand Yorkshire pint and enjoy accomplished two AA-Rosette food that covers all the bases. Look for signature starters such as chef's black pudding with parsnip mash, and main courses like baked monkfish and Parma ham.

Open all day all wk ⊕ FREE HOUSE ◀ Black Sheep, Copper Dragon, Timothy Taylor Landlord. Facilities ❦ Children's menu Children's portions Garden Parking Wi-fi Rooms 7

KIRKBYMOORSIDE — Map 19 SE68

George & Dragon Hotel

PICK OF THE PUBS

17 Market Place YO62 6AA ☎ 01751 433334
e-mail: reception@georgeanddragon.net
dir: Just off A170 between Scarborough & Thirsk. In town centre

A warm Yorkshire welcome awaits

The G&D, as it is affectionately known, is a family-owned whitewashed coaching inn in the sleepy market town of Kirkbymoorside. Its undoubted charm is due to many things – the log fire in the bar, the sheltered courtyard and fountain, the collection of cricketing, golf and rugby paraphernalia. Order a pint of Copper Dragon or Daleside and grab a seat in one of the nooks and crannies. At lunchtime, tuck into a baguette or panini. Or, if a meal in the Knight's Restaurant with its contemporary decor and leather seats suits you better, begin with Scottish smoked salmon, then enjoy oven-roasted rump of lamb with a tower of braised vegetable and sage and potato croquettes; or roast pan-fried breast of duck with seasonal greens and a classic orange sauce. The traditional Sunday carvery is hugely popular.

Open all day all wk 10.30am-11pm Bar Meals L served all wk 12-2 D served all wk 6-9 Restaurant L served all wk 12-2 D served all wk 6-9 ⊕ FREE HOUSE ◀ Greene King Abbot Ale, Copper Dragon, Daleside, Black Sheep, Guest ales. ♀ 12 Facilities Non-diners area ❦ Children's menu Children's portions Garden ☂ Parking Wi-fi ☞

KIRKHAM — Map 19 SE76

Stone Trough Inn

Kirkham Abbey YO60 7JS ☎ 01653 618713
e-mail: timstonetroughinn@live.co.uk
dir: 1.5m off A64, between York & Malton

A great reputation and a picturesque setting

Set amongst the Howardian Hills in a stunning location overlooking Kirkham Priory and the River Derwent, this free house was converted from a cottage during the early 1980s. It took its name from the base of a 12th-century cross erected by a French knight to commemorate a son killed in a riding accident. The cross has long since disappeared, but its hollowed-out base now stands at the entrance to the car park. Yorkshire ales are on offer in the pleasingly traditional interior. Food-wise, the menu includes salmon fillet in a saffron, leek and prawn sauce; and chicken wrapped in bacon with saffron rice.

Open all day all wk 11-11 (Sun 12-11) ⊕ FREE HOUSE ◀ Tetley's Cask, Timothy Taylor Landlord, Black Sheep Best Bitter, York, Cropton, Wold Top, Guest ales.
Facilities ❦ Children's menu Children's portions Garden Parking

KNARESBOROUGH — Map 19 SE35

The General Tarleton Inn ★★★★★ RR ◉◉

PICK OF THE PUBS

Boroughbridge Rd, Ferrensby HG5 0PZ ☎ 01423 340284
e-mail: gti@generaltarleton.co.uk
dir: A1(M) junct 48 at Boroughbridge, take A6055 to Knaresborough. Inn 4m on right

Award-winning food with Yorkshire roots

Just north of Knaresborough, this 18th-century coaching inn is handy for the Yorkshire Dales and was renamed in honour of General Banastre Tarleton who fought in the American War of Independence. The renovated interior retains its old beams and original log fires, while the sofas encourage guests to settle down with the seasonal menus that have helped chef-proprietor John Topham and his team earn two AA Rosettes. Championing local produce, East Coast fish is delivered daily, local vegetables arrive the day they've been picked, and the game comes from nearby shoots. The 'Food with Yorkshire Roots' menu is available in the Bar Brasserie, fine-dining restaurant, and terrace garden and courtyard. If you start with Little Moneybags, you'll experience the inn's renowned signature starter of crisp pastry seafood parcels in lobster sauce. Among the mains, look out for Goosnargh duckling and fillet of Longhorn beef. Accompanying wines can be selected from a list of 150.

Open all wk 12-3 5.30-11 Bar Meals L served all wk 12-2 D served all wk 5.30-9.15 Av main course £16 Restaurant L served Sun 12-1.45 D served Mon-Sat 6-9.15 Fixed menu price fr £18.50 Av 3 course à la carte fr £32 ⊕ FREE HOUSE ◀ Black Sheep Best Bitter, Timothy Taylor Landlord ♂ Aspall. ♀ 11 Facilities Non-diners area

Save on hotels. Book at **theAA.com/hotel**

YORKSHIRE, NORTH 507 **ENGLAND**

♦ Children's menu Children's portions Garden ⊐ Parking Wi-fi **Rooms** 13

The Red Lion Inn

DL11 6RE ☎ **01748 884218**
e-mail: rlionlangthwaite@aol.com
web: www.redlionlangthwaite.co.uk
dir: *From A6108 between Richmond & Leyburn follow Reeth signs. In Reeth follow Langthwaite sign*

Often used as a film and TV location

The Red Lion is a traditional country pub owned by the same family for 49 years. It hosts two darts teams in winter, a quoits team in summer, and bar snacks are served all year round. There are some wonderful walks in this part of the Dales and relevant books and maps are on sale in the bar. In the tiny snug there are photographs relating to the various films and TV programmes filmed at this unusually photogenic pub (including *All Creatures Great and Small*, *A Woman of Substance* and *Hold the Dream*). Ice cream, chocolates and sweets are available as well.

Open all wk 11-3 7-11 **Bar Meals** L served all wk 11-3 ⊕ FREE HOUSE ◖ Black Sheep Best Bitter & All Creatures, Worthington's Creamflow, Guinness ♂ Thatchers Gold. ₹ 9 **Facilities** Non-diners area Family room Outside area ⊐ Parking

Blacksmiths Arms

YO62 6TN ☎ **01751 417247**
e-mail: pete.hils@blacksmithslastingham.co.uk
dir: *7m from Pickering & 4m from Kirkbymoorside. A170 (Pickering to Kirkbymoorside road), follow Lastingham & Appleton-le-Moors signs*

Well loved pub on the southern fringe of the North Yorks Moors

With a cottage garden and decked outdoor seating area, this stone-built, 17th-century free house has a wonderful atmosphere. In the small front bar pewter mugs and beer pump clips hang from the low beams, and copper cooking pans decorate the open range. A snug and two delightful dining rooms complete the interior. Home-cooked dishes prepared from local supplies include Yorkshire hotpot; lamb and mint pie; and Whitby breaded scampi (also in takeaway form). Enjoy the food with Theakston's Best

Bitter or a guest ale. St Mary's Church, opposite the pub, is renowned for its Saxon crypt.

Open all day all wk **Bar Meals** L served all wk 12-5 D served all wk 6.30-8.45 Av main course £12 **Restaurant** L served all wk 12-5 D served Mon-Sat 6.30-8.45 ⊕ FREE HOUSE ◖ Theakston Best Bitter, 2 Guest ales. **Facilities** Non-diners area ♦ Children's menu Children's portions Family room Garden ⊐ Wi-fi ⛟ (notice required)

Horseshoe Inn ★★★★ INN

Main St YO18 7NL ☎ **01751 460240**
e-mail: info@horseshoelevisham.co.uk
dir: *A169, 5m from Pickering. 4m, pass Fox & Rabbit Inn on right. In 0.5m left to Lockton. Follow steep winding road to village*

Family-run pub in tranquil village

On the edge of the North York Moors National Park, here is a village pub where you can stay overnight while touring the area, perhaps by steam train from Levisham station. Charles and Toby Wood have created an inviting atmosphere that's especially apparent in the beamed and wooden-floored bar, where a gilt-edged mirror hangs above the open fire, and the real ales are from Black Sheep and Cropton. Local suppliers play a big part behind the scenes so that the kitchen can prepare hearty plates of deep-fried Whitby haddock; beef or mushroom Stroganoff with rice; and steak and ale pie.

Open all day all wk **Bar Meals** L served all wk 12-2 D served all wk 6-8.30 **Restaurant** L served all wk 12-2 D served all wk 6-8.30 ⊕ FREE HOUSE ◖ Black Sheep Best Bitter, Cropton Yorkshire Moors, Two Pints, Yorkshire Warrior & Endeavour ♂ Thatchers Gold. ₹ 12 **Facilities** Non-diners area ♣ (Bar Garden) ♦ Children's menu Children's portions Garden ⊐ Parking Wi-fi **Rooms** 9

The Queens Head ★★★★ INN

Westmoor Ln, Finghall DL8 1QZ ☎ **01677 450259**
e-mail: enquiries@queensfinghall.co.uk
dir: *From Bedale follow A684 W towards Leyburn, just after pub & caravan park turn left signed Finghall*

Dales produce is high on the list

This pretty 18th-century country inn with beams and open fires is set on a hillside above Wensleydale and there are stunning views of the countryside from the terrace. The dining room overlooks Wild Wood — believed to be one of the inspirations for Kenneth Grahame's *Wind in the Willows*. Drinkers can quaff a pint of Black Sheep by the fire and diners can create their own deli board while considering the menu, which demonstrates the kitchen team's passion for Dales produce. As well as sandwiches and pub favourites there are contemporary dishes like Indian-spiced salmon fillet; potato, pea and cheese

croquettes; and crab and ginger risotto. Spacious accommodation is located in the adjacent annexe.

Open all wk 12-3 6-close Closed: 26 Dec & 1 Jan **Bar Meals** L served all wk 12-2 D served all wk 6-9 **Restaurant** L served all wk 12-2 D served all wk 6-9 ⊕ FREE HOUSE ◖ Black Sheep Best Bitter, Theakston XB & Black Bull. ₹ 10 **Facilities** Non-diners area ♦ Children's menu Children's portions Garden ⊐ Parking ⛟ (notice required) **Rooms** 3

Sandpiper Inn

PICK OF THE PUBS

Market Place DL8 5AT ☎ **01969 622206**
e-mail: hsandpiper99@aol.com
dir: *A1 onto A684 to Leyburn*

Wensleydale market town inn

Leyburn's oldest building is this 17th-century, ivy-clad inn, although it has been a pub for only 30 years or so. Run since 1999 by Jonathan and Janine Harrison, its bar and snug offers real ales from a small army of Yorkshire breweries, and some 100 single malts. The restaurant, distinguished by a huge stone lintel above an open fireplace, oak floors and candlelit tables is where Jonathan has built on his already excellent reputation for modern British food. Such reputations, of course, require using the finest ingredients, which he does for traditional and international dishes such as Swinton Park venison with pearl barley and vegetable risotto; sea bass with shellfish sausage and light curry and apple sauce; and potato rösti with glazed balsamic tomatoes and roasted red onions. Lunch offers coq au vin; and house rib-burger. For dessert, why not one of the Sandpiper's own ice creams or sorbets?

Open 11.30-3 6.30-11 (Sun 12-2.30 6.30-10.30) Closed: Mon & occasionally Tue **Bar Meals** L served Tue-Sun 12-2.30 Av main course £17 **Restaurant** L served Tue-Sun 12-2.30 D served Tue-Thu & Sun 6.30-9, Fri-Sat 6.30-9.30 Av 3 course à la carte fr £25 ⊕ FREE HOUSE ◖ Black Sheep Best Bitter, Daleside, Copper Dragon, Archers, Yorkshire Dales ♂ Thatchers Gold. ₹ 10 **Facilities** Non-diners area ♦ Children's menu Family room Garden ⊐ Wi-fi

| LITTON | Map 18 SD97 |

Queens Arms ★★★ INN

BD23 5QJ ☎ 01756 770096
e-mail: info@queensarmslitton.co.uk
dir: N of Grassington on B6265

Stunning views of the Yorkshire Dales

This 17th-century drovers' inn is now under local ownership and an extensive refurbishment in 2012 saw the arrival of new sumptuous fabrics and comfortable chairs to enhance the original features of slate floors, open fires and beams. The pub offers a warm welcome to outdoor enthusiasts, fresh from enjoying the Yorkshire Dales countryside, as well as families enjoying Sunday lunch or afternoon tea, and locals playing darts. Cask-conditioned ales from the on-site microbrewery will soon join Goose Eye, Thwaites and Black Sheep at the bar. Locally sourced dishes include Wharfedale leg of lamb rogan josh and battered Whitby haddock.

Open all wk Mon-Fri 12-3 6-11 Sat 11-11 Sun 12-10.30
Bar Meals L served Mon-Fri 12-2, Sat 12-2.30, Sun 12-4 D served Mon-Thu 6-8, Fri-Sat 6-8.30 Av main course £10.95 ⊕ FREE HOUSE ◗ Thwaites Original, Black Sheep, Goose Eye Chinook Blonde Ö Thatchers.
Facilities Non-diners area ✿ (Bar Garden) ◗◗ Children's portions Garden ⋈ Wi-fi **Rooms** 6

| LOW ROW | Map 18 SD99 |

The Punch Bowl Inn ★★★★ INN

DL11 6PF ☎ 01748 886233
e-mail: info@pbinn.co.uk
web: www.pbinn.co.uk
dir: A1 from Scotch Corner take A6108 to Richmond. Through Richmond then right onto B6270 to Low Row

Lots on offer at this Yorkshire Dales inn

With Wainwright's Coast to Coast Walk on the doorstep, this Grade II listed Swaledale pub dates back to the 17th century. As well as open fires and antique furniture, the bar and bar stools were hand-crafted by Robert 'The Mouseman' Thompson's company during an extensive refurbishment a few years ago (see if you can spot the mice around the bar). Typical food choices include wild mushroom and thyme risotto; Gressingham duck breast with stir-fried vegetables, noodles and hoi sin sauce; and espresso crème brûlée. Local cask-conditioned ales also feature. If you would like to stay over for the Swaledale festivals, the bedrooms all have spectacular views.

The Punch Bowl Inn

Open all day all wk 11am-mdnt Closed: 25 Dec **Bar Meals** L served all wk 12-2 D served all wk 6-9 Av main course £13.50 **Restaurant** L served all wk 12-2 D served all wk 6-9 Av 3 course à la carte fr £23.50 ⊕ FREE HOUSE ◗ Theakston Best Bitter, Black Sheep Best Bitter & Riggwelter, Timothy Taylor Landlord Ö Thatchers Gold. ☗ 13 **Facilities** Non-diners area ✿ (Bar) ◗◗ Children's menu Children's portions Parking Wi-fi ⛟ (notice required) **Rooms** 11

| MALHAM | Map 18 SD96 |

The Lister Arms ★★★★ INN

PICK OF THE PUBS

See Pick of the Pubs on opposite page
See advert below

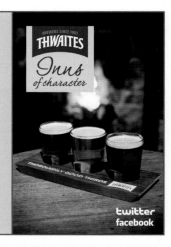

PICK OF THE PUBS

The Lister Arms ★★★★ INN

MALHAM   Map 18 SD96

BD23 4DB ☎ **01729 830330**
e-mail: relax@listerarms.co.uk
web: www.listerarms.co.uk
dir: *In village centre*

Gorgeous inn and village amidst spectacular scenery

This handsome old stone coaching inn sits amongst some of the county's most impressive limestone scenery which is riddled with caverns. Being right on the village green makes it a good place to stop for morning coffee, a pint of one of the guest ales, or Thwaites Wainwright bitter, named after Blackburn-born Alfred Wainwright, famous for his Lakeland Fells guides. History is visible wherever you look: outside, there's a traditional mounting block for horse riders, and a beautiful tiled entrance way; inside, the renovated ground floor is divided into little nooks, with original beams, flagged floors and wood burning stoves. The kitchen team serve up food that is seasonal, local and always freshly prepared, with daily 'Lister Loves' dishes displayed on a board hanging above the fireplace in the bar. For lunch try one of the Home Comforts, such as a Whitby scampi and chips; beefsteak, mushroom and Wainwright's ale pie with creamy mash, roasted root

vegetables and jug of gravy; or fettucine pasta with wild mushrooms and Harrogate blue cheese. Dinner might begin with baked goats' cheese with fresh tomato sauce, roasted peppers, white beans and olives; continue with a rib-eye steak from the chargrill or a sharing Butcher's or Fishmonger's deli boards; and finish with Bramley apple and blackberry crumble or chocolate marquise with orange crème fraîche. Children can choose from their own menu, tuck into complimentary fresh fruit and top up their soft drinks free. Well-behaved dogs, muddy boots and cycles are also happily welcomed.

Open all day all wk **Bar Meals** Av main course £12 food served all day **Restaurant** Av 3 course à la carte fr £25 food served all day ⊕ THWAITES INNS OF CHARACTER ◀ Wainwright, Original ♂ Kingstone Press. ⚲ 8 **Facilities** Non-diners area ☙ (Bar Garden) ⁛ Children's menu Children's portions Garden ⋒ Parking Wi-fi **Rooms** 9

MARTON (NEAR BOROUGHBRIDGE) Map 19 SE46

The Punch Bowl Inn NEW

YO51 9QY ☎ 01423 322519
e-mail: enquiries@thepunchbowlmartoncumgrafton.com
web: www.thepunchbowlmartoncumgrafton.com
dir: In village centre

Village pub with six eating areas

A Provenance Inn group member, the 16th-century Punch Bowl commands a central location in the village. Its beamed, wood-floored bar and tap-room's generous seating includes a settle, and there's a log fire in each of the six eating areas. The Yorkshire Plate starter features Harrogate Blue cheese, black pudding fritter, duck rillettes, beetroot salsa, Malham chorizo and griddled sourdough. Typical main dishes are seafood platter; confit shoulder of lamb; and mushroom, spinach and ricotta Wellington, with roasts and baked Cajun salmon on Sundays. Summer barbecues are held in the courtyard.

Open all day all wk **Bar Meals** L served Mon-Sat 12-2.30, Sun 12-3 D served Mon-Sat 5.30-9.30, Sun 5.30-8.30 Av main course £12.95 **Restaurant** L served Mon-Sat 12-2.30, Sun 12-3 D served Mon-Sat 5.30-9.30, Sun 5.30-8.30 Av 3 course à la carte fr £22.95 ⊕ PROVENANCE INNS ◀ Black Sheep Best Bitter, Timothy Taylor Landlord ♂ Aspall. **Facilities** Non-diners area ♣ (Bar Garden) ♦♦ Children's menu Children's portions Garden ♫ Parking Wi-fi ▭ (notice required)

MARTON (NEAR SINNINGTON) Map 19 SE78

The Appletree Country Inn NEW

YO62 6RD ☎ 01751 433189
e-mail: info@theappletreecountryinn.co.uk
dir: Between Kirkbymoorside & Malton

Re-opened pub on the way up

After it had been closed for over two years, chef/proprietor Graham Kirk bought this 18th-century inn, applied heaps of TLC and reopened it in 2011. The bar, usually propped up by happy locals, offers weekly-changing, widely-sourced cask ales, cider from Ampleforth Abbey, and wines selected by a local merchant. Graham, who says his aim is to revive forgotten British dishes, updates his menus often, with entries of, for example, fresh celeriac with Jervaulx Blue cheese and buttered walnut salad; pan-fried sea trout with East Coast crab cakes; and roast crown of pigeon. Paintings are by local countryside artist, Andrew Hutchinson.

Open 12-3 5.30-12 (Sun all day) Closed: 1-14 Jan, Mon **Bar Meals** L served Wed-Sat 12-2.30, Sun 12-7 D served Wed-Sat 5.30-9, Sun 12-7 Av main course £15 **Restaurant** L served Wed-Sat 12-2.30, Sun 12-7 D served Wed-Sat 5.30-9, Sun 12-7 Av 3 course à la carte fr £25 ⊕ FREE HOUSE ◀ Rudgate, Wold Top, York ♂ Ampleforth Abbey. **Facilities** Non-diners area ♣ (Bar Outside area) ♦♦ Children's portions Outside area ♫ Parking Wi-fi ▭ (notice required)

MASHAM Map 19 SE28

The Black Sheep Brewery

Wellgarth HG4 4EN ☎ 01765 680101 & 680100
e-mail: sue.dempsey@blacksheep.co.uk
dir: Off A6108, 9m from Ripon & 7m from Bedale

Famous brewery site for over 20 years

Set up by Paul Theakston, a member of Masham's famous brewery family, in the former Wellgarth Maltings in 1992, the complex includes an excellent visitor centre and a popular bar-cum-bistro. Go on a fascinating tour of the brewery. Next take in the wonderful views over the River Ure and surrounding countryside as you sup tip-top pints of Riggwelter and Golden Sheep; then tuck into a good plate of food, perhaps braised beef, fish pie, pan-fried lamb's liver with black pudding, mash and rich onion gravy, or a roast beef sandwich.

Open all wk 10-5 (Thu-Sat 10am-late) Closed: 25-26 Dec **Restaurant** L served Mon-Sat 12-2.30, Sun 12-3 D served Thu-Sat 6.30-9 ⊕ BLACK SHEEP BREWERY ◀ Best Bitter, Riggwelter, Ale, Golden Sheep. **Facilities** Non-diners area ♣ (Garden) ♦♦ Children's menu Children's portions Garden ♫ Parking Wi-fi ▭ (notice required)

The White Bear

Wellgarth HG4 4EN ☎ 01765 689319
e-mail: sue@whitebearmasham.co.uk
dir: Signed from A1 between Bedale & Ripon

Theakston's flagship pub in bustling market town

Theakston Brewery's flagship inn stands just a short stroll from the legendary brewhouse and market square in this bustling market town and provides the perfect base for exploring the Yorkshire Dales. Handsome and stylish, there's a snug taproom for quaffing pints of Old Peculier by the glowing fire, oak-floored lounges with deep sofas and chairs for perusing the daily papers, and an elegant dining room. Menus take in pork fillet wrapped in bacon filled with black pudding served with parsnip and English mustard purée; butternut squash and spinach curry; sausage and mash with onion gravy; and mushroom and sweet pepper risotto with parmesan crisps. Expect regular live music and 30 cask ales at the late June beer festival.

Open all day all wk **Bar Meals** L served all wk 12-9 food served all day **Restaurant** L served all wk 12-2.30 D served all wk 6-9 ⊕ FREE HOUSE/THEAKSTON ◀ Best Bitter, Black Bull Bitter, Lightfoot & Old Peculier, Caledonian Deuchars IPA. **Facilities** Non-diners area ♣ (Bar Garden) ♦♦ Children's menu Children's portions Garden ♫ Beer festival Parking Wi-fi ▭ (notice required)

MIDDLEHAM Map 19 SE18

The White Swan

Market Place DL8 4PE ☎ 01969 622093
e-mail: enquiries@whiteswanhotel.co.uk
dir: From A1, take A684 towards Leyburn then A6108 to Ripon, 1.5m to Middleham

Popular and attractive inn

Paul Klein's Tudor coaching inn stands in the cobbled market square in the shadow of Middleham's ruined castle and, like the village, is steeped in the history of the turf, with several top horseracing stables located in the area. Expect to find oak beams, flagstones and roaring log fires in the atmospheric bar, where you can quaff tip-top Black Sheep or Wensleydale ales and enjoy modern British pub food. Using quality Yorkshire produce the menu might feature shredded confit of crispy duck leg with bacon salad; chicken breast stuffed with mozzarella and sun-dried tomato, with pesto risotto; and glazed lemon tart with raspberry sauce to finish.

Open all day all wk 8am-11pm (mdnt at wknds) **Bar Meals** food served all day **Restaurant** L served all wk 8am-9.30pm (bkfst from 8am) D served all wk 8am-9.30pm (bkfst from 8am) food served all day ⊕ FREE HOUSE ◀ Black Sheep Best Bitter, John Smith's, Theakston, Wensleydale ♂ Thatchers Gold. ♥ 9 **Facilities** Non-diners area ♣ (Bar Outside area) ♦♦ Children's menu Children's portions Family room Outside area ♫ Parking Wi-fi ▭ (notice required)

MIDDLESMOOR Map 19 SE07

Crown Hotel

HG3 5ST ☎ 01423 755204
dir: Telephone for directions

Family run hotel at the top of the valley

There are great views towards Gouthwaite Reservoir from this breezy 900-ft high hilltop village with its cobbled streets. This family-run traditional free house dates back to the 17th century and is in an ideal spot for anyone following the popular Nidderdale Way. Visitors can enjoy a good pint of local beer and food by the cosy, roaring log fire, or in the sunny pub garden. A large selection of malt whiskies is also on offer.

Open Tue-Sun Closed: all day Mon, Tue-Thu L (winter) **Bar Meals** L served Tue-Sun 12-2 D served Tue-Sun 7-8.30 ⊕ FREE HOUSE ◀ Black Sheep Best Bitter, Wensleydale Bitter, Guinness. **Facilities** ♣ (Bar Restaurant Garden) ♦♦ Garden ♫ Parking **Notes** ☻

Save on hotels. Book at **theAA.com/hotel**

YORKSHIRE, NORTH 511 ENGLAND

MUKER
Map 18 SD99

The Farmers Arms

DL11 6QG ☎ 01748 886297
e-mail: enquiries@farmersarmsmuker.co.uk
dir: *From Richmond take A6108 towards Leyburn, turn right onto B6270*

A typical Dales pub in spectacular walking country

At the head of beautiful Swaledale, the pub is understandably popular with those who love the great outdoors, whatever the weather, although the obvious place to be on a sunny day is the south-facing patio, with a pint of Old Peculier. The open-fired, stone-flagged bar is muddy-boot-and-dog-friendly. Menus include lunchtime giant filled Yorkshire puddings, hot roast beef baguettes and paninis, while an evening meal could feature cod goujons; home-made creamy mustard chicken; gammon and chips; and macaroni cheese. Specials include casseroled pork in paprika sauce; and fisherman's pie. There's a separate children's menu, too.

Open all day all wk **Bar Meals** L served all wk 12-2.30 D served all wk 6-8.30 ⊕ FREE HOUSE ◀ Theakston Best Bitter & Old Peculier, John Smith's, Black Sheep, Guest ales ☼ Thatchers Gold. ⬤ 9 **Facilities** Non-diners area ❀ (Bar Restaurant Outside area) ◀ Children's menu Children's portions Outside area ⌅ Parking

NEWTON ON OUSE
Map 19 SE55

The Dawnay Arms

YO30 2BR ☎ 01347 848345
e-mail: dine@thedawnay.co.uk
dir: *From A19 follow Newton on Ouse signs*

Great riverside location

Right in the middle of a picture-perfect village, The Dawnay Arms dates back to Georgian times. It sits on the banks of the River Ouse, and its large rear garden runs down to moorings for those arriving by boat. The interior, all chunky beams and tables, hosts a great array of cask ales including Treboom, a relatively recent addition to York's renowned microbreweries; the well-chosen wine list also deserves mention. Food, British in style, might include wood pigeon 'Wellington' with celeriac, mushrooms and Madeira; baked Whitby cod with a parmesan and herb crust, and prawn and saffron risotto; pear and almond tart with custard could round things off.

Open 12-3 6-11 (Sat-Sun all day) Closed: 1st wk Jan, Mon **Bar Meals** L served Tue-Sat 12-2.30, Sun 12-6 D served Tue-Sat 6-9.30, Sun 12-6 **Restaurant** L served Tue-Sat 12-2.30, Sun 12-6 D served Tue-Sat 6-9.30, Sun 12-6 ⊕ FREE HOUSE ◀ Treboom Drum Beat, Black Sheep Best Bitter & Golden Sheep. ⬤ 12 **Facilities** Non-diners area ❀ (Bar Garden) ◀ Children's menu Children's portions Garden ⌅ Parking Wi-fi ⛟ (notice required)

NUNNINGTON
Map 19 SE67

The Royal Oak Inn

Church St YO62 5US ☎ 01439 748271
dir: *Village centre, close to Nunnington Hall*

Good food, real ales, real fires in winter

This Grade II listed, 18th-century solid stone country inn welcomes with an open-plan bar furnished with scrubbed pine and decorated with farming memorabilia, open fires in winter and fresh flowers in summer. The sign on the front door says it all: 'Real ale, real food, real people'. True to this promise, head chef Ed Woodhill uses the best local produce to create innovative interpretations of traditional dishes. Typical choices include ham hock croquette with home-made piccalilli; gorgonzola and pear chutney tart and pheasant en croûte.

Open 12-2.30 6.30-11 (Sun 12-3 6.30-11 summer 12-3 winter) Closed: Mon (ex BHs 12-2) & Tue in winter **Bar Meals** L served Tue-Sun 12-2 (booking required Sun) D served Tue-Sun 6.30-9 (summer), Tue-Sat fr 6.30 (winter) Av main course £12 **Restaurant** L served Tue-Sat 12-2, Sun 12-3 (booking required Sun) D served Tue-Sun 6.30-9 (summer), Tue-Sat fr 6.30 (winter) ⊕ FREE HOUSE ◀ Black Sheep, Wold Top, John Smith's. ⬤ 10 **Facilities** Non-diners area ❀ (Bar Restaurant Garden) ◀ Children's menu Children's portions Garden ⌅ Parking

OLDSTEAD
Map 19 SE57

The Black Swan at Oldstead
★★★★★ RR ⚜⚜⚜

PICK OF THE PUBS

See Pick of the Pubs on page 512

OSMOTHERLEY
Map 19 SE49

The Golden Lion

PICK OF THE PUBS

6 West End DL6 3AA ☎ 01609 883526
e-mail: goldenlionosmotherley@yahoo.co.uk
dir: *Telephone for directions*

Recommended for its interesting dishes

Standing in Osmotherley, the 'Gateway to the North Yorkshire Moors', the Golden Lion is a 250-year-old sandstone building. The atmosphere is warm and welcoming with open fires, a wooden bar, bench seating, whitewashed walls, mirrors and fresh flowers. As well as some 60 single malt whiskies, there are always three real ales on offer. The extensive menu ranges through basic pub grub to more refined dishes. Starters might include smoked salmon and prawn roulade; grilled aubergines filled with ratatouille; and fresh mussels in a white wine and cream sauce. Mains are along the lines of home-made chicken Kiev; sirloin steak, and fillets of plaice, supplemented by specials such as turkey roulade; duck, chestnut and thyme risotto; and sea bass with a samphire, crayfish and basil sauce. Popular desserts are raspberry ripple cheesecake, ginger sponge and crème brûlée. The pub holds a beer festival in November.

Open 12-3 6-11 Closed: 25 Dec, Mon L, Tue L **Bar Meals** L served Wed-Sun 12-2.30 D served all wk 6-9 ⊕ FREE HOUSE ◀ Timothy Taylor Landlord, York Guzzler, Salamander, Wall's Brewing Co ☼ Herefordshire. **Facilities** ❀ (Bar Restaurant Outside area) ◀ Children's menu Children's portions Outside area Beer festival Wi-fi

PATELEY BRIDGE
Map 19 SE16

The Sportsmans Arms Hotel

Wath-in-Nidderdale HG3 5PP ☎ 01423 711306
e-mail: sportsmansarms@btconnect.com
dir: *A59, B6451, hotel 2m N of Pateley Bridge*

Dales hotel in a picturesque conservation village

The Sportsmans Arms is set in beautiful Nidderdale, one of the loveliest of the Yorkshire Dales, and stands on the 53-mile, circular Nidderdale Way. Enter the hallway and find open log fires, comfortable chairs, a warm and welcoming bar and a calm, softly lit restaurant. As much of the food as possible is locally sourced: fish arrives daily from Whitby and other East Coast harbours. Always a good choice are the Nidderdale lamb, pork, beef, fresh trout and especially game (season permitting) from the Moors. The wine list offers a wide selection of styles and prices to complement any dish.

Open all wk 12-2.30 6.30-11 Closed: 25 Dec **Bar Meals** L served all wk 12-2 D served all wk 7-9 Av main course £14 **Restaurant** L served Sun 12-2 D served Mon-Sat 7-9 Fixed menu price fr £29.50 Av 3 course à la carte fr £35 ⊕ FREE HOUSE ◀ Black Sheep, Rudgate Brewery, Timothy Taylor ☼ Thatchers Gold. ⬤ 12 **Facilities** Non-diners area ❀ (Bar Garden Outside area) ◀ Children's portions Garden Outside area ⌅ Parking Wi-fi

PICK OF THE PUBS

The Black Swan at Oldstead ★★★★★ RR ⬡⬡⬡

OLDSTEAD   Map 19 SE57

Main St YO61 4BL ☎ 01347 868387
e-mail:
enquiries@blackswanoldstead.co.uk
web: www.blackswanoldstead.co.uk
dir: *A1 junct 49, A168, A19S, after 3m
left to Coxwold then Byland Abbey. In
2m left for Oldstead, pub 1m on left*

Outstanding food in rural Yorkshire

Dating back to the 16th century and set
in a sleepy hamlet below the North York
Moors, The Black Swan is owned and
run by the Banks family, who have
farmed in the village for generations. In
the bar you'll find a stone-flagged floor,
an open log fire, original wooden window
seats, soft cushions, and fittings by
Robert 'Mousey' Thompson who, in the
1930s, was a prolific maker of
traditional handcrafted English oak
furniture. Expect tip-top real ales,
cracking wines by the glass, malt
whiskies and vintage port, while the
first-class food on offer changes with
the seasons, being sourced mainly from
local farms. The same award-winning
menus are offered in the bar and in the
comfortable restaurant where Persian
rugs line an oak floor, the furniture is
antique, and candles in old brass
holders create light soft enough to be
romantic, but bright enough to read the
innovative modern country menus by.

Start perhaps with langoustine soup,
crab and cheddar croûton; or butternut
squash cannelloni, langoustine, tomato
and basil; move on to ox cheek,
cauliflower cheese, macaroni, truffle
and salsify; or halibut, Jerusalem
artichoke, squid, pink fir potato and
samphire; and finish with dark
chocolate, vanilla and pear. The
bedrooms have solid oak floors and are
furnished with quality antiques, classy
soft fabrics, and paintings. Bathrooms
are fitted with an iron roll-top bath and
a walk-in wet room shower, which
sounds like just the place to head for
after one of the pleasant walks
radiating from the front of the building
(route details are available at the bar).
Booking for meals may be required.

Open 12-3 6-11 Closed: 1wk Jan, Mon L,
Tue L, Wed L **Bar & Restaurant Meals** L
served Thu-Sun 12-2 D served all wk
6-9; 3-course fixed menu £25; lunch
6-course tasting menu £35; à la carte &
7-course tasting menus available
⬡ FREE HOUSE ◧ Black Sheep. ⬡ 14
Facilities Non-diners area ⬡ Children's
menu Children's portions Garden ⬡
Parking Wi-fi **Rooms 4**

PICKERING — Map 19 SE78

Fox & Hounds Country Inn ★★★★ INN ⊛
PICK OF THE PUBS

Sinnington YO62 6SQ ☎ 01751 431577
e-mail: fox.houndsinn@btconnect.com
dir: *3m W of town, off A170 between Pickering & Helmsley*

Great country pub atmosphere

Resident proprietors Andrew and Catherine Stephens run this friendly, 18th-century coaching inn on the edge of the North Yorks Moors. In the wood-panelled bar, under oak beams and, depending on the temperature, warmed by a double-sided log-burner called Big Bertha, a pint of Copper Dragon Best, or Anglers Reward, could be waiting, or maybe a rarely encountered whisky. Making full use of locally farmed produce, light lunches and early suppers (except Saturdays) include chargrilled minute steak and fries; smoked haddock with sauté potatoes; and various omelettes. Differing only in part, the main menu also lists roasted Gressingham duck breast; grilled salmon with saffron risotto; and savoury choux pastry with spinach, mushroom and goats' cheese. It is for these dishes and more that the restaurant has earned an AA Rosette. Turn right along the village street past the village green to an ancient packhorse bridge over the gentle River Seven (yes, Seven).

Open all wk 12-2 5.30-11 (Sat 12-2 6-11 Sun 12-2.30 6-10.30) Closed: 25-27 Dec **Bar Meals** L served all wk 12-2 D served Mon-Fri 5.30-9, Sat-Sun 6-9 Av main course £13.95 **Restaurant** L served all wk 12-2 D served all wk 6.30-9 Av 3 course à la carte fr £22.95 ⊕ FREE HOUSE ◀ Copper Dragon Best Bitter, Wold Top Anglers Reward ♂ Thatchers Gold. ♥ 9 **Facilities** Non-diners area ♦♦ Children's menu Children's portions Garden ⋈ Parking Wi-fi ▥ **Rooms** 10

The Fox & Rabbit Inn
Whitby Rd, Lockton YO18 7NQ ☎ 01751 460213
e-mail: info@foxandrabbit.co.uk
dir: *From Pickering take A169 towards Whitby. Lockton in 5m*

Reliable stop near Dalby Forest

The archetypical North Yorkshire Moors pub, all heavy orange pantiles and honey limestone dressed with creepers, set on a secluded junction at the fringe of Dalby Forest. The owning Wood brothers are keen supporters of local microbreweries, with beers from brewers Cropton and Wold Top slaking the thirst of the cyclists and ramblers with whom the pub is a favourite stop to recuperate from their exertions in the National Park. For the inner man, good solid Yorkshire pub grub like steak and Black Sheep ale pie or Whitby scampi and chips are ideal; or divert to wild mushroom and leek cannelloni.

Open all day all wk **Bar Meals** L served Mon-Thu 12-2.30, Fri-Sun 12.30-4 D served all wk 5-8.30 Av main course £11 **Restaurant** L served Mon-Thu 12-2.30, Fri-Sun 12.30-4 D served all wk 5-8.30 Av 3 course à la carte fr £20 ⊕ FREE HOUSE ◀ Black Sheep Best Bitter, Marston's Oyster Stout, Cropton, Wold Top Ales, Tetley's Smooth Flow, Guest ales ♂ Thatchers Gold. ♥ 13 **Facilities** Non-diners area ❖ (Bar Garden) ♦♦ Children's menu Children's portions Garden ⋈ Parking ▥ (notice required)

The White Swan Inn ★★★ HL ⊛
PICK OF THE PUBS

Market Place YO18 7AA ☎ 01751 472288
e-mail: welcome@white-swan.co.uk
dir: *From N: A19 or A1 to Thirsk, A170 to Pickering, left at lights, 1st right onto Market Place. Pub on left. From S: A1 or A1(M) to A64 to Malton rdbt, A169 to Pickering*

Market town inn with award-winning menu

This sturdy 16th-century coaching inn fronts the steep main street in the appealing old town of Pickering, just yards from both the fine Norman castle and the terminus station of the famous North Yorks Moors Railway. Whitby and York are within easy reach, whilst great walks thread to the secret dales feathering the moorlands of the nearby National Park. The stylish inn offers great food and comfortable accommodation; close links with top London butcher The Ginger Pig, whose farm is seven miles from the pub, means that rare-breed meat gets star billing on a seasonal menu that has wowed critics and visitors. The menu may feature gratinated king scallops with Fountain's Gold cheddar; slow roasted Ginger Pig belly pork with curly kale; chicken, pheasant and bacon fricassée, or pesto linguine with sautéed Jerusalem artichokes and roast tomatoes. Calorific puddings, Yorkshire beers like Cropton or Black Sheep, and fine wines complete the picture.

Open all day all wk **Bar Meals** L served all wk 12-2 D served all wk 6.45-9 **Restaurant** L served all wk 12-2 D served all wk 6.45-9 ⊕ FREE HOUSE ◀ Black Sheep, World Top, Copper Dragon ♂ Westons Old Rosie. ♥ 13 **Facilities** Non-diners area ❖ (Bar Garden) ♦♦ Children's menu Children's portions Garden ⋈ Parking Wi-fi ▥ (notice required) **Rooms** 21

PICKHILL — Map 19 SE38

Nags Head Country Inn ★★★★ INN ⊛⊛
PICK OF THE PUBS

YO7 4JG ☎ 01845 567391
e-mail: enquiries@nagsheadpickhill.co.uk
dir: *A1(M) junct 50, A61 towards Thirsk. Left onto B6267 signed Masham. Right signed Pickhill*

Renowned for excellent food, fine wines and real ales

For nearly 40 years the Boynton family have been welcoming visitors to their extended, former 17th-century coaching inn set in a peaceful village just off the A1 north of Thirsk. Synonymous with Yorkshire hospitality at its best, notably among weary travellers and the local racing fraternity, the inn comprises a beamed lounge and a traditional taproom bar with flagged and tiled floors, beams adorned with ties and a magpie selection of tables and chairs tucked around open fires. A terrific menu is the icing on the cake here; a small but perfectly formed taproom menu offers sandwiches and simple meals such as steak and chips with all the trimmings or Thai chicken, vegetable and noodle stir-fry. In the lounge or elegant restaurant, order mushroom and roasted garlic risotto to start, followed perhaps by corn-fed chicken with a small wing Kiev, buttered cabbage, potato dumplings and pearl barley broth. Tempting, calorific puddings seal the deal, perhaps forced Yorkshire rhubarb pithivier with frangipane and ewe's milk ice cream. If all this leaves you feeling too full to move, consider staying in one of the inn's comfortably furnished bedrooms.

Open all wk 11-11 (Sun 11-10.30) Closed: 25 Dec (drinks only available) **Bar Meals** L served Mon-Sat 12-2, Sun 12-3 D served Mon-Sat 6-9.30, Sun 5.30-8 **Restaurant** L served Mon-Sat 12-2, Sun 12-3 D served Mon-Sat 6-9.30, Sun 5.30-8 ⊕ FREE HOUSE ◀ Black Sheep Best Bitter, Theakston Old Peculier, Best Bitter & Black Bull, Rudgate Viking ♂ Thatchers Gold. ♥ 8 **Facilities** Non-diners area ♦♦ Children's menu Children's portions Garden ⋈ Parking Wi-fi ▥ (notice required) **Rooms** 13

PICTON — Map 19 NZ40

The Station Hotel
TS15 0AE ☎ 01642 700067
e-mail: info@thestationhotelpicton.co.uk
dir: *Exit A19, follow Yarm/A67 signs. Left signed Picton, approx 1.5m to pub*

Family friendly local

A reliable country local in the rich farmlands just outside the picturesque old Teesside town of Yarm. The railway still runs by, but today's visitors are car-borne, drawn to this fiercely traditional pub by well liked Yorkshire beers, including some from the Black Sheep stable and a filling menu of pub fare with a twist. The home-made dishes may include pork fillet with port and orange sauce, or oven-roasted cod with a Wensleydale cheese, lime and ginger crumb topping. An extensive specials board changes frequently. The adjoining village play area makes The Station popular with families.

Open all wk 5-11.30 (Sat 12-2.30 5-11.30 Sun 12-11.30) **Bar Meals** L served Sat 12-2.30, Sun 12-7 D served Mon-Sat 5-9, Sun 12-7 Av main course £12.70 **Restaurant** L served Sat 12-2.30, Sun 12-7 D served Mon-Sat 5-9, Sun 4-7 ⊕ FREE HOUSE ◀ Tetley's Cask & Smoothflow, Black Sheep Progress, Guinness, Guest ales ♂ Thatchers. ♥ 14 **Facilities** Non-diners area ♦♦ Children's menu Children's portions Play area Garden Parking Wi-fi ▥ (notice required)

REETH — Map 19 SE09

Charles Bathurst Inn ★★★★ INN
PICK OF THE PUBS

See Pick of the Pubs on page 514

PICK OF THE PUBS

Charles Bathurst Inn ★★★★ INN

REETH   Map 19 SE09

Arkengarthdale DL11 6EN
☎ 01748 884567
e-mail: info@cbinn.co.uk
web: www.cbinn.co.uk
dir: *A1 onto A6108 at Scotch Corner, through Richmond, left onto B6270 to Reeth. At Buck Hotel right signed Langthwaite, pass church on right, inn 0.5m on right*

Spectacular dale scenery at remote country inn

This 18th-century inn sits in possibly one of the North's finest dales, and takes its name from the son of Oliver Cromwell's physician who built it for his workers in what was once a busy lead mining area. In winter, it caters for serious ramblers tackling The Pennine Way and the Coast to Coast route, and it offers a welcome escape from the rigours of the moors and many a tale has been swapped over pints of Black Sheep or Theakston ale. The 'Terrace Room' features handcrafted tables and chairs from Robert Thompson's craftsmen in nearby Kilburn with their unique hand carved mouse on every item, watch out for them! English classics meet modern European dishes on a menu written up on the mirror hanging above the stone fireplace and the provenance is impeccable: pan-fried pigeon breast with wild mushroom fricassée followed by locally shot roast

loin of venison, crispy haggis, fondant potato and root vegetable mash. Choose the cheeseboard for the chance to taste local specialities such as mature and oak-smoked Wensleydale, and Shepherd Purse cheeses - Mrs Bell's Blue, Yorkshire Ryedale and Monk's Folly. The wine list is also excellent with well-written tasting notes. From April to September the local outdoor game of quoits can be played. The bedrooms have fabulous views overlooking the Stang and Arkengarthdale and are finished to a high standard with exposed beams, cast iron bed frames and warm colours.

Open all day all wk 11am-mdnt Closed: 25 Dec **Bar Meals** L served Mon-Fri 12-2.30, Sat-Sun 12-6 D served all wk

6-9 Av main course £13.50
Restaurant L served all wk 12-2.30 D served all wk 6-9 Av 3 course à la carte fr £23.50 ⊕ FREE HOUSE ◀ Black Sheep Best Bitter, Black Sheep Golden Sheep, Black Sheep Riggwelter, Rudgate Jorvik Blonde, Theakston. ♈ 12
Facilities Non-diners area ❄ (Bar) ♦♦ Children's menu Children's portions Play area Garden ⊼ Parking Wi-fi 🚌 (notice required) **Rooms** 19

PICK OF THE PUBS

The Anvil Inn

SAWDON   Map 17 SE98

Main St YO13 9DY ☎ 01723 859896
e-mail: info@theanvilinnsawdon.co.uk
web: www.theanvilinnsawdon.co.uk
dir: *1.5m N of Brompton-by-Sawdon, on
A170 8m E of Pickering & 6m W of
Scarborough*

Natural affinity between fine ale and fine dining

The bar, with a soaring, timbered
ceiling, dates from the early 1700s,
although back then — indeed, until 1985
— it was a blacksmith's forge, which is
why it's crammed with artefacts,
including the furnace, bellows, tools
and, of course, an anvil. Since this
sleepy village on the edge of the North
Riding Forest Park regained a pub,
everybody — locals, walkers, mountain-
bikers, Uncle Tom Cobley and all —
simply love it. Weekly-changing beers
tend to come from local microbreweries,
so if luck is on your side you may
encounter Midnight Bell, which is a mild
ale from Leeds Brewery; Wold Top's
Angler's Reward; or, ahem, Old Leg Over
from Daleside. At least 11 wines are
sold by the glass, but if none is to your
liking you may ask for something else to
be opened. Another big draw is chef-
patron Mark Wilson's modern European
cooking, typically featuring fish from the
East Coast, county-sourced meats and
locally grown fruit and vegetables, many
from the village itself. At lunchtime look
for air-cured Yorkshire ham and potato

rösti; and twice-baked soufflé of roast
shallots with Kashmir Gold saffron and
Ryedale cheese, while the evening menu
might tempt with pan-roasted breast of
guinea fowl with croquette of confit leg,
thyme and lemon risotto, sherry and
shallot jus; honey-roasted haunch of
Yorkshire venison with braised Puy
lentils and beetroot, and damson gin
syrup; or slow-braised daube of beef
with buttery mash and rich red onion
braising liquor. A mini-cellar of dessert
wines is on hand from which to choose
something to accompany warm treacle
tart with vanilla ice cream and boozy
prunes, for instance, or a plate of three
British cheeses with house chutney.

Open 12-2.30 6-11 Closed: 26 Dec, 1
Jan & varying annual holiday, Mon-Tue
Bar Meals L served Wed-Sat 12-2, Sun

12-2.30 D served Wed-Sat 6.30-9, Sun
6-8 Av main course £15 **Restaurant** L
served Wed-Sat 12-2, Sun 12-2.30 D
served Wed-Sat 6.30-9, Sun 6-8 Av 3
course à la carte fr £28 ⊕ FREE HOUSE
◾ Daleside Old Leg Over, Wold Top
Angler's Reward, Leeds Midnight Bell
Ŏ Westons Stowford Press. ♀ 11
Facilities Non-diners area ♣ Bar
Garden) ♦♦ Children's portions (Garden
⌱ Parking

RIPON   Map 19 SE37

The George at Wath ★★★★ INN ◉

Main St, Wath HG4 5EN ☎ 01765 641324
e-mail: richard@thegeorgeatwath.co.uk
dir: *From A1 (dual carriageway) N'bound turn left signed Melmerby & Wath. From A1 S'bound exit at slip road signed A61. At T-junct right (signed Ripon). Approx 0.5m turn right signed Melmerby & Wath*

Welcoming free house with award-winning food

The George at Wath, a brick-built double-fronted free house dating from the 18th century, is just three miles from the cathedral city of Ripon. This traditional Yorkshire pub retains its flagstone floors, log-burning fires and cosy atmosphere, while the contemporary dining room proffers seasonal and locally sourced ingredients for its mix of classic and bistro-style dishes: salt cod fritters could be followed by glazed gammon with chips cooked in dripping; finish with a chocolate tart, or rhubarb and custard. The George is child and dog friendly.

Open 12-3 5-11 (Sat-Sun all day) Closed: Mon & Tue L ⊕ FREE HOUSE ◀ Theakston, Rudgate. **Facilities** ☘ (Bar Garden) ♦♦ Children's menu Children's portions Garden Parking Wi-fi **Rooms** 5

The Royal Oak ★★★★ INN ◉

36 Kirkgate HG4 1PB ☎ 01765 602284
e-mail: info@royaloakripon.co.uk
dir: *In town centre*

City centre, inn with a modern feel

Built as a coaching inn, this city centre venue now has a clean, modern and open feel, with wooden floorboards in the bright, spacious bar and comfortable leather settees in the AA-Rosetted restaurant. Owned by the Timothy Taylor brewery you can obviously expect excellent ales. Lunchtime brings 'door step' sandwiches with dripping-cooked chips, and there's also a good range of pub classics like pie and mash or fish and chips. Other mains include poached salmon salad; pan-fried sea bass; handmade pea tortellini or barley risotto with squash and crispy goats' cheese. There's also an impressive board of local cheeses. Regular food and wine tasting events and modern accommodation complete the package.

Open all day all wk **Bar Meals** L served Mon-Sat 12-9, Sun 12-8 D served Mon-Sat 12-9, Sun 12-8 **Restaurant** L served Mon-Sat 12-9, Sun 12-8 D served Mon-Sat 12-9, Sun 12-8 ⊕ TIMOTHY TAYLOR & CO LTD ◀ Landlord, Best Bitter, Golden Best ♂ Westons Stowford Press. ♀ 14 **Facilities** Non-diners area ♦♦ Children's menu Children's portions Garden Parking Wi-fi 🚌 **Rooms** 6

ROBIN HOOD'S BAY   Map 19 NZ90

Laurel Inn

New Rd YO22 4SE ☎ 01947 880400
dir: *Telephone for directions*

On the winding street towards the sea

Given its location it's hardly surprising that this was once the haunt of smugglers who used a network of underground tunnels and secret passages to bring the booty ashore. Nowadays it's the haunt of holidaymakers and walkers, and the setting for this small, traditional pub which retains lots of character features, including beams and an open fire. The bar is decorated with old photographs, and an international collection of lager bottles. This popular free house serves Adnams and Theakston Old Peculier and Best Bitter.

Open all wk ⊕ FREE HOUSE ◀ Theakston Best Bitter & Old Peculier, Adnams. **Facilities** ☘ (Bar) ♦♦ Family room Wi-fi **Notes** ◉

SAWDON   Map 17 SE98

The Anvil Inn

PICK OF THE PUBS

See Pick of the Pubs on page 515

SCAWTON   Map 19 SE58

The Hare Inn

PICK OF THE PUBS

YO7 2HG ☎ 01845 597769
e-mail: liz@thehare-inn.com
dir: *Exit A170 towards Rievaulx Abbey & Scawton. Pub 1m on right*

Historic inn with a new lease of life

This pretty free house in the North Yorkshire Moors was built in the 13th century and allegedly used as a brewhouse by the monks who built Rievaulx Abbey nearby. Later, in the 17th century, ale was brewed here for local iron workers. Liz and her husband, chef-patron Paul Jackson, took over the Hare in October 2012. You'll find low-beamed ceilings and flagstone floors, a wood-burning stove offering a warm welcome in the bar, and an old-fashioned kitchen range in the dining area. Using his imagination and flair, Paul's combines the best produce with seasonal availability, and each dish demonstrates a high attention to detail and is beautifully presented. Perhaps start with hare, Yorkshire Blue, pear, walnuts, cauliflower, quince, chocolate and port; continue with loin of lamb, garlic gnocchi, sweetbread, ratatouille, red wine and salsify; and finish with lemon pannacotta, ice cream, blackberry and vanilla, or a cheeseboard. Look out for the friendly ghost!

Open Tue-Sat 12-2 6-9.30 (Sun 12-4) Closed: 2wks end of Jan beg of Feb, Mon, Sun eve (ex BHs) **Bar Meals** L served Tue-Sat 12-2, Sun 12-4 Av main course £7-£10 **Restaurant** L served Tue-Sat 12-2, Sun 12-4 D served Tue-Sat 6-9 Fixed menu price fr £20.50 Av 3 course à la

carte fr £30 ⊕ FREE HOUSE ◀ Black Sheep, Rudgate Viking, Guest ales ♂ Thatchers. ♀ 10 **Facilities** Non-diners area ☘ (Bar Garden) ♦♦ Children's menu Children's portions Garden 🚶 Parking 🚌 (notice required)

SETTLE   Map 18 SD86

The Lion at Settle ★★★★ INN

Duke St BD24 9DU ☎ 01729 822203
e-mail: relax@thelionsettle.co.uk
web: www.thelionsettle.co.uk
dir: *Telephone for directions*

Revamped Dales coaching inn

Owned by Thwaites and set in the heart of Settle's 17th-century market place, this inn's interior oozes history and atmosphere, with original inglenook fireplaces, wooden floors and a grand staircase lined with pictures that trace back through the town's history. It's a comfortable base for exploring the Dales or the spectacular Settle to Carlisle railway line. Expect decent cask ales and a classic pub menu offering freshly prepared pub favourites. Typical examples include tempura tiger prawns; traditional lamb hot pot; Whitby scampi and chips; and Bramley apple and blackberry crumble for dessert.

Open all day all wk 11-11 (Fri-Sat 11am-11.30pm Sun 12-10.30) **Bar Meals** L served Mon-Sat 12-9, Sun 12-8 D served Mon-Sat 12-9, Sun 12-8 Av main course £10.95 food served all day **Restaurant** L served Mon-Sat 12-9, Sun 12-8 D served Mon-Sat 12-9, Sun 12-8 food served all day ⊕ THWAITES INNS OF CHARACTER ◀ Original, Lancaster Bomber & Wainwright, Guest ales ♂ Kingstone Press. ♀ 9 **Facilities** Non-diners area ☘ (Bar Garden) ♦♦ Children's menu Children's portions Garden 🚶 Wi-fi 🚌 (notice required) **Rooms** 14

See advert on opposite page

Save on hotels. Book at **theAA.com/hotel**

YORKSHIRE, NORTH 517 ENGLAND

Devonshire Arms

Grassington Rd, Cracoe BD23 6LA ☎ 01756 730237
e-mail: info@devonshirecracoe.co.uk
dir: *Telephone for directions*

Old beams and warming fires in traditional inn

The original setting for the Rhylstone Ladies WI calendar, this convivial, lovingly renovated 17th-century inn is conveniently located for the Three Peaks and has excellent views of Rhylstone Fell. In the hands of experienced licensees Barbara and Nathan Hutchinson you will find character, quality and service here. A wide range of cask ales plus an extensive wine list will wash down a menu that runs from spiced whitebait with lime and paprika mayonnaise to pan-seared Yorkshire lamb rump with dauphinoise potatoes and apricot and mint gravy.

Open all day all wk 8.30am-mdnt **Bar Meals** L served all wk 8.30-8.30 D served all wk 8.30-8.30 food served all day **Restaurant** L served all wk 8.30-8.30 D served all wk 8.30-8.30 food served all day ⊕ MARSTON'S ◀ EPA & Burton Bitter, Jennings Bitter. ♟ 11
Facilities Non-diners area 🐾 (Bar Garden) ♦♦ Children's menu Children's portions Play area Garden 🅿 Parking Wi-fi 🚐 (notice required)

The Coachman Inn ★★★★ RR ⊛

Pickering Road West YO13 9PL ☎ 01723 859231
e-mail: info@coachmaninn.co.uk
dir: *From A170 in Snainton take B1258. Pub signed from A170*

Coaching inn with a rustic bar and a romantic restaurant

Built in 1776, this Grade II listed Georgian coaching inn is superbly located to make the most of coast and countryside. The Coachman holds a coveted AA Rosette for culinary excellence; food is served in the romantic candlelit Carriages Restaurant, rustic Coachman Bar or outside in the gardens and bistro courtyard. Typical dishes include pressed duck terrine or smoked haddock fishcake; followed by braised beef cheeks, mushroom and walnut hotpot pie or escalope of rose veal. Leave space for black cherry Eton mess or Blue Wensleydale pannacotta. Traditional beers are available and a wide selection of wines by the glass. Six individually designed bedrooms are available.

Open all wk 12-12 **Bar Meals** L served all wk 12-9 D served all wk 12-9 food served all day **Restaurant** L served Mon-Sat 12-9, Sun 12-3 D served Mon-Sat 12-9, Sun 4-9 food served all day ⊕ FREE HOUSE ◀ John Smith's, Wold Top, Guinness. ♟ 15
Facilities Non-diners area ♦♦ Children's menu Children's portions Garden 🅿 Parking Wi-fi **Rooms** 6

Fox & Hounds Inn

BD23 5HY ☎ 01756 760269 & 760367
e-mail: starbottonfox@aol.com
dir: *Telephone for directions*

Traditional family-run pub in the glorious Yorkshire Dales

Built as a private house some 400 years ago, this pub has been serving this picturesque limestone Yorkshire Dales village since the 1840s. Make for the bar, with its large stone fireplace, oak beams and flagged floor to enjoy a pint of Black Sheep, something from the local Yorkshire Dales brewery, or one of the wide selection of malts. Head to the dining room for home-cooked pork medallions in brandy and mustard sauce; Thai cod and prawn fishcakes; or broccoli and Stilton quiche. The area is renowned for its spectacular walks.

Open 12-3 6-11 (Sun 12-3.30 5.30-10.30) Closed: 1-22 Jan, Mon **Bar Meals** L served Tue-Sun 12-2.30

D served Tue-Sat 6-9, Sun 5.30-8 Av main course £9.50-£14.95 ⊕ FREE HOUSE ◀ Timothy Taylor Landlord, Black Sheep, Moorhouse's, Yorkshire Dales, Guest ales ⏱ Thatchers Gold. ♟ 10 **Facilities** Non-diners area ♦♦ Garden Parking 🚐

The Blackwell Ox Inn ★★★★ INN ⊛

Huby Rd YO61 1DT ☎ 01347 810328
e-mail: enquiries@blackwelloxinn.co.uk
dir: *A1237 onto B1363 to Sutton-on-the-Forest. Left at T-junct, 50yds on right*

Blending period charm with modern elegance

This inn's name celebrates a shorthorn Teeswater Ox that stood 6ft high at the crop and weighed 1,033 kilos. When the beast was slaughtered in 1779 its meat fetched £110, about £7,000 today. Built around 1823 as a private house, the pub's well-stocked bar offers Yorkshire ales like Black Sheep. The simple cooking style owes much to a North Yorkshire-focused sourcing policy for lunchtime hot and cold sandwiches, alongside mussels, chips and aïoli; and sausage and mash. The restaurant menu could list pan-roasted cod loin, rib-eye steak, and feta cheese and roast vegetable tart. The inn has a terrace for alfresco dining.

Open all wk 12-2 5.30-11 (Sun 12-10.30) Closed: 25 Dec, 1 Jan **Bar Meals** L served Mon-Sat 12-2, Sun 12-4 D served Mon-Sat 6-9.30 **Restaurant** L served Mon-Sat 12-2, Sun 12-4 D served Mon-Sat 6-9.30 ⊕ FREE HOUSE ◀ Timothy Taylor Landlord, Black Sheep Best Bitter, York Guzzler, Guinness. ♟ 14 **Facilities** Non-diners area ♦♦ Children's menu Children's portions Garden 🅿 Parking Wi-fi 🚐 (notice required) **Rooms** 7

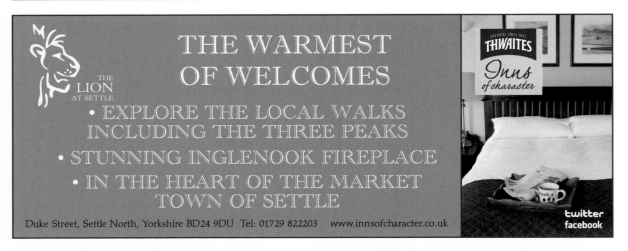

THORNTON LE DALE · Map 19 SE88

The New Inn

Maltongate YO18 7LF ☎ **01751 474226**
e-mail: enquire@the-new-inn.com
dir: *A64 N from York towards Scarborough. At Malton take A169 to Pickering. At Pickering rdbt right onto A170, 2m, pub on right*

A very warm welcome and good food

Standing at the heart of a picturesque village complete with stocks and a market cross, this family-run Georgian coaching house dates back to 1720. The old-world charm of the location is echoed inside the bar and restaurant, with real log fires and exposed beams. Enjoy well-kept Theakston Black Bull and guest ales, bitters, lagers and wines and tuck into beef and ale casserole; breast of duckling with sweet orange sauce; and chicken wrapped in Parma ham and topped with mozzarella.

Open all wk 12-2.30 5-11 (summer all day) ⊕ STAR PUBS & BARS ◀ Theakston Black Bull, Guest ales. **Facilities** ◑ Children's menu Children's portions Garden Parking Wi-fi

---

THORNTON WATLASS · Map 19 SE28

The Buck Inn ★★★ INN

PICK OF THE PUBS

HG4 4AH ☎ **01677 422461**
e-mail: innwatlass1@btconnect.com
dir: *From A1 at Leeming Bar take A684 to Bedale, B6268 towards Masham. Village in 2m*

Plenty of choice for real ale fans

Run by Michael and Margaret Fox for the past two decades, this traditional, pub has no trouble in maintaining its welcoming and relaxed atmosphere. The inn doesn't just overlook the village green and cricket pitch; players score four runs for hitting the pub wall, and six if the ball goes over the roof! Thornton Watlass is very much the quintessential village, and where Wensleydale, gateway to the Yorkshire Dales National Park, begins; this glorious area is where much of the TV series *Heartbeat* was filmed. There are three separate dining areas and the menu ranges from traditional, freshly prepared pub fare to exciting modern cuisine backed by daily changing blackboard specials. Beer drinkers have a choice of five real ales, including Masham-brewed Black Sheep. There's live jazz music most Sunday lunchtimes. Cottage-style bedrooms provide a comfortable night's sleep.

Open all wk 11am-mdnt Closed: 25 Dec eve **Bar Meals** L served Mon-Sat 12-2, Sun 12-3 D served Mon-Sat 6-9, Sun 6-8.30 **Restaurant** L served Mon-Sat 12-2, Sun 12-3 D served Mon-Sat 6-9, Sun 6-8.30 ⊕ FREE HOUSE ◀ Black Sheep Best Bitter, 4 Guest ales ♂ Thatchers Gold. **Facilities** Non-diners area ◑ Children's menu Children's portions Play area Family room Garden Parking ⊟ **Rooms** 7

WASS · Map 19 SE57

Wombwell Arms

PICK OF THE PUBS

YO61 4BE ☎ **01347 868280**
e-mail: info@wombwellarms.co.uk
dir: *From A1 take A168 to A19 junct. Take York exit, then left after 2.5m, left at Coxwold to Ampleforth. Wass 2m*

Homely inn with interesting food

Ian and Eunice Walker's whitewashed village inn sits in the shadow of the Hambleton Hills. Dating from 1620, it was built as a granary using stones from the ruins of nearby Byland Abbey. There are two oak-beamed, flagstone-floored bars, one with a huge inglenook fireplace, the other with a wood-burning stove, and the atmosphere is relaxed and informal. Locals, walkers and cyclists quaff pints of Timothy Taylor Landlord. High quality, modern British meals with a South African twist are prepared from local produce as far as possible. Tuck into decent sandwiches for lunch and choose one of the Wombwell classics for dinner; perhaps the steak, mushroom and Guinness pie with gravy and chips. Or try rooibos tea smoked chicken salad with chorizo. Leave room for the cinnamon crème brûlée with toasted almonds and fruit praline, or a plate of local cheeses.

Open all wk 12-3 6-11 (Sat 12-11 Sun 12-10.30) **Bar Meals** L served Mon-Fri 12-2, Fri-Sat 12-2.30, Sun 12-3 D served Mon-Thu 6-8.30, Fri-Sat 6-9, Sun 6-8 Av main course £11.95 **Restaurant** L served Mon-Fri 12-2, Sat 12-2.30, Sun 12-3 D served Mon-Thu 6-8.30, Fri-Sat 6-9, Sun 6-8 Fixed menu price fr £10 Av 3 course à la carte fr £16.95 ⊕ FREE HOUSE ◀ Timothy Taylor Landlord, Black Sheep Best Bitter, Guest ales. ♈ 10 **Facilities** Non-diners area ◑ Children's menu Children's portions Garden ⊟ Parking Wi-fi ⛍ (notice required)

WEST BURTON · Map 19 SE08

Fox & Hounds

DL8 4JY ☎ **01969 663111**
e-mail: the_fox_hounds@unicombox.co.uk
dir: *A468 between Hawes & Leyburn, 0.5m E of Aysgarth*

Community pub in the Dales

In a beautiful Dales setting, this is a traditional pub overlooking the large village green, which has swings and football goals, and its own hidden waterfalls. Parents can happily sit at the front and enjoy a drink while keeping an eye on their children. A proper local, the pub hosts men's and women's darts teams and a dominoes team; in summer customers play quoits out on the green. Real ales, some from the Black Sheep Brewery down the road, and home-made food prepared from fresh ingredients is served. In addition to the pizzas cooked in the pizza oven, dishes include chicken curry, steak-and-kidney pie, lasagne, steaks and other pub favourites.

Open all day all wk ⊕ FREE HOUSE ◀ Theakston Best Bitter, Black Sheep, John Smith's, Copper Dragon. **Facilities** ◑ Children's menu Children's portions Parking

---

WEST TANFIELD · Map 19 SE27

The Bruce Arms

PICK OF THE PUBS

Main St HG4 5JJ ☎ **01677 470325**
e-mail: halc123@yahoo.co.uk
dir: *On A6108 between Ripon & Masham*

Enticing menu in tranquil village inn

Handy for the glorious, undiscovered countryside of nearby Nidderdale Area of Outstanding Beauty, this homely stone-built pub sits at the heart of the extremely pretty village of West Tanfield, which stands beside a languorous loop of the River Ure; the cathedral city of Ripon, Fountains Abbey and the famous spa at Harrogate are also within easy reach. The inn's interior is a comfy mix of traditional village pub, complete with good Yorkshire-brewed ales, beams and log fires, and contemporary bistro which complements the stylish, modern European cooking of highly experienced chef-patron Hugh Carruthers. There's a regularly changing menu, formulated to make the most of locally available seasonal produce; home in on a starter of duck and black pudding terrine with quails' eggs and apple, leading to loin of venison with dauphinoise, root vegetables, beetroot and chestnuts, or fillet of halibut with sauce vierge, mash and green beans mains.

Open 12-2.30 6-9.30 (Sun 12-3.30) Closed: 2wks Feb, Mon **Bar Meals** L served Tue-Sat 12-2.30 D served Tue-Sat 6-7.30 Av main course £15 **Restaurant** L served Tue-Sat 12-2.30, Sun 12-3 D served Tue-Sat 6-9.30 Fixed menu price fr £12.95 Av 3 course à la carte fr £28.50 ⊕ FREE HOUSE ◀ Black Sheep Best Bitter, Guest ales ♂ Aspall. ♈ 10 **Facilities** Non-diners area ◑ Children's portions Outside area ⊟ Parking

Save on hotels. Book at **theAA.com/hotel**

YORKSHIRE, NORTH 519 **ENGLAND**

WEST WITTON	Map 19 SE08

The Wensleydale Heifer ★★★★★ RR ◉

PICK OF THE PUBS

Main St DL8 4LS ☎ 01969 622322
dir: *A1 to Leeming Bar junct, A684 towards Bedale for approx 10m to Leyburn, then towards Hawes, 3.5m to West Witton*

Stylish boutique restaurant with rooms

Between Leyburn and Hawes in the heart of the Yorkshire Dales National Park, this 17th-century coaching inn still looks the part, while offering plenty of modern comforts. For morning coffee and the daily newspapers there's the Whisky Lounge, which exceeds its job description by also serving Heifer Gold and Black Sheep real ales, and Aspall cider. Of the two dining experiences, the fish bar is less formal, with sea-grass flooring, wooden tables and rattan chairs. The restaurant, on the other hand, with chocolate leather chairs, linen table cloths and Doug Hyde artworks, is described by the proprietors as 'contemporary decadence'. Whichever you choose, the food is still AA Rosette quality, and often adventurous, to wit, panko-crusted (Japanese-style breadcrumbs) goats' cheese fritters; tian of Whitby crab with home-cured gravad lax; roast halibut fillet with braised beef rib; and the more prosaic roast lamb shoulder. 'Little Heifers' get their own well-considered menu.

Open all day all wk **Bar Meals** L served all wk 12.30-2.30 D served all wk 6-9.30 Av main course £20 **Restaurant** L served all wk 12.30-2.30 D served all wk 6-9.30 Fixed menu price fr £19.75 Av 3 course à la carte fr £33 ⊕ FREE HOUSE ◢ Heifer Gold, Black Sheep Ŏ Aspall. ♟ **Facilities** Non-diners area ❖ (Bar Garden) ♦ Children's menu Children's portions Garden ⋈ Parking Wi-fi 🚐 **Rooms** 13

WHITBY	Map 19 NZ81

The Magpie Café

14 Pier Rd YO21 3PU ☎ 01947 602058
e-mail: ian@magpiecafe.co.uk
dir: *Telephone for directions*

Fish focussed café

The acclaimed Magpie Café has been the home of North Yorkshire's 'best-ever fish and chips' since the late 1930s. You could pop in for a pint of Cropton, but the excellent views of the harbour from the dining room, together with the prospect of fresh seafood, could prove too much of a temptation. An exhaustive list of fish and seafood dishes is offered daily; perhaps Whitby crab pâté with French bread and home-made chutney and then seafood paella, or your choice of fish simply battered and served with chips. Desserts include classics like sherry trifle or spotted dick.

Open all day all wk Closed: 25 Dec, 6-31 Jan **Bar Meals** food served all day **Restaurant** L served all wk 11.30-9 D served all wk 11.30-9 food served all day

⊕ FREE HOUSE ◢ Cropton Scoresby Stout, The Captain Cook Slipway, Cropton Blackout. ♟ 10 **Facilities** ♦ Children's menu Children's portions Wi-fi 🚐

WIGGLESWORTH	Map 18 SD85

The Plough Inn ★★★★ INN ◉◉

BD23 4RJ ☎ 01729 840243
e-mail: info@theploughatwigglesworth.co.uk
dir: *From A65 between Skipton & Long Preston take B6478 to Wigglesworth*

Splendid country views from the restaurant

Originally a farmhouse, The Plough has been trading as a pub since 1720 and the bar of this traditional country free house features oak beams and an open fire. There are fine views of the surrounding hills from the conservatory restaurant, where the pub's precarious position on the Yorkshire/Lancashire border is reflected in the menu which features local suppliers. Typical dishes are risotto of Yorkshire blue cheese with wild mushrooms; which might be followed by fish pie topped with herb and creamed potato gratin. Leave room for the apple crumble and ice cream.

Open Wed-Sun Closed: Mon-Tue **Bar Meals** L served Wed-Sat 12-2, Sun 12-7 D served Wed-Sat 6-9, Sun 12-7 **Restaurant** L served Wed-Sat 12-2, Sun 12-7 D served Wed-Sat 12-2, Sun 12-7 ⊕ FREE HOUSE ◢ Black Sheep, Timothy Taylor Landlord, Guest ales. ♟ 9 **Facilities** Non-diners area ♦ Children's portions Outside area ⋈ Parking Wi-fi **Rooms** 9

YORK	Map 16 SE65

Blue Bell

PICK OF THE PUBS

53 Fossgate YO1 9TF ☎ 01904 654904
e-mail: robsonhardie@aol.com
dir: *In city centre*

Tucked away, quaint city pub

Its slimline frontage is easy to miss, but don't walk past this charming pub – the smallest in York – which has been serving customers in the ancient heart of the city for 200 years. In 1903 it was given a typical Edwardian makeover, and since then almost nothing has changed – so the Grade II listed interior still includes varnished wall and ceiling panelling, cast-iron tiled fireplaces, and charming old settles. The layout is original too, with the taproom at the front and the snug down a long corridor at the rear, both with servery hatches. The only slight drawback is that the pub's size leaves no room for a kitchen, so don't expect anything more complicated than lunchtime sandwiches. However, there's a good selection of real ales: no fewer than seven are usually on tap, including rotating guests. The pub has won awards for its efforts in fund-raising.

Open all day all wk **Bar Meals** L served Mon-Sat 12-2.30 ⊕ PUNCH TAVERNS ◢ Timothy Taylor Landlord, Bradfield Farmers Blonde, Roosters Yankee Ŏ Westons Traditional. **Facilities** Non-diners area ❖ (Bar) Wi-fi **Notes** ◉

Lamb & Lion Inn ★★★★ INN ◉

2-4 High Petergate YO1 7EH ☎ 01904 612078
e-mail: gm@lambandlionyork.com
dir: *From York Station, turn left. Stay in left lane, over Lendal Bridge. At lights left (Theatre Royal on right). At next lights pub on right under Bootham Bar (medieval gate)*

Right in the historical centre of York

This rambling Georgian inn has unrivalled views of nearby York Minster from its elevated beer garden. Conjoined to the medieval Bootham Bar gateway, it is furnished and styled in keeping with its grand heritage. A warren of snugs and corridors radiate from a bar offering a challenging array of beers, including Golden Mane, brewed for the inn. Equally enticing is the AA-Rosette menu, offering comforting classics ranging from a fish finger butty and steak pie to moules frites, slow-cooked lamb shank and a Yorkshire platter. Finish with chocolate brownie or knickerbocker glory. Accommodation is available.

Open all day all wk **Bar Meals** Av main course £9.95 food served all day **Restaurant** food served all day ⊕ FREE HOUSE ◢ Great Heck Golden Mane, Black Sheep Best Bitter, Copper Dragon Golden Pippin. ♟ 10 **Facilities** Non-diners area ❖ (Bar Restaurant Garden) ♦ Children's menu Children's portions Garden ⋈ Wi-fi **Rooms** 12

Lysander Arms

Manor Ln, Shipton Rd YO30 5TZ ☎ 01904 640845
e-mail: christine@lysanderarms.co.uk
dir: *Telephone for directions*

British menu and Yorkshire hospitality

This pub stands on a former RAF airfield where No. 4 Squadron's Westland Lysander aircraft were based early in World War II. Still relatively modern, which accounts for the contemporary feel of the interior, it has a long, fully air-conditioned bar with up-to-date furnishings, brick-built fireplace and large-screen TV. Brasserie restaurant meals range from 'light bites' such as Yorkshire Blue cheese and chive rarebit with pickled red cabbage to hearty meals such as steak, mushroom and ale pie or slow-cooked belly pork with crispy crackling, black pudding, creamed potatoes and roasted apple.

Open all day all wk ⊕ FREE HOUSE ◢ John Smith's Extra Smooth, York Guzzler, Wychwood Hobgoblin, Copper Dragon, Black Sheep, Theakston Ŏ Kopparberg. **Facilities** ❖ (Bar Garden) ♦ Children's menu Children's portions Play area Garden Parking Wi-fi

YORKSHIRE, SOUTH

BRADFIELD
Map 16 SK29

The Strines Inn

Bradfield Dale S6 6JE ☎ 0114 285 1247
e-mail: thestrinesinn@yahoo.co.uk
dir: *N off A57 between Sheffield & Manchester*

Popular free house overlooking reservoir

Although built as a manor house in 1275, most of the structure is 16th century; it has been an inn since 1771, the public rooms containing artefacts from its bygone days. The name apparently means 'meeting of waters' in Old English. Locally brewed Bradfield Farmers Bitter shares bar space with ambassadors from the further-flung Marston's, Jennings and Wychwood. Traditional home-made food begins with sandwiches and salads, then by way of pies and giant Yorkshire puddings arrives at mammoth mixed grill; liver and onions; and home-made butter bean stew. A play area and an enclosure for peacocks, geese and chickens are outside.

Open all wk 10.30-3 5.30-11 (Sat-Sun 10.30am-11pm; all day Apr-Oct) Closed: 25 Dec **Bar Meals** L served Mon-Fri 12-2.30, Sat-Sun 12-9 (summer all wk 12-9) D served Mon-Fri 5.30-9, Sat-Sun 12-9 (summer all wk 12-9) Av main course £8.95 ⊕ FREE HOUSE ◀ Marston's Pedigree, Jennings Cocker Hoop, Bradfield Farmers Bitter, Wychwood Hobgoblin. ♟ 10 **Facilities** Non-diners area � (Bar Garden) ♦♦ Children's menu Children's portions Play area Garden ᴲ Parking ▭ (notice required)

PENISTONE
Map 16 SE20

Cubley Hall

PICK OF THE PUBS

Mortimer Rd, Cubley S36 9DF ☎ 01226 766086
e-mail: info@cubleyhall.co.uk
dir: *M1 junct 37, A628 towards Manchester, or M1 junct 35a, A616. Hall just S of Penistone*

Impressive building with ornate, elegant decor and excellent food

Built as a farm in the 1700s, Cubley Hall was a gentleman's residence in Queen Victoria's reign and later became a children's home before being transformed into pub in 1982. In 1990 the massive, oak-beamed bar was converted into the restaurant and furnished with old pine tables, chairs and church pews, and the building was extended to incorporate the hotel, which was designed to harmonise with the original mosaic floors, ornate plaster ceilings, oak panelling and stained glass. On the edge of the Peak District National Park, the hall is reputedly haunted by Florence Lockley, who married there in 1904 and is affectionately known as Flo. Food-wise, take your pick from light bites, chalkboard specials and an extensive main menu listing pub classics and home-made pizzas. Typically, choose from a Crawshaw beefburger with all the trimmings; fish and chips; pork and leek sausages; mash and onion gravy; and chicken and mushroom carbonara.

Open all day all wk **Bar Meals** L served all wk 12-9 D served all wk 12-9 food served all day **Restaurant** L served Sun 2 sittings 12-3.30 & 3-5.30 ⊕ FREE HOUSE ◀ Tetley's Bitter, Black Sheep Best Bitter. **Facilities** Non-diners area ♦♦ Children's menu Children's portions Play area Family room Garden ᴲ Parking Wi-fi ▭ (notice required)

SHEFFIELD
Map 16 SK38

The Fat Cat

PICK OF THE PUBS

23 Alma St S3 8SA ☎ 0114 249 4801
e-mail: info@thefatcat.co.uk
dir: *Telephone for directions*

Own Kelham Island beers in Victorian pub

Built in 1832, it was known as The Alma Hotel for many years, then in 1981 it was the first Sheffield pub to introduce guest beers. The policy continues, with constantly changing, mainly microbrewery, guests from across the country, two handpumped ciders, unusual bottled beers, Belgian pure fruit juices and British country wines. The pub's own Kelham Island Brewery accounts for at least four of the 11 traditional draught real ales. The smart interior is very much that of a traditional, welcoming back-street pub, with real fires making it feel very cosy, while outside is an attractive walled garden with Victorian-style lanterns and bench seating. Except on Sunday evenings, typical home-cooked food from a simple weekly menu is broccoli cheddar pasta; Mexican mince and nachos; and savoury bean casserole. Events include the Monday quiz and curry night. Annual beer festival.

Open all wk 12-11 (Fri-Sat 12-12) Closed: 25 Dec **Bar Meals** L served Mon-Fri & Sun 12-3, Sat 12-8 D served Mon-Fri 6-8, Sat 12-8 ⊕ FREE HOUSE ◀ Timothy Taylor Landlord, Kelham Island Best Bitter & Pale Rider, Guest ales Ō Thatchers Gold. **Facilities** Non-diners area ♦♦ Children's portions Family room Garden Beer festival Parking Wi-fi ▭

Kelham Island Tavern

PICK OF THE PUBS

62 Russell St S3 8RW ☎ 0114 272 2482
e-mail: kelhamislandtav@aol.com
dir: *Just off A61 (inner ring road). Follow brown tourist signs for Kelham Island*

Real ales in a city setting

This 1830s backstreet pub was built to quench the thirst of steelmakers who lived and worked nearby. The semi-derelict pub was rescued in 2001 by Lewis Gonda and Trevor Wraith, who transformed it into a 'small gem'. The pub is in a conservation and popular walking area, with old buildings converted into stylish apartments, and The Kelham Island Museum round the corner in Alma Street telling the story of the city's industrial heritage. The real ale list is formidable: residents Barnsley Bitter, Brewers Gold and Farmers Blonde are joined by ten ever-changing

guests, as well as Westons Old Rosie cider, and a midsummer beer festival is held every year at the end of June. Constantly updated blackboards typically offer beef bourguignon; steak-and-ale pie; broccoli and cheese pie; and soups, pâtés and various bar snacks. Great in the summer, the pub has won awards for its beer garden and floral displays.

Open all day all wk 12-12 **Bar Meals** L served Mon-Sat 12-3 ⊕ FREE HOUSE ◀ Barnsley Bitter, Crouch Vale Brewers Gold, Bradfield Farmers Blonde, 10 Guest ales Ō Westons Old Rosie. **Facilities** Non-diners area ☚ (Bar Garden) ♦♦ Children's portions Family room Garden ᴲ Beer festival Cider festival Parking ▭ (notice required)

The Sheffield Tap

Platform 1B, Sheffield Station, Sheaf St S1 2BP ☎ 0114 273 7558
e-mail: info@sheffieldtap.com
dir: *Access from Sheaf St & from Platform 1B. (NB limited access from Platform 1B on Fri & Sat)*

Back on track to serve the best beers

For more than 30 years disused, derelict and vandalised, the former Edwardian refreshment room and dining rooms of Sheffield Midland Railway Station have become a much praised Grade II listed free house. Painstakingly restored to its former glory by the current custodians, with help from the Railway Heritage Trust, The Sheffield Tap is now a beer mecca offering ten real ales, one real cider, 12 keg products and more than 200 bottled beers from around the world. Food is limited to bagged bar snacks, and children are welcome until 8pm every day.

Open all day all wk Closed: 25-26 Dec, 1 Jan ⊕ FREE HOUSE ◀ Thornbridge Ō Thistly Cross. **Facilities** Non-diners area ☚ (Bar Restaurant Garden) ♦♦ Garden Wi-fi ▭ (notice required)

TOTLEY
Map 16 SK37

The Cricket Inn

PICK OF THE PUBS

See Pick of the Pubs on page 522
See advert on opposite page

the Cricket inn

Children, dogs & muddy boots welcome!

A stunning year-round destination pub bordering the Peak District and Sheffield.

Hearty homemade food includes daily seasonal specials, Sunday lunches and home-smoked meat and fish.

The Cricket Inn, Penny Lane, Totley, Sheffield S17 3AZ
T: 0114 236 5256
www.cricketinn.co.uk
@CricketInnSheff

Top 50 Gastro Pubs 2010 · MICHELIN hotels & restaurants 2009 · PubChef Food EXCELLENCE AWARDS · THE GOOD FOOD GUIDE 2009 · MICHELIN eating out in pubs 2008

Thornbridge beers and an extensive wine list available. Snuggle up next to log fires in the winter and enjoy the rolling fields in the summer, while our expert team take care of your needs.

Photography ©Jodi Hinds www.jodihinds.com

PICK OF THE PUBS

The Cricket Inn

TOTLEY   Map 16 SK37

Penny Ln, Totley S17 3AZ
☎ **0114 236 5256**
e-mail: cricket@brewkitchen.co.uk
web: www.cricketinn.co.uk
dir: *Follow A621 from Sheffield 8m. Turn
right onto Hillfoot Rd, 1st left onto
Penny Ln*

Excellent range of beers with food to match

Bordering the Peak District National
Park and tucked away down narrow
country lanes next to rolling fields and a
cricket pitch, this quintessential village
pub started life as a farmhouse. It only
became a pub in the 19th century when
it was used as a watering hole by
navvies building the nearby Totley
Tunnel on the Sheffield to Manchester
railway. Partly owned by Bakewell's
Thornbridge Brewery, the pub is run by
restaurateur Richard Smith, whose
grandfather's cousin was the landlord
when he was a child. Now a popular
seafood- and game-led gastro-pub, it
attracts Peak District walkers, whilst
dogs and children are made to feel very
welcome. Not surprisingly for a pub
owned by a brewery, the beer selection
is impressive, with four Thornbridge
ales including Wild Swan on tap as well
as a small selection of bottled Belgian
beers. The food here is seasonal and
locally sourced, with the chefs even
smoking their own meat and fish on site

every day. Snacks include black pepper
pork crackling with Bramley apple sauce
and croquettes of ham and smoked
Hawes Wensleydale cheese.
Alternatively, go for smoked haddock
and white bean cassoulet with tomatoes
and garden herb crumb; or lobster and
prawn cocktail with shaved fennel with
caper Marie Rose sauce, followed by
Portuguese-style seafood stew or seven-
hour braised ox cheek with bourguignon
garnish, pomme purée and red wine.
Desserts might include Yorkshire curd
tart with nutmeg ice cream; sticky toffee
Yorkshire parkin, clotted cream,
honeycomb ice cream; or a local
cheeseboard showcasing the likes of
Harrogate Blue, Monk's Folly and Hawes
Wensleydale. A weekday early bird menu
is particularly good value.

Open all day all wk 11-11 **Bar Meals** L
served all wk 12-9.30 D served all wk
12-9.30 Av main course £15 food served
all day **Restaurant** L served all wk
12-9.30 D served all wk 12-9.30 Fixed
menu price fr £12 food served all day
⊕ BREWKITCHEN LTD ◗ Thornbridge
Wild Swan, Lord Marples, Jaipur. ♟ 10
Facilities Non-diners area 🐾 ♟
Children's menu & portions Garden 🏕
Parking Wi-fi 🚌 (notice required)

Save on hotels. Book at theAA.com/hotel

YORKSHIRE, WEST 523 ENGLAND

YORKSHIRE, WEST

ADDINGHAM
Map 19 SE04

The Fleece
PICK OF THE PUBS

154 Main St LS29 0LY ☎ 01943 830491
e-mail: info@fleeceinnaddingham.co.uk
dir: Between Ilkley & Skipton

Chalkboards and changing menus of seriously good food

After establishing a string of successful gastro-pubs, Craig Minto returned to this 17th-century coaching inn, once owned by his father. Located where several well-tramped footpaths meet, it's popular with walkers. Food and drink is served on the front terrace and in the stone-flagged interior with its enormous fireplace, wooden settles and bar offering real ales like Copper Dragon and Ilkley. Much of the produce is local and organic, with beef and lamb coming from a nearby farm, surplus vegetables from allotment holders, and game straight from the shoot. The daily chalkboard and rolling menus offer pan-roasted chicken supreme stuffed with mushroom duxelle, buttered kale and red wine jus; sirloin of Yorkshire beef, caramelised onion and Blacksticks Blue cheese; sea bass fillets, tenderstem broccoli and brown shrimp and dill risotto; and ricotta, basil and roast pumpkin cannelloni. An on-site deli sells 'proper Yorkshire' produce, including ready meals from The Fleece's kitchen.

Open all day all wk 12-11 (Sun 12-10.30) **Bar Meals** L served Mon-Sat 12-2.15, Sun 12-8 D served Mon-Sat 5-9, Sun 12-8 **Restaurant** L served Mon-Sat 12-2.15, Sun 12-8 D served Mon-Sat 5-9, Sun 12-8 ⊕ PUNCH TAVERNS ◀ Timothy Taylor Landlord, Black Sheep, Copper Dragon, Ilkley Ŏ Westons Stowford Press. ♚ 30
Facilities Non-diners area ✿ (Bar Garden) ♦♦ Children's menu Children's portions Play area Garden ♬ Parking Wi-fi ☷ (notice required)

BRADFORD
Map 19 SE13

New Beehive Inn

171 Westgate BD1 3AA ☎ 01274 721784
e-mail: newbeehiveinn+21@btinternet.com
dir: For detailed directions contact pub

Step back in time at an inn with much character

Dating from 1901 and centrally situated with many tourist attractions nearby, this classic Edwardian inn retains its period Arts and Crafts atmosphere with five separate bars and gas lighting. It is on the national inventory list of historic pubs. Outside, with a complete change of mood, you can relax in the Mediterranean-style courtyard. The pub offers a good range of unusual real ales, such as Salamander Mudpuppy and Abbeydale Moonshine, and a selection of over 100 malt whiskies, served alongside some simple bar snacks. Music fans should attend the cellar bar, which is open at weekends and features regular live bands.

Open all day all wk ⊕ FREE HOUSE ◀ Kelham Island Best Bitter, Abbeydale Moonshine, Salamander Mudpuppy,

Ilkley Mary Jane, Saltaire Cascade Pale Ale Ŏ Westons Old Rosie. **Facilities** Non-diners area ♦♦ Family room Garden Parking Wi-fi ☷

EMLEY
Map 16 SE21

The White Horse

2 Chapel Ln HD8 9SP ☎ 01924 849823
dir: M1 junct 38, A637 towards Huddersfield. At rdbt left onto A636, then right to Emley

The hub of the community

On the old coaching route to Huddersfield and Halifax on the edge of the village, this 18th-century pub has views towards Emley Moor Mast and the surrounding countryside. The pub is popular with walkers, cyclists and locals – walking maps are available from the bar, which is warmed by a working Yorkshire range. Of the eight cask ales, four are permanent (including their own Ossett Brewery ales), and four are ever-rotating guests featuring microbreweries. A simple menu offers the likes of cod goujons, creamy garlic mushrooms, steak-and-ale pie, and mixed grill. Look to the blackboards for daily specials and desserts.

Open all wk 12-11 (Mon 4-11 Fri-Sat 12-11.30 Sun 12-10.30) **Bar Meals** L served Tue-Sat 12-2 D served Tue-Fri 5-8, Sat 5-9 **Restaurant** L served Sun 12-5 D served Tue-Fri 5-8, Sat 5-9 ⊕ FREE HOUSE ◀ Ossett Excelsior, Emley Cross & Yorkshire Blonde, Copper Dragon, Guest ales Ŏ Rotating Guest ciders. ♚ 9
Facilities Non-diners area ✿ (Bar Garden) ♦♦ Children's portions Family room Garden ♬ Parking ☷ (notice required)

HALIFAX
Map 19 SE02

Shibden Mill Inn ★★★★ INN ◉◉
PICK OF THE PUBS

See Pick of the Pubs on page 524

The Three Pigeons

1 Sun Fold, South Pde HX1 2LX ☎ 01422 347001
e-mail: threepigeons@ossett-brewery.co.uk
dir: From A629 (Skircoat Rd) in Halifax turn into Hunger Hill. Left into Union St, right into Heath View St, left into South Parade, right into Sun Fold

Character pub to enjoy Ossett beers

When Ossett Brewery took over this great little real ale pub they restored its period features to their former glory. The interior is divided into four small rooms or snugs, and each has its own character and charm. There is an amazing art deco painted ceiling in the central bar which has gained the pub its Grade II listed status. Good ales are the draw here, with Three Pigeons ale and three other beers always available. Expect live jamming sessions every Sunday night.

Open all wk 4-11 (Fri-Sat 12-12 Sun 12-11) ⊕ OSSETT BREWERY ◀ Three Pigeons, Pale Gold, Silver King, Excelsior, Yorkshire Blonde & Big Red, Guest ales

Ŏ Westons Traditional, Perry & Old Rosie.
Facilities ✿ (Bar) **Notes** ◉

HARTSHEAD
Map 16 SE12

The Gray Ox

15 Hartshead Ln WF15 8AL ☎ 01274 872845
e-mail: grayox@hotmail.co.uk
dir: M62 junct 25, A644 signed Dewsbury. Take A62, branch left signed Hartshead & Moor Top/B6119. Left to Hartshead

Hillside inn with great views and fine food

This rural inn seems to grow out of the dark gritstone hills overlooking the deep-cut Calder Valley at the fringe of the West Yorkshire Pennines. Timeless reminders of the old farmhouse it once was flicker in shadows cast from the huge log fire that warms the beamed bar where locals enjoy beers from Jennings. Rooms ramble through the old building, where the six chefs have built a grand reputation for producing fine locally-sourced dishes. Indulge in a starter of seared pigeon breast with braised celeriac, progressing then to Moroccan spiced rump of Yorkshire lamb with fragrant couscous. Booking ahead is advisable.

Open all wk 12-3.30 6-12 (Sun 12-10.30) **Bar Meals** L served Mon-Sat 12-2, Sun 12-7 D served Mon-Fri 6-9, Sat 6-9.30, Sun 12-7 Av main course £18 **Restaurant** L served Mon-Sat 12-2, Sun 12-7 D served Mon-Fri 6-9, Sat 6-9.30, Sun 12-7 Fixed menu price fr £10 Av 3 course à la carte fr £30 ⊕ MARSTON'S ◀ Jennings Cumberland Ale, Cocker Hoop, Sneck Lifter. ♚ 12 **Facilities** Non-diners area ✿ (Garden) ♦♦ Children's menu Children's portions Garden Parking Wi-fi ☷

HAWORTH
Map 19 SE03

The Old White Lion Hotel

Main St BD22 8DU ☎ 01535 642313
e-mail: enquiries@oldwhitelionhotel.com
dir: A629 onto B6142, 0.5m past Haworth Station

Charming inn in Brontë country

This traditional family-run 300-year-old coaching inn looks down onto the famous cobbled Main Street of the famous Brontë village of Haworth. In the charming bar the ceiling beams are supported by timber posts, and locals appreciatively quaff their pints of guest ale. Food is taken seriously and 'dispensed with hospitality and good measure'. Bar snacks include baguettes, salads and jackets, while a meal in the Gimmerton Restaurant might include warm Yorkshire game patties followed by slow-braised Wharfedale lamb with dauphinoise potatoes or charred breast of chicken on mixed bean and chorizo cassoulet with garlic goats' cheese dumplings.

Open all day all wk 11-11 (Sun 12-10.30) **Bar Meals** L served Mon-Fri 12-2.30, Sat-Sun all day D served Mon-Fri 6-9.30, Sat-Sun all day **Restaurant** L served Sun 12-2.30 D served all wk 7-9.30 ⊕ FREE HOUSE ◀ Tetley's Bitter, John Smith's, Local guest ales. ♚ 9
Facilities Non-diners area ♦♦ Children's menu Children's portions Parking Wi-fi ☷

PICK OF THE PUBS

Shibden Mill Inn ★★★★ INN ❀❀

HALIFAX   Map 19 SE02

Shibden Mill Fold HX3 7UL
☎ **01422 365840**
e-mail: enquiries@shibdenmillinn.com
web: www.shibdenmillinn.com
dir: *From A58 into Kell Ln. 0.5m, left into Blake Hill*

Award-winning food in renovated corn mill

The Shibden Valley used to be an important wool production area, the waters of Red Beck powering this 17th-century, former spinning mill until the industry collapsed in the late 1800s. Now it's a charming inn, with open fires, oak beams, small windows and heavy tiles, happily enjoying a more civilised existence below overhanging trees in a wooded glen that makes Halifax just down the road seem a thousand miles away. The beer garden is extremely popular, not least with beer fans who come here to sample a real ale called Shibden Mill, brewed specially for the inn, Black Sheep or one of the three guest ales. With two AA Rosettes, the restaurant attracts those who enjoy food prepared from trusted local growers and suppliers, and a seasonal menu offering newly conceived dishes and old favourites. Two starters to consider might be pan-fried pheasant breast, chestnut purée, Brussel sprout coleslaw, spiced pigeon kebab; or bouillabaisse, rouille, croûtons and Lancashire cheese.

Turn over the page for possibilities such as Round Green Farm venison Rossini; poached and roasted Todmorden rabbit; or Nettlenipper cheese and caramelised onion omelette. Among the old favourites mentioned earlier are ham hock and Denholme Honey sandwich; beer-battered Scottish haddock with dripping fat chips; and hand-made 8oz minced Yorkshire beef burger. There's also a gourmet menu of Yorkshire artisan cheeses served with home-made chutney, oat biscuits, celery and Eccles cakes, ideally accompanied by a glass of vintage port. Stay overnight in one of the individually designed luxury bedrooms, with a full Yorkshire breakfast to look forward to next morning.

Open Mon-Sat 12-11, Sun 12-10.30
Closed: 25-26 Dec eve & 1 Jan eve
Meals L served Mon-Thu 12-2, Fri-Sat 12-2.30, Sun 12-7.30 D served Mon-Thu 5.30-9, Fri 5.30-9.30, Sat 6-9.30
⊕ FREE HOUSE ◀ John Smith's, Black Sheep, Shibden Mill, 3 Guest ales. ♀ 22
Facilities Non-diners area ♦♦ Children's menu Children's portions Garden ⊼ Parking Wi-fi **Rooms** 11

| HEPWORTH | Map 16 SE10 |

The Butchers Arms

PICK OF THE PUBS

38 Towngate HD9 1TE ☎ 01484 682361
e-mail: info@thebutchersarmshepworth.co.uk
dir: A616 into Hepworth. Pub in village centre

Popular gastro-pub with an emphasis on all things local

This pretty hilltop pub is now celebrating its five-year anniversary under Yorkshire chef Tim Bilton. When he took over, it was a failing business with an uncertain future; now it is one of the region's most popular gastro-pubs. Whether it's the Black Sheep or Acorn ale served in the bustling bar or Tim's excellent modern British cuisine, the strict sourcing policy means that the majority of ingredients are from within a 75-mile radius, including some produce grown by villagers in their own gardens and allotments. In the beamed interior, enjoy toad-in-the-hole from the bar menu; things move up a gear in the restaurant, where you might find crispy pheasant rillette, Yorkshire brisket and pan-seared venison haunch steak, as well as blackboard specials. There are also cookery demonstrations and a smart outside area with decking.

Open all day all wk **Bar Meals** L served Mon-Fri 12-2, Sat-Sun all day D served Mon-Fri 5-9, Sat-Sun all day **Restaurant** L served Mon-Fri 12-2, Sat-Sun all day D served Mon-Fri 5-9, Sat-Sun all day ⊕ ENTERPRISE INNS ◀ Black Sheep, Copper Dragon, Acorn Yorkshire Pride Ö Pure North Original. ♟ 16 **Facilities** Non-diners area 🐾 (Bar Garden) 🍴 Children's portions Garden ⏞ Parking

| HOLMFIRTH | Map 16 SE10 |

Farmers Arms

2-4 Liphill Bank Rd HD9 2LR ☎ 01484 683713
e-mail: farmersarms2@gmail.com
dir: From Holmfirth take A635 (Greenfield Rd) on right signed Manchester. Left at Compo's Café. 2nd right into Liphill Bank Rd

Great ales and home-cooked food

A small village pub run with pride by Sam Page and Danielle Montgomery, The Farmers Arms sits in typical Last of the Summer Wine country. There is a welcome emphasis on real ales, with an annual beer festival every autumn and regular beers including Timothy Taylor Landlord, Greene King IPA and Bradfield Farmers Blonde. The menu appeals too; settle by the log fire and enjoy fresh dishes prepared from scratch such as smoked haddock, spring onion and mature cheddar fishcake with chunky tomato salsa; ox stew and dumplings with home-made chunky bread; and apple crumble with custard.

Open Tue-Thu 12-3 5-12 (Fri-Sun 12-12 Mon 5-12) Closed: Mon L **Bar Meals** L served Tue-Thu 12-2, Fri-Sat 12-3, Sun 12-8 D served Tue-Thu 6-9.30, Sat 5-9.30, Sun 12-8 ⊕ PUNCH TAVERNS ◀ Timothy Taylor Landlord, Bradfield Farmers Blonde, Greene King IPA, Guest ales Ö Thatchers Gold, Westons Wyld Wood Organic. ♟ 13

Facilities Non-diners area 🐾 (Bar Garden) 🍴 Children's portions Garden ⏞ Beer festival Parking Wi-fi 🚌 (notice required)

| ILKLEY | Map 19 SE14 |

Ilkley Moor Vaults

Stockeld Rd LS29 9HD ☎ 01943 607012
e-mail: info@ilkleymoorvaults.co.uk
dir: From Ilkley on A65 towards Skipton. Pub on right

Stylish pub at the start of the Dales Way

This pub was once attached to the Victorian Ilkley Moor Hotel, which burnt down in the early 1970s. Known locally as The Taps, it sits at the start of the Dales Way and near the 'old bridge' that crosses the River Wharfe. A popular and stylish establishment, it is equally good for a pint of Timothy Taylor Landlord or traditional dishes such as game terrine with chutney and toast; steak-and-kidney pie; home-made sausage with mash and gravy or home-made rice pudding with poached prunes. There's an impressive children's menu, and a great value early bird set menu if you arrive between 17:30 and 18:30.

Open 12-3 5-11 (Sat-Sun all day) Closed: Mon (ex BHs) **Bar Meals** L served Tue-Sat 12-2.30, Sun 12-7 D served Tue-Sat 6-9, Sun 12-7 **Restaurant** L served Tue-Sat 12-2.30, Sun 12-7 D served Tue-Sat 6-9, Sun 12-7 ⊕ STAR PUBS & BARS ◀ Timothy Taylor Landlord, Theakston Best Bitter, Caledonian Deuchars IPA. ♟ 9 **Facilities** Non-diners area 🐾 (Bar Garden) 🍴 Children's menu Children's portions Garden ⏞ Parking 🚌 (notice required)

| LEEDS | Map 19 SE23 |

The Cross Keys

PICK OF THE PUBS

107 Water Ln LS11 5WD ☎ 0113 243 3711
e-mail: info@the-crosskeys.com
dir: 0.5m from Leeds Station: right into Neville St, right into Water Ln. Pass Globe Rd, pub on left

Hearty British food in city centre pub with a colourful past

Built in 1802, The Cross Keys was a watering hole for local foundry workers and it's where James Watt, famed inventor of the steam engine, reputedly hired a room to spy on his competitor Matthew Murray. To learn Murray's trade secrets Watt bought drinks for foundry workers relaxing here after work. Incredibly, this historic landmark from the peak of Leeds' industrial history was closed in the 1980s and it was a tyre storage depot for a local garage until it was restored in 2005. There has been a change of hands at this city centre pub which has a country pub atmosphere. Hand-pulled pints from local microbreweries complement food recreated from long lost recipes for traditional British dishes. The best seasonal produce goes into dishes such as potted pig with toast and chutney and oxtail and bone marrow hotpot with dumplings.

Open all day all wk 12-11 (Fri-Sat 12-12 Sun 12-10.30) Closed: 25-26 Dec, 1 Jan **Bar Meals** L served Mon-Sat 12-3, Sun 12-5 D served Mon-Sat 6-10 Av main course £14.95 **Restaurant** L served Mon-Sat 12-3, Sun 12-5 D served Mon-Sat 6-10 ⊕ FREE HOUSE ◀ Kirkstall, Magic Rock, Thornbridge Ö Westons Wyld Wood Organic & Organic Pear, Aspall. ♟ 13 **Facilities** Non-diners area 🐾 (Bar Restaurant Garden) 🍴 Children's menu Children's portions Garden ⏞ Wi-fi 🚌

North Bar

24 New Briggate LS1 6NU ☎ 0113 242 4540
e-mail: info@northbar.com
dir: From rail station towards Corn Exchange, left into Briggate (main shopping area). At x-rds with The Headrow straight on into New Briggate. Bar 100mtrs on right

Beers from around the world in upbeat atmosphere

This pioneering beer bar in the heart of Leeds is heaven for beer aficionados as it serves up to 150 beers from around the globe at any one time. Since 1997 it has served over 1,000 draught beers and over 100,000 bottled beers, yet pride of place on the vast bar are hand-pumped beers from local microbreweries, notably Roosters ales. It's a trendy European-style bar, full of characters and great conversation, as well as a venue for music and local art exhibitions. Don't miss the regular beer festivals.

Open all day all wk 11am-2am Closed: 25 Dec **Bar Meals** food served all day ⊕ FREE HOUSE ◀ Kirkstall, Roosters, Thornbridge, Marble, Buxton Ö Black Rat, Oliver's. **Facilities** Non-diners area 🐾 (Bar) 🍴 Beer festival Parking Wi-fi

| LINTHWAITE | Map 16 SE11 |

The Sair Inn

Lane Top HD7 5SG ☎ 01484 842370
dir: From Huddersfield take A62 (Oldham road) for 3.5m. Left just before lights at bus stop (in centre of road) into Hoyle Ing & follow sign

Own brewed ales and welcoming atmosphere

You won't be able to eat here, but this old hilltop alehouse has enough character in its four small rooms to make up for that; three are heated by hot Yorkshire ranges in winter. Landlord Ron Crabtreee has brewed his own beers for over 25 years and they are much sought after by real ale aficionados. Imported German and Czech lagers are available, too. In summer the outside drinking area catches the afternoon sun and commands views across the Colne Valley.

Open all wk 5-11 (Sat 12-11 Sun 12-10.30) ⊕ FREE HOUSE ◀ Linfit Bitter, Special Bitter, Gold Medal, Autumn Gold, Old Eli Ö Pure North Original. **Facilities** Non-diners area 🐾 (Bar) 🍴 🚌 (notice required) **Notes** ⊗

LINTON	Map 16 SE34

The Windmill Inn

Main St LS22 4HT ☎ **01937 582209**
dir: *From A1 exit at Tadcaster/Otley junct, follow Otley signs. In Collingham follow Linton signs*

Historic pub with a diverse menu

Once the home of a long forgotten miller, this pleasant village pub is made up of small beamed rooms that have been stripped back to bare stone, presumably the original 14th-century walls. A coaching inn since the 18th century, polished antique settles, log fires, oak beams and copper-topped cast-iron tables set the scene in which to enjoy good food in the bar or restaurant. Dishes on offer include sweet chilli duck salad; sausage and mash, and fishcakes with spiced fruit couscous, salad and paprika mayonnaise. A beer festival is held in July.

Open all wk 11-3 5.30-11 (Fri-Sat 11-11 Sun 12-10.30) Closed: 1 Jan **Bar Meals** L served Mon-Fri 12-2, Sat 12-5.30, Sun 12-5.45 Av main course £8.95 **Restaurant** L served Mon-Fri 12-2, Sat 12-9, Sun 12-5.45 D served Mon-Sat 5.30-9 Fixed menu price fr £15.95 Av 3 course à la carte fr £16 ⊕ HEINEKEN ◀ Theakston Best Bitter, Greene King Ruddles County, John Smith's, Daleside. ☙12 **Facilities** Non-diners area ✿ (Bar Garden) ♦♦ Children's portions Garden ⊞ Beer festival Parking ⊨ (notice required)

MARSDEN	Map 16 SE01

The Olive Branch

Manchester Rd HD7 6LU ☎ **01484 844487**
e-mail: eat@olivebranch.uk.com
dir: *On A62 between Marsden & Slaithwaite, 6m from Huddersfield*

Highly regarded brasserie-style food

Enter this traditional 19th-century inn on a former packhorse route above the River Colne and the Huddersfield Canal and you'll find yourself in a rambling series of rooms, fire-warmed in winter. The restaurant's brasserie-style food is exemplified by starters of parfait of chicken livers, and wood pigeon with garlic risotto and chocolate sauce, while typical main dishes include Gressingham duck breast, Chateaubriand to share, and pan-fried medallions of venison. Enjoy a pint of Greenfield Dobcross Bitter from Saddleworth on the sun deck and admire the views of Marsden Moor Estate.

Open all wk Mon-Sat 5.30pm-11pm (Sun 12-10.30) Closed: 1st 2wks Jan **Bar Meals** L served Sun 12-8 Av main course £17 **Restaurant** L served Sun 12-8 D served Mon-Sat 5.30-9.30, Sun 12-8 Fixed menu price fr £20 Av 3 course à la carte fr £28 ⊕ FREE HOUSE ◀ Greenfield Dobcross Bitter & Ale. ☙12 **Facilities** Non-diners area ♦♦ Children's menu Children's portions Garden ⊞ Parking Wi-fi

---

The Riverhead Brewery Tap & Dining Room

2 Peel St HD7 6BR ☎ **01484 841270 & 844324**
e-mail: riverhead@ossett-brewery.co.uk
dir: *In town centre*

Ossett beers at their best

The River Colne cascades through the centre of this engaging little mill town, beside which stands a stone-built Victorian former co-op building. Now owned by Ossett Brewery, the pub's beers — named after reservoirs nestling in the South Pennine moors — are brewed in the microbrewery just off the bar. It's an immensely popular spot for ramblers, rail-alers and locals. Enjoy a pint in the bare-boarded, wood-rich bar, or pop upstairs to the dining room for some classic lunchtime pub grub, enhanced in the evenings by modern dishes such as medallion of turkey with spatchcock quail, herb, leek and smoked cheese polenta, and port sauce.

Open all day all wk ⊕ OSSETT BREWERY ◀ Riverhead March Haigh, Butterley Bitter, Redbrook, Black Moss Stout. **Facilities** ♦♦ Children's portions

---

RIPPONDEN	Map 16 SE01

Old Bridge Inn

Priest Ln HX6 4DF ☎ **01422 822595**
web: www.theoldbridgeinn.co.uk
dir: *In village centre by church*

Probably Yorkshire's oldest hostelry

An inn has stood by Ripponden's old bridge, and even earlier ford, since at least 1307. The lower bar is of cruck-frame construction, and the top bar retains its wattle and daub walls, partly later encased in stone. In addition to Timothy Taylor's real ales, including Dark Mild and two guests, 12 wines are offered by the glass. Expect main courses like Jamaican jerked guinea fowl with rice, peas and pickled cucumber; Bolster Moor pork pie with mushy peas; and crisp belly pork with grilled Bury black pudding, celeriac mash and roast parsnips. Seating outside overlooks the River Ryburn. Booking for meals is recommended.

Open all wk 12-3 5.30-11 (Fri-Sat 12-11.30 Sun 12-10.30) Closed: 25 Dec **Bar Meals** L served Mon-Sat 12-2, Sun 12-4 D served Mon-Sat 6.30-9.30 (booking advisable) ⊕ FREE HOUSE ◀ Timothy Taylor Landlord ,Golden Best, Best Bitter & Dark Mild, Guest ales. ☙12 **Facilities** Non-diners area ♦♦ Children's portions Garden Outside area ⊞ Parking Wi-fi

---

SHELLEY	Map 16 SE21

The Three Acres Inn

PICK OF THE PUBS

HD8 8LR ☎ **01484 602606**
e-mail: info@3acres.com
dir: *From Huddersfield take A629 then B6116, turn left for village*

Free house with a reputation for good food

Set in the rolling green countryside of the Pennines, this old drovers' inn is an ideal stopping off place for travellers heading north to the Yorkshire Dales. Over the decades, Brian Orme and Neil Truelove have built a reputation for good quality food and a welcoming atmosphere. The inn's spacious interior has a lavishly traditional feel with exposed beams and large fireplaces. On summer evenings, sit out on the deck with a pint of Black Sheep (to remind you of the drovers) or a glass of wine and soak up the fabulous views. The food served in both bar and restaurant successfully fuses traditional English with international influences. A typical three-course meal might be prawn and crayfish cocktail; roast half duckling with brioche, orange and sausage stuffing; and lemon meringue tart. A generous range of lighter meals, grills, rotisserie chickens and sandwiches makes a great lunchtime choice.

Open all wk 12-3 6-11 (Fri-Sat 12-3 5-11) Closed: 25-26 Dec eve, 1 Jan eve **Bar Meals** L served all wk 12-2 D served Sun-Thu 6.30-9.30, Fri-Sat 5.30-9.30 **Restaurant** L served all wk 12-2 D served Sun-Thu 6.30-9.30, Fri-Sat 5.30-9.30 ⊕ FREE HOUSE ◀ Timothy Taylor Landlord & Golden Best, Black Sheep, Copper Dragon. ☙19 **Facilities** ♦♦ Children's portions Garden ⊞ Parking Wi-fi

---

SOWERBY BRIDGE	Map 16 SE02

The Alma Inn & Fresco Italian Restaurant

Cotton Stones HX6 4NS ☎ **01422 823334**
e-mail: info@almainn.com
dir: *Exit A58 at Triangle between Sowerby Bridge & Ripponden. Follow signs for Cotton Stones*

Country inn with home-cooked Italian food

An old stone inn set in a dramatically beautiful location at Cotton Stones with stunning views of the Ryburn Valley. Outside seating can accommodate 200 customers, while the interior features stone-flagged floors and real fires. The cosy bar serves several ales including a guest, and a vast selection of Belgian bottled beers, each with its individual glass. The appeal of the Fresco Italian Restaurant revolves around the wood-burning pizza oven on display in the restaurant, the only one in the Calderdale area.

Open all day all wk 12-10.30 ⊕ FREE HOUSE ◀ Timothy Taylor Landlord & Golden Best, Tetley's Bitter, Guest ales. **Facilities** ✿ (Bar Garden) ♦♦ Children's portions Garden Parking Wi-fi

PICK OF THE PUBS

Ring O'Bells Country Pub & Restaurant

THORNTON　　　　Map 19 SE03

212 Hilltop Rd BD13 3QL
☎ **01274 832296**
e-mail: enquiries@theringobells.com
web: www.theringobells.com
dir: *From M62 take A58 for 5m, right onto A644. 4.5m follow Denholme signs, into Well Head Rd into Hilltop Rd*

Dining inn in sublime Pennine countryside

The pub stands in an enviable position on a broad ridge top in an area laced by old tracks trodden by pious weavers of old, who converged on this lofty eyrie to worship at the Wesleyan chapel it once was. Today's visitors can harvest vast views across the landscapes of the South Pennines, a comfy mix of pastures, copses and distant rolling moorlands stretching many miles. Ann and Clive Preston have successfully run the pub for 20 years, and their cuisine, service and professionalism have been recognised with accolades from the trade and visitors from far and wide. Refurbishment of the bar and dining area has done nothing to dilute its traditional, historical feel, enhanced by prints of the village in the 1920s on the wood-panelled walls, whilst contemporary art exhibitions take centre stage in the restaurant. The Brontë Restaurant (the famous literary family were born in nearby Thornton), once two mill workers' cottages, now has a

conservatory running its whole length, with stunning valley views. Local farmers and suppliers of meat, fish, game and vegetables know that everything will be carefully prepared and cooked by the new head chef, who creates traditional British dishes with European influences. A starter may be shredded Yorkshire lamb, spiced couscous, apricot and fig meatballs, or cauliflower and chick pea falafels, cuing up for a mains selection featuring slow-roasted rare breed belly pork with sage and onion rösti, parsnip purée, home-made black pudding and port liquor sauce; or wild mushroom, beetroot and Stilton ravioli with pickled mushrooms and shaved Berkswell cheese. The impressive wine list features over 100 bins.

Open all wk 11.30-4 5.30-11.30 (Sat-Sun 11.30-4 6.15-11.30) Closed: 25 Dec **Bar Meals** L served all wk 12-2 D served Mon-Fri 5.30-9.30, Sat-Sun 6.15-9.30 **Restaurant** L served all wk 12-2 D served all wk 5.30-9.30, Sat-Sun 6.15-9.30 ⊕ FREE HOUSE ◀ John Smith's, Courage Directors, Black Sheep. ♀ 12 **Facilities** Non-diners area ♦♦ Children's menu Children's portions Parking Wi-fi 🚐 (notice required)

THORNTON	Map 19 SE03

Ring O'Bells Country Pub & Restaurant

PICK OF THE PUBS

See Pick of the Pubs on page 527

WIDDOP	Map 18 SD93

Pack Horse Inn

HX7 7AT ☎ 01422 842803
dir: *Off A646 & A6033*

Popular with those enjoying the Pennine Way

The Pack Horse is a converted Laithe farmhouse dating from the early 1600s. Its beautiful location is just 300 yards from the Pennine Way, which makes it popular with walkers, mountain bikers, and horse riders hacking the Mary Towneley Loop. Subdued lighting, cosy log fires and historical pictures characterise the interior. Equally attractive are the home-cooked meals, a good range of real ales and a fabulous choice of 130 single malt whiskies.

Open summer 12-3 7-11 Closed: Mon & Tue-Fri L (Oct-Etr) ⊕ FREE HOUSE ◀ Theakston XB, Black Sheep Best Bitter, Copper Dragon Golden Pippin, Thwaites Lancaster Bomber. **Facilities** ✿ (Bar) ♦♦ Parking

CHANNEL ISLANDS
GUERNSEY

CASTEL	Map 24

Fleur du Jardin

PICK OF THE PUBS

Kings Mills GY5 7JT ☎ 01481 257996
e-mail: info@fleurdujardin.com
dir: *2.5m from town centre*

Recommended for its pick-your-own crab salad

Named after one of the island's most famous breeds of cow, this friendly hotel, bar and restaurant is a short stroll from Guernsey's finest sandy beaches and coastal paths. Dating from the 15th century, it has been restyled with a modern shabby-chic appeal, but historical features such as granite walls, wooden beams and fireplaces remain untouched. The low bar might require some to stoop, but that needn't hamper the enjoyment of a pint of Sunbeam, brewed by Channel Island brewery, Liberation. In the warmer months, food and drink can be taken on the attractive sun-trap terrace. Kitchen watchwords are seasonality and freshness - it isn't unusual to see a local fisherman delivering a 10lb sea bass. Expect Guernsey beef, West Coast scallops and line-caught seafood. The baguettes and wraps make good snacks, while main courses include sea bass with chorizo bolognese and crushed new potatoes; and artichoke, shallots and tomatoes on truffle linguine.

Open all day all wk **Bar Meals** L served all wk 12-2 D served all wk 6-9 **Restaurant** L served all wk 12-2 D served all wk 6-9 ⊕ FREE HOUSE ◀ Arundel, Liberation Guernsey Sunbeam, Fuller's London Pride, Guest ales ♂ Roquette. ♟ 12 **Facilities** Non-diners area ✿ (Bar Restaurant Garden) ♦♦ Children's menu Children's portions Garden ♠ Parking Wi-fi ➡ (notice required)

ST PETER PORT	Map 24

The Admiral de Saumarez ★★★ HL

Duke of Normandie Hotel, Lefebvre St GY1 2JP
☎ 01481 721431
e-mail: enquiries@dukeofnormandie.com
dir: *From harbour rdbt into St Julians Av, 3rd left into Anns Place, continue to right, up hill, left into Lefebvre St, archway entrance on right*

Maritime theme and good pub dishes

Part of the Duke of Normandie Hotel, this thoughtfully restored bar attracts a happy mix of Guernsey locals and hotel residents. It is full of architectural salvage, including old timbers (now painted with well-known amusing sayings) and maritime memorabilia. Details of the great naval victories of the Admiral himself are engraved on the tables. You can be served your refreshments out in the suntrap beer garden in warmer weather. The lunch and dinner menus proffer traditional pub favourites: local hand-picked crab cakes with red pepper dressing for a starter perhaps; continue with deep-fried goujons of local plaice with straw fries.

Open all day all wk 11am-11.30pm **Bar Meals** L served all wk 12-2 D served all wk 6-9 Av main course £8.50 **Restaurant** L served all wk 12-2 D served all wk 6-9 Fixed menu price fr £16.50 ⊕ FREE HOUSE ◀ Liberation, Morland Old Speckled Hen ♂ Rocquette. **Facilities** Non-diners area ♦♦ Children's menu Children's portions Outside area ♠ Parking ➡ **Rooms** 37

The Ship & Crown, Crow's Nest Brasserie

The Quay GY1 2NB ☎ 01481 728994
e-mail: ship_crown@hotmail.com
dir: *Opposite Crown Pier*

Waterfront pub with magnificent views

This busy Guernsey town pub and stylish brasserie occupies a historic building and boasts stunning views across the Victoria Marina to the neighbouring Channel Islands. Run by the same family for well over 30 years, The Ship & Crown pub offers one of the widest ranges of beers and ciders on the island, but it is equally well known for its all-day bar meals. The friendly Crow's Nest Brasserie specialises in fish and seafood dishes, such as king prawn and crab risotto, but there are plenty of salad and meat options too.

Open all day all wk **Bar Meals** L served all wk 11-9 D served all wk 11-9 food served all day **Restaurant** L served all wk 12-3 D served all wk 6-10 ⊕ FREE HOUSE ◀ Fuller's London Pride, Wells Bombardier, Sharp's Doom Bar, Wychwood Hobgoblin, Liberation ♂ Addlestones. ♟ 8 **Facilities** Non-diners area ♦♦ Children's menu Children's portions Parking Wi-fi ➡

JERSEY

ST AUBIN   Map 24

Old Court House Inn

St Aubin's Harbour JE3 8AB ☎ 01534 746433
e-mail: info@oldcourthousejersey.com
dir: *From Jersey Airport, right at exit, left at lights, 0.5m to St Aubin*

Harbour-side location on Jersey's stunning south coast

At low tide a path snakes across the foreshore to St Aubin's Fort, guarding the harbour overlooked by this old inn. Wizened beams and mellow stone walls testify to the building's medieval origins; its cellars were allegedly used to secrete contraband. A strong suite of seafood options feature on the menus available at the several bars and restaurant rooms here; local oysters grilled with cheese a prelude to asparagus and tiger prawn filled baked breast of chicken or a locally caught plaice. Jersey-brewed Liberation Ale is a favoured tipple; there's a beer festival too.

Open all day all wk Closed: 25 Dec, Mon (Jan-Mar) **Bar Meals** L served all wk 12.30-2.30, all day May-Aug D served Mon-Sat 7.30-10, all day May-Aug **Restaurant** L served all wk 12.30-2.30 D served all wk 7.30-10 ⊕ FREE HOUSE ◀ Courage Directors, Theakston, John Smith's, Liberation. ♀ 9 **Facilities** Non-diners area ♦♦ Children's menu Children's portions Outside area ⊼ Beer festival Wi-fi ▥ (notice required)

ST BRELADE   Map 24

The Portelet Inn

La Route de Noirmont JE3 8AJ ☎ 01534 741899
e-mail: portelet@randalls.je
dir: *Telephone for directions*

Family-friendly with carvery

Belonging to Jersey's Randalls group of privately owned public houses, the Portelet is a family-friendly pub a short walk from the coast. Since 1948, when it was transformed from a 17th-century farmhouse into the Portelet, much has changed - children can play in Pirate Pete's, while adults relax in the bar. Although kids have their own menu, the Carvery restaurant is ideal for family dining, with a menu offering Southern-fried chicken burger; prime Harmony Farm steaks; beef and dumplings; pan-roasted salmon; and Thai red chicken (or vegetable) curry. There's live entertainment on Fridays and some Saturday nights.

Open all day Closed: Tue (Jan-Mar) **Bar Meals** L served Mon-Thu 12-8.30, Fri-Sat 12-9, Sun & PH 12-8 D served Mon-Thu 12-8.30, Fri-Sat 12-9, Sun & PH 12-8 food served all day **Restaurant** L served Mon-Thu 12-8.30, Fri-Sat 12-9, Sun & PH 12-8 D served Mon-Thu 12-8.30, Fri-Sat 12-9, Sun & PH 12-8 food served all day ⊕ RANDALLS ◀ Wells Bombardier, Guest ale.
Facilities Non-diners area ♦♦ Children's menu Children's portions Play area Family room Garden ⊼ Parking Wi-fi ▥ (notice required)

ST MARTIN   Map 24

Royal Hotel

La Grande Route de Faldouet JE3 6UG ☎ 01534 856289
e-mail: johnbarker@jerseymail.co.uk
dir: *2m from Five Oaks rdbt towards St Martin. Pub on right next to St Martin's Church*

Log fires in winter, beer garden in summer

A friendly local in the heart of St Martin, this former coaching inn prides itself on offering quality food and drink. Landlord John Barker has been welcoming guests for many years. A roaring log fire in the spacious lounge warm winter visitors, and there's a sunny beer garden to enjoy during the summer months. On the menu are traditional home-made favourites such as baby rack of ribs, chicken curry, and braised lamb shank. The pub also makes its own pizzas with a variety of toppings. Burgers, filled jacket potatoes, grills and children's choices are on offer, too.

Open all day all wk **Bar Meals** L served all wk 12-2.15 D served Mon-Sat 6-8.30 **Restaurant** L served all wk 12-2.15 D served Mon-Sat 6-8.30 ⊕ RANDALLS ◀ Ringwood Best Bitter, John Smith's Smooth, Theakston Cool Cask, Guinness, Bass ☼ Westons Stowford Press. ♀ 9 **Facilities** Non-diners area ♦♦ Children's menu Children's portions Play area Garden ⊼ Parking Wi-fi ▥ (notice required)

ST MARY   Map 24

St Mary's Country Inn

La Rue des Buttes JE3 3DS ☎ 01534 482897
e-mail: stmarys@liberationpubco.com
dir: *Telephone for directions*

Smart inn with island brewed ale and global menu

Jersey's Liberation Brewery owns this appealing country inn with smart, contemporary interior. The menu offers imaginative food at reasonable prices, including roasts and grills; espetadas (Portuguese chargrilled skewered meats and fish); murgh makhani (butter chicken curry); duck cassoulet; and ale-battered cod with chunky chips. There are just three prices on the wine list, but choice extends to half-litre carafes and plenty by the glass. In the bar you'll find continental lagers, island-brewed Mary Ann and flagship cask-conditioned Liberation Ale. There's a delightful seating area outside.

Open all day all wk **Bar Meals** L served all wk 12-2.30 D served all wk 6-9 **Restaurant** L served all wk 12-2.30 D served all wk 6-9 ⊕ LIBERATION GROUP ◀ Liberation Ale, Mary Ann Special. ♀ 19 **Facilities** Non-diners area ❀ (Bar Garden) ♦♦ Children's menu Children's portions Garden ⊼ Parking Wi-fi ▥ (notice required)

ISLE OF MAN

PEEL   Map 24 SC28

The Creek Inn

Station Place IM5 1AT ☎ 01624 842216
e-mail: thecreekinn@manx.net
dir: *On quayside opposite House of Manannan Museum*

A must for ale lovers

The family-run Creek Inn occupies a plum spot on the quayside overlooked by Peel Hill. A real ale drinkers' paradise, it has locally brewed Okells ales, up to five changing guests, and a beer festival in March. Bands play every weekend, and nightly during the TT and Manx Grand Prix, when the pub becomes the town's focal point. There's a huge selection of dishes on the menu, from local fish, steaks and burgers, to vegetarian options and salads, alongside sandwiches, hot baguettes and toasties. A typical meal might be chilli and garlic crab claws followed by steak and Rory's ale pie with chips and peas.

Open all day all wk **Bar Meals** L served all wk 11-9.30 D served all wk 11-9.30 food served all day **Restaurant** L served all wk 11-9.30 D served all wk 11-9.30 food served all day ⊕ FREE HOUSE ◀ Okells Bitter & Seasonal ales, Bushy's, 4 Guest ales ☼ Thatchers Green Goblin, St Helier, Manx Apple. ♀ 12 **Facilities** Non-diners area ♦♦ Children's menu Children's portions Garden ⊼ Beer festival Parking Wi-fi ▥

PORT ERIN   Map 24 SC26

Falcon's Nest Hotel ★★ HL

The Promenade, Station Rd IM9 6AF ☎ 01624 834077
e-mail: falconsnest@enterprise.net
dir: *Follow coast road S from airport or ferry. Hotel on seafront, immediately after steam railway station*

Family-run pub-hotel with an emphasis on seafood

In the centre of Port Erin, this magnificent building overlooks a beautiful sheltered harbour and sandy beach. Head for the saloon bar, 'Ophidian's Lair', or the residents' lounge, also open to the public, to sample local ales from Okells and Bushy's, among others, and over 70 whiskies. The former ballroom has been restored and turned into a Victorian-style dining room, where local seafood dishes include local scallops known as 'queenies'. The menu also offers a roast of the day, honey-roast Manx ham, vegetable lasagne, and many gluten-free options. The carvery here is very popular too. A beer festival is held in early May.

Open all day all wk **Bar Meals** L served all wk 12-9 food served all day **Restaurant** L served all wk 12-2 D served all wk 6-9 ⊕ FREE HOUSE ◀ John Smith's, Okells, Bushy's, Guinness, Manx guest ale, Guest ales. **Facilities** Non-diners area ♦♦ Children's menu Children's portions Family room Beer festival Parking Wi-fi ▥ (notice required) **Rooms 39**

Scotland

Cairngorms

ABERDEEN, CITY OF

ABERDEEN   Map 23 NJ90

Old Blackfriars

52 Castle St AB11 5BB ☎ 01224 581922
e-mail: oldblackfriars.aberdeen@belhavenpubs.net
dir: *From rail station right into Guild St left into Market
St, at end right into Union St. Pub on right on corner of
Marishal St*

Historic Castlegate area pub with music nights

Situated in Aberdeen's historic Castlegate, this
traditional split-level city centre pub stands on the site of
property owned by Blackfriars Dominican monks, hence
the name. Inside you'll find stunning stained glass, plus
well-kept real ales (nine handpumps) and a large
selection of malt whiskies. The pub is also renowned for
excellent food and an unobtrusive atmosphere (no
background music and no television). The wide-ranging
menu has all the pub favourites and more – chicken
Balmoral, chicken tikka makhani, sweet potato curry, and
baked lasagne. There is a weekly quiz and live music
every Thursday.

Open all day all wk 10am-mdnt (Fri-Sat 10am-1am Sun
10-11) Closed: 25 Dec, 1 Jan **Bar Meals** L served all wk
12-9.30 D served all wk 12-9.30 food served all day
Restaurant L served all wk 12-9.30 D served all wk
12-9.30 food served all day ⊕ BELHAVEN ◀ Caledonian
Deuchars IPA, Inveralmond Ossian, Old Blackfriars
♨ Addlestones Cloudy. ♔ 9 **Facilities** Non-diners area ♦♦
Children's menu Family room Wi-fi

ABERDEENSHIRE

BALMEDIE   Map 23 NJ91

The Cock & Bull Bar & Restaurant ◉

Ellon Rd, Blairton AB23 8XY ☎ 01358 743249
e-mail: info@thecockandbull.co.uk
dir: *11m N of city centre, on left of A90 between Balmedie
junct & Foveran*

**Country inn with great food of impeccable
provenance**

A cast-iron range warms the bar in this creeper-clad,
stone-built coaching inn, standing quite alone in open
farmland north of Aberdeen. Conversation is easily
stimulated by local artist Irene Morrison's paintings,
assorted hanging artefacts and good beer. Affordably
priced food in the AA-Rosette restaurant uses Marine
Stewardship Council-approved white fish and Peterhead-
landed shellfish, and beef and pork from the region's
stock farms. A seasonal menu might list pork and black
pudding burger; seafood medley tagliatelle; Grampian
braised lamb shank; and half-roasted aubergine filled
with a Mediterranean vegetable casserole. Super wines
and whiskies as well.

Open all day all wk 10am-11.30pm (Sun 12-7.30) Closed:
26-27 Dec, 2-3 Jan **Bar Meals** L served Mon-Sat 10-8.45,
Sun 12-7.30 D served Mon-Sat 10-8.45, Sun 12-7.30 food
served all day **Restaurant** L served Mon-Sat 10-8.45, Sun

12-7.30 D served Mon-Sat 10-8.45, Sun 12-7.30 food
served all day ⊕ FREE HOUSE ◀ Burnside 3 Bullz Bitter
Ale, Guinness. **Facilities** Non-diners area ♦♦ Children's
menu Play area Garden ⌁ Parking Wi-fi ⊟

MARYCULTER   Map 23 NO89

Old Mill Inn

South Deeside Rd AB12 5FX ☎ 01224 733212
e-mail: info@oldmillinn.co.uk
dir: *5m W of Aberdeen on B9077*

A family-run inn with a warm welcome

This delightful family-run 200-year-old country inn
stands on the edge of the River Dee, five miles from
Aberdeen city centre. A former mill house, the
18th-century granite building has been tastefully
modernised to include a restaurant where the finest
Scottish ingredients feature on the menu: start with
marinated herring salad or black pudding parcel, then
continue with pan-roasted lamb cutlets, roast vegetable
and pesto tagliatelle, or grilled salmon fillet on sweet
potato mash. Food and drink can be enjoyed in the garden
in warmer months.

Open all day all wk **Bar Meals** L served all wk 12-2
D served all wk 5.30-9 **Restaurant** L served all wk 12-2
D served all wk 5.30-9 ⊕ FREE HOUSE ◀ Caledonian
Deuchars IPA, Timothy Taylor Landlord, Fuller's London
Pride. **Facilities** Non-diners area ♦♦ Children's menu
Children's portions Garden Parking ⊟

NETHERLEY   Map 23 NO89

The Lairhillock Inn

PICK OF THE PUBS

AB39 3QS ☎ 01569 730001
e-mail: info@lairhillock.co.uk
dir: *From Aberdeen take A90. Right towards Durris on
B9077 then left onto B979 to Netherley*

A bustling country inn serving seasonal food

First a farmhouse and then a coaching inn, the
17th-century Lairhillock stands completely alone,
surrounded by fields. Such blatant rusticity continues
inside, especially in the fine old bar with its exposed
stonework, wood panelling, settles and log fires. Menus
change every three months to keep up with the best
seasonal Scottish produce, while the daily specials prove
that the kitchen team never lets anything interesting slip
through its fingers. Thus, there will be the popular
starters of lairies gambas, which are king prawns cooked
in lime, chilli, sweet pepper and coconut sauce; and lamb
shank and Stornoway black pudding terrine. Other
delights are Cullen skink; seared breast of pheasant;
sun-blushed tomato with smoked Mull of Kintyre
cheeseburger; and baby spinach and feta cheese
cannelloni. Aberdeen Angus steaks are always a cert and
the fish, chicken and duck smoked on the premises
always find their way to the tables.

Open all day all wk Closed: 25-26 Dec, 1-2 Jan **Bar
Meals** L served all wk 12-2 D served all wk 6-9.30

Restaurant L served Sun 12-2 D served Tue-Sat 7-9.30
⊕ FREE HOUSE ◀ Timothy Taylor Landlord, Caledonian
Deuchars IPA, Guest ales. **Facilities** Non-diners area
♣ (Bar Garden) ♦♦ Children's menu Children's portions
Garden ⌁ Parking ⊟ (notice required)

OLDMELDRUM   Map 23 NJ82

The Redgarth

Kirk Brae AB51 0DJ ☎ 01651 872353
e-mail: redgarth1@aol.com
dir: *From A947 (Oldmeldrum bypass) follow signs to Golf
Club/Pleasure Park. Inn E of bypass*

Friendly, family-run inn with attractive garden

The Redgarth looks more like a house than a pub,
because that's what it was built as in 1928. It became
the Redgarth Cocktail Bar in the 1970s and has been
further altered since, but not too much. A cask-
conditioned ale, such as Highland Scapa Special or
Kelburn Pivo Estivo, or a malt whisky from Glen Garioch,
the village distillery, might precede chicken Maryland;
roast beef and Yorkshire pudding; Hungarian pork
goulash; or catch of the day. Grills are well represented
and vegetarians will very likely find a vegetable strudel or
roast butternut squash and potato flan on the menu.

Open all wk 11-3 5-11 (Fri-Sat 11-3 5-11.45) Closed:
25-26 Dec, 1-3 Jan **Bar Meals** L served all wk 12-2
D served Sun-Thu 5-9, Fri-Sat 5-9.30 **Restaurant** L
served all wk 12-2 D served Sun-Thu 5-9, Fri-Sat 5-9.30
⊕ FREE HOUSE ◀ Inveralmond Thrappledouser, Timothy
Taylor Landlord, Highland Scapa Special & Orkney Best,
Kelburn Pivo Estivo. **Facilities** Non-diners area
♣ (Garden) ♦♦ Children's menu Children's portions
Garden ⌁ Parking Wi-fi ⊟

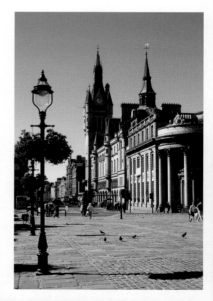

ARGYLL & BUTE

ARDUAINE   Map 20 NM71

Chartroom II Bistro ★★★ HL ◉◉

PICK OF THE PUBS

Loch Melfort Hotel PA34 4XG ☎ 01852 200233
e-mail: reception@lochmelfort.co.uk
dir: *On A816, midway between Oban & Lochgilphead*

Exceptional local seafood served here

Previously the Campbell family home, this modern bar and bistro is part of the Loch Melfort Hotel, located on the path to the NTS Arduaine Gardens with spectacular views over Asknish Bay towards Jura and beyond. Perfect for garden enthusiasts, sailors or simply those looking for tranquillity, the Chartroom II is the place to enjoy all-day drinks and home baking, as well as light lunches and suppers. It has the finest views on the West Coast and serves home-made Scottish fare including plenty of locally landed seafood, such as fantastic langoustines, lobsters and mussels; burgers; steaks, pizzas and salads. You can sit outside and enjoy a drink watching magical sunsets or sit around the fire in winter and watch the waves crashing against the rocks. The Chartroom II is family friendly and serves children's meals or smaller portions from the main menu, plus there is a playground.

Open all wk 11-10 Closed: Nov-Etr **Bar Meals** L served all wk 12-2.30 D served all wk 6-9 Av main course £10.95 ⊕ FREE HOUSE ◀ Belhaven, Fyne, Tennents ♂ Blackthorn. ⚑ 8 **Facilities** Non-diners area ♦♦ Children's menu Children's portions Play area Garden ⊼ Parking Wi-fi ▭ **Rooms** 25

CAIRNDOW   Map 20 NN11

Cairndow Stagecoach Inn ★★★ INN

PA26 8BN ☎ 01499 600286
e-mail: enq@cairndowinn.com
dir: *N of Glasgow take A82, left on A83 at Arrochar. Through Rest and be Thankful to Cairndow. Follow signs for inn*

An old coaching inn set in glorious scenery

On the upper reaches of Loch Fyne, this old coaching inn offers plenty of fine views of mountains, magnificent woodlands and rivers. Sample one of many malt whiskies in the friendly bar by the roaring fire, or idle away the time in the loch-side garden watching the oyster-catchers while sipping the local Fyne Ales. The menu in the candlelit Stables Restaurant offers steak and Fyne Ale pie; chicken breast stuffed with smoked Scottish cheddar and ham, wrapped in pancetta; roasted pepper, courgette and wild mushroom risotto; and pan-fried venison steak with shallot, mushroom and smoked bacon red wine sauce. Meals are also served all day in the bar and lounges. Accommodation is available if you would like to stay over and explore the area. On your way to the pub you should look out for Britain's tallest tree, which is taller than Nelson's Column.

Open all day all wk **Bar Meals** L served all wk 12-6 D served all wk 6-9 food served all day **Restaurant** L served all wk 12-6 D served all wk 6-9 food served all day ⊕ FREE HOUSE ◀ Fyne Hurricane Jack, Avalanche, Piper's Gold, Maverick, Jarl. **Facilities** Non-diners area ♣ (Bar Garden) ♦♦ Children's menu Children's portions Family room Garden ⊼ Parking Wi-fi ▭ (notice required) **Rooms** 18

CLACHAN-SEIL   Map 20 NM71

Tigh an Truish Inn

PICK OF THE PUBS

PA34 4QZ ☎ 01852 300242
dir: *12m S of Oban take A816. Onto B844 towards Atlantic Bridge*

Fiercely traditional pub with a waterfront beer garden

The Brunner family's 18th-century inn – right by the single-span 'Bridge over the Atlantic' at the top of Seil Sound – is not signposted from the A816, so make sure you find the turning onto the B844 (towards Easdale and on to the Isle of Luing). Roughly translated from the Gaelic, the inn's name means 'House of Trousers'. After the Battle of Culloden in 1746, the wearing of kilts was outlawed and anyone caught wearing one faced execution. Many Seil islanders defied this ruling and it was at this historic inn that they swapped their kilts for trousers before travelling to the mainland. These days people pause here for single malts, regularly changing local ales, including Atlas and Fyne ales, and a menu that brims with seafood: smoked mackerel pâté with oatcakes, breaded prawns, scampi and chips, and beer-battered haddock. For families, a separate lounge off the main bar is furnished with children's books.

Open all wk 11-11 (Mon-Fri 11-2.30 5-11 Oct-Mar) Closed: 25 Dec & 1 Jan **Bar Meals** L served all wk 12-2 D served all wk 6-8.30 (Apr-Oct) ⊕ FREE HOUSE ◀ Local guest ales. **Facilities** Non-diners area ♣ (Bar Garden) ♦♦ Children's menu Children's portions Family room Garden ⊼ Parking ▭ (notice required)

CONNEL   Map 20 NM93

The Oyster Inn

PICK OF THE PUBS

PA37 1PJ ☎ 01631 710666
e-mail: stay@oysterinn.co.uk
dir: *Telephone for directions*

A comfortable, informal inn with glorious views to Mull

Overlooking the tidal whirlpools and white water of the Falls of Lora, the 18th-century inn once served ferry passengers, the cannier among them knowing they could be 'stuck' here between ferries and thus evade Oban's Sunday licensing laws. Partly for this reason the stone-walled Ferryman's Bar next door is known as the Glue Pot; the other is that the neighbouring blacksmith boiled horses' hooves for glue – the pots still hang from the ceiling. Sadly the ferry is long gone, superseded by a modern road bridge. Reading between the lines of the jokey menu, it's clear that seafood lovers will find plenty to enjoy, from Cullen skink to West Coast mussels, oysters and scallops. In addition, there are chargrilled steaks, roast lamb, spicy chicken and a daily vegetarian dish. Tradition requires that on entering or leaving the pub, gentlemen touch the hanging glue pot, ladies wink at the Ferryman!

Open all day all wk 11am-mdnt **Bar Meals** L served all wk 12-9.30 D served all wk 12-9.30 food served all day **Restaurant** L served all wk D served all wk food served all day ⊕ FREE HOUSE ◀ Caledonian Deuchars IPA. **Facilities** Non-diners area ♣ (Bar Garden) ♦♦ Children's menu Children's portions Family room Garden ⊼ Parking Wi-fi ▭ (notice required)

CRINAN   Map 20 NR79

Crinan Hotel

PICK OF THE PUBS

PA31 8SR ☎ 01546 830261
e-mail: reservations@crinanhotel.com
dir: *From M8, at end of bridge take A82, at Tarbert left onto A83. At Inveraray follow Campbeltown signs to Lochgilphead, follow signs for A816 to Oban. 2m, left to Crinan on B841*

Stunning seafood and views at West Coast favourite

A romantic retreat in a stunning location and enjoying fabulous views across the Sound of Jura, the Crinan stands at the north end of the Crinan Canal, which connects Loch Fyne to the Atlantic Ocean. It's a long-standing place of welcome at the heart of community life in this tiny fishing village and has been run by owners Nick and Frances Ryan for over 40 years. Eat in the Crinan Seafood Bar or the Westward Restaurant. The cuisine is firmly based on the freshest seafood – it's landed daily just 50 metres from the hotel. Starters could include risotto of West Coast crab or steamed Loch Melfort mussels. For a main course perhaps choose halibut with red pepper pesto; seafood stew; or roast rack of Argyll Hill lamb. Boat trips can be arranged to the islands, and there is a classic boats regatta in the summer. Look for the 'secret garden' just behind the hotel.

Open all day all wk 11-11 Closed: 25 Dec **Bar Meals** L served all wk 12-2.30 D served all wk 6-8.30 Av main course £13 **Restaurant** D served all wk 7-9 Fixed menu price fr £45 Av 3 course à la carte fr £20 ◀ Fyne, Tennent's, Guinness, Caledonian. **Facilities** Non-diners area ♣ (Bar Garden) ♦♦ Children's menu Children's portions Garden ⊼ Parking Wi-fi ▭

DUNOON
Map 20 NS17

Coylet Inn

Loch Eck PA23 8SG ☎ **01369 840426**
e-mail: reservations@coylet-locheck.co.uk
dir: N of Dunoon on A815

Local produce in pub with loch views

Taken over in 2012 by Craig Wilson, this charming, beautifully appointed 17th-century coaching inn has a timeless quality. Located on Loch Eck's shores you wouldn't want a television or games machines to disturb your drink or meal. Well, they won't, at least not in where you can relax with a glass of wine or a pint of Piper's Gold or Highlander in peace by a real log fire. An appealing menu offers local favourites such as home-made Cullen skink soup and smoked salmon with rocket and caper salad, which might be followed by peat-smoked battered haddock and chips.

Open all day all wk **Bar Meals** L served all wk 12-2.30 D served all wk 6-8.30 **Restaurant** L served all wk 12-2.30 D served all wk 6-8.30 ⊕ FREE HOUSE ◀ Fyne Highlander & Piper's Gold, Guest ales.
Facilities Non-diners area ☘ (Bar Garden) ♦ Children's menu Children's portions Garden ⊨ Beer festival Cider festival Parking Wi-fi ▦ (notice required)

INVERARAY
Map 20 NN00

George Hotel

Main Street East PA32 8TT ☎ **01499 302111**
e-mail: info@thegeorgehotel.co.uk
dir: On A83

Family-owned gem

Built in 1776 and in the ownership of the Clark family since 1860, The George occupies a prime spot in the centre of a historic conservation town. Although there have been sensitive additions over the years, nothing detracts from the original flagstone floors and four roaring log fires. More than 100 whiskies and a range of Fyne ales are complemented by an extensive bar menu that includes traditional haggis, neeps and tatties. The restaurant showcases local produce; try the fresh potted crab followed by slow-braised lamb shank in Loch Fyne ale. The George holds beer and music festivals on the May and August Bank Holidays.

Open all day all wk 11am-1am Closed: 25 Dec **Bar Meals** food served all day **Restaurant** food served all day ⊕ FREE HOUSE ◀ Fyne. ♥ 9 **Facilities** ☘ (Bar Restaurant Garden) ♦ Children's menu Children's portions Garden ⊨ Beer festival Parking Wi-fi ▦ (notice required)

LOCHGILPHEAD
Map 20 NR88

Cairnbaan Hotel ★★★ HL ◉

PICK OF THE PUBS

Cairnbaan PA31 8SJ ☎ **01546 603668**
e-mail: info@cairnbaan.com
dir: A816 from Lochgilphead, in approx 2m take B841

Historic hotel beside the Crinan Canal

Built in 1801 to coincide with the opening of the Crinan Canal, which it overlooks, this historic hotel has been run by Darren and Christine Dobson for the past decade. Lighter meals are served from the bistro-style menu in the relaxed atmosphere of the bar, conservatory lounge, or alfresco. For a more formal occasion dine in the serene, AA-Rosetted restaurant, where the carte specialises in the use of fresh local produce, notably seafood and game. Look for starters of Tarbet landed langoustine with bread, salad and mayonnaise. Mains might include Sound of Jura scallops wrapped in pancetta with garlic butter and new potatoes. Round off, perhaps, with sticky toffee pudding with vanilla ice cream. From nearby Oban there are sailings to the islands of Mull, Coll and Tiree. Inveraray Castle is also well worth a visit, as is Dunadd Fort where the ancient kings of Scotland were crowned.

Open all wk 8am-11pm Closed: 25 Dec **Bar Meals** L served all wk 12-2.30 D served all wk 6-9.30 **Restaurant** L served all wk 12-2.30 D served all wk 6-9.30 ⊕ FREE HOUSE ◀ Local ales. ♥ 8 **Facilities** ♦ Children's menu Children's portions Garden Parking Wi-fi **Rooms** 12

LUSS
Map 20 NS39

The Inn at Inverbeg ★★★★ INN

PICK OF THE PUBS

G83 8PD ☎ **01436 860678**
e-mail: inverbeg.reception@loch-lomond.co.uk
dir: 12m N of Balloch

Top Scottish hospitality and stunning views

Today a good road skirts Loch Lomond's western shore, but it wouldn't have been so good in 1814, when this wayside inn opened its doors. Today it incorporates Mr C's Fish & Whisky Restaurant and Bar, which specialises in the obvious. Starting with the fish, expect haddock and cod, West Coast oysters, langoustines, squid, steamed mussels, tempura tiger prawns and Thai fish curry. But it offers meat dishes too, including chargrilled Buccleuch steak burger; Cajun chicken; and black pudding and haggis fritters. Mr C's other commodity is, of course, malt whiskies, more than 200 of them. If you prefer a real ale, there's Deuchars IPA, Fyne Highlander and Houston's Killellan. Live folk music is played nightly throughout the summer. Individually styled rooms are split between the inn and a sumptuous beach house right on Loch Lomond's bonnie, bonnie banks.

Open all day all wk 11-11 (Fri-Sat 11am-mdnt) **Bar Meals** L served all wk 12-9 D served all wk 12-9 Av main course £10 food served all day **Restaurant** L served all wk 12-9 D served all wk 12-9 Av 3 course à la carte fr £20

food served all day ⊕ FREE HOUSE ◀ Houston Killellan, Fyne Highlander, Caledonian Deuchars IPA. ♥ 30
Facilities Non-diners area ♦ Children's menu Children's portions ⊨ Parking Wi-fi ▦ (notice required) **Rooms** 20

PORT APPIN
Map 20 NM94

The Pierhouse Hotel & Seafood Restaurant ★★★ SHL ◉

PICK OF THE PUBS

PA38 4DE ☎ **01631 730302**
e-mail: reservations@pierhousehotel.co.uk
dir: A828 from Ballachulish to Oban. In Appin right at Port Appin & Lismore ferry sign. After 2.5m left after post office, hotel at end of road by pier

Delicious seafood on the shores of Loch Linnhe

With breathtaking views to the islands of Lismore and Mull, it would be hard to imagine a more spectacular setting for this family-run hotel and renowned seafood restaurant with one AA Rosette. Once home to the piermaster (hence the name), the distinctive whitewashed building now houses a popular bar (with 50 malt whiskies), pool room, terrace and dining area, and offers the finest seasonal Scottish seafood, meat, game and vegetables. Overlooking the pier, the Ferry Bar serves burgers and seafood dishes, with the addition of filled ciabattas at lunchtime. Meanwhile a typical three-course restaurant meal might start with Cullen skink, oysters or scallops, before progressing to grilled lobster or spinach and parmesan potato gnocchi. The tempting desserts include Pierhouse ice creams and sorbets, and vanilla crème brûlée. Twelve individually designed bedrooms include some with king-size beds and superb loch views, and a couple of family rooms.

Open all wk 11-11 Closed: 25-26 Dec **Bar Meals** L served all wk 12.30-2.30 D served all wk 6.30-9.30 Av main course £10 **Restaurant** L served all wk 12.30-2.30 D served all wk 6.30-9.30 Av 3 course à la carte fr £30 ⊕ FREE HOUSE ◀ Belhaven Best & Export, Guinness.
Facilities Non-diners area ☘ (Bar Garden) ♦ Children's menu Garden Parking ▦ **Rooms** 12

STRACHUR
Map 20 NN00

Creggans Inn ★★★ HL ◉◉

PICK OF THE PUBS

PA27 8BX ☎ **01369 860279**
e-mail: info@creggans-inn.co.uk
dir: A82 from Glasgow, at Tarbet take A83 towards Cairndow, left onto A815 to Strachur

Award-winning, family-run inn on loch shores

Since the days of Mary, Queen of Scots, this comfortable former coaching inn on Strachur Bay has enjoyed the glorious views across Loch Fyne to Inveraray. Today's hosts, Archie and Gillian MacLellan, offer two dining options: there's bistro-style MacPhunn's for a menu featuring fresh, locally sourced produce, including the loch's famed oysters, salmon and scallops. The other option is the pistachio-coloured, two-AA Rosette dining room, hung with antique prints, offering a daily-changing, fixed-price menu with main courses of caramelised rib-eye steak with garlic and green peppercorn sauce; Aberdeen Angus beefburger; and butternut squash and sun-dried tomato risotto. After dinner, as the sun sets over the waters, you may (if you can) play the baby grand piano, or simply relax with a glass of malt whisky, port, or Scottish real ale, such as Fyne Highlander. A formal terraced garden and patio both make the most of the hard-to-beat view.

Open all day all wk 11am-mdnt **Bar Meals** L served all wk 12-2.30 D served all wk 6-8.30 **Restaurant** D served all wk 7-8.30 ⊕ FREE HOUSE ◀ Fyne Highlander, Atlas Latitude, Caledonian Deuchars IPA, Harviestoun Bitter & Twisted. **Facilities** Non-diners area 🐾 (Bar Garden) 🍴 Children's menu Children's portions Garden Parking Wi-fi **Rooms** 14

TAYVALLICH   Map 20 NR78

Tayvallich Inn

PA31 8PL ☎ **01546 870282**
dir: *From Lochgilphead take A816 then B841, B8025*

Popular loch-side pub at the heart of a vibrant community

Established for over 30 years, the inn stands in a picturesque fishing village overlooking the natural harbour of Tayvallich Bay at the head of Loch Sween. There are unrivalled views, particularly from the outside area of decking, where food and a great selection of real ales can be enjoyed. Not surprisingly given the location, fresh seafood features strongly – the catch is landed from the boats right outside the front door! Lobster, crab and langoustine are available in the summer, while typical dishes in winter might be fragrant oven-baked salmon fillet with prawn and caper sauce or line-caught Tarbert haddock in batter with chips.

Open all wk all day in summer (closed 3-6 Mon-Fri in winter) Closed: 25-26 Dec, Mon (Nov-Mar) **Bar Meals** L served all wk 12-2.30 D served all wk 6-9 **Restaurant** L served all wk 12-2.30 D served all wk 6-9 ⊕ FREE HOUSE ◀ Belhaven Best, Guinness, Orkney Northern Light. 🍷 8 **Facilities** Non-diners area 🐾 (Bar Garden) 🍴 Children's menu Children's portions Garden 🚭 Parking 🚌 (notice required)

DUMFRIES & GALLOWAY

BARGRENNAN   Map 20 NX37

House O'Hill Hotel

DG8 6RN ☎ **01671 840243**
e-mail: enquiries@houseohill.co.uk
dir: *From Newton Stewart take A714 towards Girvan, 8m. Hotel signed*

Secluded location in Galloway's forested hills

At the fringe of loch-speckled Galloway Forest and beautiful Glen Trool, this contemporary, homely little hotel makes the most of its setting in Europe's first 'Dark Sky' Park. Totally renovated four years ago, the former crofter's cottage attracts cyclists and ramblers on the Southern Upland Way by offering an exceptional combination of local microbrewery beers such as Sulwath and a wide-ranging menu strong on Galloway produce. Chicken stuffed with haggis and red wine-braised venison shank are just two of the fine dishes on the hit list; seasonal specials may include skate wing. Beer festivals occur in April and September.

Open all day all wk Closed: 3-25 Jan **Bar Meals** L served all wk 12-2.45 D served all wk 6-8.45 **Restaurant** L served all wk 12-2.45 D served all wk 6-8.45 Fixed menu price fr £10 ⊕ FREE HOUSE ◀ Sulwath, Stewart's, Ayr, Fyne. **Facilities** Non-diners area 🐾 (Bar Restaurant Garden) 🍴 Children's menu Family room Garden 🚭 Beer festival Parking Wi-fi 🚌

BLADNOCH   Map 20 NX45

The Bladnoch Inn **NEW**

DG8 9AB ☎ **01988 402200**
e-mail: thebladnochinn@hotmail.co.uk
dir: *A714 S of Wigtown to Bladnoch. Inn at rdbt by river bridge*

Perfect stop for book lovers and whisky drinkers

This traditional country inn is in the heart of the Machars peninsula. A mere hip-flask's throw away is Scotland's most southerly distillery, and just down the road is Wigtown, home to some 20 bookshops. At lunchtime there are paninis, freshly baked baguettes and filled baked potatoes, while main courses include chef's signature Irish stew, wholetail scampi, gammon steak, macaroni cheese and roast of the day. Evening favourites are trio of sticky honey and mustard sausages; and haddock in salt and vinegar batter, or from the bistro menu, chicken breast stuffed with haggis; curry of the day; and steamed salmon fillet.

Open all day all wk **Bar Meals** L served all wk 12-3 D served all wk 6-9 Av main course £7.95 **Restaurant** L served all wk 12-3 ◀ Greene King, Greene King IPA Ď Kopparberg. 🍷 15 **Facilities** Non-diners area 🍴 Children's menu Children's portions Play area Outside area 🚭 Parking Wi-fi 🚌 (notice required)

ISLE OF WHITHORN   Map 20 NX43

The Steam Packet Inn

Harbour Row DG8 8LL ☎ **01988 500334**
e-mail: steampacketinn@btconnect.com
dir: *From Newton Stewart take A714, then A746 to Whithorn, then Isle of Whithorn*

Local seafood a specialty

Personally run by the Scoular family for over 20 years, this lively quayside pub stands in a picturesque village at the tip of the Machars peninsula. Sit in one of the comfortable bars and enjoy a real ale, a malt whisky or a glass of wine. Glance out of the picture windows and watch the fishermen at work, then look to the menu to sample the fruits of their labours. Extensive seafood choices - perhaps isle-landed scallops or mussels in white wine and cream - are supported by the likes of steak pie and chicken curry.

Open all day all wk 11-11 (Sun 12-11) Closed: 25 Dec, winter Tue-Thu 2.30-6 **Bar Meals** L served all wk 12-2 D served all wk 6.30-9 Av main course £10.95 **Restaurant** L served all wk 12-2 D served all wk 6.30-9 ⊕ FREE HOUSE ◀ Timothy Taylor Landlord, Guest ales. 🍷 12 **Facilities** Non-diners area 🍴 Children's menu Children's portions Garden Outside area 🚭 Parking Wi-fi 🚌

KIRKCUDBRIGHT   Map 20 NX65

Selkirk Arms Hotel

Old High St DG6 4JG ☎ **01557 330402**
e-mail: reception@selkirkarmshotel.co.uk
dir: *M74 & M6 to A75, halfway between Dumfries & Stranraer on A75*

Choice of two bars and two restaurants

In 1794, when dining at what today is a tastefully refurbished town house, Robert Burns reputedly penned and delivered *The Selkirk Grace*, which famously begins "Some hae meat and canna eat". In the bar, Sulwath Brewery's eponymous ale celebrates the occasion. A good choice of dishes is offered in both the homely lounge and bistro, with comfy sofas and a living-flame fire, and the more intimate Artistas Restaurant. Locally sourced specialities include duo of Galloway beef; chicken Kashmiri; fillet of halibut and tiger shrimps; and, for those who canna eat meat, filo nut roast parcel. Finish with cranachan parfait.

Open all day all wk **Bar Meals** L served all wk 12-2 D served all wk 6-9 Av main course £11.95 **Restaurant** L served Sun 12-2 D served all wk 7-9 ⊕ FREE HOUSE ◀ Timothy Taylor Landlord, Sulwath Selkirk Grace, Dark Horse Hetton Pale Ale, Caledonian Deuchars IPA. **Facilities** Non-diners area 🍴 Children's menu Children's portions Garden 🚭 Parking Wi-fi 🚌

MOFFAT — Map 21 NT00

Annandale Arms ★★★ HL ⊛

High St DG10 9HF ☎ 01683 220013
e-mail: margaret@annandalearmshotel.co.uk
dir: A74(M) junct 15, A701. Moffat 1m

Real ales, malt whisky and great food in the heart of Moffat

A major Moffat landmark for over 250 years, it used to be a matter of pride that this hostelry could change a coach and four in less than a minute, in which time the driver would down a pint of ale; today, Broughton Merlin deserves much more time and appreciation. The award-winning food, a mix of traditional Scottish and international dishes, is also worth pondering over: choose between locally made haggis with neeps and tatties, poacher's game pie, Annandale salmon fishcakes, steak and stout pie, and roast marinated chump of lamb with honey and cumin roast carrots and parsnips. Besides the à la carte, there are daily specials and a selection of choices from the chargrill.

Open all day all wk ⊕ FREE HOUSE ◼ Broughton Merlin ♂ Westons Stowford Press. **Facilities** ♣ (Bar Garden) ♦ Children's menu Children's portions Garden Parking Wi-fi **Rooms** 16

NEW GALLOWAY — Map 20 NX67

Cross Keys Hotel

High St DG7 3RN ☎ 01644 420494
e-mail: enquiries@thecrosskeys-newgalloway.co.uk
dir: At N end of Loch Ken, 10m from Castle Douglas on A712

Great selection of real ales and malts

This 17th-century coaching inn sits in a stunning location at the top of Loch Ken on the edge of Galloway Forest Park, a superb area for walking, fishing, birdwatching, golf, watersports and photography. Part of the hotel was once the police station and in the beamed period bar the food is served in restored, stone-walled cells. Scottish ales are supplied by the Houston and Sulwath breweries, among others. The lunch menu includes sandwiches, pizzas, pastas and burgers, while the weekly-changing dinner specials feature the likes of soy, ginger and honey beef strips with steamed egg noodles. A grill menu and early supper menu are also available.

Open 6-11.30 Closed: Sun & Tue eve winter **Bar Meals** D served all wk 6.30-8.30 Av main course £12 **Restaurant** D served all wk 6.30-8.30 ⊕ FREE HOUSE ◼ Houston, Sulwath, Guest ales ♂ Westons Stowford Press. ♥ 9 **Facilities** Non-diners area ♣ (Bar Garden) Children's menu Children's portions Garden Wi-fi ▥ (notice required)

NEWTON STEWART — Map 20 NX46

Creebridge House Hotel

Minnigaff DG8 6NP ☎ 01671 402121
e-mail: info@creebridge.co.uk
dir: From A75 into Newton Stewart, turn right over river bridge, hotel 200yds on left

Great Scottish food in a tremendous setting

In a bucolic, tranquil location between Galloway Forest Park's looming mountain and forest landscape and exquisite Wigtown Bay, patrons at this imposing 250-year-old former shooting lodge can expect to live well on the produce of this bounteous setting. Haddock and salmon arrive from the local smokery; Galloway meats from estate farms and scampi from nearby Newton Stewart all feature on the extensive menu in the elegant restaurant or Bridge's Brasserie-bar, where 30 malt whiskies and Creebridge Golden Ale are also stocked. A short walk through the 3-acre garden brings you to the River Cree, after which the hotel is named.

Open all wk 12-2 6-11.30 (Fri-Sat 12-2 6-1am) Closed: 1st 3wks Jan **Bar Meals** L served all wk 12-2 D served all wk 6-9 **Restaurant** L served all wk 12-2 D served all wk 6-9 ⊕ FREE HOUSE ◼ Caledonian Deuchars IPA, Guinness, Guest ales. **Facilities** Non-diners area ♣ (Bar Garden) ♦ Children's menu Children's portions Garden ⏜ Parking Wi-fi ▥ (notice required)

The Galloway Arms Hotel

54-58 Victoria St DG8 6DB ☎ 01671 402653
e-mail: info@gallowayarmshotel.com
dir: In town centre, opposite clock

Family-owned rural hotel

Founded 260 years ago by 6th Earl of Galloway, the hotel acted as the focus for developing the 'planted' market town of Newton Stewart, first established in the 1650s. On the banks of the River Cree, the town is well sited to explore Galloway Forest or the Machars of Whithorn, working up an appetite for traditional Scottish dishes such as chicken, leek and Highland crowdie or the prosaically-named Bonnie Prince Charlie's Balls (deep-fried haggis in Drambuie-based sauce), accompanied by a dram from the most extensive selection of malts in Galloway.

Open all day all wk 11am-mdnt ⊕ FREE HOUSE ◼ Belhaven Best & 70/- Shilling, Caledonian Deuchars IPA, Guinness. **Facilities** ♣ (Bar Garden) ♦ Children's menu Children's portions Garden Parking

---

SANDHEAD — Map 20 NX04

Tigh Na Mara Hotel

Main St DG9 9JF ☎ 01776 830210
e-mail: tighnamara@btconnect.com
dir: A75 from Dumfries towards Stranraer. Left onto B7084 to Sandhead. Hotel in village centre

Bracing sea air and long sandy beaches

Tigh na Mara means 'house by the sea', which seems appropriate for this family-run village hotel is set in the tranquil seaside village of Sandhead and boasts breathtaking views of the Sands of Luce. An extensive menu of dishes created from top-quality local ingredients might include local seafood pancakes with white wine sauce; loin of Border lamb with Lyonnaise potatoes; or poached salmon and king prawns with Chablis cream. Relax with a glass of Belhaven Best in the garden, comfortable lounge or beside the fire in the public bar.

Open all day all wk ⊕ BELHAVEN ◼ Best, Morland Old Speckled Hen. **Facilities** ♦ Children's menu Children's portions Family room Garden Parking Wi-fi

---

DUNDEE, CITY OF

BROUGHTY FERRY — Map 21 NO43

The Royal Arch Bar

285 Brook St DD5 2DS ☎ 01382 779741
dir: On A930, 3m from Dundee at Broughty Ferry rail station

Convivial local by the Tay Estuary

This long established street-corner inn is a pleasing mix of local's saloon bar, complete with stained-glass windows and an eye-catching Victorian gantry, and a well-maintained art deco lounge long ago converted from the inn's stables. The Royal Arch itself was a monument built to commemorate Queen Victoria's Dundee visit in 1863; a fragment survives on display in the bar. Dispensed from this bar are quality Scottish beers such as from local micro MōR, as well as over 50 malt whiskies; satisfying pub meals can include lamb shank in red wine or prime Scottish steak pie. Regular beer and cider festivals are held.

Open all day all wk **Bar Meals** L served Mon-Fri 11.30-2.30, Sat 11.30-8, Sun 12.30-7 D served Mon-Fri 5-8, Sat 11.30-8, Sun 12.30-7 Av main course £8 **Restaurant** L served Mon-Fri 11.30-2.30, Sat 11.30-8, Sun 12.30-7 D served Mon-Fri 5-8, Sat 11.30-8, Sun 12.30-7 Fixed menu price fr £4.50 Av 3 course à la carte fr £11 ⊕ FREE HOUSE ◼ McEwan's 80/-, Belhaven St Andrews, Caledonian Deuchars IPA, Mòr Tea, Vicar? ♂ Addlestones. ♥ 30 **Facilities** Non-diners area ♦ Children's portions Family room Garden Beer festival Cider festival Wi-fi ▥

DUNDEE · Map 21 NO43

Speedwell Bar

165-167 Perth Rd DD2 1AS ☎ 01382 667783
dir: From A92 (Tay Bridge), A991 signed Perth/A85/ Coupar Angus/A923. At Riverside rdbt 3rd exit (A991). At lights left into Nethergate signed Parking/South Tay St. Becomes Perth Rd. Pass university. Bar on right

Edwardian gem with unspoilt interior

This fine example of an unspoiled Edwardian art deco bar is worth visiting for its interior alone; all the fitments in the bar and sitting rooms are beautifully crafted mahogany – gantry, drink shelves, dado panelling and fireplace. Internal doors are all glazed with etched glass. The same family owned it for 90 years, until the present landlord's father bought it in 1995. As well as the cask-conditioned ales, 157 whiskies and imported bottles are offered. A kitchen would be good, but since the pub is listed this is impossible. Visitors are encouraged to bring their own snacks from nearby bakeries. This community pub is home to several clubs and has live Scottish music from time to time on a Tuesday.

Open all day all wk 11am-mdnt ⊕ FREE HOUSE ◀ Caledonian Deuchars IPA, Harviestoun Bitter & Twisted, Williams Bros Seven Giraffes Ö Addlestones. ♟18 **Facilities** Non-diners area ❤ (Bar) ⊨ Beer festival Wi-fi ⊨ **Notes** ⊜

EAST AYRSHIRE

DALRYMPLE · Map 20 NS31

The Kirkton Inn

1 Main St KA6 6DF ☎ 01292 560241
e-mail: kirkton@cqm.co.uk
dir: 6m SE from centre of Ayr just off A77

Welcoming village local with wholesome food

In the heart of the village of Dalrymple, this inn was built in 1879 as a coaching inn and has been providing sustenance to travellers ever since; the welcoming atmosphere makes it easy to feel at home. It's a stoutly traditional setting, with open fires and polished brasses. Eat traditional and wholesome dishes in the Coach Room in the oldest part of the building, and perhaps choose chicken and leek pie, or Kirkton burger, followed by hot chocolate fudge cake. Lighter options are soup and sandwiches. Dining is also available in another room which overlooks the River Doon.

Open all day all wk **Bar Meals** L served all wk 12-2.30 D served all wk 5-8 Av main course £8.95 **Restaurant** L served all wk 12-2.30 D served all wk 5-9 Fixed menu price fr £10.95 Av 3 course à la carte fr £10.95 ◀ John Smith's, Guinness. ♟20 **Facilities** Non-diners area ❤ (Bar Garden) ⊪ Children's menu Children's portions Play area Family room Garden ⊨ Parking Wi-fi ⊨ (notice required)

GATEHEAD · Map 20 NS33

The Cochrane Inn

45 Main Rd KA2 0AP ☎ 01563 570122
dir: From Glasgow A77 to Kilmarnock, then A759 to Gatehead

A warm welcome and hearty good food

There's a friendly, bustling atmosphere inside this traditional ivy-covered village centre pub, which sits just a short drive from the Ayrshire coast. The interior has natural stone walls adorned with gleaming brasses and log fires in winter. The menus combine British and international flavours in hearty, wholesome food. This might translate as salt and pepper squid with jalapeño salsa or smoked duck breast with apple salad, walnuts and orange dressing; then haggis, neeps and tatties; chicken stuffed with cream cheese, chorizo and garlic; or steak and sausage pie.

Open all wk 12-2.30 5.30 onwards (Sun 12-9) ⊕ FREE HOUSE ◀ John Smith's. **Facilities** ⊪ Children's menu Children's portions Garden Parking Wi-fi

SORN · Map 20 NS52

The Sorn Inn

PICK OF THE PUBS

35 Main St KA5 6HU ☎ 01290 551305
e-mail: craig@sorninn.com
dir: A70 from S; or A76 from N onto B743 to Sorn

A fusion of fine dining and brasserie-style food

The whitewashed Sorn Inn dates back to the 18th century when it was a coaching inn on the old Edinburgh to Kilmarnock route. It is now a smart gastro-pub with comfortably appointed rooms and real ales from Renfrewshire's Houston Brewery. Menus use the best of imported and seasonal ingredients. A beef rissole croquette to start strikes all the right notes with root vegetables and pea purée. Pastas and steaks from the grill are augmented by the likes of spiced aubergine and olive strudel, mint couscous, barbecued tomato chutney; and supreme of chargrilled chicken with banana rice and fruit curry sauce. If you have the appetite you could round off with a selection of Scottish cheeses; alternatively try the toasted almond pannacotta.

Open 12-2.30 6-10 (Fri 12-2.30 6-12 Sat 12-12 Sun 12-10) Closed: 2wks Jan, Mon **Bar Meals** L served Tue-Fri 12-2.30, Sat 12-9, Sun 12-8 D served Tue-Fri 6-9, Sat 12-9, Sun 12-8 Av main course £13 **Restaurant** L served Tue-Fri 12-2.30, Sat 12-9, Sun 12-8 D served Tue-Fri 6-9, Sat 12-9, Sun 12-8 Av 3 course à la carte fr £24 ⊕ FREE HOUSE ◀ John Smith's, Houston Texas, Guinness. ♟12 **Facilities** Non-diners area ❤ (Bar) ⊪ Children's menu Children's portions Outside area ⊨ Parking Wi-fi ⊨ (notice required)

EAST LOTHIAN

GULLANE · Map 21 NT48

The Old Clubhouse

East Links Rd EH31 2AF ☎ 01620 842008
dir: A198 into Gullane, 3rd right into East Links Rd, pass church, on left

Pub favourites overlooking the Gullane Links

Established in 1890 as the home of Gullane Golf Club, this building had a chequered past after the golfers moved on to larger premises, including stints as a disco and as tea rooms. In 1989 the Campanile family took the reins and it hasn't looked back. Roaring winter fires and walls crammed with golfing memorabilia make a good first impression, and the menu delivers a lengthy list of pub classics including regional specialities such as Cullen skink or Hornings haggis with Stornoway black pudding. For dessert, maybe home-made ice cream.

Open all day all wk Closed: 25 Dec & 1 Jan **Bar Meals** L served all wk 12-9.30 D served all wk 12-9.30 food served all day **Restaurant** L served all wk 12-9.30 D served all wk 12-9.30 food served all day ⊕ FREE HOUSE ◀ Timothy Taylor Landlord, Caledonian Deuchars IPA Ö Thistly Cross. ♟9 **Facilities** Non-diners area ❤ (Bar Garden) ⊪ Children's menu Children's portions Garden ⊨ Wi-fi ⊨ (notice required)

LONGNIDDRY · Map 21 NT47

The Longniddry Inn

Main St EH32 0NF ☎ 01875 852401
e-mail: info@longniddryinn.com
dir: On A198 (Main St), near rail station

Comprehensive menu choices in historic buildings

This combination of a former blacksmith's forge and four cottages on Longniddry's Main Street continues to be a popular spot. Held in high esteem locally for friendly service and good food, it offers an extensive menu featuring the likes of Stornoway black pudding and poached egg; haggis, neeps and tatties; chef's stir-fry; macaroni cheese; and chicken and combo sizzlers from the grill. In warmer weather take your pint of Belhaven Best, glass of wine or freshly ground coffee outside.

Open all day all wk Closed: 26 Dec, 1 Jan **Bar Meals** L served Mon-Sat 12-2.30 D served Mon-Sat 5-8.30 **Restaurant** L served Sun 12.30-7.30 ⊕ PUNCH TAVERNS ◀ Belhaven Best. **Facilities** Non-diners area ⊪ Children's menu Children's portions Garden Parking Wi-fi ⊨

EDINBURGH, CITY OF

EDINBURGH   Map 21 NT27

Bennets Bar

8 Leven St EH3 9LG ☎ 0131 229 5143
e-mail: bennetsbar@hotmail.co.uk
dir: *Adjacent to Kings Theatre. Telephone for detailed directions*

Unchanged interior and 120 malts to choose from

Bennets is a listed property dating from 1839 with hand-painted tiles and murals on the walls, original stained-glass windows, intricate wood carving on bar fitments and brass beer taps. It's a friendly pub, popular with performers from the adjacent Kings Theatre. The traditional bar has some contemporary twists and serves real ales, over 120 malt whiskies and a decent selection of wines. The home-made food, at a reasonable price, ranges from toasties, burgers and salads to stovies (potato and meat stew), steak pie, and Scottish fare. There's also a daily roast and traditional puddings. Coffee and tea are served all day.

Open all day all wk 11am-1am Closed: 25 Dec ⊕ IONA PUB ◀ Caledonian Deuchars IPA & 80/-, Guinness. **Facilities** ⋔ Children's menu Children's portions Family room Wi-fi

Bert's Bar

29-31 William St EH3 7NG ☎ 0131 225 5748
e-mail: bertsbar@maclay.co.uk
dir: *Telephone for directions*

Known for a love of rugby, real ales and good food

Although it has changed names a few times, Bert's has been an Edinburgh watering hole since the 1930s. Popular with rugby fans, it retains many of its original features although the food and drink offering is thoroughly modern. Enjoy a well-kept pint of Deuchars or Thistly Cross cider or order from a broad menu that offers plenty of choice. Start, perhaps, with local smoked salmon and move on to beef steak pie; Cajun chicken; curry of the day or the more traditional haggis, neeps and tatties.

Open all day all wk Closed: 25 Dec ⊕ MACLAY ◀ Caledonian Deuchars IPA, Harviestoun Bitter & Twisted, Timothy Taylor Landlord, Orkney Dark Island Ō Thistly Cross. **Facilities** ❤ (Bar) Wi-fi

The Bow Bar

80 The West Bow EH1 2HH ☎ 0131 226 7667
dir: *Telephone for directions*

A whisky and beer connoisseurs' delight

If there is one free house that reflects the history and traditions of Edinburgh's Old Town, it is The Bow Bar. With some 220 malt whiskies, eight real ales poured from traditional tall founts and 30 bottled beers, the focus may be on liquid refreshment but the range of snacks includes haggis, cheese and chilli pies and bridies (meat pastries). Tables from old train carriages and a church gantry add to the unique feel of a bar where the sound of conversation makes up for the lack of gaming machines and music. Twice a year in January and July, the pub holds ten-day long beer festivals.

Open all day all wk Closed: 25-26 Dec, 1-2 Jan **Bar Meals** L served Mon-Sat 12-3, Sun 12.30-3 ⊕ FREE HOUSE ◀ Alechemy, Tryst Ales, Stewart Edinburgh No 3 & Pentland IPA, Harviestoun Bitter & Twisted, Atlas Latitude, Fyne Avalanche & Jarl, Cairngorm Black Gold, Tempest, Thornbridge Ō Westons Stowford Press. **Facilities** Non-diners area ❤ (Bar Restaurant) Beer festival Wi-fi

The Café Royal ◉

PICK OF THE PUBS

19 West Register St EH2 2AA ☎ 0131 556 1884
e-mail: info@caferoyal.org.uk
dir: *Off Princes St, in city centre*

Hearty Scottish fare in historic building

Apart from a change of hands in June 2012, little has changed at The Café Royal since it moved across the road from its original site in 1863. Designed by local architect Robert Paterson, it is a glorious example of Victorian and Baroque, with an interior seemingly frozen in time. Elegant stained glass and fine late Victorian plasterwork dominate the building, as do irreplaceable Doulton ceramic murals in the bar and restaurant. The whole building and its interior were listed in 1970 so future generations can enjoy the unique building which still sticks to its early 19th-century roots by serving local ales such as Harviestoun Bitter & Twisted, wine, coffee and fresh oysters in the bar and restaurant. Scottish produce dominates the menu, from starters of black pudding with king scallops to mains of Balmoral chicken wrapped in bacon and stuffed with haggis.

Open all day all wk **Bar Meals** Av main course £11.50-£13.50 food served all day **Restaurant** L served all wk 12-2.30 (all day May-Sep) D served all wk 5-9.30 Fixed menu price fr £14.50 Av 3 course à la carte fr £25.50 ⊕ SPIRIT PUB COMPANY ◀ Caledonian Deuchars IPA, Kelburn Ca'Canny & Goldihops, Harviestoun Bitter & Twisted, Cairngorm Ales Ō Aspall. ♟ 9 **Facilities** Non-diners area ⋔ Wi-fi 🚌 (notice required)

Doric Tavern

PICK OF THE PUBS

15-16 Market St EH1 1DE ☎ 0131 225 1084
e-mail: info@the-doric.com
dir: *In city centre opposite Waverly Station & Edinburgh Dungeons*

Edinburgh's oldest gastro-pub

Housed in a 17th-century building, the Doric claims to be Edinburgh's oldest food-serving hostelry; certainly records show a pub on this site since 1823. Its name is taken from an old language once spoken in north-east Scotland, mainly Aberdeenshire. Conveniently located for Waverley Station, the pub is just a short walk from Princes Street and Edinburgh Castle. Public rooms include a ground-floor bar, and a wine bar and bistro upstairs. In these pleasantly informal surroundings, a wide choice of fresh, locally sourced food is prepared by the chefs on site. While supping a pint, you can nibble on marinated olives or haggis spring rolls. Mains from the grill include a Border beef rib-eye, while a chef's specials might be a home-made game pie with chargrilled asparagus. Seafood is delivered fresh each morning: haddock is deep-fried in the pub's own beer-batter and served with hand-cut chips and home-made tartare sauce.

Open all day all wk Sat-Thu 11.30-11 (Fri 11am-1am) Closed: 25-26 Dec **Bar Meals** L served all wk 12-10 D served all wk 12-10 food served all day **Restaurant** L served all wk 12-10 D served all wk 12-10 food served all day ⊕ FREE HOUSE ◀ Caledonian Deuchars IPA, Stewart's 80/-, Guinness, Guest ales. **Facilities** Non-diners area ⋔ Children's menu Children's portions Family room 🚌

The Guildford Arms

1-5 West Register St EH2 2AA ☎ 0131 556 4312
e-mail: guildfordarms@dmstewart.com
dir: *Opposite Balmoral Hotel at E end of Princes St*

Celebrated free house and galleried restaurant

Very much a destination pub, particularly during the Edinburgh Fringe; although simply missing one's train at Waverley station is reason enough to pop into this late-Victorian classic. Study the public bar's magnificent Jacobean-style ceiling at close quarters from the galleried restaurant. Here, dine on Scottish seafood; haggis, neeps and tatties; pan-fried salmon with Stornoway black pudding; or mushroom Wellington, blue cheese and caramelised red onion. Ten hand-pumps, their blue porcelain handles bearing the logo of the Stewart family, the pub's owners since 1896, declare a near-religious zeal for real ales, accentuated by two 11-day beer festivals, each featuring over 50 brews.

Open all day all wk Closed: 25-26 Dec, 1 Jan **Bar Meals** L served all wk 12-3, snacks 3-9 food served all day **Restaurant** L served Sun-Fri 12-3, Sat 12-5.30 D served Sun-Thu 5.30-9.30, Fri-Sat 5.30-10 ⊕ FREE HOUSE ◀ Harviesoun Bitter & Twisted, Fyne Jarl, Orkney Dark Island, Caledonian Deuchars IPA, rotating Stewart, Highland Ō Thistly Cross, Westons 1st Quality. ♟ 12 **Facilities** Non-diners area ❤ (Bar) Children's portions Beer festival

Halfway House

24 Fleshmarket Close EH1 1BX ☎ 0131 225 7101
e-mail: stevewhiting@straitmail.co.uk
dir: *From Royal Mile (close to x-rds with North & South bridges) into Cockburn St. Into Fleshmarket Cl, or take flight of steps off Cockburn St on right*

Edinburgh's smallest pub is an iconic institution

Hidden down one of the Old Town's 'closes' (a narrow alleyway, often with a flight of steps and enclosed by tall buildings), the cosy interior of this pub is adorned with railway memorabilia and throngs with beer aficionados supping interesting ales from Scottish microbreweries, perhaps Houston Peter's Well and Cairngorm Trade Winds. Mop up the ale with some traditional Scottish bar food made from fresh produce: Cullen skink (a smoked haddock, potato, onion and cream soup) is a house speciality. Look out for the regular beer festivals, but if beer is not your thing, then perhaps sample a few of the 40 or so whiskies behind the bar.

Open all day all wk **Bar Meals** Av main course £6.50 food served all day FREE HOUSE Stewart Pentland IPA, Harviestoun Bitter & Twisted, Cairngorm Trade Winds, Houston Peter's Well, Cromarty, Alechemy Addlestones. **Facilities** Non-diners area (Bar) Outside area Beer festival Wi-fi **Notes**

The Sheep Heid Inn NEW

AA PUB OF THE YEAR FOR SCOTLAND 2013-2014

PICK OF THE PUBS

43-45 The Causeway, Duddingston EH15 3QA
☎ 0131 661 7974
e-mail: enquiry@thesheepheidedinburgh.co.uk
dir: *A1 from city centre towards Musselburgh, at lights into Duddingston Road West, 4th right or 5th right into The Causeway*

Oldest pub in Edinburgh

There's so much history associated with Edinburgh's, and possibly Scotland's, oldest surviving pub – it was established in 1360 – that it could do with its own guidebook. The name itself is a matter of conjecture, but it probably stems from King James VI of Scotland's gift of a ram's head snuff box in 1580. Harviestoun Bitter & Twisted, from the foot of the Ochil Hills, and Deuchars occupy the real ale pumps, while food ranges from light meals and tapas-style sharers to modern British classics. The 'From the Sea' section of the menu offers smoked loin of cod; and beer-battered haddock; 'From the Land' suggests marinated sticky chicken with lemon, honey and chilli sauce; pulled beef and bacon pie with orange- and cardamom-infused carrots; and 'From the Garden' lists crispy potato, squash, olive and truffle cake. The inn is also home to Scotland's oldest skittle alley.

Open all day all wk **Bar Meals** Av main course £9.95 food served all day **Restaurant** Fixed menu price fr £7.95 Av 3 course à la carte fr £18.95 food served all day Caledonian Deuchars IPA, Harviestoun Bitter & Twisted Aspall. 20 **Facilities** Non-diners area Children's menu Children's portions Garden Beer festival Parking Wi-fi (notice required)

The Shore Bar & Restaurant

3 Shore, Leith EH6 6QW ☎ 0131 553 5080
e-mail: info@theshore.biz
dir: *Telephone for directions*

Enjoyable food at Edinburgh's bustling port

Centuries ago, a lighthouse guiding seafarers to the safety of Edinburgh's port is believed to have shared the site of this redoubtable old pub at the heart of Leith's bustling waterfront. A memorable wood-boarded interior welcomes guests keen to sample the excellent Scottish seafood for which the place is widely recognised. Monkfish cheeks with curried parsnip and pickled carrots make a fascinating entrée, coupled with mains like pork belly and scallops with butternut squash purée or perhaps a warming venison casserole. Scottish-brewed real ales are the heart of the liquid fare here. Outside seating looks out on the promenade beside the Water of Leith.

Open all wk noon-1am (Sun 12.30pm-1am) Closed: 25-26 Dec, 1 Jan **Bar Meals** L served all wk 12-6 D served all wk 6-10.30 food served all day **Restaurant** L served all wk 12-6 D served all wk 6-10.30 food served all day FREE HOUSE Belhaven 80/-, Caledonian Deuchars IPA, Guinness. 14 **Facilities** Non-diners area Children's portions Wi-fi

EDINBURGH *continued*

Whiski Bar & Restaurant

119 High St EH1 1SG ☎ **0131 556 3095**
e-mail: info@whiskibar.co.uk
web: www.whiskibar.co.uk
dir: Telephone for detailed instructions

Whisky, music and food galore on the Royal Mile

If you find yourself on Edinburgh's famous Royal Mile and in need of sustenance and a 'wee' dram, then seek out this acclaimed bar at number 119. Choose from over 300 malt whiskies (all available by the nip) and tuck into some traditional Scottish food. Served all day, the menu makes good use of Scottish Border beef and daily deliveries of seafood from local fishermen. Typically, try smoked mackerel pâté; Haggis tower with 'neeps' and mash; then cranachan for pudding. Come for the traditional Scottish music in the evening – this bar is famous for its fiddle music.

Open all day all wk Closed: 25 Dec **Bar Meals** L served Mon-Thu 10-10, Fri-Sun 10-10.30 D served Mon-Thu 10-10, Fri-Sun 10-10.30 Av main course £10 food served all day **Restaurant** L served Mon-Thu 10-10, Fri-Sun 10-10.30 D served Mon-Thu 10-10, Fri-Sun 10-10.30 Fixed menu price fr £16.95 Av 3 course à la carte fr £25 food served all day ⊕ FREE HOUSE ◀ Innis & Gunn ♨ Thistly Cross. ♀ 9 **Facilities** Non-diners area ♦♦ Children's menu Children's portions Outside area ⏢ ➡ (notice required)

See advert on page 539

RATHO	Map 21 NT17

The Bridge Inn ★★★★ INN

PICK OF THE PUBS

27 Baird Rd EH28 8RA ☎ **0131 333 1320**
e-mail: info@bridgeinn.com
dir: From Newbridge at B7030 junct, follow signs for Ratho & Edinburgh Canal Centre

Canal-side inn offering restaurant cruises

The tree-lined Union Canal between Edinburgh and the Falkirk Wheel runs past this waterside inn, once used by the early 19th-century navvies who dug the cut. In both the bar and restaurant the menu offers dishes based on local produce, including from the pub's new kitchen garden, and from its own chickens, ducks and saddleback pigs, the latter providing a rich supply of pork loin, fillet, belly and sausages. Bar favourites are fresh haddock with hand-cut chips, and pie of the week, while the restaurant features Buccleuch sirloin and fillet steaks; caramelised shoulder of hogget; smoked coley risotto; and hand-dived scallops. Scottish cask ales may include Trade Winds from Cairngorm Brewery, Dark Island from Orkney and beers from Arran. The pub's two renovated barges provide Sunday lunch, afternoon tea and dinner cruises. Children and dogs love the big grassy area outside.

Open all day all wk 11-11 (Fri-Sat 11am-mdnt) Closed: 25 Dec **Bar Meals** L served Mon-Fri 12-3, Sat 12-9, Sun 12.30-8.30 D served Mon-Fri 5.30-9, Sat 12-9, Sun 12.30-8.30 **Restaurant** L served Mon-Fri 12-3, Sat 12-9, Sun 12.30-8.30 D served Mon-Fri 5.30-9, Sat 12-9, Sun 12.30-8.30 ⊕ FREE HOUSE ◀ Caledonian Deuchars IPA, Belhaven, Guest ales ♨ Aspall. ♀ 21 **Facilities** Non-diners area ♣ (Bar Garden) ♦♦ Children's menu Children's portions Garden ⏢ Beer festival Parking Wi-fi ➡ (notice required) **Rooms** 4

FIFE

BURNTISLAND	Map 21 NT28

Burntisland Sands Hotel

Lochies Rd KY3 9JX ☎ **01592 872230**
e-mail: mail@burntislandsands.co.uk
dir: Towards Kirkcaldy, Burntisland on A921. Hotel on right before Kinghorn

Just a hop from the beach

Once a highly regarded girls' boarding school, this small, family-run hotel stands only 50 yards from an award-winning sandy beach. Visitors can expect reasonably priced meals throughout the day, including internationally themed evenings. Typical dishes served in the three dining areas include haggis, neeps and tatties; baked yellowfin sole stuffed with a smoked haddock mousse; and caramel, apple and custard pie. Relax and enjoy a Scottish ale in the bar and lounge area, perhaps on a live music night. There is also a patio garden and children can play with the rabbits in the activity area.

Open all day all wk **Bar Meals** L served Mon-Fri 12-2.30, Sat-Sun all day D served Mon-Fri 5-8.30, Sat-Sun all day **Restaurant** L served Mon-Fri 12-2.30, Sat-Sun all day D served Mon-Fri 5-8.30, Sat-Sun all day ⊕ FREE HOUSE ◀ Caledonian Deuchars IPA, Tennent's, Guinness, Belhaven Best, Guest ales. **Facilities** Non-diners area ♣ (Garden) ♦♦ Children's menu Children's portions Play area Garden ⏢ Parking Wi-fi ➡ (notice required)

EARLSFERRY	Map 21 NO40

The Golf Tavern

5 Links Rd KY9 1AW ☎ **01333 330610**
e-mail: richard@ship-elie.com
dir: From Lundin Links take A915, then A917 towards Elie. Turn right signed Earlsferry, through golf course to T-junct. Right into one-way system, pub on right near 4th tee

Free house focusing on sport and traditional food

Known to locals as the '19th', although it is close to the fourth tee on the Elie Golf Course, this pub has become the hub of Earlsferry since Richard and Jill Philip (who also run The Ship Inn, Elie; see entry) took over five years ago. Although sport is the draw here, whether it's golf, pool or live rugby on the TV, it offers something for everybody. Enjoy a pint of Deuchars IPA and order from the traditional menu that includes antipasti platters, pâté of the day, steak burger, and chicken curry. Check the blackboard for the daily specials and vegetarian options.

Open all day all wk Closed: 25 Dec **Bar Meals** L served Mon-Sat 12-2.30, Sun 12.30-3 D served Sun-Thu 6-9, Fri-Sat 6-9.30 **Restaurant** L served Mon-Sat 12-2.30, Sun 12.30-3 D served Sun-Thu 6-9, Fri-Sat 6-9.30 ⊕ FREE HOUSE ◀ Caledonian Deuchars IPA. **Facilities** Non-diners area ♣ (Bar) ♦♦ Children's menu Children's portions Wi-fi

ELIE   Map 21 NO40

The Ship Inn

The Toft KY9 1DT ☎ 01333 330246
e-mail: info@ship-elie.com
dir: *A915 & A917 to Elie. From High Street follow signs to Watersport Centre & The Toft*

Community favourite with lots going on

Sitting right on the waterfront at Elie Bay, The Ship has been a pub since 1838. The enthusiastic Philip family (who also run The Golf Tavern, Earlsferry; see entry) has run this lively free house for over 20 years. Charity and celebratory events take place throughout the year, including an Easter egg hunt. The pub has its own cricket team, which plays regular fixtures on the beach. Live music is staged, and barbecues are held in the beer garden during the summer. Together with Scottish ales, the best of local produce features on the concise menu that offers the likes of smoked haddock crêpe, and chicken and bacon salad.

Open all day all wk Closed: 25 Dec **Bar Meals** L served Mon-Sat 12-2.30, Sun 12.30-3 D served Mon-Thu 6-9, Fri-Sat 6-9.30 **Restaurant** L served Mon-Sat 12-2.30, Sun 12.30-3 D served Mon-Thu 6-9, Fri-Sat 6-9.30 ⊕ FREE HOUSE ◀ Caledonian Deuchars IPA & 80/-, Belhaven Best. **Facilities** Non-diners area ❀ (Bar Garden) ❶ Children's menu Children's portions Play area Family room Garden ﹏

ST ANDREWS   Map 21 NO51

The Inn at Lathones ★★★★ INN ⊛⊛

PICK OF THE PUBS

Largoward KY9 1JE ☎ 01334 840494
e-mail: stay@innatlathones.com
dir: *5m from St Andrews on A915*

A warm welcome awaits at this 400-year old inn

Although many people associate St Andrews purely with golf, this 400-year-old coaching inn with rooms is the exception to the rule as it doubles up as a live music venue. Lindisfarne and Curtis Stigers are among the many luminaries who perform here, and the walls display one of the best collections of music memorabilia in the country. Ancient meets modern at the inn and guests can relax in deep sofas and enjoy excellent ales from Orkney Brewery around log-burners. For the past 14 years the chefs here have been awarded two AA Rosettes; their innovative cooking of well-sourced local ingredients can be judged from starters that include game spiced terrine, or leek and Dunsyre Blue tart with mixed leaves and hazelnut dressing. Mains come up trumps, too, with roasted sea bass with mussels and prawns, lemon and fennel sauce, or slow-roasted belly of pork with sautéed wild mushrooms and pak choi. Smart, contemporary accommodation is available.

Open all day all wk 10-10 Closed: 2wks Jan **Bar Meals** food served all day **Restaurant** L served all wk 12-2.30 D served all wk 6-9.30 ⊕ FREE HOUSE ◀ Orkney Dark Island, Atlas Three Sisters, Belhaven Best. ☻ 11 **Facilities** Non-diners area ❶ Garden ﹁ Parking ﹏ **Rooms** 21

The Jigger Inn

PICK OF THE PUBS

The Old Course Hotel KY16 9SP ☎ 01334 474371
e-mail: reservations@oldcoursehotel.co.uk
dir: *M90 junct 8, A91 to St Andrews*

Perhaps golf's most famous 19th-hole

Steeped in history, The Jigger was a stationmaster's lodge in the 1800s on a railway line that disappeared many years ago. Located in the grounds of The Old Course Hotel, its close proximity to the world-famous St Andrews golf course means that it is home to some impressive golfing memorabilia. Don't be surprised if you are sharing the bar with a caddy or a golfing legend fresh from a game. Crackling open-hearth fires, traditional Scottish pub hospitality and plenty of golfing gossip are the background for a selection of Scottish beers, including St Andrews and Jigger Ale. All-day availability is one advantage of a short, simple menu that lists soups, inviting sandwiches and quenelles of haggis, neeps and tatties as starters, and continues with Jigger burger with Mull cheddar, Ayrshire bacon and fries; shepherd's pie with roasted root vegetables; pork and honey sausages on colcannon mash; and desserts such as apple and pear crumble.

Open all day all wk 11-11 (Sun 12-11) **Bar Meals** L served all wk 12-9.30 food served all day **Restaurant** D served all wk 12-9.30 ⊕ FREE HOUSE ◀ The Jigger Inn Jigger Ale, St Andrews, Guinness. ☻ 8 **Facilities** Non-diners area ❶ Garden ﹁ Parking ﹏

GLASGOW, CITY OF

GLASGOW   Map 20 NS56

Bon Accord

153 North St G3 7DA ☎ 0141 248 4427
e-mail: paul.bonaccord@ntlbusiness.com
dir: *M8 junct 19 merge onto A804 (North Street) signed Charing Cross*

An unmissable destination for malt whisky lovers

Tourists from all over the world come to the 'Bon', Paul McDonagh and son Thomas's acclaimed alehouse and malt whisky bar. The reason? To sample some of the annual tally of a thousand-plus different beers, over 40 ciders (maybe at one of the four beer and cider festivals), or the 350-strong malts collection (a far cry from the original five on offer). To line the stomach are all-day breakfasts, baguettes, giant Yorkshire puddings, chilli con carne, fish and chips, grilled steaks, chicken salads, macaroni cheese and vegetarian Glamorgan sausage (made with leek and Caerphilly).

Open all day all wk **Bar Meals** L served all wk 12-8 D served all wk 12-8 Av main course £5.95 food served all day **Restaurant** food served all day ⊕ FREE HOUSE ◀ Over 1,000 real ales per year ♂ Over 40 ciders per year. ☻ 11 **Facilities** Non-diners area ❶ Garden Outside area ﹁ Beer festival Cider festival Wi-fi ﹏

Rab Ha's

83 Hutchieson St G1 1SH ☎ 0141 572 0400
e-mail: management@rabhas.com
dir: *Telephone for directions*

A blend of Victorian character and contemporary Scottish decor

This hotel, restaurant and bar in the heart of Glasgow's revitalised Merchant City takes its name from Robert Hall, a local 19th-century character known as 'The Glasgow Glutton' who would earn a living by taking bets on the amount of food he could consume. The kitchen team prides itself on the extensive use of carefully sourced Scottish produce to create hearty Scottish dishes like breaded Scottish brie; smoked Loch Fyne trout and salmon rillette; Cullen skink; haggis, neeps and tatties; Angus sirloin steak and hand-cut chips; Rab's tomato and seafood broth; and Ailsa Craig cheese salad. The bar menu even lists haggis nachos!

Open all day all wk 12-12 (Sun 12.30-12) **Bar Meals** L served Mon-Thu 12-9, Fri-Sat 12-10, Sun 12.30-9 D served Mon-Thu 12-9, Fri-Sat 12-10, Sun 12.30-9 Av main course £9.50 food served all day **Restaurant** L served Telephone for opening times D served Wed-Sat 5-10 Fixed menu price fr £12.95 Av 3 course à la carte fr £20 ⊕ FREE HOUSE ◀ Tennent's, Blue Moon, West Brewery St Mungos, Budweiser Budvar, Belhaven Best ♂ Addlestones. **Facilities** Non-diners area ❀ (Bar Outside area) ❶ Children's portions Outside area ﹁ Wi-fi ﹏ (notice required)

GLASGOW *continued*

Stravaigin ⊛⊛

PICK OF THE PUBS

26-30 Gibson St G12 8NX ☎ 0141 334 2665
e-mail: stravaigin@btinternet.com
dir: *Telephone for directions*

Encouraging a policy of culinary curiosity

'Stravaig' is an old Scots word meaning 'to wander aimlessly with intent' which fits the Stravaigin's 'think global, eat local' philosophy perfectly. Located in a busy street close to the university, this popular bar/restaurant has picked up two AA Rosettes, and an environmental award. The modern split-level basement restaurant draws the crowds with its contemporary decor, modern art and quirky antiques. The bar offers an extensive wine list and real ales like Fyne Chip 71. Expect innovative and exciting fusion food cooked from top-notch, seasonal Scottish ingredients – the same menu is served throughout. Embracing the flavours of the world are dishes of North Indian chickpea and cumin biscuit stack; Mull cheddar and polenta cakes; Gressingham duck leg massaman curry; haggis, neeps and tatties (veggie version available too); and poppy seed and apple cake for dessert (wines are recommended with each dessert).

Open all day all wk Closed: 25 Dec, 1 Jan **Bar Meals** L served all wk 11-5 D served all wk 5-11 food served all day **Restaurant** L served Sat-Sun 12-5 D served all wk 5-11 ⊕ FREE HOUSE ◀ Caledonian Deuchars IPA, Belhaven Best, Fyne Chip 71 ♂ Westons Wyld Wood Organic Classic. ♟ 19 **Facilities** Non-diners area ♣ (Bar) ♦ Children's menu Children's portions ☴ Wi-fi

Ubiquitous Chip ⊛⊛

PICK OF THE PUBS

12 Ashton Ln G12 8SJ ☎ 0141 334 5007
e-mail: mail@ubiquitouschip.co.uk
dir: *In West End of Glasgow, off Byres Rd. Beside Hillhead subway station*

Scottish country produce in sublime city setting

Down a cobbled mews in the West End, this Glasgow stalwart has been one of the city's most celebrated eateries since 1971. The main dining area opens into a vine-covered courtyard, while upstairs is the brasserie-style, two AA Rosette restaurant. There are three drinking areas: the traditional Big Pub, serving real ales (there's a twice-yearly beer festival here too), nearly 30 wines by the glass and more than 150 malt whiskies; the Wee Bar, which lives up to its name by being possibly the 'wee-est' bar in Scotland; and the Corner Bar, which serves cocktails across a granite slab reclaimed from a mortuary. The various, frequently updated menus draw inspiration from regional Scottish dishes: venison haggis with neeps 'n tatties; Perthshire pigeon breast, golden raisin and caper salsa, port syrup and endive; Loch Melfort mussels steamed in Chip 71 broth, or grilled haunch of roe deer with chocolate crumb setting the standard, with plum and star anise cobbler to finish.

Open all day all wk 11am-1am Closed: 25 Dec, 1 Jan **Bar Meals** L served Mon-Sun 11-5 D served all wk 5-11 Av main course £14 food served all day **Restaurant** L served Mon-Sat 12-2.30, Sun 12.30-3.30 D served all wk 5-11 Fixed menu price fr £19.95 Av 3 course à la carte fr £40 ⊕ FREE HOUSE ◀ Caledonian Deuchars IPA, Fyne Chip 71 ♂ Addlestones. ♟ 29 **Facilities** Non-diners area ♣ (Bar Outside area) ♦ Children's menu Children's portions Outside area ☴ Beer festival Wi-fi ▭ (notice required)

WEST Brewery

PICK OF THE PUBS

Templeton Building, Glasgow Green G40 1AW
☎ 0141 550 0135
e-mail: info@westbeer.com
dir: *Telephone for directions*

Brewery pub with German food

This buzzy brewery pub/restaurant occupies the old Winding House of the former Templeton Carpet Factory, one of Glasgow's most unique Victorian buildings, modelled on the Doge's Palace in Venice. WEST is the only brewery in the UK to produce all of its beers according to the German Purity Law, which means they are free from artificial additives, colourings and preservatives. Look down into the brewhouse from the beer hall and watch the brewers making the lagers and wheat beers, including St Mungo, Dunkel, Munich and Hefeweizen, with equipment imported from Germany. Brewery tours are conducted on selected days of the week. The all-day menu offers German dishes like Wiener schnitzel, spätzle (Bavarian noodles with caramelised onions and melted cheese) and Nuremberg sausages served with sauerkraut. Grills, burgers and British pub grub also feature. For dessert is the adults-only Hefeweizen ice cream, made by hand and infused with their award-winning wheat beer. Brunch is available at weekends. Look out for the Oktoberfest beer festival.

Open all day all wk Closed: 25-26 Dec, 1-2 Jan **Bar Meals** L served all wk 12-5 D served all wk 5-9 **Restaurant** L served all wk 12-5 D served all wk 5-9 ⊕ FREE HOUSE ◀ WEST Munich Red. **Facilities** Non-diners area ♣ (Bar Restaurant Garden) ♦ Children's menu Children's portions Garden ☴ Beer festival ▭ (notice required)

HIGHLAND

ACHILTIBUIE — Map 22 NC00

Summer Isles Hotel & Bar

PICK OF THE PUBS

IV26 2YG ☎ 01854 622282
e-mail: info@summerisleshotel.com
dir: *Take A835 N from Ullapool for 10m, Achiltibuie signed on left, 15m to village. Hotel 1m on left*

Stunning views and peace and quiet

A wild and largely untouched landscape, where the weather can change in days from Arctic to Aegean, provides the backdrop for this highly praised hotel. Fabulous is the only word for the views out to Badentarbat Bay and the Summer Isles. The informal all-day bar serves fresh ground coffee, snacks, lunch, afternoon tea and evening meals, but note that restaurant food is not served between November and March. Where once crofters gathered to drink, today's guests are mostly locals (some of whom may well be crofters) from the scattering of houses along this remote road, plus tourists, of course. Those old farmers are remembered in Crofters' Pale, one of the bar's three An Teallach Ale Company's brews. Nearly everything you eat is home produced, locally caught or at least Scottish – scallops, lobster, langoustines, crab, halibut, turbot, salmon, venison, quail, and Shetland lamb.

Open all wk 11-11 Closed: 31 Oct-3 Apr **Bar Meals** L served all wk 12-3, soup & snacks till 5 D served all wk 6-8.30 **Restaurant** L served Apr-Oct all wk 12.30-2.30 D served Apr-Oct all wk till 8 ⊕ FREE HOUSE ◀ An Teallach Crofters' Pale Ale, Beinn Deorg. ♟ **Facilities** Non-diners area ♣ (Garden) ♦ Children's menu Children's portions Garden ☴ Parking Wi-fi ▭ (notice required)

AVIEMORE — Map 23 NH81

The Old Bridge Inn

Dalfaber Rd PH22 1PU ☎ 01479 811137
e-mail: sayhello@oldbridgeinn.co.uk
dir: *Exit A9 to Aviemore, 1st right into Ski Rd, 1st left, 1st left again in 200mtrs*

Ideal place to relax for outdoor pursuit enthusiasts

Overlooking the River Spey, this friendly pub is in an area popular for outdoor pursuits. Drink in the attractive riverside garden or in the relaxing bars warmed by a roaring log fire. Here malt whiskies naturally have their place, but not to the exclusion of excellent real ales. In winter try a warming seasonal cocktail while perusing the après-ski menu in the comfortable restaurant. After an active day, a Dalfour brown trout starter could easily be followed by roast Gressingham duck with spring onion mash and spring greens. There is a varied music programme with regular funk/soul/disco nights.

Open all day all wk 11am-mdnt (Fri-Sat 11am-1am Sun 12.30-12) ⊕ FREE HOUSE ◀ Caledonian Deuchars IPA, Cairngorm Trade Winds & Black Gold, Atlas Nimbus, Harviestoun Schiehallion ♂ Thistly Cross. **Facilities** ♦ Children's portions Garden Parking Wi-fi

CAWDOR — Map 23 NH85

Cawdor Tavern

PICK OF THE PUBS

See Pick of the Pubs on opposite page

Save on hotels. Book at **theAA.com/hotel**

HIGHLAND 543 SCOTLAND

PICK OF THE PUBS

Cawdor Tavern

CAWDOR Map 23 NH85

The Lane IV12 5XP ☎ **01667 404777**
e-mail: enquiries@cawdortavern.co.uk
web: www.cawdortavern.co.uk
dir: *A96 onto B9006, follow Cawdor
Castle signs. Tavern in village centre*

Scottish innkeeping at its best

The Tavern is tucked away in the heart
of Cawdor's pretty conservation village;
near by is the castle where Macbeth
held court. Pretty wooded countryside
slides away from the pub, offering
umpteen opportunities for rambles and
challenging cycle routes. Exercise over,
repair to this homely hostelry to enjoy
the welcoming mix of fine Scottish food
and island micro-brewery ales that
makes the pub a destination in its own
right. There's an almost baronial feel to
the bars, created from the Cawdor
Estate's joinery workshop in the 1960s.
The lounge bar's wonderful panelling
came from Cawdor Castle's dining room
as a gift from a former laird; log fires
and stoves add winter warmth, as does
the impressive choice of Orkney Brewery
beers and Highland and Island malts.
An accomplished menu balances meat,
fish, game and vegetarian options,
prepared in a modern Scottish style with
first class Scottish produce. Settle in the
delightful restaurant beneath wrought
iron Jacobean chandeliers and
contemplate starting with a trio of
Scottish puddings – black pudding,

prize haggis and white pudding layered
together and served with home-made
chutney. Next maybe a venison burger
from the grill, topped with smoked
bacon, tomato relish and melting
mozzarella. Classic sweets include
sticky toffee pudding, and chocolate
brownie with warm chocolate sauce.
Alfresco drinking and dining is possible
on the colourful patio area at the front
of the Tavern during the warm summer
months. Excellent value is a Sunday
high tea starting at 4.30pm.

Open all wk 11-3 5-11 (Sat 11am-mdnt
Sun 12.30-11) all day in summer
Closed: 25 Dec, 1 Jan **Bar Meals** L
served Mon-Sat 12-2, Sun 12.30-3 (all
day summer) D served all wk 5.30-9 (all
day summer) **Restaurant** L served Mon-

Sat 12-2, Sun 12.30-3 (all day summer)
D served all wk 5.30-9 (all day summer)
⊕ FREE HOUSE ◼ Orkney Red
MacGregor, Raven Ale, Clootie Dumpling
& Dark Island, Atlas Latitude Highland
Pilsner, Three Sisters, Nimbus &
Wayfarer ♂ Thatchers Gold. ♟ 9
Facilities Non-diners area ♥ (Bar
Outside area) ♦♦ Children'smenu &
portions Outside area ㅈ Beer festival
Parking Wi-fi ▬ (notice required)

FORTROSE — Map 23 NH75

The Anderson

PICK OF THE PUBS

Union St IV10 8TD ☎ 01381 620236
e-mail: info@theanderson.co.uk
dir: *From Inverness take A9 N signed Wick. Right onto B9161 signed Munlochy, Cromarty & A832. At T-junct right onto A832 to Fortrose*

Coastal conservation village on the Black Isle

On the beautiful Black Isle to the north of Inverness, this striking black-and-white painted pub enjoys a tranquil seaside setting; a short walk from its door passes the gaunt, ruined cathedral before happening on the picturesque harbour at Fortrose, with sweeping views across the Moray Firth. Nearby Chanonry Point lighthouse is renowned as one of the best places from which to watch the dolphins in the Firth. But why leave an inn famed for its classic range of finest Scottish microbrewery beers, vast array of Belgian beers and 230 single malts selected by American proprietor Jim Anderson? The 'global cuisine' created with freshest Scottish produce is equally comprehensive. Aberdeen beef, West Coast seafood and Highland game are amongst dishes on the daily-changing menu: seafood chowder or fried ravioli are typical starters, followed perhaps by Stornoway guinea fowl stuffed with Munro's white pudding and served with a creamy leek and cider sauce. You could finish with apple rhubarb crumble tartlet with vanilla ice cream.

Open all wk 4pm-11pm Closed: mid Nov-mid Dec **Bar Meals** D served all wk 6-9.30 **Restaurant** D served all wk 6-9.30 ⊕ FREE HOUSE ◀ Rotating ales ♂ Addlestones, Moorlands Farm. ♟ 13 **Facilities** Non-diners area ♣ (Bar Garden) ♦ Children's menu Garden ⋒ Beer festival Parking Wi-fi

FORT WILLIAM — Map 22 NN17

Moorings Hotel ★★★★ HL ◉

Banavie PH33 7LY ☎ 01397 772797
e-mail: reservations@moorings-fortwilliam.co.uk
web: www.moorings-fortwilliam.co.uk
dir: *From A82 in Fort William follow signs for Mallaig, then left onto A830 for 1m. Cross canal bridge then 1st right signed Banavie*

Canalside spot with panoramic views

The historic Caledonian Canal and Neptune's Staircase, the famous flight of eight locks, runs right beside this

modern hotel and pub. On clear days it has panoramic views towards Ben Nevis; the view is best savoured from the Upper Deck lounge bar and the bedrooms. Food, served in the nautically themed Mariners cellar bar, the lounge and the fine-dining Jacobean Restaurant, features local fish and seafood. Dishes in the bar and lounge include a trio of Highland salmon; lamb rogan josh; and banoffee pie. There is access to the canal towpath from the gardens.

Open all day all wk Closed: 24-26 Dec **Bar Meals** L served all wk 12-9.30 D served all wk 12-9.30 Av main course £12 food served all day **Restaurant** D served all wk 7-9.30 Fixed menu price fr £30 ⊕ FREE HOUSE ◀ Tetley's Bitter, Caledonian Deuchars IPA, Guinness ♂ Blackthorn. ♟ 8 **Facilities** Non-diners area ♣ (Garden) ♦ Children's menu Garden ⋒ Parking Wi-fi ⇔ (notice required) **Rooms** 27

GAIRLOCH — Map 22 NG87

The Old Inn

PICK OF THE PUBS

IV21 2BD ☎ 01445 712006
e-mail: info@theoldinn.net
dir: *Just off A832, near harbour at south end of village*

Traditional Highland coaching inn overlooking harbour

Gairloch's oldest hostelry enjoys a wonderful setting at the foot of the Flowerdale Valley with views of the Outer Hebrides. Built in 1750, it was once a changing post for horses but now attracts herds of outdoor enthusiasts, especially walkers. Owner Alastair Pearson opened the pub's very own on-site microbrewery in 2010, so expect the pints of The Slattadale, The Flowerdale, Blind Piper and The Erradale to be in tip-top condition at the bar. It's not just the beer that's home-made: the pub has its own smokery producing smoked meats, fish and cheese, and bread is baked in-house. Local fish and game feature strongly on menus that run from simple grills and hearty home-made pies to pizza and pasta dishes. Picnic tables on the large grassy area by the stream make an attractive spot for eating and enjoying the views. Dogs are welcomed with bowls, baskets and rugs to help them feel at home.

Open all day all wk 11am-mdnt (Sun 12-12) **Bar Meals** L served all wk 12-2.30, summer 12-4.30 D served all wk 5-9.30 **Restaurant** D served all wk 6-9.30 ⊕ FREE HOUSE ◀ The Old Inn The Erradale, The Flowerdale, The Slattadale, Three Sisters & Blind Piper, Adnams Southwold Bitter, An Teallach Crofters' Pale Ale, Cairngorm Trade Winds. **Facilities** Non-diners area ♣ (Bar Garden) ♦ Children's menu Children's portions Garden ⋒ Parking Wi-fi ⇔ (notice required)

GLENCOE — Map 22 NN15

Clachaig Inn

PH49 4HX ☎ 01855 811252
e-mail: frontdesk@clachaig.com
dir: *Follow Glencoe signs from A82. Inn 3m S of village*

Real craic at this legendary Highland inn

In the heart of Glencoe, against a backdrop of spectacular mountains, this famous Highland inn has welcomed climbers, hill-walkers, skiers, kayakers and regular travellers for over 300 years. Real ales (sometimes as many as 15), nearly 300 malt whiskies, good food and fresh coffee are served in all three bars, each with its own distinctive and lively character. Local dishes on offer include Stornoway black pudding; oak-smoked West Coast salmon; Highland venison burger; and vegetarian haggis, neeps 'n' tatties. As well as beer and whisky tastings, the pub also holds a Hogmanay beer festival, and two others — FebFest and OctoberFest.

Open all day all wk Closed: 24-26 Dec **Bar Meals** L served all wk 12-9 D served all wk 12-9 food served all day ⊕ FREE HOUSE ◀ Local ales (up to 15 at one time) ♂ Westons. **Facilities** Non-diners area ♣ (Bar Garden) ♦ Children's menu Children's portions Play area Family room Garden ⋒ Beer festival Parking Wi-fi ⇔

GLENUIG — Map 22 NM67

Glenuig Inn

PH38 4NG ☎ 01687 470219
e-mail: bookings@glenuig.com
dir: *From Fort William on A830 towards Mallaig. Left onto A861, 8m to Glenuig Bay*

A more spectacular setting you couldn't wish for

Completely renovated but retaining walls dating back to around 1746 and Bonnie Prince Charlie's time, the Glenuig Inn is now a popular base for sea-kayakers drawn to the stunning beaches in the Sound of Arisaig. The emphasis here is 'as local as we can get it' and this philosophy applies to the bar, where only local real ale from Cairngorm is served, and the kitchen, where menus are prepared using organic seasonal ingredients wherever possible. A typical selection might include Glenuig hot smoked salmon, followed by Skye lamb tagine or home-made venison burger, and chocolate and chilli tart to finish. The inn is commited to 'going green' in everything they do.

Open all day all wk **Bar Meals** food served all day **Restaurant** food served all day ⊕ FREE HOUSE ◀ Cairngorm Trade Winds, Black Gold & Wild Cat ♂ Thistly Cross. ♟ 9 **Facilities** Non-diners area ♣ (Bar Restaurant Garden) ♦ Children's menu Children's portions Play area Family room Garden ⋒ Parking Wi-fi

PICK OF THE PUBS

The Plockton Hotel ★★★ SHL

Harbour St IV52 8TN ☎ 01599 544274
e-mail: info@plocktonhotel.co.uk
web: www.plocktonhotel.co.uk
dir: *A87 towards Kyle of Lochalsh. At Balmacara follow Plockton signs, 7m*

Award-winning local seafood served here

After two decades of running this award-winning harbourside hotel, Dorothy and Tom Pearson retired, making way for son Alan to carry on where his parents left off. Dating from 1827, the original black fronted building is thought to have been a ships' chandlery before it was converted to serve as the village inn. Set with the mountains on one side and the deep blue waters of Loch Carron on the other, this lovely village is well known for its white-washed cottages and, of all things, palm trees. The hotel specialises in seafood – including freshly landed fish and locally caught langoustines – supplemented by Highland steaks and locally reared beef. Lunchtime features light bites, warm bloomers and toasted paninis, as well as hot main dishes ranging from Talisker whisky pâté; traditional pan-fried herring in oatmeal; or Highland burger stuffed with haggis and cheese. Evening choices might include haggis served with a tot of whisky; smoked salmon platter; or

Plockton smokies – a hot starter of flaked smoked mackerel layered with cream, cheese and tomatoes. Typical main courses include casserole of Highland venison cooked in red wine, herbs, juniper berries and redcurrant jelly; fillet of monkfish wrapped in bacon; chargrilled Aberdeen Angus steak with whisky sauce; or supreme of chicken stuffed with Argyle smoked ham and cheese. A fine range of malts is available to round off that perfect Highland day, perhaps accompanied by one of the 'basket' meals served every evening from 9pm-10pm – try the breaded scampi tails.

Open all day all wk 11am-mdnt (Sun 12.30-11) Closed: 25 Dec, 1 Jan

Bar Meals L served Mon-Sat 12-2.15, Sun 12.30-2.15 D served all wk 6-10 **Restaurant** L served Mon-Sat 12-2.15, Sun 12.30-2.15 D served all wk 6-9 🛢 FREE HOUSE ◼ Plockton Bay & Crags Ale, Houston, Cromarty Ales, Inveralmond. **Facilities** Non-diners area ♦♦ Children's menu Children's portions Family room Garden ⋒ Wi-fi **Rooms** 15

INVERGARRY Map 22 NH30

The Invergarry Inn

PH35 4HJ ☎ 01809 501206
e-mail: info@invergarryhotel.co.uk
dir: At junct of A82 & A87

In a tranquil spot, ideal for walking

A real Highland atmosphere pervades this roadside inn set in glorious mountain scenery between Fort William and Fort Augustus. Welcoming bars make it a great base from which to explore Loch Ness, Glencoe and the West Coast. Relax by the crackling log fire with a wee dram or a pint of Garry Ale, then tuck into a good meal. Perhaps try Lochaber haggis, bashit neeps and tatties to start; followed by sea bream en papillote or a succulent 10oz rib-eye Scottish beefsteak and hand-cut chips. There are, of course, excellent walks from the front door. Booking required for dinner.

Open all day all wk **Bar Meals** L served all wk 8am-9.30pm D served all wk 8am-9.30pm Av main course £15 food served all day **Restaurant** L served all wk 8am-9.30pm D served all wk 8am-9.30pm food served all day ⊕ FREE HOUSE ◀ The Invergarry Inn Garry Ale, Timothy Taylor, Guinness. **Facilities** Non-diners area ♦️ Children's menu Children's portions Family room Garden ╱ Parking

INVERIE Map 22 NG70

The Old Forge

PH41 4PL ☎ 01687 462267
e-mail: info@theoldforge.co.uk
dir: From Fort William take A830 (Road to the Isles) towards Mallaig. Take ferry from Mallaig to Inverie

Moor up for true Highland hospitality

Britain's most remote mainland pub is – ironically - only accessible by boat (unless you're in the mood for an 18-hour hike). It stands literally between heaven and hell; Loch Nevis is Gaelic for heaven and Loch Hourn is Gaelic for hell. It's popular with everyone from locals to hill walkers, and is renowned for its impromptu ceilidhs. It is also the ideal place to sample local fish and seafood and there's no better way than choosing the seafood platter of rope mussels, langoustines, oak-smoked salmon and smoked trout. Other dishes might include smoked venison salad with home-made red onion marmalade; home-made haggis lasagne; and crème brûlée for dessert. There are 12 boat moorings and a daily ferry from Mallaig. (Contact inn for details).

Open all day all wk ⊕ FREE HOUSE ◀ Guinness, Guest ales. **Facilities** ♣ (Bar Restaurant Garden) ♦️ Children's menu Children's portions Play area Family room Garden Parking Wi-fi

KYLESKU Map 22 NC23

Kylesku Hotel

PICK OF THE PUBS

IV27 4HW ☎ 01971 502231
e-mail: info@kyleskuhotel.co.uk
dir: A835, A837 & A894 to Kylesku. Hotel at end of road at Old Ferry Pier

Waterside inn with wonderful seafood

At the centre of the North West Highlands Global Geopark – 2,000 square kilometres of lochs, mountains and wild coast – and close to Britain's highest waterfall, this former 17th-century coaching inn enjoys a glorious location. Views from the bar and restaurant are truly memorable – you may catch sight of seals, dolphins, otters, eagles and terns. The fishing boats moor at the old ferry slipway to land the creel-caught seafood that forms the backbone of the daily-changing chalkboard menu. So settle down with a pint of An Teallach or Isle of Skye real ale, and ponder your choice of the morning's catch. You could start with hand-dived Summer Isles scallops with truffle celeriac purée and black pudding bonbons followed by Loch Duart salmon tempura with wasabi mayonnaise, apple and coriander salad. Meat lovers could try grilled Scottish rib eye with béarnaise, cracked pepper and chips; or roasted duck breast, fondant potato, spiced red cabbage and mandarin jus.

Open all day all wk Closed: Nov-Feb **Bar Meals** L served all wk 12-6 D served all wk 6-9 Av main course £15 food served all day **Restaurant** D served all wk 7-9 ⊕ FREE HOUSE ◀ An Teallach, Isle of Skye. ♈ 12 **Facilities** Non-diners area ♣ (Bar Restaurant Garden) ♦️ Children's menu Children's portions Garden ╱ Wi-fi

NORTH BALLACHULISH Map 22 NN06

Loch Leven Hotel

Old Ferry Rd PH33 6SA ☎ 01855 821236
e-mail: reception@lochlevenhotel.co.uk
dir: Off A82, N of Ballachulish Bridge

A hotel with one of Scotland's most idyllic views

The slipway into Loch Leven at the foot of the garden recalls the origins of this 17th-century inn as one of the Road to The Isles staging points linked to the old ferry. Sip beers from Cairngorm Brewery or a wee dram from a choice of over 60 malts while enjoying the warmth of the open fire, or make the most of the terrace and garden when the sun's out. The extraordinary location, near the foot of Glencoe and with horizons peppered by Munro peaks rising above azure sea lochs, is gifted with superb seafood from the local depths. Indulge in tiger prawn stir-fry, smoked haddock fishcake and smoked salmon with Scottish oatcakes. Adjoining the traditional bar are family and games rooms.

Open all day all wk 11-11 (Thu-Sat 11am-mdnt Sun 12.30-11) **Bar Meals** L served all wk 12-3 D served all wk 6-9 Av main course £10 **Restaurant** L served all wk 12-3 D served all wk 6-9 Fixed menu price fr £15 Av 3 course à la carte fr £20 ⊕ FREE HOUSE ◀ Cairngorm, Atlas, River

Leven. **Facilities** Non-diners area ♣ (Bar Garden) ♦️ Children's menu Children's portions Play area Family room Garden ╱ Parking Wi-fi 🚐 (notice required)

PLOCKTON Map 22 NG83

The Plockton Hotel ★★★ SHL

PICK OF THE PUBS

See Pick of the Pubs on page 545

Plockton Inn & Seafood Restaurant

PICK OF THE PUBS

See Pick of the Pubs on opposite page

SHIELDAIG Map 22 NG85

Shieldaig Bar & Coastal Kitchen ★ HL ◉◉

PICK OF THE PUBS

IV54 8XN ☎ 01520 755251
e-mail: tighaneilean@keme.co.uk
dir: Exit A896

Lochside bar and restaurant in a tiny village

In a remote and peaceful location is the famous Tigh an Eilean Hotel, of which the Shieldaig Bar & Coastal Kitchen is part. Here, the magnificent Torridon Mountains meet the western seas; offshore is Shieldaig Island, while Upper Loch Torridon is just round the corner. An abundance of wildlife is visible from this extraordinary waterside setting – otters and seals, white-tailed sea eagles, oyster catchers, pine martens to name but a few. An Teallach Brewery supplies the traditional bar, where live music and ceilidhs add a weekend buzz. The sea provides much of what appears on the menu, especially the shellfish landed daily by fishermen who employ environmentally responsible creel-fishing and hand-diving techniques. Ways of sampling this local bounty include seafood stew and fisherman's pie, while among the other dishes are home-made beefburgers and wood-fired hand-made pizzas. Outside by the loch is a courtyard with benches and tables where you can watch the spectacular sunsets.

Open all day all wk **Bar Meals** L served all wk 12-2.30 D served all wk 6-9 **Restaurant** L served all wk 12-2.30 D served all wk 6-9 ⊕ FREE HOUSE ◀ An Teallach. ♈ 8 **Facilities** Non-diners area ♦️ Children's menu Children's portions Garden ╱ Parking Wi-fi 🚐 (notice required) **Rooms** 11

Save on hotels. Book at **theAA.com/hotel**

HIGHLAND 547 SCOTLAND

PICK OF THE PUBS

Plockton Inn & Seafood Restaurant

PLOCKTON Map 22 NG83

Innes St IV52 8TW ☎ **01599 544222**
e-mail: info@plocktoninn.co.uk
web: www.plocktoninn.co.uk
dir: *A87 towards Kyle of Lochalsh. At Balmacara follow Plockton signs, 7m*

Friendly inn offering great seafood

Located in Plockton which is on Loch Carron in the West Highlands, this inn is owned and run by Mary Gollan, her brother Kenny and his partner Susan Trowbridge. The Gollans were born and bred in the village and it was actually their great-grandfather who built the attractive stone free house as a manse. The beautiful views can be enjoyed from seats on the decking outside. The ladies double up in the role of chef, while Kenny manages the bar, where you'll find winter fires, Plockton real ales from the village brewery, and a selection of over 50 malt whiskies. A meal in the reasonably formal Dining Room or more relaxed Lounge Bar is a must, with a wealth of freshly caught local fish and shellfish, West Highland beef, lamb, game and home-made vegetarian dishes on the menu, plus daily specials. The Plockton prawns (called langoustines here), which Martin the barman catches in the sea loch, are taken to Kenny's smokehouse to the rear of the building to be cured along with other seafood — the results can be

sampled in the seafood platter starter. Other starters include oysters, vegetarian antipasti and moules marinière. Among the main dishes are langoustines, served hot with garlic butter or cold with Marie Rose sauce; pan-fried hand-dived king scallops with bacon, garlic and cream; roast vegetable bake; and haggis and clapshot. Desserts include chocolate ginger torte and Scottish cheeses served with Orkney oatcakes. The public bar is alive on Tuesdays and Thursdays with music from local musicians, who are often joined by talented youngsters from the National Centre of Excellence in Traditional Music in the village.

Open all day all wk **Bar Meals** L served all wk 12-2.30 D served all wk 6-9 Av main course £10 **Restaurant** D served all wk 6-9 Av 3 course à la carte fr £23 🍺 FREE HOUSE 🍺 Greene King Abbot Ale, Fuller's London Pride, Young's Special, Plockton Crags Ale & Bay. **Facilities** Non-diners area 🐾 👬 Children's menu Children's portions Play area Garden 🎋 Parking Wi-fi 🚌 (notice required)

TORRIDON
Map 22 NG95

The Torridon Inn ★★★★ INN

PICK OF THE PUBS

IV22 2EY ☎ 01445 791242

e-mail: info@thetorridon.com

dir: *From Inverness take A9 N, then follow signs to Ullapool. Take A835 then A832. In Kinlochewe take A896 to Annat. Pub 200yds on right after village*

Idyllic location and home-cooked food

Stunning views of the rugged Torridon Mountains are guaranteed from this hostelry's location close to the loch shores. It makes it a convenient base for active types who want to walk, mountaineer, kayak or rock climb, but its cosy comfortable atmosphere and good home-cooked food very much appeal to the less active too. Created from converting old farm buildings, a stable block and buttery, the inn holds a popular ale festival in October; there's a good range of local beer on tap, such as Isle of Sky Red Cuillin, own blend Torridon Ale and Cromarty Happy Chappy, all year round, not forgetting a selection of over 80 whiskies. The kitchen prides itself on sourcing 90% of produce from within an hour's drive so you might find Isle of Ewe smoked salmon, caper and shallot dressing and toasted muffin, then chargrilled Macbeth's Highland 10oz rump steak, grilled tomato, field mushroom, battered onion ring and chips on the menu.

Open all day all wk Closed: Jan **Bar Meals** L served all wk 12-2 D served all wk 6-9 **Restaurant** L served all wk 12-2 D served all wk 6-9 ⊕ FREE HOUSE ◀ Isle of Skye Red Cuillin, Torridon Ale, Cairngorm Trade Winds, An Teallach & Crofters Pale Ale, Cromarty Happy Chappy.
Facilities Non-diners area ⚬♦ Children's menu Children's portions Play area Garden ⊼ Beer festival Parking Wi-fi ▭ (notice required) **Rooms** 12

MIDLOTHIAN

DALKEITH
Map 21 NT36

The Sun Inn ★★★★ INN ⚙

PICK OF THE PUBS

Lothian Bridge EH22 4TR ☎ 0131 663 2456

e-mail: thesuninn@live.co.uk

dir: *On A7 towards Galashiels, opposite Newbattle Viaduct*

A thoroughly modern gastro-pub

This family-run former coaching inn stands in wooded grounds close to the banks of the River Esk. The owners have blended the original fireplace, oak beams and exposed stone walls with wooden floors and feature wallpapers. Scottish cask ales have pride of place behind the bar, which also offers an extensive wine list. Food in the more formal restaurant is modern British, masterminded by owner and head chef Ian Minto and his son Craig. Locally sourced Scottish ingredients form the backbone of the menus, with lunchtime offerings including moules marinière, pheasant and ham pie, and pan-seared fillet of salmon. At dinner, smoked salmon mousse with watercress purée, smoked trout and horseradish croquettes and mustard cress could precede a main course special of confit chicken leg, fondant potato, chestnut mushrooms, smoked pancetta, artichoke purée and a red wine jus. A bright summer patio and five individually styled en suite bedrooms complete the picture.

Open all day all wk Closed: 26 Dec, 1 Jan **Bar Meals** L served Mon-Sat 12-2, Sun 12-7 D served Mon-Sat 6-9, Sun 12-7 **Restaurant** L served Mon-Sat 12-2, Sun 12-7 D served Mon-Sat 6-9, Sun 12-7 ⊕ FREE HOUSE ◀ Caledonian Deuchars IPA, Belhaven Best, Inveralmond Ŏ Addlestones. ⓟ 28 **Facilities** Non-diners area ⚬♦ Children's menu Children's portions Garden ⊼ Parking Wi-fi **Rooms** 5

PENICUIK
Map 21 NT25

The Howgate Restaurant

Howgate EH26 8PY ☎ 01968 670000

e-mail: peter@howgate.com

dir: *10m N of Peebles. 3m E of Penicuik on A6094 between Leadburn junct & Howgate*

Fine food and ales in a former dairy

Formerly the home of Howgate cheeses, this beautifully converted farm building has a fire-warmed bar offering bistro-style meals, while the candlelit restaurant serves a full carte. The kitchen uses the finest Scottish produce, especially beef and lamb, which are cooked in the charcoal grill; other options might include Howgate chicken liver and smoked bacon pâté with beetroot chutney and Scottish oatcakes; traditional Scotch beef, Belhaven and mushroom pie with hand-cut chips; and coconut bread-and-butter pudding with vanilla ice cream. There are fine beers to enjoy and an impressively produced wine list roams the globe.

Open all wk 12-2 6-9.30 Closed: 25-26 Dec, 1 Jan **Bar Meals** L served all wk 12-2 D served all wk 6-9.30 Av main course £9.95 **Restaurant** L served all wk 12-2 D served all wk 6-9.30 Av 3 course à la carte fr £25 ⊕ FREE HOUSE ◀ Belhaven Best, Hoegaarden. ⓟ 14 **Facilities** ⚬♦ Children's portions Garden ⊼ Parking Wi-fi ▭ (notice required)

ROSLIN
Map 21 NT26

The Original Rosslyn Inn ★★★★ INN

2-4 Main St EH25 9LE ☎ 0131 440 2384

e-mail: enquiries@theoriginalhotel.co.uk

dir: *Off city bypass at Straiton for A703*

A perfect escape from the city and a stone's throw from Rosslyn Chapel

Just eight miles from central Edinburgh and a short walk from Rosslyn Chapel, this family-run village inn has been in the Harris family for 38 years. Robert Burns, the famous Scottish poet, stayed here in 1787 and wrote a two verse poem for the landlady about his visit. Today you have the chance to catch up with the locals in the village bar, or relax by the fire in the lounge whilst choosing from the menu. Soups, jackets and paninis are supplemented by main course options like haggis with tatties and neeps; breaded haddock and chips; and vegetarian harvester pie. Alternatively, the Grail Restaurant offers more comprehensive dining options. There are well-equipped bedrooms, four with four-posters.

Open all day all wk **Bar Meals** L served all wk 12-9.15 D served all wk 12-9.15 Av main course £8 food served all day **Restaurant** L served all wk 12-9.15 D served all wk 12-9.15 food served all day ⊕ FREE HOUSE ◀ Belhaven Best. ⓟ 14 **Facilities** Non-diners area ⚬ (Bar Garden) ⚬♦ Children's menu Children's portions Garden ⊼ Parking Wi-fi ▭ **Rooms** 7

MORAY

FOCHABERS
Map 23 NJ35

Gordon Arms Hotel

80 High St IV32 7DH ☎ 01343 820508

e-mail: enquiries@gordonarms.co.uk

dir: *A96 approx halfway between Aberdeen & Inverness, 9m from Elgin*

Origianl character and close to the Whisky Trail

This 200-year-old former coaching inn, close to the River Spey and within easy reach of Speyside's whisky distilleries, is understandably popular with salmon fishers, golfers and walkers. The hotel makes an ideal base from which to explore this scenic corner of Scotland. The cuisine makes full use of local produce: venison, lamb and game from the uplands, fish and seafood from the Moray coast, beef from Aberdeenshire and salmon from the Spey - barely a stone's throw from the kitchen!

Open all day all wk 11-11 (Thu 11am-mdnt Fri-Sat 11am-12.30am) ⊕ FREE HOUSE ◀ Caledonian Deuchars IPA, John Smith's Extra Smooth, Guest ales. **Facilities** ⚬♦ Parking

FORRES
Map 23 NJ06

The Old Mill Inn NEW

Brodie IV36 2TD ☎ **01309 641605**
dir: *Between Nairn & Forres on A96*

Spacious, family-friendly pub and restaurant

Two areas lay claim to the Scottish Riviera title because of their unusually high (for Scotland, that is) sunshine hours; the coast between Nairn and Forres – that's here – and Galloway. A watermill until 1960, the pub has somehow managed to acquire windows, panelling and a beautiful door from a demolished stately home across the Moray Firth. There's a wide choice of food, from chargrills to boneless salmon cutlets, and from Scottish tapas to marinated rump of lamb. Delivering an ever-changing selection of Scottish real ales are the bar's five hand-pumps; many more can be tried during the June beer festival.

Open all day all wk Closed: 25-26 Dec, 1 Jan **Bar Meals** L served all wk 11.30-5 D served all wk 5-9 food served all day **Restaurant** D served Tue-Sat 5.30-9, Sun 5.30-8 🍺 Rotating Guest Ales. **Facilities** 🛉 Children's menu Children's portions Garden 🍺 Beer festival Parking Wi-fi 🚌 (notice required)

NORTH LANARKSHIRE

CUMBERNAULD
Map 21 NS77

Castlecary House Hotel

Castlecary Rd G68 0HD ☎ **01324 840233**
e-mail: enquiries@castlecaryhotel.com
dir: *A80 onto B816 between Glasgow & Stirling. 7m from Falkirk, 9m from Stirling*

Friendly, family-run hotel

Castlecary House Hotel is located close to the historic Antonine Wall and the Forth and Clyde Canal. Meals in the four lounge bars plough a traditional furrow with options such as deep-fried black pudding balls, bangers and mash, and baked gammon. Home-made puddings include sticky toffee pudding and profiteroles. More formal fare is available in Camerons Restaurant, where high tea is served on Sundays. There is an excellent selection of real ales on offer, including Arran Blonde and Harviestoun Bitter. A beer festival is held once or twice a year – contact the hotel for details.

Open all day all wk Closed: 1 Jan **Bar Meals** L served 12-9 D served 12-9 Av main course £8 food served all day **Restaurant** L served Sun 12.30-3 D served Mon-Sat 6-9.30 Fixed menu price fr £10.95 Av 3 course à la carte fr £15 ⊕ FREE HOUSE 🍺 Arran Blonde, Harviestoun Bitter & Twisted, Inveralmond Ossian's Ale, Houston Peter's Well, Caledonian Deuchars IPA. ☗ 8 **Facilities** Non-diners area 🛉 Children's menu Children's portions Garden Beer festival Parking Wi-fi 🚌

PERTH & KINROSS

GLENFARG
Map 21 NO11

The Famous Bein Inn ★★★ INN ◉

PH2 9PY ☎ **01577 830216**
e-mail: enquiries@beininn.com
dir: *From S: M90 junct 8, A91 towards Cupar. Left onto B996 to Bein Inn. From N: M90 junct 9, A912 towards Gateside*

Relaxed atmosphere and alfresco dining in warmer weather

Standing by the river in the glorious wooded Glen of Farg, this former drovers' inn is just minutes from the M90. While enjoying a refreshing pint of Inveralmond ale by the log fire or out on the sundeck, choose from the list of locally sourced and freshly prepared food served all day from midday. Awarded one AA Rosette, the Balvaird Restaurant is the place to taste rib-eye steak with peppercorn sauce, while plates in the bistro range from chicken liver parfait to coq au vin, pork belly with apple and cinnamon purée, and sticky toffee pudding with toffee sauce.

Open all day all wk Closed: 25-26 Dec ⊕ FREE HOUSE 🍺 Belhaven Best, Inveralmond, Guinness, Tennent's. **Facilities** 🛉 Children's menu Children's portions Garden Parking Wi-fi **Rooms** 11

KILLIECRANKIE
Map 23 NN96

Killiecrankie House
Hotel ★★★ SHL ◉◉

PICK OF THE PUBS

PH16 5LG ☎ **01796 473220**
e-mail: enquiries@killiecrankiehotel.co.uk
dir: *Take B8079 N from Pitlochry. Hotel in 3m*

Historic venue in stunning location

This white-painted Victorian manse gleams amidst woodland at the Pass of Killiecrankie, the gateway to The Highlands. This magnificent gorge, famed for the battle in 1689 when the Jacobites routed the forces of King William III, is a stronghold for red squirrels and a renowned birdwatching area. There are countless walks into the hills, including majestic Ben Vrackie rising behind the hotel, riverside walks and the nearby lochs in the Tummel Valley, with a garland of shapely mountains. Standing in a four-acre estate, the hotel retains much of its old character and successfully blends it with modern comforts. The cosy, wood-panelled bar is a popular haunt, while the snug sitting room opens on to a small patio. Arm yourself with a beer from the likes of Orkney or Belhaven as you study a menu that makes the most of Scotland's diverse produce and which has gained the restaurant two AA Rosettes.

Open all day all wk Closed: Jan & Feb **Bar Meals** L served all wk 12.30-2 D served all wk 6.30-8.30 **Restaurant** D served all wk 6.30-8.30 ⊕ FREE HOUSE 🍺 Orkney Red MacGregor, Caledonian Best, Belhaven Best ♂ Thistly Cross. ☗ 8 **Facilities** Non-diners area 🛉 Children's menu Garden 🍺 Parking **Rooms** 10

PITLOCHRY
Map 23 NN95

Moulin Hotel

PICK OF THE PUBS

11-13 Kirkmichael Rd, Moulin PH16 5EH
☎ **01796 472196**
e-mail: enquiries@moulinhotel.co.uk
dir: *From A9 at Pitlochry take A924. Moulin 0.75m*

Hearty local food in prime walking country

Dating from 1695, this welcoming inn located on an old drovers' road at the foot of Ben Vrackie is a popular base for walking and touring. Locals are drawn to the bar for the excellent home-brewed beers, with Ale of Atholl, Braveheart, Moulin Light, and Belhaven Best served on handpump. The interior boasts beautiful stone walls and lots of cosy niches, with blazing log fires in winter; while the courtyard garden is lovely in summer. Menus offer the opportunity to try something local such as mince and tatties; venison Braveheart (strips of local venison pan-fried with mushrooms and Braveheart beer); and Vrackie Grostel (sautéed potatoes with smoked bacon lightly herbed and topped with a fried egg). You might then round off your meal with Highland honey sponge and custard. A specials board broadens the choice further. Over 20 wines by the glass and more than 30 malt whiskies are available.

Open all day all wk 11-11 (Fri-Sat 11am-11.45pm Sun 12-11) **Bar Meals** L served all wk 12-9.30 D served all wk 12-9.30 Av main course £9 food served all day **Restaurant** D served all wk 6-9 Fixed menu price fr £23.50 Av 3 course à la carte fr £26 ⊕ FREE HOUSE 🍺 Moulin Braveheart, Old Remedial, Ale of Atholl & Moulin Light, Belhaven Best. ☗ 25 **Facilities** Non-diners area 🛉 Children's menu Children's portions Garden 🍺 Parking Wi-fi 🚌 (notice required)

RENFREWSHIRE

HOUSTON
Map 20 NS46

Fox & Hounds

South St PA6 7EN ☎ **01505 612448**
e-mail: houstonbrewerysales@gmail.com
dir: *M8 junct 29, A737 signed Irvine. Take A761 signed Bridge of Weir, then follow Houston signs. Pub in village centre*

Own microbrewery and home-made food

This welcoming old coaching inn, now changed hands, is very much at the heart of the attractive village of Houston, and pulls in the plaudits for the beers which flow from its microbrewer. The menu in the bar and restaurant displays a range of home-made dishes.

Open all day all wk 11am-mdnt (Fri-Sat 11am-1am Sun fr 12.30) **Bar Meals** L served all wk 12-5 D served Mon-Sat 5-10, Sun 5-9 food served all day **Restaurant** L served all wk 12-5 D served Mon-Sat 5-10, Sun 5-9 food served all day ⊕ FREE HOUSE ◀ Houston Killellan, Houston Peter's Well, Houston Barochan. ♟ 10 **Facilities** Non-diners area ♦♦ Children's menu Children's portions Outside area ⊼ Parking Wi-fi ▭ (notice required)

SCOTTISH BORDERS

ALLANTON
Map 21 NT85

Allanton Inn

TD11 3JZ ☎ **01890 818260**
e-mail: info@allantoninn.co.uk
dir: *From A1 at Berwick take A6105 for Chirnside (5m). At Chirnside Inn take Coldstream Rd for 1m to Allanton*

Informal dining in family-run Borders pub

Wooden floors, contemporary furnishings, artworks, subtle lighting and that all-important log fire characterise this 18th-century coaching inn. A huge silver spoon and fork dominate one wall of the modern bar, a subtle hint perhaps to study the menu, while enjoying that pint of Inveralmond Ossian. Beef may come from the family farm and the fish is fresh from Eyemouth, while receiving the garden smokehouse treatment are pork, salmon, chicken and even cheeses. Daily blackboard specials add to a regularly changing menu that typically features breast of Barbary duck, and game in season. A large garden with fruit trees overlooks open countryside.

Open all day all wk 12-11 Closed: 2wks Feb (dates vary) **Bar Meals** L served all wk 12-3 D served all wk 6-9 **Restaurant** L served all wk 12-3 D served all wk 6-9 ⊕ FREE HOUSE ◀ Inveralmond Ossian, Scottish Borders Game Bird, Harviestoun Bitter & Twisted, Fyne Piper's Gold. ♟ 10 **Facilities** Non-diners area ♦♦ Children's menu Children's portions Garden ⊼ Wi-fi

GALASHIELS
Map 21 NT43

Kingsknowes Hotel ★★★ HL

1 Selkirk Rd TD1 3HY ☎ **01896 758375**
e-mail: enquiries@kingsknowes.co.uk
dir: *Exit A7 at Galashiels/Selkirk rdbt*

Traditional food on banks of the Tweed

An imposing Scots baronial mansion dating from 1869, The Kingsknowes is set in over three acres of grounds on the banks of the Tweed with lovely views of the Eildon Hills and Abbotsford House, Sir Walter Scott's ancestral home. Meals are served in two restaurants and the Courtyard Bar, where fresh local or regional produce is used as much as possible. Typical choices include haggis on potato rösti topped with quails' eggs; and pan-fried salmon with chive and king prawn risotto. The impressive glass conservatory is the ideal place to enjoy a glass of McEwan's 70/-.

Open all day all wk Mon-Wed 12-11 (Thu-Sat noon-1am Sun 12-11) **Bar Meals** L served Mon-Fri 12-2, Sat 12-9.30, Sun 12-8.30 D served Mon-Fri 5.45-9, Sat 12-9.30, Sun 12-8.30 Av main course £11 **Restaurant** Fixed menu price fr £19.50 Av 3 course à la carte fr £25 ⊕ FREE HOUSE ◀ McEwan's 70/-, John Smith's. **Facilities** Non-diners area ♦♦ Children's menu Play area Garden Parking ▭ (notice required) **Rooms** 12

INNERLEITHEN
Map 21 NT33

Traquair Arms Hotel

Traquair Rd EH44 6PD ☎ **01896 830229**
e-mail: info@traquairarmshotel.co.uk
dir: *From A72 (Peebles to Galashiels road) take B709 for St Mary's Loch & Traquair*

A taste of Italy in the Scottish Borders

Amidst heather-covered hills stands this imposing pub-hotel with a tranquil beer garden. Expect to share it with muddy mountain bikers – downhill and cross-country trails are right on the doorstep. It's one of only two places where you can drink Traquair Bear Ale, brewed a stone's throw away at Traquair House. The bar menu has dishes such as chicken and haggis with clapshot mash and whisky sauce; Aberdeen Angus sirloin; and fish pie. In the restaurant, an unusual combination of Scottish and Italian food is prepared by the resident Italian chef. Sample dishes include Italian sausage with borlotti beans, cherry tomatoes, toasted focaccia and salad; and roast haunch of Tweed Valley venison with garlic baby potatoes, root vegetables and a redcurrant jus.

Open all day all wk Closed: 25 Dec **Bar Meals** L served Mon-Fri 12-2.30, Sat-Sun all day D served Mon-Fri 5-9, Sat-Sun all day **Restaurant** L served Mon-Fri 12-2.30, Sat-Sun all day D served Mon-Fri 5-9, Sat-Sun all day ⊕ FREE HOUSE ◀ Caledonian Deuchars IPA, Timothy Taylor Landlord, Traquair Bear Ale. **Facilities** Non-diners area 🐾 (Bar Garden) ♦♦ Children's menu Children's portions Garden ⊼ Parking Wi-fi ▭

KELSO
Map 21 NT73

The Cobbles Freehouse & Dining ◉

7 Bowmont St TD5 7JH ☎ **01573 223548**
e-mail: info@thecobbleskelso.co.uk
web: www.thecobbleskelso.co.uk
dir: *In town centre*

Accomplished food and well-kept ales

Positioned on the cobbled town square in the heart of picturesque Kelso, this attractive 19th-century coaching inn oozes character. Grab a seat by the roaring log fire in winter and enjoy single malts or the pub's own ales (The Cobbles is brewery tap for Tempest Brewing Co). The restaurant has an AA Rosette for its food and the frequently changing menu is dominated by local fish and shellfish, Border lamb, beef and pork or game in season. Influences come from far and wide, with traditional British food, modern European classics and Pacific Rim dishes rubbing shoulders on menus that offer everything from light bites to three-course meals. Bar meals range from local roe deer burgers to pan-fried fillet of salmon with braised Puy lentils. An excellent value set-price menu offers evening dishes such as sea bass with crab, lemon and pea risotto to braised shoulder of pork with ginger and plums.

Open all day all wk 11.30-11 Closed: 25-26 Dec, bar only on Mon in winter **Bar Meals** L served all wk 12-2 D served Mon-Sat 6-9, Sun 6-8 **Restaurant** L served all wk 12-2 D served Mon-Sat 6-9, Sun 6-8 ⊕ FREE HOUSE ◀ Tempest Ö Thistly Cross. **Facilities** Non-diners area ♦♦ Children's menu Children's portions Outside area ⊼ Parking Wi-fi ▭ (notice required)

Save on hotels. Book at **theAA.com/hotel**

SCOTTISH BORDERS 551 | SCOTLAND

PICK OF THE PUBS

The Wheatsheaf at Swinton

SWINTON   Map 21 NT84

Main St TD11 3JJ ☎ 01890 860257
e-mail:
reception@wheatsheaf-swinton.co.uk
web: www.wheatsheaf-swinton.co.uk
dir: *From Edinburgh A697 onto B6461.
From East Lothian A1 onto B6461*

Scottish hospitality and locally sourced food

Husband and wife team Chris and Jan Winson have built up an impressive reputation for their dining destination in this attractive village. Whether you choose to eat in the Sun Room or the Dining Room, the latter overlooking the village green, the menus feature home-made food using locally sourced produce, including daily delivered fresh seafood from Eyemouth 12 miles away, and beef from livestock raised on the surrounding Borders pastures. Also likely to appear, according to the season, are wild salmon, venison, partridge, pheasant, woodcock and duck. The bar and garden menu is likely to offer a club sandwich, steak-and-ale pie and beefburger. A restaurant meal might start with pan-seared woodland pigeon breast, Stornoway black pudding purée, crispy apple and light game jus; or home-made Thai crab cake with sweet chilli sauce. Head chef John Forrestier, from Nancy in France, specialises in fish, so a main course definitely worth considering is his baked

Dover sole with scallop mousse, clams, beurre blanc and pickled cockle salad. Alternatives might include roast Scottish venison with celeriac purée, seared poached pears, rösti potato and light beetroot and chocolate sauce; or pan-seared goats' cheese gnocchi and morel mushroom fricassée, buttered kale and truffle oil. Other regular meat dishes include oven-roast pork fillet, and slow-braised Borders beef blade. Finally, a couple of the desserts: glazed pomegranate tart and lemon sorbet; and baked Malteser cheesecake with passionfruit coulis. The bar stocks Belhaven IPA, draught Peroni, plus Stewart Brewery and Scottish Borders Brewery bottled beers. Here too is a whisky map and tasting notes to study before choosing your single malt.

Open 4-11 (Sat 12-12 Sun 12-11)
Closed: 23-24 & 26 Dec, 2-3 Jan, Mon-Fri L **Bar Meals** L served Sat 12-3, Sun 12-4 D served Mon-Sat 6-9, Sun 6-8.30 **Restaurant** L served Sat 12-3, Sun 12-4 D served Mon-Sat 6-9, Sun 6-8.30 ⊕ FREE HOUSE ◀ IPA, Belhaven, Scottish Borders Gamebird & Foxy Blonde, Stewarts Brewing Hollyrood, Peroni. ♟ 12 **Facilities** Non-diners area ♛ Garden ⋔ Parking 🚌

KIRK YETHOLM   Map 21 NT82

The Border Hotel

The Green TD5 8PQ ☎ 01573 420237
e-mail: borderhotel@aol.com
dir: From A698 in Kelso take B6352 for 7m to Kirk Yetholm

A homely place to stop awhile

Standing at the end of the 268-mile-long Pennine Way walk, this 18th-century former coaching inn is a welcoming and most hospitable place to revive after any journey, be it on foot or by car. Cracking pints of Pennine Way Bitter will slake parched throats and the traditional British menu, which features local game and farm meats, will satisfy healthy appetites. Try a rack of ribs to share ahead of saddle of local roe deer with red wine jus and mash. The stone-flagged bar has a blazing winter log fire, and the conservatory dining room looks over the patio and beer garden.

Open all day all wk **Closed:** 25 Dec **Bar Meals** L served all wk 12-2 D served all wk 6-8.45 Av main course £10 **Restaurant** L served all wk 12-2 D served all wk 6-8.45 Fixed menu price fr £10 Av 3 course à la carte fr £16.95 ⊕ FREE HOUSE ◀ Broughton Pennine Way Bitter, Scottish Borders Game Bird, Orkney Raven Ale ☼ Westons Old Rosie. ♣ 10 **Facilities** Non-diners area ♣ (Bar Garden) ♦♦ Children's menu Children's portions Play area Garden ♬ Parking Wi-fi ➡ (notice required)

MELROSE   Map 21 NT53

Burts Hotel ★★★ HL ⊛⊛

PICK OF THE PUBS

Market Square TD6 9PL ☎ 01896 822285
e-mail: enquiries@burtshotel.co.uk
dir: From A68 N of St Boswells take A6091 towards Melrose. approx 2m right signed Melrose & B6374, follow to Market Sq

Recommended for its Scottish whiskies and ales

Owned by the Henderson family for some 40 years, this 18th-century hotel stands in Melrose's picturesque market square. Due to its status as a listed building, restoration and extensions have necessarily been sympathetic, yet all the refinements of a modern first-class hotel are evident. After a day out, perhaps visiting Sir Walter Scott's Abbotsford home, settle down with one of the 80 single malts, or a pint of Caledonian Deuchars IPA. Lying in the shadow of the Eildon Hills, the town is surrounded by the rich countryside and waters which provide much of the produce used in the kitchen. The Bistro Bar's lunch and supper menu lists Teviot Smokery smoked salmon, fillet of North Sea haddock, and roast duck breast, while the restaurant has held two AA Rosettes since 1995 and offers dishes such as monkfish tail, crispy duck leg, spiced lentils, confit red peppers and curried foam. Bedrooms are appointed to a high standard, all have en suites.

Open all wk 12-2.30 5-11 **Bar Meals** L served all wk 12-2 D served all wk 6-9.30 Av main course £11.95

Restaurant L served Sat-Sun D served all wk 7-9 Av 3 course à la carte fr £36 ⊕ FREE HOUSE ◀ Caledonian Deuchars IPA & 80/-, Timothy Taylor Landlord, Fuller's London Pride, Scottish Borders Game Bird. ♣ 10 **Facilities** ♣ (Bar Garden) ♦♦ Children's portions Garden ♬ Parking Wi-fi **Rooms** 20

NEWCASTLETON   Map 21 NY48

Liddesdale ★★★★ INN

17 Douglas Square TD9 0QD ☎ 01387 375255
dir: In village centre

Set amidst beautiful countryside

This inn sits in Douglas Square at the heart of Newcastleton (sometimes referred to as Copshaw Holm), a 17th-century village planned by the third Duke of Buccleugh. An ideal base for exploring the unspoiled countryside in this area, the inn has a bar stocked with over 20 malt whiskies and a different cask-conditioned ale every week in the summer. A typical meal might include jalapeño peppers stuffed with cream cheese; haggis and pork sausages with horseradish mash and onion gravy; and sticky toffee pudding with vanilla ice cream.

Open all day all wk ⊕ FREE HOUSE ◀ Samuel Smith's ☼ Samuel Smith's Organic. **Facilities** ♦♦ Children's menu Children's portions Garden Wi-fi **Rooms** 6

ST BOSWELLS   Map 21 NT53

Buccleuch Arms Hotel

The Green TD6 0EW ☎ 01835 822243
e-mail: info@buccleucharms.com
dir: On A68, 10m N of Jedburgh. Hotel on village green

Friendly hotel serving local food

Originally an inn for the fox-hunting aristocracy, this smart and friendly country-house hotel dates from the 16th century. Set beside the village cricket pitch, it's an attractive brick and stone building with an immaculate garden. Inside, a large and comfortable lounge is warmed by a log fire in winter, while the spacious enclosed garden comes into its own during the warmer months. Local produce underpins the extensive menus which run from comfort food such as roasted breast of chicken stuffed with haggis, served with wholegrain mustard sauce and scallop potatoes to a Mexican-style burger with coleslaw and chips.

Open all day all wk 12-11 **Closed:** 25 Dec **Bar Meals** L served all wk 12-2.30 D served Sun-Thu 5.30-9, Fri-Sat 5.30-9.30 **Restaurant** L served all wk 12-2.30 D served Sun-Thu 5.30-9, Fri-Sat 5.30-9.30 ⊕ FREE HOUSE ◀ Scottish Borders Brewery Ales, Belhaven Best. **Facilities** Non-diners area ♣ (Bar Garden) ♦♦ Children's menu Children's portions Play area Garden ♬ Parking Wi-fi ➡ (notice required)

SWINTON   Map 21 NT84

The Wheatsheaf at Swinton

PICK OF THE PUBS

See Pick of the Pubs on page 551

TIBBIE SHIELS INN   Map 21 NT22

Tibbie Shiels Inn

PICK OF THE PUBS

St Mary's Loch TD7 5LH ☎ 01750 42231
e-mail: tibbieshiels@hotmail.com
dir: From Moffat take A708. Inn 14m on right

Superbly located famous old inn

The first thing any first-time visitor to this lovely whitewashed old inn between two lochs wants to know is: who was Tibbie Shiels? She was a young widow who, determined to support herself and her six bairns, took in lodgers and became the first licensee, catering in due course to Sir Walter Scott, Thomas Carlyle and Robert Louis Stevenson. Her spirit still keeps watch over the bar, which serves a real ale named after her and over 50 malt whiskies. The majority of the ingredients used in the kitchen are local, including venison, pheasant, partridge, hill-raised lamb and garden-grown herbs. Sandwiches, salads, ploughman's and paninis are all on offer, while the main menu lists Scottish smoked salmon on toasted crumpet; chicken, leek and smoked bacon pie; battered haddock and chips; and macaroni cheese. Evening events, including live music, take place throughout the year.

Open all day 8am-mdnt **Closed:** Wed **Bar Meals** L served Thu-Tue 12-3.30 D served Thu-Tue 5.30-9 **Restaurant** L served Thu-Tue 12-3.30 D served Thu-Tue 5.30-9 ⊕ FREE HOUSE ◀ Belhaven 80/-, Broughton Greenmantle Ale, Tibbie Shiels Ale & The Reiver ☼ Westons Stowford Press. **Facilities** Non-diners area ♣ (Bar Garden) ♦♦ Children's menu Children's portions Play area Garden ♬ Parking Wi-fi ➡

SOUTH AYRSHIRE

SYMINGTON   Map 20 NS33

Wheatsheaf Inn

Main St KA1 5QB ☎ 01563 830307
dir: Off A77 between Ayr & Kilmarnock

Village free house with friendly service

Close to the Royal Troon Golf Course and one of Scotland's oldest churches, this charming 17th-century free house has been run by Martin and Marnie Thompson for over 25 years. Log fires burn in every room of the former coaching inn and the interior is decorated with the work of local artists. The varied menu offers plenty of choice, with dishes like pan-fried sea bass fillet on salsa verde, and Kirsch and cherry glazed duck breast contrasting with more homely favourites such as breaded scampi with fries; desserts include fruit Pavlova. The two-course set menu is a steal.

Open all day all wk 11-11 (Fri-Sat 11am-mdnt) Closed: 1 Jan **Bar Meals** L served all wk all day D served all wk all day food served all day **Restaurant** L served all wk 12-2 D served all wk 5-9 ⊕ FREE HOUSE ◀ Belhaven Best, Morland Old Speckled Hen, Guinness.
Facilities Non-diners area ⑪ Children's menu Children's portions Garden ⴳ Parking ⛺ (notice required)

STIRLING

CALLANDER   Map 20 NN60

The Lade Inn

Kilmahog FK17 8HD ☎ 01877 330152
e-mail: info@theladeinn.com
dir: From Stirling take A84 to Callander. 1m N of Callander, left at Kilmahog Woollen Mills onto A821 towards Aberfoyle. Pub immediately on left

Warming fires in winter, a garden in summer

In the heart of the Trossachs National Park, the stone-built Lade Inn is part of the surrounding Leny Estate, built as a tearoom in 1935. First licensed in the 1960s, the family-owned and run inn is known for real ales brewed by their microbrewery at the side of the pub, and for its week-long beer festival in late August/early September. There is also an on-site real ale shop selling bottled ales from microbreweries throughout Scotland. The home-cooked menu offers many smaller portions and/or allergen-free dishes, such as gluten-free vegetable curry and dairy-free penne pasta. The beer garden with its three ponds and bird feeding station is great for families.

Open all day all wk **Bar Meals** L served Mon-Sat 12-9, Sun 12.30-9 D served Mon-Sat 12-9, Sun 12.30-9 **Restaurant** L served Mon-Sat 12-9, Sun 12.30-9 D served Mon-Sat 12-9, Sun 12.30-9 ⊕ FREE HOUSE ◀ Waylade, LadeBack & LadeOut, Belhaven Best, Tennent's ♡ Thistly Cross. ♚ 9 **Facilities** Non-diners area ✿ (Bar Garden) ⑪ Children's menu Children's portions Play area Family room Garden ⴳ Beer festival Parking Wi-fi ⛺ (notice required)

DRYMEN   Map 20 NS48

The Clachan Inn

2 Main St G63 0BG ☎ 01360 660824
e-mail: info@clachaninndrymen.co.uk
dir: Telephone for directions

Scottish hospitality stretching back over the years

Established in 1734, The Clachan is believed to be the oldest licensed pub in Scotland; this quaint white-painted cottage on the West Highland Way was once owned by Rob Roy's sister. Family-run for the past 30 years the bar stocks frequently changing guest ales while a warming log fire keeps things cosy. More comfort comes with the food — choose from pub favourites such as deep-fried potato skins with dips; jumbo sausage with baked beans and chips; and home-made toffee sponge pudding.

Open all day all wk Closed: 25 Dec & 1 Jan **Bar Meals** L served Mon-Sat 12-3.45 D served Mon-Sat 6-9.45

Restaurant L served Mon-Sat 12-3.45 D served Mon-Sat 6-9.45 ⊕ FREE HOUSE ◀ Harviestoun Bitter & Twisted, Cairngorm Trade Winds, Guinness. ♚ 9
Facilities Non-diners area ✿ (Bar) ⑪ Children's menu Children's portions Wi-fi ⛺ (notice required)

KIPPEN   Map 20 NS69

Cross Keys Hotel

Main St FK8 3DN ☎ 01786 870293
e-mail: info@kippencrosskeys.co.uk
dir: 10m W of Stirling, 20m from Loch Lomond off A811

Warming fires in winter, a garden in summer

The 300-year-old Cross Keys stands on Kippen's Main Street and offers seasonally changing menus and a good pint of Harviestoun Bitter & Twisted. The pub's welcoming interior, warmed by three log fires, is perfect for resting your feet after a walk in nearby Burnside Wood, or you can sit in the garden when the weather permits. The menu takes in beetroot, feta and walnut risotto; seafood linguine with roasted lemons; chicken with chorizo, spinach and bean broth; and a good range of pub classics, perhaps rib-eye steak, horseradish and caramelised onion sandwich or haddock and chips. Dogs are welcome in the top bar.

Open all wk 12-3 5-11 (Fri 12-3 5-1am Sat noon-1am Sun 12-12) Closed: 1 Jan ⊕ FREE HOUSE ◀ Belhaven Best, Harviestoun Bitter & Twisted, Guinness, Guest ales ♡ Addlestones. **Facilities** ✿ (Bar Garden) ⑪ Children's menu Children's portions Play area Family room Garden Parking Wi-fi

The Inn at Kippen

PICK OF THE PUBS

Fore Rd FK8 3DT ☎ 01786 870500
e-mail: info@theinnatkippen.co.uk
dir: From Stirling take A811 to Loch Lomond. 1st left at Kippen station rdbt, 1st right into Fore Rd. Inn on left

Stylish but traditional pub

Enjoy views across the Forth Valley to the Highlands from this traditional whitewashed free house in a picturesque village at the foot of the Campsie Hills. Here you can rub shoulders with the locals in the stylish bar, which provides a relaxing setting in which to savour a pint of Deuchars IPA. Warmed by roaring fires, the inn is the kind of place you'll want to linger — maybe over a meal in the bar or the more formal dining area. The menu is driven by seasonal, locally sourced ingredients. Lunch brings Italian flat bread topped with mozzarella; the chef's own special curry; and shepherd's pie. For dinner you could enjoy medallions of haggis rolled in golden crumb and served with whisky and grain mustard may; lasagne; and lemon drizzle sponge cake with cream. Typical specials include red Thai curry with egg fried rice. There's a pretty garden area for summer dining.

Open all day all wk **Bar Meals** L served all wk 12-2.30 D served all wk 5-9 Av main course £9 **Restaurant** L served Sat-Sun 12-5 D served Fri-Sun 5-9.30 Av 3 course à la carte fr £19 ⊕ FREE HOUSE ◀ Caledonian Deuchars

IPA. ♚ 9 **Facilities** Non-diners area ✿ (Bar Garden) ⑪ Children's menu Children's portions Garden ⴳ Parking Wi-fi ⛺

WEST LOTHIAN

LINLITHGOW   Map 21 NS97

Champany Inn - The Chop and Ale House ◉◉

PICK OF THE PUBS

Champany EH49 7LU ☎ 01506 834532
e-mail: reception@champany.com
dir: 2m NE of Linlithgow at junct of A904 & A803

Great steak, wine and whisky at renowned inn

Within striking distance of Edinburgh is this famous inn, a cluster of buildings including a former millhouse and farmer's bothy dating back to the 16th century. Of the two splendid restaurants, the more informal is The Chop and Ale House: so with a pint of Belhaven in hand, or a glass of their own-label South African wine, settle down to study the bistro-style menu. Beef is the big thing here — Aberdeen Angus of course — whether it be steaks or the same steak minced and formed in half-pound burgers. Starters include smoked trout mousse or salmon roulade with cream cheese and chives, while main course alternatives to steak are Scottish lamb chops or chargrilled chicken. If you can manage a dessert, red wine and winter berry jelly is on the carte. Be sure to stop in at the wine and whisky shop for a very well chosen selection of the grape and grain.

Open all wk 12-2 6.30-10 (Fri-Sun 12-10) Closed: 25-26 Dec, 1 Jan **Bar Meals** L served all wk 12-2 D served all wk 6.30-10 **Restaurant** L served all wk 12.30-2 D served all wk 6.30-10 ⊕ FREE HOUSE ◀ Belhaven. **Facilities** ⑪ Children's portions Garden ⴳ Parking

The Four Marys

65/67 High St EH49 7ED ☎ 01506 842171
e-mail: fourmaryslinlithgow@belhavenpubs.nett
dir: M9 junct 3 or junct 4, A803 to Linlithgow. Pub in town centre

Real ale paradise in historic town setting

This eye-catching building at the heart of Linlithgow became a pub only in 1981; its pedigree stretches back a further 500 years to when royalty lived at the nearby palace and the town's movers and shakers lived at the house. The eponymous Marys were ladies-in-waiting to Linlithgow-born Mary, Queen of Scots; amongst the bevvy of artefacts in the pub are materials connected to that ill-fated monarch. With striking dressed-stone walls, period and antique furnishings, the pub has forged ever higher standards for real ales in Scotland; twice-yearly beer festivals are held, whilst robust pub grub includes venison and haggis dishes.

Open all day all wk **Bar Meals** L served all wk 12-5 D served all wk 5-9 Av main course £7.99 food served all day **Restaurant** L served all wk 12-5 D served all wk 5-9

continued

LINLITHGOW *continued*

food served all day ⊕ BELHAVEN/GREENE KING
◖ Belhaven 80/- & Four Marys, Belhaven St Andrews,
Morland Old Speckled Hen, Caledonian Deuchars IPA,
Stewart Edinburgh Gold, St Andrews. ♀ 9
Facilities Non-diners area ⁙ Children's menu Children's
portions Garden Outside area Beer festival Wi-fi 🚐

SCOTTISH ISLANDS

ISLE OF COLL

ARINAGOUR   Map 22 NM25

Coll Hotel

PICK OF THE PUBS

PA78 6SZ ☎ 01879 230334
e-mail: info@collhotel.com
dir: *Ferry from Oban. Hotel at head of Arinagour Bay, 1m
from Pier (collections by arrangement)*

Great for local seafood

With stunning views over the sea to Jura and Mull Being
the Isle of Coll's only inn it is, naturally, the hub of the
island community. Come to this hotel to mingle with the
locals, soak in the atmosphere, and enjoy pints of Fyne
ale and malt whiskies. In the summer months the
fabulous garden acts as an extension to the bar or the
Gannet Restaurant; watch the yachts coming and going
while enjoying a glass of Pimm's or something from the
global wine selection. Fresh produce is landed and
delivered from around the island every day and features
on the specials board. Famed for its seafood, you'll find it
in dishes such as seared Coll crab cakes with wasabi
mayonnaise, and a pot of Connel mussels in garlic and
cream. Among the non-fish options, try the venison fillet
in redcurrant sauce or steak and ale pie.

Open all day all wk **Bar Meals** L served all wk 12-2
D served all wk 6-9 Av main course £12 **Restaurant** L
served all wk 12-2 D served all wk 6-9 Av 3 course à la
carte fr £25 ⊕ FREE HOUSE ◖ Fyne Ales Piper's Gold &
Avalanche. **Facilities** Non-diners area ⁙ Children's menu
Children's portions Play area Garden ♠ Parking Wi-fi
🚐 (notice required)

ISLE OF ISLAY

PORT CHARLOTTE   Map 20 NR25

The Port Charlotte Hotel

Main St PA48 7TU ☎ 01496 850360
e-mail: info@portcharlottehotel.co.uk
dir: *From Port Askaig take A846 towards Bowmore. Right
onto A847, through Blackrock. Take unclassified road to
Port Charlotte*

Beachside hotel displaying Scottish art

In an attractive conservation village, this sympathetically
restored Victorian hotel is perfectly positioned on the west
shore of Loch Indaal. A large conservatory opens out into
the garden and directly onto the beach. Lovers of Scottish
art will enjoy the work on display in the lounge and public

bar. Islay ales and whiskies make a great way to warm up
before enjoying menus focusing on local seafood –
perhaps half an Islay lobster or oven-baked wild halibut
steak. From the restaurant menu, try the lavender crème
brûlée for dessert.

Open all day all wk Closed: 24-26 Dec **Bar Meals** L served
all wk 12-2 D served all wk 6-9 Av main course £11.95
Restaurant L served all wk 12-2 D served all wk 6-9 Av 3
course à la carte fr £32 ⊕ FREE HOUSE ◖ Islay. ♀ 9
Facilities Non-diners area ♣ (Garden) ⁙ Children's
menu Children's portions Play area Family room Garden
Parking Wi-fi 🚐

ISLE OF MULL

DERVAIG   Map 22 NM45

The Bellachroy Hotel

PA75 6QW ☎ 01688 400314
e-mail: info@thebellachroy.co.uk
dir: *Take ferry from Oban to Craignure. A849 towards
Tobermory. Left at T-junct onto B8073 to Dervaig*

Oldest inn on Mull specialising in local seafood

Enjoying a stunning location overlooking Loch Cuin in the
pretty village of Dervaig, this historic drovers' inn is
Mull's oldest hostelry. Dating from 1608, the draw here,
apart from the character bar and the alfresco dining
terrace, are the tip-top Fyne ales – try a pint of
Highlander – the mind-boggling range of the Scottish
Islands' malt whiskies, and the fresh local produce on the
daily menus. Expect Sound of Mull scallops; roast wild
Mull venison; MacSween's haggis and Tobermory oak
smoked salmon, plus world-class langoustines, lobster,
scallops and oysters, all landed at nearby harbours.

Open all day all wk **Bar Meals** L served all wk 12-2.30
D served all wk 6-8.30 Av main course £10 **Restaurant** L
served all wk 12-2.30 D served all wk 6-8.30 Av 3 course
à la carte fr £20 ⊕ FREE HOUSE ◖ Fyne Avalanche,
Highlander. **Facilities** Non-diners area ♣ (Bar Garden) ⁙
Children's menu Children's portions Garden ♠ Parking
Wi-fi 🚐 (notice required)

ORKNEY

ST MARY'S   Map 24 HY40

The Commodore

Holm KW17 2RU ☎ 01856 781788
e-mail: enquiries@commodoreorkney.com
dir: *On A961 (Kirkwall to St Margarets Hope road)*

Locally brewed beers and Scapa Flow views

Just outside St Mary's village in Holm and only a ten-
minute drive from Kirkwall, this family-friendly pub and
restaurant enjoys stunning views over the Scapa Flow,
the Churchill Barriers and the Italian Chapel. A number of
local ales such as Highland Orkney Best are showcased
in the bar and this sourcing policy extends to the menu in
the light and airy restaurant. Bar meals of steak pie or
chicken Kiev are complemented by Westray salmon in
pastry, or Egilsay pork chops glazed with whisky, mustard
and brandy from the main menu.

Open Fri-Sat 5pm-close Closed: 26 Dec & 1-2 Jan, Sun-
Thu **Bar Meals** D served Fri-Sat from 5pm
Restaurant D served Fri-Sat from 5pm ⊕ FREE HOUSE
◖ Highland Orkney Blast, Scapa & Best, Orkney Raven
Ale & Red MacGregor ☼ Kopparberg. ♀
Facilities Non-diners area ⁙ Children's menu Children's
portions Outside area Parking Wi-fi 🚐

STROMNESS   Map 24 HY20

Ferry Inn

John St KW16 3AD ☎ 01856 850280
e-mail: info@ferryinn.com
dir: *Opposite ferry terminal*

Enjoy island ales overlooking the harbour

With its prominent harbour-front location, the Ferry Inn
has long enjoyed a reputation for local ales. The pub has
racking for a further ten local ales on top of the five
handpulls on the bar and although the beers change
regularly look out for the island's own Dark Island and
Skull Splitter. If beer isn't your thing, there are plenty of
wines and malt whiskies to choose from, as well as an
appealing menu that can include haggis and clap shot
with whisky sauce or an Orkney seafood platter.

Open all day all wk 9am-mdnt (Thu-Sat 9am-1am Sun
9.30am-mdnt) Closed: 25 Dec & 1 Jan **Bar Meals** L served
all wk 11.45-5 D served all wk 5-9.30 Av main course £9
food served all day **Restaurant** L served all wk 11.45-5
D served all wk 5-9.30 Av 3 course à la carte fr £24 food
served all day ⊕ FREE HOUSE ◖ Highland Scapa Special
& Orkney IPA, Orkney Dark Island & Skull Splitter.
Facilities Non-diners area ⁙ Children's menu Children's
portions ♠ Parking Wi-fi 🚐

ISLE OF SKYE

ARDVASAR   Map 22 NG60

Ardvasar Hotel ★★★ SHL

IV45 8RS ☎ 01471 844223
e-mail: richard@ardvasar-hotel.demon.co.uk
web: www.ardvasarhotel.com
dir: *From ferry terminal, 50yds & turn left*

Homely, welcoming and serving excellent Skye produce

Beside the road towards the southern tip of Skye, sit out
front to drink in the extraordinary views to the rocky
foreshore, Sound of Sleat and the mountains of the
Knoydart Peninsula, a ferry ride away via Mallaig. Once
you've sipped your Skye-brewed beer or local malt, retire

Save on hotels. Book at **theAA.com/hotel**

SCOTTISH ISLANDS 555 SCOTLAND

to the comfy lounge bar or dining room to indulge in some of Skye's most renowned seafood meals; the local boats may land salmon, crab, lobster or scallops. Estate venison and Aberdeen Angus beef extend the choice. Residents in the individually designed rooms can look to a fine Scottish breakfast to set another day in paradise going.

Open all day all wk 11am-mdnt (Sun 12-11) **Bar Meals** L served all wk 12-2.30 D served all wk 5-9 ⊕ FREE HOUSE ◀ Isle of Skye Red Cuillin. **Facilities** Non-diners area ♦♦ Children's menu Children's portions Garden ⊼ Parking **Rooms** 10

CARBOST
Map 22 NG33

The Old Inn and Waterfront Bunkhouse

PICK OF THE PUBS

IV47 8SR ☎ 01478 640205
e-mail: enquiries@theoldinnskye.co.uk
dir: *From Skye Bridge follow A87 N. Take A863, then B8009 to inn*

Free house attracting locals, tourists and hill walkers

The Old Inn and Waterfront Bunkhouse, on the shores of Loch Harport near the Talisker distillery, is a charming, 200-year-old island cottage very popular among the walking and climbing fraternity. Arrive early for a table on the waterside patio and savour the breathtaking views of the Cuillin Hills with a pint of Hebridean ale in hand. Inside, open fires welcome winter visitors, and live Highland music is a regular feature most weekends. The menu includes daily home-cooked specials with numerous fresh fish dishes such as local prawns and oysters, and mackerel from the loch. A typical choice could start with crispy confit duck leg salad or hot smoked salmon with Achmore crème fraîche; continue with a chargrilled Highland sirloin steak or Thai green vegetable curry; and finish with home-made rice pudding with dried apricots, raisins and toasted almonds.

Open all day all wk Mon-Fri 11am-1am (Sat 11am-12.30am Sun 12.30-11.30) **Bar Meals** L served all wk 12-9 D served all wk 12-9 food served all day **Restaurant** D served all wk food served all day ⊕ FREE HOUSE ◀ Isle of Skye Red Cuillin & Black Cuillin, Cuillin Skye Ale & Pinnacle Ale, Hebridean. **Facilities** Non-diners area ♦♦ Children's portions Family room Garden ⊼ Parking Wi-fi ▭

ISLEORNSAY
Map 22 NG71

Hotel Eilean Iarmain ★★★ SHL ◉◉

PICK OF THE PUBS

IV43 8QR ☎ 01471 833332
e-mail: hotel@eilean-iarmain.co.uk
dir: *A851, A852 right to Isleornsay harbour front*

Hebridean charm in spectacular setting

There's masses of Highland character at this well known hotel with its own pier overlooking Sleat Sound and the Knoydart Hills beyond. Step inside to find tartan carpets and stag antlers in the hallway, whilst elsewhere the decor is mainly cotton and linen chintzes with traditional furniture. More a small private hotel than a pub, the bar and restaurant ensure that the standards of food and drinks served here are exacting — the Gaelic Whiskies company is based here so sample a 'wee dram' or two. The head chef declares, 'We never accept second best, it shines through in the standard of food served in our restaurant'. Here you can try dishes like grilled pier-landed langoustines, pan-seared fillet of Eilean Iarmain Estate venison, or pepper crusted halibut fillet with a black olive tapenade. At lunchtime, a range of upmarket classics and sandwiches are also available. Half portions are served for children.

Open all day all wk 11am-11.30pm (Thu 11am-mdnt Fri 11am-1am Sat 11am-12.30am) **Bar Meals** L served 12-2 D served 5.30-9 Av main course £10.95 **Restaurant** D served 6.30-8.30 Fixed menu price fr £34.50 Av 3 course à la carte fr £39.95 ⊕ FREE HOUSE ◀ McEwan's 80/-, Isle of Skye, Guinness. **Facilities** Non-diners area ♦♦ Children's portions Garden ⊼ Parking ▭ **Rooms** 16

STEIN
Map 22 NG25

Stein Inn

Macleod's Ter IV55 8GA ☎ 01470 592362
e-mail: angus.teresa@steininn.co.uk
web: www.steininn.co.uk
dir: *A87 from Portree. In 5m take A850 for 15m. Right onto B886, 3m to T-junct. Turn left*

Skye's oldest inn amid beautiful scenery

If your travels take you to Skye, then you just have to visit the Waternish peninsula and the island's oldest inn, for

slap-bang in front of it, across a grassy foreshore, are the beautiful waters of Loch Bay. The wood-panelled bar, with peat fire a-smouldering, stocks 125 malts and Reeling Deck beer from the Isle of Skye brewery. Daily-changing menus take full advantage of the abundant fresh fish and shellfish, sheep, wild deer and Highland cattle, with choices including salmon with vermouth and tarragon sauce; pork chop with walnut and Achmore Blue cheese butter; and 'legendary' haggis toasties.

Open all day all wk 11am-mdnt Closed: 25 Dec, 1 Jan **Bar Meals** L served all wk 12-4 D served all wk 6-9.30 **Restaurant** D served all wk 6-9.30 ⊕ FREE HOUSE ◀ Isle of Skye Red Cuillin & Reeling Deck, Cairngorm Trade Winds, Caledonian Deuchars IPA, Orkney Dark Island. ₹ 9 **Facilities** Non-diners area ♣ (Bar Garden) ♦♦ Children's menu Children's portions Play area Family room Garden Parking Wi-fi ▭

SOUTH UIST

LOCHBOISDALE
Map 22 NF71

The Polochar Inn

Polochar HS8 5TT ☎ 01878 700215
e-mail: polocharinn@aol.com
dir: *W from Lochboisdale, take B888. Hotel at end of road*

Cosy island pub overlooking the Sound

Standing virtually alone overlooking the Sound of Eriskay and a prehistoric standing stone, this white-painted inn is the former change-house, where travellers waited for the ferry to Barra. Owned by sisters Morag MacKinnon and Margaret Campbell, it serves Hebridean real ales and specialises in local seafood and meats, as well as pasta dishes, all made with fresh, seasonal ingredients and served in a dining room with outstanding views of the sea. The beer garden is the ideal spot for dolphin watching and for admiring the beautiful sunsets. On summer Saturday nights the sound of live music fills the bar.

Open all day all wk 11-11 (Fri-Sat 11am-1am Sun 12.30pm-1am) **Bar Meals** L served Mon-Sat 12.30-8.30, Sun 1-8.30 (winter all wk 12-2.30) D served Mon-Sat 12.30-8.30, Sun 1-8.30 (winter all wk 5-8.30) Av main course £10 food served all day ⊕ FREE HOUSE ◀ Hebridean, Guest ales. **Facilities** Non-diners area ♦♦ Children's menu Children's portions Family room Garden ⊼ Parking Wi-fi ▭ (notice required)

Wales

Snowdonia

ANGLESEY, ISLE OF

BEAUMARIS
Map 14 SH67

Ye Olde Bulls Head
Inn ★★★★★ INN ⑨⑨⑨

PICK OF THE PUBS

Castle St LL58 8AP ☎ 01248 810329
e-mail: info@bullsheadinn.co.uk
dir: *From Britannia Road Bridge follow A545. Inn in town centre*

Historic inn on the island's coast

This 15th-century pub started life as a staging post and inn on the route to Ireland, a stone's throw from the gates of Beaumaris' medieval castle. The bar transports drinkers back to Dickensian times (the man himself stayed here), with settles, antique furnishings and artefacts, including the town's old ducking stool. The Bull's location in the midst of a rich larder of seafood and Welsh livestock farms means that the menus here are exceptional; this potential has been realised and recognised by the award of three AA Rosettes. The light and airy Brasserie has been moulded from the former stables and its menu offers a good range of modern global dishes, such as gnocchi in a tomato and garlic sauce; and lamb koftas with Moroccan couscous. Push the boat out in the intimate Loft Restaurant with spiced loin of Anglesey lamb, braised leg and shoulder, smoked potato, glazed vegetables and kidney and onion sauce. Quality accommodation is available. AA Restaurant of the Year for Wales 2013–14.

Open all day all wk Closed: 25 Dec **Bar Meals** L served Mon-Sat 12-2, Sun 12-3 **Restaurant** L served Mon-Sat 12-2, Sun 12-3 D served Brasserie all wk 6-9; Loft Restaurant Tue-Thu 7-9.30, Fri-Sat 6.30-9 Av 3 course à la carte fr £42.50 ⊕ FREE HOUSE ◀ Bass, Hancock's, Guest ales. ♚ 20 **Facilities** Non-diners area ♦♦ Children's menu Children's portions Parking Wi-fi **Rooms** 26

RED WHARF BAY
Map 14 SH58

The Ship Inn

PICK OF THE PUBS

LL75 8RJ ☎ 01248 852568
dir: *Telephone for directions*

A walkers' favourite with lovely views

Wading birds flock here to feed on the extensive sands of Red Wharf Bay, making The Ship's waterside beer garden a birdwatcher's paradise on warm days. In the Kennealy family's hands for over 40 years, the pub faces east on the lee side of a hill, sheltered from prevailing winds and catching the morning and afternoon sun perfectly. Before the age of steam, sailing ships landed cargoes here from all over the world; now the boats bring fresh Conwy Bay fish and seafood to the kitchens of this traditional free house. Real ales are carefully tended and a single menu applies to both bars and restaurant. Typical starters include a charred bundle of asparagus with a balsamic and honey dressing; and frittata of locally reared duck

egg with curried mayonnaise and seasonal salad. Move on to bangers and mash with onion gravy or a minted lamb burger with sour cream, chips and a Greek-style side salad. Other options include lunchtime sandwiches and wraps and a separate children's menu.

Open all day all wk **Bar Meals** L served all wk 12-2.30 D served all wk 6-9 **Restaurant** D served Sat-Sun ⊕ FREE HOUSE ◀ Conwy Rampart, Adnams, Guest ales ♂ Westons Wyld Wood Organic. **Facilities** Non-diners area ♦♦ Children's menu Children's portions Play area Family room Garden ⌐ Parking Wi-fi

BRIDGEND

KENFIG
Map 9 SS88

Prince of Wales Inn

CF33 4PR ☎ 01656 740356
e-mail: prince-of-wales@btconnect.com
dir: *M4 junct 37 into North Cornelly. Left at x-rds, follow signs for Kenfig & Porthcawl. Pub 600yds on right*

Inn with an intriguing history

Thought to be one of the most haunted pubs in Wales, this 16th-century stone-built free house was formerly the seat of local government for the lost city of Kenfig. Just as remarkably, it is also the only pub in Britain to have held a Sunday school continuously from 1857 to 2000. Welsh brunch, and beef and traditional Welsh ale pie are amongst the local dishes on the menu, and the daily blackboard specials are also worth attention.

Open all day all wk ⊕ FREE HOUSE ◀ Bass, Sharp's Doom Bar, Worthington's, Guest ales ♂ Tomos Watkin Taffy Apples. **Facilities** ♣ (Bar Garden) ♦♦ Children's menu Children's portions Garden Parking Wi-fi

CARDIFF

CREIGIAU
Map 9 ST08

Caesars Arms

PICK OF THE PUBS

Cardiff Rd CF15 9NN ☎ 029 2089 0486
e-mail: info@caesarsarms.co.uk
dir: *M4 junct 34, A4119 towards Llantrisant/Rhondda. Approx 0.5m right at lights signed Groesfaen. Through Groesfaen, past Dynevor Arms pub. Next left, signed Creigiau. 1m, left at T-junct, pass Creigiau Golf Course. Pub 1m on left*

Excellent local produce and fish here

Just ten miles from Cardiff, this smart dining pub and farm shop is tucked away down winding country lanes. Inside the whitewashed building, you'll find an appealing bar and dining area, and fine countryside views from the heated patio and terrace. There's much more than the excellent ales from Felinfoel Brewery. The pub has its own beehives and makes its own honey; the vegetables, herbs and salads from its gardens are used in the kitchen, and there's an in-house smokery. The inn prides itself on the vast selection of fresh fish, seafood, meat and game displayed on shaven ice. Fresh seafood is an

undoubted strength, with deliveries taken twice daily. Start with fish soup with crab and lemongrass before moving on to fresh lobster or lemon sole. Carnivores can choose from mountain lamb, plus Carmarthenshire Welsh beef and venison from the Brecon Beacons.

Open 12-2.30 6-10 (Sun 12-4) Closed: 25-26 Dec, 1 Jan, Sun eve **Bar Meals** L served Mon-Sat 12-2.30 **Restaurant** L served Mon-Sat 12-2.30, Sun 12-4 D served Mon-Sat 6-10 Fixed menu price fr £8.95 Av 3 course à la carte fr £29.95 ⊕ FREE HOUSE ◀ Felinfoel Double Dragon, Brains Smooth, Guinness ♂ Gwynt y Ddraig Orchard Gold. **Facilities** Non-diners area ♦♦ Children's portions Garden ⌐ Parking ⌂ (notice required)

GWAELOD-Y-GARTH
Map 9 ST18

Gwaelod-y-Garth Inn

Main Rd CF15 9HH ☎ 029 2081 0408 & 07855 313247
e-mail: gwaelo-dinn@btconnect.com
dir: *From M4 junct 32, N on A470, left at next exit, at rdbt turn right 0.5m. Right into village*

Friendly village pub with own ales and good walks

This stone-built hillside cottage enjoys a wonderful position on the thickly wooded flank of Garth Hill, high above Taffs Well, with great walking and stunning views such as the fairytale Victorian sham castle of Castell Coch across the vale. At the bar guest ales from as far afield as Essex and Derbyshire rub shoulders with local brews, including some from their own microbrewery Violet Cottage, along with a farm cider from Pontypridd. A pleasing selection of home-cooked pub food produces dishes of grilled sea bass fillets on braised fennel, and Welsh Black steak and ale pie with puff pastry.

Open all day all wk 11am-mdnt (Sun 12-11) **Bar Meals** L served Mon-Thu 12-2, Fri-Sat 11-9, Sun 12-3.30 D served Mon-Thu 6.30-9, Fri-Sat 11-9 **Restaurant** L served Mon-Thu 12-2, Fri-Sat 11-9, Sun 12-3.30 D served Mon-Thu 6.30-9, Fri-Sat 11-9 ⊕ FREE HOUSE ◀ Wye Valley Bitter, Swansea Three Cliffs Gold, RCH Pitchfork, Crouch Vale Brewers Gold, Thornbridge Jaipur, Gower Brewery Co, Tiny Rebel, Violet Cottage Shine On, Total Eclipse & Zig Zag ♂ Local cider, Gwynt-y-Ddraig. ♚ 10 **Facilities** Non-diners area ♣ (Bar Garden) ♦♦ Children's menu Children's portions Garden ⌐ Parking Wi-fi ⌂

PENTYRCH   Map 9 ST18

Kings Arms NEW

22 Church Rd CF15 9QF ☎ **029 2089 0202**
e-mail: kingsarmswales@hotmail.co.uk
dir: M4 junct 32, A470 (Merthyr Tydfil). Left onto B4262 signed Radyr then Pentyrch. Right at rdbt for Pentyrch. Or M4 junct 34, A4119 (dual carriageway) signed Llantrisant & Rhondda. Into right lane, right at lights signed Groes Farm. Left to Pentyrch

Traditional Welsh longhouse pub

In a leafy village on the outskirts of Cardiff, this Grade II listed pub is full of traditional features, from the flagstoned snug to the exposed lime-washed walls and log fire of the lounge. The restaurant opens out onto the lovely landscaped gardens. Local breweries Brains and Otley supply the real ales while there is also a choice of New and Old World wines. Promoting seasonal Welsh produce, the menus and daily blackboard specials could include a Severn and Wye Valley smoked mackerel focaccia sandwich; confit leg of free-range duck; and loin of pork with a sage and black pudding crust. The Sunday roasts are very popular.

Open all day all wk **Bar Meals** Av main course £11 food served all day **Restaurant** L served Mon-Sat 12-3, Sun 12-4 D served Mon-Sat 6-10 Av 3 course à la carte fr £15.50 ⊕ BRAINS ◀ Otley 03 Boss.
Facilities Non-diners area ◑ Children's menu Children's portions Garden ⌂ Parking Wi-fi ▦ (notice required)

CARMARTHENSHIRE

ABERGORLECH   Map 8 SN53

The Black Lion

SA32 7SN ☎ **01558 685271**
e-mail: georgerashbrook@hotmail.com
dir: A40 E from Carmarthen, then B4310 signed Brechfa & Abergorlech

Cosy black and white pub in charming Welsh countryside

A drive through the pretty Cothi Valley brings you to this attractive, 16th-century village pub run by George and Louise Rashbrook. Louise does all the cooking and George wisely gives her generous credit for doing so. You can eat from an extensive menu in the flagstoned bar, while the evening menu in the more modern, candlelit dining room offers beef, almond, mint and lemon casserole; mustard-stuffed chicken in bacon; scampi and chips; and mushroom, brie and cranberry Wellington. The lovely beer garden overlooks a Roman bridge.

Open 12-3 7-11 (Sat-Sun & BH all day) Closed: Mon (ex BHs) **Bar Meals** L served Tue-Sun 12-2.30 D served Tue-Sun 7-9 Av main course £8.95 **Restaurant** D served Tue-Sun 7-9 ⊕ FREE HOUSE ◀ Rhymney ᵇ Westons Stowford Press, Gwynt-y-Ddraig. **Facilities** Non-diners area ❤ (Bar Garden Outside area) ◑ Children's menu Children's portions Garden Outside area ⌂ Parking Wi-fi ▦ (notice required)

LLANDDAROG   Map 8 SN51

Butchers Arms

SA32 8NS ☎ **01267 275330**
e-mail: b5dmj@aol.com
dir: From A48 between Carmarthen & Cross Hands follow Llanddarog/B4310 signs. Pub by church in village

Pretty pub by the village church

Well into their third decade here, David and Mavis James's success story continues. David runs his kitchen with unconcealed enthusiasm, making good use of locally sourced ingredients to provide pleasing home-made food. Admire the Toby jug collection, order a pint of Felinfoel Cambrian Bitter or Celtic Pride, then contemplate a traditional lunch of beef and ale pie with chips, or in the evening honey-roast boneless duck with orange and Grand Marnier sauce; a sizzling platter of king tiger prawns in garlic butter; or mushroom Stroganoff. Most children's dishes include chips and some of the ice creams come with a novelty toy.

Open 12-3 6-11 Closed: 24-26 Dec, Sun & Mon **Bar Meals** L served Tue-Sat 12-2.30 D served Tue-Sat 6-9.30 **Restaurant** L served Tue-Sat 12-2.30 D served Tue-Sat 6-9.30 ⊕ FREE HOUSE ◀ Felinfoel Cambrian Bitter, Double Dragon, Celtic Pride. ⬤ 10
Facilities Non-diners area ◑ Children's menu Garden ⌂ Wi-fi ▦ (notice required)

LLANDEILO   Map 8 SN62

The Angel Hotel

Rhosmaen St SA19 6EN ☎ **01558 822765**
e-mail: capelbach@hotmail.com
dir: In town centre adjacent to post office

Reliable base in idyllic Welsh market town

This gabled inn commands a position near the crest of the long hill rising from Llandeilo's old bridge across the Towy, at the fringe of the Brecon Beacons National Park. Popular as both a locals' pub, with some reliable Welsh real ales and a good range of wines, and as an intimate place to dine in Y Capel Bach Bistro, an 18th-century gem tucked away at the rear of the hotel. Most diets are catered for on the ever-changing specials board and fixed price menu; perhaps deep fried squid to start, followed by venison steak or provençal vegetable bake.

Open 11.30-3 6-11 Closed: Sun **Bar Meals** L served Mon-Sat 11.30-2.30 D served Mon-Sat 6-9 Av main course £5.95 **Restaurant** L served Mon-Sat 11.30-2.30 D served Mon-Sat 6-9 Fixed menu price fr £12.95 Av 3 course à la carte fr £18 ⊕ FREE HOUSE ◀ Evan Evans, Tetley's. ⬤ 10
Facilities Non-diners area ❤ (Bar Garden) ◑ Children's menu Children's portions Garden ⌂ Wi-fi ▦ (notice required)

LLANDOVERY   Map 9 SN73

The Kings Head

1 Market Square SA20 0AB ☎ **01550 720393**
e-mail: info@kingsheadcoachinginn.co.uk
dir: M4 junct 49, A483 through Ammanford, Llandeilo onto A40 to Llandovery. Pub in town centre opposite clock tower

A family-run, former coaching inn

Overlooking the cobbled market square, this 17th-century inn, all exposed beams and crooked floors, was once the home of the Llandovery Bank, known as the Black Ox Bank. A good few menus are offered – lunchtime specials (all at £5, Mondays to Fridays), light bites, bar, carte, grills, vegetarian and children's. For your lunchtime fiver you could enjoy deep-fried fish and chips, or pork and chive sausages, while the carte offers mozzarella and spinach chicken; slow-braised Welsh lamb shank; pan-seared duck breast; and whole roast pheasant. Representing the Principality are real ales from Tomos Watkin's Swansea brewery, alongside 6X and Doom Bar.

Open all day all wk 10am-mdnt Closed: 25 Dec **Bar Meals** L served all wk 12-2.30 D served all wk 6-9.30 Av main course £10 **Restaurant** L served all wk 12-2.30 D served all wk 6-9.30 Av 3 course à la carte fr £17 ⊕ FREE HOUSE ◀ Wadworth 6X, Sharp's Doom Bar, Tomos Watkin. **Facilities** Non-diners area ❤ (Bar) ◑ Children's menu Children's portions ⌂ Parking Wi-fi ▦ (notice required)

LLANLLWNI   Map 8 SN43

Belle @ Llanllwni

SA40 9SQ ☎ **01570 480495**
e-mail: food@thebelle.co.uk
dir: Midway between Carmarthen & Lampeter on A485

Well cooked food at this cosy roadside inn

Surrounded by countryside and with stunning views, this cosy and welcoming roadside inn sits on the A485 between Carmarthen and Lampeter. Head this way on a sunny day and dine alfresco. There are two rotating ales here to enjoy along with local bottled Welsh ciders. In the dining room, smoked mackerel and new potato salad with mustard mayonnnaise may be followed by slow roast belly pork with sauté potato and pesto cream sauce; or gammon, egg and chips, finished with a sweet like winter berry bavarois with pomegranate water ice. Expect excellent ingredients including free-range local meats.

Open 12-3 5.30-11 Closed: 25-26 Dec, Mon (ex BHs) **Bar Meals** L served Wed-Sat 12-3 D served Tue-Sun 6-9.30 **Restaurant** L served Sun 12-3 D served Tue-Sun 6-9.30 ⊕ FREE HOUSE ◀ Peroni, Guinness, Guest ales ᵇ Westons Stowford Press, Gwynt y Ddraig. ⬤ 9
Facilities Non-diners area ◑ Children's menu Children's portions Outside area ⌂ Parking ▦ (notice required)

NANTGAREDIG — Map 8 SN42

Y Polyn ◉◉

PICK OF THE PUBS

SA32 7LH ☎ 01267 290000
e-mail: ypolyn@hotmail.com
dir: *From A48 follow signs to National Botanic Garden of Wales. Then follow brown signs to Y Polyn*

Stylish but never stuffy, this pub is a real find

With a trout fishery nearby, bracing walks in the Towy Valley just down the hill and the inspiring National Botanic Garden of Wales a mile or so up the road, this former tollhouse outside the attractive county town of Carmarthen is an established destination pub for lovers of Welsh food. West Wales is rapidly becoming one of the hotspots for organic and homespun cuisine, and the bounty of the local area is to the forefront in the tempting dishes that come from the modest kitchen here. "Fat equals Flavour. Live with it" is the unapologetic ethos here. Treats include ham hock hash with buttered leeks and grain mustard sauce; and lemon sole with anchovy, caper and parsley butter. Warm plum and frangipane tart or white chocolate cheesecake with poached rhubarb seal the deal. All this has gained the inn two AA Rosettes for its accomplished country-pub cooking. The excellent beers come from Pontypridd.

Open all wk 12-4 7-11 Closed: Mon, Sun eve **Bar Meals** Av main course £14.50 **Restaurant** L served Tue-Sun 12-2 D served Tue-Sat 7-9 Fixed menu price fr £12 Av 3 course à la carte fr £32.50 ⊕ FREE HOUSE ◀ Otley 01, 03 Boss. ☻12 **Facilities** Non-diners area ♦♦ Children's portions Garden ⊼ Parking Wi-fi

CEREDIGION

ABERAERON — Map 8 SN46

The Harbourmaster

PICK OF THE PUBS

Pen Cei SA46 0BT ☎ 01545 570755
e-mail: info@harbour-master.com
dir: *In Aberaeron follow Tourist Information Centre signs. Pub adjacent*

Quayside delight with great bay views

The three-storey, former harbourmaster's house on Aberaeron's Georgian quayside was built in 1811, its deep mauve walls making a fitting bookend to a row of pastel-coloured neighbours. Head for the bar in the former grain store overlooking the harbour and order a pint of Purple Moose Glaslyn, HM Best, Hallets real cider, or one of the 15 wines sold by the glass. The thoughtfully chosen shades of the interior enhance the original features, especially the beautiful spiral staircase. The kitchen makes the most of carefully sourced produce, typically appearing on the bar menu as a breakfast of Welsh rarebit and Talsarn bacon; and lunch of Cardigan Bay crab and parsley risotto; faggots, mash and peas; and stone-baked pizzas. A three-course dinner might be potted local pheasant with cognac and onion marmalade;

baked fillet of hake with butternut squash risotto; and pear and frangipane tart with chocolate ice cream.

Open all day all wk 10am-11.30pm Closed: 25 Dec **Bar Meals** L served all wk 12-2.30 D served all wk 6-9 **Restaurant** L served all wk 12-2.30 D served all wk 6.30-9 Av 3 course à la carte fr £30 ⊕ FREE HOUSE ◀ Purple Moose Glaslyn Ale, HM Best Bitter Ö Hallets Real. ☻15 **Facilities** Non-diners area ♦♦ Children's menu Children's portions ⊼ Parking Wi-fi

LLANFIHANGEL-Y-CREUDDYN — Map 9 SN67

y Ffarmers NEW

PICK OF THE PUBS

SY23 4LA ☎ 01974 261275
e-mail: bar@yffarmers.co.uk
dir: *From Aberystwyth take B4340 towards Trawsgoed. After New Cross left signed Llanfihangel-y-Creuddyn*

A rural oasis in the Welsh hills

Persevere down winding narrow lanes through stunning countryside to arrive in Llanfihangel's gorgeous open square, where you'll find listed whitewashed cottages, an imposing church and the y Ffarmers country pub. Since Rhodri and Esther (and family) took over this traditional local and spruced the place up with a contemporary feel, it has become an oasis for tip-top Welsh beer and quality pub food. Expect to find a buzzy community vibe and the place packed with local drinkers supping pints of Evan Evans or heady Gwynt y Ddraig cider, farmers from the hills and local foodies in the know. There's distinct Welsh flavour to the short monthly menus (in Welsh and English, naturally), which champion produce from local farms and artisan producers. Typically, tuck into local game pâté with home-made chutney; sea bass, cockle and laverbread cake and leek and lemon sauce, and bara brith pudding with Welsh whisky cream. Don't miss the Sunday roast lunches, or the annual tractor run in September.

Open 12-2 6-11 Closed: 2-9 Jan, Mon **Bar Meals** L served Tue-Sun 12-2 D served Tue-Sat 6-9 Av main course £11 **Restaurant** L served Tue-Sun 12-2 D served Tue-Sat 6-9 Fixed menu price fr £10 Av 3 course à la carte fr £20 ⊕ FREE HOUSE ◀ Wye Valley, Evan Evans, Felinfoel Ö Gwynt y Ddraig. **Facilities** Non-diners area ♣ (Bar Garden) ♦♦ Children's menu Children's portions Garden ⊼ ⚌ (notice required)

LLWYNDAFYDD — Map 8 SN35

The Crown Inn & Restaurant

SA44 6BU ☎ 01545 560396
e-mail: thecrowninnandrestaurant@hotmail.co.uk
dir: *Off A487 NE of Cardigan*

Time a visit for the popular carvery

Outside this traditional Welsh longhouse is a delightful, award-winning garden, while an easy walk down the lane leads to a cove with caves and National Trust cliffs. Dating from 1799, the pub has original beams, open fireplaces and a pretty restaurant. There's a carvery every Sunday and a varied menu with a good selection of dishes, including chicken liver and cognac pâté, which might be followed by lamb's liver cooked in red wine, bacon and red onion with garlic mash. Blackboard specials, a children's menu, light snacks and bar food are also available.

Open all day all wk **Bar Meals** L served all wk 12-3 D served all wk 6-9 **Restaurant** L served all wk 12-3 D served all wk 6-9 ⊕ FREE HOUSE ◀ Flowers IPA, Morland Old Speckled Hen, Cottage, Guest ales. ☻12 **Facilities** Non-diners area ♣ (Bar Garden) ♦♦ Children's menu Children's portions Play area Family room Garden ⊼ ⚌ (notice required)

TREGARON — Map 9 SN65

Y Talbot ★★★★ INN NEW

The Square SY25 6JL ☎ 01974 298208
e-mail: info@ytalbot.com
dir: *On B4343 in village centre. (NB take caution in winter on mountain road from Beulah)*

Hikers, bikers, cyclists - all welcome at this historic drovers' inn

If only the walls of this charming, 400-year-old drovers' inn could talk. They might reveal whether former US president Jimmy Carter ever boasted of 'the one that got away' during a fishing holiday here in the 1980s, or if an elephant really was buried here in 1848. Today, the beamed, slate-floored inn is recognised for its devotion to cask ales and draught ciders from Wales and The Borders - ask for a sample. In the Y Long Room restaurant the extensive regular menu offers home-made lamb cawl; roast breast of Bryn Derw chicken; confit pork belly; and fresh Cardigan Bay fish.

Open all day all wk **Bar Meals** L served all wk 12-2.30 D served all wk 6-9 Av main course £12 **Restaurant** L served all wk 12-2.30 D served all wk 6-9.30 ⊕ FREE HOUSE ◀ Purple Moose Glaslyn Ale, Felinfoel Double Dragon, Wye Valley HPA, Buckley's Best Ö Gwynt y Ddraig Happy Daze, Welsh Mountain Cider. **Facilities** Non-diners area ♣ (Bar Garden) ♦♦ Children's menu Children's portions Play area Garden ⊼ Parking Wi-fi ⚌ (notice required) **Rooms** 13

CONWY

BETWS-Y-COED   Map 14 SH75

Ty Gwyn Inn ★★★ INN

PICK OF THE PUBS

LL24 0SG ☎ 01690 710383 & 710787
e-mail: mratcl1050@aol.com
dir: *At junct of A5 & A470, 100yds S of Waterloo Bridge*

Local, seasonal food drive the menus

Located on the old London to Holyhead road, the Ty Gwyn was welcoming travellers long before Thomas Telford built his impressive cast iron Waterloo Bridge over the River Conwy opposite in 1815. The Ratcliffe family has owned and run this former coaching for the past 28 years, and now Martin (the chef for all that time) and his wife Nicola are in charge. Much of the original 17th-century character is evident inside. Real ales come from as near as Conwy's Great Orme brewery, as well as from much further afield. Martin's cooking relies heavily on quality local produce including home-grown veg. Typical dishes include a starter of creamy scrambled free-range goose egg with smoked salmon and wild garlic, and main courses such as slow-roasted suckling pig with black pudding and hazelnut stuffing and thyme scented roast root vegetables. Some of Nicola's own-designed en suite rooms have four-posters.

Open all wk 12-2 6.30-11 Closed: 24, 25 & 26 Dec, 1wk Jan **Bar Meals** L served all wk 12-2 D served all wk 6.30-9 Av main course £14.95 **Restaurant** L served all wk 12-2 D served all wk 6.30-9 Av 3 course à la carte fr £25 ⊕ FREE HOUSE ◀ Adnams Broadside, Brains The Rev. James, Morland Old Speckled Hen, Great Orme. **Facilities** ◀◗ Children's menu Children's portions Outside area ⌒ Parking Wi-fi ▭ **Rooms** 13

CAPEL CURIG   Map 14 SH75

Bryn Tyrch Inn

LL24 0EL ☎ 01690 720223
e-mail: info@bryntyrchinn.co.uk
dir: *On A5, 6m from Betws-y-Coed*

Smart inn with wonderful Snowdon views

Occupying an idyllic position in the heart of the Snowdonia National Park with breathtaking views of Snowdon and Moel Siabod, this remote hotel and bar is an ideal base for exploring the stunning mountains of the region. Welsh produce dominates the menu, which can be enjoyed in the informal bar or the terrace restaurant. Seared wood pigeon, chestnut and bacon tart, poached egg with port reduction; chargrilled rib-eye Welsh steak with hand-cut chips; and fish of the day are typical choices. Look out for hog roasts in the garden during the summer.

Open all wk (L only wknds & hols) Closed: mid Dec-27 Dec, 3-21 Jan **Bar Meals** L served wknds & hols 12-3

D served all wk 6-9 **Restaurant** L served wknds & hols 12-3 D served all wk 6-9 ⊕ FREE HOUSE ◀ Purple Moose Dark Side of the Moose, Snowdonia. **Facilities** Non-diners area ◀◗ Children's menu Children's portions Garden ⌒ Parking Wi-fi

---

Cobdens Hotel ★★ SHL

LL24 0EE ☎ 01690 720243
e-mail: info@cobdens.co.uk
dir: *On A5, 5m W of Betws-y-Coed*

Mecca for those enjoying all that Snowdonia has to offer

This 250-year-old inn sits at the foot of Moel Siabod in a beautiful mountain village deep in Snowdonia, with Snowdon itself a couple of miles down the valley. No surprise then that it's a haven for outdoor pursuit enthusiasts of all descriptions, taking refreshment, rebuilding their strength or enjoying live music in the famous Mountain Bar built into the rock face. Typical dishes include pear and endive salad with gorgonzola and walnuts; halibut steak Provençale with fine salad and new potatoes; and hearty meat options such as Welsh rib-eye steak with peppercorn sauce.

Open all day all wk 12-11 (Sun 12-10.30) Closed: 21-28 Dec, 6-20 Jan **Bar Meals** L served all wk 12-2 D served all wk 6-9 **Restaurant** L served all wk 12-2 D served all wk 6-9 ⊕ FREE HOUSE ◀ Conwy Rampart & Clogwyn Gold, Cobdens Ale, Honey Fayre, Telford Porter, Guest ales ⌂ Rosie's Perfect Pear, Triple D & Wicked Wasp. **Facilities** Non-diners area ❀ (Bar Garden) ◀◗ Children's menu Children's portions Garden ⌒ Parking Wi-fi ▭ **Rooms** 17

COLWYN BAY   Map 14 SH87

Pen-y-Bryn

PICK OF THE PUBS

Pen-y-Bryn Rd LL29 6DD ☎ 01492 533360
e-mail: pen.y.bryn@brunningandprice.co.uk
dir: *1m from A55. Follow signs to Welsh Mountain Zoo. Establishment at top of hill*

Character interior and friendly atmosphere

Looks can be deceiving. This unprepossessing 1970s building may look like a medical centre but step inside to find a handsome interior, where you'll find a friendly and chatty atmosphere with local ales and cracking pub food served throughout the day. The interior has character in spades, with oak floors, open fires, rugs, bookcases and old furniture, whilst the stunning rear garden and terrace enjoy panoramic views over the sea and the Great Orme headland. The modern British menu offers a great choice of sandwiches and lighter meals, perhaps Welsh rarebit on thick toast with chutney, or you might opt for mussels cooked in white wine, garlic and cream. Main course options range from chargrilled chicken on tagliatelle with

a spiced saffron butter sauce, to braised shoulder of lamb on crushed new potatoes with rosemary gravy. Chocolate brownie with chocolate sauce and ice cream, or lemon tart with fruit compôte will round things off nicely.

Open all day all wk Mon-Sat 12-11 (Sun 12-10.30) **Bar Meals** L served Mon-Sat 12-9.30, Sun 12-9 D served Mon-Sat 12-9.30, Sun 12-9 food served all day **Restaurant** L served Mon-Sat 12-9.30, Sun 12-9 D served Mon-Sat 12-9.30, Sun 12-9 food served all day ⊕ BRUNNING & PRICE ◀ Original, Purple Moose Snowdonia Ale, Guest ales ⌂ Aspall. ♇ 14 **Facilities** Non-diners area ◀◗ Children's menu Children's portions Garden ⌒ Beer festival Parking

CONWY   Map 14 SH77

The Groes Inn ★★★★★ INN ⊛

AA PUB OF THE YEAR FOR WALES 2013-2014

PICK OF THE PUBS

Ty'n-y-Groes LL32 8TN ☎ 01492 650545
e-mail: reception@groesinn.com
dir: *Exit A55 to Conwy, left at mini rdbt by Conwy Castle onto B5106, 2.5m inn on right*

Historic pub with views of Snowdonia

Snuggling between the easternmost summits of the Carneddau mountain range and the rich riverside pastures of the Conwy Valley, this charming creeper-clad inn - the first licensed house in Wales - has been welcoming customers since 1573. The walled town of Conwy is just two miles away and the front of the inn has magnificent views of the hills behind, which rise towards Snowdonia. Rambling rooms, beamed ceilings, careworn settles, military hats, historic cooking utensils — this inn has plenty to point out but don't expect a jukebox or pool table. Naturally there's a distinctly Welsh tilt to the menu, awarded one AA Rosette, with lamb and game from nearby estates and a varied selection of fruits of the sea brought in through Conwy's quay or Anglesey's boats; try the seafood chowder or the venison pie. Be sure to taste the beers, including the pub's very own Groes Ale.

Open all wk 12-3 6-11 **Bar Meals** L served all wk 12-2 D served all wk 6.30-9 Av main course £10 **Restaurant** L served all wk 12-2 D served all wk 6.30-9 Fixed menu price fr £15 ⊕ FREE HOUSE ◀ Groes Ale, Great Orme Welsh Black, Orme, Tetley's ⌂ Westons Stowford Press. ♇ 14 **Facilities** Non-diners area ❀ (Bar Garden) Children's menu Children's portions Family room Garden ⌒ Parking Wi-fi ▭ (notice required) **Rooms** 14

PICK OF THE PUBS

The Queens Head

LLANDUDNO JUNCTION   Map 14 SH77

Glanwydden LL31 9JP ☎ 01492 546570
e-mail: enquiries@
queensheadglanwydden.co.uk
web: www.queensheadglanwydden.co.
uk
dir: *A55 onto A470 towards Llandudno.
At 3rd rdbt right towards Penrhyn Bay,
2nd right into Glanwydden, pub on left*

A warm welcome, effortless charm and excellent service

A former AA Pub of the Year for Wales, this charming country pub is located in a pretty rural village just a five-minute drive from the Victorian seaside town of Llandudno. Once the storehouse of the Llangwestennin Parish, this early 18th-century pub is perfectly situated for country walks, cycling, or a day on the beach. The Queens Head continues to attract discerning customers with its warm welcome, effortless charm and excellent service. The stylish terrace is great for summer evenings, whilst on colder nights the relaxed atmosphere in the bar is perfect for a pre-dinner drink by the log fire; real ales include Great Orme brews, and the lip-smacking wine list with description notes on the back of the menu has plenty of choice. The dedicated kitchen makes excellent use of local produce in varied menus that might include a starter of Conwy fish soup finished with brandy and tomato;

crispy lamb and feta salad; or deep-fried Welsh brie with home-made cranberry and orange chutney. Local fish and seafood is the cornerstone of the menu and typical examples are home-made salmon and coriander fishcakes; seared Anglesey king scallops with pea purée, pancetta and rocket or monkfish and king prawn curry in a light mango and coconut sauce. Meat-lovers and vegetarians are certainly not overlooked, with the likes of home-made steak, mushroom and ale pie; grill pork loin steak in a soused prune and armagnac jus; or roasted half of Barbary duck with stir fry and noodles. Pasta, salads and vegetarian choices are also available. Booking for meals may be required.

Open all day all wk 12-10.30
Bar Meals food served all day
Restaurant food served all day
⊞ FREE HOUSE ◖ Great Orme. ♟ 10
Facilities Non-diners area Children's portions Garden ⋈ Parking
🚌 (notice required)

DOLWYDDELAN — Map 14 SH75

Elen's Castle Hotel

LL25 0EJ ☎ 01690 750207
e-mail: stay@hotelinsnowdonia.co.uk
dir: *5m S of Betws-y-Coed, follow A470*

Relaxed and welcoming atmosphere at this village hostelry

Elen's Castle was once owned by the Earl of Ancaster, who sold it to his gamekeeper. The latter opened it as a coaching inn around 1880, specialising in hunting parties. Now a family-run free house, it boasts an old-world bar with a wood-burning stove and an intimate restaurant with breathtaking views of the mountains and Lledr River. Sample dishes include chicken Cymru (succulent chicken breast served in a leek, mushroom, cream and Caerphilly cheese sauce with seasonal vegetables); and Welsh Black beefburger served with chunky chips. Water from the on-site Roman well is said to have healing properties.

Open vary by season Closed: 1st 2wks Jan, wk days in quiet winter periods **Bar Meals** D served 6.30-9 Av main course £9.50 **Restaurant** D served 6.30-9 Fixed menu price fr £25 Av 3 course à la carte fr £30 ⊕ FREE HOUSE ◀ Shepherd Neame Spitfire, Wychwood Hobgoblin, Brains, Worthington's, Black Sheep ♂ Westons Stowford Press. **Facilities** Non-diners area ♣ (Bar) ♦ Children's menu Children's portions Play area Family room Garden ⊼ Parking Wi-fi ▭ (notice required)

LLANDUDNO JUNCTION — Map 14 SH77

The Queens Head

PICK OF THE PUBS

See Pick of the Pubs on opposite page

LLANELIAN-YN-RHÔS — Map 14 SH87

The White Lion Inn

LL29 8YA ☎ 01492 515807
e-mail: info@whitelioninn.co.uk
dir: *A55 junct 22, left signed Old Colwyn, A547. At rdbt 2nd exit onto B5383 signed Betwys-yn-Rhos. In 1m turn right into Llanelian Rd, follow to village. Pub on right*

One of the oldest country inns in north Wales

Parts of this attractive family-run inn are reputed to date back over 1,200 years. It still retains its original slate floor and oak-beamed ceiling, and there is an old salt cellar by the inglenook fireplace. The Cole family have been running the inn for almost 25 years and have restored and preserved many aspects of traditional village life revolving around the pub, including reinstating the snug next to the bar. The food is traditional, home cooked, and wherever possible locally sourced, including of course, shoulder of Welsh lamb. Other dishes on the comprehensive main menu and specials board include fish stew and grilled gammon steak.

Open Tue-Fri 11.30-3 6-11 (Sat 11.30-4 6-11.30 Sun 12-10.30) Closed: Mon (ex BHs) **Bar Meals** L served Tue-Sat 12-2, Sun 12-9 D served Tue-Sat 6-9, Sun 12-9 Av main course £9.99 **Restaurant** L served Tue-Sat 12-2, Sun 12-9 D served Tue-Sat 6-9, Sun 12-9 ⊕ FREE HOUSE ◀ Marston's Pedigree, Mansfield Smooth Creamy Ale & Dark Mild, Guest ale. ☕ 11 **Facilities** Non-diners area ♦ Children's menu Children's portions Garden ⊼ Parking Wi-fi ▭ (notice required)

LLANNEFYDD — Map 14 SH97

The Hawk & Buckle Inn

LL16 5ED ☎ 01745 540249
e-mail: enquiries@hawkandbuckleinn.com
dir: *Telephone for directions*

Old inn situated high in the hills of north Wales

From high in the north Wales hills, this lovingly restored 17th-century coaching inn enjoys spectacular views across the local countryside to Blackpool Tower and beyond. The real ale selection includes The Rev. James and Conwy Celebration, and fresh local produce is used wherever possible to create dishes such as black pudding and goats' cheese stack with apple chutney; slow roasted lamb chump with mint and cranberry gravy; the 8oz Hawk burger topped with Welsh cheese and smoked bacon; or red snapper fillet with citrus butter.

Open all wk Mon-Thu 6-11 Fri-Sat 6-12 Sun 12-10.30 (extended hours during summer) **Bar & Restaurant** L served Sun 12-8 D served Mon-Sat 6-9, Sun 12-8 (extended hours during summer) ⊕ FREE HOUSE ◀ Brains The Rev. James, Purple Moose Glaslyn Ale, Conwy Celebration Ale. **Facilities** Non-diners area Outside area Parking Wi-fi

TREFRIW — Map 14 SH76

The Old Ship

High St LL27 0JH ☎ 01492 640013
e-mail: rhian.barlow@btopenworld.com
dir: *From A470 between Tal-y-Bont & Betws-y-Coed follow Trefriw signs*

A great place to end a walk

A perfect refuelling stop following a tramp in the hills, this traditional inn is situated in a peaceful village in the wooded eastern edge of the Snowdonia National Park. Warm up by the log fire with a refreshing pint of Purple Moose Glaslyn Ale and peruse the daily chalkboard menu. Using locally sourced ingredients, freshly prepared dishes take in pea and ham soup; coq au vin with creamy dauphinoise potatoes and green beans; and pub classics such as fish and chips or sausages with garlic mash and red wine gravy. For dessert, maybe dark and white chocolate cheesecake.

Open 12-3 6-11 (Sat-Sun 12-11) Closed: Mon (ex BHs) **Bar Meals** L served Tue-Fri 12-2.30, Sat-Sun 12-9 D served Tue-Fri 6-9, Sat-Sun 12-9 ⊕ FREE HOUSE ◀ Banks's Bitter, Purple Moose Glaslyn Ale, Bragdyr Nant Cwrw Coryn, Great Orme. ☕ **Facilities** Non-diners area ♦ Children's menu Children's portions Garden ⊼ Parking

DENBIGHSHIRE

LLANELIDAN — Map 15 SJ15

The Leyland Arms

LL15 2PT ☎ 01824 750822
e-mail: info@leylandarms.co.uk
dir: *Midway between Ruthin & Gwyddelwern on A494, left to Llanelidan*

Village community pub overlooking the cricket pitch

Overlooking the cricket pitch and adjacent to St Elidan church in sleepy Llanelidan, deep in the Clwydian Hill, The Leyland Arms is the heart and soul of the village. A true community pub, it's the home of the cricket team and the annual nativity play is held in the stables at the back of the pub. In summer enjoy the views from the terraced garden and hunker down by the fire in winter with a pint of Thwaites Original. Food is prepared from locally sourced ingredients and the daily menu may include warm creamed camembert, leek and chive tartlet; steak-and-kidney suet with real gravy; and bara brith bread-and-butter pudding.

Open 12-3 6-11 Closed: Mon **Bar Meals** L served Tue-Sun 12-3 D served Tue-Sat 6-9 Av main course £10 **Restaurant** L served Tue-Sun 12-2.30 D served Tue-Sun 6-9 ⊕ FREE HOUSE ◀ Thwaites Original & Triple C, Guest ale ♂ Kingstone Press. ☕ 12 **Facilities** Non-diners area ♣ (Bar Garden) ♦ Children's portions Garden ⊼ Cider festival Parking Wi-fi ▭

RHEWL — Map 15 SJ16

The Drovers Arms

Denbigh Rd LL15 2UD ☎ 01824 703163
dir: *1.3m from Ruthin on A525*

Traditional food at small village inn

A small countryside village pub whose name recalls a past written up and illustrated on storyboards displayed inside. Main courses are divided on the menu into poultry, traditional meat, fish, grills and vegetarian; examples from each section are chicken in tarragon sauce; Welsh lamb's liver and onions; Vale of Clwyd sirloin steak; home-made fish pie; and mushroom Stroganoff. Ales are from J W Lees, including Coronation Street, and can be enjoyed in the garden in summer.

Open all wk 12-3 5.30-11 (Sat 12-3 5.30-12 Sun 12-11 Jun-Sep all day) Closed: Tue L ⊕ J W LEES ◀ Bitter, Coronation Street. **Facilities** ♦ Children's menu Children's portions Play area Family room Garden Parking Wi-fi

ST ASAPH
Map 15 SJ07

The Plough Inn

The Roe LL17 0LU ☎ 01745 585080
e-mail: ploughsa@gmail.com
dir: *Exit A55 at Rhyl/St Asaph signs, left at rdbt, pub 200yds on left*

A former coaching inn combining modern and traditional

In Simon Rodenhurst's ten years at this 18th-century coaching inn, his first-floor open kitchen has prepared more than half a million meals. The bar is a quirky blend of modern and traditional, with open fires, blackboard menus, an unusual trompe l'oeil bar and real ales from north Wales; the restaurant, though very modern, retains a vaulted ceiling from its days as a ballroom. Dine here on teriyaki marinated pork fillet with couscous; confit of duck leg with sticky red cabbage and leek mash or pan fried lamb rump on beetroot mash, and help Simon towards his millionth meal. There's live music on Friday nights, as well as a cocktail bar and a wine shop.

Open all day all wk **Bar Meals** L served all wk 10-9 D served all wk 10-9 food served all day **Restaurant** L served all wk 12-9 D served all wk 12-9 ⊕ FREE HOUSE ◄ Conwy, Great Orme, Plassey. ⬤ 10 **Facilities** Non-diners area ✿ (Garden) ◀◀ Children's menu Children's portions Garden Parking Wi-fi ▭

FLINTSHIRE

BABELL
Map 15 SJ17

Black Lion Inn

CH8 8PZ ☎ 01352 720239
e-mail: theblacklioninn@btinternet.com
dir: *A55 junct 31 to Caerwys. Left at x-rds signed Babell. In 3m turn right*

Ancient coaching inn with ghostly residents

A building surely cannot survive for 700 years without acquiring ghosts – and this former coaching inn has plenty, including that of a Canadian man forever asking to come in. From its rural location, it commands mind-blowing views across an Area of Outstanding Natural Beauty. Comfy sofas and an open fire distinguish the bar, where locally-brewed cask ales complement an appealing modern British menu featuring pan-seared Scottish salmon supreme; and free-range Welsh chicken fillet with Caerfyrddin ham and melted Black Bomber cheese. Every Wednesday is pie night, the last Wednesday each month is Celtic Music Night, and there's a September beer festival.

Open all day Closed: Mon, Tue **Bar Meals** L served Wed-Sun 12-9 D served Wed-Sun 12-9 food served all day **Restaurant** L served Wed-Sun 12-9 D served Wed-Sun 12-9 food served all day ⊕ FREE HOUSE ◄ Purple Moose Myrica Gale, Black Lion Bitter, Great Orme Celtica. ⬤ 8 **Facilities** Non-diners area ◀◀ Children's menu Children's portions Play area Garden ▭ Beer festival Parking Wi-fi ▭ (notice required)

CILCAIN
Map 15 SJ16

White Horse Inn

CH7 5NN ☎ 01352 740142
e-mail: christine.jeory@btopenworld.com
dir: *From Mold take A541 towards Denbigh. After approx 6m turn left*

Traditional inn, the hub of the village life

This 400-year-old pub is the last survivor of five originally to be found in this lovely hillside village, probably because it was the centre of the local gold-mining industry in the 19th century. Today, the White Horse is popular with walkers, cyclists and horse-riders. Food here is home made by the landlord's wife using the best quality local ingredients, and is accompanied by a good range of real ales. A typical meal might start with garlic and ginger breaded prawns with curry mayonnaise, followed by home-made steak-and-kidney pie or, for a vegetarian option, three-bean smokey chilli served with basmati rice.

Open all wk 12-3 6.30-11 (Sat 12-11 Sun 12-10.30) **Bar Meals** L served Mon-Sat 12-2.15, Sun 12-3 D served all wk 7-9 ⊕ FREE HOUSE ◄ Purple Moose, Eastgate, Liverpool Organic. ⬤ 9 **Facilities** Non-diners area ✿ (Bar Garden) Garden ▭ Parking Wi-fi

MOLD
Map 15 SJ26

Glasfryn

PICK OF THE PUBS

Raikes Ln, Sychdyn CH7 6LR ☎ 01352 750500
e-mail: glasfryn@brunningandprice.co.uk
dir: *From Mold follow signs to Theatr Clwyd, 1m from town centre*

Hill views, heavenly ales and great menus

With magical views from the gardens over the Alyn Valley towards the rippling hills of the Clwydian Range Area of Outstanding Natural Beauty; this imposing dining pub was converted from a judge's country residence some years ago by the Brunning and Price group. Their hallmark style of polished wood, country and quirky prints, quality antiquey furnishing and largely wood flooring complements the Arts and Crafts style of the original building. Locals wouldn't miss its two beer festivals: the first, in March, celebrates Welsh food and drink; in October it's the turn of British Pie Week together with Champion Beers of Britain. The pub's 12 real ale pumps are the tip of the refreshment iceberg – the wine and malt whisky lists are comprehensive too. Fine pub grub is a given; there's a great range of starters and light bites, or investigate mains like slow cooked shoulder of lamb with cinnamon, cumin and chickpeas, apricot and date couscous.

Open all day all wk **Bar Meals** L served Mon-Sat 12-9.30, Sun 12-9 D served Mon-Sat 12-9.30, Sun 12-9 Av main course £9.95-£17.95 food served all day **Restaurant** L served Mon-Sat 12-9.30, Sun 12-9 D served Mon-Sat 12-9.30, Sun 12-9 food served all day ⊕ BRUNNING & PRICE ◄ Purple Moose Snowdonia Ale, Flowers Original Ŏ Aspall. ⬤ 16 **Facilities** Non-diners area ✿ (Bar Garden) ◀◀ Garden ▭ Beer festival Parking Wi-fi ▭ (notice required)

NORTHOP
Map 15 SJ26

Stables Bar Restaurant ★★★ CHH

CH7 6AB ☎ 01352 840577
e-mail: info@soughtonhall.co.uk
dir: *From A55, take A119 through Northop*

Stable block conversion makes an excellent eatery

This unusual free house dates from the 18th century and was created from Soughton Hall's stable block, and original features like the cobbled floors and roof timbers remain intact; the magnificent main house was built as a bishop's palace. The selection of real ales includes Stables Bitter, or diners can browse the wine shop for a bottle to accompany their meal. The Classic menu offers ciabatta sandwiches, platters to share and hearty main courses, while the seasonal à la carte dinner menu features perhaps chicken, chorizo and polenta croquette on red onion relish with crispy pancetta. Enjoy the gardens in summer.

Open all day all wk ⊕ FREE HOUSE ◄ Coach House Honeypot Best Bitter & Dick Turpin Premium Bitter, Plassey Bitter, Stables Bitter. **Facilities** ◀◀ Children's menu Children's portions Family room Garden Parking Wi-fi **Rooms** 15

GWYNEDD

ABERDYFI
Map 14 SN69

Penhelig Arms Hotel & Restaurant

PICK OF THE PUBS

See Pick of the Pubs on opposite page

BEDDGELERT
Map 14 SH54

Tanronnen Inn ★★★★ INN

LL55 4YB ☎ 01766 890347
e-mail: guestservice@tanronnen.co.uk
dir: *In village centre opposite river bridge*

Great hospitality at the heart of Snowdonia

Originally part of the Beddgelert Estate, this stone-built building was the stables for the passing coach trade in 1809; after conversion to a cottage, it opened as a beer house in 1830. By the end of the 19th century, it had two letting bedrooms and was serving meals for visitors. Badly damaged by flooding in 1906, the shop at the back was incorporated to provide more accommodation. Today's inn has two attractive small bars serving Robinsons ales, a large lounge with open fire, a dining room open to non-residents in which to enjoy home-cooked meals, and attractive accommodation.

Open all day all wk **Bar Meals** L served all wk 12.30-2 D served all wk 7-8 **Restaurant** L served all wk 12.30-2 D served all wk 7-8 ⊕ ROBINSONS ◄ Unicorn, Dizzy Blonde. **Facilities** Non-diners area ◀◀ Children's menu Children's portions Outside area ▭ Parking **Rooms** 7

Save on hotels. Book at **theAA.com/hotel**

GWYNEDD 565 WALES

PICK OF THE PUBS

Penhelig Arms Hotel & Restaurant

ABERDYFI　　　　Map 14 SN69

Terrace Rd LL35 0LT ☎ 01654 767215
e-mail: info@penheligarms.com
web: www.penheligarms.com
dir: *On A493, W of Machynlleth*

Small hostelry with a big reputation

This popular waterside inn has been serving travellers and locals since 1870 and offers spectacular views over the mountain-backed tidal Dyfi Estuary, a nature reserve rich in birdlife. Aberdyfi is a charming little resort with a championship golf course, and sandy beach and harbour, making it a favourite with golfers and watersports enthusiasts; the Penhelig Arms is also perfectly situated for visitors to Cader Idris, the Snowdonia National Park and several historic castles in the area. Music and TV-free, the wood-panelled and log-fire-warmed Fisherman's Bar is a cosy and friendly bolt-hole to enjoy Brains real ales and bar meals such as smoked salmon salad, roast supreme of chicken, chargrilled rump steak burger and bloomer sandwiches. The waterfront restaurant offers a more brasserie-style experience with views over the estuary and menus showcasing the abundant Welsh seafood (a Penhelig speciality) and Welsh beef and lamb. The kitchen team emphasise the freshness of ingredients and fuse local and

cosmopolitan influences in a style of cooking that allows natural flavours to shine through. A typical menu might include seared scallops, chorizo and citrus dressing; roast rack of lamb, creamed potatoes, mange-tout, port and red wine sauce; or wild mushroom raviolini with truffle oil. Leave room for apple pie with clotted cream; orange and cardamom pannacotta; or a Welsh cheese slate with biscuits, fruit cake and honey. On Sundays, expect a set menu featuring a traditional roast. Daily specials are listed on the blackboard. The short wine list is attractively priced and complements the excellent food. In warmer weather, you can sit outside on the sea wall terrace.

Open all day all wk **Bar Meals** L served all wk 12-2 D served all wk 6-9 Av main course £10.25 **Restaurant** L served all wk 12-2 D served all wk 7-9 Fixed menu price fr £15 Av 3 course à la carte fr £19 ⊕ BRAINS ◾ Bitter & The Rev. James, Guest ale ♨ Westons Stowford Press, Thatchers Katy. ♟ 20 **Facilities** Non-diners area 🐾 ♦️ Children's menu & portions Outside area ⊓ Parking Wi-fi 🚌 (notice required)

BLAENAU FFESTINIOG — Map 14 SH74

The Miners Arms

Llechwedd Slate Caverns LL41 3NB ☎ 01766 830306
e-mail: bookings@llechwedd.co.uk
dir: *From Llandudno take A470 S. Through Betwys-y-Coed, 16m to Blaenau Ffestiniog*

Replica of a Victorian miners' pub

Housed in two former miners' cottages on the site of Llechwedd Slate Caverns, this welcoming pub is a great place to finish an underground tour, where you can glimpse the life of a Victorian slate quarryman. Slate floors, open fires and staff in Victorian costume emphasise the heritage theme and this extends to the menu which includes tasty home-made soup, sandwiches, a 'traditional miner's lunch' and lobsgows, a local speciality stew that reputedly dates back to Blaenau Ffestiniog's trading links with Hamburg. Welsh treats such as bara brith (a moist fruit bread) and Welsh cakes are also available.

Open 9-5.30 Closed: winter, Mon-Fri except BHs and local school holidays **Bar Meals** L served all wk 11-3.30 ⊕ FREE HOUSE ◀ Purple Moose. **Facilities** Non-diners area ♦♦ Children's portions Play area Family room Garden 🏞 Parking 🚌

BRITHDIR — Map 14 SH71

Cross Foxes NEW

LL40 2SG ☎ 01341 421001
e-mail: hello@crossfoxes.co.uk
dir: *At junct of A470 & A487, 4m from Dolgellau*

Rejuvinated inn, certainly worth finding

How fortunate that Nicol and Dewi Gwynne bought an abandoned pub, then brilliantly transformed it. Grade II listed it may be, but what an interior! True, they've used traditional Welsh materials like slate and stone, but the effect is light years from being Welsh Traditional. In the impressive Bar & Café you'll find regional real ales and ciders and a multiplicity of teas (including one from Wales!), fresh coffees and finger sandwiches. A meal in the Grill might be lamb cawl with Caerphilly cheese; Snowdonia Ale-battered sea bass; and strawberry meringue roulade. Gaze at Cadair Idris from the large decked area.

Open all day all wk **Bar Meals** L served all wk 12-9 D served all wk 12-9 Av main course £9.95 food served all day **Restaurant** L served all wk 12-2.30 D served all wk 5.30-9 Av 3 course à la carte fr £25 ⊕ FREE HOUSE ◀ Cader Ales, Evan Evans ♂ Kingstone Press. **Facilities** Non-diners area ❀ (Bar Garden) ♦♦ Children's menu Children's portions Garden 🏞 Parking Wi-fi 🚌 (notice required)

CAERNARFON — Map 14 SH46

Black Boy Inn ★★★★ INN

Northgate St LL55 1RW ☎ 01286 673604
e-mail: office@black-boy-inn.com
web: www.black-boy-inn.com
dir: *A55 junct 9 onto A487, follow signs for Caernarfon. Within town walls between castle & Victoria Dock*

Old fashioned values in the shadow of Caernarfon Castle

Character oozes from the very fabric of this ancient gabled inn, one of the oldest in Wales (built 1522). Relax with a pint of local Snowdonia Ale in the fire-warmed, low-ceilinged rooms strewn amidst beams and struts rescued from old ships. Meat and other products are generally local, and dishes from the long menu include field mushrooms and red onion compôte; vegetable cobbler; black pudding-stuffed chicken breast; and braised lamb shank. The well-proportioned bedrooms are ideal for those wishing to explore Mount Snowdon, the Lleyn Peninsula or catch the Welsh Highland Railway.

Open all day all wk **Bar Meals** L served 12-9 D served 12-9 food served all day **Restaurant** L served 12-9 D served 12-9 food served all day ⊕ FREE HOUSE ◀ Purple Moose Snowdonia Ale, Brains The Rev. James, Hancock's. **Facilities** Non-diners area ♦♦ Children's menu Children's portions Play area Garden 🏞 Parking Wi-fi 🚌 **Rooms** 26

LLANBEDR — Map 14 SH52

Victoria Inn ★★★★ INN

LL45 2LD ☎ 01341 241213
e-mail: junevicinn@aol.com
dir: *On A496 between Barmouth and Harlech*

Close to the beach and many mountain walks

Fascinating features for pub connoisseurs are the circular wooden settle, ancient stove, grandfather clock and flagged floors in the atmospheric bar of the Victoria.

Home-made food is served in the lounge bar and restaurant, complemented by a range of Robinsons traditional ales. A children's play area has been incorporated into the well-kept garden, with a playhouse, slides and swings. Situated beside the River Artro, the Rhinog mountain range and the famous Roman Steps are right on the doorstep. If you would like to explore the area, there are five spacious and thoughtfully furnished bedrooms to stay in.

Open all day all wk 11-11 (Sun 12-10.30) ⊕ ROBINSONS ◀ Unicorn, Guest ales ♂ Westons Stowford Press. **Facilities** ♦♦ Children's menu Children's portions Play area Garden Parking **Rooms** 5

PENNAL — Map 14 SH60

Glan yr Afon/Riverside

Riverside Hotel SY20 9DW ☎ 01654 791285
e-mail: info@riversidehotel-pennal.co.uk
dir: *3m from Machynlleth on A493 towards Aberdovey. Pub on left*

Stylish 16th-century inn between sea and mountains

In the glorious Dyfi Valley close to Cader Idris and Cardigan Bay this family-run inn has slate floors, modern light oak furnishings and bold funky fabrics. There's a wood-burning stove pumping out heat in winter, Dark Side of the Moose ale on tap, and a good range of modern pub food. Relax and opt for a starter of warm duck, onion and orange salad, then a robust fish stew of king prawns and chorizo, or pork schnitzel with creamy cider and sage sauce. There's a riverside garden, with views to the hills, for summer enjoyment.

Open all wk 12-3 6-11 Closed: 25-26 Dec, 2wks Jan **Bar Meals** L served all wk 12-2 D served all wk 6-9 Av main course £13.95 **Restaurant** L served all wk 12-2 D served all wk 6-9 Fixed menu price fr £10.15 Av 3 course à la carte fr £25.50 ⊕ FREE HOUSE ◀ Sharp's Doom Bar, Purple Moose Dark Side of the Moose & Snowdonia Ale, Salopian Golden Thread, Stonehouse, Brewdog ♂ Kingstone Press. ♚ 12 **Facilities** Non-diners area ❀ (Bar Garden) ♦♦ Children's menu Children's portions Garden 🏞 Parking Wi-fi 🚌 (notice required)

TREMADOG — Map 14 SH53

The Union Inn NEW

7 Market Square LL49 9RB ☎ 01766 512748
e-mail: mail@union-inn.com
dir: *From Porthmadog follow A487. Caernarfon signs. Follow Tremadog signs. Inn on right before T-junct in village centre*

Freehold, family-run pub in historic setting

Hefty local stones were used to build this early 19th-century pub, part of a row of cottages facing the main square of Britain's first planned town. Customers can thank these stones for the snugness of the interior, not least the bar, which offers such a good choice of Welsh real ales and ciders. Home-made food is fresh, locally sourced and seasonal, with Welsh lamb and beef dishes held in particularly high regard. You'll also find authentic curries, steak and ale pie, fresh fish, scampi and vegetarian dishes, such as mushroom Stroganoff, and daily specials.

Open all wk 12-2 5.30-11.30 **Bar Meals** L served all wk 12-2 D served all wk 5.30-9 **Restaurant** L served all wk 12-2 D served all wk 5.30-9 ⊕ FREE HOUSE ◀ Purple Moose Snowdonia Ale & Madog's Ale, Great Orme, Big Bog Ö Gwynt y Ddraig Happy Daze, Dog Dancer & Farmhouse Scrumpy. **Facilities** Non-diners area ❖ (Bar Outside area) ♦♦ Children's menu Children's portions Outside area ᗒ Wi-fi ᔆ (notice required)

TUDWEILIOG   Map 14 SH23

Lion Hotel

LL53 8ND ☎ 01758 770244
e-mail: martlee.lion@gmail.com
dir: *A487 from Caernarfon onto A499 towards Pwllheli. Right onto B4417 to Nefyn, through Edern to Tudweiliog*

A reputation for value for money

Standing at a tangent to the road, beyond a garden with tables and chairs, the 300-year-old Lion has been run by the Lee family for the past 40 years. The bar features an extensive list of whiskies, alongside real ales from Big Bog, Cwrw Llyn and Purple Moose breweries, all Welsh of course. Typical pub meals include spare ribs in barbecue sauce; lamb or chicken balti; sweet chilli, prawn and cod fishcakes; and leek and mushroom crumble. Ample parking and a children's play area both help to make it popular with the many families holidaying in the beautiful Lleyn Peninsula.

Open all wk 11-3 6-11 (summer all day) **Bar Meals** L served all wk 12-2 D served all wk 6-9 Av main course £9.20 ⊕ FREE HOUSE ◀ Cwrw Llyn Brenin Enlli, Big Bog, Purple Moose, Guinness. **Facilities** Non-diners area ♦♦ Children's menu Children's portions Play area Family room Garden ᗒ Parking Wi-fi ᔆ (notice required)

WAUNFAWR   Map 14 SH55

Snowdonia Parc Brewpub & Campsite

LL55 4AQ ☎ 01286 650409 & 650218
e-mail: info@snowdonia-park.co.uk
dir: *Telephone for directions*

Own microbrewery and wholesome food

In the heart of Snowdonia, a short drive from Mount Snowdon, this popular walkers' pub is located at Waunfawr Station on the Welsh Highland Railway. There are steam trains on site (the building was originally the stationmaster's house), plus a microbrewery and campsite. Home-cooked food ranges from chicken, leek and ham pie to vegetable curry and roast Welsh beef with all the trimmings. Naturally the pub serves its own Welsh Highland Bitter along with other ales. The Welsh Highland Railway Rail Ale Festival is held in mid-May.

Open all day all wk 11-11 (Fri-Sat 11am-11.30pm) **Bar Meals** food served all day **Restaurant** food served all day ⊕ FREE HOUSE ◀ Snowdonia Welsh Highland Bitter, Summer Ale, Carmen Sutra, Cais & Gwyrfai, Corvedale Dark & Delicious, John Thompson Gold. **Facilities** Non-diners area ❖ (Bar Garden) ♦♦ Children's menu Play area Family room Garden ᗒ Beer festival Parking Wi-fi ᔆ (notice required)

MONMOUTHSHIRE

ABERGAVENNY   Map 9 SO21

Clytha Arms

PICK OF THE PUBS

See Pick of the Pubs on page 568

LLANGYBI   Map 9 ST39

The White Hart Village Inn ◉◉

PICK OF THE PUBS

NP15 1NP ☎ 01633 450258
e-mail: enquiries@thewhitehartvillageinn.com
dir: *M4 junct 25 onto B4596 (Caerleon road), through Caerleon High St, straight over rdbt into Usk Rd, continue to Llangybi*

Visitors keep coming back for the excellent cuisine

Situated in the beautiful Usk Valley in a pretty village, a warm welcome awaits at this picturesque historic inn where no less than 11 fireplaces can be found. Oliver Cromwell based himself here during local Civil War campaigns; so add a priest hole, exposed beams, precious Tudor plasterwork and a mention in TS Eliot's poem *Usk* and you've a destination to savour. Chef-patron Michael Bates offers reliable ales from the likes of Wychwood Hobgoblin, as well as a variety of ciders. Using fresh local produce, and combining exciting ingredients and complementary flavours, head chef Adam Whittle prepares dishes with the utmost attention to detail to create two-AA Rosette menus. The à la carte starts with swede velouté, truffle and honey, followed by saddle of wild rabbit, braised leg and lettuce, lemon quinoa, salsify and mustard. Finish with blood orange trifle. In summer, head outside to the extensive seating area.

Open all day 12-11 (Sun 12-10) Closed: Mon **Bar Meals** L served Tue-Sat 12-6 Av main course £7.25 food served all day **Restaurant** L served Tue-Sat 12-3, Sun 12-4 D served Tue-Sat 6-10 Fixed menu price fr £18.95 Av 3 course à la carte fr £25 ⊕ FREE HOUSE ◀ Wye Valley Butty Bach, Wychwood Hobgoblin Ö Thatchers Gold, Ty Gwyn, Gwynt y Ddraig Farmhouse Scrumpy. ♟ 15

Facilities Non-diners area ♦♦ Children's menu Children's portions Garden ᗒ Parking Wi-fi

LLANTRISANT   Map 9 ST39

The Greyhound Inn

PICK OF THE PUBS

See Pick of the Pubs on page 570
See advert on page 569

LLANVAIR DISCOED   Map 9 ST49

The Woodlands Tavern Country Pub & Dining

PICK OF THE PUBS

NP16 6LX ☎ 01633 400313
e-mail: info@thewoodlandstavern.co.uk
dir: *5m from Caldicot & Magor*

Family-run village pub with a modern menu

The Woodlands Tavern is a friendly, family-run village free house at the foot of Gray Hill, close to the Roman fortress town of Caerwent and walking trails through Wentwood Forest. A patio ensures that food and drink can be served outside in fine weather. As well as being popular with walkers, cyclists and fishermen who quench their thirsts with pints of Wye Valley, Bevan's Bitter and regularly changing guest ales, The Woodlands draws diners from far and wide for its modern British menu and daily chalkboard specials. Typically, you can tuck into goujons of Cornish plaice with tartare sauce, and follow that with braised Welsh lamb shank on mash with red wine and rosemary sauce. Fish specials appear on the blackboard: perhaps prawn and crayfish risotto or seafood linguine. The popular Sunday three-course lunch will probably feature roast sirloin of beef with Yorkshire pudding. Apple pie with creamy custard is an irresistible pud with which to finish.

Open 12-3 6-12 (Sun 12-4) Closed: 1 Jan, Sun eve, Mon **Bar Meals** L served Tue-Fri 12-2, Sat 12-2.30, Sun 12-4 D served Tue-Fri 6-9, Sat 6-9.30 **Restaurant** L served Tue-Fri 12-2, Sat 12-2.30, Sun 12-4 D served Tue-Fri 6-9, Sat 6-9.30 Fixed menu price fr £10.95 ⊕ FREE HOUSE ◀ Rhymney Bevan's Bitter, Felinfoel, Marston's & Pedigree, Wye Valley Butty Bach, Guest ales Ö Westons Old Rosie, Thatchers Gold. ♟ 10
Facilities Non-diners area ❖ (Bar Outside area) ♦♦ Children's menu Children's portions Outside area ᗒ Parking Wi-fi ᔆ (notice required)

PICK OF THE PUBS

Clytha Arms

ABERGAVENNY   Map 9 SO21

Clytha NP7 9BW ☎ 01873 840206
e-mail: theclythaarms@btinternet.com
web: www.clytha-arms.com
dir: *From A449/A40 junction (E of Abergavenny) follow Old Road Abergavenny/Clytha signs*

Friendly pub with excellent beers

Tucked away off the old Abergavenny to Raglan road, this eye-catching converted dower house stands on the edge of parkland dotted with small woods and the occasional folly. There are enchanting views from the large garden across the lush Vale of Gwent towards Blorenge Mountain and the shapely Skirrid Hill, whilst the Usk Valley Walk follows the nearby river. The main bar is full of character, with old pews, tables and rustic furnishings, as well as posters and a wood-burning stove. The pub is renowned for its range of real ales, with Wye Valley Bitter and over 300 guest ales every year supporting some great artisan ciders and perrys. Drinkers who feel the need for a little more choice can enjoy the Clytha's annual Welsh Cider Festival, or the Welsh Beer, Cheese and Music festival, held over the late May and August Bank Holiday weekends respectively. Grazers can have a simple tapas from Andrew Canning's widely fêted gastro-pub menu, or tuck into a full restaurant meal accompanied by a

choice of over 100 wines, including a white from the nearby Monnow Valley vineyard. Starters like grilled oysters with laverbread and Caerphilly; or charcuterie with celeriac salad might herald a main course of stuffed ham with cider sauce and sauté potatoes; Caerphilly and walnut stuffed aubergine with basil risotto; or wild boar and duck cassoulet. Mango brûlée with coconut ice cream is a typical choice for dessert. Local attractions include Raglan Castle, as well as golf, fishing and countryside walks.

Open 12-3 6-12 (Fri-Sun 12-12) Closed: 25 Dec, Mon L **Bar meals** & **Restaurant** L served Tue-Sun 12.30-2.30 D served Mon-Sat 7-9.30

⊕ FREE HOUSE ◀ The Kite CPA, Rhymney Bitter, Wye Valley Bitter, 4 Guest ales (300+ per year) ⚭ Gwynt y Ddraig Black Dragon, Ragan Perry, Clytha Perry. **Facilities** Non-diners area ⫯ Children's menu Children's portions Play area Garden Beer festival Cider festival Parking Wi-fi

The Greyhound Hotel & Inn

This picturesque 18th century stone-built village pub in the glorious Usk Valley offers everything you would expect from the best of country inns. In the same family hands for over 30 years, the pub's owner and chef Nick Davies and his staff are proud of its great reputation for delicious, home-cooked food, and the relaxed, friendly atmosphere. In winter, the roaring log fires and cosy bars cheer up the worst of the weather. In summer, the beautiful gardens are the perfect setting for enjoying a drink or something to eat on warmer days and evenings. Fresh, local ingredients are used in the extensive variety of meals and snacks, whenever possible. The menu includes traditional British favourites such as steak pie, fresh battered cod or liver and bacon with onions, as well as dishes like lasagne verdi, chicken curry and several vegetarian options. There are daily 'specials' and a range of mostly home-made puddings and desserts.

Sandwiches and other light snacks are available at lunchtimes. The main bar serves the three lounges, with their comfortable seating and tables. The old-fashioned Stable Bar has a tiled floor, so is ideal for muddy-booted walkers. There is a range of real ales, traditional cask and bottled beers and ciders, wines, spirits and soft drinks. The 10 en-suite rooms are located in a stone-built, two-storey, 17th century stable block next to the main building. Facilities include free wi-fi and flat screen TVs. A newly-equipped drying room is available for golfers and hikers. Competitively-priced accommodation rates include a full cooked breakfast.

Llantrissent, near Usk, Monmouthshire NP15 1LE • **Tel:** 01291 672505/673447
Website: www.greyhound-inn.com • **Email:** enquiry@greyhound-inn.com

PICK OF THE PUBS

The Greyhound Inn

LLANTRISANT　　　　Map 9 ST39

NP15 1LE ☎ 01291 672505 & 673447
e-mail: enquiry@greyhound-inn.com
web: www.greyhound-inn.com
dir: *M4 junct 24, A449 towards
Monmouth, exit at 1st junct signed Usk.
2nd left for Llantrisant. Or from
Monmouth A40, A449 exit for Usk. In Usk
left into Twyn Sq follow Llantrisant
signs. 2.5m under A449 bridge. Inn on
right*

Good food and ale in beautiful surroundings

Standing alone a little way out of
Llantrisant (Llantrissent) village, the
Greyhound was built as a traditional
Welsh longhouse in the 18th century,
before becoming an inn in 1845. It has
been in the hands of the same family for
over 30 years. The three lounges are
served by the Stable Bar, where you can
find a range of real ales including
Flowers Original, a monthly guest, and
Gwynt y Ddraig and Kingstone Press
ciders. You can also play darts, crib or
dominoes in front of the log fire. As well
as running the whole show, Nick heads
the highly-praised kitchen team, the
fruits of whose labours you can enjoy in
the candlelit dining room and
elsewhere. Among his starters are duck
spring rolls with hoisin sauce; and
deep-fried whitebait, while in addition
to several grills he offers chilli con
carne; a medium-fruity chicken curry;

battered plaice; freshly grilled local
trout; and home-made cauliflower
cheese with salad. Daily specials boards
offer unusual and seasonal dishes,
including half a dozen featuring chicken
differently styled – chasseur, coq au vin
and Véronique, for example; Welsh
venison and ale pie; pork and prunes;
lamb cutlets, lamb shank and lamb
Provençal; and salmon. Outside are two
acres of award-winning flower gardens,
a large paddock and an array of
restored outbuildings. The Usk Valley
Walk runs nearby on its 48-mile journey
between the Roman town of Caerleon
and Brecon, along the way visiting the
riverside towns of Usk and Abergavenny,
where it enters the Brecon Beacons
National Park.

Open all day 11-11 Closed: 25 & 31
Dec, 1 Jan, Sun eve **Bar Meals** L served
all wk 12-2.15 D served Mon-Sat 6-10
Restaurant L served all wk 12-2.15 D
served Mon-Sat 6-10 ⊕ FREE HOUSE
◗ Flowers Original & Bass, Greene King
Abbot Ale, Guest ale ♂ Gwynt y Ddraig,
Kingstone Press. ♟ 10 **Facilities** Non-
diners area ♦♦ Children's menu Family
room Garden ⋒ Parking Wi-fi
🚌 (notice required)

PANTYGELLI   Map 9 SO31

The Crown

Old Hereford Rd NP7 7HR ☎ **01873 853314**
e-mail: crown@pantygelli.com
dir: *Telephone for directions*

Family-run free house with fine views

A charming family-run free house dating from the 16th
century, The Crown has fine views of Skirrid, in Welsh
Ysgyrid Fawr, known also as Holy Mountain. Walkers and
cyclists love it, but it's a genuine community pub too,
serving Bass, Rhymney Bitter, Wye Valley and guest real
ales and Gwatkin cider, all ideal before or with king
prawn, lemon and dill risotto with chervil garnish; roast
duck breast with a red wine and fresh fig sauce, shredded
spring cabbage and gaufrette potato crisps; and a
dessert of sticky toffee pudding with butterscotch sauce.

Open 12-2.30 6-11 (Sat 12-3 6-11 Sun 12-3 6-10.30)
Closed: Mon L **Bar Meals** L served Tue-Sun 12-2 D served
Tue-Sat 7-9 **Restaurant** L served Tue-Sun 12-2 D served
Tue-Sat 7-9 ⊕ FREE HOUSE ◀ Rhymney Bitter, Wye Valley
HPA, Bass, Guest ales ○ Westons Stowford Press,
Gwatkin Yarlington Mill, Kingstone Press.
Facilities Non-diners area ❀ (Bar Garden) ♦ Children's
portions Garden ⌒ Parking Wi-fi

PENALLT   Map 4 SO51

The Inn at Penallt ★★★★ INN ◉

PICK OF THE PUBS

NP25 4SE ☎ **01600 772765**
e-mail: enquiries@theinnatpenallt.co.uk
web: www.theinnatpenallt.co.uk
dir: *From Monmouth take B4293 to Trellech. Approx 2m,
left at brown sign for inn. At next x-rds left. Right at war
memorial*

Magical village location high above the Wye

Standing between the village green and colourful
wildflower meadows, the inn's enviable setting
culminates with the famous Wye Gorge, blanketed in
thick woodland just beyond the village edge. Rescued
from closure a few years ago by Jackie and Andrew
Murphy, past winners of AA Pub of the Year for Wales,
their AA-Rosette standard menu is well crafted from
sustainable local produce. Nibble on olives and home-
made bread with olive oil while making your choices, and
then perhaps start with Welsh goats' cheese pannacotta;
or Madgett's Farm chicken liver and summer truffle

parfait, and follow on with the duo of Brecon venison with
parsnip purée; or the pan-roasted cod steak with crushed
pea and smoked bacon risotto. Vegetarians will surely be
tempted by the trio of vegetarian tasters – goats' cheese
beingets and cauliflower cream, wild mushroom tartlet,
and crushed pea and asparagus risotto with aged
parmesan. Desserts should not be overlooked – perhaps
the lemon scented treacle tart with ginger ice cream, or
almond and Amaretto trifle will round off what is sure to
be a memorable meal.

The Inn at Penallt

Open Tue 6-11 Wed-Fri 12-3 6-11 Sat 12-11 Sun 12-5
Closed: 1st 2wks Jan, Mon (ex BHs) **Bar Meals** L served
Wed-Sun 12-2.30 D served Tue-Sat 6-9 Av main course
£15 **Restaurant** L served Wed-Sun 12-2.30 D served Tue-
Sat 6-9 Av 3 course à la carte fr £25 ⊕ FREE HOUSE
◀ Wye Valley Butty Bach, Kingstone Classic Bitter,
Newmans Wolvers Ale ○ Ty Gwyn, Gwynt y Ddraig Black
Dragon. ▾ **Facilities** Non-diners area ❀ (Bar Garden) ♦
Children's menu Children's portions Play area Garden ⌒
Parking Wi-fi ⇔ **Rooms** 4

See advert below

RAGLAN
Map 9 SO40

The Beaufort Arms Coaching Inn & Brasserie ★★★ HL ⊛

PICK OF THE PUBS

High St NP15 2DY ☎ **01291 690412**
e-mail: enquiries@beaufortraglan.co.uk
dir: 0.5m from junct of A40 & A449 Abergavenny/
Monmouth, midway between M50 & M4

Excellent hostelry with a rich history

This grandly proportioned former coaching inn has always had strong links with nearby Raglan Castle; during the Civil War Roundhead soldiers frequented the bar during the siege of 1646. Nowadays, the place is equally popular when re-enactments are held at the castle, so it's not unusual to see men in full medieval armour tucking into a full Welsh breakfast in the brasserie. The inn has been beautifully appointed with many delightful design features, while holding strong to its traditional roots. A handsome display of fishing trophies dominates the country bar, where locals and visitors gather and chat over pints of The Rev. James. The inn offers well-kept real ales, ciders, and Belgian and German beers. Food is served in the lounge, with its carved bar, deep leather settees, and large stone fireplace ('lifted', some say, from the castle), as well as in the private dining room and brasserie. Enjoy skilfully presented modern dishes from a regularly changing menu, such as crispy crab, mushroom and leek risotto; slow roasted ginger and citrus shoulder of pork, mash, honey glazed carrots; or venison medallions, beetroot, fondant potatoes, with cinnamon, blackberry and orange jus; and steamed spiced plum pudding with crème anglaise. The weekly-changing specials board includes fresh fish from Devon.

Open all day all wk Closed: 25 Dec **Bar Meals** L served Mon-Thu 12-3, Fri-Sat 12-5 D served all wk 6-9.30 **Restaurant** L served Mon-Thu 12-3, Fri-Sat 12-5, Sun 12-4 D served Mon-Sat 6-9.30, Sun 6-8.30 ⊕ FREE HOUSE ◀ Fuller's London Pride, Brains The Rev. James, Morland Old Speckled Hen, Wye Valley Butty Bach ♨ Westons Stowford Press, Thatchers Gold. ♟ 16 **Facilities** Non-diners area ♦♦ Children's menu Children's portions Garden ⋒ Parking Wi-fi ▦ (notice required) **Rooms** 15

RHYD-Y-MEIRCH
Map 9 SO30

Goose and Cuckoo Inn

Upper Llanover NP7 9ER ☎ **01873 880277**
e-mail: llanovergoose@gmail.com
dir: From Abergavenny take A4042 towards Pontypool. Turn left after Llanover, follow signs for inn

Walkers' haven with food from the Aga

Popular with walkers, this friendly, whitewashed pub in the Brecon Beacons National Park has a garden with views of the Malvern Hills and a traditional interior with flagstoned bar area and a wood-burning stove. So, the perfect setting for a pint of well-kept Rhymney Bitter or one of the 85 single malt whiskies. All the food is home

made on the Aga by landlady Carol Dollery; typical dishes include parsnip soup; steak and ale pie; lasagne; quiche; and treacle tart. The pub hosts two beer festivals – in May and August.

Open Tue-Thu 11.30-3 7-11 (Fri-Sun all day) Closed: Mon (ex BHs) **Bar Meals** L served Tue-Sun 11.30-3 D served Tue-Sun 7-9 ⊕ FREE HOUSE ◀ Rhymney Bitter, Newmans Red Stag ♨ Kingstone Press. **Facilities** Non-diners area ♣ (Bar Garden) ♦♦ Children's portions Family room Garden ⋒ Beer festival Parking **Notes** ⊛

SHIRENEWTON
Map 9 ST49

The Carpenters Arms

Usk Rd NP16 6BU ☎ **01291 641231**
dir: M48 junct 2, A48 to Chepstow then A4661, B4235. Village 3m on left

Traditional inn in a wooded valley

Between the rivers Wye and Usk in the wooded valley of the Mounton Brook, this 400-year-old traditional country pub was formerly a smithy and carpenter's shop. Today it has four bars with flagstone floors, open fires, church pew seating and lots of old chamber pots. Home-made food is typified by Stilton stuffed mushrooms with garlic mayonnaise; chicken and leek pie with a choice of potatoes, vegetables and gravy; and home-made sticky toffee sponge pudding with caramel sauce, cream and ice cream. Daily specials might include honey-glazed duck breast with plum sauce. Traditional Sunday roasts are popular.

Open 12-3 5.30-12 (Sat 12-2.30 5-11 Sun 12-4.30) Closed: Mon L **Bar Meals** L served Tue-Sun 12-2 D served Mon-Sat 6.30-9.30 **Restaurant** L served Tue-Sun 12-2 D served Mon-Sat 6.30-9.30 ⊕ PUNCH TAVERNS ◀ Fuller's London Pride, Marstons Pedigree ♨ Gaymers. ♟ **Facilities** Non-diners area ♣ (Bar Outside area) ♦♦ Children's menu Children's portions Family room Outside area ⋒ Parking Wi-fi ▦ (notice required)

SKENFRITH
Map 9 SO42

The Bell at Skenfrith ★★★★★ RR ⊛⊛

PICK OF THE PUBS

NP7 8UH ☎ **01600 750235**
e-mail: enquiries@skenfrith.co.uk
dir: M4 junct 24 onto A449. Exit onto A40, through tunnel & lights. At rdbt take 1st exit, right at lights onto A466 towards Hereford road. Left onto B4521 towards Abergavenny, 3m on left

Award-winning inn with an organic kitchen garden

Husband-and-wife team William and Janet Hutchings create a welcoming atmosphere at this 17th-century coaching inn on the banks of the River Monnow. Character oozes from the fully restored oak bar, flagstone floors, comfortable sofas and old settles, while 11 individually decorated bedrooms, some with four-posters, provide high-quality accommodation. On draught are Wye Valley Bitter and Hereford Pale Ale, Kingstone Classic

Bitter, as well as Ty Gwyn local cider. The two AA-Rosette restaurant uses produce from the kitchen garden in its regularly changing menus and daily specials board. For lunch, you could choose fillet of lemon sole with nero pasta and bok choy. For a thoroughly satisfying three-course dinner, perhaps local game and foie gras terrine, red wine pickled carrots, fig jam and seeded bread; roasted butternut squash, caramelised red onions, chestnut gnocchi, purple sprouting broccoli, spiced seeds and sage foam; and rum and raisin rice pudding. The acclaimed wine list offers a well-chosen world selection. There are splendid views of Skenfrith Castle from the pub.

Open all day Closed: Tue Nov-Mar **Bar Meals** L served all wk 12-2.30 D served Mon-Sat 7-9.30, Sun 7-9 Av main course £15 **Restaurant** L served all wk 12-2.30 D served Mon-Sat 7-9.30, Sun 7-9 Fixed menu price fr £18 Av 3 course à la carte fr £33 ⊕ FREE HOUSE ◀ Wye Valley Bitter & HPA, Kingstone Classic Bitter ♨ Westons Stowford Press, Ty Gwyn, Local cider. ♟ 13 **Facilities** Non-diners area ♦♦ Children's menu Garden ⋒ Parking Wi-fi **Rooms** 11

TINTERN PARVA
Map 4 SO50

Fountain Inn

Trellech Grange NP16 6QW ☎ **01291 689303**
e-mail: fountaininntintern@btconnect.com
dir: From M48 junct 2 follow Chepstow then A466/Tintern signs. In Tintern turn by George Hotel for Raglan. Bear right, inn at top of hill, 2m from A466

Good food and well-kept ales at this village pub

A fine old inn dating from 1611 in lovely countryside, with a garden overlooking the Wye Valley. New owners offer several curries, including chicken Kashmiri, and fruit and vegetable Jalfrezi; and Welsh Black beef, Welsh lamb and roasted ham, all with fresh vegetables, roast potatoes, Yorkshire pudding and beer gravy. They also have a fresh fish menu with whole griddled flounder; sizzling crevettes; and beer-battered cod and chips. Their passion for real ales and ciders is evident both in the great bar line-up, and at the Easter and September beer festivals.

Open all day all wk **Bar Meals** L served Tue-Sun 12-2.30 D served all wk 6-9 **Restaurant** L served Tue-Sun 12-2.30 D served all wk 6-9 ⊕ FREE HOUSE ◀ Wychwood Hobgoblin, Brains The Rev. James, Kingstone Classic Bitter, Whittingtons Cats Whiskers, Butcombe, Mayfields, Rhymney, Hook Norton, Hereford, Ring O'Bells, Bass ♨ Thatchers Gold, Broadoak. ♟ 9 **Facilities** Non-diners area ♣ (Bar Garden) ♦♦ Children's menu Children's portions Family room Garden ⋒ Beer festival Parking Wi-fi ▦ (notice required)

Save on hotels. Book at **theAA.com/hotel**

MONMOUTHSHIRE – NEWPORT 573 WALES

TREDUNNOCK
Map 9 ST39

Newbridge on Usk ★★★★ RR ◉◉

PICK OF THE PUBS

NP15 1LY ☎ 01633 451000
e-mail: newbridgeonusk@celtic-manor.com
dir: *M4 junct 24 follow Newport signs. Right at Toby Carvery, B4236 to Caerleon. Right over bridge, through Caerleon to mini rdbt. Straight ahead onto Llangibby/ Usk road*

Lovely views of the Monmouthshire hills

With medieval Usk and Roman Caerleon on the doorstep and myriad sporting opportunities locally (including golf at Celtic Manor, owners of the inn), this smart gastro-pub with rooms offers a relaxing end to a busy day. Set above a bend in the river in the Vale of Usk, this is the latest incarnation of a hostelry that has served passers-by for 200 years. Cosy, rustic, old-world fittings meld seamlessly with contemporary comforts; on summer evenings the riverside garden is a winning place to sup a glass of Brains The Rev. James and contemplate the sunset illuminating the beautiful Monmouthshire hills. Welsh produce is used creatively in dishes worthy of two AA Rosettes, with starters like chicken and rabbit terrine; and mains of roasted loin of Welsh venison with glazed red cabbage, pressed horseradish potato, red wine jus; and fillet of cod with potato salad, Puy lentil vinaigrette and poached hen's egg.

Open all wk 11am-mdnt **Bar Meals** L served all wk 12-2.30 D served all wk 7-10 **Restaurant** L served all wk 12-2.30 D served all wk 7-10 ⊕ FREE HOUSE ◢ Brains The Rev. James & Smooth, Guest ale ♂ Tomos Watkin Taffy Apples. 🍷 12 **Facilities** Non-diners area ⚐♦ Children's menu Children's portions Garden ⊓ Parking Wi-fi ▭ Rooms 6

TRELLECH
Map 4 SO50

The Lion Inn

PICK OF THE PUBS

NP25 4PA ☎ 01600 860322
e-mail: debs@globalnet.co.uk
dir: *From A40 S of Monmouth take B4293, follow Trellech signs. From M8 junct 2, straight across rdbt, 2nd left at 2nd rdbt, B4293 to Trellech*

A traditional inn with nautical beginnings

Although best known for its food and drink, the Lion once showed true versatility by providing the best-dressed entry in the Monmouth raft race. Built in 1580 as a brewhouse and inn by a former sea captain, it consists of two rooms, both with open fires; one is a traditional bar, the other a restaurant. Debbie Zsigo has run it for 18 years and knows instinctively what works. In the bar the answer is Butcombe Bitter and Felinfoel Double Dragon, and a local cider, Springfield Red Dragon. In the restaurant she provides bar snacks, pizzas, light meals and a good range of main dishes, typically local butcher-made faggots; chicken curry; breaded plaice; and vegetarian pasta bake. There's a stream and an aviary in

the garden, and beautiful views from the suntrap courtyard. Beer festivals are in June and November and a cider one in August.

Open 12-3 6-11 (Mon 12-3 7-11 Thu 12-3 6-12 Fri-Sat 12-12 Sun 12-4.30) Closed: Sun eve **Bar Meals** L served Mon-Fri 12-2, Sat-Sun 12-2.30 D served Mon 7-9.30, Tue-Sat 6-9.30 Av main course £10 **Restaurant** L served Mon-Fri 12-2, Sat-Sun 12-2.30 D served Mon 7-9.30, Tue-Sat 6-9.30 ⊕ FREE HOUSE ◢ Butcombe Bitter, Felinfoel Double Dragon ♂ Springfield Red Dragon. **Facilities** Non-diners area ♦♦ Children's portions Garden ⊓ Beer festival Cider festival Parking ▭ (notice required)

USK
Map 9 SO30

The Nags Head Inn

Twyn Square NP15 1BH ☎ 01291 672820
e-mail: keynags@tiscali.co.uk
dir: *On A472*

Bustling old town hostelry in the Vale of Gwent

Fronting the old town square mid-way between the castle and fine priory church, parts of the inn date from the 15th century. Saunter around the old town before sampling the largely Welsh real ales here, where the same family has held-sway for 45 years, lovingly caring for the highly-traditional interior, all beams and polished tables, rural artefacts and horse-brasses. The tempting menu draws on the wealth of produce the fertile Vale of Gwent can offer; seasonal game dishes are a speciality, whilst there's a good vegetarian selection; try the cheese and leek Glamorgan sausage.

Open all wk 10.30-2.30 5-11 Closed: 25 Dec **Bar Meals** L served all wk 11.45-1.45 D served all wk 5.30-9.30 **Restaurant** L served all wk 11.45-1.45 D served all wk 5.30-9.30 ⊕ FREE HOUSE ◢ Brains Bitter, Buckley's Bitter, The Rev. James & Bread of Heaven, Sharp's Doom Bar ♂ Westons Stowford Press. 🍷 9 **Facilities** Non-diners area ⚐ (Bar Restaurant Garden) ♦♦ Children's portions Garden ⊓ Parking Wi-fi ▭

Raglan Arms ◉

PICK OF THE PUBS

Llandenny NP15 1DL ☎ 01291 690800
e-mail: raglanarms@gmail.com
dir: *From Monmouth take A449 to Raglan, left in village. From M4 take A449 exit. Follow Llandenny signs on right*

A great combination of traditional values and top cuisine

This mid 19th-century stone-built pub enjoys a pretty village location. Dine at rustic tables around the bar, where you'll find Wye Valley Bitter, or in the conservatory. In summer, head for the decked area outside and soak up the sun while you eat. Everything is freshly prepared in the kitchen – even the bread is baked here and bacon is cured on site. The menus change on a daily basis and there is a firm emphasis on locally sourced food, which is so good it holds an AA Rosette. Some dishes, such as imam bayildi with crème fraîche or vanilla and bay leaf

pannacotta with Sauternes and poached saffron pears, reflect an enthusiasm for international flavours, while others like Welsh rarebit, beef stew with dumplings, and slow-roast shoulder of Llanlowell pork, take their cues from traditional British cuisine. A Raglan hallmark is its excellent selection of British and French cheeses for dessert.

Open Tue-Fri 12-2 6.30-9 Sat 12-2.30 6.30-9.30 Sun 12-2.30 Closed: 25-27 Dec, Sun eve & Mon **Bar Meals** L served Tue-Fri 12-2, Sat-Sun 12-2.30 D served Tue-Fri 6.30-9, Sat 6.30-9.30 Av main course £12-£14 **Restaurant** L served Tue-Fri 12-2, Sat-Sun 12-2.30 D served Tue-Fri 6.30-9, Sat 6.30-9.30 Fixed menu price fr £18 Av 3 course à la carte fr £26 ⊕ FREE HOUSE ◢ Wye Valley Bitter ♂ Thatchers Gold. 🍷 18 **Facilities** Non-diners area ⚐ (Bar Garden) ♦♦ Children's portions Garden ⊓ Parking

NEWPORT

CAERLEON
Map 9 ST39

The Bell at Caerleon

Bulmore Rd NP18 1QQ ☎ 01633 420613
e-mail: thebellinn@hotmail.co.uk
dir: *M4 junct 25, B4596 signed Caerleon. In Caerleon before river bridge right onto B4238 signed Christchurch. Left into Bulmore Rd (follow brown pub sign)*

Superb range of ciders and ales

For more than 400 years this 17th-century coaching inn has stood in ancient Caerleon on the banks of the River Usk. Situated close to an ancient Roman burial ground (also believed by some to be the location of King Arthur's Camelot), the pub is particularly well known for its range of local ciders and perrys. It holds annual real ale and cider festivals with barbecues and free entertainment. Local produce drives the menu, which might include ham hock terrine with home-made chutney; seafood gratin; and venison steak with fondant potato, celery, leek and celeriac ragout and a red wine and port jus.

Open all day all wk **Bar Meals** L served Mon-Sat 12-2.30, Sun 12-4 D served all wk 6-9.30 **Restaurant** L served Mon-Sat 12-2.30, Sun 12-4 D served all wk 6-9.30 ⊕ ENTERPRISE INNS ◢ Sharp's Doom Bar, Felinfoel Double Dragon, Bath Gem, 3 Rotating ales ♂ Gwynt y Ddraig Black Dragon & Happy Daze, Hallets Real. 🍷 10 **Facilities** Non-diners area ⚐ (Bar Garden) ♦♦ Children's portions Garden ⊓ Beer festival Cider festival Parking Wi-fi ▭ (notice required)

PEMBROKESHIRE

ABERCYCH · Map 8 SN24

Nags Head Inn

SA37 0HJ ☎ 01239 841200
e-mail: samnags@hotmail.co.uk
dir: *On B4332 (Carmarthen to Newcastle Emlyn road)*

Classic Welsh riverside pub

Situated at the entrance to the enchanted valley in the famous Welsh folk tales of *Mabinogion*, this famous old inn is the first building you see over the county boundary when crossing into Pembrokeshire from the Teifi Falls at Cenarth. In one of the outbuildings the old forge still remains where the blacksmith crafted the first horse-drawn ploughs for export to America. Old Emrys ale is brewed on the premises ready for consuming in the beamed bars and riverside gardens, alongside other Welsh ales. The fine fare includes home-made cawl with cheese and crusty bread; steak, Guinness and mushroom pie; and Cardigan Bay lobster.

Open Tue-Sun Closed: Mon **Bar Meals** L served Tue-Sun 12-2 D served Tue-Sun 6-9 Av main course £10 **Restaurant** L served Tue-Sun 12-2 D served Tue-Sun 6-9 Fixed menu price fr £12.95 ⊕ FREE HOUSE ◗ Old Emrys, Nags Head Brewery. **Facilities** Non-diners area ❀ (Bar Garden) ◗◗ Children's menu Children's portions Play area Garden Parking ▄▄

AMROTH · Map 8 SN10

The New Inn

SA67 8NW ☎ 01834 812368
e-mail: paulluger@hotmail.com
dir: *A48 to Carmarthen, A40 to St Clears, A477 to Llanteg then left, follow road to seafront, turn left. 0.25m on left*

Old inn specialising in Welsh beef dishes

Originally a farmhouse, this 16th-century inn belongs to Amroth Castle Estate and has been family run for some 38 years. The pub has old-world charm with beamed ceilings, a Flemish chimney, a flagstone floor and an inglenook fireplace. It is close to the beach, with views towards Saundersfoot and Tenby from the dining room upstairs. Along with Welsh beef, home-made dishes include broccoli and cream cheese bake; pork and leek sausages; Greek salad; and minted lamb steak. There is even a toddlers' menu in addition to the children's menu. Enjoy food or drink outside on the large lawn complete with picnic benches.

Open all day all wk Mar-Oct 11-11 (Oct-Mar eve & wknds only) **Bar Meals** food served all day **Restaurant** food served all day ⊕ FREE HOUSE ◗ Sharp's Doom Bar, Hancock's, Guinness, Guest ales.
Facilities Non-diners area ❀ (Bar Garden) ◗◗ Children's menu Children's portions Family room Garden ▰ Parking ▄▄

ANGLE · Map 8 SM80

The Old Point House NEW

East Angle Bay SA71 5AS ☎ 01646 641205
e-mail: croeso@theoldpointhouse.co.uk
dir: *From Pembroke take B4320 signed Monkton & Hundleton. Right signed Angle. At T-junct left signed West Angle Bay. 1st right at pub sign on wall into narrow lane. Follow lane round bay to pub*

Remote but well worth tracking down

It's all angles round here – Angle village, Angle Bay, Angle RNLI... Indeed, the 15th-century Old Point has been the lifeboatmen's local since 1868, when their boathouse was built nearby. At its uneven-floored heart is the snug, its walls covered in old photos and memorabilia, Felinfoel Best is on handpump, and real cider comes from Honey's in Somerset. Pub food includes sandwiches, jacket potatoes, pan-fried John Dory, curried chicken, Pembrokeshire rib-eye steak, pasta bolognese and daily specials. Picnic tables at the front look across Angle Bay. The track from the village skirts the foreshore, occasionally getting cut off by spring tides.

Open all day Jul-Sep (12-3 6-10 autumn & winter) Closed: 10-31 Jan, Mon & Tue 5 Nov-1 Mar **Bar Meals** L served 12-2.30 (Mar-5 Oct) D served 6.30-8.30 (Mar-5 Oct) Av main course £10 **Restaurant** L served 12-2.30 (Mar-5 Oct) D served 6.30-8.30 (Mar-5 Oct) ⊕ FREE HOUSE ◗ Felinfoel Best Bitter ⭘ Honey's Midford Cider, Gwynt y Ddraig. **Facilities** Non-diners area ❀ (Bar Garden Outside area) ◗◗ Children's portions Garden Outside area ▰ Parking Wi-fi ▄▄ (notice required)

CAREW · Map 8 SN00

Carew Inn

SA70 8SL ☎ 01646 651267
e-mail: mandy@carewinn.co.uk
dir: *From A477 take A4075. Inn 400yds opposite castle*

One of Wales' best kept secrets

Opposite the Carew Celtic cross and Norman castle, this traditional stone-built country inn is a great place to finish the one-mile circular walk around the castle and millpond. Mandy and Rob Scourfield have celebrated 22 years here, during which time they have built a strong reputation for quality ales and home-cooked food. A meal might include home-made smoked mackerel pâté with toast; pork tenderloin with chorizo sausage in a spicy sauce, served with crispy potatoes; and home-made lemon cheesecake. There's a children's play area in the garden, which also hosts regular barbecues in the summer.

Open all day all wk 11am-mdnt (Sun 12-12) Closed: 25 Dec **Bar Meals** L served all wk 12-2.30 D served all wk 6-9 Av main course £9.95 **Restaurant** L served all wk 12-2.30 D served all wk 6-9 Av 3 course à la carte fr £23 ⊕ FREE HOUSE ◗ Worthington's, Brains The Rev. James, Guest ales. ☗ 9 **Facilities** Non-diners area ❀ (Bar Garden) ◗◗ Children's menu Children's portions Play area Garden ▰ Parking Wi-fi ▄▄ (notice required)

DALE · Map 8 SM80

Griffin Inn NEW

SA62 3RB ☎ 01646 636227
e-mail: info@griffininndale.co.uk
dir: *From end of M4 onto A48 to Carmarthen. A40 to Haverfordwest, B4327 to Dale. In Dale (with sea on left) pub on corner by slipway*

By the sea in a hidden corner of west Wales

Standing opposite the sea wall in a pretty coastal village, the Griffin offers the pleasure of roaring log fires in the winter and, in the summer, the joy of eating out on the water's edge, looking across Dale Bay. On tap in the bar you'll find The Rev. James, Buckleys Best and Evan Evans Cwrw Haf (koo-roo - it's Welsh for beer). The kitchen's sourcing policy demands that produce is both local and sustainable: for example, two village fishermen supply fresh fish and seafood from the bay. Be there when they land and you can choose from the catch.

Open all wk all day Apr-Sep (12-3 6-11 rest of year) Closed: 5-30 Nov **Bar Meals** L served all wk 12-3 D served all wk 5-9 summer, 6-9 winter **Restaurant** L served all wk 12-3 D served all wk 5-9 summer, 6-9 winter ⊕ FREE HOUSE ◗ Brains The Rev. James, Evan Evans Cwrw, Evan Evans Cwrw Haf, Buckleys Best Bitter ⭘ Westons Stowford Press. **Facilities** Non-diners area ◗◗ Children's menu Children's portions Outside area ▰ Parking Wi-fi ▄▄ (notice required)

LETTERSTON · Map 8 SM92

The Harp Inn

31 Haverfordwest Rd SA62 5UA ☎ 01348 840061
e-mail: info@theharpatletterston.co.uk
dir: *On A40, 10m from Haverfordwest, 4m from Fishguard*

Modernised hostelry in the heart of Pembrokeshire

Formerly a working farm and home to a weekly market, this 15th-century free house remained largely unchanged for 500 years. Owned by the Sandall family since 1982, the building has a stylish conservatory restaurant where diners can enjoy local favourites like Welsh fillet steak; venison Roquefort; and whole sea bass. Alternatively, the bar lunch menu offers classic pub meals including crispy battered cod and chips. Enjoy lunch with your children in the fenced garden.

Open all day all wk **Bar Meals** food served all day **Restaurant** food served all day ⊕ FREE HOUSE ◗ Tetley's, Greene King Abbot Ale ⭘ Thatchers Gold. **Facilities** Non-diners area ◗◗ Children's menu Children's portions Play area Garden Parking Wi-fi ▄▄

Save on hotels. Book at **theAA.com/hotel**

PEMBROKESHIRE 575 WALES

LITTLE HAVEN Map 8 SM81

St Brides Inn

St Brides Rd SA62 3UN ☎ 01437 781266
e-mail: kgardham@btinternet.com
dir: *From Haverfordwest take B4341 signed Broad Haven. Through Broad Haven to Little Haven*

Great walkers' refuelling stop

An ideal stop for walkers on the nearby Pembrokeshire coastal path as it runs through the seaside village of Little Haven, the St Brides Inn has the added attraction of an indoor ancient well, as well as a pretty floral beer garden. Food-wise expect the likes of deep-fried breaded camembert with warm cranberry sauce; pork loin stuffed with black pudding and served with cider sauce; and home-made rhubarb and ginger crumble. Lunchtime light bites include a bacon and black pudding bap; and pork and apple sausage and mushroom bap with fried potatoes.

Open all wk 11.30-3 5.30-11.30 (all day summer) **Bar Meals** L served all wk 12-2.30 D served all wk 6-9 **Restaurant** L served all wk 12-2.30 D served all wk 6-9 ⊕ MARSTON'S ◀ Pedigree, Banks's Bitter, Ringwood Boondoggle. ♥ 9 **Facilities** Non-diners area ♣ (Bar Garden) ♦♦ Children's menu Children's portions Garden ⌁ Wi-fi ▭ (notice required)

The Swan Inn

Point Rd SA62 3UL ☎ 01437 781880
e-mail: enquiries@theswanlittlehaven.co.uk
dir: *B4341 from Haverfordwest. In Broad Haven follow seafront/Little Haven signs 0.75m*

Popular spot in an idyllic setting

Arrive early to bag a window table and savour one of the best views in Pembrokeshire from this 200-year-old pub perched above a rocky cove overlooking St Brides Bay. This free house buzzes with chatter and contented visitors enjoying well-kept real ales and a good choice of wines in the comfortably rustic bar, furnished with old settles, polished oak tables and leather armchairs. There's also an intimate dining room, with an elegant contemporary-style restaurant upstairs; cooking is modern British, with a commitment to seasonal and local produce.

Open all day all wk 11am-mdnt Closed: 3 Jan-18 Feb, Sun out of season ⊕ FREE HOUSE ◀ Morland Old Speckled Hen, Penlon Cottage, Brains The Rev. James, Worthington's, Guinness. **Facilities** ♦♦ Children's menu Children's portions Garden Wi-fi

NEWPORT Map 8 SN03

Salutation Inn

Felindre Farchog, Crymych SA41 3UY ☎ 01239 820564
e-mail: johndenley@aol.com
web: www.salutationcountryhotel.co.uk
dir: *On A487 between Cardigan & Fishguard*

Top local produce served in former coaching inn

This tastefully modernised, 16th-century coaching inn stands on the River Nevern in the Pembrokeshire Coast National Park. Owners since 2000 are John Denley, a veteran of 20 years in restaurants in North Africa and the Middle East, and his wife Gwawr, born two miles away on the slopes of Carningli Mountain. There is an emphasis on fresh locally sourced produce for the menu, which lists home-baked ham with chips; chicken breast paprika and tagliatelle; and spinach, mozzarella and cherry tomato with pinenuts vegetarian suet pudding. Felinfoel, Brains and a local guest are on tap.

Open all day Closed: Tue in winter **Bar Meals** L served all wk 12.30-2.30 D served all wk 6.30-9 **Restaurant** L served Sun 12.30-2.30 D served Sat-Sun 7-9 ⊕ FREE HOUSE ◀ Felinfoel, Brains, Local guest ales Ŏ Thatchers Gold. **Facilities** Non-diners area ♣ (Bar Garden) ♦♦ Children's menu Children's portions Garden ⌁ Parking Wi-fi ▭ (notice required)

PORTHGAIN Map 8 SM83

The Sloop Inn

SA62 5BN ☎ 01348 831449
e-mail: matthew@sloop-inn.freeserve.co.uk
dir: *Take A487 NE from St Davids for 6m. Left at Croesgooch for 2m to Porthgain*

Cosy pub with a maritime history

Possibly the most famous pub on the north Pembrokeshire coast, The Sloop Inn is located in beautiful quarrying village of Porthgain and is especially enticing on a cold winter's day. The walls and ceilings are packed with pictures and memorabilia from nearby shipwrecks. The harbour is less than 100 yards from the door and there is a village green to the front and a large south-facing patio. With ales like Felinfoel and Greene King IPA on the pump, a varied menu includes breakfasts, snacks, pub favourites, steaks and home-caught fish.

Open all day all wk 9.30am-11pm (winter 11.30-11) Closed: 25 Dec **Bar Meals** L served all wk 12-2.30 D served all wk 6-9.30 **Restaurant** L served all wk 12-2.30 D served all wk 6-9.30 ⊕ FREE HOUSE/B G

BETTERSPOONS Ltd ◀ Cropton Yorkshire Warrior, Hancock's HB, Felinfoel, Greene King IPA Guest ale. **Facilities** Non-diners area ♦♦ Children's menu Garden ⌁ Parking Wi-fi ▭

ROSEBUSH Map 8 SN02

Tafarn Sinc

Preseli SA66 7QT ☎ 01437 532214
e-mail: briandavies2@btconnect.com
dir: *Telephone for directions*

Railway hotel maintaining its nostalgic originality

Built to serve the railway that no longer exists, this large red corrugated-iron free house stands testament to its rapid construction in 1876. This idiosyncratic establishment refuses to be modernised and boasts wood-burning stoves, a sawdust floor, and a charming garden. Set high in the Preseli Hills amid stunning scenery, it is popular with walkers, who can refuel on traditional favourites like local lamb burgers; prime Welsh sirloin steak; home-cooked ham; and Glamorgan sausages with chutney.

Open all day 12-11 Closed: Mon (ex BHs & summer) **Bar Meals** L served Tue-Sat 12-2 D served Tue-Sat 6-9 **Restaurant** L served Tue-Sat 12-2 D served Tue-Sat 6-9 ⊕ FREE HOUSE ◀ Worthington's, Tafarn Sinc, Guest ale. **Facilities** Non-diners area ♦♦ Children's menu Garden ⌁ Parking ▭ (notice required)

ST DOGMAELS Map 8 SN14

The Teifi Netpool Inn NEW

SA43 3ET ☎ 01239 612680
e-mail: pclock101@gmail.com
dir: *From A487 follow St Dogmaels signs (B4546). Left signed St Dogmaels, Llandudoch & Poppit (B4546). Left into Maeshfryd St, to end, pub on left*

Wide choice of Welsh beers and good food

Historically used by the local fishermen and the place where they sold their daily catch, this traditional pub is family run and family friendly. A little of the beaten track on the banks of the River Teifi near the village green it is worth seeking out. Beers from the Kite microbrewery near Carmarthen feature along with several Welsh guest ales, and there are beer and cider festivals held in the months of May and August. Sunday lunches are very popular and booking is recommended.

Open all day all wk **Bar Meals** L served all wk 12-7 D served all wk 12-7 Av main course £5.50 food served all day ⊕ FREE HOUSE ◀ Wye Valley Butty Bach, Kite Brewery ales Ŏ Thatchers. **Facilities** Non-diners area ♦♦ Children's menu Children's portions Play area Outside area ⌁ Beer festival Cider festival Parking Wi-fi ▭ (notice required)

PICK OF THE PUBS

The Stackpole Inn

STACKPOLE   Map 8 SR99

SA71 5DF ☎ 01646 672324
e-mail: info@stackpoleinn.co.uk
web: www.stackpoleinn.co.uk
dir: *From Pembroke take B4319, follow Stackpole signs, approx 4m*

A real find in beautiful Pembrokeshire

This traditional inn is a walker's delight, set in pristine gardens at the heart of the National Trust's Stackpole Estate and close to the spectacular Pembrokeshire coastal path. There's a rare George V postbox in the mellow stone wall outside, a survival from the time when one of the two original stone cottages was a post office. Nowadays the pub offers facilities for walkers, cyclists, fishermen and climbers, as well as those who simply prefer to relax and do nothing. Once inside, you'll find a slate bar, ceiling beams made from ash trees grown on the estate, and a wood-burning stove set within the stone fireplace. The pub's free house status means that there's always a guest beer from around the UK to accompany three Welsh ales, a couple of real ciders and a varied wine list. Local produce from the surrounding countryside and fish from the coast play a major part in the home-cooked menu. A lighter lunch menu

offers freshly baked Couronne loaves with an appetising selection of fillings that includes Welsh brie with locally cured bacon, and tuna with tarragon mayonnaise. Three-course appetites might begin with creamy Welsh blue cheese on bitter leaf salad with pickled walnuts and poached grapes, or smoked salmon on potato blini with herb crème fraîche. Main course options range from seared Welsh lamb with Moroccan couscous and tomato jus with seasonal vegetables; to wild sea bass fillet with fennel and saffron risotto. Round things off with caramelised lemon tart and passionfruit sorbet, or creamy rice pudding with cinnamon and apple.

Open all wk 12-3 6-11 Closed: Sun eve (winter) **Bar Meals** L served Mon-Sat 12-2, Sun 12-2.30 D served all wk 6.30-9 **Restaurant** L served Mon-Sat 12-2, Sun 12-2.30 D served all wk 6.30-9 🛢 FREE HOUSE 🍺 Brains The Rev. James, Felinfoel Double Dragon, Guest ale Ö Gwynt y Ddraig. 🍷 12 **Facilities** Non-diners area 👬 Children's menu Children's portions Garden 🪑 Parking Wi-fi 🚌

Save on hotels. Book at **theAA.com/hotel**

PEMBROKESHIRE – POWYS 577 WALES

ST DOGMAELS *continued*

Webley Waterfront Inn & Hotel

Poppit Sands SA43 3LN ☎ 01239 612085
e-mail: enquiries@webleyhotel.co.uk
dir: *A484 from Carmarthen to Cardigan, then to
St Dogmaels, right in village centre to Poppit Sands on
B4546*

Seafood in a magnificent setting

This long-established family business is spectacularly
situated at the start of the Pembrokeshire Coast National
Park, a haven for birdwatchers and watersports
enthusiasts. The inn offers outstanding views across the
River Teifi and Poppit Sands to Cardigan Bay, which
supplies the daily catch for the menu. King scallops with
crispy bacon and carrot purée, perhaps to start, followed
by pan-seared salmon and sautéed new potatoes. The
specials board might feature dressed lobster and crab.
Other dishes include rump steak and five bean chilli. The
bar serves Gwynt y Ddraig Welsh cider together with a
selection of ales.

Open all day all wk **Bar Meals** L served all wk 12-2.30
D served all wk 6-8.30 **Restaurant** D served all wk 6-9
⊕ FREE HOUSE ◀ Brains Buckley's Bitter, Felinfoel, Guest
ales Ŏ Gwynt y Ddraig. ▼ 8 **Facilities** Non-diners area
❀ (Bar Garden) ♦ Children's menu Children's portions
Family room Garden ⊼ Parking Wi-fi ▥

STACKPOLE   Map 8 SR99

The Stackpole Inn

PICK OF THE PUBS

See Pick of the Pubs on opposite page

TENBY   Map 8 SN10

Hope and Anchor **NEW**

Saint Julians St SA70 7AX ☎ 01834 842131
dir: *A478 or A4139 into Tenby. Into High St, becomes
Saint Julians St. Pub on left*

A popular pub with a good choice of fish dishes

Heading down towards the harbour and the beach at
Tenby and you can't miss the blue Hope and Anchor pub.
Traditionally a fishing pub it has remained popular with
locals for years and years. They offer seven real ales that
change throughout the week and the menus and special
boards feature lots of fish. Tenby mackerel, pan fried in
butter or with a Cajun seasoning; sea bass with rocket
and couscous salad; or mussels cooked with bacon,
onions, Stowford Press cider and cream; even locally
caught lobster is featured. Meat eaters might choose
peppered pork steaks; steak and ale pie; or rosemary and
garlic chicken.

Open all day all wk **Closed:** 25 Dec **Bar Meals** Av main
course £8.95 food served all day **Restaurant** food served
all day ◀ Sharp's Doom Bar, Brains The Rev. James,
Felinfoel Double Dragon Ŏ Westons Scrumpy, Old Rosie,
Vintage Cloudy, Welsh ciders. ▼ 13
Facilities Non-diners area ♦ Children's menu Children's
portions Garden ⊼ ▥ (notice required)

POWYS

BERRIEW   Map 15 SJ10

The Lion Hotel

SY21 8PQ ☎ 01686 640452
e-mail: trudi.jones@btconnect.com
dir: *5m from Welshpool on A483, right to Berriew. In
village centre*

Friendly inn with distinctive exterior

Behind the black-and-white timbered exterior of this
17th-century family-run coaching inn lie bars and dining
areas where yet more old timbers testify to its age.
Menus, based on local produce, include a starter of
ballotine of mackerel, potato and chive salad, coriander
and lemon mayo; then mains might be loin of Welsh lamb
with boulangère potatoes, or dill gnocchi with white wine
cream sauce. Yogurt pannacotta with candied orange or
a selection of Welsh farmhouse cheese finish things off
nicely. There is a separate bar area where you can enjoy a
pint of real ale from the selection on tap including
Banks's Bitter, Pedigree and Old Empire.

Open all wk 12-3 5-11 (Fri-Sat 12-11 Sun 12-3 6-10.30)
⊕ MARSTON'S ◀ Pedigree & Old Empire, Banks's Bitter,
Guest ales. **Facilities** ♦ Children's portions Parking Wi-fi

---

BRECON   Map 9 SO02

The Usk Inn ★★★★ INN

PICK OF THE PUBS

Talybont-on-Usk LD3 7JE ☎ 01874 676251
e-mail: stay@uskinn.co.uk
dir: *6m E of Brecon, just off A40 towards Abergavenny &
Crickhowell*

An ideal stop for Brecon Beacon visitors

The Usk Inn enjoys an enviable position about 300 metres
from the village centre at Talybont-on-Usk on the
picturesque Abergavenny to Brecon road. Attracting
locals and visitors to the Brecon Beacons National Park in
equal number, the inn opened in the 1840s just as the
Brecon to Merthyr railway line was being built alongside
it. Another source of custom is the Brecon to
Monmouthshire canal that passes through the village.
Over the years The Usk has been transformed from an
ordinary pub into a country inn with a restaurant and
guest rooms. Expect a choice of guest ales at the bar,
along with ciders and popular wines. The Usk's reputation
for good cooking and good value is based on the kitchen's
selection of carefully sourced ingredients, served in a
blend of traditional and modern dishes. The bedrooms are
cheerfully bright, decorated in refreshing colours.

Open all day all wk 11am-11.30pm (Sun 11-10.30)
Closed: 25-26 Dec eve **Bar Meals** L served all wk 12-2.30
Restaurant L served Sun 12-2.30 D served all wk
6.30-9.30 ⊕ FREE HOUSE ◀ Guinness, Guest ales
Ŏ Thatchers, Robinsons. ▼ 11 **Facilities** Non-diners area
♦ Children's portions Garden ⊼ Parking ▥ (notice
required) **Rooms** 10

The White Swan Inn

PICK OF THE PUBS

Llanfrynach LD3 7BZ ☎ 01874 665276
e-mail: paulowen11@yahoo.co.uk
dir: *A40, 3m E of Brecon onto B4558 follow Llanfrynach
signs*

Ambitious cooking in coaching inn with
mountain views

A change of hands in July 2012 marked a new chapter in
the history of this 17th-century coaching inn opposite the
ancient church of St Brynach. An atmospheric pub set
against the impressive backdrop of the Brecon Beacons,
it offers a warm and cosy welcome, whether you eat in the
spacious Flagstone Restaurant or the more informal bar,
which also offers a lighter snack menu and weekly
changing guest ales. The inventive menus change
monthly and all dishes are freshly prepared using locally
sourced produce. A starter of wood pigeon breast, sautéed
wild mushrooms in white truffle oil and beetroot purée
might be followed by loin of Breconshire venison, red wine
chocolate sauce, creamed celeriac, cabbage and
dauphinoise. Malaysian vegetable curry with coconut rice
and pak choi noodles is one meat-free option. Puddings
include poached pear, pistachio ice cream, peanut crunch
chocolate mousse.

Open Tue-Fri 11.30-3 6.30-11.30 (Sat-Sun all day)
Closed: 25-26 Dec, 1st 2wks Jan, Mon (ex Jun-Nov & BHs)
Bar Meals L served Tue-Fri 12-2.30, Sat-Sun all day
D served Tue-Sun 6-9, Sat-Sun all day **Restaurant** L
served Tue-Fri 12-2.30, Sat-Sun all day D served Tue-Sun
6-9, Sat-Sun all day ⊕ FREE HOUSE ◀ Sharp's Doom
Bar, Guest ales. ▼ 8 **Facilities** Non-diners area ❀ (Bar
Garden) ♦ Children's menu Children's portions Garden ⊼
Parking Wi-fi ▥ (notice required)

PICK OF THE PUBS

The Bear ★★★★ INN ❀

Brecon Rd NP8 1BW ☎ 01873 810408
e-mail: bearhotel@aol.com
web: www.bearhotel.co.uk
dir: *On A40 between Abergavenny &*
Brecon

Landmark market town pub with plenty of character

Run by the same family since 1978, this wonderful coaching inn in the charming market town of Crickhowell has been at the centre of the community since 1432 and retains bags of character. A superb old bar brims with antique furnishings on the rug-strewn floor, sheltered cobbled courtyard and memorable hanging baskets. With the lovely Usk Valley walk, nearby canal and the tops of the Black Mountains and Brecon Beacons looming large, visitors wanting peace, tranquillity and adventure seek out the comfortably appointed bedrooms, whilst the cuisine has gained an AA Rosette for the skilled chef and kitchen team. Taken in the bar or in two restaurant areas, the fare is strongly influenced by availability of local produce for which the area is widely renowned. A meal here might kick off with mussels, cream, white wine and garlic; pork and apricot terrine with apple compôte; or breast of local wood pigeon, spiced chickpea and watercress salad. Welsh Black steaks cooked to

your liking are one option when it comes to main course, but there might also be slow braised Welsh lamb shank with spring onion mash, vegetables and braising juices or seared fillet of salmon with crushed new potatoes and roast fennel. Vegetarians are well catered for and may be tempted by potato gnocchi, spinach and ricotta cream sauce. Round things off with comforting desserts such as rhubarb and custard with crystalised ginger ice cream or rum and raisin parfait. Although you could conclude with a board of local cheeses that might include Perl Wen or Smoked Caws Cenarth. Booking for meals may be required. Dogs are welcome here and there are good dog walks, short and long, all around this area.

Open all day all wk Closed: 25 Dec **Bar Meals** L served all wk 12-2 D served Mon-Sat 6-10, Sun 7-9.30 **Restaurant** L served Sun 12-2 D served Mon-Sat 6-10 🛢 FREE HOUSE ◀ Brains The Rev. James, Wye Valley Butty Bach, Hancock's HB, Guest ales ♂ Westons Stowford Press. ♟ 10 **Facilities** Non-diners area ❤ (Bar Garden) ♦♦ Children's menu Children's portions Family room Garden ⴲ Parking Wi-fi notice required)

Save on hotels. Book at **theAA.com/hotel**

POWYS 579 WALES

COEDWAY   Map 15 SJ31

The Old Hand and Diamond Inn

SY5 9AR ☎ 01743 884379
e-mail: moz123@aol.com
web: www.oldhandanddiamond.co.uk
dir: *From Shrewsbury take A458 towards Bridgnorth. Right onto B4393 signed Four Crosses. Coedway approx 5m*

One for all the family

On the Powys/Shropshire border, this 17th-century inn retains much of its original character, with exposed beams and an inglenook fireplace. Its reputation for good quality food owes much to local farmers who supply the best meats, including from rare-breed Jacob sheep. Enjoy local Shropshire Lad and guest real ales in the bar, while choosing from an extensive menu that lists chicken Caesar salad; home-made beef curry; fish of the day; and a daily vegetarian dish. Among the desserts are sticky toffee pudding and lemon crème brûlée. The beer garden has plenty of seating and a children's play area.

Open all day all wk 11am-1am **Bar Meals** L served Mon-Thu 12-2.30, Fri-Sun 12-9.30 D served Mon-Thu 6-9.30, Fri-Sun 12-9.30 **Restaurant** L served Mon-Thu 12-2.30, Fri-Sun 12-9.30 D served Mon-Thu 6-9.30, Fri-Sun 12-9.30 ⊕ FREE HOUSE ◀ Worthington's, Wood's Shropshire Lad, Guest ales. **Facilities** Non-diners area ❤ (Bar Garden) ♦♦ Children's portions Play area Garden ⊼ Parking Wi-fi ▄▄

CRICKHOWELL   Map 9 SO21

The Bear ★★★★ INN ◉

PICK OF THE PUBS

See Pick of the Pubs on opposite page

DEFYNNOG   Map 9 SN92

The Tanners Arms **NEW**

LD3 8SF ☎ 01874 638032
e-mail: info@tannersarmspub.com
dir: *From Brecon take A40 towards Llandovery. Left onto A4067 to Defynnog*

Old inn not far from the glorious Brecon Beacons

In a tiny village and overlooking open countryside, this 17th-century inn derives its name from the tannery that was once in business up the road. In the foothills of the Brecon Beacons National Park it makes a good stopping point for those setting off to explore this mountain area. The pub has real ales and ciders changing very regularly and the menus offer breaded crab claws; home-made pâté on toast as starter choices, then there's brie and artichoke quiche with roasted vegetables; 8oz gammon steak with all the trimmings; and a variety of curries ranging from vegetable korma to beef vindaloo. Lunchtime quick bites and sandwiches are offered too. June beer festival.

Open all wk 5-12 (Fri 4-12 Sat-Sun 12-12) **Bar Meals** L served Sat-Sun 12-2 D served all wk 6-9 **Restaurant** L served Sat-Sun 12-2 D served all wk 6-9 ⊕ FREE HOUSE ◀ Constantly changing ales ♂ Constantly changing ciders. **Facilities** Non-diners area ❤ (Bar Garden) ♦♦ Children's menu Children's portions Garden ⊼ Beer festival Parking Wi-fi ▄▄ (notice required)

GLANGRWYNEY   Map 9 SO21

The Bell

NP8 1EH ☎ 01873 811115
e-mail: mark.jones@hotmail.com
dir: *On A40 halfway between Abergavenny & Crickhowell*

A warm retreat in a small rural village

Real ale lovers should visit this lovely Brecon Beacons National Park pub (now in fresh hands) during the Easter or August Bank Holiday beer festivals. In fact, at any time it's the perfect destination for anyone who wants somewhere comfortable for a decent pint and something to eat. In addition to a constantly-changing selection of local ales and ciders – Gwynt y Ddraig, for example – the menu draws extensively on local produce for cockle, bacon and laverbread ravioli; Welsh steak and ale pie; wild boar with orange and apricot sauce; and beetroot and ricotta tortellini with creamy Perl Wen cheese sauce.

Open all day 12-11.30 Closed: Mon (ex holiday periods) **Bar Meals** L served Tue-Sun 12-3 D served Tue-Sun 6-9 **Restaurant** L served Tue-Sun 12-3 D served Tue-Sun 6-9 ⊕ BRAINS ◀ 4 Guest ales ♂ Westons, Gwynt y Ddraig Orchard Gold. ♟ 9 **Facilities** Non-diners area ♦♦ Children's menu Children's portions Garden ⊼ Beer festival Parking Wi-fi ▄▄ (notice required)

GLASBURY   Map 9 SO31

The Harp Inn

HR3 5NR ☎ 01497 847373
e-mail: info@theharpinn.co.uk
web: www.theharpinn.co.uk
dir: *In village centre on B4350, approx 3.5m from Hay-on-Wye*

Country pub with a long history

A pub since the 16th century, this comfortable inn overlooks the River Wye and is just a few miles from Hay-on-Wye itself. In the bar, grab a table and enjoy a pint of one of several local real ales on offer or one of the ten wines available by the glass. The tempting menu offers classics of home-made steak and Wye Valley stout pie, trio of Brian George's pork sausages and Thai green curry. Regular music events include monthly folk and Irish sessions and occasional jazz nights.

Open 12-3 6-12 Closed: Mon **Bar Meals** L served Tue-Sun 12-2 D served Tue-Sun 6.30-9 **Restaurant** L served Tue-Sun 12-2 D served Tue-Sun 6.30-9 ⊕ FREE HOUSE ◀ Wye Valley Dorothy Goodbody's Country Ale, Butty Bach ♂ Westons Stowford Press. ♟ 10 **Facilities** Non-diners area ❤ (Bar Garden) ♦♦ Children's menu Children's portions Garden ⊼ Parking Wi-fi ▄▄ (notice required)

HAY-ON-WYE
Map 9 SO24

The Old Black Lion ★★★★ INN ⊛

PICK OF THE PUBS

HR3 5AD ☎ **01497 820841**
e-mail: info@oldblacklion.co.uk
dir: *From B4348 in Hay-on-Wye into Lion St. Inn on right*

Good cooking in historic inn

Parts of this charming whitewashed inn date from the 1300s, although structurally most of it is 17th century. It is situated close to what was known as the Lion Gate, one of the original entrances to the old walled town of Hay-on-Wye. The oak-timbered bar is furnished with scrubbed pine tables, comfy armchairs and a log-burning stove – perfect for savouring a pint of Old Black Lion Ale. The inn has a long-standing reputation for its food – witness the AA Rosette – and the pretty dining room overlooking the garden terrace is where to enjoy the ham hock and foie gras terrine, piccalilli dressing and salad followed by honey and black pepper glazed chicken breast, wild mushroom, leek and pearl barley broth, smoked bacon and creamed potato. Guest rooms are available. Hay, of course, has bookshops at every turn, and it is also home to a renowned annual literary festival. Please note that only children over eight are permitted in the pub.

Open all day all wk 8am-11pm Closed: 24-26 Dec **Bar Meals** L served Mon-Fri 12-2, Sat-Sun 12-2.30 D served Sun-Thu 6.30-9, Fri-Sat 6.30-9.30 **Restaurant** L served Mon-Fri 12-2, Sat-Sun 12-2.30 D served Sun-Thu 6.30-9, Fri-Sat 6.30-9.30 ⊕ FREE HOUSE ◀ Old Black Lion Ale, Sharp's Doom Bar ♂ Westons Stowford Press. ♟ 8 **Facilities** Non-diners area Garden ⊁ Parking Wi-fi **Rooms** 10

The Three Tuns

4 Broad St HR3 5DB ☎ **01497 821855**
e-mail: info@three-tuns.com
dir: *In town centre*

Stylish town pub with a warm welcome

Despite a devastating fire a few years ago, this 16th-century, possibly older, pub has attracted an eclectic roll-call of famous, even infamous, visitors, from Jools Holland to the Great Train Robbers. In the bar is an old settle, reclaimed from the fire and restored for that welcome pint of Wye Valley Bitter or Butty Bach. The menus range from a home-made pizza, baked ciabatta or beer battered haddock and chips to choices such as vanilla fillet of turbot, crab and pea risotto, roasted white chicory and artichoke purée; and local shot mixed game casserole, herb dumplings and mustard cream.

Open 11-3 6-11 Closed: 25 Dec, Mon & Tue (winter) **Bar Meals** L served all wk 12-2 D served all wk 6-9 **Restaurant** L served all wk 12-2 D served all wk 6-9 ⊕ FREE HOUSE ◀ Wye Valley Bitter, Butty Bach ♂ Westons Old Rosie. **Facilities** Non-diners area ♦♦ Children's portions Garden ⊁ Wi-fi ⊟

LLANDRINDOD WELLS
Map 9 SO06

The Bell Country Inn

Llanyre LD1 6DY ☎ **01597 823959**
e-mail: info@bellcountryinn.co.uk
dir: *1.5m NW of Llandrindod Wells on A4081*

Contemporary comforts in lovely hill country

Overlooking the spa town of Llandrindod Wells, this thoughtfully modernised inn, originating as a drovers' overnight stop in Georgian times, is in an enviable village location in knolly hill countryside between the Rivers Wye and Ithon. Two bars and a popular restaurant offer frequently changing real ales and menus based on the best that the farms, rivers and estates of mid-Wales can offer. A classic slow-cooked shank of Welsh lamb with red wine and blackcurrant jus; home-made pie of the week or pan grilled supreme of salmon may feature, with some tasty calorific puddings to finish. Weekend specials and a pie-and-pint night add more variety.

Open 12-3 6-11.30 Closed: 1 wk in Feb, Sun eve & Mon L **Bar Meals** L served Tue-Sun 12-2 D served Mon-Sat 6-9 Av main course £9.95 **Restaurant** L served Tue-Sun 12-2 D served Mon-Sat 6-9 Av 3 course à la carte fr £28 ⊕ FREE HOUSE ◀ Guest ales. **Facilities** Non-diners area ♦♦ Children's menu Children's portions Garden Outside area ⊁ Parking Wi-fi ⊟ (notice required)

The Laughing Dog

Howey LD1 5PT ☎ **01597 822406**
dir: *From A483 between Builth Wells & Llandrindod Wells follow Howey signs. Pub in village centre*

Hints of India and family-friendly

The oldest part of this reputedly haunted, one-time drovers' pub dates from the 17th century. The kitchen sources locally for home-made British cooking, with French and Indian influences, including Welsh lamb casserole with chorizo and butter beans; sesame-baked salmon fillet with coconut and vegetable dhal; breast of chicken in pathia sauce; and Mediterranean vegetable Wellington. Among the desserts is lemon tart with minted red berry compôte. Additional attractions are the games room and dog-friendly garden.

Open 6-11 (Fri 5.30-11 Sat-Sun all day) Closed: Mon May-Aug except Royal Welsh wk **Bar Meals** L served Sun 12-2 D served Fri-Sat 6.30-9 **Restaurant** L served Sun 12-2 D served Fri-Sat 6.30-9 ⊕ FREE HOUSE ◀ Wye Valley Bitter, Newmans Wolvers Ale, The Celt Experience Celt-Bronze Ale, Felinfoel Double Dragon, Rhymney Bevan's Bitter. **Facilities** Non-diners area ♥ (Bar Garden) ♦♦ Children's portions Garden ⊁ ⊟ (notice required)

LLANFYLLIN
Map 15 SJ11

Cain Valley Hotel

High St SY22 5AQ ☎ **01691 648366**
e-mail: info@cainvalleyhotel.co.uk
dir: *From Shrewsbury & Oswestry follow signs for Lake Vyrnwy onto A490 to Llanfyllin. Hotel on right*

Traditional food in long-established hotel

A watering hole since the 17th century, this hotel offers the choice of an oak-panelled lounge bar and a heavily beamed restaurant. A full bar menu is available at lunchtime and in the evening typically offers Thai fishcakes; prawns with Marie Rose sauce, which might be followed by grilled lamb double chop with redcurrant and rosemary sauce; home-made steak and ale pie; chicken in a creamy garlic mushroom sauce. Lovers of mild ale will find Ansell's in the bar, alongside The Rev. James and Thatchers Gold cider.

Open all day all wk 11.30am-mdnt (Sun 12-11) Closed: 25 Dec **Bar Meals** L served all wk 12-2 D served all wk 7-9 **Restaurant** D served all wk 7-9 ⊕ FREE HOUSE ◀ Worthington's, Ansell's Mild, Guinness, Brains The Rev. James ♂ Thatchers Gold. **Facilities** Non-diners area ♦♦ Children's menu Children's portions ⊁ Parking Wi-fi ⊟ (notice required)

LLANGYNIDR
Map 9 SO11

The Coach & Horses

Cwmcrawnon Rd NP8 1LS ☎ **01874 730245**
e-mail: info@coachandhorses.org
dir: *Take A40 from Abergavenny towards Brecon. At Crickhowell left onto B4558 to Llangynidr (NB narrow river bridge), or from Beaufort take B4560 through Brynmawr to Llangynidr*

Enjoy local ales and food close to the Brecon Beacons

Just two minutes' walk from the nearby canal moorings and surrounded by the Brecon Beacons, this early 18th-century free house is also a popular meeting place for car club members - the car park can accommodate over 70 vehicles. Changing real ales are sourced from a 40-mile radius, and include the inn's own Llangynidr Canal Water ale. The talented chefs prepare the likes of deep-fried brie followed by home-made venison faggots with horseradish mash and a red wine sauce, finishing with chilled banana terrine. The beer garden has lovely views over the countryside, and there are beer festivals in May and July.

Open all day 12-12 Closed: Mon in winter **Bar Meals** L served all wk 12-2 D served all wk 6-9 **Restaurant** L served Mon-Sat 12-2, Sun 12-3 D served Sun 6-9 ⊕ FREE HOUSE ◀ Llangynidr Canal Water, Guest ales ♂ Westons Stowford Press, Gwynt y Ddraig. **Facilities** Non-diners area ♥ (Bar Garden) ♦♦ Children's menu Children's portions Garden ⊁ Beer festival Parking Wi-fi ⊟ (notice required)

Save on hotels. Book at **theAA.com/hotel**

POWYS 581 | WALES

PICK OF THE PUBS

The Dragon ★★★★ INN ✿

MONTGOMERY   Map 15 SO29

SY15 6PA ☎ 01686 668359
e-mail: reception@dragonhotel.com
web: www.dragonhotel.com
dir: *A483 towards Welshpool, right onto B4386 then B4385. Behind town hall*

Award-winning bistro food in a family-run inn

Set in the stunning Welsh Marches, this black-and-white timber-framed coaching inn dates back to the 1600s. It is full of historical features, including the enclosed patio which has been created from the former coach entrance, and the masonry in the bar, lounge and most bedrooms, which was allegedly removed from Montgomery Castle after its destruction by Oliver Cromwell. Husband and wife team Mark and Sue Michaels oversee the bar and kitchen respectively. Ales from the Montgomery Brewery, wines from the Penarth Vineyard and local Old Monty cider are among the refreshments on offer. Awarded an AA Rosette for its fine food for over ten years, this inn offers an excellent range of light snacks and full meals. Snack-wise, you can choose from a huge range of fillings, served in a sandwich, a baguette or a jacket potato. Ploughman's lunches and jumbo Welsh

rarebits are also on offer. If you prefer a lengthy meal, kick off with ham hock and parsley terrine, or beetroot and halloumi salad. Typical main courses range from brisket of beef, horseradish pudding, mash and onion gravy to a home-made curry. A vegetarian option might be tagliatelle with roast vegetables and tomato sauce; and a please-all children's menu, which includes pint-sized portions of many of the adult's main courses and simple meals such as sausages and chips. Twenty en suite rooms make the Dragon an ideal base for touring, walking Offa's Dyke, and fishing on the Severn. Booking for meals may be required.

Open all wk 12-11 **Bar Meals** L served all wk 12-2 D served all wk 7-9 Av main course £11 **Restaurant** L served all wk 12-2 D served all wk 7-9 Fixed menu price fr £16.50 Av 3 course à la carte fr £26 ⊞ FREE HOUSE ◀ Wood's Special Bitter, Bass, Montgomery Ö Old Monty. **Facilities** Non-diners area ♦♦ Children's menu Children's portions Outside area ⋒ Parking ➤ (notice required) **Rooms** 20

MACHYNLLETH — Map 14 SH70

Wynnstay Hotel

PICK OF THE PUBS

SY20 8AE ☎ 01654 702941
e-mail: info@wynnstay-hotel.com
dir: At junct A487 & A489. 5m from A470

Strong commitment to Welsh food

The Romans called it Maglona; today locals call this busy market town 'Mach' and it was here in the late 18th century that politician Sir Watcyn Williams-Wynne built his pied-à-terre. Now the Wynnstay, it's run by Paul Johns and his brother Gareth, a Master Chef of Great Britain dedicated to sourcing ingredients for their restaurant from within, as far as is practicable, a 50-mile radius. So should you decide to eat only dishes declaring their Welsh origin, you could choose from Bryn Derw chicken and pork terrine; Cardigan Bay fish casserole; loin of Llanfair pork with black pudding mash; and fillet of Aberdyfi sea bass. Alternatively, in the bar, try a pizza from a wood-fired oven, with a pint of Monty's Moonrise or Evan Evans Warrior. No piped music will interfere with your enjoyment, but a visiting choir might treat you to an impromptu rendition of Rhyfelgyrch gwyr Harlech.

Open all wk 12-2.30 6-11 Closed: 1wk over New Year **Restaurant** L served all wk 12-2 D served all wk 6.30-9 ⊕ FREE HOUSE ◀ Greene King IPA, The Celt Experience Celt-Golden Ale, Monty's Moonrise, Evan Evans Warrior, Guinness. ♟ 10 **Facilities** Non-diners area ❀ (Bar Outside area) ◀❙ Children's portions Outside area ⋈ Parking ⛐ (notice required)

MONTGOMERY — Map 15 SO29

The Dragon ★★★★ INN ◉

PICK OF THE PUBS

See Pick of the Pubs on page 581

NEW RADNOR — Map 9 SO26

Red Lion Inn

Llanfihangel-nant-Melan LD8 2TN ☎ 01544 350220
e-mail: theredlioninn@yahoo.co.uk
dir: A483 to Crossgates then right onto A44, 6m to pub. 3m W of New Radnor on A44

Ancient inn with a suntrap garden

Here in the wild landscape of mid-Wales is a drovers' inn that still provides water, though nowadays it's for hosing down muddy bikes, rather than for livestock to drink. The beamed lounge bar and locals' bar offer guest real ales. The traditional and modern cookery served in the two small restaurants is based on fresh, local produce such as Welsh Black beef, Welsh lamb and organic salmon. Welsh cream teas are served during the afternoon. Next door is St Michael's church, one of four so named encircling the burial place of the last Welsh dragon. According to legend, should anything happen to them the dragon will rise again.

Open 12-11.30 (Sun 12-7.30) Closed: Tue ⊕ FREE HOUSE ◀ Guest ales ♂ Westons Stowford Press. **Facilities** ◀❙ Family room Garden Parking

---

OLD RADNOR — Map 9 SO25

The Harp

PICK OF THE PUBS

LD8 2RH ☎ 01544 350655
e-mail: mail@harpinnradnor.co.uk
dir: Old Radnor signed from A44 between Kington & New Radnor

Welsh longhouse with lovely views

The Harp is a stone-built Welsh longhouse, believed to date from the 15th century, with spectacular views of the Radnor Valley. Open the simple wooden door and you step into a cosy lounge and bars with oak beams, log fires, semi-circular wooden settles and slate floors; books, board games and hop bines complete the warmly traditional appeal. Real ales from Shropshire are rotated, and an annual June beer festival is hugely popular. The food focus is on fresh and seasonal produce, and local sources are identified on the pleasingly straightforward menu. Artisan bread with rapeseed oil and balsamic dip tides you over while your choices are being prepared. Black Mountains Smokery kipper, served warm with crushed new potato and chive salad, makes a tasty starter. Welsh lamb and beef will probably feature in the main course, or grilled sea bass fillets for fish lovers. Finish with a selection of Welsh cheeses; or rhubarb with custard, fresh cream and ginger crumb.

Open Tue-Fri 6-11 (Sat-Sun 12-3 6-11) Closed: Mon (ex BHs) **Bar Meals** L served Sat-Sun 12-2.30 D served Tue-Sat 6-9 **Restaurant** L served Sat-Sun 12-2.30 D served Tue-Sat 6-9 ⊕ FREE HOUSE ◀ Three Tuns, Wye Valley, Hobsons, Ludlow, Salopian ♂ Kingston Rosy, Dunkertons, Westons Stowford Press. **Facilities** Non-diners area ❀ (Bar Garden) ◀❙ Children's portions Garden ⋈ Beer festival Parking Wi-fi

---

PAINSCASTLE — Map 9 SO14

The Roast Ox Inn **NEW**

LD2 3JL ☎ 01497 851398
dir: From Hay-on-Wye take B4351, through Clyro to Painscastle

Classic pub food in restored rural local

In stunning countryside close to Hay-on-Wye and Brecon, the Roast Ox is traditional country pub and one that was fully restored using traditional building materials and methods following a disastrous fire. Expect rustic brick floors, stone walls, old fireplaces and a classic pub atmosphere, alongside comfortable furnishings and local Wye Valley Butty Bach ale tapped straight from the barrel. The dining room was originally a blacksmith's workshop, which served the drovers on their way to market with oxen and cattle. Menus feature classic pub dishes and the Sunday roast lunches are famous locally – so it's best to book.

Open pm Jan-Mar Closed: Mon-Tue Jan-Mar **Bar Meals** L served all wk 12-2 D served all wk 6-9 **Restaurant** L served all wk 12-2 D served all wk 6-9 ⊕ FREE HOUSE ◀ Sharp's Doom Bar, Wye Valley Butty Bach ♂ Thatchers. ♟ 8 **Facilities** Non-diners area ❀ (Bar Outside area) ◀❙ Children's portions Outside area ⋈ Parking Wi-fi ⛐ (notice required)

TALGARTH — Map 9 SO13

Castle Inn

Pengenffordd LD3 0EP ☎ 01874 711353
e-mail: info@thecastleinn.co.uk
dir: 4m S of Talgarth on A479

Black Mountains pub with good real ales

This welcoming inn enjoys a spectacular location in the heart of the Black Mountains, in the Brecon Beacons National Park. It is named after the Iron Age hill fort that tops the hill behind it – Castell Dinas. Numerous walks and mountain bike routes begin and end at its door, making it popular with outdoor enthusiasts. With a good selection of real local ales, substantial pub food includes steaks, beef, lamb, venison swordfish and tuna cooked on hot rocks; chicken and leek pie; and vegetable chilli. Look out for the Black Mountains' Beast – a large black cat that has been seen by several customers!

Open Wed-Fri 6-11 (Sat-Sun 12-11) Closed: Mon-Tue ⊕ FREE HOUSE ◀ Wye Valley Butty Bach, Rhymney Bitter & Hobby Horse, Brains The Rev. James, Evan Evans, Guest ales ♂ Westons Stowford Press & Vintage, Thatchers Gold. **Facilities** ◀❙ Children's portions Garden Parking Wi-fi

---

Save on hotels. Book at **theAA.com/hotel**

POWYS 583 WALES

PICK OF THE PUBS

The Castle Coaching Inn

TRECASTLE　　　　Map 9 SN82

LD3 8UH ☎ **01874 636354**
e-mail: reservations@castle-coaching-inn.co.uk
web: www.castle-coaching-inn.co.uk
dir: *On A40, W of Brecon*

Ideal for base for walking in the Brecon Beacons

Privately owned and run by the Porter family, this Georgian coaching inn sits on the old London to Carmarthen route in the northern part of the Brecon Beacons National Park. It makes an ideal base for the pursuit of outdoor activities or, for the less energetic, the simple appreciation of mountain views, lakes, waterfalls and wildlife. The inn has lovely old fireplaces and a remarkable bow-fronted window looking out from the bar, where an open log fire burns throughout the winter. The focus on customer satisfaction makes this a relaxing hostelry, even at weekends when it becomes especially lively. Two real ales on tap change weekly, ensuring a pint in tip-top condition; wines and a good selection of Scottish and Irish whiskies are also served. While settling back to enjoy your drink and the pub's great atmosphere, take a look at the menu and specials board. Some guests prefer to stay in the bar to eat; the menu is the same both here and in the restaurant, although additional bar food includes fresh sandwiches, jackets, seafood or steak and ale pie, lamb casserole. Starters range from home-made soup of the day with crusty bread, to duck and orange pâté; deep-fried camembert; and a salmon, cod and prawn fishcake served with home-made tartare sauce. Main courses typically include Welsh sirloin steak cooked to your liking with mushrooms, cherry tomatoes and onion rings; supreme of chicken stuffed with Stilton, wrapped in bacon, with a white wine and cream sauce; and slow-roasted Welsh lamb. Desserts press all the right buttons with the likes of Belgian triple chocolate praline torte with vanilla ice cream; and lemon posset with shortbread. Outside, the peaceful terrace and garden beckon on sunny days.

Open all wk Sat-Sun 12-3 Mon-Sat 6-11 Sun 7-11 **Bar Meals** L served Sat-Sun 12-2 D served Mon-Sat 6.30-9, Sun 7-9 **Restaurant** L served Sat-Sun 12-2 D served Mon-Sat 6.30-9, Sun 7-9 ⊕ FREE HOUSE 🛢 Guest ales. **Facilities** Non-diners area 🐾 (Bar Garden) 👫 Children's menu Children's portions Garden 🎋 Parking Wi-fi

Star Inn

LD3 7YX ☎ 01874 676635
e-mail: anna@starinntalybont.co.uk
dir: *Exit A40 from Brecon towards Crickhowell, inn in 6m*

An astonishing number of beers at Brecon Beacons' pub

In the National Park, with a garden right next to the Monmouthshire & Brecon Canal, and an ever-changing choice of real ales – over 500 guests a year – Ian and Anna Bell's village pub is extremely popular, and even that could be an understatement. Beer festivals pull in even more fans in mid-June and mid-October. But, of course, there's food too, in the shape of Welsh lamb shank with chive mash and rosemary and redcurrant jus; fresh fish and chips in beer batter; and butternut squash and mushroom pie. Under-12s have their own selection and the under-2s can have mash, veg and gravy – free.

Open all wk 11.30-3 5-11 (summer Mon-Fri 11.30-11 Sat-Sun 11-11) **Bar Meals** L served Mon-Fri 12-2, Sat-Sun 12-2.30 D served all wk 6-9 (no food Sun eve Nov-Mar) **Restaurant** L served Mon-Fri 12-2, Sat-Sun 12-2.30 D served all wk 6-9 (no food Sun eve Nov-Mar) ⊕ PUNCH TAVERNS ◀ Wye Valley, Brecon Brewing, Guest ales ♂ Gwynt y Ddraig. **Facilities** Non-diners area ❖ (Bar Restaurant Garden) ♦❙ Children's menu Children's portions Garden ⊼ Beer festival Wi-fi

The Castle Coaching Inn

PICK OF THE PUBS

See Pick of the Pubs on page 583

Bunch of Grapes

Ynysangharad Rd CF37 4DA ☎ 01443 402934
e-mail: info@bunchofgrapes.org.uk
dir: *From A470 onto A4054 (Pentrebach Rd to Merthyr road) into Ynysangharad Rd*

Good beers deep in The Rhondda

Surrounded by the striking, wooded landscapes of the Rhondda Valley, landlord Nick Otley and his team revel in offering a sturdy combination of craft beers – some brewed at the eponymous Otley Brewery in the valley nearby - Welsh draught ciders and the best of the region's burgeoning fine food. A true taste of South Wales is the starter of pan-fried cockles with laverbread and leeks, maybe followed by Otley ale braised rabbit with braised chicory and Talgarth black pudding or wild venison leg braised in Otley Dark-O stout. Regular beer and food-related festivals are held; there's a deli here too.

Open all day all wk **Bar Meals** L served Mon-Thu 2.30-8, Fri 2.30-7, Sat 3-6.30 Av main course £8 food served all day **Restaurant** L served all wk 12-2.30 D served all wk 6.30-9.30 Av 3 course à la carte fr £30 ⊕ FREE HOUSE ◀ Otley O2 Croeso, Guest ales ♂ Gwynt y Ddraig, Blaengawney. **Facilities** Non-diners area ❖ (Bar Garden) ♦❙ Children's menu Children's portions Garden ⊼ Beer festival Parking

Kings Head ★★★★ INN

SA3 1HX ☎ 01792 386212
e-mail: info@kingsheadgower.co.uk
dir: *M4 junct 47, follow signs for Gower A483, 2nd exit at rdbt, right at lights onto B495 towards Old Walls, left at fork to Llangennith, pub on right*

A pub with it all, near glorious coastline

A lane to Rhossili Bay's magnificent beach starts just along from this 17th-century village inn, which still displays plenty of old beams, exposed stonework and a large open fire. The bar serves a weekly rotating schedule of real ales from the Gower Brewery, which pub landlord Chris Stevens co-founded. Much praised home-made food using local produce includes Vietnamese, Goan and Thai curries; pizzas; gourmet burgers; salt marsh lamb; and Welsh beef and venison. Comfortable and stylish accommodation is available. A beer festival is held during the last weekend of November.

Open all day all wk 9am-11pm (Sun 9am-10.30pm) **Bar Meals** L served all wk 9am-9.30pm D served all wk 9am-9.30pm Av main course £9 food served all day **Restaurant** L served all wk 9am-9.30pm D served all wk 9am-9.30pm food served all day ⊕ FREE HOUSE ◀ Gower, Guinness. **Facilities** Non-diners area ❖ (Bar Garden) ♦❙ Children's menu Children's portions Garden ⊼ Beer festival Parking ➤ **Rooms** 27

King Arthur Hotel

Higher Green SA3 1AD ☎ 01792 390775
e-mail: info@kingarthurhotel.co.uk
dir: *Just N of A4118, SW of Swansea*

A warm welcome and a delightful setting

Sheep graze on the village green opposite this charming inn set in a pretty village at the heart of the beautiful Gower Peninsula. Inside you'll find real log fires, bare wood floors and walls decorated with nautical memorabilia. Eat in the restaurant, main bar or family room, where choices range from pub favourites such as fillet of cod in a lager batter with home-made tartare sauce or a chicken fillet Kiev through to healthy salads (maybe Greek, ham or chicken Caesar). Enjoy the food with a choice of well-kept local ales, or one of 11 wines served by the glass.

Open all day all wk Closed: 25 Dec **Bar Meals** food served all day **Restaurant** L served all wk 12-2.30 D served Sun-Thu 6-9, Fri-Sat 6-9.30 ⊕ FREE HOUSE ◀ Felinfoel Double Dragon, Tomos Watkin OSB, Cottage King Arthur, Worthington's, Bass. ♟ 11 **Facilities** Non-diners area ♦❙ Children's menu Children's portions Family room Garden Parking ➤

Cross Inn

PICK OF THE PUBS

See Pick of the Pubs on page 586
See advert on opposite page

Save on hotels. Book at **theAA.com/hotel**

VALE OF GLAMORGAN 585 WALES

Cross Inn

Llanblethian, Cowbridge, Vale of Glamorgan CF71 7JF • **Tel:** 01446 772995
Website: www.crossinncowbridge.co.uk • **Email:** artherolry@aol.com

Often adored by visitors, a 17th century coaching inn set in a picturesque corner of the Vale of Glamorgan countryside on the fringe of the ancient town of Cowbridge, just a few miles from the splendid Heritage Coast. You will find a family run pub with cosy restaurant and character bar having a comfortable atmosphere and welcoming log fires.

Bar and children's meals are served in addition to the frequently changing restaurant menu where choices range from traditional curried chicken, homemade pies to steaks, seared duck breast, slow braised belly pork, trout fillet, pan fried bream and smoked haddock fillet. The food and Ales are mainly locally sourced and the kitchen and premises have been awarded Grade 5 by the Food Standards Agency for 2010/11/12 & 2013. The pub enjoys Camra recommendation and a good reputation for its range of ales as a Freehouse. With lovely hanging flower baskets, the inn has won 'in bloom awards 2010 & 2011'.

The food is supported by a wine list of regularly selected quality wine from around the world and from across the road where the oldest vineyard in Wales is located.

Outside there is a bus stop and the Inn has a good car park, many walkers visit as it is a good starting or finishing point for a perfect experience of a countryside walk. A number of walking routes are on the website that have been designed for enjoyment and lasting from 60 minutes to all day.

This old inn is dog friendly and also makes its mark with visitors as well as locals.

A great selection of real ales and friendly staff make it an ideal place to relax after a walk or cycle ride around the natural world of the numerous country lanes that meander to their junction at the *Cross Inn*.

PICK OF THE PUBS

Cross Inn

COWBRIDGE   Map 9 SS97

Church Rd, Llanblethian CF71 7JF
☎ **01446 772995**
e-mail: arthurolry@aol.com
web: www.crossinncowbridge.co.uk
dir: *B4270 from Cowbridge towards
Llantwit Major, pub 0.5m on right*

Ever popular country pub

Much loved by visitors, this 17th-century former coaching inn is set in a picturesque corner of the Vale of Glamorgan's countryside on the fringe of the ancient town of Cowbridge, just a few miles from the splendid Heritage Coast. A family-run pub, Cross Inn has a cosy restaurant and comfortable, character bar with welcoming log fires and a convivial atmosphere. The chefs take great pride in developing daily menus of essentially British food with European influences. Fresh produce is sourced from local farmers and other reliable suppliers, with fish, prime Welsh steaks, poultry and other ingredients delivered every day to supply the bar meals, children's meals and the frequently changing restaurant menu. Expect choices to include pub favourites such as home-made curried chicken, beer battered fillet of cod, pies and steaks. The regularly changing specials board features a variety of fish, meat and game dishes, and the traditional

Sunday lunch are always popular. On arriving at Cross Inn particularly noticeable are the lovely hanging flower baskets which have won the pub several awards. Dogs are very welcome, and the pub, with a good sized car park, is an ideal starting and finishing point for walkers who enjoy exploring the many delightful country walks the area has to offer.

Open all day all wk 11am-11pm **Bar Meals** L served Tue-Fri 12-2.30, Sat 12-9, Sun 12-4 D served Tue-Fri 5.30-9, Sat 12-9 Av main course £8.75 **Restaurant** L servedTue-Fri 12-2.30, Sat 12-9, Sun 12-4 D served Tue-Fri 5.30-9, Sat 12-9 Fixed menu price fr £9.95

⊕ FREE HOUSE ◧ Hancock's HB, Wye Valley Butty Bach, Evan Evans Crwr, Shepherd Neame Bishops Finger, Thornbridge Jaipur Ŏ Westons & Stowford Press, Thatchers Gold. **Facilities** Non-diners area ❖ ♦♦ Children's menu Garden ⊼ Beer festival Parking Wi-fi 🚌 (notice required)

Save on hotels. Book at **theAA.com/hotel**

VALE OF GLAMORGAN – WREXHAM 587 WALES

COWBRIDGE *continued*

Victoria Inn

Sigingstone CF71 7LP ☎ 01446 773943
e-mail: oleary445@aol.com
dir: Off B4270 in Sigingstone

An open-until-late pub found down the country lanes

Unusual white-painted tiling on the upper half of this family-owned inn makes it instantly recognisable as you drive into the village (which the Welsh call Dresigin, by the way). There are photographs, prints and antiques everywhere, while outside there's a beer garden. The Victoria isn't far from Cardiff, so beer drinkers can expect Brain's SA in the bar, with ample support in the form of Hancocks HB from Burton-on-Trent and Sharp's Doom Bar from Rock, in Cornwall. The inn is a great all rounder and does breakfasts, lunches and dinners, a daily roast and other dishes that include 'famous' salmon, sole and haddock pancake, garnished with prawns; and home-made faggots.

Open all wk 9.30-3 5.30-11.30 **Bar Meals** L served all wk 11.45-2.30 D served all wk 5.30-9 **Restaurant** L served all wk 11.45-2.30 D served all wk 5.30-9 ⊕ FREE HOUSE ◀ Hancocks HB, Worthington's Creamflow, Sharp's Doom Bar, Brains SA Smooth. **Facilities** Non-diners area ♦♦ Children's menu Garden Outside area ⋒ Parking Wi-fi ▭ (notice required)

EAST ABERTHAW   Map 9 ST06

Blue Anchor Inn

PICK OF THE PUBS

CF62 3DD ☎ 01446 750329
e-mail: blueanchor@gmail.com
dir: From Barry take A4226, then B4265 towards Llantwit Major. Follow signs, turn left for East Aberthaw. 3m W of Cardiff Airport

14th-century pub run by the same family for over 70 years

The grandfather of the present owners, Jeremy and Andrew Coleman, acquired this pretty, stone-built and heavily thatched inn in 1941, when he bought it from a large local estate. The inn has been trading almost continuously since 1380, the only break being in 2004

when a serious fire destroyed the top half of the building, forcing its closure for restoration. The interior remains warmly traditional; a warren of small rooms with low, beamed ceilings and open fires, including a large inglenook. A selection of well-kept real ales, including Wye Valley, is always on tap. An enticing range of food is offered in both the bar and the upstairs restaurant. Choose pub classics like gammon steak with egg and chips or more upmarket offerings such as pan-fried supreme of wood pigeon with red cabbage and black berry compôte followed by baked whole sea bass stuffed with herbs. A good choice is offered for Sunday lunch.

Open all day all wk 11-11 (25 Dec 12-2) **Bar Meals** L served Mon-Sat 12-2 D served Mon-Sat 6-9 Av main course £10 **Restaurant** L served Sun 12.30-2.30 D served Mon-Sat 7-9.30 ⊕ FREE HOUSE ◀ Theakston Old Peculier, Wadworth 6X, Wye Valley HPA, Brains Bitter. ♟ 9 **Facilities** Non-diners area ❀ (Bar Restaurant Garden) ♦♦ Children's menu Garden ⋒ Parking Wi-fi ▭ (notice required)

MONKNASH   Map 9 SS97

The Plough & Harrow

CF71 7QQ ☎ 01656 890209
e-mail: info@theploughmonknash.com
dir: M4 junct 35 onto dual carriageway to Bridgend. At rdbt follow St Brides sign, then brown tourist signs. Pub 3m NW of Llantwit Major

Step back in time for a warm welcome

Set in peaceful countryside on the edge of a small village with views across the fields to the Bristol Channel, this area is great for walkers attracted to the coastline. Dating back to 1383, the low, slate-roofed building was originally built as the chapter house of a monastery, although it has been a pub for 500 years. Expect an atmospheric interior, open fires, real ciders, up to eight guest ales on tap, and home-cooked food.

Open all day all wk **Bar Meals** L served Mon-Fri 12-2.30, Sat-Sun 12-5 D served Mon-Sat 6-9 Av main course £8.50 **Restaurant** L served Mon-Fri 12-2.30, Sat-Sun 12-5 D served Mon-Sat 6-9 ⊕ FREE HOUSE ◀ Shepherd Neame Spitfire, Wye Valley HPA, Hancock's HB, Bass, Guest ales ♦ Gwynt y Ddraig Happy Daze, Fiery Fox & Black Dragon. ♟ **Facilities** Non-diners area ♦♦ Children's menu Children's portions Garden ⋒ Beer festival Parking ▭ (notice required)

WREXHAM

ERBISTOCK   Map 15 SJ34

The Boat Inn **NEW**

LL13 0DL ☎ 01978 780666
e-mail: info@boatondee.com
web: www.boatondee.com
dir: A483 Whitchurch/Llangollen exit, towards Whitchurch on A539. After 2m turn right at signs for Erbistock & The Boat Inn

Local ales and modern food at riverside gem

A dead-end lane past the Victorian church leads to the 13th-century Boat, in an unrivalled position on the banks of the River Dee; there was once a ferry crossing here. Expect to find a cosy flagstoned and oak beamed bar and several rambling rooms with open fires, stone walls and charming nooks and crannies. It's a fine spot for a pint of local Weetwood Cheshire Cat and some modern pub food, best enjoyed in the glorious riverside garden. From the extensive menu choose Keralan lamb and spinach curry; or chicken, ham and leek pie, followed by warm chocolate and Guinness brownie, or opt for the chicken and lemon and thyme mayonnaise sandwich (served all afternoon).

Open all day all wk **Bar Meals** Av main course £10 food served all day **Restaurant** food served all day ⊕ FREE HOUSE ◀ Weetwood Best & Cheshire Cat, Conwy Welsh Pride ♦ Hereford Dry. ♟ 10 **Facilities** Non-diners area ❀ (Bar Garden) ♦♦ Children's menu Children's portions Garden ⋒ Parking Wi-fi

ERBISTOCK *continued*

Cross Foxes

Overton Bridge LL13 0DR ☎ 01978 780380
e-mail: cross.foxes@brunningandprice.co.uk
dir: *From Wrexham take A525 S. At Marchwiel take A528 signed Ellesmere to Erbistock*

Traditional riverside inn with a conservatory and beer garden

Smack beside the River Dee close to the Shropshire border, this spruced-up 18th-century former coaching inn offers great river views from its raised terrace and through picture-windows in the one of the light and airy dining rooms. In typical Brunning & Price style, the interior is smart and comfortable, the choice of ales wines and spirits is impressive, and the all-day food operation is not only good value but a cut above the norm. Take potted salmon and crab, lamb shank with bubble-and-squeak and rosemary sauce, and sticky toffee pudding.

Open all day all wk Closed: 25 Dec ⊕ BRUNNING & PRICE ◀ Ringwood Best Bitter, Mansfield Riding Bitter, Brakspear ⚬ Westons. **Facilities** ⋔ Children's portions Play area Garden Parking

GRESFORD	Map 15 SJ35

Pant-yr-Ochain

PICK OF THE PUBS

Old Wrexham Rd LL12 8TY ☎ 01978 853525
e-mail: pant.yr.ochain@brunningandprice.co.uk
dir: *From Chester take exit for Nantwich. Holt off A483. Take 2nd left, also signed Nantwich Holt. Turn left at 'The Flash' sign. Pub 500yds on right*

Accomplished food in elegant setting

Although there has been a building on this site since the 13th century, today's structure originally dates from the 1530s, as you can see from the Tudor wattle-and-daub walls and timber in the snug. A sweeping drive lined by majestic trees leads to this decoratively gabled manor house overlooking a lake and award-winning gardens. The interior has an inglenook fireplace and a host of nooks and crannies. The bar dispenses well-kept real ales such as Weetwood Eastgate Ale. Wine lovers too will not be disappointed by having to choose between over two dozen options. A daily-changing menu may offer a starter of smoked salmon with Bloody Mary jelly and crostini and main courses such as chicken, ham hock and leek pie; or seared calves' liver with buttered mash and red wine sauce. Chocolate and almond torte with 'Ferrero Rocher' ice cream is one dessert option.

Open all wk 12-11.30 (Sun 12-11) **Bar Meals** Av main course £11.95 food served all day **Restaurant** food served all day ⊕ FREE HOUSE/BRUNNING & PRICE ◀ Flowers Original, Brunning & Price Original Bitter, Purple Moose, Weetwood Ales Eastgate Ale ⚬ Tomas Watkin Taffy Apples, Westons Stowford Press, Aspall, Gwynt y Ddraig. ☕ 22 **Facilities** Non-diners area ❀ (Bar Garden) ⋔ Children's menu Children's portions Play area Garden ⛱ Parking Wi-fi

LLANARMON DYFFRYN CEIRIOG	Map 15 SJ13

The Hand at Llanarmon ★★★★ INN ◉
PICK OF THE PUBS

LL20 7LD ☎ 01691 600666
e-mail: reception@thehandhotel.co.uk
dir: *Exit A5 at Chirk follow B4500 for 11m. Through Ceiriog Valley to Llanarmon D C. Pub straight ahead*

Enjoyable food and well-kept real ales

Still very much at the heart of the local community, this 16th-century free house was once a stopping place for drovers and their flocks on the old drovers' road from London to Anglesey. Make the journey up the remote Ceiriog Valley in the shadow of the Berwyn Mountains, and you'll find this classic country inn with its unique dining room and 13 comfortable en suite bedrooms. Original oak beams, burnished brass and large fireplaces set the scene in the bar, where travellers and locals mingle over pints of Weetwood Cheshire Cat. The pub has established a strong reputation for no-nonsense dishes,

cooked from scratch with flair and imagination. Typical examples are spicy king prawns with lemon mayonnaise followed by ox cheek bourguignon with cabbage and horseradish mash. The same menu is served in the bar, the restaurant and on the sunny patio garden.

Open all day all wk 11-11 (Sun 12-10.30) Closed: 25 Dec **Bar Meals** L served Mon-Sat 12-2.20, Sun 12.30-2.45 D served all wk 6.30-8.45 Av main course £16 **Restaurant** L served Mon-Sat 12-2.20, Sun 12.30-2.45 D served all wk 6.30-8.45 Av 3 course à la carte fr £27 ⊕ FREE HOUSE ◀ Weetwood Cheshire Cat, Conwy Rampart. **Facilities** Non-diners area ❀ (Bar Garden) ⋔ Children's portions Garden ⛱ Parking Wi-fi ▦ (notice required) **Rooms** 13

West Arms ★★★★ INN ◉
PICK OF THE PUBS

LL20 7LD ☎ 01691 600665
e-mail: info@thewestarms.co.uk
dir: *Exit A483 or A5 at Chirk, take B4500 to Ceiriog Valley*

Off the beaten track in a secret valley

Built as a farmhouse in 1570, a century later it became a hotel known as The Eagles, before becoming a drovers' inn; nowadays it's a magnet for ramblers. Its ancient, labyrinthine rooms are full of character, with inglenook fireplaces, slate-flagged floors and aged oak beams. A great selection of real ales includes Stonehouse Brewery's Cambrian Gold and Station Bitter. Celebrity chef Grant Williams prepares dishes to AA Rosette standard using ingredients from the bountiful Ceiriog Valley and home-grown produce from the vast gardens. Some of the bar meals, such as antipasti platter, are served in both starter and main course portions, while designed solely for bowls or larger plates are bouillabaisse; Welsh lamb cutlets with sweet potato; vegetable and almond tagine; and cig ceiriog, which is a platter of meatballs, sticky chicken drumsticks, and lamb and leek koftas. The views from the gardens take some beating.

Open all day all wk **Bar Meals** L served Mon-Fri 12-2.30, Sat-Sun 12-9 D served Mon-Fri 6.30-9, Sat-Sun 12-9 Av main course £14.95 **Restaurant** L served Sun 12-6 D served all wk 7-9 Fixed menu price fr £27.95 Av 3 course à la carte fr £32.95 ⊕ FREE HOUSE ◀ Stonehouse Cambrian Gold & Station Bitter, Guinness, Guest ales ⚬ Westons Stowford Press. **Facilities** Non-diners area ❀ (Bar Garden) ⋔ Children's menu Children's portions Garden ⛱ Parking Wi-fi ▦ **Rooms** 15

Beer festivals, or their equivalent, are as old as the hills. The brewing of hops goes back to the beginning of human civilisation, and the combination of a common crop and a fermenting process that results in alcoholic liquid has long been a cause of celebration. Beer festivals officially began in Germany with the first Munich Oktoberfest in 1810. Wherever in the world beer is brewed, today and for the last few millennia, admirers, enthusiasts, aficionados – call them what you will – have gathered together to sample and praise its unique properties. It happens throughout Europe, in Australia, New Zealand, America and Canada, and annual events are held in pubs all over Britain.

Beer festivals are often occasions for the whole family, when entertainment is laid on for children as well as adults. Summer is naturally a popular season for festivals, when the action can take place outdoors, but many are held in October, traditionally harvest time. Beer festivals are sometimes large and well advertised gatherings that attract a wide following and last several days; or they might be local but none the less enthusiastic neighbourhood get-togethers.

Pubs name marked with an asterisk (*) have not confirmed the festival details for 2013-2014. For up-to-date information, please check directly with the pub.

Abbreviations

Etr Easter; **May BH** (1st Monday on May); **Spring BH** (last Monday in May); **Aug BH** (last Monday in August); **wk** week; **wknd** weekend

Public Holidays 2014

New Year's Day January 1; **Good Friday** April 18; **Easter Monday** April 21; **Early May Bank Holiday** May 5; **Spring Bank Holiday** May 26; **Summer Bank Holiday** (August Bank Holiday) August 25 (August 5 Scotland only); **St Andrew's Day** November 30 (Scotland only); **Christmas Day** December 25; **Boxing Day** December 26

ENGLAND

BEDFORDSHIRE

LINSLADE
The Globe Inn*
01525 373338

ODELL
The Bell*
01234 720254
Summer

STUDHAM
The Bell in Studham
01582 872460
Summer

BERKSHIRE

HERMITAGE
The White Horse of Hermitage*
01635 200325
Jun

KNOWL HILL
Bird In Hand Country Inn
01628 826622
Jun & Nov

MONEYROW GREEN
The White Hart
01628 621460
Aug

READING
The Flowing Spring*
0118 969 9878
Midsummer wknd (12+ real ales, live music, BBQ)

WALTHAM ST LAWRENCE
The Bell
0118 934 1788

WINKFIELD
Rose & Crown*
01344 882051

WOKINGHAM
The Broad Street Tavern
0118 977 3706
4 times a year

WOOLHAMPTON
The Rowbarge
0118 971 2213
Oct

BRISTOL
The Albion
0117 973 3522
Annually

BUCKINGHAMSHIRE

AMERSHAM
Hit or Miss Inn
01494 713109
middle wknd Jul

AYLESBURY
The King's Head
01296 718812

BEACONSFIELD
The Royal Standard of England
01494 673382

CHEDDINGTON
The Old Swan
01296 668226

CHESHAM
The Black Horse Inn
01494 784656

The Swan
01494 783075
Aug BH

CUBLINGTON
The Unicorn
01296 681261
May & Aug BHs

DENHAM
The Falcon Inn
01895 832125

DORNEY
The Palmer Arms
01628 666612
29-31 Jul

GERRARDS CROSS
The Three Oaks
01753 899016
Summer

HEDGERLEY
The White Horse
01753 643225
Etr, Spring BH & Aug BH

LACEY GREEN
The Whip Inn
01844 344060
May & Sep

LITTLE KINGSHILL
The Full Moon
01494 862397
12-14 Jul

MEDMENHAM
The Dog and Badger
01491 571362
May

MOULSOE
The Carrington Arms
01908 218050

PRESTON BISSETT
The White Hart
01280 847969
Spring BH

SEER GREEN
The Jolly Cricketers
01494 676308
Etr wknd & Aug BH

CAMBRIDGESHIRE

BALSHAM
The Black Bull Inn
01223 893844

BOURN
The Willow Tree
01954 719775

CAMBRIDGE
Cambridge Blue
01223 471680
Feb, Jun, Oct

DRY DRAYTON
The Black Horse*
01954 782600
St George's Day wknd

HEMINGFORD GREY
The Cock Pub and Restaurant
01480 463609
Aug BH wknd

HINXTON
The Red Lion Inn
01799 530601

HISTON
Red Lion
01223 564437
Etr & 1st wk Sep

OFFORD D'ARCY
The Horseshoe Inn
01480 810293
Midsummer

PETERBOROUGH
Charters Bar & East Restaurant
01733 315700
Etr Thu-Etr Mon

SPALDWICK
The George
01480 890293

STRETHAM
The Lazy Otter
01353 649780

CHESHIRE

ASTON
The Bhurtpore Inn
01270 780917
Jul (130 beers)

CHESTER
Old Harkers Arms
01244 344525
Early Feb & Oct

CHOLMONDELEY
The Cholmondeley Arms
01829 720300

KETTLESHULME
Swan Inn
01663 732943
1st wknd Sep

KNUTSFORD
The Dog Inn
01625 861421

MOBBERLEY
The Bulls Head
01565 873345
Jun

SPURSTOW
The Yew Tree Inn
01829 260274
Good Fri-Etr Mon

STOAK
The Bunbury Arms
01244 301665

SUTTON LANE ENDS
The Hanging Gate Inn*
01260 252238
May or Aug BH

CORNWALL & ISLES OF SCILLY

ALTARNUN
Rising Sun Inn
01566 86636
Mid-late Nov

BLISLAND
The Blisland Inn*
01208 850739
May

CALLINGTON
Manor House Inn
01579 362354
1st wknd Sep

CUBERT
The Smugglers' Den Inn*
01637 830209
May Day BH wknd

GWEEK
Black Swan
01326 221502
Autumn

GWITHIAN
The Red River Inn
01736 753223
Etr wknd

MARAZION
Godolphin Arms*
01736 710202

MITCHELL
The Plume of Feathers
01872 510387
May

MORWENSTOW
The Bush Inn
01288 331242

PENZANCE
The Turks Head Inn
01736 363093

POLPERRO
Old Mill House Inn
01503 272362
1st wknd Oct

ST AGNES
Driftwood Spars*
01872 552428
Mid Mar (mini beer festival) & May
Day BH wknd

ST IVES
The Watermill
01736 757912
Jun & Nov

ST MERRYN
The Cornish Arms
01841 532700
Mar (beer & mussel festival)

TRESCO (ISLES OF SCILLY)
The New Inn
01720 422849
Mid May & early Sep

TRURO
Old Ale House
01872 271122

CUMBRIA

BOOT
Brook House Inn
019467 23288
6–9 Jun

BOWLAND BRIDGE
Hare & Hounds Country Inn
015395 68333
May

BROUGHTON-IN-FURNESS
Blacksmiths Arms
01229 716824
1st wknd Oct

CARTMEL
The Cavendish Arms
015395 36240

ELTERWATER
The Britannia Inn
015394 37210
2wks mid Nov

HAWKSHEAD
Kings Arms
015394 36372

LOW LORTON
The Wheatsheaf Inn
01900 85199 & 85268
Late Mar

MILNTHORPE
The Cross Keys*
015395 62115
Annually

SEATHWAITE
Newfield Inn
01229 716208
Oct

SIZERGH
The Strickland Arms*
015395 61010
Annually

TIRRIL
Queen's Head Inn*
01768 863219
Aug (beer & sausage festival)

WASDALE HEAD
Wasdale Head Inn
019467 26229

DERBYSHIRE

ASHOVER
The Old Poets Corner
01246 590888
Mar & Oct (Thu-Sun, 40 beers & ciders, live music)

BIRCHOVER
Red Lion Inn
01629 650363
Mid Jul

BONSALL
The Barley Mow
01629 825685
3-4 annually on BHs

CASTLETON
Ye Olde Nags Head
01433 620248
Summer

CASTLETON
The Peaks Inn
01433 620247
Jul

CHINLEY
Old Hall Inn
01663 750529
3rd wknd Sep, 4th wknd Feb

DERBY
The Brunswick Inn*
01332 290677
1st wknd Oct

ELMTON
The Elm Tree
01909 721261
Mid May

EYAM
Miners Arms
01433 630853
3 each year

FENNY BENTLEY
Bentley Brook Inn
01335 350278
Spring BH

HAYFIELD
The Royal Hotel
01663 742721
1st wknd Oct

SHARDLOW
The Old Crown Inn
01332 792392
Apr & Oct

DEVON

ASHBURTON
The Rising Sun
01364 652544

BRANSCOMBE
The Fountain Head
01297 680359
Mid Jun

The Masons Arms*
01297 680300
Jul (30 ales & ciders, live music, BBQ)

BRIDFORD
The Bridford Inn
01647 252250
May & Aug

BUCKFASTLEIGH
Dartbridge Inn*
01364 642214
Annually

CLEARBROOK
The Skylark Inn
01822 853258
Aug BH

CLOVELLY
Red Lion Hotel
01237 431237
Spring BH

COCKWOOD
The Anchor Inn
01626 890203
Etr, Halloween

HONITON
The Holt
01404 47707

IDDESLEIGH
The Duke of York
01837 810253
Aug

KILMINGTON
The Old Inn
01297 32096
Spring BH Sat & Aug BH Sat

KINGS NYMPTON
The Grove Inn
01769 580406
Jul

LUTON (NEAR CHUDLEIGH)
The Elizabethan Inn
01626 775425
Jun

MEAVY
The Royal Oak Inn
01822 852944
3rd wknd Jun (real ale)

NEWTON ABBOT
The Wild Goose Inn
01626 872241
May BH wknd

PLYMTREE
The Blacksmiths Arms
01884 277474
Biannually

SANDFORD
The Lamb Inn
01363 773676

SIDMOUTH
Dukes
01395 513320
1st wk Aug

SLAPTON
The Tower Inn
01548 580216

TOTNES
Royal Seven Stars Hotel*
01803 862125

Steam Packet Inn
01803 863880
Mid May (4 days)

TRUSHAM
Cridford Inn
01626 853694

TUCKENHAY
The Maltsters Arms*
01803 732350
Annually

DORSET

BUCKHORN WESTON
Stapleton Arms
01963 370396

CHETNOLE
The Chetnole Inn
01935 872337

CORFE CASTLE
The Greyhound Inn
01929 480205
Aug BH wknd

GUSSAGE ALL SAINTS
The Drovers Inn*
01258 840084
Etr

IWERNE COURTNEY OR SHROTON
The Cricketers
01258 860421

MILTON ABBAS
The Hambro Arms
01258 880233
Jul

NORTH WOOTTON
The Three Elms
01935 812881

STUDLAND
The Bankes Arms Hotel
01929 450225
Mid Aug

WEST LULWORTH
The Castle Inn*
01929 400311
Annually

WEST STOUR
The Ship Inn*
01747 838640
Jun or Jul

WORTH MATRAVERS
The Square and Compass
01929 439229
1st Sat Oct (beer & pumpkin festival)

CO DURHAM

BARNARD CASTLE
The Morritt Arms Hotel*
01833 627232

BOLDRON
The George & Dragon Inn
01833 638215
Early May

FIR TREE
Duke of York Inn
01388 767429

FROSTERLEY
The Black Bull Inn
01388 527784

LONGNEWTON
Vane Arms
01642 580401
Oct (Blacksheep wknd), Jul (mini beer festival)

STANLEY
The Stables Pub and Restaurant
01207 288750
3rd wknd Sep

ESSEX

CASTLE HEDINGHAM
The Bell Inn
01787 460350
3rd wknd Jul, last wknd Nov

CHAPPEL
The Swan Inn*
01787 222353
Spring & Aug BH (Essex & Suffolk beers)

CHELMSFORD
Admiral J McHardy
01245 256783

CHRISHALL
The Red Cow
01763 838792
Jun-Aug

FEERING
The Sun Inn
01376 570442
End of May & Oct

FELSTED
The Swan at Felsted*
01371 820245

FULLER STREET
The Square and Compasses
01245 361477
Jun

GOLDHANGER
The Chequers Inn
01621 788203
Mar & Sep

HASTINGWOOD
Rainbow & Dove
01279 415419
Last wknd Oct (Oktoberfest inspired festival)

LITTLE BRAXTED
The Green Man
01621 891659

LITTLEBURY
The Queens Head Inn Littlebury
01799 520365
Etr

LITTLEY GREEN
The Compasses
01245 362308
2nd last wknd Aug

MARGARETTING TYE
The White Hart Inn*
01277 840478
Jul & Nov

MOUNT BURES
The Thatchers Arms
01787 227460
May & Oct

NEWNEY GREEN
The Duck Pub & Dining
01245 421894
Aug BH

STOCK
The Hoop
01277 841137

WOODHAM MORTIMER
Hurdlemakers Arms
01245 225169
Last wknd Jun (25+ real ales & ciders)

GLOUCESTERSHIRE

ALDERTON
The Gardeners Arms
01242 620257
Spring BH & 26 Dec (both 5 days)

ALMONDSBURY
The Bowl
01454 612757

BIBURY
Catherine Wheel
01285 740250
August BH

BROCKHAMPTON
Craven Arms Inn
01242 820410
2nd wknd in Jul

CHELTENHAM
The Gloucester Old Spot
01242 680321
3 times a year

The Royal Oak Inn
01242 522344
Spring BH

CLIFFORD'S MESNE
The Yew Tree
01531 820719
Oct

COATES
The Tunnel House Inn
01285 770280
1st wknd Aug

DURSLEY
The Old Spot Inn
01453 542870
3 times a year

EWEN
The Wild Duck
01285 770310
Summer

LECHLADE ON THAMES
The Trout Inn
01367 252313
25-Jun

NORTH CERNEY
Bathurst Arms
01285 831281
Jan, Apr, Jul & Oct

STONEHOUSE
The George Inn
01453 822302
Aug BH

TETBURY
The Priory Inn
01666 502251
May BH (real ale & cider)

GREATER MANCHESTER

MANCHESTER
Marble Arch
0161 832 5914

STOCKPORT
The Nursery Inn
0161 432 2044
3 times a year (8 guests on handpump)

WALMERSLEY
The Lord Raglan
0161 764 6680
Summer & Autumn

HAMPSHIRE

BALL HILL
The Furze Bush Inn
01635 253228
24-26 Dec

BEAULIEU
The Drift Inn*
023 8029 2342

BISHOP'S WALTHAM
The Hampshire Bowman
01489 892940
Jul & Dec

BRANSGORE
The Three Tuns Country Inn
01425 672232
Sep

CHALTON
The Red Lion
023 9259 2246
End Jul-beginning Aug

CHERITON
The Flower Pots Inn
01962 771318
Aug

CLANFIELD
The Rising Sun Inn
023 9259 6975

DUNBRIDGE
The Mill Arms
01794 340401
Summer

EAST BOLDRE
Turfcutters Arms
01590 612331

EAST STRATTON
Northbrook Arms
01962 774150
May BH

EXTON
The Shoe Inn
01489 877526

FORDINGBRIDGE
The Augustus John
01425 652098
May BH

HANNINGTON
The Vine at Hannington*
01635 298525
Jun

HOOK
Crooked Billet
01256 762118
Aug BH

HURSLEY
The Kings Head
01962 775208
Aug BH & Dec

LYNDHURST
New Forest Inn
023 8028 4690
2nd wknd Jul

MICHELDEVER
The Dove Inn
01962 774288

NORTH WALTHAM
The Fox
01256 397288
Late Apr

OLD BASING
The Crown
01256 321424
Annually

PETERSFIELD
The Old Drum
01730 300544

The White Horse Inn
01420 588387
Jun

ROCKFORD
The Alice Lisle
01425 474700

SELBORNE
The Selborne Arms*
01420 511247
1st wknd Oct

STOCKBRIDGE
The Three Cups Inn
01264 810527

TICHBORNE
The Tichborne Arms
01962 733760
3rd wknd in Aug

WINCHESTER
The Westgate Inn
01962 820222

The Bell Inn*
01962 865284
Summer

HEREFORDSHIRE

BODENHAM
England's Gate Inn*
01568 797286
Jul

BRINGSTY COMMON
Live and Let Live
01886 821462
Etr wknd

HOARWITHY
The New Harp Inn
01432 840900
BHs

LEOMINSTER
The Grape Vaults
01568 611404
2nd Sat Dec (Victorian Street Market day)

WELLINGTON
The Wellington
01432 830367
Jun

WOOLHOPE
The Crown Inn
01432 860468
May Day BH

HERTFORDSHIRE

ALDBURY
The Valiant Trooper
01442 851203
BHs

ARDELEY
Jolly Waggoner
01438 861350
Aug

BARLEY
The Fox & Hounds*
01763 849400
Every BH wknd

HERONSGATE
The Land of Liberty, Peace and Plenty
01923 282226
Etr, Aug BH, Xmas

PERRY GREEN
The Hoops Inn*
01279 843568
Aug

TRING
The Cow Roast Inn
01442 822287

WELWYN GARDEN CITY
The Brocket Arms
01438 820250
1st wknd Sep

KENT

CANTERBURY
The Red Lion*
01227 721339
Aug BH wknd

CHARING
The Bowl Inn
01233 712256
Mid Jul

CHILHAM
The White Horse
01227 730355
Summer

CHIPSTEAD
George & Dragon
01732 779019
Summer

DARTFORD
The Rising Sun Inn
01474 872291

FAVERSHAM
Albion Taverna
01795 591411
Early Sep, annual Hop Festival

HALSTEAD
Rose & Crown
01959 533120
Spring, Summer & Autumn

HERNHILL
The Red Lion
01227 751207
Aug BH

IDEN GREEN
The Peacock
01580 211233

LOWER HALSTOW
The Three Tuns
01795 842840
Aug BH

ROLVENDEN
The Bull
01580 241212

SMARDEN
The Chequers Inn
01233 770217

TONBRIDGE
The Little Brown Jug
01892 870318
May & Oct

LANCASHIRE

BILSBORROW
Owd Nell's Tavern
01995 640010
1st wk Sep (Oyster Festival); last wk Oct (Oktoberfest)

HEST BANK
Hest Bank Inn
01524 824339

LANCASTER
The White Cross
01524 33999
Late Apr (beer & pie festival)

The Sun Hotel and Bar
01524 66006
Summer

PARBOLD
The Eagle & Child
01257 462297
Early May BH

TOCKHOLES
The Royal Arms*
01254 705373

LEICESTERSHIRE

LONG WHATTON
The Royal Oak
01509 843694

MOUNTSORREL
The Swan Inn*
0116 230 2340
May & Aug BHs

OADBY
Cow and Plough
0116 272 0852
Quarterly

LINCOLNSHIRE

ASWARBY
The Tally Ho Inn
01529 455170
Aug BH (real ales, hog roast, live music & family fun)

BOURNE
The Wishing Well Inn
01778 422970
Aug BH

FROGNALL
The Goat
01778 347629
Jun

LINCOLN
The Victoria
01522 541000
Halloween & Winter

LITTLE BYTHAM
The Willoughby Arms
01780 410276
Aug BH

THEDDLETHORPE ALL SAINTS
Kings Head Inn*
01507 339798

LONDON

EC1
The Peasant
020 7336 7726
Apr & Nov

Ye Olde Mitre
020 7405 4751
May, Aug & Dec

The Coach & Horses
020 7278 8990

N1
The Drapers Arms
020 7619 0348
Aug

The Charles Lamb
020 7837 5040
Spring BH

NW1
The Queens*
020 7586 0408
Late Sep-early Oct (British Food Fortnight)

The Engineer*
020 7483 1890

The Prince Albert*
020 7485 0270
3-day real ale festival 2 or 3 times a year

NW3
The Holly Bush
020 7435 2892

NW5
The Lord Palmerston
020 7485 1578
Feb & Sep

NW10
William IV Bar & Restaurant*
020 8969 5944

SE1
The George Inn
020 7407 2056

SW3
Coopers Arms
020 7376 3120
May

SW6
The White Horse
020 7736 2115
4 each year (American, Great British, Old Ale & European)

SW10
The Hollywood Arms*
020 7349 7840

SW18
The Alma Tavern*
020 8870 2537
Annually (Young's mini festival)

W2
The Prince Bonaparte*
020 7313 9491
3rd wk Mar

The Cow
020 7221 5400

W14
The Albion
020 7603 2826
Etr wknd

WC2
The George*
020 7353 9638
Mar (real ale & cider)

LONDON, GREATER

CHELSFIELD
The Five Bells
01689 821044
Etr & Oct

KINGSTON UPON THAMES
The Boaters Inn
020 8541 4672
Mar

NORFOLK

BINHAM
Chequers Inn*
01328 830297

BRANCASTER STAITHE
The Jolly Sailors
01485 210314
Mid-late Jun (Norfolk Ale & Music Festival)

BURSTON
The Crown
01379 741257
2 or 3 a year

CROMER
The Red Lion Food and Rooms
01263 514964
Autumn

HEYDON
Earle Arms
01263 587376
St George's Day

HUNSTANTON
The Ancient Mariner Inn
01485 536390
Summer

HUNWORTH
The Hunny Bell
01263 712300
Aug

KING'S LYNN
The Stuart House Hotel, Bar & Restaurant
01553 772169
Jul

LARLING
Angel Inn
01953 717963
Early Aug

NORWICH
The Mad Moose Arms
01603 627687
May & Oct

THOMPSON
Chequers Inn*
01953 483360

WESTON LONGVILLE
The Parson Woodforde*
01603 881675

WINTERTON-ON-SEA
Fishermans Return
01493 393305
Aug BH

NORTHAMPTONSHIRE

EYDON
Royal Oak @ Eydon*
01327 263167

FOTHERINGHAY
The Falcon Inn*
01832 226254

NORTHAMPTON
Althorp Coaching Inn
01604 770651

OUNDLE
The Chequered Skipper
01832 273494
Twice a year

THORNBY
The Red Lion
01604 740238

TOWCESTER
The Saracens Head*
01327 350414

WADENHOE
The King's Head*
01832 720024
Aug

AYNHO
The Great Western Arms
01869 338288
1st wknd Oct

NORTHUMBERLAND

BEADNELL
The Craster Arms
01665 720272
last wknd Jul

CARTERWAY HEADS
The Manor House Inn
01207 255268

HEDLEY ON THE HILL
The Feathers Inn
01661 843607
Etr

HEXHAM
Miners Arms Inn
01434 603909

Battlesteads Hotel & Restaurant
01434 230209

MILFIELD
The Red Lion Inn
01668 216224
Last wknd Jun

SEAHOUSES
The Bamburgh Castle Inn
01665 720283
Annually

NOTTINGHAMSHIRE

BEESTON
Victoria Hotel
0115 925 4049
End Jan; Etr; last 2wks Jul (beer & music) & Oct

KIMBERLEY
The Nelson & Railway Inn
0115 938 2177
Each BH

LAXTON
The Dovecote Inn
01777 871586
3rd wknd Mar, last wknd Aug

NEWARK-ON-TRENT
The Prince Rupert*
01636 918121
Each BH

NOTTINGHAM
Ye Olde Trip to Jerusalem
0115 947 3171
2 or 3 a year

OXFORDSHIRE

BANBURY
Ye Olde Reindeer Inn
01295 264031

BLOXHAM
The Elephant & Castle
01295 720383
Early May (part of Bloxfest Music Festival)

BRIGHTWELL-CUM-SOTWELL
The Red Lion
01491 837373
Summer, 2 days (local beer & musicians)

BURFORD
The Highway Inn
01993 823661

Beer Festivals *continued*

CAULCOTT
Horse & Groom
01869 343257
Mid Jul

DORCHESTER
The George*
01865 340404

FERNHAM
The Woodman Inn
01367 820643
Annually

FRINGFORD
The Butchers Arms
01869 277363
Jun

FYFIELD
The White Hart
01865 390585

GREAT TEW
The Falkland Arms
01608 683653

HENLEY-ON-THAMES
The Cherry Tree Inn
01491 680430
Aug

KELMSCOTT
The Plough Inn
01367 253543

MARSH BALDON
Seven Stars
01865 343337
Aug BH

NORTHMOOR
The Red Lion
01865 300301

OXFORD
The Magdalen Arms
01865 243159
Annually

PISHILL
The Crown Inn
01491 638364
Late Sep

ROTHERFIELD PEPPARD
The Unicorn*
01491 628674

STANDLAKE
The Bell Inn
01865 300784
Aug

TETSWORTH
The Old Red Lion
01844 281274
Etr (mini festival)

THAME
The Thatch
01844 214340
Late Sep-early Oct (National Cask
Ale Week)

WEST HANNEY
The Plough Inn
01235 868674
May (Oxfordshire ales) & Aug BH
(champion beers of Britain)

WITNEY
The Three Horseshoes*
01993 703086
Aug BH

WYTHAM
White Hart
01865 244372
Etr

RUTLAND

LYDDINGTON
Old White Hart
01572 821703
Summer

OAKHAM
The Grainstore Brewery
01572 770065
Aug BH

SHROPSHIRE

BASCHURCH
The New Inn
01939 260335
Annually

BISHOP'S CASTLE
The Three Tuns Inn
01588 638797
2nd wknd Jul (all town pubs
involved)

CLUN
The White Horse Inn
01588 640305
1st wknd Oct

CRAVEN ARMS
The Sun Inn
01584 861239
Early Oct

MUCH WENLOCK
The George & Dragon
01952 727312
23rd April (St George's Day); late
Sep-early Oct (National Cask Ale
Week)

SHIFNAL
Odfellows Wine Bar
01952 461517
May & Sep

STOTTESDON
Fighting Cocks
01746 718270
Early Nov

WENTNOR
The Crown Inn
01588 650613
Jul

SOMERSET

BATH
The Star Inn
01225 425072
Twice annually

BISHOPSWOOD
Candlelight Inn
01460 234476

CORTON DENHAM
The Queens Arms
01963 220317

CROSCOMBE
The George Inn
01749 342306
Spring BH wknd, Oct

FRESHFORD
The Inn at Freshford*
01225 722250
Aug

HASELBURY PLUCKNETT
The White Horse at Haselbury
01460 78873

HINTON ST GEORGE
The Lord Poulett Arms
01460 73149

ILCHESTER
Ilchester Arms
01935 840220
BHs

PITNEY
The Halfway House
01458 252513
Mar

PORLOCK
The Bottom Ship*
01643 863288
1st wknd Jul (The Weir Fest)

SHEPTON BEAUCHAMP
Duke of York
01460 240314
Sep

TRISCOMBE
The Blue Ball Inn
01984 618242
1st Sat Sep (Triscombefest)

WEDMORE
The George Inn
01934 712124

WEST HUNTSPILL
Crossways Inn
01278 783756
Aug BH

WHEDDON CROSS
The Rest and Be Thankful Inn
01643 841222

STAFFORDSHIRE

BARTON-UNDER-NEEDWOOD
The Waterfront
01283 711500
1st wknd Apr

ECCLESHALL
The George
01785 850300
Etr wknd

STAFFORD
The Holly Bush Inn
01889 508234
Jun & Sep

SUMMERHILL
Oddfellows in the Boat
01543 361692

WRINEHILL
The Hand & Trumpet
01270 820048
Last wk Jan

SUFFOLK

BRANDESTON
The Queens Head
01728 685307
Jun

BURY ST EDMUNDS
The Old Cannon Brewery
01284 768769
Aug BH wknd

DUNWICH
The Ship at Dunwich
01728 648219
Spring, Summer, Autumn

ELVEDEN
Elveden Inn
01842 890876
Mid Jun (inc live bands)

FRAMLINGHAM
The Station Hotel
01728 723455
Mid Jul

HAWKEDON
The Queen's Head
01284 789218
3rd wknd Jul

LAXFIELD
The Kings Head (The Low House)*
01986 798395
May & Sep

LINDSEY TYE
The Lindsey Rose
01449 741424
1st wknd Aug

NAYLAND
Anchor Inn
01206 262313
Father's Day, Octoberfest

SIBTON
Sibton White Horse Inn
01728 660337

SNAPE
The Golden Key
01728 688510

SOMERLEYTON
The Duke's Head
01502 733931

WALBERSWICK
The Anchor
01502 722112
Mid Aug

SURREY

CARSHALTON
The Sun
020 8773 4549
Jun

CHIDDINGFOLD
The Swan Inn
01428 684688
Sep

FARNHAM
The Bat & Ball Freehouse
01252 792108
2nd wknd Jun

FETCHAM
The Bell*
01372 372624
Late Sep-early Oct (National Cask
Ale Week)

LONG DITTON
The Ditton
020 8339 0785

NEWDIGATE
The Surrey Oaks
01306 631200
Spring BH & Aug BH

TILFORD
The Duke of Cambridge
01252 792236
May (Cherryfest, beer & music)

WEST END
The Inn @ West End*
01276 858652

WINDLESHAM
The Half Moon
01276 473329

SUSSEX, EAST

ERIDGE GREEN
The Nevill Crest and Gun
01892 864209

LANGNEY
The Farm @ Friday Street
01323 766049
Jun & Aug

BLACKBOYS
The Blackboys Inn
01825 890283
Annually

COWBEECH
The Merrie Harriers
01323 833108
Aug BH (beer & music)

EAST DEAN
The Tiger Inn
01323 423209

HARTFIELD
Anchor Inn
01892 770424

ICKLESHAM
The Queen's Head
01424 814552
1st wknd Oct

SUSSEX, WEST

EAST GRINSTEAD
The Old Dunnings Mill
01342 326341
Jun & Sep

HENLEY
Duke of Cumberland Arms*
01428 652280
Mid summer (bi-annually)

KINGSFOLD
The Dog and Duck
01306 627295
Annually (charity event)

LAMBS GREEN
The Lamb Inn
01293 871336
Aug

OVING
The Gribble Inn
01243 786893
Summer & Winter

SLINDON
The Spur
01243 814216

WINEHAM
The Royal Oak*
01444 881252

WARWICKSHIRE

ALCESTER
The Holly Bush
01789 762482
Jun & Oct

EDGEHILL
The Castle Inn*
01295 670255

HUNNINGHAM
The Red Lion, Hunningham
01926 632715
Aug BH (film & beer festival)

WARWICK
The Rose & Crown
01926 411117
May

WEST MIDLANDS

BIRMINGHAM
The Old Joint Stock
0121 200 1892
Twice a year

WIGHT, ISLE OF

NITON
Buddle Inn
01983 730243
Jun & Sep

WILTSHIRE

ALDBOURNE
The Crown Inn
01672 540214
3rd wknd May & 3rd wknd Sep

The Blue Boar
01672 540237
Apr & Oct

BOX
The Quarrymans Arms
01225 743569
6 a year (mini ale weeks)

BROAD CHALKE
The Queens Head Inn*
01722 780344
Summer

BROUGHTON GIFFORD
The Fox
01225 782949
Summer

CRICKLADE
The Red Lion Inn
01793 750776
1st wknd Jun

DEVIZES
The Raven Inn*
01380 828271
Early Aug (The Wadworth Shire Horses' holiday weeks)

EAST CHISENBURY
Red Lion Freehouse
01980 671124
May BH

EDINGTON
The Three Daggers
01380 830940
Mar

HORNINGSHAM
The Bath Arms at Longleat*
01985 844308
Mid Jun

MALMESBURY
The Smoking Dog
01666 825823
Spring BH

NEWTON TONY
The Malet Arms
01980 629279
Jul

SALISBURY
Old Mill*
01722 327517
May & Oct

WARMINSTER
The George Inn
01985 840396
Aug

WORCESTERSHIRE

BECKFORD
The Beckford*
01386 881532
Oct

BEWDLEY
The Mug House Inn & Angry Chef Restaurant
01299 402543
Early May BH wknd

BRETFORTON
The Fleece Inn
01386 831173
Mid-late Oct

BROADWAY
Crown & Trumpet
01386 853202
Xmas & New Year

KNIGHTWICK
The Talbot
01886 821235
2nd wknd Oct

MALVERN
The Nag's Head
01684 574373
23rd April (St George's Day)

YORKSHIRE, NORTH

APPLETREEWICK
The Craven Arms
01756 720270
Oct (over 25 beers)

COLTON
Ye Old Sun Inn
01904 744261
Summer

CROPTON
The New Inn
01751 417330
Nov

HARDRAW
The Green Dragon Inn
01969 667392
Jun, Jul & Oct

KILBURN
The Forresters Arms Inn
01347 868386
23rd April (St George's Day)

KIRBY HILL
The Shoulder of Mutton Inn
01748 822772

MASHAM
The White Bear
01765 689319
Late Jun

OSMOTHERLEY
The Golden Lion
01609 883526
Nov

RIPON
The George at Wath*
01765 641324
BHs

YORKSHIRE, SOUTH

SHEFFIELD
The Fat Cat
0114 249 4801
Aug

Kelham Island Tavern
0114 272 2482
Late Jun wknd

YORKSHIRE, WEST

HALIFAX
The Three Pigeons*
01422 347001
May

HOLMFIRTH
Farmers Arms
01484 683713
Autumn

LEEDS
North Bar
0113 242 4540
Spring (Belgian & Dutch beers), Summer (USA beers), Autumn/Winter (German beers)

LINTON
The Windmill Inn
01937 582209
Jul

SOWERBY BRIDGE
The Alma Inn & Fresco Italian Restaurant*
01422 823334
Late Sep (Oktoberfest)

CHANNEL ISLANDS

JERSEY
ST AUBIN
Old Court House Inn
01534 746433

ISLE OF MAN

PEEL
The Creek Inn
01624 842216
Mar

PORT ERIN
Falcon's Nest Hotel
01624 834077
Early May

SCOTLAND

ARGYLL & BUTE

DUNOON
Coylet Inn
01369 840426

INVERARAY
George Hotel
01499 302111
May BH & Aug BH

CITY OF DUNDEE

BROUGHTY FERRY
The Royal Arch Bar
01382 779741
1st wknd Oct (charity event)

DUNDEE
Speedwell Bar
01382 667783
1st wknd Oct (Rotary Charity Oktoberfest)

CITY OF EDINBURGH

EDINBURGH
The Sheep Heid Inn
0131 661 7974

Halfway House
0131 225 7101

The Guildford Arms
0131 556 4312
Apr & Oct (plus monthly brewery wknds)

The Bow Bar
0131 226 7667
End Jan & end Jul (plus German Beer Festival)

RATHO
The Bridge Inn
0131 333 1320

CITY OF GLASGOW

GLASGOW
WEST Brewery
0141 550 0135
OktoberFest

Bon Accord
0141 248 4427
4 each year (90 beers &ciders)

Ubiquitous Chip
0141 334 5007
Twice a year (times vary)

DUMFRIES & GALLOWAY

BARGRENNAN
House O'Hill Hotel
01671 840243
Apr & Sep

HIGHLAND

CAWDOR
Cawdor Tavern
01667 404777

FORTROSE
The Anderson*
01381 620236
Jan (Burns Weekend Real Ale Festival), monthly mini-festivals

GLENCOE
Clachaig Inn
01855 811252
Hogmanay, FebFest & OctoberFest

TORRIDON
The Torridon Inn
01445 791242
1st wknd Oct

MORAY

FORRES
The Old Mill Inn
01309 641605
Jun

NORTH LANARKSHIRE

CUMBERNAULD
Castlecary House Hotel
01324 840233

SCOTTISH BORDERS

NEWCASTLETON
Liddesdale*
01387 375255
1st wknd Jul

STIRLING

CALLANDER
The Lade Inn
01877 330152
30 Aug-8 Sep

WEST LOTHIAN

LINLITHGOW
The Four Marys
01506 842171
last wknd May & Oct

WALES

BRIDGEND

KENFIG
Prince of Wales Inn*
01656 740356

CONWY

COLWYN BAY
Pen-y-Bryn*
01492 533360

FLINTSHIRE

BABELL
Black Lion Inn
01352 720239
April & Sep (Annual Ale Trail)

MOLD
Glasfryn
01352 750500
Mar (Welsh Food & Drink week); Oct
(Great British Pie & Champion Beers
of Britain week)

GWYNEDD

WAUNFAWR
Snowdonia Parc Brewpub &
Campsite
01286 650409
Etr wknd; usually mid May (Welsh
Highland Railway Raleail Festival)

MONMOUTHSHIRE

ABERGAVENNY
Clytha Arms
01873 840206
Spring BH

RHYD-Y-MEIRCH
Goose and Cuckoo Inn
01873 880277
End May & end Aug

TINTERN PARVA
Fountain Inn
01291 689303
Etr & Sep

TRELLECH
The Lion Inn
01600 860322
Jun & Nov

NEWPORT

CAERLEON
The Bell at Caerleon
01633 420613

PEMBROKESHIRE

ST DOGMAELS
The Teifi Netpool Inn
01239 612680
May & Aug

POWYS

DEFYNNOG
The Tanners Arms
01874 638032
Jun

GLANGRWYNEY
The Bell
01873 811115
Etr & Aug BH

LLANGYNIDR
The Coach & Horses
01874 730245
Jul

OLD RADNOR
The Harp*
01544 350655
Jun

TALYBONT-ON-USK
Star Inn
01874 676635
Mid Jun & mid Oct

RHONDDA CYNON TAFF

PONTYPRIDD
Bunch of Grapes
01443 402934
Every 2 months (20+ ales)

SWANSEA

LLANGENNITH
Kings Head
01792 386212
Last wknd Nov

VALE OF GLAMORGAN

COWBRIDGE
Cross Inn
01446 772995
Late Apr & Sep (mini Beer & cider
festival)

MONKNASH
The Plough & Harrow
01656 890209
Jun-Jul

Cider Festivals

ENGLAND

BEDFORDSHIRE

STUDHAM
The Bell in Studham
01582 872460
Summer

BERKSHIRE

HERMITAGE
The White Horse of Hermitage*
01635 200325

MONEYROW GREEN
The White Hart
01628 621460
Aug

READING
The Flowing Spring*
0118 969 9878

WINKFIELD
Rose & Crown*
01344 882051

BRISTOL

BRISTOL
The Albion
0117 973 3522
May BH

BUCKINGHAMSHIRE

CHEDDINGTON
The Old Swan
01296 668226

DENHAM
The Falcon Inn
01895 832125

MILTON KEYNES
The Swan Inn*
01908 665240

MOULSOE
The Carrington Arms
01908 218050

CAMBRIDGESHIRE

BOURN
The Willow Tree
01954 719775

HINXTON
The Red Lion Inn
01799 530601

SPALDWICK
The George
01480 890293

STRETHAM
The Lazy Otter
01353 649780

CORNWALL & ISLES OF SCILLY

GWITHIAN
The Red River Inn
01736 753223
Etr wknd

MORWENSTOW
The Bush Inn
01288 331242

ST MAWGAN
The Falcon Inn
01637 860225

TRESCO (ISLES OF SCILLY)
The New Inn
01720 422849
Jun

CUMBRIA

ULVERSTON
Farmers Arms Hotel
01229 584469

DERBYSHIRE

BAMFORD
Yorkshire Bridge Inn
01433 651361

CHINLEY
Old Hall Inn
01663 750529
3rd wknd Sep

DEVON

BRIDFORD
The Bridford Inn
01647 252250
May & Aug

KINGS NYMPTON
The Grove Inn
01769 580406
Jul

MEAVY
The Royal Oak Inn
01822 852944
Aug BH wknd, Mid Nov (cider &
bean festival)

TOTNES
Royal Seven Stars Hotel*
01803 862125

DORSET

BOURTON
The White Lion Inn
01747 840866
Ju

CHEDINGTON
Winyard's Gap Inn
01935 891244
Aug

WORTH MATRAVERS
The Square and Compass
01929 439229
1st Sat Nov

DURHAM, CO

FROSTERLEY
The Black Bull Inn
01388 527784

STANLEY
The Stables Pub and Restaurant
01207 288750
2nd wknd Dec

ESSEX

LITTLE BRAXTED
The Green Man
01621 891659

GLOUCESTERSHIRE

ALDERTON
The Gardeners Arms
01242 620257
Aug BH

CHELTENHAM
The Royal Oak Inn
01242 522344
Aug BH

The Gloucester Old Spot
01242 680321

CLIFFORD'S MESNE
The Yew Tree
01531 820719
Oct

COATES
The Tunnel House Inn
01285 770280

SHEEPSCOMBE
The Butchers Arms
01452 812113

TETBURY
The Priory Inn
01666 502251
May BH (real cider & ale)

HAMPSHIRE

BISHOP'S WALTHAM
The Hampshire Bowman
01489 892940
Jul & Dec

EAST STRATTON
Northbrook Arms
01962 774150
Sep

GUILDFORD
The Keystone*
01483 575089
Jul

LYNDHURST
New Forest Inn
023 8028 4690
Last wknd Mar

PETERSFIELD
The White Horse Inn
01420 588387
Sep

STOCKBRIDGE
The Three Cups Inn
01264 810527

HEREFORDSHIRE

HOARWITHY
The New Harp Inn
01432 840900
Aug BH

ORLETON
The Boot Inn
01568 780228
Last wknd Jul

WOOLHOPE
The Crown Inn
01432 860468

KENT

DARTFORD
The Rising Sun Inn
01474 872291

LOWER HALSTOW
The Three Tuns
01795 842840
Aug BH

LANCASHIRE

BILSBORROW
Owd Nell's Tavern
01995 640010
Last wk Jul

LEICESTERSHIRE

LONG WHATTON
The Royal Oak
01509 843694

LONDON

NW1
The Engineer*
020 7483 1890

NW5
The Lord Palmerston
020 7485 1578
23rd Apr (St George's Day)

SW10
The Hollywood Arms*
020 7349 7840

LONDON, GREATER

KINGSTON UPON THAMES
The Boaters Inn
020 8541 4672
Apr

NORFOLK

WINTERTON-ON-SEA
Fishermans Return
01493 393305

NORTHUMBERLAND

BEADNELL
The Craster Arms
01665 720272
Last wknd Jul

CARTERWAY HEADS
The Manor House Inn
01207 255268

HEDLEY ON THE HILL
The Feathers Inn
01661 843607
Aug BH

OXFORDSHIRE

FRINGFORD
The Butchers Arms
01869 277363

KELMSCOTT
The Plough Inn
01367 253543
Aug

WYTHAM
White Hart
01865 244372
Etr

RUTLAND

OAKHAM
The Grainstore Brewery
01572 770065
May BH

SOMERSET

CHEW MAGNA
The Bear and Swan
01275 331100

DUNSTER
The Stags Head Inn
01643 821229
Dec

HASELBURY PLUCKNETT
The White Horse at Haselbury
01460 78873

ILCHESTER
Ilchester Arms
01935 840220

PORLOCK

The Bottom Ship*
01643 863288
1st wknd Jul (The Weir Fest)

SHEPTON MALLET
The Three Horseshoes Inn
01749 850359

SHEPTON MONTAGUE
The Montague Inn
01749 813213

STAFFORDSHIRE

STAFFORD
The Holly Bush Inn
01889 508234
Jun & Sep

WRINEHILL
The Hand & Trumpet
01270 820048
Aug

SUFFOLK

HAWKEDON
The Queen's Head
01284 789218
3rd wknd Jul

SOMERLEYTON
The Duke's Head
01502 733931

SUSSEX, EAST

ERIDGE GREEN
The Nevill Crest and Gun
01892 864209

HARTFIELD
Anchor Inn
01892 770424

WARWICKSHIRE

ALCESTER
The Holly Bush
01789 762482
Jun & Oct

WILTSHIRE

ALDBOURNE
The Crown Inn
01672 540214
2nd week Jul

BOX
The Quarrymans Arms
01225 743569
Jul

BROUGHTON GIFFORD
The Fox
01225 782949

COLLINGBOURNE DUCIS
The Shears Inn
01264 850304
Late summer

EDINGTON
The Three Daggers
01380 830940
Sep

SHERSTON

The Rattlebone Inn
01666 840871
Jul

WORCESTERSHIRE

BRETFORTON
The Fleece Inn
01386 831173
Mid-late Oct

YORKSHIRE, NORTH

HARDRAW
The Green Dragon Inn
01969 667392
Oct

YORKSHIRE, SOUTH

SHEFFIELD
Kelham Island Tavern
0114 272 2482
Late Jun wknd

SCOTLAND

ARGYLL & BUTE

DUNOON
Coylet Inn
01369 840426

DUNDEE, CITY OF

BROUGHTY FERRY
The Royal Arch Bar
01382 779741
Last wknd Apr

GLASGOW, CITY OF

GLASGOW
Bon Accord
0141 248 4427

WALES

DENBIGHSHIRE

LLANELIDAN
The Leyland Arms
01824 750822

MONMOUTHSHIRE

TRELLECH
The Lion Inn
01600 860322
Aug

NEWPORT

CAERLEON
The Bell at Caerleon
01633 420613

PEMBROKESHIRE

ST DOGMAELS
The Teifi Netpool Inn
01239 612680
May & Aug

How to find a pub in the atlas section

Pubs are shown in the gazetteer under the name of their nearest town or village. If a pub is in a very small village, or in a remote rural area, it may appear under a larger town that is within five miles of its actual location.

The black dots in the atlas section match the location name in the gazetteer.

The county map shown opposite will help you identify the counties within each country. The county names are shown at the top of each page in the gazetteer.

The atlas section and the index that follow will help you find the towns featured in the guide.

Key to County Map

England

1 Bedfordshire
2 Berkshire
3 Bristol
4 Buckinghamshire
5 Cambridgeshire
6 Greater Manchester
7 Herefordshire
8 Hertfordshire
9 Leicestershire
10 Northamptonshire
11 Nottinghamshire
12 Rutland
13 Staffordshire
14 Warwickshire
15 West Midlands
16 Worcestershire

Scotland

17 City of Glasgow
18 Clackmannanshire
19 East Ayrshire
20 East Dunbartonshire
21 East Renfrewshire
22 Perth & Kinross
23 Renfrewshire
24 South Lanarkshire
25 West Dunbartonshire

Wales

26 Blaenau Gwent
27 Bridgent
28 Caerphilly
29 Denbighshire
30 Flintshire
31 Merthyr Tydfil
32 Monmouthshire
33 Neath Port Talbot
34 Newport
35 Rhondda Cynon Taff
36 Torfaen
37 Vale of Glamorgan
38 Wrexham

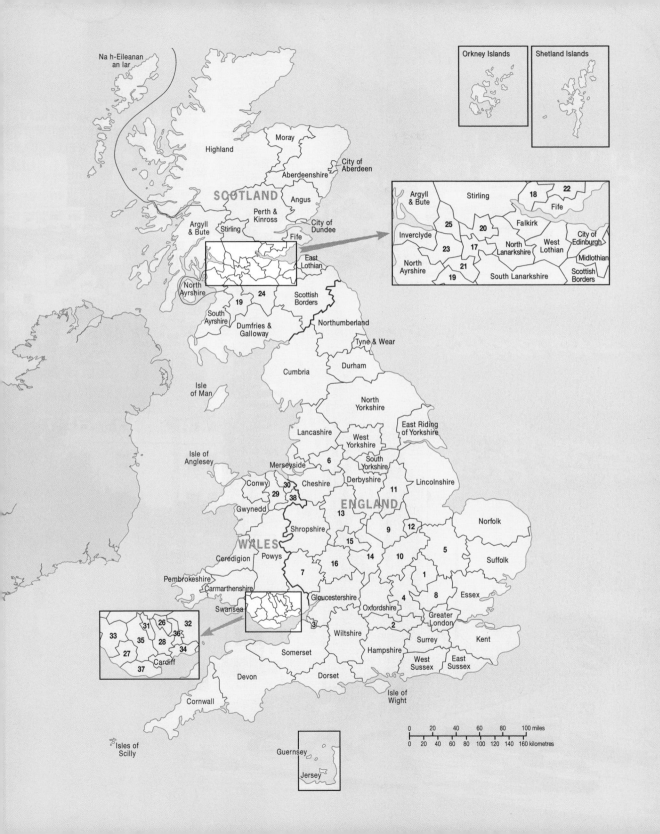

Na h-Eileanan
an Iar

Orkney Islands

Shetland Islands

Highland

Moray

SCOTLAND

Aberdeenshire

City of
Aberdeen

Angus

Perth &
Kinross

City of
Dundee

Argyll
& Bute

Stirling

Fife

East
Lothian

Argyll
& Bute

Stirling

18

22

Fife

25

20

Falkirk

Inverclyde

23

17

North
Lanarkshire

West
Lothian

City of
Edinburgh

North
Ayrshire

North
Ayrshire

19

24

Scottish
Borders

21

19

South Lanarkshire

Midlothian

Scottish
Borders

South
Ayrshire

Dumfries &
Galloway

Northumberland

Isle
of Man

Cumbria

Tyne & Wear

Durham

North
Yorkshire

East Riding
of Yorkshire

Lancashire

West
Yorkshire

Isle of
Anglesey

Merseyside

6

South
Yorkshire

Lincolnshire

Conwy

30

Cheshire

Derbyshire

11

29

38

Gwynedd

13

ENGLAND

Norfolk

Shropshire

9

12

WALES

15

5

Suffolk

Ceredigion

Powys

16

14

10

1

Pembrokeshire

7

Gloucestershire

8

Essex

Carmarthenshire

4

Swansea

3

Oxfordshire

2

Greater
London

31

26

32

Wiltshire

Surrey

Kent

33

35

28

36

34

Somerset

Hampshire

West
Sussex

East
Sussex

27

Cardiff

37

Devon

Dorset

Isle of
Wight

Cornwall

Isles of
Scilly

Guernsey

Jersey

| 0 | 20 | 40 | 60 | 80 | 100 miles |

| 0 | 20 | 40 | 60 | 80 | 100 | 120 | 140 | 160 kilometres |

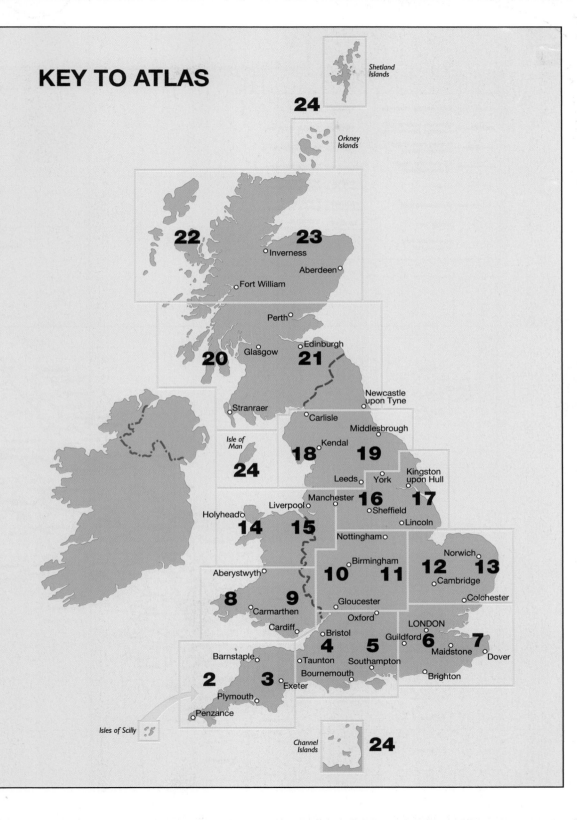

KEY TO ATLAS

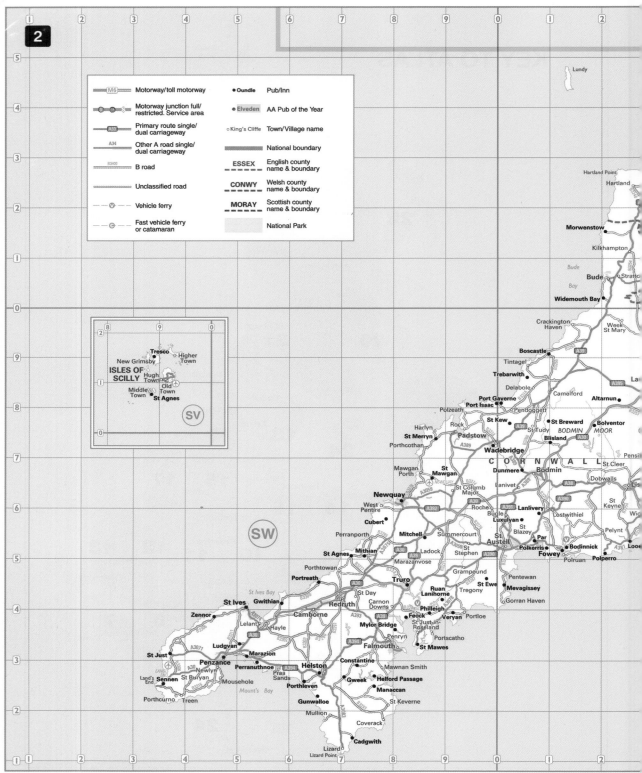

2

Legend

M6	Motorway/toll motorway
Motorway junction full/restricted. Service area	
A33	Primary route single/dual carriageway
A34	Other A road single/dual carriageway
B3400	B road
	Unclassified road
— V —	Vehicle ferry
— C —	Fast vehicle ferry or catamaran
● Oundle	Pub/Inn
● Elveden	AA Pub of the Year
○ King's Cliffe	Town/Village name
	National boundary
ESSEX	English county name & boundary
CONWY	Welsh county name & boundary
MORAY	Scottish county name & boundary
	National Park

ISLES OF SCILLY

Tresco
Higher Town
New Grimsby
Hugh Town
Old Town
Middle Town
St Agnes

SV

SW

Lundy

Hartland Point
Hartland

Morwenstow
Kilkhampton

Bude
Bay
Bude
Stratton
Widemouth Bay

Crackington Haven
Week St Mary

Boscastle
Tintagel
Trebarwith
Delabole
Camelford
Altarnun
La

Polzeath
Port Gaverne
Port Isaac
Harlyn
Rock
St Kew
Pendoggett
St Breward
Bolventor
BODMIN
Blisland
MOOR
Padstow
St Merryn
Porthcothan
Wadebridge
Pensil

Mawgan Porth
St Mawgan
Dunmere
Bodmin
St Cleer
CORNWALL

Newquay
St Columb Major
Lanivet
Dobwalls
Lis
Roche
Bugle
Lanlivery
Lostwithiel
St Keyne
West Pentire
Cubert
Luxulyan
St Blazey
Pelynt
Wi
Perranporth
Mitchell
Summercourt
St Austell
Par
Bodinnick
Ladock
St Stephen
Polkerris
Fowey
Looe
St Agnes
Mithian
Marazanvose
Polruan
Polperro

Porthtowan
Grampound
Pentewan
Portreath
Truro
St Ewe
Mevagissey
St Day
Ruan Lanihorne
Tregony
Gorran Haven
St Ives
Gwithian
Redruth
Carnon Downs
Philleigh
Zennor
Camborne
Feock
Veryan
Portloe
Lelant
Hayle
St Just-in-Roseland
Portscatho
Ludgvan
Mylor Bridge
Penryn
St Mawes
St Just
Marazion
Penzance
Falmouth
Newlyn
Perranuthnoe
Helston
Constantine
Mawnan Smith
Land's End
Sennen
St Buryan
Praa Sands
Gweek
Helford Passage
Porthcurno
Mousehole
Porthleven
Manaccan
Treen
Mount's Bay
Gunwalloe
St Keverne

Mullion

Coverack

Lizard
Cadgwith
Lizard Point

For continuation pages refer to numbered arrows

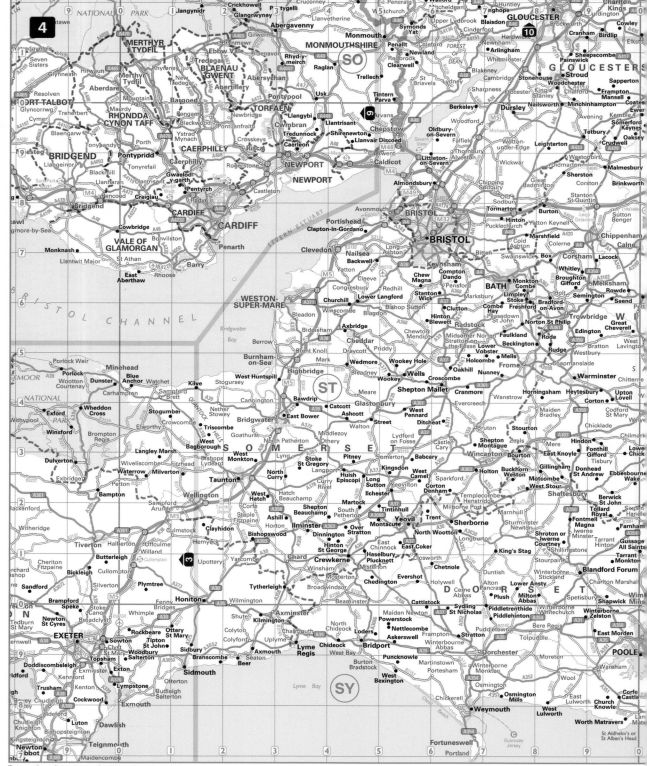

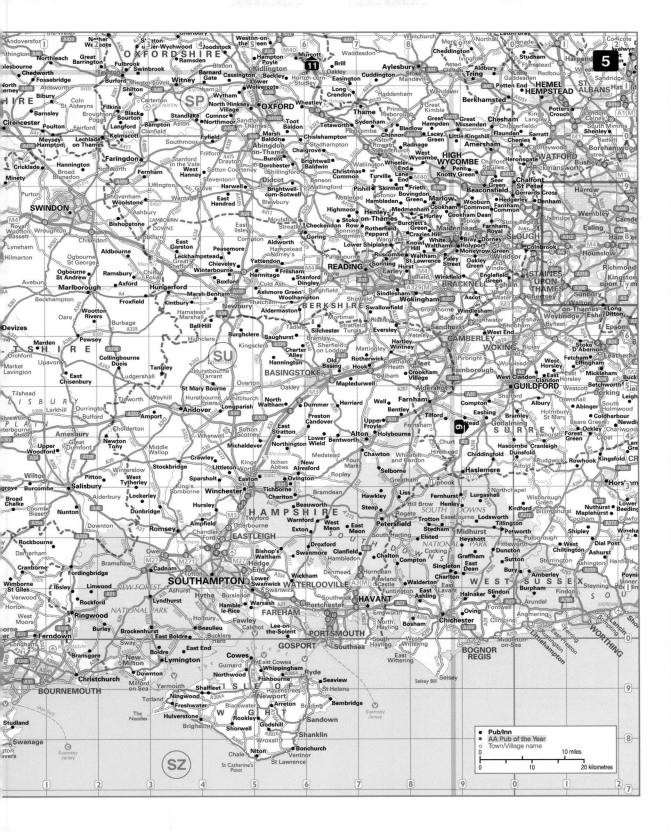

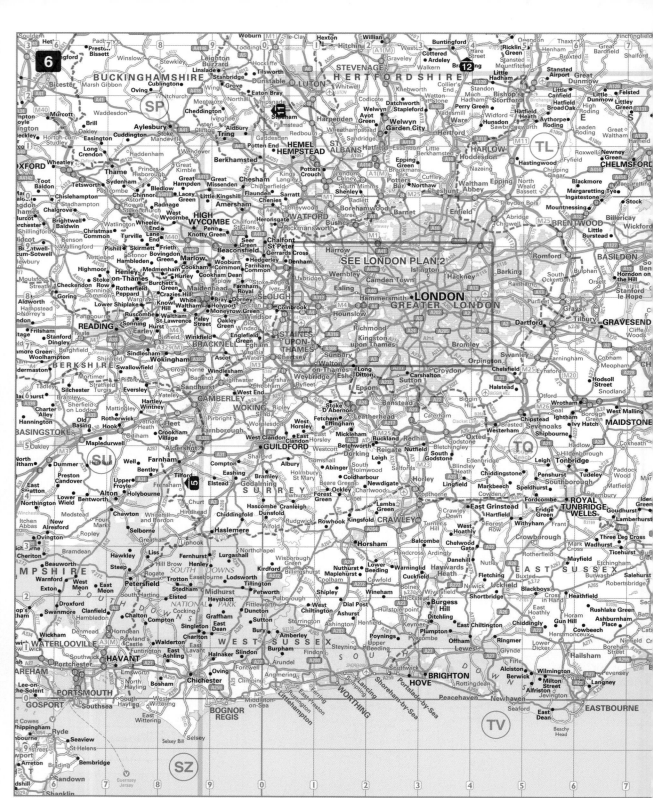

CARDIGAN BAY

Aberdyfi
Borth
Llandre
Aberystwyth
Llanfarian
Llanilar
Llanrhystud
Llansantffraid
Aberarth
Aberaeron
New Quay
Llwyndafydd
Llangranog
Aberporth
Tan-y-groes
Blaenporth
Talgarreg
Rhydowen
Temple Bar
Lampeter
C E R E D
Llanybydder

St Dogmaels
Cardigan
Llechryd
Llandysul
Abercych
Newcastle Emlyn
Llangeler
Llanllwni
SN
Llan
Abergorlech
Talley

SM
Strumble Head
Nevern
Newport
Eglwyswrw
Fishguard
PEMBROKESHIRE COAST NATIONAL PARK
MYNYDD PRESELI
Cynwyl Elfed
Brechfa

Porthgain
Letterston
Wolf's Castle
Rosebush
CARMARTHENSHIRE
Nantgaredig
Llandeilo

St David's Head
St Davids
Solva
PEMBROKESHIRE
Llandissilio
Carmarthen
Llanarthne
Llanddarog
Llandybie
Cross Hands
Newgale
Roch
Robeston Wathen
Narberth
Whitland
St Clears
Llansteffan
Pontyberem
Pontyates
An

St Brides Bay
PEMBROKESHIRE COAST NATIONAL PARK
Broad Haven
Haverfordwest
Red Roses
Laugharne
Kidwelly
Pont Abraham
Pontardd

Little Haven
Johnston
Kilgetty
Pendine
Pembrey
Burry Port
Swansea West
M4
Gorseinon

Marloes
Milford Haven
Neyland
Amroth
Saundersfoot
Pont
Llanelli
Gowerton
Dunvant

Broad Sound
Dale
Angle
Pembroke Dock
Pembroke
Carew
St Florence
Tenby
Carmarthen Bay
Pembrey
Llanrhidian
SWANSEA
Gowerton

Castlemartin
Penally
Manorbier
Llangennith
Reynoldston
Rhossili Worms Head
Bishopston

Stackpole
Bosherston
PEMBROKESHIRE COAST NATIONAL PARK
Port Einon
Oxwich

SR
SS

Pub/Inn
AA Pub of the Year
Town/Village name
10 miles
0   10   20 kilometres

Lundy
Ilfracombe
Combe Martin
Mortehoe
Lee

For continuation pages refer to numbered arrows

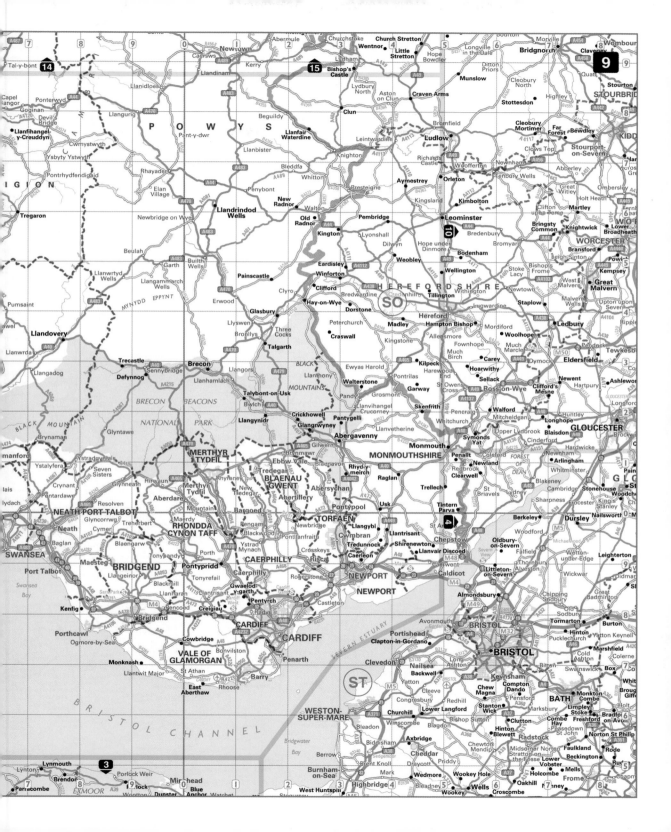

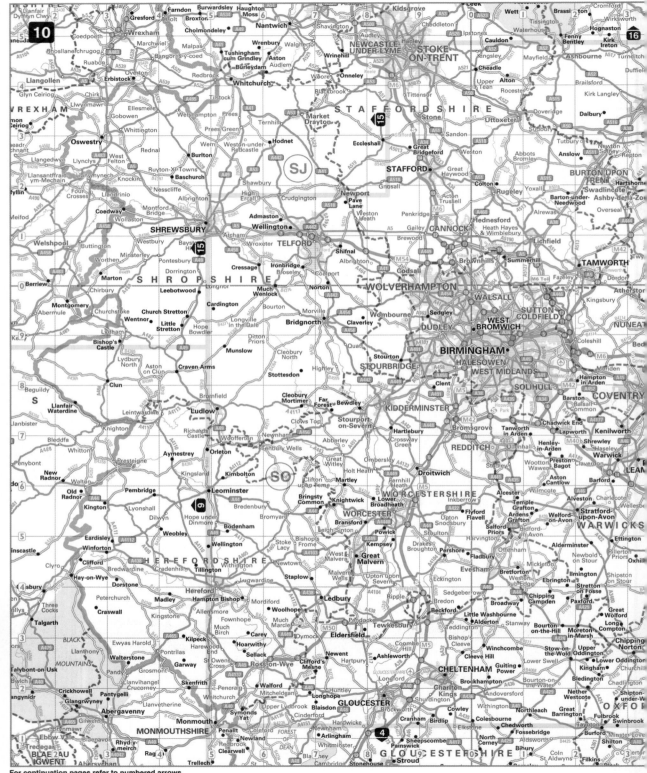

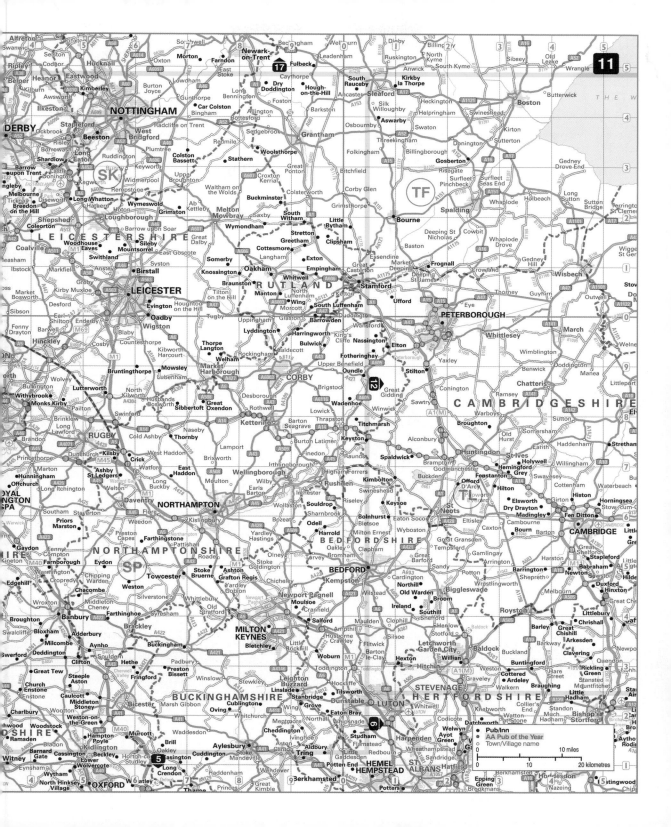

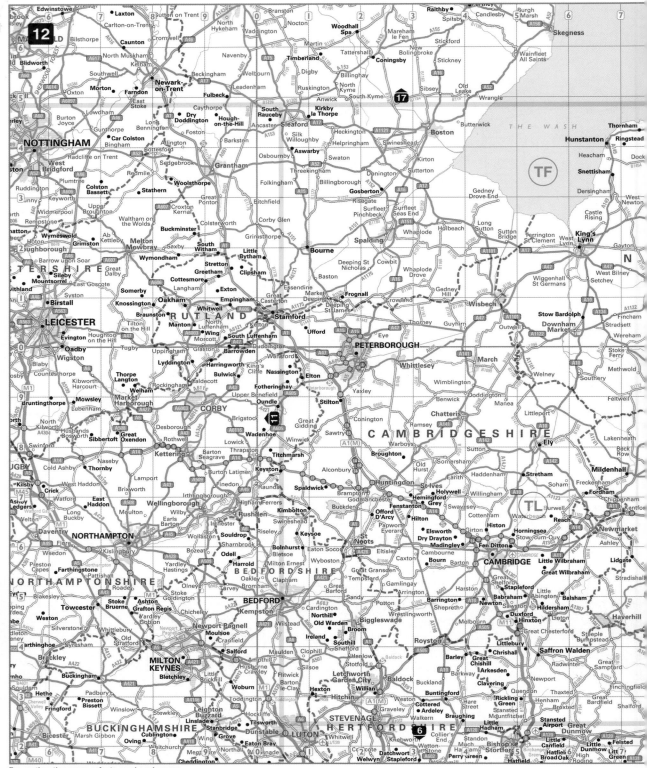

For continuation pages refer to numbered arrows

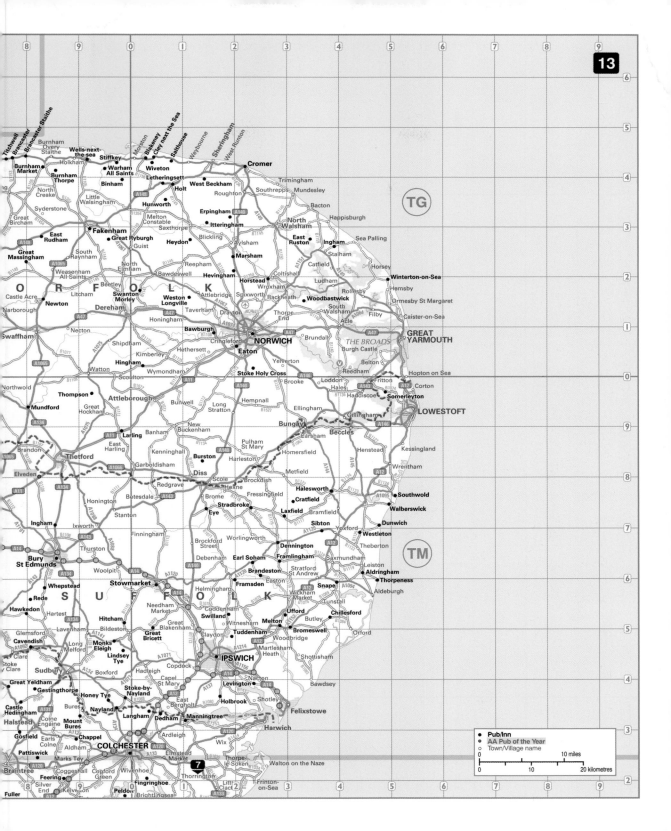

ISLE OF
ANGLESEY

Cemaes
Amlwch
Llanerchymedd
Holyhead
Llanfachraeth
Benllech
Red
Wharf Bay
Llangoed
Trearddur Bay
Pentraeth
Holy
Island
Llangefni
Beaumaris
Rhosneigr
Menai
Bridge Bangor
Llanfairfechan
Aberffraw
Llanfair
P.G.
Y Felinheli
Llanllechid
Newborough
Bethesda
Tal-y-Bont
Caernarfon
Llanrug
Trefriw
Bontnewydd
Llanberis
Waunfawr
Capel Curig
CONWY
Llandwrog
Llanwnda
Betws-y-Coed
Caernarfon
Bay
Penygroes
Rhyd-Ddu
Dolwyddelan
Clynnog-fawr
Penmachno
Pentrefoelas
SH
Beddgelert
Blaenau Ffestiniog
Cerrigydrudion
Llanaelhaearn
Prenteg
Y Maer
Morfa Nefyn
Nefyn
Tremadog
Maentwrog
Ffestiniog
Llanystumdwy
Porthmadog
Renrhyndeudraeth
Tudweiliog
Bodfuan
PENINSULA
Criccieth
Borth-y-Gest
Talsarnau
Bala
Sarn
LLEYN
Pwllheli
Trawsfynydd
SNOWDONIA
Y Rhiw
Llanbedrog
Harlech
GWYNEDD
Aberdaron
Absersoch
NATIONAL
Llanuwchllyn
Bardsey
Island
Llanbedr
PARK
Dyffryn Ardudwy
Ganllwyd
Tal-y-bont
Brithdir
Llanw
Barmouth
Dolgellau
Dinas-Mawddwy
Fairbourne
Mallwyd
Llangadfa
Llwyngwril
Corris
Cemmaes
Road
Llanbrynmair
Bryncrug
Pennal
Tywyn
Machynlleth
Carno
SN
Aberdyfi

Borth
Tal-y-bont
9
Llandre
Aberystwyth
Capel
Bangor
Ponterwyd
Llanidloes

Llandudno
Deganwy
Llandudno Junction
Rhôs-
on-Sea
Colwyn Bay
Rhy
Penmaenmawr
Conwy
Llanddulas
Abergel
Llansanffraid
Glan Conwy
Llanelian-
yn-Rhôs
Betws-
yn-Rhos
Llannefyd
Llanrwst
Llanfair
Talhaiarn
Hen
Llangernyw
Llansannan
Tal-y-Cafn
Bylchau

	Pub/Inn
•	AA Pub of the Year
○	Town/Village name

0   10 miles
0   10   20 kilometres

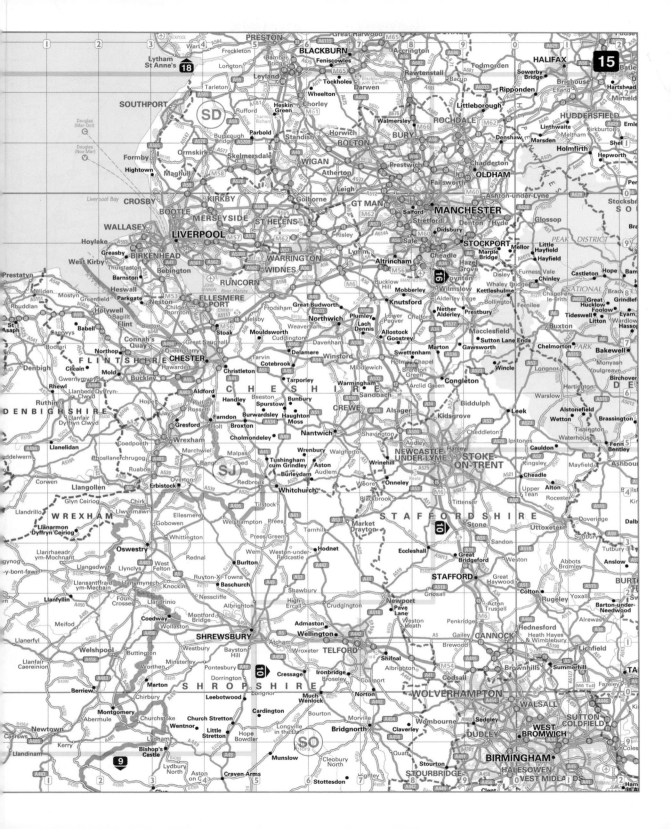

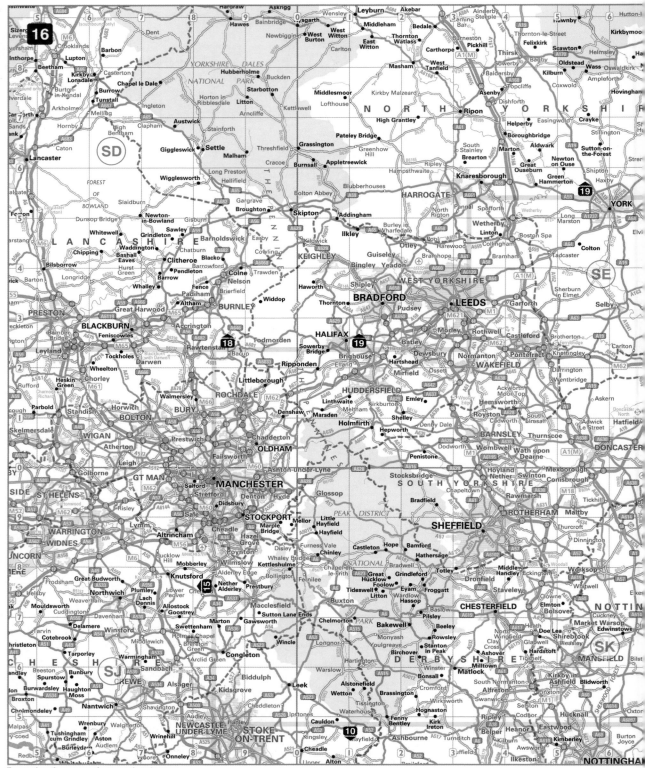

17

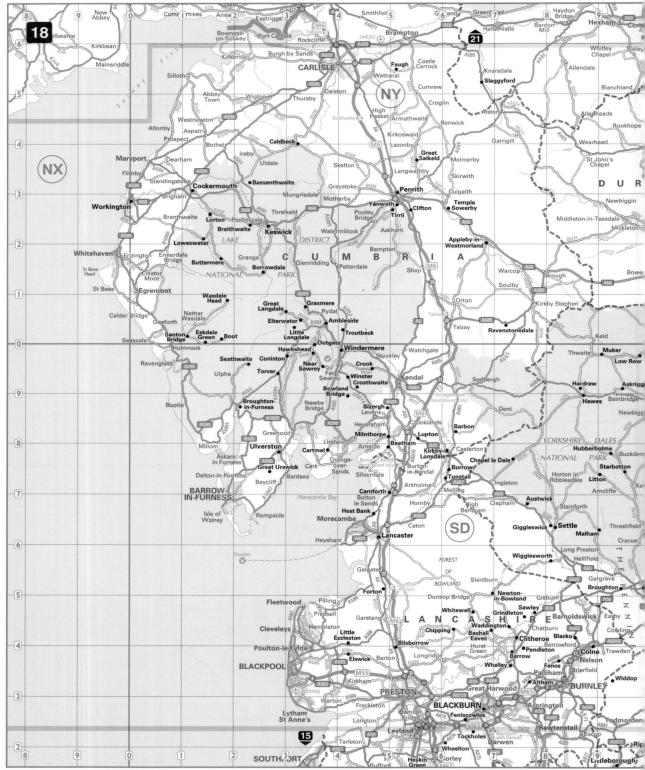

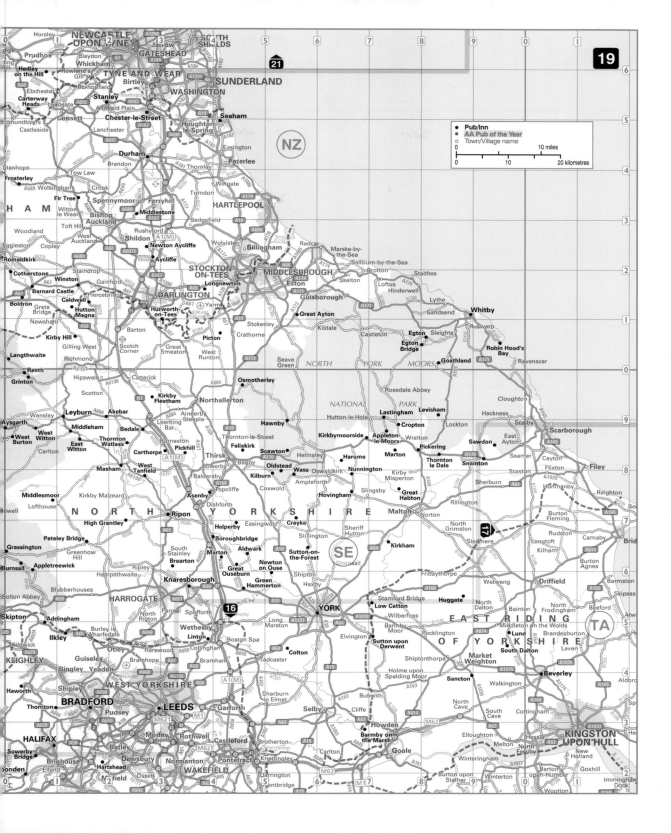

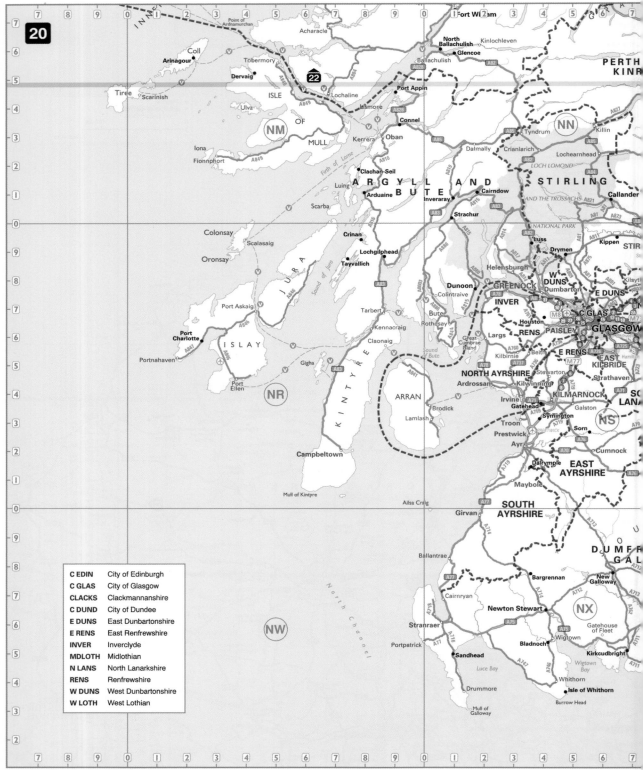

C EDIN — City of Edinburgh
C GLAS — City of Glasgow
CLACKS — Clackmannanshire
C DUND — City of Dundee
E DUNS — East Dunbartonshire
E RENS — East Renfrewshire
INVER — Inverclyde
MDLOTH — Midlothian
N LANS — North Lanarkshire
RENS — Renfrewshire
W DUNS — West Dunbartonshire
W LOTH — West Lothian

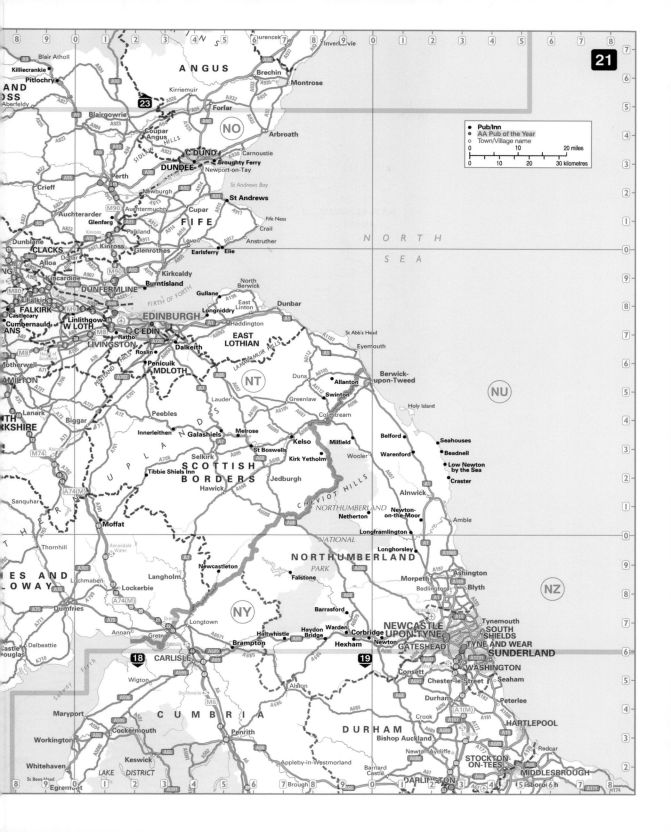

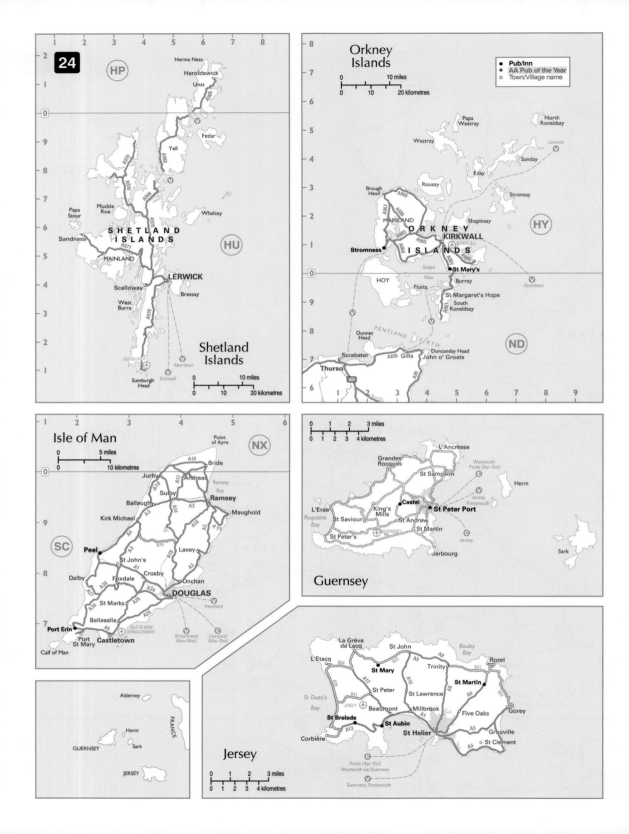

Central London

Index

Red entries are Pick of the Pubs

A

ABERAERON
The Harbourmaster 560

ABERCYCH
Nags Head Inn 574

ABERDEEN
Old Blackfriars 532

ABERDYFI
Penhelig Arms Hotel & Restaurant 564

ABERGAVENNY
Clytha Arms 567

ABERGORLECH
The Black Lion 559

ABINGER
The Stephan Langton 415
The Volunteer 415

ACHILTIBUIE
Summer Isles Hotel & Bar 542

ADDERBURY
Red Lion 335

ADDINGHAM
The Fleece 523

ADMASTON
The Pheasant Inn at Admaston 365

AKEBAR
The Friar's Head 494

ALBURY
The Drummond at Albury 415
William IV 415

ALCESTER
The Holly Bush 454

ALCISTON
Rose Cottage Inn 426

ALDBOURNE
The Blue Boar 471
The Crown Inn 471

ALDBURY
The Greyhound Inn 238
The Valiant Trooper 238

ALDERMASTON
Hinds Head 29

ALDERMINSTER
The Bell 454

ALDERTON
The Gardeners Arms 174

ALDFORD
The Grosvenor Arms 64

ALDRINGHAM
The Parrot and Punchbowl Inn
& Restaurant 400

ALDWARK
The Aldwark Arms 494

ALDWORTH
The Bell Inn 29

ALFRISTON
George Inn 426

ALLANTON
Allanton Inn 550

ALLOSTOCK
The Three Greyhounds Inn 64

ALMONDSBURY
The Bowl 174

ALSTONEFIELD
The George 394
The Watts Russell Arms 394

ALTARNUN
Rising Sun Inn 76

ALTHAM
The Walton Arms 262

ALTON
The Anchor Inn 202

ALTON
Bulls Head Inn 396

ALTRINCHAM
The Victoria 199

ALVESTON
The Baraset Barn 456

AMBERLEY
The Bridge Inn 438

AMBLESIDE
Drunken Duck Inn 92
Wateredge Inn 92

AMERSHAM
Hit or Miss Inn 39

AMPFIELD
White Horse at Ampfield 202

AMPORT
The Hawk Inn 203

AMROTH
The New Inn 574

ANDOVER
Wyke Down Country Pub & Restaurant 203

ANGLE
The Old Point House 574

ANSLOW
The Burnt Gate at Anslow 396

APPLEBY-IN-WESTMORLAND
The Royal Oak Appleby 92
Tufton Arms Hotel 94

APPLETON-LE-MOORS
The Moors Inn 494

APPLETREEWICK
The Craven Arms 494

ARDELEY
Jolly Waggoner 238

ARDENS GRAFTON
The Golden Cross 456

ARDUAINE
Chartroom II Bistro 533

ARDVASAR
Ardvasar Hotel 554

ARINAGOUR
Coll Hotel 554

ARKESDEN
Axe & Compasses 165

ARLINGHAM
The Old Passage Inn 176

ARRETON
The White Lion 467

ASCOT
The Thatched Tavern 30

ASENBY
Crab & Lobster 495

ASHBURNHAM PLACE
Ash Tree Inn 426

ASHBURTON
The Rising Sun 123

ASHBY ST LEDGERS
The Olde Coach House Inn 320

ASHCOTT
Ring O'Bells 372

ASHILL
Square & Compass 372

ASHLEWORTH
The Queens Arms 176

ASHMORE GREEN
The Sun in the Wood 30

ASHOVER
The Old Poets Corner 111

ASHTON
The Old Crown 320

ASHURST
The Fountain Inn 438

ASKERSWELL
The Spyway Inn 148

ASKRIGG
The King's Arms 495

ASTON
The Bhurtpore Inn · 64

ASTON CANTLOW
The King's Head · 456

ASWARBY
The Tally Ho Inn · 278

AUSTWICK
The Game Cock Inn · 495

AVIEMORE
The Old Bridge Inn · 542

AVONWICK
The Turtley Corn Mill · 123

AXBRIDGE
Lamb Inn · 373

AXFORD
Red Lion Inn · 472

AXMOUTH
The Harbour Inn · 123
The Ship Inn · 123

AYCLIFFE
The County · 161

AYLESBURY
The King's Head · 39

AYMESTREY
The Riverside Inn · 230

AYNHO
The Great Western Arms · 320

AYOT GREEN
The Waggoners · 238

AYSGARTH
The George & Dragon Inn · 495

AYTHORPE RODING
Axe & Compasses · 165

B

BABCARY
Red Lion · 373

BABELL
Black Lion Inn · 564

BABRAHAM
The George Inn at Babraham · 55

BACKWELL
The New Inn · 373

BAKEWELL
The Bull's Head · 111
The Monsal Head Hotel · 112

BALCOMBE
The Cowdray · 438

BALL HILL
The Furze Bush Inn · 203

BALMEDIE
The Cock & Bull Bar & Restaurant · 532

BALSHAM
The Black Bull Inn · 55

BAMFORD
Yorkshire Bridge Inn · 112

BAMPTON
Exeter Inn · 123

BAMPTON
The Romany · 335

BANBURY
The Wykham Arms · 336
Ye Olde Reindeer Inn · 336

BARBON
The Barbon Inn · 94

BARFORD
The Granville @ Barford · 456

BARGRENNAN
House O'Hill Hotel · 535

BARLEY
The Fox & Hounds · 239

BARMBY ON THE MARSH
The King's Head · 492

BARNARD CASTLE
The Morritt Arms Hotel · 161

BARNARD GATE
The Boot Inn · 336

BARNOLDBY LE BECK
The Ship Inn · 278

BARNSLEY
The Village Pub · 176

BARNSTON
Fox and Hounds · 306

BARRASFORD
The Barrasford Arms · 324

BARRINGTON
The Royal Oak · 55

BARROW
The Eagle at Barrow · 262

BARROW UPON TRENT
Ragley Boat Stop · 112

BARROWDEN
Exeter Arms · 361

BARSTON
The Malt Shovel at Barston · 464

BARTON-UNDER-NEEDWOOD
The Waterfront · 396

BASCHURCH
The New Inn · 365

BASHALL EAVES
The Red Pump Inn · 263

BASSENTHWAITE
The Pheasant · 94

BATH
The Chequers · 373
The Garricks Head · 373
The Hop Pole · 373
King William · 374
The Marlborough Tavern · 374
The Star Inn · 374

BAUGHURST
The Wellington Arms · 203

BAWBURGH
Kings Head · 307

BAWDRIP
The Knowle Inn · 374

BEACONSFIELD
The Royal Standard of England · 39

BEADNELL
The Craster Arms · 324

BEARSTED
The Oak on the Green · 245

BEAULIEU
The Drift Inn · 203

BEAUMARIS
Ye Olde Bulls Head Inn · 558

BEAUWORTH
The Milburys · 203

BECKFORD
The Beckford · 487

BECKINGTON
Woolpack Inn · 374

BECKLEY
The Abingdon Arms · 338

BEDALE
The Castle Arms Inn · 495

BEDDGELERT
Tanronnen Inn · 564

BEDFORD
The Embankment · 26
The Park Pub & Kitchen · 26
The Three Tuns · 26

BEELEY
The Devonshire Arms at Beeley · 112

BEER
Anchor Inn · 123

BEESANDS
The Cricket Inn · 124

BEESTON
Victoria Hotel · 331

BEETHAM
The Wheatsheaf at Beetham · 94

BELCHFORD
The Blue Bell Inn · 278

BELFORD
Blue Bell Hotel · 326

BEMBRIDGE
The Crab & Lobster Inn   467

BENENDEN
The Bull at Benenden   245

BENTLEY
The Bull Inn   203

BENTWORTH
The Sun Inn   206

BERKELEY
The Malt House   176

BERKHAMSTED
The Old Mill   239

BERRIEW
The Lion Hotel   577

BERWICK
The Cricketers Arms   426

BERWICK ST JOHN
The Talbot Inn   472

BETCHWORTH
The Red Lion   415

BETWS-Y-COED
Ty Gwyn Inn   561

BEVERLEY
The Ferguson Fawsitt Arms
  & Country Lodge   492
Green Dragon   493

BEWDLEY
Little Pack Horse   487
The Mug House Inn & Angry Chef
  Restaurant   487
Woodcolliers Arms   487

BIBURY
Catherine Wheel   176

BICKLEIGH
Fisherman's Cot   124

BIDDENDEN
The Three Chimneys   246

BIGBURY-ON-SEA
Pilchard Inn   124

BILSBORROW
Owd Nell's Tavern   263

BINHAM
Chequers Inn   307

BIRCHOVER
The Druid Inn   114
Red Lion Inn   114

BIRDLIP
The Golden Heart   177

BIRMINGHAM
The Old Joint Stock   464

BIRSTALL
The White Horse   273

BISHOP'S CASTLE
The Three Tuns Inn   365

BISHOP'S WALTHAM
The Hampshire Bowman   206

BISHOPSTONE
The Royal Oak   472

BISHOPSWOOD
Candlelight Inn   374

BLACK BOURTON
The Vines   338

BLACKAWTON
The Normandy Arms   124

BLACKBOYS
The Blackboys Inn   427

BLACKBURN
Clog and Billycock   263
The Millstone at Mellor   263

BLACKMORE
The Leather Bottle   165

BLACKO
Moorcock Inn   265

BLADNOCH
The Bladnoch Inn   535

BLAENAU FFESTINIOG
The Miners Arms   566

BLAISDON
The Red Hart Inn   177

BLAKENEY
The Blakeney White Horse   307
The Kings Arms   307

BLANDFORD FORUM
The Anvil Inn   148

BLEDINGTON
The Kings Head Inn   177

BLEDLOW
The Lions of Bledlow   41

BLETCHLEY
The Crooked Billet   41

BLIDWORTH
Fox & Hounds   332

BLISLAND
The Blisland Inn   76

BLOXHAM
The Elephant & Castle   338

BLUE ANCHOR
The Smugglers   375

BODENHAM
England's Gate Inn   230

BODINNICK
The Old Ferry Inn   77

BOLDRE
The Hobler Inn   206
The Red Lion   206

BOLDRON
The George & Dragon Inn   161

BOLNHURST
The Plough at Bolnhurst   26

BOLVENTOR
Jamaica Inn   77

BONCHURCH
The Bonchurch Inn   467

BONSALL
The Barley Mow   114

BOOT
Brook House Inn   94

BOROUGHBRIDGE
The Black Bull Inn   495
Crown Inn Roecliffe   497

BORROWDALE
The Langstrath Country Inn   94

BOSCASTLE
Cobweb Inn   77
The Wellington Hotel   77

BOSHAM
The Anchor Bleu   439

BOSSINGHAM
The Hop Pocket   246

BOURN
The Willow Tree   55

BOURNE
The Wishing Well Inn   278

BOURTON
The White Lion Inn   148

BOURTON-ON-THE-HILL
Horse and Groom   177

BOVINGDON GREEN
The Royal Oak   41

BOWLAND BRIDGE
Hare & Hounds Country Inn   96

BOX
The Northey   472
The Quarrymans Arms   472

BOXFORD
The Bell at Boxford   30

BRABOURNE
The Five Bells Inn   246

BRADFIELD
The Strines Inn   520

BRADFORD
New Beehive Inn   523

BRADFORD-ON-AVON
The Dandy Lion   474
The Tollgate Inn   474

BRAITHWAITE
Coledale Inn   96
The Royal Oak   96

BRAMLEY
Jolly Farmer Inn 415

BRAMPFORD SPEKE
The Lazy Toad Inn with Rooms 124

BRAMPTON
Blacksmiths Arms 96

BRANCASTER
The Ship Hotel 307

BRANCASTER STAITHE
The Jolly Sailors 307
The White Horse 309

BRANDESTON
The Queens Head 400

BRANSCOMBE
The Fountain Head 124
The Masons Arms 125

BRANSFORD
The Bear & Ragged Staff 487

BRANSGORE
The Three Tuns Country Inn 206

BRASSINGTON
Ye Olde Gate Inn 114

BRAUGHING
The Golden Fleece 239

BRAUNSTON
The Blue Ball 361

BRAUNTON
The Williams Arms 125

BRAY
The Crown Inn 30
The Hinds Head 30

BREARTON
Malt Shovel Inn 497

BRECON
The Usk Inn 577
The White Swan Inn 577

BREEDON ON THE HILL
The Three Horseshoes 274

BRENDON
Rockford Inn 125

BRETFORTON
The Fleece Inn 488

BRIDFORD
The Bridford Inn 125

BRIDGNORTH
Halfway House Inn 365

BRIDPORT
The Shave Cross Inn 148
The West Bay 149

BRIGHTON & HOVE
The Basketmakers Arms 427
The Bell 427
Preston Park Tavern 427

BRIGHTWELL BALDWIN
The Lord Nelson Inn 338

BRIGHTWELL-CUM-SOTWELL
The Red Lion 338

BRILL
The Pheasant Inn 41

BRINGSTY COMMON
Live and Let Live 230

BRINKWORTH
The Three Crowns 474

BRISTOL
The Albion 38
Cornubia 38
Highbury Vaults 39
The Kensington Arms 39
Robin Hood's Retreat 39

BRITHDIR
Cross Foxes 566

BROAD CHALKE
The Queens Head Inn 474

BROADWAY
Crown & Trumpet 488

BROCKENHURST
The Filly Inn 206

BROCKHAMPTON
Craven Arms Inn 177

BROMESWELL
The British Larder 401

BROOKLAND
Woolpack Inn 246

BROOM
The Cock 26

BROUGHTON
The Bull 497

BROUGHTON
The Crown Inn 55

BROUGHTON
Saye and Sele Arms 338

BROUGHTON GIFFORD
The Fox 474

BROUGHTON-IN-FURNESS
Blacksmiths Arms 96

BROUGHTY FERRY
The Royal Arch Bar 536

BROXTON
Egerton Arms 64

BRUNTINGTHORPE
The Joiners 274

BUCKFASTLEIGH
Dartbridge Inn 125

BUCKHORN WESTON
Stapleton Arms 149

BUCKINGHAM
The Old Thatched Inn 41

BUCKLAND
The Jolly Farmers Deli Pub & Restaurant 417

BUCKLAND MONACHORUM
Drake Manor Inn 126

BUCKMINSTER
Tollemache Arms 274

BULWICK
The Queen's Head 320

BUNBURY
The Dysart Arms 64

BUNTINGFORD
The Sword Inn Hand 239

BURCHETT'S GREEN
The Crown 30

BURCOMBE
The Ship Inn 474

BURCOT
The Chequers 338

BURFORD
The Highway Inn 339
The Inn for All Seasons 339
The Lamb Inn 339

BURGESS HILL
The Oak Barn 439

BURGHCLERE
Marco Pierre White The Carnarvon Arms 208

BURLEY
The Burley Inn 208

BURLEYDAM
The Combermere Arms 64

BURLTON
The Burlton Inn 365

BURNHAM MARKET
The Hoste 309

BURNHAM THORPE
The Lord Nelson 309

BURNHAM-ON-CROUCH
Ye Olde White Harte Hotel 165

BURNSALL
The Devonshire Fell 497
The Red Lion 499

BURNTISLAND
Burntisland Sands Hotel 540

BURPHAM
George & Dragon 440

BURROW
The Highwayman 265

BURSTON
The Crown 309

BURTON
The Old House at Home 474

BURWARDSLEY
The Pheasant Inn   64

BURY
The Squire & Horse   440

BURY ST EDMUNDS
The Nutshell   401
The Old Cannon Brewery   401
The Three Kings   401

BUTTERLEIGH
The Butterleigh Inn   126

BUTTERMERE
Bridge Hotel   96

C

CADGWITH
Cadgwith Cove Inn   77

CADNAM
Sir John Barleycorn   208

CAERLEON
The Bell at Caerleon   573

CAERNARFON
Black Boy Inn   566

CAIRNDOW
Cairndow Stagecoach Inn   533

CALDBECK
Oddfellows Arms   97

CALDWELL
Brownlow Arms   499

CALLANDER
The Lade Inn   553

CALLINGTON
Manor House Inn   77

CAMBRIDGE
The Anchor   55
Cambridge Blue   56
Free Press   56
The Old Spring   56
The Punter   56

CANTERBURY
The Chapter Arms   246
The Dove Inn   248
The Granville   248
The Red Lion   248

CAPEL CURIG
Bryn Tyrch Inn   561
Cobdens Hotel   561

CAR COLSTON
The Royal Oak   332

CARBOST
The Old Inn and Waterfront Bunkhouse   555

CARDINGTON
The Royal Oak   366

CAREW
Carew Inn   574

CAREY
Cottage of Content   230

CARNFORTH
The Longlands Inn and Restaurant   265

CARSHALTON
The Sun   305

CARTERWAY HEADS
The Manor House Inn   326

CARTHORPE
The Fox & Hounds   499

CARTMEL
The Cavendish Arms   97
The Masons Arms   97
Pig & Whistle   97

CASSINGTON
The Chequers Inn   339

CASTEL
Fleur du Jardin   528

CASTLE HEDINGHAM
The Bell Inn   167

CASTLETON
The Peaks Inn   114
Ye Olde Nags Head   114

CATCOTT
The Crown Inn   375

CATTISTOCK
Fox & Hounds Inn   149

CAULCOTT
Horse & Groom   339

CAULDON
Yew Tree Inn   396

CAUNTON
Caunton Beck   332

CAVENDISH
Bull Inn   401

CAWDOR
Cawdor Tavern   542

CHACOMBE
George and Dragon   321

CHADWICK END
The Orange Tree   464

CHAGFORD
Sandy Park Inn   126

CHALFONT ST PETER
The Greyhound Inn   41

CHALGROVE
The Red Lion Inn   340

CHALTON
The Red Lion   208

CHAPEL LE DALE
The Old Hill Inn   499

CHAPPEL
The Swan Inn   167

CHARING
The Bowl Inn   248
The Oak   248

CHARLBURY
The Bull Inn   340

CHARLTON
The Fox Goes Free   440

CHARTER ALLEY
The White Hart Inn   208

CHAWTON
The Greyfriar   208

CHEADLE
The Queens At Freehay   396

CHECKENDON
The Highwayman   340

CHEDDINGTON
The Old Swan   44

CHEDINGTON
Winyard's Gap Inn   149

CHEDWORTH
Hare & Hounds   177

CHELMORTON
The Church Inn   115

CHELMSFORD
Admiral J McHardy   167

CHELSFIELD
The Five Bells   305

CHELTENHAM
The Gloucester Old Spot   178
The Royal Oak Inn   178

CHELWOOD GATE
The Red Lion   429

CHENIES
The Red Lion   44

CHERITON
The Flower Pots Inn   209

CHESHAM
The Black Horse Inn   44
The Swan   44

CHESTER
The Brewery Tap   68
Old Harkers Arms   68

CHESTER-LE-STREET
The Moorings Hotel   161

CHESTERFIELD
Red Lion Pub & Bistro   115

CHETNOLE
The Chetnole Inn   149

CHEW MAGNA
The Bear and Swan   375
The Pony and Trap   375

Save on hotels. Book at **theAA.com/hotel**

INDEX 633

CHICHESTER
The Bull's Head · 440
The Earl of March · 440
Royal Oak Inn · 440

CHIDDINGFOLD
The Crown Inn · 417
The Swan Inn · 417

CHIDDINGLY
The Six Bells · 429

CHIDDINGSTONE
Castle Inn · 248

CHIDEOCK
The Anchor Inn · 149

CHIEVELEY
The Crab at Chieveley · 32

CHILHAM
The White Horse · 248

CHILLENDEN
The Griffins Head · 250

CHILLESFORD
The Froize Inn · 401

CHINLEY
Old Hall Inn · 115

CHINNOR
The Sir Charles Napier · 340

CHIPPING
Dog & Partridge · 265

CHIPPING CAMPDEN
The Bakers Arms · 178
Eight Bells · 178
The Kings · 180
Noel Arms Hotel · 180
Seagrave Arms · 180
The Volunteer Inn · 180

CHIPPING NORTON
The Chequers · 340

CHIPSTEAD
George & Dragon · 250

CHISELHAMPTON
Coach & Horses Inn · 342

CHOLMONDELEY
The Cholmondeley Arms · 68

CHRISHALL
The Red Cow · 167

CHRISTCHURCH
The Ship In Distress · 151

CHRISTLETON
Ring O'Bells · 68

CHRISTMAS COMMON
The Fox and Hounds · 342

CHURCH ENSTONE
The Crown Inn · 342

CHURCH KNOWLE
The New Inn · 151

CHURCH STRETTON
The Bucks Head · 366

CHURCHILL
The Crown Inn · 375

CILCAIN
White Horse Inn · 564

CIRENCESTER
The Crown of Crucis · 180
The Fleece at Cirencester · 180

CLACHAN-SEIL
Tigh an Truish Inn · 533

CLANFIELD
The Rising Sun Inn · 209

CLAPTON-IN-GORDANO
The Black Horse · 376

CLAVERING
The Cricketers · 167

CLAVERLEY
The Woodman · 366

CLAYHIDON
The Merry Harriers · 126

CLEARBROOK
The Skylark Inn · 126

CLEARWELL
The Wyndham Arms · 181

CLEEVE HILL
The Rising Sun · 181

CLENT
The Bell & Cross · 488

CLEOBURY MORTIMER
The Crown Inn · 366

CLEY NEXT THE SEA
The George Hotel · 309

CLIFFORD
The Castlefields · 231

CLIFFORD'S MESNE
The Yew Tree · 181

CLIFTON
Duke of Cumberland's Head · 342

CLIFTON
George and Dragon · 97

CLIPSHAM
The Olive Branch · 361

CLITHEROE
The Assheton Arms · 265

CLOVELLY
Red Lion Hotel · 126

CLUN
The White Horse Inn · 366

CLUTTON
The Hunters Rest · 376

COATES
The Tunnel House Inn · 181

COCKERMOUTH
The Trout Hotel · 97

COCKWOOD
The Anchor Inn · 127

COEDWAY
The Old Hand and Diamond Inn · 579

COLCHESTER
The Rose & Crown Hotel · 167

COLDHARBOUR
The Plough Inn · 417

COLEFORD
The New Inn · 127

COLEORTON
George Inn · 274

COLESBOURNE
The Colesbourne Inn · 184

COLLINGBOURNE DUCIS
The Shears Inn · 475

COLNBROOK
The Ostrich · 32

COLNE
The Alma Inn · 265

COLSTON BASSETT
The Martin's Arms · 332

COLTON
Ye Old Sun Inn · 499

COLTON
The Yorkshireman · 396

COLWYN BAY
Pen-y-Bryn · 561

COMBE HAY
The Wheatsheaf · 376

COMPTON
Coach & Horses · 440

COMPTON
The Withies Inn · 417

COMPTON DANDO
The Compton Inn · 376

CONGLETON
Egerton Arms Country Inn · 68
The Plough At Eaton · 68

CONINGSBY
The Lea Gate Inn · 280

CONISTON
The Black Bull Inn & Hotel · 98

CONNEL
The Oyster Inn · 533

CONSTANTINE
Trengilly Wartha Inn · 77

CONWY
The Groes Inn 561

COOKHAM
The White Oak 32

COOKHAM DEAN
The Chequers Brasserie 32

CORBRIDGE
The Angel of Corbridge 326

CORFE CASTLE
The Greyhound Inn 151

CORTON
The Dove Inn 475

CORTON DENHAM
The Queens Arms 376

COTEBROOK
Fox & Barrel 68

COTHERSTONE
The Fox and Hounds 162

COTTERED
The Bull at Cottered 239

COTTESMORE
The Sun Inn 362

COWBEECH
The Merrie Harriers 429

COWBRIDGE
Cross Inn 584
Victoria Inn 587

COWES
Duke of York Inn 467
The Fountain Inn 467

COWLEY
The Green Dragon Inn 184

CRAFTHOLE
The Finnygook Inn 79

CRANBORNE
The Inn at Cranborne 151

CRANBROOK
The George Hotel 250

CRANHAM
The Black Horse Inn 184

CRANLEIGH
The Richard Onslow 417

CRANMORE
Strode Arms 376

CRASTER
The Jolly Fisherman 326

CRASWALL
The Bulls Head 231

CRATFIELD
The Cratfield Poacher 403

CRAVEN ARMS
The Sun Inn 367

CRAWLEY
The Fox and Hounds 209

CRAYKE
The Durham Ox 499

CRAZIES HILL
The Horns 32

CREIGIAU
Caesars Arms 558

CRESSAGE
The Riverside Inn 367

CREWKERNE
The George Inn 378
The Manor Arms 378

CRICK
The Red Lion Inn 321

CRICKHOWELL
The Bear 579

CRICKLADE
The Red Lion Inn 475

CRINAN
Crinan Hotel 533

CROMER
The Red Lion Food and Rooms 310

CROOK
The Sun Inn 98

CROOKHAM VILLAGE
The Exchequer 209

CROPTON
The New Inn 501

CROSCOMBE
The Bull Terrier 378
The George Inn 378

CROSTHWAITE
The Punch Bowl Inn 98

CRUDWELL
The Potting Shed 475

CUBERT
The Smugglers' Den Inn 79

CUBLINGTON
The Unicorn 44

CUCKFIELD
The Talbot 440

CUDDINGTON
The Crown 44

CUMBERNAULD
Castlecary House Hotel 549

CUMNOR
Bear & Ragged Staff 342
The Vine Inn 342

D

DALBURY
The Black Cow 115

DALE
Griffin Inn 574

DALKEITH
The Sun Inn 548

DALRYMPLE
The Kirkton Inn 537

DANEHILL
The Coach and Horses 429

DARTFORD
The Rising Sun Inn 250

DARTMOUTH
Royal Castle Hotel 127

DATCHWORTH
The Tilbury 239

DEDDINGTON
Deddington Arms 342

DEDHAM
Marlborough Head Inn 168
The Sun Inn 168

DEFYNNOG
The Tanners Arms 579

DELAMERE
The Fishpool Inn 69

DENBURY
The Union Inn 127

DENHAM
The Falcon Inn 47
The Swan Inn 47

DENNINGTON
Dennington Queen 403

DENSHAW
The Rams Head Inn 199

DERBY
The Alexandra Hotel 115
The Brunswick Inn 115

DERVAIG
The Bellachroy Hotel 554

DEVIZES
The Bear Hotel 475
The Raven Inn 475

DIAL POST
The Crown Inn 443

DIDSBURY
The Metropolitan 199

DINNINGTON
Dinnington Docks 378

DITCHEAT
The Manor House Inn 378

DITCHLING
The Bull 429

DITTISHAM
The Ferry Boat 127

DODDISCOMBSLEIGH
The Nobody Inn   128

DOE LEA
Hardwick Inn   117

DOLTON
Rams Head Inn   128

DOLWYDDELAN
Elen's Castle Hotel   563

DONHEAD ST ANDREW
The Forester   476

DORCHESTER (ON THAMES)
The George   342
The White Hart   344

DORNEY
The Palmer Arms   47

DORSTONE
The Pandy Inn   231

DOWNTON
The Royal Oak   209

DROITWICH
The Chequers   488
The Honey Bee   488
The Old Cock Inn   490

DROXFORD
The Bakers Arms   210

DRY DODDINGTON
Wheatsheaf Inn   280

DRY DRAYTON
The Black Horse   56

DRYMEN
The Clachan Inn   553

DULVERTON
Woods Bar and Restaurant   379

DUMMER
The Queen Inn   210
The Sun Inn   210

DUNBRIDGE
The Mill Arms   210

DUNCTON
The Cricketers   443

DUNDEE
Speedwell Bar   537

DUNMERE
The Borough Arms   79

DUNOON
Coylet Inn   534

DUNSFOLD
The Sun Inn   418

DUNSTER
The Luttrell Arms   379
The Stags Head Inn   379

DUNWICH
The Ship at Dunwich   403

DURHAM
Victoria Inn   162

DURSLEY
The Old Spot Inn   184

DUXFORD
The John Barleycorn   56

E

EARDISLEY
The Tram Inn   231

EARL SOHAM
Victoria   403

EARLSFERRY
The Golf Tavern   540

EASHING
The Stag on the River   418

EASINGTON
Mole and Chicken   47

EAST ABERTHAW
Blue Anchor Inn   587

EAST ALLINGTON
The Fortescue Arms   128

EAST ASHLING
Horse and Groom   443

EAST BOLDRE
Turfcutters Arms   210

EAST BOWER
The Bower Inn   379

EAST CHILTINGTON
The Jolly Sportsman   429

EAST CHISENBURY
Red Lion Freehouse
                                             476

EAST CLANDON
The Queens Head   418

EAST COKER
The Helyar Arms   379

EAST DEAN
The Star & Garter   443

EAST DEAN
The Tiger Inn   429

EAST END
The East End Arms   210

EAST GARSTON
The Queen's Arms Country Inn   32

EAST GRINSTEAD
The Old Dunnings Mill   443

EAST HADDON
The Red Lion   321

EAST HENDRED
Eyston Arms   344

EAST KNOYLE
The Fox and Hounds   476

EAST MEON
Ye Olde George Inn   211

EAST MORDEN
The Cock & Bottle   151

EAST RUDHAM
The Crown Inn   310

EAST RUSTON
The Butchers Arms   310

EAST STRATTON
Northbrook Arms   211

EAST WITTON
The Blue Lion   501
The Cover Bridge Inn   501

EASTON
The Chestnut Horse   211

EATON
The Red Lion   310

EATON BRAY
The White Horse   26

EBBESBOURNE WAKE
The Horseshoe   476

EBRINGTON
The Ebrington Arms   184

ECCLESHALL
The George   397

EDGEHILL
The Castle Inn   456

EDINBURGH
Bennets Bar   538
Bert's Bar   538
The Bow Bar   538
The Café Royal   538
Doric Tavern   538
The Guildford Arms   538
Halfway House   539
The Sheep Heid Inn   539
The Shore Bar & Restaurant   539
Whiski Bar & Restaurant   540

EDINGTON
The Three Daggers   476

EDWINSTOWE
Forest Lodge   332

EFFINGHAM
The Plough   418

EGTON
The Wheatsheaf Inn   501

EGTON BRIDGE
Horseshoe Hotel   501
The Postgate   501

ELDERSFIELD
The Butchers Arms   490

ELIE
The Ship Inn   541

ELMTON
The Elm Tree 117

ELSTEAD
The Woolpack 418

ELSTED
The Three Horseshoes 444

ELSWICK
The Ship at Elswick 266

ELSWORTH
The George & Dragon 57

ELTERWATER
The Britannia Inn 98

ELTON
The Crown Inn 57

ELVEDEN
Elveden Inn 403

ELY
The Anchor Inn 57

EMLEY
The White Horse 523

EMPINGHAM
The White Horse Inn 362

ENGLEFIELD GREEN
The Fox and Hounds 418

EPPING GREEN
The Beehive 241

ERBISTOCK
The Boat Inn 587
Cross Foxes 588

ERIDGE GREEN
The Nevill Crest and Gun 431

ERPINGHAM
The Saracen's Head 310

ESKDALE GREEN
Bower House Inn 98

ETTINGTON
The Chequers Inn 457
The Houndshill 457

EVERSHOT
The Acorn Inn 151

EVERSLEY
The Golden Pot 211

EVINGTON
The Cedars 274

EWEN
The Wild Duck 186

EWHURST GREEN
The White Dog 431

EXETER
The Hour Glass 128
Red Lion Inn 128

EXFORD
The Crown Hotel 379

EXTON
Fox & Hounds 362

EXTON
The Puffing Billy 128

EXTON
The Shoe Inn 211

EYAM
Miners Arms 117

EYDON
Royal Oak @ Eydon 321

EYE
The White Horse Inn 403

F

FAKENHAM
The Wensum Lodge Hotel 310

FALSTONE
The Pheasant Inn 326

FAR FOREST
The Plough Inn 490

FARINGDON
The Lamb at Buckland 344
The Trout at Tadpole Bridge 344

FARNBOROUGH
The Inn at Farnborough 457

FARNDON
The Farndon 69

FARNDON
The Farndon Boathouse 334

FARNHAM
The Bat & Ball Freehouse 420
The Spotted Cow at Lower Bourne 420

FARNHAM
The Museum Inn 151

FARNHAM COMMON
The Foresters 47

FARNHAM ROYAL
The Emperor 47

FARTHINGHOE
The Fox 321

FARTHINGSTONE
The Kings Arms 321

FAUGH
The String of Horses Inn 98

FAULKLAND
Tuckers Grave 380

FAVERSHAM
Albion Taverna 250
Shipwright's Arms 250

FEERING
The Sun Inn 168

FELIXKIRK
The Carpenters Arms 502

FELSTED
The Swan at Felsted 168

FEN DITTON
Ancient Shepherds 57

FENCE
Fence Gate Inn 266

FENISCOWLES
Oyster & Otter 266

FENNY BENTLEY
Bentley Brook Inn 117
The Coach and Horses Inn 117

FENSTANTON
King William IV 57

FEOCK
The Punchbowl & Ladle 79

FERNDOWN
The Kings Arms 152

FERNHAM
The Woodman Inn 344

FERNHURST
The Red Lion 444

FETCHAM
The Bell 420

FILKINS
The Five Alls 346

FINGRINGHOE
The Whalebone 168

FIR TREE
Duke of York Inn 162

FISHBOURNE
The Fishbourne 468

FLADBURY
Chequers Inn 490

FLAMBOROUGH
The Seabirds Inn 493

FLAUNDEN
The Bricklayers Arms 241

FLETCHING
The Griffin Inn 431

FLYFORD FLAVELL
The Boot Inn 490

FOCHABERS
Gordon Arms Hotel 548

FONTHILL GIFFORD
The Beckford Arms 476

FONTMELL MAGNA
The Fontmell 152

FOOLOW
The Bulls Head Inn 117

FORDCOMBE
Chafford Arms 251

FORDHAM
White Pheasant · 57

FORDINGBRIDGE
The Augustus John · 211

FOREST GREEN
The Parrot Inn · 420

FORRES
The Old Mill Inn · 549

FORT WILLIAM
Moorings Hotel · 544

FORTON
The Bay Horse Inn · 266

FORTROSE
The Anderson · 544

FOSSEBRIDGE
The Inn at Fossebridge · 186

FOTHERINGHAY
The Falcon Inn · 322

FOWEY
The Ship Inn · 79

FRAMLINGHAM
The Station Hotel · 405

FRAMPTON MANSELL
The Crown Inn · 186

FRAMSDEN
The Dobermann Inn · 405

FRESHFORD
The Inn at Freshford · 380

FRESHWATER
The Red Lion · 468

FRIETH
The Prince Albert · 47

FRILSHAM
The Pot Kiln · 33

FRINGFORD
The Butchers Arms · 346

FROGGATT
The Chequers Inn · 118

FROGNALL
The Goat · 280

FROSTERLEY
The Black Bull Inn · 162

FROXFIELD
The Pelican Inn · 476

FULBECK
The Hare & Hounds · 280

FULBROOK
The Carpenters Arms · 346

FULLER STREET
The Square and Compasses · 169

FYFIELD
The White Hart · 346

G

GAIRLOCH
The Old Inn · 544

GALASHIELS
Kingsknowes Hotel · 550

GARWAY
Garway Moon Inn · 231

GATEHEAD
The Cochrane Inn · 537

GAWSWORTH
Harrington Arms · 69

GAYDON
The Malt Shovel · 458

GEORGEHAM
The Rock Inn · 129

GERRARDS CROSS
The Three Oaks · 48

GESTINGTHORPE
The Pheasant · 169

GIGGLESWICK
Black Horse Hotel · 502

GILLINGHAM
The Kings Arms Inn · 152

GLANGRWYNEY
The Bell · 579

GLASBURY
The Harp Inn · 579

GLASGOW
Bon Accord · 541
Rab Ha's · 541
Stravaigin · 542
Ubiquitous Chip · 542
WEST Brewery · 542

GLENCOE
Clachaig Inn · 544

GLENFARG
The Famous Bein Inn · 549

GLENUIG
Glenuig Inn · 544

GLOUCESTER
Queens Head · 186

GOATHLAND
Birch Hall Inn · 502

GODSHILL
The Taverners · 468

GOLDHANGER
The Chequers Inn · 169

GOODNESTONE
The Fitzwalter Arms · 251

GOOSTREY
The Crown · 69

GORING
Miller of Mansfield · 346

GOSBERTON
The Black Horse · 281

GOSFIELD
The Green Man · 169

GOUDHURST
The Goudhurst Inn · 251
Green Cross Inn · 251
The Star & Eagle · 251

GRAFFHAM
The Foresters Arms · 444

GRAFTON REGIS
The White Hart · 322

GRASMERE
The Travellers Rest Inn · 100

GRASSINGTON
Grassington House · 502

GRAVESEND
The Cock Inn · 251

GREASBY
Irby Mill · 306

GREAT AYTON
The Royal Oak · 502

GREAT BARRINGTON
The Fox · 186

GREAT BRICETT
The Veggie Red Lion · 405

GREAT BRIDGEFORD
The Mill at Worston · 397

GREAT BUDWORTH
George and Dragon · 71

GREAT CHEVERELL
The Bell Inn · 479

GREAT CHISHILL
The Pheasant · 57

GREAT HABTON
The Grapes Inn · 502

GREAT HAMPDEN
The Hampden Arms · 48

GREAT HUCKLOW
The Queen Anne Inn · 118

GREAT LANGDALE
The New Dungeon Ghyll Hotel · 100

GREAT MASSINGHAM
The Dabbling Duck · 311

GREAT MISSENDEN
The Nags Head · 48
The Polecat Inn · 48

GREAT OUSEBURN
The Crown Inn · 504

GREAT OXENDON
The George Inn · 322

GREAT RYBURGH
The Blue Boar Inn   311

GREAT SALKELD
The Highland Drove Inn and
   Kyloes Restaurant   100

GREAT TEW
The Falkland Arms   346

GREAT TOTHAM
The Bull at Great Totham   169

GREAT URSWICK
General Burgoyne   100

GREAT WILBRAHAM
The Carpenters Arms   59

GREAT WOLFORD
The Fox & Hounds Inn   458

GREAT YELDHAM
The White Hart   170

GREEN HAMMERTON
The Bay Horse Inn   504

GREETHAM
The Wheatsheaf   362

GRESFORD
Pant-yr-Ochain   588

GRIMSTON
The Black Horse   274

GRINDLEFORD
The Maynard   118

GRINDLETON
Duke of York   266

GRINTON
The Bridge Inn   504

GROVE
Grove Lock   48

GUILDFORD
The Boatman   420
The Keystone   420

GUITING POWER
The Hollow Bottom   186

GULLANE
The Old Clubhouse   537

GUN HILL
The Gun   431

GUNNISLAKE
The Rising Sun Inn   81

GUNWALLOE
The Halzephron Inn   81

GUSSAGE ALL SAINTS
The Drovers Inn   152

GWAELOD-Y-GARTH
Gwaelod-y-Garth Inn   558

GWEEK
Black Swan   81

GWITHIAN
The Red River Inn   81

H

HALESWORTH
The Queen's Head   405

HALIFAX
Shibden Mill Inn   523
The Three Pigeons   523

HALNAKER
The Anglesey Arms at Halnaker   444

HALSTEAD
Rose & Crown   252

HALTWHISTLE
Milecastle Inn   326

HAM
Hand & Flower   306

HAMBLE-LE-RICE
The Bugle   213

HAMBLEDEN
The Stag & Huntsman Inn   48

HAMPTON BISHOP
The Bunch of Carrots   231

HAMPTON IN ARDEN
The White Lion Inn   464

HAMPTON POYLE
The Bell   348

HANDLEY
The Calveley Arms   71

HANNINGTON
The Jolly Tar   479

HANNINGTON
The Vine at Hannington   213

HARBERTON
The Church House Inn   129

HARBY
Bottle & Glass   334

HARDRAW
The Green Dragon Inn   504

HARDSTOFT
The Shoulder at Hardstoft   118

HAROME
The Star Inn   504

HARRIETSHAM
The Pepper Box Inn   252

HARRINGWORTH
The White Swan   322

HARROLD
The Muntjac   27

HARTFIELD
Anchor Inn   431
The Hatch Inn   431

HARTLEBURY
The White Hart   490

HARTLEY WINTNEY
The Cricketers   213

HARTSHEAD
The Gray Ox   523

HARTSHORNE
The Mill Wheel   118

HARWELL
The Hart of Harwell   348

HASCOMBE
The White Horse   422

HASELBURY PLUCKNETT
The White Horse at Haselbury   380

HASLEMERE
The Wheatsheaf Inn   422

HASSOP
The Old Eyre Arms   118

HASTINGWOOD
Rainbow & Dove   170

HATFIELD BROAD OAK
The Duke's Head   170

HATFIELD HEATH
The Thatcher's   170

HATHERSAGE
Millstone Inn   119
The Plough Inn   119
The Scotsmans Pack Country Inn   119

HAUGHTON MOSS
The Nags Head   71

HAVANT
The Royal Oak   213

HAWES
The Moorcock Inn   504

HAWKEDON
The Queen's Head   405

HAWKHURST
The Black Pig at Hawkhurst   252
The Great House   252

HAWKLEY
The Hawkley Inn   213

HAWKSHEAD
Kings Arms   100
The Queen's Head Inn & Restaurant   100
The Sun Inn   101

HAWNBY
The Inn at Hawnby   504

HAWORTH
The Old White Lion Hotel   523

HAY-ON-WYE
The Old Black Lion   580
The Three Tuns   580

Save on hotels. Book at **theAA.com/hotel**

INDEX 639

HAYDON BRIDGE
The General Havelock Inn 326

HAYFIELD
The Royal Hotel 119

HAYTOR VALE
The Rock Inn 129

HEATHFIELD
Star Inn 433

HEDGERLEY
The White Horse 50

HEDLEY ON THE HILL
The Feathers Inn 328

HELFORD PASSAGE
The Ferryboat Inn 81

HELPERBY
The Oak Tree Inn 505

HELSTON
The Queens Arms 81

HEMEL HEMPSTEAD
Alford Arms 241

HEMINGFORD GREY
The Cock Pub and Restaurant 59

HENLEY
Duke of Cumberland Arms 444

HENLEY-IN-ARDEN
The Bluebell 458

HENLEY-ON-THAMES
The Cherry Tree Inn 348
The Five Horseshoes 348
The Little Angel 348
The Three Tuns 351
WhiteHartNettlebed 351

HEPWORTH
The Butchers Arms 525

HERMITAGE
The White Horse of Hermitage 33

HERNHILL
The Red Lion 252

HERONSGATE
The Land of Liberty, Peace and Plenty 241

HERRIARD
The Fur & Feathers 214

HESKIN GREEN
Farmers Arms 266

HEST BANK
Hest Bank Inn 267

HETHE
The Muddy Duck 351

HEVINGHAM
Marsham Arms Coaching Inn 311

HEXHAM
Battlesteads Hotel & Restaurant 328
Dipton Mill Inn 328
Miners Arms Inn 328
Rat Inn 328

HEXTON
The Raven 241

HEYDON
Earle Arms 311

HEYSHOTT
Unicorn Inn 444

HEYTESBURY
The Angel Coaching Inn 479

HIGH GRANTLEY
The Grantley Arms 505

HIGH WYCOMBE
The Sausage Tree 50

HIGHMOOR
Rising Sun 351

HIGHTOWN
The Pheasant Inn 306

HILDERSHAM
The Pear Tree Inn 59

HILTON
The Prince of Wales 59

HINDON
Angel Inn 479
The Lamb at Hindon 479

HINGHAM
The White Hart Hotel 311

HINTON
The Bull at Hinton 188

HINTON BLEWETT
Ring O'Bells 380

HINTON ST GEORGE
The Lord Poulett Arms 380

HINXTON
The Red Lion Inn 59

HISTON
Red Lion 59

HITCHAM
The White Horse Inn 406

HOARWITHY
The New Harp Inn 232

HODNET
The Bear at Hodnet 367

HODSOLL STREET
The Green Man 254

HOGNASTON
The Red Lion Inn 119

HOLBROOK
The Compasses 406

HOLCOMBE
The Holcombe Inn 380

HOLLINGBOURNE
The Dirty Habit 254

HOLMFIRTH
Farmers Arms 525

HOLSWORTHY
The Bickford Arms 129

HOLT
The Pigs 311

HOLTON
The Old Inn 382

HOLYBOURNE
The White Hart Hotel 214

HOLYPORT
The Belgian Arms 33
The George on the Green 33

HOLYWELL
The Old Ferryboat Inn 59

HONEY TYE
The Lion 406

HONITON
The Holt 129

HOOK
Crooked Billet 214
The Hogget Country Pub & Eating House 214

HOPE
Cheshire Cheese Inn 119

HORNDON ON THE HILL
Bell Inn & Hill House 170

HORNINGSEA
The Crown & Punchbowl 61

HORNINGSHAM
The Bath Arms at Longleat 480

HORSHAM
The Black Jug 446

HORSTEAD
Recruiting Sergeant 311

HOUGH-ON-THE-HILL
The Brownlow Arms 281

HOUSTON
Fox & Hounds 550

HOVINGHAM
The Malt Shovel 505
The Worsley Arms Hotel 505

HUBBERHOLME
The George Inn 505

HUGGATE
The Wolds Inn 493

HUISH EPISCOPI
Rose & Crown (Eli's) 382

HULVERSTONE
The Sun Inn at Hulverstone 468

HUNGERFORD
The Crown & Garter 33
The Pheasant Inn 34
The Swan Inn 34

HUNNINGHAM
The Red Lion, Hunningham 458

HUNSDON
The Fox and Hounds 241

HUNSTANTON
The Ancient Mariner Inn 313
The King William IV Country Inn
& Restaurant 313

HUNWORTH
The Hunny Bell 313

HURLEY
The Olde Bell Inn 34

HURSLEY
The Dolphin Inn 214
The Kings Head 216

HURST
The Green Man 34

HURWORTH-ON-TEES
The Bay Horse 162

HUTTON MAGNA
The Oak Tree Inn 163

I

IBSLEY
Old Beams Inn 216

ICKHAM
The Duke William 254

ICKLESHAM
The Queen's Head 433

IDDESLEIGH
The Duke of York 129

IDEN GREEN
The Peacock 254

IGHTHAM
The Harrow Inn 254

ILCHESTER
Ilchester Arms 382

ILFRACOMBE
The George & Dragon 130

ILKLEY
Ilkley Moor Vaults 525

ILMINGTON
The Howard Arms 458

ILMINSTER
New Inn 382

INGATESTONE
The Red Lion 171

INGHAM
The Cadogan 406

INGHAM
The Ingham Swan 313

INGHAM
Inn on the Green 281

INGLEBY
The John Thompson Inn & Brewery 119

INNERLEITHEN
Traquair Arms Hotel 550

INVERARAY
George Hotel 534

INVERGARRY
The Invergarry Inn 546

INVERIE
The Old Forge 546

IPSWICH
The Fat Cat 406

IRELAND
The Black Horse 27

IRONBRIDGE
The Malthouse 367

ISLE OF WHITHORN
The Steam Packet Inn 535

ISLEORNSAY
Hotel Eilean Iarmain 555

ITTERINGHAM
The Walpole Arms 314

IVY HATCH
The Plough at Ivy Hatch 254

K

KELMSCOTT
The Plough Inn 351

KELSO
The Cobbles Freehouse & Dining 550

KEMPSEY
Walter de Cantelupe Inn 490

KENFIG
Prince of Wales Inn 558

KENILWORTH
The Almanack 458

KESWICK
Farmers Arms 101
The George 101
The Horse & Farrier Inn 103
The Inn at Keswick 103
The Kings Head 103
Pheasant Inn 103
The Swinside Inn 103

KETTLESHULME
Swan Inn 71

KEYSOE
The Chequers 27

KEYSTON
Pheasant Inn 61

KILBURN
The Forresters Arms Inn 506

KILLIECRANKIE
Killiecrankie House Hotel 549

KILMINGTON
The Old Inn 130

KILPECK
The Kilpeck Inn 232

KILSBY
The George 322

KILVE
The Hood Arms 382

KIMBERLEY
The Nelson & Railway Inn 334

KIMBOLTON
The New Sun Inn 61

KIMBOLTON
Stockton Cross Inn 232

KING'S LYNN
The Stuart House Hotel, Bar & Restaurant 314

KING'S STAG
The Greenman 154

KINGHAM
The Kingham Plough 352

KINGS NYMPTON
The Grove Inn 131

KINGSAND
The Halfway House Inn 82

KINGSBRIDGE
The Crabshell Inn 130

KINGSDON
Kingsdon Inn 382

KINGSFOLD
The Dog and Duck 446
The Owl at Kingsfold 446

KINGSKERSWELL
Barn Owl Inn 130
Bickley Mill Inn 130

KINGSTON
The Dolphin Inn 131

KINGSTON UPON THAMES
The Boaters Inn 306

KINGTON
The Stagg Inn and Restaurant 232

KINTBURY
The Dundas Arms 34

KIPPEN
Cross Keys Hotel 553
The Inn at Kippen 553

KIRBY HILL
The Shoulder of Mutton Inn 506

KIRDFORD
The Half Moon Inn 446

Save on hotels. Book at theAA.com/hotel

INDEX 641

KIRK IRETON
Barley Mow Inn 121

KIRK YETHOLM
The Border Hotel 552

KIRKBY FLEETHAM
The Black Horse Inn 506

KIRKBY LA THORPE
Queens Head 281

KIRKBY LONSDALE
The Pheasant Inn 103
The Sun Inn 105
The Whoop Hall 105

KIRKBYMOORSIDE
George & Dragon Hotel 506

KIRKCUDBRIGHT
Selkirk Arms Hotel 535

KIRKHAM
Stone Trough Inn 506

KIRTON IN LINDSEY
The George 282

KNARESBOROUGH
The General Tarleton Inn 506

KNIGHTWICK
The Talbot 491

KNOSSINGTON
The Fox & Hounds 275

KNOTTY GREEN
The Red Lion Knotty Green 50

KNOWL HILL
Bird In Hand Country Inn 35

KNUTSFORD
The Dog Inn 71

KYLESKU
Kylesku Hotel 546

L

LACEY GREEN
The Whip Inn 50

LACH DENNIS
The Duke of Portland 71

LACOCK
The George Inn 480
Red Lion Inn 480

LAMBERHURST
The Vineyard 255

LAMBS GREEN
The Lamb Inn 446

LANCASTER
The Borough 267
Penny Street Bridge 267
The Stork Inn 267
The Sun Hotel and Bar 269
The White Cross 269

LANE END
Grouse & Ale 50

LANGFORD
The Bell at Langford 352

LANGHAM
The Shepherd and Dog 171

LANGLEY MARSH
The Three Horseshoes 383

LANGNEY
The Farm @ Friday Street 433

LANGTHWAITE
The Red Lion Inn 507

LANLIVERY
The Crown Inn 82

LAPWORTH
The Boot Inn 459

LARLING
Angel Inn 314

LASTINGHAM
Blacksmiths Arms 507

LAXFIELD
The Kings Head (The Low House) 406

LAXTON
The Dovecote Inn 334

LEAMINGTON SPA (ROYAL)
The Moorings at Myton 459

LECHLADE ON THAMES
The Trout Inn 188

LECKHAMPSTEAD
The Stag 35

LEDBURY
Prince of Wales 232
The Talbot 233
The Trumpet Inn 233

LEE-ON-THE-SOLENT
The Bun Penny 216

LEEBOTWOOD
Pound Inn 367

LEEDS
The Cross Keys 525
North Bar 525

LEEK
Three Horseshoes Inn 397

LEICESTER
The Almanack 275

LEIGH
The Greyhound Charcott 255

LEIGH
The Plough 422
The Seven Stars 422

LEIGHTERTON
The Royal Oak 188

LEOMINSTER
The Grape Vaults 233

LETHERINGSETT
The Kings Head 314

LETTERSTON
The Harp Inn 574

LEVINGTON
The Ship Inn 407

LEVISHAM
Horseshoe Inn 507

LEYBURN
The Queens Head 507
Sandpiper Inn 507

LEYSDOWN-ON-SEA
The Ferry House Inn 255

LIDGATE
The Star Inn 407

LIFTON
The Arundell Arms 131

LIMPLEY STOKE
The Hop Pole Inn 480

LINCOLN
Pyewipe Inn 282
The Victoria 282
Wig & Mitre 283

LINDSEY TYE
The Lindsey Rose 407

LINGFIELD
Hare and Hounds 422

LINLITHGOW
Champany Inn - The Chop and Ale House 553
The Four Marys 553

LINSLADE
The Globe Inn 27

LINTHWAITE
The Sair Inn 525

LINTON
The Bull Inn 255

LINTON
The Windmill Inn 526

LINWOOD
The High Corner Inn 216

LISS
The Jolly Drover 216

LITTLE BRAXTED
The Green Man 171

LITTLE BURSTEAD
The Dukes Head 171

LITTLE BYTHAM
The Willoughby Arms 283

LITTLE CANFIELD
The Lion & Lamb 171

LITTLE DUNMOW
Flitch of Bacon 172

LITTLE ECCLESTON
The Cartford Inn 269

LITTLE HADHAM
The Nags Head 241

LITTLE HAVEN
St Brides Inn 575
The Swan Inn 575

LITTLE HAYFIELD
Lantern Pike 121

LITTLE KINGSHILL
The Full Moon 50

LITTLE LANGDALE
Three Shires Inn 105

LITTLE STRETTON
The Ragleth Inn 367

LITTLE WASHBOURNE
The Hobnails Inn 188

LITTLE WILBRAHAM
Hole in the Wall 61

LITTLEBOROUGH
The White House 199

LITTLEBURY
The Queens Head Inn Littlebury 171

LITTLETON
The Running Horse 216

LITTLETON-ON-SEVERN
White Hart 188

LITTLEY GREEN
The Compasses 172

LITTON
Queens Arms 508

LITTON
Red Lion Inn 121

LIVERPOOL
The Monro 306

LLANARMON DYFFRYN CEIRIOG
The Hand at Llanarmon 588
West Arms 588

LLANBEDR
Victoria Inn 566

LLANDDAROG
Butchers Arms 559

LLANDEILO
The Angel Hotel 559

LLANDOVERY
The Kings Head 559

LLANDRINDOD WELLS
The Bell Country Inn 580
The Laughing Dog 580

LLANDUDNO JUNCTION
The Queens Head 563

LLANELIAN-YN-RHÔS
The White Lion Inn 563

LLANELIDAN
The Leyland Arms 563

LLANFAIR WATERDINE
The Waterdine 368

LLANFIHANGEL-Y-CREUDDYN
y Ffarmers 560

LLANFYLLIN
Cain Valley Hotel 580

LLANGENNITH
Kings Head 584

LLANGYBI
The White Hart Village Inn 567

LLANGYNIDR
The Coach & Horses 580

LLANLLWNI
Belle @ Llanllwni 559

LLANNEFYDD
The Hawk & Buckle Inn 563

LLANTRISANT
The Greyhound Inn 567

LLANVAIR DISCOED
The Woodlands Tavern Country Pub
& Dining 567

LLWYNDAFYDD
The Crown Inn & Restaurant 560

LOCHBOISDALE
The Polochar Inn 555

LOCHGILPHEAD
Cairnbaan Hotel 534

LOCKERLEY
Kings Arms at Lockerley 217

LODERS
Loders Arms 154

LODSWORTH
The Halfway Bridge Inn 446
The Hollist Arms 447

LONDON E1
Town of Ramsgate 285

LONDON E8
The Cat & Mutton 285

LONDON E9
The Empress 285

LONDON E14
The Grapes 285
The Gun 286

LONDON EC1
The Bleeding Heart Tavern 286
The Coach & Horses 286
The Eagle 286
The Jerusalem Tavern 286
The Peasant 287
Ye Olde Mitre 287

LONDON EC2
The Fox 287
Old Dr Butler's Head 287
The Princess of Shoreditch 286

LONDON EC4
The Black Friar 287
The Old Bank of England 288
The White Swan 288

LONDON N1
The Albion 288
The Barnsbury 288
The Charles Lamb 288
The Drapers Arms 288
The Duke of Cambridge 289
The House 289

LONDON N6
The Flask 289

LONDON NW1
The Chapel 289
The Engineer 289
The Globe 290
The Lansdowne 290
The Prince Albert 290
The Queens 290

LONDON NW3
The Holly Bush 290

LONDON NW5
The Bull and Last 290
Dartmouth Arms 290
The Lord Palmerston 291

LONDON NW6
The Salusbury Pub and Dining Room 291

LONDON NW8
The New Inn 291
The Salt House 291

LONDON NW10
William IV Bar & Restaurant 291

LONDON SE1
The Anchor & Hope 291
The Fire Station 292
The Garrison 292
The George Inn 292
The Market Porter 292

LONDON SE5
The Crooked Well 292

LONDON SE10
The Cutty Sark Tavern 292
Greenwich Union Pub 293
North Pole Bar & Restaurant 293

LONDON SE11
The Tommyfield 293

LONDON SE21
The Crown & Greyhound 293
The Rosendale 293

LONDON SE22
The Palmerston 293

LONDON SE23
The Dartmouth Arms　294

LONDON SW1
The Buckingham Arms　294
Nags Head　294
The Orange Public House & Hotel　294
The Thomas Cubitt　294
The Wilton Arms　294

LONDON SW3
The Admiral Codrington　295
The Builders Arms　295
Coopers Arms　295
The Pig's Ear　295

LONDON SW4
The Abbeville　295
The Stonhouse　295

LONDON SW6
The Atlas　296
The Harwood Arms　296
The Jam Tree　296
The Sands End Pub　296
The White Horse　296

LONDON SW10
The Hollywood Arms　296
Lots Road Pub and Dining Room　297

LONDON SW11
The Bolingbroke Pub & Dining Room　297
The Fox & Hounds　297

LONDON SW12
The Avalon　297

LONDON SW13
The Bull's Head　297
The Idle Hour　297

LONDON SW14
The Victoria　299

LONDON SW15
The Spencer　299
The Telegraph　299

LONDON SW18
The Alma Tavern　299
The Earl Spencer　299
The Roundhouse　299
The Ship Inn　301

LONDON W1
Duke of Wellington　301
French House　301
The Grazing Goat　301
The Only Running Footman　301
The Portman　301

LONDON W2
The Cow　302
The Prince Bonaparte　302
The Westbourne　302

LONDON W4
Sam's Brasserie & Bar　302
The Swan　302

LONDON W6
Anglesea Arms　302
The Dartmouth Castle　302
The Hampshire Hog　303
The Stonemasons Arms　303

LONDON W8
The Mall Tavern　303
The Scarsdale　303

LONDON W9
The Waterway　303

LONDON W11
Portobello Gold　304

LONDON W14
The Albion　304
The Cumberland Arms　304

LONDON WC1
The Bountiful Cow　304
The Lady Ottoline　304
The Lamb　304
Norfolk Arms　305

LONDON WC2
The George　305
The Seven Stars　305
The Sherlock Holmes　305

LONG COMPTON
The Red Lion　459

LONG CRENDON
The Angel Inn　51

LONG DITTON
The Ditton　422

LONG SUTTON
The Devonshire Arms　383

LONG WHATTON
The Falcon Inn　275
The Royal Oak　275

LONGFRAMLINGTON
The Anglers Arms　328

LONGHOPE
The Glasshouse Inn　188

LONGHORSLEY
Linden Tree　328

LONGNEWTON
Vane Arms　163

LONGNIDDRY
The Longniddry Inn　537

LONGPARISH
The Plough Inn　217

LOOE
The Ship Inn　82

LOW CATTON
The Gold Cup Inn　493

LOW LORTON
The Wheatsheaf Inn　105

LOW NEWTON BY THE SEA
The Ship Inn　330

LOW ROW
The Punch Bowl Inn　508

LOWER ANSTY
The Fox Inn　154

LOWER BEEDING
The Crabtree　447

LOWER BROADHEATH
The Dewdrop Inn　491

LOWER CHICKSGROVE
Compasses Inn　480

LOWER HALSTOW
The Three Tuns　255

LOWER LANGFORD
The Langford Inn　383

LOWER ODDINGTON
The Fox　188

LOWER SHIPLAKE
The Baskerville　352

LOWER SWANWICK
Old Ship　217

LOWER VOBSTER
Vobster Inn　383

LOWER WIELD
The Yew Tree　217

LOWER WOLVERCOTE
The Trout Inn　352

LOWESWATER
Kirkstile Inn　105

LUDGVAN
White Hart　82

LUDLOW
The Church Inn　368
The Clive Bar & Restaurant with Rooms　368

LUND
The Wellington Inn　493

LUPTON
The Plough Inn　105

LURGASHALL
The Noah's Ark　447

LUSS
The Inn at Inverbeg　534

LUSTLEIGH
The Cleave Pub　131

LUTON (NEAR CHUDLEIGH)
The Elizabethan Inn　131

LUTTERWORTH
The Man at Arms　275

LUXULYAN
The Kings Arms　82

LYDDINGTON
The Marquess of Exeter — 362
Old White Hart — 362

LYDFORD
Dartmoor Inn — 133

LYME REGIS
The Mariners — 154
Pilot Boat Inn — 154

LYMINGTON
Mayflower Inn — 218
The Walhampton Arms — 218

LYMPSTONE
The Globe Inn — 133

LYNDHURST
New Forest Inn — 218
The Oak Inn — 218

LYNMOUTH
Rising Sun Hotel — 133

M

MACHYNLLETH
Wynnstay Hotel — 582

MADINGLEY
The Three Horseshoes — 61

MADLEY
The Comet Inn — 233

MAIDSTONE
The Black Horse Inn — 257

MALHAM
The Lister Arms — 508

MALMESBURY
The Smoking Dog — 480
The Vine Tree — 481

MALVERN
The Inn at Welland — 491
The Nag's Head — 491
The Wyche Inn — 491

MANACCAN
The New Inn — 82

MANCHESTER
Dukes 92 — 201
Marble Arch — 201

MANNINGTREE
The Mistley Thorn — 172

MANTON
The Horse and Jockey — 363

MAPLEDURWELL
The Gamekeepers — 218

MAPLEHURST
The White Horse — 447

MARAZION
Godolphin Arms — 83

MARDEN
The Millstream — 481

MARGARETTING TYE
The White Hart Inn — 172

MARKBEECH
The Kentish Horse — 257

MARLBOROUGH
The Lamb Inn — 481

MARLDON
The Church House Inn — 133

MARLOW
The Hand & Flowers — 51
The Kings Head — 51

MARPLE BRIDGE
Hare & Hounds — 201

MARSDEN
The Olive Branch — 526
The Riverhead Brewery Tap
  & Dining Room — 526

MARSH BALDON
Seven Stars — 352

MARSH BENHAM
The Red House — 35

MARSHAM
The Plough Inn — 314

MARSHFIELD
The Catherine Wheel — 191
The Lord Nelson Inn — 191

MARTLEY
Admiral Rodney Inn — 492

MARTOCK
The Nag's Head Inn — 383

MARTON
The Davenport Arms — 71

MARTON
The Lowfield Inn — 368
The Sun Inn — 368

MARTON (NEAR BOROUGHBRIDGE)
The Punch Bowl Inn — 510

MARTON (NEAR SINNINGTON)
The Appletree Country Inn — 510

MARYCULTER
Old Mill Inn — 532

MASHAM
The Black Sheep Brewery — 510
The White Bear — 510

MATLOCK
The Red Lion — 121

MAYFIELD
The Middle House — 433

MEAVY
The Royal Oak Inn — 133

MEDMENHAM
The Dog and Badger — 51

MELBOURNE
The Melbourne Arms — 121

MELLOR
The Moorfield Arms — 201

MELLS
The Talbot Inn — 384

MELROSE
Burts Hotel — 552

MELTON
Wilford Bridge — 407

MEVAGISSEY
The Ship Inn — 83

MEYSEY HAMPTON
The Masons Arms — 191

MICHELDEVER
The Dove Inn — 220
Half Moon & Spread Eagle — 220

MICKLEHAM
King William IV — 422
The Running Horses — 424

MIDDLE HANDLEY
Devonshire Arms — 121

MIDDLEHAM
The White Swan — 510

MIDDLESMOOR
Crown Hotel — 510

MIDDLESTONE
Ship Inn — 163

MIDDLETON STONEY
Best Western The Jersey Arms — 353

MILCOMBE
The Horse & Groom Inn — 353

MILDENHALL
The Bull Inn — 407

MILFIELD
The Red Lion Inn — 330

MILLTOWN
The Nettle Inn — 122

MILNTHORPE
The Cross Keys — 105

MILTON ABBAS
The Hambro Arms — 154

MILTON KEYNES
The Swan Inn — 51

MILTON STREET
The Sussex Ox — 433

MILVERTON
The Globe — 384

MINCHINHAMPTON
The Weighbridge Inn — 191

MINETY
Vale of the White Horse Inn — 481

MITCHELL
The Plume of Feathers 83

MITHIAN
The Miners Arms 83

MOBBERLEY
The Bulls Head 72

MODBURY
California Country Inn 133

MOFFAT
Annandale Arms 536

MOLD
Glasfryn 564

MONEYROW GREEN
The White Hart 35

MONKNASH
The Plough & Harrow 587

MONKS ELEIGH
The Swan Inn 408

MONKS KIRBY
The Bell Inn 459

MONKTON COMBE
Wheelwrights Arms 384

MONTACUTE
The Kings Arms Inn 384
The Phelips Arms 384

MONTGOMERY
The Dragon 582

MORETON-IN-MARSH
The Red Lion Inn 191

MORTON
The Full Moon Inn 334

MORWENSTOW
The Bush Inn 83

MOTCOMBE
The Coppleridge Inn 154

MOULDSWORTH
The Goshawk 72

MOULSOE
The Carrington Arms 52

MOUNT BURES
The Thatchers Arms 172

MOUNTNESSING
The George & Dragon 172

MOUNTSORREL
The Swan Inn 275

MOWSLEY
The Staff of Life 276

MUCH WENLOCK
The George & Dragon 370
The Talbot Inn 370

MUKER
The Farmers Arms 511

MUNDFORD
Crown Hotel 315

MUNSLOW
The Crown Country Inn 370

MURCOTT
The Nut Tree Inn 353

MYLOR BRIDGE
The Pandora Inn 83

N

NAILSWORTH
The Britannia 191
Tipputs Inn 191

NANTGAREDIG
Y Polyn 560

NANTWICH
The Thatch Inn 72

NASSINGTON
The Queens Head Inn 322

NAYLAND
Anchor Inn 408

NEAR SAWREY
Tower Bank Arms 105

NETHER ALDERLEY
The Wizard Inn 72

NETHER WESTCOTE
The Feathered Nest Country Inn 191

NETHERLEY
The Lairhillock Inn 532

NETHERTON
The Star Inn 330

NETTLECOMBE
Marquis of Lorne 155

NEW ALRESFORD
The Bell Inn 220

NEW GALLOWAY
Cross Keys Hotel 536

NEW RADNOR
Red Lion Inn 582

NEWARK-ON-TRENT
The Prince Rupert 334

NEWCASTLETON
Liddesdale 552

NEWDIGATE
The Surrey Oaks 424

NEWENT
Kilcot Inn 193

NEWLAND
The Ostrich Inn 193

NEWNEY GREEN
The Duck Pub & Dining 173

NEWNHAM
The George Inn 257

NEWPORT
Salutation Inn 575

NEWQUAY
The Lewinnick Lodge Bar & Restaurant 83

NEWTON
Duke of Wellington Inn 330

NEWTON
The George & Dragon 315

NEWTON
The Queen's Head 62

NEWTON ABBOT
The Wild Goose Inn 133

NEWTON AYCLIFFE
Blacksmiths Arms 163

NEWTON ON OUSE
The Dawnay Arms 511

NEWTON ST CYRES
The Beer Engine 134

NEWTON STEWART
Creebridge House Hotel 536
The Galloway Arms Hotel 536

NEWTON TONY
The Malet Arms 481

NEWTON-IN-BOWLAND
Parkers Arms 269

NEWTON-ON-THE-MOOR
The Cook and Barker Inn 330

NINGWOOD
Horse & Groom 468

NITON
Buddle Inn 470

NORTH BALLACHULISH
Loch Leven Hotel 546

NORTH BOVEY
The Ring of Bells Inn 134

NORTH CERNEY
Bathurst Arms 193

NORTH CURRY
The Bird in Hand 384

NORTH FAMBRIDGE
The Ferry Boat Inn 173

NORTH HINKSEY VILLAGE
The Fishes 353

NORTH WALTHAM
The Fox 220

NORTH WOOTTON
The Three Elms 155

NORTHAMPTON
Althorp Coaching Inn 323

NORTHAW
The Sun at Northaw 241

NORTHILL
The Crown 27

NORTHINGTON
The Woolpack Inn 220

NORTHLEACH
The Wheatsheaf Inn 193

NORTHMOOR
The Red Lion 353

NORTHOP
Stables Bar Restaurant 564

NORTHWICH
The Red Lion 72

NORTHWOOD
Travellers Joy 470

NORTON
The Hundred House 370

NORTON ST PHILIP
George Inn 385

NORWICH
Adam & Eve 315
The Mad Moose Arms 315
Ribs of Beef 315

NOSS MAYO
The Ship Inn 134

NOTTINGHAM
Fellows Morton & Clayton 335
Ye Olde Trip to Jerusalem 335

NUNNEY
The George at Nunney 385

NUNNINGTON
The Royal Oak Inn 511

NUNTON
The Radnor Arms 481

NUTFIELD
The Inn on the Pond 424

NUTHURST
Black Horse Inn 447

O

OADBY
Cow and Plough 276

OAKHAM
The Finch's Arms 363
The Grainstore Brewery 363

OAKHILL
The Oakhill Inn 385

OAKLEY GREEN
The Greene Oak 35

OAKSEY
The Wheatsheaf at Oaksey 482

OCKLEY
Bryce's at The Old School House 424
The Kings Arms Inn 424

ODELL
The Bell 27

OFFCHURCH
The Stag at Offchurch 460

OFFHAM
The Blacksmiths Arms 433

OFFORD D'ARCY
The Horseshoe Inn 62

OGBOURNE ST ANDREW
Silks on the Downs 482

OLD BASING
The Crown 220

OLD RADNOR
The Harp 582

OLD WARDEN
Hare and Hounds 28

OLDBURY-ON-SEVERN
The Anchor Inn 193

OLDHAM
The Roebuck Inn 201
The White Hart Inn 201

OLDMELDRUM
The Redgarth 532

OLDSTEAD
The Black Swan at Oldstead 511

ONNELEY
The Wheatsheaf Inn 397

ORLETON
The Boot Inn 233

OSMINGTON MILLS
The Smugglers Inn 155

OSMOTHERLEY
The Golden Lion 511

OSWESTRY
The Bradford Arms 370

OTTERY ST MARY
The Talaton Inn 134

OUNDLE
The Chequered Skipper 323

OUTGATE
Outgate Inn 108

OVER STRATTON
The Royal Oak 385

OVING
The Black Boy 52

OVING
The Gribble Inn 448

OVINGTON
The Bush 220

OXFORD
The Magdalen Arms 355
The Oxford Retreat 355
The Punter 355
Turf Tavern 355

OXHILL
The Peacock 460

P

PAINSCASTLE
The Roast Ox Inn 582

PAINSWICK
The Falcon Inn 193

PALEY STREET
The Royal Oak Paley Street 35

PANTYGELLI
The Crown 571

PAR
The Britannia Inn & Restaurant 85
The Royal Inn 85

PARBOLD
The Eagle & Child 269

PARKGATE
The Boat House 72
The Ship Hotel 73

PARRACOMBE
The Fox & Goose 134

PARTNEY
Red Lion Inn 283

PATELEY BRIDGE
The Sportsmans Arms Hotel 511

PATTISWICK
The Compasses at Pattiswick 173

PAVE LANE
The Fox 370

PAXFORD
The Churchill Arms 195

PEASEMORE
The Fox at Peasemore 36

PEEL
The Creek Inn 529

PELDON
The Peldon Rose 173

PEMBRIDGE
New Inn 235

PENALLT
The Inn at Penallt 571

PENDLETON
The Swan with Two Necks 271

PENICUIK
The Howgate Restaurant 548

PENISTONE
Cubley Hall 520

Save on hotels. Book at theAA.com/hotel

INDEX 647

PENN
The Old Queens Head — 52

PENNAL
Glan yr Afon/Riverside — 566

PENRITH
Cross Keys Inn — 108

PENSHURST
The Bottle House Inn — 257
The Spotted Dog — 257

PENTYRCH
Kings Arms — 559

PENZANCE
The Coldstreamer Inn — 85
Dolphin Tavern — 85
The Turks Head Inn — 85

PERRANUTHNOE
The Victoria Inn — 85

PERRY GREEN
The Hoops Inn — 241

PERSHORE
The Defford Arms — 492

PETERBOROUGH
The Brewery Tap — 62
Charters Bar & East Restaurant — 62

PETERSFIELD
The Old Drum — 222
The Trooper Inn — 222
The White Horse Inn — 222

PETWORTH
The Angel Inn — 448

PEWSEY
The Seven Stars Inn — 482

PHILLEIGH
Roseland Inn — 86

PICKERING
Fox & Hounds Country Inn — 513
The Fox & Rabbit Inn — 513
The White Swan Inn — 513

PICKHILL
Nags Head Country Inn — 513

PICTON
The Station Hotel — 513

PIDDLEHINTON
The Thimble Inn — 155

PIDDLETRENTHIDE
The Piddle Inn — 155
The Poachers Inn — 155

PILSLEY
The Devonshire Arms at Pilsley — 122

PISHILL
The Crown Inn — 355

PITLOCHRY
Moulin Hotel — 549

PITNEY
The Halfway House — 385

PITTON
The Silver Plough — 482

PLOCKTON
The Plockton Hotel — 546
Plockton Inn & Seafood Restaurant — 546

PLUCKLEY
The Dering Arms — 257

PLUMLEY
The Smoker — 73

PLUMPTON
Half Moon — 435

PLUSH
The Brace of Pheasants — 156

PLYMOUTH
The Fishermans Arms — 134

PLYMTREE
The Blacksmiths Arms — 136

POLKERRIS
The Rashleigh Inn — 86

POLPERRO
Old Mill House Inn — 86

PONTYPRIDD
Bunch of Grapes — 584

POOLE
The Guildhall Tavern — 156
The Rising Sun — 156

PORLOCK
The Bottom Ship — 386
The Ship Inn — 386

PORT APPIN
The Pierhouse Hotel & Seafood
   Restaurant — 534

PORT CHARLOTTE
The Port Charlotte Hotel — 554

PORT ERIN
Falcon's Nest Hotel — 529

PORT GAVERNE
Port Gaverne Hotel — 86

PORT ISAAC
The Slipway — 86

PORTGATE
The Harris Arms — 136

PORTHGAIN
The Sloop Inn — 575

PORTHLEVEN
The Ship Inn — 86

PORTREATH
Basset Arms — 87

POSTBRIDGE
Warren House Inn — 136

POTTEN END
Martins Pond — 244

POTTERS CROUCH
The Holly Bush — 244

POULTON
The Falcon Inn — 195

POWERSTOCK
Three Horseshoes Inn — 156

POWICK
The Halfway House Inn — 492

POYNINGS
Royal Oak — 448

PRESTBURY
The Legh Arms — 73

PRESTON BAGOT
The Crabmill — 460

PRESTON BISSETT
The White Hart — 52

PRESTON CANDOVER
Purefoy Arms — 222

PRIORS MARSTON
The Hollybush Inn — 460

PUNCKNOWLE
The Crown Inn — 156

R

RADNAGE
The Three Horseshoes Inn — 52

RAGLAN
The Beaufort Arms Coaching Inn
   & Brasserie — 572

RAITHBY
Red Lion Inn — 283

RAMSBURY
The Bell at Ramsbury — 483

RAMSDEN
The Royal Oak — 355

RATHO
The Bridge Inn — 540

RATTERY
Church House Inn — 136

RAVENSTONEDALE
The Black Swan — 108
The Fat Lamb Country Inn — 108
The King's Head — 108

REACH
Dyke's End — 62

READING
The Flowing Spring — 36
The Shoulder of Mutton — 36

RED WHARF BAY
The Ship Inn — 558

REDE
The Plough 408

REETH
Charles Bathurst Inn 513

REYNOLDSTON
King Arthur Hotel 584

RHEWL
The Drovers Arms 563

RHYD-Y-MEIRCH
Goose and Cuckoo Inn 572

RICKLING GREEN
The Cricketers Arms 173

RINGMER
The Cock 435

RINGSTEAD
The Gin Trap Inn 315

RINGWOOD
The Star Inn 222

RIPON
The George at Wath 516
The Royal Oak 516

RIPPONDEN
Old Bridge Inn 526

ROBIN HOOD'S BAY
Laurel Inn 516

ROCKBEARE
Jack in the Green Inn 136

ROCKBOURNE
The Rose & Thistle 222

ROCKFORD
The Alice Lisle 223

RODE
The Mill at Rode 386

ROLVENDEN
The Bull 258

ROMALDKIRK
Rose & Crown 163

ROMSEY
The Cromwell Arms 223
The Three Tuns 223

ROOKLEY
The Chequers 470

ROSEBUSH
Tafarn Sinc 575

ROSLIN
The Original Rosslyn Inn 548

ROTHERFIELD PEPPARD
The Unicorn 355

ROTHERWICK
The Coach and Horses 223

ROWDE
The George & Dragon 483

ROWHOOK
The Chequers Inn 448

ROWSLEY
The Grouse & Claret 122

RUAN LANIHORNE
The Kings Head 87

RUDGE
The Full Moon at Rudge 386

RUSCOMBE
Buratta's at the Royal Oak 36

RUSHLAKE GREEN
Horse & Groom 436

RYE
The George Tap 436
Mermaid Inn 436
The Ypres Castle Inn 436

S

SAFFRON WALDEN
Old English Gentleman 174

ST AGNES
Driftwood Spars 87

ST ANDREWS
The Inn at Lathones 541
The Jigger Inn 541

ST ASAPH
The Plough Inn 564

ST AUBIN
Old Court House Inn 529

ST BOSWELLS
Buccleuch Arms Hotel 552

ST BRELADE
The Portelet Inn 529

ST BREWARD
The Old Inn & Restaurant 87

ST DOGMAELS
The Teifi Netpool Inn 575
Webley Waterfront Inn & Hotel 577

ST EWE
The Crown Inn 87

ST IVES
The Queens 87
The Sloop Inn 88
The Watermill 88

ST JUST (NEAR LAND'S END)
Star Inn 88
The Wellington 88

ST KEW
St Kew Inn 88

ST MARGARET'S BAY
The Coastguard 258

ST MARTIN
Royal Hotel 529

ST MARY
St Mary's Country Inn 529

ST MARY BOURNE
The Bourne Valley Inn 223

ST MARY'S
The Commodore 554

ST MAWES
The Victory Inn 88

ST MAWGAN
The Falcon Inn 88

ST MERRYN
The Cornish Arms 90

ST PETER PORT
The Admiral de Saumarez 528
The Ship & Crown, Crow's Nest Brasserie 528

SALCOMBE
The Victoria Inn 136

SALEHURST
Salehurst Halt 436

SALFORD
The Swan 28

SALFORD
The King's Arms 202

SALFORD PRIORS
The Bell at Salford Priors 460

SALISBURY
The Cloisters 484
Old Mill 484
The Wig and Quill 484

SALTASH
The Crooked Inn 90

SALTHOUSE
The Salthouse Dun Cow 316

SANCTON
The Star 493

SANDFORD
The Lamb Inn 138

SANDHEAD
Tigh Na Mara Hotel 536

SANDWICH
George & Dragon Inn 258

SANTON BRIDGE
Bridge Inn 108

SAPPERTON
The Bell at Sapperton 195

SARRATT
The Cock Inn 244

SAWDON
The Anvil Inn 516

SAWLEY
The Spread Eagle 271

SCAWTON
The Hare Inn 516

SEAHAM
The Seaton Lane Inn   163

SEAHOUSES
The Bamburgh Castle Inn   330
The Olde Ship Inn   331

SEATHWAITE
Newfield Inn   109

SEAVIEW
The Boathouse   470
The Seaview Hotel & Restaurant   470

SEDGLEY
Beacon Hotel & Sarah Hughes Brewery   466

SEEND
Bell Inn   484

SEER GREEN
The Jolly Cricketers   52

SELBORNE
The Selborne Arms   223

SELLING
The Rose and Crown   258

SEMINGTON
The Lamb on the Strand   484

SENNEN
The Old Success Inn   90

SETTLE
The Lion at Settle   516

SHALFLEET
The New Inn   470

SHAPWICK
The Anchor Inn   156

SHARDLOW
The Old Crown Inn   122

SHEBBEAR
The Devil's Stone Inn   138

SHEEPSCOMBE
The Butchers Arms   195

SHEFFIELD
The Fat Cat   520
Kelham Island Tavern   520
The Sheffield Tap   520

SHELLEY
The Three Acres Inn   526

SHENLEY
The White Horse, Shenley   244

SHEPTON BEAUCHAMP
Duke of York   386

SHEPTON MALLET
The Three Horseshoes Inn   386
The Waggon and Horses   388

SHEPTON MONTAGUE
The Montague Inn   388

SHERBORNE
The Kings Arms   157

SHERSTON
The Rattlebone Inn   484

SHIELDAIG
Shieldaig Bar & Coastal Kitchen   546

SHIFNAL
Odfellows Wine Bar   371

SHILTON
Rose & Crown   355

SHIPBOURNE
The Chaser Inn   258

SHIPLEY
The Countryman Inn   448
George & Dragon   448

SHIPTON-UNDER-WYCHWOOD
The Shaven Crown Hotel   357

SHIRENEWTON
The Carpenters Arms   572

SHORTBRIDGE
The Peacock Inn   437

SHORWELL
The Crown Inn   471

SHREWLEY
The Durham Ox Restaurant and
    Country Pub   462

SHREWSBURY
The Armoury   371
Lion & Pheasant Hotel   371
The Mytton & Mermaid Hotel   371

SHROTON OR IWERNE COURTNEY
The Cricketers   157

SIBBERTOFT
The Red Lion   323

SIBTON
Sibton White Horse Inn   408

SIDBURY
The Hare & Hounds   138

SIDMOUTH
Blue Ball Inn   138
Dukes   138

SILCHESTER
Calleva Arms   225

SILEBY
The White Swan   276

SINDLESHAM
The Walter Arms   36

SINGLETON
The Partridge Inn   448

SIZERGH
The Strickland Arms   109

SKENFRITH
The Bell at Skenfrith   572

SKIPTON
Devonshire Arms   517

SKIRMETT
The Frog   54

SLAGGYFORD
The Kirkstyle Inn   331

SLAPTON
The Tower Inn   141

SLINDON
The Spur   452

SMARDEN
The Chequers Inn   258

SNAINTON
The Coachman Inn   517

SNAPE
The Crown Inn   408
The Golden Key   410
Plough & Sail   410

SNETTISHAM
The Rose & Crown   316

SOMERBY
Stilton Cheese Inn   276

SOMERFORD KEYNES
The Bakers Arms   195

SOMERLEYTON
The Duke's Head   410

SONNING
The Bull Inn   36

SORN
The Sorn Inn   537

SOULDROP
The Bedford Arms   28

SOURTON
The Highwayman Inn   141

SOUTH DALTON
The Pipe & Glass Inn   494

SOUTH GODSTONE
Fox & Hounds   424

SOUTH LUFFENHAM
The Coach House Inn   363

SOUTH POOL
The Millbrook Inn   141

SOUTH RAUCEBY
The Bustard Inn & Restaurant   283

SOUTH WITHAM
Blue Cow Inn & Brewery   283

SOUTHAMPTON
The White Star Tavern, Dining & Rooms   225

SOUTHILL
The White Horse   28

SOUTHWOLD
The Crown Hotel   410
The Randolph   410

SOWERBY BRIDGE
The Alma Inn & Fresco Italian Restaurant   526

SOWTON
The Black Horse Inn 141

SPALDWICK
The George 62

SPARKWELL
The Treby Arms 141

SPARSHOLT
The Plough Inn 225

SPELDHURST
George & Dragon 259

SPREYTON
The Tom Cobley Tavern 141

SPURSTOW
The Yew Tree Inn 73

STACKPOLE
The Stackpole Inn 577

STAFFORD
The Holly Bush Inn 397

STALISFIELD GREEN
The Plough at Stalisfield Green ... 259

STAMFORD
The George of Stamford 284
The Tobie Norris 284

STANBRIDGE
The Five Bells 28

STANDLAKE
The Bell Inn 357

STANFORD DINGLEY
The Old Boot Inn 37

STANLEY
The Stables Pub and Restaurant ... 165

STANSTED AIRPORT
See Little Canfield 122

STANTON IN PEAK
The Flying Childers Inn 122

STANTON WICK
The Carpenters Arms 388

STAPLEFORD
Papillon Woodhall Arms 244

STAPLEFORD
The Rose at Stapleford 63

STAPLOW
The Oak Inn 235

STARBOTTON
Fox & Hounds Inn 517

STATHERN
Red Lion Inn 277

STAVERTON
Sea Trout Inn 142

STEDHAM
Hamilton Arms/Nava Thai Restaurant ... 452

STEEP
Harrow Inn 225

STEEPLE ASTON
The Red Lion 357

STEIN
Stein Inn 555

STIFFKEY
The Stiffkey Red Lion 316

STILTON
The Bell Inn Hotel 63

STOAK
The Bunbury Arms 73

STOCK
The Hoop 174

STOCKBRIDGE
Mayfly 225
The Peat Spade Inn 225
The Three Cups Inn 225

STOCKPORT
The Arden Arms 202
The Nursery Inn 202

STOGUMBER
The White Horse 388

STOKE BRUERNE
The Boat Inn 323

STOKE D'ABERNON
The Old Plough 425

STOKE FLEMING
The Green Dragon Inn 142

STOKE HOLY CROSS
The Wildebeest 316

STOKE ROW
Crooked Billet 357

STOKE ST GREGORY
Rose & Crown 388

STOKE-BY-NAYLAND
The Angel Inn 411
The Crown 411

STONEHOUSE
The George Inn 195

STOTTESDON
Fighting Cocks 372

STOURTON
The Fox Inn 397

STOURTON
Spread Eagle Inn 485

STOW BARDOLPH
The Hare Arms 316

STOW-ON-THE-WOLD
The Unicorn 195
White Hart Inn 197

STOWMARKET
The Buxhall Crown 411

STOWTING
The Tiger Inn 259

STRACHUR
Creggans Inn 534

STRADBROKE
The Ivy House 411

STRATFORD-UPON-AVON
The One Elm 462

STRATTON
Saxon Arms 157

STREET
The Two Brewers 388

STRETHAM
The Lazy Otter 63
The Red Lion 63

STRETTON
The Jackson Stops Country Inn ... 363

STRETTON ON FOSSE
The Plough Inn 462

STROMNESS
Ferry Inn 554

STROUD
Bear of Rodborough Hotel 197
The Ram Inn 197
Rose & Crown Inn 197
The Woolpack Inn 197

STUDHAM
The Bell in Studham 28

STUDLAND
The Bankes Arms Hotel 157

SUMMERHILL
Oddfellows in the Boat 400

SUSWORTH
The Jenny Wren Inn 284

SUTTON
The White Horse Inn 452

SUTTON LANE ENDS
The Hanging Gate Inn 73
Sutton Hall 74

SUTTON UPON DERWENT
St Vincent Arms 494

SUTTON-ON-THE-FOREST
The Blackwell Ox Inn 517

SWALLOWFIELD
The George & Dragon 37

SWANMORE
The Rising Sun 226

SWANTON MORLEY
Darbys Freehouse 318

SWERFORD
The Mason's Arms   357

SWETTENHAM
The Swettenham Arms   74

SWILLAND
Moon & Mushroom Inn   411

SWINBROOK
The Swan Inn   358

SWINDON
The Weighbridge Brewhouse   485

SWINTON
The Wheatsheaf at Swinton   552

SWITHLAND
The Griffin Inn   277

SYDENHAM
The Crown Inn   358

SYDLING ST NICHOLAS
The Greyhound Inn   157

SYMINGTON
Wheatsheaf Inn   552

SYMONDS YAT (EAST)
The Saracens Head Inn   235

T

TALGARTH
Castle Inn   582

TALYBONT-ON-USK
Star Inn   584

TAMWORTH
The Globe Inn   400

TANGLEY
The Fox Inn   226

TANWORTH IN ARDEN
The Bell Inn   462

TARPORLEY
Alvanley Arms Inn   74
The Swan, Tarporley   74

TARRANT MONKTON
The Langton Arms   157

TAUNTON
The Hatch Inn   389

TAVISTOCK
Peter Tavy Inn   142

TAYVALLICH
Tayvallich Inn   535

TEMPLE GRAFTON
The Blue Boar Inn   462

TEMPLE SOWERBY
The Kings Arms   109

TENBY
Hope and Anchor   577

TENTERDEN
White Lion Inn   259

TETBURY
Gumstool Inn   197
The Priory Inn   198
Snooty Fox Hotel   198
The Trouble House   198

TETSWORTH
The Old Red Lion   358

THAME
The James Figg   358
The Thatch   358

THEDDLETHORPE ALL SAINTS
Kings Head Inn   284

THOMPSON
Chequers Inn   318

THORNBY
The Red Lion   323

THORNHAM
Marco Pierre White The Lifeboat Inn   318
The Orange Tree   318

THORNTON
Ring O'Bells Country Pub & Restaurant   528

THORNTON LE DALE
The New Inn   518

THORNTON WATLASS
The Buck Inn   518

THORPE LANGTON
The Bakers Arms   277

THORPENESS
The Dolphin Inn   414

THREE LEG CROSS
The Bull   437

THURLESTONE
The Village Inn   142

TIBBIE SHIELS INN
Tibbie Shiels Inn   552

TICEHURST
The Bell   437

TICHBORNE
The Tichborne Arms   226

TIDESWELL
The George   122
Three Stags' Heads   122

TILFORD
The Duke of Cambridge   425

TILLINGTON
The Bell   237

TILLINGTON
The Horseguards Inn   452

TILSWORTH
The Anchor Inn   29

TIMBERLAND
The Penny Farthing Inn   284

TINTERN PARVA
Fountain Inn   572

TINTINHULL
The Crown and Victoria Inn   389

TIPTON ST JOHN
The Golden Lion Inn   142

TIRRIL
Queen's Head Inn   109

TITCHMARSH
The Wheatsheaf at Titchmarsh   323

TITCHWELL
Titchwell Manor Hotel   318

TOCKHOLES
The Royal Arms   271

TOLLARD ROYAL
King John Inn   485

TONBRIDGE
The Little Brown Jug   259

TOOT BALDON
The Mole Inn   359

TOPSHAM
Bridge Inn   142

TORCROSS
Start Bay Inn   145

TORMARTON
Best Western Compass Inn   198

TORPOINT
Edgcumbe Arms   90

TORQUAY
The Cary Arms   145

TORRIDON
The Torridon Inn   548

TORVER
Church House Inn   109

TOTLEY
The Cricket Inn   520

TOTNES
The Durant Arms   145
Royal Seven Stars Hotel   145
Rumour   145
Steam Packet Inn   145
The White Hart Bar & Restaurant   145

TOWCESTER
The Saracens Head   324

TREBARWITH
The Mill House Inn   90
The Port William   90

TREBURLEY
The Springer Spaniel   91

TRECASTLE
The Castle Coaching Inn   584

TREDUNNOCK
Newbridge on Usk   573

TREFRIW
The Old Ship 563

TREGADILLETT
Eliot Arms 91

TREGARON
Y Talbot 560

TRELLECH
The Lion Inn 573

TREMADOG
The Union Inn 566

TRENT
Rose & Crown Trent 160

TRESCO (ISLES OF SCILLY)
The New Inn 91

TRING
The Cow Roast Inn 244

TRISCOMBE
The Blue Ball Inn 389

TROTTON
The Keepers Arms 452

TROUTBECK
Queen's Head 110

TRURO
Old Ale House 91
The Wig & Pen 91

TRUSHAM
Cridford Inn 146

TUCKENHAY
The Maltsters Arms 146

TUDDENHAM
The Fountain 414

TUDELEY
The Poacher 259

TUDWEILIOG
Lion Hotel 567

TUNBRIDGE WELLS (ROYAL)
The Beacon 260
The Crown Inn 260
The Hare on Langton Green 260

TUNSTALL
The Lunesdale Arms 271

TURVILLE
The Bull & Butcher 54

TUSHINGHAM CUM GRINDLEY
Blue Bell Inn 76

TUXFORD
The Mussel & Crab 335

TYTHERLEIGH
The Tytherleigh Arms 146

U

UFFORD
The Ufford Crown 414

UFFORD
The White Hart 63

ULVERSTON
Farmers Arms Hotel 110
Old Farmhouse 110
The Stan Laurel Inn 110

UPPER FROYLE
The Hen & Chicken Inn 226

UPPER ODDINGTON
The Horse and Groom Inn 198

UPPER WOODFORD
The Bridge Inn 485

UPTON LOVELL
Prince Leopold Inn 485

USK
The Nags Head Inn 573
Raglan Arms 573

V

VERYAN
The New Inn 91

W

WADDINGTON
Waddington Arms 271

WADEBRIDGE
The Quarryman Inn 92
The Swan Hotel 92

WADENHOE
The King's Head 324

WADHURST
The Best Beech Inn 437

WALBERSWICK
The Anchor 414
The Bell Inn 414

WALDERTON
The Barley Mow 454

WALFORD
The Mill Race 237

WALMERSLEY
The Lord Raglan 202

WALTERSTONE
Carpenters Arms 237

WALTHAM ST LAWRENCE
The Bell 37

WARDEN
The Boatside Inn 331

WARENFORD
The White Swan 331

WARHAM ALL SAINTS
Three Horseshoes 318

WARMINGHAM
The Bear's Paw 76

WARMINSTER
The Angel Inn 486
The Bath Arms 486
The George Inn 486

WARNFORD
The George & Falcon 226

WARNINGLID
The Half Moon 454

WARSASH
The Jolly Farmer Country Inn 227

WARWICK
The Rose & Crown 463

WASDALE HEAD
Wasdale Head Inn 110

WASS
Wombwell Arms 518

WATERROW
The Rock Inn 389

WAUNFAWR
Snowdonia Parc Brewpub & Campsite 567

WEDMORE
The George Inn 389

WELFORD-ON-AVON
The Bell Inn 463

WELHAM
The Old Red Lion 277

WELL
The Chequers Inn 227

WELLINGTON
The Old Orleton Inn 372

WELLINGTON
The Wellington 237

WELLS
The City Arms 390
The Crown at Wells 390
The Fountain Inn & Boxer's Restaurant 390

WELLS-NEXT-THE-SEA
The Crown Hotel 319
The Globe Inn 319

WELWYN
The White Hart 245

WELWYN GARDEN CITY
The Brocket Arms 245

WENTNOR
The Crown Inn 372

WEOBLEY
Ye Olde Salutation Inn 237

WEST BAGBOROUGH
The Rising Sun Inn 390

WEST BECKHAM
The Wheatsheaf 319

WEST BEXINGTON
The Manor Hotel 160

Save on hotels. Book at theAA.com/hotel

INDEX 653

WEST BROMWICH	
The Vine	466
WEST BURTON	
Fox & Hounds	518
WEST CAMEL	
The Walnut Tree	390
WEST CHILTINGTON	
The Queens Head	454
WEST CLANDON	
The Onslow Arms	425
WEST END	
The Inn @ West End	425
WEST HANNEY	
Plough Inn	359
WEST HATCH	
The Farmers Arms	390
WEST HOATHLY	
The Cat Inn	454
WEST HORSLEY	
The King William IV	425
WEST HUNTSPILL	
Crossways Inn	391
WEST LULWORTH	
The Castle Inn	160
Lulworth Cove Inn	160
WEST MALLING	
The Farmhouse	260
WEST MEON	
The Thomas Lord	227
WEST MONKTON	
The Monkton Inn	391
WEST PENNARD	
The Apple Tree Inn	391
WEST STOUR	
The Ship Inn	160
WEST TANFIELD	
The Bruce Arms	518
WEST TYTHERLEY	
The Black Horse	227
WEST WITTON	
The Wensleydale Heifer	519
WEST WYCOMBE	
The George and Dragon Hotel	54
WESTERHAM	
The Fox & Hounds	260
Grasshopper on the Green	260
WESTLETON	
The Westleton Crown	414
WESTON	
The Crown	324
WESTON LONGVILLE	
The Parson Woodforde	319

WESTON-ON-THE-GREEN	
The Ben Jonson	359
WETTON	
Ye Olde Royal Oak	400
WEYMOUTH	
The Old Ship Inn	160
The Red Lion	160
WHALLEY	
The Three Fishes	273
WHEATLEY	
Bat & Ball Inn	359
WHEDDON CROSS	
The Rest and Be Thankful Inn	391
WHEELER END	
The Chequers Inn	54
WHEELTON	
The Dressers Arms	273
WHEPSTEAD	
The White Horse	414
WHIPPINGHAM	
The Folly	471
WHITBY	
The Magpie Café	519
WHITCHURCH	
Willeymoor Lock Tavern	372
WHITE WALTHAM	
The Beehive	37
WHITEWELL	
The Inn at Whitewell	273
WHITLEY	
Marco Pierre White The Pear Tree Inn	486
WHITSTABLE	
The Sportsman	262
WHITWELL	
The Noel @ Whitwell	363
WICKHAM	
Greens Restaurant & Bar	227
WIDDOP	
Pack Horse Inn	528
WIDECOMBE IN THE MOOR	
The Old Inn	146
The Rugglestone Inn	146
WIDEMOUTH BAY	
Bay View Inn	92
WIGGLESWORTH	
The Plough Inn	519
WILLIAN	
The Fox	245
WILMINGTON	
The Giants Rest	437
WIMBORNE ST GILES	
The Bull Inn	160

WINCHCOMBE	
The White Hart Inn and Restaurant	199
WINCHESTER	
The Bell Inn	227
The Black Boy	228
The Golden Lion	228
The Green Man	228
The Old Vine	228
The Westgate Inn	228
The Wykeham Arms	230
WINCLE	
The Ship Inn	76
WINDERMERE	
The Angel Inn	110
Eagle & Child Inn	111
WINDLESHAM	
The Half Moon	426
WINEHAM	
The Royal Oak	454
WINFORTON	
The Sun Inn	237
WING	
Kings Arms	365
WINKFIELD	
Rose & Crown	37
WINKLEIGH	
The Kings Arms	148
WINSFORD	
Royal Oak Inn	391
WINSTER	
The Brown Horse Inn	111
WINSTON	
The Bridgewater Arms	165
WINTERBORNE ZELSTON	
Botany Bay Inne	161
WINTERBOURNE	
The Winterbourne Arms	37
WINTERTON-ON-SEA	
Fishermans Return	319
WITHYBROOK	
The Pheasant	464
WITHYHAM	
The Dorset Arms	438
WITNEY	
The Fleece	359
The Three Horseshoes	359
WIVETON	
Wiveton Bell	319
WOBURN	
The Birch at Woburn	29
The Black Horse	29
The Tavistock Bar & Lounge	29
WOKINGHAM	
The Broad Street Tavern	38

WOOBURN COMMON
Chequers Inn — 54

WOODBASTWICK
The Fur & Feather Inn — 320

WOODBURY SALTERTON
The Digger's Rest — 148

WOODCHESTER
The Old Fleece — 199

WOODHALL SPA
Village Limits Country Pub, Restaurant & Motel — 284

WOODHAM MORTIMER
Hurdlemakers Arms — 174

WOODHOUSE EAVES
The Wheatsheaf Inn — 277

WOODSTOCK
The Kings Arms — 361

WOOKEY
The Burcott Inn — 394

WOOKEY HOLE
Wookey Hole Inn — 394

WOOLHAMPTON
The Rowbarge — 38

WOOLHOPE
The Butchers Arms — 238
The Crown Inn — 238

WOOLSTHORPE
The Chequers Inn — 285

WOOLSTONE
The White Horse — 361

WOOTTON RIVERS
Royal Oak — 486

WORKINGTON
The Old Ginn House — 111

WORTH MATRAVERS
The Square and Compass — 161

WRENBURY
The Dusty Miller — 76

WRINEHILL
The Crown Inn — 400
The Hand & Trumpet — 400

WROTHAM
The Bull — 262

WYE
The New Flying Horse — 262

WYMESWOLD
The Windmill Inn — 278

WYMONDHAM
The Berkeley Arms — 278

WYTHAM
White Hart — 361

Y

YANWATH
The Yanwath Gate Inn — 111

YATTENDON
The Royal Oak Hotel — 38

YEALMPTON
Rose & Crown — 148

YEOVIL
The Half Moon Inn — 394
The Masons Arms — 394

YORK
Blue Bell — 519
Lamb & Lion Inn — 519
Lysander Arms — 519

Z

ZENNOR
The Tinners Arms — 92

Acknowledgments

AA Media Ltd would like to thank the following photographers, companies and picture libraries for their assistance in the preparation of this book.

Abbreviations for the picture credits are as follows – (t) top; (b) bottom; (c) centre; (l) left; (r) right; (AA) AA World Travel Library.

01 AA/Tim Locke; 002 AA/Karl Blackwell; 003 AA/James Tims; 004 Ros Roberts/Stone; 005 © Cephas Picture Library/Alamy; 004 Courtesy of The Wild Duck; 007 AA/Chris Hill; 008 AA/Karl Blackwell; 009 AA/Rich Newton; 010t AA/Clive Sawyer; 010b Courtesy of The Eleveden; 011t Courtesy of Sheep Heid Inn, Duddingston; 011b Courtesy of The Groes Inn; 012 Bananastock; 014 Meeta K Wolff; 017 © Cultura Creative/Alamy; 018 AA/David W Robertson; 021 AA/Ian Burgum; 022tl Courtesy of Yorkshire Bridge Inn; 022cl Courtesy of The Stackpole Inn; 022tr Courtesy of The Pheasant; 022cr Courtesy of The Bear; 023 AA/Tom Mackie; 024-025 AA/Guy Edwardes; 76bl AA/Neil Coates; 237br AA/Caroline Jones; 271bl AA/David Clapp; 273br AA/James Tims; 426bl AA/James Tims; 492bl AA/Caroline Jones; 528bl AA/David Clapp; 530-531 AA/Mark Hamblin; 532br AA/Stephen Whitehorne; 556-557 AA/Steve Watkins; 589 AA/Rebecca Duke; 600 AA/Nigel Hicks.

Photographs in the gazetteer are provided by the establishments.

Every effort has been made to trace the copyright holders, and we apologise in advance for any unintentional omissions or errors. We would be pleased to apply any corrections in a following edition of this publication.

Readers' Report Form

Please send this form to:–
The Editor, The AA Pub Guide,
AA Lifestyle Guides,
13th Floor,
Fanum House,
Basingstoke RG21 4EA

e-mail: lifestyleguides@theAA.com

Please use this form to tell us about any pub or inn you have visited, whether it is in the guide or not currently listed. We are interested in the quality of food, the selection of beers and the overall ambience of the establishment.

Feedback from readers helps us to keep our guide accurate and up to date. However, if you have a complaint to make during a visit, we do recommend that you discuss the matter with the pub management there and then, so that they have a chance to put things right before your visit is spoilt.

Please note that the AA does not undertake to arbitrate between you and the pub management, or to obtain compensation or engage in protracted correspondence.

Date

Your name (BLOCK CAPITALS)

Your address (BLOCK CAPITALS)

Post code

E-mail address

Name of pub

Location

Comments

(please attach a separate sheet if necessary)

Please tick here ☐ if you DO NOT wish to receive details of AA offers or products

PTO

Readers' Report Form *continued*

Have you bought this guide before? ☐ YES ☐ NO

Do you regularly use any other pub, accommodation or food guides? ☐ YES ☐ NO
If YES, which ones?

_____

_____

What do you find most useful about The AA Pub Guide?

_____

_____

_____

Do you read the editorial features in the guide? ☐ YES ☐ NO

Do you use the location atlas? ☐ YES ☐ NO

Is there any other information you would like to see added to this guide?

_____

_____

_____

_____

What are your main reasons for visiting pubs (tick all that apply)

Food ☐   Business ☐   Accommodation ☐
Beer ☐   Celebrations ☐   Entertainment ☐
Atmosphere ☐   Leisure ☐
Other

_____

How often do you visit a pub for a meal?
more than once a week ☐
once a week ☐
once a fortnight ☐
once a month ☐
once in six months ☐